DODS

PARLIAMENTARY

COMPANION

2014

 # Dods Contacts

Do you need to contact Members of Parliament, the House of Lords or local councillors?

Dods' definitive data provides you with direct access to those who shape policy and legislation in the UK. Constantly updated to ensure the most current information is available, renting Dods data gives you full contact details of all 650 MPs 800 Peers and over 20,000 councillors.

Lists available include:

Person Type	Quantity	Cost per record
Members of Parliament	650	75p
House of Lords	806*	75p
Members of the European Parliament	736	75p
Councillors	20,000*	75p

*Subject to change

Minimum order £350 for single use; all orders are subject to VAT.

To discuss your requirements, please contact Lucy Williams on 020 7593 5644 email lucy.williams@dods.co.uk or visit www.dodsshop.co.uk

DODS
PARLIAMENTARY
COMPANION

2014

182nd year

ACKNOWLEDGEMENTS

Dods Parliamentary Companion published since 1832

Published by

Dods
Data and Reference Division
21 Dartmouth Street
London SW1H 9BP

Telephone: 020 7593 5500
E-mail: editor@dods.co.uk
www.dodspeople.com

Editor: Helen Haxell
Deputy Editor: Elizabeth Newton
Assistant Editor: Jason Lower (Civil Service)
Editorial Assistants: Imogen Dale, James Floyd
Production Manager: Roy Hodgkinson
Database Management: Kirsty Green-Armytage
Circulation: Jo Wass, Lucy Williams
Head of UK Content: Daisy Drury
Publisher (Dods Books): Martin Beck

All photographs taken at annual photoshoot in Parliament by Graham Martin
Email: graham.martin@btinternet.com
Photo of Richard Drax MP © The Dorset Echo; photo of Lord Liddle © Policy Network;
photo of Baroness Young of Hornsey © Eamonn.McCabe@btinternet.com;
photo of Lord Giddens © Nigel Stead/LSE; photo of Lord Tyler © Paul Heartfield

All general election calculations are based on the notional results compiled by Colin Rallings
and Michael Thrasher, *Media Guide to the New Constituencies* (LGC Election Centre,
University of Plymouth, for BBC, ITN, PA News and Sky News, 2007).

Typesetting by Dods
Printed in Great Britain by Polestar Wheatons, Exeter, Devon

© 2013 Dods, 21 Dartmouth Street, London SW1H 9BP
ISBN 978-1-908232-16-8   ISSN 0070-7007

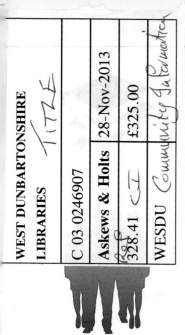
Directory.
Searchable public affairs directory in partnership with *Public Affairs News*

People.
Access senior public affairs professionals' biographies

Organisations.
Contact details available for over 3,500 public affairs-related organisations

**Dods People
Public Affairs**

Get everything in one place online at

publicaffairs.dodspeople.com

For more information and details on how to get your

organisation listed, please contact Helen Haxell on

020 7593 5673 or **publicaffairs.dodspeople@dods.co.uk**

in association with

PublicAffairs
NEWS

CONTENTS

EDITOR'S PREFACE

Dods Parliamentary Companion (DPC) was established in 1832 by Charles Dod. It has retained its original character throughout the years; however, much additional information has been included particularly to the peers section explaining membership by party, and a detailed piece on political interests and countries of interest for both members of the Houses of Parliament, supplied by MPs and Peers themselves.

Since the last edition, there have been six by-elections; two hereditary peers entered the House of Lords; an array of changes in the devolved parliament and assemblies which have seen two new MLAs, one new member of the National Assembly for Wales and three new MSPs. Biographies of the new members to the House of Commons can be viewed from page 69.

The working peers who were announced by the Queen in the summer appear in this edition, and take the total membership of the House of Lords to 832; to be seen from page 598 and the Addenda.

I would like to record my appreciation for the assistance I have received from Members and Staff of both Houses and from the ministerial offices in compiling the detailed information provided in DPC.

For further information on Dods please see our online service, Dodspeople.com and our sister publication, *Vacher's Quarterly*.

H. R. Haxell, *Editor*
September 2013

FOREWORD

Over 180 years since its first publication, *Dods Parliamentary Companion* (DPC) remains a chief source of information about Westminster and Whitehall.

I know how important it is to Members of Parliament, their researchers and civil servants, yet DPC is not only a key resource to those of us within Parliament, more importantly DPC helps to open up the functioning of Government and Parliament, the people, and their responsibilities to those outside of Westminster, the millions of people who form the electorate of our country and whom those of us in Parliament seek to serve.

I wish Dods continued success.

Ed Miliband

Rt Hon Ed Miliband MP
Leader of the Labour Party

ADDENDA

WORKING PEERAGES

LABOUR

Lord Allen of Kensington CBE

ALLEN OF KENSINGTON (Life Baron), Charles Lamb Allen; cr 2013

Non-political career: Accountant, British Steel 1974-79; Deputy audit manager, Gallaghers plc 1979-82; Director, Management Services, Grandmet International Services Ltd 1982-85; Group managing director, Compass Vending Leisure Division, Granada Group 1991-92; Granada TV: Chief executive 1992-96, Chair 1996-2006; LWT: Chief executive 1994-96, Chair 1996-2006; Chief executive: Granada Group 1996-2000, ITV plc 2004-06; Chief adviser, Home Office 2006-08; Senior adviser, Goldman Sachs Equity Partners 2008-.

Other: Chair: Granada Leisure and services 1993-2000, Boxclever 1994-2000, GMTV 1996-2000, Yorkshire TV 1997-2006; Non-executive director, Tesco plc 1999-2010; Executive chair, Granada Media/Ganada plc 2000-04; Chair: British Commonwealth Games 2000-02, Anglia TV 2000-06, Meridian TV 2000-06, ITV Digital 2001-02; Vice-chair, London Olympic Bid 2004-05; Director, London Organising Committee, Olympic Games 2005-13; Chair, Global Radio Group 2007-; Non-executive director: Endemol 2008-, Virgin Media 2008-, Get AS 2009-; Executive chair, EMI Music 2010; Chair, 2 Sisters Food Group 2011-; CBE 2003; Kt 2012; FCMA.

The Lord Allen of Kensington CBE, House of Lords, London SW1A 0PW
Tel: 020 7219 5353

CONSERVATIVE

Lord Balfe

BALFE (Life Baron), Richard Andrew Balfe; cr 2013

Son of Dr Richard Balfe and Dorothy Balfe. Married Susan Jane Honeyford (2 sons 1 daughter).

Education: Brook Secondary Modern School, Sheffield; London School of Economics (BSc social policy and administration 1971).

Non-political career: Civil servant: Crown Agents for Overseas Governments 1961-65, Foreign Office 1965-67; Research officer, Finer Committee on One Parent Families 1970-73; Political secretary, Royal Arsenal Co-operative Society 1973-79; Director, Co-operative Wholesale Society 1978-80.

Other organisations: Member, European Movement; Chair, European Parliament Members Pension Fund; Director, governing board, CERN Pension Fund; Trustee, Royal Statistical Society Pension Fund; Member, European Parliament Former Members' Association; Vice-chair, Global Democracy Initiative; Fellow, Royal Statistical Society.

Lord Balfe, House of Lords, London SW1A 0PW *Tel:* 020 7219 5353

CONSERVATIVE

Lord Bamford

BAMFORD (Life Baron), Anthony Paul Bamford; cr 2013

President, Burton on Trent Conservative Association 1987-90.

Non-political career: Chair, J C Bamford Group/JCB 1975-; Director, Tarmac 1987-95.

Other: Member: President's committee, CBI 1986-88; Design Council 1987-89; President, Agricultural Society 1987-88.

The Lord Bamford, House of Lords, London SW1A 0PW Tel: 020 7219 5353

CONSERVATIVE

Baroness Goldie

GOLDIE (Life Baroness), Annabel MacNicoll Goldie; cr 2013

Scottish Conservatives: Vice-chair 1992, Deputy Chair 1995-97, 1997-98, Chair March-July 1997, Deputy Leader 1998-2005, Leader in the Scottish Parliament 2005-11.

Other assemblies: Contested West Renfrewshire constituency 1999, 2003 and 2007, and Renfrewshire North and West constituency 2011 Scottish Parliament elections. MSP for West of Scotland region 1999-2011, and for West Scotland region since 5 May 2011: Scottish Conservatives Spokesperson for: Economy, Industry and Finance 1999-2001, Enterprise and Lifelong Learning 2001-03, Justice and Home Affairs 2003-05, Home Affairs 2005-06; Leader, Conservatives in the Scottish Parliament 2005-11; Scottish Conservatives Spokesperson for: Culture and Communities 2011-13, Constitution 2013-.

The Baroness Goldie, House of Lords, London SW1A 0PW Tel: 020 7219 5353

LABOUR

Lord Haughey

HAUGHEY (Life Baron), William Haughey; cr 2013

Married Susan 1978.

Education: St Francis; Holyrood Secondary; Springburn College.

Non-political career: Apprentice, Turner Refrigeration; Founder, City Refrigeration 1985-.

Other: Director, Celtic Football Club; Founder, City Charitable Trust; OBE 2003; Kt 2012; The Loving Cup 2001; St Mungo Prize 2006; Honorary doctorate, Glasgow Caledonian University.

Lord Haughey OBE, House of Lords, London SW1A 0PW *Tel:* 020 7219 5353
Website: www.williehaughey.com

CONSERVATIVE

Baroness Hodgson of Abinger CBE

BARONESS HODGSON OF ABINGER (Life Baroness), Fiona Ferelith Hodgson; cr 2013

Married Robin Granville Hodgson MP (now Lord Hodgson of Astley Abbotts CBE) (3 sons 1 daughter and 1 twin son deceased).

Non-political career: Former civil servant, market researcher, interior designer.

Other organisations: Chair, GAPS (Gender Action in Peace and Security) advisory group; Member, Oxfam Association; Trustee, Chalker Foundation; Patron, Afghan Connection; WPD (Widows for Peace through Democracy); Delegate, Commission on the Status of Women; Member, Wellbeing general council and appeals committee, Royal College of Obstetricians and Gynaecologists; Chair, governance board, Independent Sector Complaints and Adjudication Service; Independent Doctors Federation; Member: International Social Services UK, Farm Animal Welfare Council 1989-97, Advisory Committee on Animal Feeding stuffs 2001-04. CBE 2012.

Baroness Hodgson of Abinger CBE, House of Lords, London SW1A 0PW
Tel: 020 7219 5353

CONSERVATIVE

Lord Holmes of Richmond

HOLMES OF RICHMOND (Life Baron), Christopher Holmes; cr 2013

Son of Michael and Margaret Holmes.

Education: Harry Cheshire High School, Kidderminster; King's College, Cambridge (BA 1994).

Non-political career: Paralympic swimmer; Motivational and leadership speaker 1992-; Admitted solicitor 2004; Director, Paralympic integration, 2012 Olympic and Paralympic Games organising committee 2009-13.

Other organisations: Non-executive director: Disability Rights Commission 2002-07, UK Sport 2005-; Patron, Help for Heroes 2008-.

Awards: Six gold medals at Barcelona Olympic Games 1992; Three gold medals at Atlanta Olympic Games 1996.

Lord Holmes of Richmond, House of Lords, London SW1A 0PW *Tel:* 020 7219 5353

LIBERAL DEMOCRAT

Baroness Humphreys

HUMPHREYS (Life Baroness), Christine Mary Humphreys; cr 2013

Non-political career: Teacher; Head of vocational education.

Political career: AM for North Wales region 1999-2001: Liberal Democrats Spokesperson on Economics and Environment; President, Welsh Liberal Democrats 2007-.

Baroness Humphreys, House of Lords, London SW1A 0PW *Tel:* 020 7219 5353

GREEN

Baroness Jones of Moulsecoomb

JONES OF MOULSECOOMB (Life Baroness), Jennifer Helen Jones; cr 2013

2 daughters.

Education: Westlain Grammar, Brighton; University College, London (BSc environmental archaeology 1994).

Non-political career: Housewife with some political activism 1970-90; Archaeologist/ political activist 1991-99; Financial controller for Metro (a fire safety company) 1999-2000.

Other organisations: Member: CND, Soil Association, Friends of the Earth.

Baroness Jones of Moulsecoomb, House of Lords, London, SW1A 0PW *Tel:* 020 7219 5353

LABOUR

Baroness Kennedy of Cradley

KENNEDY OF CRADLEY (Life Baroness), Alicia Pamela Kennedy; cr 2013

Non-political career: Labour Party: Strategic adviser for campaigns, Head of field operations 2005, 2010, Deputy general secretary.

The Baroness Kennedy of Cradley, House of Lords, London, SW1A 0PW *Tel:* 020 7219 5353

CONSERVATIVE

Lord Leigh of Hurley

LEIGH OF HURLEY (Life Baron), Howard Darryl Leigh; cr 2013

Education: Economics

Non-Politcal career: Merchant banker; Chartered accountant, Deloitte Haskins & Sells; Cavendish Corporate Finance: Founder 1988, Senior partner.

Other organisations: Chair, Faculty of Corporate Finance, Institute of Chartered Accountants.

The Lord Leigh of Hurley, House of Lords, London SW1A 0PW *Tel:* 020 7219 5353

LIBERAL DEMOCRAT

Lord Palumbo of Southwark

PALUMBO OF SOUTHWARK (Life Baron), James Rudolph Palumbo; cr 2013

Son of Peter Garth Palumbo (later Lord Palumbo) and Denia Wigram. Eton College; Worcester College, Oxford.

Non-political career: Property developer; Merchant banker; Founder, Ministry of Sound 1997-

The Lord Palumbo of Southwark, House of Lords, London SW1A 0PW Tel: 020 7219 5353

LIBERAL DEMOCRAT

Lord Purvis of Tweed

PURVIS OF TWEED (Life Baron), Jeremy Purvis; cr 2013

Born 15 January 1974; Son of George Purvis, ambulance technician, and Eileen Purvis; Single.

Education: Berwick-upon-Tweed High School; Brunel University (BSc politics and modern history 1996).

Non-political career: Company director. Research assistant to Sir David Steel MP, House of Commons 1993; Parliamentary assistant: Liberal International 1994, ELDR Group, European Parliament 1995; Personal assistant to Sir David Steel MP (later Lord Steel of Aikwood) 1996-98; Director, McEwan Purvis 2001-03; Policy and strategy adviser to Willie Rennie as Leader, Scottish Liberal Democrat; Head, Devo Plus.

Political career: MSP for Tweeddale, Ettrick and Lauderdale constituency 2003-11: Scottish Liberal Democrat: Spokesperson for: Finance 2003-05, Justice 2005-07; Member, Scottish Parliament Arts Advisory Group 2007-11; Scottish Liberal Democrat: Shadow Cabinet Secretary for Education and Lifelong Learning 2007-08, Shadow Minister for Children and Early Years 2007-08, Spokesperson on Economy and Finance 2008-11.

Other: Member, Amnesty International; Scottish Council, European Movement; Selkirk Merchant Company; Rowan Tree Theatre Company.

Recreations: Classic cars, reading, painting. Member, Jensen Owners.

The Lord Purvis of Tweed, House of Lords, London SW1A 0PW *Tel:* 020 7219 5353

LIBERAL DEMOCRAT

Baroness Suttie

BARONESS SUTTIE (Life Baroness), Alison Mary Suttie; cr 2013

Education: Heriot-Watt University (BA French and Russian 1990).

Non-political career: Lecturer 1990-91; Liberal Democrat adviser, House of Commons 1991-96; Adviser, EPLD group, European Parliament; Office of Pat Cox as President of the European Parliament: Press attaché and adviser 1999-2001, Press secretary 2002-04; Head of office to leaders of the Liberal Democrats Sir Menzies Campbell and Nick Clegg 2006-10; Deputy chief of staff, Office of Nick Clegg as the Deputy Prime Minister 2010-11; Consultant 2012-.

Baroness Suttie, House of Lords, London, SW1A 0PW *Tel:* 020 7219 5353

LIBERAL DEMOCRAT

Lord Verjee CBE

VERJEE (Life Baron), Rumi Verjee; cr 2013

Education: Downing College, Cambridge (law).

Non-Political career: Founder, Domino's Pizza UK; Chair, Thomas Goode and Co.

Other organisations: Chair: Brompton Capital Ltd, Ipanema Properties; Member: World Presidents' Organization, Global Leadership Foundation, Advisory board, British Olympic Association. Fellow, Downing College, Cambridge.

CBE 2009.

The Lord Verjee CBE, House of Lords, London, SW1A 0PW *Tel:* 020 7219 5353

CONSERVATIVE

Baroness Williams of Trafford

WILLIAMS OF TRAFFORD (Life Baroness), Susan Frances Maria Williams; cr 2013

Married Alex Williams 2005 (1 son 2 daughters).

Education: La Sagesse High School, Jesmond; Huddersfield Polytechnic (BSc applied nutrition 1989).

Non-political career: Nutritionist, Action and Research into Multiple Sclerosis (ARMS) 1992-2002; Leadership consultant, Local Government Improvement and Development 2006-12; Director, North West Rail Campaign 2011-; Executive director, Atlantic Gateway 2012-.

Other organisations: Board member, Central Salford Urban Regeneration Company 2008-10; Chair (North West), Heritage Lottery Fund.

Baroness Williams of Trafford, House of Lords, London, SW1A 0PW *Tel:* 020 7219 5353

Review of the UK Parliaments and Assemblies 2012–13

The 2012-13 season was marked by classic mid-term signs of 'wait and see' politics across the UK and at national and regional levels. In former electoral cycles in the days of two-party government and opposition, the autumn of 2013 would have brought endless speculation about the date of a likely spring 2014 general election, but the Fixed Term Parliament Act takes the decision out of the Prime Minister's hands, which means that the election will almost certainly wait until May 2015. In Scotland, there remains a year to go until the September 2014 independence referendum with almost all local political activity being viewed through that particular prism. And, if it really is "the economy, stupid" which decides who governs, then the Conservative-Liberal Democrat Coalition's long waiting game for signs of the green shoots of recovery from the worldwide crash of 2008 remains the central theme defining national political action. The year to autumn 2013 saw continued sparring on the UK's relationship with the European Union, with the Conservative Party in particular restive as the UK Independence Party (UKIP) made significant electoral gains at local council level. Constitutional reform, however, appeared to have stalled, with the House of Lords remaining a significant unresolved issue and attempts to change the composition of the Commons also in tatters.

HOUSE OF COMMONS

In the House of Commons, the Coalition Government continued to operate without much question of any early dissolution of the bond between David Cameron's Conservative Party and Nick Clegg's Liberal Democrats. In many ways, this was a curious feature of the period, at least so far as the usual historical comparators are concerned. Both parties faced significant splits within their ranks, formerly a sign that a governing party would not long endure. For the Conservatives, Europe remains a toxic issue, with Same-Sex Marriage another significant source of discomfort. For the Liberal Democrats, support for Chancellor George Osborne's austerity economic policy remains a difficult line to tread, and government policy on immigration has also been a source of discontent. The continued flat-line in the polls with only 20 or so months to a general election also preys on Liberal Democrat minds, and the announcement by former schools minister Sarah Teather, until quite recently one of the party's rising younger stars, that she would stand down at the 2015 election seemed to encapsulate simultaneously concerns about where the Party is going in policy terms and how well it is likely to fare in 2015.

To cap it all, the Prime Minister, David Cameron, recalled Parliament early in September to vote on whether military action against Syria should be joined. The vote was lost (more of which later), the first time a government seeking endorsement of military action by the House had lost a vote since Lord North during the American War of Independence. Lord North's government promptly collapsed to usher in the long hegemony of Pitt the Younger; the Coalition, however, faced not even the whisper of a threat of a vote of no confidence (presumably because it would quite easily have won one). England, said Disraeli, does not love Coalitions, but it does appear willing to tolerate the present one until its expected end date.

ECONOMY

The economy continues to determine much government policy, with the talk continuing to emphasise tight belts, restraint and austerity. Chancellor Osborne's March Budget was very much a 'steady as she goes' vessel, with minor changes in taxes and pensions, some boosts for housebuilding and purchasing and for small- and medium-sized businesses, and cash cuts for almost all government departments, some of them facing significant real-terms and actual cash cuts. By the autumn, some signs of recovery were being alleged: unemployment was falling month on month and inflation remained comparatively low, for example. The new Governor of the Bank of England, Mark Carney, announced that interest rates would remain at historically low levels until unemployment fell (although the Bank's primary target remains control of inflation, which could require interest rate rises in the event of a spike driven by, say, a housing or property boom). Low rates are intended to spur both business investment and personal spending, although they are simultaneously discouraging saving.

EUROPE

The UK's relationship with the EU also remains an overarching political theme, with the Conservative Party in particular restive on the subject. Between autumn 2012 and autumn 2013, Cameron was forced to pledge to his backbenchers that a referendum on continued membership would be held during the post-2015 Parliament if he remained Prime Minister. This was not enough; a backbench Private Member's Bill, sponsored by James Wharton MP, but with the tacit support of at least the Conservative portion of the Government, has been launched in the Commons and will go into its Committee Stage in the autumn. It would give a legal guarantee that a referendum will be held during the Parliament after the next. Underlying the continued unrest are the repeatedly strong polling figures being achieved by UKIP and its ebullient leader Nigel Farage, with some polling suggesting that UKIP advances in Tory marginal seats could, even if they don't result in UKIP Westminster MPs, mean Labour slipping through the middle to take such seats and win a Commons majority. Almost inevitably, discussion of Europe also means discussion of immigration policy, with the fact that EU citizens, from the other 27 EU countries, are free to travel and work in the UK a particular bone of contention. Promises to 'tighten' border controls continue to be made, and a short-term pilot project sending out vans in a few parts of England bearing posters asking people to 'shop' illegal immigrants caused considerable controversy.

QUEEN'S SPEECH 2013

The Queen's Speech which opened the 2013-14 Parliamentary Session in May contained 15 new Bills, not all of them capable of being described as major or obvious vote-winners. The Government appeared broadly to promise more of the same, rather than a substantial eye-catching, age-defining piece of legislative change of the sort that might be expected next year in a pre-election period. There will be a Bill to restrict immigration, in an effort to appease some backbench opinion and to staunch the rising tide of UKIP. Deportation of people without a legal right to stay in the UK is expected to become easier, and businesses, landlords and the NHS are all being given new responsibility to check the status of employees, tenants and patients, not entirely to their pleasure.

Crime and anti-social behaviour are also the targets of other measures, with, among other things, forced marriage becoming a criminal offence but having your dog bite a burglar in your home will not result in your prosecution. Changes are proposed to the way the police are paid, and there are also plans to reduce probation service budgets. Post-Queen's Speech plans also emerged to privatise the Royal Mail, a challenge previously shirked even by Margaret Thatcher.

Her Majesty also announced plans to introduce a new, single-tier pension system and to increase the retirement age to 67 from 2026, eight years earlier than previously planned. Retirees will also face a new cap on the cost of social care provided for them, with protections also introduced for those whose care provider goes out of business (though this one applies only in England, because devolutionary arrangements of similar though differing sorts have already been made in Wales and Scotland).

HS2

Although some of these measures are likely to cause disagreement across the floor of both Houses, there are others likely to bring division within the ranks of, in particular, the Coalition Government parties. The High Speed Rail (Preparation) Bill is likely to be opposed by MPs whose constituencies are earmarked for new rail lines between London, Manchester and Leeds, as well as environmental campaigners. A Joint Committee is likely to hear petitions from those whose land will need to be purchased or otherwise affected if the high-speech scheme is to go ahead, linking London more quickly to other major English cities. The cost of the scheme is also likely to be the cause of much argument, with initial high estimates already on the rise. Simon Burns a Transport Minister with responsibility for HS2 resigned to run for the Deputy Speaker position vacated by Nigel Evans.

CONSTITUTIONAL REFORM AGENDA STALLED

The Deputy Prime Minister's primary responsibility is for a programme of constitutional reform, almost all of which appears to be on hold. The Liberal Democrats were sorely disappointed in 2011 by the public's failure to vote in favour of a new Alternative Vote system for Westminster elections. This year, politics has taken Lords Reform off the table yet again, and the composition of the House of Commons won't be changing this side of 2020. Few of the reforms heralded in the Coalition agreement have in fact come to pass. The non-appearance in the Queen's Speech of proposals to regulate political lobbying was hastily reversed shortly before the summer recess after a set of mini-lobbying scandals involving MPs who appeared to be receiving payments for asking questions or briefing industry, and a Lobbying Bill will be the first business of the House of Commons in October 2013 after its conference recess. However, plans to enable voters to sack miscreant MPs, popular after the 2008-09 expenses scandal, are also in the long grass. The tide of reform expected in the wake of the expenses scandal appears to have ebbed: the changes made in the appointment of chairs and members of select committees, and in how time for debate is allocated in the Chamber of the Commons appear to be it for this Parliament.

SELECT COMMITTEE WORK

That said, the revitalised Select Committee system of parliamentary scrutiny of governmental policy, expenditure and legislation continues to get good press. Elected chairs of committees such as Labour's Margaret Hodge of the Public Accounts Committee and the Conservative Andrew Tyrie of the Treasury Committee are seen as doughty interrogators without fear or favour, and Hodge, in particular, has become the scourge, among others, of high-paid managers at the BBC. The effectiveness of these Committees, most of which have the job of monitoring a single government department and commenting on its policy proposals, was debated as the Liaison Committee (a super-Committee containing the Chairs of all the major select committees) pressed the Government to give Parliament more power and influence over, for example, appointments to political or diplomatic posts. The present Parliament's Committees are chaired by and filled by MPs elected by all other MPs rather than appointed by Government Whips, as they used to be. The growing confidence they have demonstrated, and new forms of inquiry such as an extremely detailed examination of banking standards continue to raise questions about what powers and sanctions they have to make witnesses tell them the truth, and, on the other side, whether their staffing and personal inquisitive styles are sufficiently well developed to do the job. The new prominence of the Committees has, however, begun to fulfil the aim of providing parliamentarians an alternative career structure to ministerial office, and also provides some explanation of what Members are doing when not sitting on the green benches of the Commons Chamber.

The Liaison Committee, which brings together the Chairs of all the other committees to provide a strategic overview of the system, also managed a clear-eyed report on both the high-profile successes (principally over phone hacking) of the past two years, and of the areas where the committee system still needs strengthening. In particular, it was self-critical about the tendency of some MPs to seek to score partisan points rather than conduct forensic scrutiny of witnesses and about the shortcomings in questioning that have sometimes been apparent as MPs have leapt from one subject to another without following up answers fully. In a more general sense, the Committees tendency to report and make recommendations but rarely to follow them up was also pinpointed as a weakness. The Committee did, however, rule out the possibility of hiring lawyers rather than letting MPs themselves ask the questions, as happens with the US congressional committees generally held up to be more effective. The argument that MPs as the democratically elected representatives might be better placed still holds.

Questions of the effectiveness of parliamentary scrutiny were also raised in a thoughtful paper co-authored by the former clerk of the House of Commons and a senior lawyer. Sir Malcolm Jack and Richard Gordon QC raised concern that the modern Parliament faces more challenge to its authority from Courts dealing with modern EU legislation and laws such as the Human Rights Act than was the case when its powers and privileges were originally developed to deal with an over-mighty monarchy. Whether a full-scale Act setting out the reach and extent of parliamentary powers and privileges is necessary, particularly in the absence of a written UK constitution, remains under discussion. A Joint Committee of the Lords and Commons has also set out a series of changes intended to strengthen Committees and make Parliament's powers of summons and punishment clearer. What action may flow remains to become clear.

Other elements of parliamentary scrutiny have won less recent favour, notably from the Joint Committee on Human Rights, on which Lords and Commons MPs were united in criticising the Government for pushing through too much emergency legislation without sufficient time for proper scrutiny or debate.

In particular, the 2012-13 Session saw four Bills become law as emergency measures on a shortened parliamentary timetable, limiting the time for discussion, including new laws on police complaints and conduct and the succession to the Crown. The new Lobbying Bill is a further such example, given a Second Reading only a few days after publication, given three days (in which substantial amendment proved necessary) during the September sittings, and given only two more days to complete its passage in October.

INTELLIGENCE AND SECURITY COMMITTEE

Parliamentary scrutiny of the nation's security forces took a small forward step, with the Intelligence and Security Committee becoming a parliamentary rather than a government committee for the first time. It remains significantly different from other Select Committees – its chair is not elected by MPs, for example, but chosen by No. 10 (and is currently the unimpeachable Sir Malcolm Rifkind, the former Foreign Secretary).

EQUAL MARRIAGE

Homsexuality was decriminalised by the Wilson government in 1967 (at least, in England and Wales; Scotland and Northern Ireland required later, localised legislation), an Act that turned out to be one of that Government's lasting legacies. When the history of the Cameron Government comes to be written it may well be that immediate furores over Europe, immigration policy and the like will seem less long-lastingly important than the passing of the Same-Sex Marriage Bill, which obtained its Royal Assent shortly before the summer recess. In the face of opposition from substantial sections of his own party, as well as from sections of the various Churches, Cameron pressed an Act which may gain him little immediate tactical political advantage for the simple reason that he thought it the right thing to do in the 21st Century (with the possible short-term advantage that younger voters, by which we now appear to mean anyone under 50, will be less likely to think of the Conservatives as the 'nasty' Party). The outrage of opponents, widely reported as being likely to destroy Cameron's leadership of his party, gradually wilted as it became clear that he had no intention of stepping back or diluting his proposal to allow gay and lesbian partners to marry. And, in spite of vocal protests outside the Houses of Parliament as the Bill made its way through both the Houses of Commons and the Lords, there were substantial eventual majorities in both Houses in favour of the Bill.

SUCCESSION TO THE THRONE

The role of royalty was also, rarely, discussed in the Commons as the Succession to the Crown Act enabled the ascent to the Throne of a first-born daughter. The concepts of equality and monarchy have not always sat easily together, but any male born after 28 October 2011 will no longer precede an older sister. The subsequent birth of Prince George, as first-born of the Duke and the Duchess of Cambridge provided a third male heir in line for the time being, though. A curious further refinement introduced by the Bill is that the Monarch will be able in future to object to the marriages of only the first six persons in line to the throne. The Princess Eugenie may therefore thank Prince George for being now able to marry whomever she likes.

LEVESON

Lord Justice Leveson is due to give evidence in October 2013 to the Culture, Media and Sport Committee while the final result of his long inquiry into press and media ethics remains to become clear. The main political parties believed that they had struck a deal to set up a royal charter to introduce a new regulatory system for the media, less reliant on their policing themselves. But the newspaper industry has drawn up an alternative charter which is also being considered by the Privy Council. The Council will make the final decision, and in spite of opposition from most critics of media conduct, and particularly the Hacked Off group fronted by the actor Hugh Grant; which led the most high-profile opposition once media activities including the phone-hacking of both celebrities and 'ordinary' people were uncovered.

CABINET RESHUFFLE

David Cameron's long-awaited first major Cabinet reshuffle came in September 2012 (and another minor reshuffle of junior ministerial ranks was expected at time of going to press in October 2013). Mr Cameron's 2012 shift-around was slightly more sweeping than had been anticipated. He had committed himself to leaving Ministers in post long enough to get to grips with their briefs and control over their Departments. With the exception of some forced departures – Liam Fox, David Laws and Chris Huhne – that aim was achieved for nearly half the Parliament, and the suspicion is that the Government will seek to make it to the 2015 election without going through another substantial blood-letting.

These things rarely pass without trouble, though, and Mr Cameron's first reshuffle was no exception. The departures and reassignments of Cheryl Gillan (sacked as Welsh Secretary), Caroline Spelman (sacked Environment Secretary), Justine Greening (moved, apparently unwillingly, from Transport to International Development) and Baroness Warsi (moved, very publicly unwillingly, from Party Chair to a non-Cabinet role at the Foreign Office) reopened old complaints about the Coalition's absence of women at the top table. The promotions into Cabinet of Theresa Villiers (Northern Ireland) and Maria Miller (Culture) meant only four of the 23 Cabinet rank Ministers were female.

The Government was also open, in senior and junior ranks, to a suggestion, accidental or otherwise, that the products of public schools had done better than their less privileged counterparts. Jeremy Hunt, having survived numerous calls for his head over his connections with the Murdoch empire, found himself promoted to Health Secretary to everyone's surprise but his own, with Andrew Lansley demoted from Health to the administrative post of Leader of the House of Commons. Patrick McLoughlin moved from Chief Whip to Transport, with Owen Paterson switching from Northern Ireland to Environment. As well as Theresa Villiers and Maria Miller, there were three new male faces in the Cabinet, Chris Grayling as Justice Secretary, Grant Shapps as new Party Chair, and David Jones at the Wales Office. The 2013 reshuffle was widely expected to bring forward more women from the 2010 intake into junior ministerial posts.

Anticipating a reshuffle, some left before being pushed and/or to pursue other projects. Ministers Chloe Smith and John Randall both left their jobs before Cameron announced his new ministerial teams.

The Secretary of State for Scotland, Michael Moore, was replaced by his Liberal Democrat colleague Alistair Carmichael. There were a vast amount of newly appointed Parliamentary Under-Secretary of States, such as Shailesh Vara to Justice. Esther McVey was promoted at Work and Pensions and Liberal Democrat Baroness Kramer joined Transport as a Minister.

Ed Miliband updated his shadow ministerial team too with promotions for Rachel Reeves and Tristram Hunt at Work and Pensions and Education respectively.

WHIPPING AND REBELLION

The reshuffle briefly installed Andrew Mitchell as Government Chief Whip, but he had to be replaced after a few weeks due to a contested altercation with a policeman about his bicycle. The chalice he had to surrender is unquestionably a poisoned one, though, with his successor Sir George Young having had an unenviable task: the younger, sharper-elbowed, post-expenses Conservative MPs who entered the House in 2010 have proved distinctly less biddable than previous generations, and, having kicked House of Lords reform into the long grass before the summer, inflicted another embarrassment on their frontbench by voting for a reduction in the European Union budget. Although that vote was not legally binding, it was one of many signs to the Conservative part of the Coalition that the troops are not willing simply to walk through the Lobbies. Various reasons have been proposed – the fact of a narrowish majority in Coalition times; the exasperation of 2010 Tories at seeing ministerial jobs go to Liberal Democrats; the comparative absence among new Tories of 'professional' political backgrounds rather than groundings in business, law, or other careers; and a deep irritation with the older Members who were around and benefited from the discredited expenses regime. Whatever the cause, the message is clear: the Whips don't have quite the power they used to have to control the backbenches.

COMINGS AND GOINGS

There was a time when by-elections were comparatively rare, resulting largely from the death of a sitting MP; the present Parliament, though, is averaging nearly one every two months. Among the highest profile MPs leaving the House for various reasons have been Chris Huhne (prison), David Miliband (charitable work in the US), Louise Mensch (family life in the US) and Martin McGuinness (an end of double-hatting by Sinn Féin). The deaths of Croydon's Malcolm Wicks and Middlesbrough's

Sir Stuart Bell also created vacancies, and the decision of former First Minister of Wales Alun Michael and former Chair of the Parliamentary Labour Party Tony Lloyd to quit Parliament in order to stand (successfully) for the newly-created posts of Police and Crime Commissioner in their respective areas left seats to be filled in Cardiff and Manchester.

The Liberal Democrats had a glimmer of good news in holding on in Eastleigh, the seat vacated by Huhne when he pleaded guilty to perverting the course of justice by asking his wife to take speeding points for him more than a decade ago. UKIP pushed close with an unexpectedly strong second place, but the Liberal Democrats continue to hope that this is a signal that their dismal national polling ratings might be bucked in constituencies where they have bedded in over the past two decades.

In Mid Ulster, no-one was much surprised that Francie Molloy replaced the departing Martin McGuinness in a long-term Sinn Féin stronghold. And in South Shields, which the former Foreign Secretary and brother of the Labour leader, David Miliband forsook to move to New York to run the charity International Rescue, Labour were safe victors. Once again, though UKIP ran into second place, demonstrating that they can do well not only in seats in the South of England and those where Conservatives are the incumbents. South Shields also brought a glimmer of bad news for the Liberal Democrats who, albeit never expecting to do well in a Labour heartland, none the less managed to finish seventh.

A substantial number of sitting MPs are likely to stand down at the next election, and several have already made their intentions clear. Patrick Mercer, of Newark, had already announced that he would go before embarrassing newspaper stories appeared to suggest he was receiving payments for asking questions about Fiji. Eric Joyce, the former Labour MP for Falkirk will also go; Joyce was arrested in the Commons after a late-night incident at the Sports and Social Club bar. Joyce's departure also began a chain of events that left Labour leader Ed Miliband in a stand-off with the Unite Union, accused for a time of trying to rig selection of a candidate to replace Joyce in a Mid Scotland seat that Labour will lose only when pigs sprout wings.

Otherwise, most of those departing will be long-serving MPs reaching the usual retirement years – former Cabinet Ministers Bob Ainsworth and John Denham, the only double-Oscar-winning actress in British history, Glenda Jackson, and the Chair of the Justice and Liaison Committees, Sir Alan Beith, among them. Dawn Primarolo, a long-serving Labour Minister who has distinguished herself as a Deputy Speaker since 2010 will also leave.

Meantime a number of less voluntarily departed MPs will attempt to return to the House after losing their seats last time round. Most were new Labour MPs, with Mike O'Brien, Sally Keeble and Joan Ryan among former Ministers trying to get back in. Chances are that their expenses records will play some role in their opponents election planning and campaigns in what are often marginal seats, such as Hendon and Bedford.

BARONESS THATCHER OF KESTEVEN

The death of Margaret Thatcher, the UK's only female Prime Minister, at the age of 87 was announced in April. Some 23 years having passed since she was Prime Minister, she was accorded a funeral with full military honours, and a procession from Westminster to St Paul's Cathedral. There were some outbreaks of protest and celebration around parts of the country where her name remains tantamount to a swearword, and there were some effusions in the other direction from those for whom her status is unquestionably mythological. But by and large, the passage of time and her increasing frailty meant that her passing prompted some sober and well-perspectived reflection on her 11 years in office, from the strike-riven 1979 through to the Falklands War and Miner's Strike, past the privatisation of a substantial number of former national assets and financial drains, and almost to the end of the Cold War with the fall of the Berlin Wall in 1989, before her own defenestration by her senior colleagues in 1990.

LAY MEMBERS OF STANDARDS COMMITTEE

A little-noticed innovation which may have wide long-term consequences was the introduction to a House of Commons Committee some new members who had not been elected to the House. The Commons has long claimed the 'privilege' of regulating its own affairs, and the opening up of some 'lay' places on the Committee on Standards opens a small chink in that wall. What would once have been seen as the thin end of an unelected wedge passed with little comment outside Westminster itself, perhaps because, after the expenses events of 2009, most of the public would trust almost anyone more than an elected representative.

The Committee, set up to regulate MPs' behaviour and ensure that their code of conduct is adhered to, has had three non-MPs added to it as 'lay' Members. The idea is that a view from beyond the Westminster village will inform consideration of investigations into MPs' breach of standards. The lay members will participate fully in evidence taking and the consideration of draft reports, although they will not be able formally to move amendments or take part in any votes. At least one of them will have to be present when the Committee does any business.

PAYING MPS

Whilst it remains clear from the comments section of any daily newspaper that a substantial majority of the nation's voters would happily see MPs paid no salary at all and required to sleep on park benches, the honourable Members themselves continue to feel under-valued. The Independent Parliamentary Standards Authority (IPSA)'s consultation on what MPs ought to be paid found that more than two-thirds thought a substantial uprating on their £65,713 basic pay was required, with Conservative MPs on average identifying £96,740, Liberal Democrats £78,361 and Labour MPs £77,322 as appropriate figures.

Following the 2009 expenses scandal, MPs were forced to accept that they could no longer decide their own pay and conditions and set up IPSA to sup from that particular poisoned chalice. The system might not be as generous as it used to be, but at least they could console themselves that someone else would get the blame for any pay rise. Or so they thought. When IPSA announced in July that it wanted to give MPs a rise of about 11 per cent from the current £66,000 to £74,000 from 2015, all hell predictably broke loose. Once the dust had settled, though, it became clear that IPSA was offering a package which would reduce MP benefits in other areas – free meals if the Commons sits later than 7.30, for example, and reductions in or the abolition of 'resettlement' payments when they lose or quit their seats. IPSA is also playing the long game: one of the reasons the still toxic expenses problems happened was that MPs kept their headline pay artificially low by extending their income through creative expenses. Making a substantial one-off increase to a salary that fits the job might just remove the sting eventually, with future rises more in line with general pay increases. The 232 new MPs who entered the Commons in 2010 will be particularly glad not to continue to suffer the flak for a system they had no part in creating. IPSA is consulting on its new plan, and there will no doubt be another negative publicity hit for MPs to take before the question is settled.

What goes into making the ideal MP remains a moot point, too – among others, Rushanara Ali has spoken recently of the continued under-representation of both women and ethnic communities, Glenda Jackson suggested her parliamentary colleagues fall a long way short of the professional standards and dedication her former theatrical and cinematic co-stars take for granted, and Gloria de Piero, former TV journalist turned MP, bravely toured the country trying to find out why no-one likes or trust their politicians.

HOUSE OF LORDS

Reform of the House of Lords, reducing its size and introducing an element, at least, of election to one of the few entirely unelected legislative Chambers in the democratic world, was intended to be one of the defining themes of 2012-13, but Conservative opposition to plans laid by Deputy Prime Minister Nick Clegg, abetted by Labour willingness to exploit cracks in the Coalition, has once again taken the Upper House back to the future. Mr Clegg's hopes to complete the project begun in the era of Lloyd George is entirely dead for this Parliament, but there are increasing concerns about the operations of the Lords.

The Speaker of the House of Lords herself expressed that concern in *The Times* in an article suggesting that her House was "in danger of becoming a place of ridicule". Baroness D'Souza noted that "the Lords has an image problem at the best of times, being frequently portrayed as nothing but a chamber of ermine-clad, elderly political cronies". But D'Souza is also concerned that the ever-growing number of Peers being squeezed into the Lords is making its consensual procedures unworkable. There were then around 810 members of the Lords, and another 30 were added soon after she published.

The reason for new appointments is the need to balance the political composition of the Upper House after a long period of Labour Government, but the difficulty is that that rebalancing act can only be achieved by new creations as Life Peers who cannot be removed from the House no matter what reason there might be for ending their membership. There is, indeed, some disquiet that Lords who served prison sentences for expenses offences, are back in harness and again claiming the daily allowance of around £300. There is also some smirking at the Coalition pledge to reduce the cost of Westminster, a promise hard to keep when the plan to reduce the number of MPs from 650 to 600 has fallen by the wayside and the number of Lords keeps on leaping upwards. Something will eventually have to give – there simply isn't office space for the current peerage within the 19th-century Palace of Westminster and its surrounding parliamentary buildings, and the pressure for more staff for them is another headache.

With the Commons also not reducing its number as planned, that gives the UK just over 1,500 national legislators. The United States, with more than four times the population, struggles by with 535 between its Senate and House of Representatives; the Indian Parliament manages with 790 (representing a population about 20 times greater than the UK). It is probably worth noting in passing that both the Conservative and Liberal Democrat manifestos of 2010 promised cuts in the number of UK parliamentarians.

The Lords, unlike the Commons, regulates its own proceedings, rather than putting in the hand of the Speaker the power to decide who speaks or which amendments are debated, for example. The difficulty appears to be that some of the current crop of Peers would rather regulate themselves differently from how their colleagues – more courteous or more hidebound, according to taste – comported themselves in times past. The Lord Speaker identified the difficulty that daily attendance averages 479 (which rather avoids the question of what the other 350 or so are doing), leaving simply not enough time for all of them to speak as frequently as they would now wish. The absence of control from the chair or timetabling or any of the other procedural wheezes the Commons has to speed its business through means that the progress of legislation and other business in the Lords is now as painstakingly slow as Lords reform itself. The fact that Lords can't retire once appointed means that numbers will only continue to grow as an ageing population collides with Prime Ministers eager to offer patronage while also upping the number on their side of the political divide.

It is, of course, also worth remembering that the Lords has been much larger: in the days when all hereditary Peers had seats as of right, the House numbered something over 1,300. But those were the days when a chap behaved as a chap ought to, and most of them didn't turn up. The hereditaries have not, of course, quite gone from the Lords – 92 yet remain as part of the unfinished business of Tony Blair's reform of the place.

February saw one of the more peculiar rituals required by this remaining presence, a very particularly British form of 'democracy'. The death in 2012 of Earl Ferrers created a gap among the 92. As he was a Conservative Peer, his 48 remaining colleagues became the electorate to choose a replacement from among the dispossessed peerage. Some 27 candidates stood, among them the former Conservative MP and Agriculture Secretary Douglas Hogg, once famous for claiming expenses for cleaning his moat, now resplendent inheritor of the title Lord Hailsham. His Lordship was to be disappointed: Viscount Ridley, with no fewer than 24 votes in his credit column, emerged victorious in this most ruritanian of electoral battles – there is, incidentally, one other hereditary peer in the legislature, of course, although the Viscount Thurso has the unique distinction of having actually gone to the trouble of being elected there by more than his immediate colleagues, as the MP for Caithness, Sutherland and Easter Ross, John Thurso.)

The Lords was expected to provide more of a block to Same-Sex Marriage legislation than eventually turned out to be the case. Otherwise, it quietly got on with its main job of revising legislation throughout the 2012-13 season, with comparatively little ping-ponging of Bills back and forth between the two Houses.

RESTORATION AND RENEWAL

London Bridge may not be falling down, but the Palace of Westminster a little upstream may be. The Commission, the six senior MPs who act as the effective Board for Parliament, published a report in early November on the "restoration and renewal" of the 170-year-old building outlining the need for some pretty drastic and massively expensive repair work over the coming decade or two. The starkest conclusion was that if the world-famous building were not an internationally recognised symbol of the UK and of democracy, and were not a grade 1 listed building, its owners would probably pull it down and start again. Given that that is not a feasible or desirable option, the two Houses of Parliament will instead have to decide whether to move out completely to an alternative location while essential works are done, try to move out one House, probably the Lords, while works are done on half the building, or try to do the works over a 25-plus year period while keeping Parliament at work there. It will likely be a couple of years before a final decision is taken, but the catalogue of water damage, ill-documented repair work, possible mechanical and electrical failure and considerable fire risk mean that the Palace will need to undergo a major overhaul.

ELIZABETH AND BEN

Meantime, though, one of the most famous parts of the building got a new name. The Queen's Jubilee was officially marked, once again, at Westminster in September, when the Clock Tower was officially renamed the Elizabeth Tower in brief ceremony not attended by Her Majesty herself. The new name mirrors the nomenclature of the tower at the other end of the Palace, titled the Victoria Tower in commemoration of an earlier Jubilee, but will still probably be better known to the world at large by the name of the Clock Bell it houses, Big Ben.

SCOTLAND

North of the border with England, the question of Scotland's future within the United Kingdom or otherwise is the defining issue now and for at least a year to come. Scotland will go to the polls on 18 September 2014 to decide whether it wishes to return to the independence subsumed into the Union back in 1707, when Queen Anne sat on the two thrones and the Stuarts languished in France, dreaming of a return twice thereafter attempted and failed by the old and the young pretenders.

Scottish newspapers and other media are already daily filled with stories and comment about what independence would mean. The almost complete absence of interest to be found in the newspapers and media South of the Tweed might indicate that a certain mental independence has already been achieved on both sides. To date, the No campaign has had the best of it, with considerable assistance from No. 10 Downing Street and the UK Treasury from which have emanated a stream of stories, including whether a free Scotland could continue to use Sterling as its currency: the threat of Scots being forced into the tottering Euro is considered something of an Ace by the No campaign. The Westminster Government also took the unusual step of publishing a lengthy legal opinion on how Scotland and the remains of the UK would look if the Union were dissolved, and it concluded that England, Wales and Northern Ireland would, in effect, continue as the existing United Kingdom, with all the treaty obligations and memberships of the EU and UN Security Council that that implies, while Scotland would be a brand new legal entity and would have to negotiate brand new rights and obligations internationally.

No one ever made money under-estimating Scotland's First Minister Alex Salmond or his deputy Nicola Sturgeon, though, and the SNP, with a year to go, has kept its powder comparatively dry. 2014 will be the 600th anniversary of the Battle of Bannockburn (2013's anniversary of Flodden has played less part in Scotland's consciousness), and Alex Salmond will be hoping, among other things, that the hoped-for birth of a panda in Edinburgh Zoo and a successful Commonwealth Games in Glasgow will show a confident, internationalist Scotland ready to play its part in the world on its own two feet. Salmond is also keen to hold a TV debate with the Prime Minister, presumably on the basis that the sight and sound of David Cameron talking about Scotland is likely worth its weight in Yes votes.

The Electoral Commission has ruled that a simple, six-word question would be the best option for the vote. The Scottish electorate will be asked "Should Scotland be an independent country?". The SNP, in power at present in Edinburgh, had suggested the slightly less straightforward "Do you agree that

Scotland should be independent?", a question which, as Latin masters everywhere would recognise, rather invites the answer yes. Polling so far suggests that Scotland will vote no, though, including among the 16- and 17-year-olds to whom the vote has been extended for the event.

So long as Scotland does remain within the Union, however devolved, the long-thorny West Lothian question remains to be answered. The McKay Commission, set up to consider how Westminster should deal with legislation that affects England alone, produced a suggestion that Scottish MPs should no longer be able to vote on such Bills. Why, after all, should the Member for West Lothian be able to influence policy in West Bromwich when the reverse does not apply to his English counterpart. This has, in turn, again raised the question whether Scotland (and, indeed, Wales and Northern Ireland) are over-represented at Westminster when most legislation affecting the three jurisdictions is dealt with in Edinburgh, Cardiff and Belfast. Which has in turn prompted the reply that the Westminster Parliament is, after all, the UK Parliament, not the English one, and that reducing the number of MPs from the other Nation, the Principality and the Province would leave them somewhat under-represented on UK economic or foreign policy. The constitutional difficulty of mixing home rule for individual parts of the UK with a national parliament continues to perplex the finest procedural minds.

Scotland also continues to make its own legislation. The Forth Road Bridge Bill, making provision to maintain the toll bridge between Edinburgh and Fife, became the 200th Act to be passed by the Scottish Parliament since its resumption in 1999. The Bill made it on to the statute book in late June when the Great Seal of Scotland was applied after the Queen had given her Assent, another way in which legislation made in Scotland differs from the UK variety, where it is Her Majesty who has the final word.

NORTHERN IRELAND
There was but one major Bill for Northern Ireland alone in the Queen's Speech, making technical changes to how institutions, including the Assembly operate. Double-hatting, the practice by which members of the Assembly were also able to sit in other Parliaments, is to be ended formally (it has more or less ended voluntarily over the past few years). The days when, for example, Ian Paisley snr (now Lord Bannside) could sit in Stormont, Westminster and Brussels simultaneously, are past. Interestingly, the Bill includes provision preventing members at Stormont not only from sitting in the Westminster Parliament, but also from sitting in Dublin (where former Belfast MP Gerry Adams, for example, is these days a member of the Dáil, Ireland's equivalent of the House of Commons).

The Northern Ireland Assembly also wants Westminster-style 'topical' questions for Assembly Ministers, following complaints that Question Time at Stormont was too dull. Ministers have until now had advance notice of what they will be asked; the new system, also mirroring that in Scotland, will enable Members to ask questions without notice, prompting more spontaneous, and perhaps testing, replies.

The Northern Ireland marching season brought a reminder of the tensions that remain within the comparatively peaceful power-sharing as Unionist/Protestant marchers sought to take their traditional routes through predominantly Nationalist/Catholic areas.

The role of the Northern Ireland Housing Executive, and in particular the Housing Minister, Nelson McCausland, also came under the spotlight in July, when the Assembly was recalled from recess to debate allegations made in a TV programme.

Other aspects of the United Kingdom were troubling Northern Ireland as the long fade of the unionist majority had its latest impact. Belfast City Council, now more nationalist in tone, decided to join the rest of the UK in flying the Union Flag above its premises only on a set number of special days each year rather than every day. The flag is one of Northern Ireland's most potent symbols, given that the unionist and nationalist sections of the community differ over the importance of the Union Jack or the Republic of Ireland's tricolour. Protests from unionists followed in Belfast, requiring substantial police response.

Northern Ireland's electoral register also came in for some criticism, with the Electoral Commission suggesting that 400,000 voters were registered at the wrong address and the register was only about three-quarters accurate. Given the history of alleged electoral malpractice in Northern Ireland's past (vote early, vote often!), it is perhaps a counterbalancing sign of the normalisation of life and politics in the Province that this was generally attributed more to routine incompetence than to any gerrymandering by any side of the community.

WALES

Wales will also see some electoral change as a result of the draft Wales Bill, though this one was issued ahead of full parliamentary scrutiny to allow for outside views to be considered before it becomes law. As in Northern Ireland, double-hatting membership of the Cardiff Assembly and the Westminster Parliament would be prevented, and fixed terms of five years would be introduced for the National Assembly for Wales, meaning they would likely not happen at the same time as UK parliamentary elections in future.

The National Assembly's presiding officer, Rosemary Butler, expressed concern that Welsh politics receives too little attention even among the media most people in Wales read, see or listen to. It's a simple fact that Wales-based BBC and ITV news programmes receive much smaller viewership than the "national" broadcasts from London. With the doings of the Assembly largely confined to the local programming, this means that most Wales-based viewers receive largely English news.

The Assembly also concerned itself with the standards its Members are expected to maintain, after a set of recommendations from its standards commissioner. A detailed report recommends sanctions including suspension from duty and loss of pay in extreme cases of breach.

LOCAL COUNCIL RESULTS AND THE RISE OF UKIP

Politically speaking, May's local council election results were marked by a forward surge for UKIP and a further signal that the overall vote is thoroughly split. Both UKIP and the Greens stood record numbers of candidates. In addition to UKIP, Labour made substantial gains, but national vote shares were around Labour 29 per cent, Conservatives 25, UKIP 23 and the Liberal Democrats 14. Overall, in England, the Conservatives saw 1,116 councillors elected (down 335), Labour 538 (up 291), the Liberal Democrats 352 (down 124), independents 165 (up 24), UKIP 147 (up 139), the Greens 22 (up 5). As ever, the results were scanned carefully for any national significance, with the response to UKIP's rise as a serious force the main outcome.

Legislatively speaking, the Communities and Local Government Department, headed by Eric Pickles, sought to give local authorities more control over how to spend the money they raise. More freedom in how to spend most grants was permitted, and councils will soon be able to keep a share of business rates raised in their areas. This decentralising of decision-making was, of course, tempered in the short term by a set of tight local government spending settlements as a result of the national austerity drive, and with most councils maintaining council tax freezes or small rises. In that financial climate, the long-term impact of the changes, though welcome to most local councils eager for greater decentralisation of finance and decision-making, remains to become clear.

CONCLUSION

September 2013 found the major parties entering their conference seasons in slightly distracted mode. The Conservatives, in spite of losing the Syria vote, seemed in relatively united mood as signs of economic recovery began to be detected. Labour, by contrast, who had seemed to have the Government on the run over Syria, were mired in discussions about their funding by the trade unions and whispering about whether leader Ed Miliband's indifferent poll ratings made him the ideal standard bearer for the 2015 election. The Liberal Democrats, meantime, were flatlining in the polls at around just 10 per cent of the national vote, but optimistic that come 2015 they are again likely to hold the balance of power in a coalition government with one or other of the main two.

The 2013-14 legislative season is the final full one before that May 2015 election but it is not yet clear what the major themes will be, although the Education Secretary Michael Gove's attempts to reform classroom teaching and the national curriculum are likely to loom large, at least in England, with Iain Duncan Smith's benefit cutting plans (including the controversial 'bedroom tax') another clear dividing line between the Government and Opposition (and even within the Government, with some Lib Dems openly discontented on that score). The Scottish referendum in September 2014 promises to be one of the defining events of the UK election run-up, with the likelihood that Scotland will receive more control over its own affairs whether or not it chooses to break away entirely. Military action has not happened against Syria, but the question of how that conflict resolves is still an open one. Finally, the perennial itch of the UK's relationship with its European partners is unlikely to remain unscratched in a pre-election year. Finally, though, the economic situation will probably remain the defining feature of political fortune with the Government seeking continued signs of improvement before the March Budget with which George Osborne is likely to open a year-long election campaign.

Public Legislation 2012–13

Dates are of Royal Assent

Local Government Finance Act 2012 (8 November 2012)
To make provisions about: non-domestic rating, grants to local authorities, council tax, the supply of information for purposes relating to rates in Northern Ireland, and for connected purposes.

Infrastructure (Financial Assistance) Act 2012 (18 November 2012)
To make provision in relation to the giving of financial assistance in respect of the provision of infrastructure.

Civil Aviation Act 2012 (18 January 2013)
To make provision about: the regulation of operators of dominant airports, to confer functions on the Civil Aviation Authority (CAA) under competition legislation in connection with services provided at airports, aviation security, the regulation of provision of flight accommodation; to make further provision about the CAA's membership, administration and functions in relation to enforcement, regulatory burdens and the provision of information relating to aviation; and for connected purposes.

Financial Services Act 2012 (18 January 2013)
To amend the Bank of England Act 1998, the Financial Services and Markets Act 2000 and the Banking Act 2009; to make other provisions: about financial services and markets, the exercise of certain statutory functions relating to building societies, friendly societies and other mutual societies, to amend section 785 of the Companies Act 2006, and to make provision enabling the Director of Savings to provide services to other public bodies; and for connected purposes.

Prisons (Interference with Wireless Telegraphy) Act 2012 (18 January 2013)
To make provision about interference with wireless telegraphy in prisons and similar institutions.

Electoral Registration and Administration Act 2013 (1 January 2013)
To make provision for the registration of electors and the administration and conduct of elections; and to amend section 3(2)(a) of the Parliamentary Constituencies Act 1986.

European Union (Croatian Accession and Irish Protocol) Act 2013 (31 January 2103)
To make provision consequential on the treaty concerning the accession of the Republic of Croatia to the European Union, signed at Brussels on 9 December 2011, and provision consequential on the Protocol on the concerns of the Irish people on the Treaty of Lisbon, adopted at Brussels on 16 May 2012; and to make provision about the entitlement of nationals of the Republic of Croatia to enter or reside in the United Kingdom as workers.

Police (Complaints and Conduct) Act 2012 (1 February 2013)
To make provision about interviews held during certain investigations under Schedule 3 to the Police Reform Act 2002; and about the application of Part 2 of that Act to matters occurring before 1 April 2004.

Prevention of Social Housing Fraud Act 2013 (1 February 2013)
An Act to create offences and make other provisions relating to sub-letting and parting with possession of social housing; and about the investigation of social housing fraud; and for connected purposes.

Statute Law (Repeals) Act 2013 (1 February 2013)
To promote the reform of the statute law by the repeal, in accordance with recommendations of the Law Commission and the Scottish Law Commission, of certain enactments which (except in so far as their effect is preserved) are no longer of practical utility.

Trusts (Capital and Income) Act 2013 (1 February 2013)
To amend the law relating to capital and income in trusts.

Disabled Persons' Parking Badges Act 2013 (1 February 2013)
To amend section 21 of the Chronically Sick and Disabled Persons Act 1970, and for connected purposes.

European Union (Approvals) Act 2013 (1 March 2013)
To make provisions approving for the purposes of section 8 of the European Union Act 2011 certain draft decisions under Article 352 of the Treaty on the Functioning of the European Union; and to make provision approving for the purposes of section 7(3) of that Act a draft decision under Article 17(5) of the Treaty on European Union about the number of members of the European Commission.

HGV Road User Levy Act 2013 (1 March 2013)
To make provisions charging a levy in respect of the use or keeping of heavy goods vehicles on public roads in the United Kingdom, and for connected purposes.

Mental Health (Discrimination) (No. 2) Act 2013 (1 March 2013)
To make further provision about discrimination against people on the grounds of their mental health.

Prisons (Property) Act 2013 (1 March 2013)
To make provision for the destruction of certain property found in prisons and similar institutions.

Scrap Metal Dealers Act 2013 (1 March 2013)
To amend the law relating to scrap metal dealers; and for connected purposes.

Mobile Homes Act 2013 (27 March 2013)
To amend the law relating to mobile homes.

Presumption of Death Act 2013 (27 March 2013)
To make provisions in relation to the presumed death of missing persons; and for connected purposes.

Supply and Appropriation (Anticipation and Adjustments) Act 2013 (27 March 2013)
To authorise the use of resources for the years ending with 31 March 2010, 31 March 2011, 31 March 2012, 31 March 2013 and 31 March 2014; and to authorise the issue of sums out of the Consolidated Fund for the years ending with 31 March 2013 and 31 March 2014; and to appropriate the supply authorised by this Act for the years ending with 31 March 2010, 31 March 2011, 31 March 2012 and 31 March 2013.

Crime and Courts Act 2013 (29 April 2013)
To establish, and make provision about, the National Crime Agency; to abolish the Serious Organised Crime Agency and the National Policing Improvement Agency; to make provisions about the judiciary and the structure, administration, proceedings and powers of courts and tribunals, the deferred prosecution agreements, border control, drugs and driving, and for connected purposes.

Defamation Act 2013 (29 April 2013)
To amend the law of defamation.

Enterprise and Regulatory Reform Act 2013 (29 April 2013)
To make provision about: the UK Green Investment Bank, employment law; to establish and make provision about the Competition and Markets Authority and to abolish the Competition Commission and the Office of Fair Trading; to amend the Competition Act 1998 and the Enterprise Act 2002; to make provision for the reduction of legislative burdens; to make provision about copyright and rights in performances; to make provision about payments to company directors; to make provision about redress schemes relating to lettings agency work and property management work; to make provision about the supply of customer data; to make provision for the protection of essential supplies in cases of insolvency; to make provision about certain bodies established by Royal Charter; to amend section 9(5) of the Equality Act 2010; and for connected purposes.

Groceries Code Adjudicator Act 2013 (29 April 2013)
To set up a Groceries Code Adjudicator with the role of enforcing the Groceries Code and encouraging compliance with it.

Growth and Infrastructure Act 2013 (29 April 2013)
To make provision with regard to facilitating or controlling the following, namely, the provision or use of infrastructure, the carrying-out of development, and the compulsory acquisition of land; to make provision about when rating lists are to be compiled; to make provision about the rights of employees of companies who agree to be employee shareholders; and for connected purposes.

Justice and Security Act 2013 (29 April 2013)
To provide for oversight of the Security Service, the Secret Intelligence Service, the Government Communications Headquarters and other activities relating to intelligence or security matters; to make provision about closed material procedure in relation to certain civil proceedings; to prevent the making of certain court orders for the disclosure of sensitive information; and for connected purposes.

Marine Navigation (No. 2) Act 2013 (29 April 2013)
To make provision in relation to marine navigation and harbours.

Partnerships (Prosecution) (Scotland) Act 2013 (29 April 2013)
To make provision about the prosecution in Scotland of partnerships, partners and others following dissolution or changes in membership.

Public Service Pensions Act 2013 (29 April 2013)
To make provision for public service pension schemes; and for connected purposes.

Succession to the Crown Act 2013 (29 April 2013)
To make succession to the Crown not depend on gender; to make provision about Royal Marriages; and for connected purposes.

Finance Act 2013 (18 July 2013)
To grant certain duties, to alter other duties, and to amend the law relating to the National Debt and the Public Revenue, and to make further provision in connection with finance.

Marriage (Same Sex Couples) Act 2013 (18 July 2013)
To make provision for the marriage of same-sex couples in England and Wales, about gender change by married persons and civil partners, about consular functions in relation to marriage, for the marriage of armed forces personnel overseas, for permitting marriages according to the usages of belief organisations to be solemnized on the authority of certificates of a superintendent registrar, for the review of civil partnership, for the review of survivor benefits under occupational pension schemes, and for connected purposes.

Source: legislation.gov.uk

Related Politicians

The following lists those who are related and are current members of UK and European legislatures.

Claire Baker MSP and Richard Baker MSP
Spouses

Ed Balls MP and Yvette Cooper MP
Spouses

Lord Bannside and Baroness Paisley of St George's
Spouses

Lord Bannside, Baroness Paisley of St George's and Ian Paisley Jnr MP
Parents of

Alan Beith MP and Baroness Maddock
Spouses

Paul Blomfield MP and Linda McAvan MEP
Spouses

Baroness Bonham-Carter of Yarnbury and Lord Razzall
Partners

Peter Bottomley MP and Baroness Bottomley of Nettlestone
Spouses

Archbishop of Canterbury and Lord Williams of Elvel
Stepson and stepfather

Lord Chadlington and Lord Deben
Siblings

Lord Chadlington and Ben Gummer MP
Uncle of

Lord Cobbold and Earl of Lytton
Cousins

Viscount Colville of Culross and Lord Carrington
Cousins

Yvette Cooper MP and Ed Balls MP
Spouses

Jon Cruddas MP and Baroness Healy of Primrose Hill
Spouses

John Cryer MP and Rachel Reeves MP
Siblings-in-Law

Lord Deben and Lord Chadlington
Siblings

Lord Deben and Ben Gummer MP
Father and son

Lord Denham and Lord Redesdale
Cousins

Diane Dodds MEP and Nigel Dodds MP
Spouses

Frank Doran MP and Joan Ruddock MP
Spouses

Jack Dromey MP and Harriet Harman MP
Spouses

Mark Durkan MP and Mark H Durkan MLA
Uncle and nephew

Angela Eagle MP and Maria Eagle MP
Twins

Baroness Eccles of Moulton and Viscount Eccles
Spouses

Annabelle Ewing MSP and Fergus Ewing MSP
Siblings

Mark Field MP and Charlie Elphicke MP
Brothers-in-law

Ben Gummer MP and Lord Chadlington
Nephew of

Ben Gummer MP and Lord Deben
Son and father

Duncan Hames MP and Jo Swinson MP
Spouses

Harriet Harman MP and Jack Dromey MP
Spouses

Baroness Healy of Primrose Hill and Jon Cruddas MP
Spouses

Baroness Hodgson of Abinger and Lord Hodgson of Astley Abbotts
Spouses

Baroness Hollis of Higham and Lord Howarth of Newport
Partners

Stewart Hosie MP and Shona Robison MSP
Spouses

Lord Howarth of Newport and Baroness Hollis of Higham
Partners

Baroness Howe of Idlicote and Lord Howe of Aberavon
Spouses

Lord Howell of Guildford and George Osborne
Father- and son-in-law

Lord Hoyle and Lindsay Hoyle MP
Father and son

Lord Hunt of Chesterton and Tristram Hunt MP
Father and son

Lord Hurd of Westwell and Nick Hurd MP
Father and son

Nick Hurd MP and Marquess of Lothian
Son- and Father-in-law

Bernard Jenkin MP and Baroness Jenkin of Kennington
Spouses

Lord Jenkin of Roding and Bernard Jenkin MP
Father and son

Lord Jenkin of Roding and Baroness Jenkin of Kennington
Father- and daughter-in-law

Lord Kinnock and Baroness Kinnock of Holyhead
Spouses

Lord Layard and Baroness Meacher
Spouses

Huw Lewis AM and Lynne Neagle AM
Spouses

Earl of Lindsay and Lord Montagu of Beaulieu
Nephew and Uncle

Baroness Linklater of Butterstone and John Thurso MP
Cousins

Marquess of Lothian and Nick Hurd MP
Father- and son-in-law

Earl of Lytton and Lord Cobbold
Cousins

Linda McAvan MEP and Paul Blomfield MP
Spouses

Ian McCrea MLA and William McCrea MP
Son and father

Baroness McDonagh and Siobhain McDonagh MP
Siblings

Michael McMahon MSP and Siobhan McMahon MSP
Father and daughter

Baroness Maddock and Alan Beith MP
Spouses

Lord Martin of Springburn and Paul Martin MSP
Father and son

Alex Maskey MLA and Paul Maskey MP
Siblings

Michael Meacher MP and Baroness Meacher
Formerly spouses

Baroness Meacher and Lord Layard
Spouses

Lord Montagu of Beaulieu and Earl of Lindsay
Uncle and Nephew

Lynne Neagle AM and Huw Lewis AM
Spouses

Baroness Neuberger and Lord Neuberger of Abbotsbury
Siblings-in-law

George Osborne MP and Lord Howell of Guildford
Son- and father-in-law

Baroness Paisley of St George's and Lord Bannside
Spouses

Baroness Healy of Primrose Hill and Jon Cruddas MP
Spouses

Lord Palumbo and Lord Palumbo of Southwark
Father and Son

Earl Peel and Nicholas Soames MP
Brothers-in-law

Baroness Rawlings and Lord Wolfson of Sunningdale
Formerly spouses

Nick Raynsford MP and Alison Seabeck MP
Spouses

Lord Razzall and Baroness Bonham-Carter of Yarnbury
Partners

Lord Redesdale and Lord Denham
Cousins

Lord Rees-Mogg and Jacob Rees-Mogg MP
Father and son

Rachel Reeves MP and John Cryer MP
Siblings-in-Law

Shona Robison MSP and Stewart Hosie MP
Spouses

Joan Ruddock MP and Frank Doran MP
Spouses

Lord Sainsbury of Preston Candover and Lord Sainsbury of Turville
Cousins

Alison Seabeck MP and Nick Raynsford MP
Spouses

Nicholas Soames MP and Earl Peel
Brothers-in-law

Julian Sturdy MP and Robert Sturdy MEP
Son and Father

Jo Swinson MP and Duncan Hames MP
Spouses

Lord Thomas of Gresford and Baroness Walmsley
Spouses

John Thurso MP and Baroness Linklater of Butterstone
Cousins

Keith Vaz MP and Valerie Vaz MP
Siblings

Baroness Walmsley and Lord Thomas of Gresford
Spouses

Lord Williams of Elvel and Archbishop of Canterbury
Stepfather and stepson

Lord Wolfson of Aspley Guise and Lord Woflson of Sunningdale
Son and father

Lord Wolfson of Sunningdale and Baroness Rawlings
Formerly spouses

Lord Wolfson of Sunningdale and Lord Wolfson of Aspley Guise
Father and son

Parliaments of the 20th and 21st centuries

Assembled	Dissolved	Length	Ministries	Took Office
		yrs. m. d.		
VICTORIA				
3 Dec 1900	8 Jan 1906	5 1 5	{ Salisbury (Con)	6 Dec 1900
			Balfour (Con)	12 July 1902
EDWARD VII				
13 Feb 1906	10 Jan 1910	3 10 28	{ C. Bannerman (Lib)	5 Dec 1905
			Asquith (Lib)	5 April 1908
15 Feb 1910	28 Nov 1910	9 13	Asquith (Lib)	15 Feb 1910
GEORGE V				
31 Jan 1911	25 Nov 1918	7 9 25	{ Asquith (Lib)	25 May 1915
4 Feb 1919	25 Oct 1922	3 8 21	Lloyd George (Lib)	6 Dec 1916
			Coalition	
20 Nov 1922	16 Nov 1923	11 27	A. Bonar Law (Con)	23 Oct 1922
8 Jan 1924	9 Oct 1924	9 1	J. R. MacDonald (Lab)	22 Jan 1924
2 Dec 1924	10 May 1929	4 5 8	S. Baldwin (Con)	4 Nov 1924
25 June 1929	7 Oct 1931	2 3 12	J. R. MacDonald (Lab)	5 June 1929
			{ J. R. MacDonald	24 August 1931
3 Nov 1931	25 Oct 1935	3 11 22	(Nat. Govt.)	
			S. Baldwin	
26 Nov 1935			S. Baldwin	7 June 1935
			(Nat. Govt.)	
EDWARD VIII			N. Chamberlain	28 May 1937
			(Nat. Govt.)	
GEORGE VI	15 June 1945	9 6 20	W. Churchill	10 May 1940
			(Nat. Govt.)	
1 Aug 1945	3 Feb 1950	4 6 2	C. R. Attlee (Lab)	26 July 1945
1 Mar 1950	5 Oct 1951	1 7 4	C. R. Attlee (Lab)	25 Feb 1950
31 Oct 1951	6 May 1955	3 6 6	{ W. Churchill (Con)	26 Oct 1951
			A. Eden (Con)	
ELIZABETH II			A. Eden (Con)	6 April 1955
7 June 1955	18 Sept 1959	4 3 11	{ H. Macmillan (Con)	10 Jan 1957
			H. Macmillan (Con)	9 Oct 1959
20 Oct 1959	25 Sept 1964	4 11 5	A. Douglas-Home (Con)	9 Oct 1963
27 Oct 1964	10 Mar 1966	1 4 11	{ H. Wilson (Lab)	16 Oct 1964
18 Apr 1966	29 May 1970	4 1 11	H. Wilson (Lab)	1 April 1966
29 June 1970	8 Feb 1974	3 7 10	E. R. G. Heath (Con)	19 June 1970
6 Mar 1974	20 Sept 1974	6 14	H. Wilson (Lab)	4 Mar 1974
			(Minority Govt.)	
22 Oct 1974	7 April 1979	4 5 15	{ H. Wilson (Lab)	11 Oct 1974
			J. Callaghan (Lab)	5 April 1976
9 May 1979	13 May 1983	4 0 4	Mrs M. Thatcher (Con)	3 May 1979
15 June 1983	18 May 1987	3 11 3	Mrs M. Thatcher (Con)	9 June 1983
17 June 1987	16 Mar 1992	4 8 28	{ Mrs M. Thatcher (Con)	11 June 1987
			J. Major (Con)	28 Nov 1990
27 April 1992	8 April 1997	4 11 19	J. Major (Con)	10 April 1992
7 May 1997	14 May 2001	4 0 7	T. Blair (Lab)	1 May 1997
20 June 2001	11 April 2005	3 9 22	T. Blair (Lab)	7 June 2001
17 May 2005	8 April 2010	4 10 22	{ T. Blair (Lab)	5 May 2005
			G. Brown (Lab)	27 June 2007
13 May 2010			D. Cameron (Con)	
			(Coalition Govt.)	11 May 2010

Size of the House of Commons since 1801

With the Union of Great Britain and Ireland in 1801 the number of members of Parliament was fixed at 658. In 1885 the total was increased to 670, and by the Act of 1918 to 707. With the creation of the Irish Free State in 1922, the Irish representation was reduced to 13 members from Ulster, making the membership of the House of Commons 615. In 1945, owing to the division of large constituencies, the number was increased by 25 to 640. Under the Act of 1948 the number was decreased to 625. Orders passed in 1954 and 1955 increased the number to 630. As the result of redistribution and boundary changes, the total number of MPs elected at the 1979 general election was 635. The House of Commons (Redistribution of Seats) Act 1979 and the Boundary Commission reports of 1983 resulted in an increase of 15 seats after the 1983 election to 650 members. At the 1992 election, 651 Members were elected, an extra seat having been created for Milton Keynes. Reports from the Boundary Commission caused an increase to 659 at the 1997 election. This was cut to 646 for the 2005 general election, with Scotand losing 13 seats as a result of previous over representation and the creation of the Scottish Parliament. Reports from the Boundary Commission caused an increase to 650 at the 2010 election.

General Election Majorities since the Reform Act

(NB *In certain cases, such as the election of* 1910, *the Government Party had a working arrangement with other parties, which ensured them a majority in the House*)

1832	Lib	300	1924	Con	223
1835	Lib	108	1929	Lab	No majority
1837	Lib	40	1931	Nat Govt	493
1841	Con	78	1935	Nat Govt	249
1847	Lib	2	1945	Lab	146
1852	Con	8	1950	Lab	5
1857	Lib	92	1951	Con	17
1859	Lib	40	1955	Con	58
1865	Lib	62	1959	Con	100
1868	Lib	106	1964	Lab	4
1874	Con	52	1966	Lab	96
1880	Lib	176	1970	Con	30
1885	Lib	No majority	1974	(Feb) Lab	No majority
1886	Unionist	120	1974	(Oct) Lab	3
1892	Lib	No majority	(3 over all parties, 42 over Cons)		
1895	Unionist	152	1979	Con	43
1900	Unionist	135	1983	Con	144
1906	Lib	130	1987	Con	101
1910	(Jan) Lib	No majority	1992	Con	21
1910	(Dec) Lib	No majority	1997	Lab	177
1918	Coalition	249	2001	Lab	165
1922	Con	75	2005	Lab	66
1923	Con	No majority	2010	Con/Lib Dem coalition	83

Long Parliaments

The longest lived Parliaments in English history have been the Elizabethan Parliament of 1572–83, the Long Parliament of 1640–53, and the Cavalier Parliament of 1661–79. The First World War Parliament met on 31 January 1911, and was dissolved on 25 November 1918. That of the Second met 26 November 1935, and was dissolved 15 June 1945.

Prime Ministers since 1721

1721–42	Sir Robert Walpole (Whig)		1868–74	William Gladstone (Lib)
1742–43	Spencer Compton (Whig)		1874–80	Benjamin Disraeli (Con)
1743–54	Henry Pelham (Whig)		1880–85	William Gladstone (Lib)
1754–56	Duke of Newcastle (Whig)		1885–86	Marquess of Salisbury (Con)
1756–57	Duke of Devonshire (Whig)		1886	William Gladstone (Lib)
1757–62	Duke of Newcastle (Whig)		1886–92	Marquess of Salisbury (Con)
1762–63	Earl of Bute (Tory)		1892–94	William Gladstone (Lib)
1763–65	George Grenville (Whig)		1894–95	Earl of Rosebery (Lib)
1765–66	Marquess of Rockingham (Whig)		1895–1902	Marquess of Salisbury (Con)
1766–67	William Pitt (the Elder) (Whig)		1902–05	Arthur Balfour (Con)
1767–70	Duke of Grafton (Whig)		1905–08	Sir Henry Campbell-Bannerman
1770–82	Lord North (Tory)			(Lib)
1782	Marquess of Rockingham (Whig)		1908–16	Herbert Asquith (Lib)
1782–83	Earl of Shelburne (Whig)		1916–22	David Lloyd George (Lib)
1783	Duke of Portland (Coalition)			(Coalition)
1783–1801	William Pitt (the Younger) (Tory)		1922–23	Andrew Bonar Law (Con)
1801–04	Henry Addington (Tory)		1923–24	Stanley Baldwin (Con)
1804–06	William Pitt (the Younger) (Tory)		1924	Ramsay MacDonald (Lab)
1806–07	Lord Grenville (Whig)		1924–29	Stanley Baldwin (Con)
1807–09	Duke of Portland (Tory)		1929–35	Ramsay MacDonald (Lab)
1809–12	Spencer Perceval (Tory)		1935–37	Stanley Baldwin (Con) (Nat Govt)
1812–27	Earl of Liverpool (Tory)		1937–40	Neville Chamberlain (Con)
1827	George Canning (Tory)			(Nat Govt)
1827–28	Viscount Goderich (Tory)		1940–45	Winston Churchill (Con)
1828–30	Duke of Wellington (Tory)			(Coalition)
1830–34	Earl Grey (Whig)		1945–51	Clement Attlee (Lab)
1834	Viscount Melbourne (Whig)		1951–55	Winston Churchill (Con)
1834–35	Sir Robert Peel (Tory)		1955–57	Sir Anthony Eden (Con)
1835–41	Viscount Melbourne (Whig)		1957–63	Harold Macmillan (Con)
1841–46	Sir Robert Peel (Tory)		1963–64	Sir Alec Douglas-Home (Con)
1846–52	Lord John Russell (Whig)		1964–70	Harold Wilson (Lab)
1852	Earl of Derby (Con)		1970–74	Edward Heath (Con)
1852–55	Earl of Aberdeen (Lib) (Coalition)		1974–76	Harold Wilson (Lab)
1855–58	Viscount Palmerston (Lib)		1976–79	James Callaghan (Lab)
1858–59	Earl of Derby (Con)		1979–90	Margaret Thatcher (Con)
1859–65	Viscount Palmerston (Lib)		1990–97	John Major (Con)
1865–66	Earl Russell (Lib)		1997–2007	Tony Blair (Lab)
1866–68	Earl of Derby (Con)		2007–10	Gordon Brown (Lab)
1868	Benjamin Disraeli (Con)		2010–	David Cameron (Con)
				(Coalition)

Government 2

Opposition 50

The Government

The Cabinet
(Conservative/Liberal Democrat coalition)

Prime Minister, First Lord of the Treasury and Minister for the Civil Service	**David Cameron** MP (Con)
Deputy Prime Minister, Lord President of the Council	**Nick Clegg** MP (Lib Dem)
First Secretary of State, Secretary of State for Foreign and Commonwealth Affairs	**William Hague** MP (Con)
Chancellor of the Exchequer	**George Osborne** MP (Con)
Chief Secretary to the Treasury	**Danny Alexander** MP (Lib Dem)
Secretary of State for the Home Department	**Theresa May** MP (Con)
Secretary of State for Defence	**Philip Hammond** MP (Con)
Secretary of State for Business, Innovation and Skills; President of the Board of Trade	Dr **Vincent Cable** MP (Lib Dem)
Secretary of State for Work and Pensions	**Iain Duncan Smith** MP (Con)
Lord Chancellor and Secretary of State for Justice	**Chris Grayling** MP (Con)
Secretary of State for Education	**Michael Gove** MP (Con)
Secretary of State for Communities and Local Government	**Eric Pickles** MP (Con)
Secretary of State for Health	**Jeremy Hunt** MP (Con)
Leader of the House of Lords; Chancellor of the Duchy of Lancaster	**Lord Hill of Oareford** CBE (Con)
Secretary of State for Environment, Food and Rural Affairs	**Owen Paterson** MP (Con)
Secretary of State for International Development	**Justine Greening** MP (Con)
Secretary of State for Scotland	**Alistair Carmichael** MP (Lib Dem)
Secretary of State for Energy and Climate Change	**Edward Davey** MP (Lib Dem)
Secretary of State for Transport	**Patrick McLoughlin** MP (Con)
Secretary of State for Culture, Media and Sport; Minister for Women and Equalities	**Maria Miller** MP (Con)
Secretary of State for Northern Ireland	**Theresa Villiers** MP (Con)
Secretary of State for Wales	**David Jones** MP (Con)

Also attending Cabinet

Minister without portfolio	**Kenneth Clarke** QC MP (Con)
Leader of the House of Commons, Lord Privy Seal	**Andrew Lansley** CBE MP (Con)
Parliamentary Secretary to the Treasury; Chief Whip	Sir **George Young** CH MP (Con)
Minister for the Cabinet Office; Paymaster General	**Francis Maude** MP (Con)
Minister for Government Policy, Cabinet Office	**Oliver Letwin** MP (Con)
Minister of State, Cabinet Office and Department for Education	**David Laws** MP (Lib Dem)
Minister without portfolio; Chairman of the Conservative Party	**Grant Shapps** MP (Con)
Senior Minister of State (Faith and Communities), Department for Communities and Local Government and Foreign and Commonwealth Office	**Baroness Warsi** (Con)
Minister of State for Universities and Science, Department for Business, Innovation and Skills	**David Willetts** MP (Con)

attend when ministerial responsibilities on agenda

Attorney General	**Dominic Grieve** QC MP (Con)
Minister of State	**Greg Clark** MP (Con)

Departmental Ministers

Department for Business, Innovation and Skills
Secretary of State for Business, Innovation and Skills;
President of the Board of Trade | Rt Hon Dr **Vincent Cable** MP (Lib Dem)
Ministers of State | Rt Hon **David Willetts** MP (Con)
Rt Hon **Michael Fallon** MP (Con)
Lord Green of Hurstpierpoint (Con)
Matthew Hancock MP (Con)
Parliamentary Under-Secretaries of State | **Viscount Younger of Leckie** (Con)
Jo Swinson MP (Lib Dem)

Cabinet Office
Deputy Prime Minister, Lord President of the Council | Rt Hon **Nick Clegg** MP (Lib Dem)
Ministers | Rt Hon **Francis Maude** MP (Con)
Rt Hon **Oliver Letwin** MP (Con)
Ministers of State | Rt Hon **David Laws** MP (Lib Dem)
Rt Hon **Greg Clark** MP (Con)
Parliamentary Secretaries | **Nick Hurd** MP (Con)
Jo Johnson MP (Con)
Ministers without portfolio | Rt Hon **Kenneth Clarke** QC MP (Con)
Rt Hon **Grant Shapps** MP (Con)
Rt Hon **John Hayes** MP (Con)

Department for Communities and Local Government
Secretary of State for Communities and Local
Government | Rt Hon **Eric Pickles** MP (Con)
Senior Minister of State | Rt Hon **Baroness Warsi** (Con)
Parliamentary Under-Secretaries of State | **Brandon Lewis** MP (Con)
Stephen Williams MP (Lib Dem)
Nick Boles MP (Con)
Baroness Stowell of Beeston MBE (Con)
Kris Hopkins MP (Con)

Department for Culture, Media and Sport
Secretary of State for Culture, Media and Sport
(Minister for Women and Equalities) | Rt Hon **Maria Miller** MP (Con)
Parliamentary Under-Secretaries of State | Hon **Ed Vaizey** MP (Con)
Helen Grant MP (Con)
Jo Swinson MP (Lib Dem)

Ministry of Defence
Secretary of State for Defence | Rt Hon **Philip Hammond** MP (Con)
Minister of State | Rt Hon **Mark Francois** MP (Con)
Parliamentary Under-Secretaries of State | Dr **Andrew Murrison** MP (Con)
Philip Dunne MP (Con)
Lord Astor of Hever DL (Con)
Anna Soubry MP (Con)

Department for Education
Secretary of State for Education | Rt Hon **Michael Gove** MP (Con)
Ministers of State | Rt Hon **David Laws** MP (Lib Dem)
Matthew Hancock MP (Con)
Parliamentary Under-Secretaries of State | **Edward Timpson** MP (Con)
Elizabeth Truss MP (Con)
Lord Nash (Con)

Department of Energy and Climate Change

Secretary of State for Energy and Climate Change	Rt Hon **Edward Davey** MP (Lib Dem)
Ministers of State	Rt Hon **Gregory Barker** MP (Con)
	Rt Hon **Michael Fallon** MP (Con)
Parliamentary Under-Secretary of State	**Baroness Verma** (Con)

Department for Environment, Food and Rural Affairs

Secretary of State for Environment, Food and Rural Affairs	Rt Hon **Owen Paterson** MP (Con)
Parliamentary Under-Secretaries of State	**Dan Rogerson** MP (Lib Dem)
	Lord de Mauley TD (Con)
	George Eustice MP (Con)

Foreign and Commonwealth Office

First Secretary of State, Secretary of State for Foreign and Commonwealth Affairs (Foreign Secretary)	Rt Hon **William Hague** MP (Con)
Senior Minister of State	Rt Hon **Baroness Warsi** (Con)
Ministers of State	Rt Hon **David Lidington** MP (Con)
	Rt Hon **Hugo Swire** MP (Con)
	Lord Green of Hurstpierpoint (Con)
	Rt Hon **Hugh Roberston** MP (Con)
Parliamentary Under-Secretary of State	**Mark Simmonds** MP (Con)

Department of Health

Secretary of State for Health	Rt Hon **Jeremy Hunt** MP (Con)
Minister of State	**Norman Lamb** MP (Lib Dem)
Parliamentary Under-Secretaries of State	Dr **Daniel Poulter** MP (Con)
	Rt Hon **Earl Howe** (Con)
	Jane Ellison MP (Con)

Home Office

Secretary of State for the Home Department (Home Secretary)	Rt Hon **Theresa May** MP (Con)
Ministers of State	**Mark Harper** MP (Con)
	Rt Hon **Damian Green** MP (Con)
	Norman Baker MP (Lib Dem)
Parliamentary Under-Secretaries of State	**James Brokenshire** MP (Con)
	Lord Taylor of Holbeach CBE (Con)

Department for International Development

Secretary of State for International Development	Rt Hon **Justine Greening** MP (Con)
Minister of State	Rt Hon **Alan Duncan** MP (Con)
Parliamentary Under-Secretary of State	**Lynne Featherstone** MP (Lib Dem)

Ministry of Justice

Lord Chancellor and Secretary of State for Justice	Rt Hon **Chris Grayling** MP (Con)
Ministers of State	Rt Hon **Lord McNally** (Lib Dem)
	Rt Hon **Damian Green** MP (Con)
Parliamentary Under-Secretaries of State	**Shailesh Vara** MP (Con)
	Jeremy Wright MP (Con)

Law Officers

Attorney General	Rt Hon **Dominic Grieve** QC MP (Con)
Solicitor General	**Oliver Heald** MP (Con)
Advocate General for Scotland	Rt Hon **Lord Wallace of Tankerness** QC (Lib Dem)

Leader of the House of Commons

Leader of the House of Commons	Rt Hon **Andrew Lansley** CBE MP (Con)
Parliamentary Secretary	Rt Hon **Tom Brake** MP (Lib Dem)

Leader of the House of Lords

Leader of the House of Lords	Rt Hon **Lord Hill of Oareford** CBE (Con)
Deputy Leader	Rt Hon **Lord McNally** (Lib Dem)

Northern Ireland Office

Secretary of State for Northern Ireland	Rt Hon **Theresa Villiers** MP (Con)
Minister of State	Rt Hon **Andrew Robathan** MP (Con)

Privy Council Office

Lord President of the Council	Rt Hon **Nick Clegg** MP (Lib Dem)

Scotland Office

Secretary of State for Scotland	Rt Hon **Alistair Carmichael** MP (Lib Dem)
Parliamentary Under-Secretary of State	Rt Hon **David Mundell** MP (Con)

Department for Transport

Secretary of State for Transport	Rt Hon **Patrick McLoughlin** MP (Con)
Minister of State	**Baroness Kramer** (Lib Dem)
Parliamentary Under-Secretaries of State	**Stephen Hammond** MP (Con)
	Robert Goodwill MP (Con)

HM Treasury

Chancellor of the Exchequer	Rt Hon **George Osborne** MP (Con)
Chief Secretary to the Treasury	Rt Hon **Danny Alexander** MP (Lib Dem)
Financial Secretary	**Sajid Javid** MP (Con)
Exchequer Secretary	**David Gauke** MP (Con)
Economic Secretary	**Nicky Morgan** MP (Con)
Commercial Secretary	**Lord Deighton** KBE (Con)

Wales Office

Secretary of State for Wales	Rt Hon **David Jones** MP (Con)
Parliamentary Under-Secretaries of State	**Stephen Crabb** MP (Con)
	Baroness Randerson (Lib Dem)

Department for Work and Pensions

Secretary of State for Work and Pensions	Rt Hon **Iain Duncan Smith** MP (Con)
Ministers of State	**Steve Webb** MP (Lib Dem)
	Esther McVey MP (Con)
	Mike Penning MP (Con)
Parliamentary Under-Secretary of State	**Lord Freud** (Con)

Government Whips

Commons

CHIEF WHIP

Parliamentary Secretary to the Treasury   Rt Hon Sir **George Young** CH MP (Con)

DEPUTY CHIEF WHIPS

Treasurer of HM Household   **Greg Hands** MP (Con)

Comptroller of HM Household   Rt Hon **Don Foster** MP (Lib Dem)

WHIPS

Vice-Chamberlain of HM Household   Rt Hon **Desmond Swayne** TD MP (Con)

Lords Commissioner of HM Treasury   **Anne Milton** MP (Con)
Mark Lancaster TD MP (Con)
David Evennett MP (Con)
Stephen Crabb MP (Con)
Karen Bradley MP (Con)
Sam Gyimah MP (Con)

ASSISTANT WHIPS   **John Penrose** MP (Con)
Mark Hunter MP (Lib Dem)
Jenny Willott MP (Lib Dem)
Amber Rudd MP (Con)
Claire Perry MP (Con)
Gavin Barwell MP (Con)
Jo Johnson MP (Con)

Lords

CHIEF WHIP

*Captain of the Honourable Corps of the
Gentlemen-at-Arms*   Rt Hon **Baroness Anelay of St Johns** DBE (Con)

DEPUTY CHIEF WHIP

*Captain of the Queen's Bodyguard of the
Yeomen of the Guard*   **Lord Newby** OBE (Lib Dem)

WHIPS, LORDS IN WAITING   **Lord Popat** (Con)
Earl Attlee TD (Con)
Lord Gardiner of Kimble (Con)
Rt Hon **Lord Wallace of Saltaire** (Lib Dem)
Lord Ahmad of Wimbledon (Con)
Lord Bates (Con)

WHIPS, BARONESSES IN WAITING   **Baroness Northover** (Lib Dem)
Baroness Jolly (Lib Dem)

Government Spokespeople in the Lords

Leader of the House of Lords, Chancellor of the Duchy of Lancaster	Rt Hon **Lord Hill of Oareford** CBE (Con)
Deputy Leader of the House of Lords	Rt Hon **Lord McNally** (Lib Dem)
Business, Innovation and Skills	**Lord Green of Hurstpierpoint** (Con) **Viscount Younger of Leckie** (Con) **Lord Popat** (Con) **Baroness Garden of Frognal** (Lib Dem)
Cabinet Office	Rt Hon **Lord Wallace of Saltaire** (Lib Dem) **Lord Gardiner of Kimble** (Con)
Communities and Local Government	Rt Hon **Baroness Warsi** (Con) **Baroness Hanham** CBE (Con) **Lord Ahmad of Wimbledon** (Con)
Culture, Media and Sport	**Lord Gardiner of Kimble** (Con) **Baroness Northover** (Lib Dem)
Defence	**Lord Astor of Hever** DL (Con) **Baroness Garden of Frognal** (Lib Dem)
Education	**Lord Nash** (Con) **Baroness Garden of Frognal** (Lib Dem)
Energy and Climate Change	**Baroness Verma** (Con) **Lord Gardiner of Kimble** (Con)
Environment, Food and Rural Affairs	**Lord de Mauley** TD (Con) **Baroness Northover** (Lib Dem)
Foreign and Commonwealth Office	Rt Hon **Baroness Warsi** (Con) **Lord Green of Hurstpierpoint** (Con) Rt Hon **Lord Wallace of Saltaire** (Lib Dem)
Health	Rt Hon **Earl Howe** (Con) **Baroness Northover** (Lib Dem)
Home Office	**Baroness Stowell of Beeston** MBE (Con) **Earl Attlee** TD (Con)
International Development	**Baroness Northover** (Lib Dem) **Lord Ahmad of Wimbledon** (Con)
Justice	Rt Hon **Lord McNally** (Lib Dem) **Lord Ahmad of Wimbledon** (Con)
Law Officers	Rt Hon **Lord Wallace of Tankerness** QC (Lib Dem) **Earl Attlee** TD (Con)
Northern Ireland	**Baroness Randerson** (Lib Dem) **Earl Attlee** TD (Con)
Scotland	Rt Hon **Lord Wallace of Tankerness** QC (Lib Dem) **Earl Attlee** TD (Con)
Transport	**Earl Attlee** TD (Con) **Lord Popat** (Con)
HM Treasury	**Lord Deighton** KBE (Con) **Lord Newby** OBE (Lib Dem)

Wales	**Baroness Randerson** (Lib Dem)
	Earl Attlee TD (Con)
Women and Equalities	**Baroness Northover** (Lib Dem)
	Baroness Stowell of Beeston MBE (Con)
Work and Pensions	**Lord Freud** (Con)
	Baroness Stowell of Beeston MBE (Con)

Alphabetical list of Ministers and Whips
(Con/Lib Dem coalition)

AHMAD OF WIMBLEDON, Lord (Con)	Spokesperson, Departments for Communities and Local and International Development and Ministry of Justice; Whip
ALEXANDER, Rt Hon Danny (Lib Dem)	Chief Secretary to the Treasury
ANELAY OF ST JOHNS, Rt Hon Baroness (Con)	Chief Whip; Captain of the Honourable Corps of the Gentlemen-at-Arms
ASTOR OF HEVER, Lord (Con)	Parliamentary Under-Secretary of State and Spokesperson, Ministry of Defence
ATTLEE, Earl (Con)	Spokesperson, Department for Transport, Northern Ireland Office, Home Office, Law Officers, Scotland Office and Wales Office; Whip
BAKER, Norman (Lib Dem)	Minister of State, Home Office
BARKER, Rt Hon Gregory (Con)	Minister of State for Climate Change, Department of Energy and Climate Change
BARWELL, Gavin (Con)	Assistant Whip
BOLES, Nick (Con)	Parliamentary Under-Secretary of State (Planning), Department for Communities and Local Government
BRADLEY, Karen (Con)	Government Whip
BRAKE, Rt Hon Tom (Lib Dem)	Parliamentary Secretary (Deputy Leader of the House of Commons)
BROKENSHIRE, James (Con)	Parliamentary Under-Secretary of State (Crime and Security), Home Office
CABLE, Rt Hon Dr Vincent (Lib Dem)	Secretary of State for Business, Innovation and Skills; President of the Board of Trade
CAMERON, Rt Hon David (Con)	Prime Minister, First Lord of the Treasury and Minister for the Civil Service
CARMICHAEL, Rt Hon Alistair (Lib Dem)	Secretary of State for Scotland
CLARK, Rt Hon Greg (Con)	Minister of State (Cities and Constitution), Cabinet Office
CLARKE, Rt Hon Kenneth (Con)	Minister without Portfolio, Cabinet Office
CLEGG, Rt Hon Nick (Lib Dem)	Leader Liberal Democrats; Deputy Prime Minister, Lord President of the Council
CRABB, Stephen (Con)	Parliamentary Under-Secretary of State, Wales Office; Whip
DAVEY, Rt Hon Edward (Lib Dem)	Secretary of State for Energy and Climate Change
DEIGHTON, Lord (Con)	Commercial Secretary and Spokesperson, HM Treasury
DE MAULEY, Lord (Con)	Parliamentary Under-Secretary of State (Resource Management, the Local Environment and Environmental Science) and Spokesperson, Department for Environment, Food and Rural Affairs
DUNCAN, Rt Hon Alan (Con)	Minister of State, Department for International Development
DUNCAN SMITH, Rt Hon Iain (Con)	Secretary of State for Work and Pensions
DUNNE, Philip (Con)	Parliamentary Under-Secretary of State (Defence Equipment, Support and Technology), Ministry of Defence

ELLISON, Jane (Con)	Parliamentary Under-Secretary of State, Department of Health
EUSTICE, George (Con)	Parliamentary Under-Secretary of State, Department for Environment, Food and Rural Affairs
EVENNETT, David (Con)	Whip
FALLON, Rt Hon Michael (Con)	Minister of State for Business and Enterprise, Department for Business, Innovation and Skills and Minister of State for Energy, Department of Energy and Climate Change
FEATHERSTONE, Lynne (Lib Dem)	Parliamentary Under-Secretary of State, Department for International Development
FOSTER, Rt Hon Don (Lib Dem)	Deputy Chief Whip (Comptroller of HM Household)
FRANCOIS, Rt Hon Mark (Con)	Minister of State for Defence Personnel, Welfare and Veterans, Ministry of Defence
FREUD, Lord (Con)	Parliamentary Under-Secretary of State (Minister for Welfare Reform) and Spokesperson, Department for Work and Pensions
GARDINER OF KIMBLE, Lord (Con)	Spokesperson, Departments for Culture, Media and Sport and Energy and Climate Change and Cabinet Office; Whip
GAUKE, David (Con)	Exchequer Secretary, HM Treasury
GOODWILL, Robert (Con)	Parliamentary Under-Secretary of State, Department for Transport
GOVE, Rt Hon Michael (Con)	Secretary of State for Education
GRANT, Helen (Con)	Parliamentary Under-Secretary of State (Sport and Equalities), Department for Culture, Media and Sport
GRAYLING, Rt Hon Chris (Con)	Lord Chancellor and Secretary of State for Justice
GREEN, Rt Hon Damian (Con)	Minister of State for Policing and Criminal Justice, Home Office and Ministry of Justice
GREEN OF HURSTPIERPOINT, Lord (Con)	Minister of State for Trade and Investment and Spokesperson, Department for Business, Innovation and Skills and Foreign and Commonwealth Office
GREENING, Rt Hon Justine (Con)	Secretary of State for International Development
GRIEVE, Rt Hon Dominic (Con)	Attorney General
GYMIAH, Sam (Con)	Government Whip
HAGUE, Rt Hon William (Con)	First Secretary of State, Secretary of State for Foreign and Commonwealth Affairs (Foreign Secretary)
HAMMOND, Rt Hon Philip (Con)	Secretary of State for Defence
HAMMOND, Stephen (Con)	Parliamentary Under-Secretary of State, Department for Transport
HANCOCK, Matthew (Con)	Minister of State for Skills and Enterprise, Department for Business, Innovation and Skills and Education
HANDS, Greg (Con)	Deputy Chief Whip (Treasurer of HM Household)
HARPER, Mark (Con)	Minister of State for Immigration, Home Office
HAYES, Rt Hon John (Con)	Minister without Portfolio, Cabinet Office
HEALD, Oliver (Con)	Solicitor General
HILL OF OAREFORD, Rt Hon Lord (Con)	Leader of the House of Lords and Chancellor of the Duchy of Lancaster
HOPKINS, Kris (Con)	Parliamentary Under-Secretary of State, Department for Communities and Local Government

HOWE, Rt Hon Earl (Con)	Parliamentary Under-Secretary of State and Spokesperson, Department of Health
HUNT, Rt Hon Jeremy (Con)	Secretary of State for Health
HUNTER, Mark (Lib Dem)	Assistant Whip
HURD, Nick (Con)	Parliamentary Secretary (Minister for Civil Society), Cabinet Office
JAVID, Sajid (Con)	Financial Secretary, HM Treasury
JOHNSON, Jo (Con)	Parliamentary Secretary, Cabinet Office and Assistant Whip
JOLLY, Baroness (Lib Dem)	Whip
JONES, Rt Hon David (Con)	Secretary of State for Wales
KNIGHT, Rt Hon Greg (Con)	Whip (Vice-Chamberlain of HM Household)
KRAMER, Baroness (Lib Dem)	Minister of State, Department for Transport
LAMB, Norman (Lib Dem)	Minister of State for Care and Support, Department of Health
LANCASTER, Mark (Con)	Whip
LANSLEY, Rt Hon Andrew (Con)	Leader of the House of Commons, Lord Privy Seal
LAWS, Rt Hon David (Lib Dem)	Minister of State, Cabinet Office and Department for Education
LETWIN, Rt Hon Oliver (Con)	Minister for Policy, Cabinet Office
LEWIS, Brandon (Con)	Parliamentary Under-Secretary of State, Department for Communities and Local Government
LIDINGTON, Rt Hon David (Con)	Minister of State, Foreign and Commonwealth Office
McLOUGHLIN, Rt Hon Patrick (Con)	Secretary of State for Transport
McNALLY, Rt Hon Lord (Lib Dem)	Deputy Leader of the House of Lords; Minister of State and Spokesperson, Ministry of Justice; Leader, Liberal Democrats in the House of Lords
McVEY, Esther (Con)	Minister of State (Employment), Department for Work and Pensions
MAUDE, Rt Hon Francis (Con)	Minister for the Cabinet Office; Paymaster General
MAY, Rt Hon Theresa (Con)	Secretary of State for the Home Department (Home Secretary)
MILLER, Rt Hon Maria (Con)	Secretary of State for Culture, Media and Sport; Minister for Women and Equalities
MILTON, Anne (Con)	Whip
MORGAN, Nicky (Con)	Economic Secretary, HM Treasury
MUNDELL, Rt Hon David (Con)	Parliamentary Under-Secretary of State, Scotland Office
MURRISON, Dr Andrew (Con)	Parliamentary Under-Secretary of State (International Security Strategy), Ministry of Defence
NASH, Lord (Con)	Parliamentary Under-Secretary of State for Schools and Spokesperson, Department for Education
NEWBY, Lord (Lib Dem)	Deputy Chief Whip (Captain of the Queen's Bodyguard of the Yeomen of the Guard); Spokesperson, HM Treasury
NORTHOVER, Baroness (Lib Dem)	Spokesperson, Departments for Culture, Media and Sport, Environment, Food and Rural Affairs, Health, International Development, and for Women and Equalities; Whip
OSBORNE, Rt Hon George (Con)	Chancellor of the Exchequer

PATERSON, Rt Hon Owen (Con)	Secretary of State for Environment, Food and Rural Affairs
PENNING, Mike (Con)	Minister of State, Department for Work and Pensions
PENROSE, John (Con)	Assistant Whip
PERRY, Claire (Con)	Assistant Whip
PICKLES, Rt Hon Eric (Con)	Secretary of State for Communities and Local Government
POPAT, Lord (Con)	Spokesperson Departments for Business, Innovation and Skills and Transport; Whip
POULTER, Dr Daniel (Con)	Parliamentary Under-Secretary of State, Department of Health
RANDERSON, Baroness (Lib Dem)	Parliamentary Under-Secretary of State and Spokesperson, Wales Office; Spokesperson for Northern Ireland Office
ROBATHAN, Rt Hon Andrew (Con)	Minister of State, Northern Ireland Office
ROBERTSON, Rt Hon Hugh (Con)	Minister of State, Foreign and Commonwealth Office
ROGERSON, Dan (Lib Dem)	Parliamentary Under-Secretary of State, Department for Environment, Food and Rural Affairs
RUDD, Amber (Con)	Assistant Whip
SHAPPS, Rt Hon Grant (Con)	Minister without Portfolio, Cabinet Office; Chairman, Conservative Party
SIMMONDS, Mark (Con)	Parliamentary Under-Secretary of State, Foreign and Commonwealth Office
SOUBRY, Anna (Con)	Parliamentary Under-Secretary of State, Ministry of Defence
STOWELL OF BEESTON, Baroness (Con)	Parliamentary Under-Secretary of State, Department for Communities and Local Government; and Government Spokesperson, Departments for Work and Pensions, Home Office, and for Women and Equalities
SWAYNE, Rt Hon Desmond (Con)	Whip (Vice-Chamberlain of HM Household)
SWINSON, Jo (Lib Dem)	Parliamentary Under-Secretary of State (Minister for Employment Relations and Consumer Affairs), Department for Business, Innovation and Skills and Parliamentary Under-Secretary of State (Women and Equalities), Department for Culture, Media and Sport
SWIRE, Rt Hon Hugo (Con)	Minister of State, Foreign and Commonwealth Office
TAYLOR OF HOLBEACH, Lord (Con)	Parliamentary Under-Secretary of State (Criminal Information) and Home Office
TIMPSON, Edward (Con)	Parliamentary Under-Secretary of State, Department for Education
TRUSS, Elizabeth (Con)	Parliamentary Under-Secretary of State, Department for Education
VARA, Shailesh (Con)	Parliamentary Under-Secretary of State, Ministry of Justice
VAIZEY, Hon Ed (Con)	Parliamentary Under-Secretary of State (Minister for Culture, Communications and Creative Industries), Department for Culture, Media and Sport
VERMA, Baroness (Con)	Parliamentary Under-Secretary of State and Spokesperson, Department of Energy and Climate Change

VILLIERS, Rt Hon Theresa (Con)	Secretary of State for Northern Ireland
WALLACE OF SALTAIRE, Rt Hon Lord (Lib Dem)	Spokesperson, Foreign and Commonwealth Office and Cabinet Office; Whip
WALLACE OF TANKERNESS, Rt Hon Lord (Lib Dem)	Advocate General for Scotland; Spokesperson, Law Officers and Scotland Office
WARSI, Rt Hon Baroness (Con)	Senior Minister of State (Faith and Communities) and Spokesperson, Department for Communities and Local and Foreign and Commonwealth Office
WEBB, Steve (Lib Dem)	Minister of State for Pensions, Department for Work and Pensions
WILLIAMS, Stephen (Lib Dem)	Parliamentary Under-Secretary of State, Department for Communities and Local Government
WILLETTS, Rt Hon David (Con)	Minister of State for Universities and Science, Department for Business, Innovation and Skills
WILLOTT, Jenny (Lib Dem)	Assistant Whip
WRIGHT, Jeremy (Con)	Parliamentary Under-Secretary of State (Minister for Prisons and Rehabilitation), Ministry of Justice
YOUNG, Rt Hon Sir George (Con)	Parliamentary Secretary to the Treasury; Chief Whip
YOUNGER OF LECKIE, Viscount (Con)	Parliamentary Under-Secretary of State and Spokesperson, Department for Business, Innovation and Skills

Ministerial Responsibilities and Staff

Prime Minister's Office

10 Downing Street, London SW1A 2AA Tel: 020 7930 4433
Email: [initialsurname]@no10.x.gsi.gov.uk Website: www.gov.uk/number10 Twitter: @number10gov

Prime Minister, First Lord of the Treasury and Minister for the Civil Service
Rt Hon **David Cameron** MP (Con)

Parliamentary Private Secretary	Gavin Williamson MP (Con) 020 7219 7150
Chief of Staff (Political)	Ed Llewellyn OBE
Email: ellewellyn@no10.x.gsi.gov.uk
Deputy Chiefs of Staff (Political)	Oliver Dowden
Catherine Fall
Email: cfall@no10.x.gsi.gov.uk
Principal Private Secretary	Chris Martin
Email: cmartin@no10.x.gsi.gov.uk
Private Secretaries to the Prime Minister	Gus Jaspert
John Casson
Email: jcasson@no10.x.gsi.gov.uk
Kate Joseph
Dan York-Smith
Tim Kiddell
Email: tkiddell@no10.x.gsi.gov.uk
Simon Case
Military Assistant	Col. Gwyn Jenkins
Political Secretary	Stephen Gilbert
Email: sgilbert@no10.x.gsi.gov.uk
Political Private Secretary	Laurence Mann
Email: lmann@no10.x.gsi.gov.uk
Director of Communications	Craig Oliver
Email: coliver@no10.x.gsi.gov.uk
Political Press Secretary to the Prime Minister	Graeme Wilson
Head of Press (Political)	Alan Sendorek
Email: asendorek@no10.x.gsi.gov.uk
Head of Broadcasting (Political)	Michael Salter
Email: msalter@no10.x.gsi.gov.uk
Head of Strategic Communications	Ameet Gill
Email: agill@no10.x.gsi.gov.uk
Head of Events and Visits	Liz Sugg
Email: lsugg@no10.x.gsi.gov.uk
Director of External Relations	Gabby Bertin
Email: gbertin@no10.x.gsi.gov.uk
Speechwriter	Claire Foges
Email: cfoges@no10.x.gsi.gov.uk
Head of Policy Unit	Jo Johnson MP (Con) 020 7219 7125
Email: jo.johnson.mp@parliament.uk
Deputy Heads of Policy Unit	Christopher Lockwood
Patrick Rock
Email: prock@no10.x.gsi.gov.uk

Deputy Director of Policy Unit	Antonia Williams
Private Secretary to	
Jo Johnson MP	Kate Marley
Special Advisers (Policy Unit)	Ramsay Jones
	Email: rjones@no10.x.gsi.gov.uk
	Andrew Dunlop
	Email: adunlop@no10.x.gsi.gov.uk
	Daniel Korski
	Nick Seddon
	Tara Singh
	Laura Trott
	Richard Parr
Policy Advisers	Miles Gibson
	Email: mgibson@no10.x.gsi.gov.uk
	Conrad Bailey
	Tim Luke
	Email: tluke@no10.x.gsi.gov.uk

Department for Business, Innovation and Skills

1 Victoria Street, London SW1H 0ET
Tel: 020 7215 5000 Email: [firstname.surname]@bis.gsi.gov.uk   (Please note: not for ministers)
bis.correspondence@bis.gsi.gov.uk Website: www.gov.uk/bis Twitter: @bisgovuk

Secretary of State for Business, Innovation and Skills; President of the Board of Trade
Rt Hon Dr **Vincent Cable** MP (Lib Dem)

Overall responsibility for department strategy and all policies; overall responsibility for BIS budget; particular focus on business and banking issues; lead Cabinet Minister for reducing regulatory burdens across Government.

Parliamentary Private Secretary	Tessa Munt MP (Lib Dem)	020 7219 4024	
	Email: tessa.munt.mp@parliament.uk		
Special Advisers	Emily Walch	020 7215 0005	Fax: 020 7215 5468
	Email: mpst.spad@bis.gsi.gov.uk		
	Giles Wilkes	020 7215 0005	Fax: 020 7215 5468
	Email: mpst.spad@bis.gsi.gov.uk		
Principal Private Secretary	Hannah Wiskin	020 7215 5621	Fax: 020 7215 5468
	Email: mpst.cable@bis.gsi.gov.uk		
Private Secretary	Emily Hamblin	020 7215 5233	Fax: 020 7215 5468
	Email: mpst.cable@bis.gsi.gov.uk		
	cablempstcorrespondence@bis.gsi.gov.uk		

Minister of State for Universities and Science Rt Hon **David Willetts** MP (Con)

Looking across all departmental business at strategic priorities; higher education (including HEFCE and Student Loans Company); science and research (including Research Councils); life sciences; innovation; Technology Strategy Board; Energy Technologies Institute; the National Measurement Office; the Design Council; the UK Accreditation Service; the British Standards Institute; Space.

Parliamentary Private Secretary	Paul Uppal MP (Con)	020 7219 7195	Fax: 020 7219 5221
	Email: paul.uppal.mp@parliament.uk		
Special Adviser	Nick Hillman	020 7215 3077	Fax: 020 7215 5468
	Email: mpst.willettsspad@bis.gsi.gov.uk		
Private Secretary	Benedict Collins	020 7215 5568	Fax: 020 7215 5468
	Email: mpst.willetts@bis.gsi.gov.uk		

Minister of State for Business and Enterprise Rt Hon **Michael Fallon** MP (Con)

(jointly with the Department of Energy and Climate Change) Business sectors, including low carbon economy, low emission vehicles, electronics; small business, enterprise and access to finance; competitiveness and economic growth; deregulation and better regulation; regional and local economic development (including Grants for Business Investment); business support; export licensing; Royal Mail; general oversight of Shareholder Executive and its portfolios; Commons spokesman on trade and investment.

Parliamentary Private Secretary	Dr Therese Coffey MP (Con) 020 7219 7164	
	Email: therese.coffey.mp@parliament.uk	
Special Adviser	James Wild	
	Email: mpst.fallonspad@bis.gsi.gov.uk	
Private Secretary	Philip Carr	020 7215 5933 Fax: 020 7215 5551
	Email: mpst.fallon@bis.gsi.gov.uk	

Minister of State for Trade and Investment **Lord Green of Hurstpierpoint** (Con)

(jointly with Foreign and Commonwealth Office) Development and implementation of cross-government strategy for trade and inward investment; responsibility for UKTI, ECGD; oversight of FCO prosperity directorate. Supports Chancellor of the Exchequer and Financial Secretary to the Treasury on financial services and banking issues; Member of the Prime Minister's Business Advisory Group; co-ordination of European business, multilateral trade policy, single market and implementation; Spokesman for the Government on trade and investment issues in the House of Lords.

Parliamentary Private Secretary	Margot James MP (Con)	020 7219 7226 Fax: 020 7219 6434
	Email: margot.james.mp@parliament.uk	
Private Secretary	Simon Clode	020 7215 3867
	Email: mpst.green@bis.gsi.gov.uk	

Minister of State for Skills and Enterprise **Matthew Hancock** MP (Con)

(jointly with Department for Education)

Private Secretary	Athith Shetty	020 7215 5914
	Email: mpst.hancock@bis.gsi.gov.uk	

Parliamentary Under-Secretary of State **Viscount Younger of Leckie** (Con)

All BIS business in the Lords except trade and investment; intellectual property (including the IPO).

Private Secretary	Victoria Miles-Keay	020 7215 6867 Fax: 020 7215 5551
	Email: mpst.younger@bis.gsi.gov.uk	

Parliamentary Under-Secretary of State (Minister for Employment Relations and Consumer Affairs) **Jo Swinson** MP (Lib Dem)

(jointly with Department for Culture, Media and Sport covering equalities) Post Office and Postal Policy; employment relations (including Advisory, Conciliation and Arbitration Service (Acas)), consumer policy and consumer affairs; competition policy; corporate governance; company law (including Companies House); social enterprise; Insolvency Service (including company investigations).

Private Secretary	Emily Cloke	020 7215 5229 Fax: 020 7215 5551
	Email: mpst.swinson@bis.gsi.gov.uk	
Head of Parliamentary Unit	Ian Webster	020 7215 6630 Fax: 020 7799 1531
	Email: mpst.parly@bis.gsi.gov.uk	

Cabinet Office

Dover House, Whitehall, London SW1A 2AU
Tel: 020 7276 3000
Website: www.gov.uk/cabinet-office www.gov.uk/dpm Twitter: @cabinetofficeuk

Deputy Prime Minister, Lord President of the Council Rt Hon **Nick Clegg** MP (Lib Dem)

Support to the Prime Minister in the full range of Government policy and initiatives. Special responsibility for political and constitutional reform: reform of the House of Lords; overall policy responsibility for devolution, including the question on the consequences of devolution for the House of Commons; introducing legislation to provide for individual voter registration; party funding reform; Royal succession; taking forward proposals for recall of MPs; widening access to elected office, including supporting people with disabilities to become MPs; electoral policy. Policy responsibility for the Electoral Commission, Boundary Commission and Independent Parliamentary Standards Authority; joint responsibility with the Justice Secretary for Bill of Rights Commission.

Parliamentary Private Secretary	Duncan Hames MP (Lib Dem) 020 7219 7039 Email: duncan.hames.mp@parliament.uk
Head of Communications and Spokesman	James Sorene 020 7276 2544 Email: james.sorene@cabinet-office.x.gsi.gov.uk
Chief of Staff	Jonny Oates Email: spadsdpm@cabinet-office.x.gsi.gov.uk
Deputy Chief of Staff	Joanne Foster Email: spadsdpm@cabinet-office.x.gsi.gov.uk
Director of Strategy	Ryan Coetzee Email: spadsdpm@cabinet-office.x.gsi.gov.uk
Director of Communications (based at Number 10)	Lena Pietsch
Head of Political Communications (based at Number 10)	Sean Kemp
Political Speechwriter	Zena Elmahrouki
Special Advisers (Media)	James Holt Email: spadsdpm@cabinet-office.x.gsi.gov.uk James McGrory Email: spadsdpm@cabinet-office.x.gsi.gov.uk
Director of Policy Innovation and Implementation (based at Number 10)	Polly Mackenzie
Chief Policy Projects Adviser (based at Number 10)	Julian Astle Email: julian.astle@cabinet-office.x.gsi.gov.uk
Chief Economic and Business Adviser	Chris Saunders
Parliamentary Liaison and Constitutional Affairs	Matthew Hanney
Senior Home and Foreign Affairs Adviser and Co-ordinator of Policy Staff	Tim Colbourne
Special Advisers (based at Number 10)	Veena Hudson (acting) Shabnum Mustapha

Departmental Advisers
(MoD; FCO; DfID)	Monica Allen
	Email: monica.allen@cabinet-office.x.gsi.gov.uk
(DH; DWP)	Emily Frith
(Home Office; MoJ)	Alex Dziedzan
(DCLG; DEFRA; DfT)	Adam Pritchard
(Cabinet Office; DfE; DCMS)	Matt Sanders
Principal Private Secretary	Lucy Smith
	Email: psdpm@cabinet-office.x.gsi.gov.uk

Minister for the Cabinet Office; Paymaster General Rt Hon **Francis Maude** MP (Con)

Public sector efficiency and reform; civil service issues; industrial relations strategy in the public sector; the Government's transparency programme; civil contingencies; cyber security; civil society; UK Statistics; overall responsibility for Cabinet Office policy and the Department.

Parliamentary Private Secretary	Stuart Andrew MP (Con)	020 7219 7130
	Email: stuart.andrew.mp@parliament.uk	
Special Advisers	Henry Newman	020 7276 2510
	Email: psspecialadvisers@cabinet-office.gsi.gov.uk	
	Simone Finn	020 7276 2510
	Email: psspecialadvisers@cabinet-office.gsi.gov.uk	
Principal Private Secretary	Daniel Gieve	020 7276 0426 Fax: 020 7276 0514
	Email: psfrancismaude@cabinet-office.gsi.gov.uk	

Minister for Government Policy Rt Hon **Oliver Letwin** MP (Con)

The Coalition Partnership; strategic reform plans.

Parliamentary Private Secretary	Paul Maynard MP (Con)	020 7219 7017
	Email: paul.maynard.mp@parliament.uk	
Special Adviser	Martha Varney	020 7276 2500
	Email: mvarney@no10.x.gsi.gov.uk	
	martha.varney@cabinet-office.gsi.gov.uk	
Private Secretary	Guy Horsington	020 7276 0659 Fax: 020 7276 0514
	Email: psoliverletwin@cabinet-office.gsi.gov.uk	

Minister of State Rt Hon **David Laws** MP (Lib Dem)

(jointly with Department for Education)

Parliamentary Private Secretary	Simon Wright MP (Lib Dem)	020 7219 3482
	Email: simon.wright.mp@parliament.uk	
Special Adviser	Julian Astle	
	Email: jastle@no10.x.gsi.gov.uk	
	julian.astle@cabinet-office.x.gsi.gov.uk	
Private Secretary	Nick Donlevy	020 7276 6124
	Email: psdavidlaws@cabinet-office.x.gsi.gov.uk	

Minister of State (Cities and Constitution) **Greg Clark** MP (Con)

Parliamentary Secretary (Minister for Civil Society) **Nick Hurd** MP (Con)

Big Society agenda; National Citizen Service; Big Society Capital; community first/community organisers; charities; volunteering; social enterprise; Cabinet Office interest in devolution.

Private Secretary	Laura Osbaldeston	020 7276 0867 Fax: 020 7276 0514
	Email: psnickhurd@cabinet-office.gsi.gov.uk	

Parliamentary Secretary (based at No 10) **Jo Johnson** MP (Con)
Head of the Downing Street Policy Unit.

Private Secretary	Kate Marley	020 7930 4433

Minister without portfolio Rt Hon **Kenneth Clarke** QC MP (Con)
Economy adviser; trade envoy.

Parliamentary Private Secretary Ben Wallace MP (Con)   020 7219 5804   Fax: 020 7219 5901
Email: wallaceb@parliament.uk

Special Adviser   Kathryn Laing   020 7276 3104
Email: pskennethclarke@cabinet-office.gsi.gov.uk

Private Secretary   Owain Robertson   020 7276 3105   Fax: 020 7276 0514
Email: pskennethclarke@cabinet-office.gsi.gov.uk

Minister without portfolio Rt Hon **Grant Shapps** MP (Con)

Parliamentary Private Secretary Jake Berry MP (Con)   020 7219 7214
Email: jake.berry.mp@parliament.uk

Private Secretary   Rose Jeffries   020 7276 1042
Email: psgrantshapps@cabinet-office.gsi.gov.uk

Minister without portfolio Rt Hon **John Hayes** MP (Con)

Parliamentary Private Secretary Mel Stride MP (Con)   020 7219 7037
Email: mel.stride.mp@parliament.uk

Private Secretary   Kellie Hurst   020 7276 0573
Email: psjohnhayes@cabinet-office.gsi.gov.uk

Parliamentary Clerk   Stuart Doubleday   020 7276 0415   Fax: 020 7276 0514
Email: coparliamentarybranch@cabinet-office.gsi.gov.uk

Department for Communities and Local Government

Eland House, Bressenden Place, London SW1E 5DU
Tel: 030 3444 0000
Email: [firstname.lastname]@communities.gsi.gov.uk   Website: www.gov.uk/dclg
Twitter: @communitiesuk

Secretary of State for Communities and Local Government Rt Hon **Eric Pickles** MP (Con)

Overall strategic direction of Department.

Parliamentary Private Secretary John Glen MP (Con)   020 7219 7138   Fax: 020 7219 3951
Email: john.glen.mp@parliament.uk

Special Advisers   Sheridan Westlake   030 3444 3992
Email: psadvisers@communities.gsi.gov.uk

                                 Zoe Thorogood   030 3444 3992
Email: psadvisers@communities.gsi.gov.uk

Principal Private Secretary   David Hill   030 3444 3450
Email: eric.pickles@communities.gsi.gov.uk

Senior Minister of State (Faith and Communities) Rt Hon **Baroness Warsi** (Con)

(jointly with Foreign and Commonwealth Office)

Parliamentary Private Secretary Eric Ollerenshaw OBE MP
                                 (Con)   020 7219 7096
Email: eric.ollerenshaw.mp@parliament.uk

Special Adviser	Jessica Cunniffe	030 3444 3992
	Email: psadvisers@communities.gsi.gov.uk	
Private Secretary	Gillie Severin	030 3444 1938
	Email: baroness.warsi@communities.gsi.gov.uk	

Parliamentary Under-Secretary of State **Brandon Lewis** MP (Con)

Local government; fire and resilience; Thames Gateway; travellers; community pubs.

| Private Secretary | Ruth Long | 030 3444 3430 |
| | Email: psbrandonlewis@communities.gsi.gov.uk | |

Parliamentary Under-Secretary of State **Stephen Williams** MP (Lib Dem)

Parliamentary Under-Secretary of State (Planning) **Nick Boles** MP (Con)

Planning and development; local growth (supporting Minister of State for Housing); deregulation.

| Private Secretary | Fakruz Zaman | 020 3444 3480 |
| | Email: psnickboles@communities.gsi.gov.uk | |

Parliamentary Under-Secretary of State **Baroness Stowell of Beeston** MBE (Con)

Parliamentary Under-Secretary of State **Kris Hopkins** MP (Con)

Parliamentary Clerk	Chris Woolf	030 3444 3407
	Email: chris.woolf@communities.gsi.gov.uk	
Correspondence Manager	Paul B Smith	030 3444 3391
	Email: paulb.smith@communities.gsi.gov.uk	

Department for Culture, Media and Sport

Fourth Floor, 100 Parliament Street, London SW1A 2BQ
Tel: 020 7211 6000
Email: [firstname.surname]@culture.gsi.gov.uk enquiries@culture.gov.uk enquiries@geo.gsi.gov.uk
Website: www.gov.uk/dcms www.gov.uk/geo Twitter: @DCMS

Secretary of State for Culture, Media and Sport (Minister for Women and Equalities)
Rt Hon **Maria Miller** MP (Con)

Overall responsibility of Department.

Parliamentary Private Secretary	Mary Macleod MP (Con)	020 7219 7023 Fax: 020 7219 4049
	Email: mary.macleod.mp@parliament.uk	
Special Advisers	Joanna Hindley	020 7211 6010
	Email: specialadvisers@culture.gsi.gov.uk	
	Nick King	020 7211 6010
	Email: specialadvisers@culture.gsi.gov.uk	
Principal Private Secretary	To be appointed	020 7211 6243
	Email: secretaryofstate@culture.gsi.gov.uk	

Parliamentary Under-Secretary of State (Minister for Culture, Communications and Creative Industries) Hon **Ed Vaizey** MP (Con)

Broadband, spectrum and telecoms; culture; heritage and built environment; internet and creative industries; libraries; media; museums and galleries.

| Private Secretary | Hanna Johnson | 020 7211 6304 |
| | Email: minister-culture@culture.gsi.gov.uk | |

Parliamentary Under-Secretary of State (Sport and Equalities) **Helen Grant** MP (Con)

Parliamentary Under-Secretary of State (Women and Equalities) **Jo Swinson** MP (Lib Dem)
(jointly with Department for Business, Innovation and Skills)

Private Secretary	Natalie Davis	020 7215 3817	Fax: 020 7215 5551
	Email: mpst.swinson@bis.gsi.gov.uk		

Parliamentary Clerk	David Goss	020 7211 6068
	Email: david.goss@culture.gsi.gov.uk	

Ministry of Defence
Floor 5, Main Building, Whitehall, London SW1A 2HB
Tel: 020 7218 9000
Email: defencesecretary-group@mod.uk Website: www.gov.uk/mod Twitter: @DefenceHQ

Secretary of State for Defence Rt Hon **Philip Hammond** MP (Con)

Overall responsibility for the Department; operations; personnel; defence transformation; defence planning, programme and resource allocation; defence policy; international relations; nuclear programme; acquisition; parliamentary business and communications.

Parliamentary Private Secretary	Claire Perry MP (Con)	020 7219 7050	Fax: 020 7219 1385
	Email: claire.perry.mp@parliament.uk		
Special Advisers	Graham Hook	020 7218 1964	
	Email: sofs-specialadvisersgroup@mod.uk		
	Hayden Allan	020 7218 2397	
	Email: sofs-specialadvisersgroup@mod.uk		
Principal Private Secretary	Emma Davies	020 7218 2111	Fax: 020 7218 7140
	Email: defencesecretary-group@mod.uk		

Minister of State Rt Hon **Mark Francois** MP (Con)

Parliamentary Private Secretary	Damian Hinds MP (Con)	020 7219 7057
	Email: damian.hinds.mp@parliament.uk	
Private Secretary	Charles Seeley	020 7218 2452
	Email: mindpwv-privateoffice@mod.uk	

Parliamentary Under-Secretary of State (International Security Strategy)
Dr **Andrew Murrison** MP (Con)

International defence strategy and relations; defence diplomacy; international defence institutions; planning for the 2015 Strategic Defence and Security Review.

Private Secretary	Anna Platt	020 7218 2229
	Email: miniss-privateoffice@mod.uk	

Parliamentary Under-Secretary of State (Defence Equipment, Support and Technology)
Philip Dunne MP (Con)

The equipment cycle, including investment decisions, science and technology and industrial strategy; Defence Materiel Strategy; non-equipment investment programme and decisions, including IT and estates. Defence Exports.

Private Secretary	Tom Burden	020 7218 6621
	Email: mindest-privateoffice@mod.uk	

Parliamentary Under-Secretary of State **Lord Astor of Hever** DL (Con)

Department issues in the House of Lords, including defence policy, operations, personnel, equipment, and legacy issues.

Private Secretary	Alan Lawson	020 7218 7346 Fax: 020 7218 7140
	Email: usofs-privateoffice@mod.uk	

Parliamentary Under-Secretary of State **Anna Soubry** MP (Con)

Parliamentary Clerk	Teresa Andrews	020 7218 1991 Fax: 020 7218 2044
	Email: parlibranch-parliclerk@mod.uk	

Department for Education

Sanctuary Buildings, Great Smith Street, London SW1P 3BT
Tel: 0370 000 2288 (Public Communications Unit) Fax: 01928 738248
Email: [firstname.surname]@education.gsi.gov.uk ministers@education.gsi.gov.uk
Website: www.gov.uk/dfe www.education.gov.uk Twitter: @educationgovuk

Secretary of State for Education Rt Hon **Michael Gove** MP (Con)

All the Department's policies.

Parliamentary Private Secretary	Gavin Barwell MP (Con)	020 7219 2119
	Email: gavin.barwell.mp@parliament.uk	
Special Advisers	Henry de Zoete	
	Email: advisers.ps@education.gsi.gov.uk	
	Dominic Cummings (due to leave at end of 2013)	
	Email: advisers.ps@education.gsi.gov.uk	
	Tim Leunig	
	Email: advisers.ps@education.gsi.gov.uk	
	Henry Cook	
	Email: advisers.ps@education.gsi.gov.uk	
Senior Principal Private Secretary	Louise Evans	
Principal Private Secretary	Pamela Dow	
Deputy Principal Private Secretary	Elin Jones	
Private Secretaries	Elizabeth Kelly	
	Email: sec-of-state.ps@education.gsi.gov.uk	
	Vicky Woodcock	
	Email: sec-of-state.ps@education.gsi.gov.uk	

Minister of State Rt Hon **David Laws** MP (Lib Dem)

(jointly with Cabinet Office) Pupil Premium, raising attainment, narrowing the gap; teachers; school improvement, accountability, inspection; funding; admissions; raising the participation age, and financial support for young people; Ofsted; Teaching Agency and National College; child poverty and social mobility strategy.

Parliamentary Private Secretary	Simon Wright MP (Lib Dem) 020 7219 3482	
	Email: simon.wright.mp@parliament.uk	
Senior Private Secretary	Lydia Mullholland	
	Email: laws.ps@education.gsi.gov.uk	

Parliamentary Under-Secretary of State **Edward Timpson** MP (Con)

Adoption, fostering, and residential care home reform; child protection; special educational needs; family law and justice; children's services; school sport; Office of Children's Commissioner.

Private Secretary	Rafi Addlestone
	Email: timpson.ps@education.gsi.gov.uk

Parliamentary Under-Secretary of State **Elizabeth Truss** MP (Con)

Childcare and early learning; assessment, qualifications, and curriculum reform; behaviour, attendance; school food review; reducing bureaucracy; Ofqual; Standards and Testing Agency.

Private Secretary	Matthew Edwards
	Email: truss.ps@education.gsi.gov.uk

Minister of State for Skills and Enterprise **Matthew Hancock** MP (Con)

(jointly with Department for Business, Innovation and Skills).

Senior Private Secretary	Athith Shetty
	Email: hancock.ps@education.gsi.gov.uk
	mpst.hancock@bis.gsi.gov.uk

Parliamentary Under-Secretary of State for Schools **Lord Nash** (Con)

Academies and free schools, including UTCs and studio schools; school improvement and sixth form performance and improvement; school funding, including revenue and capital, pupil premium; 16-19 funding, including revenue and capital, financial support for young people, YPLA, EFA; school organisation, including new schools, competitions; school governance; extremism; sustainability; corporate issues, including spending controls and FOI.

Private Secretary	Bonnie Wang
	Email: nash.ps@education.gsi.gov.uk
Parliamentary Clerk	To be appointed

Department of Energy and Climate Change
3 Whitehall Place, London SW1A 2AW
Tel: 0300 060 4000
Email: [firstname.surname]@decc.gsi.gov.uk enquiries@decc.gsi.gov.uk Website: www.gov.uk/decc
Twitter: @deccgovuk

Secretary of State for Energy and Climate Change Rt Hon **Edward Davey** MP (Lib Dem)

Overall responsibility for Department; DECC strategy and budgets; energy market reform; carbon price; annual energy statement; energy security; National Security; DECC delivery landscape; devolved administrations.

Parliamentary Private Secretary	Steve Gilbert MP (Lib Dem)	020 7219 7153	Fax: 020 7219 4180
	Email: stephen.gilbert.mp@parliament.uk		
Special Advisers	Paul Hodgson	0300 068 5986	
	Email: ps.decc.spads@decc.gsi.gov.uk		
	Chris Nicholson	0300 068 5986	
	Email: ps.decc.spads@decc.gsi.gov.uk		
Principal Private Secretary	Ross Gribbin	0300 068 5968	
	Email: ps.decc.sos@decc.gsi.gov.uk		

Minister of State for Climate Change Rt Hon **Gregory Barker** MP (Con)

The Green Deal; CERT, CESP and ECO; energy efficiency, including its contribution to EMR; public sector energy efficiency, including greening DECC; national and international climate change; EU Environment Council; national carbon markets and EU ETS; climate science; carbon budgets; carbon reduction commitment and climate change agreements; fuel poverty, Warm Home Discount and Warm Front; promoting the interests of energy consumers; Green Investment Bank; green jobs and skills; heat, including RHI; decentralised energy and small scale renewables, including co-operative/local ownership and business rates; FITs; energy innovation, including marine energy (wave and tidal) and geothermal.

Parliamentary Private Secretary	Laura Sandys MP (Con)	020 7219 3000
	Email: laura.sandys.mp@parliament.uk	
Senior Private Secretary	Anjoum Noorani	0300 068 5981
	Email: ps.gregory.barker@decc.gsi.gov.uk	

Minister of State for Energy Rt Hon **Michael Fallon** MP (Con)

(jointly with the Department for Business, Innovation and Skills) Energy Bill; supports the Secretary of State on EMR; security of supply; International energy; CCS, gas and coal policy; nuclear policy; renewable energy deployment; grid policy including smart grids and network of recharging points; oil and gas exploration, licensing and revenues; offshore environment and decommissioning; regulation and competition in the energy sector (incl. nuclear); waste and decommissioning policy for new nuclear; resilience and emergency preparedness; Energy Council; Coal Authority; lean regulation.

Senior Private Secretary	Jessica Ayers	0300 068 5982
	Email: ps.michael.fallon@decc.gsi.gov.uk	

Parliamentary Under-Secretary of State **Baroness Verma** (Con)

Departmental performance and delivery; efficiency; managing liabilities, including coal health and the Concessionary Fuel Scheme; transparency; managing the nuclear legacy, including NDA performance and delivery (supported by the Shareholder Executive) and policy on plutonium and MOX; URENCO; Geological Disposal Facility (GDF); civil nuclear security, including responsibility for the Civil Nuclear Constabulary; smart meter; nuclear safety and regulation; nuclear non-proliferation; supports Minister of State for Climate Change on Green Deal and fuel poverty; departmental business in the Lords.

Senior Private Secretary	Stephen Burke	0300 068 5449
	Email: ps.sandip.verma@decc.gsi.gov.uk	
Parliamentary Clerk	Derek Turner	0300 068 5991
	Email: derek.turner@decc.gsi.gov.uk	

Department for Environment, Food and Rural Affairs

Nobel House, 17 Smith Square, London SW1P 3JR
Email: [firstname.surname]@defra.gsi.gov.uk defra.helpline@defra.gsi.gov.uk
Website: www.gov.uk/defra Twitter: @Defragovuk

Secretary of State for Environment, Food and Rural Affairs Rt Hon **Owen Paterson** MP (Con)

Overall responsibility for Department; represents UK at EU Agriculture and Fisheries Council, shares responsibility with Secretary of State for Energy and Climate Change for representing UK at EU Environment Council; strategy, budgets and finances; legislative programme; emergencies; EU and international relations; Environment Agency; Natural England.

Parliamentary Private Secretary	David Burrowes MP (Con)	020 7219 8144	Fax: 020 7219 5289
	Email: david.burrowes.mp@parliament.uk		

Special Advisers	Amanda Craig	020 7238 5823
	Email: ps.advisers@defra.gsi.gov.uk	
	Guy Robinson	020 7238 5823
	Email: ps.advisers@defra.gsi.gov.uk	
Principal Private Secretary	Jeremy Marlow	020 7238 5339 Fax: 020 7238 6241
	Email: secretary.state@defra.gsi.gov.uk	

Parliamentary Under-Secretary of State **Dan Rogerson** MP (Lib Dem)

Parliamentary Under-Secretary of State (Resource Management, the Local Environment and Environmental Science) **Lord de Mauley** TD (Con)

All departmental business in the House of Lords. Resource management; climate change adaptation; environmental impacts of climate change mitigation, including biofuels; environmental regulation, including deputising for the Secretary of State at EU Environment Council; sustainable development including sustainable consumption and production; waste management; local environment; air quality; noise and litter; welfare of companion and wild animals, including circuses, dangerous dogs and zoos; localism and civil society; science and research; environmental science; nanotechnology; pesticides, chemicals and industrial pollution; genetically modified organisms; plant and bee health; Royal Botanic Gardens, Kew; Food and Environment Research Agency.

Senior Private Secretary	Tonima Saha	020 7238 5535 Fax: 020 7238 6241
	Email: ps.lord.demauley@defra.gsi.gov.uk	

Parliamentary Under-Secretary of State **George Eustice** MP (Con)

Parliamentary Clerk	Deirdre Kennedy	020 7238 5455 Fax: 020 7238 6241
	Email: parlybranch@defra.gsi.gov.uk	

Foreign and Commonwealth Office
King Charles Street, Whitehall, London SW1A 2AH
Tel: 020 7008 1500
Email: [firstname.surname]@fco.gsi.gov.uk msu.correspondence@fco.gsi.gov.uk
Website: www.gov.uk/fco Twitter: @foreignoffice

First Secretary of State, Secretary of State for Foreign and Commonwealth Affairs (Foreign Secretary) Rt Hon **William Hague** MP (Con)

Overall responsibility for Foreign and Commonwealth Office.

Parliamentary Private Secretary	Keith Simpson MP (Con)	020 7219 6457
	Email: keithsimpsonmp@parliament.uk	
Special Advisers	Arminka Helic	020 7008 2117/020 7008 2312
	Email: pospads@fco.gov.uk	
	Denzil Davidson	020 7008 2117/020 7008 2312
	Email: pospads@fco.gov.uk	
Principal Private Secretary	Thomas Drew	020 7008 2059
	Email: sosfa-action@fco.gov.uk	

Senior Minister of State Rt Hon **Baroness Warsi** (Con)
(jointly with Department for Communities and Local Government)

All FCO business in the Lords; Afghanistan, Pakistan, Bangladesh; Central Asia; human rights; UN, international organisations and ICC.

Parliamentary Private Secretary	Eric Ollerenshaw OBE MP	
	(Con)	020 7219 7096
	Email: eric.ollerenshaw.mp@parliament.uk	

Special Adviser	Naweed Khan	020 7008 2577
	Email: psministerwarsiaction@fco.gsi.gov.uk	
Private Secretary	Nick Heath	020 7008 2356
	Email: psministerwarsiaction@fco.gsi.gov.uk	

Minister of State Rt Hon **David Lidington** MP (Con)

EU, including Gibraltar and SBAs; Europe, including Balkans, Ukraine, Belarus and Moldova; Russia, South Caucasus; NATO and European security; OSCE and Council of Europe; FCO relations with Parliament; communications; FCO finance; estates and security; information technology.

Parliamentary Private Secretary	Tobias Ellwood MP (Con)	020 7219 4349	Fax: 020 7219 0946
	Email: tobias.ellwood.mp@parliament.uk		
Private Secretary	Olaf Henricson-Bell	020 7008 8294	Fax: 020 7008 3731
	Email: psliddington@fco.gov.uk		

Minister of State Rt Hon **Hugo Swire** MP (Con)

Far East and South East Asia; India and Nepal; Latin America, including Dominican Republic, Haiti, and Cuba; Falklands; Australasia and Pacific; Commonwealth; Migration and Olympic and Paralympic Legacy.

Parliamentary Private Secretary	Richard Graham MP (Con)	020 7219 7077	Fax: 020 7219 2299
	Email: richard.graham.mp@parliament.uk		
Private Secretary	Fergus Eckersley	020 7008 2127	
	Email: psministerswireaction@fco.gsi.gov.uk		

Minister of State for Trade and Investment **Lord Green of Hurstpierpoint** (Con)

(jointly with Department for Business, Innovation and Skills)

FCO relations with British business; commercial economic diplomacy department; economics unit; UK Trade and Investment, Export Credits Guarantee Department (ECGD); business policy. Spokesman for the Government on trade and investment issues in the House of Lords.

Parliamentary Private Secretary	Margot James MP (Con)	020 7219 7226	Fax: 020 7219 6434
	Email: margot.james.mp@parliament.uk		
Private Secretary	Simon Clode	020 7215 3867 (Mon, Tues, Fri)/	
		020 7008 5751 (Wed, Thurs)	
	Email: mpst.green@bis.gsi.gov.uk		

Minister of State Rt Hon **Hugh Robertson** MP (Con)

Parliamentary Under-Secretary of State **Mark Simmonds** MP (Con)

Africa; Overseas Territories (not Falklands, SBAs or Gibraltar); conflict issues; climate change; international energy security; consular policy; protocol; ministerial oversight for FCO Services; the Caribbean (not including Dominican Republic, Haiti or Cuba).

Private Secretary	Benjamin Wastnage	020 7008 2173
	Email: psministersimmondsaction@fco.gsi.gov.uk	

Parliamentary Clerk	Susan Geary	020 7008 2094
	Email: prtactioninfo@fco.gsi.gov.uk	

Department of Health

Richmond House, 79 Whitehall, London SW1A 2NS
Tel: 020 7210 4850
Email: [firstname.surname]@dh.gsi.gov.uk   Website: www.gov.uk/dh   Twitter: @DHgovuk

Secretary of State for Health Rt Hon **Jeremy Hunt** MP (Con)
Overall responsibility for Department.

Parliamentary Private Secretary	Robert Wilson MP (Con)	020 7219 2498/ Fax: 020 7219 0847
		020 7219 6519
	Email: robwilsonmp@parliament.uk	
Special Adviser	Christina Robinson	020 7210 2471
	Email: specialadvisors@dh.gsi.gov.uk	
Principal Private Secretary	Kristen McLeod	020 7210 5158
	Email: kristen.mcleod@dh.gsi.gov.uk	

Minister of State for Care and Support **Norman Lamb** MP (Lib Dem)

Older people, including dementia; long-term conditions; local government, health and wellbeing boards; adult social care, including funding reform, legislation, finance, workforce, regulation; quality regulation, including relationship with CQC; healthwatch; NHS Constitution; integration; personal health budgets, personalisation; reablement, continuing care; end of life care; safeguarding; mental health, including child and adolescent mental health services; physical and learning disabilities, autism; third sector; Big Society; volunteers; carers; prison health services.

Special Adviser	Emily Frith	
	Email: emily.frith@dh.gsi.gov.uk	
Private Secretary	Diana Kirby	020 7210 4865
	Email: diana.kirby@dh.gsi.gov.uk	

Parliamentary Under-Secretary of State Dr **Daniel Poulter** MP (Con)

Nursing; patient experience; maternity services; nursing and midwifery; health visiting; school nursing; children's health and public health; Allied Health Professions: physiotherapy, occupational health and others; NHS workforce, including pay and pensions; professional regulation; health education and training, relationship with Health Education England; NHS estates and facilities; NHS IT and information strategy; relationship with NHS Information Centre; procurement; NHS Business Services Authority; NHS security management; veterans' health; patient safety, HCAIs, Mid Staffs; NHS Litigation Authority.

Private Secretary	Aurelia Valota	020 7210 5119
	Email: aurelia.valota@dh.gsi.gov.uk	

Parliamentary Under-Secretary of State (Quality) Rt Hon **Earl Howe** (Con)

Reform, including NHS Commissioning Board, Clinical Commissioning Groups, any qualified provider and choice; Primary Care, including dentistry; urgent care; NHS performance; winter planning; economic regulation and provider policy; FT pipeline and relationship with NHS Trust Development Authority; medicines, pharmacy and industry, including regulation (MHRA); NICE; research and development, Health Research Authority; innovation; Academic Health Sciences Centres; departmental management; transition; finance overall, including DH DEL and Spending Review, NHS financial performance, allocations, central budgets and Vote 2; income generation.

Private Secretary	Dr Stephen Jones	020 7210 5066
	Email: stephen.jones@dh.gsi.gov.uk	

Parliamentary Under-Secretary of State **Jane Ellison** MP (Con)

Parliamentary Private Secretary to ministerial team	Andrew Jones MP (Con) 020 7219 3000 Email: andrew.jones.mp@parliament.uk
Parliamentary Clerk	Tim Elms 020 7210 5808 Fax: 020 7210 5814 Email: tim.elms@dh.gsi.gov.uk

---

Home Office
Peel Building, 2 Marsham Street, London SW1P 4DF
Tel: 020 7035 4848
Website: www.gov.uk/home-office
Twitter: @UKHomeOffice

Secretary of State for the Home Department (Home Secretary) Rt Hon **Theresa May** MP (Con)

Overall responsibility for work of the Home Office.

Parliamentary Private Secretary	George Hollingbery MP (Con) 020 7219 7109 Email: george.hollingbery.mp@parliament.uk
Special Advisers	Fiona Cunningham 020 7035 0196 Fax: 020 7035 0900 Email: advisers@homeoffice.gsi.gov.uk
	Nick Timothy 020 7035 0196 Fax: 020 7035 0900 Email: advisers@homeoffice.gsi.gov.uk
	Stephen Parkinson 020 7035 8837 Email: advisers@homeoffice.gsi.gov.uk
Principal Private Secretary	David Oliver 020 7035 0586 Email: privateoffice.external@homeoffice.gsi.gov.uk

---

Minister of State for Immigration **Mark Harper** MP (Con)

Policy on immigration and asylum; implementation of the limit on economic migrants; responsibility for the Identity and Passport Service and the General Register Office; international and European immigration and asylum policy; border control and enforcement; exclusion orders; extradition, mutual legal assistance and judicial co-operation; parliamentary champion; correspondence champion.

Parliamentary Private Secretary	Guy Opperman MP (Con) 020 7219 7227 Fax: 020 7219 6435 Email: guy.opperman.mp@parliament.uk
Private Secretary	Andrew Jones 020 7035 8799 Fax: 0870 336 9034 Email: ministerforimmigration@homeoffice.gsi.gov.uk

---

Minister of State for Policing and Criminal Justice Rt Hon **Damian Green** MP (Con)

(jointly with Ministry of Justice) Criminal justice strategy, human rights and overall responsibility for all policing issues in the Home Office: police reform, resources and police accountability; police funding; National Policing Improvement Agency and College of Policing; police leadership; firearms policy; public order.

Parliamentary Private Secretary	David Rutley MP (Con) 020 7219 7106 Email: david.rutley.mp@parliament.uk
Private Secretary	Yasmin Brooks 020 7035 8774 Fax: 0870 336 9033 Email: yasmin.brooks@homeoffice.gsi.gov.uk

---

Minister of State **Norman Baker** MP (Lib Dem)

Parliamentary Under-Secretary of State (Crime and Security) **James Brokenshire** MP (Con)

Olympic security; international CT; cyber crime; use of DNA and reform of DNA database; forensic science service; use of powers of surveillance by local authorities; CCTV and ANPR; Freedoms Bill; organised crime, including international drugs and support on the National Crime Agency; financial crime and identity crime, including fraud and asset recovery; Home Office science, including CT science and technology; security industry; space and maritime security; EU; communications capabilities; powers of entry.

Private Secretary	Emma Ross	020 7035 8766
	Email: privateoffice.external@homeoffice.gsi.gov.uk	

Parliamentary Under-Secretary of State (Criminal Information) **Lord Taylor of Holbeach** CBE (Con)

Private Secretary	Benedict Collins	020 7035 8796 Fax: 0870 336 9036
Parliamentary Clerk	Joanne Dawes	020 7035 8838
	Email: privateoffice.external@homeoffice.gsi.gov.uk	
	parliamentaryteam@homeoffice.gsi.gov.uk	

Department for International Development

22 Whitehall, London SW1A 2EG
Tel: 020 7023 0000
Email: [firstinitial-surname]@dfid.gov.uk dfidcorrespondence@dfid.gov.uk
Website: www.gov.uk/dfid Twitter: @DFID_UK

Secretary of State for International Development Rt Hon **Justine Greening** MP (Con)

Overall responsibility for Department's business and its policies.

Parliamentary Private Secretary	Julian Smith MP (Con)	020 7219 7145
	Email: julian.smith.mp@parliament.uk	
Special Advisers	Victoria Crawford	020 7023 1602
	Email: special-advisers@dfid.gov.uk	
	Guy Levin	020 7023 1602
	Email: special-advisers@dfid.gov.uk	
Principal Private Secretary	Vel Gnanendran	020 7023 0419
	Email: pssofs@dfid.gov.uk	

Minister of State Rt Hon **Alan Duncan** MP (Con)

Asia, Middle East, Caribbean and Overseas Territories; international finance; international relations (except EU); trade; humanitarian and security; corporate performance divisions.

Parliamentary Private Secretary	Ben Gummer MP (Con)	020 7219 7090 Fax: 020 7219 3542
	Email: ben.gummer.mp@parliament.uk	
Private Secretary	Jonny Baxter	020 7023 0399
	Email: psmos@dfid.gov.uk	

Parliamentary Under-Secretary of State **Lynne Featherstone** MP (Lib Dem)

Sub-Saharan Africa; European Union; policy, including health, education, water and sanitation, governance and civil society; research and evidence; private sector development.

Private Secretary	Emily Travis	020 7023 0150
	Email: pspuss@dfid.gov.uk	
Parliamentary Clerk	Rob Foot	020 7023 0559 Fax: 020 7023 0634
	Email: p-questions@dfid.gov.uk	

Ministry of Justice

102 Petty France, London SW1H 9AJ
Tel: 020 3334 3555 Fax: 020 3334 4455
Email: [firstname.surname]@justice.gsi.gov.uk general.queries@justice.gsi.gov.uk
Website: www.gov.uk/moj Twitter: @MoJGovUK

Lord Chancellor and Secretary of State for Justice Rt Hon **Chris Grayling** MP (Con)

Overall responsibility of Department; criminal justice and penal policy strategy; judicial policy; national security justice issues; EU and international issues; Anti-corruption Champion; Claims Management Regulation Unit; non-delegate Royal, Church and Hereditary issues; Lord Lieutenant and Constitutional issues.

Parliamentary Private Secretary	Lee Scott MP (Con) Email: scottle@parliament.uk	020 7219 8326 Fax: 020 7219 0970
Special Advisers	Amy Fisher Email: amy.fisher@justice.gsi.gov.uk	020 3334 3646
	Will Gallagher Email: will.gallagher@justice.gsi.gov.uk	020 3334 3645
Principal Private Secretary	James Crawforth Email: james.crawforth@justice.gsi.gov.uk	020 3334 3657

Minister of State and Deputy Leader of the House of Lords Rt Hon **Lord McNally** (Lib Dem)

Departmental business in the House of Lords; support to Secretary of State on constitutional matters; human rights and civil liberties; freedom of information; legal aid; family justice; defamation; support to Secretary of State on EU; Crown Dependencies.

Private Secretary	Chris Beal Email: christopher.beal@justice.gsi.gov.uk	020 3334 4665 Fax: 020 3334 3692

Minister of State for Policing and Criminal Justice Rt Hon **Damian Green** MP (Con)

(jointly with Home Office) Strategic oversight of the criminal justice system, reporting jointly to the Secretary of State for Justice and Home Secretary; joint working with Home Office, Attorney General's Office and CJS agencies; criminal law, procedure and the criminal offences gateway; sponsorship of the Criminal Cases Review Commission; the Transforming Justice programme; human rights and civil liberties (jointly with Lord McNally).

Parliamentary Private Secretary	David Rutley MP (Con) Email: david.rutley.mp@parliament.uk	020 7219 7106
Private Secretary	Yasmin Brooks Email: yasmin.brooks@homeoffice.gsi.gov.uk	020 7035 8774

Parliamentary Under-Secretary of State **Shailesh Vara** MP (Con)

(Parliamentary Under-Secretary of State (Minister for Prisons and Rehabilitation) **Jeremy Wright** MP (Con)

Rehabilitation revolution; prisons and probation; youth justice; sentencing policy.

Private Secretary	Chloe Burton Email: chloe.burton@justice.gsi.gov.uk	020 3334 3686 Fax: 020 3334 3692
Parliamentary Clerk	Ann Nixon Email: ann.nixon@justice.gsi.gov.uk	020 3334 3635 Fax: 020 3334 3638

Law Officers

Attorney General's Office, 20 Victoria Street, London SW1H 0NF
Tel: 020 7271 2492 Fax: 020 7271 2430
Email: [firstname.surname]@attorneygeneral.gsi.gov.uk
correspondenceunit@attorneygeneral.gsi.gov.uk Website: www.gov.uk/ago

Attorney General Rt Hon **Dominic Grieve** QC MP (Con)

Overall responsibility for the work of the Attorney General's Office and superintended Departments (the Treasury Solicitor's Department, the Crown Prosecution Service with the Revenue and Customs Prosecution Office, the Serious Fraud Office, the Services Prosecuting Authority and HM Crown Prosecution Service Inspectorate).

Specific statutory duty to superintend the discharge of duties by the Director of Public Prosecutions (who heads the Crown Prosecution Service and the Revenue and Customs Prosecution Office) and the Director of the Serious Fraud Office; non-statutory oversight of the Services Prosecuting Authority and government prosecuting departments Government's principal legal adviser dealing with questions of international law, European Community/Union law, human rights, devolution issues, and public interest functions; questions of law arising on Bills and with issues of legal policy, legal aspects of all major international and domestic litigation involving the Government.

Parliamentary Private Secretary	Jessica Lee MP (Con)	020 7219 7067
	Email: jessica.lee.mp@parliament.uk	
Principal Private Secretary	James Gerard	020 7271 2405
	Email: james.gerard@attonerygeneral.gsi.gov.uk	

Solicitor General **Oliver Heald** MP (Con)

Deputises for Attorney General; provides support to the Attorney General in his superintendence of the Treasury Solicitor's Department, the Crown Prosecution Service, the Service Prosecuting Authority, HM Crown Prosecution Service Inspectorate and the Serious Fraud Office; provides support to the Attorney General on civil litigation and advice on civil law matters and on the public interest function.

Private Secretary	Sharmin Choudhury	020 7271 2406
	Email: sharmin.choudhury@attorneygeneral.gsi.gov.uk	

Advocate General for Scotland Rt Hon **Lord Wallace of Tankerness** QC (Lib Dem)

Office of the Advocate General for Scotland, Dover House, 66 Whitehall, London SW1A 2AU
Tel: 020 7270 6720 Fax: 020 7270 6813
Email: privateoffice@advocategeneral.gsi.gov.uk [firstname.surname]@advocategeneral.gsi.gov.uk
Website: www.oag.gov.uk

The Advocate General for Scotland is a Minister of the Crown and is one of the three UK Law Officers. Along with the Attorney General and the Solicitor General for England and Wales, the Advocate General provides legal advice to all UK Government departments on a wide range of issues including human rights, European and constitutional law. The Advocate General is also the UK Government's principal legal adviser on Scots law and its senior representative within the Scottish legal community. The Advocate General is the Minister responsible to the UK Parliament for the Office of the Advocate General.

Private Secretary	Lucy Proctor	020 7270 6720 Fax: 020 7270 6813
	Email: privateoffice@advocategeneral.gsi.gov.uk	
Parliamentary Clerk	Michael Dawes	020 7271 2490
	Email: michael.dawes@attorneygeneral.gsi.gov.uk	

Leader of the House of Commons

1 Horse Guards Road, London SW1A 2HQ
Tel: 020 7276 1005 Fax: 020 7276 1006
Email: [firstname.surname]@cabinet-office.x.gsi.gov.uk Website: www.gov.uk/government/
organisations/the-office-of-the-leader-of-the-house-of-commons

Leader of the House of Commons and Lord Privy Seal Rt Hon **Andrew Lansley** CBE MP (Con)

Government's Legislative Programme; managing the business of the House; Government's representative
in the House (House of Commons Commission); House of Commons representative in Government;
House of Commons reform and related issues; Chair of Board of Trustees for Chevening Estate.

Parliamentary Private Secretary	John Howell OBE MP (Con) 020 7219 6676 Fax: 020 7219 2606	
	Email: howelljm@parliament.uk	
Special Adviser	Chris White	020 7276 1005
	Email: leader@commonsleader.x.gsi.gov.uk	
Head of Office	Mike Winter	020 7276 1005
	Email: leader@commonsleader.x.gsi.gov.uk	

Parliamentary Secretary (Deputy Leader of the House of Commons)
Rt Hon **Tom Brake** MP (Lib Dem)

Supports the Leader in handling Government's business in the House; monitors the legislative
programme; Minister with internal responsibility for Correspondence, FOI and Green Issues.

Private Secretary	To be appointed	020 7276 1005
	Email: deputy@commonsleader.x.gsi.gov.uk	

Leader of the House of Lords

House of Lords, London SW1A 0PW
Tel: 020 7219 3200
Website: www.gov.uk/government/organisations/office-of-the-leader-of-the-house-of-lords

Leader of the House of Lords; Chancellor of the Duchy of Lancaster
Rt Hon **Lord Hill of Oareford** CBE (Con)

Principal responsibility for the strategic management and delivery of the Government's legislative
programme in the Lords; leading Government benches in the House of Lords; conduct of Government
business in the Lords with the Lords Chief Whip; repeating in the Lords statements made by the Prime
Minister in the Commons; giving guidance to the House on matters of order and procedure; taking part
in formal ceremonies in the House, such as the State Opening of Parliament; Chair, Board of Trustees
for Chequers and Dorneywood.

As Chancellor of the Duchy of Lancaster, Lord Hill is accountable to the Sovereign for the
administration of the Duchy.

Parliamentary Private Secretary	Nigel Adams MP (Con)	020 7219 7141
	Email: nigel.adams.mp@parliament.uk	
Special Advisers	James Marshall	020 7219 3200
	Email: james.marshall@cabinet-office.x.gsi.gov.uk	
	Elizabeth Plummer	020 7219 3200
	Email: elizabeth.plummer@cabinet-office.x.gsi.gov.uk plummere@parliament.uk	
	Alastair Masser	020 7219 0267
	Email: massera@parliament.uk	

Principal Private Secretary	Andrew Mackersie	020 7219 3131
	Email: psleaderofthelords@cabinet-office.x.gsi.gov.uk	
Private Secretary	Julia Labeta	020 7219 3200
	Email: psleaderofthelords@cabinet-office.x.gsi.gov.uk	

Deputy Leader of the House of Lords Rt Hon **Lord McNally** (Lib Dem)

| Private Secretary | Chris Beal | 020 3334 4665 |
| | Email: christopher.beal@justice.gsi.gov.uk | |

Northern Ireland Office
1 Horse Guards Road, London SW1A 2HQ
Tel: 028 9052 0700
Email: [firstname.surname]@nio.x.gsi.gov.uk   Website: www.gov.uk/nio

Secretary of State for Northern Ireland Rt Hon **Theresa Villiers** MP (Con)

Overseeing the Northern Ireland devolution settlement and representing Northern Ireland interests at UK Government level and UK Government interests in Northern Ireland.

Parliamentary Private Secretary	Damian Collins MP (Con)	020 7219 7072	Fax: 020 7219 2213
	Email: damian.collins.mp@parliament.uk		
Special Adviser	Jonathan Caine	020 7210 0803	Fax: 020 7210 6449
	Email: jonathan.caine@nio.x.gsi.gov.uk		
Private Secretary	Fiona McCoy	020 7210 6460/	Fax: 020 7210 6449/
		028 9052 7899	028 9052 7040
	Email: sos@nio.x.gsi.gov.uk		

Minister of State **Andrew Robathan** MP (Con)

| Parliamentary Clerk | Ben Sneddon | 020 7210 6551 |
| | Email: parly.section@nio.x.gsi.gov.uk | |

Scotland Office
Dover House, Whitehall, London SW1A 2AU
Tel: 020 7270 6741 Fax: 020 7270 6815
Email: sofsscotland@scotlandoffice.gsi.gov.uk Website: www.gov.uk/scotland-office
Twitter: @scotlandoffice

Secretary of State for Scotland Rt Hon **Alistair Carmichael** MP (Lib Dem)

Represents interests of Scotland in Cabinet, particularly with regard to reserved matters. Leads on: economic affairs; Scottish budget; Scottish fiscal position; implementation of Scotland Act 2012; UK economic policy; defence; MoD in Scotland; nuclear deterrent; industry; fisheries; food and drinks industry; agriculture; manufacturing; life sciences; constitutional affairs; primary legislation, including Queen's Speech; JMC; Libya; foreign affairs; international development; corporate services; national security; counter-terrorism; military assistance to civil powers; civil contingencies and emergency powers; broadcasting; Crown Estate.

Principal Private Secretary	Colin Faulkner	020 7270 6728	Fax: 020 7270 6815
	Email: sofsscotland@scotlandoffice.gsi.gov.uk		
Private Secretary	James Newman	0131-244 9091	
	Email: sofsscotland@scotlandoffice.gsi.gov.uk		
Diary Secretary	Claire Loughlin	020 7270 6741	Fax: 020 7270 6815
	Email: sofsscotland@scotlandoffice.gsi.gov.uk		

Parliamentary Under-Secretary of State Rt Hon **David Mundell** MP (Con)

Leads on: fatal accident enquiries (defence); veterans issues; Post Office network; Scottish banknotes; business/enterprise; insolvency; better regulation; competition issues; housing (construction industry); SMEs; broadband; creative industries; Scotland Act 1998 Orders; constitutional reform; legislative competency; elections and boundaries; electoral fraud and registration; postal voting; Boundary Commission; voting rights of prisoners; home and social affairs; welfare reform and employability; health and social care; poverty; employment; voluntary sector and charities; asylum and immigration; data and identity management; Student Loans Company; digital inclusion; sport and culture; justice; National Lottery and gambling; equalities; education and skills; energy and climate change; transmission issues; S185 Energy Act scheme; carbon capture and storage; renewables; carbon emissions reductions target; nuclear; supergrids; emissions trading; fossil fuel levy; transport.

Private Secretary	Jennifer Manton	020 7270 6806	Fax: 020 7270 6815
	Email: pusofsscotland@scotlandoffice.gsi.gov.uk		
Assistant Private Secretary and Diary Secretary	Jamie Wasley	020 7270 6816	Fax: 020 7270 6815
	Email: pusofsscotland@scotlandoffice.gsi.gov.uk		
Parliamentary Clerk	Ben Sneddon	020 7270 6746	
	Email: parly.section@nio.x.gsi.gov.uk		

Department for Transport
Great Minster House, 33 Horseferry Road, London SW1P 4DR
Tel: 0300 330 3000
Email: [firstname.surname]@dft.gsi.gov.uk Website: www.gov.uk/dft Twitter: @transportgovuk

Secretary of State for Transport Rt Hon **Patrick McLoughlin** MP (Con)

Overall responsibility for transport strategy, including economic growth and climate change; transport security; high speed rail strategy.

Parliamentary Private Secretary	Gavin Williamson MP (Con) 020 7219 7150	
	Email: gavin.williamson.mp@parliament.uk	
Special Advisers	Ben Mascall	020 7944 4377
	Email: ben.mascall@dft.gsi.gov.uk	
	Julian Glover	020 7944 4377
	Email: julian.glover@dft.gsi.gov.uk	
Principal Private Secretary	Philip West	020 7944 3011 Fax: 020 7944 4399
	Email: philip.west@dft.gsi.gov.uk	

Minister of State Rt Hon **Baroness Kramer** (Lib Dem)

Parliamentary Under-Secretary of State **Stephen Hammond** MP (Con)

Strategic roads and Highways Agency; motoring agencies; road safety and standards; freight and logistics, including lorry road user charging; maritime and dangerous goods, including Maritime and Coastguard Agency; London; Crossrail; better regulation.

Private Secretary	Tom Newman-Taylor	020 7944 4404	Fax: 020 7944 4521
	Email: tom.newman-taylor@dft.gsi.gov.uk		

Parliamentary Under-Secretary of State **Robert Goodwill** MP (Con)

Parliamentary Clerk	James Langston	020 7944 4472	Fax: 020 7944 4466
	Email: james.langston@dft.gsi.gov.uk		

HM Treasury

1 Horse Guards Road, London SW1A 2HQ
Tel: 020 7270 4558 Fax: 020 7270 4861
Email: [firstname.surname]@hmtreasury.gsi.gov.uk   (Please note: not for ministers)
public.enquiries@hmtreasury.gsi.gov.uk Website: www.gov.uk/hm-treasury Twitter: @HMTreasury

Chancellor of the Exchequer Rt Hon **George Osborne** MP (Con)

Overall responsibility for the work of the Treasury.

Parliamentary Private Secretary	Robert Wilson MP (Con)	020 7219 2498
	Email: robwilsonmp@parliament.uk	
Special Advisers	Rupert Harrison	020 7270 5013
	Email: rupert.harrison@hmtreasury.gsi.gov.uk	
	Lady Eleanor Wolfson	020 7270 5027
	Email: eleanor.wolfson@hmtreasury.gsi.gov.uk	
	Ramesh Chhabra	020 7270 5027
	Email: ramesh.chhabra@hmtreasury.gsi.gov.uk	
	Neil O'Brien	020 7270 5027
	Email: neil.o'brien@hmtreasury.gsi.gov.uk	
	Thea Rogers	020 7270 5013
	Email: thea.rogers@hmtreasury.gsi.gov.uk	
Principal Private Secretary	Clare Lombardelli	020 7270 5168
	Email: private.office@hmtreasury.gsi.gov.uk	

Chief Secretary to the Treasury Rt Hon **Danny Alexander** MP (Lib Dem)

Public expenditure including: spending reviews and strategic planning; in-year spending control; public sector pay and pensions; Annually Managed Expenditure (AME) and welfare reform; efficiency and value for money in public service; procurement; capital investment. Treasury interest in devolution.

Parliamentary Private Secretary	Lorely Burt MP (Lib Dem) 020 7219 8269 Fax: 020 7219 5199	
	Email: lorely.burt.mp@parliament.uk	
Special Advisers	Will de Peyer	020 7270 5027
	Email: william.depeyer@hmtreasury.gsi.gov.uk	
	John Foster	020 7270 5013
	Email: john.foster@hmtreasury.gsi.gov.uk	
	Julia Church	020 7270 5013 (on maternity leave)
	Email: julia.church@hmtreasury.gsi.gov.uk	
Private Secretary	William Garton	020 7270 4339
	Email: action.cst@hmtreasury.gsi.gov.uk	

Financial Secretary **Sajid Javid** MP (Con)

Financial services policy, including banking and financial services reform and regulation, financial stability, city competitiveness, wholesale and retail markets in the UK, Europe and internationally and the Financial Services Authority; banking support, including Asset Protection Scheme, Recapitalisation Fund and other schemes; bank lending; UK Financial Interests; Equitable Life; personal savings and pensions policy; Government Actuary's department; EU budget; support to the Chancellor on EU and wider international finance issues.

Private Secretary	To be appointed
	Email: fst.action@hmtreasury.gsi.gov.uk

Exchequer Secretary **David Gauke** MP (Con)

Strategic oversight of the UK tax system including direct, indirect, business and personal taxation; corporate and small business taxation, with input from Commercial Secretary; Departmental Minister for HM Revenue and Customs and the Valuation Office Agency; Lead Minister on European and international tax issues; overall responsibility for the Finance Bill.

Private Secretary	Oliver Haydon	020 7270 4349
	Email: action.xst@hmtreasury.gsi.gov.uk	

Economic Secretary **Nicky Morgan** MP (Con)

Environmental issues including taxation of transport, international climate change issues and energy issues; North Sea oil taxation; tax credits and child poverty; assists Chief Secretary on welfare reform; charities and voluntary sector; excise duties and gambling, including excise fraud and law enforcement; stamp duty land tax; ministerial responsibility for the Royal Mint; Departmental Minister for HM Treasury Group; working with the Exchequer Secretary on the Finance Bill; support to the Chief Secretary on public service pensions.

Private Secretary	To be appointed
	Email: action.est@hmtreasury.gsi.gov.uk

Commercial Secretary **Lord Deighton** KBE (Con)

Treasury spokesperson in the House of Lords; enterprise and productivity, including industrial strategy, better regulation, competition policy, infrastructure, and microeconomic reform; corporate finance, including public corporations and public private partnerships; assists the Financial Secretary on financial services and banking policy including UK Financial Investments; working with the Financial Secretary to promote the Government's financial services policies and the competitiveness of the UK; asset freezing and financial crime; foreign exchange reserves and debt management policy; National Savings and Investment; Debt Management Office.

Private Secretary	Emily Marsh	020 7270 4350
	Email: comsec.action@hmtreasury.gsi.gov.uk	
Parliamentary Clerk	Stephen Wiles	020 7270 4520 Fax: 020 7270 4325
	Email: stephen.wiles@hmtreasury.gsi.gov.uk	

Wales Office

Gwydyr House, Whitehall, London SW1A 2NP
Tel: 020 7270 0534
Email: [firstname.surname]@walesoffice.gsi.gov.uk
wales.office@walesoffice.gsi.gov.uk
Website: www.gov.uk/wales-office Twitter: @walesoffice

Secretary of State for Wales Rt Hon **David Jones** MP (Con)

Overall Strategic direction; Assembly liaison; constitutional issues, including Government of Wales Act; economy; infrastructure; business; Silk Commission; inward investment; foreign affairs, including EU; Welsh language, Royal matters.

Parliamentary Private Secretary	Daniel Kawczynski MP (Con) 020 7219 6249 Fax: 020 7219 1047	
	Email: kawczynskid@parliament.uk	
Principal Private Secretary	Stephen Hillcoat	020 7270 0550 Fax: 020 7270 0568
	Email: privateoffice@walesoffice.gsi.gov.uk	

Parliamentary Under-Secretary of State **Stephen Crabb** MP (Con)

Defence; environment; energy; welfare; transport; borders, including immigration; broadcasting; local government; law and order.

Private Secretary	Beth Adams	020 7270 0569
	Email: bethany.adams@walesoffice.gsi.gov.uk	

Parliamentary Under-Secretary of State **Baroness Randerson** (Lib Dem)

Health; education; elections; public appointments; rural affairs; equality; human trafficking (inter-departmental committee); culture, tourism; Big Society.

Private Secretary	Elizabeth Allen	020 7270 0538
	Email: elizabeth.allen2@walesoffice.gsi.gov.uk	
Parliamentary Clerk	Ben Sneddon	020 7270 0584/020 7210 6551
	Email: parly.section@nio.x.gsi.gov.uk	

Department for Work and Pensions

Caxton House, Tothill Street, London SW1H 9DA
Tel: 020 7340 4000
Website: www.gov.uk/dwp Twitter: @dwppressoffice Twitter: @MinisterDisPpl

Secretary of State for Work and Pensions Rt Hon **Iain Duncan Smith** MP (Con)

Overall departmental responsibility.

Parliamentary Private Secretary	Andrew Selous MP (Con)	020 7219 8134 Fax: 020 7219 1741
	Email: andrew.selous.mp@parliament.uk	
Special Advisers	Philippa Stroud	020 3267 5033
	Email: special-advisers@dwp.gsi.gov.uk	
	Lisa Hunter	020 3267 5033
	Email: special-advisers@dwp.gsi.gov.uk	
	Romilly Dennys	020 3267 5033
	Email: special-advisers@dwp.gsi.gov.uk	
Principal Private Secretary	Paul McComb	020 3267 5007
	Email: secretaryofstate@dwp.gsi.gov.uk	

Minister of State for Pensions **Steve Webb** MP (Lib Dem)

Pensions reform; State Pension, Single Tier, Second State Pensions and Pension Credit; The Pension, Disability and Carers Service; ageing society and extending working lives; Winter Fuel Payments; Cold Weather Payments; Welfare Benefit Uprating; private pensions; automatic enrolment into workplace pensions; automatic transters; Defined Ambition pensions; the Pensions Regulator; Pension Protection Fund; Financial Assistance Scheme; Pensions Advisory Service and Ombudsman; Child Maintenance; family policy, including flexible working, childcare, flexible parental leave; maternity benefits; Social Fund; financial inclusion; method of payment policy; reducing regulation; departmental transparency.

Private Secretary	Michael Dynan-Oakley	020 3267 5027
	Email: minister.pensions@dwp.gsi.gov.uk	

Minister of State (Employment) **Esther McVey** MP (Con)

Private Secretary	To be appointed

Minister of State **Mike Penning** MP (Con)

Private Secretary	To be appointed

Parliamentary Under-Secretary of State (Minister for Welfare Reform) **Lord Freud** (Con)

All departmental business in the House of Lords; universal credit; benefit cap; housing benefit and support for mortgage interest; employment support allowance; income support; bereavement benefit; fraud and error (including debt management); health and work; sickness absence; statutory sick pay; industrial injuries disablement benefit; employer liability compensation payments; data sharing; Social Security Advisory Committee; devolution issues; financial inclusion – credit unions.

Private Secretary	Rob Cook	020 3267 5035
	Email: minister.welfarereform@dwp.gsi.gov.uk	

Parliamentary Clerk	James Rowe	020 3267 5053 Fax: 020 3267 5086
	Email: james.rowe@dwp.gsi.gov.uk	

Ministerial Committees of the Cabinet

Banking Reform Committee
Chair: Chancellor of the Exchequer
Deputy Chair: Secretary of State for Business, Innovation and Skills

Coalition Committee
Chairs: Prime Minister; Deputy Prime Minister
Deputy Chairs: First Secretary of State, Secretary of State for Foreign and Commonwealth Affairs; Secretary of State for Energy and Climate Change

Coalition Operation and Strategic Planning Group
Chairs: Minister for Government Policy, Cabinet Office; Chief Secretary to the Treasury

Economic Affairs Committee
Chair: Chancellor of the Exchequer
Deputy Chair: Secretary of State for Business, Innovation and Skills

European Affairs Committee
Chair: First Secretary of State and Foreign Secretary
Deputy Chair: Secretary of State for Energy and Climate Change

Home Affairs Committee
Chair: Deputy Prime Minister
Deputy Chair: Lord Chancellor, Secretary of State for Justice

Local Growth Committee
Chair: Deputy Prime Minister
Deputy Chair: Chancellor of the Exchequer

National Security Council
Chair: Prime Minister
Deputy Chairs: Deputy Prime Minister, Lord President of the Council; First Secretary of State, Secretary of State for Foreign and Commonwealth Affairs

Olympic and Paralympic Legacy Committee
Chair: Prime Minister
Deputy Chairs: Deputy Prime Minister; First Secretary of State, Secretary of State for Foreign and Commonwealth Affairs

Parliamentary Business and Legislation Committee
Chair: Leader of the House of Commons
Deputy Chair: Deputy Leader of the House of Commons

Public Expenditure Committee
Chair: Chancellor of the Exchequer
Deputy Chair: Chief Secretary to the Treasury

Social Justice Committee
Chair: Secretary of State for Work and Pensions
Deputy Chair: Chief Secretary to the Treasury

Need additional copies?
Call 020 7593 5679
Visit www.dodsshop.co.uk

Parliamentary Private Secretaries

Prime Minister's Office

David Cameron, Prime Minister

Gavin Williamson
020 7219 7150

Business, Innovation and Skills

Vincent Cable, Secretary of State

Tessa Munt
020 7219 4024
Email: tessa.munt.mp@parliament.uk

David Willetts, Minister of State

Paul Uppal
020 7219 7195 Fax: 020 7219 5221
Email: paul.uppal.mp@parliament.uk

Michael Fallon, Minister of State

Therese Coffey
020 7219 7164
Email: therese.coffey.mp@parliament.uk

Lord Green of Hurstpierpoint, Minister of State

Margot James
020 7219 7226 Fax: 020 7219 6434
Email: margot.james.mp@parliament.uk

Cabinet Office

Nick Clegg, Deputy Prime Minister

Duncan Hames
020 7219 7039
Email: duncan.hames.mp@parliament.uk

Francis Maude, Minister

Stuart Andrew
020 7219 7130
Email: stuart.andrew.mp@parliament.uk

Oliver Letwin, Minister

Paul Maynard
020 7219 7017
Email: paul.maynard.mp@parliament.uk

David Laws, Minister of State

Simon Wright
020 7219 3482
Email: simon.wright.mp@parliament.uk

Kenneth Clarke, Minister without portfolio

Ben Wallace
020 7219 5804 Fax: 020 7219 5901
Email: wallaceb@parliament.uk

Grant Shapps, Minister without portfolio

Jake Berry
020 7219 7214
Email: jake.berry.mp@parliament.uk

John Hayes, Minister without portfolio

Mel Stride
020 7219 7037
Email: mel.stride.mp@parliament.uk

Communities and Local Government

Eric Pickles, Secretary of State

John Glen
020 7219 7138 Fax: 020 7219 3951
Email: john.glen.mp@parliament.uk

Baroness Warsi, Senior Minister of State

Eric Ollerenshaw
020 7219 7096
Email: eric.ollerenshaw.mp@parliament.uk

Culture, Media and Sport

Maria Miller, Secretary of State

Mary Macleod
020 7219 7023 Fax: 020 7219 4049
Email: mary.macleod.mp@parliament.uk

Defence

Mark Francois, Minister of State

Damian Hinds
020 7219 7057
Email: damian.hinds.mp@parliament.uk

Education

David Laws, Minister of State

Simon Wright
020 7219 3482
Email: simon.wright.mp@parliament.uk

Energy and Climate Change

Edward Davey, Secretary of State

Steve Gilbert
020 7219 7153 Fax: 020 7219 4180
Email: stephen.gilbert.mp@parliament.uk

Gregory Barker, Minister of State

Laura Sandys
020 7219 3000
Email: laura.sandys.mp@parliament.uk

Environment, Food and Rural Affairs

Owen Paterson, Secretary of State

David Burrowes
020 7219 8144 Fax: 020 7219 5289
Email: david.burrowes.mp@parliament.uk

Foreign and Commonwealth Office

William Hague, First Secretary of State

Keith Simpson
020 7219 6457
Email: keithsimpsonmp@parliament.uk

Baroness Warsi, Senior Minister of State

Eric Ollerenshaw
020 7219 7096
Email: eric.ollerenshaw.mp@parliament.uk

David Lidington, Minister of State

Tobias Ellwood
020 7219 4349 Fax: 020 7219 0946
Email: tobias.ellwood.mp@parliament.uk

Hugo Swire, Minister of State

Richard Graham
020 7219 7077 Fax: 020 7219 2299
Email: richard.graham.mp@parliament.uk

Lord Green of Hurstpierpoint, Minister of State

Margot James
020 7219 7226 Fax: 020 7219 6434
Email: margot.james.mp@parliament.uk

Health

Ministerial team

Andrew Jones
020 7219 3000
Email: andrew.jones.mp@parliament.uk

Home Office

Theresa May, Secretary of State

George Hollingbery
020 7219 7109
Email: george.hollingbery.mp@parliament.uk

Mark Harper, Minister of State

Guy Opperman
020 7219 7227 Fax: 020 7219 6435
Email: guy.opperman.mp@parliament.uk

Damian Green, Minister of State

David Rutley
020 7219 7106
Email: david.rutley.mp@parliament.uk

International Development

Justine Greening, Secretary of State

Julian Smith
020 7219 7145
Email: julian.smith.mp@parliament.uk

Alan Duncan, Minister of State

Ben Gummer
020 7219 7090 Fax: 020 7219 3542
Email: ben.gummer.mp@parliament.uk

Justice

Chris Grayling, Lord Chancellor and Secretary of State

Lee Scott
020 7219 8326 Fax: 020 7219 0970
Email: scottle@parliament.uk

Damian Green, Minister of State

David Rutley
020 7219 7106
Email: david.rutley.mp@parliament.uk

Law Officers

Dominic Grieve, Attorney General

Jessica Lee
020 7219 7067
Email: jessica.lee.mp@parliament.uk

Leader of the House of Commons

Andrew Lansley, Leader of the House of Commons

John Howell
020 7219 6676 Fax: 020 7219 2606
Email: howelljm@parliament.uk

Leader of the House of Lords

Lord Hill of Oareford, Leader of the House of Lords

Nigel Adams
020 7219 7141
Email: nigel.adams.mp@parliament.uk

Northern Ireland Office

Theresa Villiers, Secretary of State

Damian Collins
020 7219 7072 Fax: 020 7219 2213
Email: damian.collins.mp@parliament.uk

HM Treasury

George Osborne, Chancellor of the Exchequer

Rob Wilson
020 7219 2498

Danny Alexander, Chief Secretary to the Treasury

Lorely Burt
020 7219 8269 Fax: 020 7219 5199
Email: lorely.burt.mp@parliament.uk

Wales Office

David Jones, Secretary of State

Daniel Kawczynski
020 7219 6249 Fax: 020 7219 1047
Email: kawczynskid@parliament.uk

Work and Pensions

Iain Duncan Smith, Secretary of State

Andrew Selous
020 7219 8134 Fax: 020 7219 1741
Email: andrew.selous.mp@parliament.uk

Special Advisers

Pay 2013–14*

Pay Band	Pay Range
0	Up to £40,352
1	£40,352–£54,121
2	£52,215–£69,266
3 and Premium	£66,512–£103,263
4	£88,966–£106,864
Scheme ceiling	£142,668

* based on 2012-13 figures, 2013-14 figures were not available at time of going to press.

Prime Minister's Office

David Cameron, Prime Minister

Craig Oliver
coliver@no10.x.gsi.gov.uk
Oliver Dowden
Ed Llewellyn
ellewellyn@no10.x.gsi.gov.uk
Catherine Fall
cfall@no10.x.gsi.gov.uk
Claire Foges
cfoges@no10.x.gsi.gov.uk
Liz Sugg
lsugg@no10.x.gsi.gov.uk
Andrew Dunlop
adunlop@no10.x.gsi.gov.uk
Daniel Korski
Nick Seddon
Tara Singh
Ameet Gill
agill@no10.x.gsi.gov.uk
Michael Salter
msalter@no10.x.gsi.gov.uk
Alan Sendorek
asendorek@no10.x.gsi.gov.uk
Richard Parr
Laura Trott
Ramsay Jones
rjones@no10.x.gsi.gov.uk

Business, Innovation and Skills

Vincent Cable, Secretary of State

Giles Wilkes
020 7215 0005 Fax: 020 7215 5468
mpst.spad@bis.gsi.gov.uk
Emily Walch
020 7215 0005 Fax: 020 7215 5468
mpst.spad@bis.gsi.gov.uk

David Willetts, Minister of State

Nick Hillman
020 7215 3077 Fax: 020 7215 5468
mpst.willettsspad@bis.gsi.gov.uk

Michael Fallon, Minister of State

James Wild
mpst.fallonspad@bis.gsi.gov.uk

Cabinet Office

Nick Clegg, Deputy Prime Minister	Jonny Oates
	spadsdpm@cabinet-office.x.gsi.gov.uk
	Joanne Foster
	spadsdpm@cabinet-office.x.gsi.gov.uk
	Ryan Coetzee
	spadsdpm@cabinet-office.x.gsi.gov.uk
	Lena Pietsch
	Sean Kemp
	James McGrory
	spadsdpm@cabinet-office.x.gsi.gov.uk
	James Holt
	spadsdpm@cabinet-office.x.gsi.gov.uk
	Julian Astle
	Chris Saunders
	Tim Colbourne
	Veena Hudson
	Shabnum Mustapha
	Monica Allen
	monica.allen@cabinet-office.x.gsi.gov.uk
	Emily Frith
	Alex Dziedzan
	Adam Pritchard
	Matt Sanders
Francis Maude, Minister	Simone Finn
	020 7276 2510
	psspecialadvisers@cabinet-office.gsi.gov.uk
	Henry Newman
	020 7276 2510
	psspecialadvisers@cabinet-office.gsi.gov.uk
Oliver Letwin, Minister	Martha Varney
	020 7276 2500
	mvarney@no10.x.gsi.gov.uk
	martha.varney@cabinet-office.gsi.gov.uk
David Laws, Minister of State	Julian Astle
	jastle@no10.x.gsi.gov.uk
	julian.astle@cabinet-office.x.gsi.gov.uk
Kenneth Clarke, Minister without portfolio	Kathryn Laing
	020 7276 3104
	pskennethclarke@cabinet-office.gsi.gov.uk

Communities and Local Government

Eric Pickles, Secretary of State	Sheridan Westlake
	030 3444 3992
	psadvisers@communities.gsi.gov.uk
	Zoe Thorogood
	030 3444 3992
	psadvisers@communities.gsi.gov.uk
Baroness Warsi, Senior Minister of State	Jessica Cunniffe
	030 3444 3992
	psadvisers@communities.gsi.gov.uk

Culture, Media and Sport

Maria Miller, Secretary of State

Joanna Hindley
020 7211 6010
specialadvisers@culture.gsi.gov.uk
Nick King
020 7211 6010
specialadvisers@culture.gsi.gov.uk

Defence

Philip Hammond, Secretary of State

Graham Hook
020 7218 1964
sofs-specialadvisersgroup@mod.uk
Hayden Allan
020 7218 2397
sofs-specialadvisersgroup@mod.uk

Education

Michael Gove, Secretary of State

Henry de Zoete
advisers.ps@education.gsi.gov.uk
Dominic Cummings
(due to leave at the end of 2013)
advisers.ps@education.gsi.gov.uk
Tim Leunig
advisers.ps@education.gsi.gov.uk
Henry Cook
advisers.ps@education.gsi.gov.uk

Energy and Climate Change

Edward Davey, Secretary of State

Paul Hodgson
0300 068 5986
ps.decc.spads@decc.gsi.gov.uk
Chris Nicholson
0300 068 5986
ps.decc.spads@decc.gsi.gov.uk

Environment, Food and Rural Affairs

Owen Paterson, Secretary of State

Amanda Craig
020 7238 5823
ps.advisers@defra.gsi.gov.uk
Guy Robinson
020 7238 5823
ps.advisers@defra.gsi.gov.uk

Foreign and Commonwealth Office

William Hague, First Secretary of State

Arminka Helic
020 7008 2117/020 7008 2312
pospads@fco.gov.uk
Denzil Davidson
020 7008 2117/020 7008 2312
pospads@fco.gov.uk

Baroness Warsi, Senior Minister of State

Naweed Khan
020 7008 2577
psministerwarsiaction@fco.gsi.gov.uk

Health

Jeremy Hunt, Secretary of State

Christina Robinson
020 7210 2471
specialadvisors@dh.gsi.gov.uk

Norman Lamb, Minister of State

Emily Frith
emily.frith@dh.gsi.gov.uk

Home Office

Theresa May, Secretary of State

Fiona Cunningham
020 7035 0196 Fax: 020 7035 0900
advisers@homeoffice.gsi.gov.uk
Nick Timothy
020 7035 0196 Fax: 020 7035 0900
advisers@homeoffice.gsi.gov.uk
Stephen Parkinson
020 7035 8837
advisers@homeoffice.gsi.gov.uk

International Development

Justine Greening, Secretary of State

Victoria Crawford
020 7023 1602
special-advisers@dfid.gov.uk
Guy Levin
020 7023 1602
special-advisers@dfid.gov.uk

Justice

Chris Grayling, Lord Chancellor and Secretary of State

Amy Fisher
020 3334 3646
amy.fisher@justice.gsi.gov.uk
Will Gallagher
020 3334 3645
will.gallagher@justice.gsi.gov.uk

Leader of the House of Commons

Andrew Lansley, Leader of the House of Commons

Chris White
020 7276 1005
leader@commonsleader.x.gsi.gov.uk

Leader of the House of Lords

Lord Hill of Oareford, Leader of the House of Lords

James Marshall
020 7219 3200
james.marshall@cabinet-office.x.gsi.gov.uk
Elizabeth Plummer
020 7219 3200
elizabeth.plummer@cabinet-office.x.gsi.gov.uk
plummere@parliament.uk
Alastair Masser
020 7219 0267
massera@parliament.uk

Northern Ireland Office

Theresa Villiers, Secretary of State

Jonathan Caine
020 7210 0803 Fax: 020 7210 6449
jonathan.caine@nio.x.gsi.gov.uk

Transport

Patrick McLoughlin, Secretary of State

Ben Mascall
020 7944 4377
ben.mascall@dft.gsi.gov.uk
Julian Glover
020 7944 4377
julian.glover@dft.gsi.gov.uk

HM Treasury

George Osborne, Chancellor of the Exchequer

Rupert Harrison
020 7270 5013
rupert.harrison@hmtreasury.gsi.gov.uk
Lady Eleanor Wolfson
020 7270 5027
eleanor.wolfson@hmtreasury.gsi.gov.uk
Ramesh Chhabra
020 7270 5027
ramesh.chhabra@hmtreasury.gsi.gov.uk
Neil O'Brien
020 7270 5027
neil.o'brien@hmtreasury.gsi.gov.uk
Thea Rogers
020 7270 5013
thea.rogers@hmtreasury.gsi.gov.uk

Danny Alexander, Chief Secretary to the Treasury

Will de Peyer
020 7270 5027
william.depeyer@hmtreasury.gsi.gov.uk
John Foster
020 7270 5013
john.foster@hmtreasury.gsi.gov.uk
Julia Church (on maternity leave)
020 7270 5013
julia.church@hmtreasury.gsi.gov.uk

Work and Pensions

Iain Duncan Smith, Secretary of State

Philippa Stroud
020 3267 5033
special-advisers@dwp.gsi.gov.uk
Lisa Hunter
020 3267 5033
special-advisers@dwp.gsi.gov.uk
Romilly Dennys
020 3267 5033
special-advisers@dwp.gsi.gov.uk

Dods Contacts

Do you need to contact Members of Parliament, the House of Lords or local councillors?

Dods' definitive data provides you with direct access to those who shape policy and legislation in the UK. Constantly updated to ensure the most current information is available, renting Dods data gives you full contact details of all 650 MPs, 800 Peers and over 20,000 councillors.

Lists available include:

Person Type	Quantity	Cost per record
Members of Parliament	650	75p
House of Lords	806*	75p
Members of the European Parliament	736	75p
Councillors	20,000*	75p

*Subject to change

Minimum order £350 for single use; all orders are subject to VAT.

To discuss your requirements, please contact Lucy Williams on 020 7593 5644 email lucy.williams@dods.co.uk or visit www.dodsshop.co.uk

The Opposition

Labour (official opposition)

Shadow Cabinet

Leader of the Opposition	Rt Hon **Ed Miliband** MP
Shadow Deputy Prime Minister; Chair, Labour Party; Shadow Secretary of State for Culture, Media and Sport	Rt Hon **Harriet Harman** QC MP
Shadow Chancellor of the Exchequer	Rt Hon **Ed Balls** MP
Shadow Secretary of State for Foreign and Commonwealth Affairs (Foreign Secretary)	Rt Hon **Douglas Alexander** MP
Shadow Secretary of State for the Home Department (Home Secretary)	Rt Hon **Yvette Cooper** MP
Shadow Lord Chancellor and Secretary of State for Justice; Shadow Minister for London	Rt Hon **Sadiq Khan** MP
Opposition Chief Whip	Rt Hon **Rosie Winterton** MP
Shadow Secretary of State for Health	Rt Hon **Andy Burnham** MP
Shadow Secretary of State for Business, Innovation and Skills	**Chuka Umunna** MP
Shadow Secretary of State for Work and Pensions	**Rachel Reeves** MP
Shadow Secretary of State for Education	**Tristram Hunt** MP
Shadow Secretary of State for Defence	**Vernon Coaker** MP
Shadow Secretary of State for Communities and Local Government	Rt Hon **Hilary Benn** MP
Shadow Secretary of State for Energy and Climate Change	Rt Hon **Caroline Flint** MP
Shadow Leader of the House of Commons; Chair, National Policy Forum	**Angela Eagle** MP
Shadow Secretary of State for Transport	**Mary Creagh** MP
Shadow Secretary of State for Northern Ireland	**Ivan Lewis** MP
Shadow Secretary of State for International Development	Rt Hon **Jim Murphy** MP
Shadow Secretary of State for Scotland	**Margaret Curran** MP
Shadow Secretary of State for Wales	**Owen Smith** MP
Shadow Secretary of State for Environment, Food and Rural Affairs	**Maria Eagle** MP
Shadow Minister for the Cabinet Office	**Michael Dugher** MP
Shadow Minister without Portfolio; Deputy Chair, Labour Party	**John Trickett** MP
Shadow Minister for Women and Equalities	**Gloria De Peiro** MP
Shadow Chief Secretary to the Treasury	**Chris Leslie** MP
Shadow Leader of the House of Lords	Rt Hon **Baroness Royall of Blaisdon**
Shadow Chief Whip in the House of Lords	Rt Hon **Lord Bassam of Brighton**

Also attending Shadow Cabinet

Shadow Minister for Care and Older People	**Liz Kendall** MP
Shadow Minister for Housing	**Emma Reynolds** MP
Shadow Attorney General	**Emily Thornberry** MP
Shadow Minister without Portfolio	Dr **Lord Wood of Anfield**
Policy Review Co-ordinator	**Jon Cruddas** MP

Shadow Ministers

Business, Innovation and Skills

Shadow Secretary of State	**Chuka Umunna** MP
Shadow Ministers	**Liam Byrne** MP
	Iain Wright MP
	Toby Perkins MP
	Stella Creasy MP
	Ian Murray MP
	Lord Stevenson of Balmacara
	Lord Young of Norwood Green
	Baroness Hayter of Kentish Town
	Lord Liddle

Cabinet Office

Shadow Deputy Prime Minister	Rt Hon **Harriet Harman** QC MP
Shadow Ministers	**Michael Dugher** MP
	Jon Ashworth MP
	Chi Onwurah MP
	Lisa Nandy MP
	Dr **Lord Wood of Anfield**
	Baroness Hayter of Kentish Town
Shadow Minister without Portfolio	**Jon Trickett** MP

Communities and Local Government

Shadow Secretary of State	Rt Hon **Hilary Benn** MP
Shadow Ministers	**Emma Reynolds** MP
	Dr **Roberta Blackman-Woods** MP
	Lyn Brown MP
	Andy Sawford MP
	Lord McKenzie of Luton
	Lord Beecham

Culture, Media and Sport

Shadow Secretary of State	Rt Hon **Harriet Harman** QC MP
Shadow Ministers	**Helen Goodman** MP
	Clive Efford MP
	Baroness Jones of Whitchurch
	Lord Stevenson of Balmacara

Defence

Shadow Secretary of State	**Vernon Coaker** MP
Shadow Ministers	**Kevan Jones** MP
	Alison Seabeck MP
	Yvonne Fovargue MP
	Gemma Doyle MP
	Lord Rosser

Education
Shadow Secretary of State	**Tristram Hunt** MP
Shadow Ministers	**Kevin Brennan** MP
	Steve McCabe MP
	Rushanara Ali MP
	Lucy Powell MP
	Rt Hon **Baroness Hughes of Stretford**
	Baroness Jones of Whitchurch

Energy and Climate Change
Shadow Secretary of State	Rt Hon **Caroline Flint** MP
Shadow Ministers	**Tom Greatrex** MP
	Jonathan Reynolds MP
	Julie Elliott MP
	Baroness Worthington

Environment, Food and Rural Affairs
Shadow Secretary of State	**Maria Eagle** MP
Shadow Ministers	**Huw Irranca-Davies** MP
	Barry Gardiner MP
	Thomas Docherty MP
	Rt Hon **Lord Knight of Weymouth**

Equalities Office
Shadow Ministers	**Gloria De Piero** MP
	Sharon Hodgson MP
	Baroness Thornton

Foreign and Commonwealth Office
Shadow Foreign Secretary	Rt Hon **Douglas Alexander** MP
Shadow Ministers	Rt Hon **John Spellar** MP
	Gareth Thomas MP
	Ian Lucas MP
	Kerry McCarthy MP
	Lord Triesman
	Lord Bach
	Lord Liddle

Health
Shadow Secretary of State	Rt Hon **Andy Burnham** MP
Shadow Ministers	**Liz Kendall** MP
	Luciana Berger MP
	Andrew Gwynne MP
	Jamie Reed MP
	Rt Hon **Lord Hunt of Kings Heath** OBE
	Lord Bradley

Home Office
Shadow Home Secretary	Rt Hon **Yvette Cooper** MP
Shadow Ministers	**Jack Dromey** MP

Rt Hon **David Hanson** MP
Diana Johnson MP
Helen Jones MP
Steve Reed MP
Rt Hon **Baroness Smith of Basildon**
Lord Rosser

International Development
Shadow Secretary of State | Rt Hon **Jim Murphy** MP
Shadow Ministers | **Alison McGovern** MP
Gavin Shuker MP
Lord Collins of Highbury

Justice
Shadow Lord Chancellor and Secretary of State;
Shadow Minister for London | Rt Hon **Sadiq Khan** MP
Shadow Ministers | **Stephen Twigg** MP
Andy Slaughter MP
Jenny Chapman MP
Dan Jarvis MP
Lord Beecham
Rt Hon **Lord Falconer of Thoroton** QC

Law Officers
Shadow Attorney General | **Emily Thornberry** MP
Shadow Advocate General for Scotland | **Lord Davidson of Glen Clova** QC

Leader of the House of Commons
Shadow Leader | **Angela Eagle** MP
Shadow Deputy Leaders | **Angela Smith** MP

Leader of the House of Lords
Shadow Leader | Rt Hon **Baroness Royall of Blaisdon**
Shadow Deputy Leader | Rt Hon **Lord Hunt of Kings Heath** OBE

Northern Ireland
Shadow Secretary of State | **Ivan Lewis** MP
Shadow Ministers | **Stephen Pound** MP
Rt Hon **Lord McAvoy**

Scotland
Shadow Secretary of State | **Margaret Curran** MP
Shadow Ministers | **Russell Brown** MP
Gordon Banks MP
Rt Hon **Lord McAvoy**

Transport
Shadow Secretary of State   **Mary Creagh** MP
Shadow Ministers   **Lilian Greenwood** MP
Gordon Marsden MP
Richard Burden MP
Rt Hon **Lord Davies of Oldham**
Lord Rosser

Treasury
Shadow Chancellor of the Exchequer   Rt Hon **Ed Balls** MP
Shadow Chief Secretary   **Chris Leslie** MP
Shadow Ministers   **Cathy Jamieson** MP
Catherine McKinnell MP
Shabana Mahmood MP
Lord Eatwell
Rt Hon **Lord Davies of Oldham**
Lord Davidson of Glen Clova QC
Lord Adonis

Wales
Shadow Secretary of State   **Owen Smith** MP
Shadow Ministers   **Nia Griffith** MP
Baroness Morgan of Ely

Work and Pensions
Shadow Secretary of State   **Rachel Reeves** MP
Shadow Ministers   Rt Hon **Stephen Timms** MP
Chris Bryant MP
Gregg McClymont MP
Kate Green MP
Baroness Sherlock OBE
Lord Bradley

Opposition Commons Whips
Chief Whip   Rt Hon **Rosie Winterton**
Deputy Chief Whip   **Alan Campbell**
Assistant Chief Whip   **Mark Tami**
Whips   **Heidi Alexander**
David Hamilton
Graham Jones
Tom Blenkinsop
Susan Elan Jones
Phil Wilson
Julie Hilling
Karl Turner
Nic Dakin
Seema Malhotra
Bridget Phillipson
Stephen Doughty

Opposition Lords Spokespeople

Leader of the Opposition	Rt Hon **Baroness Royall of Blaisdon**
Deputy Leader of the Opposition	Rt Hon **Lord Hunt of Kings Heath** OBE
Business, Innovation and Skills	**Lord Stevenson of Balmacara** **Lord Young of Norwood Green** **Lord Liddle** **Baroness Hayter of Kentish Town**
Cabinet Office	**Baroness Hayter of Kentish Town** Dr **Lord Wood of Anfield**
Communities and Local Government	**Lord Beecham** **Lord McKenzie of Luton**
Culture, Media and Sport	**Baroness Jones of Whitchurch** **Lord Stevenson of Balmacara**
Defence	**Lord Rosser**
Education	Rt Hon **Baroness Hughes of Stretford** **Baroness Jones of Whitchurch**
Energy and Climate Change	**Baroness Worthington**
Environment, Food and Rural Affairs	Rt Hon **Lord Knight of Weymouth**
Equalities Office	**Baroness Thornton**
Foreign and Commonwealth Office	**Lord Triesman** **Lord Bach** **Lord Liddle**
Health	Rt Hon **Lord Hunt of Kings Heath** OBE **Lord Bradley**
Home Office	Rt Hon **Baroness Smith of Basildon** **Lord Rosser**
International Development	**Lord Collins of Highbury**
Justice	Rt Hon **Lord Falconer of Thoroton** QC **Lord Beecham**
Law Officers	**Lord Davidson of Glen Clova** QC
Northern Ireland	Rt Hon **Lord McAvoy**
Scotland	Rt Hon **Lord McAvoy**
Transport	Rt Hon **Lord Davies of Oldham** **Lord Rosser**
Treasury	**Lord Davidson of Glen Clova** QC Rt Hon **Lord Davies of Oldham** **Lord Eatwell** Rt Hon **Lord Adonis**
Wales	**Baroness Morgan of Ely**
Work and Pensions	**Baroness Sherlock** OBE **Lord Bradley**

Opposition Lords Whips

Chief Whip	Rt Hon **Lord Bassam of Brighton**
Deputy Chief Whips	**Lord Tunnicliffe** CBE
	Rt Hon **Baroness Smith of Basildon**
Senior Whips	**Lord McAvoy**
	Baroness Wheeler
Whips	**Lord Collins of Highbury**
	Lord Grantchester
	Baroness Hayter of Kentish Town
	Baroness Morgan of Ely
	Baroness Sherlock OBE
	Lord Stevenson of Balmacara
	Baroness Worthington

Crossbench

Convenor	**Lord Laming** CBE DL

Democratic Unionist Party

Parliamentary Group Leader; Constitutional Issues; Foreign Affairs; Culture, Olympics, Media and Sport	Rt Hon **Nigel Dodds** OBE
Justice and Home Affairs; House Issues; Shadow Deputy Prime Minister	Dr **William McCrea**
Defence; Energy and Climate Change	Rt Hon **Jeffrey Donaldson**
International Development; Cabinet Office	**Gregory Campbell**
Business, Innovation and Skills; Communities and Local Government; Education	**David Simpson**
Treasury	**Sammy Wilson**
Work and Pensions; Environment, Food and Rural Affairs	**Ian Paisley**
Health; Transport; Equality and Human Rights	**Jim Shannon**

Plaid Cymru (The Party of Wales)

Parliamentary Leader; Group Whip; Constitution; Defence; Environment, Food and Rural Affairs; Foreign and Commonwealth Affairs; Home Affairs; Justice	Rt Hon **Elfyn Llwyd**
Cabinet Office; Energy and Climate Change; Education; Health; International Development; Work and Pensions	**Hywel Williams**
Business, Innovation and Skills; Communities and Local Government; Culture, Olympics, Media and Sport; Transport; Treasury	**Jonathan Edwards**

Scottish National Party

Group Leader; Defence; Foreign Affairs	**Angus Robertson**
Deputy Group Leader; Treasury	**Stewart Hosie**
Chief Whip; Home Affairs; Constitution; Justice; Culture, Media and Sport	**Peter Wishart**

Trade; Energy and Climate Change; Consumer Affairs	**Mike Weir**
Transport; Tourism; Scotland Office; Deputy Prime Minister	**Angus MacNeil**
International Development; Fisheries, Environment, Food and Rural Affairs; Work and Pensions	**Dr Eilidh Whiteford**

Social Democratic and Labour Party

Leader; Chief Whip; Health; Business, Innovation and Skills; Culture, Media and Sport	**Dr Alasdair McDonnell**
Treasury; International Development; Foreign Affairs; Home Affairs and Justice; Work and Pensions	**Mark Durkan**
Political Affairs; Energy and Climate Change; Environment, Food and Rural Affairs	**Margaret Ritchie**

Ulster Unionist Party

Leader in the House of Lords	**Lord Rogan**

Salaried Parliamentarians 2013–14

On 8 February 2012 it was agreed that salaries would continue to be frozen at 2010 levels. Further to the Independent Parliamentary Standards Authority (IPSA) review of Members' pay it was announced that Members' salaries would increase by one per cent from April 2013.

House of Commons	Total salary £
Prime Minister	142,500
Cabinet Minister	134,565
Lord Chancellor	134,565
Government Chief Whip	134,565
Minister of State	98,740
Parliamentary Under-Secretary of State	89,435
Government Deputy Chief Whip	98,740
Government Whip	84,977
Assistant Government Whip	84,977
Leader of the Opposition	128,836
Opposition Chief Whip	98,740
Deputy Opposition Chief Whip	84,977
Assistant Opposition Whip	84,977
Speaker	141,504
Deputy Speaker:	
Chairman of Ways and Means	107,108
First Deputy Chairman of Ways and Means	102,098
Second Deputy Chairman of Ways and Means	102,098
Attorney General	161,510
Solicitor General	124,986
Select Committee Chair	*81,124
	†81,936
Member of Parliament	*66,396
	†67,060

House of Lords	£
Cabinet Minister	101,038
Minister of State	78,891
Parliamentary Under Secretary of State	68,710
Advocate General for Scotland	91,755
Government Chief Whip	78,891
Government Deputy Chief Whip	68,710
Government Whip	63,537
Leader of the Opposition	68,710
Opposition Chief Whip	63,537
Speaker	101,038
Chairman of Committees	84,524
Principal Deputy Chairman of Committees	79,076

The number of paid Ministerial posts is limited to 109. The Government may appoint additional Ministers; however, these will be unpaid appointments.

*April 2013 figure †April 2014 figure

ALLOWANCES

For the full guide see:
www.parliament.uk/documents/commons-finance-office/greenbook0907.pdf
Updated figures for 2013-14 from House of Commons Library Research Paper 13/33.

Figures are for annual costs unless otherwise stated.

Accommodation

Non-London area Members may claim a maximum of £20,100. MPs who do not claim for rent or mortgage payments can claim for hotel accommodation: up to £150 per night in London, or £120 per night elsewhere. In addition Members may claim £25 for subsistence costs incurred for overnight stays while on parliamentary business.

Office expenditure

Non-London area MPs may claim up to £22,750 to maintain their constituency office and provide surgeries; for London area MPs it is £25,350.

General administration

Each MP can claim up to £10,394 to cover the cost of office equipment, various services, communication costs etc.

Staffing

Costs cannot exceed £144,000 for London area MPs and £137,200 for non-London MPs. In addition Members can only employ one "connected party" (i.e. spouse, family member, business partner) unless previous arrangements were in effect prior to the introduction of the allowances scheme.

Travel

Reasonable expenses can be reimbursed for the purposes of performing parliamentary duties.

PENSIONS

NB: A review of pensions is expected by the end of 2013.

MPs' pensions

MPs' pensions are dependent on the amount of their salary that they choose to contribute. There are three options:

– accrual rate of 1/40th and a 11.9 per cent contribution from their salary;

– accrual rate of 1/50th and a 7.9 per cent contribution from their salary; or

– accrual rate of 1/60th and a 5.9 per cent contribution from their salary.

   MP's pension = accrual rate x final salary as MP x number of years served.

MPs can take up to 25 per cent of their pension as a tax-free lump sum.

Salaried parliamentarians' pensions

The Prime Minister, Lord Chancellor and Commons Speaker were entitled to a pension of half of their final office-holder's salary, regardless of length of service. However, under new arrangements made in 2008 only the Commons Speaker will receive this pension; the Prime Minister and Lord Chancellor will receive the same pension benefits as other ministers in the Commons.

An office-holder's pension for Members of the Commons is in addition to their pension as an MP, and is calculated:

   Accrual rate [set with MP's pension] x final pensionable salary x sum total of contribution factors

   Contribution factor in a year = (MP's pension contribution percentage rate x office-holder salary)

   (MP's salary pension contribution for year)

When ministerial office ends; the contribution earned is uprated in line with RPI.

PAYMENTS ON LEAVING OFFICE
Severance pay
Ministers and other paid office holders (with the exception of the Prime Minister and Commons Speaker) are entitled to a severance payment of one-quarter of their final Ministerial salary when they leave office for whatever reason.

Severance payments under £30,000 are tax and National Insurance exempt.

Winding-up allowance and resettlement grant
One-third of the sum of the current staffing provision and incidental expenses allowance is payable as a winding-up allowance at the time of a Member's retirement, defeat, or death.

The resettlement grant is payable to those who cease to be an MP at a general election. The amount is based on age and length of service, and up to £56,450 for London area MPs and £53,350 for all other MPs.

PARLIAMENT

HOUSE OF COMMONS

HOUSE OF COMMONS

London SW1A 0AA 020 7219 3000 Information Office 020 7219 4272
Website: www.parliament.uk Twitter: @UKParliament

Bulk correspondence to MPs may be delivered to Derby Gate at the Palace of Westminster, but must be stamped or franked or accompanied by a cheque for second-class postage made out to Post Office Counters. A single letter petitioning an individual MP can be delivered without postage payment by hand when the House is sitting.

Speaker and Deputy Speakers

The Speaker is the presiding officer of the Commons, whose main responsibility is to maintain order in debates and apply the rules and traditions of the House. The Chairman of Ways and Means is the principal deputy Speaker. By tradition, the Speaker, once elected, renounces party allegiance for the remainder of his or her career.

The Speaker: Rt Hon **John Bercow** MP 020 7219 5300
Chairman of Ways and Means: Rt Hon **Lindsay Hoyle** MP (Lab)
First Deputy Chairman: **To be appointed**
Second Deputy Chairman: Rt Hon **Dawn Primarolo** MP (Lab)

Speaker's Secretary: **Peter Barratt** 020 7219 4111 Email: barrattpf@parliament.uk
Speaker's Chaplain: Rev **Rose Hudson-Wilkin**

House of Commons Commission/Members Estimate Committee

The House of Commons Commission is responsible for the management of the House, including the employment of its staff and the provision of services by the departments of the House.

Chair: Rt Hon **John Bercow** MP (Speaker)
Members: Rt Hon **Andrew Lansley** CBE MP (Leader of the House) (Con)
Angela Eagle MP (Shadow Leader of the House) (Lab)
Sir **Paul Beresford** MP (Con)
Frank Doran MP (Lab)
John Thurso MP (Lib Dem)
Secretary: **Robert Twigger** 020 7219 3270

Members (MPs)

State of the Parties (September 2013)

	Total
Conservative	303
Labour	257
Liberal Democrat	56
Democratic Unionist Party	8
Scottish National Party	6
Independent	5
Sinn Féin	5
Plaid Cymru	3
Social Democratic and Labour Party	3
Alliance	1
Green Party	1
Respect	1
The Speaker	1
	650 seats

Changes since 2010 General Election

DISQUALIFICATION

Phil Woolas	Oldham East and Saddleworth – *Lab*	5 November 2010

RESIGNATIONS

Gerry Adams	Belfast West – *Sinn Féin*	26 January 2011
Eric Illsley	Barnsley Central – *Ind*	8 February 2011
Peter Soulsby	Leicester South – *Lab*	1 April 2011
Marsha Singh	Bradford West – *Lab*	2 March 2012
Louise Mensch	Corby – *Con*	29 August 2012
Tony Lloyd	Manchester Central – *Lab*	22 October 2012
Alun Michael	Cardiff South and Penarth – *Lab/Co-op*	22 October 2012
Denis MacShane	Rotherham – *Ind*	5 November 2012
Martin McGuinness	Mid Ulster – *Sinn Féin*	2 January 2013
Chris Huhne	Eastleigh – *Lib Dem*	5 February 2013
David Miliband	South Shields – *Lab*	15 April 2013

DEATHS

David Cairns	Inverclyde – *Lab*	10 May 2011
Alan Keen	Feltham and Heston – *Lab/Co-op*	10 November 2011
Malcolm Wicks	Croydon North – *Lab*	29 September 2012
Stuart Bell	Middlesbrough – *Lab*	13 October 2012

CHANGE OF PARTY

Eric Joyce	Falkirk	Labour Whip suspended February 2011, now Independent
Patrick Mercer	Newark	Resigned from the Conservative Party May 2013, now Independent
Mike Hancock	Portsmouth South	Resigned Liberal Democrat Whip June 2013, now Independent
David Ward	Bradford East	Liberal Democrat Whip withdrawn July 2013, now Independent
Nigel Evans	Ribble Valley	Resigned Conservative Whip September 2013, now Independent

BY-ELECTIONS

OLDHAM EAST AND SADDLEWORTH

13 January 2011 due to the Labour MP Phil Woolas having his Membership voided by the special election court on 5 November 2010.

Lab	Debbie Abrahams	14,718
Lib Dem	Elwyn Watkins	11,160
Con	Kashif Ali	4,481

UKIP Paul Nuttall 2,029, *BNP* Derek Adams 1,560, *Green* Peter Allen 530, *Loony* Nick "The Flying Brick" Delves 145, *Eng Dem* Stephen Morris 144, *Pirate* Loz Kaye 96, *CMEP* David Bishop 67

Lab majority 3,558 – Lab hold (4.97% from Lib Dem to Lab)
Electorate 72,788 – Total vote 34,987 – Turnout 48.07%

BARNSLEY CENTRAL

3 March 2011 due to the resignation of the Labour MP Eric Illsley.

Lab	Dan Jarvis	14,724
UKIP	Jane Collins	2,953
Con	James Hockney	1,999
BNP	Enis Dalton	1,463

Ind Tony Devoy 1,266, *Lib Dem* Dominic Carman 1,012, *Eng Dem* Kevin Riddiough 544, *Loony* Alan "Howling Laud" Hope 198, *Ind* Michael Val Davies 60

Lab majority 11,771 – Lab hold (3.02% from UKIP to Lab)
Electorate 65,471 – Total vote 24,252 – Turnout 37.04%

LEICESTER SOUTH

5 May 2011 due to the resignation of the Labour MP Sir Peter Soulsby.

Lab	Jon Ashworth	19,771
Lib Dem	Zuffar Haq	7,693
Con	Jane Hunt	5,169

UKIP Abhijit Pandya 994, *Loony* Alan "Howling Laud" Hope 553

Lab majority 12,078 – Lab hold (8.08% from Lib Dem to Lab)
Electorate 77,880 – Total vote 34,707 – Turnout 44.56%

BELFAST WEST

9 June 2011 due to the resignation of the Sinn Féin MP Gerry Adams.

Sinn Féin	Paul Maskey	16,211
SDLP	Alex Attwood	3,088
PBPA	Gerry Carroll	1,751
DUP	Brian Kingston	1,393

UUP Bill Manwaring 386, *All* Aaron McIntyre 122

Sinn Féin majority 13,123 – Sinn Féin hold (1.58% from SDLP to Sinn Féin)
Electorate 61,441 – Total vote 23,048 – Turnout 37.51%

INVERCLYDE

30 June 2011 due to the death of the Labour MP David Cairns.

Lab	Iain McKenzie	15,118
SNP	Anne McLaughlin	9,280
Con	David Wilson	2,784

Lib Dem Sophie Bridger 627, *UKIP* Mitch Sorbie 288

Lab majority 5,838 – Lab hold (8.82% from Lab to SNP)
Electorate 61,856 – Total vote 28,163 – Turnout 45.53%

FELTHAM AND HESTON

15 December 2011 due to the death of the Labour MP Alan Keen.

Lab	Seema Malhotra	12,639
Con	Mark Bowen	6,436

Lib Dem Roger Crouch 1,364, *UKIP* Andrew Charalambous 1,276, *BNP* David Furness 540, *Green* Daniel Goldsmith 426, *Eng Dem* Roger Cooper 322, *LPBP* George Hallam 128, *Bus-Pass* David Bishop 93

Lab majority 6,203 – Lab hold (8.55% from Con to Lab)
Electorate 80,813 – Total vote 23,299 – Turnout 28.83%

BRADFORD WEST

29 March 2012 due to the resignation of the Labour MP Marsha Singh.

Respect	George Galloway	18,341
Lab	Imran Hussain	8,201
Con	Jackie Whiteley	2,746

Lib Dem Jeanette Sunderland 1,505, *UKIP* Sonja McNally 1,085, *Green* Dawud Islam 481, *DN* Neil Craig 344, *Loony* Alan "Howling Laud" Hope 111

Respect majority 10,140 – Respect gain (36.42% from Lab to Respect)
Electorate 64,618 – Total vote 32,903 – Turnout 50.92%

CARDIFF SOUTH AND PENARTH

15 November 2012 due to the resignation of the Labour/Co-operative MP Alun Michael.

Lab/Co-op	Stephen Doughty	9,193
Con	Craig Williams	3,859
Lib Dem	Bablin Molik	2,103
PlC	Luke Nicholas	1,854
UKIP	Simon Zeigler	1,179

Green Anthony Slaughter 800, *SLP* Andrew Jordan 235, *Comm* Robert Griffiths 213

Lab majority 5,334 – Lab hold (8.33% from Con to Lab)
Electorate 75,764 – Total vote 19,571 – Turnout 25.83%

CORBY

15 November 2012 due to the resignation of the Conservative MP Louise Mensch.

Lab/Co-op	Andy Sawford	17,267
Con	Christine Emmett	9,476
UKIP	Margot Parker	5,108

Lib Dem Jill Hope 1,770, *BNP* Gordon Riddell 614, *Eng Dem* David Wickham 432, *Green* Jonathan Hornett 378, *Ind* Ian Gillman 212, *CLEAR* Peter Reynolds 137, *Bus-Pass* David Bishop 99, *Ind* Mozzarella 73, *YPP* Rohen Kapur 39, *Dem2015* Adam Lotun 35, *UPP* Chris Scotton 25

Lab/Co-op majority 7,791 – Lab/Co-op gain (12.63% from Con to Lab/Co-op)
Electorate 79,878 – Total vote 35,775 – Turnout 44.79%

MANCHESTER CENTRAL

15 November 2012 due to the resignation of the Labour MP Tony Lloyd.

Lab/Co-op	Lucy Powell	11,507
Lib Dem	Marc Ramsbottom	1,571

Con Matt Sephton 754, *UKIP* Christopher Cassidy 749, *Green* Tom Dylan 652, *BNP* Eddy O'Sullivan 492, *Pirate* Loz Kaye 308, *TUSC* Alex Davidson 220, *Respect* Catherine Higgins 182, *Loony* Alan "Howling Laud" Hope 78, *People* Lee Holmes 71, *Comm League* Peter Clifford 64

Lab majority 9,936 – Lab hold (16.39% from Lib Dem to Lab)
Electorate 91,692 – Total vote 16,891 – Turnout 18.42%

CROYDON NORTH

29 November 2012 due to the death of the Labour MP Malcolm Wicks.

Lab	Steve Reed	15,898
Con	Andrew Stranack	4,137

UKIP Winston McKenzie 1,400, *Lib Dem* Marisha Ray 860, *Green* Shasha Khan 855, *Respect* Lee Jasper 707, *CPA* Stephen Hammond 192, *NF* Richard Edmonds 161, *Comm* Ben Stevenson 119, *Loony* John Cartwright 110, *NineEleven* Simon Lane 66, *YPP* Robin Smith 63

Lab majority 11,761 – Lab hold (7.95% from Lab to Con)
Electorate 93,036 – Total vote 24,680 – Turnout 26.53%

MIDDLESBROUGH

29 November 2012 due to the death of the Labour MP Stuart Bell.

Lab	Andy McDonald	10,201
UKIP	Richard Elvin	1,990
Lib Dem	George Selmer	1,672
Con	Ben Houchen	1,063
Peace	Imdad Hussain	1,060

BNP Peter Foreman 328, *TUSC* John Malcolm 277, *Ind* Mark Heslehurst 275

Lab majority 8,211 – Lab hold (3.2% from UKIP to Lab)
Electorate 65,095 – Total vote 16,924 – Turnout 26%

ROTHERHAM

29 November 2012 due to the resignation of the Labour MP Denis MacShane.

Lab	Sarah Champion	9,966
UKIP	Jane Collins	4,648
BNP	Marlene Guest	1,804
Respect	Yvonne Ridley	1,778

Con Simon Wilson 1,157, *Eng Dem* David Wildgoose 703, *Ind* Simon Copley 582, *Lib Dem* Mike Beckett 451, *TUSC* Ralph Dyson 281, *Ind* Paul Dickson 51, *Ind* Clint Bristow 29

Lab majority 5,318 – Lab hold (6.94% from Lab to UKIP)
Electorate 63,420 – Total vote 21,496 – Turnout 33.89%

EASTLEIGH

28 February 2013 due to the resignation of the Liberal Democrat MP Chris Huhne.

Lib Dem	Mike Thornton	13,342
UKIP	Diane James	11,571
Con	Maria Hutchings	10,559
Lab	John O'Farrell	4,088

Ind Danny Stupple 768, *NHA* Iain Maclennan 392, *BBCP* Ray Hall 235, *Christian* Kevin Milburn 163, *Loony* Alan "Howling Laud" Hope 136, *TPP* Jim Duggan 128, *CMEP* David Bishop 72, *Eng Dem* Michael Walters 70, *TUSC* Daz Procter 62, *Wessex Reg* Colin Bex 30

Lib Dem majority 1,771 – Lib Dem hold (19.31% from Lib Dem to UKIP)
Electorate 79,004 – Total vote 41,706 – Turnout 52.79%

MID ULSTER

7 March 2013 due to the resignation of the Sinn Féin MP Martin McGuinness.

Sinn Féin	Francie Molloy	17,462
Ind	Nigel Lutton	12,781
SDLP	Patsy McGlone	6,478

All Eric Bullick 487

Sinn Féin majority 4,681 – Sinn Féin hold (19.53% from Sinn Féin to Ind)
Electorate 67,192 – Total vote 37,426 – Turnout 55.7%

SOUTH SHIELDS

2 May 2013 due to the resignation of the Labour MP David Miliband.

Lab	Emma Lewell-Buck	12,493
UKIP	Richard Elvin	5,988
Con	Karen Allen	2,857

Ind Ahmed Khan 1,331, *Ind Soc* Phil Brown 750, *BNP* Dorothy Brookes 711, *Lib Dem* Hugh Annand 352, *Loony* Alan "Howling Laud" Hope 197, *Ind* Thomas Darwood 57

Lab majority 6,505 – Lab hold (12.78% from Lab to UKIP)
Electorate 62,979 – Total vote 24,780 – Turnout 39.35%

MPs' BIOGRAPHIES

LABOUR

ABBOTT, DIANE　　Hackney North and Stoke Newington *(Majority 14,461)*

Diane Julie Abbott. Born 27 September 1953; Daughter of late Reginald Abbott, welder, and late Julie Abbott, psychiatric nurse; Married David Thompson 1991 (divorced 1993) (1 son).

Education: Harrow County Girls' Grammar School; Newnham College, Cambridge (BA history 1976).

Non-political career: Administration trainee, Home Office 1976-78; Race relations officer, National Council for Civil Liberties 1978-80; Journalist: Thames Television 1980-82, TV AM 1982-84, Freelance 1984-85; Principal press officer, Lambeth Council 1986-87. Equality officer, ACTT 1985-86; Member, RMT Parliamentary Campaigning Group 2002-.

Political career: Member for Hackney North and Stoke Newington 1987-2010, for Hackney North and Stoke Newington (revised boundary) since 6 May 2010 general election (First black female MP); Shadow Minister for Public Health 2010-13. *Select committees:* Member: Treasury and Civil Service 1989-97, Foreign Affairs 1997-2001. Member, Labour Party National Executive Committee 1994-97; Contested Labour leadership 2010. *Councils and public bodies:* Westminster City Councillor 1982-86; Former member, Greater London Assembly advisory cabinet for women and equality.

Political interests: Small businesses, education; Africa, Jamaica.

Other: Founder, Black Women Mean Business 1992-; London Schools and the Black Child. *Spectator* Speech of the Year 2008.

Recreations: Reading, cinema.

Diane Abbott MP, House of Commons, London SW1A 0AA
Tel: 020 7219 4426 *Fax:* 020 7219 4964 *Email:* chalkiasg@parliament.uk
Constituency: No constituency office *Website:* www.dianeabbott.org.uk
Twitter: @HackneyAbbott

LABOUR

ABRAHAMS, DEBBIE　　Oldham East and Saddleworth *(Majority 3,558)*

Deborah Angela Elspeth Abrahams. Born 15 September 1960; Married John Abrahams (2 daughters).

Education: Bolton Institute of Technology; Salford University (BA biochemistry and physiology 1984); Liverpool University (MS health and education 1994); Conversational French.

Non-political career: Community worker, charity, Wythenshawe; Head of healthy cities, Knowsley Council 1992-2000; Senior research fellow, IMPACT, University of London 2000-06; Director, International Health Impact Assessment Consortium, Liverpool University 2006-10. Member, Unison.

Political career: Contested Colne Valley 2010 general election. Member for Oldham East and Saddleworth since 13 January 2011 by-election; PPS to Andy Burnham as Shadow Secretary of State for Health 2011-. *Select committees:* Member Work and Pensions 2011-. Chair PLP Departmental Group for Health and Social Services 2011-; Member, Labour National Policy Forum and Joint Policy Committee. *Councils and public bodies:* Board member, Bury and Rochdale Health Authority 1998-2002; Chair, Rochdale Primary Care NHS Trust 2002-06; School governor.

Political interests: Health, education, child protection, welfare, employment, inequality; Bangladesh, Kashmir, Pakistan.

Other: Co-operative Society; Fellow, Faculty of Public Health; Chair, North West Action on Smoking and Health.

Recreations: Running, gardening, film.

Debbie Abrahams MP, House of Commons, London SW1A 0AA
Tel: 020 7219 1041 *Fax:* 020 7219 2405 *Email:* debbie.abrahams.mp@parliament.uk
Constituency: Lord Chambers, 11 Church Lane, Oldham OL1 3AN
Tel: 0161-624 4248 *Fax:* 0161-626 8572 *Email:* abrahamsd@parliament.uk
Website: www.debbieabrahams.org.uk *Twitter:* @debbie_abrahams

CONSERVATIVE

ADAMS, NIGEL
Selby and Ainsty *(Majority 12,265)*

PPS to Lord Hill of Oareford as Leader of the House of Lords and Chancellor of the Duchy of Lancaster

Born 30 November 1966; Son of Derek Adams, school caretaker, and late Isabella Adams, home help; Married Claire Robson 1992 (1 son 3 daughters).

Education: Selby High School; French, Spanish.

Non-political career: Member, Armed Forces Parliamentary Scheme (RAF) 2012-. Managing director, Advanced Digital Telecom Ltd 1993-2000; Commercial director, Yorkshire Tourist Board 2005-06; Chairman: NGC Networks Ltd 2006-, NGC Network Services Ltd 2007-.

Political career: Contested Rossendale and Darwen 2005 general election. Member for Selby and Ainsty since 6 May 2010 general election; PPS to Leaders of the House of Lords and Chancellors of the Duchy of Lancaster: Lord Strathclyde 2010-13, Lord Hill of Oareford 2013-. *Select committees:* Member: Environment, Food and Rural Affairs 2010. Deputy regional chair, Yorkshire and Humber Conservatives 2001-03; President, Selby Conservative Association 2002-04; Board member, North of England Conservative Party 2002-03; President, Conservatives at Work 2012-13. *Councils and public bodies:* Governor: Camblesforth Primary School, Selby 2002-04, Selby High School 2007-.

Political interests: Energy, Culture, media and sport, business, EFRA.

Other: Member, Yorkshire County Cricket Club Members' Committee 2004-05; Patron, Selby Hands of Hope Charity; Member: Carlton, Selby Conservative Club. Member: Yorkshire County Cricket Club, Hovingham Cricket Club, House of Lords and House of Commons Cricket Club.

Recreations: Cricket, golf, football, theatre, shooting.

Nigel Adams MP, House of Commons, London SW1A 0AA
Tel: 020 7219 7141 *Email:* nigel.adams.mp@parliament.uk
Constituency: 17 High Street, Tadcaster, North Yorkshire LS24 9AP
Tel: 01937 838088 *Website:* www.selbyandainsty.com www.nigeladams.org

CONSERVATIVE

AFRIYIE, ADAM
Windsor *(Majority 19,054)*

Born 4 August 1965; Married 2nd Tracy-Jane Newall 2005 (3 sons 1 daughter 1 stepson).

Education: Addey and Stanhope School, New Cross; Imperial College (Wye), London (BSc agricultural economics 1987).

Non-political career: Managing director (now non-executive chair), Connect Support Services 1993-; Chair, DeHavilland Information Services 1998-2005; Board member, Policy Exchange 2003-05; Non-executive chair: Adfero Ltd 2005-, Castleford Media 2010-.

Political career: Member for Windsor 2005-10, for Windsor (revised boundary) since 6 May 2010 general election; Shadow Minister for: Innovation, Universities and Skills 2007-09, Innovation and Science 2009-10; Chair, Parliamentary Office of Science and Technology (POST) 2010-. *Select committees:* Member: Science and Technology/Innovation, Universities and Skills 2005-07, Children, Schools and Families 2007-09; Chair: Members' Expenses 2011-. Chair, Tonbridge Edenbridge and Malling Association constituency branch 1999-2004; President, Conservative Technology Forum 2010-. *Councils and public bodies:* Governor, Museum of London 1999-2005.

Political interests: Mental health, simpler tax and benefits system, public policy, innovation and science.

Other: Chair (London region): Business for Sterling 1999-2004, No to the Euro campaign 2001-04; Trustee, Museum in Docklands 2003-05; Young Enterprise (North Berkshire): Chair 2005-07, Patron 2008-; National Trust; Windsor and Eton Society.

Recreations: Distance running.

Adam Afriyie MP, House of Commons, London SW1A 0AA
Tel: 020 7219 8023 *Email:* adam.afriyie.mp@parliament.uk
Constituency: No constituency office *Website:* www.adamafriyie.org *Twitter:* @AdamAfriyie

AINSWORTH, BOB
Coventry North East *(Majority 11,775)*

Robert William Ainsworth. Born 19 June 1952; Son of late Stanley and Pearl Ainsworth; Married Gloria Sandall 1974 (2 daughters).

Education: Foxford Comprehensive School, Coventry; French.

Non-political career: Sheet metal worker; Fitter with Jaguar Cars, Coventry 1971-91. Member, MSF/Unite: Shop steward 1974-80, Senior steward and secretary of joint shop stewards 1980-91, Union Branch President 1983-87.

LABOUR

Political career: Member for Coventry North East 1992-2010, for Coventry North East (revised boundary) since 6 May 2010 general election; Opposition Whip 1995-97; Government Whip 1997-2001; Parliamentary Under-Secretary of State: Department of the Environment, Transport and the Regions 2001, Home Office (Anti-drugs Co-ordination and Organised Crime) 2001-03; Deputy Chief Whip 2003-07; Ministry of Defence 2007-10: Minister of State for the Armed Forces 2007-09, Secretary of State 2009-10; Shadow Secretary of State for Defence 2010. *Select committees:* Member: Accommodation and Works 2003-05, Selection 2003-05, 2006-07, Finance and Services 2003-05, Administration 2005-07, Foreign Affairs 2010-13, Arms Export Controls 2011-13; Chair: Joint Committee on the Draft Enhanced Terrorism Prevention and Investigation Measures Bill 2012-13. *Councils and public bodies:* Coventry City Council: Councillor 1984-93, Deputy Leader 1988-91.

Political interests: Industry, environment, taxation, defence, foreign policy; France, India, Pakistan, USA.

Other: PC 2005; Bell Green Working Men's Club.

Recreations: Walking, chess, reading, gardening.

Rt Hon Bob Ainsworth MP, House of Commons, London SW1A 0AA
Tel: 020 7219 4047 *Fax:* 020 7219 2889 *Email:* ainsworthr@parliament.uk
Constituency: Bayley House, 22-23 Bayley Lane, Coventry, Warwickshire CV1 5RJ
Tel: 02476 226707 *Fax:* 02476 433401 *Email:* wisec@parliament.uk

ALDOUS, PETER
Waveney *(Majority 769)*

Born 26 August 1961; Single.

Education: Harrow School; Reading University (BSc land management 1982).

Non-political career: Chartered surveyor, private practice, Norwich and Ipswich 1983-2010.

Political career: Contested Waveney 2005 general election. Member for Waveney since 6 May 2010 general election. *Select committees:* Member: Environmental Audit 2010-. Member, Conservative Party 1998-. *Councils and public bodies:* Councillor, Waveney District Council 1999-2002; Suffolk County Council: Councillor 2001-05, Deputy Leader, Conservative Group 2002-05.

CONSERVATIVE

Political interests: Employment, transport, broadband, offshore renewables, fishing, agriculture, town planning, urban regeneration; USA.

Other: Member, Royal Institute of Chartered Surveyors; Beccles Conservative Club; Farmers' Club.

Recreations: Squash, Ipswich Town F.C, horse racing, cricket.

Peter Aldous MP, House of Commons, London SW1A 0AA
Tel: 020 7219 7182 *Email:* peter.aldous.mp@parliament.uk
Constituency: 15 Surrey Street, Lowestoft, Suffolk NR32 1LJ
Tel: 01502 359980 *Website:* www.peteraldous.com *Twitter:* @peter_aldous

ALEXANDER, DANNY
Inverness, Nairn, Badenoch and Strathspey *(Majority 8,765)*

Chief Secretary to the Treasury

Daniel Grian Alexander. Born 15 May 1972; Son of Dion and Jane Alexander; Married Rebecca Hoar 2005 (2 daughters).

Education: Lochaber High School, Fort William; St Anne's College, Oxford (BA philosophy, politics and economics 1993); Gaelic.

Non-political career: Researcher, Campaign for Freedom of Information 1991; Press officer: Scottish Liberal Democrats 1993-96, European Movement 1996-97; Election aide to Jim Wallace MP 1997; Deputy director and head of communications, European Movement 1997-99; Head of communications: Britain in Europe campaign 1999-2003, Cairngorms National Park 2004-05.

LIBERAL DEMOCRAT

Political career: Member for Inverness, Nairn, Badenoch and Strathspey since 5 May 2005 general election; Liberal Democrat: Spokesperson for Work and Pensions, especially disabled people 2005-07; Whip 2006-07; Shadow Chancellor of the Duchy of Lancaster (Spokesperson for Social Exclusion) 2007; Shadow Secretary of State for Work and Pensions 2007-08; Secretary of State for Scotland (and provides ministerial support to Deputy Prime Minister) 2010; Chief Secretary to the Treasury 2010-. *Select committees:* Member: Scottish Affairs 2005-08. Chief of Staff to Nick Clegg as Leader of the Liberal Democrats 2007-10; Chair Manifesto Group 2007-.

Political interests: Highlands and Islands issues, housing, economic policy, Europe, pensions, social security.

Other: Advisory Council Demos. PC 2010; Abernethy Angling Improvement Association. President, Strathspey Rugby Club; Patron, Ross County Cricket Club.

Recreations: Hill-walking, fishing, cricket, golf, reading, travel.

Rt Hon Danny Alexander MP, House of Commons, London SW1A 0AA
Tel: 020 7219 2300 *Fax:* 020 7219 1438 *Email:* danny.alexander.mp@parliament.uk
Constituency: 45 Huntly Street, Inverness IV3 5HR
Tel: 01463 711280 *Fax:* 01463 714960 *Email:* jamie.mackie@parliament.uk
Website: www.dannyalexander.org.uk *Twitter:* @dannyalexander

ALEXANDER, DOUGLAS   Paisley and Renfrewshire South *(Majority 16,614)*

Shadow Secretary of State for Foreign and Commonwealth Affairs (Shadow Foreign Secretary)

Douglas Garven Alexander. Born 26 October 1967; Son of Rev. Douglas Alexander and Dr Joyce Alexander; Married Jacqueline Christian 2000 (1 son 1 daughter).

Education: Park Mains High School, Erskine, Renfrewshire; Lester B. Pearson College, Vancouver, Canada; Edinburgh University (MA 1990; LLB 1993; Diploma legal practice 1994); University of Pennsylvania, USA.

LABOUR

Non-political career: Parliamentary researcher to Gordon Brown MP 1990-91; Rector's Assessor, Edinburgh University 1993-96; Solicitor: Brodies W.S. 1994-96, Digby Brown 1996-97. Member: TGWU, GMB, Community.

Political career: Contested Perth and Kinross 1995 by-election and Perth 1997 general election. Member for Paisley South 6 November 1997 by-election to 2005, for Paisley and Renfrewshire South since 5 May 2005 general election; Minister for E-Commerce and Competitiveness, Department of Trade and Industry 2001-02; Cabinet Office 2002-04: Minister of State 2002-03, Minister for the Cabinet Office and Chancellor of the Duchy of Lancaster 2003-04; Minister of State, Foreign and Commonwealth Office and Department of Trade and Industry (Trade, Investment and Foreign Affairs) 2004-05; Minister of State, Foreign and Commonwealth Office (Europe) 2005-06; Secretary of State for: Transport and for Scotland 2006-07, International Development 2007-10; Shadow Secretary of State for: International Development 2010, Work and Pensions 2010-11, Foreign and Commonwealth Affairs (Shadow Foreign Secretary) 2011-; General election campaign co-ordinator 1999-2001, 2007-.

Political interests: Constitutional reform, economic policy, employment.

Other: Notary Public. PC 2005.

Publications: Co-author, New Scotland, New Britain (1999); Telling it like it could be: the moral force of progressive politics (2005); Contributor, The Purple Book (Progress, 2011).

Recreations: Running, angling.

Rt Hon Douglas Alexander MP, House of Commons, London SW1A 0AA
Tel: 020 7219 1345 *Email:* alexanderd@parliament.uk
Constituency: 2014 Mile End Mill, Abbey Mill Business Centre, Paisley, Renfrewshire PA1 1JS
Tel: 0141-561 0333 *Fax:* 0141-561 0334 *Website:* www.douglasalexander.org.uk
Twitter: @DAlexanderMP

LABOUR

ALEXANDER, HEIDI
Lewisham East *(Majority 6,216)*

Opposition Whip

Born 17 April 1975; Daughter of Malcolm Alexander, electrician, and Elaine Alexander; Married Martin Ballantyne.

Education: Churchfields Secondary School, Swindon; Durham University (BA geography 1996; MA European urban and regional change 1999); German.

Non-political career: Researcher to Joan Ruddock MP 1999-2005; Campaign manager, Clothes Aid 2006; Director and chair, Greater London Enterprise 2007-09; Director, Lewisham Schools for the Future LEA 2007-09. Member, Unite 2009-.

Political career: Member for Lewisham East since 6 May 2010 general election; PPS to Mary Creagh as Shadow Secretary of State for Environment, Food and Rural Affairs 2010-12; Opposition Whip 2012-. *Select committees:* Member: Communities and Local Government 2010-12, Regulatory Reform 2010-, Selection 2013-. *Councils and public bodies:* London Borough of Lewisham Council: Councillor 2004-10, Deputy Mayor 2006-10, Cabinet Member for Regeneration 2006-10; Vice-President, Local Government Association 2011-.

Political interests: Housing, urban regeneration, international development.

Heidi Alexander MP, House of Commons, London SW1A 0AA
Tel: 020 7219 7099 *Fax:* 020 7219 2677 *Email:* heidi.alexander.mp@parliament.uk
Constituency: All correspondence via Westminster office
Tel: 020 8461 4733 *Email:* heidi@heidialexander.org.uk *Website:* www.heidialexander.org.uk
Twitter: @heidi_mp

LABOUR

ALI, RUSHANARA
Bethnal Green and Bow *(Majority 11,574)*

Shadow Minister for Education

Born 14 March 1975.

Education: Mulberry School; Tower Hamlets College; Oxford University (BA philosophy, politics and economics 1997).

Non-political career: Research assistant to Michael Young 1997; Parliamentary assistant to Oona King MP; Research fellow, Institute for Public Policy Research 1999-2001: Seconded to Foreign and Commonwealth Office; Communities Directorate, Home Office 2001-05; Associate director, Young Foundation 2005-.

Political career: Member for Bethnal Green and Bow since 6 May 2010 general election; Shadow Minister for: International Development 2010-13, Education 2013-. *Councils and public bodies:* Governor, Tower Hamlets College.

Other: Commissioner, London Child Poverty Commission; Chair, Tower Hamlets Summer University; Trustee, Paul Hamlyn Foundation; Member, Tate Britain Council.

Rushanara Ali MP, House of Commons, London SW1A 0AA
Tel: 020 7219 7200 *Email:* rushanara.ali.mp@parliament.uk
Constituency: No constituency office publicised *Website:* www.rushanaraali.org
Twitter: @rushanaraali

LABOUR

ALLEN, GRAHAM
Nottingham North *(Majority 8,138)*

Graham William Allen. Born 11 January 1953; Son of Bill and Edna Allen; Married Allyson 1995 (1 daughter).

Education: Forest Fields Grammar School, Nottingham; City of London Polytechnic (BA politics and economics 1975); Leeds University (MA political sociology 1977).

Non-political career: Warehouseman 1972; Research officer, Labour Party 1978-83; Local government officer 1983-84; National co-ordinator, political fund ballots 1984-86; Research and education officer, GMBATU 1986-87. Member, Unite.

Political career: Member for Nottingham North 1987-2010, for Nottingham North (revised boundary) since 6 May 2010 general election; Shadow Minister for: Social Security 1991-92, Constitutional Affairs 1992-94, Media and Broadcasting 1994-95, Transport 1995-96, Environment 1996-97; Government Whip 1997-2001; Member Speaker's Committee on the Electoral Commission 2010-. *Select committees:* Member: Public Accounts 1988-91, Selection 2000-01, Reform of the House of Commons 2009-10; Chair: Political and Constitutional Reform 2010-; Member: Liaison 2010-. Chair Labour Treasury Committee 1990-91.

Political interests: Economic policy, democratic renewal; China, Russia, USA.

Other: Fellow, Industry and Parliament Trust 1995; Chair, One Nottingham the Local Strategic Partnership 2005-09; President, Basford Hall Miners Welfare. House of Lords and House of Commons Cricket XI; Bulwell Forest Golf; Vice-President, Bulwell Cricket Club.

Publications: Reinventing Democracy (1995); The Last Prime Minister (2001); Co-author, (with Iain Duncan Smith MP) Early Intervention (2008); Author: Early Intervention: The Next Steps (independent report to HMG, 2011), Early Intervention: Smart Investment, Massive Savings (independent report to HMG, 2011).

Recreations: Playing all sports, walking, cooking, oil painting.

Graham Allen MP, House of Commons, London SW1A 0AA
Tel: 020 7219 3000
Constituency: No constituency office
Tel: 0115-975 2377 *Email:* stephensons@parliament.uk *Twitter:* @GrahamAllenMP

CONSERVATIVE

AMESS, DAVID
Southend West *(Majority 7,270)*

David Anthony Andrew Amess. Born 26 March 1952; Son of late James Amess and Maud Amess; Married Julia Arnold 1983 (1 son 4 daughters).

Education: St Bonaventure's Grammar School, Forest Gate, London; Bournemouth College of Technology (BSc economics 1974).

Non-political career: Teacher, St John Baptist Junior School, Bethnal Green, London 1970-71; Underwriter, Leslie Godwin Agency 1974-76; Accountancy personnel 1976-79; Senior consultant, Executemps Company Agency 1979-81; AA Recruitment Co 1981-87; Chair and chief executive: Accountancy Solutions 1987-90, Accountancy Group 1990-96.

Political career: Contested Newham North West 1979 general election. Member for Basildon 1983-97, for Southend West 1997-2010, for Southend West (revised boundary) since 6 May 2010 general election; PPS to: Parliamentary Under-Secretaries of State, DHSS: Edwina Currie 1987-88, Lord Skelmersdale 1988, to Michael Portillo: as Minister of State: Department of Transport 1988-90, Department of Environment 1990-92, as Chief Secretary to the Treasury 1992-94, as Secretary of State: for Employment 1994-95, for Defence 1995-97; Sponsored: Horses and Ponies Bill 1984-85, Members of Parliament (Minimum Age) Bill 1984-85, Horses, Ponies and Donkeys Bill 1987-88, Abortion (Right of Conscience) (Amendment) Bill 1988-89, British Nationality (Honorary Citizenship) Bill 1988-89, Adoption (Amendment) Bill 1989-90, Dogs Bill 1989-90, Pet Animals (Amendment) Bill 1990-91, Protection Against Cruel Tethering Act 1988, Human Fertilisation (Choice) Bill 1992-93, Voluntary Personal Security Cards Bill 1992-93, Football Matches (Violent and Disorderly Conduct) Bill 1992-93, Newly Qualified Drivers Bill 1993-94, Coercion in Family Planning (Prohibition) Bill 1994-95, Freezing of Human Embryos Bill 1995-96, Abortion (Amendment) Bill 1996-97, Reform of Quarantine Regulations Bill 1997-98, Voluntary Personal Security Cards Bill 1997-98, The Warm Homes Act 2000. *Select committees:* Member: Broadcasting 1994-97, Health 1998-2007, Chairmen's Panel/Panel of Chairs 2001-, Backbench Business 2012-. Chair, Conservative Party Committee on Health 1999; Vice-chair, Conservative Party Committee on Health and Social Services 2001; Member, Executive, 1922 Committee 2004-12. Honorary Secretary, Conservative Friends of Israel 1998-. *Councils and public bodies:* Councillor, London Borough of Redbridge Council 1982-86.

Political interests: Health, education, transport, environment, pro-life movement, animal welfare; Far East, Middle East, European Union, Pacific Basin, USA.

Other: Founder member, Wallenberg Appeal Foundation; Industry and Parliament Trust: Fellow 1994, Chair, Fellowship Committee 2007-; President, 1912 Club 1996-; Fairhaven Hospices, Salvation Army, RSPCA, Southend Fund, Mencap, Age UK, Dogs Trust. Freeman, City of London. Charity Champion awards: Animal Welfare and Environment Champion 2011, Outstanding Achievement (with Stephen Pound MP and Bob Russell MP) 2012; Carlton, St Stephen's Constitutional. Kingswood Squash and Racketball Club.

Publications: The Basildon Experience (1995); Basildon 1992: Against All Odds! (2012).

Recreations: Socialising, reading, writing, sports, modern music, keeping animals, gardening.

David Amess MP, House of Commons, London SW1A 0AA
Tel: 020 7219 3452 *Fax:* 020 7219 2245 *Email:* amessd@parliament.uk
Constituency: Iveagh Hall, 67 Leigh Road, Leigh-on-Sea, Essex SS9 1JW
Tel: 01702 472391 *Email:* swca@tory.org *Website:* www.southendwestconservatives.com
www.davidamess.co.uk

ANDERSON, DAVID
Blaydon *(Majority 9,117)*

LABOUR

Born 2 December 1953; Son of Cyril and Janet Anderson; Married Eva Jago 1973.

Education: Maltby Grammar School; Doncaster Technical College (1969-71); Durham Technical College (mining and mechanical engineering 1971-74); Moscow Higher Trade Union School (1983); Durham University (DipSocSc 1989).

Non-political career: Mechanic, National Coal Board mines 1969-89; Elderly care worker, Newcastle upon Tyne social services 1989-2004. Lay official, National Union of Mineworkers 1978-89; Unison: Lay official 1989-2005, Member, NEC board, President 2003-04; Member, TUC general council 2000-05.

Political career: Member for Blaydon 2005-10, for Blaydon (revised boundary) since 6 May 2010 general election; PPS to Bill Rammell as Minister of State: Department for Education and Skills/Innovation, Universities and Skills 2006-08, Foreign and Commonwealth Office 2008-09, Ministry of Defence 2009-10; Opposition Assistant Whip 2010-11. *Select committees:* Member: Northern Ireland Affairs 2005-10, 2011-, Procedure 2005-06, Energy and Climate Change 2009-10, North East 2009-10, Backbench Business 2010, 2012-, Environment, Food and Rural Affairs 2010-11, Regulatory Reform 2010-. Chair, Labour Friends of Iraq 2005-.

Political interests: Public services, employment, energy; Iraq, Middle East, Northern Ireland, USA.

Other: Patron: Mick Knighton Mesothelioma Research Fund, Gateshead Visible Ethnic Minorities Group; FACT (Fight All Cancers Togeher); About Turn Veterans Project. Health and Wellbeing Champion, Charity Champion Awards 2011.

Recreations: Walking, travel, football, music, driving.

David Anderson MP, House of Commons, London SW1A 0AA
Tel: 020 7219 4348 *Fax:* 020 7219 8276 *Email:* andersonda@parliament.uk
Constituency: St Cuthbert's Community Hall, Shibdon Road, Blaydon on Tyne, Tyne and Wear NE21 5PT
Tel: 0191-414 2488 *Fax:* 0191-414 2244 *Email:* stevensons@parliament.uk
Website: www.daveanderson.org.uk

ANDREW, STUART
Pudsey *(Majority 1,659)*

PPS to Francis Maude as Minister for the Cabinet Office and Paymaster General

CONSERVATIVE

Stuart James Andrew. Born 25 November 1971; Son of James Andrew and Maureen Andrew; Partnered.

Education: Ysgol David Hughes, Menai Bridge; Welsh.

Non-political career: British Heart Foundation -1998; Fundraiser, Hope House Children's Hospice 1998-2000; Head of fundraising, East Lancashire Hospice 2000-03; Fundraising manager, Martin House Children's Hospice 2003-.

Political career: Contested Wrexham 1997 general election. Member for Pudsey since 6 May 2010 general election; PPS to Francis Maude as Minister for the Cabinet Office and Paymaster General 2012-. *Select committees:* Member: Welsh Affairs 2010-12. *Councils and public bodies:* Councillor, Leeds City Council 2003-10.

Political interests: Special needs education, transport, planning, charities, health; Commonwealth, USA.

Other: Chair, The Yeadon Project; Member, Institute of Fundraising.

Recreations: Walking the Yorkshire Dales, attending gym.

Stuart Andrew MP, House of Commons, London SW1A 0AA
Tel: 020 7219 7130 *Email:* stuart.andrew.mp@parliament.uk
Constituency: The Shaw Rooms, 98 Thornhill Street, Calverley, Leeds LS28 5PD
Tel: 0113-204 7954 *Website:* www.stuartandrew.com *Twitter:* @StuartAndrewMP

CONSERVATIVE

ARBUTHNOT, JAMES
North East Hampshire *(Majority 18,597)*

James Norwich Arbuthnot. Born 4 August 1952; Son of late Sir John Sinclair-Wemyss Arbuthnot, MP for Dover 1950-64, and Lady Arbuthnot; Married Emma Broadbent 1984 (1 son 3 daughters).

Education: Eton College; Trinity College, Cambridge (BA law 1974).

Non-political career: Called to the Bar: Inner Temple 1975, Lincoln's Inn 1977.

Political career: Contested Cynon Valley 1983 general election and 1984 by-election. Member for Wanstead and Woodford 1987-97, for North East Hampshire 1997-2010, for North East Hampshire (revised boundary) since 6 May 2010 general election; PPS to: Archie Hamilton as Minister of State for the Armed Forces 1988-90, Peter Lilley as Secretary of State for Trade and Industry 1990-92; Assistant Government Whip 1992-94; Parliamentary Under-Secretary of State, Department of Social Security 1994-95; Minister of State for Procurement, Ministry of Defence 1995-97; Member, Shadow Cabinet 1997-2001: Opposition Chief Whip 1997-2001; Member, Intelligence and Security Committee 2001-05; Shadow Secretary of State for Trade 2003-05; Shadow Minister for Trade and Industry 2005. *Select committees:* Member: Joint Committee on House of Lords Reform 2002-03; Chair: Defence 2005-; Member: Liaison 2005-, Joint Committee on National Security Strategy 2010-; Chair: Armed Forces Bill 2011. Branch chair, Putney Conservative Association 1975-77; Joint deputy chair, Chelsea Conservative Association 1980-82; President, Cynon Valley Conservative Association 1983-92. *Councils and public bodies:* Councillor, Royal Borough of Kensington and Chelsea 1978-87.

Political interests: Taxation, defence, foreign affairs, law; Afghanistan, Australia, France, Germany, India, Israel, Italy, Pakistan, Russia, Taiwan, USA.

Other: Fellow, Industry and Parliament Trust 1989. PC 1998; Pratts.

Recreations: Playing guitar, skiing.

Rt Hon James Arbuthnot MP, House of Commons, London SW1A 0AA
Tel: 020 7219 4649 *Fax:* 020 7219 3910 *Email:* james.arbuthnot.mp@parliament.uk
Constituency: North East Hampshire Conservative Association, The Mount, Bounty Road, Basingstoke, Hampshire RG21 3DD
Tel: 01256 322 207 *Email:* office@nehc.org.uk *Website:* www.jamesarbuthnot.com

LABOUR

ASHWORTH, JON
Leicester South *(Majority 12,078)*

Shadow Minister for Cabinet Office

Jonathan Ashworth. Born 14 October 1978; Married Emilie Oldknow (1 daughter).

Education: Philips High School, Bury; Bury College; Durham University (BA politics and philosophy 2000).

Non-political career: Special adviser to Chief Secretaries to the Treasury 2004-07: Paul Boateng 2004-05, Des Browne 2005-06, Stephen Timms 2006-07; Deputy Political Secretary to Gordon Brown as Prime Minister 2007-10; Political Secretary to Harriet Harman as Acting Leader of the Opposition 2010; Head of party relations to Ed Miliband as Leader of the Opposition 2010-11. Unite; GMB.

Political career: Member for Leicester South since 6 May 2011 by-election; Opposition Whip 2011-13; Shadow Minister for Cabinet Office 2013-; Labour Party: Political research officer 2001, Economics and welfare policy officer 2002-04, Member, Labour Party NEC 2013-; Member, Co-operative Party.

Political interests: Economy, social security, employment, foreign affairs, international development; Australia, Bangladesh, India, Italy, Middle East, Pakistan, Somalia, USA.

Other: Saffron Lane Working Men's Club.

Recreations: Reading, cinema, boxing fan, music.

Jon Ashworth MP, House of Commons, London SW1A 0AA
Tel: 020 7219 3000 *Email:* jon.ashworth.mp@parliament.uk
Constituency: Tenth Floor, 60 Charles Street, Leicester LE1 1FB
Tel: 0116-251 1927 *Fax:* 0116-262 6329 *Website:* www.jonashworth.org
Twitter: @JonAshworth

AUSTIN, IAN

Dudley North *(Majority 649)*

Shadow Minister for Work and Pensions

Born 6 March 1965; Son of Alfred and Margaret Austin; Married Catherine Miles 1993 (2 sons 1 daughter).

Education: Dudley School; Essex University (BA government 1987).

Non-political career: Communications manager, Focus Housing 1989-94; Regional press officer, West Midlands Labour Party 1995-98; Deputy director of communications, Scottish Labour Party 1998-99; Special adviser to Gordon Brown as Chancellor of the Exchequer 1999-2005.

LABOUR

Political career: Member for Dudley North 2005-10, for Dudley North (revised boundary) since 6 May 2010 general election; PPS to Gordon Brown: as Chancellor of the Exchequer 2007, as Prime Minister 2007-08; Assistant Government Whip 2008-09; Minister for the West Midlands 2008-10; Parliamentary Under-Secretary of State, Department for Communities and Local Government 2009-10; Shadow Minister for: Communities and Local Government 2010, Sports 2010-11, Work and Pensions 2011-; *Councils and public bodies:* Councillor Dudley Borough Council 1991-95.

Political interests: Housing, training and skills, employment, manufacturing and trade.

Recreations: Football, cycling, reading.

Ian Austin MP, House of Commons, London SW1A 0AA
Tel: 020 7219 8012 *Fax:* 020 7219 4488 *Email:* austini@parliament.uk
Constituency: Turner House, 157-185 Wrens Nest Road, Dudley, West Midlands DY1 3RU
Tel: 01384 342503/4 *Fax:* 01384 342523 *Website:* www.ianaustin.co.uk
Twitter: @IanAustinMP

BACON, RICHARD

South Norfolk *(Majority 10,940)*

Richard Michael Bacon. Born 3 December 1962; Married Victoria Panton 2006 (2 sons).

Education: King's School, Worcester; London School of Economics (BSc (Econ) politics and economics 1986); German.

Non-political career: Investment banker, Barclays de Zoete Wedd 1986-89; Financial journalist, Euromoney Publications plc 1993-94; Deputy director, Management Consultancies Association 1994-96; Brunswick Public Relations 1996-99; Founder, English Word Factory 1999-.

CONSERVATIVE

Political career: Contested Vauxhall 1997 general election. Member for South Norfolk 2001-10, for South Norfolk (revised boundary) since 6 May 2010 general election; Member Public Accounts Commission 2005-. *Select committees:* Member: Public Accounts 2001-, European Scrutiny 2003-07, Unopposed Bills (Panel) 2010-. Chair, Hammersmith Conservative Association 1995-96; Co-founder, Geneva Conservative general election voluntary agency 2000.

Political interests: Public expenditure, education, health, agriculture, Europe.

Other: Member, Amnesty International. Commons Select Committee Member of the Year, *House Magazine* awards 2012.

Recreations: Music, reading, modern painting.

Richard Bacon MP, House of Commons, London SW1A 0AA
Tel: 020 7219 8301 *Email:* richardbaconmp@parliament.uk
Constituency: Grasmere, Denmark Street, Diss, Norfolk IP22 4LE
Tel: 01379 643728/01379 642769 *Fax:* 01379 642220 *Email:* reevet@parliament.uk
rigbym@parliament.uk *Website:* www.richardbacon.org.uk

BAILEY, ADRIAN

West Bromwich West *(Majority 5,651)*

Adrian Edward Bailey. Born 11 December 1945; Son of Edward Bailey, fitter, and Sylvia Bailey, née Bayliss; Married Jill Millard 1989 (1 stepson).

Education: Cheltenham Grammar School; Exeter University (BA economic history 1967); Loughborough College of Librarianship (Postgraduate Diploma librarianship 1971).

Non-political career: Librarian, Cheshire County Council 1971-82; Political organiser, Co-operative Party 1982-2000. Member, GMBATU 1982-.

LAB/CO-OP

Political career: Contested South Worcester 1970 and Nantwich February and October 1974 general elections and Wirral 1976 by-election. Member for West Bromwich West 23 November 2000 by-election to 2010, for West Bromwich West (revised boundary) since 6 May 2010 general election; PPS to John Hutton: as Chancellor of the Duchy of Lancaster 2005, as Secretary of

State for Work and Pensions 2005-06, to Hilary Armstrong as Chancellor of the Duchy of Lancaster 2006, to Ministers of State, Ministry of Defence: Adam Ingram 2006-07, Bob Ainsworth 2007. *Select committees:* Member: Northern Ireland Affairs 2001-05, Unopposed Bills (Panel) 2001-, Business, Enterprise and Regulatory Reform/Business and Enterprise/Business, Innovation and Skills 2007-09, European Scrutiny 2007-10, Quadripartite (Committees on Strategic Export Controls)/Arms Export Controls 2007-10, West Midlands 2009-10; Chair: Business, Innovation and Skills 2010-; Member: Liaison 2010-, Joint Committee on National Security Strategy 2010-. Contested Cheshire West 1979 European Parliament election. Secretary West Bromwich West Constituency Labour Party 1993-2000; Chair Parliamentary Group 2004. *Councils and public bodies:* Sandwell Borough Council: Councillor 1991-2001, Chair finance 1992-97, Deputy leader 1997-2000.

Political interests: Co-operatives and mutuals, urban regeneration, animal welfare (anti-hunting with dogs), taxation, economic policy, child protection policy; China, India, Pakistan.

Other: Action Aid, Redwings Horse Sanctuary, Staffs Bull Terrier Heritage Society, NSPCC.

Recreations: Football, swimming, walking.

Adrian Bailey MP, House of Commons, London SW1A 0AA
Tel: 020 7219 6060 *Fax:* 020 7219 1202 *Email:* baileya@parliament.uk
Constituency: Terry Duffy House, Thomas Street, West Bromwich, West Midlands BR70 6NT
Tel: 0121-569 1926 *Fax:* 0121-569 1936 *Email:* cromptonm@parliament.uk
Website: www.adrianbailey.org

LABOUR

BAIN, WILLIE   Glasgow North East *(Majority 15,942)*

William Thomas Bain. Born 29 November 1972; Son of William Bain, lift engineer, and Catherine Bain, payroll clerk.

Education: St Roch's Secondary School; Strathclyde University (LLB 1995; DipLP 1996; LLM 2004).

Non-political career: Senior lecturer, public law, London South Bank University 2004-09.

Political career: Member for Glasgow North East since 12 November 2009 by-election; PPS to Sadiq Khan as Minister of State, Department for Transport 2010; Shadow Minister for: Transport 2010, Environment, Food and Rural Affairs 2010-11, Scotland 2011-13. *Select committees:* Member: Joint Committee on Tax Law Rewrite Bills 2009-10. Secretary, Glasgow North East CLP 1999-2009 Member, Co-operative Party.

Political interests: Transport, economy, welfare state, climate change, constitutional reform, foreign affairs, human rights; China, European Union, Malawi, Sudan, South Sudan, USA.

Other: Member: Amnesty International, Progress; Fellow, RSA 2011-.

Recreations: Music, films, theatre, tennis.

Willie Bain MP, House of Commons, London SW1A 0AA
Tel: 020 7219 7527 *Email:* willie.bain.mp@parliament.uk
Constituency: Flemington House, 110 Flemington Street, Glasgow G21 4BX
Tel: 0141-557 2513 *Email:* willie@williebain.com *Website:* www.williebain.com
Twitter: @William_Bain

LIBERAL DEMOCRAT

BAKER, NORMAN   Lewes *(Majority 7,647)*

Parliamentary Under-Secretary of State, Department for Transport

Norman John Baker. Born 26 July 1957.

Education: Royal Liberty School, Gidea Park; Royal Holloway College, London University (BA German 1978); French, German.

Non-political career: Regional director, Our Price Records 1978-83; English as a foreign language teacher/lecturer 1985-97; Lib Dem environment campaigner, House of Commons 1989-90.

Political career: Contested Lewes 1992 general election. Member for Lewes 1997-2010, for Lewes (revised boundary) since 6 May 2010 general election; Liberal Democrat Spokesperson for: Environment, Food and Rural Affairs 1997-99, Millennium Dome 1998-2001, Transport 1998-99, Consumer Affairs and Broadcasting 1999-2001, Home Affairs 2001-02, Shadow Secretary of State for: Environment 2002-05, Environment, Food and Rural Affairs 2005-06; Shadow Minister for the Cabinet Office and Chancellor of the Duchy of Lancaster 2007; Shadow Secretary of State for Transport 2007-10; Parliamentary Under-Secretary of State, Department for Transport 2010-. *Select committees:* Member: Environmental Audit 1997-2000, Broadcasting 2000-01, Joint Committee on Human Rights 2001-03. *Councils and public bodies:* Lewes District Council: Councillor 1987-99, Leader 1991-97; Councillor: Glynde and Beddingham Parish Council 1987-2003, East Sussex County Council 1989-97.

Political interests: Civil liberties, environment; Sweden, Tibet.

Other: President, Tibet Society. Zurich/*Spectator* Parliamentarians of the Year Awards: Best Newcomer MP 1997, Inquisitor of the Year 2001; Opposition MP of the Year, Channel 4 2002; Lord Erskine Award, RSPCA 2003.

Publications: Various environmental texts; The Strange Death of David Kelly (Methuen, 2007).

Recreations: Music.

Norman Baker MP, House of Commons, London SW1A 0AA
Tel: 020 7219 2864 *Fax:* 020 7219 0445 *Email:* bakern@parliament.uk
Constituency: 23 East Street, Lewes, East Sussex BN7 2LJ
Tel: 01273 480281 *Fax:* 01273 480287 *Email:* normanbaker@cix.co.uk
Website: www.normanbaker.org.uk

CONSERVATIVE

BAKER, STEVE
Wycombe *(Majority 9,560)*

Steven John Baker. Born 6 June 1971; Married Beth 1996 (no children).

Education: Poltair Comprehensive School, St Austell; St Austell Sixth Form College; Southampton University (BEng aerospace systems engineering 1992); St Cross College, Oxford (MSc computer science 2000).

Non-political career: Engineer officer, Royal Air Force 1989-99. Head of consulting and product manager, DecisionSoft Ltd, Oxford 2000-01; Principal, Ambriel Consulting Ltd 2001-10; Chief technology officer, BASDA Ltd, Great Missenden 2002-07; Product development director, Core Filing Ltd, Oxford 2005-06; Chief architect, global financing and asset servicing platforms, Lehman Brothers, London 2006-08; Corporate affairs director, The Cobden Centre 2009-10.

Political career: Member for Wycombe since 6 May 2010 general election. *Select committees:* Member: Transport 2010-13. Chair, Conservative Party Committee for Public Services 2011-; Member, Executive, 1922 Committee 2012-.

Political interests: Enterprise, economics, money and banking, health, education, liberty, foreign affairs, defence, Kashmir, Pakistan.

Other: Associate consultant, Centre for Social Justice 2008-; Member, Speen Baptist Church; Chartered aerospace engineer, Royal Aeronautical Society 1999; Member, Institute of Directors; Volunteer, Wycombe Winter Night Shelter 2008-09; Royal Air Force Club.

Recreations: Skydiving, motorcycling, photography, sailing.

Steve Baker MP, House of Commons, London SW1A 0AA
Tel: 020 7219 3547/020 7219 5099 *Fax:* 020 7219 4614 *Email:* steve.baker.mp@parliament.uk
Constituency: 150a West Wycombe Road, High Wycombe, Buckinghamshire HP12 3AE
Tel: 01494 448408 *Email:* sue.hynard@parliament.uk *Website:* www.stevebaker.info
Twitter: @stevebakermp

CONSERVATIVE

BALDRY, TONY
Banbury *(Majority 18,227)*

Antony Brian Baldry. Born 10 July 1950; Son of Peter Baldry, consultant physician, and Oina Baldry, née Paterson; Married Catherine Weir 1979 (divorced 1996) (1 son 1 daughter); married Pippa Isbell 2001.

Education: Leighton Park School, Reading; Sussex University (BA social science 1972; LLB 1973; MA international development 2005); Lincoln's Inn (barrister 1975).

Non-political career: TA Officer 1971-83; Honorary Colonel RLC (TA). PA to Margaret Thatcher 1974 general election, served in her private office March-October 1975; Barrister specialising in construction law, general commercial law and international arbitration 1975-.

Political career: Contested Thurrock 1979 general election. Member for Banbury 1983-2010, for Banbury (revised boundary) since 6 May 2010 general election; PPS: to Lynda Chalker as Minister of State, FCO 1985-87, to John Wakeham: as Lord Privy Seal 1987-88, as Leader of the House 1987-89, as Lord President of The Council 1988-89, as Secretary of State for Energy 1989-90; Parliamentary Under-Secretary of State: Department of Energy 1990, Department of Environment 1990-94, Foreign and Commonwealth Office 1994-95; Minister of State, Ministry of Agriculture, Fisheries and Food 1995-97; Second Church Estates Commissioner 2010-. *Select committees:* Member: Trade and Industry 1997-2001, Liaison 2001-05, Standards and Privileges 2001; Chair: International Development 2001-05; Member: Ecclesiastical Committee 2010-, Joint Committee on the Draft Detention of Terrorist Suspects (Temporary Extension) Bills 2011. Member, Executive 1922 Committee 2001-02. Deputy chair, Conservative Group for Europe 1981-83; Chair, Conservative Parliamentary Mainstream Group 1997-2001.

Political interests: Employment, youth affairs, legal affairs, overseas aid and development, European Union, childcare; Africa, Asia, Caribbean, Middle East, North America.

Other: IPU British Group: Executive Committee Member 1997-, Treasurer 2000-01; Vice-president, National Children's Homes 1981-83; Governor, Commonwealth Institute 1997-2005; Council member: Overseas Development Institute 2003-, Chatham House 2004-. Liveryman: Merchant Taylors' Company, Stationers' and Newspaper Makers Company, Arbitrators Company, Bowyers Company. Robert Schumann Silver Medal 1978. Kt 2012; Carlton, Farmers' Club, Garrick.

Recreations: Walking, cycling, gardening, historical biography.

Sir Tony Baldry MP, House of Commons, London SW1A 0AA
Tel: 020 7219 6465 *Email:* tony.baldry.mp@parliament.uk
Constituency: Alexandra House, Church Passage, Banbury, Oxfordshire OX16 5JZ
Tel: 01295 673873 *Fax:* 01295 263376 *Website:* tonybaldry.co.uk *Twitter:* @tonybaldry

BALDWIN, HARRIETT West Worcestershire *(Majority 6,754)*

Harriett Mary Morison Baldwin. Born 2 May 1960; Daughter of Anthony Eggleston, OBE and late Jane Eggleston, née Buxton; Married 2nd James Stanley Baldwin 2004 (1 son from previous marriage 2 stepdaughters).

Education: Friends' School, Saffron Walden; Marlborough College; Lady Margaret Hall, Oxford (BA French and Russian 1982); McGill University, Montreal, Canada (MBA international finance 1985); French, Russian.

CONSERVATIVE

Non-political career: Armed Forces RAF Parliamentary Scheme. Graduate trainee, Security Pacific National Bank 1982-83; Treasury analyst, Hewlett-Packard Canada 1985-86; JP Morgan 1986-2008: Various roles/investor 1986-98, Head of currency management, Asset management division 1998-2006, Managing director 1998-2008.

Political career: Contested Stockton North 2005 general election. Member for West Worcestershire since 6 May 2010 general election; PPS to Mark Hoban as Minister of State for Employment, Department for Work and Pensions 2012-13. *Select committees:* Member: Work and Pensions 2010-12, Joint Committee on the Draft Care and Support Bill 2013.

Political interests: Pensions, economics, social enterprise, financial literacy, micro-finance, welfare reform; Cyprus, Russia.

Other: Member, NATO Parliamentary Assembly 2010-; Vice-chair, Social Investment Business 2008-12; Supporter: Centre for Social Justice, Camfed, Opportunity International; Parliamentary Champion, Save the Children; Carlton Club.

Publications: Author: Leviathan Is Still At Large (Centre for Policy Studies, 2002), Social Enterprise Zones (Conservative Policy Review, 2007), Growth, Growth, Growth, (Centre for Policy Studies, 2011), Iron Ladies (Demos, 2012).

Recreations: Canal boats, walking, cycling.

Harriett Baldwin MP, House of Commons, London SW1A 0AA
Tel: 020 7219 5487 *Fax:* 020 7219 5151 *Email:* harriett.baldwin.mp@parliament.uk
Constituency: Malvern Hills Science Park, Geraldine Road, Malvern,
Worcestershire WR14 3SZ
Tel: 01684 585165 *Website:* www.harriettbaldwin.com *Twitter:* @HBaldwinMP

BALLS, ED
Morley and Outwood *(Majority 1,101)*

Shadow Chancellor of the Exchequer

Edward Michael Balls. Born 25 February 1967; Son of Professor Michael Balls and Carolyn Balls; Married Yvette Cooper MP 1998 (2 daughters 1 son).

Education: Nottingham High School; Keble College, Oxford (scholarship, BA philosophy, politics and economics 1988); John F Kennedy School of Government, Harvard University (Kennedy scholar MPA 1990).

LAB/CO-OP

Non-political career: Teaching fellow Department of Economics, Harvard University 1989-90; Economics leader writer and columnist, *Financial Times* 1990-94; Economic adviser to Gordon Brown as Shadow Chancellor of Exchequer 1994-97; Secretary, Labour Party Economic Policy Commission 1994-97; Economic adviser to Gordon Brown as Chancellor of Exchequer 1997-99; Chief economic adviser, HM Treasury 1999-2004; Senior research fellow, Smith Institute 2004-05. Member: TGWU/Unite, Unison.

Political career: Member for Normanton 2005-10, for Morley and Outwood since 6 May 2010 general election; Economic Secretary, HM Treasury 2006-07; Secretary of State for Children, Schools and Families 2007-10; Shadow Secretary of State for: Education 2010, the Home Department (Home Secretary) 2010-11; Shadow Chancellor of the Exchequer 2011-; Contested Labour leadership 2010.

Political interests: Economic, social and international affairs, home affairs.

Other: Chair, Fabian Society 2007-08; Ran London marathon in 2012 and 2013 for Action for Stammering Children and Whizz-Kidz. Honorary doctorate, Nottingham University; Honorary fellow, Keble College, Oxford 2008. Young Financial Journalist of the Year, Wincott 1992; *e-politix* Disability Champion 2006; Parliamentarian of the Year, *Spectator* awards 2010; Parliamentarian of the Year, Political Studies award 2011. PC 2007.

Publications: Co-editor, Reforming Britain's Economic and Financial Policy (2002); World Bank Development Report (1995); Co-editor, Microeconomic Reform in Britain (2004); Co-author, Evolution and Devolution in England: How Regions Strengthen Our Towns and Cities (2006); Britain and Europe: A City Minister's Perspective (2007); Contributions to academic journals including Scottish Journal of Political Economy, World Economics and reports by Social Justice Commission and Fabian Society.

Recreations: Cooking, playing football with children.

Rt Hon Ed Balls MP, House of Commons, London SW1A 0AA
Tel: 020 7219 4115 *Email:* ed.balls.mp@parliament.uk
Constituency: Albion Chambers, Albion Street, Morley LS27 8DT
Tel: 0113-253 9466 *Fax:* 0113-204 9060 *Email:* ed@edballs.com *Website:* www.edballs.co.uk
Twitter: @EdBallsMP

BANKS, GORDON
Ochil and South Perthshire *(Majority 5,187)*

Shadow Minister for Scotland

Gordon Raymond Banks. Born 14 June 1955; Son of William Banks and Patricia Banks, née Macknight; Married Lynda Nicol 1981 (1 daughter 1 son).

Education: Lornshill Academy, Alloa; Glasgow College of Building (City and Guilds construction technology and concrete practice 1976); Stirling University (BA history and politics 2003).

LABOUR

Non-political career: Chief buyer, Barratt Developments 1976-86; Director, Cartmore Building Supply Co Ltd 1986-; Parliamentary officer to Dr Richard Simpson MSP 1999-2003; Researcher to Martin O'Neill MP 2003-06. Member, Unite.

Political career: Member for Ochil and South Perthshire since 5 May 2005 general election; PPS to James Purnell: as Minister of State, Department for Work and Pensions 2006-07, as Secretary of State for Culture, Media and Sport 2007-08; as Secretary of State for Work and Pensions 2008-09; Shadow Minister for: Business, Innovation and Skills 2010-11, Scotland 2012-.
Select committees: Member: Northern Ireland Affairs 2005-06, Scottish Affairs 2005-06, Regulatory Reform 2005-10, Unopposed Bills (Panel) 2005-13. Chair, PLP Departmental: Committee for Foreign and Commonwealth Affairs 2006-10, Group for Business, Innovation and Skills 2012. Contested Mid Scotland and Fife region 2003 Scottish Parliament election.

Political interests: Economy, Europe, environment, international development.

Other: Coeliac UK.

Recreations: Playing guitar, songwriting, football, motor sport.

Gordon Banks MP, House of Commons, London SW1A 0AA
Tel: 020 7219 8275 *Fax:* 020 7219 8693 *Email:* banksgr@parliament.uk
Constituency: 49-51 High Street, Alloa, Clackmannanshire FK10 1JF
Tel: 01259 721536 *Fax:* 01259 216761 *Email:* scotth@parliament.uk
Unit 3, Penny Lane Arcade, Church Street, Crieff, Perthshire PH7 3AE
Tel: 01764 654738 *Email:* gibsond@parliament.uk *Website:* www.gordonbanks.info
Twitter: @gordonbanksmp

BARCLAY, STEVE North East Cambridgeshire *(Majority 16,425)*

Stephen Paul Barclay. Born May 1972; Married Karen.

Education: King Edward VII School, Lancashire; Peterhouse, Cambridge (BA history 1994, MA); College of Law, Chester (1996).

Non-political career: 2nd Lieutenant, Royal Regiment of Fusiliers 1991. Trainee solicitor, Lawrence Graham Solicitors 1996-98; Company lawyer, Axa Insurance 1998-2001; Financial Services Authority 2002-06; Barclays Retail Bank 2006-10: Director of regulatory affairs 2006-08, Head of anti-money laundering and sanctions 2008-10.

CONSERVATIVE

Political career: Contested Manchester Blackley 1997 and Lancaster and Wyre 2001 general elections. Member for North East Cambridgeshire since 6 May 2010 general election. *Select committees:* Member: Public Accounts 2010-. Member, Conservative Party 1994-.

Recreations: Rugby, skydiving.

Steve Barclay MP, House of Commons, London SW1A 0AA
Tel: 020 7219 7117 *Email:* stephen.barclay.mp@parliament.uk
Constituency: Cromwell House, Wisbech Road, March, Cambridgeshire PE15 8EB
Tel: 01354 656635 *Website:* www.stevebarclay.net *Twitter:* @SteveBarclayMP

BARKER, GREGORY Bexhill and Battle *(Majority 12,880)*

Minister of State for Climate Change, Department of Energy and Climate Change

Gregory Leonard George Barker. Born 8 March 1966; Married Celeste Harrison 1992 (divorced 2008) (1 daughter 2 sons).

Education: Steyning Grammar School; Lancing College, West Sussex; Royal Holloway College, London University (BA modern history, economic history, politics 1987).

CONSERVATIVE

Non-political career: Researcher, Centre for Policy Studies 1987-89; Equity analyst, Gerrard Vivian Gray 1988-90; Director, International Pacific Securities 1990-97; Associate partner, Brunswick Group Ltd 1997-98; Head, investor communications, Siberian Oil Company 1998-2000; Director, Daric plc (Bartlett Merton) 1998-2001.

Political career: Contested Eccles 1997 general election. Member for Bexhill and Battle 2001-10, for Bexhill and Battle (revised boundary) since 6 May 2010 general election; Opposition Whip 2003-05; Shadow Minister for: the Environment 2005-08, Climate Change 2008-10; Minister of State, Department of Energy and Climate Change 2010-. *Select committees:* Member: Environmental Audit 2001-05, 2007-10, Broadcasting 2003-05. Chair: Shoreham Young Conservatives 1982-83, Royal Holloway Conservative Society 1986-87; Vice-chair: Hammersmith Conservative Association 1993-95, Wandsworth and Tooting Conservative Association 1997-98; Founding member, 2020 group 2011-.

Political interests: Environment, education, overseas development; Australia, Germany, Russia, USA.

Other: Former member, British-German Forum; Associate, Centre for Policy Studies 1988-89. Honourable Artillery Company. PC 2012; Pratt's, Bexhill Conservative Club. Bexhill Rowing Club.

Recreations: Skiing, hunting, horse racing.

Rt Hon Gregory Barker MP, House of Commons, London SW1A 0AA
Tel: 020 7219 1852 *Email:* gregory.barker.mp@parliament.uk
Constituency: 6a Amherst Road, Bexhill-on-Sea, East Sussex TN40 1QJ
Tel: 01424 736861 *Email:* enquiries@gregorybarker.com *Website:* www.gregorybarker.com
Twitter: @GregBarkerMP

CONSERVATIVE

BARON, JOHN
Basildon and Billericay *(Majority 12,398)*

John Charles Baron. Born 21 June 1959; Son of Raymond Baron and Kathleen Baron, née Whittlestone; Married Thalia Mayson, née Laird 1992 (2 daughters).

Education: Attended nine schools by 16 including: Birmingham Grammar School; Wadham Comprehensive, Crewkerne; Queen's College, Taunton, Somerset; Jesus College, Cambridge (BA history and economics 1982); Royal Military College Sandhurst 1984.

Non-political career: Captain Royal Regiment of Fusiliers 1984-87. Director: Henderson Private Investors Ltd 1987-99, Rothschild Asset Management 1999-2001.

Political career: Contested Basildon 1997 general election. Member for Billericay 2001-10, for Basildon and Billericay since 6 May 2010 general election; Shadow Minister for: Health 2002-03 (resigned over Iraq War), Health 2003-07; Opposition Whip 2007-10. *Select committees:* Member: Education and Skills 2001-02, Foreign Affairs 2010-.

Political interests: Foreign affairs, economy, civil liberties, defence, cancer.

Other: Member, Chartered Institute for Securities and Investment (MCSI); Numerous local charities.

Publications: Regular column for *Financial Times*'s Investors Chronicle; Co-author, The Future of Conservatism: Values Revisited (Biteback, 2011).

Recreations: Tennis, walking, history, cycling.

John Baron MP, House of Commons, London SW1A 0AA
Tel: 020 7219 8138 *Fax:* 020 7219 1743 *Email:* baronj@parliament.uk
Constituency: 13 Bentalls Business Park, Basildon, Essex SS14 3BN
Tel: 01268 520765 *Fax:* 01268 524009 *Email:* turnerja@parliament.uk
Website: www.johnbaron.co.uk

LABOUR

BARRON, KEVIN
Rother Valley *(Majority 5,866)*

Kevin John Barron. Born 26 October 1946; Son of late Richard Barron and Edna Barron; Married Carol McGrath 1969 (died 2008) (1 son 2 daughters).

Education: Maltby Hall Secondary Modern, near Rotherham; Sheffield University (day release, social sciences); Ruskin College, Oxford (Diploma labour studies 1977).

Non-political career: Colliery electrician and NUM trade union delegate, Maltby 1962-83. Unite.

Political career: Member for Rother Valley 1983-2010, for Rother Valley (revised boundary) since 6 May 2010 general election; PPS to Neil Kinnock as Leader of the Opposition 1985-88; Sponsored Private Member's Bills: to ban advertising and promotion of tobacco products 1993, 1994, Energy efficiency stamp duty rebate; Opposition Spokesperson for: Energy 1988-92, Employment 1993-95, Health 1995-97; Member: Intelligence and Security Committee 1997-2005, Speaker's Committee for the Independent Parliamentary Standards Authority 2010-, Speakers' Working Group on All-Party Groups 2011-12. *Select committees:* Chair: Health 2005-10; Member: Liaison 2005-; Standards and Privileges: Member 2005-10, Chair 2010-13; Chair: Privileges 2013-, Standards 2013-. Chair, PLP: Yorkshire Regional Group 1987-2010, Departmental Group for Health and Social Services 1997-2001, 2010-11.

Political interests: Energy, environment, home affairs, health, intelligence and security, international development, British film; Bulgaria, Guyana, Tanzania.

Other: Honorary Treasurer, Commonwealth Parliamentary Association (UK Branch) 2010-; Trustee, National Coal Mining Museum 2005; Patron, Safe@last (charity for runaway children and young people) 2008-; Member, General Medical Council 1999-2009; Vice-president, Royal Society of Health 2007; Honorary Fellow, Royal College of Physicians; Vice-president, Chartered Institute of Environmental Health 2008-; FRCP 2008; One World Action; BIBIC (British Institute for Brain Injured Children). PC 2001.

Recreations: Family life, football, fly fishing, photography, walking, film, lying in bed.

Rt Hon Kevin Barron MP, House of Commons, London SW1A 0AA
Tel: 020 7219 4432/020 7219 6306 *Fax:* 020 7219 5952 *Email:* barronk@parliament.uk
Constituency: 9 Lordens Hill, Dinnington, Sheffield, South Yorkshire S25 2QE
Tel: 01909 568611 *Fax:* 01909 569974 *Email:* woolleys@parliament.uk
Website: www.kevinbarronmp.com

CONSERVATIVE

BARWELL, GAVIN

Croydon Central *(Majority 2,969)*

Assistant Whip

Gavin Laurence Barwell. Born 23 January 1972; Married Karen 2001 (3 sons).

Education: Trinity School, Croydon; Trinity College, Cambridge (BA natural sciences 1993).

Non-political career: Environment desk officer, Conservative Research Department 1993-95; Special adviser to John Gummer as Secretary of State for the Environment 1995-97; Conservative Party: Press officer, CCHQ May-October 1997, Head of political section, Conservative Research Department CCHQ 1997-98, Head of local government 1998-2003, Chief operating officer 2003-06; Political consultant 2006-10.

Political career: Member for Croydon Central since 6 May 2010 general election; PPS to: Greg Clark as Minister of State for Decentralisation and Cities 2011-12, Michael Gove as Secretary of State for Education 2012-13; Assistant Whip 2013-. *Select committees:* Member: Science and Technology 2010-12, Joint Committee on the Draft House of Lords Reform Bill 2011-12. Member, Executive, 1922 Committee 2010-11. *Councils and public bodies:* Croydon Council: Councillor 1998-2010, Chief Whip 2006-07, Cabinet Member for: Resources and Customer Services 2007-08, Community Safety and Cohesion 2008-10; Chair of governors, Trinity School of John Whitgift, Croydon; Vice-President, Local Government Association 2011-.

Political interests: Education, crime, race, migration; India, USA.

Other: Member, Court of Governors, Whitgift Foundation.

Recreations: Sport – particularly football and tennis, military history, travel.

Gavin Barwell MP, House of Commons, London SW1A 0AA
Tel: 020 7219 2119 *Email:* gavin.barwell.mp@parliament.uk
Constituency: 133 Wickham Road, Shirley, Croydon CR0 8TE
Tel: 020 8663 8741 *Website:* www.gavinbarwell.com *Twitter:* @GavinBarwellMP

LABOUR

BAYLEY, HUGH

York Central *(Majority 6,451)*

Born 9 January 1952; Son of Michael Bayley, architect, and Pauline Bayley; Married Fenella Jeffers 1984 (1 son 1 daughter).

Education: Haileybury College; Bristol University (BSc politics 1974); York University (BPhil Southern African studies 1976).

Non-political career: District officer, then national officer, NALGO 1975-82; General secretary, International Broadcasting Trust 1982-86; York University 1986-92: Lecturer, social policy 1986-97, Research fellow, health economics 1987-92. TGWU 1975-82, BECTU 1982-, RMT 1992-2002.

Political career: Contested York 1987 general election. Member for York 1992-97, for City of York 1997-2010, for York Central since 6 May 2010 general election; PPS to Frank Dobson as Secretary of State for Health 1997-99; Parliamentary Under-Secretary of State, Department of Social Security 1999-2001; Temporary Deputy Speaker 2010. *Select committees:* Member: Health 1992-97, International Development 2001-, Chairmen's Panel/Panel of Chairs 2005-. Chair, PLP Departmental Committee for International Development 2002-10. *Councils and public bodies:* Councillor, London Borough of Camden 1980-86; York Health Authority 1988-90.

Political interests: Health, economic policy, environment, international development, defence, electoral reform; Africa.

Other: Member, Executive Committee, Inter-Parliamentary Union, British Group 1997-99, 2001-; Commonwealth Parliamentary Association (CPA) UK Branch: Member, Executive Committee 1997-99, 2001-, Chair 2006-08; Member, UK Delegation to North Atlantic Assembly 1997-99; Parliamentary Assembly of the Organisation for Security and Co-operation in Europe 2001-07; NATO Parliamentary Assembly: Member UK Delegation 2001-, Chair, Economics and Security Committee 2008-, Vice-President 2010-; Parliamentary Network on the World Bank: Chair 2007-10, Board member 2010-; Chair, Westminster Foundation for Democracy 2005-09; Council member, Overseas Development Institute.

Publications: The Nation's Health (1995).

Hugh Bayley MP, House of Commons, London SW1A 0AA
Tel: 020 7219 6824 *Fax:* 020 7219 0346 *Email:* hugh.bayley.mp@parliament.uk
Constituency: 59 Holgate Road, York YO24 4AA
Tel: 01904 623713 *Fax:* 01904 623260 *Website:* www.hughbayley.co.uk

BEBB, GUTO
Aberconwy *(Majority 3,398)*

Guto ap Owain Bebb. Born 9 October 1968; Son of Owain Bebb and Helen Gwyn; Married Esyllt Penri 1993 (3 sons 2 daughters).

Education: Ysgol Syr Hugh Owen, Caernarfon; Aberystwyth University (BA history 1990); Welsh.

Non-political career: Partner Egin Partnership 1993-.

Political career: Contested Ogmore 2002 by-election and Conwy 2005 general election. Member for Aberconwy since 6 May 2010 general election. *Select committees:* Member: Welsh Affairs 2010-, Members' Expenses 2011, Public Accounts 2012-. Member, Executive, 1922 Committee 2012-. Contested Conwy constituency 2003 National Assembly for Wales election.

CONSERVATIVE

Political interests: Europe, taxation, reform of the welfare state, devolution, economy, rural development, regeneration policy; Eastern Europe, Israel, North America.

Other: Member, British-American Parliamentary Group; Member, Institute of Business Consultants (IBC) 1993-.

Publications: Various in Welsh language .

Recreations: Wine, reading, music and family.

Guto Bebb MP, House of Commons, London SW1A 0AA
Tel: 020 7219 7002 *Email:* guto.bebb.mp@parliament.uk
Constituency: 1 Ashdown House, Riverside Business Park, Benarth Road, Conwy, Gwynedd LL32 8UB
Tel: 01492 583094 *Fax:* 01492 592721 *Email:* office@gutobebbmp.co.uk
Website: www.aberconwyconservatives.co.uk www.gutobebbmp.co.uk *Twitter:* @gutobebb

BECKETT, MARGARET
Derby South *(Majority 6,122)*

Margaret Mary Beckett. Born 15 January 1943; Daughter of late Cyril Jackson, carpenter, and Winifred Jackson, teacher; Married Lionel (Leo) Beckett 1979 (2 stepsons).

Education: Notre Dame High School, Manchester and Norwich; Manchester College of Science and Technology; John Dalton Polytechnic.

Non-political career: Student apprentice in metallurgy, AEI Manchester 1961-66; Experimental officer, Department of Metallurgy, Manchester University 1966-70; Industrial policy researcher, Labour Party 1970-74; Political adviser, Ministry of Overseas Development 1974; Principal researcher, Granada Television 1979-83. Member: Transport and General Workers' Union 1964-, National Union of Journalists, BECTU.

LABOUR

Political career: Contested (as Margaret Jackson) Lincoln February 1974 general election. Member for Lincoln October 1974-79. Contested Lincoln 1979 general election. Member (as Margaret Beckett) for Derby South 1983-2010, for Derby South (revised boundary) since 6 May 2010 general election; PPS to Judith Hart as Minister of Overseas Development 1974-75; Assistant Government Whip 1975-76; Parliamentary Under-Secretary of State, Department of Education and Science 1976-79; Shadow Minister, Social Security 1984-89; Shadow Chief Secretary to the Treasury 1989-92; Shadow Leader, House of Commons 1992-94; Deputy Leader, Labour Party and Opposition 1992-94; Leader of Opposition May-July 1994; Shadow Secretary of State for Health 1994-95; Shadow President of the Board of Trade 1995-97; President of the Board of Trade 1997-98; Secretary of State for Trade and Industry 1997-98; President of the Council and Leader of the House of Commons 1998-2001; Secretary of State for: Environment, Food and Rural Affairs 2001-06, Foreign and Commonwealth Affairs (Foreign Secretary) 2006-07; Minister for Housing and Planning (attending Cabinet), Department for Communities and Local Government 2008-09; Chair Intelligence and Security Committee 2008-10; Contested Speaker election 2009. *Select committees:* Chair: Modernisation of the House of Commons 1998-2001, Joint Committee on National Security Strategy 2010-. Member, Labour Party 1963-; Secretary, Trades Council and Labour Party, Swinton and Pendlebury 1968-70; Member: National Executive Committee, Labour Party 1980-81, 1985-86, 1988-97, 2011-, Tribune Group, Socialist Education Committee, Labour Women's Action Committee, Socialist Environment and Resources Association. *Councils and public bodies:* Member, Committee on Standards in Public Life 2010-.

Political interests: Industry, climate change, nuclear disarmament.

Other: Member: Amnesty International, Anti-Apartheid Movement, Fabian Society, Global Zero, Top Level Group on Nuclear non-proliferation. PC 1993; DBE 2013.

Publications: The Need For Consumer Protection (1972); The National Enterprise Board; The Nationalisation of Shipbuilding, Ship Repair and Marine Engineering; Renewing the NHS (1995); Vision for Growth – A New Industrial Strategy for Britain (1996).

Recreations: Cooking, reading, caravanning.

Margaret Beckett DBE MP, House of Commons, London SW1A 0AA
Tel: 020 7219 6662/5135/2088 *Fax:* 020 7219 4780 *Email:* beckettm@parliament.uk
Constituency: No constituency office publicised
Tel: 01332 345636 *Fax:* 01332 371306

BEGG, ANNE

Aberdeen South *(Majority 3,506)*

Margaret Anne Begg. Born 6 December 1955; Daughter of late David Begg, MBE, orthotist, and Margaret Begg, nurse; Single.

Education: Brechin High School; Aberdeen University (MA history and politics 1977); Aberdeen College of Education (Secondary Teaching Certificate 1978).

Non-political career: English and history teacher, Webster's High School, Kirriemuir 1978-88; Head of English department, Arbroath Academy 1988-97. Member: Educational Institute of Scotland (EIS) 1978-, EIS National Council 1990-95, GMB 2004-.

LABOUR

Political career: Member for Aberdeen South 1997-2005, for Aberdeen South (revised boundary) since 5 May 2005 general election; Vice-chair Speaker's Conference 2009-10. *Select committees:* Member: Scottish Affairs 1997-2001; Work and Pensions: Member 2001-10, Chair 2010-; Member: Chairmen's Panel/Panel of Chairs 2002-11, Liaison 2010-. Member, Labour Party National Executive Committee 1998-99; Vice-chair, Labour Party National Policy Forum 2006-10.

Political interests: Disability, broadcasting, welfare reform, social inclusion, genetics, pensions, energy.

Other: Patron, Access to Training and Employment; Fellow, Industry and Parliament Trust 2000; Member, General Teaching Council for Scotland. Disabled Scot of the Year 1988. DBE 2011.

Recreations: Reading, cinema, theatre, public speaking.

Dame Anne Begg DBE MP, House of Commons, London SW1A 0AA
Tel: 020 7219 2140 *Email:* anne.begg.mp@parliament.uk
Constituency: Admiral Court, Poynernook Road, Aberdeen AB11 5QX
Tel: 01224 252704 *Website:* www.annebegg.com *Twitter:* @annebegg

BEITH, ALAN

Berwick-upon-Tweed *(Majority 2,690)*

Alan James Beith. Born 20 April 1943; Son of late James Beith, foreman packer, and Joan Beith; Married Barbara Ward 1965 (died 1998) (1 son deceased 1 daughter); married Baroness Maddock 2001.

Education: King's School, Macclesfield; Balliol College, Oxford (BA philosophy, politics and economics 1964); Nuffield College, Oxford (BLitt, MA 1966); Welsh, French, Norwegian.

Non-political career: Politics lecturer, Newcastle University 1966-73. Member, Association of University Teachers.

LIBERAL DEMOCRAT

Political career: Contested Berwick-upon-Tweed 1970 general election. Member for Berwick-upon-Tweed 8 November 1973 by-election to 2010, for Berwick-upon-Tweed (revised boundary) since 6 May 2010 general election ; Chief Whip, Liberal Party 1976-87; Member House of Commons Commission 1979-97; Liberal Spokesperson for Foreign Affairs 1985-87; Alliance Spokesperson for Foreign Affairs 1987; Liberal Spokesperson for Treasury 1987; SLD Spokesperson for Treasury 1988-89; Liberal Democrat: Treasury Spokesperson 1989-94, Home Affairs Spokesperson 1994-95; Member, Intelligence and Security Committee 1994-2008; Liberal Democrat Spokesperson for: Police, Prison and Security Matters 1995-97, Home and Legal Affairs (Home Affairs) 1997-99; Contested Speaker election 2000; Liberal Democrat Spokesperson for Cabinet Office 2001-02; Member: Speaker's Committee on the Electoral Commission 2001-10; Deputy chairman Review Committee of Privy Counsellors of the Anti-terrorism, Crime and Security Act 2002-04; Contested Speaker election 2009. *Select committees:* Member: Procedure 2000-01; Liaison: Member 2003-10, Chair 2010-; Chair: Constitutional Affairs/Justice 2003-; Member: Liaison (Liaison Sub-Committee) 2006-10, Joint Committee on National Security Strategy 2010-; Liaison (National Policy Statements Sub-committee): Member 2010-12, Chair

2012-. Deputy Leader: Liberal Party 1985-88, Liberal Democrat Party 1993-2003. *Councils and public bodies:* Councillor: Hexham RDC 1969-74, Tynedale DC 1974-75.

Political interests: Parliamentary and constitutional affairs, architectural and artistic heritage; Canada, Scandinavia, Zimbabwe.

Other: Local preacher, Methodist Church 1965-; Historic Chapels Trust: Trustee 1995-, Chair 2002-; President, North of England Civic Trust 2005-; Vice-President, Northumberland and Newcastle Society 2009-; Diabetes UK; Hospice Care North Northumberland. Honorary DCL: Newcastle University 1998, Northumbria University 2010; Honorary doctorate, Earlham College, Indiana 2013. PC 1992; Kt 2008; President, National Liberal Club 2009-; Athenæum; Northern Counties, Newcastle upon Tyne.

Publications: Co-author, Case for Liberal Party and Alliance (1983); Faith and Politics (1987); A View From the North (2008).

Recreations: Music, walking, boating.

Rt Hon Sir Alan Beith MP, House of Commons, London SW1A 0AA
Tel: 020 7219 3540 *Fax:* 020 7219 5890 *Email:* alan.beith.mp@parliament.uk
Constituency: 54 Bondgate Within, Alnwick, Northumberland NE66 1JD
Tel: 01665 602901 *Fax:* 01665 604435 *Email:* alanbeith@berwicklibdems.org.uk
Website: www.alanbeith.org.uk

BELLINGHAM, HENRY   North West Norfolk *(Majority 14,810)*

Henry Campbell Bellingham. Born 29 March 1955; Married Emma Whiteley 1993 (1 son).

Education: Eton College; Magdalene College, Cambridge (BA law 1978, MA); Counsel of Legal Education 1978-79.

Non-political career: Barrister, Middle Temple 1978-87; Company director and business consultant 1997-2010.

Political career: Member for Norfolk North West 1983-97. Contested Norfolk North West 1997 general election. Member for North West Norfolk 2001-10, for North West Norfolk (revised boundary) since 6 May 2010 general election; PPS to Malcolm Rifkind as Secretary of State for Transport and for Defence and as Foreign Secretary 1991-97; Shadow Minister for: Trade and Industry (Small Business and Enterprise) 2002-03, Economic Affairs (Small Business and Enterprise) 2003-05; Opposition Whip 2005-06; Shadow Minister for Constitutional Affairs/Justice 2006-10; Parliamentary Under-Secretary of State, Foreign and Commonwealth Office (Minister for Africa, UN and overseas territories) 2010-12. *Select committees:* Member: Environment 1988-90, Northern Ireland 2001-02, Trade and Industry 2002-03. Chair, Conservative Council on Eastern Europe 1989-93.

CONSERVATIVE

Political interests: Small businesses, agriculture, defence, Northern Ireland, foreign policy, legal services; Africa, Caribbean, Overseas Territories.

Other: President, British Resorts Association 1993-97.

Recreations: Country sports, golf, cricket.

Henry Bellingham MP, House of Commons, London SW1A 0AA
Tel: 020 7219 8234 *Fax:* 020 7219 2844 *Email:* bellinghamh@parliament.uk
Constituency: First Floor, 12 London Road, King's Lynn, Norfolk PE30 5PY
Tel: 01485 600559/01553 692076 *Fax:* 01485 600292 *Website:* www.henrybellingham.com

BENN, HILARY   Leeds Central *(Majority 10,645)*

Shadow Secretary of State for Communities and Local Government

Hilary James Wedgwood Benn. Born 26 November 1953; Son of Tony Benn, MP for Bristol South East 1950-61, 1963-83 and for Chesterfield 1984-2001, and late Caroline Middleton De Camp; Married Rosalind Retey 1973 (died 1979); married Sally Clark 1982 (3 sons 1 daughter).

Education: Holland Park Comprehensive School; Sussex University (BA Russian and East European studies 1974).

LABOUR

Non-political career: Research officer and latterly head of policy and communications, MSF 1975-97; Special adviser to David Blunkett as Secretary of State for Education and Employment 1997-99. Member, Unite.

Political career: Contested Ealing North 1983 and 1987 general elections. Member for Leeds Central 10 June 1999 by-election to 2010, for Leeds Central (revised boundary) since 6 May

2010 general election; Parliamentary Under-Secretary of State: Department for International Development 2001-02, Home Office (Community and Custodial Provision) 2002-03; Department for International Development: Minister of State 2003, Secretary of State 2003-07; Secretary of State for Environment, Food and Rural Affairs 2007-10; Shadow Secretary of State for Environment, Food and Rural Affairs 2010; Shadow Leader of the House of Commons 2010-11; Member: House of Commons Commission 2010-11, Speaker's Committee for the Independent Parliamentary Standards Authority 2011-12; Shadow Secretary of State for Communities and Local Government 2011-. *Select committees:* Member: Environment, Transport and Regional Affairs 1999-2001, Environment, Transport and Regional Affairs (Environment Sub-Committee) 1999-2001. Joint vice-chair, PLP Departmental Committee for Education and Employment 2000-01. *Councils and public bodies:* London Borough of Ealing: Councillor 1979-99, Deputy Leader 1986-90, Chair, Education Committee 1986-90; Member, Association of Metropolitan Authorities Education Committee 1986-90; Chair, Association of London Authorities Education Committee 1989-90.

Political interests: International development, home affairs, education, employment, trade unions, environment, urban policy; Democratic Republic of the Congo, Sudan, USA.

Other: Minister of the Year *House Magazine* 2006, 2007; Politicians' Politician Channel 4 2006; Parliamentarian of the Year, League Against Cruel Sports 2011. PC 2003.

Publications: Contributor: Beyond 2002: Long-term policies for Labour (Profile Books, 1999), The Forces of Conservatism (IPPR, 1999), Men who made Labour (Routledge, 2006), Politics for a New Generation (IPPR, 2007), The End of the Peer Show: Responses to the Draft Bill on Lords Reform (2011).

Recreations: Watching sport, gardening.

Rt Hon Hilary Benn MP, House of Commons, London SW1A 0AA
Tel: 020 7219 5770 *Email:* hilary.benn.mp@parliament.uk
Constituency: 2 Blenheim Terrace, Leeds LS2 9JG
Tel: 0113-244 1097 *Email:* boxj@parliament.uk *Website:* www.hilarybennmp.com
Twitter: @HilaryBennMP

LABOUR

BENTON, JOE
Bootle *(Majority 21,181)*

Joseph Edward Benton. Born 28 September 1933; Son of late Thomas and Agnes Benton; Married Doris Wynne 1959 (4 daughters).

Education: St Monica's Primary and Secondary School; Bootle Technical College; Spanish.

Non-political career: RAF national service 1955-57. Apprentice fitter and turner 1949; Personnel manager Pacific Steam Navigation Company; Girobank 1982-90. Member, RMT Parliamentary Campaigning Group 2002-.

Political career: Member for Bootle 8 November 1990 by-election to 2010, for Bootle (revised boundary) since 6 May 2010 general election; Opposition Whip 1994-97. *Select committees:* Member: Chairmen's Panel/Panel of Chairs 1997-, Education and Employment 1997-99, Education and Employment (Education Sub-Committee) 1997-99, Parliamentary Privilege (Joint Committee) 1997-2000, Northern Ireland Affairs 2010-, European Scrutiny 2013. *Councils and public bodies:* Sefton Borough Council: Councillor 1970-90, Leader, Labour Group 1985-90, JP, Bootle bench 1969.

Political interests: Education, housing, local and regional government, health.

Other: Chairman of Governors, Hugh Baird College of Technology 1972-92; Member, Institute of Linguists; Affiliate Member, Institute of Personnel Management.

Recreations: Reading, listening to classical music, squash, swimming.

Joe Benton MP, House of Commons, London SW1A 0AA
Tel: 020 7219 6973 *Fax:* 020 7219 3895 *Email:* bentonj@parliament.uk
Constituency: Second Floor, St Hugh's House, Stanley Road, Bootle L20 3QQ
Tel: 0151-933 8432 *Fax:* 0151-933 4746

BENYON, RICHARD
Newbury *(Majority 12,248)*

CONSERVATIVE

Richard Henry Ronald Benyon. Born 21 October 1960; Son of Sir William and Lady Benyon; Married Zoe Robinson 2004 (2 sons and 3 sons by previous marriage).

Education: Bradfield College, Reading; Royal Agricultural College (Diploma real estate management, land economy 1987); French, some Swahili.

Non-political career: Army officer, Royal Green Jackets 1980-85. Land agent chartered surveyor 1987-; Farmer 1990-; Chair, Rural and Urban Housing Business 2001-10.

Political career: Contested Newbury 1997 and 2001 general elections. Member for Newbury 2005-10, for Newbury (revised boundary) since 6 May 2010 general election; Opposition Whip 2007-09; Shadow Minister for Environment, Food and Rural Affairs 2009-10; Parliamentary Under-Secretary of State, Department for Environment, Food and Rural Affairs (Natural Environment and Fisheries 2010-12, Natural Environment, Water and Rural Affairs 2012-13) 2010-13. *Select committees:* Member: Home Affairs 2005-07; *Ex-officio* member: Environmental Audit 2010-. *Councils and public bodies:* Newbury District Council: Councillor 1991-95, Leader, Conservative group 1994-95.

Political interests: Rural matters, social affairs, defence, health, home affairs; Africa, Northern Ireland.

Other: Founder trustee, Help for Heroes; Member, Royal Institution of Chartered Surveyors; Vice-chair, Citizens Advice 1994-; Berkshire Community Foundation 1995-2000.

Recreations: Walking, tennis, shooting, fishing, cooking.

Richard Benyon MP, House of Commons, London SW1A 0AA
Tel: 020 7219 8319 *Fax:* 020 7219 4509 *Email:* richard.benyon.mp@parliament.uk
Constituency: 6 Cheap Street, Newbury, Berkshire RG14 5DD
Tel: 01635 551070 *Fax:* 01635 569690 *Email:* mp@richardbenyon.com
Website: www.richardbenyon.com *Twitter:* @RichardBenyonMP

BERCOW, JOHN
Buckingham *(Majority 12,529)*

Speaker

THE SPEAKER

John Simon Bercow. Born 19 January 1963; Son of Brenda Bercow, née Bailey, and late Charles Bercow; Married Sally Illman 2002 (2 sons 1 daughter).

Education: Finchley Manorhill School, London; Essex University (BA government 1985).

Non-political career: Credit analyst, Hambros Bank 1987-88; Public affairs consultant, Rowland Sallingbury Casey (public affairs arm of Saatchi & Saatchi Group) 1988-95; Board director, Rowland Company 1994-95; Special adviser to: Jonathan Aitken as Chief Secretary to the Treasury 1995, Virginia Bottomley as Secretary of State for National Heritage 1995-96.

Political career: Contested Motherwell South 1987 and Bristol South 1992 general elections. Member for Buckingham 1997-2010, for Buckingham (revised boundary) since 6 May 2010 general election (Conservative 1997-2009, Speaker since 2009); Opposition Spokesperson for: Education and Employment 1999-2000, Home Affairs 2000-01; Shadow Chief Secretary to the Treasury 2001-02; Opposition Spokesperson for Work and Pensions 2002; Shadow Secretary of State for International Development 2003-04; Speaker 2009-; Ex-officio chair House of Commons Commission 2009-; Chair: Speaker's Committee on the Electoral Commission 2009-, Speaker's Committee for the Independent Parliamentary Standards Authority 2009-. *Select committees:* Member: Welsh Affairs 1997-98, Trade and Industry 1998-99, Office of the Deputy Prime Minister 2002-04, Home Affairs 2003, Office of the Deputy Prime Minister (Urban Affairs Sub-Committee) 2003-04, International Development 2004-09, Procedure 2004-05, Chairmen's Panel 2005-09, Joint Committee on Consolidation, Etc, Bills 2005-09, Quadripartite (Committees on Strategic Export Controls)/Arms Export Controls 2006-09. Member, Executive 1922 Committee 1998-99. Chair, University of Essex Conservative Association 1984-85; National chair, Federation of Conservative Students 1986; Vice-chair, Conservative Collegiate Forum 1987. *Councils and public bodies:* London Borough of Lambeth: Councillor 1986-90, Deputy Leader, Conservative Opposition 1987-89; Ex-officio chair: Boundary Commission for England 2009-, Boundary Commission for Northern Ireland 2009-, Boundary Commission for Scotland 2009-, Boundary Commission for Wales 2009-.

Political interests: Special educational needs, international development, human rights, constitutional reform; Burma, Sudan, USA, Zimbabwe.

Other: President, Commonwealth Parliamentary Association (UK Branch) 2009-; Honorary President, Inter-Parliamentary Union, British Group 2009-; Honorary President: Armed Forces Parliamentary Scheme 2009-, British-American Parliamentary Group 2009-, Hansard Society for Parliamentary Government 2009-, Parliamentary Press Gallery 2009-; President: Industry and Parliament Trust 2009-, Parliament Choir 2009-. Honorary doctorate, Essex University 2010. Backbencher to Watch, *Spectator* awards 1998; Backbencher of the Year *House Magazine* 2005; Opposition Politician of the Year, Channel 4/Hansard Society 2005; Politician of the Year, Stonewall awards 2010. PC 2009.

Publications: Turning Scotland Around (1987); Faster Moves Forward for Scotland (1987); Aiming for the Heart of Europe: A Misguided Venture (1998); Subsidiarity and the Illusion of Democratic Control (2003); How Much Common Ground (2004); Incoming Assets: Why Tories Should Change Policy on Immigration and Asylum (2005); Promote Freedom or Protect Oppressors: The Choice at the UN Review Summit (2005).

Recreations: Tennis, squash, reading, swimming, music.

Rt Hon John Bercow MP, House of Commons, London SW1A 0AA
Tel: 020 7219 4111/020 7219 5300 *Fax:* 020 7219 6901 *Email:* bercowj@parliament.uk
Constituency: Speaker's House, House of Commons, London SW1A 0AA
Tel: 020 7219 6346 *Fax:* 020 7219 0981 *Website:* www.johnbercow.co.uk

CONSERVATIVE

BERESFORD, PAUL

Mole Valley *(Majority 15,653)*

Alexander Paul Beresford. Born 6 April 1946; Son of Raymond and Joan Beresford; Married Julie Haynes (3 sons 1 daughter).

Education: Waimea College, New Zealand; Otago University, Dunedin, New Zealand (BDS 1970).

Non-political career: Dental surgeon. Member, National Farmers' Union.

Political career: Member for Croydon Central 1992-97, for Mole Valley 1997-2010, for Mole Valley (revised boundary) since 6 May 2010 general election; Parliamentary Under-Secretary of State, Department of the Environment 1994-97; Member House of Commons Commission 2010-. *Select committees:* Member: Education 1992-94, Procedure 1997-2001, Environment, Transport and Regional Affairs 2000-01, Environment, Transport and Regional Affairs (Environment Sub-Committee) 2001, Environment, Transport and Regional Affairs (Transport Sub-Committee) 2001, Transport, Local Government and the Regions 2001-02, Transport, Local Government and the Regions (Urban Affairs Sub-Committee) 2001-02, ODPM/Communities and Local Government 2002-10, ODPM/Communities and Local Government (Urban Affairs Sub-Committee) 2003-05, Finance and Services 2010-, Standards and Privileges 2010-13, Joint Committee on Security 2010-, Standards 2013-, Privileges 2013-. 1922 Committee: Secretary 2002-06, Member, Executive 2006-07. *Councils and public bodies:* London Borough of Wandsworth: Councillor 1978-94, Leader 1983-92.

Political interests: Inner cities, housing, education, health; Australia, Fiji, New Zealand, Samoa.

Other: Fellow, Industry and Parliament Trust 2002; British Dental Association; British Academy/Cosmetic Dentistry; British Endodontic Society. Kt 1990.

Recreations: DIY, reading.

Sir Paul Beresford MP, House of Commons, London SW1A 0AA
Tel: 020 7219 5018 *Email:* dukem@parliament.uk
Constituency: Mole Valley Conservative Association, 86 South Street, Dorking, Surrey RH4 2EW
Tel: 01306 883312 *Fax:* 01306 885194 *Email:* mvca@btconnect.com
Twitter: @PaulBeresfordMP

Need additional copies?

Call 020 7593 5679

Visit www.dodsshop.co.uk

BERGER, LUCIANA

Liverpool Wavertree *(Majority 7,167)*

Shadow Minister for Health

Luciana Clare Berger. Born 13 May 1981; Single.

Education: Birmingham University (BCom commerce with Spanish 2004); Birkbeck College (MSc government 2005); French, Spanish.

Non-political career: Government strategy unit, Accenture 2005-06; NHS Confederation 2006; Director, Labour Friends of Israel 2007-10. Member: USDAW, UCATT.

LAB/CO-OP

Political career: Member for Liverpool Wavertree since 6 May 2010 general election; Shadow Minister for: Climate Change 2010-13, Health 2013-. *Select committees:* Member: Business, Innovation and Skills 2010, Finance and Services 2010, Arms Export Controls 2010. Vice-chair, PLP Departmental Group for Treasury 2010. *Councils and public bodies:* Former school governor.

Political interests: Business, innovation and skills, culture, higher education; Spain.

Other: Fellow, Royal Society of Arts; Parliamentary Champion, Whizz-Kidz. Alumnus of the Year, Birmingham University 2012.

Recreations: Keeping fit, cinema.

Luciana Berger MP, House of Commons, London SW1A 0AA
Tel: 020 7219 7102 *Fax:* 020 7219 2770 *Email:* luciana.berger.mp@parliament.uk
Constituency: UCATT Building, 56 Derwent Road East, Stoneycroft, Liverpool L13 6QR
Tel: 0151-228 1628 *Fax:* 0151-228 2519 *Email:* luciana4wavertree@hotmail.co.uk
Website: www.lucianaberger.com *Twitter:* @lucianaberger

BERRY, JAKE

Rossendale and Darwen *(Majority 4,493)*

PPS to Grant Shapps as Minister without Portfolio, Cabinet Office and Chairman Conservative Party

Born 1978; Married Charlotte.

Education: Sheffield University (law); Chester College (law finals).

Non-political career: Property lawyer.

CONSERVATIVE

Political career: Member for Rossendale and Darwen since 6 May 2010 general election; PPS to Grant Shapps: as Minister of State for Housing and Local Government 2010-12, as Minister without Portfolio, Cabinet Office and Chairman Conservative Party 2012-; Member, Policy Advisory Board 2013-.

Recreations: Walking, water-skiing.

Jake Berry MP, House of Commons, London SW1A 0AA
Tel: 020 7219 7214 *Email:* jake.berry.mp@parliament.uk
Constituency: 4 Mount Terrace, Rawtenstall, Rossendale, Lancashire BB4 8SF
Tel: 01706 215547 *Website:* www.jakeberry.org *Twitter:* @JakeBerryMP

BETTS, CLIVE

Sheffield South East *(Majority 10,505)*

Clive James Charles Betts. Born 13 January 1950; Son of late Harold and Nellie Betts; Civil partner James Thomas 2011.

Education: King Edward VII School, Sheffield; Pembroke College, Cambridge (BA economics and politics 1971).

Non-political career: Economist, Trades Union Congress 1971-73; Local government economist: Derbyshire County Council 1973-74, South Yorkshire County Council 1974-86, Rotherham Borough Council 1986-91. Member, TGWU.

LABOUR

Political career: Contested Sheffield Hallam October 1974 and Louth 1979 general elections. Member for Sheffield Attercliffe 1992-2010, for Sheffield South East since 6 May 2010 general election; Opposition Whip 1996-97; Assistant Government Whip 1997-98; Government Whip 1998-2001. *Select committees:* Member: Treasury 1996-97, Selection 1997-2001, Transport, Local Government and the Regions (Urban Affairs Sub-Committee) 2001-02, Transport, Local Government and the Regions 2001-02, ODPM/Communities and Local Government 2002-10, ODPM/Communities and Local Government (Urban Affairs Sub-Committee) 2003-05, Finance and Services 2005-10, 2010-, Chairmen's Panel/Panel of Chairs 2009-, Yorkshire and the Humber 2009-10, Reform of the House of Commons 2009-10;

Chair: Communities and Local Government 2010-; Member: Liaison 2010-, Liaison (National Policy Statements Sub-committee) 2010-. Member, Labour Leader's Campaign Team with responsibility for Environment and Local Government 1995-96. *Councils and public bodies:* Sheffield City Council: Councillor 1976-92, Chair: Housing Committee 1980-86, Finance Committee 1986-88, Leader 1987-92; Vice-chair, Association of Metropolitan Authorities 1988-91; Chair, South Yorkshire Pensions Authority 1989-92; Vice-President, Local Government Association 2010-.

Political interests: Local and regional government, housing, planning, regeneration, transport; Bosnia, Iran, Middle East, Netherlands, Portugal, Serbia, Ukraine.

Other: Trustee, Parliamentary Pension Scheme; Fellow, Industry and Parliament Trust 1997; President, South East Sheffield Citizens' Advice Bureau 1998-.

Recreations: Supporting Sheffield Wednesday FC, playing squash, cricket, walking, real ale, scuba diving.

Clive Betts MP, House of Commons, London SW1A 0AA
Tel: 020 7219 5114 *Email:* clive.betts.mp@parliament.uk
Constituency: First Floor, Barkers Pool House, Burgess Street, Sheffield, South Yorkshire S1 2HF
Tel: 0114-275 7788 *Website:* www.clivebetts.com *Twitter:* @CliveBettsMP

BINGHAM, ANDREW
High Peak *(Majority 4,677)*

Andrew Russell Bingham. Born 23 June 1962; Son of late Anthony Bingham and Mary Bingham; Married Jayne Dranfield 1986 (no children).

Education: Long Lane Comprehensive, Chapel-En-Le-Frith; High Peak College of Further Education (catering 1980).

Non-political career: ARB Sales Ltd: Sales engineer 1981-83, Company director 1983-2004; Freelance engineering consultant 2004-10.

CONSERVATIVE

Political career: Contested High Peak 2005 general election. Member for High Peak since 6 May 2010 general election. *Select committees:* Member: Work and Pensions 2010-12, European Scrutiny 2013-. Association deputy chairman 2000-01; Association chairman 2001-04. *Councils and public bodies:* High Peak Borough Council: Councillor 1999-2011, Chair, Social Inclusion Committee 2003-07, Cabinet member, Community and Social Development 2007-10.

Political interests: Small business, pensions, culture media and sport.

Recreations: Sports – badminton, football and cricket.

Andrew Bingham MP, House of Commons, London SW1A 0AA
Tel: 020 7219 8479 *Fax:* 020 7219 2413 *Email:* andrew.bingham.mp@parliament.uk
Constituency: 20 Broad Walk, Buxton, Derbyshire SK17 6JR
Tel: 01298 26698 *Website:* www.andrewbingham.org.uk *Twitter:* @HighPeakAndrew

---

BINLEY, BRIAN
Northampton South *(Majority 6,004)*

Brian Arthur Roland Binley. Born 1 April 1942; Son of Phyllis and Frank Binley; Married Jacqueline Denise 1985 (1 son and 1 son by former marriage).

Education: Finedon Mulso CofE Secondary Modern, Northamptonshire.

Non-political career: Area manager Courage (central) Ltd 1976-79; National sales manager Phonotas Services Ltd 1980-87; General manager Tele Resources Ltd 1987-89; Managing director and founder BCC Marketing Services Ltd 1989-2001; Chair and co-founder Beechwood House Publishing Ltd 1993-2000; Chair BCC Marketing Services Ltd 2002-.

CONSERVATIVE

Political career: Member for Northampton South 2005-10, for Northampton South (revised boundary) since 6 May 2010 general election. *Select committees:* Member: Joint Committee on Consolidation, Etc, Bills 2005-10, Trade and Industry/Business, Enterprise and Regulatory Reform/Business and Enterprise/Business, Innovation and Skills 2006-, Crossrail Bill 2006-07, Arms Export Controls 2008-10; Chair: Joint Committee on the Rookery South (Resource Recovery Facility) Order 2012-13. National Young Conservatives organiser 1965-68; Agent, Kidderminster Conservative Association 1996-98; 1922 Committee: Executive member 2006-10, Treasurer 2010-; Treasurer, Cornerstone Group 2005-; Chair, Conservative Parliamentary Enterprise Group 2006-. *Councils and public bodies:* Northamptonshire County Council: Councillor 1997-2005, Chair finance and resources scrutiny committee 2000-05, Member of Cabinet 2005-07.

Political interests: Business, local government ; India, Iran, Israel, Maldives, Sri Lanka.

Other: Member: RSA, IOD; Freemason 1991-; Management committee member, Lowdown Northampton 2004-07; Northampton Town and Country; Northampton Conservative; Carlton.
Publications: Co-author, The Future of Conservatism: Values Revisited (Biteback, 2011).
Recreations: Northampton Town FC, Northamptonshire CCC, freemasonry, golf, opera, literature.

Brian Binley MP, House of Commons, London SW1A 0AA
Tel: 020 7219 8298 *Fax:* 020 7219 2265 *Email:* brian.binley.mp@parliament.uk
Constituency: Northampton South Conservative Association, White Lodge, 42 Billing Road, Northampton NN1 5DA
Tel: 01604 633414 *Fax:* 01604 250252 *Email:* nsca@devlinfisher.co.uk
Website: www.brianbinley.co.uk www.brianbinley.blogspot.com

BIRTWISTLE, GORDON
Burnley *(Majority 1,818)*

Born 6 September 1943; Married (2 children).
Education: Hyndburn Park Secondary Modern, Accrington; Accrington College (HNC production engineering; HNC mechanical engineering 1966).
Non-political career: Apprenticeship, Howard and Bullough, Accrington 1958; Engineering industry: Jig and tool draftsman, Machine shop methods engineer, Ran cutter grinder and supplies businesses.
Political career: Contested Burnley 1992, 1997 and 2005 general elections. Member for Burnley since 6 May 2010 general election; PPS to Danny Alexander as Chief Secretary to the Treasury 2010-12; Apprenticeship Ambassador to Business 2013-; Chair, Liberal Democrat Parliamentary Party Committee on Business, Innovation and Skills 2012-; Co-founder, Campaign for Manufacturing. Member: Labour Party 1960s-70s; SDP/Liberal Democrats 1982-.
Councils and public bodies: Former Labour councillor 1970s; Burnley Borough Council: Councillor 1983-, Chair, Leadership Scrutiny Committee, Mayor 2002-03, Leader, Liberal Democrat group, Council leader 2006-10; Vice-President, Local Government Association 2010-.
Political interests: Industry, skills and business in general; Denmark, Norway, Sweden.
Recreations: Golf, gardening, cricket.

LIBERAL DEMOCRAT

Gordon Birtwistle MP, House of Commons, London SW1A 0AA
Tel: 020 7219 7028 *Email:* gordon.birtwistle.mp@parliament.uk
Constituency: 23 St James Row, Burnley, Lancashire BB11 1EY
Tel: 01282 704430 *Email:* gbirtwistlemp@gmail.com *Website:* www.burnleylibdems.org.uk
Twitter: @GBirtwistle_MP

BLACKMAN, BOB
Harrow East *(Majority 3,403)*

Robert John Blackman. Born 26 April 1956; Son of Robert Blackman and Winifred Blackman; Married Nicola 1988 (no children).
Education: Preston Manor High School; Liverpool University (BSc physics and maths) (Union President).
Non-political career: Sales, Unisys 1979-90; British Telecom 1991-2010: Sales 1991-95, Sales tutor, training college 1995-98, Regulatory compliance manager 1998-2010. Member, Connect.
Political career: Contested Brent South 1992, Bedford 1997 and Brent North 2005 general elections. Member for Harrow East since 6 May 2010 general election. *Select committees:* Member: Communities and Local Government 2010-, Backbench Business 2012-. *Councils and public bodies:* London Borough of Brent Council: Councillor 1986-2010, Conservative Group Leader 1990-2010, Council Leader 1991-96, Deputy Council Leader 2006-10; Member, London Assembly 2004-08; Governor: Preston Manor High School, Wembley Primary School.
Political interests: Local government, science, communications, sport, public expenditure, housing, housing benefit reform and welfare reform; Azerbaijan, Brazil, India, Israel, Italy, Nepal, Sri Lanka, USA.
Other: St Luke's Hospice; Cancer Research.
Recreations: Tottenham Hotspur FC, bridge, chess, reading, cricket.

CONSERVATIVE

Bob Blackman MP, House of Commons, London SW1A 0AA
Tel: 020 7219 7082 *Fax:* 020 7219 2336 *Email:* bob.blackman.mp@parliament.uk
Constituency: 209 Headstone Lane, Harrow, HA2 6ND
Tel: 020 8421 3323 *Fax:* 020 8421 3332 *Website:* www.bobblackmanmp.com
Twitter: @bobblackmanmp

LABOUR

BLACKMAN-WOODS, ROBERTA   City of Durham *(Majority 3,067)*

Shadow Minister for Communities and Local Government

Roberta Carol Blackman-Woods. Born 16 August 1957; Daughter of late Charles and Eleanor Woods; Married Professor Tim Blackman 1986 (1 daughter).

Education: Methodist College, Belfast; Ulster University (BSc social science 1979; PhD 1989).

Non-political career: Welfare rights officer, Newcastle City Council 1982-85; Lecturer in social policy: Ulster University 1985-90, Newcastle University 1990-95; Dean of labour and social studies, Ruskin College, Oxford 1995-2000; Professor of social policy and associate dean, Northumbria University 2000-05. GMB; University and College Union.

Political career: Member for City of Durham since 5 May 2005 general election; PPS to: Hilary Armstrong as Chancellor of the Duchy of Lancaster 2006-07, Des Browne as Secretary of State for Defence 2007-08, David Lammy as Minister of State, Department for Innovation, Universities and Skills/Business, Innovation and Skills 2008-10; Deputy Minister for the North East 2008-10; Shadow Minister, Department of Business, Innovation and Skills May-October 2010; Shadow Minister for: Cabinet Office 2010-11, Communities and Local Government 2011-. *Select committees:* Member: Joint Committee on Statutory Instruments and Commons Committee on Statutory Instruments 2005-10, Education and Skills 2005-06, Innovation, Universities[, Science] and Skills/Science and Technology 2007-10. Member, PLP Departmental Committees on: Education 2005-10, International Development 2005-10, Communities and Local Government 2005-10; PLP Departmental Group for Women: Honorary Secretary 2007-08, Chair 2008-10 Vice-chair 2010-11. Chair, CLP: Newcastle East and Wallsend 1991-95, City of Durham 2003-05. *Councils and public bodies:* Councillor: Newcastle City Council 1992-95, Oxford City Council 1996-2000.

Political interests: Education, housing, international development, regeneration, planning; Afghanistan, Africa, China.

Other: Vice-chair, Commonwealth Parliamentary Association (UK Branch) 2011-.

Recreations: Music, reading, gardening.

Dr Roberta Blackman-Woods MP, House of Commons, London SW1A 0AA
Tel: 020 7219 4982 *Fax:* 020 7219 8018 *Email:* woodsr@parliament.uk
Constituency: The Miners' Hall, Redhills, Flass Street, Durham DH1 4BD
Tel: 0191-374 1915 *Fax:* 0191-374 1916 *Email:* mail@roberta.org.uk
Website: www.roberta.org.uk *Twitter:* @robertabwMP

CONSERVATIVE

BLACKWOOD, NICOLA   Oxford West and Abingdon *(Majority 176)*

Nicola Claire Blackwood. Born 16 October 1979.

Education: Home schooled; Trinity College of Music; St Anne's College, Cambridge (BA music); Emmanuel College, Cambridge (MPhil musicology).

Non-political career: Studying for DPhil in musicology, Somerville College, Oxford 2005-; Parliamentary researcher to Andrew Mitchell MP -2006; Social action manager -2007.

Political career: Member for Oxford West and Abingdon since 6 May 2010 general election. *Select committees:* Member: Home Affairs 2010-, Joint Committee on the Draft Enhanced Terrorism Prevention and Investigation Measures Bill 2012-13. Commissioner, Conservative Human Rights Commission 2006-; Social Action Manager 2007; Vice-chairman (social action), Conservative Party 2010-13. *Councils and public bodies:* Governor, Northern House School 2009-.

Political interests: Civil liberties and human rights, home affairs, international development, universities, science and environment; Afghanistan, Democratic Republic of Congo, Iran, Rwanda, Sudan.

Other: Member, advisory council, ZANE (supports Zimbabwe's pensioners).

Recreations: Music.

Nicola Blackwood MP, House of Commons, London SW1A 0AA
Tel: 020 7219 7126 *Email:* nicola.blackwood.mp@parliament.uk
Constituency: No constituency office publicised *Website:* www.nicolablackwood.com
Twitter: @NicolaBlackwood

BLEARS, HAZEL
Salford and Eccles *(Majority 5,725)*

Hazel Anne Blears. Born 14 May 1956; Daughter of Arthur and Dorothy Blears; Married Michael Halsall 1989.

Education: Wardley Grammar School; Eccles Sixth Form College; Trent Polytechnic (BA law 1977); Chester College of Law (Law Society part II 1978); French, Spanish.

Non-political career: Trainee solicitor, Salford Council 1978-80; Private practice solicitor 1980-81; Solicitor: Rossendale Council 1981-83, Wigan Council 1983-85; Principal solicitor, Manchester City Council 1985-97. Branch secretary, Unison 1981-85; Member, USDAW.

LABOUR

Political career: Contested Tatton 1987 and Bury South 1992 general elections. Member for Salford 1997-2010, for Salford and Eccles since 6 May 2010 general election; PPS to Alan Milburn: as Minister of State, Department of Health 1998, as Chief Secretary, HM Treasury 1999; Parliamentary Under-Secretary of State, Department of Health 2001-03: (Health 2001-02, Public Health 2002-03); Minister of State, Home Office 2003-06: (Crime Reduction, Policing, Community Safety and Counter-Terrorism 2003-05, Policing, Security and Community Safety 2005-06); Minister without Portfolio 2006-07; Secretary of State for Communities and Local Government 2007-09; Member Intelligence and Security Committee 2010-; North West Regional Group of Labour MPs: Chair 1998-99, 2011-, Secretary 2010-11. Member: North West Executive 1997-99, National Policy Forum 1997-2001, Leadership Campaign Team 1997-98; Labour Party Development Co-ordinator and Deputy to Ian McCartney 1998-2001; Leader, Parliamentary Campaign Team 2003-; Labour Party NEC 2004-; Chair, Labour Party 2006-07; Chair, Social Action Forum 2010-12. *Councils and public bodies:* Councillor, Salford City Council 1984-92.

Political interests: Employment, health, arts, urban regeneration, crime, security, social mobility.

Other: Chair, Salford Community Health Council 1993-97. PC 2005.

Publications: Making Healthcare Mutual (Mutuo, 2002); Communities in Control (Fabian Society, 2003); Politics of Decency (Mutuo, 2004).

Recreations: Dance, motorcycling.

Rt Hon Hazel Blears MP, House of Commons, London SW1A 0AA
Tel: 020 7219 6595 *Email:* blearsh@parliament.uk
Constituency: 201 Langworthy Road, Salford M6 5PW
Tel: 0161-925 0705 *Website:* www.hazelblears.co.uk *Twitter:* @HazelBlearsMP

BLENKINSOP, TOM
Middlesbrough South and East Cleveland *(Majority 1,677)*

Opposition Whip

Thomas Francis Blenkinsop. Born 14 August 1980; Son of Barbara and Bill Blenkinsop; Married Vicki.

Education: Newlands School FCJ, Middlesbrough; St Mary's Sixth Form College, Saltersgill, Middlesbrough; Teesside University (BSc philosophy, politics and economics 2001); Warwick University (MA continental philosophy 2002); TUC Organising Academy 2010.

LABOUR

Non-political career: Constituency researcher to Ashok Kumar MP 2002-08; Officer, Community trade union, Middlesbrough 2008-10. Member, Community.

Political career: Member for Middlesbrough South and East Cleveland since 6 May 2010 general election; Opposition Whip 2011-. *Select committees:* Member: Environment, Food and Rural Affairs 2010-12, Standards and Privileges 2010-11, Treasury 2011, Selection 2012-. Member, Co-operative Party.

Political interests: Teesside steel industry, public services, Sure Start, chemical industry, higher education, further education, manufacturing, economics, business, trade, unions, employment law; Barbados, Northern Ireland, Republic of Ireland, Italy, Qatar, Spain.

Other: Member, Fabian Society; Saltburn 500 Club.

Recreations: Middlesbrough F.C; Guisborough Town F.C.

Tom Blenkinsop MP, House of Commons, London SW1A 0AA
Tel: 020 7219 7111
Constituency: Harry Tout House, 8 Wilson Street, Guisborough TS14 6NA
Tel: 01287 610878 *Fax:* 01287 631894 *Email:* info@tomblenkinsop.com
Website: www.tomblenkinsop.com *Twitter:* @tomblenkinsop

LABOUR

BLOMFIELD, PAUL
Sheffield Central *(Majority 165)*

Born 25 August 1953; Son of Henry and Mabel Blomfield; Married Linda McAvan MEP 2000 (1 son from previous marriage).

Education: Abbeydale Boys Grammar School, Sheffield; Tadcaster Grammar School; St John's College, York (theology); Teacher training (CertEd 1976).

Non-political career: Sheffield University 1978-2010: Various posts 1978-2003, General manager, Students' Union 2003-10. Member, National Executive Committee and Vice-President, National Union of Students 1976-78; Former branch secretary, Unison; Member: Amicus/Unite, GMB.

Political career: Member for Sheffield Central since 6 May 2010 general election; PPS to Hilary Benn as: Shadow Leader of the House of Commons 2010-11, Shadow Secretary of State for Communities and Local Government 2011-. *Select committees:* Member: Business, Innovation and Skills 2010-. Chair, Labour for Democracy 2012-. Member: Co-operative Party, Labour Party 1978-; Chair, Sheffield Labour Party 1993-2008. *Councils and public bodies:* Governor, Sheffield City Polytechnic 1982-92; Sheffield City Trust: Board member 1994-2008, Chair 1997-2008.

Political interests: Universities, education, skills, housing, voluntary and community sector, financial inclusion, small businesses; Southern Africa, Burma, Kashmir, Palestine, Somaliland.

Other: Executive committee, Anti-Apartheid Movement 1978-94; Former executive member, Sheffield Race Equality Council.

Recreations: Walking, cycling, Sheffield United season ticket holder.

Paul Blomfield MP, House of Commons, London SW1A 0AA
Tel: 020 7219 3000 *Email:* paul.blomfield.mp@parliament.uk
Constituency: Unit 4, Edmund Road Business Centre, 135 Edmund Road, Sheffield S2 4ED
Tel: 0114-272 2882 *Fax:* 0114-272 2442 *Website:* www.paulblomfield.co.uk
Twitter: @paulblomfieldmp

LABOUR

BLUNKETT, DAVID
Sheffield, Brightside and Hillsborough *(Majority 13,632)*

Born 6 June 1947; Son of late Arthur and Doris Blunkett; Married Ruth Gwynneth Mitchell 1970 (divorced 1990) (3 sons); (1 son); married Dr Margaret Williams 2009 (3 stepdaughters).

Education: Royal National Normal College for the Blind; Shrewsbury Technical College; Sheffield Richmond College of Further Education (day release and evening courses); Sheffield University (BA political theory and institutions 1972); Huddersfield College of Education (PGCE 1973); Esperanto.

Non-political career: Office work, East Midlands Gas Board 1967-69; Tutor in industrial relations and politics, Barnsley College of Technology 1973-81. Shop steward, GMB EMGB 1967-69; Member: NATFHE 1973-87, Unison 1973-.

Political career: Contested Sheffield Hallam February 1974 general election. Member for Sheffield Brightside 1987-2010, for Sheffield Brightside and Hillsborough since 6 May 2010 general election; Opposition Spokesperson for Local Government 1988-92; Shadow Secretary of State for: Health 1992-94, Education 1994-95, Education and Employment 1995-97; Secretary of State for Education and Employment 1997-2001; Home Secretary 2001-04; Secretary of State for Work and Pensions 2005; Member, Labour Party National Executive Committee 1983-98; Labour Party: Vice-chair 1992-93, Chair 1993-94. *Councils and public bodies:* Councillor, Sheffield City Council 1970-88, Chair, Social Services Committee 1976-80, Leader 1980-87; Councillor, South Yorkshire County Council 1973-77; Former chair, Race Relations Forum.

Political interests: Local government, employment and welfare to work, citizenship and civil renewal; France, USA.

Other: Council member, Guide Dogs for the Blind Association; Former trustee, Community Service Volunteers; Fellow, Industry and Parliament Trust 1991; Vice-president, Alzheimer's Society 2009; Guide Dogs for the Blind. Honorary Doctorate, Haifa University, Israel 2005; Fellow, Sheffield Hallam University. PC 1997.

Publications: Building from the Bottom (1983); Democracy in Crisis – the Town Halls Respond (1987); On a Clear Day (autobiography) (1995, 2002); Politics and Progress (2001); The Blunkett Tapes – My Life in the Bear Pit (2006).

Recreations: Walking, sailing, music, poetry.

Rt Hon David Blunkett MP, House of Commons, London SW1A 0AA
Tel: 020 7219 4043 *Fax:* 020 7219 5903 *Email:* blunkettd@parliament.uk
Constituency: Second Floor, MidCity House, 17-21 Furnival Gate, Sheffield, South Yorkshire S1 4QR
Tel: 0114-273 5987 *Email:* dbconstituency@aol.com *Website:* www.davidblunkett.typepad.com

CONSERVATIVE

BLUNT, CRISPIN
Reigate *(Majority 13,591)*

Crispin Jeremy Rupert Blunt. Born 15 July 1960; Son of late Major-General Peter and Adrienne Blunt; Married Victoria Jenkins 1990 (separated) (1 son 1 daughter).

Education: Wellington College, Berkshire; Royal Military Academy, Sandhurst (commissioned 1980); University College, Durham University (BA politics 1984); Cranfield Institute of Technology (MBA 1991).

Non-political career: Army Officer 1979-90; Regimental duty 13th/18th Royal Hussars (QMO) in England, Germany and Cyprus. District agent, Forum of Private Business 1991-92; Political consultant, Politics International 1993; Special adviser to Malcolm Rifkind MP: as Secretary of State for Defence 1993-95, as Foreign Secretary 1995-97.

Political career: Contested West Bromwich East 1992 general election. Member for Reigate 1997-2010, for Reigate (revised boundary) since 6 May 2010 general election; Opposition Spokesperson for Northern Ireland 2001-02; Shadow Minister for Trade and Industry 2002-03; Opposition Whip 2004-09; Shadow Minister for National Security 2009-10; Parliamentary Under-Secretary of State, Ministry of Justice 2010-12. *Select committees:* Member: Defence 1997-2000, Environment, Transport and Regional Affairs 2000-01, Environment, Transport and Regional Affairs (Environment Sub-Committee) 2000-01, Defence 2003-04, Finance and Services 2005-09, Joint Committee on Voting Eligibilty (Prisoners) Bill 2013-. Secretary, Conservative Party Committees for: Foreign and Commonwealth Affairs 1997-2001, European Affairs 1999-2000. Executive member, 1922 Committee 2000-01; Treasurer, Conservative Parliamentary Friends of India 2001-06; Chair, Conservative Middle East Council 2003-08.

Political interests: Defence, foreign affairs, environment, energy, justice; Middle East, India, USA.

Other: Reigate Priory Cricket, MCC; House of Lords and House of Commons Cricket Club.

Recreations: Cricket, skiing, gardening.

Crispin Blunt MP, House of Commons, London SW1A 0AA
Tel: 020 7219 2254 *Fax:* 020 7219 3373 *Email:* crispinbluntmp@parliament.uk
Constituency: 83 Bell Street, Reigate, Surrey RH2 7AN
Tel: 01737 222756 *Website:* www.crispinbluntmp.com

CONSERVATIVE

BOLES, NICK
Grantham and Stamford *(Majority 14,826)*

Parliamentary Under-Secretary of State (Planning), Department for Communities and Local Government

Nicholas Edward Coleridge Boles. Born 2 November 1965; Civil partner 2011.

Education: Winchester College; Magdalen College, Oxford (BA politics, philosophy and economics 1987); John F Kennedy School of Government, Harvard University (MPP master of public policy 1989); French, German, Spanish.

Non-political career: Longwall Holdings Ltd: Chief executive 1995-2000, Chairman 2000-07; Director, Policy Exchange 2002-07.

Political career: Contested Hove 2005 general election. Member for Grantham and Stamford since 6 May 2010 general election; PPS to Nick Gibb as Minister of State for Schools 2010-12; Parliamentary Under-Secretary of State (Planning), Department for Communities and Local Government 2012-. *Select committees:* Member: Political and Constitutional Reform 2010, Standing Orders 2011-12, 2013-. *Councils and public bodies:* Westminster City Council: Councillor 1998-2002, Chair, Housing Committee 1999-2001.

Political interests: Education, local government, foreign affairs.

Other: Political fellow, Institute for Government 2010-.

Publications: Blue tomorrow (Politicos, 2001); Which Way's Up? – the Future for Coalition Britain (2010).

Recreations: Sailing, skiing, running, playing the piano.

Nick Boles MP, House of Commons, London SW1A 0AA
Tel: 020 7219 7079 *Email:* nick.boles.mp@parliament.uk
Constituency: c/o Conservative Office, North Street, Bourne, Lincolnshire PE10 9AJ
Tel: 01778 421498 *Email:* gsca@btinternet.com *Website:* www.nickbolesmp.com

CONSERVATIVE

BONE, PETER
Wellingborough *(Majority 11,787)*

Peter William Bone. Born 19 October 1952; Son of late William and Marjorie Bone; Married Jeanette Sweeney 1981 (2 sons 1 daughter).

Education: Stewards Comprehensive School, Harlow, Essex; Westcliff High School for Boys, Essex.

Non-political career: Financial director, Essex Electronics and Precision Engineering Group 1977-83; Chief executive, High Tech Electronics Company 1983-90; Managing director: Palm Travel (West) Ltd 1990-, AJWB Travel Ltd.

Political career: Contested Islwyn 1992, Pudsey 1997 and Wellingborough 2001 general elections. Member for Wellingborough 2005-10, for Wellingborough (revised boundary) since 6 May 2010 general election. *Select committees:* Member: Joint Committee on Statutory Instruments and Commons Committee on Statutory Instruments 2005-10, Trade and Industry 2005-07, Health 2007-10, Backbench Business 2010-12, Chairmen's Panel/Panel of Chairs 2010-. Member, Executive, 1922 Committee 2007-12. Contested Mid and West Wales 1994 European Parliament election. Deputy chair, Southend West Conservative Association 1977-84; Press secretary to Paul Channon MP 1982-84; Member, National Union Executive Committee 1993-96; Founder member, All Wales Conservative Policy Group (think tank). *Councils and public bodies:* Councillor, Southend-on-Sea Borough Council 1977-86; Former member, Southern Airport Management Committee.

Political interests: European Union parliamentary reform, human trafficking.

Other: Secretary, Parliament First; Fellow, Institute of Chartered Accountants of England and Wales 1976. Wellingborough Golf Club; Wellingborough Old Grammarians.

Publications: Contributor: *Daily Telegraph, The Times, Daily Express, Western Mail*; Numerous TV appearances and radio interviews.

Recreations: Running marathons for charity, cricket.

Peter Bone MP, House of Commons, London SW1A 0AA
Tel: 020 7219 8496 *Fax:* 020 7219 0301 *Email:* bonep@parliament.uk
Constituency: 21 High Street, Wellingborough, Northamptonshire NN8 4JZ
Tel: 01933 279343 *Website:* www.wellingboroughconservatives.org *Twitter:* @PeterBoneMP

CONSERVATIVE

BOTTOMLEY, PETER
Worthing West *(Majority 11,729)*

Peter James Bottomley. Born 30 July 1944; Son of Sir James Bottomley, KCMG, HM Diplomatic Service, and Barbara Bottomley, social worker; Married Virginia Garnett (later MP as Virginia Bottomley, now Baroness Bottomley of Nettlestone) 1967 (1 son 2 daughters).

Education: Comprehensive school, Washington DC; Westminster School, London; Trinity College, Cambridge (BA economics 1966, MA).

Non-political career: Industrial sales, industrial relations, industrial economics. Former member, TGWU.

Political career: Contested Greenwich, Woolwich West February and October 1974 general elections. Member for Greenwich, Woolwich West 1975 by-election to 1983, for Eltham 1983-97, for Worthing West 1997-2010, for Worthing West (revised boundary) since 6 May 2010 general election; PPS to: Cranley Onslow as Minister of State, Foreign and Commonwealth Office 1982-83, Norman Fowler as Secretary of State for Health and Social Security 1983-84; Parliamentary Under-Secretary of State: Department of Employment 1984-86, Department of Transport (Minister for Roads and Traffic) 1986-89, Northern Ireland Office (Agriculture, Environment) 1989-90; PPS to Peter Brooke as Secretary of State for Northern Ireland 1990. *Select committees:* Member: Standards and Privileges 1997-2002, Unopposed Bills (Panel) 1997-, Constitutional Affairs 2003-05, Ecclesiastical Committee, Joint Committee on the Draft Defamation Bill 2011. President, Conservative Trade Unionists 1978-80.

Countries of interest: Southern Africa, El Salvador, USA.

Other: NATO Parliamentary Assembly; Member, UK Delegation, Organisation for Security and Co-operation in Europe Parliamentary Assembly; Trustee, Christian Aid 1978-84; Chair: Family Forum 1980-82, Church of England Children's Society 1982-84; Member, Council of Nacro 1997-2003; Fellow, Industry and Parliament Trust; Trustee, Dr Busby's Trustees (Willen) Main Charity; Former Fellow, Institute of Personnel Management; Fellow, Institute of Road Safety Officers. Court Member, Drapers' Company. Gold Medal, Institute of the Motor Industry 1988. Kt 2011. Former Parliamentary swimming and occasional dinghy sailing champion.

Recreations: Children, canoeing.
Sir Peter Bottomley MP, House of Commons, London SW1A 0AA
Tel: 020 7219 5060 *Fax:* 020 7219 1212 *Email:* bottomleyp@parliament.uk
Constituency: Contact Westminster office *Twitter:* @PBottomleyMP

BRADLEY, KAREN
Staffordshire Moorlands *(Majority 6,689)*

Government Whip

Karen Anne Bradley. Born 12 March 1970; Married Neil Bradley 2001 (2 sons).
Education: Buxton Girls School, Buxton; Imperial College, London (BSc mathematics 1991).
Non-political career: Student accountant, then manager, Deloittes 1991-98; Senior manager, KPMG 1998-2004; Self-employed economic and fiscal adviser 2004-; Senior manager, KPMG 2007-.

CONSERVATIVE

Political career: Contested Manchester Withington 2005 general election. Member for Staffordshire Moorlands since 6 May 2010 general election; Assistant Government Whip 2012-13; Government Whip 2013-. *Select committees:* Member: Work and Pensions 2010-12, Procedure 2011-12, Administration 2012-. Secretary, 1922 Committee 2012.

Political interests: Economy, rural affairs, home affairs, childcare.

Other: Associate, Institute Chartered Accountants in England and Wales 1994; Member, Chartered Institute of Taxation 1995; Royal British Legion.

Recreations: Walking, cooking.

Karen Bradley MP, House of Commons, London SW1A 0AA
Tel: 020 7219 7215 *Fax:* 020 7219 6222 *Email:* karen.bradley.mp@parliament.uk
Constituency: Unit 24, The Smithfield Centre, Haywood Street, Leek, Staffordshire ST13 5JW
Tel: 01538 382421 *Fax:* 01538 382421 *Website:* www.karenbradley.co.uk
Twitter: @karen__bradley

BRADSHAW, BEN
Exeter *(Majority 2,721)*

Benjamin Peter James Bradshaw. Born 30 August 1960; Son of late Canon Peter Bradshaw and late Daphne Bradshaw, teacher; Civil partner Neal Dalgleish 2006.
Education: Thorpe St Andrew School, Norwich; Sussex University (BA German 1982); Freiburg University, Germany; German, Italian.
Non-political career: BBC 1986-97: Reporter and presenter 1986-97, Berlin correspondent during fall of Berlin Wall 1989-91, Reporter *World At One* and *World This Weekend*, Radio 4 1991-97. Member: NUJ, GMB, USDAW.

LABOUR

Political career: Member for Exeter 1997-2010, for Exeter (revised boundary) since 6 May 2010 general election; Introduced Pesticides Act (Private Member's Bill) 1998; PPS to John Denham as Minister of State, Department of Health 2000-01; Parliamentary Under-Secretary of State, Foreign and Commonwealth Office 2001-02; Parliamentary Secretary, Privy Council Office 2002-03; Department for Environment, Food and Rural Affairs 2003-07: Parliamentary Under-Secretary of State 2003-06, Minister of State (MoS) 2006-07; MoS for Health Services, Department of Health 2007-09; Minister for the South West 2007-09; Secretary of State for Culture, Media and Sport 2009-10; Shadow Secretary of State for Culture, Olympics, Media and Sport 2010. *Select committees:* Member: European Scrutiny 1998-2001, Ecclesiastical Committee 2010-, Joint Committee on Privacy and Injunctions 2011-12, Culture, Media and Sport 2012-. Labour Movement for Europe, Member: Labour Campaign for Electoral Reform, SERA, Christian Socialist Movement.

Political interests: Foreign affairs, environment, transport, modernisation of Parliament; Europe – particularly Germany and Italy, USA.

Other: Honorary fellowship, Humboldt University, Berlin. Consumer Journalist of the Year, Argos 1989; Journalist of the Year, Anglo-German Foundation 1990; News Reporter award, Sony 1993; Politician of the Year, Stonewall awards 2009. PC 2009; Whipton Labour, Exeter.

Publications: Numerous for the BBC on domestic and foreign affairs.

Recreations: Cycling, walking, cooking, music, ashtanga yoga.

Rt Hon Ben Bradshaw MP, House of Commons, London SW1A 0AA
Tel: 020 7219 6597 *Fax:* 020 7219 0950 *Email:* ben.bradshaw.mp@parliament.uk
Constituency: Labour HQ, 26b Clifton Hill, Exeter, Devon EX1 2DJ
Tel: 01392 424464 *Fax:* 01392 435523 *Website:* www.benbradshaw.co.uk
Twitter: @BenPBradshaw

CONSERVATIVE

BRADY, GRAHAM
Altrincham and Sale West *(Majority 11,595)*

Graham Stuart Brady. Born 20 May 1967; Son of John Brady, accountant, and Maureen Brady, née Birch, medical secretary; Married Victoria Lowther 1992 (1 son 1 daughter).

Education: Altrincham Grammar School; Durham University (BA law 1989).

Non-political career: Shandwick plc 1989-90; Assistant director of publications, Centre for Policy Studies 1990-92; Public affairs director, The Waterfront Partnership 1992-97.

Political career: Member for Altrincham and Sale West 1997-2010, for Altrincham and Sale West (revised boundary) since 6 May 2010 general election; PPS to Michael Ancram as Conservative Party Chairman 1999-2000; Opposition Whip 2000; Opposition Spokesperson for: Employment 2000-01, Schools 2001-03; PPS to Michael Howard as Leader of the Opposition 2003-04; Shadow Minister for Europe (resigned) 2004-07. *Select committees:* Member: Education and Employment 1997-2001, Education and Employment (Employment Sub-Committee) 1997-2001, Office of the Deputy Prime Minister 2004-05, Office of the Deputy Prime Minister (Urban Affairs Sub-Committee) 2004-05, Treasury 2007-10, Reform of the House of Commons 2009-10, Chairmen's Panel/Panel of Chairs 2009-. Joint Secretary, Conservative Party Committee for Education and Employment 1997-2000; 1922 Committee: Member, executive 1998-2000, 2007-10, Chairman 2010-. Chairman, Durham University Conservative Association 1987-88; National Union Executive Committee 1988; Chairman, Northern Area Conservative Collegiate Forum 1987-89; Vice-chairman, East Berkshire Conservative Association 1993-95. *Councils and public bodies:* Independent governor and member, audit committee, Manchester Metropolitan University 2008-11.

Political interests: Education, health, Europe; Commonwealth, Far East, British Overseas Territories.

Other: Vice-Patron, Friends of Rosie (research into children's cancer); Vice-President, Altrincham Chamber of Trade Commerce and Industry 1997-; Patron, Family Contact Line/Counselling and Family Centre; Governor, Westminster Foundation for Democracy 2009-10; Panellist, Medical Practitioners Tribunal Service 2010-; Stockdales, Genie Networks. Backbencher of the Year, *The Spectator*/Threadneedle award 2010; Carlton.

Publications: Towards an Employees' Charter – and Away From Collective Bargaining (Centre for Policy Studies, 1991); The Future of Conservatism: Values Revisited (Biteback, 2010).

Recreations: Family, gardening, reading.

Graham Brady MP, House of Commons, London SW1A 0AA
Tel: 020 7219 1260 *Fax:* 020 7219 1649 *Email:* crowthers@parliament.uk
Constituency: Altrincham and Sale West Conservative Association, Thatcher House, Delahays Farm, Green Lane, Timperley, Cheshire WA15 8QW
Tel: 0161-904 8828 *Fax:* 0161-904 8868 *Email:* office@altsaletory.demon.co.uk
Website: www.grahambradymp.co.uk *Twitter:* @grahambradyMP

LIBERAL DEMOCRAT

BRAKE, TOM
Carshalton and Wallington *(Majority 5,260)*

Parliamentary Secretary (Deputy Leader of the House of Commons)

Thomas Anthony Brake. Born 6 May 1962; Son of Michael and Judy Brake; Married Candida Goulden 1998 (1 daughter 1 son).

Education: Lycee International, St Germain-en-Laye, France; Imperial College, London (BSc physics 1983); French, Portuguese, Russian.

Non-political career: Principal consultant (IT), Cap Gemini 1983-97.

Political career: Contested Carshalton and Wallington 1992 general election. Member for Carshalton and Wallington 1997-2010, for Carshalton and Wallington (revised boundary) since 6 May 2010 general election; Liberal Democrat: Spokesperson for: Environment, Transport in London and Air Transport 1997-99, Environment, Transport, the Regions, Social Justice and London Transport 1999-2001, Whip 2000-04, Spokesperson for: Transport, Local Government and the Regions 2001-02, Transport 2002-03, Shadow Secretary of State for: International Development 2003-05, Transport 2005-06, Shadow Minister for: Communities and Local Government 2006-07, London and the Olympics 2007-10, Home Office 2008-10; Parliamentary Secretary (Deputy Leader of the House of Commons) 2012-. *Select committees:* Member: Environment, Transport and Regional Affairs 1997-2001, Environment, Transport and Regional Affairs (Environment Sub-Committee) 1997-2001, Environment, Transport and Regional Affairs

(Transport Sub-Committee) 1999-2000, Accommodation and Works 2001-03, Transport 2002-03, Home Affairs 2008-10. Chair, Liberal Democrat Parliamentary Party: Committee on Home Affairs, Justice and Equalities 2010-12, Co-Chairs Committee 2012. Spokesman on London, Liberal Democrat Party 2010-12. *Councils and public bodies:* Councillor: London Borough of Hackney 1988-90, London Borough of Sutton 1994-98.

Political interests: Environment, transport, sport, international development, home affairs; Australia, France, Portugal, Russia.

Other: Member: Amnesty International, Greenpeace; Royal British Legion; Oxfam; Bliss. PC 2011. Collingwood Athletic Club; Wallington Tennis Club.

Publications: Policing paper, 'Trusted, Professional and Effective: British policing at its best' (2012).

Recreations: Sport, film, eating.

Rt Hon Tom Brake MP, House of Commons, London SW1A 0AA
Tel: 020 7219 0924
Constituency: Kennedy House, 5 Nightingale Road, Carshalton, Surrey SM5 2DN
Tel: 020 8255 8155 *Email:* info@tombrake.co.uk *Website:* www.tombrake.co.uk
Twitter: @thomasbrake

BRAY, ANGIE
Ealing Central and Acton *(Majority 3,716)*

Angela Lavinia Bray. Born 13 October 1953; Daughter of late Benedict Bray and Patricia Bray; Partner Nigel Hugh-Smith.

Education: Downe House, Newbury, Berkshire; St Andrews University (MA medieval history 1975); London College of Printing (radio journalism).

Non-political career: Radio presenter, British Forces Broadcasting 1979-80; Radio presenter/producer/reporter/editor, LBC 1980-88; Researcher, *Right Talk* (political programme), Channel 4 1988; Head of broadcasting unit, Conservative Central Office 1989-91; Press secretary to Conservative Party chairman 1991-92; Public affairs consultant 1992-2000. Member, National Union of Journalists 1979-83.

CONSERVATIVE

Political career: Contested East Ham 1997 general election. Member for Ealing Central and Acton since 6 May 2010 general election; PPS to Francis Maude as Minister for the Cabinet Office and Paymaster General 2010-12. *Select committees:* Member: Transport 2010; Culture, Media and Sport 2012-. Kensington and Chelsea Conservative Political Forum: Chair 1999-2000, President 2000-03; Vice-President, Hammersmith and Fulham Conservative Association 2000-10; Conservative Friends of Israel; Conservative Friends of Poland; Conservative Human Rights Commission. *Councils and public bodies:* London Assembly: Member 2000-08, Member, Notting Hill Carnival Review Group 2000-08, Deputy Chair, Culture, Sport and Tourism Committee 2004-06, Leader, Conservative group 2006-07, Spokesperson for: Transport, Notting Hill Carnival, Culture, Sport and Tourism; Governor, Berrymead Junior School.

Political interests: London issues, transport, NHS, education; Italy, Middle East, Spain, USA.

Other: PDSA; Battersea Dogs' Home; Age Concern. Freedom, City of London. Ealing Lawn Tennis Club.

Recreations: History, music, travel, tennis, my dogs, cinema.

Angie Bray MP, House of Commons, London SW1A 0AA
Tel: 020 7219 7055 *Email:* angie.bray.mp@parliament.uk
Constituency: 39 Broughton Road, London W13 8QW
Tel: 020 8810 0579 *Website:* www.angiebray.co.uk *Twitter:* @AngieBrayMP

BRAZIER, JULIAN
Canterbury *(Majority 6,048)*

Julian William Hendy Brazier. Born 24 July 1953; Son of Lieutenant Colonel Peter Brazier, retired, and Patricia Brazier, née Stubbs; Married Katherine Blagden 1984 (3 sons).

Education: Wellington College, Berkshire; Brasenose College, Oxford (Scholarship BA mathematics and philosophy 1975, MA); London Business School.

Non-political career: TA officer 1972-82; Captain in 21 SAS (Artists) 1989-92. Charter Consolidated Ltd 1975-84: Economic research 1975-77, Corporate finance 1977-81, Secretary, board executive committee 1981-84; Management consultant, H B Maynard International 1984-87.

CONSERVATIVE

Political career: Contested Berwick-upon-Tweed 1983 general election. Member for Canterbury 1987-2010, for Canterbury (revised boundary) since 6 May 2010 general election; PPS to

Gillian Shephard as: Minister of State, HM Treasury 1990-92, Secretary of State for Employment 1992-93; Opposition Whip 2001-02; Shadow Minister for: Work and Pensions 2002-03, Home Affairs 2003, Foreign Affairs 2003-05, Transport (aviation and shipping) 2005-10; Co-chair, Prime Minister's Review of the Reserve Forces 2010-11. *Select committees:* Member: Defence 1997-2001, 2010-. Member, Executive, 1922 Committee 2010-12. President, Conservative Family Campaign 1995-2001; Vice-chair, Conservative Party Listening to Churches Programme 2000-03; Member, Cornerstone Group 2005-.

Political interests: Defence, foreign affairs, economics, law and order, families, countryside; Australia, Canada, Lebanon, Middle East, Russia, South Africa, USA.

Other: President, Canterbury Sea Cadets 2009-; Friends of Canterbury Cathedral and Westminster Cathedral, Afghanaid, Red Cross Landmines Appeal, Royal British Legion. Highland Park/ *The Spectator* Backbencher of the Year (jointly) 1996. TD 1993; Kent and Canterbury; East Kent and Canterbury Conservatives Club.

Publications: Co-author, Not Fit to Fight: The Cultural Subversion of the Armed Forces in Britain and America (Social Affairs Unit, 1999); Ten pamphlets on defence, social and economic issues (with Bow Group, Centre for Policy Studies and Conservative 2000).

Recreations: Cross-country running, science, philosophy.

Julian Brazier TD MP, House of Commons, London SW1A 0AA
Tel: 020 7219 3000
Constituency: Canterbury Conservative Association, PO Box 1116, Canterbury, Kent CT1 9LQ
Tel: 01227 785427 *Email:* canterbury@tory.org *Website:* www.julianbrazier.co.uk

---

LABOUR

BRENNAN, KEVIN
Cardiff West *(Majority 4,751)*

Shadow Minister for Education

Kevin Denis Brennan. Born 16 October 1959; Son of late Michael Brennan, steelworker, and Beryl Brennan, née Evans, school cook/cleaner; Married Amy Wack 1988 (1 daughter).

Education: St Alban's RC Comprehensive, Pontypool; Pembroke College, Oxford (BA philosophy, politics and economics 1982) (President Oxford Union 1982); University College of Wales, Cardiff (PGCE history 1985); Glamorgan University (MSc education management 1992); Welsh.

Non-political career: News editor, volunteer organiser Cwmbran Community Press 1982-84; Head of economics and business studies Radyr Comprehensive School 1985-94; Research officer to Rhodri Morgan MP 1995-99; Special adviser to Rhodri Morgan as First Minister National Assembly for Wales 2000-01. NUT 1984-94; TGWU/Unite 1995-; Musicians' Union 2003-.

Political career: Member for Cardiff West 2001-10, for Cardiff West (revised boundary) since 6 May 2010 general election; PPS to Alan Milburn as Chancellor of the Duchy of Lancaster 2004-05; Assistant Government Whip 2005-06; Government Whip 2006-07; Parliamentary Under-Secretary of State, Department for Children, Schools and Families 2007-08; Parliamentary Secretary, Cabinet Office 2008-09; Minister of State (Further Education, Skills, Apprenticeships and Consumer Affairs), Departments for Business, Innovation and Skills and Children, Schools and Families 2009-10; Shadow Minister for: Business, Innovation and Skills 2010, Education 2010-. *Select committees:* Member: Public Administration 2001-05, 2010-11. Member, Bevan Foundation; Chair, Cardiff West Constituency Labour Party 1998-2000; Member, Labour Campaign Electoral Reform. *Councils and public bodies:* Cardiff City Council: Councillor, Chair: Finance Committee 1993-96, Economic Scrutiny Committee 1999-2001.

Political interests: Economy, constitutional affairs, creative industries, education; Ireland, USA.

Other: Member, Fabian Society; Chair, Yes for Wales Cardiff 1997.

Recreations: Rugby, golf, reading, cricket, music, member parliamentary rock band 'MP4'.

Kevin Brennan MP, House of Commons, London SW1A 0AA
Tel: 020 7219 8156 *Email:* brennank@parliament.uk
Constituency: 33-35 Cathedral Road, Cardiff CF11 9HB
Tel: 029 2022 3207 *Email:* simmonse@parliament.uk *Website:* www.kevinbrennan.co.uk
Twitter: @KevinBrennanMP

CONSERVATIVE

BRIDGEN, ANDREW
North West Leicestershire *(Majority 7,511)*

Andrew James Bridgen. Born 28 October 1964; Married Jacqueline Cremin 2000 (2 sons).
Education: Pingle School, Swadlincote; Nottingham University (BSc biological sciences 1986); CPC road haulage operations 1991.
Non-political career: Royal Marine officer training. Managing director, AB Produce plc (market gardening business) 1988-2010.
Political career: Member for North West Leicestershire since 6 May 2010 general election. *Select committees:* Member: Regulatory Reform 2010-, Joint Committee on Draft Deregulation Bill 2013-. North West Leicestershire Conservative Association. *Councils and public bodies:* Business member, East Midlands Regional Assembly 1999-2000.
Political interests: Business and enterprise, civil liberties, law and order, armed force, transport, environment, food and rural affairs.
Other: Regional committee member: Business for Sterling, The 'No' Campaign; Institute of Directors: Member 1992-, Regional chair 1999-2003; Christians Against Poverty; Hospice Hope; National Forest; Action Deafness; Ivanhoe Club, Ashby; Carlton Club. Burton Rugby Club.
Recreations: Military history, skiing, fishing, driving, reading, country pursuits.
Andrew Bridgen MP, House of Commons, London SW1A 0AA
Tel: 020 7219 7238 *Fax:* 020 7219 6819 *Email:* andrew.bridgen.mp@parliament.uk
Constituency: 6 Elford Street, Ashby De La Zouch, Leicestershire LE65 1HH
Tel: 01530 417736 *Fax:* 01530 560896 *Email:* andrew@andrewbridgen.com
Website: www.andrewbridgen.com *Twitter:* @AndrewBridgenMP

CONSERVATIVE

BRINE, STEVE
Winchester *(Majority 3,048)*

Stephen Charles Brine. Born 28 January 1974; Married Susie (1 daughter 1 son).
Education: Bohunt Comprehensive School; Highway College, Portsmouth; Liverpool Hope University (BA history 2006) (Student Union President).
Non-political career: Journalist: BBC Radio, WGN Radio, Chicago USA; Former director, Azalea Group (public relations and marketing firm).
Political career: Member for Winchester since 6 May 2010 general election. *Select committees:* Member: Justice 2011-, Joint Committee on Voting Eligibilty (Prisoners) Bill 2013-.
Political interests: NHS, media, planning and development, justice, environment; Italy, USA.
Other: Liphook Golf Club, Hampshire.
Recreations: Football, skiing, tennis, golf, live music.
Steve Brine MP, House of Commons, London SW1A 0AA
Tel: 020 7219 7189 *Email:* steve.brine.mp@parliament.uk
Constituency: 9 Stockbridge Road, Winchester, Hampshire SO22 6RN
Tel: 01962 791110 *Website:* www.stevebrine.com *Twitter:* @sbrine

CONSERVATIVE

BROKENSHIRE, JAMES
Old Bexley and Sidcup *(Majority 15,857)*

Parliamentary Under-Secretary of State (Crime and Security), Home Office

James Peter Brokenshire. Born 8 January 1968; Son of Joan and Peter Brokenshire; Married Cathrine Anne Mamelok 1999 (2 daughters 1 son).
Education: Davenant Foundation Grammar School; Cambridge Centre for Sixth Form Studies; Exeter University (LLB 1990).
Non-political career: Trainee, solicitor, then partner, Jones Day Gouldens Solicitors 1991-2005.
Political career: Member for Hornchurch 2005-10, for Old Bexley and Sidcup since 6 May 2010 general election; Shadow Minister for Home Affairs 2006-10; Parliamentary Under-Secretary of State, Home Office: Minister for Crime Prevention 2010-11, for Crime and Security 2011-. *Select committees:* Member: Constitutional Affairs 2005-06.
Political interests: Health, housing and regeneration, law and order.
Recreations: Community radio, watching cricket, hill walking.
James Brokenshire MP, House of Commons, London SW1A 0AA
Tel: 020 7219 8400 *Fax:* 020 7219 2043 *Email:* james.brokenshire.mp@parliament.uk
Constituency: 19 Station Road, Sidcup, Kent DA15 7EB
Tel: 020 8300 3471 *Website:* www.jamesbrokenshire.com *Twitter:* @Jbrokenshire

LIBERAL DEMOCRAT

BROOKE, ANNETTE
Mid Dorset and North Poole *(Majority 269)*

Annette Lesley Brooke. Born 7 June 1947; Daughter of Ernest Kelley, bookbinder, and Edna Kelley; Married Mike Brooke 1969 (2 daughters).

Education: Romford Technical College; London School of Economics (BSc Econ 1968); Hughes Hall, Cambridge (Cert Ed 1969).

Non-political career: Open University 1971-91: Counsellor, Tutor: social sciences, economics 1969-85; Various college posts: Reading, Aylesbury, Poole, Bournemouth; Head of economics, Talbot Heath School Bournemouth 1984-94; Partner, Broadstone Minerals 1988; Owner, Gemini shop, Poole 1994-.

Political career: Member for Mid Dorset and Poole North 2001-10, for Mid Dorset and North Poole (revised boundary) since 6 May 2010 general election; Liberal Democrat: Whip 2001-03; Spokesperson for: Home Affairs 2001-04, Children 2004-10; Shadow Minister for: Education 2005-06, Families 2006-10, Young People 2007, Schools 2008-10. *Select committees:* Member: Public Administration 2001-05, Procedure 2005-06, Public Accounts 2006-08, Children, Schools and Families 2007-10, Chairmen's Panel/Panel of Chairs 2010-, Standards and Privileges 2010-13, Standards 2013, Privileges 2013. Chair, Liberal Democrat Parliamentary Party Committee on Communities and Local Government. Chair, Liberal Democrat Parliamentary Party 2013-. *Councils and public bodies:* Councillor, Poole Borough Council 1986-2003: Chair: Planning 1991-96, Education 1996-2000, Sheriff 1996-97, Mayor 1997-98; Vice-President, Local Government Association 2011-.

Political interests: Children and young people, local government, microfinance; Ghana, Kenya.

Other: Patron, Julia's House Children's Hospice 2001-; MP of the Year, Women in Public Life awards 2010. OBE 2013.

Recreations: Gym, reading, shopping with daughters.

Annette Brooke OBE MP, House of Commons, London SW1A 0AA
Tel: 020 7219 8193 *Fax:* 020 7219 1898 *Email:* brookea@parliament.uk
Constituency: 14 York Road, Broadstone, Dorset BH18 8ET
Tel: 01202 693555 *Fax:* 01202 658420 *Email:* mackayj@parliament.uk
Website: www.annettebrooke.org.uk *Twitter:* @Annette4MDNP

LABOUR

BROWN, GORDON
Kirkcaldy and Cowdenbeath *(Majority 23,009)*

James Gordon Brown. Born 20 February 1951; Son of late Rev. Dr John Brown and late Jessie Brown, née Souter; Married Sarah Macaulay 2000 (1 daughter deceased 2 sons).

Education: Kirkcaldy High School; Edinburgh University (MA 1972; PhD 1982).

Non-political career: Edinburgh University: Rector 1972-75, Temporary lecturer 1975-76; Lecturer in politics, Glasgow College of Technology 1976-80; Journalist, then editor, Current Affairs Department, Scottish Television 1980-83; Visiting fellow, Institute of Politics, Harvard University, USA 2010. Member, TGWU.

Political career: Member for Dunfermline East 1983-2005, for Kirkcaldy and Cowdenbeath since 5 May 2005 general election; Opposition Spokesperson for: Trade and Industry 1985-87, Shadow Chief Secretary to the Treasury 1987-89; Opposition Spokesman for Trade and Industry 1989-92; Shadow Chancellor of the Exchequer 1992-97; Chancellor of the Exchequer 1997-2007; Prime Minister, First Lord of the Treasury and Minister for the Civil Service June 2007-10; Member, Scottish Executive Labour Party 1977-83; Chair, Labour Party in Scotland 1983-84; Former member, National Executive Committee, Labour Party; Head, General Election Campaign (Strategy) 1999-2001; Leader, Labour Party 2007-10.

Political interests: Economic policy, employment, health, social security, Scotland.

Other: Governor, European Investment Bank 1997-2007; Commonwealth Parliamentary Association (UK Branch): Joint Honorary Treasurer (ex-officio) 1997-99, Former Joint Honorary Secretary, Vice-President 2007-10; Special envoy for global education, United Nations 2012-; Board member, World Wide Web Foundation 2010-; Convener, High Level Panel on Education, Global Campaign for Education 2010-. Parliamentarian of the Year, *The Spectator*/Highland Park 1997; Speechmaker of the Year, Channel 4 and *The House* Magazine 1999; Politician of the Year, Channel 4 2000, 2001; Politician of the Year, *GQ* 2005. PC 1996.

Publications: Co-editor, Values, Visions and Voices: An Anthology of Socialism; Co-author, John Smith: Life and Soul of the Party; Maxton; Where There is Greed; Speeches 1997-2006; Courage: Eight Portraits (2007); Britain's Everyday Heroes (2007); Beyond the Crash (2010); Change We Choose: Speeches 2007-09 (2010).

Recreations: Tennis, football, reading, writing.

Rt Hon Gordon Brown MP, House of Commons, London SW1A 0AA
Tel: 020 7219 2968 *Fax:* 020 7219 5734 *Email:* browng@parliament.uk
Constituency: Carlyle House, Carlyle Road, Kirkcaldy, Fife KY1 1DB
Tel: 01592 263792 *Website:* www.gordonbrownmp.org *Twitter:* @OfficeGSBrown

BROWN, LYN
West Ham *(Majority 22,534)*

Shadow Minister for Communities and Local Government

Lyn Carol Brown. Born 13 April 1960; Daughter of Joseph and Iris Brown; Married John Cullen 2008.

Education: Plashet Comprehensive School; Whitelands College, Roehampton (BA English and religious studies 1982).

Non-political career: Residential social worker, London Borough of Ealing Council 1984-85; Newham Voluntary Agencies, Newham 1985-87; London Borough of Waltham Forest Council 1988-2005. Unison.

LABOUR

Political career: Contested Wanstead and Woodford general election 1992. Member for West Ham 2005-10, for West Ham (revised boundary) since 6 May 2010 general election; PPS to: Phil Woolas as Minister of State, Department for Communities and Local Government 2006-07, John Denham as Secretary of State for Innovation, Universities and Skills 2007-09; Assistant Government Whip 2009-10; Opposition Whip 2010-13; Shadow Minister for Communities and Local Government 2013-. *Select committees:* Member: ODPM/Communities and Local Government 2005-07. Member, Co-operative Party. *Councils and public bodies:* London Borough of Newham: Councillor 1988-2005, Chair, Direct Services Organisation 1989-90, Chair, Leisure 1992-2002, Cabinet Member for Culture and Community 2002-05; Founder Member and Chair, London Library Development Agency 1999-2006; Chair: Cultural Services Executive, Local Government Association 2000-03, Culture and Tourism Panel, Association of London Government 2002-05; Member: London Regional Sports Board -2007, London Arts Board -2007, Museums, Libraries and Archives Council, London -2007: Judge, Golden Dagger Award 2005-07.

Political interests: Poverty, housing, libraries, local government, sexual and reproductive health, foreign affairs; Africa, Bangladesh, China, Pakistan.

Other: Member, Fabian Society.

Recreations: Walking, reading, relaxing with friends.

Lyn Brown MP, House of Commons, London SW1A 0AA
Tel: 020 7219 6999 *Fax:* 020 7219 0864 *Email:* brownl@parliament.uk
Constituency: 306 High Street, London E15 1AJ
Tel: 020 8470 3463 *Email:* lyn@lynbrown.org.uk *Website:* www.lynbrown.org.uk

BROWN, NICK
Newcastle upon Tyne East *(Majority 4,453)*

Nicholas Hugh Brown. Born 13 June 1950.

Education: Tunbridge Wells Technical High School; Manchester University (BA 1971).

Non-political career: Proctor and Gamble advertising department. Legal adviser for northern region, GMBATU 1978-83.

Political career: Member for Newcastle upon Tyne East 1983-97, for Newcastle upon Tyne East and Wallsend 1997-2010, for Newcastle upon Tyne East since 6 May 2010 general election; Opposition Frontbench Spokesperson for: Legal Affairs 1985-92, Treasury and Economic Affairs 1988-94; Deputy to Margaret Beckett as Shadow Leader of the Commons 1992-94; Opposition Spokesperson for Health 1994-95; Opposition Deputy Chief Whip 1995-97; Government Chief Whip 1997-98; Minister of Agriculture, Fisheries and Food 1998-2001; Minister of State for Work, Department of Work and Pensions 2001-03; Deputy Government Chief Whip 2007-08; Minister for the North East 2007-10; Government Chief Whip 2008-10; Shadow Parliamentary Secretary to the Treasury and Opposition Chief Whip 2010; Member Speaker's Committee for the Independent Parliamentary Standards Authority 2010-. *Select committees:* Member: Broadcasting 1994-95, Selection 1996-97, 2007-08, Administration 2007-09, Joint Committees on the: Draft Financial Services Bill 2011-12, Draft Communications Data Bill 2012-13. *Councils and public bodies:* Councillor, Newcastle upon Tyne City Council 1980-83.

Countries of interest: Australia, China, Japan, New Zealand, USA.

LABOUR

Other: Freeman, Newcastle 2001. PC 1997.

Rt Hon Nick Brown MP, House of Commons, London SW1A 0AA
Tel: 020 7219 6814 *Fax:* 020 7219 5941 *Email:* nickbrownmp@parliament.uk
Constituency: 1 Mosley Street, Newcastle upon Tyne NE1 1YE
Tel: 0191-261 1408 *Fax:* 0191-261 1409 *Website:* www.nickbrownmp.com

BROWN, RUSSELL
Dumfries and Galloway *(Majority 7,449)*

Shadow Minister for Scotland

Russell Leslie Brown. Born 17 September 1951; Son of late Howard Brown and late Muriel Brown; Married Christine Calvert 1973 (2 daughters).

Education: Annan Academy, Dumfriesshire.

Non-political career: Variety of posts, including quality inspection and production supervisor, ICI 1974-97. Transport and General Workers' Union: Member 1974-, Branch secretary and chair 1979-85.

LABOUR

Political career: Member for Dumfries 1997-2005, for Dumfries and Galloway since 5 May 2005 general election; PPS: to Leaders of the House of Lords: Lord Williams of Mostyn 2002-03, Baroness Amos 2003-05, to Alistair Darling as Secretary of State for Scotland 2005-06, to Douglas Alexander as Secretary of State for Transport and for Scotland 2006-07, to Lord Drayson as Minister of State, Ministry of Defence and Department for Business, Enterprise and Regulatory Reform 2007, to Secretaries of State for Scotland: Des Browne 2007-08, Jim Murphy 2008-10, to Gareth Thomas as Minister of State, Department for International Development 2009-10; Shadow Minister for: Defence 2010-13, Scotland 2013-. *Select committees:* Member: European Legislation 1997-98, European Scrutiny 1998-99, Scottish Affairs 1999-2001, Regulatory Reform 1999-05, Joint Committee on Consolidation, Etc, Bills 2001-10, Standards and Privileges 2001-03, Joint Committee on Conventions 2006, International Development 2010. Vicechair, PLP Scottish Regional Group 1997-2005, 2009-10. *Councils and public bodies:* Councillor: Dumfries and Galloway Regional Council 1986-96, Annandale and Eskdale District Council 1988-96, Dumfries and Galloway Unitary Council 1995-97.

Political interests: Employment, welfare state, health and safety, energy policy; European Union.

Other: Chair, Local Community Education Project 1991-97; Fellow, Industry and Parliament Trust 2004; Cancer Research UK; Macmillan Cancer.

Recreations: Sport (especially football).

Russell Brown MP, House of Commons, London SW1A 0AA
Tel: 020 7219 4429 *Fax:* 020 7219 0922 *Email:* russell.brown.mp@parliament.uk
Constituency: 13 Hanover Street, Stranraer, Dumfries and Galloway DG9 7SB
Tel: 01776 705254 *Fax:* 01776 703006 *Email:* russell@russellbrownmp.com
5 Friars Vennel, Dumfries DG1 2RQ
Tel: 01387 247902 *Fax:* 01387 247903 *Website:* www.russellbrownmp.com
Twitter: @russellbrownmp

BROWNE, JEREMY
Taunton Deane *(Majority 3,993)*

Jeremy Richard Browne. Born 17 May 1970; Son of Sir Nicholas Walker Browne and Diana Browne; Married Charlotte Callen 2004 (divorced); partner Rachel Binks (1 daughter).

Education: Bedales School, Petersfield; Nottingham University (BA politics 1992).

Non-political career: Dewe Rogerson Ltd 1994-96; Director of press and broadcasting, Liberal Democrats 1997-2000; Edelman Communications Worldwide 2000-02; Associate director, ReputationInc 2003-04.

LIBERAL DEMOCRAT

Political career: Contested Enfield Southgate 1997 general election. Member for Taunton 2005-10, for Taunton Deane since 6 May 2010 general election; Liberal Democrat: Shadow Minister for Foreign and Commonwealth Office 2005-07, Whip 2006-07, Shadow Minister for Home Affairs 2007, Shadow Chief Secretary to the Treasury 2007-10; Minister of State: Foreign and Commonwealth Office 2010-12; for Crime Prevention, Home Office 2012-13. *Select committees:* Member: Home Affairs 2005-08.

Political interests: Economy, policing, armed forces, Parkinson's disease, foreign policy; Central and South America, Asia, Australasia.

Jeremy Browne MP, House of Commons, London SW1A 0AA
Tel: 020 7219 5181 *Email:* brownej@parliament.uk
Constituency: Liberal Democrat Office, Masons House, Magdalene Street, Taunton, Somerset TA1 1SG
Tel: 01823 337874 *Fax:* 01823 339823 *Website:* www.jeremybrowne.org.uk

CONSERVATIVE

BRUCE, FIONA
Congleton *(Majority 7,063)*

Fiona Claire Bruce. Born 26 March 1957; Married Richard (2 sons).
Education: Burnley High School; Howell's School, Llandaff; Qualified solicitor 1981.
Non-political career: Senior partner, Fiona Bruce & Co LLP.
Political career: Contested Warrington South 2005 general election. Member for Congleton since 6 May 2010 general election. *Select committees:* Member: Scottish Affairs 2010-13, International Development 2012-. Commissioner, Conservative Human Rights Commission. *Councils and public bodies:* Warrington Borough Council: Councillor 2004-10, Executive Member for Finance; Former school governor.
Political interests: Small business, family, community; North Korea, Rwanda, Tanzania.
Other: Member: Law Society, Specialist Society of Trusts and Estate Practitioners. Overall winner, Women into Business Award 2005.
Publications: Co-author: There is such a thing as society (Politicos, 2002), Freedom, Responsibility and the State: Curbing Over-Mighty Government (Politeia, 2012).
Recreations: Family, countryside, theatre.
Fiona Bruce MP, House of Commons, London SW1A 0AA
Tel: 020 7219 7042 *Fax:* 020 7219 1258 *Email:* fiona.bruce.mp@parliament.uk
Constituency: Riverside, Mountbatten Way, Congleton, Cheshire CW12 1DT
Tel: 01260 274044 *Website:* www.fionabruce.mp

LIBERAL DEMOCRAT

BRUCE, MALCOLM
Gordon *(Majority 6,748)*

Malcolm Gray Bruce. Born 17 November 1944; Son of David Bruce, agricultural merchant and hotelier, and Kathleen Bruce; Married Veronica Wilson 1969 (divorced 1992) (1 son 1 daughter); married Rosemary Vetterlein 1998 (2 daughters 1 son).
Education: Wrekin College, Shropshire; St Andrews University (MA economics and political science 1966); Strathclyde University (MSc marketing 1971); CPE and Inns of Court School of Law, Gray's Inn 1995; French, German (a little).
Non-political career: Trainee journalist, *Liverpool Post* 1966-67; Boots section buyer 1968-69; Research and information officer, NE Scotland Development Authority 1971-75; Director, Noroil Publishing House (UK) Ltd. 1975-81; Joint editor/publisher, Aberdeen Petroleum Publishing 1981-84. Member, NUJ.
Political career: Contested Angus North and Mearns October 1974 and Aberdeenshire West 1979 general elections. Member for Gordon 1983-97, Gordon (revised boundary) 1997-2005, for Gordon (revised boundary) since 5 May 2005 general election; Liberal Spokesperson for Energy 1985-87; Scottish Liberal Spokesperson for Education 1986-87; Alliance Spokesperson for Employment 1987; Liberal Spokesperson for Trade and Industry 1987-88; SLD Spokesperson for Natural Resources (energy and conservation) 1988-89; Liberal Democrat Spokesperson for: the Environment and Natural Resources 1989-90, Scottish Affairs 1990-92, Trade and Industry 1992-94, the Treasury 1994-99; Chair, Liberal Democrat Parliamentary Party 1999-2001; Liberal Democrat Shadow Secretary of State for: Environment, Food and Rural Affairs 2001-02, Trade and Industry 2003-05. *Select committees:* Member: Scottish Affairs 1990-92, Trade and Industry 1992-94, Treasury 1997-99, Standards and Privileges 1999-2001; Chair: International Development 2005-; Member: Liaison 2005-, Quadripartite (Committees on Strategic Export Controls)/ Arms Export Controls 2006-, Joint Committee on National Security Strategy 2010-. Leader Scottish: Social and Liberal Democrats 1988-89, Liberal Democrats 1989-92; President Scottish Liberal Democrats 2000-. *Councils and public bodies:* Rector, Dundee University 1986-89.
Political interests: Energy, gas industry, oil industry, industrial policy, trade policy, deaf children, Scottish home rule and federalism; Balkans, Baltic States, Canada, Czech Republic, Eastern Europe, Hungary, Russia, Scandinavia, South Africa, USA, Zimbabwe.
Other: Member: UK Delegation Parliamentary Assembly of the Council of Europe/Western European Union 2000-05, Executive Committee, Inter-Parliamentary Union, British Group 2010-; Honorary Vice-President, National Deaf Children's Society; Honorary. President, Grampian Branch; Honorary Vice-President: Combined Heat and Power Association, Action on Hearing Loss; Council member, Overseas Development Institute; National Deaf Children's Society. PC 2006; Kt 2012.
Recreations: Golf, cycling, walking, theatre and music.
Rt Hon Sir Malcolm Bruce MP, House of Commons, London SW1A 0AA
Tel: 020 7219 6233 *Fax:* 020 7219 2334
Constituency: 67 High Street, Inverurie, Aberdeenshire AB51 3QJ
Tel: 01467 623413 *Fax:* 01467 624994 *Email:* info@malcolmbruce.org.uk
Website: www.malcolmbruce.org.uk *Twitter:* @malcolmbruce

LABOUR

BRYANT, CHRIS
Rhondda *(Majority 11,553)*

Shadow Minister for Work and Pensions

Christopher John Bryant. Born 11 January 1962; Son of Rees Bryant and Anne Bryant, née Goodwin; Civil partner Jared Cranney 2010.

Education: Cheltenham College; Mansfield College, Oxford (BA English 1983, MA); Ripon College, Cuddesdon (MA CertTheol 1986); French, Spanish.

Non-political career: Church of England: Ordained Deacon 1986, Priest 1987; Curate, All Saints High Wycombe 1986-89; Diocesan youth chaplain, Diocese of Peterborough 1989-91; Agent, Holborn and St Pancras Labour Party 1991-93; Local government development officer, Labour Party 1993-94; London manager, Common Purpose 1994-96; Freelance author 1996-98; Head of European Affairs, BBC 1998-2000. GMB 1991-94; MSF 1994-.

Political career: Contested Wycombe 1997 general election. Member for Rhondda since 7 June 2001 general election; PPS to: Lord Falconer of Thoroton as Lord Chancellor 2005-06, Harriet Harman as Leader of the House of Commons 2007-08; Deputy Leader of the House of Commons 2008-09; Parliamentary Under-Secretary of State, Foreign and Commonwealth Office 2009-10; Shadow Minister for: Foreign and Commonwealth Office 2010, Justice (Political and Constitutional Reform) 2010-11; Shadow Minister for: Immigration 2011-13, Work and Pensions 2013-. *Select committees:* Member: Culture, Media and Sport 2001-05, Joint Committee on House of Lords Reform 2002-10, Public Accounts 2007, Modernisation of the House of Commons 2007-10. Chair, Christian Socialist Movement 1993-98; Labour Movement for Europe: Chair 2002-07, Vice-chair 2007-. *Councils and public bodies:* London Borough of Hackney: Councillor 1993-98, Chief Whip 1994-95.

Political interests: Wales, European affairs, broadcasting, information economy; Latin America, Spain.

Other: Associate, National Youth Theatre of Great Britain. Campaigner of the Year, *Wales Yearbook* awards 2011; Politician of the Year, Stonewall awards 2011. Ferndale RFC.

Publications: Reclaiming The Ground (Hodder and Stoughton, 1993); John Smith: An Appreciation (Hodder and Stoughton, 1994); Possible Dreams (Hodder and Stoughton, 1995); Stafford Cripps: The First Modern Chancellor (Hodder and Stoughton, 1997); Glenda Jackson: The Biography (HarperCollins, 1999).

Recreations: Swimming, theatre.

Chris Bryant MP, House of Commons, London SW1A 0AA
Tel: 020 7219 8315 *Fax:* 020 7219 1792 *Email:* bryantc@parliament.uk
Constituency: Oxford House, Dunraven Street, Tonypandy, Mid Glamorgan CF40 1AU
Tel: 01443 687697/01443 687621 *Email:* morganke@parliament.uk
Website: www.chris-bryant.co.uk *Twitter:* @ChrisBryantMP

LABOUR

BUCK, KAREN
Westminster North *(Majority 2,126)*

Karen Patricia Buck. Born 30 August 1958; Married Barrie Taylor (1 son).

Education: Chelmsford High School; London School of Economics (BSc Econ, MSc Econ, MA social policy and administration).

Non-political career: Research and development worker, Outset (charity specialising in employment for disabled people) 1979-83; London Borough of Hackney: Specialist officer developing services/employment for disabled people 1983-86, Public health officer 1986-87. Member, TGWU.

Political career: Member for Regent's Park and Kensington North 1997-2010, for Westminster North since 6 May 2010 general election; Parliamentary Under-Secretary of State, Department for Transport 2005-06; Parliamentary assistant to Tony McNulty as Minister for London 2008-10; Shadow Minister for: Welfare Reform 2010-11, Education 2011-13; PPS to Ed Miliband as Leader of the Opposition 2013-. *Select committees:* Member: Social Security 1997-2001, Selection 1999-2001, Work and Pensions 2001-05, 2010, Home Affairs 2006-09, Home Affairs Sub-Committee 2008-09, Children, Schools and Families 2009-10; Chair: London 2009-10. Chair, PLP London Regional Group 1999-2010. Labour Party: Policy Directorate (Health) 1987-92, Campaign Strategy Co-ordinator 1992-99. *Councils and public bodies:* Councillor, Westminster City Council 1990-97.

Political interests: Housing, urban regeneration, health care, welfare, children, child poverty, environment and climate change.

Other: Everychild, Amnesty. MP of the Year, Women in Public Life Awards 2007.
Recreations: Music: rock, soul, jazz, opera.
Karen Buck MP, House of Commons, London SW1A 0AA
Tel: 020 7219 3000 *Fax:* 020 7219 3664 *Email:* karen.buck.mp@parliament.uk
Constituency: The Labour Party, 4g Shirland Mews, London W9 3DY
Tel: 020 8968 7999 *Fax:* 020 8960 0150 *Email:* buckk@parliament.uk
Website: www.karenbuck.org.uk *Twitter:* @KarenPBuckMP

BUCKLAND, ROBERT
South Swindon *(Majority 3,544)*

Robert James Buckland. Born 22 September 1968; Younger son of Roger and Barbara Buckland; Married Sian Pugh Reed 1997 (twin son and daughter).
Education: St Michael's School, Bryn, Llanelli; Hatfield College, Durham (BA law 1990); Inns of Court School of Law 1991.
Non-political career: Called to the Bar 1991; Barrister, Wales and Chester circuit 1992-: Iscoed Chambers, Swansea -1999, 30 Park Place, Cardiff 1999-2007, Apex Chambers 2007-, Recorder of Crown Court 2009-.

CONSERVATIVE

Political career: Contested Islwyn 1995 by-election, Preseli Pembrokeshire 1997 and South Swindon 2005 general elections. Member for South Swindon since 6 May 2010 general election. *Select committees:* Member: Justice 2010-13, Joint Committees on: Statutory Instruments 2010-, Consolidation, Etc, Bills 2010-, Works of Art 2011-12, Joint Committee on Privacy and Injunctions 2011-12, Standards 2013-, Privileges 2013-, Joint Committee on Human Rights 2013-. Secretary, 1922 Committee 2012-. Conservative Party: Constituency chair: Llanelli 1993-96, Swansea West 1999-2000; Tory Reform Group: Board Member 2000-03, Vice-President; Member: Conservative Group for Europe 2002-, Conservative Foreign Affairs Forum 2006-, Society of Conservative Lawyers, Llanelli Conservative Club, Swindon Conservative Club; Chair, Conservative Human Rights Commission. *Councils and public bodies:* Councillor, Dyfed County Council 1993-96.
Political interests: Criminal justice, constitutional affairs, foreign affairs, education; South and East Asia, Central and Eastern Europe, Israel, Middle East, Russia.
Other: Member, Criminal Bar Association; Llanelli Crossroads Scheme 1993-96; Patron, Swindon Threshold Homelessness Charity; Trustee, Hop Skip and Jump; Carlton. Glamorgan County Cricket Club; Crawshays Welsh RFC.
Recreations: Music, wine, family, church architecture, watching rugby, football and cricket.
Robert Buckland MP, House of Commons, London SW1A 0AA
Tel: 020 7219 7168 *Fax:* 020 7219 4849 *Email:* robert.buckland.mp@parliament.uk
Constituency: 1 Milton Road, Swindon, Wiltshire SN1 5JE
Tel: 01793 533393 *Fax:* 01793 533393 *Website:* www.robertbuckland.co.uk
Twitter: @robertbuckland

BURDEN, RICHARD
Birmingham, Northfield *(Majority 2,782)*

Shadow Minister for Transport

Born 1 September 1954; Son of late Kenneth Burden, engineer, and Pauline Burden, secretary; Married Jane Slowey 2001 (1 stepson 2 stepdaughters).
Education: Wallasey Technical Grammar School; Bramhall Comprehensive School, Stockport; St John's College of Further Education, Manchester; York University (BA politics 1978); Warwick University (MA industrial relations 1979).

LABOUR

Non-political career: Graduate, Armed Forces Parliamentary Scheme (Royal Navy). President, York University Students' Union 1976-77; NALGO: Branch organiser North Yorkshire 1979-81, West Midlands District Officer 1981-92. Member, TGWU 1979-; Sponsored by TGWU 1989-96.
Political career: Contested Meriden 1987 general election. Member for Birmingham Northfield 1992-2010, for Birmingham, Northfield (revised boundary) since 6 May 2010; PPS to Jeffrey Rooker: as Minister of State and Deputy Minister, Ministry of Agriculture, Fisheries and Food 1997-99, as Minister of State, Department of Social Security 1999-2001; Adviser on motor sports to Richard Caborn, as Minister of State for Sport 2002-07; Shadow Minister for Transport 2013-. *Select committees:* Member: Trade and Industry 2001-05, International Development 2005-, Quadripartite (Committees on Strategic Export Controls)/Arms Export Controls 2006-; Chair: West Midlands 2009-10. Member, Labour Party Departmental Committees for: Trade and Industry/Business, Enterprise and Regulatory Reform 1997-, Foreign Affairs 2001-, Interna-

tional Development 2005-. Founder member, Bedale Labour Party 1980; Labour Middle East Council: Executive member, Vice-chair 1994-95; Member, Co-operative Party; Labour Campaign for Electoral Reform: Chair 1996-98, Vice-chair 1998-; Labour Friends of Palestine and the Middle East 2009-: Policy chair 2009-11, Vice-chair 2011-.

Political interests: Industrial policy – especially motor and motorsport industries, poverty, health, constitution, electoral reform, regeneration, regional government, international development, community empowerment; Middle East, Europe.

Other: Joint Action for Water Services (Jaws) to oppose water privatisation: Founded 1985, Secretary 1985-90; Co-chair, Parliamentary Advisory Council on Transport Safety (PACTS) 1995-98; Fellow, Industry and Parliament Trust 1999; Member, Fabian Society; Macmillan Cancer Relief; Medical Aid for Palestinians; Kingshurst Labour, Austin Sports and Social Club; Austin Branch British Legion; Bromsgrove and District MG Owners' Club. 750 Motor.

Publications: Tap Dancing – Water, the Environment and Privatisation (1988).

Recreations: Cinema, motor racing, travel, food.

Richard Burden MP, House of Commons, London SW1A 0AA
Tel: 020 7219 2318 *Email:* richard.burden.mp@parliament.uk
Constituency: No constituency office published
Tel: 0121-477 7746 *Website:* www.richardburden.com *Twitter:* @RichardBurdenMP

BURLEY, AIDAN
Cannock Chase *(Majority 3,195)*

Born 22 January 1979; Son of Lois and Geoff Burley.

Education: King Edward VI School, Birmingham; West House School, Birmingham; St John's College, Oxford (BA theology 2001).

Non-political career: Assistant to David Willetts MP 2001; Political researcher to Philip Hammond MP 2002; Management consultant: Accenture 2002-05, Hedra/Mouchel 2005-10; Special adviser (police reform taskforce) to Nick Herbert MP 2007.

CONSERVATIVE

Political career: Member for Cannock Chase since 6 May 2010 general election; PPS to Secretaries of State for Transport: Philip Hammond 2011, Justine Greening 2011. *Select committees:* Member: Home Affairs 2010-11 Work and Pensions 2012-13. Member, Conservative Party 1997-; Vice-chair, Oxford University Conservative Association 1999-2000. *Councils and public bodies:* Councillor, London Borough of Hammersmith and Fulham Council 2006-10; Governor, St Thomas of Canterbury Primary School, Fulham 2006-07.

Political interests: Police reform, social mobility, welfare, disability issues; New Zealand, USA.

Other: The Newlife Foundation for Disabled Children, Cannock. Rugeley Rugby Club; Cannock Rugby Club; House of Commons and House of Lords Rugby XV.

Recreations: Rugby, tennis, football, cooking.

Aidan Burley MP, House of Commons, London SW1A 0AA
Tel: 020 7219 7034 *Email:* aidan.burley.mp@parliament.uk
Constituency: 6 High Green Court, Newhall Street, Cannock, Staffordshire WS11 1GR
Tel: 01543 502447 *Website:* www.aidanburleymp.org *Twitter:* @AidanBurleyMP

BURNHAM, ANDY
Leigh *(Majority 15,011)*

Shadow Secretary of State for Health

Andrew Murray Burnham. Born 7 January 1970; Son of Kenneth Burnham, telecommunications engineer, and Eileen Burnham, née Murray; Married Marie-France van Heel 2000 (1 son 2 daughters).

Education: St Aelred's RC High School, Merseyside; Fitzwilliam College, Cambridge (BA English 1991, MA); Dutch, Spanish.

LABOUR

Non-political career: Researcher to Tessa Jowell MP 1994-97; Parliamentary officer, NHS Confederation 1997; Administrator, Football Task Force 1997-98; Special adviser to Chris Smith as Secretary of State for Culture, Media, and Sport 1998-2001. TGWU 1995-; Unison 2000-.

Political career: Member for Leigh 2001-10, for Leigh (revised boundary) since 6 May 2010 general election; PPS to: David Blunkett as Home Secretary 2003-04, Ruth Kelly as Secretary of State for Education and Skills 2004-05; Parliamentary Under-Secretary of State, Home Office 2005-06; Minister of State, Department of Health (Delivery and Reform) 2006-07; Chief Secretary to the Treasury 2007-08; Secretary of State for: Culture, Media and Sport 2008-09, Health

2009-10; Election Co-ordinator 2010-11; Shadow Secretary of State for: Health 2010, 2011-, Education 2010-11. *Select committees:* Member: Health 2001-03. Joint vice-chair, PLP Departmental Committee for Trade and Industry 2002-04. Member, Co-operative Party; Contested Labour leadership 2010. *Councils and public bodies:* Chair, Supporters Direct 2002-05.
Political interests: Health, sport, media, education, crime.
Other: Campaigner of the Year, *The Spectator* awards 2012. PC 2007; Lowton Labour Club.
Publications: Football in the Digital Age (Mainstream Publishing, 1999); Supporters Direct – the Changing Face of the Football Business (Frank Cass, 2000).
Recreations: Football, cricket, rugby league, (Leigh RLFC, Everton FC).
Rt Hon Andy Burnham MP, House of Commons, London SW1A 0AA
Tel: 020 7219 8250 *Email:* andy.burnham.mp@parliament.uk
Constituency: 10 Market Street, Leigh, Lancashire WN7 1DS
Tel: 01942 682353 *Fax:* 01942 731992 *Website:* www.andyburnham.net
Twitter: @AndyBurnhamMP

CONSERVATIVE

BURNS, CONOR
Bournemouth West *(Majority 5,583)*

Born 24 September 1972; Son of Thomas Burns and Kathleen Burns, née Kennedy; Single.
Education: St Columba's College, St Albans; Southampton University (BA modern history and politics with philosophy 1994).
Non-political career: Director, Policy Research Centre for Business Ltd 1997; Company secretary, DeHavilland Global Knowledge Distribution plc 1998; Sales director, insurance company; Associate director, PLMR 2008-10.
Political career: Contested Eastleigh 2001 and 2005 general elections. Member for Bournemouth West since 6 May 2010 general election; PPS to: Hugo Swire as Minister of State, Northern Ireland Office 2010-11, Owen Paterson as Secretary of State for Northern Ireland (resigned) 2011-12. *Select committees:* Member: Education 2010, Culture, Media and Sport 2012-. Chair: Southampton University Conservative Association 1992-93, Wessex Area Conservative Students 1993-94. *Councils and public bodies:* Southampton City Council: Councillor 1999-2002, Housing and urban regeneration spokesperson 1999, Education and employment spokesperson 1999, Conservative group leader 2001-02.
Political interests: Mental health, foreign affairs, Northern Ireland, education; China, Latin America, Middle East, USA.
Other: Management team, Homestart.
Recreations: Swimming, snooker, cooking, collecting political biographies.
Conor Burns MP, House of Commons, London SW1A 0AA
Tel: 020 7219 7021 *Email:* conor.burns.mp@parliament.uk
Constituency: Bournemouth West Conservatives, 135 Hankinson Road, Bournemouth BH9 1HR
Tel: 01202 534888 *Email:* conor@localconservatives.com
Website: www.bournemouthwestconservatives.com www.conorburns.com
Twitter: @Conor_BurnsMP

CONSERVATIVE

BURNS, SIMON
Chelmsford *(Majority 5,110)*

Simon Hugh McGuigan Burns. Born 6 September 1952; Son of late Major B. S. Burns, MC and late Mrs Anthony Nash; Married Emma Clifford 1982 (divorced) (1 son 1 daughter).
Education: Christ the King School, Accra, Ghana; Stamford School, Lincolnshire; Worcester College, Oxford (BA history 1975).
Non-political career: Assistant to Sally Oppenheim MP 1975-81; Director and company secretary, What to Buy for Business Ltd 1981-83; Conference organiser, Institute of Directors 1983-87.
Political career: Contested Alyn and Deeside 1983 general election. Member for Chelmsford 1987-97, for Chelmsford West 1997-2010, for Chelmsford since 6 May 2010 general election; PPS: to Timothy Eggar as Minister of State at Departments of: Employment 1989-90, Education and Science 1990-92, Trade and Industry 1992-93, to Gillian Shephard as Minister of Agriculture, Fisheries and Food 1993-94; Assistant Government Whip 1994-95; Government

Whip 1995-96; Parliamentary Under-Secretary of State, Department of Health 1996-97; Opposition Spokesperson for: Social Security 1997-1998, Environment, Transport and the Regions (Planning, Housing and Construction) 1998-99, Health 2001-05; Shadow Minister for: Health and Education 2001-04, Health 2004-05; Opposition Whip 2005-10; Minister of State: for Health, Department of Health 2010-12, Department for Transport 2012-13. *Select committees:* Member: Health 1999-05, Public Accounts 2000-01, Armed Forces Bill 2005-06, Administration 2006-09, Selection 2007-08. 1922 Committee: Member, Executive 1999, Treasurer 1999-2001.

Political interests: Health; USA.

Other: Honorary PhD, Anglia University. PC 2011.

Recreations: Photography, American politics, reading.

Rt Hon Simon Burns MP, House of Commons, London SW1A 0AA
Tel: 020 7219 6811 *Email:* burnss@parliament.uk
Constituency: Chelmsford Conservative Association, 88 Rectory Lane, Chelmsford, Essex CM1 1RF
Tel: 01245 352872 *Website:* www.chelmsfordconservatives.com www.simonburnsmp.com

---

CONSERVATIVE

BURROWES, DAVID
Enfield Southgate *(Majority 7,626)*

PPS to Owen Paterson as Secretary of State for Environment, Food and Rural Affairs

David John Barrington Burrowes. Born 12 June 1969; Son of Mary Burrowes, née Walpole, and John Burrowes; Married Janet Coekin 1996 (4 sons 2 daughters).

Education: Highgate School, London; Exeter University (LLB 1991).

Non-political career: Shepherd Harris and Co, Enfield: Solicitor 1995-2005, Consultant 2005-.

Political career: Contested Edmonton 2001 general election. Member for Enfield Southgate 2005-10, for Enfield Southgate (revised boundary) since 6 May 2010 general election; Shadow Minister for Justice 2007-10; PPS to: Francis Maude as Minister for the Cabinet Office and Paymaster General 2010, Oliver Letwin as Minister of State, Cabinet Office 2010-12, Owen Paterson as Secretary of State for Environment, Food and Rural Affairs 2012-. *Select committees:* Member: Public Administration 2005-10, Armed Forces Bill 2005-06, Joint Committee on the Draft Legal Services Bill 2006, Joint Committee on the Draft Human Tissue and Embryos Bill 2007. Co-founder and trustee, Conservative Christian Fellowship 1990; Vice-chair, Exeter University Conservatives 1990-95; President and chair, Conservative Christian Fellowship 1990-95; Member, Executive, Enfield Southgate Conservative Association 1995-98; Member Conservative Human Rights Commission 2005-10; Deputy chair Conservative Social Justice Review's Addictions Working Party 2005-07; Chair of Trustees, Conservative Christian Fellowship 2006-. *Councils and public bodies:* London Borough of Enfield: Councillor 1994-2006, Cabinet Member for Voluntary and Community Development 2002-04.

Political interests: Criminal justice system, family policy, drugs and alcohol policy and voluntary sector, umbilical cord blood banking, treatment and research; Cyprus, Israel.

Other: Patron: Nightingale Community Hospice Trust, Street Pastors, Ascension Trust, Faith Action Magazine, Youth Crime Diversion Scheme, Enfield Good Samaritan Network, Mothers at Home Matter.

Publications: Co-author Moral Basis of Conservatism (1995); Such a Thing as Society: Maggie's Children and Volunteering, Policy Exchange (2006); Contributor to: Chapters on Addictions in 'Breakdown Britain' and 'Breakthrough Britain' (Conservative Social Justice Review 2007), From Thatcher to Cameron – the journey to Compassionate Conservatism (CCF, 2010); A better future for families (Chair, Addaction Commission Report, 2012).

Recreations: Cricket, football.

David Burrowes MP, House of Commons, London SW1A 0AA
Tel: 020 7219 8144 *Fax:* 020 7219 5289 *Email:* david.burrowes.mp@parliament.uk
Constituency: 1c Chaseville Parade, Chaseville Park Road, Winchmore Hill, London N21 1PG
Tel: 020 8360 0234 *Fax:* 020 8364 2766 *Email:* david@davidburrowes.com
Website: www.davidburrowes.com *Twitter:* @davidburrowesmp

BURSTOW, PAUL

Sutton and Cheam *(Majority 1,608)*

Paul Kenneth Burstow. Born 13 May 1962; Son of Brian Burstow, tailor, and Sheila Burstow; Married Mary Kemm 1995 (1 son 2 daughters).

Education: Glastonbury High School For Boys; Carshalton College of Further Education (business studies); South Bank Polytechnic (BA business studies).

Non-political career: Buyer, Allied Shoe Repairs 1985-86; Salesman, Kall Kwick Printers, Chiswick 1986-87; Association of Social Democrat/Liberal Democrat Councillors: Organising secretary 1987-89, Campaigns officer 1992-96, Political secretary 1996-97.

LIBERAL DEMOCRAT

Political career: Contested Sutton and Cheam 1992 general election. Member for Sutton and Cheam 1997-2010, for Sutton and Cheam (revised boundary) since 6 May 2010 general election; Liberal Democrat: Spokesperson for Disabled People 1997-98, Social Services and Community Care 1997-99, Local Government 1997-99, Older People 1999-2003; Shadow Secretary of State for Health 2003-05; Spokesperson for London 2005-06, Chief Whip 2006-10; Minister of State for Care Services, Department of Health 2010-12. *Select committees:* Member: Health 2003-04, 2005-06, Finance and Services 2006-10, Modernisation of the House of Commons 2006-07, Public Accounts 2008-10; Chair: Joint Committee on the Draft Care and Support Bill 2013. Former member: SDP/Liberal Alliance, London Regional Liberal Democrat Executive; Member, Federal Policy Committee 1988-90; Chair, Liberal Democrat Parliamentary Party 2012-. *Councils and public bodies:* London Borough of Sutton: Councillor 1986-2002, Chair, Environment Services 1988-96, Deputy Leader 1994-99.

Political interests: Environment, disability, community safety, ageing.

Other: PC 2012; National Liberal.

Recreations: Cooking, reading, cycling, walking, keeping fit.

Rt Hon Paul Burstow MP, House of Commons, London SW1A 0AA
Tel: 020 7219 1196 *Fax:* 020 7219 0974 *Email:* burstowp@parliament.uk
Constituency: 234 Gander Green Lane, Cheam, Surrey SM3 9QF
Tel: 020 8288 6550 *Fax:* 020 8288 6553 *Email:* paul@paulburstow.org.uk
Website: www.paulburstow.org.uk *Twitter:* @PaulBurstow

BURT, ALISTAIR

North East Bedfordshire *(Majority 18,942)*

Alistair James Hendrie Burt. Born 25 May 1955; Son of James Burt, doctor, and Mina Burt, teacher; Married Eve Twite 1983 (1 son 1 daughter).

Education: Bury Grammar School, Lancashire; St John's College, Oxford (BA jurisprudence 1977); French.

Non-political career: Solicitor private practice 1980-98; Executive search consultant Whitehead Mann GKR 1997-2001.

CONSERVATIVE

Political career: Member for Bury North 1983-97. Contested Bury North 1997 general election. Member for North East Bedfordshire 2001-10, for North East Bedfordshire (revised boundary) since 6 May 2010 general election; PPS to Kenneth Baker as Secretary of State for the Environment, for Education and Science and Chancellor of the Duchy of Lancaster 1985-90; Department of Social Security: Parliamentary Under-Secretary of State 1992-95, Minister of State 1992-97: and Minister for Disabled People 1995-97; Opposition Spokesperson for Education and Skills 2001-02; PPS to Leaders of the Opposition: Iain Duncan Smith 2002-03, Michael Howard 2003-05; Shadow Minister for Communities and Local Government 2005-08; Opposition Assistant Chief Whip 2008-10; Parliamentary Under-Secretary of State, Foreign and Commonwealth Office 2010-13. *Select committees:* Member: International Development 2002-03, Procedure 2001-02, Office of the Deputy Prime Minister 2002, Selection 2008-10, Administration 2009-10. Vice-President, Tory Reform Group 1985-88, 2001-; Deputy chair, Conservative Party 2007-10: Local government 2007-08, Development 2008-10. *Councils and public bodies:* Councillor, London Borough of Haringey 1982-84.

Political interests: Church affairs, trade and industry, Third World, foreign affairs, agriculture, rural affairs, disability, sport, poverty, social affairs; North Africa, North America, South Asia, Middle East.

Other: Secretary, Parliamentary Christian Fellowship 1985-97; Chair, Bow Group industry committee 1987-92; Patron, Habitat for Humanity UK 1997-; Chair, Enterprise Forum 1998-2001; Vice-president, Headway Bedford 2000-; Chair, Christians in Parliament 2002-06; Fellow, Industry and Parliament Trust 2006; Fellow, Solicitors Part 2 1980. Biggleswade AC.

Recreations: Football, modern art, walking, outdoor leisure.

Alistair Burt MP, House of Commons, London SW1A 0AA
Tel: 020 7219 8132 *Fax:* 020 7219 1740 *Email:* alistair.burt.mp@parliament.uk
Constituency: Biggleswade Conservative Club, St Andrews Street, Biggleswade,
Bedfordshire SG18 8BA
Tel: 01767 313385 *Email:* nebca@northeastbedsconservatives.com
Website: www.alistair-burt.co.uk *Twitter:* @AlistairBurtFCO

BURT, LORELY
Solihull *(Majority 175)*

PPS to Danny Alexander as Chief Secretary to the Treasury

Lorely Jane Burt. Born 10 September 1954; Daughter of Hazel Baker, née Abbiss, and Raymond Baker; Married Richard Burt 1992 (1 daughter from previous marriage 1 stepson).

Education: High Arcal Grammar School, Dudley; University College of Wales, Swansea (BSc Econ economics 1975); Open University (MBA 1997).

Non-political career: Assistant governor, Pucklechurch Remand Centre and HMP Holloway 1975-78; Personnel and training posts, Beecham, Eurocar, Forte and Mercers 1978-84; Managing director, Kudos Leisure Ltd training company 1984-97; Director: Ace Creative Enterprises Ltd marketing company 1994-99, Mansion House Group 1999-2002; Self-employed estate planning consultant 2002-05.

LIBERAL DEMOCRAT

Political career: Contested Dudley South 2001 general election. Member for Solihull 2005-10, for Solihull (revised boundary) since 6 May 2010 general election; Liberal Democrat: Whip 2005-06, Shadow Minister for: Northern Ireland 2005-06, Small Business, Women and Equality 2006-07, Business, Enterprise and Regulatory Reform 2007-09, Business, Innovation and Skills 2009-10; PPS to Danny Alexander as Chief Secretary to the Treasury 2012-. *Select committees:* Member: Treasury 2005-06, Regulatory Reform 2006-10, Joint Committee on Voting Eligibilty (Prisoners) Bill 2013-. Chair, Liberal Democrat Parliamentary Party Committee on Business, Innovation and Skills 2010-12. Contested West Midlands 2004 European Parliament election. Member Liberal Democrat: Federal Policy Committee 2002-03, West Midlands regional executive 2002-; Chair Liberal Democrat Parliamentary Party 2007-. *Councils and public bodies:* Councillor Dudley Metropolitan Borough Council 1998-2003.

Political interests: Industry, manufacturing, equalities, planning, women in enterprise, osteoporosis, funerals and bereavement, personal and company debt, management, prisons; Guinea-Bissau, Israel, Japan, Palestine, Tunisia.

Other: Methuen Trust; Fellow, Institute of Sales and Marketing Management 1998. Small Business Friendly Award, Federation of Small Businesses 2008; International Luminary Award, Women's Business Enterprise National Council 2009; Small Business Friendly Award, Federation of Small Businesses Warwickshire and Coventry region 2009.

Recreations: Theatre, cinema, socialising, food, keeping fit.

Lorely Burt MP, House of Commons, London SW1A 0AA
Tel: 020 7219 8269 *Fax:* 020 7219 5199 *Email:* lorely.burt.mp@parliament.uk
Constituency: 81 Warwick Road, Solihull, West Midlands B92 7HP
Tel: 0121-706 9593 *Fax:* 0121-706 9365 *Website:* www.lorelyburt.org.uk *Twitter:* @lorelyburt

BYLES, DAN
North Warwickshire *(Majority 54)*

Daniel Alan Byles. Born 24 June 1974; Married Prashanthi Katangoor Reddy 2007 (1 daughter).

Education: Warwick School; Leeds University (economics and management studies 1996); Royal Military Academy Sandhurst (1997); Joint Services Command and Staff College, Junior Division (2001); Nottingham Trent University (MA creative writing 2007).

Non-political career: Light Infantry (University Cadetship Commission) 1993-96; Medical support officer (left with Major rank), Royal Army Medical Corps 1996-2005. Freelance defence consultant 2005-10.

CONSERVATIVE

Political career: Member for North Warwickshire since 6 May 2010 general election. *Select committees:* Member: Energy and Climate Change 2010-. Vice-chair, Knighton Branch, South Leicester Conservatives 2006.

Political interests: Defence, economic policy, energy security, healthcare; South East Asia, China, Middle East, India.

Other: Fellow, Royal Geographical Society; Trustee and founder, the Carpe Diem Trust 2006-10. Guinness World Records: First mother and son team to row any ocean 1998, First mother and son team to reach the Magnetic North Pole 2007.

Recreations: Scuba diving, mountaineering, reading, writing, expeditions.

Dan Byles MP, House of Commons, London SW1A 0AA
Tel: 020 7219 7179 *Email:* dan.byles.mp@parliament.uk
Constituency: 8 Kingsway House, 4 King Street, Bedworth, Warwickshire CV12 8HY
Tel: 02476 315233 *Fax:* 02476 315233 *Email:* sandra.trickett@parliament.uk
Website: www.northwarksconservatives.co.uk   www.danbyles.co.uk   *Twitter:* @danielbyles

---

LABOUR

BYRNE, LIAM
Birmingham, Hodge Hill *(Majority 10,302)*

Shadow Minister for Higher Education

Liam Dominic Byrne. Born 2 October 1970; Married Sarah 1998 (2 sons 1 daughter).

Education: Burnt Mill Comprehensive, Harlow, Essex; Manchester University (BA politics and modern history); Harvard Business School, USA (Fulbright Scholar MBA).

Non-political career: Andersen Consulting 1993-96; Leader of Labour Party's Office 1996-97; N M Rothschild 1997-99; Co-founder eGS Group Ltd 2000-04. Member: National Council, NUS, Amicus.

Political career: Member for Birmingham Hodge Hill 15 July 2004 by-election to 2010, for Birmingham, Hodge Hill (revised boundary) since 6 May 2010 general election; Parliamentary Under-Secretary of State, Department of Health (Care Services) 2005-06; Minister of State, Home Office 2006-08 (Policing, Security and Community Safety 2006, Citizenship, Immigration and Nationality 2006-07, Borders and Immigration 2007-08); Minister for the West Midlands 2007-08; Minister of State, HM Treasury 2008; Minister for the Cabinet Office; Chancellor of the Duchy of Lancaster (attending Cabinet) 2008-09; Chair Council of Regional Ministers 2008-10; Chief Secretary to the Treasury 2009-10; Shadow Chief Secretary to the Treasury 2010; Shadow Minister for the Cabinet Office 2010-11; Shadow Secretary of State for Work and Pensions 2011-13; Shadow Minister for Higher Education 2013-. *Select committees:* Member: European Scrutiny 2005-10, European Standing B 2005-06. Adviser 1997 general election campaign; Policy Review Co-ordinator, Labour Party 2011-12.

Political interests: Anti-social behaviour, drugs, social policy, welfare reform, youth policy; Kashmir.

Other: Fellow, Social Market Foundation; Member: Christian Socialist Movement, Fabian Society. PC 2008.

Publications: Local Government transformed (1996); Information Age Government (1997); Cities of Enterprise, New Strategies for Full Employment (2002); A Chance to Serve? (Progress, 2002); Britain in 2020 (2003); The Fate We're In (Progress, 2003); Reinventing Government Again (2004); The Left's Agenda for Science (2004); Why Labour Won: Lessons from 2005 (Fabian Society, 2005); Powered by Politics: Reforming Parties from the Inside (2005); Power to the People, Next Steps for New Labour (Progress); From Free Movement to Fair Movement: The Immigration Debate in the UK (in Rethinking Immigration and Integration: A New Centre-Left Agenda) (Policy Network, 2007); From Choice to Control: Empowering Public Services (in Public Matters: The Renewal of the Public Realm) (2007); A Common Place (Fabian Society, 2007); Contributor, The Purple Book (Progress, 2011); Turning to Face the East (Guardian Books, 2013).

Recreations: Running, music, family.

Rt Hon Liam Byrne MP, House of Commons, London SW1A 0AA
Tel: 020 7219 6953 *Fax:* 020 7219 1431 *Email:* byrnel@parliament.uk
Constituency: No constituency office
Tel: 0121-789 7287 *Fax:* 0121-789 9824 *Website:* www.liambyrne.co.uk
Twitter: @LiamByrneMP

LIBERAL DEMOCRAT

CABLE, VINCENT
Twickenham *(Majority 12,140)*

Secretary of State for Business, Innovation and Skills; President of the Board of Trade

John Vincent Cable. Born 9 May 1943; Son of late Leonard Cable and Edith Cable; Married Dr Olympia Rebelo (died 2001) (2 sons 1 daughter); married Rachel Wenban Smith 2004.

Education: Nunthorpe Grammar School, York; Fitzwilliam College, Cambridge (BA natural science and economics 1966) (Union President); Glasgow University (PhD international economics 1973).

Non-political career: Finance officer, Kenya Treasury 1966-68; Economics lecturer, Glasgow University 1968-74; Diplomatic Service 1974-76; Deputy director, Overseas Development Institute 1976-83; Special adviser to: John Smith as Secretary of State for Trade 1979, Sir Sonny Ramphal as Commonwealth Secretary-General 1983-90; Adviser to World Commission on Environment and Development (Brundtland Commission) 1985-87; Group planning, Shell 1990-93; Head, economics programme, Chatham House 1993-95; Chief economist, Shell International 1995-97; Former visiting fellow, Nuffield College, Oxford and London School of Economics; Special professor of economics, Nottingham University 1999; Former research fellow, international economics, Royal Institute of International Affairs.

Political career: Contested Glasgow Hillhead (Labour) 1970, York (SDP/Alliance) 1983 and 1987, Twickenham (Liberal Democrat) 1992 general elections. Member for Twickenham since 1 May 1997 general election; Liberal Democrat: Spokesperson for the Treasury (EMU and The City) 1997-99, Principal Spokesperson for Trade and Industry 1999-2003, Shadow Chancellor of the Exchequer 2003-10; Secretary of State for Business, Innovation and Skills; President of the Board of Trade 2010-. *Select committees:* Member, Treasury 1998-99. Liberal Democrat Party: Deputy Leader 2006-10, Acting Leader 2007. *Councils and public bodies:* Councillor (Labour), Glasgow City Council 1971-74.

Political interests: Economic policy, development, policing, energy, environment; China, India, Kenya, Nigeria, Russia.

Other: Member, Competitiveness Council, Council of the European Union 2010-; Patron: Shooting Star Hospice, Hampton Village Tsunami Appeal, Homelink. Opposition Politician of the Year, *House Magazine* awards 2008; Politician of the Year, *Public Affairs News* awards 2008; Parliamentarian of the Year, CAB 2008; Channel 4 Political awards 2009: Political Impact award, Opposition Politician; 'I Told You So', *The Oldie* awards 2009. PC 2010; British Legion Club, Twickenham.

Publications: Wide variety of books and pamphlets including: Protectionism and Industrial Decline (1983), The New Giants: China and India (Chatham House, 1994), The World's New Fissures; The Politics of Identity (Demos, 1995), Globalisation and Global Governance (Chatham House, 1999), Multiple Identities (Demos, 2005), Public Services: Reform with a Purpose (Centre for Reform, 2005), The Storm (Atlantic, 2009), Free Radical (Atlantic, 2009), Tackling Fiscal Crisis (Reform, 2009), Moving from the financial crisis to sustainable growth (Centre Forum, 2011).

Recreations: Ballroom and Latin dancing, classical music, riding, walking.

Rt Hon Dr Vincent Cable MP, House of Commons, London SW1A 0AA
Tel: 020 7219 3000 *Email:* cablev@parliament.uk
Constituency: 2a Lion Road, Twickenham, Middlesex TW1 4JQ
Tel: 020 8892 0215 *Website:* www.vincentcable.org.uk *Twitter:* @vincecable

CONSERVATIVE

CAIRNS, ALUN
Vale of Glamorgan *(Majority 4,307)*

Alun Hugh Cairns. Born 30 July 1970; Son of Hugh Cairns, retired, and Margaret Cairns; Married Emma Turner 1996 (1 son).

Education: Ysgol Gyfun Ddwyieithog Ystalyfera; University of Wales (MBA 2001); Welsh.

Non-political career: Board Member, Reserve and Cadet Forces in Wales. Lloyd's Bank Group 1989-99: Business development consultant 1992-98, Field manager 1998-99.

Political career: Contested Gower 1997 and Vale of Glamorgan 2005 general elections. Member for Vale of Glamorgan since 6 May 2010 general election. *Select committees:* Member: Welsh Affairs 2010-11, Public Administration 2011-. Contested Bridgend constituency 1999 and 2003 National Assembly for Wales elections. AM for South Wales West region 1999-2011: Welsh Conservative: Spokesperson for: Economic Development 1999-2000, Economic

Development and Europe 2000-03, Economic Development and Transport 2003-07; Chair, Committee on Finance 2007-08; Shadow Minister for: Education and Lifelong Learning 2007-08, Local Government 2008-09, Heritage 2009-10; Spokesperson for the Economy 2009-10; Shadow Chief Whip and Business Manager 2009-10. Member: Vale of Glamorgan Conservative Association, Swansea West Conservative Association 1987-; Deputy chair, Welsh Young Conservatives 1995-96; Chaired one of William Hague's Policy Advisory Groups 1996-97; Conservative Economic Spokesperson in Wales 1997-98; Regional Policy co-ordinator, South Wales West 1998-99.

Political interests: Economy, trade and industry, SEN, culture, media and sport, defence; North and South America, South East Asia, Australasia.

Other: Motor Neurone Disease Association; Children with Special Needs; MIND in the Vale; Royal British Legion; RAF Association.

Recreations: Running, computing, skiing, gardening, shooting, squash.

Alun Cairns MP, House of Commons, London SW1A 0AA
Tel: 020 7219 7175 *Email:* alun.cairns.mp@parliament.uk
Constituency: 29 High Street, Barry, Vale of Glamorgan CF62 7EB
Tel: 01446 403814 *Fax:* 01446 403861 *Website:* www.aluncairns.co.uk *Twitter:* @AlunCairns

CAMERON, DAVID
Witney *(Majority 22,740)*

Prime Minister, First Lord of the Treasury and Minister for the Civil Service

CONSERVATIVE

David William Donald Cameron. Born 9 October 1966; Son of late Ian Cameron and Mary Cameron, née Mount; Married Samantha Sheffield 1996 (1 son 2 daughters 1 son deceased).

Education: Eton College; Brasenose College, Oxford (BA philosophy, politics, economics 1988).

Non-political career: Conservative Research Department 1988-92: Head of political section, Member Prime Minister's Question Time briefing team; Special adviser to: Norman Lamont as Chancellor of the Exchequer 1992-93, Michael Howard as Home Secretary 1993-94; Director of corporate affairs Carlton Communications plc 1994-2001.

Political career: Contested Stafford 1997 general election. Member for Witney 2001-10, for Witney (revised boundary) since 6 May 2010 general election; Shadow Minister for: Privy Council Office 2003, Local and Devolved Government Affairs 2004; Member Shadow Cabinet 2004-10; Shadow Secretary of State for Education and Skills 2005; Leader of the Opposition 2005-10; Prime Minister, First Lord of the Treasury and Minister for the Civil Service 2010-. *Select committees:* Member: Home Affairs 2001-04, Modernisation of the House of Commons 2003. Deputy Chairman Conservative Party 2003; Head of Policy Co-ordination Conservative Party 2004; Leader Conservative Party 2005-; President, Conservative Friends of America.

Other: Commonwealth Parliamentary Association (UK Branch): Vice-President 2005-, Chairman of the Branch 2011-; Patron, Atlantic Council of the UK; President, British Inter-Parliamentary Union Group; Honorary President, United Nations Association UK 2010-; Patron: History of Parliament Group, Westminster Foundation for Democracy; Trustee, The Hunterian Collection; Honorary Patron, European Union Youth Orchestra; Vice-President, Hansard Society; Honorary Governor, Ditchley Foundation; Vice-President, Civil Service Sports Council; Honorary Lords Taverner; Vice-President, National Society for Epilepsy; Trustee, Epilepsy Research UK; Sponsor, The Airey Neave Trust; Patron: Carterton Educational Trust, Mulberry Bush School, Trips, Outings and Activities for the Learning Disabled, Bampton Classical Opera, West Oxfordshire, KIDS, Lawrence Home Nursing Team, British Schools Exploring Society, Cancer Research UK Relay for Life, Witney, Motability, The Diana Award, The Peel Society, Witney United Football Club, Loomba Foundation, Ley Community, Friends of Wychwood, Abdabs Youth Theatre, St Margaret's Church, Westminster. Opening Up Politics award, Hansard Society 2007; Person of the Year, *The Times* 2010; King Abdul Aziz Medal (Saudi Arabia) 2012. PC 2005; President, United and Cecil Club. President, House of Lords and House of Commons Tennis Club.

Recreations: Tennis, cooking.

Rt Hon David Cameron MP, House of Commons, London SW1A 0AA
Tel: 020 7219 3475
Constituency: No constituency office *Website:* www.witneyconservatives.com
www.gov.uk/number10 *Twitter:* @Number10gov @David_Cameron

LABOUR

CAMPBELL, ALAN

Tynemouth *(Majority 5,739)*

Opposition Deputy Chief Whip

Born 8 July 1957; Son of Albert Campbell and Marian Campbell, née Hewitt; Married Jayne Lamont 1991 (1 son 1 daughter).

Education: Blackfyne Secondary School, Consett; Lancaster University (BA politics 1978); Leeds University (PGCE 1979); Newcastle Polytechnic (MA history 1984); Basic French.

Non-political career: Whitley Bay High School 1980-89; Hirst High School, Ashington, Northumberland: Teacher 1989-97, Head of sixth form, Head of department.

Political career: Member for Tynemouth 1997-2010, for Tynemouth (revised boundary) since 6 May 2010 general election; PPS to: Lord Macdonald of Tradeston as Minister for the Cabinet Office and Chancellor of the Duchy of Lancaster 2001-03, Adam Ingram as Minister of State, Ministry of Defence 2003-05; Assistant Government Whip 2005-06; Government Whip 2006-08; Parliamentary Under-Secretary of State (Crime Reduction), Home Office 2008-10; Shadow Minister for Home Office 2010; Opposition Deputy Chief Whip 2010-. *Select committees:* Member: Public Accounts 1997-2001, Armed Forces Bill 2005-06, Selection 2006-08, 2010-, Joint Committee on Security 2010-. Honorary Secretary and Honorary Treasurer, Northern Group of Labour MPs 1999-2005.

Political interests: Crime and policing, shipbuilding and offshore industries, fishing; Colombia, Falkland Islands.

Recreations: Family.

Alan Campbell MP, House of Commons, London SW1A 0AA
Tel: 020 7219 6619 *Fax:* 020 7219 3006 *Email:* campbellal@parliament.uk
Constituency: 99 Howard Street, North Shields, Tyne and Wear NE30 1NA
Tel: 0191-257 1927 *Fax:* 0191-257 6537 *Website:* www.alancampbellmp.co.uk

DEMOCRATIC UNIONIST PARTY

CAMPBELL, GREGORY

East Londonderry *(Majority 5,355)*

DUP Spokesperson for International Development and for Cabinet Office

Gregory Lloyd Campbell. Born 15 February 1953; Son of James Campbell and Martha Joyce, née Robinson; Married Frances Patterson 1979 (1 son 3 daughters).

Education: Londonderry Technical College; Magee College (Extra-Mural Certificate political studies 1982).

Non-political career: Civil servant 1972-82, 1986-94; Self-employed (set up publishing company) 1994-99; Director, Causeway Press.

Political career: Contested Foyle 1983, 1987, 1992 and East Londonderry 1997 general elections. Member for East Londonderry 2001-10, for East Londonderry (revised boundary) since 6 May 2010 general election; DUP Spokesperson for: Defence 2005-07, Culture, Media and Sport/ Culture, Olympics, Media and Sport 2005-12, Work and Pensions 2007-09, 2009-10, Transport 2009, International Development 2010-, Cabinet Office 2012-. *Select committees:* Member: Transport, Local Government and the Regions 2001-02, Transport, Local Government and the Regions (Transport Sub-Committee) 2001-02, Transport 2002-04, Northern Ireland Affairs 2004-09. Member: Northern Ireland Assembly 1982-86, Northern Ireland Forum for Political Dialogue 1996-98; MLA for East Londonderry 1998-2011, and for East Londonderry (revised boundary) since 5 May 2011: Minister: for Regional Development 2000-01, of Culture, Arts and Leisure 2008-09. DUP: Security Spokesman 1994; Treasurer; Senior Party Officer. *Councils and public bodies:* Councillor, Londonderry City Council 1981-2011.

Political interests: Economic development, tourism, employment, enterprise, trade and industry.

Publications: Discrimination: The Truth (1987); Discrimination: Where Now? (1993); Ulster's Verdict on the Joint Declaration (1994); Working Toward 2000 (1998).

Recreations: Football, music, reading.

Gregory Campbell MP, House of Commons, London SW1A 0AA
Tel: 020 7219 8495 *Fax:* 020 7219 1953 *Email:* fieldingm@parliament.uk
Constituency: 25 Bushmills Road, Coleraine, Co Londonderry BT52 2BP
Tel: 028 7032 7327 *Fax:* 028 7032 7328 *Email:* wilkinsonh@parliament.uk

LIBERAL DEMOCRAT

CAMPBELL, MENZIES

North East Fife *(Majority 9,048)*

Walter Menzies Campbell. Born 22 May 1941; Son of late George and Elizabeth Campbell; Married Elspeth Urquhart 1970.

Education: Hillhead High School, Glasgow; Glasgow University (MA arts 1962; LLB law 1965); Stanford University, California (Post-graduate Studies international law 1966-67).

Non-political career: Competed: 1964 (Tokyo) Olympics, 1966 Commonwealth Games (Jamaica); UK Athletics Team Captain 1965-66; UK 100 metres record holder 1967-74; Called to the Bar (Scotland) 1968; QC (Scotland) 1982; Chair, Royal Lyceum Theatre Company, Edinburgh 1984-87.

Political career: Contested Greenock and Port Glasgow February and October 1974, East Fife 1979, and North East Fife 1983 general elections. Member for North East Fife 1987-2005, for North East Fife (revised boundary) since 5 May 2005 general election; Liberal Spokesperson for Arts, Broadcasting and Sport 1987-88; Liberal Democrat: Spokesperson for: Scotland (Legal Affairs, Lord Advocate) 1987-99, Defence, Sport 1988-89, Defence and Disarmament, Sport 1989-94, Foreign Affairs and Defence, Sport 1994-97, Foreign Affairs (Defence and Europe) 1997-99, Principal Spokesperson for Defence and Foreign Affairs 1999-2001; Contested Speaker election 2000; Shadow Secretary of State for Foreign and Commonwealth Affairs 2001-06; Leader Liberal Democrat Party 2006-07; Member Intelligence and Security Committee 2010-. *Select committees:* Member: Trade and Industry 1990-92, Defence 1992-97, 1997-99, Foreign Affairs 2008-, Joint Committee on the Draft Detention of Terrorist Suspects (Temporary Extension) Bills 2011, Joint Committee on Parliamentary Privilege 2013. Chair Scottish Liberal Party 1975-77; Deputy Leader Liberal Democrat Party 2003-06; Chair, Home Rule Commission 2011-.

Political interests: Defence, foreign affairs, legal affairs, sport, arts; North America, Middle East.

Other: North Atlantic Assembly (now NATO Parliamentary Assembly): Member 1989-, Leader, UK Delegation 2010-; Member, UK Delegation, Parliamentary Assembly of OSCE 1992-97, 1999-2001; Member: Board of the British Council 1998-2002, Council of the Air League 1999-2006, Olympic Board; Member, Faculty of Advocates. Chancellor, St Andrews University 2006-. Three honorary doctorates from Scottish universities. Member to Watch, Highland Park/*The Spectator* 1996; Opposition Politician of the Year, Channel 4 2004; Opposition Politician of the Year, *House Magazine* 2004; Westminster Politician of the Year, *Herald*/Diageo 2004; Politician of the Year, *Oldie* magazine 2005; Parliamentarian of the Year, Political Studies Association 2005. CBE 1987; PC 1999; Kt 2004; CH 2013; Reform; National Liberal Club.

Recreations: All sports, theatre, music.

Rt Hon Sir Menzies Campbell CH CBE QC MP, House of Commons, London SW1A 0AA
Tel: 020 7219 6910 *Fax:* 020 7219 0559 *Email:* menzies.campbell.mp@parliament.uk
Constituency: North East Fife Liberal Democrats, 16 Millgate, Cupar, Fife KY15 5EG
Tel: 01334 656361 *Fax:* 01334 654045 *Email:* fife_office@mingcampbell.org.uk
Website: www.mingcampbell.org.uk *Twitter:* @MingCampbellMP

LABOUR

CAMPBELL, RONNIE

Blyth Valley *(Majority 6,668)*

Ronald Campbell. Born 14 August 1943; Son of Ronnie and Edna Campbell; Married Deirdre McHale 1967 (5 sons including twins 1 daughter).

Education: Ridley High School, Blyth.

Non-political career: Miner 1958-86. NUM Lodge Chairman, Bates Colliery, Blyth 1982-86; NUM Sponsored MP.

Political career: Member for Blyth Valley since 11 June 1987 general election; Parliamentary Commissioner for Administration 1987-97. *Select committees:* Member: Public Administration 1997-2001, Catering 2001-05, Health 2005-07. Chair, Northern Regional Group of Labour MPs 1999-2000. *Councils and public bodies:* Councillor: Blyth Borough Council 1969-74, Blyth Valley Council 1974-88.

Political interests: Economy, environment, employment; Africa, China, Far East, USA.

Other: Patron: ME Association, Spartans Supporters Club.

Recreations: Furniture restoration, stamp collecting, antiques.

Ronnie Campbell MP, House of Commons, London SW1A 0AA
Tel: 020 7219 4216 *Email:* ronnie.campbell.mp@parliament.uk
Constituency: 42 Renwick Road, Blyth, Northumberland NE24 2LQ
Tel: 01670 363050 *Fax:* 01670 355192

LIBERAL DEMOCRAT

CARMICHAEL, ALISTAIR
Orkney and Shetland *(Majority 9,928)*

Secretary of State for Scotland

Alexander Morrison Carmichael. Born 15 July 1965; Son of Alexander Carmichael, farmer, and Mina Carmichael, née McKay; Married Kathryn Jane Eastham 1987 (2 sons).

Education: Islay High School, Argyll; Aberdeen University (LLB Scots law 1992; Dip LP 1993); French, German.

Non-political career: Hotel manager 1984-89; Procurator fiscal depute, Procurator Fiscal Service 1993-96; Solicitor, private practice 1996-2001.

Political career: Contested Paisley South 1987 general election. Member for Orkney and Shetland since 7 June 2001 general election; Scottish Liberal Democrat Spokesperson on the Energy Review 2001-02; Liberal Democrat: Deputy Spokesperson for: Northern Ireland 2002-05, Home Affairs 2004-06, Shadow Secretary of State for: Transport 2006-07, Northern Ireland and Scotland 2007-08, 2008-10; Deputy Chief Whip (Comptroller of HM Household) 2010-13; Secretary of State for Scotland 2013-; Member, Parliamentary and Political Service Honours Committee 2012-. *Select committees:* Member: Scottish Affairs 2001-05, 2008-10 International Development 2001-02, Public Accounts 2005-06, Joint Committee on Consolidation, Etc, Bills 2008-10, Members' Allowances 2009-10, Joint Committee on Security 2010-. Member, Liberal Democrat Federal Policy Committee 2004-; Deputy leader, Scottish Liberal Democrats 2012-.

Political interests: Transport, agriculture, fishing industry, criminal justice, energy; Burma, Palestine/Israel, Uzbekistan.

Other: Amnesty International; Elder, Church of Scotland 1995-; Director, Solicitors Will Aid (Scotland) Ltd; RNLI; Amicus Lime. PC 2011.

Recreations: Amateur dramatics, music.

Rt Hon Alistair Carmichael MP, House of Commons, London SW1A 0AA
Tel: 020 7219 8181 *Fax:* 020 7219 1787 *Email:* carmichaela@parliament.uk
Constituency: Orkney: 14 Palace Road, Kirkwall, Orkney KW15 1PA
Tel: 01856 876541 *Fax:* 01856 876162 *Email:* flettb@parliament.uk
Shetland: 171 Commercial Street, Lerwick, Shetland ZE1 0HX
Tel: 01595 690044 *Fax:* 01595 690055 *Email:* wishartb@parliament.uk
Website: www.alistaircarmichael.co.uk *Twitter:* @acarmichaelmp

CONSERVATIVE

CARMICHAEL, NEIL
Stroud *(Majority 1,299)*

William Neil Carmichael. Born 15 April 1961; Son of late TLB Carmichael and E Carmichael; Married Laurence (1 son twin daughters).

Education: St Peter's School, York; Nottingham University (BA politics 1982).

Non-political career: Farmer 1982-; Business Development Strategic Impact 2002-.

Political career: Contested Leeds East 1992 and Stroud 2001 and 2005 general elections. Member for Stroud since 6 May 2010 general election. *Select committees:* Member: Environmental Audit 2010-, Education 2010-. Patron, Tory Reform Group; Deputy chairman, Conservative Europe Group. *Councils and public bodies:* Councillor, Northumberland County Council 1989-93.

Political interests: International affairs, European Union, education, rural affairs, public services, environment; Poland; Middle East.

Other: GLOBE International; Member, Royal Institute of International Affairs, Chatham House; Chairman and chief executive, Northumberland Daybreak (caring for people with learning difficulties) 1992-99.

Publications: Co-author: Who Governs the Governors? School Governance in the Twenty First Century (2011), Stronger Boards, Better Education (2012).

Recreations: Travel, golf, motor racing, environment.

Neil Carmichael MP, House of Commons, London SW1A 0AA
Tel: 020 7219 7163 *Email:* neil.carmichael.mp@parliament.uk
Constituency: 7 Bridge Street, Nailsworth, Stroud G16 0AA
Tel: 01453 751572 *Website:* www.neilcarmichael.co.uk *Twitter:* @neil_mp

CARSWELL, DOUGLAS

Clacton *(Majority 12,068)*

John Douglas Wilson Carswell. Born 3 May 1971; Son of Wilson Carswell, OBE FRCS and Margaret Carswell, née Clark; Married Clementine 2007 (1 daughter).

Education: Charterhouse, Surrey; University of East Anglia (BA history 1993); King's College, London (MA British imperial history 1994).

Non-political career: Corporate affairs manager, satellite television broadcaster, Italy 1997-99; Chief project officer INVESCO Asset Management 1999-2003.

CONSERVATIVE

Political career: Contested Sedgefield 2001 general election. Member for Harwich 2005-10, for Clacton since 6 May 2010 general election. *Select committees:* Member: Joint Committee on Human Rights 2005-08, Children, Schools and Families and predecessor 2006-08, 2009-10, Public Accounts 2009-10. Press officer Conservative Central Office 1997; Policy Unit Conservative Party 2004-05; Co-founder, Direct Democracy Group.

Political interests: Crime and policing, immigration, Britain's independence, education, NHS reform, local government finance reform, decentralisation, direct democracy and localism.

Other: Clacton Conservative Club.

Publications: Author of ten published books and pamphlets, including: Direct Democracy (2002); Paying for Localism (2004); Direct Democracy: an agenda for a new model party (2005); The Localist Papers (2007); The Plan: 12 months to renew Britain (2008); Written for *Financial Times*, *Mail on Sunday*, *Daily Mail* and *Daily Telegraph*.

Recreations: Gardening, riding, swimming, running.

Douglas Carswell MP, House of Commons, London SW1A 0AA
Tel: 020 7219 8397
Constituency: 84 Station Road, Clacton-on-Sea, Essex CO15 1SP
Tel: 01255 423112 *Email:* douglas@douglascarswell.com
Website: www.douglascarswell.com www.talkcarswell.com *Twitter:* @DouglasCarswell

CASH, WILLIAM

Stone *(Majority 13,292)*

William Nigel Paul Cash. Born 10 May 1940; Son of Paul Cash, MC (killed in action, 1944) and Moyra Roberts, née Morrison; Married Bridget Lee 1965 (2 sons 1 daughter).

Education: Stonyhurst College, Clitheroe, Lancashire; Lincoln College, Oxford (MA history); French.

Non-political career: Solicitor 1967-: Solicitor, William Cash & Company 1979-.

Political career: Member for Stafford 1984 by-election to 1997, for Stone 1997-2010, for Stone (revised boundary) since 6 May 2010 general election; Shadow Attorney General 2001-03. *Select committees:* European Scrutiny: Member 1998-2010, Chair 2010-; Member: Joint Committee on Consolidation, Etc, Bills 2005-10, Liaison 2010-, Joint Committee on Parliamentary Privilege 2013. Conservative Backbench Committee for European Affairs: Chair 1989-91, Joint vice-chair 1997-.

CONSERVATIVE

Political interests: European Union, trade and industry, media, small businesses, heritage, debt relief; East Africa, Far East, Europe, Malaysia.

Other: Founder and Chair, European Foundation 1993-; Vice-President, Conservative Small Business Bureau 1986-2000; Beefsteak, Carlton, Vincent's (Oxford), Garrick.

Publications: Against a Federal Europe (1991); Europe – The Crunch (1992); AEA – The Associated European Area (2000); John Bright: Statesman, Orator, Agitator (I.B.Tauris, 2011).

Recreations: Local history, cricket, jazz.

William Cash MP, House of Commons, London SW1A 0AA
Tel: 020 7219 6330 *Fax:* 020 7219 3935 *Email:* mcconaloguej@parliament.uk
Constituency: 50 High Street, Stone, Staffordshire ST15 8AU
Tel: 01785 811000 *Fax:* 01785 811000 *Email:* orgsec.stonecons@btconnect.com
Website: www.billcashmp.co.uk *Twitter:* @BillCashMP

LABOUR

CATON, MARTIN

Gower *(Majority 2,683,*

Martin Philip Caton. Born 15 June 1951; Son of William and Pauline Caton, retired shopkeepers; Married Bethan Evans 1996 (2 stepdaughters).
Education: Newport Grammar School, Essex; Norfolk School of Agriculture (National Certificate agriculture 1971); Aberystwyth College of Further Education (Higher National Certificate applied biology 1980).
Non-political career: Agriculture research, Welsh Plant Breeding Station, Aberystwyth 1972-84; Political researcher to David Morris MEP 1984-97. Member, GMB; Former Section Treasurer/Membership Secretary, IPCS.
Political career: Member for Gower 1997-2010, for Gower (revised boundary) since 6 May 2010 general election. *Select committees:* Member: Welsh Affairs 1997-2005, Joint Committee on Consolidation, Etc, Bills 2010-, Chairmen's Panel/Panel of Chairs 2003-, Environmental Audit 2005-. Chair Welsh Regional Group of Labour MPs 2002-. Member: Socialist Environmental Resources Association, Socialist Health Association. *Councils and public bodies:* Councillor: Mumbles Community Council 1986-90, Swansea City Council 1988-95, City and County of Swansea 1995-97.
Political interests: Environment, planning, education, European Union.
Other: Member, CND Cymru.
Recreations: Reading, walking, theatre, thinking about gardening.
Martin Caton MP, House of Commons, London SW1A 0AA
Tel: 020 7219 5111 *Email:* martin.caton.mp@parliament.uk
Constituency: 9 Pontardulais Road, Gorseinon, Swansea, West Glamorgan SA4 4FE
Tel: 01792 892100 *Fax:* 01792 892100 *Email:* daviesl@parliament.uk
Website: www.martin-caton.co.uk

LABOUR

CHAMPION, SARAH

Rotherham *(Majority 5,318)*

Sarah Deborah Champion. Born 10 July 1969; Daughter of Ronald Champion and Mary Champion, née Biggs; Divorced.
Education: Prince William Comprehensive School, Oundle; Sheffield University (BA psychology 1991); Derby University (PG Cert; Diploma psychodynamic counselling).
Non-political career: Manager, Chinese Arts Centre, Manchester; Chief executive, Bluebell Wood Children's Hospice, Dinnington 2008-12. Community.
Political career: Member for Rotherham since 29 November 2012 by-election. *Select committees:* Member: Transport 2012-.
Political interests: Welfare, health, education, social care, defence; China, East Asia, Kashmir, Palestine, South East Asia, USA.
Publications: Representing the People (1999); Made in China (2001); Vital: International Live Artists of Chinese Descent (2008).
Recreations: Endurance horse riding, gardening, food, travel.
Sarah Champion MP, House of Commons, London SW1A 0AA
Tel: 020 7219 3000 *Email:* sarah.champion.mp@parliament.uk
Constituency: Unit 35, Moorgate Crofts Business Centre, South Grove, Rotherham S60 2DH
Tel: 01709 331035 *Fax:* 01709 331036 *Website:* www.sarahchampionmp.com
Twitter: @sarahchampionMP

LABOUR

CHAPMAN, JENNY

Darlington *(Majority 3,388)*

Shadow Minister for Justice

Jennifer Chapman. Born 25 September 1973.
Education: Hummersknott School, Darlington; Brunel University (BSc psychology 1996); Durham University (MA medieval archaeology 2004).
Non-political career: Member, USDAW.
Political career: Member for Darlington since 6 May 2010 general election; Shadow Minister for Justice 2011-. *Select committees:* Member: Procedure 2010-, Joint Committee on Consolidation, Etc, Bills 2010-. *Councils and public bodies:* Darlington Council: Councillor 2007-10, Cabinet Member for Children and Young People; Governor, Branksome School; Member, Darlington Partnership Board.

Political interests: Justice, children, families, employment, transport, economy.
Other: Member, National Trust; Trustee, Darlington Rape Crisis Centre; Vice-chair, Progress 2012-; Chair of trustees, Newblood Live.
Publications: Contributor, The Purple Book (Progress, 2011).
Jenny Chapman MP, House of Commons, London SW1A 0AA
Tel: 020 7219 7046 *Email:* jenny.chapman.mp@parliament.uk
Constituency: 40a Coniscliffe Road, Darlington, Co Durham DL3 7RG
Tel: 01325 382345 *Website:* www.jennychapmanmp.co.uk *Twitter:* @JennyChapman

CONSERVATIVE

CHISHTI, REHMAN
Gillingham and Rainham *(Majority 8,680)*

Atta-Ur-Rehman Chishti. Born 4 October 1978.
Education: Fort Luton High School for Boys; Chatham Grammar School for Girls; University of Wales, Aberystwyth (law 2000); Inns of Court School of Law (Bar Vocational Course: Postgraduate Diploma law 2001); Urdu.
Non-political career: Special adviser to Benazir Bhutto 1999-2007; Called to the Bar, Lincoln's Inn 2001; Barrister, Goldsmith Chambers, London 2003-09; Special adviser to Francis Maude MP as Chair of Conservative Party 2006-07.
Political career: Contested (Labour) Horsham 2005 general election. Member for Gillingham and Rainham since 6 May 2010 general election. *Select committees:* Member: Joint Committee on Human Rights 2010-, Joint Committee on the Draft Defamation Bill 2011, Justice 2012-. *Councils and public bodies:* Medway Council: Councillor 2003-, Cabinet member for Community Safety and Enforcement 2007-10; Governor, Chatham Grammar School for Girls 2001-12.
Political interests: Law and order, criminal justice system, foreign affairs, NHS; Asia, Central America, Middle East, Pakistan, Saudi Arabia, South America, United States of America.
Other: Bar Council of England and Wales.
Recreations: Cricket, running, reading, squash, tennis.
Rehman Chishti MP, House of Commons, London SW1A 0AA
Tel: 020 7219 7075 *Email:* rehman.chishti.mp@parliament.uk
Constituency: Gillingham and Rainham Conservatives, Burden House, 200 Canterbury Street, Gillingham, Kent ME7 5XG
Tel: 01634 570118 *Website:* www.rehmanchishti.com

CONSERVATIVE

CHOPE, CHRISTOPHER
Christchurch *(Majority 15,410)*

Christopher Robert Chope. Born 19 May 1947; Son of late Judge Robert Chope and of Pamela Chope, née Durell; Married Christine Hutchinson 1987 (1 son 1 daughter).
Education: St Andrew's School, Eastbourne; Marlborough College; St Andrew's University (LLB 1970).
Non-political career: Barrister, Inner Temple 1972; Consultant, Ernst and Young 1992-98.
Political career: Member for Southampton Itchen 1983-92. Contested Southampton Itchen 1992 general elecion. Member for Christchurch 1997-2010, for Christchurch (revised boundary) since 6 May 2010 general election; PPS to Peter Brooke as Minister of State, HM Treasury 1986; Parliamentary Under-Secretary of State: Department of the Environment 1986-90, Department of Transport (Minister for Roads and Traffic) 1990-92; Opposition Spokesperson for: the Environment, Transport and the Regions 1997-98, Trade and Industry 1998-99, the Treasury 2001-02; Shadow Minister for: Transport 2002-03, Environment and Transport 2003-05. *Select committees:* Member: Trade and Industry 1999-2002, Chairmen's Panel/Panel of Chairs 2005-, Procedure 2005-10, Administration 2006-10, Political and Constitutional Reform 2010-, Standards 2013-, Privileges 2013-. Joint Secretary, Conservative Backbench Environmental Committee 1983-86; 1922 Committee: Executive member 2001-05, 2005-06, Secretary 2006-12. Member, executive committee, Society of Conservative Lawyers 1983-86; Vice-chair, Conservative Party 1997-98. *Councils and public bodies:* London Borough Wandsworth Council: Councillor 1974-83, Council Leader 1979-83; Member: Health and Safety Commission 1992-97, Local Government Commission for England 1994-95.
Other: Member, Parliamentary Delegation to Council of Europe: Chair: Migration and Refugees Committee 2011-12, Legal Affairs and Human Rights Committee 2012-; Fellow, Industry and Parliament Trust 2001. OBE 1982.
Christopher Chope OBE MP, House of Commons, London SW1A 0AA
Tel: 020 7219 5808 *Fax:* 020 7219 6938 *Email:* chopec@parliament.uk
Constituency: 18a Bargates, Christchurch, Dorset BH23 1QL
Tel: 01202 474949 *Email:* office@christchurchconservatives.com
Website: www.christchurchconservatives.com

CONSERVATIVE

CLAPPISON, JAMES
Hertsmere *(Majority 17,605)*

William James Clappison. Born 14 September 1956; Son of late Leonard Clappison, farmer, and Dorothy Clappison; Married Helen Margherita Carter 1984 (1 son 3 daughters).

Education: St Peter's School, York; The Queen's College, Oxford (BA philosophy, politics and economics 1978); Gray's Inn, London.

Non-political career: Barrister 1981-.

Political career: Contested Barnsley East 1987 general election, Bootle May and November 1990 by-elections. Member for Hertsmere since 9 April 1992 general election; PPS to Baroness Blatch as Minister of State: Department for Education 1992-94, Home Office 1994-95; Parliamentary Under-Secretary of State, Department of the Environment 1995-97; Opposition Spokesperson for: Home Affairs (Crime, Immigration and Asylums) 1997-99, Education and Employment 1999-2000; Shadow: Financial Secretary, HM Treasury 2000-01, Minister for: Work 2001-02, the Treasury 2002, Work and Pensions 2007-10. *Select committees:* Member: Health 1992-94, Home Affairs 2002-10, 2010-, Constitutional Affairs 2003-05, European Scrutiny 2007-, International Development 2010-11. Joint Secretary, Conservative Parliamentary Committees on: Education 1992-93, Health 1993-94; Member Conservative Economic Affairs/ Enterprise/Pensions/Social Affairs Policy Committee 2001-. Contested Yorkshire South 1989 European Parliament election.

Political interests: Home affairs, economic policy, health, education; Israel.

Recreations: Bridge, walking.

James Clappison MP, House of Commons, London SW1A 0AA
Tel: 020 7219 4152 *Fax:* 020 7219 0514 *Email:* tilleye@parliament.uk
Constituency: 104 High Street, London Colney, Hertfordshire AL2 1QL
Tel: 01727 828221 *Fax:* 01727 828404 *Website:* www.jamesclappison.co.uk

CONSERVATIVE

CLARK, GREG
Tunbridge Wells *(Majority 15,576)*

Minister of State (Cities and Constitution), Cabinet Office

Gregory David Clark. Born 28 August 1967; Son of John and Patricia Clark; Married Helen Fillingham 1999 (2 daughters 1 son).

Education: St Peter's Comprehensive, Middlesbrough; Magdalene College, Cambridge (BA economics 1989, MA); London School of Economics (PhD 1992).

Non-political career: Consultant, Boston Consulting Group 1991-94; Teaching and research, LSE and Open University Business School 1994-96; Commercial Policy, BBC: Chief adviser 1997-99, Controller 1999-2001; Special adviser to Ian Lang as Secretary of State for Trade and Industry 1996-97; Director of Policy, Conservative Party 2001-05.

Political career: Member for Tunbridge Wells 2005-10, for Tunbridge Wells (revised boundary) since 6 May 2010 general election; Shadow Minister for: Charities, Voluntary Bodies and Social Enterprise 2006-07, Cabinet Office 2007-08; Shadow Secretary of State for Energy and Climate Change 2008-10; Minister of State for: Decentralisation, Department for Communities and Local Government 2010-11, Cities, Departments for Communities and Local Government and Business, Innovation and Skills 2011, Decentralisation and Cities, Departments for Business, Innovation and Skills and Communities and Local Government 2011-12; Financial Secretary, HM Treasury 2012-13, Minister of State (Cities and Constitution) 2013-. *Select committees:* Member: Public Accounts 2005-07. *Councils and public bodies:* Councillor, Westminster City Council 2002-05.

Political interests: Economics, poverty, welfare reform, transport, health, housing development, energy and climate change.

Other: PC 2010.

Rt Hon Greg Clark MP, House of Commons, London SW1A 0AA
Tel: 020 7219 6977 *Email:* gregclarkmp@parliament.uk
Constituency: No constituency office publicised *Website:* www.gregclark.org
Twitter: @gregclarkmp

CLARK, KATY

North Ayrshire and Arran *(Majority 9,895)*

Kathryn Sloan Clark. Born 3 July 1967; Daughter of Dr Norman Clark and Esther Clark; 1 daughter.
Education: Kyle Academy, Ayr; Aberdeen University (LLB 1990); Edinburgh University (Diploma legal practice 1991).
Non-political career: Qualified solicitor – Scotland, England and Wales; Private practice, Edinburgh and Musselburgh -1998; Head of membership legal services, Unison 1998-2005. Member: GMB, CWU.

LABOUR

Political career: Contested Galloway and Upper Nithsdale 1997 general election. Member for North Ayrshire and Arran since 5 May 2005 general election. *Select committees:* Member: Scottish Affairs 2005-10, Procedure 2005-10, Crossrail Bill 2006-07, European Scrutiny 2006-10, Joint Committee on the Draft Human Tissue and Embryos Bill 2007, Chairmen's Panel/Panel of Chairs 2010-, Environmental Audit 2010-, Business, Innovation and Skills 2010-, Arms Export Controls 2011-. Member: Labour Party 1985-, Co-operative Party.

Political interests: Equality, human rights, economic and social justice, transport, environment.

Katy Clark MP, House of Commons, London SW1A 0AA
Tel: 020 7219 4113 *Fax:* 020 7219 4002 *Email:* clarkk@parliament.uk
Constituency: 53 Main Street, Kilbirnie, Ayrshire KA25 7BX
Tel: 01505 684127 *Fax:* 01505 684349 *Website:* www.katyclark.org.uk
Twitter: @KatyClarkMP

CLARKE, KENNETH

Rushcliffe *(Majority 15,811)*

Minister without Portfolio, Cabinet Office

Kenneth Harry Clarke. Born 2 July 1940; Son of late Kenneth Clarke, watchmaker and jeweller, and Doris Clarke; Married Gillian Edwards 1964 (1 son 1 daughter).
Education: Nottingham High School; Gonville and Caius College, Cambridge (BA law 1962; LLB 1963) (President, Cambridge Union 1963).
Non-political career: Called to the Bar 1963; Member, Midland Circuit, practising from Birmingham; QC 1980; Bencher, Gray's Inn; Deputy chair, British American Tobacco 1998-; Director: Independent News and Media (UK), Independent News and Media plc; Member, Advisory Board, Centaurus Capital.

CONSERVATIVE

Political career: Contested Mansfield Notts 1964 and 1966 general elections. Member for Rushcliffe 1970-2010, for Rushcliffe (revised boundary) since 6 May 2010 general election; PPS to Sir Geoffrey Howe as Solicitor General 1971-72; Assistant Government Whip 1972-74; Government Whip 1973-74; Opposition Spokesperson for: Social Services 1974-76, Industry 1976-79; Parliamentary Secretary, Ministry of Transport 1979-80; Parliamentary Under-Secretary of State, Department of Transport 1980-82; Minister for Health 1982-85; Paymaster General and Employment Minister 1985-87; Chancellor, Duchy of Lancaster and Minister of Trade and Industry 1987-88; Secretary of State for: Health 1988-90, Education and Science 1990-92; Home Secretary 1992-93, Chancellor of the Exchequer 1993-97; Shadow Secretary of State for Business, Enterprise and Regulatory Reform/Innovation and Skills 2009-10; Lord Chancellor and Secretary of State for Justice 2010-12; Government Anti-Corruption Champion 2010-12; Minister without Portfolio, Cabinet Office 2012-. *Select committees:* Member: Joint Committee on House of Lords Reform 2003-10; Joint Committee on Tax Law Rewrite Bills: Member 2005-09, Chair 2007-09. Chair: Cambridge University Conservative Association 1961, Federation Conservative Students 1963-65; Contested Conservative Party leadership 1997, 2001 and 2005; Chair, Democracy Task Force 2005-; President, Tory Reform Group.

Political interests: Economic policy, National Health Service.

Other: Member, Justice and Home Affairs Council, Council of the European Union 2010-12; President, Industry and Parliament Trust 2010-12. Liveryman, The Clockmakers' Company. Three honorary law doctorates; Honorary Fellow, Gonville and Caius College, Cambridge. Double Act of the Year (with Theresa May MP), *The Spectator* awards 2011; Oldie of the Year, *Oldie* awards 2012. PC 1984; Garrick.

Recreations: Birdwatching, football, cricket, jazz, Formula 1 motor racing.

Rt Hon Kenneth Clarke QC MP, House of Commons, London SW1A 0AA
Tel: 020 7219 3000 *Fax:* 020 7219 4841 *Email:* clarkek@parliament.uk
Constituency: Rushcliffe House, 17/19 Rectory Road, West Bridgford, Nottingham NG2 6BE
Tel: 0115-948 4533 *Website:* www.rushcliffeconservatives.com

LABOUR

CLARKE, TOM
Coatbridge, Chryston and Bellshill *(Majority 20,714)*

Thomas Clarke. Born 10 January 1941; Son of late James Clarke and late Mary Gordon.

Education: Columba High School, Coatbridge; Scottish College of Commerce.

Non-political career: Assistant director, Scottish Council for Educational Technology (Scottish Film Council) 1966-82. Member, GMB.

Political career: Member for Coatbridge and Airdrie 1982 by-election to 1983, for Monklands West 1983-97, for Coatbridge and Chryston 1997-2005, for Coatbridge, Chryston and Bellshill since 5 May 2005 general election; Author and Sponsor Disabled Persons (Services, Representation and Consultation) Act 1986; Shadow Minister for UK Personal Social Services 1987-92; Shadow Secretary of State for: Scotland 1992-93, International Development 1993-94; Shadow Cabinet Minister for Disabled People's Rights 1995-97; Minister of State (Film and Tourism), Department of National Heritage/for Culture, Media and Sport 1997-98; Author and Sponsor International Development (Reporting and Transparency) Act 2006. *Select committees:* Member: Administration 2008-10, Standards and Privileges 2010-13, Joint Committee on the Draft House of Lords Reform Bill 2011-12, Standards 2013-, Privileges 2013-. *Councils and public bodies:* Councillor: Coatbridge Town Council 1964-74, Monklands District Council 1974-82; Provost of Monklands 1974-82; JP 1972; President, Convention of Scottish Local Authorities 1978-80.

Political interests: Film industry, foreign affairs, disability rights, civil service, local and regional government, energy industry, international development; Africa, Central America, Asia, Eastern Europe, Gulf States, Indonesia, Peru, Philippines, South Africa, USA.

Other: Labour Member PAD Group to Iran, sponsored by Archbishop of Canterbury 1989; Led CPA delegations to Australia 2000; Observer, Peruvian election 2001; Led IPU Rwanda 2002; Led IPU Bahrain and Kuwait 2005; Fellow, Industry and Parliament Trust. Disability Champion, *ePolitix* 2003, 2009. CBE 1980; PC 1997. Coatbridge Municipal Golf.

Publications: Director of award winning amateur film Give us a Goal (1972); Joint chair, film review A Bigger Picture (1998).

Recreations: Films, walking, reading.

Rt Hon Tom Clarke CBE MP, House of Commons, London SW1A 0AA
Tel: 020 7219 6997 *Fax:* 020 7219 6094 *Email:* clarket@parliament.uk
Constituency: Municipal Buildings, Kildonan Street, Coatbridge, North Lanarkshire ML5 3LF
Tel: 01236 600800 *Fax:* 01236 600808 *Email:* hartys@parliament.uk
Website: www.tomclarke.org.uk

LIBERAL DEMOCRAT

CLEGG, NICK
Sheffield, Hallam *(Majority 15,284)*

Leader Liberal Democrats; Deputy Prime Minister, Lord President of the Council

Nicholas William Peter Clegg. Born 7 January 1967; Son of Hermance Eulalie Van Den Wall Bake and Nicholas Peter Clegg; Married Miriam Gonzalez Durantez 2000 (3 sons).

Education: Westminster School, London; Cambridge University (BA social anthropology 1989, MA); Minnesota University, USA (political philosophy) (Cambridge – Minnesota Fellowship Award 1990); College of Europe, Bruges, Belgium (Diploma European affairs 1992); Dutch, French, German, Spanish.

Non-political career: Trainee journalist, *Nation Magazine*, New York 1990; Political consultant, GJW Government Relations 1992-93; European Commission: Official 1994-96, Adviser to European Commission Vice-president Sir Leon Brittan 1996-99; Columnist, *Guardian Unlimited* 2003-06; Part-time lecturer, Sheffield University and guest lecturer, Cambridge University 2004-05.

Political career: Member for Sheffield, Hallam since 5 May 2005 general election; Liberal Democrat: Spokesperson for Foreign and Commonwealth Office 2005-06, Shadow Home Secretary 2006-07, Leader 2007-; Deputy Prime Minister, Lord President of the Council (with special responsibility for political and constitutional reform) 2010-; Member Speaker's Committee on the Electoral Commission 2010-. *Select committees:* Member Joint Committees on: Consolidation, Etc, Bills 2005-08, Tax Law Rewrite Bills 2005-08. MEP for East Midlands 1999-2004. Member, Manifesto Working Group 2013-.

Political interests: Trade and industry, education, globalisation, constitutional reform, Europe.

Other: David Thomas prize, *Financial Times* 1993; Apology of the Year, *The Spectator* awards 2012. PC 2008.

Recreations: Literature, tennis, spending time with his children, the outdoors, skiing and mountaineering.

Rt Hon Nick Clegg MP, House of Commons, London SW1A 0AA
Tel: 020 7219 3000 *Email:* nick.clegg.mp@parliament.uk
Constituency: 85 Nethergreen Road, Sheffield, South Yorkshire S11 7EH
Tel: 0114-230 9002 *Fax:* 0114-230 9614 *Email:* nickclegg@sheffieldhallam.org.uk
Website: www.nickclegg.com *Twitter:* @nick_clegg

CLIFTON-BROWN, GEOFFREY
The Cotswolds *(Majority 12,864)*

Geoffrey Robert Clifton-Brown. Born 23 March 1953; Son of Robert Clifton-Brown and late Elizabeth Clifton-Brown; Married Alexandra Peto-Shepherd 1979 (divorced 2003) (1 son 1 daughter).

Education: Eton College; Royal Agricultural College, Cirencester (ARICS); French.

Non-political career: Graduate estate surveyor, Property Services Agency, Dorchester 1975; Investment surveyor, Jones Lang Wootton 1975-79; Managing director, own farming business in Norfolk 1979-.

CONSERVATIVE

Political career: Member for Cirencester and Tewkesbury 1992-97, for Cotswold 1997-2010, for The Cotswolds since 6 May 2010 general election; PPS to Douglas Hogg as Minister of Agriculture, Fisheries and Food 1995-97; Opposition Whip 1999-2001; Opposition Spokesperson for: Environment, Food and Rural Affairs 2001, Transport, Local Government and the Regions 2001-02; Shadow Minister for: Local Government 2002-03, Local and Devolved Government 2003-04; Opposition Whip 2004-05; Assistant Chief Whip 2005; Shadow Minister for: Foreign Affairs 2005-07, Trade 2007, 2009-10 International Development 2007-10. *Select committees:* Member: Public Accounts 1997-99, Broadcasting 2000-01, Administration 2001, 2010-11, Finance and Services 2005-; Selection: Member 2005-06, Chair 2010-; Member: Liaison 2010-. Chairman: North Norfolk Constituency Association 1986-91, International Office, Conservative Party 2010-; Vice-chairman (international affairs), Conservative Party 2010-.

Political interests: Economy, taxation, foreign affairs, environment, agriculture; Brazil, China, India.

Other: Vice-chair, Euro Atlantic Group 1995-; Fellow, Industry and Parliament Trust 1996; Armed Forces Parliamentary Fellowship 1997; Fellow, Royal Institute of Chartered Surveyors (FRICS) 2002. Liveryman, Worshipful Company of Farmers. Freeman, City of London; Farmers'.

Publications: Privatisation of the State Pension – Secure Funded Provision For All (Bow Group, 1996).

Recreations: Fishing, other rural pursuits.

Geoffrey Clifton-Brown MP, House of Commons, London SW1A 0AA
Tel: 020 7219 5147 *Fax:* 020 7219 2550 *Email:* cliftonbrowng@parliament.uk
Constituency: Unit 1143, Regent Court, Gloucester Business Park, Hucclecote, Gloucestershire GL3 4AD
Tel: 01452 371630 *Fax:* 0845 009 0109 *Website:* www.cliftonbrown.co.uk

CLWYD, ANN
Cynon Valley *(Majority 9,617)*

Born 21 March 1937; Daughter of Gwilym and Elizabeth Lewis; Married Owen Roberts 1963 (died 2012).

Education: Holywell Grammar School; The Queen's School, Chester; University College of Wales, Bangor; Welsh.

Non-political career: Journalist, *Guardian*; Broadcaster, BBC. Member: NUJ, TGWU.

LABOUR

Political career: Contested Denbigh 1970 and Gloucester October 1974 general elections. Member for Cynon Valley 3 May 1984 by-election to 2010, for Cynon Valley (revised boundary) since 6 May 2010 general election; Shadow Minister of Education and Women's Rights 1987-88; Shadow Secretary of State for: International Development 1989-92, Wales 1992, National Heritage 1992-93; Opposition Spokesperson for: Employment 1993-94, Foreign Affairs 1994-95; Assistant to John Prescott as Deputy Leader of Labour Party 1994-95; Special envoy to Iraq on human rights 2003-10. *Select committees:* Member: International Development 1997-2005, Foreign Affairs 2010-, Arms Export Controls 2011-. Vice-chair PLP Departmental Committee for Foreign and Commonwealth Affairs 2002-06; Chair Parliamentary Labour Party 2005-06. European Parliament: MEP for Mid and West Wales 1979-84. Member, National Executive Committee, Labour Party 1983-84; Chair, Tribune Group 1986-87.

Political interests: Human rights, international development, animal welfare; Cambodia, Iran, Iraq, Russia, East Timor, Turkey, Vietnam.

Other: Inter-Parliamentary Union, British Group: Chair 2004-07, Vice-chair 2010-; Member, Arts Council 1975-79; Vice-chair, Welsh Arts Council 1975-79; Royal Commission on NHS 1976-79; Member, White Robe Gorsedd, Royal National Eisteddfod of Wales. Honorary Fellow: North East Wales Institute of Higher Education 1996, University of Wales, Bangor 2004; Honorary LLD, University of Wales, Carmarthen 2006. BBC/*House Magazine* Backbencher of the Year 2003; *The Spectator* Backbencher of the Year; Channel 4 Campaigning Politician of the Year 2003-04; HTV Communicator of the Year 2005. PC 2004.

Recreations: Walking, boating.

Rt Hon Ann Clwyd MP, House of Commons, London SW1A 0AA
Tel: 020 7219 6609 *Fax:* 020 7219 5943 *Email:* ann.clwyd.mp@parliament.uk
Constituency: Fourth Floor, Crown Buildings, Aberdare, Mid Glamorgan CF44 7HU
Tel: 01685 871394 *Fax:* 01685 883006 *Twitter:* @AnnClwyd

LABOUR

COAKER, VERNON

Gedling *(Majority 1,859)*

Shadow Secretary of State for Defence

Vernon Rodney Coaker. Born 17 June 1953; Son of Edwin Coaker; Married Jacqueline Heaton 1978 (1 son 1 daughter).

Education: Drayton Manor Grammar School, London; Warwick University (BA politics 1974); Trent Polytechnic (PGCE 1976).

Non-political career: Humanities teacher, Nottinghamshire: Manvers School 1976-82, Arnold Hill School 1982-89, Bramcote Park School 1989-95, Big Wood School 1995-97. Member: NUT, Unite.

Political career: Contested Gedling 1987 and 1992 general elections. Member for Gedling 1997-2010, for Gedling (revised boundary) since 6 May 2010 general election; PPS: to Stephen Timms: as Minister of State, Department of Social Security 1999, as Financial Secretary, HM Treasury 1999-2001, as Minister of State for Schools and Learners, Department for Education and Skills 2001-02, as Minister of State, Department of Trade and Industry 2002, to Estelle Morris as Secretary of State for Education and Skills 2002, to Tessa Jowell as Secretary of State for Culture, Media and Sport 2002-03; Assistant Government Whip 2003-05; Government Whip 2005-06; Home Office: Parliamentary Under-Secretary of State (Crime Reduction) 2006-08; Minister of State (Policing, Crime and Security) 2008-09; Minister of State, Department of Children, Schools and Families 2009-10; Shadow Minister for: Education 2010, Policing 2010-11; Shadow Secretary of State for Northern Ireland 2011-13, Defence 2013-. *Select committees:* Member: Social Security 1998-99, European Standing Committee B 1998. *Councils and public bodies:* Councillor, Rushcliffe Borough Council 1983-97.

Political interests: Environment, education, welfare reform, foreign policy, sport; Angola, France, Kosovo, Macedonia.

Other: Unicef.

Recreations: Sport, walking.

Vernon Coaker MP, House of Commons, London SW1A 0AA
Tel: 020 7219 6627 *Email:* vernon.coaker.mp@parliament.uk
Constituency: 2a Parkyn Road, Daybrook, Nottingham NG5 6BG
Tel: 0115-920 4224 *Fax:* 0115-920 4500 *Email:* robertsc@parliament.uk
Website: www.vernon-coaker-mp.co.uk *Twitter:* @Vernon_CoakerMP

LABOUR

COFFEY, ANN

Stockport *(Majority 6,784)*

Margaret Ann Wishart Coffey. Born 31 August 1946; Daughter of late John Brown, MBE, Flight-Lieutenant, RAF, and Marie Brown, nurse; Married 1973 (divorced 1989) (1 daughter); married Peter Saraga 1998 .

Education: Nairn Academy; Bodmin and Bushey Grammar Schools; Polytechnic of South Bank, London (BSc sociology 1967); Walsall College of Education (Postgraduate Certificate education 1971); Manchester University (MSc psychiatric social work 1977).

Non-political career: Trainee social worker, Walsall Social Services 1971-72; Social worker: Birmingham 1972-73, Gwynedd 1973-74, Wolverhampton 1974-75, Stockport 1977-82, Cheshire 1982-88; Team leader, fostering, Oldham Social Services 1988-92. Member, USDAW.

Political career: Contested Cheadle 1987 general election. Member for Stockport 1992-2010, for Stockport (revised boundary) since 6 May 2010 general election; Opposition Whip 1995-96; Opposition Spokeswoman on Health 1996-97; Joint PPS to Tony Blair as Prime Minister 1997-98; PPS to Alistair Darling as Secretary of State for: Social Security/Work and Pensions 1998-2002, Transport 2002-06, Trade and Industry 2006-07, Chancellor of the Exchequer 2007-10. *Select committees:* Member: Trade and Industry 1993-95, Modernisation of the House of Commons 2000-10, Joint Committee on the Draft House of Lords Reform Bill 2011-12. *Councils and public bodies:* Stockport Metropolitan Borough Council: Councillor 1984-92, Leader Labour Group 1988-92; Member, District Health Authority 1986-90.

Political interests: Children, health, education, town centres markets.

Other: Fellow, Industry and Parliament Trust 1994.

Recreations: Photography, drawing, cinema, swimming, reading.

Ann Coffey MP, House of Commons, London SW1A 0AA
Tel: 020 7219 4546 *Email:* ann.coffey.mp@parliament.uk
Constituency: 207a Bramhall Lane, Stockport, Cheshire SK2 6JA
Tel: 0161-483 2600 *Email:* dunbarb@parliament.uk *Website:* www.anncoffeymp.com
Twitter: @anncoffey_MP

CONSERVATIVE

COFFEY, THERESE

Suffolk Coastal *(Majority 9,128)*

PPS to Michael Fallon as Minister of State for Business and Enterprise, Department for Business, Innovation and Skills

Therese Anne Coffey. Born 18 November 1971; Daughter of late Tom Coffey and Sally Coffey.

Education: St Mary's College, Rhos-on-Sea; St Mary's College, Crosby; St Edward's College, Liverpool; University College, London (BSc 1993; PhD chemistry 1997).

Non-political career: Chartered management accountant, Mars UK Ltd 1997-2007; Finance director, Mars Drinks UK 2007-09; Property finance manager, BBC 2009-10.

Political career: Contested Wrexham 2005 general election. Member for Suffolk Coastal since 6 May 2010 general election; Board member, Parliamentary Office of Science and Technology (POST); PPS to Michael Fallon as Minister of State for Business and Enterprise, Department for Business, Innovation and Skills 2012-. *Select committees:* Member: Culture, Media and Sport 2010-12. Contested South East 2004 and 2009 European Parliament elections. Member, Conservative Party 1988-; National deputy chair, Conservative Students 1993-94; Chair, North West Hampshire Conservatives 2006-09; Deputy regional chair, South East 2009; Former member, Conservative Way Forward. *Councils and public bodies:* Councillor, Whitchurch Town Council 1999-2003.

Political interests: Rural affairs, enterprise, energy; EU, Latin America.

Other: Member, CAMRA; Water Aid; Dogs Trust.

Dr Therese Coffey MP, House of Commons, London SW1A 0AA
Tel: 020 7219 7164 *Email:* therese.coffey.mp@parliament.uk
Constituency: National Hall, Sun Lane, Woodbridge, Suffolk IP12 1EG
Tel: 01394 610045 *Website:* www.theresecoffeymp.com *Twitter:* @theresecoffey

CONSERVATIVE

COLLINS, DAMIAN

Folkestone and Hythe *(Majority 10,122)*

PPS to Theresa Villers as Secretary of State for Northern Ireland

Damian Noel Thomas Collins. Born 4 February 1974; Married Sarah Richardson 2004 (1 daughter 1 son).

Education: St Mary's High School, Herefordshire; Belmont Abbey School, Herefordshire; St Benet's Hall, Oxford (BA modern history 1996).

Non-political career: Desk officer, Conservative Party Research Department 1996-98; Press officer, Conservative Party Press Office 1998-99; Account director, M&C Saatchi 1999-2005; Managing director, Influence Communications Ltd 2005-08; Senior counsel, Lexington Communications 2008-10.

Political career: Contested Northampton North 2005 general election. Member for Folkestone and Hythe since 6 May 2010 general election; PPS to Theresa Villers as Secretary of State for Northern Ireland 2012-. *Select committees:* Member: Culture, Media and Sport 2010-12, Joint Committee on Consolidation, Etc, Bills 2010-. President, Oxford University Conservative Association 1995.

Political interests: Enterprise, economy, regeneration, social mobility, local food, creative industries, international relations.

Other: Political officer, Bow Group 2003-04; Folkestone Stop Short Project; Folkestone Youth Project; Lord's Taverners.

Publications: Conservative Revival (Politicos, 2006); The New Blue (Social Market Foundation, 2008).

Recreations: Sport (football, cricket, rugby union).

Damian Collins MP, House of Commons, London SW1A 0AA
Tel: 020 7219 7072 *Fax:* 020 7219 2213 *Email:* damian.collins.mp@parliament.uk
Constituency: 4 West Cliff Gardens, Folkestone, Kent CT20 1SP
Tel: 01303 253524 *Fax:* 01303 251061 *Email:* shepwayconservatives@btconnect.com
Website: www.damiancollins.com *Twitter:* @DamianCollins

COLVILE, OLIVER
Plymouth, Sutton and Devonport *(Majority 1,149)*

Oliver Newton Colvile. Born 26 August 1959; Single.

Education: Stowe School, Buckingham.

Non-political career: Director, small public relations company 1993-95; Account director, Rowland Sallingbury Casey 1993, 1995-96; Proprietor, Oliver Colvile & Associates 1996-2010; Director, Polity Communications 2005-. National Society of Conservative Agents 1981-93; Chair, London branch Conservative Agents 1986-87; Editor, National Society of Conservative Agents' Journal 1992-93.

CONSERVATIVE

Political career: Contested Plymouth Sutton 2001 and 2005 general elections. Member for Plymouth, Sutton and Devonport since 6 May 2010 general election. *Select committees:* Member: Northern Ireland Affairs 2010-. Agent, Conservative Party 1981-93; Battersea Conservative Association: Vice and deputy chair 1997-99, Chair, Shaftesbury branch 1997-2000. *Councils and public bodies:* Governor, St Andrew's Primary School.

Political interests: Defence, mental health, pharmacy, social care, renewable energy, fishing; France, Malawi, South Africa, Zimbabwe.

Other: Conservative Foreign Affairs Forum; Director, Enterprise Forum; Member: Federation of Small Businesses, Institute of Directors. Stonehouse Lawn Tennis Club; Surrey County Cricket Club; Plymouth Albion Rugby Club; Royal Western Yacht Club; Royal Corinthian Yacht Club; Marylebone Cricket Club.

Recreations: Cricket, rugby, horse racing.

Oliver Colvile MP, House of Commons, London SW1A 0AA
Tel: 020 7219 7219 *Email:* oliver.colvile.mp@parliament.uk
Constituency: 202 Exeter Street, Plymouth PL4 0NH
Tel: 01752 600108 *Website:* www.olivercolvile.org *Twitter:* @olivercolvile

CONNARTY, MICHAEL
Linlithgow and East Falkirk *(Majority 12,553)*

Born 3 September 1947; Son of late Patrick and Elizabeth Connarty; Married Margaret Doran 1969 (1 son 1 daughter).

Education: St Patrick's High School, Coatbridge; Stirling University (BA economics 1972); Glasgow University/Jordanhill College of Education (DCE 1975); French.

Non-political career: Stirling University: President Student Association 1970-71, Honorary President (Rector) 1983-84; Teacher economics and modern studies (secondary and special needs) 1975-92; Chair, Stirling Economic Development Co. 1987-90. EIS: Central Region President 1983-84, National Council 1984-85; Member: Unite, CWU.

LABOUR

Political career: Contested Stirling 1983 and 1987 general elections. Member for Falkirk East 1992-2005, for Linlithgow and East Falkirk since 5 May 2005 general election; PPS to Tom Clarke, as Minister of State, Department for Culture, Media and Sport 1997-98; Board member, Parliamentary Office of Science and Technology (POST) 1997-. *Select committees:* Member: Information 1997-2001; European Scrutiny: Member 1998-2006, 2010-, Chair 2006-10; Member: Liaison 2006-10. Chair, Scottish Group of Labour MPs 1998-99; Member, PLP Departmental Committees for: Department for Work and Pensions 2001-, Department for International Development 2002-, Department for Business, Innovation and Skills 2010-. Member, Labour Party Scottish Executive Committee 1981-82, 1983-92; Chair, Labour Party Scottish Local Government Committee 1988-90; Vice-chair, Labour Group, COSLA 1988-90; Chair, Stirlingshire Co-operative Party 1990-92. *Councils and public bodies:* Stirling District Council: Councillor 1977-90, Council leader 1980-90; JP 1977-90.

Political interests: Economy and enterprise, international development, European Union, industry, skills and training, youth affairs, crime, drug abuse, small businesses, human rights; Latin America, Australia, Middle East, USA.

Other: Life member: International Parliamentary Union 1992-, Commonwealth Parliamentary Association 1992-; British American Parliamentary Group 1992-; Parliamentary Assembly of the Council of Europe: Member 2010-, Member, Education, Culture and Science Committee 2010-, Chair, Sub-Committee on Education, Youth and Sport 2012-; Member, Socialist Education Association 1978-; Vice-chair, Scottish Medical Aid for Palestinians 1988-95; Fellow, Industry and Parliament Trust 1994; Chair, Board of Scottish National Jazz Orchestra 2006-.

Recreations: Family, jazz and classical music, reading, walking.

Michael Connarty MP, House of Commons, London SW1A 0AA
Tel: 020 7219 5071 *Fax:* 020 7219 2541 *Email:* michael.connarty.mp@parliament.uk
Constituency: 5 Kerse Road, Grangemouth, Stirlingshire FK3 8HQ
Tel: 01324 474832 *Fax:* 01324 666811 *Email:* westj@parliament.uk
62 Hopetoun Street, Bathgate, West Lothian EH48 4PD
Tel: 01506 676711 *Fax:* 01506 676722 *Email:* rankiny@parliament.uk
Website: www.mconnartymp.com

LABOUR

COOPER, ROSIE   West Lancashire *(Majority 4,343)*

Rosemary Elizabeth Cooper. Born 5 September 1950; Daughter of William and Rose Cooper; Single.

Education: Bellerive Convent Grammar School; Liverpool University.

Non-political career: Concept Design Partnership & W Cooper Limited 1973-80; The Littlewoods Organisation 1980-2001: Merchandiser 1980-92, Public relations manager 1994-95, Group corporate communications manager 1995-2000, Seconded as project manager for government task force on equal pay 1999-2001. USDAW.

Political career: Contested (as Liberal) Knowsley North 1986 by-election and (as Liberal/Alliance) 1987 general election, and (as Liberal Democrat) Liverpool Broadgreen 1992 general election. Member (Labour) for West Lancashire since 5 May 2005 general election; PPS to: Lord Rooker as Minister of State, Department for Environment, Food and Rural Affairs 2006-07, Ben Bradshaw: as Minister of State, Department for Health 2007-09, as Secretary of State for Culture, Media and Sport 2009-10. *Select committees:* Member: European Scrutiny 2005-06, Northern Ireland Affairs 2005-10, Justice 2007-08, North West 2009-10, Justice 2010, Health 2010-, Administration 2010-12, Unopposed Bills (Panel) 2013-. Honorary Secretary, PLP Departmental Committee for Northern Ireland 2005-10. Contested North West region 2004 European Parliament election. Member: Liberal Party/Liberal Democrats -1999, Labour Party 1999-. *Councils and public bodies:* Liverpool City Council (Liberal/Liberal Democrat 1973-1999, Labour 1999-2000): Councillor 1973-2000, Lord Mayor 1992-93, Labour spokesperson for housing 1999-2000, Honorary Alderman 2011; Member and vice-chair, Liverpool Health Authority 1994-96; Chair, Liverpool Women's Hospital NHS Foundation Trust 1996-2005.

Political interests: Health, disability equality, housing; Dominican Republic, Haiti, Northern Ireland, USA.

Other: Director Merseyside Centre for Deaf People 1973-2004; Cosmopolitan Housing Association 1994-2011.

Recreations: Theatre, music, cinema, community affairs.

Rosie Cooper MP, House of Commons, London SW1A 0AA
Tel: 020 7219 3000 *Email:* rosie.cooper.mp@parliament.uk
Constituency: Suite 108, Malthouse Business Centre, 48 Southport Road, Ormskirk, Lancashire L39 1QR
Tel: 01695 570094 *Fax:* 01695 570094 *Email:* rosie@rosiecooper.net
Website: www.rosiecooper.net *Twitter:* @rosie4westlancs

LABOUR

COOPER, YVETTE
Normanton, Pontefract and Castleford *(Majority 10,979)*

Shadow Secretary of State for Home Department (Home Secretary)

Born 20 March 1969; Daughter of Tony Cooper, former leader Engineers and Managers Association, and June Cooper; Married Ed Balls (now MP) 1998 (2 daughters 1 son).

Education: Eggars Comprehensive; Balliol College, Oxford (BA philosophy, politics and economics 1990); Harvard University (Kennedy Scholar 1991); London School of Economics (MSc economics 1995).

Non-political career: Economic researcher for John Smith MP 1990-92; Domestic policy specialist, Bill Clinton presidential campaign 1992; Policy adviser to Labour Treasury teams 1992-94; Economic columnist/Leader writer, *The Independent* 1995-97. Member: TGWU, GMB.

Political career: Member for Pontefract and Castleford 1997-2010, for Normanton, Pontefract and Castleford since 6 May 2010 general election; Parliamentary Under-Secretary of State, Department of Health (Public Health) 1999-2002; Parliamentary Secretary, Lord Chancellor's Department 2002-03; Office of the Deputy Prime Minister/Department for Communities and Local Government 2003-08: Parliamentary Under-Secretary of State 2003-05, Minister of State (Minister for Housing and Planning) 2005-07, Minister for Housing (attending cabinet) 2007-08; Chief Secretary to the Treasury 2008-09; Secretary of State for Work and Pensions 2009-10; Shadow Secretary of State for: Work and Pensions 2010, Foreign and Commonwealth Affairs (Foreign Secretary) 2010-11; Shadow Minister for Women and Equalities 2010-13; Shadow Secretary of State for Home Department (Home Secretary) 2011-. *Select committees:* Member: Education and Employment 1997-99, Education and Employment (Employment Sub-Committee) 1997-99.

Political interests: Unemployment, coal industry, poverty, equal opportunities; USA.

Other: PC 2007.

Rt Hon Yvette Cooper MP, House of Commons, London SW1A 0AA
Tel: 020 7219 5080 *Email:* coopery@parliament.uk
Constituency: 1 York Street, Castleford, West Yorkshire WF10 1RB
Tel: 01977 553388 *Fax:* 01977 559753 *Website:* www.yvettecooper.com
Twitter: @YvetteCooperMP

LABOUR

CORBYN, JEREMY
Islington North *(Majority 12,401)*

Jeremy Bernard Corbyn. Born 26 May 1949; Son of David Corbyn and Naomi Corbyn; (3 sons).

Education: Adams Grammar School, Newport, Shropshire; Spanish.

Non-political career: Full-time organiser, National Union of Public Employees (NUPE) 1975-83; Also worked for Tailor and Garment workers and AUEW; NUPE sponsored MP; Member, RMT Parliamentary Campaigning Group 2002-.

Political career: Member for Islington North since 9 June 1983 general election. *Select committees:* Member: Social Security 1991-97, London 2009-10, Justice 2011-. Member, Socialist Campaign Group. *Councils and public bodies:* Councillor, Haringey Borough Council 1974-84: Chair: Community Development 1975-78, Public Works 1978-79, Planning 1980-81.

Political interests: People of Islington, Stop the War, Liberation, welfare state, NHS, socialism, human rights, anti-racism, anti-imperialism and internationalism, transport safety, environment; Africa, Chagos Islands, Middle East, Latin America.

Other: Member, Executive Committee, Inter-Parliamentary Union, British Group.

Recreations: Running, railways.

Jeremy Corbyn MP, House of Commons, London SW1A 0AA
Tel: 020 7219 3545 *Fax:* 020 7219 2328 *Email:* corbynj@parliament.uk
Constituency: 86 Durham Road, London N7 7DU
Tel: 020 7561 7488 *Website:* www.jeremycorbyn.org.uk *Twitter:* @jeremycorbyn

CONSERVATIVE

COX, GEOFFREY
Torridge and West Devon *(Majority 2,957)*

Charles Geoffrey Cox. Born 30 April 1960; Son of Michael and Diane Cox; Married Patricia Macdonald 1985 (1 daughter 2 sons).

Education: King's College, Taunton; Downing College, Cambridge (BA English and law 1981).

Non-political career: Barrister, Thomas More Chambers 1982-2001; Standing counsel to Mauritius 1996-2000; QC 2003. Member, National Farmers' Union.

Political career: Contested Torridge and West Devon 2001 general election. Member for Torridge and West Devon 2005-10, for Torridge and West Devon (revised boundary) since 6 May 2010 general election. *Select committees:* Member: Environment, Food and Rural Affairs 2006-10, Standards and Privileges 2010-13, Standards 2013-, Privileges 2013-.

Political interests: Agriculture, education, defence, legal and constitutional issues; Mauritius.

Recreations: Reading, walking dogs, swimming, countryside .

Geoffrey Cox QC MP, House of Commons, London SW1A 0AA
Tel: 020 7219 4719 *Fax:* 020 7219 4307 *Email:* coxg@parliament.uk
Constituency: 2 Bridge Chambers, Lower Bridge Street, Bideford, Devon EX39 2BU
Tel: 01237 459001 *Fax:* 01237 459003 *Email:* tellgeoffrey@geoffreycox.co.uk
Website: www.geoffreycox.co.uk *Twitter:* @Geoffrey_Cox

CONSERVATIVE

CRABB, STEPHEN
Preseli Pembrokeshire *(Majority 4,605)*

Parliamentary Under-Secretary of State, Wales Office; Government Whip

Born 20 January 1973; Married Béatrice Monnier 1996 (1 son 1 daughter).

Education: Tasker Milward VC School, Haverfordwest; Bristol University (BSc politics 1995); London Business School (MBA 2004); French, Welsh learner.

Non-political career: Research assistant to Andrew Rowe MP 1995-96; Parliamentary affairs officer, National Council for Voluntary Youth Services 1996-98; Policy and campaign manager, London Chamber of Commerce 1998-2002; Self-employed marketing consultant 2002-05.

Political career: Contested Preseli Pembrokeshire 2001 general election. Member for Preseli Pembrokeshire 2005-10, for Preseli Pembrokeshire (revised boundary) since 6 May 2010 general election; Assistant Government Whip 2010-12; Parliamentary Under-Secretary of State, Wales Office 2012-; Government Whip 2012-. *Select committees:* Member: Welsh Affairs 2005-07, International Development 2007-09, Treasury 2008-09. Chair: North Southwark and Bermondsey Conservative Association 1998-2000, Conservative Party Human Rights Commission 2007-.

Political interests: International development, trade, dairy industry and energy; Africa, France, India, Middle East, USA.

Other: Patron: Haverfordwest Mencap 2005-, Pembrokeshire Care Society, 2012; Balfour, Haverfordwest, Haverfordwest County AFC.

Recreations: Rugby, long distance running, cooking, family.

Stephen Crabb MP, House of Commons, London SW1A 0AA
Tel: 020 7219 6518 *Fax:* 020 7219 0907 *Email:* stephen.crabb.mp@parliament.uk
Constituency: Suite 1, 20 Upper Market Street, Haverfordwest, Pembrokeshire SA61 1QA
Tel: 01437 767555 *Email:* jonesad@parliament.uk *Website:* www.stephencrabb.com
Twitter: @scrabbmp

LABOUR

CRAUSBY, DAVID
Bolton North East *(Majority 4,084)*

David Anthony Crausby. Born 17 June 1946; Son of late Thomas Crausby, factory worker/club steward, and Kathleen Crausby, cotton worker; Married Enid Noon 1965 (2 sons).

Education: Derby Grammar School, Bury; Bury Technical College.

Non-political career: Shop steward/works convenor, AEEU 1968-97; Full-time works convenor 1978-97; Chair, Amicus (AEEU) Group 2001-; Secretary, Unite Group 2010-.

Political career: Contested Bury North 1987 and Bolton North East 1992 general elections. Member for Bolton North East 1997-2010, for Bolton North East (revised boundary) since 6 May 2010 general election. *Select committees:* Member: Administration 1997-2001, Social Security 1999-2001, Defence 2001-10, Quadripartite (Committees on Strategic Export Controls)/Arms Export Controls 2006-10; Chair: North West 2009-10; Member: Chairmen's Panel/

Panel of Chairs 2010-. Member, Labour Party Departmental Committees for: Foreign and Commonwealth Affairs 1997-2001, Social Security 1997-2001, Trade and Industry 1997-2001; North West Regional Group PLP: Vice-chair 2000-01, Chair 2001-02. *Councils and public bodies:* Bury Council: Councillor 1979-92, Chair of Housing 1985-92.

Political interests: Industrial relations, pensions, housing, defence; Bermuda, Canada, New Zealand.

Other: Commons Speech of the Year, *House Magazine* awards 2011.

Recreations: Football, cinema, walking.

David Crausby MP, House of Commons, London SW1A 0AA
Tel: 020 7219 4092 *Fax:* 020 7219 3713 *Email:* crausbyd@parliament.uk
Constituency: 426 Blackburn Road, Bolton, Lancashire BL1 8NL
Tel: 01204 303340 *Website:* www.davidcrausby.co.uk

CREAGH, MARY
Wakefield *(Majority 1,613)*

Shadow Secretary of State for Transport

Mary Helen Creagh. Born 2 December 1967; Daughter of Thomas and Elizabeth Creagh; Married Adrian Pulham 2001 (1 son 1 daughter).

Education: Bishop Ullathorne RC Comprehensive, Coventry; Pembroke College, Oxford (BA modern languages (French/Italian) 1990); London School of Economics (MSc European studies 1997); French, Italian, Spanish.

LABOUR

Non-political career: Stagiare, Socialist group, European Parliament 1990; Assistant to Stephen Hughes MEP 1991; Press officer: European Youth Forum 1991-95, London Enterprise Agency 1995-97; Lecturer, entrepreneurship, Cranfield School of Management 1997-2005. GMB: Member 1991-95, 2003-, Chair, Brussels branch 1992-95; Member, Unison 2004-.

Political career: Member for Wakefield 2005-10, for Wakefield (revised boundary) since 6 May 2010 general election; PPS: to Ministers of State, Department of Health: Andy Burnham 2006-07, Lord Warner 2006, to Andy Burnham: as Chief Secretary to the Treasury 2007-08, as Secretary of State for Culture, Media and Sport 2008-09; Assistant Government Whip 2009-10; Shadow Minister for Public Health 2010; Opposition Whip 2010; Shadow Secretary of State for: Environment, Food and Rural Affairs 2010-13, Transport 2013-. *Select committees:* Member: Joint Committee on Human Rights 2005-07, Finance and Services 2007-10, Yorkshire and the Humber 2009. *Councils and public bodies:* London Borough of Islington: Councillor 1998-2005, Leader, Labour group 2000-04.

Political interests: Europe, employment, social policy, disability issues, Irish community, human rights, children's issues, environment; Burundi, Democratic Republic of Congo, Rwanda, Sudan.

Other: Member: European Movement 1995-, Fabian Society 1995-, Oxfam 1995-, RNID 1996-, Amnesty International 1997- Trustee, Rathbone Training 1997-2004; Member, Ectopic Pregnancy Trust 2001-; Member Higher Education Academy 2002-.

Recreations: Family, yoga, cycling, swimming, food.

Mary Creagh MP, House of Commons, London SW1A 0AA
Tel: 020 7219 6984/020 7219 8766 *Fax:* 020 7219 4257 *Email:* creaghm@parliament.uk
Constituency: 20-22 Cheapside, Wakefield, West Yorkshire WF1 2TF
Tel: 01924 386124 *Fax:* 01924 299723 *Email:* mary@marycreagh.co.uk
Website: www.marycreagh.co.uk *Twitter:* @MaryCreagh_MP

CREASY, STELLA
Walthamstow *(Majority 9,478)*

Shadow Minister for Business, Innovation and Skills

Stella Judith Creasy. Born 1977.

Education: Colchester County High School; Magdalene College, Cambridge (psychology); London School of Economics (PhD psychology).

Non-political career: Researcher to Douglas Alexander MP, Charles Clarke MP and Ross Cranston MP; Deputy director, Involve; Head of campaigns, Scout Association. Member, Unite.

LAB/CO-OP

Political career: Member for Walthamstow since 6 May 2010 general election; Member Public Accounts Commission 2011-; PPS to Andy Burnham as Shadow Secretary of State for Education 2011; Shadow Minister for: Crime Prevention 2011-13, Business, Innovation and Skills 2013-.

Select committees: Member: Public Accounts 2010-11. Member: SERA, Labour Women's Network, Co-operative Party. *Councils and public bodies:* Waltham Forest Council: Councillor 2002-05, Former Deputy Mayor, Interim mayor 2003.

Other: Fabian Society. Campaigner of the Year, *Spectator* awards 2011; Campaign of the Year, *PoliticsHome* awards 2012.

Recreations: Indie music, American TV crime drama, cake, pub quizzes.

Dr Stella Creasy MP, House of Commons, London SW1A 0AA
Tel: 020 7219 6980
Constituency: Walthamstow Labour Party, 23 Orford Road, Walthamstow, London E17 9NL
Tel: 020 8521 1223 *Email:* stella@workingforwalthamstow.org.uk
Website: www.workingforwalthamstow.org.uk *Twitter:* @stellacreasy

CROCKART, MIKE
Edinburgh West *(Majority 3,803)*

Michael Crockart. Born 19 March 1966; Married (2 sons).

Education: Perth High School; Edinburgh University (BSc social services 1987).

Non-political career: Police constable, Lothians and Borders Police 1990-98; Standard Life Assurance: Systems developer 1998-2005, Lead business service developer 2006-07, IT project manager 2007-10.

LIBERAL DEMOCRAT

Political career: Contested Edinburgh North and Leith 2005 general election. Member for Edinburgh West since 6 May 2010 general election; PPS to Michael Moore as Secretary of State for Scotland (resigned) 2010. *Select committees:* Member: Joint Committee on Human Rights 2011-12, Business, Innovation and Skills 2012-, Joint Committee on the Draft Enhanced Terrorism Prevention and Investigation Measures Bill 2012-13, Scottish Affairs 2012-. Co-chair, Liberal Democrat Parliamentary Party Committee on Energy and Climate Change 2012-. Contested Edinburgh North and Leith constituency 2007 Scottish Parliament election. Convener, Edinburgh West Liberal Democrats 2009.

Recreations: Photography, classical music.

Mike Crockart MP, House of Commons, London SW1A 0AA
Tel: 020 7219 2691 *Fax:* 020 7219 2096 *Email:* mike.crockart.mp@parliament.uk
Constituency: 185 St John's Road, Edinburgh EH12 7SL
Tel: 0131-339 0339 *Fax:* 0131-476 7101 *Website:* www.mikecrockartmp.com
Twitter: @CrockartMP

CROUCH, TRACEY
Chatham and Aylesford *(Majority 6,069)*

Tracey Elizabeth Anne Crouch. Born 24 July 1975.

Education: Folkestone Grammar School for Girls; Hull University (BA law and politics 1996).

Non-political career: Researcher to Rt Hon Michael Howard MP 1996-98; Public affairs manager, Harcourt 1998-2000; Senior public affairs manager, Westminster Strategy 2000-03; Chief of staff to: Damian Green MP 2003, Rt Hon David Davis MP 2003-05; Norwich Union/Aviva 2005-10: Senior political adviser 2005-07, Head of public affairs 2007-10.

CONSERVATIVE

Political career: Member for Chatham and Aylesford since 6 May 2010 general election. *Select committees:* Member: Culture, Media and Sport 2012-. Member, Executive, 1922 Committee 2010-12; Secretary, Backbench Public Services Committee. Conservative Co-operative Movement.

Political interests: Home affairs, education, sport, economic affairs, health and social care.

Other: Member, UK Delegation, Organisation for Security and Co-operation in Europe Parliamentary Assembly. FA coaching level 1 2006; Manager, Meridian Girls FC.

Recreations: Sport, music, reading.

Tracey Crouch MP, House of Commons, London SW1A 0AA
Tel: 020 7219 7203 *Email:* tracey.crouch.mp@parliament.uk
Constituency: 6-8 Revenge Road, Lordswood, Chatham, Kent ME5 8UD
Tel: 01634 673180 *Website:* www.traceycrouch.org *Twitter:* @tracey_crouch

LABOUR

CRUDDAS, JON
Dagenham and Rainham *(Majority 2,630)*

Policy Review Co-ordinator, Labour Party

Jonathan Cruddas. Born 7 April 1962; Son of John Cruddas, sailor, and Pat Cruddas, housewife; Married Anna Healy, later Baroness Healy of Primrose Hill, 1992 (1 son).

Education: Oaklands RC Comprehensive, Portsmouth; Warwick University 1981-88 (BSc economics; MA industrial relations; PhD industrial and business studies); University of Wisconsin, USA Visiting fellow 1987-88.

Non-political career: Policy officer Labour Party Policy Directorate 1989-94; Chief assistant to General Secretary Labour Party 1994-97; Deputy political secretary Prime Minister's political office Downing Street 1997-2001. TGWU 1989-2001: Branch secretary 1992-94.

Political career: Member for Dagenham 2001-10, for Dagenham and Rainham since 6 May 2010 general election. *Select committees:* Member: Public Accounts 2003-05. Honorary Secretary, PLP London Regional Group 2005-10. Policy Review Co-ordinator, Labour Party 2012-.

Political interests: Labour law, industrial economy, economic regeneration, housing, the far right, community cohesion.

Other: Dagenham Working Men's Club, Dagenham Royal Naval Association. White Hart Dagenham Angling Society.

Recreations: Golf, angling.

Jon Cruddas MP, House of Commons, London SW1A 0AA
Tel: 020 7219 8161 *Fax:* 020 7219 1756 *Email:* cruddasj@parliament.uk
Constituency: 50-52 New Road, Dagenham RM9 6YS
Tel: 020 8984 7854 *Email:* mullanem@parliament.uk *Website:* www.joncruddas.org.uk
Twitter: @JonCruddasMP

LABOUR

CRYER, JOHN
Leyton and Wanstead *(Majority 6,416)*

John Robert Cryer. Born 11 April 1964; Son of late Bob Cryer, MP for Keighley 1974-83 and Bradford South 1987-94, and Ann Cryer, née Place, MP for Keighley 1997-2010; Married Narinder Bains 1994 (divorced 2011) (2 sons 1 daughter); married Ellie Reeves 2012.

Education: Oakbank School, Keighley; Hatfield Polytechnic (BA literature and history 1985); London College of Printing (Postgraduate Certificate print journalism 1988).

Non-political career: Journalist: *Tribune* 1992-96; *Morning Star* 1989-92; Freelance journalist, 1992-97: *Labour Briefing* (editor), *Guardian, GPMU Journal, T&G Record*; Lloyd's of London Publications; Political officer: ASLEF 2005-06, Unite 2006-10. Member: TGWU 1986-, NUJ 1988-, UCATT 1997-.

Political career: Member for Hornchurch 1997-2005. Contested Hornchurch 2005 general election. Member for Leyton and Wanstead since 6 May 2010 general election. *Select committees:* Member: Deregulation and Regulatory Reform 1997-2002, Treasury 2010-11. Member, Labour Party Departmental Committees for: Education and Employment 1997-2001, Parliamentary Affairs 1997-2001, Trade and Industry 1997-2001; Member, PLP Committee 2003-05, 2010-; Secretary, Labour Against the European Superstate 2004-05; Contested PLP chairman election 2012; Chair, Labour for a Referendum. Member, Executive of Labour Euro Safeguards Committee; Press officer, Defend Clause Four Campaign 1995; Member, Co-operative Party; Secretary, Labour Against the Euro.

Political interests: Employment, social security, education, further education, European Union, health, economic policy, industry, energy policy, transport; Australia, India, USA.

Other: Member: CND, Amnesty International, Transport on Water, Tibet Support Group, Keighley and Worth Valley Railway, RAF Hornchurch Association; Member, British Board of Boxing Control 1997-99; First Step Nursery, Hornchurch; St Francis Hospice, Havering; Child Poverty Action Group; St Francis Foundation for Animal Welfare; Islamic Relief; East Africa Flood Apeal; Leyton Royal British Legion; Patron, Carefree Kids Waltham Forest; Patron, Box4Life Leyton; Recovery Resoucres Foundation, Leytonstone. Member: House of Commons Cricket Club, House of Commons Rugby Club, House of Commons Boxing Club.

Publications: Co-author with Ann Cryer, Boldness be my Friend: Remembering Bob Cryer MP (1996); Many articles mainly in political publications.

Recreations: Swimming, reading, sport, old cars, cinema, cycling, triathlons.

John Cryer MP, House of Commons, London SW1A 0AA
Tel: 020 7219 7100 *Email:* john.cryer.mp@parliament.uk
Constituency: 6 Gainsborough Road, Leytonstone, London E11 1HR
Tel: 020 8989 5249 *Website:* www.johncryermp.co.uk

LABOUR

CUNNINGHAM, ALEX
Stockton North *(Majority 6,676)*

Alexander Cunningham. Born 1 May 1955; Son of John and Jean Cunningham; Married Evaline 1977 (2 sons).

Education: Branksome Comprehensive, Darlington; Queen Elizabeth Sixth Form; Darlington College of Technology (Certificate journalism 1976).

Non-political career: Journalist: *Darlington and Stockton Times* 1974-76, *The Mail*, Hartlepool 1976-77, Radio Tees 1977-79, Radio Clyde 1979, *Evening Gazette* 1979-84; Public relations officer, British Gas 1984-89; Transco: Communications adviser 1995-2000; Head of communications 2000-02; Managing director, Tees Valley Communicators Ltd 2002-10. National Union of Journalists: Member 1974-80, Father of Chapel 1977-79; Member, National Union of Public Employees/Unison 1980-.

Political career: Member for Stockton North since 6 May 2010 general election; PPS to Sadiq Khan as Shadow Lord Chancellor and Secretary of State for Justice 2011-. *Select committees:* Member: Work and Pensions 2010-11, Armed Forces Bill 2011, Education 2011-, LASPO Bill Committee 2012. Stockton North CLP: Press officer 1984-2010, Vice-chair, secretary 1985-95, Chair 1995-2000; Member, Co-operative Party 1986-. *Councils and public bodies:* Cleveland County Council: Councillor 1989-96, Vice-chair Education Committee 1990-96, Chair, Standing Advisory Council for Religious Education 1989-96; Councillor, Stockton Borough Council 1999-2010; Chair, Stockton Children's Trust; Board member, Arts Council England North East 2002-08; Board member and chair, North East Libraries and Archives Council (later MLA North East) 2003-09; Council member, Museums, Libraries and Archives Council 2008-09; Non-executive director, North Tees and Hartlepool NHS Trust.

Political interests: Children's services, education, health, leisure, culture, energy, carers, poverty; France, Palestine.

Other: Member, Socialist Education Association 1984-; Eastern Ravens Trust; Awayout; Daisychain. Patron, Stockton Rugby Club.

Recreations: Sport, reading, travel.

Alex Cunningham MP, House of Commons, London SW1A 0AA
Tel: 020 7219 7157 *Email:* alex.cunningham.mp@parliament.uk
Constituency: Stockton Business Centre, Brunswick Street, Stockton on Tees TS18 1DW
Tel: 01642 345291 *Fax:* 01642 345132 *Email:* robert.cook@parliament.uk
Website: www.alexcunninghammp.com *Twitter:* @ACunninghamMP

LABOUR

CUNNINGHAM, JAMES
Coventry South *(Majority 3,845)*

James Dolan Cunningham. Born 4 February 1941; Son of Adam and Elizabeth Cunningham; Married Marion Podmore 1985 (1 son 1 daughter 1 stepson 1 stepdaughter).

Education: Columba High School, Coatbridge; Tillycoultry College, Ruskin Courses (Labour movement, industrial law).

Non-political career: Engineer Rolls-Royce 1965-88. Shop steward, MSF 1968-88.

Political career: Member for Coventry South East 1992-97, for Coventry South 1997-2010, for Coventry South (revised boundary) since 6 May 2010 general election; PPS to Mike O'Brien: as Solicitor General 2005-07, as Minister of State: Department for Work and Pensions 2007-08, Department of Energy and Climate Change 2008-09, Department of Health 2009-10. *Select committees:* Member: Home Affairs 1993-97, Trade and Industry 1997-2001, Chairmen's Panel 1998-2001, Constitutional Affairs 2003-05, Office of the Deputy Prime Minister 2005, Procedure 2005-06, Standards and Privileges 2010. Chair PLP: Departmental Committee for the Treasury 1999-2010, West Midlands Regional Group 2005-10. Chair, Coventry South East CLP 1977-79. *Councils and public bodies:* Coventry City Council: Councillor 1972-92, Council Leader 1988-92.

Political interests: Economic policy, European Union, industrial relations, NHS; Eastern Europe, Russia, USA.

Recreations: Walking, reading, historical buildings.

James Cunningham MP, House of Commons, London SW1A 0AA
Tel: 020 7219 6362 *Fax:* 020 7219 4907 *Email:* eleanorm.connolly@parliament.uk
Constituency: Ground Floor, Rear of Queens House, 16 Queens Road, Coventry, Warwickshire CV1 3EG
Tel: 024 7655 3159 *Email:* gannond@parliament.uk *Website:* www.jimcunningham.org.uk

LABOUR

CUNNINGHAM, TONY

Workington *(Majority 4,575)*

Thomas Anthony Cunningham. Born 16 September 1952; Son of late Daniel Cunningham, docker, and Bessie Cunningham, née Lister; Married Anne Margaret Gilmore 1984 (1 daughter 1 son 1 stepdaughter 1 stepson).

Education: Workington Grammar School; Liverpool University (BA history and politics 1975); Didsbury College (PGCE 1976); TESL; Some Swahili.

Non-political career: Teacher: Alsager Comprehensive School 1976-80, Mikunguni Trade School, Zanzibar 1980-82, Netherhall School, Maryport 1983-94; Chief executive, Human Rights NGO 1999-2000. NUT: Member 1976-94, Local secretary 1985-94; AEEU 1993-.

Political career: Member for Workington 2001-10, for Workington (revised boundary) since 6 May 2010 general election; PPS to Elliot Morley as Minister of State, Department for Environment, Food and Rural Affairs 2003-05; Assistant Government Whip 2005-08; Government Whip 2008-10; Opposition Assistant Chief Whip 2010-11; Shadow Minister for International Development 2011-13. *Select committees:* Member: European Scrutiny 2001-04, Catering 2001-05, Selection 2006-12, Joint Committee on Security 2011. European Parliament: MEP for Cumbria and North Lancashire 1994-99. Contested North West region 1999 European Parliament election. *Councils and public bodies:* Allerdale Borough Council: Councillor 1987-94, Leader 1992-94.

Political interests: Third World, education, tourism, sport, small businesses; Sub-Saharan Africa.

Other: UN Office for Disaster Risk Reduction (UNISDR); Patron: Mines Advisory Group 1994-, Voluntary Services Overseas (VSO) 1994-; Macmillan Nurses. Kt 2012; Station Road Working Men's Club.

Recreations: Sport, running, reading, Workington RFC .

Sir Tony Cunningham MP, House of Commons, London SW1A 0AA
Tel: 020 7219 6905 *Fax:* 020 7219 1245 *Email:* cunninghamt@parliament.uk
Constituency: Moss Bay House, 40 Peart Road, Derwent Howe, Workington, Cumbria CA14 3YT
Tel: 01900 65815 *Fax:* 01900 68348 *Email:* smithjmt@parliament.uk
Website: www.tonycunningham.org.uk

LABOUR

CURRAN, MARGARET

Glasgow East *(Majority 11,840)*

Shadow Secretary of State for Scotland

Margaret Patricia Curran. Born 24 November 1958; Daughter of late James Curran, labourer, and late Rose Curran, cleaner; Married Robert Murray (2 sons).

Education: Our Lady and St Francis Secondary School, Glasgow; Glasgow University (MA history and economic history 1981); Dundee College (Postgraduate Certificate community education 1982).

Non-political career: Social work department, Strathclyde Regional Council: Welfare rights officer 1982-83, Community worker 1983-87, Senior community worker 1987-89; Lecturer in community education, Strathclyde University 1989-99. Member: Communication Workers' Union, Unite.

Political career: Contested Glasgow East by-election 24 July 2008. Member for Glasgow East since 6 May 2010 general election; Shadow Minister for Disabled People 2010-11; Shadow Secretary of State for Scotland 2011-. *Select committees:* Member: Work and Pensions 2010. Scottish Parliament: MSP for Glasgow Baillieston constituency 1999-2011: Convener, Social Inclusion, Housing and Voluntary Sector Committee 1999-2000; Scottish Labour: Deputy Whip 1999-2000; Deputy Minister for Social Justice 2000-02; Minister for: Social Justice 2002-03, Communities 2003-04, Parliamentary Business 2004-07; Shadow Cabinet Secretary: for Justice 2007, for Health and Wellbeing 2007-08, without Portfolio with special responsibility for Policy Development 2008-09. Former chair, Scottish Organisation of Labour Students; Election agent to Mohammad Sarwar 1997 general election; Member, Scottish Labour Women's Caucus.

Political interests: Social inclusion, community empowerment, women's issues, poverty, employment, pensions and welfare; Ireland, Scotland, USA.

Other: Member, Amnesty International; Women's Aid; Oxfam. Scottish Politician of the Year 2004, *The Herald*.

Publications: Book references in community education journals.

Recreations: Films, books, country music, theatre.

Margaret Curran MP, House of Commons, London SW1A 0AA
Tel: 020 7219 8102 *Fax:* 020 7219 6656 *Email:* margaret.curran.mp@parliament.uk
Constituency: Academy House, 1346 Shettleston Road, Glasgow G32 9AT
Tel: 0141-778 8993 *Email:* rachel.mcgee@parliament.uk *Website:* margaretcurran.org
Twitter: @Margaret_Curran

DAKIN, NIC

Scunthorpe *(Majority 2,549)*

Opposition Whip

LABOUR

Nicholas Dakin. Born 10 July 1955; Son of Royston and Elsie Dakin; Married Audrey (3 children).

Education: Stonehill High School, Leicestershire; Longslade Upper School, Leicestershire; Hull University (history 1976; MEd 1987); King's College, London (PGCE 1977); French, Swedish.

Non-political career: English teacher, Greatfield High School, Hull 1977-79; Teacher of English as a foreign language in Gävle, Sweden 1979-81; John Leggott College 1982-2010: Vice-principal 2004-07; Principal 2007-10. Member: National Union of Teachers, GMB.

Political career: Member for Scunthorpe since 6 May 2010 general election; Opposition Whip 2011-. *Select committees:* Member: Education 2010-11, Procedure 2011-. Vice-chair, PLP Departmental Group for DPM/Constitutional Affairs 2010-. *Councils and public bodies:* North Lincolnshire Council: Councillor, Chair, Education 1996-97, Council Leader 1997-2003, Leader, Labour Group 2003-07.

Political interests: Education, manufacturing, conservation, arts, economic policy, debt advice and support; Finland, Sweden.

Other: Yorkshire Forward: Board member 2003-07, Deputy chair 2004-06. Scunthorpe Squash Club.

Recreations: Scunthorpe United F.C, squash, walking, travel.

Nic Dakin MP, House of Commons, London SW1A 0AA
Tel: 020 7219 7139 *Email:* nic.dakin.mp@parliament.uk
Constituency: 18a Ethel Court, Scunthorpe, North Lincolnshire DN15 6RP
Tel: 01724 842000 *Email:* lorraine.yeadon@parliament.uk *Website:* www.nicdakin.com
Twitter: @NicDakinMP

DANCZUK, SIMON

Rochdale *(Majority 889)*

LABOUR

Simon Christopher Danczuk. Born 24 October 1966; Son of Kevin and Christine Danczuk; Married (2 children and 2 children from previous marriage).

Education: Gawthorpe Comprehensive School, Padiham; Lancaster University (BA Hons economics and sociology 1991).

Non-political career: Production worker, Main Gas, Padiham 1982-86; Labourer, ICI Factory, Darwen 1986-88; Barman, ICI Sports and Social Club, Darwen 1988-91; Research assistant, Sociology Department, Lancaster University 1991-93; Research officer, Bolton Bury Training and Enterprise Council 1993-95; Research consultant, Opinion Research Corporation International 1995-97; Research co-ordinator, Big Issue in the North Trust 1997-98; Media and public relations officer, Big Issue in the North 1998-99; Director, Vision Twentyone 1999-2011. Member: AEU 1982-86, GMB 1987-.

Political career: Member for Rochdale since 6 May 2010 general election; PPS to Chuka Umunna as Shadow Secretary of State for Business, Innovation and Skills 2011-. *Select committees:* Member: Communities and Local Government 2010-. Secretary, Rossendale and Darwen Labour Party 1991-93; Member, Regional Board, North West Labour Party 1993-2007; Chairman, Labour Friends of Palestine. *Councils and public bodies:* Councillor, Blackburn with Darwen Council 1993-2001.

Political interests: Social and economic regeneration, environment, housing, local government; Bangladesh, Kashmir, Pakistan, Palestine.

Other: Rochdale Labour Club; Wellfield Working Men's Club; Brickcroft Social Club. Milnrow Cricket Club; Rochdale Bowling Club; Rochdale Football Supporters Trust;.

Simon Danczuk MP, House of Commons, London SW1A 0AA
Tel: 020 7219 3000 *Email:* simon.danczuk.mp@parliament.uk
Constituency: 26 St Mary's Gate, Rochdale OL16 1DZ
Tel: 01706 750135 *Website:* www.simondanczuk.com *Twitter:* @simondanczuk

LABOUR

DARLING, ALISTAIR
Edinburgh South West *(Majority 8,447)*

Alistair Maclean Darling. Born 28 November 1953; Married Margaret McQueen Vaughan 1986 (1 son 1 daughter).

Education: Loretto School; Aberdeen University (LLB 1976).

Non-political career: Solicitor 1978-82; Advocate 1984-.

Political career: Member for Edinburgh Central 1987-2005, for Edinburgh South West since 5 May 2005 general election; Opposition Spokesperson for: Home Affairs 1988-92, Treasury, Economic Affairs and the City 1992-96; Sponsored Solicitors (Scotland) Act 1988 (Private Member's Bill); Shadow Chief Secretary to the Treasury 1996-97; Chief Secretary to the Treasury 1997-98; Secretary of State for: Social Security/Work and Pensions 1998-2002, Transport 2002-06, Scotland 2003-06, Trade and Industry 2006-07; Chancellor of the Exchequer 2007-10; Shadow Chancellor of the Exchequer 2010; Member, Labour Party's Economic Commission 1994-97; Chair, Better Together Campaign 2012-. *Councils and public bodies:* Lothian Regional Council: Councillor 1982-87, Chair, Lothian Region Transport Committee 1986-87.

Political interests: Transport, education, health, economic policy, constitution.

Other: Governor European Investment Bank 2007-10. Backbencher of the Year, *The Spectator* awards 2012. PC 1997.

Publications: Back from the Brink: 1,000 days at No. 11 (2011).

Rt Hon Alistair Darling MP, House of Commons, London SW1A 0AA
Tel: 020 7219 4584 *Email:* alistair.darling.mp@parliament.uk
Constituency: CBC House, 24 Canning Street, Edinburgh EH3 8EG
Tel: 0131-272 2727 *Website:* www.alistairdarlingmp.org.uk

LIBERAL DEMOCRAT

DAVEY, EDWARD
Kingston and Surbiton *(Majority 7,560)*

Secretary of State for Energy and Climate Change

Edward Jonathon Davey. Born 25 December 1965; Son of late John Davey, solicitor, and late Nina Davey, née Stanbrook, teacher; Married Emily Gasson 2005 (1 son).

Education: Nottingham High School; Jesus College, Oxford (BA philosophy, politics and economics 1988); Birkbeck College, London (MSc economics 1993).

Non-political career: Senior economics adviser to Liberal Democrat MPs 1989-93; Management consultant, Omega Partners 1993-97; Director, Omega Partners Postal 1996-97.

Political career: Member for Kingston and Surbiton 1997-2010, for Kingston and Surbiton (revised boundary) since 6 May 2010 general election; Liberal Democrat: London Whip 1997-2000; Spokesperson for: the Treasury (Public Spending and Taxation) 1997-99, Economy 1999-2001, London 2000-03; Shadow Chief Secretary to the Treasury 2001-02, Spokesperson for Office of the Deputy Prime Minister 2002-05; Shadow Secretary of State for: Education and Skills 2005-06, Trade and Industry 2006, Chief of Staff to Sir Menzies Campbell as Leader of the Liberal Democrats 2006-07; Shadow Secretary of State for Foreign and Commonwealth Affairs 2007-10; Parliamentary Under-Secretary of State (Minister for Employment Relations, Consumer and Postal Affairs), Department for Business, Innovation and Skills 2010-12; Secretary of State for Energy and Climate Change 2012-. *Select committees:* Member: Procedure 1997-2000, Treasury 1999-2001, Treasury (Treasury Sub-Committee) 1999-2001. Chair, Costing Group (costing all policies for manifesto) 1992 and 1997 general elections; Member, Federal Policy Committee 1994-95; Liberal Democrat Policy Group (Economics, Tax and Benefits and Transport); Member, Association of Liberal Democrat Councillors; Chair, Campaigns and Communications Committee 2006-09.

Political interests: Taxation, economics, internet, employment, environment, modernisation of Parliament; Latin America.

Other: Patron: Jigsaw, Kingston Special Needs Project; Goodwill Ambassador for Children of Peace; Trustee, Kidsout. Royal Humane Society Honourable Testimonial; Chief Constable, London Transport Police Commendation 1994; Royal Humane Society 1994; Double Act of the Year (with John Hayes MP), *The Spectator* awards 2012. PC 2012.

Publications: Making MPs Work for our Money: Reforming Budget Scrutiny (Centre for Reform), 2000.

Recreations: Music, walking, swimming.

Rt Hon Edward Davey MP, House of Commons, London SW1A 0AA
Tel: 020 7219 3512 *Fax:* 020 7219 0250 *Email:* daveye@parliament.uk
Constituency: Liberal Democrats, 21 Berrylands Road, Surbiton, Surrey KT5 8QX
Tel: 020 8288 0161 *Fax:* 020 8972 1088 *Email:* edward@edwarddavey.co.uk
Website: www.edwarddavey.co.uk *Twitter:* @eddaveykands

LABOUR

DAVID, WAYNE
Caerphilly *(Majority 10,755)*

Born 1 July 1957; Son of David Haydn David, teacher, and Edna David, née Jones, housewife; Married Catherine Thomas 1991 (divorced 2007).

Education: Cynffig Comprehensive School, Kenfig Hill, Mid Glamorgan; University College, Cardiff (BA history and Welsh history 1979; PGCE further education 1983); University College, Swansea (economic history research 1979-82).

Non-political career: History teacher, Brynteg Comprehensive School 1983-85; Tutor organiser, Workers' Educational Association South Wales District 1985-89; Policy adviser, youth policy, Wales Youth Agency 1999-2001. Member: MSF 1983-2004, AEEU 1998-2004, Amicus 2004-07, Unite 2007-.

Political career: Member for Caerphilly 2001-10, for Caerphilly (revised boundary) since 6 May 2010 general election; Team PPS, Ministry of Defence 2005; PPS to Adam Ingram as Minister of State, Ministry of Defence 2005-06; Assistant Government Whip 2007-08; Parliamentary Under-Secretary of State, Wales Office 2008-10; Shadow Minister for: Wales 2010, Europe 2010-11, Justice (Political and Constitutional Reform) 2011-13; PPS to Ed Miliband as Leader of the Opposition 2013-. *Select committees:* Member: European Scrutiny 2001-07, Standards and Privileges 2004-05, Joint Committee on Conventions 2006, Welsh Affairs 2007. Honorary Secretary PLP: Departmental Committee for Work and Pensions 2002-08, Welsh Regional Group 2003-07. European Parliament: MEP for South Wales 1989-94, for South Wales Central 1994-99: Vice-president, Socialist Group 1994-98, Leader, European Parliamentary Labour Party 1994-98; Contested Rhondda constituency 1999 National Assembly for Wales election. Ex-officio Member of Labour Party NEC 1994-98. *Councils and public bodies:* Cefn Cribwr Community Council: Councillor 1985-91, Chair 1986-87.

Political interests: European affairs, economy, education, devolution, constitution; Belgium, Bulgaria, Poland.

Other: Vice-president, Cardiff UN Association 1989-; President: Aber Valley Male Voice Choir 2001-, Council for Wales of Voluntary Youth Services 2002-, Caerphilly Local History Society 2006-. Fellow, Cardiff University 1995; Bargoed Labour Club.

Publications: Contributor: The Future of Europe, Problems and Issues for the 21st Century (1996); Remaining True (biography of Ness Edwards MP) (2006).

Recreations: Music, playing the oboe.

Wayne David MP, House of Commons, London SW1A 0AA
Tel: 020 7219 8152 *Fax:* 020 7219 1751 *Email:* wayne.david.mp@parliament.uk
Constituency: BTM Community Council Offices, Newport Road, Bedwas, Caerphilly, Mid Glamorgan CF83 8YB
Tel: 029 2088 1061 *Fax:* 029 2088 1954 *Email:* jonesli@parliament.uk
Website: www.waynedavid.labour.co.uk *Twitter:* @WayneDavidMP

LAB/CO-OP

DAVIDSON, IAN
Glasgow South West *(Majority 14,671)*

Ian Graham Davidson. Born 8 September 1950; Son of Graham Davidson and Elizabeth Crowe; Married Morag Christine Ann Mackinnon 1978 (1 son 1 daughter).

Education: Jedburgh Grammar School; Galashiels Academy; Edinburgh University (MA); Jordanhill College.

Non-political career: Sabbatical Chair National Association of Labour Students 1973-74; Researcher for Janey Buchan, MEP 1978-85; Project manager Community Service Volunteers 1985-92. Member, ASTMS/MSF/Amicus/Unite.

Political career: Member for Glasgow Govan 1992-97, for Glasgow Pollok 1997-2005, for Glasgow South West since 5 May 2005 general election. *Select committees:* Member: Selection 1997-99, Public Accounts 1997-2010; Scottish Affairs: Member 2005-10, Chair 2010-; Member: Liaison 2010-. Member, Labour Party Departmental Committees for: Defence 1997-, International Development 1997-, Trade and Industry 1997-. Member, Co-operative Party; Secretary: Tribune Group, Trade Union Group of Labour MPs 1998-2002; Chair, Co-operative Parliamentary Group 1998-99; Founder and Chair, Labour Against the Euro 2002-; Chair, Scottish Regional Group of Labour MPs 2003-04; Contested Scottish Labour deputy leadership election 2011. *Councils and public bodies:* Strathclyde Regional Council: Councillor 1978-92, Chair, Education Committee 1986-92.

Political interests: Local and regional government, international development, local economic development, defence, co-operative movement, trade and industry, trade unions, shipbuilding, Europe, poverty, Euro (against); Africa, Europe, Commonwealth, USA, Japan, British Overseas Territories.

Other: Club Captain, Commons and Lords RFC.
Recreations: Family, sport, distance running, swimming, rugby.
Ian Davidson MP, House of Commons, London SW1A 0AA
Tel: 020 7219 3610 *Fax:* 020 7219 2238 *Email:* iandavidsonmp@parliament.uk
Constituency: 3 Kilmuir Drive, Glasgow G46 8BW
Tel: 0141-621 2216 *Fax:* 0141-621 4217 *Website:* www.iandavidsonmp.com
Twitter: @IanDavidsonMP

DAVIES, DAVID
Monmouth *(Majority 10,425)*

David Thomas Charles Davies. Born 27 July 1970; Son of Peter and Kathleen Davies; Married 2003 (2 daughters 1 son).
Education: Bassaleg Comprehensive, Newport; HGV class one; German, Hungarian, Welsh.
Non-political career: Served as a gunner with 104 Air Defence Regiment, Territorial Army, Raglan Barracks, Newport. British Steel Corporation 1988-89; Youth hostel manager, USA; Casual work in Australia 1989-91; Manager, Burrow Heath Ltd (forwarder and tea importers) 1991-99; Special Constable, British Transport Police 2007-.

CONSERVATIVE

Political career: Contested Bridgend 1997 general election. Member for Monmouth since 5 May 2005 general election. *Select committees:* Welsh Affairs: Member 2005-10, Chair 2010-; Member: Home Affairs 2007-10, Home Affairs Sub-Committee 2008-09, Liaison 2010-, Liaison (National Policy Statements Sub-committee) 2010-. National Assembly for Wales: AM for Monmouth constituency 1999-2007: Deputy Leader/Business Secretary 1999; Chief Whip 1999-2001. Organiser for anti-Assembly 'No' Campaign 1997; Campaign manager for Rod Richards as leader of Welsh Conservative Party 1998.
Political interests: Home affairs, including prisons and sentencing, policing, Welsh affairs; China, Germany, Iran.
Other: Member, UK delegation, Parliamentary Assembly of the Council of Europe; Honorary member: Rotary Club of Usk and District, Institution of Royal Engineers; President, Welsh Amateur Boxing Association; Combat Stress; The Richard Hunt Foundation; Chepstow Mencap; Chepstow Conservative Club; Abergavenny Conservative Club; Usk Conservative Club; Monmouth Conservative Club. Torfaen Warriors Boxing Club; Chepstow Amateur Boxing Club.
Recreations: Surfing, history, languages, boxing.
David Davies MP, House of Commons, London SW1A 0AA
Tel: 020 7219 8360 *Email:* david.davies.mp@parliament.uk
Constituency: The Grange, 16 Maryport Street, Usk, Monmouthshire NP15 1AB
Tel: 01291 672817 *Fax:* 01291 672737 *Website:* www.david-daviesmp.co.uk
Twitter: @davidtcdavies

DAVIES, GERAINT
Swansea West *(Majority 504)*

Geraint Richard Davies. Born 3 May 1960; Son of David Davies, civil servant, and Betty Davies; Married Dr Vanessa Fry 1991 (3 daughters).
Education: Llanishen Comprehensive, Cardiff; JCR President, Jesus College, Oxford (BA philosophy, politics and economics 1982).
Non-political career: Sales and marketing trainee; Group product manager, Unilever 1982-88; Marketing manager, Colgate Palmolive Ltd 1988-89; Managing director, Pure Crete Ltd 1989-97; Chair, Flood Risk Management Wales, Environment Agency 2005-. Member, GMB.

LAB/CO-OP

Political career: Contested Croydon South 1987 and Croydon Central 1992 general elections. Member for Croydon Central 1997-2005. Contested Croydon Central 2005 general election. Member for Swansea West since 6 May 2010 general election; Team PPS, Department for Constitutional Affairs 2003-05; Introduced: Regulation of Childcare Providers Bill 2003, Physical Punishment of Children (prohibition) Bill 2003, Regulation of Hormone Disrupting Chemicals Bill 2004, School Meals and Nutrition Bill 2005, Credit Card Regulation (child pornography) Bill 2010. *Select committees:* Member: Public Accounts 1997-2003, Welsh Affairs 2010-, Standing Orders 2011-, Unopposed Bills (Panel) 2011-, European Scrutiny 2013-. Chair, PLP Departmental Committee for Environment, Transport and the Regions 1997-2004; Member, PLP Departmental Committees for: National Heritage/Culture, Media and Sport 1997-98, Trade and Industry 1997-2001, Treasury 1998-2001; Vice-chair, PLP Departmental: Committee for Transport 2004-05, Group for Justice 2010-. Chair, Labour Finance and Industry Group 1998-2005;

Member, Co-operative Party. *Councils and public bodies:* Councillor, Croydon Council 1986-97: Chair, Housing Committee 1994-96, Council Leader 1996-97; Governor, Dylan Thomas Community School.

Political interests: Treasury, trade and industry, housing, children's issues, transport, environment, human rights, equality; Crete, Wales.

Other: Parliamentary ambassador, NSPCC; Amnesty International; WWF (UK). Royal Humane Society Award for saving a man's life.

Recreations: Family, singing.

Geraint Davies MP, House of Commons, London SW1A 0AA
Tel: 020 7219 7166 *Email:* geraint.davies.mp@parliament.uk
Constituency: 31 High Street, Swansea SA1 1LG
Tel: 01792 475943 *Email:* info@geraintdavies.org *Website:* www.geraintdavies.org.uk
Twitter: @GeraintDaviesMP

DAVIES, GLYN
Montgomeryshire *(Majority 1,184)*

Edward Glyn Davies. Born 16 February 1944; Married (4 children).

Education: Llanfair Caerinian High School; University College of Wales, Aberyswyth (Diploma international law and relations 1995); Welsh.

Non-political career: Principal, T E Davies & Son (livestock farmers) 1976-. Member: National Farmers' Union, Farmers Union of Wales.

Political career: Contested Montgomeryshire 1997 general election. Member for Montgomeryshire since 6 May 2010 general election; PPS to Cheryl Gillan as Secretary of State for Wales 2010-12. *Select committees:* Member: Welsh Affairs 2010, 2012-. Contested Montgomeryshire constituency 1999 and 2003, and Mid and West Wales region 2007 National Assembly for Wales elections; AM for Mid and West Wales region 1999-2007: Conservative spokesperson for: Agriculture and the Rural Economy 1999, Finance 1999-2001, Culture, Media, Sport and the Welsh Language 2001-03, Local Government, Environment and Planning 2003-05, Finance, Rural Affairs, Environment and Planning/Finance 2005-06. *Councils and public bodies:* Montgomeryshire District Council: Councillor 1979-89, Chair 1985-89, Chair, Planning Committee 1982-87, Chair, Finance Committee 1987-89; Development Board for Rural Wales: Member 1986-, Chair 1989-94; Member: Welsh Development Agency 1989-94, Welsh Tourist Board 1989-94.

CONSERVATIVE

Political interests: Energy policy, Welsh affairs, social care.

Other: Member: RSPB, National Trust, Montgomeryshire Wildlife Trust, Wildfowl and Wetlands Trust, CLA; President, Campaign for the Protection of Rural Wales 2007-10; President, Montgomery Branch, Parkinsons Disease Society 2006-.

Recreations: Sport and fitness, countryside issues, family, house and garden.

Glyn Davies MP, House of Commons, London SW1A 0AA
Tel: 020 7219 7112 *Email:* glyn.davies.mp@parliament.uk
Constituency: 20 High Street, Welshpool, Powys SY21 7JP
Tel: 01938 552315/01938 554037 *Email:* pamela.williams@parliament.uk
Website: www.glyn-davies.co.uk *Twitter:* @GlynDaviesMP

DAVIES, PHILIP
Shipley *(Majority 9,944)*

Philip Andrew Davies. Born 5 January 1972; Son of Peter Davies and Marlyn Lifsey; Married Deborah Hemsley 1994 (separated) (2 sons).

Education: Old Swinford Hospital School, Stourbridge; Huddersfield University (BA historical and political studies 1993).

Non-political career: Asda Stores: Management training scheme 1995-97, Deputy customer services manager 1997, Customer relations manager 1997-98, Call centre manager 1998-99, Customer service project manager 2000-04, Senior marketing manager 2004-05.

CONSERVATIVE

Political career: Contested Colne Valley 2001 general election. Member for Shipley 2005-10, for Shipley (revised boundary) since 6 May 2010 general election. *Select committees:* Member: Culture, Media and Sport 2006-, Modernisation of the House 2007-10, Backbench Business 2010-12, Chairmen's Panel/Panel of Chairs 2010-, Joint Committee on Privacy and Injunctions 2011-12. Member, Executive, 1922 Committee 2006-12. Secretary, 92 Group.

Political interests: Law and order, Europe, education; USA.

Other: Readers' Representative of the Year, *The Spectator* awards 2011.

Recreations: Horseracing, cricket, football, rugby league.

Philip Davies MP, House of Commons, London SW1A 0AA
Tel: 020 7219 8264 *Fax:* 020 7219 8389 *Email:* daviesp@parliament.uk
Constituency: Shipley Conservatives Association, 76 Otley Road, Shipley,
West Yorkshire BD18 3SA
Tel: 01274 592248 *Email:* philipdavies@shipleyconservatives.fsnet.co.uk
Website: www.philip-davies.org.uk *Twitter:* @PhilipDaviesMP

CONSERVATIVE

DAVIS, DAVID
Haltemprice and Howden *(Majority 11,602)*

David Michael Davis. Born 23 December 1948; Son of late Ronald and Elizabeth Davis; Married
Doreen Cook 1973 (1 son 2 daughters).

Education: Bec Grammar School; Warwick University (BSc molecular science, computing science 1971); London Business School (MSc business studies 1973); Harvard Business School
(AMP 1985).

Non-political career: Joined Tate & Lyle 1974; Finance director, Manbré & Garton 1976-80;
Managing director, Tate & Lyle Transport 1980-82; President, Redpath-Labatt joint venture 1982-
84; Tate & Lyle 1984-87: Strategic planning director 1984-87, Non-executive director 1987-90.

Political career: Member for Boothferry 1987-97, for Haltemprice and Howden from 1997 to 18
June 2008 and 11 July 2008 by-election to 2010, for Haltemprice and Howden (revised boundary) since 6 May 2010 general election; PPS to Francis Maude as Financial Secretary to Treasury
1988-90; Assistant Government Whip 1990-93; Parliamentary Secretary, Office of Public Service and Science 1993-94; Minister of State, Foreign and Commonwealth Office 1994-97;
Shadow Deputy Prime Minister with responsibility for the Cabinet Office 2002-03; Shadow Secretary of State for Home, Constitutional and Legal Affairs 2003-04; Shadow Home Secretary
2003-08. *Select committees:* Chair: Public Accounts 1997-2001; Member: Liaison 1998-2001.
Contested Conservative Party leadership 2001; Party Chairman 2001-02; Member, Conservative
Policy Board 2001-03; Contested Conservative Party leadership 2005.

Political interests: Health, law and order, industry, agriculture.

Other: PC 1997.

Publications: How to Turn Round a Company (1988); The BBC Viewer's Guide to Parliament
(1989); Co-author, The Future of Conservatism: Values Revisited (Biteback, 2011).

Recreations: Mountaineering, flying light aircraft, writing.

Rt Hon David Davis MP, House of Commons, London SW1A 0AA
Tel: 020 7219 5900 *Fax:* 020 7219 4183 *Email:* david.davis.mp@parliament.uk
Constituency: Spaldington Court, Spaldington, Howden, East Yorkshire DN14 7NG
Tel: 01430 430365 *Website:* www.daviddavismp.com

CONSERVATIVE

DE BOIS, NICK
Enfield North *(Majority 1,692)*

Geoffrey Nicholas de Bois. Born 23 February 1959; Son of late WG Col John de Bois, DFM and
late Paula de Bois; Married Vanessa Coleman 1982 (divorced) (1 son 3 daughters); married
Helen Seaman 2009.

Education: Culford School, Bury St Edmunds; Cambridge College of Arts and Technology
(HND business studies 1981).

Non-political career: Public relations manager, Advertising Standards Authority 1982-84;
Rapier Design Group: Managing director 1984-2010, Chairman 1991-2010.

Political career: Contested Stalybridge and Hyde 1997 and Enfield North 2001 and 2005 general elections. Member for Enfield North since 6 May 2010 general election. *Select committees:*
Member: Public Administration 2010-11, Justice 2011-. Secretary, 1922 Committee 2012-. Member, Conservative Party 1992-; Deputy Chair, Huntington Conservative Association 1992-97.

Political interests: Crime and policing, small- and medium-sized enterprises, trade and exports,
healthcare, justice, home affairs; Asia, Pacific, USA.

Other: Alternate Member, UK Delegation, Organisation for Security and Co-operation in
Europe Parliamentary Assembly; Institute of Directors 1991-2004; Confederation of British
Industry 2002-04; Macmillan Cancer Support; NSPCC; Breakthrough Breast Cancer.

Recreations: Travel, Liverpool FC, keen rugby fan and gym enthusiast.

Nick de Bois MP, House of Commons, London SW1A 0AA
Tel: 020 7219 7066 *Email:* nick.debois.mp@parliament.uk
Constituency: 605 Hertford Road, Enfield, Middlesex EN3 6UP
Tel: 01992 678255 *Website:* www.nickdebois.com *Twitter:* @nickdebois

DENHAM, JOHN
Southampton Itchen *(Majority 192)*

John Yorke Denham. Born 15 July 1953; Son of Edward and Beryl Denham; Married Ruth Eleanore Dixon 1979 (divorced) (1 son 1 daughter); Partner Sue Littlemore (1 son).

Education: Woodroffe Comprehensive School, Lyme Regis; Southampton University (BSc chemistry 1974); President Student's Union 1976-77.

Non-political career: Advice worker, Energy Advice Agency, Durham 1977-78; Transport campaigner, Friends of the Earth 1978-79; Head of youth affairs, British Youth Council 1979-83; Campaigner, War on Want 1984-88; Consultant to various voluntary organisations 1988-92. Member, Amicus (MSF).

LABOUR

Political career: Contested Southampton Itchen 1983 and 1987 general elections. Member for Southampton Itchen 1992-2010, for Southampton Itchen (revised boundary) since 6 May 2010 general election; Opposition Spokesperson for Social Security 1995-97; Department of Social Security: Parliamentary Under-Secretary of State 1997-98, Minister of State 1998-99; Minister of State: Department of Health 1999-2001, Home Office 2001-03; Secretary of State for: Innovation, Universities and Skills 2007-09, Communities and Local Government 2009-10; Shadow Secretary of State for: Communities and Local Government 2010, Business, Innovation and Skills 2010-11; PPS to Ed Miliband as Leader of the Opposition 2011-13. *Select committees:* Chair: Home Affairs 2003-07; Member: Liaison 2003-07, Liaison (Liaison Sub-Committee) 2003-07. *Councils and public bodies:* Councillor, Hampshire County Council 1981-89; Southampton City Council: Councillor 1989-92, Chair, Housing Committee 1990-92; Vice-President, Local Government Association 2010-11.

Other: Fellow, Industry and Parliament Trust 1996. PC 2000.

Recreations: Cooking, walking, music, football, rugby, cricket.

Rt Hon John Denham MP, House of Commons, London SW1A 0AA
Tel: 020 7219 0067 *Email:* denhamj@parliament.uk
Constituency: 20-22 Southampton Street, Southampton, Hampshire SO15 2ED
Tel: 023 8033 9807 *Fax:* 023 8033 9907 *Email:* john@johndenham.org.uk
Website: www.johndenham.org.uk *Twitter:* @JohnDenhamMP

DE PIERO, GLORIA
Ashfield *(Majority 192)*

Shadow Minister for Women and Equalities

Born 21 December 1972; Married James Robinson 2012.

Education: Yorkshire Martyrs School, Bradford; Bradford and Ilkley College; Westminster University (BA social science 1996); London University (MSc social and political theory 2001).

Non-political career: *Jonathan Dimbleby,* ITV 1997-98; BBC: *On the Record* 1998-2002, *Politics Show* 2002-03; Political correspondent, GMTV 2003-10. Member: Unite, GMB.

LABOUR

Political career: Member for Ashfield since 6 May 2010 general election; Shadow Minister for: Culture 2010-11, Crime Prevention 2011-13, Women and Equalities 2013-.

Political interests: Mental health, crime, regeneration, anti-social behaviour.

Recreations: Swimming, karaoke.

Gloria De Piero MP, House of Commons, London SW1A 0AA
Tel: 020 7219 7004 *Email:* gloria.depiero.mp@parliament.uk
Constituency: 8 Station Street, Kirkby-in-Ashfield, Nottinghamshire NG17 7AR
Tel: 01623 720399 *Website:* www.gloria-de-piero.co.uk *Twitter:* @gloriadepieromp

DINENAGE, CAROLINE
Gosport *(Majority 14,413)*

Caroline Julia Dinenage. Born 28 October 1971; Daughter of Fred Dinenage, tv presenter; Married Carlos (2 sons).

Education: Wykeham House, Fareham; Oaklands RC Comprehensive, Waterlooville; University of Wales, Swansea (BA English and politics); French.

Non-political career: Member, Armed Forces Parliamentary Scheme. Director, Recognition Express.

CONSERVATIVE

Political career: Contested Portsmouth South 2005 general election. Member for Gosport since 6 May 2010 general election. *Select committees:* Member: Science and Technology 2012-13, Business, Innovation and Skills 2012-. *Councils and public bodies:* Councillor, Winchester District Council 1998-2003.

Political interests: Defence (particularly supporting service families), business and industry, sport; China, Falkland Islands, Gibraltar, Hong Kong, India.

Other: Member, NATO Parliamentary Assembly; Parliamentary ambassador, England Netball; Vice-President, RSPCA; Save the Children.

Recreations: Portsmouth F.C, netball, skiing.

Caroline Dinenage MP, House of Commons, London SW1A 0AA
Tel: 020 7219 7078/020 7219 0198 *Fax:* 020 7219 6874
Email: caroline.dinenage.mp@parliament.uk
Constituency: 167 Stoke Road, Gosport, Hampshire PO12 1SE
Tel: 023 9252 2121 *Fax:* 023 9252 0900 *Website:* www.caroline4gosport.co.uk
Twitter: @cj_dinenage

CONSERVATIVE

DJANOGLY, JONATHAN
Huntingdon *(Majority 10,819)*

Jonathan Simon Djanogly. Born 3 June 1965; Son of Sir Harry Djanogly, CBE and Carol Djanogly; Married Rebecca Silk 1991 (1 son 1 daughter).

Education: University College School, London; Oxford Polytechnic (BA law and politics 1987); Guildford College of Law (law finals 1988); ICAEW (corporate finance qualification).

Non-political career: Partner: SJ Berwin LLP Solicitors 1988-2009, Mail order retail business 1994-2002.

Political career: Contested Oxford East 1997 general election. Member for Huntingdon 2001-10, for Huntingdon (revised boundary) since 6 May 2010 general election; Shadow Minister for Home, Constitutional and Legal Affairs 2004-05; Shadow Solicitor General 2005-10; Shadow Minister for Trade and Industry/Business, Enterprise and Regulatory Reform/Business, Innovation and Skills 2005-10 (Corporate Governance 2006-09, Business 2009-10); Parliamentary Under-Secretary of State, Ministry of Justice 2010-12. *Select committees:* Member: Trade and Industry 2001-05, Joint Committee on Statutory Instruments 2001-02. Chair, Oxford Polytechnic Conservative Association 1986-87; Vice-chair, Westminster North Conservative Association 1993-94. *Councils and public bodies:* Westminster City Council: Councillor 1994-2001, Chair: Traffic Committee 1995-96, Contracts 1996-97, Social Services Committee 1998-99, Environment Committee 1999-2000.

Political interests: Small businesses, trade, environment, rural affairs, transport, planning.

Other: Chairman, Pembroke VCT plc 2013-.

Recreations: Sport, arts, theatre, reading histories and biographies, Britain's countryside and heritage.

Jonathan Djanogly MP, House of Commons, London SW1A 0AA
Tel: 020 7219 2367 *Fax:* 020 7219 0476 *Email:* jonathan.djanogly.mp@parliament.uk
Constituency: HCCA, 8 Stukeley Road, Huntingdon, Cambridgeshire PE29 6XG
Tel: 01480 437840 *Fax:* 01480 453012 *Email:* hollandn@parliament.uk
Website: www.jonathandjanogly.com *Twitter:* @JDjanogly

LAB/CO-OP

DOBBIN, JIM
Heywood and Middleton *(Majority 5,971)*

James Dobbin. Born 26 May 1941; Son of William Dobbin, miner, and Catherine Dobbin, née McCabe, mill worker; Married Pat Russell 1964 (2 sons 2 daughters).

Education: St Columba's RC High, Cowdenbeath; St Andrew's RC High, Kirkcaldy; Napier College, Edinburgh (BSc bacteriology, virology 1970).

Non-political career: Microbiologist, NHS 1966-94. Member, Unite.

Political career: Contested Bury North 1992 general election. Member for Heywood and Middleton 1997-2010, for Heywood and Middleton (revised boundary) since 6 May 2010 general election. *Select committees:* Member: European Scrutiny 1998-2013, Joint Committee on Consolidation, Etc, Bills 2001-, Communities and Local Government 2007-09, Chairmen's Panel/Panel of Chairs 2010-, Transport 2010-. Member PLP Departmental Committees for: Environment, Transport and the Regions 1997-2004, Health 1997-2004, Northern Ireland 1997-2004; Honorary Treasurer, North West Regional Group of Labour MPs 1999-2004. Chair, Rochdale District Labour Party 1980-81: Executive Member, Rochdale Constituency Labour Party 1986-87. *Councils and public bodies:* Rochdale Metropolitan Borough Council: Councillor 1983-92, 1994-97, Chairman of Housing 1986-90, Leader of Labour Group 1994-96, Council Leader 1996-97.

Political interests: Local and regional government, health, housing, transport, small businesses, life issues, involuntary tranquiliser addiction, child health/immunisation; Africa, America (North and South), Spain.

Other: Substitute member, Parliamentary Assembly of the Council of Europe 2010-13; Member, Parliamentary Assembly of the Council of Europe 2010-; Vice-chair of Public Health Subcommittee; Fellow, Industry and Parliament Trust 2001; Fellow, Institute of Medical Lab Sciences. Knight of St Gregory (Papal Order) 2008.

Recreations: Walking, football.

Jim Dobbin MP, House of Commons, London SW1A 0AA
Tel: 020 7219 4530 *Fax:* 020 7219 2696 *Email:* dobbinj@parliament.uk
Constituency: 45 York Street, Heywood, Lancashire OL10 4NN
Tel: 01706 361135 *Fax:* 01706 625703 *Email:* lambertc@parliament.uk
Twitter: @jimdobbinmp

DOBSON, FRANK
Holborn and St Pancras *(Majority 9,942)*

Frank Gordon Dobson. Born 15 March 1940; Son of late James Dobson, railwayman, and Irene Dobson; Married Dr Janet Alker 1967 (1 daughter 2 sons).

Education: Archbishop Holgate's Grammar School, York; London School of Economics (BSc (Econ) 1962).

Non-political career: Worked at HQ of: CEGB 1962-70, Electricity Council 1970-75; Assistant Secretary, Office of Local Ombudsman 1975-79. RMT.

LABOUR

Political career: Member for Holborn and St Pancras 1979-2010, for Holborn and St Pancras (revised boundary) since 6 May 2010 general election; Opposition Spokesperson for Education 1981-83; Shadow Health Minister 1983-87; Shadow Leader, House of Commons and Campaigns Co-ordinator 1987-89; Shadow Secretary of State for: Energy 1989-92, Employment 1992-93, Transport 1993-94; Shadow Minister for London 1993-97; Shadow Secretary of State for Environment 1994-97; Secretary of State for Health 1997-99. *Select committees:* Member: Administration 2005-08, 2010. Chair PLP Civil Liberties Committee 2006-. *Councils and public bodies:* Governor, Argyle Primary School 1966-; Camden Borough Council: Councillor 1971-76, Leader 1973-75; Chair, Coram's Field and the Harmsworth Memorial Playground 1978-; Member, Court, University of York 2001-; Governor, Royal Veterinary College 2002-; Member, London School of Hygiene and Tropical Medicine 2008-; Governor, Coram Foundation 2008-.

Political interests: Central London, transport, energy, redistribution of wealth, government reform; South Africa, Bangladesh, Canada.

Other: Chair, Network South Africa 2004; Trustee, Covent Garden Community Centre. Honorary Fellow: Birkbeck College, London University 2010; Royal College of Physicians 2010. PC 1997.

Recreations: Walking, theatre, watching cricket and football.

Rt Hon Frank Dobson MP, House of Commons, London SW1A 0AA
Tel: 020 7219 5840 *Fax:* 020 7219 6956 *Email:* patelm@parliament.uk
Constituency: No constituency office *Website:* www.frankdobson.co.uk

DOCHERTY, THOMAS
Dunfermline and West Fife *(Majority 5,470)*

Shadow Minister for Environment, Food and Rural Affairs

Born 28 January 1975; Married Katie McCulloch 2004.

Education: Studying at Open University (history degree).

Non-political career: Research assistant to Scott Barrie MSP 1999-2002; Public affairs officer, BNFL 2002-05; Network Rail 2006-07; Account director, communications consultancy 2007-10.

LABOUR

Political career: Contested Tayside North 2001 general election. Member for Dunfermline and West Fife since 6 May 2010 general election; PPS to Angela Eagle as Shadow Leader of the House of Commons 2011-13; Shadow Deputy Leader of the House of Commons 2013; Shadow Minister for Environment, Food and Rural Affairs 2013-. *Select committees:* Member: Environment, Food and Rural Affairs 2010-13, Administration 2010-, Defence 2010-, Procedure 2010-, Armed Forces Bill 2010-11, Arms Export Controls 2011, 2012-, Joint Committee on Parliamentary Privilege 2013. Contested South of Scotland region 2003 Scottish Parliament election. Chair, Dunfermline and West Fife Labour Party.

Recreations: Dunfermline Athletic F.C.

Thomas Docherty MP, House of Commons, London SW1A 0AA
Tel: 020 7219 3000 *Email:* thomas.docherty.mp@parliament.uk
Constituency: East End Park, Halbeath Road, Dunfermline, Fife KY12 7RB
Tel: 01383 626669 *Website:* www.thomasdocherty.org.uk *Twitter:* @Thomas_Docherty

DEMOCRATIC UNIONIST PARTY

DODDS, NIGEL
Belfast North *(Majority 2,224)*

DUP Parliamentary Group Leader; Spokesperson for Constitutional Issues, for Foreign Affairs and for Culture, Olympics, Media and Sport

Nigel Alexander Dodds. Born 20 August 1958; Son of late Joseph Dodds, civil servant, and Doreen Dodds, née McMahon; Married Diane Harris (later MLA as Diane Dodds, now MEP) 1985 (2 sons 1 daughter).

Education: Portora Royal School, Enniskillen; St John's College, Cambridge (BA law 1980); Queen's University, Belfast Institute of Professional Legal Studies (Cert PLS 1981); French.

Non-political career: Barrister 1981-83; European Parliament Secretariat (non-attached members) 1984-96; Member of Senate, Queen's University, Belfast 1985-93.

Political career: Contested East Antrim 1992 general election. Member for Belfast North 2001-10, for Belfast North (revised boundary) since 6 May 2010 general election; DUP Chief Whip 2001-08; DUP Spokesperson for: Treasury 2005-07, Work and Pensions 2005-07, Business of the House 2005-10, Justice 2007-10, Business, Enterprise and Regulatory Reform 2007-10; DUP Parliamentary Group Leader 2010-; Spokesperson for: Reform and Constitutional Agenda/Constitutional Issues 2010-, Foreign Affairs 2010-, Culture, Olympics, Media and Sport 2012-. *Select committees:* Member: Members' Allowances 2009-10, Joint Committee on Statutory Instruments and Commons Committee on Statutory Instruments 2009-10. Member Northern Ireland Forum for Political Dialogue 1996-98; MLA for Belfast North 1998-2010: Minister of: Social Development 1999-2000, 2001-02, Enterprise, Trade and Investment 2007-08, Finance and Personnel 2008-09. DUP: Secretary 1992-2008, Deputy Leader 2008-. *Councils and public bodies:* Belfast City Council: Councillor 1985-2010, Lord Mayor of Belfast 1988-89, 1991-92, Vice-President, Association of Local Authorities of Northern Ireland 1989-90.

Political interests: European affairs, constitution, social policy; The Commonwealth, USA.

Other: Member, Executive Committee, Inter-Parliamentary Union, British Group. OBE 1997; PC 2010.

Rt Hon Nigel Dodds OBE MP, House of Commons, London SW1A 0AA
Tel: 020 7219 8419 *Fax:* 020 7219 2347 *Email:* doddsn@parliament.uk
Constituency: 39 Shore Road, Belfast BT15 3PG
Tel: 028 9077 4774 *Fax:* 028 9077 7685 *Email:* ndodds@dup-belfast.co.uk
Website: www.nigeldodds.co.uk *Twitter:* @NigelDoddsMP

SINN FÉIN

DOHERTY, PAT
West Tyrone *(Majority 10,685)*

Patrick Doherty. Born 18 July 1945; Married (2 sons 3 daughters).
Education: St Joseph's College, Lochwinnoch.
Non-political career: Site engineer 1975.

Political career: Contested West Tyrone 1997 general election. Member for West Tyrone since 7 June 2001 general election; Contested Donegal North East 1989 Dáil general election, 1996 by-election and 1997 general election, Connaught/Ulster 1989 and 1994 European Parliament elections. MLA for West Tyrone 1998-2012: Chair, Assembly Committee on Enterprise, Trade and Investment 1999-2002, Sinn Féin Spokesperson for Agriculture, Member, Assembly Commission 2009-11, Sinn Féin Spokesperson for Regional Development 2011-12, Deputy chair, Assembly Committee on Regional Development 2011-12, Assembly Private Secretary to Michelle O'Neill as Minister of Agriculture and Rural Development 2011-12. Sinn Féin: Activist 1970-84, Elections director 1984-85, National organiser 1985-88, Vice-president 1988-2009, Leader, delegation to Dublin Forum for Peace and Reconciliation 1994-96, Member, Castle Buildings talks team 1997-98; Member, Oireachtas Good Friday Agreement Implementation Committee.

Political interests: Irish national self-determination; Ireland, Scotland.

Other: Founder member, Local Credit Union 1992.

Recreations: Walking, reading, building stone walls.

Pat Doherty MP, House of Commons, London SW1A 0AA
Tel: 020 7219 8159 *Email:* dohertyp@parliament.uk
Constituency: 1a Melvin Road, Strabane, Co Tyrone BT82 9AE
Tel: 028 7188 6464 *Fax:* 028 7188 0120 *Email:* patsf.doherty@gmail.com
Website: www.westtyronesinnfein.com
4 James Street, Omagh, Co Tyrone BT78 1DH
Tel: 028 8225 3040

**DEMOCRATIC
UNIONIST PARTY**

DONALDSON, JEFFREY

Lagan Valley *(Majority 10,486)*

DUP Spokesperson for Defence and for Energy and Climate Change

Jeffrey Mark Donaldson. Born 7 December 1962; Son of James and Sarah Anne Donaldson; Married Eleanor Cousins 1987 (2 daughters).

Education: Kilkeel High School; Castlereagh College (Diploma electrical engineering 1982); French.

Non-political career: Ulster Defence Regiment 1980-85. Agent to Enoch Powell MP 1983-84; Personal assistant to Sir James Molyneaux MP 1984-85; Partner, financial services and estate agency business 1986-96. Former member, AEEU.

Political career: Member for Lagan Valley 1997-2010, for Lagan Valley (revised boundary) since 6 May 2010 general election (UUP May 1997 to January 2004, DUP since January 2004); Ulster Unionist Spokesperson for: Trade and Industry 1997-2000, Environment, Transport and the Regions 2000-01, Treasury 2001-02, Transport, Local Government and the Regions 2001-02, Work and Pensions 2001-03, Defence 2002-03, Trade and Industry 2002-03; DUP Spokesperson for: Education 2004-05, Defence 2004-05, 2007-, Transport 2005-07, 2009-10, International Development 2005-07, Home Office 2007-10, Equality 2010-12, Energy and Climate Change 2010-. *Select committees:* Member: Northern Ireland Affairs 1997-2000, Environment, Transport and Regional Affairs 2000-01, Environment, Transport and Regional Affairs (Transport Sub-Committee) 2000-01, Regulatory Reform 2001-05, Joint Committee on Statutory Instruments 2001-06, Transport 2004-07, 2009-10, Defence 2010-, Arms Export Controls 2011-12, 2013-. Member: Northern Ireland Assembly (UUP) 1985-86, Northern Ireland Forum 1996-98; MLA for Lagan Valley 2003-10 (UUP November 2003 to 15 January 2004, DUP 15 January 2004 to 2010): Junior Minister, Office of the First Minister and Deputy First Minister 2008-09; Member, Northern Ireland Assembly Committees on: Education 2007-08, Chairpersons' Liaison Group 2007-08; Chair, Northern Ireland Assembly Committee on Assembly and Executive Review 2007-08; Member, Northern Ireland Assembly Committees on: Public Accounts 2009-10, Justice 2010. Ulster Unionist Council: Honorary Secretary 1988-2000, Vice-president 2000-03; Resigned from UUP 15 January 2004. Party officer, Democratic Unionist Party 2004-. *Councils and public bodies:* Alderman, Lisburn City Council 2005-10; Member, Northern Ireland Policing Board 2007-08.

Political interests: Christian values, constitution, transport, defence, international development; Cyprus, Ethiopia, Israel, Moldova, Northern Ireland, South Africa, USA.

Other: Member: Presbyterian Church, Loyal Orange Order, Constitutional Monarchy Association, Regimental Association of the Ulster Defence Regiment; Trustee, Royal Ulster Rifles Association; Chairman, Causeway Institute for Peace-building and Conflict Resolution; Care and Tear Fund. PC 2007.

Recreations: Hill-walking, reading, local history, church.

Rt Hon Jeffrey Donaldson MP, House of Commons, London SW1A 0AA
Tel: 020 7219 3407 *Fax:* 020 7219 2347 *Email:* jeffrey.donaldson.mp@parliament.uk
Constituency: The Old Town Hall, 29 Castle Street, Lisburn, Co Antrim BT27 4DH
Tel: 028 9266 8001 *Fax:* 028 9267 1845 *Email:* jeffreydonaldsonmp@laganvalley.net
Website: www.jeffreydonaldsonmp.org *Twitter:* @J_Donaldson_MP

LABOUR

DONOHOE, BRIAN

Central Ayrshire *(Majority 12,007)*

Brian Harold Donohoe. Born 10 September 1948; Son of late George and Catherine Donohoe; Married Christine Pawson 1973 (2 sons).

Education: Irvine Royal Academy; Kilmarnock Technical College (National Certificate engineering 1972).

Non-political career: Apprentice engineer, Ailsa Shipyard 1965-70; Draughtsman/engineer, Hunterston Nuclear Power Station 1970-77; Draughtsman, ICI Organics Division 1977-81; District officer, NALGO 1981-92. Convenor, Political and Education Committee, TASS 1969-81; Secretary, Irvine Trades Council 1973-82; District officer, NALGO 1981-92; Member, TGWU Parliamentary Campaigning Group 1992-; Member, Unite Parliamentary Campaigning Group 2010.

Political career: Member for Cunninghame South 1992-2005, for Central Ayrshire since 5 May 2005 general election; PPS to Lord Adonis at Department for Transport 2008-10: as Minister of State 2008-09, as Secretary of State 2009-10. *Select committees:* Member: Environment, Transport and Regional Affairs 1997-2001, Environment, Transport and Regional Affairs (Environment Sub-Committee) 1997-2001, Environment, Transport and Regional Affairs (Transport Sub-

Committee) 1997-2001, Transport, Local Government and the Regions 2001-02, Transport, Local Government and the Regions (Transport Sub-Committee) 2001-02, Transport 2002-05, Administration 2005-10. Chair: Scottish Group of Labour MPs 1997-98, PLP Departmental Group for Transport 2004-. Treasurer, Cunninghame South Constituency Labour Party 1983-91. *Councils and public bodies:* Chair: Cunninghame Industrial Development Committee 1975-85, North Ayrshire and Arran Local Health Council 1977-79.

Political interests: Health, local and regional government, transport, small businesses; Indonesia, Malaysia, Singapore, Taiwan, USA.

Other: Industry and Parliament Trust: Fellow 1995, 2001, Trustee 2010-; Thrive: Board member 2003-, Vice-chair 2010-.

Recreations: Gardening.

Brian Donohoe MP, House of Commons, London SW1A 0AA
Tel: 020 7219 6230 *Fax:* 020 7219 5388 *Email:* brian.donohoe.mp@parliament.uk
Constituency: 17 Townhead, Irvine, Ayrshire KA12 0BL
Tel: 01294 276844 *Fax:* 01294 313463 *Email:* brownrm@parliament.uk
Website: www.briandonohoemp.co.uk

DORAN, FRANK
Aberdeen North *(Majority 8,361)*

Born 13 April 1949; Son of Francis Doran and Betty Hedges Doran; Married Patricia Govan 1967 (divorced) (2 sons); married Joan Ruddock MP 2010.

Education: Ainslie Park Secondary School; Leith Academy; Dundee University (LLB 1975).

Non-political career: Solicitor 1977-88. Member, GMB 1983-.

Political career: Member for Aberdeen South 1987-92. Contested Aberdeen South 1992 general election. Member for Aberdeen Central 1997-2005, for Aberdeen North since 5 May 2005 general election; Opposition Spokesperson for Energy 1988-92; PPS to Ian McCartney as Minister of State: Department of Trade and Industry 1997-99, Cabinet Office 1999-2001; Member House of Commons Commission 2010-. *Select committees:* Member: Culture, Media and Sport 2001-05, Finance and Services 2005-10; Chair: Administration 2005-10; Member: Liaison 2005-10; Chair: Works of Art 2011-. Contested North East Scotland 1984 European Parliament election. Secretary: GMB Westminster Parliamentary Group 2001-, Trade Union Group of Labour MPs 2001-.

LABOUR

Political interests: Energy, childcare, families, mental health, employment.

Other: Founder member, Scottish Legal Action Group 1974; Chair, Dundee Association for Mental Health 1979-82; Fellow, Industry and Parliament Trust 1990; Aberdeen Trades Council.

Recreations: Cinema, art, football, sport.

Frank Doran MP, House of Commons, London SW1A 0AA
Tel: 020 7219 3481 *Fax:* 020 7219 0682 *Email:* doranf@parliament.uk
Constituency: 69 Dee Street, Aberdeen AB11 6EE
Tel: 01224 252715 *Fax:* 01224 252716 *Email:* dilloni@parliament.uk
Website: www.frankdoran.org.uk

DORRELL, STEPHEN
Charnwood *(Majority 15,029)*

Stephen James Dorrell. Born 25 March 1952; Son of late Philip Dorrell, company director; Married Penelope Anne Taylor 1980 (3 sons 1 daughter).

Education: Uppingham School, Rutland; Brasenose College, Oxford (BA law 1973); German, French.

Non-political career: Director, family business 1975-87, 1997-.

Political career: Contested Kingston-upon-Hull East October 1974 general election. Member for Loughborough 1979-97, for Charnwood 1997-2010, for Charnwood (revised boundary) since 6 May 2010 general election; PPS to Peter Walker as Secretary of State for Energy 1983-87; Assistant Government Whip 1987-88; Government Whip 1988-90; Parliamentary Under-Secretary of State, Department of Health 1990-92; Financial Secretary, HM Treasury 1992-94; Secretary of State for: National Heritage 1994-95, Health 1995-97; Member Shadow Cabinet 1997-98: Shadow Secretary of State for Education and Employment 1997-98. *Select committees:* Honorary Member: Public Accounts 1992-94, Member: Joint Committee on Consolidation, Etc, Bills 2005-; Chair: Health 2010-; Member: Liaison 2010-. Chair, Conservative Party Committee for Education and Employment 1997-98. Patron, Tory Reform Group. *Councils and public bodies:* Chairman, Millennium Commission 1994-95.

CONSERVATIVE

Political interests: Health, economics, education.
Other: PC 1994.
Recreations: Reading, walking.
Rt Hon Stephen Dorrell MP, House of Commons, London SW1A 0AA
Tel: 020 7219 4472 *Fax:* 020 7219 5838 *Email:* stephen.dorrell.mp@parliament.uk
Constituency: 768 Melton Road, Thurmaston, Leicester LE4 8BD
Tel: 0116-260 8700 *Email:* info@stephendorrell.org.uk *Website:* www.stephendorrell.org.uk

DORRIES, NADINE
Mid Bedfordshire *(Majority 15,152)*

Nadine Vanessa Dorries. Born 21 May 1957; Daughter of Sylvia and George Bargery; Married
Paul Dorries 1984 (divorced) (3 daughters).
Education: Halewood Grange Comprehensive, Liverpool; Warrington District School of Nursing.
Non-political career: Former nurse; Businesswoman; Director, BUPA; Adviser to Oliver
Letwin MP 2002-05.
Political career: Contested Hazel Grove 2001 general election (as Nadine Bargery). Member
for Mid Bedfordshire 2005-10, for Mid Bedfordshire (revised boundary) since 6 May 2010 gen-
CONSERVATIVE eral election. *Select committees:* Member: Education and Skills 2005-06, Science and Technol-
ogy 2007, Innovation, Universities[, Science] and Skills/Science and Technology 2007-10,
Energy and Climate Change 2009-10, Health 2010-11, Chairmen's Panel/Panel of Chairs 2010-.
Conservative Whip suspended November 2012-May 2013.
Political interests: Law and order, social structure, health, rural affairs; Angola, Zambia.
Recreations: Family, friends, walking, reading, dogs.
Nadine Dorries MP, House of Commons, London SW1A 0AA
Tel: 020 7219 5928 *Fax:* 020 7219 6428 *Email:* dorriesn@parliament.uk
Constituency: No constituency office publicised *Website:* www.dorries.org
Twitter: @NadineDorriesMP

DOUGHTY, STEPHEN
Cardiff South and Penarth *(Majority 5,334)*

Opposition Whip

Stephen John Doughty. Born 15 April 1980; Single.
Education: Llantwit Major Comprehensive School, Vale of Glamorgan; Lester B Pearson
United World College, Victoria, Canada; Corpus Christi College, Oxford (BA); St Andrews Uni-
versity (MLitt); French, Welsh (basic).
Non-political career: Policy and campaigns adviser, World Vision 2004-06; Head of UK and
EU government relations, Oxfam 2006-09; Head of health and education campaign, Oxfam
LAB/CO-OP International 2010-11; Head, Oxfam Cymru 2011-12; Special adviser to Douglas Alexander as
Secretary of State for International Development 2009-10. Member: GMB, Unison.
Political career: Member for Cardiff South and Penarth since 15 November 2012 by-election;
PPS to Rachel Reeves as Shadow Chief Secretary to the Treasury 2013-; Opposition Whip 2013-.
Select committees: Member: Welsh Affairs 2012-. Member: Labour Party, Co-operative Party.
Political interests: Economy and finance, foreign affairs, defence, international development,
energy and climate change; Afghanistan, Africa, Bangladesh, Canada, EU, India, Israel, Paki-
stan, Palestine, Somalia/Somaliland, USA, Yemen.
Other: Christian Socialist Movement; Progress; Fabian Society.
Recreations: Cardiff City FC, Welsh rugby union, singing, surfing, sailing, walking.
Stephen Doughty MP, House of Commons, London SW1A 0AA
Tel: 020 7219 5348 *Email:* stephen.doughty.mp@parliament.uk
Constituency: Ground Floor, Mount Stuart House, Mount Stuart Square, Cardiff Bay CF10 5FQ
Tel: 029 2054 2072 *Website:* www.stephendoughty.org.uk *Twitter:* @SDoughtyMP

LABOUR

DOWD, JIM
Lewisham West and Penge *(Majority 5,828)*

James Patrick Dowd. Born 5 March 1951; Son of late James and Elfriede Dowd; Single.
Education: Sedgehill Comprehensive School, London; London Nautical School.
Non-political career: Apprentice telephone engineer, GPO (now BT) 1967-72; Station manager, Heron Petrol Stations Ltd. 1972-73; Telecommunications engineer, Plessey Company 1973-92. Member: POEU 1967-72, MSF/Unite 1973-2010, GMB 1990-.
Political career: Contested Beckenham 1983 and Lewisham West 1987 general elections. Member for Lewisham West 1992-2010, for Lewisham West and Penge since 6 May 2010 general election; Opposition Whip for London 1993-95; Opposition Spokesperson for Northern Ireland 1995-97; Government Whip 1997-2001. *Select committees:* Member: Health 2001-10, Science and Technology 2012-. *Councils and public bodies:* London Borough of Lewisham: Councillor 1974-94, Deputy Leader 1984-86, Mayor 1992; Member, Lewisham and North Southwark District Health Authority.
Political interests: NHS, transport, economic policy, industrial policy, environment, housing, animal welfare, human rights, education; Italy, Taiwan, UAE.
Other: Member, several animal welfare organisations; Fellow, Industry and Parliament Trust 1996; Bromley Labour Club.
Recreations: Music, reading, theatre, Cornwall.
Jim Dowd MP, House of Commons, London SW1A 0AA
Tel: 020 7219 4617 *Fax:* 020 7219 2686 *Email:* dowdj@parliament.uk
Constituency: 43 Sunderland Road, Forest Hill, London SE23 2PS
Tel: 020 8699 2001 *Fax:* 020 8699 2001 *Website:* www.jimdowd.org.uk

LAB/CO-OP

DOYLE, GEMMA
West Dunbartonshire *(Majority 17,408)*

Shadow Minister for Defence

Born 1981; Daughter of Edward Doyle, retired telecommunications engineer, and Maria Doyle, primary teacher; Married 2012.
Education: Our Lady and St Patrick's High, Dumbarton; Glasgow University (MA European civilisation 2006).
Non-political career: Caseworker and parliamentary assistant to numerous MSPs 2001-06; Conference development manager 2006-07; Conference producer, Institute of Mechanical Engineers 2007-08; Political officer, Parliamentary Labour Party 2008-10. Member, Unite.
Political career: Member for West Dunbartonshire since 6 May 2010 general election; Shadow Minister for Defence 2010-. *Select committees:* Member: Energy and Climate Change 2010, Administration 2010, Armed Forces Bill 2011. Chair, PLP Departmental Group for Defence 2010. Member, Co-operative Party.
Political interests: Employment, energy, defence, regeneration; Bosnia, Croatia, Eastern Europe, Montenegro.
Gemma Doyle MP, House of Commons, London SW1A 0AA
Tel: 020 7219 3000 *Email:* gemma.doyle.mp@parliament.uk
Constituency: 11 Castle Street, Dumbarton G82 1QS
Tel: 01389 734214 *Fax:* 01389 761498 *Email:* info@gemmadoyle.org.uk
Unit B13, Whitecrook Business Centre, Whitecrook Street, Clydebank G81 1QF
Tel: 0141-952 3177 *Fax:* 0141-952 5872 *Website:* www.gemmadoyle.org.uk
Twitter: @GemmaWDMP

CONSERVATIVE

DOYLE-PRICE, JACKIE
Thurrock *(Majority 92)*

Jacqueline Doyle-Price. Born 5 August 1969; Daughter of Brian and Kathleen Doyle-Price; Single.
Education: Notre Dame RC, Sheffield; Durham University (BA economics and politics 1991).
Non-political career: Administrative officer, South Yorkshire Police 1992; Parliamentary officer, City of London Corporation 1993-2000; Assistant private secretary to Rt Hon the Lord Mayor of the City of London 2000-05; Associate, Financial Services Authority 2005.
Political career: Contested Sheffield Hillsborough 2005 general election. Member for Thurrock since 6 May 2010 general election. *Select committees:* Member: Public Accounts 2010-. Treasurer, National Association of Conservative Graduates 1994-97; Chair, Lewisham Deptford Constituency Association 1997-98; Constituency officer, Greenwich and Woolwich Conservatives 2006-07.

Political interests: Welfare, foreign affairs, vocational education, financial services, transport; Bosnia and Herzegovina, Croatia, Serbia.

Other: Freeman, City of London; Grays Conservative; RAFA Grays.

Recreations: Theatre, reading, film, watching soaps.

Jackie Doyle-Price MP, House of Commons, London SW1A 0AA
Tel: 020 7219 7171 *Fax:* 020 7219 4924 *Email:* jackie.doyleprice.mp@parliament.uk
Constituency: 2 Orsett Business Centre, Stanford Road, Grays, Essex RM16 3BX
Tel: 01375 802029 *Website:* www.jackiedoyleprice.com *Twitter:* @JackieDP

DRAX, RICHARD
South Dorset *(Majority 7,443)*

Richard Grosvenor Plunkett-Ernle-Erle Drax. Born 29 January 1958; Divorced Zara (2 daughters 2 sons); married Elsebet.

Education: Harrow School; Royal Agricultural College, Cirencester (Diploma of Membership rural land management 1990); Westminster Press (Diploma journalism 1995).

Non-political career: Officer, Coldstream Guards 1978-87. Journalist: *Yorkshire Evening Press* 1991-96, *TyneTees, Calendar, Daily Telegraph* 1996-97; Journalist/Reporter, *BBC South Today*, *BBC Solent* 1997-2006.

CONSERVATIVE

Political career: Member for South Dorset since 6 May 2010 general election. *Select committees:* Member: Environment, Food and Rural Affairs 2010-.

Political interests: Defence.

Other: Patron, Cherry Tree Nursery 2006.

Recreations: Sailing, golf, skiing.

Richard Drax MP, House of Commons, London SW1A 0AA
Tel: 020 7219 7051 *Email:* richard.drax.mp@parliament.uk
Constituency: SDCA, Chesil House, Dorset Green Technology Park, Winfrith Newburgh, Dorchester DT2 8ZB
Tel: 01305 851900 *Fax:* 01308 851900
Website: www.southdorsetconservatives.com richarddrax.com

DROMEY, JACK
Birmingham, Erdington *(Majority 3,277)*

Shadow Minister for Home Office

Born 29 September 1948; Married Harriet Harman (now MP) 1982 (2 sons 1 daughter).

Education: Cardinal Vaughan Grammar School; French.

Non-political career: Chair for 15 years, Joint Industrial Council, Ministry of Defence. Secretary: South East Regional Council, TUC, Brent Trades Council 1976-78; Transport and General Workers' Union 1978-2003: Has served at all levels of the union from district officer to national organiser, Deputy general secretary 2003-08; Deputy general secretary, Unite 2008-.

LABOUR

Political career: Member for Birmingham, Erdington since 6 May 2010 general election; Shadow Minister for: Communities and Local Government 2010-13, Home Office 2013-. *Select committees:* Member: Business, Innovation and Skills 2010-11, Regulatory Reform 2010-. Chair, PLP Departmental Group for Business, Innovation and Skills 2010. Treasurer, Labour Party 2004-10. *Councils and public bodies:* Founder member, Greater London Enterprise Board.

Political interests: Workers' rights (including equalities and the Vulnerable Workers' Agenda), manufacturing, housing, transport, international development (including supply chain ethical trading).

Other: Global Organising Alliance; Former executive council member and chair, National Council for Civil Liberties.

Recreations: Music, gym, walking, family.

Jack Dromey MP, House of Commons, London SW1A 0AA
Tel: 020 7219 0903 *Fax:* 020 7219 0477 *Email:* jack.dromey.mp@parliament.uk
Constituency: 77 Mason Road, Birmingham B24 9EH
Tel: 0121-350 6077 *Website:* www.jackdromey.org *Twitter:* @JackDromeyMP

CONSERVATIVE

DUDDRIDGE, JAMES
Rochford and Southend East *(Majority 11,050)*

James Philip Duddridge. Born 26 August 1971; Son of Philip and Jenny Duddridge; Married Kathryn (Katy) Thompson 2004 (2 sons 1 daughter).

Education: Crestwood School, Eastleigh, Hampshire; Huddersfield New College; Wells Blue School; Essex University (BA government 1993).

Non-political career: Research assistant to Bernard Jenkin MP 1991-93; Retail and merchant banking, Barclays Bank 1993-2002: Barclays Bank of Swaziland 1995-96, Barclays Bank Head Office 1996, Sales director, Banque Belgolaise, Ivory Coast 1997-98, National sales manager, Barclays 1998-2001; Service delivery director, Barclays Bank Botswana 2001-02; Account director and consultant, YouGov 2000-05; Director, Okavango Ltd 2002-05.

Political career: Contested Rother Valley 2001 general election. Member for Rochford and Southend East 2005-10, for Rochford and Southend East (revised boundary) since 6 May 2010 general election; Opposition Whip 2008-10; Government Whip 2010-12. *Select committees:* Member: Environment, Food and Rural Affairs 2005-07, International Development 2006-08, Strategic Export Controls (Quadripartite Committee)/Arms Export Controls 2007-08; Chair: Regulatory Reform 2012-; Member: Liaison 2013-, Joint Committee on Draft Deregulation Bill 2013-. Chair, Wells Young Conservatives 1989-91; Campaigns department, Conservative Central Office 1989-91; Chair, Essex University Conservative Students 1990-91; General election campaign manager to Stephen Shakespeare, Colchester 1997; Adviser, Lady Miller Postal Services Bill 1999; Executive committee member, Conservative Way Forward 2000-01.

Political interests: African politics, pensions; Botswana, Ivory Coast, South Africa, Swaziland, Zimbabwe.

Other: Member: Executive committee, British Group Inter-Parliamentary Union 2005-06, Commonwealth Parliamentary Association; Student representative, Huddersfield Police Forum 1987-88; Member, Bow Group 1999-; Speaker, Westminster Foundation for Democracy 2003-04; Member, Chartered Institute of Bankers 1993-2002; Associate member, Market Research Society 2003-05.

Recreations: Running, cycling, Southampton FC, Southend United FC.

James Duddridge MP, House of Commons, London SW1A 0AA
Tel: 020 7219 4830
Constituency: Suite 1, Strand House, 742 Southchurch Road, Southend-on-Sea, Essex SS1 2PS
Tel: 01702 616135 *Fax:* 01702 619071 *Email:* james@jamesduddridge.com
Website: www.jamesduddridge.com *Twitter:* @JamesDuddridge

LABOUR

DUGHER, MICHAEL
Barnsley East *(Majority 11,090)*

Shadow Minister for the Cabinet Office

Michael Vincent Dugher. Born 26 April 1975; Married Joanna (2 daughters 1 son).

Education: McAuley RC School, Doncaster; Nottingham University (BA politics 1997).

Non-political career: Head of policy, Amalgamated Engineering and Electrical Union (AEEU) 1998-2001; Special adviser to: Stephen Byers MP as Secretary of State for Transport, Local Government and the Regions (subsequently Department for Transport) 2001-02, Geoffrey Hoon MP: as Secretary of State for Defence 2003-05, as Lord Privy Seal and Leader of the House of Commons 2005-06; UK director, political relations, EDS 2006-07; Special adviser to Geoffrey Hoon MP as Chief Whip 2007-08; Chief political spokesman to Gordon Brown as the Prime Minister 2008-10. Unite; Unison.

Political career: Contested Skipton and Ripon 2001 general election. Member for Barnsley East since 6 May 2010 general election; Shadow Minister for Defence 2010-11; PPS to Ed Miliband as Leader of the Opposition 2011; Shadow Minister without Portfolio, Cabinet Office 2011-13; Shadow Minister for the Cabinet Office 2013-. *Select committees:* Member: Public Administration 2010-12. Vice-chair, Labour Party; Executive member, BAPG

Political interests: Economy, defence, health, transport, work and pensions, education; Republic of Ireland, Israel, USA.

Other: Member, Hoyland and District branch, Royal British Legion; Patron: Wombwell Operatic Society, Barnsley Independent Alzheimer's and Dementia Support Group, Worsbrough Brass 2013-.

Publications: Co-author (with John Spellar MP), Fools Gold: Dispelling the Myth of the Tory Economic Legacy (Progress, 1999); Chapter for 'Dictionary of Labour Biography' (Politicos, 2001).

Recreations: History, music, watching football.

Michael Dugher MP, House of Commons, London SW1A 0AA
Tel: 020 7219 7006 *Email:* michael.dugher.mp@parliament.uk
Constituency: West Bank House, West Street, Hoyland, Barnsley S74 9EE
Tel: 01226 743483 *Website:* www.michaeldugher.co.uk *Twitter:* @MichaelDugherMP

DUNCAN, ALAN

Rutland and Melton *(Majority 14,000)*

Minister of State, Department for International Development

Alan James Carter Duncan. Born 31 March 1957; Son of late Wing-Commander James Duncan, OBE, and Anne Duncan, née Carter; Civil partner James Dunseath 2008.

Education: Merchant Taylors' School, Northwood; St John's College, Oxford (BA philosophy, politics and economics 1979) (President, Oxford Union 1979); Harvard University (Kennedy Scholar 1981-82).

CONSERVATIVE

Non-political career: Graduate trainee, Shell International Petroleum 1979-81; Marc Rich & Co 1981-88; Oil trader and adviser to governments and companies on oil supply, shipping and refining 1989-92; Visiting Fellow, St Antony's College, Oxford 2002-03.

Political career: Contested Barnsley West and Penistone 1987 general election. Member for Rutland and Melton 1992-2010, for Rutland and Melton (revised boundary) since 6 May 2010 general election; PPS to Dr Brian Mawhinney: as Minister of State, Department of Health 1993-94, as Chairman Conservative Party 1995-97; Parliamentary Political Secretary to William Hague as Leader of the Conservative Party 1997-98; Opposition Spokesperson for: Health 1998-99, Trade and Industry 1999-2001, Foreign and Commonwealth Affairs 2001-03; Shadow Secretary of State for: Constitutional Affairs 2003-04, International Development 2004-05, Transport 2005, Trade and Industry/Business, Enterprise and Regulatory Reform 2005-09, Shadow Leader of the House of Commons 2009; Member House of Commons Commission 2009; Shadow Minister for Prisons 2009-10; Minister of State, Department for International Development 2010-. *Select committees:* Member: Social Security 1992-95. Joint Secretary, Conservative Parliamentary Committee on the Environment 1992-94; Chairman, Conservative Constitutional Affairs Committee 1992-94. Vice-chair, Conservative Party 1997-98.

Political interests: International trade, international economics; Middle East, Pakistan.

Other: Liveryman, Merchant Taylors' Company. Freeman, City of London. PC 2010; Beefsteak.

Publications: Co-author: Bearing the Standard: Themes for a Fourth Term (CPC pamphlet, 1991), Who Benefits? Reinventing Social Security, An End to Illusions (1993), Saturn's Children: How the State Devours Liberty, Prosperity and Virtue (1995); Beware Blair (1997).

Recreations: Shooting, skiing.

Rt Hon Alan Duncan MP, House of Commons, London SW1A 0AA
Tel: 020 7219 5204 *Fax:* 020 7219 2529 *Email:* alan.duncan.mp@parliament.uk
Constituency: No constituency office publicised *Website:* www.alanduncan.org.uk

DUNCAN SMITH, IAIN

Chingford and Woodford Green *(Majority 12,963)*

Secretary of State for Work and Pensions

George Iain Duncan Smith. Born 9 April 1954; Son of late Group Captain W. G. G. Duncan Smith, DSO, DFC, and Pamela Duncan Smith, née Summers; Married Hon. Elizabeth Fremantle 1982 (2 sons 2 daughters).

Education: HMS Conway (Cadet School); Universita per Stranieri, Perugia, Italy; RMA Sandhurst; Dunchurch College of Management; Italian.

CONSERVATIVE

Non-political career: Commissioned, Scots Guards 1975-81; Active service in: Northern Ireland 1976, Rhodesia/Zimbabwe 1979-80; ADC to Major-General Sir John Acland, KCB, CBE, Commander of Commonwealth Monitoring Force in Zimbabwe 1979-81. GEC Marconi 1981-88; Director: Bellwinch Property 1988-89, Publishing Director Jane's Information Group 1989-92.

Political career: Contested Bradford West 1987 general election. Member for Chingford 1992-97, for Chingford and Woodford Green 1997-2010, for Chingford and Woodford Green (revised boundary) since 6 May 2010 general election; Member, Shadow Cabinet 1997-2003; Shadow Secretary of State for: Social Security 1997-99, Defence 1999-2001; Leader of the Opposition 2001-03; Secretary of State for Work and Pensions 2010-. *Select committees:* Member: Health

1993-95, Administration 1993-97, Standards and Privileges 1995-97. Joint Secretary, Conservative Parliamentary Committees on: Foreign Affairs 1992-97, Defence 1995-96; Former vice-chair, European Affairs Committee; Chair, Conservative Party Committee for Social Security 1997-99. Vice-chair, Fulham Conservative Association 1991; Chair, Conservative Policy Board 2001-03; Leader, Conservative Party 2001-03.

Political interests: Finance, small businesses, transport, defence, environment, social policy.

Other: Member, Employment, Social Affairs, Health and Consumer Affairs Council, Council of the European Union 2010-; Founder and Patron, Centre for Social Justice 2004-; Patron, Haven House Childrens Hospice; Trustee, Whitefields School Community Trust; Haven House Foundation; Whitefields Community Trust. Freeman, City of London 1993. Commons Minister of the Year, *House Magazine* awards 2011. PC 2001.

Publications: Co-author Who Benefits? Reinventing Social Security; Game, Set and Match? (Maastricht); Facing the Future (Defence and Foreign and Commonwealth Affairs); 1994 and Beyond; A Response to Chancellor Kohl; A Race against time, Europe's growing vulnerability to missile attack (2002); The Devil's Tune (Robson Books, 2003).

Recreations: Cricket, rugby, tennis, sport in general, painting, theatre, family, shooting, fishing.

Rt Hon Iain Duncan Smith MP, House of Commons, London SW1A 0AA
Tel: 020 7219 2667 *Fax:* 020 7219 4867 *Email:* nashj@parliament.uk
Constituency: Chingford and Woodford Green Conservative Association, 64a Station Road, Chingford, London E4 7BA
Tel: 020 8524 4344 *Fax:* 020 8523 9697 *Email:* cwgca@tory.org
Website: www.iainduncansmith.org

DUNNE, PHILIP
Ludlow *(Majority 9,749)*

Parliamentary Under-Secretary of State (Defence Equipment, Support and Technology), Ministry of Defence

Philip Martin Dunne. Born 14 August 1958; Son of Sir Thomas Dunne and Henrietta Dunne, née Crawley; Married Domenica Fraser 1989 (2 sons 2 daughters).

Education: Eton College; Keble College, Oxford (BA philosophy, politics and economics 1980, MA).

CONSERVATIVE

Non-political career: Graduate trainee to senior manager, S G Warburg & Co Ltd 1980-88; Partner, Gatley Farms 1987-; Ottakar's plc: Co-founder director (non-executive) 1987-2006, Chair (non-executive) 1998-2006; Director of corporate development, James Gulliver Associates 1988-90; Partner, Phoenix Securities and successor 1991-2001; Managing director, Donaldson, Lufkin and Jenette 1997-2001; Chair (non-executive), Baronsmead VCT 4 plc 2001-10; Director, Ruffer Investment Management Limited and Ruffer LLP 2002-09 (non-executive 2005-09). NFU 1987-.

Political career: Member for Ludlow since 5 May 2005 general election; Opposition Whip 2008-10; Assistant Government Whip 2010-12; Parliamentary Under-Secretary of State (Defence Equipment, Support and Technology), Ministry of Defence 2012-. *Select committees:* Member: Work and Pensions 2005-06, Public Accounts 2006-09; Treasury 2007-08. Deputy chair, International Office and Conservatives Abroad, Conservative Party 2008-10. *Councils and public bodies:* South Shropshire District Council: Councillor 2001-07, Conservative group leader 2003-05.

Political interests: Agriculture, business (especially small business), economy, financial services, health, international affairs, local government; Hong Kong, Middle East, USA.

Other: Non-executive director, Juvenile Diabetes Research Foundation 1998-2005; Director, Moor Park Charitable Trust 2001-07; Governor, Westminster Foundation for Democracy 2008-10; Member, Country Land and Business Association; Trustee: Henry Hewes Almshouse, Ludlow Town Walls, William Penny Brookes Foundation, M.A Walker Charitable Trust; Whites. Church Stretton Golf Club.

Recreations: Country sports, skiing, travel.

Philip Dunne MP, House of Commons, London SW1A 0AA
Tel: 020 7219 2388 *Fax:* 020 7219 0788 *Email:* philip.dunne.mp@parliament.uk
Constituency: 54 Broad Street, Ludlow, Shropshire SY8 1GP
Tel: 01584 872187 *Fax:* 01584 876345 *Email:* philipdunne@ludlowconservatives.com
Website: www.philipdunne.com

DURKAN, MARK
Foyle *(Majority 4,824)*

SDLP Spokesperson for Treasury, for International Development, for Foreign Affairs, for Home Affairs and Justice and for Work and Pensions

John Mark Durkan. Born 26 June 1960; Son of late Brendan Durkan, police officer, and late Isobel Durkan; Married Jackie Green 1993 (1 daughter).

Education: St Columb's College, Derry; Queen's University, Belfast (politics); Ulster University (public policy management).

SOCIAL DEMOCRATIC AND LABOUR PARTY

Non-political career: Deputy President, Union of Students in Ireland 1982-84; Parliamentary Assistant to John Hume MP 1984-98.

Political career: Member for Foyle 2005-10, for Foyle (revised boundary) since 6 May 2010 general election; SDLP Spokesperson for: Finance -2010, International Development, Foreign Affairs, Home Affairs and Justice, Treasury 2010-, Work and Pensions 2010-; Member: Forum for Peace and Reconciliation (Dublin) 1994-96, Northern Ireland Forum for Political Dialogue 1996-98; Northern Ireland Assembly: MLA for Foyle 1998-2010: Minister of Finance and Personnel 1999-2001, Deputy First Minister 2001-02; Member Preparation for Government Committee 2006-07. Chair, SDLP 1990-95; Member: SDLP Talks Team: Brooke/Mayhew Talks 1991-92, Castle Buildings Talks 1996-98; Leader, SDLP 2001-10. *Councils and public bodies:* Councillor, Derry City Council 1993-2000; Member: Northern Ireland Housing Council 1993-95, Western Health and Social Services Council 1993-2000.

Political interests: Justice and human rights, international development, healthcare, children's rights; Colombia, Malawi, Middle East, South Africa, South Sudan, Sudan.

Recreations: Spending time with daughter, Manchester United F.C.

Mark Durkan MP, House of Commons, London SW1A 0AA
Tel: 020 7219 5096 *Fax:* 020 7219 2694 *Email:* mark.durkan.mp@parliament.uk
Constituency: 23 Bishop Street, Derry, Co Derry BT48 6PR
Tel: 028 7136 0700 *Fax:* 028 7136 0808 *Email:* m.durkan@sdlp.ie
Website: www.markdurkan.ie *Twitter:* @markdurkan

EAGLE, ANGELA
Wallasey *(Majority 8,507)*

Shadow Leader of the House of Commons; Chair, National Policy Forum

Born 17 February 1961; Daughter of André Eagle, printworker, and late Shirley Eagle, dressmaker and student; Civil partner Maria Exall 2008.

Education: Formby High School; St John's College, Oxford (BA philosophy, politics and economics 1983).

Non-political career: Researcher, then national press officer, COHSE 1984-92. Member: COHSE, National Union of Journalists, Unison.

LABOUR

Political career: Member for Wallasey 1992-2010, for Wallasey (revised boundary) since 6 May 2010 general election; Opposition Whip 1996-97; Parliamentary Under-Secretary of State: Department of the Environment, Transport and the Regions (Minister for Green Issues and Regeneration) 1997-98, Department of Social Security 1998-2001, Home Office 2001-02; Exchequer Secretary, HM Treasury 2007-09; Minister of State (Minister for Pensions and the Ageing Society), Department for Work and Pensions 2009-10; Shadow Minister for Treasury 2010; Shadow Chief Secretary to the Treasury 2010-11; Shadow Leader of the House of Commons 2011-; Member: House of Commons Commission 2011-, Speaker's Committee for the Independent Parliamentary Standards Authority 2012-. *Select committees:* Member: Public Accounts 1995-97, 2002-03, 2007-09, Treasury 2003-07, Treasury (Treasury Sub-Committee) 2003-10. Active at branch, women's section, general committee levels in Crosby Constituency 1978-80; Chair: Oxford University Fabian Club 1980-83, National Conference of Labour Women 1991; Vice-chair, PLP 2005-; Member, Labour Party NEC 2005-; Chair, National Policy Forum 2012-.

Political interests: Economic policy, NHS, politics of sport.

Other: Member, British Film Institute.

Publications: Columnist and regular contributor to Tribune.

Recreations: Chess, cricket, cinema.

Angela Eagle MP, House of Commons, London SW1A 0AA
Tel: 020 7219 3843/020 7219 5057 *Email:* eaglea@parliament.uk
Constituency: Sherlock House, 6 Manor Road, Liscard, Wallasey, Wirral CH45 4JB
Tel: 0151-637 1979 *Fax:* 0151-638 5861 *Website:* www.angelaeaglemp.co.uk
Twitter: @angelaeagle

LABOUR

EAGLE, MARIA
Garston and Halewood *(Majority 16,877)*

Shadow Secretary of State for Envrionment, Food and Rural Affairs

Born 17 February 1961; Daughter of André Eagle, printworker, and late Shirley Eagle, dressmaker and student.

Education: Formby High School; Pembroke College, Oxford (BA philosophy, politics and economics 1983); College of Law, London (Common Professional Exam, Law Society Finals 1990).

Non-political career: Voluntary sector 1983-90; Articles of clerkship, Brian Thompson & Partners, Liverpool 1990-92; Goldsmith Williams, Liverpool 1992-95; Senior Solicitor, Steven Irving & Co, Liverpool 1994-97. Member, GMB.

Political career: Contested Crosby 1992 general election. Member for Liverpool Garston 1997-2010, for Garston and Halewood since 6 May 2010 general election; PPS to John Hutton as Minister of State, Department of Health 1999-2001; Parliamentary Under-Secretary of State: Department for Work and Pensions (Minister for Disabled People) 2001-05, Department for Education and Skills 2005-06 (Minister for Children and Families 2005-06, for Young People 2006), Northern Ireland Office 2006-07; Ministry of Justice 2007-10: Parliamentary Under-Secretary of State 2007-09, Minister of State 2009-10; Government Equalities Office 2008-10: Parliamentary Under-Secretary of State 2008-09, Minister of State (Deputy Minister for Women and Equality) 2009-10; Shadow Solicitor General 2010; Shadow Minister for Justice 2010; Shadow Secretary of State for: Transport 2010-13, Environment, Food and Rural Affairs 2013-. *Select committees:* Member: Public Accounts 1997-99. Campaigns organiser and press officer, Merseyside West Euro Constituency Labour Party 1983-84; Constituency Labour Party secretary, press officer and political education officer 1983-85; Campaigns organiser Crosby 1993-96.

Political interests: Transport, housing, employment; Australia, Nicaragua, USA.

Other: Fellow, Industry and Parliament Trust 2001. Played cricket for Lancashire as a Junior; Played chess for England and Lancashire.

Publications: Co-author, High Time or High Tide for Labour Women.

Recreations: Cinema, chess, cricket.

Maria Eagle MP, House of Commons, London SW1A 0AA
Tel: 020 7219 0551 *Email:* eaglem@parliament.uk
Constituency: Unit House, Speke Boulevard, Liverpool, Merseyside L24 9HZ
Tel: 0151-448 1167 *Website:* www.mariaeaglemp.co.uk *Twitter:* @Meaglemp

PLAID CYMRU

EDWARDS, JONATHAN
Carmarthen East and Dinefwr *(Majority 3,481)*

Plaid Cymru Spokesperson for Business, Innovation and Skills, for Communities and Local Government, for Culture, Olympics, Media and Sport, for Transport and for Treasury

David Jonathan Edwards. Born 26 April 1976; Married Emma Edwards (2012).

Education: Ysgol Gymraeg Rhydaman; Ysgol Gyfun Maes yr Yrfa; University of Wales, Aberystwyth (history and politics); Post-graduate Degree (international history); Welsh.

Non-political career: Chief of staff to Rhodri Glyn Thomas AM and Adam Price MP; National Campaigns Directorate, Plaid Cymru 2005-07; Citizens Advice Cymru 2007-10.

Political career: Member for Carmarthen East and Dinefwr since 6 May 2010 general election; Plaid Cymru Spokesperson for: Business, Innovation and Skills 2010-, Communities and Local Government 2010-, Culture, Olympics, Media and Sport 2010-, Transport 2010-, Treasury 2010-. *Select committees:* Member: Welsh Affairs 2010-. *Councils and public bodies:* Councillor, Carmarthen Town Council; Sheriff of Carmarthen Town.

Political interests: Social justice, foreign affairs.

Other: Penygroes cricket team.

Recreations: Cricket, Swansea City F.C.

Jonathan Edwards MP, House of Commons, London SW1A 0AA
Tel: 020 7219 3000 *Email:* jonathan.edwards.mp@parliament.uk
Constituency: 37 Wind Street, Ammanford, Carmarthenshire SA18 3DN
Tel: 01269 597677 *Fax:* 01269 591334 *Website:* www.jonathanedwards.org.uk
Twitter: @JonathanPlaid

LABOUR

EFFORD, CLIVE

Eltham *(Majority 1,663)*

Shadow Minister for Culture, Media and Sport

Clive Stanley Efford. Born 10 July 1958; Son of Stanley Efford, retired civil servant, and Mary Efford, née Caldwell; Married Gillian Vallins 1981 (3 daughters).

Education: Walworth Comprehensive School; Southwark Further Education College.

Non-political career: Youth and community worker assistant to warden, Pembroke College Mission 1976; Partner family-owned jewellery and watch repair business 1981-85; Taxi driver 1987-97. Member, T&GWU: Member, Passenger Transport Committee of T&G; Represented T&G on London Taxi Board.

Political career: Contested Eltham 1992 general election. Member for Eltham 1997-2010, for Eltham (revised boundary) since 6 May 2010 general election; Presented two bills in Parliament on energy efficiency and energy conservation; Assistant to Tony McNulty as Minister for London 2008-10; PPS to Ministers of State, Department for Communities and Local Government: Margaret Beckett 2008-09, John Healey 2009; Shadow Minister for: Home Office 2010-11, Culture, Media and Sport 2011-. *Select committees:* Member: Procedure 1997-2001, Standing Orders 1999-2000, Transport 2002-09, London 2009-10, Communities and Local Government 2010-11. Vice-chair, London Group of Labour MPs 2001-07; Honorary Secretary, PLP Departmental Committee for Transport 2006-10. Member, Labour Friends of India. *Councils and public bodies:* London Borough of Greenwich: Councillor 1986-98, Chair: Social Services 1989-90, Health and Environment 1992-96, Secretary Labour Group 1986-87, Chief Whip Labour Group 1990-92; Chair Eltham area planning and transport committee 1992-97.

Political interests: Welfare state, health, transport, education, environment, local and regional government, energy conservation, energy efficiency, energy from waste, waste management, recycling, social housing.

Other: Chair of trustees, Samuel Montagu Youth Club; Trustee, Greenwich Community College Trust; Eltham Hill CIU Club.

Recreations: Football (FA Preliminary Coachers Club).

Clive Efford MP, House of Commons, London SW1A 0AA
Tel: 020 7219 4057 *Email:* effordc@parliament.uk
Constituency: 132 Westmount Road, Eltham, London SE9 1UT
Tel: 020 8850 5744 *Email:* clive@cliveefford.org.uk *Website:* www.cliveefford.org.uk
Twitter: @Cliveefford

LABOUR

ELLIOTT, JULIE

Sunderland Central *(Majority 6,725)*

Shadow Minister for Energy and Climate Change

Born 29 July 1963; Daughter of Laura Smith and late Harold Smith; 4 children.

Education: Whitburn Junior School; Seaham Northlea Comprehensive; Newcastle Polytechnic (Degree government and public policy).

Non-political career: Organiser, Labour Party 1993-98; Regional officer, National Asthma Campaign 1998-99; Political officer, GMB 1999-2010. Former secretary and treasurer, Northern Trade Union Liaison Organisation.

Political career: Member for Sunderland Central since 6 May 2010 general election; PPS to Caroline Flint as Shadow Secretary of State for: Communities and Local Government 2010-11, Energy and Climate Change 2011-13; Shadow Minister for Energy and Climate Change 2013-. *Select committees:* Member: European Scrutiny 2010-, Business, Innovation and Skills 2011-. Member, Labour Party 1984-; Agent, Tynemouth 1997 general election; Former chair, Labour North Board. *Councils and public bodies:* Former governor and chair, Whitburn Comprehensive School.

Political interests: Employment and skills, regeneration, health inequalities, education.

Other: Vice-chair, Progress 2012-.

Recreations: Walking, baking, Rugby Union.

Julie Elliott MP, House of Commons, London SW1A 0AA
Tel: 020 7219 7165 *Fax:* 020 7219 4597 *Email:* julie.elliott.mp@parliament.uk
Constituency: 10 Norfolk Street, Sunderland SR1 1EA
Tel: 0191-565 5327 *Fax:* 0191-565 9848 *Website:* www.julie4sunderland.co.uk
Twitter: @JulieElliottMP

ELLIS, MICHAEL
Northampton North *(Majority 1,936)*

Michael Tyrone Ellis. Born 13 October 1967.

Education: Wellingborough School, Northamptonshire; Buckingham University (LLB 1993); Inns of Court School of Law (Bar Vocational Course 1993).

Non-political career: Called to the Bar, Middle Temple 1993; Barrister, Clarendon Chambers, Northampton 1993-2010.

Political career: Member for Northampton North since 6 May 2010 general election. *Select committees:* Member: Joint Committee on Statutory Instruments 2010-, Home Affairs 2011-, Unopposed Bills (Panel) 2011-, Joint Committee on the Draft Communications Data Bill 2012-13. *Councils and public bodies:* Councillor, Northamptonshire County Council 1997-2001.

Political interests: Justice, home affairs, constitution, foreign affairs; Israel, USA.

Other: President, Commonwealth Jewish Council 2012-; Carlton.

Recreations: Gym, theatre.

CONSERVATIVE

Michael Ellis MP, House of Commons, London SW1A 0AA
Tel: 020 7219 7220 *Fax:* 020 7219 6375 *Email:* michael.ellis.mp@parliament.uk
Constituency: 78 St George's Avenue, Northampton NN2 6JF
Tel: 01604 858539 *Fax:* 01604 712372 *Website:* www.michaelellis.co.uk
Twitter: @Michael_Ellis1

ELLISON, JANE
Battersea *(Majority 5,977)*

Parliamentary Under-Secretary of State, Department of Health

Jane Elizabeth Ellison. Born 1964; Partner John.

Education: Oxford University (BA politics, philosophy and economics).

Non-political career: John Lewis Partnership, London: Manager, customer direct marketing, Senior manager, customer magazine, *Source.*

Political career: Contested Pendle 2005 general election. Member for Battersea since 6 May 2010 general election. Parliamentary Under-Secretary of State, Department of Health 2013-. *Select committees:* Member: Backbench Business 2010-, Work and Pensions 2012-. Member, Conservative Party 1983-; Vice-President, Tory Reform Group; Member, Policy Advisory Board 2013-. *Councils and public bodies:* Former councillor, London Borough of Barnet Council; Governor, Honeywell Junior and Infants School, Battersea.

Political interests: Social exclusion, public transport, public services.

Other: Member, Battersea Society; Friend of Battersea Park; Trustee, Sing for Pleasure.

Recreations: Walking, singing in choir.

CONSERVATIVE

Jane Ellison MP, House of Commons, London SW1A 0AA
Tel: 020 7219 7010 *Email:* jane.ellison.mp@parliament.uk
Constituency: 1-3 Summerstown, London SW17 0QB
Tel: 020 8944 2065 *Website:* www.janeellison.net *Twitter:* @janeellisonmp

ELLMAN, LOUISE
Liverpool Riverside *(Majority 14,173)*

Louise Joyce Ellman. Born 14 November 1945; Daughter of late Harold and Anne Rosenberg; Married Geoffrey Ellman 1967 (1 son 1 daughter).

Education: Manchester High School for Girls; Hull University (BA sociology 1967); York University (MPhil social administration 1972).

Non-political career: Open University tutor/further education lecturer. Member, TGWU/Unite.

Political career: Member for Liverpool Riverside 1997-2010, for Liverpool Riverside (revised boundary) since 6 May 2010 general election. *Select committees:* Member: Environment, Transport and Regional Affairs 1997-2001, Environment, Transport and Regional Affairs (Environment Sub-Committee) 1997-2001, Transport, Local Government and the Regions 2001-02, Transport, Local Government and the Regions (Transport Sub-Committee) 2001-02, Transport, Local Government and the Regions (Urban Affairs Sub-Committee) 2001-02; Transport: Member 2002-08, Chair 2008-; Member: Liaison 2008-, Liaison (National Policy Statements Sub-committee) 2009-. Member, Co-operative Party; Vice-chair, Labour Friends of Israel. *Councils and public bodies:* Lancashire County Council: Councillor 1970-97, Council Leader 1981-97; Councillor, West Lancashire District Council 1974-87; Vice-chair, Lancashire Enterprises 1982-97; Founder chair, Northwest Regional Association 1991-93; Vice-President, Local Government Association 2011-.

LAB/CO-OP

Political interests: Regional policy, local government, transport, public services, arts; Middle East.

Other: Chair, Jewish Labour Movement 2004-.

Louise Ellman MP, House of Commons, London SW1A 0AA
Tel: 020 7219 5210 *Email:* louise.ellman.mp@parliament.uk alex.mayes@parliament.uk
Constituency: 515 The Cotton Exchange Building, Old Hall Street, Liverpool, Merseyside L3 9LQ
Tel: 0151-236 2969 *Fax:* 0151-236 4301 *Email:* lloydju@parliament.uk carneyr@parliament.uk
Website: www.louiseellman.co.uk *Twitter:* @LouiseEllman

CONSERVATIVE

ELLWOOD, TOBIAS
Bournemouth East *(Majority 7,728)*

PPS to David Lidington as Minister of State, Foreign and Commonwealth Office

Tobias Martin Ellwood. Born 12 August 1966; Son of Peter and Dr Caroline Ellwood; Married Hannah Ryan 2005 (1 son).

Education: Vienna International School, Austria; Loughborough University of Technology (BA design and technology 1990) (Student Union President); City University Business School (MBA 1998); Kennedy School of Government, Harvard University, USA (Senior Executive Course national and international studies 2009); German.

Non-political career: Territorial Army. Army officer, Royal Green Jackets 1991-96, served in Northern Ireland, Cyprus, Kuwait, Germany, Gibraltar and Bosnia; Researcher to Tom King MP 1996-97; Senior business development manager: London Stock Exchange 1998-2002, Allen and Overy 2002-04.

Political career: Contested Worsley 2001 general election. Member for Bournemouth East 2005-10, for Bournemouth East (revised boundary) since 6 May 2010 general election; Opposition Whip 2005-07; Shadow Minister for Culture, Media and Sport 2007-10; PPS to: Liam Fox as Secretary of State for Defence 2010-11, David Lidington as Minister of State, Foreign and Commonwealth Office 2011-. *Select committees:* Member: Environmental Audit 2005-06, Armed Forces Bill 2011. Chair, Conservative Insight 2000; Branch chair, South West Hertfordshire Conservative Association 1998-2003. *Councils and public bodies:* Councillor: Aldbury Parish Council 1996-99, Dacorum Borough Council 1999-2003; Governor, Queen's Park Infant School, Bournemouth.

Political interests: Defence, education, environment, tourism; Afghanistan, Iraq, Middle East, USA, Yemen.

Other: CBI London Council 2000; Treasurer, Bow Group 2000; Member, Atlantic Council; Caring Canines, Crumbs Café, Dorset Education Bus.

Publications: Introduction to the Conservative Party Post-Conflict Reconstruction.

Recreations: Volleyball, windsurfing, saxophone, theatre.

Tobias Ellwood MP, House of Commons, London SW1A 0AA
Tel: 020 7219 4349 *Fax:* 020 7219 0946 *Email:* tobias.ellwood.mp@parliament.uk
Constituency: Boscombe Conservative Club, Haviland Road West, Boscombe, Bournemouth, Dorset BH1 4JW
Tel: 01202 397047 *Fax:* 01202 397047 *Email:* becaoffice@btconnect.com
Website: www.bournemoutheastconservatives.com www.tobiasellwood.com
Twitter: @TobiasEllwoodMP

CONSERVATIVE

ELPHICKE, CHARLIE
Dover *(Majority 5,274)*

Charles Brett Anthony Elphicke. Born 14 March 1971; Married Natalie Ross Pears 1996 (1 son 1 daughter).

Education: Felsted School, Essex; Nottingham University (LLB 1993); Inns of Court School of Law (Bar Finals 1994).

Non-political career: Formerly ran printing business; Called to the Bar, Middle Temple 1994; Solicitor: Supreme Court of England and Wales, Cameron, McKenna and Wilde Sapte 1996-2001; Partner, Reed Smith 2001-05; Partner and head of European tax, Hunton & Williams Solicitors 2006-10.

Political career: Contested St Albans 2001 general election. Member for Dover since 6 May 2010 general election. *Select committees:* Member: Public Administration 2010-, Joint Committee on Consolidation, Etc, Bills 2010-. Member, Executive, 1922 Committee 2010-12. Chair, Dulwich and West Norwood Conservatives 1999-2000. *Councils and public bodies:* Councillor, London Borough of Lambeth Council 1994-98.

Political interests: Poverty alleviation, wealth creation, transport, tax fairness.

Other: Research fellow, Centre for Policy Studies; Member, Law Society of England and Wales. Freeman of the City of London. Overall Winner, BCS Chartered Institute of IT MP Web Awards 2010.

Publications: Author, Centre for Policy Studies publications: Ending Pensioner Poverty (2003), (with William Norton) SAINTS can get Britain saving again (2005), The Case for Reducing Business Taxes (2006), The tax double whammy: more tax costs more than you think (2006), Robin Hood or Sheriff of Nottingham? Winners and losers from tax and benefit reform over the last 10 years (2006), Where has your pay rise gone? (2006), Are you better off now than you were four years ago? (2007), Why do we feel so broke? (2008), Uh-Oh, We're In Trouble (2008); Ten Points for Growth (2011); Lower, Simpler, Stronger Business Taxes (2013).

Recreations: Sailing, walking by the sea, spending time with family.

Charlie Elphicke MP, House of Commons, London SW1A 0AA
Tel: 020 7219 7052 *Email:* charlie.elphicke.mp@parliament.uk
Constituency: c/o Dover and Deal Conservative Association, 54 The Strand, Walmer, Deal, Kent CT14 7DP
Tel: 01304 379669 *Email:* charlie@elphicke.com *Website:* www.elphicke.com
Twitter: @charlieelphicke

ENGEL, NATASCHA North East Derbyshire *(Majority 2,445)*

LABOUR

Born 9 April 1967; Daughter of Christina Sheehan and Achaz Engel; Married David Salisbury Jones 2001 (divorced) (3 sons).

Education: Kent College, Canterbury; King's School, Canterbury; King's College, London (BA German and Portuguese 1990); Westminster University (MA technical and specialist translation 1992); German, Portuguese, Spanish.

Non-political career: Journalist, *Dover Express* 1990; English and German teacher, Spain 1990-92; Teletext subtitler for ITV and Channel 5 1993-96; Organiser, Trade Union Congress Organising Academy 1996-97; Trade union liaison officer, Labour Party 1997-2001; Programme director, Smith Institute 2001-02; Ballot co-ordinator, Trade Union Political Fund 2002-03. Member: GMB/UCATT.

Political career: Member for North East Derbyshire 2005-10, for North East Derbyshire (revised boundary) since 6 May 2010 general election; PPS to: Peter Hain as Secretary of State for Work and Pensions 2007-08, Liam Byrne as Minister for the Cabinet Office and Chancellor of the Duchy of Lancaster 2008-09, John Denham as Secretary of State for Communities and Local Government 2009-10. *Select committees:* Member: Work and Pensions 2005-07, Reform of the House of Commons 2009-10; Chair: Backbench Business 2010-; Member: Liaison 2010-. Labour Party: National trade union policy co-ordinator 1998-2000, National trade union general election co-ordinator 2000-01.

Political interests: Parliamentary reform, Europe, park homes, planning reforms, youth, welfare rights; Germany, Spain, USA.

Other: Fabian Society; Amnesty International; YMCA; British Youth Council. Commons Backbencher of the Year, *House Magazine* awards 2011.

Publications: Several pamphlets including: Shop Stewards' Pocket Policy Guide, Trade Union Links with the Labour Party, Rights Won By Unions, Age of Regions, Learning to Organise.

Recreations: Sports.

Natascha Engel MP, House of Commons, London SW1A 0AA
Tel: 020 7219 1015 *Email:* natascha.engel.mp@parliament.uk
Constituency: 62 Market Street, Eckington, Derbyshire S21 4JH
Tel: 01246 439018 *Email:* maggie.flude@parliament.uk
Website: www.nataschaengelmp.wordpress.com

LABOUR

ESTERSON, BILL

Sefton Central *(Majority 3,862)*

William Roffen Esterson. Born 27 October 1966; Son of Derek and Joyce Esterson; Married Caroline (1 son 1 daughter).

Education: Rochester Mathematical School; Leeds University (BSc maths and philosophy 1990); French, German.

Non-political career: Director, training consultancy 1995-2010. Unite; USDAW.

Political career: Member for Sefton Central since 6 May 2010 general election; PPS to Stephen Twigg as Shadow Secretary of State for Education 2011-13. *Select committees:* Member: Environment, Food and Rural Affairs 2010-11, Education 2010-, Joint Committee on the Draft House of Lords Reform Bill 2011-12, Unopposed Bills (Panel) 2011-, Communities and Local Government 2011-13, Joint Committee on the Rookery South (Resource Recovery Facility) Order 2012-13. Chair, PLP Departmental Group for Education 2010-12. *Councils and public bodies:* Medway Council: Councillor 1995-2010, Labour Spokesperson for Children's Services.

Political interests: Children's service.

Other: Formby Hockey Club.

Recreations: Playing hockey and cricket.

Bill Esterson MP, House of Commons, London SW1A 0AA
Tel: 020 7219 4403 *Email:* bill.esterson.mp@parliament.uk
Constituency: 29 Liverpool Road North, Maghull, Merseyside L31 2HB
Tel: 0151-531 8433 *Website:* www.billesterson.org.uk *Twitter:* @BillEstersonMP

CONSERVATIVE

EUSTICE, GEORGE

Camborne and Redruth *(Majority 66)*

Parliamentary Under-Secretary of State, Department for Environment, Food and Rural Affairs

Charles George Eustice. Born 28 September 1971; Son of Paul Eustice and Adele Eustice.

Education: Truro Cathedral School; Truro School; Cornwall College, Poole; Writtle College, Chelmsford.

Non-political career: Trevaskis Fruit Farm; Conservative Party: Campaign director, anti-Euro 'No Campaign' 1999-2003; Head of press, 2005 general election 2003-05; Press Secretary to Conservative Leader David Cameron 2005-07; External relations co-ordinator, Conservative HQ 2008-09; Associate director, Portland PR 2009-10.

Political career: Member for Camborne and Redruth since 6 May 2010 general election. *Select committees:* Member: Environment, Food and Rural Affairs 2010-, Joint Committee on Privacy and Injunctions 2011-12. Member, Executive, 1922 Committee 2012-13. Contested South West region (UKIP) 1999 European Parliament election. Member: UKIP 1998-99, Conservative Party 2003-; Member, Policy Advisory Board 2013-; Parliamentary Under-Secretary of State, Department for Environment, Food and Rural Affairs 2013-.

Political interests: Farming, environment, Europe, regeneration.

Other: Columnist, *PR Week*.

George Eustice MP, House of Commons, London SW1A 0AA
Tel: 020 7219 7032 *Email:* george.eustice.mp@parliament.uk
Constituency: 1 Trevenson Street, Camborne, Cornwall TR14 8JD
Tel: 01209 713355 *Email:* camborneredruthconservatives@googlemail.com
Website: www.georgeeustice.co.uk

LAB/CO-OP

EVANS, CHRIS

Islwyn *(Majority 12,215)*

Christopher James Evans. Son of late Michael Evans and Lynne Evans.

Education: Porth County Comprehensive; Pontypridd College; Trinity College, Carmarthen (BA History).

Non-political career: Manager, bookmaker 1998-2001; Lloyds TSB Bank plc 2001-03; Marketing, Glamorgan University 2003-04; Official, Union of Finance Staff 2004; Parliamentary researcher to Don Touhig MP 2006-10. Member, Unite.

Political career: Contested Cheltenham 2005 general election. Member for Islwyn since 6 May 2010 general election. *Select committees:* Member: Justice 2010-12, Joint Committees on: the Draft Defamation Bill 2011, the Draft Enhanced Terrorism Prevention and Investigation Measures Bill 2012-13; Member: Environmental Audit 2012-. Member, Co-operative Party.

Political interests: Justice, finance, welfare; China, France, Germany, Greece, USA.

Other: Member, Fabian Society.

Recreations: Watching sports, running, reading.
Chris Evans MP, House of Commons, London SW1A 0AA
Tel: 020 7219 7091 *Email:* chris.evans.mp@parliament.uk
Constituency: 6 Woodfieldside Business Park, Penmaen Road, Pontllanfraith, Blackwood,
Gwent NP12 2DG
Tel: 01495 231990 *Website:* www.chrisevansmp.co.uk

EVANS, GRAHAM
Weaver Vale *(Majority 991)*

Graham Thomas Evans. Born 10 November 1963; Son of Gordon Evans and Violet Evans (née
Payne); Married Cheryl 1995 (1 daughter 2 sons).

Education: Poynton County High School; Manchester Metropolitan University (BA business
studies 2000); Postgraduate Diploma marketing management.

Non-political career: BAe Systems; Sun Chemical; Hewlett Packard; UK managing director,
Italian manufacturing company.

CONSERVATIVE

Political career: Contested Worsley 2005 general election. Member for Weaver Vale since 6
May 2010 general election. *Select committees:* Member: Administration 2011-13, Work and
Pensions 2012-. Member, Executive, 1922 Committee 2012-. North West Area Officer, Conser-
vative Party. *Councils and public bodies:* Macclesfield Borough Council: Councillor 2000-09,
Chair, Community Development Committee.

Political interests: Education, policing, defence, science, healthcare, welfare; China, Israel,
USA.

Other: Member, Countryside Alliance; Member, Institute of Directors; Royal British Legion.

Recreations: Football (Manchester United), running, British history, cricket.

Graham Evans MP, House of Commons, London SW1A 0AA
Tel: 020 7219 7183 *Fax:* 020 7219 5079 *Email:* mail@grahamevansmp.com
Constituency: The Bungalow, Sheath Street, Northwich, Cheshire CW9 5BH
Tel: 01606 350 323 *Email:* help@grahamevansmp.com *Website:* www.grahamevansmp.com
Twitter: @GrahamEvansMP

EVANS, JONATHAN
Cardiff North *(Majority 194)*

Jonathan Peter Evans. Born 2 June 1950; Son of David and Harriet Evans; Married Margaret
Thomas 1975 (2 daughters 1 son).

Education: Lewis School, Pengram; Howardian High School, Cardiff; Law Society's College of
Law, Guildford and London; French.

Non-political career: Leo Abse and Cohen solicitors: Trainee 1968-73, Solicitor 1973-87, Managing partner 1987-92; Eversheds, London: Insurance director 1997-99, Consultant (corporate
and regulatory insurance) 1999-2009; Director: NFU Mutual Insurance 2000-10, Country
Mutual Insurance Brokers 2003-05; Chairman: Pearl Group Ltd 2005-09, Phoenix Life companies 2009-.

CONSERVATIVE

Political career: Contested Ebbow Vale February and October 1974, Wolverhampton North
East 1979 and Brecon and Radnor 1987 general elections. Member for Brecon and Radnor
1992-97. Contested Brecon and Radnor 1997 general election. Member for Cardiff North since
6 May 2010 general election; PPS to Michael Mates as Minister of State for Northern Ireland
1992-94; Minister for Corporate and Consumer Affairs, Department of Trade and Industry
1994-95; Parliamentary Secretary, Lord Chancellor's Department 1995-96; Under-Secretary
of State for Wales 1996-97; MEP for Wales 1999-2009: Conservative EP Leader 2001-05;
Member: Japan Delegation 1999-2004, Economic and Monetary Affairs Committee 1999-
2009; Chair, United States Delegation 2004-09; Spokesperson on Modernisation of EU Competition Policy; Member, Conference of Delegation Chairmen 2004-09; Co-chair, Transatlantic Legislators Dialogue 2005-09; Chair, Advisory board, Transatlantic Economic Council
2007-09. Chair, Cardiff Central Young Conservatives 1968; Vice-chair, Wales Conservative
Political Centre 1974-76; Member, Conservative Working Party on Devolution in Wales 1975;
Chair, Welsh Conservative Parliamentary Candidates 1985-90; Conservative Spokesperson for
Wales 1997-98; Vice-President, Tory Reform Group; Board member, Conservative Party
2002-05; Chair: Association of Conservative Clubs 2006-, Parliamentary Mainstream 2010-.
Councils and public bodies: Deputy Chairman, Welsh Housing Federation (Housing for
Wales) 1988-92.

Political interests: Economic and monetary affairs, trade and industry, building societies and housing, financial services, cooperatives and mutuals, promotion of the Arts; Austria, China, Czech Republic, France, Japan, Slovakia, Slovenia, USA.

Other: Council of Europe: Member, 2013-, Co-Rapporteur on Albania 2013-; Fellow, Royal Society of Arts 1995; Member, Law Society; Fellow, Institute of Welsh Affairs 2007-; National Society for the Prevention of Cruelty to Children; Welsh National Sports Centre for the Disabled; Carlton; Cardiff and County Club; County Conservative Club; Fairwater Conservative Club; Gough Constitutional Club; Ystradgynlais. Cardiff Athletic Club (rugby section).

Recreations: Watching Cardiff City, rugby, music, family, reading.

Jonathan Evans MP, House of Commons, London SW1A 0AA
Tel: 020 7219 7205 *Email:* jonathan.evans.mp@parliament.uk
Constituency: 54 Old Church Road, Whitchurch, Cardiff CF14 1AB
Tel: 029 2061 3539 *Email:* vivienne.ward@parliament.uk *Website:* www.jonathanevans.co.uk
Twitter: @JonathanEvansMP

EVANS, NIGEL
Ribble Valley *(Majority 14,769)*

INDEPENDENT

Nigel Martin Evans. Born 10 November 1957; Son of late Albert Evans and Betty Evans; Single.

Education: Dynevor School, Swansea; University College of Wales, Swansea (BA politics 1979); French, Russian (poor).

Non-political career: Management family retail newsagent and convenience store 1979-90; Worked on three US presidential elections in New York, Florida and California.

Political career: Contested Swansea West 1987 general election and Pontypridd 1989 and Ribble Valley 1991 by-elections. Member for Ribble Valley 1992-2010, for Ribble Valley (revised boundary) since 6 May 2010 general election; PPS: to David Hunt: as Secretary of State for Employment 1993-94, as Chancellor of the Duchy of Lancaster 1994-95, to Tony Baldry as Minister of State, Ministry of Agriculture, Fisheries and Food 1995-96, to William Hague as Secretary of State for Wales 1996-97; Opposition Spokesperson for: Scotland and Wales 1997-99, Wales 1999-2001; Shadow Secretary of State for Wales 2001-03; First Deputy Chairman, Ways and Means and Deputy Speaker 2010-13. *Select committees:* Member: Welsh Affairs 2003-05, Trade and Industry 2003-05, Culture, Media and Sport 2005-09, International Development 2009-10; Chairmen's Panel/Panel of Chairs: Member 2009-10, Ex-officio member 2010-13. Chair Conservative Welsh Parliamentary Candidates Policy Group 1990; President Conservative North West Parliamentary Candidates Group 1991; Secretary North West Conservative MPs 1992-97; Vice-chair: Conservative Party (Wales) 1999-2001, Conservative Party (Conservatives Abroad) 2004-05; Resigned from Conservative Party September 2013. *Councils and public bodies:* West Glamorgan County Council: Councillor 1985-91, Deputy Leader, Conservative Group 1990-91.

Political interests: Education, small businesses, US elections, local and regional government, defence, agriculture, international politics, European affairs, telecommunications, space; Australia, Bahrain, Caribbean, Egypt, Europe, Far East, Gibraltar, India, USA.

Other: British Inter-Parliamentary Union: Treasurer 2005-08, Vice-chair 2008-10; Member, executive, Commonwealth Parliamentary Association 2005-; Member: Council of Europe 2006, Western European Union 2006-; UK chair Technological and Aerospace committee; Honorary Treasurer, Commonwealth Parliamentary Association (UK Branch) 2010; Fellow, Industry and Parliament Trust 1998; Adviser, Arensky Chamber Orchestra; Honorary President, British Youth Council; Macmillan. Honorary LLD Swansea University 2012; Carlton; countryclubuk.com; RAC; Groucho.

Recreations: Tennis, swimming, running, theatre, cinema, arts, music.

Nigel Evans MP, House of Commons, London SW1A 0AA
Tel: 020 7219 6939 *Fax:* 020 7219 2568 *Email:* evansn@parliament.uk
Constituency: 9 Railway View, Clitheroe, Lancashire BB7 2HA
Tel: 01200 425939 *Fax:* 01200 422904 *Email:* ribblevalley@tory.org
Website: www.nigel-evans.org.uk *Twitter:* @nigelevansmp

VACHER'S QUARTERLY
The most up-to-date contact details throughout the year
Call 020 7593 5644 or visit www.dodsshop.co.uk

CONSERVATIVE

EVENNETT, DAVID
Bexleyheath and Crayford *(Majority 10,344)*

Government Whip

David Anthony Evennett. Born 3 June 1949; Son of late Norman Evennett and late Irene Evennett, née Turner; Married Marilyn Smith 1975 (2 sons).

Education: Buckhurst Hill County High School; London School of Economics (BSc Econ economics 1971; MSc Econ politics 1972).

Non-political career: Schoolmaster, Ilford County High School 1972-74; Marine insurance broker, Lloyds 1974-81; Member, Lloyds 1976-92; Director, Lloyds Underwriting Agency 1982-91; Commercial liaison manager, Bexley College 1997-2001; Consultant, J&H Marsh and McLennan (UK) then Marsh (UK) Ltd 1998-2000; Freelance lecturer 2001-05.

Political career: Contested Hackney South and Shoreditch 1979 general election. Member for Erith and Crayford 1983-97. Contested Bexleyheath and Crayford 1997 and 2001 general elections. Member for Bexleyheath and Crayford since 5 May 2005 general election; PPS to: Baroness Blatch as Minister of State for Education 1992-93, John Redwood as Secretary of State for Wales 1993-95, Baroness Blatch and David Maclean as Ministers of State, Home Office 1995-96, Gillian Shephard as Secretary of State for Education and Employment 1996-97; Opposition Whip 2005-09; Shadow Minister for: Innovation, Universities and Skills 2009, Universities and Skills 2009-10; PPS to Michael Gove as Secretary of State for Education 2010-12; Government Whip (Lord Commissioner of HM Treasury) 2012-. *Select committees:* Member: Education and Skills 2005-06, Selection 2012-. *Councils and public bodies:* Councillor, London Borough of Redbridge 1974-78.

Political interests: Education, economy, transport, London; Australia, Austria, Canada, Italy, New Zealand, Sweden, USA.

Other: Bexleyheath Conservative Club.

Recreations: Travel, reading, cinema, family.

David Evennett MP, House of Commons, London SW1A 0AA
Tel: 020 7219 8403 *Fax:* 020 7219 2163 *Email:* david.evennett.mp@parliament.uk
Constituency: 17 Church Road, Bexleyheath, Kent DA7 4DD *Website:* www.davidevennett.com
Twitter: @davidevennett

CONSERVATIVE

FABRICANT, MICHAEL
Lichfield *(Majority 17,683)*

Michael Louis David Fabricant. Born 12 June 1950; Son of late Isaac Fabricant and Helena Fabricant, née Freed; Single.

Education: Brighton, Hove and Sussex Grammar School, Brighton; Loughborough University (BSc economics and law 1973); Sussex University (MSc systems and econometrics 1974); Oxford University/London University/University of Southern California, Los Angeles, USA (PhD econometrics and economic forecasting 1975-78); Dutch, French, German, Hebrew (basic), Russian (basic).

Non-political career: Staff, then freelance radio broadcaster and journalist 1968-80; Economist and founder director, leading broadcast and communications group, manufacturing and commissioning electronics equipment to radio stations to 48 countries 1980-91; Adviser, Home Office on broadcasting matters; Adviser to foreign governments on establishment and management of radio stations, including Russian Federation 1980-91; Has lived and worked extensively in Europe, Africa, the Far East, former Soviet Union, and USA.

Political career: Contested South Shields 1987 general election. Member for Mid Staffordshire 1992-97, for Lichfield 1997-2010, for Lichfield (revised boundary) since 6 May 2010 general election; Presented Bills to strengthen economic and political ties between UK, USA, Canada, Australia and New Zealand; Promoted legislation to encourage flying of Union Flag and to force Government to undertake and publish regular financial cost-benefit analyses of Britain's membership of European Union; PPS to Michael Jack as Financial Secretary to the Treasury 1996-97; Shadow Minister for: Trade and Industry 2003, Economic Affairs 2003-05; Opposition Whip 2005-10; Government Whip 2010-12. *Select committees:* Member: Culture, Media and Sport 1997-99, Home Affairs 1999-2001, Catering 1999-2001, Liaison 2001-03; Chair: Information 2001-03; Member: Finance and Services 2001-04, Culture, Media and Sport 2001-05, Administration 2009-10, Selection 2010-12. Member, Executive, 1922 Committee 2001-03. Chair, Brighton Pavilion Conservative Association 1985-88; Member, Conservative Way Forward; Associate member, European Research Group; Member, Conservative Against a Federal Europe; Chair, Conservative Friends of America 2007-10; Vice-chairman (parliamentary campaigning), Conservative Party 2012-.

Political interests: Broadcasting and media, business, defence, engineering, enterprise, exports, foreign affairs, heritage, industry, inland waterways, international aid and development, international trade, internet, manufacturing, police and security issues, science and technology, technology, telecommunications, trade and industry; Australia, Eastern Europe, Middle East, USA, Wales.

Other: Member: Inter-Parliamentary Union, Commonwealth Parliamentary Association; Member: Council of the Institution of Electrical Engineers 1996-2000, Senate of the Engineering Council 1996-2002; Director, Engineering and Technology Board 2002-06; CEng; FIET; FRSA; Cancer Research; Rottingdean (Sussex).

Recreations: Reading, music, fell-walking, skiing and listening to the omnibus edition of *The Archers*.

Michael Fabricant MP, House of Commons, London SW1A 0AA
Tel: 020 7219 5022 *Email:* michael.fabricant.mp@parliament.uk
Constituency: No constituency office publicised *Website:* www.michael.fabricant.mp.co.uk
Twitter: @Mike_Fabricant

FALLON, MICHAEL   Sevenoaks *(Majority 17,515)*

Minister of State for Business and Enterprise, Department for Business, Innovation and Skills and Minister of State for Energy, Department of Energy and Climate Change

Michael Cathel Fallon. Born 14 May 1952; Son of late Martin Fallon, OBE, FRICS, and Hazel Fallon; Married Wendy Payne 1986 (2 sons).

Education: Epsom College, Surrey; St Andrews University (MA classics and ancient history 1974).

CONSERVATIVE

Non-political career: European Educational Research Trust 1974-75; Conservative Research Department 1975-79 (seconded to Opposition Whips Office, House of Lords 1975-77, EEC Desk Officer 1977-79); Secretary, Lord Home's Committee on Future of the House of Lords 1977-78; Joint managing director, European Consultants Ltd 1979-81; Assistant to Baroness Elles MEP 1979-83; Director, Quality Care Homes plc 1992-97; Chief executive, Quality Care Developments Ltd 1996-97; Director: Just Learning Ltd 1996-2009, Bannatyne Fitness Ltd 1999-2000, Just Learning Holdings 2001-09, Just Learning Development Ltd 2001-09, Careshare Ltd 2003-09, Collins Stewart Tullet plc 2004-06, Tullett Prebon plc 2006-12, Attendo AB 2008-12.

Political career: Contested Darlington March 1983 by-election. Member for Darlington 1983-92. Contested Darlington 1992 general election. Member for Sevenoaks 1997-2010, for Sevenoaks (revised boundary) since 6 May 2010 general election; PPS to Cecil Parkinson as Secretary of State for Energy 1987-88; Assistant Government Whip 1988-90; Government Whip May-July 1990; Parliamentary Under-Secretary of State, Department of Education and Science 1990-92; Opposition Frontbench Spokesperson for: Trade and Industry June-December 1997, the Treasury December 1997-98; Minister of State for: Business and Enterprise, Department for Business, Innovation and Skills 2012-, Energy, Department of Energy and Climate Change 2013-. *Select committees:* Member: Treasury 1999-2012, Treasury (Treasury Sub-Committee) 1999-2001; Chair: Treasury (Treasury Sub-Committee) 2001-10. Member, Executive 1922 Committee 2005-07; Deputy chair, Conservative Party 2010-12. *Councils and public bodies:* Member: Higher Education Funding Council 1992-97, Deregulation Task Force 1994-97.

Political interests: Constitution, public sector, education, Treasury.

Other: Member, Advisory Council, Social Market Foundation 1994-2000; Non-executive director, International Care and Relief 1998-2003; Board member, Centre for Policy Studies 2009-; President, Royal London Society for the Blind 2010-. PC 2012; Academy Club.

Publications: Brighter Schools (Social Market Foundation, 1993); Putting Social Mobility Back Into Britain (NTB, 2007).

Recreations: Skiing, opera, visiting classical sites.

Rt Hon Michael Fallon MP, House of Commons, London SW1A 0AA
Tel: 020 7219 6482 *Fax:* 020 7219 6791 *Email:* michael.fallon.mp@parliament.uk
Constituency: Becket House, 13 Vestry Road, Sevenoaks, Kent TN14 5EL
Tel: 01732 452261 *Email:* office@sevenoakstory.org.uk
Website: www.sevenoaksconservatives.org www.michaelfallonmp.org.uk

LABOUR

FARRELLY, PAUL
Newcastle-under-Lyme *(Majority 1,552)*

Christopher Paul Farrelly. Born 2 March 1962; Son of late Thomas Farrelly and Anne Farrelly, née King; Married Victoria Perry 1998 (1 son 2 daughters).

Education: Wolstanton County Grammar School; Marshlands Comprehensive, Newcastle-Under-Lyme; St Edmund Hall, Oxford (BA philosophy, politics and economics 1984); French, German, Italian.

Non-political career: Manager, corporate finance division, Barclays De Zoete Wedd Ltd 1984-90; Reuters Ltd 1990-95: Correspondent, News editor; Deputy city and business editor, *Independent on Sunday* 1995-97; City editor, *The Observer* 1997-2001. Unite; Unity.

Political career: Contested Chesham and Amersham 1997 general election. Member for Newcastle-under-Lyme since 7 June 2001 general election. *Select committees:* Member: Joint Committee on Consolidation, Etc, Bills 2001-, European Standing Committee B 2003-05, Science and Technology 2003-05, Unopposed Bills (Panel) 2004-, Culture, Media and Sport 2005-, Joint Committee on Privacy and Injunctions 2011-12. Member, Co-operative Party; Vice-chair, Hornsey and Wood Green CLP 1994-95; Newcastle-under-Lyme CLP 1998-2006: Campaign co-ordinator and organiser, Political education officer; Member: Socialist Education Association, Labour Party Irish Society.

Political interests: Education, health, employment, trade and industry, regeneration, investment, European affairs, pensions, crime; Australia, China, France, Germany, Hungary, Iceland, Ireland, Italy, Japan, New Zealand, Norway, Russia.

Other: Member: Amnesty International, Greenpeace. Trentham RUFC; Finchley RFC; House of Commons and House of Lords RUFC.

Publications: Editor, Hammer of the Left by John Golding (2003).

Recreations: Rugby, football, writing, biography, history, architecture.

Paul Farrelly MP, House of Commons, London SW1A 0AA
Tel: 020 7219 8391 *Fax:* 020 7219 1986 *Email:* paul.farrelly.mp@parliament.uk
Constituency: Waterloo Buildings, 79-81 Dunkirk, Newcastle-under-Lyme, Staffordshire ST5 2SW
Tel: 01782 715033 *Fax:* 01782 613174 *Email:* hopwoodc@parliament.uk
Website: www.paulfarrelly.com

LIBERAL DEMOCRAT

FARRON, TIM
Westmorland and Lonsdale *(Majority 12,264)*

President Liberal Democrat Party

Timothy James Farron. Born 27 May 1970; Son of Chris Farron and late Susan Farron, née Trenchard; Married Rosie Cantley 2000 (2 daughters 2 sons).

Education: Lostock Hall High School, Preston, Lancashire; Runshaw Tertiary College, Leyland; Newcastle University (BA politics 1991).

Non-political career: Lancaster University: Adult education officer 1992-96, Student support officer 1996-98, Faculty administrator 1998-2002; Head of faculty administration St Martin's College, (Ambleside, Lancaster, Carlisle) 2002-05. Association of University Teachers 1995-.

Political career: Contested North West Durham 1992, South Ribble 1997 and Westmorland and Lonsdale 2001 general elections. Member for Westmorland and Lonsdale 2005-10, for Westmorland and Lonsdale (revised boundary) since 6 May 2010 general election; Liberal Democrat: Spokesperson for Youth Affairs 2005-06; PPS to Sir Menzies Campbell as Leader of the Liberal Democrats 2006-07; Shadow Minister for: Home Affairs 2007, Countryside 2007-08; Shadow Secretary of State for Environment, Food and Rural Affairs 2008-10. *Select committees:* Member: Education and Skills 2005-06, Environmental Audit 2006-07, European Scrutiny 2010-. Chair, Liberal Democrat Policy Committee on International Affairs 2010-11. Contested North West England 1999 European Parliament election. President, Liberal Democrat Party 2010-; Member, Manifesto Working Group 2013-. *Councils and public bodies:* Councillor: Lancashire County Council 1993-2000, South Ribble Borough Council 1995-99, South Lakeland District Council 2004-08.

Political interests: Education, rural affairs, youth work, health, crime and policing, social care.

Other: Member, Amnesty International 1993-; President, Kendal and South Westmorland Liberal Club; Liberal Democrat Christian Forum; Cumbria Wildlife; Lakes Line User Group.

Recreations: Fell-walking, running, cycling, football, watching Blackburn Rovers, music.

Tim Farron MP, House of Commons, London SW1A 0AA
Tel: 020 7219 8498 *Fax:* 020 7219 2810 *Email:* farron@parliament.uk
Constituency: Acland House, Yard 2, Stricklandgate, Kendal, Cumbria LA9 4ND
Tel: 01539 723403 *Fax:* 01539 740800 *Email:* tim@timfarron.co.uk
Website: www.timfarron.co.uk *Twitter:* @timfarron

FEATHERSTONE, LYNNE   Hornsey and Wood Green *(Majority 6,875)*

Parliamentary Under-Secretary of State, Department for International Development

Lynne Choona Featherstone. Born 20 December 1951; Daughter of late Joseph Woolf and Gladys Ryness; Married Stephen Featherstone 1982 (divorced 2002) (2 daughters).

Education: South Hampstead High School, London; Oxford Polytechnic (Diploma communications and design 1974); French.

LIBERAL DEMOCRAT

Non-political career: Graphic designer, London and Australia 1974-77; Freelance designer 1977-80; Managing director, Inhouse Outhouse Design 1980-87; Strategic design consultant 1987-97; Director, Ryness Electrical Supplies Ltd 1991-2002.

Political career: Contested Hornsey and Wood Green 1997 and 2001 general elections. Member for Hornsey and Wood Green since 5 May 2005 general election; Liberal Democrat: Spokesperson for: Home Affairs 2005-06, London 2006-07, Shadow Secretary of State for International Development 2006-07; Shadow Minister for Youth and Equalities 2008-10; Parliamentary Under-Secretary of State: (Minister for Equalities), Home Office and Government Equalities Office 2010-12, Department for International Development 2012-. *Select committees:* Member: Environmental Audit 2005-06. *Councils and public bodies:* London Borough of Haringey Council: Councillor 1998-2006, Leader of Opposition 1998-2003; London Assembly: Member 2000-05, Chair, Assembly Committee on Transport 2000-05; Member, Metropolitan Police Authority 2000-05.

Political interests: Transport, policing, equalities; Afghanistan, Africa, EU, India, Nepal, Pakistan, USA.

Other: Unsung Hero award, *Daily Mail* 2002; Best Campaign Website, Orange Digital award 2010.

Publications: Marketing and Communications Techniques for Architects (Longman, 1992).

Recreations: Writing poetry, film.

Lynne Featherstone MP, House of Commons, London SW1A 0AA
Tel: 020 7219 8401 *Fax:* 020 7219 0008 *Email:* featherstonel@parliament.uk
Constituency: 62 High Street, London N8 7BX
Tel: 020 8340 5459 *Fax:* 020 8340 5459 *Email:* lynne@lynnefeatherstone.org
Website: www.lynnefeatherstone.org *Twitter:* @lfeatherstone

FIELD, FRANK   Birkenhead *(Majority 15,195)*

Born 16 July 1942; Son of late Walter Field.

Education: St Clement Danes Grammar School, London; Hull University (BSc economics 1963).

Non-political career: Teacher in further education 1964-69; Director: Child Poverty Action Group 1969-79, Low Pay Unit 1974-80; Non-executive director, Medicash 2003-.

Political career: Contested Buckinghamshire South 1966 general election. Member for Birkenhead 1979-2010, for Birkenhead (revised boundary) since 6 May 2010 general election; Opposition Spokesperson for Education 1980-81; Minister of State, Department of Social Security (Welfare Reform) 1997-98; Leads Independent Review on Poverty and Life Chances 2010-. *Select committees:* Chair: Social Security 1990-97; Member: Public Accounts 2002-05, Ecclesiastical Committee. *Councils and public bodies:* Councillor, Hounslow Borough Council 1964-68; DL 2011.

LABOUR

Political interests: Poverty and income redistribution, church affairs; Poland.

Other: Chair: Churches Conservation Trust 2001-07, King James Bible Trust 2007-12; Trustee, Cathedral Fabrics Commission for England; Chair, The Birkenhead Education Trust. Three honorary doctorates; Two honorary fellowships. PC 1997.

Publications: Publications on low pay, poverty and social issues since 1971; Neighbours From Hell (2003); Attlee's Great Contemporaries (2009); Saints and Heroes (2010); Contributor, The Purple Book (Progress, 2011).

Rt Hon Frank Field MP, House of Commons, London SW1A 0AA
Tel: 020 7219 5193 *Fax:* 020 7219 0601 *Email:* fieldf@parliament.uk
Constituency: No constituency office
Tel: 0800 028 0293 *Website:* www.frankfield.co.uk *Twitter:* @frankfieldteam

FIELD, MARK
Cities of London and Westminster *(Majority 11,076)*

Mark Christopher Field. Born 6 October 1964; Son of late Major Peter Field and Ulrike Field, née Peipe; Married Michèle Acton 1994 (divorced 2006); married Victoria Elphicke 2007 (1 son 1 daughter).

Education: Reading School; St Edmund Hall, Oxford (BA law 1987, MA) (JCR President); College of Law, Chester (Solicitors' Finals 1988).

Non-political career: Trainee solicitor 1988-90; Solicitor, Freshfields 1990-92; Employment consultant 1992-94; Director and co-owner, Kellyfield Consulting 1994-2001; Member, advisory board, London School of Commerce 2005-; Adviser: Ellwood & Atfield 2011-, Cains (lawyer) 2011-.

CONSERVATIVE

Political career: Contested Enfield North 1997 general election. Member for Cities of London and Westminster 2001-10, for Cities of London and Westminster (revised boundary) since 6 May 2010 general election; Opposition Whip 2003-04; Shadow Minister for London 2003-05; Shadow Financial Secretary to the Treasury 2005; Shadow Minister for Culture 2005-06; Member Intelligence and Security Committee 2010-. *Select committees:* Member: Constitutional Affairs 2003-04, Procedure 2008-10. Association/ward officer, Kensington and Chelsea and Islington North Associations 1989-99. *Councils and public bodies:* Councillor, Royal London Borough of Kensington and Chelsea 1994-2002.

Political interests: Economy, financial services, small businesses, foreign affairs, security, employment; Germany, India, USA.

Other: Liveryman, Merchant Taylors' Company. Freeman, City of London; City of London Club (honorary); Carlton (honorary); RAC (honorary).

Publications: Contributing Chapters to: A Blue Tomorrow (Politicos, 2001), Reforming the City (Forum Press, 2009); Various and regular articles for national newspapers on financial services, pensions and economic issues; Regular contributor to BBC Radio 4 *Westminster Hour*, Sky News, BBC 2 *Daily Politics*, ITV *Late Debate*; Author, Between the Crashes: Reflections and Insights on UK Politics and Global Economics in the Aftermath of the Financial Crisis (Biteback, 2013).

Recreations: Football, cricket, popular/rock music, walking in London, history of London.

Mark Field MP, House of Commons, London SW1A 0AA
Tel: 020 7219 8155 *Fax:* 020 7219 1980 *Email:* fieldm@parliament.uk
Constituency: 90 Ebury Street, London SW1W 9QD
Tel: 020 7730 8181 *Fax:* 020 7730 4520 *Email:* office@westminsterconservatives.co.uk
Website: www.markfieldmp.com *Twitter:* @MarkFieldMP

FITZPATRICK, JIM
Poplar and Limehouse *(Majority 6,030)*

James Fitzpatrick. Born 4 April 1952; Son of James Fitzpatrick and Jean Fitzpatrick, née Stones; Married Jane Lowe 1980 (divorced) (1 son 1 daughter); married Dr Sheila Hunter 2003.

Education: Holyrood Secondary, Glasgow; Limited French, German, Spanish and Bangla.

Non-political career: Trainee, Tytrak Ltd, Glasgow 1970-73; Driver, Mintex Ltd, London 1973-74; Firefighter, London Fire Brigade 1974-97. Fire Brigades Union: Member 1974-97, Member, National Executive Council 1988-97.

LABOUR

Political career: Member for Poplar and Canning Town 1997-2010, for Poplar and Limehouse since 6 May 2010 general election; PPS to Alan Milburn as Secretary of State for Health 1999-2001; Assistant Government Whip 2001-03; Government Whip (Vice-Chamberlain of HM Household) 2003-05; Parliamentary Under-Secretary of State: Office of the Deputy Prime Minister 2005-06, Department of Trade and Industry (Employment Relations, Postal Services, London) 2006-07, Department for Transport (Minister for Aviation, Shipping and Road Safety) 2007-09; Minister of State, Department for Environment, Food and Rural Affairs (Minister for Food, Farming and the Environment) 2009-10; Shadow Minister for: Environment, Food and Rural Affairs 2010, Transport 2010-13. *Select committees:* Member: Selection 2003-05. Honorary Treasurer, PLP London Regional Group 1999-2001. Member: SNP 1969-70, Labour Party - 1977, Socialist Workers' Party 1978, Labour Party 1983-; Agent for Jo Richardson MP 1987; Member, London Labour Executive 1988-97; Chair: Barking Constituency Labour Party 1988-90, Greater London Labour Party 1991-97.

Political interests: Poverty, regeneration, racism, fire, animal welfare, transport; Bangladesh.

Other: Patron: Richard House Trust, Daneford Trust, Sreeper Village Orphanage, Bangladesh, Neighbours in Poplar, SS Robin, Ragged School Trust, London Waterways. Worshipful Company of Shipwrights. Freeman, City of London. Fire Brigade Long Service and Good Conduct Medal (HMQ) 1994. Honorary President, Millwall Rugby Football Club; Honorary Vice-President, Millwall Bowls; Honorary President Poplar, Blackwall and District Rowing Club.

Recreations: Reading, TV/film, West Ham United FC.

Jim Fitzpatrick MP, House of Commons, London SW1A 0AA
Tel: 020 7219 5085/020 7219 6215 *Fax:* 020 7219 2776
Email: jim.fitzpatrick.mp@parliament.uk
Constituency: Trussler Hall, 78 Grundy Street, London E14 6DR
Tel: 020 7536 0562 *Fax:* 020 7536 0572 *Website:* www.jimfitzpatrickmp.org
Twitter: @FitzMP

FLELLO, ROBERT
Stoke-on-Trent South *(Majority 4,130)*

Robert Charles Douglas Flello. Born 14 January 1966; Son of Valerie Flello, née Hughes, and Alfred Flello; Partner Karen Clarke.

Education: King's Norton Boys' School; University of Wales, Bangor (BSc chemistry 1987); Some French and Italian.

Non-political career: Executive officer, Inland Revenue 1987-89; Tax consultant, Price Waterhouse 1989-94; Manager, Arthur Andersen 1994-2000; Director, Platts Flello Ltd 2000-03; Chief executive officer, Malachi Community Trust 2003-04. Member: Unite, Unity, USDAW.

LABOUR

Political career: Member for Stoke-on-Trent South 2005-10, for Stoke-on-Trent South (revised boundary) since 6 May 2010 general election; PPS: to Lord Falconer of Thoroton as Lord Chancellor 2006-07, to Hazel Blears: as Minister without Portfolio 2007, as Secretary of State for Communities and Local Government 2007-09, to Bob Ainsworth as Secretary of State for Defence 2009-10; Shadow Minister for Justice 2010-13. *Select committees:* Member: Science and Technology 2005-07, Finance and Services 2010-. *Councils and public bodies:* Councillor, Birmingham City Council 2002-04.

Political interests: Employment, home affairs, Treasury matters, transport, defence, special needs education, environmental sustainability, justice for Colombia; Colombia, Cyprus, Italy, Norway.

Recreations: Motorbike riding, reading especially ancient history, cooking, visiting castles, exploring historical sites particularly Roman and Greek.

Robert Flello MP, House of Commons, London SW1A 0AA
Tel: 020 7219 3000 *Email:* flellor@parliament.uk
Constituency: Travers Court, City Road, Fenton, Stoke-on-Trent, Staffordshire ST4 2PY
Tel: 01782 844810 *Website:* www.robertflello.com *Twitter:* @RobFlelloMP

FLINT, CAROLINE
Don Valley *(Majority 3,595)*

Shadow Secretary of State for Energy and Climate Change

Caroline Louise Flint. Born 20 September 1961; Daughter of late Wendy Flint, née Beasley, clerical/shop employee; Married Saief Zammel (divorced) (1 son 1 daughter); married Phil Cole 2001 (1 stepson).

Education: Twickenham Girls School; Richmond Tertiary College; University of East Anglia (BA American history/literature and film studies 1983).

LABOUR

Non-political career: Graduate, Armed Forces Parliamentary Scheme. Management trainee, Greater London Council/Inner London Education Authority 1984-85; Policy officer, ILEA 1985-87; Head, Women's Unit, National Union of Students 1988-89; Lambeth Council 1989-93: Equal opportunities officer 1989-91, Welfare and staff development officer 1991-93; Senior researcher/political officer, GMB Trade Union 1994-97. Former shop steward: NALGO at GLC/ILEA, GMB at Lambeth Council; Member: GMB, Community.

Political career: Member for Don Valley 1997-2010, for Don Valley (revised boundary) since 6 May 2010 general election; Joint PPS to Ministers of State, Foreign and Commonwealth Office 1999-2001; PPS: to Peter Hain as Minister of State: Department of Trade and Industry 2001, Foreign and Commonwealth Office 2001-02, to John Reid: as Minister without Portfolio and Party Chair 2002-03, as Leader of the House of Commons and President of the Council 2003; Parliamentary Under-Secretary of State (PUSS), Home Office 2003-05; Department of Health 2005-07: PUSS (Public Health) 2005-06, Minister of State (MoS) (Public Health) 2006-07; MoS, Department for Work and Pensions (Minister for Employment and Welfare Reform) 2007-08; Minister for Yorkshire and the Humber 2007-08; Minister for Housing and Planning (attending Cabinet), Department for Communities and Local Government 2008; MoS, Foreign and Commonwealth Office (Europe) 2008-09; Shadow Secretary of State for: Communities and Local Government 2010-11, Energy and Climate Change 2011-. *Select committees:* Member: Education and Employment 1997-99, Education and Employment (Education Sub-Committee) 1997-99, Administration 2001-05, Modernisation of the House of Commons 2003. National Women's Officer, Labour Students 1983-85; Executive Member, Labour Co-ordinating Committee 1984-85; Chair, Brentford and Isleworth Constituency Labour Party 1991-95; Facilitator, Labour National Policy Forums 1994-97; Associate Editor, *Renewal* 1995-2000; Labour Party adviser to Police Federation of England and Wales 1999; Member, Trade Union Group of Labour MPs; Labour Friends of Israel; Friends of Labour Students; Labour Women's Network. *Councils and public bodies:* School Governor, Strand on the Green Primary 1992-96.

Political interests: Employment, childcare, welfare to work, crime, education, housing.

Other: Member: Inter-Parliamentary Union 1997-, British American Parliamentary Group 1997-; Chair Working For Childcare 1991-95; Board member: Sure Start Denaby Main Partnership 2000-03, Doncaster Early Years Development and Childcare Partnership 2001-03; President, Denaby Utd FC 2001-02; Member: Fabian Society, Progress. PC 2008.

Publications: Contributor, The Purple Book (Progress, 2011); The Power Book (LGIU, SERA, The Co-op Party, 2012).

Recreations: Cinema, family and friends.

Rt Hon Caroline Flint MP, House of Commons, London SW1A 0AA
Tel: 020 7219 4407 *Fax:* 020 7219 1277 *Email:* caroline.flint.mp@parliament.uk
Constituency: Meteor House, First Avenue, Auckley, Doncaster, South Yorkshire DN9 3GA
Tel: 01302 623330 *Fax:* 01302 775099 *Website:* www.carolineflintdonvalley.com
Twitter: @carolineflintmp

FLYNN, PAUL
Newport West *(Majority 3,544)*

Paul Philip Flynn. Born 9 February 1935; Son of late James and late Kathleen Flynn; Married 2nd Samantha Cumpstone 1985 (1 stepson 1 stepdaughter and 1 son and 1 daughter (deceased) from previous marriage).

Education: St Illtyd's College, Cardiff; University College of Wales, Cardiff; Welsh.

Non-political career: Chemist, steel industry 1962-83; Broadcaster, Gwent Community Radio 1983-84; Research officer for Llewellyn Smith MEP 1984-87.

LABOUR

Political career: Contested Denbigh October 1974 general election. Member for Newport West since 11 June 1987 general election; Opposition Spokesman on: Health and Social Security 1988-89, Social Security 1989-90; Board member, Parliamentary Office of Science and Technology (POST) 1997-. *Select committees:* Member: Welsh Affairs 1997-98, Environmental Audit 2003-05, Public Administration 2005-, Political and Constitutional Reform 2011-. Secretary, Welsh Group of Labour MPs 1997-2000. *Councils and public bodies:* Councillor: Newport Council 1972-81, Gwent County Council 1974-83.

Political interests: Health, medicinal and illegal drugs, social security, pensions, animal welfare, devolution, Welsh affairs, constitutional reform, modernisation of Parliament; Afghanistan, Azerbaijan, Baltic States, Eastern Europe, Hungary, Israel, Romania.

Other: Member, UK Delegation to Council of Europe and Western European Union 1997-. Campaign for Freedom of Information award 1991; Backbencher of the Year (jointly), Highland Park/*The Spectator* 1996; Best Website of an Elected Representative, *New Statesman* 2000; MP Website Awards for Design, BCS 2008; MP of the Year, *Welsh Yearbook* 2009.

Publications: Commons Knowledge. How to be a Backbencher (1997); Baglu Mlaen (Staggering Forward, 1998); Dragons Led by Poodles (1999); The Unusual Suspect (2010); How to be an MP (Biteback, 2012); Clockwinder Who Wouldn't Say No (Biteback, 2012).

Recreations: Local history, photography.

Paul Flynn MP, House of Commons, London SW1A 0AA
Tel: 020 7219 3478 *Fax:* 020 7219 2433
Constituency: No constituency office
Tel: 01633 262348 *Fax:* 01633 760532 *Email:* paulflynnmp@talk21.com
Website: www.paulflynnmp.co.uk *Twitter:* @Paulflynnmp

FOSTER, DON
Bath *(Majority 11,883)*

Deputy Chief Whip (Comptroller of HM Household)

LIBERAL DEMOCRAT

Donald Michael Ellison Foster. Born 31 March 1947; Son of late John Foster, vicar, and late Iris Foster, née Ellison; Married Victoria Pettegree 1968 (1 son 1 daughter).

Education: Lancaster Royal Grammar School; Keele University (BSc physics and psychology 1969; CEd 1969); Bath University (MEd 1981); French (enthusiastic).

Non-political career: Science teacher, Sevenoaks School, Kent 1969-75; Science project director, Resources for Learning Development Unit, Avon LEA 1975-80; Education lecturer, Bristol University 1980-89; Management consultant, Pannell Kerr Forster 1989-92.

Political career: Contested (Liberal/Alliance) Bristol East 1987 general election. Member (Lib Dem) for Bath 1992-2010, for Bath (revised boundary) since 6 May 2010 general election; Liberal Democrat: Spokesperson for: Education 1992-95, Education and Employment 1995-97; Principal Spokesperson for: Environment, Transport, the Regions and Social Justice 1999-2001, Transport, Local Government and the Regions 2001-02, Shadow Secretary of State for: Transport 2002-03, Culture, Media and Sport 2003-10; Sponsored Live Music Act 2012; Parliamentary Under-Secretary of State, Department for Communities and Local Government 2012-13; Deputy Chief Whip (Comptroller of HM Household) 2013-. *Select committees:* Member: Education and Employment 1996-99, Education and Employment (Education Sub-Committee) 1997-99. Chair, Liberal Democrat Parliamentary Party Committee on Culture, Media and Sport 2010-12. President, Liberal Democrat Youth and Students 1993-95. *Councils and public bodies:* Councillor, Avon County Council 1981-89; Executive, Association of County Councils 1985-89; Joint Honorary President, British Youth Council 1992-99.

Political interests: Education, local and regional government, transport, culture, media, sport and tourism; Africa.

Other: Vice-chair, British Association for Central and Eastern Europe 1994-97; Trustee, Open School and Education Extra 1993-99; National Campaign for Nursery Education: Vice-chair 1993-99, President 1999-2001; President, British Association for Early Childhood Education 1998-2002; Governor, Westminster Foundation for Democracy 2010-; Member, Olympic Board 2010-; CPhys; MInstP; Water Aid. Honorary Fellow, Bath College of High Education 1995. Sports Parliamentarian of the Year 2011. PC 2010; National Liberal.

Publications: Resource-based Learning in Science (1979); Science With Gas (1981); Co-author: Aspects of Science (1984), Reading About Science (1984), Nuffield Science (1986); Teaching Science 11-13 (1987); From the Three Rs to the Three Cs (2003); Numerous educational and political articles and pamphlets.

Recreations: Classical music, travel, sport.

Rt Hon Don Foster MP, House of Commons, London SW1A 0AA
Tel: 020 7219 4805 *Fax:* 020 7219 2695 *Email:* fosterd@parliament.uk
Constituency: 31 James Street West, Bath, Somerset BA1 2BT
Tel: 01225 338973 *Fax:* 01225 463630 *Website:* www.donfoster.co.uk
Twitter: @DonFosterMP

FOVARGUE, YVONNE
Makerfield *(Majority 12,490)*

Shadow Minister for Defence

LABOUR

Yvonne Helen Fovargue. Born 29 November 1956; Daughter of late Kenneth Gibbon and late Irene Gibbon; Married Paul Kenny 2009 (1 daughter).

Education: Sale Girls Grammar School; Leeds University (BA English 1978); Manchester City College (PGCE English and religious studies 1979); NVQ strategic management level 5 2003.

Non-political career: Housing department, Manchester City Council: Housing information manager 1979-82, Estate manager 1982-86; Newton le Willows Citizens Advice Bureau/St Helen's District Citizens Advice Bureau: Manager 1986-92, Chief executive 1992-2010. Member 1979-: NALGO, NUPE ASTMS, Amicus, Unite, USDAW.

Political career: Member for Makerfield since 6 May 2010 general election; Opposition Whip 2011-13; Shadow Minister for: Transport 2013, Defence 2013-. *Select committees:* Member: Health 2010-11, Joint Committee on Consolidation, Etc, Bills 2010-, Selection 2012-13. Vice-chair, PLP Departmental Group for Work and Pensions 2010-. Vice-chair, Warrington South CLP 2008-10. *Councils and public bodies:* Councillor, Warrington Borough Council 2004-10.

Political interests: Third sector, consumer credit and debt, employment law, health, legal aid.

Other: Member, Mensa; Trustee and board member, St Helens CVS 2001-10.

Recreations: Reading, theatre, music.

Yvonne Fovargue MP, House of Commons, London SW1A 0AA
Tel: 020 7219 3000 *Email:* yvonne.fovargue.mp@parliament.uk
Constituency: Wigan Investment Centre, Waterside Drive, Wigan WN3 5BA
Tel: 01942 824029 *Fax:* 01942 492746 *Website:* www.yvonnefovargue.com
Twitter: @Y_FovargueMP

FOX, LIAM

North Somerset *(Majority 7,862)*

CONSERVATIVE

Born 22 September 1961; Son of William Fox, teacher, and Catherine Fox; Married Jesme Baird 2005.

Education: St Bride's High School, East Kilbride; Glasgow University (MB, ChB 1983; MROGP 1989).

Non-political career: General practitioner, Beaconsfield, Buckinghamshire and Nailsea, North Somerset; Divisional surgeon, St John's Ambulance, Buckinghamshire.

Political career: Contested Roxburgh and Berwickshire 1987 general election. Member for Woodspring 1992-2010, for North Somerset since 6 May 2010 general election; PPS to Michael Howard as Home Secretary 1993-94; Assistant Government Whip 1994-95; Government Whip 1995-96; Parliamentary Under-Secretary of State, Foreign and Commonwealth Office 1996-97; Opposition Spokesperson for: Constitutional Affairs, Scotland and Wales 1997-99; Member Shadow Cabinet 1998-2010: Shadow Secretary of State for Health 1999-2003, Shadow Foreign Secretary 2005, Shadow Secretary of State for Defence 2005-10; Secretary of State for Defence 2010-11. *Select committees:* Member: Scottish Affairs 1992-93. Chair, Conservative Health/Social Services Policy Committee 2001-. Chair, West of Scotland Young Conservatives 1983; National vice-chair, Scottish Young Conservatives 1983-84; Secretary, West Country Conservative Members' Committee 1992-93; Co-chair, Conservative Party 2003-05; Contested Conservative Party leadership 2005.

Political interests: Health, economic policy, foreign affairs; USA.

Other: President, Glasgow University Club 1982-83; Guest of US State Department, involving study of drug abuse problems in USA, and Republican Party campaigning techniques 1985; Member, Central Committee, Families for Defence 1987-89. World Debating Competition, Toronto (Individual speaking prize) 1982; Best Speaker's Trophy, Glasgow University 1983. PC 2010.

Publications: Making Unionism Positive (1988).

Recreations: Tennis, swimming, cinema, theatre.

Rt Hon Dr Liam Fox MP, House of Commons, London SW1A 0AA
Tel: 020 7219 4198 *Email:* douglasi@parliament.uk
Constituency: 71 High Street, Nailsea, North Somerset BS48 1AW
Tel: 01275 790090 *Fax:* 01275 790091 *Email:* admin@northsomersetconservatives.com
Website: www.northsomersetconservatives.com www.liamfoxmp.co.uk
Twitter: @LiamFoxMP

FRANCIS, HYWEL

Aberavon *(Majority 11,039)*

LABOUR

David Hywel Francis. Born 6 June 1946; Son of David Francis, miners' union official, and Catherine Francis, housewife; Married Mair Price 1968 (1 daughter 2 sons (1 deceased)).

Education: Whitchurch Grammar School, Cardiff; University College of Wales, Swansea (BA history 1968; PhD 1978); Welsh.

Non-political career: Organisation department assistant, Trade Union Congress 1971-72; University College of Wales, Swansea 1972-99: Senior research assistant 1972-74, Department of Adult Continuing Education: Tutor and lecturer 1974-86, Director 1987-99, Professor 1992-99, Emeritus Professor; Special adviser to Paul Murphy MP as Secretary of State for Wales 1999-2000; Fellow, National Centre for Public Policy University of Wales, Swansea 2000-01. Member: AUT 1974-2001, ISTC Community 2000-.

Political career: Member for Aberavon since 7 June 2001 general election; Sponsored Carers (Equal Opportunities) Act 2004. *Select committees:* Welsh Affairs: Member 2001-10, Chair 2005-10; Member: European Standing Committee B 2003-05, Liaison 2005-, Liaison (National Policy Statements Sub-committee) 2009-10; Chair: Joint Committee on Human Rights 2010-. Contested South Wales West region 1999 National Assembly for Wales election.

Political interests: Carers' rights, disability rights, citizenship, European affairs, lifelong learning, steel, coal; China, Cuba, France, Italy, South Africa, Venezuela.

Other: Vice-president, Friends of Cyprus; Member Gorsedd of National Eisteddfod 1986; Fellow, Royal Society of the Arts 1988; Founder and trustee, Bevan Foundation 2000-; Member, Down's Syndrome Association; Trustee: Bevan Foundation 2001-, Paul Robeson Wales Trust 2001-; Vice-president, Carers UK; President: Côr Meibion Aberafan, Port Talbot Town Cricket Club, Welsh Miners' Museum, Seven Sisters RFC; Honorary life member, SNAC; Vice-president, Aberavon RFC; Honorary Parliamentary Patron, National Institute for Adult Continuing Education 2005-; Fellow, Royal Historical Society; Cronfa Sam Francis, Downs' Syndrome Association. Honorary DLitt, Swansea University. Campaigner of the Year Award, ITV Wales (2006). Aberavon RFC; Briton Ferry Steel Cricket Club; Port Talbot Cricket Club; Seven Sisters RFC.

Publications: Co-author, The Fed: A history of the South Wales miners in the Twentieth Century (Lawrence and Wishart, 1980, 1998); Miners against Fascism (Lawrence and Wishart, 1984, 2004, 2012); Co-editor, Communities and their Universities (Lawrence and Wishart, 1996); Wales: A learning country (Welsh Centre for Lifelong Learning, 1999); History on Our Side: Wales and the 1984-85 Miners' Strike (2009).

Recreations: Walking, cycling, swimming, cinema, reading, writing.

Dr Hywel Francis MP, House of Commons, London SW1A 0AA
Tel: 020 7219 8121 *Fax:* 020 7219 6223 *Email:* francish@parliament.uk
Constituency: Unit 7, Water Street Business Centre, Gwyn Terrace, Aberavon SA12 6LG
Tel: 01639 897660 *Fax:* 01639 891725 *Website:* www.hywelfrancis.co.uk

---

CONSERVATIVE

FRANCOIS, MARK

Rayleigh and Wickford *(Majority 22,338)*

Minister of State for Defence Personnel, Welfare and Veterans, Ministry of Defence

Mark Gino Francois. Born 14 August 1965; Son of Reginald Francois, engineer, and Anna Francois, née Carloni, cook; Married Karen Thomas 2000 (divorced 2006).

Education: St Nicholas Comprehensive School, Basildon; Bristol University (BA history 1986); King's College, London (MA war studies 1987).

Non-political career: TA 1983-89, Commissioned 1985. Management trainee, Lloyds Bank 1987; Market Access International (public affairs consultancy) 1988-95: Consultant, Director; Public affairs consultant, Francois Associates 1996-2001.

Political career: Contested Brent East 1997 general election. Member for Rayleigh 2001-10, for Rayleigh and Wickford since 6 May 2010 general election; Opposition Whip 2002-04; Shadow Economic Secretary 2004-05; Shadow Paymaster General 2005-07; Shadow Minister for Europe 2007-10; Government Whip (Vice-Chamberlain of HM Household) 2010-12; Minister of State for Defence Personnel, Welfare and Veterans, Ministry of Defence 2012-. *Select committees:* Member: Environmental Audit 2001-05, European Standing Committee A 2002-05, Selection 2010-12, Administration 2010-12, Armed Forces Bill 2011. *Councils and public bodies:* Councillor, Basildon District Council 1991-95.

Political interests: Defence, local and regional government, housing, environment.

Other: Member, Royal United Services Institute for Defence Studies 1991-; President: Friends of Holy Trinity Church, Rayleigh 2002-, Rayleigh Division, St John Ambulance 2002-; Patron, Rayleigh Branch of Royal British Legion 2002-; President: Rayleigh Brass Band 2006-, Wyvern Community Transport 2008-; Patron, Rayleigh Bowls Club 2011-; National Patron, Cruse Bereavement Care. Member, Worshipful Company of Wheelwrights 2003-. Freeman, City of London 2004. PC 2010; Carlton; Rayleigh Conservative Club.

Recreations: Reading, sports, military history, travel.

Rt Hon Mark Francois MP, House of Commons, London SW1A 0AA
Tel: 020 7219 8287 *Fax:* 020 7219 1858 *Email:* mark.francois.mp@parliament.uk
Constituency: 25 Bellingham Lane, Rayleigh, Essex SS6 7ED
Tel: 01268 742044 *Fax:* 01268 741833
Email: enquiries@rayleighandwickfordconservatives.com
Website: www.rayleighandwickfordconservatives.com www.markfrancoismp.com

CONSERVATIVE

FREEMAN, GEORGE
Mid Norfolk *(Majority 13,856)*

George William Freeman. Born 12 July 1967; Son of Arthur Freeman, National Hunt jockey and trainer, and Joanna Philipson; Married Eleanor Holmes (1 son 1 daughter).

Education: Radley College, Oxfordshire; Girton College, Cambridge (BA geography 1989); French.

Non-political career: Parliamentary officer, National Farmers Union 1990-92; Founder, The Local Identity Agency 1992-97; Director, Early Stage Ventures, Merlin Ventures 1997-2001; Chief executive officer, Amedis Pharmaceuticals 2001-03; Director, 4D Biomedical 2003-11; Adviser to Norwich Research Park Venture Fund 2007-10; Non-executive director, Elsoms Seeds Ltd.

Political career: Contested Stevenage 2005 general election. Member for Mid Norfolk since 6 May 2010 general election; PPS to Gregory Barker as Minister of State for Climate Change, Department of Energy and Climate Change 2010-12; Adviser on Life Sciences to David Willetts as Minister of State for Universities and Science 2011-. *Select committees:* Member: Communities and Local Government 2010. Founding member, 2020 group 2011-. *Councils and public bodies:* Governor, Bevington Primary School 1995-96; Board member, Greater Cambridge Partnership 2005-10.

Political interests: Constitution, crime, civil society, localism, rural economy, universities and innovation, biotechnology, healthcare reform; France, USA.

Other: Co-founder, Businesswise Learn to Earn 1995-97; Trustee, Cambridge Union Society 2005-09; Norfolk Club. Rob Roy Boat Club.

Recreations: Sailing, horseracing, hill walking, rowing.

George Freeman MP, House of Commons, London SW1A 0AA
Tel: 020 7219 1940 *Email:* george.freeman.mp@parliament.uk
Constituency: Wayland House, High Street, Watton, Thetford, Norfolk IP25 6AR
Tel: 01953 880215 *Email:* george@georgefreeman.co.uk *Website:* www.georgefreeman.co.uk
Twitter: @Freeman_george

CONSERVATIVE

FREER, MIKE
Finchley and Golders Green *(Majority 5,809)*

Michael Freer. Born 29 May 1960; Civil partnership 2007.

Education: Chadderton Grammar School, Manchester; St Aidan's School, Carlisle.

Non-political career: Retail catering industry; Retail gaming industry; Relationship director, Barclays Bank plc; Self-employed consultant.

Political career: Contested Harrow West 2005 general election. Member for Finchley and Golders Green since 6 May 2010 general election. *Select committees:* Member: Communities and Local Government 2010-11, Scottish Affairs 2010-13, Work and Pensions 2013-. Conservative Friends of Cyprus; Conservative Friends of Israel; Friend of British-Asian Conservative Link; Conservative Muslim Forum. *Councils and public bodies:* London Borough of Barnet Council: Councillor 1990-94, 2001-10, Council Leader 2006-09; Non-executive director, London Development Agency 2008-10; Vice-President, Local Government Association 2011-.

Political interests: Breast cancer screening, local government funding, local government reform, dementia, reducing cost of central government; Cyprus, Israel, Middle East, USA.

Other: Member, Friends of Windsor Open Space; Chair, Barnet Multi-faith Forum.

Recreations: Cycling, reading.

Mike Freer MP, House of Commons, London SW1A 0AA
Tel: 020 7219 7071 *Fax:* 020 7219 2211 *Email:* mike.freer.mp@parliament.uk
Constituency: Finchley and Golders Green Conservatives, 212 Ballards Lane, Finchley, London N3 2LX
Tel: 020 8445 5875 *Website:* www.finchleyconservatives.com www.mikefreer.com
Twitter: @mikefreermp

CONSERVATIVE

FULLBROOK, LORRAINE
South Ribble *(Majority 5,554)*

Born 1959; Married Mark.

Non-political career: Former press and media adviser; Consultant 2000-.

Political career: Contested South Ribble 2005 general election. Member for South Ribble since 6 May 2010 general election. *Select committees:* Member: Home Affairs 2010-. *Councils and public bodies:* Hart District Council: Councillor 2002-04, Leader 2003-04.

Political interests: Law and order, economy, immigration, EU.

Recreations: Reading, collecting advertising memorabilia, travel.

Lorraine Fullbrook MP, House of Commons, London SW1A 0AA
Tel: 020 7219 7217 *Email:* lorraine.fullbrook.mp@parliament.uk
Constituency: Office of Lorraine Fullbrook MP, Unit 6, Enterprise House, Meadowcroft Business Park, Pope Lane, Whitestake, Lancashire PR4 4BA
Email: info@lorrainefullbrook.com *Website:* www.lorrainefullbrook.com

CONSERVATIVE

FULLER, RICHARD
Bedford *(Majority 1,353)*

Richard Quentin Fuller. Born 30 May 1962.

Education: Bedford Modern School; Oxford University (BA philosophy, politics and economics 1981); Harvard Business School (MBA 1987).

Non-political career: Partner: LEK Consulting, Investcorp Technology Ventures.

Political career: Contested Bedford 2005 general election. Member for Bedford since 6 May 2010 general election. *Select committees:* Member: Regulatory Reform 2012-. Chair, Oxford University Conservative Association 1983; National chair, Young Conservatives 1985-87; Patron, Tory Reform Group.

Political interests: Social enterprise, entrepreneurship, small business, education, economic development in West Africa; Bangladesh, South Korea, Nigeria, USA.

Other: President, Bedfordshire Blue Raiders (American football).

Richard Fuller MP, House of Commons, London SW1A 0AA
Tel: 020 7219 7012 *Email:* richard.fuller.mp@parliament.uk
Constituency: 135 Midland Road, Bedford MK40 1DN
Tel: 01234 261487 *Website:* www.richardfuller.org.uk

CONSERVATIVE

GALE, ROGER
North Thanet *(Majority 13,528)*

Roger James Gale. Born 20 August 1943; Son of Richard Gale, solicitor, and Phyllis Gale, née Rowell; Married Wendy Bowman 1964 (divorced 1967); married Susan Sampson 1971 (divorced 1980) (1 daughter); married Susan Marks 1980 (2 sons).

Education: Thomas Hardye School, Dorchester; Guildhall School of Music and Drama (LGSM&D 1963); French (working).

Non-political career: Advanced post-graduate, Parliament and Armed Forces Scheme. Freelance broadcaster 1963-; Programme director, Radio Scotland 1965; Personal assistant to general manager, Universal Films 1971-72; Freelance reporter, BBC Radio London 1972-73; Producer: Radio 1 *Newsbeat*, BBC Radio 4 *Today* 1973-76; Director, BBC Children's Television 1976-79; Senior producer, Children's Television, Thames TV; Editor, Teenage Unit; Producer special projects, Thames TV 1979-83. Member: National Union of Journalists -2005, Equity, BECTU -2005.

Political career: Contested Birmingham Northfield 1982 by-election. Member for North Thanet 1983-2010, for North Thanet (revised boundary) since 6 May 2010 general election; PPS to Ministers of State for the Armed Forces: Archibald Hamilton 1992-93, Jeremy Hanley 1993-94. *Select committees:* Member: Home Affairs 1990-92, Broadcasting 1997-2005, Chairmen's Panel/Panel of Chairs 1997-, Procedure 2007-. Vice-chair, Conservative Party Committee for Culture, Media and Sport (Media) 1997-2001. President, Conservative Animal Welfare; Vice-chair: Holborn and St Pancras Conservative Association 1971-72, Conservative Party 2001-03. *Councils and public bodies:* Special constable, British Transport Police 2004-07.

Political interests: Education, animal welfare, media, broadcasting, tourism, leisure industry, licensed trade; Africa (Southern and Western), Cuba, Cyprus, Mongolia, Tunisia.

Other: Delegate: Council of Europe 1987-89, 2011-, Western European Union 1987-89; International Election Observer: Armenia, Botswana, The Gambia, Georgia, Ghana, Kenya, Macedonia, Mongolia, Mozambique, South Africa, Ukraine; Vice-President, St John (Herne Bay); President,

Herne Bay Air Cadets; Honorary Member, British Veterinary Association; Lord's Taverners; Fellow, Industry and Parliament Trust; Chairman, Try Angle Awards Foundation; Patron, Animals Worldwide; SPANA (Society for the Protection of Animals Abroad: Chairman, Trustee; LGSM&D; Christian Children's Fund; Dogs Trust; Animal Health Trust; Scouts; St John Ambulance; RNLI; Animals Worldwide; SPANA (Society for the Protection of Animals Abroad). Freeman, City of London. RSPCA Richard Martin Award for Outstanding Contribution to Animal Welfare. Kt 2012; Farmer's; Royal College of Defence Studies. Royal Temple Yacht.

Recreations: Swimming, sailing.

Sir Roger Gale MP, House of Commons, London SW1A 0AA
Tel: 020 7219 4087/07623 978479 (pager) *Email:* galerj@parliament.uk
Constituency: The Old Forge, 215a Canterbury Road, Birchington, Kent CT7 9AH
Tel: 01843 848588 (am) *Fax:* 01843 844856 *Email:* suzy@galemail.com
Website: www.rogergale.co.uk

GALLOWAY, GEORGE Bradford West *(Majority 10,140)*

Born 16 August 1954; Son of George, engineering worker, and Sheila Galloway, née Reilly, factory worker; Married Elaine Fyffe 1979 (divorced 1999) (1 daughter); married Dr Amineh Abu-Zayyad 2000 (divorced); partner Rima Husseini (2 sons); married Putri Gayatri Pertiwi 2012.

Education: Harris Academy, Dundee.

Non-political career: General labourer, Garden Works, Dundee 1972; Production worker, Michelin Tyres 1973; Labour organiser, Dundee East and West Constituencies 1977-83; General secretary, War on Want 1983-87; Presenter, *A Free World*, Al-Mayadeen TV, Beirut 2012-. Member, TGWU 1973-; Sponsored by TGWU 1987-96.

**RESPECT – THE
UNITY COALITION**

Political career: Member for Glasgow Hillhead 1987-97, for Glasgow Kelvin 1997-2005 (Independent Labour October 2003 to January 2004, Respect January 2004 to May 2005), for Bethnal Green and Bow 2005-10. Contested Poplar and Limehouse 2010 general election. Member for Bradford West since 29 March 2012 by-election. *Select committees:* Member: Broadcasting 1997-99, 2000. Contested Glasgow region (1) 2011 Scottish Parliament election. Chair, Scottish Labour Party 1980-81.

Political interests: Foreign affairs, defence; Bangladesh, Cuba, Iraq, Kashmir, Pakistan, Palestine, Scotland, Venezuela.

Other: Founder and Chair, Emergency Committee on Iraq and Palestine (ECIP) 1991-; Vice-president, Stop the War Coalition. Hilal-i-Quaid-Azam for services to the restoration of democracy in Pakistan 1990; Hilal-i-Pakistan for services to the people of Kashmir 1996; Kashmir Centres Europe Kashmir Award for work, efforts, support and services to the Kashmir cause 1998; Parliamentary Debater of the Year, *The Spectator* 2003; Groucho.

Publications: Co-author, Downfall: The Ceausescus and the Romanian Revolution (1989); I'm Not The Only One (2004); The Fidel Castro Handbook (2006); Open Season: The Neil Lennon Story (2011).

Recreations: Football, sport, films, music.

George Galloway MP, House of Commons, London SW1A 0AA
Tel: 020 7219 0867 *Fax:* 020 7219 7769 *Email:* george.galloway.mp@parliament.uk
Constituency: 2 Grattan Road, Bradford BD1 2LU
Tel: 01274 738269/07902 312641 *Email:* ggoffice2012@gmail.com
Website: www.votegeorgegalloway.com *Twitter:* @georgegalloway

GAPES, MIKE Ilford South *(Majority 11,287)*

Michael John Gapes. Born 4 September 1952; Son of late Frank Gapes, postal worker, and Emily Gapes, office worker.

Education: Buckhurst Hill County High School; Fitzwilliam College, Cambridge (MA economics 1975); Middlesex Polytechnic, Enfield (Diploma industrial relations 1976); French.

Non-political career: Voluntary Service Overseas teacher, Swaziland 1971-72; Secretary, Cambridge Students' Union 1973-74; Chair, National Organisation of Labour Students 1976-77; National student organiser, Labour Party 1977-80; Research officer, Labour Party International Department 1980-88; Senior international officer, Labour Party 1988-92. Member, TGWU.

LAB/CO-OP

Political career: Contested Ilford North 1983 general election. Member for Ilford South since 9 April 1992 general election; PPS to: Paul Murphy as Minister of State, Northern Ireland Office 1997-99, Lord Rooker as Minister of State, Home Office 2001-02. *Select committees:* Foreign

Affairs: Member 1992-97, 2010-, Chair 2005-10; Member: Defence 1999-2001, 2003-05, Liaison 2005-10, Quadripartite (Committees on Strategic Export Controls)/Arms Export Controls 2006-, Joint Committee on National Security Strategy 2010. Vice-chair, PLP Departmental Committee for Defence 1992-94, 1996-97; Chair, PLP Departmental: Committee for Children and the Family 1993-95, Group for Foreign and Commonwealth Affairs 2010-. Member, Labour National Policy Forum and Joint Policy Committee 1996-2005; Chair, Co-operative Party, Parliamentary Group 2000-01; Trade union liaison officer, London Group of Labour MPs 2001-05.

Political interests: Defence, international affairs, European Union, economic policy, education, mental health.

Other: Vice-President, Council of European National Youth Committees 1977-79; Member: NATO Parliamentary Assembly 2002-05, 2010-, OSCE Parliamentary Assembly 2005-10; Treasurer, Inter-Parliamentary Union, British Group 2010-; President, Redbridge United Chinese Association 1992-; Vice-President, Redbridge Chamber of Commerce 1992-; Member, Redbridge Racial Equality Council 1992-; Council member: Royal Institute of International Affairs 1996-99, Voluntary Service Overseas 1997-2010; Trustee, Parkside Community Association 1999-2010; Chair, Westminster Foundation for Democracy 2002-05; Fellow, Industry and Parliament Trust 2005; Ilford and Woodford Royal Airforce Association; Webb Memorial Trust; Shelter; Oxfam; Voluntary Service Overseas; Cardiac Risk in the Young. Vice-President, Ilford Football Club; West Ham United Supporters' Club.

Recreations: Watching football at West Ham, blues and jazz music.

Mike Gapes MP, House of Commons, London SW1A 0AA
Tel: 020 7219 6485 *Email:* mike.gapes.mp@parliament.uk
Constituency: No constituency office publicised *Website:* www.mikegapes.org.uk
Twitter: @MikeGapes

LABOUR

GARDINER, BARRY
Brent North *(Majority 8,028)*

Shadow Minister for Natural Environment and Fisheries

Barry Strachan Gardiner. Born 10 March 1957; Son of late John Flannegan Gardiner, general manager Kelvin Hall, and late Sylvia Strachan, doctor; Married Caroline Smith 1979 (3 sons 1 daughter).

Education: Haileybury College, Hertford; St Andrews University (MA philosophy 1983); Harvard University (J. F. Kennedy Scholarship 1984); Cambridge University (research 1984-87); French, Russian.

Non-political career: Partner, Mediterranean Average Adjusting Co 1987-97; Occasional lecturer, Academy of National Economy, Moscow, Russia 1992-96. Member: MSF, GMB.

Political career: Member for Brent North 1997-2010, for Brent North (revised boundary) since 6 May 2010 general election; PPS to Beverley Hughes as Minister of State, Home Office 2002-04; Parliamentary Under-Secretary of State: Northern Ireland Office 2004-05, Department of Trade and Industry 2005-06, Minister for Biodiversity, Landscape and Rural Affairs, Department for Environment, Food and Rural Affairs 2006-07; Prime Minister's Special Envoy for Forestry 2007-08; PPS to Lord Mandelson as Secretary of State for Business, Enterprise and Regulatory Reform/Business, Innovation and Skills 2009-10; Leader of the Opposition's Special Envoy for Climate Change and the Environment 2011-; Shadow Minister for Natural Environment and Fisheries 2013-. *Select committees:* Member: Procedure 1997-2001, Broadcasting 1998-2001, Public Accounts 1999-2002, Joint Committee on Consolidation of Bills Etc 2001-10, Energy and Climate Change 2010-, Environment, Food and Rural Affairs 2011-. Chair, PLP Departmental Committee for Culture, Media and Sport 2002-04; Vice-chair, PLP Departmental: Committee for the Treasury 2002-04, Group for Energy and Climate Change 2010-; Chair, PLP Departmental Group for Environment, Food and Rural Affairs 2010-. Member, Labour Finance and Industry Group; Former vice-chair, Labour Friends of Israel; Chair, Labour Friends of India 1999-2002, 2008-. *Councils and public bodies:* Cambridge City Council: Councillor 1988-94, Chair of Finance, Mayor 1992-93.

Political interests: Chinese community in the UK, economic policy, trade and industry, education, foreign affairs, environment, climate change, India-UK relations; Brazil, China, India, Russia, Sri Lanka.

Other: Chairman of the Board, GLOBE International Ltd (Global Legislators Organisation); Fellow, The Linnean Society; Associate, Chartered Insurance Institute; Fellow, The Linnean Society; Move It!; Fryent Country Park. Member, Shipwrights' Company. Freeman, City of London.

Publications: Various articles on shipping and maritime affairs; Articles on political philosophy in *Philosophical Quarterly*; Articles on Energy Policy and the Environment.

Recreations: Walking, music, reading philosophy, bird-watching, singing, opera.

Barry Gardiner MP, House of Commons, London SW1A 0AA
Tel: 020 7219 4046 *Fax:* 020 7219 2495 *Email:* barry.gardiner.mp@parliament.uk
Constituency: No constituency office *Website:* www.barrygardinermp.com
Twitter: @BarryGardiner

GARNIER, EDWARD
Harborough *(Majority 9,797)*

Edward Henry Garnier. Born 26 October 1952; Son of late Colonel William d'Arcy Garnier, and Hon. Mrs Garnier; Married Anna Mellows 1982 (2 sons 1 daughter).

Education: Wellington College, Berkshire; Jesus College, Oxford (BA modern history 1974, MA); College of Law, London; French.

Non-political career: Barrister; Called to the Bar, Middle Temple 1976; QC 1995; Assistant Recorder 1998; Recorder 2000; Northern Ireland Bar 2010 Bencher: Middle Temple 2001, Inn Court of Northern Ireland 2010.

CONSERVATIVE

Political career: Contested Hemsworth 1987 general election. Member for Harborough 1992-2010, for Harborough (revised boundary) since 6 May 2010 general election; PPS to: Alastair Goodlad and David Davis as Ministers of State, Foreign and Commonwealth Office 1994-95, Sir Nicholas Lyell as Attorney-General and Sir Derek Spencer as Solicitor-General 1995-97, Roger Freeman as Chancellor of the Duchy of Lancaster 1996-97; Shadow Minister, Lord Chancellor's Department 1997-99; Shadow Attorney General 1999-2001; Shadow Minister for: Home Affairs 2005-07, Justice 2007-09; Shadow Attorney General 2009-10; Solicitor General 2010-12. *Select committees:* Member: Home Affairs 1992-95. Member, Executive, 1922 Committee 2002-05. Treasurer, Macleod Group of Conservative MPs 1995-97; Chair, Executive Committee, Society of Conservative Lawyers 2003-.

Political interests: Agriculture, defence, foreign affairs, education, constitutional affairs.

Other: Director, Great Britain-China Centre 1998-2010; Trustee, China-Oxford Scholarship Fund 2006-10; Foreign Affairs Forum: Secretary 1988-92, Vice-chair 1992-; Visiting Parliamentary Fellow, St Antony's College, Oxford 1996-97; Advisory Board, Samaritans 2013-. Kt 2012; White's, Pratt's, Vincent's (Oxford).

Publications: Co-author Bearing the Standard: Themes for a Fourth Term (1991); Facing the Future (1993); Contributor to Halsbury's Laws of England (4th edition, 1985).

Recreations: Shooting, cricket, tennis, skiing, opera, biographical research.

Sir Edward Garnier QC MP, House of Commons, London SW1A 0AA
Tel: 020 7219 4034 *Email:* edward.garnier.mp@parliament.uk
Constituency: 24 Nelson Street, Market Harborough, Leicestershire LE16 9AY
Tel: 01858 464146 *Fax:* 01858 410013 *Email:* office@harboroughconservatives.com
Website: www.harboroughconservatives.com www.edwardgarnier.co.uk

GARNIER, MARK
Wyre Forest *(Majority 2,643)*

Mark Robert Timothy Garnier. Born 26 February 1963; Son of late Peter Garnier, motoring writer, and Patricia Garnier, née Dowden, journalist; Married Caroline Joyce 2001 (2 sons 1 daughter).

Education: Charterhouse, Surrey.

Non-political career: Manager, Swiss Bank Corporation 1982-89; Managing director, South China Securities (UK) Ltd 1989-95; Executive director, Daiwa Europe Ltd 1995-96; Executive, L.C.F Edmond de Rothschild Securities 1996-97; Executive director, Bear Stearns 1998; Self-employed hedge fund adviser 1999-2005; Partner, CGR Capital LLP 2006-09; Senior partner, Severn Capital LLP 2009-.

CONSERVATIVE

Political career: Contested Wyre Forest 2005 general election. Member for Wyre Forest since 6 May 2010 general election. *Select committees:* Member: Treasury 2010-, Parliamentary Commission on Banking Standards 2012-13. Deputy chairman (membership), Forest of Dean Conservative Association 2003-04. *Councils and public bodies:* Councillor, Forest of Dean District Council 2003-07.

Political interests: Health issues, rural interests, transport, economic issues.

Other: Fellow: Securities and Investment Institute, Chartered Securities Institute; Chairman, Investment Committee, Coachmakers of London. Court assistant, Worshipful Company of Coachmakers and Coach Harness Makers of London. Freeman of the City of London; Royal Automobile Club; Carlton Club. North London Rifle Club.

Recreations: Historic aviation, historic motorsport, full-bore target rifle, shooting, fishing, photography, writing, skiing.

Mark Garnier MP, House of Commons, London SW1A 0AA
Tel: 020 7219 7198 *Email:* mark.garnier.mp@parliament.uk
Constituency: 9a Lower Mill Street, Kidderminster, Worcestershire DY11 6UU
Tel: 01562 746771 *Website:* www.markgarnier.co.uk *Twitter:* @Mark4wyreForest

GAUKE, DAVID
South West Hertfordshire *(Majority 14,920)*

Exchequer Secretary, HM Treasury

David Michael Gauke. Born 8 October 1971; Son of Jim Gauke and Susan Hall; Married Rachel Rank 2000 (3 sons).

Education: Northgate High School, Ipswich; St Edmund Hall, Oxford (BA law 1993); College of Law, Chester (legal practice course 1995).

Non-political career: Parliamentary research assistant to Barry Legg MP 1993-94; Trainee solicitor and solicitor, Richards Butler 1995-99; Solicitor, Macfarlanes 1999-2005.

CONSERVATIVE

Political career: Contested Brent East 2001 general election. Member for South West Hertfordshire 2005-10, for South West Hertfordshire (revised boundary) since 6 May 2010 general election; Shadow Exchequer Secretary to the Treasury 2007-10; Exchequer Secretary, HM Treasury 2010-. *Select committees:* Member: Procedure 2005-07, Treasury 2006-07, Joint Committee on Tax Law Rewrite Bills 2009. Deputy chair, Brent East Conservative Association 1998-2000; Member: Conservative Friends of Israel 2000-; Centre for Policy Studies 2003-.

Political interests: Education, Europe, tax, the economy.

Other: Law Society 1997; Friends of Watersmeet 2004-; Hospice of St Francis; Iain Rennie Hospice at Home; The Peace Hospice (Watford); Rickmansworth Conservative Club; Tring Conservative Club.

Recreations: Football, cricket, country walks.

David Gauke MP, House of Commons, London SW1A 0AA
Tel: 020 7219 4459 *Fax:* 020 7219 4759 *Email:* gauked@parliament.uk
Constituency: South West Hertfordshire Conservative Association, Scots Bridge House, Scots Hill, Rickmansworth, Hertfordshire WD3 3BB
Tel: 01923 771781 *Fax:* 01923 779471 *Email:* david@davidgauke.com
Website: www.davidgauke.com

GEORGE, ANDREW
St Ives *(Majority 1,719)*

Andrew Henry George. Born 2 December 1958; Son of Reginald George, horticulturist, and Diana George, née Petherick, teacher and musician; Married Jill Elizabeth Marshall 1987 (1 son 1 daughter).

Education: Helston Grammar School; Helston School; Sussex University (BA cultural and community studies 1980); University College, Oxford (MSc agricultural economics 1981); Cornish (little), French (little).

Non-political career: Agriculture Work; Research and writing; Charity worker for various rural community development bodies, Nottinghamshire, Cornwall; Deputy director, Cornwall Rural Community Council 1994-97.

LIBERAL DEMOCRAT

Political career: Contested St Ives 1992 general election. Member for St Ives 1997-2010, for St Ives (revised boundary) since 6 May 2010 general election; Liberal Democrat Shadow Minister for: Fisheries 1997-2005; Disabilities 1999-2001; PPS to Charles Kennedy as Leader of the Liberal Democrat Party 2001-02; Liberal Democrat Shadow: Minister for Food and Rural Affairs 2002-05, Secretary of State for International Development 2005-06. *Select committees:* Member: Agriculture 1997-2000, Communities and Local Government 2007-10, Health 2010-. Chair, Liberal Democrat Parliamentary Party Committee on Energy and Climate Change; Environment, Food and Rural Affairs 2010-12.

Political interests: International development, Cornwall, economic development, housing, fishing industry, agriculture, social exclusion, devolution, small nations, anti-racism, domestic violence, immigration, environment, gypsy, Romany, travellers, minority groups, health services and health professions, global TB; All small nations, Africa, Canada, Greece, Sri Lanka, Yemen.

Other: Chair: Grocery Market Action Group, Marbles Reunited (Restitution of the Pantheon Marbles); Supporter of Third World development, environmental, anti poverty and anti-racial discrimination charities. House of Commons and House of Lords Cricket Club; House of Commons and House of Lords Rugby Club; House of Commons Football Team; Leedstown Cricket Club.

Publications: Planning – A Guide (1986); The Natives are Revolting Down in the Cornwall Theme Park (1986); Homes for Locals (1987); Cornwall at the Crossroads (1989); Co-author, A Vision of Cornwall (1995); A View from the Bottom Left-hand Corner (Patten Press, 2002).

Recreations: Cricket, football, rugby, tennis, swimming, writing, walking, Cornish culture, cycling, gardening, drawing, singing, poetry, poultry keeping.

Andrew George MP, House of Commons, London SW1A 0AA
Tel: 020 7219 4588 *Fax:* 020 7219 5572 *Email:* andrew.george.mp@parliament.uk
Constituency: Trewella, 18 Mennaye Road, Penzance, Cornwall TR18 4NG
Tel: 01736 360020 *Fax:* 01736 332866 *Email:* andrew@andrewgeorge.org.uk
Website: www.andrewgeorge.org.uk *Twitter:* @AndrewGeorgeLD

GIBB, NICK

Bognor Regis and Littlehampton *(Majority 13,063)*

Nicholas John Gibb. Born 3 September 1960; Son of late John Gibb, civil engineer, and Eileen Gibb, schoolteacher; Single.

Education: Maidstone Boys' Grammar School, Kent; Roundhay School, Leeds; Thornes House School, Wakefield; Durham University (BA law 1981).

Non-political career: Chartered accountant, specialising in taxation, KPMG, London 1984-97.

Political career: Contested Stoke-on-Trent Central 1992 general election and Rotherham 1994 by-election. Member for Bognor Regis and Littlehampton 1997-2010, for Bognor Regis and Littlehampton (revised boundary) since 6 May 2010 general election; Opposition Spokesperson for: the Treasury December 1998-99, Trade and Industry 1999-2001, Transport, Local Government and the Regions 2001; Shadow Minister for: Education and for Young People 2005, Schools 2005-10; Minister of State for Schools, Department for Education 2010-12. *Select committees:* Member: Social Security 1997-98, Treasury 1998, Treasury (Treasury Sub-Committee) 1998, Public Accounts 2001-03, Education and Skills 2003-05; Chair: Joint Committee on Voting Eligibilty (Prisoners) Bill 2013-. Member, Policy Advisory Board 2013-.

CONSERVATIVE

Political interests: Economics, taxation, education, social security; Israel, USA.

Other: Fellow, Institute of Chartered Accountants in England and Wales.

Recreations: Long-distance running, skiing.

Nick Gibb MP, House of Commons, London SW1A 0AA
Tel: 020 7219 6374 *Fax:* 020 7219 1395 *Email:* gibbn@parliament.uk
Constituency: 2 Flansham Business Centre, Hoe Lane, Bognor Regis, West Sussex PO22 8NJ
Tel: 01243 587016

GILBERT, STEVE

St Austell and Newquay *(Majority 1,312)*

PPS to Edward Davey as Secretary of State for Energy and Climate Change

Stephen David John Gilbert. Born 6 November 1976; Son of Jackie Bull and David Gilbert.

Education: Fowey Community School, Cornwall; St Austell College; Aberystwyth University (BScEcon international politics 1998); London School of Economics (MScEcon international relations 2000).

Non-political career: Parliamentary assistant to Lembit Öpik MP 1998; Research and media assistant to Robin Teverson MEP 1998-99; Account executive, PPS 2000-02; Public affairs manager: IMA 2002-04, Fidelity Investments 2004-05; Account manager, Deborah Clark Associates 2005-07.

LIBERAL DEMOCRAT

Political career: Member for St Austell and Newquay since 6 May 2010 general election; PPS to Edward Davey as Secretary of State for Energy and Climate Change 2012-. *Select committees:* Member: Communities and Local Government 2010-13. Chair, Liberal Democrat Parliamentary Party Committee on International Affairs (Defence) 2011-12. Member, Liberal Democrats 1992-. *Councils and public bodies:* Councillor: Restormel Borough Council 1998-2002, London Borough of Haringey Council 2002-06.

Political interests: Communities, affordable housing, environment, civil liberties; East Europe, MENA region.

Other: Member, UK Parliamentary Delegation to NATO; Member, Chartered Institute of Public Relations. St Austell Rugby Club.

Recreations: Cinema, gym, travel.

Steve Gilbert MP, House of Commons, London SW1A 0AA
Tel: 020 7219 7153 *Fax:* 020 7219 4180 *Email:* stephen.gilbert.mp@parliament.uk
Constituency: c/o St Austell and Newquay Lib Dems, 10 South Street, St Austell, Cornwall PL25 5BH
Tel: 01726 63443 *Fax:* 01726 68457 *Email:* steve@stevegilbert.info
Website: www.stevegilbert.info *Twitter:* @stephen_gilbert

SINN FÉIN

GILDERNEW, MICHELLE   Fermanagh and South Tyrone *(Majority 4)*

Born 28 March 1970; Married Jimmy (2 sons 1 daughter).

Education: St Catherine's College, Armagh; Ulster University, Coleraine.

Political career: Member for Fermanagh and South Tyrone since 7 June 2001 general election; MLA for Fermanagh and South Tyrone 1998-2012: Sinn Féin Spokesperson for: Social Development, Women's issues, Member, Preparation for Government Committee 2006-07, Minister of Agriculture and Rural Development 2007-11, Chair, Assembly Committee on Health, Social Services and Public Safety 2011-12, Sinn Féin Spokesperson for Health 2011-12. Sinn Féin: Member, Inter-Party talks team; Press officer 1997; Head of London office 1997-98.

Political interests: Housing, rural affairs, education.

Other: Aghaloo GFC.

Michelle Gildernew MP, House of Commons, London SW1A 0AA
Tel: 020 7219 8162 *Fax:* 020 7219 6107 *Email:* gildernewm@parliament.uk
Constituency: Thomas Clarke House, 60 Irish Street, Dungannon, Co Tyrone BT70 1QD
Tel: 028 8772 2776 *Email:* michelle.gildernew@sinn-fein.ie *Twitter:* @gildernewmp

CONSERVATIVE

GILLAN, CHERYL   Chesham and Amersham *(Majority 16,710)*

Cheryl Elise Kendall Gillan. Born 21 April 1952; Daughter of late Adam Gillan, company director, and late Mona Gillan; Married John Coates Leeming 1985.

Education: Cheltenham Ladies' College; College of Law; Chartered Institute of Marketing.

Non-political career: International Management Group 1977-84; Director, British Film Year 1984-86; Senior marketing consultant, Ernst and Young 1986-91; Marketing director, Kidsons Impey 1991-93; Consultant PKF 1999-2005.

Political career: Member for Chesham and Amersham 1992-2010, for Chesham and Amersham (revised boundary) since 6 May 2010 general election; PPS to Viscount Cranborne as Leader of the House of Lords and Lord Privy Seal 1994-95; Parliamentary Under-Secretary of State, Department of Education and Employment 1995-97; Shadow Minister for: Trade and Industry 1997-98, Foreign and Commonwealth Affairs 1998-2001, International Development 1998-2001; Opposition Whip 2001-03; Shadow Minister for Home Affairs 2003-05; Shadow Secretary of State for Wales 2005-10; Secretary of State for Wales 2010-12. *Select committees:* Member: Science and Technology 1992-95, Procedure 1994-95, Public Accounts 2003-04. Contested Greater Manchester Central 1989 European Parliament election.

Political interests: Industry, space, international affairs, defence, education, employment; China, Commonwealth, Europe, Hungary, Japan, Pacific Rim, Poland, former Soviet Union, USA.

Other: Member Executive Committee, Commonwealth Parliamentary Association (CPA) UK Branch 1998-: UK Representative British Islands and Mediterranean region 1999-2004, international treasurer 2004-06; Member: NATO Parliamentary Assembly 2003-05, Council of Europe 2012-; Chair, Bow Group 1987-88; FCIM. Member, Worshipful Company of Marketors. Freeman, City of London. MP of the Year, *Wales Yearbook* awards 2011. PC 2010; RAC.

Recreations: Golf, music, gardening.

Rt Hon Cheryl Gillan MP, House of Commons, London SW1A 0AA
Tel: 020 7219 4061 *Fax:* 020 7219 2762 *Email:* cheryl.gillan.mp@parliament.uk
Constituency: 7a Hill Avenue, Amersham, Buckinghamshire HP6 5BD
Tel: 01494 721577 *Email:* shawmj@parliament.uk *Website:* www.cherylgillan.co.uk
Twitter: @CherylGillanMP

LABOUR

GILMORE, SHEILA
Edinburgh East *(Majority 9,181)*

Born 1 October 1949; Daughter of Harry Hawthorne and Elizabeth McDonald; Married Brian Gilmore 1969 (3 sons 1 daughter).

Education: George Watson's College, Edinburgh; Kent University (history and politics 1970); Edinburgh University (law 1977).

Non-political career: Teacher, Glasgow 1971-73; Lawyer, solicitor's firm, Edinburgh 1977-2001.

Political career: Member for Edinburgh East since 6 May 2010 general election; PPS to Jon Trickett as Shadow Minister for the Cabinet Office 2011-. *Select committees:* Member: Political and Constitutional Reform 2010-, Work and Pensions 2011-. Chair PLP Departmental Group for Work and Pensions 2011-. Contested Edinburgh Pentlands constituency 2007 Scottish Parliament election. Election agent to Nigel Griffiths MP 1992-2005. *Councils and public bodies:* Councillor, Edinburgh City Council 1991-2007.

Political interests: Employment, Incapacity Benefit, Employment and Support Allowance, disabilities, housing, women's issues.

Recreations: Cycling, reading.

Sheila Gilmore MP, House of Commons, London SW1A 0AA
Tel: 020 7219 7062 *Email:* sheila.gilmore.mp@parliament.uk
Constituency: 84 Niddrie Mains Road, Edinburgh EH16 4DT
Tel: 0131-661 7522 *Website:* www.sheilagilmore.co.uk *Twitter:* @SheilaGilmoreMP

LABOUR

GLASS, PATRICIA
North West Durham *(Majority 7,612)*

Born February 1956; Married Bob (2 children).

Education: St Leonards RC School, Durham; New College, Durham; Sunderland University (BEd); Northumbria University (MSc).

Non-political career: Local education authorities 1973-2006; Government adviser on education 2006-10. GMB.

Political career: Member for North West Durham since 6 May 2010 general election; PPS to Maria Eagle as Shadow Secretary of State for Transport 2011-. *Select committees:* Member: Education 2010-.

Political interests: Education, transport; Africa, Eastern Europe.

Other: Fabian Society; Co-operative Society.

Patricia Glass MP, House of Commons, London SW1A 0AA
Tel: 020 7219 7054 *Fax:* 020 7219 1652 *Email:* pat.glass.mp@parliament.uk
Constituency: 1 Gledstone House, 26 Newmarket Street, Consett, Co Durham DH8 5LQ
Tel: 01207 501782 *Fax:* 01207 501791 *Website:* www.patglassmp.org.uk
Twitter: @PatGlassMP

GLEN, JOHN
Salisbury *(Majority 5,966)*

PPS to Eric Pickles as Secretary of State for Communities and Local Government

John Philip Glen. Born 1 April 1974; Son of Philip Glen, nursery man, and Thalia Glen, hairdresser; Married Emma O'Brien 2008 (1 stepson 1 stepdaughter).

Education: King Edward's School, Bath; Mansfield College, Oxford (BA modern history 1996, MA) (Student Union President); Judge Institute, Cambridge (MBA 2003).

CONSERVATIVE

Non-political career: Parliamentary researcher to Michael Bates MP and Gary Streeter MP 1996-97; Strategy consultant, Andersen Consulting 1997-2004: Head of political section, Office of William Hague MP as Leader of the Opposition (on secondment) 2000-01; Research Department, Conservative Party: Deputy director 2004-05, Director 2005-06; Senior adviser to global head of strategy, Accenture 2006-10; Director, Walton Bates 2007-.

Political career: Contested Plymouth Devonport 2001 general election. Member for Salisbury since 6 May 2010 general election; PPS to Eric Pickles as Secretary of State for Communities and Local Government 2012-. *Select committees:* Member: Defence 2010-12, Arms Export Controls 2010-12. *Councils and public bodies:* JP, Westminster 2006-12.

Political interests: Policy development, youth issues, armed forces, foreign affairs, education, health; Maldives, Uganda, USA.

Other: Board member, Centre for Policy Studies 2009-10; Chippenham Constitutional Club; National Club.

Recreations: Church, family, eating out, friends.

John Glen MP, House of Commons, London SW1A 0AA
Tel: 020 7219 7138 *Fax:* 020 7219 3951 *Email:* john.glen.mp@parliament.uk
Constituency: The Morrison Hall, 12 Brown Street, Salisbury, Wiltshire SP1 1HE
Tel: 01722 323050 *Fax:* 01722 327080 *Website:* www.johnglenmp.com
Twitter: @JohnGlenMP

GLINDON, MARY
North Tyneside *(Majority 12,884)*

Mary Theresa Glindon. Born 13 January 1957; Daughter of Margaret and Cecil Mulgrove; Married Raymond Glindon 2000 (1 daughter 1 stepson 1 stepdaughter).

Education: Sacred Heart Grammar School, Fenham, Newcastle upon Tyne; Newcastle upon Tyne Polytechnic (BSc sociology 1979).

Non-political career: Clerical officer, civil service 1980-85; Administrator, local government 1987-88; Administrator/community development/manager, Centre for Unemployment 1988-2004; Administrator, NHS call centre 2005; Trainee dispenser, NHS 2005-06; Travel sales adviser, call centre 2006; Sales assistant, department store 2006-08; Administration officer, Department for Work and Pensions and Child Maintenance and Enforcement Commission 2008-10. Member: North Tyneside Trades Union Council, GMB.

LABOUR

Political career: Member for North Tyneside since 6 May 2010 general election. *Select committees:* Member: Environment, Food and Rural Affairs 2010-, Unopposed Bills (Panel) 2011-, Communities and Local Government 2013-. Member, Labour Party 1990-; Former constituency chair and vice-chair -2010. *Councils and public bodies:* Councillor, North Tyneside Council 1995-2010; Deputy Mayor 1998-99, Mayor 1999-2000.

Political interests: Employment, housing, health, environment, older people's issues; Middle East.

Other: Founding member and treasurer, Battle Hill Community Development Project 1983-; Kettlewell Education Trust; Parliamentary patron, YMCA; Ambassador for Scouts.

Recreations: Travel, history, walking.

Mary Glindon MP, House of Commons, London SW1A 0AA
Tel: 020 7219 3000 *Fax:* 020 7219 3272 *Email:* mary.glindon.mp@parliament.uk
Constituency: Suites 1 & 2, Salisbury House, 2 Buddle Street, Wallsend NE28 6EH
Tel: 0191-234 2493 *Website:* www.northtynesidelabour.co.uk www.maryglindonmp.co.uk

GODSIFF, ROGER
Birmingham, Hall Green *(Majority 3,799)*

Roger Duncan Godsiff. Born 28 June 1946; Son of late George Godsiff, chargehand/fitter, and Gladys Godsiff; Married Julia Morris 1977 (1 son 1 daughter).

Education: Catford Comprehensive School, London.

Non-political career: Banking 1965-70; Political officer, APEX 1970-88; Senior research officer, GMB 1988-91; Chair (unpaid), South of England Foundation 2001-; Director (unpaid), Syrian Society -2011. Member of, and sponsored by, GMB.

LABOUR

Political career: Contested Birmingham Yardley 1983 general election. Member for Birmingham Small Heath 1992-97, for Birmingham Sparkbrook and Small Heath 1997-2010, for Birmingham, Hall Green since 6 May 2010 general election; Member, Co-operative Party. *Councils and public bodies:* London Borough of Lewisham: Councillor 1971-90, Mayor 1977.

Political interests: European Union, foreign affairs, sport, recreation, immigration; America, Asia, Middle East, Indian sub-continent, Japan.

Other: Member, Executive Committee, IPU 1999; Fellow, Industry and Parliament Trust 1994; Chair, Charlton Athletic Community Trust 2002-. Member, Charlton Athletic Supporters Club.

Recreations: Sport in general, particularly football.

Roger Godsiff MP, House of Commons, London SW1A 0AA
Tel: 020 7219 5191 *Fax:* 020 7219 2221 *Email:* godsiffr@parliament.uk
Constituency: 62 Horse Shoes Lane, Sheldon, Birmingham B26 3HY
Tel: 0121-603 2299 *Fax:* 0121-603 2299 *Email:* novellm@parliament.uk
Website: www.rogergodsiffmp.co.uk *Twitter:* @RogerGodsiff

LABOUR

GOGGINS, PAUL
Wythenshawe and Sale East *(Majority 7,575)*

Paul Gerard Goggins. Born 16 June 1953; Son of John Goggins and late Rita Goggins; Married Wyn Bartley 1977 (2 sons 1 daughter).

Education: St Bede's College, Manchester; Ushaw College, Durham 1971-73; Birmingham Polytechnic (Certificate residential care of children and young people 1976); Manchester Polytechnic (Certificate of Qualification in Social Work 1982).

Non-political career: Child care worker, Liverpool Catholic Social Services 1974-75; Officer-in-charge, local authority children's home, Wigan 1976-84; Project director, NCH Action For Children, Salford 1984-89; National director, Church Action On Poverty 1989-97. Member, TGWU/Unite.

Political career: Member for Wythenshawe and Sale East since 1 May 1997 general election; PPS: to John Denham as Minister of State: Department of Social Security 1998-99, Department of Health 1999-2000; to David Blunkett: as Secretary of State for Education and Employment 2000-01, as Home Secretary 2001-03; Parliamentary Under-Secretary of State: Home Office 2003-06, Northern Ireland Office (NIO) 2006-07; Minister of State, NIO 2007-10; Shadow Minister for: Cabinet Office 2010, Northern Ireland 2010; Member Intelligence and Security Committee 2010-. *Select committees:* Member: Social Security 1997-98, Joint Committee on the Draft Detention of Terrorist Suspects (Temporary Extension) Bills 2011. *Councils and public bodies:* Councillor, Salford City Council 1990-98.

Political interests: Poverty, unemployment, housing, transport, global poverty, community regeneration, counter-terrorism; Colombia, Ireland.

Other: Chair of trustees, Cardinal Hume Centre, Honorary President, Wythenshawe Mobile 1997-; Member, CAFOD Board 2000-03; Trustee, Russian European Trust 2001-03. PC 2009.

Recreations: Watching Manchester City F.C, walking, singing.

Rt Hon Paul Goggins MP, House of Commons, London SW1A 0AA
Tel: 020 7219 5865 *Email:* paul.goggins.mp@parliament.uk
Constituency: Unit A, Etrop Court, 25 Rowlands Way, Wythenshawe, Manchester M22 5RG
Tel: 0161-499 7900 *Fax:* 0161-499 7911 *Website:* www.paulgoggins.org

CONSERVATIVE

GOLDSMITH, ZAC
Richmond Park *(Majority 4,091)*

Frank Zacharias Robin Goldsmith. Born 20 January 1975; Son of Sir James Goldsmith and Lady Annabel Vane-Tempest-Stewart; Married Sheherazade Ventura-Bentley 1999 (divorced 2010) (1 son 2 daughters); married Alice Rothschild 2013.

Education: Eton College.

Non-political career: Redefining Progress, San Francisco, USA 1994-95; International Society for Ecology and Culture 1995-97; Editor, *Ecologist* 1997-2007.

Political career: Member for Richmond Park since 6 May 2010 general election. *Select committees:* Member: Environmental Audit 2010-. Deputy chair, Quality of Life Policy Group, Conservative Party 2005-07.

Political interests: The environment, democratic reform, health, small business.

Other: Beacon Prize for Young Philanthropist of the Year 2003; International Environmental Leadership, Global Green Award 2004; Richmond Green Champion 2010; Politician of the Year, Business Leaders Award 2011.

Publications: Author, The Constant Economy (Atlantic Books, 2009); Co-author, Freedom, Responsibility and the State: Curbing Over-Mighty Government (Politeia, 2012).

Zac Goldsmith MP, House of Commons, London SW1A 0AA
Tel: 020 7219 3000
Constituency: 372 Upper Richmond Road West, London SW14 7JU
Tel: 020 8939 0321 *Fax:* 020 8939 0331 *Email:* zac@zacgoldsmith.com
Website: www.zacgoldsmith.com *Twitter:* @ZacGoldsmith

LABOUR

GOODMAN, HELEN
Bishop Auckland *(Majority 5,218)*

Shadow Minister for Culture, Media and Sport

Helen Catherine Goodman. Born 2 January 1958; Daughter of Alan and Hanne Goodman; Married Charles Seaford 1988 (2 children).

Education: Lady Manners School, Bakewell; Somerville College, Oxford (BA philosophy, politics and economics 1979).

Non-political career: Research assistant to Phillip Whitehead MP 1979-80; Civil servant, HM Treasury, ending as Head of Strategy Unit 1980-97; Adviser Czechoslovak Prime Minister's Office 1990-91; Director, Commission on Future of Multi Ethnic Britain 1998; Head of strategy Children's Society 1998-2002; Chief executive, National Association of Toy and Leisure Libraries 2002-05. FDA branch secretary, HM Treasury 1986-88; GMB.

Political career: Member for Bishop Auckland 2005-10, for Bishop Auckland (revised boundary) since 6 May 2010 general election; PPS to Harriet Harman as Minister of State, Ministry of Justice 2007; Parliamentary Secretary, Office of the Leader of the House of Commons 2007-08; Assistant Government Whip 2008-09; Parliamentary Under-Secretary of State, Department for Work and Pensions 2009-10; Shadow Minister for: Work and Pensions 2010, Justice 2010-11, Culture, Media and Sport 2011-. *Select committees:* Member: Public Accounts 2005-07, Joint Committee on the Draft Climate Change Bill 2007, Ecclesiastical Committee 2010-, Procedure 2010-. Chair Camden Co-operative Party 1997-98; Member National Policy Forum 2005-07.

Political interests: Economics, environment, children, international development, human rights; Czech Republic, Denmark.

Recreations: Cooking, family.

Helen Goodman MP, House of Commons, London SW1A 0AA
Tel: 020 7219 4346 *Fax:* 020 7219 0444 *Email:* goodmanh@parliament.uk
Constituency: 1 Cockton Hill Road, Bishop Auckland, Co Durham DL14 6EN
Tel: 01388 603075 *Fax:* 01388 603075 *Website:* www.helengoodman.co.uk
Twitter: @HelenGoodmanMP

CONSERVATIVE

GOODWILL, ROBERT
Scarborough and Whitby *(Majority 8,130)*

Parliamentary Under-Secretary of State, Department for Transport

Born 31 December 1956; Son of Robert Goodwill and Joan Goodwill; Married Maureen Short 1987 (2 sons 1 daughter).

Education: Bootham School, York; Newcastle University (BSc agriculture 1979); German.

Non-political career: Farmer 1979-. Member, then branch chairman, National Farmers Union.

Political career: Contested Redcar 1992 and North West Leicestershire 1997 general elections. Member for Scarborough and Whitby since 5 May 2005 general election; Opposition Whip 2006-07; Shadow Minister for Transport 2007-10; Assistant Government Whip 2010-12; Government Whip (Lord Commissioner of HM Treasury) 2012-13; Parliamentary Under-Secretary of State, Department for Transport 2013-. *Select committees:* Member: Transport 2005-06. European Parliament: Contested Cleveland and Richmond 1994 and Yorkshire (South) 1998 elections; MEP for Yorkshire and the Humber 1999-2004: Deputy Conservative leader 2003-04.

Political interests: Agriculture, fisheries, environment, transport; Belarus, Moldova, Ukraine.

Other: Patron, National Traction Engine Trust; Farmers.

Recreations: Steam ploughing, travel.

Robert Goodwill MP, House of Commons, London SW1A 0AA
Tel: 020 7219 8268 *Fax:* 020 7219 8108 *Email:* robert.goodwill.mp@parliament.uk
Constituency: 21 Huntriss Row, Scarborough, North Yorkshire YO11 2ED
Tel: 01723 365656 *Fax:* 01723 362577 *Website:* www.robertgoodwill.co.uk

CONSERVATIVE

GOVE, MICHAEL
Surrey Heath *(Majority 17,289)*

Secretary of State for Education

Michael Andrew Gove. Born 26 August 1967; Son of Ernest and Christine Gove; Married Sarah Vine 2001 (1 daughter 1 son).

Education: Robert Gordon's College, Aberdeen; Lady Margaret Hall, Oxford (BA English 1988).

Non-political career: Reporter, *Press and Journal*, Aberdeen 1989; Researcher/reporter, Scottish Television 1990-91; Reporter, BBC News and Current Affairs 1991-96; *The Times:* Writer and editor 1996-2005, Writer 2005-. National Union of Journalists 1989-.

Political career: Member for Surrey Heath since 5 May 2005 general election; Shadow Minister for Housing 2005-07; Shadow Secretary of State for Children, Schools and Families 2007-10; Secretary of State for Education 2010-. *Select committees:* Member: European Scrutiny 2005-07.

Political interests: Education, crime, terrorism.

Other: Member, Education, Youth, Culture and Sport Council, Council of the European Union 2010-; Chair, Policy Exchange 2003-05. Minister of the Year, *The Spectator* awards 2011. PC 2010; Garrick.

Publications: Michael Portillo – The Future of the Right (Fourth Estate, 1995); The Price of Peace (CPS, 2000); Celsius 7/7 (Weidenfeld-Nicolson, 2005).

Rt Hon Michael Gove MP, House of Commons, London SW1A 0AA
Tel: 020 7219 3000 *Fax:* 020 7219 4829 *Email:* michael.gove.mp@parliament.uk
Constituency: Curzon House, Church Road, Windlesham, Surrey GU20 6BH
Tel: 01276 472468 *Fax:* 01276 451602 *Email:* office@shca.org.uk
Website: www.michaelgove.com

GRAHAM, RICHARD Gloucester *(Majority 2,420)*

PPS to Hugo Swire as Minister of State, Foreign and Commonwealth Office, Trade Envoy for Indonesia

Born 4 April 1958; Married Anthea 1989 (1 daughter 2 sons).

Education: Christ Church College, Oxford (BA history 1979); Certificate investment management (IMC); Bahasa Indonesia, Cantonese, French, Malay, Mandarin, Swahili, Tagalog.

Non-political career: Airline manager, Cathay Pacific Airways and John Swire & Sons 1980-86; Diplomat, HM Diplomatic Service 1986-92: First secretary, Nairobi High Commission, First secretary, Peking Embassy, Trade Commissioner, China, HM Consul, Macau; Investment manager 1992-2009: Director, Baring Asset Management, Director, Greater China Fund Inc 1994-2004, Head of Institutional and International Business, Baring Asset Management.

CONSERVATIVE

Political career: Member for Gloucester since 6 May 2010 general election; PPS to: Lord Howell of Guildford as Minister of State and Government Spokesperson, Foreign and Commonwealth Office 2010-12, Hugo Swire as Minister of State, Foreign and Commonwealth Office 2012-. *Select committees:* Member: Work and Pensions 2010. Contested South West England 2004 European Parliament election. *Councils and public bodies:* Cotswold District Council: Councillor 2003-07, Chair, Overview and Scrutiny Committee.

Countries of interest: China, Indonesia.

Other: Chair, British Chamber of Commerce, Shanghai; Vice-chair, Board of Airline Representatives in the Philippines; Former member, Executive Council, China-Britain Business Council; Member: Pensions Group, International Financial Services Ltd, London, RAF Association; Director, Care for Children Ltd; Trustee, Gloucestershire Community Foundation 2008-. Gloucester City Winget Cricket Club; Marylebone Cricket Club.

Recreations: Cricket, squash.

Richard Graham MP, House of Commons, London SW1A 0AA
Tel: 020 7219 7077 *Fax:* 020 7219 2299 *Email:* richard.graham.mp@parliament.uk
Constituency: Second Floor, St Peters House, 2 College Street, Gloucester GL1 2NE
Tel: 01452 501167 *Website:* www.richardgraham.org

GRANT, HELEN Maidstone and The Weald *(Majority 5,889)*

Parliamentary Under-Secretary of State (Sport and Equalities), Department for Culture, Media and Sport

Born 28 September 1961; Daughter of Dr Gladys Spedding and Dr Julius Okuboye, both retired; Married Simon Grant 1991 (2 sons).

Education: St Aidans Comprehensive School, Carlisle; Trinity Comprehensive School, Carlisle; Hull University (LLB 1982); College of Law, Guildford (Solicitors Finals 1984).

CONSERVATIVE

Non-political career: Articled clerk, Cartmell Mawson & Maine, Carlisle 1985-87; Assistant solicitor, Hempsons, London 1987-88; Fayers & Co, London: Associate solicitor 1988-92, Equity partner 1992-94; Maternity sabattical 1994-95; Consultant solicitor, T G Baynes & Co, Kent 1995-96; Senior partner/owner, Grants Solicitors LLP 1996-.

Political career: Member for Maidstone and The Weald since 6 May 2010 general election; Parliamentary Under-Secretary of State: (Women and Equalities), Department for Culture, Media and Sport and Ministry of Justice 2012-13, (Minister for Victims and the Courts), Ministry of Justice 2012-13; Parliamentary Under-Secretary of State (Sport and Equalities) 2013-. *Select committees:* Member: Justice 2010-11. Member, Labour Party 2004-05; Conservative Party: Member 2006-, Deputy Chair, diversity group, Croydon Central and Croydon South Conservative Federation 2006-08, Special adviser to Oliver Letwin MP as Chair of Party Policy Review 2006-10, Member: Social Mobility Task Force 2007-08, The Society of Conservative Lawyers. *Councils and public bodies:* Non-executive director, Croydon NHS Primary Care Trust 2005-07.

Political interests: Justice, business and enterprise, crime, law and order, women, children and families, social mobility; Chagos Islands/Diego Garcia, India, Nigeria.

Other: Member, Bow Group; Centre for Social Justice: Member, Family Division Policy Group 2006-, Member, Family Law Reform Commission 2007-; Law Society: Member 1985-, Member: Family Law Panel 2000-, Equalities and Diversities Committee 2008-09; Member, Resolution 1997-; President, Maidstone Museums Foundation 2008-; Patron, Tomorrow's People, Maidstone 2009-, Honorary Vice-President, MENCAP Trust, Maidstone; Carlton Club. Kingswood Lawn Tennis Club.

Publications: State of the Nation/Fractured Families (Centre for Social Justice, 2006); Breakthrough Britain (Centre for Social Justice, 2007); Every Family Matters (Centre for Social Justice, 2009).

Recreations: Tennis, movies, family life, sporting events.

Helen Grant MP, House of Commons, London SW1A 0AA
Tel: 020 7219 7107 *Fax:* 020 7219 2806 *Email:* helen.grant.mp@parliament.uk
Constituency: Maidstone and The Weald Conservative Association, 3 Albion Place, Maidstone, Kent ME14 5DY
Tel: 01622 769898 *Fax:* 01622 764427 *Website:* www.helengrant.org *Twitter:* @HelenGrantMP

GRAY, JAMES North Wiltshire *(Majority 7,483)*

CONSERVATIVE

James Whiteside Gray. Born 7 November 1954; Son of late Very Revd John R. Gray, Moderator of General Assembly of Church of Scotland, and Dr Sheila Gray; Married Sarah Ann Beale 1980 (divorced) (2 sons 1 daughter); married Mrs Philippa Mayo 2009 (1 stepson, 2 stepdaughters).

Education: Glasgow High School; Glasgow University (MA history 1975); Christ Church, Oxford (history thesis 1975-77); French.

Non-political career: Honourable Artillery Company (TA) 1978-84; Armed Forces Parliamentary Scheme (Army): Member 1998, Post-Graduate Scheme 2000; Member, HAC Court of Assistants 2002-07; Royal College of Defence Studies 2003. Management trainee, P&O 1977-78; Anderson Hughes & Co Ltd (Shipbrokers) 1978-84; Baltic Exchange: Member 1978-91, Director 1989-91, Pro Bono Member 1997-; Managing director, GNI Freight Futures Ltd, Senior Manager, GNI Ltd (Futures Brokers) 1984-92; Special adviser to Secretaries of State for Environment: Michael Howard MP 1992-93, John Gummer MP 1993-95; Director, Westminster Strategy 1995-96. Union of Country Sports Workers.

Political career: Contested Ross, Cromarty and Skye 1992 general election. Member for North Wiltshire 1997-2010, for North Wiltshire (revised boundary) since 6 May 2010 general election; Opposition Whip 2000-01; Opposition Spokesman for Defence 2001-02; Shadow Minister for: Environment, Food and Rural Affairs 2002-03, Environment and Transport 2003-05; Shadow Secretary of State for Scotland May 2005. *Select committees:* Member: Environment, Transport and Regional Affairs 1997-2000, Broadcasting 2001-03, Regulatory Reform 2005-10, Environment, Food and Rural Affairs 2007-10, Chairmen's Panel/Panel of Chairs 2010-, Finance and Services 2010-, Procedure 2010-. Chair, Conservative Rural Affairs Group 2003-04; Vice-chair, Conservative Backbench Foreign Affairs and Defence Committee 2010-. Deputy Chair, Wandsworth Tooting Conservative Association 1994-96.

Political interests: Countryside, agriculture, defence, environment, foreign affairs; Afghanistan, America, Arctic, Antarctica, China, Mongolia, Nepal, Sri Lanka.

Other: Parliamentary delegate to Council of Europe and Western European Union 2007-10; Vice-President, HAC Saddle Club; President, Chippenham Multiple Sclerosis Society; President, Association of British Riding Schools; International League for the Protection of Horses; MS Society; RNID. Member, Honourable Artillery Company. Freeman, City of London 1978; President, Chippenham Constitutional Club 2000-; Wootton Bassett Conservative Club; Pratt's. Member, Avon Vale Foxhounds.

Publications: Financial Risk Management in the Shipping Industry (1985); Futures and Options for Shipping (1987) (Lloyds of London Book Prize winner); Shipping Futures (1990); Crown v Parliament: Who decides on Going to War (2003).

Recreations: Riding horses, heritage and local history.

James Gray MP, House of Commons, London SW1A 0AA
Tel: 020 7219 6237 *Fax:* 020 7219 1163 *Email:* jamesgraymp@parliament.uk
Constituency: No constituency office publicised *Website:* www.jamesgray.org
Twitter: @jamesgraymp

GRAYLING, CHRIS
Epsom and Ewell *(Majority 16,134)*

Lord Chancellor and Secretary of State for Justice

Christopher Stephen Grayling. Born 1 April 1962; Son of John and Elizabeth Grayling; Married Susan Dillistone 1987 (1 son 1 daughter).

Education: Royal Grammar School, High Wycombe; Sidney Sussex College, Cambridge (BA history 1984); French.

Non-political career: BBC News: Trainee 1985-86, Producer 1986-88; Programme editor, *Business Daily*, Channel 4 1988-91; Business development manager BBC Select 1991-93; Director: Charterhouse Prods Ltd 1993, Workhouse Ltd 1993-95, SSVC Group 1995-97; Change consultant and European marketing director Burson Marsteller 1997-2001.

CONSERVATIVE

Political career: Contested Warrington South 1997 general election. Member for Epsom and Ewell 2001-10, for Epsom and Ewell (revised boundary) since 6 May 2010 general election; Opposition Whip 2002; Shadow Spokesperson for Health 2002-03; Shadow Minister for: Public Services, Health and Education 2003-04, Higher Education 2004-05, Health 2005; Shadow Leader of the House of Commons 2005; Ex-officio member House of Commons' Commission 2005; Shadow Secretary of State for: Transport 2005-07, Work and Pensions 2007-09; Shadow Home Secretary 2009-10; Minister of State for Employment, Department for Work and Pensions 2010-12; Lord Chancellor and Secretary of State for Justice 2012-. *Select committees:* Member: Transport, Local Government and the Regions 2001-02, Transport, Local Government and the Regions (Transport Sub-Committee) 2001-02, Transport, Local Government and the Regions (Urban Affairs Sub-Committee) 2001-02, Transport 2002, Modernisation of the House of Commons 2005-06. *Councils and public bodies:* Councillor, London Borough of Merton 1998-2002.

Political interests: Transport, welfare reform, pensions, home affairs.

Other: Member, Corporation of Merton College 1999-2001; Chair, Epsom Victim Support 2001-07; President, Industry and Parliament Trust 2012-. PC 2010.

Publications: The Bridgwater Heritage (1983); A Land Fit for Heroes (1985); Co-author, Just Another Star? (1987).

Recreations: Golf, cricket, football.

Rt Hon Chris Grayling MP, House of Commons, London SW1A 0AA
Tel: 020 7219 8194 *Fax:* 020 7219 1763 *Email:* graylingc@parliament.uk
Constituency: 212 Barnett Wood Lane, Ashtead, Surrey KT21 2DB
Tel: 01372 271036 *Fax:* 01372 270906 *Email:* martinverdinosv@parliament.uk
Website: www.chrisgrayling.net

GREATREX, TOM
Rutherglen and Hamilton West *(Majority 21,002)*

Shadow Minister for Energy and Climate Change

Thomas James Greatrex. Born 30 September 1974; Son of late Simon Greatrex and Brenda Greatrex, née King; Married Laura 2003 (twin daughters).

Education: Judd School, Tonbridge; London School of Economics (BSc economics, government and law 1996).

Non-political career: Researcher, Opposition Whips Office 1996-97; Special adviser to Nick Brown MP: as Chief Whip 1997-98, as Minister of Agriculture, Fisheries and Food 1998-99; Regional officer, GMB 1999-2004; Head of policy and public affairs, East Dunbartonshire Council 2004-06; Corporate affairs director, NHS 24 2006-07; Special adviser to Secretaries of State for Scotland: Douglas Alexander MP 2007, Des Browne MP 2007-08, Jim Murphy MP 2008-10. Member, GMB.

LAB/CO-OP

Political career: Member for Rutherglen and Hamilton West since 6 May 2010 general election; Shadow Minister for: Scotland 2010-11, Energy and Climate Change 2011-. *Select committees:* Member: Energy and Climate Change 2010, Procedure 2010-. Vice-chair, PLP Departmental Group for Northern Ireland 2010-.

Political interests: Manufacturing, economic policy, energy policy, constitution, Northern Ireland; Brazil, China, India, Italy, Malawi, Malaysia, Portugal.

Other: Blantyre Miners Welfare Club.

Recreations: Fulham F.C, cinema.

Tom Greatrex MP, House of Commons, London SW1A 0AA
Tel: 020 7219 8974 *Email:* tom.greatrex.mp@parliament.uk
Constituency: Blantyre Miners Community Resource Centre, 3 Calder Street, Blantyre, Lanarkshire G72 0AU
Tel: 01698 821380 *Website:* www.tomgreatrex.org *Twitter:* @tomgreatrexmp

GREEN, DAMIAN
Ashford *(Majority 17,297)*

Minister of State for Policing and Criminal Justice, Home Office and Ministry of Justice

Damian Howard Green. Born 17 January 1956; Son of Howard Green and late Audrey Green; Married Alicia Collinson 1988 (2 daughters).

Education: Reading School; Balliol College, Oxford (BA philosophy, politics and economics 1977, MA) (President, Oxford Union 1977); French.

CONSERVATIVE

Non-political career: Financial journalist, BBC Radio 1978-82; Business producer, *Channel 4 News* 1982-84; News editor, business news, *The Times* 1984-85; Business editor, *Channel 4 News* 1985-87; Programme presenter and city editor, *Business Daily* 1987-92; Special adviser, Prime Minister's Policy Unit 1992-94; Self-employed public affairs consultant 1995-97.

Political career: Contested Brent East 1992 general election. Member for Ashford 1997-2010, for Ashford (revised boundary) since 6 May 2010 general election; Opposition Spokesperson for: Education and Employment 1998-99, Environment 1999-2001; Shadow Secretary of State for: Education and Skills 2001-03, Transport 2003-04; Shadow Minister for Immigration 2005-10; Minister of State for: Immigration, Home Office 2010-12, Policing and Criminal Justice, Home Office and Ministry of Justice 2012-. *Select committees:* Member: Culture, Media and Sport 1997-98, Procedure 1997-98, Home Affairs 2004-05, Treasury 2005-06. Chair, Conservative Education Policy Committee 2001-03; Member, Executive, 1922 Committee 2004-05. Vice-President, Tory Reform Group 1997-; Chair, Conservative Parliamentary Mainstream Group 2003-10.

Political interests: Economic policy, foreign affairs, media, education, employment, rural affairs; France, Georgia, Italy, Moldova.

Other: Member, SPUC; President, Find a Voice. PC 2012.

Publications: ITN Budget Fact Book (1984, 1985, 1986); A Better BBC (1990); The Cross-Media Revolution (1995); Communities in the Countryside (1996); Regulating the Media in the Digital Age (1997); 21st Century Conservatism (1998); The Four Failures of the New Deal (1999); Better Learning (2002); More than Markets (2003); Co-author, Controlling Economic Migration (2006).

Recreations: Football, cricket, opera, cinema.

Rt Hon Damian Green MP, House of Commons, London SW1A 0AA
Tel: 020 7219 3518 *Fax:* 020 7219 0904 *Email:* damian.green.mp@parliament.uk
Constituency: c/o Hardy House, The Street, Bethersden, Ashford, Kent TN26 3AG
Tel: 01233 820454 *Fax:* 01233 820111 *Email:* ashfordconservatives@btconnect.com
Website: www.damiangreenmp.org.uk *Twitter:* @damiangreenmp

GREEN, KATE
Stretford and Urmston *(Majority 8,935)*

Shadow Minister for Work and Pensions

Katherine Anne Green. Born 2 May 1960; Divorced.

Education: Currie High School; Edinburgh University (LLB 1982).

Non-political career: Various roles, Barclays Bank 1982-97; Whitehall and Industry Group (on secondment), Home Office 1997-99; Director, National Council for One Parent Families 2000-04; Chief executive, Child Poverty Action Group 2004-09. Member: Unite 2000-, GMB 2009-, USDAW 2009-.

LABOUR

Political career: Contested Cities of London and Westminster 1997 general election. Member for Stretford and Urmston since 6 May 2010 general election; Shadow Minister for: Equalities Office 2011-13, Work and Pensions 2013-. *Select committees:* Member: Work and Pensions

2010-11. Chair, PLP Departmental Group for Women 2011. Member, Labour Party 1990-. *Councils and public bodies:* Magistrate, City of London 1993-2009; Member, National Employment Panel 2001-07; Member, then Chair, London Child Poverty Commission 2006-09. **Political interests:** Employment, exclusion, poverty, criminal justice; United Kingdom.

Other: Trustee: The Avenues Youth Project 1998-2003, End Child Poverty 2000-09, Family and Parenting Institute 2000-07, Institute for Fiscal Studies 2006-09; Member, Fawcett Society 2006-; Trustee, Friends Provident Foundation 2007-09; Member, Fabian Society 2009-; Trustee, Webb Memorial Trust 2010-. Freeman, City of London. OBE 2005.

Kate Green OBE MP, House of Commons, London SW1A 0AA
Tel: 020 7219 7162 *Fax:* 0207 219 4561 *Email:* kate.green.mp@parliament.uk
Constituency: Stretford and Urmston Labour Party, The Morris Hall, 9 Atkinson Road, Urmston, Manchester M41 9AD
Tel: 0161-749 9120 *Fax:* 0161-749 9121 *Website:* www.kategreen.org *Twitter:* @KateGreenSU

CONSERVATIVE

GREENING, JUSTINE
Putney *(Majority 10,053)*

Secretary of State for International Development

Born 30 April 1969; Single.

Education: Oakwood Comprehensive School, Rotherham, Yorkshire; Thomas Rotherham College, Rotherham; Southampton University (BSc business economics and accounting 1990); London Business School (MBA 2000); French.

Non-political career: Audit assistant, PriceWaterhouse 1991-94; Audit assistant manager, Revisuisse PriceWaterhouse 1995-96; Finance manager, SmithKline Beecham, 1996-2001; Business strategy manager, GlaxoSmithKline, 2001-02; Sales and marketing finance manager, Centrica 2002-05.

Political career: Contested Ealing, Acton and Shepherd's Bush 2001 general election. Member for Putney 2005-10, for Putney (revised boundary) since 6 May 2010 general election; Shadow Minister for: the Treasury 2007-09, Communities and Local Government 2009-10; Economic Secretary, HM Treasury 2010-11; Secretary of State for: Transport 2011-12; International Development 2012-. *Select committees:* Member: Work and Pensions 2005-07, Public Accounts 2010-11. Vice-chair (Youth), Conservative Party 2005-10. *Councils and public bodies:* Councillor, Epping Town Council 1998-2002.

Political interests: Vocational education, youth crime, environment, economy, transport.

Other: Bow Group: Member 1998-, Political officer 1999-2000; Associate, Institute of Chartered Accountants in England and Wales 1994. People's Choice Award, Women in Public Life Awards 2011. PC 2011.

Publications: *A Wholly Healthy Britain* in A Blue Tomorrow (2000).

Recreations: Swimming, cycling.

Rt Hon Justine Greening MP, House of Commons, London SW1A 0AA
Tel: 020 7219 8300 *Email:* greeningj@parliament.uk
Constituency: 3 Summerstown, London SW17 0BQ
Tel: 020 8946 4557 *Website:* www.justinegreeningmp.co.uk *Twitter:* @JustineGreening

LABOUR

GREENWOOD, LILIAN
Nottingham South *(Majority 1,772)*

Shadow Minister for Transport

Lilian Rachel Greenwood. Born 26 March 1966; Daughter of Harry Greenwood, lecturer, and Patricia Greenwood, typist; Married Ravi Subramanian 2008 (3 daughters).

Education: Canon Slade, Bolton; St Catharine's College, Cambridge (BA economics and social and political science 1987); Southbank University, London (MSc sociology and social policy 1991).

Non-political career: Research officer: Local Authority Conditions of Service Advisory Board 1988-89, Civil and Public Services Association 1989-92; Trade union organiser, latterly regional head of campaigns and policy, Unison 1992-2010. NALGO 1988-89, GMB 1989-92, NUPE/ Unison 1992-.

Political career: Member for Nottingham South since 6 May 2010 general election; Opposition Assistant Whip 2010-11; Shadow Minister for Transport 2011-. *Select committees:* Member: Transport 2010, Regulatory Reform 2010-. Member, Co-operative Party.

Political interests: Transport, employment rights, pensions; Kashmir.
Other: Member: Fabian Society, Compass 2007-. Holme Pierrepont Running Club.
Recreations: Running, walking, cinema, reading.
Lilian Greenwood MP, House of Commons, London SW1A 0AA
Tel: 020 7219 6517 *Fax:* 020 7219 3442 *Email:* lilian.greenwood.mp@parliament.uk
Constituency: First Floor, 12 Regent Street, Nottingham NG1 5BQ
Tel: 0115-711 7000 *Website:* www.liliangreenwood.co.uk *Twitter:* @LilianGreenwood

GRIEVE, DOMINIC
Beaconsfield *(Majority 21,782)*

Attorney General

Dominic Charles Roberts Grieve. Born 24 May 1956; Son of late W. P. Grieve, QC, MP for Soli-hull 1964-83, and late Evelyn Grieve, née Mijouain; Married Caroline Hutton 1990 (2 sons and 1 son deceased).
Education: Westminster School, London; Magdalen College, Oxford (BA modern history 1978, MA 1989); Central London Polytechnic (Diploma law 1980); French.
Non-political career: Territorial Army 1981-83. Called to the Bar 1980; Bencher, Middle Temple 2004; QC 2008; Honorary Recorder, Royal Borough of Kingston on Thames.

CONSERVATIVE

Political career: Contested Norwood 1987 general election. Member for Beaconsfield 1997-2010, for Beaconsfield (revised boundary) since 6 May 2010 general election; Opposition Spokesperson for: Constitutional Affairs and Scotland 1999-2001, Home Office 2001-03; Shadow Attorney General 2003-09; Shadow Home Secretary 2008-09; Shadow Secretary of State for Justice 2009-10; Attorney General 2010-. *Select committees:* Member: Joint Committee on Statutory Instruments 1997-2001, Environmental Audit 1997-2001. President, Oxford University Conservative Association 1977; Society of Conservative Lawyers: Chair: Research Committee 1992-95, Finance and General Purposes 2006-. *Councils and public bodies:* Councillor, London Borough of Hammersmith and Fulham 1982-86.
Political interests: Law and order, environment, defence, foreign affairs, European Union, constitution; France, India, Luxembourg.
Other: Vice-chair/director, Hammersmith and Fulham MIND 1986-89; Lay visitor to police stations 1990-96; Council member, Luxembourg Society; Member: London Diocesan Synod of Church of England 1994-2000, John Muir Trust; Governor, The Ditchley Foundation 2010-; Vice-chair, Franco-British Council 2011-; President, Franco-British Society 2011-; Vice-President, The English Clergy Association 2012-. Opposition Politician of the Year, *House Magazine* 2005; Politician of the Year, *The Spectator* 2005; Politicians' Politician of the Year, Channel 4 2006. PC 2010.
Recreations: Mountaineering, skiing, scuba diving, fell-walking, architecture and art.
Rt Hon Dominic Grieve QC MP, House of Commons, London SW1A 0AA
Tel: 020 7219 6220 *Email:* dominic.grieve.mp@parliament.uk
Constituency: Disraeli House, 12 Aylesbury End, Beaconsfield, Buckinghamshire HP9 1LW
Tel: 01494 673745 *Fax:* 01494 670428 *Email:* office@beaconsfieldconservatives.co.uk
Website: www.beaconsfieldconservatives.co.uk www.dominicgrieve.org.uk

GRIFFITH, NIA
Llanelli *(Majority 4,701)*

Shadow Minister for Wales

Nia Rhiannon Griffith. Born 4 December 1956; Daughter of Professor T Gwynfor Griffith, professor of Italian and member of Gorsedd of Bards, and Dr Rhiannon Griffith, née Howell, medical doctor; Married Richard Leggett 1982 (divorced) (no children).
Education: Newland High School, Hull; Somerville College, Oxford (BA modern languages 1979); University College of North Wales, Bangor (PGCE 1980); French, Italian, Spanish, Welsh.

LABOUR

Non-political career: Language teacher 1980-92, 1997-2005; Education adviser 1992-97; Estyn schools inspector 1992-97; Head of modern languages, Morriston Comprehensive School, Swansea 1997-2005; Chair, Carmarthenshire Youth Project 1998-2005. National Union of Teachers; USDAW.
Political career: Member for Llanelli since 5 May 2005 general election; PPS: at Department for Environment, Food and Rural Affairs 2007-08, to Harriet Harman: as Minister for Women and Equality 2008-10, as Acting Leader of the Opposition 2010; Shadow Minister for: Business,

Innovation and Skills 2010-11, Wales 2011-. *Select committees:* Member: European Scrutiny 2005-07, 2010-, Welsh Affairs 2005-10, 2011-, Joint Committee on Human Rights 2006-07, Joint Committee on the Draft Climate Change Bill 2007. Chair: PLP Welsh Regional Group 2007-08, PLP Departmental Group for Environment, Food and Rural Affairs 2010; Vice-chair, PLP Departmental Group for Energy and Climate Change 2010. Secretary, Carmarthenshire County Labour Party 1994-99, 2004-05; Chair, Carmarthen West and South Pembrokeshire Constituency Labour Party 1999-2000. *Councils and public bodies:* Carmarthen Town Council: Councillor 1987-99, Sheriff 1997, Deputy mayor 1998.

Political interests: Environment, Europe, community issues, cycling, industry, energy, equalities; France, Italy, Spain.

Other: Member, Amnesty International.

Publications: Co-author Ciao BK3 Italian textbook (Nelson, 1990); 100 ideas for teaching languages (Continuum Press, 2005).

Recreations: Arts, European cinema, music, cycling.

Nia Griffith MP, House of Commons, London SW1A 0AA
Tel: 020 7219 4903 *Fax:* 020 7219 4560 *Email:* nia.griffith.mp@parliament.uk
Constituency: 6 Queen Victoria Road, Llanelli, Dyfed SA15 2TL
Tel: 01554 756374 *Fax:* 01554 741183 *Website:* www.niagriffith.org.uk
Twitter: @NiaGriffithMP

CONSERVATIVE

GRIFFITHS, ANDREW

Burton *(Majority 6,304)*

Andrew James Griffiths. Born 19 October 1970; Son of Bob Griffiths and Harriet Griffiths; Single.

Education: High Arcal School, Dudley.

Non-political career: Family engineering business; Manager, Halifax plc; Chief of staff to Jonathan Evans MEP 1999; Farming adviser to Neil Parish MEP -2004; Chief of staff to: Rt Hon Theresa May MP 2004-06, Hugo Swire MP 2006-07, Eric Pickles MP 2007-10.

Political career: Contested Dudley North 2001 general election. Member for Burton since 6 May 2010 general election. *Select committees:* Member: Political and Constitutional Reform 2010-. Contested West Midlands region 2004 European Parliament election.

Political interests: Drugs and alcohol rehabilitation, the brewery and pub industry, manufacturing; America, China, Kashmir, Pakistan.

Recreations: Sport, architecture, music.

Andrew Griffiths MP, House of Commons, London SW1A 0AA
Tel: 020 7219 7029 *Fax:* 020 7219 0911 *Email:* andrew.griffiths.mp@parliament.uk
Constituency: Gothard House, 9 St Paul's Square, Burton-upon-Trent, Staffordshire DE14 2EF
Tel: 01283 564934 *Website:* www.andrewgriffithsmp.com *Twitter:* @agriffithsmp

CONSERVATIVE

GUMMER, BEN

Ipswich *(Majority 2,079)*

PPS to Alan Duncan as Minister of State, Department for International Development

Benedict Michael Gummer. Born 19 February 1978; Son of John Gummer, former MP, now Lord Deben (qv), and Penelope Gummer, née Gardner; Single.

Education: Tonbridge School, Kent; Peterhouse College, Cambridge (BA history 2000, MA).

Non-political career: Businessman and writer.

Political career: Member for Ipswich since 6 May 2010 general election; Parliamentary adviser to Lord Feldman as Conservative Party co-chairman 2012-; PPS to Alan Duncan as Minister of State, Department for International Development 2012-. *Select committees:* Member: Regulatory Reform 2010-12, Justice 2010-12.

Political interests: Education, prison reform, tax reform, fiscal policy.

Other: Member, UK Delegation, Organisation for Security and Co-operation in Europe Parliamentary Assembly.

Publications: The Scourging Angel: The Black Death in the British Isles (Bodley Head, 2009).

Ben Gummer MP, House of Commons, London SW1A 0AA
Tel: 020 7219 7090 *Fax:* 020 7219 3542 *Email:* ben.gummer.mp@parliament.uk
Constituency: 9 Fore Street, Ipswich, Suffolk IP4 1JW
Tel: 01473 232883 *Email:* ben@bengummer.com *Website:* www.bengummer.com
Twitter: @ben4ipswich

GWYNNE, ANDREW

Denton and Reddish *(Majority 9,831)*

Shadow Minister for Health

Andrew John Gwynne. Born 4 June 1974; Son of Richard Gwynne and Margaret Gwynne, née Ridgway; Married Allison Dennis 2003 (2 sons 1 daughter).

Education: Egerton Park Community High School, Denton; North East Wales Institute of Higher Education, Wrexham (HND business and finance 1995); Salford University (BA politics and contemporary history 1998).

LABOUR

Non-political career: Assistant to European Declarative System (EDS) programme manager ICL 1990-92; National Computing Centre, Y2K team 1999-2000; Researcher for Andrew Bennett MP 2000-05; European co-ordinator for Arlene McCarthy MEP 2000-01. Unite (formerly AEEU and Amicus) 2000-.

Political career: Member for Denton and Reddish 2005-10, for Denton and Reddish (revised boundary) since 6 May 2010 general election; PPS to: Baroness Scotland of Asthal as Minister of State, Home Office 2005-07, Jacqui Smith as Home Secretary 2007-09, Ed Balls as Secretary of State for Children, Schools and Families 2009-10; Shadow Minister for: Transport 2010-11, Health 2011-. *Select committees:* Member: Procedure 2005-10, Court of Referees 2007-10. PLP North West Regional Group: Vice-chair 2008-09, Chair 2009-11. Chair, Denton and Reddish Constituency Labour Party 1998-2004; Member, Co-operative Party 2000-; Chair, Labour Friends of Israel 2007-10. *Councils and public bodies:* Tameside MBC: Councillor 1996-2008, Chair: Denton and Audenshaw District Assembly 1998-2001, Resources and community services scrutiny panel 2003-04.

Political interests: Education and skills, regeneration, local government, environment, transport; China, Commonwealth, India, Israel/Palestinian Authority, Latin America, USA.

Other: Member, Christian Socialist Movement 2000-; Patron, Tameside Homestart; Trustee, Charities of Thomas Moores; President, Denton and Audenshaw Carnival Association; Denton Labour Club; Stockport Labour Club.

Recreations: Reading, computing, history, family.

Andrew Gwynne MP, House of Commons, London SW1A 0AA
Tel: 020 7219 4708 *Fax:* 020 7219 4548 *Email:* gwynnea@parliament.uk
Constituency: Town Hall, Market Street, Denton, Greater Manchester M34 2AP
Tel: 0161-320 1504 *Fax:* 0161-320 1503 *Website:* www.andrewgwynne.co.uk
Twitter: @gwynnemp

GYIMAH, SAM

East Surrey *(Majority 16,874)*

Assistant Whip

Samuel Phillip Gyimah. Born 10 August 1976; Married Dr Nicola Black.

Education: Achimota Secondary School, Ghana; Freman College, Hertfordshire; Somerville College, Oxford (BA philosophy, politics and economics 1999) (Union President 1997).

Non-political career: Investment banker, Goldman Sachs 1999-2003; Entrepreneur 2003-10.

Political career: Member for East Surrey since 6 May 2010 general election; Member Speaker's Committee on the Electoral Commission 2010-12; PPS to David Cameron as Prime Minister 2012-13; Assistant Whip 2013-. *Select committees:* Member: International Development 2011-12. *Councils and public bodies:* School governor, London 2004-07.

CONSERVATIVE

Political interests: Small business, higher education, international development.

Other: Former board member, Nacro; Chair, Bow Group 2007; Member, development board, Somerville College, Oxford; Vice-President, National Centre for Young People with Epilepsy. CBI Entrepreneur of the Future 2005.

Publications: Editor, From the Ashes...The Future of the Conservative Party (2005) Co-author with Nesta, Beyond the Banks.

Sam Gyimah MP, House of Commons, London SW1A 0AA
Tel: 020 7219 3504 *Fax:* 020 7219 1808
Constituency: East Surrey Conservative Association, 2 Hoskins Road, Oxted, Surrey RH8 9HT
Tel: 01883 715782 *Fax:* 01883 730576 *Email:* sam@samgyimah.com admin@esca.org.uk
Website: www.samgyimah.com *Twitter:* @SamGyimah

CONSERVATIVE

HAGUE, WILLIAM
Richmond (Yorkshire) *(Majority 23,336)*

First Secretary of State, Secretary of State for Foreign and Commonwealth Affairs (Foreign Secretary)

William Jefferson Hague. Born 26 March 1961; Son of Nigel and Stella Hague; Married Ffion Jenkins 1997.

Education: Wath-upon-Dearne Comprehensive School, Yorkshire; Magdalen College, Oxford (BA philosophy, politics and economics 1982) (President, Oxford Union 1981); INSEAD Business School, France 1985-86.

Non-political career: Shell UK 1982-83; McKinsey and Company 1983-88; Political adviser to Sir Geoffrey Howe as Chancellor of the Exchequer and Leon Brittan as Chief Secretary to the Treasury 1983; Political and economic adviser, JCB 2001-; Non-executive director, AES Engineering 2001-09; Member, Political Council of Terra Firma Capital Partners 2001-; Non-executive director, AMT Sybex 2003-09.

Political career: Contested Wentworth 1987 general election. Member for Richmond (Yorkshire) 23 February 1989 by-election to 2010, for Richmond (Yorkshire) (revised boundary) since 6 May 2010 general election; PPS to Norman Lamont as Chancellor of the Exchequer 1990-93; Department of Social Security: Joint Parliamentary Under-Secretary of State 1993-94, Minister of State for Social Security and Disabled People 1994-95; Secretary of State for Wales 1995-97; Leader of the Opposition 1997-2001; Shadow Foreign Secretary and Senior Member of the Shadow Cabinet 2005-10; First Secretary of State, Secretary of State for Foreign and Commonwealth Affairs (Foreign Secretary) 2010-. *Select committees:* Member: Joint Committee on House of Lords Reform 2002-05. President Oxford University Conservative Association 1981; Leader Conservative Party June 1997-2001.

Political interests: Agriculture, economic policy.

Other: International Democrat Union, Global Alliance of Conservative, Christian Democrat and like-minded parties: Chair 1999-2002, Deputy Chair 2002-05, Assistant chair 2005-; Vice-President, Commonwealth Parliamentary Association (UK Branch) 2010-; Council of the European Union: Member: Foreign Affairs Council 2010-, General Affairs Council 2010-; Fellow, Royal Society of Literature. *The Spectator*/Highland Park Parliamentarian of the Year 1998; National Book Awards History Book of the Year for biography of Pitt the Younger 2005; Threadneedle/*The Spectator* Speech of the Year 2007. PC 1995; Beefsteak, Carlton, Buck's, Pratt's, Budokwai, Mark's.

Publications: Speaking with Conviction (Conservative Policy Forum, 1998); I Will Give you Back your Country (Conservative Policy Forum, 2000); Biography of William Pitt the Younger (2004); Biography of William Wilberforce (2007).

Recreations: Walking, sailing, cross country, skiing, judo.

Rt Hon William Hague MP, House of Commons, London SW1A 0AA
Tel: 020 7219 4611 *Email:* haguew@parliament.uk
Constituency: Unit 1, Omega Business Village, Thurston Road, Northallerton, North Yorkshire DL6 2NJ
Tel: 01609 779093 *Fax:* 01609 778172 *Twitter:* @WilliamJHague

LABOUR

HAIN, PETER
Neath *(Majority 9,775)*

Peter Gerald Hain. Born 16 February 1950; Son of Walter and Adelaine Hain; Married Patricia Western 1975 (divorced 2002) (2 sons); married Elizabeth Haywood 2003.

Education: Pretoria Boys High School, South Africa; Emanuel School, Wandsworth, London; Queen Mary College, London University (BSc economics and political science 1973); Sussex University (MPhil political science 1976).

Non-political career: Head of research, Union of Communication Workers 1976-91. Member, GMB.

Political career: Contested Putney 1983 and 1987 general elections. Member for Neath 4 April 1991 by-election to 2010, for Neath (revised boundary) since 6 May 2010 general election; Opposition Whip 1995-96; Opposition Spokesperson for Employment 1996-97; Parliamentary Under-Secretary of State, Welsh Office 1997-99; Minister of State: Foreign and Commonwealth Office 1999-2001, Department of Trade and Industry (Energy and Competitiveness) 2001, Foreign and Commonwealth Office (Europe) 2001-02; Government representative European Union Convention 2002-03; Secretary of State for Wales 2002-08; Leader of the House of Commons and Lord Privy Seal 2003-05; Secretary of State for: Northern Ireland 2005-07, Work and Pensions 2007-08, Wales 2009-10; Shadow Secretary of State for Wales 2010-12. *Select committees:* Chair: Modernisation of the House of Commons 2003-05. Leader, Young Liberals 1971-73; Member: Labour Party 1977-, Labour Party NEC 2011-12; Chair, National Policy Forum 2010-12.

Political interests: Social justice, democratic renewal, including Lords reform, electoral reform and devolution, environmental policy, including renewable energy, foreign affairs; Southern Africa, Spain.

Other: Former member, Anti-Apartheid Movement; Chair, 'Stop the Seventy Tour' (which disrupted the South African rugby tour, and stopped the South African cricket tour to Britain) 1969-70; Founder, *Anti-Nazi League* 1977; Director, *Tribune* Newspaper 1991-97; Founder, Unite Against Fascism 2005; Honorary President, Unite Against Fascism, Wales 2009-; Non-executive independent director, Cluff Gold 2013-; Non-executive director, Amara Mining PCC 2013-. Welsh Politician of the Year, *am.pm* 2006; Welsh MP of the Year, BBC 2007. PC 2001; Royal British Legion, Resolven; Resolven Rugby Club; Ynysygerwn Cricket; Neath Rugby Football; Neath AFC; Ospreys.

Publications: 17 books including: Ayes to the Left: A future for socialism (Lawrence and Wishart, 1995), Mandela (Spruce, 2010), Autobiography, Outside In (Biteback, 2012).

Recreations: Rugby, soccer, cricket, motor racing, rock and folk music.

Rt Hon Peter Hain MP, House of Commons, London SW1A 0AA
Tel: 020 7219 3925 *Fax:* 020 7219 3816 *Email:* hainp@parliament.uk
Constituency: 39 Windsor Road, Neath, West Glamorgan SA11 1NB
Tel: 01639 630152 *Fax:* 01639 641196 *Website:* www.peterhain.org *Twitter:* @peterhain

HALFON, ROBERT
Harlow *(Majority 4,925)*

CONSERVATIVE

Robert Henry Halfon. Born 22 March 1969; Son of Clement and Jenny Halfon; Partner Vanda Colombo.

Education: Highgate School, London; Exeter University (BA politics 1991; MA Russian and East European politics 1992).

Non-political career: Parliamentary researcher to a number of Conservative MPs including Harold Elliston MP and Michael Fabricant MP 1992-94; Head of research, Market Access Ltd 1994-98; Policy Analyst, APCO UK 1998-2000; Political director, Renewing One Nation, Conservative Central Office 2000-01; Chief of staff to Oliver Letwin MP 2001-05; Political director/consultant, Conservative Friends of Israel 2005-10; Self-employed consultant 2005-10. Member, Prospect.

Political career: Contested Harlow 2001 and 2005 general elections. Member for Harlow since 6 May 2010 general election. *Select committees:* Member: Public Administration 2010-. 1922 Committee: Member, Executive 2010-, Member, Sub Committee for Campaigning. Chair: Western Area Conservative Students 1987-90, Exeter University Conservative Association 1989-90; Deputy Chair, Vauxhall Conservative Association 1998-2000; Member, Conservative Way Forward; Vice-chair, Conservative Friends of Azerbaijan; Officer, Conservative Friends of Israel 2010-. *Councils and public bodies:* Councillor, Roydon Parish Council 2005-11; Member, Skills Commission.

Political interests: Apprenticeships, Big Society, community cohesion, education, green belt, housing, information technology, Islamism, literacy, mobile technology, social action, terrorism, trade unions; Azerbaijan, Brazil, Iraq (Kurdistan region), Israel, Libya, Sri Lanka, Russia, USA.

Other: Fellow, Royal Society of Arts; Member: Co-operative Society, Advisory Board, Centre for Social Justice, British Horological Institute, Institute of Journalists, Freedom Association; Patron, Harlow Homestart; President, St Johns Ambulance, Harlow; Co-operative trustee, Harlow Employability. National Conservative Excellence Award for Social Action 2008; United and Cecil Club; Royal British Legion, Harlow; Great Parndon Community Association; Maypole Social Club, Harlow; East India Club.

Publications: Retreat or Reform (Institute for European Defence and Strategic Studies, 1994); Corporate Irresponsibility (Social Affairs Unit, 1998); Numerous articles in various publications and written chapters for: From the Ashes: The Future of the Conservative Party (Bow Group, 2005), The Last Moral Force, The New Blue (Social Market Foundation, 2008), Encyclopedia of Soviet Union and Eastern Europe (by Bogdan Szjakowski, 1994).

Recreations: Chelsea FC, countryside, horology, travelling, mobile technology.

Robert Halfon MP, House of Commons, London SW1A 0AA
Tel: 020 7219 7223
Constituency: Harlow Enterprise Hub, Kao-Hockham Building, Edinburgh Way, Harlow, Essex CM20 2NQ
Tel: 01279 311451 *Email:* halfon4harlow@roberthalfon.com *Website:* www.roberthalfon.com www.roberthalfon.blogspot.com *Twitter:* @halfon4harlowMP

LIBERAL DEMOCRAT

HAMES, DUNCAN
Chippenham *(Majority 2,470)*

PPS to Nick Clegg as Deputy Prime Minister and Lord President of the Council

Duncan John Hames. Born 16 June 1977; Married Jo Swinson MP 2011.

Education: Watford Boys' Grammar School; New College, Oxford (BA philosophy, politics and economics 1998).

Non-political career: Recruitment, Northwich Park Hospital 1995; Business consultant, Deloitte Consulting 1998-2004; Director, Chippenham Consultants Limited 2005-10.

Political career: Contested Tottenham 2000 by-election and Watford 2001 and Westbury 2005 general elections. Member for Chippenham since 6 May 2010 general election; PPS to: Sarah Teather as Minister of State for Children and Families 2010-11, Chris Huhne as Secretary of State for Energy and Climate Change 2011-12, Ed Davey as Secretary of State for Energy and Climate Change February-September 2012, Nick Clegg as Deputy Prime Minister and Lord President of the Council 2012-; Vice-president, Liberal Democrat Youth and Students 2000-02; Member, Federal Finance and Administration Committee 2001; Chair, Federal Policy Committee 2012-; Member, Manifesto Working Group 2013-. *Councils and public bodies:* Governor, Westwood with Ilford School 2002-06; Councillor, West Wiltshire District Council 2003-07; South West England Regional Development Agency: Board member 2003-09, Chair, Audit Committee 2008-09; Board member, Culture South West 2006-08; Governor, George Ward School 2006-10.

Political interests: Financial education, renewable energy, digital society; China, Israel-Palestine, South Sudan.

Other: Associate, CIMA.

Duncan Hames MP, House of Commons, London SW1A 0AA
Tel: 020 7219 7039 *Email:* duncan.hames.mp@parliament.uk
Constituency: Avonbridge House, Bath Road, Chippenham, Wiltshire SN15 2BB
Tel: 01249 454110 *Fax:* 01249 454115 *Email:* duncan@duncanhames.org.uk
Website: www.duncanhames.org.uk *Twitter:* @duncanhames

LABOUR

HAMILTON, DAVID
Midlothian *(Majority 10,349)*

Opposition Whip

Born 24 October 1950; Son of David Hamilton and Agnes Gardner; Married Jean Trench Macrae 1969 (2 daughters).

Education: Dalkeith High School.

Non-political career: Armed Forces Parliamentary Scheme 2002-10. Miner, National Coal Board 1965-84; Unemployed 1984-87; Employment training scheme supervisor, Midlothian Council 1987-89; Placement and training officer, Craigmillar Festival Society 1989-92; Chief executive, Craigmillar Opportunities Trust 1992-2000. NUM 1965-87, 2001-: Monktonhall Colliery: Delegate, 1976-87, Joint union chair 1981-87; TGWU 1987-2000.

Political career: Member for Midlothian 2001-05, for Midlothian (revised boundary) since 5 May 2005 general election; PPS to Ed Miliband as Secretary of State for Energy and Climate Change 2008-10; Opposition Whip 2010-. *Select committees:* Member: Broadcasting 2001-05, Procedure 2001-05, Scottish Affairs 2003-05, 2007-08, Work and Pensions 2003-05, European Scrutiny 2005-07, Defence 2005-10. PLP Scottish Regional Group: Vice-chair 2005-06, Chair 2007-08. *Councils and public bodies:* Midlothian Council: Councillor 1995-2001, Convenor, Strategic Services Committee 1995-2001; Convention of Scottish Local Authorities (COSLA): Chair, Economic Development, Planning and Transport Committee 1997-99; Chair, Midlothian Innovation Technology Trust 2002-.

Political interests: Defence, energy, biotechnology; Cyprus, EU, Gibraltar, USA.

Other: Chair, Midlothian Innovation Technology Trust 2002-; Director: Gullane Miners' Home 2004-09, Scottish Mining Museum 2009-12; Dalkeith Miners Welfare; Honorary President, Midlothian Artists.

Recreations: Films, theatre, grandchildren.

David Hamilton MP, House of Commons, London SW1A 0AA
Tel: 020 7219 8257 *Fax:* 020 7219 2532 *Email:* david.hamilton.mp@parliament.uk
Constituency: PO Box 11, 95 High Street, Dalkeith, Midlothian EH22 1AX
Tel: 0131-654 1585 *Fax:* 0131-654 1586 *Website:* www.davidhamiltonmp.com
Twitter: @davidhamiltonmp

LABOUR

HAMILTON, FABIAN

Leeds North East *(Majority 4,545)*

Fabian Uziell-Hamilton. Born 12 April 1955; Son of late Mario Uziell-Hamilton, solicitor, and late Adrianne Uziell-Hamilton (Her Honour Judge Uziell-Hamilton); Married Rosemary Ratcliffe 1980 (1 son 2 daughters).

Education: Brentwood School, Essex; York University (BA social sciences 1977); French.

Non-political career: Taxi driver 1978-79; Graphic designer 1979-94; Consultant and dealer, Apple Macintosh computer systems 1994-97. Member: SLADE 1978-82, NGA 1982-91, GPMU 1991-2005, Amicus 2005-07, Unite 2007-.

Political career: Contested Leeds North East 1992 general election. Member for Leeds North East 1997-2010, for Leeds North East (revised boundary) since 6 May 2010 general election; PPS to Rachel Reeves as Shadow Chief Secretary to the Treasury 2012-13. *Select committees:* Member: Administration 1997-2001, Foreign Affairs 2001-10, Quadripartite (Committees on Strategic Export Controls)/Arms Export Controls 2006-10, Political and Constitutional Reform 2010-, Joint Committee on National Security Strategy 2010-, International Development 2013-, Arms Exports Controls 2013-. Vice-chair, PLP Departmental Group for Home Affairs 2010-. Member, Co-operative Party 1981-; Member, Labour Friends of Israel 1997-. *Councils and public bodies:* Councillor, Leeds City Council 1987-98: Chair: Race Equality Committee 1988-94, Economic Development Committee 1994-96, Education Committee 1996-97.

Political interests: Education, transport, small businesses, anti-racism, international development, alternative fuels, foreign affairs, holocaust education, prison health, hospices and palliative care; Southern Africa, Caribbean, Cyprus, Europe, Iceland, Indian sub-continent, Iran, Japan, Kashmir, Korea, Middle East, Russia, Tibet, Turkey.

Other: Member, Executive Committee, Inter-Parliamentary Union, British Group; Member: Fabian Society 1990-, Jewish Labour Movement; St Gemmas Hospice; Childline; Practical Actions; Refugee Education, Training and Advisory Service; St George's Crypt, Leeds.

Recreations: Film, opera, cycling, computers, photography.

Fabian Hamilton MP, House of Commons, London SW1A 0AA
Tel: 020 7219 3493 *Fax:* 020 7219 5540 *Email:* fabian.hamilton.mp@parliament.uk
Constituency: 335 Roundhay Road, Leeds LS8 4HT
Tel: 0113-249 6600 *Fax:* 0113-235 9866 *Email:* fabian@leedsne.co.uk
Website: www.leedsne.co.uk *Twitter:* @fabianhamilton

CONSERVATIVE

HAMMOND, PHILIP

Runnymede and Weybridge *(Majority 16,509)*

Secretary of State for Defence

Born 4 December 1955; Son of Bernard Hammond, civil engineer and local government officer; Married Susan Williams-Walker 1991 (2 daughters 1 son).

Education: Shenfield School, Brentwood, Essex; University College, Oxford (MA politics, philosophy and economics 1977).

Non-political career: Assistant to Chair, then marketing manager, Speywood Laboratories Ltd 1977-81; Director, Speywood Medical Ltd 1981-83; Established and ran medical equipment manufacturing and distribution companies 1983-94; Director various medical equipment manufacturing companies 1983-96; Director, Castlemead Ltd 1984-; Partner, CMA Consultants 1993-95; Director, Castlemead Homes Ltd 1994-2004; Consultant to Government of Malawi 1995-97; Director, Consort Resources Ltd 1999-2003.

Political career: Contested Newham North East 1994 by-election. Member for Runnymede and Weybridge since 1 May 1997 general election; Opposition Spokesperson for: Health and Social Services 1998-2001, Trade and Industry 2001-02; Shadow Minister for Local and Devolved Government Affairs 2002-05; Shadow Chief Secretary to the Treasury 2005; Shadow Secretary of State for Work and Pensions 2005-07; Shadow Chief Secretary to the Treasury 2007-10; Secretary of State for: Transport 2010-11, Defence 2011-. *Select committees:* Member: Unopposed Bills (Panel) 1997-2004, Environment, Transport and Regional Affairs 1998, Environment, Transport and Regional Affairs (Transport Sub-Committee) 1998, Trade and Industry 2002. Secretary, Conservative Party Committee for Health 1997-98. Chair, East Lewisham Conservative Association 1989-96; Member, Executive Council, Greater London Area 1989-96.

Political interests: Economic policy, international trade, European Union, defence, social security, transport, housing and planning, energy, health; Southern and Eastern Africa, Germany, Italy, Latin America.

Other: White Lodge, Chertsey. PC 2010; Carlton.

Recreations: Travel, cinema, walking.

Rt Hon Philip Hammond MP, House of Commons, London SW1A 0AA
Tel: 020 7219 4055 *Fax:* 020 7219 5851 *Email:* philip.hammond.mp@parliament.uk
Constituency: Runnymede, Spelthorne and Weybridge, Conservative Association, 55 Cherry
Orchard, Staines, Middlesex TW18 2DQ
Tel: 01784 453544 *Fax:* 01784 466109 *Email:* office@runnymedeweybridgeconservatives.com
Website: www.runnymedeweybridgeconservatives.com

HAMMOND, STEPHEN
Wimbledon *(Majority 11,408)*

Parliamentary Under-Secretary of State, Department for Transport

Stephen William Hammond. Born 4 February 1962; Son of Bryan Hammond and Janice Hammond; Married Sally Brodie 1991 (1 daughter).

Education: King Edward VI School, Southampton; Richard Hale School, Hertford; Queen Mary College, London University (BSc econ 1982).

Non-political career: Trainee analyst, Reed Stenhouse Investment Services 1983-85; Fund manager, Canada Life 1987-88; Stockbroker, UBS Philips and Drew 1987-91; Director: UK equities, Dresdner Kleinwort Benson Securities 1991-98, Pan European research, Commerzbank Securities 1998-2001.

CONSERVATIVE

Political career: Contested North Warwickshire 1997 and Wimbledon 2001 general elections. Member for Wimbledon since 5 May 2005 general election; Shadow Minister for Transport 2005-10; PPS to Eric Pickles as Secretary of State for Communities and Local Government 2010-12; Parliamentary Under-Secretary of State, Department for Transport 2012-. *Select committees:* Member: Regulatory Reform 2005-08. Chair, Stevenage Conservatives 1991-94; Member, Executive, Eastern Area 1992-94; Chair, Wimbledon Conservative Association 2001-03; Member, 2020 Group. *Councils and public bodies:* Merton Borough Council: Councillor 2002-06, Environment spokesman 2002-04, Deputy group leader 2004-06.

Political interests: Economics, financial affairs, transport, foreign affairs; China, EU, India, Portugal, Sri Lanka, USA.

Other: Wimbledon Society; Associate, Society of Investment Analysts 1985; Macmillan Cancer. Royal Wimbledon Golf Club; Wimbledon Hockey Club.

Recreations: Reading, sport, relaxing with family, cooking.

Stephen Hammond MP, House of Commons, London SW1A 0AA
Tel: 020 7219 3401 *Fax:* 020 7219 0462 *Email:* hammonds@parliament.uk
Constituency: Wimbledon Conservative Association, c/o 1 Summerstown, London SW17 0BQ
Tel: 020 8944 2905 *Email:* agent@wimbledonconservatives.co.uk
Website: www.stephenhammondmp.co.uk *Twitter:* @SHammondMP

HANCOCK, MATTHEW
West Suffolk *(Majority 13,050)*

Minister of State for Skills and Enterprise, Departments for Business, Innovation and Skills and Education

Born 2 October 1978; Married Martha 2006 (2 sons 1 daughter).

Education: King's School, Chester; West Cheshire College; Exeter College, Oxford (BA politics, philosophy and economics 1999); Christ College, Cambridge (Master's economics 2003).

Non-political career: Border Business Systems, Farndon; Economist, Bank of England 2000-05; Chief of staff to George Osborne MP 2005-10.

CONSERVATIVE

Political career: Member for West Suffolk since 6 May 2010 general election; Parliamentary Under-Secretary of State, Departments for Business, Innovation and Skills and Education 2012-13; Minister of State for Skills and Enterprise, Department for Business, Innovation and Skills and Education 2013-. *Select committees:* Member: Public Accounts 2010-12, Standards and Privileges 2010-12. Member, Conservative Party 1999-.

Political interests: Economics, racing, education; India, UK, USA.

Other: Cancer Research UK; Founder, Dom Pardey Charitable Trust; Racing Welfare.

Publications: Various Bank of England publications.

Recreations: Walking, cooking, cricket.

Matthew Hancock MP, House of Commons, London SW1A 0AA
Tel: 020 7219 7186 *Email:* matthew.hancock.mp@parliament.uk
Constituency: Unit 8, Swan Lane Business Park, Exning, Newmarket, Suffolk CB8 7FN
Tel: 01638 576692 *Email:* office@westsuffolkconservatives.com
Website: www.westsuffolkconservatives.com www.matthewhancock.co.uk
Twitter: @matthancockmp

HANCOCK, MIKE

Portsmouth South *(Lib Dem Majority 5,200)*

INDEPENDENT

Michael Thomas Hancock. Born 9 April 1946; Son of Thomas Hancock and Margaret Hancock, née Cole; Married Jacqueline Elliott 1967 (1 son 1 daughter).

Education: Copnor and Portsea School, Hampshire.

Non-political career: Director, BBC Daytime; District officer, Hampshire, Isle of Wight and Channel Islands Mencap 1989-97.

Political career: Contested Portsmouth South (SDP) 1983 general election. Member (SDP) for Portsmouth South 14 June 1984 by-election to 1987. Contested Portsmouth South (as SDP/Alliance) 1987 and (as Lib Dem) 1992 general elections. Member for Portsmouth South 1997-2010, for Portsmouth South (revised boundary) since 6 May 2010 general election; Liberal Democrat Spokesperson for: Foreign Affairs, Defence and Europe (Defence) 1997-99, Environment, Transport, the Regions and Social Justice (Planning) 2000-01. *Select committees:* Member: Public Administration 1997-99, Defence 1999-2011, Chairmen's Panel/Panel of Chairs 2000-13. Contested Wight and Hampshire South 1994 European Parliamentary election. Member: Labour Party 1968-81, Social Democrat Party 1981-87, Liberal Democrat Party 1987-; Resigned Liberal Democrat Whip June 2013. *Councils and public bodies:* Portsmouth City Council: Councillor 1971-, Leader, Liberal Democrat Group 1989-97; Hampshire County Council: Councillor 1973-97, Opposition Leader 1977-81, 1989-93, Leader 1993-97; Vice-chair, Portsmouth Docks 1992-2002; Vice-President, Local Government Association 2010-.

Political interests: European affairs, defence, sport; Moldova, Romania, Russia, Ukraine.

Other: Chair Liberal Group Council of Europe; Leader Liberal Group Western European Union; NATO Parliamentary Assembly; Chair, Southern Branch, NSPCC 1989-92; Trustee, Royal Marine Museum; Mencap; Save the Children; Animal Aid; NAVS; Christian Aid. CBE 1992.

Publications: Council of Europe Report on International Abduction of Children by One of the Parents (2002).

Recreations: Supporter Portsmouth Football Club.

Mike Hancock CBE MP, House of Commons, London SW1A 0AA
Tel: 020 7219 1102 *Fax:* 020 7219 2496 *Email:* hancockm@parliament.uk
Constituency: 1a Albert Road, Southsea, Hampshire PO5 2SE
Tel: 02392 861055 *Fax:* 02392 830530 *Email:* portsmouthldp@cix.co.uk
Website: www.mikehancock.co.uk

HANDS, GREG

Chelsea and Fulham *(Majority 16,722)*

Deputy Chief Whip (Treasurer of HM Household)

CONSERVATIVE

Gregory William Hands. Born 14 November 1965; Son of Edward and Mavis Hands; Married Irina Hundt 2005 (1 daughter 1 son).

Education: Dr Challoner's Grammar School, Amersham; Robinson College, Cambridge (BA modern history 1989); Czech, French, German.

Non-political career: Banker 1989-97.

Political career: Member for Hammersmith and Fulham 2005-10, for Chelsea and Fulham since 6 May 2010 general election; Shadow Minister for the Treasury 2009-10; PPS to George Osborne as Chancellor of the Exchequer 2010-11; Assistant Government Whip 2011-13; Deputy Chief Whip (Treasurer of HM Household) 2013-. *Select committees:* Member: ODPM/Communities and Local Government 2006-08, European Scrutiny 2007-10, Communities and Local Government 2009-10. *Councils and public bodies:* Hammersmith and Fulham Borough Council: Councillor 1998-2006: Leader, Conservative group 1999-2003; Prison visitor, HMP Wormwood Scrubs 2002-04.

Political interests: Finance, foreign affairs, housing, local government; Central and Eastern Europe, Germany, Ireland, North Korea, Russia and ex-USSR.

Other: Trustee, Brunswick Club for Young People 2003-; Carlton Club.

Recreations: Playing and watching football, local history, British, German and Soviet history, photography.

Greg Hands MP, House of Commons, London SW1A 0AA
Tel: 020 7219 0809 *Fax:* 020 7219 6801
Constituency: Contact Westminster office
Email: mail@greghands.com *Website:* www.greghands.com *Twitter:* @greghands

HANSON, DAVID

Delyn *(Majority 2,272)*

Shadow Minister for Home Office

David George Hanson. Born 5 July 1957; Son of late Brian Hanson, fork lift driver, and Glenda Hanson, wages clerk; Married Margaret Mitchell 1986 (2 sons 2 daughters).

Education: Verdin Comprehensive School, Winsford, Cheshire; Hull University (BA drama 1978; Cert Ed 1980).

Non-political career: Vice-president, Hull University Students' Union 1978-79; Trainee, Co-operative Union 1980-81; Manager, Plymouth Co-operative 1981-82; Various posts with Spastics Society 1982-89; Director, Re-Solv (Society for the Prevention of Solvent Abuse) 1989-92. USDAW; Unite.

LABOUR

Political career: Contested Eddisbury 1983 and Delyn 1987 general elections. Member for Delyn since 9 April 1992 general election; PPS to Alastair Darling as Chief Secretary to the Treasury 1997-98; Assistant Government Whip 1998-99; Parliamentary Under-Secretary of State, Wales Office 1999-2001; PPS to Tony Blair as Prime Minister 2001-05; Minister of State: Northern Ireland Office 2005-07, Ministry of Justice 2007-09, Home Office 2009-10; Shadow Exchequer Secretary 2010-11; Shadow Minister for: Policing 2011-13, Home Office 2013-. *Select committees:* Member: Welsh Affairs 1992-95. Contested Cheshire West 1984 European Parliament election. Member, Leadership Campaign Team 1994-97. *Councils and public bodies:* Vale Royal Borough Council: Councillor 1983-91, Labour Leader, Council Leader 1989-91; Councillor, Northwich Town Council 1987-91.

Political interests: Foreign affairs, heritage, local and regional government, solvent abuse; South Africa, Cyprus.

Other: Fellow, Industry and Parliament Trust 1998; Executive member, Commonwealth Parliamentary Association 2010-; Re-Solv (Preventing Solvent Abuse); Flint Life Boats; Flint Abbeyfield Society. PC 2007.

Recreations: Football, cinema, family.

Rt Hon David Hanson MP, House of Commons, London SW1A 0AA
Tel: 020 7219 5064 *Fax:* 020 7219 2671 *Email:* david.hanson.mp@parliament.uk
Constituency: 64 Chester Street, Flint, Flintshire CH6 5DH
Tel: 01352 763159 *Fax:* 01352 730140 *Email:* robbinsh@parliament.uk
Website: www.davidhanson.org.uk *Twitter:* @DavidHansonMP

HARMAN, HARRIET

Camberwell and Peckham *(Majority 17,187)*

Shadow Deputy Prime Minister; Chair, Labour Party; Shadow Secretary of State for Culture, Media and Sport

Born 30 July 1950; Daughter of late John Bishop Harman and Anna Harman; Married Jack Dromey (now MP) 1982 (2 sons 1 daughter).

Education: St Paul's Girls' School, London; York University (BA politics 1978).

Non-political career: Legal officer, National Council for Civil Liberties 1978-82; QC 2001. Member, Unite (TGWU sector).

LABOUR

Political career: Member for Peckham 1982 by-election to 1997, for Camberwell and Peckham 1997-2010, for Camberwell and Peckham (revised boundary) since 6 May 2010 general election; Member, Public Accounts Commission; Shadow Minister, Social Services 1984, 1985-87; Spokesperson for Health 1987-92; Shadow Chief Secretary to the Treasury 1992-94; Shadow Secretary of State for: Employment 1994-95, Health 1995-96, Social Security 1996-97; Secretary of State for Social Security and Minister for Women 1997-98; Solicitor General 2001-05; Minister of State, Department for Constitutional Affairs/Ministry of Justice 2005-07; Leader of the House of Commons and Lord Privy Seal 2007-10; Ex-officio member House of Commons Commission 2007-10; Minister for Women and Equality 2007-10; Member Speaker's Committee for the Independent Parliamentary Standards Authority 2009-10; Acting Leader of the Opposition 2010; Deputy Leader of the Opposition/Shadow Deputy Prime Minister 2010-; Shadow

Secretary of State for: International Development 2010-11, Culture, Media and Sport 2011-. *Select committees:* Chair Modernisation of the House of Commons 2007-10. Member, Labour Party National Executive Committee 1993-98; Deputy Leader Labour Party 2007-; Chair Labour Party 2007-; Acting Leader Labour Party 2010. *Councils and public bodies:* Chair, Childcare Commission 1999-.

Political interests: Women, social services, provision for under-fives, law, domestic violence, civil liberties.

Other: PC 1997.

Rt Hon Harriet Harman QC MP, House of Commons, London SW1A 0AA
Tel: 020 7219 4218 *Fax:* 020 7219 4877 *Email:* harmanh@parliament.uk
Constituency: No constituency office *Website:* www.harrietharman.org
Twitter: @HarrietHarman

CONSERVATIVE

HARPER, MARK
Forest of Dean *(Majority 11,064)*

Minister of State for Immigration, Home Office

Mark James Harper. Born 26 February 1970; Son of James and Jane Harper; Married Margaret Whelan 1999.

Education: Headlands School, Swindon, Wiltshire Swindon College; Brasenose College, Oxford (BA philosophy, politics and economics 1991).

Non-political career: Auditor, KPMG 1991-95; Intel Corporation (UK) Ltd: Senior finance analyst 1995-97, Finance manager 1997-2000, Operations manager 2000-02; Own accountancy practice 2002-05.

Political career: Contested Forest of Dean 2001 general election. Member for Forest of Dean since 5 May 2005 general election; Shadow Minister for: Defence 2005-07, Work and Pensions (Disabled People) 2007-10; Parliamentary Secretary (Minister for Political and Constitutional Reform), Cabinet Office 2010-12; Minister of State for Immigration, Home Office 2012-. *Select committees:* Member: Administration 2005-06, Work and Pensions 2009. South Swindon Conservative Association: Treasurer 1993-98, Deputy chair 1998.

Political interests: Education, special needs education, law and order, health, defence; Israel, Turkey, USA.

Other: ACA 1995.

Recreations: Walking the dogs, travel, cinema.

Mark Harper MP, House of Commons, London SW1A 0AA
Tel: 020 7219 5056 *Fax:* 020 7219 0937 *Email:* mark.harper.mp@parliament.uk
Constituency: 35 High Street, Cinderford, Gloucestershire GL14 2SL
Tel: 01594 823482 *Fax:* 01594 823623 *Website:* www.markharper.org *Twitter:* @Mark_J_Harper

CONSERVATIVE

HARRINGTON, RICHARD
Watford *(Majority 1,425)*

Born 4 November 1957; Married Jessie 1983 (2 sons).

Education: Leeds Grammar School; Keble College, Oxford (MA law and jurisprudence 1979).

Non-political career: Assistant to managing director, Waitrose; Founder, now non-executive director, Harvington Properties 1983-; Managing director, then chairman, holiday resort company 1990-2000.

Political career: Member for Watford since 6 May 2010 general election. *Select committees:* Member: International Development 2010-12. Conservative Party: Treasurer 2008-10, Vice-chairman, Target Seats 2012-. *Councils and public bodies:* Governor, University College School, Hampstead 2000-.

Political interests: Youth unemployment, local transport infrastructure, business and enterprise, treasury; Kashmir, Middle East, Pakistan.

Other: Chair, executive board, Conservative Friends of Israel; Fundraising chair and trustee, Variety Club Children's Society 1998-2001; Oriental Club; Oxhey Conservative Club; Watford Town and Country Club.

Recreations: Cinema, watching football.

Richard Harrington MP, House of Commons, London SW1A 0AA
Tel: 020 7219 7180 *Email:* richard.harrington.mp@parliament.uk
Constituency: 30 The Avenue, Watford, Hertfordshire WD17 4AE
Tel: 01923 296790 *Email:* richard@richardharrington.org.uk
Website: www.richardharrington.org.uk *Twitter:* @Richard4Watford

CONSERVATIVE

HARRIS, REBECCA

Castle Point *(Majority 7,632)*

Rebecca Elizabeth Harris. Born 22 December 1967; Daughter of Philip and Louise Harris; Married Frank Skelton 1999 (1 son).

Education: London School of Economics (BSc government).

Non-political career: Marketing director, Philimore and Co (publisher) 1997-2007; Campaign officer, Conservative Research Department; Special adviser to Tim Yeo MP 2003-10.

Political career: Member for Castle Point since 6 May 2010 general election. *Select committees:* Member: Business, Innovation and Skills 2010-, Joint Committee on the Draft Enhanced Terrorism Prevention and Investigation Measures Bill 2012-13, Regulatory Reform 2012-. Campaign coordinator, Conservative Campaign HQ 2000-01; North West London area officer, Conservative Party 2007-08; Vice-chairman (youth), Conservative Party 2013-. *Councils and public bodies:* Chichester District Council: Councillor 1999-2003, Deputy chair, scrutiny committee 1999-2003.

Political interests: Small business, education and skills, planning.

Other: Hadleigh Conservative Club; Canvey Island Conservative Club; Benfleet Conservative Club.

Recreations: Gardening, walking.

Rebecca Harris MP, House of Commons, London SW1A 0AA
Tel: 020 7219 7206 *Email:* rebecca.harris.mp@parliament.uk
Constituency: c/o Castle Point Conservatives, Bernard Braine House, 8 Green Road, Benfleet, Essex SS7 5JT
Tel: 01268 792992 *Fax:* 01268 792992 *Email:* office@castlepointconservatives.com
Twitter: @RebeccaHarrisMP

LABOUR

HARRIS, TOM

Glasgow South *(Majority 12,658)*

Thomas Harris. Born 20 February 1964; Son of Tom Harris, lorry/taxi driver, and Rita Harris, née Ralston, office clerk; Married Carolyn Moffat 1998 (3 sons, 1 from previous marriage).

Education: Garnock Academy, Kilbirnie, Ayrshire; Napier College, Edinburgh (HND journalism 1986).

Non-political career: Trainee reporter, *East Kilbride News* 1986-88; Reporter, *Paisley Daily Express* 1988-90; Press officer: Scottish Labour Party 1990-92, Strathclyde Regional Council 1993-96; Senior media officer, Glasgow City Council 1996; Public relations manager, East Ayrshire Council 1996-98; Chief public relations and marketing officer, Strathclyde Passenger Transport Executive 1998-2001. Member: National Union of Journalists 1984-97, Unison 1997-2004, Amicus/Unite 2004-.

Political career: Member for Glasgow Cathcart 2001-05, for Glasgow South since 5 May 2005 general election; PPS to: John Spellar as Minister of State, Northern Ireland Office 2003-05, Patricia Hewitt as Secretary of State for Health 2005-06; Parliamentary Under-Secretary of State, Department for Transport 2006-08; Shadow Minister for Environment, Food and Rural Affairs 2012-13. *Select committees:* Member: Science and Technology 2001-04, Transport 2010-12, Administration 2010, 2013-. Chair, PLP Departmental Committee for Northern Ireland 2005-07. Member, Labour Friends of Israel; Contested Scottish Labour leadership election 2011.

Political interests: Welfare reform, economy, foreign affairs, immigration and asylum, transport; Iraq, Israel, Northern Ireland, USA.

Other: Railway Benefit Fund.

Publications: Why I'm Right...And Everyone Else Is Wrong (2011).

Recreations: Astronomy, cinema, hillwalking.

Tom Harris MP, House of Commons, London SW1A 0AA
Tel: 020 7219 8237 *Fax:* 020 7219 1769 *Email:* tomharrismp@parliament.uk
Constituency: Cathcart Old Parish Chruch, 119 Carmunnock Road, Glasgow G44 5UU
Tel: 0141-637 1962 *Website:* www.tomharris.org.uk *Twitter:* @TomHarrisMP

HART, SIMON
Carmarthen West and South Pembrokeshire *(Majority 3,423)*

Simon Anthony Hart. Born 15 August 1963; Married Abigail Holland 1998 (1 son 1 daughter).
Education: Radley College, Oxfordshire; Royal Agriculture College, Cirencester (Diploma rural estate management 1984).
Non-political career: Territorial Army. Chartered surveyor, Knight, Frank & Rutley 1986-88; Associated to sole principal, Llewellyn Humphreys 1988-98; Associate land agent, Balfour, Burd & Benson 1998-99; Countryside Alliance 1999-2010: Campaigns director 1999-2003, Chief executive 2003-10.

CONSERVATIVE

Political career: Member for Carmarthen West and South Pembrokeshire since 6 May 2010 general election. *Select committees:* Member: Political and Constitutional Reform 2010-, Welsh Affairs 2012-. Member, Executive, 1922 Committee 2012-.
Political interests: Rural affairs, small business; Falkland Islands.
Other: Member, Countryside Alliance; Associate, Royal Institute of Chartered Surveyors 1985; Farmers Club. Cresselly Cricket Club.
Recreations: Cricket, all aspects of country sports.
Simon Hart MP, House of Commons, London SW1A 0AA
Tel: 020 7219 7228 *Email:* simon.hart.mp@parliament.uk
Constituency: 15 St John Street, Whitland, Carmarthenshire SA34 0AN
Tel: 01994 342002 *Website:* www.simon-hart.com

HARVEY, NICK
North Devon *(Majority 5,821)*

Nicholas Barton Harvey. Born 3 August 1961; Son of Frederick Harvey, civil servant, and Christine Harvey, teacher; Married Kate Fox 2003 (1 daughter 1 son).
Education: Queen's College, Taunton; Middlesex Polytechnic (BA business studies 1983) (President Students' Union 1981-82); French.
Non-political career: Communications and marketing executive: Profile PR Ltd 1984-86, Dewe Rogerson Ltd 1986-91; Communications Consultant 1991-. Former member, National Union of Journalists.

LIBERAL DEMOCRAT

Political career: Contested Enfield Southgate (Liberal/Alliance) 1987 general election. Member for North Devon 1992-2010, for North Devon (revised boundary) since 6 May 2010 general election; Liberal Democrat Spokesperson for: Transport 1992-94, Trade and Industry 1994-97, Constitution (English Regions) 1997-99, Health 1999-2001, Culture, Media and Sport 2001-03; Member, House of Commons Commission 2005-10; Liberal Democrat Shadow Secretary of State for Defence 2006-10; Member Speaker's Committee for the Independent Parliamentary Standards Authority 2009-10; Minister of State for the Armed Forces, Ministry of Defence 2010-12. *Select committees:* Member: Trade and Industry 1994-95, European Scrutiny 2004-05, Home Affairs 2005-06, Standards and Privileges 2005-10, Standards 2013-, Privileges 2013-. National vice-chair, Union of Liberal Students 1981-82; Chair: Candidates Committee 1993-98, Campaigns and Communications 1994-99.
Political interests: Economics, European Union, defence, foreign policy.
Other: UK member: Council of Europe 2005-07, Western European Union 2005-07; Vice-President, Federation of Economic Development Authorities (FEDA) 2000-. Honorary Doctorate, Middlesex University 2000. Kt 2012.
Recreations: Travel, football, walking, music.
Sir Nick Harvey MP, House of Commons, London SW1A 0AA
Tel: 020 7219 6232 *Fax:* 020 7219 2683 *Email:* pagep@parliament.uk
Constituency: The Castle Centre, Barnstaple, Devon EX31 1DR
Tel: 01271 328631 *Fax:* 01271 345664 *Email:* mail@nickharveymp.com
Website: www.nickharveymp.com

CONSERVATIVE

HASELHURST, ALAN
Saffron Walden *(Majority 15,242)*

Alan Gordon Barraclough Haselhurst. Born 23 June 1937; Son of late John Haselhurst and Alice Haselhurst, née Barraclough; Married Angela Bailey 1977 (2 sons 1 daughter).

Education: King Edward VI School, Birmingham; Cheltenham College; Oriel College, Oxford.

Non-political career: Secretary, treasurer, librarian, Oxford Union Society 1959-60; Executive, chemicals and plastics industry 1960-70; Public affairs consultant 1974-97.

Political career: Member for Middleton and Prestwich 1970-February 1974. Contested Middleton and Prestwich February 1974 general election. Member for Saffron Walden 7 July 1977 by-election to 2010, for Saffron Walden (revised boundary) since 6 May 2010 general election; PPS to Mark Carlisle as Secretary of State, Education and Science 1979-81; Chairman Ways and Means and Deputy Speaker 1997-2010; Contested Speaker elections 2000, 2009. *Select committees:* Ex-officio chair: Chairmen's Panel 1997-2010; Ex-officio member: Court of Referees 1997-2010, Standing Orders 1998-2010, Unopposed Bills (Panel) 2000-10; Member: Finance and Services 2008-, Liaison 2010-, Ecclesiastical Committee 2010-; Chair: Administration 2010-; Member: Works of Art 2011-. President, Oxford University Conservative Association 1958; National Chair, Young Conservative Movement 1966-68; Deputy Chair, Conservative Group for Europe 1982-85.

Political interests: Education, aerospace, aviation, youth affairs, European Union, agriculture, community development; Commonwealth countries, USA.

Other: Chair, Commonwealth Youth Exchange Council 1978-81; Commonwealth Parliamentary Association, Chair: UK branch 2010-, International Executive Committee 2011-; Fellow, Industry and Parliament Trust 1982; Chair of trustees, Community Projects Foundation 1986-97. Kt 1995; PC 1999; MCC. Member, executive committee, Essex County Cricket Club 1996-2008.

Publications: Occasionally Cricket (Queen Anne Press, 1999); Eventually Cricket (Queen Anne Press, 2001); Incidentally Cricket (Queen Anne Press, 2003); Accidentally Cricket (Professional and Higher Partnership, 2009); Unusually Cricket (Professional and Higher Partnership, 2010).

Recreations: Hi-fi, watching cricket, gardening.

Rt Hon Sir Alan Haselhurst MP, House of Commons, London SW1A 0AA
Tel: 020 7219 5214 *Fax:* 020 7219 5600 *Email:* alan.haselhurst.mp@parliament.uk
Constituency: The Old Armoury, Saffron Walden, Essex CB10 1JN
Tel: 01799 506349 *Fax:* 01799 506047 *Email:* office@saffronwaldenconservatives.org.uk
Website: www.saffronwaldenconservatives.com www.siralanhaselhurst.net

LABOUR

HAVARD, DAI
Merthyr Tydfil and Rhymney *(Majority 4,056)*

David Stewart Havard. Born 7 February 1950; Son of late Eileen Havard, shop worker, and Ted Havard, miner; Married Julia Watts 1986 (divorced).

Education: Secondary modern school, Treharris; Grammar Technical, Quakers Yard, Edwardsville; Comprehensive school, Afon Taf; St Peter's College, Birmingham (Certificate in Education); Warwick University (MA industrial relations).

Non-political career: MSF full time officer: Studies tutor 1971-75, Researcher 1975-79, Education 1975-82, Official 1989-, Delegation leader: Wales Labour Party, Conferences; Wales secretary. Amicus.

Political career: Member for Merthyr Tydfil and Rhymney 2001-10, for Merthyr Tydfil and Rhymney (revised boundary) since 6 May 2010 general election. *Select committees:* Member: European Standing Committee C, Regulatory Reform 2001-05, Defence 2003-10, 2010-, Panel of Chairs 2011-. Vice-chair, PLP Departmental Committee for Defence 2006-10. Former member, Wales Labour Party Joint Policy Committee.

Political interests: Education, lifelong learning, health, cancer and blood, industrial relations and working conditions.

Other: Alternate Member, UK Delegation, Organisation for Security and Co-operation in Europe Parliamentary Assembly. Merthyr Town FC; Treharris Mini Rugby; Merthyr Rugby Juniors.

Publications: Contributor to academic publications on trade union and economic development.

Recreations: Hillwalking, horse riding, birdwatching, Commons and Lords Rugby team.

Dai Havard MP, House of Commons, London SW1A 0AA
Tel: 020 7219 8255 *Fax:* 020 7219 1449 *Email:* dai.havard.mp@parliament.uk
Constituency: Unit 4, Triangle Business Park, Pentrebach, Merthyr Tydfil, Mid Glamorgan CF48 4TQ
Tel: 01685 379247 *Fax:* 01685 387563 *Email:* toomeyd@parliament.uk
Website: www.daihavardmp.co.uk

CONSERVATIVE

HAYES, JOHN

South Holland and The Deepings *(Majority 21,880)*

Minister without Portfolio, Cabinet Office

John Henry Hayes. Born 23 June 1958; Son of late Henry Hayes and Lily Hayes; Married Susan Hopewell 1997 (2 sons).

Education: Colfe's Grammar School, London; Nottingham University (BA politics 1980; PGCE history/English 1982); Some Italian and Spanish.

Non-political career: Data Base Ltd IT company 1983-99: Director 1986-97, Non-executive director 1997-99; Associate professor, American University in London 2005-10. Associate member, Association of Teachers and Lecturers.

Political career: Contested Derbyshire North East 1987 and 1992 general elections. Member for South Holland and The Deepings 1997-2010, for South Holland and The Deepings (revised boundary) since 6 May 2010 general election; Shadow Minister for Schools 2000-01; Opposition Pairing Whip 2001-02; Shadow Minister for: Agriculture, Fisheries and Food 2002-03, Local and Devolved Government (Housing and Planning) 2003-05, Transport 2005, Vocational Education 2005-09, Lifelong Learning, Further and Higher Education 2009, Universities and Skills 2009-10; Minister of State for: Further Education, Skills and Lifelong Learning, Departments for Business, Innovation and Skills and Education 2010-12, Energy, Department of Energy and Climate Change 2012-13; Minister without Portfolio (Senior Adviser to the Prime Minister), Cabinet Office 2013-. *Select committees:* Member: Agriculture 1997-99, Education and Employment 1998-99,1999-2000, Education and Employment (Education Sub-Committee) 1999-2000, Selection 2001-02, Administration 2001-02. Joint vice-chair, Conservative Party Committee for Education and Employment 1997-99; Conservative Party Committee for Agriculture, Fisheries and Food: Joint secretary 1998-99, Secretary 1999-2000. Former chair, Young Conservatives; Vice-chair: Conservatives Against Federal Europe, Conservative Party 1999-2000; Member, 1992 Group; Joint chair, Cornerstone Group 2004-. *Councils and public bodies:* Councillor, Nottinghamshire County Council 1985-98.

Political interests: Education, elections and campaigning, political ideas and philosophy, local government, agriculture, commerce and industry, energy, welfare of elderly and disabled people; England, Italy, Spain, USA.

Other: Countryside member, NFU; Countryside Alliance, SPUC; Patron, Headway Cambridgeshire; Chair, British Caribbean Association 2009-; Headway, various local charities in South Lincolnshire. Charity Champion award 2008; Double Act of the Year (with Ed Davey MP), *The Spectator* awards 2012; Commons Minister of the Year, *House Magazine* awards 2012. PC 2013; Carlton; Spalding Club; Spalding Gentlemen's Society.

Publications: Representing Rural Britain – Blair's Bogus Claim (Conservative Policy Forum, 2000); Answer the Question: Prime Ministerial Accountability and the Rule of Parliament (Politica, 2000); Tony B. Liar (Conservative Party, 2001); The Right to Own: Conservative Action on Housing (Conservative Party, 2004); The Right Homes in the Right Places (Conservative Party, 2005); Being Conservative: A Cornerstone of Policies to Revive Tory Britain (Cornerstone Group, 2005); Towards a Virtuous Circle of Learning (NIACE, 2006); Towards a Gold Standard for Craft, Guaranteeing Professional Apprenticeships (Centre for Policy Studies, 2007); From Social Engineering to Social Aspiration: Strategies to Broaden Access to Higher Education (UALL/Birkbeck, 2008).

Recreations: The arts (particularly English painting, poetry and prose), good food and wine, many sports (including boxing), studying the past, gardening, making jam, antiques, architecture and aesthetics.

Rt Hon John Hayes MP, House of Commons, London SW1A 0AA
Tel: 020 7219 1389 *Fax:* 020 7219 2273 *Email:* hayesj@parliament.uk
Constituency: 10 Broad Street, Spalding, Lincolnshire PE11 1TB
Tel: 01775 711534 *Fax:* 01775 713905 *Email:* davieshm@parliament.uk

CONSERVATIVE

HEALD, OLIVER

North East Hertfordshire *(Majority 15,194)*

Solicitor General

Born 15 December 1954; Son of late J A Heald, chartered engineer, and late Joyce Heald, née Pemberton, teacher; Married Christine Whittle 1979 (1 son 2 daughters).

Education: Reading School; Pembroke College, Cambridge (MA law 1976); French, German.

Non-political career: Barrister, Middle Temple 1977-; Bencher 2013; QC.

Political career: Contested Southwark and Bermondsey 1987 general election. Member for North Hertfordshire 1992-97, for North East Hertfordshire 1997-2010, for North East Hertfordshire (revised boundary) since 6 May 2010 general election; PPS to: Sir Peter Lloyd as Minister of State, Home Office 1994, William Waldegrave as Minister of Agriculture, Fisheries and Food 1994-95; Sponsored Private Member's Bill: Insurance Companies (Reserves) Act 1995; Parliamentary Under-Secretary of State, Department of Social Security 1995-97; Opposition Whip 1997-2000; Opposition Spokesperson for: Home Affairs 2000-01, Health 2001-02; Shadow Minister for Work and Pensions 2002-03; Shadow Leader of the House 2003-05; Member House of Commons' Commission 2003-05; Shadow Secretary of State for Constitutional Affairs 2004-07; Shadow Chancellor of the Duchy of Lancaster 2005-07; Solicitor General 2012-. *Select committees:* Member: Administration 1998-2000, Modernisation of the House of Commons 2003-05, Work and Pensions 2007-12, Selection 2009-10, Standards and Privileges 2010-12, Ecclesiastical Committee 2010-12, Joint Committee on the Draft House of Lords Reform Bill 2011-12. Chair, North Hertfordshire Conservative Association 1984-86; Southwark and Bermondsey Conservative Association: President 1993-98, Patron 1998-; Chairman: Executive Society of Conservative Lawyers 2008-12, Executive Parliamentary Resources Unit. *Councils and public bodies:* Member, Committee on Standards in Public Life 2008-12.

Political interests: Industrial relations, environment, law and order, pensions.

Other: Member, Council of Europe 2008-12.

Publications: Co-author, Auditing the New Deal: What Figures for the Future (Politeia, 2004); A Reformed Second Chamber: Building a Better House (Society of Conservative Lawyers, 2012).

Recreations: Sport, family.

Oliver Heald MP, House of Commons, London SW1A 0AA
Tel: 020 7219 6354 *Email:* oliver.heald.mp@parliament.uk
Constituency: No constituency address publicised *Website:* www.oliverhealdmp.com

LABOUR

HEALEY, JOHN

Wentworth and Dearne *(Majority 13,920)*

Born 13 February 1960; Son of Aidan Healey, prison service, and Jean Healey, teacher; Married Jackie Bate 1993 (1 son).

Education: Lady Lumley's Comprehensive School, Pickering; St Peter's School, York; Christ's College, Cambridge (Scholar; BA 1982).

Non-political career: Journalist/deputy editor, *House Magazine* 1983-84; Disability campaigner for three national charities 1984-90; Tutor, Open University Business School 1989-92; Campaigns manager, Issue Communications 1990-92; Head of communications, MSF Union 1992-94; Campaigns and communications director, Trades Union Congress 1994-97. Member, GMB.

Political career: Contested Ryedale 1992 general election. Member for Wentworth 1997-2010, for Wentworth and Dearne since 6 May 2010 general election; PPS to Gordon Brown as Chancellor of the Exchequer 1999-2001; Parliamentary Under-Secretary of State, Department for Education and Skills (Adult Skills) 2001-02; HM Treasury 2002-07: Economic Secretary 2002-05, Financial Secretary 2005-07; Minister of State, Department for Communities and Local Government 2007-10: Minister for Local Government 2007-09, Minister for Housing (attending Cabinet) 2009-10; Member Speaker's Committee on the Electoral Commission -2009; Shadow Minister for Housing 2010; Shadow Secretary of State for Health 2010-11. *Select committees:* Member: Education and Employment 1997-99, Education and Employment (Employment Sub-Committee) 1997-99, Public Accounts 2005-07, Joint Committee on Tax Law Rewrite Bills 2005-09. *Councils and public bodies:* Vice-President, Local Government Association 2010-11.

Political interests: Employment, trade unions, economy, tax, industrial relations, disability, local and regional government; Australia, USA.

Other: Rotherham Hospice. PC 2008.

Recreations: Family.

Rt Hon John Healey MP, House of Commons, London SW1A 0AA
Tel: 020 7219 6359 *Fax:* 020 7219 2451 *Email:* healeyj@parliament.uk
Constituency: 79 High Street, Wath-upon-Dearne, Rotherham, South Yorkshire S63 7QB
Tel: 01709 875943 *Fax:* 01709 874207 *Website:* www.johnhealeymp.co.uk
Twitter: @JohnHealey_MP

HEATH, DAVID
Somerton and Frome *(Majority 1,817)*

David William St John Heath. Born 16 March 1954; Son of Eric Heath and late Pamela Heath; Married Caroline Netherton 1987 (1 son 1 daughter).
Education: Millfield School, Somerset; St John's College, Oxford (MA physiological sciences 1976); City University, London (ophthalmic optics 1979); French (basic).
Non-political career: Qualified optician in practice 1979-85; Parliamentary consultant, Worldwide Fund for Nature 1990-91; Consultant to various NGOs/charities; Member, Audit Commission 1994-97.

LIBERAL DEMOCRAT

Political career: Contested Somerton and Frome 1992 general election. Member for Somerton and Frome 1997-2010, for Somerton and Frome (revised boundary) since 6 May 2010 general election; Liberal Democrat Spokesperson for: Foreign Affairs 1997-99, Agriculture, Rural Affairs and Fisheries 1999-2001, Work and Pensions 2001-02, Science 2001-03, Lord Chancellor's Department/Department for Constitutional Affairs 2002-06, Home Office 2002-05, Science 2004; Shadow Leader of the House 2005-07; Spokesperson for Cabinet Office 2006-07; Shadow Secretary of State for Justice and Lord Chancellor 2007-08; Shadow Leader of the House of Commons 2009-10; Parliamentary Secretary (Deputy Leader of the House of Commons) 2010-12; Minister of State for Agriculture and Food, Department for Environment, Food and Rural Affairs 2012-13. *Select committees:* Member: Foreign Affairs 1997-99, Standards and Privileges 2001-05, Science and Technology 2001-03, Modernisation of the House of Commons 2005-06, Court of Referees 2007-10, Justice 2008-10. Member: Liberal Party National Executive 1988-89, Liberal Democrats Federal Executive 1990-92, 1993-95; Chair, Liberal Democrat Commission on Privacy 2008-10. *Councils and public bodies:* Somerset County Council: Councillor 1985-97, Council Leader 1985-89; Chair, Avon and Somerset Police Authority 1993-96.
Political interests: Education, local and regional government, rural affairs, environment, home affairs, constitutional affairs; Balkans, Europe, France, USA.
Other: Member Council of Local Authorities and Regions of Europe 1993-97; Parliamentary Assembly of the Organisation for Security and Co-operation in Europe (OSCE): Member 1997-2010, Leader, Liberal Group 2009-10; Member, Witham Friary Friendly Society; Vice-chair: Committee of Local Police Authorities 1993-97, Association of County Councils 1994-97; Member, Academic Council of Wilton Park 2002-10; FADO; Honorary Fellow, College of Optometrists. CBE 1989.
Recreations: Cricket, rugby football, until recently pig breeding.
David Heath CBE MP, House of Commons, London SW1A 0AA
Tel: 020 7219 6245 *Fax:* 020 7219 5939 *Email:* david.heath.mp@parliament.uk
Constituency: 17 Bath Street, Frome, Somerset BA11 1DN
Tel: 01373 473618 *Fax:* 01373 455152 *Email:* davidheath@davidheath.co.uk
Website: www.davidheath.co.uk *Twitter:* @DavidHeathMP

HEATON-HARRIS, CHRISTOPHER
Daventry *(Majority 19,188)*

Born 28 November 1967; Son of David and Ann Heaton-Harris; Married Jayne Carlow 1990 (2 daughters).
Education: Tiffin Grammar School for Boys, Kingston-upon-Thames, Surrey.
Non-political career: Various positions, What 4 Ltd (wholesale fresh produce company) 1989-99; Owner, Whistle Blower Ltd 2009-10.
Political career: Contested Leicester South 1997 general election and 2004 by-election. Member for Daventry since 6 May 2010 general election. *Select committees:* Member: Public Accounts

CONSERVATIVE

2010-, European Scrutiny 2010-. European Parliament: MEP for East Midlands 1999-2009: Founder member, Campaign for Parliamentary Reform 2001, Chief Whip, EP Conservatives 2001-04, Member: Budgetary Control Committee 1999-2004, Delegation for relations with the NATO Parliamentary Assembly 2002-09, Central America Delegation 2004-09, Internal Market and Consumer Protection Committee 2004-07, 2008-09, Culture and Education Committee 2007-09.

Political interests: Economic policy, campaign strategy, defence, education, youth policy, Europe, sport; Australia, China, Uganda, USA.
Other: Member, Executive Committee, Inter-Parliamentary Union, British Group 2010-12; President, Sports Intergroup 2002-09; Chair, Friends of Football 2003-06.
Recreations: Football referee, sport.
Christopher Heaton-Harris MP, House of Commons, London SW1A 0AA
Tel: 020 7219 7048 *Fax:* 020 7219 1375 *Email:* chris.heatonharris.mp@parliament.uk
Constituency: 78 St George's Avenue, Northampton, Northamptonshire NN2 6JF
Tel: 01604 859721 *Fax:* 01604 859329 *Email:* agent@wnc.uk.com
Website: www.daventryconservatives.com www.heatonharris.com *Twitter:* @chhcalling

HEMMING, JOHN
Birmingham, Yardley *(Majority 3,002)*

John Alexander Melvin Hemming. Born 16 March 1960; Son of Melvin John and Doreen Hemming; Married Christine Margaret Richards 1981 (2 daughters 1 son); partner Emily Cox (1 daughter).
Education: King Edward's School, Birmingham; Magdalen College, Oxford (BA atomic, nuclear and theoretical physics 1981, MA).
Non-political career: Founder and senior partner, John Hemming and Company 1983; Founder: Marketnet 1994, Music Mercia International 1997. Member, Musicians' Union 1997.

LIBERAL DEMOCRAT

Political career: Contested Birmingham Hall Green 1983, Birmingham Small Heath 1987, Birmingham Yardley 1992, 1997 and 2001 general elections. Member for Birmingham Yardley 2005-10, for Birmingham, Yardley (revised boundary) since 6 May 2010 general election. *Select committees:* Member: Regulatory Reform 2005-, Procedure 2006-, Joint Committee on the Draft Legal Services Bill 2006, Modernisation of the House of Commons 2008-10, Backbench Business 2010-, Joint Committee on Statutory Instruments 2010-, Standing Orders 2011-, Joint Committee on Draft Deregulation Bill 2013-. *Councils and public bodies:* Birmingham City Council: Councillor 1990-2007, Deputy leader 2004-05, Liberal Democrat group leader 2004-07.
Political interests: Energy, family policy, law and order, health.
Recreations: Jazz piano.
John Hemming MP, House of Commons, London SW1A 0AA
Tel: 020 7219 4345 *Fax:* 020 7219 0152 *Email:* hemmingj@parliament.uk
Constituency: 1772 Coventry Road, Birmingham B26 1PB
Tel: 0121-722 3417 *Fax:* 0121-722 3437 *Email:* john.hemming@jhc.co.uk
Website: john.hemming.name *Twitter:* @johnhemmingmp

HENDERSON, GORDON
Sittingbourne and Sheppey *(Majority 12,383)*

Gordon Leonard Henderson. Born 27 January 1948; Son of William and Shirley Henderson; Married Louise Crowder 1994 (1 son 2 daughters).
Education: Fort Luton High School for Boys; Rochester Mathematical School.
Non-political career: Manager, Woolworths 1964-79; Self-employed restaurateur 1979-83; Senior contracts officer, GEC Marconi Avionics 1983-93; Operations manager, Beams UK 1993-2007; Management consultant 2008-.

CONSERVATIVE

Political career: Contested Luton South 2001 and Sittingbourne and Sheppey 2005 general elections. Member for Sittingbourne and Sheppey since 6 May 2010 general election. *Select committees:* Member: Regulatory Reform 2010-. Member: Conservative Party, Conservative Friends of Israel. *Councils and public bodies:* Deputy leader, Conservative group, Swale Borough Council 1986-90, 1991-95; Member, Kent Police Authority 1989-93; Councillor, Kent County Council 1989-93.
Political interests: Law and order, defence, business; Southern Africa, India, Israel.
Other: Former director, Swale Community Action Project; Chairman, Litter Angels Ltd; Director, Halfway Conservative Hall Ltd; Demelza House (children's hospice); Danny Boy Trust; Sheerness Conservative Club.
Recreations: Reading, writing, football.
Gordon Henderson MP, House of Commons, London SW1A 0AA
Tel: 020 7219 7144 *Email:* gordon.henderson.mp@parliament.uk
Constituency: Top Floor, Unit 10, Periwinkle Court Business Centre, Milton Regis, Sittingbourne, Kent ME10 2JZ
Tel: 01795 423199 *Email:* jess.mcmahon@parliament.uk
Website: www.blinkss.co.uk www.gordonhendersonmp.org.uk

LAB/CO-OP

HENDRICK, MARK

Preston *(Majority 7,733)*

Mark Phillip Hendrick. Born 2 November 1958; Son of Brian Hendrick, timber worker, and Jennifer Hendrick, née Chapman, clerk/typist; Married Yu Yannan 2008.

Education: Salford Grammar School; Liverpool Polytechnic (BSc electrical and electronic engineering 1982); Manchester University (MSc computer science 1985, CertEd 1992); Volkshochschule, Hanau, Germany ('Zertifikat Deutsch als Fremdsprache'); CEng; German (fluent).

Non-political career: Student engineer, Ministry of Defence 1979; Work student, AEG Telefunken 1981; Science and Engineering Research Council 1982-84, 1985-88; Lecturer in electronics and software design, Stockport college 1990-94. Member, GMB.

Political career: Member for Preston 23 November 2000 by-election to 2010, for Preston (revised boundary) since 6 May 2010 general election; PPS: to Margaret Beckett: as Secretary of State for Environment, Food and Rural Affairs 2003-06, as Foreign Secretary 2006-07, to Jack Straw as Lord Chancellor and Secretary of State for Justice 2007-08, to Ivan Lewis as Minister of State, Foreign and Commonwealth Office 2009-10; Opposition Whip 2010-12. *Select committees:* Member: European Scrutiny 2001-04, International Development 2009-10, Foreign Affairs 2012-. European Parliament: MEP for Lancashire Central 1994-99. Chair, Eccles Constituency Labour Party 1990-94; Member, Preston and District Co-operative Party 1994-; Chair, Labour/Co-operative Parliamentary Group 2005-06. *Councils and public bodies:* Salford City Council: Councillor 1987-95, Representative as an alternate director, Manchester Airport plc 1987-94.

Political interests: Foreign affairs, defence, European affairs, economic and industrial affairs, international development; China, Germany, Hungary, Japan, Poland, USA.

Other: Member, UK Delegation, Organisation for Security and Co-operation in Europe Parliamentary Assembly; RSPCA, CAFOD; Deepdale Labour. Penwortham Sports and Social.

Publications: Changing States: A Labour Agenda for Europe (Mandarin Paperbacks, 1996); The euro and Co-operative Enterprise: Co-operating with the euro (Co-operative Press Ltd, 1998).

Recreations: Football, boxing, chess, travel, foreign languages.

Mark Hendrick MP, House of Commons, London SW1A 0AA
Tel: 020 7219 4791 *Fax:* 020 7219 5220 *Email:* mark.hendrick.mp@parliament.uk
Constituency: PTMC, Marsh Lane, Preston, Lancashire PR1 8UQ
Tel: 01772 883575 *Fax:* 01772 887188 *Email:* warhurste@parliament.uk
Website: www.prestonmp.co.uk

CONSERVATIVE

HENDRY, CHARLES

Wealden *(Majority 17,179)*

Born 6 May 1959; Son of late Charles Hendry and Margaret Hendry; Married Sallie Moores, née Smith 1995 (2 sons 1 stepson 1 stepdaughter).

Education: Rugby School; Edinburgh University (BCom business studies 1981); German.

Non-political career: Account director, Ogilvy and Mather PR 1982-88; Special adviser to: John Moore as Secretary of State for Social Services 1988, Antony Newton: as Minister of Trade and Industry 1988-89, as Secretary of State for Social Security 1989-90; Burson-Marsteller: Senior counsellor, public affairs 1990-92, Associate director, public relations; Agenda Group: Chief executive 1999-2001, Non-executive chair 2001-04; Director, Incredi Bull Ideas 2003-04.

Political career: Contested Clackmannan 1983 and Mansfield 1987 general elections. Member for High Peak 1992-97. Contested High Peak 1997 general election. Member for Wealden 2001-10, for Wealden (revised boundary) since 6 May 2010 general election; PPS to: William Hague and Lord Mackay of Ardbrecknish as Ministers of State, Department of Social Security 1994-95, Gillian Shephard as Secretary of State for Education and Employment 1995; Opposition Whip 2001-02; Shadow Minister for: Young People 2002-05, Higher Education 2005, Trade and Industry/Business, Enterprise and Regulatory Reform 2005-08 (Energy, Science and Technology 2006-07, Energy, Industry and Postal Affairs 2007-08), Energy 2008-10; Minister of State, Department of Energy and Climate Change 2010-12; Trade envoy to Azerbaijan, Kazakhstan and Turkmenistan 2012-. *Select committees:* Member: Procedure 1992-95, European Standing Committee B 1992-95, Northern Ireland Affairs 1994-97, Culture, Media and Sport 2003-04, Energy and Climate Change 2009-10. President, Edinburgh University Conservative Association 1979-80; Vice-chair: Scottish Federation of Conservative Students 1980-81, Battersea Conservative Association 1981-83, Conservative Party 1995-97; Chief of staff to Leader of Opposition 1997; Head of business liaison, Conservative Party 1997-99; Deputy chair, Conservative Party 2003-05; Patron, Tory Reform Group.

Political interests: Trade and industry, youth policy, training, urban regeneration, social affairs, housing, homelessness, rural affairs, agriculture; Europe, Russia, Southern Africa, USA.

Other: Trustee, Drive for Youth 1989-98; Joint Honorary President, British Youth Council 1992-97; Development board member, Tusk Force 1992-98; Patron, The Big Issue Foundation 1995-2010; UK Youth Parliament: Trustee 2002-10, Co-chair 2006-.

Recreations: Tennis, skiing, family, opera, rugby, travel.

Charles Hendry MP, House of Commons, London SW1A 0AA
Tel: 020 7219 8238 *Fax:* 020 7219 1977 *Email:* charles.hendry.mp@parliament.uk
Constituency: Wealden Conservative Association, The Granary, Bales Green Farm, Arlington, East Sussex BN27 6SH
Tel: 01323 489289 *Fax:* 01323 484847 *Email:* office@sabineassociates.co.uk
jeanette@eandwconservatives.com *Website:* wealdenconservatives.com
www.charleshendry.co.uk

LABOUR

HEPBURN, STEPHEN
Jarrow *(Majority 12,908)*

Born 6 December 1959; Son of Peter and Margaret Hepburn; Single.

Education: Springfield Comprehensive, Jarrow; Newcastle University (BA politics).

Non-political career: Labourer, South Tyneside Metropolitan Borough Council; Research assistant to Don Dixon MP. Member, UCATT.

Political career: Member for Jarrow 1997-2010, for Jarrow (revised boundary) since 6 May 2010 general election. *Select committees:* Member: Administration 1997-2001, Defence 1999-2001, Accommodation and Works 2003-05, Northern Ireland Affairs 2004-, Administration 2009-10. *Councils and public bodies:* South Tyneside Council: Councillor 1985-, Chair Finance Committee 1989-90, Deputy Leader 1990-97.

Political interests: Small businesses.

Other: Supporter, St Clare's Hospice; Neon CIU, Jarrow, Iona Catholic Club, Hebburn. President, Jarrow FC; Patron, Jarrow Roofing FC.

Recreations: Football.

Stephen Hepburn MP, House of Commons, London SW1A 0AA
Tel: 020 7219 4134 *Email:* hepburns@parliament.uk
Constituency: 141 Tedco Business Centre, Viking Industrial Estate, Jarrow, Tyne and Wear NE32 3DT
Tel: 0191-420 0648 *Fax:* 0191-489 7531 *Email:* hepburn4jarrow@btinternet.com

CONSERVATIVE

HERBERT, NICK
Arundel and South Downs *(Majority 16,691)*

Nicholas Le Quesne Herbert. Born 7 April 1963; Son of Michael and Judy Le Q Herbert; Civil partner Jason Eades 2008.

Education: Haileybury College, Hertford; Magdalene College, Cambridge (BA law and land economy 1985).

Non-political career: British Field Sports Society 1990-96: Director of political affairs 1992-96 (co-founder Countryside Movement); Chief executive, Business for Sterling 1998-2000 (founder of the 'No' Campaign); Director, Reform 2002-05.

Political career: Contested Berwick-upon-Tweed 1997 general election. Member for Arundel and South Downs 2005-10, for Arundel and South Downs (revised boundary) since 6 May 2010 general election; Shadow Minister for Police Reform 2005-07; Shadow Secretary of State for: Justice 2007-09, Environment, Food and Rural Affairs 2009-10; Minister of State for Policing and Criminal Justice, Home Office and Ministry of Justice 2010-12. *Select committees:* Member: Home Affairs 2005-06.

Political interests: Rural affairs, public services, the economy.

Other: PC 2010.

Recreations: Watching cricket, racing, country sports, cinema, theatre, opera.

Rt Hon Nick Herbert MP, House of Commons, London SW1A 0AA
Tel: 020 7219 4080 *Fax:* 020 7219 1295 *Email:* herbertn@parliament.uk
Constituency: No constituency office
Email: nick@nickherbert.com *Website:* www.nickherbert.com *Twitter:* @nickherbertmp

INDEPENDENT

HERMON, SYLVIA
North Down *(Majority 14,364)*

Sylvia Eileen Hermon. Born 11 August 1955; Daughter of Robert and Mary Paisley; Married Sir John Hermon, OBE QPM 1988 (died 2008) (2 sons).

Education: Dungannon High School for Girls; Aberstwyth University, Wales (LLB 1977); Chester College of Law (Part II Solicitors' Qualifying Examinations 1978); French, German.

Non-political career: Lecturer, European, international and constitutional law, Queen's University, Belfast 1978-88.

Political career: Member for North Down since 7 June 2001 general election (UUP 2001 to March 2010, Independent since March 2010); UUP Spokesperson for: Home Affairs 2001-05, Trade and Industry 2001-02, Youth and Women's Issues 2001-05, Culture, Media and Sport 2002-05. *Select committees:* Member: Northern Ireland Affairs 2005-. Author and committee member addressing Patten Report, also of Criminal Justice Review 2000; Ulster Unionist Executive 1999; Constituency chair, North Down Unionist Constituency Association 2001-03; Resigned from the UUP March 2010, now sits as an Independent.

Political interests: Policing, human rights, European affairs, health, education; India, Republic of Ireland, Russia.

Other: Honorary member: Donaghadee Rotary Club, Bangor Club of Soroptomists International; Patron, Evergreens; Marie Curie Cancer Care; The Alzheimer's Society; RNLI; RUC GC Foundation.

Publications: A Guide to EEC Law in Northern Ireland (SLS Legal Publications (NI), 1986).

Recreations: Swimming, ornithology.

Sylvia Hermon MP, House of Commons, London SW1A 0AA
Tel: 020 7219 8491 *Fax:* 020 7219 1969 *Email:* sylvia.hermon.mp@parliament.uk
Constituency: 17a Hamilton Road, Bangor, Co Down BT20 4LF
Tel: 028 9127 5858 *Fax:* 028 9127 5747 *Email:* jamisons@parliament.uk
Website: www.sylviahermon.org

LABOUR

HEYES, DAVID
Ashton under Lyne *(Majority 9,094)*

David Alan Heyes. Born 2 April 1946; Son of Harold Heyes, police officer, and Lilian Heyes, née Crowe; Married Judith Egerton-Gallagher 1968 (1 son 1 daughter).

Education: Blackley Technical High School, Manchester; Open University (BA social sciences 1987).

Non-political career: Local government officer: Manchester City Council 1962-74, Greater Manchester Council 1974-86, Oldham Metropolitan Borough Council 1987-90; Self-employed computer graphics 1990-95; Deputy district manager, Manchester Citizens Advice Bureau service 1995-2001. Member, Unison (formerly NALGO) 1962-.

Political career: Member for Ashton under Lyne since 7 June 2001 general election. *Select committees:* Member: Public Administration 2001-, Communities and Local Government 2010-. *Councils and public bodies:* Oldham Metropolitan Borough Council: Councillor 1992-2004: Secretary, Labour Group 1993-2000, Chair, Personnel Committee 1994-2000.

Political interests: Social exclusion, health, education, work and pensions, local and regional government.

Other: Development worker, Voluntary Action Manchester 1993-95.

David Heyes MP, House of Commons, London SW1A 0AA
Tel: 020 7219 8129 *Fax:* 020 7219 1738 *Email:* heyesd@parliament.uk
Constituency: St Michael's Court, St Michael's Square, Stamford Street, Ashton-Under-Lyne, Lancashire OL6 6XN
Tel: 0161-331 9307 *Fax:* 0161-330 9420

DO YOU NEED THIS INFORMATION ONLINE?
visit www.dodspeople.com or call 020 7593 5675
to register for a free trial

LAB/CO-OP

HILLIER, MEG
Hackney South and Shoreditch *(Majority 14,288)*

Born 14 February 1969; Married Joe Simpson 1997 (1 son 2 daughters).
Education: Portsmouth High School; St Hilda's College, Oxford (BA philosophy, politics and economics 1990); City University, London (Diploma newspaper journalism 1991).
Non-political career: Reporter, *South Yorkshire Times* 1991; Petty officer, P&O European Ferries 1992; Public relations officer, Newlon Housing Group 1993; *Housing Today*: Reporter 1994-95, Features editor 1995-98; Freelance journalist 1998-2000. TGWU/Unite.
Political career: Member for Hackney South and Shoreditch 2005-10, for Hackney South and Shoreditch (revised boundary) since 6 May 2010 general election; PPS to Ruth Kelly as Secretary of State for Communities and Local Government 2006-07; Parliamentary Under-Secretary of State (Identity), Home Office 2007-10; Shadow Minister for Home Office 2010; Shadow Secretary of State for Energy and Climate Change 2010-11. *Select committees:* Member: Northern Ireland Affairs 2005-06, Public Accounts 2011-. Vice-chair, PLP Departmental Group for Women 2011-13. Member, Co-operative Party; Chair, parliamentary group, Co-operative Party 2010-11. *Councils and public bodies:* London Borough of Islington: Councillor 1994-2002, Chair, Neighbourhood Services Committee 1995-97, Mayor 1998-99; Member, London Assembly (for North East London) 2000-04; Board member, Transport for London 2004-05.
Countries of interest: West and East Africa, Ghana, Nigeria, Turkey.
Other: Member, Fabian Society; Trustee, War Memorials Trust 2001-.
Meg Hillier MP, House of Commons, London SW1A 0AA
Tel: 020 7219 5325 *Fax:* 020 7219 8768 *Email:* meghilliermp@parliament.uk
Constituency: No constituency office *Website:* www.meghillier.com *Twitter:* @Meg_HillierMP

LABOUR

HILLING, JULIE
Bolton West *(Majority 92)*

Opposition Whip

Julie Ann Hilling. Daughter of Penelope and Arthur Hilling.
Education: Cedars School, Leighton Buzzard; Nottingham University (BSc chemistry); Manchester Polytechnic (Diploma youth and community work); French.
Non-political career: Community worker: St Ann's Tenant and Residents Association 1977-79, Sneinton Heritage Community Association 1979-81; Youth worker: St Helens Borough Council 1982-88, Wigan Council 1988-2004; North West learning organiser, NASUWT 2004-06; North West senior regional organiser, Transport Salaried Staffs' Association 2006-10. National President, Community of Youth Workers Union 1991-99; Member: Unite, TSSA.
Political career: Member for Bolton West since 6 May 2010 general election; PPS to Shadow Equalities Office 2010-12; Opposition Whip 2012-. *Select committees:* Member: Transport 2010-12, Standards and Privileges 2011-12. Former vice-chair, Bolton West Constituency Labour Party.
Political interests: Transport, education, young people, care of older people and the disabled; Kashmir, Palestine.
Other: Vice-President, Socialist Educational Association; Honorary President, British Youth Council; Ambassador, Girlguiding; Parliamentary Patron, YMCA.
Julie Hilling MP, House of Commons, London SW1A 0AA
Tel: 020 7219 7020 *Email:* julie.hilling.mp@parliament.uk
Constituency: The Old Surgery, 108 Market Street, Westhoughton BL5 3AZ
Tel: 01942 813468 *Fax:* 01942 841617 *Website:* www.juliehilling.org.uk
Twitter: @JulieHillingMP

CONSERVATIVE

HINDS, DAMIAN
East Hampshire *(Majority 13,497)*

PPS to Mark Francois as Minister of State for Defence Personnel, Welfare and Veterans, Ministry of Defence

Damian Patrick George Hinds. Born 27 November 1969; Son of Frank Hinds and Bebe Hinds; Married Jacqui Morel 2007 (2 daughters 1 son).
Education: St Ambrose Grammar, Altrincham; Trinity College, Oxford (BA philosophy, politics and economics 1992).
Non-political career: Research analyst, Mercer Management Consulting 1992-95; Various marketing and commercial management roles, Holiday Inn/Bass plc 1995-2003; Freelance adviser to the hotel trade 2003-05, 2007-10; Strategy director, Greene King plc 2005-07.

Political career: Contested Stretford and Urmston 2005 general election. Member for East Hampshire since 6 May 2010 general election; PPS to Mark Francois as Minister of State for Defence Personnel, Welfare and Veterans, Ministry of Defence 2012-. *Select committees:* Member: Education 2010-12.

Political interests: Social mobility, education, welfare, affordable credit, financial inclusion.

Other: Chairman, Bow Group 2001-02; Volunteer, The Prince's Trust 2002-08.

Publications: Co-author, Power to the People (Bow Group, 1998); Editor, The Ideas Book 2000 (Bow Group, 1999); Co-editor, Go Zones: Policies for the Places Politics Forgot (Bow Group, 2004); Co-author, Seven Key Truths About Social Mobility (APPG report on Social Mobility, 2012); Contributor, Unlocking Local Leadership on Climate Change (Green Alliance, 2012).

Recreations: Music.

Damian Hinds MP, House of Commons, London SW1A 0AA
Tel: 020 7219 7057 *Email:* damian.hinds.mp@parliament.uk
Constituency: 14a Butts Road, Alton, Hampshire GU34 1ND
Tel: 01420 84122 *Website:* www.damianhinds.com *Twitter:* @damian57

HOBAN, MARK

Fareham *(Majority 17,092)*

Mark Gerard Hoban. Born 31 March 1964; Son of Tom Hoban, general manager, and Maureen Hoban, née Orchard; Married Fiona Barrett 1994.

Education: St Leonards RC School, Durham; London School of Economics (BSc Econ 1985).

Non-political career: Pricewaterhouse Coopers 1985-2001: Chartered accountant, Manager 1990-92, Senior manager 1992-2001.

CONSERVATIVE

Political career: Contested South Shields 1997 general election. Member for Fareham since 7 June 2001 general election; Opposition Whip 2002-03; Shadow Minister for: Public Services, Health and Education 2003-04, Education 2004-05, Treasury 2005-10; Financial Secretary, HM Treasury 2010-12; Minister of State for Employment, Department for Work and Pensions 2012-13. *Select committees:* Member: Science and Technology 2001-03, European Standing Committee A 2001-05. General election campaign manager 1987, 1992; Political vice-chair, Southampton Itchen Conservative Association 1991-93.

Political interests: Economy, trade and industry, education, health.

Other: Honorary Vice-President, Society of Maritime Industries -2010; Associate, Institute of Chartered Accountants of England and Wales 1988. Liveryman, Fruiterers' Company 2003-. Freeman, City of London 2003.

Recreations: Cooking, reading, travel, entertaining.

Mark Hoban MP, House of Commons, London SW1A 0AA
Tel: 020 7219 8191 *Email:* hobanm@parliament.uk
Constituency: 14 East Street, Fareham, Hampshire PO16 0BN
Tel: 01329 233573 *Email:* help@markhoban.com *Website:* www.markhoban.com

HODGE, MARGARET

Barking *(Majority 16,555)*

Margaret Eve Hodge. Born 8 September 1944; Daughter of Hans and Lisbeth Oppenheimer; Married Andrew Watson 1968 (divorced 1978) (1 son 1 daughter); married Henry Hodge 1978 (later Mr Justice Hodge, he died 2009) (2 daughters).

Education: Bromley High School; Oxford High School; London School of Economics (BSc economics 1966); German, French, Italian.

Non-political career: Teaching and market research 1966-73; Senior consultant, Price Waterhouse 1992-94. Member, Unison.

LABOUR

Political career: Member for Barking 1994 by-election to 2010, for Barking (revised boundary) since 6 May 2010 general election; Parliamentary Under-Secretary of State, Department for Education and Employment (Employment and Equal Opportunities) 1998-2001; Minister of State: Department for Education and Skills 2001-05: (Lifelong Learning and Higher Education 2001-03, Lifelong Learning, Further and Higher Education 2003, Children, Young People and Families 2003-05), Department for Work and Pensions (Employment and Welfare Reform) 2005-06, Department of Trade and Industry (Industry and the Regions) 2006-07, Department for Culture, Media and Sport 2007-08, 2009-10 (Culture, Creative Industries and Tourism 2007-08, Culture and Tourism 2009-10); Shadow Minister for Culture, Media and Sport 2010; Chair, Public

Accounts Commission 2010-. *Select committees:* Member: Education and Employment 1996-97, Deregulation 1996-97, Liaison 1997-98, 2010-, Chair: Education and Employment (Education Sub-Committee) 1997-98, Public Accounts 2010-. Progress; Member, Labour Party Local Government Committee 1983-92; Chair, London Group of Labour MPs 1995-98; Labour Women's Network; Chair, Fabian Executive Committee 1997-98. *Councils and public bodies:* London Borough of Islington: Councillor 1973-94, Chair, Housing Committee 1975-79, Leader 1982-92; Chair, Association of London Authorities 1984-92; Member, Home Office Advisory Committee on Race Relations 1988-92.

Political interests: Education, economy, local and regional government, housing, inner cities, democratic reform, London government; Nepal.

Other: Director: University College, Middlesex Hospitals; Governor, London School of Economics 1990-2001; Vice-chair, AMA 1991-92; Fellow, Industry and Parliament Trust 1996. Honorary Fellow University of North London; Honorary DCL City 1993. Inquisitor of the Year, *The Spectator* awards 2012, Parliamentarian of the Year Award, Political Studies Association 2012. MBE 1978; PC 2003.

Publications: Quality, Equality and Democracy; Beyond the Town Hall; Fabian pamphlet on London Government, Not Just the Flower Show; Numerous articles.

Recreations: Family, opera, piano, travel, cooking.

Rt Hon Margaret Hodge MBE MP, House of Commons, London SW1A 0AA
Tel: 020 7219 6666 *Email:* hodgem@parliament.uk
Constituency: 102 North Street, Barking, Essex IG11 8LA
Tel: 020 8594 1333 *Fax:* 020 8594 1131
Email: margarethodge@hotmail.co.uk *Website:* margaret-hodge.co.uk
Twitter: @margarethodge

LABOUR

HODGSON, SHARON Washington and Sunderland West *(Majority 11,458)*

Shadow Minister for Women and Equalities

Born 1 April 1966; Daughter of Joan Cohen, née Wilson; Married Alan Hodgson 1990 (1 son 1 daughter).

Education: Heathfield Senior High School, Gateshead; Newcastle College (HEFC English 1997); TUC, National Education Centre (Open College Network Diploma labour party organising 2000).

Non-political career: Payroll/account clerk, Tyneside Safety Glass, Team Valley Trading Estate, Gateshead 1982-88; Personnel, Northern Rock Building Society, Gosforth 1988-92; Payroll administrator, Burgess Microswitch, Team Valley Trading Estate, Gateshead 1992-94; Charity administrator, The Total Learning Challenge (educational charity), Newcastle 1998-99; Regional organiser, Labour North 1999-2000; Constituency organiser, Mitcham and Morden CLP 2000-02; Labour link co-ordinator, London, Unison 2002-05. Member: GMB 1999-2007, Unite 2007-, CWU 2008-.

Political career: Member for Gateshead East and Washington West 2005-10, for Washington and Sunderland West since 6 May 2010 general election; PPS to: Liam Byrne as Minister of State, Home Office 2006-07, Bob Ainsworth as Minister of State, Ministry of Defence 2007-08, Dawn Primarolo as Minister of State, Department of Health 2008-09; Sponsored Special Educational Needs (Information) Act 2008; Assistant Government Whip 2009-10; Opposition Whip 2010; Shadow Minister for: Education 2010-13, Women and Equalities 2013-. *Select committees:* Member: Regulatory Reform 2005-10, European Scrutiny 2006, Court of Referees 2007-10, Children, Schools and Families 2007-10, North East 2009-10, Ecclesiastical Committee. Honorary Secretary, PLP Departmental Committee for the Treasury 2006-10. Women's officer, Tyne Bridge CLP 1998-2000; Constituency secretary, Mitcham and Morden CLP 2002-05.

Political interests: North/South divide, employment (especially youth and green jobs), education (especially special educational needs), health (especially cancer issues), child poverty, fuel poverty, free school meals, childcare and early intervention.

Other: Member: Fabian Society 2004-, Christian Socialist Movement 2005-; Board member, Basketball Foundation.

Recreations: Reading, cinema, cooking, shopping, travel, family.

Sharon Hodgson MP, House of Commons, London SW1A 0AA
Tel: 020 7219 5160 *Fax:* 020 7219 4493 *Email:* sharon.hodgson.mp@parliament.uk
Constituency: Suites 1 and 1a, Vermont House, Concord, Washington, Tyne and Wear NE37 2SQ
Tel: 0191-417 2000 *Email:* brownjea@parliament.uk *Website:* www.sharonhodgson.org
Twitter: @SharonHodgsonMP

HOEY, KATE
Vauxhall *(Majority 10,651)*

Catharine Letitia Hoey. Born 21 June 1946; Daughter of Thomas and Letitia Hoey; Single.

Education: Belfast Royal Academy; Ulster College of Physical Education (Diploma teaching 1964); City of London College, London (BSc economics 1968).

Non-political career: Lecturer, Southwark College 1972-76; Senior lecturer, Kingsway College 1976-85; Educational adviser to Arsenal Football Club 1985-89. Member, GMB.

Political career: Contested Dulwich 1983 and 1987 general elections. Member for Vauxhall 15 June 1989 by-election to 2010, for Vauxhall (revised boundary) since 6 May 2010; Opposition Spokesperson for Citizen's Charter and Women 1992-93; PPS to Frank Field as Minister of State, Department of Social Security 1997-98; Parliamentary Under-Secretary of State: Home Office (Metropolitan Police, European Union, Judicial Co-operation) 1998-99, Department for Culture, Media and Sport (Minister for Sport) 1999-2001. *Select committees:* Member: Broadcasting 1991-97, Social Security 1994-97, Science and Technology 2004-05, Northern Ireland Affairs 2007-10, 2010-. *Councils and public bodies:* Councillor: Hackney Borough Council 1978-82, Southwark Borough Council 1988-89.

LABOUR

Political interests: Sport, foreign affairs, housing, countryside; Angola, Bosnia, Oman, Tibet, Zimbabwe.

Other: Chair, Countryside Alliance 2005-; Honorary Vice-President: Surrey County Cricket Club, British Wheelchair Basketball Association; Honorary President, British Pistol Club; Trustee, Outward Bound Trust. *The Spectator/*Highland Park Debater of the Year Award 1998; University of Ulster Distinguished Graduate 2000.

Publications: Occasional articles on sport in the press.

Kate Hoey MP, House of Commons, London SW1A 0AA
Tel: 020 7219 5989 *Fax:* 020 7219 5985 *Email:* hoeyk@parliament.uk
Constituency: No constituency office *Website:* www.katehoey.com *Twitter:* @hoeykateMP

HOLLINGBERY, GEORGE
Meon Valley *(Majority 12,125)*

PPS to Theresa May as Home Secretary

George Michael Edward Hollingbery. Born 12 October 1963; Married Janette Marie White (1 son 2 daughters).

Education: Radley College, Oxfordshire; Lady Margaret Hall, Oxford (BA human sciences 1985); The Wharton School, Pennsylvania (MBA 1991).

Non-political career: Stockbroker, Robert Fleming Securities 1985-89; Non-executive director and shareholder, Lister Bestcare Ltd 1991-95; Director and founder, Pet Depot Ltd 1994-99; Chairman and founder, Companion Care Veterinary Group 1998-2001.

CONSERVATIVE

Political career: Contested Winchester 2005 general election. Member for Meon Valley since 6 May 2010 general election; PPS to Theresa May as Home Secretary 2012-. *Select committees:* Member: Communities and Local Government 2010-12, Works of Art 2011-. Member, Executive, 1922 Committee February-September 2012. Deputy chairman, Winchester Conservative Association 1999-2001; Chairman, Winchester campaign team 2001 general election. *Councils and public bodies:* Winchester City Council: Councillor 1999-, Deputy leader, Conservative group, Council Deputy Leader 2006-08.

Political interests: Countryside issues, entrepreneurship, education, local government; Chile, China, USA.

Other: Founder and chairman: Alresford Golden Jubilee Celebrations, Alresford Millennium Trail Group, "A night for Naomi" 2000 (local hospice appeal), "Another night for Naomi" 2005.

Recreations: Field sports, modern garden design, modern crafts.

George Hollingbery MP, House of Commons, London SW1A 0AA
Tel: 020 7219 7109 *Email:* george.hollingbery.mp@parliament.uk
Constituency: No constituency office publicised
Tel: 01962 734076 *Website:* www.georgehollingbery.com *Twitter:* @Ghollingbery

VACHER'S QUARTERLY
The most up-to-date contact details throughout the year
Call 020 7593 5644 or visit www.dodsshop.co.uk

CONSERVATIVE

HOLLOBONE, PHILIP
Kettering *(Majority 9,094)*

Philip Thomas Hollobone. Born 7 November 1964; Son of Thomas and Patricia Hollobone; Married Donna Cooksey 2001 (1 son 1 daughter).

Education: Dulwich College, London; Lady Margaret Hall, Oxford (BA modern history and economics 1987, MA).

Non-political career: Soldier and paratrooper, Territorial Army 1984-93. Industry research analyst, various 1987-2003.

Political career: Contested Lewisham East 1997 and Kettering 2001 general elections. Member for Kettering 2005-10, for Kettering (revised boundary) since 6 May 2010 general election. *Select committees:* Member: Crossrail Bill 2006-07, Transport 2006-10, Backbench Business 2010-12, Chairmen's Panel/Panel of Chairs 2010-. Chair, Bromley and Chislehurst Conservative Association 1999; Deputy chair, Kettering Constituency Conservative Association 2002-. *Councils and public bodies:* Councillor: London Borough of Bromley 1990-94, Kettering Borough Council 2003-.

Philip Hollobone MP, House of Commons, London SW1A 0AA
Tel: 020 7219 8373 *Fax:* 020 7219 8802 *Email:* philip.hollobone.mp@parliament.uk
Constituency: No constituency office publicised

CONSERVATIVE

HOLLOWAY, ADAM
Gravesham *(Majority 9,312)*

Adam James Harold Holloway. Born July 1965; Son of Revd Roger Holloway, OBE and Anne Holloway, née Alsopp; Single.

Education: Cranleigh School, Surrey; Magdalene College, Cambridge (MA); Imperial College, London (MBA 1998); Royal Military Academy Sandhurst (Commissioned 1987).

Non-political career: Commissioned, Grenadier Guards 1987-92. Presenter: World in Action, Granada TV 1992-93; Senior reporter: ITN 1993-97, *Tonight with Trevor McDonald* 2000-01, Contributions to ITN/Sky News, Iraq War 2003.

Political career: Member for Gravesham since 5 May 2005 general election; PPS to David Lidington as Minister of State, Foreign and Commonwealth Office (resigned) 2010-11. *Select committees:* Member: Defence 2006-10, 2012- Arms Export Controls 2009-11. Deputy chairman, Conservative Middle East Council 2010-.

Political interests: Defence, crime.

Other: Trustee: Christian Aid 1997-2001, Map Action 2002-; Parliamentary chairman, Council for Arab British Understanding. Backbencher of the Year, *The Spectator* awards 2011; Gravesend Conservative Club; Northfleet Conservative Club; Pratts.

Publications: In Blood Stepp'd in Too Far: Towards a realistic policy for Afghanistan (Centre for Policy Studies, 2009); The Failure of British Political and Military Leadership in Basra (First Defence, 2010).

Adam Holloway MP, House of Commons, London SW1A 0AA
Tel: 020 7219 8402 *Fax:* 020 7219 2871 *Email:* hollowaya@parliament.uk
Constituency: No constituency office
Tel: 01474 332097 *Website:* www.adamholloway.co.uk

LABOUR

HOOD, JIM
Lanark and Hamilton East *(Majority 13,478)*

James Hood. Born 16 May 1948; Son of late William Hood, miner, and Bridget Hood; Married Marion Stewart McCleary 1967 (1 son 1 daughter).

Education: Lesmahagow Higher Grade School; Coatbridge College; Nottingham University/ WEA (economics, industrial relations and communication).

Non-political career: Armed Forces Parliamentary Scheme. Mining engineer 1964-87. Member, National Union of Mineworkers 1964-: Official 1973-87, Leader of Nottinghamshire striking miners in 1984-85 national miners' strike; Member, AEEU/Amicus/Unite 1996-.

Political career: Member for Clydesdale 1987-2005, for Lanark and Hamilton East since 5 May 2005 general election. *Select committees:* Member: Liaison 1992-2006, Defence 1997-2001, Chairmen's Panel/Panel of Chairs 1997-; European Scrutiny: Chair 1998-2006, Member 2006-07. *Councils and public bodies:* Councillor, Newark and Sherwood District Council 1979-87.

Political interests: NHS, home affairs, agriculture, environment, energy, housing, education, alcohol abuse and under-age drinking, defence; Europe.

Other: Member, UK Delegation to the NATO Parliamentary Assembly 2005-10; Member, Parliamentary Assembly to: Council of Europe 2008-, Western European Union 2008-10; Fellow, Industry and Parliament Trust.

Recreations: Gardening, reading, writing.

Jim Hood MP, House of Commons, London SW1A 0AA
Tel: 020 7219 4585 *Fax:* 020 7219 5872 *Email:* hoodj@parliament.uk
Constituency: c/o Council Offices, South Vennel, Lanark ML11 7JT
Tel: 01555 673177 *Fax:* 01555 673188 *Email:* davidsonh@parliament.uk
Website: www.jimhoodmp.org.uk *Twitter:* @Jamesho514

HOPKINS, KELVIN
Luton North *(Majority 7,520)*

Kelvin Peter Hopkins. Born 22 August 1941; Son of late Professor Harold Hopkins FRS, physicist and mathematician, and Joan Frost, medical secretary; Married Patricia Langley 1965 (1 son 1 daughter).

Education: Queen Elizabeth's Grammar School, High Barnet; Nottingham University (BA politics, economics and mathematics with statistics); French (basic).

Non-political career: TUC Economic Department 1969-70, 1973-77; Policy and research officer, NALGO/Unison 1977-94. Delegate, Luton Trades Union Council; Member: GMB, CWU.

LABOUR

Political career: Contested Luton North 1983 general election. Member for Luton North 1997-2010, for Luton North (revised boundary) since 6 May 2010 general election. *Select committees:* Former member: European Standing Committee B; Member: Broadcasting 1999-2001, Public Administration 2002-10, 2011-, Crossrail Bill 2006-07, European Scrutiny 2007-, Transport 2010, Joint Committee on Draft Deregulation Bill 2013-. Chair, PLP Departmental Group for DPM/Constitutional Affairs 2010-. Vice-chair, Central Region Labour Party 1995-96. *Councils and public bodies:* Councillor, Luton Borough Council 1972-76; Governor, Luton Sixth Form College 1993-.

Political interests: Economic policy, employment, transport, European Union, arts; France, Sweden.

Other: Chair of Governors, Luton College of Higher Education 1985-89; Member, Mary Seacole House, Luton; Fellow, Industry and Parliament Trust 2000. Honorary Fellow: Luton University 1993, University of Bedfordshire 2010.

Publications: Various NALGO publications.

Recreations: Music, wine, collecting antique glassware.

Kelvin Hopkins MP, House of Commons, London SW1A 0AA
Tel: 020 7219 6670 *Fax:* 020 7219 0957 *Email:* hopkinsk@parliament.uk
Constituency: 3 Union Street, Luton, Bedfordshire LU1 3AN
Tel: 01582 488208 *Fax:* 01582 480990 *Website:* www.kelvinhopkinsmp.com

HOPKINS, KRIS
Keighley *(Majority 2,940)*

Parliamentary Under-Secretary of State, Department for Communities and Local Government

Kristan Frederick Hopkins. Born 8 June 1963; 1 daughter.

Education: Leeds University (Degree communications and cultural studies).

Non-political career: Duke of Wellington's Regiment. Former part-time media and communications lecturer, including Trinity and All Saints College, Leeds.

CONSERVATIVE

Political career: Contested Leeds West 2001 and Halifax 2005 general elections. Member for Keighley since 6 May 2010 general election; PPS to Andrew Robathan as Minister of State for the Armed Forces, Ministry of Defence 2012-13; Parliamentary Under-Secretary of State, Department for Communities and Local Government 2013-. *Select committees:* Member: Northern Ireland Affairs 2011-12. *Councils and public bodies:* Bradford Council: Councillor 1998-2010, Deputy leader 2004-06, Council leader 2006-10, Conservative group leader 2006-10.

Political interests: Education, health, housing, community cohesion, local government.

Recreations: Walking, running, photography.

Kris Hopkins MP, House of Commons, London SW1A 0AA
Tel: 020 7219 3000 *Email:* kris.hopkins.mp@parliament.uk
Constituency: Churchill House, North Street, Keighley, West Yorkshire BD21 3AF
Tel: 01535 211152 *Website:* www.krishopkins.co.uk

LIBERAL DEMOCRAT

HORWOOD, MARTIN
Cheltenham *(Majority 4,920)*

Martin Charles Horwood. Born 12 October 1962; Son of Don Horwood and Nina Horwood, née Edge; Married Dr Shona Arora 1995 (1 daughter 1 son).

Education: Cheltenham College; The Queen's College, Oxford (BA modern history 1984).

Non-political career: Account executive, Ted Bates Advertising 1985-86; Director of development, British Humanist Association 1986-88; Creative co-ordinator, Help the Aged 1988-90; Donor marketing manager, Oxfam 1990-95; Director of communications and fundraising, Oxfam (India) 1995-96; Director of fundraising, Alzheimer's Society 1996-2001; Senior consultant then head of consultancy, Target Direct Marketing 2001-05. TGWU 1990-95; MSF/Amicus/Unite 1996-2013.

Political career: Contested Oxford East 1992 and Cities of London and Westminster 2001 general elections. Member for Cheltenham 2005-10, for Cheltenham (revised boundary) since 6 May 2010 general election; Liberal Democrat: Spokesman on the Charities Bill 2005-06, Shadow Minister for Environment 2006-10. *Select committees:* Member: ODPM/Communities and Local Government 2005-07, Environmental Audit 2007-10, Joint Committee on Privacy and Injunctions 2011-12. Chair, Liberal Democrat: Parliamentary Party Committee on Transport 2010-11, Parliamentary Party Committee on International Affairs (FCO, MoD and DFID) 2011-. President, Oxford Student Liberal Society 1983; Chair: Union of Liberal Students 1984-85, Liberal Information Network (LINk) 1987-90; Vice-President, Green Liberal Democrats 2007-. *Councils and public bodies:* Councillor, Vale of White Horse District Council 1991-95.

Political interests: Sustainable development, environment, international affairs, mutual/social ownership, tribal peoples, NHS; India, Tibet.

Other: Member: World Development Movement 1988-, Survival International 1992-, Alzheimer's Society 1996-, Amnesty International 1999-; Trustee, Fight for Sight 2002-08; Member: Friends of the Holst Birthplace Museum 2005-, Campaign to Protect Rural England 2006-; Patron, Cheltenham Open Door 2006-; Member, Cheltenham Civic Society 2007-; Trustee: Gloucestershire County Association for the Blind 2008-, Emthonjeni Trust 2011-; Institute of Fundraising 1996-2005. Animal Welfare Champion 2009.

Recreations: Cycling, drawing, astronomy, geneaology.

Martin Horwood MP, House of Commons, London SW1A 0AA
Tel: 020 7219 4784 *Fax:* 020 7219 1185 *Email:* martin.horwood.mp@parliament.uk
Constituency: 16 Hewlett Road, Cheltenham, Gloucestershire GL52 6AA
Tel: 01242 224889 *Fax:* 01242 256658 *Website:* www.martinhorwood.net
Twitter: @MartinChelt

SCOTTISH NATIONAL PARTY

HOSIE, STEWART
Dundee East *(Majority 1,821)*

SNP Deputy Leader Parliamentary Group; Spokesperson for Treasury

Born 3 January 1963; Son of R A Hosie, architectural ironmonger, and E A Hosie, bookkeeper; Married Shona Robison (later MSP) 1997 (1 daughter).

Education: Carnoustie High School; Bell Street Tech (HD computer studies 1981); Dundee College of Technology 1981.

Non-political career: Group IS manager MIH 1988-93; Systems analyst various organisations 1993-96; Year 2000/EMU project manager Stakis plc/Hilton 1996-2000; Various project management posts 2000-05. MSF 1992.

Political career: Contested Kirkcaldy 1992 and 1997 general elections. Member for Dundee East since 5 May 2005 general election; SNP Spokesperson for: Treasury 2005-, Women 2005-07, Home Affairs 2005-07, Economy 2005-07; SNP: Deputy leader parliamentary group 2007-; Chief Whip 2007-13. *Select committees:* Member: Treasury 2010-. Contested Kirkcaldy constituency 1999 Scottish Parliament election. SNP youth convener 1986-89; SNP national secretary 1999-2003; Organisation convener 2003-05.

Political interests: Economic development, job creation.

Other: Endorsed by the Save the Scottish Regiments Campaign.

Recreations: Football, hill-walking, rugby.

Stewart Hosie MP, House of Commons, London SW1A 0AA
Tel: 020 7219 8164 *Fax:* 020 7219 6716 *Email:* hosies@parliament.uk
Constituency: SNP Parliamentary Offices, 8 Old Glamis Road, Dundee DD3 8HP
Tel: 01382 623200 *Fax:* 01382 903205 *Email:* hosie@dundeesnp.org stewart@stewarthosie.com
95 High Street, Carnoustie, Angus DD7 9EA
Website: stewart.dundeesnp.org *Twitter:* @StewartHosieMP

HOWARTH, GEORGE

Knowsley *(Majority 25,686)*

George Edward Howarth. Born 29 June 1949; Son of late George Howarth and Eleanor Howarth; Married Julie Rodgers 1977 (2 sons 1 daughter).

Education: Schools in Huyton; Liverpool Polytechnic (BA social sciences 1977).

Non-political career: Engineering apprentice 1966-70; Engineer 1970-75; Teacher 1977-82; Co-operative Development Services 1980-82; Chief executive, Wales Co-operative Centre 1982-86. Unite.

LABOUR

Political career: Member Knowsley North 13 November 1986 by-election to 1997, for Knowsley North and Sefton East 1997-2010, for Knowsley since 6 May 2010 general election; Opposition Spokesperson for: the Environment 1989-92, Environmental Protection 1993-94, Home Affairs 1994-97; Parliamentary Under-Secretary of State: Home Office 1997-99, Northern Ireland Office 1999-2001; Member Intelligence and Security Committee 2008-. *Select committees:* Member: Public Accounts 2002-03, Modernisation of the House of Commons 2005-10; Chair: Armed Forces Bill 2005-06; Member: Joint Committee on Conventions 2006, Chairmen's Panel/ Panel of Chairs 2009-, Finance and Services 2012-. Chair, Knowsley South Labour Party 1981-85; Secretary, Knowsley Borough District Labour Party 1977-80; Member, North West Region Executive, Labour Party 1981-84. *Councils and public bodies:* Councillor Huyton Urban District Council 1971-75; Knowsley Borough Council: Councillor 1975-86, Deputy Leader 1982-83.

Political interests: Housing, environment, crime, disorder; Middle East, South Africa.

Other: Chair, Knowsley Skills Academy. PC 2005.

Recreations: Coarse fishing, family, reading.

Rt Hon George Howarth MP, House of Commons, London SW1A 0AA
Tel: 020 7219 6902 *Fax:* 020 7219 0495 *Email:* george.howarth.mp@parliament.uk
Constituency: Lathom House, North Mersey Business Centre, Woodward Road, Kirkby, Merseyside L33 7UY
Tel: 0151-546 9918 *Fax:* 0151-546 9918 *Website:* www.georgehowarth.org.uk

HOWARTH, GERALD

Aldershot *(Majority 5,586)*

James Gerald Douglas Howarth. Born 12 September 1947; Son of late Mary Howarth and late James Howarth, company director; Married Elizabeth Squibb 1973 (1 daughter 2 sons).

Education: Bloxham School, Banbury; Southampton University (BA English 1969); French (some), German (reasonable).

Non-political career: Commissioned RAFVR 1968. Assistant manager, loan syndication Bank of America International Ltd 1971-77; European Arab Bank 1977-81: Manager and personal assistant to group managing director 1979, Manager, loan syndications 1980; Loan syndication

CONSERVATIVE

manager responsible for arranging project and other loans in Africa, Middle East and South America, Standard Chartered Bank plc 1981-83; Joint managing director, Taskforce Communications 1993-95. Member, National Union of Seamen 1966.

Political career: Member for Cannock and Burntwood 1983-92. Contested Cannock and Burntwood 1992 general election. Member for Aldershot 1997-2010, for Aldershot (revised boundary) since 6 May 2010 general election; PPS: to Michael Spicer: as Parliamentary Under-Secretary of State, Department of Energy 1987-90, as Minister of State, Department of the Environment 1990; to Sir George Young as Minister of State, Department of the Environment 1990-91, to Margaret Thatcher 1991-92; Shadow Minister for Defence 2002-10; Parliamentary Under-Secretary of State (International Security Strategy), Ministry of Defence 2010-12. *Select committees:* Member: Home Affairs 1997-2001, Defence 2001-03, Armed Forces Bill 2005-06. Joint vice-chairman, Conservative Party Committee for Environment, Transport and Regions 1997-99; Joint secretary, Conservative Party Committee for Defence 1999-2001; Member, Executive, 1922 Committee 2000-02; Vice-chairman: Conservative Party Home Affairs Committee 2000-02, Conservative Home Affairs/Constitutional/Culture, Media and Sport Policy Committee 2001-02. Member, Greater London Area CPC Advisory Committee; Vice-chair, City Conservative Forum 1981-84; Founder member, No Turning Back Group; Chair, 92 Group of Conservative MPs 2001-07, 2013-. *Councils and public bodies:* Councillor, London Borough of Hounslow 1982-83.

Political interests: Aerospace, aviation, defence, media, privatisation; Brazil, Chile, Germany, Malaysia, Russia.

Other: General Secretary, Society for Individual Freedom 1969-71; Director, Freedom Under Law 1973-77; President, Air Display Association Europe 2002-; Council member, Air League 2005-10, 2013-; Fellow, Industry and Parliament Trust; Trustee, Vulcan to the Sky 2006-;

Trustee, British Forces Foundation; Joint Patron, Aerobility (The British Disabled Flying Association); RNLI, ACET, RAF Benevolent Fund. Liveryman, Guild of Air Pilots and Air Navigators. Parliamentary Pilot of the Year, Britannia Airways 1988. Kt 2012; Aldershot Conservative, Liveryman Club.

Publications: Co-author, No Turning Back (1985), and further publications by the Group.

Recreations: Flying, tennis, DIY, shooting, family.

Sir Gerald Howarth MP, House of Commons, London SW1A 0AA
Tel: 020 7219 5650 *Fax:* 020 7219 1198 *Email:* geraldhowarth@parliament.uk
Constituency: Conservative Club (not for correspondence), Victoria Road, Aldershot, Hampshire GU11 1JX
Tel: 01252 323637 *Fax:* 01252 323637 *Email:* aldershotca@tory.org
Website: www.geraldhowarth.org *Twitter:* @geraldhowarth

HOWELL, JOHN
Henley *(Majority 16,588)*

PPS to Andrew Lansley as Leader of the House of Commons and Lord Privy Seal

John Michael Howell. Born 27 July 1955; Son of Alexander and Gladys Howell; Married Alison Parker 1987 (1 son 2 daughters).

Education: Battersea Grammar School, London; Edinburgh University (MA archaeology 1978); St John's College, Oxford (DPhil prehistoric archaeology 1981).

CONSERVATIVE

Non-political career: Ernst & Young 1987-96; Business presenter, BBC World Service Television 1996-97; Director: Fifth World Productions Ltd 1996-2003, Media Presentation Consultants Ltd 2005-08.

Political career: Member for Henley 26 June 2008 by-election to 2010, for Henley (revised boundary) since 6 May 2010 general election; PPS to: Greg Clark as Minister of State for Decentralisation 2010-11, Leaders of the House of Commons and Lords Privy Seal: Sir George Young 2010-12, Andrew Lansley 2012-. *Select committees:* Member: Work and Pensions 2009-10. *Councils and public bodies:* Oxfordshire County Council: Councillor 2004-09, Cabinet member for Change Management 2005-08; Vice-President, Local Government Association 2010-11.

Political interests: Rural issues, social policy, local government, foreign affairs; Central and Eastern Europe, South Asia.

Other: OBE 2000; Leander Club, Henley.

Publications: Neolithic Northern France (1983); Understanding Eastern Europe: the context of change (1994).

Recreations: Music, theatre.

John Howell OBE MP, House of Commons, London SW1A 0AA
Tel: 020 7219 6676 *Fax:* 020 7219 2606 *Email:* howelljm@parliament.uk
Constituency: PO Box 84, Watlington, Oxfordshire OX49 5XD
Tel: 01491 613072 *Email:* angie.paterson@parliament.uk *Website:* www.johnhowellmp.com
Twitter: @JohnHowellMP

HOYLE, LINDSAY
Chorley *(Majority 2,593)*

Chairman, Ways and Means and Deputy Speaker

Lindsay Harvey Hoyle. Born 10 June 1957; Son of Doug Hoyle, former MP, now Lord Hoyle (qv) and late Pauline Hoyle; Married Lynda Fowler (divorced 1982); married Catherine Swindley (2 daughters).

Education: Lords College, Bolton; Horwich FE; Bolton TIC (City & Guilds Construction).

Non-political career: Honorary Colonel, D(64) Medical Squadron, 5 General Services. Company director. Shop steward; Member, Amicus/MSF/Unite.

LABOUR

Political career: Member for Chorley 1997-2010, for Chorley (revised boundary) since 6 May 2010 general election; Parliamentary assistant to Beverley Hughes as Minister for the North West 2008-10; Chairman, Ways and Means and Deputy Speaker 2010-. *Select committees:* Member: Catering 1997-2005, Trade and Industry/Business, Enterprise and Regulatory Reform/ Business and Enterprise/Business, Innovation and Skills 1998-2010, European Scrutiny 2005-10, Quadripartite (Committees on Strategic Export Controls) 2006-07; Ex-officio member: Chairmen's Panel/Panel of Chairs 2010-13; Member: Finance and Services 2010-; Chair: Panel of Chairs 2013-. Joint vice-chair, PLP Departmental Committee for Defence 1997-2001. *Councils* *and public bodies:* Councillor, Adlington Town Council 1980-98; Chorley Borough Council: Councillor 1980-98, Chair, Economic Development and Deputy Leader 1994-97, Mayor of Chorley 1997-98.

Political interests: Trade and industry, sport, defence, small businesses, agriculture; British Overseas Territories, Falkland Islands, Gibraltar.

Other: Armed Forces Parliamentary Scheme (Royal Marines) 1998-; Trustee, History of Parliament Trust; Member, Cuerdon Valley Trust; President, Chorley Mencap. PC 2013. Member: Adlington Cricket Club, Chorley Cricket Club.

Recreations: Cricket, Rugby League.

Rt Hon Lindsay Hoyle MP, House of Commons, London SW1A 0AA
Tel: 020 7219 3515 *Fax:* 020 7219 3831 *Email:* gaskillm@parliament.uk
Constituency: 35-39 Market Street, Chorley, Lancashire PR7 2SW
Tel: 01257 271555 *Fax:* 01257 277462 *Email:* goreb@parliament.uk
Website: www.lindsayhoylemp.com *Twitter:* @LindsayHoyle_MP

LIBERAL DEMOCRAT

HUGHES, SIMON
Bermondsey and Old Southwark *(Majority 8,530)*

Deputy Leader, Liberal Democrats

Simon Henry Ward Hughes. Born 17 May 1951; Son of late James Hughes and Sylvia Hughes, née Ward; Single.

Education: Llandaff Cathedral School, Cardiff; Christ College, Brecon; Selwyn College, Cambridge (BA law 1973, MA); Inns of Court School of Law; College of Europe, Bruges (Certificate in Higher European Studies 1975); French.

Non-political career: Barrister; Called to the Bar, Inner Temple 1974; In practice 1978-.

Political career: Member (Liberal 1983-88, Liberal Democrat since 1988) for Southwark and Bermondsey February 1983 by-election to 1997, for North Southwark and Bermondsey 1997-2010, for Bermondsey and Old Southwalk since 6 May 2010 general election; Liberal Spokesperson for the Environment 1983-88; Liberal Democrat: Spokesperson for: Health 1988, London 1988-97, Deputy Chief Whip 1989-99; Spokesperson for: Education, Science and Training 1988-92, Church of England 1988-97, Environment and Natural Resources 1992-94, Urban Affairs and Young People 1994-97, Health 1995-99, Home and Legal Affairs 1999-2003, London 2003-04; Shadow: Office of the Deputy Prime Minister 2005, Attorney General 2005-07, Secretary of State for Constitutional Affairs/Justice 2006-07, Leader of the House of Commons 2007-09, Secretary of State for Energy and Climate Change 2009-10; Member, Speakers' Working Group on All-Party Groups 2011-12. *Select committees:* Member: Accommodation and Works 1992-97, Joint Committee on Conventions 2006, Modernisation of the House of Commons 2007-10, Ecclesiastical Committee 2010-, Joint Committee on Human Rights 2012-. Chair, Liberal Democrat Policy Committee on Communities and Local Government 2010-11. Chair, Liberal Party's Home Affairs Panel 1977-83; President, National League of Young Liberals 1986-92; Liberal Democrat Youth and Students: Vice-President 1983-86, President 1992-; Vice-chair, Southwark and Bermondsey Liberal Association 1981-83; President, Liberal Democrats 2004-08; Contested Liberal Democrat leadership 1999, 2006; Deputy Leader, Liberal Democrats 2010-. *Councils and public bodies:* Liberal Democrat London mayoral candidate 2004.

Political interests: Human rights, civil liberties, youth affairs, social affairs, housing, environment; Commonwealth, southern Africa, west Africa, latin America, eastern Europe, Cyprus, South Africa .

Other: Trainee, EEC, Brussels 1976; Trainee and member, Secretariat, Directorate and Commission on Human Rights, Council of Europe, Strasbourg 1976-77; Chair, Thames Festival Trust. Honorary Fellow, South Bank University. PC 2011; Redriff (Rotherhithe).

Publications: Co-author, Human Rights in Western Europe – The Next 30 Years (1981); The Prosecutorial Process in England and Wales (1981); Across the Divide – Liberal Values for Defence and Disarmament (1986); Pathways to Power (1992); Who Goes Where – Asylum: Opportunity not Crisis (2002); Co-author, Beyond Blair (2006).

Recreations: Music, theatre, history, sport (Millwall Football Club, Glamorgan County Cricket Club and Wales rugby football union), the countryside and open air.

Rt Hon Simon Hughes MP, House of Commons, London SW1A 0AA
Tel: 020 7219 6256 *Fax:* 020 7219 6567
Constituency: 4 Market Place, London, London SE16 3UQ
Tel: 020 7232 2557 *Email:* simon@simonhughes.org.uk *Website:* www.simonhughes.org.uk
Twitter: @SimonHughesMP

CONSERVATIVE

HUNT, JEREMY

South West Surrey *(Majority 16,318)*

Secretary of State for Health

Jeremy Richard Streynsham Hunt. Born 1 November 1966; Son of Admiral Sir Nicholas Hunt and Meriel Hunt; Married Lucia Guo 2009 (1 son 1 daughter).

Education: Charterhouse, Surrey; Magdalen College, Oxford (BA philosophy, politics and economics 1988, MA); French, Japanese.

Non-political career: Management consultant, Outram Cullinan and Co 1988-89; English teacher, Japan 1990-91; Founder and managing director, Hotcourses Ltd 1991-2005.

Political career: Member for South West Surrey 2005-10, for South West Surrey (revised boundary) since 6 May 2010 general election; Shadow Minister for Disabled People 2005-07; Shadow Secretary of State for Culture, Media and Sport 2007-10; Secretary of State for: Culture, Olympics, Media and Sport 2010-12; Health 2012-. *Select committees:* Member: International Development 2005-06. *Councils and public bodies:* Ex-officio member, Olympic Board -2012.

Political interests: Education, international development, philanthropy; Africa, Japan.

Other: Member, Education, Youth, Culture and Sport Council, Council of the European Union 2010-12; Founder and trustee, The Hotcourses Foundation 2004-. PC 2010.

Recreations: Latin music and dance.

Rt Hon Jeremy Hunt MP, House of Commons, London SW1A 0AA
Tel: 020 7219 6813 *Email:* huntj@parliament.uk
Constituency: South West Surrey Conservative Association, 2 Royal Parade, Tilford Road, Hindhead, Surrey GU26 6TD
Tel: 01428 609416 *Fax:* 01428 607498 *Website:* www.jeremyhunt.org *Twitter:* @Jeremy_Hunt

LABOUR

HUNT, TRISTRAM

Stoke-on-Trent Central *(Majority 5,565)*

Shadow Secretary of State for Education

Tristram Julian William Hunt. Born 31 May 1974; Son of Julian Hunt, now Lord Hunt of Chesterton (qv), and Marylla Shephard; Married Juliet Thornback (2004) (1 son 2 daughters).

Education: University College School, London; Trinity College, Cambridge (BA history 1995); Chicago University (Post-graduate Fellowship); Cambridge University (PhD Victorian civic pride 2000).

Non-political career: Senior researcher, Labour Party election campaign 1997; Special adviser, Department of Trade and Industry 1998-2001; Research fellow, Institute for Public Policy Research 2001; Associate fellow, Centre for History and Economics, King's College, Cambridge 2001-02; Radio and television broadcaster 2001-; History lecturer, Queen Mary University, London 2003-. Member, Unite.

Political career: Member for Stoke-on-Trent Central since 6 May 2010 general election; Shadow Minister for Education 2013; Shadow Secretary of State for Education 2013-. *Select committees:* Member: Political and Constitutional Reform 2010-, Joint Committee on the Draft House of Lords Reform Bill 2011-12, Works of Art 2012-, Joint Committee on Parliamentary Privilege 2013.

Political interests: Education, urban regeneration, constitutional reform, manufacturing, heritage and arts, energy security; China, India.

Other: Trustee, Heritage Lottery Fund; Fellow, Royal Historical Society; Trustee, History of Parliament Trust; Vice-chair, Progress.

Publications: Numerous publications in academic journals; Author: The English Civil War: At First Hand (Weidenfeld and Nicolson, 2002); Building Jerusalem: The Rise and Fall of the Victorian City (Weidenfeld and Nicolson, 2004), The Frock-Coated Communist: The Revolutionary Life of Friedrich Engels (Penguin, 2009); Contributor, The Purple Book (Progress, 2011).

Dr Tristram Hunt MP, House of Commons, London SW1A 0AA
Tel: 020 7219 1179 *Email:* tristram.hunt.mp@parliament.uk
Constituency: 88 Lonsdale Street, Stoke ST4 4DP
Tel: 01782 410455 *Email:* tristramhunt@parliament.uk *Website:* www.tristramhunt.com
Twitter: @TristramHuntMP

HUNTER, MARK
Cheadle *(Majority 3,272)*

Assistant Government Whip

Mark James Hunter. Born 25 July 1957; Son of A.B. Hunter and late E.M. Hunter; Married Lesley Graham 1997 (1 daughter 1 son).

Education: Audenshaw Grammar School, Manchester.

Non-political career: Advertising manager, Associated Newspapers; Business development manager, Guardian Media Group.

LIBERAL DEMOCRAT

Political career: Contested Ashton-under-Lyne 1987 and Stockport 2001 general elections. Member for Cheadle 14 July 2005 by-election to 2010, for Cheadle (revised boundary) since 6 May 2010 general election; Liberal Democrat Shadow Minister for: Office of the Deputy Prime Minister 2005-06, Home Affairs 2006-07, Foreign and Commonwealth Office 2007; PPS to Nick Clegg as Leader of the Liberal Democrats 2007-10; Liberal Democrat Shadow Minister for Transport 2008-10; Assistant Government Whip 2010-. *Select committees:* Member: Trade and Industry/Business, Enterprise and Regulatory Reform/Business and Enterprise 2005-08, Quadripartite (Committees on Strategic Export Controls)/Arms Export Controls 2007-08, Selection 2010-, Administration 2011-. *Councils and public bodies:* Councillor, Tameside Metropolitan Borough Council (MBC) 1980-89; Stockport MBC: Councillor 1996-06, Chair, Education Committee 1997-2001, Deputy Leader 2001-02, Leader 2002-05; Vice-President, Local Government Association 2010-11.

Political interests: Local government, human rights, international affairs.

Other: National Trust; Amnesty International; CAMRA; Honorary President, Stockport Parkinsons Disease Society.

Recreations: Lifelong Manchester City fan, reading, theatre, eating out.

Mark Hunter MP, House of Commons, London SW1A 0AA
Tel: 020 7219 3889 *Fax:* 020 7219 0813 *Email:* hunterm@parliament.uk
Constituency: Hillson House, 3 Gill Bent Road, Cheadle Hulme, Cheadle, Stockport, Cheshire SK8 7LE
Tel: 0161-486 1359 *Fax:* 0161-486 9005 *Email:* info@cheadle-libdems.org.uk
Website: www.markhunter.org.uk *Twitter:* @markhuntermp

HUPPERT, JULIAN
Cambridge *(Majority 6,792)*

Julian Leon Huppert. Born 21 July 1978; Son of Professor Felicia Huppert, professor of psychology, and Professor Herbert Huppert FRS, professor of theoretical geophysics; Partner Dr Caroline Wright.

Education: Perse School, Cambridge; Trinity College, Cambridge (BA MSci natural sciences 2000, MA); Cambridge University (PhD biological chemistry 2005); Some French.

Non-political career: Team member, review of Bulgarian education policy, Organisation for Economic Co-operation and Development 2000; Business analyst, Monis Software Ltd 2000-01; Director and chief executive officer, Cambridge Laboratory Innovations 2003-05; Postdoctoral researcher, Trinity College, Cambridge: Wellcome Trust Sanger Institute 2005-07, Unilever Centre for Molecular Science Informatics, Cambridge University 2007-08; Academic fellow (Research Councils UK), Computational Biology, Cambridge University 2007-12; Director of studies, Clare College, Cambridge 2009-10; Fellow, Clare College 2009-, University Lecturer, University of Cambridge 2012-.

LIBERAL DEMOCRAT

Political career: Contested Huntingdon 2005 general election. Member for Cambridge since 6 May 2010 general election; Board member, Parliamentary Office of Science and Technology (POST). *Select committees:* Member: Home Affairs 2010-, Joint Committees on: Human Rights 2010-11, the Draft Defamation Bill 2011, the Draft Communications Data Bill 2012-13. Cochair, Liberal Democrat Parliamentary Party Committees on: Transport 2011-12, Home Affairs, Justice and Equalities 2012-. Member, Manifesto Working Group 2013-. *Councils and public bodies:* Cambridgeshire County Council: Councillor 2001-09, Leader, Liberal Democrat group 2004-07; Vice-President, Local Government Association 2010-.

Political interests: Science, internationalism, human rights, DNA database, civil liberties, education, transport, evidence-based policy, UN and foreign affairs, wellbeing, environment, climate change.

Other: Chair and founder, Cambridge WorldMUN Trust 2000-11; Friends of Stourbridge Common; Liberty: Member, National Council Member 2009-; Member: Electoral Reform Society, CTC, Dignity in Dying, British Humanist Association, Campaign for Science and Engineering; Royal Society of Chemistry: Member 2005-, Fellow 2012-; Member, Institute of Physics 2007-.

Publications: Numerous publications in peer-reviewed scientific journals; Contributor, Unlocking Local Leadership on Climate Change (Green Alliance, 2012).

Recreations: Cycling, music, climbing, walking.
Dr Julian Huppert MP, House of Commons, London SW1A 0AA
Tel: 020 7219 0647 *Email:* julian.huppert.mp@parliament.uk
Constituency: 16 Signet Court, Cambridge CB5 8LA
Tel: 01223 304421 *Fax:* 01223 312148 *Email:* julianhuppertmp@gmail.com
Website: www.julianhuppert.org.uk *Twitter:* @julianhuppert

CONSERVATIVE

HURD, NICK
Ruislip, Northwood and Pinner *(Majority 19,060)*

Parliamentary Secretary (Minister for Civil Society), Cabinet Office

Nicholas Richard Hurd. Born 13 May 1962; Son of Douglas Hurd, MP 1974-97, now Lord Hurd of Westwell (qv), and Tatiana Hurd, née Eyre; Married Kim Richards 1988 (divorced) (2 sons 2 daughters); married Lady Clare Kerr (daughter of Most Hon the Marquess of Lothian QC DL (qv)) 2010 (1 daughter).

Education: Eton College; Exeter College, Oxford (BA classics 1984).

Non-political career: Investment manager, Morgan Grenfell 1985-90; Corporate finance executive, Crown Communications 1990-92; Managing director, Passport Magazine Directories 1992-94; Flemings Bank (Brazil-based) 1995-99; Director, Band-X Ltd 2001-06; Founder, Small Business Network 2002; Chief of staff to Tim Yeo MP 2003-05; Non-executive director, Sancroft Ltd 2008-10.

Political career: Member for Ruislip Northwood 2005-10, for Ruislip, Northwood and Pinner since 6 May 2010 general election; Opposition Whip 2007-08; Sponsored Sustainable Communities Act 2007; Shadow Minister for Charities[, Social Enterprise and Volunteering] 2008-10; Parliamentary Secretary (Minister for Civil Society), Cabinet Office 2010-. *Select committees:* Member: Environmental Audit 2005-10, Joint Committee on the Draft Climate Change Bill 2007. *Councils and public bodies:* Governor, Coteford Junior School.

Political interests: Environment, community, penal reform, health; Brazil, China.

Other: Member, Vote No to the EU Constitution Campaign; Trustee, Greenhouse Schools Project.

Recreations: Sport, music.

Nick Hurd MP, House of Commons, London SW1A 0AA
Tel: 020 7219 1053 *Fax:* 020 7219 4854 *Email:* nick.hurd.mp@parliament.uk
Constituency: 32 High Street, Northwood, Middlesex HA6 1BN
Tel: 01923 822876 *Fax:* 01923 841514 *Email:* annrnca@aol.com *Website:* www.nickhurd.com
Twitter: @nickhurdmp

LABOUR

IRRANCA-DAVIES, HUW
Ogmore *(Majority 13,246)*

Shadow Minister for Environment, Food and Rural Affairs

Ifor Huw Irranca-Davies. Born 22 January 1963; Son of Gethin Davies and Teresa Davies, née Griffiths; Married Joanna Irranca 1990 (3 sons).

Education: Gowerton Comprehensive School; Crewe and Alsager College of Higher Education (BA combined studies 1986); Swansea Institute of Higher Education (MSc European leisure resort management 1996); Welsh.

Non-political career: Leisure facility management 1986-96: Lliw Valley Borough Council, Community Leisure Management Ltd, London Borough of Southwark, Cardiff Institute of Higher Education, Swansea College; Senior lecturer and course director, business faculty, Swansea Institute of Higher Education 1996-2002. Member: UCATT, GMB.

Political career: Contested Brecon and Radnorshire 2001 general election. Member for Ogmore 14 February 2002 by-election to 2010, for Ogmore (revised boundary) since 6 May 2010 general election; PPS: to Jane Kennedy as Minister of State: Northern Ireland Office 2003-04, Department for Work and Pensions 2004-05, to Tessa Jowell as Secretary of State for Culture, Media and Sport 2005-06; Assistant Government Whip 2006-07; Parliamentary Under-Secretary of State: Wales Office 2007-08, Department for Environment, Food and Rural Affairs 2008-10 (Minister for the Natural and Marine Environment 2008-10, for Wildlife and Rural Affairs 2008-09); Shadow Minister for: Environment, Food and Rural Affairs 2010, 2011-, Energy 2010-11. *Select committees:* Member: Joint Committee on Statutory Instruments 2002-04, Procedure 2002-05. Vice-president, Neath Constituency Labour Party 2001-02; Secretary, Ystalyfera branch 1999-2002.

Political interests: Social justice, community regeneration, devolution, international development, European Union; China, Middle East, Northern Ireland.

Other: President, Garw Valley Ladies' Choir; Vice-President, Maesteg Amateur Operatic Society; President, Pencoed and District Choral Society; Vice-President, Y Bont; President: Ogmore Valley Silver Band, Glamorgan area Ramblers Cymru; Vice-President, Ramblers Association Wales; Patron, Maesteg Gleemen; Tenovus (National Cancer Charity). Environmental Parliamentarian of the Year, CIWEM 2012. Vice-President, Maesteg Cricket Club; Patron, Maesteg RFC.

Recreations: Hill-walking, cycling, most sport, family.

Huw Irranca-Davies MP, House of Commons, London SW1A 0AA
Tel: 020 7219 4027 *Email:* irrancadaviesh@parliament.uk
Constituency: Unit 2, 112-113 Commercial Street, Maesteg, Mid Glamorgan CF34 9DL
Tel: 01656 737777   *Website:* www.huwirranca-davies.org.uk   *Twitter:* @IrrancaDaviesMP

JACKSON, GLENDA   Hampstead and Kilburn *(Majority 42)*

Glenda May Jackson. Born 9 May 1936; Daughter of Harry and Joan Jackson; Married Roy Hodges 1958 (divorced 1976) (1 son).

Education: West Kirby County Grammar School for Girls; RADA.

Non-political career: Actress: Plays include: *The Idiot* 1962, *Love's Labour's Lost*, *Hamlet* 1965, *Three Sisters* 1967, *Hedda Gabler* 1975; Films include: *Women in Love*, *Mary, Queen of Scots*, *A Touch of Class*; Television includes *Elizabeth R* 1971; Member, Royal Shakespeare Company 1963-67, 1979-80.

LABOUR

Political career: Member for Hampstead and Highgate 1992-2010, for Hampstead and Kilburn since 6 May 2010 general election; Opposition Spokeswoman on Transport 1996-97; Parliamentary Under-Secretary of State, Department of the Environment, Transport and the Regions 1997-99; Resigned in July 1999 reshuffle. *Select committees:* Member: Work and Pensions 2010-. *Councils and public bodies:* Member, advisory cabinet for homelessness, Greater London Assembly 2000-04.

Political interests: Overseas aid and development, housing, environment.

Other: Member: Anti-Apartheid Movement, Amnesty International, Has campaigned for: Oxfam, Shelter, Friends of the Earth. Best film actress awards: Variety Clubs of Great Britain 1971, 1975, 1978, NY Film critics 1971, Oscar 1971, 1974. CBE 1978.

Recreations: Cooking, gardening, reading Jane Austen.

Glenda Jackson CBE MP, House of Commons, London SW1A 0AA
Tel: 020 7219 4008 *Fax:* 020 7219 2112 *Email:* jacksong@parliament.uk
Constituency: No constituency office *Website:* www.glenda-jackson.co.uk
Twitter: @glendajacksonmp

JACKSON, STEWART   Peterborough *(Majority 4,861)*

Stewart James Jackson. Born 31 January 1965; Son of Sylvia and Raymond Jackson; Married Sarah O'Grady 1999 (1 daughter).

Education: London Nautical School, Southwark, London; Chatham House Grammar School, Ramsgate, Kent; Royal Holloway College, London University (BA economics and public administration 1988); University of West London (MA human resource management 2001).

Non-political career: Business banking manager, Lloyds Bank plc 1993-96; Retail branch manager, Lloyds TSB Group 1996-98; Business services manager, Aztec training and enterprise council for South West London 1998-2000; Business adviser, human resources, Business Link for London 2000-05. Member, Lloyds TSB Group Union 1989-98.

CONSERVATIVE

Political career: Contested Brent South 1997 and Peterborough 2001 general elections. Member for Peterborough 2005-10, for Peterborough (revised boundary) since 6 May 2010 general election; Opposition Whip 2007-08; Shadow Minister for Communities and Local Government 2008-10; PPS to Owen Paterson as Secretary of State for Northern Ireland 2010-11. *Select committees:* Member: Regulatory Reform 2005-10, Health 2006-07, Public Accounts 2012-. Deputy chair, Ealing North Conservative Association 1998-2000. *Councils and public bodies:* Councillor, London Borough of Ealing 1990-98; Vice-President, Local Government Association 2010-.

Political interests: Housing, planning, home affairs, regeneration, Europe; Kashmir, Pakistan, South America, USA.

Other: Inter-Parliamentary Union, British Group: Member, Executive Committee, Vice-chair 2011-; Board of Trustees, London City YMCA 1993-98; Good Neighbours Scheme, Peterborough Salvation Army 2005-; Management board, New Local Government Network 2010-13;

Member, Chartered Institute of Personnel and Development 2001-; BLISS – Premature Birth Charity; SHINE; Action Medical Research; Tourettes Action; Peterborough Conservative Club; Carlton Club.

Recreations: Reading, travel, theatre, cinema, cycling.

Stewart Jackson MP, House of Commons, London SW1A 0AA
Tel: 020 7219 5046 *Email:* stewart.jackson.mp@parliament.uk
Constituency: Peterborough Conservative Association, 193 Dogsthorpe Road, Peterborough, Cambridgeshire PE1 3AT
Tel: 01733 891080 *Email:* stewart@peterboroughconservatives.com
Website: www.peterboroughconservatives.com www.stewartjackson.org.uk
Twitter: @SJacksonMP

JAMES, MARGOT

Stourbridge *(Majority 5,164)*

PPS to Lord Green of Hurstpierpoint as Minister of State for Trade and Investment, Department for Business, Innovation and Skills and Foreign and Commonwealth Office

Born 1958; Partner Jay.

Education: Millfield School, Somerset; London School of Economics (BSc economics and government).

CONSERVATIVE

Non-political career: Maurice James Industries; Researcher to Sir Anthony Durant MP; Press officer, Conservative Central Office; Co-founder and director, Shire Health 1986-99; Ogilvy & Mather: Head of European healthcare, Regional president, pharmaceutical division 2005-.

Political career: Contested Holborn and St Pancras 2005 general election. Member for Stourbridge since 6 May 2010 general election; Parliamentary aide to Lord Green of Hurstpierpoint as Minister of State for Trade and Investment January-September 2012; PPS to Lord Green of Hurstpierpoint as Minister of State for Trade and Investment, Department for Business, Innovation and Skills and Foreign and Commonwealth Office 2012-. *Select committees:* Member: Business, Innovation and Skills 2010-12, Arms Export Controls 2010-12, Joint Committee on the Draft Care and Support Bill 2013. Chair, London School of Economics Conservative Association; Vice-chair (women's issues), Conservative Party 2005-10. *Councils and public bodies:* Non-executive director, Parkside NHS Trust 1998-2003; Councillor, Kensington and Chelsea Borough Council 2006-08.

Political interests: Business, health, older people, education, prison reform.

Other: Trustee, Abantu; Mentor: Prince's Trust, Young Enterprise. Communicator of the Year 1997.

Recreations: Cooking, theatre, travel, opera.

Margot James MP, House of Commons, London SW1A 0AA
Tel: 020 7219 7226 *Fax:* 020 7219 6434 *Email:* margot.james.mp@parliament.uk
Constituency: 15-17 Lawn Avenue, Stourbridge, West Midlands DY8 3UR
Tel: 01384 370574 *Fax:* 01384 370441 *Website:* www.margotjames.com
Twitter: @margotjamesmp

JAMES, SIÂN

Swansea East *(Majority 10,838)*

Siân Catherine James. Born 24 June 1959; Daughter of Melbourne and Martha Griffiths; Married Martin James 1976 (2 children).

Education: Cefn Saeson Comprehensive School, Cimla, Neath; University of Wales, Swansea (BsCon Welsh language 1989); Welsh.

Non-political career: Field officer, National Federation of Young Farmers' Clubs 1990-91; Save the Children 1991-94; Deputy public affairs manager, National Trust 1994-98; Communications manager, Securicor 1998-99; Lobbyist, Association of Train Operating Companies 1999-2003; Director, Welsh Women's Aid 2003-05.

LABOUR

Political career: Member for Swansea East since 5 May 2005 general election. *Select committees:* Member: Welsh Affairs 2005-10, 2010-, Procedure 2005-10, Crossrail Bill 2006-07, Constitutional Affairs/Justice 2006-11, Administration 2010. *Councils and public bodies:* Councillor, Neath Town Council 2004.

Political interests: Social exclusion, public transport, work and pensions issues, Welsh affairs, children and young people, domestic abuse; Burma, Cuba, Portugal, Slovakia.

Recreations: Reading, antiques, model railways, vintage coach prams.

Siân James MP, House of Commons, London SW1A 0AA
Tel: 020 7219 3000/020 7219 1666 *Email:* jamessc@parliament.uk
Constituency: 485 Llangyfelach Road, Brynhyfryd, Swansea SA5 9EA
Tel: 01792 455089

JAMIESON, CATHY
Kilmarnock and Loudoun *(Majority 12,378)*

Shadow Economic Secretary

Born 3 November 1956; Daughter of Robert Jamieson, retired motor mechanic, and Mary Jamieson, retired office administrator; Married Ian Sharpe 1976 (1 son).

Education: James Hamilton Academy, Kilmarnock; Glasgow School of Art (BA fine art 1979); Goldsmith's College, London (Post-graduate Higher Diploma art 1980); Glasgow University (CQSW 1983); Glasgow Caledonian University (Certificate management 1996).

LAB/CO-OP

Non-political career: Strathclyde Regional Council: Trainee social worker 1980-81; Social worker 1983-86; Community intermediate treatment worker 1986-88; Senior intermediate treatment worker 1988-92; Principal officer, Who Cares? Scotland 1992-99. Transport and General Workers' Union (TGWU)/Unite: Member, Former chair, Unite Group of Labour MSPs; Member, USDAW.

Political career: Member for Kilmarnock and Loudoun since 6 May 2010 general election; Shadow Economic Secretary 2011-. *Select committees:* Member: Scottish Affairs 2010-11, Environment, Food and Rural Affairs 2011-12, Culture, Media and Sport 2011, Members' Expenses 2011-. Scottish Parliament: MSP for Carrick, Cumnock and Doon Valley constituency 1999-2011: Scottish Labour Minister for: Education and Young People 2001-03, Justice 2003-07; Member, Scottish Parliamentary Bureau 2007-08; Shadow Minister for Parliamentary Business 2007; Acting Shadow First Minister 2007, 2008; Shadow Cabinet Secretary for: Health and Wellbeing 2008-09, Housing and Regeneration 2009. Various positions at local branch and constituency level 1980-99 including: Chair, Cunninghame South Constituency Labour Party; Vice-chair, South of Scotland Euro Constituency Labour Party; Election agent for Alex Smith MEP 1994; Member, Labour's: Scottish Executive 1996-99, 2000-08, National Executive 1998; Vice-chair, Scottish Co-operative Party 1998-99; Labour Party in the Scottish Parliament: Deputy Leader 2000-08, Interim Leader 2007, 2008; Contested Scottish Labour Leader in the Scottish Parliament election 2008; Chair, parliamentary group, Co-operative Party 2011-.

Political interests: Co-operative movement, voluntary sector, social economy, workers' rights, anti-poverty, children, criminal justice; Cuba, Palestine, Western Sahara, Tibet.

Other: Trustee, Barony A Frame; Who Cares? Scotland; Woodcraft Folk; Patron: Cumnock Osteoporosis Group, Girvan Youth Trust.

Publications: Various publications in professional/political journals and magazines.

Recreations: Kilmarnock FC, art, photography, Ayrshire history.

Cathy Jamieson MP, House of Commons, London SW1A 0AA
Tel: 020 7219 8456 *Email:* cathy.jamieson.mp@parliament.uk
Constituency: 32 Grange Street, Kilmarnock KA1 2DD
Tel: 01563 522361 *Website:* www.cathyjamieson.com *Twitter:* @cathyjamieson

JARVIS, DAN
Barnsley Central *(Majority 11,771)*

Shadow Minister for Justice

Dan Owen Woolgar Jarvis. Born 30 November 1972; Married Caroline (died 2010) (1 son 2 daughters).

Education: Rushcliffe Comprehensive, Nottingham; Aberystwyth University (international politics and strategic studies); Royal Military Academy, Sandhurst.

Non-political career: Major, Parachute Regiment 1996-2011. Unite; Unison.

LABOUR

Political career: Member for Barnsley Central since 3 March 2011 by-election; Shadow Minister for: Culture, Media and Sport 2011-13, Justice 2013-. *Select committees:* Member: Business, Innovation and Skills 2010-11. Chair, PLP Departmental Group for Business, Innovation and Skills 2011.

Political interests: Defence and security, policing and immigration, business, innovation and skills, health, sport, countryside, cancer, education and literacy; Afghanistan, Nepal, Pakistan.

Other: Vice-chair, Progress 2011-. MBE (mil) 2011.

Recreations: Parliamentary Mountaineering Group.

Dan Jarvis MBE MP, House of Commons, London SW1A 0AA
Tel: 020 7219 1082 *Email:* dan.jarvis.mp@parliament.uk
Constituency: Corporate Mailroom, PO Box 634, Barnsley S70 9GG
Tel: 01226 787893 *Website:* www.danjarvismp.co.uk *Twitter:* @DanJarvisMP

JAVID, SAJID
Bromsgrove *(Majority 11,308)*

Financial Secretary, HM Treasury

Born 5 December 1969; Married Laura (4 children).

Education: Downend School, Bristol; Filton Technical College, Bristol; Exeter University (economics and politics 1991); Punjabi, Urdu.

Non-political career: Vice-president, Chase Manhattan Bank; Managing director, Deutsche Bank; Board member, Deutsche Bank International (Asia) Ltd; Investment partner, JP Morgan Partners LLC; Businessman.

CONSERVATIVE

Political career: Member for Bromsgrove since 6 May 2010 general election; PPS to: John Hayes as Minister of State for Further Education, Skills and Lifelong Learning 2010-11, George Osborne as Chancellor of the Exchequer 2011-12; Economic Secretary, HM Treasury 2012-13; Financial Secretary, HM Treasury 2013-. *Select committees:* Member Work and Pensions 2010; Ex-officio Member Public Accounts 2012-. *Councils and public bodies:* Former governor, Normand Croft Community School.

Political interests: Civil liberties, free enterprise, defence, welfare policy.

Other: Trustee: Westminster Children's Society, London Early Years Foundation.

Publications: Contributor, There is Such a Thing as Society (2002).

Recreations: Gym, running, hiking, cricket.

Sajid Javid MP, House of Commons, London SW1A 0AA
Tel: 020 7219 7027 *Fax:* 020 7219 0930 *Email:* sajid.javid.mp@parliament.uk
Constituency: Rear Office, 18 High Street, Bromsgrove, Worcestershire B61 8HQ
Tel: 01527 872135 *Email:* mary.marsh@parliament.uk *Website:* www.sajidjavid.com
Twitter: @SajidJavid

JENKIN, BERNARD
Harwich and North Essex *(Majority 11,447)*

Bernard Christison Jenkin. Born 9 April 1959; Son of Charles Jenkin, MP for Wanstead and Woodford 1964-87, now Baron Jenkin of Roding (qv), and Alison Graham; Married Anne Strutt, now Baroness Jenkin of Kennington (qv), 1988 (2 sons).

Education: Highgate School, London; William Ellis School, London; Corpus Christi College, Cambridge (BA English literature 1982) (President, Cambridge Union Society 1982); French (conversational).

Non-political career: Ford Motor Co Ltd 1983-86; Venture capital manager, 3i plc 1986-88; **CONSERVATIVE** Manager, Legal and General Ventures Ltd 1989-92; Adviser, Legal and General Group plc 1992-95.

Political career: Contested Glasgow Central 1987 general election. Member for North Colchester 1992-97, for North Essex 1997-2010, for Harwich and North Essex since 6 May 2010 general election; PPS to Michael Forsyth as Secretary of State for Scotland 1995-97; Opposition Spokesperson for: Constitutional Affairs, Scotland and Wales 1997-98, Environment, Transport and the Regions (Roads and Environment) 1998; Shadow Minister for Transport 1998-2001; Member, Shadow Cabinet 1999-2003; Shadow Secretary of State for: Defence 2001-03, The Regions 2003-05; Shadow Minister for Energy 2005. *Select committees:* Member: European Standing Committee B 1992-97, Social Security 1993-97, Defence 2006-10, Arms Export Controls 2008-10; Chair: Public Administration 2010-; Member: Liaison 2010-, Unopposed Bills (Panel) 2010-, Joint Committee on Parliamentary Privilege 2013. Conservative Backbench Committees: Vice-chair, Smaller Businesses 1992-95, Secretary, Foreign Affairs 1994-95; Member, Executive, 1922 Committee 2010-. Deputy chair (candidates), Conservative Party 2005-06. *Councils and public bodies:* Governor, Central Foundation Girls' School ILEA 1985-89.

Political interests: Economic policy, trade, European Union, defence, foreign affairs, good governance, the Civil Service; Afghanistan, Chile, France, Georgia, Germany, India, Iraq, New Zealand, Pakistan, Russia, Singapore, USA.

Other: Governor, London Goodenough Trust for Overseas Graduates 1992-2001; Council member, St Paul's Cathedral 2006-; Vice-President, Combat Stress 2009-; Vice-chair and trustee, Parliament Choir; Action Aid, BASC, National Trust, British Paralympic Association, Students Partnership Worldwide; Colchester Conservative Constitutional Club.

Publications: Maastricht: Game Set and Match? (1993); Who Benefits: Reinventing Social Security (1993); A Conservative Europe: 1994 and beyond (1994); Fairer Business Rates (1996); A Defence Policy for the UK: Matching Commitments and Resources (2007).

Recreations: Sailing, music (especially opera), fishing, family, DIY.

Bernard Jenkin MP, House of Commons, London SW1A 0AA
Tel: 020 7219 4029 *Fax:* 020 7219 5963 *Email:* bernard.jenkin.mp@parliament.uk
Constituency: Harwich and North Essex Conservatives Association, Unit C2, East Gores Farm, Salmons Lane, Coggeshall, Colchester, Essex CO6 1RZ
Email: info@hneca.co.uk *Website:* www.bernardjenkinmp.com *Twitter:* @bernardjenkin

LABOUR

JOHNSON, ALAN   Kingston upon Hull West and Hessle *(Majority 5,742)*

Alan Arthur Johnson. Born 17 May 1950; Son of late Stephen Johnson and Lillian Johnson; Married Judith Cox 1968 (divorced) (1 son 2 daughters); married Laura Patient 1991 (1 son).

Education: Sloane Grammar School, Chelsea.

Non-political career: Postman 1968-87; Communication Workers Union: Local officer, Slough 1974-81, Branch official 1976, Executive Council 1981-87, National officer 1987-93, General Secretary 1993-95; Member, General Council, Trades Union Congress 1993-95; Executive member, Postal, Telegraph and Telephone International 1993-97; Director, Unity Bank Trust plc 1993-97; Joint general secretary, Communication Workers Union 1995-97. Member, Communication Workers' Union.

Political career: Member for Kingston upon Hull West and Hessle 1997-2010, for Kingston upon Hull West and Hessle (revised boundaries) since 6 May 2010 general election; PPS to Dawn Primarolo at HM Treasury: as Financial Secretary 1997-99, as Paymaster General 1999; Department of Trade and Industry 1999-2003: Parliamentary Under-Secretary of State (Competitiveness) 1999-2001, Minister of State 2001-03: (Employment Relations and Regions 2001-02, Employment Relations, Industry and the Regions 2002-03); Minister of State, Department for Education and Skills (Lifelong Learning, Further and Higher Education) 2003-04; Secretary of State for: Work and Pensions 2004-05, Trade and Industry 2005-06, Education and Skills 2006-07, Health 2007-09; Secretary of State for the Home Office (Home Secretary) 2009-10; Shadow Secretary of State for the Home Office (Shadow Home Secretary) 2010; Shadow Chancellor of the Exchequer 2010-11. *Select committees:* Member: Trade and Industry 1997-98. Member: Southern Regional Executive of Labour Party 1981-87, Member Labour Party National Executive Committee 1995-97, Labour Campaign for Electoral Reform.

Political interests: Education, electoral reform, employment, Post Office.

Other: Member, World Executive, Postal, Telegraph and Telephone International 1993-97. PC 2003.

Publications: This Boy – A Memoir of a Childhood (Bantam Press, 2013).

Recreations: Tennis, cooking, reading, radio, music, football.

Rt Hon Alan Johnson MP, House of Commons, London SW1A 0AA
Tel: 020 7219 6637/020 7219 1305 *Email:* johnsona@parliament.uk
Constituency: Goodwin Resource Centre, Icehouse Road, Hull, Humberside HU3 2HQ
Tel: 01482 219211 *Fax:* 01482 219211 *Email:* windlet@parliament.uk
Website: www.alanjohnson.org

LABOUR

JOHNSON, DIANA   Kingston upon Hull North *(Majority 641)*

Shadow Minister for Crime and Security

Diana Ruth Johnson. Born 25 July 1966; Daughter of late Eric and Ruth Johnson.

Education: Sir John Deane's Sixth Form College, Cheshire; Northwich County Grammar School for Girls, Cheshire; Queen Mary College, London University (LLB 1989); Council for Legal Education (law finals 1991).

Non-political career: Volunteer/locum lawyer, Tower Hamlets Law Centre 1991-94; Employment, immigration and education lawyer, North Lewisham Law Centre 1995-99; Employment lawyer, Paddington Law Centre 1999-2002; National Officer, FDA Trade Union 2002-03. Member: Unite, Unison.

Political career: Contested Brentwood and Ongar 2001 general election. Member for Hull North 2005-10, for Kingston upon Hull North since 6 May 2010 general election; PPS to Stephen Timms: as Minister of State, Department for Work and Pensions 2005-06, as Chief Secretary to the Treasury 2006-07; Assistant Government Whip 2007-09; Parliamentary Under-Secretary of State for Schools, Department for Children, Schools and Families 2009-10; Shadow Minister for: Health 2010, Home Office 2010-11, Crime and Security 2011-. *Select committees:* Member: Public Accounts 2005. Member: Co-operative Party, Labour Women's Network. *Councils and public bodies:* London Borough of Tower Hamlets: Councillor 1994-2002, Chair: Social services 1997-2000, Social services and health scrutiny panel 2000-02; Legal visiting member, Mental Health Act Commission 1995-98; Member: London Assembly 2003-04, Metropolitan Police Authority 2003-04; Non-executive director: Newham Healthcare Trust 1998-2001, Tower Hamlets PCT 2001-05.

Political interests: Employment rights, health, education, animal welfare, policing; Colombia, Denmark, Jordan.

Other: Member: Fawcett Society, Amnesty International, Fabian Society.

Recreations: Cinema, theatre, Hull City FC.

Diana Johnson MP, House of Commons, London SW1A 0AA
Tel: 020 7219 5647 *Fax:* 020 7219 0959 *Email:* johnsond@parliament.uk
Constituency: Sycamore Suite, Community Enterprise Centre, Cottingham Road, Hull, Humberside HU5 2DH
Tel: 01482 319135 *Fax:* 01482 319137 *Website:* www.dianajohnson.co.uk
Twitter: @DianaJohnsonMP

CONSERVATIVE

JOHNSON, GARETH
Dartford *(Majority 10,628)*

Gareth Alan Johnson. Born 12 October 1969; Son of Alan Johnson, retired milkman, and Ruth Johnson; Married Wendy Morris 1997 (1 son 1 daughter).

Education: Dartford Grammar School; University of the West of England (Post-graduate Diploma law); College of Law (legal practice course 1995).

Non-political career: Legal adviser, Magistrates Court Service 1988-98; Solicitor, Gary Jacobs Mehta & Co 1997-2002; Assistant solicitor, then solicitor, Thomas Boyd Whyte 2002-.

Political career: Contested Lewisham West 2001 and Dartford 2005 general elections. Member for Dartford since 6 May 2010 general election. *Select committees:* Member: Science and Technology 2012, Justice 2013-. *Councils and public bodies:* London Borough of Bexley Council: Councillor 1998-2002, Cabinet Member for Policy and Resources 1998-2002; Board of Governors, Dartford Grammar Girls School.

Political interests: Home affairs, environment; USA.

Other: Member, Executive Committee, Inter-Parliamentary Union, British Group; Member, Law Society; Dartford Conservative Club.

Recreations: Cricket, rugby.

Gareth Johnson MP, House of Commons, London SW1A 0AA
Tel: 020 7219 7047 *Email:* gareth.johnson.mp@parliament.uk
Constituency: Dartford Civic Offices, Home Gardens, Dartford, Kent DA1 1DR
Tel: 01322 225958 *Website:* www.garethjohnsonmp.co.uk

CONSERVATIVE

JOHNSON, JO
Orpington *(Majority 17,200)*

Parliamentary Secretary, Cabinet Offic; Assistant Government Whip

Joseph Edmund Johnson. Born 1971; Son of Stanley Johnson and Charlotte Johnson, née Fawcett; Married Amelia Gentleman (2 children).

Education: European School, Uccle, Brussels; Hall School, Hampstead; Eton College; Balliol College, Oxford (BA modern history 1994); INSEAD (MBA 2000); Institut d'Etudes Europennes, Universite Libre de Bruxelles (Licence Speciale 1995); French.

Non-political career: Corporate financial, Deutsche Bank; *Financial Times* 1997-: Lex column 1997, Paris correspondent 2001-04, Bureau chief, South Asia 2005-08, Head of Lex 2008-, Associate editor.

Political career: Member for Orpington since 6 May 2010 general election; PPS to Mark Prisk as Minister of State for Business and Enterprise 2011-12; Assistant Government Whip 2012-; Parliamentary Secretary, Cabinet Office (Head of Number Ten Policy Unit) 2013-. *Select committees:* Member: Public Accounts 2010-12. Chair, Policy Advisory Board 2013-.

Political interests: Business, finance; France, India.

Publications: Co-author, The Man Who Tried To Buy The World (2003); Co-editor, Reconnecting Britain and India: Ideas for an Enhanced Partnership (2011).

Jo Johnson MP, House of Commons, London SW1A 0AA
Tel: 020 7219 7125 *Email:* jo.johnson.mp@parliament.uk
Constituency: Orpington Conservative Association, 6 Sevenoaks Road, Orpington, Kent BR6 9JJ
Tel: 01689 820347 *Website:* www.jo-johnson.com *Twitter:* @JoJohnsonMP

JONES, ANDREW
Harrogate and Knaresborough *(Majority 1,039)*

PPS to Health ministerial team

Andrew Hanson Jones. Born 28 November 1963; Single.

Education: Bradford Grammar School; Leeds University (BA English 1985).

Non-political career: Marketing manager: Kingfisher plc 1985-88, 1996-98; Going Places plc 1989-96, Marketing Store; Account director, M&C Saatchi 1998-2000; Sales and marketing director, Bettys and Taylors of Harrogate.

CONSERVATIVE

Political career: Contested Harrogate and Knaresborough 2001 general election. Member for Harrogate and Knaresborough since 6 May 2010 general election; PPS to: Mark Prisk as Minister of State for Business and Enterprise 2010-11, Justine Greening as Secretary of State for Transport 2011-12, Andrew Mitchell as Parliamentary Secretary to the Treasury and Chief Whip September-October 2012, Department of Health ministerial team 2013-. *Select committees:* Member: Regulatory Reform 2010-. Member, Conservative Party 1987-. *Councils and public bodies:* Harrogate Borough Council: Councillor 2003-11, Cabinet Member, Resources 2006-10.

Political interests: Renewable energy, recycling.

Other: Chair, Bow Group 1998-99. Member, Yorkshire County Cricket Club.

Recreations: Cricket, walking, theatre, music.

Andrew Jones MP, House of Commons, London SW1A 0AA
Tel: 020 7219 3000 *Email:* andrew.jones.mp@parliament.uk
Constituency: 57 East Parade, Harrogate, North Yorkshire HG1 5LQ
Tel: 01423 529614 *Website:* www.andrewjonesmp.co.uk *Twitter:* @AndrewJonesMP

JONES, DAVID
Clwyd West *(Majority 6,419)*

Secretary of State for Wales

David Ian Jones. Born 22 March 1952; Son of late Bryn Jones and Elspeth Jones, née Savage-Williams; Married Sara Tudor 1982 (2 sons).

Education: Ruabon Grammar School, Wrexham; University College London (LLB law 1973); Chester College of Law; French, Welsh.

Non-political career: Senior partner, David Jones & Company, Llandudno 1985-2005.

CONSERVATIVE

Political career: Contested Conwy 1997 and City of Chester 2001 general elections. Member for Clwyd West 2005-10, for Clwyd West (revised boundary) since 6 May 2010 general election; Shadow Minister for Wales 2006-10; Wales Office: Parliamentary Under-Secretary of State 2010-12, Secretary of State for Wales 2012-. *Select committees:* Member: Welsh Affairs 2005-10. Contested North Wales region 1999 National Assembly for Wales election. AM (replacement) for North Wales 2002-03. Chair, Conwy Conservative Association 1998-99; Patron, Chinese Conservative Group.

Political interests: Law and order, constitution, Welsh affairs, countryside; China, Middle East.

Other: Member, Law Society; Honorary life fellow, Cancer Research UK. PC 2012.

Recreations: Travel.

Rt Hon David Jones MP, House of Commons, London SW1A 0AA
Tel: 020 7219 8070 *Fax:* 020 7219 0142 *Email:* jonesdi@parliament.uk
Constituency: 3 Llewelyn Road, Colwyn Bay, Clwyd LL29 7AP
Tel: 01492 535845 *Fax:* 01492 534157 *Email:* bryan.george@parliament.uk
Website: www.davidjonesmp.co.uk davidjonesblog.com *Twitter:* @DavidJonesMP

LABOUR

JONES, GRAHAM
Hyndburn *(Majority 3,090)*

Opposition Whip

Graham Peter Jones. Born 3 March 1966.

Education: St Christopher's CoE High School; University of Central Lancashire (Degree applied social studies 1992); Graphic design.

Political career: Member for Hyndburn since 6 May 2010 general election; Opposition Whip 2010-; *Councils and public bodies:* Hyndburn Borough Council: Councillor 2002-10, Leader, Labour group 2006-10; Councillor, Lancashire County Council 2009-.

Recreations: Blackburn Rovers, football, golf.

Graham Jones MP, House of Commons, London SW1A 0AA
Tel: 020 7219 7089 *Fax:* 020 7219 2492 *Email:* graham.jones.mp@parliament.uk
Constituency: 50 Abbey Street, Accrington BB5 1EE
Tel: 01254 382283 *Fax:* 01254 398089 *Website:* hhgrahamjones.blogspot.com
Twitter: @GrahamJones_MP

LABOUR

JONES, HELEN
Warrington North *(Majority 6,771)*

Shadow Minister for Home Office

Helen Mary Jones. Born 24 December 1954; Daughter of late Robert Jones and Mary Scanlan; Married Michael Vobe 1988 (1 son).

Education: Ursuline Convent, Chester; University College, London (BA English); Chester College; Liverpool University (MEd); Manchester Metropolitan University; French.

Non-political career: English teacher; Development officer, MIND; Justice and peace officer, Liverpool Archdiocese; Solicitor. Member: USDAW, Unite.

Political career: Contested Shropshire North 1983 and Ellesmere Port and Neston 1987 general elections. Member for Warrington North 1997-2010, for Warrington North (revised boundary) since 6 May 2010 general election; PPS to Dawn Primarolo as Minister of State, Department of Health 2007-08; Assistant Government Whip 2008-09; Government Whip 2009-10; Shadow Minister for Justice 2010; Opposition Whip 2010; Shadow Deputy Leader of the House of Commons 2010-11; Shadow Minister for: Communities and Local Government 2011-13, Home Office 2013-. *Select committees:* Member: Catering 1997-98, Public Administration 1998-2000, Standing Orders 1999-2000, 2001-10, 2011-, Education and Employment 1999-2001, Education and Employment (Education Sub-Committee) 1999-2001, Unopposed Bills (Panel) 1999-2010, Education and Skills 2003-07, Administration 2005-07, Selection 2009-10, Joint Committee on Security 2010-11. Honorary Secretary, PLP Departmental Committee for Home Affairs 2002-06. Contested Lancashire Central 1984 European Parliament election. *Councils and public bodies:* Councillor, Chester City Council 1984-91.

Political interests: Education, health; Africa, England, Finland, Ireland, Italy, Norway, Scotland, Uganda, Wales.

Recreations: Gardening, reading, cooking.

Helen Jones MP, House of Commons, London SW1A 0AA
Tel: 020 7219 4048 *Email:* jonesh@parliament.uk
Constituency: Suite 9, Gilbert Wakefield House, 67 Bewsey Street, Warrington, Cheshire WA2 7JQ
Tel: 01925 232480 *Fax:* 01925 232239 *Twitter:* @HelenJonesMP

LABOUR

JONES, KEVAN
North Durham *(Majority 12,076)*

Shadow Minister for Defence

Kevan David Jones. Born 25 April 1964.

Education: Portland Comprehensive, Worksop, Nottinghamshire; Newcastle upon Tyne Polytechnic (BA government and public policy 1985); University of Southern Maine, USA.

Non-political career: Parliamentary assistant to Nick Brown MP 1985-89; GMB: Political officer 1989-2001, Regional organiser 1992-99, Senior organiser 1999-2001. GMB.

Political career: Member for North Durham 2001-10, for North Durham (revised boundary) since 6 May 2010 general election; Parliamentary Under-Secretary of State (Minister for Veterans), Ministry of Defence 2008-10; Shadow Minister for Defence 2010-. *Select committees:* Member: Defence 2001-09, Administration 2005-09, 2010-13, Armed Forces Bill 2005-06,

2011. Member PLP Parliamentary Affairs Committee 2006-. Northern Region Labour Party: Chair 1998-2000, Vice-chair 2000-. *Councils and public bodies:* Newcastle City Council: Councillor 1990-2001, Chair Public Health 1993-97, Chief Whip 1994-2000, Chair Development and Transport 1997-2001.

Political interests: Regeneration, transport, employment, regional policy, local and regional government, defence; Afghanistan, Iraq, Poland, United Arab Emirates, USA.

Other: Patron, Chester Le Street Mind 2001-. Speech of the Year (with Charles Walker MP), *The Spectator* awards 2012; Opposition Frontbencher of the Year, *House Magazine* awards 2012; Sacriston Working Men's Club.

Recreations: Golf.

Kevan Jones MP, House of Commons, London SW1A 0AA
Tel: 020 7219 8219 *Fax:* 020 7219 1759 *Email:* kevanjonesmp@parliament.uk
Constituency: Fulforth Centre, Front Street, Sacriston, Co Durham DH7 6JT
Tel: 0191-371 8834 *Fax:* 0191-371 8834 *Website:* www.kevanjonesmp.org.uk
Twitter: @KevanJonesMP

JONES, MARCUS
Nuneaton *(Majority 2,069)*

Marcus Charles Jones. Born 5 April 1974; Son of Brian Jones, signwriter, and Jean Jones, legal cashier; Married Suzanne 2004 (1 son 1 daughter).

Education: St Thomas More School, Nuneaton; King Edward VI College.

Non-political career: Conveyancing manager, Tustain Jones & Co, Solicitors 1999-2010.

Political career: Member for Nuneaton since 6 May 2010 general election. *Select committees:* Member: Backbench Business 2012-, Administration 2012-. *Councils and public bodies:* Nuneaton and Bedworth Borough Council: Councillor 2005-10, Leader, Conservative group 2006-09, Council Leader 2008-09.

CONSERVATIVE

Political interests: Economy, business and skills, local government.

Recreations: Family, watching Coventry City FC, angling.

Marcus Jones MP, House of Commons, London SW1A 0AA
Tel: 020 7219 7123 *Fax:* 020 7219 3483 *Email:* marcus.jones.mp@parliament.uk
Constituency: 13-17 Hollybush House, Bond Gate, Nuneaton, Warwickshire CV11 4AR
Tel: 024 7634 8482 *Fax:* 024 7634 8482 *Website:* www.marcusjones.org.uk

JONES, SUSAN ELAN
Clwyd South *(Majority 2,834)*

Opposition Whip

Born 1 June 1968; Daughter of Richard Jones, retired steelworks costs clerk, and Eirlys Jones, retired medical secretary.

Education: Grango Comprehensive School, Rhosllannerchrugog; Ruabon School Sixth Form; Bristol University (BA English 1989); Cardiff University (MA applied English language studies 1992); Welsh, some French, German and Japanese.

LABOUR

Non-political career: English teacher: Tomakomai English School, Japan 1990-91, Atsuma Board of Education, Japan 1992-94; Corporate development fundraiser, Muscular Dystrophy Campaign 1995-96; Fundraiser, USPG 1997-2002; Director, Caris Haringey 2002-05; Fundraising executive, Housing Justice 2005-10. Member, MSF Voluntary Sector branch 1996-.

Political career: Contested Surrey Heath 1997 general election. Member for Clwyd South since 6 May 2010 general election; PPS to Harriet Harman as Shadow Secretary of State for International Development 2010-11; Opposition Whip 2011-. *Select committees:* Member: Welsh Affairs 2010-12. Chair, Bristol University Labour Club 1986-87; Member, National Committee, Labour Students 1989-90. *Councils and public bodies:* London Borough of Southwark Council: Councillor 2006-09, Deputy Labour Group leader 2007-09.

Political interests: Charities, rural communities, economic development, Welsh language, crime.

Other: Member: Christian Socialist Movement 2006-, Church in Wales; Honorary Vice-President, Stiwt Theatre, Rhosllannerchrugog.

Recreations: Classical music.

Susan Elan Jones MP, House of Commons, London SW1A 0AA
Tel: 020 7219 0920 *Email:* susan.jones.mp@parliament.uk
Constituency: Enterprise Centre, Well Street, Cefn Mawr, Wrexham LL14 3AL
Tel: 01978 824288 *Website:* www.susanelanjones.co.uk

LABOUR

JOWELL, TESSA
Dulwich and West Norwood *(Majority 9,365)*

Tessa Jane Helen Douglas Jowell. Born 17 September 1947; Daughter of Dr Kenneth Palmer and Rosemary Palmer, radiographer; Married Roger Jowell 1970 (divorced 1977); married David Mills 1979 (1 son 1 daughter 3 stepchildren).

Education: St Margaret's School, Aberdeen; Aberdeen University (MA); Edinburgh University; Goldsmith's College, London University; French.

Non-political career: Child care officer, London Borough of Lambeth 1969-71; Psychiatric social worker, Maudsley Hospital 1972-74; Assistant director, MIND 1974-86; Director: Community care special action project, Birmingham 1987-90, Joseph Rowntree Foundation, Community Care Programme 1990-92; Senior visiting research fellow: Policy Studies Institute 1987-90, King's Fund Institute 1990-92; Visiting Fellow, Nuffield College, Oxford 1993-2003. Member: Unite, Amicus.

Political career: Contested Ilford North 1978 by-election and 1979 general election. Member for Dulwich 1992-97, for Dulwich and West Norwood 1997-2010, for Dulwich and West Norwood (revised boundary) since 6 May 2010 general election; Opposition Whip 1994-95; Opposition Spokesperson for: Women 1995-96, Health 1994-95, 1996-97; Minister of State: Department of Health (Minister for Public Health) 1997-99, Department for Education and Employment (Minister for Employment, Welfare to Work and Equal Opportunities) 1999-2001; Minister for Women 1999-2001; Department for Culture, Media and Sport: Secretary of State 2001-07: Minister for: Women 2005-06, the Olympics 2005-07, the Olympics and London; Paymaster General (also attending Cabinet, reporting to Prime Minister, based in Cabinet Office) 2007-08, the Olympics; Paymaster General 2008-10; Minister for the Cabinet Office 2009-10; Minister for London 2009-10; Shadow Minister for: the Cabinet Office 2010, 2011, London and the Olympics 2010-12. *Select committees:* Member: Social Security 1992, Health 1992-94. *Councils and public bodies:* Councillor, London Borough of Camden Council 1971-86; Vice-chair, then chair, Social Services Committee, Association of Metropolitan Authorities 1978-86; Central Council for Training and Education in Social Work (CCETSW) 1980s; Mental Health Act Commission 1985-90; Chair, Millennium Commission.

Political interests: Young people, political engagement; China, India, Italy.

Other: Governor, National Institute for Social Work 1985-97; Member, Olympic Board; Trustee: Amelia Ward Prize Fund, Tennis Foundation 2013; Vice-President, Royal Television Society 2013; Ditchley Park: Trustee 2011, Council of Management 2013; Member, Expert Resource Group, Havard School for Public Health, Ministerial Health Leaders' Forum 2013; Senior Fellow, Institute for Government 2012; Homestart; Magic Bus India. Freedom, London Borough of Southwark 2012. PC 1998; DBE 2012.

Publications: Various articles on social policy; Contributor, The Purple Book (Progress, 2011).

Recreations: Family, reading, walking.

Rt Hon Dame Tessa Jowell DBE MP, House of Commons, London SW1A 0AA
Tel: 020 7219 3409 *Fax:* 020 7219 2702 *Email:* jowellt@parliament.uk
Constituency: All correspondence via Westminster Office *Website:* www.tessajowell.net
Twitter: @jowellt

INDEPENDENT

JOYCE, ERIC
Falkirk *(Lab Majority 7,843)*

Eric Stuart Joyce. Born 13 October 1960; Son of late Leslie Joyce and Sheila McKay, née Christie; Married Rosemary Jones 1991 (twin daughters).

Education: Perth Academy; Stirling University (BA religious studies 1986); Royal Military Academy, Sandhurst 1987; Bath University (MA education 1994); Keele University (MBA education 1995).

Non-political career: Private, Black Watch Regiment 1978-81; Officer 1987-99. Commission for Racial Equality 1999-2000. Member, Unison.

Political career: Member for Falkirk West 21 December 2000 by-election to 2005, for Falkirk since 5 May 2005 general election; PPS: to Mike O'Brien as Minister of State: Foreign and Commonwealth Office 2003-04, Department of Trade and Industry 2004-05, to Margaret Hodge as Minister of State: Department for Work and Pensions 2005-06, Department of Trade and Industry 2006, to John Hutton as Secretary of State for: Work and Pensions 2006-07, Business, Enterprise and Regulatory Reform 2007-08, Defence 2008-09, to Bob Ainsworth as Secretary of State for Defence (resigned) 2009; Shadow Minister for Northern Ireland 2010. *Select committees:* Member: Scottish Affairs 2001-03, Procedure 2001-05, Public Accounts 2010, Joint Committee on Privacy and Injunctions 2011-12, Unopposed Bills (Panel) 2011-13. Labour Whip suspended February 2012; Resigned from Labour Party March 2012.

Political interests: Foreign affairs, international development (especially education issues), defence, trade and industry (especially oil and gas, GM crops), higher education, asylum and immigration; Argentina, China, Democratic Republic of Congo, Turkey, USA.

Other: Executive member, Fabian Society 1998-; Fellow, Industry and Parliament Trust 2004; Camelon Labour Club.

Publications: Arms and the Man – Renewing the Armed Services (Fabian Society, 1997); Now's the Hour: New Thinking for Holyrood (Fabian Society, 1999).

Recreations: Climbing, judo, most sports.

Eric Joyce MP, House of Commons, London SW1A 0AA
Tel: 020 7219 2779 *Fax:* 020 7219 2090 *Email:* eric.joyce.mp@parliament.uk
Constituency: 37 Church Walk, Denny FK6 6DF
Tel: 01324 823200 *Fax:* 01324 823200 *Email:* mcintyrem@parliament.uk
Website: www.ericjoyce.co.uk *Twitter:* @ericjoyce

KAUFMAN, GERALD Manchester Gorton *(Majority 6,703)*

Gerald Bernard Kaufman. Born 21 June 1930; Son of Louis and Jane Kaufman.

Education: Leeds Grammar School; The Queen's College, Oxford (MA philosophy, politics and economics 1953).

Non-political career: Assistant general secretary, Fabian Society 1954-55; Political staff, *Daily Mirror* 1955-64; Political correspondent, *New Statesman* 1964-65; Parliamentary press liaison officer, Labour Party 1965-70. Member: GMB, National Union of Journalists.

LABOUR

Political career: Contested Bromley 1955 and Gillingham 1959 general elections. Member for Ardwick 1970-83, for Manchester Gorton 1983-2010, for Manchester Gorton (revised boundary) since 6 May 2010 general election; Parliamentary Under-Secretary of State for the Environment 1974-75; Department of Industry 1975-79: Parliamentary Under-Secretary 1975, Minister of State 1975-79; Opposition Frontbench Spokesperson for the Environment 1979-80; Shadow Environment Secretary 1980-83; Shadow Home Secretary 1983-87; Shadow Foreign Secretary 1987-92; Member Speaker's Committee on the Electoral Commission 2010-; Longest serving Labour MP June 2010-. *Select committees:* Member: Liaison 1992-2005; Chair: National Heritage 1992-97, Culture, Media and Sport 1997-2005; Member: Speaker's Committee on the Electoral Commission 2010-. Member, Labour Party National Executive 1991-92. *Councils and public bodies:* Member, Royal Commission on Lords Reform 1999-2000.

Other: Member, Fabian Society. PC 1978; Hilal-i-Pakistan 1999; Kt 2004. President, Gorton and District Sunday Football League.

Publications: Co-author, How to Live Under Labour (1964); Editor, The Left (1966); To Build the Promised Land (1973); How to Be a Minister (1980, 1997); Editor, Renewal (1983); My Life in the Silver Screen (1985); Inside the Promised Land (1986); Meet Me In St Louis (1994).

Recreations: Cinema, theatre, opera, concerts, travel.

Rt Hon Sir Gerald Kaufman MP, House of Commons, London SW1A 0AA
Tel: 020 7219 5145 *Fax:* 020 7219 6825 *Email:* kaufmang@parliament.uk
Constituency: No constituency office
Tel: 0161-248 0073 *Fax:* 0161-248 0073 *Email:* searsb@parliament.uk

KAWCZYNSKI, DANIEL Shrewsbury and Atcham *(Majority 7,944)*

PPS to David Jones as Secretary of State for Wales

Daniel Robert Kawczynski. Born 24 January 1972; Son of Leonard and Halina Kawczynski; Married Kate Lumb 2000 (divorced) (1 daughter).

Education: St George's College, Weybridge; Stirling University (BA business studies with French 1994); French, Polish.

Non-political career: Sales account manager telecommunications, BT, Cable & Wireless, Xerox 1994-2004; Owner/joint manager, equestrian centre and livery stables.

CONSERVATIVE

Political career: Contested Ealing Southall 2001 general election. Member for Shrewsbury and Atcham since 5 May 2005 general election; PPS to: Jim Paice as Minister of State for Agriculture and Food 2010-12, Richard Benyon as Parliamentary Under-Secretary of State (Natural Environment and Fisheries), Department for Environment, Food and Rural Affairs 2010-12, David Jones as Secretary of State for Wales 2012-. *Select committees:* Member: Environment, Food and Rural Affairs 2005-07, Justice 2007-09, International Development 2008-10. Chairman Stirling University Conservative Association 1991-93.

Political interests: Agriculture, foreign affairs; Libya, Mauritania, Saudi Arabia.

Other: Honorary President Shrewsbury Parkinson's Society.

Recreations: Golf, vegetable and fruit growing.

Daniel Kawczynski MP, House of Commons, London SW1A 0AA
Tel: 020 7219 6249 *Fax:* 020 7219 1047 *Email:* kawczynskid@parliament.uk
Constituency: Unit 1, Benbow Business Park, Harlescott Lane, Shrewsbury, Shropshire SY1 3FA
Tel: 01743 466477 *Fax:* 01743 465774 *Email:* mail@daniel4shrewsbury.co.uk
Website: www.daniel4shrewsbury.co.uk

KEELEY, BARBARA   Worsley and Eccles South *(Majority 4,337)*

Barbara Mary Keeley. Born 26 March 1952; Daughter of Edward and Joan Keeley; Married Colin Huggett 1985.

Education: Mount St Mary's College, Leeds; Salford University (BSc politics and contemporary history 1994).

Non-political career: IBM UK Limited: Systems programmer 1983, Field systems engineer 1983-87, Field systems engineering manager 1987-89; Consultant and adviser in community regeneration 1989-94, 1995-2001; Area manager, Business in the Community North West 1994-95; Consultant, Princess Royal Trust for Carers 2001-05; Research on policy issues related to primary health care for Princess Royal Trust 2003-05. GMB.

LABOUR

Political career: Member for Worsley 2005-10, for Worsley and Eccles South since 6 May 2010 general election; PPS: to Jim Murphy: as Parliamentary Secretary, Cabinet Office 2006, as Minister of State, Department for Work and Pensions 2006-07, to Harriet Harman as Minister for Women 2007-08; Assistant Government Whip 2008-09; Deputy Leader of the House of Commons 2009-10; Shadow Deputy Leader of the House of Commons 2010; Shadow Minister for: Health 2010, Communities and Local Government 2010-11; PPS to Ed Balls as Shadow Chancellor of the Exchequer 2011-. *Select committees:* Member: Constitutional Affairs 2005-06, Finance and Services 2006-10, Health 2011-, Joint Committee on the Draft Care and Support Bill 2013. PLP Women's Committee: Honorary Secretary 2006-07, Chair 2007-08. *Councils and public bodies:* Trafford Borough Council: Councillor 1995-2004, Vice-chair, social services 1995-97, Cabinet member 1997-99, 2000-04; Director, Trafford's pathfinder Children's Trust 2002-04.

Political interests: Health and social care, carers, women in sport; European Union, Israel/Middle East, Tibet.

Other: Member: Amnesty International, Fabian Society.

Publications: Co-author: Carers Speak Out (2002), Primary Carers (2003).

Recreations: Jogging, swimming, live music.

Barbara Keeley MP, House of Commons, London SW1A 0AA
Tel: 020 7219 8025 *Fax:* 020 7219 3847 *Email:* keeleyb@parliament.uk
Constituency: First Floor, 37 Manchester Road, Walkden, Greater Manchester M28 3NS
Tel: 0161-799 4159 *Fax:* 0161-799 5829 *Website:* www.barbarakeeley.co.uk
Twitter: @KeeleyMP

KELLY, CHRIS   Dudley South *(Majority 3,856)*

Born 1978.

Education: Wolverhampton Grammar School; Oxford Brookes University (BA history and politics 1999); Business School, Imperial College London (MBA 2003).

Non-political career: Oxford University Officer Training Corp 1996-98. Keltruck Ltd, West Bromwich 1999-2002: Marketing executive 1999-2000, Marketing manager 2000-02; Parliamentary assistant to Michael Howard MP 2004-05; Keltruck Ltd, West Bromwich 2004-: Non-executive director 2004-05, Marketing director 2006-.

CONSERVATIVE

Political career: Member for Dudley South since 6 May 2010 general election. *Select committees:* Member: European Scrutiny 2010-. Member, Conservative Party 1996-.

Other: Executive officer, International Young Democrat Union 2004-05.

Recreations: Sport, travel.

Chris Kelly MP, House of Commons, London SW1A 0AA
Tel: 020 7219 7053
Constituency: No constituency office publicised
Tel: 01384 211041 *Email:* office@chriskelly.mp *Website:* www.dudleyconservatives.com
www.chriskelly.mp

KENDALL, LIZ
Leicester West *(Majority 4,017)*

Shadow Minister for Care and Older People

Elizabeth Louise Kendall. Born 1971.

Education: Watford Grammar School for Girls; Cambridge University (history).

Non-political career: Special adviser to Harriet Harman MP: as Shadow Secretary of State for Social Security 1996-97, as Secretary of State for Social Security and Minister for Women 1997-98; Research fellow, King's Fund; Associate director, health, social care and children's early years, Institute for Public Policy Research; Director, Maternity Alliance; Special adviser to Patricia Hewitt MP as Secretary of State for: Trade and Industry and Minister for Women and Equality 2004-05, Health 2005-07; Director, Ambulance Service Network 2007-09. Member, Unite.

LABOUR

Political career: Member for Leicester West since 6 May 2010 general election; Shadow Minister for Health (Care and Older People 2011-) 2010-. *Select committees:* Member: Education 2010. Chair, PLP Departmental Group for Education 2010. Member: Labour Party 1992-, Co-operative Party.

Political interests: Employment, care for the elderly, early years services, NHS.

Other: Member, Fabian Society; Vice-chair, Progress.

Publications: Contributor, The Purple Book (Progress, 2011).

Liz Kendall MP, House of Commons, London SW1A 0AA
Tel: 020 7219 3000 *Email:* liz.kendall.mp@parliament.uk
Constituency: 42 Narborough Road, Leicester LE3 0BQ
Tel: 0116-204 4980 *Fax:* 0116-204 4989 *Website:* www.lizkendall.org *Twitter:* @leicesterliz

KENNEDY, CHARLES
Ross, Skye and Lochaber *(Majority 13,070)*

Charles Peter Kennedy. Born 25 November 1959; Son of Ian Kennedy, crofter, and late Mary MacVarish MacEachen; Married Sarah Gurling 2002 (separated 2010) (1 son).

Education: Lochaber High School, Fort William; Glasgow University (MA politics, philosophy and English 1982); Indiana University (1982-83).

Non-political career: President, Glasgow University Union 1980-81; Winner, British Observer Mace Debating Tournament 1982; Journalist with BBC Highland, Inverness 1982.

LIBERAL DEMOCRAT

Political career: Member (SDP 1983-92, Liberal Democrat since 1992) for Ross, Cromarty and Skye 1983-97, for Ross, Skye and Inverness West 1997-2005, for Ross, Skye and Lochaber since 5 May 2005 general election; Alliance Spokesman for Social Security 1987; SDP Spokesman for: Scotland and Social Security 1987-88, Trade and Industry 1988-89; Liberal Democrat Spokesman for: Health 1989-92, European Union Affairs 1992-97, Agriculture, Fisheries, Food and Rural Affairs 1997-99; Leader, Liberal Democrat Party 1999-2006. *Select committees:* Member: Standards and Privileges 1997-99, Works of Art 2011-. Chair: Glasgow University Social Democratic Club 1979-80, SDP Scotland 1986-88; President, Liberal Democrat Party 1990-94; Former member, Liberal Democrat: Federal Executive Committee, Policy Committee; Leader 1999-2006. *Councils and public bodies:* Rector, Glasgow University 2008-.

Political interests: Scotland, social policy, broadcasting, European Union.

Other: Vice-President, Liberal International 2006-; President, European Movement 2008-; Member, Scottish Crofters Foundation; Highland Hospice. Rector, Glasgow University 2008, 2011-. Doctorate, Glasgow University 2001. *The Spectator*: Member to Watch 1989, Politician of the Year 2004. PC 1999; National Liberal.

Publications: The Future of Politics (2000); Associate editor, The House Magazine 2006-.

Recreations: Reading, writing, music, swimming, golf, journalism, broadcasting.

Rt Hon Charles Kennedy MP, House of Commons, London SW1A 0AA
Tel: 020 7219 0356 *Fax:* 020 7219 4881 *Email:* kennedyc@parliament.uk
Constituency: 5 MacGregor's Court, Dingwall, Ross and Cromarty IV15 9HS
Tel: 01349 862152 *Fax:* 01349 866829 *Email:* charles@highlandlibdems.org.uk
Website: www.highlandlibdems.org.uk www.charleskennedy.org.uk
Twitter: @charles_kennedy

LABOUR

KHAN, SADIQ
Tooting *(Majority 2,524)*

Shadow Lord Chancellor and Secretary of State for Justice; Shadow Minister for London

Sadiq Aman Khan. Born 8 October 1970; Son of late Amanullah Ahmed Khan and Sehrun Nisa Khan; Married Saadiya Ahmad 1994 (2 daughters).

Education: Ernest Bevin Secondary Comprehensive, London; University of North London (LLB 1992); College of Law, Guildford (Law Society Finals 1993); Urdu, Hindi.

Non-political career: Christian Fisher Solicitors: Trainee solicitor 1993-95, Solicitor 1995-98, Partner 1998-2000; Visiting lecturer, University of North London and London Metropolitan University 1998-2004; Equity partner, Christian Fisher Khan Solicitors 2000-02; Equity partner and co-founder, Christian Khan Solicitors 2002-04. Member: GMB, Unison, CWU group of Labour MPs.

Political career: Member for Tooting 2005-10, for Tooting (revised boundary) since 6 May 2010 general election; PPS to Jack Straw as Leader of the House of Commons 2007; Assistant Government Whip 2007-08; Parliamentary Under-Secretary of State, Department for Communities and Local Government 2008-09; Minister of State, Department for Transport (attending cabinet) 2009-10; Shadow Secretary of State for Transport 2010; Shadow Lord Chancellor and Secretary of State for Justice (with responsibility for political and constitutional reform) 2010-; Shadow Minister for London 2013-. *Select committees:* Member: Public Accounts 2005-07. Chair, PLP Departmental Committee for Home Affairs 2006-07. Member, Labour Party NEC 2012-. *Councils and public bodies:* Wandsworth Borough Council: Councillor 1994-2006, Deputy leader, Labour group 1996-2001, Honorary Alderman; Governor: Fircroft Primary School 1994-, Gatton Primary School 2004-.

Political interests: Social justice, crime, international affairs, public services.

Other: Founder, Human Rights Lawyers Association; Vice-chair: Law Society 1993-, Legal Action Group 1999-2004; Chair: Liberty 2001-04, Legal affairs committee, Muslim Council of Britain 2004-05; Patron, Progress 2005-; Vice-chair: Fabian Society, Executive Committee 2006-, Friends of the Earth; Chair, Fabian Society 2009-; Patron, Polka Theatre Company; Fellow, Industry and Parliament Trust; Windsor Fellowship 1992; Esso Law Bursary 1992; Society of Black Lawyers Bursary 1992; Sweet & Maxwell Law Prize 1993; *The Spectator* Newcomer of Year 2005; *Muslim News* Award for Citizenship 2008. PC 2009.

Publications: Challenging Racism (Lawrence and Wishart, 2003); Police Misconduct: Legal Remedies (Legal Action Group, 2005); Fairness not Favours – How to reconnect with British Muslims (Fabian Society, 2009); Articles in various publications on legal matters and policing.

Recreations: Playing and watching sports, cinema, family, friends, local community.

Rt Hon Sadiq Khan MP, House of Commons, London SW1A 0AA
Tel: 020 7219 6967 *Fax:* 020 7219 6477 *Email:* sadiqkhanmp@parliament.uk
Constituency: 273 Balham High Road, London SW17 7BD
Tel: 020 8682 2897 *Fax:* 020 8682 3416 *Email:* office@tootinglabour.org.uk
Website: www.sadiqkhan.org.uk *Twitter:* @SadiqKhan

CONSERVATIVE

KIRBY, SIMON
Brighton Kemptown *(Majority 1,328)*

Simon Gerard Kirby. Born 22 December 1964; Son of Mrs J.D. Kirby and Mr G.L. Kirby; Married Elizabeth 1992 (2 daughters 4 sons).

Education: Hastings Grammar School; Open University (BSc mathematical modelling 1995).

Non-political career: Managing director, C-Side Ltd 1993-2001.

Political career: Member for Brighton Kemptown since 6 May 2010 general election; PPS to Hugh Robertson as Minister of State for Sport and Tourism, Department for Culture, Media and Sport 2012-13. *Select committees:* Member: Environmental Audit 2010-11, Business, Innovation and Skills 2010-12, Administration 2011-12. Member, Executive, 1922 Committee May-September 2012. Vice-chair, Bexhill and Battle Conservatives 2005-06. *Councils and public bodies:* Councillor: East Sussex County Council 1992-93, 2005-09, Brighton Borough Council 1995-97, Brighton and Hove City Council 1996-99, Mid Sussex District Council 1999-2001.

Political interests: Business, older people, HIV and AIDS; South America, China, USA.

Other: Carlton Club.

Recreations: Brighton and Hove Albion Football Club, Whitehawk Football Club, Brighton Rugby Club.

Simon Kirby MP, House of Commons, London SW1A 0AA
Tel: 020 7219 7024 *Email:* simon.kirby.mp@parliament.uk
Constituency: 370 South Coast Road, Telscombe Cliffs, East Sussex BN10 7ES
Tel: 01273 589178 *Email:* info@simonkirby.org *Website:* www.simonkirby.org
Twitter: @SimonKirbyMP

CONSERVATIVE

KNIGHT, GREG
East Yorkshire *(Majority 13,486)*

Gregory Knight. Born 4 April 1949; Son of Albert Knight, company director, and Isabel Knight, née Bell.

Education: Alderman Newton's Grammar School, Leicester; College of Law, London; College of Law, Guildford (solicitor 1973).

Non-political career: Solicitor 1973-89, 1997-2001; Business consultant 1997-2001.

Political career: Member for Derby North 1983-97. Contested Derby North 1997 general election. Member for Yorkshire East 2001-10, for East Yorkshire (revised boundary) since 6 May 2010 general election; PPS to David Mellor as Minister of State: Foreign and Commonwealth Office 1987-88, Department of Health 1988-89; Assistant Government Whip 1989-90; Government Whip 1990-93; Government Deputy Chief Whip 1993-96; Minister of State Department of Trade and Industry 1996-97; Deputy Shadow Leader of the House 2002-03; Shadow Minister for: Culture, Media and Sport 2003, Environment and Transport 2003-05, Transport 2005; Government Whip (Vice-Chamberlain of HM Household) 2012-13. *Select committees:* Member: Broadcasting 1993-96, Finance and Services 1993-96, Modernisation of the House of Commons 2001-03, 2005-10, Procedure: Member 2005, Chair 2005-12; Member: Liaison 2006-12, Administration 2006-10, Standards and Privileges 2009-10, Reform of the House of Commons 2009-10, Joint Committee on the Draft Detention of Terrorist Suspects (Temporary Extension) Bills 2011, Finance and Services 2013-. Chair, Leicester and Leicestershire Young Conservatives 1972-73; Vice-chair, Conservative Parliamentary Candidates Association 1997-2001. *Councils and public bodies:* Councillor: Leicester City Council 1976-79, Leicestershire County Council 1977-83.

Political interests: Consumer issues, information technology, music, arts, home affairs; USA.

Other: British-American Parliamentary Group: Executive Committee Member 2001-08, Treasurer 2008-; The Law Society. PC 1995; Bridlington Conservative.

Publications: Co-author, Westminster Words (1988); Honourable Insults (1990); Parliamentary Sauce (1993); Right Honourable Insults (1998); Naughty Graffiti (2005); Dishonourable Insults (2011).

Recreations: Classic and vintage cars, music, member parliamentary rock band 'MP4'.

Rt Hon Greg Knight MP, House of Commons, London SW1A 0AA
Tel: 020 7219 8417 *Email:* sothcottt@parliament.uk
Constituency: 18 Exchange Street, Driffield, East Yorkshire YO25 6LJ
Tel: 0845 090 0203 *Email:* secretary@gregknight.com
Website: www.eyorksconservatives.com www.gregknight.com *Twitter:* @gregknightmp

CONSERVATIVE

KWARTENG, KWASI
Spelthorne *(Majority 10,019)*

Kwasi Alfred Addo Kwarteng. Born 26 May 1975; Son of Alfred Kwasi Kwarteng, economist, and Charlotte Kwarteng, barrister; Single.

Education: Eton College (King's Scholar; Newcastle Scholar); Trinity College, Cambridge (BA classics and history 1996, MA; PhD British history 2000); Kennedy Scholar, Harvard University, USA 1997; Birkbeck College, London (Post-graduate Certificate economics 2000); Certificate investment management 2005; Basic Arabic, French, German, Italian.

Non-political career: Financial analyst: Investment banking 2000-04, Fund management 2004-06; Freelance journalist and author 2006-.

Political career: Contested Brent East 2005 general election. Member for Spelthorne since 6 May 2010 general election. *Select committees:* Member: Transport 2010-13.

Political interests: Economy and finance, transport; Africa, Middle East.

Other: Chair, Bow Group 2005-06; Trustee, History of Parliament Trust.

Publications: Author: Ghosts of Empire (Bloomsbury, 2011), Gridlock Nation (Biteback, 2011); Co-author: (with Chris Skidmore MP), After the Coalition (Biteback, 2011), (with Priti Patel MP, Dominic Raab MP, Chris Skidmore MP and Elizabeth Truss MP) Britannia Unchained: Global Lessons for Growth and Prosperity (Palgrave Macmillan, 2012).

Recreations: Music, foreign languages, travel.

Kwasi Kwarteng MP, House of Commons, London SW1A 0AA
Tel: 020 7219 4017 *Fax:* 020 7219 5852 *Email:* kwasi.kwarteng.mp@parliament.uk
Constituency: Spelthorne Conservative Association, 55 Cherry Orchard, Staines, Middlesex TW18 2SQ
Tel: 01784 453544 *Website:* www.kwart2010.com *Twitter:* @kwasikwarteng

LAING, ELEANOR
Epping Forest *(Majority 15,131)*

Eleanor Fulton Laing. Born 1 February 1958; Daughter of late Matthew Pritchard and Betty Pritchard, née McFarlane; Married Alan Laing 1983 (divorced 2003) (1 son).

Education: St Columba's School, Kilmacolm, Renfrewshire; Edinburgh University (BA 1982; LLB) (First woman Union President); French.

Non-political career: Practised law in Edinburgh, City of London and industry 1983-89; Special adviser to John MacGregor MP: as Secretary of State for Education 1989-90, as Leader of the House of Commons 1990-92, as Secretary of State for Transport 1992-94.

CONSERVATIVE

Political career: Contested Paisley North 1987 general election. Member for Epping Forest 1997-2010, for Epping Forest (revised boundary) since 6 May 2010 general election; Opposition Whip 1999-2000; Opposition Spokesperson for: Constitutional Affairs and Scotland 2000-01, Education and Skills 2001-03; Shadow Minister for: Children 2003, Women 2004-07; Shadow Secretary of State for Scotland 2005; Shadow Minister for: Women and Equality 2005-07, Justice 2007-10; Special Representative to Gibraltar 2010-; Member: Speakers' Working Group on All-Party Groups 2011-12, Speaker's Committee on the Electoral Commission 2012-.
Select committees: Member: Education and Employment 1997-98, Education and Employment (Employment Sub-Committee) 1997-98, Environment, Transport and Regional Affairs 1998-99, Environment, Transport and Regional Affairs (Transport Sub-Committee) 1998-99, Office of the Deputy Prime Minister 2004-05, Office of the Deputy Prime Minister (Urban Affairs Sub-Committee) 2004-05, Political and Constitutional Reform 2010-, Joint Committee on Human Rights 2010, Joint Committee on the Draft House of Lords Reform Bill 2011-12, Joint Committee on Parliamentary Privilege 2013, Scottish Affairs 2013-. Chair, Conservative Party Committee for Home Affairs and Constitution. Chairman, Society of Conservative Lawyers.

Political interests: Education, transport, economic policy, constitution, devolution; Australia, Gibraltar, New Zealand, Uganda, USA.

Recreations: Theatre, music, golf.

Eleanor Laing MP, House of Commons, London SW1A 0AA
Tel: 020 7219 2086 *Fax:* 020 7219 0079 *Email:* eleanor.laing.mp@parliament.uk
Constituency: Thatcher House, 4 Meadow Road, Loughton, Essex IG10 4HX
Tel: 020 8508 6608 *Fax:* 020 8508 8099 *Email:* efca@btinternet.com
Website: www.eleanorlaing.com

LAMB, NORMAN
North Norfolk *(Majority 11,626)*

Minister of State for Care and Support, Department of Health

Norman Peter Lamb. Born 16 September 1957; Son of late Hubert Lamb, professor of climatology, and Beatrice Lamb, née Milligan, nurse; Married Mary Green 1984 (2 sons).

Education: George Abbot School, Guildford, Surrey; Wymondham College, Wymondham, Norfolk; Leicester University (LLB 1980); Qualified solicitor 1984.

Non-political career: Norwich City Council: Trainee solicitor 1982-84, Senior assistant solicitor 1984-85; Steele and Company Norfolk: Solicitor 1986-87, Partner 1987-2001; Consultant 2001-06.

LIBERAL DEMOCRAT

Political career: Contested North Norfolk 1992 and 1997 general elections. Member for North Norfolk 2001-10, for North Norfolk (revised boundary) since 6 May 2010 general election; Liberal Democrat Spokesperson for: International Development 2001-02, the Treasury 2002-05,

Shadow Secretary of State for Trade and Industry 2005-06; Chief of Staff to Sir Menzies Campbell as Leader of the Liberal Democrats 2006; Liberal Democrat Shadow Secretary of State for Health 2006-10; Chief Parliamentary and Political Adviser to the Deputy Prime Minister 2010-12; PPS to Nick Clegg as Deputy Prime Minister, Lord President of the Council 2010-12; Assistant Whip 2010-12; Parliamentary Under-Secretary of State (Minister for Employment Relations, Consumer and Postal Affairs), Department for Business, Innovation and Skills 2012; Minister of State for Care and Support, Department of Health 2012-. *Select committees:* Member: Treasury 2003-05, Treasury (Treasury Sub-Committee) 2003-10. Chair, Tottenham Liberals 1980-81; Norwich South Liberals 1985-87. *Councils and public bodies:* Norwich City Council: Councillor 1987-91, Group leader 1989-91.

Political interests: Health, employment, social affairs, constitution, environment, international development; South Africa, USA.

Other: Norfolk Air Ambulance; Benjamin Foundation; Norfolk and Norwich Association for the Blind; Wells Hospital; About with Friends. President's Award, Royal College of Psychiatrists 2011. Norwich City Football Club.

Publications: Remedies in the Employment Tribunal (Sweet and Maxwell, 1998); The NHS: a liberal blueprint (CentreForum).

Recreations: Walking, football, cycling.

Norman Lamb MP, House of Commons, London SW1A 0AA
Tel: 020 7219 0542 *Fax:* 020 7219 1963 *Email:* lambn@parliament.uk
Constituency: Unit 4, North Walsham Garden Centre, Nursery Drive, Norwich Road,
North Walsham, Norfolk NR28 0DR
Tel: 01692 403752 *Website:* www.normanlamb.org.uk *Twitter:* @normanlamb

---

LABOUR

LAMMY, DAVID   Tottenham *(Majority 16,931)*

David Lindon Lammy. Born 19 July 1972; Son of Rosalind Lammy, council officer; Married Nicola Green 2005 (2 children).

Education: The King's School, Peterborough; School of Oriental and African Studies, London University (LLB 1993); Harvard Law School, USA (LLM 1997).

Non-political career: Barrister, 3 Serjeants Inn, Philip Naughton QC 1994-96; Attorney, Howard Rice Nemerovsky Canada Falk & Rabkin 1997-98; Barrister, D J Freeman 1998-2000. Member, Amicus branch of Unite.

Political career: Member for Tottenham since 22 June 2000 by-election; PPS to Estelle Morris as Secretary of State for Education and Skills 2001-02; Parliamentary Under-Secretary of State: Department of Health 2002-03, Department for Constitutional Affairs 2003-05, Department for Culture, Media and Sport 2005-07, Department for Innovation, Universities and Skills (DIUS) (Skills) 2007-08; Minister of State (Higher Education and Intellectual Property) DIUS/Department for Business, Innovation and Skills 2008-10; Shadow Minister for Higher Education 2010. *Select committees:* Member: Public Administration 2001, Procedure 2001, Ecclesiastical Committee 2010-, Works of Art 2011-, Joint Committee on the Draft Defamation Bill 2011. Member: Society of Labour Lawyers, Christian Socialist Movement. *Councils and public bodies:* Member: Archbishops' Council 1999-2002, London Assembly 2000.

Political interests: Health, Treasury (regeneration), arts and culture, education, international development, gambling, intellectual property, sport; Africa, Latin America, Caribbean, USA.

Other: ActionAid: Trustee 2000-06, Honorary Ambassador 2006-; Patron: Peace Alliance, boys2MEN, Haringey Shed, Oxford Access Scheme, Into University, London Nightline; Honorary president, Haringey Borough Swimming Club; Honorary vice-president, Haringey Advisory Group on Alcohol; President, Tottenham Community Festival; Ovarian Cancer Action; Member, Fabian Society. Honorary Doctorate of Law, University of East London 2004. PC 2008; The Honourable Society of Lincoln's Inn.

Publications: Leading Together (2002); Out of the Ashes (2011).

Recreations: Film, live music, Tottenham Hotspur FC.

Rt Hon David Lammy MP, House of Commons, London SW1A 0AA
Tel: 020 7219 0767 *Fax:* 020 7219 0357 *Email:* lammyd@parliament.uk
Constituency: No constituency office *Website:* www.davidlammy.co.uk
Twitter: @DavidLammy

CONSERVATIVE

LANCASTER, MARK
Milton Keynes North *(Majority 8,961)*

Government Whip

John Mark Lancaster. Born 12 May 1970; Son of Revd Ron Lancaster, MBE and Kath Lancaster; Married Katherine Reader 1995 (divorced); (1 daughter).

Education: Kimbolton School, Huntingdon; Buckingham University (BSc business studies 1991); Exeter University (MBA 1994); French, Nepali.

Non-political career: Officer Royal Engineers 1988-90; Lt Colonel Royal Engineers (TA) 1990-. Director, Kimbolton Fireworks Ltd 1990-2005.

Political career: Contested Nuneaton 2001 general election. Member for Milton Keynes North East 2005-10, for Milton Keynes North since 6 May 2010 general election; Opposition Whip 2006-07; Shadow Minister for International Development 2007-10; PPS to Andrew Mitchell as Secretary of State for International Development 2010-12; Government Whip 2012-. *Select committees:* Member: Office of the Deputy Prime Minister 2005-06, Defence 2006, Communities and Local Government 2008-09, International Development 2009-10, Armed Forces Bill 2011. *Councils and public bodies:* Huntingdon District Council: Councillor 1995-99, Chair, Leisure Committee 1996-99.

Political interests: Defence, international development, commerce; China, India, Nepal, USA.

Other: Vice-chair: British Fireworks Association 1999-2006, MK SNAP 2004-; Patron, Willen Hospice 2006-; Parliamentary adviser, Royal Society of Chemistry. Member, Worshipful Company of Fanmakers. Hon DSc, Buckingham University 2007. TD 2002; United and Cecil Club; Army & Navy. House of Commons and House of Lords Cricket Club; Associate member, MCC.

Publications: Contributor, Fireworks Principles and Practice (Chemical Publishing, 1999).

Recreations: Cricket, football, collecting classic British motorcycles.

Mark Lancaster TD MP, House of Commons, London SW1A 0AA
Tel: 020 7219 8414 *Fax:* 020 7219 6685 *Email:* officeofmarklancaster@parliament.uk
Constituency: Suite 102, Milton Keynes Business Centre, Foxhunter Drive, Linford Wood MK14 6GD
Tel: 01908 686830 *Fax:* 01908 686831 *Website:* www.lancaster4mk.com
Twitter: @MarkLancasterMP

CONSERVATIVE

LANSLEY, ANDREW
South Cambridgeshire *(Majority 7,838)*

Leader of the House of Commons, Lord Privy Seal

Andrew David Lansley. Born 11 December 1956; Son of Thomas Lansley, OBE, and Irene Lansley; Married Marilyn Biggs 1985 (divorced 2001) (3 daughters); married Sally Low 2001 (1 daughter 1 son).

Education: Brentwood School, Essex; Exeter University (BA politics 1979) (President, Guild of Students 1977-78).

Non-political career: Department of [Trade and] Industry 1979-87: Private secretary to Norman Tebbit as Secretary of State for Trade and Industry 1984-85; Principal private secretary to Norman Tebbit as Chancellor of the Duchy of Lancaster 1985-87; British Chambers of Commerce 1987-90: Policy director 1987-89, Deputy director-general 1989-90; Director Conservative Research Department 1990-95; Director Public Policy Unit 1995-97.

Political career: Member for South Cambridgeshire 1997-2010, for South Cambridgeshire (revised boundary) since 6 May 2010 general election; Member Shadow Cabinet 1999-2001: Shadow Minister for the Cabinet Office and Policy Renewal 1999-2001; Shadow Chancellor of the Duchy of Lancaster 1999-2001; Member Shadow Cabinet 2003-10: Shadow Secretary of State for Health 2003-10; Secretary of State for Health 2010-12; Leader of the House of Commons, Lord Privy Seal 2012-; Member: House of Commons Commission 2012-, Speaker's Committee for the Independent Parliamentary Standards Authority 2012-, Public Accounts Commission 2012-. *Select committees:* Member: Health 1997-98, Trade and Industry 2001-04. Vice-chair, Conservative Party (with responsibility for policy renewal) 1998-99.

Political interests: Health, local and regional government, economic policy, trade and industry; Egypt, France, Germany, Israel, Japan, South Africa, USA.

Other: Patron: ASPIRE (Spinal injury), Headway (Acquired Brain injury); Member, National Union Executive Committee 1990-95. CBE 1996; PC 2010.

Publications: A Private Route (1988); Co-author Conservatives and the Constitution (1997); Do the right thing – Why Conservatives must achieve greater fairness and diversity in candidate selection (2002); Extending the Reach (2003).

Recreations: Spending time with my children, films, biography, history, cricket.

Rt Hon Andrew Lansley CBE MP, House of Commons, London SW1A 0AA
Tel: 020 7219 3000 *Email:* lansleya@parliament.uk
Constituency: 153 St Neots Road, Hardwick, Cambridge CB3 7QJ
Tel: 01954 212707 *Website:* www.andrewlansley.co.uk

LATHAM, PAULINE
Mid Derbyshire *(Majority 11,292)*

Pauline Elizabeth Latham. Born 4 February 1948; Married Derek Latham 1968 (1 daughter 2 sons).

Education: Bramcote Hills Technical Grammar School.

Non-political career: Proprietor, Humble plc 1976-87; Director, Michael St Development 1982-95; Founder member and chair, Grant Maintained Schools Advisory Committee -2004.

Political career: Contested Broxtowe 2001 general election. Member for Mid Derbyshire since 6 May 2010 general election. *Select committees:* Member: International Development 2010-. Secretary, 1922 Sub-committee on Foreign Affairs, Defence and International Development. Contested East Midlands 1999 and 2004 European Parliament elections. *Councils and public bodies:* Councillor: Derbyshire County Council 1987-2002, Derby City Council 1992-96, 1998-2010; Mayor of Derby 2007-08; Governor and chair of governors, Ecclesbourne School.

CONSERVATIVE

Political interests: Education, international development, health (Cancer and Type 1 Diabetes); Africa.

Other: Vice-chair, Commonwealth Parliamentary Association (UK Branch) 2011-; Free the Children: Trustee, Board Member; Patron, Women's Work. OBE 1995.

Recreations: Horse riding, walking, travel.

Pauline Latham OBE MP, House of Commons, London SW1A 0AA
Tel: 020 7219 7110 *Email:* pauline.latham.mp@parliament.uk
Constituency: The Old Station, Station Road, Spondon, Derby DE21 7NE
Tel: 01332 676679 *Website:* www.paulinelatham.co.uk *Twitter:* @Pauline_Latham

LAVERY, IAN
Wansbeck *(Majority 7,031)*

Born 6 January 1963; Son of John Lavery, miner, and Patricia Lavery; Married Hilary (2 sons).

Education: Ashington High School; New College, Durham (HNC mining engineering).

Non-political career: Miner, National Coal Board: Lynemouth Colliery 1980, Ellington Colliery 1980-92; National Union of Mine Workers: General Secretary, Northumberland Area 1992-2002, National President 2002-. National Union of Mineworkers: Member 1980-, Representative, Ellington Colliery 1986-92; Member, GMB.

Political career: Member for Wansbeck since 6 May 2010 general election; PPS to Harriet Harman: as Deputy Leader and Chair, Labour Party; Deputy Leader of the Opposition; Shadow Secretary of State for International Development 2010-11, as Shadow Deputy Prime Minister, Chair, Labour Party, and Shadow Secretary of State for Culture, Media and Sport 2011-12. *Select committees:* Member: Northern Ireland Affairs 2010-11, Regulatory Reform 2010-, Energy and Climate Change 2010-, Joint Committee on Draft Deregulation Bill 2013-. Member, Ashington Town branch, Labour Party; Executive committee member, Wansbeck CLP. *Councils and public bodies:* Former councillor, Wansbeck District Council.

LABOUR

Political interests: Local regeneration, employment, energy, climate change, poverty, internationalism, sport; Foreign and Commonwealth affairs.

Other: International Energy Miners Organisation; Chair: Ashington Community Football Club, Hirst Welfare Centre, Ashington Group – The Pitmen Painters; Trustee: Northumberland Aged Miners Homes Association, North East Area Miners Trust, Woodhorn Museum, North East CISWO Trust.

Recreations: History, walking, horse and greyhound racing, Newcastle United FC, all sports.

Ian Lavery MP, House of Commons, London SW1A 0AA
Tel: 020 7219 3000 *Email:* ian.lavery.mp@parliament.uk
Constituency: 7 Esther Court, Wansbeck Business Park, Ashington, Northumberland NE63 8AP
Tel: 01670 852494 *Fax:* 01670 818262 *Website:* www.ianlavery.co.uk *Twitter:* @IanLaveryMP

LIBERAL DEMOCRAT

LAWS, DAVID
Yeovil *(Majority 13,036)*

Minister of State, Cabinet Office and Department for Education

David Anthony Laws. Born 30 November 1965; Son of D.A. Laws and Mrs M.T. Davies.

Education: St George's College, Weybridge; King's College, Cambridge (Scholar BA economics 1987).

Non-political career: Vice-president, JP Morgan and Company 1987-92; Barclays de Zoete Wedd Ltd 1992-94: Managing director, Head US Dollar and Sterling treasuries 1992-94; Member, Investment Committee, Stanhope Capital 2011-.

Political career: Contested Folkestone and Hythe 1997 general election. Member for Yeovil 2001-10, for Yeovil (revised boundary) since 6 May 2010 general election; Liberal Democrat: Spokesman for Defence 2001-02; Shadow Chief Secretary to the Treasury 2002-05; Shadow Secretary of State for: Work and Pensions 2005-07, Children, Schools and Families 2007-10; Chief Secretary to the Treasury 2010; Minister of State: Department for Education 2012-, Cabinet Office 2012-. *Select committees:* Member: Treasury 2001-03, Treasury (Treasury Sub-Committee) 2001-03, Joint Committee on the Draft Financial Services Bill 2011-12. Liberal Democrat Parliamentary Party: Economics adviser 1994-97, Director of Policy and Research 1997-99; Chair, Manifesto Working Group 2013-.

Political interests: Economy, education, pensions, public service reform; Egypt, Ethiopia, France, Jordan.

Other: Winner 1984 Observer Mace National Schools Debating Competition. PC 2010.

Publications: Co-editor (with Paul Marshall), The Orange Book (2004); Author, 22 Days in May – The Birth of the Lib Dem-Conservative Coalition (2010).

Recreations: Running, reading, desert regions.

Rt Hon David Laws MP, House of Commons, London SW1A 0AA
Tel: 020 7219 8413 *Fax:* 020 7219 8188 *Email:* lawsd@parliament.uk
Constituency: 5 Church Street, Yeovil, Somerset BA20 1HB
Tel: 01935 425025/01935 423284 *Fax:* 01935 433652 *Email:* enquiries@yeovil-libdems.org.uk
Website: www.yeovil-libdems.org.uk

LAB/CO-OP

LAZAROWICZ, MARK
Edinburgh North and Leith *(Majority 1,724)*

Marek Jerzy Lazarowicz. Born 8 August 1953; Son of Jerzy Witold Lazarowicz and Ivy Lazarowicz, née Eacott; Married Caroline Elizabeth Johnston 1993 (1 daughter 3 sons).

Education: St Benedicts School, London; St Andrews University (MA moral philosophy and medieval history 1976); Edinburgh University (LLB 1992); Diploma Legal Practice 1993.

Non-political career: Organiser, Scottish Education and Action for Development 1978-80, 1982-86; General secretary, British Youth Council Scotland 1980-82; Advocate 1996-. TGWU 1978-.

Political career: Contested Edinburgh Pentlands 1987 and 1992 general elections. Member for Edinburgh North and Leith 2001-05, for Edinburgh North and Leith (revised boundary) since 5 May 2005 general election; PPS to David Cairns as Minister of State, Scotland Office 2007-08; Prime Minister's Special Representative on Carbon Trading 2008-10; Shadow Minister for International Development 2010-11. *Select committees:* Member: Scottish Affairs 2001-03, Regulatory Reform 2002-05, Environment, Food and Rural Affairs 2002-05, Modernisation of the House of Commons 2005-10, Environmental Audit 2007-, Joint Committee on the Draft Climate Change Bill 2007. Vice-chair, PLP Departmental Committee for the Cabinet Office 2002-03; Chair, PLP Departmental Committee for Parliamentary Affairs 2006-10. Vice-convener, Scottish Parliament Cross-Party Tackling Debt Group 2007-11. Member, Co-operative Party; Chair, Scottish Labour Party 1989-90; Member: Socialist Environment and Resources Association (SERA), SERA Parliamentary Group; Chair, Co-operative Party Parliamentary Group 2008-09. *Councils and public bodies:* City of Edinburgh District Council: Councillor 1980-96, Council Leader 1986-93; Councillor, City of Edinburgh Council 1999-2001.

Political interests: Environment, transport, consumer issues, co-operative issues, constitution, finance, economy, small businesses, international development.

Publications: Co-author The Scottish Parliament: An Introduction (T and T Clark, 1st edition 1999, 2nd edition 2000, 3rd edition 2004); Various articles, papers and pamphlets on political and legal issues.

Recreations: Jogging, walking, cycling.

Mark Lazarowicz MP, House of Commons, London SW1A 0AA
Tel: 020 7219 8222 *Fax:* 020 7219 1761 *Email:* mark.lazarowicz.mp@parliament.uk
Constituency: 5 Croall Place, Edinburgh EH7 4LT
Tel: 0131-557 0577 *Fax:* 0131-557 5759 *Website:* www.marklazarowicz.org.uk
Twitter: @marklazarowicz

LEADSOM, ANDREA
South Northamptonshire *(Majority 20,478)*

Andrea Jacqueline Leadsom. Born 13 May 1963; Daughter of Judy Crompton and Richard Salmon; Married Ben Leadsom 1993 (2 sons 1 daughter).

Education: Tonbridge Girls Grammar; Warwick University (political science 1984); French.

Non-political career: Various roles, BZW 1987-93; Financial institutions director, Barclays Bank 1991-97; Managing director, De Putron (funds management) 1997-99; Head of corporate governance, Invesco Perpetual 1999-2009.

CONSERVATIVE

Political career: Contested Knowsley South 2005 general election. Member for South Northamptonshire since 6 May 2010 general election. *Select committees:* Member: Treasury 2010-. *Councils and public bodies:* Councillor, South Oxfordshire District Council 2003-07.

Political interests: Economy, early years development, bank reform.

Other: Oxford Parent Infant Project: Chair 2001-09, Trustee; Launching Northamptonshire Parent Infant Project (NORPIP). Newcomer of the Year, *The Spectator* awards 2012.

Andrea Leadsom MP, House of Commons, London SW1A 0AA
Tel: 020 7219 7149 *Fax:* 020 7219 4045 *Email:* andrea.leadsom.mp@parliament.uk
Constituency: 78 St George's Avenue, Northampton NN2 6JF
Tel: 01604 859721 *Website:* www.andrealeadsom.com *Twitter:* @andrealeadsom

LEE, JESSICA
Erewash *(Majority 2,501)*

PPS to Dominic Grieve as Attorney General

Jessica Katherine Lee. Born 17 April 1976.

Education: Loughborough High School for Girls; Royal Holloway, University of London (BA history and politics 1997); College of Law, London (CPE 1999; BVC 2000).

Non-political career: Armed Forces Parliamentary Scheme 2010-. Called to the Bar, Middle Temple 2000; 42 Bedford Row, London 2001-08, St Mary's Chamber, Nottingham 2008-10.

CONSERVATIVE

Political career: Contested Camberwell and Peckham 2005 general election. Member for Erewash since 6 May 2010 general election; PPS to Dominic Grieve as Attorney General 2010-. *Select committees:* Member: Justice 2010. Member, Conservative Party 1991-.

Political interests: Child protection, academy schools, SMEs, manufacturing, justice; Gibraltar, Malta, USA.

Recreations: Cooking, reading, theatre.

Jessica Lee MP, House of Commons, London SW1A 0AA
Tel: 020 7219 7067 *Email:* jessica.lee.mp@parliament.uk
Constituency: 73 Derby Road, Long Eaton, Derbyshire NG10 1LU
Tel: 0115-972 2419 *Website:* www.jessicaleemp.com *Twitter:* @JessicaLeeMP

LEE, PHILLIP
Bracknell *(Majority 15,704)*

Phillip James Lee. Born 28 September 1970; Single.

Education: Sir William Borlase's Grammar School, Marlow; King's College, London (BSc human biology 1993); Keble College, Oxford (MSc biological anthropology 1994); St Mary's Hospital Medical School, Imperial College, London (MBBS 1999).

Non-political career: St Mary's Hospital, London; Wexham Park Hospital, Slough; Stoke Mandeville Hospital, Aylesbury; GP, Thames Valley.

CONSERVATIVE

Political career: Contested Blaenau Gwent 2005 general election. Member for Bracknell since 6 May 2010 general election; Board member, Parliamentary Office of Science and Technology (POST). *Select committees:* Member: Energy and Climate Change 2010-, Administration 2010-12. Executive member, Conservative Friends of Bangladesh; Vice-chair, Conservative Middle East Council. *Councils and public bodies:* Councillor, Beaconsfield Town Council 2001-02.

Political interests: Science, energy security policy, space industry; Middle East, Norway.

Other: Member, General Medical Council. Old Grumblers Cricket Club; Marlow Waterski Club.

Recreations: Skiing, football, rugby union.

Dr Phillip Lee MP, House of Commons, London SW1A 0AA
Tel: 020 7219 1270 *Email:* phillip.lee.mp@parliament.uk
Constituency: 10 Milbanke Court, Milbanke Way, Western Road, Bracknell,
Berkshire RG12 1RP
Tel: 01344 868894 *Email:* phillip@phillip-lee.com *Website:* www.phillip-lee.com
Twitter: @DrPhillipLeeMP

LIBERAL DEMOCRAT

LEECH, JOHN
Manchester Withington *(Majority 1,850)*

Born 11 April 1971; Son of Rev. John and Jean Leech; Partner Catherine Kilday.

Education: Manchester Grammar School; Loreto College, Manchester; Brunel University (BSc history and politics 1994).

Non-political career: Assistant restaurant manager, McDonald's 1995-97; Customer relations, RAC Ltd 1998-2005.

Political career: Member for Manchester Withington 2005-10, for Manchester Withington (revised boundary) since 6 May 2010 general election; Liberal Democrat Shadow Minister for Transport 2006-10. *Select committees:* Member: Transport 2005-13, Culture, Media and Sport 2013-. Chair, Liberal Democrat Parliamentary Party Committee on Culture, Media and Sport 2012-. *Councils and public bodies:* Manchester City Council: Councillor 1998-2008, Deputy leader, Liberal Democrat Group 2003-05.

Political interests: Housing, planning, transport.

Recreations: Amateur dramatics, football.

John Leech MP, House of Commons, London SW1A 0AA
Tel: 020 7219 1534 *Fax:* 020 7219 0442 *Email:* john.leech.mp@parliament.uk
Constituency: 8 Gawsworth Avenue, East Didsbury, Manchester M20 5NF
Tel: 0161-434 3334 *Fax:* 0161-434 3206 *Email:* leechj@parliament.uk
Website: www.johnleechmp.wordpress.com *Twitter:* @johnleechmcr

CONSERVATIVE

LEFROY, JEREMY
Stafford *(Majority 5,460)*

Jeremy John Elton Lefroy. Born 30 May 1959; Married Janet Mackay 1985 (1 son 1 daughter).

Education: Highgate School, London; King's College, Cambridge (BA classics 1980); German, Swahili.

Non-political career: Armed Forces Parliamentary Scheme 2010-11, 2011-12. Foreman, Ford Motor Company 1980-81; Trainee accountant, Arthur Andersen 1981-84; Finance manager/ director, Cowan de Groot plc 1984-86; Finance manager, EDM Schluter Ltd 1986-88; General manager/managing director, African Coffee Company Ltd, Tanzania 1989-2000; Director and part-owner, African Speciality Products Ltd 2000-.

Political career: Contested Newcastle-under-Lyme 2005 general election. Member for Stafford since 6 May 2010 general election. *Select committees:* Member: International Development 2010-. Contested West Midlands 2004 European Parliament election. Treasurer, Newcastle-under-Lyme Conservative Association 2003-06. *Councils and public bodies:* Newcastle-under-Lyme Borough Council: Councillor 2003-07, Shadow finance and resources spokesman 2004-06, Cabinet member for finance and resources 2006-07.

Political interests: Sustainable development and enterprise, urban regeneration, environment, small business, health; Kenya, Switzerland, Tanzania, Uganda.

Other: Director, Tanzania Coffee Board 1997-99; Chair: Tanzania Coffee Association 1997-99, Parliamentary Network of the World Bank and IMF; Trustee, Donald Mackay Trust 1987-; Member and Trustee, Conservative Christian Fellowship 2002-; Chair, Equity for Africa 2003-; ACA 1984; Institute of Chartered Accountants in England and Wales 1984-.

Recreations: Playing and writing music, hill-walking, sport.

Jeremy Lefroy MP, House of Commons, London SW1A 0AA
Tel: 020 7219 7154 *Fax:* 020 7219 4186 *Email:* jeremy.lefroy.mp@parliament.uk
Constituency: Unit 15, Pearl House, Anson Court, Staffordshire Technology Park, Beaconside, Stafford ST18 0GB
Tel: 01785 252477 *Website:* www.jeremylefroymp.co.uk *Twitter:* @JeremyLefroyMP

LEIGH, EDWARD

Gainsborough *(Majority 10,559)*

Edward Julian Egerton Leigh. Born 20 July 1950; Son of late Sir Neville Leigh, former Clerk to the Privy Council; Married Mary Goodman 1984 (3 sons 3 daughters).

Education: Oratory School, Reading, Berkshire; French Lycee, London; Durham University (BA history 1972) (Union President); French.

Non-political career: Member, Conservative Research Department 1973-75; Principal correspondence secretary to Margaret Thatcher as Leader of the Opposition 1976-77; Barrister, Inner Temple 1977-.

CONSERVATIVE

Political career: Contested Teesside, Middlesbrough October 1974 general election. Member for Gainsborough and Horncastle 1983-97, for Gainsborough 1997-2010, for Gainsborough (revised boundary) since 6 May 2010 general election; PPS to John Patten as Minister of State, Home Office 1990; Parliamentary Under-Secretary of State, Department of Trade and Industry 1990-93; Public Accounts Commission: Member -2010, 2011, Chair 2011-; Financial adviser to the Treasury 2010-11. *Select committees:* Member: Social Security 1997-2000; Public Accounts: Member 2000-01, Chair 2001-10; Member: Liaison 2001-10, Chairmen's Panel/Panel of Chairs 2010-, Members' Expenses 2011-. Vice-chair, Conservative Party Committees for: Foreign and Commonwealth Affairs 1997-2001, Social Security 1997-2001; Chair, Conservative Party Committee for Foreign Affairs. Member, governing council, Conservative Christian Fellowship; Chair, Cornerstone Group 2004-. *Councils and public bodies:* Councillor: Richmond Borough Council 1974-78, GLC 1977-81; Chair National Council for Civil Defence 1979-83; Director Coalition For Peace Through Security 1981-83.

Political interests: Defence, foreign affairs, agriculture, families.

Other: Delegate, Parliamentary Assembly of the Council of Europe; Fellow, Industry and Parliament Trust 1983; Veteran member, Honourable Artillery Company; Vice-chairman, The Catholic Union of Great Britain; Fellow Institute of Arbitrators 1999-; CAFOD; Malteser International. Knight of Honour and Devotion Sovereign Military Order of Malta; Kt 2013.

Publications: Right Thinking (1982); Onwards from Bruges (1989); Choice and Responsibility – The Enabling State (1990); The Nation that Forgot God (2009); Monastery of the Mind (2012).

Recreations: Walking, reading, swimming.

Sir Edward Leigh MP, House of Commons, London SW1A 0AA
Tel: 020 7219 6480 *Email:* edward.leigh.mp@parliament.uk
Constituency: 1 Rasen Hub, 20 Union Street, Market Rasen LN8 3AA
Website: www.edwardleigh.org.uk *Twitter:* @Eleigh_MP

LESLIE, CHARLOTTE

Bristol North West *(Majority 3,274)*

Charlotte Ann Leslie. Born 11 August 1978; Daughter of Ian Leslie and Jane Leslie.

Education: Badminton School, Bristol; Millfield School, Somerset; Balliol College, Oxford (BA classics 2001).

Non-political career: BBC television and independent companies 2002-04; Former adviser to David Willetts MP 2006-07; Editor, *Crossbow* 2006-08; Former education adviser, The Young Foundation 2008; Public affairs officer, National Autistic Society 2008; Education associate, Portland PR 2009.

CONSERVATIVE

Political career: Member for Bristol North West since 6 May 2010 general election. *Select committees:* Member: Education 2010-, Health 2013-. Former policy adviser, Public Services Policy Review Report, Conservative Party.

Political interests: Education, health, Big Society and volunteering, sport, EU Referendum, beer and pubs; Africa (sub-Saharan), China, Middle East.

Other: Member, Bow Group.

Publications: More Good School Places (Policy Exchange, 2005); The Invisible Children (Bow Group, 2007); SEN – The Truth About Inclusion (Bow Group, 2008); Towards a Royal College of Teaching (2013).

Recreations: Surfing, writing, drawing, swimming, boxing training.

Charlotte Leslie MP, House of Commons, London SW1A 0AA
Tel: 020 7219 7026 *Fax:* 020 7219 0921 *Email:* charlotte.leslie.mp@parliament.uk
Constituency: 184 Henleaze Road, Bristol BS9 4NE
Tel: 0117-962 9427 *Fax:* 0117-923 8153 *Website:* www.charlotteleslie.com
Twitter: @CLeslieMP

LAB/CO-OP

LESLIE, CHRIS

Nottingham East *(Majority 6,969)*

Shadow Chief Secretary to the Treasury

Christopher Michael Leslie. Born 28 June 1972; Son of Michael and Dania Leslie; Married Nicola (1 daughter).

Education: Bingley Grammar School; Leeds University (BA politics and parliamentary studies 1994; MA industrial and labour studies 1996).

Non-political career: Office administrator 1994-96; Political research assistant 1996-97; Director, New Local Government Network 2005-10. Member: TGWU, GMB.

Political career: Member for Shipley 1997-2005. Contested Shipley 2005 general election. Member for Nottingham East since 6 May 2010 general election; PPS to Lord Falconer as Minister of State, Cabinet Office 1998-2001; Parliamentary Secretary, Cabinet Office 2001-02; Parliamentary Under-Secretary of State for: Local Government and the Regions, Office of the Deputy Prime Minister 2002-03, Department for Constitutional Affairs 2003-05; Shadow Financial Secretary 2010-13; Shadow Chief Secretary to the Treasury 2013-. *Select committees:* Member: Public Accounts 1997-98. Member, Labour Party Departmental Committees for: Environment, Transport and the Regions 1997-2001, the Treasury 1997-2001. *Councils and public bodies:* Councillor, Bradford City Council 1994-98.

Political interests: Industrial policy, economic policy, environment, local and regional government; Kashmir.

Other: Trustee: Consumer Credit Counselling Service, Credit Action.

Recreations: Travel, tennis, cinema, art.

Chris Leslie MP, House of Commons, London SW1A 0AA
Tel: 020 7219 3000 *Email:* chris.leslie@parliament.uk
Constituency: Ground Floor, 12 Regent Street, Nottingham NG1 5BQ
Tel: 0115-711 7666 *Email:* josie.tanvir@parliament.uk *Website:* www.chrisleslie.org
Twitter: @ChrisLeslieMP

CONSERVATIVE

LETWIN, OLIVER

West Dorset *(Majority 3,923)*

Minister for Government Policy, Cabinet Office

Born 19 May 1956; Son of late Professor William Letwin and late Dr Shirley Robin Letwin; Married Isabel Davidson 1984 (1 son 1 daughter).

Education: Eton College; Trinity College, Cambridge (BA history 1978, MA; PhD philosophy 1982); London Business School; French, Italian.

Non-political career: Visiting fellow (Procter Fellow), Princeton University, USA 1980-81; Research fellow, Darwin College, Cambridge 1981-82; Special adviser to Sir Keith Joseph as Secretary of State for Education 1982-83; Special adviser, Prime Minister's Policy Unit 1983-86; N. M. Rothschild & Son, Merchant Bank: Manager 1986, Assistant director 1987, Director 1991-2003, Managing director 2003, Non-executive director 2005-09.

Political career: Contested Hackney North 1987 and Hampstead and Highgate 1992 general elections. Member for West Dorset since 1 May 1997 general election; Opposition Spokesperson for Constitutional Affairs, Scotland and Wales 1998-99; Shadow Financial Secretary 1999-2000; Shadow Chief Secretary to the Treasury 2000-01; Shadow Home Secretary 2001-03; Shadow Secretary of State for Economic Affairs and Shadow Chancellor of the Exchequer 2003-05; Shadow Secretary of State for Environment, Food and Rural Affairs 2005; Cabinet Office: Minister of State 2010-12, Minister for Government Policy 2012-. *Select committees:* Member: Deregulation 1998-99, European Standing Committee B 1998. Member, Conservative Disability Group; Chairman: Conservative Policy Review 2005-10, Conservative Research Department 2005-10; Conservative Policy Forum (CDF) 2010-.

Other: Fellow, Royal Society of Arts; Joseph Weld Hospice. PC 2002.

Publications: Ethics, Emotion and the Unity of the Self (1985); Aims of Schooling (1986); Privatising the World (1989); Drift to Union (1989); The Purpose of Politics (1999); Plus articles and reviews in learned and popular journals.

Recreations: Skiing, sailing, tennis, reading, writing books.

Rt Hon Oliver Letwin MP, House of Commons, London SW1A 0AA
Tel: 020 7219 3000 *Email:* letwino@parliament.uk
Constituency: Chapel House, Dorchester Road, Maiden Newton, Dorset DT2 0BG
Tel: 01308 456891/01300 321188 *Fax:* 01300 321233
Email: anthonystanley@westdorsetconservatives.com *Website:* www.oliverletwinmp.com

LEWELL-BUCK, EMMA　　　South Shields *(Majority 6,505)*

Born 8 November 1978; Daughter of Linda and David Lewell; Married Simon Buck.

Education: St Joseph's Comprehensive; Northumbria University (BA politics and media studies); Durham University (MSW social work).

Non-political career: Child protection social worker. GMB.

Political career: Member for South Shields since 2 May 2013 by-election. *Select committees:* Member: Environment, Food and Rural Affairs 2013-. Member, Co-operative. *Councils and public bodies:* South Tyneside Council: Councillor 2004-13, Lead Member for Adult Social Care and Support Services.

LABOUR

Emma Lewell-Buck MP, House of Commons, London SW1A 0AA
Tel: 020 7219 4468 *Email:* emma.lewell-buck.mp@parliament.uk
Constituency: Ede House, 143 Westoe Road, South Shields, Tyne and Wear NE33 3PD
Tel: 0191-427 1240 *Website:* www.southshieldslabour.org.uk *Twitter:* @EmmaLewellBuck

LEWIS, BRANDON　　　Great Yarmouth *(Majority 4,276)*

Parliamentary Under-Secretary of State, Department for Communities and Local Government

Brandon Kenneth Lewis. Born 20 June 1971; Son of Jack and Lynn Lewis; Married Justine Rappolt 1999 (1 son 1 daughter).

Education: Forest School, Snaresbrook; Buckingham University (BSc economics 1993; LLB 1996); King's College, London (LLM commercial law 1998); Inns of Court, School of Law (Bar Vocational Course).

CONSERVATIVE

Non-political career: Director: Woodlands Schools Ltd 2001-, i5 Consulting Ltd -2010.

Political career: Contested Sherwood 2001 general election. Member for Great Yarmouth since 6 May 2010 general election; Parliamentary Under-Secretary of State, Department for Communities and Local Government 2012-. *Select committees:* Member: Regulatory Reform 2010-12, Work and Pensions 2010-12. *Councils and public bodies:* Brentwood Borough Council: Councillor 1998-2009, Leader 2004-09.

Political interests: Tourism, local government, coastal erosion, business, transport; Italy, USA.

Other: Fellowship, British Triathlon Federation; Member, Institute of Directors 2001-07; Member, Lords Taverner's; Carlton Club. Born2Tri; Hemsby Cricket Club.

Recreations: Running, cycling, swimming, reading.

Brandon Lewis MP, House of Commons, London SW1A 0AA
Tel: 020 7219 7231 *Email:* justine.duggan@parliament.uk
Constituency: Sussex Road Business Centre, Sussex Road, Gorleston-on-Sea, Norfolk NR31 6PF
Tel: 01493 652928 *Email:* office@brandonlewis.org *Website:* www.brandonlewis.co
Twitter: @BrandonLewis

LEWIS, IVAN　　　Bury South *(Majority 3,292)*

Shadow Secretary of State for Northern Ireland

Born 4 March 1967; Son of Joe Lewis and late Gloria Lewis; Married Juliette Fox 1990 (divorced) (2 sons).

Education: William Hulme Grammar School; Stand College; Bury Further Education College.

Non-political career: Co-ordinator, Contact Community Care Group 1986-89; Community care manager, Jewish Social Services 1989-92; Chief executive, Manchester Jewish Federation 1992-97. Member, Unite.

LABOUR

Political career: Member for Bury South 1997-2010, for Bury South (revised boundary) since 6 May 2010 general election; PPS to Stephen Byers as Secretary of State for Trade and Industry 1999-2001; Parliamentary Under-Secretary of State, Department for Education and Skills 2001-05: (for Young People and Learning 2001-02, for Adult Learning and Skills 2002, for Young People and Adult Skills 2002-03, for Skills and Vocational Education 2003-05); Economic Secretary, HM Treasury 2005-06; Parliamentary Under-Secretary of State: Department of Health (Care Services) 2006-08, Department for International Development 2008-09; Minister of State, Foreign and Commonwealth Office 2009-10; Shadow Minister for Foreign and Commonwealth Office 2010; Shadow Secretary of State for: Culture, Media and Sport 2010-11, International Development 2011-13, Northern Ireland 2013-. *Select committees:* Member: Deregulation 1997-99, Health 1999. Chair, Bury South Labour Party 1991-96; Vice-chair, Labour Friends of Israel 1997-2001. *Councils and public bodies:* Councillor, Bury Metropolitan Borough Council 1990-98.

Political interests: Health, crime, education, international development, culture, media and sport; Democratic Republic of the Congo, Middle East, Rwanda, USA.

Other: Founder member, Co-ordinator and Chair, Contact Community Care Group 1986-92; Chair, Bury MENCAP 1989-92; Trustee, Holocaust Educational Trust.

Publications: Contributor, The Purple Book (Progress, 2011).

Recreations: Walking, reading, supporting Manchester City FC.

Ivan Lewis MP, House of Commons, London SW1A 0AA
Tel: 020 7219 2609 *Email:* lewisi@parliament.uk
Constituency: 381 Bury New Road, Prestwich, Manchester M25 1AW
Tel: 0161-773 5500 *Fax:* 0161-773 7959 *Email:* ivanlewis@burysouth.fsnet.co.uk
Website: www.ivanlewis.org.uk *Twitter:* @IvanLewis_MP

CONSERVATIVE

LEWIS, JULIAN   New Forest East *(Majority 11,307)*

Julian Murray Lewis. Born 26 September 1951; Son of late Samuel Lewis and late Hilda Lewis.

Education: Dynevor School, Swansea; Balliol College, Oxford (BA philosophy and politics, MA 1977); St Antony's College, Oxford (DPhil strategic studies 1981); Doctoral research (strategic studies) 1975-77, 1978-81.

Non-political career: Seaman, HM Royal Naval Reserve 1979-82. Secretary, Campaign for Representative Democracy 1977-78; Research director and director, Coalition for Peace Through Security 1981-85; Director, Policy Research Associates 1985-; Deputy director, Conservative Research Department 1990-96; Visiting senior research fellow, Centre for Defence Studies, Department of War Studies, King's College, London.

Political career: Contested Swansea West 1983 general election. Member for New Forest East 1997-2010, for New Forest East (revised boundary) since 6 May 2010 general election; Opposition Whip 2001-02; Shadow Minister for: Defence 2002-04, 2005-10, the Cabinet Office 2004-05; Member Intelligence and Security Committee 2010-. *Select committees:* Member: Welsh Affairs 1998-2001, Defence 2000-01. Secretary, Conservative Parliamentary Defence Committee 1997-2001; Vice-chair, Conservative Parliamentary Committees for: European Affairs 2000-01, Foreign and Commonwealth Affairs 2000-01; Member Executive, 1922 Committee 2001. Treasurer, Oxford University Conservative Association 1971; Secretary, Oxford Union 1972.

Political interests: Defence, security, foreign affairs, European affairs; Western Europe, Central and Eastern Europe, Russia.

Other: Joint organiser of campaign against militant infiltration of the Labour Party 1977-78. Trench Gascoigne prize winner 2005, 2007; Royal College of Defence Studies prize winner 2006; Athenæum, Honorary president Totton Conservative.

Publications: Changing Direction: British Military Planning for Post-War Strategic Defence 1942-1947 (1988, 2003, 2008); Who's Left? An Index of Labour MPs and Left-Wing Causes 1985-1992 (1992); Labour's CND Cover-Up (1992); The Liberal Democrats: The Character of Their Politics (1993); What's Liberal? Liberal Democrat Quotations and Facts (1996); Racing Ace – The Fights and Flights of 'Kink' Kinkead DSO, DSC*, DFC* (2011).

Recreations: History, fiction, films, music, photography.

Dr Julian Lewis MP, House of Commons, London SW1A 0AA
Tel: 020 7219 4179
Constituency: 3 The Parade, Southampton Road, Cadnam, Hampshire SO40 2NG
Tel: 023 8081 4817 *Website:* www.julianlewis.net

CONSERVATIVE

LIDDELL-GRAINGER, IAN   Bridgwater and West Somerset *(Majority 9,249)*

Ian Richard Peregrine Liddell-Grainger. Born 23 February 1959; Son of late David Liddell-Grainger, farmer, and Ann Grainger; Married Jill Nesbitt 1985 (1 son 2 daughters).

Education: Millfield School, Somerset; South of Scotland Agricultural College, Edinburgh (National Certificate agriculture 1978).

Non-political career: Major Fusiliers TA. Family farm, Berwickshire 1980-85; Managing director, property management and development companies group 1985-2000.

Political career: Contested Torridge and Devon West 1997 general election. Member for Bridgwater 2001-10, for Bridgwater and West Somerset since 6 May 2010 general election. *Select committees:* Member: Public Administration 2001-10, Scottish Affairs 2002-05, Environment, Food and Rural Affairs 2003-05, Crossrail Bill 2006-07, Environmental Audit 2007-10, Joint Committee on Statutory Instruments 2010-, Works of Art 2011-. Contested Tyne and Wear 1994 European Parliament election. Member, Conservative Agricultural Forum 1992-97; President, Tyne Bridge Conservative Association 1993-96. *Councils and public bodies:* Councillor: Tynedale District Council 1989-95, Northern Area Council 1992-95.

Political interests: Business, economy, defence, rural affairs, farming, taxation, education, health, energy; Africa especially South Africa, Hong Kong, Singapore, Switzerland, USA, Vietnam.

Other: Member, Executive Committee: Commonwealth Parliamentary Association, Inter-Parliamentary Union, British Group; RNLI; Macmillans; BIBIC; Help for Heroes.

Recreations: Walking, travel, family, gardening, vigorous debate.

Ian Liddell-Grainger MP, House of Commons, London SW1A 0AA
Tel: 020 7219 8149 *Email:* ianlg@parliament.uk
Constituency: 16 Northgate, Bridgwater, Somerset TA6 3EU
Tel: 01278 458383 *Website:* www.liddellgrainger.org.uk

LIDINGTON, DAVID

Aylesbury *(Majority 12,618)*

Minister of State, Foreign and Commonwealth Office

David Roy Lidington. Born 30 June 1956; Son of Roy and Rosa Lidington; Married Helen Parry 1989 (4 sons).

Education: Haberdashers' Aske's School, Hertfordshire; Sidney Sussex College, Cambridge (MA history; PhD).

Non-political career: British Petroleum 1983-86; Rio Tinto Zinc 1986-87; Special adviser to Douglas Hurd MP: as Home Secretary 1987-89, as Foreign Secretary 1989-90; Senior consultant, Public Policy Unit 1991-92.

CONSERVATIVE

Political career: Contested Vauxhall 1987 general election. Member for Aylesbury since 9 April 1992 general election; Sponsored Chiropractors Act 1994; PPS to: Michael Howard as Home Secretary 1994-97, William Hague as Leader of the Opposition 1997-99; Opposition Spokesperson for Home Affairs 1999-2001; Shadow Financial Secretary 2001-02; Shadow Minister for Agriculture and the Fisheries 2002; Shadow Secretary of State for: Environment, Food and Rural Affairs 2002-03, Northern Ireland 2003-07; Shadow Minister for Foreign and Commonwealth Affairs 2007-10; Minister of State, Foreign and Commonwealth Office 2010-. *Select committees:* Member: Education 1992-96. Chair, International Office and Conservatives Abroad -2010.

Other: PC 2011; Aylesbury Conservative Club.

Recreations: History, choral singing, reading.

Rt Hon David Lidington MP, House of Commons, London SW1A 0AA
Tel: 020 7219 3432 *Fax:* 020 7219 2564 *Email:* david.lidington.mp@parliament.uk
Constituency: 100 Walton Street, Aylesbury, Buckinghamshire HP21 7QP
Tel: 01296 482102 *Fax:* 01296 398481 *Email:* office@aylesburyconservatives.com
Website: www.davidlidington.co.uk *Twitter:* @DLidington

LILLEY, PETER

Hitchin and Harpenden *(Majority 15,271)*

Peter Bruce Lilley. Born 23 August 1943; Son of Arnold Lilley and Lilian Lilley, née Elliott; Married Gail Ansell 1979.

Education: Dulwich College, London; Clare College, Cambridge (BA natural sciences and economic sciences 1965); French.

Non-political career: Economic adviser in developing countries 1966-72; Investment adviser on North Sea oil and other energy industries 1972-84; Partner, W Greenwell & Co 1979-86; Director: Great Western Resources Ltd 1985-87, Greenwell Montague Stockbrokers 1986-87 (head, oil

CONSERVATIVE

investment department), JP Morgan Claverhouse Investment Trust 1997-2008, Idox plc 2002-, Melchior Japan Investment Trust 2006-10; Non-executive director and vice-chairman, Tethys Petroleum Ltd 2006-.

Political career: Contested Haringey, Tottenham October 1974 general election. Member for St Albans 1983-97, for Hitchin and Harpenden 1997-2010, for Hitchin and Harpenden (revised boundary) since 6 May 2010 general election; Joint PPS to: Lord Bellwin as Minister of State and William Waldegrave as Parliamentary Under-Secretary of State, Department of Environment 1984, Nigel Lawson, as Chancellor of the Exchequer 1984-87; Economic Secretary to the Treasury 1987-89; Financial Secretary to the Treasury 1989-90; Secretary of State for: Trade and Industry 1990-92, Social Security 1992-97; Member, Shadow Cabinet and Shadow Chancellor of the Exchequer 1997-98; Deputy Leader of the Opposition (with overall responsibility for development of party policy) 1998-99. *Select committees:* Chair: Joint Committee on the Draft Financial Services Bill 2011-12; Member: Energy and Climate Change 2012-. Chairman, Conservative Party Committee for Finance 1997-98. Consultant director, Conservative Research Department 1979-83; Contested Leadership of the Conservative Party June 1997; Chair, Globalisation and Global Poverty Policy Group 2006-07; Member, Policy Advisory Board 2013-. *Councils and public bodies:* Member, School of Management Advisory Board, Southampton University 2002-12.

Political interests: Economic policy, European Union, education, race relations; Central Asia, France.

Other: Trustee, Parliamentary Contributory Pension Fund; Chair: House of Commons Members Fund, Bow Group 1973-75; Stairways (Mencap) Harpenden. Honorary LLD, University of Hertfordshire. PC 1990; Carlton, Beefsteak.

Publications: You Sincerely Want to Win? – Defeating Terrorism in Ulster (1972); Lessons for Power (1974); Co-author Delusions of Income Policy (1977); Contributor End of the Keynesian Era (1980); Thatcherism, the Next Generation (1989); The Mais Lecture Benefits and Costs: Securing the Future of the Social Security (1993); Patient Power (Demos, 2000); Common Sense on Cannabis (Social Market Foundation, 2001); Taking Liberties (Adam Smith Institute, 2002); Save Our Pensions (Social Market Foundation, 2003); Identity Crisis (Bow Group, 2004); Too Much of a Good Thing (Centre for Policy Studies, 2005); Tony Duke of York (Bow Group, 2006); In It Together – Report of Commission on Global Poverty (Conservative Party, 2007); Paying for Success (Policy Exchange, 2008).

Recreations: Mending ancient walls.

Rt Hon Peter Lilley MP, House of Commons, London SW1A 0AA
Tel: 020 7219 4577 *Fax:* 020 7219 3840 *Email:* lilleyp@parliament.uk
Constituency: Riverside House, 1 Place Farm, Wheathampstead, Hertfordshire AL4 8SB
Tel: 01582 834344 *Fax:* 01582 834884 *Email:* feedback@peterlilley.co.uk
tory_herts@btconnect.com *Website:* www.peterlilley.co.uk *Twitter:* @PeterLilleyMP

LIBERAL DEMOCRAT

LLOYD, STEPHEN
Eastbourne *(Majority 3,435)*

Stephen Anthony Christopher Lloyd. Born 15 June 1957; Son of late John Lloyd, shipping director, and late Nuala Lloyd, nurse; Married Patricia 1993 (divorced 2001); Partner Cherine Markill.

Education: St George's College, Weybridge.

Non-political career: Commodity broker, Cominco UK Ltd 1977-80; Actor 1981-82; Proprietor, Radio Production Company 1983-90; Membership and campaigns manager, Hearing Concern 1990-92; Freelance campaigns and business development co-ordinator, various leading charities 1992-98; Business development director and head of diversity services, Grass Roots Group plc 1998-2005; Freelance business development consultant, including Grass Roots Group, Federation of Small Business 2005-10.

Political career: Contested Beaconsfield 2001 and Eastbourne 2005 general elections. Member for Eastbourne since 6 May 2010 general election. *Select committees:* Member: Work and Pensions 2010-. Chair, Liberal Democrat Parliamentary Party Committee on Northern Ireland 2012-. Maidenhead Liberal Democrats: Chair 2000-02, Membership secretary, Chilterns region 2000-02.

Political interests: Small business, apprenticeships, employment, disability, microfinance, town centre regeneration.

Other: Electoral Reform Society; Liberal Democrat Business Forum; Greenpeace; Amnesty International; Member, Federation of Small Businesses; Trustee, RNID 1994-98; Patron: Hearing Link, Families for Autism, Wellmind.

Publications: Age of Opportunity (Liberal Democrats) 2000 Challenge of Disability (Grass Roots Group) 1998.

Recreations: Reading, classic movies, eating out.

Stephen Lloyd MP, House of Commons, London SW1A 0AA
Tel: 020 7219 7061 *Email:* stephen.lloyd.mp@parliament.uk
Constituency: 100 Seaside Road, Eastbourne, East Sussex BN21 3PF
Tel: 01323 733030 *Email:* stephen@stephenlloyd.org.uk
Website: www.eastbournelibdems.co.uk www.stephenlloyd.org.uk

LLWYD, ELFYN
Dwyfor Meirionnydd *(Majority 6,367)*

Plaid Cymru Parliamentary Leader; Group Whip; Spokesperson for Constitution, for Defence, for Environment, Food and Rural Affairs, for Foreign and Commonwealth Affairs, for Home Affairs and for Justice

Born 26 September 1951; Son of late Huw Meirion and Hefina Hughes; Married Eleri, née Llwyd 1974 (1 son 1 daughter).

Education: Dyffryn Conwy School; Llanrwst Grammar School; University College of Wales, Aberystwyth (LLB 1974); College of Law, Chester (Solicitor 1977); Gray's Inn 1997; Welsh.

PLAID CYMRU

Non-political career: Solicitor 1977-97; President, Gwynedd Law Society 1990-91; Barrister, Gray's Inn 1997-. PCS: Member, Vice-chair, Parliamentary Group, Chair, Justice Unions Parliamentary Group.

Political career: Member for Meirionnydd Nant Conwy 1992-2010, for Dwyfor Meirionnydd since 6 May 2010 general election; Plaid Cymru: Spokesperson for: Transport 1992-94, Trade and Industry 1992-94; Parliamentary Whip 1995-2001, Parliamentary Spokesperson for: Northern Ireland 1997-99, Housing 1997-2005, Local Government 1997-2006, Tourism 1997-2005, Home Affairs 1999-; Leader, Plaid Cymru Parliamentary Party 1999-; Plaid Cymru Spokesperson for: Defence 2001-06, 2009-, Foreign and Commonwealth Affairs 2004-, Constitutional Affairs 2005-06, Environment, Food and Rural Affairs 2005-; Group Whip 2005-; Plaid Cymru Spokesperson for: Business, Enterprise and Regulatory Reform 2006-09, Justice 2007-, Energy and Climate Change 2009-10, Cabinet Office 2009-10, Constitution 2010-. *Select committees:* Member: Welsh Affairs 1992-97, 1998-2001, Standards and Privileges 2005-10, Reform of the House of Commons 2009-10, Justice 2010-, Joint Committee on Privacy and Injunctions 2011-12. Member, Plaid Cymru Policy Cabinet 1994-, Parliamentary Leader 1997-. *Councils and public bodies:* Council member, National Library of Wales.

Political interests: Civil liberties, agriculture, tourism, home affairs; Greece, Scotland, Spain, USA, Wales.

Other: Member, Parliamentary Panel, UNICEF 1993-; Council member, University of Wales, Aberystwyth 1992; Parliamentary Friend, NSPCC Wales 1994; Patron, Abbeyfield Wales 1994; Honorary member, Gorsedd of Bards 1998; Fellow, Institute of Welsh Affairs; Chair: Dolgellau Hatchery Trust, Executive Committee, National Eisteddfod, Bala 2009; Vice-President, Llangollen International Eisteddfod; President, Three Peaks Yacht Race 2013-; NSPCC; Children in Wales; Urdd Gobaith Cymru; Tenovus; Air Ambulance Wales. Parliamentary Campaigner of the Year, *HTV/Wales Year Book* 2010. PC 2011. President: Estimaner Angling Association, Betwsy-Coed Football Club, Llanuwchllyn Football Club, Bala Rugby Club; Vice-President, Dolgellau Old Grammarians' Rugby Club.

Recreations: Pigeon breeding, choral singing, rugby, fishing.

Rt Hon Elfyn Llwyd MP, House of Commons, London SW1A 0AA
Tel: 020 7219 3555 *Fax:* 020 7219 2633 *Email:* elfyn.llwyd.mp@parliament.uk
Constituency: Angorfa, Heol Meurig, Dolgellau, Gwynedd LL40 1LN
Tel: 01341 422661 *Email:* jenkinssh@parliament.uk *Website:* www.elfynllwyd.plaidcymru.org

LONG, NAOMI
Belfast East *(Majority 1,533)*

Naomi Rachel Long. Born 13 December 1971; Daughter of Olive Johnston and James Johnston; Married Michael Long 1995.

Education: Bloomfield Collegiate; Queen's University, Belfast (MEng civil engineering 1994).

Non-political career: Graduate engineer, Parkman (NI) Ltd 1994-96; Queens University, Belfast 1996-99; Mulholland and Doherty Consulting Engineers 1999-2000.

Political career: Contested Belfast East 2005 general election. Member for Belfast East since 6 May 2010 general election; Member Speaker's Committee on the Electoral Commission 2010-. *Select committees:* Member: Northern Ireland Affairs 2010-. Northern Ireland Assembly: MLA for Belfast East 2003-10: Member, Preparation for Government Committee 2006; Alliance Spokesperson for Office of First Minister and Deputy First Minister 2007-10. Alliance Party: Member 1994-, Deputy Leader 2006-; Spokesperson for: Education 1998-2006, Regional Development 2005-10, Cohesion 2007-, Victims Issues 2007-. *Councils and public bodies:* Belfast City Council: Councillor 2001-10, Alliance Group Leader, Member, Belfast District Policing Partnership Board, Lord Mayor of Belfast 2009-10.

ALLIANCE

Political interests: Religious freedom, human rights, international development, conflict resolution.

Other: Graduate member, Institution of Civil Engineers.

Naomi Long MP, House of Commons, London SW1A 0AA
Tel: 020 7219 7013/020 7219 2340 *Fax:* 020 7219 0451 *Email:* naomi.long.mp@parliament.uk
Constituency: 56 Upper Newtownards Road, Belfast BT4 3EL
Tel: 028 9047 2004 *Fax:* 028 9065 6408 *Email:* belfast.east@allianceparty.org
Website: www.naomilong.com *Twitter:* @naomi_long

LOPRESTI, JACK
Filton and Bradley Stoke *(Majority 6,914)*

Giacomo Lopresti. Born 23 August 1969; Married Lucy Cope 1992 (2 sons 1 daughter).

Education: Brislington Secondary School.

Non-political career: Gunner, 266 Battery, Royal Artillery; Served with 29 Commando Regiment RA in Helmand Province, Afghanistan autumn 2008 to winter 2009. Estate agent 1998-2001; Independent mortgage broker 2001-05; Regional development manager, Treasurer's Department, Conservative Party 2005-07.

Political career: Contested Bristol East 2001 general election. Member for Filton and Bradley Stoke since 6 May 2010 general election. *Select committees:* Member: Northern Ireland Affairs 2010-, Armed Forces Bill 2011. Contested South West region 2004 European Parliament election. *Councils and public bodies:* Councillor, Bristol City Council 1999-2007.

CONSERVATIVE

Political interests: Defence, foreign affairs, social mobility; Afghanistan, USA.

Other: Member: International Churchill Society, General George Patton Historical Society.

Recreations: Running half-marathons.

Jack Lopresti MP, House of Commons, London SW1A 0AA
Tel: 020 7219 7070 *Email:* jack.lopresti.mp@parliament.uk
Constituency: 27 The Courtyard, Woodlands, Bradley Stoke, Bristol BS32 4NH
Tel: 01454 617783 *Website:* www.jacklopresti.com *Twitter:* @JackLoprestiMP

LORD, JONATHAN
Woking *(Majority 6,807)*

Jonathan George Caladine Lord. Born 17 September 1962; Son of the late His Honour John Lord and Ann Lord, née Caladine; Married Caroline Commander 2000 (1 son 1 daughter).

Education: Shrewsbury School; Kent School, Connecticut, USA; Merton College, Oxford (BA modern history 1985, MA).

Non-political career: Bates Dorland; AP Lintas; Ogilvy and Mather; Director, Saatchi and Saatchi 1998-2000; Marketing consultant.

CONSERVATIVE

Political career: Contested Oldham West and Royton 1997 general election. Member for Woking since 6 May 2010 general election; Sponsored Sports Ground Safety Authority Act 2011; President, Oxford University Conservative Association 1983; Campaign manager to Anne Milton MP 2005 general election; Chairman, Guildford Conservative Association 2006-10; Deputy chairman, Surrey Area Conservatives 2007-09. *Councils and public bodies:* Westminster City Council: Councillor 1994-2002, Council Deputy Leader 1998-2000; Councillor, Surrey County Council 2009-11.

Political interests: Culture, media and sport, business; USA.

Other: Patron, Home-Start, Woking.

Recreations: Cricket, theatre, walking.

Jonathan Lord MP, House of Commons, London SW1A 0AA
Tel: 020 7219 6913 *Email:* jonathan.lord.mp@parliament.uk
Constituency: Woking Conservatives, Churchill House, Chobham Road, Woking, Surrey GU21 4AA
Tel: 01483 773384 *Website:* www.jonathanlord.co.uk

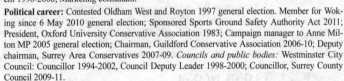

LOUGHTON, TIM

East Worthing and Shoreham *(Majority 11,105)*

CONSERVATIVE

Timothy Paul Loughton. Born 30 May 1962; Son of Reverend Michael Loughton and Pamela Loughton; Married Elizabeth MacLauchlan 1992 (1 son 2 daughters).

Education: The Priory School, Lewes; Warwick University (BA classical civilisation 1983); Clare College, Cambridge (Research Mesopotamian archaeology 1983-84).

Non-political career: Montagu Loebl Stanley/Flemings London: Fund manager 1984-, Director 1992-2000; General election PA to Tim Eggar MP 1987. Formerly BIFU.

Political career: Contested Sheffield Brightside 1992 general election. Member for East Worthing and Shoreham 1997-2010, for East Worthing and Shoreham (revised boundary) since 6 May 2010 general election; Opposition Spokesman for: Regeneration, Poverty, Regions, Housing 2000-01; Health 2001-03; Shadow Minister for: Health 2003-07, Children 2003-10; Children's Bill 2004; Childcare Bill 2006; Adoption and Children Bill 2006; Mental Health Bill 2007; Children and Young Person's Bill 2008; Children, Schools and Families Bill 2010; Parliamentary Under-Secretary of State for Children and Families, Department for Education 2010-12. *Select committees:* Member: Environmental Audit 1997-2001, European Standing committee C 1999-2001. Chairman, Lewes Young Conservatives 1978; Vice-chairman: Sussex Young Conservatives 1979, Lewes Constituency Conservative Association 1979, South East Area Young Conservatives 1980; Secretary, Warwick University Conservative Association 1981-82; Vice-chairman, Battersea Conservative Association 1990-91; Member, London Area Conservative Executive Committee 1993-96; Life Vice-President, Sheffield Brightside Constituency Association 1993-; Deputy chairman, Battersea Constituency Conservative Association 1994-96; Executive Committee Member, Selsdon Group 1994-2003; Member, Carlton Club Political Committee 1994-2004; Chairman, Conservative Disability Group 1998-2006; Member, Shoreham Conservative Club.

Political interests: Finance, foreign affairs, home affairs, education (special needs), environmental taxation, environment and housing, disability, animal welfare, health, children's issues; Indian sub-continent, Latin America, Middle East.

Other: Member: CPA, IPU; Member, Patron, President, Vice-president numerous Worthing and West Sussex organisations; Lecturer, English Wine and Stock Exchange; Member, Bow Group 1985-92; MSi(Dip); St Barnabas Hospice; Ropetackle Centre Trust; Adur Special Needs Project; Parley Online; President, Shoreham Conservative Club. Patron, Worthing Hockey; Captain, Lords and Commons Hockey Team; President, Adur Athletic; Member: Commons and Lords Ski team, Commons and Lords Tennis team.

Recreations: Skiing, tennis, hockey, wine, archaeology, classics.

Tim Loughton MP, House of Commons, London SW1A 0AA
Tel: 020 7219 4471 *Fax:* 020 7219 0461 *Email:* loughtont@parliament.uk
Constituency: Haverfield House, 4 Union Place, Worthing, West Sussex BN11 1LG
Tel: 01903 235168 *Fax:* 01903 219755 *Email:* eastworthingandshoreham@tory.org
Website: www.timloughton.com *Twitter:* @timloughton

LOVE, ANDY

Edmonton *(Majority 9,613)*

LAB/CO-OP

Andrew McCulloch Love. Born 21 March 1949; Son of late James Love and Olive Love; Married Ruth Rosenthal 1983.

Education: Greenock High School; Strathclyde University (BSc physics 1973).

Non-political career: Armed Forces Parliamentary Scheme 2011-. Parliamentary officer, Co-operative Party 1993-97. TGWU/Unite: Member, Branch chair 1980-83; National executive member, NACO 1989-92.

Political career: Contested Edmonton 1992 general election. Member for Edmonton 1997-2010, for Edmonton (revised boundary) since 6 May 2010 general election; PPS: to Jacqui Smith as Minister of State: Department of Health 2001-03, Department of Trade and Industry 2003-05, to John Healey as Minister of State, Department for Communities and Local Government 2008-09. *Select committees:* Member: Public Accounts 1997-2001, Regulatory Reform 1999-05, Treasury 2005-, Parliamentary Commission on Banking Standards 2012-13. Member, PLP Departmental Committee for Trade and Industry 1997-2001, 2003-05; PLP Departmental Group for Treasury: Member 1997-2010, Chair 2010-; PLP Departmental Committees: Vice-chair, ODPM/Communities and Local Government 2002-10, Member, International Development 2005-10. Chair: Hornsey and Wood Green Labour Party 1987-89, Policy Committee Greater London Labour Party 1992-94; Secretary, Co-operative Parliamentary Group 1999-2001. *Councils and public bodies:* Councillor, London Borough of Haringey 1980-86.

Political interests: Housing, regeneration, mutuality, the economy; Cyprus, Lebanon, Mexico, Sri Lanka.

Other: Vice-chair, North London Further Education College 1987-90; Trustee, Industrial Common Ownership Fund (ICOF) 1996-; Vice-patron: Heal Cancer Charity, Helen Rollason Cancer Appeal 1999-; Patron, Nightingale Hospice Trust 2001-; Fellow: Royal Society of Arts, Industry and Parliament Trust 2004; Association of Chartered Institute of Secretaries: Member 1996, Fellow 2000; RSA. Muswell Hill Golf Club.

Recreations: History, opera, cinema, golf.

Andy Love MP, House of Commons, London SW1A 0AA
Tel: 020 7219 6377 *Fax:* 020 7219 6623 *Email:* andy.love.mp@parliament.uk
Constituency: Broad House, 205 Fore Street, Edmonton, London N18 2TZ
Tel: 020 8803 0574 *Fax:* 020 8807 1673 *Email:* andylovemp@aol.com
Website: www.andylovemp.com

GREEN PARTY

LUCAS, CAROLINE
Brighton Pavilion *(Majority 1,252)*

Born 9 December 1960; Married Richard Savage 1991 (2 sons).

Education: Malvern Girls' College; Exeter University (BA English literature 1983; PhD English and women's studies 1989); Kansas University, USA (Scholarship 1983-84); Journalism (Diploma 1987); French.

Non-political career: Oxfam: Press officer 1989-91, Communications officer, Asia desk 1991-94, Policy adviser on trade and environment 1994-97, Team leader, Trade and investment, Policy department 1998-99; Policy adviser on trade and investment, Department for International Development 1997-98; Author.

Political career: Contested Oxford East 1992 general election. Member for Brighton Pavilion since 6 May 2010 general election. *Select committees:* Member: Environmental Audit 2010-. European Parliament: MEP for South East 1999-2010: Intergroup on the Welfare and Conservation of Animals: Vice-president 2004-09, President 2009-10. Green Party: National press officer 1987-89, Co-chair, party council 1989-90, Member, regional council 1997-99, Leader 2008-12. *Councils and public bodies:* Councillor, Oxfordshire County Council 1993-97.

Political interests: Animal welfare, environment, social justice, green economy, climate change, drugs policy, equalities and human rights; Burma, Palestine.

Other: Vice-president, Stop the War Coalition; Member, national council, Campaign for Nuclear Disarmament; Board member, International Forum on Globalisation; Matron, Women's Environmental Network; Vice-President, RSPCA. Michael Kay Award for Animal Welfare 2006; Michael Kay Award for Services to European Animal Welfare, RSPCA 2006; *Observer* Ethical Politician of the Year 2007, 2009, 2010; MP of the Year, Women in Public Life Awards 2011.

Publications: Co-author, Writing for Women (Oxford University Press, 1989); Reforming World Trade (Oxfam, 1996); Co-author: With Ruth Mayne: Global Trade and the Rise of New Social Issues (Routledge, 1999), Watchful in Seattle: WTO Threats to Public Services, Food and the Environment (1999); With Mike Woodin: The Euro or a Sustainable Future for Britain (2000); With Colin Hines: From Seattle to Nice: Challenging the Free Trade Agenda at the Heart of Enlargement (2000), Stopping the Great Food Swap: Relocalising Europe's Food Supply (2001); With Mike Woodin: Green Alternatives to Globalisation: A Manifesto (Pluto, 2004).

Recreations: Gardening, country walks.

Dr Caroline Lucas MP, House of Commons, London SW1A 0AA
Tel: 020 7219 7025 *Email:* caroline.lucas.mp@parliament.uk
Constituency: Brighton Media Centre, 15-17 Middle Street, Brighton BN1 1AA
Email: brightonoffice@parliament.uk *Website:* www.carolinelucas.com
Twitter: @CarolineLucas

LUCAS, IAN
Wrexham *(Majority 3,658)*

Shadow Minister for Foreign and Commonwealth Office

Ian Colin Lucas. Born 18 September 1960; Son of Colin Lucas, process engineer, and Alice Lucas, cleaner; Married Norah Sudd 1986 (1 daughter 1 son).

Education: Greenwell Comprehensive School, Gateshead; Royal Grammar School, Newcastle upon Tyne; New College, Oxford (BA jurisprudence 1982); College of Law, Christleton law (Solicitor's Final Exam 1983); German.

LABOUR

Non-political career: Russell-Cooke Potter and Chapman Solicitors: Articled clerk, Assistant solicitor 1983-86; Solicitor's Admission 1985; Assistant solicitor: Percy Hughes and Roberts 1986-87, Lees Moore and Price 1987-89, Roberts Moore Nicholas Jones 1989-92, DR Crawford 1992-97; Principal, Crawford Lucas 1997-2000; Partner, Stevens Lucas, Oswestry 2000-01. Amicus/MSF, Unite 1996-.

Political career: Contested Shropshire North 1997 general election. Member for Wrexham since 7 June 2001 general election; PPS to: Bill Rammell as Minister of State, Department for Education and Skills 2005-06, Liam Byrne as Minister of State, Home Office 2007-08; Assistant Government Whip 2008-09; Parliamentary Under-Secretary of State, Department for Business, Innovation and Skills 2009-10; Shadow Minister for the Digital Economy, Departments for: Business, Innovation and Skills 2010-11, Culture, Media and Sport 2011; Shadow Minister for Foreign and Commonwealth Office (Africa and Middle East) 2011-. *Select committees:* Member: Environmental Audit 2001-03, Procedure 2001-02, Transport 2003-05, Public Accounts 2007. Honorary Treasurer, PLP Welsh Regional Group 2005-08. Chair, Wrexham Labour Party 1992-93; Vice-chair, North Shropshire Labour Party 1993-2000; Society of Labour Lawyers 1996-. *Councils and public bodies:* Member, Gresford Community Council 1987-91.

Political interests: Economy, European affairs, health, education, environment, manufacturing; Germany, Japan, Lesotho, USA.

Other: Chair, Committee member, Homeless in Oswestry Action Project 1993-2000; Member, Fabian Society 2000-; Patron: Dynamic Wrexham (for children with disabilities) 2001-, The Venture Wrexham (children and young people's charity) 2001-; Fellow, Industry and Parliament Trust 2005.

Recreations: History, film, football, cricket, painting.

Ian Lucas MP, House of Commons, London SW1A 0AA
Tel: 020 7219 8346 *Fax:* 020 7219 1948 *Email:* lucasi@parliament.uk
Constituency: Vernon House, 41 Rhosddu Road, Wrexham, Clwyd LL11 2NS
Tel: 01978 355743 *Fax:* 01978 310051 *Website:* www.ianlucas.co.uk *Twitter:* @IanCLucas

LUFF, PETER
Mid Worcestershire *(Majority 15,864)*

Peter James Luff. Born 18 February 1955; Son of late Thomas Luff, master printer, and late Joyce Luff; Married Julia Jenks 1982 (1 son 1 daughter).

Education: Windsor Grammar School; Corpus Christi College, Cambridge (BA economics 1976, MA); French (rusty).

Non-political career: Member, Armed Forces Parliamentary Scheme (Royal Navy) 1996, 2002. Research assistant to Peter Walker MP 1977-80; Head of private office to Edward Heath MP 1980-82; Company secretary, family stationery business, Luff & Sons Ltd -1987; Account director, director and managing director, Good Relations Public Affairs Ltd 1982-87; Special adviser

CONSERVATIVE

to Lord Young of Graffham as Secretary of State for Trade and Industry 1987-89; Senior consultant, Lowe Bell Communications 1989-90; Assistant managing director, Good Relations Ltd 1990-92.

Political career: Contested Holborn and St Pancras 1987 general election. Member for Worcester 1992-97, for Mid Worcestershire 1997-2010, for Mid Worcestershire (revised boundary) since 6 May 2010 general election; PPS to: Tim Eggar as Minister of State, Department of Trade and Industry 1993-96, Lord Mackay of Clashfern as Lord Chancellor 1996-97, Ann Widdecombe as Minister for Prisons, Home Office 1996-97; Opposition Whip 2000-05; Assistant Chief Whip 2002-05; Parliamentary Under-Secretary of State (Defence Equipment, Support and Technology), Ministry of Defence 2010-12. *Select committees:* Member: Welsh Affairs 1992-97, Consolidation Etc Joint Bills Committee 1995-97, Liaison 1997-2000; Chair: Agriculture 1997-2000; Member: Information 2001-05, Selection 2002-05, Administration 2002-06; Chair: Trade and Industry/Business, Enterprise and Regulatory Reform/Business and Enterprise/Business,

Innovation and Skills 2005-10; Member: Liaison 2005-10, Quadripartite (Committees on Strategic Export Controls)/Arms Export Controls 2006-09, Liaison (National Policy Statements Sub-committee) 2009-10, Liaison Sub-Committee 2010, Joint Committee on National Security Strategy 2010. Member, Executive 1922 Committee 2005-10. Chair, Conservative Parliamentary Friends of India 2001-05.

Political interests: Business issues, performing arts, defence; China, Falkland Islands, France, India, Israel, Mongolia, Turkey.

Other: Member, Joseph Rowntree Inquiry into Planning for Housing 1992-94; Patron: Conservative Students 1995-98, Worcestershire ME Support Group; Vice-President: Severn Valley Railway 1997-, Evesham Rowing Club 1997-, Droitwich Canals Trust 1997-; Worcester Birmingham Canal Society 2001-; Chair, Worcester Cathedral Council 2002-08; Honorary Fellow, Chartered Institute of Public Relations; Water Aid, St Mungo's, Worcester Cathedral, LAMDA. Worcestershire County Cricket.

Publications: Supporting Excellence – Funding Dance and Drama Students (Bow Group, 1995).

Recreations: Theatre, photography, shooting, diving, reading.

Peter Luff MP, House of Commons, London SW1A 0AA
Tel: 020 7219 3000 *Email:* peter.luff.mp@parliament.uk
Constituency: No constituency office publicised
Tel: 01905 763952 *Website:* www.peterluff.org.uk *Twitter:* @PeterJLuff

LUMLEY, KAREN
Redditch *(Majority 5,821)*

Karen Elizabeth Lumley. Born 28 March 1964; Daughter of Derek and Sylvia (both deceased); Married Richard Lumley 1984 (1 son 1 daughter).

Education: Rugby High School for Girls; East Warwickshire College of Further Education (business studies); French.

Non-political career: Member Armed Forces Parliamentary Scheme. Trainee accountant, Ford Motor Company 1982-84; Assistant accountant, John Bull Group 1984-85; Company secretary, RKL Geological Services Ltd 1989-.

CONSERVATIVE

Political career: Contested Delyn 1997 and Redditch 2001 and 2005 general elections. Member for Redditch since 6 May 2010 general election. *Select committees:* Member: Welsh Affairs 2010-, Transport 2012-. Contested Delyn constituency 1999 National Assembly for Wales election. Deputy chair: Welsh Young Conservatives 1986-87, Welsh Conservative Party 1999-2000. *Councils and public bodies:* Group leader, Wrexham Borough Council 1991-96; Councillor: Clwyd County Council 1993-96, Redditch Borough Council 2001-03; Trustee, Vaynor First School, Redditch.

Political interests: Education, health, foreign affairs; Bosnia, Macedonia, Maldives, Montenegro, Serbia, Ukraine.

Recreations: Cooking, knitting, reading.

Karen Lumley MP, House of Commons, London SW1A 0AA
Tel: 020 7219 7133 *Email:* karen.lumley.mp@parliament.uk
Constituency: Grosvenor House, Prospect Hill, Redditch B97 4DL
Tel: 01527 591334 *Email:* karen@tellkaren.com *Website:* www.tellkaren.com

McCABE, STEVE
Birmingham, Selly Oak *(Majority 3,482)*

Shadow Minister for Education

Stephen James McCabe. Born 4 August 1955; Son of James and Margaret McCabe; Married Lorraine Lea Clendon 1991 (divorced) (1 son 1 daughter).

Education: Port Glasgow, Senior Secondary; Moray House College, Edinburgh (Diploma social studies 1977; Certificate Qualification Social Work 1977); Bradford University (MA social work 1986).

LABOUR

Non-political career: Social work with young offenders 1977-85; Lecturer in social work, North East Worcestershire College 1989-91; Part-time researcher, British Association of Social Workers 1989-91; Part-time child protection social worker 1989-91; Central Council for Education in Social Work 1991-97. Member: MSF, Unite; Shop steward, NALGO 1978-82.

Political career: Member for Birmingham Hall Green 1997-2010, for Birmingham, Selly Oak since 6 May 2010 general election; PPS to Charles Clarke: as Secretary of State for Education and Skills 2003-04, as Home Secretary 2004-05; Assistant Government Whip 2006-07; Government Whip 2007-10; Opposition Whip 2010; Shadow Minister for Education 2013-. *Select* *committees:* Member: Deregulation 1997-99, Northern Ireland Affairs 1998-2003, Joint Committee on House of Lords Reform 2003-10, Home Affairs 2005-06, 2010-. Chair, PLP Departmental Group for Home Affairs 2006, 2010-. *Councils and public bodies:* Birmingham City Council: Councillor 1990-98, Chair, Transportation Committee 1993-96.

Political interests: Community care, transport, economic issues, police and security issues.

Other: Local Cricket Club.

Recreations: Reading, football, hill walking.

Steve McCabe MP, House of Commons, London SW1A 0AA
Tel: 020 7219 3509 *Fax:* 020 7219 0367 *Email:* mccabes@parliament.uk
Constituency: No constituency office
Tel: 0121-443 3878 *Fax:* 0121-441 4779 *Website:* www.stevemccabe-mp.org.uk
Twitter: @steve_mccabe

McCANN, MICHAEL   East Kilbride, Strathaven and Lesmahagow *(Majority 14,503)*

Born 2 January 1964; Son of Charles and Bridget McCann; Married Tracy Thomson 1989 (1 son 1 daughter).

Education: St Brides High School, East Kilbride; St Andrews High School.

Non-political career: Armed Forces Parliamentary Scheme. Civil servant, Overseas Development Administration/Department for International Development 1982-92; Scottish officer, Civil and Public Services Association 1992-98; Deputy Scottish secretary, Public and Commercial Services Union 1998-2008; Senior parliamentary researcher to Adam Ingram MP 2008-10. Elected member, Civil and Public Services Association 1982-92; Member, GMB 1992-.

LABOUR

Political career: Member for East Kilbride, Strathaven and Lesmahagow since 6 May 2010 general election; PPS to Liam Byrne as Shadow Secretary of State for Work and Pensions 2011-. *Select committees:* Member: International Development 2010-. Chair, PLP Departmental Group for International Development 2010-. Member, Labour Party 1987-; Secretary, East Kilbride, Strathaven and Lesmahagow CLP 2004-. *Councils and public bodies:* South Lanarkshire Council: Councillor 1999-2010, Council Deputy Leader 2007-10.

Political interests: Energy policy, international aid, foreign affairs; Africa, Europe, USA.

Other: Member, Parkinson's Disease Society.

Recreations: Golf, music.

Michael McCann MP, House of Commons, London SW1A 0AA
Tel: 020 7219 7058 *Email:* michael.mccann.mp@parliament.uk
Constituency: Civic Centre, Andrew Street, East Kilbride G74 1AB
Tel: 01355 239642 *Website:* www.michaelmccann.org.uk *Twitter:* @michaelmccannMP

McCARTHY, KERRY   Bristol East *(Majority 3,722)*

Shadow Minister for Foreign and Commonwealth Office

Kerry Gillian McCarthy. Born 26 March 1965; Daughter of Oliver Haughney and Sheila Rix; Single.

Education: Denbigh High School, Luton; Luton Sixth Form College; Liverpool University (BA Russian, politics and linguistics 1986); Law Society (CPE and final solicitors examinations 1992).

Non-political career: Legal assistant, South Bedfordshire Magistrates Court 1986-88; Litigation assistant, Neves Solicitors, Luton 1988-89; Trainee solicitor, Wilde Sapte 1992-94; Legal manager, Abbey National Treasury Services 1994-96; Senior counsel, debt markets, Merrill Lynch Europe plc 1996-99; Lawyer, Labour Party 2001; Regional director, Britain in Europe campaign 2002-04; Head of public policy, The Waterfront Partnership 2004-05. TGWU 1994-2007; Unite 2007-.

LABOUR

Political career: Member for Bristol East 2005-10, for Bristol East (revised boundary) since 6 May 2010 general election; PPS to: Rosie Winterton as Minister of State, Department of Health 2007, Douglas Alexander as Secretary of State for International Development 2007-09; Assistant Government Whip 2009-10; Shadow Minister for Work and Pensions 2010; Opposition Whip 2010; Shadow Economic Secretary 2010-11; Shadow Minister for Foreign and Commonwealth Office 2011-. *Select committees:* Member: Treasury 2005-07, South West 2009-10. Chair, PLP South West Regional Group 2007-09. Chair, Luton North Constituency Labour Party 1994-96; Secretary, Luton North CLP 1996-99; National Policy Forum 1998-2005; Economic Policy

Commission 1998-2005. *Councils and public bodies:* Luton Borough Council: Councillor 1995-96, 1999-2003, Chair of housing and cabinet member 1999-2001; Director, London Luton Airport 1999-2003.

Political interests: Environment, food policy, poverty, foreign affairs; Latin America, Asia, Jordan, Russia, Somaliland/Somalia.

Other: Member: Howard League for Penal Reform, Labour Animal Welfare Society; Patron, FoodCycle; Board member, UnConvention; Vice-President, League Against Cruel Sports; Member, The Law Society 1994-99. Technology/Social Media User of the Year, *House Magazine* awards 2011; St George Labour.

Recreations: Travel, scuba diving, music.

Kerry McCarthy MP, House of Commons, London SW1A 0AA
Tel: 020 7219 4510 *Email:* kerry.mccarthy.mp@parliament.uk
Constituency: 326a Church Road, St George, Bristol BS5 8AJ
Tel: 0117-939 9901 *Fax:* 0117-939 9902 *Email:* kerry.mccarthy.mp@parliament.uk
Website: www.kerrymccarthymp.org *Twitter:* @kerryMP

McCARTNEY, JASON
Colne Valley *(Majority 4,837)*

Jason Alexander McCartney. Born 29 January 1968; Divorced (2 daughters).

Education: Lancaster Royal Grammar School; RAF College, Cranwell (officer training 1988); Leeds Trinity (Post-graduate Diploma broadcast journalism 1997).

Non-political career: Officer, Royal Air Force 1988-97. Journalist, BBC Radio 1997-98; Broadcast journalist, ITV Yorkshire 1998-2007; Senior lecturer: Broadcast journalism, Leeds Trinity 2007-08, Journalism, Leeds Metropolitan University 2008-. National Union of Journalists: Former member, Father of Chapel, ITV Yorkshire 2005-07.

CONSERVATIVE

Political career: Member for Colne Valley since 6 May 2010 general election. *Select committees:* Member: Transport 2013-. Member, Executive, 1922 Committee 2013-.

Political interests: Military, crime, broadcasting, sport, pensions.

Other: Member: UK Delegation, NATO Parliamentary Assembly, NATO Defence and Security Committee; Royal British Legion; Honorary President, RAFA, Huddersfield; Governor, SportsAid 2004-; RAF club; Huddersfield Town Supporters' Trust. Yorkshire County Cricket Club; Huddersfield Town Supporters' Trust.

Publications: Co-author, Freedom, Responsibility and the State: Curbing Over-Mighty Government (Politeia, 2012).

Recreations: Cricket, tennis, Huddersfield Town FC, days out with my daughters.

Jason McCartney MP, House of Commons, London SW1A 0AA
Tel: 020 7219 7041 *Fax:* 020 7219 6474 *Email:* jason.mccartney.mp@parliament.uk
Constituency: Upperbridge House, 24 Huddersfield Road, Holmfirth HD9 2JS
Tel: 01484 688364/01484 688378 *Website:* www.jasonmccartney.com
Twitter: @JasonMcCartney

McCARTNEY, KARL
Lincoln *(Majority 1,058)*

Karl Ian McCartney. Born 25 October 1968; Son of John and Brenda McCartney; Married Cordelia Pyne 1999 (2 sons).

Education: Birkenhead School for Boys; Neston High School; Willink School, Burghfield Common; St David's University College (BA geography 1991) (Student Union President 1991-92); Kingston University Business School (MBA 1998); French, Welsh (basic).

Non-political career: Armed Forces Parliamentary Scheme (RAF) 2011-; Combined Cadet Force School (RAF). Hasbro UK 1992-93; Agent and researcher, Conservative Central Office 1993-96; Corporate affairs, Corporation of London 1996-2001; Director, MLS Ltd (Consultancy) 2000-; Public relations manager, Norton Rose 2001; London Communications Agency 2002-03; Campaign director, Sir Keith Park Memorial Campaign 2007-.

CONSERVATIVE

Political career: Contested Lincoln 2005 general election. Member for Lincoln since 6 May 2010 general election. *Select committees:* Member: Unopposed Bills (Panel) 2011-, Transport 2012-. Member, Executive, 1922 Committee 2012-. *Councils and public bodies:* Wrotham Parish Council 1999-2004; Magistrate: Dartford and Gravesham 1999-2002, Maidstone 2002-04, Lincoln 2004-10; Upper Witham Internal Drainage Board 2007-11; Witham Third District Internal Drainage Board 2008-11; Member, Court: Lincoln University 2011-, Hull University 2011-.

Political interests: Small business, education, sport, transport, military matters, crime and the judiciary; The Commonwealth, Italy, New Zealand, Northern Ireland, Scotland, Wales.
Other: Trustee, Friends of Wrotham St Georges 1999-; Patron: MNDA, Lincolnshire branch, St John's Ambulance; MISM 1994-, AMBA 1997-, MIPR 1998-; Fundraiser, RSPCA 1993-98; Board member, Servol 1997-98; Adviser, Prince's Youth Business Trust 1997-2001; Volunteer, High Hopes 1999-2003; Nomad Trust, Lincoln; Cooke & Connell charity, Lincoln; Bomber Command Memorial Campaign; Sir Keith Park Memorial Campaign; St. Barnardos, Lincolnshire. Freedom of the City of London 1999. Westminster Wanderers (legends) Football Club; Westminster Lobbyists XV; The Fighting Pilgrims, SDUC Oldboys XI; House of Commons Football, Rugby, Cricket and Shooting Clubs.
Recreations: Football, rugby, cricket, snowboarding, croquet, golf, hill walking, classic cars, shooting.
Karl McCartney MP, House of Commons, London SW1A 0AA
Tel: 020 7219 7221 *Fax:* 020 7219 1964 *Email:* karl.mccartney.mp@parliament.uk
Constituency: c/o Lincoln Conservatives, 1a Farrier Road, Lincoln LN6 3RU
Tel: 01522 687261 *Fax:* 01522 687261 *Email:* info@lincolnconservatives.co.uk
Website: www.lincolnconservatives.co.uk www.karlmccartney.co.uk *Twitter:* @karlmccartney

McCLYMONT, GREGG Cumbernauld, Kilsyth and Kirkintilloch East *(Majority 13,755)*

Shadow Minister for Work and Pensions

Born 3 June 1976; Son of H.F. McClymont and Sheila McClymont, nee McGalliard.
Education: Cumbernauld High School; Glasgow University (MA history 1997); Pennsylvania University, USA (MA history 1998); St John's College, Oxford (PhD 2006).
Non-political career: History fellow, St Hugh's College, Oxford 2007-. Unite; Community.
Political career: Member for Cumbernauld, Kilsyth and Kirkintilloch East since 6 May 2010 general election; Opposition Whip 2011; Shadow Minister for Work and Pensions 2011-. *Select committees:* Member: Science and Technology 2010-12, Business, Innovation and Skills 2010. Chair PLP Departmental Group for Business, Innovation and Skills 2011.
Other: Honorary MA, St Hugh's College, Oxford 2007. Mansfield Road F.C.
Recreations: Football.
Gregg McClymont MP, House of Commons, London SW1A 0AA
Tel: 020 7219 7045 *Email:* gregg.mcclymont.mp@parliament.uk
Constituency: Lennox House, Lennox Road, Cumbernauld, Seafar G67 1LL
Tel: 01236 457788 *Website:* www.greggmcclymont.com *Twitter:* @greggmcclymont

LABOUR

McCREA, WILLIAM South Antrim *(Majority 1,183)*

DUP Shadow Deputy Prime Minister; Spokesperson for Justice and Home Affairs and for House Issues

Robert Thomas William McCrea. Born 6 August 1948; Son of late Robert Thomas McCrea, farmer, and late Sarah McCrea; Married Anne McKnight 1971 (2 sons 3 daughters).
Education: Cookstown Grammar School; Marietta Bible College, Ohio, USA (doctorate of divinity 1989); Theological College of Free Presbyterian Church of Ulster.
Non-political career: Civil servant, Northern Ireland Department of Health and Social Services 1966-82; Director, Daybreak Recording Company 1981-; Gospel recording artist.
Political career: Member for Mid Ulster 1983 to 17 December 1985 (resigned seat in protest against Anglo-Irish Agreement), 23 January 1986 by-election to 1997. Contested Mid Ulster 1997 general election. Member for South Antrim 21 September 2000 by-election to 2001. Contested South Antrim 2001 general election. Member for South Antrim 2005-10, for South Antrim (revised boundary) since 6 May 2010 general election; Member, Public Accounts Commission - 2011; DUP: Spokesperson for: Environment, Food and Rural Affairs 2005-10, Local Government 2009-10; Shadow Leader of the House/House Issues 2009-; Spokesperson for Justice and Home Affairs 2010-; Shadow Deputy Prime Minister 2012-. *Select committees:* Member: Chairmen's Panel/Panel of Chairs 2006-, Joint Committee on the Draft House of Lords Reform Bill 2011-12. Northern Ireland Assembly: Member 1982-86; Member, Northern Ireland Forum for Political Dialogue 1996-98; MLA for Mid Ulster 1998-2007, for South Antrim 2007-10: DUP Spokesperson for Environment 1998, Chair, Committee on Environment 1999-2002, Deputy

DEMOCRATIC UNIONIST PARTY

Whip, DUP Assembly Group, Member, Preparation for Government Committee 2006-07, Chair, Committee on Agriculture and Rural Development 2007-09. Vice-chair, DUP Central Executive Committee 1998-; Member, DUP Environmental Policy Group 1998-; Chair, DUP Group on Review of Public Administration, Northern Ireland 2006-. *Councils and public bodies:* Board of Governors, Magherafelt High School; Magherafelt District Council: Councillor 1973-2010, Chair 1977-81, 2002-03.

Political interests: Agriculture, health, elderly issues, environment, special needs education, planning; USA.

Other: Member: Woodland Trust, The Loyal Orange Order, Royal Black Institution and Apprentice Boys of Derry; Autism Northern Ireland (PAPA); RSPB Northern Ireland.

Publications: In His Pathway – The Story of the Reverend William McCrea (1980).

Recreations: Gospel music, horse riding.

Dr William McCrea MP, House of Commons, London SW1A 0AA
Tel: 020 7219 8525 *Fax:* 020 7219 2347 *Email:* william.mccrea.mp@parliament.uk
Constituency: 5-7 School Street, The Square, Ballyclare, Co Antrim BT39 9BE
Tel: 028 9334 2727 *Fax:* 028 9334 2707

LABOUR

McDONAGH, SIOBHAIN Mitcham and Morden *(Majority 13,666)*

Siobhain Ann McDonagh. Born 20 February 1960; Daughter of Breda McDonagh, née Doogue, psychiatric nurse, and Cumin McDonagh, building labourer; Single, no children.

Education: Holy Cross Convent, New Malden; Essex University (BA government 1981).

Non-political career: Clerical officer, DHSS 1981-83; Housing Benefits assistant 1983-84; Receptionist, Homeless Persons Unit, London Borough of Wandsworth 1984-86; Housing adviser 1986-88; Development co-ordinator, Battersea Church Housing Trust 1988-97. Member, GMB.

Political career: Contested Mitcham and Morden 1987 and 1992 general elections. Member for Mitcham and Morden 1997-2010, for Mitcham and Morden (revised boundary) since 6 May 2010 general election; PPS to John Reid: as Secretary of State for Defence 2005-06, as Home Secretary 2006-07; Assistant Government Whip 2007-08. *Select committees:* Member: Social Security 1997-98, Health 2000-05, Unopposed Bills (Panel) 2004-, London 2009-10, Education 2012-. *Councils and public bodies:* Councillor, London Borough of Merton 1982-97: Chair, Housing Committee 1990-95.

Political interests: Health, housing, quality of life, welfare reform.

Other: Member: South Mitcham Community Centre, Colliers Wood Community Centre, Grenfell Housing Association, Merton MIND; Vice-President, QUIT (smoking cessation charity); Trustee, Mitcham Garden Village.

Recreations: Travel, friends, music.

Siobhain McDonagh MP, House of Commons, London SW1A 0AA
Tel: 020 7219 4678 *Email:* mcdonaghs@parliament.uk
Constituency: 1 Crown Road, Morden, Surrey SM4 5DD
Tel: 020 8542 4835 *Fax:* 020 8544 0377 *Website:* www.siobhainmcdonagh.org.uk
Twitter: @SiobhainMP

LABOUR

McDONALD, ANDY Middlesbrough *(Majority 8,211)*

Andrew Joseph McDonald. Married Sally (children).

Non-political career: Head of office and senior serious injury solicitor, Thompsons Solicitors, Middlesbrough.

Political career: Member for Middlesbrough since 29 November 2012 by-election. *Select committees:* Member: Justice 2012-. *Councils and public bodies:* Councillor, Middlesbrough Council 1995-99; Governor: Abingdon Primary School 1995-2010, Middlesbrough College 2012-.

Other: Former chair, Davison Trust, Middlesbrough; Chair, Teeside branch, Headway; Former chair and secretary, Military Special Interest Group, Association of Personal Injury Lawyers.

Andy McDonald MP, House of Commons, London SW1A 0AA
Tel: 020 7219 4995 *Email:* andy.mcdonald.mp@parliament.uk
Constituency: No constituency office *Twitter:* @AndyMcDonaldMP

McDONNELL, ALASDAIR
Belfast South *(Majority 5,926)*

Leader, Social Democratic and Labour Party; SDLP Chief Whip and Spokesperson for Health; Business, Innovation and Skills; Culture, Media and Sport

Born 1 September 1949; Son of late Charles McDonnell and late Margaret McDonnell, née McIlhatton; Married Olivia Nugent 1998 (2 daughters 2 sons).

Education: St McNissis College, Garron Tower, Co Antrim; University College Dublin Medical School (MB, BCh, BAO 1974).

SOCIAL DEMOCRATIC AND LABOUR PARTY

Non-political career: Junior hospital doctor, Belfast 1975-79; Full-time GP 1979-99; Part-time GP 1999-2009; Partner, Arrow Travel. Member, BMA.

Political career: Contested (National Democrat) North Antrim 1970 general election, (SDLP) Belfast South 1979 general election, 1982 by-election, 1983, 1987, 1992, 1997 and 2001 general elections. Member for Belfast South 2005-10, for Belfast South (revised boundary) since 6 May 2010 general election; SDLP Spokesperson for: Employment and Learning 2005-07, Economic Development 2005-07, Education 2005-08, Health 2005-, Enterprise, Trade and Investment 2007-08, Europe 2008-10, Enterprise and Regulatory Reform 2008-09, Innovation and Universities 2008-09, Northern Ireland Affairs 2008-10, Business, Innovation and Skills 2009-, Culture, Media and Sport 2010-; SDLP Chief Whip 2010-. *Select committees:* Member: Northern Ireland Affairs 2005-. Member Northern Ireland Forum for Political Dialogue 1996; Northern Ireland Assembly: MLA for Belfast South 1998-2011, and for Belfast South (revised boundary) since 5 May 2011; Member Preparation for Government Committee 2006-07; SDLP Spokesperson for: Enterprise, Trade and Development 2007-11, Enterprise, Trade and Investment 2011-12. Social Democratic and Labour Party: Deputy Leader 2004-10, Leader 2011-. *Councils and public bodies:* Belfast City Council: Councillor 1977-81, 1985-2001, Deputy Mayor of Belfast 1995-96.

Political interests: Urban renewal, economic reconstruction, job creation, information technology, biotechnology, renewable energy; Atlantic Canada, France, Germany, Netherlands, Serbia and Balkans, USA.

Other: Member, British-Irish Parliamentary Assembly; Director, Medevol.

Dr Alasdair McDonnell MP, House of Commons, London SW1A 0AA
Tel: 020 7219 8510 *Fax:* 020 7219 2832 *Email:* mcdonnella@parliament.uk
Constituency: 120a Ormeau Road, Belfast BT7 2EB
Tel: 028 9024 2474 *Fax:* 028 9043 9935 *Website:* www.alasdairmcdonnell.com
Twitter: @alasdairmcd_mp

McDONNELL, JOHN
Hayes and Harlington *(Majority 10,824)*

John Martin McDonnell. Born 8 September 1951; Son of late Robert and Elsie McDonnell; Married Marilyn Cooper 1971 (divorced 1987) (2 daughters); married Cynthia Pinto 1995 (1 son).

Education: Great Yarmouth Grammar School, Burnley Technical College; Brunel University (BSc government and politics); Birkbeck College, London University (MSc politics and sociology); French.

Non-political career: Shopfloor production worker 1968-73; Assistant head, social insurance department, National Union of Mineworkers 1977-78; Researcher, TUC 1978-82; Head of policy unit, London Borough of Camden 1985-87; Chief Executive: Association of London Authorities 1987-95, Association of London Government 1995-97. Former Shop Steward, Unison; Co-ordinator, RMT Parliamentary Group 2002-; Chair: Bakers and Allied Workers Union Parliamentary Group, PCS Parliamentary Group; Member: Justice Trade Unions Group, ASLEF Parliamentary Group; Secretary: FBU Group, NUJ Group, Justice Unions Group.

LABOUR

Political career: Contested Hayes and Harlington 1992 general election. Member for Hayes and Harlington 1997-2010, for Hayes and Harlington (revised boundary) since 6 May 2010 general election. *Select committees:* Member: Deregulation and Regulatory Reform 1999-2002, Unopposed Bills (Panel) 1999-2004. Member Labour Party: Committee on Ireland, CND; Chair: Labour Representation Committee, Socialist Campaign Group of MPs; Member Unison Group; Chair: RMT Group, PCS Group; Secretary: FBU Group, Justice Trade Unionist Group, NUJ Group. *Councils and public bodies:* Councillor GLC 1981-86: Chair Finance Committee 1982-85, Deputy Leader 1984-85.

Political interests: Economics, local and regional government, Irish affairs, environment, aviation, public administration; Gambia, Iran, Ireland, Kenya, Lango, Nulo Mountains, Punjab, Somalia, Tanzania.

Other: Chair: Britain and Ireland Human Rights Centre, Hands Off Venezuela Group, Hands Off People of Iran; Treasurer Liberation; Chair, Friends of Lake Farm Country Park; Member: Friends of Ireland – Coalition in support of Belfast Agreement, London Wildlife Trust, Hayes Irish Society, Hayes and Harlington History Society, Hayes and Harlington Community Development Forum, Hayes and Harlington Canal Society; Harlington Hospice; Hayes and Harlington Workingmen's. Hillingdon Outdoor Activities Centre; Wayfarer Sailing Association; Vice-president, Hayes Football Club; Patron, Hayes Cricket Club.

Publications: Editor, Labour Herald; Another World is Possible: a manifesto for 21st century socialism.

Recreations: Sailing, football refereeing, cycling, gardening, theatre, cinema.

John McDonnell MP, House of Commons, London SW1A 0AA
Tel: 020 7219 6908 *Email:* mcdonnellj@parliament.uk
Constituency: Pump Lane, Hayes, Middlesex UB3 3NB
Tel: 020 8569 0010 *Fax:* 020 8569 0109 *Website:* www.john-mcdonnell.net
Twitter: @johnmcdonnellMP

LABOUR

McFADDEN, PAT
Wolverhampton South East *(Majority 6,593)*

Patrick Bosco McFadden. Born 26 March 1965; Son of James and Annie McFadden; Married (1 son 1 daughter).

Education: Holyrood Secondary School, Glasgow; Edinburgh University (MA politics 1988).

Non-political career: Adviser to Donald Dewar MP as Scottish Affairs Spokesperson 1988-93; Speechwriter and policy adviser to John Smith MP as Labour Party Leader 1993; Policy adviser to Tony Blair MP as Labour Party Leader and political secretary to him as Prime Minister 1994-2005. Member, Community.

Political career: Member for Wolverhampton South East 2005-10, for Wolverhampton South East (revised boundary) since 6 May 2010 general election; Parliamentary Secretary, Cabinet Office 2006-07; Minister of State (Employment Relations and Postal Affairs 2007-09), Department for Business, Enterprise and Regulatory Reform/Business, Innovation and Skills 2007-10 (attending Cabinet 2009-10); Shadow Secretary of State for Business, Innovation and Skills 2010. *Select committees:* Member: Treasury 2011-, Parliamentary Commission on Banking Standards 2012-13.

Other: PC 2008.

Recreations: Reading and sport.

Rt Hon Pat McFadden MP, House of Commons, London SW1A 0AA
Tel: 020 7219 4036 *Email:* mcfaddenp@parliament.uk
Constituency: Crescent House, Broad Street, Bilston, West Midlands WV14 0BZ
Tel: 01902 405762 *Fax:* 01902 402381 *Website:* www.patmcfadden.com
Twitter: @patmcfaddenmp

LABOUR

McGOVERN, ALISON
Wirral South *(Majority 531)*

Shadow Minister for International Development

Born December 1980; Daughter of Mike McGovern, British Rail telecoms engineer, and Ann McGovern, nurse; Married Ashwin Kumar (1 daughter).

Education: Wirral Grammar School; University College, London (BA philosophy).

Non-political career: Researcher, House of Commons 2002-06; Public affairs manager: Network Rail 2006-08, The Art Fund 2008-09, Creativity, Culture and Education 2009. Member, Unite.

Political career: Member for Wirral South since 6 May 2010 general election; PPS to Gordon Brown MP 2010-13; Opposition Whip 2013; Shadow Minister for International Development 2013-. *Select committees:* Member: International Development 2010-13, Works of Art 2011-. *Councils and public bodies:* London Borough of Southwark Council: Councillor 2006-10, Deputy Leader, Labour group -2010.

Political interests: Employment, arts and culture, regeneration, international development, economy; India.

Other: Trustee, South London Gallery 2006-10; Vice-chair, Progress 2012-.

Alison McGovern MP, House of Commons, London SW1A 0AA
Tel: 020 7219 7190 *Email:* alison.mcgovern.mp@parliament.uk
Constituency: 99 New Chester Road, New Ferry, Wirral, Merseyside CH62 4RA
Tel: 0151-645 6590 *Email:* alison@alisonmcgovern.org.uk
Website: www.alisonmcgovern.org.uk *Twitter:* @Alison_McGovern

McGOVERN, JIM
Dundee West *(Majority 7,278)*

James Christopher McGovern. Born 17 November 1956; Son of Thomas and Alice McGovern; Married Norma Ward 1991 (1 son 1 daughter).

Education: Lawside Roman Catholic Academy, Dundee; Telford College, Edinburgh (City and Guilds glazing craft 1976).

Non-political career: Glazier: Lindsay and Scott 1973-87, Dundee District Council 1987-97; GMB official 1997-2005. GMB.

LABOUR

Political career: Member for Dundee West since 5 May 2005 general election; PPS to Pat McFadden as Minister of State, Department for Business, Enterprise and Regulatory Reform 2007-08. *Select committees:* Member: Scottish Affairs 2005-07, 2008-. Chair, PLP Scotland Group. *Councils and public bodies:* Councillor, Tayside Regional Council 1994-96.

Political interests: Employment rights, human rights, the economy, Scotland; Colombia, Cuba, Ireland, Palestine, Poland, Spain.

Recreations: Reading, gym, watching football.

Jim McGovern MP, House of Commons, London SW1A 0AA
Tel: 020 7219 4938 *Fax:* 020 7219 4812 *Email:* mcgovernj@parliament.uk
Constituency: 7 West Wynd (off Perth Road), Dundee DD1 4JQ
Tel: 01382 322100 *Fax:* 01382 322696 *Website:* www.jimmcgovern.co.uk
Twitter: @JimMcGovernMP

McGUIRE, ANNE
Stirling *(Majority 8,304)*

Anne Catherine McGuire. Born 26 May 1949; Daughter of late Albert Long, railway signalman, and late Agnes Long, shop worker; Married Len McGuire 1972 (1 son 1 daughter).

Education: Our Lady of St Francis Secondary, Glasgow; Glasgow University (MA politics with history 1971); Notre Dame College of Education (Diploma secondary education 1975).

Non-political career: Supply teacher, history/modern studies 1982-84; Development worker/senior manager, Community Service Volunteers 1984-93; Depute director, Scottish Council for Voluntary Organisations 1993-97. National executive, GMB 1987-91.

LABOUR

Political career: Member for Stirling 1997-2005, for Stirling (revised boundary) since 5 May 2005 general election; PPS to Donald Dewar as Secretary of State for Scotland December 1997-98; Assistant Government Whip 1998-2001; Government Whip 2001-02; Parliamentary Under-Secretary of State: Scotland Office 2002-05, Department for Work and Pensions (Minister for Disabled People) 2005-08; PPS to Ed Miliband as Leader of the Opposition 2010-11; Member Public Accounts Commission 2011-; Shadow Minister for Work and Pensions 2011-13. *Select committees:* Member: Public Accounts 2010-11. Member, Labour Party Scottish Executive 1984-97; Chair, Labour Party Scotland 1992-93. *Councils and public bodies:* Councillor, Strathclyde Regional Council 1980-82.

Political interests: European Union, rural development, urban regeneration; China, Germany, USA.

Other: Strathcarron Hospice. PC 2008.

Recreations: Reading, walking, watching football.

Rt Hon Anne McGuire MP, House of Commons, London SW1A 0AA
Tel: 020 7219 5014 *Fax:* 020 7219 0792 *Email:* anne.mcguire.mp@parliament.uk
Constituency: 22 Viewfield Street, Stirling FK8 1UA
Tel: 01786 446515 *Fax:* 01786 446513 *Website:* www.annemcguiremp.org.uk
Twitter: @AnneMcGuireMP

CONSERVATIVE

McINTOSH, ANNE
Thirsk and Malton *(Majority 11,281)*

Anne Caroline Ballingall McIntosh. Born 20 September 1954; Daughter of late Dr Alastair McIntosh, medical practitioner, and late Grethe-Lise McIntosh; Married John Harvey 1992.

Education: Harrogate Ladies' College; Edinburgh University (LLB 1977); Åarhus University, Denmark (European law 1978); French, Danish, Spanish, German, Italian.

Non-political career: Trainee, EEC Competition Directorate, Brussels 1978; Legal adviser, Didier & Associates, Brussels 1979-80; Apprentice, Scottish Bar, Edinburgh 1980-82; Admitted to Faculty of Advocates 1982; Advocate, practising with European Community Law Office, Brussels 1982-83; Adviser, European Democratic Group, principally on Transport, Youth Education, Culture, Tourism, Relations with Scandinavia, Austria and Yugoslavia 1983-89.

Political career: Contested Workington 1987 general election. Member for Vale of York 1997-2010, for Thirsk and Malton since 27 May 2010; Opposition Spokesperson for Culture, Media and Sport 2001-02; Shadow Minister for: Transport 2002-03, Environment and Transport 2003-05, Foreign Affairs 2005, Work and Pensions 2005-06, Children, Young People and Families 2006-07, Environment, Food and Rural Affairs 2007-10. *Select committees:* Member: Environment, Transport and Regional Affairs 1999-2001, Environment, Transport and Regional Affairs (Transport Sub-Committee) 1999-2001, European Standing Committee C 1999-2001, European Scrutiny 2000-03, Transport, Local Government and the Regions (Transport Sub-Committee) 2001-02, Transport, Local Government and the Regions (Urban Affairs Sub-Committee) 2001-02, Transport, Local Government and the Regions 2001-02, Transport 2003-05; Environment, Food and Rural Affairs: Member 2007-10, Chair 2010-; Member: Chairmen's Panel/Panel of Chairs 2010-, Liaison 2010-, Liaison (National Policy Statements Sub-committee) 2010-. Joint vice-chair, Conservative Party Committee for Social Security 1999-. European Parliament: MEP for Essex North East 1989-94, and for Essex North and Suffolk South 1994-99: Bureau member, European People's Party 1994-97. Executive member 1922 Committee 2000-01. *Councils and public bodies:* Member, Faculty of Advocates 1982-.

Political interests: Transport, tourism, legal affairs, environment, farming and animal husbandry; Central and Eastern Europe, Scandinavia.

Other: President, Anglia Enterprise in Europe 1989-99; Co-chair, European Transport Safety Council 1994-99; President, Yorkshire First – Enterprise in Yorkshire; Member: Yorkshire Agricultural Society, Anglo-Danish Society; Vice-President, National Eye Research (Yorkshire) Advisory Board; Patron, Thirsk Museum Society; Fellow, Industry and Parliament Trust 1995; Graduate, Armed Forces Parliamentary Scheme, Royal Navy 2000; Vice-President, North Yorkshire Moore Railway. Honorary Doctorate of Laws Anglia Polytechnic University 1997; Yorkshire Agricultural Society; Royal Over-seas League; Royal Automobile Club.

Recreations: Swimming, reading, cinema.

Anne McIntosh MP, House of Commons, London SW1A 0AA
Tel: 020 7219 3541 *Fax:* 020 7219 0972 *Email:* mcintosha@parliament.uk
Constituency: Thirsk and Malton Conservative Association, 109 Town Street, Old Malton, North Yorkshire YO17 7HD
Tel: 01845 523835 *Email:* info@thirskandmaltonconservatives.com
Website: thirskandmaltonconservatives.com www.annemcintosh.org.uk
Twitter: @AnneMcIntoshMP

LABOUR

McKECHIN, ANN
Glasgow North *(Majority 3,898)*

Born 22 April 1961; Daughter of late William McKechin and Anne McKechin, née Coyle; Single.

Education: Sacred Heart High School, Paisley; Paisley Grammar School; Strathclyde University (LLB Scots law 1981).

Non-political career: Solicitor 1983-; Pacitti Jones Solicitors, Glasgow 1986-2000: Solicitor, Partner 1990-2000. TGWU/Unite.

Political career: Member for Glasgow Maryhill 2001-05, for Glasgow North since 5 May 2005 general election; PPS to Jacqui Smith as Minister of State: Department of Trade and Industry 2005, Department for Education and Skills 2005; Parliamentary Under-Secretary of State, Scotland Office 2008-10; Shadow Minister for Scotland 2010; Shadow Secretary of State for Scotland 2010-11. *Select committees:* Member: Scottish Affairs 2001-05, Standing Orders 2001-10, Information 2001-05, International Development 2005-09, 2010, Business, Innovation and Skills 2011-, Arms Export Controls 2012-. Vice-chair, PLP Departmental Committee for International Development 2002-08; Chair, PLP Scottish Regional Group 2008. Contested West of Scotland region 1999 Scottish Parliament election. Glasgow Kelvin Labour Party: Constituency secretary 1995-98, Women's officer 2000-01; Manifesto Group Chair for International Development Policy 2007-08; Member, Co-operative Party. *Councils and public bodies:* Vice-chair, Westminster Foundation for Democracy 2012-.

Political interests: International development, economics, small businesses; Africa, Rwanda.

Other: Member: Steering Committee WTO Parliamentary Conference 2003-06, Delegation to NATO Parliamentary Assembly 2005-08; World Development Movement 1998-2004: Scottish representative 1998-2001, Council member 1999-2004; Member, management board: Mercycorps Scotland 2003-08, World Development Trust 2004-08; Fellow, Industry and Parliament Trust 2005; Governor, Westminster Foundation for Democracy 2012-; Law Society of Scotland.

Recreations: Dance, films, art history.

Ann McKechin MP, House of Commons, London SW1A 0AA
Tel: 020 7219 8239 *Fax:* 020 7219 1770 *Email:* ann.mckechin.mp@parliament.uk
Constituency: 154 Raeberry Street, Glasgow G20 6EA
Tel: 0141-946 1300 *Fax:* 0141-946 1412 *Email:* sarah.thoms@parliament.uk
Website: www.annmckechinmp.net *Twitter:* @AnnMcKechinMP

McKENZIE, IAIN   Inverclyde *(Majority 5,838)*

Born 4 April 1959; Son of Adam and Isobel McKenzie; Married (2 children).

Education: Greenock High School; James Watt College (HND quality assurance 2000).

Non-political career: Apprentice mechanic HGV; Various roles, finally procurement officer, IBM 1981-2009; Wise Group 2009-10. Member, Unite.

Political career: Member for Inverclyde since 30 June 2011 by-election. *Select committees:* Member: Scottish Affairs 2011-13, Environment, Food and Rural Affairs 2012-. *Councils and public bodies:* Inverclyde Council: Councillor 2003-, Education Convenor, Convenor, Policy and Resources Committee, Council Leader 2011; Member: Association for Public Service Excellence (APSE), Convention of Scottish Local Authorities, Inverclyde Alliance Board; Board member, River Clyde Homes 2008-11.

LABOUR

Political interests: Europe, employment; Brazil, China, Spain.

Recreations: Running, football.

Iain McKenzie MP, House of Commons, London SW1A 0AA
Tel: 020 7219 8446 *Email:* iain.mckenzie.mp@parliament.uk
Constituency: The Parliamentary Office, 20 Union Street, Greenock, Renfrewshire PA16 8JL
Tel: 01475 791820 *Fax:* 01475 791821 *Website:* www.iainmckenziemp.co.uk
Twitter: @inverclydeMP

McKINNELL, CATHERINE   Newcastle upon Tyne North *(Majority 3,414)*

Shadow Exchequer Secretary

Born 8 June 1976; Daughter of John and Agnes Grady; Married Rhys (2 children).

Education: Sacred Heart Comprehensive School, Fenham, Newcastle upon Tyne; Edinburgh University (MA politics and history 2000); Northumbria University (Postgraduate Diploma law and common professional examination 2002); Italian.

Non-political career: Employment solicitor, Newcastle. Unite.

LABOUR

Political career: Member for Newcastle upon Tyne North since 6 May 2010 general election; Shadow Solicitor General 2010-11; Shadow Minister for Education 2011-12; Shadow Exchequer Secretary 2012-. *Select committees:* Member: Political and Constitutional Reform 2010.

Political interests: Regional development, manufacturing, economy, women and children, international development, justice and legal aid, apprenticeships; Italy.

Other: Northumbrian Association; Tyneside Irish Centre; MS Society; CAFOD. British Military Fitness.

Recreations: Swimming, travel.

Catherine McKinnell MP, House of Commons, London SW1A 0AA
Tel: 020 7219 7115 *Email:* catherine.mckinnell.mp@parliament.uk
Constituency: No constituency office publicised
Tel: 0191-229 0352 *Website:* www.catherinemckinnellmp.co.uk *Twitter:* @CatMcKinnellMP

CONSERVATIVE

MACLEOD, MARY
Brentford and Isleworth *(Majority 1,958)*

PPS to Maria Miller as Secretary of State for Culture, Media and Sport and Minister for Women and Equalities

Education: Glasgow University.

Non-political career: Management consultant, Andersen Consulting; Policy adviser, HM The Queen's private office, Buckingham Palace 1998-99; Managing director, MCG 2002-; Policy adviser to David Willetts MP.

Political career: Contested Ross, Skye and Inverness West 1997 general election. Member for Brentford and Isleworth since 6 May 2010 general election; PPS to: Nick Herbert as Minister of State for Policing, Home Office and Ministry of Justice 2010-12, Maria Miller as Secretary of State for Culture, Media and Sport and Minister for Women and Equalities 2012-. *Select committees:* Member: Home Affairs 2010. Member, Conservative Party 1992-; Deputy Chairman, Kensington and Chelsea Conservative Association 2003-06; Chair, Conservative Candidates Association 2005-09; Member, Conservative Women's Advisory Board 2005-09. *Councils and public bodies:* School governor, Holland Park Secondary School 2005-10; Trustee, Holland Park School Trust 2008-; Advisory Board, Learning for Life 2008-.

Other: Ambassador, ActionAid.

Recreations: Sport, music, art, reading, clay pigeon shooting.

Mary Macleod MP, House of Commons, London SW1A 0AA
Tel: 020 7219 7023 *Fax:* 020 7219 4049 *Email:* mary.macleod.mp@parliament.uk
Constituency: 433 Chiswick High Road, Chiswick, London W4 4AU
Tel: 020 8994 7203 *Website:* www.marymacleod.com *Twitter:* @MaryMacleodMP

CONSERVATIVE

McLOUGHLIN, PATRICK
Derbyshire Dales *(Majority 13,866)*

Secretary of State for Transport

Patrick Allan McLoughlin. Born 30 November 1957; Son of Patrick Alphonsos McLoughlin; Married Lynne Newman 1984 (1 son 1 daughter).

Education: Cardinal Griffin Comprehensive School, Cannock; Staffordshire College of Agriculture.

Non-political career: Agricultural worker 1974-79; Various positions with National Coal Board (including underground) 1979-86.

Political career: Contested Wolverhampton South East 1983 general election. Member for West Derbyshire 8 May 1986 by-election to 2010, for Derbyshire Dales since 6 May 2010 general election; PPS to: Angela Rumbold as Minister of State, Department of Education 1987-88, Lord Young of Graffham as Secretary of State for Trade and Industry 1988-89; Parliamentary Under-Secretary of State, Department of Transport (Minister for Aviation and Shipping) 1989-92; Joint Parliamentary Under-Secretary of State, Department of Employment 1992-93; Parliamentary Under-Secretary of State, Department of Trade and Industry (Trade and Technology) 1993-94; Assistant Government Whip 1995-96; Government Whip 1996-97; Opposition Pairing Whip 1997-98; Opposition Deputy Chief Whip 1998-2005; Opposition Chief Whip 2005-10; Parliamentary Secretary to the Treasury 2010-12; Chief Whip 2010-12; Member, Parliamentary and Political Service Honours Committee 2012; Secretary of State for Transport 2012-. *Select committees:* Member: Broadcasting 1994-95, Selection 1997-2001, Finance and Services 1998-2005, Accommodation and Works 2001-05, Modernisation of the House of Commons 2004-05, Selection 2005, Administration 2005. National vice-chair, Young Conservatives 1982-84. *Councils and public bodies:* Councillor: Cannock Chase District Council 1980-87, Staffordshire County Council 1981-87.

Political interests: Agriculture, education.

Other: PC 2005.

Rt Hon Patrick McLoughlin MP, House of Commons, London SW1A 0AA
Tel: 020 7219 3511 *Email:* patrick.mcloughlin.mp@parliament.uk
Constituency: No constituency office

SCOTTISH NATIONAL PARTY

MacNEIL, ANGUS
Na h-Eileanan An Iar *(Majority 1,885)*

SNP Spokesperson for Transport, for Tourism, for Scotland Office and for Deputy Prime Minister's Portfolio

Angus Brendan MacNeil. Born 21 July 1970; Son of Iain MacNeil, postman and crofter, and late Clare MacNeil, district nurse; Married Jane Douglas 1998 (3 daughters).

Education: Castlebay Secondary School, Isle of Barra; Nicolson Institute, Stornoway, Isle of Lewis; Strathclyde University (BEng civil engineering 1992); Jordanhill College (PGCE primary teaching and bilingualism 1996); Gaelic, Irish gaelic.

Non-political career: Civil engineer, Lilley Construction Ltd, Edinburgh 1992-93; Radio reporter, BBC, Inverness 1993-95; Primary teacher, Salen Primary School, Mull 1996-98; Gaelic development officer, Lochaber 1998-99; Education lecturer (part-time), Inverness College 1999-.

Political career: Contested Inverness East, Nairn and Lochaber 2001 general election. Member for Na h-Eileanan An Iar since 5 May 2005 general election; SNP Spokesperson for: Transport 2005-, Environment 2005-07, Tourism 2005-, Fishing 2005-10, Food and Rural Affairs 2005-10, Work and Pensions 2007-08, Scotland Office 2008-, Deputy Prime Minister's Portfolio 2013-. *Select committees:* Member: Scottish Affairs 2005-09. Convener Lochaber branch SNP 1999.

Political interests: Economics of Small States; Norway, Iceland, Faroe Islands.

Other: Amnesty International, Voluntary Services Overseas (VSO).

Recreations: Football, sailing, fishing.

Angus MacNeil MP, House of Commons, London SW1A 0AA
Tel: 020 7219 8476 *Fax:* 020 7219 6111 *Email:* macneila@parliament.uk
Constituency: 31 Bayhead Street, Stornoway, Isle of Lewis, Outer Hebrides HS1 2DU
Tel: 01851 702272 *Fax:* 01851 701767 *Email:* macdonaldrm@parliament.uk
Twitter: @AngusMacNeilMP

CONSERVATIVE

McPARTLAND, STEPHEN
Stevenage *(Majority 3,578)*

Stephen Anthony McPartland. Born 9 August 1976; Married Emma.

Education: Liverpool College; Liverpool University (BA history 1997); Liverpool John Moores University (MSc technology management 1998).

Non-political career: Agent, North East Hertfordshire Conservative Association 2001-08; Membership director, British American Business (American Chamber of Commerce) 2008-10.

Political career: Member for Stevenage since 6 May 2010 general election. *Select committees:* Member: Science and Technology 2011-12.

Political interests: Healthcare (particularly cancer treatment and respiratory diseases), education, satellite technology, international trade, policing, addiction treatment, urban regeneration, government procurement of IT projects; China, India, UK, USA.

Other: Asthma UK; Trustee: The Living Room, Turn the Tide.

Recreations: Reading, keeping fit, cinema.

Stephen McPartland MP, House of Commons, London SW1A 0AA
Tel: 020 7219 7156 *Email:* stephen.mcpartland.mp@parliament.uk
Constituency: Currently moving offices
Website: www.stephenmcpartland.co.uk *Twitter:* @SMcPartlandMP

LABOUR

MACTAGGART, FIONA
Slough *(Majority 5,523)*

Fiona Margaret Mactaggart. Born 12 September 1953; Daughter of late Sir Ian Mactaggart and late Rosemary Belhaven.

Education: Cheltenham Ladies' College; London University: King's College (BA English 1975), Goldsmiths' College (Postgraduate Certificate teaching 1987), Institute of Education (MA 1993).

Non-political career: Vice-president, National Secretary, National Union of Students 1978-81; Press and public relations officer, National Council for Voluntary Organisations 1981; General secretary, Joint Council for the Welfare of Immigrants 1982-86; Primary school teacher 1987-92; Public relations officer, private property company 1992; Lecturer in primary education Institute of Education 1992-97. Member: NUJ 1981, ASTMS 1981, TGWU 1982-86, NUT 1987-92, AUT 1992-97, GMB 1997-.

Political career: Member for Slough 1997-2010, for Slough (revised boundary) since 6 May 2010 general election; PPS to Chris Smith as Secretary of State for Culture, Media and Sport December 1997-2001; Parliamentary Under-Secretary of State, Home Office 2003-06: (Race Equality, Community Policy and Civil Renewal 2003-05, Offender Management and Criminal Justice 2005-06); Shadow Minister for Equalities Office 2010-11. *Select committees:* Member: Public Administration 1997-98, Education and Skills/Children, Schools and Families 2006-10, Joint Committee on Human Rights 2009-10, Health 2010, Public Accounts 2011-. Honorary secretary, PLP Departmental Committee for Home Affairs 1997-99, 2000-02; PLP Departmental Group for Women: Chair 2001-03, 2008-10, 2011-, Vice-chair 2007-08. Member, National Policy Forum. *Councils and public bodies:* London Borough of Wandsworth: Councillor 1986-90, Leader, Labour Group 1988-90.

Political interests: Human rights, civil liberties, home affairs, education, arts, health.

Other: Chair, Liberty 1994-96, Editorial Board, Renewal; Chair, Commonweal Housing 2007-; Member, advisory committee, Parliament Choir. Society Champion, Charity Champion Awards 2011.

Recreations: Walking, talking, reading, the arts, watching television, going to the theatre, opera, museums and galleries.

Fiona Mactaggart MP, House of Commons, London SW1A 0AA
Tel: 020 7219 3416 *Fax:* 020 7219 0989 *Email:* mactaggartf@parliament.uk
Constituency: 52 High Street, Chalvey, Slough, Berkshire SL1 2SQ
Tel: 01753 518161 *Fax:* 01753 550293 *Email:* fiona.mactaggart@gmail.com
Website: www.fionamactaggart.org.uk *Twitter:* @fionamacmp

CONSERVATIVE

McVEY, ESTHER
Wirral West *(Majority 2,436)*

Minister of State (Employment), Department for Work and Pensions

Esther Louise McVey. Born 24 October 1967; Daughter of James and Barbara McVey.

Education: Belvedere School, Liverpool; Queen Mary and Westfield, London (LLB 1990); City University, London (Post-graduate Course radio journalism 1991); John Moore's University, Liverpool (MSc corporate governance 2009, winner North of England Excellence Award).

Non-political career: Director, JG McVey & Co Ltd 2000-06; Managing director, Making It (UK) Ltd 2002-10; Founder, Winning Women 2003-10.

Political career: Contested Wirral West 2005 general election. Member for Wirral West since 6 May 2010 general election; PPS to Chris Grayling as Minister of State for Employment 2010-12; Department for Work and Pensions: Parliamentary Under-Secretary of State (Minister for Disabled People) 2012-13, Minister of State (Employment) 2013-.

Political interests: Law and order and sentencing, transport, education, city regeneration.

Other: Board member: Madeleine McCann Fund 2007-08, North West Women's Enterprise Forum 2008-10; Patron: Wirral Holistic Therapeutic Cancer Care, Full of Life (charity for disabled children and their families); Ambassador, Action Medical Research; Member, NCH.

Recreations: Theatre, cinema, walking.

Esther McVey MP, House of Commons, London SW1A 0AA
Tel: 020 7219 7191 *Email:* esther.mcvey.mp@parliament.uk
Constituency: The Parade, Hoylake Community Centre, Hoyle Road, Hoylake, Wirral CH47 3AG
Tel: 0151-632 4348 *Email:* officeofesthermcveymp@parliament.uk
Website: www.esthermcvey.com *Twitter:* @esthermcveymp

LABOUR

MAHMOOD, KHALID
Birmingham, Perry Barr *(Majority 11,908)*

Born 13 July 1961.

Non-political career: Former engineer. AEEU; Former adviser Danish International Trade Union.

Political career: Member for Birmingham Perry Barr 2001-10, for Birmingham, Perry Bar (revised boundary) since 6 May 2010 general election; PPS to Tony McNulty as Minister of State: Department for Transport 2004-05, Home Office 2005-06. *Select committees:* Member: Broadcasting 2001-05, Home Affairs 2009-10. Local Constituency Labour Party: Secretary, Vice-chair; Member: Socialist Health Association, Socialist Education Association; Labour Finance and Industry Group: National member, Midlands branch executive member. *Councils and public bodies:* Birmingham City Council 1990-93: Councillor, Chair Race Relations.

Political interests: Community relations, British industry, international trade, terrorism.

Other: Adviser President of Olympic Council Asia; Member governing body: Neighbourhood forum, South Birmingham CHC.

Khalid Mahmood MP, House of Commons, London SW1A 0AA
Tel: 020 7219 8141 *Fax:* 020 7219 1745 *Email:* mahmoodk@parliament.uk
Constituency: 18 Heathfield Road, Handsworth, Birmingham B19 1HB
Tel: 0121-356 8264/8 *Fax:* 0121-356 8278 *Website:* www.khalidmahmoodmp.co.uk

MAHMOOD, SHABANA
Birmingham, Ladywood *(Majority 10,105)*

Shadow Minister for HM Treasury

Born 17 September 1980; Daughter of Zubaida and Mahmood Ahmed.

Education: Small Heath School, Birmingham; King Edward VI Camp Hill School for Girls; Lincoln College, Oxford (BA law 2002); Inns of Court School of Law (Bar Vocational Course 2003); Basic French, fluent Mirpuri and Urdu.

Non-political career: Barrister: 12 King's Bench Walk 2003-04, Berrymans Lace Mawer 2004-08.

LABOUR

Political career: Member for Birmingham, Ladywood since 6 May 2010 general election; Shadow Minister for: Home Office 2010-11, Business, Innovation and Skills (Higher Education) 2011-13, Business, Innovation and Skills (Universities and Science) 2013-, HM Treasury 2013-. *Select committees:* Member: Work and Pensions 2010.

Shabana Mahmood MP, House of Commons, London SW1A 0AA
Tel: 020 7219 7818 *Email:* shabana.mahmood.mp@parliament.uk
Constituency: No constituency office
Tel: 0121-551 2869 *Fax:* 0121-551 7852 *Website:* www.shabanamahmood.org
Twitter: @shabanamahmood

MAIN, ANNE
St Albans *(Majority 2,305)*

Anne Margaret Main. Born 17 May 1957; Daughter of Rita and late George Wiseman; Married Stephen Tonks 1978 (died 1991) (1 son 2 daughters); married Andrew Main 1995 (1 son).

Education: Bishop of Llandaff Secondary School, Cardiff; University College of Wales, Swansea (BA English 1978); Sheffield University (PGCE 1979); French.

Non-political career: Teaching and family 1979-80; Home-maker 1980-90; Carer for terminally ill husband 1990-91; Single parent and supply teacher 1991-95. NUT 1979-80.

CONSERVATIVE

Political career: Member for St Albans 2005-10, for St Albans (revised boundary) since 6 May 2010 general election. *Select committees:* Member: ODPM/Communities and Local Government 2005-10, Energy and Climate Change 2009-10, Chairmen's Panel/Panel of Chairs 2010-. Chair and founder, Conservative Friends of Bangladesh.

Political interests: Environment, education, health; Bangladesh.

Other: Member, International League for the Protection of Horses 1999-; St Albans Civic Society 2003-; Fellow, Industry and Parliament Trust 2007; Governor, Westminster Foundation for Democracy 2010-11; Supporter, Grove House Hospice charity; Patron, Macmillan; Conservative Women's Club; St Albans Conservative Club; Beaconsfield Conservative Club.

Recreations: Dog walking, art, reading, food and wine.

Anne Main MP, House of Commons, London SW1A 0AA
Tel: 020 7219 8270 *Fax:* 020 7219 3058 *Email:* maina@parliament.uk
Constituency: 104 High Street, London Colney, St Albans, Hertfordshire AL2 1QL
Tel: 01727 825100 *Fax:* 01727 828404 *Email:* agent@stalbansconservatives.com
Website: www.annemain.com

Need additional copies?
Call 020 7593 5679

Visit www.dodsshop.co.uk

LABOUR

MALHOTRA, SEEMA

Feltham and Heston *(Majority 6,203)*

Opposition Whip

Born 7 August 1972; Daughter of Sushil Kumar Malhotra, retired engineer and small business-man, and Usha Malhotra, retired teacher; Married Sushil Saluja 2005.

Education: Green School, Isleworth; Warwick University (politics and philosophy 1994) (schol-arship, University of Massachusetts, Amhurst, USA 1992-93); Aston University (business IT 1995); German (some), Hindi, Punjabi.

Non-political career: Management consultant, Accenture 1995-2003; Consultant 2004-05; Senior manager, PriceWaterhouseCoopers 2003-07; Adviser to: Liam Byrne: as Minister for the West Midlands 2007-08, as Chair of the Council of Regional Ministers 2008-09, Ian Austin as Minister for the West Midlands 2008-09; Adviser to the Video Games industry on child safety agenda 2008; Programme leader, cross-government programme to increase diversity in public appointments 2009-10; Political adviser to Harriet Harman as Acting Leader of the Opposition May-October 2010; Strategic programme adviser, UKIE May-November 2011. Unite: Member, Chair, South Thames Community Branch 2007-11.

Political career: Member for Feltham and Heston since 15 December 2011 by-election; PPS to Yvette Cooper as Shadow Secretary of State for Home Department (Home Secretary); Shadow Minister for Women and Equalities 2012; Opposition Whip 2013-. *Select committees:* Member: Justice 2012-. Chair, PLP Departmental Group for Business, Innovation and Skills 2012-. Mem-ber, Co-operative Party.

Political interests: Business and entrepreneurship, civil and criminal justice, public administra-tion, youth offending, apprenticeships, aviation, gender and equalities, British-American rela-tions, policing, women offenders, community banking, women and business, diversity on public boards; China, India, Middle East.

Other: Chair, Young Fabians 1999-2000; Fabian Society: Executive member 2000-, Chair 2005-06, Founder and director, Fabian Women's Network 2005-; Fellow, British American Project; Fellow, Royal Society of Arts; Trustee, Swanswell 2011-. Shortlisted, Asian Women of Achieve-ment awards 2006.

Publications: Contributor: Dictionary of Labour Biography (Politico's, 2001), From the Work-house to Welfare (Fabian Society and Webb Memorial Trust, 2009).

Recreations: Running, cinema, music, gardening, playing the guitar.

Seema Malhotra MP, House of Commons, London SW1A 0AA
Tel: 020 7219 8957 *Fax:* 020 7219 2578 *Email:* seema.malhotra.mp@parliament.uk
Constituency: No constituency office *Website:* www.seemamalhotra.com
Twitter: @SeemaMalhotra1

LABOUR

MANN, JOHN

Bassetlaw *(Majority 8,215)*

Born 10 January 1960; Son of James Mann and Brenda Cleavin; Married Joanna White 1986 (2 daughters 1 son).

Education: Bradford Grammar School; Manchester University (BA Econ 1982); ITD Diploma 1992; French, German.

Non-political career: Head research and education AEU 1988-90; National training officer TUC 1990-95; Liaison officer National Trade Union and Labour Party 1995-2000; Director Abraxas Communications Ltd 1998-2002. AEEU 1985-.

Political career: Member for Bassetlaw 2001-10, for Bassetlaw (revised boundary) since 6 May 2010 general election; PPS: to Richard Caborn as Minister for Sport 2005-07, to Tessa Jowell as Minister for: the Olympics and London 2007-08, the Olympics 2008, the Olympics and Paymas-ter General 2009. *Select committees:* Member: Information 2001-05, Treasury 2003-05, 2009-, Treasury (Treasury Sub-Committee) 2003-10, Unopposed Bills (Panel) 2004-. Contested East Midlands 1999 European Parliament election. *Councils and public bodies:* Councillor London Borough of Lambeth 1986-90.

Political interests: Small businesses, training, economic regeneration, sport, drugs.

Other: Fellow, Industry and Parliament Trust 2003; MIPD; IPD, YHA, Manton Miners.

Publications: Labour and Youth: The Missing Generation (Fabian Society, 1985); Heroin in Bas-setlaw (2002); The Real Deal (Fabian Society, 2006); The Bassetlaw Anti-Social Behaviour Hand-book (2007); Co-Writer, Antisemitism in European Football: A scar on the beautiful game (2008); Miner Compensation – The Legal Complaints Service and the Coal Health Compensation Scheme (2009); What every Parent and Grandparent Needs to Know about Drugs and Alcohol (2009).

Recreations: Football, cricket, fellwalking and mountaineering.

John Mann MP, House of Commons, London SW1A 0AA
Tel: 020 7219 8345 *Fax:* 020 7219 5965 *Email:* mannj@parliament.uk
Constituency: 68a Carlton Road, Worksop, Nottinghamshire S80 1PH
Tel: 01909 506 200 *Fax:* 01909 532447 *Email:* whitej@parliament.uk
Website: www.johnmannmp.com *Twitter:* @johnmannmp

MARSDEN, GORDON
Blackpool South *(Majority 1,852)*

Shadow Minister for Transport

Born 28 November 1953; Son of late George Henry and Joyce Marsden.

Education: Stockport Grammar School; New College, Oxford (MA history 1976); London University (PhD research in combined historical studies 1976-80); Harvard University (Kennedy Scholarship 1978-79); French, German.

Non-political career: Open University tutor/associate lecturer, arts faculty 1977-97; Public relations consultant 1980-85; Chief public affairs adviser to English Heritage 1984-85; Editor: *History Today* 1985-97, *New Socialist* 1989-90. Member, GMB.

LABOUR

Political career: Contested Blackpool South 1992 general election. Member for Blackpool South 1997-2010, for Blackpool South (revised boundary) since 6 May 2010 general election; PPS to: Lord Irvine of Lairg as Lord Chancellor 2001-03, Tessa Jowell as Secretary of State for Culture, Media and Sport 2003-05, John Denham as Secretary of State for Communities and Local Government 2009-10; Shadow Minister for: Communities and Local Government 2010, Business, Innovation and Skills 2010-13, Transport 2013-. *Select committees:* Member: Deregulation 1997-99, Ecclesiastical Committee 1997-, Education and Employment 1998-2001, Education and Employment (Education Sub-Committee) 1998-2001, Education and Skills 2005-07, Innovation, Universities[, Science] and Skills/Science and Technology 2007-10. Convenor, Labour Seaside Group of MPs 1997-2010; Honorary Secretary, PLP Departmental Committee for Culture, Media and Sport 2005-10; Chair, PLP North West Regional Group 2006-07. Chair, Seaside and Coastal Towns Manifesto Group 2007-10. *Councils and public bodies:* Member, National Skills Commission 2006-.

Political interests: Heritage, education, international affairs, social affairs, disability, human rights; Caribbean, Eastern Europe, North Africa, Russia, USA.

Other: Member, Fabian Society 1975-: Chair, Young Fabians 1980-81; Judge, Ford Conservation Awards UK 1990-97; Board member, Institute of Historical Research 1996-2001; President, British Resorts and Destinations Association 1998-: Chair, Research and and Public Committee 2000-01; President, Blackpool Disability Services 2000-; Trustee, Dartmouth Street Trust; Board member: History Today Trust, Gareth Butler Trust; Trustee, History of Parliament Trust. Gibbs Prize in History 1975; Kennedy Scholar, Harvard 1978-79; Parliamentary Fellow, St Antony's College, Oxford 2003; Centenary Fellowship, Historical Association 2006.

Publications: Editor, Victorian Values (1990, 1998); Contributor to The History Debate (1990); Low Cost Socialism (1997); Contributor The English Question (Fabian Society, 2000); International History of Censorship (2001).

Recreations: Theatre, early music and medieval culture, swimming, heritage sites, architecture.

Gordon Marsden MP, House of Commons, London SW1A 0AA
Tel: 020 7219 1262 *Fax:* 020 7219 5859 *Email:* gordonmarsdenmp@parliament.uk
Constituency: 304 Highfield Road, Blackpool, Lancashire FY4 3JX
Tel: 01253 344143 *Fax:* 01253 344940 *Website:* www.gordonmarsden.co.uk
Twitter: @gordonmarsdenmp

MASKEY, PAUL
Belfast West *(Majority 13,123)*

Paul John Maskey. Born 10 June 1967; Son of Alex and Teresa Maskey; Married Patricia (2 children).

Education: Edmund Rice College; Irish.

Political career: Member for Belfast West since 9 June 2011 by-election; Northern Ireland Assembly: MLA for Belfast West 2007-11, and for Belfast West (revised boundary) 2011-12: Deputy chair, Enterprise, Trade and Investment Committee 2007-08, Chair, Public Accounts Committee 2008-12; Sinn Féin: Deputy Whip, Spokesperson for: Public Accounts, Governance 2011-12. *Councils and public bodies:* Belfast City Council: Councillor 2001-09, Leader, Sinn Féin Group -2009.

SINN FÉIN

Political interests: Poverty; Basque Country, Italy.

Other: Board member: Upper Andersonstown Community Forum, Greater Andersonstown Neighbourhood Partnership; Fáilte Feirste Thiar.

Recreations: Walking, five-a-side football.

Paul Maskey MP, House of Commons, London SW1A 0AA
Tel: 020 7219 3000
Constituency: c/o 53 Falls Road, Belfast BT12 4PD
Tel: 028 9034 7350 *Fax:* 028 9034 7360 *Email:* westbelfastmp@sinnfein.ie
Website: www.sinnfeinbelfast.com *Twitter:* @PaulMaskeyMP

CONSERVATIVE

MAUDE, FRANCIS
Horsham *(Majority 11,460)*

Minister for the Cabinet Office; Paymaster General

Francis Anthony Aylmer Maude. Born 4 July 1953; Son of late Angus Maude, former MP, later Baron Maude of Stratford-upon-Avon, PC (Life Peer), author and journalist, and late Lady Maude; Married Christina Hadfield 1984 (2 sons 3 daughters).

Education: Abingdon School; Corpus Christi, Cambridge (MA history 1976) (Hulse Prize and Avory Studentship); College of Law (Forster Boulton Prize and Inner Temple Law Scholarship 1977).

Non-political career: Called to Bar, Inner Temple 1977; Practising barrister 1977-85; Head of global privatisation, Salomon Bros International 1992-93; Managing director, global privatisation, Morgan Stanley & Co Ltd 1993-97; Chair, Deregulation Task Force 1993-97; Benfield Group plc: Non-executive director 1999-, Deputy chair 2003-08; Non-executive director, Businesses for Sale Company plc 2000-02; Chair: Prestbury Holdings plc 2002-08, Jubilee Investment Trust plc 2003-07, The Mission Marketing Group 2006-09.

Political career: Member for North Warwickshire 1983-92. Contested North Warwickshire 1992 general election. Member for Horsham 1997-2010, for Horsham (revised boundary) since 6 May 2010 general election; PPS to Peter Morrison as Minister of State for Employment 1984; Government Whip 1985-87; Parliamentary Under-Secretary of State, Department of Trade and Industry 1987-89; Minister of State, Foreign and Commonwealth Office 1989-90; Financial Secretary to the Treasury 1990-92; Member, Shadow Cabinet 1997-2001: Shadow Secretary of State: for National Heritage 1997, for Culture, Media and Sport 1997-98; Shadow Chancellor of the Exchequer 1998-2000; Shadow Secretary of State for Foreign and Commonwealth Affairs 2000-01; Shadow Minister for the Cabinet Office and Shadow Chancellor of the Duchy of Lancaster 2007-10; Minister for the Cabinet Office; Paymaster General 2010-. *Select committees:* Member: Public Accounts 1990-92. Member, Executive 1922 Committee 1997; Chair, Conservative Party Committees for: Culture, Media and Sport 1997-98, Finance 1998-2000 European Affairs 2000-01, Foreign and Commonwealth Affairs 2000-01. Chair, Conservative Party 2005-07. *Councils and public bodies:* Councillor, Westminster City Council 1978-84; Chair of governors, Abingdon School 1994-2003.

Other: PC 1992.

Recreations: Skiing, reading, opera.

Rt Hon Francis Maude MP, House of Commons, London SW1A 0AA
Tel: 020 7219 2494 *Fax:* 020 7219 2990 *Email:* francismaudemp@parliament.uk
Constituency: Gough House, Madeira Avenue, Horsham, West Sussex RH12 1RL
Tel: 01403 242000 *Fax:* 01403 210600 *Website:* www.francismaude.com

CONSERVATIVE

MAY, THERESA
Maidenhead *(Majority 16,769)*

Secretary of State for the Home Office (Home Secretary)

Theresa Mary May. Born 1 October 1956; Daughter of late Rev Hubert and Zaidee Brasier; Married Philip May 1980.

Education: Wheatley Park Comprehensive School, Holton, Oxfordshire; St Hugh's College, Oxford (BA geography 1977, MA); French (basic).

Non-political career: Various posts latterly senior adviser, international affairs, Association for Payment Clearing Services 1985-97.

Political career: Contested North West Durham 1992 general election and Barking 1994 by-election. Member for Maidenhead 1997-2010, for Maidenhead (revised boundary) since 6 May 2010 general election; Opposition Spokeswoman for Education and Employment (schools, disabled people and women) 1998-99; Member Shadow Cabinet 1999-2010: Spokeswoman for

Women's Issues 1999-2001, Shadow Secretary of State for: Education and Employment 1999-2001, Transport, Local Government and the Regions 2001-02, Transport 2002, Environment and Transport 2003-04, the Family 2004-05, Culture, Media and Sport 2005; Shadow Leader of the House of Commons 2005-09; Member House of Commons Commission 2006-09; Shadow Minister for Women 2007-10; Shadow Secretary of State for Work and Pensions 2009-10; Secretary of State for the Home Office (Home Secretary) 2010-; Minister for Women and Equalities 2010-12. *Select committees:* Member: Education and Employment 1997-98, Education and Employment (Education Sub-Committee) 1997-99, Modernisation of the House of Commons 2006-10. Joint secretary, Conservative Party Committee for Home Affairs 1997-98; Chair, Conservative Transport/Local Government/Planning Policy Committee 2001-02. Chair: Conservative Disability Group 1997-98, Conservative Party 2002-03. *Councils and public bodies:* Councillor, London Borough of Merton 1986-94.

Other: Patron: National Rheumatoid Arthritis Society, Electric Eels, Alexander Devine Children's Hospice, Project Rainbow, Friends of St Andrew's Church (Sonning), Mission Direct; Fellow, Royal Geographical Society; Trustee, Maidenhead Civic Society; Patron, League of Friends of St Marks Hospital. *The Spectator* awards: Double Act of the Year (with Kenneth Clarke MP) 2011, Minister of the Year 2012. PC 2003; Maidenhead Conservative.

Recreations: Walking, cooking.

Rt Hon Theresa May MP, House of Commons, London SW1A 0AA
Tel: 020 7219 5206 *Fax:* 020 7219 1145 *Email:* mayt@parliament.uk
Constituency: c/o Maidenhead Conservative Association, 2 Castle End Farm, Ruscombe, Berkshire RG10 9XQ
Tel: 0118-934 5433 *Email:* office@maidenheadconservatives.com *Website:* www.tmay.co.uk

---

MAYNARD, PAUL Blackpool North and Cleveleys *(Majority 2,150)*

PPS to Oliver Letwin as Minister for Government Policy, Cabinet Office

Paul Christopher Maynard. Born 16 December 1975.

Education: St Ambrose College, Altrincham; University College, Oxford (BA modern history 1997); French, German.

Non-political career: Researcher, Hodgart Temporal 1997-99; Health policy officer, Conservative Party 1999-2002; Head of home affairs, Conservative Research Department 2001-02; Senior researcher, Reform 2003; Special adviser to Dr Liam Fox MP 2003-07.

CONSERVATIVE

Political career: Contested Twickenham 2005 general election. Member for Blackpool North and Cleveleys since 6 May 2010 general election; PPS to Oliver Letwin as Minister for Government Policy, Cabinet Office 2012-. *Select committees:* Member: Transport 2010-12. Vice-chair, Weaver Vale Conservative Association 1997-99.

Political interests: Education, social policy; Australia, Bosnia and Herzegovina, Germany, Moldova.

Other: Society Champion, Charity Champion awards 2012.

Paul Maynard MP, House of Commons, London SW1A 0AA
Tel: 020 7219 7017 *Email:* paul.maynard.mp@parliament.uk
Constituency: 16 Queen Street, Blackpool FY1 1PD
Tel: 01253 473071 *Website:* www.paulmaynard.co.uk *Twitter:* @PaulMaynardMP

MEACHER, MICHAEL Oldham West and Royton *(Majority 9,352)*

Michael Hugh Meacher. Born 4 November 1939; Son of late George Meacher and Dorris Meacher, née Foxell; Married Molly Reid 1962 (divorced 1987, later Baroness Meacher (qv)) (2 sons 2 daughters); married Lucianne Sawyer, née Craven 1988.

Education: Berkhamsted School, Hertfordshire; New College, Oxford (BA Greats 1962); London School of Economics (Diploma social administration 1963).

Non-political career: Secretary, Danilo Dolci Trust 1964; Sembal research fellow in social gerontology, Essex University 1965-66; Lecturer in social administration: York University 1966-69, London School of Economics 1970; Visiting professor to Department of Sociology, Surrey University 1980-86. Member, Unison.

LABOUR

Political career: Contested Colchester 1966 general election and Oldham West 1968 by-election. Member for Oldham West 1970-97, for Oldham West and Royton 1997-2010, for Oldham West and Royton (revised boundary) since 6 May 2010 general election; Parliamentary Under-Secretary of State: Department of Industry 1974-75, Department of Health and Social Security 1975-76, Department of Trade 1976-79; Member Shadow Cabinet 1983-97: Principal Opposition Front-bench Spokesperson for: Health and Social Security 1983-87, Employment 1987-89, Social Security 1989-92, Overseas Development and Co-operation 1992-93, Citizen's Charter and Science 1993-94, Transport 1994-95, Education and Employment 1995-96, Environmental Protection 1996-97; Minister of State: Department of the Environment, Transport and the Regions (Environment) 1997-2001, Department for Environment, Food and Rural Affairs 2001-03 (Environment 2001-02, Environment and Agri-Environment 2002-03). *Select committees:* Member: Environmental Audit 1997-2003. Contested Deputy Leadership, Labour Party 1983; Member, Labour Party National Executive Committee 1983-89; Contested Leadership, Labour Party 2007.

Political interests: Economics and social policy, redistribution of income and wealth, industrial democracy, civil liberties, housing, democracy and accountability.

Other: First Base (housing charity for young people); Fellow, Industry and Parliament Trust 1989; Macmillan Cancer; Motor Neurone Disease Association. Honorary Freeman, Borough of Oldham. PC 1997.

Publications: The Care of Old People (Fabian Society, 1969); Taken For A Ride: Special Residential Homes for the Elderly Mentally Infirm: A Study of Separatism in Social Policy (1972); Socialism with a Human Face – the Political Economy in the 1980s (1982); Diffusing Power – The Key to Socialist Revival (1992); Destination of the Species (2010); Numerous articles and pamphlets on social and economic policy.

Recreations: Sport, music, reading, photography (camcorder).

Rt Hon Michael Meacher MP, House of Commons, London SW1A 0AA
Tel: 020 7219 4532/020 7219 6461 *Fax:* 020 7219 5945 *Email:*
michael.meacher.mp@parliament.uk
Constituency: 11 Church Lane, Oldham, Greater Manchester OL1 3AN
Tel: 0161-626 5779 *Fax:* 0161-626 8572 *Email:* buckleysd@parliament.uk
Website: www.michaelmeacher.info *Twitter:* @michaelmeacher

LABOUR

MEALE, ALAN
Mansfield *(Majority 6,012)*

Joseph Alan Meale. Born 31 July 1949; Son of late Albert Meale and Elizabeth Meale; Married Diana Gilhespy 1983 (1 son (deceased) 1 daughter).

Education: St Joseph's Roman Catholic School, Bishop Auckland; Durham University; Ruskin College, Oxford; Sheffield Hallam University.

Non-political career: Author and editor; Development officer; Researcher for MPs Barbara Castle, Tony Benn, Dennis Skinner, Albert Booth, Joan Maynard, John Prescott; Parliamentary and political adviser to Michael Meacher as Spokesperson for Health and Social Security 1984-87. National employment development officer, NACRO 1977-80; Assistant to Ray Buckton, General Secretary of ASLEF 1979-84.

Political career: Member for Mansfield 1987-2010, for Mansfield (revised boundary) since 6 May 2010 general election; Opposition Whip 1992-94; PPS to John Prescott: as Deputy Leader of the Labour Party 1994-97, as Deputy Prime Minister and Secretary of State for the Environment, Transport and the Regions 1997-98; Parliamentary Under-Secretary of State, Department of the Environment, Transport and the Regions 1998-99; Adviser to Richard Caborn, as Minister of State for Sport 2002-05. *Select committees:* Member: Home Affairs 1990-92, Court of Referees 1999-2001; Chair: Crossrail Bill 2006-07; Member: Panel of Chairs 2011-, Joint Committee on Voting Eligibilty (Prisoners) Bill 2013-. Chair PLP East Midlands and Central Groups 1988-95. Former officer, national and local Labour Party; Member, Co-operative Party. *Councils and public bodies:* Deputy leader, Newton Aycliffe Town Council 1974-79; Governor Portland Training College 1988-.

Political interests: Home affairs, European affairs, transport, health, social security, drug abuse, human rights, environment, poverty, sport, unemployment, media, music, armed forces welfare; Cyprus, Europe, France, Ireland.

Other: Former executive member: Commonwealth Parliamentary Association (CPA), Inter-Parliamentary Union (IPU); Member, UK Delegation Parliamentary Assembly of the Council of Europe (CoE)/Western European Union 2000-: Representative Kyoto Protocol 2001-09, CoE President CTTs Environment, Agriculture, Local and Regional Democracy: First Vice-President 2001-08, President 2008-, Chair, CoE Sustainable Development 2002-04, UK Government Whip CoE Delegation 2007-, Acting Leader, UK Delegation 2010-; Chair, CPA Cyprus Group (British Section) 2007-; Fellow, Industry and Parliament Trust 1993; Board member, Portland Training College 1987-2010; Member, War Pensions Board 1989-97; Parliamentary Representative,

SSAFA 1990-94; Commissioner, Commonwealth War Graves 2003-11; Member, Labour Research Trust; Guide Dogs. Freeman, State of Louisiana, USA; Freeman, City of: Mansfield, Ohio, USA; Morphou, Cyprus. Honorary Senatorship of Louisiana, USA; Kt 2011; Honorary Citizen Morphou, Cyprus.

Recreations: Environment, reading, writing, arts, politics, sports, European affairs, Cyprus, Mansfield Town AFC, thoroughbred horses.

Sir Alan Meale MP, House of Commons, London SW1A 0AA
Tel: 020 7219 4159 *Email:* mealea@parliament.uk
Constituency: 85 West Gate, Mansfield, Nottinghamshire NG18 1RT
Tel: 01623 660531 *Fax:* 01623 420495 *Website:* www.alanmeale.co.uk

MEARNS, IAN   Gateshead *(Majority 12,549)*

James Ian Mearns. Born 21 April 1957; Son of James Mearns and Agnes Mearns, née Watson; Partner Anne (1 son 1 daughter from previous marriage).

Education: St Mary's Technical School, Newcastle upon Tyne.

Non-political career: Northern Gas 1974-85. Member: Unite, Unison.

Political career: Member for Gateshead since 6 May 2010 general election; PPS to Ivan Lewis as Shadow Secretary of State for International Development 2011-13. *Select committees:* Member: Education 2010-, Backbench Business 2010-. Chair PLP Departmental Group for Communities and Local Government 2011-. *Councils and public bodies:* Gateshead Council: Councillor 1983-2010, Former Cabinet Member for: Education 1993-2002, Lifelong Learning, Adult Social Care, Jobs and Employment; Council Deputy Leader 2002-10; Council representative, Local Government Association; Member: Association of North East Councils, North East Regional Authority; Former chair of governors: Kelvin Grove Primary School, Gateshead, Thomas Hepburn Community Comprehensive, Felling; Vice-President, Local Government Association 2010-.

LABOUR

Political interests: Education, local government, regional development, health, transport; Kurdistan (Iraq).

Other: Patron, Redheugh Boys Club; President, Trinity Community Association, Gateshead; Honorary Member, Royal Engineers; Saltwell Social Club; Gateshead Corporation; Tyneside Irish Centre; Parliamentary Sports and Social Club.

Recreations: Sports – football, cricket.

Ian Mearns MP, House of Commons, London SW1A 0AA
Tel: 020 7219 7074 *Email:* ian.mearns.mp@parliament.uk
Constituency: 12 Regent Terrace, Gateshead NE8 1LU
Tel: 0191-477 0651 *Fax:* 0191-477 7383 *Website:* www.ianmearns.org.uk
Twitter: @IanMearnsMP

MENZIES, MARK   Fylde *(Majority 13,185)*

Mark Andrew Menzies. Born 18 May 1971; Single (no children).

Education: Keil School, Dumbarton; Glasgow University (MA economic and social history 1994).

Non-political career: Graduate trainee, Marks & Spencer 1994-95; Marketing executive, Asda supermarkets 1995-2008; Senior marketing executive, Morrisons supermarkets 2008-10.

Political career: Contested Glasgow Govan 2001 and Selby 2005 general elections. Member for Fylde since 6 May 2010 general election; PPS to: Charles Hendry as Minister of State, Department of Energy and Climate Change 2010-12, Mark Prisk as Minister of State for Housing, Department for Communities and Local Government 2012-13. *Select committees:* Member: Scottish Affairs 2010. Member, Conservative Party 1987-.

CONSERVATIVE

Political interests: Energy, defence, food retailing; Australia, Middle East, USA.

Other: Social innovation marketing award, IGD/Unilever 2007.

Recreations: Skiing, walking, film.

Mark Menzies MP, House of Commons, London SW1A 0AA
Tel: 020 7219 7073 *Fax:* 020 7219 2235 *Email:* mark.menzies.mp@parliament.uk
Constituency: Office of Mark Menzies MP, 28 Orchard Road, Lytham St Annes, Lancashire FY8 1PF
Tel: 01253 729846 *Website:* www.markmenzies.org.uk

INDEPENDENT

MERCER, PATRICK

Newark *(Con Majority 16,152)*

Patrick John Mercer. Born 26 June 1956; Son of late Eric Mercer, Bishop of Exeter, and Rosemary Mercer, née Denby; Married Catriona Beaton 1990 (1 son).

Education: King's School, Chester; Exeter College, Oxford (BA modern history 1980, MA); Royal Military Academy, Sandhurst (commission 1975); Staff College (psc 1988); French, Serbo-Croat.

Non-political career: Regular Army officer, Worcestershire and Sherwood Foresters Regiment 1974-98: Head of strategy, Army Training and Recruiting Agency 1997-98, Commanding battalion in Bosnia, Canada, Tidworth, Operational service in the Balkans and Ulster; Reporter, BBC Radio 4 *Today* Programme 1999; Freelance journalist 2000-01; Member, King's College London mission to East Timor 2000.

Political career: Member for Newark 2001-10, for Newark (revised boundary) since 6 May 2010 general election; Shadow Minister for Homeland Security 2003-07. *Select committees:* Member: Defence 2001-03, Home Affairs 2007-10; Chair: Home Affairs Sub-Committee 2008-09; Member: Ecclesiastical Committee 2010-. Resigned from the Conservative Party May 2013.

Political interests: Agriculture, prisons, defence, Northern Ireland, home affairs; Ukraine, Russia, Israel, Serbia, Bosnia.

Other: Honorary Colonel, Nottinghamshire Army Cadet Force; President, Newark Patriotic Fund. Mentioned in Despatches 1983, Gallantry commendation 1991. MBE 1993; OBE 1997; Newark Working Men's, Newark Conservative.

Publications: Give Them a Volley and Charge (Spellmount, 1997); Inkermann: The Soldier's Battle (Osprey, 1997); To Do and Die (Harper Collins, 2009); Dust and Steel (Harper Collins, 2009); Red Runs the Helmand (Harper Collins, 2012).

Recreations: Painting, walking, bird-watching, history, country sports.

Patrick Mercer OBE MP, House of Commons, London SW1A 0AA
Tel: 020 7219 8225 *Fax:* 020 7219 1962 *Email:* barkerep@parliament.uk
Constituency: 29a London Road, Newark, Nottinghamshire NG24 1TN
Tel: 01636 612837 *Fax:* 01636 676312 *Email:* graysj@parliament.uk

CONSERVATIVE

METCALFE, STEPHEN

South Basildon and East Thurrock *(Majority 5,772)*

Stephen James Metcalfe. Born 9 January 1966; Son of late David Metcalfe and Valerie Metcalfe; Married Angela Giblett 1988 (1 son 1 daughter).

Education: Loughton School; Buckhurst Hill County High School.

Non-political career: Driver, Metloc Printers 1984-85; Order clerk, Burrup Mathison, London 1985-86; Metloc Printers Ltd (family business): Sales executive 1986-87, Studio manager 1987-92, Director 1992-2011.

Political career: Contested Ilford South 2005 general election. Member for South Basildon and East Thurrock since 6 May 2010 general election. *Select committees:* Member: Science and Technology 2010-. Deputy chairman, Essex Area Conservatives 2002-06; Member: Conservative Friends of Israel 2006-, Conservative Christian Fellowship 2006-. *Councils and public bodies:* Epping Forest District Council: Customer service e-government and ICT 2003-06, Customer service including waste management portfolio holder 2006-07.

Political interests: Economy, small business, foreign policy, science and technology, education; Africa, China, Middle East, USA.

Other: Founder, Wasters Wine Society; President, Northlands Park Community Centre, Basildon 2008-; United and Cecil Club. Woodford Rugby Club.

Recreations: Theatre, wine tasting, travel.

Stephen Metcalfe MP, House of Commons, London SW1A 0AA
Tel: 020 7219 7009 *Fax:* 020 7219 0306 *Email:* stephen.metcalfe.mp@parliament.uk
Constituency: South Basildon and East Thurrock Conservatives, 2 Orsett Business Centre, Stanford Road, Grays, Essex RM16 1BX
Tel: 01268 200430 *Website:* www.stephenmetcalfemp.com

LABOUR

MILIBAND, ED
Doncaster North *(Majority 10,909)*

Leader, Labour Party; Leader of the Opposition

Edward Samuel Miliband. Born 24 December 1969; Son of Ralph Miliband and Marion Miliband, née Kozak; Married Justine Thornton 2011 (2 sons).

Education: Corpus Christi College, Oxford (BA philosophy, politics and economics); London School of Economics (MSc Econ).

Non-political career: Television journalist; Speechwriter and researcher to: Harriet Harman 1993, Gordon Brown as Shadow Chancellor of the Exchequer 1994-97; HM Treasury: Special adviser to Gordon Brown as Chancellor of the Exchequer 1997-2002, Chair, Council of Economic Advisers 2004-05; Fellow and lecturer in government, Harvard University 2002-04. TGWU/USDAW.

Political career: Member for Doncaster North 2005-10, for Doncaster North (revised boundary) since 6 May 2010 general election; Parliamentary Secretary, Cabinet Office 2006-07; Minister for the Cabinet Office; Chancellor of the Duchy of Lancaster 2007-08; Secretary of State for Energy and Climate Change 2008-10; Shadow Secretary of State for Energy and Climate Change 2010; Leader of the Opposition 2010-; Leader, Labour Party 2010-.

Other: PC 2007.

Publications: Contributor, The Purple Book (Progress, 2011).

Rt Hon Ed Miliband MP, House of Commons, London SW1A 0AA
Tel: 020 7219 4778 *Email:* ed.miliband.mp@parliament.uk
Constituency: Hutton Business Centre, Bridge Works, Bentley, Doncaster, South Yorkshire DN5 9QP
Tel: 01302 875462 *Website:* www.edmiliband.org *Twitter:* @Ed_Miliband

LABOUR

MILLER, ANDREW
Ellesmere Port and Neston *(Majority 4,331)*

Andrew Peter Miller. Born 23 March 1949; Son of late Ernest and Daphne Miller; Married Frances Keeble 1975 (2 sons 1 daughter).

Education: Hayling Island Secondary School; Highbury Technical College; London School of Economics (Diploma industrial relations 1977).

Non-political career: Technician, Portsmouth Polytechnic (analyst in geology) 1967-76; Regional official, MSF (formerly ASTMS) 1977-92. Member, MSF 1968-.

Political career: Member for Ellesmere Port and Neston 1992-2010, for Ellesmere Port and Neston (revised boundary) since 6 May 2010 general election; PPS to Ministers, Department of Trade and Industry 2001-05; Member, First Steps Team working with the Foreign Office to promote relations with EU and prospective EU member states with specific responsibility for Hungary and Malta 2001-10; Board member, Parliamentary Office of Science and Technology (POST). *Select committees:* Member: Science and Technology 1992-97, Information 1992-2001, Joint Committee on Human Rights 2001; Chair: Regulatory Reform 2005-10; Member: Liaison 2005-, Joint Committee on Conventions 2006; Chair: Science and Technology 2010-. Member, North West Regional Executive Committee 1984-92; President, Computing for Labour 1993-; Chair: Leadership Campaign Team 1997-98, North West Group of Labour MPs 1997-98; Member, Scientists for Labour 1997-.

Political interests: Industry, economic policy, science and technology, communications and information technology, pensions; China, Europe, Hungary, Malta, USA.

Other: Patron: Road Peace, Chester Childbirth Trust, Parents Against Drug Abuse; Fellow, Industry and Parliament Trust 1995. Officers' Cross of the Order of Merit (Hungary) 2004. Vice-President: Alvanley Cricket Club, Chester and Ellesmere Port Athletics Club.

Recreations: Walking, photography, tennis, cricket.

Andrew Miller MP, House of Commons, London SW1A 0AA
Tel: 020 7219 3580 *Fax:* 020 7219 3796 *Email:* millera@parliament.uk
Constituency: Whitby Hall Lodge, Stanney Lane, Ellesmere Port, Cheshire CH65 6QY
Tel: 0151-357 3019 *Fax:* 0151-356 8226 *Website:* www.andrew-miller-mp.co.uk
Twitter: @APMiller1949

CONSERVATIVE

MILLER, MARIA
Basingstoke *(Majority 13,176)*

Secretary of State for Culture, Media and Sport; Minister for Women and Equalities

Maria Frances Lewis Miller. Born 26 March 1964; Daughter of John and June Lewis; Married Iain Miller 1990 (1 daughter 2 sons).

Education: Brynteg Comprehensive, Bridgend; London School of Economics (BSc economics 1985).

Non-political career: Advertising executive, Grey Advertising Ltd 1985-90; Marketing manager, Texaco 1990-94; Company director: Grey Advertising Ltd 1995-99, The Rowland Company/PR21 1999-2003.

Political career: Contested Wolverhampton North East 2001 general election. Member for Basingstoke 2005-10, for Basingstoke (revised boundary) since 6 May 2010 general election; Shadow Minister for: Education 2005-06, Family Welfare, including Child Support Agency 2006-07, Families 2007-10; Parliamentary Under-Secretary of State (Minister for Disabled People), Department for Work and Pensions 2010-12; Secretary of State for Culture, Media and Sport 2012-; Minister for Women and Equalities 2012-. *Select committees:* Member: Trade and Industry 2005-06, Children, Schools and Families 2007. President, Wolverhampton North East Conservative Association 2001-07; Chair, Wimbledon Conservative Association 2002-03.

Political interests: Housing, education, media; Canada.

Other: Rising Star, *House Magazine* awards 2012. PC 2012.

Recreations: Cycling.

Rt Hon Maria Miller MP, House of Commons, London SW1A 0AA
Tel: 020 7219 5749 *Email:* foxlc@parliament.uk
Constituency: The Mount, Bounty Road, Basingstoke, Hampshire RG21 3DD
Tel: 01256 322207 *Email:* agent@nehc.org.uk *Website:* www.mariamiller.co.uk
Twitter: @MariaMillerMP

CONSERVATIVE

MILLS, NIGEL
Amber Valley *(Majority 536)*

Nigel John Mills. Born 1974; Single.

Education: Loughborough Grammar School; Newcastle University (classics 1996).

Non-political career: Accountant: PriceWaterhouseCoopers 1996-2008, Deloitte LLP 2008-10.

Political career: Member for Amber Valley since 6 May 2010 general election. *Select committees:* Member: Administration 2010-, Northern Ireland Affairs 2011-, Work and Pensions 2012-. Deputy chair, Amber Valley Conservative Association. *Councils and public bodies:* Amber Valley Borough Council: Councillor 2004-11, Chair, scrutiny committee; Councillor, Heanor and Loscoe Town Council 2007-11.

Political interests: Employment, crime, anti-social behaviour, education, taxation.

Other: Institute of Chartered Accountants in England and Wales.

Recreations: Sport.

Nigel Mills MP, House of Commons, London SW1A 0AA
Tel: 020 7219 7233 *Email:* nigel.mills.mp@parliament.uk
Constituency: Thomas Henry House, Suite 101, 1-5 Church Street, Ripley, Derbyshire DE5 3BU
Tel: 01773 744341 *Fax:* 01773 744341 *Website:* www.nigelmillsmp.com

CONSERVATIVE

MILTON, ANNE
Guildford *(Majority 7,782)*

Government Whip

Anne Frances Milton. Born 3 November 1955; Married Dr Graham Henderson (3 sons 1 daughter).

Education: Haywards Heath Grammar School, Sussex; St Bartholomew's Hospital, London (RGN 1977); Polytechnic of the South Bank, London (Diploma district nursing 1982).

Non-political career: St Bartholomew's Hospital, London: Staff nurse 1977-78, Research nurse 1978-81; District nursing sister, City and Hackney Health Authority 1981-83; Nursing sister, St Thomas Hospital 1983-85; Medical adviser to: East London and City Health Authority 1985-2000, Social housing providers 1994-2004. Former shop steward, Royal College of Nursing 1970s.

Political career: Member for Guildford 2005-10, for Guildford (revised boundary) since 6 May 2010 general election; Shadow Minister for: Tourism 2006-07, Health 2007-10; Parliamentary

Under-Secretary of State (Public Health), Department of Health 2010-12; Government Whip 2012-. *Select committees:* Member: Health 2005-06, Selection 2012-. *Councils and public bodies:* Reigate Borough Council: Councillor 1999-2004, Leader, Conservative group 2001-03.

Recreations: Gardening, reading, family.

Anne Milton MP, House of Commons, London SW1A 0AA
Tel: 020 7219 8392 *Fax:* 020 7219 5239 *Email:* anne.milton.mp@parliament.uk
Constituency: 17a Home Farm, Loseley Park, Guildford, Surrey GU3 1HS
Tel: 01483 300330 *Fax:* 01483 300321 *Website:* www.annemilton.com
Twitter: @AnneMiltonMP

MITCHELL, ANDREW   Sutton Coldfield *(Majority 17,005)*

Andrew John Bower Mitchell. Born 23 March 1956; Son of Sir David Mitchell, MP 1964-97, and Pamela Mitchell; Married Sharon Bennet 1985 (2 daughters).

Education: Rugby School; Jesus College, Cambridge (MA history 1978) (Union President 1978); French.

Non-political career: UN Peacekeeping Forces Cyprus: 1st Royal Tank Regiment (SSLC). International and corporate finance Lazard Brothers and Company Ltd 1979-87; Lazard Brothers: Consultant 1987-92, Director 1997-2009; Director: Miller Insurance Group 1997-2001, Financial Dynamics Holdings 1997-2002; Senior strategy adviser: Boots 1997-2000, Andersen Consulting/Accenture 1997-2009; Director, Commer Group 1998-2002; Supervisory board member, The Foundation 1999-2009.

CONSERVATIVE

Political career: Contested Sunderland South 1983 general election. Member for Gedling 1987-97. Contested Gedling 1997 general election. Member for Sutton Coldfield 2001-10, for Sutton Coldfield (revised boundary) since 6 May 2010 general election; PPS to: William Waldegrave as Minister of State, Foreign and Commonwealth Office 1988-90, John Wakeham as Secretary of State for Energy 1990-92; Assistant Government Whip 1992-93; Government Whip 1993-95; Parliamentary Under-Secretary of State, Department of Social Security 1995-97; Shadow Minister for: Economic Affairs 2003-04, Home Affairs 2004-05; Shadow Secretary of State for International Development 2005-10; Secretary of State for International Development 2010-12; Parliamentary Secretary to the Treasury September-October 2012; Chief Whip September-October 2012; Member, Parliamentary and Political Service Honours Committee September-October 2012. *Select committees:* Member: Work and Pensions 2001-03, Modernisation of the House of Commons 2002-04, Parliamentary and Political Service Honours Committee 2012-. Chair, Cambridge University Conservative Association 1977; Secretary, One Nation Group of Conservative MPs 1989-92, 2005-; Vice-chair, Conservative Party (candidates) 1992-93.

Political interests: International development, health, defence, economy; Africa, Far East, USA.

Other: Council SOS SAHEL 1992-2010; English Speaking Union Council International Debate Council 1998-2010; Council of management, GAP 1999-2006; Alexandra Rose Charity: Vice-chair 1999-2010, Trustee 2010-. Liveryman, Vintners' Company. PC 2010; Chair, Coningsby Club 1984-85.

Recreations: Music, cycling, skiing, walking.

Rt Hon Andrew Mitchell MP, House of Commons, London SW1A 0AA
Tel: 020 7219 8516 *Fax:* 020 7219 1981 *Email:* andrew.mitchell.mp@parliament.uk
Constituency: Sutton Coldfield Conservative Association, 36 High Street, Sutton Coldfield, West Midlands B72 1UP
Tel: 0121-354 2229 *Fax:* 0121-321 1762 *Email:* info@sutton-coldfield-tories.org.uk
Website: www.suttoncoldfieldconservatives.com www.andrew-mitchell-mp.co.uk

MITCHELL, AUSTIN   Great Grimsby *(Majority 714)*

Austin Vernon Mitchell. Born 19 September 1934; Son of Richard Vernon and Ethel Mary Mitchell; Married Patricia Dorothea Jackson (divorced) (2 daughters); married Linda Mary McDougall (1 son 1 daughter).

Education: Woodbottom Council School; Bingley Grammar School, Yorkshire; Manchester University (BA history 1956, MA 1957); Nuffield College, Oxford (MA, DPhil 1963); French.

Non-political career: Lecturer in history, Otago University, Dunedin, New Zealand 1959-63; Senior lecturer in politics, University of Canterbury, Christchurch, NZ 1963-67; Official fellow, Nuffield College, Oxford 1967-69; Journalist: Yorkshire Television 1969-71, BBC 1972, Yorkshire Television 1973-77; Programme controller Penine Radio 1975-77; Political commentator, Sky Television's Target programme 1989-98; Associate editor, *House Magazine.* GMB, NUJ.

LABOUR

Political career: Member for Grimsby 1977 by-election to 1983, for Great Grimsby 1983-2010, for Great Grimsby (revised boundary) since 6 May 2010 general election; PPS to John Fraser as Minister of State for Prices and Consumer Protection 1977-79; Opposition Whip 1979-85; Opposition Spokesperson for Trade and Industry 1988-89; Member Public Accounts Commission 1997-. *Select committees:* Member: Agriculture 1997-2001, Environment, Food and Rural Affairs 2001-05, Public Accounts 2005-, Yorkshire and the Humber 2009-10. Vice-chair Labour Campaign for Electoral Reform; Chair: Labour Euro-Safeguards Campaign, Labour Economic Policy Group.

Political interests: Economics, media, fishing industry, agriculture, poverty, accountancy, legal reform, European Union, electoral reform, constitutional reform, small businesses; Canada, China, France, Germany, Hong Kong, Iceland, New Zealand, Nigeria.

Other: Vice-chair, Hansard Society; Member: Advisory Council, National Fishing Heritage Centre, Hairdressing Council 1979-; Vice-President, Federation of Economic Development Authorities (FEDA); President, Debating Group; Fellow, Industry and Parliament Trust; Chair, Yorkshire and Humber Seafood Group 2007-; Member, Royal Institute of International Affairs; Harbour Place, Grimsby; Grimsby Women's Refuge. Order of New Zealand 2001.

Publications: New Zealand Politics in Action (1962); Government by Party (1966); Whigs in Opposition, 1815-30 (1969); Politics and People in New Zealand (1970); Half Gallon Quarter Acre Pavlova – Paradise (1974); Can Labour Win Again (1979); Yes Maggie there is an Alternative; Westminster Man (1982); The Case for Labour (1983); Four Years in the Death of the Labour Party (1983); Yorkshire Jokes (1988); Teach Thissen Tyke (1988); Britain, Beyond the Blue Horizon (1989); Competitive Socialism (1989); Accounting for Change (1993); Election '45 (1995); Corporate Governance Matters (1996); The Common Fisheries Policy, End or Mend? (1996); Co-author Last Time: Labour's Lessons from the Sixties (1997); Farewell My Lords (1999); Co-author Parliament in Pictures (1999); Pavlova Paradise Revisited (2002); Yorkshire Sayings (2005).

Recreations: Photography, contemplating exercise.

Austin Mitchell MP, House of Commons, London SW1A 0AA
Tel: 020 7219 4559 *Fax:* 020 7219 4843 *Email:* mitchellav@parliament.uk
Constituency: 13 Bargate, Grimsby, Humberside DN34 4SS
Tel: 01472 342145 *Fax:* 01472 251484 *Email:* bentonjo@parliament.uk
Website: www.austinmitchell.org *Twitter:* @AVMitchell2010

SINN FÉIN

MOLLOY, FRANCIE
Mid Ulster *(Majority 4,681)*

Francis Joseph Molloy. Born 16 December 1950; Son of late Arthur Molloy and Annie, née Daly; Married Ann Mulgrew 1971 (2 sons 2 daughters).

Education: St Patrick's Intermediate, Dungannon; FELDEN Government Training Centre (engineering 1967); Ulster University; Newry Further Education College (Foundation Studies humanities).

Non-political career: Trainee fitter welder, Feldon GTC 1966-67; Fitter/welder/sales, Ulster Plant (later Powerscreen) 1967-74; Self-employed welder/light engineer 1978-81. Former member, AEWU.

Political career: Member for Mid Ulster since 7 March 2013 by-election; Contested Northern Ireland region 1994 European Parliament election; Member: Northern Ireland Forum for Political Dialogue 1996, Sinn Féin Talks Team, Castle Buildings Talks 1997-98; MLA for Mid Ulster 1998-2013: Chair Assembly Committee on Finance and Personnel 1999-2002, Deputy Speaker 2006-11, Sinn Féin Spokesperson for: Victims, Families and Poverty 2011-12; Principal Deputy Speaker 2011-13; Sinn Féin Spokesperson for Environment 2012-13. *Councils and public bodies:* Councillor 1985-2011: Dungannon District Council, Dungannon and South Tyrone Borough Council, Mayor 2001, 2005, Deputy mayor 2003.

Political interests: Housing, rural affairs; South Africa.

Other: Member, Committee of the Regions 2010-13. Clonmore Emmetts Gaelic FC.

Recreations: Painting, art, mainly water colour, organic gardening, Spanish civil war.

Francie Molloy MP, House of Commons, London SW1A 0AA
Tel: 020 7219 3000
Constituency: 26 Burn Road, Cookstown, Co Tyrone BT80 8DN
Tel: 028 8676 5850 *Email:* sinnfeincookstown@yahoo.com *Twitter:* @FrancieMolloy

MOON, MADELEINE
Bridgend *(Majority 2,263)*

LABOUR

Born 27 March 1950; Daughter of Albert Ironside and Hilda Ironside; Married Stephen Moon 1983 (1 son).

Education: Whinney Hill School; Durham Girls Grammar School; Madeley College, Staffordshire (Cert Ed 1971); Keele University (BEd 1972); Cardiff University (CQSW, Dip SW 1980).

Non-political career: Social services directorate, Mid Glamorgan County Council 1980-86; Contracting officer, City and County of Swansea and senior social work practitioner 1996-2002; Residential care home inspector, Care Standards Inspectorate for Wales 2002-05. GMB, Unison.

Political career: Member for Bridgend 2005-10, for Bridgend (revised boundary) since 6 May 2010 general election; PPS to: Jim Knight as Minister of State, Department for Children, Schools and Families 2007-08, Lord Hunt of Kings Heath as Minister of State, Department of Energy and Climate Change 2009-10. *Select committees:* Member: Environment, Food and Rural Affairs 2005-07, Welsh Affairs 2005-06, Defence 2009-. Vice-chair, PLP Welsh Regional Group 2008-10. *Councils and public bodies:* Porthcawl Town Council 1990-2000: Councillor, Mayor 1992-93, 1995-96; Councillor, Bridgend Borough Council 1991-2004; Bridgend representative: Sports Council for Wales, Tourism South and West Wales; Chair, British Resorts Association 1999-2001.

Political interests: Environment, health and social welfare, care for people with disabilities and old people, police, prisons, suicide, defence, women's role in public life, RAF; Afghanistan, Central Asia, China, Colombia, Israel, Palestinian Territories, Pakistan.

Other: Member, NATO Parliamentary Assembly 2010-.

Recreations: Theatre, film, reading, walking.

Madeleine Moon MP, House of Commons, London SW1A 0AA
Tel: 020 7219 0814 *Fax:* 020 7219 6488 *Email:* moonm@parliament.uk
Constituency: 47 Nolton Street, Bridgend, Vale of Glamorgan CF31 3AA
Tel: 01656 750002 *Fax:* 01656 660081 *Website:* www.madeleinemoonmp.com

MOORE, MICHAEL
Berwickshire, Roxburgh and Selkirk *(Majority 5,675)*

LIBERAL DEMOCRAT

Michael Kevin Moore. Born 3 June 1965; Son of Reverend W. Haisley Moore, Church of Scotland minister, and Jill Moore, physiotherapist; Married Alison Louise Hughes 2004 (1 daughter).

Education: Strathallan School; Jedburgh Grammar School; Edinburgh University (MA politics and modern history 1987).

Non-political career: Research assistant to Archy Kirkwood MP 1987-88; Coopers and Lybrand, Edinburgh 1988-97: Manager, Corporate Finance Practice 1993-97.

Political career: Member for Tweeddale, Ettrick and Lauderdale 1997-2005, for Berwickshire, Roxburgh and Selkirk since 5 May 2005 general election; Liberal Democrat: Spokesperson for: Scotland 1997-99, 2001, Transport 1999-2001; Shadow Minister for Foreign Affairs 2001-05; Shadow Secretary of State for: Defence 2005-06, Foreign and Commonwealth Affairs 2006-07, International Development 2007-10, Northern Ireland and Scotland 2008; Secretary of State for Scotland 2010-13. *Select committees:* Member: Scottish Affairs 1997-99, Armed Forces Bill 2005-06. Campaign chair, 1999 and 2003 Scottish Parliament elections; Parliamentary Group Convener 2000-01; Scottish MP representative, Liberal Democrat Policy Committee 2001-02; Scottish Liberal Democrats: Deputy leader 2002-10, Acting leader 2008.

Political interests: Transport, textiles, Europe, corporate social responsibility, foreign affairs, defence, international development; Afghanistan, Kosovo.

Other: Member, NATO Parliamentary Assembly, UK delegation 2007-10; Member, Amnesty International; Governor and vice-chair, Westminster Foundation for Democracy 2002-05; Board member, Scotland in Europe 2003-06; Parliamentary visiting fellow, St Anthony's College, Oxford 2003-04; Council member, Royal Institute of International Affairs 2004-10; Member, advisory council: British Council 2005-08, John Smith Memorial Trust 2007-10; Fellow, Institute of Chartered Accountants of Scotland 1991. PC 2010. Jed-Forest Rugby Club.

Recreations: Rugby, hill-walking, music, films.

Rt Hon Michael Moore MP, House of Commons, London SW1A 0AA
Tel: 020 7219 2236 *Fax:* 020 7219 0263 *Email:* michaelmooremp@parliament.uk
Constituency: Parliamentary Office, 11 Island Street, Galashiels, Borders TD1 1NZ
Tel: 01896 663650 *Fax:* 01896 663655 *Website:* www.michaelmoore.org.uk
Twitter: @MichaelMooreMP

CONSERVATIVE

MORDAUNT, PENNY
Portsmouth North *(Majority 7,289)*

Penelope Mary Mordaunt. Born 4 March 1973; Daughter of John Mordaunt and Jennifer Snowden.

Education: Oaklands RC Comprehensive School, Waterlooville; Reading University (philosophy) (President Students' Union).

Non-political career: Royal Navy Reservist. Magician's assistant to Will Ayling, President of Magic Circle; Head of foreign press, George W Bush's presidential campaign 2000; Former communications director: London Borough of Kensington and Chelsea Council, Freight Transport Association, National Lottery; Director of strategy, policy and partnerships, Diabetes UK; Associate, Hanover.

Political career: Contested Portsmouth North 2005 general election. Member for Portsmouth North since 6 May 2010 general election. *Select committees:* Member: European Scrutiny 2010-13, Defence 2010-, Arms Export Controls 2011-, Joint Committee on Privacy and Injunctions 2011-12. Member, Executive, 1922 Committee 2012-. *Councils and public bodies:* Commissioner, Commission on Assisted Dying 2010-.

Political interests: Care and quality of life for the elderly, healthcare, defence, the arts, space; India, USA.

Other: British Astronomical Association.

Recreations: Painting, astronomy, Burmese cats.

Penny Mordaunt MP, House of Commons, London SW1A 0AA
Tel: 020 7219 7129 *Fax:* 020 7219 3592 *Email:* penny.mordaunt.mp@parliament.uk
Constituency: 379 London Road, Portsmouth, Hampshire PO2 9LD
Tel: 023 9269 7266 *Fax:* 023 9269 9578 *Email:* info@pennymordaunt.com
Website: www.pennymordaunt.com *Twitter:* @pennymordauntmp

LABOUR

MORDEN, JESSICA
Newport East *(Majority 1,650)*

Jessica Elizabeth Morden. Born 29 May 1968; Daughter of Mick and Margaret Morden; Partner Sion Ffrancon Jones (1 daughter 1 son).

Education: Croesyceiliog Comprehensive School; Birmingham University (BA history 1989).

Non-political career: Labour Party organiser; Political assistant to Llew Smith MEP; Constituency assistant to Huw Edwards MP; General Secretary, Welsh Labour Party 1999-2005. Member GMB.

Political career: Member for Newport East since 5 May 2005 general election; PPS to Secretaries of State for Wales: Peter Hain 2007-08, 2009-10, Paul Murphy 2008-09; PPS to Shadow Secretaries of State for Wales: Peter Hain 2011-12, Owen Smith 2012-. *Select committees:* Member: Constitutional Affairs/Justice 2005-10, Modernisation of the House of Commons 2005-06, Welsh Affairs 2005-07, 2010-.

Political interests: Anti-social behaviour, electoral issues, police, children, steel industry.

Recreations: Cinema, gym.

Jessica Morden MP, House of Commons, London SW1A 0AA
Tel: 020 7219 6213 *Fax:* 020 7219 6196 *Email:* mordenj@parliament.uk
Constituency: Suite 2, Seventh Floor, Clarence House, Clarence Place, Newport, Monmouthshire NP19 7AA
Tel: 01633 841725 *Fax:* 01633 841727 *Website:* www.jessicamorden.com
Twitter: @jessicamordenmp

CONSERVATIVE

MORGAN, NICKY
Loughborough *(Majority 3,744)*

Economic Secretary, HM Treasury

Nicola Ann Morgan. Born 10 October 1972; Married Jonathan Morgan 2000 (1 son).

Education: Surbiton High School, Kingston-upon-Thames; St Hugh's College, Oxford (BA law 1993, MA); Legal Practice Course 1994.

Non-political career: Trainee/assistant solicitor, Theodore Goddard 1994-97; Assistant solicitor, Allen & Overy 1998-2002; Corporate professional support lawyer, Travers Smith 2002-10.

Political career: Contested Islington South and Finsbury 2001 and Loughborough 2005 general elections. Member for Loughborough since 6 May 2010 general election; PPS to David Willetts as

Minister of State for Universities and Science 2010-12; Assistant Government Whip 2012-13; Economic Secretary, HM Treasury 2013-. *Select committees:* Member: Business, Innovation and Skills 2010. Chair, Wessex Young Conservatives 1995-97; Vice-chair, Battersea Conservatives 1997-99. **Political interests:** Business, financial services, economy, higher education, mental health; Bangladesh.

Other: Vice-chairman, Indo British Trade Council; Founder, Bluelist Organisation 2002-04; Member, Law Society; RNIB; Mind; Rethink; Rainbows Hospice; Carpenters Arms; World Vision.

Recreations: Choral singing, cookery, reading, theatre, cinema, running.

Nicky Morgan MP, House of Commons, London SW1A 0AA
Tel: 020 7219 7224 *Email:* nicky.morgan.mp@parliament.uk
Constituency: 3/3a Nottingham Road, Loughborough, Leicestershire LE11 1ER
Tel: 01509 262723 *Email:* jane.hunt@parliament.uk *Website:* www.nickymorgan.com
Twitter: @nickymorgan01

LABOUR

MORRICE, GRAEME
Livingston *(Majority 10,791)*

Born 23 February 1959.
Education: Broxburn Academy; Napier University (SHND business studies 1978).
Non-political career: Member, Unite.
Political career: Member for Livingston since 6 May 2010 general election; PPS to: John Denham as Shadow Secretary of State for Business, Innovation and Skills 2010-11, Margaret Curran as Shadow Secretary of State for Scotland 2012-13, Harriet Harman as Shadow Deputy Prime Minister; Chair, Labour Party; Shadow Secretary of State for Culture, Media and Sport 2013-. *Select committees:* Member: Scottish Affairs 2011-12, Scottish Affairs 2013-. Member, Co-operative Party. *Councils and public bodies:* West Lothian Council (previously West Lothian District Council): Councillor 1987-2012; Leader, Labour Group 1992-2010, Council Leader 1995-2007; Executive Spokesperson for Resources and Capacity, Convention of Scottish Local Authorities (COSLA).
Political interests: Education, NHS, local government.
Recreations: Reading, art, listening to music, playing the guitar.

Graeme Morrice MP, House of Commons, London SW1A 0AA
Tel: 020 7219 3000 *Email:* graeme.morrice.mp@parliament.uk
Constituency: Geddes House, Kirkton North Road, Livingston, West Lothian EH54 6GU
Tel: 01506 410109 *Fax:* 01506 411041 *Website:* www.graememorricemp.co.uk

CONSERVATIVE

MORRIS, ANNE MARIE
Newton Abbot *(Majority 523)*

Born 5 July 1957; Daughter of Margaret Agg and late John Backes; Partner Roger.
Education: Bryanston School, Dorset; Hertford College, Oxford (BA jurisprudence 1980); College of Law, London (Law Society finals 1981); Open University (MBA 1997); Harvard University (leadership programme 2004); School of Coaching, Strathclyde University (Diploma executive coaching 2007); French.
Non-political career: Trainee solicitor, Withers, London 1981-83; Corporate finance lawyer, Norton Rose, London 1983-85; Corporate commercial banking lawyer, Crossman Block, London 1985; Asset finance lawyer, Sinclair Roche & Temerley, Singapore 1986-88; Allen & Overy, London: Corporate finance lawyer 1988-90, Head of education and training 1990-93; Director of professional and business development, Baker & McKenzie 1993-95; Director of marketing and business development, Simmons & Simmons 1995-97; Marketing director, tax and legal services, PricewaterhouseCoopers 1997-99; Global marketing director: Ernst & Young 1999-2002, Linklaters 2002-05; Managing director, Manteion Ltd 2005-.
Political career: Member for Newton Abbot since 6 May 2010 general election. *Select committees:* Member: Work and Pensions 2012-. *Councils and public bodies:* Councillor, West Sussex County Council 2005-07; Associate Governor, Rydon Primary School, Kingsteignton; Governor, Newton Abbot College.
Political interests: Micro and small businesses, health and the NHS, the elderly, education, vocational training and apprenticeships.

Other: Member: Devon and Cornwall Board, Institute of Directors 2001-, Federation of Small Businesses; Fellow, Chartered Institute of Marketing 2002; Dame Hannah Roger Trust at Seale-Hayne.

Recreations: Horseriding.

Anne Marie Morris MP, House of Commons, London SW1A 0AA
Tel: 020 7219 3000 *Fax:* 020 7219 6578 *Email:* annemarie.morris.mp@parliament.uk
Constituency: 2 Salisbury House, Salisbury Road, Newton Abbot, Devon TQ12 2DF
Tel: 01626 386277 *Website:* www.annemariemorris.co.uk *Twitter:* @AMMorrisMP

CONSERVATIVE

MORRIS, DAVID
Morecambe and Lunesdale *(Majority 866)*

Born 3 January 1966; Son of Lieutenant Commander Alan Morris, retired Royal Navy, and Vera Morris; Divorced (2 sons).

Education: St Andrews School, Bahamas; Lowton High School.

Non-political career: Honorary Lieutenant Commander, Royal Navy (Armed Forces Parliamentary Scheme). Song writer and session guitar player, music industry; Former managing director, David Morris Hairdressing; Commercial property investor, northern England.

Political career: Contested Blackpool South 2001 and Carmarthen West and South Pembrokeshire 2005 general elections. Member for Morecambe and Lunesdale since 6 May 2010 general election. *Select committees:* Member: Science and Technology 2010-12, 2012- Administration 2012-. Chair, Conservative Friends of Nuclear Energy.

Political interests: Nuclear energy, small business, maritime affairs; Bahamas, Hong Kong.

Other: Government-appointed member, National Hairdressing Council.

Recreations: Playing and collecting guitars, classic cars.

David Morris MP, House of Commons, London SW1A 0AA
Tel: 020 7219 7234 *Email:* david.morris.mp@parliament.uk
Constituency: Office 204, Riverway House, Morecambe Road, Lancaster,
Lancashire LA1 2RX
Tel: 01524 841225 *Website:* www.davidmorrismp.co.uk *Twitter:* @MPDavidMorris

LABOUR

MORRIS, GRAHAME
Easington *(Majority 14,982)*

Grahame Mark Morris. Born 13 March 1961; Son of late Richard Morris, colliery electrician, and Constance Morris, pit canteen worker; Married Michelle Hughes 1986 (2 sons).

Education: Peterlee Howletch Secondary School; Newcastle College (BTEC Ordinary National Certificate); Newcastle Polytechnic (BTEC Higher National Certificate medical laboratory sciences).

Non-political career: Medical laboratory scientific officer, Sunderland Royal Infirmary 1980-87; Researcher and constituency caseworker to John Cummings MP 1987-2010. Member, Unite.

Political career: Member for Easington since 6 May 2010 general election; PPS to: Meg Hillier as Shadow Secretary of State for Energy and Climate Change 2010-11, Rachel Reeves as Shadow Chief Secretary to the Treasury 2011-12. *Select committees:* Member: Health 2010-, Joint Committee on the Draft Care and Support Bill 2013, Unopposed Bills (Panel) 2013-. Member, Labour Party 1976-; Secretary, Easington Constituency Labour Party 1996-2006. *Councils and public bodies:* Councillor, Easington District Council 1987-2003; Non-executive director, City Hospitals Sunderland NHS Trust 1997-2005.

Political interests: NHS, local government, economic regeneration, public health, housing; China, Cuba, Venezuela.

Other: Haswell and District MENCAP; Easington Riding for the Disabled; World Vision; Shelter; Dogs Trust; Peterlee Labour Club; Murton Victoria (CIU); Easington Colliery Workingmen's Club CIU; Southside Social Club, Easington Village.

Grahame Morris MP, House of Commons, London SW1A 0AA
Tel: 020 7219 1283 *Email:* grahame.morris.mp@parliament.uk
Constituency: The Glebe Centre Annex, Durham Place, Murton, Seaham,
Co Durham SR7 9BX
Tel: 0191-526 2828 *Website:* www.grahamemorrismp.co.uk *Twitter:* @grahamemorris

CONSERVATIVE

MORRIS, JAMES
Halesowen and Rowley Regis *(Majority 2,023)*

James George Morris. Born 4 February 1967; Married (1 son 1 daughter).

Education: Nottingham High School; Birmingham University (English literature); Oxford University (Postgraduate research); Cranfield School Management (MBA).

Non-political career: Managing director: 1996-2001, Vice-Versa Ltd 2001-06; Director, Mind the Gap 2003-08; Chief executive officer, Localis 2008-10.

Political career: Member for Halesowen and Rowley Regis since 6 May 2010 general election. *Select committees:* Member: Communities and Local Government 2010-.

Political interests: Localism, local government, foreign affairs.

Publications: Change Starts Small (2004); Big Ideas (2008); Million Vote Mandate (2008); Can Localism Deliver? (2009); The Bottom Line (2009); For Good Measure (2010); Co-author, Freedom, Responsibility and the State: Curbing Over-Mighty Government (Politeia, 2012).

Recreations: Cricket, family, theatre, music.

James Morris MP, House of Commons, London SW1A 0AA
Tel: 020 7219 8715 *Fax:* 020 7219 1429 *Email:* james.morris.mp@parliament.uk
Constituency: Trinity Point, New Road, Halesowen B63 3HY
Tel: 0121-550 6777 *Email:* lisa.townsend@parliament.uk *Website:* www.jamesmorrismp.com
Twitter: @JamesMorrisMP

CONSERVATIVE

MOSLEY, STEPHEN
City of Chester *(Majority 2,583)*

Stephen James Mosley. Born 22 June 1972; Married Caroline Smith 1997 (1 son 1 daughter).

Education: King Edward's School, Birmingham; Nottingham University (BSc chemistry 1993).

Non-political career: IBM (UK) Ltd 1993-97; Director: Weblong Ltd 1997-2010, Streamfolder Ltd 2004-10, Severn Industrial Estates Ltd 2004-10.

Political career: Member for City of Chester since 6 May 2010 general election. *Select committees:* Member: Science and Technology 2010-, Joint Committee on the Draft Communications Data Bill 2012-13. *Councils and public bodies:* Chester City Council: Councillor 2000-09, Council Deputy Leader 2007-09; Governor: Queens Park High School, Chester 2001-06, Overleigh St Mary's CoE Primary School, Chester 2005-; Councillor, Cheshire County Council 2005-09; Member, Cheshire Fire and Rescue Authority 2008-09.

Political interests: Local government, science and technology, business; Central and Southern Africa.

Other: Director, Abbeyfield (Chester) Society 2000-07.

Stephen Mosley MP, House of Commons, London SW1A 0AA
Tel: 020 7219 7207 *Email:* stephen.mosley.mp@parliament.uk
Constituency: Unionist Buildings, Nicholas Street, Chester CH1 2NX
Tel: 01244 458120 *Email:* stephen@chestermp.com *Website:* www.chestermp.com
Twitter: @mp4chester

CONSERVATIVE

MOWAT, DAVID
Warrington South *(Majority 1,553)*

David John Mowat. Born 20 February 1957; Son of John and Pat Mowat; Married Veronica 1983 (1 son 3 daughters).

Education: Lawrence Sheriff Grammar School, Rugby; Imperial College, London (civil engineering 1978).

Non-political career: Cadet pilot officer. Chartered accountant, Arthur Andersen; Accenture 1981-2006: Various roles, Partner 1989-2006, Global industry managing partner – energy 2000-06.

Political career: Member for Warrington South since 6 May 2010 general election; Board member, Parliamentary Office of Science and Technology (POST); PPS to Greg Clark as Financial Secretary 2012-13. *Select committees:* Member: Scottish Affairs 2010-12, Joint Committee on the Draft Financial Services Bill 2011-12. *Councils and public bodies:* Councillor, Macclesfield Borough Council 2007-08.

Political interests: Nuclear policy, energy policy, devolution, economy and business, occupational pensions; Russia.

Other: Member, Politea 2005-08; Chair, Fairbridge, Greater Manchester 2005-08; Member: ACA 1981, Institute of Petroleum 1998; Warrington club.

Publications: Co-author, Freedom, Responsibility and the State: Curbing Over-Mighty Government (Politeia, 2012).

Recreations: Golf, chess, rugby, sailing.

David Mowat MP, House of Commons, London SW1A 0AA
Tel: 020 7219 7178 *Fax:* 020 7219 5067 *Email:* david.mowat.mp@parliament.uk
Constituency: Warrington South Conservative Association, 1 Stafford Road, Warrington WA4 6RP
Tel: 01925 231267 *Fax:* 01925 575299 *Email:* wsca@talktalk.net
Website: www.davidmowat.org

MUDIE, GEORGE
Leeds East *(Majority 10,293)*

George Edward Mudie. Born 6 February 1945; Married (2 children).

Education: Local state schools.

Non-political career: Trade union official.

Political career: Member for Leeds East 1992-2010, for Leeds East (revised boundary) since 6 May 2010 general election; Opposition Whip 1994-97; Pairing and Accommodation Whip 1995-97; Deputy Chief Whip 1997-98; Parliamentary Under-Secretary of State, Department for Education and Employment (Lifelong Learning) 1998-99; Assistant Government Whip 2009-10; Opposition Whip 2010. *Select committees:* Member: Accommodation and Works 1992-98, Public Accounts 1994-95, Selection 1995-99, Finance and Services 1997-99, Treasury 2001-09, 2010-, Treasury (Treasury Sub-Committee) 2001-10, Joint Committee on Tax Law Rewrite Bills 2009; Chair: Joint Committee on Statutory Instruments 2010-; Member: Liaison 2010-, Backbench Business 2010-12, Joint Committee on the Draft Financial Services Bill 2011-12. *Councils and public bodies:* Former Leader, Leeds City Council.

LABOUR

Other: Harehills Labour Club.

Recreations: Watching football.

George Mudie MP, House of Commons, London SW1A 0AA
Tel: 020 7219 5889 *Email:* mudieg@parliament.uk
Constituency: The Former Presbytery, Our Lady of Good Counsel, Rosgill Drive, Leeds LS14 6QY
Tel: 0113-232 3266 *Fax:* 0113-232 3853 *Email:* george@gmudie.fsnet.co.uk
Website: www.leedslabour.org.uk

MULHOLLAND, GREG
Leeds North West *(Majority 9,103)*

Gregory Thomas Mulholland. Born 31 August 1970; Son of John and Maureen Mulholland; Married Raegan Hatton 2004 (3 daughters).

Education: St Ambrose College, Altrincham; York University (BA politics 1991; MA public administration and public policy 1995).

Non-political career: Account handler (sales promotion and events), several leading agencies 1997-2002.

Political career: Member for Leeds North West 2005-10, for Leeds North West (revised boundary) since 6 May 2010 general election; Liberal Democrat Shadow Minister for: International Development 2005-06, Schools 2006-07, Health 2007-10. *Select committees:* Member: Work and Pensions 2005-10, Public Administration 2010-. Chair, Liberal Democrat Parliamentary Party Committee on Work and Pensions 2012-. Executive member, Edinburgh Central 2001; Vice-chair, Leeds North West 2003-05. *Councils and public bodies:* Councillor, Leeds City Council 2003-05: Leeds District Spokesperson, METRO (West Yorkshire Passenger Transport Authority) 2004-05.

LIBERAL DEMOCRAT

Political interests: Education, higher education, international development, public transport, work and pensions, social care; Developing world, USA.

Other: Member, Amnesty International; Supporter: CAFOD, TIDAL (Trade Injustice Debt Action Leeds); Institute of Sales Promotion 1999; Adel War Memorial Association; Otley Pub Club.

Recreations: Hillwalking, watching football and rugby league, skiing, travel, real ale, fitness.

Greg Mulholland MP, House of Commons, London SW1A 0AA
Tel: 020 7219 3833 *Email:* greg.mulholland.mp@parliament.uk
Constituency: Wainwright House, 12 Holt Park Centre, Holt Road, Leeds LS16 7SR
Tel: 0113-226 6519 *Fax:* 0113-226 2237 *Email:* info@gregmulholland.org
Website: www.gregmulholland.org *Twitter:* @GregMulholland1

CONSERVATIVE

MUNDELL, DAVID   Dumfriesshire, Clydesdale and Tweeddale *(Majority 4,194)*

Parliamentary Under-Secretary of State, Scotland Office

David Gordon Mundell. Born 27 May 1962; Son of Dorah Mundell, hotelier; Married Lynda Carmichael 1987 (divorced) (2 sons 1 daughter).

Education: Lockerbie Academy; Edinburgh University (LLB 1984); Strathclyde University Business School (MBA 1991); French, German.

Non-political career: Solicitor, Maxwell Waddell 1987-89; Corporate lawyer, Biggart Baillie & Gifford, Glasgow 1989-91; BT Scotland: Group legal adviser 1991-98, Head of national affairs 1998-99.

Political career: Member for Dumfriesshire, Clydesdale and Tweeddale since 5 May 2005 general election; Shadow Secretary of State for Scotland 2005-10; Parliamentary Under-Secretary of State, Scotland Office 2010-. *Select committees:* Member: Scottish Affairs 2005-10. Contested Dumfries constituency 1999 and 2003 Scottish Parliament elections. MSP for South of Scotland region 1999-2005. Chairman, Scottish Conservative and Unionist Party 2011-. *Councils and public bodies:* Councillor: Annandale and Eskdale District Council 1984-86, Dumfries and Galloway Council 1986-87.

Political interests: Business, commerce, rural affairs; Sierra Leone, USA.

Other: Member: Dyspraxia Foundation, Law Society of Scotland 1986-, Law Society 1992-. PC 2010.

Rt Hon David Mundell MP, House of Commons, London SW1A 0AA
Tel: 020 7219 4895 *Fax:* 020 7219 2707 *Email:* david.mundell.mp@parliament.uk
Constituency: 2 Holm Street, Moffat, Dumfriesshire DG10 9EB
Tel: 01683 222746 *Fax:* 01683 222796 *Email:* david@davidmundell.com
Website: www.davidmundell.com *Twitter:* @DavidMundellMP

LAB/CO-OP

MUNN, MEG   Sheffield Heeley *(Majority 5,807)*

Margaret Patricia Munn. Born 24 August 1959; Daughter of late Reginald Munn, representative, and Lillian Munn, née Seward, retired nurse tutor; Married Dennis Bates 1989.

Education: Rowlinson Comprehensive School, Sheffield; York University (BA languages 1981); Nottingham University (MA social work 1986); Certificate of Qualification in social work 1986; Open University (Certificate management studies 1995; Diploma management studies 1997); French, German, Italian, Spanish.

Non-political career: Social work assistant, Berkshire County Council 1981-84; Nottinghamshire County Council: Social worker 1986-90, Senior social worker 1990-92; District manager, Barnsley Metropolitan Council 1992-96; Children's services manager, Wakefield Metropolitan District Council 1996-99; Assistant director, City of York Council 1999-2000. Unison (and its predecessor) 1981-96; GMB 1997-2006; USDAW 2004-.

Political career: Member for Sheffield Heeley 2001-10, for Sheffield Heeley (revised boundary) since 6 May 2010 general election; Team PPS Department for Education and Skills 2003-04; PPS to Margaret Hodge as Minister of State, Department for Education and Skills 2004-05; Parliamentary Under-Secretary of State: Department of Trade and Industry 2005-06, Department for Communities and Local Government (Women and Equality) 2006-07, Foreign and Commonwealth Office 2007-08. *Select committees:* Member: Procedure 2001-02, Education and Skills 2001-03. Chair, PLP Women's Committee 2003-05. Member, Co-operative Party 1975-; Chair, Co-operative Parliamentary Group 2004-05. *Councils and public bodies:* Councillor, Nottingham City Council 1987-91.

Political interests: Social welfare, social affairs, co-operative issues, European affairs, small businesses, women, technology, child protection; France, Germany, Iraq.

Other: Westminster Foundation for Democracy: Chair 2008-10, Vice-chair 2010-12; Chartered Management Institute 2012.

Publications: Co-editor, Family Fortunes: the New Politics of Childhood (Fabian Society, 2004); Contributed essay in Labour Looks to Israel (Labour Friends of Israel, 2005); Foreword to Diversity and the Economy (Smith Institute, 2006); President's Address to the Co-operative Congress (Co-operatives UK, 2006); Contributed essay in Making the Progressive Case for Israel (Labour Friends of Israel, 2011); Vetting and Disclosures: Getting it right in practice (Child Protection APPG/NSPCC, 2011); Editor, Unlocking Potential: Perspectives on Women in Science, Engineering and Technology (Smith Institute, 2011); Making Care Proceedings Better for Children (Child Proection APPG/NSPCC, 2013).

Recreations: Tennis, swimming, reading.

Meg Munn MP, House of Commons, London SW1A 0AA
Tel: 020 7219 8316 *Email:* meg.munn.mp@parliament.uk
Constituency: PO Box 4333, Sheffield, South Yorkshire S8 2EY
Tel: 0114-258 2010 *Website:* www.megmunnmp.org.uk *Twitter:* @MegMunnMP

LIBERAL DEMOCRAT

MUNT, TESSA
Wells *(Majority 800)*

PPS to Vince Cable as Secretary of State for Business, Innovation and Skills

Tessa Jane Munt. Born 16 October 1959; Married Martin Munt 1992 (separated) (1 son 1 daughter 1 stepdaughter).

Education: Reigate County School for Girls; Sutton High School.

Non-political career: Lecturer, South East Essex College of Arts and Technology 1992-94; Administrator, Holiday Explorers 1994; Supply teacher, Samuel Ward Upper School, Haverhill 1994-95; Community resource unit manager, Suffolk social services 1994-96; Personal assistant to Phil Edmonds 1996-98; Fee-earner: Franks Charlesly and Co 1996-98, Jay Benning and Pelts 1998-99, Forsters 1999-2006.

Political career: Contested South Suffolk 2001 general election, Ipswich 2001 by-election and Wells 2005 general election. Member for Wells since 6 May 2010 general election; PPS to Vince Cable as Secretary of State for Business, Innovation and Skills 2012-. *Select committees:* Member: Education 2010-12, Administration 2010-. Parliamentary Candidates Association: Vice-chair 2003-09, Patron 2009-; Member, Federal Executive 2005-09.

Political interests: Education, prison service, domestic violence, children and families, planning, the environment, Isle of Man; Africa.

Other: Burnham on Sea and Highbridge Twinning Association; Wedmore Twinning Association; Wells Twinning Association; Member: Greenpeace, Friends of the Earth, IFAW, CND, EIA, Sedgemoor Peace Group, Amnesty International, Save the Children, Somerset Tourism Association, Wedmore Green Group, Sustainable Axbridge Network, Street Society, Shepton Mallet Society, Wedmore Society; Counsellor and speaker, Childline 2000-; Speaker, Environmental Investigation Agency 2000-.

Recreations: Listening to music, East African history, cinema, reading, cooking for friends.

Tessa Munt MP, House of Commons, London SW1A 0AA
Tel: 020 7219 4024 *Email:* tessa.munt.mp@parliament.uk
Constituency: Hodge's Chambers, Cheddar Road, Wedmore, Somerset BS28 4EH
Tel: 01934 710748 *Website:* www.tessamunt.org.uk *Twitter:* @tessamunt

SINN FÉIN

MURPHY, CONOR
Newry and Armagh *(Majority 8,331)*

Conor Terence Murphy. Born 10 July 1963; Married Catherine (1 son 1 daughter).

Education: St Colman's College, Newry; Ulster University (BA humanities); Queen's University, Belfast (MA).

Political career: Contested Newry and Armagh 2001 general election. Member for Newry and Armagh since 5 May 2005 general election; Northern Ireland Assembly: MLA for Newry and Armagh 1998-2012: Deputy chair, Assembly Committee on Public Accounts 2002, Member, Preparation for Government Committee 2006-07, Minister for Regional Development 2007-11, Chair, Assembly Committee on Finance and Personnel 2011-12, Sinn Féin Spokesperson for Economy 2011-12. *Councils and public bodies:* Councillor, Newry and Mourne District Council 1989-97.

Other: Manages Cumann Na Meirleach Ard Mhaca Theas, project for ex-prisoners, South Armagh.

Conor Murphy MP, House of Commons, London SW1A 0AA
Tel: 020 7219 8534 *Fax:* 020 7219 6107 *Email:* murphyc@parliament.uk
Constituency: 1 Kilmorey Terrace, Patrick Street, Newry, Co Down BT35 6DW
Tel: 028 3026 1693 *Fax:* 028 3026 8283 *Website:* www.newryarmaghsf.com
Twitter: @conormurphymp

LABOUR

MURPHY, JIM
East Renfrewshire *(Majority 10,420)*

Shadow Secretary of State for International Development

James Murphy. Born 23 August 1967; Son of Jim Murphy, pipe-fitter, and Anne Murphy, secretary; Married Claire Cook (1 daughter 2 sons).

Education: Bellarmine Secondary School, Glasgow; Milnerton High School, Cape Town, South Africa.

Non-political career: President: NUS (Scotland) 1992-94, NUS 1994-96; Director, Endsleigh Insurance 1994-96; Project manager, Scottish Labour Party 1996-97. Member, GMB.

Political career: Member for Eastwood/East Renfrewshire (renamed 2005) since 1 May 1997 general election; PPS to Helen Liddell as Secretary of State for Scotland 2001-02; Assistant Government Whip 2002-03; Government Whip 2003-05; Parliamentary Secretary, Cabinet Office 2005-06; Minister of State: Department for Work and Pensions (Employment and Welfare Reform) 2006-07, Foreign and Commonwealth Office (Europe) 2007-08; Secretary of State for Scotland 2008-10; Shadow Secretary of State for: Scotland 2010, Defence 2010-13, International Development 2013-. *Select committees:* Member: Public Accounts 1999-2001. Labour Friends of Israel: Vice-chair 1997-2001, Chair 2001-02; Member, Co-operative Party.

Political interests: Economy, employment, international affairs, defence, consumer issues, sport; Southern Africa, Middle East.

Other: Commons Minister of the Year, *House Magazine* 2008. PC 2008. Bonnington Golf.

Recreations: Football, travelling in Scotland and Ireland, cinema, horse-racing, golf.

Rt Hon Jim Murphy MP, House of Commons, London SW1A 0AA
Tel: 020 7219 4615 *Email:* jimmurphymp@parliament.uk
Constituency: Suite 4/5, 1 Spiersbridge Way, Thornliebank, East Renfrewshire G46 8NG
Tel: 0141-620 6310 *Website:* www.jimmurphymp.com *Twitter:* @jimmurphymp

LABOUR

MURPHY, PAUL
Torfaen *(Majority 9,306)*

Paul Peter Murphy. Born 25 November 1948; Son of late Ronald Murphy and late Marjorie Murphy; Single.

Education: St Francis School, Abersychan; West Monmouth School, Pontypool; Oriel College, Oxford (MA modern history 1970); French (basic).

Non-political career: Management trainee, CWS 1970-71; Lecturer in government, Ebbw Vale College of Further Education 1971-87; Visiting Parliamentary Fellow, St Anthony's College, Oxford 2006-07. Member, TGWU-Unite.

Political career: Contested Wells 1979 general election. Member for Torfaen since 11 June 1987 general election; Opposition Spokesman on: Welsh Affairs 1988-94, Northern Ireland 1994-95, Foreign Affairs 1995, Defence, Disarmament and Arms Control 1995-97; Minister of State, Northern Ireland Office (Minister for Political Development) 1997-99; Secretary of State for: Wales 1999-2002, Northern Ireland 2002-05; Chairman, Intelligence and Security Committee 2005-08; Secretary of State for Wales 2008-09. *Select committees:* Member: Joint Committee on National Security Strategy 2010-. Chair, PLP Departmental Committee for Northern Ireland 2010-. Secretary, Torfaen Constituency Labour Party 1971-87; Chair, Welsh Group of Labour MPs 1996-97. *Councils and public bodies:* Torfaen Borough Council: Councillor 1973-87, Chair, Finance Committee 1976-86.

Political interests: Local and regional government, wales, education, housing, foreign affairs; France, Ireland, Northern Ireland.

Other: Vice-chair, British-American Parliamentary Group 2004-05, 2007-09; British-Irish Parliamentary Assembly: Co-chair 2006-07, 2009-10, Vice-chair 2010-; Vice-chair, Franco-British Friendship Group. Honorary Fellow, Oriel College, Oxford 2001; Parliamentary Visiting Fellow, St Antony's College, Oxford 2006-07; Honorary Fellow, Glyndŵr University, Wrexham 2009-. Knight of St Gregory (Papal Order); PC 1999; KCMCO; Oxford and Cambridge Club.

Recreations: Classical music, cooking.

Rt Hon Paul Murphy MP, House of Commons, London SW1A 0AA
Tel: 020 7219 3463 *Fax:* 020 7219 3819 *Email:* paul.murphy.mp@parliament.uk
Constituency: 73 Upper Trosnant Street, Pontypool, Torfaen, Gwent NP4 8AU
Tel: 01495 750078 *Fax:* 01495 752584 *Website:* www.paulmurphymp.co.uk

MURRAY, IAN

Edinburgh South *(Majority 316)*

Shadow Minister for Business, Innovation and Skills

Born 10 August 1976; Son of Lena Murray and late James Brownlie Murray; Partner Hannah Woolfson.

Education: Wester Hailes Education Centre; Edinburgh University (MA social policy and law 1997).

Non-political career: Royal Blind Asylum 1996-97; Aegon UK 1998-99; Operations director, Internet TV station 1999-2001; Managing director, 100mph Events Ltd 2001-; Partner, Alibi Bars 2005-11. Member, USDAW.

Political career: Member for Edinburgh South since 6 May 2010 general election; PPS to Ivan Lewis as Shadow Secretary of State for Culture, Media and Sport 2010-11; Shadow Minister for Business, Innovation and Skills 2011-. *Select committees:* Member: Environmental Audit 2010-12, Business, Innovation and Skills 2010-11, Arms Export Controls 2010-12. Vice-chair, PLP Departmental Group for Culture, Olympics, Media and Sport 2010-. Member: Labour Party, Co-operative Party; Campaign manager, Edinburgh Pentlands, 2001 general election. *Councils and public bodies:* Councillor, Edinburgh City Council 2003-10.

Political interests: Education, services for disabled people, social justice, equal opportunities, environment, conservation, business; South America, Middle East, Nepal, USA.

Other: Member, Fabian Society; Trustee, Great War Memorial Committee; McCrae's Battalion Trust 2007-; Fellow, Industry and Parliament Trust 2011-; Supporter: Care for the Wild, Amnesty International.

Recreations: Sport, reading, cooking.

Ian Murray MP, House of Commons, London SW1A 0AA
Tel: 020 7219 7064 *Email:* ian.murray.mp@parliament.uk
Constituency: 31 Minto Street, Edinburgh EH9 2BT
Tel: 0131-662 4520 *Email:* ian@ianmurraymp.co.uk *Website:* www.ianmurraymp.co.uk
Twitter: @ianmurraymp

MURRAY, SHERYLL

South East Cornwall *(Majority 3,220)*

Born 4 February 1956; Married Neil (died 2011) (1 son 1 daughter).

Education: Torpoint Comprehensive School.

Political career: Member for South East Cornwall since 6 May 2010 general election. *Select committees:* Member: Environmental Audit 2010-12, Environmental, Food and Rural Affairs 2012-. Member, Executive, 1922 Committee 2012-. *Councils and public bodies:* Former councillor, Cornwall County Council; Caradon District Council: Councillor, Leader, Conservative group.

Political interests: Environment, tourism, Royal Navy; America, Middle East, UK.

Other: Animal Welfare Champion, Charity Champion awards 2012.

Recreations: Formula One Motor Sport.

Sheryll Murray MP, House of Commons, London SW1A 0AA
Tel: 020 7219 3000 *Email:* sheryll.murray.mp@parliament.uk
Constituency: Windsor Place, Liskeard, Cornwall PL14 4BH
Tel: 01579 344428 *Email:* sheryll@sheryllmurray.com *Website:* www.sheryllmurray.com
Twitter: @sheryllmurray

MURRISON, ANDREW

South West Wiltshire *(Majority 10,367)*

Parliamentary Under-Secretary of State (International Security Strategy), Ministry of Defence

Andrew William Murrison. Born 24 April 1961; Son of William Murrison and Marion Murrison, née Horn; Married Jennifer Munden 1994 (5 daughters).

Education: Harwich High School; The Harwich School; Bristol University (MB CHB 1984; MD 1995); Cambridge University (DPH medicine 1996); French.

Non-political career: Surgeon Commander Royal Navy 1981-2000; Royal Naval Reserve 2000-: Served in Iraq (Operation Telic II) 2003. Principal medical officer, HM Naval Base Portsmouth 1996-99; Staff officer, Commander-In-Chief Fleet 1999-2000; Locum consultant occupational physician, Gloucestershire Royal Hospital and GP 2000-01.

Political career: Member for Westbury 2001-10, for South West Wiltshire since 6 May 2010 general election; Shadow Minister for: Public Services, Health and Education 2003-04, Health 2004-07, Defence 2007-10; PPS to Andrew Lansley as Secretary of State for Health 2010-12; Prime Minister's Special Representative for the Centenary Commemoration of the First World War 2011-; Parliamentary Under-Secretary of State (International Security Strategy), Ministry of Defence 2012-. *Select committees:* Member: Science and Technology 2001-05.

Political interests: Health, defence; Morocco, Iraq.

Other: Royal British Legion. Gilbert Blane Medal 1994; Warminster Conservative Club; Royal British Legion, Warminster Branch; Vice-president, Trowbridge White Ensign Association; Westbury Lions.

Publications: Tommy this an' Tommy that: the military covenant (Biteback, 2011).

Recreations: Sailing, skiing.

Dr Andrew Murrison MP, House of Commons, London SW1A 0AA
Tel: 020 7219 8337 *Email:* murrisona@parliament.uk
Constituency: Suite 1, Holloway House, Epsom Square, White Horse Business Park, Trowbridge, Wiltshire BA14 0XG
Tel: 01225 358584 *Fax:* 01225 358583 *Email:* packerj@parliament.uk
Website: www.andrewmurrison.co.uk *Twitter:* @murrisonMP

NANDY, LISA
Wigan *(Majority 10,487)*

Shadow Minister for Cabinet Office

LABOUR

Lisa Eva Nandy. Born 9 August 1979; Daughter of Dipak Nandy, academic and founding director of the Runnymede Trust, and Luise Nandy, television producer.

Education: Parrs Wood Comprehensive School, Manchester; Holy Cross Sixth Form College, Bury; Newcastle University (BA politics 2001); Birkbeck University, London (MSc government, policy and politics 2005).

Non-political career: Parliamentary assistant to Neil Gerrard MP 2001-03; Policy researcher, Centrepoint 2003-05; Policy adviser, Children's Society 2005-10. Member: Unite, CWU.

Political career: Member for Wigan since 6 May 2010 general election; PPS to Tessa Jowell as Shadow Minister for London and the Olympics 2011-12; Shadow Minister for: Children and Families 2012-13, Cabinet Office 2013-. *Select committees:* Member: Education 2010-12. Vice-chair, PLP Departmental Group for Communities and Local Government 2010-11. Member, Wigan Labour Party. *Councils and public bodies:* London Borough of Hammersmith and Fulham Council: Councillor 2006-10, Shadow Cabinet Member for Housing and Regeneration; Governor, Brackenbury Primary School 2002-.

Political interests: International corporate responsibility, children, poverty, low pay; Colombia.

Other: Director, Lyric Theatre, Hammersmith 2006-10; Member, Amnesty International.

Publications: Author: Waiting in Line: Young Refugees in the Labour Market (Centrepoint, 2003), Bed and Breakfast: Unfit Housing for Young People (Centrepoint, 2005), With Nicola Clarke, Living on the Edge of Despair (The Children's Society, 2008).

Recreations: Rugby league, theatre and the arts.

Lisa Nandy MP, House of Commons, London SW1A 0AA
Tel: 020 7219 7188 *Fax:* 020 7219 5152 *Email:* lisa.nandy.mp@parliament.uk
Constituency: Room S46, Second Floor, Wigan Investment Centre, Waterside Drive, Wigan WN3 5BA
Tel: 01942 242047 *Fax:* 01942 239451 *Website:* www.lisanandy.co.uk *Twitter:* @lisanandy

NASH, PAMELA
Airdrie and Shotts *(Majority 12,408)*

LABOUR

Born 24 June 1984.

Education: St Margaret's School, Airdrie; Glasgow University.

Non-political career: Boots plc; Parliamentary researcher to John Reid MP.

Political career: Member for Airdrie and Shotts since 6 May 2010 general election; PPS to: Ann McKechin as Shadow Secretary of State for Scotland 2011, Shaun Woodward as Shadow Secretary of State for Northern Ireland 2011, Margaret Curran as Shadow Secretary of State for Scotland 2011-12, Vernon Coaker as Shadow Secretary of State for Northern Ireland 2011-13. *Select committees:* Member: Science and Technology 2010-, Scottish Affairs 2012-. Former member, Scottish Youth Parliament.

Other: Parliamentary officer, Young Fabians 2009-.
Pamela Nash MP, House of Commons, London SW1A 0AA
Tel: 020 7219 7003 *Email:* pamela.nash.mp@parliament.uk
Constituency: 100 Stirling Street, Airdrie ML6 0AS
Tel: 01236 753795 *Fax:* 01236 752930 *Website:* www.pamelanash.com *Twitter:* @pamela_nash

NEILL, ROBERT
Bromley and Chislehurst *(Majority 13,900)*

CONSERVATIVE

Robert James Macgillivray Neill. Born 24 June 1952; Son of John Neill and Elsie Neill, née Coombs; Married Daphne White 2009.
Education: Abbs Cross School, Havering; London School of Economics (LLB law 1973); French.
Non-political career: Trainee dealer, London Stock Exchange 1974; Barrister in private practice (specialising in criminal law) 1975-2006; Called to the Irish Bar 1990.
Political career: Contested Dagenham 1983 and 1987 general elections. Member for Bromley and Chislehurst 29 June 2006 by-election to 2010, for Bromley and Chislehusrt (revised boundary) since 6 May 2010 general election; Shadow Minister for Communities and Local Government 2007-10 (Local Government 2009-10); Parliamentary Under-Secretary of State, Department for Communities and Local Government 2010-12. *Select committees:* Member: Constitutional Affairs/Justice 2006-10, Justice 2012-13. Greater London Conservatives: Deputy chairman 1993-96, Chair 1996-99; Conservative Party: Deputy chairman (local government) 2008-10, Vice-chairman (local government) 2012-. *Councils and public bodies:* London Borough of Havering: Councillor 1974-90, Chief whip and chairman of Environment and Social Services Committees; GLC Councillor for Romford 1985-86; Leader, London Fire and Civil Defence Authority 1985-87; Greater London Authority: Member 2000-08, Leader, Conservative group 2000-02; Non-executive board director, North East London Strategic Health Authority 2002-06; Board member, London Regional Arts Council 2003-07.
Political interests: Policing and criminal justice, local government, environment, arts; France, Hungary, Ireland, Italy, Spain, Switzerland.
Other: Member: Committee of the Regions 2002-08, Parliamentary Assembly, Council of Europe 2012-; Member: Royal Opera House Trust, Friends of English National Opera; Carlton Club.
Recreations: Theatre, travel, opera, sailing.
Robert Neill MP, House of Commons, London SW1A 0AA
Tel: 020 7219 8169 *Fax:* 020 7219 8089 *Email:* bob.neill.mp@parliament.uk
Constituency: Bromley and Chislehurst Conservative Association, 5 White Horse Hill, Chislehurst, Kent BR7 6DG
Tel: 020 8295 2639 *Email:* office@bromleyconservatives.com *Website:* www.bobneillmp.co.uk

NEWMARK, BROOKS
Braintree *(Majority 16,121)*

CONSERVATIVE

Brooks Phillip Victor Newmark. Born 8 May 1958; Son of late Howard and Gilda Newmark; Married Lucy Keegan 1985 (4 sons 1 daughter).
Education: Bedford School; Harvard College, Harvard University, USA (BA history 1980); Worcester College, Oxford (Postgraduate Research politics 1980-82); Harvard Business School (MBA finance 1984).
Non-political career: Vice-president, Shearson Lehman Brothers Inc 1984-87; Director: Newmark Brothers Ltd 1987-92, Stellican Ltd 1992-98; Partner, Apollo Management LP 1998-2005.
Political career: Contested Newcastle upon Tyne Central 1997 and Braintree 2001 general elections. Member for Braintree 2005-10, for Braintree (revised boundary) since 6 May 2010 general election; Opposition Whip 2007-10; Government Whip 2010-12. *Select committees:* Member: Science and Technology 2005-07, Treasury 2006-07, 2012-, Finance and Services 2009-11. Chairman: Southwark and Bermondsey Conservative Association 1990-93, Women2Win 2005-.
Political interests: Economic policy, special needs education, poverty reduction and international development, foreign policy, women's issues; China, India, Middle East, USA.
Other: Director, Harvard University Alumni Association 2005-; Founder, A Partner in Education. Worshipful Company of Broderers. Freeman, City of London; Beefsteak, Boodle's, Cresta, White's; Chairman, United & Cecil Club 2010-.
Publications: Direct Democracy: An Agenda for a New Model Party (2005); Simply Red: The True State of the Public Finances (Centre for Policy Studies, 2006); The Price of Irresponsibility (Centre for Policy Studies, 2008); The Hidden Debt Bombshell (Centre for Policy Studies, 2009).

Recreations: Football (Newcastle United supporter), running, skiing.

Brooks Newmark MP, House of Commons, London SW1A 0AA
Tel: 020 7219 3464 *Fax:* 020 7219 5245 *Email:* brooks.newmark.mp@parliament.uk
Constituency: Avenue Lodge, The Avenue, Witham, Essex CM8 2DL
Tel: 01376 512386 *Fax:* 01376 516475 *Email:* theoffice@braintreeconservatives.co.uk
Website: www.brooksnewmark.com *Twitter:* @TweetBrooks

NEWTON, SARAH   Truro and Falmouth *(Majority 435)*

Sarah Louise Newton. Married Alan Newton (1 son 2 daughters).

Education: Falmouth School.

Non-political career: Marketing, Citibank then American Express.

Political career: Member for Truro and Falmouth since 6 May 2010 general election; Board member, Parliamentary Office of Science and Technology (POST). *Select committees:* Member: Administration 2010-12, Science and Technology 2012-. Former vice-chair and chair, Wimbledon Conservative Association; Deputy chairman, Conservative Party 2012-. *Councils and public bodies:* Former councillor, London Borough of Merton Council.

CONSERVATIVE

Political interests: Ageing population, rural affairs, sustainable energy.

Other: Director, International Longevity Centre; Fellow, Royal Society of Arts; Co-director, Riverside Shelter for Homeless, New York City; Age Concern England.

Recreations: Sailing, skiing, bee-keeping.

Sarah Newton MP, House of Commons, London SW1A 0AA
Tel: 020 7219 7174 *Email:* sarah.newton.mp@parliament.uk
Constituency: 18 Lemon Street, Truro, Cornwall TR1 2LZ
Tel: 01872 274760 *Website:* www.sarahnewton.org.uk *Twitter:* @SarahNewtonMP

NOKES, CAROLINE   Romsey and Southampton North *(Majority 4,156)*

Caroline Fiona Ellen Nokes. Born 26 June 1972; Daughter of Roy Perry, former MEP, and Veronica Haswell; Married Marc Anthony Nokes 1995 (1 daughter).

Education: La Sagesse Convent, Romsey; Peter Symonds' College, Winchester; Sussex University (BA government and politics 1994); French.

Non-political career: Political researcher to Roy Perry MEP 1994-2004; Consultant, Euro/Arab affairs 2004; Chief executive, National Pony Society 2008-09.

Political career: Contested Southampton Itchen 2001 and Romsey 2005 general elections. Member for Romsey and Southampton North since 6 May 2010 general election. *Select committees:* Member: Environmental Audit 2010-, Works of Art 2011-. *Councils and public bodies:* Test Valley Borough Council: Councillor 1999-2011, Leisure portfolio holder 2001-10.

CONSERVATIVE

Political interests: Agriculture, sport, environment.

Other: Vice-president, Romsey Hospital Appeal 2001.

Recreations: Skiing, riding.

Caroline Nokes MP, House of Commons, London SW1A 0AA
Tel: 020 7219 7218 *Email:* caroline.nokes.mp@parliament.uk
Constituency: Room 4, 13 Market Place, Romsey SO51 8NA
Tel: 01794 521155 *Email:* caroline@romseyconservatives.co.uk
Website: www.carolinenokes.com *Twitter:* @carolinenokes

NORMAN, JESSE   Hereford and South Herefordshire *(Majority 2,481)*

Alexander Jesse Norman. Born 23 June 1962; Married Kate 1992 (2 sons 1 daughter).

Education: Merton College, Oxford (BA classics 1985); University College, London (MPhil philosophy 1999; PhD 2003).

Non-political career: Project director, educational charity, eastern Europe 1988-91; Director, BZW (Barclays de Zoete Wedd) 1991-97; Teaching fellow and lecturer, University College, London 1999-2003; Conservative Research Department 2004-05; Policy adviser to: George Osborne as Shadow Chancellor of the Exchequer 2005, Philip Hammond as Shadow Secretary of State for Work and Pensions 2005-07; Executive director, Policy Exchange 2005-06.

CONSERVATIVE

Political career: Member for Hereford and South Herefordshire since 6 May 2010 general election. *Select committees:* Member: Treasury 2010-, Joint Committees on: Consolidation, Etc,

Bills 2010-, the Draft Enhanced Terrorism Prevention and Investigation Measures Bill 2012-13. Chair, Conservative Co-operative Movement; Member, Policy Advisory Board April-September 2013. *Councils and public bodies:* Former school governor.

Political interests: Big Society, economy, public services, PFI, human rights.

Other: Founder, schoolsfirst.org.uk; Member, advisory board, Roundhouse; Vice-President: Ross-on-Wye Horticultural Society, Herefordshire and Gloucestershire Canal Trust, Hereford Musical Theatre Company; Patron: Kindle Centre, Hereford City, Friends of St Mary's, Ross-on-Wye, Herefordshire Mind, Hereford Music Pool, Riding for the Disabled, Herefordshire, St Martin's Church Roof Appeal, Hereford, Number 1 Ledbury Road, Hereford. Parliamentarian of the Year, *The Spectator* awards 2012; Commons Backbencher of the Year, *House Magazine* awards 2012. Westfields Football Club.

Publications: Author: The Achievements of Michael Oakeshott (Gerald Duckworth & Co, 1993), After Euclid (University of Chicago Press, 2005), Compassionate Conservatism (Policy Exchange, 2006); From Here to Fraternity (Centre Forum, 2007); Compassionate Economics (Policy Exchange, 2008); Churchill's Legacy (Liberty, 2009); The Big Society (University of Buckingham Press, 2010) Edmund Burke: Philosopher, Politician, Prophet (William Collins, 2013).

Recreations: Music, sports, theatre.

Jesse Norman MP, House of Commons, London SW1A 0AA
Tel: 020 7219 7084 *Email:* jesse.norman.mp@parliament.uk
Constituency: Suite 3, Penn House, Broad Street, Hereford HR4 9AP
Tel: 01432 276422 *Website:* www.jesse4hereford.com *Twitter:* @jesse_norman

CONSERVATIVE

NUTTALL, DAVID
Bury North *(Majority 2,243)*

David John Nuttall. Born 25 March 1962; Son of Roy Nuttall and late Kathleen Nuttall; Married Susan Smith 2004.

Education: Aston Comprehensive School, Rotherham; London University external student (LLB 1987); Law Society Finals Qualified Solicitor 1990; Notarial Examinations Qualified Notary 1998.

Non-political career: Taylor Son & Co/Taylors: Trainee legal executive 1980-90, Qualified solicitor 1990, Partner 1990-98, Senior partner 1998-2006; Notary Public, Nuttalls Notaries 2006-10.

Political career: Contested Sheffield Hillsborough 1997, Morecambe and Lunesdale 2001 and Bury North 2005 general elections. Member for Bury North since 6 May 2010 general election. *Select committees:* Member: Procedure 2010-. Contested Yorkshire and the Humber 1999 European Parliament election. Member, Conservative Party 1980-; Chair, South Yorkshire Conservatives 2001-04. *Councils and public bodies:* Rotherham Metropolitan Borough Council: Councillor 1992-96, 2004-06, Opposition leader 1995-96.

Political interests: Home affairs, law and order, small business, European Union.

Other: Fellow, Institute of Legal Executives 1988; Member, Notaries Society; Salisbury Conservative Club, Bury. Yorkshire County Cricket Club; Ramsbottom Cricket Club; Tottington Sports Club.

Recreations: Walking, watching sport especially football and cricket, bird-watching.

David Nuttall MP, House of Commons, London SW1A 0AA
Tel: 020 7219 7030 *Fax:* 020 7219 2409 *Email:* david.nuttall.mp@parliament.uk
Constituency: 15 St Mary's Place, Bury, Lancashire BL9 0DZ
Tel: 0161-797 5007 *Email:* nabila.afilal@parliament.uk *Website:* www.david.nuttall.info
Twitter: @DavidNuttallMP

CONSERVATIVE

O'BRIEN, STEPHEN
Eddisbury *(Majority 13,255)*

Stephen Rothwell O'Brien. Born 1 April 1957; Son of David O'Brien, retired businessman, and Rothy O'Brien, retired shop owner and nurse; Married Gemma Townshend 1986 (2 sons 1 daughter).

Education: Loreto School, Mombasa, Kenya; Handbridge School, Chester; Sedbergh School, Cumbria (music scholar); Emmanuel College, Cambridge (BA law 1979, MA); College of Law, Chester (Professional Qualification 1980); French.

Non-political career: Armed Forces Parliamentary Scheme (Army) 2001-03, 2005-07. Freshfields, London: Articles 1981-83, Senior Managing Solicitor 1983-88; Redland plc 1988-98: Group secretary and director of Strategy and Corporate Affairs, Director of UK and overseas operations, Member, Group Executive Committee, Deputy chairman, Redland Tile and Brick

(Northern Ireland 1995-98), Executive director, Redland Clay Tile (Mexico 1994-98); International business consultant 1998-2010; Parliamentary adviser to: Institute of Chartered Secretaries and Administrators 2000-10, Manufacturing Technologies Association 2005-10.

Political career: Member for Eddisbury 22 July 1999 by-election to 2010, for Eddisbury (revised boundary) since 6 May 2010 general election; Private Member's Bill, Honesty in Food Labelling 1999-2000, re-introduced 2002-03; PPS to Michael Ancram as Chairman of the Conservative Party 2000-01; Opposition Whip 2001-02; Shadow Financial Secretary to the Treasury 2002; Shadow Paymaster General 2002-03; Shadow Secretary of State for Industry 2003-05; Shadow Minister for: Education and Skills 2005, Health and Social Care 2005-10; Parliamentary Under-Secretary of State, Department for International Development 2010-12; Prime Minister's Envoy and Special Representative to the Sahel 2012-. *Select committees:* Member: Education and Employment (Education Sub-Committee) 1999-2001, Environment, Food and Rural Affairs 2001. Secretary: Conservative Industry Group 2000-02, Conservative Northern Ireland Group 1999-2002. Chairman, Chichester Conservative Association 1998-99; Executive committee member, Westminster Candidates Association 1998-99; Conservative Business Liaison Unit (construction sector lead) 1998-2001; Member, National Membership Committee of the Conservative Party 1999-2001.

Political interests: Economy, trade and industry, agriculture and the rural economy, health, housing, infrastructure, transport, Northern Ireland, foreign affairs, education, constitutional affairs, international development; Africa, Australia, Canada, European countries, Ireland, Latin America, USA.

Other: Member: British-Irish Inter-Parliamentary Body 2000-10, International Parliamentary Union 2006-, Commonwealth Parliamentary Association 1999-; Non-executive director, Cambridge University Careers Service 1992-99; Member, CBI South East Regional Council 1995-98; Chairman, Public and Parliamentary Affairs Committee BMP (UK Building Materials Producers) 1995-99; Non-executive director, City of London Sinfonia 2001-; Board Trustee, Liverpool School of Tropical Medicine 2006-10, 2013-; Non-executive director, Small Business Research Trust 2006-08; Chairman, Malaria Consortium (UK) 2007-10; Board Trustee, Innovative Vector Control Consortium 2008-10; Member, Law Society; Global Advocate, Roll Back Malaria; Fellow, Institute of Chartered Secretaries and Administrators; FCIS. PC 2013; Winsford Constitutional and Conservative, Cheshire Pitt Club.

Recreations: Music (piano), fell-walking.

Rt Hon Stephen O'Brien MP, House of Commons, London SW1A 0AA
Tel: 020 7219 6315/020 7219 5173 *Fax:* 020 7219 0584 *Email:* obriens@parliament.uk
Constituency: Eddisbury Conservative Association, 4 Church Walk, High Street, Tarporley, Cheshire CW6 0AJ
Tel: 01829 733243 *Fax:* 01829 733243 *Email:* office@eddisburyconservatives.co.uk
Website: www.eddisburyconservatives.co.uk www.stephenobrien.org.uk

LABOUR

O'DONNELL, FIONA

East Lothian *(Majority 12,258)*

Born 27 January 1960; Daughter of Gladys and Patrick Kenny; Divorced (3 sons including twins and 1 daughter).

Education: Lochaber High School, Fort William.

Non-political career: Voluntary sector – mental health, housing, disability, children and families; Public policy; Campaigner and development officer, Scottish Labour Party -2010. Member, GMB.

Political career: Member for East Lothian since 6 May 2010 general election; Shadow Minister for Environment, Food and Rural Affairs 2011-12. *Select committees:* Member: Scottish Affairs 2010-11, International Development 2012-, Arms Export Controls 2012-13, Standards 2013-, Privileges 2013-. *Councils and public bodies:* Former: School board member, Community councillor, Scone.

Political interests: International development, employment, welfare, social inclusion, carers, education.

Other: Member, RSPB.

Fiona O'Donnell MP, House of Commons, London SW1A 0AA
Tel: 020 7219 7059 *Email:* fiona.odonnell.mp@parliament.uk
Constituency: 65 High Street, Tranent, East Lothian EH33 1LN
Tel: 01875 824779 *Website:* www.fionaodonnellmp.org *Twitter:* @FionaODonnellMP

CONSERVATIVE

OFFORD, MATTHEW
Hendon *(Majority 106)*

Matthew James Offord. Born 3 September 1969; Married Claire Rowles 2010.

Education: Amery Hill School, Alton; Nottingham Trent University (BA photography 1992); Lancaster University (MA environment, culture and society 2000); King's College London (PhD rural governance and economic redevelopment).

Non-political career: Media analyst, Medialink Communications 1995-96; Political adviser: Conservative Central Office 1996-97, Local Government Association 1997; Political analyst, BBC 2001-10.

Political career: Contested Barnsley East and Mexborough 2001 general election. Member for Hendon since 6 May 2010 general election. *Select committees:* Member: Environmental Audit 2012-. Chair, Hendon Conservative Association 2004-. *Councils and public bodies:* London Borough of Barnet Council: Councillor 2002-, Council deputy leader, Cabinet member for: Environment and Transport, Community Safety, Community Engagement.

Countries of interest: Sub-Saharan Africa, Cyprus, Israel, Middle East, Sri Lanka.

Other: Member, The Association of European Parliamentarians for Africa; Fellow, Royal Geographical Society. Welsh Harp's Seahorse Sailing Club.

Recreations: Sailing, scuba diving.

Dr Matthew Offord MP, House of Commons, London SW1A 0AA
Tel: 020 7219 7083 *Email:* matthew.offord.mp@parliament.uk
Constituency: 120 Bunns Lane, Mill Hill, London NW7 2AS
Tel: 020 3114 2131 *Website:* www.matthewofford.co.uk *Twitter:* @HendonMP

CONSERVATIVE

OLLERENSHAW, ERIC
Lancaster and Fleetwood *(Majority 333)*

PPS to Baroness Warsi as Senior Minister of State (Faith and Communities), Department for Communities and Local Government and Foreign and Commonwealth Office

Born 26 March 1950; Son of Mr E and Mrs B Ollerenshaw; Single.

Education: Hyde County Grammar School; London School of Economics (BSc (Econ) 1971).

Non-political career: History teacher 1973-2010.

Political career: Contested Heywood and Middleton 1992 general election. Member for Lancaster and Fleetwood since 6 May 2010 general election; PPS to Baroness Warsi: as Minister Without Portfolio and Chairman Conservative Party 2010-12, as Senior Minister of State (Faith and Communities), Department for Communities and Local Government and Foreign and Commonwealth Office 2012-. *Select committees:* Member: Standards and Privileges 2010. Member, The 40 Group. *Councils and public bodies:* Inner London Education Authority: Member 1986-90, Opposition Leader 1988-90; Hackney Borough Council: Member 1990-2008, Leader, Conservative group 1998-2008, Joint Leader of Council 2000-01; Greater London Assembly: Member 2000-04, Leader, Conservative group; Former member: Metropolitan Police Authority, Great Ormond Street Hospital School Board, London Fire and Emergency Planning Authority; Vice-President, Local Government Association 2010-11.

Political interests: Education, local government, housing, energy; Azerbaijan, Pakistan, Turkey.

Other: Trustee, Future First (education charity). OBE.

Recreations: Reading, keeping fit, listening to music.

Eric Ollerenshaw OBE MP, House of Commons, London SW1A 0AA
Tel: 020 7219 7096 *Email:* eric.ollerenshaw.mp@parliament.uk
Constituency: The Village Centre, 59 High Street, Great Eccleston, Lancashire PR3 0YB
Tel: 01995 672975 *Email:* lancasterwyre@tory.org *Website:* www.ericollerenshaw.com

---

LABOUR

ONWURAH, CHI
Newcastle upon Tyne Central *(Majority 7,466)*

Shadow Minister for the Cabinet Office

Chinyelu Susan Onwurah. Born 12 April 1965; Daughter of Kathleen Onwurah, née Roche, and Dr Moses Onwurah.

Education: Kenton School; Imperial College, London (BEng electrical engineering 1987); Manchester Business School (MBA 2002); French.

Non-political career: Nortel 1987-95; Cable & Wireless 1995-99; Director of product strategy, Global Telesystems UK 1999-2000; Director of market development, Teligent 2000-01; Partner, Hammatan Ventures 2001-04; Head of telecoms technology, OFCOM 2004-10. Member, Unite.

Political career: Member for Newcastle upon Tyne Central since 6 May 2010 general election; Shadow Minister for Business, Innovation and Skills (Innovation, Science and Digital Infrastructure) 2010-13; Board member, Parliamentary Office of Science and Technology (POST); Shadow Minister for the Cabinet Office 2013-. *Select committees:* Member: Business, Innovation and Skills 2010. Member, Labour Party 1981-.

Political interests: Education, technology, manufacturing, international development, trade, social mobility; China, France, Nigeria, South Africa.

Other: Former national executive member: Anti-Apartheid Movement, Action for South Africa (ACTSA); Member, Chatham House; Open University Business School; Institute of Engineering Technology; Fellow, Institute of Engineering and Technology; Action for South Africa.

Recreations: Reading, music, country walks.

Chi Onwurah MP, House of Commons, London SW1A 0AA
Tel: 020 7219 7114 *Email:* chi.onwurah.mp@parliament.uk
Constituency: Unit 24, 7-15 Pink Lane, Newcastle upon Tyne NE1 5DW
Tel: 0191-232 5838 *Email:* carol.stanners@parliament.uk *Website:* www.chionwurahmp.com
Twitter: @ChiOnwurah

CONSERVATIVE

OPPERMAN, GUY
Hexham *(Majority 5,788)*

PPS to Mark Harper as Minister of State for Immigration, Home Office

Guy Thomas Opperman. Born 18 May 1965; Son of Michael and Julie Opperman; Partner Karen.

Education: Harrow School; Lille University, France (Diploma 1984); Buckingham University (LLB 1987); Bar Vocational Course 1989; French.

Non-political career: Farmer near Arusha, Tanzania 1987-88; Director (unpaid), TD Chrome Ltd (family engineering business) -2010; Called to the Bar, Middle Temple 1989; Barrister, 3 Paper Buildings 1991-2010; Adviser to Michael Ancram as Shadow Secretary of State for Foreign and Commonwealth Affairs 2001-05.

Political career: Contested North Swindon 1997 and Caernarfon 2005 general elections. Member for Hexham since 6 May 2010 general election; PPS to Mark Harper as Minister of State for Immigration, Home Office 2012-. *Select committees:* Member: Unopposed Bills (Panel) 2011-. *Councils and public bodies:* Councillor, Marlborough, Wiltshire 1995-99.

Political interests: Prison reform and sentencing, health, fuel poverty, tourism, apprenticeships and youth training, equal pay, Northumberland.

Other: Member, Countryside Alliance; Help for Heroes; Injured Jockeys Fund; Save the Children; Tynedale Activities for Children; Children with Leukaemia; Great North Air Ambulance Service. Bar Pro Bono Award for Services to Victim Support 2007; Pro Bono Champion Award for services to Pro Bono and local community hospital campaign 2009; Albert Edward Club, Hexham.

Publications: 150 journalist articles; Author, Doing Time: Prisons in the 21st Century (Bretwalda Books, 2012).

Recreations: Cricket, amateur steeplechase jockey.

Guy Opperman MP, House of Commons, London SW1A 0AA
Tel: 020 7219 7227 *Fax:* 020 7219 6435 *Email:* guy.opperman.mp@parliament.uk
Constituency: Hexham Conservatives, 1 Meal Market, Hexham, Northumberland NE46 1NF
Tel: 01434 603777 *Fax:* 01434 601659 *Email:* hexham@tory.org
Website: www.hexhamconservatives.co.uk www.guyopperman.blogspot.com
Twitter: @GuyOppermanMP

CONSERVATIVE

OSBORNE, GEORGE
Tatton *(Majority 14,487)*

Chancellor of the Exchequer

George Gideon Oliver Osborne. Born 23 May 1971; Son of Sir Peter George Osborne, Bt, founder and chairman Osborne and Little plc, and Felicity Osborne, née Loxton-Peacock; Married Hon Frances Howell, daughter of Lord Howell of Guildford (qv), 1998 (1 son 1 daughter).

Education: St Paul's School, London; Davidson College, North Carolina USA (Dean Rusk Scholarship) 1990; Magdalen College, Oxford (Scholarship, BA modern history 1993, MA); French.

Non-political career: Freelance journalist *Sunday* and *Daily Telegraph* 1993; Head of political section Conservative Research Department 1994-95; Special adviser Ministry of Agriculture, Fisheries and Food 1995-97; Political Office, 10 Downing Street 1997; Secretary Shadow Cabinet 1997-2001; Political secretary to William Hague MP as Leader of Opposition 1997-2001.

Political career: Member for Tatton 2001-10, for Tatton (revised boundary) since 6 May 2010 general election; Member Public Accounts Commission 2002-05; Opposition Whip 2003; Shadow Minister for Economic Affairs 2003-04; Shadow Chief Secretary of the Treasury 2004-05; Shadow Chancellor of the Exchequer 2005-10; Chancellor of the Exchequer 2010-. *Select committees:* Member: Public Accounts 2001-04, Transport 2002-03. General election campaign co-ordinator 2007-.

Other: Vice-President, East Cheshire Hospice. PC 2010.

Recreations: Cinema, theatre, walking, observing American politics.

Rt Hon George Osborne MP, House of Commons, London SW1A 0AA
Tel: 020 7219 8214 *Fax:* 020 7219 6372 *Email:* george.osborne.mp@parliament.uk
Constituency: Tatton Conservative Association, Manchester Road, Knutsford, Cheshire WA16 0LT
Tel: 01565 873037 *Fax:* 01565 873039 *Website:* www.georgeosborne4tatton.com
Twitter: @George_Osborne

LABOUR

OSBORNE, SANDRA
Ayr, Carrick and Cumnock *(Majority 9,911)*

Sandra Currie Osborne. Born 23 February 1956; Daughter of Thomas Clark, labourer, and Isabella Clark, shop worker, meat factory worker, cleaner and laundry worker; Married Alastair Osborne 1982 (2 daughters).

Education: Camphill Senior Secondary, Paisley; Anniesland College; Jordanhill College (Diploma community education 1990); Strathclyde University (Diploma equality and discrimination 1991; MSc equality and discrimination 1992).

Non-political career: Counsellor, Women's Aid 1983-94. TGWU: Member, Former branch secretary.

Political career: Member for Ayr 1997-2005, for Ayr, Carrick and Cumnock since 5 May 2005 general election; PPS: to Ministers of State for Scotland: Brian Wilson 1999-2001, George Foulkes 2001-02, to Helen Liddell as Secretary of State for Scotland 2002-03. *Select committees:* Member: Information 1997-2000, Scottish Affairs 1998-99, European Scrutiny 2004-10, 2011-13, Foreign Affairs 2005-10, 2013-, Defence 2010-13, Armed Forces Bill 2011, Panel of Chairs 2011-. Scottish Regional Group of Labour MPs: Vice-chair 1998-99, Chair 1999-2000; Vice-chair, PLP Departmental Group for Foreign and Commonwealth Affairs 2010-. *Councils and public bodies:* Councillor, Kyle and Carrick District Council 1990-95; South Ayrshire Council: Councillor 1995-97, Convener, Community Services (Housing and Social Work) 1996-97.

Political interests: Women, housing, poverty; Afghanistan, Colombia, Iran, Palestine.

Other: Women's Aid.

Recreations: Reading and television.

Sandra Osborne MP, House of Commons, London SW1A 0AA
Tel: 020 7219 3000 *Email:* osbornes@parliament.uk
Constituency: Parliamentary Office, 139 Main Street, Ayr KA8 8BX
Tel: 01292 262906 *Website:* www.sandraosborne.co.uk

CONSERVATIVE

OTTAWAY, RICHARD
Croydon South *(Majority 15,818)*

Richard Geoffrey James Ottaway. Born 24 May 1945; Son of late Professor Christopher Ottaway and Grace Ottaway; Married Nicola Kisch 1982.

Education: Backwell School, Somerset; Bristol University (LLB 1974).

Non-political career: Royal Navy Officer 1961-70; Royal Naval Reserve 1971-82. Admitted solicitor 1977, specialising in international, maritime and commercial law; Partner, William A. Crump & Son 1981-87; Director, Coastal States Petroleum (UK) Ltd 1988-95.

Political career: Member for Nottingham North 1983-87. Contested Nottingham North 1987 general election. Member for Croydon South 1992-2010, for Croydon South (revised boundary) since 6 May 2010 general election; PPS: to Ministers of State, Foreign and Commonwealth Office 1985-87, to Michael Heseltine: as President of the Board of Trade and Secretary of State for Trade and Industry 1992-95, as Deputy Prime Minister and First Secretary of State 1995; Government Whip 1995-97; Opposition Whip June-November 1997; Opposition Spokesperson for: Local Government and London 1997-99, Defence 1999-2000, Treasury 2000-01; Shadow Secretary of State for the Environment 2004; Member, Intelligence and Security Committee 2005-10. *Select committees:* Member: Procedure 1996-97, Standards and Privileges 2001-04; Foreign Affairs: Member 2003-04, Chair 2010-; Member: Defence 2004-05, Liaison 2010-, Arms Export Controls 2010-11, Joint Committee on National Security Strategy 2010-. Vice-chair, 1922 Committee 2005-10. Vice-chair, Conservative Party (with responsibility for local government) 1998-99; Chair, executive committee, Society of Conservative Lawyers 2000-03; Board member, Conservative Party 2006-10.

Political interests: Defence, foreign affairs, world population; Singapore.

Other: Freeman, City of London. Royal London Yacht Club. PC 2013.

Publications: Papers on international and maritime law, global pollution, London, privatisation, debt and international fraud.

Recreations: Yacht racing, jazz.

Rt Hon Richard Ottaway MP, House of Commons, London SW1A 0AA
Tel: 020 7219 6392 *Fax:* 020 7219 2256 *Email:* ottawayr@parliament.uk
Constituency: Croydon South Conservative Association, 36 Brighton Road, Purley, Surrey CR8 2LG
Tel: 020 8660 0491 *Fax:* 020 8763 9686 *Email:* croydonconservatives@tory.org
Website: www.richardottaway.com

LABOUR

OWEN, ALBERT
Ynys Môn *(Majority 2,461)*

Born 10 August 1959; Son of late William Owen and Doreen, née Wood; Married Angela Margaret Magee 1983 (2 daughters).

Education: Holyhead County Comprehensive School, Anglesey; Coleg Harlech (Diploma industrial relations 1994); York University (BA politics 1997); Welsh.

Non-political career: Merchant seafarer 1976-92; Welfare rights and employment adviser 1995-97; Centre manager Isle of Anglesey County Council 1997-2001. RMT 1976-92: Health and safety officer 1985-87, Ferry sector national panel 1987-92; NUS 1992-97: Welfare officer 1992-94; Unison 1997-2001.

Political career: Member for Ynys Môn since 7 June 2001 general election. *Select committees:* Member: Welsh Affairs 2001-05, 2006-10, Accommodation and Works 2001-05, Energy and Climate Change 2010-, Chairmen's Panel/Panel of Chairs 2010-. Contested Ynys Môn constituency 1999 National Assembly for Wales election. Constituency Labour Party: Treasurer 1991-92, Vice-chair 1992-96; Press officer 1996-2000. *Councils and public bodies:* Councillor Holyhead Town Council 1997-99.

Political interests: Welsh affairs, welfare, economic development; Ireland, Cyprus, Malta/Gozo.

Other: Director Homeless project 1998-; Member: Institute of Welsh Affairs 1999-2001, Management committee WEA North Wales 1999-2001; Chair Anglesey Regeneration Partnership 2000-01; Cancer Research. Holyhead Sailing Club.

Recreations: Cycling, walking, cooking, gardening.

Albert Owen MP, House of Commons, London SW1A 0AA
Tel: 020 7219 8415 *Fax:* 020 7219 1951 *Email:* albert.owen.mp@parliament.uk
Constituency: 18a Thomas Street, Holyhead, Anglesey LL65 1RR
Tel: 01407 765750 *Fax:* 01407 764336 *Twitter:* @AlbertOwenMP

CONSERVATIVE

PAICE, JIM

South East Cambridgeshire *(Majority 5,946)*

James Edward Thornton Paice. Born 24 April 1949; Son of late Edward Paice and late Winifred Paice; Married Ava Patterson 1973 (2 sons).

Education: Framlingham College, Suffolk; Writtle Agricultural College (National Diploma agriculture 1970); French (very basic).

Non-political career: Farm manager 1970-73; Farmer and contractor 1973-79; Framlingham Management and Training Services Ltd: Training manager, later general manager 1979-87, Non-executive director 1987-89; Director, United Framlingham Farmers Ltd 1989-94.

Political career: Contested Caernarvon 1979 general election. Member for South East Cambridgeshire 1987-2010, for South East Cambridgeshire (revised boundary) since 6 May 2010 general election; PPS: to Baroness Trumpington as Minister of State, Ministry of Agriculture, Fisheries and Food 1989-90, to John Gummer: as Minister of Agriculture, Fisheries and Food 1990-93, as Secretary of State for the Environment 1993-94; Parliamentary Under-Secretary of State: Department of Employment 1994-95, Department for Education and Employment 1995-97; Opposition Spokesperson for: Agriculture, Fisheries and Food 1997-2001, Home Affairs 2001-03; Shadow Minister for: Home, Constitutional and Legal Affairs 2003-04, Home Affairs 2004; Shadow Secretary of State for Agriculture, Fisheries and Food 2004-05; Shadow Minister for: Agriculture 2005-10, Agriculture and Rural Affairs 2006-10; Minister of State for Agriculture and Food, Department for Environment, Food and Rural Affairs 2010-12. *Select committees:* Member: Scottish Affairs 2013-. *Councils and public bodies:* Suffolk Coastal District Council: Councillor 1976-87, Chair 1982-83.

Political interests: Small businesses, employment, agriculture, rural affairs, training, waste management; Europe, New Zealand.

Other: UK delegate, EEC Council of Young Farmers 1974-78; Fellow, Industry and Parliament Trust 1990; Council member, Ely Cathedral 2002-10; Trustee, Game Conservancy Trust 2003-07, 2008-10; Fellow, Writtle University College; Game Conservancy Trust. PC 2010; Kt 2012.

Recreations: Shooting, conservation.

Rt Hon Sir Jim Paice MP, House of Commons, London SW1A 0AA
Tel: 020 7219 1347 *Fax:* 020 7219 3804 *Email:* james.paice.mp@parliament.uk
Constituency: No constituency office publicised *Website:* www.jamespaicemp.com

**DEMOCRATIC
UNIONIST PARTY**

PAISLEY, IAN

North Antrim *(Majority 12,558)*

DUP Spokesperson for Work and Pensions and for Environment, Food and Rural Affairs

Ian Richard Kyle Paisley. Born 12 December 1966; Son of the Rt Hon Rev. Dr Ian Paisley, former MP, MEP and MLA, now Lord Bannside, and Eileen Paisley, née Cassells, now Baroness Paisley of St George's; Married Fiona Currie 1990 (2 daughters 2 sons).

Education: Shaftesbury House College; Methodist College, Belfast; Queen's University, Belfast (BA modern history 1989; MSc Irish politics 1992).

Non-political career: Researcher, author and political assistant.

Political career: Member for North Antrim since 6 May 2010 general election; DUP Spokesperson for: Work and Pensions 2010-, Environment, Food and Rural Affairs 2010-. *Select committees:* Member: Northern Ireland Affairs 2010-. Member Northern Ireland Forum for Political Dialogue 1996-98; MLA for North Antrim 1998-2010: Member, Preparation for Government Committee 2006-07; Junior Minister, Office of First and Deputy First Minister 2007-08; Chair, Agriculture and Rural Development Committee 2009-10. *Councils and public bodies:* Lay visitor, Police Holding Centres for the Police Authority 1996-2001; Member, Northern Ireland Policing Board 2001-07, 2008-10.

Political interests: Justice, Europe, agriculture, policing, foreign policy; Africa, China, Middle East, USA.

Other: British Motorcycle Federation; Fellow, University of Maryland School of Leadership, Washington DC, USA. Royal Humane Society for Life Saving 1999.

Publications: Reasonable Doubt – The Case for the UDR4; Echoes; Peace Deal; Ian Paisley – A Life in Photographs.

Recreations: Rugby, reading, motor racing, collector of 19th century cartoons and political caricatures, motorcycling.

Ian Paisley MP, House of Commons, London SW1A 0AA
Tel: 020 7219 7116 *Fax:* 020 7219 2996 *Email:* ian.paisley.mp@parliament.uk
Constituency: 9-11 Church Street, Ballymena BT43 6DD
Tel: 028 2564 1421 *Fax:* 028 2564 7296 *Email:* info@ianpaisleymp.co.uk irkpj@yahoo.co.uk
Website: www.ianpaisleymp.co.uk

PARISH, NEIL
Tiverton and Honiton *(Majority 9,320)*

Neil Quentin Gordon Parish. Born 26 May 1956; Married Sue Edwards 1981 (1 son 1 daughter).
Education: Brymore School; Taunton College.
Non-political career: Former farmer and businessman.
Political career: Member for Tiverton and Honiton since 6 May 2010 general election. *Select committees:* Member: Environment, Food and Rural Affairs 2010-. Chair, Conservative Party Committee for Environment. MEP for South West 1999-2009: Conservative agriculture spokesperson, President, Animal Welfare Intergroup, Chair: Australia and New Zealand Delegation 2004-07, Agriculture and Rural Development Committee 2007-09. Chair, Bridgwater Conservative Assocation 1997-99. *Councils and public bodies:* Sedgemoor District Council: Councillor 1983-95, Deputy Leader 1989-95; Councillor, Somerset County Council 1989-93.

CONSERVATIVE

Political interests: Regional policy, animal welfare, agriculture; China, Israel, Slovenia, Zimbabwe.
Other: Election monitor, Zimbabwe 2000.
Recreations: Swimming, music, country life, Brains Trust, debating.

Neil Parish MP, House of Commons, London SW1A 0AA
Tel: 020 7219 7172 *Fax:* 020 7219 5005 *Email:* neil.parish.mp@parliament.uk
Constituency: 9c Mill Park Industrial Estate, White Cross Road, Woodbury Salterton, Exeter, Devon EX5 1EL
Tel: 01395 233503 *Fax:* 01395 233903 *Email:* neil@neilparish.co.uk
Website: www.neilparish.co.uk

PATEL, PRITI
Witham *(Majority 15,196)*

Born 29 March 1972; Married.
Education: Westfield Girls School, Watford; Keele University (BA economics 1994); Essex University (Diploma British government and politics 1995).
Non-political career: Head of Media and Communications, Referendum Party 1995-97; Conservative Research Department 1997; Deputy press secretary to William Hague MP 1997-2000; Associate director, Shandwick 2000-03; Corporate relations manager, Diageo 2003-08; Director, corporate communications, Weber Shandwick 2007-10.

CONSERVATIVE

Political career: Contested Nottingham North 2005 general election. Member for Witham since 6 May 2010 general election. *Select committees:* Member: Members' Expenses 2011-, Public Administration 2011-, Joint Committee on Draft Deregulation Bill 2013-. Member, Executive, 1922 Committee 2010-. Elected member, Conservative Party Board.
Political interests: Trade, business, the economy, Europe, law and order, immigration; Africa, Asia, India, Middle East.
Other: Trustee, Crossroads Care, Braintree and Witham; Brainwave, Witham (a children's charity); Homestart, Witham; Royal British Legion, Witham.
Publications: Co-author (with Kwasi Kwarteng MP, Dominic Raab MP, Chris Skidmore MP and Elizabeth Truss MP), Britannia Unchained: Global Lessons for Growth and Prosperity (Palgrave Macmillan, 2012).
Recreations: Horse racing, cricket, travel, music.

Priti Patel MP, House of Commons, London SW1A 0AA
Tel: 020 7219 3528 *Fax:* 020 7219 5192 *Email:* withammp@parliament.uk
Constituency: Witham Conservative Association, Avenue Lodge, The Avenue, Witham, Essex CM8 2LD *Website:* www.priti4witham.com

CONSERVATIVE

PATERSON, OWEN
North Shropshire *(Majority 15,828)*

Secretary of State for Environment, Food and Rural Affairs

Owen William Paterson. Born 24 June 1956; Son of late Alfred and Cynthia Paterson; Married Hon. Rose Ridley 1980 (2 sons 1 daughter).

Education: Radley College, Oxfordshire; Corpus Christi College, Cambridge (MA history 1978); French, German.

Non-political career: British Leather Co Ltd: Sales director 1985-93, Managing director 1993-99.

Political career: Contested Wrexham 1992 general election. Member for North Shropshire since 1 May 1997 general election; Opposition Whip 2000-01; PPS to Iain Duncan Smith as Leader of the Opposition 2001-03; Shadow Minister for: Environment, Food and Rural Affairs 2003-05, Transport 2005-07; Shadow Secretary of State for Northern Ireland 2007-10; Secretary of State for: Northern Ireland 2010-12, Environment, Food and Rural Affairs 2012-. *Select committees:* Member: Welsh Affairs 1997-2001, European Standing Committee A 1998-2001, Welsh Grand Committee 1998-2000 European Scrutiny 1999-2000, Agriculture 2000-01. Conservative Party Committees: Joint Vice-chair, Environment, Transport and Regions 1999-2001, Joint Secretary, European Affairs 1999-2001, Secretary, Foreign and Commonwealth Affairs 1999-2001. Member: 92 Group 1997-, Conservative Friends of Israel 1997-, Conservative Way Forward 1997-, Conservative 2000 1997-; Vice-President, Conservatives Against a Federal Europe 1998-2001, Member: No Turning Back Group 1998-, Executive, 1922 Committee 2000.

Political interests: Trade, industry, agriculture, foreign affairs, economy, social justice, Northern Ireland; China, Western and Eastern Europe, India, USA.

Other: President, Cotance (European Tanners' Confederation) 1996-98; Member: Inter-Parliamentary Union 1997-, Commonwealth Parliamentary Association 1997-; Member, Advisory Board, European Foundation 1998-; Director, Orthopaedic Institute Ltd, Oswestry; Member, Countryside Alliance; Orthopaedic Institute Ltd, Gobowen; Royal Irish Regiment Benevolent Fund; Midlands Centre for Spinal Injuries; Ellesmere Community Care Centre Trust. Liveryman, Leathersellers' Company. PC 2010. Patron, Oswestry Cricket Club; Member, Shropshire Cricket Club.

Rt Hon Owen Paterson MP, House of Commons, London SW1A 0AA
Tel: 020 7219 5185 *Fax:* 020 7219 3955 *Email:* patersono@parliament.uk
Constituency: No constituency office
Tel: 01978 710073 *Fax:* 01978 710667 *Email:* rose@myoceanemail.co.uk
Website: www.owenpaterson.org.uk

CONSERVATIVE

PAWSEY, MARK
Rugby *(Majority 6,000)*

Mark Julian Francis Pawsey. Born 16 January 1957; Son of James Pawsey, MP for Rugby 1979-83, Rugby and Kenilworth 1983-97, and Cynthia Pawsey; Married Tracy Harris 1984 (2 sons 2 daughters).

Education: Lawrence Sheriff Grammar School, Rugby; Reading University (estate management 1978); French.

Non-political career: Member, Armed Forces Parliamentary Scheme. Trainee surveyor, Strutt and Parker 1978-79; Account manager, Autobar Vending Supplies Ltd 1979-82; Managing director, Central Catering Supplies Ltd 1982-.

Political career: Contested Nuneaton 2005 general election. Member for Rugby since 6 May 2010 general election. *Select committees:* Member: Communities and Local Government 2010-. *Councils and public bodies:* Councillor, Rugby Borough Council 2002-07.

Political interests: Planning, environment, local government, trade; Rwanda.

Other: Chairman, Commons and Lords RFC; Old Laurentian RFC.

Recreations: Village life, rugby, wine appreciation.

Mark Pawsey MP, House of Commons, London SW1A 0AA
Tel: 020 7219 7136 *Email:* mark.pawsey.mp@parliament.uk
Constituency: Albert Buildings, 2 Castle Mews, Rugby CV21 2XL
Tel: 01788 579499 *Website:* www.markpawsey.org.uk *Twitter:* @markpawsey

LABOUR

PEARCE, TERESA

Erith and Thamesmead *(Majority 5,703)*

Born 1 February 1955; Daughter of Arthur Farrington, shoe repairer, and Josephine Farrington, book-keeper/clerk; Single (2 daughters).

Education: St Thomas More; Basic French.

Non-political career: Senior manager, Tax Investigations Team, PriceWaterhouseCoopers 1999-2009. Member, GMB.

Political career: Member for Erith and Thamesmead since 6 May 2010 general election. *Select committees:* Member: Work and Pensions 2010-, Treasury 2011-, Unopposed Bills (Panel) 2013-. Member, National Constitutional Committee 1996-2008. *Councils and public bodies:* Councillor, London Borough of Bexley Council 1998-2002.

Political interests: Tax reform, children in care.

Recreations: Cinema, reading, travel.

Teresa Pearce MP, House of Commons, London SW1A 0AA
Tel: 020 7219 6936 *Fax:* 020 7219 2190 *Email:* teresa.pearce.mp@parliament.uk
Constituency: 315 Bexley Road, Erith DA8 3EX
Tel: 01322 342991 *Website:* www.teresapearce.org.uk *Twitter:* @tpearce003

CONSERVATIVE

PENNING, MIKE

Hemel Hempstead *(Majority 13,406)*

Minister of State, Department for Work and Pensions

Michael Allan Penning. Born 28 September 1957; Son of Freda and Brian Penning; Married Angela Louden 1988 (2 daughters).

Education: Appleton Comprehensive School, Benfleet, Essex; King Edmund Comprehensive School, Rochford, Essex.

Non-political career: Soldier, Grenadier Guards 1974-80; Royal Army Medical Corps (RAMC) 1980-81; Fire officer, Essex Fire and Rescue Services 1982-88; Freelance political journalist, Express Newspapers and News International 1988-92; Politics and journalism lecturer, UK and USA 1992-2005; Journalist and media adviser to six Shadow Cabinet members 1996-2004; Deputy chief press spokesperson, Conservative Central Office 2000-04. Member FBU 1982-.

Political career: Contested Thurrock 2001 general election. Member for Hemel Hempstead 2005-10, for Hemel Hempstead (revised boundary) since 6 May 2010 general election; Shadow Minister for Health 2007-10; Parliamentary Under-Secretary of State, Department for Transport 2010-12; Minister of State, Northern Ireland Office 2012-13, Department for Work and Pensions 2013-. *Select committees:* Member: Health 2005-07. Member, Executive, 1922 Committee 2006-07. Director, Conservatives Against a Federal Europe 1995; General election campaign manager, Rochford and Southend East 1997.

Political interests: Constitution, single currency (against), health, home affairs, defence; Gibraltar.

Other: British Legion. GSM (Northern Ireland).

Recreations: Rugby Union, football, coarse fishing, golf.

Mike Penning MP, House of Commons, London SW1A 0AA
Tel: 020 7219 3000 *Email:* penningm@parliament.uk
Constituency: The Bury, Queensway, Hemel Hempstead, Hertfordshire HP1 1HR
Tel: 01442 251126 *Email:* mike@penning4hemel.com *Website:* www.mikepenning.com

CONSERVATIVE

PENROSE, JOHN

Weston-Super-Mare *(Majority 2,691)*

Assistant Whip

John David Penrose. Born 22 June 1964; Son of late David Penrose and Anna Penrose, now Lawrie; Married Diana (Dido) Harding 1995 (2 daughters).

Education: Ipswich School, Suffolk; Downing College, Cambridge (BA law 1986); Columbia University, USA (MBA 1991); French, German.

Non-political career: Risk manager, JP Morgan 1986-90; Management consultant, McKinsey and Company 1992-94; Commercial director, academic books division, Thomson Publishing 1995-96; Managing director, schools publishing, Europe, Pearson plc 1996-2000; Non-executive director, Logotron Ltd 2008-11.

Political career: Contested Ealing Southall 1997 and Weston-Super-Mare 2001 general elections. Member for Weston-Super-Mare 2005-10, for Weston-Super-Mare (revised boundary) since 6 May 2010 general election; PPS to Oliver Letwin as Chair, Conservative Policy Review 2006-09; Shadow Minister for: Business, Enterprise and Regulatory Reform 2009, Business

2009-10; Parliamentary Under-Secretary of State (Minister for Tourism and Heritage), Department for Culture, Media and Sport 2010-12; Assistant Whip 2013-. *Select committees:* Member: Work and Pensions 2005-09, Regulatory Reform 2009-10, Administration 2012-. Treasurer, Leyton and Wanstead Conservative Association 1993-95.

Political interests: Drug addiction, pensions, environment, education, international development.

Other: Research secretary, Bow Group 1998-99; President, Weston Abbeyfields Nursing (charity); President: Weston Conservative Club, Weston Constitutional Club.

Publications: Members' Rights (The Bow Group, 1997); Better Regulation (Conservative Party, 2009); UK Tourism Policy (UK Government, 2010); We Deserve Better (2013).

Recreations: Fishing, beekeeping.

John Penrose MP, House of Commons, London SW1A 0AA
Tel: 020 7219 5310 *Email:* penrosej@parliament.uk
Constituency: 24-26 Alexandra Parade, Weston-Super-Mare, Somerset BS23 1QX
Tel: 01934 613841 *Fax:* 01934 632955 *Email:* beauperec@parliament.uk
Website: www.johnpenrose.org *Twitter:* @JohnPenroseNews

CONSERVATIVE

PERCY, ANDREW
Brigg and Goole *(Majority 5,147)*

Born 1977.
Education: York University.
Non-political career: History teacher; MP's researcher; Part-time primary teacher. Member, National Association of Schoolmasters Union of Woman Teachers (NASUWT).
Political career: Member for Brigg and Goole since 6 May 2010 general election. *Select committees:* Member: Procedure 2010-11, Regulatory Reform 2010-, Standing Orders 2011-, Northern Ireland Affairs 2012-, Health 2012-. *Councils and public bodies:* School governor.
Political interests: Education; Canada, Commonwealth, Far East, Israel, USA.
Other: Supporter: Countryside Alliance, Campaign Against Political Correctness.

Andrew Percy MP, House of Commons, London SW1A 0AA
Tel: 020 7219 3000 *Email:* andrew.percy.mp@parliament.uk
Constituency: 81-83 Pasture Road, Goole, East Yorkshire DN14 6BP
Tel: 01405 767969 *Email:* brigg.goole@gmail.com *Website:* www.andrewpercy.org
Twitter: @andrewpercy

LABOUR

PERKINS, TOBY
Chesterfield *(Majority 549)*

Shadow Minister for Business, Innovation and Skills

Matthew Toby Perkins. Born 12 August 1970; Son of V.F Perkins and late Teresa Perkins, both university lecturers; Married Susan Francis 1996 (1 son 1daughter).
Education: Trinity School, Leamington Spa; Silverdale School, Sheffield.
Non-political career: Telephone sales, CCS Media 1991-95; Recruitment consultant/area manager, Prime Time Recruitment 1995-2002; Business owner, Club Rugby (internet sports firm) 2005-. Member, Amicus/Unite 2005-.
Political career: Member for Chesterfield since 6 May 2010 general election; Shadow Minister for: Education 2010-11, Business, Innovation and Skills 2011-. *Select committees:* Member: Communities and Local Government 2010, Joint Committee on Statutory Instruments 2010-. Chair, PLP Departmental Group for Communities and Local Government 2010-11. Member: Labour Party, Co-operative Party. *Councils and public bodies:* Councillor, Chesterfield Borough Council 2003-11; Director, Families First Nursery 2007-11.
Political interests: Sport and youth involvement, small businesses, crime, jobs and regeneration.
Other: Founder, Chesterfield Flood Victims Appeal 2007-09; Vice-chair, Progress 2012-. Former player, Chesterfield Rugby Club; Coach, Sheffield Tigers Rugby Club.
Recreations: Rugby (qualified coach).

Toby Perkins MP, House of Commons, London SW1A 0AA
Tel: 020 7219 2320 *Email:* toby.perkins.mp@parliament.uk
Constituency: 113 Saltergate, Chesterfield, Derbyshire S40 1NF
Tel: 01246 386286 *Website:* www.tobyperkins.org.uk *Twitter:* @tobyperkinsmp

CONSERVATIVE

PERRY, CLAIRE
Devizes *(Majority 13,005)*

Assistant Whip

Claire Louise Perry. Born 3 April 1964; Daughter of Joanna and David Richens, both retired; Married Clayton Perry 1996 (seperated 2013) (1 son 2 daughters).

Education: Nailsea Comprehensive School; Oxford University (BA geography 1985); Harvard Business School (MBA 1990).

Non-political career: Analyst, Bank of America 1985-88; Consultant, McKinsey and Company 1990-94; Various roles, Credit Suisse First Boston 1994-2000; Volunteer fundraiser 2002-04; Policy adviser to George Osborne MP 2007-09.

Political career: Member for Devizes since 6 May 2010 general election; PPS to Philip Hammond as Secretary of State for Defence 2011-13; Chair, Independent Parliamentary Inquiry into Online Child Protection -2012; Adviser to the Prime Minister on Preventing the Sexualisation and Commercialisation of Childhood 2012-; Assistant Whip 2013-. *Select committees:* Member: Justice 2010-11. Member, Conservative Party 2006-; Founding member: 2020 group 2011-, Conservative Women's Forum. *Councils and public bodies:* Governor: Wellington Academy, St John's School, Marlborough.

Political interests: Economy, education, defence, justice, international development, child protection.

Recreations: Reading, walking, cycling, gardening.

Claire Perry MP, House of Commons, London SW1A 0AA
Tel: 020 7219 7050 *Fax:* 020 7219 1385 *Email:* claire.perry.mp@parliament.uk
Constituency: Renelec House, 46 New Park Street, Devizes, Wiltshire SN10 1DT
Tel: 01380 729358 *Email:* tamara.reay@parliament.uk *Website:* www.claireperry.org.uk
Twitter: @claire4devizes

CONSERVATIVE

PHILLIPS, STEPHEN
Sleaford and North Hykeham *(Majority 19,905)*

Stephen James Phillips. Born 9 March 1970; Son of late Stewart Phillips, civil servant, and Janice Phillips; Married Fiona Parkin 1998 (divorced 2013) (1 son 2 daughters).

Education: Canford School, Dorset; Oriel College, Oxford (BCL law 1991; MA 1992).

Non-political career: 2nd Lt, 14/20th King's Hussars, subsequently Welsh Guards 1988-91. Called to the Bar, Lincoln's Inn 1993; Barrister, 7 King's Bench Walk, London 1993-; QC 2009; Recorder, South East Circuit 2009-.

Political career: Member for Sleaford and North Hykeham since 6 May 2010 general election. *Select committees:* Member: European Scrutiny 2010-, Joint Committee on the Draft Defamation Bill 2011. Member, Conservative Party 1988-.

Political interests: Foreign affairs, home affairs, justice.

Other: Cavalry and Guards.

Recreations: Getting muddy.

Stephen Phillips QC MP, House of Commons, London SW1A 0AA
Tel: 020 7219 7146/020 7219 6487 *Email:* stephen.phillips.mp@parliament.uk
Constituency: Sleaford and North Hykham Conservatives, 6 Market Place, Sleaford, Lincolnshire NG34 7SD
Tel: 01529 419000 *Fax:* 01529 419019 *Email:* admin@snhca.co.uk
Website: www.stephenphillips.org.uk

LABOUR

PHILLIPSON, BRIDGET
Houghton and Sunderland South *(Majority 10,990)*

Opposition Whip

Bridget Maeve Phillipson. Born 19 December 1983; Daughter of Clare Phillipson, director of domestic violence charity; Married Lawrence Dimery 2009 (1 daughter).

Education: St Robert of Newminster School and Sixth Form College, Washington; Hertford College, Oxford (BA modern history 2005); French, Spanish.

Non-political career: Sunderland City Council 2005-07; Women's refuge manager, Wearside Women in Need 2007-10. Member, GMB 2005-.

Political career: Member for Houghton and Sunderland South since 6 May 2010 general election; Member Speaker's Committee on the Electoral Commission 2010-; PPS to Jim Murphy as Shadow Secretary of State for Defence 2010-13; Opposition Whip 2013-. *Select committees:* Member: Home Affairs 2010-, Speaker's Committee on the Electoral Commission 2010-, Procedure 2010-11. Member, Labour Party 1998-; Former chair, Oxford University Labour Club; North East representative, National Policy Forum.

Political interests: Housing, women and equalities, UK software industry, jobs, economy.

Recreations: Dog walking, reading, history, music.

Bridget Phillipson MP, House of Commons, London SW1A 0AA
Tel: 020 7219 7087 *Fax:* 020 7219 2419 *Email:* bridget.phillipson.mp@parliament.uk
Constituency: 1 and 1a Wylam Place, Mill Pit, Shiney Row, Houghton-le-Spring, Tyne and
Wear DH4 4JT
Tel: 0191-385 7994 *Fax:* 0191-385 5941 *Website:* www.bridgetphillipson.com
Twitter: @bphillipsonmp

CONSERVATIVE

PICKLES, ERIC
Brentwood and Ongar *(Majority 16,921)*

Secretary of State for Communities and Local Government

Eric Jack Pickles. Born 20 April 1952; Son of late Jack Pickles and Constance Pickles; Married
Irene 1976.

Education: Greenhead Grammar School, Keighley, Yorkshire; Leeds Polytechnic.

Non-political career: Industrial trainer.

Political career: Member for Brentwood and Ongar 1992-2010, for Brentwood and Ongar (revised
boundary) since 6 May 2010 general election; Opposition Spokesperson for Social Security 1998-
2001; Shadow Minister for Transport 2001-02; Shadow Secretary of State for: Local Government
and the Regions 2002-03, Local Government 2003-05; Shadow Minister for Local Government
2005-07; Shadow Secretary of State for Communities and Local Government 2007-09; Secretary
of State for Communities and Local Government 2010-. *Select committees:* Member: Environment,
Transport and Regional Affairs 1997-98, Environment, Transport and Regional Affairs (Transport
Sub-Committee) 1997-98. Member, Conservative Party National Union Executive Committee
1975-97; National chair, Young Conservatives 1980-81; Member: Conservative Party National
Local Government Advisory Committee 1985-, One Nation Forum 1987-91; Deputy leader, Con-
servative Group on Association of Metropolitan Authorities 1989-91; Local government editor,
Newsline 1990-92; Conservative Party: Vice-chair 1993-97, Deputy chair (local government)
2005-07, Chair 2009-10. *Councils and public bodies:* Bradford Metropolitan District Council:
Councillor 1979-91, Leader, Conservative Group 1987-91; Member, Yorkshire Regional Health
Authority 1982-90; Chair: Joint Committee Against Racism 1982-87, National Local Government
Advisory Committee 1992-95; Vice-President, Local Government Association 1997-2010.

Political interests: Housing, health, social services, local government; Eastern Europe, India,
Poland, USA.

Other: PC 2010; Carlton.

Recreations: Films, opera, bird watching, golf.

Rt Hon Eric Pickles MP, House of Commons, London SW1A 0AA
Tel: 020 7219 4428 *Fax:* 020 7219 2783 *Email:* picklese@parliament.uk
Constituency: No constituency office *Website:* www.ericpickles.com *Twitter:* @EricPickles

CONSERVATIVE

PINCHER, CHRISTOPHER
Tamworth *(Majority 6,090)*

Christopher John Pincher. Born 24 September 1969; Son of John Pincher and Sandra Pincher;
Single.

Education: Ounsdale School, Staffordshire; London School of Economics (BSc (Econ) government and history 1991).

Non-political career: Manager, Accenture 1993-2010.

Political career: Contested Warley 1997 and Tamworth 2005 general elections. Member for
Tamworth since 6 May 2010 general election. *Select committees:* Member: Energy and Climate
Change 2010-, Armed Forces Bill 2011, Standing Orders 2011-. Member, Conservative Party
1987-; Treasurer, Conservative Friends of Azerbaijan.

Political interests: Home affairs, defence, education, energy; Azerbaijan, Middle East, Latvia,
Russia, USA.

Other: Macmillan charity; Ambassador, Tamworth in the Community; Travellers' Club.

Recreations: Literature and biography, golf, the turf, history, Formula 1, horse racing.

Christopher Pincher MP, House of Commons, London SW1A 0AA
Tel: 020 7219 7169 *Email:* christopher.pincher.mp@parliament.uk
Constituency: 23 Albert Road, Tamworth, Staffordshire B79 7JS
Tel: 01827 312778 *Website:* www.christopherpincher.com *Twitter:* @ChrisPincher

POULTER, DANIEL
Central Suffolk and North Ipswich *(Majority 13,786)*

Parliamentary Under-Secretary of State, Department of Health

Daniel Leonard James Poulter. Born 30 October 1978.

Education: Bristol University (LLB Hons); Guys and St Thomas' School of Medicine (MBBS); King's College, London (AKC).

Non-political career: Speciality registrar, obstetrics and gynaecology 2008-10; NHS hospital doctor 2010-.

Political career: Member for Central Suffolk and North Ipswich since 6 May 2010 general election; Parliamentary Under-Secretary of State, Department of Health 2012-. *Select committees:* Member: Health 2011-12, Joint Committee on the Draft House of Lords Reform Bill 2011-12. *Councils and public bodies:* Councillor, Hastings Borough Council 2006-07; Deputy Leader, Reigate and Banstead Council 2008-10.

Political interests: Health, rural affairs, pensions, older people, voluntary sector, overseas development; Australasia, West Indies.

Other: Member, British Medical Association -2012; Supporter, Help the Heroes; Set up medical and lifestyle advice clinics for homeless; Raised money for victims of domestic violence. Guy's Hospital Rugby Club.

Publications: Published author in field of women's health.

Recreations: Cricket, rugby, golf, fishing.

Dr Daniel Poulter MP, House of Commons, London SW1A 0AA
Tel: 020 7219 7038 *Fax:* 020 7219 1192 *Email:* daniel.poulter.mp@parliament.uk
Constituency: The Business Centre, Earl Soham, Suffolk IP13 7SA
Tel: 01728 685148 *Email:* mail@centralsuffolk.co.uk *Website:* www.drdanielpoulter.com

POUND, STEPHEN
Ealing North *(Majority 9,301)*

Shadow Minister for Northern Ireland

Stephen Pelham Pound. Born 3 July 1948; Son of late Pelham Pound, journalist, and late Dominica Pound, teacher; Married Maggie Griffiths 1976 (1 son 1 daughter).

Education: Hertford Grammar School; London School of Economics (Diploma industrial relations 1979; BSc economics 1982) (Sabbatical President of Union 1981-82).

Non-political career: Armed Forces Parliamentary Scheme (Navy). Seaman 1964-66; Bus conductor 1966-68; Hospital porter 1969-79; Student 1979-84; Housing officer 1984-97. Branch Secretary, 640 Middlesex Branch, COHSE 1975-79; Branch Officer, TGWU (ACTS) 1990-96.

Political career: Member for Ealing North 1997-2010, for Ealing North (revised boundary) since 6 May 2010 general election; PPS to Hazel Blears: as Minister of State, Home Office 2005-06, as Minister without Portfolio 2006-07, to Stephen Timms: as Minister of State, Department for Business, Enterprise and Regulatory Reform 2007-08, as Minister of State, Department for Work and Pensions 2008, as Financial Secretary, HM Treasury 2008-09, to Sadiq Khan as Minister of State, Department for Transport 2009, to Stephen Timms as Financial Secretary, HM Treasury 2010; Opposition Assistant Whip 2010; Shadow Minister for Northern Ireland 2010-. *Select committees:* Member: Broadcasting 1997-2001, Northern Ireland Affairs 1999-2010, Standards and Privileges 2003-05. Member, Labour Party Departmental Committee for Environment, Transport and the Regions 1997-2001. *Councils and public bodies:* London Borough of Ealing: Councillor 1982-98, Mayor 1995-96.

Countries of interest: Armenia, Assyria, Ireland, Poland, Ukraine.

Other: Outstanding Achievement (with David Amess MP and Bob Russell MP), Charity Champion awards 2012; St Joseph's Catholic Social, Hanwell. Fulham FC Supporters Club.

Recreations: Watching football, playing cricket, snooker, jazz, gardening, collecting comics.

Stephen Pound MP, House of Commons, London SW1A 0AA
Tel: 020 7219 4312 *Fax:* 020 7219 5982 *Email:* steve.pound.mp@parliament.uk
Constituency: No constituency office *Website:* www.stevepound.org.uk

LAB/CO-OP

POWELL, LUCY
Manchester Central *(Majority 9,936)*

Shadow Minister for Education

Lucy Maria Powell. Born 10 October 1974; Married James (1 daughter 1 stepson).

Education: Parrs Wood High School, Manchester; Xaverian Sixth Form; Oxford University (chemistry); King's College, London.

Non-political career: Labour Party, London, general election campaign 1997; Parliamentary assistant to Beverley Hughes MP; Director, Britain in Europe; Project manager, National Endowment for Science, Technology and the Arts (NESTA) 2007-10; Campaign manager, Ed Miliband Labour Party Leadership Campaign 2010; Deputy chief of staff to Ed Miliband as Labour Party Leader 2010-12.

Political career: Contested Manchester Withington 2010 general election. Member for Manchester Central since 15 November 2012 by-election. Shadow Minster for Education 2013-. *Select committees:* Member: Transport 2012-.

Political interests: Education, health, environment, foreign policy, regeneration, economic development, innovation and skills.

Recreations: Manchester City F.C.

Lucy Powell MP, House of Commons, London SW1A 0AA
Tel: 020 7219 3000 *Email:* lucy.powell.mp@parliament.uk
Constituency: No constituency office published
Tel: 0161-232 0872 *Fax:* 0161-232 1865 *Email:* contact@lucypowell.org.uk
Website: lucypowell.org.uk *Twitter:* @LucyMPowell

LABOUR

PRIMAROLO, DAWN
Bristol South *(Majority 4,734)*

Second Deputy Chairman, Ways and Means and Deputy Speaker

Born 2 May 1954; Née Gasson: married Michael Primarolo 1972 (divorced) (1 son); married Thomas Ducat 1990.

Education: Thomas Bennett Comprehensive School, Crawley; Bristol Polytechnic (BA social science 1984).

Non-political career: Secretary 1972-73; Secretary and advice worker, Law Centre, East London; Secretary, Avon County Council 1975-78; Voluntary work 1978-81; Mature student 1981-87. Member, Unison.

Political career: Member for Bristol South 1987-2010, for Bristol South (revised boundary) since 6 May 2010 general election; Opposition Spokesperson for: Health 1992-94, Treasury and Economic Affairs 1994-97; HM Treasury: Financial Secretary 1997-99, Paymaster General 1999-2007; Minister of State: for Public Health, Department of Health 2007-09, for Children, Young People and Families, Department for Children, Schools and Families 2009-10; Shadow Minister for Children 2010; Second Deputy Chairman, Ways and Means and Deputy Speaker 2010-. *Select committees:* Member: Public Accounts 1997-98; Ex-officio member: Chairmen's Panel/Panel of Chairs 2010-. *Councils and public bodies:* Councillor, Avon County Council 1985-87.

Political interests: Education, housing, social security, health, economic policy, equal opportunities.

Other: PC 2002.

Rt Hon Dawn Primarolo MP, House of Commons, London SW1A 0AA
Tel: 020 7219 3000 *Email:* dawn.primarolo.mp@parliament.uk
Constituency: PO Box 1002, Bristol, Gloucestershire BS99 1WH
Tel: 0117-909 0063 (10am-1pm) *Website:* www.bristolsouthlabourparty.org.uk
www.dawnprimarolo.co.uk

CONSERVATIVE

PRISK, MARK
Hertford and Stortford *(Majority 15,437)*

Mark Michael Prisk. Born 12 June 1962; Son of Michael Prisk, chartered surveyor, and Irene Prisk, née Pearce; Married Lesley Titcomb 1989.

Education: Truro School, Cornwall; Reading University (BSc land management 1983).

Non-political career: Graduate surveyor, Knight Frank 1983-85; Derrick Wade & Waters 1985-91: Senior surveyor 1985-89, Director 1989-91; Principal: The Mark Prisk Connection 1991-97, mp², consultancy 1997-2001.

Political career: Contested Newham North West 1992 and Wansdyke 1997 general elections. Member for Hertford and Stortford 2001-10, for Hertford and Stortford (revised boundary) since 6 May 2010 general election; Shadow Financial Secretary 2002-03; Shadow Paymaster General

2003-04; Opposition Whip 2004-05; Shadow Minister for: Business and Enterprise 2005-09, Business 2009-10; Minister of State for: Business and Enterprise, Department for Business, Innovation and Skills 2010-12, Housing, Department for Communities and Local Government 2012-13. *Select committees:* Member: Welsh Affairs 2001-05, Regulatory Reform 2008-09, Speaker's Committee on the Electoral Commission 2013-. Secretary, Conservative Defence/Foreign Affairs Policy Committee 2001-02. Chair, Reading University Conservatives 1981-82; National vice-chair, Federation of Conservative Students 1982-83; Deputy chair, Hertfordshire Area 1999-2000; Member, Conservative Business Relations Board 2006-.

Political interests: Defence, education, planning, development, small businesses; China, Italy, Russia, USA.

Other: Member, Prince's Trust; Founding chair, Youth For Peace Through NATO 1983-86; Founder, East Hertfordshire Business Forum; Chair, Hertfordshire Countryside Partnership; Creator, Charter for Hertfordshire's Countryside; Member, Royal Institute of Chartered Surveyors; Vice-President, First Defence 2004-10; Trustee, Industry and Parliamentary Trust 2007-10.

Publications: Eternal Vigilance, The Defence of a Free Society (First Defence, 2003).

Recreations: Music, piano, rugby, cricket, theatre, architecture, choral singing.

Mark Prisk MP, House of Commons, London SW1A 0AA
Tel: 020 7219 6358 *Email:* hunterj@parliament.uk
Constituency: Hertford and Stortford Conservatives, Room GLO4, Harlow Enterprise Hub, Kao Hockham Building, Edinburgh Way, Harlow, Essex CM20 2NQ
Tel: 01279 312196 *Email:* hertfordandstortford@tory.org *Website:* www.markprisk.com
Twitter: @PriskMark

PRITCHARD, MARK   The Wrekin *(Majority 9,450)*

Mark Andrew Pritchard. Born 22 November 1966; Son of late Frank Pritchard and Romona Pritchard; Married Sondra Spaeth 1997.

Education: Afan Comprehensive School, Cymmer, Glamorgan; Aylestone School, Hereford; Regents Theological College; London Guildhall University (MA marketing management; Post-Graduate Diploma marketing).

Non-political career: Royal Military Police 2008. Parliamentary researcher 1993-05; Director and founder 1998-2005: Pritchard Communications Ltd, Next Steps Market Research Ltd.

Political career: Contested Warley 2001 general election. Member for The Wrekin 2005-10, for The Wrekin (revised boundary) since 6 May 2010 general election. *Select committees:* Member: Environmental Audit 2005-07, Work and Pensions 2006-09, Welsh Affairs 2007-10, Transport 2009-10, Joint Committee on National Security Strategy 2010-, International Development 2012-, Panel of Chairs 2012-. Joint secretary, Conservative Parliamentary: Defence Committee -2005, Foreign Affairs Committee -2005; Secretary, 1922 Committee 2010-12. National board member, Conservative Councillors Association 2002; Conservative Party Human Rights Commission 2006-; Deputy chairman, International Office, Conservative Party 2010-12. *Councils and public bodies:* Councillor, Harrow Council 1993-94; Woking Borough Council: Councillor 2000-03, Chair, Economic Committee.

Political interests: Defence, cyber-security, homeland security, foreign relations, counter-terrorism, animal welfare and conservation; Africa, Latin America, Asean region, India, Israel, USA.

Other: UK chair, Parliamentarians for Global Action; Member, Executive Committee: Commonwealth Parliamentary Association, Inter-Parliamentary Union; British American Parliamentary Group: Executive member, Vice-chair 2010-; Member, UK parliamentary delegation to NATO 2010-; Vice-chair, Inter-Parliamentary Union, British Group 2010-11; Bow Group Council 1994; Member, Miniature Schnauzer Club of Great Britain; Oliver Twist Club; Member: Chartered Institute of Marketing, Institute of Public Relations, Market Research Society; Great Ormond Street Children's Hospital; Various orphanage charities; Founder, The Music Charity; Carlton Club.

Recreations: Walking, skiing, writing, animal welfare, tennis, writing comedy.

Mark Pritchard MP, House of Commons, London SW1A 0AA
Tel: 020 7219 8494 *Fax:* 020 7219 5969 *Email:* pritchardm@parliament.uk
Constituency: 25 Church Street, Wellington, Shropshire TF1 1DG
Tel: 01952 256080 *Fax:* 01952 256080 *Website:* www.markpritchard.com
Twitter: @MPritchardMP

PUGH, JOHN
Southport *(Majority 6,024)*

John David Pugh. Born 28 June 1948; Son of James and Patricia Pugh; Married Annette Sangar 1971 (1 son 3 daughters).

Education: Prescott Grammar School; Maidstone Grammar School; Durham University (BA philosophy 1971); Liverpool University (MA logic 1974; MEd 1981); Nottingham University (MPhil theology 1984); Manchester University (PhD logic 1995).

Non-political career: Head of social studies, Salesian High School, Bootle 1972-83; Head of philosophy and religious studies, Merchant Taylors' Boys' School, Crosby 1983-2001.

LIBERAL DEMOCRAT

Political career: Member for Southport since 7 June 2001 general election; Liberal Democrat: Spokesperson for Education 2002-05, Shadow Minister for: Transport 2005-06, Health 2006-07, Treasury 2008-10, Health 2009-10; Member Public Accounts Commission 2011-. *Select committees:* Member: Transport, Local Government and the Regions 2001-02, Transport, Local Government and the Regions (Transport Sub-Committee) 2001-02, Transport, Local Government and the Regions (Urban Affairs Sub-Committee) 2001-02, ODPM/Communities and Local Government 2002-03, ODPM/Communities and Local Government (Urban Affairs Sub-Committee) 2003, ODPM/Communities and Local Government 2005-10, Crossrail Bill 2006-07, Public Accounts 2006-10, Communities and Local Government 2013-. Chair, Liberal Democrat Parliamentary Party Committee on Health and Social Care 2010-. Chair, Southport Liberal Democrat Association 1984-87. *Councils and public bodies:* Councillor, Sefton Metropolitan Borough Council 1987-2001: Former member, Merseyside Police Authority; Member, Merseyside Partnership.

Political interests: Local and regional government, elderly, education, transport, health.

Publications: Christian Understanding of God (1990).

Recreations: Philosophy society Liverpool University, weightlifting, reading, football, computers.

Dr John Pugh MP, House of Commons, London SW1A 0AA
Tel: 020 7219 8318 *Fax:* 020 7219 1794 *Email:* pughj@parliament.uk
Constituency: 35 Shakespeare Street, Southport, Lancashire PR8 5AB
Tel: 01704 533555 *Fax:* 01704 884160 *Website:* www.johnpugh.org.uk *Twitter:* @johnpughmp

QURESHI, YASMIN
Bolton South East *(Majority 8,634)*

Born 5 July 1963; Daughter of Mohammad Qureshi, civil engineer, and Sakina Beg, primary school teacher; Married Nadeem Ashraf Butt 2008.

Education: Westfield School; South Bank Polytechnic, London (BA law 1984); Council of Legal Education (Barrister Exams 1985); University College, London (Masters law); Punjabi, Urdu.

Non-political career: Called to the Bar, Lincoln's Inn 1985; Barrister 1987-: Crown prosecutor, Crown Prosecution Service 1987-2000; United Nations Mission in Kosovo, Judicial Affairs Department Co-ordinator, Criminal Law Unit 2000-01, Department director 2001-02; Crown prosecutor, Crown Prosecution Service 2004-08; Human rights adviser to Mayor of London, Ken Livingstone 2004-08; Barrister: 2 Kings Bench Walk Chambers, London 2004-08, Kenworthy's Chambers 2008-. Member: First Division Association, Union of Shop, Distributive and Allied Workers (USDAW), GMB.

LABOUR

Political career: Contested Brent East 2005 general election. Member for Bolton South East since 6 May 2010 general election. *Select committees:* Member: Justice 2010-, Political and Constitutional Reform 2011, Joint Committee on Privacy and Injunctions 2011-12. Vice-chair, PLP Departmental Group for Women 2013-. Labour Party: Watford Constituency Labour Party: Secretary, Treasurer, Regional delegate to area, Delegate to Labour group.

Political interests: Crime, education, young people.

Other: Former chair, Human Rights and Civil Liberties Working Group, Association of Muslim Lawyers; Former president, Pakistan Club (UK); British Institute of Human Rights; Society of Labour Lawyers; Fabian Society: Member, Former chair, Watford and District branch; Voluntary legal work for the Free Representation Unit; Bolton Labour Socialist Club.

Recreations: Reading.

Yasmin Qureshi MP, House of Commons, London SW1A 0AA
Tel: 020 7219 7019 *Email:* yasmin.qureshi.mp@parliament.uk
Constituency: c/o Bolton Labour Party, 60 St Georges Road, Bolton, Lancashire BL1 2DD
Tel: 01204 371202 *Website:* www.yasminqureshi.org.uk *Twitter:* @YasminQureshiMP

CONSERVATIVE

RAAB, DOMINIC
Esher and Walton *(Majority 18,593)*

Dominic Rennie Raab. Born 25 February 1974; Married Erika (1 son).

Education: Dr Challoner's Grammar School, Amersham; Lady Margaret Hall, Oxford (law); Jesus College, Cambridge (Master's law).

Non-political career: Lawyer, Linklaters; Foreign and Commonwealth Office 2000-06: British Embassy, The Hague 2003-06; Chief of staff to: David Davis MP 2006-08, Dominic Grieve MP 2008-10.

Political career: Member for Esher and Walton since 6 May 2010 general election. *Select committees:* Member: Joint Committee on Human Rights 2010-13.

Political interests: Civil liberties, human rights, industrial relations, economy; Far East, Latin America, Middle East.

Other: Member, Law Society; Esher Neighbourhood Fund. Clive Parry Prize for international law; Newcomer of the Year, *The Spectator* awards 2011.

Publications: Author, The Assault on Liberty (Fourth Estate, 2009); Co-author (with Kwasi Kwarteng MP, Priti Patel MP, Chris Skidmore MP and Elizabeth Truss MP), Britannia Unchained: Global Lessons for Growth and Prosperity (Palgrave Macmillan, 2012).

Recreations: Travel, boxing, theatre.

Dominic Raab MP, House of Commons, London SW1A 0AA
Tel: 020 7219 7069 *Email:* dominic.raab.mp@parliament.uk
Constituency: No constituency office publicised
Email: ursula.henry@parliament.uk *Website:* www.dominicraab.com domraab.blogspot.com

CONSERVATIVE

RANDALL, JOHN
Uxbridge and South Ruislip *(Majority 11,216)*

Alexander John Randall. Born 5 August 1955; Son of late Alec Randall, company director, and late Joyce Randall, née Gore; Married Katherine Gray 1986 (2 sons 1 daughter).

Education: Merchant Taylors' School, Northwood; School of Slavonic and East European Studies, London University (BA Serbo-Croat 1979); French, Russian, Serbo-Croat.

Non-political career: Randall's of Uxbridge: Sales assistant 1973-79, Buyer 1979, Director 1980-, Managing director 1988-97; Tour leader, Birdquest Holidays and Limosa Holidays as specialist ornithologist 1986-97.

Political career: Member for Uxbridge 31 July 1997 by-election to 2010, for Uxbridge and South Ruislip since 6 May 2010 general election; Opposition Whip 2000-03, 2003-05; Opposition Assistant Chief Whip 2005-10; Deputy Chief Whip (Treasurer of HM Household) 2010-13. *Select committees:* Member: Deregulation 1997-2001, Environment, Transport and Regional Affairs 1998-2000, Environment, Transport and Regional Affairs (Environment Sub-Committee) 1998-2000, Transport 2003-05, Finance and Services 2005-06, Selection 2005-07, Administration 2007-09, Members' Allowances 2009-10; Chair: Joint Committee on Security 2010-; Member: Selection 2012-. Uxbridge Conservative Association: Honorary Treasurer 1994, Chair 1994-97.

Political interests: Environment, trade and industry, foreign affair s, transport; Balkans, Caucasus, Russia.

Other: Chair, Uxbridge Retailers' Association -1997. PC 2010; Uxbridge Conservative. Member: Uxbridge Cricket Club, Uxbridge Rugby Football Club, Saracens Rugby Football Club, Middlesex County Cricket Club.

Recreations: Local history, ornithology, theatre, opera, travel, music (plays piano), cricket, football, rugby.

Rt Hon John Randall MP, House of Commons, London SW1A 0AA
Tel: 020 7219 6885 *Email:* john.randall.mp@parliament.uk
Constituency: No constituency office
Email: randall162@aol.com *Website:* www.johnrandallmp.com

LABOUR

RAYNSFORD, NICK
Greenwich and Woolwich *(Majority 10,153)*

Wyvill Richard Nicolls Raynsford. Born 28 January 1945; Son of late Wyvill and Patricia Raynsford; Married Anne Jelley 1968 (divorced 2011) (3 daughters); Married Alison Seabeck MP 2012.

Education: Repton School, Derby; Sidney Sussex College, Cambridge (BA history 1966, MA); Chelsea School of Art (Diploma art and design 1972).

Non-political career: Director: SHAC, the London Housing Aid Centre 1976-86, Raynsford and Morris 1987-92. Member GMB.

Political career: Member for Fulham 1986 by-election to 1987. Contested Fulham 1987 general election. Member for Greenwich 1992-97, for Greenwich and Woolwich 1997-2010, for Greenwich and Woolwich (revised boundary) since 6 May 2010 general election; PPS to Roy Hattersley as Deputy Leader Labour Party 1986-87; Opposition Spokesperson for: Transport and London 1993-94, Housing, Construction and London 1994-97; Department of the Environment, Transport and the Regions 1997-2001: Parliamentary Under-Secretary of State 1997-99, Minister of State (Housing and Planning) 1999-2001; Minister of State Department for Transport, Local Government and the Regions (Local Government and the Regions) 2001-02; Minister of State: Office of the Deputy Prime Minister 2002-05: (Local Government and the Regions 2002-03, Local and Regional Government 2003-05). *Select committees:* Member: Members' Expenses 2011-. *Councils and public bodies:* Councillor, London Borough of Hammersmith and Fulham 1971-75.

Political interests: Housing, social policy, transport, environment; Europe.

Other: Chair, Centre for Public Scrutiny 2007-; President: Youthbuild UK 2008-, National Home Improvement Council 2008-; Trustee, London Open House 2009-. PC 2001.

Publications: A Guide to Housing Benefit (1982); Contributor to journals including Building.

Recreations: Photography, walking, golf.

Rt Hon Nick Raynsford MP, House of Commons, London SW1A 0AA
Tel: 020 7219 5895 *Fax:* 020 7219 2619 *Email:* nick.raynsford.mp@parliament.uk
Constituency: 32 Woolwich Road, London SE10 0JU *Website:* www.nickraynsford.org.uk

CONSERVATIVE

RECKLESS, MARK
Rochester and Strood *(Majority 9,953)*

Mark John Reckless. Born 6 December 1970; Married Catriona Brown 2011.

Education: Marlborough College; Oxford University (BA philosophy, politics and economics); Columbia Business School, New York USA (MBA); College of Law (LLB).

Non-political career: Economist: Warburgs 1993-97, Booz Allen Hamilton 1999-2001; Conservative Party Policy Unit 2002-04; Called to the Bar, Lincoln's Inn 2007.

Political career: Contested Medway 2001 and 2005 general elections. Member for Rochester and Strood since 6 May 2010 general election. *Select committees:* Member: Home Affairs 2010-. *Councils and public bodies:* Councillor, Medway Council 2007-11; Member, Kent Police Authority 2007-11.

Political interests: Economy, home affairs, education, policing.

Other: Top three economists, *Sunday Times* and *Institutional Investor* 1996 and 1997.

Publications: The Euro: Bad for Business 1998.

Recreations: Walking, running.

Mark Reckless MP, House of Commons, London SW1A 0AA
Tel: 020 7219 7135 *Email:* mark.reckless.mp@parliament.uk
Constituency: Suite 6, 4a Castle View Mews, Castle Hill, Rochester, Kent ME1 1LA
Tel: 01634 409917 *Website:* www.markreckless.com *Twitter:* @MarkReckless

CONSERVATIVE

REDWOOD, JOHN
Wokingham *(Majority 13,492)*

John Alan Redwood. Born 15 June 1951; Son of William Redwood and Amy Redwood, née Champion; Married Gail Chippington 1974 (divorced 2004) (1 son 1 daughter).

Education: Kent College, Canterbury; Magdalen College, Oxford (BA modern history 1971, MA); St Antony's College, Oxford (DPhil modern history 1975); French, Spanish.

Non-political career: Fellow, All Souls College, Oxford 1972-87, 2003-05, 2007-; Tutor and lecturer 1972-73; Investment analyst, Robert Fleming & Co. 1974-77; N. M. Rothschild: Bank clerk 1977-78, Manager 1978-79, Assistant director 1979-80, Director, investment division 1980-83, Overseas corporate finance director and head of international (non-UK) privatisation 1986-87; Head, Prime Minister's policy unit 1983-85; Norcros plc: Director 1985-89, Chair

1987-89; Chair, Hare Hatch Holdings 1999-2008; Visiting professor, Middlesex University Business School 2000-; Chair, Concentric plc 2003-08; Non-executive chair, Evercore Pan-Asset Management Ltd 2008-09.

Political career: Contested Southwark Peckham 1981 by-election. Member for Wokingham 1987-2010, for Wokingham (revised boundary) since 6 May 2010 general election; Department of Trade and Industry: Parliamentary Under-Secretary of State for Corporate Affairs 1989-90, Minister of State 1990-92; Minister for Local Government 1992-93; Secretary of State for Wales 1993-95; Member Shadow Cabinet 1997-2000: Shadow Secretary of State for: Trade and Industry 1997-99, Environment, Transport and the Regions 1999-2000; Member, Shadow Cabinet 2004-05: Shadow Secretary of State for Deregulation 2004-05; Chair, Conservative Party Committees for: Trade and Industry 1997-99, Environment, Transport and the Regions 1999-2000, Economic Affairs 2010-. Contested Leadership of Conservative Party 1995 and 1997; Chair: No Turning Back Group 2001-, Policy Review on Economic Competitiveness 2005-10. *Councils and public bodies:* Councillor, Oxfordshire County Council 1973-77; Governor, Oxford Polytechnic 1973-77.

Political interests: Popular capitalism, European affairs, constitution, Euro, transport, economy; China, India, USA.

Other: Member, Chartered Institute for Securities and Investment; Various local and educational charities. PC 1993. House of Lords and House of Commons Cricket Club.

Publications: Reason, Ridicule and Religion (Thames & Hudson, 1976); Public Enterprise in Crisis (Blackwell, 1980); Going for Broke (Blackwell, 1984); Popular Capitalism (Routledge, 1987); The Global Marketplace (HarperCollins, 1993); Our Currency, Our Country (Penguin, 1997); Several books and articles, especially on wider ownership and popular capitalism; The Death of Britain (Macmillan, 1999); Stars and Strife (Macmillan, 2001); Just Say No (Politicos, 2001); Third Way Which Way? (Middlesex, 2002); Singing the Blues (Politicos, 2004); Superpower Struggles (Palgrave, 2005); I Want To Make A Difference, But I Don't Like Politics (Politicos, 2006); After the Credit Crisis (Middlesex, 2009).

Recreations: Village cricket, water sports.

Rt Hon John Redwood MP, House of Commons, London SW1A 0AA
Tel: 020 7219 4205 *Fax:* 020 7219 0377 *Email:* john.redwood.mp@parliament.uk
Constituency: 30 Rose Street, Wokingham, Berkshire RG40 1XU
Tel: 0118-962 9501 *Fax:* 0118-962 9323 *Email:* andrea.wca30@ntlbusiness.com
Website: www.johnredwoodsdiary.com *Twitter:* @JohnRedwood

LABOUR

REED, JAMIE
Copeland *(Majority 3,833)*

Shadow Minister for Health

Jamieson Ronald Reed. Born 4 August 1973; Son of Ronald and Gloria Reed; Married (3 sons 1 daughter).

Education: Whitehaven School; Manchester Metropolitan University (BA English 1994); Leicester University (MA mass communication 2000).

Non-political career: Researcher, European Parliament 1995-97; Adviser, Labour Group Cumbria County Council 1997-2000; Manager, TU and Community Sellafield Campaign 2000-01; Public affairs, BNFL 2001-05. GMB.

Political career: Member for Copeland 2005-10, for Copeland (revised boundary) since 6 May 2010 general election; PPS to: Tony McNulty as Minister of State, Home Office 2006-08, Harriet Harman as Leader of the House of Commons 2008-10; Shadow Minister for: Environment, Food and Rural Affairs 2010-11, Health 2011-. *Select committees:* Member: Environment, Food and Rural Affairs 2005-07, Regulatory Reform 2005-10.

Political interests: Energy, climate change, local economic regeneration, Anglo-American relations; EU, Israel/Palestine, Middle East, USA.

Recreations: American literature, modern history, football, fell walking, Whitehaven RLFC.

Jamie Reed MP, House of Commons, London SW1A 0AA
Tel: 020 7219 4706 *Fax:* 020 7219 4870 *Email:* reedjr@parliament.uk
Constituency: Phoenix Enterprise Centre, Phoenix House, Jacktrees Road, Cleator Moor, Cumbria CA25 5BD
Tel: 01946 816723 *Fax:* 01946 816743 *Email:* andersenj@parliament.uk
Website: www.jamiereedmp.com *Twitter:* @JReedMP

LABOUR

REED, STEVE

Croydon North *(Majority 11,761)*

Shadow Minster for the Home Office

Stephen Mark Ward Reed. Born November 1963.

Non-political career: Member: Unite, GMB.

Political career: Member for Croydon North since 29 November 2012 by-election. Shadow Minster for the Home Office 2013-. *Select committees:* Member: Public Administration 2012-. Chair, PLP Departmental Group for Education 2013-. Member: Labour Party, Co-operative Party. *Councils and public bodies:* London Borough of Lambeth Council: Councillor 1998-12, Leader 2006-12; Member, London Enterprise Panel 2012-.

Other: Fellow, Royal Society for the encouragement of Arts, Manufactures and Commerce.

Steve Reed MP, House of Commons, London SW1A 0AA
Tel: 020 7219 7297 *Email:* steve.reed.mp@parliament.uk
Constituency: 908 London Road, Thornton Heath CR7 7PE
Tel: 020 8665 1214 *Website:* www.stevereedmp.co.uk *Twitter:* @SteveReedMP

CONSERVATIVE

REES-MOGG, JACOB

North East Somerset *(Majority 4,914)*

Jacob William Rees-Mogg. Born 24 May 1969; Son of late William Rees-Mogg, later Lord Rees-Mogg, and Gillian Rees-Mogg, née Morris; Married Helena de Chair 2007 (3 sons 1 daughter).

Education: Eton College; Trinity College, Oxford (BA history).

Non-political career: *Daily Telegraph* 1989; Conservative Central Office Research Department 1990; J. Rothschild 1991-93; Director, Lloyd George Management 1993-2007; Somerset Capital Management 2007-.

Political career: Contested Central Fife 1997 and the Wrekin 2001 general elections. Member for North East Somerset since 6 May 2010 general election. *Select committees:* Member: Procedure 2010-, European Scrutiny 2010-, Works of Art 2013-. President Oxford University Conservative Association 1990; Cities of London and Westminster Conservative Association: Treasurer 1997-, Chair.

Political interests: Treasury, Europe/Eurosceptic; China, Far East, India.

Publications: Co-author, Freedom, Responsibility and the State: Curbing Over-Mighty Government (Politeia, 2012).

Recreations: History, cricket.

Hon Jacob Rees-Mogg MP, House of Commons, London SW1A 0AA
Tel: 020 7219 7118 *Email:* jacob.reesmogg.mp@parliament.uk
Constituency: North East Somerset Conservative Association, Rear of 16 High Street, Keynsham, Bristol BS31 1DQ
Tel: 0117-987 2313 *Fax:* 0117-987 2322 *Email:* jacob@northeastsomersetconservatives.co.uk
Website: www.northeastsomersetconservatives.co.uk www.jacobreesmogg.com

CONSERVATIVE

REEVELL, SIMON

Dewsbury *(Majority 1,526)*

Simon Justin Reevell. Born 2 March 1966; Son of Stephen and Jean; Married Louise.

Education: Boston Spa Comprehensive School; Manchester Polytechnic (Degree economics 1987); Polytechnic of Central London (Diploma law 1989); Inns of Court School of Law (Bar Vocational Course 1990).

Non-political career: Former army officer. Called to the Bar, Lincoln's Inn 1990; Barrister, 39 Park Square Chambers, Leeds 1990-.

Political career: Member for Dewsbury since 6 May 2010 general election. *Select committees:* Member: Scottish Affairs 2010-. Chair, Beverley and Holderness Conservative Association.

Other: Alternate Member, UK Delegation, Organisation for Security and Co-operation in Europe Parliamentary Assembly; Supporter: RNLI, Help for Heroes, Dog's Trust.

Publications: Co-author, Freedom, Responsibility and the State: Curbing Over-Mighty Government (Politeia, 2012).

Recreations: Tennis.

Simon Reevell MP, House of Commons, London SW1A 0AA
Tel: 020 7219 7210 *Email:* simon.reevell.mp@parliament.uk
Constituency: 5 Northgate, Dewsbury, West Yorkshire WF13 1DS
Tel: 01924 465008 *Website:* www.simonreevell.com *Twitter:* @simonreevell

REEVES, RACHEL

Leeds West *(Majority 7,016)*

Shadow Secretary of State for Work and Pensions

Rachel Jane Reeves. Born 13 February 1979; Daughter of Graham and Sally Reeves, both teachers; Married 2010 (1 daughter).

Education: Cator Park School; New College, Oxford (BA philosophy, politics and economics 2000); London School of Economics (MSc economics 2004).

Non-political career: Economist: Bank of England 2000-02; British Embassy, Washington DC 2002-03; Bank of England 2004-06, Halifax Bank of Scotland 2006-. Amicus/MSF/Unite: Member 1998-; Youth representative, Southern Region 1999-2000, Political representative, Southern Region 2001-02, National political committee 2004-06, Yorkshire political committee 2006-.

LABOUR

Political career: Contested Bromley and Chislehurst 2005 general election and 2006 by-election. Member for Leeds West since 6 May 2010 general election; Shadow Minister for Pensions 2010-11; Shadow Chief Secretary to the Treasury 2011-13; Shadow Secretary of State for Work and Pensions 2013-. *Select committees:* Member: Business, Innovation and Skills 2010. Vice-chair, PLP Departmental Group for Transport 2010-. *Councils and public bodies:* Governor: Kirkstall Valley Primary School 2006-10, West Leeds High School 2007-09.

Political interests: Economy, education; China, Japan, USA.

Other: Amnesty International 1996-; Fawcett Society 1998-; Fabian Society 1998-; Board: Leeds Healthy Living Network 2008-, Bramley and Rodley Community Action 2008-10; Patron: Bramley Elderly Action 2010-, June Hancock Mesothelioma Research Fund; Trustee, Bramley and Rodley Community Action 2008-.

Publications: How do financial markets react to central bank communication?, Journal of Political Economy (2006); Why Vote Labour? (2010); Contributor, The Purple Book (Progress, 2011).

Recreations: Tennis, swimming, cycling, reading.

Rachel Reeves MP, House of Commons, London SW1A 0AA
Tel: 020 7219 3000 *Email:* rachel.reeves.mp@parliament.uk
Constituency: Unit 10, Armley Park Court, Stanningley Road, Leeds LS12 2AE
Tel: 0113-263 0411 *Fax:* 0113-263 0411 *Email:* rreevesmp@gmail.com
Website: www.rachelreeves.net *Twitter:* @RachelReevesMP

REID, ALAN

Argyll and Bute *(Majority 3,431)*

Born 7 August 1954; Son of James Reid and Catherine Reid, née Steele; Single.

Education: Prestwick Academy; Ayr Academy; Strathclyde University (BSc maths 1975); Jordanhill College (teacher training qualification 1976); Bell College (computer data processing 1979).

Non-political career: Maths teacher 1976-77; Computer programmer, Strathclyde Regional Council 1977-85; Computer project programmer, Glasgow University 1985-. EIS 1976-77; NALGO 1977-85; AUT 1985-2001.

LIBERAL DEMOCRAT

Political career: Contested Paisley South 1990 by-election, 1992 general election, and Dumbarton 1997 general election. Member for Argyll and Bute 2001-05, for Argyll and Bute (revised boundary) since 5 May 2005 general election; Liberal Democrat: Whip 2002-05, Spokesperson for Scotland 2004-05, Shadow Minister for: Trade and Industry 2005-06, Information Technology 2005-06, Northern Ireland 2006-10, Scotland 2007-10, Whip 2009-10. *Select committees:* Member: Broadcasting 2001-05, Scottish Affairs 2010-. Chair, Liberal Democrat Parliamentary Party Committee on Transport 2012-. Scottish Liberal Democrats 1981-: Vice-convener 1994-98, Member executive committee; Election agent to George Lyon Scottish Parliament election 1999. *Councils and public bodies:* Renfrew District Council 1988-96: Councillor, Group secretary.

Political interests: Environment, employment, fuel tax, health, fishing industry, local issues, elderly, farming, rural development, international affairs.

Recreations: Chess, football, walking, reading, television.

Alan Reid MP, House of Commons, London SW1A 0AA
Tel: 020 7219 8127 *Fax:* 020 7219 1737 *Email:* reida@parliament.uk
Constituency: 95 Alexandra Parade, Dunoon, Argyll PA23 8AL
Tel: 01369 704840 *Fax:* 01369 701212 *Email:* alan.reid@aandb-libdems.org
Website: www.alanreid.org

LABOUR

REYNOLDS, EMMA
Wolverhampton North East *(Majority 2,484)*

Shadow Minister for Housing

Emma Elizabeth Reynolds. Born 2 November 1977.

Education: Perton Middle School; Codsall High School; Wulfrun College; Wadham College, Oxford (BA politics, philosophy and economics 2000); French, Italian, Spanish.

Non-political career: Intern, British High Commission, Pakistan summer 1999; English teacher, France, Spain and Argentina; Information officer, Enlargement Information Centre, European Commission 2000-01; Policy researcher, Small Business Europe, Brussels 2001-04; Political adviser, Party of European Socialists, Brussels 2004-06; Special adviser to Geoff Hoon MP: as Minister for Europe 2006-07, as Chief Whip 2007-08; Senior consultant (part-time), Cogitamus Ltd 2009-10. Member, GMB 2002.

Political career: Member for Wolverhampton North East since 6 May 2010 general election; Shadow Minister for Foreign and Commonwealth Office 2010-13; Shadow Minister for Housing 2013-. *Select committees:* Member: Foreign Affairs 2010, Arms Export Controls 2010-11.

Political interests: Foreign affairs, public services, economy, welfare state, manufacturing, skills; EU, India, Latin America, Pakistan, USA.

Recreations: Running, cinema, reading, swimming, tennis.

Emma Reynolds MP, House of Commons, London SW1A 0AA
Tel: 020 7219 6919 *Email:* emma.reynolds.mp@parliament.uk
Constituency: 492a Stafford Road, Wolverhampton, West Midlands WV10 6AN
Tel: 01902 397698 *Fax:* 01902 397538 *Website:* www.emmareynolds.org.uk
Twitter: @EmmaReynoldsMP

LAB/CO-OP

REYNOLDS, JONATHAN
Stalybridge and Hyde *(Majority 2,744)*

Shadow Minster for Energy and Climate Change

Jonathan Neil Reynolds. Born 28 August 1980; Son of Keith Reynolds, fireman, and Judith Reynolds; Married Claire (1 son 1 daughter).

Education: Houghton Kepier Comprehensive School; Sunderland City College; Manchester University (BA politics and modern history 2001); BPP Law School, Manchester (2009).

Non-political career: Political assistant to James Purnell MP; Trainee solicitor, Addleshaw Goddard, Manchester; Former columnist, Progress online magazine. Member: Unite, USDAW.

Political career: Member for Stalybridge and Hyde since 6 May 2010 general election; Opposition Assistant Whip 2010-11; PPS to Ed Miliband as Leader of the Opposition 2011-13; Shadow Minister for Energy and Climate Change 2013-. *Select committees:* Member: Science and Technology 2010-12, Finance and Services 2010-12, Standing Orders 2011-. Member: National Executive Committee, Labour Party 2003-05, Co-operative Party. *Councils and public bodies:* Tameside Council: Councillor 2007-, Cabinet Secretary Without Portfolio (Policy and Corporate Performance), Deputy chair, Longdendale and Hattersley District Assembly; Governor: Hollingworth Primary School, Longdendale Language College.

Political interests: Transport, defence, economy, manufacturing, social care; Middle East, Germany, Turkey.

Other: Vice-chair, Progress -2012; National Autistic Society.

Recreations: Football, history, music, gardening.

Jonathan Reynolds MP, House of Commons, London SW1A 0AA
Tel: 020 7219 7155 *Email:* jonathan.reynolds.mp@parliament.uk
Constituency: Hyde Town Hall, Market Street, Hyde SK14 1AL
Tel: 0161-367 8077 *Email:* jonathan@jonathanreynolds.org.uk
Website: www.jonathanreynolds.org.uk *Twitter:* @jreynoldsmp

CONSERVATIVE

RIFKIND, MALCOLM
Kensington *(Majority 8,616)*

Malcolm Leslie Rifkind. Born 21 June 1946; Married Edith Steinberg 1970 (1 son 1 daughter).

Education: George Watson's College, Edinburgh; Edinburgh University (LLB 1966; MSc 1970).

Non-political career: Lecturer, University College of Rhodesia 1967-68; Called to the Scottish Bar 1970; QC (Scotland) 1985.

Political career: Contested Edinburgh Central 1970 general election. Member for Edinburgh Pentlands 1974-97. Contested Edinburgh Pentlands 1997 and 2001 general elections. Member for Kensington and Chelsea 2005-10, for Kensington since 6 May 2010 general election; Opposition front bench spokesperson for Scottish Affairs 1975-76; Minister for Home Affairs and the Environment, Scottish Office 1979-82; Foreign and Commonwealth Office: Parliamentary

Under-Secretary of State 1982-83, Minister of State 1983-86; Secretary of State for: Scotland 1986-90, Transport 1990-92, Defence 1992-95, Foreign and Commonwealth Affairs 1995-97; Shadow Secretary of State for Work and Pensions 2005; Chair Intelligence and Security Committee 2010-. *Select committees:* Member: Joint Committee on Conventions 2006; Chair: Standards and Privileges 2009-10; Member: Liaison 2010, Joint Committee on National Security Strategy 2010-. Honorary secretary, Parliamentary Group of Conservative Friends of Israel 1976-79; Joint secretary, Conservative Foreign and Commonwealth Affairs Committee 1977-79. Honorary President, Scottish Young Conservatives 1976-77; Honorary Secretary, Federation of Conservative Students 1977-79; President, Scottish Conservative Party 1997-2002; Patron, Tory Reform Group. *Councils and public bodies:* Member, Edinburgh Town Council 1970-74.

Other: Member Queen's Bodyguard for Scotland, Royal Company of Archers 1993; Honorary Colonel, 162 Movement Control Regiment, RLC (V). PC 1986; KCMG 1997; New Club, Pratt's, White's.

Recreations: Field sports.

Rt Hon Sir Malcolm Rifkind KCMG MP, House of Commons, London SW1A 0AA
Tel: 020 7219 5683 *Fax:* 020 7219 4213 *Email:* shaylorc@parliament.uk
Constituency: 1a Chelsea Manor Street, London SW3 5RP
Tel: 020 7352 0102 *Fax:* 020 7351 5885 *Email:* jonathan@kcfc.org.uk
Website: www.malcolmrifkind.com

RIORDAN, LINDA
Halifax *(Majority 1,472)*

Linda June Riordan. Born 31 May 1953; Daughter of John Foulds Haigh and Alice Haigh; Married Alan Riordan 1979 (died 2007).

Education: J.H.Whitley Secondary Modern School, Illingworth, Yorkshire; Bradford University (BSc politics and history 1997); Spanish.

Non-political career: Midland Bank; Private secretary to Alice Mahon MP 2001-05. Unite.

LAB/CO-OP

Political career: Member for Halifax 2005-10, for Halifax (revised boundary) since 6 May 2010 general election. *Select committees:* Member: Environmental Audit 2005-10, Crossrail Bill 2006-07, Procedure 2006-10, Justice 2008-12, Chairmen's Panel/Panel of Chairs 2010-, European Scrutiny 2013-. Co-operative Party. *Councils and public bodies:* Councillor Calderdale Metropolitan Borough Council 1995-2006.

Political interests: Transport, culture, media and sport, justice; Ireland, Kashmir, Moldova, Palestine.

Other: Member, UK Delegation, Organisation for Security and Co-operation in Europe Parliamentary Assembly.

Recreations: Reading, swimming, theatre.

Linda Riordan MP, House of Commons, London SW1A 0AA
Tel: 020 7219 5399 *Fax:* 020 7219 1513 *Email:* riordanl@parliament.uk
Constituency: 2-4 Shaw Lodge House, Halifax, West Yorkshire HX3 9ET
Tel: 01422 251800 *Fax:* 01422 251888 *Website:* www.lindariordanmp.com
Twitter: @Linda_Riordan

RITCHIE, MARGARET
South Down *(Majority 8,412)*

SDLP Spokesperson for Political Affairs; Energy and Climate Change; Environment, Food and Rural Affairs

Born 25 March 1958; Daughter of late John Ritchie and late Rose Ritchie, née Drumm; Single.

Education: St Mary's High School; Queen's University Belfast (BA geography and political science 1979); Post-graduate qualification, administrative management.

Non-political career: Assistant to Eddie McGrady MP 1987-2003.

SOCIAL DEMOCRATIC AND LABOUR PARTY

Political career: Member for South Down since 6 May 2010 general election; Spokesperson for: Political Affairs 2010-, Energy and Climate Change 2010-, Environment, Food and Rural Affairs 2010-. *Select committees:* Member: Environment, Food and Rural Affairs 2012-. Member, Northern Ireland Forum 1996; MLA for South Down 2003-11, and for South Down (revised boundary) 2011-12: SDLP Spokesperson for Regional Development 2003-07, Minister for Social Development 2007-10. Social Democratic and Labour Party: Member 1980-, Member General Council, International Secretary -2007, Leader 2010-11. *Councils and public bodies:* Down District Council: Councillor 1985-2009, Chair 1993-94.

Political interests: Health, environment, Europe, provision facilities for the young, economy, regional development; Belgium, France.

Other: Alternate member, EU Committee of the Regions 2005-09.

Recreations: Walking, reading.

Margaret Ritchie MP, House of Commons, London SW1A 0AA
Tel: 020 7219 7147/020 7219 8510 *Fax:* 020 7219 4037 *Email:*
margaret.ritchie.mp@parliament.uk
Constituency: 32 Saul Street, Downpatrick, Co Down BT 30 6NQ
Tel: 028 4461 2882 *Fax:* 028 4461 9574 *Email:* m.ritchie@sdlp.ie
Website: www.margaretritchie.com *Twitter:* @MRitchieMP

CONSERVATIVE

ROBATHAN, ANDREW — South Leicestershire *(Majority 15,524)*

Minister of State, Northern Ireland Office

Andrew Robert George Robathan. Born 17 July 1951; Son of late Douglas Robathan and Sheena Robathan, née Gimson; Married Rachael Maunder 1991 (1 son 1 daughter).

Education: Merchant Taylors' School, Northwood; Oriel College, Oxford (BA modern history 1973, MA); RMA, Sandhurst; Army Staff College (psc 1984); French, German (colloquial).

Non-political career: Regular Army officer, Coldstream Guards and SAS 1974-89; Rejoined Army for Gulf War January-April 1991. BP 1991-92.

Political career: Member for Blaby 1992-2010, for South Leicestershire since 6 May 2010 general election; PPS to Iain Sproat as Minister of State, Department of National Heritage 1995-97; Shadow Minister for: Trade and Industry 2002-03, International Development 2003, Defence 2004-05; Opposition Deputy Chief Whip 2005-10; Ministry of Defence: Parliamentary Under-Secretary of State (Defence Personnel, Welfare and Veterans) 2010-12, Minister of State for: the Armed Forces 2012-13, Northern Ireland Office 2013-. *Select committees:* Member: International Development 1997-2002, 2003-04, Administration 2005-07, Selection 2006-10, Armed Forces Bill 2011. Chair, Conservative Parliamentary Committee on Defence 1994-95; Vice-chair: Conservative Parliamentary Committee on Northern Ireland 1994-2002, Conservative Defence/Foreign Affairs Policy Committee 2001-02; Member, Executive, 1922 Committee 2001-02, 2003-04. *Councils and public bodies:* Councillor, London Borough of Hammersmith and Fulham 1990-92.

Political interests: International development, environment, transport, defence, Northern Ireland; Africa, Indian Sub-Continent, Middle East.

Other: Chairman, Halo Trust 2003-06. Freeman, Merchant Taylors' Company. Freeman, City of London. PC 2010; Special Forces Club, Pratts.

Recreations: Mountain walking, skiing, wildlife, shooting.

Rt Hon Andrew Robathan MP, House of Commons, London SW1A 0AA
Tel: 020 7219 3459 *Fax:* 020 7219 0096 *Email:* thompsondm@parliament.uk
Constituency: 51 Main Street, Broughton Astley, Leicestershire LE9 6RE
Tel: 01455 283594 *Fax:* 01455 286159 *Email:* southleicscons@btconnect.com

SCOTTISH NATIONAL PARTY

ROBERTSON, ANGUS — Moray *(Majority 5,590)*

SNP Westminster Group Leader; SNP Spokesperson for Foreign Affairs and Defence

Angus Struan Carolus Robertson. Born 28 September 1969.

Education: Broughton High School, Edinburgh; Aberdeen University (MA politics and international relations 1991); German, French.

Non-political career: News editor, Austrian Broadcasting Corporation 1991-99; Reporter, BBC Austria 1992-99; Contributor: National Public Radio USA, Radio Telefís Eireann, Ireland, Deutsche Welle, Germany; Consultant in media skills, presentation skills and political affairs with Communications Skills International (CSI) 1994-2001. National Union of Journalists.

Political career: Member for Moray 2001-05, for Moray (revised boundary) since 5 May 2005 general election; SNP Spokesperson for: Foreign Affairs and for Defence 2001-, Europe and for Office of the Deputy Prime Minister 2005-07; SNP Westminster Group: Deputy Leader 2005-07, Leader 2007-. *Select committees:* Member: European Scrutiny 2001-10. Contested Midlothian constituency 1999 Scottish Parliament election. Member, National Executive Young Scottish Nationalists 1986; National organiser, Federation of Student Nationalists 1988; Member, SNP International Bureau; Deputy SNP spokesperson for Constitutional and External Affairs 1998-99; European policy adviser, SNP Group, Scottish Parliament.

Political interests: Scottish independence, international and European affairs, defence, whisky, oil, fishing, sustainable development and youth issues; Armenia, Austria, Azerbaijan, Georgia, Germany, Ireland, Norway, USA.

Other: Member, UK Delegation, Organisation for Security and Co-operation in Europe Parliamentary Assembly.

Recreations: Sport, current affairs, history, travel, socialising, cinema, whisky tasting.

Angus Robertson MP, House of Commons, London SW1A 0AA
Tel: 020 7219 8259 *Fax:* 020 7219 1781 *Email:* robertsona@parliament.uk
Constituency: Moray Parliamentary Office, 9 Wards Road, Elgin, Morayshire IV30 1NL
Tel: 01343 551111 *Fax:* 01343 556355 *Email:* moraymp@googlemail.com
Website: www.angusrobertson.org *Twitter:* @MorayMP

ROBERTSON, HUGH
Faversham and Mid Kent *(Majority 17,088)*

Minister of State, Foreign and Commonwealth Office

Hugh Michael Robertson. Born 9 October 1962; Son of George Robertson, retired headmaster, and June Robertson, née McBryde; Married Anna Copson 2002 (1 son).

Education: King's School, Canterbury; Reading University (BSc land management 1985); Royal Military Academy Sandhurst (Commissioned 1986).

Non-political career: Army officer, Life Guards, serving in Northern Ireland, Gulf War and Bosnia 1985-95. Schroder Investment Management 1995-2001: Assistant director 1999-2001; Special adviser on security to Shadow Northern Ireland Secretary 1998-2001.

CONSERVATIVE

Political career: Member for Faversham and Mid Kent 2001-10, for Faversham and Mid Kent (revised boundary) since 6 May 2010 general election; Opposition Whip 2002-04; Opposition Spokesperson for Sport 2004-05; Shadow Minister for Sport and for Olympics 2005-10; Department for Culture, Media and Sport: Parliamentary Under-Secretary of State (Minister for Sport and the Olympics) 2010-12, Minister of State for: Sport and Tourism 2012-13, Foreign and Commonwealth Office 2013-.

Political interests: Defence, foreign affairs, fruit farming, sport, Olympics; Balkans, Middle East, Syria.

Other: Fellow, Royal Geographical Society; Governor, Westminster Foundation for Democracy 2005-08. Armourers and Brasiers Prize 1986. Sultan of Brunei's Personal Order of Merit 1992; PC 2012; Cavalry and Guards; Pratts. Playing member, MCC.

Recreations: Cricket, hockey.

Rt Hon Hugh Robertson MP, House of Commons, London SW1A 0AA
Tel: 020 7219 2643 *Fax:* 020 7219 1765 *Email:* jenkinsv@parliament.uk
Constituency: 11 The Square, Lenham, Kent ME17 2PQ
Tel: 01622 851616 *Fax:* 01622 850294 *Email:* staintonjamesa@parliament.uk
Website: www.hughrobertson.org.uk

ROBERTSON, JOHN
Glasgow North West *(Majority 13,611)*

John Webster Robertson. Born 17 April 1952; Son of Charles Robertson and Agnes Millen Robertson, née Webster; Married Eleanor Munro 1973 (3 daughters).

Education: Shawlands Academy; Langside College (ONC electrical engineering 1983); Stow College (HNC electrical engineering 1985).

Non-political career: Armed Forces Parliamentary Scheme. GPO/Post Office/British Telecom/ BT 1969-2000: Technical officer 1973-87, Special faults investigation officer 1987-91, Customer service manager 1991-95, Field manager 1995-99, Local customer manager 1999-2000. Member: NCU/POEU/CWU 1969-91, STE/Connect/Prospect 1991-2012; Political and education officer, Glasgow branch, CWU/NCU 1986-90; Chair, West of Scotland, Connect 1997-2000; Member, Amicus/Unite 2004-.

LABOUR

Political career: Member for Glasgow Anniesland 23 November 2000 by-election to 2005, for Glasgow North West since 5 May 2005 general election; PPS: to Kim Howells as Minister of State, Foreign and Commonwealth Office 2005-08, to Yvette Cooper: as Chief Secretary to the Treasury 2008-09, as Secretary of State for Work and Pensions 2009-10, as Shadow Home Secretary 2010-. *Select committees:* Member: Scottish Affairs 2001-05, European Scrutiny 2003-05, Energy and Climate Change 2009-, Chairmen's Panel/Panel of Chairs 2010-. Election agent to Donald Dewar MP, MSP 1993-2000; Chair, Anniesland constituency Labour party 1995-2000; Secretary: Glasgow Group of MPs 2001-06, Scottish Parliamentary Labour Party 2004-.

Political interests: International development, defence, work and pensions, Scottish affairs, communications, foreign affairs, music, nuclear energy; Angola, Australia, Iran, Japan, Mexico, Nigeria, USA.

Other: Commonwealth Parliamentary Association: Member 2000-, Member, Executive Committee 2010-; Member: Executive Committee, Inter-Parliamentary Union, British Group 2000-, British-American Parliamentary Group 2000-, British-Irish Parliamentary Assembly 2001-, NATO Parliamentary Assembly 2010-. Cambus Athletic Football Club; Garrowhill Cricket Club; Old Kilpatrick Bowling Club.

Recreations: Reading, music, football, cricket, golf.

John Robertson MP, House of Commons, London SW1A 0AA
Tel: 020 7219 6964 *Fax:* 020 7219 1096 *Email:* john.robertson.mp@parliament.uk
Constituency: 131 Dalsetter Avenue, Drumchapel, Glasgow G15 8TE
Tel: 0141-944 7298 *Fax:* 0141-944 7121 *Email:* jrmpoffice@btinternet.com
Website: www.john-robertson.co.uk *Twitter:* @JohnRobertsonMP

ROBERTSON, LAURENCE
Tewkesbury *(Majority 6,310)*

Laurence Anthony Robertson. Born 29 March 1958; Son of James Robertson, former colliery electrician, and Jean Robertson, née Larkin; Married Susan Lees 1989 (2 stepdaughters).

Education: St James' Church of England Secondary School; Farnworth Grammar School; Bolton Institute of Higher Education (Diploma management services 1979).

Non-political career: Warehouse assistant 1976-77; Work study engineer 1977-83; Industrial management consultant 1983-89; Factory owner 1987-88; Charity fundraising, public relations and special events consultant 1988-.

CONSERVATIVE

Political career: Contested Makerfield 1987 and Ashfield 1992 general elections. Member for Tewkesbury 1997-2010, for Tewkesbury (revised boundary) since 6 May 2010 general election; Opposition Whip 2001-03; Shadow Minister for: Trade and Industry 2003, Economic Affairs 2003-05, Northern Ireland 2005-10. *Select committees:* Member: Environmental Audit 1997-99, Joint Committee on Consolidation of Bills Etc 1997-2001, Social Security 1999-2001, European Scrutiny 1999-2002, Education and Skills 2001; Chair: Northern Ireland Affairs 2010-; Member: Liaison 2010-. Former member: Conservative 2000 Foundation, Conservative Way Forward; Vice-chair, Association of Conservative Clubs 1997-2000.

Political interests: Overseas aid, constitution, European affairs, education, economic policy, law and order, countryside, Northern Ireland; African countries, particularly Ethiopia, UK, USA.

Other: Co-chairman, British-Irish Parliamentary Association 2011-; Fellow Industry and Parliament Trust 2001; Overseas Aid charities; charities linked to horse racing.

Publications: Europe: The Case Against Integration (1991); The Right Way Ahead (1995).

Recreations: Horses and horseracing, golf, other sports (completed six marathons), reading, writing, countryside.

Laurence Robertson MP, House of Commons, London SW1A 0AA
Tel: 020 7219 4196 *Fax:* 020 7219 2325 *Email:* robertsonl@parliament.uk
Constituency: 22 High Street, Tewkesbury, Gloucestershire GL20 5AL
Tel: 01684 291640 *Fax:* 01684 291759 *Email:* calwaym@parliament.uk
Website: www.laurencerobertsonmp.com

ROBINSON, GEOFFREY
Coventry North West *(Majority 6,288)*

Born 25 May 1938; Son of late Robert Robinson and late Dorothy Robinson, née Skelly; Married Marie Elena Giorgio 1967 (1 daughter 1 son).

Education: Emanuel School, London; Clare College, Cambridge; Yale University, USA; French, Italian, German.

Non-political career: Research assistant, Labour Party 1965-68; Senior executive, Industrial Reorganisation Corporation 1968-70; Financial controller, British Leyland 1970-72; Managing director, Leyland Innocenti 1972-73; Chief executive, Jaguar Cars Coventry 1974-75; Chief executive (unpaid), Triumph Motorcycles (Meriden) Ltd 1978-80; Director, West Midlands Enterprise Board 1982-85; Chief executive, TransTec plc 1986-97. Member, T&G.

LABOUR

Political career: Member for Coventry North West 4 March 1976 by-election to 2010, for Coventry North West (revised boundary) since 6 May 2010 general election; Opposition Frontbench Spokesperson for: Science 1982-83, Trade and Industry and Regional Affairs 1983-87; Paymaster General, HM Treasury 1997-98.

Political interests: Industry, economic policy, new technology; France, Germany, Italy, USA.
Publications: The Unconventional Minister: My Life in New Labour.
Recreations: Motorcars, gardens, architecture, football.
Geoffrey Robinson MP, House of Commons, London SW1A 0AA
Tel: 020 7219 4083 *Fax:* 020 7219 0984 *Email:* robinsong@parliament.uk
Constituency: Transport House, Short Street, Coventry, Warwickshire CV1 2LS
Tel: 024 7625 7870 *Fax:* 024 7625 7813 *Website:* www.labourincoventry.org.uk

---

ROGERSON, DAN
North Cornwall *(Majority 2,981)*

Parliamentary Under-Secretary of State, Department for Environment, Food and Rural Affairs

Daniel John Rogerson. Born 23 July 1975; Son of Stephen and Patricia Rogerson; Married Heidi Purser 1999 (2 sons 1 daughter).
Education: St Mary's School, Bodmin; Bodmin College, Cornwall; University of Wales, Aberystwyth (BSc politics 1996).

LIBERAL DEMOCRAT

Non-political career: Research assistant, Bedford Borough Council 1996-98; Administrative officer, De Montfort University 1998-2002; Campaigns officer, Devon and Cornwall Liberal Democrats 2002-04. Unison 1996-97.
Political career: Contested North East Bedfordshire 2001 general election. Member for North Cornwall 2005-10, for North Cornwall (revised boundary) since 6 May 2010 general election; Liberal Democrat: Shadow Minister for: Environment, Food and Rural Affairs 2005-06, Office of the Deputy Prime Minister/Communities and Local Government 2006-07; Whip 2007-10; Shadow Minister for: the Arts, Culture and Heritage 2007, Communities and Local Government 2007-10; Parliamentary Under-Secretary of State, Department for Environment, Food and Rural Affairs 2013-. *Select committees:* Member: Environment, Food and Rural Affairs 2005-. Chair, Liberal Democrat Parliamentary Party Committee on Education, Families and Young People 2010-. Member, Association of Liberal Democrat Councillors 1998-. *Councils and public bodies:* Bedford Borough Council: Councillor 1999-2002, Deputy leader, Liberal Democrat group 2000-02.
Political interests: Local services, local taxation, minority languages, housing, dairy industry, waste, muscular dystrophy, packaging industry, rural affairs, education, young people; Canada, Georgia, Latvia.
Other: Trustee, History of Parliament Trust; Camelford Liberal; St Lawrence's Social.
Recreations: Blues music, collecting books of Liberal historical interest, reading.
Dan Rogerson MP, House of Commons, London SW1A 0AA
Tel: 020 7219 4707 *Fax:* 020 7219 1018
Constituency: 4 Tower Street, Launceston, Cornwall PL15 8BQ
Tel: 01566 777123 *Fax:* 01566 772122 *Email:* contact@danrogerson.org
Website: www.danrogerson.org

ROSINDELL, ANDREW
Romford *(Majority 16,954)*

Andrew Richard Rosindell. Born 17 March 1966; Son of Frederick Rosindell, tailor, and Eileen Clark, pianist; Single.
Education: Marshalls Park Comprehensive School, Romford.
Non-political career: Armed Forces Parliamentary Scheme: Royal Marines 2002-03, RAF 2004-06, Army 2009-13. Central Press Features London 1984-86; Freelance journalist 1986-97; Parliamentary researcher to Vivian Bendall MP 1986-97; Director and international director, European Foundation 1997-2001.

CONSERVATIVE

Political career: Contested Glasgow Provan 1992 and Thurrock 1997 general elections. Member for Romford 2001-10, for Romford (revised boundary) since 6 May 2010 general election; Opposition Whip 2005-07; Shadow Minister for Home Affairs (Animal Welfare) 2007-10. *Select committees:* Member: Regulatory Reform 2001-05, Joint Committee on Statutory Instruments 2002-03, Constitutional Affairs 2004-05, Foreign Affairs 2010-, Panel of Chairs 2010-. Member, National Union Executive Committee, Conservative Party 1986-88, 1992-94; Chairman, Greater London Young Conservatives 1987-88; International secretary, Young Conservatives United Kingdom 1991-98; Chairman: National Young Conservatives 1993-94, Romford Conservative Association 1998-2001, Conservative Friends of Gibraltar 2002-; Member, Conservative Christian Fellowship; Vice-chair (campaigning), Conservative Party 2004-05; Chairman, Conservative Friends of Australia and New Zealand 2010-. *Councils and public bodies:* London Borough of Havering: Councillor 1990-2002, Alderman 2007-; Chairman, North Romford Community Area Forum 1998-2002.

Political interests: Foreign and international relations, European affairs, law and order, defence, local and regional government, animal welfare; Australia, British Overseas Territories and Crown Dependencies, Canada, Eastern Europe, Gulf States, Liechtenstein, New Zealand, Nordic countries, Switzerland, USA.

Other: Chairman, European Young Conservatives 1993-97; Executive member, International Democrat Union 1994-2002, Chair, International Young Democrat Union 1998-2002; Member, Executive Committee: Commonwealth Parliamentary Association 2010-, Inter-Parliamentary Union, British Group 2010-; Westminster Foundation for Democracy: Governor 2010, Board Member 2010-; Fellow, Industry and Parliament Trust. Freeman, City of London; Romford Conservative and Constitutional; Royal Air Forces Association; Romford Royal British Legion.

Publications: Co-author, Defending Our Great Heritage (1993).

Recreations: Staffordshire bull terrier "Buster", travel, philately, history.

Andrew Rosindell MP, House of Commons, London SW1A 0AA
Tel: 020 7219 8475/8499 *Email:* andrew.rosindell.mp@parliament.uk
Constituency: Margaret Thatcher House, 85 Western Road, Romford RM1 3LS
Tel: 01708 766700 *Email:* andrew@rosindell.com *Website:* www.rosindell.com
Twitter: @AndrewRosindell

LABOUR

ROTHERAM, STEVE
Liverpool Walton *(Majority 19,818)*

Steven Philip Rotheram. Born 4 November 1961; Son of Dorothy and Harry Rotheram; Married Sandra 1989 (1 son 2 daughters).

Education: Ruffwood Comprehensive; Kirkby Further Education College (building studies 1995); Studying for MA in contemporary urban renaissance.

Non-political career: Construction sector 1978-89; Instructor 1989-2001; Director: SIP Property Development LLP, SPR Consultants. Member, UCATT (UCATT-supported MP).

Political career: Member for Liverpool Walton since 6 May 2010 general election. *Select committees:* Member: Communities and Local Government 2011, Culture, Media and Sport 2011-. Chair, PLP Departmental Group for Culture, Olympics, Media and Sport 2010-. Member, Labour Party National Executive Committee 2012-. *Councils and public bodies:* Councillor, Liverpool City Council 2002-11; Former Lord Mayor of Liverpool.

Political interests: Construction industry, further education, apprenticeships; France.

Other: Member: St George's Hall Trust, Liverpool Institute of Performing Arts, Fazakerley 9/10 Credit Union, The Social Academy, St George's Hall Trust; Liverpool Lord Mayor's Charity. Speech of the Year, *PoliticsHome* awards 2012.

Recreations: Football (Liverpool FC season ticket holder), theatre.

Steve Rotheram MP, House of Commons, London SW1A 0AA
Tel: 020 7219 7101 *Email:* steve.rotheram.mp@parliament.uk
Constituency: 330 Rice Lane, Walton, Liverpool L9 2BL
Tel: 0151-525 5025 *Email:* gary.booth@parliament.uk *Website:* www.steverorerammp.org.uk
Twitter: @SteveRotheramMP

LABOUR

ROY, FRANK
Motherwell and Wishaw *(Majority 16,806)*

Born 29 August 1958; Son of late James Roy, settler manager, and Esther McMahon, home help; Married Ellen Foy 1977 (1 son 1 daughter).

Education: St Joseph's High School, Motherwell; Our Lady's High School, Motherwell; Motherwell College (HNC marketing 1994); Glasgow Caledonian University (BA consumer and management studies 1994).

Non-political career: Steelworker, Ravenscraig 1977-91; Personal assistant to Helen Liddell MP 1994-97. Shop steward, ISTC 1983-90; Member, Community Union.

Political career: Member for Motherwell and Wishaw 1997-2005, for Motherwell and Wishaw (revised boundary) since 5 May 2005 general election; PPS: to Helen Liddell as Minister of State, Scottish Office 1998-99, to Secretaries of State for Scotland: Dr John Reid 1999-2001, Helen Liddell 2001; Sponsor Aviation Offences Act 2003; Assistant Government Whip 2005-06; Government Whip 2006-10; Opposition Whip 2010. *Select committees:* Member: Social Security 1997-98, Defence 2001-05, Selection 2008-10, Foreign Affairs 2010-. Election agent to Dr Jeremy Bray MP 1987-92.

Political interests: Employment, social welfare, foreign affairs; Europe, USA.

Other: Vice-President, Federation of Economic Development Authorities (FEDA).
Recreations: Football, reading, music.

Frank Roy MP, House of Commons, London SW1A 0AA
Tel: 020 7219 6467 *Fax:* 020 7219 8233 *Email:* frank.roy.mp@parliament.uk
Constituency: 265 Main Street, Wishaw, Lanarkshire ML2 7NE
Tel: 01698 303040 *Fax:* 01698 303060 *Website:* www.frankroy.org.uk *Twitter:* @frankroymp

ROY, LINDSAY
Glenrothes *(Majority 16,448)*

Lindsay Allan Roy. Born 19 January 1949; Son of John Roy, railway signalman, and Margaret Roy, nurse; Married Irene Elizabeth 1972 (1 daughter 2 sons).
Education: Perth Academy; Edinburgh University (BSc geography 1970); French.
Non-political career: Teacher, then principal teacher of modern studies, Queen Anne High School, Dunfermline, Fife 1972-83; Assistant rector, Kircaldy High School, Fife 1983-86; Depute rector, Glenwood High School, Glenrothes, Fife 1986-89; Rector: Inverkeithing High School, Fife 1989-2007, Kirkcaldy High School 2008. Member, GMB 2009-.

LABOUR

Political career: Member for Glenrothes since 6 November 2008 by-election; PPS to Tessa Jowell as Minister for the Cabinet Office and Paymaster General 2009-10. *Select committees:* Member: Scottish Affairs 2009-, Public Administration 2010-. Vice-chair, PLP Departmental Group for Education 2010-. *Councils and public bodies:* Associate assessor, HM Inspectorate of Education 1996-2008.
Political interests: Education, health and welfare, economy, foreign policy, international development; Argentina, China, Finland, New Zealand, South Africa, Thailand, Uganda.
Other: Management board member, Carnegie College 1997-2006; Church Elder, St Columba's Church, Glenrothes; Trustee, John MacDougall Mesothelioma Trust; Fellow, Royal Society for the Arts 2004-; Headteachers' Association of Scotland/School Leaders Scotland: Member, Executive 2003-, President 2004-05; International Confederation of Principals: Scotland representative 2006-, Executive member; Member, Scottish Literacy Commission 2008-09; Christian Aid; Cancer Research; Heart Foundation; Diabetes UK. CBE 2004; Rotary Club, Glenrothes.
Recreations: Five-a-side football, mountain biking, mountain climbing, angling, reading.

Lindsay Roy CBE MP, House of Commons, London SW1A 0AA
Tel: 020 7219 8273 *Email:* lindsay.roy.mp@parliament.uk
Constituency: 83a Woodside Way, Glenrothes, Fife KY7 5DW
Tel: 01592 751549 *Fax:* 01592 758662 *Email:* lroymp@parliament.uk
Website: www.lroymp.org.uk *Twitter:* @LindsayRoyMP

RUANE, CHRIS
Vale of Clwyd *(Majority 2,509)*

Christopher Shaun Ruane. Born 18 July 1958; Son of late Michael Ruane, labourer, and Esther Ruane; Married Gill Roberts 1994 (2 daughters).
Education: Blessed Edward Jones Comprehensive, Rhyl; University College of Wales, Aberystwyth (BSc (Econ) history and politics 1979); Liverpool University (PGCE 1980); Welsh (learner).
Non-political career: Primary school teacher Ysgol Mair, Rhyl 1982-97, Deputy head 1991-97. National Union of Teachers: School Rep 1982-97, President, West Clwyd 1991, Vale of Clwyd 1997.

LABOUR

Political career: Contested Clwyd North West 1992 general election. Member for Vale of Clwyd 1997-2010, for Vale of Clwyd (revised boundary) since 6 May 2010 general election; PPS: to Peter Hain as Secretary of State for Wales 2002-07, to Caroline Flint: as Minister of State, Department for Work and Pensions 2007-08, as Minister for Housing, Department for Communities and Local Government 2008, to David Miliband as Foreign Secretary 2009-10; PPS to Ed Balls: as Shadow Home Secretary 2010-11, as Shadow Chancellor 2011; Opposition Whip 2011-13. *Select committees:* Member: Welsh Affairs 1999-2002, Joint Committee on Statutory Instruments and Commons Committee on Statutory Instruments 2009-10, Home Affairs 2013-. PLP Welsh Regional Group: Vice-chair 2007-08, Chair 2008-. Member, Labour Group of Seaside MPs 1997-; Chair, North Wales Group of Labour MPs 2002-. *Councils and public bodies:* Councillor, Rhyl Town Council 1988-99.
Political interests: Regeneration of seaside towns, housing, electoral registration, anti-poverty, environment, tourism, mindfulness; Belize, Ireland, Vietnam.

Other: Member, British-Irish Parliamentary Assembly; Member, Steering Group forming Vale of Clwyd Credit Union; Founder member, Rhyl Anti Apartheid 1987; Rhyl Environmental Association: Founder member 1988, President; Founder member, Rhyl and District Amnesty International Group 1989; Chair, Rhyl City Strategy Consortium; Fellow, Industry and Parliament Trust 2001; President, North Wales Ramblers Association 2008-.

Recreations: Cooking, walking, reading, humour.

Chris Ruane MP, House of Commons, London SW1A 0AA
Tel: 020 7219 6378 *Email:* ruanec@parliament.uk
Constituency: 25 Kinmel Street, Rhyl, Clwyd LL18 1AH
Tel: 01745 354626 *Fax:* 01745 334827 *Website:* www.chrisruane.org *Twitter:* @chrisruanemp

RUDD, AMBER
Hastings and Rye *(Majority 1,993)*

Assistant Whip

Amber Augusta Rudd. Born 1 August 1963; Divorced (1 son 1 daughter).

Education: Queen's College, London; Edinburgh University (MA history 1986); French, German, Italian.

Non-political career: JPMorgan, London 1986-87; Director: Lawnstone Ltd 1988-97, MacArthur and Co 1997-99; Chief executive officer, Investors Noticeboard Ltd 1999-2001; Consultant, I-Search Ltd 2001-03; Columnist, *Corporate Financier* 2003-; Managing director and senior consultant, Lawnstone Ltd 2003-10.

CONSERVATIVE

Political career: Contested Liverpool Garston 2005 general election. Member for Hastings and Rye since 6 May 2010 general election; PPS to George Osborne as Chancellor of the Exchequer 2012-13; Assistant Whip 2013-. *Select committees:* Member: Environment, Food and Rural Affairs 2010-12.

Political interests: Welfare, transport, Department for Environment Food and Rural Affairs, economy.

Other: Substitute member, Parliamentary Assembly of the Council of Europe 2010-12; Trustee, The Snowdon Awards Scheme; Director, Susan Smith Blackburn Prize; Carlton.

Recreations: Theatre, cinema.

Amber Rudd MP, House of Commons, London SW1A 0AA
Tel: 020 7219 7229 *Email:* amber.rudd.mp@parliament.uk
Constituency: Creative Media Centre, 45 Robertson Street, Hastings, East Sussex TN34 1HL
Tel: 01424 205435 *Fax:* 01424 205401 *Email:* louisem.sargent@parliament.uk
Website: www.amberrudd.co.uk *Twitter:* @AmberRuddMP

RUDDOCK, JOAN
Lewisham Deptford *(Majority 12,499)*

Born 28 December 1943; Daughter of late Kenneth Anthony and Eileen Anthony; Married Keith Ruddock 1963 (separated 1990, he died 1996); married Frank Doran MP 2010.

Education: Pontypool Grammar School for Girls; Imperial College, London University (BSc botany 1965).

Non-political career: Director: research and publications, Shelter, National Campaign for Homeless 1968-73, Oxford Housing Aid Centre 1973-77; Special programmes officer (Manpower Services Commission) for unemployed young people, Berkshire County Council 1977-79; Manager, Citizens Advice Bureau, Reading 1979-86. Member, Unite.

LABOUR

Political career: Contested Newbury 1979 general election. Member for Lewisham Deptford 1987-2010, for Lewisham Deptford (revised boundary) since 6 May 2010 general election; Private Member's Bill on flytipping – Control of Pollution Act (amendment) 1989; Opposition Spokesperson for: Transport 1989-92, Home Affairs 1992-94, Environmental Protection 1994-97; Parliamentary Under-Secretary of State for Women 1997-98; Promoted: Ten-Minute-Rule Bill 1999, Prophylactic Mastectomy Registry Presentation Bill 1999, Organic Food and Farming Targets Bill 1999, Ten-Minute-Rule Bill 2000, Sex Discrimination (Amendment) No. 2, Ten-Minute-Rule Bill 2002, Waste Bill, Private Member's Bill – Municipal Waste, Recycling Bill 2003, (Household Waste Recycling Act 2003); Parliamentary Under-Secretary of State: Department for Environment, Food and Rural Affairs 2007-08, Department of Energy and Climate Change (DECC) 2008-09; Minister of State, DECC 2009-10; Shadow Minister for Energy and Climate Change 2010. *Select committees:* Member: Modernisation of the House of Commons 2001-05, Environment, Food and Rural Affairs 2003-05, International Development 2005-07. Vice-chair, PLP Women's Committee 2005-07; Honorary Treasurer, PLP London Regional Group 2005-08.

Political interests: Environment, Women, Foreign Affairs; Afghanistan, Palestine.
Other: Member, British Delegation to Council of Europe and Western European Union 1988-89; Inter-Parliamentary Union 2001-; Chair, CND 1981-85; ARCS 1965; FRSA 2012. Honorary Fellow: Goldsmith's College, London University; Laban, London. PC 2010; DBE 2012.
Recreations: Travel, music, gardening.
Rt Hon Dame Joan Ruddock MP, House of Commons, London SW1A 0AA
Tel: 020 7219 4513 *Fax:* 020 7219 6045 *Email:* joan.ruddock.mp@parliament.uk
Constituency: No constituency office publicised
Tel: 020 8691 5992/020 8691 1400 (Casework) *Fax:* 020 8691 8242
Website: www.joanruddock.org

RUFFLEY, DAVID
Bury St Edmunds *(Majority 12,380)*

David Laurie Ruffley. Born 18 April 1962; Son of Jack Ruffley, solicitor, and Yvonne Ruffley, née Harris; Single.
Education: Bolton Boys' School; Queens' College, Cambridge (BA law 1985).
Non-political career: Clifford Chance Solicitors, London 1985-91; Special adviser to Ken Clarke MP: as Secretary of State for Education and Science 1991-92, as Home Secretary 1992-93, as Chancellor of the Exchequer 1993-96; Strategic Economic Consultant to the Conservative Party 1996-97.

CONSERVATIVE

Political career: Member for Bury St Edmunds 1997-2010, for Bury St Edmunds (revised boundary) since 6 May 2010 general election; Opposition Whip 2004-05; Shadow Minister for: Work and Pensions 2005-07, Home Affairs 2007-10. *Select committees:* Member: Public Administration 1997-99, Treasury 1998-2004, 2005-06, 2010-, Joint Committee on the Draft Financial Services Bill 2011-12. Member, Executive, 1922 Committee 2003-04; Deputy Chairman, Economic Affairs Backbench Committee 2010-.
Political interests: Treasury, welfare reform, home affairs; Central Asia, Middle East, USA.
Other: Patron: West Suffolk Voluntary Association for the Blind, Bury and District Football League, Alzheimer's Society West Suffolk Branch, Bury St Edmunds Town Trust; Unpaid adviser to Grant Maintained Schools Foundation 1996-97; Fellow, British American Project 2002-; USA Department of State International Visitor Programme, Trade and Economic Development 2003; Member, advisory council, Centre for Policy Studies 2003-; Pratt's. Bury St Edmunds Golf Club.
Recreations: Football, cinema, golf, thinking.
David Ruffley MP, House of Commons, London SW1A 0AA
Tel: 020 7219 2880 *Fax:* 020 7219 3998 *Email:* ruffleyd@parliament.uk
Constituency: 10 Hatter Street, Bury St Edmunds, Suffolk IP33 1LZ
Email: info@telldavidruffley.com *Website:* www.davidruffleymp.com

RUSSELL, BOB
Colchester *(Majority 6,982)*

Robert Edward Russell. Born 31 March 1946; Son of late Ewart Russell and late Muriel Russell, née Sawdy; Married Audrey Blandon 1967 (twin sons 1 daughter 1 daughter deceased).
Education: St Helena Secondary Boys, Colchester; North-East Essex Technical College (Proficiency Certificate, National Council for the Training of Journalists 1966).
Non-political career: Trainee reporter, *Essex County Standard* and *Colchester Gazette* 1963-66; News editor, *Braintree and Witham Times* 1966-68; Editor, *Maldon and Burnham Standard* 1968-69; Sub-editor: London *Evening News* 1969-72, London *Evening Standard* 1972-73; Press officer, BT Eastern Region 1973-85; Publicity information officer, Essex University 1986-97. Branch secretary, North-Essex, National Union of Journalists 1967-68.

LIBERAL DEMOCRAT

Political career: Member for Colchester 1997-2010, for Colchester (revised boundary) since 6 May 2010 general election; Liberal Democrat: Spokesperson for: Home and Legal Affairs 1997-99, Sport 1999-2005; Whip 1999-2002, 2003-06, Shadow Minister for Defence 2005-10, Whip 2006-10; Member Speaker's Committee for the Independent Parliamentary Standards Authority 2010-. *Select committees:* Member: Home Affairs 1998-2005, 2006-10 Catering 2000-01, Regulatory Reform 2005-06, Armed Forces Bill 2005-06, 2011, Chairmen's Panel 2009-10, Administration 2010-11, Defence 2011-. Member: Labour Party 1966, SDP May 1981, Liberal Democrats since formation. *Councils and public bodies:* Colchester Borough Council: Councillor 1971-2002, Mayor 1986-87, Council Leader 1987-91, Honorary Alderman 2002.
Political interests: Environment, local and regional government, sport, transport, animal welfare, voluntary sector, youth organisations, defence; St Helena.

Other: Member: Oxfam, East of England Co-operative Society, Colchester Credit Union, Scout Association, National Trust, Essex Village Trust; Fellow, Industry and Parliament Trust 2005; Colchester Stars Cycle Speedway; St Mary Magdalen Hospital Almshouse Charity, Colchester. Journalists Prize, NEETC 1965; Outstanding Achievement (with David Amess MP and Stephen Pound MP), Charity Champion awards 2012. Kt 2012.

Recreations: Local history, walking, camping.

Sir Bob Russell MP, House of Commons, London SW1A 0AA
Tel: 020 7219 5150 *Email:* susan.hislop@parliament.uk
Constituency: Magdalen Hall, Wimpole Road, Colchester, Essex CO1 2DE
Tel: 01206 506600 *Fax:* 01206 506610 *Email:* info@bobrussell.org.uk
Website: www.bobrussell.org.uk

CONSERVATIVE

RUTLEY, DAVID
Macclesfield *(Majority 11,959)*

PPS to Damian Green as Minister of State for Policing and Criminal Justice, Home Office and Ministry of Justice

David Henry Rutley. Born 7 March 1961; Son of John Rutley and Birthe Anderson; Married Rachel (4 children).

Education: The Priory School, Lewes; London School of Economics (BSc Econ 1985); Harvard Business School (MBA 1989).

Non-political career: Business development director, PepsiCo International 1991-94; Special adviser 1994-96: Cabinet office, Ministry of Agriculture, HM Treasury; Director of business effectiveness, Safeway Stores 1996-2000; ASDA stores 2000-05: Director of Financial Services, Director of E-commerce; Sales and marketing director, Halifax General Insurance 2005-07; Barclays Bank 2008-10: Business consultant 2008-09, Marketing director 2009-10.

Political career: Contested St Albans 1997 general election. Member for Macclesfield since 6 May 2010 general election; PPS to Damian Green as Minister of State for: Immigration, Home Office 2010-12, Policing and Criminal Justice, Home Office and Ministry of Justice 2012-. *Select committees:* Member: Treasury 2010.

Political interests: Economy, business, home affairs, rural issues, community groups; China, Denmark, Slovenia, USA.

Other: Trustee, Kids Count 1988; Member: British Mountaineering Council, RSPB, National Trust; Many charities in Macclesfield including: NSPCC (East Cheshire Branch), Macclesfield Silk Museum Trust, Just Drop In, Macclesfield Community Garden Centre, Poynton Royal British Legion Concert Band.

Recreations: Spending time with family, walking and climbing in the Peak District, mountaineering, fishing, ornithology.

David Rutley MP, House of Commons, London SW1A 0AA
Tel: 020 7219 7106 *Email:* david.rutley.mp@parliament.uk
Constituency: c/o Macclesfield Conservative Association, West Bank Road, Macclesfield, Cheshire SK10 3BT
Tel: 01625 422848 *Fax:* 01625 617066 *Email:* mcatory@btconnect.com
Website: www.macclesfieldconservatives.com www.davidrutley.org.uk
Twitter: @DavidRutleyMP

LIBERAL DEMOCRAT

SANDERS, ADRIAN
Torbay *(Majority 4,078)*

Adrian Mark Sanders. Born 25 April 1959; Son of late John Sanders, insurance official, and Helen Sanders, nurse; Married Alison Nortcliffe 1991.

Education: Torquay Boys' Grammar School.

Non-political career: Parliamentary officer, Liberal Democrat Whips' Office 1989-90; Association of Liberal Democrat Councillors 1990-92; Policy officer, National Council for Voluntary Organisations 1992-93; Assistant to Paddy Ashdown MP as Liberal Democrat Party Leader 1992-93; Southern Association of Voluntary Action Groups for Europe 1993-97.

Political career: Contested Torbay 1992 general election. Member for Torbay 1997-2010, for Torbay (revised boundary) since 6 May 2010 general election; Liberal Democrat: Whip 1997-2001, Spokesperson for: Housing 1997-2001, Environment, Transport, the Regions and Social Justice 1999-2001, Transport, Local Government and the Regions (Local Government) 2001-02, Tourism 2002-05, Whip 2006-10: Deputy Chief Whip 2006-10. *Select committees:* Member:

Joint Committee on Consolidation of Bills Etc 1997-2001, Office of the Deputy Prime Minister 2003-05, Office of the Deputy Prime Minister (Urban Affairs Sub-Committee) 2003-05, Culture, Media and Sport 2005-13, Selection 2006-10, Modernisation of the House of Commons 2006-08, Transport 2013-. Contested Devon and East Plymouth 1994 European Parliament election. Vice-President, National League of Young Liberals 1985; Political secretary, Devon and Cornwall Regional Liberal Party 1983-84; Information officer, Association of Liberal Councillors 1986-89. *Councils and public bodies:* Councillor, Torbay Borough Council 1984-86.

Political interests: Local and regional government, voluntary sector, tourism, diabetes; Australasia, Indian sub-continent, USA.

Other: Member: CPA 1997-, IPU 1997-, British American Parliamentary Group 1997-; Vice-chair, Commonwealth Parliamentary Association (UK Branch) 2010-11; Diabetes UK; Paignton Preservation Society.

Recreations: Football, music.

Adrian Sanders MP, House of Commons, London SW1A 0AA
Tel: 020 7219 6304 *Fax:* 020 7219 1128 *Email:* sandersa@parliament.uk
Constituency: 69 Belgrave Road, Torquay, Devon TQ2 5HZ
Tel: 01803 200036 *Fax:* 01803 200031 *Website:* www.adriansanders.org
Twitter: @AdrianSandersMP

CONSERVATIVE

SANDYS, LAURA
South Thanet *(Majority 7,617)*

PPS to Gregory Barker as Minister of State for Climate Change, Department of Energy and Climate Change

Laura Jane Sandys. Born 1964; Daughter of late Duncan Sandys, former MP, later Lord Duncan-Sandys, and Marie-Claire, née Schmitt; Married Randolph Kent.

Education: Cambridge University (MSt international relations).

Non-political career: Parliamentary officer, Consumers Association; Owned two businesses, specialising in marketing, campaigning and communications; Senior research associate, Centre for Defence Studies, King's College, London; Consultant, Baku-Ceyhan Pipeline Project, Government of Georgia.

Political career: Member for South Thanet since 6 May 2010 general election; Member Speaker's Committee for the Independent Parliamentary Standards Authority 2010-; PPS to Gregory Barker as Minister of State for Climate Change, Department of Energy and Climate Change 2012-. *Select committees:* Member: Energy and Climate Change 2010-12, Joint Committee on the Draft House of Lords Reform Bill 2011-12, Ecclesiastical Committee 2012-. Member: Quality of Life Taskforce, Conservative Party, Democracy Taskforce, Conservative Party; Patron, Tory Reform Group.

Political interests: Small businesses, care of the elderly, defence policy, green economy, food security, trade.

Other: Deputy chair, Civic Trust; Trustee, Open University; Chair, Open Democracy; Vice-President, Protect Kent; Director: Policy Connect, Open Democracy; President, Kent Federation of Amenity Societies.

Laura Sandys MP, House of Commons, London SW1A 0AA
Tel: 020 7219 3000 *Email:* laura.sandys.mp@parliament.uk
Constituency: 16a Grange Road, Ramsgate CT11 9LR
Tel: 01843 589434 *Email:* laura@sandys.org.uk *Website:* www.telllaura.org.uk
Twitter: @LauraSandysMP

LABOUR

SARWAR, ANAS
Glasgow Central *(Majority 10,551)*

Born 14 March 1983; Son of Mohammed Sarwar, MP 1997-2010, and Perveen Sarwar; Married (2 sons).

Education: Hutchesons' Grammar School, Glasgow; Glasgow University; Urdu.

Non-political career: Dentist, NHS, Glasgow. Member: Unite, Community.

Political career: Member for Glasgow Central since 6 May 2010 general election. *Select committees:* Member: International Development 2010-12, Arms Export Controls 2010-12. Vice-chair, PLP Departmental Group for International Development 2010-12. Contested Glasgow region (1) 2007 Scottish Parliament election. Member, Labour Party 1999-; Deputy Leader, Scottish Labour 2011-.

Political interests: The economy, foreign policy, international development, work and pensions; Scotland.

Other: Founder and former co-ordinator, Y-Vote; Former vice-chair, Progress; International Rescue Committee.

Anas Sarwar MP, House of Commons, London SW1A 0AA
Tel: 020 7219 7076 *Email:* anas.sarwar.mp@parliament.uk
Constituency: 9 Scotland Street, Glasgow G5 8NB
Tel: 0141-429 6027 *Website:* www.anassarwar.org *Twitter:* @AnasSarwar

SAWFORD, ANDY
Corby *(Majority 7,791)*

Shadow Minister for Communities and Local Government

LAB/CO-OP

Andrew Sawford. Born 15 March 1976; Son of Phil Sawford, MP for Kettering 1997-2005, and Rosemary Sawford, née Stokes; Married Jo (2 children).

Education: Montsaye Comprehensive, Rothwell, Northamptonshire; Durham University (history 1997).

Non-political career: Office of Phil Hope MP; Director: Small consultancy business, Connect Public Affairs 2003-08; Chief executive, Local Government Information Unit 2008-12; Chair, Local Energy Ltd. Community; Unite.

Political career: Member for Corby since 15 November 2012 by-election; PPS to Stephen Twigg as Shadow Secretary of State for Education 2013-; Shadow Minister for Communities and Local Government 2013-. *Select committees:* Member: Communities and Local Government 2012-. Member: Labour Party, Co-operative Party.

Political interests: Education and skills, health, employment.

Other: Director: Centre for Public Scrutiny, Centre for Public Service Partnerships; Fellow, Royal Society of Arts.

Andy Sawford MP, House of Commons, London SW1A 0AA
Tel: 020 7219 6134 *Email:* andy.sawford.mp@parliament.uk
Constituency: Grosvenor House, George Street, Corby, Northamptonshire NN17 1QB
Tel: 01536 264194 *Website:* www.andysawford.wordpress.com *Twitter:* @AndySawford

SCOTT, LEE
Ilford North *(Majority 5,404)*

PPS to Chris Grayling as Lord Chancellor and Secretary of State for Justice

CONSERVATIVE

Born 6 April 1956; Son of late Sydney and Renne Scott; Married Estelle Dombey, née King 1987 (3 daughters 2 sons).

Education: Clarks College, Ilford, Essex; College of Distributive Trades, London.

Non-political career: Director, Scott and Fishell 1972-82; Selfridges 1975-80; Tatung 1980-82; Sales executive: Toshiba 1982-84, ITT 1984-86, NKR 1986-88; Campaign director/provincial director, United Jewish Israel Appeal 1988-98; Director, Scott Associates 1998-.

Political career: Contested Waveney 2001 general election. Member for Ilford North 2005-10, for Ilford North (revised boundary) since 6 May 2010 general election; PPS to: Philip Hammond as Secretary of State for Transport (resigned) 2010, Chris Grayling as Lord Chancellor and Secretary of State for Justice 2012-. *Select committees:* Member: Transport 2005-08, Health 2007-10, Panel of Chairs 2011-12. Deputy chair (political), Ilford North CC 1998-99; Essex area chairman, Conservative Friends of Israel 2001-. *Councils and public bodies:* London Borough of Redbridge: Councillor 1998-2006, Cabinet member for regeneration and the community 2002.

Political interests: Trade and industry, community issues, transport, the Tamil community; Middle East, Sri Lanka.

Other: Committee member, Victim Support Redbridge 1999-.

Recreations: Music, reading, sport.

Lee Scott MP, House of Commons, London SW1A 0AA
Tel: 020 7219 8326 *Fax:* 020 7219 0970 *Email:* scottle@parliament.uk
Constituency: 9 Sevenways Parade, Gants Hill, Ilford, Essex IG2 6XH
Website: www.leescott.co.uk

MPs' BIOGRAPHIES [S] **333**

LABOUR

SEABECK, ALISON

Plymouth, Moor View *(Majority 1,588)*

Shadow Minister for Defence

Alison Jane Seabeck. Born 20 January 1954; Daughter of Lilian Ward, née Lomas, and late Michael John Ward, MP for Peterborough October 1974-79; Married Denis Seabeck 1975 (divorced 2007) (2 daughters); Married Nick Raynsford MP 2012.

Education: Harold Hill Grammar School, Romford; North East London Polytechnic (general studies).

Non-political career: Member, Armed Forces Parliamentary Scheme. Various posts including Marks and Spencer management trainee, employment consultant, PA to college of further education principal; Parliamentary assistant to Roy Hattersley MP 1987-92; Adviser to Nick Raynsford MP 1992-2005. Member: Amicus/Unite, GMB.

Political career: Member for Plymouth Devonport 2005-10, for Plymouth, Moor View since 6 May 2010 general election; PPS to Geoff Hoon as Minister of State for Europe 2006-07; Assistant Government Whip 2007-08; PPS to Geoff Hoon as Secretary of State for Transport 2008-09; Shadow Minister for: Housing 2010-11, Defence 2011-. *Select committees:* Member: ODPM/Communities and Local Government 2005-06, Regulatory Reform 2005-07, Communities and Local Government 2009-10; Chair: South West 2009-10; Member: Backbench Business 2010, Defence 2010. Vice-chair, PLP Departmental Committee for ODPM/Communities and Local Government 2005-10; Chair, PLP South West Regional Group 2007, 2009-10; Vice-chair, PLP Departmental Group for Transport 2010-. Member: Labour Women's Network, South London Co-operative Party 2001-06, South West Co-operative Party 2006-.

Political interests: Local government, construction, housing, defence; Australia, Europe, India, Pakistan.

Other: Member, Fawcett Society; Parliamentary convener, London Housing Group 2006-07; Patron: Devon Lupus Group 2006-, 47th Plymouth Scouts 2006-09, Plymouth YMCA.

Recreations: Travelling, swimming, reading, gardening, photography.

Alison Seabeck MP, House of Commons, London SW1A 0AA
Tel: 020 7219 6431 *Fax:* 020 7219 0883 *Email:* alison.seabeck.mp@parliament.uk
Constituency: No constituency office publicised
Tel: 01752 365617 *Email:* jamessi@parliament.uk *Website:* www.alisonseabeck.org.uk
Twitter: @AlisonSeabeck

CONSERVATIVE

SELOUS, ANDREW

South West Bedfordshire *(Majority 16,649)*

PPS to Iain Duncan Smith as Secretary of State for Work and Pensions

Andrew Edmund Armstrong Selous. Born 27 April 1962; Son of Commander Gerald Selous and Miranda Selous, née Casey; Married Harriet Marston 1993 (3 daughters).

Education: Eton College; London School of Economics (BSc Econ industry and trade 1984); French, German.

Non-political career: TA officer, Honourable Artillery Company, Royal Regiment of Fusiliers 1981-94. Director, CNS Electronics Ltd 1988-94; Underwriter, Great Lakes Re (UK) plc 1991-2001.

Political career: Contested Sunderland North 1997 general election. Member for South West Bedfordshire since 7 June 2001 general election; PPS to Michael Ancram as Shadow Foreign Secretary 2004; Opposition Whip 2004-06; Shadow Minister for Work and Pensions 2006-10; PPS to Iain Duncan Smith as Secretary of State for Work and Pensions 2010-. *Select committees:* Member: Work and Pensions 2001-05, Ecclesiastical Committee 2010-. Chair, Conservative Christian Fellowship 2001-06.

Political interests: Trade and industry, families, defence, homelessness; Australia, Nicaragua, USA.

Other: ACII 1993; Chartered Insurer 1998; Community family trusts; Parkinsons UK; Homestart; Leighton Linslade Homeless; Brain Tumour Action; Leighton Buzzard Conservative, Dunstable Conservative.

Recreations: Family, walking, tennis, bridge.

Andrew Selous MP, House of Commons, London SW1A 0AA
Tel: 020 7219 8134 *Fax:* 020 7219 1741 *Email:* andrew.selous.mp@parliament.uk
Constituency: 6c Princes Street, Dunstable, Bedfordshire LU6 3AX
Tel: 01582 662821 *Fax:* 01582 476619 *Website:* www.andrewselous.org.uk
Twitter: @Andrew_SelousMP

**DEMOCRATIC
UNIONIST PARTY**

SHANNON, JIM
Strangford *(Majority 5,876)*

DUP Spokesperson for Health, for Transport and for Equality and Human Rights

Richard James Shannon. Born 25 March 1955; Son of Richard and Moira Shannon, both retired; Married Sandra George 1987 (3 sons).

Education: Coleraine Academical Institution (1971); Ulster-Scots.

Non-political career: Ulster Defence Regiment 1973-75, 1976-77; Royal Artillery, TA 1977-88. Self-employed pork retailer 1985-. Member: Mid Ards Branch, Ulster Farmers' Union, Transport and General Workers' Union (TGWU) 1976-85.

Political career: Member for Strangford since 6 May 2010 general election; DUP Spokesperson for: Health 2010-, Transport 2010-, Equality and Human Rights 2012-; Member Northern Ireland Forum for Political Dialogue 1996-98; MLA for Strangford 1998-2010. *Councils and public bodies:* Ards Borough Council: Councillor 1985-2010, Mayor 1991-92.

Political interests: Farming, fishing, environment, Ulster-Scots; Scotland, USA.

Other: Secretary, Loyal Orange Institution, Kircubbin LOL 1900; Registrar, Royal Black Perceptory Ballywater No 675; Comber, Apprentice Boys of Derry; Member: British Association Shooting and Conservation, Countryside Alliance NI, Royal British Legion, Greyabbey Branch, National Trust; NSPCC; Action Cancer. General Service Medal, Ulster Defence Regiment. Carrowdore Shooting Club.

Recreations: Fieldsports, football.

Jim Shannon MP, House of Commons, London SW1A 0AA
Tel: 020 7219 7160 *Fax:* 020 7219 2347 *Email:* jim.shannon.mp@parliament.uk
Constituency: 34a Frances Street, Newtownards, Co Down BT23 7DN
Tel: 028 9182 7990 *Fax:* 028 9182 7991

CONSERVATIVE

SHAPPS, GRANT
Welwyn Hatfield *(Majority 17,423)*

Minister without Portfolio, Cabinet Office; Chairman, Conservative Party

Grant V Shapps. Born 14 September 1968; Son of Tony and Beryl Shapps; Married Belinda Goldstone 1997 (1 son twin son and daughter).

Education: Watford Boys' Grammar School; Cassio College, Watford (OND business and finance 1987); Manchester Polytechnic (HND business and finance 1989).

Non-political career: Sales executive, Nashua Gestetner 1989-90; Printhouse Corporation: Founder 1990-, Chairman 2000-.

Political career: Contested North Southwark and Bermondsey 1997 and Welwyn Hatfield 2001 general elections. Member for Welwyn Hatfield since 5 May 2005 general election; Shadow Minister for Housing (attending Shadow Cabinet) 2007-10; Minister of State for Housing and Local Government, Department for Communities and Local Government 2010-12; Member Speaker's Committee on the Electoral Commission 2010-12; Minister without Portfolio, Cabinet Office 2012-. *Select committees:* Member: Public Administration 2005-07. Branch chair, Barnhill, Brent North 1995-99; Member: Conservative Friends of Israel 1995, Selsdon Group 1996, Conservative Foreign Affairs Forum 1996; Vice-President, North Southwark and Bermondsey Association 1997; Vice-chair, (Campaigning) Conservative Party 2005-09; Chairman, Conservative Party 2012-.

Political interests: Health, education, home affairs, foreign affairs.

Other: Isabel Hospice; Resolve; Hertfordshire Action on Disability; Mixed Group. MP Contribution to Central Lobby, *PoliticsHome* awards 2012. PC 2010.

Rt Hon Grant Shapps MP, House of Commons, London SW1A 0AA
Tel: 020 7219 8497 *Email:* shappsg@parliament.uk
Constituency: Welwyn Hatfield Conservative Association, Maynard House, The Common, Hatfield, Hertfordshire AL10 0NF
Tel: 01707 262632 *Fax:* 01707 263892 *Email:* sandra@welhatconservatives.com
Website: www.shapps.com *Twitter:* @grantshapps @ToryChairman

---

CONSERVATIVE

SHARMA, ALOK

Reading West *(Majority 6,004)*

Born 7 September 1967; Married (2 daughters).
Education: Blue Coat School, Reading; Salford University (BSc applied physics with electronics 1988); Institute of Chartered Accountants in England and Wales (ACA 1991).
Non-political career: Chartered accountant; Accountancy and corporate finance advice.
Political career: Member for Reading West since 6 May 2010 general election; PPS to Mark Hoban as Financial Secretary 2010-12. *Select committees:* Member: Science and Technology 2010-11. Conservative Party: Member 1978-, Vice-chairman (BME communities) 2012-.
Political interests: Trade, industry, finance; India, Pakistan, Sweden.
Other: Former chair, economic affairs committee, Bow Group; Fellow, Royal Society for the encouragement of Arts, Manufacturing and Commerce; Member, Institute of Chartered Accountants in England and Wales.
Alok Sharma MP, House of Commons, London SW1A 0AA
Tel: 020 7219 7131 *Email:* alok.sharma.mp@parliament.uk
Constituency: 16c Upton Road, Tilehurst, Reading, Berkshire RG30 4BJ
Tel: 0118-941 3803 *Website:* www.aloksharma.co.uk

LABOUR

SHARMA, VIRENDRA

Ealing Southall *(Majority 9,291)*

Virendra Kumar Sharma. Born 5 April 1947; Married Nirmala (1 son 1 daughter).
Education: London School of Economics (MA 1979); Punjabi, Hindi, Urdu.
Non-political career: Day services manager, London Borough of Hillingdon 1996-2007. Member, Transport and General Workers' Union (TGWU)/Unite.
Political career: Member for Ealing Southall 17 July 2007 by-election to 2010, Ealing Southall (revised boundary) since 6 May 2010 general election; PPS to Phil Woolas as Minister of State, Home Office and HM Treasury 2008-09. *Select committees:* Member: Joint Committee on Human Rights 2007-10, 2010-, Justice 2007-09, International Development 2009-10, Health 2010-. Labour Party National Ethnic Minorities Officer 1986-92. *Councils and public bodies:* Councillor London Borough of Ealing 1982-: Former Mayor.
Countries of interest: Bangladesh, Canada, Cyprus, India, Mauritius, Nepal, Pakistan, Sri Lanka, USA.
Other: Member, Indian Workers Association; Age UK.
Virendra Sharma MP, House of Commons, London SW1A 0AA
Tel: 020 7219 6080 *Fax:* 020 7219 3969 *Email:* sharmav@parliament.uk
Constituency: 112a The Green, Southall, Middlesex UB2 4BQ
Tel: 020 8571 1003 *Fax:* 020 8571 9991 *Website:* www.virendrasharma.com
Twitter: @VirendraSharma

LAB/CO-OP

SHEERMAN, BARRY

Huddersfield *(Majority 4,472)*

Barry John Sheerman. Born 17 August 1940; Son of late Albert Sheerman and Florence Sheerman, née Pike; Married Pamela Brenchley 1965 (1 son 3 daughters).
Education: Hampton Grammar School; Kingston Technical College (economics and politics); London School of Economics (BSc economics 1965); London University (MSc political sociology 1967); French.
Non-political career: Lecturer, University College of Wales, Swansea 1966-79. Member: AUT, Amicus.
Political career: Contested Taunton October 1974 general election. Member for Huddersfield East 1979-83, for Huddersfield 1983-2010, for Huddersfield (revised boundary) since 6 May 2010 general election; Opposition Spokesperson for: Employment and Education 1983-88, Home Affairs 1988-92, Disabled People's Rights 1992-94; Chair Cross-Party Advisory Group on Preparation for EMU 1998-; Vice-chair Joint Pre-Legislative Committee Investigating the Financial Services and Markets Bill 1998-; Chair Cross-Party Advisory Group to Chancellor of the Exchequer on European Economic Reform. *Select committees:* Chair: Education and Employment (Education Sub-Committee) 1999-2001; Member: Liaison 1999-2010, Education and Employment (Employment Sub-Committee) 2000-01; Chair: Education and Skills/Children, Schools and Families 2001-10; Member: Liaison (Liaison Sub-Committee) 2002-10. Member, Co-operative Party; Chair, Labour Forum for Criminal Justice. *Councils and public bodies:* Councillor, Loughor and Lliw Valley Unitary District Council 1972-79.

Political interests: Trade, industry, finance, further education, education, economy, social enterprise and entrepreneurship; European Union, Kenya, South America, USA.

Other: World Bank Business Partnership for Development Global Road Safety Partnership (GRSP); Chair: Parliamentary Advisory Council on Transport Safety 1981-, National Educational Research and Development Trust; Fellow, Industry and Parliament Trust 1982, 1996; Chair: Urban Mines 1995-, Networking for Industry/Policy Connect 1995-, Schools to Work; Governor, London School of Economics 1995-; Director and trustee, National Children's Centre; Chair, John Clare Education and Environment Trust 2004-; FRSA, FRGS, City and Guilds Institute; National Children's Centre; John Clare Trust; Dominic Rogers Trust. Two honorary doctorates. Member, Royal Commonwealth Club.

Publications: Co-author, Harold Laski: A Life on the Left (1993).

Recreations: Walking, biography, films, social entrepreneurship.

Barry Sheerman MP, House of Commons, London SW1A 0AA
Tel: 020 7219 5037 *Fax:* 020 7219 2404 *Email:* sheermanb@parliament.uk
Constituency: Office F18, The Media Centre, 7 Northumberland Street, Huddersfield,
West Yorkshire HD1 1RL
Tel: 01484 487970 *Email:* osullivang@parliament.uk *Website:* www.barrysheerman.co.uk
Twitter: @bsheermanmp

CONSERVATIVE

SHELBROOKE, ALEC
Elmet and Rothwell *(Majority 4,521)*

Alec Edward Shelbrooke. Born 10 January 1976; Son of Cllr Derek Shelbrooke and Patricia Shelbrooke JP, both retired teachers; Married Susan Shelbrooke.

Education: St George's CoE Comprehensive School, Gravesend; Brunel University (BSc mechanical engineering 1998).

Non-political career: Project Manager, Leeds University 1999-2010. Member, MSF/Unite 1999-2010.

Political career: Contested Wakefield 2005 general election. Member for Elmet and Rothwell since 6 May 2010 general election; PPS to: Theresa Villiers as Minister of State, Department for Transport 2010-12, Mike Penning as Minister of State, Northern Ireland Office 2012-13; Deputy Chair, Elmet Conservative Association 2001-04. *Councils and public bodies:* Councillor, Leeds City Council 2004-10.

Political interests: Foreign affairs, transport, welfare, international aid; Middle East, USA.

Other: Member: Institute of Mechanical Engineers 1994-, Association of Project Managers 2001-11; Martin House; Lee's Smile; Carlton.

Recreations: Football, motor racing, cricket, music, reading.

Alec Shelbrooke MP, House of Commons, London SW1A 0AA
Tel: 020 7219 3000 *Email:* alec.shelbrooke.mp@parliament.uk
Constituency: First Floor, 43 Market Place, Wetherby, Leeds LS22 6LN
Tel: 01937 589002 *Email:* conservatives@elmetandrothwell.com
Website: www.elmetandrothwell.com www.alecshelbrooke.co.uk *Twitter:* @AlecShelbrooke

CONSERVATIVE

SHEPHERD, RICHARD
Aldridge-Brownhills *(Majority 15,266)*

Richard Charles Scrimgeour Shepherd. Born 6 December 1942; Son of late Alfred Shepherd and Davida Shepherd, née Wallace.

Education: Isleworth Grammar School, Middlesex; London School of Economics (BSc 1964; MSc 1967); John Hopkins School of Advanced International Studies (Diploma economics 1965).

Non-political career: Aide to Peter Walker MP 1970; Director, Partridges (retail food business), London 1972-; Underwriter, Lloyd's 1974-94; Personal assistant to Edward Taylor MP (Glasgow Cathcart) October 1974 general election.

Political career: Contested Nottingham East February 1974 general election. Member for Aldridge-Brownhills 1979-2010, for Aldridge-Brownhills (revised boundary) since 6 May 2010 general election; Introduced four Private Member's Bills: The Crown Immunity Bill 1986, Protection of Official Information Bill 1988, The Referendum Bill 1992, Public Interest Disclosure Bill; Contested Commons Speaker election 2000, 2009. *Select committees:* Member: Modernisation of the House of Commons 1997-2010, Public Administration 1997-2000, Joint Committee on Human Rights 2001-. Secretary, European Affairs, Industry Committees 1980-81; Vice-chair,

Conservative Party Committee for Constitutional Affairs, Scotland and Wales 1997-. Conservative Whip suspended Nov 1994-March 1995 (voted against Government on European Communities (Finance) Bill). *Councils and public bodies:* Member: South East Economic Planning Council 1970-74, Court of Governors, London School of Economics.
Political interests: Freedom of information, abuse of executive power, EU.
Other: Co-Chair, Campaign for Freedom of Information. *The Spectator:* Backbencher of the Year 1987, Parliamentarian of the Year 1995; Campaign for Freedom of Information 1988. Knighted 2013; Beefsteak, Chelsea Arts, Garrick.
Sir Richard Shepherd MP, House of Commons, London SW1A 0AA
Tel: 020 7219 5004 *Fax:* 020 7219 0083 *Email:* shepherdr@parliament.uk
Constituency: 82 Walsall Road, Aldridge, Walsall, West Midlands WS9 0JW
Tel: 01922 452228 *Fax:* 01922 452228 *Email:* ald-browncons@tory.org

LABOUR

SHERIDAN, JIM   Paisley and Renfrewshire North *(Majority 15,280)*

James Sheridan. Born 24 November 1952; Married Jean McDowell 1977 (1 son 1 daughter).
Education: St Pius Secondary School.
Non-political career: Print room assistant, Beaverbrook Newspapers 1967-70; Semi-skilled painter, Barcley Curle 1970-74; M/C operator, Bowater Containers 1974-79; Semi-skilled painter, Yarrow Shipbuilders 1982-84; Material handler, Pilkington Optronics 1984-99. TGWU 1984-: Convener 1984-99, Stand down official 1998-99.
Political career: Member for West Renfrewshire 2001-05, for Paisley and Renfrewshire North since 5 May 2005 general election; Team PPS, Ministry of Defence 2005-06 (resigned over Lebanon conflict). *Select committees:* Member: Information 2001-04, Broadcasting 2003-05, Public Accounts 2003-05, Armed Forces Bill 2005-06, International Development 2007-09, Chairmen's Panel/Panel of Chairs 2009-, Culture, Media and Sport 2010-. PLP Scottish Regional Group: Vice-chair 2008, Chair 2008-10. *Councils and public bodies:* Renfrewshire Council: Councillor 1999-2003, Chair, Scrutiny Board.
Political interests: Employment rights, welfare, defence, social affairs and foreign affairs; Cyprus, Nigeria, Saudi Arabia.
Other: Inchinnan Community Association.
Recreations: Keep fit, golf, football.
Jim Sheridan MP, House of Commons, London SW1A 0AA
Tel: 020 7219 8314 *Email:* sheridanj@parliament.uk
Constituency: Mirren Court Three, Ground Floor, 123 Renfrew Road, Paisley, Renfrewshire PA3 4EA
Tel: 0141-847 1457 *Fax:* 0141-847 1395 *Email:* enquiries@jimsheridanmp.org.uk
Website: www.jimsheridanmp.org.uk *Twitter:* @JimSheridanMP

LAB/CO-OP

SHUKER, GAVIN   Luton South *(Majority 2,329)*

Shadow Minister for International Development

Gavin Paul Shuker. Born 10 October 1981; Married Lucie 2007.
Education: Icknield High School; Luton Sixth Form College; Girton College, Cambridge (BA social and political science 2003).
Non-political career: Associate pastor, City Life Church, Cambridge 2003-06; Charity worker, Fusion UK 2003-08; Endis Ltd 2008-10; Church leader, City Life Church, Luton 2006-. Member, USDAW.
Political career: Member for Luton South since 6 May 2010 general election; PPS to Sadiq Khan as Shadow Lord Chancellor and Secretary of State for Justice 2010-11; Shadow Minister for: Environment, Food and Rural Affairs 2011-13, International Development 2013-. *Select committees:* Member: Transport 2010-11.
Political interests: Political engagement, electoral reform, child poverty, student funding, transport policy (especially rail), international development, debt reduction, civil liberties; Bangladesh, India, Ireland, Pakistan, Poland, Portugal.
Recreations: Cooking, real ale, church, formula one.
Gavin Shuker MP, House of Commons, London SW1A 0AA
Tel: 020 7219 1130 *Email:* gavin.shuker.mp@parliament.uk
Constituency: 3 Union Street, Luton, Bedfordshire LU1 3AN
Tel: 01582 457774 *Fax:* 01582 480990 *Email:* office@gavinshuker.org
Website: www.gavinshuker.org *Twitter:* @gavinshuker

CONSERVATIVE

SIMMONDS, MARK
Boston and Skegness *(Majority 12,426)*

Parliamentary Under-Secretary of State, Foreign and Commonwealth Office

Mark Jonathan Mortlock Simmonds. Born 12 April 1964; Son of Neil Mortlock Simmonds, teacher, and Mary Griffith Simmonds, née Morgan, teacher; Married Lizbeth Hanomancin-Garcia 1994 (2 daughters 1 son).

Education: Worksop College, Nottinghamshire; Trent Polytechnic (BSc urban estate surveying 1986).

Non-political career: Surveyor, Savills 1986-88; Partner, Strutt and Parker 1988-96; Director, Hillier Parker 1997-99; Chair, MSb Ltd 1999-.

Political career: Contested Ashfield 1997 general election. Member for Boston and Skegness 2001-10, for Boston and Skegness (revised boundary) since 6 May 2010 general election; Shadow Minister for: Public Services, Health and Education 2003-04, Education 2004, Foreign Affairs 2004-05, International Development 2005-07, Health 2007-10; PPS to Caroline Spelman as Secretary of State for Environment, Food and Rural Affairs 2010-12; Parliamentary Under-Secretary of State, Foreign and Commonwealth Office 2012-. *Select committees:* Member: Environmental Audit 2001-03, Education and Skills 2001-03. *Councils and public bodies:* London Borough of Wandsworth 1990-94: Councillor, Chair: Property Committee 1991-92, Housing Committee 1992-94.

Political interests: Economy, education, agriculture, foreign affairs, health; Latin America.

Recreations: Reading, history, rugby, tennis, family.

Mark Simmonds MP, House of Commons, London SW1A 0AA
Tel: 020 7219 8143 *Fax:* 020 7219 1746 *Email:* mark.simmonds.mp@parliament.uk
Constituency: 5 Church Close, Boston, Lincolnshire PE21 6NA
Tel: 01205 751414 *Fax:* 01205 751414 *Website:* www.marksimmonds.org
Twitter: @MarkJSimmonds

DEMOCRATIC UNIONIST PARTY

SIMPSON, DAVID
Upper Bann *(Majority 3,361)*

DUP Spokesperson for Business, Innovation and Skills, for Communities and Local Government, and for Education

Thomas David Simpson. Born 16 February 1959; Married Elaine Elizabeth (1 adopted son 2 adopted daughters).

Education: Killicomaine High School; College of Business Studies, Belfast.

Non-political career: Food manufacturing industry; Senior partner, Universal Meat Company.

Political career: Contested Upper Bann 2001 general election. Member for Upper Bann since 5 May 2005 general election; DUP Spokesperson for: Trade and Industry 2005-07, Young People 2007-10, Transport 2007-09, International Development 2007-10, Business, Innovation and Skills 2009-, Communities and Local Government 2010-, Education 2012-. *Select committees:* Member: Joint Committee on Statutory Instruments and Commons Committee on Statutory Instruments 2006-09, Transport 2007-09, Northern Ireland Affairs 2009-. Northern Ireland Assembly: MLA for Upper Bann 2003-10; Chair, Committee on Social Development 2008-09. DUP: Vice-President; Vice-Chairman: Victims Committee, Council Association; Chairman, Upper Bann Constituency Association. *Councils and public bodies:* Craigavon Borough Council: Councillor 2001-10, Deputy Mayor 2003-04, Mayor 2004-05; Member, Northern Ireland Policing Board 2007-08.

Political interests: History of politics; Africa, Israel.

Other: Deputy Master, Loughall District Loyal Orange Order.

David Simpson MP, House of Commons, London SW1A 0AA
Tel: 020 7219 8533 *Fax:* 020 7219 2347 *Email:* simpsond@parliament.uk
Constituency: 13 Thomas Street, Portadown BT62 3NP
Tel: 028 3833 2234 *Fax:* 028 3833 2123 *Email:* davidsimpson@upperbanndup.co.uk
Website: www.davidsimpsonmp.co.uk

CONSERVATIVE

SIMPSON, KEITH
Broadland *(Majority 7,292)*

PPS to William Hague as First Secretary of State, Secretary of State for Foreign and Commonwealth Affairs

Keith Robert Simpson. Born 29 March 1949; Son of Harry Simpson and Jean Simpson, née Day; Married Pepita Hollingsworth 1984 (1 son).

Education: Thorpe Grammar School, Norfolk; Hull University (BA history 1970); King's College, University of London.

Non-political career: Honorary Colonel Royal Military Police TA 1998-2007. Senior lecturer in war studies, RMA Sandhurst 1973-86; Head of foreign affairs and defence section, Conservative Research Department 1987-88; Special adviser to George Younger MP and Tom King MP as Secretaries of State for Defence 1988-90; Director, Cranfield Security Studies Institute, Cranfield University 1991-97.

Political career: Contested Plymouth Devonport 1992 general election. Member for Mid Norfolk 1997-2010, for Broadland since 6 May 2010 general election; Opposition Spokesperson for Defence 1998-99; Opposition Whip 1999-2001; Opposition Spokesperson for Environment, Food and Rural Affairs 2001-02; Shadow Minister for: Defence 2002-05, Foreign Affairs 2005-10; PPS to William Hague as First Secretary of State, Secretary of State for Foreign and Commonwealth Affairs 2010-. *Select committees:* Member: European Standing Committee A 1998, Environment, Food and Rural Affairs 2001-02. Joint Secretary Conservative Party Committee for Defence 1997-99. National vice-chair, Federation of Conservative Students 1971-72; Chair, Conservative History Group 2003-. *Councils and public bodies:* Member: Royal United Services Institute for Defence Studies, British Commission for Military History, Lord Chancellor's Advisory Panel on the National Archives; Parliamentary Commissioner, Commonwealth War Graves Commission 2008-.

Political interests: Foreign affairs, defence, education, farming, countryside; France, Germany, Gulf States, Israel, Jordan, Poland, Saudi Arabia, Syria, USA.

Other: Council member, SSAFA 1997-2002; Trustee, History of Parliament Trust 2005-; Macmillan Cancer Relief.

Publications: The Old Contemptibles (1981); Joint editor, A Nations in Arms (1985); History of the German Army (1985); Editor, The War the Infantry Knew 1914-1919 (1986).

Recreations: Stroking cats, reading, restaurants, cinema, malt whiskies, observing ambitious people.

Keith Simpson MP, House of Commons, London SW1A 0AA
Tel: 020 7219 6457 *Email:* keithsimpsonmp@parliament.uk
Constituency: Broadland Conservative Association, The Stable, Church Farm, Attlebridge, Norfolk NR9 5ST
Tel: 01603 865763 *Fax:* 01603 865762 *Email:* organiser@broadlandconservatives.org.uk
Website: www.keithsimpson.com

CONSERVATIVE

SKIDMORE, CHRIS
Kingswood *(Majority 2,445)*

Christopher James Skidmore. Born 17 May 1981.

Education: Bristol Grammar School; Oxford University (history).

Non-political career: *Western Daily Press*; *People* magazine; Researcher, *Great Tales of English History*; University tutor, Bristol University; Author.

Political career: Member for Kingswood since 6 May 2010 general election. *Select committees:* Member: Health 2010-13, Education 2012-. Conservative Party: Member 1996-, Adviser on education, Director, Public Services Improvement Group.

Political interests: Health, education, social care, disability.

Other: Chair, Bow Group; Fellow, Royal Society of Arts; Fellow, Royal Historical Society.

Publications: Author: Edward VI: The Lost King (Weidenfeld, 2007), Death and the Virgin (Weidenfeld, 2010); Co-author: (with Kwasi Kwarteng MP) After the Coalition (BiteBack, 2011), (with Kwasi Kwarteng MP, Priti Patel MP, Dominic Raab MP and Elizabeth Truss MP) Britannia Unchained: Global Lessons for Growth and Prosperity (Palgrave Macmillan, 2012).

Chris Skidmore MP, House of Commons, London SW1A 0AA
Tel: 020 7219 7094 *Email:* chris.skidmore.mp@parliament.uk
Constituency: 47 High Street, Kingswood, Bristol BS15 4AA
Tel: 0117-908 1524 *Website:* www.chrisskidmore.com *Twitter:* @chrisskidmoremp

LABOUR

SKINNER, DENNIS
Bolsover *(Majority 11,182)*

Dennis Edward Skinner. Born 11 February 1932; Son of Edward Skinner; Married Mary Parker 1960 (died) (1 son 2 daughters).

Education: Tupton Hall Grammar School, Clay Cross, Derbyshire; Ruskin College, Oxford.

Non-political career: Miner 1949-70. President, Derbyshire Miners 1966-70.

Political career: Member for Bolsover 1970-2010, for Bolsover (revised boundary) since 6 May 2010 general election; President, North East Derbyshire Constituency Labour Party 1968-71; National Executive Committee, Labour Party: Member 1978-92, 1994-98, 1999-, Vice-chair 1987-88, Chair 1988-89. *Councils and public bodies:* Councillor: Clay Cross UDC 1960-70, Derbyshire County Council 1964-70; Former President, Derbyshire UDC Association.

Political interests: Inland waterways, energy, economic policy, environment, anti-Common Market, Third World.

Other: Parliamentarian of the Year 2010, Political Studies Association.

Recreations: Cycling, tennis, athletics (watching).

Dennis Skinner MP, House of Commons, London SW1A 0AA
Tel: 020 7219 5107 *Fax:* 020 7219 0028 *Email:* skinnerd@parliament.uk
Constituency: 1 Elmhurst Close, South Normanton, Alfreton, Derbyshire DE55 3NF
Tel: 01773 581027

LABOUR

SLAUGHTER, ANDY
Hammersmith *(Majority 3,549)*

Shadow Minister for Justice

Andrew Francis Slaughter. Born 29 September 1960; Son of Alfred Slaughter and Marie Slaughter; Single.

Education: Latymer Upper School, London; Exeter University (BA English 1982).

Non-political career: Barrister specialising in housing and personal injury law 1993-. GMB; Unite.

Political career: Contested Uxbridge 1997 by-election. Member for Ealing, Acton and Shepherd's Bush 2005-10, for Hammersmith since 6 May 2010 general election; PPS to: Stephen Ladyman as Minister of State, Department for Transport 2005-07, Lord Jones of Birmingham as Minister of State, Foreign and Commonwealth Office and Department for Business, Enterprise and Regulatory Reform 2007-08, Lord Malloch-Brown as Minister of State, Foreign and Commonwealth Office 2007-09; Shadow Minister for Justice 2010-. *Select committees:* Member: Regulatory Reform 2005-07, Children, Schools and Families 2007-09, Court of Referees 2007-10, Communities and Local Government 2009-10, London 2009-10, Joint Committee on Human Rights 2010. Vice-chair, PLP London Regional Group 2007-10. *Councils and public bodies:* Governor William Morris Sixth Form 1994-; London Borough of Hammersmith and Fulham: Councillor 1986-2006, Council leader 1996-2005.

Political interests: International affairs, housing, education, health, transport; Bahrain, Caribbean, Egypt, Middle East, Palestine, Spain, Tunisia.

Other: Management committee, Hammersmith and Fulham Community Law Centre 1990-.

Andy Slaughter MP, House of Commons, London SW1A 0AA
Tel: 020 7219 4990 *Fax:* 020 7381 5074 *Email:* slaughtera@parliament.uk
Constituency: 28 Greyhound Road, London W6 8NX
Tel: 020 7610 1950 *Fax:* 020 7381 5074 *Email:* andy@andyslaughter.com
Website: www.andyslaughter.co.uk *Twitter:* @hammersmithandy

LABOUR

SMITH, ANDREW
Oxford East *(Majority 4,581)*

Andrew David Smith. Born 1 February 1951; Son of late David Smith and Georgina Smith; Married Valerie Lambert 1976 (1 son).

Education: Reading Grammar School; St John's College, Oxford (BA economics, politics 1972; BPhil sociology 1974).

Non-political career: Member relations officer, Oxford and Swindon Co-op Society 1979-87. Member, Union Shop, Distributive and Allied Workers.

Political career: Contested Oxford East 1983 general election. Member for Oxford East 1987-2010, for Oxford East (revised boundary) since 6 May 2010 general election; Opposition Spokesperson for Education 1988-92; Opposition Frontbench Spokesperson for Treasury and Economic Affairs 1992-96; Shadow Chief Secretary to the Treasury 1994-96; Shadow Secretary of State for

Transport 1996-97; Minister of State, Department for Education and Employment (Minister for Employment, Welfare to Work and Equal Opportunities) 1997-99; Chief Secretary to the Treasury 1999-2002; Secretary of State for Work and Pensions 2002-04. *Select committees:* Member: South East 2009-10. *Councils and public bodies:* Councillor, Oxford City Council 1976-87.

Political interests: Car industry, education, retail industry, housing, employment.

Other: Chair of governors, Oxford Polytechnic/Oxford Brookes University 1987-93; Pathway Workshop. Honorary Doctorate, Oxford Brookes University. PC 1997; Blackbird Leys Community Association. President, Blackbird Leys Boys and Girls Football Club.

Recreations: Gardening, walking, windsurfing.

Rt Hon Andrew Smith MP, House of Commons, London SW1A 0AA
Tel: 020 7219 5102 *Email:* smithad@parliament.uk
Constituency: Unit A, Bishop Mews, Transport Way, Oxford OX4 6HD
Tel: 01865 595790 *Fax:* 01865 595799 *Email:* andrewsmith.mp@gmail.com
Website: www.andrewsmithmp.org.uk *Twitter:* @OxfordLabourMP

LABOUR

SMITH, ANGELA
Penistone and Stocksbridge *(Majority 3,049)*

Shadow Deputy Leader of the House of Commons

Angela Christine Smith. Born 16 August 1961; Daughter of Tom and Pat Smith; Married Steven Wilson 2005 (1 stepson 1 stepdaughter).

Education: Toll Bar Secondary School, Waltham; Nottingham University (BA English studies 1990); Newnham College, Cambridge (PhD 1994).

Non-political career: Medical secretary, National Health Service 1979-84; Secretary, Barclays Bank 1984-87; English lecturer, Dearne Valley College 1994-2003. Unison; GMB.

Political career: Member for Sheffield Hillsborough 2005-10, for Penistone and Stocksbridge since 6 May 2010 general election; PPS to Yvette Cooper: as Minister of State, ODPM/Department for Communities and Local Government 2005-08, as Chief Secretary to the Treasury 2008; Opposition Assistant Whip 2010-11; Shadow Deputy Leader of the House of Commons 2011-. *Select committees:* Member: Regulatory Reform 2005-07, Court of Referees 2007-10, Transport 2009-10, Procedure 2010-11, Administration 2010-12. Member, Labour Party National Executive Committee 2010-11. *Councils and public bodies:* Sheffield City Council: Councillor, 1996-2005, Chair of Finance 1998-99, Cabinet Member for Education 2002-05; Member, Regional Education and Skills Commission 2002-05; Chair, 14-19 Board, Sheffield First for Learning and Work 2002-05.

Political interests: Education, skills agenda, environment and conservation, transport; Balkans, Finland.

Other: RSPB; Wildlife Trust; Woodland Trust; Ramblers Association; IFAW; League Against Cruel Sports. Constituency MP of the Year, *House Magazine* awards 2011.

Recreations: Hill-walking, cooking.

Angela Smith MP, House of Commons, London SW1A 0AA
Tel: 020 7219 6713 *Fax:* 020 7219 8598 *Email:* smithac@parliament.uk
Constituency: The Arc, Town Hall, Manchester Road, Stocksbridge, Sheffield, South Yorkshire S36 2DT
Tel: 0114-283 1855 *Fax:* 0114-283 1850 *Email:* wilsonst@parliament.uk
Website: www.angelasmith-mp.org.uk *Twitter:* @angelasmithmp

CONSERVATIVE

SMITH, CHLOE
Norwich North *(Majority 3,901)*

Chloe Rebecca Smith. Born 17 May 1982; Daughter of David Smith, furniture designer and maker, and Claire Smith, teacher.

Education: Methwold High School, Norfolk; Swaffham Sixth Form College, Norfolk; York University (BA English literature 2004); French.

Non-political career: Business consultant, Deloitte 2004-09.

Political career: Member for Norwich North 23 July 2009 by-election to 2010, for Norwich North (revised boundary) since 6 May 2010 general election; Assistant Government Whip 2010-11; Economic Secretary, HM Treasury 2011-12; Parliamentary Secretary (Minister for Political and Constitutional Reform), Cabinet Office 2012-13. *Select committees:* Member: Work and

Pensions 2009-10, Public Accounts 2011-12. Member: Conservative Friends of Israel 2001-, Conservative Party Implementation Team 2008-09, Tory Reform Group 2009-. *Councils and public bodies:* Honorary Vice-President, Norfolk Association of Local Councils 2009-; School governor, Heartsease Primary School, Norwich 2010-12; Member: Hellesdon High School Academy Trust 2012-, Advisory board, Norwich Business School.

Political interests: Work and pensions, public services, efficiency, electoral engagement.

Other: Patron, YMCA Norfolk 2009-; Honorary Vice-President, Norfolk and Norwich Novi Sad Association 2009-; Patron, Blue Ribbon Foundation.

Recreations: Arts, including theatre and drawing; sports, including cycling, badminton.

Chloe Smith MP, House of Commons, London SW1A 0AA
Tel: 020 7219 8449
Constituency: Diamond House, Vulcan Road, Norwich NR6 6AQ
Tel: 01603 414756 *Email:* chloe@chloesmith.org.uk *Website:* www.chloesmith.org.uk
Twitter: @chloesmithmp

CONSERVATIVE

SMITH, HENRY
Crawley *(Majority 5,928)*

Henry Edward Millar Smith. Born 14 May 1969; Son of late John Smith and Josephine Smith; Married Jennifer Ricks 1994 (1 son 1 daughter).

Education: Frensham Heights, Farnham; University College London (BA philosophy 1991).

Non-political career: Property investment business.

Political career: Contested Crawley 2001 and 2005 general elections. Member for Crawley since 6 May 2010 general election. *Select committees:* Member: European Scrutiny 2010-. *Councils and public bodies:* West Sussex County Council: Councillor 1997-2010, Council leader 2003-10; Councillor, Crawley Borough Council 2002-04; Vice-President, Local Government Association 2011-.

Political interests: Local government, foreign policy; British Overseas Territories, USA.

Other: Flag Institute.

Publications: Co-author, Direct Democracy: An Agenda for a New Model Party (2005).

Recreations: Vexillology, skiing.

Henry Smith MP, House of Commons, London SW1A 0AA
Tel: 020 7219 7043 *Fax:* 020 7219 1653 *Email:* henry.smith.mp@parliament.uk
Constituency: Unit 4, Crawley Business Centre, Stephenson Way, Three Bridges, Crawley, West Sussex RH10 1TN
Tel: 01293 934554 *Email:* steve.aldridge@parliament.uk *Website:* www.henrysmith.info
Twitter: @HenrySmithMP

CONSERVATIVE

SMITH, JULIAN
Skipton and Ripon *(Majority 9,950)*

PPS to Justine Greening as Secretary of State for International Development

Julian Richard Smith. Born 30 August 1971; Married Amanda.

Education: Balfron High School; Millfield School, Somerset; Birmingham University (BA English and history 1993); French.

Non-political career: Squash coach, Perpignan; Landscape Promotions 1993-94; The Bird Moore Partnership 1994-99; Arq International, London: Founder and managing director 1999-2010, Non-executive director 2010-11.

Political career: Member for Skipton and Ripon since 6 May 2010 general election; PPS to: Alan Duncan as Minister of State, Department for International Development 2010-12, Justine Greening as Secretary of State for International Development 2012-. *Select committees:* Member: Scottish Affairs 2010. Deputy chair, Bethnal Green and Bow Conservatives 2008-09.

Political interests: Business, education, welfare, universities and skills, agriculture.

Other: Junior international squash player.

Recreations: Violin and piano.

Julian Smith MP, House of Commons, London SW1A 0AA
Tel: 020 7219 7145 *Email:* julian.smith.mp@parliament.uk
Constituency: 7 Gargrave Road, Broughton, Skipton BD23 3AQ
Website: www.juliansmithmp.com *Twitter:* @juliansmithmp

LABOUR

SMITH, NICK

Blaenau Gwent *(Majority 10,516)*

Nicholas Desmond John Smith. Born 14 January 1960; Son of William and Alma Smith; Divorced (2 daughters).

Education: Tredegar Comprehensive School; Coventry University (BA history, politics and international relations 1981); Birkbeck College, London (MSc economic change 1991).

Non-political career: Constituency organiser to Frank Dobson MP 1989-91; Organiser, Wales Labour Party 1991-93; Head of membership development, Labour Party 1993-98; Consultant, international campaigning 1998-2000; Campaign manager, public policy, NSPCC 2000-04; Secretary general, European Parliamentary Labour Party 2005-06; Director, policy and partnerships, Royal College of Speech and Language Therapists 2006-. AEEU; Transport and General Workers' Union; GMB; Community; Unite.

Political career: Member for Blaenau Gwent since 6 May 2010 general election; PPS to Douglas Alexander as Shadow Secretary of State for: Work and Pensions 2010-11, Foreign and Commonwealth Office 2011-. *Select committees:* Member: Public Accounts 2010-. Election agent to Emily Thornberry MP 2005. *Councils and public bodies:* London Borough of Camden Council: Former councillor, Member, then executive member, Education 2003-05.

Political interests: Economic development, health, children; China, India, Nepal, USA.

Other: Alternate Member, UK Delegation, Organisation for Security and Co-operation in Europe Parliamentary Assembly; Member: Aneurin Bevan Society, Tribune, Fabian Society; Fellow, Royal Geographical Society.

Recreations: Hiking, singing, reading, chess.

Nick Smith MP, House of Commons, London SW1A 0AA
Tel: 020 7219 7018 *Fax:* 020 7219 0565 *Email:* nick.smith.mp@parliament.uk
Constituency: 23 Beaufort Street, Brynmawr, Gwent NP23 4AQ
Tel: 01495 313167 *Fax:* 01495 310541 *Website:* www.nicksmithmp.com
Twitter: @BlaenauGwentMP

LABOUR

SMITH, OWEN

Pontypridd *(Majority 2,785)*

Shadow Secretary of State for Wales

Born 2 May 1970; Married Liz (2 sons 1 daughter).

Education: Coed-y-Lan Comprehensive, Pontypridd; Barry Boys Comprehensive, Barry; Sussex University (history and French); French.

Non-political career: BBC Radio and TV Producer, including BBC Radio 4 *Today* and BBC Wales *Dragon's Eye* 1992-2002; Special adviser to Paul Murphy MP: as Secretary of State for Wales 2002, as Secretary of State for Northern Ireland 2002-05; Head of policy and government affairs, Pfizer 2005-08; Director of health economic and corporate affairs, Amgen UK & Ireland 2008-10. Unite; GMB.

Political career: Contested Blaenau Gwent 2006 by-election. Member for Pontypridd since 6 May 2010 general election; Shadow Minister for Wales 2010-11; Shadow Exchequer Secretary 2011-12; Shadow Secretary of State for Wales 2012-. *Select committees:* Member: Welsh Affairs 2010-11.

Political interests: Economic affairs, industrial policy, equality, health, constitutional reform; France, Ireland, Wales.

Other: Llantrisant Working Men's Club.

Recreations: Family, reading, fishing and Pontyclun RFC.

Owen Smith MP, House of Commons, London SW1A 0AA
Tel: 020 7219 7128/020 7219 1287 *Email:* owen.smith.mp@parliament.uk
Constituency: Office of Owen Smith MP, GMB House, Morgan Street, Pontypridd CF37 2DS
Tel: 01443 401122 *Website:* www.owensmithmp.com *Twitter:* @OwenSmithMP

LIBERAL DEMOCRAT

SMITH, ROBERT
West Aberdeenshire and Kincardine *(Majority 3,684)*

Born 15 April 1958; Son of late Sir (William) Gordon Smith, Bt, VRD, and Diana, Lady Smith; Married Fiona Anne Cormack MD 1993 (3 daughters).

Education: Merchant Taylors' School, Northwood; Aberdeen University (BSc).

Non-political career: Family estate manager until 1997.

Political career: Contested (SDP/Liberal Alliance) Aberdeen North 1987 general election. Member for West Aberdeenshire and Kincardine 1997-2005, for West Aberdeenshire and Kincardine (revised boundary) since 5 May 2005 general election; Liberal Democrat: Whip 1999-2001, Spokesperson for: Scotland 1999-2001, Trade and Industry 2005-06, Energy 2005-06, Deputy Chief Whip 2001-06, Deputy Shadow Leader of the House 2007-10; Whip 2008-10. *Select committees:* Member: Scottish Affairs 1999-2001, European Standing Committee A 2000-01, Procedure 2001-10, Trade and Industry 2001-05, Unopposed Bills (Panel) 2001-10, Standing Orders 2001-10, Accommodation and Works 2003-05, International Development 2007-09, Energy and Climate Change 2009-, Joint Committee on Consolidation, Etc, Bills 2010-. *Councils and public bodies:* General Council Assessor, Aberdeen University 1994-98; Councillor, Aberdeenshire Council 1995-97; Vice-convener, Grampian Joint Police Board 1995-97; JP 1997.

Political interests: Energy, oil and gas industry, energy efficiency, fuel poverty, post offices, broadband provision, rural affairs, international development; Afghanistan, Burma, China, Zimbabwe.

Other: Member: IPU, CPA; Alternate Member, UK Delegation, Organisation for Security and Co-operation in Europe Parliamentary Assembly; Director, Grampian Transport Museum 1995-97; Member, Electoral Reform Society.

Recreations: Hill-walking, sailing.

Sir Robert Smith Bt MP, House of Commons, London SW1A 0AA
Tel: 020 7219 5106 *Fax:* 020 7219 4526 *Email:* robert.smith.mp@parliament.uk
Constituency: Banchory Business Centre, Burn O'Bennie Road, Banchory AB31 5ZU
Tel: 01330 826549

CONSERVATIVE

SOAMES, NICHOLAS
Mid Sussex *(Majority 7,402)*

Arthur Nicholas Winston Soames. Born 12 February 1948; Son of late Baron and Lady Soames; Married Catherine Weatherall 1981 (divorced 1988) (1 son); married Serena Smith 1993 (1 daughter 1 son).

Education: Eton College; Mons Officer Cadet School 1966; French.

Non-political career: Lieutenant, 11th Hussars 1967-72; Honorary Colonel: Bristol University Officers Training Corps 2006-11, 'C' Squadron (KSY) Royal Yeomanry 2011-. Equerry to Prince of Wales 1970-72; Stockbroker 1972-74; PA to: Sir James Goldsmith 1974-76, US Senator Mark Hatfield 1976-78; Assistant director, Sedgwick Group 1979-81; Senior adviser, MARSH.

Political career: Contested Dumbartonshire Central 1979 general election. Member for Crawley 1983-97, for Mid Sussex 1997-2010, for Mid Sussex (revised boundary) since 6 May 2010 general election; PPS to: John Gummer as Minister of State for Employment and Chairman of the Conservative Party 1984-86, Nicholas Ridley as Secretary of State for the Environment 1987-89; Joint Parliamentary Secretary, Ministry of Agriculture, Fisheries and Food 1992-94; Minister of State for the Armed Forces, Ministry of Defence 1994-97; Shadow Secretary of State for Defence 2003-05: Member Shadow Cabinet 2004-05. *Select committees:* Member: Public Administration 1999, Joint Committee on Consolidation of Bills Etc 2001-10, Standards and Privileges 2006-10, Administration 2013-. Secretary, Conservative Foreign Affairs Committee 1986-87; Member, Executive, 1922 Committee 2000-03, 2005-06, 2010-12. President, Conservative Middle East Council 2007-; Patron, Tory Reform Group.

Political interests: Defence, foreign affairs, trade and industry, aerospace, aviation, agriculture and countryside matters; Europe, Middle East, USA.

Other: Council member, RUSI; Trustee, Amber Foundation. Vintners' Company. PC 2011; White's, Turf, Pratt's. President, Haywards Heath Rugby Football Club.

Recreations: Country pursuits, racing.

Rt Hon Nicholas Soames MP, House of Commons, London SW1A 0AA
Tel: 020 7219 4143 *Fax:* 020 7219 2998 *Email:* nicholas.soames.mp@parliament.uk
Constituency: 5 Hazelgrove Road, Haywards Heath, West Sussex RH16 3PH
Tel: 01444 452590 *Fax:* 01444 415766 *Email:* info@msca.org.uk
Website: www.midsussexconservatives.com www.nicholassoames.org.uk

CONSERVATIVE

SOUBRY, ANNA
Broxtowe *(Majority 389)*

Parliamentary Under-Secretary of State, Ministry of Defence

Anna Mary Soubry. Born 7 December 1956; 2 daughters.

Education: Hartland Comprehensive School, Worksop; Birmingham University (law); Bar Finals.

Non-political career: Trainee reporter, Alloa; Presenter and reporter, *North Tonight*, Grampian TV; Presenter and reporter, Central TV: *Central News East, Central Weekend, Heart of the Country*; Barrister 1995-. Former Shop Steward, National Union of Journalists.

Political career: Contested Gedling 2005 general election. Member for Broxtowe since 6 May 2010 general election; PPS to Simon Burns as Minister of State for Health 2010-12; Parliamentary Under-Secretary of State: (Public Health), Department of Health 2012-13, Ministry of Defence 2013-. *Select committees:* Member: Justice 2010. *Councils and public bodies:* Rector, Stirling University.

Political interests: Justice, home affairs, health.

Recreations: Gardening, cooking, watching cricket, rugby and football.

Anna Soubry MP, House of Commons, London SW1A 0AA
Tel: 020 7219 3000 *Email:* anna.soubry.mp@parliament.uk
Constituency: Barton House, 61 High Road, Chilwell, Nottingham NG9 4AJ
Tel: 0115-943 6507 *Fax:* 0115-943 0950 *Website:* www.annasoubry.org.uk
Twitter: @Anna_SoubryMP

LABOUR

SPELLAR, JOHN
Warley *(Majority 10,756)*

Shadow Minister for Foreign and Commonwealth Office

John Francis Spellar. Born 5 August 1947; Son of late William Spellar and Phyllis Spellar; Married Anne Wilmot 1981 (died 2003) (1 daughter).

Education: Dulwich College, London; St Edmund's Hall, Oxford (BA philosophy, politics and economics 1969).

Non-political career: National officer, Electrical, Electronic, Telecommunication and Plumbing Union 1969-97.

Political career: Contested Bromley 1970 general election. Member for Birmingham Northfield 28 October 1982 by-election to June 1983. Contested Birmingham Northfield 1983 and 1987 general elections. Member for Warley West 1992-97, for Warley 1997-2010, for Warley (revised boundary) since 6 May 2010 general election; Opposition Whip 1992-94; Opposition Spokesperson for: Northern Ireland 1994-95, Defence, Disarmament and Arms Control 1995-97; Ministry of Defence: Parliamentary Under-Secretary of State 1997-99, Minister of State for the Armed Forces 1999-2001; Minister for Transport: Department of Transport, Local Government and the Regions 2001-02, Department for Transport 2002-03; Minister of State, Northern Ireland Office 2003-05; Government Whip 2008-10; Opposition Deputy Chief Whip 2010; Shadow Minister for Foreign and Commonwealth Office 2010-. *Select committees:* Member: Joint Committee on Conventions 2006, Finance and Services 2009-10, Selection 2010, Joint Committee on Security 2010, Administration 2010-13.

Political interests: Energy, electronics industry, motor industry, construction industry, defence; Australia, Israel, USA.

Other: PC 2001; Rowley Regis and Blackheath Labour Club; Brand Hall Labour Club.

Recreations: Gardening.

Rt Hon John Spellar MP, House of Commons, London SW1A 0AA
Tel: 020 7219 0674 *Fax:* 020 7219 2113 *Email:* john.spellar.mp@parliament.uk
Constituency: Brandhall Labour Club, Tame Road, Oldbury, West Midlands B68 0JT
Tel: 0121-423 2933 *Fax:* 0121-423 2933 *Email:* john.spellar@btconnect.com
Website: www.johnspellar.labour.co.uk *Twitter:* @spellar

CONSERVATIVE

SPELMAN, CAROLINE

Meriden *(Majority 16,253)*

Caroline Alice Spelman. Born 4 May 1958; Daughter of late Marshall Cormack and Helen Cormack; Married Mark Spelman 1987 (2 sons 1 daughter).

Education: Herts and Essex Grammar School for Girls, Bishops Stortford; Queen Mary College, London (BA European studies 1980); French, German.

Non-political career: Sugar beet commodity secretary, National Farmers Union 1981-84; Deputy director, International Confederation of European Beetgrowers, Paris 1984-89; Research fellow, Centre for European Agricultural Studies 1989-93; Director, Spelman, Cormack and Associates 1989-2010.

Political career: Contested Bassetlaw 1992 general election. Member for Meriden 1997-2010, for Meriden (revised boundary) since 6 May 2010 general election; Opposition Whip 1998-99; Board member Parliamentary Office of Science and Technology (POST) 1997-2001; Opposition Spokesperson for: Health 1999-2001, Women's Issues 1999-2001; Shadow Secretary of State for International Development 2001-03; Shadow Minister for Women 2001-04; Shadow Secretary of State for: the Environment 2003-04, Local and Devolved Government Affairs 2004-05, Office of the Deputy Prime Minister/Communities and Local Government 2005-07, 2009-10; Secretary of State for Environment, Food and Rural Affairs 2010-12. *Select committees:* Member: Science and Technology 1997-98. Member, Conservative Agriculture Policy Committee 2001-04. Co-opted member, executive committee, Conservative Women's National Council; Member, board of directors, governing council, Conservative Christian Fellowship; Advisory board member, Women2Win; Chair, Conservative Party 2007-09.

Political interests: Environment, agriculture, international development; Brazil, France, Germany, Portugal.

Other: Council of the European Union: Member: Agriculture and Fisheries Council 2010-12, Environment Council 2010-12; Patron: Domestic Violence Refuge (MABL), Drug Rehabilitation Charity (WELCOME); Chair, Parliamentary Chair; Vice-chair, Tearfund. PC 2010. Member: Lords and Commons Tennis Group, Lords and Commons Hockey Club.

Publications: The non-food uses of agricultural raw materials (CABI, 1991); A Green and Pleasant Land (Bow Group, 1994).

Recreations: Tennis, cooking, gardening.

Rt Hon Caroline Spelman MP, House of Commons, London SW1A 0AA
Tel: 020 7219 4189 *Fax:* 020 7219 0378
Constituency: 631 Warwick Road, Solihull, West Midlands B91 1AR
Tel: 0121-711 7029 *Email:* caroline@carolinespelman.com
Website: www.carolinespelman.com

SPENCER, MARK

Sherwood *(Majority 214)*

Mark Steven Spencer. Born 20 January 1970; Son of Cyril and Dorothy Spencer; Married Claire (1 son 1 daughter).

Education: Colonel Frank Seeley School, Calverton; Shuttleworth Agricultural College, Bedfordshire (farming course; National Certificate agriculture).

Non-political career: Farmer; Proprietor: Spring Lane Farm Shop, Floralands Garden Village, Lambley.

CONSERVATIVE

Political career: Member for Sherwood since 6 May 2010 general election. *Select committees:* Member: Environmental Audit 2010-. *Councils and public bodies:* Councillor, Gedling District Council 2003-11; Nottinghamshire County Council: Councillor 2005-13, Shadow Spokesperson for Community Safety and Partnerships 2006-13; Member, East Midlands Regional Assembly 2009-10.

Political interests: Rural affairs, education, health, employment, business; UK.

Other: National Federation of Young Farmers' Clubs: Chair 2000, Member; Royal Agricultural Society of England: Trustee, Associate 2005, Honorary show director 2007-09, Fellow 2010; Trustee, The Core Centre, Calverton; Fellow, Royal Agricultural Societies; Nottingham Breast Institute; NORSACA.

Recreations: Family, farming, socialising.

Mark Spencer MP, House of Commons, London SW1A 0AA
Tel: 020 7219 7143 *Email:* mark.spencer.mp@parliament.uk
Constituency: Sherwood Constituency Office, Room 3, Under One Roof, 3a Vine Terrace, Hucknall, Nottingham NG15 7HN
Tel: 0115-968 1186 *Website:* www.markspencermp.com *Twitter:* @MarkSpencerMP

CONSERVATIVE

STANLEY, JOHN
Tonbridge and Malling *(Majority 18,178)*

John Paul Stanley. Born 19 January 1942; Married Susan Giles 1968 (1 son 1 daughter 1 son deceased).

Education: Repton School, Derby; Lincoln College, Oxford.

Non-political career: Conservative Research Department 1967-68; Research Associate, Institute for Strategic Studies 1968-69; Rio Tinto-Zinc Corp. Ltd 1969-79.

Political career: Contested Newton 1970 general election. Member for Tonbridge and Malling since 28 February 1974 general election; PPS to Margaret Thatcher as Leader of the Opposition 1976-79; Minister for Housing and Construction 1979-83; Minister for the Armed Forces 1983-87; Minister of State, Northern Ireland Office 1987-88. *Select committees:* Member: Foreign Affairs 1992-, Quadripartite (Committees on Strategic Export Controls)/Arms Export Controls 2006-11; Chair: Arms Export Controls 2011-; Member: Arms Exports Controls 2013-.

Other: Commonwealth Parliamentary Association (CPA): UK Branch: Member, Executive Committee 1999-, Honorary Treasurer 2007-10; Member, Executive Committee, Inter-Parliamentary Union, British Group. PC 1984; Kt 1988.

Recreations: Music and the arts, sailing.

Rt Hon Sir John Stanley MP, House of Commons, London SW1A 0AA
Tel: 020 7219 5977 *Email:* john.stanley.mp@parliament.uk
Constituency: 91 High Street, West Malling, Maidstone, Kent ME19 6NA
Tel: 01732 842794 *Fax:* 01732 873960 *Website:* www.tcconservatives.com

STEPHENSON, ANDREW
Pendle *(Majority 3,585)*

Andrew George Stephenson. Born 17 February 1981; Son of Malcolm Stephenson and Ann Stephenson.

Education: Poynton County High School; Royal Holloway, University of London (BSc business management 2002).

Non-political career: Partner, Stephenson and Threader 2002-10.

Political career: Member for Pendle since 6 May 2010 general election; National deputy chairman, Conservative Future 2001-02; Chairman, Tatton Conservative Association 2006; Conservative Party: Vice-chairman (youth) 2010-11, Vice-chairman (Conservative Future) 2011-13. *Councils and public bodies:* Councillor, Macclesfield Borough Council 2003-07.

Political interests: Environment, small business, education, health, economy, local government; America, Bosnia, Canada, Pakistan.

Other: Patron, SELRAP (Skipton East Lancashire Railway Action Partnership) 2010-; President, Nelson Brass Band 2010-; Colne British Legion; Earby Conservative Club; Barnoldswick Conservative Club.

Recreations: Manchester City FC, walking, food and drink.

Andrew Stephenson MP, House of Commons, London SW1A 0AA
Tel: 020 7219 7222 *Fax:* 020 7219 6385 *Email:* andrew.stephenson.mp@parliament.uk
Constituency: 9 Cross Street, Nelson, Lancashire BB9 7EN
Tel: 01282 614748 *Website:* www.pendleconservatives.com
www.andrewstephensonmp.co.uk *Twitter:* @Andrew4Pendle

CONSERVATIVE

STEVENSON, JOHN
Carlisle *(Majority 853)*

Andrew John Stevenson. Born 1963; Married Tracey Stevenson.

Education: Aberdeen Grammar School; Dundee University (BA history and politics); College of Law, Chester.

Non-political career: Trainee solicitor, Dickinson Dees, Newcastle upon Tyne 1990; Solicitor, now partner, Bendles, Carlisle.

Political career: Member for Carlisle since 6 May 2010 general election. *Select committees:* Member: Joint Committee on the Draft House of Lords Reform Bill 2011-12, Communities and Local Government 2012-. Chair: Carlisle Conservative Association, Penrith and the Border Conservative Association, North Cumbria Conservatives. *Councils and public bodies:* Councillor, Carlisle City Council 1999-2010.

Countries of interest: Israel.

Other: Member, Law Society; Eden Valley Hospice. Committee member, Chatsworth Tennis Club.

Publications: Co-author, Freedom, Responsibility and the State: Curbing Over-Mighty Government (Politeia, 2012).

Recreations: Golf, running, sport.

John Stevenson MP, House of Commons, London SW1A 0AA
Tel: 020 7219 3000 *Email:* john.stevenson.mp@parliament.uk
Constituency: 2 Currie Street, Carlisle, Cumbria CA1 1HH
Tel: 01228 550684 *Email:* office@johnstevensonmp.co.uk
Website: www.johnstevensonmp.co.uk *Twitter:* @JohnStevensonMP

CONSERVATIVE

STEWART, BOB
Beckenham *(Majority 17,784)*

Robert Alexander Stewart. Born 7 July 1949; Son of Jock Stewart, MC and Joan Stewart; Married Claire Podbielski 1994 (4 children; 2 children from first marriage).

Education: Chigwell School; Royal Military Academy Sandhurst 1969; Wales University (international politics 1977); Army Staff College 1980-81; Joint Services Staff College 1987-88.

Non-political career: Regular officer (infantry officer-colonel) British Army, Cheshire Regiment 1969-96: Served in Northern Ireland, British UN Commander, Bosnia 1992-93, Policy chief, Supreme HQ Allied Powers Europe, Belgium -1996; Senior consultant, Hill & Knowlton 1997-98; Managing director, WorldSpace 1999-2001; Freelance writer and lecturer 2002-.

Political career: Member for Beckenham since 6 May 2010 general election. *Select committees:* Member: Defence 2010-, Arms Export Controls 2011-.

Political interests: Defence, veteran service personnel, disabled children; Eastern Europe, Middle East, Northern Ireland.

Other: Member, UK Delegation, Organisation for Security and Co-operation in Europe Parliamentary Assembly; President, Action for Armed Forces; Vice-president, UKNDA; Patron, ELIFAR. DSO 1993; Army and Navy.

Publications: Broken Lives (1993); Leadership Under Pressure (2009).

Bob Stewart MP, House of Commons, London SW1A 0AA
Tel: 020 7219 7011 *Email:* bob.stewart.mp@parliament.uk
Constituency: No constituency office *Website:* www.bobstewartmp.com

CONSERVATIVE

STEWART, IAIN
Milton Keynes South *(Majority 5,201)*

Iain Aitken Stewart. Born 18 September 1972; Son of James Stewart and Leila Stewart.

Education: Hutchesons' Grammar School, Glasgow; Exeter University (BA politics 1993); Chartered Management Institute (Diploma management 2006).

Non-political career: Trainee chartered accountant, Coopers and Lybrand 1993-94; Head of research, Scottish Conservative Party 1994-98; Parliamentary Resources Unit, House of Commons: Deputy director 1998-2001, Director 2001-06; Associate, Odgers Berndtson 2006-10.

Political career: Contested Milton Keynes South West 2001 and 2005 general elections. Member for Milton Keynes South since 6 May 2010 general election. *Select committees:* Member: Transport 2010-. Contested Glasgow Rutherglen constituency 1999 Scottish Parliament election. *Councils and public bodies:* Councillor, Shenley Brook End and Tattenhoe Parish Council 2005-11.

Political interests: Constitution, economy, transport, energy security, education.

Other: Founder member, Atlantic Bridge 1999; Patron, Milton Keynes City Orchestra; Bletchley Conservative; President, Stony Stratford Conservative 2007-.

Publications: It's Our Money! Who Spends it? (London Scottish Tory Club, 2004) The Scottish Constitution – In Search of a New Settlement (Policy Institute, 2007).

Recreations: Opera, good food, wine and whisky, gym, running marathons.

Iain Stewart MP, House of Commons, London SW1A 0AA
Tel: 020 7219 7230 *Email:* iain.stewart.mp@parliament.uk
Constituency: Suite 102, Milton Keynes Business Centre, Foxhunter Drive, Linford Wood MK14 6GD
Tel: 01908 686830 *Fax:* 01908 686831 *Website:* www.ias4mks.com *Twitter:* @iainastewart

STEWART, RORY
Penrith and The Border *(Majority 11,241)*

Born 3 January 1973; Son of Mr and Mrs Brian Thomas Webster Stewart; Married Shoshana Clark 2012.

Education: Eton College; Balliol College, Oxford (BA politics, philosophy and economics, MA); French, Indonesian, Persian (Dari), conversational Urdu and Serbo-Croatian.

Non-political career: 2nd Lieutenant, Black Watch. Foreign and Commonwealth Office 1995-2000; Second Secretary, British Embassy, Jakarta, Indonesia 1997, British Representative, Montenegro 1999-2000; Walked across Pakistan, Iran, Afghanistan, India and Nepal 2000-02; Deputy governorate co-ordinator, Amara, Iraq 2003; Senior adviser, Nasiriyah, Iraq 2004; Founder and chief executive, Turquoise Mountain 2006-10; Ryan Family professor, practice of human rights and director, Carr Centre for Human Rights Policy, Harvard University 2008-10.

CONSERVATIVE

Political career: Member for Penrith and The Border since 6 May 2010 general election. *Select committees:* Member: Foreign Affairs 2010-.

Political interests: Local democracy, rural affairs, broadband, foreign affairs; Asia, EU, Middle East.

Other: Member, UK Delegation, Organisation for Security and Co-operation in Europe Parliamentary Assembly; Executive chairman, Turquoise Mountain Foundation 2006-10. Royal Society of Literature Oondaatje Award 2004; Camino del Cid 2008; Radio France Award 2009; Livingstone Medal, Royal Scottish Geographical Society 2010. OBE 2004.

Publications: Author: The Places in Between (Picador, 2004), The Prince of the Marshes (Harcourt, 2006), Occupational Hazards: My Time Governing in Iraq (Picador, 2006).

Recreations: Walking.

Rory Stewart OBE MP, House of Commons, London SW1A 0AA
Tel: 020 7219 7127 *Email:* rory.stewart.mp@parliament.uk
Constituency: No constituency office
Email: rory@rorystewart.co.uk *Website:* www.rorystewart.co.uk *Twitter:* @RoryStewartUK

STRAW, JACK
Blackburn *(Majority 9,856)*

John Whitaker Straw. Born 3 August 1946; Son of late Walter Straw, insurance clerk, and Joan Straw, nursery teacher; Married Anthea Weston (divorced 1978) (1 daughter deceased); married Alice Perkins 1978 (1 son 1 daughter).

Education: Brentwood School, Essex; Leeds University (LLB 1967); Inns of Court School of Law 1972.

Non-political career: President, National Union of Students 1969-71; Called to the Bar, Inner Temple 1972; Practised as Barrister 1972-74; Special adviser to: Barbara Castle as Secretary of State for Social Services 1974-76, Peter Shore as Secretary of State for the Environment 1976-77; Member, staff of Granada Television *World in Action* 1977-79; Master of Bench of Inner Temple 1997; Consultant, ED&F Man 2011-. Member, GMB.

LABOUR

Political career: Contested Tonbridge and Malling February 1974 general election. Member for Blackburn 1979-2010, for Blackburn (revised boundary) since 6 May 2010 general election; Opposition Spokesperson for: Treasury and Economic Affairs 1980-83, Environment 1983-87; Shadow Education Secretary 1987-92; Shadow Environment Secretary 1992-94; Shadow Home Secretary 1994-97; Home Secretary 1997-2001; Foreign Secretary 2001-06; Leader of the House of Commons 2006-07; Ex-officio Member House of Commons Commission 2006-07; Lord Chancellor and Secretary of State for Justice 2007-10; Member Speaker's Committee on the Electoral Commission -2010; Shadow Lord Chancellor and Secretary of State for Justice 2010; Acting Shadow Deputy Prime Minister 2010; Chair, Speakers' Working Group on All-Party Groups 2011-12. *Select committees:* Chair: Modernisation of the House of Commons 2006-07. Member, Labour Party National Executive Committee 1994-95. *Councils and public bodies:* Councillor, Islington Borough Council 1971-78; ILEA: Member 1971-74, Deputy Leader 1973.

Political interests: Education, taxation, economic policy, local and regional government, police, foreign affairs, European Union; Iran, Turkey.

Other: Vice-President, Commonwealth Parliamentary Association (UK Branch) 2010-; Member of Council, Lancaster University 1989-92; Governor, Blackburn College 1990-; Pimlico School: Governor 1994-2000, Chair 1995-98; President, Industry and Parliament Trust 2007-10; Visiting fellow, Nuffield College, Oxford 1990-98; Visiting professor in public policy, University College, London 2012-. Fellow, Royal Statistical Society 1995-; Honorary LLD: Leeds University 1999, Brunel University 2007. *House Magazine* Minister of the Year 2006. PC 1997; Order of the Republic Medal of Turkey (2012). Honorary Vice-President, Blackburn Rovers FC 1998-.

Publications: Policy and Ideology (1993); Last Man Standing: Memoirs of a Political Survivor (Macmillan, 2012); Aspects of Law Reform: An Insider's Perspective (Hamlyn, 2013).

Recreations: Cooking, walking, music, watching Blackburn Rovers.

Rt Hon Jack Straw MP, House of Commons, London SW1A 0AA
Tel: 020 7219 5070 *Fax:* 020 7219 2310 *Email:* strawj@parliament.uk
Constituency: Richmond Chambers, Richmond Terrace, Blackburn, Lancashire BB1 7AS
Tel: 01254 52317 *Fax:* 01254 682213 *Email:* jack.straw@blackburnlabour.org
Website: blackburnlabour.org

STREETER, GARY
South West Devon *(Majority 15,874)*

Gary Nicholas Streeter. Born 2 October 1955; Son of Kenneth Streeter, farmer, and Shirley Streeter; Married Janet Stevens 1978 (1 son 1 daughter).

Education: Tiverton Grammar School; King's College, London (LLB 1977).

Non-political career: Solicitor; Partner, Foot and Bowden, Plymouth, (specialist in company and employment law) 1984-98.

CONSERVATIVE

Political career: Member for Plymouth Sutton 1992-97, for South West Devon 1997-2010, for South West Devon (revised boundary) since 6 May 2010 general election; PPS to: Sir Derek Spencer as Solicitor General 1993-95, Sir Nicholas Lyell as Attorney General 1994-95; Assistant Government Whip 1995-96; Parliamentary Secretary, Lord Chancellor's Department 1996-97; Opposition Spokesperson for: Foreign Affairs 1997-98, Europe 1997-98; Shadow Secretary of State for International Development 1998-2001; Shadow Minister for Foreign Affairs 2003-04; Member Speaker's Committee on the Electoral Commission 2010-. *Select committees:* Member: Office of the Deputy Prime Minister 2002-04, Office of the Deputy Prime Minister (Urban Affairs Sub-Committee) 2003-04, Home Affairs 2005-10, Chairmen's Panel/Panel of Chairs 2009-, Joint Committee on Security 2010-, Ecclesiastical Committee 2010-. Chair, board of directors, governing council, Conservative Christian Fellowship; Vice-chair, Conservative Party 2001-02; Chair, Conservative Party: Human Rights Commission 2005-07, International Office 2005-08. *Councils and public bodies:* Plymouth City Council: Councillor 1986-92, Chair, Housing Committee 1989-91.

Political interests: Law and order, family moral and social affairs, developing world; Middle East, North Korea.

Other: Chair, Westminster Foundation for Democracy 2010-.

Recreations: Watching cricket and rugby, family.

Gary Streeter MP, House of Commons, London SW1A 0AA
Tel: 020 7219 5033 *Fax:* 020 7219 2414 *Email:* deans@parliament.uk
Constituency: Old Newnham Farm, Plymouth, Devon PL7 5BL
Tel: 01752 335666 *Fax:* 01752 338401 *Email:* mail@garystreeter.co.uk
Website: www.garystreeter.co.uk

STRIDE, MEL
Central Devon *(Majority 9,230)*

PPS to John Hayes as Minister without Portfolio, Cabinet Office

Melvyn John Stride. Born 30 September 1961; Son of Mel Stride and Barbara Stride; Married Michelle King Hughes 2006 (3 daughters).

Education: Portsmouth Grammar School; St Edmund Hall, Oxford (BA politics, philosophy and economics 1984) (President Oxford Union 1984).

Non-political career: Founder and ex-director, Venture Marketing Group 1987-2007. Member, Amicus 2006-10.

CONSERVATIVE

Political career: Member for Central Devon since 6 May 2010 general election; PPS to John Hayes as Minister: of State for Further Education, Skills and Lifelong Learning 2011-12, of State for Energy, Department of Energy and Climate Change 2012-13, without Portfolio, Cabinet Office 2013-. *Select committees:* Member: Northern Ireland Affairs 2010-11. Oxford University Conservative Association: Member 1981-84, President 1982.

Political interests: Education, welfare reform, social justice; USA.

Other: Commission for Social Justice Working Group 2006-07; Oxford Union Society: Member 1981-, President 1984; Member, Association of Professional Tourist Guides 2006; Pilot's licence 1990; Registered blue badge guide 2005. Guide of the Year 2005; Carlton; RAC.

Recreations: History, walking, spending time with family.

Mel Stride MP, House of Commons, London SW1A 0AA
Tel: 020 7219 7037 *Email:* mel.stride.mp@parliament.uk
Constituency: 2a Manaton Court, Manaton Close, Matford Business Park, Exeter EX2 8PF
Tel: 01392 823306 *Website:* www.melstridemp.com

LABOUR

STRINGER, GRAHAM
Blackley and Broughton *(Majority 12,303)*

Graham Eric Stringer. Born 17 February 1950; Son of late Albert Stringer, railway clerk, and late Brenda Stringer, shop assistant; Married Kathryn Carr 1999 (1 son 1 stepson 1 stepdaughter).

Education: Moston Brook High School; Sheffield University (BSc chemistry 1971).

Non-political career: Analytical chemist; Chair of Board, Manchester Airport plc 1996-97. Branch officer and shop steward, MSF; Member, Amicus/Unite.

Political career: Member for Manchester Blackley 1997-2010, for Blackley and Broughton since 6 May 2010 general election; Parliamentary Secretary, Cabinet Office 1999-2001; Government Whip 2001-02. *Select committees:* Member: Environment, Transport and Regional Affairs 1997-99, Environment, Transport and Regional Affairs (Transport Sub-Committee) 1997-99, Transport 2002-10, Modernisation of the House of Commons 2006, Science and Technology 2006-07, 2010-, Innovation, Universities[, Science] and Skills 2007-10, Transport 2011-, Justice 2013-. Vice-chair, PLP Departmental Committee for Transport 2006-10. *Councils and public bodies:* Manchester City Council: Councillor 1979-98, Leader 1984-96.

Political interests: Urban regeneration, House of Lords reform, revitalising local democracy, aviation and airports, bus regulation, science policy, justice policy.

Other: Honorary RNCM. Member: Manchester Tennis and Racquet Club, Cheetham Hill Cricket Club.

Recreations: Real tennis, squash.

Graham Stringer MP, House of Commons, London SW1A 0AA
Tel: 020 7219 5235 *Email:* stringerg@parliament.uk
Constituency: North Manchester Sixth Form College, Rochdale Road, Manchester M9 4AF
Tel: 0161-202 6600 *Fax:* 0161-202 6626 *Email:* graham.stringer.mp@parliament.uk

LABOUR

STUART, GISELA
Birmingham, Edgbaston *(Majority 1,274)*

Gisela Gschaider Stuart. Born 26 November 1955; Daughter of late Martin Gschaider and Liane Krompholz; Married Robert Scott Stuart 1980 (divorced 2000) (2 sons); married Derek Scott 2010 (died 2012).

Education: Staatliche Realschule, Vilsbiburg, Bavaria; Manchester Polytechnic (business studies 1979); London University (LLB 1992); German.

Non-political career: Deputy director, London Book Fair 1983; Translator; Lawyer and lecturer, Worcester College of Technology and Birmingham University 1992-97. Member, Amicus.

Political career: Member for Birmingham Edgbaston 1997-2010, for Birmingham, Edgbaston (revised boundary) since 6 May 2010 general election; PPS to Paul Boateng as Minister of State, Home Office 1998-99; Parliamentary Under-Secretary of State, Department of Health 1999-2001; Parliamentary representative Convention on Future of Europe 2002-04. *Select committees:* Member: Social Security 1997-98, Foreign Affairs 2001-10, Joint Committee on Conventions 2006, Defence 2010-, Arms Export Controls 2010-11, Joint Committee on Privacy and Injunctions 2011-12. Chair, PLP Departmental Group for Defence 2011-.

Political interests: Pension law, constitutional reform, European Union.

Other: Member, advisory board, Birmingham University Business School; Board member, External System London University; Trustee, Henry Jackson Society; Fellow, Industry and Parliament Trust 2002. Honorary Doctorate, Aston University. Bundesverdienstkreuz, Germany.

Publications: The Making of Europe's Constitution (Fabian Society, 2003); Editor, *The House Magazine* 2005-.

Gisela Stuart MP, House of Commons, London SW1A 0AA
Tel: 020 7219 4853 *Fax:* 020 7219 0317 *Email:* stuartg@parliament.uk
Constituency: No constituency office publicised
Tel: 0121-454 5430 *Fax:* 0121-454 3167 *Website:* www.giselastuartmp.co.uk
Twitter: @GiselaStuart

CONSERVATIVE

STUART, GRAHAM
Beverley and Holderness *(Majority 12,987)*

Graham Charles Stuart. Born 12 March 1962; Son of late Dr Peter Stuart and Joan Stuart; Married Anne Crawshaw 1989 (2 daughters).

Education: Glenalmond College, Perthshire; Selwyn College, Cambridge (law/philosophy 1985).

Non-political career: Sole proprietor, Go Enterprises 1984-2010; Director, CSL Publishing Ltd 1987-.

Political career: Contested Cambridge 2001 general election. Member for Beverley and Holderness 2005-10, for Beverley and Holderness (revised boundary) since 6 May 2010 general election. *Select committees:* Member: Environmental Audit 2006-10, Joint Committee on the Draft Climate Change Bill 2007, Education and Skills/Children, Schools and Families 2007-10; Chair: Education 2010-; Member: Liaison 2010-. Chairman, Cambridge University Conservative Association 1985; Board member, Conservative Party 2006-10. *Councils and public bodies:* Cambridge City Council: Councillor 1998-2004, Leader, Conservative Group 2000-04.

Political interests: Education, older people, mental health, welfare, economics, community hospitals, climate change; Brazil, China, India, Mexico, South Africa.

Other: Chair: CHANT (Community Hospitals Acting Nationally Together) 2005-10, East Riding Health Action Group 2007-09; Vice-President, GLOBE International 2007-; Chair, Rural Fair Share -2011.

Recreations: Sailing, cricket, motor cycling, triathlon.

Graham Stuart MP, House of Commons, London SW1A 0AA
Tel: 020 7219 4340 *Email:* graham.stuart.mp@parliament.uk
Constituency: 9 Cross Street, Beverley, East Yorkshire HU17 9AX
Tel: 01482 679687 *Fax:* 01482 861667 *Email:* graham@grahamstuart.com
Website: www.grahamstuart.com *Twitter:* @grahamstuart

LIBERAL DEMOCRAT

STUNELL, ANDREW
Hazel Grove *(Majority 6,371)*

Robert Andrew Stunell. Born 24 November 1942; Son of late Robert Stunell and Trixie Stunell; Married Gillian Chorley 1967 (3 sons 2 daughters).

Education: Surbiton Grammar School; Manchester University (architecture RIBA Pt. II exemption 1963); Liverpool Polytechnic; (Some) German, French.

Non-political career: Architectural assistant: CWS Manchester 1965-67, Runcorn New Town 1967-81; Freelance architectural assistant 1981-85; Association of Liberal Democrat Councillors: Various posts including political secretary 1985-97, Head of Service 1989-96. Member, NALGO: New Towns Whitley Council 1977-81.

Political career: Contested City of Chester 1979, 1983, 1987, Hazel Grove 1992 general elections. Member for Hazel Grove 1997-2010, for Hazel Grove (revised boundary) since 6 May 2010 general election; Liberal Democrat: Spokesperson for Energy 1997-2005, Deputy Chief Whip 1997-2001, Chief Whip 2001-06, Shadow Secretary of State for Office of the Deputy Prime Minister/Communities and Local Government 2006-07; Parliamentary Under-Secretary of State, Department for Communities and Local Government 2010-12. *Select committees:* Member: Broadcasting 1997-2000, Modernisation of the House of Commons 1997-2006, Procedure 1997-2001, Unopposed Bills (Panel) 1997-2001, Standing Orders 1998-2001, Finance and Services 2001-06, Selection 2001-06, International Development 2009-10, Arms Export Controls 2009-10. Member, Liberal Democrat Federal: Executive Committee 2001-06, Conference Committee 2001-06; Chair, Local Election Campaign 2007-12. *Councils and public bodies:* Councillor: Chester City Council 1979-90, Cheshire County Council 1981-91; Vice-chair, Association of County Councils 1985-90; Councillor, Stockport Metropolitan Borough Council 1994-2002; Vice-president, Local Government Association 1997-2010.

Political interests: Local democracy and regional devolution, Third World, race relations, energy, climate change.

Other: President, Goyt Valley Rail Users Association; Vice-president, Macclesfield Canal Society 1998-; North West Constitutional Convention 1999-; Fellow, Industry and Parliament Trust 2000; President, Marple Civic Society 2012-. OBE 1995; PC 2012; Kt 2013.

Publications: Budgeting For Real (1984, 1994, 1999); Life In The Balance (1986); Thriving In The Balance (1995); Open Active & Effective (1995); Local Democracy Guaranteed (1996); Energy – Clean and Green to 2050 (1999); Nuclear Waste – Cleaning up the Mess (2001).

Recreations: Theoretical astronomy, camping, table tennis.

Rt Hon Sir Andrew Stunell OBE MP, House of Commons, London SW1A 0AA
Tel: 020 7219 5136 *Fax:* 020 7219 2302 *Email:* andrew.stunell.mp@parliament.uk
Constituency: 34 Stockport Road, Romiley, Stockport SK6 3AA
Tel: 0161-406 7070 *Fax:* 0161-494 2425 *Email:* enquiries@andrewstunell.org.uk
Website: www.andrewstunell.org.uk

STURDY, JULIAN
York Outer *(Majority 3,688)*

Julian Charles Sturdy. Born 1971; Son of Robert Sturdy MEP and Elizabeth Hommes; Married Victoria (1 son 1 daughter).

Education: Harper Adams University (agriculture).

Non-political career: Farming and property business.

Political career: Contested Scunthorpe 2005 general election. Member for York Outer since 6 May 2010 general election; PPS to Simon Burns as Minister of State, Department for Transport 2012-13. *Select committees:* Member: Transport 2010-12. *Councils and public bodies:* Councillor, Harrogate Borough Council 2002-07; Governor, educational foundation of local school.

CONSERVATIVE

Other: Director, Harrogate District Community Transport.

Julian Sturdy MP, House of Commons, London SW1A 0AA
Tel: 020 7219 7199 *Email:* julian.sturdy.mp@parliament.uk
Constituency: York Conservatives, 1 Ash Street, York YO26 4ZB
Tel: 01904 784847 *Website:* www.juliansturdy.co.uk

SUTCLIFFE, GERRY
Bradford South *(Majority 4,622)*

Gerard Sutcliffe. Born 13 May 1953; Son of Henry and Margaret Sutcliffe; Married Maria Holgate 1972 (3 sons).

Education: Cardinal Hinsley Grammar School, Bradford.

Non-political career: Salesperson 1969-72; Display advertising, *Bradford Telegraph and Argus* 1972-75; Field printers, Bradford 1975-80. Deputy Branch Secretary, SOGAT/GPMU 1980-94; Member: Yorkshire and Humberside Trade Union Friends of Labour, Regional TUC.

LABOUR

Political career: Member for Bradford South 9 June 1994 by-election to 2010, for Bradford South (revised boundary) since 6 May 2010 general election; PPS: to Harriet Harman as Secretary of State for Social Security and Minister for Women 1997-98, to Stephen Byers: as Chief Secretary, HM Treasury July-December 1998, as Secretary of State for Trade and Industry 1999; Assistant Government Whip 1999-2001; Government Whip 2000-03; Parliamentary Under-Secretary of State: Department of Trade and Industry 2003-06: (Employment Relations, Competition and Consumers 2003-04, Employment Relations, Consumers and Postal Services 2004-05, Employment Relations and Consumer Affairs 2005-06), Home Office/Ministry of Justice (Criminal Justice and Offender Management) 2006-07, Department for Culture, Media and Sport (Minister for Sport) 2007-10; Shadow Minister for: Culture, Media and Sport 2010, Security and Counter Terrorism 2010-11. *Select committees:* Member: Public Accounts 1996-98, Unopposed Bills (Panel) 1997-99, Selection 2001-03, Culture, Media and Sport 2011-. Vice-chair, PLP Yorkshire Regional Group 1997-2010. *Councils and public bodies:* Bradford City Council: Councillor 1982-94, Leader 1992-94.

Political interests: Employment, local and regional government; Azerbaijan, Bangladesh, Brazil, European Union, India, Pakistan, Qatar.

Other: Patron: Catholic Housing Aid (CHAS), Police Community Clubs of Great Britain; Director, Responsible Gambling Trust; Honorary Fellow, Bradford College. Honorary Chairman, Bradford Bulls RLFC.

Recreations: Sport, music.

Gerry Sutcliffe MP, House of Commons, London SW1A 0AA
Tel: 020 7219 3247 *Fax:* 020 7219 1227 *Email:* sutcliffeg@parliament.uk
Constituency: Gumption Business Centre, Glydegate, Bradford, West Yorkshire BD5 0BQ
Tel: 01274 288688 *Fax:* 01274 288689 *Website:* www.gerrysutcliffe.org.uk
Twitter: @GSutcliffeMP

LIBERAL DEMOCRAT

SWALES, IAN

Redcar *(Majority 5,214)*

Ian Cameron Swales. Born 5 April 1953; Son of Harry Swales and Elizabeth Swales, née Doig; Married Patricia Thew 1972 (2 sons 1 daughter).
Education: Ashville College, Harrogate; Manchester University (BSc chemical engineering) 1973; FCCA 1977.
Non-political career: Yorkshire Electricity 1973-78; Various roles, to Global Head of Leadership Development, ICI 1978-99; Training and consultancy business 1999-.
Political career: Contested Redcar 2005 general election. Member for Redcar since 6 May 2010 general election. *Select committees:* Member: Public Accounts 2010-, European Scrutiny 2010-. Member, SDP/Liberal Democrats 1981-.
Political interests: Business, public spending, pensions and benefits, environment and green industry, steel industry, chemical industry, social justice; Slovakia.
Recreations: Walking, reading, travel, cooking.
Ian Swales MP, House of Commons, London SW1A 0AA
Tel: 020 7219 7132 *Email:* ian.swales.mp@parliament.uk
Constituency: Room 103, Innovation Centre, Vienna Court, Kirkleatham Business Park, Redcar, North Yorkshire TS10 5SH
Tel: 01642 777940 *Email:* ian@ianswales.com *Website:* www.ianswales.com
Twitter: @iswales

CONSERVATIVE

SWAYNE, DESMOND

New Forest West *(Majority 16,896)*

Government Whip (Vice-Chamberlain of HM Household)

Desmond Angus Swayne. Born 20 August 1956; Son of George Swayne and Elisabeth Swayne, née Gibson; Married Moira Teek 1987 (1 son 2 daughters).
Education: Bedford School; St Mary's College, St Andrews University (MA theology 1980); Spanish and French (rusty).
Non-political career: Major, Territorial Army. Schoolmaster, A-level economics: Charterhouse 1980-81, Wrekin College 1982-87; Risk management systems manager, Royal Bank of Scotland 1988-96.
Political career: Contested Pontypridd 1987 and West Bromwich West 1992 general elections. Member for New Forest West 1997-2010, for New Forest West (revised boundary) since 6 May 2010 general election; Opposition Whip 2002-03; Opposition Spokesperson for: Health 2001, Defence 2001-02; Shadow Minister for: International Affairs 2003-04, Northern Ireland 2004; PPS to: Michael Howard as Leader of the Opposition 2004-05, David Cameron: as Leader of the Opposition 2005-10, as Prime Minister 2010-12; Government Whip 2012-13; Government Whip (Vice-Chamberlain of HM Household) 2013-. *Select committees:* Member: Scottish Affairs 1997-2001, Social Security 1999-2001, Procedure 2002-05, Defence 2005-06, Ecclesiastical Committee -2010, Administration 2012-.
Other: Member, Countryside Alliance. TD; PC 2011; Cavalry and Guards. Serpentine Swimming Club.
Recreations: Territorial Army.
Rt Hon Desmond Swayne TD MP, House of Commons, London SW1A 0AA
Tel: 020 7219 4886 *Fax:* 020 7219 0901 *Email:* swayned@parliament.uk
Constituency: 4 Cliff Crescent, Marine Drive, Barton-on-Sea, New Milton, Hampshire BH25 7EB
Tel: 01425 629844 *Fax:* 01425 621898 *Email:* desmondswayne@hotmail.com
Website: www.desmondswaynemp.com

LIBERAL DEMOCRAT

SWINSON, JO

East Dunbartonshire *(Majority 2,184)*

Parliamentary Under-Secretary of State (Minister for Employment Relations and Consumer Affairs), Department for Business, Innovation and Skills and Parliamentary Under-Secretary of State (Women and Equalities), Department for Culture, Media and Sport

Born 5 February 1980; Daughter of Peter and Annette Swinson; Married Duncan Hames MP 2011.
Education: Douglas Academy, Milngavie; London School of Economics (BSc management 2000); French.
Non-political career: Marketing executive and manager, Emap's Viking FM 2000-02; Marketing manager, Spaceandpeople Ltd 2002-04; Development officer, UK Public Health Association Scotland 2004-05.

Political career: Contested Hull East 2001 general election. Member for East Dunbartonshire since 5 May 2005; Liberal Democrat: Spokesperson for Culture, Media and Sport 2005-06; Whip 2005-06; Shadow Secretary of State for Scotland 2006-07; Shadow Minister for: Women and Equalities 2007, Foreign and Commonwealth Office 2008-10; PPS to: Vincent Cable as Secretary of State for Business, Innovation and Skills and President of the Board of Trade 2010-12, Nick Clegg as Deputy Prime Minister, Lord President of the Council 2012; Parliamentary Under-Secretary of State: (Minister for Employment Relations and Consumer Affairs), Department for Business, Innovation and Skills 2012-, (Women and Equalities), Department for Culture, Media and Sport 2012-. *Select committees:* Member: Environmental Audit 2007-10. Contested Strathkelvin and Bearsden constituency 2003 Scottish Parliament election. Liberal Democrat Youth and Students: Secretary 1998-99, Vice-chair 1999-2000, Vice-chair, campaigns 2000-01; Vice-chair, Haltemprice and Howden Liberal Democrats 2000; Member, Federal Executive 2002; Vice-chair, Gender Balance Taskforce 2003-06; Chair: Campaign for Gender Balance 2007-08, Women's Policy Working Group 2008-09; Deputy leader, Scottish Liberal Democrats 2010-12; Chair, Federal Policy Committee 2012-; Member, Manifesto Working Group 2013-.

Political interests: Quality of life and wellbeing, climate change, allergy, foreign affairs, corporate social responsibility; Chechnya, India, Kosovo, Romania, Sierra Leone.

Other: Member: Amnesty International 1998-, New Economics Foundation 2003-, Friends of the Earth, Unlock Democracy; Trustee, Help a Local Child 2001-02; Ran Great North Run for Diabetes UK 2006; Ran Loch Ness Marathon for Anaphylaxis Campaign 2007; Moonwalk for breast cancer charity walk the walk 2008; Glasgow half-marathon for Beatson Pebble Appeal 2009; Ran London Marathon for Leukaemia and Lymphoma Research 2011.

Recreations: Hiking, reading, running.

Jo Swinson MP, House of Commons, London SW1A 0AA
Tel: 020 7219 8088 *Fax:* 020 7219 0555 *Email:* jo.swinson.mp@parliament.uk
Constituency: 126 Drymen Road, Bearsden, Glasgow G61 3RB
Tel: 0141-943 1568 *Fax:* 0141-943 1564 *Website:* www.joswinson.org.uk *Twitter:* @joswinson

CONSERVATIVE

SWIRE, HUGO

East Devon *(Majority 9,114)*

Minister of State, Foreign and Commonwealth Office

Hugo George William Swire. Born 30 November 1959; Son of late Humphrey Swire and of Dowager, Marchioness Townshend, née Montgomerie; Married Sasha Nott 1996 (2 daughters).

Education: Eton College; St Andrews University (1978-79); Royal Military Academy Sandhurst.

Non-political career: Commissioned, 1st Battalion Grenadier Guards 1980-83; Joint managing director, International News Services and Prospect Films 1983-85; Financial consultant, Streets Financial Ltd 1985-87; Head of development, National Gallery 1988-92; Sotheby's: Deputy director 1992-97, Director 1997-2003; Non-executive director, then non-executive chair, PhotoMe International plc 2005-10; Non-executive director, Symphony Environmental Technologies plc 2008-10.

Political career: Contested Greenock and Inverclyde 1997 general election. Member for East Devon 2001-10, for East Devon (revised boundary) since 6 May 2010 general election; PPS to Theresa May as chairman of the Conservative Party 2003; Opposition Whip 2003-04; Shadow Minister for the Arts 2004-05; Shadow Secretary of State for Culture, Media and Sport 2005-07; Chair, Speakers' Advisory Committee on Works of Art 2005-10; Minister of State: Northern Ireland Office 2010-12, Foreign and Commonwealth Office 2012-. *Select committees:* Member: Northern Ireland Affairs 2002-05.

Political interests: Defence, foreign affairs, culture, pensioners; Bosnia, Lebanon, Oman, Qatar, Slovenia, United Arab Emirates.

Other: Council member, RNLI; Fund for Refugees in Slovenia; Jurassic Coast Trust; Fellow, Royal Society of Arts 1993; Children's Hospice, South West. PC 2011; White's, Pratt's, Beefsteak; President, Exmouth Conservative Club.

Recreations: Gardening, walking, bee keeping.

Rt Hon Hugo Swire MP, House of Commons, London SW1A 0AA
Tel: 020 7219 8173 *Fax:* 020 7219 1895 *Email:* hugo.swire.mp@parliament.uk
Constituency: 9c Mill Road Industrial Estate, White Cross Road, Woodbury Salterton, Exeter, Devon EX5 1EL
Tel: 01395 233503 *Email:* office@eastdevonconservatives.org.uk
Website: www.hugoswire.org.uk *Twitter:* @hugoswire

CONSERVATIVE

SYMS, ROBERT

Poole *(Majority 7,541)*

Robert Andrew Raymond Syms. Born 15 August 1956; Son of Raymond Syms, builder, and Mary Syms, teacher; Married Nicola Guy 1991 (divorced 1999); married Fiona Mellersh 2000 (separated 2007) (1 daughter 1 son).

Education: Colston's School, Bristol.

Non-political career: Director, family building, plant hire and property group, Chippenham, Wiltshire 1978-.

Political career: Contested Walsall North 1992 general election. Member for Poole 1997-2010, for Poole (revised boundary) since 6 May 2010 general election; PPS to Michael Ancram as Chair Conservative Party 1999-2000; Opposition Spokesperson for Environment, Transport and Regions 1999-2001; Opposition Whip 2003; Shadow Minister for: Local and Devolved Government Affairs 2003-05, Local Government 2005-07; Assistant Government Whip 2012-13. *Select committees:* Member: Health 1997-2000, 2007-10, Procedure 1998-99, Transport 2002-03, Liaison 2010-13; Chair: Regulatory Reform 2010-12; Member: Joint Committee on the Draft Detention of Terrorist Suspects (Temporary Extension) Bills 2011. Joint Vice-chair, Conservative Party Committee for Constitutional Affairs, Scotland and Wales 1997-99. North Wiltshire Conservative Association: Treasurer 1982-84, Deputy chair 1983-84, Chair 1984-86; Vice-chair, Conservative Party 2001-03. *Councils and public bodies:* Councillor: North Wiltshire District Council 1983-87, Wiltshire County Council 1985-97; Member, Wessex Regional Health Authority 1988-90.

Political interests: Economic policy, constitution, local and regional government; USA, most of English speaking world.

Other: Member: North Wiltshire Enterprise Agency 1986-90, Calne Development Project Trust 1986-97; Fellow, Chartered Institute of Building.

Recreations: Reading, music.

Robert Syms MP, House of Commons, London SW1A 0AA
Tel: 020 7219 4601 *Fax:* 020 7219 6867 *Email:* symsr@parliament.uk guyn@parliament.uk
Constituency: Poole Conservative Association, 38 Sandbanks Road, Poole, Dorset BH14 8BX
Tel: 01202 739922 *Fax:* 01202 739944 *Email:* symsr@pooleconservatives.org
Website: www.robertsymsmp.com

LABOUR

TAMI, MARK

Alyn and Deeside *(Majority 2,919)*

Opposition Assistant Chief Whip

Mark Richard Tami. Born 3 October 1962; Son of Michael Tami and Patricia Tami; Married Sally Ann Daniels 1994 (2 sons).

Education: Enfield Grammar School; Swansea University (BA history 1985).

Non-political career: AEEU: Head of research and communications 1992-99, Head of policy 1999-2001. Member: AEEU Amicus 1986-, TUC General Council 1999-2001.

Political career: Member for Alyn and Deeside since 7 June 2001 general election; PPS to John Healey as Financial Secretary to the Treasury 2005-06; Assistant Government Whip 2007-10; Opposition Whip 2010-11; Opposition Assistant Chief Whip 2011-. *Select committees:* Member: Northern Ireland Affairs 2001-05, European Standing Committee B 2003-05, Joint Committee on Tax Law Rewrite Bills 2005-07, Joint Committee on Human Rights 2007, Selection 2010-, Works of Art 2011-12, Joint Committee on Security 2011-, Administration 2012-. Vice-chair PLP Welsh Regional Group 2005-07. Treasurer, Labour Friends of Australia.

Political interests: Manufacturing, aerospace, animal welfare.

Other: Glamorgan County Cricket.

Recreations: Football (Norwich City), cricket, fishing, antiques.

Mark Tami MP, House of Commons, London SW1A 0AA
Tel: 020 7219 8174 *Fax:* 020 7219 1943 *Email:* tamim@parliament.uk
Constituency: 70 High Street, Connocks Quay, Flintshire, Clwyd CH5 4DD
Tel: 01244 819854 *Fax:* 01244 823548 *Website:* www.marktami.co.uk

CONSERVATIVE

TAPSELL, PETER

Louth and Horncastle *(Majority 13,871)*

Peter Hannay Bailey Tapsell. Born 1 February 1930; Son of late Eustace Tapsell and late Jessie Tapsell, née Hannay; Married The Hon. Cecilia Hawke 1963 (divorced 1971) (1 son deceased); married Gabrielle Mahieu 1974.

Education: Tonbridge School, Kent; Merton College, Oxford (BA modern history 1953, MA; Diploma economics 1954).

Non-political career: Subaltern Army national service in Middle East 1948-50; Royal Sussex Regiment; Honorary Life member, 6th Squadron RAF 1971. Conservative research department 1954-57; Personal assistant to Anthony Eden as Prime Minister 1955; Partner, James Capel and Co (stockbrokers) 1960-90; Adviser to central banks and international companies 1960-.

Political career: Contested Wednesbury February 1957 by-election. Member for Nottingham West 1959-64. Contested Nottingham West 1964 general election. Member for Horncastle 1966-83, for Lindsey East 1983-97, for Louth and Horncastle 1997-2010, for Louth and Horncastle (revised boundary) since 6 May 2010 general election; Opposition Frontbench Spokesperson for: Foreign and Commonwealth Affairs 1976-77, Treasury and Economic Affairs 1977-78; Longest serving Conservative MP 2001-; Father of the House 2010-. *Select committees:* Member: Unopposed Bills (Panel) 2004-.

Political interests: Foreign affairs, economics, finance, defence; Africa, Asia.

Other: Member: International Investment Advisory Board to Brunei Government 1976-83, Trilateral Commission 1979-98, Business Advisory Council of the UN 2001-04; Chair, British-Caribbean Association 1963-64; Vice-President, Tennyson Society 1966-; Council member, Institute of Fiscal Studies 1983-2005; Trustee, Oxford Union Society 1985-93; Honorary Deputy chair, Mitsubishi Trust Oxford Foundation 1988-; Member, London Stock Exchange 1957-90. Honorary Postmaster, Merton College, Oxford 1953; Honorary Fellow, Merton College, Oxford 1989. *The Spectator*: Backbencher of the Year 1993, Parliamentarian of the Year 2004. Brunei Dato 1971; Kt 1985; PC 2011; Athenæum, Carlton, Hurlingham.

Recreations: Overseas travel, walking in mountains, reading history.

Rt Hon Sir Peter Tapsell MP, House of Commons, London SW1A 0AA
Tel: 020 7219 4477 *Fax:* 020 7219 0976
Constituency: Cannon Street House, Cannon Street, Louth, Lincolnshire LN11 9NL
Tel: 01507 609840 *Fax:* 01507 608091

LIBERAL DEMOCRAT

TEATHER, SARAH

Brent Central *(Majority 1,345)*

Sarah Louise Teather. Born 1 June 1974.

Education: Leicester Grammar School; St John's College, Cambridge (BA pharmacology 1996).

Non-political career: Science policy officer Royal Society 1998-2001; Science policy consultant Technopolis Ltd 2001-02; Policy analyst Macmillan Cancer Relief 2002-03.

Political career: Contested Finchley and Golders Green 2001 general election. Member for Brent East 18 September 2003 by-election to 2010, for Brent Central since 6 May 2010 general election; Liberal Democrat: Spokesperson for: Health 2003-04, London 2004-05; Shadow Minister for Communities and Local Government 2005; Shadow to Office of the Deputy Prime Minister 2005-06; Shadow Secretary of State for Education and Skills/Innovation, Universities and Skills 2006-07; Shadow Secretary of State for Business, Enterprise and Regulatory Reform 2007-08; Shadow Minister for Housing 2008-10; Minister of State for Children and Families, Department for Education 2010-12; *Councils and public bodies:* Councillor, London Borough of Islington 2002-03.

Political interests: Health, housing, Guantanamo Bay, civil liberties, children, SEN/disability, child poverty, family policy, immigration, asylum, poverty; Middle East.

Other: Patron: PLIAS, Silver Star. Opposition Parliamentarian of the Year 2009, Asian Voice.

Recreations: Singing, music.

Sarah Teather MP, House of Commons, London SW1A 0AA
Tel: 020 7219 8147 *Fax:* 020 7219 0041 *Email:* teathers@parliament.uk
Constituency: 70 Walm Lane, Willesden Green, London NW2 4RA
Tel: 020 8459 0455 *Fax:* 020 8830 3280 *Website:* www.sarahteather.org.uk

LAB/CO-OP

THOMAS, GARETH
Harrow West *(Majority 3,143)*

Shadow Minister for Foreign and Commonwealth Office

Gareth Richard Thomas. Born 15 July 1967.

Education: Hatch End High School; Lowlands College; University College of Wales, Aberystwyth (BSc (Econ) politics 1988); University of Greenwich (PGCE 1992); King's College, London (MA imperial and Commonwealth studies 1996).

Non-political career: Member, Amicus.

Political career: Member for Harrow West 1997-2010, for Harrow West (revised boundary) since 6 May 2010 general election; PPS to Charles Clarke: as Minister of State, Home Office 1999-2001, as Minister without Portfolio and Party Chair 2001-02, as Secretary of State for Education and Skills 2002-03; Sponsored Private Member's Bill, Industrial and Provident Societies Act 2002; Parliamentary Under-Secretary of State: Department for International Development 2003-08, Department for Business, Enterprise and Regulatory Reform (Trade and Consumer Affairs) 2007-08; Minister of State (Trade, Investment and Consumer Affairs/Trade, Development and Consumer Affairs), Departments for: Business, Enterprise and Regulatory Reform 2008-09, International Development 2008-10; Shadow Minister for: International Development 2010, Treasury 2010, Business, Innovation and Skills 2010-11, Cabinet Office 2011-13, Foreign and Commonwealth Office 2013-; Shadow Deputy Minister for London 2013-. *Select committees:* Member: Environmental Audit 1997-99. Vice-chair, PLP Departmental Committee for Culture, Media and Sport 2000-04; Honorary Secretary, PLP Departmental Committee for Trade and Industry 2000-04. Member, SERA; Chair, Co-operative Party 2000-. *Councils and public bodies:* London Borough of Harrow: Councillor 1990-97, Labour Group Whip 1996-96; Vice-chair, Association of Local Government Social Services Committee.

Political interests: Energy, mutuals, health, environment; Europe, India, Norway, Pakistan, Sri Lanka.

Other: Member, Fabian Society; Fellow, Industry and Parliament Trust 2003; United Services Club, Pinner.

Publications: At the Energy Crossroads Policies for a Low Carbon Economy (Fabian Society, 2001); From Margins to Mainstream – Making Social Responsibility Part of Corporate Culture (2002).

Recreations: Canoeing, running, rugby union.

Gareth Thomas MP, House of Commons, London SW1A 0AA
Tel: 020 7219 4243 *Fax:* 020 7219 1154 *Email:* gareth.thomas.mp@parliament.uk
Constituency: 132 Blenheim Road, West Harrow, Middlesex HA2 7AA
Tel: 020 8861 6300 *Email:* gareth.thomas@harrowlabour.org *Website:* www.gareththomas.org
Twitter: @GarethThomasMP

LABOUR

THORNBERRY, EMILY
Islington South and Finsbury *(Majority 3,569)*

Shadow Attorney General

Born 27 July 1960; Daughter of late Sallie Thornberry and Cedric Thornberry; Married Christopher Nugee 1992 (1 daughter 2 sons).

Education: Church of England Secondary Modern, Guildford; Burlington Danes, Shepherd's Bush, London; Kent University, Canterbury (BA law 1982).

Non-political career: Member, Mike Mansfield's Chambers: Tooks Court 1985. Member, Unite (TGWU sector) 1985-.

Political career: Member for Islington South and Finsbury since 5 May 2005 general election; PPS to Joan Ruddock as Minister of State, Department of Energy and Climate Change 2009-10; Shadow Minister for: Energy and Climate Change 2010, Health 2010-11; Shadow Attorney General 2011-. *Select committees:* Member: Environmental Audit 2005-07, Joint Committee on the Draft Legal Services Bill 2006, Communities and Local Government 2006-09.

Political interests: Housing, environment, poverty, equality; Middle East.

Other: Society of Labour Lawyers 1983; Friends of the Earth 1990; The Fawcett Society; Fabian Society.

Recreations: Family, cycling, travel.

Emily Thornberry MP, House of Commons, London SW1A 0AA
Tel: 020 7219 5676 *Fax:* 020 7219 5955 *Email:* thornberrye@parliament.uk
Constituency: 65 Barnsbury Street, Islington, London N1 1EJ
Tel: 020 7697 9307 *Fax:* 020 7697 4587 *Email:* emilythornberrymp@parliament.uk
Website: www.emilythornberry.com *Twitter:* @emilythornberry

LIBERAL DEMOCRAT

THORNTON, MIKE
Eastleigh *(Majority 1,771)*

Michael Thornton. Born 1 May 1952; Son of Peter and Rosamond Thornton; Married Peta (1 daughter).

Education: Manchester Polytechnic (law 1973); French.

Non-political career: Hotel Manager; Marketing Manager, Wholesale News 1987-96; Independent Financial Adviser 1996-2002; Business Development Manager 2004-08, 2011-13; Local Business Bank Manager 2008-11. Former Member, Unite.

Political career: Member for Eastleigh since 28 February 2013 by-election; *Councils and public bodies:* Councillor, Eastleigh Borough Council 2007-; Bishopstoke Parish Council.

Other: Children's Society. Bishopstoke Tennis Club, New Community Table Tennis Club.

Recreations: Countryside walks, tennis, squash, table tennis.

Mike Thornton MP, House of Commons, London SW1A 0AA
Tel: 020 7219 7334 *Email:* mike.thornton.mp@parliament.uk
Constituency: 109a Leigh Road, Eastleigh SO50 9DR
Tel: 023 8062 0007 *Email:* mike@mikethornton.org.uk *Website:* www.eastleighlibdems.org.uk
Twitter: @Mike4Eastleigh

LIBERAL DEMOCRAT

THURSO, JOHN
Caithness, Sutherland and Easter Ross *(Majority 4,826)*

Sir John Archibald Sinclair, Viscount Thurso. Born 10 September 1953; Son of late Robin, 2nd Viscount Thurso, and Margaret, née Robertson; Married Marion Ticknor, née Sage 1976 (2 sons 1 daughter).

Education: Eton College; Westminster Technical College (HCIMA membership exam 1974); French.

Non-political career: Managing director: Lancaster Hotel 1981-85, Cliveden House Ltd 1985-93; Non-executive director, Savoy Hotel plc 1993-98; Managing director, Fitness and Leisure Holdings Ltd 1995-2001; Chair: Thurso Fisheries Ltd 1995-, Scrabster Harbour Trust 1996-2001; Director: Profile Recruitment and Management Ltd 1996-2002, Walker Greenbank plc 1997-2002, Anton Mosiman Ltd 1997-2002; Chair, International Wine and Spirit Competition 1999-; Deputy chair, Millennium and Copthorn's Hotels plc 2002-09.

Political career: Member for Caithness, Sutherland and Easter Ross 2001-05, for Caithness, Sutherland and Easter Ross (revised boundary) since 5 May 2005 general election. (First former hereditary member of House of Lords to become an MP); Liberal Democrat Whip 2001-02; Scottish Liberal Democrat Spokesperson for Tourism 2001-05; Liberal Democrat: Spokesperson for Scotland 2001-06, Shadow Secretary of State for: Transport 2003-05, Scotland 2003-06, Business, Enterprise and Regulatory Reform 2008-09, Business, Innovation and Skills 2009-10; Member House of Commons Commission 2010-. *Select committees:* Member: Culture, Media and Sport 2001-05, Administration 2005-10, Treasury 2006-, Liaison 2010-; Chair: Finance and Services 2010-; Member: Joint Committee on the Draft House of Lords Reform Bill 2011-12, Parliamentary Commission on Banking Standards 2012-13. Chair, Liberal Democrat Parliamentary Party Committees on: Scotland 2010-, Constitutional and Political Reform 2012-. Member, Liberal Democrat Party Federal Policy Committee 1999-2001.

Political interests: Tourism, House of Lords reform, treasury, financial services, banking reform, energy.

Other: Chair: Bucks Game Conservancy 1990-92, BHA Clubs Panel 1992-96, Master Innholders Association 1995-97; President, Licensed Victuallers Schools 1996-97; President and Fellow, Tourism Society 1999-; Patron: Hotel Catering and International Management Association 1997-2003, Institute of Management Services 1998-; President, Academy of Food and Wine Service 1998-; Chair, UK Springboard Festival Year 2000; Trustee: Castle of Mey Trust, La Foundation pour la Formation Hoteliere (Zurich); FHCIMA 1991; FInstD 1997. Liveryman, Innholders' Company 1997. Freeman, City of London 1991. Honorary DBA, Oxford Brookes University 2004. Succeeded his father 1995 as 3rd Viscount Thurso and 6th Bt of Ulbster; Brook's, New Edinburgh.

Publications: Tourism Tomorrow (1998).

John Thurso MP, House of Commons, London SW1A 0AA
Tel: 020 7219 1752 *Fax:* 020 7219 3797 *Email:* john.thurso.mp@parliament.uk
Constituency: No constituency office
Email: john@johnthurso.org.uk *Website:* www.johnthurso.org.uk

LABOUR

TIMMS, STEPHEN
East Ham *(Majority 27,826)*

Shadow Minister for Employment

Stephen Creswell Timms. Born 29 July 1955; Son of late Ronald Timms, engineer, and Margaret Timms, retired school teacher; Married Hui-Leng Lim 1986.

Education: Farnborough Grammar School, Hampshire; Emmanuel College, Cambridge (MA mathematics 1977; MPhil operational research 1978); German.

Non-political career: Computer and telecommunications industry; Logica Ltd 1978-86; Ovum Ltd 1986-94. Member, Unite.

Political career: Member for Newham North East from 9 June 1994 by-election to 1997, for East Ham 1997-2010, for East Ham (revised boundary) since 6 May 2010 general election; PPS to Andrew Smith as Minister of State, Department for Education and Employment 1997-98; Joint PPS to Marjorie Mowlam as Secretary of State for Northern Ireland 1998; Department of Social Security 1998-99: Parliamentary Under-Secretary of State 1998-99, Minister of State 1999; Financial Secretary, HM Treasury 1999-2001; Minister of State: Department for Education and Skills (School Standards) 2001-02, Department of Trade and Industry (Energy, E-Commerce and Postal Services) 2002-04; Financial Secretary, HM Treasury 2004-05; Minister of State Department for Work and Pensions (Pensions Reform) 2005-06; Chief Secretary to the Treasury 2006-07; Minister of State (Competitiveness), Department for Business, Enterprise and Regulatory Reform 2007-08; Minister of State, Department for Work and Pensions 2008; Financial Secretary, HM Treasury 2008-10; Parliamentary Under-Secretary of State, Department for Business, Innovation and Skills (Digital Britain) 2009-10; Shadow Financial Secretary 2010; Shadow Minister for: Business, Innovation and Skills 2010, Employment 2010-. *Select committees:* Member: Treasury 1996-97, Public Accounts 2004-05, Joint Committee on Tax Law Rewrite Bills 2009-10. Christian Socialist Movement: Joint vice-chair 1995-98, Chair 2012-; Vice-chair, Labour Party Faith Groups 2007-. *Councils and public bodies:* London Borough of Newham: Councillor 1984-97, Leader of the Council 1990-94; Board Member, East London Partnership (now East London Business Alliance) 1990-2006; Stratford Development Partnership 1992-94.

Political interests: Economic policy, urban regeneration, telecommunications, employment, Christian socialism; Germany, Singapore.

Other: Fellow, Industry and Parliament Trust 1997; Trustee, Traidcraft Foundation 2011-. Honorary doctorate. PC 2006.

Publications: Broadband Communications: The Commercial Impact (1987).

Recreations: Cycling, walking.

Rt Hon Stephen Timms MP, House of Commons, London SW1A 0AA
Tel: 020 7219 4000 *Fax:* 020 7219 2949 *Email:* timmss@parliament.uk
Constituency: No constituency office
Email: stephen@stephentimms.org.uk *Website:* www.stephentimms.org.uk
Twitter: @stephenctimms

CONSERVATIVE

TIMPSON, EDWARD
Crewe and Nantwich *(Majority 6,046)*

Parliamentary Under-Secretary of State, Department for Education

Anthony Edward Timpson. Born 26 December 1973; Son of John Timpson and Alexandra Timpson; Married Julia Still 2002 (1 son 2 daughters).

Education: Uppingham School, Rutland; Durham University (BA politics 1996); Law conversion; College of Law, London (LLB 1997).

Non-political career: Called to the Bar 1999; Non-practising family law barrister.

Political career: Member for Crewe and Nantwich 22 May 2008 by-election to 2010, for Crewe and Nantwich (revised boundary) since 6 May 2010 general election; PPS to Theresa May as Home Secretary 2010-12; Parliamentary Under-Secretary of State, Department for Education 2012-. *Select committees:* Member: Children, Schools and Families 2008-10, Joint Committee on Human Rights 2008-10. Campaign co-ordinator, Eddisbury Conservative Association 2006-07.

Political interests: Crime, family, education, children in care, fostering and adoption.

Other: Patron: Supported Community Business, Crewe; Home Start, Central Cheshire. Worshipful Company of Pattenmakers.

Recreations: Marathons, travel, writing, cricket, football.

Edward Timpson MP, House of Commons, London SW1A 0AA
Tel: 020 7219 8027 *Email:* timpsone@parliament.uk
Constituency: 30 Victoria Street, Crewe CW1 2JE
Tel: 01270 501725 *Website:* www.edwardtimpson.com

TOMLINSON, JUSTIN

North Swindon *(Majority 7,060)*

Justin Paul Tomlinson. Born 5 November 1976; Son of Vera and Paul Tomlinson; Married Jo Wheeler 2012.

Education: Harry Cheshire High School, Kidderminster; Oxford Brookes University (BA business 1999).

Non-political career: Sales and marketing manager, First Leisure 1999-2000; Marketing executive, Point to Point 2000; Director, TB Marketing Solutions Ltd 2000-10.

Political career: Contested North Swindon 2005 general election. Member for North Swindon since 6 May 2010 general election. *Select committees:* Member: Joint Committee on Consolidation, Etc, Bills 2010-, Unopposed Bills (Panel) 2011-, Public Accounts 2012-. Chair, Oxford Brookes University Conservative Students' Association 1995-99; Deputy chair, North Swindon Conservative Association 2000-04; National chair, Conservative Future 2002-03. *Councils and public bodies:* Swindon Borough Council: Councillor 2000-10, Cabinet member 2003-08.

Political interests: Business, financial education, development, local government, sport, consumer issues, young entrepreneurs.

Other: Honorary President, Swindon British Heart Foundation. Swindon Town Supporters Trust; Swindon Supermarine Football Club.

Recreations: Football, cricket, cinema, video games.

Justin Tomlinson MP, House of Commons, London SW1A 0AA
Tel: 020 7219 7167 *Email:* justin.tomlinson.mp@parliament.uk
Constituency: Swindon Conservative MPs' Office, First Floor, 1 Milton Road, Swindon SN1 5JE
Tel: 01793 533393 *Website:* www.justintomlinson.com *Twitter:* @jtomlinsonmp

TREDINNICK, DAVID

Bosworth *(Majority 5,032)*

David Arthur Stephen Tredinnick. Born 19 January 1950; Son of late Stephen Tredinnick and late Evelyn Tredinnick, née Wates; Married Rebecca Shott 1983 (Divorced 2008) (1 son 1 daughter).

Education: Eton College; Mons Officer Cadet School; Graduate School of Business Cape Town University (MBA 1975); St John's College, Oxford (MLitt 1987).

Non-political career: 2nd Lieutenant Grenadier Guards 1968-71. Trainee, E. B. Savory Milln & Co. (Stockbrokers) 1972-73; Account executive, Quadrant Int. 1974; Salesman, Kalle Infotech UK 1976; Sales manager, Word Right Word Processing 1977-78; Consultant, Baird Communications NY 1978-79; Marketing manager, QI Europe Ltd 1979-81; Malden Mitcham Properties: Manager 1981-87, Director.

Political career: Contested Cardiff South and Penarth 1983 general election. Member for Bosworth 1987-2010, for Bosworth (revised boundary) since 6 May 2010 general election; PPS to Sir Wyn Roberts as Minister of State, Welsh Office 1991-94. *Select committees:* Member: Liaison 1997-2005; Chair: Joint Committee on Statutory Instruments 1997-2005; Member: Health 2010-, Science and Technology 2013-. Member, Executive, 1922 Committee 2002-05.

Political interests: Complementary and alternative medicine, health care, diet and nutrition, foreign affairs, home affairs, police, law and order, environment; Eastern Europe.

Other: Chair, British Atlantic Group of Young Politicians 1989-91; Future of Europe Trust 1991-95.

Recreations: Golf, skiing, tennis, windsurfing, sailing.

David Tredinnick MP, House of Commons, London SW1A 0AA
Tel: 020 7219 4514 *Fax:* 020 7219 4901 *Email:* tredinnickd@parliament.uk
Constituency: Bosworth Conservative Association, 10a Priory Walk, Hinckley, Leicestershire LE10 1HU
Tel: 01455 635741 *Fax:* 01455 612023
Website: www.bosworthconservatives.com www.davidtredinnickmp.com

LABOUR

TRICKETT, JON
Hemsworth *(Majority 9,844)*

Shadow Minister without Portfolio; Deputy Chair, Labour Party

Jon Hedley Trickett. Born 2 July 1950; Son of Laurence and Rose Trickett; Married Sarah Balfour 1993 (1 son 2 daughters).

Education: Roundhay School, Leeds; Hull University (BA politics); Leeds University (MA political sociology); French.

Non-political career: Plumber/builder 1974-86. Member: GMB, RMT Parliamentary Campaigning Group 2002-.

Political career: Member for Hemsworth 1 February 1996 by-election to 2010, for Hemsworth (revised boundary) since 6 May 2010 general election; PPS to Peter Mandelson: as Minister without Portfolio 1997-98, as Secretary of State for Trade and Industry July-December 1998; PPS to Gordon Brown as Prime Minister 2008-10; Shadow Minister of State for Cabinet Office 2010-11; Shadow Minister for the Cabinet Office 2011-13; Shadow Minister without Portfolio 2013-; Deputy Chair, Labour Party 2013-. *Select committees:* Member: Unopposed Bills (Panel) 1997-2013, Education and Employment 2001, Education and Employment (Employment Sub-Committee) 2001, Public Accounts 2001-06, Public Administration 2010. Secretary PLP Departmental Committee for Health and Social Services 2005-08. *Councils and public bodies:* Leeds City Council: Councillor 1984-96, Leader of the Council 1989-96.

Political interests: Economic policy, finance, industry, sport; Middle East, France, USA.

Other: British Cycling Federation. Member: British Cycling Federation, West Riding Sailing Club; Honorary Life Member, Cyclists' Touring Club.

Recreations: Cycle racing, windsurfing.

Jon Trickett MP, House of Commons, London SW1A 0AA
Tel: 020 7219 5074 *Fax:* 020 7219 2133 *Email:* trickettj@parliament.uk
Constituency: 1a Highfield Road, Hemsworth, Pontefract, West Yorkshire WF9 4DP
Tel: 01977 722290 *Fax:* 01977 722290 *Email:* jtrickett@jontrickett.org.uk
Website: www.jontrickett.org.uk *Twitter:* @jon_trickett

CONSERVATIVE

TRUSS, ELIZABETH
South West Norfolk *(Majority 13,140)*

Parliamentary Under-Secretary of State, Department for Education

Elizabeth Mary Truss. Born 26 July 1975; Daughter of John Truss and Priscilla Truss; Married Hugh O'Leary 2000 (2 daughters).

Education: Roundhay School, Leeds; Merton College, Oxford (BA philosophy, politics and economics 1996).

Non-political career: Commercial analyst, Shell International 1996-2000; Director, financial analysis, Cable and Wireless 2000-05; Managing director, political division, Communication Group 2006-07; Deputy director, Reform 2007-09.

Political career: Contested Hemsworth 2001 and Calder Valley 2005 general elections. Member for South West Norfolk since 6 May 2010 general election; Parliamentary Under-Secretary of State, Department for Education 2012-. *Select committees:* Member: Justice 2010-12. Member, Conservative Party 1996-; Chair, Lewisham Deptford Conservative Association 1998-2000. *Councils and public bodies:* Councillor, London Borough of Greenwich Council 2006-10.

Political interests: Economy, education, food.

Other: Member, Chartered Institute of Management Accountants. Minister to Watch, *The Spectator* awards 2012.

Publications: Co-author (with Kwasi Kwarteng MP, Priti Patel MP, Dominic Raab MP and Chris Skidmore MP), Britannia Unchained: Global Lessons for Growth and Prosperity (Palgrave Macmillan, 2012).

Recreations: Film, food, design.

Elizabeth Truss MP, House of Commons, London SW1A 0AA
Tel: 020 7219 7151 *Fax:* 020 7219 4109 *Email:* elizabeth.truss.mp@parliament.uk
Constituency: The Limes, 32 Bridge Street, Thetford, Norfolk IP24 3AG
Tel: 01842 757345 *Website:* www.elizabethtruss.com *Twitter:* @trussliz

CONSERVATIVE

TURNER, ANDREW
Isle of Wight *(Majority 10,527)*

Andrew John Turner. Born 24 October 1953; Son of Eustace Turner, schoolmaster, and Joyce Turner, née Lowe, schoolmistress; Partner Carole Dennett.

Education: Rugby School; Keble College, Oxford (BA geography 1976, MA); Birmingham University (PGCE 1977); Henley Management College.

Non-political career: Teacher economics and geography, comprehensive schools 1977-84; Specialist, education, trade and industry, Conservative Research Department 1984-86; Special adviser to Norman Fowler as Secretary of State for Social Services 1986-88; Director, Grant-Maintained Schools Foundation 1988-97; Education consultant 1997-2001; Deputy director, Education Unit, Institute of Economic Affairs 1998-2000; Head of policy and resources, education department, London Borough of Southwark 2000-01.

Political career: Contested Hackney South and Shoreditch 1992 and Isle of Wight 1997 general elections. Member for Isle of Wight since 7 June 2001 general election; Sponsored Animal Welfare (Journey to Slaughter) Bill 2001; Shadow Minister for Charities 2005-06. *Select committees:* Member: Education and Skills 2001-05, Justice 2008-10, Political and Constitutional Reform 2010-, Chairmen's Panel/Panel of Chairs 2010-. Member, Executive, 1922 Committee 2001-03, 2006-12; Vice-chair: Conservative Education Policy Committee 2001-02, Conservative Home Affairs Public Services Policy Group 2002-03. Contested Birmingham East 1994 European Parliament election. Appointee party education policy groups for general elections 1987, 1992, 2001; Vice-President, Association of Conservative Clubs 2002-05; Vice-chair (campaigning), Conservative Party 2003-05. *Councils and public bodies:* Councillor, Oxford City Council 1979-96; Sheriff of Oxford 1994-95.

Political interests: Education, social services, economy, constitution.

Recreations: Walking, old movies, avoiding gardening.

Andrew Turner MP, House of Commons, London SW1A 0AA
Tel: 020 7219 8490 *Fax:* 020 7219 0174
Constituency: The Riverside Centre, The Quay, Newport, Isle of Wight PO30 2QR
Tel: 01983 530808 *Fax:* 01983 822266 *Email:* mail@islandmp.org islandmp.org

TURNER, KARL
Kingston upon Hull East *(Majority 8,597)*

Opposition Whip

Born 15 April 1971; Son of Ken Turner, trade unionist, and Pat Turner.

Education: Bransholme High School; Hull College; Hull University (law 2004).

Non-political career: Youth training scheme, Hull City Council; Self-employed antiques dealer; Called to the Bar, Middle Temple 2005; Barrister: Max Gold Partnership, Hull 2005-09, Wilberforce Chambers, Hull 2009-. Member: Unison, GMB.

LABOUR

Political career: Member for Kingston upon Hull East since 6 May 2010 general election; Opposition Whip 2013-. *Select committees:* Member: Justice 2010-13, Home Affairs 2012-13.

Political interests: Justice, jobs, welfare, home affairs; Sri Lanka.

Karl Turner MP, House of Commons, London SW1A 0AA
Tel: 020 7219 7088 *Email:* karl.turner.mp@parliament.uk
Constituency: 1181 Holderness Road, Hull HU8 9EA
Tel: 01482 781019 *Website:* www.karlturnermp.org.uk *Twitter:* @KarlTurnerMP

LABOUR

TWIGG, DEREK
Halton *(Majority 15,504)*

John Derek Twigg. Born 9 July 1959; Son of Kenneth and Irene Twigg; Married Mary Cassidy 1988 (1 son 1 daughter).

Education: Bankfield High School, Widnes; Halton College of Further Education (1978).

Non-political career: Civil servant, Department for Education and Employment 1975-96. Member GMB.

Political career: Member for Halton 1997-2010, for Halton (revised boundary) since 6 May 2010 general election; PPS: to Helen Liddell: as Minister of State, Department of the Environment, Transport and the Regions 1999, as Minister of State, Department of Trade and Industry 1999-2001, to Stephen Byers as Secretary of State for Transport, Local Government and the Regions 2001-02; Assistant Government Whip 2002-03, Government Whip 2003-04; Parliamentary Under-Secretary of State: Department for Education and Skills 2004-05, Department for

Transport 2005-06, Ministry of Defence (Minister for Veterans) 2006-08; Shadow Minister for Health 2010-11. *Select committees:* Member: Public Accounts 1998-99, Children, Schools and Families 2009-10, Joint Committee on Voting Eligibilty (Prisoners) Bill 2013-, Defence 2013-. *Councils and public bodies:* Councillor: Cheshire County Council 1981-85; Halton Borough Council 1983-97.

Political interests: Economy, education, health and poverty, defence; Greece.

Recreations: Various sporting activities, hill walking, military history.

Derek Twigg MP, House of Commons, London SW1A 0AA
Tel: 020 7219 1039 *Fax:* 020 7219 3642 *Email:* derek.twigg.mp@parliament.uk
Constituency: Bridge Business Centre (not for correspondence), Suite E, Cheshire House, Gorsey Lane, Widnes, Cheshire WA8 0RP
Tel: 0151-424 7030 *Fax:* 0151-423 8535 *Website:* www.derektwigg.org.uk

LAB/CO-OP

TWIGG, STEPHEN
Liverpool West Derby *(Majority 18,467)*

Shadow Minister Political and Constitutional Reform

Born 25 December 1966; Son of Ian David Twigg and late Jean Barbara Twigg; Civil Partnership.

Education: Southgate Comprehensive; Balliol College, Oxford (BA politics and economics 1988); French.

Non-political career: President, National Union of Students; Parliamentary officer: Amnesty International UK, NCVO; Research assistant to Margaret Hodge MP; Political consultant, Rowland Sallingbury Casey; General Secretary, Fabian Society 1996-97; Director: Foreign Policy Centre 2005-, Special projects, Aegis Trust 2005-. Member, Amicus-MSF.

Political career: Member for Enfield Southgate 1997-2005. Contested Enfield Southgate 2005 general election. Member for Liverpool West Derby since 6 May 2010 general election; Parliamentary Secretary, Privy Council Office 2001-02; Department for Education and Skills 2002-05: Parliamentary Under-Secretary of State 2002-04: for Young People and Learning 2002, for Schools 2002-04, Minister of State 2004-05; Shadow Minister for Foreign Commonwealth Office 2010-11; Shadow Secretary of State for Education 2011-13; Shadow Minister Political and Constitutional Reform 2013-. *Select committees:* Member: Modernisation of the House of Commons 1998-2000, Education and Employment 1999-2001, Education and Employment (Employment Sub-Committee) 1999-2001. Honorary Secretary, Labour Party Departmental Committee for Foreign and Commonwealth Affairs 1997-99; Member, Labour Party Departmental Committees for: Education and Employment 1997-2001, Home Affairs 1997-2001; Member, Departmental Committee for Education and Skills 2001-05. Chair: Labour Campaign for Electoral Reform -2001, Labour Friends of Israel -2001. *Councils and public bodies:* London Borough of Islington Council: Councillor 1992-97, Chief Whip 1994-96, Deputy Leader 1996; Governor: Merryhills Primary School, Southgate School, Middlesex University Court.

Political interests: Education, electoral reform, local and regional government, foreign affairs; Africa, Middle East.

Other: Member: Amnesty International, Stonewall, Holocaust Educational Trust, League Against Cruel Sports; Honorary President, British Youth Council; Patron, Principal Theatre Company; Honorary President, Progress 2011-; Chicken Shed Theatre Company; National Liberal. Southgate Cricket.

Publications: Co-author, The Cross We Bear: Electoral Reform in Local Government (1997); Contributor, The Purple Book (Progress, 2011).

Stephen Twigg MP, House of Commons, London SW1A 0AA
Tel: 020 7219 4158 *Email:* stephen.twigg.mp@parliament.uk
Constituency: 229 Eaton Road, Liverpool L12 2AG
Tel: 0151-230 0853 *Website:* www.stephentwiggmp.co.uk *Twitter:* @StephenTwigg

---

DO YOU NEED THIS INFORMATION ONLINE?
visit www.dodspeople.com or call 020 7593 5675
to register for a free trial

TYRIE, ANDREW
Chichester *(Majority 15,877)*

Andrew Guy Tyrie. Born 15 January 1957; Son of the late Derek and Patricia Tyrie.

Education: Felsted School, Essex; Trinity College, Oxford (BA philosophy, politics and economics 1979, MA); College of Europe, Bruges (Diploma economics 1980); Wolfson College, Cambridge (MPhil international relations 1981); French.

Non-political career: Group head office, British Petroleum 1981-83; Adviser to Chancellors of the Exchequer: Nigel Lawson 1986-89, John Major 1989-90; Fellow, Nuffield College, Oxford 1990-91; Senior economist, European Bank for Reconstruction and Development 1992-97.

CONSERVATIVE

Political career: Contested Houghton and Washington 1992 general election. Member for Chichester since 1 May 1997 general election; Public Accounts Commission: Member 1997, Chair 2011; Shadow Financial Secretary 2003-04; Shadow Paymaster General 2004-05. *Select committees:* Member: Joint Committee on Consolidation of Bills Etc 1997-2001, Public Administration 1997-2001; Treasury: Member 2001-03, 2009-10, Chair 2010-; Member: Treasury (Treasury Sub-Committee) 2001-04, Constitutional Affairs/Justice 2005-10, Joint Committee on Conventions 2006, Joint Committee on Draft Constitution Renewal Bill 2008, Reform of the House of Commons 2009-10; Joint Committee on Tax Law Rewrite Bills: Member 2009-10, Chair 2010; Member: Liaison 2010-; Chair: Parliamentary Commission on Banking Standards 2012-13. Member, Executive, 1922 Committee 2005-06.

Political interests: European Union, economic policy, constitutional reform, international affairs.

Other: Member, Inter-Parliamentary Union 1999-. *The Spectator* awards: Backbencher of the Year 2000, 2009, Select Committee Chairman of the Year 2011; RAC; Garrick. MCC; Chichester Yacht Club; Goodwood Golf and Country Clubs.

Publications: Various works on economic and monetary union in Europe and other European issues; The Prospects for Public Spending (1996); Reforming the Lords: a Conservative Approach (Conservative Policy Forum, 1998); Sense on EMU (1998); Co-author, Leviathan at Large: The New Regulator for the Financial Markets (Centre for Policy Studies, 2000); Mr Blair's Poodle: An Agenda for Reviving the House of Commons (2000); Back from the Brink (2001); Co-author, Statism by Stealth: New Labour, New Collectivism (Centre for Policy Studies, 2002); Axis of Anarchy: America, Britain and the New World Order after Iraq (2003); Mr Blair's Poodle goes to War: The House of Commons, Congress and Iraq (Centre for Policy Studies, 2004); Pruning the Politicians: The Case for a smaller House of Commons (2004); The Conservative Party's proposals for the funding of political parties (2006); One Nation Again (One Nation Group, 2006); An Elected Second Chamber: A Conservative View (Constitution Unit, 2009); Extraordinary Rendition: Closing the Gap (2009); After the Age of Abundance (Centre for Policy Studies, 2011); The IMF and the Eurozone (Centre for Policy Studies, 2012); Neither Just nor Secure: The Justice and Security Bill (Centre for Policy Studies, 2013).

Recreations: Golf, walking.

Andrew Tyrie MP, House of Commons, London SW1A 0AA
Tel: 020 7219 6371 *Fax:* 020 7219 0625 *Email:* andrew.tyrie.mp@parliament.uk
Constituency: St John's House, St John's Street, Chichester, West Sussex PO19 1UU
Tel: 01243 783519 *Email:* office@chichesterconservatives.com
Website: www.andrewtyrie.com

UMUNNA, CHUKA
Streatham *(Majority 3,259)*

Shadow Secretary of State for Business, Innovation and Skills

Chuka Harrison Umunna. Born 17 October 1978.

Education: St Dunstan's College, Catford; Manchester University (LLB English and French law 2001); Nottingham Law School 2002.

Non-political career: Trainee solicitor/solicitor, Herbert Smith LLP 2002-06; Solicitor, Rochman Landau 2006-10. Member: GMB, Unite.

LABOUR

Political career: Member for Streatham since 6 May 2010 general election; PPS to Ed Miliband as Leader of the Opposition 2010-11; Shadow Minister for Business, Innovation and Skills 2011; Shadow Secretary of State for Business, Innovation and Skills 2011-. *Select committees:* Member: Treasury 2010-11. Member, Labour Party 1997-; Vice-chair, Streatham Labour Party 2004-08; Member, BAME Labour 2006-.

Political interests: Economy, employment, equality, education, home affairs and justice, climate change, community and youth engagement.

Other: Member, Fabian Society 1998-; Management committee member, Compass 2003-; Trustee, Generation Next Foundation; Member: Law Society Roll of Solicitors 2004-, Employment Lawyers Association 2004-; Trustee, Anthony Bourne Foundation.

Publications: Founder and former editor, TMP Online 2007-08.

Chuka Umunna MP, House of Commons, London SW1A 0AA
Tel: 020 7219 2115 *Email:* chuka.umunna.mp@parliament.uk
Constituency: 3a Mount Ephraim Road, Streatham, London SW16 1NQ
Tel: 020 8769 5063 *Website:* www.chuka.org.uk *Twitter:* @ChukaUmunna

UPPAL, PAUL
Wolverhampton South West *(Majority 691)*

PPS to David Willetts as Minister of State for Universities and Science, Department for Business, Innovation and Skills

Paul Singh Uppal. Born 14 June 1967; Son of Surjit and Balbir Uppal; Married Kashmir Uppal 1991 (1 son 2 daughters).

Education: Harborne Hill Comprehensive; Warwick University (politics 1989).

Non-political career: Runs own business.

CONSERVATIVE

Political career: Contested Birmingham Yardley 2005 general election. Member for Wolverhampton South West since 6 May 2010 general election; PPS to David Willetts as Minister of State for Universities and Science, Department for Business, Innovation and Skills 2012-. *Select committees:* Member: Environmental Audit 2011-, Joint Committee on the Rookery South (Resource Recovery Facility) Order 2012-13. Member, Policy Advisory Board 2013-.

Political interests: Crime, business relations with India and the Middle East, foreign affairs, male health, organ donation; India, USA.

Recreations: Running, reading, spending time with his children.

Paul Uppal MP, House of Commons, London SW1A 0AA
Tel: 020 7219 7195 *Fax:* 020 7219 5221 *Email:* paul.uppal.mp@parliament.uk
Constituency: Gresham Chambers, Second Floor, 14 Lichfield Street, Wolverhampton, West Midlands WV1 1DG
Tel: 01902 712134 *Fax:* 01902 238931 *Website:* www.pauluppal.co.uk *Twitter:* @pauluppalmp

VAIZEY, ED
Wantage *(Majority 13,547)*

Parliamentary Under-Secretary of State (Minister for Culture, Communications and Creative Industries), Department for Culture, Media and Sport

Edward Henry Butler Vaizey. Born 5 June 1968; Son of late Lord Vaizey of Greenwich and of Marina Vaizey, CBE; Married Alexandra Holland 2005 (1 son 1 daughter).

Education: St Paul's School, London; Merton College, Oxford (BA modern history 1989, MA); City University (Diploma law 1992); Inns of Court School of Law.

CONSERVATIVE

Non-political career: Desk officer, Conservative Research Department 1989-91; Called to the Bar, Middle Temple 1993; Barrister specialising in family law and child care 1994-96; Director: Public Policy Unit 1996-97, Politics International 1997-98; Director and partner, Consolidated Communications 1998-2003; Freelance journalist 2001-; Speechwriter to Michael Howard MP as Leader of the Opposition 2003-05.

Political career: Contested Bristol East 1997 general election. Member for Wantage 2005-10, for Wantage (revised boundary) since 6 May 2010 general election; Shadow Minister for the Arts 2006-10; Parliamentary Under-Secretary of State (Minister for Culture, Communications and Creative Industries), Departments for: Business, Innovation and Skills 2010-11, Culture, Media and Sport 2010-. *Select committees:* Member: Modernisation of the House of Commons 2005-07, Environmental Audit 2006-07. Election aide to Iain Duncan Smith MP 2001 general election; Deputy chair, Conservative Globalisation and Global Poverty Policy Group 2006.

Political interests: Arts, architecture, energy, science and technology, environment; India, Israel, Middle East, USA.

Other: Honorary Fellow, Royal Institute of British Architects 2011; Samaritans.

Publications: Editor: A Blue Tomorrow (Politicos, 2001), The Blue Book on Health (Politicos, 2002), The Blue Book on Transport (Politicos, 2002).

Recreations: Horse riding, football.

Hon Ed Vaizey MP, House of Commons, London SW1A 0AA
Tel: 020 7219 6350 *Fax:* 020 7219 2718 *Email:* ed.vaizey.mp@parliament.uk
Constituency: Oxfordshire Conservatives, 8 Gorwell, Watlington, Oxfordshire OX49 5QE
Tel: 01491 612852 *Fax:* 01491 612001 *Email:* matthew.barber@oxfordshireconservatives.com
Website: www.oxfordshireconservatives.com www.vaizey.com *Twitter:* @edvaizey

VARA, SHAILESH
North West Cambridgeshire *(Majority 16,677)*

Parliamentary Under-Secretary of State, Ministry of Justice

Shailesh Lakhman Vara. Born 4 September 1960; Son of Lakhman Arjan Vara and Savita, née Gadher; Married Beverley Fear 2002 (2 sons).

Education: Aylesbury Grammar School; Brunel University (LLB).

Non-political career: Articled: Richards Butler 1988-90 (in Hong Kong 1989-90), Solicitor: Crossman Block 1991-92, Payne Hicks Beach 1992-93, CMS Cameron McKenna 1994-2001.

CONSERVATIVE

Political career: Contested Birmingham Ladywood 1997 and Northampton South 2001 general elections. Member for North West Cambridgeshire 2005-10, for North West Cambridgeshire (revised boundary) since 6 May 2010 general election; Shadow Deputy Leader of the House 2006-10; Assistant Government Whip 2010-12; Parliamentary Under-Secretary of State, Ministry of Justice 2013-. *Select committees:* Member: Environment, Food and Rural Affairs 2005-06, Administration 2010-11, Finance and Services 2011-13. Society of Conservative Lawyers: Treasurer 2001-04, Vice-chair, Executive Committee 2006-09; Vice-chair, Conservative Party 2001-05; Chair, Conservative Parliamentary Friends of India 2008-10; Vice-chair, Conservative China Parliamentary Group 2009-10.

Other: Honorary Fellow, Brunel University 2010-. Vice-president, Huntingdonshire County Cricket Club 2007-.

Recreations: Cricket, theatre, taekwondo.

Shailesh Vara MP, House of Commons, London SW1A 0AA
Tel: 020 7219 6050 *Email:* shailesh.vara.mp@parliament.uk
Constituency: North West Cambridgeshire Conservative Association, The Old Barn, Hawthorn Farm, Ashton, Stamford, Lincolnshire PE9 3BA
Tel: 01733 380089 *Fax:* 01780 749379 *Email:* nwcca@tory.org
Website: www.shaileshvara.com

VAZ, KEITH
Leicester East *(Majority 14,082)*

Nigel Keith Anthony Standish Vaz. Born 26 November 1956; Son of late Merlyn Verona Vaz, teacher, and late Anthony Xavier Vaz, manager; Married Maria Fernandes 1993 (1 son 1 daughter).

Education: St Joseph's Convent, Aden; Latymer Upper School, Hammersmith; Gonville and Caius College, Cambridge (BA law 1979, MA, MCFI 1988); College of Law, London.

Non-political career: London Borough of Richmond: Articled Clerk 1980-82, Solicitor 1982; Senior solicitor, London Borough of Islington 1982-85; Solicitor: Highfields and Belgrave Law Centre 1985-87, North Leicester Advice Centre 1986-87. Member, Unison 1985-.

LABOUR

Political career: Contested Richmond and Barnes 1983 general election. Member for Leicester East 1987-2010, for Leicester East (revised boundary) since 6 May 2010 general election; Opposition Frontbench Spokesperson for the Environment 1992-97; Promoter Race Relations Remedies Act 1994; PPS: to John Morris as Attorney General 1997-99, to Solicitors General Lord Falconer of Thoroton 1997-98, Ross Cranston 1998-99; Parliamentary Secretary, Lord Chancellor's Department 1999; Minister of State, Foreign and Commonwealth Office (Minister for Europe) 1999-2001. *Select committees:* Home Affairs: Member 1987-92, Chair 2007-; Member: Constitutional Affairs 2003-07, Liaison 2007-, Joint Committee on National Security Strategy 2010-, Administration 2012-. Joint vice-chair, PLP Departmental Committee for International Development 1997-2000. Contested Surrey West 1984 and 1994 European Parliament elections. Labour Party Race Action Group: Chair 1983-2000, Patron 2000-; Chair, Unison Group 1990-99; Vice-chair, Tribune Group 1992; Labour Party Regional Executive 1994-96; Chair, National Ethnic Minority Taskforce 2006-; Member, Labour Party National Executive Committee 2007-; Vice-chair, Women's, Race and Equality Committee; Trustee, Labour Party Pensions Regulator 2008-. *Councils and public bodies:* Vice-chair, British Council 1998-99; Governor, Commonwealth Institute 1998-99.

Political interests: Education, legal services, local and regional government, race relations, urban policy, small businesses; Bangladesh, India, Oman, Pakistan, Yemen.

Other: Member, Executive Committee Inter-Parliamentary Union 1993-94; EU Ambassador for Year of Inter-Cultural Dialogue 2008; President, Leicester and South Leicestershire RSPCA 1988-99; Member, National Advisory Committee, Crime Concern 1989-93; Patron, Gingerbread 1990-; Fellow, Industry and Parliament Trust 1993; Joint patron, UN Year of Tolerance 1995; Founder patron, Naz Project, London 1999-; Patron, Asian Donors Appeal 2000-; Founder patron, Silver Star Appeal 2006. Medal of Honour, President of Yemen on behalf of the people of Yemen 2004; PC 2006; Safari (Leicester).

Publications: Columnist: Tribune, Catholic Herald; Co-author, Law Reform Now (1996).

Recreations: Tennis.

Rt Hon Keith Vaz MP, House of Commons, London SW1A 0AA
Tel: 020 7219 4605 *Fax:* 020 7219 3922 *Email:* vazk@parliament.uk
Constituency: Casework Centre, 292 Victoria Road East, Leicester LE5 0LF
Tel: 0116-246 0163 *Fax:* 0116-246 1135 *Website:* www.keithvazmp.com
Twitter: @keith_vazMP

LABOUR

VAZ, VALERIE
Walsall South *(Majority 1,755)*

Valerie Carol Marian Vaz. Born 7 December 1954; Daughter of late Merlyn Verona Vaz, teacher, and late Anthony Xavier Vaz, personnel manager; Married Paul Townsend 1992 (1 daughter).

Education: Twickenham County Grammar School; Bedford College, London University (BSc biochemistry 1978); Sidney Sussex College, Cambridge (Research animal nutrition 1978-79); College of Law, London (common professional examination 1981; solicitors final examination 1982); French (basic).

Non-political career: Trainee solicitor, Herbert Smith; Lawyer: London Borough of Brent, London Borough of Hammersmith and Fulham; Presenter, Network East, BBC; Townsend Vaz Solicitors; Deputy district judge (part-time), Midlands and Oxford Circuits; Solicitor, Government Legal Service, Treasury Solicitors Department 2001-10; On secondment, Ministry of Justice 2008-09. Member, USDAW.

Political career: Contested Twickenham 1987 general election. Member for Walsall South since 6 May 2010 general election. *Select committees:* Member: Health 2010-, Regulatory Reform 2010-. Vice-chair, PLP Departmental Group for Business, Innovation and Skills 2010-. Contested East Midlands 1999 European Parliament election. *Councils and public bodies:* London Borough of Ealing Council: Councillor 1986-90, Deputy Council Leader 1988-89; Member, Ealing Health Authority 1986-89; School governor 1986-90.

Political interests: Health, science and technology, legal and constitutional affairs, music; South Asia, Burma, Yemen.

Other: Member, National Trust; Friend, Kew Gardens; Law Society.

Publications: Author, Obesity and Diabetes Programmes in England: Capturing the State of Play in July 2011.

Recreations: Music – play piano, gardening, walking.

Valerie Vaz MP, House of Commons, London SW1A 0AA
Tel: 020 7219 7176 *Fax:* 020 7219 5054 *Email:* valerie.vaz.mp@parliament.uk
Constituency: 114a Lichfield Street, Walsall WS1 1SZ
Tel: 01922 635835 *Website:* www.valerievazmp.co.uk *Twitter:* @Valerie_VazMP

CONSERVATIVE

VICKERS, MARTIN
Cleethorpes *(Majority 4,298)*

Martin John Vickers. Born 13 September 1950; Son of Norman and Winifred Vickers, née Watson; Married Ann 1981 (1 daughter).

Education: Havelock School; Grimsby College; Lincoln University (BA politics 2004).

Non-political career: Printing industry; Retail industry.

Political career: Contested Cleethorpes 2005 general election. Member for Cleethorpes since 6 May 2010 general election. *Select committees:* Member: Procedure 2012-, Transport 2013-. Constituency agent to Edward Leigh MP 1994-2010. *Councils and public bodies:* North East Lincolnshire Council: Councillor, Cabinet Member for Environmental Services -2011.

Political interests: Constitution, local government, regeneration issues, energy policy, transport.

Publications: Contributor: Freedom, Responsibility and the State: Curbing Over-Mighty Government (Politeia, 2012), Unlocking Local Leadership on Climate Change (Green Alliance, 2012).

Recreations: Reading, football, cricket, travel, railways, music, religion.

Martin Vickers MP, House of Commons, London SW1A 0AA
Tel: 020 7219 7212 *Email:* martin.vickers.mp@parliament.uk
Constituency: 62 St Peter's Avenue, Cleethorpes DN35 8HP
Tel: 01472 603554 *Email:* mvickersmp@gmail.com *Website:* www.martinvickers.co.uk
Twitter: @MartinVickersMP

VILLIERS, THERESA

Chipping Barnet *(Majority 11,927)*

Secretary of State for Northern Ireland

Theresa Anne Villiers. Born 5 March 1968; Daughter of late George and Virginia Villiers; Married Sean Wilken 1999 (divorced).

Education: Francis Holland School, London; Bristol University (LLB 1990); Jesus College, Oxford University (BCL 1991); Inns of Court School of Law (1992).

Non-political career: Barrister Lincoln's Inn 1994-95; Lecturer in law King's College, London University 1995-99.

CONSERVATIVE

Political career: Member for Chipping Barnet 2005-10, for Chipping Barnet (revised boundary) since 6 May 2010 general election; Shadow Chief Secretary to the Treasury 2005-07; Shadow Secretary of State for Transport 2007-10; Minister of State, Department for Transport 2010-12; Secretary of State for Northern Ireland 2012-. *Select committees:* Member: Environmental Audit 2005-06. European Parliament: MEP for London 1999-2005: Deputy leader, Conservatives group 2001-02.

Political interests: Transport, economic policy, business, deregulation, information technology, animal welfare, financial services, environment; Cyprus, Israel.

Other: President: Friends of Barnet Hospital, Barnet Borough Talking Newspapers, Barnet Old People's Welfare. PC 2010. Middlesex County Cricket Club.

Publications: European Tax harmonisation: The Impending Threat; Co-author, Waiver, Variation and Estoppel (Chancery Wiley Law Publications, 1998).

Rt Hon Theresa Villiers MP, House of Commons, London SW1A 0AA
Tel: 020 7219 3000
Constituency: 163 High Street, Barnet, Hertfordshire EN5 5SU
Tel: 020 8449 7345 *Fax:* 020 8449 7346 *Email:* theresa@theresavilliers.co.uk
Website: www.theresavilliers.co.uk

WALKER, CHARLES

Broxbourne *(Majority 18,804)*

Charles Ashley Rupert Walker. Born 11 September 1967; Son of Carola Chataway, née Ashton, and late Timothy Walker; Married Fiona Newman 1995 (1 daughter 2 sons).

Education: American School of London; University of Oregon, USA (BSc politics and American history 1990).

Non-political career: Communications director, CSG (Corporate Services Group) plc 1997-2001; Director: Blue Arrow Ltd 1999-2001, LSM Processing Ltd 2002-04, Debitwise 2004. Amicus.

CONSERVATIVE

Political career: Contested Ealing North 2001 general election. Member for Broxbourne since 5 May 2005 general election; Member Speaker's Committee for the Independent Parliamentary Standards Authority 2010-. *Select committees:* Member: Scottish Affairs 2005-10, Public Administration 2007-11, Chairmen's Panel/Panel of Chairs 2010-, Standing Orders 2011-; Chair: Prodecure 2012-; Member: Liaison 2012-. Vice-chair: Lewisham East Conservatives 1992-93, Battersea Conservatives 2002-03; 1922 Committee: Member, Executive 2006-10, Vice-chair 2010-; Member, Conservative Party Board 2010-. *Councils and public bodies:* Councillor, Wandsworth Borough Council 2002-06; Vice-President, Local Government Association 2010-.

Political interests: Employment, taxation, the economy, mental health.

Other: Patron, Isabelle Hospice. *The Spectator* awards: Speech of the Year 2011, Speech of the Year (with Kevan Jones MP) 2012; Best Contribution to the *House Magazine, House Magazine* awards 2012.

Recreations: Fishing, watching cricket.

Charles Walker MP, House of Commons, London SW1A 0AA
Tel: 020 7219 0338 *Fax:* 020 7219 0505 *Email:* charles.walker.mp@parliament.uk
Constituency: 57-59 High Street, Hoddesdon, Hertfordshire EN11 8TQ
Tel: 01992 479972 *Fax:* 01992 479973 *Email:* broxbourne@tory.org
Website: www.charleswalker.org

CONSERVATIVE

WALKER, ROBIN
Worcester *(Majority 2,982)*

Robin Caspar Walker. Born 12 April 1978; Son of late Peter Walker, MP for Worcester 1961-92, later Lord Walker of Worcester, and Tessa Pout; Married Charlotte Keenan 2011.

Education: St Paul's School, London; Balliol College, Oxford (BA ancient and modern history 2000).

Non-political career: Member, Armed Forces Parliamentary Scheme (RAF). Intern, Office of the chairman of the House Ways and Means Committee, Washington DC, September 2000; Chief executive, Property Map Ltd 2000-01; Research executive, i-Search Ltd 2001-03; Finsbury Group (Financial Communications): Executive 2003-04, Senior executive 2004-06, Associate partner 2006-09, Partner 2009-10.

Political career: Member for Worcester since 6 May 2010 general election. *Select committees:* Member: Welsh Affairs 2011-12, Business, Innovation and Skills 2012-, Arms Exports Controls 2013-. Volunteer assistant to: Stephen Dorrell MP, general election campaign 1997, Worcester Conservative Association, general election campaign 2001; Press officer to Oliver Letwin MP 2005 general election; Member: Conservative Middle East Council, Tory Reform Group.

Political interests: Education, health, police, foreign affairs, defence, business; Canada, India, Italy, Latin America, Middle East, South Africa, USA, Zambia.

Other: Commonwealth Parliamentary Association; Inter-Parliamentary Union; Member, TRG 1997-; St Richard's Hospice, Worcester; Carlton Club: Member 1996-, Member and deputy treasurer, Political Committee 2000-04; Member, Young Members Committee 2004-07. Worcester County Cricket Club; Worcester Warriors RFC.

Recreations: Walking, reading, travel, writing, watching cricket and rugby.

Robin Walker MP, House of Commons, London SW1A 0AA
Tel: 020 7219 7196 *Email:* robin.walker.mp@parliament.uk
Constituency: Office of Robin Walker MP, Guildhall, High Street, Worcester WR1 2EY
Tel: 01905 22401 *Email:* kate.dixon@parliament.uk *Website:* www.walker4worcester.com

CONSERVATIVE

WALLACE, BEN
Wyre and Preston North *(Majority 15,844)*

PPS to Kenneth Clarke as Minister without portfolio, Cabinet Office

Robert Ben Lobban Wallace. Born 15 May 1970; Married Liza Cooke 2001 (2 sons 1 daughter).

Education: Millfield School, Somerset; Royal Military Academy, Sandhurst (Commission 1991); French, German.

Non-political career: Army officer, Scots Guards 1991-98: Mentioned in Despatches 1991, Service in Northern Ireland, Central America, Cyprus, Germany; Intelligence 1994-95. RGS&H advertising agency, Boston, USA 1988; Ski instructor, Austrian National Ski School 1988-89; EU and overseas director, Qinetiq 2003-05.

Political career: Member for Lancaster and Wyre 2005-10, for Wyre and Preston North since 6 May 2010 general election; Shadow Minister for Scotland 2007-10; PPS to Kenneth Clarke: as Lord Chancellor and Secretary of State for Justice 2010-12, as Minister without portfolio, Cabinet Office 2012-. *Select committees:* Member: Scottish Affairs 2005-10. Contested West Aberdeenshire and Kincardine constituency 1999 Scottish Parliament election. MSP for North East Scotland region 1999-2003: Conservative Party Health Spokesperson.

Political interests: Foreign policy, intelligence, home affairs, health, security, sport; Iran, Italy, Middle East, Romania, Russia, USA.

Other: Member, Queen's Bodyguard of Scotland, Royal Archers 2007-.

Recreations: Sailing, skiing, racing, motorsport.

Ben Wallace MP, House of Commons, London SW1A 0AA
Tel: 020 7219 5804 *Fax:* 020 7219 5901 *Email:* wallaceb@parliament.uk
Constituency: Great Eccleston Village Centre, 59 High Street, Great Eccleston,
Lancashire PR3 0YB
Tel: 01995 672977 *Website:* www.benwallacemp.com

LABOUR

WALLEY, JOAN
Stoke-on-Trent North *(Majority 8,235)*

Joan Lorraine Walley. Born 23 January 1949; Daughter of late Arthur and late Mary Emma Walley; Married Jan Ostrowski 1981 (2 sons).

Education: Biddulph Grammar School, Staffordshire; Hull University (BA social administration 1970); University College of Wales, Swansea (Diploma community work development 1975); German.

Non-political career: Member, Armed Forces Parliamentary Scheme (RAF). Alcoholics recovery project 1970-73; Local government officer: Swansea City Council 1974-78, Wandsworth Council 1978-79; NACRO development officer 1979-82. Member: Unison, Unity.

Political career: Member for Stoke-on-Trent North 1987-2010, for Stoke-on-Trent North (revised boundary) since 6 May 2010 general election; Opposition Spokesperson on: Environmental Protection and Development 1988-90, Transport 1990-95. *Select committees:* Member: Trade and Industry 1995-97, 1997-98, Environmental Audit 1997-2010, Chairmen's Panel 2008-10, West Midlands 2009-10; Chair: Environmental Audit 2010-; Member: Liaison 2010-, Liaison (National Policy Statements Sub-committee) 2010-, Members' Expenses 2011-. Member: SERA, SEA. *Councils and public bodies:* Lambeth Council: Councillor 1981-85, Chair, Health and Consumer Services Committee.

Political interests: Environment, health, small businesses; Eastern Europe.

Other: Vice-President, Institute Environmental Health Officers; President: West Midlands Home and Water Safety Council, City of Stoke on Trent Primary School Sports Association; Fellow, Industry and Parliament Trust 1990. DUniv, Staffordshire University 2007; Fegg Hayes Sports and Social.

Recreations: Walking, swimming, music, football.

Joan Walley MP, House of Commons, London SW1A 0AA
Tel: 020 7219 4524 *Fax:* 020 7219 4397 *Email:* walleyj@parliament.uk
Constituency: Unit 5, Burslem Enterprise Centre, Moorland Road, Burslem, Stoke-on-Trent, Staffordshire ST6 1JN
Tel: 01782 577900 *Fax:* 01782 836462 *Email:* landona@parliament.uk
Website: www.joanwalleymp.org.uk

CONSERVATIVE

WALTER, ROBERT
North Dorset *(Majority 7,625)*

Robert John Walter. Born 30 May 1948; Married Sally Middleton 1970 (died 1995) (2 sons 1 daughter); married Feride Alp 2011.

Education: Lord Weymouth School, Warminster; Aston University, Birmingham (BSc 1971).

Non-political career: Former farmer; Sheep farm, South Devon; Member, London Stock Exchange 1983-86; Director and Vice-President, Aubrey G Lanston and Co 1986-97.

Political career: Contested Bedwelty 1979 general election. Member for North Dorset 1997-2010, for North Dorset (revised boundary) since 6 May 2010 general election; Opposition Spokesperson for Constitutional Affairs (Wales) 1999-2001; Introduced: Sex Discrimination (Amendment) Bill 2000, Restricted Byways Bill 2004, House of Commons (Participation) Bill 2006. *Select committees:* Member: Unopposed Bills (Panel) 1997-, Health 1997-99, European Standing Committee B 1998-2005, European Scrutiny 1999, International Development 2001-03, Treasury 2003-05, Treasury (Treasury Sub-Committee) 2003-05. Chair: Aston University Conservative Association 1967-69, Westbury Constituency Young Conservative 1973-76, Conservative Foreign Affairs Forum 1986-88; Member: Carlton Club Political Committee 1991-99, National Union Executive Committee 1992-95; Conservative Group for Europe: Chair 1992-95, Vice-President 1997-2000; Member, Executive 1922 Committee 2002-05. *Councils and public bodies:* Chair of governors, Tachbrook School 1980-99.

Political interests: Agriculture, international affairs, human rights.

Other: Former chair, European Democrat Forum; British-Irish Parliamentary Assembley: Member 1997-, Vice-chair 2012-; Chair, European Affairs Committee 2006-; Assembly of Western European Union: Member 2001-11, President, European Security and Defence Assembly 2009-11; President, Federated Group of Christian Democrats and European Democrats; Parliamentary Assembly of Council of Europe: Member 2001-, Leader, UK Delegation 2010-, Vice-President 2011-, President, European Democrat Group 2011-; Chair, Inter-Parliamentary Union, British Group 2010-. Liveryman, Worshipful Company of Needlemakers 1983. Freeman, City of London 1993. DLitt, Aston University (2011); Blandford Constitutional. Vice-President, North Dorset Rugby Club.

Recreations: Sailing.

Robert Walter MP, House of Commons, London SW1A 0AA
Tel: 020 7219 6981 *Fax:* 020 7219 2608 *Email:* robert.walter.mp@parliament.uk
Constituency: The Stables, White Cliff Gardens, Blandford Forum, Dorset DT11 7BU
Tel: 01258 452585 *Fax:* 01258 459614 *Website:* www.bobwaltermp.com

WARD, DAVID
Bradford East *(Lib Dem Majority 365)*

Born 24 June 1953; Married Jacqueline Ann 1984 (2 sons).

Education: Boston Grammar School; North Kesteven Grammar School; Trent Polytechnic (accountancy 1977); Bradford University (MBA 1981; MPhil 1984); Leicester University (MSc training 1986).

Non-political career: Accountant, Lincolnshire County Council 1971-79; Leeds Metropolitan University: Principal lecturer 1985-2004, Bradford sports partnership manager (on secondment) 2004-. Unison (NALGO): Member 1971-79, Branch treasurer 1977-79; Member, NAFTHE 1985-2010.

LIBERAL DEMOCRAT

Political career: Contested Bradford North 1990 by-election and 1992, 2001 and 2005 general elections. Member for Bradford East since 6 May 2010 general election. *Select committees:* Member: Business, Innovation and Skills 2010-12, Education 2012-. Liberal Democrat Whip withdrawn July-September 2013. *Councils and public bodies:* Bradford Metropolitan District Council: Councillor 1984-, Education portfolio holder 2000-04, Deputy Leader, Liberal Democrat Group 2004-10, Chair, Bradford North Area Committee 2005-10; Vice-president, Local Government Association 2010-.

Political interests: Education, community cohesion.

Other: Director, Bantams Community Programme 2005-.

Recreations: Football.

David Ward MP, House of Commons, London SW1A 0AA
Tel: 020 7219 3000 *Fax:* 020 7219 6204 *Email:* david.ward.mp@parliament.uk
Constituency: 458-460 Killinghall Road, Bradford, West Yorkshire BD2 4SL
Tel: 01274 458010 *Fax:* 01274 458011 *Email:* david@davidward.org.uk
Website: davidward4bradford.org.uk *Twitter:* @DavidWardMP

WATKINSON, ANGELA
Hornchurch and Upminster *(Majority 16,371)*

Angela Eileen Watkinson. Born 18 November 1941; Daughter of Edward Ellicott and Maisie Ellicott, née Thompson; Married Roy Watkinson 1961 (divorced) (1 son 2 daughters).

Education: Wanstead County High School; Anglia University (HNC public administration 1989); French, German, Swedish.

Non-political career: Bank of New South Wales 1958-64; Family career break 1964-76; Special school secretary, Essex County Council 1976-88; London Borough of Barking and Dagenham Council: Clerk to school governing bodies 1988, Committee clerk 1988-89; Committee manager, Basildon District Council 1989-94.

CONSERVATIVE

Political career: Member for Upminster 2001-10, for Hornchurch and Upminster since 6 May 2010 general election; Opposition Whip 2002-04; Shadow Minister for: Health and Education 2004, Education 2004-05; Local Government Affairs and Communities 2005; Opposition Whip 2005-10; Government Whip 2010-12. *Select committees:* Member: Home Affairs 2001-02, European Scrutiny 2002-03, Selection 2010-12. Secretary, Conservative Education Policy Committee 2001-02. Member: Monday Club 1996-2001, Conservative Way Forward Group 1998-; Vice-President, Billericay Conservative Association 1999-2001; Member: Conservative Christian Fellowship 1999-, Conservative Friends of Israel 2001-. *Councils and public bodies:* Councillor, Group secretary, Committee chair: London Borough of Havering 1994-98, Essex County Council 1997-2001; Vice-President, Local Government Association 2012; Member, Committee on Standards in Public Life 2012-.

Political interests: Education, law and order, families, European affairs, constitution, local and regional government, sustainable resources, dance; Egypt, Israel, Qatar, Sweden, USA.

Other: Member, Parliamentary Assembley of the Council of Europe 2004-05, 2013-; Patron, Romford Autistic Group Support 2007; Ambassador for Guiding; President, Havering Branch, Diabetes UK 2007; R.O.S.E. (Realistic Opportunities for Supported Employment); Add+Up. DBE 2013.

Recreations: Working, family, travel, reading, music, dining, crosswords, sudoku, visiting stately homes and gardens, animal sanctuaries, theatre, ballet.

Dame Angela Watkinson DBE MP, House of Commons, London SW1A 0AA
Tel: 020 7219 8267 *Email:* angela.watkinson.mp@parliament.uk
Constituency: 23 Butts Green Road, Hornchurch RM11 2JS
Tel: 01708 475252/01708 444750 *Website:* www.angelawatkinsonmp.com

WATSON, TOM
West Bromwich East *(Majority 6,696)*

LABOUR

Thomas Anthony Watson. Born 8 January 1967; Son of Anthony Watson, trade union official, and Linda Watson, née Pearce, social worker; Married Siobhan Corby 2000 (separated) (1 son 1 daughter).

Education: King Charles I School, Kidderminster.

Non-political career: Marketing officer, Save the Children 1987-88; Account executive, advertising agency 1988-90; Development officer, Labour Party 1993-97; Political officer, AEEU 1997-2001. Member, AEEU 1995-.

Political career: Member for West Bromwich East 2001-10, for West Bromwich East (revised boundary) since 6 May 2010 general election; PPS to Dawn Primarolo as Paymaster General, HM Treasury 2003-04; Assistant Government Whip 2004-05; Government Whip 2005-06; Parliamentary Under-Secretary of State, Ministry of Defence (Minister for Veterans) 2006; Assistant Government Whip 2007-08; Parliamentary Secretary, Cabinet Office 2008-09. *Select committees:* Member: Home Affairs 2001-03, Culture, Media and Sport 2009-12. National Development Officer (Youth), Labour Party 1993-97; Member, Labour Party NEC; Deputy Chair, Labour Party 2011-13; Campaign Co-ordinator 2011-13.

Political interests: Culture, media, manufacturing, digital policy; Australia, Japan, USA.

Other: Fellow, Industry and Parliament Trust 2006; Cystic Fibrosis Trust. Commons Select Committee Member of the Year, *House Magazine* awards 2011; MP of the Year, *PoliticsHome* awards 2012; West Bromwich Labour, Friar Park Labour.

Publications: Co-author: Votes for All (Fabian Society pamphlet, 2000), Dial M for Murdoch (2012).

Recreations: Supporter West Bromwich Albion FC, gardening, film.

Tom Watson MP, House of Commons, London SW1A 0AA
Tel: 020 7219 8123 *Fax:* 020 7219 1943 *Email:* tom.watson.mp@parliament.uk
Constituency: Terry Duffy House, 1 Towns Street, West Bromwich, West Midlands B70 6NT
Tel: 0121-569 1904 *Fax:* 0121-553 2043 *Website:* www.tom-watson.co.uk
Twitter: @tom_watson

WATTS, DAVID
St Helens North *(Majority 13,101)*

LABOUR

David Leonard Watts. Born 26 August 1951; Son of Leonard and Sarah Watts; Married Avril Davies 1972 (2 sons).

Education: Seel Road Secondary Modern School.

Non-political career: Labour Party organiser; Research assistant to: Angela Eagle MP 1992-93, John Evans MP 1993-97. Shop steward, United Biscuits AEU.

Political career: Member for St Helens North 1997-2010, for St Helens North (revised boundary) since 6 May 2010 general election; PPS: to John Spellar: as Minister of State, Ministry of Defence 1999-2001, as Minister of Transport, Department for Transport, Local Government and the Regions 2001-02, as Minister of State, Department for Transport 2002-03, to John Prescott as Deputy Prime Minister 2003-05; Government Whip 2005-10; Opposition Whip 2010. *Select committees:* Member: Finance and Services 1997-2001, 2005-06, Foreign Affairs 2010-12, Administration 2010-, Arms Export Controls 2011-12. Chair: PLP North West Regional Group 2000-01, Parliamentary Labour Party 2012-. *Councils and public bodies:* St Helens Metropolitan Borough Council: Councillor 1979-97, Leader 1993-97; Vice-chair, Association of Metropolitan Authorities.

Political interests: Regional policy, education, training.

Other: UK President, Euro Group of Industrial Regions 1989-93.

Recreations: Watching football and rugby, reading.

David Watts MP, House of Commons, London SW1A 0AA
Tel: 020 7219 6325 *Fax:* 020 7219 0913 *Email:* wattsd@parliament.uk
Constituency: Sixth Floor, Century House, Hardshaw Street, St Helens, Merseyside WA10 1QU
Tel: 01744 21336 *Fax:* 01744 21343 *Email:* davewattsmp@hotmail.com

CONSERVATIVE

WEATHERLEY, MIKE

Hove *(Majority 1,868)*

Michael Richard Weatherley. Born 2 July 1957; Married 2nd Adriana Alves 2003 (divorced) (2 sons 1 daughter from previous marriage).

Education: Kent College, Canterbury; South Bank Polytechnic (BA business studies 1979); French, Portuguese (not fluent).

Non-political career: Group finance and administration director, Cash Bases Group Ltd 1994-2000; Group finance controller, Pete Waterman Ltd 2000-05, Vice-president, Finance and Administration (Europe), Motion Picture Licensing Company Ltd 2007-.

Political career: Contested Barking 2001 and Brighton Pavilion 2005 general elections. Member for Hove since 6 May 2010 general election. Adviser to the Prime Minister on Intellectual Property 2013-. *Select committees:* Member: Administration 2010-12, Justice 2013-. *Councils and public bodies:* Councillor, Crawley Borough Council 2006-07.

Political interests: Music, film, small business; Brazil, Europe.

Other: Round Table: Area chairman, Sussex 1996-97, National Executive 1997-98, President, Brighton 1998-2002; Fellow, Chartered Management Accountant 1988; Chartered marketer.

Recreations: Skiing, football (qualified referee), rock music.

Mike Weatherley MP, House of Commons, London SW1A 0AA
Tel: 020 7219 7216 *Email:* mike.weatherley.mp@parliament.uk
Constituency: Contact Westminster office *Website:* www.mikeweatherleymp.com
Twitter: @mike_weatherley

LIBERAL DEMOCRAT

WEBB, STEVE

Thornbury and Yate *(Majority 7,116)*

Minister of State for Pensions, Department for Work and Pensions

Steven John Webb. Born 18 July 1965; Son of Brian and Patricia Webb; Married Helen Edwards 1993 (1 daughter 1 son).

Education: Dartmouth High School, Birmingham; Hertford College, Oxford (BA philosophy, politics and economics 1983).

Non-political career: Researcher then programme director, Institute for Fiscal Studies 1986-95; Special adviser to Social Security Select Committee 1986-95; University of Bath: Professor of social policy 1995-, Visiting professor 1997-.

Political career: Member for Northavon 1997-2010, for Thornbury and Yate since 6 May 2010 general election; Liberal Democrat: Spokesperson for Social Security and Welfare (Pensions) 1997-99; Principal Spokesperson for Social Security 1999-2001; Shadow Secretary of State for: Work and Pensions 2001-05, Health 2005-06; Chair of the Election Manifesto Team 2006-07; Shadow Secretary of State for Environment, Food and Rural Affairs 2007-08; Shadow Minister for Countryside 2008; Shadow Secretary of State for: Energy and Climate Change 2008-09, Work and Pensions 2009-10; Minister of State for Pensions, Department for Work and Pensions 2010-. *Select committees:* Member: Ecclesiastical Committee -2010. Member, Liberal Democrats 1992-; Member: Costings Group, Policy Committee, Manifesto Committee, Economic Recovery Group.

Political interests: Social affairs, welfare, Third World, internet.

Other: Member: Oxfam, Amnesty International, World Development Movement, Commission on Social Justice.

Publications: Include: Beyond The Welfare State (1990), Co-author For Richer, For Poorer (1994), Inequality in the UK (1997).

Recreations: Internet, occasional church organist, armchair supporter of West Bromwich Albion.

Steve Webb MP, House of Commons, London SW1A 0AA
Tel: 020 7219 4378 *Email:* webbs@parliament.uk
Constituency: Poole Court, Poole Court Drive, Yate, Bristol, Gloucestershire BS37 5PP
Tel: 01454 322100 *Fax:* 01454 866515 *Email:* steve@stevewebb.org.uk
Website: www.stevewebb.org.uk *Twitter:* @stevewebb1

SCOTTISH NATIONAL PARTY

WEIR, MIKE

Angus *(Majority 3,282)*

SNP Spokesperson for Trade, for Energy and Climate Change and for Consumer Affairs

Michael Fraser Weir. Born 24 March 1957; Son of James Weir, electrician, and Elizabeth Weir, née Fraser, hospital cook; Married Anne Jack 1985 (2 daughters).

Education: Arbroath High School; Aberdeen University (LLB 1979).

Non-political career: Solicitor: Charles Wood and Son 1981-83, Myers and Wills 1983-84; Solicitor and partner, J and DG Shiell 1984-2001.

Political career: Contested Aberdeen South 1987 general election. Member for Angus 2001-05, for Angus (revised boundary) since 5 May 2005 general election; SNP Spokesperson for: Trade and Industry 2004, Health 2004, Environment 2004, Work and Pensions 2005-07, Trade 2005-, Industry and Energy 2005-13, Environment 2007-13 Energy and Climate Change 2013-, Consumer Affairs 2013-. *Select committees:* Member: Scottish Affairs 2001-05, Trade and Industry/ Business, Enterprise and Regulatory Reform/Business and Enterprise 2005-09, Chairmen's Panel/ Panel of Chairs 2005-10, Energy and Climate Change 2009-10. *Councils and public bodies:* Angus District Council 1984-88: Councillor, Convener General Purposes Committee 1984-88.

Political interests: Disability, European affairs, rural affairs, international and sustainable development, climate change, environment, energy, industry/business.

Other: Law Society of Scotland 1981.

Recreations: History, organic gardening.

Mike Weir MP, House of Commons, London SW1A 0AA
Tel: 020 7219 8125 *Email:* mike.weir.mp@parliament.uk
Constituency: 16 Brothock Bridge, Arbroath, Angus DD11 1NG
Tel: 01241 874522 *Website:* www.angussnp.org *Twitter:* @mikeweirsnp

CONSERVATIVE

WHARTON, JAMES

Stockton South *(Majority 332)*

James Stephen Wharton. Born 16 February 1984.

Education: Yarm School; Durham University (LLB 2005).

Non-political career: Solicitor, BHP Law 2006-10.

Political career: Member for Stockton South since 6 May 2010 general election. *Select committees:* Member: Public Accounts 2010-12. Constituency chair 2002-06.

Political interests: Education, young people, law and order; Sri Lanka.

Other: Law society; United & Cecil Club.

Recreations: Countryside, walking, eating out, friends and family.

James Wharton MP, House of Commons, London SW1A 0AA
Tel: 020 7219 7236 *Fax:* 020 7219 6546 *Email:* james.wharton.mp@parliament.uk
Constituency: Suite 6, DTV Business Centre, Orde Wingate Way, Stockton on Tees TS19 0GD
Tel: 01642 636235 *Fax:* 01642 636234 *Email:* james@jameswharton.co.uk
Website: www.jameswharton.co.uk

CONSERVATIVE

WHEELER, HEATHER

South Derbyshire *(Majority 7,128)*

Heather Kay Wheeler. Born 14 May 1959; Daughter of Mr C.P.C. Wilkinson, retired civil servant, and Mrs F.M. Wilkinson, retired primary teacher; Married Bob Wheeler 1986 (1 daughter).

Education: Grey Coat Hospital Secondary School, London.

Non-political career: Manager, Rics Ins Brokers 1979-87; Company secretary and director, Bretby Inns Ltd 1997-2006; Professional indemnity insurance broker, Lloyd's.

Political career: Contested Coventry South 2001 and 2005 general elections. Member for South Derbyshire since 6 May 2010 general election. *Select committees:* Member: Standards and Privileges 2010-13, Communities and Local Government 2011-, Standards 2013-, Privileges 2013-. Member, Executive, 1922 Committee 2012-. Various posts, Putney and South Derbyshire Conservative Association 1976-99. *Councils and public bodies:* Councillor, London Borough of Wandsworth Council 1982-86; South Derbyshire District Council: Councillor 1995-, Leader, Conservative group 2002-10, Council Leader 2007-10; Vice-President, Local Government Association 2011-.

Political interests: Affordable housing, economic regeneration; China, Japan, Taiwan.

Other: Association of Chartered Insurance Institute 1985.

Recreations: Watching sport, DIY, the Archers.

Heather Wheeler MP, House of Commons, London SW1A 0AA
Tel: 020 7219 1184 *Email:* heather.wheeler.mp@parliament.uk
Constituency: The Nissen Hut Offices, Church Street, Swadlincote, Derbyshire DE11 8LF
Tel: 01283 225365 *Twitter:* @HeatherWheeler

WHITE, CHRIS
Warwick and Leamington *(Majority 3,513)*

Christopher White. Born 28 April 1967.

Education: Comprehensive school; Manchester University.

Non-political career: MG Rover, Longbridge; Freelance public relations consultant.

Political career: Contested Birmingham Hall Green 2001 and Warwick and Leamington 2005 general elections. Member for Warwick and Leamington since 6 May 2010 general election; Sponsored Public Services (Social Value) Act 2012. *Select committees:* Member: International Development 2010-, Arms Export Controls 2010-. *Councils and public bodies:* Councillor, Warwick District Council 2007-; Governor, Myton School.

CONSERVATIVE

Other: Trustee, Victim Support.

Chris White MP, House of Commons, London SW1A 0AA
Tel: 020 7219 7201 *Fax:* 020 7219 5495 *Email:* chris.white.mp@parliament.uk
Constituency: 43a Clemens Street, Leamington Spa CV31 2DP
Tel: 01926 315888 *Website:* www.chriswhitemp.com *Twitter:* @chriswhite_mp

WHITEFORD, EILIDH
Banff and Buchan *(Majority 4,027)*

SNP Spokesperson for International Development, for Fisheries, for Environment, Food and Rural Affairs and for Work and Pensions

Born 24 April 1969; Daughter of Douglas Whiteford and Kathleen MacLeod; Married Stephen Smith.

Education: Banff Academy; Glasgow University (MA English and Scottish literature 1991; PhD Scottish literature 1998); Guelph University, Ontario (MA English language and literature 1994).

SCOTTISH NATIONAL PARTY

Non-political career: Assistant to Alex Salmond MP 1992; Tutor in Scottish studies, Newbattle Abbey College 1995-97; Part-time lecturer, Scottish literature, Glasgow University 1995-97; Assistant to: Allan Macartney MEP 1998, Ian Hudghton MEP 1998-99, Irene McGugan MSP 1999; Academic development officer and lecturer, Scottish literature, Glasgow University and Newbattle Abbey College 1999-2001; Co-ordinator, Scottish Carers' Alliance 2001-03; Campaign manager, Oxfam Scotland 2003-09.

Political career: Member for Banff and Buchan since 6 May 2010 general election; SNP Spokesperson for: International Development 2010-, Fishing, Food and Rural Affairs 2010-13, Work and Pensions 2010-, Fisheries 2013-, Environment, Food and Rural Affairs 2013-. *Select committees:* Member: Scottish Affairs 2010-. Member, SNP 1986-.

Political interests: Social policy, agriculture and fisheries, international development; Scotland.

Recreations: Music, reading.

Dr Eilidh Whiteford MP, House of Commons, London SW1A 0AA
Tel: 020 7219 7005 *Email:* eilidh.whiteford.mp@parliament.uk
Constituency: Office 7, Burnside Business Centre, Burnside Road, Peterhead,
Aberdeenshire AB42 3AW
Tel: 01779 822022 *Fax:* 01779 822025 *Website:* www.eilidhwhiteford.info

WHITEHEAD, ALAN
Southampton Test *(Majority 2,413)*

Alan Patrick Vincent Whitehead. Born 15 September 1950; Married Sophie Wronska 1979 (1 son 1 daughter).

Education: Isleworth Grammar School, Middlesex; Southampton University (BA politics and philosophy 1973; PhD political science 1976); French.

Non-political career: Outset: Deputy director 1976-79, Director 1979-83; Director BIIT 1983-92; Professor of public policy Southampton Institute 1992-97. Member, Unison (formerly NUPE).

Political career: Contested Southampton Test 1983, 1987 and 1992 general elections. Member for Southampton Test 1997-2010, for Southampton Test (revised boundary) since 6 May 2010 general election; Joint PPS to David Blunkett as Secretary of State for Education and Employ-

LABOUR

ment 1999-2000; PPS to Baroness Blackstone as Minister for Education and Employment 1999-2001; Parliamentary Under-Secretary of State, Department for Transport, Local Government and the Regions 2001-02. *Select committees:* Member: Environment, Transport and Regional Affairs 1997-99, Environment, Transport and Regional Affairs (Environment Sub-Committee) 1997-99, Constitutional Affairs/Justice 2003-10, Standards and Privileges 2005-13, Joint Committee on the Draft Climate Change Bill 2007, Energy and Climate Change 2009-, Environmental Audit 2010-, Standards 2013-, Privileges 2013-. Chair: PLP Departmental Committee for Local Government 1998-2001, PLP Departmental Group for Energy and Climate Change 2010-; Vice-chair, PLP Departmental Group for Environment, Food and Rural Affairs 2010-. Member, Labour Party National Policy Forum 1999-2001, 2010-; Chair, Manifesto Group Local Government 2007-; Sustainable Communities Policy Commission, National Policy Forum. *Councils and public bodies:* Southampton City Council: Councillor 1980-92, Leader 1984-92.

Political interests: Environment, local and regional government, higher education, education, constitution, transport, energy; France, Lithuania, Poland.

Other: Director/board member: Southampton Environment Centre, Third Age Centre, Southampton. Visiting professor, Southampton Institute 1997-.

Recreations: Football (playing and watching), writing, tennis.

Dr Alan Whitehead MP, House of Commons, London SW1A 0AA
Tel: 020 7219 5517 *Fax:* 020 7219 0918 *Email:* whiteheada@parliament.uk
Constituency: 20-22 Southampton Street, Southampton, Hampshire SO15 1ED
Tel: 02380 231942 *Fax:* 02380 231943 *Email:* alan@alan-whitehead.org.uk
Website: www.alan-whitehead.org.uk alansenergyblog.wordpress.com
Twitter: @alanwhiteheadmp

WHITTAKER, CRAIG Calder Valley *(Majority 6,431)*

Born 30 August 1962; Son of late Frank Whittaker and Marjorie Whittaker; Divorced (1 son 2 daughters); married Elaine Wilkinson 2011.

Education: Belmont High School, New South Wales, Australia; Tighes Hill College, New South Wales, Australia.

Non-political career: Armed Forces Parliamentary Scheme 2010-11. Director, Kezdem PTY Ltd, New South Wales, Australia 1991; Branch manager, Wilkinsons Home and Garden Stores 1992-98; General manager, PC World Dixons Store Group 1998-2009.

CONSERVATIVE

Political career: Member for Calder Valley since 6 May 2010 general election. *Select committees:* Member: Education 2010-, Unopposed Bills (Panel) 2011-, Joint Committee on the Draft Communications Data Bill 2012-13. Constituency agent 2005 general election; Chair, Calder Valley Conservative Association 2005-06. *Councils and public bodies:* Councillor, Heptonstall Parish Council 1998-2003; Calderdale Metropolitan Borough Council: Councillor 2003-04, 2007-11, Cabinet member, Children and Young Peoples Services 2007-10.

Political interests: Education, children, aged care; Australia, Kenya, New Zealand, Tanzania.

Other: Treasurer, Heptonstall Festival Committee 1996-2000; Chairman, TLC (Together for Looked-After Children).

Publications: Co-author, Freedom, Responsibility and the State: Curbing Over-Mighty Government (Politeia, 2012).

Recreations: Sailing, reading.

Craig Whittaker MP, House of Commons, London SW1A 0AA
Tel: 020 7219 7031 *Fax:* 020 7219 1192 *Email:* craig.whittaker.mp@parliament.uk
Constituency: First Floor, Spring Villa, 16 Church Lane, Brighouse, West Yorkshire HD6 1AT
Tel: 01484 711260 *Fax:* 01484 718288 *Email:* office@craigwhittakermp.co.uk
Website: www.craigwhittakermp.co.uk *Twitter:* @CraigWhi2kermp

WHITTINGDALE, JOHN Maldon *(Majority 19,407)*

John Flasby Lawrance Whittingdale. Born 16 October 1959; Son of late John Whittingdale and Margaret Whittingdale; Married Ancilla Murfitt 1990 (divorced 2008) (1 son 1 daughter).

Education: Winchester College; University College, London (BSc economics 1982).

Non-political career: Head of political section, Conservative Research Department 1982-84; Special adviser to Secretaries of State for Trade and Industry: Norman Tebbit MP, Leon Brittan MP and Paul Channon MP 1984-87; Manager, N M Rothschild & Sons 1987; Political secretary to Margaret Thatcher as Prime Minister 1988-90; Private secretary to Margaret Thatcher MP 1990-92.

CONSERVATIVE

Political career: Member for South Colchester and Maldon 1992-97, for Maldon and Chelmsford East 1997-2010, for Maldon since 6 May 2010 general election; PPS to Eric Forth as Minister of State for: Education 1994-95, Education and Employment 1994-96; Opposition Whip 1997-98; Opposition Spokesperson for the Treasury 1998-99; Parliamentary Private Secretary to William Hague as Leader of Opposition 1999-2001; Shadow Secretary of State for: Trade and Industry 2001-02, Culture, Media and Sport 2002-03, Agriculture, Fisheries and Food 2003-04, Culture, Media and Sport 2004-05. *Select committees:* Member: Health 1993-97, Information 1997-98, Trade and Industry 2001; Chair: Culture, Media and Sport 2005-; Member: Liaison 2005-; Joint Committee on Privacy and Injunctions: Member 2011, Chair 2011-12. 1922 Committee: Member, Executive 2005-06, Vice-chair 2006-. Member: 92 Group, No Turning Back Group; Member: Executive, Conservative Way Forward 2005-10, Conservative Party Board 2006-10.

Political interests: Broadcasting and media; Armenia, China, Georgia, Israel, Japan, Korea, Malaysia, Russia, Ukraine, USA.

Other: Member, Executive Committee, Inter-Parliamentary Union, British Group 2010-; Fellow: Industry and Parliament Trust 1996, Royal Society of Arts 2008-; Council member, Freedom Association 2008-. Inquisitor of the Year, *The Spectator* awards 2011. OBE 1990; Essex. Captain, House of Commons Rifle Team 2010-.

Publications: New Policies for the Media (1995).

Recreations: Cinema, music.

John Whittingdale OBE MP, House of Commons, London SW1A 0AA
Tel: 020 7219 3557 *Fax:* 020 7219 2522 *Email:* john.whittingdale.mp@parliament.uk
Constituency: 19 High Street, Maldon, Essex CM9 5PE
Tel: 01621 855663 *Email:* m.c.c.a@btconnect.com *Website:* www.johnwhittingdale.org.uk

WIGGIN, BILL
North Herefordshire *(Majority 9,887)*

CONSERVATIVE

William David Wiggin. Born 4 June 1966; Son of Sir Jerry Wiggin and Mrs Rosie Dale Harris; Married Camilla Chilvers 1999 (2 sons 1 daughter).

Education: Eton College; University College of North Wales (BA economics 1988).

Non-political career: Trader UBS 1991-93; Associate director, currency options sales, Dresdner Kleinwort Benson 1994-98; Manager, structured products, Commerzbank 1998-2001.

Political career: Contested Burnley 1997 general election. Member for Leominster 2001-10, for North Herefordshire since 6 May 2010 general election; Shadow Minister for Environment, Food and Rural Affairs 2003; Shadow Secretary of State for Wales 2003-05; Shadow Minister for Environment, Food and Rural Affairs 2005-09; Opposition Whip 2009-10; Assistant Government Whip 2010-12. *Select committees:* Member: Welsh Affairs 2001-03, Transport, Local Government and the Regions 2001-02, Environment, Food and Rural Affairs 2002-05. Secretary, Conservative Agricultural/Rural Affairs Policy Committee 2001-03; Member, Executive, 1922 Committee 2002-03. Contested North West region 1999 European Parliamentary election. Vice-chair, Hammersmith and Fulham Conservative Association 1995-97. *Councils and public bodies:* Governor, Hammersmith and West London College 1995-98.

Political interests: Defence, agriculture, Treasury, environment.

Other: Trustee, Violet Eveson Charitable Trust. Goldsmiths' Company. Freeman, City of London; Hurlingham, Annabels, Pratt's, Rankin.

Recreations: Motorcycles, country sports, Hereford cattle.

Bill Wiggin MP, House of Commons, London SW1A 0AA
Tel: 020 7219 8175/020 7219 2394 *Fax:* 020 7219 1893 *Email:* bill.wiggin.mp@parliament.uk
Constituency: North Herefordshire Conservative Association office, 8 Corn Square, Leominster, Herefordshire HR6 8LR
Tel: 01568 612565 *Fax:* 01568 610320 *Website:* www.billwiggin.com

---

VACHER'S QUARTERLY

The most up-to-date contact details throughout the year

Call 020 7593 5644 or visit www.dodsshop.co.uk

CONSERVATIVE

WILLETTS, DAVID
Havant *(Majority 12,160)*

Minister of State for Universities and Science, Department for Business, Innovation and Skills

David Lindsay Willetts. Born 9 March 1956; Son of John and Hilary Willetts; Married Hon. Sarah Butterfield 1986 (1 son 1 daughter).

Education: King Edward's School, Birmingham; Christ Church, Oxford (BA philosophy, politics and economics 1978); German (fluent).

Non-political career: HM Treasury 1978-84: Private secretary to Nicholas Ridley MP as Financial Secretary 1981-82, Principal, Monetary Policy Division 1982-84; Prime Minister's Downing Street Policy Unit 1984-86; Director of Studies, Centre for Policy Studies 1987-92; Consultant director, Conservative Research Department 1987-92; Director: Retirement Security Ltd 1988-94, Electra Corporate Ventures Ltd 1988-94; Governor, Ditchley Foundation 1998-; Visiting Fellow, Nuffield College, Oxford 1999-2006; Member, Global Commission on Ageing 2000-; Visiting Fellow, Cass Business School 2004-07.

Political career: Member for Havant 1992-2010, for Havant (revised boundary) since 6 May 2010 general election; PPS to Sir Norman Fowler as Chairman of Conservative Party 1993-94; Assistant Government Whip 1994-95; Government Whip July-November 1995; Parliamentary Secretary, Office of Public Service 1995-96; Paymaster General, Office of Public Service July-December 1996; Opposition Spokesman for Employment 1997-98; Shadow Secretary of State for: Education and Employment 1998-99, Social Security 1999-2001, Work and Pensions 2001-05, and Welfare Reform 2004-05, Trade and Industry 2005, Education and Skills/Innovation, Universities and Skills 2005-09; Shadow Minister for Universities and Skills 2009-10; Minister of State for Universities and Science, Department for Business, Innovation and Skills 2010-. *Select committees:* Member: Social Security 1992-93. Member Conservative Economic Affairs/ Enterprise/Pensions/Social Affairs Policy Committee 2001-. Chair, Conservative Research Department 1997; Member, Conservative Policy Board 2001-; Head of policy co-ordination, Conservative Party 2003-04. *Councils and public bodies:* Member: Lambeth and Lewisham Family Practitioners' Committee 1987-90, Parkside Health Authority 1988-90, Social Security Advisory Committee 1989-92.

Political interests: Economic policy, health, social security, education; Germany, USA.

Other: Member, Competitiveness Council, Council of the European Union 2010-. PC 2010; Hurlingham.

Publications: Modern Conservatism (1992); Civic Conservatism (1994); Blair's Gurus (1996); Why Vote Conservative (1997); Welfare to Work (1998); After the Landslide (1999); Browned-off: What's Wrong with Gordon Brown's Social Policy (2000); Co-author, Tax Credits: Do They Add Up? (2002); Left Out, Left Behind (2003); Old Europe? Demographic Change and Pension Reform (2003); Conservatives in Birmingham (2008); The Pinch – How the baby boomers took their children's future – and why they should give it back (Atlantic Books, 2010).

Recreations: Swimming, reading, cycling.

Rt Hon David Willetts MP, House of Commons, London SW1A 0AA
Tel: 020 7219 4570 *Fax:* 020 7219 2567 *Email:* willettsd@parliament.uk
Constituency: c/o Havant Conservative Association, 19 South Street, Havant, Hampshire PO9 1BU
Tel: 02392 499746 *Fax:* 02392 498753 *Email:* david@davidwilletts.co.uk

PLAID CYMRU

WILLIAMS, HYWEL
Arfon *(Majority 1,455)*

Plaid Cymru Spokesperson for Cabinet Office, for Energy and Climate Change, for Education, for Health, for International Development and for Work and Pensions

Born 14 May 1953; Son of Robert Williams and Jennie Page Williams, shopkeepers; Divorced (3 daughters); Married Dr Myfanwy Davies 2010 (1 son).

Education: Glan y Môr School, Pwllheli; University of Wales: Cardiff (BSc psychology 1974), Bangor (CQSW social work 1979); Welsh.

Non-political career: Social worker: Mid Glamorgan County Council 1974-76, Gwynedd County Council 1976-84; North Wales Social Work Practice Centre, University of Wales, Bangor 1985-94: Project worker 1985-94, Head of centre 1991-94; Freelance lecturer consultant and author social work and social policy 1994-2001. NALGO 1974-84; NUPE 1974-84; UCAC 1984-94.

Political career: Member for Caernarfon 2001-10, for Arfon since 6 May 2010 general election; Plaid Cymru Spokesperson for: Work and Pensions 2001-, Health 2001-, Disability 2001-05, International Development 2004-, Culture, Media and Sport 2005-06, Education and Skills/Children, Schools and Families 2005-10, Treasury 2006-07, Defence 2007-09, Transport 2007-09, Cabinet Office 2010-, Energy and Climate Change 2010-, Education 2010-. *Select committees:* Member: European Standing Committee B 2002-04, Welsh Affairs 2004-05, Chairmen's Panel/Panel of Chairs 2005-, Science and Technology 2012-, Works of Art 2012-. Contested Clwyd South constituency 1999 National Assembly for Wales election. Policy developer social security and policy for older people, Plaid Cymru 1999-2001; Plaid Cymru policy cabinet 1999-2001.

Political interests: Social affairs, social security, social work, language issues, international development.

Other: North Wales Air Ambulance; Kidney Wales.

Publications: Geirfa Gwaith Cymdeithasol/A Social Work Vocabulary (University of Wales Press, 1988); General editor Geirfa Gwaith Plant/Child Care Terms (UWP, 1993); Gwaith Cymdeithasol a'r Iaith Gymraeg/Social Work and the Welsh Language (UWP/CCETSW); Llawlyfr Hyfforddi a Hyfforddwyr/An Index of Trainers and Training (AGWC, 1994); Gofal – Pecyn Adnoddau a Hyfforddi Gofal yn y Gymuned yng Nghymru/A Training and Resource Pack for Community Care in Wales (CCETSW Cymru, 1998).

Recreations: Reading, cinema, walking, kite flying.

Hywel Williams MP, House of Commons, London SW1A 0AA
Tel: 020 7219 5021 *Fax:* 020 7219 3705 *Email:* hywel.williams.mp@parliament.uk
Constituency: 8 Castle Street, Caernarfon, Gwynedd LL55 1SE
Tel: 01286 672076 *Fax:* 01286 672003 *Website:* www.hywelwilliams.plaidcymru.org
Twitter: @hywelwilliamsmp

WILLIAMS, MARK
Ceredigion *(Majority 8,324)*

Mark Fraser Williams. Born 24 March 1966; Son of Ronald and Pauline Williams; Married Helen Wyatt 1997 (2 daughters and twin son and daughter).

Education: Richard Hale School, Hertford; University College of Wales, Aberystwyth (BSc politics and economics 1987); Plymouth University (PGCE primary education 1993).

Non-political career: Constituency assistant to Geraint Howells MP 1987-92; Primary school teacher: Madron Daniel School, Cornwall 1993-96, Forches Cross School, Barnstaple, Devon 1996-2000; Deputy head teacher, Llangors Church in Wales School, nr Brecon 2000-05. Member, National Association of Schoolmasters/Union of Women Teachers (NASUWT) 1993.

LIBERAL DEMOCRAT

Political career: Contested Monmouth 1997 general election, Ceredigion 2000 by-election and 2001 general election. Member for Ceredigion 2005-10, for Ceredigion (revised boundary) since 6 May 2010 general election; Liberal Democrat Shadow Minister for: Education 2005-06, Wales 2006-10, Innovation, Universities and Skills 2007. *Select committees:* Member: Welsh Affairs 2005-. Chair, Liberal Democrat Parliamentary Party Committees on: Constitutional and Political Reform 2010-12, Wales 2012-. Research assistant, Liberal/Liberal Democrat Peers 1987-92; Member, Welsh Liberal Democrats Executive 1991-92; President, Ceredigion Liberal Democrats 1998-2000; Member, Welsh Liberal Democrats Campaign Committee 2000.

Political interests: Education, rural affairs, human rights, devolution; Iran, Nigeria.

Other: Member: Greenpeace, Countryside Alliance; Member, General Teaching Council of Wales.

Recreations: Reading, political biographies, gardening, fresh air.

Mark Williams MP, House of Commons, London SW1A 0AA
Tel: 020 7219 8469 *Email:* williamsmf@parliament.uk
Constituency: 32 North Parade, Aberystwyth, Ceredigion SY23 2NF
Tel: 01970 627721 *Website:* www.markwilliams.org.uk *Twitter:* @mark4ceredigion

---

Need additional copies?
Call 020 7593 5679
Visit www.dodsshop.co.uk

WILLIAMS, ROGER
Brecon and Radnorshire *(Majority 3,747)*

Roger Hugh Williams. Born 22 January 1948; Son of Morgan Glyn and Eirlys Williams; Married Penelope James 1973 (1 daughter 1 son).

Education: Christ College, Brecon, Powys; Selwyn College, Cambridge (BA agriculture 1969).

Non-political career: Farmer 1969-. Former chair, Brecon and Radnorshire National Farmers Union; Member, Farmers Union of Wales.

LIBERAL DEMOCRAT

Political career: Member for Brecon and Radnorshire since 7 June 2001 general election; Liberal Democrat: Spokesperson/Shadow Minister for Rural Affairs 2002-05, 2006-10; Whip 2004-07; Shadow Secretary of State for Wales 2007-10; Whip 2008-10. *Select committees:* Member: Welsh Affairs 2001-05, Environment, Food and Rural Affairs 2005-10, Science and Technology 2010-. Chair, Liberal Democrat Parliamentary Party Committees on: Wales 2010-12, Environment, Food and Rural Affairs 2012-. Contested Carmarthen West and South Pembrokeshire constituency 1999 National Assembly for Wales election. Deputy leader, Welsh Liberal Democrats. *Councils and public bodies:* Councillor, Powys County Council 1981-2001; Member, Development Board for Rural Wales 1989-97; Chair: Mid Wales Agri-Food Partnership, Brecon Beacons National Park 1991-95; Lay school inspector.

Political interests: Agriculture, education, economic development; Afghanistan, Egypt, Mali.

Other: Member, UK Delegation, Organisation for Security and Co-operation in Europe Parliamentary Assembly; Member, Country Landowners and Business Association. CBE 2013.

Recreations: Sport, walking, nature conservation.

Roger Williams CBE MP, House of Commons, London SW1A 0AA
Tel: 020 7219 8145 *Fax:* 020 7219 1747 *Email:* williamsr@parliament.uk
Constituency: 4 Watergate, Brecon, Powys LD3 9AN
Tel: 01874 625739 *Fax:* 01874 625635 *Email:* info@rogerwilliams.org.uk
Website: www.rogerwilliams.org.uk *Twitter:* @RogerWilliamsMP

WILLIAMS, STEPHEN
Bristol West *(Majority 11,366)*

Stephen Roy Williams. Born 11 October 1966; Son of late Malcolm Williams, road worker, and Diana Williams, née Evans, school dinner lady and waitress; Single.

Education: Mountain Ash Comprehensive School, Glamorgan; Bristol University (BA history 1988).

Non-political career: Graduate trainee up to supervisor, Coopers and Lybrand, Bristol 1988-95; Tax manager: Kraft Jacobs Suchard Ltd, Cheltenham Head Office 1995, Grant Thornton, Cheltenham Office 1996-98, Grant Thornton, Bristol Office 1998-2001, Orange plc 2001-02, Wincanton plc 2002-03, RAC plc 2004-05.

LIBERAL DEMOCRAT

Political career: Contested Bristol South 1997 and Bristol West 2001 general elections. Member for Bristol West 2005-10, for Bristol West (revised boundary) since 6 May 2010 general election; Liberal Democrat: Shadow Minister for: Health 2005-06, Further and Higher Education 2006-07, Children, Schools and Families 2007; Shadow Secretary of State for Innovation, Universities and Skills 2007-10. *Select committees:* Member: Education and Skills/Children, Schools and Families 2005-08, Public Accounts 2005-06, Political and Constitutional Reform 2010-, Members' Expenses 2011-. Chair, Liberal Democrat Parliamentary Party Committee on Treasury 2010-; Convenor, Liberal Democrat Parliamentary Parties Group of Chairs. Chair, Bristol University SDP/Liberal Club 1986-87; Constituency secretary, Cynon Valley SDP 1986-88. *Councils and public bodies:* Deputy Leader/Group Chair, Liberal Democrat Group, Avon County Council 1993-96; Bristol City Council: Councillor 1995-99, Leader, Liberal Democrat Group/Shadow Council Leader 1995-97.

Political interests: Taxation, education, preventive healthcare, transport, civil rights, arts, Europe; China, all EU members and candidates for entry, India, Israel, Palestine, USA.

Other: Member, Chartered Institute of Taxation. World Health Organisation medal for anti-tobacco campaigning 2013.

Publications: Getting Your Share of the Banks (Centre Forum 2011); Contributed Chapter, The Green Book (2013).

Recreations: Art galleries, historic sites, theatre, cinema, eating out, postcard collecting, genealogy.

Stephen Williams MP, House of Commons, London SW1A 0AA
Tel: 020 7219 8416 *Fax:* 020 7219 4802 *Email:* stephen.williams.mp@parliament.uk
Constituency: PO Box 2500, Bristol BS6 9AH
Tel: 0117-942 3494 *Fax:* 0117-942 6925 *Website:* www.stephenwilliams.org.uk
www.stephenwilliamsmp.wordpress.com *Twitter:* @SWilliamsMP

WILLIAMSON, CHRIS
Derby North *(Majority 613)*

Christopher Williamson. Born 16 September 1956; Son of late George and Eileen Williamson. **Education:** Castle Donington High School; Sir Thomas More School, Allenton; Leicester Polytechnic (CQSW). **Non-political career:** Bricklayer 1973-78; Market trader 1978-79; Social worker 1981-87; Welfare rights officer 1987-2002. **Political career:** Member for Derby North since 6 May 2010 general election; Shadow Minister for Communities and Local Government 2010-13. *Select committees:* Member: Communities and Local Government 2010. Member, Labour Party 1976-. *Councils and public bodies:* Derby City Council: Councillor 1991-2011, Council Leader; Member: General Assembly, Local Government Association 2006-10, State of the City Forum, Derby City Partnership 2009-10. **Political interests:** Poverty, animal welfare, urban regeneration, environment, climate change, local government community empowerment; Cuba, Ecuador, Scandinavian countries, Venezuela. **Other:** League Against Cruel Sports: Member 1976-, Chair 1984-94, Trustee. **Recreations:** Cycling, walking, watching Derby County.

Chris Williamson MP, House of Commons, London SW1A 0AA
Tel: 020 7219 7049 *Fax:* 020 7219 1383 *Email:* chris.williamson.mp@parliament.uk
Constituency: 9a Theatre Walk, Westfield Centre, Derby DE1 2NG
Tel: 01332 205126 *Website:* www.chriswilliamson.org *Twitter:* @ChriswMP

LABOUR

WILLIAMSON, GAVIN
South Staffordshire *(Majority 16,590)*

PPS to David Cameron as Prime Minister

Gavin Alexander Williamson. Born 25 June 1976; Married Joanne (2 daughters). **Education:** Raincliffe Comprehensive School; Bradford University (BSc social sciences 1997). **Non-political career:** Businessman; Managing director, architecture design company; Ran and owned a pottery company. **Political career:** Contested Blackpool North and Fleetwood 2005 general election. Member for South Staffordshire since 6 May 2010 general election; PPS to Hugo Swire as Minister of State, Northern Ireland Office 2011-12; Acting PPS to Owen Paterson as Secretary of State for Northern Ireland July-September 2012; PPS to: Patrick McLoughlin as Secretary of State for Transport 2012-13, David Cameron as Prime Minister 2013-. *Select committees:* Member: Northern Ireland Affairs 2010-11. Former chair, Staffordshire Conservative Students; Deputy chair, Staffordshire Conservatives; Chair, Stoke-on-Trent Conservative Association; Vice-chair, Derbyshire Dales Conservative Association. *Councils and public bodies:* Councillor, North Yorkshire County Council 2001-05. **Political interests:** Manufacturing and industry, design, MoD, Commonwealth affairs, green belt; China, Japan, Korea, Sierra Leone. **Other:** Member, British Irish Parliamentary Assembly; Executive member, Commonwealth Parliamentary Association. **Recreations:** Pottery, time with family, books, architecture, cars.

Gavin Williamson MP, House of Commons, London SW1A 0AA
Tel: 020 7219 7150 *Email:* gavin.williamson.mp@parliament.uk
Constituency: Jubilee House, 59 Wolverhampton Road, Codsall, South Staffordshire, Staffordshire WV8 1PL
Email: gavin@gavinwilliamson.org *Website:* www.gavinwilliamson.org
Twitter: @GWilliamsonMP

CONSERVATIVE

WILLOTT, JENNY
Cardiff Central *(Majority 4,576)*

Assistant Government Whip

Jennifer Nancy Willott. Born 29 May 1974; Daughter of Brian and Alison Willott; Married Andrew Poole 2009 (2 sons). **Education:** Wimbledon High School; Uppingham School; St Mary's College, Durham (BA classics 1996); London School of Economics (MSc Econ development studies 1997); French, Spanish. **Non-political career:** Researcher and proposal writer, Adithi NGO, Bihar, India 1995; Head of office, Lembit Öpik MP 1997-2000; Researcher, Liberal Democrat group, National Assembly

LIBERAL DEMOCRAT

for Wales 2000-01; Project administrator, Barnardo's, Derwen project 2001; Head of advocacy, Unicef UK 2001-03; Head, Victim Support, South Wales 2003-05.

Political career: Contested Cardiff Central 2001 general election. Member for Cardiff Central since 5 May 2005 general election; Liberal Democrat: Shadow Minister for Youth Affairs 2006-07; Whip 2006-08; Deputy Chief Whip 2006-08, Shadow Minister for Justice 2008; Shadow Secretary of State for Work and Pensions 2008-09; Shadow Chancellor of the Duchy of Lancaster 2009-10; PPS to Chris Huhne as Secretary of State for Energy and Climate Change (resigned) 2010; Assistant Government Whip 2012-. *Select committees:* Member: Work and Pensions 2005-10, Public Administration 2005-10. Chair, Liberal Democrat Parliamentary Party Committee on Work and Pensions 2010-12. Member, Manifesto Working Group 2013-. *Councils and public bodies:* Councillor, London Borough of Merton 1998-2000.

Political interests: International development, children's issues, crime and disorder, work and pensions; India.

Other: Unicef UK; Shelter; Cancer Research; Ty Hafan Children's Hospice.

Recreations: Travelling, music, reading.

Jenny Willott MP, House of Commons, London SW1A 0AA
Tel: 020 7219 8418 *Fax:* 020 7219 0694 *Email:* willottj@parliament.uk
Constituency: 38 The Parade, Roath, Cardiff CF24 3AD
Tel: 029 2046 2276 *Email:* jenny@jennywillott.com *Website:* www.jennywillott.com
Twitter: @jennywillott

LABOUR

WILSON, PHIL

Sedgefield *(Majority 8,696)*

Opposition Whip

Philip Wilson. Born 31 May 1959; Son of Ivy and Bernard Wilson; Partner Margaret Brown since 1999 (2 children 3 stepchildren).

Education: Trimdon Secondary Modern; Sedgefield Comprehensive School.

Non-political career: Shop assistant; Civil Service clerical worker; Aide to Tony Blair MP 1987-94; Researcher to Stephen Hughes MEP 1989; Labour Party organiser and assistant general secretary 1994-99; Public relations consultant: Brunswick 1999-2002, Fellows Associates 2002-07. Member: USDAW 1977-78, CPSA 1978-87, TGWU 1986-, GMB 1994-.

Political career: Member for Sedgefield 19 July 2007 by-election to 2010, for Sedgefield (revised boundary) since 6 May 2010 general election; PPS: to Vernon Coaker as Minister of State: Home Office 2008-09, Department for Children, Schools and Families 2009, to Andy Burnham as Secretary of State for Health 2009-10; Opposition Whip 2010-. *Select committees:* Member: Public Accounts 2007-10, Regulatory Reform 2007-10, North East 2009-10. Honorary secretary/treasurer, PLP Northern Regional Group 2007-10.

Political interests: Regional development, sustainable communities, education; USA.

Recreations: Reading, jazz, history.

Phil Wilson MP, House of Commons, London SW1A 0AA
Tel: 020 7219 4966 *Email:* phil.wilson.mp@parliament.uk
Constituency: 4 Beveridge Walkway, Newton Aycliffe, Co Durham DL5 4EE
Tel: 01325 324827 *Email:* brownmar@parliament.uk *Website:* www.philwilsonmp.co.uk
Twitter: @PhilWilsonMP

CONSERVATIVE

WILSON, ROBERT

Reading East *(Majority 7,605)*

PPS to George Osborne as Chancellor of the Exchequer

Born 4 January 1965; Married Jane (4 children).

Education: Wallingford School, Oxfordshire; Reading University (BA history).

Non-political career: Entrepreneur in health and telecommunications.

Political career: Contested Bolton North East 1997 general election. Member for Reading East 2005-10, for Reading East (revised boundary) since 6 May 2010 general election; Shadow Minister for Higher Education 2007-09; Opposition Whip 2009-10; PPS to: Jeremy Hunt as Secretary of State for: Culture, Olympics, Media and Sport 2010-12, Health 2012-13, George Osborne as Chancellor of the Exchequer 2013-. *Select committees:* Member: Education and Skills 2005-07, Procedure 2005-08, Innovation, Universities[, Science] and Skills/Science and Technology 2007-10. *Councils and public bodies:* Councillor, Reading Borough Council 1992-96, 2003-06.

Political interests: Crime, education, immigration.

Publications: 5 Days to Power (2010).

Recreations: Cricket, family.

Robert Wilson MP, House of Commons, London SW1A 0AA
Tel: 020 7219 2498/020 7219 6519 *Fax:* 020 7219 0847 *Email:* robwilsonmp@parliament.uk
Constituency: 12a South View Park, Marsack Street, Reading, Berkshire RG4 5AF
Tel: 0118-375 9785 *Email:* office@readingeastconservatives.com
Website: www.robwilsonmp.com *Twitter:* @RobWilson_RDG

WILSON, SAMMY
East Antrim *(Majority 6,770)*

DUP Spokesperson for Treasury

Samuel Wilson. Born 4 April 1953; Son of Alexander and Mary Wilson.

Education: Methodist College, Belfast; Queen's University, Belfast (BA economics and politics 1975); Stranmillis College, Belfast (DipEd 1976).

Non-political career: Head of economics, Grosvenor Grammar School, Belfast 1975-83.

DEMOCRATIC UNIONIST PARTY

Political career: Contested Strangford 1992 and East Antrim 2001 general elections. Member for East Antrim 2005-10, for East Antrim (revised boundary) since 6 May 2010 general election; DUP Spokesperson for: Education and Skills 2003-07, Housing 2005-07, Communities and Local Government 2007-09, Children, Schools and Families 2007-10, Innovation, Universities and Skills 2007-09, Treasury 2009-, Education 2010-12. *Select committees:* Member: Northern Ireland Affairs 2005-09, Transport 2009. Northern Ireland Assembly: Member Northern Ireland Forum for Political Dialogue 1996, MLA for Belfast East 1998-2003, for East Antrim 2003-11, and for East Antrim (revised boundary) since 5 May 2011: Minister of: Environment 2008-09, Finance and Personnel 2009-13. DUP press officer 1982-96. *Councils and public bodies:* East Belfast City Council: Councillor 1981-2010, Lord Mayor 1986-87, 2000-01; Member, Northern Ireland Policing Board 2001-06.

Political interests: Social issues, policing, education; America, China.

Publications: The Carson Trail (1982); The Unionist Case – The Forum Report Answered (1984); Data Response Questions in Economics (1995).

Recreations: Gardening, motorbikes.

Sammy Wilson MP, House of Commons, London SW1A 0AA
Tel: 020 7219 8523 *Fax:* 020 7219 3671 *Email:* barronj@parliament.uk
Constituency: East Antrim DUP, 116 Main Street, Larne, Co Antrim BT40 1RG
Tel: 028 2826 7722 *Fax:* 028 2826 9922 *Website:* www.sammywilson.org

WINNICK, DAVID
Walsall North *(Majority 990)*

David Julian Winnick. Born 26 June 1933; Son of late Eugene and Rose Winnick; Married Bengisu Rona 1968 (divorced) (1 son).

Education: London School of Economics (Diploma social administration 1974).

Non-political career: Army national service 1951-53. Tribune: Progress chaser, Advertisement manager 1963-66; United Kingdom Immigrants Advisory Service 1970-79: Chair 1984-90. Association of Professional, Executive, Clerical and Computer Staff (APEX): Member, Executive Council 1978-88, Vice-President 1983-88.

LABOUR

Political career: Contested Harwich 1964 general election. Member for Croydon South 1966-70. Contested Croydon South 1970 and Croydon Central October 1974 general elections and Walsall North 1976 by-election. Member for Walsall North 1979-2010, for Walsall North (revised boundary) since 6 May 2010 general election. *Select committees:* Member: Environment 1979-83, Home Affairs 1983-87, 1997-, Procedure 1989-97. *Councils and public bodies:* Councillor, London Borough of: Willesden Council 1959-64, Brent Council 1964-66.

Other: British-Irish Inter-Parliamentary Body: Member 1990-2005, British co-chair 1997-2005.

Recreations: Reading, theatre, films, walking.

David Winnick MP, House of Commons, London SW1A 0AA
Tel: 020 7219 5003 *Fax:* 020 7219 0215 *Email:* winnickd@parliament.uk
Constituency: 47 Field Road, Bloxwich, Walsall, West Midlands WS3 3JD
Tel: 01922 492084 *Website:* www.davidwinnick.webs.com

LABOUR

WINTERTON, ROSIE

Doncaster Central *(Majority 6,229)*

Opposition Chief Whip

Rosalie Winterton. Born 10 August 1958; Daughter of late Gordon and Valerie Winterton, teachers.

Education: Doncaster Grammar School; Hull University (BA history 1979).

Non-political career: Constituency personal assistant to John Prescott MP 1980-86; Parliamentary officer: Southwark Council 1986-88, Royal College of Nursing 1988-90; Managing director, Connect Public Affairs 1990-94; Head of private office, John Prescott MP as Deputy Leader of Labour Party 1994-97. Transport and General Workers' Union: Branch officer 1998-99, Chair, Parliamentary Group 1998-99; Member, Unite.

Political career: Member for Doncaster Central 1997-2010, for Doncaster Central (revised boundary) since 6 May 2010 general election; Parliamentary Secretary, Lord Chancellor's Department 2001-03; Minister of State: Department of Health 2003-07, Department for Transport 2007-08; Minister for Yorkshire and the Humber 2008-10; Minister of State: (Pensions and the Ageing Society), Department for Work and Pensions 2008-09, (Regional Economic Development and Co-ordination) Departments for Business, Innovation and Skills and for Communities and Local Government 2009-10; Shadow Leader of the House of Commons and Lord Privy Seal 2010; Shadow Minister for Women 2010; Member: House of Commons Commission 2010, Speaker's Committee for the Independent Parliamentary Standards Authority 2010-11; Opposition Chief Whip 2010-; Member, Parliamentary and Political Service Honours Committee 2012-. *Select committees:* Member: Standing Committees: Transport Bill January 2000, Finance Bill April 2000; Member, Speaker's Committee on the Electoral Commission 2009-10, Parliamentary and Political Service Honours Committee 2012-.

Political interests: Regional policy, employment, transport, housing, home affairs.

Other: Member, Amnesty International; Patron: Doncaster Housing for Young People (DHYP), Darts Doncaster Community Arts, South Yorkshire Centre for Inclusive Living (SYCIL), Home Start Doncaster. PC 2006; Doncaster Trades and Labour Club; Intake Social Club; Doncaster Catholic Club. Green Wyvern Sailing Club.

Recreations: Sailing, reading.

Rt Hon Rosie Winterton MP, House of Commons, London SW1A 0AA
Tel: 020 7219 3000 *Email:* rosie.winterton.mp@parliament.uk
Constituency: Doncaster Trades, 19 South Mall, Frenchgate, Doncaster,
South Yorkshire DN1 1LL
Tel: 01302 326297 *Fax:* 01302 342921 *Website:* www.rosiewinterton.co.uk

SCOTTISH NATIONAL PARTY

WISHART, PETER

Perth and North Perthshire *(Majority 4,379)*

SNP Chief Whip and Spokesperson for Home Affairs, for the Constitution, for Justice and for Culture, Media and Sport

Born 9 March 1962; Son of late Alex Wishart, former dockyard worker, and Nan Irvine, retired teacher; Married Carrie Lindsay 1990 (separated 2003) (1 son).

Education: Queen Anne High School, Dunfermline; Moray House College of Education (Dip CommEd 1984).

Non-political career: Musician, Big Country 1981; Community worker, Central Region 1984-85; Musician, Runrig 1985-2001. Musicians Union 1985-.

Political career: Member for North Tayside 2001-05, for Perth and North Perthshire since 5 May 2005 general election; SNP Chief Whip 2001-07; SNP Spokesperson for: Transport 2001-05, Rural Affairs 2001-05, Culture, Media and Sport 2001-, Constitution 2005-07, 2012-, Overseas Aid 2005-07, Home Affairs 2007-, Justice 2007-, International Development 2007-10; SNP Chief Whip 2013-. *Select committees:* Member: Catering 2004-05, Administration 2005-08, Scottish Affairs 2009-10, Works of Art 2011-12. Member: National Council 1997-, NEC 1999-2006; Executive vice-convener, fundraising, SNP 1999-2001.

Political interests: Arts and culture, international development, justice and equality; Southern Africa, Germany, Scandinavia.

Other: Director, Fast Forward Positive Lifestyle 1992-2001; Campaign Committee, Scotland Against Drugs 1997-99.

Recreations: Music, hillwalking, travel, member parliamentary rockband 'MP4'.

Peter Wishart MP, House of Commons, London SW1A 0AA
Tel: 020 7219 8303 *Email:* wishartp@parliament.uk
Constituency: 35 Perth Street, Blairgowrie, Perthshire PH10 6DL
Tel: 01250 876576 *Fax:* 01250 876991
9 York Place, Perth, Perthshire PH2 8EP
Tel: 01738 639598 *Fax:* 01738 587637 *Website:* www.petewishartmp.com
Twitter: @PeteWishart

WOLLASTON, SARAH   Totnes *(Majority 4,927)*

Born 1962; Married Adrian (1 son 2 daughters).

Education: Tal Handaq Service Children's School, Malta; Watford Grammar School for Girls; Guys Hospital Medical School (BSc pathology 1983; MB 1986).

Non-political career: Forensic medical examiner, police 1996-2001; GP, Chagford Health Centre 1999-2010; Trainer, Peninsula Medical School 2001-10; Teacher, Exeter Postgraduate Centre -2010; Examiner, Royal College of General Practitioners.

Political career: Member for Totnes since 6 May 2010 general election. *Select committees:* Member: Health 2010-, Joint Committee on the Draft Care and Support Bill 2013.

CONSERVATIVE

Political interests: NHS, alcohol related problems, bovine TB, rural communities.

Other: Patron, Devon Rape Crisis Centre; Member, Royal College of General Practitioners 1992; Fellow, Higher Education Academy 2007; Children and Families in Grief.

Recreations: Cross-country running, tandeming.

Dr Sarah Wollaston MP, House of Commons, London SW1A 0AA
Tel: 020 7219 4064 *Fax:* 020 7219 5019 *Email:* sarah.wollaston.mp@parliament.uk
Constituency: Above Totnes Conservative Club, Station Road, Totnes, Devon TQ9 5HW
Tel: 01803 868378 *Fax:* 01803 868378 *Email:* nina.smith@parliament.uk
Website: www.drsarah.org.uk *Twitter:* @drwollastonmp

WOOD, MIKE   Batley and Spen *(Majority 4,406)*

Michael Wood. Born 3 March 1946; Son of late Rowland Wood, foundry worker, and late Laura Wood, retired cleaner; Married 2nd Christine O'Leary 1999 (1 son 1 daughter from previous marriage 2 stepdaughters).

Education: Nantwich and Acton Grammar School, Nantwich, Cheshire; Salisbury/Wells Theological College (Cert Theol 1974); Leeds University (CQSW 1981); Leeds Polytechnic (BA history and politics 1989).

Non-political career: Probation officer, social worker, community worker 1965-97. Member, GMB.

LABOUR

Political career: Contested Hexham 1987 general election. Member for Batley and Spen 1997-2010, for Batley and Spen (revised boundary) since 6 May 2010 general election. *Select committees:* Member: Broadcasting 1997-98, Procedure 2010-11. Member, Labour Friends of India 1997-. *Councils and public bodies:* Kirklees Metropolitan District Council: Councillor 1980-88, Deputy Leader 1986-87.

Political interests: Poverty, housing, transport, environmental issues and world development, small businesses; France, Indian Sub-continent.

Other: Kirkwood Hospice.

Recreations: Sport, music, ornithology, walking.

Mike Wood MP, House of Commons, London SW1A 0AA
Tel: 020 7219 4125 *Email:* woodm@parliament.uk
Constituency: Tom Myers House, 9 Cross Crown Street, Cleckheaton,
West Yorkshire BD19 3HW
Tel: 01274 335233 *Fax:* 01274 335235 *Website:* www.mikewood.org.uk

---

DO YOU NEED THIS INFORMATION ONLINE?
visit www.dodspeople.com or call 020 7593 5675
to register for a free trial

LAB/CO-OP

WOODCOCK, JOHN

Barrow and Furness *(Majority 5,208)*

John Zak Woodcock. Born 14 October 1978; Married Mandy Telford (2 daughters).

Education: Tapton Secondary School, Sheffield; Edinburgh University (MA English literature and history).

Non-political career: Journalist, *Scotsman*; Head, safeguarding vulnerable people, Crime and Policing Group, Home Office 2003-07; Special adviser to: John Hutton MP: as Chancellor of the Duchy of Lancaster and Minister for the Cabinet Office 2005, as Secretary of State for Work and Pensions 2005-07, as Secretary of State for Business, Enterprise and Regulatory Reform 2007-08, Gordon Brown MP as Prime Minister on political press issues 2009.

Political career: Member for Barrow and Furness since 6 May 2010 general election; Shadow Minister for Transport 2010-13. *Select committees:* Member: Defence 2010, Arms Export Controls 2010. Vice-chair, PLP Departmental Group for Defence 2010-11. Chair, Labour Friends of Israel 2011-. *Councils and public bodies:* Governor, Walney School.

Political interests: Civil nuclear power, manufacturing industry.

Other: Vice-chair, Progress. Sports Parliamentarian of the Year, Sport and Recreation Alliance 2011.

Publications: Columnist, *PR Week*; Contributor, The Purple Book (Progress, 2011).

Recreations: Barrow Athletic F.C, Barrow Raiders, Sheffield Wednesday F.C.

John Woodcock MP, House of Commons, London SW1A 0AA
Tel: 020 7219 7008 *Fax:* 020 7219 0170 *Email:* john.woodcock.mp@parliament.uk
Constituency: 22 Hartington Street, Barrow-in-furness, Cumbria LA14 5SL
Tel: 01229 431204 *Website:* www.johnwoodcock.org *Twitter:* @JWoodcockMP

LABOUR

WOODWARD, SHAUN

St Helens South and Whiston *(Majority 14,122)*

Shaun Anthony Woodward. Born 26 October 1958; Son of Dennis Woodward and Joan Woodward, née Nunn; Married Camilla Sainsbury 1987 (1 son 3 daughters).

Education: Bristol Grammar School; Jesus College, Cambridge (MA English literature 1982).

Non-political career: BBC TV News and Current Affairs 1982-98; Director of communications, Conservative Party 1991-92. Member, Amicus/Unite.

Political career: Member (Conservative May 1997 to December 1999, Labour since December 1999) for Witney 1997-2001, for St Helens South 2001-10, for St Helens South and Whiston since 6 May 2010 general election; Conservative Opposition Spokesperson for Environment, Transport and the Regions 1999; Parliamentary Under-Secretary of State: Northern Ireland Office 2005-06, Department for Culture, Media and Sport (Minister for Creative Industries and Tourism) 2006-07; Secretary of State for Northern Ireland 2007-10; Shadow Secretary of State for Northern Ireland 2010-11. *Select committees:* Member: Broadcasting 1997-99, European Scrutiny 1998-99, Foreign Affairs 1999, Broadcasting 2000-01, Joint Committee on Human Rights 2001-05. *Councils and public bodies:* Member, Foundation Board, RSC 1998-2002, Director: English National Opera 1998-2001, Marine Stewardship Council 1998-2001.

Political interests: Finance, environment, education, culture, children's issues, European affairs, race relations and civil rights, regeneration, international development, works of art; Australia, China, France, Germany, Italy, USA.

Other: Trustee, Childline -2005; Vice-President, St Helens District Council for Voluntary Service; Honorary President, St Helens Millennium Centre; Member, Fundraising Council, Southwark Cathedral 2011-; Trustee, Human Dignity Trust 2012-; Hamptons International Film Festival: Advisory board, Honorary chair 2013-; LAMDA: Deputy chair 2013-, Chairman, Capital Campaign 2013-. Visiting professor, Queen Mary and Westfield College, London University; Visiting fellow, John F. Kennedy School of Government, Harvard University. PC 2007.

Publications: Co-author: Tranquillisers (1983), Ben: The Story of Ben Hardwick (1984), Drugwatch (1985).

Recreations: Opera, tennis, reading, gardening, architecture.

Rt Hon Shaun Woodward MP, House of Commons, London SW1A 0AA
Tel: 020 7219 2680 *Email:* woodwardsh@parliament.uk
Constituency: Sixth Floor, Century House, Hardshaw Street, St Helens, Merseyside WA10 1QW
Tel: 01744 24226 *Fax:* 01744 24306 *Email:* grunewaldb@parliament.uk

LABOUR

WRIGHT, DAVID
Telford *(Majority 978)*

Born 22 December 1966; Son of Kenneth Wright and Heather Wright, née Wynn; Married Lesley Insole 1996.

Education: Wrockwardine Wood Comprehensive School, Telford, Shropshire; New College, Telford, Shropshire; Wolverhampton Polytechnic (BA humanities 1988).

Non-political career: Housing strategy manager, Sandwell Metropolitan Borough Council 1988-2001. Member, Unite.

Political career: Member for Telford 2001-10, for Telford (revised boundary) since 6 May 2010 general election; PPS: to Rosie Winterton as Minister of State, Department of Health 2004-05, to David Miliband: as Minister of Communities and Local Government 2005-06, as Secretary of State for Environment, Food and Rural Affairs 2006, to John Hutton as Secretary of State for Work and Pensions 2006, to Jane Kennedy as Financial Secretary to the Treasury 2007-08; Assistant Government Whip 2009-10; Opposition Whip 2010-11. *Select committees:* Member: Administration 2001-02, 2013- Environmental Audit 2001-05, Procedure 2001-05, Communities and Local Government 2007, 2009, Selection 2010-12, Armed Forces Bill 2011, Joint Committee on the Draft Communications Data Bill 2012-13. *Councils and public bodies:* Councillor, Wrekin District Council 1989-97; Oakengates Town Council 1989-2000: Councillor, Former chair.

Political interests: Housing and regeneration, regional development, sports development, heritage, poverty; Brazil, France, Hungary, Japan, USA.

Other: Dogs Trust; Member: Wrockwardine Wood and Trench Labour, Dawley Social.

Recreations: Football (Telford United), local history.

David Wright MP, House of Commons, London SW1A 0AA
Tel: 020 7219 8331 *Fax:* 020 7219 1979 *Email:* wrightda@parliament.uk
Constituency: 35b High Street, Dawley, Telford, Shropshire TF4 2EX
Tel: 01952 507747 *Fax:* 01952 506064 *Email:* info@fromtelfordfortelford.com
Website: www.davidwrightmp.org.uk *Twitter:* @DavidWrightMP

LABOUR

WRIGHT, IAIN
Hartlepool *(Majority 5,509)*

Shadow Minister for Business, Innovation and Skills

Iain David Wright. Born 9 May 1972; Son of Mervyn Wright, factory shift manager, and Linda Wright, née Harland, hairdresser; Married Tiffiny Lee Shanley 1995 (3 sons 1 daughter).

Education: Manor Comprehensive School, Hartlepool; Hartlepool Sixth Form College, Hartlepool; University College, London (BA history 1994, MA 1995).

Non-political career: Audit manager, Enterprise Risk Services Deloitte & Touche 1996-2003; Governance manager, OneNorthEast (Regional Development Agency) 2003-04. Member, GMB.

Political career: Member for Hartlepool since 30 September 2004 by-election; PPS to Rosie Winterton as Minister of State, Department of Health 2005-06; Parliamentary Under-Secretary of State: Department for Communities and Local Government 2007-09, Department for Children, Schools and Families (14-19 Reform and Apprenticeships) 2009-10; Shadow Minister for: Education 2010-11, Business, Innovation and Skills (Competitiveness and Enterprise) 2011-13, Business, Innovation and Skills (Competitiveness, Enterprise, Digital Infrastrucure and Space) 2013-. *Select committees:* Member: European Standing Committee A 2004-05, Public Administration 2005-06, Modernisation of the House of Commons 2006-08, Public Accounts 2007, Finance and Services 2010-. Honorary Secretary/Honorary Treasurer, PLP Northern Regional Group 2005-07. Treasurer, Hartlepool CLP 2002-04; Board member, Labour North 2003-04; Chair, Labour Friends of Israel 2005-06. *Councils and public bodies:* Councillor, Hartlepool Borough Council 2002-04: Cabinet Member for Performance Management 2003-04.

Political interests: Economics, regeneration; China, Latin America, Middle East.

Other: ICAEW.

Recreations: Music, history, Hartlepool United Football Club.

Iain Wright MP, House of Commons, London SW1A 0AA
Tel: 020 7219 5587 *Email:* iain.wright.mp@parliament.uk
Constituency: 23 South Road, Hartlepool, Cleveland TS26 9HD
Tel: 01429 224403 *Fax:* 01429 864775 *Website:* www.iainwrightmp.org.uk
Twitter: @IainWrightMP

CONSERVATIVE

WRIGHT, JEREMY
Kenilworth and Southam *(Majority 12,552)*

Parliamentary Under-Secretary of State (Minister for Prisons and Rehabilitation), Ministry of Justice

Jeremy Paul Wright. Born 24 October 1972; Son of John and Audrey Wright; Married Yvonne Salter 1998 (1 daughter 1 son).

Education: Taunton School, Somerset; Trinity School, New York City, USA; Exeter University (LLB law 1995); Inns of Court School of Law (Bar Vocational Course 1996).

Non-political career: Barrister, specialising in criminal law 1996-.

Political career: Member for Rugby and Kenilworth 2005-10, for Kenilworth and Southam since 6 May 2010 general election; Opposition Whip 2007-10; Government Whip 2010-12; Parliamentary Under-Secretary of State (Minister for Prisons and Rehabilitation), Ministry of Justice 2012-. *Select committees:* Member: Constitutional Affairs 2005-07. Chair, Warwick and Leamington Conservative Association 2002-03.

Political interests: Criminal justice, education, foreign affairs, dementia; USA.

Recreations: Travel, golf, James Bond films.

Jeremy Wright MP, House of Commons, London SW1A 0AA
Tel: 020 7219 2008 *Fax:* 020 7219 0024 *Email:* jeremy.wright.mp@parliament.uk
Constituency: Jubilee House, Smalley Place, Kenilworth, Warwickshire CV8 1QG
Tel: 01926 853650 *Fax:* 01926 854615 *Email:* barnespa@parliament.uk
Website: www.jeremywrightmp.co.uk

LIBERAL DEMOCRAT

WRIGHT, SIMON
Norwich South *(Majority 310)*

PPS to David Laws as Minister of State, Cabinet Office and Department for Education

Simon James Wright. Born 15 September 1979; Married Rosalind.

Education: Dereham Neatherd High School; Imperial College, London (BSc mathematics); Kings College, London (PGCE).

Non-political career: Former maths teacher; Campaigns and communications officer to Norman Lamb MP.

Political career: Member for Norwich South since 6 May 2010 general election; PPS to: Sarah Teather as Minister of State for Children and Families, Department for Education 2011-12, David Laws as Minister of State, Cabinet Office and Department for Education 2012-. *Select committees:* Member: Environmental Audit 2010-. Agent to Norman Lamb MP 2005 general election. *Councils and public bodies:* Former councillor, North Norfolk District Council.

Recreations: Music.

Simon Wright MP, House of Commons, London SW1A 0AA
Tel: 020 7219 3482 *Email:* simon.wright.mp@parliament.uk
Constituency: 2 Douro Place, Norwich NR2 4BG
Tel: 01603 627660 *Email:* office@simonwright.org.uk *Website:* www.simonwright.org.uk
Twitter: @SimonWrightMP

CONSERVATIVE

YEO, TIM
South Suffolk *(Majority 8,689)*

Timothy Stephen Kenneth Yeo. Born 20 March 1945; Son of late Dr Kenneth Yeo and Norah Yeo; Married Diane Pickard 1970 (1 son 2 daughters).

Education: Charterhouse, Surrey; Emmanuel College, Cambridge (MA history 1968).

Non-political career: Member, Cambridge University Air Squadron 1965-67. Assistant treasurer, Bankers Trust Company 1970-73; Director, Worcester Engineering Co. Ltd 1975-86; Chief executive, Spastics Society 1980-83; Chair: Univent plc 1995-2009, Genus plc 2002-04; Columnist, *Financial Times* 2004-08; Director, ITI Energy Ltd 2006-; Chair: AFC Energy plc 2007-, Eco City Vehicles plc 2007-; Director, Groupe Eurotunnel SA 2007-; Chair, TMO Renewables 2010-.

Political career: Contested Bedwelty February 1974 general election. Member for South Suffolk 1983-2010, for South Suffolk (revised boundary) since 6 May 2010 general election; PPS to Douglas Hurd: as Home Secretary 1988-89, as Foreign and Commonwealth Secretary 1989-90; Joint Parliamentary Under-Secretary of State: Department of the Environment 1990-92, Department of Health 1992-93; Minister of State, Department of the Environment 1993-94; Opposition

Spokesperson for Environment, Transport and the Regions 1997-98; Shadow Minister of Agriculture, Fisheries and Food 1998-2001; Shadow Secretary of State for: Culture, Media and Sport 2001-02, Trade and Industry 2002-03, Public Services, Health and Education 2003-04, Environment and Transport 2004-05. *Select committees:* Member: Treasury 1996-97, Culture, Media and Sport 2005-06; Chair: Environmental Audit 2005-10; Member: Liaison 2006-, Joint Committee on the Draft Climate Change Bill 2007; Chair: Energy and Climate Change 2010-; Member: Liaison (National Policy Statements Sub-committee) 2010-, Joint Committee on National Security Strategy 2010-. Chair, Conservative Party Committee for Agriculture, Fisheries and Food 1998-2001. Vice-chair, Conservative Party (with responsibility for Local Government) 1998; Patron, Tory Reform Group.

Political interests: Health, economic policy, environment, charity reform, rural affairs; Tanzania.

Other: Trustee, Tanzania Development Trust 1980-97; Chair, Charities VAT Reform Group 1981-88; Vice-President, International Voluntary Service 1984; Fellow, Industry and Parliament Trust 1985; President, Charities Tax Reform Group 1988-90; Chair, Council of Victoria University, Kampala, Uganda 2011-; President, Renewable Energy Association 2012-; The Children's Trust. Royal St George's (Sandwich); Royal and Ancient Golf Club, St Andrews; MCC; Sunningdale Golf.

Publications: Public Accountancy and Acquisition of Charities (1983); Golf correspondent, *Country Life* 1994-2006; Green Gold (2010).

Recreations: Golf, skiing.

Tim Yeo MP, House of Commons, London SW1A 0AA
Tel: 020 7219 6353 *Fax:* 020 7219 4857 *Email:* timyeomp@parliament.uk
Constituency: 4 Byford Road, Sudbury, Suffolk CO10 2YG
Tel: 01787 312363 *Email:* peter@ss-ca.org.uk *Website:* www.timyeo.org.uk

---

CONSERVATIVE

YOUNG, GEORGE
North West Hampshire *(Majority 18,583)*

Parliamentary Secretary to the Treasury; Chief Whip

George Samuel Knatchbull Young. Born 16 July 1941; Son of late Sir George Young, 5th Bt, CMG, and Elizabeth Young, née Knatchbull-Hugessen; Married Aurelia Nemon-Stuart 1964 (2 sons 2 daughters).

Education: Eton College; Christ Church, Oxford (BA philosophy, politics and economics 1963, MA); Surrey University (MPhil economics 1971).

Non-political career: Economic adviser Post Office 1969-74.

Political career: Member for Ealing Acton February 1974-97, for North West Hampshire 1997-2010, for North West Hampshire (revised boundary) since 6 May 2010 general election; Opposition Whip 1976-79; Parliamentary Under-Secretary of State: Department of Health and Social Services 1979-81, Department of Environment 1981-86; Government Whip 1990; Department of Environment: Minister for Housing and Planning 1990-93, Minister for Housing, Inner Cities and Construction 1993-94; Financial Secretary, HM Treasury 1994-95; Secretary of State for Transport 1995-97; Member Shadow Cabinet 1997-2000: Shadow Secretary of State for Defence 1997-98; Shadow Leader of the House of Commons 1998-99; Shadow Chancellor of the Duchy of Lancaster 1998-99; Shadow Leader of the House of Commons and Constitutional Affairs 1999-2000; Contested Speaker election 2000, 2009; Shadow Leader of the House of Commons 2009-10; Member: House of Commons Commission 2009-12, Speaker's Committee for the Independent Parliamentary Standards Authority 2009-12; Leader of the House of Commons, Lord Privy Seal 2010-12; Member Public Accounts Commission 2010-12; Parliamentary Secretary to the Treasury 2012-; Chief Whip 2012-; Member Parliamentary and Political Service Honours Committee 2012-. *Select committees:* Member: Public Accounts 1994-95, Modernisation of the House of Commons 1998-2000, Selection 2001-09; Chair: Standards and Privileges 2001-09; Member: Liaison 2001-09, Liaison (Liaison Sub-Committee) 2002-09, Reform of the House of Commons 2009. Chair Conservative Party: Committee for Defence 1997-98, Constitution Committee 1998-2000. Patron, Tory Reform Group. *Councils and public bodies:* Councillor: London Borough of Lambeth 1968-71, GLC 1970-73.

Political interests: Housing, disability, health education, constitutional reform.

Other: Trustee: Guinness Trust 1986-90, Foundations Independent Living Trust 2002-. Resurrection of the Year, *The Spectator* awards 2012. 6th Baronet, created 1813, succeeded his father 1960; PC 1993; CH 2012.

Publications: Tourism – Blessing or Blight (1970).

Recreations: Bicycling, opera.

Rt Hon Sir George Young CH MP, House of Commons, London SW1A 0AA
Tel: 020 7219 6665 *Email:* george.young.mp@parliament.uk
Constituency: 2 Church Close, Andover, Hampshire SP10 1DP
Tel: 01264 401401 *Email:* sirgeorge@sirgeorgeyoung.org.uk
Website: www.sirgeorgeyoung.org.uk

ZAHAWI, NADHIM

Stratford-on-Avon *(Majority 11,346)*

Born 2 June 1967; Married Lana (2 sons).

Education: King's College School, Wimbledon; University College, London (BSc chemical engineering).

Non-political career: European marketing director, Smith and Brooks Ltd; Co-founder and chief executive officer, YouGov 2000-10.

CONSERVATIVE

Political career: Contested Erith and Thamesmead 1997 general election. Member for Stratford-on-Avon since 6 May 2010 general election. *Select committees:* Member: Business, Innovation and Skills 2010-, Arms Export Controls 2010-, Joint Committee on Privacy and Injunctions 2011-12. Founding member, 2020 group 2011-. *Councils and public bodies:* Councillor, London Borough of Wandsworth Council 1994-2006; Governor: Chartfield Delicate School 2002-04, Brandlehow Primary School.

Political interests: Business, foreign affairs; Middle East.

Other: Chair, Police Consultative Committee, Putney; Patron, Peace One Day.

Recreations: Horseriding and show jumping.

Nadhim Zahawi MP, House of Commons, London SW1A 0AA
Tel: 020 7219 7159 *Fax:* 020 7219 4462 *Email:* nadhim.zahawi.mp@parliament.uk
Constituency: First Floor, 3 Trinity Street, Stratford-upon-Avon, Warwickshire CV37 6BL
Tel: 01789 264362/01789 292723 *Email:* nadhim@zahawi.com
Website: www.stratfordconservatives.com www.zahawi.com *Twitter:* @nadhimzahawi

ANALYSIS OF MPs

Committees and Offices

MPs' Political Interests

For precise details of individuals' stated interests, see relevant biography. The interests listed are supplied by MPs themselves.

Animals

See also:
Animal rights and welfare

Business and finance

See also:
Business banking and finance
Economic development
Economy
Enterprise
Euro and EMU
Exports
Financial services
Globalisation
Investment
Manufacturing
Pensions
Retail industry
Rural economy
Small businesses
Tax
Transatlantic trade

Communities, planning and local government

See also:
Community cohesion
Community safety
Conservation areas
Construction industry
Homelessness
Housing
Local government
London government
London
Planning
Regeneration
Rural communities
Sustainable communities
Town planning
Urban renewal

Culture, recreation and sport

See also:
Architecture
Creative industries
Culture and creativity
Cycling
Dance
Design
Films and film-making
Heritage
Music
Olympics 2012 (not participation)
Performing arts
Sports development
Tourism

Defence and security

See also:
British armed forces
Terrorism
Veterans

Education and skills

See also:
Child care
Further and higher education
Skills and competences
Special educational needs
Universities
Youth services

Employment and welfare

See also:
Apprenticeships
Benefits
Child poverty
Employment rights
Equal opportunities in employment
Lifelong learning
Pay
Trade unions
Unemployment and jobseeking
Youth training schemes

Energy and Utilities

See also:
Climate change
Coal
Energy from waste
Environmental impact of energy
Nuclear power
Renewables
Telecommunications

Environment, food and rural affairs

See also:
Agriculture
Bovine TB
Environmental issues
Environmental sustainability
Fisheries
Recycling

Rural environment
Sustainable development
Waste management

Government, politics and public administration

See also:
Constitution
Constitutional reform
Democracy and elections
Devolved government
Electoral reform
Northern Ireland
Policy-making
Political parties
Public administration
Public services
Reform of public services
Regional policy
Scottish independence
Scotland
Wales
Women in public life

Healthcare and pharmaceuticals

See also:
Addiction
Alcohol abuse
Breast cancer screening
Care for the elderly
Children in care
Community hospitals
Dementia
Diet and nutrition
Disabilities
Disabled children
Health and social care professionals
Health education
Health inequalities
Healthcare
Mental health
National Health Service (NHS)
Older people
Parkinson's disease
Rehabilitation therapy
Social care
Solvent abuse

Home affairs

See also:
Charities and volunteers
Child protection
Children and families
Citizenship
Consumer rights
Crime

Crime and punishment
Domestic violence
Immigration, migration and nationality
Justice system
Legal services
Police
Police reform
Prisons
Race relations
Racism
Refugees and asylum seekers
Religion
Sentencing
Social inclusion
Young offenders
Youth justice

Information and communications

See also:
Broadband
Information and communication technology
Internet
Libraries
Media and regulatory policy
Post Office

International affairs

See also:
Europe
European affairs
European Union
European Union enlargement
Foreign policy
Human rights
Humanitarian aid
International development and aid
Poverty
Sexual health
Transatlantic relations

Science and technology

See also:
Astronomy and space
Biotechnology
Engineering
Genetics
Medical science

Transport and infrastructure

See also:
Aerospace
Airport expansion
Alternative fuels
Boats and ships
Cars
Maritime industries
Public transport

Laurence Robertson	Con	p324	Alan Campbell	Lab	p118
Geoffrey Robinson	Lab	p324	Neil Carmichael	Con	p120
Lindsay Roy	Lab	p327	Douglas Carswell	Con	p121
Amber Rudd	Con	p328	Martin Caton	Lab	p122
David Ruffley	Con	p329	James Clappison	Con	p124
David Rutley	Con	p330	Nick Clegg	Lib Dem	p126
Barry Sheerman	Lab/Co-op	p335	Vernon Coaker	Lab	p128
Mark Simmonds	Con	p338	Ann Coffey	Lab	p128
Dennis Skinner	Lab	p340	Geoffrey Cox	Con	p133
Chloe Smith	Con	p341	Tracey Crouch	Con	p135
Andrew Stephenson	Con	p347	John Cryer	Lab	p136
Iain Stewart	Con	p348	Alex Cunningham	Lab	p137
Jack Straw	Lab	p349	Tony Cunningham	Lab	p138
Graham Stuart	Con	p352	Nic Dakin	Lab	p139
Robert Syms	Con	p356	Alistair Darling	Lab	p140
Peter Tapsell	Con	p357	Wayne David	Lab	p141
Stephen Timms	Lab	p360	Philip Davies	Con	p143
Justin Tomlinson	Con	p361	Jim Dowd	Lab	p152
Jon Trickett	Lab	p362	Jackie Doyle-Price	Con	p152
Elizabeth Truss	Con	p362	Clive Efford	Lab	p159
Andrew Turner	Con	p363	Julie Elliott	Lab	p159
Derek Twigg	Lab	p363	Tobias Ellwood	Con	p161
Andrew Tyrie	Con	p365	Graham Evans	Con	p164
Chuka Umunna	Lab	p365	Nigel Evans	Ind	p165
Martin Vickers	Con	p368	David Evennett	Con	p166
Theresa Villiers	Con	p369	Michael Fallon	Con	p167
Charles Walker	Con	p369	Paul Farrelly	Lab	p168
Heather Wheeler	Con	p375	Tim Farron	Lib Dem	p168
Bill Wiggin	Con	p378	Caroline Flint	Lab	p171
David Willetts	Con	p379	Don Foster	Lib Dem	p173
Gavin Williamson	Con	p382	Roger Gale	Con	p177
Iain Wright	Lab	p388	Mike Gapes	Lab/Co-op	p178
Tim Yeo	Con	p389	Barry Gardiner	Lab	p179
			Edward Garnier	Con	p180

Education and skills

Diane Abbott	Lab	p69	David Gauke	Con	p181
Debbie Abrahams	Lab	p69	Nick Gibb	Con	p182
Peter Aldous	Con	p71	Michelle Gildernew	Sinn Féin	p183
David Amess	Con	p74	Cheryl Gillan	Con	p183
Richard Bacon	Con	p77	Patricia Glass	Lab	p184
Gregory Barker	Con	p82	John Glen	Con	p184
Gavin Barwell	Con	p84	Michael Gove	Con	p187
Hilary Benn	Lab	p87	Damian Green	Con	p191
Joe Benton	Lab	p88	Justine Greening	Con	p192
Paul Beresford	Con	p90	Ben Gummer	Con	p194
Roberta Blackman-Woods	Lab	p94	Andrew Gwynne	Lab	p195
Paul Blomfield	Lab	p96	Robert Halfon	Con	p197
Nick Boles	Con	p97	Fabian Hamilton	Lab	p199
Graham Brady	Con	p100	Matthew Hancock	Con	p200
Angie Bray	Con	p101	Mark Harper	Con	p203
Kevin Brennan	Lab	p102	Rebecca Harris	Con	p204
Robert Buckland	Con	p109	Alan Haselhurst	Con	p206
Andy Burnham	Lab	p110	Dai Havard	Lab	p206
Conor Burns	Con	p111	John Hayes	Con	p207
			David Heath	Lib Dem	p209

Heritage

Home affairs

Human rights

Willie Bain	*Lab*	p78
Norman Baker	*Lib Dem*	p78
John Baron	*Con*	p83
John Bercow	*Speaker*	p89
Nicola Blackwood	*Con*	p94
David Blunkett	*Lab*	p96
Andrew Bridgen	*Con*	p103
Katy Clark	*Lab*	p125
Ann Clwyd	*Lab*	p127
Stephen Crabb	*Con*	p133
Mary Creagh	*Lab*	p134
Geraint Davies	*Lab/Co-op*	p142
Jim Dowd	*Lab*	p152
George Freeman	*Con*	p176
Steve Gilbert	*Lib Dem*	p182
Helen Goodman	*Lab*	p187
Harriet Harman	*Lab*	p202
Sylvia Hermon	*Ind*	p213
Simon Hughes	*Lib Dem*	p223
Mark Hunter	*Lib Dem*	p225
Julian Huppert	*Lib Dem*	p225
Sajid Javid	*Con*	p230
Elfyn Llwyd	*PlC*	p255
Naomi Long	*All*	p255
Caroline Lucas	*Green*	p258
Jim McGovern	*Lab*	p267
Fiona Mactaggart	*Lab*	p271
Gordon Marsden	*Lab*	p275
Michael Meacher	*Lab*	p277
Alan Meale	*Lab*	p278
Dominic Raab	*Con*	p315
Gavin Shuker	*Lab/Co-op*	p337
Sarah Teather	*Lib Dem*	p357
Emily Thornberry	*Lab*	p358
Robert Walter	*Con*	p371
Mark Williams	*Lib Dem*	p380
Stephen Williams	*Lib Dem*	p381
Shaun Woodward	*Lab*	p387

Humanitarian aid

Laurence Robertson	*Con*	p324

Immigration, migration and nationality

Gavin Barwell	*Con*	p84
Douglas Carswell	*Con*	p121
Lorraine Fullbrook	*Con*	p177
Andrew George	*Lib Dem*	p181
Roger Godsiff	*Lab*	p185
Dan Jarvis	*Lab*	p229
Susan Elan Jones	*Lab*	p235
Dan Rogerson	*Lib Dem*	p325
Sarah Teather	*Lib Dem*	p357
Hywel Williams	*PlC*	p379
Robert Wilson	*Con*	p383
Shaun Woodward	*Lab*	p387

Information and communications

Andrew Miller	*Lab*	p281
John Robertson	*Lab*	p323
Robert Smith	*Lib Dem*	p344

Information and communication technology

Robert Halfon	*Con*	p197
Greg Knight	*Con*	p241
Alasdair McDonnell	*SDLP*	p265
Stephen McPartland	*Con*	p271
John Spellar	*Lab*	p345
Theresa Villiers	*Con*	p369

International affairs

Neil Carmichael	*Con*	p120
Jeremy Corbyn	*Lab*	p132
James Duddridge	*Con*	p154
Philip Dunne	*Con*	p156
Mike Gapes	*Lab/Co-op*	p178
Cheryl Gillan	*Con*	p183
Mark Hunter	*Lib Dem*	p225
Julian Huppert	*Lib Dem*	p225
Sadiq Khan	*Lab*	p240
Ian Lavery	*Lab*	p245
Angus MacNeil	*SNP*	p271
Gordon Marsden	*Lab*	p275
Jim Murphy	*Lab*	p293
Richard Ottaway	*Con*	p303
Mark Pritchard	*Con*	p313
Alan Reid	*Lib Dem*	p319
Andy Slaughter	*Lab*	p340
Andrew Tyrie	*Con*	p365
Robert Walter	*Con*	p371

International development and aid

Heidi Alexander	*Lab*	p73
Jon Ashworth	*Lab*	p76
Tony Baldry	*Con*	p79
Gordon Banks	*Lab*	p81
Gregory Barker	*Con*	p82
Kevin Barron	*Lab*	p83
Hugh Bayley	*Lab*	p84
Hilary Benn	*Lab*	p87
John Bercow	*Speaker*	p89
Roberta Blackman-Woods	*Lab*	p94
Nicola Blackwood	*Con*	p94
Tom Brake	*Lib Dem*	p100
Richard Burden	*Lab*	p109
Alistair Burt	*Con*	p113
Tom Clarke	*Lab*	p126
Ann Clwyd	*Lab*	p127
Michael Connarty	*Lab*	p130
Tony Cunningham	*Lab*	p138
Ian Davidson	*Lab/Co-op*	p141
Jeffrey Donaldson	*DUP*	p149
Stephen Doughty	*Lab/Co-op*	p151

Philip Dunne	Con	p156
Clive Efford	Lab	p159
Louise Ellman	Lab/Co-op	p160
Nigel Evans	Ind	p165
Don Foster	Lib Dem	p173
Mark Francois	Con	p175
Mike Freer	Con	p176
Andrew Gwynne	Lab	p195
Greg Hands	Con	p201
David Hanson	Lab	p202
John Hayes	Con	p207
John Healey	Lab	p208
David Heath	Lib Dem	p209
David Heyes	Lab	p213
Margaret Hodge	Lab	p215
John Howell	Con	p222
Mark Hunter	Lib Dem	p225
Kevan Jones	Lab	p234
Marcus Jones	Con	p235
Andrew Lansley	Con	p244
Chris Leslie	Lab/Co-op	p250
Brandon Lewis	Con	p251
John McDonnell	Lab	p265
Theresa May	Con	p276
Ian Mearns	Lab	p279
Graeme Morrice	Lab	p287
Grahame Morris	Lab	p288
James Morris	Con	p289
Stephen Mosley	Con	p289
Paul Murphy	Lab	p293
Robert Neill	Con	p296
Mark Pawsey	Con	p306
Eric Pickles	Con	p310
John Pugh	Lib Dem	p314
Andrew Rosindell	Con	p325
Bob Russell	Lib Dem	p329
Adrian Sanders	Lib Dem	p330
Alison Seabeck	Lab	p333
Henry Smith	Con	p342
Andrew Stephenson	Con	p347
Jack Straw	Lab	p349
Graham Stringer	Lab	p351
Gerry Sutcliffe	Lab	p353
Robert Syms	Con	p356
Justin Tomlinson	Con	p361
Stephen Twigg	Lab/Co-op	p364
Keith Vaz	Lab	p367
Martin Vickers	Con	p368
Angela Watkinson	Con	p372
Alan Whitehead	Lab	p376

London government

Margaret Hodge	Lab	p215

London

Angie Bray	Con	p101
Jeremy Corbyn	Lab	p132
Frank Dobson	Lab	p147
David Evennett	Con	p166

Manufacturing

Ian Austin	Lab	p77
Tom Blenkinsop	Lab	p95
Nic Dakin	Lab	p139
Jack Dromey	Lab	p153
Michael Fabricant	Con	p166
Tom Greatrex	Lab/Co-op	p190
Andrew Griffiths	Con	p194
Ian Lucas	Lab	p259
Catherine McKinnell	Lab	p269
Michael Moore	Lib Dem	p285
Chi Onwurah	Lab	p301
Emma Reynolds	Lab	p320
Mark Tami	Lab	p356
Tom Watson	Lab	p373

Maritime industries

David Morris	Con	p288

Media

Nigel Adams	Con	p70
Kevin Barron	Lab	p83
Anne Begg	Lab	p86
Steve Brine	Con	p103
Chris Bryant	Lab	p108
Andy Burnham	Lab	p110
William Cash	Con	p121
Michael Fabricant	Con	p166
Don Foster	Lib Dem	p173
Roger Gale	Con	p177
Damian Green	Con	p191
Gerald Howarth	Con	p221
Charles Kennedy	Lib Dem	p239
Jason McCartney	Con	p262
Alan Meale	Lab	p278
Maria Miller	Con	p282
Austin Mitchell	Lab	p283
Linda Riordan	Lab/Co-op	p321
John Whittingdale	Con	p377

Medical science

Oliver Colvile	Con	p130
Paul Flynn	Lab	p172
David Tredinnick	Con	p361

Mental health

Adam Afriyie	Con	p70
Conor Burns	Con	p111
Gloria De Piero	Lab	p145
Frank Doran	Lab	p150
Mike Gapes	Lab/Co-op	p178

Dan Jarvis	Lab	p229
Diana Johnson	Lab	p231
David Jones	Con	p233
Andrew Lansley	Con	p244
Steve McCabe	Lab	p260
Stephen McPartland	Con	p271
Seema Malhotra	Lab	p274
Madeleine Moon	Lab	p285
Robert Neill	Con	p296
David Nuttall	Con	p298
Priti Patel	Con	p305
Mark Reckless	Con	p316
Laurence Robertson	Con	p324
Andrew Rosindell	Con	p325
Jack Straw	Lab	p349
Gary Streeter	Con	p350
David Tredinnick	Con	p361
Robin Walker	Con	p370
Angela Watkinson	Con	p372
James Wharton	Con	p375
Jenny Willott	Lib Dem	p382
Sammy Wilson	DUP	p384

Police reform

Aidan Burley	Con	p110

Policy-making

Katy Clark	Lab	p125
John Glen	Con	p184
Julian Huppert	Lib Dem	p225

Political parties

Jeremy Corbyn	Lab	p132
Ian Davidson	Lab/Co-op	p141
Cathy Jamieson	Lab/Co-op	p229
Sammy Wilson	DUP	p384

Post Office

Alan Johnson	Lab	p231

Poverty

Lyn Brown	Lab	p105
Richard Burden	Lab	p109
Alistair Burt	Con	p113
Greg Clark	Con	p124
Yvette Cooper	Lab	p132
Alex Cunningham	Lab	p137
Margaret Curran	Lab	p138
Ian Davidson	Lab/Co-op	p141
Charlie Elphicke	Con	p161
Frank Field	Lab	p169
Jim Fitzpatrick	Lab	p170
Paul Goggins	Lab	p186
Kate Green	Lab	p191
Cathy Jamieson	Lab/Co-op	p229
Ian Lavery	Lab	p245
Caroline Lucas	Green	p258

Kerry McCarthy	Lab	p261
Paul Maskey	Sinn Féin	p275
Alan Meale	Lab	p278
Austin Mitchell	Lab	p283
Lisa Nandy	Lab	p295
Brooks Newmark	Con	p296
Sandra Osborne	Lab	p302
Chris Ruane	Lab	p327
Sarah Teather	Lib Dem	p357
Chris Williamson	Lab	p382
Mike Wood	Lab	p386
David Wright	Lab	p388

Prisons

David Davies	Con	p142
Ben Gummer	Con	p194
Fabian Hamilton	Lab	p199
Patrick Mercer	Ind	p280
Madeleine Moon	Lab	p285
Tessa Munt	Lib Dem	p292
Guy Opperman	Con	p301

Public administration

Sarah Champion	Lab	p122
Chris Evans	Lab/Co-op	p163
Naomi Long	All	p255
John McDonnell	Lab	p265
Seema Malhotra	Lab	p274
David Simpson	DUP	p338

Public services

David Anderson	Lab	p75
Tom Blenkinsop	Lab	p95
Neil Carmichael	Con	p120
Jane Ellison	Con	p160
Louise Ellman	Lab/Co-op	p160
Nick Herbert	Con	p212
Sadiq Khan	Lab	p240
Jesse Norman	Con	p297
Emma Reynolds	Lab	p320
Chloe Smith	Con	p341

Public transport

Jane Ellison	Con	p160
Siân James	Lab	p228
Greg Mulholland	Lib Dem	p290

Race relations

Peter Lilley	Con	p253
Andrew Stunell	Lib Dem	p352
Keith Vaz	Lab	p367

Racism

Jim Fitzpatrick	Lab	p170
Andrew George	Lib Dem	p181

Recycling

Clive Efford	Lab	p159
Andrew Jones	Con	p233

Unemployment and jobseeking

Yvette Cooper	*Lab*	p132
Paul Goggins	*Lab*	p186
Alan Meale	*Lab*	p278

Universities

Paul Blomfield	*Lab*	p96

Urban renewal

Peter Aldous	*Con*	p71
Heidi Alexander	*Lab*	p73
Adrian Bailey	*Lab/Co-op*	p77
Hilary Benn	*Lab*	p87
Hazel Blears	*Lab*	p95
Karen Buck	*Lab*	p108
Charles Hendry	*Con*	p211
Tristram Hunt	*Lab*	p224
Jeremy Lefroy	*Con*	p248
Alasdair McDonnell	*SDLP*	p265
Anne McGuire	*Lab*	p267
Stephen McPartland	*Con*	p271
Graham Stringer	*Lab*	p351
Stephen Timms	*Lab*	p360
Keith Vaz	*Lab*	p367
Chris Williamson	*Lab*	p382

Veterans

Bob Stewart	*Con*	p348

Wales

Chris Bryant	*Lab*	p108
David Davies	*Con*	p142
Paul Flynn	*Lab*	p172
Siân James	*Lab*	p228
David Jones	*Con*	p233
Paul Murphy	*Lab*	p293
Albert Owen	*Lab*	p303

Waste management

Clive Efford	*Lab*	p159
Jim Paice	*Con*	p304

Women issues

Lorely Burt	*Lib Dem*	p114

Margaret Curran	*Lab*	p138
Sheila Gilmore	*Lab*	p184
Helen Grant	*Con*	p188
Harriet Harman	*Lab*	p202
Barbara Keeley	*Lab*	p238
Seema Malhotra	*Lab*	p274
Madeleine Moon	*Lab*	p285
Meg Munn	*Lab/Co-op*	p291
Brooks Newmark	*Con*	p296
Sandra Osborne	*Lab*	p302
Joan Ruddock	*Lab*	p328

Young offenders

Seema Malhotra	*Lab*	p274

Youth affairs

Tony Baldry	*Con*	p79
Liam Byrne	*Lab*	p115
Michael Connarty	*Lab*	p130
Stephen Crabb	*Con*	p133
Natascha Engel	*Lab*	p162
John Glen	*Con*	p184
Richard Harrington	*Con*	p203
Alan Haselhurst	*Con*	p206
Christopher Heaton-Harris	*Con*	p209
Charles Hendry	*Con*	p211
Julie Hilling	*Lab*	p214
Simon Hughes	*Lib Dem*	p223
Tessa Jowell	*Lab*	p236
Toby Perkins	*Lab*	p308
Yasmin Qureshi	*Lab*	p314
Angus Robertson	*SNP*	p322
Dan Rogerson	*Lib Dem*	p325
Bob Russell	*Lib Dem*	p329
Chuka Umunna	*Lab*	p365
James Wharton	*Con*	p375

Youth justice

Justine Greening	*Con*	p192

Youth training schemes

Tim Farron	*Lib Dem*	p168

MPs' Countries of Interest

For precise details of individuals' stated interests, see relevant biography. The interests listed are supplied by MPs themselves.

Afghanistan

James Arbuthnot	Con	p76
Roberta Blackman-Woods	Lab	p94
Nicola Blackwood	Con	p94
Stephen Doughty	Lab/Co-op	p151
Tobias Ellwood	Con	p161
Lynne Featherstone	Lib Dem	p169
Paul Flynn	Lab	p172
James Gray	Con	p189
Dan Jarvis	Lab	p229
Bernard Jenkin	Con	p230
Kevan Jones	Lab	p234
Jack Lopresti	Con	p256
Madeleine Moon	Lab	p285
Michael Moore	Lib Dem	p285
Sandra Osborne	Lab	p302
Joan Ruddock	Lab	p328
Robert Smith	Lib Dem	p344
Roger Williams	Lib Dem	p381

Africa

Diane Abbott	Lab	p69
Tony Baldry	Con	p79
Hugh Bayley	Lab	p84
Henry Bellingham	Con	p87
Richard Benyon	Con	p89
Roberta Blackman-Woods	Lab	p94
Paul Blomfield	Lab	p96
Peter Bottomley	Con	p98
Lyn Brown	Lab	p105
Alistair Burt	Con	p113
Ronnie Campbell	Lab	p119
William Cash	Con	p121
Tom Clarke	Lab	p126
Jeremy Corbyn	Lab	p132
Stephen Crabb	Con	p133
Tony Cunningham	Lab	p138
Ian Davidson	Lab/Co-op	p141
Jim Dobbin	Lab/Co-op	p146
Stephen Doughty	Lab/Co-op	p151
James Duddridge	Con	p154
Lynne Featherstone	Lib Dem	p169
Don Foster	Lib Dem	p173
Roger Gale	Con	p177
Andrew George	Lib Dem	p181
Peter Hain	Lab	p196
Fabian Hamilton	Lab	p199
Philip Hammond	Con	p199
Gordon Henderson	Con	p210
Charles Hendry	Con	p211
Meg Hillier	Lab/Co-op	p214

Simon Hughes	Lib Dem	p223
Jeremy Hunt	Con	p224
Cathy Jamieson	Lab/Co-op	p229
Helen Jones	Lab	p234
Kwasi Kwarteng	Con	p241
David Lammy	Lab	p243
Pauline Latham	Con	p245
Charlotte Leslie	Con	p249
Michael McCann	Lab	p261
Ann McKechin	Lab	p268
Gordon Marsden	Lab	p275
Stephen Metcalfe	Con	p280
Andrew Mitchell	Con	p283
Stephen Mosley	Con	p289
Tessa Munt	Lib Dem	p292
Jim Murphy	Lab	p293
Stephen O'Brien	Con	p298
Matthew Offord	Con	p300
Ian Paisley	DUP	p304
Priti Patel	Con	p305
Mark Pritchard	Con	p313
Andrew Robathan	Con	p322
Laurence Robertson	Con	p324
David Simpson	DUP	p338
Peter Tapsell	Con	p357
Stephen Twigg	Lab/Co-op	p364
Peter Wishart	SNP	p385

Angola

Vernon Coaker	Lab	p128
Nadine Dorries	Con	p151
Kate Hoey	Lab	p217
John Robertson	Lab	p323

Antarctica

James Gray	Con	p189

Argentina

Eric Joyce	Ind	p236
Lindsay Roy	Lab	p327

Armenia

Stephen Pound	Lab	p311
Angus Robertson	SNP	p322
John Whittingdale	Con	p377

Asia

Tony Baldry	Con	p79
Jeremy Browne	Lib Dem	p106
Robert Buckland	Con	p109
Alistair Burt	Con	p113
Dan Byles	Con	p114
Alun Cairns	Con	p116
Sarah Champion	Lab	p122

Rehman Chishti	Con	p123
Tom Clarke	Lab	p126
Nick de Bois	Con	p144
Roger Godsiff	Lab	p185
John Howell	Con	p222
Peter Lilley	Con	p253
Kerry McCarthy	Lab	p261
Madeleine Moon	Lab	p285
Priti Patel	Con	p305
David Ruffley	Con	p329
Rory Stewart	Con	p349
Peter Tapsell	Con	p357
Valerie Vaz	Lab	p368

Australia

James Arbuthnot	Con	p76
Jon Ashworth	Lab	p76
Gregory Barker	Con	p82
Paul Beresford	Con	p90
Tom Brake	Lib Dem	p100
Julian Brazier	Con	p101
Nick Brown	Lab	p105
Michael Connarty	Lab	p130
John Cryer	Lab	p136
Maria Eagle	Lab	p158
Nigel Evans	Ind	p165
David Evennett	Con	p166
Michael Fabricant	Con	p166
Paul Farrelly	Lab	p168
John Healey	Lab	p208
Christopher Heaton-Harris	Con	p209
Eleanor Laing	Con	p242
Paul Maynard	Con	p277
Mark Menzies	Con	p279
Stephen O'Brien	Con	p298
John Robertson	Lab	p323
Andrew Rosindell	Con	p325
Alison Seabeck	Lab	p333
Andrew Selous	Con	p333
John Spellar	Lab	p345
Tom Watson	Lab	p373
Craig Whittaker	Con	p377
Shaun Woodward	Lab	p387

Austria

Jonathan Evans	Con	p164
David Evennett	Con	p166
Angus Robertson	SNP	p322

Azerbaijan

Bob Blackman	Con	p93
Paul Flynn	Lab	p172
Robert Halfon	Con	p197
Eric Ollerenshaw	Con	p300
Christopher Pincher	Con	p310
Angus Robertson	SNP	p322
Gerry Sutcliffe	Lab	p353

Bahamas

David Morris	Con	p288

Bahrain

Nigel Evans	Ind	p165
Andy Slaughter	Lab	p340

Bangladesh

Debbie Abrahams	Lab	p69
Jon Ashworth	Lab	p76
Lyn Brown	Lab	p105
Simon Danczuk	Lab	p139
Frank Dobson	Lab	p147
Stephen Doughty	Lab/Co-op	p151
Jim Fitzpatrick	Lab	p170
Richard Fuller	Con	p177
George Galloway	Respect	p178
Anne Main	Con	p273
Nicky Morgan	Con	p286
Virendra Sharma	Lab	p335
Gavin Shuker	Lab/Co-op	p337
Gerry Sutcliffe	Lab	p353
Keith Vaz	Lab	p367

Barbados

Tom Blenkinsop	Lab	p95

Belarus

Robert Goodwill	Con	p187

Belgium

Wayne David	Lab	p141
Margaret Ritchie	SDLP	p321

Belize

Chris Ruane	Lab	p327

Bermuda

David Crausby	Lab	p133

Bosnia and Herzegovina

Clive Betts	Lab	p91
Gemma Doyle	Lab/Co-op	p152
Jackie Doyle-Price	Con	p152
Kate Hoey	Lab	p217
Karen Lumley	Con	p260
Paul Maynard	Con	p277
Patrick Mercer	Ind	p280
Andrew Stephenson	Con	p347
Hugo Swire	Con	p355

Brazil

Bob Blackman	Con	p93
Geoffrey Clifton-Brown	Con	p127
Barry Gardiner	Lab	p179
Tom Greatrex	Lab/Co-op	p190
Gerald Howarth	Con	p221
Nick Hurd	Con	p226
Iain McKenzie	Lab	p269
Caroline Spelman	Con	p346

Graham Stuart	Con	p352		David Lammy	Lab	p243
Gerry Sutcliffe	Lab	p353		Gordon Marsden	Lab	p275
Mike Weatherley	Con	p374		Daniel Poulter	Con	p311
David Wright	Lab	p388		Andy Slaughter	Lab	p340

British Overseas Territories

Chile

Henry Bellingham	Con	p87		George Hollingbery	Con	p217
Graham Brady	Con	p100		Gerald Howarth	Con	p221
Jeremy Corbyn	Lab	p132		Bernard Jenkin	Con	p230
Ian Davidson	Lab/Co-op	p141		**China**		
Helen Grant	Con	p188		Graham Allen	Lab	p73
Lindsay Hoyle	Lab	p222		Adrian Bailey	Lab/Co-op	p77
Andrew Rosindell	Con	p325		Willie Bain	Lab	p78
Henry Smith	Con	p342		Roberta Blackman-Woods	Lab	p94

Bulgaria

				Lyn Brown	Lab	p105
Kevin Barron	Lab	p83		Nick Brown	Lab	p105
Wayne David	Lab	p141		Conor Burns	Con	p111

Burma/Myanmar

				Dan Byles	Con	p114
John Bercow	Speaker	p89		Vincent Cable	Lib Dem	p116
Paul Blomfield	Lab	p96		Ronnie Campbell	Lab	p119
Alistair Carmichael	Lib Dem	p120		Sarah Champion	Lab	p122
Siân James	Lab	p228		Geoffrey Clifton-Brown	Con	p127
Caroline Lucas	Green	p258		David Davies	Con	p142
Robert Smith	Lib Dem	p344		Caroline Dinenage	Con	p145
Valerie Vaz	Lab	p368		Chris Evans	Lab/Co-op	p163

Burundi

				Graham Evans	Con	p164
Mary Creagh	Lab	p134		Jonathan Evans	Con	p164
				Paul Farrelly	Lab	p168

Cambodia

				Hywel Francis	Lab	p174
Ann Clwyd	Lab	p127		Barry Gardiner	Lab	p179

Canada

				Cheryl Gillan	Con	p183
Alan Beith	Lib Dem	p86		Richard Graham	Con	p188
Julian Brazier	Con	p101		James Gray	Con	p189
Malcolm Bruce	Lib Dem	p107		Tom Greatrex	Lab/Co-op	p190
David Crausby	Lab	p133		Andrew Griffiths	Con	p194
Frank Dobson	Lab	p147		Andrew Gwynne	Lab	p195
Stephen Doughty	Lab/Co-op	p151		Duncan Hames	Lib Dem	p198
David Evennett	Con	p166		Stephen Hammond	Con	p200
Andrew George	Lib Dem	p181		Christopher Heaton-Harris	Con	p209
Alasdair McDonnell	SDLP	p265		Mark Hendrick	Lab/Co-op	p211
Maria Miller	Con	p282		George Hollingbery	Con	p217
Austin Mitchell	Lab	p283		Tristram Hunt	Lab	p224
Stephen O'Brien	Con	p298		Nick Hurd	Con	p226
Andrew Percy	Con	p308		Huw Irranca-Davies	Lab	p226
Dan Rogerson	Lib Dem	p325		David Jones	Con	p233
Andrew Rosindell	Con	p325		Tessa Jowell	Lab	p236
Virendra Sharma	Lab	p335		Eric Joyce	Ind	p236
Andrew Stephenson	Con	p347		Simon Kirby	Con	p240
Robin Walker	Con	p370		Mark Lancaster	Con	p244

Caribbean

				Charlotte Leslie	Con	p249
Tony Baldry	Con	p79		Peter Luff	Con	p259
Henry Bellingham	Con	p87		Anne McGuire	Lab	p267
Nigel Evans	Ind	p165		Iain McKenzie	Lab	p269
Fabian Hamilton	Lab	p199		Stephen McPartland	Con	p271

Seema Malhotra	*Lab*	p274
Stephen Metcalfe	*Con*	p280
Andrew Miller	*Lab*	p281
Austin Mitchell	*Lab*	p283
Madeleine Moon	*Lab*	p285
Grahame Morris	*Lab*	p288
Brooks Newmark	*Con*	p296
Chi Onwurah	*Lab*	p301
Ian Paisley	*DUP*	p304
Neil Parish	*Con*	p305
Owen Paterson	*Con*	p306
Mark Prisk	*Con*	p312
John Redwood	*Con*	p316
Jacob Rees-Mogg	*Con*	p318
Rachel Reeves	*Lab*	p319
Lindsay Roy	*Lab*	p327
David Rutley	*Con*	p330
Nick Smith	*Lab*	p343
Robert Smith	*Lib Dem*	p344
Graham Stuart	*Con*	p352
Heather Wheeler	*Con*	p375
John Whittingdale	*Con*	p377
Stephen Williams	*Lib Dem*	p381
Gavin Williamson	*Con*	p382
Sammy Wilson	*DUP*	p384
Shaun Woodward	*Lab*	p387
Iain Wright	*Lab*	p388

Colombia

Alan Campbell	*Lab*	p118
Mark Durkan	*SDLP*	p157
Robert Flello	*Lab*	p171
Paul Goggins	*Lab*	p186
Diana Johnson	*Lab*	p231
Jim McGovern	*Lab*	p267
Madeleine Moon	*Lab*	p285
Lisa Nandy	*Lab*	p295
Sandra Osborne	*Lab*	p302

Commonwealth

Stuart Andrew	*Con*	p75
Graham Brady	*Con*	p100
Ian Davidson	*Lab/Co-op*	p141
Nigel Dodds	*DUP*	p148
Cheryl Gillan	*Con*	p183
Andrew Gwynne	*Lab*	p195
Alan Haselhurst	*Con*	p206
Simon Hughes	*Lib Dem*	p223
Karl McCartney	*Con*	p262
Andrew Percy	*Con*	p308

Congo, Democratic Republic of

Hilary Benn	*Lab*	p87
Nicola Blackwood	*Con*	p94

Mary Creagh	*Lab*	p134
Eric Joyce	*Ind*	p236
Ivan Lewis	*Lab*	p251

Croatia

Gemma Doyle	*Lab/Co-op*	p152
Jackie Doyle-Price	*Con*	p152

Cuba

Hywel Francis	*Lab*	p174
Roger Gale	*Con*	p177
George Galloway	*Respect*	p178
Siân James	*Lab*	p228
Cathy Jamieson	*Lab/Co-op*	p229
Jim McGovern	*Lab*	p267
Grahame Morris	*Lab*	p288
Chris Williamson	*Lab*	p382

Cyprus

Harriett Baldwin	*Con*	p80
David Burrowes	*Con*	p112
Jeffrey Donaldson	*DUP*	p149
Robert Flello	*Lab*	p171
Mike Freer	*Con*	p176
Roger Gale	*Con*	p177
David Hamilton	*Lab*	p198
Fabian Hamilton	*Lab*	p199
David Hanson	*Lab*	p202
Simon Hughes	*Lib Dem*	p223
Andy Love	*Lab/Co-op*	p257
Alan Meale	*Lab*	p278
Matthew Offord	*Con*	p300
Albert Owen	*Lab*	p303
Virendra Sharma	*Lab*	p335
Jim Sheridan	*Lab*	p337
Theresa Villiers	*Con*	p369

Czech Republic

Malcolm Bruce	*Lib Dem*	p107
Jonathan Evans	*Con*	p164
Helen Goodman	*Lab*	p187

Denmark

Gordon Birtwistle	*Lib Dem*	p93
Helen Goodman	*Lab*	p187
Diana Johnson	*Lab*	p231
David Rutley	*Con*	p330

East Timor

Ann Clwyd	*Lab*	p127

Eastern Europe

Guto Bebb	*Con*	p85
Malcolm Bruce	*Lib Dem*	p107
Robert Buckland	*Con*	p109
Tom Clarke	*Lab*	p126
James Cunningham	*Lab*	p137
Gemma Doyle	*Lab/Co-op*	p152
Michael Fabricant	*Con*	p166

Paul Flynn	*Lab*	p172
Steve Gilbert	*Lib Dem*	p182
Greg Hands	*Con*	p201
John Howell	*Con*	p222
Simon Hughes	*Lib Dem*	p223
Julian Lewis	*Con*	p252
Anne McIntosh	*Con*	p268
Gordon Marsden	*Lab*	p275
Owen Paterson	*Con*	p306
Eric Pickles	*Con*	p310
Andrew Rosindell	*Con*	p325
Bob Stewart	*Con*	p348
David Tredinnick	*Con*	p361
Joan Walley	*Lab*	p371

Ecuador

Chris Williamson	*Lab*	p382

Egypt

Nigel Evans	*Ind*	p165
Andrew Lansley	*Con*	p244
David Laws	*Lib Dem*	p246
Andy Slaughter	*Lab*	p340
Angela Watkinson	*Con*	p372
Roger Williams	*Lib Dem*	p381

El Salvador

Peter Bottomley	*Con*	p98

England

John Hayes	*Con*	p207
Helen Jones	*Lab*	p234

Ethiopia

Jeffrey Donaldson	*DUP*	p149
David Laws	*Lib Dem*	p246
Laurence Robertson	*Con*	p324

Europe

Ben Bradshaw	*Lab*	p99
Robert Buckland	*Con*	p109
Richard Burden	*Lab*	p109
William Cash	*Con*	p121
Ian Davidson	*Lab/Co-op*	p141
Nigel Evans	*Ind*	p165
Cheryl Gillan	*Con*	p183
Fabian Hamilton	*Lab*	p199
Greg Hands	*Con*	p201
David Heath	*Lib Dem*	p209
Charles Hendry	*Con*	p211
Jim Hood	*Lab*	p218
John Howell	*Con*	p222
Julian Lewis	*Con*	p252
Michael McCann	*Lab*	p261
Anne McIntosh	*Con*	p268
Alan Meale	*Lab*	p278
Andrew Miller	*Lab*	p281
Stephen O'Brien	*Con*	p298

Jim Paice	*Con*	p304
Owen Paterson	*Con*	p306
Nick Raynsford	*Lab*	p316
Frank Roy	*Lab*	p326
Alison Seabeck	*Lab*	p333
Nicholas Soames	*Con*	p344
Gareth Thomas	*Lab/Co-op*	p358
Mike Weatherley	*Con*	p374

European Union

David Amess	*Con*	p74
Willie Bain	*Lab*	p78
Russell Brown	*Lab*	p106
Neil Carmichael	*Con*	p120
Therese Coffey	*Con*	p129
Stephen Doughty	*Lab/Co-op*	p151
Lynne Featherstone	*Lib Dem*	p169
David Hamilton	*Lab*	p198
Stephen Hammond	*Con*	p200
Barbara Keeley	*Lab*	p238
Charles Kennedy	*Lib Dem*	p239
Jamie Reed	*Lab*	p317
Emma Reynolds	*Lab*	p320
Barry Sheerman	*Lab/Co-op*	p335
Rory Stewart	*Con*	p349
Gerry Sutcliffe	*Lab*	p353
Stephen Williams	*Lib Dem*	p381

Falkland Islands

Alan Campbell	*Lab*	p118
Caroline Dinenage	*Con*	p145
Simon Hart	*Con*	p205
Lindsay Hoyle	*Lab*	p222
Peter Luff	*Con*	p259

Faroe Islands

Angus MacNeil	*SNP*	p271

Fiji

Paul Beresford	*Con*	p90

Finland

Nic Dakin	*Lab*	p139
Helen Jones	*Lab*	p234
Lindsay Roy	*Lab*	p327
Angela Smith	*Lab*	p341

France

Bob Ainsworth	*Lab*	p71
James Arbuthnot	*Con*	p76
David Blunkett	*Lab*	p96
Tom Brake	*Lib Dem*	p100
Vernon Coaker	*Lab*	p128
Oliver Colvile	*Con*	p130
Stephen Crabb	*Con*	p133
Alex Cunningham	*Lab*	p137
Chris Evans	*Lab/Co-op*	p163
Jonathan Evans	*Con*	p164

Helen Jones	Lab	p234
John McDonnell	Lab	p265
Jim McGovern	Lab	p267
Alan Meale	Lab	p278
Paul Murphy	Lab	p293
Robert Neill	Con	p296
Stephen O'Brien	Con	p298
Albert Owen	Lab	p303
Stephen Pound	Lab	p311
Linda Riordan	Lab/Co-op	p321
Angus Robertson	SNP	p322
Chris Ruane	Lab	p327
Gavin Shuker	Lab/Co-op	p337
Owen Smith	Lab	p343

Israel

James Arbuthnot	Con	p76
Guto Bebb	Con	p85
Brian Binley	Con	p92
Bob Blackman	Con	p93
Robert Buckland	Con	p109
David Burrowes	Con	p112
Lorely Burt	Lib Dem	p114
Alistair Carmichael	Lib Dem	p120
James Clappison	Con	p124
Jeffrey Donaldson	DUP	p149
Stephen Doughty	Lab/Co-op	p151
Michael Dugher	Lab	p154
Michael Ellis	Con	p160
Graham Evans	Con	p164
Paul Flynn	Lab	p172
Don Foster	Lib Dem	p173
Mike Freer	Con	p176
Nick Gibb	Con	p182
Andrew Gwynne	Lab	p195
Robert Halfon	Con	p197
Duncan Hames	Lib Dem	p198
Mark Harper	Con	p203
Tom Harris	Lab	p204
Gordon Henderson	Con	p210
Barbara Keeley	Lab	p238
Andrew Lansley	Con	p244
Peter Luff	Con	p259
Patrick Mercer	Ind	p280
Madeleine Moon	Lab	p285
Matthew Offord	Con	p300
Neil Parish	Con	p305
Andrew Percy	Con	p308
Mark Pritchard	Con	p313
Jamie Reed	Lab	p317
David Simpson	DUP	p338
Keith Simpson	Con	p339
John Spellar	Lab	p345
John Stevenson	Con	p347
Ed Vaizey	Con	p366

Theresa Villiers	Con	p369
Angela Watkinson	Con	p372
John Whittingdale	Con	p377
Stephen Williams	Lib Dem	p381

Italy

James Arbuthnot	Con	p76
Jon Ashworth	Lab	p76
Bob Blackman	Con	p93
Tom Blenkinsop	Lab	p95
Ben Bradshaw	Lab	p99
Angie Bray	Con	p101
Steve Brine	Con	p103
Jim Dowd	Lab	p152
David Evennett	Con	p166
Paul Farrelly	Lab	p168
Robert Flello	Lab	p171
Hywel Francis	Lab	p174
Tom Greatrex	Lab/Co-op	p190
Damian Green	Con	p191
Nia Griffith	Lab	p193
Philip Hammond	Con	p199
John Hayes	Con	p207
Helen Jones	Lab	p234
Brandon Lewis	Con	p251
Karl McCartney	Con	p262
Catherine McKinnell	Lab	p269
Paul Maskey	Sinn Féin	p275
Robert Neill	Con	p296
Mark Prisk	Con	p312
Geoffrey Robinson	Lab	p324
Robin Walker	Con	p370
Ben Wallace	Con	p370
Shaun Woodward	Lab	p387

Jamaica

Diane Abbott	Lab	p69

Japan

Nick Brown	Lab	p105
Lorely Burt	Lib Dem	p114
Ian Davidson	Lab/Co-op	p141
Jonathan Evans	Con	p164
Paul Farrelly	Lab	p168
Cheryl Gillan	Con	p183
Roger Godsiff	Lab	p185
Fabian Hamilton	Lab	p199
Mark Hendrick	Lab/Co-op	p211
Jeremy Hunt	Con	p224
Andrew Lansley	Con	p244
Ian Lucas	Lab	p259
Rachel Reeves	Lab	p319
John Robertson	Lab	p323
Tom Watson	Lab	p373
Heather Wheeler	Con	p375
John Whittingdale	Con	p377

Gavin Williamson	Con	p382	Stephen O'Brien	Con	p298
David Wright	Lab	p388	Mark Pritchard	Con	p313
Jordan			Dominic Raab	Con	p315
Diana Johnson	Lab	p231	Emma Reynolds	Lab	p320
David Laws	Lib Dem	p246	Mark Simmonds	Con	p338
Kerry McCarthy	Lab	p261	Robin Walker	Con	p370
Keith Simpson	Con	p339	Iain Wright	Lab	p388
Kashmir			**Latvia**		
Debbie Abrahams	Lab	p69	Christopher Pincher	Con	p310
Steve Baker	Con	p79	Dan Rogerson	Lib Dem	p325
Paul Blomfield	Lab	p96	**Lebanon**		
Liam Byrne	Lab	p115	Julian Brazier	Con	p101
Sarah Champion	Lab	p122	Andy Love	Lab/Co-op	p257
Simon Danczuk	Lab	p139	Hugo Swire	Con	p355
George Galloway	Respect	p178	**Lesotho**		
Lilian Greenwood	Lab	p192	Ian Lucas	Lab	p259
Andrew Griffiths	Con	p194	**Libya**		
Fabian Hamilton	Lab	p199	Daniel Kawczynski	Con	p237
Richard Harrington	Con	p203	**Liechtenstein**		
Julie Hilling	Lab	p214	Andrew Rosindell	Con	p325
Stewart Jackson	Con	p227	**Lithuania**		
Chris Leslie	Lab/Co-op	p250	Alan Whitehead	Lab	p376
Linda Riordan	Lab/Co-op	p321	**Luxembourg**		
Kenya			Dominic Grieve	Con	p193
Annette Brooke	Lib Dem	p104	**Former Yugoslav Republic of Macedonia**		
Vincent Cable	Lib Dem	p116	Vernon Coaker	Lab	p128
Jeremy Lefroy	Con	p248	Karen Lumley	Con	p260
John McDonnell	Lab	p265	**Malawi**		
Barry Sheerman	Lab/Co-op	p335	Willie Bain	Lab	p78
Craig Whittaker	Con	p377	Oliver Colvile	Con	p130
Korea, North			Mark Durkan	SDLP	p157
Greg Hands	Con	p201	Tom Greatrex	Lab/Co-op	p190
Gary Streeter	Con	p350	**Malaysia**		
Korea, South			William Cash	Con	p121
Richard Fuller	Con	p177	Brian Donohoe	Lab	p149
Kosovo			Tom Greatrex	Lab/Co-op	p190
Vernon Coaker	Lab	p128	Gerald Howarth	Con	p221
Michael Moore	Lib Dem	p285	John Whittingdale	Con	p377
Jo Swinson	Lib Dem	p354	**Maldives**		
Latin America			Brian Binley	Con	p92
Chris Bryant	Lab	p108	John Glen	Con	p184
Conor Burns	Con	p111	Karen Lumley	Con	p260
Therese Coffey	Con	p129	**Mali**		
Michael Connarty	Lab	p130	Roger Williams	Lib Dem	p381
Jeremy Corbyn	Lab	p132	**Malta**		
Edward Davey	Lib Dem	p140	Jessica Lee	Con	p247
Andrew Gwynne	Lab	p195	Andrew Miller	Lab	p281
Philip Hammond	Con	p199	Albert Owen	Lab	p303
Simon Hughes	Lib Dem	p223	**Mauritania**		
David Lammy	Lab	p243	Daniel Kawczynski	Con	p237
Tim Loughton	Con	p257			
Kerry McCarthy	Lab	p261			

Serbia

Clive Betts	*Lab*	p91
Jackie Doyle-Price	*Con*	p152
Karen Lumley	*Con*	p260
Alasdair McDonnell	*SDLP*	p265
Patrick Mercer	*Ind*	p280

Sierra Leone

David Mundell	*Con*	p291
Jo Swinson	*Lib Dem*	p354
Gavin Williamson	*Con*	p382

Singapore

Brian Donohoe	*Lab*	p149
Bernard Jenkin	*Con*	p230
Ian Liddell-Grainger	*Con*	p252
Richard Ottaway	*Con*	p303
Stephen Timms	*Lab*	p360

Slovakia

Jonathan Evans	*Con*	p164
Siân James	*Lab*	p228
Ian Swales	*Lib Dem*	p354

Slovenia

Jonathan Evans	*Con*	p164
Neil Parish	*Con*	p305
David Rutley	*Con*	p330
Hugo Swire	*Con*	p355

Somalia

Jon Ashworth	*Lab*	p76
Paul Blomfield	*Lab*	p96
Stephen Doughty	*Lab/Co-op*	p151
Kerry McCarthy	*Lab*	p261
John McDonnell	*Lab*	p265

South Africa

Julian Brazier	*Con*	p101
Malcolm Bruce	*Lib Dem*	p107
Tom Clarke	*Lab*	p126
Oliver Colvile	*Con*	p130
Frank Dobson	*Lab*	p147
Jeffrey Donaldson	*DUP*	p149
Mark Durkan	*SDLP*	p157
Hywel Francis	*Lab*	p174
David Hanson	*Lab*	p202
George Howarth	*Lab*	p221
Simon Hughes	*Lib Dem*	p223
Norman Lamb	*Lib Dem*	p242
Andrew Lansley	*Con*	p244
Ian Liddell-Grainger	*Con*	p252
Francie Molloy	*Sinn Féin*	p284
Chi Onwurah	*Lab*	p301
Lindsay Roy	*Lab*	p327
Graham Stuart	*Con*	p352
Robin Walker	*Con*	p370

South America

Jeremy Browne	*Lib Dem*	p106
Alun Cairns	*Con*	p116
Rehman Chishti	*Con*	p123
Jim Dobbin	*Lab/Co-op*	p146
Stewart Jackson	*Con*	p227
Ian Murray	*Lab*	p294
Barry Sheerman	*Lab/Co-op*	p335

South Sudan

Willie Bain	*Lab*	p78
Mark Durkan	*SDLP*	p157
Duncan Hames	*Lib Dem*	p198

Spain

James Arbuthnot	*Con*	p76
Luciana Berger	*Lab/Co-op*	p91
Tom Blenkinsop	*Lab*	p95
Angie Bray	*Con*	p101
Chris Bryant	*Lab*	p108
Jim Dobbin	*Lab/Co-op*	p146
Natascha Engel	*Lab*	p162
Nia Griffith	*Lab*	p193
Peter Hain	*Lab*	p196
John Hayes	*Con*	p207
Elfyn Llwyd	*PIC*	p255
Jim McGovern	*Lab*	p267
Iain McKenzie	*Lab*	p269
Robert Neill	*Con*	p296
Andy Slaughter	*Lab*	p340

Sri Lanka

Brian Binley	*Con*	p92
Bob Blackman	*Con*	p93
Barry Gardiner	*Lab*	p179
Andrew George	*Lib Dem*	p181
James Gray	*Con*	p189
Robert Halfon	*Con*	p197
Stephen Hammond	*Con*	p200
Andy Love	*Lab/Co-op*	p257
Matthew Offord	*Con*	p300
Lee Scott	*Con*	p332
Virendra Sharma	*Lab*	p335
Gareth Thomas	*Lab/Co-op*	p358
Karl Turner	*Lab*	p363
James Wharton	*Con*	p375

Sudan

Willie Bain	*Lab*	p78
Hilary Benn	*Lab*	p87
John Bercow	*Speaker*	p89
Nicola Blackwood	*Con*	p94
Mary Creagh	*Lab*	p134
Mark Durkan	*SDLP*	p157

Sweden

| Norman Baker | *Lib Dem* | p78 |
| Gordon Birtwistle | *Lib Dem* | p93 |

Nic Dakin	Lab	p139	Karen Lumley	Con	p260
David Evennett	Con	p166	Patrick Mercer	Ind	p280
Kelvin Hopkins	Lab	p219	Stephen Pound	Lab	p311
Alok Sharma	Con	p335	John Whittingdale	Con	p377
Angela Watkinson	Con	p372	**United Arab Emirates**		
Switzerland			Jim Dowd	Lab	p152
Jeremy Lefroy	Con	p248	Kevan Jones	Lab	p234
Ian Liddell-Grainger	Con	p252	Hugo Swire	Con	p355
Robert Neill	Con	p296	**United Kingdom**		
Syria			Kate Green	Lab	p191
Hugh Robertson	Con	p323	Matthew Hancock	Con	p200
Keith Simpson	Con	p339	Stephen McPartland	Con	p271
Taiwan			Sheryll Murray	Con	p294
James Arbuthnot	Con	p76	Laurence Robertson	Con	p324
Brian Donohoe	Lab	p149	Mark Spencer	Con	p346
Jim Dowd	Lab	p152	**United States of America**		
Heather Wheeler	Con	p375	Bob Ainsworth	Lab	p71
Tanzania			Peter Aldous	Con	p71
Kevin Barron	Lab	p83	Graham Allen	Lab	p73
Fiona Bruce	Con	p107	David Amess	Con	p74
Jeremy Lefroy	Con	p248	David Anderson	Lab	p75
John McDonnell	Lab	p265	Stuart Andrew	Con	p75
Craig Whittaker	Con	p377	James Arbuthnot	Con	p76
Tim Yeo	Con	p389	Jon Ashworth	Lab	p76
Thailand			Willie Bain	Lab	p78
Lindsay Roy	Lab	p327	Gregory Barker	Con	p82
Tunisia			Gavin Barwell	Con	p84
Lorely Burt	Lib Dem	p114	Hilary Benn	Lab	p87
Roger Gale	Con	p177	John Bercow	Speaker	p89
Andy Slaughter	Lab	p340	Bob Blackman	Con	p93
Turkey			David Blunkett	Lab	p96
Ann Clwyd	Lab	p127	Crispin Blunt	Con	p97
Fabian Hamilton	Lab	p199	Peter Bottomley	Con	p98
Mark Harper	Con	p203	Ben Bradshaw	Lab	p99
Meg Hillier	Lab/Co-op	p214	Angie Bray	Con	p101
Eric Joyce	Ind	p236	Julian Brazier	Con	p101
Peter Luff	Con	p259	Kevin Brennan	Lab	p102
Eric Ollerenshaw	Con	p300	Steve Brine	Con	p103
Jonathan Reynolds	Lab/Co-op	p320	Nick Brown	Lab	p105
Jack Straw	Lab	p349	Malcolm Bruce	Lib Dem	p107
Uganda			Aidan Burley	Con	p110
John Glen	Con	p184	Conor Burns	Con	p111
Christopher Heaton-Harris	Con	p209	Simon Burns	Con	p111
Helen Jones	Lab	p234	Ronnie Campbell	Lab	p119
Eleanor Laing	Con	p242	Sarah Champion	Lab	p122
Jeremy Lefroy	Con	p248	Rehman Chishti	Con	p123
Lindsay Roy	Lab	p327	Tom Clarke	Lab	p126
Ukraine			Michael Connarty	Lab	p130
Clive Betts	Lab	p91	Rosie Cooper	Lab	p131
Robert Goodwill	Con	p187	Yvette Cooper	Lab	p132
Mike Hancock	Ind	p201	Stephen Crabb	Con	p133
			John Cryer	Lab	p136
			James Cunningham	Lab	p137

Keith Simpson	Con	p339
Henry Smith	Con	p342
Nick Smith	Lab	p343
Nicholas Soames	Con	p344
John Spellar	Lab	p345
Mel Stride	Con	p350
Robert Syms	Con	p356
Jon Trickett	Lab	p362
Paul Uppal	Con	p366
Ed Vaizey	Con	p366
Robin Walker	Con	p370
Ben Wallace	Con	p370
Angela Watkinson	Con	p372
Tom Watson	Lab	p373
John Whittingdale	Con	p377
David Willetts	Con	p379
Stephen Williams	Lib Dem	p381
Phil Wilson	Lab	p383
Sammy Wilson	DUP	p384
Shaun Woodward	Lab	p387
David Wright	Lab	p388
Jeremy Wright	Con	p389

Uzbekistan

Alistair Carmichael	Lib Dem	p120

Venezuela

Hywel Francis	Lab	p174
George Galloway	Respect	p178
Grahame Morris	Lab	p288
Chris Williamson	Lab	p382

Vietnam

Ann Clwyd	Lab	p127
Ian Liddell-Grainger	Con	p252
Chris Ruane	Lab	p327

Wales

Geraint Davies	Lab/Co-op	p142
Michael Fabricant	Con	p166
Helen Jones	Lab	p234
Elfyn Llwyd	PlC	p255
Karl McCartney	Con	p262
Owen Smith	Lab	p343

Yemen

Stephen Doughty	Lab/Co-op	p151
Tobias Ellwood	Con	p161
Andrew George	Lib Dem	p181
Keith Vaz	Lab	p367
Valerie Vaz	Lab	p368

Zambia

Nadine Dorries	Con	p151
Robin Walker	Con	p370

Zimbabwe

Alan Beith	Lib Dem	p86
John Bercow	Speaker	p89
Malcolm Bruce	Lib Dem	p107
Oliver Colvile	Con	p130
Kate Hoey	Lab	p217
Neil Parish	Con	p305
Robert Smith	Lib Dem	p344

MPs by UK Regions

England

Eastern

Basildon and Billericay	John Baron	Con
South Basildon and East Thurrock	Stephen Metcalfe	Con
Bedford	Richard Fuller	Con
Mid Bedfordshire	Nadine Dorries	Con
North East Bedfordshire	Alistair Burt	Con
South West Bedfordshire	Andrew Selous	Con
Braintree	Brooks Newmark	Con
Brentwood and Ongar	Eric Pickles	Con
Broadland	Keith Simpson	Con
Broxbourne	Charles Walker	Con
Bury St Edmunds	David Ruffley	Con
Cambridge	Julian Huppert	Lib Dem
North East Cambridgeshire	Steve Barclay	Con
North West Cambridgeshire	Shailesh Vara	Con
South Cambridgeshire	Andrew Lansley	Con
South East Cambridgeshire	Jim Paice	Con
Castle Point	Rebecca Harris	Con
Chelmsford	Simon Burns	Con
Clacton	Douglas Carswell	Con
Colchester	Bob Russell	Lib Dem
Epping Forest	Eleanor Laing	Con
Great Yarmouth	Brandon Lewis	Con
Harlow	Robert Halfon	Con
Harwich and North Essex	Bernard Jenkin	Con
Hemel Hempstead	Mike Penning	Con
Hertford and Stortford	Mark Prisk	Con
North East Hertfordshire	Oliver Heald	Con
South West Hertfordshire	David Gauke	Con
Hertsmere	James Clappison	Con
Hitchin and Harpenden	Peter Lilley	Con
Huntingdon	Jonathan Djanogly	Con
Ipswich	Ben Gummer	Con
Luton North	Kelvin Hopkins	Lab
Luton South	Gavin Shuker	Lab/Co-op
Maldon	John Whittingdale	Con
Mid Norfolk	George Freeman	Con
North Norfolk	Norman Lamb	Lib Dem
North West Norfolk	Henry Bellingham	Con
South Norfolk	Richard Bacon	Con
South West Norfolk	Elizabeth Truss	Con
Norwich North	Chloe Smith	Con
Norwich South	Simon Wright	Lib Dem
Peterborough	Stewart Jackson	Con
Rayleigh and Wickford	Mark Francois	Con
Rochford and Southend East	James Duddridge	Con
Saffron Walden	Alan Haselhurst	Con
St Albans	Anne Main	Con
Southend West	David Amess	Con
Stevenage	Stephen McPartland	Con

Central Suffolk and North Ipswich	Daniel Poulter	Con
Suffolk Coastal	Therese Coffey	Con
South Suffolk	Tim Yeo	Con
West Suffolk	Matthew Hancock	Con
Thurrock	Jackie Doyle-Price	Con
Watford	Richard Harrington	Con
Waveney	Peter Aldous	Con
Welwyn Hatfield	Grant Shapps	Con
Witham	Priti Patel	Con

East Midlands

Amber Valley	Nigel Mills	Con
Ashfield	Gloria De Piero	Lab
Bassetlaw	John Mann	Lab
Bolsover	Dennis Skinner	Lab
Boston and Skegness	Mark Simmonds	Con
Bosworth	David Tredinnick	Con
Broxtowe	Anna Soubry	Con
Charnwood	Stephen Dorrell	Con
Chesterfield	Toby Perkins	Lab
Corby	Andy Sawford	Lab/Co-op
Daventry	Christopher Heaton-Harris	Con
Derby North	Chris Williamson	Lab
Derby South	Margaret Beckett	Lab
Derbyshire Dales	Patrick McLoughlin	Con
Mid Derbyshire	Pauline Latham	Con
North East Derbyshire	Natascha Engel	Lab
South Derbyshire	Heather Wheeler	Con
Erewash	Jessica Lee	Con
Gainsborough	Edward Leigh	Con
Gedling	Vernon Coaker	Lab
Grantham and Stamford	Nick Boles	Con
Harborough	Edward Garnier	Con
High Peak	Andrew Bingham	Con
Kettering	Philip Hollobone	Con
Leicester East	Keith Vaz	Lab
Leicester South	Jon Ashworth	Lab
Leicester West	Liz Kendall	Lab
North West Leicestershire	Andrew Bridgen	Con
South Leicestershire	Andrew Robathan	Con
Lincoln	Karl McCartney	Con
Loughborough	Nicky Morgan	Con
Louth and Horncastle	Peter Tapsell	Con
Mansfield	Alan Meale	Lab
Newark	Patrick Mercer	Ind*
Northampton North	Michael Ellis	Con
Northampton South	Brian Binley	Con
South Northamptonshire	Andrea Leadsom	Con
Nottingham East	Chris Leslie	Lab/Co-op
Nottingham North	Graham Allen	Lab
Nottingham South	Lilian Greenwood	Lab
Rushcliffe	Kenneth Clarke	Con
Rutland and Melton	Alan Duncan	Con

*Elected as Conservative

Sherwood	Mark Spencer	Con
Sleaford and North Hykeham	Stephen Phillips	Con
South Holland and The Deepings	John Hayes	Con
Wellingborough	Peter Bone	Con

London

Barking	Margaret Hodge	Lab
Battersea	Jane Ellison	Con
Beckenham	Bob Stewart	Con
Bermondsey and Old Southwark	Simon Hughes	Lib Dem
Bethnal Green and Bow	Rushanara Ali	Lab
Old Bexley and Sidcup	James Brokenshire	Con
Bexleyheath and Crayford	David Evennett	Con
Brent Central	Sarah Teather	Lib Dem
Brent North	Barry Gardiner	Lab
Brentford and Isleworth	Mary Macleod	Con
Bromley and Chislehurst	Robert Neill	Con
Camberwell and Peckham	Harriet Harman	Lab
Carshalton and Wallington	Tom Brake	Lib Dem
Chelsea and Fulham	Greg Hands	Con
Chingford and Woodford Green	Iain Duncan Smith	Con
Chipping Barnet	Theresa Villiers	Con
Croydon Central	Gavin Barwell	Con
Croydon North	Steve Reed	Lab
Croydon South	Richard Ottaway	Con
Dagenham and Rainham	Jon Cruddas	Lab
Dulwich and West Norwood	Tessa Jowell	Lab
Ealing Central and Acton	Angie Bray	Con
Ealing North	Stephen Pound	Lab
Ealing Southall	Virendra Sharma	Lab
East Ham	Stephen Timms	Lab
Edmonton	Andy Love	Lab/Co-op
Eltham	Clive Efford	Lab
Enfield North	Nick de Bois	Con
Enfield Southgate	David Burrowes	Con
Erith and Thamesmead	Teresa Pearce	Lab
Feltham and Heston	Seema Malhotra	Lab
Finchley and Golders Green	Mike Freer	Con
Greenwich and Woolwich	Nick Raynsford	Lab
Hackney North and Stoke Newington	Diane Abbott	Lab
Hackney South and Shoreditch	Meg Hillier	Lab/Co-op
Hammersmith	Andy Slaughter	Lab
Hampstead and Kilburn	Glenda Jackson	Lab
Harrow East	Bob Blackman	Con
Harrow West	Gareth Thomas	Lab/Co-op
Hayes and Harlington	John McDonnell	Lab
Hendon	Matthew Offord	Con
Holborn and St Pancras	Frank Dobson	Lab
Hornchurch and Upminster	Angela Watkinson	Con
Hornsey and Wood Green	Lynne Featherstone	Lib Dem
Ilford North	Lee Scott	Con
Ilford South	Mike Gapes	Lab/Co-op
Islington North	Jeremy Corbyn	Lab
Islington South and Finsbury	Emily Thornberry	Lab

Kensington	Malcolm Rifkind	Con
Kingston and Surbiton	Edward Davey	Lib Dem
Lewisham Deptford	Joan Ruddock	Lab
Lewisham East	Heidi Alexander	Lab
Lewisham West and Penge	Jim Dowd	Lab
Leyton and Wanstead	John Cryer	Lab
Cities of London and Westminster	Mark Field	Con
Mitcham and Morden	Siobhain McDonagh	Lab
Orpington	Jo Johnson	Con
Poplar and Limehouse	Jim Fitzpatrick	Lab
Putney	Justine Greening	Con
Richmond Park	Zac Goldsmith	Con
Romford	Andrew Rosindell	Con
Ruislip, Northwood and Pinner	Nick Hurd	Con
Streatham	Chuka Umunna	Lab
Sutton and Cheam	Paul Burstow	Lib Dem
Tooting	Sadiq Khan	Lab
Tottenham	David Lammy	Lab
Twickenham	Vincent Cable	Lib Dem
Uxbridge and South Ruislip	John Randall	Con
Vauxhall	Kate Hoey	Lab
Walthamstow	Stella Creasy	Lab/Co-op
West Ham	Lyn Brown	Lab
Westminster North	Karen Buck	Lab
Wimbledon	Stephen Hammond	Con

North East

Berwick-upon-Tweed	Alan Beith	Lib Dem
Bishop Auckland	Helen Goodman	Lab
Blaydon	David Anderson	Lab
Blyth Valley	Ronnie Campbell	Lab
Darlington	Jenny Chapman	Lab
City of Durham	Roberta Blackman-Woods	Lab
North Durham	Kevan Jones	Lab
North West Durham	Patricia Glass	Lab
Easington	Grahame Morris	Lab
Gateshead	Ian Mearns	Lab
Hartlepool	Iain Wright	Lab
Hexham	Guy Opperman	Con
Houghton and Sunderland South	Bridget Phillipson	Lab
Jarrow	Stephen Hepburn	Lab
Middlesbrough	Andy McDonald	Lab
Middlesbrough South and East Cleveland	Tom Blenkinsop	Lab
Newcastle upon Tyne Central	Chi Onwurah	Lab
Newcastle upon Tyne East	Nick Brown	Lab
Newcastle upon Tyne North	Catherine McKinnell	Lab
Redcar	Ian Swales	Lib Dem
Sedgefield	Phil Wilson	Lab
South Shields	Emma Lewell-Buck	Lab
Stockton North	Alex Cunningham	Lab
Stockton South	James Wharton	Con
Sunderland Central	Julie Elliott	Lab

Tynemouth	Alan Campbell	Lab
North Tyneside	Mary Glindon	Lab
Wansbeck	Ian Lavery	Lab
Washington and Sunderland West	Sharon Hodgson	Lab

North West

Altrincham and Sale West	Graham Brady	Con
Ashton under Lyne	David Heyes	Lab
Barrow and Furness	John Woodcock	Lab/Co-op
Birkenhead	Frank Field	Lab
Blackburn	Jack Straw	Lab
Blackley and Broughton	Graham Stringer	Lab
Blackpool North and Cleveleys	Paul Maynard	Con
Blackpool South	Gordon Marsden	Lab
Bolton North East	David Crausby	Lab
Bolton South East	Yasmin Qureshi	Lab
Bolton West	Julie Hilling	Lab
Bootle	Joe Benton	Lab
Burnley	Gordon Birtwistle	Lib Dem
Bury North	David Nuttall	Con
Bury South	Ivan Lewis	Lab
Carlisle	John Stevenson	Con
Cheadle	Mark Hunter	Lib Dem
City of Chester	Stephen Mosley	Con
Chorley	Lindsay Hoyle	Lab
Congleton	Fiona Bruce	Con
Copeland	Jamie Reed	Lab
Crewe and Nantwich	Edward Timpson	Con
Denton and Reddish	Andrew Gwynne	Lab
Eddisbury	Stephen O'Brien	Con
Ellesmere Port and Neston	Andrew Miller	Lab
Fylde	Mark Menzies	Con
Garston and Halewood	Maria Eagle	Lab
Halton	Derek Twigg	Lab
Hazel Grove	Andrew Stunell	Lib Dem
Heywood and Middleton	Jim Dobbin	Lab/Co-op
Hyndburn	Graham Jones	Lab
Knowsley	George Howarth	Lab
West Lancashire	Rosie Cooper	Lab
Lancaster and Fleetwood	Eric Ollerenshaw	Con
Leigh	Andy Burnham	Lab
Liverpool Riverside	Louise Ellman	Lab/Co-op
Liverpool Walton	Steve Rotheram	Lab
Liverpool Wavertree	Luciana Berger	Lab/Co-op
Liverpool West Derby	Stephen Twigg	Lab/Co-op
Macclesfield	David Rutley	Con
Makerfield	Yvonne Fovargue	Lab
Manchester Central	Lucy Powell	Lab/Co-op
Manchester Gorton	Gerald Kaufman	Lab
Manchester Withington	John Leech	Lib Dem
Morecambe and Lunesdale	David Morris	Con
Oldham East and Saddleworth	Debbie Abrahams	Lab
Oldham West and Royton	Michael Meacher	Lab

Pendle	Andrew Stephenson	Con
Penrith and The Border	Rory Stewart	Con
Preston	Mark Hendrick	Lab/Co-op
South Ribble	Lorraine Fullbrook	Con
Ribble Valley	Nigel Evans	Ind*
Rochdale	Simon Danczuk	Lab
Rossendale and Darwen	Jake Berry	Con
St Helens North	David Watts	Lab
St Helens South and Whiston	Shaun Woodward	Lab
Salford and Eccles	Hazel Blears	Lab
Sefton Central	Bill Esterson	Lab
Southport	John Pugh	Lib Dem
Stalybridge and Hyde	Jonathan Reynolds	Lab/Co-op
Stockport	Ann Coffey	Lab
Stretford and Urmston	Kate Green	Lab
Tatton	George Osborne	Con
Wallasey	Angela Eagle	Lab
Warrington North	Helen Jones	Lab
Warrington South	David Mowat	Con
Weaver Vale	Graham Evans	Con
Westmorland and Lonsdale	Tim Farron	Lib Dem
Wigan	Lisa Nandy	Lab
Wirral South	Alison McGovern	Lab
Wirral West	Esther McVey	Con
Workington	Tony Cunningham	Lab
Worsley and Eccles South	Barbara Keeley	Lab
Wyre and Preston North	Ben Wallace	Con
Wythenshawe and Sale East	Paul Goggins	Lab

South East

Aldershot	Gerald Howarth	Con
Arundel and South Downs	Nick Herbert	Con
Ashford	Damian Green	Con
Aylesbury	David Lidington	Con
Banbury	Tony Baldry	Con
Basingstoke	Maria Miller	Con
Beaconsfield	Dominic Grieve	Con
Bexhill and Battle	Gregory Barker	Con
Bognor Regis and Littlehampton	Nick Gibb	Con
Bracknell	Phillip Lee	Con
Brighton Kemptown	Simon Kirby	Con
Brighton Pavilion	Caroline Lucas	Green
Buckingham	John Bercow	Speaker
Canterbury	Julian Brazier	Con
Chatham and Aylesford	Tracey Crouch	Con
Chesham and Amersham	Cheryl Gillan	Con
Chichester	Andrew Tyrie	Con
Crawley	Henry Smith	Con
Dartford	Gareth Johnson	Con
Dover	Charlie Elphicke	Con
Eastbourne	Stephen Lloyd	Lib Dem
Eastleigh	Mike Thornton	Lib Dem
Epsom and Ewell	Chris Grayling	Con

*Elected as Conservative

Esher and Walton	Dominic Raab	Con
Fareham	Mark Hoban	Con
Faversham and Mid Kent	Hugh Robertson	Con
Folkestone and Hythe	Damian Collins	Con
Gillingham and Rainham	Rehman Chishti	Con
Gosport	Caroline Dinenage	Con
Gravesham	Adam Holloway	Con
Guildford	Anne Milton	Con
East Hampshire	Damian Hinds	Con
North East Hampshire	James Arbuthnot	Con
North West Hampshire	George Young	Con
Hastings and Rye	Amber Rudd	Con
Havant	David Willetts	Con
Henley	John Howell	Con
Horsham	Francis Maude	Con
Hove	Mike Weatherley	Con
Isle of Wight	Andrew Turner	Con
Lewes	Norman Baker	Lib Dem
Maidenhead	Theresa May	Con
Maidstone and The Weald	Helen Grant	Con
Meon Valley	George Hollingbery	Con
Milton Keynes North	Mark Lancaster	Con
Milton Keynes South	Iain Stewart	Con
Mole Valley	Paul Beresford	Con
New Forest East	Julian Lewis	Con
New Forest West	Desmond Swayne	Con
Newbury	Richard Benyon	Con
Oxford East	Andrew Smith	Lab
Oxford West and Abingdon	Nicola Blackwood	Con
Portsmouth North	Penny Mordaunt	Con
Portsmouth South	Mike Hancock	Ind*
Reading East	Robert Wilson	Con
Reading West	Alok Sharma	Con
Reigate	Crispin Blunt	Con
Rochester and Strood	Mark Reckless	Con
Romsey and Southampton North	Caroline Nokes	Con
Runnymede and Weybridge	Philip Hammond	Con
Sevenoaks	Michael Fallon	Con
Sittingbourne and Sheppey	Gordon Henderson	Con
Slough	Fiona Mactaggart	Lab
Southampton Itchen	John Denham	Lab
Southampton Test	Alan Whitehead	Lab
Spelthorne	Kwasi Kwarteng	Con
East Surrey	Sam Gyimah	Con
Surrey Heath	Michael Gove	Con
South West Surrey	Jeremy Hunt	Con
Mid Sussex	Nicholas Soames	Con
North Thanet	Roger Gale	Con
South Thanet	Laura Sandys	Con
Tonbridge and Malling	John Stanley	Con
Tunbridge Wells	Greg Clark	Con
Wantage	Ed Vaizey	Con
Wealden	Charles Hendry	Con

*Elected as Liberal Democrat

Winchester	Steve Brine	Con
Windsor	Adam Afriyie	Con
Witney	David Cameron	Con
Woking	Jonathan Lord	Con
Wokingham	John Redwood	Con
East Worthing and Shoreham	Tim Loughton	Con
Worthing West	Peter Bottomley	Con
Wycombe	Steve Baker	Con

South West

Bath	Don Foster	Lib Dem
Bournemouth East	Tobias Ellwood	Con
Bournemouth West	Conor Burns	Con
Bridgwater and West Somerset	Ian Liddell-Grainger	Con
Bristol East	Kerry McCarthy	Lab
Bristol North West	Charlotte Leslie	Con
Bristol South	Dawn Primarolo	Lab
Bristol West	Stephen Williams	Lib Dem
Camborne and Redruth	George Eustice	Con
Cheltenham	Martin Horwood	Lib Dem
Chippenham	Duncan Hames	Lib Dem
Christchurch	Christopher Chope	Con
North Cornwall	Dan Rogerson	Lib Dem
South East Cornwall	Sheryll Murray	Con
The Cotswolds	Geoffrey Clifton-Brown	Con
Devizes	Claire Perry	Con
Central Devon	Mel Stride	Con
East Devon	Hugo Swire	Con
North Devon	Nick Harvey	Lib Dem
South West Devon	Gary Streeter	Con
Mid Dorset and North Poole	Annette Brooke	Lib Dem
North Dorset	Robert Walter	Con
South Dorset	Richard Drax	Con
West Dorset	Oliver Letwin	Con
Exeter	Ben Bradshaw	Lab
Filton and Bradley Stoke	Jack Lopresti	Con
Forest of Dean	Mark Harper	Con
Gloucester	Richard Graham	Con
Kingswood	Chris Skidmore	Con
Newton Abbot	Anne Marie Morris	Con
Plymouth, Moor View	Alison Seabeck	Lab
Plymouth, Sutton and Devonport	Oliver Colvile	Con
Poole	Robert Syms	Con
St Austell and Newquay	Steve Gilbert	Lib Dem
St Ives	Andrew George	Lib Dem
Salisbury	John Glen	Con
North Somerset	Liam Fox	Con
North East Somerset	Jacob Rees-Mogg	Con
Somerton and Frome	David Heath	Lib Dem
Stroud	Neil Carmichael	Con
North Swindon	Justin Tomlinson	Con
South Swindon	Robert Buckland	Con
Taunton Deane	Jeremy Browne	Lib Dem

Tewkesbury	Laurence Robertson	Con
Thornbury and Yate	Steve Webb	Lib Dem
Tiverton and Honiton	Neil Parish	Con
Torbay	Adrian Sanders	Lib Dem
Torridge and West Devon	Geoffrey Cox	Con
Totnes	Sarah Wollaston	Con
Truro and Falmouth	Sarah Newton	Con
Wells	Tessa Munt	Lib Dem
Weston-Super-Mare	John Penrose	Con
North Wiltshire	James Gray	Con
South West Wiltshire	Andrew Murrison	Con
Yeovil	David Laws	Lib Dem

West Midlands

Aldridge-Brownhills	Richard Shepherd	Con
Birmingham, Edgbaston	Gisela Stuart	Lab
Birmingham, Erdington	Jack Dromey	Lab
Birmingham, Hall Green	Roger Godsiff	Lab
Birmingham, Hodge Hill	Liam Byrne	Lab
Birmingham, Ladywood	Shabana Mahmood	Lab
Birmingham, Northfield	Richard Burden	Lab
Birmingham, Perry Barr	Khalid Mahmood	Lab
Birmingham, Selly Oak	Steve McCabe	Lab
Birmingham, Yardley	John Hemming	Lib Dem
Bromsgrove	Sajid Javid	Con
Burton	Andrew Griffiths	Con
Cannock Chase	Aidan Burley	Con
Coventry North East	Bob Ainsworth	Lab
Coventry North West	Geoffrey Robinson	Lab
Coventry South	James Cunningham	Lab
Dudley North	Ian Austin	Lab
Dudley South	Chris Kelly	Con
Halesowen and Rowley Regis	James Morris	Con
Hereford and South Herefordshire	Jesse Norman	Con
North Herefordshire	Bill Wiggin	Con
Kenilworth and Southam	Jeremy Wright	Con
Lichfield	Michael Fabricant	Con
Ludlow	Philip Dunne	Con
Meriden	Caroline Spelman	Con
Newcastle-under-Lyme	Paul Farrelly	Lab
Nuneaton	Marcus Jones	Con
Redditch	Karen Lumley	Con
Rugby	Mark Pawsey	Con
Shrewsbury and Atcham	Daniel Kawczynski	Con
North Shropshire	Owen Paterson	Con
Solihull	Lorely Burt	Lib Dem
Stafford	Jeremy Lefroy	Con
Staffordshire Moorlands	Karen Bradley	Con
South Staffordshire	Gavin Williamson	Con
Stoke-on-Trent Central	Tristram Hunt	Lab
Stoke-on-Trent North	Joan Walley	Lab
Stoke-on-Trent South	Robert Flello	Lab
Stone	William Cash	Con

Stourbridge	Margot James	Con
Stratford-on-Avon	Nadhim Zahawi	Con
Sutton Coldfield	Andrew Mitchell	Con
Tamworth	Christopher Pincher	Con
Telford	David Wright	Lab
Walsall North	David Winnick	Lab
Walsall South	Valerie Vaz	Lab
Warley	John Spellar	Lab
Warwick and Leamington	Chris White	Con
North Warwickshire	Dan Byles	Con
West Bromwich East	Tom Watson	Lab
West Bromwich West	Adrian Bailey	Lab/Co-op
Wolverhampton North East	Emma Reynolds	Lab
Wolverhampton South East	Pat McFadden	Lab
Wolverhampton South West	Paul Uppal	Con
Worcester	Robin Walker	Con
Mid Worcestershire	Peter Luff	Con
West Worcestershire	Harriett Baldwin	Con
The Wrekin	Mark Pritchard	Con
Wyre Forest	Mark Garnier	Con

Yorkshire and Humberside

Barnsley Central	Dan Jarvis	Lab
Barnsley East	Michael Dugher	Lab
Batley and Spen	Mike Wood	Lab
Beverley and Holderness	Graham Stuart	Con
Bradford East	David Ward	Lib Dem
Bradford South	Gerry Sutcliffe	Lab
Bradford West	George Galloway	Respect
Brigg and Goole	Andrew Percy	Con
Calder Valley	Craig Whittaker	Con
Cleethorpes	Martin Vickers	Con
Colne Valley	Jason McCartney	Con
Dewsbury	Simon Reevell	Con
Don Valley	Caroline Flint	Lab
Doncaster Central	Rosie Winterton	Lab
Doncaster North	Ed Miliband	Lab
Elmet and Rothwell	Alec Shelbrooke	Con
Great Grimsby	Austin Mitchell	Lab
Halifax	Linda Riordan	Lab/Co-op
Haltemprice and Howden	David Davis	Con
Harrogate and Knaresborough	Andrew Jones	Con
Hemsworth	Jon Trickett	Lab
Huddersfield	Barry Sheerman	Lab/Co-op
Kingston upon Hull East	Karl Turner	Lab
Kingston upon Hull North	Diana Johnson	Lab
Kingston upon Hull West and Hessle	Alan Johnson	Lab
Keighley	Kris Hopkins	Con
Leeds Central	Hilary Benn	Lab
Leeds East	George Mudie	Lab
Leeds North East	Fabian Hamilton	Lab
Leeds North West	Greg Mulholland	Lib Dem
Leeds West	Rachel Reeves	Lab

Morley and Outwood	Ed Balls	Lab/Co-op
Normanton, Pontefract and Castleford	Yvette Cooper	Lab
Penistone and Stocksbridge	Angela Smith	Lab
Pudsey	Stuart Andrew	Con
Richmond (Yorkshire)	William Hague	Con
Rother Valley	Kevin Barron	Lab
Rotherham	Sarah Champion	Lab
Scarborough and Whitby	Robert Goodwill	Con
Scunthorpe	Nic Dakin	Lab
Selby and Ainsty	Nigel Adams	Con
Sheffield, Brightside and Hillsborough	David Blunkett	Lab
Sheffield Central	Paul Blomfield	Lab
Sheffield, Hallam	Nick Clegg	Lib Dem
Sheffield Heeley	Meg Munn	Lab/Co-op
Sheffield South East	Clive Betts	Lab
Shipley	Philip Davies	Con
Skipton and Ripon	Julian Smith	Con
Thirsk and Malton	Anne McIntosh	Con
Wakefield	Mary Creagh	Lab
Wentworth and Dearne	John Healey	Lab
York Central	Hugh Bayley	Lab
York Outer	Julian Sturdy	Con
East Yorkshire	Greg Knight	Con

Northern Ireland

East Antrim	Sammy Wilson	DUP
North Antrim	Ian Paisley	DUP
South Antrim	William McCrea	DUP
Belfast East	Naomi Long	All
Belfast North	Nigel Dodds	DUP
Belfast South	Alasdair McDonnell	SDLP
Belfast West	Paul Maskey	Sinn Féin
North Down	Sylvia Hermon	Ind
South Down	Margaret Ritchie	SDLP
Fermanagh and South Tyrone	Michelle Gildernew	Sinn Féin
Foyle	Mark Durkan	SDLP
Lagan Valley	Jeffrey Donaldson	DUP
East Londonderry	Gregory Campbell	DUP
Newry and Armagh	Conor Murphy	Sinn Féin
Strangford	Jim Shannon	DUP
West Tyrone	Pat Doherty	Sinn Féin
Mid Ulster	Francie Molloy	Sinn Féin
Upper Bann	David Simpson	DUP

Scotland

Aberdeen North	Frank Doran	Lab
Aberdeen South	Anne Begg	Lab
West Aberdeenshire and Kincardine	Robert Smith	Lib Dem
Airdrie and Shotts	Pamela Nash	Lab
Angus	Mike Weir	SNP
Argyll and Bute	Alan Reid	Lib Dem
Ayr, Carrick and Cumnock	Sandra Osborne	Lab
Central Ayrshire	Brian Donohoe	Lab

North Ayrshire and Arran	Katy Clark	Lab
Banff and Buchan	Eilidh Whiteford	SNP
Berwickshire, Roxburgh and Selkirk	Michael Moore	Lib Dem
Caithness, Sutherland and Easter Ross	John Thurso	Lib Dem
Coatbridge, Chryston and Bellshill	Tom Clarke	Lab
Cumbernauld, Kilsyth and Kirkintilloch East	Gregg McClymont	Lab
Dumfries and Galloway	Russell Brown	Lab
Dumfriesshire, Clydesdale and Tweeddale	David Mundell	Con
East Dunbartonshire	Jo Swinson	Lib Dem
West Dunbartonshire	Gemma Doyle	Lab/Co-op
Dundee East	Stewart Hosie	SNP
Dundee West	Jim McGovern	Lab
Dunfermline and West Fife	Thomas Docherty	Lab
East Kilbride, Strathaven and Lesmahagow	Michael McCann	Lab
Edinburgh East	Sheila Gilmore	Lab
Edinburgh North and Leith	Mark Lazarowicz	Lab/Co-op
Edinburgh South	Ian Murray	Lab
Edinburgh South West	Alistair Darling	Lab
Edinburgh West	Mike Crockart	Lib Dem
Falkirk	Eric Joyce	Ind*
North East Fife	Menzies Campbell	Lib Dem
Glasgow Central	Anas Sarwar	Lab
Glasgow East	Margaret Curran	Lab
Glasgow North	Ann McKechin	Lab
Glasgow North East	Willie Bain	Lab
Glasgow North West	John Robertson	Lab
Glasgow South	Tom Harris	Lab
Glasgow South West	Ian Davidson	Lab/Co-op
Glenrothes	Lindsay Roy	Lab
Gordon	Malcolm Bruce	Lib Dem
Inverclyde	Iain McKenzie	Lab
Inverness, Nairn, Badenoch and Strathspey	Danny Alexander	Lib Dem
Kilmarnock and Loudoun	Cathy Jamieson	Lab/Co-op
Kirkcaldy and Cowdenbeath	Gordon Brown	Lab
Lanark and Hamilton East	Jim Hood	Lab
Linlithgow and East Falkirk	Michael Connarty	Lab
Livingston	Graeme Morrice	Lab
East Lothian	Fiona O'Donnell	Lab
Midlothian	David Hamilton	Lab
Moray	Angus Robertson	SNP
Motherwell and Wishaw	Frank Roy	Lab
Na h-Eileanan An Iar	Angus MacNeil	SNP
Ochil and South Perthshire	Gordon Banks	Lab
Orkney and Shetland	Alistair Carmichael	Lib Dem
Paisley and Renfrewshire North	Jim Sheridan	Lab
Paisley and Renfrewshire South	Douglas Alexander	Lab
Perth and North Perthshire	Peter Wishart	SNP
East Renfrewshire	Jim Murphy	Lab
Ross, Skye and Lochaber	Charles Kennedy	Lib Dem
Rutherglen and Hamilton West	Tom Greatrex	Lab/Co-op
Stirling	Anne McGuire	Lab

*Elected as Labour

Wales

Aberavon	Hywel Francis	Lab
Aberconwy	Guto Bebb	Con
Alyn and Deeside	Mark Tami	Lab
Arfon	Hywel Williams	PlC
Blaenau Gwent	Nick Smith	Lab
Brecon and Radnorshire	Roger Williams	Lib Dem
Bridgend	Madeleine Moon	Lab
Caerphilly	Wayne David	Lab
Cardiff Central	Jenny Willott	Lib Dem
Cardiff North	Jonathan Evans	Con
Cardiff South and Penarth	Stephen Doughty	Lab/Co-op
Cardiff West	Kevin Brennan	Lab
Carmarthen East and Dinefwr	Jonathan Edwards	PlC
Carmarthen West and South Pembrokeshire	Simon Hart	Con
Ceredigion	Mark Williams	Lib Dem
Clwyd South	Susan Elan Jones	Lab
Vale of Clwyd	Chris Ruane	Lab
Clwyd West	David Jones	Con
Cynon Valley	Ann Clwyd	Lab
Delyn	David Hanson	Lab
Dwyfor Meirionnydd	Elfyn Llwyd	PlC
Vale of Glamorgan	Alun Cairns	Con
Gower	Martin Caton	Lab
Islwyn	Chris Evans	Lab/Co-op
Llanelli	Nia Griffith	Lab
Merthyr Tydfil and Rhymney	Dai Havard	Lab
Monmouth	David Davies	Con
Montgomeryshire	Glyn Davies	Con
Neath	Peter Hain	Lab
Newport East	Jessica Morden	Lab
Newport West	Paul Flynn	Lab
Ogmore	Huw Irranca-Davies	Lab
Pontypridd	Owen Smith	Lab
Preseli Pembrokeshire	Stephen Crabb	Con
Rhondda	Chris Bryant	Lab
Swansea East	Siân James	Lab
Swansea West	Geraint Davies	Lab/Co-op
Torfaen	Paul Murphy	Lab
Wrexham	Ian Lucas	Lab
Ynys Môn	Albert Owen	Lab

Election statistics by party, gender and region

The following tables list all members in the House of Commons as of 12 September 2013 in the year they were elected. If an MP had a period out of parliament, the newly-elected year will appear not the original year that they were elected, an exception to this rule is David Davis he is allocated to 1987 when he was first elected.

Political party

	By-election*	%	1966	%	1970	%	Feb-74	%	1979	%	1983	%	1987	%	1992	%	1997	%	2001	%	2005	%	2010	%	Total
Con	11	3.63	1	0.33	1	0.33	2	0.66	2	0.66	7	2.3	7	2.30	19	6.27	28	9.24	26	8.58	52	17.16	147	48.51	303
Lab	38	14.79	–	–	3	1.17	–	–	5	1.95	5	1.95	14	5.45	21	8.17	48	18.68	24	9.34	32	12.45	67	26.07	257
Lib/Lib Dem	5	8.93	–	–	–	–	–	–	–	–	2	3.57	1	1.79	2	3.57	13	23.21	8	14.29	15	26.79	10	17.86	56
DUP	–	–	–	–	–	–	–	–	–	–	–	–	–	–	–	–	1	12.50	2	25.00	3	37.50	2	25.00	8
SNP	–	–	–	–	–	–	–	–	–	–	–	–	–	–	–	–	–	–	3	50.00	2	33.33	1	16.67	6
Sinn Féin	2	40.00	–	–	–	–	–	–	–	–	–	–	–	–	1	20.00	–	–	2	40.00	1	20.00	–	–	5
Ind	1	33.33	–	–	–	–	–	–	–	–	–	–	–	–	–	–	1	33.33	2	40.00	–	–	–	–	5
PlC	–	–	–	–	–	–	–	–	–	–	–	–	–	–	1	33.33	–	–	1	33.33	–	–	1	33.33	3
SDLP	–	–	–	–	–	–	–	–	–	–	–	–	–	–	–	–	–	–	–	–	2	66.67	1	33.33	3
Alliance	–	–	–	–	–	–	–	–	–	–	–	–	–	–	–	–	–	–	–	–	–	–	1	100.00	1
Green	–	–	–	–	–	–	–	–	–	–	–	–	–	–	–	–	–	–	–	–	–	–	1	100.00	1
Respect	1	100.00	–	–	–	–	–	–	–	–	–	–	–	–	–	–	–	–	–	–	–	–	–	–	1
Speaker	–	–	–	–	–	–	–	–	–	–	–	–	–	–	–	–	1	100.00	–	–	–	–	–	–	1
Total	**58**	**8.92**	**1**	**0.15**	**4**	**0.62**	**2**	**0.31**	**7**	**1.08**	**14**	**2.15**	**22**	**3.38**	**44**	**6.77**	**92**	**14.15**	**68**	**10.46**	**108**	**16.62**	**230**	**35.38**	**650**

Gender

	By-election*	%	1966	%	1970	%	Feb-74	%	1979	%	1983	%	1987	%	1992	%	1997	%	2001	%	2005	%	2010	%	Total
Male	47	9.25	1	0.20	4	0.01	2	0.39	7	1.38	13	2.56	18	3.54	39	7.68	74	14.57	62	12.20	77	15.16	159	31.30	503
Female	11	7.80	–	–	–	–	–	–	–	–	1	0.71	4	2.84	5	3.55	18	12.77	6	4.26	30	21.28	72	51.06	147
Total	**58**	**8.92**	**1**		**4**		**2**		**7**		**14**		**22**		**44**		**92**		**68**		**107**		**231**		**650**

*Earliest by-election that returned a sitting MP was in 1973.

N.B. No current Members were first elected in the general election of October 1974.

UK Region

	By-election*	%	1966	%	1970	%	Feb-74	%	1979	%	1983	%	1987	%	1992	%	1997	%	2001	%	2005	%	2010	%	Total
Eastern	2	3.45	–	–	–	–	–	–	–	–	3	5.17	2	3.45	5	8.62	6	10.34	9	15.52	11	18.97	20	34.48	58
East Midlands	3	6.52	1	2.17	2	4.35	–	–	1	2.17	2	4.35	4	8.70	3	6.52	2	4.35	3	6.52	4	8.70	21	45.65	46
London	12	16.44	–	–	–	–	–	–	1	1.37	1	1.37	2	2.74	7	9.59	13	17.81	4	5.48	16	21.92	17	23.29	73
North East	5	17.24	–	–	–	–	–	–	–	–	1	3.45	1	3.45	–	–	2	6.90	1	3.45	4	13.79	15	51.72	29
North West	8	10.67	–	–	2	2.67	–	–	2	2.67	–	–	–	–	4	5.33	16	21.33	5	6.67	7	9.33	31	41.33	75
South East	3	3.57	–	–	–	–	2	2.38	–	–	3	3.57	4	4.76	5	5.95	18	21.43	7	8.33	12	14.29	30	35.71	84
South West	–	–	–	–	–	–	–	–	–	–	–	–	1	1.82	5	9.09	11	20.00	5	9.09	10	18.18	23	41.82	55
West Midlands	4	6.78	–	–	–	–	–	–	2	3.39	–	–	1	1.69	7	11.90	4	6.78	6	10.17	9	15.25	26	44.07	59
Yorkshire and Humberside	8	14.81	–	–	–	–	–	–	1	1.85	1	1.85	2	3.70	3	5.56	8	14.81	2	3.70	11	20.37	18	33.33	54
Northern Ireland	2	11.11	–	–	–	–	–	–	–	–	–	–	–	–	–	–	1	5.56	5	27.78	6	33.33	4	22.22	18
Scotland	7	11.86	–	–	–	–	–	–	–	–	3	5.08	3	5.08	3	5.08	9	15.25	11	18.64	8	13.56	15	25.42	59
Wales	4	10.00	–	–	–	–	–	–	–	–	–	–	2	5.00	2	5.00	2	5.00	10	25.00	9	22.50	11	27.50	40
Total	**58**	**8.92**	**1**	**0.15**	**4**	**0.62**	**2**	**0.31**	**7**	**1.08**	**14**	**2.15**	**22**	**3.38**	**44**	**6.77**	**92**	**14.15**	**68**	**10.46**	**107**	**16.46**	**231**	**35.54**	**650**

*Earliest by-election that returned a sitting MP was in 1973.

N.B. No current Members were first elected in the general election of October 1974.

Constituencies, MPs and Majorities

ENGLAND	533
SCOTLAND	59
WALES	40
NORTHERN IRELAND	18
	TOTAL 650

England

			Majority	%
Aldershot	Gerald Howarth	Con	5,586	12.28
Aldridge-Brownhills	Richard Shepherd	Con	15,266	39.33
Altrincham and Sale West	Graham Brady	Con	11,595	23.4
Amber Valley	Nigel Mills	Con	536	1.16
Arundel and South Downs	Nick Herbert	Con	16,691	29.76
Ashfield	Gloria De Piero	Lab	192	0.4
Ashford	Damian Green	Con	17,297	31.29
Ashton under Lyne	David Heyes	Lab	9,094	23.56
Aylesbury	David Lidington	Con	12,618	23.69
Banbury	Tony Baldry	Con	18,227	32.32
Barking	Margaret Hodge	Lab	16,555	36.27
Barnsley Central	Dan Jarvis	Lab	11,771	48.54
Barnsley East	Michael Dugher	Lab	11,090	28.82
Barrow and Furness	John Woodcock	Lab/Co-op	5,208	11.78
Basildon and Billericay	John Baron	Con	12,398	29.74
South Basildon and East Thurrock	Stephen Metcalfe	Con	5,772	12.87
Basingstoke	Maria Miller	Con	13,176	25.95
Bassetlaw	John Mann	Lab	8,215	16.52
Bath	Don Foster	Lib Dem	11,883	25.19
Batley and Spen	Mike Wood	Lab	4,406	8.6
Battersea	Jane Ellison	Con	5,977	12.23
Beaconsfield	Dominic Grieve	Con	21,782	41.45
Beckenham	Bob Stewart	Con	17,784	37.21
Bedford	Richard Fuller	Con	1,353	2.99
Mid Bedfordshire	Nadine Dorries	Con	15,152	27.56
North East Bedfordshire	Alistair Burt	Con	18,942	34.05
South West Bedfordshire	Andrew Selous	Con	16,649	32.73
Bermondsey and Old Southwark	Simon Hughes	Lib Dem	8,530	19.04
Berwick-upon-Tweed	Alan Beith	Lib Dem	2,690	6.98
Bethnal Green and Bow	Rushanara Ali	Lab	11,574	22.52
Beverley and Holderness	Graham Stuart	Con	12,987	24.38
Bexhill and Battle	Gregory Barker	Con	12,880	23.54
Old Bexley and Sidcup	James Brokenshire	Con	15,857	34.73
Bexleyheath and Crayford	David Evennett	Con	10,344	23.89
Birkenhead	Frank Field	Lab	15,195	42.5
Birmingham, Edgbaston	Gisela Stuart	Lab	1,274	3.06
Birmingham, Erdington	Jack Dromey	Lab	3,277	9.19
Birmingham, Hall Green	Roger Godsiff	Lab	3,799	7.74

			Majority	%
Birmingham, Hodge Hill	Liam Byrne	Lab	10,302	24.02
Birmingham, Ladywood	Shabana Mahmood	Lab	10,105	27.91
Birmingham, Northfield	Richard Burden	Lab	2,782	6.64
Birmingham, Perry Barr	Khalid Mahmood	Lab	11,908	28.13
Birmingham, Selly Oak	Steve McCabe	Lab	3,482	7.46
Birmingham, Yardley	John Hemming	Lib Dem	3,002	7.32
Bishop Auckland	Helen Goodman	Lab	5,218	12.66
Blackburn	Jack Straw	Lab	9,856	20.87
Blackley and Broughton	Graham Stringer	Lab	12,303	35.81
Blackpool North and Cleveleys	Paul Maynard	Con	2,150	5.29
Blackpool South	Gordon Marsden	Lab	1,852	5.25
Blaydon	David Anderson	Lab	9,117	20.23
Blyth Valley	Ronnie Campbell	Lab	6,668	17.27
Bognor Regis and Littlehampton	Nick Gibb	Con	13,063	27.87
Bolsover	Dennis Skinner	Lab	11,182	25.39
Bolton North East	David Crausby	Lab	4,084	9.4
Bolton South East	Yasmin Qureshi	Lab	8,634	21.68
Bolton West	Julie Hilling	Lab	92	0.19
Bootle	Joe Benton	Lab	21,181	51.11
Boston and Skegness	Mark Simmonds	Con	12,426	28.78
Bosworth	David Tredinnick	Con	5,032	9.26
Bournemouth East	Tobias Ellwood	Con	7,728	17.52
Bournemouth West	Conor Burns	Con	5,583	13.38
Bracknell	Phillip Lee	Con	15,704	30.08
Bradford East	David Ward	Lib Dem	365	0.9
Bradford South	Gerry Sutcliffe	Lab	4,622	12.13
Bradford West	George Galloway	Respect	10,140	30.82
Braintree	Brooks Newmark	Con	16,121	32.73
Brent Central	Sarah Teather	Lib Dem	1,345	2.94
Brent North	Barry Gardiner	Lab	8,028	15.22
Brentford and Isleworth	Mary Macleod	Con	1,958	3.62
Brentwood and Ongar	Eric Pickles	Con	16,921	33.36
Bridgwater and West Somerset	Ian Liddell-Grainger	Con	9,249	16.95
Brigg and Goole	Andrew Percy	Con	5,147	11.71
Brighton Kemptown	Simon Kirby	Con	1,328	3.1
Brighton Pavilion	Caroline Lucas	Green	1,252	2.41
Bristol East	Kerry McCarthy	Lab	3,722	8.25
Bristol North West	Charlotte Leslie	Con	3,274	6.49
Bristol South	Dawn Primarolo	Lab	4,734	9.76
Bristol West	Stephen Williams	Lib Dem	11,366	20.49
Broadland	Keith Simpson	Con	7,292	13.83
Bromley and Chislehurst	Robert Neill	Con	13,900	31.5
Bromsgrove	Sajid Javid	Con	11,308	21.86
Broxbourne	Charles Walker	Con	18,804	41.1
Broxtowe	Anna Soubry	Con	389	0.74
Buckingham	John Bercow	Speaker	12,529	25.36
Burnley	Gordon Birtwistle	Lib Dem	1,818	4.33
Burton	Andrew Griffiths	Con	6,304	12.63
Bury North	David Nuttall	Con	2,243	4.98
Bury South	Ivan Lewis	Lab	3,292	6.8
Bury St Edmunds	David Ruffley	Con	12,380	21.06
Calder Valley	Craig Whittaker	Con	6,431	12.38
Camberwell and Peckham	Harriet Harman	Lab	17,187	36.62

			Majority	%
Camborne and Redruth	George Eustice	Con	66	0.16
Cambridge	Julian Huppert	Lib Dem	6,792	13.51
North East Cambridgeshire	Steve Barclay	Con	16,425	31.51
North West Cambridgeshire	Shailesh Vara	Con	16,677	28.54
South Cambridgeshire	Andrew Lansley	Con	7,838	13.25
South East Cambridgeshire	Jim Paice	Con	5,946	10.3
Cannock Chase	Aidan Burley	Con	3,195	7
Canterbury	Julian Brazier	Con	6,048	12.27
Carlisle	John Stevenson	Con	853	2.02
Carshalton and Wallington	Tom Brake	Lib Dem	5,260	11.42
Castle Point	Rebecca Harris	Con	7,632	16.92
Charnwood	Stephen Dorrell	Con	15,029	28.03
Chatham and Aylesford	Tracey Crouch	Con	6,069	13.84
Cheadle	Mark Hunter	Lib Dem	3,272	6.21
Chelmsford	Simon Burns	Con	5,110	9.35
Chelsea and Fulham	Greg Hands	Con	16,722	41.75
Cheltenham	Martin Horwood	Lib Dem	4,920	9.3
Chesham and Amersham	Cheryl Gillan	Con	16,710	31.8
City of Chester	Stephen Mosley	Con	2,583	5.51
Chesterfield	Toby Perkins	Lab	549	1.2
Chichester	Andrew Tyrie	Con	15,877	27.9
Chingford and Woodford Green	Iain Duncan Smith	Con	12,963	29.96
Chippenham	Duncan Hames	Lib Dem	2,470	4.71
Chipping Barnet	Theresa Villiers	Con	11,927	23.48
Chorley	Lindsay Hoyle	Lab	2,593	5.19
Christchurch	Christopher Chope	Con	15,410	31.13
Clacton	Douglas Carswell	Con	12,068	27.93
Cleethorpes	Martin Vickers	Con	4,298	9.53
Colchester	Bob Russell	Lib Dem	6,982	15.1
Colne Valley	Jason McCartney	Con	4,837	8.73
Congleton	Fiona Bruce	Con	7,063	13.88
Copeland	Jamie Reed	Lab	3,833	8.94
Corby	Andy Sawford	Lab/Co-op	7,791	21.78
North Cornwall	Dan Rogerson	Lib Dem	2,981	6.35
South East Cornwall	Sheryll Murray	Con	3,220	6.48
The Cotswolds	Geoffrey Clifton-Brown	Con	12,864	23.43
Coventry North East	Bob Ainsworth	Lab	11,775	27.03
Coventry North West	Geoffrey Robinson	Lab	6,288	13.43
Coventry South	James Cunningham	Lab	3,845	8.31
Crawley	Henry Smith	Con	5,928	12.45
Crewe and Nantwich	Edward Timpson	Con	6,046	11.82
Croydon Central	Gavin Barwell	Con	2,969	5.95
Croydon North	Steve Reed	Lab	11,761	47.65
Croydon South	Richard Ottaway	Con	15,818	28
Dagenham and Rainham	Jon Cruddas	Lab	2,630	5.92
Darlington	Jenny Chapman	Lab	3,388	7.89
Dartford	Gareth Johnson	Con	10,628	21.19
Daventry	Christopher Heaton-Harris	Con	19,188	36.99
Denton and Reddish	Andrew Gwynne	Lab	9,831	26
Derby North	Chris Williamson	Lab	613	1.36
Derby South	Margaret Beckett	Lab	6,122	14.78
Derbyshire Dales	Patrick McLoughlin	Con	13,866	29.58

			Majority	%
Mid Derbyshire	Pauline Latham	Con	11,292	23.8
North East Derbyshire	Natascha Engel	Lab	2,445	5.19
South Derbyshire	Heather Wheeler	Con	7,128	14.12
Devizes	Claire Perry	Con	13,005	28.03
Central Devon	Mel Stride	Con	9,230	17.11
East Devon	Hugo Swire	Con	9,114	17.09
North Devon	Nick Harvey	Lib Dem	5,821	11.32
South West Devon	Gary Streeter	Con	15,874	31.77
Dewsbury	Simon Reevell	Con	1,526	2.82
Don Valley	Caroline Flint	Lab	3,595	8.25
Doncaster Central	Rosie Winterton	Lab	6,229	14.88
Doncaster North	Ed Miliband	Lab	10,909	26.21
Mid Dorset and North Poole	Annette Brooke	Lib Dem	269	0.57
North Dorset	Robert Walter	Con	7,625	14.07
South Dorset	Richard Drax	Con	7,443	14.77
West Dorset	Oliver Letwin	Con	3,923	6.83
Dover	Charlie Elphicke	Con	5,274	10.45
Dudley North	Ian Austin	Lab	649	1.68
Dudley South	Chris Kelly	Con	3,856	10.08
Dulwich and West Norwood	Tessa Jowell	Lab	9,365	19.34
City of Durham	Roberta Blackman-Woods	Lab	3,067	6.62
North Durham	Kevan Jones	Lab	12,076	29.42
North West Durham	Patricia Glass	Lab	7,612	17.34
Ealing Central and Acton	Angie Bray	Con	3,716	7.84
Ealing North	Stephen Pound	Lab	9,301	19.39
Ealing Southall	Virendra Sharma	Lab	9,291	21.5
Easington	Grahame Morris	Lab	14,982	42.83
East Ham	Stephen Timms	Lab	27,826	54.67
Eastbourne	Stephen Lloyd	Lib Dem	3,435	6.58
Eastleigh	Mike Thornton	Lib Dem	1,771	4.25
Eddisbury	Stephen O'Brien	Con	13,255	29.12
Edmonton	Andy Love	Lab/Co-op	9,613	23.61
Ellesmere Port and Neston	Andrew Miller	Lab	4,331	9.78
Elmet and Rothwell	Alec Shelbrooke	Con	4,521	8.09
Eltham	Clive Efford	Lab	1,663	3.95
Enfield North	Nick de Bois	Con	1,692	3.79
Enfield Southgate	David Burrowes	Con	7,626	17.11
Epping Forest	Eleanor Laing	Con	15,131	32.39
Epsom and Ewell	Chris Grayling	Con	16,134	29.21
Erewash	Jessica Lee	Con	2,501	5.25
Erith and Thamesmead	Teresa Pearce	Lab	5,703	13.36
Esher and Walton	Dominic Raab	Con	18,593	34
Exeter	Ben Bradshaw	Lab	2,721	5.2
Fareham	Mark Hoban	Con	17,092	31.37
Faversham and Mid Kent	Hugh Robertson	Con	17,088	36.51
Feltham and Heston	Seema Malhotra	Lab	6,203	26.62
Filton and Bradley Stoke	Jack Lopresti	Con	6,914	14.3
Finchley and Golders Green	Mike Freer	Con	5,809	12.27
Folkestone and Hythe	Damian Collins	Con	10,122	19.14
Forest of Dean	Mark Harper	Con	11,064	22.66
Fylde	Mark Menzies	Con	13,185	30.12
Gainsborough	Edward Leigh	Con	10,559	21.39

			Majority	%
Garston and Halewood	Maria Eagle	Lab	16,877	39.24
Gateshead	Ian Mearns	Lab	12,549	32.73
Gedling	Vernon Coaker	Lab	1,859	3.85
Gillingham and Rainham	Rehman Chishti	Con	8,680	18.55
Gloucester	Richard Graham	Con	2,420	4.75
Gosport	Caroline Dinenage	Con	14,413	30.62
Grantham and Stamford	Nick Boles	Con	14,826	28.04
Gravesham	Adam Holloway	Con	9,312	19.66
Great Grimsby	Austin Mitchell	Lab	714	2.16
Great Yarmouth	Brandon Lewis	Con	4,276	9.9
Greenwich and Woolwich	Nick Raynsford	Lab	10,153	24.54
Guildford	Anne Milton	Con	7,782	13.98
Hackney North and Stoke Newington	Diane Abbott	Lab	14,461	30.89
Hackney South and Shoreditch	Meg Hillier	Lab/Co-op	14,288	33.01
Halesowen and Rowley Regis	James Morris	Con	2,023	4.59
Halifax	Linda Riordan	Lab/Co-op	1,472	3.36
Haltemprice and Howden	David Davis	Con	11,602	23.76
Halton	Derek Twigg	Lab	15,504	37.4
Hammersmith	Andy Slaughter	Lab	3,549	7.45
East Hampshire	Damian Hinds	Con	13,497	26.26
North East Hampshire	James Arbuthnot	Con	18,597	35.06
North West Hampshire	George Young	Con	18,583	34.81
Hampstead and Kilburn	Glenda Jackson	Lab	42	0.08
Harborough	Edward Garnier	Con	9,797	17.8
Harlow	Robert Halfon	Con	4,925	11.19
Harrogate and Knaresborough	Andrew Jones	Con	1,039	1.94
Harrow East	Bob Blackman	Con	3,403	7.05
Harrow West	Gareth Thomas	Lab/Co-op	3,143	6.78
Hartlepool	Iain Wright	Lab	5,509	14.35
Harwich and North Essex	Bernard Jenkin	Con	11,447	23.33
Hastings and Rye	Amber Rudd	Con	1,993	3.99
Havant	David Willetts	Con	12,160	27.61
Hayes and Harlington	John McDonnell	Lab	10,824	25.22
Hazel Grove	Andrew Stunell	Lib Dem	6,371	15.14
Hemel Hempstead	Mike Penning	Con	13,406	27.07
Hemsworth	Jon Trickett	Lab	9,844	22.4
Hendon	Matthew Offord	Con	106	0.23
Henley	John Howell	Con	16,588	30.96
Hereford and South Herefordshire	Jesse Norman	Con	2,481	5.12
North Herefordshire	Bill Wiggin	Con	9,887	20.75
Hertford and Stortford	Mark Prisk	Con	15,437	27.84
North East Hertfordshire	Oliver Heald	Con	15,194	30.13
South West Hertfordshire	David Gauke	Con	14,920	26.23
Hertsmere	James Clappison	Con	17,605	37.13
Hexham	Guy Opperman	Con	5,788	13.29
Heywood and Middleton	Jim Dobbin	Lab/Co-op	5,971	12.91
High Peak	Andrew Bingham	Con	4,677	9.27
Hitchin and Harpenden	Peter Lilley	Con	15,271	27.85
Holborn and St Pancras	Frank Dobson	Lab	9,942	18.09
Hornchurch and Upminster	Angela Watkinson	Con	16,371	30.57
Hornsey and Wood Green	Lynne Featherstone	Lib Dem	6,875	12.44
Horsham	Francis Maude	Con	11,460	20.5

			Majority	%
Houghton and Sunderland South	Bridget Phillipson	Lab	10,990	28.73
Hove	Mike Weatherley	Con	1,868	3.74
Huddersfield	Barry Sheerman	Lab/Co-op	4,472	10.99
Kingston upon Hull East	Karl Turner	Lab	8,597	25.09
Kingston upon Hull North	Diana Johnson	Lab	641	1.92
Kingston upon Hull West and Hessle	Alan Johnson	Lab	5,742	18.19
Huntingdon	Jonathan Djanogly	Con	10,819	19.89
Hyndburn	Graham Jones	Lab	3,090	7.2
Ilford North	Lee Scott	Con	5,404	11.45
Ilford South	Mike Gapes	Lab/Co-op	11,287	21.9
Ipswich	Ben Gummer	Con	2,079	4.42
Isle of Wight	Andrew Turner	Con	10,527	14.96
Islington North	Jeremy Corbyn	Lab	12,401	27.75
Islington South and Finsbury	Emily Thornberry	Lab	3,569	8.16
Jarrow	Stephen Hepburn	Lab	12,908	33.19
Keighley	Kris Hopkins	Con	2,940	6.13
Kenilworth and Southam	Jeremy Wright	Con	12,552	25.88
Kensington	Malcolm Rifkind	Con	8,616	24.34
Kettering	Philip Hollobone	Con	9,094	19.19
Kingston and Surbiton	Edward Davey	Lib Dem	7,560	13.2
Kingswood	Chris Skidmore	Con	2,445	5.1
Knowsley	George Howarth	Lab	25,686	57.3
West Lancashire	Rosie Cooper	Lab	4,343	8.94
Lancaster and Fleetwood	Eric Ollerenshaw	Con	333	0.78
Leeds Central	Hilary Benn	Lab	10,645	28.35
Leeds East	George Mudie	Lab	10,293	27.15
Leeds North East	Fabian Hamilton	Lab	4,545	9.54
Leeds North West	Greg Mulholland	Lib Dem	9,103	20.88
Leeds West	Rachel Reeves	Lab	7,016	18.05
Leicester East	Keith Vaz	Lab	14,082	29.26
Leicester South	Jon Ashworth	Lab	12,078	34.8
Leicester West	Liz Kendall	Lab	4,017	11.19
North West Leicestershire	Andrew Bridgen	Con	7,511	14.44
South Leicestershire	Andrew Robathan	Con	15,524	28.4
Leigh	Andy Burnham	Lab	15,011	31.61
Lewes	Norman Baker	Lib Dem	7,647	15.25
Lewisham Deptford	Joan Ruddock	Lab	12,499	30.08
Lewisham East	Heidi Alexander	Lab	6,216	14.83
Lewisham West and Penge	Jim Dowd	Lab	5,828	12.88
Leyton and Wanstead	John Cryer	Lab	6,416	15.88
Lichfield	Michael Fabricant	Con	17,683	34.23
Lincoln	Karl McCartney	Con	1,058	2.31
Liverpool Riverside	Louise Ellman	Lab/Co-op	14,173	36.39
Liverpool Walton	Steve Rotheram	Lab	19,818	57.45
Liverpool Wavertree	Luciana Berger	Lab/Co-op	7,167	18.84
Liverpool West Derby	Stephen Twigg	Lab/Co-op	18,467	51.36
Cities of London and Westminster	Mark Field	Con	11,076	29.8
Loughborough	Nicky Morgan	Con	3,744	7.07
Louth and Horncastle	Peter Tapsell	Con	13,871	27.42
Ludlow	Philip Dunne	Con	9,749	19.98
Luton North	Kelvin Hopkins	Lab	7,520	17.44
Luton South	Gavin Shuker	Lab/Co-op	2,329	5.5

			Majority	%
Macclesfield	David Rutley	Con	11,959	23.85
Maidenhead	Theresa May	Con	16,769	31.17
Maidstone and The Weald	Helen Grant	Con	5,889	12.02
Makerfield	Yvonne Fovargue	Lab	12,490	28.43
Maldon	John Whittingdale	Con	19,407	40.47
Manchester Central	Lucy Powell	Lab/Co-op	9,936	58.82
Manchester Gorton	Gerald Kaufman	Lab	6,703	17.4
Manchester Withington	John Leech	Lib Dem	1,850	4.1
Mansfield	Alan Meale	Lab	6,012	12.4
Meon Valley	George Hollingbery	Con	12,125	23.61
Meriden	Caroline Spelman	Con	16,253	31.1
Middlesbrough	Andy McDonald	Lab	8,211	48.52
Middlesbrough South and East Cleveland	Tom Blenkinsop	Lab	1,677	3.62
Milton Keynes North	Mark Lancaster	Con	8,961	16.61
Milton Keynes South	Iain Stewart	Con	5,201	9.39
Mitcham and Morden	Siobhain McDonagh	Lab	13,666	31.07
Mole Valley	Paul Beresford	Con	15,653	28.75
Morecambe and Lunesdale	David Morris	Con	866	1.99
Morley and Outwood	Ed Balls	Lab/Co-op	1,101	2.25
New Forest East	Julian Lewis	Con	11,307	22.56
New Forest West	Desmond Swayne	Con	16,896	35.47
Newark	Patrick Mercer	Ind*	16,152	31.46
Newbury	Richard Benyon	Con	12,248	20.88
Newcastle-under-Lyme	Paul Farrelly	Lab	1,552	3.58
Newcastle upon Tyne Central	Chi Onwurah	Lab	7,466	21.76
Newcastle upon Tyne East	Nick Brown	Lab	4,453	11.73
Newcastle upon Tyne North	Catherine McKinnell	Lab	3,414	7.74
Newton Abbot	Anne Marie Morris	Con	523	1.08
Mid Norfolk	George Freeman	Con	13,856	27.26
North Norfolk	Norman Lamb	Lib Dem	11,626	23.37
North West Norfolk	Henry Bellingham	Con	14,810	30.94
South Norfolk	Richard Bacon	Con	10,940	19.86
South West Norfolk	Elizabeth Truss	Con	13,140	26.7
Normanton, Pontefract and Castleford	Yvette Cooper	Lab	10,979	23.69
Northampton North	Michael Ellis	Con	1,936	4.8
Northampton South	Brian Binley	Con	6,004	15.37
South Northamptonshire	Andrea Leadsom	Con	20,478	34.01
Norwich North	Chloe Smith	Con	3,901	9.15
Norwich South	Simon Wright	Lib Dem	310	0.65
Nottingham East	Chris Leslie	Lab/Co-op	6,969	20.96
Nottingham North	Graham Allen	Lab	8,138	23.68
Nottingham South	Lilian Greenwood	Lab	1,772	4.34
Nuneaton	Marcus Jones	Con	2,069	4.62
Oldham East and Saddleworth	Debbie Abrahams	Lab	3,558	10.17
Oldham West and Royton	Michael Meacher	Lab	9,352	21.67
Orpington	Jo Johnson	Con	17,200	35.09
Oxford East	Andrew Smith	Lab	4,581	8.84
Oxford West and Abingdon	Nicola Blackwood	Con	176	0.31
Pendle	Andrew Stephenson	Con	3,585	7.93
Penistone and Stocksbridge	Angela Smith	Lab	3,049	6.54
Penrith and The Border	Rory Stewart	Con	11,241	24.89
Peterborough	Stewart Jackson	Con	4,861	10.77

* Elected as Conservative

			Majority	%
Plymouth, Moor View	Alison Seabeck	Lab	1,588	3.82
Plymouth, Sutton and Devonport	Oliver Colvile	Con	1,149	2.61
Poole	Robert Syms	Con	7,541	15.86
Poplar and Limehouse	Jim Fitzpatrick	Lab	6,030	12.72
Portsmouth North	Penny Mordaunt	Con	7,289	16.46
Portsmouth South	Mike Hancock	Ind*	5,200	12.56
Preston	Mark Hendrick	Lab/Co-op	7,733	23.69
Pudsey	Stuart Andrew	Con	1,659	3.37
Putney	Justine Greening	Con	10,053	24.59
Rayleigh and Wickford	Mark Francois	Con	22,338	42.58
Reading East	Robert Wilson	Con	7,605	15.18
Reading West	Alok Sharma	Con	6,004	12.61
Redcar	Ian Swales	Lib Dem	5,214	12.41
Redditch	Karen Lumley	Con	5,821	13.2
Reigate	Crispin Blunt	Con	13,591	27.14
South Ribble	Lorraine Fullbrook	Con	5,554	10.78
Ribble Valley	Nigel Evans	Ind†	14,769	28.21
Richmond Park	Zac Goldsmith	Con	4,091	6.89
Richmond (Yorkshire)	William Hague	Con	23,336	43.58
Rochdale	Simon Danczuk	Lab	889	1.93
Rochester and Strood	Mark Reckless	Con	9,953	20.72
Rochford and Southend East	James Duddridge	Con	11,050	26.47
Romford	Andrew Rosindell	Con	16,954	36.34
Romsey and Southampton North	Caroline Nokes	Con	4,156	8.48
Rossendale and Darwen	Jake Berry	Con	4,493	9.5
Rother Valley	Kevin Barron	Lab	5,866	12.52
Rotherham	Sarah Champion	Lab	5,318	24.74
Rugby	Mark Pawsey	Con	6,000	12.62
Ruislip, Northwood and Pinner	Nick Hurd	Con	19,060	37.85
Runnymede and Weybridge	Philip Hammond	Con	16,509	34.22
Rushcliffe	Kenneth Clarke	Con	15,811	29.37
Rutland and Melton	Alan Duncan	Con	14,000	25.3
Saffron Walden	Alan Haselhurst	Con	15,242	27.97
St Albans	Anne Main	Con	2,305	4.35
St Austell and Newquay	Steve Gilbert	Lib Dem	1,312	2.77
St Helens North	David Watts	Lab	13,101	29.26
St Helens South and Whiston	Shaun Woodward	Lab	14,122	30.5
St Ives	Andrew George	Lib Dem	1,719	3.74
Salford and Eccles	Hazel Blears	Lab	5,725	13.73
Salisbury	John Glen	Con	5,966	12.29
Scarborough and Whitby	Robert Goodwill	Con	8,130	16.48
Scunthorpe	Nic Dakin	Lab	2,549	6.88
Sedgefield	Phil Wilson	Lab	8,696	21.58
Sefton Central	Bill Esterson	Lab	3,862	7.94
Selby and Ainsty	Nigel Adams	Con	12,265	23.68
Sevenoaks	Michael Fallon	Con	17,515	35.39
Sheffield, Brightside and Hillsborough	David Blunkett	Lab	13,632	34.89
Sheffield Central	Paul Blomfield	Lab	165	0.4
Sheffield, Hallam	Nick Clegg	Lib Dem	15,284	29.81
Sheffield Heeley	Meg Munn	Lab/Co-op	5,807	14.17
Sheffield South East	Clive Betts	Lab	10,505	25.28
Sherwood	Mark Spencer	Con	214	0.44

* elected as Liberal Democrat   † elected as Conservative

			Majority	%
Shipley	Philip Davies	Con	9,944	20.05
Shrewsbury and Atcham	Daniel Kawczynski	Con	7,944	14.96
North Shropshire	Owen Paterson	Con	15,828	30.46
Sittingbourne and Sheppey	Gordon Henderson	Con	12,383	25.44
Skipton and Ripon	Julian Smith	Con	9,950	18.13
Sleaford and North Hykeham	Stephen Phillips	Con	19,905	33.39
Slough	Fiona Mactaggart	Lab	5,523	11.52
Solihull	Lorely Burt	Lib Dem	175	0.32
North Somerset	Liam Fox	Con	7,862	13.54
North East Somerset	Jacob Rees-Mogg	Con	4,914	9.58
Somerton and Frome	David Heath	Lib Dem	1,817	2.99
South Holland and The Deepings	John Hayes	Con	21,880	43.55
South Shields	Emma Lewell-Buck	Lab	6,505	26.25
Southampton Itchen	John Denham	Lab	192	0.43
Southampton Test	Alan Whitehead	Lab	2,413	5.45
Southend West	David Amess	Con	7,270	16.65
Southport	John Pugh	Lib Dem	6,024	13.71
Spelthorne	Kwasi Kwarteng	Con	10,019	21.14
Stafford	Jeremy Lefroy	Con	5,460	10.85
Staffordshire Moorlands	Karen Bradley	Con	6,689	15.24
South Staffordshire	Gavin Williamson	Con	16,590	32.85
Stalybridge and Hyde	Jonathan Reynolds	Lab/Co-op	2,744	6.68
Stevenage	Stephen McPartland	Con	3,578	8
Stockport	Ann Coffey	Lab	6,784	17.3
Stockton North	Alex Cunningham	Lab	6,676	16.89
Stockton South	James Wharton	Con	332	0.66
Stoke-on-Trent Central	Tristram Hunt	Lab	5,565	17.09
Stoke-on-Trent North	Joan Walley	Lab	8,235	20.43
Stoke-on-Trent South	Robert Flello	Lab	4,130	10.33
Stone	William Cash	Con	13,292	28.1
Stourbridge	Margot James	Con	5,164	10.91
Stratford-on-Avon	Nadhim Zahawi	Con	11,346	22.41
Streatham	Chuka Umunna	Lab	3,259	6.93
Stretford and Urmston	Kate Green	Lab	8,935	19.82
Stroud	Neil Carmichael	Con	1,299	2.24
Central Suffolk and North Ipswich	Daniel Poulter	Con	13,786	25.76
Suffolk Coastal	Therese Coffey	Con	9,128	16.57
South Suffolk	Tim Yeo	Con	8,689	16.87
West Suffolk	Matthew Hancock	Con	13,050	27.09
Sunderland Central	Julie Elliott	Lab	6,725	15.76
East Surrey	Sam Gyimah	Con	16,874	30.8
Surrey Heath	Michael Gove	Con	17,289	31.76
South West Surrey	Jeremy Hunt	Con	16,318	28.45
Mid Sussex	Nicholas Soames	Con	7,402	13.23
Sutton and Cheam	Paul Burstow	Lib Dem	1,608	3.3
Sutton Coldfield	Andrew Mitchell	Con	17,005	33.55
North Swindon	Justin Tomlinson	Con	7,060	13.99
South Swindon	Robert Buckland	Con	3,544	7.47
Tamworth	Christopher Pincher	Con	6,090	13.1
Tatton	George Osborne	Con	14,487	31.97
Taunton Deane	Jeremy Browne	Lib Dem	3,993	6.86
Telford	David Wright	Lab	978	2.36

			Majority	%
Tewkesbury	Laurence Robertson	Con	6,310	11.67
North Thanet	Roger Gale	Con	13,528	31.15
South Thanet	Laura Sandys	Con	7,617	16.55
Thirsk and Malton	Anne McIntosh	Con	11,281	29.52
Thornbury and Yate	Steve Webb	Lib Dem	7,116	14.73
Thurrock	Jackie Doyle-Price	Con	92	0.2
Tiverton and Honiton	Neil Parish	Con	9,320	16.95
Tonbridge and Malling	John Stanley	Con	18,178	35.37
Tooting	Sadiq Khan	Lab	2,524	4.97
Torbay	Adrian Sanders	Lib Dem	4,078	8.28
Torridge and West Devon	Geoffrey Cox	Con	2,957	5.3
Totnes	Sarah Wollaston	Con	4,927	10.28
Tottenham	David Lammy	Lab	16,931	41.25
Truro and Falmouth	Sarah Newton	Con	435	0.89
Tunbridge Wells	Greg Clark	Con	15,576	30.89
Twickenham	Vincent Cable	Lib Dem	12,140	20.29
Tynemouth	Alan Campbell	Lab	5,739	10.88
North Tyneside	Mary Glindon	Lab	12,884	27.69
Uxbridge and South Ruislip	John Randall	Con	11,216	24.8
Vauxhall	Kate Hoey	Lab	10,651	24.51
Wakefield	Mary Creagh	Lab	1,613	3.62
Wallasey	Angela Eagle	Lab	8,507	20.35
Walsall North	David Winnick	Lab	990	2.73
Walsall South	Valerie Vaz	Lab	1,755	4.27
Walthamstow	Stella Creasy	Lab/Co-op	9,478	22.95
Wansbeck	Ian Lavery	Lab	7,031	18.34
Wantage	Ed Vaizey	Con	13,547	23.99
Warley	John Spellar	Lab	10,756	27.91
Warrington North	Helen Jones	Lab	6,771	15.26
Warrington South	David Mowat	Con	1,553	2.82
Warwick and Leamington	Chris White	Con	3,513	7.15
North Warwickshire	Dan Byles	Con	54	0.11
Washington and Sunderland West	Sharon Hodgson	Lab	11,458	30.53
Watford	Richard Harrington	Con	1,425	2.57
Waveney	Peter Aldous	Con	769	1.5
Wealden	Charles Hendry	Con	17,179	31.21
Weaver Vale	Graham Evans	Con	991	2.25
Wellingborough	Peter Bone	Con	11,787	22.78
Wells	Tessa Munt	Lib Dem	800	1.43
Welwyn Hatfield	Grant Shapps	Con	17,423	35.5
Wentworth and Dearne	John Healey	Lab	13,920	33
West Bromwich East	Tom Watson	Lab	6,696	17.58
West Bromwich West	Adrian Bailey	Lab/Co-op	5,651	15.56
West Ham	Lyn Brown	Lab	22,534	47.48
Westminster North	Karen Buck	Lab	2,126	5.33
Westmorland and Lonsdale	Tim Farron	Lib Dem	12,264	23.78
Weston-Super-Mare	John Penrose	Con	2,691	5.1
Wigan	Lisa Nandy	Lab	10,487	23.67
North Wiltshire	James Gray	Con	7,483	15.34
South West Wiltshire	Andrew Murrison	Con	10,367	21.11
Wimbledon	Stephen Hammond	Con	11,408	24
Winchester	Steve Brine	Con	3,048	5.44

			Majority	%
Windsor	Adam Afriyie	Con	19,054	38.36
Wirral South	Alison McGovern	Lab	531	1.33
Wirral West	Esther McVey	Con	2,436	6.17
Witham	Priti Patel	Con	15,196	32.38
Witney	David Cameron	Con	22,740	39.28
Woking	Jonathan Lord	Con	6,807	12.86
Wokingham	John Redwood	Con	13,492	24.7
Wolverhampton North East	Emma Reynolds	Lab	2,484	7.09
Wolverhampton South East	Pat McFadden	Lab	6,593	18.86
Wolverhampton South West	Paul Uppal	Con	691	1.71
Worcester	Robin Walker	Con	2,982	6.08
Mid Worcestershire	Peter Luff	Con	15,864	31.11
West Worcestershire	Harriett Baldwin	Con	6,754	12.46
Workington	Tony Cunningham	Lab	4,575	11.63
Worsley and Eccles South	Barbara Keeley	Lab	4,337	10.35
East Worthing and Shoreham	Tim Loughton	Con	11,105	22.89
Worthing West	Peter Bottomley	Con	11,729	23.82
The Wrekin	Mark Pritchard	Con	9,450	20.51
Wycombe	Steve Baker	Con	9,560	19.8
Wyre and Preston North	Ben Wallace	Con	15,844	30.81
Wyre Forest	Mark Garnier	Con	2,643	5.18
Wythenshawe and Sale East	Paul Goggins	Lab	7,575	18.53
Yeovil	David Laws	Lib Dem	13,036	22.77
York Central	Hugh Bayley	Lab	6,451	13.86
York Outer	Julian Sturdy	Con	3,688	6.91
East Yorkshire	Greg Knight	Con	13,486	26.27

Scotland

			Majority	%
Aberdeen North	Frank Doran	Lab	8,361	22.13
Aberdeen South	Anne Begg	Lab	3,506	8.14
West Aberdeenshire and Kincardine	Robert Smith	Lib Dem	3,684	8.14
Airdrie and Shotts	Pamela Nash	Lab	12,408	34.56
Angus	Mike Weir	SNP	3,282	8.63
Argyll and Bute	Alan Reid	Lib Dem	3,431	7.58
Ayr, Carrick and Cumnock	Sandra Osborne	Lab	9,911	21.56
Central Ayrshire	Brian Donohoe	Lab	12,007	27.29
North Ayrshire and Arran	Katy Clark	Lab	9,895	21.4
Banff and Buchan	Eilidh Whiteford	SNP	4,027	10.46
Berwickshire, Roxburgh and Selkirk	Michael Moore	Lib Dem	5,675	11.56
Caithness, Sutherland and Easter Ross	John Thurso	Lib Dem	4,826	16.73
Coatbridge, Chryston and Bellshill	Tom Clarke	Lab	20,714	49.6
Cumbernauld, Kilsyth and Kirkintilloch East	Gregg McClymont	Lab	13,755	33.36
Dumfries and Galloway	Russell Brown	Lab	7,449	14.25
Dumfriesshire, Clydesdale and Tweeddale	David Mundell	Con	4,194	9.12
East Dunbartonshire	Jo Swinson	Lib Dem	2,184	4.55
West Dunbartonshire	Gemma Doyle	Lab/Co-op	17,408	41.1
Dundee East	Stewart Hosie	SNP	1,821	4.48
Dundee West	Jim McGovern	Lab	7,278	19.56
Dunfermline and West Fife	Thomas Docherty	Lab	5,470	11.16

			Majority	%
East Kilbride, Strathaven and Lesmahagow	Michael McCann	Lab	14,503	28.42
Edinburgh East	Sheila Gilmore	Lab	9,181	22.99
Edinburgh North and Leith	Mark Lazarowicz	Lab/Co-op	1,724	3.63
Edinburgh South	Ian Murray	Lab	316	0.72
Edinburgh South West	Alistair Darling	Lab	8,447	18.54
Edinburgh West	Mike Crockart	Lib Dem	3,803	8.17
Falkirk	Eric Joyce	Ind*	7,843	15.42
North East Fife	Menzies Campbell	Lib Dem	9,048	22.53
Glasgow Central	Anas Sarwar	Lab	10,551	34.41
Glasgow East	Margaret Curran	Lab	11,840	36.75
Glasgow North	Ann McKechin	Lab	3,898	13.13
Glasgow North East	Willie Bain	Lab	15,942	54.05
Glasgow North West	John Robertson	Lab	13,611	38.16
Glasgow South	Tom Harris	Lab	12,658	31.51
Glasgow South West	Ian Davidson	Lab/Co-op	14,671	46.04
Glenrothes	Lindsay Roy	Lab	16,448	40.54
Gordon	Malcolm Bruce	Lib Dem	6,748	13.82
Inverclyde	Iain McKenzie	Lab	5,838	20.77
Inverness, Nairn, Badenoch and Strathspey	Danny Alexander	Lib Dem	8,765	18.59
Kilmarnock and Loudoun	Cathy Jamieson	Lab/Co-op	12,378	26.53
Kirkcaldy and Cowdenbeath	Gordon Brown	Lab	23,009	50.17
Lanark and Hamilton East	Jim Hood	Lab	13,478	28.9
Linlithgow and East Falkirk	Michael Connarty	Lab	12,553	24.33
Livingston	Graeme Morrice	Lab	10,791	22.5
East Lothian	Fiona O'Donnell	Lab	12,258	24.9
Midlothian	David Hamilton	Lab	10,349	26.34
Moray	Angus Robertson	SNP	5,590	13.61
Motherwell and Wishaw	Frank Roy	Lab	16,806	42.84
Na h-Eileanan An Iar	Angus MacNeil	SNP	1,885	12.79
Ochil and South Perthshire	Gordon Banks	Lab	5,187	10.27
Orkney and Shetland	Alistair Carmichael	Lib Dem	9,928	51.16
Paisley and Renfrewshire North	Jim Sheridan	Lab	15,280	34.9
Paisley and Renfrewshire South	Douglas Alexander	Lab	16,614	41.44
Perth and North Perthshire	Peter Wishart	SNP	4,379	9.06
East Renfrewshire	Jim Murphy	Lab	10,420	20.33
Ross, Skye and Lochaber	Charles Kennedy	Lib Dem	13,070	37.46
Rutherglen and Hamilton West	Tom Greatrex	Lab/Co-op	21,002	44.62
Stirling	Anne McGuire	Lab	8,304	17.71

* elected as Labour

Wales

			Majority	%
Aberavon	Hywel Francis	Lab	11,039	35.61
Aberconwy	Guto Bebb	Con	3,398	11.3
Alyn and Deeside	Mark Tami	Lab	2,919	7.3
Arfon	Hywel Williams	PlC	1,455	5.56
Blaenau Gwent	Nick Smith	Lab	10,516	32.39
Brecon and Radnorshire	Roger Williams	Lib Dem	3,747	9.63
Bridgend	Madeleine Moon	Lab	2,263	5.89
Caerphilly	Wayne David	Lab	10,755	27.73
Cardiff Central	Jenny Willott	Lib Dem	4,576	12.62

			Majority	%
Cardiff North	Jonathan Evans	Con	194	0.41
Cardiff South and Penarth	Stephen Doughty	Lab/Co-op	5,334	27.25
Cardiff West	Kevin Brennan	Lab	4,751	11.58
Carmarthen East and Dinefwr	Jonathan Edwards	PlC	3,481	9.14
Carmarthen West and South Pembrokeshire	Simon Hart	Con	3,423	8.44
Ceredigion	Mark Williams	Lib Dem	8,324	21.72
Clwyd South	Susan Elan Jones	Lab	2,834	8.16
Vale of Clwyd	Chris Ruane	Lab	2,509	7.05
Clwyd West	David Jones	Con	6,419	16.81
Cynon Valley	Ann Clwyd	Lab	9,617	32.11
Delyn	David Hanson	Lab	2,272	6.13
Dwyfor Meirionnydd	Elfyn Llwyd	PlC	6,367	21.98
Vale of Glamorgan	Alun Cairns	Con	4,307	8.83
Gower	Martin Caton	Lab	2,683	6.43
Islwyn	Chris Evans	Lab/Co-op	12,215	35.14
Llanelli	Nia Griffith	Lab	4,701	12.53
Merthyr Tydfil and Rhymney	Dai Havard	Lab	4,056	12.61
Monmouth	David Davies	Con	10,425	22.37
Montgomeryshire	Glyn Davies	Con	1,184	3.5
Neath	Peter Hain	Lab	9,775	26.28
Newport East	Jessica Morden	Lab	1,650	4.78
Newport West	Paul Flynn	Lab	3,544	8.91
Ogmore	Huw Irranca-Davies	Lab	13,246	38.15
Pontypridd	Owen Smith	Lab	2,785	7.58
Preseli Pembrokeshire	Stephen Crabb	Con	4,605	11.6
Rhondda	Chris Bryant	Lab	11,553	37.1
Swansea East	Siân James	Lab	10,838	33.1
Swansea West	Geraint Davies	Lab/Co-op	504	1.41
Torfaen	Paul Murphy	Lab	9,306	24.69
Wrexham	Ian Lucas	Lab	3,658	11.08
Ynys Môn	Albert Owen	Lab	2,461	7.13

Northern Ireland

			Majority	%
East Antrim	Sammy Wilson	DUP	6,770	22.1
North Antrim	Ian Paisley	DUP	12,558	29.49
South Antrim	William McCrea	DUP	1,183	3.46
Belfast East	Naomi Long	All	1,533	4.43
Belfast North	Nigel Dodds	DUP	2,224	5.97
Belfast South	Alasdair McDonnell	SDLP	5,926	17.25
Belfast West	Paul Maskey	Sinn Féin	13,123	56.94
North Down	Sylvia Hermon	Ind	14,364	42.82
South Down	Margaret Ritchie	SDLP	8,412	19.64
Fermanagh and South Tyrone	Michelle Gildernew	Sinn Féin	4	0.01
Foyle	Mark Durkan	SDLP	4,824	12.63
Lagan Valley	Jeffrey Donaldson	DUP	10,486	28.59
East Londonderry	Gregory Campbell	DUP	5,355	15.26
Newry and Armagh	Conor Murphy	Sinn Féin	8,331	18.55
Strangford	Jim Shannon	DUP	5,876	18.02
West Tyrone	Pat Doherty	Sinn Féin	10,685	28.39
Mid Ulster	Francie Molloy	Sinn Féin	4,681	12.51
Upper Bann	David Simpson	DUP	3,361	8.06

Most Vulnerable Constituencies

Constituencies have been classed as vulnerable if their majority is less than 15 per cent following the 2010 general election or any subsequent by-elections.

				Majority	%
1	Fermanagh and South Tyrone	Michelle Gildernew	Sinn Féin	4	0.01
2	Hampstead and Kilburn	Glenda Jackson	Lab	42	0.08
3	North Warwickshire	Dan Byles	Con	54	0.11
4	Camborne and Redruth	George Eustice	Con	66	0.16
5	Bolton West	Julie Hilling	Lab	92	0.19
6	Thurrock	Jackie Doyle-Price	Con	92	0.2
7	Hendon	Matthew Offord	Con	106	0.23
8	Oxford West and Abingdon	Nicola Blackwood	Con	176	0.31
9	Solihull	Lorely Burt	Lib Dem	175	0.32
10	Ashfield	Gloria De Piero	Lab	192	0.4
11	Sheffield Central	Paul Blomfield	Lab	165	0.4
12	Cardiff North	Jonathan Evans	Con	194	0.41
13	Southampton Itchen	John Denham	Lab	192	0.43
14	Sherwood	Mark Spencer	Con	214	0.44
15	Mid Dorset and North Poole	Annette Brooke	Lib Dem	269	0.57
16	Norwich South	Simon Wright	Lib Dem	310	0.65
17	Stockton South	James Wharton	Con	332	0.66
18	Edinburgh South	Ian Murray	Lab	316	0.72
19	Broxtowe	Anna Soubry	Con	389	0.74
20	Lancaster and Fleetwood	Eric Ollerenshaw	Con	333	0.78
21	Truro and Falmouth	Sarah Newton	Con	435	0.89
22	Bradford East	David Ward	Lib Dem	365	0.9
23	Newton Abbot	Anne Marie Morris	Con	523	1.08
24	Amber Valley	Nigel Mills	Con	536	1.16
25	Chesterfield	Toby Perkins	Lab	549	1.2
26	Wirral South	Alison McGovern	Lab	531	1.33
27	Derby North	Chris Williamson	Lab	613	1.36
28	Swansea West	Geraint Davies	Lab/Co-op	504	1.41
29	Wells	Tessa Munt	Lib Dem	800	1.43
30	Waveney	Peter Aldous	Con	769	1.5
31	Dudley North	Ian Austin	Lab	649	1.68
32	Wolverhampton South West	Paul Uppal	Con	691	1.71
33	Kingston upon Hull North	Diana Johnson	Lab	641	1.92
34	Rochdale	Simon Danczuk	Lab	889	1.93
35	Harrogate and Knaresborough	Andrew Jones	Con	1,039	1.94
36	Morecambe and Lunesdale	David Morris	Con	866	1.99
37	Carlisle	John Stevenson	Con	853	2.02
38	Great Grimsby	Austin Mitchell	Lab	714	2.16
39	Stroud	Neil Carmichael	Con	1,299	2.24
40	Weaver Vale	Graham Evans	Con	991	2.25
41	Morley and Outwood	Ed Balls	Lab/Co-op	1,101	2.25
42	Lincoln	Karl McCartney	Con	1,058	2.31
43	Telford	David Wright	Lab	978	2.36
44	Brighton Pavilion	Caroline Lucas	Green	1,252	2.41
45	Watford	Richard Harrington	Con	1,425	2.57
46	Plymouth, Sutton and Devonport	Oliver Colvile	Con	1,149	2.61
47	Walsall North	David Winnick	Lab	990	2.73
48	St Austell and Newquay	Steve Gilbert	Lib Dem	1,312	2.77
49	Dewsbury	Simon Reevell	Con	1,526	2.82

				Majority	%
50	Warrington South	David Mowat	Con	1,553	2.82
51	Brent Central	Sarah Teather	Lib Dem	1,345	2.94
52	Somerton and Frome	David Heath	Lib Dem	1,817	2.99
53	Bedford	Richard Fuller	Con	1,353	2.99
54	Birmingham, Edgbaston	Gisela Stuart	Lab	1,274	3.06
55	Brighton Kemptown	Simon Kirby	Con	1,328	3.1
56	Sutton and Cheam	Paul Burstow	Lib Dem	1,608	3.3
57	Halifax	Linda Riordan	Lab/Co-op	1,472	3.36
58	Pudsey	Stuart Andrew	Con	1,659	3.37
59	South Antrim	William McCrea	DUP	1,183	3.46
60	Montgomeryshire	Glyn Davies	Con	1,184	3.5
61	Newcastle-under-Lyme	Paul Farrelly	Lab	1,552	3.58
62	Middlesbrough South and East Cleveland	Tom Blenkinsop	Lab	1,677	3.62
63	Brentford and Isleworth	Mary Macleod	Con	1,958	3.62
64	Wakefield	Mary Creagh	Lab	1,613	3.62
65	Edinburgh North and Leith	Mark Lazarowicz	Lab/Co-op	1,724	3.63
66	St Ives	Andrew George	Lib Dem	1,719	3.74
67	Hove	Mike Weatherley	Con	1,868	3.74
68	Enfield North	Nick de Bois	Con	1,692	3.79
69	Plymouth, Moor View	Alison Seabeck	Lab	1,588	3.82
70	Gedling	Vernon Coaker	Lab	1,859	3.85
71	Eltham	Clive Efford	Lab	1,663	3.95
72	Hastings and Rye	Amber Rudd	Con	1,993	3.99
73	Manchester Withington	John Leech	Lib Dem	1,850	4.1
74	Eastleigh	Mike Thornton	Lib Dem	1,771	4.25
75	Walsall South	Valerie Vaz	Lab	1,755	4.27
76	Burnley	Gordon Birtwistle	Lib Dem	1,818	4.33
77	Nottingham South	Lilian Greenwood	Lab	1,772	4.34
78	St Albans	Anne Main	Con	2,305	4.35
79	Ipswich	Ben Gummer	Con	2,079	4.42
80	Belfast East	Naomi Long	All	1,533	4.43
81	Dundee East	Stewart Hosie	SNP	1,821	4.48
82	East Dunbartonshire	Jo Swinson	Lib Dem	2,184	4.55
83	Halesowen and Rowley Regis	James Morris	Con	2,023	4.59
84	Nuneaton	Marcus Jones	Con	2,069	4.62
85	Chippenham	Duncan Hames	Lib Dem	2,470	4.71
86	Gloucester	Richard Graham	Con	2,420	4.75
87	Newport East	Jessica Morden	Lab	1,650	4.78
88	Northampton North	Michael Ellis	Con	1,936	4.8
89	Tooting	Sadiq Khan	Lab	2,524	4.97
90	Bury North	David Nuttall	Con	2,243	4.98
91	Kingswood	Chris Skidmore	Con	2,445	5.1
92	Weston-Super-Mare	John Penrose	Con	2,691	5.1
93	Hereford and South Herefordshire	Jesse Norman	Con	2,481	5.12
94	Wyre Forest	Mark Garnier	Con	2,643	5.18
95	Chorley	Lindsay Hoyle	Lab	2,593	5.19
96	North East Derbyshire	Natascha Engel	Lab	2,445	5.19
97	Exeter	Ben Bradshaw	Lab	2,721	5.2
98	Blackpool South	Gordon Marsden	Lab	1,852	5.25
99	Erewash	Jessica Lee	Con	2,501	5.25
100	Blackpool North and Cleveleys	Paul Maynard	Con	2,150	5.29

			Majority	%
101 Torridge and West Devon	Geoffrey Cox	Con	2,957	5.3
102 Westminster North	Karen Buck	Lab	2,126	5.33
103 Winchester	Steve Brine	Con	3,048	5.44
104 Southampton Test	Alan Whitehead	Lab	2,413	5.45
105 Luton South	Gavin Shuker	Lab/Co-op	2,329	5.5
106 City of Chester	Stephen Mosley	Con	2,583	5.51
107 Arfon	Hywel Williams	PlC	1,455	5.56
108 Bridgend	Madeleine Moon	Lab	2,263	5.89
109 Dagenham and Rainham	Jon Cruddas	Lab	2,630	5.92
110 Croydon Central	Gavin Barwell	Con	2,969	5.95
111 Belfast North	Nigel Dodds	DUP	2,224	5.97
112 Worcester	Robin Walker	Con	2,982	6.08
113 Keighley	Kris Hopkins	Con	2,940	6.13
114 Delyn	David Hanson	Lab	2,272	6.13
115 Wirral West	Esther McVey	Con	2,436	6.17
116 Cheadle	Mark Hunter	Lib Dem	3,272	6.21
117 North Cornwall	Dan Rogerson	Lib Dem	2,981	6.35
118 Gower	Martin Caton	Lab	2,683	6.43
119 South East Cornwall	Sheryll Murray	Con	3,220	6.48
120 Bristol North West	Charlotte Leslie	Con	3,274	6.49
121 Penistone and Stocksbridge	Angela Smith	Lab	3,049	6.54
122 Eastbourne	Stephen Lloyd	Lib Dem	3,435	6.58
123 City of Durham	Roberta Blackman-Woods	Lab	3,067	6.62
124 Birmingham, Northfield	Richard Burden	Lab	2,782	6.64
125 Stalybridge and Hyde	Jonathan Reynolds	Lab/Co-op	2,744	6.68
126 Harrow West	Gareth Thomas	Lab/Co-op	3,143	6.78
127 Bury South	Ivan Lewis	Lab	3,292	6.8
128 West Dorset	Oliver Letwin	Con	3,923	6.83
129 Taunton Deane	Jeremy Browne	Lib Dem	3,993	6.86
130 Scunthorpe	Nic Dakin	Lab	2,549	6.88
131 Richmond Park	Zac Goldsmith	Con	4,091	6.89
132 York Outer	Julian Sturdy	Con	3,688	6.91
133 Streatham	Chuka Umunna	Lab	3,259	6.93
134 Berwick-upon-Tweed	Alan Beith	Lib Dem	2,690	6.98
135 Cannock Chase	Aidan Burley	Con	3,195	7
136 Harrow East	Bob Blackman	Con	3,403	7.05
137 Vale of Clwyd	Chris Ruane	Lab	2,509	7.05
138 Loughborough	Nicky Morgan	Con	3,744	7.07
139 Wolverhampton North East	Emma Reynolds	Lab	2,484	7.09
140 Ynys Môn	Albert Owen	Lab	2,461	7.13
141 Warwick and Leamington	Chris White	Con	3,513	7.15
142 Hyndburn	Graham Jones	Lab	3,090	7.2
143 Alyn and Deeside	Mark Tami	Lab	2,919	7.3
144 Birmingham, Yardley	John Hemming	Lib Dem	3,002	7.32
145 Hammersmith	Andy Slaughter	Lab	3,549	7.45
146 Birmingham, Selly Oak	Steve McCabe	Lab	3,482	7.46
147 South Swindon	Robert Buckland	Con	3,544	7.47
148 Pontypridd	Owen Smith	Lab	2,785	7.58
149 Argyll and Bute	Alan Reid	Lib Dem	3,431	7.58
150 Newcastle upon Tyne North	Catherine McKinnell	Lab	3,414	7.74
151 Birmingham, Hall Green	Roger Godsiff	Lab	3,799	7.74

			Majority	%
152 Ealing Central and Acton	Angie Bray	Con	3,716	7.84
153 Darlington	Jenny Chapman	Lab	3,388	7.89
154 Pendle	Andrew Stephenson	Con	3,585	7.93
155 Sefton Central	Bill Esterson	Lab	3,862	7.94
156 Stevenage	Stephen McPartland	Con	3,578	8
157 Upper Bann	David Simpson	DUP	3,361	8.06
158 Elmet and Rothwell	Alec Shelbrooke	Con	4,521	8.09
159 West Aberdeenshire and Kincardine	Robert Smith	Lib Dem	3,684	8.14
160 Aberdeen South	Anne Begg	Lab	3,506	8.14
161 Clwyd South	Susan Elan Jones	Lab	2,834	8.16
162 Islington South and Finsbury	Emily Thornberry	Lab	3,569	8.16
163 Edinburgh West	Mike Crockart	Lib Dem	3,803	8.17
164 Bristol East	Kerry McCarthy	Lab	3,722	8.25
165 Don Valley	Caroline Flint	Lab	3,595	8.25
166 Torbay	Adrian Sanders	Lib Dem	4,078	8.28
167 Coventry South	James Cunningham	Lab	3,845	8.31
168 Carmarthen West and South Pembrokeshire	Simon Hart	Con	3,423	8.44
169 Romsey and Southampton North	Caroline Nokes	Con	4,156	8.48
170 Batley and Spen	Mike Wood	Lab	4,406	8.6
171 Angus	Mike Weir	SNP	3,282	8.63
172 Colne Valley	Jason McCartney	Con	4,837	8.73
173 Vale of Glamorgan	Alun Cairns	Con	4,307	8.83
174 Oxford East	Andrew Smith	Lab	4,581	8.84
175 Newport West	Paul Flynn	Lab	3,544	8.91
176 Copeland	Jamie Reed	Lab	3,833	8.94
177 West Lancashire	Rosie Cooper	Lab	4,343	8.94
178 Perth and North Perthshire	Peter Wishart	SNP	4,379	9.06
179 Dumfriesshire, Clydesdale and Tweeddale	David Mundell	Con	4,194	9.12
180 Carmarthen East and Dinefwr	Jonathan Edwards	PlC	3,481	9.14
181 Norwich North	Chloe Smith	Con	3,901	9.15
182 Birmingham, Erdington	Jack Dromey	Lab	3,277	9.19
183 Bosworth	David Tredinnick	Con	5,032	9.26
184 High Peak	Andrew Bingham	Con	4,677	9.27
185 Cheltenham	Martin Horwood	Lib Dem	4,920	9.3
186 Chelmsford	Simon Burns	Con	5,110	9.35
187 Milton Keynes South	Iain Stewart	Con	5,201	9.39
188 Bolton North East	David Crausby	Lab	4,084	9.4
189 Rossendale and Darwen	Jake Berry	Con	4,493	9.5
190 Cleethorpes	Martin Vickers	Con	4,298	9.53
191 Leeds North East	Fabian Hamilton	Lab	4,545	9.54
192 North East Somerset	Jacob Rees-Mogg	Con	4,914	9.58
193 Brecon and Radnorshire	Roger Williams	Lib Dem	3,747	9.63
194 Bristol South	Dawn Primarolo	Lab	4,734	9.76
195 Ellesmere Port and Neston	Andrew Miller	Lab	4,331	9.78
196 Great Yarmouth	Brandon Lewis	Con	4,276	9.9
197 Dudley South	Chris Kelly	Con	3,856	10.08
198 Oldham East and Saddleworth	Debbie Abrahams	Lab	3,558	10.17
199 Ochil and South Perthshire	Gordon Banks	Lab	5,187	10.27
200 Totnes	Sarah Wollaston	Con	4,927	10.28
201 South East Cambridgeshire	Jim Paice	Con	5,946	10.3

			Majority	%
202 Stoke-on-Trent South	Robert Flello	Lab	4,130	10.33
203 Worsley and Eccles South	Barbara Keeley	Lab	4,337	10.35
204 Dover	Charlie Elphicke	Con	5,274	10.45
205 Banff and Buchan	Eilidh Whiteford	SNP	4,027	10.46
206 Peterborough	Stewart Jackson	Con	4,861	10.77
207 South Ribble	Lorraine Fullbrook	Con	5,554	10.78
208 Stafford	Jeremy Lefroy	Con	5,460	10.85
209 Tynemouth	Alan Campbell	Lab	5,739	10.88
210 Stourbridge	Margot James	Con	5,164	10.91
211 Huddersfield	Barry Sheerman	Lab/Co-op	4,472	10.99
212 Wrexham	Ian Lucas	Lab	3,658	11.08
213 Dunfermline and West Fife	Thomas Docherty	Lab	5,470	11.16
214 Leicester West	Liz Kendall	Lab	4,017	11.19
215 Harlow	Robert Halfon	Con	4,925	11.19
216 Aberconwy	Guto Bebb	Con	3,398	11.3
217 North Devon	Nick Harvey	Lib Dem	5,821	11.32
218 Carshalton and Wallington	Tom Brake	Lib Dem	5,260	11.42
219 Ilford North	Lee Scott	Con	5,404	11.45
220 Slough	Fiona Mactaggart	Lab	5,523	11.52
221 Berwickshire, Roxburgh and Selkirk	Michael Moore	Lib Dem	5,675	11.56
222 Cardiff West	Kevin Brennan	Lab	4,751	11.58
223 Preseli Pembrokeshire	Stephen Crabb	Con	4,605	11.6
224 Workington	Tony Cunningham	Lab	4,575	11.63
225 Tewkesbury	Laurence Robertson	Con	6,310	11.67
226 Brigg and Goole	Andrew Percy	Con	5,147	11.71
227 Newcastle upon Tyne East	Nick Brown	Lab	4,453	11.73
228 Barrow and Furness	John Woodcock	Lab/Co-op	5,208	11.78
229 Crewe and Nantwich	Edward Timpson	Con	6,046	11.82
230 Maidstone and The Weald	Helen Grant	Con	5,889	12.02
231 Bradford South	Gerry Sutcliffe	Lab	4,622	12.13
232 Battersea	Jane Ellison	Con	5,977	12.23
233 Finchley and Golders Green	Mike Freer	Con	5,809	12.27
234 Canterbury	Julian Brazier	Con	6,048	12.27
235 Aldershot	Gerald Howarth	Con	5,586	12.28
236 Salisbury	John Glen	Con	5,966	12.29
237 Calder Valley	Craig Whittaker	Con	6,431	12.38
238 Mansfield	Alan Meale	Lab	6,012	12.4
239 Redcar	Ian Swales	Lib Dem	5,214	12.41
240 Hornsey and Wood Green	Lynne Featherstone	Lib Dem	6,875	12.44
241 Crawley	Henry Smith	Con	5,928	12.45
242 West Worcestershire	Harriett Baldwin	Con	6,754	12.46
243 Mid Ulster	Francie Molloy	Sinn Féin	4,681	12.51
244 Rother Valley	Kevin Barron	Lab	5,866	12.52
245 Llanelli	Nia Griffith	Lab	4,701	12.53
246 Portsmouth South	Mike Hancock	Ind*	5,200	12.56
247 Reading West	Alok Sharma	Con	6,004	12.61
248 Merthyr Tydfil and Rhymney	Dai Havard	Lab	4,056	12.61
249 Cardiff Central	Jenny Willott	Lib Dem	4,576	12.62
250 Rugby	Mark Pawsey	Con	6,000	12.62
251 Burton	Andrew Griffiths	Con	6,304	12.63
252 Foyle	Mark Durkan	SDLP	4,824	12.63
253 Bishop Auckland	Helen Goodman	Lab	5,218	12.66

* Elected as Liberal Democrat

			Majority	%
254 Poplar and Limehouse	Jim Fitzpatrick	Lab	6,030	12.72
255 Na h-Eileanan An Iar	Angus MacNeil	SNP	1,885	12.79
256 Woking	Jonathan Lord	Con	6,807	12.86
257 South Basildon and East Thurrock	Stephen Metcalfe	Con	5,772	12.87
258 Lewisham West and Penge	Jim Dowd	Lab	5,828	12.88
259 Heywood and Middleton	Jim Dobbin	Lab/Co-op	5,971	12.91
260 Tamworth	Christopher Pincher	Con	6,090	13.1
261 Glasgow North	Ann McKechin	Lab	3,898	13.13
262 Kingston and Surbiton	Edward Davey	Lib Dem	7,560	13.2
263 Redditch	Karen Lumley	Con	5,821	13.2
264 Mid Sussex	Nicholas Soames	Con	7,402	13.23
265 South Cambridgeshire	Andrew Lansley	Con	7,838	13.25
266 Hexham	Guy Opperman	Con	5,788	13.29
267 Erith and Thamesmead	Teresa Pearce	Lab	5,703	13.36
268 Bournemouth West	Conor Burns	Con	5,583	13.38
269 Coventry North West	Geoffrey Robinson	Lab	6,288	13.43
270 Cambridge	Julian Huppert	Lib Dem	6,792	13.51
271 North Somerset	Liam Fox	Con	7,862	13.54
272 Moray	Angus Robertson	SNP	5,590	13.61
273 Southport	John Pugh	Lib Dem	6,024	13.71
274 Salford and Eccles	Hazel Blears	Lab	5,725	13.73
275 Gordon	Malcolm Bruce	Lib Dem	6,748	13.82
276 Broadland	Keith Simpson	Con	7,292	13.83
277 Chatham and Aylesford	Tracey Crouch	Con	6,069	13.84
278 York Central	Hugh Bayley	Lab	6,451	13.86
279 Congleton	Fiona Bruce	Con	7,063	13.88
280 Guildford	Anne Milton	Con	7,782	13.98
281 North Swindon	Justin Tomlinson	Con	7,060	13.99
282 North Dorset	Robert Walter	Con	7,625	14.07
283 South Derbyshire	Heather Wheeler	Con	7,128	14.12
284 Sheffield Heeley	Meg Munn	Lab/Co-op	5,807	14.17
285 Dumfries and Galloway	Russell Brown	Lab	7,449	14.25
286 Filton and Bradley Stoke	Jack Lopresti	Con	6,914	14.3
287 Hartlepool	Iain Wright	Lab	5,509	14.35
288 North West Leicestershire	Andrew Bridgen	Con	7,511	14.44
289 Thornbury and Yate	Steve Webb	Lib Dem	7,116	14.73
290 South Dorset	Richard Drax	Con	7,443	14.77
291 Derby South	Margaret Beckett	Lab	6,122	14.78
292 Lewisham East	Heidi Alexander	Lab	6,216	14.83
293 Doncaster Central	Rosie Winterton	Lab	6,229	14.88
294 Isle of Wight	Andrew Turner	Con	10,527	14.96
295 Shrewsbury and Atcham	Daniel Kawczynski	Con	7,944	14.96

50 Safest Constituencies

			Majority	%
1 Manchester Central	Lucy Powell	Lab/Co-op	9,936	58.82
2 Liverpool Walton	Steve Rotheram	Lab	19,818	57.45
3 Knowsley	George Howarth	Lab	25,686	57.3
4 Belfast West	Paul Maskey	Sinn Féin	13,123	56.94
5 East Ham	Stephen Timms	Lab	27,826	54.67
6 Glasgow North East	Willie Bain	Lab	15,942	54.05
7 Liverpool West Derby	Stephen Twigg	Lab/Co-op	18,467	51.36

				Majority	%
8	Orkney and Shetland	Alistair Carmichael	Lib Dem	9,928	51.16
9	Bootle	Joe Benton	Lab	21,181	51.11
10	Kirkcaldy and Cowdenbeath	Gordon Brown	Lab	23,009	50.17
11	Coatbridge, Chryston and Bellshill	Tom Clarke	Lab	20,714	49.6
12	Barnsley Central	Dan Jarvis	Lab	11,771	48.54
13	Middlesbrough	Andy McDonald	Lab	8,211	48.52
14	Croydon North	Steve Reed	Lab	11,761	47.65
15	West Ham	Lyn Brown	Lab	22,534	47.48
16	Glasgow South West	Ian Davidson	Lab/Co-op	14,671	46.04
17	Rutherglen and Hamilton West	Tom Greatrex	Lab/Co-op	21,002	44.62
18	Richmond (Yorkshire)	William Hague	Con	23,336	43.58
19	South Holland and The Deepings	John Hayes	Con	21,880	43.55
20	Motherwell and Wishaw	Frank Roy	Lab	16,806	42.84
21	Easington	Grahame Morris	Lab	14,982	42.83
22	North Down	Sylvia Hermon	Ind	14,364	42.82
23	Rayleigh and Wickford	Mark Francois	Con	22,338	42.58
24	Birkenhead	Frank Field	Lab	15,195	42.5
25	Chelsea and Fulham	Greg Hands	Con	16,722	41.75
26	Beaconsfield	Dominic Grieve	Con	21,782	41.45
27	Paisley and Renfrewshire South	Douglas Alexander	Lab	16,614	41.44
28	Tottenham	David Lammy	Lab	16,931	41.25
29	West Dunbartonshire	Gemma Doyle	Lab/Co-op	17,408	41.1
30	Broxbourne	Charles Walker	Con	18,804	41.1
31	Glenrothes	Lindsay Roy	Lab	16,448	40.54
32	Maldon	John Whittingdale	Con	19,407	40.47
33	Aldridge-Brownhills	Richard Shepherd	Con	15,266	39.33
34	Witney	David Cameron	Con	22,740	39.28
35	Garston and Halewood	Maria Eagle	Lab	16,877	39.24
36	Windsor	Adam Afriyie	Con	19,054	38.36
37	Glasgow North West	John Robertson	Lab	13,611	38.16
38	Ogmore	Huw Irranca-Davies	Lab	13,246	38.15
39	Ruislip, Northwood and Pinner	Nick Hurd	Con	19,060	37.85
40	Ross, Skye and Lochaber	Charles Kennedy	Lib Dem	13,070	37.46
41	Halton	Derek Twigg	Lab	15,504	37.4
42	Beckenham	Bob Stewart	Con	17,784	37.21
43	Hertsmere	James Clappison	Con	17,605	37.13
44	Rhondda	Chris Bryant	Lab	11,553	37.1
45	Daventry	Christopher Heaton-Harris	Con	19,188	36.99
46	Glasgow East	Margaret Curran	Lab	11,840	36.75
47	Camberwell and Peckham	Harriet Harman	Lab	17,187	36.62
48	Faversham and Mid Kent	Hugh Robertson	Con	17,088	36.51
49	Liverpool Riverside	Louise Ellman	Lab/Co-op	14,173	36.39
50	Romford	Andrew Rosindell	Con	16,954	36.34

Women MPs 1945–2010 general elections

	Conservative	Labour*	Liberal/ Liberal Democrat	Others	Total
1945	1	21	1	1	24
1950	6	14	1	0	21
1951	6	11	0	0	17
1955	10	14	0	0	24
1959	12	13	0	0	25
1964	11	18	0	0	29
1966	7	19	0	0	26
1970	15	10	0	1	26
1974 (Feb)	9	13	0	1	23
1974 (Oct)	7	18	0	2	27
1979	8	11	0	0	19
1983	13	10	0	0	23
1987	17	21	2	1	41
1992	20	37	2	1	60
1997	13	101	3	3	120
2001	14	95	5	4	118
2005	17	98	9	3	128
2010	49	81	7	6	143

* Includes Labour/Co-operative

Women MPs (147) (September 2013)

ABBOTT Diane	Lab	Hackney North and Stoke Newington
ABRAHAMS Debbie	Lab	Oldham East and Saddleworth
ALEXANDER Heidi	Lab	Lewisham East
ALI Rushanara	Lab	Bethnal Green and Bow
BALDWIN Harriett	Con	West Worcestershire
BECKETT Margaret	Lab	Derby South
BEGG Anne	Lab	Aberdeen South
BERGER Luciana	Lab/Co-op	Liverpool Wavertree
BLACKMAN-WOODS Roberta	Lab	City of Durham
BLACKWOOD Nicola	Con	Oxford West and Abingdon
BLEARS Hazel	Lab	Salford and Eccles
BRADLEY Karen	Con	Staffordshire Moorlands
BRAY Angie	Con	Ealing Central and Acton
BROOKE Annette	Lib Dem	Mid Dorset and North Poole
BROWN Lyn	Lab	West Ham
BRUCE Fiona	Con	Congleton
BUCK Karen	Lab	Westminster North
BURT Lorely	Lib Dem	Solihull
CHAMPION Sarah	Lab	Rotherham
CHAPMAN Jenny	Lab	Darlington
CLARK Katy	Lab	North Ayrshire and Arran
CLWYD Ann	Lab	Cynon Valley
COFFEY Ann	Lab	Stockport
COFFEY Therese	Con	Suffolk Coastal

COOPER Rosie	*Lab*	West Lancashire
COOPER Yvette	*Lab*	Normanton, Pontefract and Castleford
CREAGH Mary	*Lab*	Wakefield
CREASY Stella	*Lab/Co-op*	Walthamstow
CROUCH Tracey	*Con*	Chatham and Aylesford
CURRAN Margaret	*Lab*	Glasgow East
DE PIERO Gloria	*Lab*	Ashfield
DINENAGE Caroline	*Con*	Gosport
DORRIES Nadine	*Con*	Mid Bedfordshire
DOYLE Gemma	*Lab/Co-op*	West Dunbartonshire
DOYLE-PRICE Jackie	*Con*	Thurrock
EAGLE Angela	*Lab*	Wallasey
EAGLE Maria	*Lab*	Garston and Halewood
ELLIOTT Julie	*Lab*	Sunderland Central
ELLISON Jane	*Con*	Battersea
ELLMAN Louise	*Lab/Co-op*	Liverpool Riverside
ENGEL Natascha	*Lab*	North East Derbyshire
FEATHERSTONE Lynne	*Lib Dem*	Hornsey and Wood Green
FLINT Caroline	*Lab*	Don Valley
FOVARGUE Yvonne	*Lab*	Makerfield
FULLBROOK Lorraine	*Con*	South Ribble
GILDERNEW Michelle	*Sinn Féin*	Fermanagh and South Tyrone
GILLAN Cheryl	*Con*	Chesham and Amersham
GILMORE Sheila	*Lab*	Edinburgh East
GLASS Patricia	*Lab*	North West Durham
GLINDON Mary	*Lab*	North Tyneside
GOODMAN Helen	*Lab*	Bishop Auckland
GRANT Helen	*Con*	Maidstone and The Weald
GREEN Kate	*Lab*	Stretford and Urmston
GREENING Justine	*Con*	Putney
GREENWOOD Lilian	*Lab*	Nottingham South
GRIFFITH Nia	*Lab*	Llanelli
HARMAN Harriet	*Lab*	Camberwell and Peckham
HARRIS Rebecca	*Con*	Castle Point
HERMON Sylvia	*Ind*	North Down
HILLIER Meg	*Lab/Co-op*	Hackney South and Shoreditch
HILLING Julie	*Lab*	Bolton West
HODGE Margaret	*Lab*	Barking
HODGSON Sharon	*Lab*	Washington and Sunderland West
HOEY Kate	*Lab*	Vauxhall
JACKSON Glenda	*Lab*	Hampstead and Kilburn
JAMES Margot	*Con*	Stourbridge
JAMES Siân	*Lab*	Swansea East
JAMIESON Cathy	*Lab/Co-op*	Kilmarnock and Loudoun
JOHNSON Diana	*Lab*	Kingston upon Hull North
JONES Helen	*Lab*	Warrington North
JONES Susan Elan	*Lab*	Clwyd South
JOWELL Tessa	*Lab*	Dulwich and West Norwood
KEELEY Barbara	*Lab*	Worsley and Eccles South
KENDALL Liz	*Lab*	Leicester West
LAING Eleanor	*Con*	Epping Forest
LATHAM Pauline	*Con*	Mid Derbyshire
LEADSOM Andrea	*Con*	South Northamptonshire
LEE Jessica	*Con*	Erewash

LESLIE Charlotte	Con	Bristol North West
LEWELL-BUCK Emma	Lab	South Shields
LONG Naomi	All	Belfast East
LUCAS Caroline	Green	Brighton Pavilion
LUMLEY Karen	Con	Redditch
McCARTHY Kerry	Lab	Bristol East
McDONAGH Siobhain	Lab	Mitcham and Morden
McGOVERN Alison	Lab	Wirral South
McGUIRE Anne	Lab	Stirling
McINTOSH Anne	Con	Thirsk and Malton
McKECHIN Ann	Lab	Glasgow North
McKINNELL Catherine	Lab	Newcastle upon Tyne North
MACLEOD Mary	Con	Brentford and Isleworth
MACTAGGART Fiona	Lab	Slough
McVEY Esther	Con	Wirral West
MAHMOOD Shabana	Lab	Birmingham, Ladywood
MAIN Anne	Con	St Albans
MALHOTRA Seema	Lab	Feltham and Heston
MAY Theresa	Con	Maidenhead
MILLER Maria	Con	Basingstoke
MILTON Anne	Con	Guildford
MOON Madeleine	Lab	Bridgend
MORDAUNT Penny	Con	Portsmouth North
MORDEN Jessica	Lab	Newport East
MORGAN Nicky	Con	Loughborough
MORRIS Anne Marie	Con	Newton Abbot
MUNN Meg	Lab/Co-op	Sheffield Heeley
MUNT Tessa	Lib Dem	Wells
MURRAY Sheryll	Con	South East Cornwall
NANDY Lisa	Lab	Wigan
NASH Pamela	Lab	Airdrie and Shotts
NEWTON Sarah	Con	Truro and Falmouth
NOKES Caroline	Con	Romsey and Southampton North
O'DONNELL Fiona	Lab	East Lothian
ONWURAH Chi	Lab	Newcastle upon Tyne Central
OSBORNE Sandra	Lab	Ayr, Carrick and Cumnock
PATEL Priti	Con	Witham
PEARCE Teresa	Lab	Erith and Thamesmead
PERRY Claire	Con	Devizes
PHILLIPSON Bridget	Lab	Houghton and Sunderland South
POWELL Lucy	Lab/Co-op	Manchester Central
PRIMAROLO Dawn	Lab	Bristol South
QURESHI Yasmin	Lab	Bolton South East
REEVES Rachel	Lab	Leeds West
REYNOLDS Emma	Lab	Wolverhampton North East
RIORDAN Linda	Lab/Co-op	Halifax
RITCHIE Margaret	SDLP	South Down
RUDD Amber	Con	Hastings and Rye
RUDDOCK Joan	Lab	Lewisham Deptford
SANDYS Laura	Con	South Thanet
SEABECK Alison	Lab	Plymouth, Moor View
SMITH Angela	Lab	Penistone and Stocksbridge
SMITH Chloe	Con	Norwich North

SOUBRY Anna	*Con*	Broxtowe
SPELMAN Caroline	*Con*	Meriden
STUART Gisela	*Lab*	Birmingham, Edgbaston
SWINSON Jo	*Lib Dem*	East Dunbartonshire
TEATHER Sarah	*Lib Dem*	Brent Central
THORNBERRY Emily	*Lab*	Islington South and Finsbury
TRUSS Elizabeth	*Con*	South West Norfolk
VAZ Valerie	*Lab*	Walsall South
VILLIERS Theresa	*Con*	Chipping Barnet
WALLEY Joan	*Lab*	Stoke-on-Trent North
WATKINSON Angela	*Con*	Hornchurch and Upminster
WHEELER Heather	*Con*	South Derbyshire
WHITEFORD Eilidh	*SNP*	Banff and Buchan
WILLOTT Jenny	*Lib Dem*	Cardiff Central
WINTERTON Rosie	*Lab*	Doncaster Central
WOLLASTON Sarah	*Con*	Totnes

DO YOU NEED THIS INFORMATION ONLINE?
visit www.dodspeople.com or call 020 7593 5675
to register for a free trial

MPs by Age
(Ages as at 1 September 2013)

	Conservative	%	Labour	%	Lib Dem	%	Other	%	Total	%
Under 30	1	0.3	2	0.8	0	0.0	0	0.0	3	0.5
30–39	33	10.9	31	12.1	8	14.5	1	2.9	73	11.2
40–49	111	36.6	48	18.7	14	25.5	7	20.0	180	27.7
50–59	105	34.7	86	33.5	18	32.7	17	48.6	226	34.8
60–69	42	13.9	71	27.6	11	20.0	10	28.6	134	20.6
70–79	10	3.3	16	6.2	4	7.3	0	0.0	30	4.6
Over 80	1	0.3	3	1.2	0	0.0	0	0.0	4	0.6
	303		257		55		35		650	
Average age	**50.5**		**54.3**		**52.7**		**53.9**		**52.4**	

MPs who have not supplied date of birth

Chris Evans (Lab/Co-op)
Julie Hilling (Lab)
Andy McDonald (Lab)

Mary Macleod (Con)
Sarah Newton (Con)

Pamela Nash	29	*Lab*	Stella Creasy	35/36	*Lab/Co-op*
Bridget Phillipson	29	*Lab*	Ben Gummer	35	*Con*
James Wharton	29	*Con*	Julian Huppert	35	*Lib Dem*
Anas Sarwar	30	*Lab*	Charlotte Leslie	35	*Con*
Gemma Doyle	31/32	*Lab/Co-op*	Andrew Percy	35/36	*Con*
Gavin Shuker	31	*Lab/Co-op*	Emma Reynolds	35	*Lab*
Chloe Smith	31	*Con*	Robin Walker	35	*Con*
Luciana Berger	32	*Lab/Co-op*	Steve Gilbert	36	*Lib Dem*
Alison McGovern	32	*Lab*	Duncan Hames	36	*Lib Dem*
Shabana Mahmood	32	*Lab*	Justin Tomlinson	36	*Con*
Chris Skidmore	32	*Con*	Jonathan Edwards	37	*PlC*
Andrew Stephenson	32	*Con*	Sam Gyimah	37	*Con*
Nicola Blackwood	33	*Con*	Jessica Lee	37	*Con*
Tom Blenkinsop	33	*Lab*	Gregg McClymont	37	*Lab*
Stephen Doughty	33	*Lab/Co-op*	Catherine McKinnell	37	*Lab*
Jonathan Reynolds	33	*Lab/Co-op*	Stephen McPartland	37	*Con*
Jo Swinson	33	*Lib Dem*	Paul Maynard	37	*Con*
Simon Wright	33	*Lib Dem*	Ian Murray	37	*Lab*
Jon Ashworth	34	*Lab*	Andy Sawford	37	*Lab/Co-op*
Jake Berry	34/35	*Con*	Alec Shelbrooke	37	*Con*
Aidan Burley	34	*Con*	Gavin Williamson	37	*Con*
Rehman Chishti	34	*Con*	Heidi Alexander	38	*Lab*
Matthew Hancock	34	*Con*	Rushanara Ali	38	*Lab*
Chris Kelly	34/35	*Con*	Tracey Crouch	38	*Con*
Emma Lewell-Buck	34	*Lab*	Thomas Docherty	38	*Lab*
Lisa Nandy	34	*Lab*	Michael Dugher	38	*Lab*
Daniel Poulter	34	*Con*	Zac Goldsmith	38	*Con*
Rachel Reeves	34	*Lab*	Tom Greatrex	38	*Lab/Co-op*
Chuka Umunna	34	*Lab*	Kwasi Kwarteng	38	*Con*
John Woodcock	34	*Lab/Co-op*	Nigel Mills	38/39	*Con*

Lucy Powell	38	*Lab/Co-op*	Phillip Lee	42	*Con*
Dan Rogerson	38	*Lib Dem*	John Leech	42	*Lib Dem*
Elizabeth Truss	38	*Con*	Brandon Lewis	42	*Con*
Steve Brine	39	*Con*	Mark Menzies	42	*Con*
Dan Byles	39	*Con*	George Osborne	42	*Con*
Jenny Chapman	39	*Lab*	Mark Reckless	42	*Con*
Damian Collins	39	*Con*	Julian Smith	42	*Con*
John Glen	39	*Con*	Karl Turner	42	*Lab*
Andrew Gwynne	39	*Lab*	Karen Bradley	43	*Con*
Tristram Hunt	39	*Lab*	Jeremy Browne	43	*Lib Dem*
Marcus Jones	39	*Con*	Andy Burnham	43	*Lab*
Dominic Raab	39	*Con*	Alun Cairns	43	*Con*
Sarah Teather	39	*Lib Dem*	David Davies	43	*Con*
Edward Timpson	39	*Con*	Tim Farron	43	*Lib Dem*
Jenny Willott	39	*Lib Dem*	Michelle Gildernew	43	*Sinn Féin*
Willie Bain	40	*Lab*	Mark Harper	43	*Con*
Conor Burns	40	*Con*	Damian Hinds	43	*Con*
Stephen Crabb	40	*Con*	Sajid Javid	43	*Con*
Gloria De Piero	40	*Lab*	Gareth Johnson	43	*Con*
Dan Jarvis	40	*Lab*	Mark Lancaster	43	*Con*
Penny Mordaunt	40	*Con*	Angus MacNeil	43	*SNP*
Nicky Morgan	40	*Con*	Ed Miliband	43	*Lab*
Jamie Reed	40	*Lab*	Greg Mulholland	43	*Lib Dem*
Iain Stewart	40	*Con*	Matthew Offord	43	*Con*
Rory Stewart	40	*Con*	Toby Perkins	43	*Lab*
Jeremy Wright	40	*Con*	Stephen Phillips	43	*Con*
Danny Alexander	41	*Lib Dem*	Christopher Pincher	43	*Con*
Stuart Andrew	41	*Con*	Angus Robertson	43	*SNP*
Steve Barclay	41	*Con*	Owen Smith	43	*Lab*
Gavin Barwell	41	*Con*	Mark Spencer	43	*Con*
Therese Coffey	41	*Con*	Ben Wallace	43	*Con*
Philip Davies	41	*Con*	Guto Bebb	44	*Con*
Caroline Dinenage	41	*Con*	Robert Buckland	44	*Con*
George Eustice	41	*Con*	David Burrowes	44	*Con*
David Gauke	41	*Con*	Sarah Champion	44	*Lab*
Jo Johnson	41/42	*Con*	Yvette Cooper	44	*Lab*
Daniel Kawczynski	41	*Con*	Jackie Doyle-Price	44	*Con*
Liz Kendall	41/42	*Lab*	Justine Greening	44	*Con*
David Lammy	41	*Lab*	Robert Halfon	44	*Con*
Chris Leslie	41	*Lab/Co-op*	Meg Hillier	44	*Lab/Co-op*
Naomi Long	41	*All*	Jack Lopresti	44	*Con*
Seema Malhotra	41	*Lab*	Karl McCartney	44	*Con*
Stephen Mosley	41	*Con*	Jacob Rees-Mogg	44	*Con*
Caroline Nokes	41	*Con*	Grant Shapps	44	*Con*
Priti Patel	41	*Con*	Henry Smith	44	*Con*
Julian Sturdy	41/42	*Con*	Eilidh Whiteford	44	*SNP*
Iain Wright	41	*Lab*	Douglas Alexander	45	*Lab*
Steve Baker	42	*Con*	James Brokenshire	45	*Con*
Liam Byrne	42	*Lab*	Mary Creagh	45	*Lab*
Douglas Carswell	42	*Con*	Michael Ellis	45	*Con*
James Duddridge	42	*Con*	Rebecca Harris	45	*Con*
Charlie Elphicke	42	*Con*	Christopher Heaton-Harris	45	*Con*
Andrew Griffiths	42	*Con*	Susan Elan Jones	45	*Lab*
Sadiq Khan	42	*Lab*	Jason McCartney	45	*Con*

Esther McVey	45	Con	Alistair Carmichael	48	Lib Dem
Jessica Morden	45	Lab	Jonathan Djanogly	48	Con
Alok Sharma	45	Con	Jane Ellison	48/49	Con
Ed Vaizey	45	Con	Mark Field	48	Con
Theresa Villiers	45	Con	Mark Francois	48	Con
Charles Walker	45	Con	Philip Hollobone	48	Con
Nigel Adams	46	Con	Adam Holloway	48	Con
Ed Balls	46	Lab/Co-op	Stewart Jackson	48	Con
Graham Brady	46	Con	Simon Kirby	48	Con
David Cameron	46	Con	Kerry McCarthy	48	Lab
Greg Clark	46	Con	Pat McFadden	48	Lab
Katy Clark	46	Lab	Michael Moore	48	Lib Dem
Nick Clegg	46	Lib Dem	Chi Onwurah	48	Lab
Simon Danczuk	46	Lab	Guy Opperman	48	Con
Natascha Engel	46	Lab	Laura Sandys	48/49	Con
Bill Esterson	46	Lab	Steve Webb	48	Lib Dem
George Freeman	46	Con	Robert Wilson	48	Con
Michael Gove	46	Con	John Cryer	49	Lab
Jeremy Hunt	46	Con	Graham Evans	49	Con
Ivan Lewis	46	Lab	Tom Harris	49	Lab
Paul Maskey	46	Sinn Féin	Mark Hoban	49	Con
James Morris	46	Con	George Hollingbery	49	Con
Jim Murphy	46	Lab	Andrew Jones	49	Con
Ian Paisley	46	DUP	Kevan Jones	49	Lab
Mark Pritchard	46	Con	Karen Lumley	49	Con
Gareth Thomas	46	Lab/Co-op	Michael McCann	49	Lab
Stephen Twigg	46	Lab/Co-op	Maria Miller	49	Con
Paul Uppal	46	Con	John Penrose	49	Con
Tom Watson	46	Lab	Claire Perry	49	Con
Chris White	46	Con	Steve Reed	49	Lab
Stephen Williams	46	Lib Dem	Mark Simmonds	49	Con
David Wright	46	Lab	John Stevenson	49/50	Con
Nadhim Zahawi	46	Con	Richard Bacon	50	Con
Gregory Barker	47	Con	John Bercow	50	Speaker
Nick Boles	47	Con	Jeffrey Donaldson	50	DUP
Mike Crockart	47	Lib Dem	Julie Elliott	50	Lab
Edward Davey	47	Lib Dem	Mark Garnier	50	Con
Tobias Ellwood	47	Con	Simon Hart	50	Con
Robert Flello	47	Lab	Nick Herbert	50	Con
Lilian Greenwood	47	Lab	Kris Hopkins	50	Con
Greg Hands	47	Con	Martin Horwood	50	Lib Dem
Sharon Hodgson	47	Lab	Stewart Hosie	50	SNP
Diana Johnson	47	Lab	Huw Irranca-Davies	50	Lab
Graham Jones	47	Lab	Ian Lavery	50	Lab
David Laws	47	Lib Dem	Andrea Leadsom	50	Con
Stephen Metcalfe	47	Con	Jonathan Lord	50	Con
David Morris	47	Con	Conor Murphy	50	Sinn Féin
Simon Reevell	47	Con	Yasmin Qureshi	50	Lab
Andrew Rosindell	47	Con	Hugh Robertson	50	Con
Bill Wiggin	47	Con	Amber Rudd	50	Con
Mark Williams	47	Lib Dem	Mark Tami	50	Lab
Adam Afriyie	48	Con	Sarah Wollaston	50/51	Con
Ian Austin	48	Lab	Andrew Bingham	51	Con
Andrew Bridgen	48	Con	Tom Brake	51	Lib Dem

Chris Bryant	51	Lab		John Healey	53	Lab
Paul Burstow	51	Lib Dem		John Hemming	53	Lib Dem
Jon Cruddas	51	Lab		Stephen Hepburn	53	Lab
Paul Farrelly	51	Lab		Charles Kennedy	53	Lib Dem
Caroline Flint	51	Lab		Siobhain McDonagh	53	Lab
Liam Fox	51	Con		John Mann	53	Lab
Richard Fuller	51	Con		Tessa Munt	53	Lib Dem
Helen Grant	51	Con		Fiona O'Donnell	53	Lab
Chris Grayling	51	Con		Nick Smith	53	Lab
Stephen Hammond	51	Con		Hugo Swire	53	Con
Nick Hurd	51	Con		Emily Thornberry	53	Lab
Tim Loughton	51	Con		John Whittingdale	53	Con
David Mundell	51	Con		John Baron	54	Con
Jesse Norman	51	Con		Oliver Colvile	54	Con
David Nuttall	51	Con		Margaret Curran	54	Lab
Mark Prisk	51	Con		Nick de Bois	54	Con
Steve Rotheram	51	Lab		Andrew George	54	Lib Dem
David Ruffley	51	Con		Mark Hendrick	54	Lab/Co-op
Andrew Selous	51	Con		Charles Hendry	54	Con
Mel Stride	51	Con		Margot James	54/55	Con
Graham Stuart	51	Con		Siân James	54	Lab
Craig Whittaker	51	Con		Bernard Jenkin	54	Con
Peter Wishart	51	SNP		Jeremy Lefroy	54	Con
Debbie Abrahams	52	Lab		Ian Liddell-Grainger	54	Con
Peter Aldous	52	Con		Iain McKenzie	54	Lab
Richard Benyon	52	Con		Graeme Morrice	54	Lab
Neil Carmichael	52	Con		Meg Munn	54	Lab/Co-op
Angela Eagle	52	Lab		Albert Owen	54	Lab
Maria Eagle	52	Lab		Adrian Sanders	54	Lib Dem
Nick Gibb	52	Con		David Simpson	54	DUP
William Hague	52	Con		Derek Twigg	54	Lab
Nick Harvey	52	Lib Dem		Heather Wheeler	54	Con
Eric Joyce	52	Ind		Phil Wilson	54	Lab
Caroline Lucas	52	Green		Shaun Woodward	54	Lab
Ian Lucas	52	Lab		Karen Buck	55	Lab
Ann McKechin	52	Lab		Nigel Dodds	55	DUP
Khalid Mahmood	52	Lab		Richard Drax	55	Con
Grahame Morris	52	Lab		Philip Dunne	55	Con
Andrew Murrison	52	Con		Clive Efford	55	Lab
David Rutley	52	Con		Nigel Evans	55	Ind
Andy Slaughter	52	Lab		Helen Goodman	55	Lab
Angela Smith	52	Lab		Richard Graham	55	Con
Shailesh Vara	52	Con		Richard Harrington	55	Con
Harriett Baldwin	53	Con		John Hayes	55	Con
Crispin Blunt	53	Con		Eleanor Laing	55	Con
Ben Bradshaw	53	Lab		Norman Lamb	55	Lib Dem
Kevin Brennan	53	Lab		Patrick McLoughlin	55	Con
Lyn Brown	53	Lab		Brooks Newmark	55	Con
Geoffrey Cox	53	Con		Mike Penning	55	Con
Geraint Davies	53	Lab/Co-op		Margaret Ritchie	55	SDLP
Mark Durkan	53	SDLP		Laurence Robertson	55	Con
Mike Freer	53	Con		Frank Roy	55	Lab
Lorraine Fullbrook	53/54	Con		Chris Ruane	55	Lab
Kate Green	53	Lab		Robert Smith	55	Lib Dem

Caroline Spelman	55	Con	Desmond Swayne	57	Con
Rosie Winterton	55	Lab	Robert Syms	57	Con
Norman Baker	56	Lib Dem	David Willetts	57	Con
Roberta Blackman-Woods	56	Lab	Gordon Banks	58	Lab
Fiona Bruce	56	Con	Henry Bellingham	58	Con
Alan Campbell	56	Lab	Alistair Burt	58	Con
James Clappison	56	Con	Lorely Burt	58	Lib Dem
Wayne David	56	Lab	Alex Cunningham	58	Lab
Nadine Dorries	56	Con	Nic Dakin	58	Lab
Alan Duncan	56	Con	James Gray	58	Con
Yvonne Fovargue	56	Lab	Fabian Hamilton	58	Lab
Barry Gardiner	56	Lab	Oliver Heald	58	Con
Mary Glindon	56	Lab	Sylvia Hermon	58	Ind
Robert Goodwill	56	Con	John Howell	58	Con
Nia Griffith	56	Lab	Helen Jones	58	Lab
David Hanson	56	Lab	Peter Luff	58	Con
Lindsay Hoyle	56	Lab	Steve McCabe	58	Lab
Mark Hunter	56	Lib Dem	Anne McIntosh	58	Con
Cathy Jamieson	56	Lab/Co-op	Teresa Pearce	58	Lab
Andrew Lansley	56	Con	John Randall	58	Con
Stephen Lloyd	56	Lib Dem	Jim Shannon	58	DUP
Jim McGovern	56	Lab	Stephen Timms	58	Lab
Anne Main	56	Con	Valerie Vaz	58	Lab
Theresa May	56	Con	Diane Abbott	59	Lab
Ian Mearns	56	Lab	David Anderson	59	Lab
Anne Marie Morris	56	Con	Hilary Benn	59	Lab
David Mowat	56	Con	Angie Bray	59	Con
Stephen O'Brien	56	Con	Richard Burden	59	Lab
Mark Pawsey	56	Con	Alistair Darling	59	Lab
Anna Soubry	56	Con	Iain Duncan Smith	59	Con
Andrew Tyrie	56	Con	George Galloway	59	Respect
Keith Vaz	56	Lab	David Heath	59	Lib Dem
Mike Weatherley	56	Con	Fiona Mactaggart	59	Lab
Mike Weir	56	SNP	Gordon Marsden	59	Lab
Chris Williamson	56	Lab	Dawn Primarolo	59	Lab
Anne Begg	57	Lab	Alan Reid	59	Lib Dem
Bob Blackman	57	Con	Alison Seabeck	59	Lab
Hazel Blears	57	Lab	John Thurso	59	Lib Dem
Patricia Glass	57	Lab	Andrew Turner	59	Con
Damian Green	57	Con	Graham Allen	60	Lab
Dominic Grieve	57	Con	Paul Blomfield	60	Lab
Philip Hammond	57	Con	Peter Bone	60	Con
Oliver Letwin	57	Con	Julian Brazier	60	Con
David Lidington	57	Con	Simon Burns	60	Con
Patrick Mercer	57	Ind	Gregory Campbell	60	DUP
Anne Milton	57	Con	Geoffrey Clifton-Brown	60	Con
Andrew Mitchell	57	Con	Vernon Coaker	60	Lab
Sheryll Murray	57	Con	Tony Cunningham	60	Lab
Sandra Osborne	57	Lab	John Denham	60	Lab
Neil Parish	57	Con	Mike Gapes	60	Lab/Co-op
Owen Paterson	57	Con	Edward Garnier	60	Con
Lee Scott	57	Con	Paul Goggins	60	Lab
Gary Streeter	57	Con	Mark Lazarowicz	60	Lab/Co-op
Gisela Stuart	57	Lab	Francis Maude	60	Con

Linda Riordan	60	Lab/Co-op	David Tredinnick	63	Con
Jim Sheridan	60	Lab	Jon Trickett	63	Lab
Gerry Sutcliffe	60	Lab	Jeremy Corbyn	64	Lab
Ian Swales	60	Lib Dem	David Davis	64	Con
David Ward	60	Lib Dem	Brian Donohoe	64	Lab
Hywel Williams	60	PlC	Frank Doran	64	Lab
Sammy Wilson	60	DUP	Jack Dromey	64	Lab
Bob Ainsworth	61	Lab	David Evennett	64	Con
David Amess	61	Con	George Howarth	64	Lab
James Arbuthnot	61	Con	Greg Knight	64	Con
Hugh Bayley	61	Lab	Andy Love	64	Lab/Co-op
Russell Brown	61	Lab	Alasdair McDonnell	64	SDLP
Stephen Dorrell	61	Con	Anne McGuire	64	Lab
Michael Fallon	61	Con	Alan Meale	64	Lab
Lynne Featherstone	61	Lib Dem	Andrew Miller	64	Lab
Jim Fitzpatrick	61	Lab	Paul Murphy	64	Lab
Cheryl Gillan	61	Con	Jim Paice	64	Con
David Jones	61	Con	Lindsay Roy	64	Lab
Barbara Keeley	61	Lab	Keith Simpson	64	Con
Julian Lewis	61	Con	Bob Stewart	64	Con
Elfyn Llwyd	61	PlC	Joan Walley	64	Lab
John McDonnell	61	Lab	Michael Connarty	65	Lab
Robert Neill	61	Con	Gordon Henderson	65	Con
Eric Pickles	61	Con	Jim Hood	65	Lab
John Robertson	61	Lab	Gerald Howarth	65	Con
Mike Thornton	61	Lib Dem	Tessa Jowell	65	Lab
Gordon Brown	62	Lab	Pauline Latham	65	Con
Martin Caton	62	Lab	William McCrea	65	DUP
Rosie Cooper	62	Lab	Stephen Pound	65	Lab
Ian Davidson	62	Lab/Co-op	John Pugh	65	Lib Dem
Jim Dowd	62	Lab	Nicholas Soames	65	Con
David Hamilton	62	Lab	Robert Walter	65	Con
Simon Hughes	62	Lib Dem	Roger Williams	65	Lib Dem
Francie Molloy	62	Sinn Féin	Kevin Barron	66	Lab
John Redwood	62	Con	David Blunkett	66	Lab
Andrew Robathan	62	Con	Annette Brooke	66	Lib Dem
Andrew Smith	62	Lab	Christopher Chope	66	Con
Martin Vickers	62	Con	Don Foster	66	Lib Dem
David Watts	62	Lab	Virendra Sharma	66	Lab
Alan Whitehead	62	Lab	John Spellar	66	Lab
Tony Baldry	63	Con	Adrian Bailey	67	Lab/Co-op
Clive Betts	63	Lab	Paul Beresford	67	Con
Nick Brown	63	Lab	Ann Coffey	67	Lab
Jonathan Evans	63	Con	David Crausby	67	Lab
Michael Fabricant	63	Con	Louise Ellman	67	Lab/Co-op
Sheila Gilmore	63	Lab	Hywel Francis	67	Lab
Peter Hain	63	Lab	Roger Godsiff	67	Lab
Harriet Harman	63	Lab	Mike Hancock	67	Ind
Dai Havard	63	Lab	David Heyes	67	Lab
Alan Johnson	63	Lab	Kate Hoey	67	Lab
Edward Leigh	63	Con	Malcolm Rifkind	67	Con
Madeleine Moon	63	Lab	Bob Russell	67	Lib Dem
Eric Ollerenshaw	63	Con	Jack Straw	67	Lab
Graham Stringer	63	Lab	Mike Wood	67	Lab

Malcolm Bruce	68	*Lib Dem*		Menzies Campbell	72	*Lib Dem*
Pat Doherty	68	*Sinn Féin*		Tom Clarke	72	*Lab*
Margaret Hodge	68	*Lab*		James Cunningham	72	*Lab*
George Mudie	68	*Lab*		Jim Dobbin	72	*Lab/Co-op*
Richard Ottaway	68	*Con*		Kelvin Hopkins	72	*Lab*
Nick Raynsford	68	*Lab*		George Young	72	*Con*
Tim Yeo	68	*Con*		William Cash	73	*Con*
Gordon Birtwistle	69	*Lib Dem*		Kenneth Clarke	73	*Con*
Peter Bottomley	69	*Con*		Frank Dobson	73	*Lab*
Glyn Davies	69	*Con*		Michael Meacher	73	*Lab*
Joan Ruddock	69	*Lab*		Barry Sheerman	73	*Lab/Co-op*
Margaret Beckett	70	*Lab*		Geoffrey Robinson	75	*Lab*
Alan Beith	70	*Lib Dem*		Ann Clwyd	76	*Lab*
Vincent Cable	70	*Lib Dem*		Alan Haselhurst	76	*Con*
Ronnie Campbell	70	*Lab*		Glenda Jackson	77	*Lab*
Roger Gale	70	*Con*		Paul Flynn	78	*Lab*
Peter Lilley	70	*Con*		Austin Mitchell	78	*Lab*
Richard Shepherd	70	*Con*		Joe Benton	79	*Lab*
Andrew Stunell	70	*Lib Dem*		David Winnick	80	*Lab*
Brian Binley	71	*Con*		Dennis Skinner	81	*Lab*
Frank Field	71	*Lab*		Gerald Kaufman	83	*Lab*
John Stanley	71	*Con*		Peter Tapsell	83	*Con*
Angela Watkinson	71	*Con*				

MPs by Party

Conservative

ADAMS Nigel
AFRIYIE Adam
ALDOUS Peter
AMESS David
ANDREW Stuart
ARBUTHNOT James
BACON Richard
BAKER Steve
BALDRY Tony
BALDWIN Harriett
BARCLAY Steve
BARKER Gregory
BARON John
BARWELL Gavin
BEBB Guto
BELLINGHAM Henry
BENYON Richard
BERESFORD Paul
BERRY Jake
BINGHAM Andrew
BINLEY Brian
BLACKMAN Bob
BLACKWOOD Nicola
BLUNT Crispin
BOLES Nick
BONE Peter
BOTTOMLEY Peter
BRADLEY Karen
BRADY Graham
BRAY Angie
BRAZIER Julian
BRIDGEN Andrew
BRINE Steve
BROKENSHIRE James
BRUCE Fiona
BUCKLAND Robert
BURLEY Aidan
BURNS Conor
BURNS Simon
BURROWES David
BURT Alistair
BYLES Dan
CAIRNS Alun
CAMERON David
CARMICHAEL Neil
CARSWELL Douglas
CASH William
CHISHTI Rehman
CHOPE Christopher

CLAPPISON James
CLARK Greg
CLARKE Kenneth
CLIFTON-BROWN Geoffrey
COFFEY Therese
COLLINS Damian
COLVILE Oliver
COX Geoffrey
CRABB Stephen
CROUCH Tracey
DAVIES David
DAVIES Glyn
DAVIES Philip
DAVIS David
DE BOIS Nick
DINENAGE Caroline
DJANOGLY Jonathan
DORRELL Stephen
DORRIES Nadine
DOYLE-PRICE Jackie
DRAX Richard
DUDDRIDGE James
DUNCAN Alan
DUNCAN SMITH Iain
DUNNE Philip
ELLIS Michael
ELLISON Jane
ELLWOOD Tobias
ELPHICKE Charlie
EUSTICE George
EVANS Graham
EVANS Jonathan
EVENNETT David
FABRICANT Michael
FALLON Michael
FIELD Mark
FOX Liam
FRANCOIS Mark
FREEMAN George
FREER Mike
FULLBROOK Lorraine
FULLER Richard
GALE Roger
GARNIER Edward
GARNIER Mark
GAUKE David
GIBB Nick
GILLAN Cheryl
GLEN John

GOLDSMITH Zac
GOODWILL Robert
GOVE Michael
GRAHAM Richard
GRANT Helen
GRAY James
GRAYLING Chris
GREEN Damian
GREENING Justine
GRIEVE Dominic
GRIFFITHS Andrew
GUMMER Ben
GYIMAH Sam
HAGUE William
HALFON Robert
HAMMOND Philip
HAMMOND Stephen
HANCOCK Matthew
HANDS Greg
HARPER Mark
HARRINGTON Richard
HARRIS Rebecca
HART Simon
HASELHURST Alan
HAYES John
HEALD Oliver
HEATON-HARRIS
Christopher
HENDERSON Gordon
HENDRY Charles
HERBERT Nick
HINDS Damian
HOBAN Mark
HOLLINGBERY George
HOLLOBONE Philip
HOLLOWAY Adam
HOPKINS Kris
HOWARTH Gerald
HOWELL John
HUNT Jeremy
HURD Nick
JACKSON Stewart
JAMES Margot
JAVID Sajid
JENKIN Bernard
JOHNSON Gareth
JOHNSON Jo
JONES Andrew
JONES David

JONES Marcus
KAWCZYNSKI Daniel
KELLY Chris
KIRBY Simon
KNIGHT Greg
KWARTENG Kwasi
LAING Eleanor
LANCASTER Mark
LANSLEY Andrew
LATHAM Pauline
LEADSOM Andrea
LEE Jessica
LEE Phillip
LEFROY Jeremy
LEIGH Edward
LESLIE Charlotte
LETWIN Oliver
LEWIS Brandon
LEWIS Julian
LIDDELL-GRAINGER Ian
LIDINGTON David
LILLEY Peter
LOPRESTI Jack
LORD Jonathan
LOUGHTON Tim
LUFF Peter
LUMLEY Karen
McCARTNEY Jason
McCARTNEY Karl
McINTOSH Anne
MACLEOD Mary
McLOUGHLIN Patrick
McPARTLAND Stephen
McVEY Esther
MAIN Anne
MAUDE Francis
MAY Theresa
MAYNARD Paul
MENZIES Mark
METCALFE Stephen
MILLER Maria
MILLS Nigel
MILTON Anne
MITCHELL Andrew
MORDAUNT Penny
MORGAN Nicky
MORRIS Anne Marie
MORRIS David
MORRIS James
MOSLEY Stephen
MOWAT David
MUNDELL David
MURRAY Sheryll

MURRISON Andrew
NEILL Robert
NEWMARK Brooks
NEWTON Sarah
NOKES Caroline
NORMAN Jesse
NUTTALL David
O'BRIEN Stephen
OFFORD Matthew
OLLERENSHAW Eric
OPPERMAN Guy
OSBORNE George
OTTAWAY Richard
PAICE Jim
PARISH Neil
PATEL Priti
PATERSON Owen
PAWSEY Mark
PENNING Mike
PENROSE John
PERCY Andrew
PERRY Claire
PHILLIPS Stephen
PICKLES Eric
PINCHER Christopher
POULTER Daniel
PRISK Mark
PRITCHARD Mark
RAAB Dominic
RANDALL John
RECKLESS Mark
REDWOOD John
REES-MOGG Jacob
REEVELL Simon
RIFKIND Malcolm
ROBATHAN Andrew
ROBERTSON Hugh
ROBERTSON Laurence
ROSINDELL Andrew
RUDD Amber
RUFFLEY David
RUTLEY David
SANDYS Laura
SCOTT Lee
SELOUS Andrew
SHAPPS Grant
SHARMA Alok
SHELBROOKE Alec
SHEPHERD Richard
SIMMONDS Mark
SIMPSON Keith
SKIDMORE Chris
SMITH Chloe

SMITH Henry
SMITH Julian
SOAMES Nicholas
SOUBRY Anna
SPELMAN Caroline
SPENCER Mark
STANLEY John
STEPHENSON Andrew
STEVENSON John
STEWART Bob
STEWART Iain
STEWART Rory
STREETER Gary
STRIDE Mel
STUART Graham
STURDY Julian
SWAYNE Desmond
SWIRE Hugo
SYMS Robert
TAPSELL Peter
TIMPSON Edward
TOMLINSON Justin
TREDINNICK David
TRUSS Elizabeth
TURNER Andrew
TYRIE Andrew
UPPAL Paul
VAIZEY Ed
VARA Shailesh
VICKERS Martin
VILLIERS Theresa
WALKER Charles
WALKER Robin
WALLACE Ben
WALTER Robert
WATKINSON Angela
WEATHERLEY Mike
WHARTON James
WHEELER Heather
WHITE Chris
WHITTAKER Craig
WHITTINGDALE John
WIGGIN Bill
WILLETTS David
WILLIAMSON Gavin
WILSON Robert
WOLLASTON Sarah
WRIGHT Jeremy
YEO Tim
YOUNG George
ZAHAWI Nadhim

Labour

ABBOTT Diane
ABRAHAMS Debbie
AINSWORTH Bob
ALEXANDER Douglas
ALEXANDER Heidi
ALI Rushanara
ALLEN Graham
ANDERSON David
ASHWORTH Jon
AUSTIN Ian
BAIN Willie
BANKS Gordon
BARRON Kevin
BAYLEY Hugh
BECKETT Margaret
BEGG Anne
BENN Hilary
BENTON Joe
BETTS Clive
BLACKMAN-WOODS
  Roberta
BLEARS Hazel
BLENKINSOP Tom
BLOMFIELD Paul
BLUNKETT David
BRADSHAW Ben
BRENNAN Kevin
BROWN Gordon
BROWN Lyn
BROWN Nick
BROWN Russell
BRYANT Chris
BUCK Karen
BURDEN Richard
BURNHAM Andy
BYRNE Liam
CAMPBELL Alan
CAMPBELL Ronnie
CATON Martin
CHAMPION Sarah
CHAPMAN Jenny
CLARK Katy
CLARKE Tom
CLWYD Ann
COAKER Vernon
COFFEY Ann
CONNARTY Michael
COOPER Rosie
COOPER Yvette
CORBYN Jeremy
CRAUSBY David
CREAGH Mary

CRUDDAS Jon
CRYER John
CUNNINGHAM Alex
CUNNINGHAM James
CUNNINGHAM Tony
CURRAN Margaret
DAKIN Nic
DANCZUK Simon
DARLING Alistair
DAVID Wayne
DENHAM John
DE PIERO Gloria
DOBSON Frank
DOCHERTY Thomas
DONOHOE Brian
DORAN Frank
DOWD Jim
DROMEY Jack
DUGHER Michael
EAGLE Angela
EAGLE Maria
EFFORD Clive
ELLIOTT Julie
ENGEL Natascha
ESTERSON Bill
FARRELLY Paul
FIELD Frank
FITZPATRICK Jim
FLELLO Robert
FLINT Caroline
FLYNN Paul
FOVARGUE Yvonne
FRANCIS Hywel
GARDINER Barry
GILMORE Sheila
GLASS Patricia
GLINDON Mary
GODSIFF Roger
GOGGINS Paul
GOODMAN Helen
GREEN Kate
GREENWOOD Lilian
GRIFFITH Nia
GWYNNE Andrew
HAIN Peter
HAMILTON David
HAMILTON Fabian
HANSON David
HARMAN Harriet
HARRIS Tom
HAVARD Dai
HEALEY John

HEPBURN Stephen
HEYES David
HILLING Julie
HODGE Margaret
HODGSON Sharon
HOEY Kate
HOOD Jim
HOPKINS Kelvin
HOWARTH George
HOYLE Lindsay
HUNT Tristram
IRRANCA-DAVIES Huw
JACKSON Glenda
JAMES Siân
JARVIS Dan
JOHNSON Alan
JOHNSON Diana
JONES Graham
JONES Helen
JONES Kevan
JONES Susan Elan
JOWELL Tessa
KAUFMAN Gerald
KEELEY Barbara
KENDALL Liz
KHAN Sadiq
LAMMY David
LAVERY Ian
LEWELL-BUCK Emma
LEWIS Ivan
LUCAS Ian
McCABE Steve
McCANN Michael
McCARTHY Kerry
McCLYMONT Gregg
McDONAGH Siobhain
McDONALD Andy
McDONNELL John
McFADDEN Pat
McGOVERN Alison
McGOVERN Jim
McGUIRE Anne
McKECHIN Ann
McKENZIE Iain
McKINNELL Catherine
MACTAGGART Fiona
MAHMOOD Khalid
MAHMOOD Shabana
MALHOTRA Seema
MANN John
MARSDEN Gordon
MEACHER Michael

MEALE Alan
MEARNS Ian
MILIBAND Ed
MILLER Andrew
MITCHELL Austin
MOON Madeleine
MORDEN Jessica
MORRICE Graeme
MORRIS Grahame
MUDIE George
MURPHY Jim
MURPHY Paul
MURRAY Ian
NANDY Lisa
NASH Pamela
O'DONNELL Fiona
ONWURAH Chi
OSBORNE Sandra
OWEN Albert
PEARCE Teresa
PERKINS Toby
PHILLIPSON Bridget
POUND Stephen
PRIMAROLO Dawn
QURESHI Yasmin

RAYNSFORD Nick
REED Jamie
REED Steve
REEVES Rachel
REYNOLDS Emma
ROBERTSON John
ROBINSON Geoffrey
ROTHERAM Steve
ROY Frank
ROY Lindsay
RUANE Chris
RUDDOCK Joan
SARWAR Anas
SEABECK Alison
SHARMA Virendra
SHERIDAN Jim
SKINNER Dennis
SLAUGHTER Andy
SMITH Andrew
SMITH Angela
SMITH Nick
SMITH Owen
SPELLAR John
STRAW Jack
STRINGER Graham

STUART Gisela
SUTCLIFFE Gerry
TAMI Mark
THORNBERRY Emily
TIMMS Stephen
TRICKETT Jon
TURNER Karl
TWIGG Derek
UMUNNA Chuka
VAZ Keith
VAZ Valerie
WALLEY Joan
WATSON Tom
WATTS David
WHITEHEAD Alan
WILLIAMSON Chris
WILSON Phil
WINNICK David
WINTERTON Rosie
WOOD Mike
WOODWARD Shaun
WRIGHT David
WRIGHT Iain

Labour/Co-operative

BAILEY Adrian
BALLS Ed
BERGER Luciana
CREASY Stella
DAVIDSON Ian
DAVIES Geraint
DOBBIN Jim
DOUGHTY Stephen
DOYLE Gemma
ELLMAN Louise

EVANS Chris
GAPES Mike
GREATREX Tom
HENDRICK Mark
HILLIER Meg
JAMIESON Cathy
LAZAROWICZ Mark
LESLIE Chris
LOVE Andy
MUNN Meg

POWELL Lucy
REYNOLDS Jonathan
RIORDAN Linda
SAWFORD Andy
SHEERMAN Barry
SHUKER Gavin
THOMAS Gareth
TWIGG Stephen
WOODCOCK John

Liberal Democrat

ALEXANDER Danny
BAKER Norman
BEITH Alan
BIRTWISTLE Gordon
BRAKE Tom
BROOKE Annette
BROWNE Jeremy
BRUCE Malcolm
BURSTOW Paul
BURT Lorely
CABLE Vincent
CAMPBELL Menzies
CARMICHAEL Alistair
CLEGG Nick

CROCKART Mike
DAVEY Edward
FARRON Tim
FEATHERSTONE Lynne
FOSTER Don
GEORGE Andrew
GILBERT Steve
HAMES Duncan
HARVEY Nick
HEATH David
HEMMING John
HORWOOD Martin
HUGHES Simon
HUNTER Mark

HUPPERT Julian
KENNEDY Charles
LAMB Norman
LAWS David
LEECH John
LLOYD Stephen
MOORE Michael
MULHOLLAND Greg
MUNT Tessa
PUGH John
REID Alan
ROGERSON Dan
RUSSELL Bob
SANDERS Adrian

SMITH Robert
STUNELL Andrew
SWALES Ian
SWINSON Jo
TEATHER Sarah

THORNTON Mike
THURSO John
WARD David
WEBB Steve
WILLIAMS Mark

WILLIAMS Roger
WILLIAMS Stephen
WILLOTT Jenny
WRIGHT Simon

Democratic Unionist Party

CAMPBELL Gregory
DODDS Nigel
DONALDSON Jeffrey

McCREA William
PAISLEY Ian
SHANNON Jim

SIMPSON David
WILSON Sammy

Independent

EVANS Nigel
HANCOCK Mike

HERMON Sylvia
JOYCE Eric

MERCER Patrick

Scottish National Party

HOSIE Stewart
MacNEIL Angus

ROBERTSON Angus
WEIR Mike

WHITEFORD Eilidh
WISHART Peter

Sinn Féin

DOHERTY Pat
GILDERNEW Michelle

MASKEY Paul
MOLLOY Francie

MURPHY Conor

Plaid Cymru

EDWARDS Jonathan

LLWYD Elfyn

WILLIAMS Hywel

Social Democratic and Labour Party

DURKAN Mark

McDONNELL Alasdair

RITCHIE Margaret

Alliance

LONG Naomi

Green Party

LUCAS Caroline

Respect – The Unity Coalition

GALLOWAY George

The Speaker

BERCOW John

Need additional copies?

Call 020 7593 5679

Visit www.dodsshop.co.uk

Select Committees

Each Department of State is shadowed by a Select Committee. In addition to these departmentally related select committees there are committees with responsibilities cutting across a range of government departments (Public Accounts, Public Administration, Environmental Audit, Human Rights, Statutory Instruments, European Scrutiny, Regulatory Reform, etc.) and a number of committees which concern themselves with the running of the House.

Departmental Committees

Committees on Arms Export Controls

The Committees on Arms Export Controls consist of four select committees meeting concurrently: Business, Innovation and Skills; Defence; Foreign Affairs; and International Development. All members of the four committees can attend; the committees have designated the following members to attend meetings of the Committees on Arms Export Controls.

Tel: 020 7219 3267 Fax: 020 7219 5365
Email: caeccom@parliament.uk
www.parliament.uk/caeccom

Sir John Stanley (Chair)	*Con*
Business, Innovation and Skills:	
Katy Clark	*Lab*
Ann McKechin	*Lab*
Robin Walker	*Con*
Nadhim Zahawi	*Con*
Defence:	
Thomas Docherty	*Lab*
Jeffrey Donaldson	*DUP*
Penny Mordaunt	*Con*
Bob Stewart	*Con*
Foreign Affairs:	
Ann Clwyd	*Lab*
Mike Gapes	*Lab/Co-op*
International Development:	
Sir Malcolm Bruce	*Lib Dem*
Richard Burden	*Lab*
Fabian Hamilton	*Lab*
Sir John Stanley	*Con*
Chris White	*Con*

Staff: Keith Neary (Clerk), Duma Langton (Committee Specialist), Alex Paterson (Media Officer), Jacqui Cooksey (Committee Assistant)

Business, Innovation and Skills

Tel: 020 7219 5777 Fax: 020 7219 2731
Email: biscom@parliament.uk
www.parliament.uk/bis

Adrian Bailey (Chair)	*Lab/Co-op*
Brian Binley	*Con*
Paul Blomfield	*Lab*
Katy Clark	*Lab*
Mike Crockart	*Lib Dem*
Caroline Dinenage	*Con*

Julie Elliott	*Lab*
Rebecca Harris	*Con*
Ann McKechin	*Lab*
Robin Walker	*Con*
Nadhim Zahawi	*Con*

Staff: James Davies (Clerk), Amelia Aspden (Second Clerk), Peter Stam, Josephine Willows (Committee Specialists), David Foster (Media Officer), Ian Hook (Senior Committee Assistant), Pam Morris (Committee Assistant), Henry Ayi-Hyde (Committee Support Assistant)

Communities and Local Government

Tel: 020 7219 4972 Fax: 020 7219 6101
Email: clgcom@parliament.uk
www.parliament.uk/clg

Clive Betts (Chair)	*Lab*
Bob Blackman	*Con*
Simon Danczuk	*Lab*
Mary Glindon	*Lab*
David Heyes	*Lab*
James Morris	*Con*
Mark Pawsey	*Con*
Dr John Pugh	*Lib Dem*
Andy Sawford	*Lab/Co-op*
John Stevenson	*Con*
Heather Wheeler	*Con*

Staff: Glenn McKee (Clerk), Sarah Heath (Second Clerk), Stephen Habberley, Kevin Maddison (Committee Specialists), David Foster (Media Officer), Emma McIntosh (Senior Committee Assistant), Mandy Sullivan (Committee Assistant), Stewart McIllvenna (Committee Support Assistant)

Culture, Media and Sport

Tel: 020 7219 6188 Fax: 020 7219 2031
Email: cmscom@parliament.uk
www.parliament.uk/cmscom

John Whittingdale (Chair)	*Con*
Ben Bradshaw	*Lab*
Angie Bray	*Con*
Conor Burns	*Con*
Tracey Crouch	*Con*
Philip Davies	*Con*
Paul Farrelly	*Lab*
John Leech	*Lib Dem*

Steve Rotheram   *Lab*
Jim Sheridan   *Lab*
Gerry Sutcliffe   *Lab*
Staff: Elizabeth Flood (Clerk), Grahame Danby (Second Clerk), Kevin Candy (Inquiry Manager), Jessica Bridges-Palmer (Media Officer), Emily Gregory (Senior Committee Assistant), Keely Bishop (Committee Assistant)

Defence

Tel: 020 7219 5745 Fax: 020 7219 6952
Email: defcom@parliament.uk
www.parliament.uk/defcom

James Arbuthnot (Chair)   *Con*
Julian Brazier   *Con*
Thomas Docherty   *Lab*
Jeffrey Donaldson   *DUP*
Dai Havard   *Lab*
Adam Holloway   *Con*
Madeleine Moon   *Lab*
Penny Mordaunt   *Con*
Sir Bob Russell   *Lib Dem*
Bob Stewart   *Con*
Gisela Stuart   *Lab*
Derek Twigg   *Lab*
Staff: Alda Barry, James Rhys (Clerks), Dougie Wands (Second Clerk), Ian Thomson (Committee Specialist), Karen Jackson (Audit Adviser), Alex Paterson (Media Officer), Chris Randall (Senior Committee Assistant), Rowena Macdonald, Carolyn Bowes (Committee Assistants), Sumati Sowamber (Committee Support Assistant)

Education

Tel: 020 7219 6181 Fax: 020 7219 0848
Email: educom@parliament.uk
www.parliament.uk/education-committee

Graham Stuart (Chair)   *Con*
Neil Carmichael   *Con*
Alex Cunningham   *Lab*
Bill Esterson   *Lab*
Patricia Glass   *Lab*
Charlotte Leslie   *Con*
Siobhain McDonagh   *Lab*
Ian Mearns   *Lab*
Chris Skidmore   *Con*
David Ward   *Lib Dem*
Craig Whittaker   *Con*
Staff: Lynn Gardner (Clerk), Geraldine Alexander (Second Clerk), Emma Gordon (Committee Specialist), Hannah Pearce (Media Officer), Ameet Chudasama (Senior Committee Assistant), Caroline McElwee (Committee Assistant), Paul Hampson (Committee Support Assistant)

Energy and Climate Change

Tel: 020 7219 2569 Fax: 020 7219 1362
Email: ecc@parliament.uk
www.parliament.uk/ecc

Tim Yeo (Chair)   *Con*
Dan Byles   *Con*
Barry Gardiner   *Lab*
Ian Lavery   *Lab*
Dr Phillip Lee   *Con*
Peter Lilley   *Con*
Albert Owen   *Lab*
Christopher Pincher   *Con*
John Robertson   *Lab*
Sir Robert Smith   *Lib Dem*
Dr Alan Whitehead   *Lab*
Staff: Sarah Hartwell-Naguib (Clerk), To be appointed (Second Clerk), Alfred Gathorne-Hardy, Tom Leveridge (Committee Specialists), Nick Davies (Media Officer), Shane Pathmanathan (Senior Committee Assistant), Jonathan Wright (Committee Assistant), Joe Strawson (Committee Support Assistant)

Environment, Food and Rural Affairs

Tel: 020 7219 5774 Fax: 020 7219 2094
Email: efracom@parliament.uk
www.parliament.uk/efracom

Anne McIntosh (Chair)   *Con*
Richard Drax   *Con*
Barry Gardiner   *Lab*
Mary Glindon   *Lab*
Emma Lewell-Buck   *Lab*
Iain McKenzie   *Lab*
Sheryll Murray   *Con*
Neil Parish   *Con*
Margaret Ritchie   *SDLP*
Staff: David Weir (Clerk), Dr Anna Dickson (Second Clerk), Sarah Coe (Senior Committee Specialist), Philip Jones (Committee Specialist), Hannah Pearce (Media Officer), Clare Genis (Senior Committee Assistant), Owen James (Committee Assistant), Sayeda Begum (Committee Support Assistant)

Foreign Affairs

Tel: 020 7219 6105 Fax: 020 7219 5365
Email: foraffcom@parliament.uk
www.parliament.uk/facom

Richard Ottaway (Chair)   *Con*
John Baron   *Con*
Sir Menzies Campbell   *Lib Dem*

Ann Clwyd	Lab
Mike Gapes	Lab/Co-op
Mark Hendrick	Lab/Co-op
Sandra Osborne	Lab
Andrew Rosindell	Con
Frank Roy	Lab
Sir John Stanley	Con
Rory Stewart	Con

Staff: Kenneth Fox (Clerk), Peter McGrath (Second Clerk), Brigid Fowler, Zoe Oliver Watts (Committee Specialists), Alex Paterson (Media Officer), Louise Glen (Senior Committee Assistant), Vanessa Hallinan (Committee Assistant)

Health

Tel: 020 7219 5466 Fax: 020 7219 5171
Email: healthcom@parliament.uk
www.parliament.uk/healthcom

Stephen Dorrell (Chair)	Con
Rosie Cooper	Lab
Andrew George	Lib Dem
Barbara Keeley	Lab
Charlotte Leslie	Con
Grahame Morris	Lab
Andrew Percy	Con
Virendra Sharma	Lab
David Tredinnick	Con
Valerie Vaz	Lab
Dr Sarah Wollaston	Con

Staff: David Lloyd (Clerk), Martyn Atkins (Second Clerk), Laura Daniels, Stephen Aldhouse (Committee Specialists), Hannah Pearce (Media Officer), Frances Allingham (Senior Committee Assistant), Ronnie Jefferson (Committee Assistant)

Home Affairs

Tel: 020 7219 3276
Email: homeaffcom@parliament.uk
www.parliament.uk/homeaffairscom

Keith Vaz (Chair)	Lab
Nicola Blackwood	Con
James Clappison	Con
Michael Ellis	Con
Lorraine Fullbrook	Con
Dr Julian Huppert	Lib Dem
Steve McCabe	Lab
Bridget Phillipson	Lab
Mark Reckless	Con
Chris Ruane	Lab
David Winnick	Lab

Staff: Tom Healey (Clerk), Rob Cope (Second Clerk), Ellie Scarnell (Committee Specialist), Alex Paterson (Media Officer), Andy Boyd (Senior Committee Assistant), Michelle Garratty (Committee Assistant), Iwona Hankin (Committee Support Assistant)

International Development

Tel: 020 7219 1223 Fax: 020 7219 2891
Email: indcom@parliament.uk
www.parliament.uk/indcom

Sir Malcolm Bruce (Chair)	Lib Dem
Hugh Bayley	Lab
Fiona Bruce	Con
Richard Burden	Lab
Fabian Hamilton	Lab
Pauline Latham	Con
Jeremy Lefroy	Con
Michael McCann	Lab
Fiona O'Donnell	Lab
Mark Pritchard	Con
Chris White	Con

Staff: David Harrison (Clerk), Chloë Challender (Senior Committee Specialist), Rob Page (Committee Specialist), Judith Goodall (Inquiry Manager), Hannah Pearce (Media Officer), Anita Fuki (Senior Committee Assistant), Annabel Goddard (Committee Assistant), Paul Hampson (Committee Support Assistant)

Justice

Tel: 020 7219 8196 Fax: 020 7219 0843
Email: justicecom@parliament.uk
www.parliament.uk/justicecom

Sir Alan Beith (Chair)	Lib Dem
Steve Brine	Con
Rehman Chishti	Con
Jeremy Corbyn	Lab
Nick de Bois	Con
Gareth Johnson	Con
Elfyn Llwyd	PlC
Andy McDonald	Lab
Seema Malhotra	Lab
Yasmin Qureshi	Lab
Graham Stringer	Lab
Mike Weatherley	Con

Staff: Nick Walker (Clerk), Sarah Petit (Second Clerk), Helen Kinghorn (Legal Specialist), Gemma Buckland (Public Policy Specialist), Nick Davies (Media Officer), Ana Ferreira (Senior Committee Assistant), Miguel Boo Fraga (Committee Assistant), Holly Knowles (Committee Support Assistant)

Northern Ireland Affairs

Tel: 020 7219 2173
Email: northircom@parliament.uk
www.parliament.uk/niacom

Laurence Robertson (Chair)	Con
David Anderson	Lab
Joe Benton	Lab
Oliver Colvile	Con
Stephen Hepburn	Lab
Lady Sylvia Hermon	Ind
Kate Hoey	Lab
Naomi Long	All
Jack Lopresti	Con
Dr Alasdair McDonnell	SDLP
Nigel Mills	Con
Ian Paisley	DUP
Andrew Percy	Con
David Simpson	DUP

Staff: Mike Clark (Clerk), Jessica Bridges-Palmer (Media Officer), Edward Faulkner (Senior Committee Assistant), Ravi Abhayaratne (Committee Support Assistant)

Science and Technology

Tel: 020 7219 2793/4 Fax: 020 7219 0896
Email: scitechcom@parliament.uk
www.parliament.uk/science

Andrew Miller (Chair)	Lab
Jim Dowd	Lab
Stephen Metcalfe	Con
David Morris	Con
Stephen Mosley	Con
Pamela Nash	Lab
Sarah Newton	Con
Graham Stringer	Lab
David Tredinnick	Con
Hywel Williams	PlC
Roger Williams	Lib Dem

Staff: Stephen McGinness (Clerk), Jessica Montgomery (Second Clerk), Xameerah Malik (Senior Committee Specialist), Victoria Charlton (Committee Specialist), Nick Davies (Media Officer), Darren Hackett (Senior Committee Assistant), Julie Storey (Committee Assistant), Henry Ayi-Hyde (Committee Support Assistant)

Scottish Affairs

Tel: 020 7219 6123 Fax: 020 7219 1362
Email: scotaffcom@parliament.uk
www.parliament.uk/scotaffcom

Ian Davidson (Chair)	Lab/Co-op
Mike Crockart	Lib Dem
Eleanor Laing	Con
Jim McGovern	Lab
Graeme Morrice	Lab

Pamela Nash	Lab
Sir Jim Paice	Con
Simon Reevell	Con
Alan Reid	Lib Dem
Lindsay Roy	Lab
Dr Eilidh Whiteford	SNP

Staff: Rebecca Davies, Rhiannon Hollis (Clerks), Duma Langton (Committee Specialist), Jessica Bridges-Palmer (Media Officer), Gabrielle Hill (Senior Committee Assistant), Ravi Abhayaratne (Committee Support Assistant)

Transport

Tel: 020 7219 6263 Fax: 020 7219 0909
Email: transcom@parliament.uk
www.parliament.uk/transcom

Louise Ellman (Chair)	Lab/Co-op
Sarah Champion	Lab
Jim Dobbin	Lab/Co-op
Karen Lumley	Con
Jason McCartney	Con
Karl McCartney	Con
Lucy Powell	Lab/Co-op
Adrian Sanders	Lib Dem
Iain Stewart	Con
Graham Stringer	Lab
Martin Vickers	Con

Staff: Mark Egan (Clerk), Farrah Bhatti (Second Clerk), Richard Jeremy (Committee Specialist), Hannah Pearce (Media Officer), Adrian Hitchins (Senior Committee Assistant), Stewart McIllvenna (Committee Assistant)

Treasury

Tel: 020 7219 5769 Fax: 020 7219 2069
Email: treascom@parliament.uk
www.parliament.uk/treascom

Andrew Tyrie (Chair)	Con
Mark Garnier	Con
Stewart Hosie	SNP
Andrea Leadsom	Con
Andy Love	Lab/Co-op
Pat McFadden	Lab
John Mann	Lab
George Mudie	Lab
Brooks Newmark	Con
Jesse Norman	Con
Teresa Pearce	Lab
David Ruffley	Con
John Thurso	Lib Dem

Staff: Christopher Stanton (Clerk), Lydia Menzies (Second Clerk), Jay Sheth, Adam Wales (Senior Economists), Matthew Manning (Committee Specialist), James Abbott (Media Officer), Steven Price (Senior Committee Assistant), Lisa Stead (Committee Assistant)

Welsh Affairs

Tel: 020 7219 3264 Fax: 020 7219 0300
Email: welshcom@parliament.uk
www.parliament.uk/welshcom

David Davies (Chair)	Con
Guto Bebb	Con
Geraint Davies	Lab/Co-op
Glyn Davies	Con
Stephen Doughty	Lab/Co-op
Jonathan Edwards	PlC
Nia Griffith	Lab
Simon Hart	Con
Siân James	Lab
Karen Lumley	Con
Jessica Morden	Lab
Mark Williams	Lib Dem

Staff: Marek Kubala (Clerk), Anwen Rees (Committee Specialist), Jessica Bridges-Palmer (Media Officer), Alison Mara (Senior Committee Assistant), Baris Tufekci (Committee Assistant)

Work and Pensions

Tel: 020 7219 5833 Fax: 020 7219 0580
Email: workpencom@parliament.uk
www.parliament.uk/workpencom

Dame Anne Begg (Chair)	Lab
Debbie Abrahams	Lab
Jane Ellison	Con
Graham Evans	Con
Mike Freer	Con
Sheila Gilmore	Lab
Glenda Jackson	Lab
Stephen Lloyd	Lib Dem
Nigel Mills	Con
Anne Marie Morris	Con
Teresa Pearce	Lab

Staff: Carol Oxborough (Clerk), To be appointed (Second Clerk), James Clarke, Daniela Silcock (Committee Specialists), David Foster (Assistant Media Officer), Emma Sawyer (Senior Committee Assistant), Hannah Beattie (Committee Assistant)

Joint Committees

See Lords and Commons Joint Select Committees on p1100

Committees on Private Bills

Court of Referees

The Court of Referees is a committee of senior backbenchers, assisted by the Speaker's Counsel, which decides on cases involving the right of any petitioner to make a challenge to a Private Bill (known as *locus standi*). The three Deputy Speakers and the Counsel to the Speaker are *ex-officio* members.

Members are still to be appointed.

Tel: 020 7219 3257

Staff: Simon Patrick (Clerk), Michael Carpenter (Speaker's Counsel (ex-officio))

Standing Orders

When the Examiners of Petitions for Private Bills decide that Standing Orders relating to Private Business have not been complied with in relation to an individual bill, the Standing Orders Committee (appointed for the duration of a Parliament) decides whether or not to dispense with the Standing Order(s) under question. The three Deputy Speakers are *ex-officio* members.

Tel: 020 7219 3771
Email: howes@parliament.uk

Nick Boles	Con
Geraint Davies	Lab/Co-op
John Hemming	Lib Dem

Helen Jones	Lab
Andrew Percy	Con
Christopher Pincher	Con
Jonathan Reynolds	Lab/Co-op
Charles Walker	Con

Staff: Sara Howe (Clerk)

Committee on Unopposed Bills (Panel)

Private bills, which in a given period have not been petitioned against, are referred to an Unopposed Bills Committee, which is appointed at the start of each Session. As a rule, this is chaired by either the First or Second Deputy Chairman. Four members from the Unopposed Bills Panel are selected to be part of individual Unopposed Bill committees. The three Deputy Speakers are *ex-officio* members.

Tel: 020 7219 3771
Email: howes@parliament.uk

Richard Bacon	Con
Adrian Bailey	Lab/Co-op
Sir Peter Bottomley	Con
Rosie Cooper	Lab
Geraint Davies	Lab/Co-op
Michael Ellis	Con
Bill Esterson	Lab
Paul Farrelly	Lab
Mary Glindon	Lab

Bernard Jenkin	Con	Teresa Pearce	Lab
Karl McCartney	Con	Sir Peter Tapsell	Con
Siobhain McDonagh	Lab	Justin Tomlinson	Con
John Mann	Lab	Robert Walter	Con
Grahame Morris	Lab	Craig Whittaker	Con
Guy Opperman	Con	*Staff*: Sara Howe (Clerk)	

Other Committees

Environmental Audit

Tel: 020 7219 5776
Email: eacom@parliament.uk
www.parliament.uk/eacom

Joan Walley (Chair)	Lab
Peter Aldous	Con
Richard Benyon	Con
Neil Carmichael	Con
Martin Caton	Lab
Katy Clark	Lab
Chris Evans	Lab/Co-op
Zac Goldsmith	Con
Mark Lazarowicz	Lab/Co-op
Dr Caroline Lucas	Green
Caroline Nokes	Con
Dr Matthew Offord	Con
Mark Spencer	Con
Paul Uppal	Con
Dr Alan Whitehead	Lab
Simon Wright	Lib Dem

Staff: Simon Fiander (Clerk), Nick Beech (Second Clerk), Lee Nicholson (Committee Specialist), Nick Davies (Media Officer), Andrew Wallace (Senior Committee Assistant), Anna Browning (Committee Assistant), Sayeda Begum (Committee Support Assistant)

European Scrutiny

Tel: 020 7219 3292 Fax: 020 7219 2509
Email: escom@parliament.uk
www.parliament.uk/escom

William Cash (Chair)	Con
Andrew Bingham	Con
James Clappison	Con
Michael Connarty	Lab
Geraint Davies	Lab/Co-op
Julie Elliott	Lab
Tim Farron	Lib Dem
Nia Griffith	Lab
Christopher Heaton-Harris	Con
Kelvin Hopkins	Lab
Chris Kelly	Con
Stephen Phillips	Con
Hon Jacob Rees-Mogg	Con
Linda Riordan	Lab/Co-op
Henry Smith	Con
Ian Swales	Lib Dem

Staff: Sarah Davies (Clerk), Terry Byrne, Leigh Gibson, David Griffiths, Peter Harborne (Clerk Advisers), Paul Hardy (Counsel for European Legislation), Joanne Dee (Assistant Legal Adviser), Alex Paterson (Media Officer), Hannah Finer (Assistant to the Clerk), Julie Evans (Senior Committee Assistant), John Graddon, Alex Hunter, Jane Lauder (Committee Assistants), Paula Saunderson (Office Support Assistant)

Members' Expenses

Tel: 020 7219 3299 Fax: 020 7219 2622
Email: cme@parliament.uk
www.parliament.uk/business/committees/
committees-a-z/commons-select/members-
expenses/

Adam Afriyie (Chair)	Con
Guto Bebb	Con
Cathy Jamieson	Lab/Co-op
Sir Edward Leigh	Con
Priti Patel	Con
Nick Raynsford	Lab
Joan Walley	Lab
Stephen Williams	Lib Dem

Staff: Bob Twigger (Clerk), Lee Bridges (Media Officer), Louise Sargent (Committee Assistant)

Political and Constitutional Reform

Tel: 020 7219 6287 Fax: 020 7219 2681
Email: pcrc@parliament.uk
www.parliament.uk/pcrc

Graham Allen (Chair)	Lab
Christopher Chope	Con
Paul Flynn	Lab
Sheila Gilmore	Lab
Andrew Griffiths	Con
Fabian Hamilton	Lab
Simon Hart	Con
Dr Tristram Hunt	Lab
Eleanor Laing	Con
Andrew Turner	Con
Stephen Williams	Lib Dem

Staff: Joanna Dodd (Clerk), Adele Brown (Senior Committee Specialist), Emma Fitzsimmons (Committee Specialist), Jessica Bridges-Palmer (Media Officer), Tony Catinella (Senior Committee Assistant), Jim Lawford (Committee Assistant)

Privileges

Tel: 020 7219 3259/3310 Fax: 020 7219 6864
Email: privileges@parliament.uk
www.parliament.uk/business/committees/
committees-a-z/commons-select/privileges

Kevin Barron (Chair)	Lab
Sir Paul Beresford	Con
Robert Buckland	Con
Christopher Chope	Con
Tom Clarke	Lab
Geoffrey Cox	Con
Sir Nick Harvey	Lib Dem
Fiona O'Donnell	Lab
Heather Wheeler	Con
Dr Alan Whitehead	Lab

Staff: Eve Samson (Clerk), Danielle Nash (Second Clerk), Liz Parratt (Media Officer), Christine McGrane (Committee Assistant)

Procedure

Tel: 020 7219 3318 Fax: 020 7219 2269
Email: proccom@parliament.uk
www.parliament.uk/proccom
Twitter: @CommonsProcCom

Charles Walker (Chair)	Con
Jenny Chapman	Lab
Nic Dakin	Lab
Thomas Docherty	Lab
Sir Roger Gale	Con
Helen Goodman	Lab
James Gray	Con
Tom Greatrex	Lab/Co-op
John Hemming	Lib Dem
David Nuttall	Con
Hon Jacob Rees-Mogg	Con
Martin Vickers	Con

Staff: Huw Yardley (Clerk), Margaret McKinnon (Second Clerk), Liz Parratt (Media Officer), Jim Camp (Committee Assistant)

Public Accounts

The Economic Secretary to HM Treasury is an *ex-officio* member.
Tel: 020 7219 5708 Fax: 020 7219 2782
Email: pubaccom@parliament.uk
www.parliament.uk/pac

Margaret Hodge (Chair)	Lab
Richard Bacon	Con
Steve Barclay	Con
Guto Bebb	Con
Jackie Doyle-Price	Con
Christopher Heaton-Harris	Con
Meg Hillier	Lab/Co-op
Stewart Jackson	Con

Member (ex-officio):

Nicky Morgan	Con
Fiona Mactaggart	Lab
Austin Mitchell	Lab
Nick Smith	Lab
Ian Swales	Lib Dem
Justin Tomlinson	Con

Staff: Adrian Jenner (Clerk), Alex Paterson (Media Officer), Claire Cozens (Committee Specialist), Sonia Draper (Senior Committee Assistant), Ian Blair (Committee Assistant), James McQuade (Committee Assistant)

Public Administration

Tel: 020 7219 5730 Fax: 020 7219 2681
Email: pasc@parliament.uk
www.parliament.uk/pasc

Bernard Jenkin (Chair)	Con
Alun Cairns	Con
Charlie Elphicke	Con
Paul Flynn	Lab
Robert Halfon	Con
David Heyes	Lab
Kelvin Hopkins	Lab
Greg Mulholland	Lib Dem
Priti Patel	Con
Steve Reed	Lab
Lindsay Roy	Lab

Staff: Emily Commander, Catherine Tyack (Clerks), Rebecca Short (Second Clerk), Alexandra Meakin (Committee Specialist), Jessica Bridges-Palmer (Media Officer), Paul Simpkin (Senior Committee Assistant), Su Panchanathan (Committee Assistant)

Regulatory Reform

Tel: 020 7219 5908 Fax: 020 7219 2731
Email: regrefcom@parliament.uk
www.parliament.uk/regrefcom

James Duddridge (Chair)	Con
Heidi Alexander	Lab
David Anderson	Lab
Andrew Bridgen	Con
Jack Dromey	Lab
Richard Fuller	Con
Lilian Greenwood	Lab
Rebecca Harris	Con
John Hemming	Lib Dem
Gordon Henderson	Con
Andrew Jones	Con
Ian Lavery	Lab
Andrew Percy	Con
Valerie Vaz	Lab

Staff: James Davies (Clerk), Amelia Aspden (Second Clerk), Peter Brooksbank, Peter Davis (Legal Advisers), Ian Hook (Senior Committee Assistant), Pam Morris (Committee Assistant)

Selection

To nominate or propose Members to serve on General and Select Committees of the House of Commons. The Committee's decisions are recorded in the Votes and Proceedings on a daily basis.

Tel: 020 7219 3254

Geoffrey Clifton-Brown (Chair)	Con
Heidi Alexander	Lab
Tom Blenkinsop	Lab
Alan Campbell	Lab
David Evennett	Con
Mark Hunter	Lib Dem
Anne Milton	Con
John Randall	Con
Mark Tami	Lab

Staff: Kate Emms (Clerk), Daniel Moeller (Committee Assistant)

Standards

Tel: 020 7219 3259/3310 Fax: 020 7219 6864
Email: standards@parliament.uk
www.parliament.uk/business/committees/committees-a-z/commons-select/standards

Kevin Barron (Chair)	Lab
Sir Paul Beresford	Con
Robert Buckland	Con
Christopher Chope	Con
Tom Clarke	Lab
Geoffrey Cox	Con
Sir Nick Harvey	Lib Dem
Fiona O'Donnell	Lab
Heather Wheeler	Con
Dr Alan Whitehead	Lab

Lay Members:
Sharon Darcy
Peter Jinman
Walter Radar

Staff: Eve Samson (Clerk), Danielle Nash (Second Clerk), Liz Parratt (Media Officer), Christine McGrane (Committee Assistant)

Internal Committees

Administration

Tel: 020 7219 2471 Fax: 020 7219 2622
Email: ac@parliament.uk
www.parliament.uk/ac

Sir Alan Haselhurst (Chair)	Con
Karen Bradley	Con
Thomas Docherty	Lab
Tom Harris	Lab
Mark Hunter	Lib Dem
Marcus Jones	Con
Nigel Mills	Con
David Morris	Con
Tessa Munt	Lib Dem
John Penrose	Con
Nicholas Soames	Con
Desmond Swayne	Con
Mark Tami	Lab
Keith Vaz	Lab
David Watts	Lab
David Wright	Lab

Staff: Helen Wood (Clerk), Elizabeth Bolton (Second Clerk), Anikka Weerasinghe (Media Officer), Jennifer Kelly (Committee Assistant)

Backbench Business

Tel: 020 7219 3731
Email: bbcom@parliament.uk
www.parliament.uk/bbcom

Natascha Engel (Chair)	Lab

David Amess	Con
David Anderson	Lab
Bob Blackman	Con
Jane Ellison	Con
John Hemming	Lib Dem
Marcus Jones	Con
Ian Mearns	Lab

Staff: Robin James (Clerk), To be appointed (Second Clerk), Gary Calder (Media Officer), Michael Everett (Committee Assistant)

Finance and Services

Tel: 020 7219 3299 Fax: 020 7219 2622
Email: twiggerrj@parliament.uk
www.parliament.uk/fsc

John Thurso (Chair)	Lib Dem
Sir Paul Beresford	Con
Clive Betts	Lab
Geoffrey Clifton-Brown	Con
Robert Flello	Lab
James Gray	Con
Sir Alan Haselhurst	Con
George Howarth	Lab
Lindsay Hoyle	Lab
Greg Knight	Con
Iain Wright	Lab

Staff: Bob Twigger (Clerk), Louise Sargent (Committee Assistant)

Liaison

Tel: 020 7219 5675 Fax: 020 7219 6952
Email: liaisoncommittee@parliament.uk
www.parliament.uk/liaisoncom

Sir Alan Beith (Chair)	*Lib Dem*
Graham Allen	*Lab*
James Arbuthnot	*Con*
Adrian Bailey	*Lab/Co-op*
Kevin Barron	*Lab*
Dame Anne Begg	*Lab*
Clive Betts	*Lab*
Sir Malcolm Bruce	*Lib Dem*
William Cash	*Con*
Geoffrey Clifton-Brown	*Con*
Ian Davidson	*Lab/Co-op*
David Davies	*Con*
Stephen Dorrell	*Con*
James Duddridge	*Con*
Louise Ellman	*Lab/Co-op*
Natascha Engel	*Lab*
Dr Hywel Francis	*Lab*
Sir Alan Haselhurst	*Con*
Margaret Hodge	*Lab*
Bernard Jenkin	*Con*
Anne McIntosh	*Con*
Andrew Miller	*Lab*
George Mudie	*Lab*
Richard Ottaway	*Con*
Laurence Robertson	*Con*
Graham Stuart	*Con*
John Thurso	*Lib Dem*
Andrew Tyrie	*Con*
Keith Vaz	*Lab*
Charles Walker	*Con*
Joan Walley	*Lab*
John Whittingdale	*Con*
Tim Yeo	*Con*

Staff: Andrew Kennon, Philippa Helme (Clerks), Mark Hutton (Clerk (National Policy Statements Sub-Committee)), Liz Parratt (Media Officer), Katie Phelan-Molloy (Senior Committee Assistant), Susan Ramsay (Committee Assistant)

National Policy Statements Sub-Committee

Sir Alan Beith (Chair)	*Lib Dem*
Clive Betts	*Lab*
David Davies	*Con*
Louise Ellman	*Lab/Co-op*
Anne McIntosh	*Con*
Joan Walley	*Lab*
Tim Yeo	*Con*

Panel of Chairs

The Panel of Chairs comprises the Chairman of Ways and Means, the Deputy Chairmen of Ways and Means, and not fewer than ten Members

nominated by the Speaker. Members of the Panel chair debates in Westminster Hall and act as the chairs of Public Bill Committees and other general committees. They may also act as temporary chairs of committees of the whole House when requested by the Chairman of Ways and Means.

Tel: 020 7219 3257
Email: pbohoc@parliament.uk

Lindsay Hoyle (Chair)	*Lab*
Ex-officio Members:	
Nigel Evans	*Ind*
Dawn Primarolo	*Lab*
Members:	
David Amess	*Con*
Hugh Bayley	*Lab*
Joe Benton	*Lab*
Clive Betts	*Lab*
Peter Bone	*Con*
Graham Brady	*Con*
Annette Brooke	*Lib Dem*
Martin Caton	*Lab*
Christopher Chope	*Con*
Katy Clark	*Lab*
David Crausby	*Lab*
Philip Davies	*Con*
Jim Dobbin	*Lab/Co-op*
Nadine Dorries	*Con*
Sir Roger Gale	*Con*
James Gray	*Con*
Dai Havard	*Lab*
Philip Hollobone	*Con*
Jim Hood	*Lab*
George Howarth	*Lab*
Sir Edward Leigh	*Con*
Dr William McCrea	*DUP*
Anne McIntosh	*Con*
Anne Main	*Con*
Sir Alan Meale	*Lab*
Sandra Osborne	*Lab*
Albert Owen	*Lab*
Mark Pritchard	*Con*
Linda Riordan	*Lab/Co-op*
John Robertson	*Lab*
Andrew Rosindell	*Con*
Jim Sheridan	*Lab*
Gary Streeter	*Con*
Andrew Turner	*Con*
Charles Walker	*Con*
Mike Weir	*SNP*
Hywel Williams	*PlC*

Staff: Simon Patrick (Secretary)

Officers and Officials

Office of the Chief Executive

Tel: 020 7219 1707

Clerk of the House and Chief Executive: Sir Robert Rogers KCB 020 7219 3758
Head of Office and Secretary to the Management Board: Matthew Hamlyn 020 7219 1707
Private Secretary to the Clerk: Ben Williams
Director of Internal Audit: Paul Dillon-Robinson
Head of Central Communications: Marianne Cwynarski
Central Communications Manager: Vasilis Gialias
Corporate Risk Management Facilitator: Rachel Harrison
Strategy, Planning and Performance Manager: Jane Hough
Parliamentary Programme and Project Assurance: Jane Rumsam

Department of Chamber and Committee Services

Tel: 020 7219 8232

Clerk Assistant and Director General: David Natzler 020 7219 3311
Director of Departmental Services: Tom Goldsmith 020 7219 8428
Human Resources Enquiries: Soraya Ounssi 020 7219 2904

Media and Communications Service (Select Committees)

Head: Liz Parratt 020 7219 1708
Select Committee Media Officers: James Abbott 020 7219 2003, Jessica Bridges-Palmer 020 7219
0724, Nick Davies 020 7219 3297, David Foster 020 7219 7556, Alex Paterson 020 7219 1589,
Hannah Pearce 020 7219 8430

Overseas Office

Tel: 020 7219 3728
Email: overseasoffice@parliament.uk

Principal Clerk: Crispin Poyser 020 7219 3728
Delegation Secretaries: Jyoti Chandola 020 7219 3293, Nick Wright 020 7219 3293

National Parliament Office, Brussels

National Parliament Representative: Ed Beale
Deputy National Parliament Representative: Sarah Clarkson

Chamber Business Directorate

Clerk of Legislation: Jacqy Sharpe 020 7219 3255
Clerk of Bills, Examiner of Petitions for Private Bills and Taxing Officer: Simon Patrick 020 7219 3257

Public Bill Office

Clerks: Kate Emms, John-Paul Flaherty, Georgina Holmes-Skelton, Steven Mark, David Slater

Private Bill Office

Clerk of Private Bills: Neil Caulfield

Journal Office

Tel: 020 7219 3252/020 7219 3361
Email: journaloffice@parliament.uk

Clerk of the Journals: Liam Laurence-Smyth 020 7219 3315
Clerks: Richard Cooke, Margaret McKinnon, Huw Yardley, Mark Etherton, Elizabeth Hunt, Lloyd Owen

Table Office

Tel: 020 7219 3305
Email: tableoffice@parliament.uk
Principal Clerk: Paul Evans
Clerks: Eliot Barrass, Judith Boyce, Tracey Jessup, Dr Robin James, Richard Ward

Editorial Supervisor of the Vote

Supervisor: Lynn Lewis

Vote Office

Deliverer of the Vote: Catherine Fogarty 020 7219 4220
Deputy Deliverer of the Vote: Owen Sweeney

Committee Directorate

Tel: 020 7219 3267/020 7219 4300

Clerk of Committees: Andrew Kennon 020 7219 3313
Principal Clerk of Select Committees and Deputy Head of Committee Office:
Philippa Helme 020 7219 2712
Clerk of Domestic Committees: Bob Twigger 020 7219 3299
Principal Clerks: Mark Hutton 020 7219 1341, Colin Lee 020 7219 0477,
Christopher Stanton 020 7219 3285
Head of Scrutiny Unit: Jessica Mulley 020 7219 8370
Head of Media and Communications (Select Committees): Liz Parratt 020 7219 1708

Official Report Directorate (Hansard)

Tel: 020 7219 4786/020 7219 5290

Editor: Lorraine Sutherland
Deputy Editor: Alex Newton

Parliamentary Broadcasting

Parliamentary Press Gallery enquiries: 020 7219 4700
Tel: 020 7219 4975/020 7219 6758
Director: John Angeli 020 7219 5848

Serjeant at Arms Directorate

Tel: 020 7219 3030

Serjeant at Arms: Lawrence Ward
Deputy Serjeant at Arms: Richard Latham
Assistant Serjeant at Arms: Lesley Scott

Office of Speaker's Counsel

Reporting directly to Chief Executive

Tel: 020 7219 3877

Speaker's Counsel: Michael Carpenter
Counsel for European Legislation: Paul Hardy
Counsel for Domestic Legislation: Peter Davis
Deputy Counsel: Peter Brooksbank, Daniel Greenberg
Assistant Counsel: Helen Emes

Department of Information Services

Tel: 020 7219 3666
Email: helibrary@parliament.uk
Librarian and Director General: John Pullinger 020 7219 4315

Director of Service Delivery: Dr John Benger
Director of Public Information: Edward Wood
Director of Information Management: Steve Wise
Director of Public Engagement: Aileen Walker
Director of Research: Adam Mellows-Facer
Curator of Works of Art: Malcolm Hay
Head of Central Support Services: Grahame Allen
Head of Office Services: Gabrielle Hughes
Head of Library Resources Section: Susannah Foulis
Heads of Information and Data Management Section: Gini Griffin, Catherine Meredith
Head of Public Engagement and Learning: Tom O'Leary
Head of Public Information and Outreach: Clare Cowan
Head of Visitor Services: Deborah Newman
Head of Online Services: Tracy Green
Head of Reference Services Section: Dora Clark
Reference Services Section: Amina Gual, John Prince, Chris Sear
Deposited Papers and Resource Manager: Laura McDonald

Research Sections

Head of Business and Transport Section: Tim Edmonds
Researchers: Louise Butcher, Douglas Pyper, Antony Seely, Djuna Thurley
Acting Head of Economic Policy and Statistics Section: Lorna Booth
Researchers: Daniel Harari, Feargal McGuiness, Christopher Rhodes, Gavin Thompson,
Dominic Webb, Daniel Zaczkiewicz
Head of Home Affairs Section: Pat Strickland
Researchers: John Bardens, Jacqueline Beard, Lorraine Conway, Catherine Fairbairn, Gabrielle Garton-
Grimwood, Melanie Gower, Sally Lipscombe, Philip Ward PhD, John Woodhouse
Head of International Affairs and Defence Section: Vaughne Miller
Researchers: Louisa Brooke-Holland, Arabella Lang, Dr Jon Lunn, Clare Mills, Ben Smith
Head of Parliament and Constitution Section: Lucinda Maer
Researchers: Paul Bowers PhD, Oonagh Gay, Richard Kelly, Mark Sandford, Isobel White
Head of Science and Environment Section: Patsy Richards
Researchers: Elena Ares PhD, Oliver Bennett, Emma Downing, Edward White
Head of Social and General Statistics Section: Richard Cracknell
Researchers: Paul Bolton, Aliyah Dar, Rachael Harker, Oliver Hawkins, Matthew Keep, Rod McInnes,
Tom Rutherford
Head of Social Policy Section: Christine Gillie OBE
Researchers: Manjit Gheera, Susan Hubble, Tim Jarrett, Steven Kennedy, Robert Long, Tom Powell,
Wendy Wilson
Head of Research and Library Central Team: Gavin Berman

Parliamentary Office of Science and Technology (POST)

Tel: 020 7219 2840
Website: www.parliament.uk/post

Chair: Adam Afriyie MP
Vice-chair: Professor Lord Winston
Director: Dr Christopher Tyler
Board Members: Professor Frances Balkwill, Dr Therese Coffey MP, Michael Connarty MP,
Sir David Davies CBE, Lord Haskel, Dr Julian Huppert MP, Professor Lord Krebs FRS, Dr Phillip Lee MP,
Andrew Miller MP, David Mowat MP, Sarah Newton MP, Professor Jim Norton, Chi Onwurah MP,
Lord Oxburgh KBE, Professor Ekhard Salje

Media and Communications Service (Chamber and Corporate)

Parliamentary Press Gallery enquiries: 020 7219 4700
General enquiries: 020 7219 0969

Head of Media and Communications: Lee Bridges 020 7219 0969
Photography and visuals: Catherine Bebbington 020 7219 1640, Jessica Taylor 020 7219 0898
Media Officers: Jeremy Brevitt 020 7219 0969, Gary Calder 020 7219 1123,
Anikka Weerasinghe 020 7219 0849

House of Commons Information Office

Tel: 020 7219 4272 Fax: 020 7219 5839
Email: hcinfo@parliament.uk Website: www.parliament.uk

Head of Office: Clare Cowan
Office Manager: Lynne Preece

Houses of Parliament Shop

Tel: 020 7219 3890
Email: shop@parliament.uk
Manager: Sheila Mitchell 020 7219 3812

Department of Facilities

Tel: 020 7219 4755

Director-General: John Borley 020 7219 6551
Head of the Executive Office: Fiona Channon
Director of Facilities Finance: Philip Collins
Director of Business Management: Della Herd

Parliamentary Estates Directorate

Parliamentary Director of Estates: Mel Barlex 020 7219 2455
Deputy Director and Head of Projects: Christine Sillis
Principal Estates Manager: Helen Arkell
Head of Director's Office: Robert Whiteway
Head of Fire, Safety and Environment: Charlotte Simmonds
Head of Maintenance and Operations: Lester Benjamin
Head of Programme and Planning Management: Steve Beck

Catering and Retail

Tel: 020 7219 5303

Director of Catering: Richard Tapner-Evans 020 7219 3686/020 7219 5305
Executive Chef: Mark Hill 020 7219 1444
Operations Manager: Robert Gibbs 020 7219 0355

Accommodation Services

Director: James Robertson OBE

Department of Human Resources and Change

Director-General: Andrew Walker
Head of Information Rights and Information Security: Victoria Payne
Head of Safety, Health and Welfare Services: Marianne McDougall
Head of Personnel Advice Service: Dapo Coker
Travel Office Manager: Kate White

Business Management and Delivery
Director: Janet Rissen

HR Policy and Strategy
Director: To be appointed

Change Directorate
Director: Selven Naicker

Department of Finance
Director: Myfanwy Barrett

Financial Management Directorate
Director: Chris Ridley

Pensions Unit
Head of Pensions: Lucy Tindal

Commercial Services Directorate
Director: Veronica Daly

Associated Offices

Parliamentary Information and Communications Technology Service
Tel: 020 7219 4063
Director of PICT: Joan Miller
Director of Operations and Member Services: Matthew Taylor
Director of Programmes and Project Development: Rebecca Elton
Director of Resources: Fergus Reid
Director of Technology: Steve O'Connor
Director of Network Programme: Innis Montgomery

Parliamentary Commissioner for Standards
c/o House of Commons, London SW1A 0AA
Tel: 020 7219 0320 Fax: 020 7219 0490
Email: standardscommissioner@parliament.uk Website: www.parliament.uk/pcs
Parliamentary Commissioner for Standards: Kathryn Hudson

Parliamentary Security
Reporting directly to chief executives and Speakers of both Houses of Parliament
Parliamentary Security Director: Paul Martin

Political Offices

Government
Leader of the House of Commons' Office 020 7219 4040
Chief Whip's Office 020 7219 4400

Whips' Assistants Office
Chief Clerk: Claire Scott 020 7219 0057
Whips' Assistants:
Janet Costello 020 7219 4333
John John 020 7219 1351
Michael McCarthy 020 7219 4334/020 7219 3612
Emma McEwan 020 7219 4773
Harriet Reece 020 7219 4333
Paul Renwick 020 7219 4333
Emma Wilde 020 7219 4333

Official Opposition
Leader's Office 020 7219 4778
Opposition Chief Whip's Office 020 7219 4770
Head of Parliamentary Support: Roland Hunt 020 7219 0009
Deputy Head of Parliamentary Support: Russell Tatam 020 7219 4770
Whips' Assistants:
Joanna Jackson 020 7219 2786
Lee Jeffery 020 7219 1225

Democratic Unionist Party
Group Leader's Office 020 7219 8419
Whips' Assistant and Parliamentary Office: Margaret McKee 020 7219 5679 Fax: 020 7219 2347

Scottish National Party
Leader's Office 020 7219 8259
Chief of Staff: Luke Skipper 020 7219 4500 Email: skipperl@parliament.uk
Head of Communications: Stewart Easton
Head of Research: Lloyd Abou-Khater 020 7219 8231 Email: aboukhaterl@parliament.uk
Press Officer: Catriona Matheson

Plaid Cymru
Leader's Office 020 7219 3555
Whip's Office Manager: Rhian Medi Roberts 020 7219 5021
Senior Researcher: Delyth Jewell 020 7219 1900
Researcher: Emyr Williams 020 7219 6883
Press Officer: Elin Roberts 020 7219 6422

Social Democratic and Labour Party
Leader's Office 020 7219 8528
Chief Whip's Office 020 7219 8528
Parliamentary Officer: Andrew McCullough 020 7219 8528
Email: andrew.mccullough@parliament.uk

GENERAL ELECTION 2010

Electoral Information

The Representation of the People Act 1983 sets out the timetable for parliamentary elections. In the case of a parliamentary general election, the last day for the delivery of nomination papers is the sixth day after the date of the proclamation summoning the new Parliament, and the poll is held in every constituency on the eleventh day after the last day for delivery of nomination papers.

In the case of a by-election, the last day for the delivery of nomination papers is fixed by the Returning Officer and must be not earlier than the third day after the date of publication of the notice of election nor later than the seventh day after that on which the writ is received. Polling takes place on the day fixed by the Returning Officer, which is not earlier than the ninth nor later than the eleventh day after the last day for delivery of nomination papers. In calculating election timetables Sundays, Saturdays, Christmas Eve, Christmas Day, Good Friday, bank holidays and days appointed for public thanksgiving or mourning are disregarded.

Parliamentary Franchise

A person resident in the United Kingdom is entitled to be entered on the register of electors if he or she is:
* resident in the constituency
* not subject to any legal incapacity to vote (age apart)
* a British or other qualifying Commonwealth citizen or a citizen of the Republic of Ireland
* is at least 18 years of age (or will become 18 during the currency of the register)
* applies to vote to the Registration Officer no later than 11 working days before polling day.

British citizens resident abroad may also register and vote in parliamentary elections for up to 15 years after leaving the UK. HM Forces can register while serving.

Since 1999 hereditary peers, who were previously barred from voting in general elections, have been allowed to do so if they no longer sit in the Lords.

Parliamentary Candidates

A candidate must be at least 18 years old and a citizen of the United Kingdom, Commonwealth or Republic of Ireland and have indefinite leave to remain in the UK.

Since 1999 hereditary peers who no longer sit in the House of Lords have been allowed to stand as candidates for the Commons.

Each candidate must deposit £500 with the Returning Officer at the time of nomination, refunded if elected, or polls over 5 per cent of votes cast.

The current maximum expenditure which may be incurred by a candidate is £7,150 plus, in a county constituency, 7p and, in a borough constituency, 5p per registered elector. The sum in the case of a by-election is £100,000.

The Returning Officer's expenses are paid by the Treasury.

Number of Voters

In December 2012 there was a total of 46,353,900 names on the electoral registers for the United Kingdom.

England	38,837,300
Scotland	3,985,300
Wales	2,301,100
Northern Ireland	1,230,200

Parties with seats in the House of Commons

All	Alliance	**Lib Dem**	Liberal Democrat
Con	Conservative	**PlC**	Plaid Cymru
DUP	Democratic Unionist Party	**SDLP**	Social Democratic and Labour Party
Green	Green Party	**Sinn Féin**	Sinn Féin
Ind	Independent	**SNP**	Scottish National Party
Lab	Labour	**Speaker**	The Speaker
Lab/Co-op	Labour/Co-operative		

Parties with candidates in the General Election

AC Animals Count; **All** Alliance; **Animal** The Animal Protection Party; **Anti-War** Fight For An Anti-War Government; **Apol Dem** Apolitical Democrats; **ATSP** All The South Party; **AWL** Alliance for Workers' Liberty; **AWP** Anticapitalists – Workers Power; **BCM** Basingstoke Common Man; **Beer** Reduce Tax on Beer; **BEP** Blue Environment Party; **Best** Best of a Bad Bunch; **Better Britain** A Better Britain For All; **BNP** British National Party; **Brent North Ind** Brent North Needs An Independent MP; **Brom Ind Con** Bromsgrove Independent Conservative; **Bus-Pass** Bus-Pass Elvis Party; **Christian** Christian Party; **CIP** Campaign for Independent Politicians; **Clause 28** Clause 28 Children's Protection Christian Democrats; **CMGB** Christian Movement for Great Britain; **CNBPG** Community Need Before Private Greed; **Comm** Communist Party; **Comm GB** Communist Party of Great Britain; **Comm League** Communist League; **Common Good** The Common Good; **Con** Conservative; **Corn Dem** Cornish Democrats; **CPA** Christian People's Alliance; **CSP** Common Sense Party; **CURE** Citizens for Undead Rights and Equality; **Currency** Virtue Currency Cognitive Appraisal Party; **DDCP** Direct Democracy (Communist) Party; **Deficit** Cut The Deficit Party; **Dem Lab** Democratic Labour Party; **DN** Democratic Nationalists; **DUP** Democratic Unionist Party; **EIP** English Independence Party; **Eng Dem** English Democrats - Putting England First; **EPA** Equal Parenting Alliance; **Essex** Peoples Party Essex; **Expense** A Vote Against MP Expense Abuse; **FDP** Fancy Dress Party; **FR** for Freedom and Responsibility; **GMVY** Go Mad and Vote for Yourself; **Green** Green Party; **Green Soc** Alliance for Green Socialism; **Humanity** Humanity; **Impact** Impact Party; **Ind** Independent; **Ind EACPS** Independent Ealing Acton Communities Public Services; **Ind Fed UK** Independents Federation UK; **Ind KHHC** Independent Kidderminster Hospital and Health Concern; **Integrity** Integrity UK; **IZB** Islam Zinda Baad Platform; **JACP** Justice and Anti-Corruption Party; **JOT** The Joy of Talk; **JP** Justice Party; **Lab** Labour; **Lab/Co-op** Labour/Co-operative; **Land Power** Land is Power; **Lib** Liberal; **Lib Dem** Liberal Democrat; **Libertarian** Libertarian Party; **Lincs Ind** Lincolnshire Independents; **LLPBPP** Local Liberals People Before Politics Party; **Loony** Official Monster Raving Loony Party; **LTT** Lawfulness Trustworthiness and Transparency; **Mac Ind** Macclesfield Independent; **Magna Carta** The Magna Carta Party; **MCCP** Magna Carta Conservation Party Great Britain; **Mebyon Kernow** Mebyon Kernow; **Medway** Medway Independent Party; **MEP** Middle England Party; **MRP** Money Reform Party; **NCDMV** No Candidate Deserves My Vote; **NF** National Front; **NICCF** New Independent Conservative Chelsea and Fulham; **NLP** National Liberal Party; **NMB** New Millennium Bean Party; **Nobody** Nobody Party; **NP** The New Party; **NRP** Nationwide Reform Party; **NSOPS** Northampton - Save Our Public Services; **PBPA** People Before Profit Alliance; **Pirate** Pirate Party; **PlC** Plaid Cymru; **PNDP** Peoples National Democratic Party; **Reform 2000** Reform 2000; **Respect** Respect - The Unity Coalition; **Restoration** Restoration Party; **RRG** Radical Reform Group; **SACL** Scotland Against Crooked Lawyers; **SAP** Socialist Alternative Party; **Science** Science Party; **Scrap** Scrap Members Allowances; **SDLP** Social Democratic and Labour Party; **SDP** Social Democratic Party; **SEP** Socialist Equality Party; **SIG** Staffordshire Independent Group; **Sinn Féin** Sinn Féin; **SJP** Scottish Jacobite Party; **SKGH** Save King George Hospital; **SLP** Socialist Labour Party; **SMRA** Solihull and Meriden Residents Association; **Snouts** Get Snouts Out The Trough; **SNP** Scottish National Party; **Socialist** Socialist; **SOTBTH** Support Our Troops Bring Them Home; **Speaker** The Speaker; **SSP** Scottish Socialist Party; **Tamsin** Tamsin Omond to the Commons; **Tendring** Tendring First; **TPP** The Peace Party - non-violence, justice, environment; **True English** The True English (Poetry) Party; **Trust** The Trust Party; **TUSC** Trade Unionist and Socialist Coalition; **TUV** Traditional Unionist Voice; **UCUNF** Ulster Conservatives and Unionists– New Force; **UKIP** UK Independence Party; **Unity** Unity For Peace And Socialism; **UV** United Voice; **WCP** Welsh Christian Party; **Wessex Reg** Wessex Regionalists; **WRP** Workers' Revolutionary Party; **You** You Party; **Youth** The Youth Party; **YRDPL** Your Right to Democracy Party Limited.

ABERAVON

(No boundary changes)

		%	+/-%
Francis, H. Lab*	16,073	51.9	-8.0
Davies, K. Lib Dem	5,034	16.2	2.5
Jones, C. Con	4,411	14.2	4.1
Nicholls-Jones, P. PlC	2,198	7.1	-4.7
Edwards, K. BNP	1,276	4.1	
Tutton, A. Ind	919	3.0	
Beany, C. NMB	558	1.8	
Callan, J. UKIP	489	1.6	
Lab majority	11,039	35.61	
Electorate	50,838		
Turnout	31,002	60.98	

Lab hold (5.3% from Lab to Lib Dem)

ABERCONWY

(New constituency)

		%
Bebb, G. Con	10,734	35.7
Hughes, R. Lab	7,336	24.4
Priestley, M. Lib Dem	5,786	19.3
Edwards, P. PlC	5,341	17.8
Wieteska, M. UKIP	632	2.1
Wynne Jones, L. Christian	137	0.5
Con majority	3,398	11.3
Electorate	44,593	
Turnout	30,058	67.41

Con gain (notional 7.6% from Lab to Con)

ABERDEEN NORTH

(No boundary changes)

		%	+/-%
Doran, F. Lab*	16,746	44.3	2.0
Strathdee, J. SNP	8,385	22.2	0.0
Thomas, K. Lib Dem	7,001	18.5	-5.3
Whyte, S. Con	4,666	12.4	3.0
Jones, R. BNP	635	1.7	
Robertson, E. SSP	268	0.7	-1.2
Lab majority	8,361	22.13	
Electorate	64,808		
Turnout	37,777	58.29	

Lab hold (1% from SNP to Lab)

ABERDEEN SOUTH

(No boundary changes)

		%	+/-%
Begg, A. Lab*	15,722	36.5	-0.2
Sleigh, J. Lib Dem	12,216	28.4	-5.1
Harvie, A. Con	8,914	20.7	3.6
McDonald, M. SNP	5,102	11.8	2.0
Ross, S. BNP	529	1.2	
Reekie, R. Green	413	1.0	-0.9
Green, R. SACL	138	0.3	
Lab majority	3,506	8.14	
Electorate	64,031		
Turnout	43,083	67.28	

Lab hold (2.5% from Lib Dem to Lab)

WEST ABERDEENSHIRE AND KINCARDINE

(No boundary changes)

		%	+/-%
Smith, R. Lib Dem*	17,362	38.4	-7.8
Johnstone, A. Con	13,678	30.2	1.9
Robertson, D. SNP	7,086	15.7	4.4
Williams, G. Lab	6,159	13.6	0.5
Raikes, G. BNP	513	1.1	
Atkinson, A. UKIP	397	0.9	
Lib Dem majority	3,684	8.14	
Electorate	66,110		
Turnout	45,256	68.46	

Lib Dem hold (4.9% from Lib Dem to Con)

*Member of last Parliament

AIRDRIE AND SHOTTS

(No boundary changes)

		%	+/-%
Nash, P. Lab	20,849	58.1	-0.7
Coyle, S. SNP	8,441	23.5	7.1
Whitfield, R. Con	3,133	8.7	-1.1
Love, J. Lib Dem	2,898	8.1	-3.3
McGeechan, J. Ind	528	1.5	
Lab majority	12,408	34.56	
Electorate	62,364		
Turnout	35,905	57.57	

Lab hold (3.9% from Lab to SNP)

ALDERSHOT

(Boundary changes)

		%
Howarth, G. Con*	21,203	46.6
Collett, A. Lib Dem	15,617	34.3
Slater, J. Lab	5,489	12.1
Snare, R. UKIP	2,041	4.5
Cowd, G. EIP	803	1.8
Brimicombe, J. Christian	231	0.5
Con majority	5,586	12.28
Electorate	71,465	
Turnout	45,484	63.65

Con hold (notional 1.4% from Con to Lib Dem)

ALDRIDGE-BROWNHILLS

(Boundary changes)

		%
Shepherd, R. Con*	22,913	59.0
Hussain, A. Lab	7,647	19.7
Jenkins, I. Lib Dem	6,833	17.6
Macnaughton, K. Green	847	2.2
Gray, S. Christian	394	1.0
Con majority	15,266	39.33
Electorate	58,970	
Turnout	38,811	65.81

Con hold (notional 11.9% from Lab to Con)

ALTRINCHAM AND SALE WEST

(Boundary changes)

		%
Brady, G. Con*	24,176	48.8
Brophy, J. Lib Dem	12,581	25.4
Ross, T. Lab	11,073	22.4
Bullman, K. UKIP	1,563	3.2
Con majority	11,595	23.4
Electorate	71,254	
Turnout	49,549	69.54

Con hold (notional 0.9% from Con to Lib Dem)

ALYN AND DEESIDE

(No boundary changes)

		%	+/-%
Tami, M. Lab*	15,804	39.5	-9.2
Gallagher, W. Con	12,885	32.2	7.0
Brighton, P. Lib Dem	7,308	18.3	0.9
Jones, M. PlC	1,549	3.9	0.2
Walker, J. BNP	1,368	3.4	
Howson, J. UKIP	1,009	2.5	-0.1
Lab majority	2,919	7.3	
Electorate	60,931		
Turnout	40,012	65.67	

Lab hold (8.1% from Lab to Con)

AMBER VALLEY

(Boundary changes)

		%
Mills, N. Con	17,746	38.5
Mallaber, J. Lab*	17,210	37.4
Snowdon, T. Lib Dem	6,636	14.4
Clarke, M. BNP	3,195	6.9

Ransome, S. UKIP	906	2.0
'Thing, S. Loony	265	0.6
Con majority	536	1.16
Electorate	70,171	
Turnout	46,058	65.64

Con gain (notional 6.8% from Lab to Con)

ANGUS

(No boundary changes)

		%	+/-%
Weir, M. SNP*	15,020	39.5	5.9
Costa, A. Con	11,738	30.9	1.5
Hutchens, K. Lab/Co-op	6,535	17.2	-0.7
Samani, S. Lib Dem	4,090	10.8	-6.7
Gray, M. UKIP	577	1.5	
SNP majority	3,282	8.63	
Electorate	62,860		
Turnout	38,022	60.49	

SNP hold (2.2% from Con to SNP)

EAST ANTRIM

(Boundary changes)

		%
Wilson, S. DUP*	13,993	45.7
McCune, R. UCUNF	7,223	23.6
Lynch, G. All	3,377	11.0
McMullan, O. Sinn Féin	2,064	6.7
McCamphill, J. SDLP	2,019	6.6
Morrison, S. TUV	1,826	6.0
DUP majority	6,770	22.1
Electorate	60,204	
Turnout	30,640	50.89

DUP hold (notional 0.2% from UCUNF to DUP)

NORTH ANTRIM

(Boundary changes)

		%
Paisley, I. DUP	19,672	46.2
Allister, J. TUV	7,114	16.7
McKay, D. Sinn Féin	5,265	12.4
Armstrong, I. UCUNF	4,634	10.9
O'Loan, D. SDLP	3,738	8.8
Dunlop, J. All	1,368	3.2
Cubitt, L. Ind	606	1.4
DUP majority	12,558	29.49
Electorate	73,338	
Turnout	42,579	58.06

DUP hold (notional 13.6% from DUP to TUV)

SOUTH ANTRIM

(Boundary changes)

		%
McCrea, W. DUP*	11,536	33.8
Empey, R. UCUNF	10,353	30.3
McLaughlin, M. Sinn Féin	4,729	13.9
Byrne, M. SDLP	2,955	8.7
Lawther, A. All	2,607	7.6
Lucas, M. TUV	1,829	5.4
DUP majority	1,183	3.46
Electorate	63,054	
Turnout	34,143	54.15

DUP hold (notional 3.6% from DUP to UCUNF)

ARFON

(New constituency)

		%
Williams, H. PlC*	9,383	35.9
Pugh, A. Lab	7,928	30.3
Millar, R. Con	4,416	16.9
Green, S. Lib Dem	3,666	14.0
Williams, E. UKIP	685	2.6
PlC majority	1,455	5.56
Electorate	41,198	
Turnout	26,156	63.49

PlC gain (notional 3.7% from Lab to PlC)

ARGYLL AND BUTE

(No boundary changes)

		%	+/-%
Reid, A. Lib Dem*	14,292	31.6	-4.8
Mulvaney, G. Con	10,861	24.0	0.6
Graham, D. Lab	10,274	22.7	0.3
Mackenzie, M. SNP	8,563	18.9	3.4
Morrison, E. Green	789	1.8	
Doyle, G. Ind	272	0.6	
Black, J. SJP	156	0.4	
Lib Dem majority	3,431	7.58	
Electorate	67,165		
Turnout	45,293	67.44	

Lib Dem hold (2.7% from Lib Dem to Con)

ARUNDEL AND SOUTH DOWNS

(Boundary changes)

		%
Herbert, N. Con*	32,333	57.6
Deedman, D. Lib Dem	15,642	27.9
Lunnon, T. Lab	4,835	8.6
Bower, S. UKIP	3,172	5.7
Con majority	16,691	29.76
Electorate	76,835	
Turnout	56,085	72.99

Con hold (notional 3% from Lib Dem to Con)

ASHFIELD

(Boundary changes)

		%
De Piero, G. Lab	16,239	33.7
Zadrozny, J. Lib Dem	16,047	33.3
Hickton, G. Con	10,698	22.2
Holmes, E. BNP	2,781	5.8
Ellis, T. Eng Dem	1,102	2.3
Coleman, T. UKIP	933	1.9
Smith, E. Ind	396	0.8
Lab majority	192	0.4
Electorate	77,379	
Turnout	48,257	62.36

Lab hold (notional 17.2% from Lab to Lib Dem)

ASHFORD

(Boundary changes)

		%
Green, D. Con*	29,878	54.1
Took, C. Lib Dem	12,581	22.8
Clark, C. Lab	9,204	16.7
Elenor, J. UKIP	2,508	4.5
Campkin, S. Green	1,014	1.8
Con majority	17,297	31.29
Electorate	81,271	
Turnout	55,278	68.02

Con hold (notional 2.3% from Con to Lib Dem)

ASHTON UNDER LYNE

(Boundary changes)

		%
Heyes, D. Lab*	18,604	48.2
Kennedy, S. Con	9,510	24.6
Larkin, P. Lib Dem	5,703	14.8
Lomas, D. BNP	2,929	7.6
McManus, A. UKIP	1,686	4.4
Lab majority	9,094	23.56
Electorate	68,525	
Turnout	38,597	56.33

Lab hold (notional 7.4% from Lab to Con)

AYLESBURY
(*Boundary changes*)

		%
Lidington, D. Con*	27,736	52.1
Lambert, S. Lib Dem	15,118	28.4
White, K. Lab	6,695	12.6
Adams, C. UKIP	3,613	6.8
Con majority	12,618	23.69
Electorate	77,844	
Turnout	53,273	68.44

Con hold (notional 2.1% from Lib Dem to Con)

AYR, CARRICK AND CUMNOCK
(*No boundary changes*)

		%	+/-%
Osborne, S. Lab*	21,632	47.1	1.8
Grant, W. Con	11,721	25.5	2.4
Brodie, C. SNP	8,276	18.0	4.9
Taylor, J. Lib Dem	4,264	9.3	-4.8
Lab majority	9,911	21.56	
Electorate	73,320		
Turnout	45,959	62.68	

Lab hold (0.3% from Lab to Con)

CENTRAL AYRSHIRE
(*No boundary changes*)

		%	+/-%
Donohoe, B. Lab*	20,950	47.6	1.3
Golden, M. Con	8,943	20.3	-1.8
Mullen, J. SNP	8,364	19.0	7.4
Chamberlain, A. Lib Dem	5,236	11.9	-4.1
McDaid, J. SLP	422	1.0	-0.1
Lab majority	12,007	27.29	
Electorate	68,352		
Turnout	44,002	64.38	

Lab hold (1.5% from Con to Lab)

NORTH AYRSHIRE AND ARRAN
(*No boundary changes*)

		%	+/-%
Clark, K. Lab*	21,860	47.3	3.4
Gibson, P. SNP	11,965	25.9	7.9
Lardner, P. Con	7,212	15.6	-2.7
Cole-Hamilton, G. Lib Dem	4,631	10.0	-6.4
McDaid, L. SLP	449	1.0	0.3
Lab majority	9,895	21.4	
Electorate	74,223		
Turnout	46,243	62.3	

Lab hold (2.3% from Lab to SNP)

BANBURY
(*Boundary changes*)

		%
Baldry, T. Con*	29,703	52.7
Rundle, D. Lib Dem	11,476	20.4
Sibley, L. Lab	10,773	19.1
Fairweather, D. UKIP	2,806	5.0
White, A. Green	959	1.7
Edwards, R. Ind	524	0.9
Con majority	18,227	32.32
Electorate	84,379	
Turnout	56,399	66.84

Con hold (notional 1.5% from Lib Dem to Con)

BANFF AND BUCHAN
(*No boundary changes*)

		%	+/-%
Whiteford, E. SNP	15,868	41.2	-9.9
Buchan, J. Con	11,841	30.8	11.4
Reynolds, G. Lab	5,382	14.0	2.0
Milne, G. Lib Dem	4,365	11.3	-2.0
Payne, R. BNP	1,010	2.6	
SNP majority	4,027	10.46	
Electorate	64,300		
Turnout	38,513	59.9	

SNP hold (10.7% from SNP to Con)

*Member of last Parliament

BARKING
(*Boundary changes*)

		%
Hodge, M. Lab*	24,628	54.0
Marcus, S. Con	8,073	17.7
Griffin, N. BNP	6,620	14.5
Carman, D. Lib Dem	3,719	8.2
Maloney, F. UKIP	1,300	2.9
Hargreaves, G. Christian	482	1.1
Forbes, J. Green	317	0.7
Dowling, C. Loony	82	0.2
Darwood, T. Ind	77	0.2
Sijuwola, D. Restoration	45	0.1
Lab majority	16,555	36.27
Electorate	73,864	
Turnout	45,649	61.8

Lab hold (notional 1.6% from Con to Lab)

BARNSLEY CENTRAL
(*Boundary changes*)

		%
Illsley, E. Lab*	17,487	47.2
Wiggin, C. Lib Dem	6,394	17.3
Tempest, P. Con	6,388	17.2
Sutton, I. BNP	3,307	8.9
Silver, D. UKIP	1,727	4.7
Wood, D. Ind	732	2.0
Devoy, T. Ind	610	1.6
Robinson, T. SLP	356	1.0
Lab majority	11,093	29.91
Electorate	65,441	
Turnout	37,087	56.67

Lab hold (notional 4.2% from Lab to Lib Dem)

BARNSLEY EAST
(*New constituency*)

		%
Dugher, M. Lab	18,059	46.9
Brown, J. Lib Dem	6,969	18.1
Hockney, J. Con	6,329	16.5
Porter, C. BNP	3,301	8.6
Watson, T. UKIP	1,731	4.5
Hogan, K. Ind	712	1.9
Devoy, E. Ind	684	1.8
Capstick, K. SLP	601	1.6
Lab majority	11,090	28.82
Electorate	68,395	
Turnout	38,474	56.25

Lab hold (notional 14.1% from Lab to Lib Dem)

BARROW AND FURNESS
(*Boundary changes*)

		%
Woodcock, J. Lab/Co-op	21,226	48.0
Gough, J. Con	16,018	36.2
Rabone, B. Lib Dem	4,424	10.0
Smith, J. UKIP	841	1.9
Ashburner, M. BNP	840	1.9
Loynes, C. Green	530	1.2
Greaves, B. Ind	245	0.6
Lab/Co-op majority	5,208	11.78
Electorate	68,943	
Turnout	44,210	64.13

Lab/Co-op hold (notional 0.4% from Lab/Co-op to Con)

BASILDON AND BILLERICAY
(*New constituency*)

		%
Baron, J. Con*	21,922	52.6
Davies, A. Lab	9,584	23.0
Hibbs, M. Lib Dem	6,538	15.7
Bateman, I. BNP	1,934	4.6
Broad, A. UKIP	1,591	3.8
Con majority	12,398	29.74
Electorate	65,515	
Turnout	41,683	63.62

Con hold (notional 9.2% from Lab to Con)

SOUTH BASILDON AND EAST THURROCK
(New constituency)

		%
Metcalfe, S. Con	19,624	43.8
Smith, A. Lab/Co-op*	13,852	30.9
Williams, G. Lib Dem	5,977	13.3
Smith, K. UKIP	2,639	5.9
Roberts, C. BNP	2,518	5.6
X, N. Ind	125	0.3
Con majority	5,772	12.87
Electorate	71,874	
Turnout	44,835	62.38

Con gain (notional 7.5% from Lab/Co-op to Con)

BASINGSTOKE
(Boundary changes)

		%
Miller, M. Con*	25,590	50.4
Shaw, J. Lib Dem	12,414	24.5
Pepperell, F. Lab	10,327	20.3
Howell, S. UKIP	2,076	4.1
Saul, S. BCM	247	0.5
Con majority	13,176	25.95
Electorate	75,472	
Turnout	50,772	67.27

Con hold (notional 4.5% from Lib Dem to Con)

BASSETLAW
(Boundary changes)

		%
Mann, J. Lab*	25,018	50.3
Girling, K. Con	16,803	33.8
Dobbie, D. Lib Dem	5,570	11.2
Hamilton, A. UKIP	1,779	3.6
Whitehurst, G. Ind	407	0.8
Lab majority	8,215	16.52
Electorate	76,513	
Turnout	49,725	64.99

Lab hold (notional 0.7% from Lab to Con)

BATH
(Boundary changes)

		%
Foster, D. Lib Dem*	26,651	56.5
Richter, F. Con	14,768	31.3
Ajderian, H. Lab	3,251	6.9
Lucas, E. Green	1,120	2.4
Warrender, E. UKIP	890	1.9
Hewett, S. Christian	250	0.5
Onymous, A. Ind	69	0.2
Geddis, S. Ind	56	0.1
Craig, R. ATSP	31	0.1
Lib Dem majority	11,883	25.19
Electorate	69,378	
Turnout	47,169	67.99

Lib Dem hold (notional 5.8% from Con to Lib Dem)

BATLEY AND SPEN
(Boundary changes)

		%
Wood, M. Lab*	21,565	42.1
Small, J. Con	17,159	33.5
Bentley, N. Lib Dem	8,095	15.8
Exley, D. BNP	3,685	7.2
Blakeley, M. Green	605	1.2
Lab majority	4,406	8.6
Electorate	76,738	
Turnout	51,242	66.78

Lab hold (notional 2.5% from Lab to Con)

BATTERSEA
(Boundary changes)

		%
Ellison, J. Con	23,103	47.3
Linton, M. Lab*	17,126	35.0
Moran, L. Lib Dem	7,176	14.7
Evans, G. Green	559	1.1
MacDonald, C. UKIP	505	1.0
Salmon, H. Ind	168	0.4
Fox, T. Ind	155	0.3
Con majority	5,977	12.23
Electorate	74,311	
Turnout	48,879	65.78

Con gain (notional 6.5% from Lab to Con)

BEACONSFIELD
(Boundary changes)

		%
Grieve, D. Con*	32,053	61.0
Edwards, J. Lib Dem	10,276	19.6
Miles, J. Lab	6,135	11.7
Gray-Fisk, D. UKIP	2,597	5.0
Bailey, J. Green	768	1.5
Cowen, A. Expense	475	0.9
Baron, Q. Ind	191	0.4
Con majority	21,782	41.45
Electorate	74,982	
Turnout	52,548	70.08

Con hold (notional 4.7% from Lib Dem to Con)

BECKENHAM
(Boundary changes)

		%
Stewart, B. Con	27,597	57.7
Jenkins, S. Lib Dem	9,813	20.5
Egan, D. Lab	6,893	14.4
Brolly, O. UKIP	1,551	3.3
Tonks, R. BNP	1,001	2.1
Garrett, A. Green	608	1.3
Cheeseman, D. Eng Dem	223	0.5
Con majority	17,784	37.21
Electorate	66,219	
Turnout	47,796	72.18

Con hold (notional 3.2% from Con to Lib Dem)

BEDFORD
(Boundary changes)

		%
Fuller, R. Con	17,546	38.8
Hall, P. Lab*	16,193	35.8
Vann, H. Lib Dem	8,957	19.8
Adkin, M. UKIP	1,136	2.5
Dewick, W. BNP	757	1.7
Foley, B. Green	393	0.9
Bhandari, S. Ind	120	0.3
Con majority	1,353	2.99
Electorate	68,530	
Turnout	45,201	65.96

Con gain (notional 5.5% from Lab to Con)

MID BEDFORDSHIRE
(Boundary changes)

		%
Dorries, N. Con*	28,815	52.4
Jack, L. Lib Dem	13,663	24.9
Reeves, D. Lab	8,108	14.8
Hall, B. UKIP	2,826	5.1
Bailey, M. Green	773	1.4
Cooper, J. Eng Dem	712	1.3
Con majority	15,152	27.56
Electorate	76,023	
Turnout	54,983	72.32

Con hold (notional 2.2% from Lib Dem to Con)

NORTH EAST BEDFORDSHIRE
(Boundary changes)

		%
Burt, A. Con*	30,989	55.7
Pitt, M. Lib Dem	12,047	21.7
Brown, E. Lab	8,957	16.1
Capell, B. UKIP	2,294	4.1
Seeby, I. BNP	1,265	2.3
Con majority	18,942	34.05
Electorate	78,060	
Turnout	55,635	71.27

Con hold (notional 2.5% from Lib Dem to Con)

SOUTH WEST BEDFORDSHIRE
(No boundary changes)

		%	+/-%
Selous, A. Con*	26,815	52.7	4.6
Cantrill, R. Lib Dem	10,166	20.0	3.2
Bone, J. Lab	9,948	19.6	-10.5
Newman, M. UKIP	2,142	4.2	0.0
Tolman, M. BNP	1,703	3.4	
Con majority	16,649	32.73	
Electorate	76,559		
Turnout	50,873	66.45	

Con hold (0.7% from Lib Dem to Con)

BELFAST EAST
(Boundary changes)

		%
Long, N. All	12,839	37.1
Robinson, P. DUP*	11,306	32.7
Ringland, T. UCUNF	7,305	21.1
Vance, D. TUV	1,856	5.4
Ó Donnghaile, N. Sinn Féin	817	2.4
Muldoon, M. SDLP	365	1.1
All majority	1,533	4.43
Electorate	59,007	
Turnout	34,612	58.66

All gain (notional 22.9% from DUP to All)

BELFAST NORTH
(Boundary changes)

		%
Dodds, N. DUP*	14,812	39.8
Kelly, G. Sinn Féin	12,588	33.8
Maginness, A. SDLP	4,544	12.2
Cobain, F. UCUNF	2,837	7.6
Webb, B. All	1,809	4.9
McAuley, M. Ind	403	1.1
DUP majority	2,224	5.97
Electorate	65,504	
Turnout	37,233	56.84

DUP hold (notional 5% from DUP to Sinn Féin)

BELFAST SOUTH
(Boundary changes)

		%
McDonnell, A. SDLP*	14,026	40.8
Spratt, J. DUP	8,100	23.6
Bradshaw, P. UCUNF	5,910	17.2
Lo, A. All	5,114	14.9
McGibbon, A. Green	1,036	3.0
SDLP majority	5,926	17.25
Electorate	59,524	
Turnout	34,359	57.72

SDLP hold (notional 8.4% from DUP to SDLP)

BELFAST WEST
(Boundary changes)

		%
Adams, G. Sinn Féin*	22,840	69.9
Attwood, A. SDLP	5,261	16.1
Humphrey, W. DUP	2,436	7.5

*Member of last Parliament

Manwaring, B. UCUNF	1,000	3.1
Hendron, M. All	596	1.8
Sinn Féin majority	17,579	53.79
Electorate	59,522	
Turnout	32,682	54.91

Sinn Féin hold (notional 0.6% from SDLP to Sinn Féin)

BERMONDSEY AND OLD SOUTHWARK
(New constituency)

		%
Hughes, S. Lib Dem	21,590	48.2
Shawcross, V. Lab	13,060	29.2
Morrison, L. Con	7,638	17.1
Tyler, S. BNP	1,370	3.1
Chance, T. Green	718	1.6
Kirkby, A. Ind	155	0.4
Freeman, S. Ind	120	0.3
Lib Dem majority	8,530	19.04
Electorate	77,628	
Turnout	44,792	57.7

Lib Dem hold (notional 1.5% from Lab to Lib Dem)

BERWICK-UPON-TWEED
(Boundary changes)

		%
Beith, A. Lib Dem*	16,806	43.6
Trevelyan, A. Con	14,116	36.6
Strickland, A. Lab	5,061	13.1
Weatheritt, M. UKIP	1,243	3.2
Mailer, P. BNP	1,213	3.1
Lib Dem majority	2,690	6.98
Electorate	56,578	
Turnout	38,523	68.09

Lib Dem hold (notional 8.3% from Lib Dem to Con)

BERWICKSHIRE, ROXBURGH AND SELKIRK
(No boundary changes)

		%	+/-%
Moore, M. Lib Dem*	22,230	45.3	3.5
Lamont, J. Con	16,555	33.7	4.9
Miller, I. Lab	5,003	10.2	-5.7
Wheelhouse, P. SNP	4,497	9.2	0.6
Fowler, S. UKIP	595	1.2	-0.1
Black, C. SJP	134	0.3	
Lib Dem majority	5,675	11.56	
Electorate	73,826		
Turnout	49,084	66.49	

Lib Dem hold (0.7% from Lib Dem to Con)

BETHNAL GREEN AND BOW
(Boundary changes)

		%
Ali, R. Lab	21,784	42.4
Masroor, A. Lib Dem	10,210	19.9
Miah, A. Respect	8,532	16.6
Khan, Z. Con	7,071	13.8
Marshall, J. BNP	1,405	2.7
Bakht, F. Green	856	1.7
Brooks, P. Ind	277	0.5
Van Terheyden, A. Pirate	213	0.4
Hikmat, H. UV	209	0.4
Choudhury, M. Ind	100	0.2
Malik, A. Ind	71	0.1
Lab majority	11,574	22.52
Electorate	81,243	
Turnout	51,390	63.25

Lab gain (notional 0.2% from Lib Dem to Lab)

BEVERLEY AND HOLDERNESS
(Boundary changes)

		%
Stuart, G. Con*	25,063	47.0
Dobson, C. Lib Dem	12,076	22.7
Saunders, I. Lab	11,224	21.1
Whitelam, N. BNP	2,080	3.9
Horsfield, A. UKIP	1,845	3.5

Rigby, B. Green	686	1.3
Hughes, R. Ind	225	0.4
Con majority	12,987	24.38
Electorate	79,318	
Turnout	53,278	67.17

Con hold (notional 1.6% from Lib Dem to Con)

BEXHILL AND BATTLE

(Boundary changes)		%
Barker, G. Con*	28,147	51.4
Varrall, M. Lib Dem	15,267	27.9
Royston, J. Lab	6,524	11.9
Wheeler, S. Trust	2,699	4.9
Jackson, N. BNP	1,950	3.6
Con majority	12,880	23.54
Electorate	81,032	
Turnout	54,725	67.54

Con hold (notional 4% from Con to Lib Dem)

BEXLEYHEATH AND CRAYFORD

(Boundary changes)		%
Evennett, D. Con*	21,794	50.3
Dawber, H. Lab	11,450	26.4
Scott, K. Lib Dem	5,502	12.7
James, S. BNP	2,042	4.7
Dunford, J. UKIP	1,557	3.6
Griffiths, J. Eng Dem	466	1.1
Ross, A. Green	371	0.9
Con majority	10,344	23.89
Electorate	65,582	
Turnout	43,299	66.02

Con hold (notional 5.8% from Lab to Con)

BIRKENHEAD

(Boundary changes)		%
Field, F. Lab*	22,082	61.8
Gilbert, A. Con	6,887	19.3
Kelly, S. Lib Dem	6,554	18.3
Lab majority	15,195	42.5
Electorate	62,773	
Turnout	35,749	56.95

Lab hold (notional 2.9% from Lab to Con)

BIRMINGHAM, EDGBASTON

(Boundary changes)		%
Stuart, G. Lab*	16,894	40.6
Alden, D. Con	15,620	37.5
Harmer, R. Lib Dem	6,387	15.3
Lloyd, T. BNP	1,196	2.9
Warwick, G. UKIP	732	1.8
Simpson, P. Green	469	1.1
Takhar, H. Impact	146	0.4
Fernando, C. Christian	127	0.3
Lab majority	1,274	3.06
Electorate	68,573	
Turnout	41,659	60.75

Lab hold (notional 0.5% from Lab to Con)

BIRMINGHAM, ERDINGTON

(Boundary changes)		%
Dromey, J. Lab	14,869	41.7
Alden, R. Con	11,592	32.5
Holtom, A. Lib Dem	5,742	16.1
McHugh, K. BNP	1,815	5.1
Foy, M. UKIP	842	2.4
Tomkins, T. Ind	240	0.7
Williams, T. NF	229	0.7
Gray, T. Christian	217	0.6
Lab majority	3,277	9.19
Electorate	66,405	
Turnout	35,660	53.7

Lab hold (notional 10.4% from Lab to Con)

BIRMINGHAM, HALL GREEN

(Boundary changes)		%
Godsiff, R. Lab*	16,039	32.7
Yaqoob, S. Respect	12,240	24.9
Evans, J. Lib Dem	11,988	24.4
Barker, J. Con	7,320	14.9
Blumenthal, A. UKIP	950	1.9
Gardner, A. Ind	190	0.4
Lab majority	3,799	7.74
Electorate	76,580	
Turnout	49,082	64.09

Lab hold (notional 17.3% from Lab to Respect)

BIRMINGHAM, HODGE HILL

(Boundary changes)		%
Byrne, L. Lab*	22,077	51.5
Khan, T. Lib Dem	11,775	27.4
Parekh, S. Con	4,936	11.5
Lumby, R. BNP	2,333	5.4
Rafiq, W. UKIP	714	1.7
Johnson, P. SDP	637	1.5
Lab majority	10,302	24.02
Electorate	75,040	
Turnout	42,898	57.17

Lab hold (notional 3.5% from Lib Dem to Lab)

BIRMINGHAM, LADYWOOD

(Boundary changes)		%
Mahmood, S. Lab	19,950	55.1
Khan, A. Lib Dem	9,845	27.2
Ghani, N. Con	4,277	11.8
Booth, C. UKIP	902	2.5
Beck, P. Green	859	2.4
Lab majority	10,105	27.91
Electorate	73,646	
Turnout	36,200	49.15

Lab hold (notional 2.3% from Lib Dem to Lab)

BIRMINGHAM, NORTHFIELD

(Boundary changes)		%
Burden, R. Lab*	16,841	40.2
Huxtable, K. Con	14,059	33.6
Dixon, M. Lib Dem	6,550	15.6
Orton, L. BNP	2,290	5.5
Borthwick, J. UKIP	1,363	3.3
Pearce, S. Green	406	1.0
Rodgers, D. Common Good	305	0.7
Lab majority	2,782	6.64
Electorate	71,338	
Turnout	41,886	58.71

Lab hold (notional 6.6% from Lab to Con)

BIRMINGHAM, PERRY BARR

(Boundary changes)		%
Mahmood, K. Lab*	21,142	49.9
Hamilton, K. Lib Dem	9,234	21.8
Norton, W. Con	8,960	21.2
Ward, M. UKIP	1,675	4.0
Tyrrell, J. SLP	527	1.3
Hey-Smith, D. Christian	507	1.2
Lab majority	11,908	28.13
Electorate	71,304	
Turnout	42,338	59.38

Lab hold (notional 4% from Lib Dem to Lab)

BIRMINGHAM, SELLY OAK
(Boundary changes)

		%
McCabe, S. Lab*	17,950	38.5
Dawkins, N. Con	14,468	31.0
Radcliffe, D. Lib Dem	10,371	22.2
Orton, L. BNP	1,820	3.9
Burgess, J. UKIP	1,131	2.4
Burn, J. Green	664	1.4
Leeds, S. Christian	159	0.4
Lab majority	3,482	7.46
Electorate	74,805	
Turnout	46,667	62.38

Lab hold (notional 4.8% from Lab to Con)

BIRMINGHAM, YARDLEY
(Boundary changes)

		%
Hemming, J. Lib Dem*	16,162	39.4
Kelly, L. Lab	13,160	32.1
Jenkins, M. Con	7,836	19.1
Lumby, T. BNP	2,153	5.3
Duffen, G. UKIP	1,190	2.9
Morris, P. NF	349	0.9
Lib Dem majority	3,002	7.32
Electorate	72,321	
Turnout	40,989	56.68

Lib Dem hold (notional 0.01% from Lab to Lib Dem)

BISHOP AUCKLAND
(Boundary changes)

		%
Goodman, H. Lab*	16,023	38.9
Harrison, B. Con	10,805	26.2
Wilkes, M. Lib Dem	9,189	22.3
Walker, A. BNP	2,036	5.0
Zair, S. LLPBPP	1,964	4.8
Brothers, D. UKIP	1,119	2.7
Lab majority	5,218	12.66
Electorate	68,368	
Turnout	41,209	60.28

Lab hold (notional 7.2% from Lab to Con)

BLACKBURN
(Boundary changes)

		%
Straw, J. Lab*	21,751	46.1
Law-Riding, M. Con	11,895	25.2
English, P. Lib Dem	6,918	14.7
Evans, R. BNP	2,158	4.6
Irfanullah, B. Ind	1,424	3.0
Anwar, B. UKIP	942	2.0
Astley, G. Ind	238	0.5
Sharp, J. Ind	173	0.4
Lab majority	9,856	20.87
Electorate	72,331	
Turnout	47,217	65.28

Lab hold (notional 0.7% from Con to Lab)

BLACKLEY AND BROUGHTON
(New constituency)

		%
Stringer, G. Lab*	18,563	54.0
Edsberg, J. Con	6,260	18.2
Hobhouse, W. Lib Dem	4,861	14.2
Adams, D. BNP	2,469	7.2
Phillips, K. Respect	996	2.9
Willescroft, B. UKIP	894	2.6
Zaman, S. Christian	161	0.5
Lab majority	12,303	35.81
Electorate	69,489	
Turnout	34,354	49.44

Lab hold (notional 6.8% from Lab to Con)

*Member of last Parliament

BLACKPOOL NORTH AND CLEVELEYS
(New constituency)

		%
Maynard, P. Con	16,964	41.7
Martin, P. Lab	14,814	36.5
Greene, B. Lib Dem	5,400	13.3
Hopwood, R. UKIP	1,659	4.1
Clayton, J. BNP	1,556	3.8
Davies, T. Loony	198	0.5
Con majority	2,150	5.29
Electorate	66,017	
Turnout	40,649	61.57

Con gain (notional 6.9% from Lab to Con)

BLACKPOOL SOUTH
(Boundary changes)

		%
Marsden, G. Lab*	14,449	41.0
Bell, R. Con	12,597	35.7
Holt, D. Lib Dem	5,082	14.4
Goodwin, R. BNP	1,482	4.2
Howitt, H. UKIP	1,352	3.8
Tun, S. Integrity	230	0.7
Lab majority	1,852	5.25
Electorate	63,027	
Turnout	35,252	55.93

Lab hold (notional 6.2% from Lab to Con)

BLAENAU GWENT
(Boundary changes)

		%
Smith, N. Lab	16,974	52.3
Davies, D. Ind*	6,458	19.9
Smith, M. Lib Dem	3,285	10.1
Stevenson, L. Con	2,265	7.0
Davies, R. PIC	1,333	4.1
King, A. BNP	1,211	3.7
Kocan, M. UKIP	488	1.5
O'Connell, A. SLP	381	1.2
Lab majority	10,516	32.39
Electorate	52,442	
Turnout	32,466	61.91

Lab gain (notional 29.1% from Ind to Lab)

BLAYDON
(Boundary changes)

		%
Anderson, D. Lab*	22,297	49.5
Bradbury, N. Lib Dem	13,180	29.3
Hall, G. Con	7,159	15.9
McFarlane, K. BNP	2,277	5.1
Lab majority	9,117	20.23
Electorate	67,808	
Turnout	45,070	66.47

Lab hold (notional 3.2% from Lib Dem to Lab)

BLYTH VALLEY
(No boundary changes)

		%	+/-%
Campbell, R. Lab*	17,156	44.4	-10.1
Reid, J. Lib Dem	10,488	27.2	-3.7
Flux, B. Con	6,412	16.6	2.8
Fairbairn, S. BNP	1,699	4.4	
Condon, J. UKIP	1,665	4.3	
Elliott, B. Ind	819	2.1	
White, A. Eng Dem	327	0.9	
Lab majority	6,668	17.27	
Electorate	62,900		
Turnout	38,615	61.39	

Lab hold (3.2% from Lab to Lib Dem)

BOGNOR REGIS AND LITTLEHAMPTON
(*Boundary changes*)

		%
Gibb, N. Con*	24,087	51.4
McDougall, S. Lib Dem	11,024	23.5
Jones, M. Lab	6,508	13.9
Denny, D. UKIP	3,036	6.5
Moffat, A. BNP	1,890	4.0
Briggs, M. Ind	235	0.5
Con majority	13,063	27.87
Electorate	72,648	
Turnout	46,863	64.51

Con hold (notional 2.3% from Lib Dem to Con)

BOLSOVER
(*Boundary changes*)

		%
Skinner, D. Lab*	21,994	49.9
Rowley, L. Con	10,812	24.6
Hawksworth, D. Lib Dem	6,821	15.5
Radford, M. BNP	2,640	6.0
Calladine, R. UKIP	1,721	3.9
Lab majority	11,182	25.39
Electorate	73,088	
Turnout	44,042	60.26

Lab hold (notional 11.2% from Lab to Con)

BOLTON NORTH EAST
(*Boundary changes*)

		%
Crausby, D. Lab*	19,870	45.7
Dunleavy, D. Con	15,786	36.3
Ankers, P. Lib Dem	5,624	12.9
Johnson, N. UKIP	1,815	4.2
Armston, N. You	182	0.4
Lab majority	4,084	9.4
Electorate	66,850	
Turnout	43,445	64.99

Lab hold (notional 1.3% from Lab to Con)

BOLTON SOUTH EAST
(*Boundary changes*)

		%
Qureshi, Y. Lab	18,782	47.2
Morgan, A. Con	10,148	25.5
O'Hanlon, D. Lib Dem	6,289	15.8
Spink, S. BNP	2,012	5.1
Sidaway, I. UKIP	1,564	3.9
Johnson, A. Green	614	1.6
Syed, N. CPA	195	0.5
Lab majority	8,634	21.68
Electorate	69,467	
Turnout	39,828	57.33

Lab hold (notional 5.7% from Lab to Con)

BOLTON WEST
(*Boundary changes*)

		%
Hilling, J. Lab	18,327	38.4
Williams, S. Con	18,235	38.2
Pearcey, J. Lib Dem	8,177	17.1
Lamb, H. UKIP	1,901	4.0
Mann, R. Green	545	1.1
Jones, J. Ind	254	0.5
Bagnall, D. You	137	0.3
Lab majority	92	0.19
Electorate	71,282	
Turnout	47,780	67.03

Lab hold (notional 5.9% from Lab to Con)

BOOTLE
(*Boundary changes*)

		%
Benton, J. Lab	27,426	66.2
Murray, J. Lib Dem	6,245	15.1
Qureshi, S. Con	3,678	8.9

Nuttall, P. UKIP	2,514	6.1
Stewart, C. BNP	942	2.3
Glover, P. TUSC	472	1.1
Lab majority	21,181	51.11
Electorate	71,422	
Turnout	41,439	58.02

Lab hold (notional 1.7% from Lab to Lib Dem)

BOSTON AND SKEGNESS
(*Boundary changes*)

		%
Simmonds, M. Con*	21,325	49.4
Kenny, P. Lab	8,899	20.6
Smith, P. Lib Dem	6,371	14.8
Pain, C. UKIP	4,081	9.5
Owens, D. BNP	2,278	5.3
Wilson, P. Ind	171	0.4
Con majority	12,426	28.78
Electorate	67,186	
Turnout	43,178	64.27

Con hold (notional 7% from Lab to Con)

BOSWORTH
(*Boundary changes*)

		%
Tredinnick, D. Con*	23,132	42.5
Mullaney, M. Lib Dem	18,100	33.3
Palmer, R. Lab	8,674	16.0
Ryde, J. BNP	2,458	4.5
Veldhuizen, D. UKIP	1,098	2.0
Lampitt, J. Eng Dem	615	1.1
Brooks, M. Science	197	0.4
Con majority	5,032	9.26
Electorate	77,296	
Turnout	54,365	70.33

Con hold (notional 5.9% from Con to Lib Dem)

BOURNEMOUTH EAST
(*Boundary changes*)

		%
Ellwood, T. Con	21,320	48.3
Northover, L. Lib Dem	13,592	30.8
Stokes, D. Lab	5,836	13.2
Hughes, D. UKIP	3,027	6.9
Humphrey, S. Ind	249	0.6
Con majority	7,728	17.52
Electorate	71,125	
Turnout	44,108	62.01

Con hold (notional 1.7% from Lib Dem to Con)

BOURNEMOUTH WEST
(*Boundary changes*)

		%
Burns, C. Con	18,808	45.1
Murray, A. Lib Dem	13,225	31.7
Carr-Brown, S. Lab	6,171	14.8
Glover, P. UKIP	2,999	7.2
Taylor, H. Ind	456	1.1
Con majority	5,583	13.38
Electorate	71,753	
Turnout	41,737	58.17

Con hold (notional 2.9% from Lib Dem to Con)

BRACKNELL
(*Boundary changes*)

		%
Lee, P. Con	27,327	52.4
Earwicker, R. Lib Dem	11,623	22.3
Piasecki, J. Lab	8,755	16.8
Barter, M. UKIP	2,297	4.4
Burke, M. BNP	1,253	2.4
Young, D. Green	821	1.6
Haycocks, D. Scrap	60	0.1
Con majority	15,704	30.08
Electorate	76,888	
Turnout	52,209	67.9

Con hold (notional 1% from Con to Lib Dem)

BRADFORD EAST
(New constituency)

		%
Ward, D. Lib Dem	13,637	33.5
Rooney, T. Lab*	13,272	32.6
Riaz, M. Con	10,860	26.7
Poynton, N. BNP	1,854	4.6
Hussain, R. Ind	375	0.9
Shields, P. Ind	237	0.6
Robinson, G. NF	222	0.6
Lib Dem majority	365	0.9
Electorate	65,116	
Turnout	40,657	62.44

Lib Dem gain (notional 7.6% from Lab to Lib Dem)

BRADFORD SOUTH
(Boundary changes)

		%
Sutcliffe, G. Lab*	15,682	41.1
Palmer, M. Con	11,060	29.0
Griffiths, A. Lib Dem	6,948	18.2
Sutton, S. BNP	2,651	7.0
Illingworth, J. UKIP	1,339	3.5
Lewthwaite, J. DN	315	0.8
Lab majority	4,622	12.13
Electorate	63,580	
Turnout	38,118	59.95

Lab hold (notional 5.9% from Lab to Con)

BRADFORD WEST
(Boundary changes)

		%
Singh, M. Lab*	18,401	45.1
Iqbal, Z. Con	12,638	31.0
Hall-Matthews, D. Lib Dem	4,732	11.6
Sampson, J. BNP	1,370	3.4
Ali, A. Respect	1,245	3.0
Ford, D. Green	940	2.3
Smith, J. UKIP	812	2.0
Craig, N. DN	438	1.1
Lab majority	5,763	14.11
Electorate	62,519	
Turnout	40,830	65.31

Lab hold (notional 2.9% from Con to Lab)

BRAINTREE
(Boundary changes)

		%
Newmark, B. Con	25,901	52.6
Edwards, B. Lab	9,780	19.9
Jarvis, S. Lib Dem	9,247	18.8
Ford, M. UKIP	2,477	5.0
Hooks, P. BNP	1,080	2.2
Blench, D. Green	718	1.5
Con majority	16,121	32.73
Electorate	71,163	
Turnout	49,257	69.22

Con hold (notional 6.7% from Lab to Con)

BRECON AND RADNORSHIRE
(No boundary changes)

		%	+/-%
Williams, R. Lib Dem*	17,929	46.1	1.4
Davies, S. Con	14,182	36.5	1.9
Lloyd, C. Lab	4,096	10.5	-4.4
Davies, J. PlC	989	2.5	-1.1
Easton, C. UKIP	876	2.3	0.4
Robinson, D. Green	341	0.9	
Green, J. Christian	222	0.6	
Offa, L. Loony	210	0.5	
Lib Dem majority	3,747	9.63	
Electorate	54,177		
Turnout	38,896	71.79	

Lib Dem hold (0.3% from Lib Dem to Con)

*Member of last Parliament

BRENT CENTRAL
(New constituency)

		%
Teather, S. Lib Dem*	20,026	43.7
Butler, D. Lab*	18,681	40.8
Rajput, S. Con	5,067	11.1
Ali, S. Green	668	1.5
Williams, E. Christian	488	1.1
Duale, A. Respect	230	0.5
McCastree, D. Ind	163	0.4
Lib Dem majority	1,345	2.94
Electorate	74,046	
Turnout	45,785	61.83

Lib Dem gain (notional 11% from Lab to Lib Dem)

BRENT NORTH
(Boundary changes)

		%
Gardiner, B. Lab*	24,514	46.5
Patel, H. Con	16,486	31.3
Allie, J. Lib Dem	8,879	16.8
Malik, A. Ind	734	1.4
Francis, M. Green	725	1.4
Webb, S. UKIP	380	0.7
Vamadeva, J. Brent North Ind	333	0.6
Tailor, A. Eng Dem	247	0.5
Lab majority	8,028	15.22
Electorate	83,896	
Turnout	52,750	62.88

Lab hold (notional 2.4% from Lab to Con)

BRENTFORD AND ISLEWORTH
(Boundary changes)

		%
Macleod, M. Con	20,022	37.0
Keen, A. Lab*	18,064	33.4
Dakers, A. Lib Dem	12,718	23.5
Hargreaves, J. UKIP	863	1.6
Hunt, J. Green	787	1.5
Winnett, P. BNP	704	1.3
Cunningham, D. Eng Dem	230	0.4
Bhatti, A. Christian	210	0.4
Pillai, E. CPA	99	0.2
Vanneck-Surplice, T. Ind	68	0.1
Con majority	1,958	3.62
Electorate	82,024	
Turnout	54,070	65.92

Con gain (notional 5.9% from Lab to Con)

BRENTWOOD AND ONGAR
(Boundary changes)

		%
Pickles, E. Con*	28,793	56.8
Kendall, D. Lib Dem	11,872	23.4
Benzing, H. Lab	4,992	9.8
McGough, M. UKIP	2,037	4.0
Morris, P. BNP	1,447	2.9
Barnecutt, J. Green	584	1.2
Tilbrook, R. Eng Dem	491	1.0
Sapwell, J. Ind	263	0.5
Attfield, D. Ind	113	0.2
Con majority	16,921	33.36
Electorate	69,309	
Turnout	50,719	73.18

Con hold (notional 3.1% from Lib Dem to Con)

BRIDGEND
(Boundary changes)

		%
Moon, M. Lab*	13,931	36.3
Baker, H. Con	11,668	30.4
Morgan, W. Lib Dem	8,658	22.5
Thomas, N. PlC	2,269	5.9
Urch, B. BNP	1,020	2.7
Fulton, D. UKIP	801	2.1
Lab majority	2,263	5.89
Electorate	58,700	
Turnout	38,425	65.46

Lab hold (notional 6% from Lab to Con)

BRIDGWATER AND WEST SOMERSET
(New constituency)

		%
Liddell-Grainger, I. Con*	24,675	45.2
Butt Philip, T. Lib Dem	15,426	28.3
Pearce, K. Lab	9,332	17.1
Hollings, P. UKIP	2,604	4.8
Treanor, D. BNP	1,282	2.4
Graham, C. Green	859	1.6
Cudlipp, B. Ind	315	0.6
Con majority	9,249	16.95
Electorate	84,541	
Turnout	54,558	64.53

Con hold (notional 2.9% from Con to Lib Dem)

BRIGG AND GOOLE
(Boundary changes)

		%
Percy, A. Con	19,680	44.8
Cawsey, I. Lab*	14,533	33.1
Nixon, R. Lib Dem	6,414	14.6
Wright, N. UKIP	1,749	4.0
Ward, S. BNP	1,498	3.4
Con majority	5,147	11.71
Electorate	67,345	
Turnout	43,943	65.25

Con gain (notional 9.8% from Lab to Con)

BRIGHTON KEMPTOWN
(Boundary changes)

		%
Kirby, S. Con	16,217	37.9
Burgess, S. Lab/Co-op	14,889	34.8
Williams, J. Lib Dem	7,691	18.0
Duncan, B. Green	2,330	5.5
Chamberlain-Webber, J. UKIP	1,384	3.2
Hill, D. TUSC	194	0.5
Con majority	1,328	3.1
Electorate	66,164	
Turnout	42,770	64.64

Con gain (notional 4% from Lab/Co-op to Con)

BRIGHTON PAVILION
(Boundary changes)

		%
Lucas, C. Green	16,238	31.3
Platts, N. Lab	14,986	28.9
Vere, C. Con	12,275	23.6
Millam, B. Lib Dem	7,159	13.8
Carter, N. UKIP	948	1.8
Fyvie, I. SLP	148	0.3
Kara, S. CURE	61	0.1
Atreides, L. Ind	19	0.0
Green majority	1,252	2.41
Electorate	74,373	
Turnout	51,915	69.8

Green gain (notional 8.4% from Lab to Green)

BRISTOL EAST
(Boundary changes)

		%
McCarthy, K. Lab*	16,471	36.5
Shafi, A. Con	12,749	28.3
Popham, M. Lib Dem	10,993	24.4
Jenkins, B. BNP	1,960	4.3
Collins, P. UKIP	1,510	3.4
Vowles, G. Green	803	1.8
Wright, S. Eng Dem	347	0.8
Lynch, R. TUSC	184	0.4
Lab majority	3,722	8.25
Electorate	69,448	
Turnout	45,107	64.95

Lab hold (notional 4.6% from Lab to Con)

BRISTOL NORTH WEST
(Boundary changes)

		%
Leslie, C. Con	19,115	37.9
Harrod, P. Lib Dem	15,841	31.4
Townend, S. Lab	13,059	25.9
Upton, R. UKIP	1,175	2.3
Carr, R. Eng Dem	635	1.3
Dunn, A. Green	511	1.0
Con majority	3,274	6.49
Electorate	73,469	
Turnout	50,454	68.67

Con gain (notional 0.6% from Con to Lib Dem)

BRISTOL SOUTH
(Boundary changes)

		%
Primarolo, D. Lab*	18,600	38.4
Wright, M. Lib Dem	13,866	28.6
Lloyd Davies, M. Con	11,086	22.9
Chidsey, C. BNP	1,739	3.6
McNamee, C. UKIP	1,264	2.6
Bolton, C. Green	1,216	2.5
Clarke, C. Eng Dem	400	0.8
Baldwin, T. TUSC	206	0.4
Lab majority	4,734	9.76
Electorate	78,579	
Turnout	48,510	61.73

Lab hold (notional 7.6% from Lab to Lib Dem)

BRISTOL WEST
(Boundary changes)

		%
Williams, S. Lib Dem*	26,593	48.0
Smith, P. Lab	15,227	27.5
Yarker, N. Con	10,169	18.3
Knight, R. Green	2,090	3.8
Lees, C. UKIP	655	1.2
Kushlick, D. Ind	343	0.6
Baker, J. Eng Dem	270	0.5
Lib Dem majority	11,366	20.49
Electorate	82,728	
Turnout	55,459	67.04

Lib Dem hold (notional 9% from Lab to Lib Dem)

BROADLAND
(New constituency)

		%
Simpson, K. Con*	24,338	46.2
Roper, D. Lib Dem	17,046	32.3
Barron, A. Lab	7,287	13.8
Agnew, S. UKIP	2,382	4.5
Crowther, E. BNP	871	1.7
Curran, S. Green	752	1.4
Con majority	7,292	13.83
Electorate	72,445	
Turnout	52,730	72.79

Con hold (notional 0.1% from Con to Lib Dem)

BROMLEY AND CHISLEHURST
(Boundary changes)

		%
Neill, R. Con*	23,569	53.4
Webber, S. Lib Dem	9,669	21.9
Kirby, C. Lab	7,295	16.5
Jenner, E. UKIP	1,451	3.3
Savage, R. BNP	1,070	2.4
Robertson, R. Green	607	1.4
Cheeseman, J. Eng Dem	376	0.9
Con majority	13,900	31.5
Electorate	65,427	
Turnout	44,131	67.45

Con hold (notional 5.1% from Lib Dem to Con)

BROMSGROVE
(*No boundary changes*)

		%	+/-%
Javid, S. Con	22,558	43.6	-8.3
Burden, S. Lab	11,250	21.8	-8.1
Ling, P. Lib Dem	10,124	19.6	4.6
Morson, S. UKIP	2,950	5.7	1.7
Kriss, A. Brom Ind Con	2,182	4.2	
Wainwright, E. BNP	1,923	3.7	
France, M. Ind	336	0.7	
Wheatley, K. Ind	307	0.6	
Con majority	11,308	21.86	
Electorate	73,086		
Turnout	51,728	70.78	

Con hold (0.1% from Con to Lab)

BROXBOURNE
(*No boundary changes*)

		%	+/-%
Walker, C. Con*	26,844	58.7	4.9
Watson, M. Lab	8,040	17.6	-7.9
Witherick, A. Lib Dem	6,107	13.3	1.1
McCole, S. BNP	2,159	4.7	0.0
Harvey, M. UKIP	1,890	4.1	0.5
Lemay, D. Eng Dem	618	1.4	
Con majority	18,804	41.1	
Electorate	71,391		
Turnout	45,755	64.09	

Con hold (6.4% from Lab to Con)

BROXTOWE
(*Boundary changes*)

		%
Soubry, A. Con	20,585	39.0
Palmer, N. Lab*	20,196	38.3
Watts, D. Lib Dem	8,907	16.9
Shore, M. BNP	1,422	2.7
Cobb, C. UKIP	1,194	2.3
Mitchell, D. Green	423	0.8
Con majority	389	0.74
Electorate	72,042	
Turnout	52,788	73.27

Con gain (notional 2.6% from Lab to Con)

BUCKINGHAM
(*Boundary changes*)

		%
Bercow, J. Speaker*	22,860	46.3
Stevens, J. Ind	10,331	20.9
Farage, N. UKIP	8,401	17.0
Phillips, P. Ind	2,394	4.8
Martin, D. Ind	1,270	2.6
Mozar, L. BNP	980	2.0
Dale, C. Loony	856	1.7
Howard, G. Ind	435	0.9
Hews, D. Christian	369	0.8
Watts, A. Ind	332	0.7
Strutt, S. Deficit	107	0.2
Speaker majority	12,529	25.36
Electorate	74,989	
Turnout	49,402	65.88

Speaker hold (notional 13% from Ind to Speaker)

BURNLEY
(*No boundary changes*)

		%	+/-%
Birtwistle, G. Lib Dem	14,932	35.6	12.0
Cooper, J. Lab	13,114	31.3	-7.1
Ali, R. Con	6,950	16.6	5.8
Wilkinson, S. BNP	3,747	8.9	-1.3
Brown, A. Ind	1,876	4.5	
Wignall, J. UKIP	929	2.2	1.3
Hennessey, A. Ind	297	0.7	
Lib Dem majority	1,818	4.33	
Electorate	66,015		
Turnout	41,970	63.58	

Lib Dem gain (9.6% from Lab to Lib Dem)

*Member of last Parliament

BURTON
(*Boundary changes*)

		%
Griffiths, A. Con	22,188	44.4
Smeeth, R. Lab	15,884	31.8
Rodgers, M. Lib Dem	7,891	15.8
Hewitt, A. BNP	2,409	4.8
Lancaster, P. UKIP	1,451	2.9
Con majority	6,304	12.63
Electorate	74,874	
Turnout	49,932	66.69

Con gain (notional 8.7% from Lab to Con)

BURY NORTH
(*Boundary changes*)

		%
Nuttall, D. Con	18,070	40.1
Khan, M. Lab	15,827	35.1
Baum, R. Lib Dem	7,645	17.0
Maude, J. BNP	1,825	4.0
Evans, S. UKIP	1,282	2.9
Brison, B. Ind	181	0.4
Lambert, G. Pirate	131	0.3
Con majority	2,243	4.98
Electorate	66,759	
Turnout	45,067	67.51

Con gain (notional 5% from Lab to Con)

BURY SOUTH
(*Boundary changes*)

		%
Lewis, I. Lab	19,508	40.3
Wiseman, M. Con	16,216	33.5
D'Albert, V. Lib Dem	8,796	18.2
Purdy, J. BNP	1,743	3.6
Chadwick, P. UKIP	1,017	2.1
Morris, V. Eng Dem	494	1.0
Heron, G. Green	493	1.0
Lab majority	3,292	6.8
Electorate	73,544	
Turnout	48,379	65.78

Lab hold (notional 8% from Con to Lab)

BURY ST EDMUNDS
(*Boundary changes*)

		%
Ruffley, D. Con*	27,899	47.5
Chappell, D. Lib Dem	15,519	26.4
Hind, K. Lab	9,776	16.6
Howlett, J. UKIP	3,003	5.1
Ereira-Guyer, M. Green	2,521	4.3
Con majority	12,380	21.06
Electorate	84,716	
Turnout	58,797	69.4

Con hold (notional 2.8% from Con to Lib Dem)

CAERPHILLY
(*Boundary changes*)

		%
David, W. Lab*	17,377	44.8
Caulfield, M. Con	6,622	17.1
Whittle, L. PlC	6,460	16.7
David, K. Lib Dem	5,688	14.7
Reid, L. BNP	1,635	4.2
Jenkins, T. UKIP	910	2.4
Lab majority	10,755	27.73
Electorate	62,731	
Turnout	38,787	61.83

Lab hold (notional 6.5% from Lab to Con)

CAITHNESS, SUTHERLAND AND EASTER ROSS
(No boundary changes)

		%	+/-%
Thurso, J. Lib Dem*	11,907	41.3	-9.1
MacKay, J. Lab	7,081	24.6	3.7
Urquhart, J. SNP	5,516	19.1	5.8
Graham, A. Con	3,744	13.0	2.8
Campbell, G. Ind	520	1.8	
Lib Dem majority	4,826	16.73	
Electorate	47,263		
Turnout	28,848	61.04	

Lib Dem hold (6.4% from Lib Dem to Lab)

CALDER VALLEY
(Boundary changes)

		%
Whittaker, C. Con	20,397	39.3
Booth, S. Lab	13,966	26.9
Myers, H. Lib Dem	13,037	25.1
Gregory, J. BNP	1,823	3.5
Burrows, G. UKIP	1,173	2.3
Sweeny, K. Green	858	1.7
Cole, T. Ind	194	0.4
Greenwood, B. Ind	175	0.3
Rogan, P. Eng Dem	157	0.3
Con majority	6,431	12.38
Electorate	76,903	
Turnout	51,939	67.54

Con gain (notional 7.6% from Lab to Con)

CAMBERWELL AND PECKHAM
(Boundary changes)

		%
Harman, H. Lab*	27,619	58.9
Blango, C. Lib Dem	10,432	22.2
Stranack, A. Con	6,080	13.0
Jones, J. Green	1,361	2.9
Robby Munilla, Y. Eng Dem	435	0.9
Ogunleye, J. WRP	211	0.5
Sharkey, M. SLP	184	0.4
Francis, D. Ind	93	0.2
Robbins, S. Ind	87	0.2
Knox, P. Ind	82	0.2
Mountford, J. AWL	75	0.2
Lab majority	17,187	36.62
Electorate	78,627	
Turnout	46,938	59.7

Lab hold (notional 3.1% from Lab to Lib Dem)

CAMBORNE AND REDRUTH
(New constituency)

		%
Eustice, G. Con	15,969	37.5
Goldsworthy, J. Lib Dem*	15,903	37.4
Robinson, J. Lab	6,945	16.3
Elliott, D. UKIP	2,152	5.1
Jenkin, L. Mebyon Kernow	775	1.8
McPhee, E. Green	581	1.4
Hawkins, R. SLP	168	0.4
Con majority	66	0.16
Electorate	63,975	
Turnout	42,570	66.54

Con gain (notional 5.2% from Lib Dem to Con)

CAMBRIDGE
(Boundary changes)

		%
Huppert, J. Lib Dem	19,621	39.0
Hillman, N. Con	12,829	25.5
Zeichner, D. Lab	12,174	24.2
Juniper, T. Green	3,804	7.6
Burkinshaw, P. UKIP	1,195	2.4
Booth, M. TUSC	362	0.7
Old, H. Ind	145	0.3
Lib Dem majority	6,792	13.51
Electorate	75,366	
Turnout	50,288	66.73

Lib Dem hold (notional 7% from Lib Dem to Con)

NORTH EAST CAMBRIDGESHIRE
(Boundary changes)

		%
Barclay, S. Con	26,862	51.5
Spenceley, L. Lib Dem	10,437	20.0
Roberts, P. Lab	9,274	17.8
Talbot, R. UKIP	2,791	5.4
Clapp, S. BNP	1,747	3.4
Jordan, D. Ind	566	1.1
Murphy, G. Eng Dem	387	0.8
Con majority	16,425	31.51
Electorate	73,224	
Turnout	52,132	71.2

Con hold (notional 0.8% from Lib Dem to Con)

NORTH WEST CAMBRIDGESHIRE
(Boundary changes)

		%
Vara, S. Con*	29,425	50.4
Wilkins, K. Lib Dem	12,748	21.8
York, C. Lab	9,877	16.9
Brown, R. UKIP	4,826	8.3
Goldspink, S. Eng Dem	1,407	2.4
Con majority	16,677	28.54
Electorate	88,851	
Turnout	58,441	65.77

Con hold (notional 2.6% from Lib Dem to Con)

SOUTH CAMBRIDGESHIRE
(Boundary changes)

		%
Lansley, A. Con	27,995	47.3
Kindersley, S. Lib Dem	20,157	34.1
Sadiq, T. Lab	6,024	10.2
Page, R. Ind	1,968	3.3
Davies-Green, H. UKIP	1,873	3.2
Saggers, S. Green	1,039	1.8
Con majority	7,838	13.25
Electorate	78,995	
Turnout	59,162	74.89

Con hold (notional 2.5% from Con to Lib Dem)

SOUTH EAST CAMBRIDGESHIRE
(Boundary changes)

		%
Paice, J. Con*	27,629	47.9
Chatfield, J. Lib Dem	21,683	37.6
Cowan, J. Lab	4,380	7.6
Monk, A. UKIP	2,138	3.7
Sedgwick-Jell, S. Green	766	1.3
Woollard, G. Ind	517	0.9
Bell, D. CPA	489	0.9
Con majority	5,946	10.3
Electorate	83,068	
Turnout	57,724	69.49

Con hold (notional 2.7% from Con to Lib Dem)

CANNOCK CHASE
(Boundary changes)

		%
Burley, A. Con	18,271	40.0
Woodward, S. Lab	15,076	33.0
Hunt, J. Lib Dem	7,732	16.9
McKenzie, M. UKIP	2,168	4.8
Majorowicz, T. BNP	1,580	3.5
Turville, R. Ind	380	0.8
Jenkins, R. Snouts	259	0.6
Walters, M. Ind	93	0.2
Con majority	3,195	7
Electorate	74,508	
Turnout	45,647	61.26

Con gain (notional 14% from Lab to Con)

CANTERBURY
(*Boundary changes*)

		%
Brazier, J. Con*	22,050	44.8
Voizey, G. Lib Dem	16,002	32.5
Samuel, J. Lab	7,940	16.1
Farmer, H. UKIP	1,907	3.9
Meaden, G. Green	1,137	2.3
Belsey, A. MRP	173	0.4
Con majority	6,048	12.27
Electorate	74,121	
Turnout	49,282	66.49

Con hold (notional 5.4% from Con to Lib Dem)

CARDIFF CENTRAL
(*No boundary changes*)

		%	+/-%
Willott, J. Lib Dem*	14,976	41.3	-8.3
Rathbone, J. Lab	10,400	28.7	-5.5
Robson, K. Con	7,799	21.5	12.3
Williams, C. PIC	1,246	3.4	-0.1
Davies, S. UKIP	765	2.1	1.0
Coates, S. Green	575	1.6	
Saunders, R. TUSC	162	0.5	
Beech, M. Loony	142	0.4	
Mathias, A. Ind	86	0.2	
Lib Dem majority	4,576	12.62	
Electorate	61,162		
Turnout	36,254	59.28	

Lib Dem hold (1.4% from Lib Dem to Lab)

CARDIFF NORTH
(*No boundary changes*)

		%	+/-%
Evans, J. Con	17,860	37.4	1.0
Morgan, J. Lab*	17,666	37.0	-1.9
Dixon, J. Lib Dem	8,724	18.3	-0.4
Rhys, L. PIC	1,588	3.3	-0.9
Gwyn, L. UKIP	1,130	2.4	1.2
Von Ruhland, C. Green	362	0.8	
Thomson, D. WCP	300	0.6	
Con majority	194	0.41	
Electorate	65,553		
Turnout	47,703	72.77	

Con gain (1.5% from Lab to Con)

CARDIFF SOUTH AND PENARTH
(*Boundary changes*)

		%
Michael, A. Lab/Co-op*	17,262	38.8
Hoare, S. Con	12,553	28.2
Hannigan, D. Lib Dem	9,875	22.2
Aslam, F. PIC	1,851	4.2
Ziegler, S. UKIP	1,145	2.6
Burke, G. Ind	648	1.5
Townsend, M. Green	554	1.3
Bate, C. Christian	285	0.7
Griffiths, R. Comm	196	0.5
Lab/Co-op majority	4,709	10.59
Electorate	73,908	
Turnout	44,467	60.17

Lab/Co-op hold (notional 6% from Lab/Co-op to Con)

CARDIFF WEST
(*Boundary changes*)

		%
Brennan, K. Lab*	16,894	41.2
Jones-Evans, A. Con	12,143	29.6
Hitchinson, R. Lib Dem	7,186	17.5
Islam, M. PIC	2,868	7.0
Henessey, M. UKIP	1,117	2.7
Griffiths, J. Green	750	1.8
Lab majority	4,751	11.58
Electorate	62,787	
Turnout	41,043	65.37

Lab hold (notional 5.3% from Lab to Con)

*Member of last Parliament

CARLISLE
(*Boundary changes*)

		%
Stevenson, J. Con	16,589	39.2
Boaden, M. Lab	15,736	37.2
Hughes, N. Lib Dem	6,567	15.5
Stafford, P. BNP	1,086	2.6
Owen, M. UKIP	969	2.3
Reardon, J. Green	614	1.5
Metcalfe, J. TUSC	376	0.9
Howe, P. Ind	263	0.6
Con majority	853	2.02
Electorate	65,263	
Turnout	42,300	64.81

Con gain (notional 7.7% from Lab to Con)

CARMARTHEN EAST AND DINEFWR
(*Boundary changes*)

		%
Edwards, J. PIC	13,546	35.6
Gwyther, C. Lab	10,065	26.4
Morgan, A. Con	8,506	22.3
Powell, W. Lib Dem	4,609	12.1
Atkinson, J. UKIP	1,285	3.4
PIC majority	3,481	9.14
Electorate	52,385	
Turnout	38,088	72.71

PIC hold (notional 4.2% from PIC to Lab)

CARMARTHEN WEST AND SOUTH PEMBROKESHIRE
(*Boundary changes*)

		%
Hart, S. Con	16,649	41.0
Ainger, N. Lab*	13,226	32.6
Gossage, J. Lib Dem	4,890	12.1
Dixon, J. PIC	4,232	10.4
Clarke, R. UKIP	1,146	2.8
Langen, H. Ind	364	0.9
Con majority	3,423	8.44
Electorate	58,108	
Turnout	40,574	69.83

Con gain (notional 6.9% from Lab to Con)

CARSHALTON AND WALLINGTON
(*Boundary changes*)

		%
Brake, T. Lib Dem*	22,180	48.2
Andrew, K. Con	16,920	36.8
Khan, S. Lab	4,015	8.7
Day, F. UKIP	1,348	2.9
Lewis, C. BNP	1,100	2.4
Dow, G. Green	355	0.8
Lib Dem majority	5,260	11.42
Electorate	66,524	
Turnout	46,040	69.21

Lib Dem hold (notional 4.2% from Con to Lib Dem)

CASTLE POINT
(*No boundary changes*)

		%	+/-%
Harris, R. Con	19,806	43.9	-3.2
Spink, B. Ind	12,174	27.0	
Ware-Lane, J. Lab	6,609	14.7	-15.0
D'Cruz, B. Lib Dem	4,232	9.4	-0.7
Howell, P. BNP	2,205	4.9	
Con majority	7,632	16.92	
Electorate	67,286		
Turnout	45,099	67.03	

Con hold (15.1% from Con to Ind)

CENTRAL AYRSHIRE – see under Ayrshire

CENTRAL DEVON – see under Devon

CENTRAL SUFFOLK AND NORTH IPSWICH –
see under Suffolk

CEREDIGION

(Boundary changes)		%
Williams, M. Lib Dem*	19,139	50.0
James, P. PIC	10,815	28.2
Evetts, L. Con	4,421	11.5
Boudier, R. Lab	2,210	5.8
Williams, E. UKIP	977	2.5
Kiersch, L. Green	696	1.8
Lib Dem majority	8,324	21.72
Electorate	58,464	
Turnout	38,321	65.55

Lib Dem hold (notional 10.6% from PIC to Lib Dem)

CHARNWOOD

(Boundary changes)		%
Dorrell, S. Con*	26,560	49.5
Webber-Jones, R. Lib Dem	11,531	21.5
Goodyer, E. Lab	10,536	19.6
Duffy, C. BNP	3,116	5.8
Storier, M. UKIP	1,799	3.4
Con majority	15,029	28.03
Electorate	74,473	
Turnout	53,626	72.01

Con hold (notional 0.1% from Con to Lib Dem)

CHATHAM AND AYLESFORD

(Boundary changes)		%
Crouch, T. Con	20,230	46.1
Shaw, J. Lab*	14,161	32.3
McClintock, J. Lib Dem	5,832	13.3
McCarthy-Stewart, C. BNP	1,365	3.1
Newton, S. UKIP	1,314	3.0
Varnham, S. Eng Dem	400	0.9
Arthur, D. Green	396	0.9
Smith, M. Christian	109	0.3
Con majority	6,069	13.84
Electorate	67,964	
Turnout	43,861	64.54

Con gain (notional 11.1% from Lab to Con)

CHEADLE

(Boundary changes)		%
Hunter, M. Lib Dem*	24,717	47.0
Jeffreys, B. Con	21,445	40.7
Miller, M. Lab	4,920	9.3
Moore, T. UKIP	1,430	2.7
Lib Dem majority	3,272	6.21
Electorate	72,479	
Turnout	52,656	72.65

Lib Dem hold (notional 0.6% from Lib Dem to Con)

CHELMSFORD

(New constituency)		%
Burns, S. Con*	25,207	46.1
Robinson, S. Lib Dem	20,097	36.8
Dixon, P. Lab	5,980	10.9
Wedon, K. UKIP	1,527	2.8
Bateman, M. BNP	899	1.6
Thomson, A. Green	476	0.9
Breed, C. Eng Dem	254	0.5
Sherman, B. Beer	153	0.3
Con majority	5,110	9.35
Electorate	77,525	
Turnout	54,635	70.47

Con hold (notional 0.1% from Lib Dem to Con)

CHELSEA AND FULHAM

(New constituency)		%
Hands, G. Con*	24,093	60.2
Hilton, A. Lab	7,371	18.4
Hazell, D. Lib Dem	6,473	16.2
Stephenson, J. Green	671	1.7
Gittos, T. UKIP	478	1.2
McDonald, B. BNP	388	1.0
Courtenay, R. NICCF	196	0.5
Roseman, G. Eng Dem	169	0.4
Spickernell, G. BEP	17	0.1
Con majority	16,722	41.75
Electorate	66,257	
Turnout	40,048	60.44

Con hold (notional 6% from Lab to Con)

CHELTENHAM

(Boundary changes)		%
Horwood, M. Lib Dem*	26,659	50.4
Coote, M. Con	21,739	41.1
Green, J. Lab	2,703	5.1
Bowman, P. UKIP	1,192	2.3
Hanks, D. Loony	493	0.9
Lib Dem majority	4,920	9.3
Electorate	78,998	
Turnout	52,883	66.94

Lib Dem hold (notional 4.3% from Con to Lib Dem)

CHESHAM AND AMERSHAM

(Boundary changes)		%
Gillan, C. Con*	31,658	60.3
Starkey, T. Lib Dem	14,948	28.4
Gajadharsingh, A. Lab	2,942	5.6
Stevens, A. UKIP	2,129	4.1
Wilkins, N. Green	767	1.5
Con majority	16,710	31.8
Electorate	70,332	
Turnout	52,550	74.72

Con hold (notional 2.3% from Lib Dem to Con)

CITY OF CHESTER

(Boundary changes)		%
Mosley, S. Con	18,995	40.5
Russell, C. Lab*	16,412	35.0
Jewkes, E. Lib Dem	8,930	19.1
Weddell, A. UKIP	1,225	2.6
Abrams, G. Eng Dem	594	1.3
Barker, T. Green	535	1.1
Whittingham, J. Ind	99	0.2
Con majority	2,583	5.51
Electorate	70,131	
Turnout	46,853	66.81

Con gain (notional 3.9% from Lab to Con)

CHESTERFIELD

(Boundary changes)		%
Perkins, T. Lab	17,891	39.0
Holmes, P. Lib Dem*	17,342	37.8
Abbott, C. Con	7,214	15.7
Phillips, D. UKIP	1,432	3.1
Jerram, I. Eng Dem	1,213	2.6
Kerr, D. Green	600	1.3
Daramy, J. Ind	147	0.3
Lab majority	549	1.2
Electorate	71,271	
Turnout	45,924	64.44

Lab gain (notional 3.8% from Lib Dem to Lab)

CHICHESTER
(Boundary changes)

		%
Tyrie, A. Con*	31,427	55.2
Lury, M. Lib Dem	15,550	27.3
Holland, S. Lab	5,937	10.4
Moncrieff, A. UKIP	3,873	6.8
Con majority	15,877	27.9
Electorate	81,576	
Turnout	56,916	69.77

Con hold (notional 3.8% from Lib Dem to Con)

CHINGFORD AND WOODFORD GREEN
(Boundary changes)

		%
Duncan Smith, I. Con*	22,743	52.6
Arakelian, C. Lab	9,780	22.6
Seeff, G. Lib Dem	7,242	16.7
Leppert, J. BNP	1,288	3.0
Jones, N. UKIP	1,133	2.6
Craig, L. Green	650	1.5
Above, N. Ind	202	0.5
White, B. Ind	68	0.2
Con majority	12,963	29.96
Electorate	64,831	
Turnout	43,262	66.73

Con hold (notional 1.2% from Lab to Con)

CHIPPENHAM
(New constituency)

		%
Hames, D. Lib Dem	23,970	45.7
Emmanuel-Jones, W. Con	21,500	41.0
Lovell, G. Lab	3,620	6.9
Reid, J. UKIP	1,783	3.4
Simpkins, M. BNP	641	1.2
Fletcher, S. Green	446	0.9
Maguire, J. Eng Dem	307	0.6
Sexton, R. Christian	118	0.2
Lib Dem majority	2,470	4.71
Electorate	72,106	
Turnout	52,443	72.73

Lib Dem hold (notional 0% from Con to Lib Dem)

CHIPPING BARNET
(Boundary changes)

		%
Villiers, T. Con*	24,700	48.6
Welfare, D. Lab	12,773	25.1
Barber, S. Lib Dem	10,202	20.1
Fluss, J. UKIP	1,442	2.8
Tansley, K. Green	1,021	2.0
Clayton, P. Ind	470	0.9
Con majority	11,927	23.48
Electorate	77,798	
Turnout	50,797	65.29

Con hold (notional 5.7% from Lab to Con)

CHORLEY
(Boundary changes)

		%
Hoyle, L. Lab*	21,515	43.1
Cullens, A. Con	18,922	37.9
Fenn, S. Lib Dem	6,957	13.9
Hogan, N. UKIP	2,021	4.0
Curtis, C. Ind	359	0.7
Lab majority	2,593	5.19
Electorate	70,976	
Turnout	49,922	70.34

Lab hold (notional 5.6% from Lab to Con)

*Member of last Parliament

CHRISTCHURCH
(Boundary changes)

		%
Chope, C. Con*	27,888	56.3
Hurll, M. Lib Dem	12,478	25.2
Deeks, R. Lab	4,849	9.8
Williams, D. UKIP	4,201	8.5
Con majority	15,410	31.13
Electorate	68,859	
Turnout	49,507	71.9

Con hold (notional 0.1% from Con to Lib Dem)

CITIES OF LONDON AND WESTMINSTER – see under London

CITY OF CHESTER – see under Chester

CITY OF DURHAM – see under Durham

CLACTON
(New constituency)

		%
Carswell, D. Con*	22,867	52.9
Henderson, I. Lab	10,799	25.0
Green, M. Lib Dem	5,577	12.9
Taylor, J. BNP	1,975	4.6
Allen, T. Tendring	1,078	2.5
Southall, C. Green	535	1.2
Humphrey, C. Ind	292	0.7
Con majority	12,068	27.93
Electorate	67,194	
Turnout	43,204	64.3

Con hold (notional 9.7% from Lab to Con)

CLEETHORPES
(Boundary changes)

		%
Vickers, M. Con	18,939	42.0
McIsaac, S. Lab*	14,641	32.5
Morland, M. Lib Dem	8,192	18.2
Harness, S. UKIP	3,194	7.1
Con majority	4,298	9.53
Electorate	70,273	
Turnout	45,093	64.17

Con gain (notional 7.8% from Lab to Con)

CLWYD SOUTH
(Boundary changes)

		%
Jones, S. Lab	13,311	38.3
Bell, J. Con	10,477	30.2
Roberts, B. Lib Dem	5,965	17.2
Ryder, J. PlC	3,009	8.7
Hynes, S. BNP	1,100	3.2
Powell, N. UKIP	819	2.4
Lab majority	2,834	8.16
Electorate	53,768	
Turnout	34,723	64.58

Lab hold (notional 5.8% from Lab to Con)

VALE OF CLWYD
(Boundary changes)

		%
Ruane, C. Lab*	15,017	42.2
Wright, M. Con	12,508	35.1
Penlington, P. Lib Dem	4,472	12.6
Wyn-Jones, C. PlC	2,068	5.8
Si'Ree, I. BNP	827	2.3
Turner, T. UKIP	515	1.5
Butler, M. Green Soc	127	0.4
Lab majority	2,509	7.05
Electorate	55,781	
Turnout	35,589	63.8

Lab hold (notional 3.6% from Lab to Con)

CLWYD WEST
(*Boundary changes*)

		%
Jones, D. Con*	15,833	41.5
Hutton, D. Lab	9,414	24.7
Gruffydd, L. PIC	5,864	15.4
Jones, M. Lib Dem	5,801	15.2
Nicholson, W. UKIP	864	2.3
Griffiths, D. WCP	239	0.6
Blakesley, J. Ind	96	0.3
Con majority	6,419	16.81
Electorate	57,913	
Turnout	38,178	65.92

Con hold (notional 8.3% from Lab to Con)

COATBRIDGE, CHRYSTON AND BELLSHILL
(*No boundary changes*)

		%	+/-%
Clarke, T. Lab*	27,728	66.4	2.1
McGlinchey, F. SNP	7,014	16.8	3.3
Elder, K. Lib Dem	3,519	8.4	-3.5
Houston, F. Con	3,374	8.1	0.9
Lab majority	20,714	49.6	
Electorate	70,067		
Turnout	41,766	59.61	

Lab hold (0.6% from Lab to SNP)

COLCHESTER
(*Boundary changes*)

		%
Russell, B. Lib Dem*	22,151	47.9
Quince, W. Con	15,169	32.8
Newell, J. Lab	5,680	12.3
Pitts, J. UKIP	1,350	2.9
Chaney, S. BNP	705	1.5
Lynn, P. Green	694	1.5
Bone, E. Eng Dem	335	0.7
Noble, G. Essex	35	0.1
Shaw, P. Ind	20	0.1
Lib Dem majority	6,982	15.1
Electorate	74,064	
Turnout	46,240	62.43

Lib Dem hold (notional 0.3% from Lib Dem to Con)

COLNE VALLEY
(*Boundary changes*)

		%
McCartney, J. Con	20,440	36.9
Turner, N. Lib Dem	15,603	28.2
Abrahams, D. Lab	14,589	26.3
Fowler, B. BNP	1,893	3.4
Roberts, M. UKIP	1,163	2.1
Ball, C. Green	867	1.6
Grunsell, J. TUSC	741	1.3
Con majority	4,837	8.73
Electorate	80,060	
Turnout	55,401	69.2

Con gain (notional 0.2% from Lib Dem to Con)

CONGLETON
(*No boundary changes*)

		%	+/-%
Bruce, F. Con	23,250	45.7	0.5
Hirst, P. Lib Dem	16,187	31.8	5.1
Bryant, D. Lab	8,747	17.2	-10.4
Slaughter, L. UKIP	2,147	4.2	
Edwards, P. Ind	276	0.5	
Rothwell, P. Ind	94	0.2	
Parton, A. Ind	79	0.2	
Con majority	7,063	13.88	
Electorate	73,696		
Turnout	50,878	69.04	

Con hold (2.3% from Con to Lib Dem)

COPELAND
(*Boundary changes*)

		%
Reed, J. Lab*	19,699	46.0
Whiteside, C. Con	15,866	37.0
Hollowell, F. Lib Dem	4,365	10.2
Jefferson, C. BNP	1,474	3.4
Caley-Knowles, E. UKIP	994	2.3
Perry, J. Green	389	0.9
Lab majority	3,833	8.94
Electorate	63,266	
Turnout	42,857	67.74

Lab hold (notional 2.2% from Lab to Con)

CORBY
(*No boundary changes*)

		%	+/-%
Bagshawe, L. Con	22,886	42.1	2.3
Hope, P. Lab/Co-op*	20,991	38.6	-4.3
Wilson, J. Lib Dem	7,834	14.4	1.7
Davies, R. BNP	2,525	4.7	
Con majority	1,895	3.49	
Electorate	78,026		
Turnout	54,345	69.65	

Con gain (3.3% from Lab/Co-op to Con)

NORTH CORNWALL
(*Boundary changes*)

		%
Rogerson, D. Lib Dem*	22,512	48.0
Flynn, S. Con	19,531	41.6
O'Connor, M. UKIP	2,300	4.9
Hulme, J. Lab	1,971	4.2
Willett, J. Mebyon Kernow	530	1.1
Lib Dem majority	2,981	6.35
Electorate	67,844	
Turnout	46,923	69.16

Lib Dem hold (notional 0.3% from Lib Dem to Con)

SOUTH EAST CORNWALL
(*Boundary changes*)

		%
Murray, S. Con	22,390	45.1
Gillard, K. Lib Dem	19,170	38.6
Sparling, M. Lab	3,507	7.1
McWilliam, S. UKIP	3,083	6.2
Creagh-Osborne, R. Green	826	1.7
Holmes, R. Mebyon Kernow	641	1.3
Con majority	3,220	6.48
Electorate	71,288	
Turnout	49,689	69.7

Con gain (notional 9.1% from Lib Dem to Con)

COVENTRY NORTH EAST
(*Boundary changes*)

		%
Ainsworth, B. Lab*	21,384	49.1
Noonan, H. Con	9,609	22.1
Field, R. Lib Dem	7,210	16.6
Gower, T. BNP	1,863	4.3
Nellist, D. SAP	1,592	3.7
Forbes, C. UKIP	1,291	3.0
Lebar, R. CMGB	434	1.0
Lab majority	11,775	27.03
Electorate	73,035	
Turnout	43,563	59.65

Lab hold (notional 5.5% from Lab to Con)

COVENTRY NORTH WEST
(*Boundary changes*)

		%
Robinson, G. Lab*	19,936	42.6
Ridley, G. Con	13,648	29.2
McKee, V. Lib Dem	8,344	17.8
Sheppard, E. BNP	1,666	3.6
Nattrass, M. UKIP	1,295	2.8
Clarke, J. Ind	640	1.4
Wood, J. Green	497	1.1
Downes, N. SAP	370	0.8
Sidhu, W. CMGB	164	0.4
Lab majority	6,288	13.43
Electorate	72,871	
Turnout	46,806	64.23

Lab hold (notional 4% from Lab to Con)

COVENTRY SOUTH
(Boundary changes)

		%
Cunningham, J. Lab*	19,197	41.5
Foster, K. Con	15,352	33.2
Patton, B. Lib Dem	8,278	17.9
Taylor, M. UKIP	1,767	3.8
Griffiths, J. TUSC	691	1.5
Gray, S. Green	639	1.4
Lab majority	3,845	8.31
Electorate	73,652	
Turnout	46,268	62.82

Lab hold (notional 3.4% from Lab to Con)

CRAWLEY
(No boundary changes)

		%	+/-%
Smith, H. Con	21,264	44.6	5.8
Oxlade, C. Lab	15,336	32.2	-6.8
Vincent, J. Lib Dem	6,844	14.4	-1.1
Trower, R. BNP	1,672	3.5	0.5
French, C. UKIP	1,382	2.9	0.7
Smith, P. Green	598	1.3	
Khan, A. JP	265	0.6	0.1
Hubner, A. Ind	143	0.3	
Con majority	5,928	12.45	
Electorate	72,781		
Turnout	47,625	65.44	

Con gain (6.3% from Lab to Con)

CREWE AND NANTWICH
(Boundary changes)

		%
Timpson, E. Con*	23,420	45.8
Williams, D. Lab	17,374	34.0
Wood, R. Lib Dem	7,656	15.0
Clutton, J. BNP	1,414	2.8
Williams, P. BNP	1,043	2.0
Parsons, M. Ind	177	0.4
Con majority	6,046	11.82
Electorate	77,461	
Turnout	51,133	66.01

Con gain (notional 13.7% from Lab to Con)

CROYDON CENTRAL
(Boundary changes)

		%
Barwell, G. Con	19,657	39.4
Ryan, G. Lab/Co-op	16,688	33.4
Lambell, P. Lib Dem	6,553	13.1
Pelling, A. Ind*	3,239	6.5
Le May, C. BNP	1,448	2.9
Atkinson, R. UKIP	997	2.0
Golberg, B. Green	581	1.2
Gitau, J. Christian	264	0.5
Cartwright, J. Loony	192	0.4
Castle, M. Ind	138	0.3
Con majority	2,969	5.95
Electorate	76,349	
Turnout	49,911	65.37

Con gain (notional 3.3% from Lab/Co-op to Con)

CROYDON NORTH
(Boundary changes)

		%
Wicks, M. Lab*	28,949	55.8
Hadden, J. Con	12,466	24.0
Jerome, G. Lib Dem	7,226	13.9
Khan, S. Green	1,017	2.0
Serter, J. UKIP	891	1.7
Williams, N. Christian	586	1.1
Shaikh, M. Respect	272	0.5
Stevenson, B. Comm	160	0.3
Seyed Mohamed, M. Ind	111	0.2
Lab majority	16,483	31.78
Electorate	85,216	
Turnout	51,873	60.87

Lab hold (notional 0.2% from Con to Lab)

*Member of last Parliament

CROYDON SOUTH
(Boundary changes)

		%
Ottaway, R. Con*	28,684	50.8
Rix, S. Lib Dem	12,866	22.8
Avis, J. Lab	11,287	20.0
Bolter, J. UKIP	2,504	4.4
Ross, G. Green	981	1.7
Con majority	15,818	28
Electorate	81,303	
Turnout	56,488	69.48

Con hold (notional 1.8% from Con to Lib Dem)

CUMBERNAULD, KILSYTH AND KIRKINTILLOCH EAST
(No boundary changes)

		%	+/-%
McClymont, G. Lab	23,549	57.1	6.1
Hepburn, J. SNP	9,794	23.8	1.9
Ackland, R. Lib Dem	3,924	9.5	-5.1
Fraser, S. Con	3,407	8.3	1.4
O'Neill, W. SSP	476	1.1	-1.7
Lab majority	13,755	33.36	
Electorate	64,037		
Turnout	41,232	64.39	

Lab hold (2.1% from SNP to Lab)

CYNON VALLEY
(Boundary changes)

		%
Clwyd, A. Lab*	15,681	52.4
Davies, D. PlC	6,064	20.3
Thacker, L. Lib Dem	4,120	13.8
Ash, J. Con	3,010	10.1
Hughes, F. UKIP	1,001	3.4
Lab majority	9,617	32.11
Electorate	50,650	
Turnout	29,948	59.13

Lab hold (notional 8.7% from Lab to PlC)

DAGENHAM AND RAINHAM
(New constituency)

		%
Cruddas, J. Lab*	17,813	40.1
Jones, S. Con	15,183	34.2
Barnbrook, M. BNP	4,952	11.2
Bourke, J. Lib Dem	3,806	8.6
Litwin, C. UKIP	1,569	3.5
Kennedy, G. Ind	308	0.7
Watson, P. Christian	305	0.7
Rosaman, D. Green	296	0.7
Lab majority	2,630	5.92
Electorate	69,764	
Turnout	44,398	63.64

Lab hold (notional 4.9% from Lab to Con)

DARLINGTON
(Boundary changes)

		%
Chapman, J. Lab	16,891	39.3
Legard, E. Con	13,503	31.4
Barker, M. Lib Dem	10,046	23.4
Foster, A. BNP	1,262	2.9
Bull, C. UKIP	1,194	2.8
Lab majority	3,388	7.89
Electorate	68,168	
Turnout	42,959	63.02

Lab hold (notional 9.1% from Lab to Con)

DARTFORD
(*Boundary changes*)

		%
Johnson, G. Con	24,428	48.7
Adams, J. Lab	13,800	27.5
Willis, J. Lib Dem	7,361	14.7
Rogers, G. Eng Dem	2,178	4.3
Palmer, R. UKIP	1,842	3.7
Tindame, S. Ind	264	0.5
Crockford, J. FDP	207	0.4
Con majority	10,628	21.19
Electorate	76,271	
Turnout	50,162	65.77

Con gain (notional 11.5% from Lab to Con)

DAVENTRY
(*Boundary changes*)

		%
Heaton-Harris, C. Con	29,252	56.4
McGlynn, C. Lib Dem	10,064	19.4
Corazzo, P. Lab	8,168	15.8
Broomfield, J. UKIP	2,333	4.5
Bennett-Spencer, A. Eng Dem	1,187	2.3
Whiffen, S. Green	770	1.5
Con majority	19,188	36.99
Electorate	71,452	
Turnout	51,871	72.6

Con hold (notional 0.7% from Con to Lib Dem)

DELYN
(*No boundary changes*)

		%	+/-%
Hanson, D. Lab	15,083	40.7	-4.9
Sandbach, A. Con	12,811	34.6	8.5
Brereton, B. Lib Dem	5,747	15.5	-2.3
Ryder, P. PlC	1,844	5.0	-2.4
Matthys, J. BNP	844	2.3	
Haigh, A. UKIP	655	1.8	0.2
Lab majority	2,272	6.13	
Electorate	53,470		
Turnout	37,041	69.27	

Lab hold (6.7% from Lab to Con)

DENTON AND REDDISH
(*Boundary changes*)

		%
Gwynne, A. Lab*	19,191	50.8
Searle, J. Con	9,360	24.8
Broadhurst, S. Lib Dem	6,727	17.8
Robinson, W. UKIP	2,060	5.5
Dennis, J. Ind	297	0.8
Lab majority	9,831	26
Electorate	64,181	
Turnout	37,808	58.91

Lab hold (notional 6.3% from Lab to Con)

DERBY NORTH
(*Boundary changes*)

		%
Williamson, C. Lab	14,896	33.0
Mold, S. Con	14,283	31.6
Care, L. Lib Dem	12,638	28.0
Cheeseman, P. BNP	2,000	4.4
Ransome, E. UKIP	829	1.8
Gale, D. Ind	264	0.6
Geraghty, D. Pirate	170	0.4
Lab majority	613	1.36
Electorate	71,474	
Turnout	45,212	63.26

Lab hold (notional 7.4% from Lab to Con)

DERBY SOUTH
(*Boundary changes*)

		%
Beckett, M. Lab*	17,851	43.1
Perschke, J. Con	11,729	28.3

		%
Batey, D. Lib Dem	8,430	20.4
Fowke, S. UKIP	1,821	4.4
Graves, A. Ind	1,357	3.3
Lab majority	6,122	14.78
Electorate	70,999	
Turnout	41,434	58.36

Lab hold (notional 9.3% from Lab to Con)

DERBYSHIRE DALES
(*New constituency*)

		%
McLoughlin, P. Con*	24,378	52.0
Naitta, J. Lib Dem	10,512	22.4
Swindell, C. Lab	9,061	19.3
Guiver, I. UKIP	1,779	3.8
Stockell, J. Green	772	1.6
Delves, N. Loony	228	0.5
Y'Mech, A. Humanity	50	0.1
Con majority	13,866	29.58
Electorate	63,376	
Turnout	46,875	73.96

Con hold (notional 3.7% from Lib Dem to Con)

MID DERBYSHIRE
(*New constituency*)

		%
Latham, P. Con	22,877	48.2
Dhindsa, H. Lab	11,585	24.4
McIntosh, S. Lib Dem	9,711	20.5
Allsebrook, L. BNP	1,698	3.6
Kay, T. UKIP	1,252	2.6
Seerius, R. Loony	219	0.5
Con majority	11,292	23.8
Electorate	66,074	
Turnout	47,439	71.8

Con hold (notional 5.6% from Lab to Con)

NORTH EAST DERBYSHIRE
(*Boundary changes*)

		%
Engel, N. Lab*	17,948	38.1
Merriman, H. Con	15,503	32.9
Bull, R. Lib Dem	10,947	23.2
Bush, J. UKIP	2,636	5.6
Lab majority	2,445	5.19
Electorate	71,398	
Turnout	47,139	66.02

Lab hold (notional 8.6% from Lab to Con)

SOUTH DERBYSHIRE
(*Boundary changes*)

		%
Wheeler, H. Con	22,935	45.4
Edwards, M. Lab	15,807	31.3
Diouf, A. Lib Dem	8,012	15.9
Jarvis, P. BNP	2,193	4.3
Swabey, C. UKIP	1,206	2.4
Liversuch, P. SLP	266	0.5
Con majority	7,128	14.12
Electorate	70,608	
Turnout	50,490	71.51

Con gain (notional 9.8% from Lab to Con)

DEVIZES
(*Boundary changes*)

		%
Perry, C. Con	25,519	55.0
Hornby, F. Lib Dem	12,514	27.0
Ali, J. Lab	4,711	10.2
Bryant, P. UKIP	2,076	4.5
Fletcher, M. Green	813	1.8
Houlden, M. Ind	566	1.2
Coome, N. Libertarian	141	0.3
Con majority	13,005	28.03
Electorate	67,379	
Turnout	46,400	68.86

Con hold (notional 0.3% from Con to Lib Dem)

CENTRAL DEVON
(New constituency)

		%
Stride, M. Con	27,737	51.4
Hutty, P. Lib Dem	18,507	34.3
Macdonald, M. Lab	3,715	6.9
Edwards, R. UKIP	2,870	5.3
Matthews, C. Green	1,044	1.9
Con majority	9,230	17.11
Electorate	71,203	
Turnout	53,959	75.78

Con hold (notional 6.1% from Lib Dem to Con)

EAST DEVON
(Boundary changes)

		%
Swire, H. Con*	25,662	48.1
Robathan, P. Lib Dem	16,548	31.0
Manson, G. Lab	5,721	10.7
Amor, M. UKIP	4,346	8.2
Pavey, S. Green	815	1.5
Con majority	9,114	17.09
Electorate	73,109	
Turnout	53,322	72.93

Con hold (notional 1.1% from Con to Lib Dem)

NORTH DEVON
(Boundary changes)

		%
Harvey, N. Lib Dem*	24,305	47.3
Milton, P. Con	18,484	36.0
Crowther, S. UKIP	3,720	7.2
Cann, M. Lab	2,671	5.2
Knight, L. Green	697	1.4
Marshall, G. BNP	614	1.2
Cann, R. Ind	588	1.1
Vidler, N. Eng Dem	146	0.3
Sables, G. Comm GB	96	0.2
Lib Dem majority	5,821	11.32
Electorate	74,508	
Turnout	51,403	68.99

Lib Dem hold (notional 0.3% from Con to Lib Dem)

SOUTH WEST DEVON
(Boundary changes)

		%
Streeter, G. Con*	27,908	55.9
Pascoe, A. Lib Dem	12,034	24.1
Pollard, L. Lab	6,193	12.4
Williams, H. UKIP	3,084	6.2
Brean, V. Green	641	1.3
Con majority	15,874	31.77
Electorate	70,813	
Turnout	49,965	70.56

Con hold (notional 5.6% from Lib Dem to Con)

DEWSBURY
(Boundary changes)

		%
Reevell, S. Con	18,898	34.9
Malik, S. Lab*	17,372	32.1
Hutchinson, A. Lib Dem	9,150	16.9
Iqbal, K. Ind	3,813	7.0
Roberts, R. BNP	3,265	6.0
Cruden, A. Green	849	1.6
Felse, M. Eng Dem	661	1.2
Con majority	1,526	2.82
Electorate	78,910	
Turnout	54,167	68.64

Con gain (notional 5.8% from Lab to Con)

*Member of last Parliament

DON VALLEY
(Boundary changes)

		%
Flint, C. Lab*	16,472	37.8
Stephens, M. Con	12,877	29.6
Simpson, E. Lib Dem	7,422	17.0
Toseland, E. BNP	2,112	4.8
Shaw, W. UKIP	1,904	4.4
Aston, B. Eng Dem	1,756	4.0
Williams, M. Ind	887	2.0
Lab majority	3,595	8.25
Electorate	72,597	
Turnout	43,559	60

Lab hold (notional 10.6% from Lab to Con)

DONCASTER CENTRAL
(Boundary changes)

		%
Winterton, R. Lab	16,569	39.6
Davies, G. Con	10,340	24.7
Wilson, P. Lib Dem	8,795	21.0
Parramore, L. Eng Dem	1,816	4.3
Bettney, J. BNP	1,762	4.2
Andrews, M. UKIP	1,421	3.4
Pickles, S. Ind	970	2.3
Williams, D. CURE	72	0.2
Lab majority	6,229	14.88
Electorate	72,985	
Turnout	41,864	57.36

Lab hold (notional 8.7% from Lab to Con)

DONCASTER NORTH
(Boundary changes)

		%
Miliband, E. Lab*	19,637	47.2
Brodie, S. Con	8,728	21.0
Sanderson, E. Lib Dem	6,174	14.8
Chambers, P. BNP	2,818	6.8
Crawshaw, W. Eng Dem	2,148	5.2
Andrews, L. UKIP	1,797	4.3
Rawcliffe, B. TUSC	181	0.4
Lab majority	10,909	26.21
Electorate	71,681	
Turnout	41,622	58.07

Lab hold (notional 2.8% from Lab to Con)

MID DORSET AND NORTH POOLE
(Boundary changes)

		%
Brooke, A. Lib Dem*	21,100	45.0
King, N. Con	20,831	44.4
Brown, D. Lab	2,748	5.9
Evans, D. UKIP	2,109	4.5
Lib Dem majority	269	0.57
Electorate	64,660	
Turnout	46,878	72.5

Lib Dem hold (notional 6.3% from Lib Dem to Con)

NORTH DORSET
(Boundary changes)

		%
Walter, R. Con*	27,640	51.0
Gasson, E. Lib Dem	20,015	36.9
Bunney, M. Lab	2,910	5.4
Nieboer, J. UKIP	2,812	5.2
Hayball, A. Green	546	1.0
Monksummers, R. Loony	218	0.4
Con majority	7,625	14.07
Electorate	73,741	
Turnout	54,212	73.52

Con hold (notional 2.8% from Lib Dem to Con)

SOUTH DORSET
(No boundary changes)

		%	+/-%
Drax, R. Con	22,667	45.0	7.2
Knight, J. Lab*	15,224	30.2	-11.3
Kayes, R. Lib Dem	9,557	19.0	3.3
Hobson, M. UKIP	2,034	4.0	0.8
Heatley, B. Green	595	1.2	
Kirkwood, A. GMVY	233	0.5	
Con majority	7,443	14.77	
Electorate	73,838		
Turnout	50,399	68.26	

Con gain (9.3% from Lab to Con)

WEST DORSET
(No boundary changes)

		%	+/-%
Letwin, O. Con*	27,287	47.5	1.1
Farrant, S. Lib Dem	23,364	40.7	-1.1
Bick, S. Lab	3,815	6.6	-1.1
Chisholm, O. UKIP	2,196	3.8	1.8
Greene, S. Green	675	1.2	-0.6
Con majority	3,923	6.83	
Electorate	76,869		
Turnout	57,418	74.7	

Con hold (1.1% from Lib Dem to Con)

DOVER
(Boundary changes)

		%
Elphicke, C. Con	22,174	43.9
Prosser, G. Lab*	16,900	33.5
Brigden, J. Lib Dem	7,962	15.8
Matcham, V. UKIP	1,747	3.5
Whiting, D. BNP	1,104	2.2
Walters, M. Eng Dem	216	0.4
Clark, D. CPA	200	0.4
Lee-Delisle, G. Ind	82	0.2
Con majority	5,274	10.45
Electorate	71,833	
Turnout	50,471	70.26

Con gain (notional 10.4% from Lab to Con)

NORTH DOWN
(No boundary changes)

		%	+/-%
Hermon, S. Ind*	21,181	63.1	
Parsley, I. UCUNF	6,817	20.3	
Farry, S. All	1,876	5.6	-2.0
Kilpatrick, K. TUV	1,634	4.9	
Agnew, S. Green	1,043	3.1	
Logan, L. SDLP	680	2.0	-1.1
Parker, V. Sinn Féin	250	0.8	0.1
Ind majority	14,364	42.82	
Electorate	60,698		
Turnout	33,543	55.26	

Ind gain (21.1% from UCUNF to Ind)

SOUTH DOWN
(Boundary changes)

		%
Ritchie, M. SDLP	20,648	48.2
Ruane, C. Sinn Féin	12,236	28.6
Wells, J. DUP	3,645	8.5
McCallister, J. UCUNF	3,093	7.2
McConnell, I. TUV	1,506	3.5
Enright, C. Green	901	2.1
Griffin, D. All	560	1.3
SDLP majority	8,412	19.64
Electorate	70,784	
Turnout	42,840	60.52

SDLP hold (notional 0.1% from SDLP to Sinn Féin)

DUDLEY NORTH
(Boundary changes)

		%
Austin, I. Lab*	14,923	38.6
Brown, G. Con	14,274	36.9
Beckett, M. Lib Dem	4,066	10.5
Davis, M. UKIP	3,267	8.4
Griffiths, K. BNP	1,899	4.9
Inman, K. NF	173	0.5
Lab majority	649	1.68
Electorate	71,050	
Turnout	38,695	54.46

Lab hold (notional 4.7% from Lab to Con)

DUDLEY SOUTH
(Boundary changes)

		%
Kelly, C. Con	16,449	43.0
Harris, R. Lab	12,593	32.9
Bramall, J. Lib Dem	5,989	15.7
Rowe, P. UKIP	3,132	8.2
Con majority	3,856	10.08
Electorate	61,090	
Turnout	38,257	62.62

Con gain (notional 9.5% from Lab to Con)

DULWICH AND WEST NORWOOD
(Boundary changes)

		%
Jowell, T. Lab*	22,461	46.4
Mitchell, J. Lib Dem	13,096	27.1
Adegoke, K. Con	10,684	22.1
Collins, S. Green	1,266	2.6
Jones, E. UKIP	707	1.5
Lab majority	9,365	19.34
Electorate	72,817	
Turnout	48,422	66.5

Lab hold (notional 0.9% from Lab to Lib Dem)

DUMFRIES AND GALLOWAY
(No boundary changes)

		%	+/-%
Brown, R. Lab*	23,950	45.8	4.7
Duncan, P. Con	16,501	31.6	-3.8
Wood, A. SNP	6,419	12.3	0.1
Brodie, R. Lib Dem	4,608	8.8	0.5
Wright, B. UKIP	695	1.3	
Lab majority	7,449	14.25	
Electorate	74,584		
Turnout	52,271	70.08	

Lab hold (4.3% from Con to Lab)

DUMFRIESSHIRE, CLYDESDALE AND TWEEDDALE
(No boundary changes)

		%	+/-%
Mundell, D. Con*	17,457	38.0	1.9
Beamish, C. Lab/Co-op	13,263	28.9	-3.4
Bhatia, C. Lib Dem	9,080	19.8	-0.5
Orr, A. SNP	4,945	10.8	1.6
McKeane, S. UKIP	637	1.4	0.4
Ballance, A. Green	510	1.1	
Con majority	4,194	9.12	
Electorate	66,627		
Turnout	45,962	68.98	

Con hold (2.6% from Lab/Co-op to Con)

EAST DUNBARTONSHIRE
(No boundary changes)

		%	+/-%
Swinson, J. Lib Dem*	18,551	38.6	-3.2
Galbraith, M. Lab	16,367	34.1	1.0
Nolan, M. Con	7,431	15.5	-1.0
White, I. SNP	5,054	10.5	4.7
Beeley, J. UKIP	545	1.1	
Lib Dem majority	2,184	4.55	
Electorate	63,795		
Turnout	48,043	75.31	

Lib Dem hold (2.1% from Lib Dem to Lab)

WEST DUNBARTONSHIRE

(No boundary changes)

		%	+/-%
Doyle, G. Lab/Co-op	25,905	61.1	9.3
McCormick, G. SNP	8,497	20.1	-1.6
Watt, H. Lib Dem	3,434	8.1	
McIntyre, M. Con	3,242	7.7	1.2
Sorbie, M. UKIP	683	1.6	0.8
McGavigan, K. SLP	505	1.2	
Lab/Co-op majority	17,408	41.1	
Electorate	66,086		
Turnout	42,360	64.1	

Lab/Co-op hold (5.5% from SNP to Lab/Co-op)

DUNDEE EAST

(No boundary changes)

		%	+/-%
Hosie, S. SNP*	15,350	37.8	0.6
Murray, K. Lab	13,529	33.3	-2.9
Bustin, C. Con	6,177	15.2	2.4
Sneddon, C. Lib Dem	4,285	10.5	-0.8
Baird, S. Green	542	1.3	
Arthur, M. UKIP	431	1.1	0.3
Gorrie, A. SSP	254	0.6	-0.7
SNP majority	1,821	4.48	
Electorate	65,471		
Turnout	40,640	62.07	

SNP hold (1.8% from Lab to SNP)

DUNDEE WEST

(No boundary changes)

		%	+/-%
McGovern, J. Lab*	17,994	48.4	3.9
Barrie, J. SNP	10,716	28.8	-1.2
Barnett, J. Lib Dem	4,233	11.4	-3.0
Stewart, C. Con	3,461	9.3	1.0
McBride, A. Ind	365	1.0	
McFarlane, J. TUSC	357	1.0	
Lab majority	7,278	19.56	
Electorate	63,013		
Turnout	37,202	59.04	

Lab hold (2.5% from SNP to Lab)

DUNFERMLINE AND WEST FIFE

(No boundary changes)

		%	+/-%
Docherty, T. Lab	22,639	46.2	-1.2
Rennie, W. Lib Dem*	17,169	35.0	14.9
McCall, J. SNP	5,201	10.6	-8.3
Hacking, B. Con	3,305	6.7	-3.6
Inglis, O. UKIP	633	1.3	-0.2
Lab majority	5,470	11.16	
Electorate	73,590		
Turnout	49,026	66.62	

Lab hold (8.2% from Lib Dem to Lab)

CITY OF DURHAM

(No boundary changes)

		%	+/-%
Blackman-Woods, R. Lab*	20,496	44.3	-2.7
Woods, C. Lib Dem	17,429	37.6	-2.0
Varley, N. Con	6,146	13.3	3.9
Musgrave, R. BNP	1,153	2.5	
Coghill-Marshall, N. UKIP	856	1.9	
Collings, J. Ind	172	0.4	
Lab majority	3,067	6.62	
Electorate	68,832		
Turnout	46,313	67.28	

Lab hold (0.4% from Lab to Lib Dem)

NORTH DURHAM

(Boundary changes)

		%
Jones, K. Lab*	20,698	50.4
Skelton, D. Con	8,622	21.0
Lindley, I. Lib Dem	8,617	21.0
Molloy, P. BNP	1,686	4.1
Reid, B. UKIP	1,344	3.3
Lab majority	12,076	29.42
Electorate	67,544	
Turnout	41,040	60.76

Lab hold (notional 8.9% from Lab to Con)

NORTH WEST DURHAM

(Boundary changes)

		%
Glass, P. Lab	18,539	42.2
Temple, O. Lib Dem	10,927	24.9
Tempest, M. Con	8,766	20.0
Stelling, W. Ind	2,472	5.6
Stewart, M. BNP	1,852	4.2
McDonald, A. UKIP	1,259	2.9
Lab majority	7,612	17.34
Electorate	70,350	
Turnout	43,900	62.4

Lab hold (notional 8.3% from Lab to Lib Dem)

DWYFOR MEIRIONNYDD

(New constituency)

		%
Llwyd, E. PlC*	12,814	44.2
Baynes, S. Con	6,447	22.3
Humphreys, A. Lab	4,021	13.9
Churchman, S. Lib Dem	3,538	12.2
Hughes, L. Ind	1,310	4.5
Wykes, F. UKIP	776	2.7
PlC majority	6,367	21.98
Electorate	45,354	
Turnout	28,968	63.87

PlC hold (notional 7.3% from PlC to Con)

EALING CENTRAL AND ACTON

(New constituency)

		%
Bray, A. Con	17,944	37.9
Mahfouz, B. Lab	14,228	30.0
Ball, J. Lib Dem	13,041	27.5
Carter, J. UKIP	765	1.6
Edwards, S. Green	737	1.6
Fernandes, S. Christian	295	0.6
Akaki, S. Ind EACPS	190	0.4
Con majority	3,716	7.84
Electorate	70,251	
Turnout	47,418	67.5

Con gain (notional 5% from Lab to Con)

EALING NORTH

(Boundary changes)

		%
Pound, S. Lab*	24,023	50.1
Gibb, I. Con	14,722	30.7
Lucas, C. Lib Dem	6,283	13.1
Furness, D. BNP	1,045	2.2
De Wulverton, I. UKIP	685	1.4
Warleigh-Lack, C. Green	505	1.1
Ljubisic, P. Christian	415	0.9
Lab majority	9,301	19.39
Electorate	73,104	
Turnout	47,966	65.61

Lab hold (notional 0.4% from Con to Lab)

EALING SOUTHALL

(Boundary changes)

		%
Sharma, V. Lab*	22,024	51.0
Singh, G. Con	12,733	29.5
Bakhai, N. Lib Dem	6,383	14.8
Basu, S. Green	705	1.6
Anil, M. Christian	503	1.2
Chaggar, S. Eng Dem	408	1.0
Lab majority	9,291	21.5
Electorate	66,970	
Turnout	43,224	64.54

Lab hold (notional 8.4% from Lab to Con)

*Member of last Parliament

EASINGTON
(Boundary changes)

		%
Morris, G. Lab	20,579	58.8
Saville, T. Lib Dem	5,597	16.0
Harrison, R. Con	4,790	13.7
Dunn, C. BNP	2,317	6.6
Aiken, M. UKIP	1,631	4.7
Lab majority	14,982	42.83
Electorate	63,879	
Turnout	34,977	54.76

Lab hold (notional 7.8% from Lab to Lib Dem)

EAST ANTRIM – see under Antrim

EAST DEVON – see under Devon

EAST DUNBARTONSHIRE – see under Dunbartonshire

EAST HAM
(Boundary changes)

		%
Timms, S. Lab*	35,471	69.7
Shea, P. Con	7,645	15.0
Brice, C. Lib Dem	5,849	11.5
O'Connor, B. Eng Dem	822	1.6
Maciejowska, J. Green	586	1.2
Lab majority	27,826	54.67
Electorate	95,790	
Turnout	50,902	53.14

Lab hold (notional 7.4% from Con to Lab)

EAST HAMPSHIRE – see under Hampshire

EAST KILBRIDE, STRATHAVEN AND LESMAHAGOW
(No boundary changes)

		%	+/-%
McCann, M. Lab	26,241	51.4	2.7
McKenna, J. SNP	11,738	23.0	5.1
Simpson, G. Con	6,613	13.0	3.0
Loughton, J. Lib Dem	5,052	9.9	-6.6
Robb, K. Green	1,003	2.0	-1.3
Houston, J. Ind	299	0.6	0.3
Lab majority	14,503	28.42	
Electorate	76,534		
Turnout	51,032	66.68	

Lab hold (1.2% from Lab to SNP)

EAST LONDONDERRY – see under Londonderry

EAST LOTHIAN – see under Lothian

EAST RENFREWSHIRE – see under Renfrewshire

EAST SURREY – see under Surrey

EAST WORTHING AND SHOREHAM – see under Worthing

EAST YORKSHIRE – see under Yorkshire

EASTBOURNE
(Boundary changes)

		%
Lloyd, S. Lib Dem	24,658	47.3
Waterson, N. Con*	21,223	40.7
Brinson, D. Lab	2,497	4.8
Shing, S. Ind	1,327	2.5
Needham, R. UKIP	1,305	2.5
Poulter, C. BNP	939	1.8

Baldry, M. Ind	101	0.2
Gell, K. Ind	74	0.2
Lib Dem majority	3,435	6.58
Electorate	77,840	
Turnout	52,197	67.06

Lib Dem gain (notional 5.8% from Lab to Lib Dem)

EASTLEIGH
(Boundary changes)

		%
Huhne, C. Lib Dem*	24,966	46.5
Hutchings, M. Con	21,102	39.3
Barraclough, L. Lab	5,153	9.6
Finch, R. UKIP	1,933	3.6
Pewsey, T. Eng Dem	249	0.5
Stone, D. Ind	154	0.3
Low, K. NLP	93	0.2
Lib Dem majority	3,864	7.19
Electorate	77,436	
Turnout	53,725	69.38

Lib Dem hold (notional 3% from Con to Lib Dem)

EDDISBURY
(Boundary changes)

		%
O'Brien, S. Con*	23,472	51.6
Thompson, R. Lib Dem	10,217	22.4
Merrick, P. Lab	9,794	21.5
Dodman, C. UKIP	1,931	4.3
Con majority	13,255	29.12
Electorate	72,100	
Turnout	45,523	63.14

Con hold (notional 0.1% from Lib Dem to Con)

EDINBURGH EAST
(No boundary changes)

		%	+/-%
Gilmore, S. Lab	17,314	43.4	3.4
Kerevan, S. SNP	8,133	20.4	3.4
Hope, B. Lib Dem	7,751	19.4	-5.0
Donald, M. Con	4,358	10.9	0.6
Harper, R. Green	2,035	5.1	-0.6
Clark, G. TUSC	274	0.7	
Lab majority	9,181	22.99	
Electorate	60,945		
Turnout	39,934	65.52	

Lab hold (0.01% from SNP to Lab)

EDINBURGH NORTH AND LEITH
(No boundary changes)

		%	+/-%
Lazarowicz, M. Lab/Co-op*	17,740	37.4	3.2
Lang, K. Lib Dem	16,016	33.8	4.6
McGill, I. Con	7,079	14.9	-3.7
Cashley, C. SNP	4,568	9.6	-0.5
Joester, K. Green	1,062	2.2	-3.6
Hein, J. Lib	389	0.8	
Black, W. TUSC	233	0.5	
Jacobsen, D. SLP	141	0.3	
Macintyre, C. Ind	128	0.3	
Lab/Co-op majority	1,724	3.63	
Electorate	69,207		
Turnout	47,435	68.54	

Lab/Co-op hold (0.7% from Lab/Co-op to Lib Dem)

EDINBURGH SOUTH
(No boundary changes)

		%	+/-%
Murray, I. Lab	15,215	34.7	1.5
Mackintosh, F. Lib Dem	14,899	34.0	1.7
Hudson, N. Con	9,452	21.5	-2.5
Howat, S. SNP	3,354	7.6	1.5
Burgess, S. Green	881	2.0	-1.2
Lab majority	316	0.72	
Electorate	59,362		
Turnout	43,879	73.92	

Lab hold (0.1% from Lab to Lib Dem)

EDINBURGH SOUTH WEST

(No boundary changes)

		%	+/-%
Darling, A. Lab*	19,473	42.8	3.0
Rust, J. Con	11,026	24.2	0.9
McKay, T. Lib Dem	8,194	18.0	-3.0
Stewart, K. SNP	5,530	12.1	1.6
Cooney, C. Green	872	1.9	-1.5
Fox, C. SSP	319	0.7	-0.6
Bellamy, C. Comm League	48	0.1	
Lab majority	8,447	18.54	
Electorate	66,361		
Turnout	45,550	68.64	

Lab hold (1% from Con to Lab)

EDINBURGH WEST

(No boundary changes)

		%	+/-%
Crockart, M. Lib Dem	16,684	35.8	-13.6
Day, C. Lab	12,881	27.7	9.1
Geddes, S. Con	10,767	23.1	3.7
Cleland, S. SNP	6,115	13.1	4.0
Lib Dem majority	3,803	8.17	
Electorate	65,159		
Turnout	46,562	71.46	

Lib Dem hold (11.3% from Lib Dem to Lab)

EDMONTON

(Boundary changes)

		%
Love, A. Lab/Co-op*	21,665	53.2
Charalambous, A. Con	12,052	29.6
Kilbane-Dawe, I. Lib Dem	4,252	10.4
Freshwater, R. UKIP	1,036	2.5
Johnson, J. Green	516	1.3
Basarik, E. Reform 2000	379	0.9
Morrison, C. Christian	350	0.9
McLean, D. Ind	127	0.3
Lab/Co-op majority	9,613	23.61
Electorate	57,074	
Turnout	40,711	71.33

Lab/Co-op hold (notional 2.4% from Lab/Co-op to Con)

ELLESMERE PORT AND NESTON

(Boundary changes)

		%
Miller, A. Lab*	19,750	44.6
Penketh, S. Con	15,419	34.8
Aspinall, D. Lib Dem	6,663	15.1
Crocker, H. UKIP	1,619	3.7
Starkey, J. Ind	782	1.8
Lab majority	4,331	9.78
Electorate	63,509	
Turnout	44,298	69.75

Lab hold (notional 3.1% from Lab to Con)

ELMET AND ROTHWELL

(New constituency)

		%
Shelbrooke, A. Con	23,778	42.6
Lewis, J. Lab	19,257	34.5
Golton, S. Lib Dem	9,109	16.3
Clayton, S. BNP	1,802	3.2
Oddy, D. UKIP	1,593	2.9
Nolan, C. Ind	250	0.5
Con majority	4,521	8.09
Electorate	77,724	
Turnout	55,873	71.89

Con gain (notional 9.8% from Lab to Con)

ELTHAM

(Boundary changes)

		%
Efford, C. Lab*	17,416	41.3
Gold, D. Con	15,753	37.4

*Member of last Parliament

Toole, S. Lib Dem	5,299	12.6
Woods, R. BNP	1,745	4.2
Adams, R. UKIP	1,011	2.4
Hayles, A. Green	419	1.0
Tibby, M. Eng Dem	217	0.5
Graham, A. Ind	104	0.3
Lab majority	1,663	3.95
Electorate	62,590	
Turnout	42,141	67.33

Lab hold (notional 1.8% from Lab to Con)

ENFIELD NORTH

(Boundary changes)

		%
de Bois, N. Con	18,804	42.1
Ryan, J. Lab*	17,112	38.3
Smith, P. Lib Dem	5,403	12.1
Avery, T. BNP	1,228	2.8
Jones, M. UKIP	938	2.1
Linton, B. Green	489	1.1
Williams, A. Christian	161	0.4
Weald, R. Eng Dem	131	0.3
Athow, A. WRP	96	0.2
Daniels, G. Ind	91	0.2
Con majority	1,692	3.79
Electorate	57,758	
Turnout	44,651	77.31

Con hold (notional 0.7% from Lab to Con)

ENFIELD SOUTHGATE

(Boundary changes)

		%
Burrowes, D. Con*	21,928	49.2
Charalambous, B. Lab	14,302	32.1
Khan, J. Lib Dem	6,124	13.7
Krakowiak, P. Green	632	1.4
Brock, R. UKIP	505	1.1
Mukhopadhyay, A. Ind	391	0.9
Billoo, S. Respect	174	0.4
Weald, B. Eng Dem	173	0.4
Malakounides, M. Ind	88	0.2
Sturgess, J. Better Britain	35	0.1
Con majority	7,626	17.11
Electorate	55,521	
Turnout	44,573	80.28

Con hold (notional 7.2% from Lab to Con)

EPPING FOREST

(Boundary changes)

		%
Laing, E. Con*	25,148	53.8
Haigh, A. Lib Dem	10,017	21.4
Curtis, K. Lab	6,641	14.2
Richardson, P. BNP	1,982	4.3
Smith, A. UKIP	1,852	4.0
Pepper, S. Green	659	1.4
Burelli, K. Eng Dem	285	0.6
Con majority	15,131	32.39
Electorate	72,186	
Turnout	46,718	64.72

Con hold (notional 1.1% from Con to Lib Dem)

EPSOM AND EWELL

(Boundary changes)

		%
Grayling, C. Con*	30,868	55.9
Lees, J. Lib Dem	14,734	26.7
Montgomery, C. Lab	6,538	11.8
Wallace, E. UKIP	2,549	4.6
Ticher, P. RRG	266	0.5
Con majority	16,134	29.21
Electorate	79,908	
Turnout	55,242	69.13

Con hold (notional 2.1% from Con to Lib Dem)

EREWASH

(Boundary changes)

		%
Lee, J. Con	18,805	39.4
Pidgeon, C. Lab	16,304	34.2
Garnett, M. Lib Dem	8,343	17.5
Bailey, M. BNP	2,337	4.9
Sutton, J. UKIP	855	1.8
Fletcher, L. Green	534	1.1
Wilkins, L. Ind	464	1.0
Con majority	2,501	5.25
Electorate	69,655	
Turnout	47,683	68.46

Con gain (notional 10.4% from Lab to Con)

ERITH AND THAMESMEAD

(Boundary changes)

		%
Pearce, T. Lab	19,068	44.7
Bloom, C. Con	13,365	31.3
Cunliffe, A. Lib Dem	5,116	12.0
Saunders, K. BNP	2,184	5.1
Perrin, P. UKIP	1,139	2.7
Williams, L. Eng Dem	465	1.1
Akinoshun, A. Ind	438	1.0
Cordle, S. CPA	379	0.9
Powley, M. Green	322	0.8
Lab majority	5,703	13.36
Electorate	70,756	
Turnout	42,673	60.31

Lab hold (notional 6.4% from Lab to Con)

ESHER AND WALTON

(No boundary changes)

		%	+/-%
Raab, D. Con	32,134	58.8	13.2
Blackman, L. Lib Dem	13,541	24.8	-4.7
Eldergill, F. Lab	5,829	10.7	-8.7
Collignon, B. UKIP	1,783	3.3	0.0
Popham, T. Ind	378	0.7	
Chinnery, J. Loony	341	0.6	-0.6
Kearsley, M. Eng Dem	307	0.6	
Lear, A. Best	230	0.4	
Con majority	18,593	34	
Electorate	75,338		
Turnout	54,691	72.59	

Con hold (9% from Lib Dem to Con)

EXETER

(Boundary changes)

		%
Bradshaw, B. Lab*	19,942	38.1
Foster, H. Con	17,221	32.9
Oakes, G. Lib Dem	10,581	20.2
Crawford, K. UKIP	1,930	3.7
Gale, C. Lib	1,108	2.1
Black, P. Green	792	1.5
Farmer, R. BNP	673	1.3
Lab majority	2,721	5.2
Electorate	77,158	
Turnout	52,330	67.82

Lab hold (notional 6% from Lab to Con)

FALKIRK

(No boundary changes)

		%	+/-%
Joyce, E. Lab*	23,207	45.6	-5.1
McNally, J. SNP	15,364	30.2	8.9
Mackie, K. Con	5,698	11.2	1.3
Leach, K. Lib Dem	5,225	10.3	-5.7
Goldie, B. UKIP	1,283	2.5	
Lab majority	7,843	15.42	
Electorate	81,869		
Turnout	50,868	62.13	

Lab hold (7% from Lab to SNP)

FAREHAM

(No boundary changes)

		%	+/-%
Hoban, M. Con*	30,037	55.1	5.6
Bentley, A. Lib Dem	12,945	23.8	2.1
Carr, J. Lab	7,719	14.2	-11.4
Richards, S. UKIP	2,235	4.1	1.2
Doggett, P. Green	791	1.5	
Jenkins, J. Eng Dem	618	1.1	
Con majority	17,092	31.37	
Electorate	75,915		
Turnout	54,477	71.76	

Con hold (1.7% from Lib Dem to Con)

FAVERSHAM AND MID KENT

(Boundary changes)

		%
Robertson, H. Con*	26,250	56.1
Naghi, D. Lib Dem	9,162	19.6
Rehal, A. Lab	7,748	16.6
Larkins, S. UKIP	1,722	3.7
Valentine, T. Green	890	1.9
Kemp, G. NF	542	1.2
Davidson, H. Loony	398	0.9
Con majority	17,088	36.51
Electorate	66,425	
Turnout	46,804	70.46

Con hold (notional 1.6% from Lib Dem to Con)

FELTHAM AND HESTON

(Boundary changes)

		%
Keen, A. Lab/Co-op*	21,174	43.3
Bowen, M. Con	16,516	33.8
Wilson, M. Lib Dem	6,679	13.7
Donnelly, J. BNP	1,714	3.5
Shadbolt, J. UKIP	992	2.0
Anstis, E. Green	530	1.1
Tripathi, D. Ind	505	1.0
Khaira, A. Ind	180	0.4
Williams, R. Ind	168	0.4
Linley, M. WRP	78	0.2
Lab/Co-op majority	4,658	9.52
Electorate	79,989	
Turnout	48,909	61.14

Lab/Co-op hold (notional 4.9% from Lab/Co-op to Con)

FERMANAGH AND SOUTH TYRONE

(No boundary changes)

		%	+/-%
Gildernew, M. Sinn Féin*	21,304	45.3	7.5
Connor, R. Ind	21,300	45.3	
McKinney, F. SDLP	3,574	7.6	-7.1
Kamble, V. All	437	0.9	
Stevenson, J. Ind	188	0.4	
Sinn Féin majority	4	0.01	
Electorate	67,908		
Turnout	47,066	69.31	

Sinn Féin hold (18.9% from Sinn Féin to Ind)

NORTH EAST FIFE

(No boundary changes)

		%	+/-%
Campbell, M. Lib Dem*	17,763	44.2	-7.8
Briggs, M. Con	8,715	21.7	2.2
Hood, M. Lab	6,869	17.1	4.4
Campbell, R. SNP	5,685	14.2	3.8
Scott-Hayward, M. UKIP	1,032	2.6	1.2
Lib Dem majority	9,048	22.53	
Electorate	62,771		
Turnout	40,156	63.97	

Lib Dem hold (5% from Lib Dem to Con)

FILTON AND BRADLEY STOKE
(New constituency)

		%
Lopresti, J. Con	19,686	40.7
Boulton, I. Lab	12,772	26.4
Tyzack, P. Lib Dem	12,197	25.2
Knight, J. UKIP	1,506	3.1
Scott, D. BNP	1,328	2.8
Lucas, J. Green	441	0.9
Johnson, R. Christian	199	0.4
None-of-the-Above Vote, Z. Ind	172	0.4
Con majority	6,914	14.3
Electorate	69,003	
Turnout	48,336	70.05

Con hold (notional 6.4% from Lab to Con)

FINCHLEY AND GOLDERS GREEN
(Boundary changes)

		%
Freer, M. Con	21,688	45.8
Moore, A. Lab	15,879	33.5
Edge, L. Lib Dem	8,036	17.0
Cummins, S. UKIP	817	1.7
Lyven, D. Green	737	1.6
Con majority	5,809	12.27
Electorate	77,198	
Turnout	47,355	61.34

Con hold (notional 5.8% from Lab to Con)

FOLKESTONE AND HYTHE
(Boundary changes)

		%
Collins, D. Con	26,109	49.4
Beaumont, L. Lib Dem	15,987	30.2
Worsley, D. Lab	5,719	10.8
McKenna, F. UKIP	2,439	4.6
Williams, H. BNP	1,662	3.1
Kemp, P. Green	637	1.2
Plumstead, D. Ind	247	0.5
Con majority	10,122	19.14
Electorate	78,005	
Turnout	52,879	67.79

Con hold (notional 2.6% from Con to Lib Dem)

FOREST OF DEAN
(No boundary changes)

		%	+/-%
Harper, M. Con*	22,853	46.8	6.1
Hogan, B. Lab	11,789	24.1	-12.3
Coleman, C. Lib Dem	10,676	21.9	4.8
Congdon, T. UKIP	2,522	5.2	2.8
Greenwood, J. Green	923	1.9	-0.2
Con majority	11,064	22.66	
Electorate	68,419		
Turnout	48,820	71.35	

Con hold (9.2% from Lab to Con)

FOYLE
(Boundary changes)

		%
Durkan, M. SDLP*	16,922	44.3
Anderson, M. Sinn Féin	12,098	31.7
Devenney, M. DUP	4,489	11.8
McCann, E. PBPA	2,936	7.7
Harding, D. UCUNF	1,221	3.2
McGrellis, K. All	223	0.6
SDLP majority	4,824	12.63
Electorate	65,843	
Turnout	38,190	58

SDLP hold (notional 0.2% from SDLP to Sinn Féin)

FYLDE
(Boundary changes)

		%
Menzies, M. Con	22,826	52.1
Winlow, B. Lib Dem	9,641	22.0
Robinson, L. Lab	8,624	19.7

*Member of last Parliament

Bleeker, M. UKIP	1,945	4.5
Mitchell, P. Green	654	1.5
Con majority	13,185	30.12
Electorate	65,926	
Turnout	43,771	66.39

Con hold (notional 4.2% from Con to Lib Dem)

GAINSBOROUGH
(Boundary changes)

		%
Leigh, E. Con*	24,266	49.2
O'Connor, P. Lib Dem	13,707	27.8
McMahon, J. Lab	7,701	15.6
Pearson, S. UKIP	2,065	4.2
Porter, M. BNP	1,512	3.1
Con majority	10,559	21.39
Electorate	72,939	
Turnout	49,366	67.68

Con hold (notional 1.8% from Lib Dem to Con)

GARSTON AND HALEWOOD
(New constituency)

		%
Eagle, M. Lab*	25,493	59.3
Keaveney, P. Lib Dem	8,616	20.0
Downey, R. Con	6,908	16.1
Hammond, T. UKIP	1,540	3.6
Raby, D. Respect	268	0.6
Lab majority	16,877	39.24
Electorate	71,312	
Turnout	43,007	60.31

Lab hold (notional 5.7% from Lib Dem to Lab)

GATESHEAD
(New constituency)

		%
Mearns, I. Lab	20,712	54.0
Hindle, F. Lib Dem	8,163	21.3
Anderson, H. Con	5,716	14.9
Scott, K. BNP	1,787	4.7
Tennant, J. UKIP	1,103	2.9
Redfern, A. Green	379	1.0
Brunskill, E. TUSC	266	0.7
Walton, D. Christian	131	0.4
Lab majority	12,549	32.73
Electorate	66,492	
Turnout	38,343	57.67

Lab hold (notional 4% from Lab to Lib Dem)

GEDLING
(Boundary changes)

		%
Coaker, V. Lab*	19,821	41.1
Laughton, B. Con	17,962	37.2
Bateman, J. Lib Dem	7,350	15.2
Adcock, S. BNP	1,598	3.3
Marshall, D. UKIP	1,459	3.0
Lab majority	1,859	3.85
Electorate	71,946	
Turnout	48,259	67.08

Lab hold (notional 2.9% from Lab to Con)

GILLINGHAM AND RAINHAM
(New constituency)

		%
Chishti, R. Con	21,624	46.2
Clark, P. Lab*	12,944	27.7
Stamp, A. Lib Dem	8,484	18.1
Oakley, R. UKIP	1,515	3.2
Ravenscroft, B. BNP	1,149	2.5
Lacey, D. Eng Dem	464	1.0
Marchant, T. Green	356	0.8
Bryan, G. Ind	141	0.3
Meegan, G. Medway	109	0.2
Con majority	8,680	18.55
Electorate	70,814	
Turnout	46,792	66.08

Con gain (notional 9.3% from Lab to Con)

VALE OF GLAMORGAN
(Boundary changes)

		%
Cairns, A. Con	20,341	41.7
Davies, A. Lab	16,034	32.9
Parrott, E. Lib Dem	7,403	15.2
Johnson, I. PlC	2,667	5.5
Mahoney, K. UKIP	1,529	3.1
Thomas, R. Green	457	0.9
Harrold, J. Christian	236	0.5
Con majority	4,307	8.83
Electorate	70,262	
Turnout	48,757	69.39

Con gain (notional 6.1% from Lab to Con)

GLASGOW CENTRAL
(No boundary changes)

		%	+/-%
Sarwar, A. Lab	15,908	51.9	3.8
Saeed, O. SNP	5,357	17.5	2.7
Young, C. Lib Dem	5,010	16.3	-1.4
Bradley, J. Con	2,158	7.0	0.8
Whitelaw, A. Green	800	2.6	-2.3
Holt, I. BNP	616	2.0	-0.4
Nesbitt, J. SSP	357	1.2	-2.8
Urquhart, R. UKIP	246	0.8	
Archibald, F. Pirate	128	0.4	
Lab majority	10,551	34.41	
Electorate	60,105		
Turnout	30,665	51.02	

Lab hold (0.6% from SNP to Lab)

GLASGOW EAST
(No boundary changes)

		%	+/-%
Curran, M. Lab	19,797	61.5	0.9
Mason, J. SNP*	7,957	24.7	7.7
Ward, K. Lib Dem	1,617	5.0	-6.8
Khan, H. Con	1,453	4.5	-2.4
Finnie, J. BNP	677	2.1	
Curran, F. SSP	454	1.4	-2.1
Thackeray, A. UKIP	209	0.7	
Lab majority	11,840	36.75	
Electorate	61,865		
Turnout	32,214	52.07	

Lab hold (19.1% from SNP to Lab)

GLASGOW NORTH
(No boundary changes)

		%	+/-%
McKechin, A. Lab*	13,181	44.4	5.2
Gordon, K. Lib Dem	9,283	31.3	3.9
Grady, P. SNP	3,530	11.9	-1.0
Boyle, E. Con	2,089	7.0	-1.7
Bartos, M. Green	947	3.2	-4.4
Main, T. BNP	296	1.0	
McCormack, A. TUSC	287	1.0	
Lab majority	3,898	13.13	
Electorate	51,490		
Turnout	29,682	57.65	

Lab hold (0.6% from Lib Dem to Lab)

GLASGOW NORTH EAST
(No boundary changes)

		%	+/-%
Bain, W. Lab*	20,100	68.1	
McAllister, B. SNP	4,158	14.1	-3.4
Baxendale, E. Lib Dem	2,262	7.7	
Davidson, R. Con	1,569	5.3	
Hamilton, W. BNP	798	2.7	-0.5
Campbell, G. TUSC	187	0.6	
McVey, K. SSP	179	0.6	-4.3
Berrington, J. SLP	156	0.5	-13.6
Lab majority	15,942	54.05	
Electorate	59,861		
Turnout	29,497	49.28	

Lab gain (7.4% from SNP to Lab)

GLASGOW NORTH WEST
(No boundary changes)

		%	+/-%
Robertson, J. Lab*	19,233	53.9	4.8
McKee, N. Lib Dem	5,622	15.8	-3.8
Park, M. SNP	5,430	15.2	1.5
Sullivan, R. Con	3,537	9.9	0.4
Crawford, M. Green	882	2.5	-1.4
McLean, S. BNP	699	2.0	
Livingstone, M. Comm	179	0.5	
Lab majority	13,611	38.16	
Electorate	60,997		
Turnout	35,664	58.47	

Lab hold (4.3% from Lib Dem to Lab)

GLASGOW SOUTH
(No boundary changes)

		%	+/-%
Harris, T. Lab*	20,736	51.6	4.5
Fleming, M. SNP	8,078	20.1	7.5
Mustapha, S. Lib Dem	4,739	11.8	-7.2
Rankin, D. Con	4,592	11.4	-1.1
Campbell, M. Green	961	2.4	-2.0
Coyle, M. BNP	637	1.6	
Smith, B. TUSC	351	0.9	
Lab majority	12,658	31.51	
Electorate	65,069		
Turnout	40,172	61.74	

Lab hold (1.5% from Lab to SNP)

GLASGOW SOUTH WEST
(No boundary changes)

		%	+/-%
Davidson, I. Lab/Co-op*	19,863	62.3	2.2
Stephens, C. SNP	5,192	16.3	1.0
Nelson, I. Lib Dem	2,870	9.0	-2.6
Forrest, M. Con	2,084	6.5	0.8
Sheridan, T. TUSC	931	2.9	
Orr, D. BNP	841	2.6	
Lab/Co-op majority	14,671	46.04	
Electorate	58,191		
Turnout	31,869	54.77	

Lab/Co-op hold (0.6% from SNP to Lab/Co-op)

GLENROTHES
(No boundary changes)

		%	+/-%
Roy, L. Lab*	25,247	62.2	10.4
Alexander, D. SNP	8,799	21.7	-1.6
Wills, H. Lib Dem	3,108	7.7	-5.0
Low, S. Con	2,922	7.2	0.1
Seunarine, K. UKIP	425	1.1	-0.1
Lab majority	16,448	40.54	
Electorate	67,765		
Turnout	40,568	59.87	

Lab hold (11% from SNP to Lab)

GLOUCESTER
(Boundary changes)

		%
Graham, R. Con	20,267	39.8
Dhanda, P. Lab*	17,847	35.0
Hilton, J. Lib Dem	9,767	19.2
Smith, M. UKIP	1,808	3.5
Platt, A. Eng Dem	564	1.1
Meloy, B. Green	511	1.0
Con majority	2,420	4.75
Electorate	79,321	
Turnout	50,965	64.25

Con gain (notional 8.9% from Lab to Con)

GORDON
(No boundary changes)

		%	+/-%
Bruce, M. Lib Dem*	17,575	36.0	-9.0
Thomson, R. SNP	10,827	22.2	6.2
Crockett, B. Lab	9,811	20.1	-0.1
Thomson, R. Con	9,111	18.7	1.0
Edwards, S. Green	752	1.5	
Jones, E. BNP	699	1.4	
Lib Dem majority	6,748	13.82	
Electorate	73,420		
Turnout	48,825	66.5	

Lib Dem hold (7.6% from Lib Dem to SNP)

GOSPORT
(No boundary changes)

		%	+/-%
Dinenage, C. Con	24,300	51.6	7.0
Hylands, R. Lib Dem	9,887	21.0	4.4
Giles, G. Lab	7,944	16.9	-14.5
Rice, A. UKIP	1,496	3.2	-1.0
Bennett, B. BNP	1,004	2.1	
Shaw, B. Eng Dem	622	1.3	
Smith, C. Green	573	1.2	-1.7
Smith, D. Ind	493	1.1	
Read, C. Ind	331	0.7	
Hart, B. Ind	289	0.6	
Con majority	14,413	30.62	
Electorate	72,797		
Turnout	47,074	64.66	

Con hold (1.3% from Lib Dem to Con)

GOWER
(Boundary changes)

		%
Caton, M. Lab*	16,016	38.4
Davies, B. Con	13,333	31.9
Day, M. Lib Dem	7,947	19.1
Price, D. PlC	2,760	6.6
Jones, A. SOTBTH	963	2.3
Triggs, G. UKIP	652	1.6
Lab majority	2,683	6.43
Electorate	61,696	
Turnout	41,737	67.65

Lab hold (notional 5.3% from Lab to Con)

GRANTHAM AND STAMFORD
(Boundary changes)

		%
Boles, N. Con	26,552	50.2
Bisnauthsing, H. Lib Dem	11,726	22.2
Bartlett, M. Lab	9,503	18.0
Robinson, C. BNP	2,485	4.7
Wells, A. UKIP	1,604	3.0
Horn, M. Lincs Ind	929	1.8
Con majority	14,826	28.04
Electorate	78,008	
Turnout	52,874	67.78

Con hold (notional 1.2% from Con to Lib Dem)

GRAVESHAM
(No boundary changes)

		%	+/-%
Holloway, A. Con*	22,956	48.5	5.0
Smith, K. Lab	13,644	28.8	-13.3
Arrowsmith, A. Lib Dem	6,293	13.3	2.6
Clark, G. UKIP	2,265	4.8	2.9
Uncles, S. Eng Dem	1,005	2.1	0.7
Crawford, R. Green	675	1.4	
Dartnell, A. Ind	465	1.0	
Con majority	9,312	19.66	
Electorate	70,200		
Turnout	47,376	67.49	

Con hold (9.1% from Lab to Con)

*Member of last Parliament

GREAT GRIMSBY
(Boundary changes)

		%
Mitchell, A. Lab*	10,777	32.6
Ayling, V. Con	10,063	30.4
De Freitas, A. Lib Dem	7,388	22.4
Hudson, H. UKIP	2,043	6.2
Fyfe, S. BNP	1,517	4.6
Brown, E. Ind	835	2.5
Howe, A. PNDP	331	1.0
Lab majority	714	2.16
Electorate	62,427	
Turnout	33,048	52.94

Lab hold (notional 10.5% from Lab to Con)

GREAT YARMOUTH
(No boundary changes)

		%	+/-%
Lewis, B. Con	18,571	43.0	4.9
Wright, A. Lab*	14,295	33.1	-12.4
Partridge, S. Lib Dem	6,188	14.3	3.3
Baugh, A. UKIP	2,066	4.8	0.5
Tann, B. BNP	1,421	3.3	
Biggart, L. Green	416	1.0	
McMahon-Morris, M. LTT	100	0.2	
Con majority	4,276	9.9	
Electorate	70,315		
Turnout	43,204	61.44	

Con gain (8.6% from Lab to Con)

GREENWICH AND WOOLWICH
(Boundary changes)

		%
Raynsford, N. Lab*	20,262	49.0
Drury, S. Con	10,109	24.4
Lee, J. Lib Dem	7,498	18.1
Rustem, L. BNP	1,151	2.8
Hewett, A. Green	1,054	2.5
Adeleye, E. Christian	443	1.1
Wresniwiro, T. Eng Dem	339	0.8
Kasab, O. TUSC	267	0.7
Alingham, T. Ind	65	0.2
Lab majority	10,153	24.54
Electorate	65,489	
Turnout	41,368	63.17

Lab hold (notional 5.2% from Lab to Con)

GUILDFORD
(Boundary changes)

		%
Milton, A. Con*	29,618	53.2
Doughty, S. Lib Dem	21,836	39.2
Shand, T. Lab	2,812	5.1
Manzoor, M. UKIP	1,021	1.8
Morris, J. TPP	280	0.5
Con majority	7,782	13.98
Electorate	77,082	
Turnout	55,662	72.21

Con hold (notional 6.9% from Lib Dem to Con)

HACKNEY NORTH AND STOKE NEWINGTON
(Boundary changes)

		%
Abbott, D. Lab*	25,553	54.6
Angus, K. Lib Dem	11,092	23.7
Caplan, D. Con	6,759	14.4
Sellwood, M. Green	2,133	4.6
Hargreaves, M. Christian	299	0.6
Moore, S. Ind	258	0.6
Knapp, K. Loony	182	0.4
Shaer, P. Ind	96	0.2
Williams, A. Ind	61	0.1
Pope-de-Locksley, J. Magna Carta	28	0.1
Lab majority	14,461	30.89
Electorate	73,906	
Turnout	46,811	63.34

Lab hold (notional 2.5% from Lib Dem to Lab)

HACKNEY SOUTH AND SHOREDITCH
(*Boundary changes*)

		%
Hillier, M. Lab/Co-op*	23,888	55.2
Raval, D. Lib Dem	9,600	22.2
Nayyar, S. Con	5,800	13.4
Lane, P. Green	1,493	3.5
King, M. UKIP	651	1.5
Rae, B. Lib	539	1.3
Williams, J. Christian	434	1.0
Sen, N. DDCP	202	0.5
Davies, P. Comm League	110	0.3
De La Haye, D. Ind	95	0.2
Tuckett, J. Ind	26	0.1
Spinks, M. Ind	20	0.1
Lab/Co-op majority	14,288	33.01
Electorate	72,841	
Turnout	43,279	59.42

Lab/Co-op hold (notional 0.8% from Lib Dem to Lab/Co-op)

HALESOWEN AND ROWLEY REGIS
(*Boundary changes*)

		%
Morris, J. Con	18,115	41.1
Hayman, S. Lab	16,092	36.5
Tibbetts, P. Lib Dem	6,515	14.8
Baddeley, D. UKIP	2,824	6.4
Thompson, D. Ind	433	1.0
Con majority	2,023	4.59
Electorate	61,090	
Turnout	44,120	72.22

Con gain (notional 7.1% from Lab to Con)

HALIFAX
(*Boundary changes*)

		%
Riordan, L. Lab/Co-op*	16,278	37.2
Allott, P. Con	14,806	33.8
Wilson, E. Lib Dem	8,335	19.0
Bates, T. BNP	2,760	6.3
Park, D. Ind	722	1.6
Sangha, J. UKIP	654	1.5
Lab/Co-op majority	1,472	3.36
Electorate	70,380	
Turnout	43,797	62.23

Lab/Co-op hold (notional 2.7% from Lab/Co-op to Con)

HALTEMPRICE AND HOWDEN
(*Boundary changes*)

		%
Davis, D. Con*	24,486	50.2
Neal, J. Lib Dem	12,884	26.4
Marten, D. Lab	7,630	15.6
Cornell, J. BNP	1,583	3.3
Robinson, J. Eng Dem	1,485	3.0
Oakes, S. Green	669	1.4
Con majority	11,602	23.76
Electorate	70,254	
Turnout	48,822	69.49

Con hold (notional 6.6% from Lib Dem to Con)

HALTON
(*Boundary changes*)

		%
Twigg, D. Lab*	23,843	57.5
Jones, B. Con	8,339	20.1
Harasiwka, F. Lib Dem	5,718	13.8
Taylor, A. BNP	1,563	3.8
Moore, J. UKIP	1,228	3.0
Craig, J. Green	647	1.6
Lab majority	15,504	37.4
Electorate	68,846	
Turnout	41,452	60.21

Lab hold (notional 2.9% from Lab to Con)

HAMMERSMITH
(*New constituency*)

		%
Slaughter, A. Lab*	20,810	43.7
Bailey, S. Con	17,261	36.2
Emerson, M. Lib Dem	7,567	15.9
Miles, R. Green	696	1.5
Crichton, V. UKIP	551	1.2
Searle, J. BNP	432	0.9
Brennan, S. Ind	135	0.3
Lab majority	3,549	7.45
Electorate	72,348	
Turnout	47,666	65.88

Lab hold (notional 0.5% from Lab to Con)

EAST HAMPSHIRE
(*Boundary changes*)

		%
Hinds, D. Con	29,137	56.7
Carew, A. Lib Dem	15,640	30.4
Edbrooke, J. Lab	4,043	7.9
McGuinness, H. UKIP	1,477	2.9
Williams, M. Eng Dem	710	1.4
Jerrard, D. JACP	310	0.6
Con majority	13,497	26.26
Electorate	72,262	
Turnout	51,403	71.13

Con hold (notional 6.6% from Lib Dem to Con)

NORTH EAST HAMPSHIRE
(*Boundary changes*)

		%
Arbuthnot, J. Con*	32,075	60.5
Coulson, D. Lib Dem	13,478	25.4
Jones, B. Lab	5,173	9.8
Duffin, R. UKIP	2,213	4.2
Con majority	18,597	35.06
Electorate	72,196	
Turnout	53,044	73.47

Con hold (notional 4.5% from Lib Dem to Con)

NORTH WEST HAMPSHIRE
(*Boundary changes*)

		%
Young, G. Con*	31,072	58.2
McCann, T. Lib Dem	12,489	23.4
Evans, S. Lab	6,980	13.1
Oram, S. UKIP	2,751	5.2
Con majority	18,583	34.81
Electorate	75,701	
Turnout	53,381	70.52

Con hold (notional 4.6% from Lib Dem to Con)

HAMPSTEAD AND KILBURN
(*New constituency*)

		%
Jackson, G. Lab*	17,332	32.7
Philp, C. Con	17,290	32.6
Fordham, E. Lib Dem	16,491	31.1
Campbell, B. Green	759	1.4
Nielsen, M. UKIP	408	0.8
Moore, V. BNP	328	0.6
Omond, T. Tamsin	123	0.2
Alcantara, G. Ind	91	0.2
Lab majority	42	0.08
Electorate	80,373	
Turnout	53,048	66

Lab hold (notional 6.7% from Lab to Con)

HARBOROUGH
(Boundary changes)

		%
Garnier, E. Con*	26,894	48.9
Haq, Z. Lib Dem	17,097	31.1
McKeever, K. Lab	6,981	12.7
Dickens, G. BNP	1,715	3.1
King, M. UKIP	1,462	2.7
Ball, D. Eng Dem	568	1.0
Stephenson, J. Ind	228	0.4
Con majority	9,797	17.8
Electorate	77,917	
Turnout	55,027	70.62

Con hold (notional 4.7% from Lib Dem to Con)

HARLOW
(Boundary changes)

		%
Halfon, R. Con	19,691	44.7
Rammell, B. Lab*	14,766	33.5
White, D. Lib Dem	5,990	13.6
Butler, E. BNP	1,739	4.0
Croft, J. UKIP	1,591	3.6
Adeeko, O. Christian	101	0.2
Con majority	4,925	11.19
Electorate	67,583	
Turnout	44,020	65.13

Con gain (notional 5.9% from Lab to Con)

HARROGATE AND KNARESBOROUGH
(Boundary changes)

		%
Jones, A. Con	24,305	45.4
Kelley, C. Lib Dem	23,266	43.5
McNerney, K. Lab	3,413	6.4
Gill, S. BNP	1,094	2.0
Upex, J. UKIP	1,056	2.0
Con majority	1,039	1.94
Electorate	74,760	
Turnout	53,548	71.63

Con gain (notional 9.1% from Lib Dem to Con)

HARROW EAST
(Boundary changes)

		%
Blackman, B. Con	21,435	44.4
McNulty, T. Lab*	18,032	37.3
Boethe, N. Lib Dem	6,850	14.2
Pandya, A. UKIP	896	1.9
Atkins, M. Green	793	1.6
Con majority	3,403	7.05
Electorate	71,510	
Turnout	48,302	67.55

Con gain (notional 7% from Lab to Con)

HARROW WEST
(Boundary changes)

		%
Thomas, G. Lab/Co-op*	20,111	43.4
Joyce, R. Con	16,968	36.6
Noyce, C. Lib Dem	7,458	16.1
Crossman, H. UKIP	954	2.1
Langley, R. Green	625	1.4
Lab/Co-op majority	3,143	6.78
Electorate	68,554	
Turnout	46,331	67.58

Lab/Co-op hold (notional 5.7% from Lab/Co-op to Con)

HARTLEPOOL
(No boundary changes)

		%	+/-%
Wright, I. Lab*	16,267	42.4	-9.0
Wright, A. Con	10,758	28.0	16.6
Clark, R. Lib Dem	6,533	17.0	-13.3

*Member of last Parliament

Allison, S. UKIP	2,682	7.0	3.5
Bage, R. BNP	2,002	5.2	
Lab majority	5,509	14.35	
Electorate	68,927		
Turnout	38,388	55.69	

Lab hold (12.8% from Lab to Con)

HARWICH AND NORTH ESSEX
(New constituency)

		%
Jenkin, B. Con*	23,001	46.9
Raven, J. Lib Dem	11,554	23.6
Barrenger, D. Lab	9,774	19.9
Anselmi, S. UKIP	2,527	5.2
Robey, S. BNP	1,065	2.2
Fox, C. Green	909	1.9
Thompson Bates, P. Ind	170	0.4
Con majority	11,447	23.33
Electorate	70,743	
Turnout	49,076	69.37

Con hold (notional 0.02% from Con to Lib Dem)

HASTINGS AND RYE
(Boundary changes)

		%
Rudd, A. Con	20,468	41.0
Foster, M. Lab*	18,475	37.0
Perry, N. Lib Dem	7,825	15.7
Smith, A. UKIP	1,397	2.8
Prince, N. BNP	1,310	2.6
Bridger, R. Eng Dem	339	0.7
Con majority	1,993	3.99
Electorate	77,030	
Turnout	49,929	64.82

Con gain (notional 3.3% from Lab to Con)

HAVANT
(Boundary changes)

		%
Willetts, D. Con*	22,433	51.0
Payton, A. Lib Dem	10,273	23.3
Smith, R. Lab	7,777	17.7
Keiran, G. UKIP	2,611	5.9
Addams, F. Eng Dem	809	1.8
Con majority	12,160	27.61
Electorate	69,671	
Turnout	44,038	63.21

Con hold (notional 1.8% from Lab to Con)

HAYES AND HARLINGTON
(Boundary changes)

		%
McDonnell, J. Lab*	23,377	54.5
Seaman-Digby, S. Con	12,553	29.3
Khalsa, S. Lib Dem	3,726	8.7
Forster, C. BNP	1,520	3.5
Cripps, A. NF	566	1.3
Dixon, C. Eng Dem	464	1.1
Lee, J. Green	348	0.8
Shahzad, A. Christian	83	0.2
Lab majority	10,824	25.22
Electorate	74,197	
Turnout	42,916	57.84

Lab hold (notional 1.7% from Lab to Con)

HAZEL GROVE
(Boundary changes)

		%
Stunell, A. Lib Dem*	20,485	48.7
Abercorn, A. Con	14,114	33.5
Scorer, R. Lab	5,234	12.4
Whittaker, J. UKIP	2,148	5.1
Lib Dem majority	6,371	15.14
Electorate	63,085	
Turnout	42,078	66.7

Lib Dem hold (notional 2.4% from Lib Dem to Con)

HEMEL HEMPSTEAD
(Boundary changes)

		%
Penning, M. Con*	24,721	49.9
Grayson, R. Lib Dem	11,315	22.9
Orhan, A. Lab	10,295	20.8
Price, J. BNP	1,615	3.3
Alexander, D. UKIP	1,254	2.5
Young, M. Ind	271	0.6
Con majority	13,406	27.07
Electorate	74,479	
Turnout	49,526	66.5

Con hold (notional 1.9% from Lib Dem to Con)

HEMSWORTH
(Boundary changes)

		%
Trickett, J. Lab*	20,506	46.7
Myatt, A. Con	10,662	24.3
Belmore, A. Lib Dem	5,667	12.9
Womersley, I. Ind	3,946	9.0
Kitchen, I. BNP	3,059	7.0
Lab majority	9,844	22.4
Electorate	72,554	
Turnout	43,948	60.57

Lab hold (notional 7.1% from Lab to Con)

HENDON
(Boundary changes)

		%
Offord, M. Con	19,635	42.2
Dismore, A. Lab*	19,529	42.0
Harris, M. Lib Dem	5,734	12.3
Lambert, R. UKIP	958	2.1
Newby, A. Green	518	1.1
Con majority	106	0.23
Electorate	78,923	
Turnout	46,547	58.98

Con gain (notional 4.1% from Lab to Con)

HENLEY
(Boundary changes)

		%
Howell, J. Con*	30,054	56.1
Crick, A. Lib Dem	13,466	25.1
McKenzie, R. Lab	5,835	10.9
Hughes, L. UKIP	1,817	3.4
Stevenson, M. Green	1,328	2.5
Bews, J. BNP	1,020	1.9
Con majority	16,588	30.96
Electorate	73,123	
Turnout	53,587	73.28

Con hold (notional 1.9% from Lib Dem to Con)

HEREFORD AND SOUTH HEREFORDSHIRE
(New constituency)

		%
Norman, J. Con	22,366	46.2
Carr, S. Lib Dem	19,885	41.0
Roberts, P. Lab	3,506	7.2
Smith, V. UKIP	1,638	3.4
Oliver, J. BNP	986	2.0
Con majority	2,481	5.12
Electorate	72,021	
Turnout	48,453	67.28

Con gain (notional 3.8% from Lib Dem to Con)

NORTH HEREFORDSHIRE
(New constituency)

		%
Wiggin, B. Con*	24,631	51.7
Hurds, L. Lib Dem	14,744	31.0
Sabharwal, N. Lab	3,373	7.1
Oakton, J. UKIP	2,701	5.7

		%
Norman, F. Green	1,533	3.2
King, J. Ind	586	1.2
Con majority	9,887	20.75
Electorate	66,946	
Turnout	47,637	71.16

Con hold (notional 3.8% from Con to Lib Dem)

HERTFORD AND STORTFORD
(Boundary changes)

		%
Prisk, M. Con*	29,810	53.8
Lewin, A. Lib Dem	14,373	25.9
Terry, S. Lab	7,620	13.8
Sodey, D. UKIP	1,716	3.1
Harris, R. BNP	1,297	2.3
Xenophontos, L. Ind	325	0.6
Adams, M. Ind	236	0.4
Con majority	15,437	27.84
Electorate	78,360	
Turnout	55,457	70.77

Con hold (notional 2% from Con to Lib Dem)

NORTH EAST HERTFORDSHIRE
(Boundary changes)

		%
Heald, O. Con*	26,995	53.5
Annand, H. Lib Dem	11,801	23.4
Kirkman, D. Lab	8,291	16.4
Smyth, A. UKIP	2,075	4.1
Bland, R. Green	875	1.7
Campbell, R. Ind	209	0.4
Ralph, D. YRDPL	143	0.3
Reichardt, P. Ind	36	0.1
Con majority	15,194	30.13
Electorate	72,200	
Turnout	50,425	69.84

Con hold (notional 1.2% from Lib Dem to Con)

SOUTH WEST HERTFORDSHIRE
(Boundary changes)

		%
Gauke, D. Con*	30,773	54.1
Townsend, C. Lib Dem	15,853	27.9
Mann, H. Lab	6,526	11.5
Benson, M. UKIP	1,450	2.5
Gates, D. BNP	1,302	2.3
Hannaway, J. Ind	846	1.5
Con majority	14,920	26.23
Electorate	78,248	
Turnout	56,878	72.69

Con hold (notional 4.6% from Lib Dem to Con)

HERTSMERE
(No boundary changes)

		%	+/-%
Clappison, J. Con*	26,476	55.8	2.8
Russell, S. Lab	8,871	18.7	-8.4
Rowlands, A. Lib Dem	8,210	17.3	-1.0
Rutter, D. UKIP	1,712	3.6	
Seabrook, D. BNP	1,397	3.0	
Krishna-Das, A. Green	604	1.3	
Con majority	17,605	37.13	
Electorate	73,057		
Turnout	47,410	64.89	

Con hold (5.6% from Lab to Con)

HEXHAM
(Boundary changes)

		%
Opperman, G. Con	18,795	43.2
Duffield, A. Lib Dem	13,007	29.9
Tinnion, A. Lab	8,253	19.0
Ford, S. Ind	1,974	4.5
Hawkins, Q. BNP	1,205	2.8
Moss, C. Ind	249	0.6
Con majority	5,788	13.29
Electorate	60,360	
Turnout	43,543	72.14

Con hold (notional 1.7% from Con to Lib Dem)

HEYWOOD AND MIDDLETON
(*Boundary changes*)

		%
Dobbin, J. Lab/Co-op*	18,499	40.0
Holly, M. Con	12,528	27.1
Hobhouse, W. Lib Dem	10,474	22.6
Greenwood, P. BNP	3,239	7.0
Cecil, V. UKIP	1,215	2.6
Lee, C. Ind	170	0.4
Lab/Co-op majority	5,971	12.91
Electorate	80,171	
Turnout	46,251	57.69

Lab/Co-op hold (notional 6.8% from Lab/Co-op to Con)

HIGH PEAK
(*Boundary changes*)

		%
Bingham, A. Con	20,587	40.8
Bisknell, C. Lab	15,910	31.6
Stevens, A. Lib Dem	10,993	21.8
Hall, S. UKIP	1,690	3.4
Allen, P. Green	922	1.8
Dowson, L. Ind	161	0.3
Alves, T. Ind	74	0.2
Con majority	4,677	9.27
Electorate	71,458	
Turnout	50,436	70.58

Con gain (notional 6.5% from Lab to Con)

HITCHIN AND HARPENDEN
(*Boundary changes*)

		%
Lilley, P. Con*	29,869	54.5
Quinton, N. Lib Dem	14,598	26.6
de Botton, O. Lab	7,413	13.5
Wilkinson, G. UKIP	1,663	3.0
Wise, R. Green	807	1.5
Henderson, M. Ind	109	0.2
Byron, S. CURE	108	0.2
Hannah, E. YRDPL	90	0.2
Rigby, P. Ind	50	0.1
Con majority	15,271	27.85
Electorate	73,851	
Turnout	54,842	74.26

Con hold (notional 2.5% from Lib Dem to Con)

HOLBORN AND ST PANCRAS
(*Boundary changes*)

		%
Dobson, F. Lab*	25,198	45.9
Shaw, J. Lib Dem	15,256	27.8
Lee, G. Con	11,134	20.3
Bennett, N. Green	1,480	2.7
Carlyle, R. BNP	779	1.4
Spencer, M. UKIP	587	1.1
Chapman, J. Ind	96	0.2
Susperregi, M. Eng Dem	75	0.1
Meek, I. Ind	44	0.1
Lab majority	9,942	18.09
Electorate	85,437	
Turnout	54,951	64.32

Lab hold (notional 0.4% from Lab to Lib Dem)

HORNCHURCH AND UPMINSTER
(*New constituency*)

		%
Watkinson, A. Con*	27,469	51.3
McGuirk, K. Lab	11,098	20.7
Chilvers, K. Lib Dem	7,426	13.9
Whelpley, W. BNP	3,421	6.4
Webb, L. UKIP	2,848	5.3
Collins, M. Green	542	1.0
Durant, D. Ind	305	0.6
Olukotun, J. Christian	281	0.5
Con majority	16,371	30.57
Electorate	78,547	
Turnout	53,546	68.17

Con hold (notional 7.1% from Lab to Con)

*Member of last Parliament

HORNSEY AND WOOD GREEN
(*No boundary changes*)

		%	+/-%
Featherstone, L. Lib Dem*	25,595	46.3	3.1
Jennings, K. Lab	18,720	33.9	-4.3
Merrin, R. Con	9,174	16.6	3.9
McAskie, P. Green	1,261	2.3	-2.7
De Roche, S. Ind	201	0.4	
Kapur, R. Ind	91	0.2	
Lib Dem majority	6,875	12.44	
Electorate	78,748		
Turnout	55,287	70.21	

Lib Dem hold (3.7% from Lab to Lib Dem)

HORSHAM
(*Boundary changes*)

		%
Maude, F. Con*	29,447	52.7
Newman, G. Lib Dem	17,987	32.2
Skudder, A. Lab	4,189	7.5
Aldridge, H. UKIP	2,839	5.1
Fitter, N. Green	570	1.0
Lyon, S. Christian	469	0.8
Duggan, J. TPP	253	0.5
Kissach, D. Ind	87	0.2
Con majority	11,460	20.5
Electorate	77,564	
Turnout	55,907	72.08

Con hold (notional 0.6% from Con to Lib Dem)

HOUGHTON AND SUNDERLAND SOUTH
(*New constituency*)

		%
Phillipson, B. Lab	19,137	50.0
Oliver, R. Con	8,147	21.3
Boyle, C. Lib Dem	5,292	13.8
Wakefield, C. Ind	2,462	6.4
Allen, K. BNP	1,961	5.1
Elvin, R. UKIP	1,022	2.7
Lab majority	10,990	28.73
Electorate	68,729	
Turnout	38,251	55.65

Lab hold (notional 8.5% from Lab to Con)

HOVE
(*Boundary changes*)

		%
Weatherley, M. Con	18,294	36.7
Barlow, C. Lab*	16,426	32.9
Elgood, P. Lib Dem	11,240	22.5
Davey, I. Green	2,568	5.2
Perrin, P. UKIP	1,206	2.4
Ralfe, B. Ind	85	0.2
Con majority	1,868	3.74
Electorate	72,086	
Turnout	49,908	69.23

Con gain (notional 2.4% from Lab to Con)

HUDDERSFIELD
(*Boundary changes*)

		%
Sheerman, B. Lab/Co-op*	15,725	38.7
Tweed, K. Con	11,253	27.7
Blanchard, J. Lib Dem	10,023	24.6
Cooper, A. Green	1,641	4.0
Firth, R. BNP	1,563	3.9
Cooney, P. TUSC	319	0.8
Lab/Co-op majority	4,472	10.99
Electorate	66,318	
Turnout	40,679	61.34

Lab/Co-op hold (notional 7.2% from Lab/Co-op to Con)

KINGSTON UPON HULL EAST
(*Boundary changes*)

		%
Turner, K. Lab	16,387	47.8
Wilcock, J. Lib Dem	7,790	22.7
Mackay, C. Con	5,667	16.5
Hookem, M. UKIP	2,745	8.0
Uttley, J. NF	880	2.6
Burton, M. Eng Dem	715	2.1
Lab majority	8,597	25.09
Electorate	67,530	
Turnout	34,270	50.75

Lab hold (notional 5.4% from Lab to Lib Dem)

KINGSTON UPON HULL NORTH
(*Boundary changes*)

		%
Johnson, D. Lab*	13,044	39.1
Healy, D. Lib Dem	12,403	37.1
Aitken, V. Con	4,365	13.1
Mainprize, J. BNP	1,443	4.3
Barlow, P. UKIP	1,358	4.1
Deane, M. Green	478	1.4
Cassidy, M. Eng Dem	200	0.6
Lab majority	641	1.92
Electorate	64,082	
Turnout	33,392	52.11

Lab hold (notional 12.2% from Lab to Lib Dem)

KINGSTON UPON HULL WEST AND HESSLE
(*Boundary changes*)

		%
Johnson, A. Lab*	13,378	42.4
Ross, M. Lib Dem	7,636	24.2
Shores, G. Con	6,361	20.2
Horden, K. UKIP	1,688	5.3
Scott, E. BNP	1,416	4.5
Mawer, P. Eng Dem	876	2.8
Gibson, K. TUSC	150	0.5
Lab majority	5,742	18.19
Electorate	59,264	
Turnout	31,567	53.27

Lab hold (notional 7.9% from Lab to Lib Dem)

HUNTINGDON
(*Boundary changes*)

		%
Djanogly, J. Con*	26,516	48.8
Land, M. Lib Dem	15,697	28.9
Cox, A. Lab	5,982	11.0
Curtis, I. UKIP	3,258	6.0
Salt, J. Ind	1,432	2.6
Clare, J. Green	652	1.2
Jug, L. Loony	548	1.0
Holliman, C. Animal	181	0.3
Con majority	10,819	19.89
Electorate	83,557	
Turnout	54,400	65.11

Con hold (notional 2.1% from Con to Lib Dem)

HYNDBURN
(*Boundary changes*)

		%
Jones, G. Lab	17,531	40.9
Buckley, K. Con	14,441	33.7
Rankine, A. Lib Dem	5,033	11.7
Shapcott, D. BNP	2,137	5.0
Barker, G. UKIP	1,481	3.5
Logan, K. CPA	795	1.9
Gormley, K. Green	463	1.1
Reid, C. Eng Dem	413	1.0
Hall, C. Ind	378	0.9
Lab majority	3,090	7.2
Electorate	67,221	
Turnout	42,887	63.8

Lab hold (notional 3.3% from Lab to Con)

ILFORD NORTH
(*Boundary changes*)

		%
Scott, L. Con*	21,506	45.5
Klein, S. Lab	16,102	34.1
Berhanu, A. Lib Dem	5,966	12.6
Warville, D. BNP	1,545	3.3
Van Der Stighelen, H. UKIP	871	1.9
Allen, C. Green	572	1.2
Hampson, R. Christian	456	1.0
Con majority	5,404	11.45
Electorate	72,372	
Turnout	47,215	65.24

Con hold (notional 3.7% from Lab to Con)

ILFORD SOUTH
(*No boundary changes*)

		%	+/-%
Gapes, M. Lab/Co-op*	25,301	49.1	0.4
Boutle, T. Con	14,014	27.2	0.0
Al-Samerai, A. Lib Dem	8,679	16.8	-3.6
Chowdhry, W. Green	1,319	2.6	
Murray, T. UKIP	1,132	2.2	0.6
Jestico, J. SKGH	746	1.5	
Lab/Co-op majority	11,287	21.9	
Electorate	86,220		
Turnout	51,544	59.78	

Lab/Co-op hold (0.2% from Con to Lab/Co-op)

INVERCLYDE
(*No boundary changes*)

		%	+/-%
Cairns, D. Lab*	20,993	55.9	5.3
Nelson, I. SNP	6,577	17.5	-2.0
Hutton, S. Lib Dem	5,007	13.3	-3.6
Wilson, D. Con	4,502	12.0	1.8
Campbell, P. UKIP	433	1.1	
Lab majority	14,416	38.36	
Electorate	59,209		
Turnout	37,583	63.48	

Lab hold (3.6% from SNP to Lab)

INVERNESS, NAIRN, BADENOCH AND STRATHSPEY
(*No boundary changes*)

		%	+/-%
Alexander, D. Lib Dem*	19,172	40.7	0.4
Robb, M. Lab	10,407	22.1	-8.8
Finnie, J. SNP	8,803	18.7	5.1
Ferguson, J. Con	6,278	13.3	3.0
Boyd, D. Christian	835	1.8	
MacLeod, D. Green	789	1.7	-0.7
Durrance, R. UKIP	574	1.2	
McDonald, G. TUSC	135	0.3	
Fraser, C. JOT	93	0.2	
Lib Dem majority	8,765	18.59	
Electorate	72,528		
Turnout	47,146	65	

Lib Dem hold (4.6% from Lab to Lib Dem)

IPSWICH
(*Boundary changes*)

		%
Gummer, B. Con	18,371	39.1
Mole, C. Lab*	16,292	34.7
Dyson, M. Lib Dem	8,556	18.2
Streatfield, C. UKIP	1,365	2.9
Boater, D. BNP	1,270	2.7
Glover, T. Green	775	1.6
Christofi, K. Christian	149	0.3
Turtill, P. Ind	93	0.2
Wainman, S. Ind	70	0.2
Con majority	2,079	4.42
Electorate	75,770	
Turnout	47,008	62.04

Con gain (notional 8.1% from Lab to Con)

ISLE OF WIGHT
(No boundary changes)

		%	+/-%
Turner, A. Con*	32,810	46.6	-2.1
Wareham, J. Lib Dem	22,283	31.7	2.3
Chiverton, M. Lab	8,169	11.6	-5.5
Tarrant, M. UKIP	2,435	3.5	0.0
Clynch, G. BNP	1,457	2.1	
Dunsire, I. Eng Dem	1,233	1.8	
Keats, B. Green	931	1.3	
Martin, P. MEP	616	0.9	
Harris, P. Ind	175	0.3	
Randle-Jolliffe, P. Ind	89	0.1	
Corby, E. Ind	66	0.1	-0.7
Con majority	10,527	14.96	
Electorate	109,922		
Turnout	70,376	64.02	

Con hold (2.2% from Con to Lib Dem)

ISLINGTON NORTH
(No boundary changes)

		%	+/-%
Corbyn, J. Lab*	24,276	54.3	3.4
Jamieson-Ball, R. Lib Dem	11,875	26.6	-3.1
Berrill-Cox, A. Con	6,339	14.2	2.4
Dixon, E. Green	1,348	3.0	-4.0
Lennon, D. UKIP	716	1.6	
Lab majority	12,401	27.75	
Electorate	68,119		
Turnout	44,688	65.6	

Lab hold (3.3% from Lib Dem to Lab)

ISLINGTON SOUTH AND FINSBURY
(No boundary changes)

		%	+/-%
Thornberry, E. Lab*	18,407	42.1	2.4
Fox, B. Lib Dem	14,838	33.9	-4.2
Cox, A. Con	8,449	19.3	4.5
Humphreys, J. Green	710	1.6	-3.1
McDonald, R. UKIP	701	1.6	0.1
Dodds, J. Eng Dem	301	0.7	
Deboo, R. AC	149	0.3	
Lab majority	3,569	8.16	
Electorate	67,649		
Turnout	43,725	64.64	

Lab hold (3.3% from Lib Dem to Lab)

ISLWYN
(Boundary changes)

		%
Evans, C. Lab/Co-op	17,069	49.1
Thomas, D. Con	4,854	14.0
Lewis, S. PlC	4,518	13.0
Ali, A. Lib Dem	3,597	10.3
Rees, D. Ind	1,495	4.3
Voisey, J. BNP	1,320	3.8
Crew, J. UKIP	936	2.7
Taylor, P. Ind	901	2.6
Lab/Co-op majority	12,215	35.14
Electorate	55,292	
Turnout	34,760	62.87

Lab/Co-op hold (notional 9.1% from Lab/Co-op to Con)

JARROW
(Boundary changes)

		%
Hepburn, S. Lab*	20,910	53.8
Milburn, J. Con	8,002	20.6
Appleby, T. Lib Dem	7,163	18.4
Swaddle, A. BNP	2,709	7.0
Lab majority	12,908	33.19
Electorate	64,350	
Turnout	38,897	60.45

Lab hold (notional 6.4% from Lab to Con)

*Member of last Parliament

KEIGHLEY
(Boundary changes)

		%
Hopkins, K. Con	20,003	41.8
Thomas, J. Lab	17,063	35.6
Fekri, N. Lib Dem	7,059	14.7
Brons, A. BNP	1,962	4.1
Latham, P. UKIP	1,470	3.1
Smith, S. NF	135	0.3
Con majority	2,940	6.13
Electorate	65,893	
Turnout	47,922	72.73

Con gain (notional 8.3% from Lab to Con)

KENILWORTH AND SOUTHAM
(New constituency)

		%
Wright, J. Con*	25,945	53.5
Rock, N. Lib Dem	13,393	27.6
Milton, N. Lab	6,949	14.3
Moore, J. UKIP	1,214	2.5
Harrison, J. Green	568	1.2
Rukin, J. Ind	362	0.8
Con majority	12,552	25.88
Electorate	64,362	
Turnout	48,508	75.37

Con hold (notional 1.2% from Con to Lib Dem)

KENSINGTON
(New constituency)

		%
Rifkind, M. Con*	17,595	49.7
Gurney, S. Lab	8,979	25.4
Meltzer, R. Lib Dem	6,872	19.4
Pearson, C. UKIP	754	2.1
Ebrahimi-Fardouee, M. Green	753	2.1
Adams, E. Green Soc	197	0.6
Con majority	8,616	24.34
Electorate	66,257	
Turnout	35,398	53.43

Con hold (notional 5.1% from Lab to Con)

KETTERING
(Boundary changes)

		%
Hollobone, P. Con*	23,247	49.1
Sawford, P. Lab	14,153	29.9
Nelson, C. Lib Dem	7,498	15.8
Skinner, C. BNP	1,366	2.9
Hilling, D. Eng Dem	952	2.0
Bishop, D. Bus-Pass	112	0.2
Con majority	9,094	19.19
Electorate	68,824	
Turnout	47,383	68.85

Con hold (notional 9.4% from Lab to Con)

KILMARNOCK AND LOUDOUN
(No boundary changes)

		%	+/-%
Jamieson, C. Lab/Co-op	24,460	52.4	5.3
Leslie, G. SNP	12,082	25.9	-1.7
McAlpine, J. Con	6,592	14.1	2.8
Tombs, S. Lib Dem	3,419	7.3	-3.8
Lab/Co-op majority	12,378	26.53	
Electorate	74,131		
Turnout	46,658	62.94	

Lab/Co-op gain (3.5% from SNP to Lab/Co-op)

KINGSTON AND SURBITON
(Boundary changes)

		%
Davey, E. Lib Dem*	28,428	49.6
Whately, H. Con	20,868	36.5
Freedman, M. Lab	5,337	9.3

Greensted, J. UKIP	1,450	2.5
Walker, C. Green	555	1.0
Drummer, M. Loony	247	0.4
May, T. Christian	226	0.4
Lib Dem majority	7,560	13.2
Electorate	81,115	
Turnout	57,262	70.59

Lib Dem hold (notional 2.5% from Lib Dem to Con)

KINGSTON UPON HULL EAST – see under Hull

KINGSTON UPON HULL NORTH – see under Hull

KINGSTON UPON HULL WEST AND HESSLE – see under Hull

KINGSWOOD
(Boundary changes)

		%
Skidmore, C. Con	19,362	40.4
Berry, R. Lab*	16,917	35.3
FitzHarris, S. Lib Dem	8,072	16.8
Dowdney, N. UKIP	1,528	3.2
Carey, M. BNP	1,311	2.7
Foster, N. Green	383	0.8
Blundell, M. Eng Dem	333	0.7
Con majority	2,445	5.1
Electorate	66,361	
Turnout	47,942	72.24

Con gain (notional 9.4% from Lab to Con)

KIRKCALDY AND COWDENBEATH
(No boundary changes)

		%	+/-%
Brown, G. Lab*	29,559	64.5	6.4
Chapman, D. SNP	6,550	14.3	-0.2
Mainland, J. Lib Dem	4,269	9.3	-3.7
Paterson, L. Con	4,258	9.3	-1.0
Adams, P. UKIP	760	1.7	0.4
Archibald, S. Ind	184	0.4	
MacLaren of MacLaren, D. Ind	165	0.4	
Jackson, D. Land Power	57	0.1	
Lab majority	23,009	50.17	
Electorate	73,534		
Turnout	45,862	62.37	

Lab hold (3.3% from SNP to Lab)

KNOWSLEY
(New constituency)

		%
Howarth, G. Lab*	31,650	70.6
Clucas, F. Lib Dem	5,964	13.3
Dunne, D. Con	4,004	8.9
Greenhalgh, S. BNP	1,895	4.2
Rundle, A. UKIP	1,145	2.6
Lab majority	25,686	57.3
Electorate	79,266	
Turnout	44,826	56.55

Lab hold (notional 0.4% from Lab to Lib Dem)

LAGAN VALLEY
(Boundary changes)

		%
Donaldson, J. DUP*	18,199	49.6
Trimble, D. UCUNF	7,713	21.0
Lunn, T. All	4,174	11.4
Harbinson, K. TUV	3,154	8.6
Heading, B. SDLP	1,835	5.0
Butler, P. Sinn Féin	1,465	4.0
DUP majority	10,486	28.59
Electorate	65,257	
Turnout	36,678	56.21

DUP hold (notional 3.4% from DUP to UCUNF)

LANARK AND HAMILTON EAST
(No boundary changes)

		%	+/-%
Hood, J. Lab*	23,258	49.9	3.9
Adamson, C. SNP	9,780	21.0	3.2
McGavigan, C. Con	6,981	15.0	2.2
Herbison, D. Lib Dem	5,249	11.3	-7.4
McFarlane, D. Ind	670	1.4	0.5
Sale, R. UKIP	616	1.3	0.3
Lab majority	13,478	28.9	
Electorate	74,773		
Turnout	46,634	62.37	

Lab hold (0.3% from SNP to Lab)

WEST LANCASHIRE
(No boundary changes)

		%	+/-%
Cooper, R. Lab*	21,883	45.1	-2.7
Owens, A. Con	17,540	36.1	2.3
Gibson, J. Lib Dem	6,573	13.5	-0.4
Noone, D. UKIP	1,775	3.6	1.6
Cranie, P. Green	485	1.0	
Braid, D. Clause 28	217	0.5	-0.2
Lab majority	4,343	8.94	
Electorate	73,835		
Turnout	48,568	65.78	

Lab hold (2.5% from Lab to Con)

LANCASTER AND FLEETWOOD
(New constituency)

		%
Ollerenshaw, E. Con	15,404	36.0
Grunshaw, C. Lab	15,071	35.2
Langhorn, S. Lib Dem	8,167	19.1
Dowding, G. Green	1,888	4.4
McGlade, F. UKIP	1,020	2.4
Kent, D. BNP	938	2.2
Riley, K. Ind	213	0.5
Con majority	333	0.78
Electorate	67,379	
Turnout	42,773	63.48

Con gain (notional 4.8% from Lab to Con)

LEEDS CENTRAL
(Boundary changes)

		%
Benn, H. Lab*	18,434	49.1
Taylor, M. Lib Dem	7,789	20.8
Lamb, A. Con	7,541	20.1
Meeson, K. BNP	3,066	8.2
Procter, D. Ind	409	1.1
One-Nil, W. Ind	155	0.4
Lab majority	10,645	28.35
Electorate	81,266	
Turnout	37,542	46.2

Lab hold (notional 4.8% from Lab to Lib Dem)

LEEDS EAST
(Boundary changes)

		%
Mudie, G. Lab*	19,056	50.3
Anderson, B. Con	8,763	23.1
Tear, A. Lib Dem	6,618	17.5
Brown, T. BNP	2,947	7.8
Davies, M. Green Soc	429	1.1
Lab majority	10,293	27.15
Electorate	64,698	
Turnout	37,906	58.59

Lab hold (notional 5.5% from Lab to Con)

LEEDS NORTH EAST
(*Boundary changes*)

		%
Hamilton, F. Lab*	20,287	42.6
Lobley, M. Con	15,742	33.0
Choudhry, A. Lib Dem	9,310	19.5
Hendon, W. UKIP	842	1.8
Redmond, T. BNP	758	1.6
Foote, C. Green Soc	596	1.3
Lab majority	4,545	9.54
Electorate	67,899	
Turnout	47,664	70.2

Lab hold (notional 3% from Lab to Con)

LEEDS NORTH WEST
(*Boundary changes*)

		%
Mulholland, G. Lib Dem*	20,653	47.4
Mulligan, J. Con	11,550	26.5
Blake, J. Lab	9,132	21.0
Bulmer, G. BNP	766	1.8
Thackray, M. UKIP	600	1.4
Hemingway, M. Green	508	1.2
Procter, A. Eng Dem	153	0.4
Bavage, T. Green Soc	121	0.3
Lib Dem majority	9,103	20.88
Electorate	65,399	
Turnout	43,589	66.65

Lib Dem hold (notional 5.4% from Con to Lib Dem)

LEEDS WEST
(*Boundary changes*)

		%
Reeves, R. Lab	16,389	42.2
Coleman, R. Lib Dem	9,373	24.1
Marjoram, J. Con	7,641	19.7
Beverley, J. BNP	2,377	6.1
Blackburn, D. Green	1,832	4.7
Miles, J. UKIP	1,140	2.9
Lab majority	7,016	18.05
Electorate	67,453	
Turnout	38,878	57.64

Lab hold (notional 10.4% from Lab to Lib Dem)

LEICESTER EAST
(*Boundary changes*)

		%
Vaz, K. Lab*	25,804	53.6
Hunt, J. Con	11,722	24.4
Asghar, A. Lib Dem	6,817	14.2
Gilmore, C. BNP	1,700	3.5
Taylor, M. Green	733	1.5
Ransome, F. UKIP	725	1.5
Sadiq, A. Unity	494	1.0
Lab majority	14,082	29.26
Electorate	72,986	
Turnout	48,120	65.93

Lab hold (notional 4.8% from Lab to Con)

LEICESTER SOUTH
(*Boundary changes*)

		%
Soulsby, P. Lab*	21,479	45.5
Gill, P. Lib Dem	12,671	26.8
Grant, R. Con	10,066	21.3
Waudby, A. BNP	1,418	3.0
Dixey, D. Green	770	1.6
Lucas, C. UKIP	720	1.5
Lab majority	8,808	18.65
Electorate	77,175	
Turnout	47,223	61.19

Lab hold (notional 4.9% from Lib Dem to Lab)

*Member of last Parliament

LEICESTER WEST
(*Boundary changes*)

		%
Kendall, L. Lab	13,745	38.3
Harvey, C. Con	9,728	27.1
Coley, P. Lib Dem	8,107	22.6
Reynolds, G. BNP	2,158	6.0
Ingall, S. UKIP	883	2.5
Forse, G. Green	639	1.8
Huggins, S. Ind	181	0.5
Score, S. TUSC	157	0.4
Dyer, S. Pirate	113	0.3
Bowley, D. Ind	108	0.3
Lab majority	4,017	11.19
Electorate	64,900	
Turnout	35,908	55.33

Lab hold (notional 7.6% from Lab to Con)

NORTH WEST LEICESTERSHIRE
(*No boundary changes*)

		%	+/-%
Bridgen, A. Con	23,147	44.5	8.6
Willmott, R. Lab	15,636	30.1	-15.3
Reynolds, P. Lib Dem	8,639	16.6	4.6
Meller, I. BNP	3,396	6.5	3.4
Green, M. UKIP	1,134	2.2	-1.1
Con majority	7,511	14.44	
Electorate	71,217		
Turnout	52,027	73.05	

Con gain (11.9% from Lab to Con)

SOUTH LEICESTERSHIRE
(*New constituency*)

		%
Robathan, A. Con*	27,000	49.4
Ayesh, A. Lib Dem	11,476	21.0
Gimson, S. Lab	11,392	20.9
Preston, P. BNP	2,721	5.0
Williams, J. UKIP	1,988	3.6
Con majority	15,524	28.4
Electorate	76,633	
Turnout	54,656	71.32

Con hold (notional 1% from Lib Dem to Con)

LEIGH
(*Boundary changes*)

		%
Burnham, A. Lab*	24,295	51.2
Awan, S. Con	9,284	19.6
Blackburn, C. Lib Dem	8,049	16.9
Chadwick, G. BNP	2,724	5.7
Lavelle, M. UKIP	1,535	3.2
Bradbury, N. Ind	988	2.1
Dainty, T. Ind	320	0.7
Hessell, R. Christian	137	0.3
Lab majority	15,011	31.61
Electorate	75,903	
Turnout	47,494	62.57

Lab hold (notional 4.9% from Lab to Con)

LEWES
(*Boundary changes*)

		%
Baker, N. Lib Dem*	26,048	52.0
Sugarman, J. Con	18,401	36.7
Koundarjian, H. Lab	2,508	5.0
Charlton, P. UKIP	1,728	3.5
Murray, S. Green	729	1.5
Lloyd, D. BNP	594	1.2
Soucek, O. Ind	80	0.2
Lib Dem majority	7,647	15.25
Electorate	68,708	
Turnout	50,149	72.99

Lib Dem hold (notional 2.4% from Lab to Lib Dem)

LEWISHAM DEPTFORD

(Boundary changes)		%
Ruddock, J. Lab*	22,132	53.3
Langley, T. Lib Dem	9,633	23.2
Townsend, G. Con	5,551	13.4
Johnson, D. Green	2,772	6.7
Page, I. SAP	645	1.6
Martin, M. CPA	487	1.2
Lab majority	12,499	30.08
Electorate	67,058	
Turnout	41,546	61.96

Lab hold (notional 3.7% from Lab to Lib Dem)

LEWISHAM EAST

(Boundary changes)		%
Alexander, H. Lab	17,966	42.9
Pattisson, P. Lib Dem	11,750	28.0
Clamp, J. Con	9,850	23.5
Reed, R. UKIP	771	1.8
Cotterell, P. Green	624	1.5
Rose, J. Eng Dem	426	1.0
Hallam, G. CNBPG	332	0.8
Lab majority	6,216	14.83
Electorate	65,926	
Turnout	41,923	63.59

Lab hold (notional 6.4% from Lab to Lib Dem)

LEWISHAM WEST AND PENGE

(New constituency)		%
Dowd, J. Lab*	18,501	40.9
Feakes, A. Lib Dem	12,673	28.0
Phillips, C. Con	11,489	25.4
Staveley, P. UKIP	1,117	2.5
Phoenix, R. Green	931	2.1
Hammond, S. CPA	317	0.7
Lab majority	5,828	12.88
Electorate	69,022	
Turnout	45,233	65.53

Lab hold (notional 3.1% from Lab to Lib Dem)

LEYTON AND WANSTEAD

(Boundary changes)		%
Cryer, J. Lab	17,511	43.4
Qureshi, F. Lib Dem	11,095	27.5
Northover, E. Con	8,928	22.1
Wood, G. UKIP	1,080	2.7
Gunstock, A. Green	562	1.4
Clift, J. BNP	561	1.4
Bhatti, S. Christian	342	0.9
Levin, M. Ind Fed UK	80	0.2
Lab majority	6,416	15.88
Electorate	63,541	
Turnout	40,396	63.57

Lab hold (notional 2.6% from Lab to Lib Dem)

LICHFIELD

(Boundary changes)		%
Fabricant, M. Con*	28,048	54.3
Jackson, I. Lib Dem	10,365	20.1
Hyden, S. Lab	10,230	19.8
Maunder, K. UKIP	2,920	5.7
Con majority	17,683	34.23
Electorate	72,586	
Turnout	51,652	71.16

Con hold (notional 0.7% from Lib Dem to Con)

LINCOLN

(Boundary changes)		%
McCartney, K. Con	17,163	37.5
Merron, G. Lab*	16,105	35.2
Shore, R. Lib Dem	9,256	20.2
West, R. BNP	1,367	3.0

Smith, N. UKIP	1,004	2.2
Coleman, E. Eng Dem	604	1.3
Walker, G. Ind	222	0.5
Con majority	1,058	2.31
Electorate	73,540	
Turnout	45,806	62.29

Con gain (notional 5.9% from Lab to Con)

LINLITHGOW AND EAST FALKIRK

(No boundary changes)		%	+/-%
Connarty, M. Lab*	25,634	49.7	2.1
Smith, T. SNP	13,081	25.4	1.9
Glenn, S. Lib Dem	6,589	12.8	-2.5
Stephenson, A. Con	6,146	11.9	0.1
Lab majority	12,553	24.33	
Electorate	80,907		
Turnout	51,586	63.76	

Lab hold (0.1% from SNP to Lab)

LIVERPOOL RIVERSIDE

(Boundary changes)		%
Ellman, L. Lab/Co-op*	22,998	59.0
Marbrow, R. Lib Dem	8,825	22.7
Wu, K. Con	4,243	10.9
Crone, T. Green	1,355	3.5
Stafford, P. BNP	706	1.8
Gaskell, P. UKIP	674	1.7
Lab/Co-op majority	14,173	36.39
Electorate	74,539	
Turnout	38,948	52.25

Lab/Co-op hold (notional 0.2% from Lib Dem to Lab/Co-op)

LIVERPOOL WALTON

(Boundary changes)		%
Rotheram, S. Lab	24,709	71.6
Moloney, P. Lib Dem	4,891	14.2
Marsden, A. Con	2,241	6.5
Stafford, P. BNP	1,104	3.2
Nugent, J. UKIP	898	2.6
Manwell, J. CPA	297	0.9
Ireland, D. TUSC	195	0.6
Lab majority	19,818	57.45
Electorate	62,612	
Turnout	34,497	55.1

Lab hold (notional 1.3% from Lib Dem to Lab)

LIVERPOOL WAVERTREE

(Boundary changes)		%
Berger, L. Lab/Co-op	20,132	52.9
Eldridge, C. Lib Dem	12,965	34.1
Garnett, A. Con	2,830	7.5
Miney, N. UKIP	890	2.4
Lawson, R. Green	598	1.6
Singleton, K. SLP	200	0.5
McEllenborough, S. BNP	150	0.4
Dunne, F. Ind	149	0.4
Lab/Co-op majority	7,167	18.84
Electorate	62,518	
Turnout	38,033	60.84

Lab/Co-op hold (notional 5% from Lib Dem to Lab/Co-op)

LIVERPOOL WEST DERBY

(Boundary changes)		%
Twigg, S. Lab/Co-op	22,953	63.9
Twigger, P. Lib Dem	4,486	12.5
Radford, S. Lib	3,327	9.3
Hall, P. Con	3,311	9.2
Jones, H. UKIP	1,093	3.0
Andersen, K. SLP	614	1.7
Lab/Co-op majority	18,467	51.36
Electorate	63,082	
Turnout	35,953	56.99

Lab/Co-op hold (notional 3% from Lib Dem to Lab/Co-op)

LIVINGSTON
(No boundary changes)

		%	+/-%
Morrice, G. Lab	23,215	48.4	-2.6
Bardell, L. SNP	12,424	25.9	4.4
Dundas, C. Lib Dem	5,316	11.1	-4.3
Adamson-Ross, A. Con	5,158	10.8	0.6
Orr, D. BNP	960	2.0	
Forrest, A. UKIP	443	0.9	
Hendry, A. SSP	242	0.5	-1.3
Slavin, J. Ind	149	0.3	
Lab majority	10,791	22.5	
Electorate	75,924		
Turnout	47,967	63.18	

Lab hold (6.7% from SNP to Lab)

LLANELLI
(No boundary changes)

		%	+/-%
Griffith, N. Lab*	15,916	42.4	-4.4
Davies, M. PlC	11,215	29.9	3.5
Salmon, C. Con	5,381	14.3	0.7
Edwards, M. Lib Dem	3,902	10.4	-2.4
Marshall, A. UKIP	1,047	2.8	
Lab majority	4,701	12.53	
Electorate	55,637		
Turnout	37,510	67.42	

Lab hold (4% from Lab to PlC)

CITIES OF LONDON AND WESTMINSTER
(Boundary changes)

		%
Field, M. Con*	19,264	51.8
Rowntree, D. Lab	8,188	22.0
Smith, N. Lib Dem	7,574	20.4
Chase, D. Green	778	2.1
Weston, P. UKIP	664	1.8
Roseman, F. Eng Dem	191	0.5
Delderfield, D. Ind	98	0.3
Nunn, J. Pirate	90	0.3
Mad, C. Ind	84	0.2
Con majority	11,076	29.8
Electorate	66,489	
Turnout	37,168	55.9

Con hold (notional 3.4% from Lab to Con)

EAST LONDONDERRY
(Boundary changes)

		%
Campbell, G. DUP*	12,097	34.5
Ó hOisín, C. Sinn Féin	6,742	19.2
McAuley, L. UCUNF	6,218	17.7
Conway, T. SDLP	5,399	15.4
Ross, W. TUV	2,572	7.3
Fitzpatrick, B. All	1,922	5.5
DUP majority	5,355	15.26
Electorate	63,220	
Turnout	35,086	55.5

DUP hold (notional 4.2% from DUP to Sinn Féin)

EAST LOTHIAN
(No boundary changes)

		%	+/-%
O'Donnell, F. Lab	21,919	44.5	3.1
Veitch, M. Con	9,661	19.6	3.7
Ritchie, S. Lib Dem	8,288	16.8	-8.0
Sharp, A. SNP	7,883	16.0	2.9
Mackenzie, J. Green	862	1.8	-0.7
Lloyd, J. UKIP	548	1.1	0.4
Lab majority	12,258	24.9	
Electorate	73,348		
Turnout	49,221	67.11	

Lab hold (0.3% from Lab to Con)

*Member of last Parliament

LOUGHBOROUGH
(Boundary changes)

		%
Morgan, N. Con	21,971	41.5
Reed, A. Lab/Co-op*	18,227	34.4
Willis, M. Lib Dem	9,675	18.3
Stafford, K. BNP	2,040	3.9
Foden, J. UKIP	925	1.8
Con majority	3,744	7.07
Electorate	77,505	
Turnout	52,947	68.31

Con gain (notional 5.5% from Lab/Co-op to Con)

LOUTH AND HORNCASTLE
(Boundary changes)

		%
Tapsell, P. Con*	25,065	49.6
Martin, F. Lib Dem	11,194	22.1
Mountain, P. Lab	8,760	17.3
Green, J. BNP	2,199	4.3
Nurse, P. UKIP	2,183	4.3
Simpson, D. Ind	576	1.1
Mair, C. Eng Dem	517	1.0
Con majority	13,871	27.42
Electorate	77,650	
Turnout	50,580	65.14

Con hold (notional 0.8% from Lib Dem to Con)

LUDLOW
(No boundary changes)

		%	+/-%
Dunne, P. Con*	25,720	52.7	7.8
Kidd, H. Lib Dem	15,971	32.7	-7.8
Hunt, A. Lab	3,272	6.7	-3.9
Gill, C. UKIP	2,127	4.4	2.7
Evans, C. BNP	1,016	2.1	
Morrish, J. Green	447	0.9	-0.9
Powell, A. Loony	179	0.4	
Con majority	9,749	19.98	
Electorate	66,632		
Turnout	48,794	73.23	

Con hold (7.8% from Lib Dem to Con)

LUTON NORTH
(Boundary changes)

		%
Hopkins, K. Lab*	21,192	49.2
Brier, J. Con	13,672	31.7
Martins, R. Lib Dem	4,784	11.1
Brown, C. UKIP	1,564	3.6
Rose, S. BNP	1,316	3.1
Hall, S. Green	490	1.1
Lab majority	7,520	17.44
Electorate	65,645	
Turnout	43,107	65.67

Lab hold (notional 0.5% from Con to Lab)

LUTON SOUTH
(Boundary changes)

		%
Shuker, G. Lab/Co-op	14,725	34.8
Huddleston, N. Con	12,396	29.3
Hussain, Q. Lib Dem	9,567	22.6
Rantzen, E. Ind	1,872	4.4
Blakey, T. BNP	1,299	3.1
Lawman, C. UKIP	975	2.3
Rhodes, S. Ind	463	1.1
Scheimann, M. Green	366	0.9
Hall, J. Ind	264	0.6
Choudhury, F. Ind	130	0.3
Lathwell, S. Ind	84	0.2
Sweeney, F. WRP	75	0.2
Lab/Co-op majority	2,329	5.5
Electorate	65,837	
Turnout	42,335	64.3

Lab/Co-op hold (notional 4.6% from Lab/Co-op to Con)

MACCLESFIELD
(*Boundary changes*)

		%
Rutley, D. Con	23,503	46.9
Barlow, R. Lib Dem	11,544	23.0
Heald, A. Lab	10,164	20.3
Murphy, B. Mac Ind	2,590	5.2
Smith, J. UKIP	1,418	2.8
Knight, J. Green	840	1.7
Con majority	11,959	23.85
Electorate	73,427	
Turnout	50,139	68.28

Con hold (notional 3.1% from Con to Lib Dem)

MAIDENHEAD
(*Boundary changes*)

		%
May, T. Con*	31,937	59.4
Hill, T. Lib Dem	15,168	28.2
McDonald, P. Lab	3,795	7.1
Wight, K. UKIP	1,243	2.3
Rait, T. BNP	825	1.5
Forbes, P. Green	482	0.9
Prior, P. FR	270	0.5
Con majority	16,769	31.17
Electorate	72,844	
Turnout	53,807	73.87

Con hold (notional 7.8% from Lib Dem to Con)

MAIDSTONE AND THE WEALD
(*Boundary changes*)

		%
Grant, H. Con	23,491	47.9
Carroll, P. Lib Dem	17,602	35.9
Seeruthun, R. Lab/Co-op	4,769	9.7
Kendall, G. UKIP	1,637	3.4
Jeffery, S. Green	655	1.3
Butler, G. NF	643	1.3
Simmonds, H. Christian	131	0.3
Con majority	5,889	12.02
Electorate	71,041	
Turnout	49,003	68.98

Con hold (notional 8.5% from Con to Lib Dem)

MAKERFIELD
(*Boundary changes*)

		%
Fovargue, Y. Lab	20,700	47.1
Ali, I. Con	8,210	18.7
Crowther, D. Lib Dem	7,082	16.1
Brierley, R. Ind	3,424	7.8
Haslam, K. BNP	3,229	7.4
Mather, J. Ind	1,126	2.6
Lab majority	12,490	28.43
Electorate	73,813	
Turnout	43,930	59.52

Lab hold (notional 10% from Lab to Con)

MALDON
(*New constituency*)

		%
Whittingdale, J. Con*	28,661	59.8
Tealby-Watson, E. Lib Dem	9,254	19.3
Nandanwar, S. Lab	6,070	12.7
Pryke, J. UKIP	2,446	5.1
Blain, L. BNP	1,464	3.1
Con majority	19,407	40.47
Electorate	70,587	
Turnout	47,954	67.94

Con hold (notional 0.4% from Con to Lib Dem)

MANCHESTER CENTRAL
(*Boundary changes*)

		%
Lloyd, T. Lab*	21,059	52.6
Ramsbottom, M. Lib Dem	10,620	26.5
Rahuja, S. Con	4,704	11.8
Trebilcock, T. BNP	1,636	4.1
O'Donovan, G. Green	915	2.3
Weatherill, N. UKIP	607	1.5
Sinclair, R. SLP	153	0.4
Cartwright, J. Ind	120	0.3
Leff, J. WRP	59	0.2
Skelton, R. SEP	54	0.1
Lab majority	10,439	26.06
Electorate	90,110	
Turnout	40,065	44.46

Lab hold (notional 6.2% from Lab to Lib Dem)

MANCHESTER GORTON
(*Boundary changes*)

		%
Kaufman, G. Lab*	19,211	49.9
Afzal, Q. Lib Dem	12,508	32.5
Healy, C. Con	4,224	11.0
Hall, J. Green	1,048	2.7
Zulfikar, M. Respect	507	1.3
Reissmann, K. TUSC	337	0.9
Harrison, P. Christian	254	0.7
Dobson, T. Pirate	236	0.6
Lab majority	6,703	17.4
Electorate	75,933	
Turnout	38,530	50.74

Lab hold (notional 1.1% from Lab to Lib Dem)

MANCHESTER WITHINGTON
(*Boundary changes*)

		%
Leech, J. Lib Dem*	20,110	44.6
Powell, L. Lab	18,260	40.5
Green, C. Con	5,005	11.1
Candeland, B. Green	798	1.8
Gutfreund-Walmsley, B. UKIP	608	1.4
Zalzala, Y. Ind	147	0.3
Farmer, M. Ind	57	0.1
Lib Dem majority	1,850	4.1
Electorate	74,371	
Turnout	45,128	60.68

Lib Dem hold (notional 1.4% from Lab to Lib Dem)

MANSFIELD
(*Boundary changes*)

		%
Meale, A. Lab*	18,753	38.7
Critchlow, T. Con	12,741	26.3
Wyatt, M. Lib Dem	7,469	15.4
Camilleri, P. Ind	4,339	9.0
Hamilton, D. UKIP	2,985	6.2
Hill, R. BNP	2,108	4.3
Lab majority	6,012	12.4
Electorate	80,069	
Turnout	48,479	60.55

Lab hold (notional 9.5% from Lab to Con)

MEON VALLEY
(*New constituency*)

		%
Hollingbery, G. Con	28,818	56.1
Leffman, L. Lib Dem	16,693	32.5
Linsley, H. Lab	3,266	6.4
Harris, S. UKIP	1,490	2.9
Harris, P. Eng Dem	582	1.1
Coats, S. Animal	255	0.5
Quar, G. Ind	134	0.3
Con majority	12,125	23.61
Electorate	70,487	
Turnout	51,349	72.85

Con hold (notional 9.4% from Lib Dem to Con)

MERIDEN
(Boundary changes) %

Spelman, C. Con*	26,956	51.6
Williams, E. Lab	10,703	20.5
Slater, S. Lib Dem	9,278	17.8
O'Brien, F. BNP	2,511	4.8
Allcock, B. UKIP	1,378	2.6
Stanton, E. Green	678	1.3
Sinclaire, N. SMRA	658	1.3
Con majority	16,253	31.1
Electorate	82,228	
Turnout	52,268	63.56

Con hold (notional 7.9% from Lab to Con)

MERTHYR TYDFIL AND RHYMNEY
(Boundary changes) %

Havard, D. Lab*	14,007	43.6
Kitcher, A. Lib Dem	9,951	30.9
Hill, M. Con	2,412	7.5
Tovey, C. Ind	1,845	5.7
Jones, G. PlC	1,621	5.0
Barnes, R. BNP	1,173	3.6
Brown, A. UKIP	872	2.7
Cowdell, A. SLP	195	0.6
Lab majority	4,056	12.61
Electorate	54,715	
Turnout	32,156	58.77

Lab hold (notional 16.9% from Lab to Lib Dem)

MID BEDFORDSHIRE – see under Bedfordshire

MID DERBYSHIRE – see under Derbyshire

MID DORSET AND NORTH POOLE – see under Dorset

MID NORFOLK – see under Norfolk

MID SUSSEX – see under Sussex

MID ULSTER – see under Ulster

MID WORCESTERSHIRE – see under Worcestershire

MIDDLESBROUGH
(Boundary changes) %

Bell, S. Lab*	15,351	45.8
Foote-Wood, C. Lib Dem	6,662	19.9
Walsh, J. Con	6,283	18.8
McTigue, J. Ind	1,969	5.9
Ferguson, M. BNP	1,954	5.8
Parker, R. UKIP	1,236	3.7
Lab majority	8,689	25.92
Electorate	65,148	
Turnout	33,517	51.45

Lab hold (notional 6.5% from Lab to Lib Dem)

MIDDLESBROUGH SOUTH AND EAST CLEVELAND
(Boundary changes) %

Blenkinsop, T. Lab	18,138	39.2
Bristow, P. Con	16,461	35.6
Emmerson, N. Lib Dem	7,340	15.9
Lightwing, S. UKIP	1,881	4.1
Gatley, S. BNP	1,576	3.4
Allen, M. Ind	818	1.8
Lab majority	1,677	3.62
Electorate	72,666	
Turnout	46,271	63.68

Lab hold (notional 7.4% from Lab to Con)

*Member of last Parliament

MIDLOTHIAN
(No boundary changes) % +/-%

Hamilton, D. Lab*	18,449	47.0	1.5
Beattie, C. SNP	8,100	20.6	3.7
Laird, R. Lib Dem	6,711	17.1	-9.1
Callander, J. Con	4,661	11.9	2.5
Baxter, I. Green	595	1.5	
Norrie, G. UKIP	364	0.9	
McCleery, G. Ind	196	0.5	
Duncan, W. TUSC	166	0.4	
Lab majority	10,349	26.34	
Electorate	61,387		
Turnout	39,292	64.01	

Lab hold (1.1% from Lab to SNP)

MILTON KEYNES NORTH
(New constituency) %

Lancaster, M. Con*	23,419	43.4
Pakes, A. Lab/Co-op	14,458	26.8
Hope, J. Lib Dem	11,894	22.1
Phillips, M. UKIP	1,772	3.3
Hamilton, R. BNP	1,154	2.1
Francis, A. Green	733	1.4
Lennon, J. CPA	206	0.4
Fensome, M. Loony	157	0.3
Vyas, A. Ind	95	0.2
Con majority	8,961	16.61
Electorate	82,432	
Turnout	53,965	65.47

Con gain (notional 9.2% from Lab/Co-op to Con)

MILTON KEYNES SOUTH
(New constituency) %

Stewart, I. Con	23,034	41.6
Starkey, P. Lab*	17,833	32.2
Jones, P. Lib Dem	9,787	17.7
Pinto, P. UKIP	2,074	3.8
Tait, M. BNP	1,502	2.7
Deacon, K. Green	774	1.4
Nti, S. CPA	245	0.5
Worth, J. NRP	84	0.2
Con majority	5,201	9.39
Electorate	86,559	
Turnout	55,416	64.02

Con gain (notional 6.2% from Lab to Con)

MITCHAM AND MORDEN
(Boundary changes) %

McDonagh, S. Lab*	24,722	56.2
Hampton, M. Con	11,056	25.1
Coman, L. Lib Dem	5,202	11.8
Martin, T. BNP	1,386	3.2
Mills, A. UKIP	857	2.0
Roy, S. Green	381	0.9
Alagaratnam, R. Ind	155	0.4
Redgrave, E. Ind	38	0.1
Lab majority	13,666	31.07
Electorate	65,939	
Turnout	43,989	66.71

Lab hold (notional 0.5% from Lab to Con)

MOLE VALLEY
(Boundary changes) %

Beresford, P. Con*	31,263	57.4
Humphreys, A. Lib Dem	15,610	28.7
Dove, J. Lab	3,804	7.0
Jones, L. UKIP	2,752	5.1
Sedgwick, R. Green	895	1.6
Con majority	15,653	28.75
Electorate	72,297	
Turnout	54,448	75.31

Con hold (notional 2.2% from Lib Dem to Con)

MONMOUTH

(No boundary changes)

		%	+/-%
Davies, D. Con*	22,466	48.2	1.4
Sandison, H. Lab	12,041	25.8	-11.1
Blakebrough, M. Lib Dem	9,026	19.4	6.6
Clark, J. PlC	1,273	2.7	0.6
Rowe, D. UKIP	1,126	2.4	1.2
Millson, S. Green	587	1.3	
Con majority	10,425	22.37	
Electorate	64,538		
Turnout	46,594	72.2	

Con hold (6.2% from Lab to Con)

MONTGOMERYSHIRE

(Boundary changes)

		%
Davies, G. Con	13,976	41.3
Öpik, L. Lib Dem*	12,792	37.8
Fychan, H. PlC	2,802	8.3
Colbourne, N. Lab/Co-op	2,407	7.1
Rowlands, D. UKIP	1,128	3.3
Ellis, M. NF	384	1.1
Lawson, B. Ind	324	1.0
Con majority	1,184	3.5
Electorate	46,766	
Turnout	33,871	72.43

Con gain (notional 13.1% from Lib Dem to Con)

MORAY

(No boundary changes)

		%	+/-%
Robertson, A. SNP*	16,273	39.6	3.1
Ross, D. Con	10,683	26.0	4.1
Green, K. Lab	7,007	17.1	-3.3
Paterson, J. Lib Dem	5,956	14.5	-4.7
Gatt, D. UKIP	1,085	2.6	
SNP majority	5,590	13.61	
Electorate	65,924		
Turnout	41,070	62.3	

SNP hold (0.5% from SNP to Con)

MORECAMBE AND LUNESDALE

(Boundary changes)

		%
Morris, D. Con	18,035	41.5
Smith, G. Lab*	17,169	39.5
Jones, L. Lib Dem	5,791	13.3
Knight, M. UKIP	1,843	4.2
Coates, C. Green	598	1.4
Con majority	866	1.99
Electorate	69,576	
Turnout	43,518	62.55

Con gain (notional 6.9% from Lab to Con)

MORLEY AND OUTWOOD

(New constituency)

		%
Balls, E. Lab/Co-op*	18,365	37.5
Calvert, A. Con	17,264	35.3
Monaghan, J. Lib Dem	8,186	16.7
Beverley, C. BNP	3,535	7.2
Daniel, D. UKIP	1,506	3.1
Lab/Co-op majority	1,101	2.25
Electorate	74,200	
Turnout	48,941	65.96

Lab/Co-op hold (notional 9.4% from Lab/Co-op to Con)

MOTHERWELL AND WISHAW

(No boundary changes)

		%	+/-%
Roy, F. Lab*	23,910	61.0	3.5
Fellows, M. SNP	7,104	18.1	1.7
Douglas, S. Lib Dem	3,840	9.8	-2.2

		%	+/-%
Gilroy, P. Con	3,660	9.3	0.1
Gunnion, R. TUSC	609	1.6	
Lab majority	16,806	42.84	
Electorate	66,918		
Turnout	39,227	58.62	

Lab hold (0.9% from SNP to Lab)

NA H-EILEANAN AN IAR

(No boundary changes)

		%	+/-%
MacNeil, A. SNP*	6,723	45.6	0.7
MacSween, D. Lab	4,838	32.8	-1.6
Murray, M. Ind	1,412	9.6	
Davis, J. Lib Dem	1,097	7.4	-0.5
Norquay, S. Con	647	4.4	0.0
SNP majority	1,885	12.79	
Electorate	21,780		
Turnout	14,743	67.69	

SNP hold (1.2% from Lab to SNP)

NEATH

(Boundary changes)

		%
Hain, P. Lab*	17,172	46.2
Llywelyn, A. PlC	7,397	19.9
Little, F. Lib Dem	5,535	14.9
Owens, E. Con	4,847	13.0
Green, M. BNP	1,342	3.6
Bevan, J. UKIP	829	2.2
Lab majority	9,775	26.28
Electorate	57,295	
Turnout	37,189	64.91

Lab hold (notional 4.6% from Lab to PlC)

NEW FOREST EAST

(Boundary changes)

		%
Lewis, J. Con*	26,443	52.8
Scriven, T. Lib Dem	15,136	30.2
Sopowski, P. Lab	4,915	9.8
Day, P. UKIP	2,518	5.0
Golden, B. Green	1,024	2.0
Con majority	11,307	22.56
Electorate	72,858	
Turnout	50,113	68.78

Con hold (notional 3.2% from Lib Dem to Con)

NEW FOREST WEST

(Boundary changes)

		%
Swayne, D. Con*	27,980	58.7
Plummer, M. Lib Dem	11,084	23.3
Hurne, J. Lab	4,666	9.8
Lyon, M. UKIP	2,783	5.8
Richards, J. Green	1,059	2.2
Con majority	16,896	35.47
Electorate	68,332	
Turnout	47,638	69.72

Con hold (notional 0.6% from Con to Lib Dem)

NEWARK

(Boundary changes)

		%
Mercer, P. Con*	27,590	53.7
Campbell, I. Lab	11,438	22.3
Jenkins, P. Lib Dem	10,246	20.0
Irvine, T. UKIP	1,954	3.8
Con majority	16,152	31.46
Electorate	71,755	
Turnout	51,340	71.55

Con hold (notional 4.6% from Lab to Con)

NEWBURY
(Boundary changes)

		%
Benyon, R. Con*	33,057	56.4
Rendel, D. Lib Dem	20,809	35.5
Cooper, H. Lab	2,505	4.3
Black, D. UKIP	1,475	2.5
Hollister, A. Green	490	0.8
Burgess, B. Ind	158	0.3
Yates, D. Apol Dem	95	0.2
Con majority	12,248	20.88
Electorate	79,144	
Turnout	58,645	74.1

Con hold (notional 7.2% from Lib Dem to Con)

NEWCASTLE UPON TYNE CENTRAL
(Boundary changes)

		%
Onwurah, C. Lab	15,694	45.8
Kane, G. Lib Dem	8,228	24.0
Holder, N. Con	6,611	19.3
Booth, K. BNP	2,302	6.7
Davies, M. UKIP	754	2.2
Pearson, J. Green	568	1.7
Lab majority	7,466	21.76
Electorate	60,507	
Turnout	34,304	56.69

Lab hold (notional 0.6% from Lab to Lib Dem)

NEWCASTLE UPON TYNE EAST
(New constituency)

		%
Brown, N. Lab*	17,043	44.9
Taylor, W. Lib Dem	12,590	33.2
Llewellyn, D. Con	6,068	16.0
Spence, A. BNP	1,342	3.5
Gray, A. Green	620	1.6
Levy, M. Comm GB	177	0.5
Lab majority	4,453	11.73
Electorate	64,487	
Turnout	37,978	58.89

Lab hold (notional 4.6% from Lab to Lib Dem)

NEWCASTLE UPON TYNE NORTH
(Boundary changes)

		%
McKinnell, C. Lab	17,950	40.7
Beadle, R. Lib Dem	14,536	33.0
Parkinson, S. Con	7,966	18.1
Gibson, T. BNP	1,890	4.3
Proud, I. UKIP	1,285	2.9
Heyman, A. Green	319	0.7
Lab majority	3,414	7.74
Electorate	67,110	
Turnout	44,087	65.69

Lab hold (notional 4.6% from Lab to Lib Dem)

NEWCASTLE-UNDER-LYME
(No boundary changes)

		%	+/-%
Farrelly, P. Lab*	16,393	37.9	-7.1
Jenrick, R. Con	14,841	34.3	9.5
Jones, N. Lib Dem	8,466	19.6	0.8
Nixon, D. UKIP	3,491	8.1	4.5
Lab majority	1,552	3.58	
Electorate	69,433		
Turnout	43,303	62.37	

Lab hold (8.3% from Lab to Con)

NEWPORT EAST
(No boundary changes)

		%	+/-%
Morden, J. Lab*	12,744	37.0	-8.2
Townsend, E. Lib Dem	11,094	32.2	8.5
Parry, D. Con	7,918	23.0	19.1
Jones, K. BNP	1,168	3.4	

*Member of last Parliament

Cross, F. PlC	724	2.1	
Rowlands, D. UKIP	677	2.0	-1.0
Screen, L. SLP	123	0.4	-0.5
Lab majority	1,650	4.78	
Electorate	54,305		
Turnout	34,486	63.5	

Lab hold (8.3% from Lab to Lib Dem)

NEWPORT WEST
(No boundary changes)

		%	+/-%
Flynn, P. Lab*	16,389	41.2	-3.5
Williams, M. Con	12,845	32.3	2.8
German, V. Lib Dem	6,587	16.6	-1.3
Windsor, T. BNP	1,183	3.0	
Moelwyn Hughes, H. UKIP	1,144	2.9	0.5
Rees, J. PlC	1,122	2.8	-0.8
Bartolotti, P. Green	450	1.1	-0.4
Lab majority	3,544	8.91	
Electorate	62,111		
Turnout	39,775	64.04	

Lab hold (3.2% from Lab to Con)

NEWRY AND ARMAGH
(No boundary changes)

		%	+/-%
Murphy, C. Sinn Féin*	18,857	42.0	1.1
Bradley, D. SDLP	10,526	23.4	-1.4
Kennedy, D. UCUNF	8,558	19.1	5.2
Irwin, W. DUP	5,764	12.8	
Frazer, W. Ind	656	1.5	
Muir, A. All	545	1.2	
Sinn Féin majority	8,331	18.55	
Electorate	74,308		
Turnout	44,906	60.43	

Sinn Féin hold (1.3% from SDLP to Sinn Féin)

NEWTON ABBOT
(New constituency)

		%
Morris, A. Con	20,774	43.0
Younger-Ross, R. Lib Dem*	20,251	41.9
Canavan, P. Lab	3,387	7.0
Hooper, J. UKIP	3,088	6.4
Lindsey, C. Green	701	1.5
Sharp, K. Ind	82	0.2
Con majority	523	1.08
Electorate	69,319	
Turnout	48,359	69.76

Con gain (notional 5.8% from Lib Dem to Con)

MID NORFOLK
(Boundary changes)

		%
Freeman, G. Con	25,123	49.4
Newman, D. Lib Dem	11,267	22.2
Hughes, E. Lab	8,857	17.4
Coke, R. UKIP	2,800	5.5
Birt, T. Green	1,457	2.9
Kelly, C. BNP	1,261	2.5
Con majority	13,856	27.26
Electorate	74,260	
Turnout	50,831	68.45

Con hold (notional 0.04% from Con to Lib Dem)

NORTH NORFOLK
(Boundary changes)

		%
Lamb, N. Lib Dem	27,554	55.4
Ivory, T. Con	15,928	32.0
Harris, P. Lab	2,896	5.8
Baker, M. UKIP	2,680	5.4
Boswell, A. Green	508	1.0
Mann, S. Ind	95	0.2
Lib Dem majority	11,626	23.37
Electorate	67,851	
Turnout	49,737	73.3

Lib Dem hold (notional 3% from Con to Lib Dem)

NORTH WEST NORFOLK
(*Boundary changes*)

		%
Bellingham, H. Con*	25,916	54.1
Summers, W. Lib Dem	11,106	23.2
Sood, M. Lab	6,353	13.3
Gray, J. UKIP	1,841	3.9
Fleming, D. BNP	1,839	3.9
de Whalley, M. Green	745	1.6
Con majority	14,810	30.94
Electorate	73,207	
Turnout	47,865	65.38

Con hold (notional 2.1% from Con to Lib Dem)

SOUTH NORFOLK
(*Boundary changes*)

		%
Bacon, R. Con*	27,133	49.3
Howe, J. Lib Dem	16,193	29.4
Castle, M. Lab	7,252	13.2
Heasley, E. UKIP	2,329	4.2
Mitchell, H. BNP	1,086	2.0
Willcott, J. Green	1,000	1.8
Con majority	10,940	19.86
Electorate	76,179	
Turnout	55,077	72.3

Con hold (notional 3.2% from Lib Dem to Con)

SOUTH WEST NORFOLK
(*Boundary changes*)

		%
Truss, E. Con	23,753	48.3
Gordon, S. Lib Dem	10,613	21.6
Smith, P. Lab	9,119	18.5
Hipsey, K. UKIP	3,061	6.2
Pearce, D. BNP	1,774	3.6
Allen, L. Green	830	1.7
Con majority	13,140	26.7
Electorate	74,235	
Turnout	49,214	66.29

Con hold (notional 0.5% from Lib Dem to Con)

NORMANTON, PONTEFRACT AND CASTLEFORD
(*New constituency*)

		%
Cooper, Y. Lab*	22,293	48.1
Pickles, N. Con	11,314	24.4
Rush, C. Lib Dem	7,585	16.4
Thewlis-Hardy, G. BNP	3,864	8.3
Allen, G. Ind	1,183	2.6
Lab majority	10,979	23.69
Electorate	82,240	
Turnout	46,344	56.35

Lab hold (notional 12.5% from Lab to Con)

NORTH ANTRIM – see under Antrim

NORTH AYRSHIRE AND ARRAN – see under Ayrshire

NORTH CORNWALL – see under Cornwall

NORTH DEVON – see under Devon

NORTH DORSET – see under Dorset

NORTH DOWN – see under Down

NORTH DURHAM – see under Durham

NORTH EAST BEDFORDSHIRE – see under Bedfordshire

NORTH EAST CAMBRIDGESHIRE – see under Cambridgeshire

NORTH EAST DERBYSHIRE – see under Derbyshire

NORTH EAST FIFE – see under Fife

NORTH EAST HAMPSHIRE – see under Hampshire

NORTH EAST HERTFORDSHIRE – see under Hertfordshire

NORTH EAST SOMERSET – see under Somerset

NORTH HEREFORDSHIRE – see under Herefordshire

NORTH NORFOLK – see under Norfolk

NORTH SHROPSHIRE – see under Shropshire

NORTH SOMERSET – see under Somerset

NORTH SWINDON – see under Swindon

NORTH THANET – see under Thanet

NORTH TYNESIDE – see under Tyneside

NORTH WARWICKSHIRE – see under Warwickshire

NORTH WEST CAMBRIDGESHIRE – see under Cambridgeshire

NORTH WEST DURHAM – see under Durham

NORTH WEST HAMPSHIRE – see under Hampshire

NORTH WEST LEICESTERSHIRE – see under Leicestershire

NORTH WEST NORFOLK – see under Norfolk

NORTH WILTSHIRE – see under Wiltshire

NORTHAMPTON NORTH
(*Boundary changes*)

		%
Ellis, M. Con	13,735	34.0
Keeble, S. Lab*	11,799	29.2
Simpson, A. Lib Dem	11,250	27.9
Beasley, R. BNP	1,316	3.3
MacArthur, J. UKIP	1,238	3.1
Lochmuller, T. Green	443	1.1
Fitzpatrick, E. Ind	334	0.8
Webb, T. Christian	98	0.3
Mildren, M. Ind	58	0.2
Con majority	1,936	4.8
Electorate	61,850	
Turnout	40,364	65.26

Con gain (notional 6.9% from Lab to Con)

NORTHAMPTON SOUTH
(*Boundary changes*)

		%
Binley, B. Con*	15,917	40.8
Loakes, C. Lab	9,913	25.4
Varnsverry, P. Lib Dem	7,579	19.4
Clarke, T. Ind	2,242	5.7
Clark, D. UKIP	1,897	4.9
Sills, K. Eng Dem	618	1.6
Hawkins, J. Green	363	0.9
Green, D. NSOPS	325	0.8
Willsher, K. Ind	65	0.2
Costello, L. Scrap	59	0.2
Con majority	6,004	15.37
Electorate	63,105	
Turnout	39,064	61.9

Con gain (notional 9.6% from Lab to Con)

SOUTH NORTHAMPTONSHIRE
(*New constituency*)

		%
Leadsom, A. Con	33,081	55.0
Collins, S. Lib Dem	12,603	20.9
May, M. Lab	10,380	17.2
Mahoney, B. UKIP	2,406	4.0
Tappy, T. Eng Dem	735	1.2
Rock, M. Green	685	1.1
Con majority	20,478	34.01
Electorate	82,033	
Turnout	60,210	73.4

Con hold (notional 0.2% from Con to Lib Dem)

NORWICH NORTH
(*Boundary changes*)

		%
Smith, C. Con*	17,280	40.6
Cook, J. Lab/Co-op	13,379	31.4
Stephen, D. Lib Dem	7,783	18.3
Tingle, G. UKIP	1,878	4.4
Goldfinch, J. Green	1,245	2.9
Richardson, T. BNP	747	1.8
Holden, B. Ind	143	0.3
Holland, A. Christian	118	0.3
Con majority	3,901	9.15
Electorate	64,814	
Turnout	42,613	65.75

Con gain (notional 12.9% from Lab/Co-op to Con)

NORWICH SOUTH
(*Boundary changes*)

		%
Wright, S. Lib Dem	13,960	29.3
Clarke, C. Lab*	13,650	28.7
Little, A. Con	10,902	22.9
Ramsay, A. Green	7,095	14.9
Emmens, S. UKIP	1,145	2.4
Heather, L. BNP	697	1.5
Polley, G. WRP	102	0.2
Lib Dem majority	310	0.65
Electorate	73,649	
Turnout	47,621	64.66

Lib Dem gain (notional 4% from Lab to Lib Dem)

NOTTINGHAM EAST
(*Boundary changes*)

		%
Leslie, C. Lab/Co-op	15,022	45.2
Boote, S. Lib Dem	8,053	24.2
Lamont, E. Con	7,846	23.6
Wolfe, P. UKIP	1,138	3.4
Hoare, B. Green	928	2.8
Sardar, P. Christian	125	0.4
Lab/Co-op majority	6,969	20.96
Electorate	58,705	
Turnout	33,245	56.63

Lab/Co-op hold (notional 1.9% from Lab/Co-op to Lib Dem)

*Member of last Parliament

NOTTINGHAM NORTH
(*Boundary changes*)

		%
Allen, G. Lab*	16,646	48.5
Curtis, M. Con	8,508	24.8
Ball, T. Lib Dem	5,849	17.0
Brindley, B. BNP	1,944	5.7
Marriott, I. UKIP	1,338	3.9
Lab majority	8,138	23.68
Electorate	63,240	
Turnout	34,360	54.33

Lab hold (notional 8.7% from Lab to Con)

NOTTINGHAM SOUTH
(*Boundary changes*)

		%
Greenwood, L. Lab	15,209	37.2
Holland, R. Con	13,437	32.9
Sutton, T. Lib Dem	9,406	23.0
Woodward, T. BNP	1,140	2.8
Browne, K. UKIP	967	2.4
Butcher, M. Green	630	1.6
Lab majority	1,772	4.34
Electorate	67,441	
Turnout	40,857	60.58

Lab hold (notional 7.4% from Lab to Con)

NUNEATON
(*Boundary changes*)

		%
Jones, M. Con	18,536	41.4
Innes, J. Lab	16,467	36.8
Jebb, C. Lib Dem	6,846	15.3
Findley, M. BNP	2,797	6.3
Con majority	2,069	4.62
Electorate	67,837	
Turnout	44,758	65.98

Con gain (notional 7.2% from Lab to Con)

OCHIL AND SOUTH PERTHSHIRE
(*No boundary changes*)

		%	+/-%
Banks, G. Lab*	19,131	37.9	6.6
Ewing, A. SNP	13,944	27.6	-2.2
Michaluk, G. Con	10,342	20.5	-1.0
Littlejohn, G. Lib Dem	5,754	11.4	-1.9
Bushby, D. UKIP	689	1.4	0.8
Charles, H. Green	609	1.2	-0.9
Lab majority	5,187	10.27	
Electorate	75,115		
Turnout	50,525	67.26	

Lab hold (4.4% from SNP to Lab)

OGMORE
(*Boundary changes*)

		%
Irranca-Davies, H. Lab*	18,644	53.7
Moore, E. Con	5,398	15.6
Radford, J. Lib Dem	5,260	15.2
Clark, D. PlC	3,326	9.6
Thomas, K. BNP	1,242	3.6
Passey, C. UKIP	780	2.3
Lab majority	13,246	38.15
Electorate	55,527	
Turnout	34,718	62.52

Lab hold (notional 4.3% from Lab to Con)

OLD BEXLEY AND SIDCUP
(*Boundary changes*)

		%
Brokenshire, J. Con*	24,625	53.9
Everitt, R. Lab	8,768	19.2
Borrowdale, D. Lib Dem	6,996	15.3
Brooks, J. BNP	2,132	4.7
Coburn, D. UKIP	1,532	3.4

Cheeseman, E. Eng Dem	520	1.1
Hemming-Clarke, J. Ind	393	0.9
Rooks, J. Green	371	0.8
Dynamite, N. Loony	155	0.3
Con majority	15,857	34.73
Electorate	66,055	
Turnout	45,664	69.13

Con hold (notional 6.4% from Lab to Con)

OLDHAM EAST AND SADDLEWORTH
(Boundary changes)		%
Woolas, P. Lab*	14,186	31.7
Watkins, E. Lib Dem	14,083	31.5
Ali, K. Con	11,773	26.3
Stott, A. BNP	2,546	5.7
Bentley, D. UKIP	1,720	3.9
Nazir, G. Christian	212	0.5
Lab majority	103	0.23
Electorate	72,557	
Turnout	44,724	61.64

Lab hold (notional 5.1% from Lab to Lib Dem)

OLDHAM WEST AND ROYTON
(Boundary changes)		%
Meacher, M. Lab*	19,503	45.2
Ghafoor, K. Con	10,151	23.5
Alcock, M. Lib Dem	8,193	19.0
Joines, D. BNP	3,049	7.1
Roberts, H. UKIP	1,387	3.2
Miah, S. Respect	627	1.5
Lab majority	9,352	21.67
Electorate	72,359	
Turnout	43,163	59.65

Lab hold (notional 2.8% from Lab to Con)

ORKNEY AND SHETLAND
(No boundary changes)		%	+/-%
Carmichael, A. Lib Dem*	11,989	61.8	10.4
Cooper, M. Lab	2,061	10.6	-3.5
Mowat, J. SNP	2,042	10.5	0.2
Nairn, F. Con	2,032	10.5	-2.8
Smith, R. UKIP	1,222	6.3	3.9
Lib Dem majority	9,928	51.16	
Electorate	33,085		
Turnout	19,407	58.66	

Lib Dem hold (6.9% from Lab to Lib Dem)

ORPINGTON
(Boundary changes)		%
Johnson, J. Con	29,200	59.6
McBride, D. Lib Dem	12,000	24.5
Morgan, S. Lab	4,400	9.0
Greenhough, M. UKIP	1,360	2.8
Culnane, M. BNP	1,241	2.5
Galloway, T. Green	511	1.1
Snape, C. Eng Dem	199	0.4
Con majority	17,200	35.09
Electorate	67,732	
Turnout	49,021	72.37

Con hold (notional 12.1% from Lib Dem to Con)

OXFORD EAST
(Boundary changes)		%
Smith, A. Lab*	21,938	42.3
Goddard, S. Lib Dem	17,357	33.5
Argar, E. Con	9,727	18.8
Dhall, S. Green	1,238	2.4
Gasper, J. UKIP	1,202	2.3

O'Sullivan, D. SEP	116	0.2
Crawford, R. EPA	73	0.2
Lab majority	4,581	8.84
Electorate	81,903	
Turnout	51,819	63.27

Lab hold (notional 4.1% from Lib Dem to Lab)

OXFORD WEST AND ABINGDON
(Boundary changes)		%
Blackwood, N. Con	23,906	42.2
Harris, E. Lib Dem*	23,730	41.9
Stevens, R. Lab	5,999	10.6
Williams, P. UKIP	1,518	2.7
Goodall, C. Green	1,184	2.1
Mann, K. Animal	143	0.3
Con majority	176	0.31
Electorate	80,883	
Turnout	56,599	69.98

Con gain (notional 6.9% from Lib Dem to Con)

PAISLEY AND RENFREWSHIRE NORTH
(No boundary changes)		%	+/-%
Sheridan, J. Lab*	23,613	53.9	8.3
MacLaren, M. SNP	8,333	19.0	0.3
Campbell, A. Con	6,381	14.6	1.0
Dobson, R. Lib Dem	4,597	10.5	-7.7
Pearson, G. Ind	550	1.3	
Rollo, C. SSP	233	0.5	-1.0
Lab majority	15,280	34.9	
Electorate	63,704		
Turnout	43,781	68.73	

Lab hold (4% from SNP to Lab)

PAISLEY AND RENFREWSHIRE SOUTH
(No boundary changes)		%	+/-%
Alexander, D. Lab*	23,842	59.5	7.0
Doig, A. SNP	7,228	18.0	0.5
McCaskill, G. Con	3,979	9.9	1.5
Ghai, A. Lib Dem	3,812	9.5	-8.1
Mack, P. Ind	513	1.3	0.8
Kerr, J. SSP	375	0.9	-1.1
Hendry, W. Ind	249	0.6	0.2
Lab majority	16,614	41.44	
Electorate	61,197		
Turnout	40,094	65.52	

Lab hold (3.3% from SNP to Lab)

PENDLE
(No boundary changes)		%	+/-%
Stephenson, A. Con	17,512	38.7	7.2
Prentice, G. Lab*	13,927	30.8	-6.1
Anwar, A. Lib Dem	9,095	20.1	-2.9
Jackman, J. BNP	2,894	6.4	0.2
Cannon, G. UKIP	1,476	3.3	1.5
Masih, R. Christian	141	0.3	
Con majority	3,585	7.93	
Electorate	66,422		
Turnout	45,199	68.05	

Con gain (6.6% from Lab to Con)

PENISTONE AND STOCKSBRIDGE
(New constituency)		%
Smith, A. Lab*	17,565	37.7
Pitfield, S. Con	14,516	31.2
Cuthbertson, I. Lib Dem	9,800	21.0
James, P. BNP	2,207	4.7
French, G. UKIP	1,936	4.2
McEnhill, P. Eng Dem	492	1.1
Lab majority	3,049	6.54
Electorate	68,480	
Turnout	46,599	68.05

Lab hold (notional 7.5% from Lab to Con)

PENRITH AND THE BORDER
(Boundary changes)

		%
Stewart, R. Con	24,071	53.3
Thornton, P. Lib Dem	12,830	28.4
Cannon, B. Lab	5,834	12.9
Stanyer, J. UKIP	1,259	2.8
Davidson, C. BNP	1,093	2.4
Con majority	11,241	24.89
Electorate	64,484	
Turnout	45,168	70.05

Con hold (notional 0.3% from Con to Lib Dem)

PERTH AND NORTH PERTHSHIRE
(No boundary changes)

		%	+/-%
Wishart, P. SNP*	19,118	39.5	5.9
Lyburn, P. Con	14,739	30.5	0.2
Glackin, J. Lab	7,923	16.4	-2.3
Barrett, P. Lib Dem	5,954	12.3	-3.8
Taylor, D. Trust	534	1.1	
SNP majority	4,379	9.06	
Electorate	76,007		
Turnout	48,333	63.59	

SNP hold (2.9% from Con to SNP)

PETERBOROUGH
(Boundary changes)

		%
Jackson, S. Con*	18,133	40.2
Murphy, E. Lab	13,272	29.4
Sandford, N. Lib Dem	8,816	19.5
Fox, F. UKIP	3,007	6.7
King, R. Eng Dem	770	1.7
Radic, F. Green	523	1.2
Swallow, J. Ind	406	0.9
Con majority	4,861	10.77
Electorate	70,278	
Turnout	45,119	64.2

Con hold (notional 0.9% from Lab to Con)

PLYMOUTH, MOOR VIEW
(New constituency)

		%
Seabeck, A. Lab*	15,433	37.1
Groves, M. Con	13,845	33.3
Bonar, S. Lib Dem	7,016	16.9
Wakeham, B. UKIP	3,188	7.7
Cook, R. BNP	1,438	3.5
Miller, W. Green	398	1.0
Marchesi, D. SLP	208	0.5
Lab majority	1,588	3.82
Electorate	68,062	
Turnout	41,619	61.15

Lab hold (notional 7.8% from Lab to Con)

PLYMOUTH, SUTTON AND DEVONPORT
(New constituency)

		%
Colvile, O. Con	15,050	34.2
Gilroy, L. Lab/Co-op*	13,901	31.6
Evans, J. Lib Dem	10,829	24.6
Leigh, A. UKIP	2,854	6.5
Brown, A. Green	904	2.1
Gerrish, B. Ind	233	0.5
Hawkins, R. SLP	123	0.3
Con majority	1,149	2.61
Electorate	72,938	
Turnout	44,033	60.37

Con gain (notional 6.9% from Lab/Co-op to Con)

PONTYPRIDD
(Boundary changes)

		%
Smith, O. Lab	14,220	38.7
Powell, M. Lib Dem	11,435	31.1
Gonzalez, L. Con	5,932	16.1

*Member of last Parliament

Bellin, I. PlC	2,673	7.3
Bevan, D. UKIP	1,229	3.4
Parsons, S. SLP	456	1.3
Watson, D. Christian	365	1.0
Matthews, J. Green	361	1.0
Lab majority	2,785	7.58
Electorate	58,205	
Turnout	36,746	63.13

Lab hold (notional 13.3% from Lab to Lib Dem)

POOLE
(Boundary changes)

		%
Syms, R. Con*	22,532	47.4
Eades, P. Lib Dem	14,991	31.5
Sanderson, J. Lab	6,041	12.7
Wellstead, N. UKIP	2,507	5.3
Holmes, D. BNP	1,188	2.5
Northover, I. Ind	177	0.4
Con majority	7,541	15.86
Electorate	72,641	
Turnout	47,539	65.44

Con hold (notional 0.8% from Lib Dem to Con)

POPLAR AND LIMEHOUSE
(New constituency)

		%
Fitzpatrick, J. Lab*	18,679	39.4
Archer, T. Con	12,649	26.7
Galloway, G. Respect*	8,160	17.2
Fryer, J. Lib Dem	5,209	11.0
Lochner, W. UKIP	565	1.2
Osborne, A. Eng Dem	470	1.0
Smith, C. Green	449	1.0
Mahmud, K. Ind	293	0.6
Hoque, M. Ind	167	0.4
Thornton, J. Ind	59	0.1
Lab majority	6,030	12.72
Electorate	74,955	
Turnout	47,413	63.26

Lab hold (notional 0.9% from Con to Lab)

PORTSMOUTH NORTH
(Boundary changes)

		%
Mordaunt, P. Con	19,533	44.1
McCarthy-Fry, S. Lab/Co-op*	12,244	27.7
Sanders, D. Lib Dem	8,874	20.1
Fitzgerald, M. UKIP	1,812	4.1
Knight, D. Eng Dem	1,040	2.4
Maclennan, I. Green	461	1.1
Tosh, M. TUSC	154	0.4
Con majority	7,289	16.46
Electorate	70,329	
Turnout	44,272	62.95

Con gain (notional 8.6% from Lab/Co-op to Con)

PORTSMOUTH SOUTH
(Boundary changes)

		%
Hancock, M. Lib Dem*	18,921	45.7
Drummond, F. Con	13,721	33.1
Ferrett, J. Lab	5,640	13.6
Martin, C. UKIP	876	2.1
Crompton, G. BNP	873	2.1
Dawes, T. Green	716	1.7
DuCane, I. Eng Dem	400	1.0
Cummings, L. JACP	117	0.3
Lib Dem majority	5,200	12.56
Electorate	70,242	
Turnout	41,417	58.96

Lib Dem hold (notional 2.3% from Con to Lib Dem)

PRESELI PEMBROKESHIRE
(Boundary changes) %

Crabb, S. Con*	16,944	42.7
Rees, M. Lab	12,339	31.1
Tregoning, N. Lib Dem	5,759	14.5
Jones-Davies, H. PlC	3,654	9.2
Lawson, R. UKIP	906	2.3
Con majority	4,605	11.6
Electorate	57,400	
Turnout	39,682	69.13

Con hold (notional 5% from Lab to Con)

PRESTON
(Boundary changes) %

Hendrick, M. Lab/Co-op*	15,668	48.0
Jewell, M. Lib Dem	7,935	24.3
Warner-O'Neill, N. Con	7,060	21.6
Muirhead, R. UKIP	1,462	4.5
Ambroze, G. Christian	272	0.8
Tayya, K. Ind	108	0.3
Lab/Co-op majority	7,733	23.69
Electorate	61,187	
Turnout	32,637	53.34

Lab/Co-op hold (notional 2.5% from Lab/Co-op to Lib Dem)

PUDSEY
(Boundary changes) %

Andrew, S. Con	18,874	38.4
Hanley, J. Lab	17,215	35.0
Matthews, J. Lib Dem	10,224	20.8
Gibson, I. BNP	1,549	3.2
Dews, D. UKIP	1,221	2.5
Con majority	1,659	3.37
Electorate	69,257	
Turnout	49,174	71

Con gain (notional 7.6% from Lab to Con)

PUTNEY
(Boundary changes) %

Greening, J. Con*	21,223	51.9
King, S. Lab	11,170	27.3
Sandbach, J. Lib Dem	6,907	16.9
Mackenzie, B. Green	591	1.5
Darby, P. BNP	459	1.1
Wareham, H. UKIP	435	1.1
Con majority	10,053	24.59
Electorate	63,371	
Turnout	40,882	64.51

Con hold (notional 9.9% from Lab to Con)

RAYLEIGH AND WICKFORD
(New constituency) %

Francois, M. Con*	30,257	57.7
Gaszczak, S. Lib Dem	7,919	15.1
Le-Surf, M. Lab	7,577	14.4
Hayter, J. Eng Dem	2,219	4.2
Callaghan, T. UKIP	2,211	4.2
Evennett, A. BNP	2,160	4.1
Con majority	22,338	42.58
Electorate	75,661	
Turnout	52,459	69.33

Con hold (notional 2.1% from Lib Dem to Con)

READING EAST
(Boundary changes) %

Wilson, R. Con*	21,269	42.5
Epps, G. Lib Dem	13,664	27.3
Dodds, A. Lab	12,729	25.4
Pitfield, A. UKIP	1,086	2.2
White, R. Green	1,069	2.1
Lloyd, J. Ind	111	0.2
Turberville, M. Ind	57	0.1
Con majority	7,605	15.18
Electorate	74,932	
Turnout	50,103	66.86

Con hold (notional 2% from Lib Dem to Con)

READING WEST
(Boundary changes) %

Sharma, A. Con	20,523	43.1
Sarkar, N. Lab	14,519	30.5
Benson, D. Lib Dem	9,546	20.1
Hay, B. UKIP	1,508	3.2
Thomas, H. CSP	852	1.8
Windisch, A. Green	582	1.2
Con majority	6,004	12.61
Electorate	72,121	
Turnout	47,628	66.04

Con gain (notional 12% from Lab to Con)

REDCAR
(Boundary changes) %

Swales, I. Lib Dem	18,955	45.1
Baird, V. Lab*	13,741	32.7
Mastin, S. Con	5,790	13.8
Bulmer, M. UKIP	1,875	4.5
Broughton, K. BNP	1,475	3.5
Walter, H. TUSC	127	0.3
Lib Dem majority	5,214	12.41
Electorate	67,127	
Turnout	42,008	62.58

Lib Dem gain (notional 21.8% from Lab to Lib Dem)

REDDITCH
(Boundary changes) %

Lumley, K. Con	19,138	43.4
Smith, J. Lab*	13,317	30.2
Lane, N. Lib Dem	7,750	17.6
Davis, A. UKIP	1,497	3.4
Ingram, A. BNP	1,394	3.2
White, K. Green	393	0.9
Schittone, V. Eng Dem	255	0.6
Beverley, S. Christian	101	0.2
Swansborough, P. Ind	100	0.2
Fletcher, D. Nobody	73	0.2
Con majority	5,821	13.2
Electorate	66,537	
Turnout	44,090	66.26

Con gain (notional 9.2% from Lab to Con)

REIGATE
(Boundary changes) %

Blunt, C. Con*	26,688	53.3
Kulka, J. Lib Dem	13,097	26.1
Hull, R. Lab	5,672	11.3
Fox, J. UKIP	2,089	4.2
Brown, K. BNP	1,345	2.7
Essex, J. Green	1,087	2.2
Con majority	13,591	27.14
Electorate	71,604	
Turnout	50,086	69.95

Con hold (notional 0.9% from Lib Dem to Con)

EAST RENFREWSHIRE
(No boundary changes) % +/-%

Murphy, J. Lab*	25,987	50.7	6.9
Cook, R. Con	15,567	30.4	0.6
MacDonald, G. Lib Dem	4,720	9.2	-9.0
Archer, G. SNP	4,535	8.8	2.0
MacKay, D. UKIP	372	0.7	
Lab majority	10,420	20.33	
Electorate	66,249		
Turnout	51,258	77.37	

Lab hold (3.2% from Con to Lab)

554 GENERAL ELECTION 2010

RHONDDA
(No boundary changes)

		%	+/-%
Bryant, C. Lab*	17,183	55.2	-12.6
Davies, G. PlC	5,630	18.1	2.2
Wasley, P. Lib Dem	3,309	10.6	0.2
Howe, P. Ind	2,599	8.3	
Henderson, J. Con	1,993	6.4	0.9
John, T. UKIP	358	1.1	
Lab majority	11,553	37.1	
Electorate	51,554		
Turnout	31,143	60.41	

Lab hold (7.4% from Lab to PlC)

SOUTH RIBBLE
(Boundary changes)

		%
Fullbrook, L. Con	23,396	45.4
Borrow, D. Lab*	17,842	34.6
Fisher, P. Lib Dem	7,271	14.1
Duxbury, D. UKIP	1,895	3.7
Gauci, R. BNP	1,054	2.0
Con majority	5,554	10.78
Electorate	75,822	
Turnout	51,528	67.96

Con gain (notional 8.1% from Lab to Con)

RIBBLE VALLEY
(Boundary changes)

		%
Evans, N. Con*	26,298	50.2
Foster, P. Lab	11,529	22.0
Knox, A. Lib Dem	10,732	20.5
Rush, S. UKIP	3,496	6.7
Johnson, T. Ind	232	0.5
Con majority	14,769	28.21
Electorate	77,789	
Turnout	52,360	67.31

Con hold (notional 6.6% from Lab to Con)

RICHMOND (YORKSHIRE)
(Boundary changes)

		%
Hague, W. Con*	33,541	62.6
Meredith, L. Lib Dem	10,205	19.1
Driver, E. Lab	8,150	15.2
Rowe, L. Green	1,516	2.8
Con majority	23,336	43.58
Electorate	80,563	
Turnout	53,547	66.47

Con hold (notional 0.6% from Lib Dem to Con)

RICHMOND PARK
(Boundary changes)

		%
Goldsmith, Z. Con	29,461	49.6
Kramer, S. Lib Dem*	25,370	42.7
Tunnicliffe, E. Lab	2,979	5.0
Dul, P. UKIP	669	1.1
Page, J. Green	572	1.0
May, S. CPA	133	0.2
Hill, C. Ind	84	0.2
Con majority	4,091	6.89
Electorate	77,751	
Turnout	59,398	76.4

Con gain (notional 7% from Lib Dem to Con)

ROCHDALE
(Boundary changes)

		%
Danczuk, S. Lab	16,699	36.2
Rowen, P. Lib Dem*	15,810	34.3
Dean, M. Con	8,305	18.0
Jackson, C. NF	2,236	4.8

*Member of last Parliament

Denby, C. UKIP	1,999	4.3
Salim, M. IZB	545	1.2
Whitehead, J. Ind	313	0.7
Lab majority	889	1.93
Electorate	78,952	
Turnout	46,158	58.46

Lab hold (notional 0.8% from Lib Dem to Lab)

ROCHESTER AND STROOD
(New constituency)

		%
Reckless, M. Con	23,604	49.1
Murray, T. Lab	13,651	28.4
Juby, G. Lib Dem	7,800	16.2
Sands, R. Eng Dem	2,182	4.5
Marchant, S. Green	734	1.5
Con majority	9,953	20.72
Electorate	73,758	
Turnout	48,044	65.14

Con hold (notional 9.8% from Lab to Con)

ROCHFORD AND SOUTHEND EAST
(Boundary changes)

		%
Duddridge, J. Con*	19,509	46.7
Bonavia, K. Lab	8,459	20.3
Longley, G. Lib Dem	8,084	19.4
Moyies, J. UKIP	2,405	5.8
Strobridge, G. BNP	1,856	4.5
Vaughan, A. Green	707	1.7
Chytry, A. Ind	611	1.5
Con majority	11,050	26.47
Electorate	71,467	
Turnout	41,741	58.41

Con hold (notional 6.3% from Lab to Con)

ROMFORD
(Boundary changes)

		%
Rosindell, A. Con*	26,031	55.8
Voller, R. Lab	9,077	19.5
Duffett, H. Lib Dem	5,572	11.9
Bailey, R. BNP	2,438	5.2
Batten, G. UKIP	2,050	4.4
Thorogood, P. Eng Dem	603	1.3
Haines, G. Green	447	1.0
Hyde, P. Ind	151	0.3
Sturman, D. Ind	112	0.3
Con majority	16,954	36.34
Electorate	71,305	
Turnout	46,658	65.43

Con hold (notional 3.9% from Lab to Con)

ROMSEY AND SOUTHAMPTON NORTH
(New constituency)

		%
Nokes, C. Con	24,345	49.7
Gidley, S. Lib Dem*	20,189	41.2
Beg, A. Lab	3,116	6.4
Meropoulos, J. UKIP	1,289	2.6
Con majority	4,156	8.48
Electorate	68,227	
Turnout	49,029	71.86

Con gain (notional 5.5% from Lib Dem to Con)

ROSS, SKYE AND LOCHABER
(No boundary changes)

		%	+/-%
Kennedy, C. Lib Dem*	18,335	52.6	-6.1
McKendrick, J. Lab	5,265	15.1	0.2
Stephen, A. SNP	5,263	15.1	5.5
Cameron, D. Con	4,260	12.2	2.2
Scott, E. Green	777	2.2	-1.1

Anderson, P. UKIP	659	1.9	0.4
Campbell, R. Ind	279	0.8	
Lib Dem majority	13,070	37.46	
Electorate	51,836		
Turnout	34,886	67.3	

Lib Dem hold (3.1% from Lib Dem to Lab)

ROSSENDALE AND DARWEN
(Boundary changes) %

Berry, J. Con	19,691	41.7
Anderson, J. Lab*	15,198	32.1
Sheffield, B. Lib Dem	8,541	18.1
Duthie, D. UKIP	1,617	3.4
Bryan, K. NF	1,062	2.3
Johnson, M. Eng Dem	663	1.4
Melia, T. Impact	243	0.5
Sivieri, M. Ind	113	0.2
Con majority	4,493	9.5
Electorate	73,229	
Turnout	47,277	64.56

Con gain (notional 8.9% from Lab to Con)

ROTHER VALLEY
(Boundary changes) %

Barron, K. Lab*	19,147	40.9
Donaldson, L. Con	13,281	28.4
Paxton, W. Lib Dem	8,111	17.3
Blair, W. BNP	3,606	7.7
Dowdall, T. UKIP	2,613	5.6
Lab majority	5,866	12.52
Electorate	72,847	
Turnout	46,852	64.32

Lab hold (notional 8% from Lab to Con)

ROTHERHAM
(Boundary changes) %

MacShane, D. Lab*	16,741	44.5
Whiteley, J. Con	6,279	16.7
Taylor, R. Lib Dem	5,994	15.9
Guest, M. BNP	3,906	10.4
Thirlwall, P. Ind	2,366	6.3
Vines, C. UKIP	2,220	5.9
Lab majority	10,462	27.82
Electorate	63,563	
Turnout	37,601	59.16

Lab hold (notional 8.3% from Lab to Con)

RUGBY
(New constituency) %

Pawsey, M. Con	20,901	44.0
King, A. Lab	14,901	31.3
Roodhouse, J. Lib Dem	9,434	19.8
Badrick, M. BNP	1,375	2.9
Sandison, R. Green	451	1.0
Milford, B. UKIP	406	0.9
Con majority	6,000	12.62
Electorate	68,914	
Turnout	47,560	69.01

Con gain (notional 8.9% from Lab to Con)

RUISLIP, NORTHWOOD AND PINNER
(New constituency) %

Hurd, N. Con*	28,866	57.3
MacDonald, A. Lab	9,806	19.5
Papworth, T. Lib Dem	8,345	16.6
Pontey, J. UKIP	1,351	2.7
Edward, I. NF	899	1.8
Lee, G. Green	740	1.5
Akhtar, R. Christian	198	0.4
Con majority	19,060	37.85
Electorate	70,873	
Turnout	50,357	71.05

Con hold (notional 3.6% from Lab to Con)

RUNNYMEDE AND WEYBRIDGE
(No boundary changes) % +/-%

Hammond, P. Con*	26,915	55.8	4.6
Falconer, A. Lib Dem	10,406	21.6	3.8
Greenwood, P. Lab	6,446	13.4	-9.6
Micklethwait, T. UKIP	3,146	6.5	2.6
Gould, J. Green	696	1.4	-1.3
Sammons, D. Ind	541	1.1	
Con majority	16,509	34.22	
Electorate	72,566		
Turnout	48,239	66.48	

Con hold (0.4% from Lib Dem to Con)

RUSHCLIFFE
(Boundary changes) %

Clarke, K. Con*	27,470	51.0
Khan, K. Lib Dem	11,659	21.7
Clayworth, A. Lab	11,128	20.7
Faithfull, M. UKIP	2,179	4.0
Mallender, R. Green	1,251	2.3
Con majority	15,811	29.37
Electorate	72,955	
Turnout	53,834	73.79

Con hold (notional 0.7% from Con to Lib Dem)

RUTHERGLEN AND HAMILTON WEST
(No boundary changes) % +/-%

Greatrex, T. Lab/Co-op	28,566	60.7	5.2
Horne, G. SNP	7,564	16.1	2.2
Robertson, I. Lib Dem	5,636	12.0	-6.3
Macaskill, M. Con	4,540	9.6	1.3
Murdoch, J. UKIP	675	1.4	0.4
Lab/Co-op majority	21,002	44.62	
Electorate	76,408		
Turnout	47,072	61.61	

Lab/Co-op hold (1.5% from SNP to Lab/Co-op)

RUTLAND AND MELTON
(Boundary changes) %

Duncan, A. Con*	28,228	51.0
Hudson, G. Lib Dem	14,228	25.7
Morgan, J. Lab	7,893	14.3
Baker, P. UKIP	2,526	4.6
Addison, K. BNP	1,757	3.2
Higgins, L. Ind	588	1.1
Con majority	14,000	25.3
Electorate	77,185	
Turnout	55,330	71.68

Con hold (notional 3.7% from Con to Lib Dem)

SAFFRON WALDEN
(Boundary changes) %

Haselhurst, A. Con*	30,155	55.3
Wilcock, P. Lib Dem	14,913	27.4
Light, B. Lab	5,288	9.7
Lord, R. UKIP	2,288	4.2
Mitchell, C. BNP	1,050	1.9
Hossain, R. Green	735	1.4
Con majority	15,242	27.97
Electorate	76,035	
Turnout	54,498	71.67

Con hold (notional 3.4% from Lib Dem to Con)

SALFORD AND ECCLES
(New constituency)

		%
Blears, H. Lab*	16,655	39.9
Owen, N. Lib Dem	10,930	26.2
Sephton, M. Con	8,497	20.4
Wingfield, T. BNP	2,632	6.3
O'Dwyer, D. UKIP	1,084	2.6
Henry, D. TUSC	730	1.8
Morris, S. Eng Dem	621	1.5
Carvath, R. Ind	384	0.9
Lab majority	5,725	13.73
Electorate	75,483	
Turnout	41,702	55.25

Lab hold (notional 9.4% from Lab to Lib Dem)

SALISBURY
(Boundary changes)

		%
Glen, J. Con	23,859	49.2
Radford, N. Lib Dem	17,893	36.9
Gann, T. Lab	3,690	7.6
Howard, F. UKIP	1,392	2.9
Witheridge, S. BNP	765	1.6
Startin, N. Green	506	1.1
Arthur, K. Ind	257	0.5
Holme, J. Ind	119	0.3
Con majority	5,966	12.29
Electorate	67,431	
Turnout	48,524	71.96

Con hold (notional 3.6% from Con to Lib Dem)

SCARBOROUGH AND WHITBY
(No boundary changes)

		%	+/-%
Goodwill, R. Con*	21,108	42.8	1.8
David, A. Lab	12,978	26.3	-12.0
Exley-Moore, T. Lib Dem	11,093	22.5	6.5
James, M. UKIP	1,484	3.0	1.0
Scott, T. BNP	1,445	2.9	
Cluer, D. Green	734	1.5	-1.1
Popple, P. Ind	329	0.7	
Boddington, J. Green Soc	111	0.2	
Con majority	8,130	16.48	
Electorate	75,470		
Turnout	49,328	65.36	

Con hold (6.9% from Lab to Con)

SCUNTHORPE
(Boundary changes)

		%
Dakin, N. Lab	14,640	39.5
Johnson, C. Con	12,091	32.6
Poole, N. Lib Dem	6,774	18.3
Collins, J. UKIP	1,686	4.5
Ward, D. BNP	1,447	3.9
Hurst, N. Green	396	1.1
Lab majority	2,549	6.88
Electorate	63,089	
Turnout	37,076	58.77

Lab hold (notional 9.2% from Lab to Con)

SEDGEFIELD
(Boundary changes)

		%
Wilson, P. Lab*	18,141	45.0
Mahapatra, N. Con	9,445	23.4
Thompson, A. Lib Dem	8,033	19.9
Walker, M. BNP	2,075	5.2
Gregory, B. UKIP	1,479	3.7
Gittins, P. Ind	1,049	2.6
Lab majority	8,696	21.58
Electorate	64,728	
Turnout	40,298	62.26

Lab hold (notional 11.6% from Lab to Con)

*Member of last Parliament

SEFTON CENTRAL
(New constituency)

		%
Esterson, B. Lab	20,307	41.8
Jones, D. Con	16,445	33.8
Clein, R. Lib Dem	9,656	19.9
Harper, P. UKIP	2,055	4.2
Lab majority	3,862	7.94
Electorate	67,511	
Turnout	48,639	72.05

Lab hold (notional 2% from Lab to Con)

SELBY AND AINSTY
(New constituency)

		%
Adams, N. Con	25,562	49.4
Marshall, J. Lab	13,297	25.7
Holvey, T. Lib Dem	9,180	17.7
Haley, D. UKIP	1,635	3.2
Lorriman, D. BNP	1,377	2.7
Glynn, G. Eng Dem	677	1.3
Con majority	12,265	23.68
Electorate	72,804	
Turnout	51,803	71.15

Con hold (notional 9.7% from Lab to Con)

SEVENOAKS
(Boundary changes)

		%
Fallon, M. Con*	28,076	56.7
Bullion, A. Lib Dem	10,561	21.3
Siddorn, G. Lab	6,541	13.2
Heath, C. UKIP	1,782	3.6
Golding, P. BNP	1,384	2.8
Uncles, L. Eng Dem	806	1.6
Ellis, M. Ind	258	0.5
Con majority	17,515	35.39
Electorate	69,591	
Turnout	49,493	71.12

Con hold (notional 3.1% from Lib Dem to Con)

SHEFFIELD CENTRAL
(Boundary changes)

		%
Blomfield, P. Lab	17,138	41.2
Scriven, P. Lib Dem	16,973	40.8
Lee, A. Con	4,206	10.1
Creasy, J. Green	1,556	3.7
Smith, T. BNP	903	2.2
Shaw, J. UKIP	652	1.6
Rodgers, R. Ind	40	0.1
Lab majority	165	0.4
Electorate	67,554	
Turnout	41,609	61.59

Lab hold (notional 7.4% from Lab to Lib Dem)

SHEFFIELD HALLAM
(Boundary changes)

		%
Clegg, N. Lib Dem*	27,324	53.3
Bates, N. Con	12,040	23.5
Scott, J. Lab	8,228	16.1
James, N. UKIP	1,195	2.3
Barnard, S. Green	919	1.8
Wildgoose, D. Eng Dem	586	1.1
Fitzpatrick, M. Ind	429	0.8
Green, R. Christian	250	0.5
Adshead, M. Loony	164	0.3
Lib Dem majority	15,284	29.81
Electorate	68,798	
Turnout	51,263	74.51

Lib Dem hold (notional 6.8% from Con to Lib Dem)

SHEFFIELD HEELEY
(Boundary changes)   %

Munn, M. Lab/Co-op*	17,409	42.5
Clement-Jones, S. Lib Dem	11,602	28.3
Crampton, A. Con	7,081	17.3
Beatson, J. BNP	2,260	5.5
Arnott, C. UKIP	1,530	3.7
Roberts, G. Green	989	2.4
Lab/Co-op majority	5,807	14.17
Electorate	65,571	
Turnout	40,980	62.5

Lab/Co-op hold (notional 9.3% from Lab/Co-op to Lib Dem)

SHEFFIELD SOUTH EAST
(New constituency)   %

Betts, C. Lab*	20,169	48.5
Smith, G. Lib Dem	9,664	23.3
Bonson, N. Con	7,202	17.3
Hartigan, C. BNP	2,345	5.7
Arnott, J. UKIP	1,889	4.5
Andrew, S. Comm GB	139	0.3
Lab majority	10,505	25.28
Electorate	67,068	
Turnout	41,547	61.95

Lab hold (notional 9% from Lab to Lib Dem)

SHEFFIELD, BRIGHTSIDE AND HILLSBOROUGH
(New constituency)   %

Blunkett, D. Lab*	21,400	54.8
Harston, J. Lib Dem	7,768	19.9
Sharp, J. Con	4,468	11.4
Sheldon, J. BNP	3,026	7.8
Sullivan, P. UKIP	1,596	4.1
Bowler, M. TUSC	656	1.7
Lab majority	13,632	34.89
Electorate	67,740	
Turnout	39,069	57.67

Lab hold (notional 10.8% from Lab to Lib Dem)

SHERWOOD
(Boundary changes)   %

Spencer, M. Con	19,211	39.2
Oldknow, E. Lab	18,997	38.8
Moore, K. Lib Dem	7,283	14.9
North, J. BNP	1,754	3.6
Parker, M. UKIP	1,490	3.0
Swan, R. Ind	219	0.5
Con majority	214	0.44
Electorate	71,443	
Turnout	49,021	68.62

Con gain (notional 8.2% from Lab to Con)

SHIPLEY
(Boundary changes)   %

Davies, P. Con*	24,002	48.4
Hinchcliffe, S. Lab	14,058	28.4
Harris, J. Lib Dem	9,890	19.9
Warnes, K. Green	1,477	3.0
Con majority	9,944	20.05
Electorate	67,689	
Turnout	49,600	73.28

Con hold (notional 9.5% from Lab to Con)

SHREWSBURY AND ATCHAM
(No boundary changes)   %   +/-%

Kawczynski, D. Con*	23,313	43.9	6.3
West, C. Lib Dem	15,369	28.9	6.2
Tandy, J. Lab/Co-op	10,915	20.6	-13.4
Lewis, P. UKIP	1,627	3.1	0.4

Whittall, J. BNP	1,168	2.2	
Whittaker, A. Green	565	1.1	-1.2
Gollings, J. Impact	88	0.2	
Con majority	7,944	14.96	
Electorate	75,446		
Turnout	53,118	70.41	

Con hold (0.1% from Lib Dem to Con)

NORTH SHROPSHIRE
(No boundary changes)   %   +/-%

Paterson, O. Con*	26,692	51.4	2.1
Croll, I. Lib Dem	10,864	20.9	1.3
McLaughlan, I. Lab	9,406	18.1	-7.7
List, S. UKIP	2,432	4.7	-0.1
Reddall, P. BNP	1,667	3.2	
Boulding, S. Green	808	1.6	
Con majority	15,828	30.46	
Electorate	78,930		
Turnout	51,960	65.83	

Con hold (0.4% from Lib Dem to Con)

SITTINGBOURNE AND SHEPPEY
(Boundary changes)   %

Henderson, G. Con	24,313	50.0
Harrison, A. Lab	11,930	24.5
Nevols, K. Lib Dem	7,934	16.3
Davison, I. UKIP	2,610	5.4
Tames, L. BNP	1,305	2.7
Young, M. Loony	319	0.7
Cassidy, D. Ind	158	0.3
Con majority	12,383	25.44
Electorate	75,781	
Turnout	48,671	64.23

Con hold (notional 12.7% from Lab to Con)

SKIPTON AND RIPON
(Boundary changes)   %

Smith, J. Con	27,685	50.5
Flynn, H. Lib Dem	17,735	32.3
Hazelgrove, C. Lab	5,498	10.0
Mills, R. UKIP	1,909	3.5
Allen, B. BNP	1,403	2.6
Bell, R. Ind	315	0.6
Gilligan, D. Youth	95	0.2
Leakey, R. Currency	84	0.2
Con majority	9,950	18.13
Electorate	77,360	
Turnout	54,875	70.93

Con hold (notional 2.7% from Con to Lib Dem)

SLEAFORD AND NORTH HYKEHAM
(Boundary changes)   %

Phillips, S. Con	30,719	51.5
Harding-Price, D. Lib Dem	10,814	18.1
Normington, J. Lab	10,051	16.9
Overton, M. Ind	3,806	6.4
Doughty, R. UKIP	2,163	3.6
Clayton, M. BNP	1,977	3.3
Con majority	19,905	33.39
Electorate	85,450	
Turnout	59,609	69.76

Con hold (notional 0.4% from Lib Dem to Con)

SLOUGH
(Boundary changes)   %

Mactaggart, F. Lab*	21,884	45.6
Coad, D. Con	16,361	34.1
Tucker, C. Lib Dem	6,943	14.5
Mason-Apps, P. UKIP	1,517	3.2
Kennet, M. Green	542	1.1
Chaudhary, S. Christian	495	1.0
Lab majority	5,523	11.52
Electorate	86,328	
Turnout	47,955	55.55

Lab hold (notional 4.2% from Lab to Con)

SOLIHULL
(*Boundary changes*)

		%
Burt, L. Lib Dem*	23,635	42.8
Throup, M. Con	23,460	42.5
Merrill, S. Lab	4,891	8.9
Terry, A. BNP	1,624	3.0
Ison, J. UKIP	1,200	2.2
Watts, N. SMRA	319	0.6
Lib Dem majority	175	0.32
Electorate	76,288	
Turnout	55,230	72.4

Lib Dem gain (notional 0.3% from Con to Lib Dem)

NORTH SOMERSET
(*New constituency*)

		%
Fox, L. Con*	28,549	49.2
Mathew, B. Lib Dem	20,687	35.6
Parry-Hearn, S. Lab	6,448	11.1
Taylor, S. UKIP	2,257	3.9
Con majority	7,862	13.54
Electorate	77,306	
Turnout	58,051	75.09

Con hold (notional 1% from Lib Dem to Con)

NORTH EAST SOMERSET
(*New constituency*)

		%
Rees-Mogg, J. Con	21,130	41.2
Norris, D. Lab*	16,216	31.6
Coleshill, G. Lib Dem	11,433	22.3
Sandell, P. UKIP	1,754	3.4
Jay, M. Green	670	1.3
Con majority	4,914	9.58
Electorate	68,933	
Turnout	51,279	74.39

Con hold (notional 4.6% from Lab to Con)

SOMERTON AND FROME
(*Boundary changes*)

		%
Heath, D. Lib Dem*	28,793	47.5
Rees-Mogg, A. Con	26,976	44.5
Oakensen, D. Lab	2,675	4.4
Harding, B. UKIP	1,932	3.2
Warry, T. Ind	236	0.4
Lib Dem majority	1,817	2.99
Electorate	81,548	
Turnout	60,690	74.42

Lib Dem hold (notional 0.9% from Con to Lib Dem)

SOUTH ANTRIM – see under Antrim

SOUTH BASILDON AND EAST THURROCK – see under Basildon

SOUTH CAMBRIDGESHIRE – see under Cambridgeshire

SOUTH DERBYSHIRE – see under Derbyshire

SOUTH DORSET – see under Dorset

SOUTH DOWN – see under Down

SOUTH EAST CAMBRIDGESHIRE – see under Cambridgeshire

SOUTH EAST CORNWALL – see under Cornwall

SOUTH HOLLAND AND THE DEEPINGS
(*Boundary changes*)

		%
Hayes, J. Con*	29,639	59.0
Conroy, J. Lib Dem	7,759	15.4
Gould, G. Lab	7,024	14.0
Fairman, R. UKIP	3,246	6.5
Harban, R. BNP	1,796	3.6
Baxter, A. Green	724	1.5
Con majority	21,880	43.55
Electorate	76,243	
Turnout	50,240	65.89

Con hold (notional 0.3% from Con to Lib Dem)

SOUTH LEICESTERSHIRE – see under Leicestershire

SOUTH NORFOLK – see under Norfolk

SOUTH NORTHAMPTONSHIRE – see under Northamptonshire

SOUTH RIBBLE – see under Ribble

SOUTH SHIELDS
(*Boundary changes*)

		%
Miliband, D. Lab*	18,995	51.9
Allen, K. Con	7,886	21.5
Psallidas, S. Lib Dem	5,189	14.2
Watson, D. BNP	2,382	6.5
Ford, S. Green	762	2.1
Kaikavoosi, S. Ind	729	2.0
Thompson, V. Ind	316	0.9
Navabi, S. Ind	168	0.5
Nettleship, R. Anti-War	91	0.3
Lab majority	11,109	30.33
Electorate	63,294	
Turnout	36,629	57.87

Lab hold (notional 6.4% from Lab to Con)

SOUTH STAFFORDSHIRE – see under Staffordshire

SOUTH SUFFOLK – see under Suffolk

SOUTH SWINDON – see under Swindon

SOUTH THANET – see under Thanet

SOUTH WEST BEDFORDSHIRE – see under Bedfordshire

SOUTH WEST DEVON – see under Devon

SOUTH WEST HERTFORDSHIRE – see under Hertfordshire

SOUTH WEST NORFOLK – see under Norfolk

SOUTH WEST SURREY – see under Surrey

SOUTH WEST WILTSHIRE – see under Wiltshire

SOUTHAMPTON ITCHEN
(*Boundary changes*)

		%
Denham, J. Lab*	16,326	36.7
Smith, R. Con	16,134	36.3
Goodall, D. Lib Dem	9,256	20.8

*Member of last Parliament

Kebbell, A. UKIP	1,928	4.3
Spottiswoode, J. Green	600	1.4
Cutter, T. TUSC	168	0.4
Lab majority	192	0.43
Electorate	74,532	
Turnout	44,516	59.73

Lab hold (notional 10.3% from Lab to Con)

SOUTHAMPTON TEST

(Boundary changes)		%
Whitehead, A. Lab*	17,001	38.4
Moulton, J. Con	14,588	32.9
Callaghan, D. Lib Dem	9,865	22.3
Hingston, P. UKIP	1,726	3.9
Bluemel, C. Green	881	2.0
Sanderson, C. Ind	126	0.3
Lab majority	2,413	5.45
Electorate	71,931	
Turnout	44,301	61.59

Lab hold (notional 6.9% from Lab to Con)

SOUTHEND WEST

(Boundary changes)		%
Amess, D. Con*	20,086	46.0
Welch, P. Lib Dem	12,816	29.4
Flynn, T. Lab	5,850	13.4
Cockrill, G. UKIP	1,714	3.9
Gladwin, T. BNP	1,333	3.1
Bolton, B. Green	644	1.5
Velmurugan, D. Ind	617	1.4
Phillips, T. Eng Dem	546	1.3
Con majority	7,270	16.65
Electorate	66,918	
Turnout	43,668	65.26

Con hold (notional 2.8% from Con to Lib Dem)

SOUTHPORT

(No boundary changes)		%	+/-%
Pugh, J. Lib Dem*	21,707	49.4	3.2
Porter, B. Con	15,683	35.7	-1.3
Conalty, J. Lab	4,116	9.4	-3.4
Durrance, T. UKIP	2,251	5.1	3.3
Lib Dem majority	6,024	13.71	
Electorate	67,200		
Turnout	43,924	65.36	

Lib Dem hold (2.2% from Con to Lib Dem)

SPELTHORNE

(No boundary changes)		%	+/-%
Kwarteng, K. Con	22,261	47.0	-3.3
Chapman, M. Lib Dem	12,242	25.8	8.8
Tyler-Moore, A. Lab	7,789	16.4	-10.8
Browne, C. UKIP	4,009	8.5	3.9
Swinglehurst, I. Ind	314	0.7	
Littlewood, R. Best	244	0.5	
Couchman, P. TUSC	176	0.4	
Gore, J. CIP	167	0.4	
Leon-Smith, G. Ind	102	0.2	
Con majority	10,019	21.14	
Electorate	70,749		
Turnout	47,396	66.99	

Con hold (6.1% from Con to Lib Dem)

ST ALBANS

(Boundary changes)		%
Main, A. Con*	21,533	40.6
Walkington, S. Lib Dem	19,228	36.3
Mills, R. Lab	9,288	17.5

Stocker, J. UKIP	2,028	3.8
Easton, J. Green	758	1.4
Con majority	2,305	4.35
Electorate	70,058	
Turnout	52,990	75.64

Con hold (notional 3.7% from Con to Lib Dem)

ST AUSTELL AND NEWQUAY

(New constituency)		%
Gilbert, S. Lib Dem	20,189	42.7
Righton, C. Con	18,877	39.9
Jameson, L. Lab	3,386	7.2
Cole, D. Mebyon Kernow	2,007	4.3
Medway, C. UKIP	1,757	3.7
Fitton, J. BNP	1,022	2.2
Lib Dem majority	1,312	2.77
Electorate	75,232	
Turnout	47,301	62.87

Lib Dem hold (notional 4.8% from Lib Dem to Con)

ST HELENS NORTH

(Boundary changes)		%
Watts, D. Lab*	23,041	51.5
Greenall, P. Con	9,940	22.2
Beirne, J. Lib Dem	8,992	20.1
Robinson, G. UKIP	2,100	4.7
Whatham, S. SLP	483	1.1
Lab majority	13,101	29.26
Electorate	74,985	
Turnout	44,776	59.71

Lab hold (notional 4.6% from Lab to Con)

ST HELENS SOUTH AND WHISTON

(New constituency)		%
Woodward, S. Lab*	24,364	52.6
Spencer, B. Lib Dem	10,242	22.1
Allen, V. Con	8,209	17.7
Winstanley, J. BNP	2,040	4.4
Sumner, J. UKIP	1,226	2.6
Lab majority	14,122	30.5
Electorate	77,975	
Turnout	46,299	59.38

Lab hold (notional 1.9% from Lib Dem to Lab)

ST IVES

(Boundary changes)		%
George, A. Lib Dem*	19,619	42.7
Thomas, D. Con	17,900	38.9
Latimer, P. Lab	3,751	8.2
Faulkner, M. UKIP	2,560	5.6
Andrewes, T. Green	1,308	2.9
Rogers, J. Corn Dem	396	0.9
Reed, S. Mebyon Kernow	387	0.9
Lib Dem majority	1,719	3.74
Electorate	64,574	
Turnout	45,991	71.22

Lib Dem hold (notional 10.4% from Lib Dem to Con)

STAFFORD

(Boundary changes)		%
Lefroy, J. Con	22,047	43.8
Kidney, D. Lab*	16,587	33.0
Stamp, B. Lib Dem	8,211	16.3
Goode, R. UKIP	1,727	3.4
Hynd, R. BNP	1,103	2.2
Shone, M. Green	564	1.1
Con majority	5,460	10.85
Electorate	70,667	
Turnout	50,323	71.21

Con gain (notional 7.4% from Lab to Con)

STAFFORDSHIRE MOORLANDS
(Boundary changes)

		%
Bradley, K. Con	19,793	45.1
Atkins, C. Lab*	13,104	29.9
Jebb, H. Lib Dem	7,338	16.7
Povey, S. UKIP	3,580	8.2
Con majority	6,689	15.24
Electorate	62,071	
Turnout	43,886	70.7

Con hold (notional 5.7% from Lab to Con)

SOUTH STAFFORDSHIRE
(Boundary changes)

		%
Williamson, G. Con	26,834	53.1
McElduff, K. Lab	10,244	20.3
Fellows, S. Lib Dem	8,427	16.7
Nattrass, M. UKIP	2,753	5.5
Bradnock, D. BNP	1,928	3.8
Morris, A. Ind	254	0.5
Con majority	16,590	32.85
Electorate	73,849	
Turnout	50,496	68.38

Con hold (notional 1.1% from Lab to Con)

STALYBRIDGE AND HYDE
(Boundary changes)

		%
Reynolds, J. Lab/Co-op	16,189	39.4
Adlard, R. Con	13,445	32.8
Potter, J. Lib Dem	6,965	17.0
Jones, A. BNP	2,259	5.5
Cooke, J. UKIP	1,342	3.3
Bergan, R. Green	679	1.7
Lab/Co-op majority	2,744	6.68
Electorate	69,608	
Turnout	41,049	58.97

Lab/Co-op hold (notional 8.5% from Lab/Co-op to Con)

STEVENAGE
(Boundary changes)

		%
McPartland, S. Con	18,491	41.3
Taylor, S. Lab	14,913	33.3
Davies, J. Lib Dem	7,432	16.6
Mason, M. UKIP	2,004	4.5
Green, M. BNP	1,007	2.3
Vickers, C. Eng Dem	366	0.8
Phillips, S. NCDMV	327	0.7
Cox, D. Ind	80	0.2
Ralph, A. YRDPL	31	0.1
Con majority	3,578	8
Electorate	68,937	
Turnout	44,752	64.92

Con gain (notional 8% from Lab to Con)

STIRLING
(No boundary changes)

		%	+/-%
McGuire, A. Lab*	19,558	41.7	5.7
Dalrymple, B. Con	11,254	24.0	-1.1
Lindsay, A. SNP	8,091	17.3	4.7
Reed, G. Lib Dem	6,797	14.5	-6.2
Ruskell, M. Green	746	1.6	-1.4
Henke, P. UKIP	395	0.8	0.4
Lab majority	8,304	17.71	
Electorate	66,080		
Turnout	46,902	70.98	

Lab hold (3.4% from Con to Lab)

STOCKPORT
(Boundary changes)

		%
Coffey, A. Lab*	16,697	42.6
Holland, S. Con	9,913	25.3
Bodsworth, S. Lib Dem	9,778	24.9

*Member of last Parliament

Warner, D. BNP	1,201	3.1
Kelly, M. UKIP	862	2.2
Barber, P. Green	677	1.7
Lab majority	6,784	17.3
Electorate	63,536	
Turnout	39,217	61.72

Lab hold (notional 5.8% from Lab to Con)

STOCKTON NORTH
(Boundary changes)

		%
Cunningham, A. Lab	16,923	42.8
Galletley, I. Con	10,247	25.9
Latham, P. Lib Dem	6,342	16.1
Macpherson, J. BNP	1,724	4.4
Cook, F. Ind*	1,577	4.0
Parkin, G. UKIP	1,556	3.9
Saul, I. Eng Dem	1,129	2.9
Lab majority	6,676	16.89
Electorate	66,752	
Turnout	39,537	59.23

Lab hold (notional 8.4% from Lab to Con)

STOCKTON SOUTH
(Boundary changes)

		%
Wharton, J. Con	19,577	38.9
Taylor, D. Lab*	19,245	38.2
Bell, J. Lib Dem	7,600	15.1
Sinclair, N. BNP	1,553	3.1
Braney, P. UKIP	1,471	2.9
Hossack, Y. Ind	536	1.1
Strike, T. Christian	302	0.6
Con majority	332	0.66
Electorate	73,840	
Turnout	50,332	68.16

Con gain (notional 7.1% from Lab to Con)

STOKE-ON-TRENT CENTRAL
(Boundary changes)

		%
Hunt, T. Lab	12,604	38.7
Redfern, J. Lib Dem	7,039	21.6
Bhatti, N. Con	6,833	21.0
Darby, S. BNP	2,502	7.7
Lovatt, C. UKIP	1,402	4.3
Breeze, P. Ind	959	3.0
Elsby, G. Ind	399	1.2
Ward, B. Ind	303	0.9
Walker, A. Ind	295	0.9
Wright, M. TUSC	133	0.4
Lab majority	5,565	17.09
Electorate	61,003	
Turnout	32,567	53.39

Lab hold (notional 8.4% from Lab to Lib Dem)

STOKE-ON-TRENT NORTH
(Boundary changes)

		%
Walley, J. Lab*	17,815	44.2
Large, A. Con	9,580	23.8
Fisher, J. Lib Dem	7,120	17.7
Baddeley, M. BNP	3,196	7.9
Locke, G. UKIP	2,485	6.2
Lab majority	8,235	20.43
Electorate	72,054	
Turnout	40,304	55.94

Lab hold (notional 8.8% from Lab to Con)

STOKE-ON-TRENT SOUTH
(Boundary changes)

		%
Flello, R. Lab*	15,446	38.7
Rushton, J. Con	11,316	28.3
Ali, Z. Lib Dem	6,323	15.8

Coleman, M. BNP	3,762	9.4
Barlow, M. UKIP	1,363	3.4
Follows, T. SIG	1,208	3.0
Breeze, M. Ind	434	1.1
Lab majority	4,130	10.33
Electorate	68,032	
Turnout	39,962	58.74

Lab hold (notional 6.2% from Lab to Con)

STONE

(Boundary changes)		%
Cash, W. Con*	23,890	50.5
Tinker, C. Lib Dem	10,598	22.4
Lewis, J. Lab	9,770	20.7
Illsley, A. UKIP	2,481	5.3
Hoppe, D. Green	490	1.0
Con majority	13,292	28.1
Electorate	67,062	
Turnout	47,309	70.55

Con hold (notional 0.8% from Con to Lib Dem)

STOURBRIDGE

(Boundary changes)		%
James, M. Con	20,153	42.6
Waltho, L. Lab*	14,989	31.7
Bramall, C. Lib Dem	7,733	16.4
Westrop, M. UKIP	2,103	4.5
Weale, R. BNP	1,696	3.6
Duckworth, W. Green	394	0.8
Nicholas, A. Ind	166	0.4
Con majority	5,164	10.91
Electorate	70,122	
Turnout	47,317	67.48

Con gain (notional 6.9% from Lab to Con)

STRANGFORD

(Boundary changes)		%
Shannon, J. DUP	14,926	45.8
Nesbitt, M. UCUNF	9,050	27.8
Girvan, D. All	2,828	8.7
Hanna, C. SDLP	2,164	6.6
Williams, T. TUV	1,814	5.6
Coogan, M. Sinn Féin	1,161	3.6
Haig, B. Green	562	1.7
DUP majority	5,876	18.02
Electorate	60,539	
Turnout	32,600	53.85

DUP hold (notional 7.7% from DUP to UCUNF)

STRATFORD-ON-AVON

(Boundary changes)		%
Zahawi, N. Con	26,052	51.5
Turner, M. Lib Dem	14,706	29.1
Johnston, R. Lab	4,809	9.5
Parsons, B. UKIP	1,846	3.6
Jones, G. BNP	1,097	2.2
Basnett, N. Ind	1,032	2.0
Varga, K. Green	527	1.1
Bishop, F. Eng Dem	473	0.9
Con majority	11,346	22.41
Electorate	69,517	
Turnout	50,637	72.84

Con hold (notional 0.8% from Con to Lib Dem)

STREATHAM

(Boundary changes)		%
Umunna, C. Lab	20,037	42.6
Nicholson, C. Lib Dem	16,778	35.7
Bhansali, R. Con	8,578	18.2
Findlay, R. Green	861	1.8

Macharia, G. Christian	237	0.5
Polenceus, J. Eng Dem	229	0.5
Lepper, P. WRP	117	0.3
Lab majority	3,259	6.93
Electorate	74,531	
Turnout	47,059	63.14

Lab hold (notional 5.3% from Lab to Lib Dem)

STRETFORD AND URMSTON

(Boundary changes)		%
Green, K. Lab	21,821	48.4
Williams, A. Con	12,886	28.6
Cooke, S. Lib Dem	7,601	16.9
Owen, D. UKIP	1,508	3.4
Westbrook, M. Green	916	2.0
Jacob, S. Christian	178	0.4
Lab majority	8,935	19.82
Electorate	70,091	
Turnout	45,084	64.32

Lab hold (notional 0.7% from Lab to Con)

STROUD

(Boundary changes)		%
Carmichael, N. Con	23,679	40.8
Drew, D. Lab/Co-op*	22,380	38.5
Andrewartha, D. Lib Dem	8,955	15.4
Whiteside, M. Green	1,542	2.7
Parker, S. UKIP	1,301	2.2
Lomas, A. Ind	116	0.2
Con majority	1,299	2.24
Electorate	78,305	
Turnout	58,087	74.18

Con gain (notional 2% from Lab/Co-op to Con)

CENTRAL SUFFOLK AND NORTH IPSWICH

(Boundary changes)		%
Poulter, D. Con	27,125	50.7
Aalders-Dunthorne, A. Lib Dem	13,339	24.9
Joshi, B. Lab	8,636	16.1
Philpot, R. UKIP	2,361	4.4
Stringer, A. Green	1,452	2.7
Trevitt, M. Ind	389	0.7
Vass, R. NP	118	0.2
Con majority	13,786	25.76
Electorate	75,786	
Turnout	53,514	70.61

Con hold (notional 0.7% from Lib Dem to Con)

SUFFOLK COASTAL

(Boundary changes)		%
Coffey, T. Con	25,475	46.3
Cooper, D. Lib Dem	16,347	29.7
Leeder, A. Lab	8,812	16.0
Bush, S. UKIP	3,156	5.7
Fulcher, R. Green	1,103	2.0
Con majority	9,128	16.57
Electorate	77,072	
Turnout	55,081	71.47

Con hold (notional 2.9% from Con to Lib Dem)

SOUTH SUFFOLK

(Boundary changes)		%
Yeo, T. Con*	24,550	47.7
Bennett, N. Lib Dem	15,861	30.8
Bishton, E. Lab	7,368	14.3
Campbell Bannerman, D. UKIP	3,637	7.1
Con majority	8,689	16.87
Electorate	72,498	
Turnout	51,503	71.04

Con hold (notional 1.6% from Lib Dem to Con)

WEST SUFFOLK
(Boundary changes)

		%
Hancock, M. Con	24,312	50.5
Brooks-Gordon, B. Lib Dem	11,262	23.4
Ahmed, O. Lab	7,089	14.7
Smith, I. UKIP	3,085	6.4
Johns, R. BNP	1,428	3.0
Appleby, A. Ind	540	1.1
Young, C. CPA	373	0.8
Con majority	13,050	27.09
Electorate	74,374	
Turnout	48,170	64.77

Con hold (notional 2.3% from Con to Lib Dem)

SUNDERLAND CENTRAL
(New constituency)

		%
Elliott, J. Lab	19,495	45.7
Martin, L. Con	12,770	29.9
Dixon, P. Lib Dem	7,191	16.9
McCaffrey, J. BNP	1,913	4.5
Featonby-Warren, P. UKIP	1,094	2.6
Lab majority	6,725	15.76
Electorate	74,485	
Turnout	42,682	57.3

Lab hold (notional 4.9% from Lab to Con)

EAST SURREY
(No boundary changes)

		%	+/-%
Gyimah, S. Con	31,007	56.6	0.8
Lee, D. Lib Dem	14,133	25.8	2.1
Rodda, M. Lab	4,925	9.0	-5.7
Windsor, H. UKIP	3,770	6.9	2.5
Hogbin, M. Loony	422	0.8	
Pratt, S. Ind	383	0.7	
Con majority	16,874	30.8	
Electorate	76,855		
Turnout	54,780	71.28	

Con hold (0.7% from Con to Lib Dem)

SURREY HEATH
(No boundary changes)

		%	+/-%
Gove, M. Con*	31,326	57.5	6.3
Hilliar, A. Lib Dem	14,037	25.8	-2.9
Willey, M. Lab	5,552	10.2	-6.4
Stroud, M. UKIP	3,432	6.3	
Con majority	17,289	31.76	
Electorate	78,107		
Turnout	54,432	69.69	

Con hold (4.6% from Lib Dem to Con)

SOUTH WEST SURREY
(Boundary changes)

		%
Hunt, J. Con*	33,605	58.6
Simpson, M. Lib Dem	17,287	30.1
Mollet, R. Lab	3,419	6.0
Meekins, R. UKIP	1,486	2.6
Allan, C. Green	690	1.2
Hamilton, H. BNP	644	1.1
Leighton, L. Pirate	94	0.2
Price, A. Ind	34	0.1
Con majority	16,318	28.45
Electorate	76,501	
Turnout	57,357	74.98

Con hold (notional 8.6% from Lib Dem to Con)

MID SUSSEX
(Boundary changes)

		%
Soames, N. Con*	28,329	50.6
Tierney, S. Lib Dem	20,927	37.4

*Member of last Parliament

Boot, D. Lab	3,689	6.6
Montgomery, M. UKIP	1,423	2.5
Brown, P. Green	645	1.2
Minihane, S. BNP	583	1.1
Thunderclap, B. Loony	259	0.5
Con majority	7,402	13.23
Electorate	77,199	
Turnout	55,955	72.48

Con hold (notional 0.3% from Lib Dem to Con)

SUTTON AND CHEAM
(Boundary changes)

		%
Burstow, P. Lib Dem*	22,156	45.5
Stroud, P. Con	20,548	42.2
Allen, K. Lab	3,376	6.9
Clarke, J. BNP	1,014	2.1
Pickles, D. UKIP	950	2.0
Hickson, P. Green	246	0.5
Dodds, J. Eng Dem	106	0.2
Connolly, M. CPA	52	0.1
Cullip, M. Libertarian	41	0.1
Hammond, B. Ind Fed UK	19	0.0
Lib Dem majority	1,608	3.3
Electorate	66,658	
Turnout	48,697	73.05

Lib Dem hold (notional 1.5% from Lib Dem to Con)

SUTTON COLDFIELD
(Boundary changes)

		%
Mitchell, A. Con*	27,303	53.9
Pocock, R. Lab	10,298	20.3
Brighton, R. Lib Dem	9,117	18.0
Grierson, M. BNP	1,749	3.5
Siddall-Jones, E. UKIP	1,587	3.1
Rooney, J. Green	535	1.1
Con majority	17,005	33.55
Electorate	74,489	
Turnout	50,685	68.04

Con hold (notional 3.4% from Lab to Con)

SWANSEA EAST
(No boundary changes)

		%	+/-%
James, S. Lab*	16,819	51.4	-5.2
Speht, R. Lib Dem	5,981	18.3	-1.8
Holliday, C. Con	4,823	14.7	4.7
Jones, D. PlC	2,181	6.7	-0.2
Bennett, C. SOTBTH	1,715	5.2	
Rogers, D. UKIP	839	2.6	0.4
Young, T. Green	318	1.0	-0.6
Lab majority	10,838	33.1	
Electorate	59,823		
Turnout	32,741	54.73	

Lab hold (1.7% from Lab to Lib Dem)

SWANSEA WEST
(No boundary changes)

		%	+/-%
Davies, G. Lab/Co-op	12,335	34.6	-7.1
May, P. Lib Dem	11,831	33.2	4.3
Kinzett, R. Con	7,407	20.8	4.8
Roberts, H. PlC	1,437	4.0	-2.5
Bateman, A. SOTBTH	910	2.5	
Jenkins, T. UKIP	716	2.0	0.2
Ross, K. Green	404	1.1	-1.1
McCloy, I. Ind	374	1.1	
Williams, R. TUSC	179	0.5	
Lab/Co-op majority	504	1.41	
Electorate	61,334		
Turnout	35,654	58.13	

Lab/Co-op gain (5.7% from Lab/Co-op to Lib Dem)

NORTH SWINDON
(*Boundary changes*)

		%
Tomlinson, J. Con	22,408	44.4
Agarwal, V. Lab	15,348	30.4
Lock, J. Lib Dem	8,668	17.2
Halden, S. UKIP	1,842	3.7
Bates, R. BNP	1,542	3.1
Hughes, B. Green	487	1.0

Con majority	7,060	13.99
Electorate	78,384	
Turnout	50,465	64.38

Con gain (notional 10.1% from Lab to Con)

SOUTH SWINDON
(*Boundary changes*)

		%
Buckland, R. Con	19,687	41.5
Snelgrove, A. Lab*	16,143	34.0
Hooton, D. Lib Dem	8,305	17.5
Tingey, R. UKIP	2,029	4.3
Miles, J. Green	619	1.3
Kirk, A. Christian	176	0.4
Evans, K. Ind	160	0.3

Con majority	3,544	7.47
Electorate	72,619	
Turnout	47,425	65.31

Con gain (notional 5.5% from Lab to Con)

TAMWORTH
(*No boundary changes*)

		%	+/-%
Pincher, C. Con	21,238	45.7	8.8
Jenkins, B. Lab*	15,148	32.6	-10.2
Pinkett, J. Lib Dem	7,516	16.2	2.1
Smith, P. UKIP	2,253	4.8	2.1
Detheridge, C. Christian	235	0.5	

Con majority	6,090	13.1
Electorate	71,962	
Turnout	46,482	64.59

Con gain (9.5% from Lab to Con)

TATTON
(*Boundary changes*)

		%
Osborne, G. Con*	24,687	54.5
Lomax, D. Lib Dem	10,200	22.5
Jackson, R. Lab	7,803	17.2
Flannery, S. Ind	2,243	5.0
Gibson, M. True English	298	0.7

Con majority	14,487	31.97
Electorate	65,689	
Turnout	45,317	68.99

Con hold (notional 1.1% from Lib Dem to Con)

TAUNTON DEANE
(*New constituency*)

		%
Browne, J. Lib Dem*	28,531	49.0
Formosa, M. Con	24,538	42.1
Jevon, M. Lab	2,967	5.1
McIntyre, T. UKIP	2,114	3.6

Lib Dem majority	3,993	6.86
Electorate	82,507	
Turnout	58,234	70.58

Lib Dem hold (notional 1.8% from Con to Lib Dem)

TELFORD
(*Boundary changes*)

		%
Wright, D. Lab*	15,974	38.6
Biggins, T. Con	14,996	36.3
Bennion, P. Lib Dem	6,399	15.5

Allen, D. UKIP	2,428	5.9
Spencer, P. BNP	1,513	3.7

Lab majority	978	2.36
Electorate	65,061	
Turnout	41,379	63.6

Lab hold (notional 6.3% from Lab to Con)

TEWKESBURY
(*Boundary changes*)

		%
Robertson, L. Con*	25,472	47.1
Cameron, A. Lib Dem	19,162	35.5
Emmerson, S. Lab	6,253	11.6
Jones, B. UKIP	2,230	4.1
Sidford, M. Green	525	1.0
Ridgeon, G. Loony	319	0.6

Con majority	6,310	11.67
Electorate	76,655	
Turnout	54,051	70.51

Con hold (notional 4.1% from Con to Lib Dem)

NORTH THANET
(*Boundary changes*)

		%
Gale, R. Con*	22,826	52.6
Britton, M. Lab	9,298	21.4
Murphy, L. Lib Dem	8,400	19.4
Parker, R. UKIP	2,819	6.5

Con majority	13,528	31.15
Electorate	68,602	
Turnout	43,426	63.3

Con hold (notional 7.9% from Lab to Con)

SOUTH THANET
(*Boundary changes*)

		%
Sandys, L. Con	22,043	47.9
Ladyman, S. Lab*	14,426	31.4
Bucklitsch, P. Lib Dem	6,935	15.1
Shonk, T. UKIP	2,529	5.5

Con majority	7,617	16.55
Electorate	70,045	
Turnout	46,023	65.7

Con hold (notional 7.4% from Lab to Con)

THE COTSWOLDS
(*Boundary changes*)

		%
Clifton-Brown, G. Con*	29,075	53.0
Collins, M. Lib Dem	16,211	29.5
Dempsey, M. Lab	5,886	10.7
Blake, A. UKIP	2,292	4.2
Lister, K. Green	940	1.7
Steel, A. Ind	428	0.8

Con majority	12,864	23.43
Electorate	76,729	
Turnout	54,903	71.55

Con hold (notional 5.7% from Lab to Con)

THE WREKIN – see under Wrekin

THIRSK AND MALTON
(*New constituency*)

		%
McIntosh, A. Con*	20,167	52.8
Keal, H. Lib Dem	8,886	23.3
Roberts, J. Lab	5,169	13.5
Horton, T. UKIP	2,502	6.5
Clark, J. Lib	1,418	3.7

Con majority	11,281	29.52
Electorate	76,231	
Turnout	38,215	50.13

Con hold (notional 1.8% from Con to Lib Dem)

THORNBURY AND YATE
(New constituency)

		%
Webb, S. Lib Dem*	25,032	51.8
Riddle, M. Con	17,916	37.1
Egan, R. Lab	3,385	7.0
Knight, J. UKIP	1,709	3.5
Beacham, T. Ind Fed UK	126	0.3
Clements, A. Ind	58	0.1
Lib Dem majority	7,116	14.73
Electorate	64,092	
Turnout	48,321	75.39

Lib Dem hold (notional 4.4% from Lib Dem to Con)

THURROCK
(Boundary changes)

		%
Doyle-Price, J. Con	16,869	36.7
Morris, C. Lab	16,777	36.5
Davis, C. Lib Dem	4,901	10.7
Colgate, E. BNP	3,618	7.9
Broad, C. UKIP	3,390	7.4
Araba, A. Christian	266	0.6
Con majority	92	0.2
Electorate	77,758	
Turnout	45,989	59.14

Con gain (notional 6.6% from Lab to Con)

TIVERTON AND HONITON
(Boundary changes)

		%
Parish, N. Con	27,614	50.2
Underwood, J. Lib Dem	18,294	33.3
Whitlock, V. Lab	4,907	8.9
Stanbury, D. UKIP	3,277	6.0
Connor, C. Green	802	1.5
Con majority	9,320	16.95
Electorate	76,808	
Turnout	54,976	71.58

Con hold (notional 4% from Lab to Con)

TONBRIDGE AND MALLING
(No boundary changes)

		%	+/-%
Stanley, J. Con*	29,723	57.8	5.1
Simpson, L. Lib Dem	11,545	22.5	3.0
Griffiths, D. Lab	6,476	12.6	-11.2
Waller, D. UKIP	1,911	3.7	
Dawe, S. Green	764	1.5	
Easter, M. NF	505	1.0	
Rogers, L. Eng Dem	390	0.8	
Con majority	18,178	35.37	
Electorate	71,790		
Turnout	51,389	71.58	

Con hold (1% from Lib Dem to Con)

TOOTING
(Boundary changes)

		%
Khan, S. Lab*	22,038	43.4
Clarke, M. Con	19,514	38.5
Butt, N. Lib Dem	7,509	14.8
McDonald, S. UKIP	624	1.2
Vickery, R. Green	609	1.2
John-Richards, S. Ind	190	0.4
Paul, S. Christian	171	0.3
Lab majority	2,524	4.97
Electorate	73,840	
Turnout	50,740	68.72

Lab hold (notional 3.6% from Lab to Con)

*Member of last Parliament

TORBAY
(Boundary changes)

		%
Sanders, A. Lib Dem*	23,126	47.0
Wood, M. Con	19,048	38.7
Pedrick-Friend, D. Lab	3,231	6.6
Parrott, J. UKIP	2,628	5.3
Conway, A. BNP	709	1.4
Moss, S. Green	468	1.0
Lib Dem majority	4,078	8.28
Electorate	76,155	
Turnout	49,246	64.67

Lib Dem hold (notional 1.1% from Con to Lib Dem)

TORFAEN
(No boundary changes)

		%	+/-%
Murphy, P. Lab*	16,847	44.7	-12.1
Burns, J. Con	7,541	20.0	4.3
Morgan, D. Lib Dem	6,264	16.6	0.9
ab Elis, R. PlC	2,005	5.3	-0.9
Noble, J. BNP	1,657	4.4	
Wildgust, F. Ind	1,419	3.8	
Dunn, G. UKIP	862	2.3	-0.9
Turner-Thomas, R. Ind	607	1.6	-0.5
Clarke, O. Green	438	1.2	
Lab majority	9,306	24.69	
Electorate	61,183		
Turnout	37,686	61.6	

Lab hold (8.2% from Lab to Con)

TORRIDGE AND WEST DEVON
(Boundary changes)

		%
Cox, G. Con*	25,230	45.2
Symons, A. Lib Dem	22,273	39.9
Julian, R. UKIP	3,021	5.4
Jones, D. Lab	2,917	5.2
Simmons, C. Green	1,050	1.9
Baker, N. BNP	766	1.4
Con majority	2,957	5.3
Electorate	77,360	
Turnout	55,804	72.14

Con hold (notional 0.03% from Con to Lib Dem)

TOTNES
(Boundary changes)

		%
Wollaston, S. Con	21,940	45.8
Brazil, J. Lib Dem	17,013	35.5
Whitty, C. Lab	3,538	7.4
Beer, J. UKIP	2,890	6.0
Somerville, L. Green	1,181	2.5
Turner, M. BNP	624	1.3
Drew, S. Ind	390	0.8
Hopwood, S. Ind	267	0.6
Con majority	4,927	10.28
Electorate	67,962	
Turnout	47,911	70.5

Con hold (notional 2.3% from Lib Dem to Con)

TOTTENHAM
(No boundary changes)

		%	+/-%
Lammy, D. Lab*	24,128	58.8	1.1
Schmitz, D. Lib Dem	7,197	17.5	0.8
Sullivan, S. Con	6,064	14.8	1.3
Sutton, J. TUSC	1,057	2.6	
Gray, A. Green	980	2.4	-2.2
McKenzie, W. UKIP	466	1.1	
Watson, N. Ind	265	0.7	
Kadara, A. Christian	262	0.6	
Thompson, S. Ind	143	0.4	
Carr, E. Ind	125	0.3	
Lab majority	16,931	41.25	
Electorate	68,834		
Turnout	41,044	59.63	

Lab hold (0.1% from Lib Dem to Lab)

TRURO AND FALMOUTH
(New constituency)

		%
Newton, S. Con	20,349	41.7
Teverson, T. Lib Dem	19,914	40.8
Mackenzie, C. Lab	4,697	9.6
Blakeley, H. UKIP	1,911	3.9
Rich, L. Mebyon Kernow	1,039	2.1
Wright, I. Green	858	1.8
Con majority	435	0.89
Electorate	70,527	
Turnout	48,841	69.25

Con gain (notional 5.1% from Lib Dem to Con)

TUNBRIDGE WELLS
(Boundary changes)

		%
Clark, G. Con*	28,302	56.1
Hallas, D. Lib Dem	12,726	25.2
Heather, G. Lab	5,448	10.8
Webb, V. UKIP	2,054	4.1
Dawe, H. Green	914	1.8
McBride, A. BNP	704	1.4
Bradbury, F. Ind	172	0.4
Con majority	15,576	30.89
Electorate	73,855	
Turnout	50,420	68.27

Con hold (notional 2.8% from Lib Dem to Con)

TWICKENHAM
(No boundary changes)

		%	+/-%
Cable, V. Lib Dem*	32,483	54.3	2.7
Thomas, D. Con	20,343	34.0	1.7
Tomlinson, B. Lab	4,583	7.7	-3.7
Gilbert, B. UKIP	868	1.5	0.0
Roest, S. Green	674	1.1	-1.7
Hurst, C. BNP	654	1.1	
Cole, H. CURE	76	0.1	
Armstrong, P. Magna Carta	40	0.1	
Lib Dem majority	12,140	20.29	
Electorate	80,569		
Turnout	59,846	74.28	

Lib Dem hold (0.5% from Con to Lib Dem)

TYNEMOUTH
(Boundary changes)

		%
Campbell, A. Lab*	23,860	45.2
Morton, W. Con	18,121	34.4
Appleby, J. Lib Dem	7,845	14.9
Brooke, D. BNP	1,404	2.7
Payne, N. UKIP	900	1.7
Erskine, J. Green	538	1.0
Lab majority	5,739	10.88
Electorate	77,046	
Turnout	52,756	68.47

Lab hold (notional 0.4% from Lab to Con)

NORTH TYNESIDE
(Boundary changes)

		%
Glindon, M. Lab	23,505	50.5
Ord, D. Lib Dem	10,621	22.8
Mohindra, G. Con	8,514	18.3
Burrows, J. BNP	1,860	4.0
Blake, C. UKIP	1,306	2.8
Batten, B. NF	599	1.3
Lab majority	12,884	27.69
Electorate	79,070	
Turnout	46,529	58.85

Lab hold (notional 4.8% from Lab to Lib Dem)

WEST TYRONE
(No boundary changes)

		%	+/-%
Doherty, P. Sinn Féin*	18,050	48.0	9.5
Buchanan, T. DUP	7,365	19.6	2.0
Hussey, R. UCUNF	5,281	14.0	
Byrne, J. SDLP	5,212	13.8	4.9
Bower, M. All	859	2.3	
McClean, C. Ind	508	1.4	
Sinn Féin majority	10,685	28.39	
Electorate	61,148		
Turnout	37,632	61.54	

Sinn Féin hold (3.8% from DUP to Sinn Féin)

MID ULSTER
(No boundary changes)

		%	+/-%
McGuinness, M. Sinn Féin*	21,239	51.6	4.5
McCrea, I. DUP	5,876	14.3	-9.0
Quinn, T. SDLP	5,826	14.2	-3.1
Overend, S. UCUNF	4,509	11.0	
Millar, W. TUV	2,995	7.3	
Butler, I. All	397	1.0	
Sinn Féin majority	15,363	37.34	
Electorate	64,594		
Turnout	41,139	63.69	

Sinn Féin hold (6.7% from DUP to Sinn Féin)

UPPER BANN
(No boundary changes)

		%	+/-%
Simpson, D. DUP*	14,000	33.6	-3.7
Hamilton, H. UCUNF	10,639	25.5	
O'Dowd, J. Sinn Féin	10,237	24.6	3.8
Kelly, D. SDLP	5,276	12.7	-0.2
Heading, B. All	1,231	3.0	0.8
DUP majority	3,361	8.06	
Electorate	74,732		
Turnout	41,681	55.77	

DUP hold (14.6% from UCUNF to DUP)

UXBRIDGE AND SOUTH RUISLIP
(New constituency)

		%
Randall, J. Con*	21,758	48.1
Garg, S. Lab	10,542	23.3
Cox, M. Lib Dem	8,995	19.9
Neal, D. BNP	1,396	3.1
Wadsworth, G. UKIP	1,234	2.7
Harling, M. Green	477	1.1
Cooper, R. Eng Dem	403	0.9
McAllister, F. NF	271	0.6
Con majority	11,216	24.8
Electorate	73,908	
Turnout	45,222	61.19

Con hold (notional 3.4% from Lab to Con)

VALE OF CLWYD – see under Clwyd

VALE OF GLAMORGAN – see under Glamorgan

VAUXHALL
(Boundary changes)

		%
Hoey, K. Lab*	21,498	49.5
Pidgeon, C. Lib Dem	10,847	25.0
Chambers, G. Con	9,301	21.4
Healy, J. Green	708	1.6
Navarro, J. Eng Dem	289	0.7
Martin, L. Christian	200	0.5
Lambert, D. Socialist	143	0.3
Drinkall, J. AWP	109	0.3
Kapetanos, J. Animal	96	0.2
Lab majority	10,651	24.51
Electorate	74,811	
Turnout	43,458	58.09

Lab hold (notional 0.02% from Lab to Lib Dem)

WAKEFIELD

(Boundary changes)

		%
Creagh, M. Lab*	17,454	39.2
Story, A. Con	15,841	35.6
Smith, D. Lib Dem	7,256	16.3
Senior, I. BNP	2,581	5.8
Hawkins, M. Green	873	2.0
Harrop, M. Ind	439	1.0
Lab majority	1,613	3.62
Electorate	70,835	
Turnout	44,538	62.88

Lab hold (notional 6.9% from Lab to Con)

WALLASEY

(Boundary changes)

		%
Eagle, A. Lab*	21,578	51.6
Fraser, L. Con	13,071	31.3
Pitt, S. Lib Dem	5,693	13.6
Snowden, D. UKIP	1,205	2.9
Mwaba, E. Ind	107	0.3
Lab majority	8,507	20.35
Electorate	65,915	
Turnout	41,795	63.41

Lab hold (notional 1.8% from Lab to Con)

WALSALL NORTH

(Boundary changes)

		%
Winnick, D. Lab*	13,385	36.9
Clack, H. Con	12,395	34.2
Fazal, N. Lib Dem	4,754	13.1
Woodall, C. BNP	2,930	8.1
Hazell, E. UKIP	1,737	4.8
Smith, P. Dem Lab	842	2.3
Shakir, B. Christian	144	0.4
Lab majority	990	2.73
Electorate	64,771	
Turnout	36,273	56

Lab hold (notional 9% from Lab to Con)

WALSALL SOUTH

(Boundary changes)

		%
Vaz, V. Lab	16,211	39.4
Hunt, R. Con	14,456	35.1
Sinha, M. Lib Dem	5,880	14.3
Bennett, D. UKIP	3,449	8.4
Khan, G. Christian	482	1.2
Mulla, M. Ind	404	1.0
Lab majority	1,755	4.27
Electorate	64,851	
Turnout	41,136	63.43

Lab hold (notional 8.3% from Lab to Con)

WALTHAMSTOW

(Boundary changes)

		%
Creasy, S. Lab/Co-op	21,252	51.5
Ahmed, F. Lib Dem	11,774	28.5
Hemsted, A. Con	5,734	13.9
Chisholm-Benli, J. UKIP	823	2.0
Perrett, D. Green	767	1.9
Taaffe, N. TUSC	279	0.7
Mall, A. Christian	248	0.6
Warburton, P. Ind	117	0.3
Lab/Co-op majority	9,478	22.95
Electorate	64,625	
Turnout	41,297	63.9

Lab/Co-op hold (notional 0.1% from Lab/Co-op to Lib Dem)

*Member of last Parliament

WANSBECK

(No boundary changes)

		%	+/-%
Lavery, I. Lab	17,548	45.8	-9.1
Reed, S. Lib Dem	10,517	27.4	1.2
Storey, C. Con	6,714	17.5	2.6
Finlay, S. BNP	1,418	3.7	
Stokoe, L. UKIP	974	2.5	
Best, N. Green	601	1.6	-1.8
Reid, M. Ind	359	0.9	
Flynn, M. Christian	142	0.4	
Lab majority	7,031	18.34	
Electorate	61,782		
Turnout	38,334	62.05	

Lab hold (5.1% from Lab to Lib Dem)

WANTAGE

(Boundary changes)

		%
Vaizey, E. Con*	29,284	51.9
Armitage, A. Lib Dem	15,737	27.9
Mitchell, S. Lab	7,855	13.9
Jones, J. UKIP	2,421	4.3
Twine, A. Green	1,044	1.9
Con majority	13,547	23.99
Electorate	80,833	
Turnout	56,461	69.85

Con hold (notional 4.3% from Lib Dem to Con)

WARLEY

(Boundary changes)

		%
Spellar, J. Lab*	20,240	52.5
Parmar, J. Con	9,484	24.6
Keating, E. Lib Dem	5,929	15.4
Harvey, N. UKIP	2,617	6.8
Lab majority	10,756	27.91
Electorate	62,751	
Turnout	38,539	61.42

Lab hold (notional 2% from Lab to Con)

WARRINGTON NORTH

(Boundary changes)

		%
Jones, H. Lab*	20,135	45.4
Campbell, P. Con	13,364	30.1
Eccles, D. Lib Dem	9,196	20.7
Scott, A. Ind	1,516	3.4
Lab majority	6,771	15.26
Electorate	70,473	
Turnout	44,376	62.97

Lab hold (notional 6.6% from Lab to Con)

WARRINGTON SOUTH

(Boundary changes)

		%
Mowat, D. Con	19,641	35.7
Bent, N. Lab	18,088	32.9
Crotty, J. Lib Dem	15,094	27.4
Ashington, J. UKIP	1,624	3.0
Davies, S. Green	427	0.8
Con majority	1,553	2.82
Electorate	79,182	
Turnout	55,007	69.47

Con gain (notional 6% from Lab to Con)

WARWICK AND LEAMINGTON

(Boundary changes)

		%
White, C. Con	20,876	42.5
Plaskitt, J. Lab*	17,363	35.4
Beddow, A. Lib Dem	8,977	18.3
Lenton, C. UKIP	926	1.9

Davison, I. Green	693	1.4
Cullinane, J. Ind	197	0.4
Con majority	3,513	7.15
Electorate	67,800	
Turnout	49,128	72.46

Con gain (notional 8.8% from Lab to Con)

NORTH WARWICKSHIRE
(Boundary changes)

		%
Byles, D. Con	18,993	40.1
O'Brien, M. Lab*	18,939	40.0
Martin, S. Lib Dem	5,481	11.6
Holmes, J. BNP	2,106	4.5
Fowler, S. UKIP	1,335	2.8
Lane, D. Eng Dem	411	0.9
Con majority	54	0.11
Electorate	70,138	
Turnout	47,361	67.53

Con gain (notional 5% from Lib Dem to Con)

WASHINGTON AND SUNDERLAND WEST
(New constituency)

		%
Hodgson, S. Lab*	19,615	52.3
Cuthbert, I. Con	8,157	21.7
Andras, P. Lib Dem	6,382	17.0
McDonald, I. BNP	1,913	5.1
Hudson, L. UKIP	1,267	3.4
Lab majority	11,458	30.53
Electorate	68,910	
Turnout	37,528	54.46

Lab hold (notional 11.6% from Lab to Con)

WATFORD
(Boundary changes)

		%
Harrington, R. Con	19,291	34.8
Brinton, S. Lib Dem	17,866	32.3
Ward, C. Lab*	14,750	26.6
Emerson, A. BNP	1,217	2.2
Eardley, G. UKIP	1,199	2.2
Brandon, I. Green	885	1.6
Con majority	1,425	2.57
Electorate	80,798	
Turnout	55,410	68.58

Con gain (notional 2.1% from Lib Dem to Con)

WAVENEY
(Boundary changes)

		%
Aldous, P. Con	20,571	40.2
Blizzard, B. Lab*	19,802	38.7
Dean, A. Lib Dem	6,811	13.3
Tyler, J. UKIP	2,684	5.2
Elliott, G. Green	1,167	2.3
Barfe, L. Ind	106	0.2
Con majority	769	1.5
Electorate	78,532	
Turnout	51,229	65.23

Con gain (notional 6.8% from Lab to Con)

WEALDEN
(Boundary changes)

		%
Hendry, C. Con*	31,090	56.5
Bowers, C. Lib Dem	13,911	25.3
Blackmore, L. Lab	5,266	9.6
Docker, D. UKIP	3,319	6.0
Jonas, D. Green	1,383	2.5
Con majority	17,179	31.21
Electorate	76,537	
Turnout	55,038	71.91

Con hold (notional 2.8% from Lib Dem to Con)

WEAVER VALE
(Boundary changes)

		%
Evans, G. Con	16,953	38.5
Stockton, J. Lab	15,962	36.2
Hampson, P. Lib Dem	8,196	18.6
Marsh, C. BNP	1,063	2.4
Remfry, P. UKIP	1,018	2.3
Thorp, H. Green	338	0.8
Cooksley, M. Ind	270	0.6
Reynolds, T. Ind	133	0.3
Charlton, W. Ind	57	0.1
Con majority	991	2.25
Electorate	67,269	
Turnout	44,061	65.5

Con gain (notional 8.1% from Lab to Con)

WELLINGBOROUGH
(Boundary changes)

		%
Bone, P. Con	24,918	48.2
Buckland, J. Lab	13,131	25.4
Barron, K. Lib Dem	8,848	17.1
Haynes, A. UKIP	1,636	3.2
Walker, R. BNP	1,596	3.1
Spencer, T. Eng Dem	530	1.0
Hornett, J. Green	480	0.9
Crofts, P. TUSC	249	0.5
Donaldson, G. Ind	240	0.5
Lavin, M. Ind	33	0.1
Con majority	11,787	22.78
Electorate	76,846	
Turnout	51,734	67.32

Con hold (notional 10.8% from Lab to Con)

WELLS
(Boundary changes)

		%
Munt, T. Lib Dem	24,560	43.9
Heathcoat-Amory, D. Con*	23,760	42.5
Merryfield, A. Lab/Co-op	4,198	7.5
Baynes, J. UKIP	1,711	3.1
Boyce, H. BNP	1,004	1.8
Briton, C. Green	631	1.1
Lib Dem majority	800	1.43
Electorate	79,432	
Turnout	55,963	70.45

Lib Dem gain (notional 3.6% from Con to Lib Dem)

WELWYN HATFIELD
(No boundary changes)

		%	+/-%
Shapps, G. Con*	27,894	56.8	7.4
Hobday, M. Lab	10,471	21.3	-14.9
Zukowskyj, P. Lib Dem	8,010	16.3	2.2
Platt, D. UKIP	1,643	3.4	
Weston, J. Green	796	1.6	
Parker, N. Ind	158	0.3	
Con majority	17,423	35.5	
Electorate	72,058		
Turnout	49,079	68.11	

Con hold (11.1% from Lab to Con)

WENTWORTH AND DEARNE
(New constituency)

		%
Healey, J. Lab*	21,316	50.5
Donelan, M. Con	7,396	17.5
Love, N. Lib Dem	6,787	16.1
Wilkinson, J. UKIP	3,418	8.1
Baldwin, G. BNP	3,189	7.6
Lab majority	13,920	33
Electorate	72,586	
Turnout	42,187	58.12

Lab hold (notional 7.5% from Lab to Con)

WEST ABERDEENSHIRE AND KINCARDINE –
see under Aberdeenshire

WEST BROMWICH EAST
(Boundary changes) %

Watson, T. Lab*	17,657	46.4
Thompson, A. Con	10,961	28.8
Garrett, I. Lib Dem	4,993	13.1
Lewin, T. BNP	2,205	5.8
Cowles, M. Eng Dem	1,150	3.0
Grey, S. UKIP	984	2.6
Lab majority	6,696	17.58
Electorate	62,668	
Turnout	38,089	60.78

Lab hold (notional 7.7% from Lab to Con)

WEST BROMWICH WEST
(Boundary changes) %

Bailey, A. Lab/Co-op*	16,263	44.8
Hardie, A. Con	10,612	29.2
Smith, S. Lib Dem	4,336	11.9
Green, R. BNP	3,394	9.3
Ford, M. UKIP	1,566	4.3
Lab/Co-op majority	5,651	15.56
Electorate	64,859	
Turnout	36,319	56

Lab/Co-op hold (notional 7.7% from Lab/Co-op to Con)

WEST DORSET – see under Dorset

WEST DUNBARTONSHIRE – see under
Dunbartonshire

WEST HAM
(Boundary changes) %

Brown, L. Lab*	29,422	62.0
Morris, V. Con	6,888	14.5
Pierce, M. Lib Dem	5,392	11.4
Gain, S. CPA	1,327	2.8
Malik, K. Ind	1,245	2.6
Davidson, M. NF	1,089	2.3
Gandy, K. UKIP	766	1.6
Lithgow, J. Green	645	1.4
Agbogun-Toko, G. Ind	177	0.4
Lab majority	22,534	47.48
Electorate	85,313	
Turnout	47,458	55.63

Lab hold (notional 3.9% from Con to Lab)

WEST LANCASHIRE – see under Lancashire

WEST SUFFOLK – see under Suffolk

WEST TYRONE – see under Tyrone

WEST WORCESTERSHIRE – see under
Worcestershire

WESTMINSTER NORTH
(New constituency) %

Buck, K. Lab*	17,377	43.6
Cash, J. Con	15,251	38.2
Blackburn, M. Lib Dem	5,513	13.8
Smith, T. Green	478	1.2
Curry, S. BNP	334	0.8
Badzak, J. UKIP	315	0.8

*Member of last Parliament

Bahaijoub, A. Ind	101	0.3
Roseman, E. Eng Dem	99	0.3
Fajardo, G. Christian	98	0.3
Dharamsey, A. Ind	32	0.1
Lab majority	2,126	5.33
Electorate	66,739	
Turnout	39,895	59.78

Lab hold (notional 0.6% from Lab to Con)

WESTMORLAND AND LONSDALE
(Boundary changes) %

Farron, T. Lib Dem*	30,896	59.9
McKeever, G. Con	18,632	36.1
Todd, J. Lab	1,158	2.3
Mander, J. UKIP	801	1.6
Lib Dem majority	12,264	23.78
Electorate	66,988	
Turnout	51,569	76.98

Lib Dem hold (notional 11% from Con to Lib Dem)

WESTON-SUPER-MARE
(Boundary changes) %

Penrose, J. Con*	23,356	44.3
Bell, M. Lib Dem	20,665	39.2
Bradley, D. Lab	5,772	10.9
Spencer, P. UKIP	1,406	2.7
Parsons, P. BNP	1,098	2.1
Peverelle, J. Eng Dem	275	0.5
Satch, S. Ind	144	0.3
Con majority	2,691	5.1
Electorate	78,487	
Turnout	52,771	67.24

Con hold (notional 0.4% from Lib Dem to Con)

WIGAN
(Boundary changes) %

Nandy, L. Lab	21,404	48.3
Winstanley, M. Con	10,917	24.6
Clayton, M. Lib Dem	6,797	15.3
Freeman, A. UKIP	2,516	5.7
Mather, C. BNP	2,506	5.7
Lab majority	10,487	23.67
Electorate	75,407	
Turnout	44,302	58.75

Lab hold (notional 7.7% from Lab to Con)

NORTH WILTSHIRE
(Boundary changes) %

Gray, J. Con*	25,114	51.5
Evemy, M. Lib Dem	17,631	36.1
Hughes, J. Lab	3,239	6.7
Bennett, C. UKIP	1,908	3.9
Chamberlain, P. Green	599	1.2
Allnatt, P. Ind	208	0.4
Con majority	7,483	15.34
Electorate	66,315	
Turnout	48,774	73.55

Con hold (notional 0% from Lib Dem to Con)

SOUTH WEST WILTSHIRE
(New constituency) %

Murrison, A. Con*	25,321	51.6
Carbin, T. Lib Dem	14,954	30.5
Rennison, R. Lab	5,613	11.4
Cuthbert-Murray, M. UKIP	2,684	5.5
Black, C. Ind	446	0.9
Con majority	10,367	21.11
Electorate	71,647	
Turnout	49,109	68.54

Con hold (notional 1.1% from Lib Dem to Con)

WIMBLEDON
(Boundary changes)

		%
Hammond, S. Con*	23,257	48.9
Sheehan, S. Lib Dem	11,849	24.9
Judge, A. Lab	10,550	22.2
McAleer, M. UKIP	914	1.9
Thacker, R. Green	590	1.3
Martin, D. Christian	235	0.5
Con majority	11,408	24
Electorate	65,723	
Turnout	47,539	72.33

Con hold (notional 0.4% from Lib Dem to Con)

WINCHESTER
(Boundary changes)

		%
Brine, S. Con	27,155	48.4
Tod, M. Lib Dem	24,107	43.0
Davies, P. Lab	3,051	5.5
Penn-Bull, J. UKIP	1,139	2.0
Lancaster, M. Eng Dem	503	0.9
Con majority	3,048	5.44
Electorate	73,805	
Turnout	56,060	75.96

Con gain (notional 9.1% from Lib Dem to Con)

WINDSOR
(Boundary changes)

		%
Afriyie, A. Con*	30,172	60.8
Tisi, J. Lib Dem	11,118	22.4
Jhund, A. Lab	4,910	9.9
Rye, J. UKIP	1,612	3.3
Phillips, P. BNP	950	1.9
Wall, D. Green	628	1.3
Hooper, P. Ind	198	0.4
Con majority	19,054	38.36
Electorate	69,511	
Turnout	49,672	71.46

Con hold (notional 8% from Lib Dem to Con)

WIRRAL SOUTH
(Boundary changes)

		%
McGovern, A. Lab	16,276	40.6
Clarke, J. Con	15,745	39.3
Saddler, J. Lib Dem	6,611	16.5
Scott, D. UKIP	1,274	3.2
Lab majority	531	1.33
Electorate	56,099	
Turnout	40,055	71.4

Lab hold (notional 4% from Lab to Con)

WIRRAL WEST
(Boundary changes)

		%
McVey, E. Con	16,726	42.3
Davies, P. Lab	14,290	36.2
Reisdorf, P. Lib Dem	6,630	16.8
Griffiths, P. UKIP	899	2.3
Kirwan, D. Ind	506	1.3
James, D. CSP	321	0.8
Con majority	2,436	6.17
Electorate	55,050	
Turnout	39,505	71.76

Con hold (notional 2.3% from Lab to Con)

WITHAM
(New constituency)

		%
Patel, P. Con	24,448	52.1
Phelps, M. Lib Dem	9,252	19.7

Spademan, J. Lab	8,656	18.4
Hodges, D. UKIP	3,060	6.5
Abbott, J. Green	1,419	3.0
Con majority	15,196	32.38
Electorate	66,969	
Turnout	46,924	70.07

Con hold (notional 1.1% from Con to Lib Dem)

WITNEY
(Boundary changes)

		%
Cameron, D. Con*	33,973	58.7
Barnes, D. Lib Dem	11,233	19.4
Goldberg, J. Lab	7,511	13.0
MacDonald, S. Green	2,385	4.1
Tolstoy-Miloslavsky, N. UKIP	2,001	3.5
Hope, A. Loony	234	0.4
Wesson, P. Ind	166	0.3
Cook, J. Ind	151	0.3
Bex, C. Wessex Reg	62	0.1
Barschak, A. Ind	53	0.1
Con majority	22,740	39.28
Electorate	78,766	
Turnout	57,886	73.49

Con hold (notional 6.3% from Lib Dem to Con)

WOKING
(No boundary changes)

		%	+/-%
Lord, J. Con	26,551	50.2	2.9
Sharpley, R. Lib Dem	19,744	37.3	4.4
Miller, T. Lab	4,246	8.0	-8.2
Burberry, R. UKIP	1,997	3.8	0.9
Roxburgh, J. TPP	204	0.4	
Temple, R. MCCP	44	0.1	
Con majority	6,807	12.86	
Electorate	73,837		
Turnout	52,919	71.67	

Con hold (0.7% from Con to Lib Dem)

WOKINGHAM
(Boundary changes)

		%
Redwood, J. Con*	28,754	52.6
Bray, P. Lib Dem	15,262	27.9
Davidson, G. Lab	5,516	10.1
Ashwell, M. Ind	2,340	4.3
Zebedee, A. UKIP	1,664	3.0
Bisset, M. Green	567	1.0
Owen, P. Loony	329	0.6
Smith, R. Ind	96	0.2
Con majority	13,492	24.7
Electorate	76,386	
Turnout	54,620	71.51

Con hold (notional 4.6% from Lib Dem to Con)

WOLVERHAMPTON NORTH EAST
(Boundary changes)

		%
Reynolds, E. Lab	14,448	41.2
Rook, J. Con	11,964	34.1
Ross, C. Lib Dem	4,711	13.4
Patten, S. BNP	2,296	6.6
Valdmanis, P. UKIP	1,138	3.3
Bhatoe, S. SLP	337	1.0
Lab majority	2,484	7.09
Electorate	58,931	
Turnout	35,041	59.46

Lab hold (notional 9% from Lab to Con)

WOLVERHAMPTON SOUTH EAST
(Boundary changes) %

McFadden, P. Lab*	16,505	47.2
Wood, K. Con	9,912	28.4
Whitehouse, R. Lib Dem	5,277	15.1
Fanthom, G. UKIP	2,675	7.7
Handa, S. Ind	338	1.0
Lab majority	6,593	18.86
Electorate	59,884	
Turnout	34,963	58.38

Lab hold (notional 8.9% from Lab to Con)

WOLVERHAMPTON SOUTH WEST
(Boundary changes) %

Uppal, P. Con	16,344	40.5
Marris, R. Lab*	15,653	38.8
Lawrence, R. Lib Dem	6,430	15.9
Mobberley, A. UKIP	1,487	3.7
Barry, R. EPA	246	0.6
Con majority	691	1.71
Electorate	58,845	
Turnout	40,323	68.52

Con gain (notional 3.5% from Lab to Con)

WORCESTER
(No boundary changes) % +/-%

Walker, R. Con	19,358	39.5	4.5
Foster, M. Lab*	16,376	33.4	-8.4
Alderson, J. Lib Dem	9,525	19.4	3.2
Bennett, J. UKIP	1,360	2.8	0.4
Kirby, S. BNP	1,219	2.5	0.4
Stephen, L. Green	735	1.5	-0.5
Robinson, A. Pirate	173	0.4	
Nielsen, P. Ind	129	0.3	
Christian-Brookes, A. Ind	99	0.2	
Con majority	2,982	6.08	
Electorate	72,835		
Turnout	49,073	67.38	

Con gain (6.4% from Lab to Con)

MID WORCESTERSHIRE
(Boundary changes) %

Luff, P. Con*	27,770	54.5
Rowley, M. Lib Dem	11,906	23.4
Lunn, R. Lab	7,613	14.9
White, J. UKIP	3,049	6.0
Matthews, G. Green	593	1.2
Con majority	15,864	31.11
Electorate	72,145	
Turnout	50,996	70.69

Con hold (notional 0.02% from Lib Dem to Con)

WEST WORCESTERSHIRE
(Boundary changes) %

Baldwin, H. Con	27,213	50.2
Burt, R. Lib Dem	20,459	37.8
Barber, P. Lab	3,661	6.8
Bovey, C. UKIP	2,119	3.9
Victory, M. Green	641	1.2
Con majority	6,754	12.46
Electorate	72,807	
Turnout	54,200	74.44

Con hold (notional 3.2% from Lib Dem to Con)

WORKINGTON
(Boundary changes) %

Cunningham, T. Lab*	17,865	45.4
Pattinson, J. Con	13,290	33.8

*Member of last Parliament

Collins, S. Lib Dem	5,318	13.5
Wingfield, M. BNP	1,496	3.8
Lee, S. UKIP	876	2.2
Logan, R. Eng Dem	414	1.1
Lab majority	4,575	11.63
Electorate	59,607	
Turnout	39,339	66

Lab hold (notional 5.7% from Lab to Con)

WORSLEY AND ECCLES SOUTH
(New constituency) %

Keeley, B. Lab*	17,892	42.7
Lindley, I. Con	13,555	32.4
Gadsden, R. Lib Dem	6,883	16.4
Townsend, A. UKIP	2,037	4.9
Whitelegg, P. Eng Dem	1,334	3.2
Lab majority	4,337	10.35
Electorate	72,473	
Turnout	41,884	57.79

Lab hold (notional 7.6% from Lab to Con)

EAST WORTHING AND SHOREHAM
(Boundary changes) %

Loughton, T. Con*	23,458	48.4
Doyle, J. Lib Dem	12,353	25.5
Benn, E. Lab	8,087	16.7
Glennon, M. UKIP	2,984	6.2
Board, S. Green	1,126	2.3
Maltby, C. Eng Dem	389	0.8
Con majority	11,105	22.89
Electorate	74,001	
Turnout	48,507	65.55

Con hold (notional 1.7% from Lib Dem to Con)

WORTHING WEST
(Boundary changes) %

Bottomley, P. Con*	25,416	51.6
Thorpe, H. Lib Dem	13,687	27.8
Ross, I. Lab	5,800	11.8
Wallace, J. UKIP	2,924	5.9
Aherne, D. Green	996	2.0
Dearsley, S. Christian	300	0.6
Con majority	11,729	23.82
Electorate	80,859	
Turnout	49,249	60.91

Con hold (notional 1.5% from Lib Dem to Con)

THE WREKIN
(Boundary changes) %

Pritchard, M. Con*	21,922	47.6
Kalinauckas, P. Lab	12,472	27.1
Cameron-Daw, A. Lib Dem	8,019	17.4
Hurst, M. UKIP	2,050	4.5
Harwood, S. BNP	1,505	3.3
Con majority	9,450	20.51
Electorate	65,544	
Turnout	46,078	70.3

Con hold (notional 8.8% from Lab to Con)

WREXHAM
(No boundary changes) % +/-%

Lucas, I. Lab*	12,161	36.8	-8.8
Rippeth, T. Lib Dem	8,503	25.8	2.3
Hughes, G. Con	8,375	25.4	5.5
Jones, A. PlC	2,029	6.2	0.5
Roberts, M. BNP	1,134	3.4	0.4
Humberstone, J. UKIP	774	2.3	
Lab majority	3,658	11.08	
Electorate	50,872		
Turnout	33,017	64.9	

Lab hold (5.6% from Lab to Lib Dem)

WYCOMBE
(Boundary changes)

		%
Baker, S. Con	23,423	48.5
Guy, S. Lib Dem	13,863	28.7
Lomas, A. Lab	8,326	17.3
Wiseman, J. UKIP	2,123	4.4
Khokar, M. Ind	228	0.5
Fitton, D. Ind	188	0.4
Con majority	9,560	19.8
Electorate	74,175	
Turnout	48,294	65.11

Con hold (notional 4.8% from Con to Lib Dem)

WYRE AND PRESTON NORTH
(New constituency)

		%
Wallace, B. Con*	26,877	52.3
Gallagher, D. Lib Dem	11,033	21.5
Smith, C. Lab	10,932	21.3
Cecil, N. UKIP	2,466	4.8
Con majority	15,844	30.81
Electorate	70,201	
Turnout	51,426	73.26

Con hold (notional 3.9% from Con to Lib Dem)

WYRE FOREST
(Boundary changes)

		%
Garnier, M. Con	18,793	36.8
Taylor, R. Ind KHHC*	16,150	31.6
Knowles, N. Lab	7,298	14.3
Farmer, N. Lib Dem	6,040	11.8
Wrench, M. UKIP	1,498	2.9
Howells, G. BNP	1,120	2.2
Con majority	2,643	5.18
Electorate	76,713	
Turnout	51,034	66.53

Con gain (notional 7.3% from Ind KHHC to Con)

WYTHENSHAWE AND SALE EAST
(No boundary changes)

		%	+/-%
Goggins, P. Lab*	17,987	44.0	-8.1
Clowes, J. Con	10,412	25.5	3.3
Eakins, M. Lib Dem	9,107	22.3	0.8
Todd, B. BNP	1,572	3.8	
Cassidy, C. UKIP	1,405	3.4	0.3
Worthington, L. TUSC	268	0.7	
Lab majority	7,575	18.53	
Electorate	79,923		
Turnout	40,887	51.16	

Lab hold (5.7% from Lab to Con)

YEOVIL
(Boundary changes)

		%
Laws, D. Lib Dem*	31,843	55.6
Davis, K. Con	18,807	32.9
Skevington, L. Lab	2,991	5.2
Pearson, N. UKIP	2,357	4.1
Baehr, R. BNP	1,162	2.0
Lib Dem majority	13,036	22.77
Electorate	82,314	
Turnout	57,241	69.54

Lib Dem hold (notional 2.7% from Con to Lib Dem)

YNYS MÔN
(No boundary changes)

		%	+/-%
Owen, A. Lab*	11,490	33.3	-1.3
Rees, D. PIC	9,029	26.2	-4.9
Ridge-Newman, A. Con	7,744	22.4	11.4
Wood, M. Lib Dem	2,592	7.5	0.7
Rogers, P. Ind	2,225	6.5	-8.2
Gill, E. UKIP	1,201	3.5	2.5
Owen, D. Christian	163	0.5	
Lab majority	2,461	7.13	
Electorate	50,075		
Turnout	34,514	68.92	

Lab hold (1.8% from PIC to Lab)

YORK CENTRAL
(New constituency)

		%
Bayley, H. Lab*	18,573	39.9
Wade Weeks, M. Con	12,122	26.1
Vassie, C. Lib Dem	11,694	25.1
Chase, A. Green	1,669	3.6
Kelly, J. BNP	1,171	2.5
Abbott, P. UKIP	1,100	2.4
Vee, E. Loony	154	0.3
Lab majority	6,451	13.86
Electorate	76,439	
Turnout	46,549	60.9

Lab hold (notional 6% from Lab to Con)

YORK OUTER
(New constituency)

		%
Sturdy, J. Con	22,912	42.9
Kirk, M. Lib Dem	19,224	36.0
Alexander, J. Lab	9,108	17.1
Morris, J. UKIP	1,100	2.1
Smurthwaite, C. BNP	956	1.8
Con majority	3,688	6.91
Electorate	75,937	
Turnout	53,375	70.29

Con gain (notional 3.7% from Lib Dem to Con)

EAST YORKSHIRE
(Boundary changes)

		%
Knight, G. Con*	24,328	47.4
Adamson, R. Lib Dem	10,842	21.1
Rounding, P. Lab	10,401	20.3
Daniels, C. UKIP	2,142	4.2
Pudsey, B. BNP	1,865	3.6
Allerston, R. SDP	914	1.8
Jackson, M. Green	762	1.5
Con majority	13,486	26.27
Electorate	80,105	
Turnout	51,328	64.08

Con hold (notional 0.1% from Con to Lib Dem)

State of the parties

	2010 General Election	2005 General Election
Conservative	306	198
Labour*	258	355
Liberal Democrat	57	62
Democratic Unionist Party	8	9
Scottish National Party	6	6
Sinn Fein	5	5
Social Democratic Labour Party	3	3
Plaid Cymru	3	3
Alliance	1	2
Green	1	0
Independent	1	0
Ulster Unionist Party	0	1
Respect	0	1
The Speaker	1	1
TOTAL	**650**	**646**

*Includes Labour/Co-operative MPs.

Share of the vote

	Total Seats	Total Votes	% of votes
Con	306	10,703,864	36.1
Lab	258	8,609,462	29.0
Lib Dem	57	6,836,761	23.0
UKIP	0	921,913	3.1
BNP	0	552,305	1.9
SNP	6	491,386	1.7
Green	1	285,616	1.0
Ind	1	231,870	0.8
Sinn Féin	5	171,942	0.6
DUP	8	168,216	0.6
PlC	3	165,394	0.6
SDLP	3	110,970	0.4
UCUNF	0	102,361	0.3
England	0	64,826	0.2
All	1	42,762	0.1
Respect	0	33,251	0.1
TUV	0	26,300	0.1
Speaker	1	22,860	0.1
Other	0	142,490	0.5
TOTAL	**650**	**29,684,549**	**65.1**

Share of the vote by region
England
EASTERN

	Total Seats	Total Votes	% of Votes
Con	52	1,356,739	47.12
Lib Dem	4	692,932	24.07
Lab	2	564,581	19.61
UKIP	0	123,437	4.29
BNP	0	59,505	2.07
Green	0	42,677	1.48
Ind	0	26,108	0.91
England	0	8,390	0.29
Tendring	0	1,078	0.04
CPA	0	862	0.03
Christian	0	635	0.02
Loony	0	548	0.02
TUSC	0	362	0.01
NCDMV	0	327	0.01
YRDPL	0	264	0.01
Animal	0	181	0.01
WRP	0	175	0.01
Beer	0	153	0.01
NP	0	118	0.00
CURE	0	108	0.00
LTT	0	100	0.00
Essex	0	35	0.00
TOTAL	**58**	**2,879,315**	**67.3**

EAST MIDLANDS

	Total Seats	Total Votes	% of Votes
Con	31	915,933	41.18
Lab	15	661,813	29.76
Lib Dem	0	462,988	20.82
UKIP	0	72,659	3.27
BNP	0	69,706	3.13
Ind	0	16,680	0.75
Green	0	11,667	0.52
England	0	8,641	0.39
Lincs Ind	0	929	0.04
Loony	0	712	0.03
Unity	0	494	0.02
TUSC	0	406	0.02
NSOPS	0	325	0.01
Pirate	0	283	0.01
SLP	0	266	0.01
Christian	0	223	0.01
Science	0	197	0.01
Bus-Pass	0	112	0.01
Scrap	0	59	0.00
Humanity	0	50	0.00
TOTAL	**46**	**2,224,143**	**67.00**

LONDON

	Total Seats	Total Votes	% of Votes
Lab	38	1,245,637	36.62
Con	28	1,174,568	34.53
Lib Dem	7	751,561	22.10
UKIP	0	59,452	1.75
Green	0	54,316	1.60
BNP	0	45,902	1.35
Respect	0	17,368	0.51
Ind	0	14,590	0.43
England	0	9,076	0.27
Christian	0	8,272	0.24
NF	0	2,825	0.08
CPA	0	2,794	0.08
TUSC	0	1,603	0.05
Loony	0	858	0.03
SKGH	0	746	0.02
SAP	0	645	0.02
Lib	0	539	0.02
WRP	0	502	0.01
Reform 2000	0	379	0.01
Brent North Ind	0	333	0.01
CNBPG	0	332	0.01
Pirate	0	303	0.01
UV	0	209	0.01
Green Soc	0	197	0.01
NICCF	0	196	0.01
Ind EACPS	0	190	0.01
SLP	0	184	0.01
Comm	0	160	0.00
AC	0	149	0.00
Socialist	0	143	0.00
Tamsin	0	123	0.00
Comm League	0	110	0.00
AWP	0	109	0.00
Ind Fed UK	0	99	0.00
Animal	0	96	0.00
CURE	0	76	0.00
AWL	0	75	0.00
Magna Carta	0	66	0.00
Restoration	0	45	0.00
Libertarian	0	41	0.00
Better Britain	0	35	0.00
BEP	0	17	0.00
TOTAL	**73**	**3,394,921**	**64.60**

NORTH EAST

	Total Seats	Total Votes	% of Votes
Lab	25	518,261	43.55
Con	2	282,347	23.72
Lib Dem	2	280,468	23.57
BNP	0	51,940	4.36
UKIP	0	34,896	2.93

	Total Seats	Total Votes	% of Votes
Ind	0	15,669	1.32
Green	0	3,787	0.32
LLPBPP	0	1,964	0.17
England	0	1,456	0.12
NF	0	599	0.05
Christian	0	575	0.05
TUSC	0	393	0.03
Comm GB	0	177	0.01
TOTAL	**29**	**1,192,532**	**61**

NORTH WEST

	Total Seats	Total Votes	% of Votes
Lab	47	1,292,978	39.47
Con	22	1,038,967	31.71
Lib Dem	6	707,716	21.60
UKIP	0	103,782	3.17
BNP	0	70,032	2.14
Ind	0	20,188	0.62
Green	0	17,046	0.52
England	0	4,533	0.14
Lib	0	3,327	0.10
NF	0	3,298	0.10
Mac Ind	0	2,590	0.08
Respect	0	2,398	0.07
TUSC	0	2,378	0.07
SLP	0	1,450	0.04
Christian	0	1,355	0.04
CPA	0	1,287	0.04
IZB	0	545	0.02
Pirate	0	367	0.01
CSP	0	321	0.01
You	0	319	0.01
True English	0	298	0.01
Impact	0	243	0.01
Integrity	0	230	0.01
Clause 28	0	217	0.01
Loony	0	198	0.01
WRP	0	59	0.00
SEP	0	54	0.00
TOTAL	**75**	**3,276,176**	**62.40**

SOUTH EAST

	Total Seats	Total Votes	% of Votes
Con	74	2,118,035	49.32
Lib Dem	4	1,124,777	26.19
Lab	4	697,495	16.24
UKIP	0	177,269	4.13
Green	1	62,124	1.45
BNP	0	30,618	0.71
Ind	0	26,865	0.63
Speaker	1	22,860	0.53

SOUTH EAST Cont.

	Total Seats	Total Votes	% of Votes
England	0	15,442	0.36
Loony	0	3,315	0.08
Trust	0	2,699	0.06
Christian	0	2,104	0.05
NF	0	1,690	0.04
CSP	0	852	0.02
EIP	0	803	0.02
TPP	0	737	0.02
TUSC	0	692	0.02
CPA	0	651	0.02
MEP	0	616	0.01
Expense	0	475	0.01
Best	0	474	0.01
JACP	0	427	0.01
Animal	0	398	0.01
FR	0	270	0.01
RRG	0	266	0.01
JP	0	265	0.01
BCM	0	247	0.01
FDP	0	207	0.00
MRP	0	173	0.00
CIP	0	167	0.00
SLP	0	148	0.00
SEP	0	116	0.00
Medway	0	109	0.00
Deficit	0	107	0.00
Apol Dem	0	95	0.00
Pirate	0	94	0.00
NLP	0	93	0.00
NRP	0	84	0.00
EPA	0	73	0.00
Wessex Reg	0	62	0.00
CURE	0	61	0.00
Scrap	0	60	0.00
MCCP	0	44	0.00
TOTAL	**84**	**4,294,159**	**67.98**

SOUTH WEST

	Total Seats	Total Votes	% of Votes
Con	36	1,187,637	42.82
Lib Dem	15	962,954	34.72
Lab	4	426,910	15.39
UKIP	0	123,910	4.47
Green	0	31,517	1.14
BNP	0	20,866	0.75
Ind	0	6,135	0.22
Meb Ker	0	5,379	0.19
England	0	3,277	0.12
Lib	0	1,108	0.04
Loony	0	1,030	0.04
Christian	0	743	0.03

	Total Seats	Total Votes	% of Votes
SLP	0	499	0.02
Corn Dem	0	396	0.01
TUSC	0	390	0.01
GMVY	0	233	0.01
Libertarian	0	141	0.01
Ind Fed UK	0	126	0.00
Comm GB	0	96	0.00
ATSP	0	31	0.00
TOTAL	**55**	**2,773,378**	**69.25**

WEST MIDLANDS

	Total Seats	Total Votes	% of Votes
Con	33	1,044,081	39.54
Lab	24	808,114	30.61
Lib Dem	2	540,160	20.46
UKIP	0	106,273	4.02
BNP	0	72,806	2.76
Ind KHHC	0	16,150	0.61
Green	0	14,996	0.57
Respect	0	12,240	0.46
Ind	0	8,676	0.33
Christian	0	2,366	0.09
England	0	2,289	0.09
Brom Ind Con	0	2,182	0.08
SAP	0	1,962	0.07
SIG	0	1,208	0.05
SMRA	0	977	0.04
SLP	0	864	0.03
Dem Lab	0	842	0.03
TUSC	0	824	0.03
NF	0	751	0.03
SDP	0	637	0.02
CMGB	0	598	0.02
Common Good	0	305	0.01
EPA	0	246	0.01
Impact	0	234	0.01
Loony	0	179	0.01
Pirate	0	173	0.01
Nobody	0	73	0.00
TOTAL	**59**	**2,640,206**	**64.75**

YORKSHIRE AND HUMBERSIDE

	Total Seats	Total Votes	% of Votes
Lab	32	826,537	34.35
Con	19	790,062	32.83
Lib Dem	3	552,570	22.96
BNP	0	104,177	4.33
UKIP	0	67,322	2.80
Ind	0	21,032	0.87
Green	0	20,824	0.87
England	0	11,722	0.49

YORKSHIRE AND HUMBERSIDE cont.

	Total Seats	Total Votes	% of Votes
TUSC	0	2,047	0.09
Lib	0	1,418	0.06
Green Soc	0	1,257	0.05
Respect	0	1,245	0.05
NF	0	1,237	0.05
SLP	0	957	0.04
SDP	0	914	0.04
DN	0	753	0.03
PNDP	0	331	0.01
Loony	0	318	0.01
Christian	0	250	0.01
Comm GB	0	139	0.01
Youth	0	95	0.00
Currency	0	84	0.00
CURE	0	72	0.00
TOTAL	**54**	**2,405,363**	**62.94**

Northern Ireland

	Total Seats	Total Votes	% of Votes
Sinn Féin	5	171,942	25.52
DUP	8	168,216	24.96
SDLP	3	110,970	16.47
UCUNF	0	102,361	15.19
Ind	1	47,778	7.09
All	1	42,762	6.35
TUV	0	26,300	3.90
Green	0	3,542	0.53
TOTAL	**18**	**673,871**	**57.64**

Scotland

	Total Seats	Total Votes	% of Votes
Lab	41	1,035,535	42.00
SNP	6	491,386	19.93
Lib Dem	11	465,471	18.88
Con	1	412,765	16.74
UKIP	0	17,223	0.70
Green	0	16,827	0.68
BNP	0	8,910	0.36
Ind	0	6,479	0.26
SSP	0	3,157	0.13
TUSC	0	2,217	0.09
SLP	0	1,673	0.07
Solidarity	0	1,126	0.05
Christian	0	835	0.03
Trust	0	534	0.02
Lib	0	389	0.02
SJP	0	290	0.01
Comm	0	179	0.01
SACL	0	138	0.01

Total Seats	Total Votes		% of Votes
Pirate	0	120	0.00
JOT	0	93	0.00
Land Power	0	57	0.00
Comm League	0	48	0.00
TOTAL	**59**	**2,465,452**	**63.95**

Wales

	Total Seats	Total Votes	% of Votes
Lab	26	531,601	36.24
Con	8	382,730	26.09
Lib Dem	3	295,164	20.12
PlC	3	165,394	11.28
UKIP	0	35,690	2.43
Ind	0	21,670	1.48
BNP	0	17,843	1.22
Green	0	6,293	0.43
SOTBTH	0	3,588	0.24
Christian	0	1,408	0.10
SLP	0	1,155	0.08
NMB	0	558	0.04
WCP	0	539	0.04
NF	0	384	0.03
Loony	0	352	0.02
TUSC	0	341	0.02
Comm	0	196	0.01
Green Soc	0	127	0.01
TOTAL	**40**	**1,465,033**	**65.73**

Seats which changed parties

Changes are based on notional election results, thus Solihull is shown as changing parties even though its MP represented the predecessor seat in the 2005 parliament. In addition, as changes are based on notional 2005 general election results, Norwich North is shown as changing parties, although the Conservatives gained it from Labour in a by-election; similarly Glasgow East does not appear as a change in party as a by-election gain was reversed at the general election. North Down is listed as the sitting MP changed her party during the course of the last parliament.

	2005	2010
Aberconwy*	Lab	Con
Amber Valley*	Lab	Con
Arfon*	Lab	PlC
South Basildon and East Thurrock*	Lab/Co-op	Con
Battersea*	Lab	Con
Bedford*	Lab	Con
Belfast East*	DUP	Alliance
Bethnal Green and Bow*	Respect	Lab
Blackpool North and Cleveleys*	Lab	Con
Blaenau Gwent*	Ind	Lab
Bradford East*	Lab	Lib Dem
Brent Central*	Lab	Lib Dem
Brentford and Isleworth*	Lab	Con

Notional holder after boundary changes

	2005	*2010*
Brigg and Goole*	Lab	Con
Brighton Pavilion*	Lab	Green
Bristol North West*	Lab	Con
Broxtowe*	Lab	Con
Burnley	Lab	Lib Dem
Burton*	Lab	Con
Bury North*	Lab	Con
Calder Valley*	Lab	Con
Camborne and Redruth*	Lib Dem	Con
Cannock Chase*	Lab	Con
Cardiff North	Lab	Con
Carlisle*	Lab	Con
Carmarthen West and South Pembrokeshire*	Lab	Con
Chatham and Aylesford*	Lab	Con
City of Chester*	Lab	Con
Chesterfield*	Lib Dem	Lab
Cleethorpes*	Lab	Con
Colne Valley*	Lab	Con
Corby	Lab/Co-op	Con
South East Cornwall*	Lib Dem	Con
Crawley	Lab	Con
Crewe and Nantwich*	Lab	Con
Darford*	Lab	Con
South Derbyshire*	Lab	Con
Dewsbury*	Lab	Con
South Dorset	Lab	Con
Dover*	Lab	Con
North Down	UUP	Ind
Dudley South*	Lab	Con
Ealing Central and Acton*	Lab	Con
Eastbourne*	Con	Lib Dem
Elmet and Rothwell*	Lab	Con
Enfield North*	Lab	Con
Erewash*	Lab	Con
Filton and Bradley Stoke*	Lab	Con
Finchley and Golders Green*	Lab	Con
Gillingham and Rainham*	Lab	Con
Gloucester*	Lab	Con
Great Yarmouth	Lab	Con
Halesowen and Rowley Regis*	Lab	Con
Harlow*	Lab	Con
Harrow East*	Lab	Con
Hastings and Rye*	Lab	Con
Hendon*	Lab	Con
Hereford and South Herefordshire*	Lib Dem	Con
High Peak*	Lab	Con
Hove*	Lab	Con
Hyndburn*	Lab	Con
Ipswich*	Lab	Con
Keighley*	Lab	Con
Kingswood*	Lab	Con
Lancaster and Fleetwood*	Lab	Con
North West Leicestershire	Lab	Con

	2005	*2010*
Lincoln*	Lab	Con
Loughborough*	Lab/Co-op	Con
Milton Keynes North*	Lab	Con
Milton Keynes South*	Lab	Con
Montgomeryshire*	Lib Dem	Con
Morecambe and Lunesdale*	Lab	Con
Newton Abbot*	Lib Dem	Con
Northampton North*	Lab	Con
Northampton South*	Lab	Con
Norwich North*	Lab	Con
Norwich South*	Lab	Lib Dem
Nuneaton*	Lab	Con
Oxford West and Abingdon*	Lib Dem	Con
Pendle	Lab	Con
Plymouth, Sutton and Devonport*	Lab/Co-op	Con
Portsmouth North*	Lab/Co-op	Con
Pudsey*	Lab	Con
Reading West*	Lab	Con
Redcar*	Lab	Lib Dem
Redditch*	Lab	Con
South Ribble*	Lab	Con
Richmond Park*	Lib Dem	Con
Romsey and Southampton North*	Lib Dem	Con
Rossendale and Darwen*	Lab	Con
Rugby*	Lab	Con
Sherwood*	Lab	Con
Stafford *	Lab	Con
Staffordshire Moorlands*	Lab	Con
Stevenage*	Lab	Con
Stockton South*	Lab	Con
Stourbridge*	Lab	Con
Stroud*	Lab/Co-op	Con
North Swindon*	Lab	Con
South Swindon*	Lab	Con
Tamworth*	Lab	Con
South Thanet*	Lab	Con
Thurrock*	Lab	Con
Truro and Falmouth*	Lib Dem	Con
Warrington South*	Lab	Con
Warwick and Leamington*	Lab	Con
North Warwickshire*	Lab	Con
Watford*	Lab	Con
Waveney*	Lab	Con
Weaver Vale*	Lab	Con
Wells*	Con	Lib Dem
Winchester*	Lib Dem	Con
Wolverhampton South West*	Lab	Con
Worcester	Lab	Con
Wyre Forest*	Ind KHHC	Con
York Outer*	Lib Dem	Con

Notional holder after boundary changes

Results in vulnerable Conservative seats

	% majority 2005	*Result*	*Swing*
Sittingbourne and Sheppey*	0.05	Con hold	12.7% from Lab to Con
Clwyd West*	0.14	Con hold	8.3% from Lab to Con
Guildford*	0.17	Con hold	6.9% from Lib Dem to Con
Solihull*	0.25	Lib Dem gain	0.3% from Con to Lib Dem
Hemel Hempstead*	0.36	Con hold	1.9% from Lib Dem to Con
Kettering*	0.39	Con hold	9.4% from Lab to Con
North East Somerset*	0.46	Con hold	4.6% from Lab to Con
Croydon Central*	0.72	Con hold	3.3% from Lab to Con
Shipley*	0.97	Con hold	9.5% from Lab to Con
Rochester and Strood*	1.14	Con hold	9.8% from Lab to Con
Wellingborough*	1.25	Con hold	10.8% from Lab to Con
Eastbourne*	1.41	Lib Dem gain	5.8% from Con to Lib Dem
Gravesham	1.45	Con hold	9.1% from Lab to Con
Wirral West*	1.51	Con hold	2.3% from Lab to Con
Preseli Pembrokeshire*	1.53	Con hold	5% from Lab to Con
Reading East*	1.71	Con hold	2% from Lib Dem to Con
South Thanet*	1.76	Con hold	7.4% from Lab to Con
Scarborough and Whitby	2.65	Con hold	6.9% from Lab to Con
Enfield Southgate*	2.72	Con hold	7.2% from Lab to Con
The Wrekin*	2.85	Con hold	8.8% from Lab to Con
St Albans*	2.94	Con hold	3.7% from Con to Lib Dem
Shrewsbury and Atcham	3.59	Con hold	0.1% from Lib Dem to Con
Staffordshire Moorlands*	3.86	Con hold	5.7% from Lab to Con
Dumfriesshire, Clydesdale and Tweeddale	3.89	Con hold	2.6% from Lab to Con
Ilford North*	4.14	Con hold	3.7% from Lab to Con
Weston-Super-Mare*	4.26	Con hold	0.4% from Lib Dem to Con
Forest of Dean	4.3	Con hold	9.2% from Lab to Con
Selby and Ainsty*	4.31	Con hold	9.7% from Lab to Con
Ludlow	4.36	Con hold	7.8% from Lib Dem to Con
West Dorset	4.62	Con hold	1.1% from Lib Dem to Con
Putney*	4.8	Con hold	9.9% from Lab to Con
Meon Valley*	4.91	Con hold	9.4% from Lib Dem to Con
Central Devon*	4.99	Con hold	6.1% from Lib Dem to Con
Torridge and West Devon*	5.37	Con hold	No swing
Wimbledon*	5.69	Con hold	0.4% from Lib Dem to Con
Wells*	5.74	Lib Dem gain	3.6% from Con to Lib Dem
Totnes*	5.76	Con hold	2.3% from Lib Dem to Con
West Worcestershire*	6.03	Con hold	3.2% from Lib Dem to Con
Beverley and Holderness*	6.23	Con hold	1.6% from Lib Dem to Con
Basingstoke*	6.27	Con hold	4.5% from Lib Dem to Con

Results in vulnerable Labour seats

	% majority 2005	*Result*	*Swing*
Gillingham and Rainham*	0.03	Con gain	9.3% from Lab to Con
Crawley	0.09	Con gain	6.3% from Lab to Con
Rochdale*	0.35	Lab hold	0.8 from Lib Dem to Lab
Harlow*	0.58	Con gain	5.9% from Lab to Con

	% majority 2005	Result	Swing
Finchley and Golders Green*	0.7	Con gain	5.8% from Lab to Con
Oxford East*	0.73	Lab hold	4.1% from Lib Dem to Lab
Portsmouth North*	0.77	Con gain	8.6% from Lab to Con
Battersea*	0.81	Con gain	6.5% from Lab to Con
Edinburgh South	0.95	Lab hold	0.1% from Lab to Lib Dem
Hove*	1	Con gain	2.4% from Lab to Con
Hampstead and Kilburn*	1.14	Lab hold	6.7% from Lab to Con
Ochil and South Perthshire	1.47	Lab hold	4.4% from SNP to Lab
Islington South and Finsbury	1.56	Lab hold	3.3% from Lib Dem to Lab
Filton and Bradley Stoke*	1.58	Con gain	6.4% from Lab to Con
Milton Keynes North*	1.71	Con gain	9.2% from Lab to Con
Arfon*	1.82	PlC gain	3.7% from Lab to PlC
Stroud*	1.85	Con gain	2.1% from Lab to Con
Dartford*	1.9	Con gain	11.5% from Lab to Con
South Basildon and East Thurrock*	2.14	Con gain	7.5% from Lab to Con
Ealing Central and Acton*	2.16	Con gain	5% from Lab to Con
City of Chester*	2.2	Con gain	3.9% from Lab to Con
Watford*	2.33	Con gain	6.1% from Lab to Con
Enfield North*	2.35	Con gain	0.7% from Lab to Con
Colne Valley*	2.51	Con gain	6.5% from Lib Dem to Con
Cardiff North	2.53	Con gain	6.5% from Lab to Con
Hastings and Rye*	2.54	Con gain	3.3% from Lab to Con
Calder Valley*	2.73	Con gain	7.6% from Lab to Con
Stourbridge*	2.92	Con gain	6.9% from Lab to Con
Milton Keynes South*	3.04	Con gain	6.2% from Lab to Con
Corby	3.13	Con gain	3.3% from Lab to Con
Aberdeen South	3.24	Lab hold	2.5% from Lib Dem to Lab
Vale of Glamorgan*	3.37	Con gain	6.1% from Lab to Con
South Swindon*	3.5	Con gain	5.5% from Lab to Con
Ynys Môn	3.5	Lab hold	1.8% from PlC to Lab
South Dorset	3.73	Con gain	9.3% from Lab to Con
Northampton South*	3.78	Con gain	9.6% from Lab to Con
High Peak*	3.8	Con gain	6.5% from Lab to Con
Loughborough*	3.88	Con gain	5.5% from Lab to Con
Aberconwy*	3.93	Con gain	7.6% from Lab to Con
Birmingham, Edgbaston*	4.01	Lab hold	0.5% from Lab to Con

Results in vulnerable Liberal Democrat seats

	% majority 2005	Result	Swing
York Outer*	0.44	Con gain	3.7% from Lib Dem to Con
Romsey and Southampton North*	0.46	Con gain	5.5% from Lib Dem to Con
Ceredigion*	0.61	Lib Dem hold	10.6% from PlC to Lib Dem
Cheltenham*	0.66	Lib Dem hold	4.3% from Con to Lib Dem
Eastleigh*	1.12	Lib Dem hold	3% from Con to Lib Dem
Somerton and Frome*	1.12	Lib Dem hold	0.9% from Con to Lib Dem
Manchester Withington*	1.39	Lib Dem hold	1.4% from Lab to Lib Dem
Westmorland and Lonsdale*	1.7	Lib Dem hold	11% from Con to Lib Dem

Notional holder after boundary changes

	% majority 2005	Result	Swing
Hereford and South Herefordshire*	2.39	Con gain	3.8% from Lib Dem to Con
Bristol West*	2.55	Lib Dem hold	9% from Lab to Lib Dem
Carshalton and Wallington *	2.93	Lib Dem hold	4.2% from Con to Lib Dem
Taunton Deane*	3.3	Lib Dem hold	1.8% from Con to Lib Dem
Chippenham*	4.7	Lib Dem hold	No swing
Leeds North West*	4.96	Lib Dem hold	5.4% from Con to Lib Dem
Hornsey and Wood Green	5.06	Lib Dem hold	3.7% from Lab to Lib Dem
Torbay*	6.01	Lib Dem hold	1.1% from Con to Lib Dem
Sutton and Cheam*	6.22	Lib Dem hold	1.5% from Lib Dem to Con
Chesterfield*	6.36	Lab gain	3.8% from Lib Dem to Lab
North Cornwall*	6.87	Lib Dem hold	0.3% from Lib Dem to Con

Result in vulnerable SDLP seat

	% majority 2005	Result	Swing
Belfast South*	0.5	SDLP hold	8.4% from DUP to SDLP

Results in vulnerable SNP seats

	% majority 2005	Result	Swing
Dundee East	0.97	SNP hold	1.8% from Lab to SNP
Perth and North Perthshire	3.31	SNP hold	2.9% from Con to SNP
Angus	4.2	SNP hold	2.2% from Con to SNP

Result in vulnerable Respect seat

	% majority 2005	Result	Swing
Bethnal Green and Bow*	2.1	Lab gain	14.1% from Respect to Lab

*Notional holder after boundary changes

New MPs

(232 MPs who did not serve in the 2005 Parliament, 5 of whom had been MPs in earlier Parliaments)

ADAMS, Nigel	Con	Selby and Ainsty
ALDOUS, Peter	Con	Waveney
ALEXANDER, Heidi	Lab	Lewisham East
ALI, Rushanara	Lab	Bethnal Green and Bow
ANDREW, Stuart	Con	Pudsey
BAKER, Steve	Con	Wycombe
BALDWIN, Harriett	Con	West Worcestershire
BARCLAY, Steve	Con	North East Cambridgeshire
BARWELL, Gavin	Con	Croydon Central
BEBB, Guto	Con	Aberconwy
BERGER, Luciana	Lab/Co-op	Liverpool Wavertree
BERRY, Jake	Con	Rossendale and Darwen
BINGHAM, Andrew	Con	High Peak
BIRTWISTLE, Gordon	Lib Dem	Burnley
BLACKMAN, Bob	Con	Harrow East
BLACKWOOD, Nicola	Con	Oxford West and Abingdon
BLENKINSOP, Tom	Lab	Middlesbrough South and East Cleveland
BLOMFIELD, Paul	Lab	Sheffield Central
BOLES, Nick	Con	Grantham and Stamford
BRADLEY, Karen	Con	Staffordshire Moorlands
BRAY, Angie	Con	Ealing Central and Acton
BRIDGEN, Andrew	Con	North West Leicestershire
BRINE, Steve	Con	Winchester
BRUCE, Fiona	Con	Congleton
BUCKLAND, Robert	Con	South Swindon
BURLEY, Aidan	Con	Cannock Chase
BURNS, Conor	Con	Bournemouth West
BYLES, Dan	Con	North Warwickshire
CAIRNS, Alun	Con	Vale of Glamorgan
CARMICHAEL, Neil	Con	Stroud
CHAPMAN, Jenny	Lab	Darlington
CHISHTI, Rehman	Con	Gillingham and Rainham
COFFEY, Therese	Con	Suffolk Coastal
COLLINS, Damian	Con	Folkestone and Hythe
COLVILE, Oliver	Con	Plymouth, Sutton and Devonport
CREASY, Stella	Lab/Co-op	Walthamstow
CROCKART, Mike	Lib Dem	Edinburgh West
CROUCH, Tracey	Con	Chatham and Aylesford
CRYER, John*	Lab	Leyton and Wanstead
CUNNINGHAM, Alex	Lab	Stockton North
CURRAN, Margaret	Lab	Glasgow East
DAKIN, Nic	Lab	Scunthorpe
DANCZUK, Simon	Lab	Rochdale
DAVIES, Geraint*	Lab/Co-op	Swansea West
DAVIES, Glyn	Con	Montgomeryshire
DE BOIS, Nick	Con	Enfield North
DE PIERO, Gloria	Lab	Ashfield
DINENAGE, Caroline	Con	Gosport
DOCHERTY, Thomas	Lab	Dunfermline and West Fife
DOYLE, Gemma	Lab/Co-op	West Dunbartonshire
DOYLE-PRICE, Jackie	Con	Thurrock
DRAX, Richard	Con	South Dorset
DROMEY, Jack	Lab	Birmingham, Erdington
DUGHER, Michael	Lab	Barnsley East
EDWARDS, Jonathan	PlC	Carmarthen East and Dinefwr

*MP in earlier Parliament

ELLIOTT, Julie	*Lab*	Sunderland Central
ELLIS, Michael	*Con*	Northampton North
ELLISON, Jane	*Con*	Battersea
ELPHICKE, Charlie	*Con*	Dover
ESTERSON, Bill	*Lab*	Sefton Central
EUSTICE, George	*Con*	Camborne and Redruth
EVANS, Christopher	*Lab/Co-op*	Islwyn
EVANS, Graham	*Con*	Weaver Vale
EVANS, Jonathan*	*Con*	Cardiff North
FOVARGUE, Yvonne	*Lab*	Makerfield
FREEMAN, George	*Con*	Mid Norfolk
FREER, Mike	*Con*	Finchley and Golders Green
FULLBROOK, Lorraine	*Con*	South Ribble
FULLER, Richard	*Con*	Bedford
GARNIER, Mark	*Con*	Wyre Forest
GILBERT, Steve	*Lib Dem*	St Austell and Newquay
GILMORE, Sheila	*Lab*	Edinburgh East
GLASS, Patricia	*Lab*	North West Durham
GLEN, John	*Con*	Salisbury
GLINDON, Mary	*Lab*	North Tyneside
GOLDSMITH, Zac	*Con*	Richmond Park
GRAHAM, Richard	*Con*	Gloucester
GRANT, Helen	*Con*	Maidstone and The Weald
GREATREX, Tom	*Lab/Co-op*	Rutherglen and Hamilton West
GREEN, Kate	*Lab*	Stretford and Urmston
GREENWOOD, Lilian	*Lab*	Nottingham South
GRIFFITHS, Andrew	*Con*	Burton
GUMMER, Ben	*Con*	Ipswich
GYIMAH, Sam	*Con*	East Surrey
HALFON, Robert	*Con*	Harlow
HAMES, Duncan	*Lib Dem*	Chippenham
HANCOCK, Matthew	*Con*	West Suffolk
HARRINGTON, Richard	*Con*	Watford
HARRIS, Rebecca	*Con*	Castle Point
HART, Simon	*Con*	Carmarthen West and South Pembrokeshire
HEATON-HARRIS, Christopher	*Con*	Daventry
HENDERSON, Gordon	*Con*	Sittingbourne and Sheppey
HILLING, Julie	*Lab*	Bolton West
HINDS, Damian	*Con*	East Hampshire
HOLLINGBERY, George	*Con*	Meon Valley
HOPKINS, Kris	*Con*	Keighley
HUNT, Tristram	*Lab*	Stoke-on-Trent Central
HUPPERT, Julian	*Lib Dem*	Cambridge
JAMES, Margot	*Con*	Stourbridge
JAMIESON, Cathy	*Lab/Co-op*	Kilmarnock and Loudoun
JAVID, Sajid	*Con*	Bromsgrove
JOHNSON, Gareth	*Con*	Dartford
JOHNSON, Jo	*Con*	Orpington
JONES, Andrew	*Con*	Harrogate and Knaresborough
JONES, Graham	*Lab*	Hyndburn
JONES, Marcus	*Con*	Nuneaton
JONES, Susan Elan	*Lab*	Clwyd South
KELLY, Chris	*Con*	Dudley South
KENDALL, Liz	*Lab*	Leicester West
KIRBY, Simon	*Con*	Brighton Kemptown
KWARTENG, Kwasi	*Con*	Spelthorne
LATHAM, Pauline	*Con*	Mid Derbyshire
LAVERY, Ian	*Lab*	Wansbeck
LEADSOM, Andrea	*Con*	South Northamptonshire
LEE, Jessica	*Con*	Erewash

LEE, Phillip	Con	Bracknell
LEFROY, Jeremy	Con	Stafford
LESLIE, Charlotte	Con	Bristol North West
LESLIE, Chris*	Lab/Co-op	Nottingham East
LEWIS, Brandon	Con	Great Yarmouth
LLOYD, Stephen	Lib Dem	Eastbourne
LONG, Naomi	All	Belfast East
LOPRESTI, Jack	Con	Filton and Bradley Stoke
LORD, Jonathan	Con	Woking
LUCAS, Caroline	Green	Brighton Pavilion
LUMLEY, Karen	Con	Redditch
MCCANN, Michael	Lab	East Kilbride, Strathaven and Lesmahagow
MCCARTNEY, Jason	Con	Colne Valley
MCCARTNEY, Karl	Con	Lincoln
MCCLYMONT, Gregg	Lab	Cumbernauld, Kilsyth and Kirkintilloch East
MCGOVERN, Alison	Lab	Wirral South
MCKINNELL, Catherine	Lab	Newcastle upon Tyne North
MACLEOD, Mary	Con	Brentford and Isleworth
MCPARTLAND, Stephen	Con	Stevenage
MCVEY, Esther	Con	Wirral West
MAHMOOD, Shabana	Lab	Birmingham, Ladywood
MAYNARD, Paul	Con	Blackpool North and Cleveleys
MEARNS, Ian	Lab	Gateshead
MENSCH, Louise	Con	Corby
MENZIES, Mark	Con	Fylde
METCALFE, Stephen	Con	South Basildon and East Thurrock
MILLS, Nigel	Con	Amber Valley
MORDAUNT, Penny	Con	Portsmouth North
MORGAN, Nicky	Con	Loughborough
MORRICE, Graeme	Lab	Livingston
MORRIS, Anne Marie	Con	Newton Abbot
MORRIS, David	Con	Morecambe and Lunesdale
MORRIS, Grahame	Lab	Easington
MORRIS, James	Con	Halesowen and Rowley Regis
MOSLEY, Stephen	Con	City of Chester
MOWAT, David	Con	Warrington South
MUNT, Tessa	Lib Dem	Wells
MURRAY, Ian	Lab	Edinburgh South
MURRAY, Sheryll	Con	South East Cornwall
NANDY, Lisa	Lab	Wigan
NASH, Pamela	Lab	Airdrie and Shotts
NEWTON, Sarah	Con	Truro and Falmouth
NOKES, Caroline	Con	Romsey and Southampton North
NORMAN, Jesse	Con	Hereford and South Herefordshire
NUTTALL, David	Con	Bury North
O'DONNELL, Fiona	Lab	East Lothian
OFFORD, Matthew	Con	Hendon
OLLERENSHAW, Eric	Con	Lancaster and Fleetwood
ONWURAH, Chi	Lab	Newcastle upon Tyne Central
OPPERMAN, Guy	Con	Hexham
PAISLEY, Ian	DUP	North Antrim
PARISH, Neil	Con	Tiverton and Honiton
PATEL, Priti	Con	Witham
PAWSEY, Mark	Con	Rugby
PEARCE, Teresa	Lab	Erith and Thamesmead
PERCY, Andrew	Con	Brigg and Goole
PERKINS, Toby	Lab	Chesterfield
PERRY, Claire	Con	Devizes
PHILLIPS, Stephen	Con	Sleaford and North Hykeham

*MP in earlier Parliament

PHILLIPSON, Bridget	Lab	Houghton and Sunderland South
PINCHER, Christopher	Con	Tamworth
POULTER, Daniel	Con	Central Suffolk and North Ipswich
QURESHI, Yasmin	Lab	Bolton South East
RAAB, Dominic	Con	Esher and Walton
RECKLESS, Mark	Con	Rochester and Strood
REES-MOGG, Jacob	Con	North East Somerset
REEVELL, Simon	Con	Dewsbury
REEVES, Rachel	Lab	Leeds West
REYNOLDS, Emma	Lab	Wolverhampton North East
REYNOLDS, Jonathan	Lab/Co-op	Stalybridge and Hyde
RITCHIE, Margaret	SDLP	South Down
ROTHERAM, Steve	Lab	Liverpool Walton
RUDD, Amber	Con	Hastings and Rye
RUTLEY, David	Con	Macclesfield
SANDYS, Laura	Con	South Thanet
SARWAR, Anas	Lab	Glasgow Central
SHANNON, Jim	DUP	Strangford
SHARMA, Alok	Con	Reading West
SHELBROOKE, Alec	Con	Elmet and Rothwell
SHUKER, Gavin	Lab/Co-op	Luton South
SKIDMORE, Chris	Con	Kingswood
SMITH, Henry	Con	Crawley
SMITH, Julian	Con	Skipton and Ripon
SMITH, Nick	Lab	Blaenau Gwent
SMITH, Owen	Lab	Pontypridd
SOUBRY, Anna	Con	Broxtowe
SPENCER, Mark	Con	Sherwood
STEPHENSON, Andrew	Con	Pendle
STEVENSON, John	Con	Carlisle
STEWART, Bob	Con	Beckenham
STEWART, Iain	Con	Milton Keynes South
STEWART, Rory	Con	Penrith and The Border
STRIDE, Mel	Con	Central Devon
STURDY, Julian	Con	York Outer
SWALES, Ian	Lib Dem	Redcar
TOMLINSON, Justin	Con	North Swindon
TRUSS, Elizabeth	Con	South West Norfolk
TURNER, Karl	Lab	Kingston upon Hull East
TWIGG, Stephen*	Lab/Co-op	Liverpool West Derby
UMUNNA, Chuka	Lab	Streatham
UPPAL, Paul	Con	Wolverhampton South West
VAZ, Valerie	Lab	Walsall South
VICKERS, Martin	Con	Cleethorpes
WALKER, Robin	Con	Worcester
WARD, David	Lib Dem	Bradford East
WEATHERLEY, Mike	Con	Hove
WHARTON, James	Con	Stockton South
WHEELER, Heather	Con	South Derbyshire
WHITE, Chris	Con	Warwick and Leamington
WHITEFORD, Eilidh	SNP	Banff and Buchan
WHITTAKER, Craig	Con	Calder Valley
WILLIAMSON, Chris	Lab	Derby North
WILLIAMSON, Gavin	Con	South Staffordshire
WOLLASTON, Sarah	Con	Totnes
WOODCOCK, John	Lab/Co-op	Barrow and Furness
WRIGHT, Simon	Lib Dem	Norwich South
ZAHAWI, Nadhim	Con	Stratford-on-Avon

*MP in earlier Parliament

Defeated MPs

76: 51 Labour, 6 Lab/Co-op, 2 Conservative, 9 Lib Dem, 4 Ind, 1 DUP, 1 SNP, 1 Ind KHHC, 1 Respect

AINGER, Nick	Lab	Carmarthen West and South Pembrokeshire
ANDERSON, Janet	Lab	Rossendale and Darwen
ATKINS, Charlotte	Lab	Staffordshire Moorlands
BAIRD, Vera	Lab	Redcar
BARLOW, Celia	Lab	Hove
BERRY, Roger	Lab	Kingswood
BLIZZARD, Bob	Lab	Waveney
BORROW, David	Lab	South Ribble
BUTLER, Dawn	Lab	Brent South
CAWSEY, Ian	Lab	Brigg and Goole
CLARK, Paul	Lab	Gillingham
CLARKE, Charles	Lab	Norwich South
COOK, Frank	Ind	Stockton North
DAVIES, Dai	Ind	Blaenau Gwent
DHANDA, Parmjit	Lab	Gloucester
DISMORE, Andrew	Lab	Hendon
DREW, David	Lab/Co-op	Stroud
FOSTER, Michael Jabez	Lab	Hastings and Rye
FOSTER, Michael John	Lab	Worcester
GALLOWAY, George	Respect	Bethnal Green and Bow
GIDLEY, Sandra	Lib Dem	Romsey
GILROY, Linda	Lab/Co-op	Plymouth Sutton
GOLDSWORTHY, Julia	Lib Dem	Falmouth and Camborne
HALL, Patrick	Lab	Bedford
HARRIS, Evan	Lib Dem	Oxford West and Abingdon
HEATHCOAT-AMORY, David	Con	Wells
HOLMES, Paul	Lib Dem	Chesterfield
HOPE, Phil	Lab/Co-op	Corby
JENKINS, Brian	Lab	Tamworth
KEEBLE, Sally	Lab	Northampton North
KEEN, Ann	Lab	Brentford and Isleworth
KIDNEY, David	Lab	Stafford
KNIGHT, Jim*	Lab	South Dorset
KRAMER, Susan	Lib Dem	Richmond Park
LADYMAN, Stephen	Lab	South Thanet
LINTON, Martin	Lab	Battersea
MCCARTHY-FRY, Sarah	Lab/Co-op	Portsmouth North
MCISAAC, Shona	Lab	Cleethorpes
MCNULTY, Tony	Lab	Harrow East
MALIK, Shahid	Lab	Dewsbury
MALLABER, Judy	Lab	Amber Valley
MARRIS, Rob	Lab	Wolverhampton South West
MASON, John	SNP	Glasgow East
MERRON, Gillian	Lab	Lincoln
MOLE, Chris	Lab	Ipswich
MORGAN, Julie	Lab	Cardiff North
NORRIS, Dan	Lab	Wansdyke
O'BRIEN, Mike	Lab	North Warwickshire
ÖPIK, Lembit	Lib Dem	Montgomeryshire
PALMER, Nick	Lab	Broxtowe
PELLING, Andrew	Ind	Croydon Central
PLASKITT, James	Lab	Warwick and Leamington
PRENTICE, Gordon	Lab	Pendle
PROSSER, Gwyn	Lab	Dover
RAMMELL, Bill	Lab	Harlow

Awarded life peerage in dissolution honours (see p1035 for Peer names)

REED, Andy	Lab/Co-op	Loughborough
RENNIE, Willie	Lib Dem	Dunfermline and West Fife
ROBINSON, Peter	DUP	Belfast East
ROONEY, Terry	Lab	Bradford North
ROWEN, Paul	Lib Dem	Rochdale
RUSSELL, Christine	Lab	City of Chester
RYAN, Joan	Lab	Enfield North
SHAW, Jonathan	Lab	Chatham and Aylesford
SMITH, Geraldine	Lab	Morecambe and Lunesdale
SMITH, Jacqui	Lab	Redditch
SMITH, Angela*	Lab/Co-op	Basildon
SNELGROVE, Anne	Lab	South Swindon
SPINK, Bob	Ind	Castle Point
STARKEY, Phyllis	Lab	Milton Keynes South West
TAYLOR, Dari	Lab	Stockton South
TAYLOR, Richard	Ind KHHC	Wyre Forest
WALTHO, Lynda	Lab	Stourbridge
WARD, Claire	Lab	Watford
WATERSON, Nigel	Con	Eastbourne
WRIGHT, Anthony David	Lab	Great Yarmouth
YOUNGER-ROSS, Richard	Lib Dem	Teignbridge

Retired MPs

(149, of whom 20 given life peerages)

AINSWORTH, Peter	Con	East Surrey
ANCRAM, Michael	Con	Devizes
ARMSTRONG, Hilary*	Lab	North West Durham
ATKINSON, Peter	Con	Hexham
AUSTIN, John	Lab	Erith and Thamesmead
BARRETT, John	Lib Dem	Edinburgh West
BATTLE, John	Lab	Leeds West
BLACKMAN, Liz	Lab	Erewash
BOSWELL, Timothy*	Con	Daventry
BREED, Colin	Lib Dem	South East Cornwall
BROWNE, Des*	Lab	Kilmarnock and Loudoun
BROWNING, Angela*	Con	Tiverton and Honiton
BURGON, Colin	Lab	Elmet
BUTTERFILL, John	Con	Bournemouth West
BYERS, Stephen	Lab	North Tyneside
CABORN, Richard	Lab	Sheffield Central
CHALLEN, Colin	Lab	Morley and Rothwell
CHAPMAN, Ben	Lab	Wirral South
CHAYTOR, David	Ind	Bury North
CLAPHAM, Michael	Lab	Barnsley West and Penistone
CLELLAND, David	Lab	Tyne Bridge
COHEN, Harry	Lab	Leyton and Wanstead
CONWAY, Derek	Ind	Old Bexley and Sidcup
CORMACK, Patrick	Con	South Staffordshire
COUSINS, Jim	Lab	Newcastle upon Tyne Central
CRYER, Ann	Lab	Keighley
CUMMINGS, John	Lab	Easington
CURRY, David	Con	Skipton and Ripon
CURTIS-THOMAS, Claire	Lab	Crosby
DAVIES, Quentin*	Lab	Grantham and Stamford
DEAN, Janet	Lab	Burton
DEVINE, Jim	Ind	Livingston
ENNIS, Jeff	Lab	Barnsley East and Mexborough
ETHERINGTON, Bill	Lab	Sunderland North
FISHER, Mark	Lab	Stoke-on-Trent Central

FOLLETT, Barbara	Lab	Stevenage
FRASER, Christopher	Con	South West Norfolk
GEORGE, Bruce	Lab	Walsall South
GERRARD, Neil	Lab	Walthamstow
GOODMAN, Paul	Con	Wycombe
GREENWAY, John	Con	Ryedale
GRIFFITHS, Nigel	Lab	Edinburgh South
GROGAN, John	Lab	Selby
GUMMER, John*	Con	Suffolk Coastal
HALL, Mike	Lab	Weaver Vale
HEAL, Sylvia	Lab	Halesowen and Rowley Regis
HENDERSON, Doug	Lab	Newcastle upon Tyne North
HEPPELL, John	Lab	Nottingham East
HESFORD, Stephen	Lab	Wirral West
HEWITT, Patricia	Lab	Leicester West
HILL, Keith	Lab	Streatham
HOGG, Douglas	Con	Sleaford and North Hykeham
HOON, Geoffrey	Lab	Ashfield
HORAM, John	Con	Orpington
HOWARD, Michael*	Con	Folkestone and Hythe
HOWARTH, David	Lib Dem	Cambridge
HOWELLS, Kim	Lab	Pontypridd
HUGHES, Beverley*	Lab	Stretford and Urmston
HUMBLE, Joan	Lab	Blackpool North and Fleetwood
HUTTON, John*	Lab	Barrow and Furness
IDDON, Brian	Lab	Bolton South East
INGRAM, Adam	Lab	East Kilbride, Strathaven and Lesmahagow
JACK, Michael	Con	Fylde
JONES, Lynne	Lab	Birmingham Selly Oak
JONES, Martyn	Lab	Clwyd South
KEETCH, Paul	Lib Dem	Hereford
KELLY, Ruth	Lab	Bolton West
KEMP, Fraser	Lab	Houghton and Washington East
KENNEDY, Jane	Lab	Liverpool Wavertree
KEY, Robert	Con	Salisbury
KILFOYLE, Peter	Lab	Liverpool Walton
KIRKBRIDE, Julie	Con	Bromsgrove
LAIT, Jacqui	Con	Beckenham
LAXTON, Bob	Lab	Derby North
LEPPER, David	Lab/Co-op	Brighton Pavilion
LEVITT, Tom	Lab	High Peak
LORD, Michael	Con	Central Suffolk and North Ipswich
MCAVOY, Thomas*	Lab/Co-op	Rutherglen and Hamilton West
MCCAFFERTY, Christine	Lab	Calder Valley
MCCARTNEY, Ian	Lab	Makerfield
MCFALL, John*	Lab/Co-op	West Dunbartonshire
MCGRADY, Eddie	SDLP	South Down
MACKAY, Andrew	Con	Bracknell
MCKENNA, Rosemary	Lab	Cumbernauld, Kilsyth and Kirkintilloch East
MACKINLAY, Andrew	Lab	Thurrock
MACLEAN, David	Con	Penrith and The Border
MALINS, Humfrey	Con	Woking
MAPLES, John*	Con	Stratford-on-Avon
MARSHALL-ANDREWS, Robert	Lab	Medway
MARTLEW, Eric	Lab	Carlisle
MATES, Michael	Con	East Hampshire
MILBURN, Alan	Lab	Darlington
MOFFAT, Anne	Lab	East Lothian

*Awarded life peerage in dissolution honours (see p1065 for Peer names)

MOFFATT, Laura	Lab	Crawley
MORAN, Margaret	Lab	Luton South
MORLEY, Elliot	Ind	Scunthorpe
MOSS, Malcolm	Con	North East Cambridgeshire
MOUNTFORD, Kali	Lab	Colne Valley
MULLIN, Chris	Lab	Sunderland South
MURPHY, Denis	Lab	Wansbeck
NAYSMITH, Doug	Lab/Co-op	Bristol North West
OATEN, Mark	Lib Dem	Winchester
O'HARA, Edward	Lab	Knowsley South
OLNER, Bill	Lab	Nuneaton
PAISLEY, Ian*	DUP	North Antrim
PEARSON, Ian	Lab	Dudley South
POPE, Greg	Lab	Hyndburn
PRENTICE, Bridget	Lab	Lewisham East
PRESCOTT, John*	Lab	Hull East
PRICE, Adam	PlC	Carmarthen East and Dinefwr
PURCHASE, Ken	Lab/Co-op	Wolverhampton North East
PURNELL, James	Lab	Stalybridge and Hyde
REID, John*	Lab	Airdrie and Shotts
SPRING, Richard	Con	West Suffolk
SALMOND, Alex	SNP	Banff and Buchan
SALTER, Martin	Lab	Reading West
SARWAR, Mohammad	Lab	Glasgow Central
SHORT, Clare	Ind	Birmingham Ladywood
SIMON, Siôn	Lab	Birmingham Erdington
SIMPSON, Alan	Lab	Nottingham South
SMITH, John	Lab	Vale of Glamorgan
SOUTHWORTH, Helen	Lab	Warrington South
SPICER, Michael*	Con	West Worcestershire
STEEN, Anthony	Con	Totnes
STEWART, Ian	Lab	Eccles
STOATE, Howard	Lab	Dartford
STRANG, Gavin	Lab	Edinburgh East
TAYLOR, Ian	Con	Esher and Walton
TAYLOR, Matthew*	Lib Dem	Truro and St Austell
TIPPING, Paddy	Lab	Sherwood
TODD, Mark	Lab	South Derbyshire
TOUHIG, Don*	Lab/Co-op	Islwyn
TRUSWELL, Paul	Lab	Pudsey
TURNER, Des	Lab	Brighton Kemptown
TURNER, Neil	Lab	Wigan
USSHER, Kitty	Lab	Burnley
VIGGERS, Peter	Con	Gosport
VIS, Rudi	Lab	Finchley and Golders Green
WAREING, Robert	Ind	Liverpool West Derby
WIDDECOMBE, Ann	Con	Maidstone and The Weald
WILLIAMS, Alan	Lab	Swansea West
WILLIAMS, Betty	Lab	Conwy
WILLIS, Phil*	Lib Dem	Harrogate and Knaresborough
WILLS, Michael*	Lab	North Swindon
WILSHIRE, David	Con	Spelthorne
WINTERTON, Ann	Con	Congleton
WINTERTON, Nicholas	Con	Macclesfield
WRIGHT, Tony Wayland	Lab	Cannock Chase
WYATT, Derek	Lab	Sittingbourne and Sheppey

*Awarded life peerage in dissolution honours (see p1065 for Peer names)

HOUSE OF LORDS

House of Lords

London SW1A 0PW 020 7219 3000 Peers' message service: 020 7219 5353
Information Office: 020 7219 3107 Website: www.parliament.uk Twitter: @UKHouseofLords
Bulk correspondence to Members may be delivered to Derby Gate at the Palace of Westminster, but
must be stamped or franked or accompanied by a cheque for second-class postage made out to Post
Office Counters.

Membership

Since the passing of the House of Lords Act, 1999, the majority of members, almost 700, are life peers.
The minority of life peers who are Lords of Appeal in Ordinary became Justices of the Supreme Court
of the United Kingdom from October 2009, forfeiting their right to participate in the Lords. The
Archbishops of Canterbury and York and the Bishops of London, Durham and Winchester are
ex-officio members of the Lords, while the remaining 21 Bishops who are members sit by rotation
according to seniority; these are known as Lords Spiritual.

Ninety-two hereditary peers still sit by virtue of election by their fellow peers. In addition, some
hereditary peers have been created life peers, of whom 11 remain.

There are two hereditary office holders who are members of the House under the House of Lords Act,
1999: the Duke of Norfolk as Earl Marshal, and the Marquess of Cholmondeley as Lord Great
Chamberlain.

Speaker and Deputies

Lord Speaker

Baroness D'Souza

Deputy Speakers

Several Lords are appointed to act as Speaker of the House of Lords in the absence of the Lord Speaker.

Baroness Anelay of St Johns (Con)
Lord Bassam of Brighton (Lab/Co-op)
Lord Brougham and Vaux (Con)
Lord Colwyn (Con)
Lord Faulkner of Worcester (Lab)
Baroness Fookes (Con)
Lord Geddes (Con)
Baroness Gibson of Market Rasen (Lab)
Baroness Gould of Potternewton (Lab)
Baroness Harris of Richmond (Lib Dem)
Lord Haskel (Lab)

Baroness Hooper (Con)
Baroness McIntosh of Hudnall (Lab)
Countess of Mar (CB)
Baroness Morris of Bolton (Con)
Baroness Pitkeathley (Lab)
Lord Roper (Lib Dem)
Lord Sewel (NA)
Viscount Simon (Lab)
Lord Skelmersdale (Con)
Viscount Ullswater (Con)

Chairman and Deputy Chairmen

Lords are appointed by the House to fill the offices of Chairman and Principal Deputy Chairman of
Committees. The Chairman is chairman *ex-officio* of all committees of the House.

Chairman of Committees:
Lord Sewel (NA)
Principal Deputy Chairman of Committees:
Lord Boswell of Aynho (NA)
Deputy Chairmen:
Baroness Andrews (Lab)
Baroness Anelay of St Johns (Con)
Lord Bassam of Brighton (Lab/Co-op)
Lord Bates (Con)
Lord Bichard (CB)

Lord Brougham and Vaux (Con)
Lord Colwyn (Con)
Lord Faulkner of Worcester (Lab)
Baroness Fookes (Con)
Lord Geddes (Con)
Baroness Gibson of Market Rasen (Lab)
Baroness Harris of Richmond (Lib Dem)
Lord Haskel (Lab)
Baroness Hooper (Con)
Baroness McIntosh of Hudnall (Lab)

Baroness Morris of Bolton (Con)
Baroness Pitkeathley (Lab)
Viscount Simon (Lab)

Lord Skelmersdale (Con)
Viscount Ullswater (Con)

House of Lords Appointments Commission

Room G5, Ground Floor, 1 Horse Guards Road, London SW1A 2HQ
Tel: 020 7271 0843
Email: enquiry@lordsappointments.gsi.gov.uk Website: lordsappointments.independent.gov.uk

The Appointments Commission is a non-statutory advisory non-departmental public body. It has two main functions: to make recommendations for non-party-political peers and to vet for propriety nominations for peerages, including those from the political parties.

Chair: **Lord Kakkar** (CB)
Independent Members: **Baroness Campbell of Surbiton** DBE (CB), Prof Dame **Joan Higgins** DBE, Dr **John Low** CBE
Political Party Nominees: Rt Hon **Lord Howard of Lympne** CH QC (Con), **Baroness Scott of Needham Market** (Lib Dem), **Lord Hart of Chilton** (Lab)
Secretary: **Clare Salters**

Members (Peers)

Party affiliation (October 2013)

	Total
Labour	232 *
Conservative	225
Crossbench	197
Liberal Democrat	101
Other	60 †
Democratic Unionist Party	4
Plaid Cymru	2
UK Independence Party	2
Ulster Unionist Party	2
Liberal Democrat Independent	1
Conservative Independent	1
Green Party	1
Independent Conservative	1
Independent Labour	1
Independent Liberal Democrat	1
Independent Ulster Unionist	1
	832 seats

* Includes 15 Labour/Co-operative peers.
† Includes the Lord Speaker, Lords Spiritual, independents and peers who have not declared any party affiliation.

Summary (October 2013)

Life Peers	720
Hereditary Peers	103 ‡
Archbishops and Bishops	20 §

‡ Includes 11 who sit as Life Peers.

§Bishop of Ripon and Leeds is to retire after Easter recess and will be replaced by the Rt Rev. James Langstaff the Bishop of Rochester. Bishop of Wakefield is to retire after Easter recess and will be replaced by the Rt Rev. Stephen Conway the Bishop of Ely.

NB: Please note Bishops of St Albans, Carlisle, Southwell and Nottingham, Peterborough, Portsmouth, and Chelmsford have no biographies as they were not introduced to the House of Lords at the time of going to press. Bishop of Southwell and Nottingham is to be introduced as the Bishop of Durham in early 2014.

Changes since last edition

NEW MEMBERS

Lord Deighton (*Con*)	1 November 2012
Lord Williams of Oystermouth (*CB*)	11 January 2013
Bishop of Coventry (*NA*)	15 January 2013
Lord Nash (*Con*)	21 January 2013
Viscount Ridley (*Con*)	6 February 2013
Baroness Lane-Fox of Soho (*CB*)	25 March 2013
Lord Berkeley of Knighton (*CB*)	26 March 2013
Bishop of Truro (*NA*)	22 April 2013
Lord Livingston of Parkhead (*Con*)	12 July 2013
Bishop of Sheffield (*NA*)	15 July 2013
Lord Borwick (*Con*)	17 July 2013
Lord King of Lothbury (*CB*)	19 July 2013
Baroness Grender (*Lib Dem*)	4 September 2013
Lord Horam (*Con*)	4 September 2013
Lord Mendelsohn (*Lab*)	5 September 2013
Lord Wrigglesworth (*Lib Dem*)	5 September 2013
Baroness Lawrence of Clarendon (*Lab*)	6 September 2013
Baroness Manzoor (*Lib Dem*)	6 September 2013
Baroness Bakewell of Hardington Mandeville (*Lib Dem*)	9 September 2013
Lord Bourne of Aberystwyth (*Con*)	9 September 2013
Baroness Neville-Rolfe (*Con*)	10 September 2013
Lord Whitby (*Con*)	10 September 2013
Lord Carrington of Fulham (*Con*)	11 September 2013
Lord Finkelstein (*Con*)	11 September 2013
Lord Paddick (*Lib Dem*)	12 September 2013
Lord Sherbourne of Didsbury (*Con*)	12 September 2013
Lord Holmes of Richmond CBE (*Con*)	13 September 2913
Lord Purvis of Tweed (*Lib Dem*)	13 September 2013
Baroness Hodgson of Abinger (*Con*)	16 September 2013
Lord Leigh of Hurley (*Con*)	16 September 2013
Lord Verjee CBE (*Lib Dem*)	17 September 2013
Baroness Suttie (*Lib Dem*)	17 September 2013
Lord Haughey OBE (*Lab*)	18 September 2013
Baroness Humphreys (*Lib Dem*)	18 September 2013
Lord Balfe (*Con*)	19 September 2013
Baroness Kennedy of Cradley (*Lab*)	19 September 2013
Baroness Jones of Moulsecoomb (*Green*)	19 September 2013
Baroness Williams of Trafford (*Con*)	19 September 2013
Lord Allen of Kensington (*Lab*)	2 October 2013
Lord Palumbo of Southwark (*Lib Dem*)	2 October 2013
Lord Bamford (*Con*)	3 October 2013
Baroness Goldie (*Con*)	3 October 2013

DEATHS

Lord Lofthouse of Pontefract (*Lab*)	1 November 2012
Earl Ferrers (*Con*)	13 November 2012
Lord McCarthy (*NA*)	18 November 2012
Lord Rees-Mogg (*CB*)	29 December 2012
Lord King of West Bromwich (*Lab*)	9 January 2013
Baroness Thatcher (*Con*)	8 April 2013
Lord Northfield (*NA*)	26 April 2013

Lord Reay (*Con*)	10 May 2013
Lord Gilbert (*Lab*)	2 June 2013
Lord Fraser of Carmyllie (*Con*)	22 June 2013
Lord Campbell of Alloway (*Con*)	30 June 2013
Lord Chitnis (*CB*)	12 July 2013
Lord Hayhoe (*Con*)	7 September 2013

CHANGE OF PARTY

Lord Rennard	Whip withdrawn March 2013
	previously Lib Dem, now Lib Dem Ind
Lord Ahmed	Resigned May 2013
	previously Lab, now Non-Affiliated
Lord Mackay of Drumadoon	Retired College of Justice in Scotland
	previously Non-Affiliated, now Crossbench
Lord Cunningham of Felling	Whip withdrawn June 2013
	previously Lab, now Non-Affiliated
Lord Laird	Resigned June 2013
	previously UUP, now Non-Affiliated
Lord Mackenzie of Framwellgate	Whip withdrawn June 2013
	previously Lab, now Non-Affiliated
Lord Hope of Craighead	Retired as Supreme Justice
	previously Non-Affiliated, now Crossbench
Lord Judge	Retired as Lord Chief Justice of England and Wales
	previously Non-Affiliated, now Crossbench

RETIREMENT

Lord Bramall (CB)	24 April 2013

PEERAGE PENDING

Rt Hon Sir John Thomas*

*Rt Hon Sir John Thomas will be introduced as a full member to the House of Lords at a later date, he will then be automatically disqualified and illegible to vote as he assumes his role as the Lord Chief Justice of England and Wales.

Peers' Biographies

ABERDARE, LORD

ABERDARE (5th Baron, UK), Alastair John Lyndhurst Bruce; cr. 1873. Born 2 May 1947; Son of Morys George Lyndhurst Bruce, 4th Baron Aberdare, and Sarah, née Dashwood; Married Elizabeth Foulkes 1971 (1 son 1 daughter).

Education: Eton College; Christ Church, Oxford (MA literae humaniores 1972); French.

Non-political career: IBM UK 1969-91; Partner, Bruce Naughton Wade (public affairs management consultants) 1991-99; Director: ProbusBNW Ltd (corporate reputation consultants) 1999-2009, WALTZ Programmes Ltd, learning to work 2009-.

CROSSBENCH

Political career: *House of Lords:* Elected hereditary peer 2009-. Member Information 2012-. *Councils and public bodies:* Trustee: National Botanic Garden of Wales 1994-2006; National Library of Wales 2012-; DL, Dyfed 2009.

Political interests: Arts, culture and heritage, education and skills, trade and technology, small businesses and entrepreneurship; China, Kenya, Russia, USA, Wales.

Other: Trustee, St John Cymru-Wales 2008-; Vice-President, Public Monuments and Sculpture Association 2011-; FRSA; FRGS. Honorary Fellow, Cardiff University 2008. MCC.

Publications: Translator and editor, Hector Berlioz: The Musical Madhouse (University of Rochester Press, 2003).

Recreations: Wales, classical music, especially Berlioz, crosswords, family.

The Lord Aberdare, House of Lords, London SW1A 0PW
Tel: 020 7219 6861 *Email:* aberdarea@parliament.uk *Email:* alastair@aberdares.co.uk

ADAMS OF CRAIGIELEA, BARONESS

ADAMS OF CRAIGIELEA (Life Baroness), (Katherine Patricia) Irene Adams; cr 2005. Born 27 December 1947; Married Allen Adams 1968 (MP 1979-90, died 1990) (1 son 2 daughters).

Education: Stanley Green High School, Paisley.

Political career: *House of Commons:* MP (Labour) for Paisley North 29 November 1990 by-election to 2005. Member Chairmen's Panel 1998-2005; Chair Scottish Affairs 2001-05. *House of Lords:* Raised to the peerage as Baroness Adams of Craigielea, of Craigielea in Renfrewshire 2005. *Councils and public bodies:* Councillor: Paisley Town Council 1970, Renfrew District Council 1974-78, Strathclyde Regional Council 1979-84; JP.

LABOUR

Recreations: Reading, walking.

The Baroness Adams of Craigielea, House of Lords, London SW1A 0PW
Tel: 020 7219 6536

ADDINGTON, LORD

ADDINGTON (6th Baron, UK), Dominic Bryce Hubbard; cr. 1887. Born 24 August 1963; Son of 5th Baron; Married Elizabeth Ann Morris 1999.

Education: The Hewett School, Norwich; Aberdeen University (MA history 1988).

Non-political career: Charity fundraiser and counsellor, Apex Trust 1991-94; Consultant, Milton Broadway, Events Company 1996-99.

Political career: *House of Lords:* First entered House of Lords 1986; Liberal Democrat Spokesperson for: Work and Social Services/Pensions (Disability) 1994-2009, Culture, Media and Sport (Sport) 1995-2010; Elected hereditary peer 1999-; Liberal Democrat: Whip 2002-10, Deputy Chief Whip 2005-10, Spokesperson for Defence 2007-10. Member: Merits of Statutory Instruments 2003-07, Procedure 2005-08, Hybrid Instruments 2011, 2012-13, Olympic and Paralympic Legacy 2013-.

LIBERAL DEMOCRAT

Political interests: Education, prison reform, disabilities, sport.

Other: Vice-President: British Dyslexia Association, UK Sports Association (Sport for those with learning disabilities); Patron, Adult Dyslexia Organisation; Apex Trust: Fundraiser 1990-, Vice-President 2001-; Aberdeen University Student Hardship Fund; National Liberal. Vice-President: Lonsdale Sporting Club, Lakenham Hewett Rugby Club; Playing Captain Commons and Lords Rugby Football Club.

Recreations: Rugby football, portrait painting.

The Lord Addington, House of Lords, London SW1A 0PW
Tel: 020 7219 4443 *Email:* addingtond@parliament.uk

CROSSBENCH

ADEBOWALE, LORD

ADEBOWALE (Life Baron), Victor Olufemi Adebowale; cr 2001. Born 21 July 1962; Son of Grace Adebowale and Ezekiel Adebowale; Married Tracey Jones (1 son 1 daughter).

Education: Thornes House School, Wakefield; Tavistock Institute (Postgraduate Diploma advanced organisational consulting); City University (MA advanced organisational consulting 2008).

Non-political career: Housing administration, London Borough of Newham 1983-86; Management posts, housing associations 1986-90; Director, alcohol recovery project 1990-95; Chief executive, Centre Point (youth social exclusion charity) 1995-2001; Member: Social Exclusion Unit Policy Action, National Employment Panel, New Deal Task Force 1997-2007; Chief executive, Turning Point 2001-; Visiting Professor, Lincoln University. Member, Unison.

Political career: *House of Lords:* Raised to the peerage as Baron Adebowale, of Thornes in the County of West Yorkshire 2001. *Councils and public bodies:* Commission Employment and Skills 2007; Board member, Audit Commission -2012; President, Community Practitioners' and Health Visitors' Association; Council member, Social Enterprise Coalition -2009; Board member, NHS England; Vice-President, Local Government Association.

Political interests: Poverty, regeneration, arts; Italy, Nigeria, USA.

Other: Director: Leadership in Mind Ltd, THP Ltd, 360 action Ltd; Patron: Tomorrow's Project, Nursing Council on Alcohol, CARE International Foundation, National College for School Leadership, ROTA, International Philosophy and Psychiatry, Social Enterprise UK; Centre for Inclusion and Diversity, Bradford University, Equalities National Council; Urban Development (Music); Honorary Fellow, Royal College of Psychiatry; Sunningdale fellow. Chancellor, Lincoln University. Four honorary doctorates; Three honorary fellowships. CBE 2000.

Recreations: Poetry writing, reading, music, kites.

The Lord Adebowale CBE, House of Lords, London SW1A 0PW
Tel: 020 7219 8704 *Email:* adebowalev@parliament.uk
Tel: 020 7481 7600 *Fax:* 020 7481 7620 *Email:* victor@leadershipinmind.co.uk
Twitter: @Voa1234

LABOUR

ADONIS, LORD

Opposition Spokesperson for Treasury

ADONIS (Life Baron), Andrew Adonis; cr 2005. Born 22 February 1963; Married Kathryn Davies 1994 (1 son 1 daughter).

Education: Kingham Hill School, Oxford; Keble College, Oxford (BA modern history 1984); Christ Church, Oxford (DPhil 1988).

Non-political career: Headquarters Secretariat, British Gas Corporation 1984-85; Research student, Nuffield College, Oxford 1985-86; Fellow, politics, Nuffield College, Oxford 1988-91; Journalist, *Financial Times* 1991-96: Political columnist, *Observer* 1996-98; Prime Minister's Policy Unit 1998-2005: Head of Policy 2001-03; Director, Institute for Government 2010-; Non-executive director, Dods Group plc 2011-.

Political career: *House of Lords:* Raised to the peerage as Baron Adonis, of Camden Town in the London Borough of Camden 2005. Parliamentary Under-Secretary of State and Government Spokesperson for Department for Education and Skills/Children, Schools and Families (Schools and Learners) 2005-08; Department for Transport 2008-10: Minister of State and Government Spokesperson 2008-09, Secretary of State 2009-10; Opposition Spokesperson for Treasury 2012-. *Other:* Adviser to Policy Review on Industrial Strategy, Labour Party 2012-. *Councils and public bodies:* Councillor, Oxford City Council 1987-91.

Other: Chair, Progress 2012-. Peer of the Year, Channel 4 Political awards 2009. PC 2009.

Publications: Parliament Today (1990); Making Aristocracy Work: the peerage and the political system in Britain 1884-1914 (1993); Co-Author, A Conservative Revolution?: the Thatcher-Reagan decade in perspective (1994); Failure in British Government: the politics of the poll tax (1994); A Class Act: the myth of Britain's classless society (1997); Co-editor, Roy Jenkins: a retrospective (2004); Contributor, The Purple Book (Progress, 2011); Five Days in May: The Coalition and Beyond (Biteback, 2013).

Rt Hon the Lord Adonis, House of Lords, London SW1A 0PW
Tel: 020 7219 5353 *Twitter:* @Andrew_Adonis

CROSSBENCH

AFSHAR, BARONESS

AFSHAR (Life Baroness), Haleh Afshar; cr 2007. Born 21 May 1944; Daughter of Pouran and Professor Hussan Afshar; Married Maurice, later Professor, Dodson 1974 (1 daughter 1 son).

Education: Davis College, Brighton; St Martin's School, Solihull; York University (BA social sciences 1967); Strasbourg University (Diploma comparative European Community law 1972); Department of Land Economy, Cambridge (PhD 1974); French, Persian.

Non-political career: Researcher, Rural Research Centre, Tehran; Journalist, *Kayhan International* daily newspaper, Tehran 1971-74; Lecturer in development, Bradford University 1976-85; York University 1985-: Deputy director and lecturer in health economics 1985-87, Department of politics and centre for women's studies 1987-: Professor 1999-; Visiting professor: Strasbourg University International Faculty of Comparative Law 1986-, Women's studies, Strathclyde University 1993-98; Founder member and chair, Muslim Women's Network 2002-. Member, AUT 1975-.

Political career: *House of Lords:* Raised to the peerage as Baroness Afshar, of Heslington in the County of North Yorkshire 2007.

Political interests: Feminism; France, India, Iran, Islamic countries.

Other: Member and various posts numerous organisations, especially concerned with women, particularly ethnic minority women, and education, including: Deputy chair, British Council's Gender and Development Task Force 2001-03, UN Associations' Services: Chair, board of trustees 2001-04, President 2004-; Commissioner, UK Drug Policy Commission 2006; Fellow, Academy of Social Sciences. Honorary doctorate, Exeter University 2011. OBE 2005.

Publications: Books: (as Homa Omid) Islam and the Post- Revolutionary State in Iran (Macmillan, 1994), Islam and Feminisms, an Iranian case study (Macmillan, 1998), Co-author, Women in Later Life: Exploring Race and Ethnicity (Open University Press, 2008); Reports: "Women and poverty" in Women and Development (International Development Committee, Seventh Report, 1999), Pamphlet, Democracy and Islam (Hansard Society, 2006); Edited volumes: Iran , A Revolution in Turmoil (Macmillan, 1985, reprinted 1989), Women, Work and Ideology In The Third World (Tavistock, 1985), Women, State and Ideology (Macmillan, 1987), Co-editor, Women, Poverty and Ideology (Macmillan, 1989), Women Development and Survival in the Third World (Longman 1991), Co-editor, Women and Adjustment Policies in The Third World (Macmillan, 1992), Women in the Middle East: Perceptions, Realities and Struggles for Liberation (Macmillan, 1993), Co-editor, The Dynamics of Race and Gender: some Feminist Interventions (Taylor and Francis 1994, reprinted 1995), Women and Politics in the Third World (Routledge, 1996), Co-editor, Empowering Women for Development (Booklinks Corporation, Hyderabad, 1997), Women and Empowerment, Illustrations from the Third World (Macmillan, 1998), Co-editor: Women and Globalization and Fragmentation in the Developing World (Macmillan, 1999), Development, Women, and War (Oxfam, 2004); Authored many papers in academic journals and contributed chapters to books, mainly on women, feminism, politics and Iran.

Recreations: Reading, opera.

The Baroness Afshar OBE, House of Lords, London SW1A 0PW
Tel: 020 7219 5353 *Email:* afsharh@parliament.uk
Department of Politics, York University, York YO10 5DD *Tel:* 01904 433554 *Fax:* 01904 433563
Email: haa1@york.ac.uk

CONSERVATIVE

AHMAD OF WIMBLEDON, LORD

Government Spokesperson, Departments for Communities and Local Government and International Development and Ministry of Justice; Government Whip

AHMAD OF WIMBLEDON (Life Baron), Tariq Mahmood Ahmad; cr 2011. Born 3 April 1968; Son of Ch. Mansoor and Amtul Matin Ahmad, nee Mir; Married Siddiquea Masud 2011 (1 son 1 daughter).

Education: Rutlish School, London; South Bank Polytechnic, London (BA business 1990); Hindi, Punjabi, Urdu.

Non-political career: NatWest Group 1991-2000: Corporate Banking Executive 1991-94, Manager: Market Intelligence 1994-97, European Strategy 1997-99, Senior manager, Corporate Banking and Financial Markets 1999-2000; Alliance Bernstein: Vice-President, Marketing director 2000-04; Strategy and marketing director and head of Russia and CIS, Sucden Financial 2004-.

Political career: *House of Commons:* Contested (Conservative) Croydon North 2005 general election. *House of Lords:* Raised to the peerage as Baron Ahmad of Wimbledon, of Wimbledon in the London Borough of Merton 2011. Party Whip 2012; Government Whip 2012-; Government Spokesperson for: Communities and Local Government 2012-, International Development 2012-,

Justice 2012-. *Other:* Deputy chairman, Wimbledon Conservative Association 1997-2002; Member, Conservative Friends of India 2003-; Vice-chairman (Cities), Conservative Party 2008-10; Parliamentary chairman, Conservative Friends of Pakistan 2011-. *Councils and public bodies:* Member, Merton Racial Equality Council 1994-97; London Borough of Merton Council: Councillor 2002-12, Opposition Spokesperson on Environment and Regeneration 2002-06, Cabinet Member: Environment and Transport 2006-08, Community Safety and Engagement 2008-09; School Governor, Wimbledon Park School 2003-06; Deputy Chairman, London Councils Transport and Environment Committee 2006-08.

Political interests: Foreign affairs, EU, international development, city and financial affairs; Bangladesh, China, India, Indonesia, Israel, Middle East, Pakistan, Russia, USA.

Other: National Vice-President, AMYA-UK 2000-09; Associate, Institute of Financial Services; Member, Institute of Directors; Associate, Chartered Institute of Bankers 1995; Humanity First, Conservative Friends of Bangladesh, Save the Children. Glory of India Award 2010.

Recreations: Gym, tennis, voluntary work.

The Lord Ahmad of Wimbledon, House of Lords, London SW1A 0PW
Tel: 020 7219 2807 *Email:* ahmadt@parliament.uk *Website:* www.tariqahmad.com
Twitter: @tariqahmadbt

AHMED, LORD

NON-AFFILIATED

AHMED (Life Baron), Nazir Ahmed; cr. 1998. Born 24 April 1957; Son of late Haji Sain Mohammed and Rashem Bibi; Married Sakina Bibi 1974 (2 sons 1 daughter).

Education: Spurley Hey Comprehensive School, Rotherham; Thomas Rotherham College, Rotherham; Sheffield Hallam University (BA public administration 1992); Punjabi, Urdu.

Non-political career: Ran chain of fish and chip shops and mini-markets 1978-85; Marble mining in Kashmir 1985-87; Business development manager, Kilnhurst Business Park 1991-; Property development 2007-; Chairman, Blackhorn Properties Ltd. Member, USDAW; Chair, Sheffield Private Branch 1996-98; Member, Political Committee 1996-98.

Political career: *House of Lords:* Raised to the peerage as Baron Ahmed, of Rotherham in the County of South Yorkshire 1998. *Other:* Chair, South Yorkshire Labour Party 1994-98; Vice-chair, South Yorkshire Euro-constituency Party 1996-98; Administrative suspension from Labour Party April-June 2012; Labour Whip suspended March 2013; Resigned from the Labour Party May 2013. *Councils and public bodies:* Councillor, Rotherham Metropolitan Borough Council 1990-2000; JP, Rotherham 1992-2000; Founder, British Muslim Councillors Forum 1992-98.

Political interests: Human rights, Kashmiri right of self-determination, conflict resolution, race relations, relations with Muslim countries, dialogue of civilisation, education, immigration, minorities' rights, private diplomacy, release of british teacher Gillian Gibbons; China, Middle East, North Africa, Pakistan, Russia, South Asia, USA.

Other: Member: Inter-Parliamentary Union 1998-, Commonwealth Parliamentary Association 1998-; Patron, Jammu and Kashmir Human Rights Commission 1998, Al-Shifa, Pakistan 1999-2013; Head of British Muslim Peace and Recognition Initiative in Darfur 2007-; FACE Advice Centre, Rotherham 1992-2000; Al-Hamd Trust-International Disabled Network 1994-98; Member, Kashmir Policy Group 1995-2008; Unity Centre, Rotherham 1996-98; Alma Hospital Trust 1998-; Patron: British Hujjaj Association 1999-, SAARC Foundation 1999-2008, Kashmiri Journalist Association Mirpur 1999-2008, Mirpur Friendship Association 2000-07, Khattak Medical College, Pakistan 2000-06, Yemeni Development Foundation, UK 2000-06, Layton Rehmatula Trust, Pakistan 2002-13, Chinese Muslim Charity, Kuwait 2002-08, SAHARA, Pakistan 2002-11, Al-Hijrah School; Board member, Board of Trustees, Jinnah Institute (London) 2003-06; President, South Yorkshire Victim Support 2003-08; Chair, Joseph Interfaith Foundation 2006-13; Patron: Response International 2005-11, Concordis International 2006-; UK Consultative, Maimonides Foundation 2007-09; Board member, British Heart Foundation 2007-10; Muslim Chaplains Association 2010-13; Rehab UK Trust 2010-13; Trustee: Fazaldad Human Rights Organisation, Zindagi Trust – Charity for underprivileged children, Joseph Interfaith Foundation - 2013; Board member, British Institute of Technology and e-Commerce; Magistrates Association 1992-2000; Young Pakistani Doctors' Association 1999-2009; Patron, Kashmiri and Pakistani Professional Association 2000-08; Muslim Aid, Islamic Relief, SAARC Foundation UK, Human Appeal International, Sahara Foundation, Muslim Hands, A Better Tomorrow School in Mirpur, Pakistan. Chancellor, British Institute of Technology and Ecommerce 2010-13. Honorary doctorate United Ukraine 2004; Member, Commonwealth Club 2009-13.

Recreations: Reading, travel, volleyball.

The Lord Ahmed, House of Lords, London SW1A 0PW
Tel: 020 7219 1396 *Fax:* 020 7219 1384 *Email:* ahmedn@parliament.uk
Twitter: @LordNazirAhmed

LIBERAL DEMOCRAT

ALDERDICE, LORD

Convener of the Liberal Democrat Peers

ALDERDICE (Life Baron), John Thomas Alderdice; cr. 1996. Born 28 March 1955; Son of late Reverend David Alderdice and Annie Alderdice, née Shields; Married Joan Hill 1977 (2 sons 1 daughter).

Education: Ballymena Academy, County Antrim; Queen's University, Belfast (MB BCh BAO 1978).

Non-political career: Consultant psychiatrist in psychotherapy, Belfast Health and Social Care Trust 1988-2010; Executive Medical Director, South and East Belfast Health and Social Services Trust 1993-97; President, Artis (Europe) Ltd 2009-; Senior research fellow, Harris Manchester College, Oxford University 2012-; Research associate, School of Social Anthropology, Oxford University 2013-.

Political career: *House of Commons:* Contested (Alliance Party) Belfast East 1987 and 1992 general elections. *House of Lords:* Raised to the peerage as Baron Alderdice, of Knock in the City of Belfast 1996. Liberal Democrat Spokesperson for Health 2010; Convener of the Crossbench Liberal Democrat Peers 2010-; Liberal Democrat Spokesperson for Northern Ireland. Member: Procedure 2003-05, House 2010-, Liaison 2010-, Mental Capacity Act 2005 2013-. Chair, Liberal Democrat: Policy Committee on Health and Social Care 2010-11 Parliamentary Party Committee on Northern Ireland 2011-. *Other:* Leader, Alliance Delegation, Forum for Peace and Reconciliation, Dublin Castle 1994-97; Member, Northern Ireland Forum 1996-98; Leader, Alliance Delegation to Northern Ireland Multiparty Talks 1996-98; MLA for Belfast East 1998-2004: Speaker of the Northern Ireland Assembly 1998-2004. Alliance Party: Executive Committee 1984-98: Chair, Policy Committee 1985-87; Party Vice-chair 1987, Party Leader 1987-98; European Liberal Democrat and Reform Party: Executive Committee 1987-2003, Treasurer 1995-99, Vice-President 1999-2003; Liberal International: Deputy President 2000-05, President 2005-09. *Councils and public bodies:* Councillor, Belfast City Council 1989-97; Member: Belfast Education and Library Board 1993-97, Committee on Standards in Public Life 2010-.

Political interests: Northern Ireland, psychoanalysis, terrorism and political conflict resolution, mental health; Middle East.

Other: Member, Commonwealth Parliamentary Association (President Northern Ireland Assembly Branch) 2000-04; Commissioner: Independent Monitoring Commission 2003-11, Commonwealth Commission on Respect and Understanding 2006-07; Patron, Northern Ireland Institute of Human Relations; President, Westminster Pastoral Foundation; Trustee, Ulster Museum 1993-97; Chairman, World Education of Scientists Permanent Monitoring Panel on Motivations for Terrorism; Joint chairman, International Dialogue Initiative 2009-; Chair of trustees, National Liberal Club, London 2012-; FRCPsych 1997; Vice-President National Benevolent Fund for the Aged; President Westminster Pastoral Foundation; Patron Youth Access UK. Freeman, City of Baltimore, USA 1991. Faculty of Medicine, Queen's University, Belfast: Honorary Lecturer 1991-99, Honorary Senior Lecturer 1999; Honorary Fellow, Royal College of Physicians of Ireland 1997; Honorary Professor, Faculty of Medicine, University of San Marcos, Peru 1999; Honorary Fellow, Royal College of Psychiatrists 2001; Honorary Affiliate, British Psychoanalytical Society 2001; Visiting Professor, Department of Psychiatry, University of Virginia, USA 2006-; Two honorary doctorates. Galloway Medal (National Schizophrenia Fellowship, NI) 1987; John F Kennedy Profiles in Courage Award 1998; W Averell Harriman Democracy Award 1998; Silver Medal Congress of Peru 1999, 2004; Medal of Honour College of Medicine, Peru 1999; KCFO (Knight Commander Royal Order of Francis I) 2002; World Federation of Scientists Ettore Majorana Erice Prize 2005; International Psychoanalytic Association's 2005 Award for Extraordinarily Meritorious Service to Psychoanalysis; National Liberal, Ulster Reform (Belfast).

Publications: Various professional articles on eating disorders, psychotherapy and ethics, the psychology of intractable conflict and terrorism, the psychology of fundamentalism, many political papers, articles and book chapters.

Recreations: Reading, music, gastronomy.

The Lord Alderdice, House of Lords, London SW1A 0PW
Tel: 020 7219 5050 *Email:* alderdicej@parliament.uk
55 Knock Road, Belfast BT5 6LB *Website:* www.lordalderdice.com *Twitter:* @AlderdiceLord

ALLAN OF HALLAM, LORD

ALLAN OF HALLAM (Life Baron), Richard Beecroft Allan; cr 2010. Born 11 February 1966; Son of John Allan, retired, and Elizabeth Allan, doctor's receptionist; Married Louise Netley 1991 (1 daughter) (divorced).

Education: Oundle School, Northamptonshire; Pembroke College, Cambridge (BA archaeology and anthropology 1988); Bristol Polytechnic (MSc information technology 1990); French, Spanish.

Non-political career: Field archaeologist in: Britain, France and Netherlands 1984-85, Ecuador 1988-89; Computer manager: Avon FHSA 1991-95, FHS 1995-97; Director of government affairs, Europe, Cisco 2005-09; Director of policy, Europe, Facebook 2009-.

LIBERAL DEMOCRAT

Political career: *House of Commons:* MP (Lib Dem) for Sheffield Hallam 1997-2005. Board member, Parliamentary Office of Science and Technology (POST) 1997-2001; Liberal Democrat Spokesperson for: Home and Legal Affairs (Community Relations and Urban Affairs) 1997-99, Education and Employment (Employment and Information Technology) 1999-2001, Trade and Industry (Information Technology) 2001-02, Cabinet Office (Information Technology) 2002-05. Member: Home Affairs 1997-98, Liaison 1998-2005, Finance and Services 1998-2001 Chair: Information 1998-2001, Member: Education and Employment 2000-01, Education and Employment (Employment Sub-Committee) 2001, Information 2001-05, Liaison (Liaison Sub-Committee) 2002-05, Public Accounts 2003-05. *House of Lords:* Raised to the peerage as Baron Allan of Hallam, of Ecclesall in the County of South Yorkshire 2010. *Councils and public bodies:* Avon County Council: Councillor 1993-95, Deputy Leader, Liberal Democrats group; Councillor, Bath City Council 1994-95.

Political interests: Information technology, heritage, home affairs, education; Kenya, Latin America especially Ecuador and Colombia, USA.

Other: Board member, Sheffield City Trust 1999-2005.

Recreations: Visiting sites of natural beauty and historical interest, walking.

The Lord Allan of Hallam, House of Lords, London SW1A 0PW
Tel: 020 7219 5353 *Email:* allanr@parliament.uk

ALLEN OF KENSINGTON, LORD – *Please see Addenda Page x*

ALLENBY OF MEGIDDO, VISCOUNT

ALLENBY OF MEGIDDO (3rd Viscount, UK), Michael Jaffray Hynman Allenby; cr. 1919. Born 20 April 1931; Son of 2nd Viscount; Married Sara Wiggin 1965 (1 son).

Education: Eton College; RMA, Sandhurst.

Non-political career: Commissioned 11th Hussars as 2nd Lieutenant 1951; Served Malaya and Cyprus, as ADC to Governor 1956-58; Brigade Major, 51 Brigade, Hong Kong 1967-70; Commanded The Royal Yeomanry (TA) 1974-77; GSO1 Instructor, Nigerian Staff College, Kaduna, Nigeria 1977-79. Director, Quickrest Ltd 1987-91.

CROSSBENCH

Political career: *House of Lords:* First entered House of Lords 1984; Deputy Speaker 1997-2008; Deputy Chairman of Committees 1997-2008; Elected hereditary peer 1999-. Member: House of Lords Offices 1997-99, Procedure 1999-2002, Personal Bills 2003-09, Administration and Works 2005-09.

Political interests: Defence, animal welfare, racing and bloodstock; Middle East.

Other: Chair, International League for Protection of Horses 1997-99; The Victory.

Recreations: Horses, sailing, photography.

The Viscount Allenby of Megiddo, House of Lords, London SW1A 0PW
Tel: 020 7219 3497 *Fax:* 020 7219 0670/020 7219 5179
Fax: 01256 762689*Email:* michael.allenby@btopenworld.com

ALLI, LORD

ALLI (Life Baron), Waheed Alli; cr. 1998. Born 16 November 1964; Partner.

Education: Norbury Manor School, south London; Stanley Technical High School.

Non-political career: Research Wootton Publications Ltd 1982-85; Head of investment research, Save and Prosper Investment 1985-88; United Trade Press Ltd 1988-91: Marketing director 1988-89, Publisher 1989-91; Management consultant, Bacon and Woodrow 1991-92; Managing director, Planet 24 Productions Ltd 1992-99; Director, Carlton Media Group 1999-2000; Non-executive director, ShineLimited 2000-; Chairman, Chorion plc 2002-11.

LABOUR

Political career: *House of Lords:* Raised to the peerage as Baron Alli, of Norbury in the London Borough of Croydon 1998.

Other: Patron: Skillset (The national training organisation for Broadcast, Film, Video and Multimedia), Family Planning Association, Naz Foundation, The Albert Kennedy Trust; Director, Elton John Aids Foundation; Vice-President, Unicef UK; National Youth Theatre London Academy.

The Lord Alli, House of Lords, London SW1A 0PW
Tel: 020 7219 8537 *Email:* alliw@parliament.uk

ALLIANCE, LORD

ALLIANCE (Life Baron), David Alliance; cr. 2004. Born 15 June 1932; Son of Eliyahou Alliance and Ashouri Sarehi; Divorced (2 sons 1 daughter).

Education: Etahad School, Iran.

Non-political career: Chair, N Brown Group plc 1968-2012; Founder, Coats Viyella plc (now Coats plc) 1986: Group chief executive 1975-90, Chair 1989-99; Chair, Tootal Group 1991-99.

Political career: *House of Lords:* Raised to the peerage as Baron Alliance, of Manchester in the County of Greater Manchester 2004.

LIBERAL DEMOCRAT

Other: CBIM 1985. Three honorary doctorates; Two honorary fellowships. CBE 1984; Kt 1989.

Recreations: Art, persian poetry, music.

The Lord Alliance CBE, House of Lords, London SW1A 0PW
Tel: 020 7219 5353

ALTON OF LIVERPOOL, LORD

ALTON OF LIVERPOOL (Life Baron), David Patrick Paul Alton; cr. 1997. Born 15 March 1951; Son of late Frederick Alton, car worker, and Bridget Mulroe; Married Elizabeth Bell 1988 (3 sons 1 daughter).

Education: Edmund Campion School, Hornchurch; Christ's College, Liverpool (Teaching Certificate history and divinity 1972).

Non-political career: Primary school teacher 1972-74, then with children with special needs 1974-79; Visiting fellowship, School of Philosophy and Public Affairs and St Mary's College, St Andrews University 1996-97; Professor of citizenship, Liverpool John Moores University 1997-; Honorary Professor Yanbian University of Science and Technology (China) 2012.

CROSSBENCH

Political career: *House of Commons:* Contested Liverpool Edge Hill February and October 1974 general elections. MP for Liverpool Edge Hill 1979-83, and for Liverpool Mossley Hill 1983-97 (Liberal 1979-88, Liberal Democrat 1988-97). Liberal Chief Whip 1985-87; Party Spokesperson on several portfolios. *House of Lords:* Raised to the peerage as Baron Alton of Liverpool, of Mossley Hill in the County of Merseyside 1997. *Other:* National President, National League of Young Liberals 1976; Chair: Liberal Policy Committee 1981-83, Candidates Committee 1984-87. *Councils and public bodies:* Liverpool City Council: Councillor 1972-80, Chair, Housing Committee, Deputy Leader of Council 1978; Councillor, Merseyside County Council 1973-77; Vice-President, Local Government Association 2010-.

Political interests: Pro-life, environment, housing, inner cities, refugees, human rights, Northern Ireland, citizenship; Equatorial Africa, China, Indian sub-continent, North Korea, Sudan, Tibet.

Other: Member: Inter-Parliamentary Union, Commonwealth Parliamentary Association; Patron, vice-president, chair numerous charities, especially those concerned with children, ethics and human rights; Trustee: Chesterton Institute, Pyongyang University of Science and Technology, North Korea, Christian Heritage Centre; Bernard Braine Memorial Fund; Life hospice for dying children, Zoe's Place, NSPCC, St Francis House, Jubilee Action, Jospice, CAFOD. Knights of St Columba Michael Bell award for services to the life cause 1997; Advocates International award for human rights work 2004; Mystery of Life award for human rights work 2009. Knight of the Sacred Military Constantinian Order of St George 2002; Knight Commander Order of St Gregory 2008. Supporter, Liverpool Football Club.

Publications: What Kind of Country (1987); Whose Choice Anyway – the Right to Life (1988); Faith in Britain (1991); Signs of Contradiction (1996); Life After Death (1997); Citizen Virtues (1998); Citizen 2000 (2000); Pilgrim Ways (2001); Passion and Pain (2003); Abortion: Heart of the Matter (2005); Euthanasia: Heart of the Matter (2005); Building Bridges: Is There Hope for North Korea? (2013).

Recreations: Walking, reading, theatre, gardening.

The Lord Alton of Liverpool, House of Lords, London SW1A 0PW
Tel: 020 7219 3551 *Fax:* 020 7219 3551 *Email:* altond@parliament.uk
Foundation for Citizenship, Liverpool John Moores University, 2 Rodney Street, Liverpool L3 5UX
Tel: 0151-231 3852 *Fax:* 0151-231 3852 *Email:* davidalton@mail.com
Website: www.davidalton.net

NON-AFFILIATED

AMOS, BARONESS

AMOS (Life Baroness), Valerie Ann Amos; cr. 1997. Born 13 March 1954; Daughter of Michael and Eunice Amos.

Education: Townley Grammar School for Girls; Warwick University (BA sociology 1976); Birmingham University (MA cultural studies 1977); University of East Anglia (doctoral research).

Non-political career: With London Boroughs: Lambeth 1981-82, Camden 1983-85, Hackney 1985-89: Head of training, Head of management services; Chief executive, Equal Opportunities Commission 1989-94; Director, Amos Fraser Bernard 1995-98; Non-executive director: Travant Capital Partners 2007-09, Titanium Resources Group 2008-09; High Commissioner to Australia 2009-11; Under-Secretary-General, Office of the Co-ordination of Humanitarian Affairs, United Nations 2010-.

Political career: *House of Lords:* Raised to the peerage as Baroness Amos, of Brondesbury in the London Borough of Brent 1997. Government Whip 1998-2001; Government Spokesperson for: Social Security 1998-2001, International Development 1998-2007, Women's Issues 1998-2001; Parliamentary Under-Secretary of State and Government Spokesperson, Foreign and Commonwealth Office 2001-03; Secretary of State for International Development 2003; Government Spokesperson for Northern Ireland Office 2003-05; Leader of the House of Lords and Lord President of the Council 2003-07; On leave of absence. Member: Selection 2000-07, House 2003-07, Liaison 2003-07, Privileges 2003-07, Procedure 2003-07. *Councils and public bodies:* Council member, Institute of Employment Studies 1993-98; Chair, board of governors, Royal College of Nursing Institute 1994-98.

Countries of interest: Sub-Saharan Africa, Caribbean, China, India.

Other: Director, Hampstead Theatre 1995-98; Chair, Royal African Society 2008-09; Deputy chair, Runnymede Trust 1990-98; Trustee, Institute of Public Policy Research 1994-98; Non-executive director, UCLH Trust; Chair, Afiya Trust 1996-98; Trustee: Voluntary Services Overseas (VSO) 1997-98, Project Hope 1997-98. Honorary professorship; 12 honorary doctorates. Peer of the Year, Women in Public Life Awards 2007. PC 2003.

Rt Hon the Baroness Amos, House of Lords, London SW1A 0PW
Tel: 020 7219 5353 *Email:* amosv@parliament.uk *Twitter:* @ValerieAmos
Tel: +1 212 963 2738 *Email:* amosv@un.org

LABOUR

ANDERSON OF SWANSEA, LORD

ANDERSON OF SWANSEA (Life Baron), Donald Anderson; cr 2005. Born 17 June 1939; Son of late David Anderson, fitter and late Eva Anderson, née Mathias; Married Dr Dorothy Trotman 1963 (3 sons).

Education: Bishop Gore Grammar School, Swansea; University College of Wales, Swansea (BA modern history and politics 1960); Inns of Court School of Law 1966-69; French, German.

Non-political career: HM Diplomatic Service 1960-64; Lecturer in US and comparative government, University College of Wales, Swansea 1964-66; Called to the Bar, Inner Temple 1969-; Barrister, South Eastern Circuit 1970-97. Former member: TGWU, NUR/RMT, AUT, FDA, FSBAA, Bar.

Political career: *House of Commons:* MP (Labour) for Monmouth 1966-70, for Swansea East October 1974-2005. PPS: to Minister of Defence (Administration) 1969-70, to Sam Silkin as Attorney General 1974-79; Opposition Frontbench Spokesperson for: Foreign and Commonwealth Affairs 1983-92, Defence, Disarmament and Arms Control 1993-94, Shadow Solicitor General 1994-96. Chair: Welsh Affairs 1981-83; Member: Chairman's Panel 1994-97; Chair: Foreign Affairs 1997-2005. *House of Lords:* Raised to the peerage as Baron Anderson of Swansea, of Swansea in the County of West Glamorgan 2005. Co-opted member EU Sub-committee C (Foreign Affairs, Defence and Development Policy) 2006-10; Member EU Sub-committee E: (Justice and Institutions) 2011-12, (Justice, Institutions and Consumer Protection) 2012-. Vice-chair, PLP Departmental Group for Foreign and Commonwealth Affairs 2010-. *Other:* Welsh Labour Group: Vice-chair 1969-70, Chair 1977-78. *Councils and public bodies:* Councillor, Royal Borough of Kensington and Chelsea 1970-75; Vice-President, Institute of Environmental Health Officers 1984-95; DL, West Glamorgan 2006-.

Political interests: Wales, foreign affairs, law, transport; Africa particularly South Africa, Central Europe and Balkans, EU, France, Germany, Norway.

Other: Commonwealth Parliamentary Association (CPA) UK Branch: Member, Executive Committee 1983-2012, Vice-chair 1987-88, 2007-08, 2010-11, Treasurer 1990-93, Special Representative 1989-90, Chair 1997-2001; Co-founder and Senior Vice-President, Association of European Parliamentarians for Africa (AWEPA) (Southern) 1984-97; Inter-Parliamentary Union: Member, Vice-chair 1985-88, Treasurer 1988-90, 1993-95; UK Delegation to North Atlantic Assembly: Member 1992-2005, Leader 1997-2001, Leader of Socialist Group 1997-2001; Organisation for Security and Co-operation in Europe: Member 1997-2001, Leader UK delegation 1997-98; Executive Committee Member: Inter-Parliamentary Union British Group 1983-2001, 2005-06, 2007-, British-American Parliamentary Group 2006-, UK Delegation to Council of Europe and WEU Assembly 2008-; Director, Campaign for a Political Europe 1966-67; Former board member, World Vision; Former president, Swansea Association for the Single Homeless 1975-81; President, Gower Society 1976-78; Chair, Parliamentary Campaign for the Homeless and Rootless 1984-90; Chair: Parliamentary Christian Fellowship 1993-95, National Prayer Breakfast 1994, Anglo-Israel Association 2005-08; Board member, Mercy Ships 2005-12; President: Swansea Male Choir 1990-2007, Morriston Big Band; Patron, Morriston Ladies Choir; Vice-President, Morriston Orpheus Choir; Swansea Harriers; President: HAFOD Brotherhood, 32nd Rhyddings Scout Group; Vice-president: Morriston Rotary Club, Swansea Business Club; Honorary Fellowship, Sussex University 1985, Honorary Fellowship, Swansea Metropolitan University 2005; Honorary Parliamentary Fellow, St Antony's College, Oxford University 1999-2000; Churches in London and Swansea. Freeman: City and County of Swansea 2000, City of London 2006. Honorary Fellow, University of Swansea 1985-2000; Visiting Parliamentary Fellow, St Antony's College, Oxford 1999-2000; Honorary Fellow Swansea Metropolitan University 2006. Commander's Cross, Order of Merit (Federal Republic of Germany) 1986; PC 2001; Medal of the Foreign Minister of Slovakia 2004; Chevalier de la Légion d'Honneur (France) 2005; Order of Merit of Republic of Hungary 2007. Bonymaen RFC; Ospreys RFC.

Recreations: Walking, church work.

Rt Hon the Lord Anderson of Swansea, House of Lords, London SW1A 0PW
Tel: 020 7219 6562/020 7219 2870 *Fax:* 020 7219 8602 *Email:* trotmang@parliament.uk

---

LABOUR

ANDREWS, BARONESS

ANDREWS (Life Baroness), (Elizabeth) Kay Andrews; cr. 2000. Born 16 May 1943; Married Professor Roy MacLeod 1970 (divorced 1992).

Education: Lewis School for Girls, Hengoed, Ystradmynach; University College of Wales, Aberystwyth (BA international politics 1964); Sussex University (MA political sociology 1966; DPhil history and social studies of science 1975).

Non-political career: Fellow, Science Policy Research Unit, Sussex University 1968-70; Parliamentary Clerk 1970-85; Policy adviser to Neil Kinnock as Leader of the Opposition 1985-92; Founder and director, Education Extra 1992-2002.

Political career: *House of Lords:* Raised to the peerage as Baroness Andrews, of Southover in the County of East Sussex 2000. Government Whip 2002-05; Government Spokesperson for: Health 2002-05, Work and Pensions 2002-05, Education and Skills 2003-05, Parliamentary Under-Secretary of State and Government Spokesperson, Office of the Deputy Prime Minister/Department for Communities and Local Government 2005-09; Deputy Chair of Committees 2012-, Deputy Speaker 2012. Member: Delegated Powers and Regulatory Reform 2010-, Leader's Group on the Working Practices of the House of Lords 2010-11, Joint Committee on the Draft House of Lords Reform Bill 2011-12, Mental Capacity Act 2005 2013-, Joint Committee on the Draft Deregulation Bill 2013-. *Councils and public bodies:* Chair, English Heritage 2009-13.

Political interests: Education and social policy, international development, cultural policy, science policy; Latin America.

Other: Chair, English Heritage 2009-13; Fellow, Royal Society of Arts; Continyou. Honorary Doctor of Laws, Sussex University 2012. OBE 1998.

Publications: Articles and books on science and education policy, social policy and out of school learning; Extra Learning (Kogan Page, 2001).

Recreations: Music, mountains, museums.

The Baroness Andrews OBE, House of Lords, London SW1A 0PW
Tel: 020 7219 8656 *Email:* andrewsk@parliament.uk

CONSERVATIVE

ANELAY OF ST JOHNS, BARONESS

Government Chief Whip

ANELAY OF ST JOHNS (Life Baroness) Joyce Anne Anelay; cr. 1996. Born 17 July 1947; Daughter of late Stanley and Annette Clarke; Married Richard Anelay QC 1970.

Education: Enfield County School; Bristol University (BA history 1968); London University Institute of Education (CertEd 1969); Brunel University (MA public and social administration 1982).

Non-political career: History teacher, St David's School, Ashford, Middlesex 1969-74.

Political career: *House of Lords:* Raised to the peerage as Baroness Anelay of St Johns, of St Johns in the County of Surrey 1996. Opposition Whip 1997-98; Opposition Spokesperson for:

Agriculture 1997-98, Social Security 1997-99, Home Affairs 1997-98, 2002-07, Culture, Media and Sport 1998-2002, Legal Affairs 2003-04, Opposition Chief Whip 2007-10; Deputy Speaker 2008-; Deputy Chairman of Committees 2008-; Government Chief Whip 2010-. Member: Procedure 1997-2000, 2007-, Selection 2007-, Administration and Works 2007-, Privileges/Privileges and Conduct 2007-, Sub-committee on Leave of Absence 2011-13. *Other:* Chair, South East Area Conservative Women's Committee 1987-90; Member, National Union Executive Committee Conservative Party 1987-97, Vice-chair, South East Area Executive Committee 1990-93; Chair, Women's National Committee 1993-96; Vice-President, National Union 1996-97. *Councils and public bodies:* Member, Social Security Appeal Tribunal 1983-96; JP, North West Surrey 1985-97; Member: Social Security Advisory Committee for Great Britain and Northern Ireland 1989-96, Women's National Commission 1991-94, Child Support Appeal Tribunal 1993-96; President, World Travel Market 2003-08.

Political interests: Social security, home affairs.

Other: President, Woking Citizens' Advice Bureau 1996-2010; Trustee, UNICEF UK 2004-07. Honorary DSocSci, Brunel 1997. OBE 1990; DBE 1995; PC 2009; Carlton. Woking Golf.

Recreations: Golf, reading.

Rt Hon the Baroness Anelay of St Johns DBE, House of Lords, London SW1A 0PW
Tel: 020 7219 3132 *Fax:* 020 7219 6837 *Email:* holgovernmentwhips@parliament.uk

ARCHER OF WESTON-SUPER-MARE, LORD

NON-AFFILIATED

ARCHER OF WESTON-SUPER-MARE (Life Baron), Jeffrey Howard Archer; cr. 1992. Born 15 April 1940; Son of late William and Lola Archer; Married Mary Doreen Weeden (later DBE) 1966 (2 sons).

Education: Wellington School, Somerset; Brasenose College, Oxford (Dip Ed 1963).

Non-political career: Athletics Blues 1963-65; Gymnastics Blue 1963; Represented Great Britain in athletics 1966; Author, playwright and amateur auctioneer.

Political career: *House of Commons:* MP (Conservative) for Louth 1969-74. Contested Louth February 1974 general election. *House of Lords:* Raised to the peerage as Baron Archer of Weston-Super-Mare, of Mark in the County of Somerset 1992. *Other:* Deputy chair, Conservative Party 1985-86; President, Conservative Party London Clubs 1998-99. *Councils and public bodies:* Councillor, Greater London Council 1966-70.

Political interests: Art, sport, 2012 olympics; Australia, India.

Other: The Archer Charitable Trust. President, Somerset AAA 1973-99; Vice-President, Cambridge City RFU; President, World Snooker Association 1997-99.

Publications: Plays: Beyond Reasonable Doubt (1987), Exclusive (1990), The Accused (2000); Novels/short stories: Not a Penny More, Not a Penny Less (1975); Shall We Tell the President? (1977); Kane and Abel (1979); A Quiver Full of Arrows (short stories, 1980); The Prodigal Daughter (1982); First Among Equals (1984); A Matter of Honour (1986); A Twist in the Tale (short stories, 1988); As the Crow Flies (1991); Honour Among Thieves (1993); Twelve Red Herrings (short stories, 1994); The Fourth Estate (1996); Collected Short Stories (1997); The Eleventh Commandment (1998); To Cut a Long Story Short (short stories, 2000); A Prison Diary – Volume I: Hell (2002); Sons of Fortune (2003); A Prison Diary – Volume II: Purgatory (2003); A Prison Diary – Volume III: Heaven (2004); False Impression (2006); Cat O'Nine Tales (short stories, 2006); The Gospel According to Judas (2007); A Prisoner of Birth (2008); Paths of Glory (2009); Rewrite of Kane and Abel (2009); And Thereby Hangs a Tale (short stories, 2010); Only Time Will Tell (2011); The Sins of the Father (2012); Best Kept Secret (2013).

Recreations: Theatre, cricket, auctioneering, art.

The Lord Archer of Weston-Super-Mare, House of Lords, London SW1A 0PW
Tel: 020 7219 5353
The Penthouse, Peninsula Heights, 93 Albert Embankment, London SE1 7TY *Tel:* 020 7735 0077 *Fax:* 020 7582 2330 *Email:* questions@jeffreyarcher.co.uk *Website:* www.jeffreyarcher.com *Twitter:* @Jeffrey_Archer

LABOUR

ARMSTRONG OF HILL TOP, BARONESS

ARMSTRONG OF HILL TOP (Life Baroness), Hilary Jane Armstrong; cr 2010. Born 30 November 1945; Daughter of late Ernest Armstrong, MP for Durham North West 1966-87, and Hannah Armstrong; Married Dr Paul Corrigan 1992.

Education: Monkwearmouth Comprehensive School, Sunderland; West Ham College of Technology (BSc sociology 1967); Birmingham University (Diploma social work 1970); Swahili (rusty).

Non-political career: Voluntary Services Overseas (VSO) teaching in Kenya 1967-69; Social worker, Newcastle Social Services 1970-73; Community worker, Southwick Neighbourhood Action Project 1973-75; Lecturer in community and youth work, Sunderland Polytechnic 1975-86; Secretary/researcher for Ernest Armstrong MP 1986-87. Chair ASTMS Northern Division Council 1981-88;.

Political career: *House of Commons:* MP for North West Durham 1987-2010. Opposition Spokesperson for Education 1988-92; PPS to John Smith as Leader of the Opposition 1992-94; Opposition Spokesperson for: Treasury and Economic Affairs 1994-95, The Environment and London 1995-97; Minister of State, Department of the Environment, Transport and the Regions 1997-2001; Government Chief Whip 2001-06; Minister for the Cabinet Office and Social Exclusion; Chancellor of the Duchy of Lancaster 2006-07. Member: Education 1998. Chair, PLP Northern Regional Group 2009-10. *House of Lords:* Raised to the peerage as Baroness Armstrong of Hill Top, of Crook in the County of Durham 2010. Member: Adoption Legislation 2012-13, Soft Power and the UK's Influence 2013-. *Other:* Member, Labour Party National Executive Committee 1992-94, 1996-2006. *Councils and public bodies:* Councillor, Durham County Council 1985-88; Vice-chair, British Council 1994-97; Non-executive director, Co. Durham and Darlington Foundation Hospital Trust.

Political interests: Regional development, world development, education, environment, social exclusion and social enterprise; Central Africa, Kenya, South Africa, Tanzania, Uganda.

Other: NCH Action for Children: Member NCH Board 1985-91, Vice-president 1991-97; Member, UNICEF National Committee 1995-97; Patron, Revolving Doors 2007-; Chair, Tony Blair Sports Foundation 2007, Trustee, Africa Governance Initiative 2008-, Board member, Emmaus 2008-11; The Cyrenians (Tyneside): Board member 2008-, Chair 2010-; Board member, Voluntary Services Overseas (VSO) International 2008-11; Board member, Voluntary Services Overseas (VSO) UK 2011-; Chair, Voluntary Services Overseas (VSO) Federation Council 2011- Ambassador Action for Children 2008-; Chair Community Energy Solutions 2009-13; Honorary degree, Sunderland University. PC 1999.

Recreations: Theatre, reading, football.

Rt Hon the Baroness Armstrong of Hill Top, House of Lords, London SW1A 0PW
Tel: 020 7219 5353 *Email:* armstrongh@parliament.uk

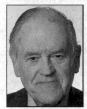

CROSSBENCH

ARMSTRONG OF ILMINSTER, LORD

ARMSTRONG OF ILMINSTER (Life Baron), Robert Temple Armstrong; cr. 1988. Born 30 March 1927; Son of late Sir Thomas Armstrong, musician, and late Hester Muriel, née Draper; Married Serena Chance 1953 (divorced 1985, she died 1994) (2 daughters); married (Mary) Patricia Carlow 1985.

Education: Dragon School, Oxford; Eton College (King's Scholar); Christ Church, Oxford (Scholar) (BA classical mods 1947, literae humaniores 1949, MA); Honorary Student, Christ Church, Oxford 1985; French.

Non-political career: Assistant principal, HM Treasury 1950-55; Private secretary to: Reginald Maudling MP as Economic Secretary to the Treasury 1953-54, Rab Butler MP as Chancellor of the Exchequer 1954-55; Principal, HM Treasury 1955-57; Secretary, Radcliffe Committee on Working of Monetary System 1957-59; Principal, HM Treasury 1959-64; Secretary, Armitage Committee on Pay of Postmen 1964; Assistant secretary: Cabinet Office 1964-66, Treasury 1967-68; Principal Private Secretary to Roy Jenkins MP as Chancellor of the Exchequer 1968; Under-Secretary (Home Finance), Treasury 1968-70; Principal Private Secretary to Edward Heath and Harold Wilson MPs as Prime Minister 1970-75; Home Office: Deputy Under-Secretary of State 1975-77, Permanent Under-Secretary of State 1977-79; Secretary of the Cabinet 1979-87; Head of the Home Civil Service 1981-87; Lucas Industries PLC 1985-92; Inchcape PLC 1988-95; N.M. Rothschild and Sons 1988-97; Shell Transport and Trading PLC 1988-97; British-American Tobacco PLC 1988-97; RTZ PLC 1988-97; Director, Royal Opera House 1988-93; Carlton Television Ltd 1991-95; IAM Gold Ltd 1996-2003; Chair: Biotechnology Investments Ltd 1989-2000, Bristol and West plc (formerly Building Society) 1993-97; Forensic Investigative Associates plc 1997-2003; Director: Bank of Ireland 1997-2001, 3i Bioscience Investment Trust plc 2000-01; Member, Advisory Panel, E-Clear (UK) plc 2007-08.

Political career: *House of Lords:* Raised to the peerage as Baron Armstrong of Ilminster, of Ashill in the County of Somerset 1988. Member: EU Sub-committee A (Economic and Financial Affairs) 2000-03, Merits of Statutory Instruments 2003-07, Review of the BBC Charter 2005-06, Delegated Powers and Regulatory Reform 2007-10, Joint Committees on: Pre-legislative Scrutiny of Constitutional Renewal Bill 2008, the Draft Detention of Terrorist Suspects (Temporary Extension) Bills 2011, the Draft Communications Data Bill 2012-13.

Political interests: Arts, museums and galleries, public service, constitutional matters; Canada, France, USA.

Other: Council member, Musicians Benevolent Fund; Royal United Kingdom Benevolent Association; Council of Honour, Royal Academy of Music; Fellow of Eton College 1979-94; Chair: Board of Trustees, V&A Museum 1988-98, Hestercombe Gardens Trust 1996-2007, Leeds Castle Foundation 2001-07; Trustee, Derek Hill Foundation 2002-; Chair, Sir Edward Heath Charitable Foundation 2005-13; Trustee, Wells Cathedral School Foundation 2007-12; Musicians Benevolent Fund. Honorary Member, Salters' Company. Freeman, City of London. Chancellor, Hull University 1994-2006. Honorary LLD, University of Hull. CB 1974; CVO 1975; KCB 1978; GCB 1983; Brooks's, Garrick.

Recreations: Music.

The Lord Armstrong of Ilminster GCB CVO, House of Lords, London SW1A 0PW
Tel: 020 7219 4983 *Email:* armstrongr@parliament.uk

ARRAN, EARL OF

ARRAN (9th Earl of, I), Arthur Desmond Colquhoun Gore; cr. 1762; 9th Viscount Sudley and Baron Saunders (I) 1758; 5th Baron Sudley (UK) 1884; 11th Bt of Castle Gore (I) 1662. Born 14 July 1938; Son of 8th Earl; Married Eleanor Van Cutsem 1974 (2 daughters).

Education: Eton College; Balliol College, Oxford (BA English literature 1960, MA).

Non-political career: Served Grenadier Guards, national service, commissioned 1958-60. Assistant manager, *Daily Mail* 1972-73; Managing director, Clark Nelson 1973-74; Assistant general manager, *Daily Express* and *Sunday Express* 1974; Director, Waterstone & Co Ltd 1984-87; Parliamentary consultant to the waste industry 1995-; Non-executive director: HMV (EMI) 1995-98, SWEL (the Economy and Inward Investment of the West Country), Bonham's (Auctioneers) 1998-2001, Weather World 2005-.

Political career: *House of Lords:* First entered House of Lords 1983. Sits as Baron Sudley; Government Whip 1987-89; Government Spokesperson for: Home Office, Department for Education and Science and Department of Health and Social Security 1987-89, Department of the Environment 1988-89; Parliamentary Under-Secretary of State: Ministry of Defence (Armed Forces) 1989-92, Northern Ireland Office 1992-94, Department of the Environment 1994; Government Deputy Chief Whip 1994-1995; Elected hereditary peer 1999-. EU Sub-committee D (Environment and Agriculture): Member 2007-08, Co-opted member 2008-10; Member: EU Sub-committee D (Agriculture, Fisheries and Environment) 2010-12, Olympic and Paralympic Legacy 2013-.

Political interests: Media, charity, sport, foreign affairs.

Other: President, Children's Country Holidays Fund 1999; Trustee, Chelsea Physic Garden; Turf, Beefsteak, Pratt's, White's.

Recreations: Tennis, golf, croquet, shooting and gardening.

The Earl of Arran, House of Lords, London SW1A 0PW
Tel: 020 7219 5353

ASHCROFT, LORD

ASHCROFT (Life Baron), Michael Anthony Ashcroft; cr. 2000. Born 4 March 1946; Son of Frederic Ashcroft and Mary Lavinia Long; Married Wendy Mahoney 1972 (divorced 1984) (2 sons 1 daughter); married Susi Anstey 1986.

Education: King Edward VI Grammar School, Norwich; Royal Grammar School, High Wycombe; Mid Essex Technical College, Chelmsford.

Non-political career: Chairman and chief executive officer, ADT Ltd 1977-97; Chairman, BCB Holdings Ltd 1987-2010; Non-executive director, Tyco International 1997-2002; Belize Ambassador to the UN 1998-2000.

Political career: *House of Lords:* Raised to the peerage as Baron Ashcroft, of Chichester in the County of West Sussex 2000. Government adviser, Military Bases in Cyprus (Unpaid) 2011-; Prime Minister's Special Representative for Veterans' Transition 2012-. *Other:* Treasurer, International Democratic Union 2007-; Conservative Party: Senior Party Treasurer 1998-2001, Vice-chair 2005-10, Deputy chair 2005-10 (Conservative future 2005-07, target seats and opinion research 2005-10).

Other: Chairman: Lord Ashcroft Foundation, Crimestoppers, Prospect Education (technology) Trust; Vice-patron, Intelligence Corps Museum; Trustee: Cleveland Clinic, Imperial War Museum Foundation; President and trustee, West India Committee; Ambassador, SkillForce. Chancellor, Anglia Ruskin University 2001-. Honorary doctorate, Anglia Ruskin University 1999. KCMG 2000; PC 2012.

Publications: Smell the Coffee – A Wake-up Call for the Conservative Party (Politicos, 2005); Dirty Politics, Dirty Times: My Fight with Wapping and New Labour (MAA Publishing, 2005); Victoria Cross Heroes (Headline Review, 2006); Special Forces Heroes (Headline Review, 2008); Minority Verdict – The Conservative Party, the Voters and the 2010 election (Biteback, 2010); George Cross Heroes (Headline Review, 2010); Degrees of Separation (Biteback, 2012); It's Not You, It's Them (Biteback, 2012); Armed Forces and Society (Biteback, 2012); Heroes of the Skies (Headline, 2012).

Recreations: Collecting Victoria Crosses, boating, writing.

Rt Hon the Lord Ashcroft KCMG, House of Lords, London SW1A 0PW
Tel: 020 7219 5353 *Website:* www.lordashcroft.com *Twitter:* @lordashcroft

ASHDOWN OF NORTON-SUB-HAMDON, LORD

ASHDOWN OF NORTON-SUB-HAMDON (Life Baron), Jeremy John Ashdown; cr. 2001. Born 27 February 1941; Son of late Lieutenant Colonel John W. R. D. Ashdown; Married Mary Jane Donne Courtenay 1961 (1 son 1 daughter).

Education: Bedford School; Hong Kong Language School (Chinese (Mandarin) 1967-70).

Non-political career: Royal Marines Officer (Captain) 1959-72 with Commando Units in Far East, Middle East and Belfast; Commanded Unit of Special Boat Service in Far East. 1st class interpreter, Chinese; First Secretary, UK Mission (Foreign Office) to UN in Geneva 1971-76; **LIBERAL DEMOCRAT** Westland Helicopters, Yeovil 1976-78; Morlands, Yeovil 1978-81; Youth officer, Dorset County Council 1981-83; UN High Representative for Bosnia and Herzegovina 2002-06.

Political career: *House of Commons:* Contested Yeovil 1979 general election. MP (Liberal/Liberal Democrat) for Yeovil 1983-2001. Liberal Spokesperson for Trade and Industry 1985-87; Alliance Spokesperson for Education and Science 1987; Liberal Spokesperson for Education and Science 1987-88; Spokesperson for Northern Ireland 1988-92; Leader, Liberal Democrats 1988-99. *House of Lords:* Raised to the peerage as Baron Ashdown of Norton-sub-Hamdon, of Norton-sub-Hamdon in the County of Somerset 2001. *Other:* Chair of the Liberal Democrat's 2015 general election campaign 2012-.

Political interests: Youth affairs, foreign affairs, defence, industry, new technology, nation building; Western Balkans.

Other: Hope and Homes for Children. PC 1989; KBE 2000; GCMG 2006; National Liberal.

Publications: Citizens' Britain: A Radical Agenda for the 1990s (1989); Beyond Westminster: Finding Hope in Britain (1992); The Ashdown Diaries (2000, 2001); Swords and Ploughshares – bringing peace to the 21st century (Orion, 2007); A Fortunate Life (2009).

Recreations: Gardening, classical music, hill-walking, wine-making.

Rt Hon the Lord Ashdown of Norton-sub-Hamdon GCMG KBE, House of Lords,
London SW1A 0PW
Tel: 020 7219 8726 *Email:* ashdownp@parliament.uk *Twitter:* @paddyashdown

ASHTON OF HYDE, LORD

ASHTON OF HYDE (4th Baron, UK), Thomas Henry Ashton; cr. 1911. Born 18 July 1958; Son of late 3rd Baron and Pauline Trewlove Ashton, née Brackenbury; Married Emma Allinson 1987 (4 daughters).

Education: Eton College; Trinity College, Oxford (BA 1980, MA).

Non-political career: Royal Hussars (PWO); Lieutenant, Royal Wessex Yeomanry. Barclays Bank 1981-82; CT Bowring Reinsurance Ltd 1982-90; Vice-President, Guy Carpenter & Company 1990-92; Director: C.T Bowring Reinsurance Ltd 1992-93, D.P Mann Ltd 1996-99; Faraday **CONSERVATIVE** Underwriting Ltd: Director 1999-, Chief executive officer 2005-; Faraday Reinsurance Company Ltd: Director 2002-, Chief executive officer 2005-; Council member, Lloyd's 2010-.

Political career: *House of Lords:* Elected hereditary peer 2011-.

Other: Joint master, Heythrop Hunt 2007-09.

The Lord Ashton of Hyde, House of Lords, London SW1A 0PW
Tel: 020 7219 5353 *Email:* ashtont@parliament.uk

ASHTON OF UPHOLLAND , BARONESS

ASHTON OF UPHOLLAND (Life Baroness), Catherine Margaret Ashton; cr 1999. Born 20 March 1956; Daughter of late Harold and Clare Ashton; Married Peter Kellner 1988 (1 son 1 daughter 1 stepson 2 stepdaughters).

Education: Upholland Grammar School; Bedford College, London University (BSc Econ 1977); French.

NON-AFFILIATED

Non-political career: Administrative officer, CND 1977-79; The Coverdale Organisation 1979-81; Central Council for Education and Training in Social Work 1981-83; Director of community development and public affairs, Business in the Community 1983-89; Public policy adviser 1989-, seconded by London First to Home Office 1998-99; Director, Political Context 1996-98; Adviser, Lattice Foundation 2000-01; European Commission: Commissioner for Trade 2008-09, High Representative for Foreign Affairs and Security Policy, and Vice-President and External Relations Commissioner 2009-; Chair, steering board, European Defence Agency 2009-.

Political career: *House of Lords:* Raised to the peerage as Baroness Ashton of Upholland, of St Albans in the County of Hertfordshire 1999. Parliamentary Under-Secretary of State and Government Spokesperson, Department for Education and Skills 2001-04 (also Department for Work and Pensions 2002-04); Government Spokesperson for Children 2003-04; Parliamentary Under-Secretary of State and Government Spokesperson, Department for Constitutional Affairs/Ministry of Justice 2004-07; Leader of the House of Lords and Lord President of the Council 2007-08; Government Spokesperson for: Cabinet Office 2008, Equality 2008; On leave of absence 2008-. Member: Selection 2007-08, Liaison 2007-08, Privileges 2007-08, House 2007-08, Procedure 2007-08. *Councils and public bodies:* Chair, Hertfordshire Health Authority 1998-2001.

Other: Trustee, Verulamium Museum 2000-; Vice-president National Council for One Parent Families 1998-2001. *House Magazine* Minister of the Year 2005; Channel 4 Peer of the Year 2005; Stonewall Politician of the Year 2006. PC 2006; Royal Commonwealth Society.

Rt Hon the Baroness Ashton of Upholland , House of Lords, London SW1A 0PW
Tel: 020 7219 5353

ASTOR, VISCOUNT

ASTOR (4th Viscount, UK), William Waldorf Astor; cr. 1917; 4th Baron Astor (UK) 1916. Born 27 December 1951; Son of 3rd Viscount and Honorary Sarah Norton, daughter of 6th Baron Grantley; Married Annabel Sheffield, née Jones 1976 (2 sons 1 daughter).

Education: Eton College.

Non-political career: Citibank, New York 1970-72; Observer, USA 1972; Westminster Press 1973-74; Director: UK and US Property and Investment Companies 1974-84, Blakeney Hotels and Cliveden Hotels 1984-90; Director: Chorion 1996-2011, Networkers 2006-, Silvergate Media 2011-.

CONSERVATIVE

Political career: *House of Lords:* First entered House of Lords 1972; Government Whip 1990-93; Government Spokesperson for: Department of Environment 1990-91, Home Office 1991-92, Department of National Heritage 1992-93; Parliamentary Under-Secretary of State: Department of Social Security 1993-94, Department of National Heritage 1994-95; Opposition Spokesperson for: Home Office 1997-2001; Elected hereditary peer 1999-; Opposition Spokesperson for: Education and Employment 1999-2001, Transport, Local Government and the Regions 2001-02, Transport 2002-05, Culture, Media and Sport 2005-06.

Other: Trustee, Stanley Spencer Gallery, Cookham; White's.

The Viscount Astor, House of Lords, London SW1A 0PW
Tel: 020 7219 4139 *Email:* astorw@parliament.uk
44 Grosvenor Gardens Mews South, London SW1W OLB

ASTOR OF HEVER, LORD

Parliamentary Under-Secretary of State and Government Spokesperson, Ministry of Defence

ASTOR OF HEVER (3rd Baron, UK), John Jacob Astor; cr. 1956. Born 16 June 1946; Son of 2nd Baron, and late Lady Irene Haig, daughter of Field Marshal 1st Earl Haig; Married Fiona Harvey 1970 (divorced 1990) (3 daughters); married Honorary Elizabeth Mackintosh 1990 (1 son 1 daughter).

Education: Eton College; French.

CONSERVATIVE

Non-political career: Lieutenant, Life Guards 1966-70; Honorary Colonel 101 (City of London) Engineer Regiment 2005-10.

Political career: *House of Lords:* First entered House of Lords 1984; Opposition Whip 1998-2010; Elected hereditary peer 1999-; Opposition Spokesperson for: Defence 2003-10, Foreign and Commonwealth Office 2003-10, International Development 2003-10; Parliamentary Under-Secretary of State and Government Spokesperson, Ministry of Defence 2010-; Government Whip 2010-11. *Other:* Member of Executive, Association of Conservative Peers 1996-98. *Councils and public bodies:* DL Kent 1996-.

Political interests: France, motorsport industry, defence; France, USA.

Other: Chair, Council of the Order of St John for Kent 1987-97; Patron: Edenbridge Music and Arts Trust 1989-2010, Kent Youth Trust 1994-2010; President: Earl Haig Branch, Royal British Legion 1994-2010, Motorsport Industry Association 1995-2010, RoSPA 1996-99, Eden Valley Museum Trust 1998-2010; Patron, Aquarian Opera 1999-2010; Royal British Legion, Kent 2002-07; President, Kent County Agricultural Society 2006-10; Patron, Conservatives in Paris; President, Tunbridge Wells International Music Festival 2009-10; Trustee: Astor of Hever Trust 1986-, Astor Foundation 1988-2008, Rochester Cathedral Trust 1988-2010, Canterbury Cathedral Trust 1992-2007. Member, Goldsmiths' Company; White's, Farmer's.

The Lord Astor of Hever DL, House of Lords, London SW1A 0PW
Tel: 020 7219 5475 *Email:* astorjj@parliament.uk

ATTENBOROUGH, LORD

ATTENBOROUGH (Life Baron), Richard Samuel Attenborough; cr. 1993. Born 29 August 1923; Son of late Frederick Attenborough; Married Sheila Sim 1945 (1 son 2 daughters).

Education: Wyggeston Grammar School, Leicester; Leverhulme scholarship to Royal Academy of Dramatic Art.

Non-political career: Served RAF 1943-46. Actor, producer and director; Appeared in a number of productions on the London stage including: *Brighton Rock* 1943, *The Mousetrap* 1952-54, *The Rape of the Belt* 1957-58; Film appearances include: *In Which We Serve, Brighton Rock, London Belongs to Me, The Guinea Pig, Morning Departure, The Ship That Died of Shame, I'm Alright Jack, The League of Gentlemen, The Angry Silence* (also co-produced), *The Dock Brief, The Great Escape, Seance On a Wet Afternoon* (also produced, BAFTA Award), *Guns at Batasi* (BAFTA Award), *The Flight of the Phoenix, The Sand Pebbles* (Hollywood Golden Globe), *Dr Dolittle* (Hollywood Golden Globe), *10 Rillington Place, The Chess Players, Jurassic Park, Miracle on 34th Street, Lost World, Elizabeth I*; Produced: *Whistle Down the Wind, The L-Shaped Room*; Directed: *Young Winston* (Hollywood Golden Globe), *A Bridge Too Far, Magic, A Chorus Line*; Produced and directed: *Oh! What a Lovely War* (BAFTA Award, Hollywood Golden Globe), *Gandhi* (8 Oscars, 5 BAFTA Awards, 5 Hollywood Golden Globes), *Cry Freedom, Chaplin, Shadowlands* (BAFTA Award); *In Love and War; Grey Owl*; Capital Radio: Chair 1972-92, Life President 1992-; Chair, Goldcrest Films and Television Ltd 1982-87; Channel Four Television: Chair 1987-92, Deputy Chair 1980-86.

LABOUR

Political career: *House of Lords:* Raised to the peerage as Baron Attenborough, of Richmond upon Thames in the London Borough of Richmond upon Thames 1993. On leave of absence October 2012-.

Political interests: Arts, education, disability, underdeveloped countries.

Other: Member, chair, president numerous organisations in arts, theatre, film including: Actors' Charitable Trust: Chairman 1956-88, President 1988-; Muscular Dystrophy Group of Great Britain: Vice-President 1962-71, President 1971-; Royal Academy of Dramatic Art: Council member 1963-, Chair 1970-; National Film and TV School: Governor 1970-81, President 1997-; Trustee: King George V Fund for Actors and Actresses 1973-, Help a London Child 1975-, Tate Gallery 1976-82, 1994-96; UK Trustees Waterford-Kamhlaba School Swaziland: Chair 1976-, Governor 1987-; Trustee, Motability 1977-; President, The Gandhi Foundation 1983-; Trustee, Tate Foundation 1986-; Patron, Goodwill Ambassador for Unicef 1987-; European Script Fund: Chair 1988-96, Honorary President 1996-; Combined Theatrical Charities Appeals Council: President 1988-, Chair 1964-88; President, Arts for Health 1989-; Patron, Richard Attenborough Centre for Disability and the Arts, Leicester University 1990-; Fellow: BAFTA 1983, BFI 1992; Muscular Dystrophy Group of Great Britain, The Actors' Charitable Trust. Freeman, City of Leicester 1990. Sussex University: Pro-Chancellor 1970-, Chancellor 1998-. Ten honorary doctorates and fellowships. *Evening Standard* Film Award, 40 years service to British Cinema 1983; Martin Luther King Jr Peace Prize 1983; European Film Awards Award of Merit for Humanitarianism in Film Making 1988; Shakespeare Prize for Outstanding Contribution to European Culture 1992; Praemium Imperiale 1998; BBC/BAFTA Lifetime Achievement Award 1999; EMMA Award 2001. CBE 1967; Kt 1976; Padma Bhushan, India 1983; Commandeur, Ordre des Arts et des Lettres (France) 1985; Chevalier, Legion d'Honneur (France) 1988; Garrick, Beefsteak. Director, Chelsea Football Club 1969-82, Life Vice-President 1993-.

Publications: In Search of Gandhi (1982); Co-author Richard Attenborough's Chorus Line (1986); Cry Freedom, A Pictorial Record (1987).

Recreations: Collecting paintings and sculpture, listening to music, watching football and reading the newspapers.

The Lord Attenborough CBE, House of Lords, London SW1A 0PW
Tel: 020 7219 5353
Old Friars, Richmond Green, Richmond upon Thames, Surrey TW9 1NH *Tel:* 020 8940 7234
Twitter: @Lord_Dickie_CBE

ATTLEE, EARL

CONSERVATIVE

Government Spokesperson, Department for Transport, Northern Ireland Office, Home Office, Law Officers, Scotland Office and Wales Office; Government Whip

ATTLEE (3rd Earl, UK), John Richard Attlee; cr. 1955; Viscount Prestwood. Born 3 October 1956; Son of 2nd Earl; Married Celia Plummer 1993 (divorced); married Terese Ahern 2008.

Education: Stowe School, Buckinghamshire.

Non-political career: Major, REME TA, All Arms Pool of Watchkeepers; Operation Lodestar 1997-98; Operation Telic (Iraq) 2003. President, The Heavy Transport Association 1994-2008; In-Country director (Rwanda), British Direct Aid 1995-96.

Political career: *House of Lords:* First entered House of Lords 1994; Opposition Whip 1997-99; Opposition Spokesperson for: Defence June-Oct 1997, Transport 1997, Northern Ireland 1997, 1998-1999, Defence 1998-2001, 2002-03, Trade and Industry 1998-99, Transport 1999-2001, 2002-03; Elected hereditary peer 1999-; Opposition Whip 2002-05; Opposition Spokesperson for: Energy 2003-04, Office of the Deputy Prime Minister 2004-05, Transport 2007-10, Maritime and Shipping 2007-10; Opposition Whip 2007-10; Government Whip 2010-; Government Spokesperson for: International Development 2010, Northern Ireland 2010-, Transport 2010-, Communities and Local Government 2010-12, Home Office (Immigration) 2010-, Wales 2012-, Law Officers 2013-, Scotland 2013-. Member: Statutory Instruments Joint Committee 2007-08, Partnerships (Prosecution) (Scotland) Bill 2013-.

Political interests: Overseas aid and development, engineering, defence, transport.

Other: TD.

Recreations: Restoration and operation of classic commericial and military vehicles.

The Earl Attlee, House of Lords, London SW1A 0PW
Tel: 020 7219 6071 *Fax:* 020 7219 5979 *Email:* attleej@parliament.uk

AVEBURY, LORD

LIBERAL DEMOCRAT

AVEBURY (4th Baron, UK), Eric Reginald Lubbock; cr. 1900; 7th Bt of Lamas (UK) 1806. Born 29 September 1928; Son of late Honorary Maurice Lubbock, son of 1st Baron, PC, DL, and late Honorary Mary Stanley; Married Kina Maria O'Kelly de Gallagh 1953 (2 sons 1 daughter) (divorced 1983); married Lindsay Stewart 1985 (1 son).

Education: Upper Canada College, Toronto; Harrow School; Balliol College, Oxford (BA engineering 1949).

Non-political career: Second Lieutenant, Welsh Guards 1949-51. Rolls-Royce aero-engine division 1951-55; Production Engineering Ltd (Management consultant) 1955-60; Charterhouse Group 1960-62; Director, C.L. Projects Ltd 1968-.

Political career: *House of Commons:* MP (Liberal) for Orpington 1962-70. Liberal Whip 1963-70. *House of Lords:* First entered House of Lords 1971; Elected hereditary peer 1999-; Liberal Democrat Spokesperson for: Race Relations and Immigration 1971-83, Foreign and Commonwealth Affairs 1998-2010: with special responsibility for Africa 2004-10, Home Office (civil liberties) 2005-10. Member: House of Lords Offices Library and Computers Sub-committee 2001-05, Religious Offences 2002-03; EU Sub-committee F (Home Affairs): Member 2003-07, 2010-12, Co-opted member 2008-10; Member: Intergovernmental Organisations 2007-08, EU Sub-committee F (Home Affairs, Health and Education) 2012-13, Joint Committee on Statutory Instruments 2013-. *Councils and public bodies:* Member: Speaker's Conference on Electoral Law 1963-65, Royal Commission on Standards of Conduct in Public Life 1975-76; President, ACERT (Advisory Council on the Education of Romany and other Travellers) 1990-; Chairman, Department for Education Stakeholder Group on Gypsies, Romanies and Travellers 2009-.

Political interests: Human rights, Gypsies, prisons, alcohol harm, asylum and immigration; Afghanistan, Bahrain, Bangladesh, Burma, Colombia, East Timor, Eritrea, Ethiopia, Indonesia, Libya, Malaysia, Mali, Mexico, Nigeria, Pakistan, Peru, Saudi Arabia, Sierra Leone, Somalia, Sri Lanka, Yemen, Zimbabwe.

Other: Secretary, the Silbury Fund; Chair, Maurice Lubbock Memorial Fund; President: Fluoridation Society 1972-84, Conservation Society 1973-81, London Bach Society, Steinitz Bach Players 1984-95; Patron, Angulimala, Buddhist Prison Chaplaincy 1990-; TAPOL (Indonesian Human Rights) 1993-; Patron: Kurdish Human Rights Project 1993-, British Campaign for East Timor 1994-; Vice-President, Steinitz Bach Players 1995-; Chair: Cameroon Campaign Group 2003-, Peru Support Group 2004-; Co-chair, Chittagong Hill Tracts Commission, Bangladesh 2005-; Chair, Bangladesh International Foundation 2007-; MInstMechE 1966; FBCS; CEng. Hilal-i-Quaid-i-Azam (Pakistan) 1990.

Publications: The Energy Crisis – Growth, Stability or Collapse (1973); Alcohol – Politics and Practicalities (1981); Authority and Accountability (1986); Desolated and Profaned (1992); A Desolation called Peace (1993); Iran: The Subjection of Women (1995); Iran: State of Terror (1996); A Positive Legal Duty: the liberation of the people of East Timor in Self Determination, ed Donald Clark and Roloo William (MacMillan, 1996); Iran: Fatal Writ (2000).

The Lord Avebury, House of Lords, London SW1A 0PW
Tel: 020 7219 3438
26 Flodden Road, London SE5 9LH *Tel:* 020 7274 4617
Email: ericavebury@gmail.com my-silbury.co.uk *Twitter:* @EricAvebury

---

LABOUR

BACH, LORD

Opposition Spokesperson for Foreign and Commonwealth Office

BACH (Life Baron), William Stephen Goulden Bach; cr. 1998. Born 25 December 1946; Son of late Stephen Bach CBE and late Joan Bach; Married Caroline Jones 1984 (1 daughter and 2 children from previous marriage).

Education: Westminster School; New College, Oxford (BA English 1968).

Non-political career: Called to the Bar, Middle Temple 1972, Tenant Barristers' Chambers 1975-2000, Head of Chambers 1996-99; Served on a number of circuit and local court and bar committees over many years. Member, TGWU/Unite 1977-.

Political career: *House of Commons:* Contested (Labour) Gainsborough 1979 and Sherwood 1983 and 1987 general elections. *House of Lords:* Raised to the peerage as Baron Bach, of Lutterworth in the County of Leicestershire 1998. Government Whip 1999-2000; Government Spokesperson for: Home Office 1999-2000, Lord Chancellor's Department 1999-2000, Education and Employment 1999-2000; Parliamentary Secretary, Lord Chancellor's Department 2000-01; Parliamentary Under-Secretary of State and Government Spokesperson, Ministry of Defence (Minister for Defence Procurement) 2001-05; Parliamentary Under-Secretary of State and Government Spokesperson, Department for Environment, Food and Rural Affairs 2005-06; Government Whip 2007-08; Government Spokesperson for: Business, Enterprise and Regulatory Reform 2007-08, Justice 2007-10, HM Treasury 2007-08, Foreign and Commonwealth Office 2008; Parliamentary Under-Secretary of State, Ministry of Justice 2008-10; Opposition Spokesperson for: Justice 2010-12, Foreign and Commonwealth Office 2013-. Member: European Communities Sub-committee E (Laws and Institutions) 1998-99, Draft Legal Services Bill Joint Committee 2006; Co-opted member European Union Sub-committee D (Environment and Agriculture) 2006-07. *Other:* Executive committee member, Society of Labour Lawyers; Elected member, Labour Party: National Policy Forum 1998-99, Economic Policy Commission 1998-99; Member, Co-operative Party; Chair and co-founder, Society of Labour Lawyers, East Midlands; Chair: Harborough District Labour Party 1989-95, 2007-, Northants and Blaby Euro Constituency GC 1992-99, South Leicestershire Constituency Labour Party 2007-. *Councils and public bodies:* Leicester City Council: Councillor 1976-87, Chief Whip, Labour Group 1981-83; Councillor, Lutterworth Town Council 1991-99; Mayor, Lutterworth 1993-94; Harborough District Council: Councillor 1995-99, Chair, Contracts Services Committee 1995-97; Chief Whip, Labour Group 1995-98.

Political interests: Crime and criminal justice, local government, sport, foreign affairs, defence and security, social welfare law; Latin America, Chile, India, Italy, Portugal, Spain, USA.

Other: Leicester University: Council member 1980-99, Court member 1980-; Member, Fabian Society; Vice-chair, Cotesbach Education Trust; Trustee, LawWorks; Patron, Coventry Law Centre. Honorary degree, Leicester University. Peer of the Year, *House Magazine* awards 2012. Leicester City FC; Leicestershire CCC; Founder Member and President, Walcote Cricket Club.

Recreations: Playing and watching football and cricket, supporting Leicester City FC, American crime writing.

The Lord Bach, House of Lords, London SW1A 0PW
Tel: 020 7219 6389 *Fax:* 020 7219 2146 *Email:* bachw@parliament.uk *Twitter:* @FightBach

BAKER OF DORKING, LORD

BAKER OF DORKING (Life Baron), Kenneth Wilfred Baker; cr. 1997. Born 3 November 1934; Son of late Wilfred Baker, OBE; Married Mary Gray-Muir 1963 (1 son 2 daughters).

Education: St Paul's School, London; Magdalen College, Oxford (BA history 1958) (Union Secretary 1958).

Non-political career: National service 1953-55 (Lieutenant in Gunners). Chair, Teather & Greenwood plc 2003-07; Non-executive director, Stanley Leisure plc (now called Genting UK) 2001-; Chair, Graphite Resources Ltd 2007-12.

CONSERVATIVE   **Political career:** *House of Commons:* Contested Poplar 1964 and Acton 1966 general elections. MP (Conservative) for Acton 1968-70, St Marylebone 1970-83 and Mole Valley 1983-97. PPS to Minister of State, Department of Employment 1970-72; Parliamentary Secretary, Civil Service Department 1972-74; Minister of State for Industry and Information Technology 1981-84; Minister for Local Government 1984-85; Secretary of State for: Environment 1985-86, Education and Science 1986-89; Chancellor of the Duchy of Lancaster 1989-90; Home Secretary 1990-92. *House of Lords:* Raised to the peerage as Baron Baker of Dorking, of Iford in the County of East Sussex 1997. Chair Information 2003-07; Member House 2007-12. *Other:* Chairman, Conservative Party 1989-90; Honorary Life member, Tory Reform Group. *Councils and public bodies:* Councillor, Twickenham Borough Council 1960-62.

Political interests: Education, history, information technology; UK.

Other: Chair: Hansard Society 1978-81, Museum of British History 1995-2005; President Royal London Society for the Blind 2000-10; Trustee: Cartoon AG Trust 2003-, Booker Prize Foundation 2005-; President Old Pauline Club 2007-09; Chair, Edge Foundation 2008-; Trustee, Baker Dearing Educational Trust 2003-; City & Guilds Fellowship Diploma 2012; The Cartoon Museum. Honorary Degree, Richmond College, The American University in London. PC 1984; CH 1992; Athenæum, Garrick.

Publications: I Have No Gun But I Can Spit (1980); London Lines (1982); The Faber Book of English History in Verse (1988); Unauthorised Versions: Poems and their Parodies (1990); The Faber Book of Conservatism (1993); The Turbulent Years: My Life in Politics (1993); The Prime Ministers – An Irreverent Political History in Cartoons (1995); Kings and Queens: An Irreverent Cartoon History of the British Monarchy (1996); The Faber Book of War Poetry (1996); Children's English History in Verse (2000); The Faber Book of Landscape Poetry (2000); George IV: A Life in Caricature (2005); George III: A Life in Caricature (2007); GK Chesterton Poems (2007); George Washingtons War in Contemporary Caricature and Print (2009); 14-18: A New Vision for Secondary Education (2013).

Recreations: Collecting books, collecting political cartoons.

Rt Hon the Lord Baker of Dorking CH, House of Lords, London SW1A 0PW
Tel: 020 7219 4434 *Email:* bakerk@parliament.uk

BAKEWELL, BARONESS

BAKEWELL (Life Baroness), Joan Dawson Bakewell; cr 2011. Born 16 April 1933; Daughter of John Rowlands and Rose Bland; Married Michael Bakewell 1955 (divorced 1972) (1 son 1 daughter); married Jack Emery (divorced 2001).

Education: Stockport High School for Girls; Newnham College, Cambridge (BA history and economics).

Non-political career: TV presenter: *Sunday Break* 1962, *Home at 4.30* 1964, *Meeting Point* 1964, *The Second Sex* 1964, *Late Night Line Up* 1965-72, *The Youthful Eye* 1968, *Moviemakers*

LABOUR   *at the National Film Theatre* 1971, *Film 72* 1972, *Film 73* 1973, *For the Sake of Appearance, Where is Your God?, Who Cares?, and the Affirmative Way* (series) 1973, *Holiday* (series) 1974-78, *Thank You, Ron* (documentary) 1974, *What's it All About?* (series) 1974, *Fairest Fortune and Edinburgh Festival Report* 1974, *Time Running Out* (series) 1974, *The Shakespeare Business* (series) 1976, *The Brontë Business* (series) 1976, *Generation to Generation* (series) 1976, *Reports Action* (series) 1976-79, *My Dad with the Children* 1977, *Arts UK: OK?* 1980, *The Heart of the Matter* 1988-2000, *Travels with Persner* 1998, *My Generation* 2000, *Taboo* (series) 2001; TV critic, *The Times* 1978-81; Radio presenter: *Away From it All* 1978-79, *PM* 1979-81, *Artist of the Week* 1998-2000, *Belief* 2001-, *Midsummer Sins* 2004, *There and Back* (play); *Brontës: The Private Faces* (theatre), Edinburgh Festival 1979; Arts correspondent, BBC 1981-87; Columnist, *Sunday Times* 1988-90; Chair, *The Brains Trust*, BBC 1998-2001; Columnist: *Guardian* 2003-05, *Independent* 2006-.

Political career: *House of Lords:* Raised to the peerage as Baroness Bakewell, of Stockport in the County of Greater Manchester 2011. Member Communications 2012-.

Political interests: Women's rights, the elderly, the arts; Brazil, India, Turkey.

Other: President, Society of Arts Publicists 1984-90; Council member, Aldeburgh Foundation 1985-99; British Film Institute: Governor 1994-2003, Deputy chair 1997-99, Chair 1999-2003; Board member, Royal National Theatre 1996-2003; Chair, Shared Experience 2004-12; National chair, Campaign for the Arts 2004-12; President, Birkbeck College 2013-; Honorary FRCA 1994; Breast Cancer Care; Women for Refugee Women; British Humanist Association; English Pen; Fawcett Society; Amnesty International. Newnham College, Cambridge: Associate 1980-91, Associate fellow 1984-87; Honorary Fellow, Royal Holloway and Bedford New College 1997; Honorary DLitt, Queen Margaret University College, Edinburgh 2005; Honorary professor, Department of Film and Media, Stirling University 2006-; Honorary DLitt: Chester 2007, University of Arts, London 2008, Staffordshire University 2009, Lancaster University 2010, Newcastle University 2011, The Open University 2010, Essex University 2011, Manchester Metropolitan University 2013. Journalist of the Year, Stonewall awards 2009 Richard Dimbleby Award, BAFTA 1994. CBE 1999; DBE 2008.

Publications: Co-author, The New Priesthood: British Television Today (1970); A Fine and Private Place (1977); The Complete Traveller (1977); The Heart of Heart of the Matter (1996); The Centre of the Bed (autobiography, 2003); Belief (2005); The View from Here (2006); All the Nice Girls (2009).

Recreations: Cinema, theatre, travel.

The Baroness Bakewell DBE, House of Lords, London SW1A 0PW
Tel: 020 7219 2921
Email: joanbakewell@googlemail.com *Twitter:* @JDBakewell

BAKEWELL OF HARDINGTON MANDEVILLE, BARONESS

BAKEWELL OF HARDINGTON MANDEVILLE (Life Baroness), Catherine Mary Bakewell; cr 2013.

Political career: *House of Lords:* Raised to the peerage as Baroness Bakewell of Hardington Mandeville, of Hardington Mandeville in the County of Somerset 2013. *Councils and public bodies:* Somerset County Council: Councillor 1993-2013, Leader 2001-07; Councillor, South Somerset District Council 2009-.

Other: Local Government Association.

LIBERAL DEMOCRAT The Baroness Bakewell of Hardington Mandeville MBE, House of Lords, London SW1A 0PW
Tel: 020 7219 5353

BALDWIN OF BEWDLEY, EARL

BALDWIN OF BEWDLEY (4th Earl, UK), Edward Alfred Alexander Baldwin; cr. 1937; Viscount Corvedale. Born 3 January 1938; Son of 3rd Earl and late Joan Elspeth, née Tomes; Married Sarah James 1970 (died 2001) (3 sons).

Education: Eton College; Trinity College, Cambridge (BA modern languages and law 1961, MA; CertEd 1970); French, German.

Non-political career: Army national service 1956-58; 2nd Lieutenant, Intelligence Corps 1957-58. German and French teacher: Christ's Hospital 1970-74, Hemel Hempstead School 1974-77;

CROSSBENCH Education officer: Leicestershire 1978-80, Oxfordshire 1980-87.

Political career: *House of Lords:* First entered House of Lords 1976; Elected hereditary peer 1999-. Co-opted member Science and Technology Sub-committee I (Complementary and Alternative Medicine) 2000. *Councils and public bodies:* Member, Research Council for Complementary Medicine 1989-91; Chair, British Acupuncture Accreditation Board 1990-98.

Political interests: Complementary medicine, medicine, environment, education.

Other: MCC.

Publications: Co-editor Baldwin Papers: A Conservative Statesman, 1908-1947 (2004).

Recreations: Mountains, tennis, music.

The Earl Baldwin of Bewdley, House of Lords, London SW1A 0PW
Tel: 020 7219 5353
2 Scholar Place, Cumnor Hill, Oxford OX2 9RD *Tel:* 01865 865318 *Fax:* 01865 865318

BALFE, LORD – *Please see Addenda Page x*

BALLYEDMOND, LORD

BALLYEDMOND (Life Baron), Edward Enda Haughey; cr. 2004. Born 5 January 1944; Son of Edward Haughey and Rose Traynor; Married Mary Gordon Young 1972 (2 sons 1 daughter).
Education: Christian Brothers School, Dundalk.

Non-political career: Chair, Norbrook Laboratories and Norbrook Holdings BV 1980-; Director and adviser, Bank of Ireland 1987-; Chair: Ballyedmond Castle Farms Ltd 1991-, Haughey Airports 2000-, Haughey Air 2000-.

CONSERVATIVE

Political career: *House of Lords:* Raised to the peerage as Baron Ballyedmond, of Mourne in the County of Down 2004. *Councils and public bodies:* Board member, Warrenpoint Harbour Authority 1986-89.

Other: Member, Senate of Ireland 1994-2002: Government spokesperson for Northern Ireland; Member: Forum for Peace and Reconciliation 1996-97, British-Irish Inter-Parliamentary Body 1997-2002; Trustee: Dublin City University 1995-, Royal College of Veterinary Surgeons 2001-. Honorary Doctor of Law, National University of Ireland 1997; Honorary Fellow, Royal College of Surgeons in Ireland 1998; Honorary Associate, Royal College of Veterinary Surgeons 2004; Honorary Doctor of Science, University of Ulster 2008. OBE 1987; Order of Bernardo O'Higgins (Chile) 1995; Honorary Consul for Chile 1997; Savage Club, London; Reform Club, Belfast; Kildare ST and University Club, Dublin.

Recreations: Shooting.

The Lord Ballyedmond OBE, House of Lords, London SW1A 0PW
Tel: 020 7219 8216
Tel: 028 3026 9824 *Fax:* 028 3026 9981 *Email:* chairman@norbrook.co.uk

BAMFORD, LORD – *Please see Addenda Page x*

BANNSIDE, LORD

BANNSIDE (Life Baron), Ian Richard Kyle Paisley; cr 2010. Born 6 April 1926; Son of late Rev J Kyle Paisley; Married Eileen Emily Cassells (now Baroness Paisley of St George's) 1956 (twin sons 3 daughters).
Education: Ballymena Model School; Ballymena Technical High School; South Wales Bible College; Reformed Presbyterian Theological College, Belfast.

Non-political career: Ordained 1946; Minister, Martyrs Memorial Free Presbyterian Church 1946-; Editor, *Revitalist* 1951; Moderator, Free Presbyterian Church of Ulster 1951-2007; Editor, *Protestant Telegraph* 1966-.

DEMOCRATIC UNIONIST PARTY

Political career: *House of Commons:* MP for North Antrim 18 June 1970 general election to 17 December 1985 (resigned seat in protest against Anglo-Irish Agreement) and 23 January 1986 by-election to 2010. DUP Spokesperson for: Constitutional Affairs 1970-2005, Foreign and Commonwealth Affairs 2005-10, Europe 2005-09. *House of Lords:* Raised to the peerage as Baron Bannside, of North Antrim in the County of Antrim 2010. On leave of absence June 2013-. *Other:* Parliament of Northern Ireland (Stormont): MP (Protestant Unionist) for Bannside 1970-72, Leader of Opposition 1972; Member: Northern Ireland Assembly 1973-74, 1982-86, Northern Ireland Constitutional Convention 1975-76; MEP for Northern Ireland 1979-2004; Member Northern Ireland Forum for Political Dialogue 1996-98; Northern Ireland Assembly: MLA for North Antrim 1998-2011: Chair Committee on Agriculture and Rural Development 1999-2002, First Minister 2007-08. Leader (co-founder), Democratic Unionist Party 1971-2008.

Political interests: Foreign affairs, religious affairs, constitution.

Other: Co-chairman, World Congress of Fundamentalists 1978; President, Whitefield College of the Bible, Laurencetown 1980; Patron, Martyrs' Memorial Missionary Fund; Margaret Newton Trust. Honorary Doctorate of Divinity, Bob Jones University, Greenville, South Carolina 1966. Oldie of the Year, *Oldie* awards 2008. PC 2005.

Recreations: History, antiquarian book collecting.

Rt Hon the Lord Bannside, House of Lords, London SW1A 0PW
Tel: 020 7219 5353 *Website:* www.ianpaisley.org

CROSSBENCH

BARBER OF TEWKESBURY, LORD

BARBER OF TEWKESBURY (Life Baron), Derek Coates Barber; cr. 1992. Born 17 June 1918; Son of late Thomas Smith-Barber and Elsie Isobel Coates; Divorced 1981 (1 son 1 daughter); married Rosemary Jennifer Brougham Pearson 1983.

Education: Royal Agricultural College, Cirencester.

Non-political career: Served in Second World War (invalided). Farmer in Gloucestershire; Various posts, Ministry of Agriculture, Fisheries and Food 1946-72; Environment consultant to Humberts, Chartered Surveyors 1972-93; Chairman, Countryside Commission 1981-91.

Political career: *House of Lords:* Raised to the peerage as Baron Barber of Tewkesbury, of Gotherington in the County of Gloucestershire 1992. On leave of absence April 2011-. Member: European Community Sub-committee D (Agriculture, Fisheries and Consumer Protection) 1993-96, Sustainable Development 1994-96. *Councils and public bodies:* Councillor, Cheltenham Rural District Council 1948-52.

Political interests: Farming, forestry, environment; Middle East.

Other: Posts in numerous countryside, agricultural and ornithological organisations, including: Royal Society for the Protection of Birds: Chair 1976-81, President 1990-91; President, Royal Agricultural Society of England 1991; Honorary Fellow, Royal Agricultural Society of England 1986; FRAgS 1991; FIAgrM 1992; FRAC 2000; Brooke Hospital for Animals (Cairo); St Dunstan's/Blind Veterans. Honorary DSc, Bradford University 1986. Bledisloe Gold Medal for distinguished service to UK agriculture 1967; RSPB Gold Medal for services to bird conservation 1982; RASE Gold Medal for services to agriculture 1991; Massey-Ferguson Award for Services to agriculture. Kt 1984.

Publications: Joint author books on agriculture as well as contributing to journals on farming and wildlife, including: Farming for Profits (1964).

Recreations: Birds, farming, fieldsports.

The Lord Barber of Tewkesbury, House of Lords, London SW1A 0PW
Tel: 020 7219 5353

LIBERAL DEMOCRAT

BARKER, BARONESS

BARKER (Life Baroness); Elizabeth Jean Barker; cr. 1999. Born 31 January 1961.

Education: Dalziel High School, Motherwell; Broadway School, Oldham; Southampton University (BSc (SocSci) psychology 1982).

Non-political career: Age Concern England 1982-2008: Project co-ordinator, Opportunities for Volunteering Programme 1983-88, Grants officer 1988-92, Field officer 1992-2008; Management consultant to Age Concern organisations; Owner, Third Sector Business (management consultancy) 2008-; Head of business development, SeeTheDifference.org 2010.

Political career: *House of Lords:* Raised to the peerage as Baroness Barker, of Anagach in Highland 1999. Liberal Democrat Spokesperson for: Pensions 2000-02, Social Services 2000-04, Health 2004-10. Member Mental Capacity Act 2005 2013-. *Other:* Union of Liberal Students: Member 1979-83, Chair 1982-83; Member: Liberal Party National Executive 1982-83, Liberal Assembly Committee 1984-97, Federal Policy Committee 1997-2003; Chair, Liberal Democrat Federal Conference Committee 1997-2004; Member: The Future of Social Services Policy Working Group, Freedom and Fairness for Women Policy Working Group, Working Group – An Age of Opportunity, It's About Freedom – Liberal Democracy Policy Working Group, Liberal Democrat Federal Executive 2004; Chair, Policy Working Group on: Poverty and Inequality 2006-07, The Future of the Voluntary Sector 2010-11. *Councils and public bodies:* Vice-President, Local Government Association 2010-.

Political interests: Health, social services, ageing, civil liberties; India, Kenya, Nigeria.

Other: Patron, Spare Tyre Theatre Company; Trustee, Andy Lawson Memorial Fund; SeeTheDifference.org; Map Action.

The Baroness Barker, House of Lords, London SW1A 0PW
Tel: 020 7219 2955 *Email:* barkere@parliament.uk

DO YOU NEED THIS INFORMATION ONLINE?
visit www.dodspeople.com or call 020 7593 5675
to register for a free trial

BARNETT, LORD

LABOUR

BARNETT (Life Baron), Joel Barnett; cr. 1983. Born 14 October 1923; Son of late Louis and Ettie Barnett; Married Lilian Goldstone 1949 (1 daughter).

Education: Manchester Central High School; Accountancy, correspondence course.

Non-political career: RASC 1939-45. Senior partner, J. C. Allen & Co (now Hacker Young) 1954-74; Vice-chair, BBC 1986-93; Chair, British Screen Finance Ltd 1986-97; Member, International Advisory Board, Unisys Inc. 1989-96; Chair: Education Broadcasting Services Trust Ltd 1993-2008, Origin (UK) Ltd (later Atos Origin (UK) Ltd.) 1996-2007, Mercury Recycling Ltd (later Mercury Recycling Group plc) 1996-, Helping Hands plc 1997-98; Previously chairman and director of a number of public limited companies.

Political career: *House of Commons:* Contested Runcorn 1959 general election. MP (Labour) for Heywood and Royton 1964-83. Chief Secretary to the Treasury 1974-79; Member of Cabinet 1977-79. Chair Public Accounts 1979-83. *House of Lords:* Raised to the peerage as Baron Barnett, of Heywood and Royton in Greater Manchester 1983. Opposition Spokesperson for Treasury Affairs 1983-86. Chair European Communities Sub-committee A (Economic and Financial Affairs, Trade and External Relations) 1995-97, 1997-98; Member: European Communities 1997-2000, Monetary Policy of the Bank of England/Economic Affairs 1998-2001, Economic Affairs 2001-05, House 2003-07, Economic Affairs Sub-committee on Finance Bill 2004-08, Finance Bill Sub-committee 2008-10. *Councils and public bodies:* Councillor, Prestwich Council 1956-59; JP, Manchester Bench 1960; Chair, Building Society Ombudsman Council 1986-96; President, Royal Institute of Public Administration 1988-91; Chair, Mansfield 1993-97.

Political interests: Finance, economics; Europe, Israel, Middle East, USA.

Other: Trustee, Victoria and Albert Museum 1983-97; Chair, Hansard Society 1984-90; Trustee: Open University Foundation 1995-2003, Global Warming Foundation; Member, Fabian Society; Member ACCA; Strathclyde University; Heathlands Village Prestwich. Honorary LLD, Strathclyde University 1983; Honorary Fellow, Birkbeck College, London University. PC 1975.

Publications: Inside the Treasury (1982).

Recreations: Walking, reading, theatre, good food, watching Manchester United.

Rt Hon the Lord Barnett, House of Lords, London SW1A 0PW
Tel: 020 7219 5440 *Email:* barnettj@parliament.uk

BASSAM OF BRIGHTON, LORD

Shadow Chief Whip

LAB/CO-OP

BASSAM OF BRIGHTON (Life Baron), (John) Steven Bassam; cr. 1997. Born 11 June 1953; Son of late Sydney Stevens and of Enid Bassam; Partner Jill Whittaker (1 son 2 daughters 1 son deceased).

Education: Clarton Secondary Modern School for Boys; Sussex University (BA history 1975); Kent University (MA social work 1979).

Non-political career: Social worker, East Sussex County Council 1976-77; Legal adviser, North Lewisham Law Centre 1979-83; Research officer, Camden Council 1983-84; Head of environmental health, Trading Standards AMA 1988-97; Consultant adviser, KPMG Capital 1997-99. Member, Unison.

Political career: *House of Commons:* Contested (Lab) Brighton Kemptown 1987 general election. *House of Lords:* Raised to the peerage as Baron Bassam of Brighton, of Brighton in the County of East Sussex 1997. Parliamentary Under-Secretary of State, Home Office 1999-2001; Government Spokesperson for: Home Office 1999-2008, Cabinet Office 2001-07; Government Whip 2001-08; Government Spokesperson for: Lord Chancellor's Department 2001-04, Office of the Deputy Prime Minister/Communities and Local Government 2002-04, 2005-07, 2008, Attorney General's Office 2005-08, Transport 2007-08, Culture, Media and Sport 2008; Government Chief Whip 2008-10; Deputy Speaker 2008-; Deputy Chairman of Committees 2008-; Shadow Chief Whip 2010-. Member: Administration and Works 2008-12, Procedure 2008-, Selection 2008-, Privileges/Privileges and Conduct 2009-, Sub-committee on Leave of Absence 2011-13. *Councils and public bodies:* Brighton Borough Council: Councillor 1983-97, Leader 1987-96; Brighton and Hove Council: Councillor 1996-99, Leader 1996-99; Head of Environmental Health and Consumer Issues, Local Government Association 1997-99.

Political interests: Local government, housing, home affairs, culture, education, political strategy, environment; Australia, India, Spain, USA.

Other: Laura Martin Trust (Homelessness Charity). Fellow, Brighton College 2002. Alumni Fellow, Sussex University 2001. PC 2009. Preston Village Cricket Club.

Recreations: Cricket, walking, running.
Rt Hon the Lord Bassam of Brighton, House of Lords, London SW1A 0PW
Tel: 020 7219 4918/07876 478160 *Fax:* 020 7219 6837 *Email:* bassams@parliament.uk
Longstone, 25 Church Place, Brighton BN2 5JN *Tel:* 01273 609473
Email: stevebassam@msn.com *Twitter:* @SteveTheQuip

BATES, LORD

Government Whip

BATES (Life Baron), Michael Walton Bates; cr 2008. Born 26 May 1961; Son of John MacLennan Bates and Ruth Bates, née Walton; Married Carole Whitfield 1983 (divorced 2008) (2 sons); married Xuelin 2012.

Education: Heathfield Senior High School, Gateshead; Gateshead College (Diploma business studies 1982); Saïd Business School, Oxford (MBA Wadham College 1998).

CONSERVATIVE

Non-political career: Trainee salesman, Gresham Life Assurance 1983; Agency inspector, Clerical Medical Investment Group 1983-87; Investment adviser: Hogg Robinson (benefit consultants) 1986-87, Joseph Nelson (fund management) 1987-91; Assistant director, Godwins (pension consultants and actuaries) 1991; Oxford Analytica International Group 1998-2007: Senior vice-president 1998-99, Director of consultancy and research 1999-2005, Head of operations 2004-05, Director 2004-06, Senior adviser 2006-07; Managing director, Walton Bates (management consultants) Ltd 2006-11; Non-executive director, Vardy Group 2006-10; Non-executive chair: Scholes & Brown Asset Management 2008-11, 55 Plus Ltd 2010-11; Chairman, International Property Awards 2013-.

Political career: *House of Commons:* Contested Tynebridge 1987 general election and Langbaurgh 1991 by-election. MP (Conservative) for Langbaurgh 1992-97. Contested Middlesbrough South and Cleveland East 1997 general election. PPS to Ministers of State: Nicholas Scott, Department of Social Security 1992-93, Sir John Wheeler, Northern Ireland Office 1994; Assistant Government Whip 1994-95; Government Whip 1995-96; Paymaster General, Office of Public Services 1996-97. *House of Lords:* Raised to the peerage as Baron Bates, of Langbaurgh in the County of North Yorkshire 2008. Opposition Whip 2009-10; Opposition Spokesperson for: Cabinet Office 2009-10, Communities and Local Government 2009-10, Energy and Climate Change 2009, Children, Schools and Families 2009-10; Deputy Chair of Committees 2013-; Government Whip 2013-. Member: Leader's Group on the Working Practices of the House of Lords 2010-11, Partnerships (Prosecution) (Scotland) Bill 2013-, Olympic and Paralympic Legacy 2013-. *Other:* Young Conservatives: Member, National Advisory Committee 1984-87, Chair, Northern Area 1984-87; Deputy chair, Conservative Party 2007-10; Project director, Campaign North 2007-10. *Councils and public bodies:* Member, Business Advisory Forum Saïd Business School, Oxford 1999-2011; Vice-President, Local Government Association 2010-11; Member, Higher Education Council.

Political interests: Education, foreign policy, business and enterprise; Albania, China, Croatia, Greece, Japan, Korea, USA.

Other: Open Fields Awards, Olympic Truce Foundation 2012.

Recreations: Cinema, walking, Newcastle United Football Club, Forumula 1 motor racing.

The Lord Bates, House of Lords, London SW1A 0PW
Tel: 020 7219 5353 *Email:* batesm@parliament.uk
Website: lordsoftheblog.net/category/lord-bates *Twitter:* @bateslord

BEECHAM, LORD

Opposition Spokesperson for Communities and Local Government and for Justice

BEECHAM (Life Baron), Jeremy Hugh Beecham; cr 2010. Born 17 November 1944; Son of Lawrence Beecham and Florence Beecham; Married Brenda Woolf 1968 (died 2010) (1 son 1 daughter).

Education: Royal Grammar School, Newcastle upon Tyne; University College, Oxford (BA jurisprudence 1965, MA).

LABOUR

Non-political career: Solicitor 1968; Partner, Allan Henderson Beecham & Peacock/Beecham Peacock 1968-2002; Director, Northern Development Company 1986-91; Consultant, Beecham Peacock 2002-11.

Political career: *House of Commons:* Contested (Labour) Tynemouth 1970 general election. *House of Lords:* Raised to the peerage as Baron Beecham, of Benwell and Newcastle upon Tyne in the County of Tyne and Wear 2010. Opposition Spokesperson for: Communities and Local Government 2010-, Health 2010-12, Justice 2012-. *Other:* Chair, Oxford University Labour Club 1964; Labour Party: Member: National Executive Committee/Shadow Cabinet Working Party on

Future of Local Government 1984-87, Joint Policy Committee 1992-; National Executive Committee: Member 1998-2010, Chair 2005-06. *Councils and public bodies:* Newcastle upon Tyne City Council: Councillor 1967-, Leader 1977-94; Commissioner, English Heritage 1983-87; Association of Metropolitan Authorities: Deputy chair 1984-86, Vice-chair 1986-91 Chair 1991-97; Vice-chair, Northern Regional Councils Association 1986-91; DL, Tyne and Wear 1995; Local Government Association: Chair 1995-2004, Vice-chair 2004-, Vice-President 2010-.

Political interests: Local government, social policy, health, criminal justice, legal aid, regional policy, environment; Israel.

Other: President: Bura 1995-2009, Age Concern Newcastle 1995-, Newcastle Choral Society 1995; Vice-President, Newcastle CVS; Trustee, Trusthouse Charitable Foundation 1999-; Vice-President, Community Foundation 2000-; Member, advisory board, Harold Hartog School of Government, Tel Aviv 2005-; New Israel Fund: Board member 2007-, Vice-chair 2009-. Honorary Freeman, Newcastle upon Tyne 1995. Honorary Fellow, Northumbria University 1989; Honorary DCL, Newcastle University 1992. Kt 1994.

Recreations: Reading, music.

The Lord Beecham, House of Lords, London SW1A 0PW
Tel: 020 7219 5353 *Email:* beechamj@parliament.uk *Twitter:* @JeremyBeecham

CONSERVATIVE

BELL, LORD

BELL (Life Baron), Timothy John Leigh Bell; cr. 1998. Born 18 October 1941; Son of late Arthur Bell and of Greta Bell; Married 2nd Virginia Wallis Hornbrook 1988 (1 son 1 daughter).

Education: Queen Elizabeth's Grammar School, Barnet.

Non-political career: ABC Television 1959-61; Colman Prentis and Varley 1961-63; Hobson Bates 1963-66; Geers Gross 1966-70; Managing director, Saatchi and Saatchi 1970-75; Chair and managing director, Saatchi and Saatchi Compton 1975-85; Special adviser: to Chairman, National Coal Board 1984-86, to South Bank Board 1985-86; Group chief executive, Lowe Howard-Spink Campbell Ewald 1985-87; Deputy chair, Lowe Hoard-Spink and Bell 1987-89; Chair: Lowe Bell Communications 1987-, Chime Communications plc 1994-.

Political career: *House of Lords:* Raised to the peerage as Baron Bell, of Belgravia in the City of Westminster 1998. *Other:* Chair, Conservative Party Keep the £ Campaign 1999-. *Councils and public bodies:* Governor, British Film Institute 1983-86.

Other: Council member, Royal Opera House 1982-85; Charity Projects: Chair 1984-93, President 1993-; Director, Centre for Policy Studies 1989-92; FIPA, FIPR; Save The Children Fund, BACUP Living with Cancer. Kt 1990. Prince Edward Yacht Club Sydney, RAC.

Recreations: Golf, music.

The Lord Bell, House of Lords, London SW1A 0PW
Tel: 020 7219 5353
14 Curzon Street, London W1J 5HN *Tel:* 020 7495 4044 *Fax:* 020 7491 9860
Email: lord.bell@bell-pottinger.co.uk

LIBERAL DEMOCRAT

BENJAMIN, BARONESS

BENJAMIN (Life Baroness), Floella Karen Yunies Benjamin; cr 2010. Born 23 September 1949; Daughter of Roy and Veronica Benjamin; Married Keith Taylor 1980 (1 son 1 daughter).

Education: Penge Girls' School.

Non-political career: Chief Accountant's Office, Barclays Bank 1967-69; Actress: Appeared in a number of productions on the stage including: *Hair* 1970-72, *Jesus Christ Superstar* 1972-74, *Black Mikado* 1974-75, *The Husband-in-Law* 1976; Television appearances include: *Within These Walls* 1973-75, *Playschool* 1976-88, *Playaway* 1976-82, *Angels* 1978-80, *Gentle Touch* 1980, *Bergerac* 1980, *Fast Forward* 1983-85, *Sarah Jane Adventures* 2007-10, *Mama Mirabelle's Home Movies* 2007-09, *Chuggington* 2010-13; *CBeebies Bedtime Stories* 2010 Film appearances include: *Black Joy* 1977, *Run Fatboy Run* 2007; Floella Benjamin Productions Ltd: Founder 1987, Chief executive 1998-; Floella Food and Drink Ltd 2004-12; Vice-president, Royal Television Society. Equity.

Political career: *House of Lords:* Raised to the peerage as Baroness Benjamin, of Beckenham in the County of Kent 2010. Member EU Sub-committee F (Home Affairs, Health and Education) 2013-. Chair, Liberal Democrat Parliamentary Party Committee on Culture, Media and Sport 2012. *Councils and public bodies:* Governor, Dulwich College 2001-11; Member, Content Board, Ofcom 2003-06; Deputy Lieutenant, Greater London 2008-; Chair of Governors, Isle of Sheppey Academy 2009-11.

Political interests: Children and young people, media, culture and arts, sport, education, diversity, equality; All Caribbean countries, France, Ghana, South Korea, South Africa, USA. **Other:** BAFTA: Council member 1990-2001, Vice-chair 1998-99, Chair, television 1999-2000; President, Elizabeth R Commonwealth Broadcasting Fund 1995-; Governor: National Film and Television School 1995-, Commonwealth Institute 1998-2006; Vice-president, Barnardo's 2000-; President, Ramblers' Association 2008-10; Patron, British Association of Play Therapists 2009-; Trustee, Sparks 2009-; Vice President, Barnardo's; Trustee, Sparks; Patron, Sickle Cell Society; NSPCC; Patron, BAPT. Chancellor, Exeter University 2006-. DLitt Exeter University. RTS award 2004; Special Lifetime Achievement award, BAFTA 2004; J.M. Barrie Award, Action for Children's Arts 2012. OBE 2001.

Publications: Author of numerous children's books; Written over 25 books including: Autobiographies: Coming to England (1995), The Arms of Britannia (2010), Sea of Tears (2011).

Recreations: Running, golf, singing, photography, walking, cooking.

The Baroness Benjamin OBE, House of Lords, London SW1A 0PW
Tel: 020 7219 8901 *Email:* benjaminf@parliament.uk
Website: www.floellabenjamin.com *Twitter:* @FloellaBenjamin

BERKELEY, LORD

BERKELEY (18th Baron, E), Anthony Fitzhardinge Gueterbock; cr. 1421; (Life Baron) Baron Gueterbock 2000. Born 20 September 1939; Son of late Brigadier Ernest Adolphus Leopold Gueterbock and late Honorary Cynthia Ella Gueterbock; Married Diana (Dido) Townsend 1965 (2 sons 1 daughter); married Rosalind Clarke 1999 (divorced 2011).

Education: Eton College; Trinity College, Cambridge (MA mechanical sciences 1961); French, German.

Non-political career: Civil engineer, Sir Alexander Gibb and Partners 1961-67; George Wimpey plc 1967-87; Public affairs manager, Eurotunnel 1987-95; Chair: Piggyback Consortium 1995-98, Rail Freight Group 1997-; European Rail Freight Association: Board member 2007-, President 2009-11.

Political career: *House of Lords:* Created a life peer as Baron Gueterbock, of Cranford in the London Borough of Hillingdon 2000. First entered House of Lords 1992; Opposition Spokesperson for Transport 1996-97; Opposition Whip 1996-97. Member European Union 1997-2001. *Councils and public bodies:* President, UK Maritime Pilots' Association; Harbour commissioner, Port of Fowey.

Political interests: Transport, environment; European Union member states.

Other: Board member, Plymouth Marine Laboratory Ltd; MICE; FRSA; FCILT; Honorary FIMechE. Honorary degree, Brighton University. OBE 1989.

Recreations: Sailing, skiing.

The Lord Berkeley OBE, House of Lords, London SW1A 0PW
Tel: 020 7219 0611/07710 431542 *Email:* berkeleyafg@parliament.uk

BERKELEY OF KNIGHTON, LORD

BERKELEY of KNIGHTON (Life Baron), Michael Fitzhardinge Berkeley; cr 2013. Born 29 May 1948; Married Deborah Coltman-Rogers (1 daughter).

Education: The Oratory School; Royal Academy of Music.

Non-political career: Phlebotomist, St Bartholomew's Hospital 1969-71; Presentation Assistant, LWT 1973; Announcer, BBC Radio 3 1974-79; Associate Composer, Scottish Chamber Orchestra 1979; Joint Artistic Director, Spitalfields Festival 1994-97; Artistic Director, Cheltenham Festival 1995-2004; Associate Composer, BBC National Orchestra of Wales 2001-08; Radio Presenter.

Political career: *House of Lords:* Raised to the peerage as Baron Berkeley of Knighton, of Knighton in the County of Powys 2013. *Councils and public bodies:* General Advisory Council, BBC 1990-95.

Other: Member: Executive committee, Association of Professional Composers 1982-84, New music sub-committee, Arts Council of Great Britain 1984-86, Central music advisory committee, BBC 1986-90; Music panel adviser, Arts Council 1986-90; Visiting professor, Huddersfield University 1991-94; Governor, National Youth Orchestra 1994-96; Director, Britten-Pears Foundation 1996-2009; Member, Board of Directors, Royal Opera House, Covent Garden 1996-2001; Chair, Royal Ballet 2003-. CBE 2012.

Publications: The Music Pack (1994).

The Lord Berkeley of Knighton CBE, House of Lords, London SW1A 0PW
Tel: 020 7219 5353 *Twitter:* @MichaelBerkele2

CONSERVATIVE

BERRIDGE, BARONESS

BERRIDGE (Life Baroness), Elizabeth Rose Berridge; cr 2011. Born 22 March 1972. **Education:** Catmose College, Rutland; Emmanuel College (BA law 1995). **Non-political career:** Barrister, Kings Chambers 1996-2005. **Political career:** *House of Commons:* Contested (Conservative) Stockport 2005 general election. *House of Lords:* Raised to the peerage as Baroness Berridge, of the Vale of Catmose in the County of Rutland 2011. Member: Joint Committee on Statutory Instruments 2010-12, Joint Committee on Human Rights 2011-. Member, Joint Committee on Statutory Instruments 2011-. *Other:* Director, Conservative Christian Fellowship, CCHQ 2005-11.

Political interests: Multiculturalism, policing, human rights, religious freedom; Ghana, Iraq, Nigeria, Trinidad and Tobago.

Other: Trustee: Kainos Community, Chair, Advisory Council, FRRME; Director, British Future; Advisory Board, Theos.

Recreations: Tennis, Swimming.

The Baroness Berridge, House of Lords, London SW1A 0PW
Tel: 020 7219 8943 *Email:* berridgee@parliament.uk
Email: oneilldm@parliament.uk *Website:* www.baronessberridge.com *Twitter:* @BaronessEB

CROSSBENCH

BEST, LORD

BEST (Life Baron), Richard Stuart Best; cr. 2001. Born 22 June 1945; Son of late Walter Best, DL, JP and late Frances Best, née Chignell; Married Belinda Stemp 1978 (2 daughters 2 sons). **Education:** Shrewsbury School; Nottingham University (BA social administration 1967). **Non-political career:** Chief executive: British Churches Housing Trust 1970-73, National Federation of Housing Associations 1973-88, Joseph Rowntree Foundation 1988-2006, Joseph Rowntree Housing Trust 1988-2006.

Political career: *House of Lords:* Raised to the peerage as Baron Best, of Godmanstone in the County of Dorset 2001. Chair House of Lords Audit Committee 2004-09; Member: Joint Committee on the Charities Bill 2004, Economic Affairs 2007-12, Economic Affairs Finance Bill Sub Committee 2009-, Information 2013-, Olympic and Paralympic Legacy 2013-. *Councils and public bodies:* Commissioner, Rural Development Commission 1989-98; Chair, Hull Partnership Liaison Board 2003-05; Member, Audit Commission's Advisory Board on Housing, Communities and Environment 2003-10; President, Local Government Association 2005-; Chair: Westminster Housing Commission 2005-06, Hanover Housing Association 2006-, Office of Public Management's Public Interest Council 2007-12; Vice-president, Town and Country Planning Association 2007-; Deputy chair, Standards Committee, Westminster City Council 2008-12; Chair: Commission on Housing in Northern Ireland 2009-10, The Property Ombudsman 2009-, Housing for an Ageing Population 2009, CLG/LGA Housing Commission 2010; DL, North Yorkshire 2012-.

Political interests: Housing, regeneration, social policy.

Other: Chair, International Board, South East European Research Centre; Member, NCVO Advisory Council 2001-; Royal Society of Arts: Trustee 2006-12, Treasurer 2009-12; President, Continuing Care Conference 2002-; Chair, The Giving Forum 2005-11; Patron, Housing Associations Charitable Trust 2007-; Honorary Fellow RIBA 2001; Honorary Life Member, Chartered Institute of Housing 2003. Honorary degrees: Sheffield University 2006, York University 2008. Parliamentarian of the Year, CAB 2010; UK Social Policy Association Award 2012. OBE 1988; Travellers Club; Farmers Club.

Publications: Contributor to various books and numerous articles for magazines and journals.

The Lord Best OBE, House of Lords, London SW1A 0PW
Tel: 020 7219 6799 *Email:* best@parliament.uk

CROSSBENCH

BEW, LORD

BEW (Life Baron), Paul Anthony Elliott; cr 2007. Born 22 January 1950; Son of Dr Kenneth Bew and Dr Mary Bew, née Leahy; Married Dr Greta Jones 1977 (1 son).

Education: Campbell College, Belfast; Pembroke College, Cambridge (BA modern history, MA; PhD 1974).

Non-political career: Humanities lecturer, Ulster College 1975-79; Queen's University, Belfast 1979-: European and American history lecturer 1979-84, Politics lecturer 1984-87, Reader, politics 1987-91, Professor of politics 1991-.

Political career: *House of Lords:* Raised to the peerage as Baron Bew, of Donegore in the County of Antrim 2007. Member Joint Committees on: the Draft Defamation Bill 2011, Parliamentary Privilege 2013. *Councils and public bodies:* Chair, Committee on Standards in Public Life September 2013-.

Political interests: Nationalism, foreign policy, education.

Other: Chairman: British-Irish Association, Anglo-Israel Association; MRIA. Honorary Fellow, Pembroke College, Cambridge.

Recreations: Five-a-side football.

The Lord Bew, House of Lords, London SW1A 0PW
Tel: 020 7219 5353
Department of Politics, Queen's University, 21 University Square, Belfast BT7 1NN
Tel: 028 9097 3660 *Fax:* 028 9097 5048 *Email:* p.bew@qub.ac.uk

BHATIA, LORD

NON-AFFILIATED

BHATIA (Life Baron), Amirali Alibhai Bhatia; cr. 2001. Born 18 March 1932; Married Nurbanu Amersi Kanji 1954 (3 daughters).

Education: Schools in Tanzania and India.

Non-political career: Chair and managing director, Forbes Campbell International Ltd 1980-2001; Director, Casley Finance Ltd 1985-2001.

Political career: *House of Lords:* Raised to the peerage as Baron Bhatia, of Hampton in the London Borough of Richmond upon Thames 2001. Suspended from membership October 2010-June 2011. Member Religious Offences 2002-03.

Countries of interest: Africa, Bangladesh, India, Middle East, Pakistan, Sri Lanka.

Other: Chair, The Forbes Trust 1985-; Chair and Co-founder, Ethnic Minority Foundation 1999-2009; British Muslim Research Centre; British Edutrust Foundation; Vice-chair, India800 Foundation; FRSA; Oxfam, Ethnic Minority Foundation. UK Charity Awards Personality of the Year 2001; Beacon Prize 2003. OBE 1997; Commonwealth Club, Institute of Directors.

Recreations: Swimming, walking, reading, music.

The Lord Bhatia OBE, House of Lords, London SW1A 0PW
Tel: 020 7219 5652 *Email:* bhatiaa@parliament.uk
Forbes House, 9 Artillery Lane, London E1 7LP *Tel:* 020 7377 8484 *Fax:* 020 7377 0032
Email: abhatia@casley.co.uk

BHATTACHARYYA, LORD

LABOUR

BHATTACHARYYA (Life Baron), Sushantha Kumar Bhattacharyya; cr. 2004. Born 6 June 1940; Son of Sudhir Bhattacharyya and Hemanalini, née Chakraborty; Married Brigid Carmel Rabbitt 1981 (3 daughters).

Education: IIT, Kharagpur (BTech mechanical engineering 1960); Birmingham University (MSc engineering production and management 1965; PhD engineering production 1970).

Non-political career: Production/industrial management, Lucas Industries Ltd 1961-67; Department of engineering, Birmingham University 1977-80; Professor of manufacturing and director, Warwick Manufacturing Group, Warwick University 1980-; Non-executive director, Technology Rover Group 1986-92; Member: National Consumer Council 1990-93, Council for Science and Technology 1993-2003; Scientific adviser to South Africa government.

Political career: *House of Lords:* Raised to the peerage as Baron Bhattacharyya, of Moseley in the County of West Midlands 2004. Co-opted member Science and Technology Sub-committee I (Waste Reduction) 2007-08.

Political interests: Manufacturing, education, industry, innovation; China, India, Singapore, Turkey.

Other: Trustee, Institute for Public Policy Research 1997; FIEE 1975; FREng 1991; FILT 1996; CCMI 2003; Fellow, RSA. Honorary DUniv, University of Surrey 1992; Honorary DSc, UTM Malaysia 1997; Honorary Doctor of Business Administration, Hong Kong Polytechnic University 2003; Honorary DSc, Birmingham University 2004. IEE Mensforth Gold Medal 1998; Sir Robert Lawrence Award, Institute of Logistics and Transport 1999; President of India Padma Bhusan 2002; IIT Kharagpur Distinguished Alumnus Award 2005. CBE 1997; Kt 2003; Athenæum.

Recreations: Family, flying, cricket.

Professor the Lord Bhattacharyya CBE, House of Lords, London SW1A 0PW
Tel: 020 7219 2363 *Email:* senhn@parliament.uk
Warwick Manufacturing Group, Warwick University, Coventry CV4 7AL *Tel:* 024 7652 3155
Fax: 024 7652 4027 *Email:* m.black@warwick.ac.uk

BICHARD, LORD

BICHARD (Life Baron), Michael George Bichard; cr 2010. Born 31 January 1947; Son of George and Nora Bichard; Married Gillian Guy 2008.

Education: King Edward VI Grammar School, Southampton; Manchester University (LLB, Hon Fellow 1968); Birmingham University (Master's social science 1973).

Non-political career: Solicitor; Chief executive: London Borough of Brent Council 1980-86, Gloucestershire County Council 1986-90, Social Security Benefits Agency 1990-95; Permanent secretary: Department for Employment 1995, Department for Education and Employment 1995-2001; Rector, London Institute/University of the Arts, London 2001-08; Chair, Rathbone Training Ltd 2001-08; Non-executive director, Reed Executive plc 2002-04; Director, River and Rowing Museum Foundation 2002-; Non-executive chair, RSe Consulting 2003-08; Chair: Soham Murders Inquiry 2004, Legal Services Commission 2005-08, Design Council 2008-12; Institute for Government: Director 2008-10, Senior fellow 2010-12.

CROSSBENCH

Political career: *House of Lords:* Raised to the peerage as Baron Bichard, of Nailsworth in the County of Gloucestershire 2010. Member, Leader's Group Reforming Working Practices 2010-11; Deputy Chair of Committees 2012-. Member: Leader's Group on the Working Practices of the House of Lords 2010-11, Secondary Legislation Scrutiny 2012-, Public Service and Demographic Change 2012-13. *Councils and public bodies:* Vice-President, Local Government Association 2011-.

Political interests: Social policy, education, public service reform, child protection.

Other: Member, Economic and Social Research Council 1989-92; Chair, Film Club 2007-; Henley Business School Strategy Board 2008-; Vice-chair, Shakespeare's Globe. Honorary Doctorates: Leeds Metropolitan University, Birmingham University, Bradford University, Middlesex University, Southampton Solent University, Cranfield University, Gloucestershire University. KCB 1999.

Recreations: Food, gardening, Manchester United FC.

The Lord Bichard KCB, House of Lords, London SW1A 0PW
Tel: 020 7219 5353 *Email:* m.bichard@btinternet.com

BILIMORIA, LORD

BILIMORIA (Life Baron), Karan Faridoon Bilimoria; cr 2006. Born 26 November 1961; Son of late Lt General Faridoon Noshir Bilimoria PVSM ADC and Yasmin Bilimoria; Married Heather Walker 1993 (2 sons 2 daughters).

Education: Hebron School, Lushington Hall, Ooty, India; Indian Institute of Management and Commerce, Osmania University, Hyderabad, India (BComm 1981); School of Business Studies, City of London Polytechnic (Diploma accounting 1982); ACA 1986; Sidney Sussex College, Cambridge (BA law 1988, MA) (Vice-president, Cambridge Union 1988); Cranfield University School of Management 1998; London Business School 2008; Harvard Business School 2011; French, Hindi.

CROSSBENCH

Non-political career: Trainee and qualified chartered accountant, Ernst & Young 1982-86; Consulting accountant, Crevsale Ltd, London 1988; Sales and marketing director, European Accounting Focus magazine 1989; Cobra Beer: Founder 1989, Chief executive 1989-2007, Chair 2007-09; Founder, General Bilimoria Wines 1989-; Founder and publishing director, *Tandoori Magazine* 1994-2003; UK Chair, Indo British Partnership 2003-09; Non-executive director, Brake Brothers Ltd 2004-07; Visiting entrepreneur, Cambridge University 2004-; Member, advisory board, Boston Analytics, Boston, USA 2005-10; Senior independent director and non-executive director, Booker Group plc 2007-; Visiting Professor, London Metropolitan University 2009; Chairman: Cobra Beer Partnership Limited 2009-, Molson Coors Cobra India Pvt Ltd 2011-; Vice-chair, Asian Business Association 2003-08.

Political career: *House of Lords:* Raised to the peerage as Baron Bilimoria, of Chelsea in the Royal Borough of Kensington and Chelsea 2006. Member: Economic Affairs Finance Bill Sub-Committee 2011, Sub-committee on Economic Affairs Finance Bill 2012-. *Councils and public bodies:* Member: New Deal Task Force, Department for Education and Employment 1999-2001, National Employment Panel 2001-07; Representative DL, Hounslow 2005-10; DL, Greater London 2001-; Deputy President, London Chamber of Commerce 2008-10.

Political interests: Manufacturing and industry, armed forces, defence, economic affairs, business and finance, banking, higher education and universities, inter faith, capital and financial markets, culture and creativity, SMEs; Commonwealth, India.

Other: Member, Prime Minister of India's Global Advisory Council 2009-; Trustee, Cobra Foundation; Chair, Advisory Board, Loomba Foundation 2001-; President's Committee, London First 2002-06; Member, Advisory Board: Judge Business School, Cambridge University, Birmingham Business School, Cranfield School of Management; Vice-chair, Asian Business Association 2003-08; Ditchley Foundation; Governor 2004-11, Council member 2011-; Member: UK-India Round Table 2005-, Asia Task Force 2005-10; Trustee, British Cardiac Research Trust 2006-; Deputy president, London Chamber of Commerce and Industry 2008-10; Commissioner, Royal Hospital, Chelsea 2006-12; Enterprise Leader, Princes Trust 2008-; Member, HRH The Duke of York's Business Advisory Council 2006-09; UK-India Business Council: Chair 2007-09, President 2009-; Trustee, St Paul's Catherdral Foundation 2011-; Patron, Pratham UK 2008-; Member, World President's Organization 2012-; FCA 2002; Fellow, Institute of Directors 2005-; Companion, Chartered Management Institute 2005-; Honorary Life Fellow, RSA 2004; Honorary Fellow, Sidney Sussex College, Cambridge University 2009-; Patron, Rethink Severe Mental Illness 2003-; Trustee, British Cardiac Research Trust 2006-; Patron, Child in Need India (CINI) UK 2008-. Liveryman: Drapers' Company City of London 2008-, Brewers' Company City of London 2008-, Worshipful Company of Chartered Accountants in England and Wales 2010-. Freeman, City of London. Chancellor, Thames Valley University 2005-10. Five honorary doctorates; Honorary Fellow, Sidney Sussex College, Cambridge 2007. Numerous, including: Asian of the Year 2002; Asian Achievers Awards Entrepreneur of the Year 2003; London Chamber of Commerce and Industry Entrepreneur of the Year 2003; RSA Albert Medal 2004; London Chamber of Commerce and Industry Business Person of the Year 2004; Institute of Chartered Accountants in England and Wales Outstanding Achievement Award 2005; Pravasi Bharti Samman, India 2008; Cranfield School of Management Entrpreneur Alumnus of the Year 2008. Non-resident Indian Millennium Honour 2001; CBE 2004; Secunderabad Club; Hawks' Club, Cambridge; University Pitt Club, Cambridge; Kelvin Grove Club, Cape Town, South Africa; Carlton Club. Delhi Gymkhana; Delhi Golf Club; Guards Polo Club, Ascot.

Publications: Bottled for Business (Capstone, 2007); Against the Grain (Capstone, 2009).

Recreations: Reading, current affairs, travel, art, music, theatre, tennis, horse riding, golf, scuba diving, sailing.

The Lord Bilimoria CBE DL, House of Lords, London SW1A 0PW
Tel: 020 7219 6040 *Fax:* 020 7219 5979 *Email:* bilimoria@parliament.uk
Cobra Beer Partnership Limited, 41-44 Great Queen Street, London WC2B 5AD *Tel:* 020 7788 2889 *Email:* karan.bilimoria@cobrabeerpartnership.com

BILLINGHAM, BARONESS

BILLINGHAM (Life Baroness), Angela Theodora Billingham; cr. 2000. Born 31 July 1939; Daughter of late Theodore and Eva Case; Married Peter Billingham 1962 (died 1992) (2 daughters).

Education: Aylesbury Grammar School; College of Education (London); Department of Education, Oxford University (MEd).

Non-political career: Teacher 1960-90; Examiner for Education Board 1990-95; Chair, Catalyst Corby urban regeneration company 2001-07. Member: NUT, GMB.

LABOUR

Political career: *House of Commons:* Contested (Labour) Banbury 1992 general election. *House of Lords:* Raised to the peerage as Baroness Billingham, of Banbury in the County of Oxfordshire 2000. Opposition Spokesperson for Culture, Media and Sport 2010-13. Member: European Union 2000-05, EU Sub-committee D (Environment, Agriculture, Public Health and Consumer Protection/Environment and Agriculture) 2000-05, Draft Climate Change Bill Joint Committee 2007, Information 2008-10; Co-opted member EU Sub-committee F (Home Affairs) 2009-10, Member Olympic and Paralympic Legacy 2013-. Vice-chair PLP Departmental Committee for Culture, Media and Sport 2005-06. *Other:* MEP for Northamptonshire and Blaby 1994-99: Chief Whip, Socialist Group. *Councils and public bodies:* Councillor: Banbury Borough Council 1970-74; Cherwell District Council 1974-84: Leader of Labour Group; Mayor of Banbury 1976; JP 1976-; Councillor, Oxfordshire County Council 1993-94.

Political interests: Europe, education, health, sport, urban regeneration, planning; European Union, India, USA.

Other: Patron: Supporters Direct (football and all professional sport), CSCS (Centre for supporting comprehensive education in the UK); Chair: Banbury and District Sport for the Disabled, Early Education; Member, advisory board, Save the Children; Chair: Northampton Osteoporosis, Council for the Advancement of Arts, Recreation and Education (CAARE); One World, Oxfam, Imperial Cancer.

Recreations: Family, tennis, cinema, bridge, gardening.

The Baroness Billingham, House of Lords, London SW1A 0PW
Tel: 020 7219 5481 *Email:* a.billingham77@btinternet.com

BILSTON, LORD

BILSTON (Life Baron), Dennis Turner; cr 2005. Born 26 August 1942; Son of late Thomas Turner and Mary Turner; Married Patricia Narroway 1976 (1 son 1 daughter).

Education: Stonefield Secondary School, Bilston; Bilston College of Further Education.

Non-political career: Director, Springvale Co-operative, sports, social and leisure centre 1981-2007. Chair, Midlands Iron and Steel Trades Confederation Conference 1974-76.

Political career: *House of Commons:* Contested Halesowen and Stourbridge February and October 1974 general elections. MP (Labour) for Wolverhampton South East 1987-2005. Opposition Whip 1992-97; PPS to Secretaries of State for International Development: Clare Short 1997-2003, Baroness Amos 2003. Chair: Catering 1997-2005. *House of Lords:* Raised to the peerage as Baron Bilston, of Bilston in the County of West Midlands 2005. Member Ecclesiastical Committee 2010-. *Other:* Co-operative Party: Member, Chair, Parliamentary Group 1991-93. *Councils and public bodies:* Wolverhampton Borough Council: Councillor 1966-86, Deputy Leader 1980-86; Councillor, West Midlands County Council 1973-86; Director, Black Country Co-operative Development Agency 1983-88; Former Vice-President, Local Government Association.

LAB/CO-OP

Political interests: Education, social services, housing, international development, small businesses; British Overseas Territories, Commonwealth, South Africa.

Other: Member, Executive Committee Inter-Parliamentary Union (British Branch); Commonwealth Parliamentary Association (Commonwealth Parliamentary Association) UK Branch: Member, Executive Committee 1999-, Vice-chair; President: Wolverhampton Deaf Children's Society 1987-, Bilston Community Association 1993-; Friday Night Domino League; Chair, Wolverhampton Fair Trade Partnership 2003-; Trustee-Secretary, Bradley Old People's Trust; Patron: Wolverhampton Interfaith and Faith Regeneration Network; Wolverhampton Orpheus Male Voice Choir; NSPCC, Oxfam, Scope. Freeman, City of Wolverhampton. Honorary Doctorate, Wolverhampton University 2005; New Springvale Sports and Social (Bilston).

Recreations: Tasting traditional ales, all card games.

The Lord Bilston, House of Lords, London SW1A 0PW
Tel: 020 7219 4210
Aubyn, 14 King Street, Bradley, Bilston WV14 8PQ *Tel:* 01902 491822

BIRMINGHAM, LORD BISHOP OF

BIRMINGHAM (9th Bishop of), David Andrew Urquhart. Born 14 April 1952.

Education: Croftinloan School, Perthshire; Rugby School; Ealing Business School (BA 1977); Wycliffe Hall, Oxford (1984).

Non-political career: Volunteer, Uganda 1971; BP plc 1972-82; Ordained Deacon 1984; Priest 1985; Curate, St Nicholas, Kingston-upon-Hull 1984-87; Vicar: Drypool 1987-92, Holy Trinity, Coventry 1992-2000; Honorary Canon, Coventry Cathedral 1999-2000; Bishop Suffragen of Birkenhead 2000-06; Prelate of the Most Distinguished Order of St Michael and St George 2005-; Archbishop of Canterbury's Envoy to China 2005-; Bishop of Birmingham 2006-.

NON-AFFILIATED

Political career: *House of Lords:* Entered House of Lords 2010. *Councils and public bodies:* Governor, Rugby School 2001-; Chair, Ridley Hall Council, Cambridge 2011-.

Political interests: Local government, economy, foreign affairs; China, DR Congo, Malawi.

Other: Chair: Church Mission Society 1994-2008, Chester Diocese Education Board 2001-06; Trustee, Hippodrome Theatre, Birmingham 2009-; Church Mission Society; Institut Pan-Africain deSanté Communitaire, DR Congo. Hon Freeman, Metropolitan Borough of Wirral 2006. Honorary DD Birmingham University 2009; Athenæum. Jesters.

Recreations: Rugby fives, Scottish hill-walking.

Rt Rev the Lord Bishop of Birmingham, House of Lords, London SW1A 0PW
Tel: 020 7219 5353
Bishop's Croft, Old Church Road, Harborne, Birmingham B17 0BG *Tel:* 0121-427 1163
Fax: 0121-426 1322 *Email:* bishop@birmingham.anglican.org
christine@birmingham.anglican.org *Website:* www.birmingham.anglican.org

CROSSBENCH

BIRT, LORD

BIRT (Life Baron), John Birt; cr. 2000. Born 10 December 1944; Son of late Leo and Ida Birt; Married Jane Lake 1965 (divorced 2006) (1 son 1 daughter); married Eithne Wallis, CB 2006.
Education: St Mary's College, Liverpool; St Catherine's College, Oxford (BA engineering science 1966, MA).
Non-political career: Granada TV 1968-70: Producer, *Nice Time* 1968-69, Joint editor, *World in Action* 1969-70; London Weekend Television 1971-87: Producer, *The Frost Programme* 1971-72, Executive producer, *Weekend World* 1972-74, Head of current affairs 1974-77, Producer, *The Nixon Interviews* 1977, Controller of features and current affairs 1977-81, Director of programmes 1981-87; BBC 1987-2000: Deputy Director-General 1987-92, Director-General 1992-2000; Visiting Fellow, Nuffield College, Oxford 1991-99; Chairman, Lynx Capital Ventures 2000-04; Strategy adviser to Tony Blair as Prime Minister 2000-05; Adviser, McKinsey's Global Media Practice 2000-05; Member, Cabinet Office Strategy Board 2003-05; PayPal (Europe) Ltd, an eBay subsidiary: Non-executive director 2004, Chair 2010-; Non-executive director, Infinis 2006-; Eutelsat: Non-executive director 2006-, Vice-chairman 2012-; Adviser: Terra Firma 2006, Capgemini 2006-10; Chairman: Waste Recycling Group 2006, Maltby Capital (EMI Holding Company) 2008-10.
Political career: *House of Lords:* Raised to the peerage as Baron Birt, of Liverpool in the County of Merseyside 2000.
Political interests: Broadcasting, digital Britain, crime, transport, constitution, humanism, energy, public sector management, London; China, Japan, South Africa, USA.
Other: Member, Wilton Park Academic Council 1980-83; Royal Television Society: Fellow 1989, Vice-president 1994-2001. Two honorary university fellowships, three honorary doctorates. Emmy Award, US National Academy of Television, Arts and Sciences 1995. Kt 1998; Groucho.
Publications: The Harder Path (2002).
Recreations: Walking, cinema, football.
The Lord Birt, House of Lords, London SW1A 0PW
Tel: 020 7219 8705 *Email:* birtj@parliament.uk
Fielden House, 13 Little College Street, London SW1P 3SH

CONSERVATIVE

BLACK OF BRENTWOOD, LORD

BLACK OF BRENTWOOD (Life Baron), Guy Vaughan Black; cr 2010. Born 6 August 1964; Son of Thomas and Monica Black (both deceased); Civil partner Mark Bolland 2006.
Education: Brentwood School, Essex; Peterhouse, Cambridge (BA history 1985, MA).
Non-political career: Graduate trainee, corporate banking division, BZW 1985-86; Desk officer, Conservative Research Department 1986-89; Special adviser to Rt Hon John Wakeham MP as Secretary of State for Energy 1989-92; Account director, Westminster Strategy 1992-94; Associate director, Lowe Bell Good Relations 1994-96; Director, Press Complaints Commission 1996-2003; Press secretary to Rt Hon Michael Howard MP as Leader of the Opposition 2004-05; Director of Media, Conservative Central Office 2004-05; Telegraph Media Group: Corporate affairs director 2005-09, Executive director 2009-.
Political career: *House of Lords:* Raised to the peerage as Baron Black of Brentwood, of Brentwood in the County of Essex 2010. Member: Information 2011-, Joint Committee on Privacy and Injunctions 2011-12. *Other:* Member, Association of Conservative Peers. *Councils and public bodies:* Councillor, Brentwood District Council 1988-92.
Political interests: Media and creative industries, health, education, energy, animal welfare; Commonwealth, Italy.
Other: Director, Advertising Standards Board of Finance 2005-; Press Standards Board of Finance: Director 2006-, Chair 2009-; Trustee: Imperial War Museum 2007-, Sir Edward Heath's Charitable Foundation 2006-10, Royal College of Music 2009-; Chair, Commonwealth Press Union Media Trust 2009-; Fellow, Royal Society of Arts; President: London Press Club 2012-, The Printing Charity 2013-; Member, Chartered Institute of Public Relations; Cats Protection; National Osteoporosis Society.
Recreations: Music, history.
The Lord Black of Brentwood, House of Lords, London SW1A 0PW
Tel: 020 7219 5353 *Email:* blackgv@parliament.uk

NON-AFFILIATED

BLACK OF CROSSHARBOUR, LORD

BLACK OF CROSSHARBOUR (Life Baron), Conrad Moffat Black; cr 2001. Born 25 August 1944; Son of George M Black and Jean Elizabeth Riley; Married Shirley Gail Hishon 1978 (divorced 1992) (2 sons 1 daughter); married Barbara Amiel 1992.

Education: Carleton University, Canada (BA history and political science 1965); Laval University, Canada (LLL law 1970); McGill University, Canada (MA history 1973).

Non-political career: Chair, Sterling Newspapers Ltd 1971-; President, Argus Corporation Ltd 1978-79; Chair: Argus Corporation Ltd 1979-2005, Telegraph Group Ltd, London 1985-2003, Hollinger Inc, USA 1985-2003, Hollinger Inc, Canada 1986-2004.

Political career: *House of Lords:* Raised to the peerage as Baron Black of Crossharbour, of Crossharbour in the London Borough of Tower Hamlets 2001. On leave of absence June 2012-.

Countries of interest: Canada.

Other: Hudson Institute; International Institute of Strategic Studies; Trilateral Commission on Foreign Relations (New York); National Interest (Washington); Nixon Centre (Washington); Member, Advisory Committee Jubilee Appeal for Veterans; Honorary Chairman, Black Family Foundation. Four honorary doctorates from Canadian universities. Order of Canada 1990; PC (Canada) 1992; Knight Commander of the Order of St Gregory the Great (Holy See) 2001; Athenæum, Beefsteak, Garrick, Whites, Century (New York), Everglades (Palm Beach, Florida), Beach (Palm Beach, Florida), Toronto (Toronto), York (Toronto), Mount Royal (Montreal), University (Montreal).

Publications: Duplessis (1976) revised as Render unto Caesar (1998); A Life in Progress (1993); Franklin Delano Roosevelt, Champion of Freedom (2003); The Invincible Quest: The Life of Richard Milhous Nixon (2007); A Matter of Principle (2011); Flight of the Eagle: The Strategic History of the United States (2013).

The Lord Black of Crossharbour OC, House of Lords, London SW1A 0PW
Tel: 020 7219 5353
c/o 9 Montague Gardens, London W3 9PT *Tel:* 07973 861155 *Email:* cmb@blackam.net, 3044 Bloor St West, Suite 296, Toronto Ontario M8X 2Y8, Canada *Tel:* +1 416 241 7758 *Fax:* +1 416 241 5026 *Email:* jmaida@blackam.net

LABOUR

BLACKSTONE, BARONESS

BLACKSTONE (Life Baroness), Tessa Ann Vosper Blackstone; cr. 1987. Born 27 September 1942; Daughter of late Geoffrey Blackstone and late Joanna Blackstone, née Vosper; Married Tom Evans 1963 (divorced 1975) (1 son 1 daughter).

Education: Ware Grammar School; London School of Economics (BScSoc sociology 1964; PhD 1969); Some French and German.

Non-political career: Associate lecturer, Enfield College 1965-66; Assistant lecturer then lecturer, Department of Social Administration, London School of Economics 1966-75; Fellow, Centre for Studies in Social Policy 1972-74; Adviser, Central Policy Review Staff, Cabinet Office 1975-78; Professor of educational administration, University of London Institute of Education 1978-83; Deputy education officer (resources), Inner London Education Authority 1983-86; Fellow, Policy Studies Institute 1987; Master, Birkbeck College, London University 1987-97; Non-executive director: Thames Television, VT Group 2004-10, Mott MacDonald 2005-08.

Political career: *House of Lords:* Raised to the peerage as Baroness Blackstone, of Stoke Newington in the County of Greater London 1987. Opposition Spokesperson for: Education and Science 1988-96, Treasury Matters 1990-91; Principal Opposition Spokesperson for Education and Science 1990-92; Opposition Spokesperson for Trade and Industry 1992-96; Principal Opposition Spokesperson for Foreign Affairs 1992-97; Minister of State and Government Spokesperson for: Department for Education and Employment (Minister of State for Education and Employment) 1997-2001, Department for Culture, Media and Sport (Minister of State for the Arts) 2001-03. Member: Public Service and Demographic Change 2012-13, Economic Affairs 2013-. *Councils and public bodies:* Chair, BBC General Advisory Council 1987-91; Chair and founder member, Institute for Public Policy Research 1988-97; Chair, British Library 2010-.

Political interests: Education, social policy, foreign affairs, arts; France, India, Palestine, USA.

Other: Co-chair, France-British Council 2013-; Royal Opera House: Board member 1987-97, 2009-, Chair, Ballet Board 1991-97, Chair, Education and Access Committee 2011-; Trustee, Natural History Museum 1992-97; Chair: Royal Institute of British Architects Trust 2003-10, Great Ormond Street Hospital Trust 2009-, British Library 2010-, Orbit Group 2013-; Vice-president, Voluntary Services Overseas (VSO); Patron, Why Me?. Vice-chancellor, University of Greenwich 2004-11. 12 honorary doctorates; Three honorary fellowships. Lifetime Award for Higher Education, *The Times* Higher Education awards 2011. PC 2001.

Publications: A Fair Start (1971); Co-author: Students in Conflict (1967), The Academic Labour Market (1974), Educational Policy and Educational Inequality (1982), Disadvantage and Education (1982), Response to Adversity (1983), Inside the Think Tank: Advising the Cabinet 1971-84 (1988); Author, Prison and Penal Reform (1992); Co-edited, Race Relations in Britain (1998).

Recreations: Tennis, walking, ballet, opera, cinema.

Rt Hon the Baroness Blackstone, House of Lords, London SW1A 0PW
Tel: 020 7219 5409 *Email:* blackstonet@parliament.uk
The British Library, 96 Euston Road, London NW1 2DB *Tel:* 020 7412 7262

CONSERVATIVE

BLACKWELL, LORD

BLACKWELL (Life Baron), Norman Roy Blackwell; cr. 1997. Born 29 July 1952; Son of Albert and Frances Blackwell; Married Brenda Clucas 1974 (3 sons 2 daughters).

Education: Latymer Upper School, London; Royal Academy of Music (Junior Exhibitioner); Trinity College, Cambridge (BA natural sciences 1973, MA); Wharton Business School, University of Pennsylvania (AM, MBA 1975; PhD finance and economics 1976).

Non-political career: Plessey Company 1976-78; McKinsey & Co 1978-95: Partner 1984-95; Prime Minister's Policy Unit: Special adviser 1986-87, Head 1995-97; Director: Group Development, NatWest Group 1997-2000, Dixons Group 2000-03; Special adviser, KPMG Corporate Finance 2000-08; Director: The Corporate Services Group 2000-06, SEGRO plc (formerly Slough Estates) 2001-10, SmartStream Technologies Ltd 2001-06; Chair, Akers Biosciences Inc 2002-03; Director, Standard Life Assurance 2003-12; Chair, Interserve plc 2006-; Director: Halma plc 2010-, Lloyds Banking Group plc 2012-; Chair, Scottish Widows Group Ltd 2012-.

Political career: *House of Lords:* Raised to the peerage as Baron Blackwell, of Woodcote in the County of Surrey 1997. Member: Joint Committee on Tax Simplification 2001-, EU Sub-committee A (Economic and Financial Affairs) 2003-07, Economic Affairs Sub-committee on the Finance Bill 2004-10, European Union 2005-08, Joint Committee on Tax Law Rewrite Bills 2005-10; EU Sub-committee E (Law and Institutions): Member 2007-08, Co-opted member 2008-10; Member: Delegated Powers and Regulatory Reform 2008-13, EU Sub-committee E (Justice and Institutions) 2010-12, Secondary Legislation Scrutiny 2013-. *Councils and public bodies:* Board Member: Office of Fair Trading 2003-10, OFCOM 2009-.

Political interests: Economic policy and taxation, public services, European Union.

Other: Office of Communications: Non-Executive Board Member 2009-, Member, Content Board 2012-, Chair: Centre for Policy Studies 2000-09, Global Vision 2007-09; Carlton, Royal Automobile.

Publications: Funding the Basic State Pension (CPS, 2001); Towards Smaller Government (CPS, 2001); Better Healthcare for all (CPS, 2002); A defining moment? – the European Constitutional Convention (CPS, 2003); Freedom annd Responsibility: A manifesto for a smaller state, bolder nation! (CPS, 2003); What if Britain says No to the EU Constitution? (CPS, 2004); Better Schools and Hospitals – Why parent and patient choice will work (CPS, 2004); Sleepwalking into an EU Legal System (CPS, 2006); From principle to policy – an outline manifesto (CPS, 2006); Three cheers for selection – How Grammar Schools help the poor (CPS, 2007).

Recreations: Classical music, walking.

The Lord Blackwell, House of Lords, London SW1A 0PW
Tel: 020 7219 8672 *Email:* blackwelln@parliament.uk
Tel: 07785 932703 *Fax:* 01372 725896 *Email:* blackwelln@parliament.uk

CROSSBENCH

BLAIR OF BOUGHTON, LORD

BLAIR OF BOUGHTON (Life Baron), Ian Warwick Blair; cr 2010. Born 19 March 1953; Married Felicity White 1980 (1 son 1 daughter).

Education: Wrekin College, Shropshire; Harvard High School, Los Angeles, USA; Christ Church, Oxford (BA English language and literature 1974, MA).

Non-political career: Metropolitan Police: Police Constable, Sergeant, then Inspector (uniform and CID) 1974-85, Detective Chief Inspector, CID, Kentish Town 1985-88, Manager, Crime Investigation Project 1988-89, Superintendent, Kensington Division 1989-91, Chief Superintendent and Staff Officer to HM Chief Inspector of Constabulary, Home Office 1991-93, Officer in charge of Operation Gallery 1993-96; Thames Valley Police: Assistant Chief Constable 1994-97, Deputy Chief Constable 1997-98; Chief Constable, Surrey Police 1998-2000; Metropolitan Police: Deputy Commissioner 2000-05, Commissioner 2005-08.

Political career: *House of Lords:* Raised to the peerage as Baron Blair of Boughton, of Boughton in the County of Cheshire 2010. Member EU Sub-committee E (Justice, Institutions and Consumer Protection) 2013-. *Councils and public bodies:* Commissioner, Commission on Assisted Dying 2010-.

Countries of interest: India.

Other: Visiting fellow: International Centre for Advanced Studies, New York University 1998, Nuffield College, Oxford 2001; Visiting Professor, John Jay College 2010; Chairman, Thames Valley Partnership; Trustee: St Paul's Cathedral Foundation, Shakespeare's Globe, Woolf Foundation for the study of Abrahamic Faiths, The Longford Trust. QPM 1998; Kt 2003; Athenæum.

Publications: Author: Investigating Rape: A New Approach for Police (1985); Policing Controversy (Profile Books, 2009).

Recreations: Theatre, opera, skiing.

The Lord Blair of Boughton QPM, House of Lords, London SW1A 0PW
Tel: 020 7219 5353

CONSERVATIVE

BLENCATHRA, LORD

BLENCATHRA (Life Baron), David John Maclean; cr 2011. Born 16 May 1953.

Education: Fortrose Academy; Aberdeen University.

Non-political career: Director, Cayman Islands Government Office, London 2011-.

Political career: *House of Commons:* MP (Conservative) for Penrith and The Border 1983 by-election to 2010. Assistant Government Whip 1987-89; Government Whip 1988-89; Parliamentary Secretary, Ministry of Agriculture, Fisheries and Food 1989-92; Minister of State: Department of the Environment 1992-93, Home Office 1993-97; Opposition Chief Whip 2001-03, 2003-05; Member House of Commons Commission 2006. Chair: Joint Committee on Statutory Instruments 2006; Member: Liaison 2006. *House of Lords:* Raised to the peerage as Baron Blencathra, of Penrith in the County of Cumbria 2011. Member: EU Sub-committee F: (Home Affairs) 2011-12, (Home Affairs, Health and Education) 2012-, Procedure 2012-; Chair Joint Committee on the Draft Communications Data Bill 2012-13.

Other: PC 1995.

Rt Hon the Lord Blencathra, House of Lords, London SW1A 0PW
Tel: 020 7219 5353

LABOUR

BLOOD, BARONESS

BLOOD (Life Baroness), May Blood; cr. 1999. Born 26 May 1938; Daughter of late William and Mary Blood; Single.

Education: Linfield Secondary, Belfast.

Non-political career: Cutting supervisor, Blackstaff Mill 1952-90; Community worker, Great Shankill Partnership 1990-98. Member, TGWU: Shop steward 1968-90, Senior steward 1980-90, Regional committee 1980, 1990.

Political career: *House of Lords:* Raised to the peerage as Baroness Blood, of Blackwatertown in the County of Armagh 1999.

Political interests: Women's issues, low pay, working class issues, family, children.

Other: Citizen's Global Circle, Boston; Chair: Great Shankill Surestart, Integrated Education Fund, Impact Training, Ulster Historical Society; Barnados; NI Integrated Fund; Centre Point; Art Ability (NI). Honorary doctorates: Ulster University 1998, Queens University, Belfast 2001, Open University 2002; Fellow, National College Dublin 2004. Catherine Dunpfy Peace Global Citizens Awards 1997; Frank Cousins Peace Award 1999; Irish Woman of the Year 2006; Grassroots Diplomat Award 2012. MBE 1995.

Publications: Autobiography, Watch My Lips, I'm Speaking (Gill & Macmillan, 2008).

Recreations: Reading, gardening.

The Baroness Blood MBE, House of Lords, London SW1A 0PW
Tel: 020 7219 8700 *Email:* bloodm@parliament.uk
Alessie Centre, 60 Shankhill Road, Belfast BT13 2BD *Tel:* 028 9087 4000 *Fax:* 028 9087 4009
Email: wendy@earlyyears.org.uk

CONSERVATIVE

BLYTH OF ROWINGTON, LORD

BLYTH OF ROWINGTON (Life Baron), James Blyth; cr. 1995. Born 8 May 1940; Son of Daniel and Jane Blyth; Married Pamela Campbell Dixon 1967 (1 daughter and 1 son deceased).
Education: Spiers School; Glasgow University (BA history 1963, MA); Competent French.
Non-political career: Mobil Oil Company 1963-69; General Foods Ltd 1969-71; Mars Ltd 1971-74; General manager, Lucas Batteries Ltd 1974-77, Lucas Aerospace Ltd 1977-81; Head of defence sales, Ministry of Defence 1981-85; Non-executive director, Imperial Group plc 1984-86; Managing director, Plessey Electronic Systems 1985-86; Chief Executive, The Plessey Co plc 1986-87; Non-executive director, Cadbury-Schweppes plc 1986-90; Boots Company plc: Director and chief executive 1987-2000, Deputy Chair 1994-98, Chair 1998-2000; Non-executive director: British Aerospace 1990-94, Anixter Inc 1995-; Director, NatWest Group 1998-2000; Diageo plc: Director 1999-, Chair 2000-08; Greenhill and Company: Senior adviser 2000-02, 2007-, Partner 2002-07; Vice-chair, Middlebrook Pharmaceuticals Inc 2008-10.
Political career: *House of Lords:* Raised to the peerage as Baron Blyth of Rowington, of Rowington in the County of Warwickshire 1995. On leave of absence March 2013-. *Councils and public bodies:* Governor, London Business School 1987-96; Chair, Advisory panel on Citizen's Charter 1991-97.
Political interests: Business, economics, pensions; Central and Latin America, Middle East, USA.
Other: President, Middle East Association 1988-93; Patron, Combined Services Winter Sports Association 1997-2002. Liveryman, Coachmakers' and Coach Harness Makers' Company. Honorary LLD, Nottingham University 1992; Honorary Fellow, London Business School 1997. Kt 1985; East India Club; Devonshire; Sports and Public Schools; RAC; Caledonian Club. The Queen's Club; Blackwell Golf Club.
Recreations: Skiing, tennis, paintings, theatre, horses, golf.
The Lord Blyth of Rowington, House of Lords, London SW1A 0PW
Tel: 020 7219 5353
Email: blyth08@googlemail.com

LABOUR

BOATENG, LORD

BOATENG (Life Baron), Paul Yaw Boateng; cr 2010. Born 14 June 1951; Son of Kwaku Boateng, barrister, and Eleanor Boateng, teacher; Married Janet Alleyne 1980 (2 sons 3 daughters).
Education: Achimota School, Ghana; Accra Academy, Ghana; Apsley Grammar School, Ghana; Bristol University (LLB 1972); College of Law (solicitor 1975); French (colloquial).
Non-political career: Solicitor 1975; Barrister-at-law; High Commissioner, South Africa 2005-09; Advisory Board, Aegis; Chair, advisory board, Aventa Capital Partners; Member: Health policy advisory board, Gilead Sciences Inc, Non-executive director, 4G Africa AG, Director, Akyen Law and Advisory Science Ltd. Member GMB.
Political career: *House of Commons:* Contested Hertfordshire West 1983 general election. MP (Labour) for Brent South 1987-2005. Opposition Frontbench Spokesman on: Treasury and Economic Affairs 1989-92, Lord Chancellor's Department 1992-97; Parliamentary Under-Secretary of State, Department of Health 1997-98; Home Office: Minister of State (Minister for Criminal Policy) 1998-99, Minister of State and Deputy Home Secretary 1999-2001; Minister for Young People 2000-01; HM Treasury 2001-05: Financial Secretary 2001-02, Chief Secretary 2002-05. Member: Public Accounts 2001-02. *House of Lords:* Raised to the peerage as Baron Boateng, of Akyem in the Republic of Ghana and of Wembley in the London Borough of Brent 2010. *Other:* Member: Labour Party NEC Human Rights sub-committee 1979-83, Labour Party Joint Committee on Crime and Policing 1984-86. *Councils and public bodies:* Member Greater London Council 1981-86: Chair, Police Committee 1981-86, Vice-chair, Ethnic Minority Committee 1981-86; Trustee, Museum of London 2009-; Board of Governors, London School of Economics 2011.
Political interests: Home affairs, housing, inner cities, overseas aid and development, environment, children and young people's policy; Africa, Caribbean, Southern Africa, USA.
Other: Chair: Afro-Caribbean Education Resource Project 1978-84, Westminster Community Relations Council 1979-81; Legal adviser, Scrap Sus Campaign 1977-81; Home Office Advisory Council on Race Relations 1981-86; World Council of Churches Commission on programme to combat racism 1984-91; Vice-Moderator 1984-91; Police Training Council 1981-85; Executive NCCL 1980-86; Governor, Police Staff College Bramshill 1981-84; Board of English National Opera 1984-97; Governor, Ditchley Park 2007-11; Board of Governors, English Speaking Union 2009-; Board member, Food for The Hungry 2009-; Trustee, Duke of Edinburgh International Youth Award 2009-; Board of Governors, Museum of London 2010-; Member, Gray's Inn. D.L., Lincoln College, Philadelphia, USA; LLD, Bristol University. PC 1999.

Publications: Contributor Reclaiming the Ground; Introduction to Sense and Sensibility: The Complete Jane Austen.

Recreations: Family, swimming, opera.

Rt Hon the Lord Boateng, House of Lords, London SW1A 0PW
Tel: 020 7219 5353 *Email:* boatengp@parliament.uk

BONHAM-CARTER OF YARNBURY, BARONESS

Deputy Convener of the Liberal Democrat Peers

BONHAM-CARTER OF YARNBURY (Life Baroness), Jane Bonham Carter; cr. 2004. Born 20 October 1957; Daughter of Mark Bonham Carter and Leslie Nast; Partner Lord Razzall.

Education: St Paul's Girls' School, London; University College, London (BA philosophy).

Non-political career: Producer, BBC Television's *Panorama* and *Newsnight* 1988-93; Editor, *A Week in Politics*, Channel Four 1993-96; Director of communications, Liberal Democrat Party 1996-98; Independent television producer, Brook Lapping Productions 1998-2004; Associate, Brook Lapping Productions, Ten Alps plc 2004-09.

LIBERAL DEMOCRAT

Political career: *House of Commons:* Co-chair, Liberal Democrat Parliamentary Party Committee on Culture, Media and Sport. *House of Lords:* Raised to the peerage as Baroness Bonham-Carter of Yarnbury, of Yarnbury in the County of Wiltshire 2004. Liberal Democrat Spokesperson for Culture, Media and Sport (Broadcasting and the Arts) 2004-10; Deputy Convener of the Liberal Democrat Peers 2010-; Trade envoy to Mexico 2012-. Member: EU Sub-committee F (Home Affairs) 2004-07, Review of the BBC Charter 2005-06, Communications 2007-10, Joint Committee on Privacy and Injunctions 2011-12, EU Sub-committee C: (Foreign Affairs, Defence and Development Policy) 2010-12, (External Affairs) 2012-. Chair, Liberal Democrat Parliamentary Party Committee on Culture, Media and Sport 2010-. *Other:* Member, Liberal Democrats Campaigns and Communications Committee 1998-2006.

Countries of interest: America, Ethiopia, Italy, Zimbabwe.

Other: Advisory committee, Centre Forum 1998-; Council member, Britain in Europe 1998-2005; Member, Referendum Campaign team 2004-05; Trustee, The Lowry 2011-; Board member, National Campaign for the Arts 2010-12; Member RAPt Rehabilitation of Addicted Prisoners Trust 1999-; The Groucho Club; The Electric.

The Baroness Bonham-Carter of Yarnbury, House of Lords, London SW1A 0PW
Tel: 020 7219 2717 *Email:* bonhamcarterj@parliament.uk anna.sharkey@parliament.uk
Email: janebonhamcarter@aol.com

BOOTHROYD, BARONESS

BOOTHROYD (Life Baroness), Betty Boothroyd; cr. 2001. Born 8 October 1929; Daughter of late Archibald and Mary Boothroyd; Single.

Education: Dewsbury College of Commerce and Art.

Non-political career: Personal/political assistant to: Barbara Castle MP 1956-58, Lord Walston as Minister of State, Foreign and Commonwealth Office 1962-73; Legislative assistant, US congressman Silvio O Conte 1960-62.

CROSSBENCH

Political career: *House of Commons:* Contested Leicester South East 1957 by-election, Peterborough 1959 general election, Nelson and Colne 1968 by-election and Rossendale 1970 general election. MP (Labour) for West Bromwich 1973-74, for West Bromwich West (Labour 1974-92, Speaker 1992-2000) 1974-2000. Assistant Government Whip 1974-76; Second Deputy Chairman of Ways and Means and Deputy Speaker 1987-92; Speaker 1992-2000; Chairman, House of Commons Commission 1992-2000. *House of Lords:* Raised to the peerage as Baroness Boothroyd, of Sandwell in the County of West Midlands 2001. *Other:* Member European Parliament 1975-77. *Councils and public bodies:* Member, National Executive Committee, Labour Party 1981-87. Councillor, Hammersmith Borough Council 1965-68.

Political interests: Constitutional affairs; Commonwealth.

Other: Vice-President, Commonwealth Parliamentary Association (UK Branch); Patron: Memorial to the Women of World War Two, Friends of the Elderly, The London Trust, The Silver Trust, Commonwealth Countries League, CHICKS (Country Holidays for Inner City Kids), National Benevolent Fund for the Aged. Worshipful Company of: Feltmakers 1994, Glovers of London 2001 (Special Member), Lightmongers 2001 (Special Member), Grocers 2005 (Honorary Member). Freeman: Metropolitan Borough of Sandwell, Metropolitan Borough of Kirklees, City of London. Chancellor, Open University 1994-2006. Ten honorary degrees, including Oxford, Cambridge and St Andrews; Honorary Master of the Bench, Middle Temple 2011. *The*

Spectator: Parliamentarian of the Year Award 1992, Personality of the Year 1993, Communicator of the Year 1994; Lifetime Achievement, *House Magazine* awards 2012. PC 1992; OM 2005; Reform Club, University Women's Club.

Publications: The Autobiography Betty Boothroyd (2001).

Recreations: Gardening.

Rt Hon the Baroness Boothroyd OM, House of Lords, London SW1A 0PW
Tel: 020 7219 8673 *Email:* boothroyd@parliament.uk

LABOUR

BORRIE, LORD

BORRIE (Life Baron), Gordon Johnson Borrie; cr. 1995. Born 13 March 1931; Son of Stanley Borrie; Married Dorene Toland 1960 (died 2010).

Education: John Bright Grammar School, Llandudno; Manchester University (LLB 1950; LLM 1952).

Non-political career: National Service with Army Legal Services, HQ British Commonwealth Forces in Korea 1952-54. Barrister-at-Law and Harmsworth Scholar of the Middle Temple; Called to the Bar, Middle Temple 1952, Bencher 1980; Practised as barrister in London 1954-57; Lecturer and later senior lecturer, College of Law 1957-64; Birmingham University: Senior lecturer in law 1965-68, Professor of English law and director, Institute of Judicial Administration 1969-76, Dean, Faculty of law 1974-76, Hon professor of law 1989-; Director-General of Fair Trading 1976-92; QC 1986; Director: Woolwich Building Society 1992-2000, Three Valleys Water 1992-2003; President, Institute of Trading Standards Administration 1992-97; Director: Mirror Group 1993-99, TeleWest 1994-2001; Chair, Direct Marketing Authority 1997-2001; Director, Vivendi Water 1998-2003.

Political career: *House of Commons:* Contested (Labour) Croydon North East 1955 and Ilford South 1959 general elections. *House of Lords:* Raised to the peerage as Baron Borrie, of Abbots Morton in the County of Hereford and Worcester 1995. Member: European Union 1997-2000, European Union Sub-committee E (Law and Institutions) 1996-2000, 2004-06, Refreshment 2003-07; Co-opted member European Union Sub-committee E (Law and Institutions) 2006-07; Member Consumer Insurance (Disclosure and Representations) Bill 2011-12. *Councils and public bodies:* Member, Parole Board for England and Wales 1971-74; Chair: Commission on Social Justice 1992-94, Advertising Standards Authority 2001-07, Council of the Property Ombudsman 2007-09.

Other: Fellow: Chartered Institute of Arbitrators, Royal Society of Arts. Seven honorary law doctorates. Kt 1982; Garrick, Reform, Pratt's.

Publications: Commercial Law (1962); Co-author: The Consumer, Society and the Law (1963), Law of Contempt (1973); The Development of Consumer Law and Policy (Hamlyn Lectures) (1984).

Recreations: Gastronomy, playing the piano, travel.

The Lord Borrie QC, House of Lords, London SW1A 0PW
Tel: 020 7219 5125
Manor Farm, Abbots Morton, Worcestershire WR7 4NA *Tel:* 01386 792330,
4 Brick Court, Temple, London EC4Y 9AD *Tel:* 020 7353 4434 *Email:* g.borrie@btinternet.com

CONSERVATIVE

BORWICK, LORD

BORWICK (5th Baron, UK) Geoffrey Robert James (Jamie) Borwick; cr 1922; 5th Bt of Eden Lacy (UK) 1916. Born 7 March 1955; Son of late Honorary Robin Sandbach Borwick; Married Lady Victoria Lorne Peta 1981 (3 sons 1 daughter).

Education: Eton College.

Non-political career: Sir Robert McAlpine & Sons Ltd 1972-81; Non-executive director, Hansa Trust plc 1984-2012; Manganese Bronze Holdings plc: Chief executive officer 1987-2001, Chair 2001-03; Chair, Federated Trust Corporation Ltd 1987-.

Political career: *House of Lords:* Elected hereditary peer 2013-.

Political interests: Business, economy, planning, transport; USA.

Other: Trustee: Federated Foundation 1985-, British Lung Foundation 2001-08, 2011-, Royal Brompton and Harefield Charity 2012-; Fellow, Ewing Foundation; Garrick.

Recreations: Travel, swimming, walking.

The Lord Borwick, House of Lords, London SW1A 0PW
Tel: 020 7219 5823 *Email:* borwickgr@parliament.uk
1 Love Lane, London EC2V 7YN *Tel:* 020 7776 9000

BOSWELL OF AYNHO, LORD

BOSWELL OF AYNHO (Life Baron), Timothy Eric Boswell; cr 2010. Born 2 December 1942; Son of late Eric Boswell and Joan Boswell; Married Helen Delahay, née Rees 1969 (3 daughters). **Education:** Marlborough College, Wiltshire; New College, Oxford (BA classics 1965, MA; Diploma agricultural economics 1966); French, German, Italian.

Non-political career: Conservative Research Department 1966-73: Head, economic section 1970-73; Farmer 1974-87; Part-time special adviser to Minister of Agriculture 1984-86. Chair, Leicestershire, Northamptonshire and Rutland NFU County Branch 1983.

NON-AFFILIATED

Political career: *House of Commons:* Contested Rugby February 1974 general election. MP (Conservative) for Daventry 1987-2010. PPS to Peter Lilley as Financial Secretary to Treasury 1989-90; Assistant Government Whip 1990-92; Government Whip 1992; Parliamentary Under-Secretary of State, Department for Education 1992-95; Parliamentary Secretary, Ministry of Agriculture, Fisheries and Food 1995-97; Opposition Spokesperson for: the Treasury 1997, Trade and Industry 1997-99, Education 1999-2001, Work and Pensions (People with Disabilities) 2001; Shadow Minister for: Education and Skills (People with Disabilities) 2002-03, Home, Constitutional and Legal Affairs 2003-04, Home Affairs 2004, Work and Pensions 2004-06, and Welfare Reform 2004-05; PPS to Francis Maude as Chairman, Conservative Party 2005-07. Member: Innovation, Universities[, Science] and Skills/Science and Technology 2007-10. Member, Executive, 1922 Committee 2007-10. *House of Lords:* Raised to the peerage as Baron Boswell of Aynho, of Aynho in the County of Northamptonshire 2010. Principal Deputy Chairman of Committees 2012-. Chair European Union 2012-. *Other:* Chair, Daventry Constituency Conservative Association 1979-83; Acting Chairman, Milton Keynes Conservatives 2009-10. *Councils and public bodies:* Member, Agriculture and Food Research Council 1988-90; DL, Northamptonshire 2010-.

Political interests: Agriculture, finance, European Union, education, equalities; Europe.

Other: Perry Foundation: Council member 1967-90, President 1984-90; Governor: University of Wales Institute, Cardiff 2007-12, Northampton University 2010-12; Fellow, City and Guilds Institutes; Farmers' Club.

Recreations: Shooting.

The Lord Boswell of Aynho, House of Lords, London SW1A 0PW
Tel: 020 7219 7291 *Email:* boswellte@parliament.uk

BOTTOMLEY OF NETTLESTONE, BARONESS

BOTTOMLEY OF NETTLESTONE (Life Baroness), Virginia Hilda Brunette Maxwell Bottomley; cr 2005. Born 12 March 1948; Daughter of late W. John Garnett, CBE; Married Peter Bottomley (now MP, later Sir Peter) 1967 (1 son 2 daughters).

Education: Putney High School; Essex University (BA sociology); London School of Economics (MSc social administration 1975).

Non-political career: Behavioural scientist 1971-84; Executive director, Odgers Berndston (executive search) 2000-; Member, Supervisory Board, Akzo Nobel NV 2000-12; NED; BUPA 2007-13; Non-executive director, Smith & Nephew 2012-.

CONSERVATIVE

Political career: *House of Commons:* Contested Isle of Wight 1983 general election. MP (Conservative) for South West Surrey 1984 by-election to 2005. PPS: to Chris Patten as Minister of State: Department of Education and Science 1985-86, Overseas Development Administration 1986-87, to Sir Geoffrey Howe as Foreign Secretary 1987-88; Parliamentary Under-Secretary of State, Department of Environment 1988-89; Minister of State, Department of Health 1989-92; Secretary of State for: Health 1992-95, National Heritage 1995-97. *House of Lords:* Raised to the peerage as Baroness Bottomley of Nettlestone, of St Helens in the County of Isle of Wight 2005. *Councils and public bodies:* Magistrate, Inner London Juvenile Courts 1975-84; Chairman, Lambeth Juvenile Court 1980-84; Governor, London School of Economics 1985-; Chair, Millennium Commission 1995-97; Government Co-chair, Women's National Commission 1991-92; Vice-chair, British Council 1997-2001; Governor, University of the Arts, London 1999-2004; DL, Surrey 2006; Sheriff of Hull 2013-.

Political interests: Health, universities, prison reform, diversity, business enterprise, regulatory reform, children and family policy; China, India, Japan, Netherlands.

Other: Fellow, Industry and Parliament Trust 1987; Council member: Ditchley Foundation 1991-, Prince of Wales International Business Leaders Forum 2002-09; Lay Canon, Guildford Cathedral 2002-; President: Farnham Castle (Centre for International Briefing) 2003-, Abbeyfield Society 2004-09; International Chamber of Commerce, UK Advisory Council 2004-; Advisory Council, Cambridge Judge Business School 2004-09; Trustee, *The Economist* 2005-. Freeman, City of London 1988. Pro-chancellor, Surrey University 2005-; Chancellor, Hull University 2006-. Honorary LLD, Portsmouth University 1993; Honorary doctorate, Aston University. PC 1992; Athenæum.

Publications: Various articles on criminal justice, poverty, children and corporate governance.
Recreations: Grandchildren.
Rt Hon the Baroness Bottomley of Nettlestone DL, House of Lords, London SW1A 0PW
Tel: 020 7219 5060 *Email:* bottomleyv@parliament.uk

CONSERVATIVE

BOURNE OF ABERYSTWYTH, LORD

BOURNE OF ABERYSTWYTH (Life Baron), Nicholas Henry Bourne; cr 2013. Born 1 January 1952; Son of late John Morgan Bourne, systems engineer, and late Joan Mary Bourne, housewife. **Education:** King Edward VI School, Chelmsford; University College of Wales, Aberystwyth (LLB law 1973; LLM 1976); Trinity College, Cambridge (LLM 1975); Honourable Society of Gray's Inn (Barrister-at-Law 1976); French.

Non-political career: Supervisor in law, St Catharine's College, Cambridge 1974-82; Personal assistant to Kenneth Baker MP 1979; Principal, Chart University Tutors Ltd 1979-88; Company secretary, Chart Foulks Lynch plc 1984-88; Assistant to Peter Morrison MP 1987; Director of studies, Holborn Law Tutors Ltd 1988-91; Senior lecturer in law, South Bank University 1991-92; Dean, Swansea Law School 1992-96; Assistant principal, Swansea Institute 1996-98; Visiting lecturer, Hong Kong University 1996-. Former member, NATFHE.

Political career: *House of Commons:* Contested Chesterfield 1983 general election and 1984 by-election and Worcester 1997 general election. *House of Lords:* Raised to the peerage as Baron Bourne of Aberystwyth, of Aberystwyth in the County of Ceredigion and of Wethersfield in the County of Essex 2013. *Other:* Contested Brecon and Radnorshire constituency 1999 and 2003 National Assembly for Wales elections. AM for Mid and West Wales region 1999-2011: Leader, Conservative Group in the National Assembly 1999-2011, Welsh Conservative Spokesperson for: Finance 1999, 2001-02, 2006-07, Europe and Constituional Affairs 2007-09, Leader of the Official Opposition 2007-11, Shadow Minister for: Finance 2008-11, Heritage 2010. Contested Mid and West Wales region 2011 National Assembly for Wales election. *Councils and public bodies:* Member: North East Thames Regional Health Authority 1990-92, West Glamorgan Health Authority 1994-97, Doctor and Dentist Review Body 1998-99, Silk Commission 2011-13, Commission on Public Service Governance and Delivery 2013.

Political interests: Foreign affairs, economy, education, health, constitutional issues; France, Greece, India, Malaysia.

Other: Patron, Kidney Wales; Member, Institute of Directors; BHF; NSPCC; Society of Authors, United Oxford and Cambridge University.

Publications: Various company law and business law text books; Editor of a series of legal text books.

Recreations: Badminton, squash, tennis, walking, theatre, cinema.

Professor the Lord Bourne of Aberystwyth, House of Lords, London SW1A 0PW
Tel: 020 7219 5353

CONSERVATIVE

BOWNESS, LORD

BOWNESS (Life Baron), Peter Spencer Bowness; cr. 1996. Born 19 May 1943; Son of late Hubert Bowness and of Doreen Bowness; Married Marianne Hall 1969 (divorced 1983) (1 daughter); married Patricia Cook 1984 (1 stepson). **Education:** Whitgift School, Croydon; Law Society School of Law, College of Law.

Non-political career: Admitted Solicitor 1966; Partner, Weightman Sadler, Solicitors, Purley, Surrey 1970-2002; Notary Public 1977; Consultant, Streeter Marshall Solicitors, Warlingham/Purley/Croydon 2002-11.

Political career: *House of Lords:* Raised to the peerage as Baron Bowness, of Warlingham in the County of Surrey and of Croydon in the London Borough of Croydon 1996. Opposition Spokesperson for Local Government 1997-98; House of Lords representative to Convention to Draft an EU Charter of Fundamental Rights 1999-2000. Chair Draft Local Government (Organisation and Standards) Bill Joint Committee 1999; Member: EU Sub-committee C (Common Foreign and Security Policy) 2000-03, Chinook ZD567 2001-02, Joint Committee on Human Rights 2002-06, 2008-12, European Union 2003-07; Chair EU Sub-committee C (Foreign Affairs, Defence and Development Policy) 2003-06; EU Sub-committee E (Law and Institutions): Co-opted Member 2006-09, Co-opted Chair 2009-10; Member European Union 2009-; Chair EU Sub-committee E: (Justice and Institutions) 2010-12, (Justice, Institutions and Consumer Protection) 2012-13; Member EU Sub-committee D (Agriculture, Fisheries, Environment and Energy) 2013-. *Councils and public bodies:* London Borough of Croydon Council: Councillor 1968-98, Leader 1976-94, Mayor

1979-80; Deputy chair, Association of Metropolitan Authorities 1978-80; Chair, London Boroughs Association 1978-94; DL, Greater London 1981-; Member: Audit Commission 1983-95, London Residuary Body 1985-93, National Training Task Force 1989-92.

Political interests: Local government, London; Europe (particularly Balkans and Baltics), Caucasus.

Other: Member, UK Delegation to: Congress of Regional and Local Authorities of Europe (Council of Europe) 1990-98, Committee of the Regions of the EU 1994-98; Member: Inter-Parliamentary Union, UK Delegation, Organisation for Security and Co-operation in Europe Parliamentary Assembly 2007-. Freeman, City of London 1984; Honorary Freeman, London Borough of Croydon 2002. CBE 1981; Kt 1987.

Recreations: Travel, gardening.

The Lord Bowness CBE DL, House of Lords, London SW1A 0PW
Tel: 020 7219 2575 *Email:* bownessp@parliament.uk

CROSSBENCH

BOYCE, LORD

BOYCE (Life Baron), Michael Cecil Boyce; cr. 2003. Born 2 April 1943; Son of late Commander Hugh Boyce DSC RN and late Madeleine Boyce, née Manley; Married Harriette Fletcher 1971 (separated 1994, divorced 2005) (1 son 1 daughter); married Fleur Rutherford, née Smith 2006.

Education: Hurstpierpoint College; Britannia Royal Naval College, Dartmouth.

Non-political career: Royal Navy 1961-2003: Served HM Submarines Anchorite, Valiant and Conqueror 1965-72; Commanded HM Submarines: Oberon 1973-74, Opossum 1974-75, Superb 1979-81, HMS Brilliant 1983-84; Captain Submarine Sea Training 1984-86; Royal College of Defence Studies 1988; Senior Naval Officer, Middle East 1989; Director, Naval Staff Duties 1989-91; Flag Officer Sea Training 1991-92, Surface Flotilla 1992-95; Commander Anti-Submarine Warfare Striking Force 1992-94; Second Sea Lord and Commander-in-Chief Naval Home Command 1995-97; Commander-in-Chief Fleet and Eastern Atlantic Area and Commander Naval Forces North Western Europe 1977-98; First Sea Lord and Chief of Naval Staff 1988-2001; Chief of the Defence Staff 2001-03; Colonel Commandant Special Boat Service 2003-. Non-executive director: WS Atkins plc 2004-13, VT Group plc 2004-10; Honorary Master of the Bench, Middle Temple 2012-.

Political career: *House of Lords:* Raised to the peerage as Baron Boyce, of Pimlico in the City of Westminster 2003. European Union Sub-committee C (Foreign Affairs, Defence and Development Policy): Member 2005-06, Co-opted member 2006-08. *Councils and public bodies:* DL, Greater London.

Other: Officers Association: President 2003-11, Senior President 2009-11; President, St John Ambulance (London District) 2003-11; Patron: Sail 4 Cancer 2003-, Submarine Association 2003-, Trafalgar Woods 2004-; UK Defence Forum; Vice-Patron, Tall Ships Youth Trust; President, Royal Navy Submarine Museum 2005-; Vice-President, Forces Pension Society 2006-; Elder Brother, Trinity House 2007-; Chair, Council White Ensign Association 2007-10; Chair and trustee, RNLI 2008-13; Chair, HMS Victory Preservation Company 2012-; Honorary Bencher, Middle Temple 2012-. Draper's Company: Master Warden 2013-. Freeman, City of London. Honorary doctorates: Portsmouth University 2005, Canterbury Christ Church University 2011-. OBE 1982; KCB 1995; GCB 1999; KStJ 2002; Commander, Legion of Merit (USA) 2003; Lord Warden and Admiral of the Cinque Ports and Constable of Dover Castle 2004-; King of Arms Order of the Bath 2009-; KG 2011; Naval and Military; Garrick. RNSA; RYA; Jester; West Withering Windsurfing Club; Queen's.

Recreations: Tennis, real tennis, squash, windsurfing, opera.

Admiral the Lord Boyce KG GCB OBE DL, House of Lords, London SW1A 0PW
Tel: 020 7219 8714

NON-AFFILIATED

BOYD OF DUNCANSBY, LORD

BOYD OF DUNCANSBY (Life Baron), Colin David Boyd; cr 2006. Born 7 June 1953; Son of Dr David Boyd and Bette Boyd, née Mutch; Married Fiona McLeod 1979 (2 sons 1 daughter).

Education: Wick High School; George Watson's College, Edinburgh; Manchester University (BA Econ 1974); Edinburgh University (LLB 1976).

Non-political career: Solicitor 1978-82; Advocate, Scotland 1983-2007; Legal associate, Royal Town Planning Institute 1990; Advocate depute 1993-95; QC (Scotland) 1995; Scottish Executive: Solicitor General for Scotland 1997-2000, Lord Advocate for Scotland 2000-06; Commissioner, Northern Lighthouse Board 1997-2006; Consultant and head of public law, Dundas & Wilson CS LLP 2007-; Honorary Professor of Law, Glasgow University; Senator of the College of Justice in Scotland 2012-.

Political career: *House of Lords:* Raised to the peerage as Baron Boyd of Duncansby, of Duncansby in Caithness 2006. As a senior member of the judiciary, disqualified from participation 2012-. Member: Delegated Powers and Regulatory Reform 2007-10, EU Sub-committee E (Justice and Institutions) 2010-12. *Councils and public bodies:* Member, Commission on Scottish Devolution 2008-09.

Political interests: Constitutional affairs, criminal justice, planning and built environment.

Other: Fellow: Legal Associate Royal Town Planning Institute; Writer to the Signet; Royal Society of Arts. PC 2000.

Recreations: Watching rugby, reading, walking.

Rt Hon the Lord Boyd of Duncansby QC, House of Lords, London SW1A 0PW
Tel: 020 7219 5353

BRABAZON OF TARA, LORD

BRABAZON OF TARA (3rd Baron, UK), Ivon Anthony Moore-Brabazon; cr. 1942. Born 20 December 1947; Son of 2nd Baron, CBE; Married Harriet Frances de Courcy Hamilton 1979 (1 son 1 daughter).

Education: Harrow School.

Non-political career: Member, Stock Exchange 1972-84.

Political career: *House of Lords:* First entered House of Lords 1977; Government Whip 1984-86; Government Spokesperson for: Transport 1984-85, Trade and Industry, Treasury and Energy 1985-86; Parliamentary Under-Secretary of State, Department of Transport 1986-89; Minister of State: Foreign and Commonwealth Office 1989-90, Department of Transport 1990-92; Opposition Spokesperson for Transport 1998-2000; Elected hereditary peer 1999-; Principal Deputy Chairman of Committees 2001-02; Chairman of Committees 2002-12; Deputy Speaker 2002-12. House of Lords' Offices/House: Member 2001-03, 2006-12, Chair 2003-06, Procedure: Member 2001-03, 2010-11, Chair 2003-10, 2011-12; Chair: European Union 2001-02, Hybrid Instruments 2003-12, Liaison 2003-12, Personal Bills 2003-09, Privileges/Privileges and Conduct 2003-12, Selection 2003-12, Standing Orders (Private Bills) 2003-12, Administration and Works 2003-10, 2011-12, Refreshment 2008-12, Sub-committee on Leave of Absence 2011-12, Joint Committee on Parliamentary Privilege 2013, Hybrid Instruments 2013-. *Councils and public bodies:* DL, Isle of Wight 1993-.

Political interests: Transport; Switzerland.

Other: President, United Kingdom Warehousing Association 1992-; Deputy chair, Foundation for Sport and the Arts 1992-2012; Shipwrecked Mariners' Society: Council member 1993-2011, Vice-President 2011-; President, Natural Gas Vehicles Association 1995-97; Institute of the Motor Industry: Deputy President 1997-98, Fellow 1997-, President 1998-2004, Vice-President 2008-; President, British International Freight Association 1997-98; Shipwrecked Mariners' Society. PC 2013; Royal Yacht Squadron (Cowes).

Recreations: Sailing, golf.

Rt Hon the Lord Brabazon of Tara DL, House of Lords, London SW1A 0PW
Tel: 020 7219 6796 *Email:* brabazoni@parliament.uk

BRADLEY, LORD

BRADLEY (Life Baron), Keith John Charles Bradley; cr 2006. Born 17 May 1950; Son of late John Bradley and late Mrs Beatrice Harris; Married Rhona Graham 1987 (2 sons 1 daughter).

Education: Bishop Vesey's Grammar School, Sutton Coldfield; Manchester Polytechnic (BA social science 1976); York University (MPhil social policy 1978).

Non-political career: Charles Impey and Co, chartered accountants 1969-73; Research officer, Manchester City Council Housing Department 1978-81; Secretary, Stockport Community Health Council 1981-87; Manchester University: Special adviser to president and vice-chancellor 2005-10, Associate vice-president 2010-. Member, Unite.

Political career: *House of Commons:* MP (Labour) for Manchester Withington 1987-2005. Opposition Spokesperson for: Social Security 1991-96, Transport 1996-97; Parliamentary Under-Secretary of State, Department of Social Security 1997-98; Deputy Chief Whip 1998-2001; Minister of State, Home Office 2001-02. *House of Lords:* Raised to the peerage as Baron Bradley, of Withington in the County of Greater Manchester 2006. Member House 2007-10. *Other:* Member: Co-operative Party, Labour Party. *Councils and public bodies:* Manchester City Council: Councillor 1983-88, Chair, Environment and Consumer Services Committee 1984-88; City Council Director: Manchester Ship Canal Co 1984-87, Manchester Airport plc 1984-87; Non-executive chair, Manchester, Salford and Trafford Lift Company 2007-; Council member, Medical Protection Society 2007-; Non-executive chair, Christie Hospital NHS Foundation Trust 2011-.

Political interests: Local and regional government, housing, health, pensions, poverty, sport; China, France, USA.
Other: Trustee: Centre for Mental Health 2011-, Prison Reform Trust 2011-; Chair, Christie Hospital Charitable Funds Committee. PC 2001.
Publications: The Bradley Report [a review of people with mental health problems or learning disabilities in the criminal justice system] (Department of Health, 2009).
Recreations: All sports, theatre, cinema.
Rt Hon the Lord Bradley, House of Lords, London SW1A 0PW
Tel: 020 7219 4207 *Email:* bradleykj@parliament.uk
Tel: 0161-275 3963 *Fax:* 0161-275 8863 *Email:* keith.bradley@manchester.ac.uk
Twitter: @LordBradley

BRADSHAW, LORD

BRADSHAW (Life Baron), William Peter Bradshaw; cr. 1999. Born 9 September 1936; Son of late Leonard Bradshaw and Ivy Bradshaw; Married Jill Hayward 1957 (died 2002) (1 son 1 daughter); married Diana Ayris 2003.
Education: Slough Grammar School; Reading University (BA political economy 1957, MA 1960); Little French.
Non-political career: National Service 1957-59. British Railways/Rail 1959-85: Management trainee, Western Region 1959-62, Various appointments, London and West of England Division 1962-73, Divisional manager, Liverpool 1973-75, Chief operating manager, London Midland

LIBERAL DEMOCRAT (LM) Region, Crewe 1976, Deputy general manager, LM Region 1977, Chief operations manager, BR Headquarters 1978-80, Director, Policy Unit 1980-83, General manager, Western Region 1983-85, Professor of transport management, Salford University 1986-92; Chair, Ulsterbus and Citybus Ltd Belfast 1987-93; Special adviser to Transport Select Committee 1992-97. Transport Salaried Staffs Association 1961-77.
Political career: *House of Commons:* Co-chair, Liberal Democrat Transport Group. *House of Lords:* Raised to the peerage as Baron Bradshaw, of Wallingford in the County of Oxfordshire 1999. Liberal Democrat Spokesperson for Transport 2001-10. Co-opted member EU Sub-committee B (Internal Market) 2007-10; Member EU Sub-committee B (Internal Market, Energy and Transport) 2010-12. Chair, Liberal Democrat Parliamentary Party Committee on Transport 2010-. *Councils and public bodies:* Councillor, Oxfordshire County Council 1993-2008, Thames Valley Police Authority: Member 1993-95, 1997-2008, Vice-chair 1999-2003; Member: Commission for Integrated Transport -2001, British Railways Board (Shadow Strategic Rail Authority) 1999-2001.
Political interests: Transport, environment, planning, police.
Other: President, Friends of the Ridgeway; National Trust; Salvation Army. Honorary Fellow, Wolfson College, Oxford; National Liberal Club.
Publications: Many chapters and articles on transport issues.
Recreations: Growing hardy perennial plants.
Professor the Lord Bradshaw, House of Lords, London SW1A 0PW
Tel: 020 7219 8621 *Email:* bradshaww@parliament.uk
Tel: 01491 839142 *Fax:* 01491 839142 *Email:* billbradshaw@btinternet.com

BRAGG, LORD

BRAGG (Life Baron), Melvyn Bragg; cr. 1998. Born 6 October 1939; Son of Stanley and Mary Bragg; Married Marie-Elisabeth Roche 1961 (died 1971) (1 daughter); married Catherine Haste 1973 (1 son 1 daughter).
Education: Nelson-Thomlinson Grammar School, Wigton; Wadham College, Oxford (BA modern history 1961, MA); French.
Non-political career: BBC radio and TV producer 1961-67; Novelist 1964-; Writer and broadcaster 1967-; Presenter, BBC TV series: Melvyn Bragg on Class and Culture, BBC 2012, *2nd*

LABOUR *House* 1973-77, *Read All About It* 1975-77; The Mystery of Mary Magdalene 2013, The Most Dangerous Man in Tudor England 2013; Presenter and editor: *The South Bank Show*, ITV 1978-2010, *The South Bank Show*, Sky Arts 2012-, *Start the Week*, Radio 4 1988-98; London Weekend Television: Controller of Arts 1990-, Head of Arts 1982-90; Border Television: Chair 1990-95, Deputy Chair 1985-90; Governor, London School of Economics 1997; Radio 4: *In Our Time* 1998-, *Rates of English* 1999-2001, *The Value of Culture* 2013.
Political career: *House of Lords:* Raised to the peerage as Baron Bragg, of Wigton in the County of Cumbria 1998. Member Communications 2010-13. *Councils and public bodies:* DL, Cumbria 2003.
Political interests: Broadcasting, universities, the arts, countryside; France, USA.

Other: Chair, Literature Panel of Arts Council 1977-80; President: Cumbrians for Peace 1982-86, Northern Arts 1983-87, National Campaign for the Arts 1986-, MIND 2001-11; Chair, RNIB Talking Books Appeal 2000-05; Fellow: Royal Society of Literature, Royal Television Society; Honorary fellow: Royal Society, British Academy; BAFTA; MIND; RNIB; St. Mungo's. Chancellor, Leeds University 1999-. 12 honorary doctorates; Four honorary fellowships. Royal Television Society Gold Medal; John Llewllyn-Rhys Memorial Award for *Without a City Wall*; PEN Awards for Fiction for *The Hired Man*; Outstanding Contribution to Television, Richard Dimbleby award 1987; Best Musical (*The Hired Man*), Ivor Novello award 1985; Numerous prizes for *The South Bank Show* including four Prix Italias; Television and Radio Industries Club (TRIC) award: Radio Programme of the Year for *Start the Week* 1990, Radio Personality of the Year for *Start the Week* 1991; WHS Literary award for *The Soldier's Return*; Viewers and Listeners Broadcaster of the Year 2007-08; Bafta Fellowship 2010; Media Brief Award 2010; Outstanding Achievement South Bank Show Awards 2010; Garrick.

Publications: For Want of a Nail (1965); The Second Inheritance (1966); Without a City Wall (1968); The Hired Man (1969); A Place in England (1970); The Nerve (1971); Josh Lawton (1972); The Silken Net (1974); A Christmas Child (1976); Speak for England (1976); Mardi Gras (musical 1976); Orion (TV play 1977); Autumn Manoeuvres (1978); Kingdom Come (1980); Love and Glory (1983); Land of the Lakes (1983); Laurence Olivier (1984); The Hired Man (musical 1984); The Maid of Buttermere (1987); Rich: The Life of Richard Burton (1988); A Time to Dance (1990); Crystal Rooms (1992); King Lear in New York (play 1992); The Seventh Seal: a study of Ingmar Bergman (1993); Credo (1996); On Giants' Shoulders (1998); The Soldier's Return (1999); A Son of War (2001); Crossing the Lines (2003); The Adventure of English (2003); 12 Books that Changed the World; Remember Me (2008); In Our Time (2009); Final Cut: The South Bank Show (2010); The Book of Books: The Radical Impact of the King James Bible 1611-2011 (Hodder & Stoughton, 2011); Screenplays: Isadora, Jesus Christ Superstar, Clouds of Glory, Grace and Mary.

Recreations: Walking, books.

The Lord Bragg, House of Lords, London SW1A 0PW
Tel: 020 7219 8741
12 Hampstead Hill Gardens, London NW3 2PL *Tel:* 020 3475 5571 *Fax:* 020 3475 5572 *Email:* melvyn.bragg@dcptv.co.uk

BRENNAN, LORD

BRENNAN (Life Baron), Daniel Joseph Brennan; cr. 2000. Born 19 March 1942; Son of late Daniel and Mary Brennan; Married Pilar Sanchez 1968 (4 sons).

Education: St Bede's Grammar School, Bradford; Manchester University (LLB 1964).

Non-political career: Called to the Bar, Gray's Inn 1967 (Bencher 1993); Crown Court Recorder 1982-; QC 1985; Member, Criminal Injuries Compensation Board 1989-97; Deputy High Court Judge 1994-; Chair, General Council of the Bar 1999; Independent assessor to Home Office on Miscarriages of Justice 2001-.

LABOUR

Political career: *House of Lords:* Raised to the peerage as Baron Brennan, of Bibury in the Country of Gloucestershire 2000.

Other: Councillor, International Bar Association; President: Catholic Union of Great Britain 2001-, Consortium for Street Children; FRSA. Two honorary doctorates. QC 1985; Cruz de Honor of the Order of St Raimond de Penafort (Spain) 2000; Garrick.

Publications: General editor, Bullen and Leake on Pleadings (2003).

The Lord Brennan QC, House of Lords, London SW1A 0PW
Tel: 020 7219 5353
Matrix Chambers, Griffin Building, Gray's Inn, London WC1R 5LN *Tel:* 020 7404 3447
Fax: 020 7404 3448 *Email:* danbrennan@matrixlaw.co.uk

BRIDGEMAN, VISCOUNT

BRIDGEMAN (3rd Viscount, UK), Robin John Orlando Bridgeman; cr. 1929. Born 5 December 1930; Son of late Brigadier Honorary Geoffrey Bridgeman, MC, FRCS, second son of 1st Viscount; Married Victoria Turton 1966 (3 sons 1 son deceased).

Education: Eton College.

Non-political career: 2nd Lieutenant, The Rifle Brigade 1950-51. Partner, Henderson Crosthwaite and Co., Stockbrokers 1973-86; Director: The Bridgeman Art Library Limited 1972-, Guinness Mahon and Co. Ltd 1988-90, Nestor-BNA plc 1988-2000.

CONSERVATIVE

Political career: *House of Lords:* First entered House of Lords 1982; Opposition Whip 1998-2010; Elected hereditary peer 1999-; Opposition Spokesperson for: Home Affairs 2001-10,

Northern Ireland 2001-07, 2009-10. Member: Information 2010-11, EU Sub-committees: G (Social Policies and Consumer Protection) 2011-12, F (Home Affairs, Health and Education) 2012-. *Councils and public bodies:* Reed's School: Chair of Governors 1994-2002, Joint life president 2002-.

Political interests: Health, social services, environment, home affairs, local government.

Other: Chairman, Friends of Lambeth Palace Library 1992-2008; Special Trustee, Hammersmith and Queen Charlotte's Hospital Authority 1992-2000; Trustee, Music at Winchester 1995-2006; Treasurer: Florence Nightingale Aid in Sickness Trust 1995-2006, New England Company 1996-2006; Chairman: Hospital of St John and St Elizabeth 1999-2007, CORESS 2006-12; Trustee, Parliament Choir 2011-; MCC. Sovereign Military Order of Malta, Knight, 1995; Beefsteak, Pitt.

Recreations: Gardening, music, shooting.

The Viscount Bridgeman, House of Lords, London SW1A 0PW
Tel: 020 7219 0663 *Fax:* 020 7219 0753 *Email:* bridgemanr@parliament.uk
19 Chepstow Road, London W2 5BP *Tel:* 020 7727 5400 *Fax:* 020 7792 9178

BRIDGES, LORD

BRIDGES (2nd Baron, UK), Thomas Edward Bridges; cr. 1957. Born 27 November 1927; Son of 1st Baron, KG, PC, GCB, GCVO, MC, and late Honorary Katharine Dianthe Farrer, daughter of 2nd Baron Farrer; Married Rachel Bunbury 1953 (died 2005) (2 sons 1 daughter).

Education: Eton College; New College, Oxford (MA modern history 1951).

Non-political career: National service commission in Royal Signals 1946-48. HM Foreign/Diplomatic Service 1951-87: Served in Bonn, Berlin, Rio de Janeiro, Athens and Moscow; Private Secretary (Overseas Affairs) to Rt Hon Edward Heath as Prime Minister 1972-74; Royal College of Defence Studies 1975; Minister (Commercial), Washington DC Embassy 1976-79; Deputy Secretary, Foreign and Commonwealth Office 1979-82; Ambassador to Italy 1983-87; Non-executive director, Consolidated Gold Fields plc 1988-90; Independent Board Member, Securities and Futures Authority Ltd 1989-97; Director, British Rail (Anglia) 1989-92.

CROSSBENCH

Political career: *House of Lords:* First entered House of Lords 1969; Elected hereditary peer 1999-; On leave of absence March 2011-. *Councils and public bodies:* Vice-president, Council for National Parks 2000-.

Countries of interest: Germany, Italy.

Other: Chair, UK National Committee for UNICEF 1989-97; British-Italian Society: Chair 1991-97, Honorary vice-president 1998-; President, Dolmetsch Foundation (promotion early music); Member, Hon Committee, William Walton Trust 2000-; FRSA; National Trust, Unicef. GCMG 1988; Athenæum.

The Lord Bridges GCMG, House of Lords, London SW1A 0PW
Tel: 020 7219 5353
The Old Rectory, Berwick St John, Shaftesbury, Dorset SP7 0EY *Tel:* 020 3375 7261

BRIGGS, LORD

BRIGGS (Life Baron), Asa Briggs; cr. 1976. Born 7 May 1921; Son of late William Walker Briggs; Married Susan Banwell 1955 (2 sons 2 daughters).

Education: Keighley Grammar School; Sidney Sussex College, Cambridge (BA history 1941); London School of Economics (BSc Econ 1941, (external, in parallel)).

Non-political career: Cryptographer, Bletchley Park 1943-45; Professor of modern history, Leeds University 1955-61; Professor of history, Sussex University 1961-76; Provost, Worcester College, Oxford 1976-91.

CROSSBENCH

Political career: *House of Lords:* Raised to the peerage as Baron Briggs, of Lewes in the County of East Sussex 1976. On leave of absence June 2012-. *Councils and public bodies:* Chairman: Committee on Nursing 1970-72, Advisory board, Redundant Churches 1983-88, Commonwealth of Learning Board 1988-93.

Political interests: Education, social policy; France, Portugal, USA.

Other: Vice-chair of Council, United Nations University 1974-80; Chair: European Institute of Education and Social Policy, Paris 1976-84, Eurydice Consultative Committee 1996-2002; Trustee, Glyndebourne Arts Trust 1966-91; Member, Civic Trust 1976-86; Chair, Trustees of the Royal Pavilion, Brighton 1981-2007; Honorary President: Social History Society, Victorian Society, Ephemera Society; Fellow: British Academy, American Academy of Arts and Sciences. Member, Spectacle Makers Company. Vice-chancellor, Sussex University 1967-76; Chancellor, Open

University 1979-94. Marconi Medal for Services to the study of Broadcasting 1975; French Academy Medal for Architecture 1982; Wolfson History Prize 2000; Norton Medlicott Medal – Lifetime Award for History, The Historical Assocation 2010; Pepys Medal for Ephemera Studies 2011; Outstanding Achievement Award for Services to Archives; Gold Medal, Sussex University 2012.

Publications: Various historical works including six volumes on history of British broadcasting; Michael Young, Social Entrepreneur (2001); A History of Longmans and Their Books, 1724-1990 (2008); Secret Days: Code Breaking at Bletchley Park (2011); Special Relationships: People and Places (Frontline Books, 2012).

Recreations: Memories of travels past.

The Lord Briggs, House of Lords, London SW1A 0PW
Tel: 020 7219 5353 *Email:* lady.briggs@googlemail.com

BRINTON, BARONESS

BRINTON (Life Baroness), Sarah (Sal) Virginia Brinton; cr 2011. Born 1 April 1955; Daughter of late Tim Brinton, MP 1979-87, and Jane-Mari Shearing, née Coningham; Married Tim Whittaker 1983 (2 sons 1 daughter 2 wards – 1 boy 1 girl).

Education: Benenden, Cranbrook; Central School of Speech and Drama (1973); London College of Secretaries (1974); Churchill College, Cambridge (BA 1984, MA); Conversational French.

Non-political career: Floor manager, BBC radio and television 1974-81; Venture capitalist 1984-90; Bursar: Lucy Cavendish College, Cambridge 1992-97, Selwyn College, Cambridge 1997-2002; Consultant, IDeA 2003-06; Director, Association of Universities in the East of England 2006-11.

LIBERAL DEMOCRAT

Political career: *House of Commons:* Contested Cambridgeshire South East 1997 and 2001 and Watford 2005 and 2010 general elections. *House of Lords:* Raised to the peerage as Baroness Brinton, of Kenardington in the County of Kent 2011. *Other:* Liberal Democrats, Education and Higher Education Working Group 1993-97; Federal Conference Committee: Member 2004-08, 2010-, Vice-chair 2010-; Federal Policy Committee: Member 2004-08, 2010-, Vice-chair 2006-08; Schools Working Group 2008-; Member, Manifesto Working Group 2013-. *Councils and public bodies:* Cambridgeshire County Council 1993-2004: Councillor 1993-2004, Education portfolio holder 1993-97, Leader, Liberal Democrat group 1997-2004; East of England Development Agency: Board Member 1999-2004, Deputy Chair 2002-04; Chair, Cambridgeshire Learning and Skills Council 2000-06.

Political interests: Education, economic development; France, Palestine.

Other: St Johns Innovation Centre, Cambridge 1992-2010; Director and trustee, Christian Blind Mission 2003-; Director: UFI Charitable Trust 2003-, East of England International 2006-11; Member: Institute of Directors RSA. Honorary Doctorate Anglia Ruskin University (for services to education and skills) 2003. East Anglian Entrepreneurial Businesswoman of the Year 1997.

Recreations: Theatre, football, cooking and swimming.

The Baroness Brinton, House of Lords, London SW1A 0PW
Tel: 020 7219 3234 *Email:* brintons@parliament.uk *Twitter:* @SalBrinton

BRISTOL, LORD BISHOP OF

BRISTOL (55th Bishop of), Michael Arthur Hill. Born 17 April 1949; Married Anthea Longridge (1 son 4 daughters).

Education: North Cheshire College of Further Education (Diploma business studies); Brasted Place Theological College, Westerham, Kent; Ridley Hall, Cambridge (General Ordination Examination); Fitzwilliam College, Cambridge (Postgraduate Certificate theology).

Non-political career: Printing industry 1968-72; Member, Scargill House Community (Christian community and conference centre) 1972-73; Ordained deacon 1997, priest 1978; Curate: St Mary

NON-AFFILIATED

Magdalene, Addiscombe, Surrey 1977-80, St Paul, Slough, Buckinghamshire 1980-83; St Leonard, Chesham Bois, Buckinghamshire: Priest-in-charge 1983-90, Rector 1990-92; Rural dean, Amersham, Buckinghamshire 1990-92; Archdeacon of Berkshire 1992-98; Area bishop of Buckingham 1998-2003; Bishop of Bristol 2003-.

Political career: *House of Lords:* Entered House of Lords 2009.

Rt Rev the Lord Bishop of Bristol, House of Lords, London SW1A 0PW
Tel: 020 7219 5353
The Bishop of Bristol's Office, 58a High Street, Winterbourne, Bristol BS36 1JQ
Tel: 01454 777728 *Email:* bishop@bristoldiocese.org *Twitter:* @bishopmikehill

BRITTAN OF SPENNITHORNE, LORD

CONSERVATIVE

BRITTAN OF SPENNITHORNE (Life Baron), Leon Brittan; cr. 2000. Born 25 September 1939; Son of late Dr Joseph Brittan and Rebecca Brittan; Married Diana Peterson 1980 (2 stepdaughters).

Education: Haberdashers' Aske's School; Trinity College, Cambridge (BA English and law 1961, MA) (President of Cambridge Union 1960); Yale University, USA (Henry Fellow 1961-62); French, German.

Non-political career: Called to the Bar, Inner Temple 1962; QC 1978; Bencher 1983; European Commission 1989-99: Vice-President: Competition 1989-93, External Affairs 1995-99, Commissioner for External Economic Affairs and Trade Policy 1993-95; Vice-chairman, UBS Warburg/ UBS Investment Bank 2000-10, 2011-; Consultant, Herbert Smith 2000-06; Unilever: Advisory director 2000-04, Non-executive director 2004-10; Distinguished visiting scholar, Yale University 2000-03; Adviser, Teijin Advisory Board 2009-; Member, International Advisory Board, Total SA.

Political career: *House of Commons:* Contested North Kensington 1966 and 1970 general elections. MP (Conservative) for Cleveland and Whitby February 1974-83, for Richmond, North Yorkshire 1983-88. Minister of State, Home Office 1979-81; Chief Secretary to the Treasury 1981-83; Home Secretary 1983-85; Secretary of State for Trade and Industry 1985-86. *House of Lords:* Raised to the peerage as Baron Brittan of Spennithorne, of Spennithorne in the County of North Yorkshire 2000. Government trade adviser 2010-11. *Other:* Chair: Cambridge University Conservative Association 1960, Society of Conservative Lawyers 1986-88, Conservative Group for Europe 2000-03; President: Conservative Group for Europe 2004-07, Richmond Conservative Association 2011-. *Councils and public bodies:* DL.

Political interests: European affairs, economic affairs, home affairs, legal and constitutional issues; Far East (especially China), Israel, USA.

Other: Bow Group: Chairman 1964-65, Editor, *Crossbow* 1966-68. Chancellor, Teesside University 1993-2005. Seven honorary doctorates from England and Korea. QC 1978; PC 1981; Kt 1989; White's, Pratt's. MCC.

Publications: Defence and Arms Control in a Changing Era (1988); European Competition Policy (1992); The Europe We Need (1994); A Diet of Brussels (2000).

Recreations: Opera, art, cricket, walking.

Rt Hon the Lord Brittan of Spennithorne QC DL, House of Lords, London SW1A 0PW
Tel: 020 7219 5353
UBS Investment Bank, 1 Finsbury Avenue, London EC2M 2PP *Tel:* 020 7568 6305 *Fax:* 020 7568 6520 *Email:* leon.brittan@ubs.com

BROERS, LORD

CROSSBENCH

BROERS (Life Baron), Alec Nigel Broers; cr. 2004. Born 17 September 1938; Son of late Alec Broers and Constance Broers, née Cox; Married Marie Phelan 1964 (2 sons).

Education: Geelong Church of England Grammar School, Australia; Melbourne University, Australia (BSc physics 1959, electronics 1960); Gonville and Caius College, Cambridge (BA mechanical sciences 1962; PhD electrical engineering 1965; ScD 1991).

Non-political career: IBM 1965-84: Research staff, TJ Watson Research Center 1965-81, Manager: Photon and electron optics 1977-81, Advanced development East Fishkill Laboratory 1982-84, Member, corporate technical committee, corporate headquarters 1984; Cambridge University: Professor of electrical engineering 1984-96, Professor emeritus 1996-, Fellow, Trinity College 1985-90, Churchill College: Fellow 1990-, Master 1990-96, Vice-chancellor 1996-2003.

Political career: *House of Lords:* Raised to the peerage as Baron Broers, of Cambridge in the County of Cambridgeshire 2004. Chair Science and Technology 2004-07; Member Science and Technology Sub-committees: II (Energy Efficiency) 2004-08, I (Scientific Aspects of Ageing) 2005-07; [Co-opted] member Science and Technology Sub-committee II (Genomic Medicine) 2008-09; Member Science and Technology 2009-13; Chair Science and Technology Sub-committee I (Radioactive Waste Management: a further update) 2010; Member Science and Technology Sub-committee I 2012-13. *Councils and public bodies:* President, Royal Academy of Engineering 2001-06; Member: Board of Trustees, American University of Shaijah, Singapore, One-North Resource Advisory Board, AIST (Japanese Instutite of Advanced Industrial Science and technology); Chair, Board of Diamond Light Source.

Political interests: Energy, industry, education; Australia, USA.

Other: Trustee: British Museum, Needham Research Institute; Foreign associate, US National Academy of Engineering; Foreign member: Chinese Academy of Engineering, American Philosophical Society; Honorary Fellow, Australian Academy of Technological Sciences and Engineering; FIEE 1984; FREng 1985; FRS 1986; FIME; FIinstP; FMedSci 2004. Numerous honorary doctorates and fellowships. American Institute of Physics Prize for Industrial Applications of Physics 1981; IEEE Cledo Brunetti Award 1985; Prince Philip Medal of Royal Academy of Engineering 2001. Kt 1998; Athenæum.

Publications: Numerous papers and book chapters on electron microscopy, micro-electronics and nanotechnology; Reith Lectures – Triumph of Technology (Cambridge University Press, 2005).

Recreations: Sailing, skiing, listening to music.

Professor the Lord Broers, House of Lords, London SW1A 0PW
Tel: 020 7219 5353 *Email:* anb1000@cam.ac.uk

LABOUR

BROOKE OF ALVERTHORPE, LORD

BROOKE OF ALVERTHORPE (Life Baron), Clive Brooke; cr. 1997. Born 21 June 1942; Son of John and Mary Brooke; Married Lorna Roberts 1967.

Education: Thornes House School, Wakefield.

Non-political career: Inland Revenue Staff Federation: Assistant Secretary 1964-82, Deputy General Secretary 1982-88, General Secretary 1988-95; Joint General Secretary, Public Services Tax and Commerce Union 1996-98; Member, TUC: General Council 1989-96, Executive Committee 1993-96; Senior strategic adviser, Accenture plc 1997-2010; Self-employed consultant 1997-2010. Member, Public and Commercial Services Union.

Political career: *House of Lords:* Raised to the peerage as Baron Brooke of Alverthorpe, of Alverthorpe in the County of West Yorkshire 1997. Chair European Communities Sub-committee B (Energy, Industry and Transport) 1999-2002; Member Information 2005-09; EU Sub-committee D (Environment and Agriculture): Member 2007, Co-opted member 2008-10; Member: Crossrail Bill 2008, EU Sub-committee B: (Internal Market, Energy and Transport) 2010-12, (Internal Market, Infrastructure and Employment) 2012-. Vice-chair, PLP Departmental Groups for: Cabinet Office 1998-2010, Home Affairs 2010, Transport 2010-. *Councils and public bodies:* Member: House of Commons Speaker's Commission on Citizenship 1988, Council of Churches for Britain and Ireland Enquiry into Unemployment and the Future of Work 1995-97, Pensions Compensation Board 1996-2005; Government Partner Director, NATS Limited 2001-06.

Political interests: Employment, transport, drug and alcohol issues; Sweden.

Other: Member: Inter-Parliamentary Union, Commonwealth Parliamentary Association; Trustee: Community Service Volunteers 1989-, Duke of Edinburgh's Study Conference 1993-; Institute for Public Policy Research: Trustee 1997-2010, Policy advisory council 2010-; Trustee, London Dorchester Committee Trust; Member, Fabian Society; Patron: European Association for the Treatment of Addiction (UK) 2001-, Sparrow Foundation 2002-; Trustee, Action on Addiction 2002-13; Patron: Federation of Drug and Alcohol Practitioners 2003-, Kenward Trust 2008-, Everyman Project 2010-; FRSA; Save The Children, Amnesty International, Cancer Research UK.

Recreations: Community services, politics, church affairs, sailing, painting in oil, walking my two Cairn Terriers.

The Lord Brooke of Alverthorpe, House of Lords, London SW1A 0PW
Tel: 020 7219 0478 *Fax:* 020 7219 5979 *Email:* brookec@parliament.uk

CONSERVATIVE

BROOKE OF SUTTON MANDEVILLE, LORD

BROOKE OF SUTTON MANDEVILLE (Life Baron), Peter Leonard Brooke; cr 2001. Born 3 March 1934; Son of late Baroness Brooke of Ystradfellte, DBE and late Lord Brooke of Cumnor PC CH; Married Joan Smith 1964 (died 1985) (3 sons and 1 son deceased); married Lindsay Allinson 1991.

Education: Marlborough College, Wiltshire; Balliol College, Oxford (BA mods and greats 1957, MA 1961); Harvard Business School (MBA 1959); Commonwealth (Harkness) Fund Fellow, Harvard; French.

Non-political career: Royal Engineers. Research associate, IMEDE, Lausanne 1960-61; Swiss correspondent, *Financial Times* 1960-61; Spencer Stuart Management Consultants 1961-79; Served in: New York 1969-71, Brussels 1971-72, Chair 1974-79.

Political career: *House of Commons:* MP (Conservative) for City of London and Westminster South 1977-97, and for Cities of London and Westminster 1997-2001. Government Whip 1979-83; Parliamentary Under-Secretary of State, Department of Education and Science 1983-85; HM Treasury: Minister of State 1985-87, Paymaster General 1987-89; Secretary of State for: Northern Ireland 1989-92, National Heritage 1992-94. Chair: Northern Ireland Affairs 1997-2001. *House of Lords:* Raised to the peerage as Baron Brooke of Sutton Mandeville, of Sutton Mandeville in the County of Wiltshire 2001. Member: Delegated Powers and Regulatory Reform 2003-07, Privileges/Privileges and Conduct 2005-, Procedure 2005-07, Selection 2005-07. *Other:* Chairman, Conservative Party 1987-89; Board member, Conservative Party 2004-06; Chairman, Association of Conservative Peers 2004-06. *Councils and public bodies:* Chair: Churches Conservation Trust 1995-98, Building Societies Ombudsman Council 1996-2001.

Political interests: Education, treasury, Northern Ireland, national heritage; USA, Commonwealth (especially St Helena, Sarawak).

Other: Member British-Irish Inter Parliamentary Body 1997-2007; Wordsworth Trust 1975-: Trustee 1975-2001, Fellow 2001-; President: British Antique Dealers Association 1995-2005, Conference on Training in Architechtural Conservation 1995-2013, British Art Market Federation 1996-; Fellow, Society of Antiquaries 1998; Founding Master, Guild of Arts Scholars, Collectors and Dealers (now the Company of Arts Scholars) 2006; Trustee: Marlburian Club 1977-2007, Cusichaca Trust 1978-98, MEMO 2009-; Multifarious, through two Trusts under CAF umbrella. Member, Drapers' Company. Freeman, City of London. Pro-chancellor, London University 2002-06. Senior Fellow, Royal College of Art 1987; Presentation Fellow, King's College, London 1989; Honorary Fellow: Queen Mary and Westfield College, London University 1996, University of Wales, Lampeter; Three honorary doctorates including the London University. PC 1988; CH 1992; Beefsteak, Brooks's, City Livery, MCC, Coningsby (lately President), St. Andrew's Youth Club (lately President). I Zingari.

Recreations: Churches, conservation, cricket, visual arts.

Rt Hon the Lord Brooke of Sutton Mandeville CH, House of Lords, London SW1A 0PW
Tel: 020 7219 2150 *Email:* brookep@parliament.uk

CROSSBENCH

BROOKEBOROUGH, VISCOUNT

BROOKEBOROUGH (3rd Viscount, UK), Alan Henry Brooke; cr. 1952; 7th Bt of Colebrooke (UK) 1822. Born 30 June 1952; Son of 2nd Viscount, PC; Married Janet Cooke 1980.

Education: Harrow School; Millfield School, Somerset; Royal Agricultural College, Cirencester 1978.

Non-political career: Commission, 17th/21st Lancers 1971; Ulster Defence Regiment 1977, Royal Irish Regiment 1992; Lieutenant-Colonel 1993; Honorary Colonel, 4th/5th Battalion, The Royal Irish Rangers 1997-2008. Non-executive director: Green Park Health Care Trust 1993-2001, Basel International (Jersey); Personal Lord in Waiting to HM The Queen 1997-; Board member, Northern Ireland Policing Board 2001-06.

Political career: *House of Lords:* First entered House of Lords 1987; Elected hereditary peer 1999-. Member: European Communities 1998-2002, Procedure 2003-05; Co-opted member EU Sub-committee D (Environment and Agriculture) 2006-10; Member EU Sub-committee A (Economic and Financial Affairs) 2012-. *Councils and public bodies:* Co. Fermanagh: DL 1987-2012, High Sheriff 1995, Lord-Lieutenant 2012-.

Political interests: Northern Ireland, agriculture, tourism, defence, health; Europe, UK.

Other: Vice-President, Somme Association 1990-; President, Army Benevolent Fund, Northern Ireland 1995-; Fellow, Industry and Parliament Trust 1999; Member, Duke of Edinburgh Award Advisory Council, Northern Ireland; President, Northern Ireland Outward Bound Association; Military, cancer and disabled; Cavalry and Guards, Pratt's, Farmers'.

Recreations: Shooting, fishing, gardening, sailing.

The Viscount Brookeborough, House of Lords, London SW1A 0PW
Tel: 020 7219 1668
Colebrooke Park, Brookeborough, Enniskillen, Co. Fermanagh BT94 4DW *Tel:* 028 8953 1402
Fax: 028 8953 1312 *Email:* ahb@colebrooke.info *Website:* www.colebrooke.info

LABOUR

BROOKMAN, LORD

BROOKMAN (Life Baron), David Keith Brookman; cr. 1998. Born 3 January 1937; Son of George Brookman MM and Blodwin Brookman; Married Patricia Worthington 1958 (3 daughters).

Education: Nantyglo Grammar School, Gwent.

Non-political career: RAF national service 1955-57. Steel worker, Richard Thomas and Baldwin, Ebbw Vale 1953-55, 1957-73; Iron and Steel Trades Confederation: Divisional organiser 1973-85, Assistant General Secretary 1985-93, General Secretary 1993-99; Board Member, British Steel (Industry)/UK Steel Enterprise 1993-. Member: Trades Union Congress Educational Advisory Committee for Wales 1976-82, Trades Union Congress 1992-99; National TU Steel Co-ordinating Committee: Member 1991-99, Chair 1993-99.

Political career: *House of Lords:* Raised to the peerage as Baron Brookman, of Ebbw Vale in the County of Gwent 1998. *Other:* Member, Labour Party: Executive Committee, Wales 1982-85, National Constitutional Committee 1987-91, NEC 1991-92. *Councils and public bodies:* Governor, Gwent College of Higher Education 1980-84; Member: Joint Industrial Council for Slag Industry 1985-93, British Steel: Joint Accident Prevention Advisory Committee 1985-93, Advisory Committee on Education and Training 1986-93, Joint Secretary British Steel: Strip Trade Board 1993-98, Joint Standing Committee 1993-98, European Works Council 1996-99.

Political interests: Employment law, manufacturing, sport.

Other: Executive Council, European Metalworkers Federation 1985-95; International Metalworkers' Federation: Honorary Secretary (British Section) 1993-99, President, Iron, Steel and Non-Ferrous Metals Department 1993-99; Member, European Coal and Steel Community Consultative Committee 1993-2002; World Cancer Research Fund, NSPCC, British Heart Foundation; Union Jack Club.

Recreations: Cricket, rugby, reading, keep-fit, golf.

The Lord Brookman, House of Lords, London SW1A 0PW
Tel: 020 7219 8633 *Fax:* 020 7219 5979

LABOUR

BROOKS OF TREMORFA, LORD

BROOKS OF TREMORFA (Life Baron), John Edward Brooks; cr. 1979. Born 12 April 1927; Son of Edward George Brooks; Married 1948 (divorced 1956) (1 son 1 daughter); married Margaret Pringle 1958 (2 sons).

Education: Coleg Harlech.

Political career: *House of Commons:* Contested (Labour) Barry February and October 1974 general elections. *House of Lords:* Raised to the peerage as Baron Brooks of Tremorfa, of Tremorfa in the County of Glamorgan 1979. Opposition Spokesperson for Defence 1980-81. *Other:* Secretary, Cardiff South East Labour Party 1966-84; Parliamentary agent to James Callaghan MP 1970 and 1979 general elections; Chair, Labour Party, Wales 1978-79. *Councils and public bodies:* South Glamorgan County Council: Councillor 1973-93, Leader 1973-77, 1986-92, Chair 1981-82; Member, Cardiff Bay Development Corporation 1987-96; DL, South Glamorgan 1994-.

Other: British Boxing Board of Control: Steward 1986-, Chair 2000-04, President 2004-07; Chair: Welsh Sports Hall of Fame 1988-2010, Sportsmatch Wales 1992-94; Welsh Sports Hall of Fame. Honorary Fellowship, University of Wales Institute, Cardiff.

Recreations: Reading, most sports.

The Lord Brooks of Tremorfa DL, House of Lords, London SW1A 0PW
Tel: 020 7219 3191

CONSERVATIVE

BROUGHAM AND VAUX, LORD

BROUGHAM AND VAUX (5th Baron, UK), Michael John Brougham; cr. 1860. Born 2 August 1938; Son of 4th Baron; Married Olivia Gray 1963 (divorced 1967, she died 1986) (1 daughter); married Catherine Gulliver 1969 (divorced 1981) (1 son).

Education: Lycée Jaccard, Lausanne, Switzerland; Millfield School, Somerset; Northampton Institute of Agriculture.

Political career: *House of Lords:* First entered House of Lords 1967; Deputy Chair of Committees 1993-97, 1997-; Deputy Speaker 1995-; Elected hereditary peer 1999-. Member: Statutory Instruments Joint Committee 2001-07, Information 2003-07, Standing Orders (Private Bills) -2003, Refreshment 2007-12, Administration and Works 2009-. *Other:* Vice-chair Association of Conservative Peers 1998-2002, 2003-10.

Political interests: Road safety, transport, motor industry, aviation; France, Spain.

Other: Royal Society for the Prevention of Accidents: President 1986-89, Vice-President 1999-; Chair, The Tax Payers' Society 1989-91; Fellow, Industry and Parliament Trust 1990, 1993; Chair, European Secure Vehicle Alliance 1992-; President, National Health Safety Groups Council/ Safety Groups UK 1994-; Honorary Vice-President, Institute of Occupational Safety and Health 2008-. CBE 1995.

Recreations: Photography, bridge, shooting.

The Lord Brougham and Vaux CBE, House of Lords, London SW1A 0PW
Tel: 020 7219 5353 *Fax:* 020 7219 5979
11 Westminster Gardens, Marsham Street, London SW1P 4JA

BROWN OF EATON-UNDER-HEYWOOD, LORD

BROWN OF EATON-UNDER-HEYWOOD (Life Baron), Simon Denis Brown; cr. 2004. Born 9 April 1937; Son of late Denis Baer Brown and Edna Brown, née Abrahams; Married Jennifer Buddicom 1963 (2 sons 1 daughter).

Education: Stowe School, Buckinghamshire; Worcester College, Oxford (BA law 1960).

Non-political career: Army national service 1955-57. Barrister 1961; Recorder 1979-84; First Junior Treasury Counsel, Common Law 1979-84; Judge of the High Court of Justice Queen's Bench Division 1984-92; President, Security Service Tribunal 1989-2000; Lord Justice of Appeal 1992-2004; President, Intelligence Services Tribunal 1995-2000, Intelligence Services Commissioner 2000-04; Vice-president, Court of Appeal Civil Division 2001-03; Lord of Appeal in Ordinary 2004-09; Justice of the Supreme Court of the United Kingdom 2009-12.

CROSSBENCH

Political career: *House of Lords:* Raised to the peerage as Baron Brown of Eaton-under-Heywood, of Eaton-under-Heywood in the County of Shropshire 2004. Lord of Appeal in Ordinary 2004-09; As Justice of the Supreme Court, disqualified from participation 2009-12. Member European Union 2005-07; Chair European Union Sub-committee E (Law and Institutions) 2005-07; Member Privileges and Conduct 2013-.

Political interests: The law and constitution.

Other: Butcher's Company. Honorary Fellow, Worcester College, Oxford 1993-; Visitor, Pembroke College, Cambridge 2010; High Steward, University, Oxford 2011-12; Visitor, St Hugh's College, Oxford 2011-. Kt 1984; PC 1992; Garrick, Denham Golf.

Recreations: Golf, reading, theatre.

Rt Hon the Lord Brown of Eaton-under-Heywood, House of Lords, London SW1A 0PW
Tel: 020 7219 8261 *Email:* sdbrown@blueyonder.co.uk

BROWNE OF BELMONT, LORD

BROWNE OF BELMONT (Life Baron), Wallace Hamilton Browne; cr 2006. Born 29 October 1947; Son of Gerald Browne and Phyllis Hamilton Browne; Married.

Education: Campbell College, Belfast; Queen's University, Belfast (BSc zoology 1970).

Non-political career: A-level biology teacher, Rainey Endowed School, Magherafelt 1970-2000. Member, NASUWT (retirement association).

Political career: *House of Lords:* Raised to the peerage as Baron Browne of Belmont, of Belmont in the County of Antrim 2006. *Other:* Northern Ireland Assembly: MLA for East Belfast 2007-11: Chair Committee on Procedures 2010-11. *Councils and public bodies:* Councillor Belfast City Council 1985-2011: Alderman 1993, Lord Mayor 2005-06; High Sheriff of Belfast 2002.

DEMOCRATIC UNIONIST PARTY

Political interests: Education, Northern Ireland affairs, Balkan affairs; Brazil, Canada, Croatia, France, Germany, Italy, Montenegro, Serbia.

Other: Trustee Somme Association, Northern Ireland.

Recreations: Golf, football, cricket, rugby.

The Lord Browne of Belmont, House of Lords, London SW1A 0PW
Tel: 020 7219 5353 *Fax:* 020 7219 2347 *Email:* brownew@parliament.uk

BROWNE OF LADYTON, LORD

BROWNE OF LADYTON (Life Baron), Desmond Henry Browne; cr 2010. Born 22 March 1952; Son of late Peter Browne, process worker, and of Maureen Browne, catering manageress; Married Maura Taylor 1983 (2 sons).

Education: Saint Michael's Academy, Kilwinning; Glasgow University (LLB 1973).

Non-political career: Qualified as solicitor 1976; Called to Scottish Bar 1993. Member, Unison.

Political career: *House of Commons:* Contested Argyll and Bute 1992 general election. MP for Kilmarnock and Loudoun 1997-2005, for Kilmarnock and Loudon (revised boundary) 2005-10. PPS to: Donald Dewar as Secretary of State for Scotland 1998-99, Adam Ingram as Minister of State, Northern Ireland Office 2000; Parliamentary Under-Secretary of State, Northern Ireland Office 2001-03; Minister of State: Department for Work and Pensions (Work) 2003-04, Home Office (Citizenship, Immigration and Nationality) 2004-05; Chief Secretary to the Treasury 2005-06; Secretary of State for: Defence 2006-08, Scotland 2007-08; Prime Minister's Special Envoy to Sri Lanka 2009-10. Member: Northern Ireland Affairs 1997-98, Public Administration 1999-2000, Joint Committee on Human Rights 2001-09, Joint Committee on National Security Strategy 2010.

LABOUR

House of Lords: Raised to the peerage as Baron Browne of Ladyton, of Ladyton in Ayrshire and Arran 2010. Opposition Spokesperson for Scotland 2011-12. Member Partnerships (Prosecution) (Scotland) Bill 2013-.

Political interests: Legal affairs, human rights, disability, education, Northern Ireland, constitution, international affairs; Afghanistan, Burundi, Colombia, Rwanda, South Africa.

Other: Member, Scottish Council For Civil Liberties 1976-; Council member, Law Society of Scotland 1988-92; Chair, Scottish Child Law Centre 1988-92; Fellow, Industry and Parliament Trust 2002. PC 2005.

Publications: Report for Lord MacAulay's Working Party on the Prison System (1990).

Recreations: Sports, football, tennis, swimming, reading, computing.

Rt Hon the Lord Browne of Ladyton, House of Lords, London SW1A 0PW
Tel: 020 7219 4501 *Email:* browned@parliament.uk

BROWNE OF MADINGLEY, LORD

CROSSBENCH

Lead Non-Executive Director, Cabinet Office Board

BROWNE OF MADINGLEY (Life Baron), Edmund John Phillip Browne; cr 2001. Born 20 February 1948; Single.

Education: King's School, Ely; St John's College, Cambridge (BA physics 1969, MA); Stanford University, USA (MS business 1980).

Non-political career: BP plc 1966-2007: Exploration and production posts in USA, UK and Canada 1969-83, Group treasurer and chief executive, BP Finance International 1984-86, Executive vice-president and chief financial officer, BP America and chief executive officer (CEO), Standard Oil Production Company 1986-89, CEO, BP Exploration, London 1989-91, Managing director, British Petroleum Company plc 1991-95, Group chief executive 1995-2007; Numerous non-executive directorships, including Intel Corporation -2006 and Goldman Sachs -2007; Partner, Riverstone LLC 2007-; Chair: Mubadala International Oil and Gas Advisory Board, Accenture Global Energy Board, Cuadrilla Resource Holdings Ltd, Stanhope Capital Advisory Board; Member: Deutsche Bank Advisory Board for Climate Change, Deutsche Bank Europe Advisory Board, Letterone Petroleum Ltd, Schlumberger Business Consulting Advisory Group, PCCW Group of Advisers; Former adviser, Fidelity International; Non-executive Director, Cabinet Office 2010-.

Political career: *House of Lords:* Raised to the peerage as Baron Browne of Madingley, of Cambridge in the County of Cambridgeshire 2001. Lead Non-Executive Director, Cabinet Office Board 2010-. EU Sub-committee A (Economic and Financial Affairs and International Trade): Co-opted member 2008-10, Member 2010-11. *Councils and public bodies:* Vice-President, Prince of Wales Business Leaders Forum 1997-2007; Council member, Foundation for Science and Technology; President, British Association for Advancement of Science -2008.

Political interests: Arts, culture, education, energy, environment.

Other: Chair: International Advisory Board, Blavatnik School of Government, Performance Theatre Advisory Group, Queen Elizabeth Prize for Enginneering Foundation; Board of trustees, Tate Galleries: Trustee 2007-, Chair 2009-; Vice-president, Flora and Fauna International; Senior fellow, St Anthony's College, Oxford; Elder Brother, Corporation of Trinity House; President, Royal Academy of Engineering 2006-11; Chair, Independent Review of Higher Education Funding and Student Finance 2009-10; Trustee: British Museum 1995-2005; Eisenhower Fellowships; Chair of Advisory Board, Judge Business School, Cambridge -2010; Chair, Independent Review of Higher Education Funding and Student Finance 2009-; Emeritus chairman, Stanford University Graduate School of Business; Fellow, American Academy of Arts and Sciences; Honorary member, School of Economics and Management, Tsinghua University Beijing; Co-chair, International Advisory Board, Russian Museum; Chair: Queen Elizabeth prize Foundation, John Browne Charitable Trust; Member: Blavatinik School of Government Foundation, Needham Resarch Institute, Cambridge China Development Trust, Cambridge Foundation, Jewish Museum and Tolerance Centre, Russia; FREng; FRS; FIMM; FInstP; FInstPet. 17 honorary doctorates from UK, western European, Russian and US universities; Nine honorary fellowships. Royal Academy of Engineering Prince Philip medal for outstanding contribution to engineering 1999; *Management Today* Most Admired CEO 1999-2002; Institute of Energy Melchett Medal 2001; Institute of Management Gold Medal 2001; Institution of Chemical Engineers Commemorative Medal 2003; British American Business Inc Channing Corporate Citizen Award 2004; World Petroleum Congress Dewhurst Award 2005. Kt 1998.

Publications: Seven Elements that have Changed the World (2013) Beyond Business (2010).

Recreations: Opera, photography, pre-Columbian art, 17th- and 18th-century printed works.

The Lord Browne of Madingley, House of Lords, London SW1A 0PW
Tel: 020 7219 5353
Email: spaynter@riverstonellc.com *Twitter:* @lordjohnbrowne

BROWNE-WILKINSON, LORD

BROWNE-WILKINSON (Life Baron), Nicolas Christopher Henry Browne-Wilkinson; cr. 1991. Born 30 March 1930; Son of late Canon A. R. Browne-Wilkinson; Married Ursula de Lacy Bacon 1955 (died 1987) (3 sons 2 daughters); married Mrs Hilary Tuckwell 1990.

Education: Lancing College, West Sussex; Magdalen College, Oxford (BA jurisprudence 1979).

CROSSBENCH

Non-political career: Called to the Bar, Lincoln's Inn 1953, Bencher 1977; Junior Counsel: to Registrar of Restrictive Trading Agreements 1964-66, to Attorney-General in Charity Matters 1966-72, in bankruptcy to Department of Trade and Industry 1966-72; QC 1972; Judge of the Courts of Appeal of Jersey and Guernsey 1976-77; Judge of the High Court, Chancery Division 1977-83; President, Employment Appeal Tribunal 1981-83; Lord Justice of Appeal 1983-85; President, Senate of the Inns of Court and the Bar 1984-86; Vice-Chancellor of the Supreme Court 1985-91.

Political career: *House of Lords:* Raised to the peerage as Baron Browne-Wilkinson, of Camden in the London Borough of Camden 1991. Lord of Appeal in Ordinary 1991-2000; Senior Law Lord 1998-2000; Member Review Committee of Privy Counsellors of the Anti-terrorism, Crime and Security Act 2002-03; On leave of absence October 2012-March 2013. Chair Privileges Lords' Interests Sub-committee 2003-05; Member Privileges 2003-07.

Other: Honorary Fellow: St Edmund Hall, Oxford 1987, Magdalen College, Oxford 1993; American College of Trial Lawyers; University of East Anglia 2000. PC 1983.

Recreations: Gardening, music.

Rt Hon the Lord Browne-Wilkinson, House of Lords, London SW1A 0PW
Tel: 020 7219 5353

BROWNING, BARONESS

BROWNING (Life Baroness), Angela Frances Browning; cr 2010. Born 4 December 1946; Daughter of late Thomas Pearson and late Linda Chamberlain; Married David Browning 1968 (2 sons).

Education: Westwood Grammar School; Reading College of Technology; Bournemouth College of Technology.

CONSERVATIVE

Non-political career: Teacher, home economics, adult education 1968-74; Auxiliary nurse 1976-77; Self-employed consultant, manufacturing industry 1977-85; Management consultant specialising in training, corporate communications and finance 1985-94; Director, Small Business Bureau 1985-94; Chair, Women Into Business 1988-92; Member, Department of Employment Advisory Committee for Women's Employment 1989-92.

Political career: *House of Commons:* Contested Crewe and Nantwich 1987 general election. MP (Conservative) for Tiverton 1992-97, for Tiverton and Honiton 1997-2010. PPS to Michael Forsyth as Minister of State, Department of Employment 1993-94; Parliamentary Secretary, Ministry of Agriculture, Fisheries and Food 1994-97; Opposition Spokesperson on Education and Employment (Education and Disability) 1997-98; Member, Shadow Cabinet 1999-2001: Shadow Secretary of State for Trade and Industry 1999-2000, Shadow Leader of the House 2000-01. Member: Agriculture 1992-93, Modernisation of the House of Commons 2000-01, Public Accounts 2004-06, 2007-10, Standards and Privileges 2004-06. *House of Lords:* Raised to the peerage as Baroness Browning, of Whimple in the County of Devon 2010. Government Spokesperson, Home Office 2011; Minister of State for Crime Prevention and Anti-Social Behaviour Reduction, Home Office 2011. Member: Liaison 2012-, Mental Capacity Act 2005 2013-. *Other:* Conservative Party: Vice-chair 2001-05; Deputy chair (organisation and campaigning) 2005-07. *Councils and public bodies:* Government co-chair, Women's National Commission 1995-97; Electoral Commissioner 2010-12.

Political interests: Small businesses, education (special needs), mental health, learning disabilities.

Other: Vice-president: National Autistic Society, Institute of Sales and Marketing Management 1997-; National vice-president, Alzheimer's Society 1997-; Patron, Research Autism; Fellow, Institute of Sales and Marketing Management.

Recreations: Theatre, cooking.

The Baroness Browning, House of Lords, London SW1A 0PW
Tel: 020 7219 5353

LIBERAL DEMOCRAT

BURNETT, LORD

BURNETT (Life Baron), John Patrick Aubone Burnett; cr 2006. Born 19 September 1945; Son of late Lt-Col Aubone Burnett OBE and Joan Burnett, née Bolt; Married Elizabeth Sherwood, née de la Mare 1971 (2 sons 2 daughters).

Education: Ampleforth College, Yorkshire; Royal Marines Commando Training Centre; Britannia Royal Naval College, Dartmouth; College of Law, London.

Non-political career: Royal Marines 1964-70: Troop Commander, 42 Commando in Borneo and Singapore, Troop Commander and Company Second-in-Command, 40 Commando in Far East and Middle East. Farmer 1976-98; Solicitor 1975; Partner, senior partner Burd Pearse solicitors, Okehampton, Devon 1976-97. Member, NFU.

Political career: *House of Commons:* Contested Torridge and West Devon 1987 general election. MP (Liberal Democrat) for Torridge and West Devon 1997-2005. Spokesperson for: Home and Legal Affairs 1997-2004, Solicitor General's Department 2004-05. *House of Lords:* Raised to the peerage as Baron Burnett, of Whitchurch in the County of Devon 2006. Liberal Democrat Spokesperson for: Planning 2007-09, Environment, Food and Rural Affairs 2009-10. Co-opted member EU Sub-committee E (Law and Institutions) 2006-10.

Political interests: Economic policy, defence, agriculture.

Other: Member: Law Society, Devon and Exeter Law Society, Law Society's Revenue (Tax) Law Committee 1984-96, Council of Devon Cattle Breeders' Association, Royal Marine Association, Royal British Legion.

Recreations: Breeding Devon cattle, walking, sport.

The Lord Burnett, House of Lords, London SW1A 0PW
Tel: 020 7219 8730

CROSSBENCH

BURNS, LORD

BURNS (Life Baron), Terence Burns; cr. 1998. Born 13 March 1944; Son of Patrick and Doris Burns; Married Anne Powell 1969 (1 son 2 daughters).

Education: Houghton-le-Spring Grammar School; Manchester University (BA economics 1965).

Non-political career: London Business School (LBS): Research posts 1965-70, Lecturer in economics 1970-74, Senior lecturer in economics 1974-79, Director, LBS Centre for Economic Forecasting 1976-79, Professor of economics 1979, Fellow 1989; Member, HM Treasury Academic Panel 1976-79; Chief Economic Adviser to HM Treasury and Head of Government Economic Service 1980-91; Visiting Fellow, Nuffield College, Oxford 1989-97; Permanent Secretary, HM Treasury 1991-98; Non-executive director: Legal and General Group plc 1999-2001, Pearson plc 1999-2010; British Land Company plc 2000-05; Chair: Glas Cymru (Welsh Water) 2001-10, Santander UK plc (formerly Abbey National plc) 2002-; Marks and Spencer plc: Deputy chair 2005-06, Chair 2006-07; Channel 4 Television Corporation: Chairman Designate 2009-10, Chair 2010-.

Political career: *House of Lords:* Raised to the peerage as Baron Burns, of Pitshanger in the London Borough of Ealing 1998. Chair Financial Services and Markets Joint Committee 1999. *Councils and public bodies:* Non-executive member, Office for Budget Responsibility 2012-.

Other: Society of Business Economists: Vice-President 1985-98, President 1998-; Fellow, London Business School 1989-; Vice-President, Royal Economic Society 1992-; Board Member, Manchester Business School 1992-98; Non-executive director, Queens Park Rangers FC 1996-2001; Royal Academy of Music: Governor 1998-2002, Chair of governing body 2002-; Monteverdi Choir and Orchestra: Trustee 1998-2001, Chair of trustees 2001-07; Chair, National Lottery Commission 2000-01; Member, Hansard Society Commission on Scrutiny Role of Parliament 1999-; Chair, Committee of Inquiry into Hunting with Dogs in England and Wales 2000; Governor, National Institute of Economic and Social Research; Chair, Independent Adviser on BBC Charter Review 2003-04. Four honorary degrees. Kt 1983; GCB 1995; Reform.

Recreations: Watching football, music, golf.

The Lord Burns GCB, House of Lords, London SW1A 0PW
Tel: 020 7219 0312 *Email:* burnst@parliament.uk
Santander UK plc, Santander House, 2 Triton Square, Regent's Place, London NW1 3AN
Tel: 020 7756 5550 *Fax:* 020 7756 5644 *Email:* terry.burns@santander.co.uk

BUSCOMBE, BARONESS

BUSCOMBE (Life Baroness), Peta Jane Buscombe; cr. 1998. Born 12 March 1954; Married Philip John Buscombe 1980 (twin sons 1 daughter).

Education: Hinchley Wood School, Surrey; Rosebery Grammar School, Epsom; Inns of Court School of Law; Columbia Law School, New York.

Non-political career: Called to the Bar, Inner Temple 1977; Director, R Buxton textile marketing company 1977-79; Legal adviser, Dairy Trade Federation 1979-80; Barclays Bank 1980-84: Legal counsel, New York, Head office lawyer and inspector, London; Legal adviser and assistant secretary, Institute of Practitioners in Advertising 1984-87; Non-executive director, Three Valleys plc 2006-; Chief executive, Advertising Association 2007-; Director: Advertising Standards Board of Finance 2007-, Committee of Advertising Practice 2007-.

Political career: *House of Commons:* Contested (Conservative) Slough 1997 general election. *House of Lords:* Raised to the peerage as Baroness Buscombe, of Goring in the County of Oxfordshire 1998. Opposition Spokesperson for: Law Officers and Lord Chancellor's Department/Legal Affairs 1999-2005, Social Security 1999-2001, Trade and Industry 1999-2000, 2001; Cabinet Office 2000-01, Home Office 2001-02, Culture, Media and Sport 2002-05, Education and Skills 2005-07. Member: EU Sub-committee B (Internal Market, Infrastructure and Employment) 2012-13, Inquiries Act 2005 2013-. *Other:* Vice-chair, Conservative Party 1997-99; President, Slough Conservative Association 1997-2001; Patron, Inns of Court School of Law Conservative Association. *Councils and public bodies:* Councillor, South Oxfordshire District Council 1995-99; Chair, Press Complaints Commission 2009-11.

Political interests: Law and order, trade and industry, legal affairs.

Other: Foundation for International and Commercial Arbitration and Alternative Dispute Resolution; Member Inter-Parliamentary Union; NSPCC; Patron PALS (Partnership for Active Leisure Scheme); Vice-President, The Henley Society; Ambassador, The Guide Association; Chair, The Samaritans advisory board.

Recreations: Gardening, riding, tennis, theatre, cinema, shooting.

The Baroness Buscombe, House of Lords, London SW1A 0PW
Tel: 020 7219 5356 *Email:* buscombep@parliament.uk

BUTLER OF BROCKWELL, LORD

BUTLER OF BROCKWELL (Life Baron) (Frederick Edward) Robin Butler; cr. 1998. Born 3 January 1938; Son of late Bernard and Nora Butler; Married Gillian Galley 1962 (1 son 2 daughters).

Education: Harrow School; University College, Oxford (BA literae humaniores 1961, MA).

Non-political career: Civil Service 1961-98: HM Treasury (HMT) 1961-72: Private secretary to Niall MacDermot as Financial Secretary to Treasury 1964-65; Secretary Budget Committee 1965-69; Seconded to Cabinet Office as Member Central Policy Review Staff 1971-72; Private secretary to Prime Ministers: Edward Heath 1972-74, Harold Wilson 1974-75; HMT 1975-82: Assistant Secretary-General, Expenditure Intelligence Division 1975-77, Under Secretary, General Expenditure Policy Group 1977-80, Principal Establishment Officer 1980-82; Principal Private Secretary to Rt Hon Margaret Thatcher as Prime Minister 1982-85; Second Permanent Secretary, Public Expenditure, HMT 1985-87; Secretary of the Cabinet and Head of the Home Civil Service 1988-98; Master, University College, Oxford 1998-2008; Non-executive director: ICI plc 1998-2008, HSBC Holdings plc 1998-2008; Member, Marsh and McLennan International Advisory Board 2005-09; Chair, Kings Health Partners Academic Health Science Centre 2009-.

Political career: *House of Lords:* Raised to the peerage as Baron Butler of Brockwell, of Herne Hill in the London Borough of Lambeth 1998. Member: Intelligence and Security Committee 2010-, Parliamentary and Political Service Honours Committee 2012-. Member: Delegated Powers and Regulatory Reform 2009-13, Leader's Group on the Working Practices of the House of Lords 2010-11, Procedure 2012-, Parliamentary and Political Service Honours Committee 2012-. *Councils and public bodies:* Member, Royal Commission on the Reform of the House of Lords 1999; Chair, Review of Intelligence on Weapons of Mass Destruction 2004.

Political interests: Higher education, civil service, constitutional matters.

Other: Chair of Governors: Harrow School 1988-91, Dulwich College 1997-2003; Visitor, Ashmolean Museum 2001-08; Trustee, Rhodes Trust 2002-09. The Salters' Company: Honorary Member, Master 2011-12. Six honorary degrees from UK and US universities; Honorary Fellow, King's College, London. CVO 1986; KCB 1988; GCB 1992; KG 2003; PC 2004; Athenæum, Brooks's, Beefsteak, Anglo-Belgian. MCC; Dulwich and Sydenham Golf Club; St Enodoc Golf Club.

Recreations: Competitive games.

Rt Hon the Lord Butler of Brockwell KG GCB CVO, House of Lords, London SW1A 0PW
Tel: 020 7219 5353

BUTLER-SLOSS, BARONESS

BUTLER-SLOSS (Life Baroness), (Ann) Elizabeth Oldfield Butler-Sloss; cr 2006. Born 10 August 1933; Daughter of Sir Cecil Havers, High Court Judge Queen's Bench Division and Lady Havers, née Enid Snelling; Married Joseph Butler-Sloss 1958 (2 sons 1 daughter).

Education: Wycombe Abbey School; French.

Non-political career: Barrister Inner Temple 1955; Practising barrister 1955-70; Registrar Principal Registry of Probate/Family Division 1970-79; High Court Judge Family Division 1979-88; Lord Justice of Appeal 1988-99; President Family Division 1999-2005.

CROSSBENCH

Political career: *House of Commons:* Contested (Conservative) Lambeth, Vauxhall 1959 general election. *House of Lords:* Raised to the peerage as Baroness Butler-Sloss, of Marsh Green in the County of Devon 2006. Member: Merits of Statutory Instruments 2007-12, Ecclesiastical Committee 2010-, Statutory Instruments Committee 2010; Chair Adoption Legislation 2012-13. *Councils and public bodies:* Chair: Cleveland Child Abuse Inquiry 1987-88, Security Commission 1995-2005; Commission on Appointment of Archbishop of Canterbury 2002.

Political interests: Education, children, family, intelligence/security, Commonwealth, legal issues, human trafficking, interfaith relations, Forced Marriages Commission 2013; Hong Kong, India, Kenya, Malaysia, Pakistan, Singapore.

Other: Former chair, St Paul's Cathedral Council; Governor, Coram and Merchant Taylors School; Inner Temple: Bencher, Treasurer 1998; Vice-President, Devon Hospice Care; President, Devon Branch National Trust, Patron, Grandparents' Association; Visitor, St Hilda's College, Oxford; Trustee: Muzaffarabad Earthquake Appeal, Human Trafficking Foundation; Honorary FCP; FCPaed; FCPsych; FSM. Honorary Freeman Merchant Taylors. Freeman, City of London. Chancellor, University of West of England 1993-2011. 18 honorary degrees; Honorary, fellow: King's College, London, St Hilda's College, Oxford, Peterhouse Cambridge, Corpus Christi College, Cambridge. DBE 1979; PC 1988; GBE 2005; RSM; Landsdowne.

Rt Hon the Baroness Butler-Sloss GBE, House of Lords, London SW1A 0PW
Tel: 020 7219 4044 *Email:* butlerslosse@parliament.uk

BYFORD, BARONESS

BYFORD (Life Baroness), Hazel Byford; cr. 1996. Born 14 January 1941; Daughter of late Sir Cyril Osborne, Conservative MP for Louth 1945-69, and Lady Osborne, CBE; Married Charles Byford 1962 (1 daughter and 1 son deceased).

Education: St Leonard's School, St Andrews; Moulton Agricultural College, Northampton.

Non-political career: Former poultry farmer.

Political career: *House of Lords:* Raised to the peerage as Baroness Byford, of Rothley in the County of Leicestershire 1996. Opposition Whip 1997-98; Opposition Spokesperson for: Agriculture December 1998-2002, Environment 1998-2003, Food, Farming and Rural Affairs 1998-2007. Member EU Sub-committee D: (Agriculture, Fisheries and Environment) 2010-12, (Agriculture, Fisheries, Environment and Energy) 2012-13, 2013-. *Other:* Chairman, National Committee, Conservative Women 1990-93; President, National Union of Conservative and Unionist Associations 1996-97. *Councils and public bodies:* Member: Transport Users' Consultative Committee 1989-94, Rail Users' Consultative Committee 1994-95; Associate member, Royal Agricultural Society 2003-.

CONSERVATIVE

Political interests: Agriculture, countryside and rural issues.

Other: WRVS Leicestershire 1961-96, County Organiser 1972-76; Patron: VIRSA 1998-2003, Institute of Agricultural Secretaries and Administrators 2000-09, Rural Stress Information Network 2001-06, National Farm Attractions Network 2002-08; Fellow, Industry and Parliament Trust 2002; Lay Canon of Leicester Cathedral 2003-; Honorary associate, British Veterinary Association 2003; President: Concordia 2004-09, Guild of Agricultural Journalists 2004-07; Honorary associate, Royal College of Veterinary Surgeons 2006; President: Lincolnshire Agricultural Society 2006, Leicestershire Clubs for Young People 2006-, Royal Association of Dairy Farmers 2007-10; Patron, Women's Farming Union 2007; President: LEAF, Royal Smithfield Club 2010; Fellow, Royal Agricultural Society of England. Worshipful Company of Farmers. Honorary Doctorate (business administration) Lincoln University 2007; Doctor of Science, Nottingham Trent University 2008; Honorary Doctor of Laws, Leicester 2010. DBE 1994; Farmers' Club.

Recreations: Golf, reading, bridge.

The Baroness Byford DBE, House of Lords, London SW1A 0PW
Tel: 020 7219 3095 *Email:* byfordh@parliament.uk

CAITHNESS, EARL OF

CAITHNESS (20th Earl of, S), Malcolm Ian Sinclair; cr. 1455; Lord Berriedale; 15th Bt of Canisbay (NS) 1631. Born 3 November 1948; Son of 19th Earl; Married Diana Caroline Coke 1975 (died 1994) (1 son 1 daughter); married Leila Jenkins 2004 (divorced).

Education: Marlborough College, Wiltshire; Royal Agricultural College, Cirencester.

Non-political career: Savills 1972-78; Brown and Mumford 1978-80; Director of various companies 1980-84; Consultant, Rickett Tinne Property Consultants, and other companies 1994-.

CONSERVATIVE

Political career: *House of Lords:* First entered House of Lords 1969; Government Spokesperson for DHSS 1984-85; Government Whip 1984-85; Government Spokesperson for Scotland 1984-86; Parliamentary Under-Secretary of State, Department of Transport 1985-86; Minister of State: Home Office 1986-88; Department of Environment 1988-89; Paymaster General and Treasury Minister 1989-90; Minister of State: Foreign and Commonwealth Office 1990-92, Department of Transport 1992-94; Elected hereditary peer 1999-. Member: EU Sub-committee F (Home Affairs) 2003-07, Draft Climate Change Bill Joint Committee 2007; Co-opted member EU Sub-committee D (Environment and Agriculture) 2008-10; Member: EU Sub-committee D: (Agriculture, Fisheries and Environment) 2010-12, (Agriculture, Fisheries, Environment and Energy) 2012-13, EU Sub-committee A (Economic and Financial Affairs) 2013-.

Other: Chief executive, Clan Sinclair Trust; Queen Elizabeth Castle of Mey Trust; Caithness Archaeological Trust; FRICS. PC 1990.

Rt Hon the Earl of Caithness, House of Lords, London SW1A 0PW
Tel: 020 7219 5442 *Email:* caithness@parliament.uk

CAMERON OF DILLINGTON, LORD

CAMERON OF DILLINGTON (Life Baron), Ewen James Hanning Cameron; cr. 2004. Born 24 November 1949; Son of Major Allan and Elizabeth Cameron; Married Caroline Ripley 1975 (3 sons 1 daughter).

Education: Harrow School; Oxford University (BA modern history 1972, MA).

Non-political career: Manager, Dillington Estate, Somerset 1971-; Chair, Orchard Media Ltd 1989-99; President, Somerset Young Farmers 1990-91; Director, Village Retail Services Association 1992-99; National president, Country Land and Business Association 1995-97; Member, Round Table for Sustainable Development 1997-2000; Chair: Let's Go Travel Ltd 1998-2006, Countryside Agency 1999-2004, Government's rural advocate for England 2000-04, Airport Direct Travel Ltd 2006-; Royal Bath and West Society: President 2006-07, Director 2008-.

CROSSBENCH

Political career: *House of Lords:* Raised to the peerage as Baron Cameron of Dillington, of Dillington in the County of Somerset 2004. Member: EU Sub-committee D (Environment and Agriculture) 2005-09, Administration and Works 2009-, EU Sub-committee D: (Agriculture, Fisheries and Environment) 2010-12, (Agriculture, Fisheries, Environment and Energy) 2012-, European Union 2012-. *Councils and public bodies:* High Sheriff of Somerset 1986-87; DL, Somerset 1989.

Political interests: Countryside, EU agriculture, environment, rural affairs, food and agriculture in developing world; (Agriculture in) Sub-Saharan Africa.

Other: Fellow, Royal Agricultural Societies 1995; Chair, Somerset Strategic Partnership 2004-11; Trustee, Lawes Agricultural Trust 2005-; FRICS 1992-. Exeter University 2003. Kt 2003.

Recreations: Golf, windsurfing, shooting.

The Lord Cameron of Dillington, House of Lords, London SW1A 0PW
Tel: 020 7219 2530 *Email:* camerone@parliament.uk
Dillington Farms, Ilminster, Somerset TA19 9EG *Tel:* 01460 57075 *Fax:* 01460 53627

CAMERON OF LOCHBROOM, LORD

CAMERON OF LOCHBROOM (Life Baron), Kenneth John Cameron; cr. 1984. Born 11 June 1931; Son of late Honorary Lord Cameron, KT, DSC; Married Jean Murray 1964 (2 daughters).

Education: The Edinburgh Academy; Corpus Christi, Oxford (MA history 1955); Edinburgh University (LLB 1958).

Non-political career: Served RNVR 1950-62; Commissioned 1951. Called to the Scottish Bar 1958; QC (Scot) 1972; Advocate Depute 1981-84; Senator, College of Justice in Scotland 1989-2003.

CROSSBENCH

Political career: *House of Lords:* Raised to the peerage as Baron Cameron of Lochbroom, of Lochbroom in the District of Ross and Cromarty 1984. Lord Advocate 1984-89. *Councils and public bodies:* President, Pensions Appeal Tribunal (Scotland) 1976-84.

Political interests: Law, arts.

Other: Fellow, Royal Society of Edinburgh; Chair, Royal Fine Art Commission for Scotland 1995-2005. Honorary Fellow: Royal Scottish Academy, Royal Incorporation of Architects in Scotland. QC (Scot) 1972; PC 1984; New Club (Edinburgh).

Recreations: Fishing, music, sailing.

Rt Hon the Lord Cameron of Lochbroom QC, House of Lords, London SW1A 0PW
Tel: 020 7219 5353

CROSSBENCH

CAMPBELL OF LOUGHBOROUGH, BARONESS

CAMPBELL OF LOUGHBOROUGH (Life Baroness), Susan Catherine Campbell; cr 2008. Born 10 October 1948.

Education: Long Eaton Grammar School, Derbyshire; Bedford College of Further Education; Leicester University (Advanced DipEd, MEd 1975).

Non-political career: Physical education (PE) teacher, Whalley Range High School, Manchester 1970-72; Director of PE, Leicester University 1972-76; Lecturer, Department of PE and Sports Science, Loughborough University 1976-80; East Midlands Regional officer, Sports Council 1980-84; National Coaching Foundation 1984-95: Deputy chief executive 1984, Chief executive 1985-95; Youth Sport Trust 1995-: Chief executive 1995-2005, Chair 2005-; PE adviser to Departments for Culture, Media and Sport and for Education and Science 2000-04; UK Sport 2003-13: Reform chair 2003-05, Chair 2005-13.

Political career: *House of Lords:* Raised to the peerage as Baroness Campbell of Loughborough, of Loughborough in the County of Leicestershire 2008.

Countries of interest: Africa, Asia.

Other: Chair, Commonwealth Advisory Board on Sport 2004-08; Trustee, International Development through Sport. MBE 1991; CBE 2003.

Recreations: Competitive squash and hockey, kayaking, golf, tennis, cycling.

The Baroness Campbell of Loughborough CBE, House of Lords, London SW1A 0PW
Tel: 020 7219 5353 *Email:* sue.campbell@youthsporttrust.org

CROSSBENCH

CAMPBELL OF SURBITON, BARONESS

CAMPBELL OF SURBITON (Life Baroness), Jane Susan Campbell; cr 2007. Born 19 April 1959; Daughter of Ronald Campbell, engineer, and Jessie Campbell, nursery nurse; Married Roger Symes 2000.

Education: Hereward College, Coventry; Hatfield Polytechnic (BA history 1979); Sussex University (MA political history 1982).

Non-political career: Equal opportunities liaison officer, Greater London Council 1984-86; Disability training development officer, London Boroughs Joint Disability Committee 1986-87; Principal disability adviser, Hounslow Council 1987-88; Director of training, London Boroughs Disability Resource Team 1988-94; Freelance consultant 1994-96; Co-director, National Centre for Independent Living 1996-2000; Chair, Social Care Institute for Excellence 2001-05.

Political career: *House of Lords:* Raised to the peerage as Baroness Campbell of Surbiton, of Surbiton in the Royal Borough of Kingston upon Thames 2007. Independent member, House of Lords Appointments Commission 2008-; Disability adviser, Department for Work and Pensions and Department of Health 2007-12. Member Joint Committee on Human Rights 2010-12. *Councils and public bodies:* Chair, British Council of Disabled People 1991-95; Governor, National Institute Social Work 1995-2001; Commissioner, Disability Rights Commission 2000-06; Chair, Disability Committee and Commissioner Commission for Equality and Human Rights 2006-09.

Political interests: Health and social care, social policy, medical ethics, independent living, equality and human rights, disability rights, end of life issues; Sweden.

Other: Founder and co-director, Not Dead Yet UK 2006-; President, National Disability Archive (Shape, London) 2013-; Disability Rights UK; Power International. Honorary LLD, Bristol University 2002; Hon Doctorate: Sheffield Hallam University 2003, Birmingham University 2009. Lifetime Achievement Award, Liberty Human Rights Awards, 2012. MBE 2000; DBE 2006.

Publications: With Mike Oliver, Disability Politics (Routledge, 1996); Contributor, Disabled People and the Right to Life (Routledge, 2008).

Recreations: Theatre, cinema, reading, gardening.

The Baroness Campbell of Surbiton DBE, House of Lords, London SW1A 0PW
Tel: 020 7219 5124 *Email:* campbelljs@parliament.uk *Website:* www.livingwithdignity.info

LABOUR

CAMPBELL-SAVOURS, LORD

CAMPBELL-SAVOURS (Life Baron), Dale Norman Campbell-Savours; cr 2001. Born 23 August 1943; Son of late John Lawrence and Cynthia Lorraine Campbell-Savours; Married Gudrun Kristin Runolfsdottir 1970 (3 sons).

Education: Keswick School; The Sorbonne, Paris.

Non-political career: Company director, clock and metal component manufacturing company.

Political career: *House of Commons:* Contested Darwen February and October 1974 general elections and Workington 1976 by-election. MP (Labour) for Workington 1979-2001. Opposition Frontbench Spokesperson for: Development and Co-operation 1991-92, Food, Agriculture and Rural Affairs 1992-94 (resigned from frontbench because of ill health). *House of Lords:* Raised to the peerage as Baron Campbell-Savours, of Allerdale in the County of Cumbria 2001. Member: Administration and Works 2007-12, Liaison 2010-; Procedure: Alternate member 2010-12, Member 2012-; Member House 2012-. *Councils and public bodies:* Councillor, Ramsbottom Urban District Council 1972-74.

Political interests: Investigative political and social work, education and health reform, industrial democracy, Member of Cumbria Remuneration Panel.

Other: Patron: Cumbria Deaf Association, The Rural Academy Cumbria; President: Allerdale Mind, Cumberland County League; Labour Club, Workington.

Publications: The Case for the Supplementary Vote (1990); The Case for The University of the Lakes (1995).

Recreations: Trout fishing, music.

The Lord Campbell-Savours, House of Lords, London SW1A 0PW
Tel: 020 7219 3513/07836 206108

NON-AFFILIATED

CANTERBURY, LORD ARCHBISHOP OF

CANTERBURY (105th Archbishop of), Justin Portal Welby. Born 6 January 1956; Son of late Gavin Welby and Jane Welby (now Lady Williams of Elvel); Married Caroline 1979 (2 sons 3 daughters 1 daughter deceased).

Education: Eton College; Trinity College, Cambridge (BA 1978); St John's College, Durham (BA 1991); French.

Non-political career: Project finance manager, Société Nationale Elf Aquitaine, Paris 1978-83; Treasurer, Elf UK 1983-84; Group Treasurer, Enterprise Oil plc 1984-89; Ordained: Deacon 1992, Priest 1993; Curate, All Saints, Chilvers Coton, Nuneaton 1992-95; Rector: St James', Southam 1995-2002, St Michael and All Angels, Ufton 1996-2002; Coventry Cathedral: Co-director, International Ministry and Canon Residentiary 2002-05, Sub-Dean and Canon for Reconciliation Ministry 2005-07; Dean of Liverpool 2007-11; Bishop of Durham 2011-13; Archbishop of Canterbury 2013-.

Political career: *House of Lords:* Entered House of Lords 2011. Member Parliamentary Commission on Banking Standards 2012-13. *Councils and public bodies:* Southam College: Parent governor 1996-2002, Chair of governors 1998-2002; South Warwickshire General Hospitals NHS Trust: Non-executive director 1998-2000, Chair 2000-02.

Countries of interest: Burundi, DR Congo, France, Israel, Kenya, Nigeria, Palestine.

Other: Association Internationale pour l'Enseignement Social Chrétien; Honorary Fellow, Association of Corporate Treasurers; Diocesan Trust; Pershaw, Nashdom and Elmore Trust. Skinners. Peer of the Year, *The Spectator* awards 2012. PC 2013; Athenæum, Liverpool.

Publications: Can Companies Sin? (Grove Books, 1992); Various articles in The Treasurer magazine, and numerous other articles on risk management, finance, and on reconciliation; Various chapters in books on reconciliation, conflict management.

Recreations: Sailing, reading, travel.

Most Rev and Rt Hon the Archbishop of Canterbury, House of Lords, London SW1A 0PW
Tel: 020 7219 5353 *Email:* welbypj@parliament.uk
Lambeth Palace, London SE1 7JU *Tel:* 020 7898 1472 *Email:* jack.palmer@churchofengland.org
Twitter: @ABCJustin

CROSSBENCH

CAREY OF CLIFTON, LORD

CAREY OF CLIFTON (Life Baron), George Leonard Carey; cr 2002. Born 13 November 1935; Son of late George and Ruby Carey; Married Eileen Harmsworth Hood 1960 (2 sons 2 daughters). **Education:** Bifrons School, Barking; King's College, London (PhD); London College of Divinity (ALCD, BD, MTh).

Non-political career: Royal Air Force 1954-56. Curate of St Mary's, Islington 1962-66; Lecturer: Oakhill Theological College 1966-70, St John's College, Nottingham; Occasional teacher at Nottingham University 1970-75; Vicar of St Nicholas Church, Durham 1975-82; Principal, Trinity Theological College, Bristol 1982-87; Bishop of Bath and Wells 1987-91; Archbishop of Canterbury 1991-2002.

Political career: *House of Lords:* Raised to the peerage as Baron Carey of Clifton, of Clifton in the City and Council of Bristol 2002. First entered the House of Lords as Archbishop of Canterbury 1991. *Councils and public bodies:* Chair: United Church Schools Trust, Foundation for Reconciliation in the Middle East.

Countries of interest: Israel, Palestine, Sudan.

Other: President, World Conference for Religion and Peace; Honorary President, International Council for Christians and Jews; Chairman, World Faiths Development Dialogue; International Sports Promotion Society; Vice-President, Tearfund; Fellow: King's College, London, Christchurch University College, Canterbury, Library of Congress; Tearfund. Honorary Liveryman, The Scriveners' Company. Freeman: City of London, Bath, Wells. 12 honorary doctorates. PC 1991; Royal Victorian Chain 2002; Athenæum, RSOL.

Publications: I Believe in Man (1975); God Incarnate (1976); Co-author, The Great Acquittal (1980); The Church in the Market Place (1984); The Meeting of the Waters (1985); The Gate of Glory (1986); The Message of the Bible (1986); The Great God Robbery (1989); I Believe (1991); Sharing a Vision (1993); Spiritual Journey (1994); Co-author, My Journey, Your Journey (1996); Canterbury Letters to the Future (1998); Jesus 2000 (1999); Know The Truth (memoirs, 2004); We Don't Do God (2012).

Recreations: Family life, music, poetry, reading, walking.

Rt Rev and Rt Hon the Lord Carey of Clifton, House of Lords, London SW1A 0PW
Tel: 020 7219 5353 *Email:* carey.george01@gmail.com *Website:* glcarey.co.uk

LIBERAL DEMOCRAT

CARLILE OF BERRIEW, LORD

CARLILE OF BERRIEW (Life Baron), Alexander Charles Carlile; cr. 1999. Born 12 February 1948; Married Frances Soley 1968 (divorced) (3 daughters); married Alison Levitt QC 2007 (2 stepdaughters).

Education: Epsom College; King's College, London University (LLB, AKC 1969); Council of Legal Education.

Non-political career: Called to the Bar, Gray's Inn 1970, Bencher 1992; QC 1984; Crown Court Recorder 1986-; Honorary Recorder of City of Hereford 1996-2009; Independent Reviewer of Terrorism Legislation 2001-10; Deputy High Court Judge 1998-; Chair: Competition Appeals Tribunal 2005-13, Lloyd's Enforcement Board.

Political career: *House of Commons:* Contested (Lib) Flint East, February 1974 and 1979 general elections. MP for Montgomery 1983-97 (Lib 1983-88, Lib Dem 1988-97). Liberal Spokesperson for Home Affairs, Law 1985-88; Alliance Spokesperson for Legal Affairs 1987; SLD Spokesperson for Foreign Affairs 1988-89; Liberal Democrat Spokesperson for: Legal Affairs 1989-90, Trade and Industry 1990-92, Wales 1992-97, Employment 1992-94, Health 1994-95, Justice, Home Affairs and Immigration 1995-97. *House of Lords:* Raised to the peerage as Baron Carlile of Berriew, of Berriew in the County of Powys 1999. Liberal Democrat Spokesperson for Mental Health and Disability 2007-10. Chair Mental Health Bill Joint Committee 2005-06; Member Delegated Powers and Regulatory Reform 2010-12. *Other:* Chair, Welsh Liberal Party 1980-82; Leader, Welsh Liberal Democrat Party 1992-97; President, Liberal Democrats Wales 1997-99. *Councils and public bodies:* Lay member, General Medical Council 1989-99; Member, Advisory Council on Public Records 1989-95; Chairman (part-time), Competition Appeals Tribunal 2005-13; Deputy Chief Steward, City of Hereford 2009-.

Political interests: Home affairs, agriculture, legal affairs, United Nations, arts, Wales, mental health, medical profession; South Asia, Central and Eastern Europe.

Other: Patron: National Depression Campaign, Concord Prison Trust, No Panic; Council member, White Ensign Association; Fellow: Institute of Advanced Legal Studies, Industry and Parliament Trust 1989; President, Howard League for Penal Reform 2006-13; Board member, Royal Medical Benevolent Institution (Epsom College); Fellow, Royal Society of Arts; Hope House Children's

Hospice, NACRO, Unicef, Rekindle, Howard League for Penal Reform, White Ensign Association. Fellow, King's College, London 2003; Honorary LLD: Glamorgan University 2009, Hungarian Institute of Criminology 2010, Manchester Metropolitan University 2011. QC 1984; CBE 2012; Athenæum. President, Berriew Football Club.

Publications: Too Serious a Thing (National Assembly for Wales review of safety of children in the NHS, 2002); Various articles and reports on Terrorism; If all do their duty they need not fear harm (Report for the Howard League on Children in Custody, 2006).

Recreations: Family, politics, theatre, food, Association Football.

The Lord Carlile of Berriew QC CBE, House of Lords, London SW1A 0PW
Tel: 020 7219 5535 *Email:* carlilea@parliament.uk
9-12 Bell Yard, London WC2A 2LF *Tel:* 020 7400 1800

CARRINGTON, LORD

CARRINGTON (6th Baron, I), Peter Alexander Rupert Carington; cr. 1796; 6th Baron Carrington (GB) 1797; (Life) Baron Carington of Upton 1999. Born 6 June 1919; Son of 5th Baron, DL, and late Honorary Sybil Marion Colville, daughter of 2nd Viscount Colville of Culross; Married Iona McClean 1942 (died 2009) (1 son 2 daughters).

Education: Eton College; RMC, Sandhurst 1937-38.

Non-political career: Major, Grenadier Guards, served North West Europe 1940-46. UK High Commissioner in Australia 1956-59; Chairman, GEC 1983-84; Honorary Bencher, Middle Temple 1983-; Secretary-General, NATO 1984-88; Chairman, Christies International plc 1988-93; Director, The Telegraph plc 1990-2004; Chairman, EC Peace Conference on Yugoslavia 1991-92.

CONSERVATIVE

Political career: *House of Lords:* Created a life peer as Baron Carington of Upton, of Upton in the County of Nottinghamshire 1999. Succeeded his father 1938; Eligible to take his seat 1940; First entered House of Lords 1945; Joint Parliamentary Secretary, Ministry of Agriculture and Fisheries 1951-54; Parliamentary Secretary, Ministry of Defence 1954-56; First Lord of the Admiralty 1959-63; Minister without Portfolio and Leader of the House of Lords 1963-1964; Leader of Opposition 1964-70, 1974-79; Secretary of State for Defence 1970-74; Minister of Aviation Supply 1971-74; Opposition Whip 1947-51; Secretary of State for: Energy January-February 1974, Foreign and Commonwealth Affairs 1979-82. *Other:* Chairman, Conservative Party 1972-74. *Councils and public bodies:* JP, Bucks 1948; DL, Bucks 1951.

Other: Vice-President, Commonwealth Parliamentary Association (UK Branch); Trustee: The Dulverton Trust 1981-, Cambridge Commonwealth Trust 1982-; Chairman of trustees, Victoria and Albert Museum 1983-88; President, The Pilgrims 1983-2002; Elder Brother, Trinity House 1984; Trustee: The Royal Fine Art Commission 1987-, Daiwa Anglo Japanese Foundation 1989, Winston Churchill Memorial Trust -2001; President, Voluntary Services Overseas (VSO) 1993-98; Hope and Homes for Children, Treloar Trust. Chancellor, Reading University 1992-. Honorary LLD, Cambridge 1981; Honorary Fellow, St Antony's College, Oxford 1982; 12 honorary degrees from universities in the United Kingdom and abroad. MC 1945; PC 1959; CH 1983; Chancellor of the Order of St Michael and St George 1984-94; KG 1985; GCMG 1988; Chancellor of the Most Noble Order of the Garter 1994-2013; Pratt's, White's.

Publications: Reflect on Things Past (autobiography, 1988).

Rt Hon the Lord Carrington KG GCMG CH MC DL, House of Lords, London SW1A 0PW
Tel: 020 7219 5353
The Courtyard, Manor Farm, Church End, Bledlow, Buckinghamshire HP27 9PD
Tel: 01844 273508/01844 274991 *Fax:* 01844 274991 *Email:* lordc@carington.co.uk

CARRINGTON OF FULHAM, LORD

CARRINGTON (Life Baron), Matthew Hadrian Marshall Carrington; cr 2013. Born 19 October 1947; Son of Walter and Dilys Carrington.

Education: The Lycee, London; Imperial College, London.

Non-political career: Production foreman 1969-72; Banker 1974-87.

Political career: *House of Commons:* Contested Tottenham 1979 general election and Fulham 1986 by-election. MP (Conservative) for Fulham 1987-97. PPS to: John Patten as Minister of State, Home Office 1990-92, Earl Ferrers as Minister of State, Home Office 1990-92, John Patten

CONSERVATIVE as Secretary of State for Education 1992-94. *House of Lords:* Raised to the peerage as Baron Carrington of Fulham, of Fulham in the London Borough of Hammersmith and Fulham 2013.

The Lord Carrington, House of Lords, London SW1A 0PW
Tel: 020 7219 5353

CARSWELL, LORD

CARSWELL (Life Baron), Robert Douglas Carswell; cr. 2004. Born 28 June 1934; Son of late Alan Carswell and Nance Carswell; Married Romayne Ferris 1961 (2 daughters).

Education: Royal Belfast Academical Institution; Pembroke College, Oxford (BA classics and law 1956, MA); Chicago University Law School (Doctor of Jurisprudence 1958).

Non-political career: Barrister, Northern Ireland 1957; QC (NI) 1971; Barrister, Gray's Inn 1972; Counsel to Attorney General for Northern Ireland 1970-71; Senior Crown Counsel in Northern Ireland 1979-84; Judge of the High Court of Justice Northern Ireland 1984-93; Lord Justice of Appeal Supreme Court of Judicature Northern Ireland 1993-97; Lord Chief Justice of Northern Ireland 1997-2004.

Political career: *House of Lords:* Raised to the peerage as Baron Carswell, of Killeen in the County of Down 2004. Lord of Appeal in Ordinary 2004-09. Joint Committee on Consolidation, Etc, Bills: Chair 2009-11, 2012-, Member 2011-12.

Political interests: Legal and constitutional matters, Northern Ireland.

Other: Chancellor, Dioceses of Armagh, Down and Dromore 1990-97. Honorary doctorate; Hon Fellow, Pembroke College, Oxford 1984. Kt 1988; PC 1993; Ulster Reform Club, Belfast.

Publications: Trustee Acts (Northern Ireland) (1964).

Recreations: Golf, hill-walking.

Rt Hon the Lord Carswell QC, House of Lords, London SW1A 0PW
Tel: 020 7219 5353 *Email:* carswellr@parliament.uk

CARTER OF BARNES, LORD

CARTER OF BARNES (Life Baron), Stephen Andrew Carter; cr 2008. Born 12 February 1964; Married Anna Maria Gorman 1992 (1 son 1 daughter).

Education: Currie High School, Edinburgh; Aberdeen University (LLB 1987); Harvard University (AMP 1997).

Non-political career: Managing director and chief executive, J Walter Thompson Ltd 1992-2000; Chief operating officer and managing director, ntl UK and Ireland 2000-02; Chief executive officer, Office of Communications (OFCOM) 2003-07; Group chief executive, Brunswick Group LLP 2007-08; Chief of strategy and principal adviser to Prime Minister 2008; Chief marketing, strategy and communications officer, EVP solutions division, Alcatel-Lucent, Paris 2010-.

Political career: *House of Lords:* Raised to the peerage as Baron Carter of Barnes, of Barnes in the London Borough of Richmond upon Thames 2008. Parliamentary Under-Secretary of State and Government Spokesperson: Department for Business, Enterprise and Regulatory Reform/ Business, Innovation and Skills (Minister for Communications, Technology and Broadcasting) 2008-09, Department for Culture, Media and Sport 2008-09; On leave of absence July 2011-13.

Other: Vice-President, Unicef 2005-; Governor and Chairman, Ashridge Business Management School 2005-. CBE 2007.

The Lord Carter of Barnes CBE, House of Lords, London SW1A 0PW
Tel: 020 7219 5353 *Email:* carterst@parliament.uk
Informa plc, Informa House, 30-32 Mortimer Street, London W1W 7RE *Tel:* 020 7017 5771

CARTER OF COLES, LORD

CARTER OF COLES (Life Baron), Patrick Robert Carter; cr. 2004. Born 9 February 1946; Married Julia Bourne 1969 (2 daughters).

Education: Brentwood School, Essex; Durham University (BA economics, economic history 1967).

Non-political career: Hambros Bank Ltd 1967-70; Director: Whitecross Equipment Ltd 1970-75, MAI Ltd 1975-85, Westminster Healthcare plc 1975-99; Chair, Sport England 2002-06.

Political career: *House of Lords:* Raised to the peerage as Baron Carter of Coles, of Westmill in the County of Hertfordshire 2004. EU Sub-committee D (Environment and Agriculture): Co-opted member 2009, Chair 2009-10; Member European Union 2010-; Chair EU Sub-committee D: (Agriculture, Fisheries and Environment) 2010-12, (Agriculture, Fisheries, Environment and Energy) 2012-13; Member EU Sub-committee A (Economic and Financial Affairs) 2013-.

Councils and public bodies: Non-executive member: Prisons Board/Strategy Board for Correctional Services 1998-2002, Home Office General Board 2002-06; Chair: National Athletics

Review, Review of Payroll Services, Criminal Records Bureau, Review of Offender Services 2006, Review of Pathology 2008, Review of Courts Estate 2009, Competition and Co-operation Panel.

Other: Member, Productivity Panel 2000-; Chair: Commonwealth Games 2002, English National Stadium 2002.

Recreations: Reading, walking, skiing, gardening, opera.

The Lord Carter of Coles, House of Lords, London SW1A 0PW
Tel: 020 7219 3342
Tel: 020 7839 1789 *Fax:* 020 7270 5233 *Email:* pippa.morgan@mckesson.co.uk

CONSERVATIVE

CATHCART, EARL

CATHCART (7th Earl, UK), Charles Alan Andrew Cathcart; cr. 1814; 7th Viscount Cathcart and Baron Greenock (UK) 1807; 16th Lord Cathcart (S) c.1442. Born 30 November 1952; Son of Major-General 6th Earl and Rosemary Smyth-Osbourne; Married Vivien Skinner 1981 (1 son 1 daughter).

Education: Eton College.

Non-political career: Command Scots Guards 1972-75. Chartered accountant: Whinney Murray 1976-79, Ernst and Whinney 1979-83 (ICAEW 1981); Director and Lloyd's underwriter: Gardner Mountain and Capel-cure Agencies 1983-94, Murray Lawrence Members Agencies 1995-96; Director, Reinsurance Group of America (UK) 1996-2011; Chairman, Equator Films Plc (now Handmade Films Ltd) 1998-2004; Finance director, Vivien Greenock Ltd 2001-; Director, Spring Gardens Eggs Ltd.

Political career: *House of Lords:* First entered House of Lords 1999; Elected hereditary peer 2007-; Opposition Whip 2007-10; Opposition Spokesperson for: Communities and Local Government 2007-10, Environment, Food and Rural Affairs 2007-10, Northern Ireland 2007-09, Scotland 2009-10. Councils and public bodies: Councillor, Breckland District Council 1998-2007.

Political interests: Rural affairs, environment, energy; UK.

Other: Member, Queen's Bodyguards for Scotland, Royal Company of Archers; ICAEW.

Recreations: Skiing, sailing, country pursuits.

The Earl Cathcart, House of Lords, London SW1A 0PW
Tel: 020 7219 5422 *Email:* cathcartc@parliament.uk

CONSERVATIVE

CAVENDISH OF FURNESS, LORD

CAVENDISH OF FURNESS (Life Baron), Richard Hugh Cavendish; cr. 1990. Born 2 November 1941; Son of late Captain Richard Edward Osborne Cavendish, DL; Married Grania Caulfeild 1970 (1 son 2 daughters).

Education: Eton College.

Non-political career: International merchanting and banking in London 1961-71; Chairman, Holker Estate Group of Companies 1971-; Commissioner for the Historic Buildings and Monuments Commission (English Heritage) 1992-98; Director, UK Nirex Ltd 1993-99.

Political career: *House of Lords:* Raised to the peerage as Baron Cavendish of Furness, of Cartmel in the County of Cumbria 1990. Government Whip 1990-92. *Other:* Chair, Morecambe and Lonsdale Conservative Association 1975-78; Member, Association of Conservative Peers. *Councils and public bodies:* Councillor, Cumbria County Council 1985-90; High Sheriff of Cumbria 1978; DL, Cumbria 1988.

Political interests: Environment, local issues, industry, foreign affairs, drug and alcohol rehabilitation, agriculture, forestry, palliative care, national hunt racing.

Other: Trustee, St Mary's Hospice, Ulverston 1987-2009; Fellow, Royal Society of Arts 1988; Chair, Lancashire and Cumbria Foundation for Medical Research 1994-. Liveryman, Fishmongers' Company; Brooks's, White's, Pratt's, Beefsteak.

Recreations: Gardening, National Hunt racing, shooting, reading, travel, fishing.

The Lord Cavendish of Furness DL, House of Lords, London SW1A 0PW
Tel: 020 7219 5353
Holker Hall, Cark-in-Cartmel, Cumbria LA11 7PL *Tel:* 01539 558220 *Fax:* 01539 558776
Email: cavendish@holker.co.uk

CHADLINGTON, LORD

CONSERVATIVE

CHADLINGTON (Life Baron), Peter Selwyn Gummer; cr. 1996. Born 24 August 1942; Son of late Rev Canon Selwyn Gummer and late Sybille Selwyn Gummer, née Mason; Married Lucy Dudley-Hill 1982 (3 daughters 1 son).

Education: King's School, Rochester; Selwyn College, Cambridge (BA moral sciences tripos 1964, MA).

Non-political career: Portsmouth and Sunderland Newspaper Group Ltd 1964-65; Viyella International 1965-66; Hodgkinson and Partners 1966-67; Industrial and Commercial Finance Corporation 1967-74; Shandwick International plc 1974-2000: Founder and chief executive 1974-94, Chairman 1994-2000; Non-executive director, CIA Group plc 1990-94; Chairman, Marketing Group of GB 1993-95; Halifax Building Society/plc: Non-executive director, London Bonds 1990-94, Non-executive director 1994-2001; Chairman, International Public Relations 1998-2000; Director: Black Box Music Ltd 1999-2001, Walbrook Club 1999-2004; Chairman, Hotcourses Ltd 2000-04; Huntsworth plc: Chief executive 2000-05, Sept 2005-, Executive chairman May-Sept 2005; Director, Hill Hay Saddle Ltd 2002-; Non-executive director, Britax Childcare Holdings Ltd 2005-11.

Political career: *House of Lords:* Raised to the peerage as Baron Chadlington, of Dean in the County of Oxfordshire 1996. Member: European Union Sub-committee B (Energy, Industry and Transport) 2000-03, Information 2005-06. *Councils and public bodies:* Member: NHS Policy Board 1991-95, Arts Council of England 1991-96; Chairman: National Lottery Advisory Board for Arts and Film 1994-96, Royal Opera House 1996-97; Council member, Cheltenham Ladies College 1998-2003; Non-executive director, Oxford Resources 1999-2002; Non-executive chairman, guideforlife.com 2000-02.

Other: Chairman, Understanding Industry Trust 1991-96; Trustee, Atlantic Partnership 1999-; Board of Trustees, American University 1999-2001; Action on Addiction: Trustee 1999-2000, Chairman 2000-07; Governor, The Ditchley Foundation 2008; Committee member, British Heart Foundation Mending Broken Hearts Appeal 2010-; Chairman, LAPADA (professional art and antique dealers' trade association) 2011-; FRSA; FIPR; Action on Addiction. Freeman, City of London. Honorary Fellow, Bournemouth University 1999-. *PR Week* Award for outstanding individual contribution to public relations 1984; Institute of Public Relations Presidents' Medal 1988; Ernst & Young Entrepreneur of the Year, Master Entrepreneur London Region 2008; White's, Garrick, Carlton, Walbrook. MCC.

Publications: Various articles and booklets on public relations.

Recreations: Opera, rugby, cricket.

The Lord Chadlington, House of Lords, London SW1A 0PW
Tel: 020 7219 5172
15-17 Huntsworth Mews, London NW1 6DD *Tel:* 020 7298 6583 *Fax:* 020 7493 3048
Email: lordchadlington@huntsworth.com

CHALFONT, LORD

NON-AFFILIATED

CHALFONT (Life Baron), (Alun) Arthur Gwynne Jones; cr. 1964. Born 5 December 1919; Son of late Arthur Gwynne Jones; Married Mona Mitchell 1948 (died 2008) (1 daughter deceased).

Education: West Monmouth School; School of Slavonic Studies, London University (BA Russian language 1955).

Non-political career: Commissioned as 2nd Lieutenant in South Wales Borderers 1940; Served in Burma, Cyprus, Malaya and East Africa; Various intelligence appointments; Graduate of: Army Staff College 1950, Joint Service Staff College 1958; Resigned commission as Brevet Lieutenant-Colonel in 1961 upon appointment to *The Times*; Honorary Colonel, University of Wales Officer Training Corps 1992-95. Defence correspondent, *The Times* 1961-64; Foreign editor, *New Statesman* 1970-71; Director: Shandwick plc 1979-94, IBM (UK) 1983-90, Lazard Bros & Co Ltd 1983-91; Chair, Vickers Shipbuilding and Engineering Ltd 1987-95; Deputy chair, Independent Broadcasting Authority 1989-90; Chair: Radio Authority 1991-95, Marlborough Stirling 1994-99; Director, Television Corporation 1996-2001; Chair, Southern Mining Corp 1997-99.

Political career: *House of Lords:* Raised to the peerage as Baron Chalfont, of Llantarnam, in the County of Monmouth 1964. Minister of State for Foreign Affairs 1964-70; Opposition Spokesperson on Defence and Foreign Affairs 1970-73; On leave of absence. Member: House of Lords Offices 2000-02, Procedure 2003-05.

Political interests: Defence, foreign affairs; China, Russia.

Other: President: Hispanic and Luso Brazilian Council 1972-79, European Atlantic Group 1983-90; FRSA. Member, Paviors' Company. Freeman, City of London. MC 1957; OBE (Mil) 1961; PC 1964; Grand Officer, Order of the Southern Cross (Brazil) 1976; Garrick. Llanelli RFC.

Publications: Several books including: The Great Commanders (1973); Montgomery of Alamein (1976); Waterloo: A Battle of Three Armies (1979); Star Wars (1985); Defence of the Realm (1987); By God's Will (1989); The Shadow of My Hand (2000).
Recreations: Music.
Rt Hon the Lord Chalfont OBE MC, House of Lords, London SW1A 0PW
Tel: 020 7219 5353

CHALKER OF WALLASEY, BARONESS

CHALKER OF WALLASEY (Life Baroness), Lynda Chalker; cr. 1992. Born 29 April 1942; Daughter of late Sidney Bates and late Marjorie Randell; Married Eric Chalker 1967 (divorced 1973); married Clive Landa 1981 (divorced 2003).
Education: Roedean School, Sussex; Heidelberg University (technical German 1961); London University; Central London Polytechnic (statistics 1965).
Non-political career: Honorary Colonel, Royal Logistic Corps (156 Transport Regiment NW) 1995-2001. Statistician, Unilever's Research Bureau Ltd 1963-69; Market researcher, Shell Mex and BP 1969-72; Executive director (International), Opinion Research International Ltd 1972-74; Adviser, Barclays Bank International 1976-79; Independent Consultant on Africa and Development 1997-; Chair, Africa Matters Limited 1997-; Director: Unilever plc 1998-2007, Group Five Construction Pty (SA) 2001-2012.

CONSERVATIVE

Political career: *House of Commons:* MP (Conservative) for Wallasey February 1974-92. Contested Wallasey 1992 general election. Parliamentary Under-Secretary of State Department of Health and Social Security 1979-82, Department of Transport: Parliamentary Under-Secretary of State 1982-83, Minister of State 1983-86; Minister of State, Foreign and Commonwealth Office 1986-97, Deputy to Foreign Secretary 1987-97, Minister for Overseas Development 1989-92. *House of Lords:* Raised to the peerage as Baroness Chalker of Wallasey, of Leigh-on-Sea in the County of Essex 1992. Minister of Overseas Development and Minister for Africa and Commonwealth, Foreign and Commonwealth Office 1992-97. *Other:* National vice-chair, Young Conservatives 1970-71; Honorary Life member, Tory Reform Group. *Councils and public bodies:* Member, BBC Advisory Committee 1974-76.
Political interests: Voluntary sector, European co-operation, Africa, overseas development, trade, transport, construction; Sub-Saharan Africa, Egypt, Jordan.
Other: Adviser, World Bank 1997-2005; Co-ordinator, Presidential International Investment Council for Nigeria 2001-; Member: Kenyan National Economic and Social Council 2004-09, Ugandan Presidential Investment Round Table 2004-, Tanzania National Business Council 2004-; Fellow, Royal Statistical Society; Chair, Medicines for Malaria Venture 2006-11; Trustee: Global Leadership Foundation, Investment Climate Facility for Africa; Royal Geographical Society; London School of Hygiene and Tropical Medicine; Institute of Highways and Transportation; Royal Statistical Society; British Executive Services Overseas, Intermediate Technology Development Group, African Medical Research Foundation, British Red Cross, Red R, Water Aid. Nine honorary degrees. PC 1987; Royal Overseas League, St James.
Publications: Police in Retreat (1968); Unhappy Families (1972); We're Richer than We Think (1978); Africa – Turning the Tide (1989).
Recreations: Theatre, cooking, gardening, jazz.
Rt Hon the Baroness Chalker of Wallasey, House of Lords, London SW1A 0PW
Tel: 020 7219 5098 *Fax:* 020 7976 4999
Africa Matters Limited, King's Scholars House, 230 Vauxhall Bridge Road, London SW1V 1AU
Tel: 020 7976 6850 *Fax:* 020 7976 4999 *Email:* pa@africamatters.com

CHANDOS, VISCOUNT

CHANDOS (3rd Viscount, UK), Thomas Orlando Lyttelton; cr. 1954; (Life) Baron Lyttelton of Aldershot 2000. Born 12 February 1953; Son of 2nd Viscount; Married Arabella Sarah Bailey 1985 (2 sons 1 daughter).
Education: Eton College; Worcester College, Oxford (BA).
Non-political career: Director: Kleinwort Benson 1985-93, Botts & Company Limited 1993-98, Capital and Regional Properties plc 1993-, Cine-UK Limited 1995-, Video Networks Limited 1996-99, Chair: Lopex plc 1997-99, Mediakey plc 1998-2000, Capital and Regional plc 2000-; Director: Global Natural Energy plc 2000-, Northbridge (UK) Limited 2001-.

LABOUR

Political career: *House of Lords:* Created a life peer as Baron Lyttelton of Aldershot, of Aldershot in the County of Hampshire 2000. First entered House of Lords 1982; Formerly SDP Spokesperson for Finance and Trade; Opposition Spokesperson on Treasury and Economic Affairs 1995-97. Member Works of Art 2003-07.

Other: Director, English National Opera 1995-; Trustee: 21st Century Learning Initiative 1995-, Education Low-Priced Sponsored Texts 1996-99; Governor, National Film and Television School 1996-2001; President, National Kidney Research Fund 2001-; Director, Social Market Foundation 2001-.

The Viscount Chandos, House of Lords, London SW1A 0PW
Tel: 020 7219 6307
Northbridge UK Ltd, 9 Park Place, London SW1A 1LP

NON-AFFILIATED

CHESTER, LORD BISHOP OF

CHESTER (40th Bishop of), Peter Robert Forster. Born 16 March 1950; Son of Thomas and Edna Forster; Married Elisabeth Stevenson 1978 (2 sons 2 daughters).

Education: Tudor Grange Grammar School for Boys, Solihull; Merton College, Oxford (MA chemistry 1973); Edinburgh University (BD theology 1977; PhD 1985).

Non-political career: Assistant Curate, Mossley Hill Parish Church, Liverpool 1980-82; Senior Tutor, St John's College, Durham 1983-91; Vicar, Beverley Minster 1991-96; Bishop of Chester 1996-.

Political career: *House of Lords:* Entered House of Lords 2001. Member: Joint Committee on Privacy and Injunctions 2011-12; Administration and Works 2013-. *Councils and public bodies:* Chair of Council, University of Chester; Chair of Governors, Ellesmere Port Academy.

Countries of interest: The Congo, Solomon Islands, Vanuatu.

Recreations: Gardening, crafts, hens.

Rt Rev Dr the Lord Bishop of Chester, House of Lords, London SW1A 0PW
Tel: 020 7219 5353 *Email:* bpchester@chester.anglican.org
Bishop's House, Abbey Square, Chester CH1 2JD *Tel:* 01244 350864
Email: bpchester@chester.anglican.org

LIBERAL DEMOCRAT

CHIDGEY, LORD

CHIDGEY (Life Baron), David William George Chidgey; cr 2005. Born 9 July 1942; Son of Major Cyril and Winifred Chidgey; Married April Idris-Jones 1964 (1 son 2 daughters).

Education: Brune Park County High School, Gosport; Portsmouth Polytechnic (Dip CivilEng 1965, CEng); Portsmouth Naval College; Graduate, Institute of Mechanical Engineers; French.

Non-political career: Consulting civil engineer; Senior civil engineer, Hampshire County Council 1964-73; Brian Colquhoun and Partners 1973-93: Associate partner 1988-93, Projects director, West Africa and South East Asia 1978-87, Managing director, Ireland 1981-88; Chief consultant to Dublin Transport Authority 1987-88; Associate director and projects director, Central Southern England Thorburn Colquhoun 1994.

Political career: *House of Commons:* Contested Eastleigh (Lib Dem) 1992 general election. MP (Lib Dem) for Eastleigh 1994 by-election to 2005. Liberal Democrat Spokesperson for: Employment 1994-95, Transport 1995-97, Trade and Industry 1997-99, Foreign Affairs 1999-2005. Member: Accomodation and Works 1998-2001, Standards and Privileges 2001, Foreign Affairs 1999-2005, Chairman's Panel 2001-05, Joint Committee on Human Rights 2003-05. *House of Lords:* Raised to the peerage as Baron Chidgey, of Hamble-le-Rice in the County of Hampshire 2005. Liberal Democrat Spokesperson for: Defence (Royal Navy, Defence Procurement) 2005-06, International Development and for the Foreign and Commonwealth Office (Africa) -2010. Co-opted member EU Sub-committee C (Foreign Affairs, Defence and Development Policy) 2006-10. Chair, Liberal Democrat Parliamentary Party Committee on International Affairs (International Development) 2010-. *Other:* Contested (SLD) Hampshire Central 1988 by-election and 1989 European Parliament election. Regional chair, Hampshire and Wight Liberal Democrats 1992-94; Joint founder and president, Association of Liberal Democrat Engineers and Applied Scientists. *Councils and public bodies:* Councillor, Winchester City Council 1987-91.

Political interests: Foreign affairs, international development, transport, built environment; Africa, Pacific Rim and South East Asia, Indian sub-continent, Middle East, Europe.

Other: AWEPA (European Parliamentarians with Africa): UK Parliament Representative 2007-, Director, Governing Council 2010-, Political co-ordinator for aid effectiveness, SADC region 2011-; Member, advisory board, UK Transatlantic Leadership Academy SLLF/Europe 2007-12; Chair, international advisory board, CPSU (Commonwealth Policy Studies Unit) 2008-12; Member, advisory board, TI (UK) 2008-; Delegate, Parliamentary Assembly Council of Europe and Western European Union 2009-11; Fellow: Institution of Civil Engineers, Institution of Engineers of Ireland, Institution of Highways and Transportation, Association of Consulting Engineers of

Ireland, Industry and Parliament Trust 1999; Member, The Chartered Institute of Transport; Companion, Royal Aeronautical Society; Save The Children. Liveryman Worshipful Company of Carmen. Freedom: City of London 1997, Borough of Eastleigh 2005; National Liberal.
Recreations: Reading, walking, following cricket.
The Lord Chidgey, House of Lords, London SW1A 0PW
Tel: 020 7219 6944 *Fax:* 020 7219 5436 *Email:* chidgeyd@parliament.uk

NON-AFFILIATED

CHOLMONDELEY, MARQUESS OF

CHOLMONDELEY (7th Marquess of, UK), David George Philip Cholmondeley; cr. 1815; 10th Earl of Cholmondeley (E) 1706; 7th Earl of Rocksavage (UK) 1815; 10th Viscount Malpas (E) 1706; 11th Viscount Cholmondeley (I) 1661; 10th Baron Cholmondeley (E) 1689; 10th Baron Newburgh (GB) 1716; 10th Baron Newborough (I) 1715. Born 27 June 1960; Son of 6th Marquess, GCVO, MC, DL; Married Rose Hanbury 2009 (twin sons).
Education: Eton College; Sorbonne.
Non-political career: Page of Honour to HM The Queen 1974-76; Joint Hereditary Lord Great Chamberlain of England (acting for the reign of Queen Elizabeth II) 1990-.
Political career: *House of Lords:* First entered House of Lords 1990; On leave of absence.
Other: KCVO 2007.
Most Hon the Marquess of Cholmondeley KCVO, House of Lords, London SW1A 0PW
Tel: 020 7219 5353
Houghton Hall, King's Lynn, Norfolk PE31 6UA *Tel:* 01829 720202

CROSSBENCH

CHORLEY, LORD

CHORLEY (2nd Baron, UK), Roger Richard Edward Chorley; cr. 1945. Born 14 August 1930; Son of 1st Baron, QC; Married Ann Elizabeth Debenham 1964 (2 sons).
Education: Stowe School, Buckinghamshire; Gonville and Caius College, Cambridge (BA natural sciences and economics 1953).
Non-political career: Coopers and Lybrand 1954-90: Partner 1967-89.
Political career: *House of Lords:* First entered House of Lords 1978; Elected hereditary peer 2001-. *Councils and public bodies:* Member: Royal Commission on the Press 1974-77, Ordnance Survey Review Committee 1978-79, Top Salaries Review Body 1981-91, Ordnance Survey Advisory Board 1982-85.
Political interests: Heritage, countryside, environment.
Other: Board member, Royal National Theatre 1980-91; Chair, Committee on Handling of Geographic Information 1985-87; Patron, British Mountaineering Council 1985-; President, Royal Geographical Society 1987-90; Member, Natural Environment Research Council 1988-94; Chair, National Trust 1991-96; Deputy chair, British Council 1991-99; Vice-President: Friends of the Lake District 1993-, Campaign for National Parks 1995-; Fellow, Institute of Chartered Accountants 1959; Honorary Fellow, Royal Institute of Chartered Surveyors 1995. Four honorary degrees; Alpine.
Recreations: Mountains.
The Lord Chorley, House of Lords, London SW1A 0PW
Tel: 020 7219 5353

LABOUR

CHRISTOPHER, LORD

CHRISTOPHER (Life Baron), Anthony (Tony) Martin Grosvenor Christopher; cr. 1998. Born 25 April 1925; Son of late George and Helen Christopher; Married Adela Thompson 1962.
Education: Cheltenham Grammar School; Westminster College of Commerce.
Non-political career: RAF 1944-48. Articled Pupil Agricultural Valuers, Gloucester 1941-44; Inland Revenue 1948-57; Civil Service Building Society: Director 1958-87, Chair 1978-87; General Secretary, Inland Revenue Staff Federation 1976-88; TUC General Council: Member 1976-89, Chair 1988-89; TU Fund Managers Ltd: Director 1981-2013, Chair 1983-2013; Director, Birmingham Midshires Building Society 1987-88; Industrial and Public Affairs Consultant 1988-.
Political career: *House of Lords:* Raised to the peerage as Baron Christopher, of Leckhampton in the County of Gloucestershire 1998. Member: Consolidation, Etc, Bills Joint Committee 2000-, Audit 2003-06, European Union Sub-committee D (Environment and Agriculture) 2005-06, Tax Law Rewrite Bills Joint Committee 2007-09. *Councils and public bodies:* Member, Inner London Probation and After-care Committee 1966-79; Chair, NACRO 1973-98; Member: Tax Reform

Committee 1974-80, Royal Commission on Distribution of Income and Wealth 1978-79, Independent Broadcasting Authority 1978-83; Chair, Tyre Industry Economic Development Council 1983-86; Member: Council of Institute of Manpower Studies 1984-89, Economic and Social Research Council 1985-88; Vice-President, Building Societies Association 1985-90; Member: General Medical Council 1989-94, Audit Commission 1989-95, Broadcasting Complaints Commission 1989-97.

Political interests: Agriculture, financial services, pensions, penal affairs and policy, economics, industry, the elderly; Africa, China, Egypt.

Other: Members' Auditor, International Confederation of Free Trades Unions 1983-2007; Trustee: Trades Union Unit Trust Charitable Trust 1981-, Commonwealth Trades Union Council Charitable Trust 1985-89, Save The Children Fund 1985-90; Institute for Public Policy Research: Trustee 1989-94, Treasurer 1990-94; Trustee, Douglas Houghton Memorial Fund 1998-; FRSA 1989. CBE 1984; Beefsteak, Wig and Pen.

Publications: Co-author: Policy for Poverty (1970); The Wealth Report (1979); The Wealth Report 2 (1982).

Recreations: Gardening, dog walking.

The Lord Christopher CBE, House of Lords, London SW1A 0PW
Tel: 020 7219 6162
TU Fund Managers Ltd, Congress House, Great Russell Street, London WC1B 3LQ
Tel: 020 7637 7114 *Fax:* 020 7637 7057

CLANCARTY, EARL OF

CLANCARTY (9th Earl of, I), Nicholas Power Richard Le Poer Trench; cr. 1803; 9th Viscount Dunlo (I), 1800; 8th Viscount Clancarty (UK) 1823; 9th Baron Kilconnel (I) 1797; 8th Baron Trench (UK) 1815; 8th Marquess of Heusden in the Netherlands 1818. Born 1 May 1952; Son of late Hon Power Edward Ford Le Poer (Terry) Trench and late Jocelyn Louise (Joy) Courtney; Married Victoria Frances Lambert 2005 (1 daughter).

Education: Westminster School; Ashford County Grammar School; Plymouth Polytechnic (BA geography and geology 1975); University of Colorado, USA (MA geography 1978); Sheffield Polytechnic (BA fine art 1987); French, German.

CROSSBENCH

Non-political career: Artist and writer; Company secretary, Dysart Press.

Political career: *House of Lords:* First entered House of Lords 1995. Sits as Viscount Clancarty; Elected hereditary peer 2010-.

Political interests: Arts and cultural issues, welfare, education; France, Germany, Netherlands.

The Earl of Clancarty, House of Lords, London SW1A 0PW
Tel: 020 7219 8929 *Email:* clancartyn@parliament.uk *Twitter:* @NickClancarty

CLARK OF CALTON, BARONESS

CLARK OF CALTON (Life Baroness), Lynda Margaret Clark; cr 2005. Born 26 February 1949.

Education: Queen's College, St Andrews University (LLB 1970); Edinburgh University (PhD 1975).

Non-political career: Dundee University: Part-time tutor 1971-73, Lecturer in jurisprudence 1973-76; Advocate, Scots Bar 1977-89; QC 1989-99 in practice at Scots Bar; Called to the English Bar 1990; Governing bencher, Inner Temple 2000; Senator of the College of Justice in Scotland 2006-.

NON-AFFILIATED

Political career: *House of Commons:* Contested North East Fife 1992 general election. MP (Labour) for Edinburgh Pentlands 1997-2005. Advocate General for Scotland 1999-2005. *House of Lords:* Raised to the peerage as Baroness Clark of Calton, of Calton in the City of Edinburgh 2005. Advocate General for Scotland 2005-06; Lord of Appeal 2006-08; As a senior member of the judiciary, disqualified from participation 2006-.

Political interests: Constitutional reform, justice system, health, education, pensions.

Other: Former member: Scottish Legal Aid Board, Edinburgh University Court. QC (Scot) 1989.

The Baroness Clark of Calton QC, House of Lords, London SW1A 0PW
Tel: 020 7219 5353

LABOUR

CLARK OF WINDERMERE, LORD

CLARK OF WINDERMERE (Life Baron), David George Clark; cr. 2001. Born 19 October 1939; Son of George Clark; Married Christine Kirkby 1970 (1 daughter).

Education: Windermere Grammar School; Manchester University (BA economics 1963, MSc 1965) Sheffield University (PhD 1978).

Non-political career: Forester 1956-57; Laboratory worker in textile mill 1957-59; Student teacher, Salford 1959-60; President, University of Manchester Union 1963-64; Lecturer in public administration, Salford University 1965-70; Chair, Forestry Commission 2001-10. Member, Unison.

Political career: *House of Commons:* Contested Manchester Withington division 1966 general election. MP (Labour) for Colne Valley 1970-74, for South Shields 1979-2001. Opposition Spokesperson for: Agriculture, Fisheries and Food 1972-74, Defence 1980-81, Environment 1981-87, Food, Agricultural and Rural Affairs 1987-92, Defence, Disarmament and Arms Control 1992-97; Chancellor of the Duchy of Lancaster 1997-98. *House of Lords:* Raised to the peerage as Baron Clark of Windermere, of Windermere in the County of Cumbria 2001. Member Joint Committee on National Security Strategy 2013-. Vice-chair, PLP Departmental Group for Defence 2010-. *Councils and public bodies:* DL, Cumbria 2006.

Political interests: Open spaces, forestry, defence, security.

Other: UK Delegation of the North Atlantic Assembly 1980-2005: Member 1980-97, 1998-2005, Leader 2001-05; Executive member, National Trust 1980-94; Patron, Vindolanda Trust 1983-; Trustee, History of Parliament Trust 1986-; Director, Carlisle United AFC; Fellow, University of Cumbria. Freeman, Borough of South Tyneside 1998. Honorary Fellow, Cumbria University 2009. PC 1997. Director, Carslile United AFC 2002-.

Publications: Industrial Manager (1966); Colne Valley: Radicalism to Socialism (1981); Victor Grayson: Labour's Lost Leader (1985); We Do Not Want The Earth (1992); The Labour Movement in Westmorland (2012).

Recreations: Gardening, fell-walking, reading, watching football.

Rt Hon the Lord Clark of Windermere DL, House of Lords, London SW1A 0PW
Tel: 020 7219 2558 *Email:* clarkd@parliament.uk

LABOUR

CLARKE OF HAMPSTEAD, LORD

CLARKE OF HAMPSTEAD (Life Baron), Anthony James Clarke; cr. 1998. Born 17 April 1932; Son of Henry Clarke and Elizabeth Clarke; Married Josephine Turner 1954 (1 son 1 daughter).

Education: St Dominic's Roman Catholic School, Kentish Town; Ruskin College, Oxford (Correspondence course trade union studies).

Non-political career: National Service, Royal Signals 1950-52; TA and Army Emergency Reserve 1952-68. Post Office: Telegraph boy, Postman, Postman higher grade (sorter); Union of Postal Workers (UPW): Full-time trade union officer 1979-93, Editor, UPW journal *The Post* 1979, Deputy General Secretary 1981-93. Branch Secretary, UPW 1962-69; Member: London Trades Council 1965-69 (EC Member 1967-68), TUC Disputes Panel 1972-93, TUC South East Regional Council 1974-79, London Council of Post Office Unions 1975-79, Midlands Council of Post Office Unions 1975-79; President, TU Friends of Israel.

Political career: *House of Commons:* Contested (Labour) Camden Hampstead February and October 1974 general elections. *House of Lords:* Raised to the peerage as Baron Clarke of Hampstead, of Hampstead in the London Borough of Camden 1998. *Other:* Member: Executive Committee, Labour Friends of Israel 1972-2001, Labour Party National Executive Committee 1983-93, St Albans Labour Party 1986-2013; Chair, Labour Party 1992-93. *Councils and public bodies:* Councillor, London Borough of Camden 1971-78.

Political interests: Overseas aid and development, industrial relations.

Other: Organiser and Lecturer, Postal and Telegraph International, Malaysia and India; Trustee, Post Office Pension Funds 1991-97; Governor, Westminster Foundation for Democracy 1992-98; Founder member, One World Action; RAF Museum. Knight of St Gregory (Papal Order) 1994; CBE 1998.

Recreations: Arsenal FC, *The Archers*, reading.

The Lord Clarke of Hampstead CBE, House of Lords, London SW1A 0PW
Tel: 020 7219 1379 *Email:* clarkeaj@parliament.uk

NON-AFFILIATED

CLARKE OF STONE-CUM-EBONY, LORD

CLARKE OF STONE-CUM-EBONY (Life Baron), Anthony Peter Clarke; cr 2009. Born 13 May 1943; Son of late Harry Clarke and Isobel Clarke, née Kay; Married Rosemary Adam 1968 (2 sons 1 daughter).

Education: Oakham School, Rutland; King's College, Cambridge (BA economics, law, MA).

Non-political career: Called to the Bar, Middle Temple 1965; QC 1979; Recorder 1985-92; Bencher Middle Temple 1987; Judge Queen's Bench Division High Court of Justice 1993-98; Admiralty Judge 1993-98; Lord Justice of Appeal 1998-2005; Head of Civil Justice 2005-09; Master of the Rolls 2005-09; Justice of the Supreme Court of the United Kingdom 2009-.

Political career: *House of Lords:* Raised to the peerage as Baron Clarke of Stone-cum-Ebony, of Stone-cum-Ebony in the County of Kent 2009. As Justice of the Supreme Court, disqualified from participation 2009-.

Other: Honorary Doctor of Laws: Exeter University 2006, Kent University 2009, Hull University 2009. Kt 1993; PC 1998.

Recreations: Bridge, tennis, golf, holidays.

Rt Hon the Lord Clarke of Stone-cum-Ebony, House of Lords, London SW1A 0PW
Tel: 020 7219 5353
Supreme Court of the United Kingdom, Parliament Square, London SW1P 3BD *Tel:* 020 7960 1966 *Fax:* 020 7960 1961 *Email:* jackie.sears@supremecourt.gsi.gov.uk

LIBERAL DEMOCRAT

CLEMENT-JONES, LORD

CLEMENT-JONES (Life Baron), Timothy Francis Clement-Jones; cr. 1998. Born 26 October 1949; Son of late Maurice Clement-Jones and Margaret Clement-Jones, née Hudson; Married Dr Vicky Yip 1973 (died 1987); married Jean Whiteside 1994 (1 son).

Education: Haileybury College, Hertford; Trinity College, Cambridge (MA economics and law 1971); French, German.

Non-political career: Solicitor; Head of legal services, London Weekend Television 1980-83; Legal director, Grand Metropolitan Retailing 1984-86; Group company secretary and legal adviser, Kingfisher plc 1986-95; Chair: Context Group Ltd 1997-2009, Upstream (government and media relation practice of DLA Piper Rudick Gray Cary) 1999-2006; Partner, DLA Piper The Global Law Firm 1999-; Co-chair, DLA Piper Global Government Relations 2006-09; London Managing Partner, DLA Piper 2011-.

Political career: *House of Lords:* Raised to the peerage as Baron Clement-Jones, of Clapham in the London Borough of Lambeth 1998. Liberal Democrat Spokesperson for: Health 1998-2004, Culture, Media and Sport 2004-10; Member, Speakers' Working Group on All-Party Groups 2011-12. Member Communications 2010-. *Other:* Chair, Association of Liberal Lawyers 1981-86; Member, Liberal Democrat National Executive 1988-98; Chair, Liberal Democrat Party Federal Finance Committee 1991-98; Director, Liberal Democrat Campaign for the European Parliamentary elections 1994; Chair, London mayoral and Assembly campaign 2000, 2004; Federal Treasurer, Liberal Democrats 2005-10.

Political interests: Cancer, inner cities, autism, crime prevention, creative industries, intellectual property, higher education; Central Asia, China, Iraq, Turkey, UAE.

Other: Trustee, Cancerbackup 1986-2008; Chairman and director, Crime Concern 1988-99; Member, Council London Lighthouse 1989-93; Director, Brixton City Challenge 1994-98; Patron, Tymes Trust; Director, British America Business Inc; Member, 48 Group Club (promotion of relations with China); Chair: Treehouse (charity for autistic children) 2001-08, Lambeth Crime Prevention Trust 2004-09, Council, School of Pharmacy, London University 2008-12; President, Ambitious About Autism 2011-; Member of Council, University College London 2012-; Trustee: Space for Giants, Barbican Centre Trust 2012-; Fellow, Public Relations Consultants Association; Law Society of England and Wales; FRSA; FIPR. Freeman, City of London. Honorary Fellow, UCL School of Pharmacy. CBE 1988; Arts.

Recreations: Travelling, eating, talking, reading, walking, the arts.

The Lord Clement-Jones CBE, House of Lords, London SW1A 0PW
Tel: 020 7219 5353 *Email:* clementjonest@parliament.uk
DLA Piper UK LLP, 3 Noble Street, London EC2V 7EE *Tel:* 020 7796 6169
Email: tim.clement-jones@dlapiper.com *Website:* www.lordclementjones.org

LABOUR

CLINTON-DAVIS, LORD

CLINTON-DAVIS (Life Baron), Stanley Clinton Clinton-Davis; cr. 1990. Born 6 December 1928; Son of Sidney and Lily Davis; Married Frances Lucas 1954 (1 son 3 daughters).

Education: Hackney Downs School, London Mercers' School, London; King's College, London University (LLB 1950).

Non-political career: Admitted solicitor 1953; Senior Partner Clintons/Clinton Davis & Co; European Commissioner for Environment Policy, Nuclear Safety and Transport 1985-89; Chairman, UNEP Sasakawa Award Committee 1989-2005; Member, panel of judges, Seatrade Awards; Former consultant on European law and affairs with S. J. Berwin & Co. solicitors. Member, GMB; Former trustee, NUMAST.

Political career: *House of Commons:* Contested Portsmouth, Langstone 1955 and Yarmouth 1959 and 1964 general elections. MP (Labour) for Hackney Central 1970-83. Parliamentary Under-Secretary of State, Department of Trade 1974-79; Opposition Spokesperson for: Trade, Prices and Consumer Protection 1979-81, Foreign Affairs 1981-83. *House of Lords:* Raised to the peerage as Baron Clinton-Davis, of Hackney in the London Borough of Hackney 1990. Opposition Spokesperson for Transport 1990-97; Supporting Spokesperson for: Trade and Industry 1990-96, Foreign Affairs 1990-97; Minister of State, Department of Trade and Industry (Minister for Trade) 1997-98. Member: Liaison 2001-05, EU Sub-committee E (Law and Institutions) 2003-07, Joint Committee on Statutory Instruments 2009-13, EU Sub-committee B: (Internal Market, Energy and Transport) 2010-12, (Internal Market, Infrastructure and Employment) 2012-, Inquiries Act 2005 2013. Vice-chair, Labour Party Departmental Committee for Legal and Constitutional Affairs 2004-10. *Other:* Member, executive council, National Association of Labour Student Organisations 1949-50; Former Joint President, Society of Labour Lawyers. *Councils and public bodies:* London Borough of Hackney: Councillor 1959-71, Mayor 1968-69, Former chair of social services.

Political interests: Transport, environment, foreign affairs, law, civil liberties, international trade; Commonwealth, Europe, Israel, South Africa, USA.

Other: Member, Parliamentary Assembly of Council of Europe and Assembly of Western European Union 2000-02; Former president: Hackney branch, Multiple Sclerosis Society, Aviation Environment Federation, UK Pilots (Marine Association); Former vice-president, Chartered Institute of Environmental Health; Former chair, Packaging Council; Former member: Royal Overseas League, Board of Deputies of British Jews; Former president, London Maritime Association; Vice-president, Institute of Export; British Airline Pilots Association: President 1980-2011, Honorary Life President 2011-; Chair: Advisory Committee on Protection of the Sea 1984-85, 1989-97, Refugee Council 1989-97; President, Association of Municipal Authorities 1992-97; Fellow, Chartered Institution of Water and Environmental Management; Fellow: Queen Mary and Westfield College, University of London 1992, King's College London, Queen Mary College 2003. Honorary Doctorate, Polytechnic University of Bucharest 1993; Honorary ACA Degree; Honorary Doctorate, University of North London/Metropolitan University 2000. First Eurogroup medal for Animal Welfare 1988. Grand Cross, Order of Leopold II (Belgium) for services to the EC 1990; PC 1998. Hendon Golf Club.

Recreations: Association football, golf, reading political biographies.

Rt Hon the Lord Clinton-Davis, House of Lords, London SW1A 0PW
Tel: 020 7219 5353 *Fax:* 020 7219 5979
Email: clintondavis200@btinternet.com

CROSSBENCH

COBBOLD, LORD

COBBOLD (2nd Baron, UK), David Antony Fromanteel Lytton Cobbold; cr. 1960. Born 14 July 1937; Son of 1st Baron, KG, PC, GCVO, DL, and Lady Hermione Bulwer-Lytton, daughter of 2nd Earl of Lytton, KG, PC, GCSI, GCIE, DL; Married Christine Stucley 1961 (3 sons 1 daughter).

Education: Eton College; Trinity College, Cambridge (BA moral sciences 1960).

Non-political career: Pilot Officer, RAF national service 1955-57. Bank of London and South America 1962-72; Responsible for upkeep and public opening of Knebworth House, Hertfordshire 1970-2001; Chairman, Lytton Enterprises Ltd, Knebworth 1971-: Treasurer, Finance for Industry Ltd 1974-79; Manager, Treasury Division BP Finance International 1979-87; Director, Hill Samuel Bank Ltd 1988-89; Head of Treasury and Financial Markets, TSB England and Wales plc and Hill Samuel Bank Ltd 1988-89; Managing director, Gaiacorp UK Ltd 1989-94; Director: Close Brothers Group plc 1993-2000, Stevenage Leisure Ltd 1998-2000.

Political career: *House of Commons:* Contested (Liberal) Bishop Auckland October 1974 general election. *House of Lords:* First entered House of Lords 1987; Elected hereditary peer 2000-. Member: Advisory Panel on Works of Art 2003-05, European Union Sub-committee A (Economic and Financial Affairs) 2003-07. *Other:* Contested Hertfordshire 1979 European Parliament election. *Councils and public bodies:* Historic Houses Association: Member, Executive Committee 1974-97, Treasurer 1988-97; President, Knebworth Twinning Association 1990-; Member, Association for Monetary Union in Europe 1991-2002; President, University of Hertfordshire Development Committee 1991-2005; Member, Board of Governors, University of Hertfordshire 1993-2005; Governor, European Union of Historic Houses Association 1993-97; DL, Hertfordshire 1993-.

Political interests: Historic buildings, drugs policy, planning policy; China, European Union, India.

Other: Fellow, Association of Corporate Treasurers 1983-; Chairman, Stevenage Community Trust 1991-2006; Trustee, Pilgrim Trust 1993-2010; Director: Shuttleworth Trust 1998-2000, English Sinfonia Ltd 1998-2000; Trustee, Knebworth House Education and Preservation Trust 2001-; Fellow, University of Hertfordshire 2006-.

Recreations: Theatre, travel.

The Lord Cobbold DL, House of Lords, London SW1A 0PW
Tel: 020 7219 6887 *Email:* david@parkgatehouse.net

CONSERVATIVE

COE, LORD

COE (Life Baron), Sebastian Newbold Coe; cr. 2000. Born 29 September 1956; Son of late Peter and Angela Coe; Married Nicola McIrvine 1990 (2 sons 2 daughters); married Carole Annett, née Smith 2011.

Education: Tapton Secondary Modern School, Sheffield; Abbeydale Grange School; Loughborough University (BSc economics and social history 1979).

Non-political career: Athlete; Associate member, Academy of Sport (France) 1982; Sports Council: Member 1983-89, Vice-chair 1986-89; Member, Health Education Authority 1987-92; Steward, British Boxing Board of Control 1994-; Member, Athletes and Medical Commission of International Olympic Committee 1997; Private Secretary to William Hague as Leader of the Opposition 1997-2001; President, Amateur Athletics Association 2000-03; Sports columnist, *Daily Telegraph*; Founding member, Laureus World Sports Academy 2000; Global adviser to Nike 2001-; Athletics commentator, Channel 7, Australia; London 2012 Olympic Bid: Vice-chair 2003-04, Chair 2004-05; Chair, LOCOG (London Organising Committee of the Olympic Games and Paralympic Games) 2005-13; Vice President IAAF (International Association of Athletics Federations); Ex-officio member, Olympic Board; Chair: Sports Honours Committee 2011, British Olympic Association 2012-; The Complete Leisure Group Ltd; Executive chair, CSM Sport and Entertainment LLP.

Political career: *House of Commons:* MP (Conservative) for Falmouth and Camborne 1992-97. PPS: to Roger Freeman: as Minister of State for Defence Procurement 1994-95, as Chancellor of the Duchy of Lancaster and Minister of Public Service 1995-96, to Nicholas Soames as Minister of State for the Armed Forces 1994-95, to Michael Heseltine as First Secretary of State and Deputy Prime Minister 1995-96; Assistant Government Whip 1996-97. *House of Lords:* Raised to the peerage as Baron Coe, of Ranmore in the County of Surrey 2000. Olympics legacy ambassador 2012-.

Political interests: Health, foreign affairs, education, environment, economy, voluntary movement.

Other: Progressive Supranucleur Palsy Association (PSP). Pro-Chancellor Loughborough University. Honorary DSc, Hull University 1988; Honorary LLD, Sheffield University; Honorary Fellow, UWIC. Gold 1,500m and silver 800m medals at Moscow Olympic Games 1980 and Los Angeles Olympic Games 1984; European Champion for 800m Stuttgart 1986; Set nine world records; BBC Sports Personality of the Year 1979; Sportswriters' Sportsman of the Year: 1979, 1980, 1981, 1984; Lifetime Achievement Award, BBC Sports Personality of the Year 2012. MBE 1982; OBE 1990; KBE 2006; CH 2013; Carlton Club; East India Club.

Publications: Autobiography, Running My Life (Hodder & Stoughton, 2012).

Recreations: Jazz, theatre, reading.

The Lord Coe CH KBE, House of Lords, London SW1A 0PW
Tel: 020 7219 5353 *Twitter:* @sebcoe

COHEN OF PIMLICO, BARONESS

LABOUR

COHEN OF PIMLICO (Life Baroness), Janet Cohen; cr. 2000. Born 4 July 1940; Daughter of late George Neel and Mary Neel; Married James Cohen 1971 (2 sons 1 daughter).

Education: South Hampstead High School, London; Newnham College, Cambridge (BA law 1962) (Associate Fellow 1988-91); Good French, some German.

Non-political career: Articled clerk, Frere Cholmeley 1963-65; Admitted solicitor 1965; Consultant: ABT Associates, USA 1965-67, John Laing Construction 1968-69; Department of Trade and Industry: Principal 1969-78, Assistant secretary 1978-82; Charterhouse Bank Ltd: Assistant director 1982-88, Director 1988-2000; Chair, Café Pelican Ltd 1984-90; Yorkshire Building Society: Director 1991-94, Vice-chair 1994-99; BPP Holdings: Non-executive director 1994-2002, Non-executive chair 2002-06; Non-executive director: Waddington plc 1994-97, London and Manchester Assurance 1997-98, ISI Ltd 1998-2002, United Assurance 1999-2000, Defence Logistics Organisation 1999-2005, London Stock Exchange 2001-13; Vice-chair, Borsa Italiana 2001-14; Non-executive director: Management Consulting Group plc 2003-10, Freshwater UK plc 2007-09, Invisco Media Holdings 2007-09. Member, First Division Association 1969-82.

Political career: *House of Lords:* Raised to the peerage as Baroness Cohen of Pimlico, in the City of Westminster 2000. Member: Tax Law Rewrite Bills Joint Committee 2001-07, European Union 2006-10; Chair EU Sub-committee A (Economic and Financial Affairs) 2006-10; Member: Small-and Medium-Sized Enterprises 2012-13, Joint Committee on the Draft Communications Data Bill 2012-13. *Councils and public bodies:* Governor, BBC 1994-99.

Political interests: Finance, City affairs; France, Germany, Italy, New Zealand.

Other: Chair, Cambridge Arts Theatre 2007-; President, BPP University College 2008-13; Cambridge Arts Theatre Trust. Chancellor, BPP University 2013-. Honorary DLitt, Humberside 1995; Honorary fellow: St Edmunds College, Cambridge, Lucy Cavendish College, Cambridge.

Publications: As Janet Neel: Death's Bright Angel (1988); Death on Site (1989); Death of a Partner (1991); Death among the Dons (1993); A Timely Death (1999); To Die For (1998); O Gentle Death (2000); Ticket to Ride (2005); As Janet Cohen: The Highest Bidder (1992); Children of a Harsh Winter (1994).

Recreations: Writing, hill-walking.

The Baroness Cohen of Pimlico, House of Lords, London SW1A 0PW
Tel: 020 7219 5353 *Email:* janet@bnsjcohen.com

COLLINS OF HIGHBURY, LORD

Opposition Whip; Opposition Spokesperson for International Development

LABOUR

COLLINS OF HIGHBURY (Life Baron), Raymond Edward Harry Collins; cr 2011. Born 21 December 1954; Son of late Harry and Isobel Collins; Civil Partner Rafael Ballesteros 2005.

Education: Matthew Arnold School, Staines; Richmond College; Kent University, Canterbury (BA industrial relations and politics 1980); Conversational Spanish.

Non-political career: Transport and General Workers' Union/Unite: Assistant librarian 1972-74, Specialist assistant, Education 1974-77, Policy adviser and special assistant to General Secretary 1980-84, National administrative officer 1984-99, Assistant General Secretary 1999-2008. Member: TGWU/Unite 1972-, Branch Committee, Staff Negotiating Committee.

Political career: *House of Lords:* Raised to the peerage as Baron Collins of Highbury, of Highbury in the London Borough of Islington 2011. Opposition Whip 2011-; Opposition Spokesperson for: Work and Pensions 2012-13, International Development 2013-. *Other:* Labour Party: Member 1970-, Member, National Policy Forum 1997-2003, Elected Member, National Constitution Committee 2001-08, General Secretary 2008-11. *Councils and public bodies:* Governing Body, Ruskin College, Oxford.

Political interests: Equality, international affairs, justice and opportunity; South America, Spain.

Other: Director, Lionel Cook Memorial Fund 2008-; Member, Ruskin College Governing Council; Stonewall; Patron, Positive East.

Recreations: Arsenal FC, cinema, reading, swimming.

The Lord Collins of Highbury, House of Lords, London SW1A 0PW
Tel: 020 7219 1675 *Fax:* 020 7219 0699 *Email:* collinsr@parliament.uk
Twitter: @Lord_Collins

NON-AFFILIATED

COLLINS OF MAPESBURY, LORD

COLLINS OF MAPESBURY (Life Baron), Lawrence Antony Collins; cr 2009. Born 7 May 1941; Son of Sol and Phoebe Collins; Married Sara Shamni 1982 (divorced 2003) (1 son 1 daughter); married Patti Langton 2013.

Education: City of London School; Downing College, Cambridge (BA 1963); Columbia University, New York (LLM 1965).

Non-political career: Solicitor 1968; Herbert Smith solicitors: Partner 1971-2000, Head of Litigation and Arbitration Department 1995-98; Visiting professor, Queen Mary College, London 1982-; QC 1997; Deputy High Court Judge 1997-2000; High Court Judge Chancery Division, High Court of Justice 2000-07; Bencher Inner Temple 2001; Lord Justice of Appeal 2007-09; Justice of the Supreme Court of the United Kingdom 2009-11; Professor of law, Faculty of Laws, University College Lonon 2011-; Non-Permanent Judge, Hong Kong Court of Final Appeal 2011; Arbitrator member, Essex Court Chambers 2012-.

Political career: *House of Lords:* Raised to the peerage as Baron Collins of Mapesbury, of Hampstead Town in the London Borough of Camden 2009. Lord of Appeal in Ordinary 2009-; As Justice of the Supreme Court, disqualified from participation 2009-11. *Councils and public bodies:* Member, Department for Constitutional Affairs/Ministry of Justice Advisory Committee on Private International Law 2004-.

Other: Member, Institut de Droit International 1989; Honorary Member, Society of Legal Scholars 1993; Fellow, British Academy 1994; Honorary Life Member, Law Society 2000; Vice-President, British Institute of International and Coparative Law 2011-. Wolfson College Cambridge: Fellow 1975-, Honorary Fellow 2009-; Honorary LLD (Cambridge) 1994; Honorary Fellow, Downing College Cambridge 2000; Honorary LLD, College of Law 2008. Kt 2000; PC 2007.

Publications: General editor, Dicey & Morris/Dicey, Morris & Collins Conflict of Laws 1987-; Essays in International Litigation and the Conflict of Laws (1994); European Community Law in the United Kingdom (1st ed 1975, 4th ed 1990).

Rt Hon the Lord Collins of Mapesbury QC, House of Lords, London SW1A 0PW
Tel: 020 7219 5353

CROSSBENCH

COLVILLE OF CULROSS, VISCOUNT

COLVILLE OF CULROSS (5th Viscount, UK), Charles Mark Townshend Colville; cr. 1902; 14th Lord Colville of Culross (S) 1604; 5th Baron Colville of Culross (UK) 1885. Born 5 September 1959; Son of late 4th Viscount and Mary Colville, née Webb-Bowen.

Education: Rugby School; Durham University (BA history 1981); French, Russian.

Non-political career: Former reporter: *Ludlow Advertiser, Worcester Evening News, Weekend World,* LWT; BBC: *Newsnight, Money Programme,* Senior director of science and history documentaries, including: *Mutant Mouse* (also wrote) 2004, *Incredible Human Journey* 2009, *How The Earth Made Us* (also produced) 2010, *Horizon, Normans, Orbit.* BECTU.

Political career: *House of Lords:* Elected hereditary peer 2011-.

Political interests: Media, science, foreign affairs; China, Japan, Russia.

Recreations: Theatre, trees, learning Russian.

The Viscount Colville of Culross, House of Lords, London SW1A 0PW
Tel: 020 7219 5353 *Email:* colvillec@parliament.uk

CONSERVATIVE

COLWYN, LORD

COLWYN (3rd Baron, UK), (Ian) Anthony Hamilton-Smith; cr. 1917; 3rd Bt of Colwyn Bay (UK) 1912. Born 1 January 1942; Son of 2nd Baron; Married Sonia Morgan 1964 (divorced 1976) (1 son 1 daughter); married Nicola Tyers 1977 (2 daughters).

Education: Cheltenham College; St Bartholomew's Hospital and Royal Dental Hospital, London University (BDS London University 1966, LDS, RCS (England) 1966).

Non-political career: Dental practice 1965-2005; Non-executive director, Medical Protection Society 1989-2002; Chair, Dental Protection Ltd 1995-2001; Non-executive director, Project Hope 1996-2001; Bandleader, Lord Colwyn Organisation; Chair: RAW FM (Radio) 1998-99, Banbury Local Radio 2003-05, Campbell, Montague International 2005-08, Dental sedation practice 2005-08. Member, Musicians' Union 1966-.

Political career: *House of Lords:* First entered House of Lords 1967; Elected hereditary peer 1999-; Deputy Chairman of Committees 2007-; Deputy Speaker 2008-; Contested Lord Speaker election 2011. Member: Administration and Works Sub-committee 1997-2003, Finance and Staff

Sub-committee 1997-2003; Chair Refreshment Sub-committee 1997-2003; Co-opted member: Science and Technology Sub-committee I (Complementary and Alternative Medicine) 2000, EU Sub-committee G (Social Policy and Consumer Affairs) 2003-07; Member: Science and Technology 2006-10, Science and Technology Sub-committees: I (Allergy) 2007, II (Genomic Medicine) 2008-09, Refreshment 2012-. *Other:* Member, Conservative Medical Society; Executive member, Association of Conservative Peers 2004-10.

Political interests: Health, dentistry, complementary medicine, arts, sport, cycling.

Other: FDI Federation Dentaire International; Member, Royal Society of Medicine; President, Natural Medicines Society 1988-2005; Member, Eastman Research Institute Trust 1990-2001; President: Huntington's Disease Association 1991-98, Society for Advancement of Anaesthesia in Dentistry 1993-98, Arterial Health Foundation 1993-2004, Metropolitan Branch, British Dental Association 1994-95; Council member, Medical Protection Society 1994-2001; Fellow, Industry and Parliament Trust 2000; Trustee, Portman Estates 2004-08; Fellow, Institute of Directors 1999-2001; Fellowship, British Dental Association 2005; Macmillan; Fight for Sight; AF Foundation (Atrial Fibrillation). CBE 1989; Ronnie Scott's; 606 Club. Life member: Cheltenham Rugby Club, Colwyn Bay Rugby Club, Hennerton Golf Club, Leander.

Recreations: Bandleader, music, riparian pursuits, golf, rugby.

The Lord Colwyn CBE, House of Lords, London SW1A 0PW
Tel: 020 7219 3184 *Fax:* 020 7219 0318 *Email:* colwyna@parliament.uk

CONDON, LORD

CONDON (Life Baron) Paul Leslie Condon; cr 2001. Born 10 March 1947; Son of late Patrick and Beryl Condon; Married Janet Workman 1969 (2 sons 1 daughter).

Education: Summerbee Secondary Modern School, Bournemouth; St Peter's College, Oxford (BA jurisprudence 1972, MA).

Non-political career: Police service 1967-2000: Assistant Chief Constable of Kent 1984-87, Metropolitan Police 1987-88: Deputy Assistant Commissioner 1987-88, Assistant Commissioner 1988-89; Chief Constable of Kent 1989-93; Commissioner, Metropolitan Police 1993-2000; Director, International Cricket Council anti-corruption unit 2000-.

CROSSBENCH

Political career: *House of Lords:* Raised to the peerage as Baron Condon, of Langton Green in the County of Kent 2005. *Councils and public bodies:* Deputy Lieutenant, Kent 2000-.

Other: QPM 1989; Knighthood 1994.

Recreations: Swimming, walking, reading, cricket.

The Lord Condon QPM DL, House of Lords, London SW1A 0PW
Tel: 020 7219 3617

COPE OF BERKELEY, LORD

COPE OF BERKELEY (Life Baron), John Ambrose Cope; cr. 1997. Born 13 May 1937; Son of late George Cope, MC, FRIBA; Married Djemila Payne 1969 (2 daughters).

Education: Oakham School, Rutland.

Non-political career: National Service (Commissioned RA) 1955-57, subsequently TA. Chartered accountant.

Political career: *House of Commons:* Contested Woolwich East 1970 general election. MP (Conservative) for Gloucestershire South February 1974-83 and for Northavon 1983-97. Government

CONSERVATIVE

Whip 1979-83; Deputy Chief Whip 1983-87; Minister of State for: Employment with special responsibility for Small Firms 1987-89, Northern Ireland Office 1989-90; Paymaster General, HM Treasury 1992-94. *House of Lords:* Raised to the peerage as Baron Cope of Berkeley, of Berkeley in the County of Gloucestershire 1997. Opposition Spokesperson for: Northern Ireland 1997-98, Home Affairs 1998-2001; Opposition Chief Whip 2001-07; Deputy Chairman of Committees 2001-07; Deputy Speaker 2002-08. Member: Procedure 2000-02, House of Lords Offices 2001-02, House of Lords Offices Administration and Works Sub-committee/committee 2001-07, Liaison 2003-09, Privileges 2005-07, Sub-committee on Lords' Interests 2008-10, Joint Committee on National Security Strategy 2010-12, Sub-committee on Lords' Conduct 2010-; Chair Small- and Medium- Sized Enterprises 2012-13; Member House 2013-. *Other:* Conservative Party: Deputy Chair 1990-92, Honorary Joint Treasurer 1991-92; Trustee, Conservative Party Archive at Bodleian Library.

Political interests: Small businesses; Palestine.

Other: Member, UK Parliamentary Delegation to Council of Europe and Western European Union 1995-97; British-Irish Parliamentary Assembly: UK Member 2008-11, British co-chair 2010-11; Commissioner, Royal Hospital Chelsea 1992-94; Patron, Friends of Royal National Hospital for Rheumatic Diseases; Trustee, War Memorials Trust; Institute of Chartered Accountants in England and Wales; FCA. PC 1988; Kt 1991; Carlton; Pratts; Beefsteak; Tudor House (Chipping Sodbury). Bentley Drivers' Club, Rolls-Royce Enthusiasts Club.

Recreations: A 1939 Bentley motor car, church bell ringing.

Rt Hon the Lord Cope of Berkeley, House of Lords, London SW1A 0PW
Tel: 020 7219 2249 *Fax:* 020 7219 0753 *Email:* copej@parliament.uk

CONSERVATIVE

CORMACK, LORD

CORMACK (Life Baron), Patrick Thomas Cormack; cr 2010. Born 18 May 1939; Son of late Thomas Cormack, local government officer; Married Kathleen McDonald 1967 (2 sons).

Education: St James' Choir School, Grimsby; Havelock School, Grimsby; Hull University (BA English and history 1961); French (basic).

Non-political career: Industrial consultant; Second master, St James' Choir School, Grimsby 1961-66; Training and education officer, Ross Group Ltd 1966-67; Assistant housemaster, Wrekin College, Shropshire 1967-69; Head of history, Brewood Grammar School, Staffordshire 1969-70; Associate editor, *Time and Tide* 1977-79; *The House Magazine*: Chairman editorial board 1979-, Editor 1983-2005, Life president 2005-; Company director, Historic House Hotels 1980-88, Aitken Dott 1984-90; Visiting lecturer, University of Texas 1984; St Antony's College, Oxford: Visiting parliamentary fellowship 1994, Senior member 1995-; Visiting senior lecturer, Hull University 1994-; *First* magazine: International president 1994-, President 2004-.

Political career: *House of Commons:* Contested (Conservative) Bolsover 1964 and Grimsby 1966 general elections. MP for Cannock 1970-74, for South West Staffordshire 1974-83, for South Staffordshire 1983-2010. PPS to Joint Parliamentary Secretaries, Department of Health and Social Security 1970-73; Deputy Shadow Leader of the House of Commons 1997-2000; Contested Speaker election 2000; Opposition Spokesman for Constitutional Affairs 1997-2000; Member House of Commons Commission 2002-05; Contested Speaker election 2009. Member: Ecclesiastical Committee 1970-2010, Lord Chancellor's Advisory Committee on Public Records 1982-87, Accommodation and Works 1987-2001, Modernisation of the House of Commons 1997-98, Joint Committee on Parliamentary Privilege 1997-2000, Foreign Affairs 2001-03, Standing Orders 2001-10, Joint Committee on Human Rights 2001, Joint Committee on Consolidation Etc Bills 2001-09; Chair: Northern Ireland Affairs 2005-10; Member: Liaison 2005-10. Chairman: Conservative Parliamentary Arts and Heritage Committee 1979-83, Conservative Party's Advisory Committee on Arts and Heritage 1987-99; Member, Executive, 1922 Committee 2002-05. *House of Lords:* Raised to the peerage as Baron Cormack, of Enville in the County of Staffordshire 2010. Member Works of Art 2012-13. *Councils and public bodies:* Member, Council of Historical Association 1963-66; Founder and vice-chairman, Heritage in Danger 1974-97; Member, Historic Buildings Council 1979-84; Chairman, Council for Independent Education 1980-95; Royal Commission on Historical Manuscripts/National Archives 1981-2004; Member, General Synod of the Church of England 1995-2005; Governor, English Speaking Union 1999-2006; DL, Staffordshire 2011.

Political interests: Arts, heritage, defence and NATO, Parliamentary history, education, electoral reform, industrial relations, human rights; Bosnia, Croatia, Finland, Lithuania, Netherlands, former Soviet Union, USA.

Other: Vice-chairman, De Burght Conference; Commonwealth Parliamentary Association (CPA) UK Branch 1970: Member, executive committee 1997-99, Joint vice-chairman 1999-2000, Treasurer 2000-03; Member, Council for Peace in the Balkans 1992-2000; Historic Churches Preservation Trust/National Churches Trust: Trustee 1973-, Vice-President 2004-; Society of Antiquaries: Fellow 1978, Vice-President 1994-98; History of Parliament Trust: Member 1979-, Trustee 1983-, Chairman 2001-; Member, Institute of Journalists 1979-89; Museum of Garden History 1980-2000; Member, Council of Winston Churchill Memorial Trust 1983-93; President, Staffordshire Historic Buildings Trust 1992-; Vice-President, Lincolnshire Historic Churches Trust 1997-; Director, Parliamentary Broadcasting Unit 1997-2010; President: Staffordshire Historic Churches Trust 1998-2012, Staffordshire Parks and Gardens Trust 2006-, Prayer Book Society 2011-; Chairman: Campaign for an Effective Second Chamber 2002-, Historic Lincoln Trust 2012; Society of Antiquaries 1978-; Royal Historical Society 2010-; Honorary Fellow Historical Association 2010; Save The Children; Historic Churches Preservation Trust; RNLI; Aid to the Church in Need. Member, Worshipful Company of Glaziers; Company of Art Scholars. Freeman, City of London 1980. Honorary Fellow: Historical Association 2010, Golden Jubilee Parliamentarians, the Political Studies Association 2010; Honorary doctorate: D. Litt. Hull University 2011, Doctor of Laws

Catholic University of America 2011. Political Studies Jubilee Award 2011. Honorary Citizen of Texas 1985; Kt 1995; Commander of the Order of the Lion (Finland) 1998; Athenæum; Honorary member, The Arts Club.

Publications: Heritage in Danger (1976); Right Turn (1978); Westminster: Palace and Parliament (1981); Castles of Britain (1982); Wilberforce – The Nation's Conscience (1983); English Cathedrals (1984); Responsible Capitalism (2009).

Recreations: Walking, talking, fighting Philistines.

The Lord Cormack, House of Lords, London SW1A 0PW
Tel: 020 7219 5353

LABOUR

CORSTON, BARONESS

CORSTON (Life Baroness), Jean Ann Corston; cr 2005. Born 5 May 1942; Daughter of late Laurie Parkin, trade union official, and late Eileen Parkin; Married Christopher Corston 1961 (1 son 1 daughter); married Professor Peter Townsend 1985 (died 2009).

Education: Yeovil Girls' High School; Open University; London School of Economics (LLB 1989); Inns of Court School of Law 1989-90.

Non-political career: Barrister. Member, Unite.

Political career: *House of Commons:* MP (Labour) for Bristol East 1992-2005. PPS to David Blunkett as Secretary of State for Education and Employment 1997-2000. Chair: Joint Committee on Human Rights 2001-05; Member: Agriculture 1992-95, Home Affairs 1995-97. Co-chair, Parliamentary Labour Party Women's Group 1992-97; Chair, PLP Children and Family Group 1995-97. *House of Lords:* Raised to the peerage as Baroness Corston, of St George in the County and City of Bristol 2005. Member: Liaison 2009-13, Joint Committee on Privacy and Injunctions 2011-12; EU Sub-committee E (Justice, Institutions and Consumer Protection): Member 2012-13, Chair 2013-; Member European Union 2013-. *Other:* Regional organiser, South West Region Labour Party 1981-85; Assistant national agent, Labour Party, London 1985-86; Secretary, Labour Party Annual Conference Arrangements 1985-86; Parliamentary Labour Party: Deputy chair 1997-2001, Chair 2001-05.

Political interests: Equal opportunities, disability, human rights, complementary medicine; India, Kenya, USA.

Other: Member, Executive Committee, Commonwealth Parliamentary Association UK Branch 1999-2005, 2010-11; Chair, Commonwealth Women Parliamentarians 2000; Fellow, Royal Society of Arts; Vice-chair and trustee, Parliament Choir 2011-. PC 2003.

Publications: The Corston Report (Home Office, 2007).

Recreations: Gardening, reading.

Rt Hon the Baroness Corston, House of Lords, London SW1A 0PW
Tel: 020 7219 4575 *Email:* corstonj@parliament.uk

LIBERAL DEMOCRAT

COTTER, LORD

COTTER (Life Baron), Brian Joseph Cotter; cr 2006. Born 24 August 1936; Son of late Michael Cotter and late Mary Cotter; Married Eyleen Wade 1963 (2 sons 1 daughter).

Education: Downside School, Somerset; London Polytechnic (business studies).

Non-political career: National Service, 1956-58. Plasticable Ltd 1990-2003: Sales manager, Managing director.

Political career: *House of Commons:* Contested Weston-Super-Mare 1992 general election. MP (Liberal Democrat) for Weston-Super-Mare 1997-2005. Liberal Democrat Spokesperson for Small Businesses 1997-2005. *House of Lords:* Raised to the peerage as Baron Cotter, of Congresbury in the County of Somerset 2006. Liberal Democrat Spokesperson for: Small Business 2006-10, Skills 2007-10. Co-opted member EU Sub-committee G (Social Policy and Consumer Affairs) 2008-10; Member EU Sub-committees: G (Social Policies and Consumer Protection) 2010-12, B (Internal Market, Infrastructure and Employment) 2013-. *Councils and public bodies:* Councillor, Woking Borough Council 1986-90.

Political interests: Business, tourism, foreign affairs, youth affairs, apprenticeships and skills; China, Ireland, Rwanda.

Other: MIND, Oxfam, Cafod, Survivors' Fund (Rwandan Widows Charity).

Publications: Creating an Entrepreneurial Culture (2001).

Recreations: Reading, walking, gardening, films.

The Lord Cotter, House of Lords, London SW1A 0PW
Tel: 020 7219 8271 *Email:* cotterb@parliament.uk

CONSERVATIVE

COURTOWN, EARL OF

COURTOWN (9th Earl of, I), James Patrick Montagu Burgoyne Winthrop Stopford; cr. 1762; Viscount Stopford; 9th Baron Courtown (I) 1758; 8th Baron Saltersford (GB) 1796. Born 19 March 1954; Son of 8th Earl, OBE, TD; Married Elisabeth Dunnett 1985 (1 son 2 daughters).

Education: Eton College; Berkshire College of Agriculture; Royal Agricultural College, Cirencester.

Non-political career: Land agent: Bruton Knowles, Gloucester 1987-90, John German, Shrewsbury 1990-93.

Political career: *House of Lords:* First entered House of Lords 1975. Sits as Baron Saltersford; Government Spokesperson for the Home Office, Scotland and Transport 1995-97; Government Whip 1995-97; Opposition Whip 1997-2000; Elected hereditary peer 1999-. Member: Bodmin Moor Commons Bill 1994, EU Sub-committees: G (Social Policies and Consumer Protection) 2011-12, D (Agriculture, Fisheries, Environment and Energy) 2012-13.

Political interests: Agriculture, environment, property, landscape industry, West Country; Ireland, Switzerland.

Recreations: Skiing, gardening.

The Earl of Courtown, House of Lords, London SW1A 0PW
Tel: 020 7219 3129 *Email:* courtownp@parliament.uk
Website: www.lordcourtown.com *Twitter:* @LordCourtown

CROSSBENCH

COUSSINS, BARONESS

COUSSINS (Life Baroness), Jean Elizabeth Coussins; cr 2007. Born 26 October 1950; Daughter of Jessica Coussins, née Hughes, and Walter Coussins; Divorced (1 son 2 daughters).

Education: Godolphin and Latymer Girls' School, London; Newnham College, Cambridge (BA modern and medieval languages 1973, MA); French, Spanish.

Non-political career: Secretary, United Nations Association 1973-75; Women's rights officer, National Council for Civil Liberties 1975-80; Deputy director, Child Poverty Action Group 1980-83; Senior education officer, Inner London Education Authority 1983-88; Commission for Racial Equality 1988-96: Director: Social policy 1988-94, Equality assurance 1994-96; Chief executive officer, Portman Group 1996-2006; Independent consultant on corporate responsibility 2006-.

Political career: *House of Lords:* Raised to the peerage as Baroness Coussins, of Whitehall Park in the London Borough of Islington 2007. Member: Information 2007-12, EU Sub-committee C (External Affairs) 2013-. *Councils and public bodies:* Member: DTI Crime Prevention Panel 1999, Scottish Ministerial Advisory Group on Alcohol Problems 2001-06, Advisory council, British Board of Film Classification 2002-05, Advertising Standards Authority 2003-09, Alcohol Education and Research Council 2004-07, Better Regulation Commission 2004-07; Governor, Channing School 2007-12.

Political interests: Modern languages, corporate social responsibility, regulation, social justice and equal opportunity, international affairs, UN; Latin America especially Chile and Peru, Cuba, EU, France, South Africa, Spain.

Other: Member, Advisory Panel on Corporate Responsibility, Camelot 2010-; President, Money Advice Trust 2010-; Vice-President, Chartered Institute of Linguists 2010-; President, Peru Support Group 2012-; Associate Fellow, Newnham College Cambridge 2003-05; Honorary Fellow, University College London 2010-. Fulham Football Club.

Recreations: Family, travel, food, swimming, football, crosswords.

The Baroness Coussins, House of Lords, London SW1A 0PW
Tel: 020 7219 8532 *Email:* coussinsj@parliament.uk

NON-AFFILIATED

COVENTRY, LORD BISHOP OF

COVENTRY (9th Bishop of), Christopher Cocksworth. Born 12 January 1959; Son of late Stanley Cocksworth and Auriol Cocksworth; Married Charlotte Pytches 1979 (5 sons).

Education: Forest School for Boys, Horsham; Manchester University (BA theology 1980; PhD 1989); Didsbury School of Education (PGCE 1981); German.

Non-political career: Teacher, King Edward's School, Witley 1981-84; Doctoral research 1986-88; Ordained deacon 1988; Assistant curate, Christ Church, Epsom 1988-92; Ordained priest 1989; Chaplain, Royal Holloway and Bedford New College 1992-97; Director, Southern Theological Education and Training Scheme 1997-2001; Honorary Canon, Guildford Cathedral 2000-01; Principal, Ridley Hall, Cambridge 2001-08; Bishop of Coventry 2008-.

Political career: *House of Lords:* Entered House of Lords 2013.

Political interests: Education, international affairs, reconciliation, beginning and end of life issues; Germany, Israel, Jordan, Nigeria, Palestine, Syria.

Other: Member, House of Bishops' Standing Committee; Chair: Joint Implementation Commission for the Anglican Methodist Covenant, Faith and Order Commission of the Church of England; Trustee, Dresden Trust; Society for the Study of Theology; Society for the Study of Liturgy; Patron to numerous charities. Doctor of Divinity, University of London.

Publications: Numerous articles on the Church; Evangelical Eucharistic Thought in the Church of England (CUP, 1993); Co-author, An Anglican Companion (CHP/SPCK 1996); Holy, Holy, Holy: Worshipping the Trinitatian God (DLT, 1997); Co-author, Being a Priest Today (Cantebury Press-SCM, 2004); Holding Together: Gospel, Church and Spirit - the Essentials of Christian Identity (Canterbury Press-SCM, 2008).

Recreations: Organic fruit and vegetable growing.

Rt Rev Dr the Lord Bishop of Coventry, House of Lords, London SW1A 0PW
Tel: 020 7219 5353
Bishop's House, 23 Davenport Road, Coventry CV5 6PW *Tel:* 024 7667 2244
Fax: 024 7671 3271 *Email:* bishop@bishop-coventry.org *Website:* www.coventry.anglican.org

---

COX, BARONESS

COX (Life Baroness), Caroline Anne Cox; cr. 1983. Born 6 July 1937; Daughter of late Robert McNeill Love and Dorothy Borland; Married Dr Murray Cox 1959 (died 1997) (2 sons 1 daughter).

Education: Channing School, Highgate, London; London Hospital (SRN 1958) London University external student (BSc Soc 1967, MSc Econ 1969).

Non-political career: Staff nurse, Edgware General Hospital 1960; North London Polytechnic: Lecturer, senior lecturer and principal lecturer 1969-74, Head, Department of Sociology 1974-77; Director, Nursing Education Research Unit, Chelsea College, London University 1977-84; Royal College of Nursing: Fellow, Vice-President 1990-; Chief executive officer, Humanitarian Aid Relief Trust (HART) 2005-.

CROSSBENCH

Political career: *House of Lords:* Raised to the peerage as Baroness Cox, of Queensbury in Greater London 1983. Government Whip 1985; Deputy Speaker 1986-2005; Deputy Chair of Committees 1986-2004.

Political interests: Human rights, humanitarian aid, education, health, nursing; Armenia, Burma, Indonesia, North Korea, Poland, Nigeria, Sri Lanka, Sudan, East Timor, Uganda.

Other: Director, Educational Research Trust 1982-2011; Patron: Medical Aid for Poland Fund 1983-, Physicians for Human Rights, UK 1990-; Standing Conference on Women's Organisations 1990-; Vice-President, Girl Guides Association 1995-; Honorary vice-chair, International Islamic Christian Organisation for Reconciliation and Reconstruction 2002-; Patron, Christian Solidarity Worldwide UK 2006-; Vice-President, Liverpool School of Tropical Medicine 2006-; Honorary FRCN; Honorary FRCS 1997; MERLIN. Chancellor: Bournemouth University 1992-2001, Liverpool Hope University 2006-13. 14 honorary doctorates and fellowships. Wilberforce Award 1995; Fridej of Nansen International Foundation Award 2004; International Mother Teresa Award 2005. Commander Cross of the Order of Merit of the Republic of Poland 1990; Mkhitar Gosh Medal (Armenia) 2005; Polish Solidarity Movement Medal 2005; Royal Overseas League.

Publications: Author of numerous publications on education and health care, including: Co-editor, A Sociology of Medical Practice (1975); Co-author, The Rape of Reason: The Corruption of the Polytechnic of North London (1975); The Right to Learn (1982); Sociology: A Guide for Nurses, Midwives and Health Visitors (1983); Editor, Trajectories of Despair: Misdiagnosis and Maltreatment of Soviet Orphans (1991); Co-author: Ethnic Cleansing in Progress: War in Nagorno Karabakh (1993), Made to Care: The Case for Residential and Village Communities for People with a Mental Handicap (1995), The 'West', Islam and Islamism: Is Ideological Islam Compatible With Liberal Democracy? (2003, 2006); Cox's Book of Modern Saints and Martyrs (Continuum, 2006); This Immoral Trade: Slavery in the 21st Century (Monarch, 2006); The Very Stones Cry Out: The Persecuted Church: Pain, Passion and Praise (Continuum, 2011).

Recreations: Campanology, hill walking, tennis.

The Baroness Cox, House of Lords, London SW1A 0PW
Tel: 020 7219 8638
3 Arnellan House, 146 Slough Lane, Kingsbury, London NW9 8XJ *Tel:* 020 8204 7336
Fax: 020 8204 5661 *Email:* caroline.cox@hart-uk.org *Website:* www.hart-uk.org

CROSSBENCH

CRAIG OF RADLEY, LORD

CRAIG OF RADLEY (Life Baron), David Brownrigg Craig; cr. 1991. Born 17 September 1929; Son of late Major Francis Brownrigg Craig and Hannah Olivia (Olive) Craig; Married June Derenburg 1955 (1 son 1 daughter).

Education: Radley College; Lincoln College, Oxford (BA pure maths 1951, MA).

Non-political career: Commissioned into RAF 1951; Flying instructor on Meteors and Hunter pilot in Fighter Command 1953-55; CO, No. 35 Squadron 1963-65; Military Assistant to Chief of the Defence Staff 1965-68; Group Captain 1968; Station CO, RAF College, Cranwell 1968-70; ADC to HM The Queen 1969-71; Director, Plans and Operations, HQ Far East Command 1970-71; OC, RAF Akrotiri (Cyprus) 1972-73; Assistant Chief of Air Staff (Operations) Ministry of Defence 1975-78; Air Officer Commanding No 1 Group 1978-80; Vice-Chief of Air Staff 1980-82; Air Officer Commanding-in-Chief Strike Command and Commander-in-Chief UK Air Forces 1982-85; Chief of the Air Staff 1985-88; Air ADC to HM The Queen 1985-88; Marshal of the Royal Air Force 1988; Chief of the Defence Staff 1988-91.

Political career: *House of Lords:* Raised to the peerage as Baron Craig of Radley, of Helhoughton in the County of Norfolk 1991. Convenor of Crossbench Peers 1999-2004. Member: Privileges 2000-04, Liaison 2000-04, 2013- Procedure 2000-04, Selection 2000-04, House 2002-04, 2007-13, Administration and Works 2002-04, Information 2004-07.

Political interests: Defence.

Other: Vice-chair, RAF Benevolent Fund 1991-; President: (RAF) The "Not Forgotten" Association 1993-, RAF Club 2002-12; FRAeS; King Edward VII's Hospital for Officers. Honorary Fellow, Lincoln College, Oxford 1984; Honorary DSc, Cranfield Institute of Technology 1988. OBE (Mil) 1967; CB 1978; KCB 1981; GCB (Mil) 1984.

Recreations: Fishing, shooting, woodwork.

Marshal of the Royal Air Force the Lord Craig of Radley GCB, House of Lords, London SW1A 0PW
Tel: 020 7219 2200 *Email:* craigd@parliament.uk

CROSSBENCH

CRAIGAVON, VISCOUNT

CRAIGAVON (3rd Viscount, UK), Janric Fraser Craig; cr. 1927; 3rd Bt of Craigavon (UK) 1918. Born 9 June 1944; Son of 2nd Viscount.

Education: Eton College; London University (BA; BSc).

Non-political career: Chartered accountant.

Political career: *House of Lords:* First entered House of Lords 1974; Elected hereditary peer 1999-. Member Hybrid Instruments 1993-97, 1999-2005; Alternate member Procedure 2010-.

Countries of interest: Netherlands, Nordic countries.

Other: Member, Executive Committee, Anglo-Austrian Society. Commander of the Order of the Lion (Finland) 1998; Commander of the Royal Order of the Polar Star (Sweden) 1999; Knight of the Order of Dannebrog (Denmark) 2006; Commander of the Royal Norwegian Order of Merit 2010.

The Viscount Craigavon, House of Lords, London SW1A 0PW
Tel: 020 7219 3881
54 Westminster Mansions, 1 Little Smith Street, London SW1P 3DQ *Tel:* 020 7222 1949

CONSERVATIVE

CRATHORNE, LORD

CRATHORNE (2nd Baron, UK), (Charles) James Dugdale; cr. 1959; 2nd Bt of Crathorne (UK) 1945. Born 12 September 1939; Son of 1st Baron, PC, TD; Married Sylvia Montgomery 1970 (died 2009) (1 son 2 daughters).

Education: Eton College; Trinity College, Cambridge (MA fine arts 1963).

Non-political career: Impressionist painting department, Sotheby & Co. 1963-66; Assistant to president, Parke-Bernet Galleries, New York 1966-69; Independent fine art consultancy, James Dugdale & Associates/James Crathorne & Associates 1969-; Lecture tours to the USA 1969-; Director, Blakeney Hotels Ltd 1979-96; Lecture series *Aspects of England*, in Metropolitan Museum, New York 1981; Australian bicentennial lecture tour 1988; Director: Woodhouse Securities Ltd 1988-99, Cliveden plc 1996-99, Cliveden Ltd 1999-2002, Hand Picked Hotels 2000-01.

Political career: *House of Lords:* First entered House of Lords 1977; Elected hereditary peer 1999-. Works of Art: Member 1983-2004, 2012-13, Chair 2003-07. *Other:* Member, Conservative

Advisory Group on Arts and Heritage 1988-99. *Councils and public bodies:* Council, RSA 1982-88; DL, County of Cleveland 1983-96; Member, University Court of Leeds University 1985-97; President, Cleveland and North Yorkshire Magistrates' Association 1997-2003; County of North Yorkshire: DL 1996-98, Lord Lieutenant 1999-; JP 1999-; Member: University Court of York 1999-, University Court of Hull 1999-; President, Cleveland and South Durham Magistrates' Association 2003-.

Political interests: Visual and performing arts, country houses; India, USA.

Other: Trustee, Georgian Theatre Royal, Richmond, Yorkshire 1970-; Fellow, Royal Society of Arts 1972; Captain Cook Birthplace Museum Trust: Trustee 1978-, Chair 1993-; Editorial Board, *House Magazine* 1983-; Georgian Group: Executive Committee 1985-, Chair 1990-99, President 1999-; President: Yarm Civic Society 1987-, Cleveland Family History Society 1988-, Cleveland Sea Cadets 1988-; Hambleton District of Council for the Protection of Rural England 1988-; Trustee, Yorkshire Regional Committee, National Trust 1988-94; Vice-President, Cleveland Wildlife Trust 1989-; Patron: Attingham Trust for Study of British Country House 1990-, Cleveland Community Foundation 1990-2004; Trustee, National Heritage Memorial Fund 1992-95; Joint Committee of National Amenity Societies: Deputy chair 1993-96, Chair 1996-99; Vice-President, Public Monuments and Sculpture Association 1997-; President, Cleveland Search and Rescue Team 1998-; Patron, Friends of Public Record Office 1998-; President: North Yorkshire County Scout Council 1999-, St John Ambulance North Yorkshire and Teesside 1999-; Yorkshire and Humberside (Reserve Forces and Cadets' Association RFCA: Vice-President 1999-, President 2006-09; Patron, British Red Cross North Yorkshire Branch 1999-; Vice-President, North of England (RFCA) 2001-; Patron, Tees Valley Community Foundation 2004-; Fellow, Society of Antiquaries 2009. KStJ 1999; Queen's Golden Jubilee Medal 2002; Queen's Diamond Jubilee Medal 2012; KCVO 2013; Brooks's, Pratts, Garrick.

Publications: Articles in The Connoisseur and Apollo; Edouard Vuillard (1967); Co-author: Tennant's Stalk (1973), A Present from Crathorne (1989); Cliveden, the Place and the People (1995); The Royal Crescent Book of Bath (1998); Co-Photographer, Parliament in Pictures (1999).

Recreations: Photography, jazz, collecting, country pursuits, travel.

The Lord Crathorne, House of Lords, London SW1A 0PW
Tel: 020 7219 5224 *Email:* crathornej@parliament.uk
Crathorne House, Yarm, North Yorkshire TS15 0AT *Tel:* 01642 700431
Email: james.crathorne@btconnect.com *Website:* www.nyll.org.uk

CONSERVATIVE

CRAWFORD AND BALCARRES, EARL OF

CRAWFORD (29th Earl of, S), cr. 1398, AND BALCARRES (12th Earl of, S), cr. 1651; Robert Alexander Lindsay; Lord Lindsay of Crawford before 1143. Lord Lindsay (S) 1633; Lord Balniel (S) 1651; 5th Baron Wigan (UK) 1826; (Life) Baron Balniel 1974. Born 5 March 1927; Son of 28th Earl, KT, GBE; Married Ruth Meyer-Bechtler 1949 (2 sons 2 daughters).

Education: Eton College; Trinity College, Cambridge.

Non-political career: Grenadier Guards 1945-48. Director, National Westminster Bank 1975-89; Vice-chair, Sun Alliance & London Insurance 1975-91; Director, Scottish American Investment Trust 1978-88; Lord Chamberlain to HM Queen Elizabeth the Queen Mother 1992-2002.

Political career: *House of Commons:* MP (Conservative) for Hertford 1955-74, for Welwyn and Hatfield March-October 1974. Contested Welwyn and Hatfield October 1974 general election. PPS to Henry Brooke: as Financial Secretary to the Treasury 1955-56, as Minister of Housing and Local Government 1956-59; Principal Opposition Frontbench Spokesperson for Health and Social Security 1967-70; Minister of State: Defence 1970-72, Ministry of Foreign and Commonwealth Affairs 1972-74. *House of Lords:* Created a life peer as Baron Balniel, of Pitcorthie in the County of Fife 1974. First entered House of Lords 1975; On leave of absence 2013-. *Councils and public bodies:* President, Rural District Council Association for England and Wales 1959-65; Chair, National Association for Mental Health 1963-70; DL, Fife 1976-2002; Chair, Historic Buildings Council for Scotland 1976-83; First Commissioner of the Crown Estate 1980-85; Chair: Royal Commission on the Ancient and Historical Monuments of Scotland 1985-95, Board of the National Library of Scotland 1991-2000.

Other: Honorary Fellow: Royal Incorporation of Architects in Scotland 1993, National Library of Scotland 2012. Premier Earl of Scotland on Union Roll; Head of the House of Lindsay; PC 1972; KT 1996; GCVO 2002.

Rt Hon the Earl of Crawford and Balcarres KT GCVO, House of Lords, London SW1A 0PW
Tel: 020 7219 5353

LABOUR

CRAWLEY, BARONESS

CRAWLEY (Life Baroness), Christine Mary Crawley; cr. 1998. Born 9 January 1950; Daughter of Thomas Louis Quinn and Joan Ryan; Married (1 son 2 daughters, including twins).

Education: Notre Dame Girls School, Plymouth; Digby Stuart Teacher Training College, Roehampton, London.

Non-political career: Former teacher and youth theatre leader, Oxfordshire. Member: MSF, Unison.

Political career: *House of Commons:* Contested Staffordshire South East 1983 general election. *House of Lords:* Raised to the peerage as Baroness Crawley, of Edgbaston in the County of West Midlands 1998. Government Whip 2002-08; Government Spokesperson for: Defence 2002-08, Foreign and Commonwealth Office 2002-05, International Development 2002-04, Transport 2004-05, Education and Skills/Children, Schools and Families and for Innovation, Universities and Skills 2005-08, Transport 2007-08, Northern Ireland 2007-08, International Development 2008; Government Whip 2009-10; Opposition Spokesperson for: Communities and Local Government 2010, Foreign and Commonwealth Office 2010, Health 2010; Opposition Deputy Chief Whip 2010-12. Member: European Union -2000, European Union Sub-committee A (Economic and Financial Affairs, Trade and External Relations) 2000-01, Refreshment 2011-12. *Other:* European Parliament: MEP for Birmingham East 1984-99: Chair, Women's Rights Committee 1989-94. Member: Co-operative Party, Labour Movement in Europe. *Councils and public bodies:* Former Town and District Councillor in South Oxfordshire; Chair: Women's National Commission 1999-2002, West Midlands Regional Cultural Consortium 1999-2002; President, Trading Standards Institute 2009-.

Political interests: Women's rights, equal opportunities, European Union.

Other: Member: Amnesty International, Fabian Society; Fellow, Royal Society of Arts.

Recreations: Latin American literature, amateur dramatics, attending local football matches in Birmingham.

The Baroness Crawley, House of Lords, London SW1A 0PW
Tel: 020 7219 4650 *Fax:* 020 7219 6837 *Email:* crawleyc@parliament.uk
Email: ccrawley@enterprise.net

CRICKHOWELL, LORD

CRICKHOWELL (Life Baron), Roger Nicholas Edwards; cr. 1987. Born 25 February 1934; Son of late Ralph Edwards, CBE, FSA; Married Ankaret Healing 1963 (1 son 2 daughters).

Education: Westminster School; Trinity College, Cambridge (BA history 1952, MA).

Non-political career: National service (Second Lieutenant) Royal Welch Fusiliers; Lieutenant, TA. Member of Lloyds 1963-2002; Chair: ITNET plc 1996-2004, HTV Group Ltd 1997-2002; Former director: William Brandts Ltd and Associated Companies, A L Sturge Holdings Ltd, PA International & Sturge Underwriting Agency Ltd, Associated British Ports Holdings plc, Anglesey Mining plc; Globtik Tankers Ltd; HTV Group 1987-97 Committee of Automobile Association 1988-98.

CONSERVATIVE

Political career: *House of Commons:* MP (Conservative) for Pembroke 1970-87. Secretary of State for Wales 1979-87. *House of Lords:* Raised to the peerage as Baron Crickhowell, of Pont Esgob in the Black Mountains and County of Powys 1987. Member Procedure 2000-03; Co-opted member EU Sub-committee D (Environment, Agriculture, Public Health and Consumer Protection/Environment and Agriculture) 2000-05; Member Joint Committees on: Draft Communications Bill 2002, Constitutional Reform Bill (HL); Co-opted member EU Sub-committee C (Foreign Affairs, Defence and Development Policy) 2006-10; Member: Draft Climate Change Bill Joint Committee 2007, Science and Technology 2007-12, Science and Technology Sub-committee I 2007-10 (Waste Reduction 2007-08, Nanotechnologies and food 2008-10), Constitution 2010-. *Councils and public bodies:* Chair: National Rivers Authority Advisory Committee 1988-89, National Rivers Authority 1989-96.

Political interests: Environment, economic policy, urban policies, arts, broadcasting.

Other: President: Cardiff University of Wales 1988-98, South East Wales Arts Association 1988-94; Chair, Cardiff Bay Opera House Trust 1993-97; Fellow, RSA. Fishmongers' Company. Honorary Fellow, Cardiff University; Honorary Doctor of Law, Glamorgan University. PC 1979; Brooks's.

Publications: Opera House Lottery – Zaha Hadid and The Cardiff Bay Opera House (1997); Westminster, Wales and Water (1999); The Rivers Join (2009).

Rt Hon the Lord Crickhowell, House of Lords, London SW1A 0PW
Email: crickhowelln@parliament.uk
4 Henning Street, London SW11 3DR

CROSSBENCH

CRISP, LORD

CRISP (Life Baron), (Edmund) Nigel Ramsay Crisp; cr. 2006. Born 14 January 1952; Married Siân Jenkins 1976 (1 daughter 1 son).

Education: Uppingham School, Rutland; St John's College, Cambridge (BA moral sciences 1973, MA).

Non-political career: Deputy director, Halewood Community Council 1973-77; Production manager, Trebor plc 1977-81; Director, Cambridgeshire Community Council 1981-86; General manager, East Berkshire Health Authority 1986-88; Wexham Park Hospital and Heatherwood Hospital 1988-92: Chief executive 1992-93; Chief executive, Oxford Radcliffe Hospital 1993-97; Regional director: South Thames Regional Office 1997-98, London Regional Office 1999-2000; Permanent Secretary for Health and Chief Executive, National Health Service, Department of Health 2000-06.

Political career: *House of Lords:* Raised to the peerage as Baron Crisp, of Eaglescliffe in the County of Durham 2006. Member Merits of Statutory Instruments 2007-09.

Countries of interest: Developing world.

Other: Honorary Professor, London School of Hygiene and Tropical Medicine; Senior Fellow, Institute for Health Care Improvement. KCB 2003.

Recreations: Countryside.

The Lord Crisp KCB, House of Lords, London SW1A 0PW
Tel: 020 7219 3873 *Email:* crisp@parliament.uk

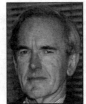

CROSSBENCH

CULLEN OF WHITEKIRK, LORD

CULLEN OF WHITEKIRK (Life Baron), (William) Douglas Cullen; cr. 2003. Born 18 November 1935; Son of late Sheriff K D Cullen and G M Cullen; Married Rosamond Downer 1961 (2 sons 2 daughters).

Education: Dundee High School; St Andrews University (MA classics 1957); Edinburgh University (LLB 1960).

Non-political career: Called to Scottish Bar 1960; Standing junior counsel to HM Customs and Excise 1970-73; QC (Scotland) 1973; Advocate-Depute 1978-81; Senator College of Justice in Scotland 1986-2005; Lord Justice Clerk and President of the Second Division of Court of Session 1997-2001; Lord Justice General of Scotland and Lord President of the Court of Session 2001-05; Justice of the Civil and Commercial Court of Qatar 2007-.

Political career: *House of Lords:* Raised to the peerage as Baron Cullen of Whitekirk, of Whitekirk in East Lothian 2003. Lord of Appeal 2003-08. Chair Partnerships (Prosecution) (Scotland) Bill 2013-; Member Constitution 2013-. *Councils and public bodies:* Chair, Medical Appeal Tribunal 1977-86; Court of Inquiry into Piper Alpha disaster 1988-90; Review of Business of Outer House of Court of Session 1995; Tribunal of Inquiry into shootings at Dunblane Primary School 1996; Ladbroke Grove Rail Inquiry 1999-2001; Review of Fatal Accident Inquiry Legislation 2008-09.

Other: President: Sacro 2000-, Saltire Society 2005-11; Faculty of Advocates; Honorary FRCS Edinburgh; FRCP Edinburgh. Chancellor, University of Abertay Dundee 2009-. Six honorary doctorates; Honorary FREng 1995; Honorary Bencher Inner Temple 2001; Inn of Northern Ireland 2002. FRSE 1993. PC 1997; KT 2008; Caledonian; New Club (Edinburgh).

Recreations: Gardening, natural history.

Rt Hon the Lord Cullen of Whitekirk KT, House of Lords, London SW1A 0PW
Tel: 020 7219 5353

CONSERVATIVE

CUMBERLEGE, BARONESS

CUMBERLEGE (Life Baroness), Julia Frances Cumberlege; cr. 1990. Born 27 January 1943; Daughter of Dr L.U. Camm and M.G.G. Camm; Married Patrick Cumberlege 1961 (3 sons).

Education: Convent of the Sacred Heart, Tunbridge Wells.

Non-political career: Executive director, MJM Healthcare Solutions 1997-2001; Non-executive director, Huntsworth plc 2001-03; Consultant, Quo Health 2001-05; Founded Cumberlege Connections April 2001; Director, Assuring Better Practice (UK) Ltd 2004-07; South East Water plc 2006-08.

Political career: *House of Lords:* Raised to the peerage as Baroness Cumberlege, of Newick in the County of East Sussex 1990. Joint Parliamentary Under-Secretary of State, Department of Health 1992-97; Opposition Spokesperson for Health 1997. Member Draft Mental Health Bill Joint Committee 2004-05. *Councils and public bodies:* Lewes District Council: Councillor 1966-79, Leader 1977-78; Councillor, East Sussex County Council 1974-85: Chair, Social Services Committee

1979-82; Chair, Brighton Health Authority 1981-88; Member, Press Council 1984-90; Chair, Review of Community Nursing for England (Report: Neighbourhood Nursing) 1985, DL, East Sussex 1986-; Member, DHSS Expert Advisory Group on AIDS 1987-89, Chair, South West Thames Regional Health Authority 1988-92; Vice-President, Royal College of Nursing 1989-; Member, NHS Policy Board for England 1989-97; Council member, UK Central Council for Nursing, Midwifery and Health Visiting 1989-92; Vice-Lord Lieutenant, East Sussex 1992; Chair: Review of Maternity Services for England (Report: Changing Childbirth) 1993, St George's Medical School Council 2000-06; Council member, Sussex University 2001-09; Vice-President, Royal College of Midwives.

Political interests: Local government, National Health Service, media, education.

Other: Various posts several organisations and charities, particularly related to health; Senior Associate, King's Fund; Patron, National Childbirth Trust; Fellow, Royal Society of Arts 1989; Trustee: Chailey Heritage School, Leeds Castle Foundation 2005-; Chair, National Association of Health Authorities 1987-88; Fellow: Royal College of Physicians 2006, Royal College of General Practitioners 2006, Royal College of Nursing 2010, Royal College of Obstetrics and Gynacology 2012. Five honorary doctorates. CBE 1985; Royal Society of Medicine.

Recreations: Other people's gardens, bicycling.

The Baroness Cumberlege CBE DL, House of Lords, London SW1A 0PW
Tel: 020 7219 5353 *Email:* cumberlegej@parliament.uk

CUNNINGHAM OF FELLING, LORD

CUNNINGHAM OF FELLING (Life Baron), (Jack) John Anderson Cunningham; cr 2005. Born 4 August 1939; Son of late Andrew and Freda Cunningham; Married Maureen Appleby 1964 (1 son 2 daughters).

Education: Jarrow Grammar School; Bede College, Durham University (BSc chemistry 1962; PhD 1966).

Non-political career: Research fellow, Durham University 1966-68. Full-time officer, GMWU 1969-70.

NON-AFFILIATED

Political career: *House of Commons:* MP (Labour) for Whitehaven 1970-83, for Copeland 1983-2005. PPS to James Callaghan as Foreign Secretary and Prime Minister 1974-76; Parliamentary Under-Secretary for Energy 1976-79; Shadow Environment Secretary 1983-89; Shadow Leader of the House 1989-92; Shadow Secretary of State for: Foreign and Commonwealth Affairs 1992-94, Trade and Industry 1994-95, National Heritage 1995-97; Minister of Agriculture, Fisheries and Food 1997-98; Minister for the Cabinet Office, and Chancellor of the Duchy of Lancaster 1998-99. Chair Joint Committee on House of Lords Reform 2002-05. *House of Lords:* Raised to the peerage as Baron Cunningham of Felling, of Felling in the County of Tyne and Wear 2005. Chair Conventions Joint Committee 2006; Member: Science and Technology Sub-committee I: (Nanotechnologies and food) 2008-10, (Radioactive Waste Management: a further update) 2010, Science and Technology 2009-13; Science and Technology Sub-committee I 2012-13. *Other:* General Election Campaign Co-ordinator 1989-92; Labour Whip withdrawn June 2013. *Councils and public bodies:* DL Cumbria 1991; Commissioner Millennium Commission 1998-99.

Political interests: Regional policy, environment, foreign affairs, industry, energy; China, Europe, Japan, South Africa, USA.

Other: Chairman, UK-Japan 21 Century Group 2004-11; Fellow, Industry and Parliament Trust 1981. PC 1993.

Recreations: Fell-walking, gardening, music, reading, fishing, theatre.

Rt Hon the Lord Cunningham of Felling DL, House of Lords, London SW1A 0PW
Tel: 020 7219 5222

CURRIE OF MARYLEBONE, LORD

CURRIE OF MARYLEBONE (Life Baron), David Anthony Currie; cr. 1996. Born 9 December 1946; Son of late Kennedy Currie and Marjorie Currie; Married Shaziye Gazioglu 1975 (divorced 1992) (2 sons); married Angela Dumas 1995 (1 stepson).

Education: Battersea Grammar School; Manchester University (BSc maths 1968); Birmingham University (MSocSci Econs 1971); London University (PhD economics 1978).

Non-political career: Economist, Hoare Govett 1971-72; Lecturer, reader and professor of economics, Queen Mary College, London University 1972-88; Visiting scholar, International Monetary Fund 1987; London Business School: Professor of economics 1988-2000, Research dean 1989-92, Governor 1989-95, 1999-2000, Deputy principal 1992-95, Deputy dean, External Rela-

CROSSBENCH

Queen's Anniversary Prize in Higher and Further Education 2001; Hamdan Award for Medical Research Excellence 2004; Scientific Achievement Award, Armenian Medical World Congress, New York 2009; Distinguished Graduates Medal, Royal College of Surgeons, Ireland 2009. KBE 2002; PC 2009.

Publications: Over 800 peer reviewed articles in academic journals.

Rt Hon Professor the Lord Darzi of Denham KBE, House of Lords, London SW1A 0PW
Tel: 020 7219 5416

Department of Surgery and Cancer, Tenth Floor QEQM Building, St Mary's Hospital Campus, Imperial College London, Praed Street, London W2 1NY *Tel:* 020 3312 1310 *Fax:* 020 3312 6950 *Email:* ejanz@imperial.ac.uk *Website:* www1.imperial.ac.uk/medicine/people/a.darzi

DAVIDSON OF GLEN CLOVA, LORD

Shadow Advocate General for Scotland and Opposition Spokesperson for Law Officers and for Treasury

DAVIDSON OF GLEN CLOVA (Life Baron), Neil Forbes Davidson; cr 2006. Born 13 September 1950; Son of John and Flora Davidson; Married Regina Sprissler 1980.

Education: Stirling University (BA economics 1971); Bradford University (MSc international business 1972); Edinburgh University (LLB 1977; LLM 1979).

LABOUR

Non-political career: Faculty of Advocates 1979; Standing Junior Counsel to: Registrar General 1982-88, Departments of Health and Social Security 1988-93; Barrister Inner Temple, London 1990; QC (Scot) 1993; Solicitor General for Scotland 2000-01; Director City Disputes Panel 1993-2000; Advocate, Axiom Advocates.

Political career: *House of Lords:* Raised to the peerage as Baron Davidson of Glen Clova, of Glen Clova in Angus 2006. Advocate General for Scotland 2006-10; Government Spokesperson for Scotland 2008-10; Shadow Advocate General for Scotland and Opposition Spokesperson for Law Officers 2010-; Opposition Spokesperson for: Treasury 2010-, Scotland 2010-12.

Countries of interest: China.

Other: Chair, Human Rights Committee, Faculty of Advocates 1997-2000. DUniv, Stirling University 2012.

The Lord Davidson of Glen Clova QC, House of Lords, London SW1A 0PW
Tel: 020 7219 5353
Email: lord.davidson@axiomadvocates.com

DAVIES OF ABERSOCH, LORD

DAVIES OF ABERSOCH (Life Baron), (Evan) Mervyn Davies; cr 2009. Born 21 November 1952; Son of late Richard Davies and Margaret Davies; Married Jeanne Gammie 1979 (1 son 1 daughter).

Education: Rydal School, Colwyn Bay; Harvard Business School (PMD 1989); Welsh.

Non-political career: Senior credit officer, Citibank 1983-93; Standard Chartered plc and predecessors 1993-2009: Director 1997-2009, Director, Hong Kong 1997-2001, Group chief executive 2001-06, Chair 2006-09; Vice-chair and partner, Corsair Capital 2010-; Non-executive chairman, **LABOUR** PineBridge Investments Ltd 2010-; Chair, advisory board, Moelis & Co 2010-; Non-executive director: Bharti Airtel Ltd 2010-, Diageo plc 2010-; Chairman, Chime Communications 2012-.

Political career: *House of Lords:* Raised to the peerage as Baron Davies of Abersoch, of Abersoch in the County of Gwynedd 2009. Minister of State and Government Spokesperson, Department for Business, Enterprise and Regulatory Reform/Business, Innovation and Skills and Foreign and Commonwealth Office (Minister for Trade, Investment and Small Business) 2009-10. *Councils and public bodies:* Chair, Council, University of Wales, Bangor; JP, Hong Kong.

Political interests: Labour, free trade, equality; Africa, Asia, Middle East.

Other: Former chair: British Chamber of Commerce, Hong Kong, Hong Kong Association of Banks; Fellow, Institute of Bankers; Trustee Royal Academy; Breakthrough Breast Cancer; Hope House Children's Hospice. CBE 2002; Shek O. Abersoch GC; Morla Nefyn GC.

Recreations: Soccer, skiing, golf, music, Welsh art.

The Lord Davies of Abersoch CBE, House of Lords, London SW1A 0PW
Tel: 020 7219 5353

DAVIES OF COITY, LORD

DAVIES OF COITY (Life Baron), (David) Garfield Davies; cr. 1997. Born 24 June 1935; Son of late David and Lizzie Davies; Married Marian Jones 1960 (4 daughters).

Education: Heolgam Secondary Modern School; Bridgend Technical College (part-time).

Non-political career: RAF national service 1956-58. Junior operative, electrical apprentice and electrician, British Steel Corporation, Port Talbot 1950-69; Union of Shop, Distributive and Allied Workers: Area organiser, Ipswich 1969-73, Deputy division officer, London/Ipswich 1973-78, National officer, Manchester 1978-85, General Secretary 1986-97. TUC: Member, General Council 1986-97, Chairman, International Committee 1992-94; Spokesperson on International Affairs 1994-97.

LAB/CO-OP

Political career: *House of Lords:* Raised to the peerage as Baron Davies of Coity, of Penybont in the County of Mid Glamorgan 1997. Member Ecclesiastical Committee 2005-. *Councils and public bodies:* Councillor, Penybont RDC 1966-69; JP, Ipswich 1972-78; Member, Employment Appeal Tribunal 1990-2006; Governor, Birmingham College of Food, Tourism and Creative Studies 1995-99.

Political interests: Health service, education, industrial relations; British Overseas Territories, Central America.

Other: Member: Executive Board, International Confederation of Free Trade Unions 1992-97, Executive Committee, European Trade Union Confederation 1992-97, Inter-Parliamentary Union 1997-, Commonwealth Parliamentary Association 1997-; Trustee, People's National Museum -2009; Vice-President, Commercial Travellers Benevolent Institute -2007; President: Sea Shell Trust, Manchester East Scout Council, Stockport County FC Independent Supporters Club, (Wales) UK Kidney Research, Royal School for the Deaf, Manchester, Kidney Research UK; Christian Aid; NCH. CBE 1996; Reform. Lancashire CCC; Stockport County AFC.

Recreations: Most sports, swimming, family, reading.

The Lord Davies of Coity CBE, House of Lords, London SW1A 0PW
Tel: 020 7219 6932
64 Dairyground Road, Bramhall, Stockport, Cheshire SK7 2QW *Tel:* 0161-439 9548

DAVIES OF OLDHAM, LORD

Opposition Spokesperson for Transport and for Treasury

DAVIES OF OLDHAM (Life Baron), Bryan Davies; cr. 1997. Born 9 November 1939; Son of late George and Beryl Davies; Married Monica Shearing 1963 (2 sons 1 daughter).

Education: Redditch High School; University College, London (BA history 1961); Institute of Education (PGCE 1962); London School of Economics (BSc economics 1968).

Non-political career: History teacher, Latymer School, London 1962-65; History and social science lecturer, Middlesex Polytechnic, Enfield 1965-74. Divisional executive officer, NATFHE 1967-74; Member, Transport and General Workers' Union/Unite 1979-.

LABOUR

Political career: *House of Commons:* Contested Norfolk Central 1966 general election. MP (Labour) for Enfield North 1974-1979. Contested Newport West 1983 general election. MP (Labour) for Oldham Central and Royton 1992-97. Assistant Government Whip 1978-79; Opposition Spokesperson for: Education 1993-95, Education and Employment 1995-97. *House of Lords:* Raised to the peerage as Baron Davies of Oldham, of Broxbourne in the County of Hertfordshire 1997. Government Whip 2000-03; Government Spokesperson for: Home Office 2000-02, Education and Skills 2001-03, Culture, Media and Sport 2001-08, Transport 2002-07, Trade and Industry 2003-04; Deputy Chief Whip (Captain, the Queen's Body Guard of the Yeomen of the Guard) 2003-10; Government Spokesperson for: Cabinet Office 2007-08, Treasury 2007-08, Environment, Food and Rural Affairs 2008, Scotland 2008, Wales 2008-10; Parliamentary Under-Secretary of State and Government Spokesperson, Department for Environment, Food and Rural Affairs 2009-10; Opposition Spokesperson for: Transport 2010-, Treasury 2010-, Wales 2010-13. Member: Refreshment 2005-08, 2009-11, Joint Committee on Security 2010. *Other:* Secretary, Parliamentary Labour Party and Shadow Cabinet 1979-92. *Councils and public bodies:* Member, Medical Research Council 1977-79; Chair, Further Education Funding Council 1998-2000.

Political interests: Economic policy, employment, training, education, arts, transport; Nepal, Sri Lanka.

Other: President, Royal Society for the Prevention of Accidents 1999-2000; Oxfam. Honorary Doctorate, Middlesex University 1996. PC 2007.

Recreations: Sport, literature.

Rt Hon the Lord Davies of Oldham, House of Lords, London SW1A 0PW
Tel: 020 7219 1475 *Email:* daviesb@parliament.uk *Email:* bm.davies@ntlworld.com

DAVIES OF STAMFORD, LORD

DAVIES OF STAMFORD (Life Baron), John Quentin Davies; cr 2010. Born 29 May 1944; Son of late Dr M I Davies, general practitioner, and Thelma Davies; Married Chantal Tamplin 1983 (2 sons).

Education: Leighton Park School, Reading; Gonville and Caius College, Cambridge (BA history 1966, MA); Harvard University, USA (Frank Knox Fellow); French, German, Italian, Russian.

Non-political career: HM Diplomatic Service 1967-74: 3rd Secretary, FCO 1967-69, 2nd Secretary, Moscow 1969-72, 1st Secretary, FCO 1972-74; Manager then assistant director, Morgan Grenfell & Co Ltd 1974-78; Director General and President, Morgan Grenfell France 1978-81; Director, main board, Morgan Grenfell Co Ltd and certain group subsidiaries 1981-87, Consultant 1987-93; Consultant, National Westminster Securities plc 1993-99; Dewe Rogerson International 1987-94; Société Genérale d'Entreprises 1999-2000; Consultant Royal Bank of Scotland 1999-2002; Director: Vinci 2003-08, Vinci UK 2003-08; Lloyd's of London: Director, Member of the Council 2004-07.

LABOUR

Political career: *House of Commons:* Contested (Conservative) Birmingham Ladywood 1977 by-election. MP for Stamford and Spalding 1987-97, for Grantham and Stamford 1997-2010 (Conservative 1987 to June 2007, Labour 2007-10). PPS to Angela Rumbold as Minister of State: Department of Education and Science 1988-90, Home Office 1990-91; Shadow Minister for Pensions 1998-99; Shadow Paymaster General 1999-2000; Shadow Minister for Defence 2000-01; Shadow Secretary of State for Northern Ireland 2001-03; Parliamentary Under-Secretary of State (Minister for Defence Equipment and Support), Ministry of Defence 2008-10. Member: Standards and Privileges 1995-97, Standards and Privileges 1997-98, Treasury 1997-98, European Scrutiny 1998, International Development 2003-07, Joint Committee on Tax Law Rewrite Bills 2007-09, Regulatory Reform 2007-10. Secretary, Conservative Parliamentary Committees on: Finance 1991-97, Trade and Industry 1991-95; Vice-chair, Conservative Party Committee for Trade and Industry 1995-98; Chair, Conservative Group for Europe 2006-07. *House of Lords:* Raised to the peerage as Baron Davies of Stamford, of Stamford in the County of Lincolnshire 2010. Member: Selection 2011, Joint Committee on the Draft Detention of Terrorist Suspects (Temporary Extension) Bills 2011, Consumer Insurance (Disclosure and Representations) Bill 2011-12, Joint Committee on Parliamentary Privilege 2013, EU Sub-committee A (Economic and Financial Affairs) 2013-.

Political interests: Defence, trade and industry, finance, agriculture, health, welfare, pensions, overseas development; EU, Russia, USA.

Other: Parliamentary adviser, Chartered Institute of Taxation 1993-2008; Fellow, Industry and Parliament Trust 1995; Trustee and member, Executive Committee, Council for Economic Policy Research 1996-2008. Liveryman, Goldsmiths' Company; Beefsteak, Brooks's, Travellers', RAF Club.

Publications: Britain and Europe: A Conservative View (1996); Co-author, Report of Inquiry into National Recognition of our Armed Forces (2008).

Recreations: Reading, walking, skiing, travel.

The Lord Davies of Stamford, House of Lords, London SW1A 0PW
Tel: 020 7219 5353 *Email:* daviesq@parliament.uk

DEAN OF THORNTON-LE-FYLDE, BARONESS

DEAN OF THORNTON-LE-FYLDE (Life Baroness), Brenda Dean; cr. 1993. Born 29 April 1943; Daughter of Hugh and Lillian Dean; Married Keith McDowall CBE 1988 (2 stepdaughters).

Education: Stretford High School for Girls.

Non-political career: SOGAT: Administrative secretary 1959-72, Assistant secretary, Manchester Branch 1972-76, Secretary, Manchester Branch 1976-83, Member, National Executive Council 1977-83, President, SOGAT '82 1983-91; Deputy general secretary, Graphical, Paper and Media Union 1991-92; Non-executive director: George Wimpey plc 2003-07, Dawson Holdings plc 2003-10; Chair, Covent Garden Market Authority 2005-13; Partnership director, National Air Traffic Services 2006-; Non-executive director, Taylor Wimpey plc 2007-13. Member: TUC General Council 1985-92, Graphical, Paper and Media Union 1959-.

LABOUR

Political career: *House of Lords:* Raised to the peerage as Baroness Dean of Thornton-le-Fylde, of Eccles in the County of Greater Manchester 1993. Opposition Spokesperson for: Employment 1994-96, National Heritage 1996-97; Opposition Whip 1996-97; Member, Committee of Inquiry into Future of Higher Education 1996-97; House of Lords Appointments Commission 2000-10. Co-opted member European Communities Sub-committee B (Energy, Industry and Transport) 1995-97, 1997-98. *Councils and public bodies:* Council member: Association for Business Sponsorship of the Arts 1990-96, City University 1991-96; Governor, Ditchley Foundation 1992-; Member: Armed Forces Pay Review Body 1993-94, Press Complaints Commission 1993-98, Broadcasting Complaints Commission 1993-94; Board member, Council, London School of Economics 1994-99; Council member, Open University 1995-98; Chair: Housing Corporation 1997-2003, Armed Forces Pay Review Body 1999-2004; Member: Senior Salaries Review Body 1999-2004, Royal Commission on the Reform of the House of Lords 1999; Council member, Nottingham University 2012-.

Political interests: Industry, media, women's issues, pensions, housing, defence; Australia, China, South Africa, USA.

Other: Industry and Parliament Trust: Trustee 1997-2009, Fellow 1998; Member, General Insurance Standards Council 1999-2005, Chair, Freedom to Fly Coalition 2002-04; President, Abbeyfield Society 2012-; Trustee, Thomson Foundation; FRSA. Liveryman, Worshipful Company of Stationers and Newspaper Makers. Freeman, City of London. Ten honorary degrees; Honorary Fellow, Preston Polytechnic, Lancashire 1991. PC 1998; Reform Club. Royal Cornwall Yacht Club.

Recreations: Watching cricket and rugby.

Rt Hon the Baroness Dean of Thornton-le-Fylde, House of Lords, London SW1A 0PW
Tel: 020 7219 6907 *Fax:* 020 7219 0549 *Email:* deanb@parliament.uk

DEAR, LORD

CROSSBENCH

DEAR (Life Baron), Geoffrey James Dear; cr 2006. Born 20 September 1937; Son of late Cecil Dear and Violet Dear, née Mackney; Married Judith Stocker 1958 (died 1996) (1 son 2 daughters); married Alison Martin Jones 1998.

Education: Fletton Grammar School, Huntingdonshire; University College, London (Bramshill Scholarship, LLB 1968).

Non-political career: Mid-Anglia Constabulary 1965; Assistant Chief Constable (operations), Nottinghamshire 1972-80; Seconded as director of command training, Bramshill Police College 1975-77; Metropolitan Police 1980-85: Personnel and training 1981-84, Operations 1984-85; Chief Constable, West Midlands Police 1985-90; HM Inspector of Constabulary 1990-97; Honorary Bencher Gray's Inn 2008; Non-executive chair, Blue Star Capital plc.

Political career: *House of Lords:* Raised to the peerage as Baron Dear, of Willersey in the County of Gloucestershire 2006. EU Sub-committee F (Home Affairs): Co-opted member 2007-09, Member 2009-12; Member: European Union 2009-, EU Sub-committee A (Economic and Financial Affairs) 2012-, Joint Committee on the Rookery South (Resource Recovery Facility) Order 2012-13. *Councils and public bodies:* DL, West Midlands 1985-96; DL, Worcestershire 1996-; Vice-Lord Lieutenant, Worcestershire 1998-2001.

Countries of interest: India, USA.

Other: Trustee: The Country Trust 1987-2012, Police Rehabilitation Trust 1991-; Police Foundation 2008-13; World Horse Welfare 2010-; Fellow, University College, London; Honorary fellow, Birmingham University. Queen's Commendation for Bravery 1979; QPM 1982; Kt 1997; East India Club; Special Forces Club. Vice-President, Warwickshire County Cricket Club.

Recreations: Country sports, cricket, rugby football, gardening, music, literature.

The Lord Dear QPM, House of Lords, London SW1A 0PW
Tel: 020 7219 3576 *Email:* deargj@parliament.uk

DEBEN, LORD

CONSERVATIVE

DEBEN (Life Baron), John Selwyn Gummer; cr 2010. Born 26 November 1939; Son of late Rev Canon Selwyn Gummer and late Sybille Gummer, née Mason; Married Penelope Gardner 1977 (2 sons 2 daughters).

Education: King's School, Rochester; Selwyn College, Cambridge (BA history 1961, MA 1971) (Union President 1962); French (reasonable).

Non-political career: Editor, Business Publications 1962-64; Editor-in-Chief, Max Parrish & Oldbourne Press 1964-66; Director, Shandwick Publishing Co 1966-81; BPC Publishing: Special assistant to chairman 1967, Publisher, special projects 1967-69, Editorial co-ordinator 1969-70; Siemssen Hunter Ltd: Director 1973-80, Chairman 1979-80; Chairman: Selwyn Shandwick International 1976-81, Sancroft International Ltd (corporate responsibility consultants) 1997-, Marine Stewardship Council 1997-2006; Vivendi UK/Veolia Water UK: Director 1997-, Chairman 2004-; Chairman, Valpak Ltd 1998-; International Commission on Consumption 1998-2005; Association of Professional Financial Advisers (formerly Association of Independent Financial Advisers) 2003-; Chairman, Zeroc Holdings Ltd 2008-; Non-executive directorships, including: Catholic Herald, Castle Trust 2011-; Chairman, Committee on Climate Change 2012-.

Political career: *House of Commons:* Contested Greenwich 1964 and 1966 general elections. MP (Conservative) for Lewisham West 1970-February 1974. Contested Lewisham West February 1974 general election. MP for Eye 1979-83, for Suffolk Coastal 1983-2010. PPS: to Jim Prior as Minister of Agriculture, Fisheries and Food 1971-72, to Patrick Jenkin as Secretary of State for Social Services 1979-81; Government Whip 1981-83; Parliamentary Under-Secretary of State, Department of Employment 1983; Minister of State, Department of Employment 1983-84; Paymaster General 1984-85; Minister of State, Ministry of Agriculture, Fisheries and Food 1985-88; Minister for Local Government 1988-89; Minister of Agriculture, Fisheries and Food 1989-93; Secretary of State for the Environment 1993-97. Member: Ecclesiastical Committee. *House of Lords:* Raised to the peerage as Baron Deben, of Winston in the County of Suffolk 2010. *Other:* Chair, Cambridge University Conservative Association 1961; Conservative Party: Vice-chair 1972-74, Chair 1983-85; Chair, Conservative Group for Europe 1997-2000. *Councils and public bodies:* Councillor, Inner London Education Authority 1967-70.

Political interests: Energy, environment, European affairs, business, industry, consumers.

Other: Member, General Synod of Church of England for St Edmundsbury and Ipswich Diocese 1978-92. PC 1985.

Publications: When the Coloured People Come (1966); The Permissive Society (1971); Co-author The Christian Calendar (1974); Faith in Politics (1987).

Recreations: Architecture, walking.

Rt Hon the Lord Deben, House of Lords, London SW1A 0PW
Tel: 020 7219 5353
46 Queen Anne's Gate, London SW1H 9AP *Tel:* 020 7960 7900 *Email:* secretariat@sancroft.com

CROSSBENCH

DEECH, BARONESS

DEECH (Life Baroness), Ruth Lynn Deech; cr 2005. Born 29 April 1943; Daughter of Josef Fraenkel and Dora, née Rosenfeld; Married Dr John Deech 1967 (1 daughter).

Education: Christ's Hospital, Hertford; St Anne's College, Oxford (BA law 1965, MA); Brandeis University, USA (MA Jewish studies 1966).

Non-political career: Called to the Bar Inner Temple 1967 (later Honorary Bencher); St Anne's College, Oxford: Fellow and law tutor 1970-91, Principal 1991-2004; Appointed Queens Counsel 2013.

Political career: *House of Lords:* Raised to the peerage as Baroness Deech, of Cumnor in the County of Oxfordshire 2005. Member: Merits of Statutory Instruments 2007-10, Draft Human Tissue and Embryos Bill Joint Committee 2007, Communications 2010-. *Councils and public bodies:* Chair, Human Fertilisation and Embryology Authority 1994-2002; BBC Governor 2002-06; Independent Adjudicator for Higher Education 2004-08; Gresham Professor of Law 2008-12; Chair, Bar Standards Board 2009-.

Political interests: Higher education, family law, broadcasting, reproductive technology; Israel, Poland, USA.

Other: Oxford Philomusica; Fellow: Royal Society of Medicine, International Society of Family Law. Liveryman, Drapers' Company. Pro-vice-chancellor, Oxford University 2001-04. Honorary LLD: Strathclyde University 2003, Richmond American International University 2006, Ben Gurion University, Israel 2012. DBE 2002.

Publications: Co-editor, Biomedicine, the Family and Human Rights (Kluwer, 2002); From IVF to Immortality (OUP, 2007).

Recreations: Opera, travel, after-dinner speaking.

The Baroness Deech DBE, House of Lords, London SW1A 0PW
Tel: 020 7219 5353 *Email:* deechr@parliament.uk
Bar Standards Board, 289-293 High Holborn, London WC1V 7HZ *Tel:* 020 7611 1444
Fax: 020 7831 9217 *Email:* ruth.deech@st-annes.ox.ac.uk
Website: www.law.ox.ac.uk/people/profile.php?who=deechr
lordsoftheblog.net/category/baroness-deech *Twitter:* @BaronessDeech

CONSERVATIVE

DEIGHTON, LORD

Commercial Secretary and Government Spokesperson, HM Treasury

DEIGHTON (Life Baron), Paul Clive Deighton; cr 2012. Born 18 January 1956; Son of late Walter Deighton and late Mabel King; Married Alison Klebanoff 1985 (2 sons).

Education: Wallington County Grammar School for Boys; Trinity College, Cambridge (BA economics 1978).

Non-political career: Bank of America 1978-81; Security Pacific 1981-83; Goldman Sachs 1983-2006: Investment Banking Division 1983-93, Head, Controllers Department, New York 1993-96, Partner and managing director 1996-2000, European Chief Operating Officer 2000-06, Member, European Management Committee 2000-06; Chief executive officer, LOCOG 2006-12.

Political career: *House of Lords:* Raised to the peerage as Lord Deighton, of Carshalton in the County of Surrey 2012. Commercial Secretary and Government Spokesperson, HM Treasury 2013-.

Other: Board member, England Rugby 2015 (organising body for the Rugby World Cup) 2013-. Honorary Doctorate, Sheffield Hallam University. KBE 2013.

The Lord Deighton KBE, House of Lords, London SW1A 0PW
Tel: 020 7219 5353

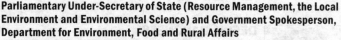

CONSERVATIVE

DE MAULEY, LORD

Parliamentary Under-Secretary of State (Resource Management, the Local Environment and Environmental Science) and Government Spokesperson, Department for Environment, Food and Rural Affairs

DE MAULEY (7th Baron, UK), Rupert Charles Ponsonby; cr. 1838. Born 30 June 1957; Son of late Colonel Hon Thomas Maurice Ponsonby, TD, DL, younger son of 5th Baron; Married Hon Lucinda Royle 2002.

Education: Eton College.

Non-political career: Lt Col, The Royal Wessex Yeomanry (Commanded) 2003-04; Colonel Commandant, The Yeomanry (Honorary) 2011-. Director, Samuel Montagu & Co Ltd 1990-93; Standard Chartered Merchant Bank Asia Ltd 1994-99; Joint chairman and chief executive, FixIT Worldwide Ltd 1999-2006.

Political career: *House of Lords:* Elected hereditary peer 2005-; Opposition Whip 2005-10; Opposition Spokesperson for: Trade and Industry/Business, Enterprise and Regulatory Reform/Business, Innovation and Skills 2005-10, Cabinet Office 2006-09, Energy and Climate Change 2008-09, Innovation, Universities and Skills 2008-09, Children, Schools and Families 2008-09, Treasury 2009-10; Government Whip 2010-12; Government Spokesperson for: Business, Innovation and Skills 2010-12, Home Office 2010, HM Treasury 2010-12, Environment, Food and Rural Affairs 2010-, Work and Pensions 2011-12; Parliamentary Under-Secretary of State (Resource Management, the Local Environment and Environmental Science), Department for Environment, Food and Rural Affairs 2012-. Member: Joint Committee on Security 2010-12, Consumer Insurance (Disclosure and Representations) Bill 2011-12.

Countries of interest: South east Asia, China, Europe.

Other: President: UK Council, Reserve Forces and Cadets Associations 2010-, Society for the Protection of Animals Abroad 2010-; Institute of Chartered Accountants in England and Wales; FCA 1990. TD.

Recreations: Country sports, woodland management.

The Lord de Mauley TD, House of Lords, London SW1A 0PW
Tel: 020 7219 5353 *Email:* demauley@parliament.uk

DENHAM, LORD

DENHAM (2nd Baron, UK), Bertram Stanley Mitford Bowyer; cr. 1937; 10th Bt of Denham (E) 1660; 2nd Bt of Weston Underwood (UK) 1933. Born 3 October 1927; Son of 1st Baron, MC; Married Jean McCorquodale 1956 (3 sons 1 daughter).

Education: Eton College; King's College, Cambridge (BA English literature 1951).

Non-political career: Countryside Commissioner 1993-99.

Political career: *House of Lords:* First entered House of Lords 1948; Government Whip 1961-64, 1970-72; Opposition Whip 1964-70; Deputy Chief Whip 1972-74; Opposition Deputy Chief Whip 1974-78; Opposition Chief Whip 1978-79; Government Chief Whip 1979-91; Extra Lord in Waiting to HM The Queen 1998-; Elected hereditary peer 1999-.

CONSERVATIVE

Political interests: Machinery of Government.
Other: PC 1981; KBE 1991; Pratt's, Garrick.
Publications: The Man Who Lost His Shadow (1979); Two Thyrdes (1983); Foxhunt (1988); Black Rod (1997); A Thing of Shreds and Patches (a read anthology of own selection of light verse, 2000); Victorian Plums (CD including The Hunting of the Snark, The Rubaiyat of Omar Khayyam and the Ballad of Reading Gaol).
Recreations: Field sports.

Rt Hon the Lord Denham KBE, House of Lords, London SW1A 0PW
Tel: 020 7219 6056 *Fax:* 020 7219 6056
The Laundry Cottage, Weston Underwood, Olney, Buckinghamshire MK46 5JZ
Tel: 01234 711535

DERBY, LORD BISHOP OF

DERBY (7th Bishop of) Alastair Llewellyn John Redfern. Born 1 September 1948; Son of Victor and Audrey Redfern; Married Jane Straw 1974 (died 2004) (2 daughters); married Caroline Boddington 2006.

Education: Bicester School; Christ Church College, Oxford (BA modern history 1970, MA 1974); Trinity College, Cambridge (BA theology 1974, MA 1979); Westcott House, Cambridge; Queen's College, Birmingham; Bristol University (PhD theology 2001).

NON-AFFILIATED

Non-political career: Curate, Wolverhampton 1976-79; Ripon College, Cuddesdon: Lecturer, church history 1979-87, Vice-principal 1985-87; Director, Oxford Institute for Church and Society 1979-83; Curate, All Saints, Cuddesdon 1983-87; Canon Theologian, Bristol Cathedral 1987-97; Diocesan Director of Training 1991-97; Bishop Suffragan of Grantham 1997-2005; Dean of Stamford 1997-2005; Canon and Prebendary, Lincoln Cathedral 2000-05; Bishop of Derby 2005-.

Political career: *House of Lords:* Entered House of Lords 2010.
Countries of interest: Diocesan links with church of North India.
Other: Chair, Multi-Faith Centre, Derby 2005-; Trustee, Derbyshire Community Foundation 2005-; Member, Community and Cohesion Group, Derby 2005-; Vice-President, Arkwright Society 2008-; Patron, Derby Arts Festival 2008-; Co-chair, Interfaith Network 2009-; House of Bishops; General Synod; Trustee, Christian Aid.
Publications: Ministry and Priesthood (1999); Being Anglican (2000); Growing the Kingdom: The Letter to the Hebrews as a Resource for Mission (2009); Thomas Hobbes and the Limits of Democracy (2009); Public Space and Private Faith: A Challenge to the Churches (2009); Community and Conflict (2011); Out of the Depths (2012); The Leadership of the People of God (2013).
Recreations: Walking, reading, published author, cycling.

Rt Rev Dr the Lord Bishop of Derby, House of Lords, London SW1A 0PW
Tel: 020 7219 5353 *Email:* redferna@parliament.uk
The Bishop's House, 6 King Street, Duffield, Belper DE56 4EU *Tel:* 01332 840132
Fax: 01332 840397 *Email:* bishop@bishopofderby.org

DESAI, LORD

DESAI (Life Baron), Meghnad Jagdishchandra Desai; cr. 1991. Born 10 July 1940; Son of late Jagdishchandra and Mandakini Desai; Married Gail Wilson 1970 (1 son 2 daughters) (divorced 2004); married Kishwar Ahluwalia, née Rosha 2004.

Education: Sayaji High School, Baroda; Premier High School, Bombay; University of Bombay (BA economics 1958, MA 1960); University of Pennsylvania (PhD economics 1964); French, Gujarati, Hindi, Marathi, Sanskrit.

LABOUR

Non-political career: Associate specialist, Department of Agricultural Economics, University of California, Berkeley 1963-65; London School of Economics 1965-: Lecturer in economics 1965-77, Senior lecturer 1977-80, Reader 1980-83, Professor 1983-2004, Convenor, Economics Department 1987-90, Head, Development Studies Institute 1990-95, Director, Centre for the Study of Global Governance 1992-2003; Professor Emeritus 2003-.

Political career: *House of Lords:* Raised to the peerage as Baron Desai, of St Clement Danes in the City of Westminster 1991. Opposition Whip 1991-94; Opposition Spokesperson for: Health 1991-93, Treasury and Economic Affairs 1992-93; Contested Lord Speaker election 2011. Member: Science and Technology 1991-92, European Community, Sub Committee A (Economic and Financial Affairs, Trade and External Relations) 1995-99, Delegated Powers Scrutiny 2001-05, Speakership of the House 2003, Merits of Statutory Instruments 2003-04, Intergovernmental Organisations 2007-08.

Political interests: Economic policy, education, development; Australia, Bangladesh, Brazil, Canada, China, India, Malaysia, Mauritius, Pakistan, Sierra Leone, Singapore, Sri Lanka, USA.
Other: Member: Executive Committee, Inter-Parliamentary Union British Group 1995-2003, Marshall Aid Commission 1998-2002; Member: One World Action; Association of University Teachers; FRSA. Five honorary doctorates; Honorary Fellow, London School of Economics 2005. Pravasi Bharatiya Purnskar Award for Overseas Indians of Distinction granted by Indian Government 2004; Padma Bhushan awarded by the Government of India 2008.
Publications: Several on economics.
Recreations: Reading, writing, cricket.
Professor the Lord Desai, House of Lords, London SW1A 0PW
Tel: 020 7219 5066 *Fax:* 020 7219 5787 *Email:* desaim@parliament.uk

DHOLAKIA, LORD

DHOLAKIA (Life Baron), Navnit Dholakia; cr. 1997. Born 4 March 1937; Son of Permananddas Mulji Dholakia and Shantabai Permananddas Dholakia; Married Ann McLuskie 1967 (2 daughters).
Education: Indian public schools in Moshi, Arusha, Tabora and Morogoro in Tanzania; Institute of Science, Bhavnager, Gujarat, India; Brighton Technical College; Gujarari, Hindi, Swahili.
Non-political career: Medical laboratory technician, Southlands Hospital, Shoreham-by-Sea 1960-66; Development officer, National Committee for Commonwealth Immigrants 1966-68; Community Relations Commission: Senior development officer 1968-74, Principal officer and

LIBERAL DEMOCRAT secretary 1974-76; Commission for Racial Equality 1976-94: Head, administration of justice section 1984-94; Member, Police Complaints Authority 1994-98.

Political career: *House of Lords:* Raised to the peerage as Baron Dholakia, of Waltham Brooks in the County of West Sussex 1997. Liberal Democrat: Spokesperson for Home Affairs 1998-2007, Deputy Chief Whip 1998-2002; Member, House of Lords Appointments Commission 2000-10; Deputy Leader, Liberal Democrat Peers 2004-; Liberal Democrat Spokesperson for Communities 2007-10. Co-opted member European Communities Sub-committee F (Social Affairs, Education and Home Affairs) 1997-2000; Member: House of Lords Offices, Sub-committee on Lords' Interests 2008-10, Sub-committee on Lords' Conduct 2010-, Joint Committee on Voting Eligibilty (Prisoners) Bill 2013-. *Other:* Chair: Brighton Young Liberals 1959-62, Brighton Liberal Association 1962-64; Secretary, Race and Community Relations Panel, Liberal Party 1969-74; Member: Liberal Democrat Federal Policy Committee 1996-97, Federal Executive Committee; President: Liberal Democrat Party 2000-04, Liberal Democrat Federal Conference Committee 2001-. *Councils and public bodies:* Councillor, County Borough of Brighton 1961-64; Member: Lord Hunt's Committee on Immigration and Youth Service 1967-69, Board of Visitors, HM Prison Lewes 1978-95; JP, Mid Sussex 1978; Member: Home Office Inter-departmental Committee on Racial Attacks and Harassment 1987-92, Sussex Police Authority 1991-94, Ethnic Minority Advisory Committee of Judicial Studies Board 1992-96; DL, West Sussex 1999-; Member: Lord Carlisle's Committee on Parole Systems Review, Home Secretary's Race Forum 1999-; Vice-chair, Policy Research Institute on Ageing and Ethnicity; Member, Governing Body, Commonwealth Institute 1999-; Trustee, Police Foundation 2004-; Member, Prime Minister's Advisory Committee on Business Appointments.
Political interests: Home affairs; East Africa, south east Asia, India.
Other: Member, Executive Committee: Inter-Parliamentary Union, British Group, Commonwealth Parliamentary Association; Patron, vice-patron and trustee numerous organisations, particularly those concerned with ethnic minorities; National Association of Care and Resettlement of Offenders: Council member 1984-, Chairman 1998-, President, Chair, Race Issues Advisory Committee 1989-; Council member: Save The Children Fund 1986-99, Howard League of Penal Reform 1992-2002; Editorial Board, *The Howard Journal of Criminology* 1993-; President, Nacro; Vice-President, Mental Health Foundation; Governor, Commonwealth Institute 1998-2005; Melvin Jones Fellowship, Lions Club. Honorary Doctor of Laws: Hertfordshire University 2009, York University 2010, East London University 2010. Asian of the Year 2000; Pravasi Bharatiya Samman Award (Government of India) 2003; Pride of India Award 2004, 2005. OBE 1994; PC 2010.
Publications: Various articles on criminal justice matters.
Recreations: Photography, travel, gardening, cooking exotic dishes.
Rt Hon The Lord Dholakia OBE DL, House of Lords, London SW1A 0PW
Tel: 020 7219 5203/020 7219 1608 *Fax:* 020 7219 3423 *Email:* dholakian@parliament.uk

LABOUR

DIXON, LORD

DIXON (Life Baron), Donald Dixon; cr. 1997. Born 6 March 1929; Son of late Albert Dixon, shipyard worker; Married Doreen Morad 1979 (1 son 1 daughter).
Education: Ellison Street Elementary School, Jarrow.
Non-political career: Royal Engineers 1947-49. Ship carpenter 1944-79. Member and branch secretary, GMWU.
Political career: *House of Commons:* MP (Labour) for Jarrow 1979-97. Opposition Deputy Chief Whip 1987-96. *House of Lords:* Raised to the peerage as Baron Dixon, of Jarrow in the County of Tyne and Wear 1997. Member Administration and Works 2003-06. *Other:* Chair, Northern Group Labour MPs 1989. *Councils and public bodies:* Councillor: Jarrow Borough Council 1963-74, South Tyneside Metropolitan District Council 1974-81; DL, Tyne and Wear 1997-.
Political interests: Trade unions, ships and shipbuilding, maritime affairs, housing, transport, social services; Commonwealth, Cyprus.
Other: Patron: Blissability South Tyneside 2001-, Sight Service Gateshead and South Tyneside 2001-. Freeman: Jarrow 1972, South Tyneside 1997. PC 1996.
Recreations: Football, reading, boxing.
Rt Hon the Lord Dixon DL, House of Lords, London SW1A 0PW
Tel: 020 7219 4124 *Email:* dixond@parliament.uk
1 Hillcrest, Jarrow, Tyne and Wear NE32 4DP *Tel:* 0191-489 7635 *Fax:* 0191-489 7635
Email: dondixon1@sky.com

CONSERVATIVE

DIXON-SMITH, LORD

DIXON-SMITH (Life Baron), Robert William Dixon-Smith; cr. 1993. Born 30 September 1934; Son of late Dixon and Alice Smith; Married Georgina Cook 1960 (1 son 1 daughter).
Education: Oundle School, Northamptonshire; Writtle Agricultural College, Essex.
Non-political career: Second Lieutenant, King's Dragoon Guards (National Service) 1956-57. Farmer.
Political career: *House of Lords:* Raised to the peerage as Baron Dixon-Smith, of Bocking in the County of Essex 1993. Opposition Spokesperson for: Environment, Transport and the Regions (Local Government) December 1998-2001, Home Affairs 2001-02, Environment 2003-07, Communities and Local Government 2007-09. Member: Science and Technology 1994-97, 2012-, European Communities 1994-97, Communications 2010-. *Councils and public bodies:* Essex County Council: Councillor 1965-93, Chair 1986-89; DL, Essex 1986; Chair, Association of County Councils 1992-93.
Political interests: Agriculture, environment, transport.
Other: Writtle Agricultural College: Governor 1967-94, Chair 1973-85, Fellow; Anglia Polytechnic University (formerly Anglia Polytechnic): Governor 1973-2000, Chair of Governors 1993-94; Fellow, Industry and Parliament Trust 1998. Liveryman, Farmers' Company 1990. Honorary Doctorate, Anglia Polytechnic University.
Recreations: Country sports, golf.
The Lord Dixon-Smith DL, House of Lords, London SW1A 0PW
Tel: 020 7219 5351
Houchins, Coggeshall, Colchester, Essex CO6 1RT *Tel:* 01376 561448

CONSERVATIVE

DOBBS, LORD

DOBBS (Life Baron), Michael John Dobbs; cr 2010. Born November 1948; Son of Eric and Eileen Dobbs.
Education: Hertford Grammar School; Christ Church, Oxford (BA); Fletcher School of Law and Diplomacy (MA, MALD, PhD).
Non-political career: Government special adviser 1981-87; Deputy chairman, Saatchi & Saatchi 1983-86, 1988-91; Presenter, *Despatch Box*, BBC 1999-2001.
Political career: *House of Lords:* Raised to the peerage as Baron Dobbs, of Wylye in the County of Wiltshire 2010. Member Joint Committee on Privacy and Injunctions 2011-12. *Other:* Conservative Party: Chief of Staff 1986-87, Joint deputy chairman 1994-95.
Political interests: Constitution, foreign affairs, arts; China, Middle East, USA.
Other: Royal Automobile.

Publications: House of Cards (1989); Wall Games (1990); Last Man to Die (1991) To Play the King (1992); The Touch of Innocents (1994); The Final Cut (1995); Goodfellowe MP (1996); The Buddha of Brewer Street (1998); Whispers of Betrayal (2000); Winston's War (2002); Never Surrender (2003); Churchill's Hour (2004); Churchill's Triumph (2005); First Lady (2006); The Lord's Day (2007); The Edge of Madness (2008); The Reluctant Hero (2009); Old Enemies (2010); A Sentimental Traitor (2012); A Ghost at the Door (2013).

The Lord Dobbs, House of Lords, London SW1A 0PW
Tel: 020 7219 5353 *Email:* dobbsm@parliament.uk *Website:* www.michaeldobbs.com
Twitter: @michael_dobbs

LABOUR

DONAGHY, BARONESS

DONAGHY (Life Baroness), Rita Margaret Donaghy; cr 2010. Born 9 October 1944; Married James Donaghy 1968 (died 1986); married Ted Easen-Thomas 2000.

Education: Leamington College for Girls; Durham University (BA English language and literature 1967).

Non-political career: Technical assistant, National Union of Teachers 1967-68; Institute of Education, London University: Assistant registrar 1968-84, Permanent secretary, Students' Union 1984-2000; Chair, Advisory, Conciliation and Arbitration Service 2000-07. Member: National Executive Committee, NALGO/Unison 1973-2000, General council, Trades Union Congress 1987-2000; President: NALGO 1989-90, Trades Union Congress 2000.

Political career: *House of Lords:* Raised to the peerage as Baroness Donaghy, of Peckham in the London Borough of Southwark 2010. *Councils and public bodies:* Member, Low Pay Commission 1997-2000; Committee on Standards in Public Life: Member 2001-07, Interim chair 2007; Chair, Department of Work and Pensions Inquiry into Fatal Construction Accidents 2009.

Other: Non-executive director, King's College Hospital NHS Trust 2005-; Fellow, Chartered Institute of Personnel and Development 2002. OBE 1998; CBE 2005.

The Baroness Donaghy CBE, House of Lords, London SW1A 0PW
Tel: 020 7219 5353

LABOUR

DONOUGHUE, LORD

DONOUGHUE (Life Baron), Bernard Donoughue; cr. 1985. Born 8 September 1934; Son of late Thomas Donoughue; Married Carol Goodman 1959 (divorced 1989) (2 sons 2 daughters); married The Honorary Sarah, Lady Berry 2009.

Education: Campbell Secondary Modern School, Northampton; Northampton Grammar School; Lincoln College, Oxford (BA history 1957); Harvard University, USA (1958-59); Nuffield College, Oxford (DPhil 1963).

Non-political career: Editorial staff, *The Economist* 1959-60; Senior research officer, Political and Economic Planning Institute 1960-63; Senior lecturer, London School of Economics 1963-74; Senior policy adviser to Prime Ministers: Harold Wilson 1974-76, James Callaghan 1976-79; Development director, Economist Intelligence Unit 1979-81; Assistant editor, *The Times* 1981-82; Head of research and investment policy, Grieveson Grant and Co. 1982-86; Head of international research and director, Kleinwort Grieveson Securities Ltd 1986-88; Executive vice-chair, LBI 1988-91; Director, Towcester Racecourse Ltd 1992-97; Visiting Professor of Government, LSE 2000-03. Member, GMBW.

Political career: *House of Lords:* Raised to the peerage as Baron Donoughue, of Ashton in the County of Northamptonshire 1985. Opposition Spokesperson for: Energy 1991-92, Treasury Affairs 1991-92, National Heritage 1992-97; Parliamentary Secretary, Ministry of Agriculture, Fisheries and Food (Minister for Farming and the Food Industry) 1997-99. *Councils and public bodies:* Member: Sports Council 1965-71, Commission of Enquiry into Association Football 1966-68, LSE Court of Governors 1968-97; Consultant member, Horse Industry Confederation 1999-2003; British Horseracing Board: Member, Committee on VAT 2000-03, Commission of Enquiry into Stable and Stud Staff 2003-04; Member, London Arts Board 1992-97; Vice-President, Comprehensive Schools Association 2000-08; Chair: Starting Price Regulatory Board 2003-, Future Funding of Racing Group 2005-, Review of Regulation of Greyhound Racing 2007-08.

Political interests: Arts, finance, sport; France, Ireland, Italy.

Other: London Symphony Orchestra: Chair Executive 1979-91, Patron 1989-95, Associate 2000-; Member: Dorneywood Trust, Victoria County History of Northamptonshire; World Horse Welfare. Honorary Fellow, Lincoln College, Oxford; Honorary LLD, Leicester; Honorary Fellow: LSE, Northampton University; Pratt's; Farmers'; 1795 Club.

Publications: Books on history and politics including: Trade Unions in a Changing Society (1963); British Politics and the American Revolution (1964); Herbert Morrison (1973); Prime Minister (1987); The Heat of the Kitchen (2003); Downing Street Diaries, Vol 1, Harold Wilson (2005); Downing Street Diaries, Vol 2, James Callaghan (2008).
Recreations: Music, theatre, sport.
The Lord Donoughue, House of Lords, London SW1A 0PW
Tel: 020 7219 5353

DOOCEY, BARONESS

DOOCEY (Life Baroness), (Elizabeth) Dee Doocey; cr 2010. Born 2 May 1948; Daughter of Joseph and Sheila O'Keefe; Married James Doocey (1 son).
Non-political career: Liberal Democrat Party: Finance director, Financial adviser; Group managing director, international fashion company; Management consultant.
Political career: *House of Lords:* Raised to the peerage as Baroness Doocey, of Hampton in the London Borough of Richmond upon Thames 2010. Coalition representative, Criminal Justice Board, Home Office. Member: Refreshment 2012-, Joint Committee on the Draft Enhanced Terrorism Prevention and Investigation Measures Bill 2012-13, Olympic and Paralympic Legacy 2013. *Other:* Election Agent to Dr Vincent Cable, Twickenham 1992-. *Councils and public bodies:* Richmond-upon-Thames Borough Council: Councillor 1986-94, Chair, Housing Committee; Member, London Assembly 2004-12: Chair, Economy, Culture and Sport Committee 2004-10, 2011-12, Assembly Chair 2010-11, Assembly Deputy Chair 2011-12; Metropolitan Police Authority: Member 2005-12, Chair, Finances and Resources Committee 2011-12; Member, Home Office Olympic Security Board 2008-12.
Political interests: Police, economic development, housing, people with disabilities, ending child trafficking, culture, sport, tourism, Olympic legacy; Ireland, USA.
Other: OBE.
The Baroness Doocey OBE, House of Lords, London SW1A 0PW
Tel: 020 7219 0926 *Email:* dooceyd@parliament.uk

LIBERAL DEMOCRAT

DRAKE, BARONESS

DRAKE (Life Baroness), Jean Lesley Patricia Drake; cr 2010. Born 16 January 1948.
Non-political career: Research officer, NUPE; Assistant general secretary, Civil and Public Services Association 1978-85; Deputy general secretary, National Communications Union 1985-95; Deputy general secretary (telecommunications and financial services), Communication Workers' Union 1996-2008. Trades Union Congress: Member, general council and executive committee 1986-2008, President 2004-05.
Political career: *House of Lords:* Raised to the peerage as Baroness Drake, of Shene in the County of Surrey 2010. Member: Joint Committee on the Draft Financial Services Bill 2011-12, Small- and Medium-Sized Enterprises 2012-13. Vice-chair, PLP Departmental Group for Work and Pensions 2010-. *Councils and public bodies:* Member, Employment Tribunal 1988-2001; Commissioner, Equal Opportunities Commission 2000-07; Member, Employment Appeals Tribunal 2001-; Board member, Sector Skills Development Agency 2001-08; Member, Pensions Commission 2002-06; Non-executive board member, Pension Protection Fund 2004-; Supervisory board member, Union Moderation Fund (BERR) 2005-; Commissioner, Equal and Human Rights Commission 2006-09; Chair, Railway Pensions Commission 2006-08; Personal Accounts Delivery Authority: Member 2007-08, Acting chair 2008-; Governor, Pensions Policy Institute.
Other: Trustee: Alliance and Leicester Group Pension Fund 1991-, O2 Pension Trustee Company 2003-; Non-executive director, Communication Workers' Friendly Society -2010. OBE; CBE.
The Baroness Drake CBE, House of Lords, London SW1A 0PW
Tel: 020 7219 5353

LABOUR

Need additional copies?

Call 020 7593 5679

Visit www.dodsshop.co.uk

LABOUR

DRAYSON, LORD

DRAYSON (Life Baron), Paul Rudd Drayson; cr. 2004. Born 5 March 1960; Son of Michael Rudd and Ruth Irene Drayson; Married Elspeth Jane Bellhouse 1994 (2 daughters 3 sons).

Education: St Dunstan's College, London; Aston University (BSc production engineering 1982; PhD robotics 1985).

Non-political career: Undergraduate engineer, BL Cars 1978-82; Development engineer, Trebor Group 1982-86; Managing director, Lambourn Food Co 1986-91; Founder and managing director, Genisys Development Ltd 1991-95; Chief executive, Powerject Pharmaceuticals plc 1993-2003; Chairman, BioIndustry Association 2001-02; Entrepreneur in Residence, Said Business School, Oxford University 2003-05.

Political career: *House of Lords:* Raised to the peerage as Baron Drayson, of Kensington in the Royal Borough of Kensington and Chelsea 2004. Ministry of Defence: Government Spokesperson 2005-07, Parliamentary Under-Secretary of State 2005-07, Minister of State (MoS) (Minister for Defence Equipment and Support) 2007; MoS (Business and Regulatory Reform), Department for Business, Enterprise and Regulatory Reform 2007; MoS (Science and Innovation) and Government Spokesperson, Department for Innovation, Universities and Skills/Business, Innovation and Skills (attending Cabinet) 2008-10; MoS (Strategic Defence Acquisition Reform) and Government Spokesperson, Ministry of Defence 2009-10. Member: Science and Technology Committee 2004-05, Information 2005-09, Science and Technology Sub-committee I (Scientific Aspects of Ageing) 2005.

Political interests: Science, business innovation, entrepreneurship; France.

Other: Trustee, Drayson Foundation; Oxford Children's Hospital (Chairman Campaign 2002-05). PC 2008; Salle d'Armes.

Recreations: Motor racing, sword fencing.

Rt Hon the Lord Drayson, House of Lords, London SW1A 0PW
Tel: 020 7219 4147 *Email:* draysonp@parliament.uk
Nether Lypiatt Manor, Nether Lypiatt, Nr Stroud, Gloucestershire GL6 7LS
Twitter: @lorddrayson

LORD SPEAKER

D'SOUZA, BARONESS

Lord Speaker

D'SOUZA (Life Baroness), Frances Gertrude Claire D'Souza; cr. 2004. Born 18 April 1944; Daughter of Robert Russell and Pauline Russell, née Parmet; Married Stanislaus D'Souza 1959 (divorced 1974) (2 daughters); married Martin Griffiths 1985 (divorced 1994); remarried Stanislaus D'Souza 2003 (died 2011).

Education: St Mary's School, Princethorpe; University College, London (BSc anthropology 1970); Lady Margaret Hall, Oxford (DPhil evolutionary models 1976).

Non-political career: Ford Foundation research fellow in comparative physiology, Nuffield Institute of Comparative Medicine 1973-77; Part-time lecturer, London School of Economics 1973-80; Senior lecturer, department of humanities, Oxford Polytechnic 1977-80; Founder director and research director, International Relief and Development Institute 1977-85; Independent research consultant for UN, Save the Children Fund, Ford Foundation 1985-88; Research fellow, Overseas Development Administration 1988-89; Executive director, Article 19 anti-censorship organisation 1989-98; Redress Trust: Director 2003-04, Consultant 2004-06.

Political career: *House of Lords:* Raised to the peerage as Baroness D'Souza, of Wychwood in the County of Oxfordshire 2004. Convenor of the Crossbench Peers 2007-11; Lord Speaker 2011-. Member Procedure 2005-; Co-opted member European Union Sub-committee F (Home Affairs) 2006-07; Member: Selection 2007-11, Liaison 2007-11, Administration and Works 2007-11, Privileges/Privileges and Conduct 2007-11, 2011-12; House: Member 2007-11, Chair 2011-; Member Joint Committee on Security 2010-11.

Political interests: Human rights and development; Afghanistan, China, Iran, North Korea, Laos, Nordic countries, Southern Africa (SADC countries), Vietnam.

Other: President, Commonwealth Parliamentary Association (UK Branch) 2011-; Honorary President, Inter-Parliamentary Union, British Group 2011-; Co-founder, Marefat High School, Kabul, Afghanistan 2002-12; President: Hansard Society 2011-, Industry and Parliament Trust 2011-, Parliament Choir 2011-, PICTFOR 2011-; The Redress Trust; Child in Need India. CMG 1999; PC 2009.

Recreations: Music (opera, string quartets, jazz and flamenco).

Rt Hon the Baroness D'Souza CMG, House of Lords, London SW1A 0PW
Tel: 020 7219 6444 (Lord Speaker's Office) *Fax:* 020 7219 2075 *Email:* lordspeaker@parliament.uk

DUBS, LORD

DUBS (Life Baron), Alfred Dubs; cr. 1994. Born 5 December 1932; Married (1 son 1 daughter).
Education: London School of Economics (BSc Econ).
Non-political career: Former local government officer; Chief executive, Refugee Council 1988-95; Deputy chair, ITC 2000; Chair: Broadcasting Standards Commission 2001-03, Appeals Panel, Association of Energy Suppliers 2004-. Member, TGWU.

LABOUR

Political career: *House of Commons:* Contested Cities of London and Westminster 1970 and Hertfordshire South February and October 1974 general elections. MP (Labour) for Battersea South 1979-83, for Battersea 1983-87. Contested Battersea 1987 and 1992 general elections. Opposition Spokesperson for Home Affairs 1983-87. *House of Lords:* Raised to the peerage as Baron Dubs, of Battersea in the London Borough of Wandsworth 1994. Opposition Whip 1995-97; Opposition Spokesperson for: The Environment (Health and Safety) 1996-97, Energy 1996-97; Parliamentary Under-Secretary of State, Northern Ireland Office (Minister for Environment and Agriculture) 1997-99; Chair Labour Party in Lords 2000-05. Member European Union 2003-06; Procedure: Member 2005-07, Alternate member 2007-10; Co-opted member European Union Sub-committee F (Home Affairs) 2006-07; Member: Human Rights Joint Committee 2007-12, Communications 2012-. Vice-chair: PLP Departmental Committee for Culture, Media and Sport -2005, PLP Departmental Groups for: Justice 2010-, Northern Ireland 2010-, DPM/Constitutional Affairs 2011-. *Other:* Member, Co-operative Party. *Councils and public bodies:* Councillor, Westminster City Council 1971-78; Chair, Westminster Community Relations Council 1972-77; Member, Kensington, Chelsea and Westminster Area Health Authority 1975-78; Broadcasting Standards Council: Member 1988-94, Deputy Chairman 1994-97; Non-executive director, Pathfinder NHS Trust 1995-97.

Political interests: Civil liberties, penal reform, race relations, immigration, health service, Ireland, human rights.

Other: Member: Executive Committee, British Group, Inter-Parliamentary Union, UK Delegation, Organisation for Security and Co-operation in Europe Parliamentary Assembly; Trustee, Action Aid 1989-97; Chair, Liberty 1990-92; Trustee, Immigration Advisory Service 1992-97; Chair, Fabian Society 1993-94; Fellow, Industry and Parliament Trust 2003; Trustee, Open University 2004-09; Patron, Naz Project London.

Publications: Lobbying: An Insider's Guide to the Parliamentary Process (1989).
Recreations: Walking in the Lake District.
The Lord Dubs, House of Lords, London SW1A 0PW
Tel: 020 7219 3590 *Fax:* 020 7219 3981 *Email:* dubsa@parliament.uk

DUNDEE, EARL OF

DUNDEE (12th Earl of, S), Alexander Henry Scrymgeour; cr. 1660; Viscount Dudhope (S) 1641; Lord Scrymgeour (S) 1641; Lord Inverkeithing (S) 1660; Baron Glassary (UK) 1954. Born 5 June 1949; Son of 11th Earl, PC, DL; Married Siobhan Mary Llewellyn 1979 (1 son 3 daughters).
Education: Eton College; St Andrews University.
Political career: *House of Commons:* Contested (Conservative) Hamilton 1978 by-election. *House of Lords:* First entered House of Lords 1983; Government Whip 1986-89; Government Spokesperson for: Education 1986-88, Scottish Affairs 1986-89, Home Affairs and for Energy 1987-89; Elected hereditary peer 1999-. Member: Joint Committee on Consolidation, Etc, Bills 2000-05, 2006-, EU Sub-committee G (Social Policy and Consumer Affairs) 2003-07; EU Sub-committee D (Environment and Agriculture): Member 2007-08, Co-opted member 2008-10; Member: EU Sub-committee D (Agriculture, Fisheries and Environment) 2010-12, Public Service and Demographic Change 2012-13. *Councils and public bodies:* Deputy Lieutenant, Fife.

CONSERVATIVE

Other: UK delegate, Organisation for Security and Co-operation in Europe 1992-97; Member: Council of Europe parliament 1992-99, Western European parliament 1992-99; Fellow, Industry and Parliament Trust 2002. Hereditary Banner Bearer for Scotland; White's, New (Edinburgh).
The Earl of Dundee, House of Lords, London SW1A 0PW
Tel: 020 7219 6781

DO YOU NEED THIS INFORMATION ONLINE?
visit www.dodspeople.com or call 020 7593 5675
to register for a free trial

LIBERAL DEMOCRAT

DYKES, LORD

DYKES (Life Baron), Hugh John Maxwell Dykes; cr. 2004. Born 17 May 1939; Son of Richard and Doreen Dykes; Married Susan Smith 1965 (divorced 2000) (2 sons and 1 son deceased); partner Sarah.

Education: Weston-Super-Mare Grammar School; College de Normandie, France; Pembroke College, Cambridge (MA economics 1963); Speaks many European languages.

Non-political career: Assistant to Edward Heath MP as Leader of the Conservative Party 1965-66; Partner, Simon and Coates stockbrokers 1968-78; Founder shareholder, Dewe Rogerson Ltd 1972-98; Associate member, Quilter Goodison stockbrokers 1978-87; Group director, Far East Division of Dixons plc 1985-90; EU special adviser to Rogers and Wells 1990-97; Member, Securities Institute (MSI) 1993-2003.

Political career: *House of Commons:* Contested Tottenham 1966 and Harrow East 1997 general elections. MP (Conservative) for Harrow East 1970-97. PPS to: Lord Lambton at Ministry of Defence 1971-72, Kenneth Baker as Civil Service Minister in Cabinet Office 1972-74; Chief Sponsor, Heavy Commercial Vehicles Act (Dykes Act) 1973. *House of Lords:* Raised to the peerage as Baron Dykes, of Harrow Weald in the London Borough of Harrow 2004. Liberal Democrat Spokesperson for: Foreign and Commonwealth Affairs (Europe) 2005-10, Environment, Food and Rural Affairs (CAP Reform) 2006-10. Member Statutory Instruments Joint Committee 2005-09; Co-opted member EU Sub-committee C (Foreign Affairs, Defence and Development Policy) 2005-06; EU Sub-committee B (Internal Market): Co-opted member 2006-07, Member 2007-10; Member: European Union 2007-12, EU Sub-committee E (Justice and Institutions) 2010-12, (Justice, Institutions and Consumer Protection) 2012-. *Other:* European Parliament: MEP (Conservative) 1974-76; Contested (Lib Dem) London region 1999 European Parliament election. Joined Liberal Democrat Party after 1997 election.

Political interests: EU, economics, taxation, transport; China, Europe, South Africa, USA.

Other: Chair, UK-European Movement 1990-96; Official International EU Observer to first South African Elections 1994; Chair, Mid-Atlantic Club 2002-05; European-Atlantic Group: Chair 2005-08, President 2008-10; Vice-president, British German Association; Governor, North London Collegiate School 1981-97; President, League of Friends Royal National Orthopaedic Hospital 1986-97; Visiting Fellow, European Institution, London School of Economics 1998-2003. Freedom, City of London 1979. Order of Merit (Germany) 1991; Medaille pour l'Europe (Luxembourg) 1993; Légion d'Honneur (France) 2004; Life member, Harrow Rugby Club; Garrick; Beefsteak.

Publications: Many articles and pamphlets on foreign affairs and Europe; Co-author, Britain on the Edge (2012).

Recreations: Music, theatre, swimming, travel, languages.

The Lord Dykes, House of Lords, London SW1A 0PW
Tel: 020 7219 2729 *Email:* dykesh@parliament.uk

CROSSBENCH

EAMES, LORD

EAMES (Life Baron), Robert Henry Alexander Eames; cr. 1995. Born 27 April 1937; Son of Revd. William and Mary Eames; Married Ann Christine Daly OBE 1966 (2 sons).

Education: Belfast Royal Academy; Methodist College, Belfast; Queen's University, Belfast (LLB 1957, PhD ecclesiastical and constitutional law 1963, LLD 1990); Trinity College, Dublin (divinity test 1963).

Non-political career: Research scholar and tutor, Faculty of Laws, Queen's University, Belfast 1960-63; Curate assistant, Bangor Parish Church 1963-66; Rector of St Dorothea's, Belfast 1966-74; Examining Chaplain to Bishop of Down 1973; Rector St Mark's, Dundela 1974-75; Bishop of Derry and Raphoe 1975-80; Bishop of Down and Dromore 1980-86; Archbishop of Armagh and Primate of All Ireland and Metropolitan 1986-2006; Honorary Bencher, Lincoln's Inn 1998; Senior Primate of Anglican Communion 2000-06.

Political career: *House of Lords:* Raised to the peerage as Baron Eames, of Armagh in the County of Armagh 1995. Member: Works of Art 2006-07, Privileges/Privileges and Conduct 2007-, Consolidation of Private/Public Bills 2007-; Co-opted member EU Sub-committee G (Social Policy and Consumer Affairs) 2007-10; Chair Leader's Group on the Code of Conduct 2009; Member: Joint Committee on Consolidation, Etc, Bills 2009-, EU Sub-committee G (Social Policies and Consumer Protection) 2010-12, Merits of Statutory Instruments/Secondary Legislation Scrutiny 2010-. *Councils and public bodies:* Select Preacher, Oxford University 1987; Chair: Commission on Communion and Women in the Episcopate (Eames Commission) 1988-, Commission on Inter-Anglican Relations (Virginia Report) 1988-; Select Preacher, Cambridge University 1990; Chair, Inter-Anglican Theological and Doctrinal Commission 1991; Select Preacher, Edinburgh University 1993; Chair, Inter-Anglican Finance Committee 1997-2005; Select Preacher, St Andrews University 2001-; Chair, Lambeth Commission Communion (Windsor Report) 2003-04; Co-chair: Consultative Commission on Northern Ireland's Past 2007-08, Consultative Group on Legacy of Northern Ireland Conflict 2008-09 (Co-chairman, Report 2009); Member, Independent Police Commission in England and Wales 2012-.

Political interests: Northern Ireland, social issues, community care, broadcasting; Middle and Far East, North Korea, South Korea, USA.

Other: Member, Anglican International Consultative Council; Member, Institute of Advanced Motorists 1965-; Life Member, Royal Yachting Association 1973-; Governor, Church Army 1985-88; Chair: Board of Governors, Royal School, Armagh 1986-2006, Armagh Observatory and Planetarium 1986-2006; Council member, St George's House, Windsor 2008-; Various church-based trusts; Christian Aid; Save the Children; RNLI. Member, Livery Company of Carmen. Freeman: City of London 1989, City of Armagh 2007. Eleven honorary doctorates from British, Irish and US universities, including Hon LLD Queen's University, Belfast 1990. Archbishop of Canterbury's award for Outstanding Service to the International Anglican Communion 2006. OM 2007; Kildare Street and University (Dublin), Athenæum, London. Member, Strangford Lough Yacht Club, Co Down; Carrickfergus Marina, Co Antrim.

Publications: A Form of Worship for Teenagers (1965); The Quiet Revolution – Irish Disestablishment (1970); Through Suffering (1973); Thinking through Lent (1978); Through Lent (1984); Chains to be Broken (1992); Biography Nobody's Fool (McCreery, 2004); Contributor to: Irish Legal Quarterly, Criminal Law Review, New Divinity, Cambridge Law Review, Conflict, Freedom and Religion (2008).

Recreations: Sailing, rugby union, reading, travel.

Rt Rev the Lord Eames OM, House of Lords, London SW1A 0PW
Tel: 020 7219 5353 *Email:* robin.eames@yahoo.co.uk

EATON, BARONESS

CONSERVATIVE

EATON (Life Baroness), (Ellen) Margaret Eaton; cr 2010. Daughter of John and Evelyn Midgley; Married John Eaton 1969 (1 son 1 daughter).

Education: Hanson Grammar School; Balls Park Teacher Training College; German.

Non-political career: Former teacher.

Political career: *House of Lords:* Raised to the peerage as Baroness Eaton, of Cottingley in the County of West Yorkshire 2010. Member: Merits of Statutory Instruments/Secondary Legislation Scrutiny 2011-13, Adoption Legislation 2012-13, Joint Committee on the Draft Care and Support Bill 2013. *Other:* Conservative Party Local Government Committee. *Councils and public bodies:* Bradford Metropolitan Borough Council: Councillor 1986-, Leader, Conservative Group 1995-2006, Council Leader 2000-06; Former chair: Bradford Local Strategic Partnership Board, Bradford Cultural Consortium; Former co-chair, Bradford Safer Communities Partnership; Director: Bradford Centre Regeneration Company, Leeds Bradford International Airport; Member, Yorkshire and Humber Assembly; Local Government Association: Vice-chair, Conservative Group, Chair, Conservative Group, Chair 2008-11, Vice-President 2011-; DL.

Political interests: Education, children's services; Eastern Europe, Germany.

Other: Member, Committee of the Regions 2003-06; Council of Europe 2012-; FRSA; Honorary Lay Canon Bradford Cathedral; Near Neighbours; Angelus Foundation; Candlelighters. Fellow, Bradford College; University of Bradford. Lifetime Achievement Award, Variety Club. OBE; DBE 2010; United; Cecil.

The Baroness Eaton DBE, House of Lords, London SW1A 0PW
Tel: 020 7219 6380 *Email:* eatonm@parliament.uk

EATWELL, LORD

Opposition Spokesperson for Treasury

EATWELL (Life Baron), John Leonard Eatwell; cr. 1992. Born 2 February 1945; Son of late Harold Eatwell and Mary Eatwell; Married Hélène Seppain 1970 (divorced 2002) (2 sons 1 daughter); married Mrs Susan Digby 2006.

Education: Headlands Grammar School, Swindon; Queens' College, Cambridge (BA economics 1967, MA); Harvard University (PhD economics 1975).

LABOUR

Non-political career: Teaching fellow, Graduate School of Arts and Sciences, Harvard University 1968-69; Research fellow, Queens' College, Cambridge 1969-70; Fellow, Trinity College, Cambridge 1970-96; Faculty of Economics and Politics, Cambridge University: Assistant lecturer 1975-77, Lecturer 1977-2002; Visiting professor of economics, New School for Social Research, New York 1982-96; Economic adviser to Neil Kinnock as Leader of the Labour Party 1985-92; Chair, Extemporary Dance Theatre 1990; Non-executive director: Anglia Television Group Ltd 1994-2001, Cambridge Econometrics Ltd 1996-2007; President, Queens' College, Cambridge 1997-; Director: Cambridge Endowment for Research in Finance, and Professor of Financial Policy, Cambridge University 2002-12, SAV Credit Ltd 2007-. Member, Association of University Teachers.

Political career: *House of Lords:* Raised to the peerage as Baron Eatwell, of Stratton St Margaret in the County of Wiltshire 1992. Opposition Spokesperson for: Trade and Industry 1992-96, Treasury and Economic Affairs 1992-93; Principal Opposition Spokesperson for Treasury and Economic Affairs 1993-97; Opposition Spokesperson for Treasury 2010-. Member: Economic Affairs 2008-10, Consumer Insurance (Disclosure and Representations) Bill 2011-12. *Councils and public bodies:* Director, Securities and Futures Authority 1997-2002; Chair: British Screen 1997-2000, British Library 2001-06; Commissioner, Jersey Financial Services Commission 2010-.

Political interests: Economics, trade and industry, arts.

Other: Institute for Public Policy Research: Trustee 1988-, Secretary 1988-97, Chair 1997-2001; Governor, Contemporary Dance Trust 1991-95; Director, Arts Theatre Trust, Cambridge 1991-98; Chair, Crusaid, the national fundraiser for AIDS 1993-98; Director, Royal Opera House 1998-2006; Chair: Commercial Radio Companies Association 2000-04, British Library 2001-06; Director, Cambridge Endowment for Research in Finance 2002-12; Governor, Royal Ballet School 2003-06; Chair, Royal Opera House Pension Fund Trustees 2007-; Commissioner, Jersey Financial Services Commission 2010-; Director, SAV Credit Ltd 2010-; Harvard Club of New York City. House of Lords and House of Commons RUFC.

Publications: Co-author An Introduction to Modern Economics (1973); Whatever happened to Britain? (1982); Co-author Keynes's Economics and the Theory of Value and Distribution (1983); The New Palgrave: A Dictionary of Economics, 4 vols (1987); The New Palgrave Dictionary of Money and Finance, 3 vols (1992); Editor Global Unemployment: Loss of Jobs in the '90s (1996); Co-author Not Just Another Accession: The Political Economy of EU Enlargement to the East (1997); Understanding Globalisation: The Nation-State, Democracy and Economic Policies in the New Epoch (1998); Global Finance at Risk: The Case for International Regulation (2000); Hard Budgets and Soft States: Social Policy Choices in Central and Eastern Europe (2000); Articles in scientific journals and other collected works.

Recreations: Classical and contemporary dance, rugby union football.

The Lord Eatwell, House of Lords, London SW1A 0PW
Tel: 020 7219 6947
The President's Lodge, Queens' College, Cambridge CB3 9ET *Tel:* 01223 335532
Fax: 01223 335555 *Email:* president@queens.cam.ac.uk

CONSERVATIVE

ECCLES, VISCOUNT

ECCLES (2nd Viscount, UK), John Dawson Eccles; cr. 1964; 2nd Baron Eccles (UK) 1962. Born 20 April 1931; Son of 1st Viscount and late Honorary Sybil Dawson, daughter of 1st Viscount Dawson of Penn; Married Diana Sturge (later Baroness Eccles of Moulton) 1955 (1 son 3 daughters).

Education: Winchester College; Magdalen College, Oxford (BA philosophy, politics and economics 1954).

Non-political career: National service 1st Battalion KRRC (60th Rifles) 2nd Lieutenant. Head Wrightson 1954; Director, Nuclear Power Group 1968-74; Head Wrightson & Co Ltd: Managing director 1968-77, Chair 1976-77; Director: Glynwed International plc 1972-96, Investors in Industry plc (3i) 1974-88, Davy International Ltd 1977-81; Commonwealth Development Corporation: Member 1982-85, General manager and subsequently chief executive 1985-94; Chair, Chamberlin & Hill plc 1982-2004; Member, Industrial Development Advisory Board 1989-93; Courtaulds Textiles plc: Director 1992-2000, Chair 1995-2000; Chair, Acker Deboeck corporate psychologists 1994-2004.

Political career: *House of Lords:* First entered House of Lords 1999; Elected hereditary peer 2005-. Member: Information 2005-07, Merits of Statutory Instruments 2005-09, Delegated Powers and Regulatory Reform 2007-10, Adoption Legislation 2012-13, EU Sub-committee E (Justice, Institutions and Consumer Protection) 2012-. *Councils and public bodies:* Monopolies and Mergers Commission: Member 1976-85, Deputy chair 1981-85.

Political interests: Economy, education, Third World development, museums and the arts, secondary legislation, local government; Third World.

Other: Chair: Board of Trustees, Royal Botanical Gardens, Kew 1983-91, Hospital for Tropical Diseases Foundation 2000-, Bowes Museum Trust, Co Durham 2000-08; Council member, Eccles Centre for American Studies, British Library 2003-. Honorary DSc, Cranfield Institute of Technology 1989. CBE 1985; Brooks's.

Recreations: Arts, gardening, bridge.

The Viscount Eccles CBE, House of Lords, London SW1A 0PW
Tel: 020 7219 5353 *Email:* ecclesj@parliament.uk

ECCLES OF MOULTON, BARONESS

ECCLES OF MOULTON (Life Baroness), Diana Catherine Eccles; cr. 1990. Born 4 October 1933; Daughter of late Raymond and Margaret Sturge; Married Honorary John Eccles 1955 (later 2nd Viscount Eccles) (1 son 3 daughters).

Education: St James's School, West Malvern; Open University (BA 1978).

Non-political career: Voluntary work, Middlesbrough Community Council 1955-58; Partner in graphic design business 1963-77; Vice-chair, National Council for Voluntary Organisations 1981-87; Director: Tyne Tees Television 1986-94, J. Sainsbury plc 1986-95, Yorkshire Electricity Group plc 1990-97, National and Provincial Building Society 1991-96, Times Newspapers Holdings Ltd 1998-, Opera North 1998-2011, London Clinic 2003-08.

CONSERVATIVE

Political career: *House of Lords:* Raised to the peerage as Baroness Eccles of Moulton, of Moulton in the County of North Yorkshire 1990. Member: Animals in Scientific Procedures 2001-02, EU Sub-committee B (Internal Market) 2003-07, Pre-legislative Scrutiny on Mental Health Bill 2005-, Communications 2007-10, Intergovernmental Organisations 2007-08, EU Sub-committee F (Home Affairs) 2010-12, Joint Committee on Statutory Instruments 2010-12, European Union 2012-, EU Sub-committees: C (External Affairs) 2012-13, E (Justice, Institutions and Consumer Protection) 2013-. *Councils and public bodies:* Member, North Eastern Electricity Board 1974-85; Durham University Council: Lay Member 1981-, Vice-chair 1985-2004; Chair, Tyne Tees Television Programme Consultative Council 1982-84; Member: Advisory Council on Energy Conservation (Department of Energy) 1982-84, Widdicombe Inquiry into Local Government 1985-86, Home Office Advisory Panel on Licences for Experimental Community Radio 1985-86, British Rail Eastern Board 1986-92, Teesside Urban Development Corporation 1987-98; Chair, Ealing District Health Authority 1988-93; Member, Unrelated Live Transplant Regulatory Authority 1990-99; Chair, Ealing, Hammersmith and Hounslow Health Authority 1993-2000; DL, North Yorkshire 1998-2008.

Other: Member, UK Delegation, Council of Europe 2010-; Trustee: Charities Aid Foundation 1982-89, York Minster Trust Fund 1989-99, 2006-09; Member, British Heart Foundation 1989-98. Honorary DCL, Durham 1995.

The Viscountess Eccles, Lady Eccles of Moulton DL, House of Lords, London SW1A 0PW
Tel: 020 7219 5353 *Email:* ecclesd@parliament.uk

EDEN OF WINTON, LORD

EDEN OF WINTON (Life Baron), John Benedict Eden; cr 1983; 9th Bt of West Auckland (E) 1672; 7th Bt of Maryland (GB) 1776. Born 15 September 1925; Son of Sir Timothy Eden, 8th and 6th Bt; Married Belinda Pascoe 1958 (divorced 1974) (2 sons 2 daughters); married Margaret Ann, Viscountess Strathallan, née Gordon 1977.

Education: Eton College; St Paul's School, USA.

Non-political career: Served British and Indian Armies 1943-47; Lieutenant, Rifle Brigade, seconded to 2nd King Edward VIIth's Own Goorkha Rifles and The Gilgit Scouts. Former tree and shrub nurseryman; Former, chairman of various plcs; Chairman, Lady Eden's School Ltd 1974-2001; Member, Timken Company International Advisory Board 1974-2001.

CONSERVATIVE

Political career: *House of Commons:* Contested Paddington North 1953 by-election. MP (Conservative) for Bournemouth West 1954-83. Opposition Spokesman for Power 1968-70; Minister of State, Ministry of Technology June-October 1970; Minister for Industry 1970-72; Minister of Posts and Telecommunications 1972-74; Sponsored Copyright Act 1983. Chair: European Affairs 1976-79, Home Affairs 1981-83. Former officer, Executive, 1922 Committee. *House of Lords:* Raised to the peerage as Baron Eden of Winton, of Rushyford in the County of Durham 1983. *Other:* Honorary life vice-president, Association of Conservative Clubs; President: Wessex Area Conservatives 1974-77, Wessex Area Young Conservatives 1978-80; Assistant to Margaret Thatcher 1983 general election. *Councils and public bodies:* Vice-president, National Chamber of Trade 1968-78; President, Independent Schools Association 1969-71; Chairman, The British Lebanese Association 1990-98; Vice-President, International Tree Foundation -1998.

Political interests: Conservation, rainforests; Cameroon, Lebanon, Sri Lanka.

Other: Member: Western European Union 1960-62, Council of Europe 1960-62 (Rapporteur, Cultural Affairs Committee), NATO Parliamentarians 1962-66; Chairman, The Royal Armouries Board of Trustees 1986-94; The Rainforest Foundation; The Jane Goodall Institute. Honorary Freeman: Annapolis, Maryland, USA 1976, Bournemouth 1984. PC 1972; Boodle's, Pratt's.

Recreations: Gardening, trees.

Rt Hon the Lord Eden of Winton, House of Lords, London SW1A 0PW
Tel: 020 7219 5353 *Email:* edenj@parliament.uk

CONSERVATIVE

EDMISTON, LORD

EDMISTON (Life Baron), Robert Norman Edmiston; cr 2011. Born 6 October 1946; Son of Vivian Edmiston and Margaret Edmiston, née Grostate; Married Tracie Spicer 1998 (1 son 2 daughters).

Education: Abbs Cross Technical High School, Hornchurch; Barking Region College of Technology.

Non-political career: Bank clerk, English Scottish & Australian Bank 1964-66; Treasury clerk, Chrysler International SA Treasury 1966-67; Financial analyst, Ford Motor Company 1967-70; Chrysler (UK) Ltd 1970-74: Senior analyst 1970-71, Capital planning manager 1971-72, Economic research analyst 1972, Financial analysis and administration manager 1972-74; Jensen Motors Ltd 1974-76: Financial controller and company secretary 1974-75, Finance director 1975-76; Part-owner, Jensen Parts & Service Ltd 1976-80; Owner: International Motors Ltd 1980-88, I.M. Group Ltd 1988-, I.M. Finance Ltd 1988-, I.M. Properties plc 1992-.

Political career: *House of Lords:* Raised to the peerage as Baron Edmiston, of Lapworth in the County of Warwickshire 2011.

Political interests: Business, social issues.

Other: Founder, Christian Vision; Chartered Institute of Management Accountants: Associate 1974, Fellow 1991.

Recreations: Golf, skiing, tennis, playing guitar, scuba.

The Lord Edmiston, House of Lords, London SW1A 0PW
Tel: 020 7219 5353

LABOUR

ELDER, LORD

ELDER (Life Baron), Thomas Murray Elder; cr. 1999. Born 9 May 1950.

Education: Kirkcaldy High School; Edinburgh University (MA economic history).

Non-political career: Bank of England 1972-80; Research assistant to Shadow Secretary of State for Trade and Industry 1980-84; Labour Party Scotland 1984-92, General Secretary 1988-92; Chief of Staff to John Smith MP as Leader of the Labour Party 1992-94; Special adviser, Scottish Office 1997-99.

Political career: *House of Commons:* Contested (Labour) Ross, Cromarty and Skye 1983 general election. *House of Lords:* Raised to the peerage as Baron Elder, of Kirkcaldy in Fife 1999. Member: Monetary Policy of the Bank of England/Economic Affairs 2000-05, Refreshment 2008-13.

Recreations: Walking, reading, opera.

The Lord Elder, House of Lords, London SW1A 0PW
Tel: 020 7219 8512

PLAID CYMRU

ELIS-THOMAS, LORD

ELIS-THOMAS (Life Baron), Dafydd Elis-Thomas; cr. 1992. Born 18 October 1946; Son of Rev William Ellis Thomas and Eirlys Thomas; Married Elen Williams 1970 (divorced) (3 sons); married Mair Parry Jones 1993.

Education: Ysgol Dyffryn Conwy; University College of Wales (PhD); Welsh.

Non-political career: Tutor in Welsh studies, Coleg Harlech 1971-74; Lecturer: University College of North Wales, Bangor, Aberystwyth, Cardiff, Open University; Broadcaster on BBC Wales, HTV, S4C, Radio Wales; Consultant to 1999: S4C, Welsh Development Agency, Rural Initiative Programme, Assembly of European Regions, Government of Catalonia; Chairman, Screen Wales; Director and deputy chair, Cynefin Environmental; Director and chair, New Media Agency; Director: Oriel Mostyn, National Botanical Gardens, MFM Marcher.

Political career: *House of Commons:* Contested Conway 1970 general election. MP (Plaid Cymru) for Meirionnydd February 1974-83, for Meirionnydd Nant Conwy 1974-92. *House of Lords:* Raised to the peerage as Baron Elis-Thomas, of Nant Conwy in the County of Gwynedd

1992. Member: European Communities 1997-98, European Communities Sub-committee C (Environment, Public Health and Consumer Protection) 1997-98. *Other:* National Assembly for Wales: AM for Meirionnydd Nant Conwy 1999-2007, for Dwyfor Meirionnydd constituency since 3 May 2007: Presiding Officer 1999-2011, Chair Assembly Committee on Environment and Sustainability 2011-, Plaid Cymru Spokesperson for: Environment, Energy and Planning 2011-12, Rural Affairs, Fisheries and Food 2012-13, Spokesperson for Transport and Society 2013-. Plaid Cymru: President 1984-91, Contested leadership election 2012; Whip withdrawn 18-20 July 2012.

Political interests: Rural affairs, environment, constitutional affairs; Wales.

Other: President, Commonwealth Parliamentary Association (Wales Branch) 1999-2011; President: Hay-on-Wye Literature Festival, University of Wales, Bangor 2001-, Ramblers Association in Wales -1999, Snowdonia National Park Society -1999, Abbeyfield -1999; Member: Welsh Arts Council -1999, Welsh Film Council -1999, Welsh Film Board -1999, Wales Committee of National Trust; BBC General Consultative Council -1999; Chair, Welsh Language Board 1993-96, 1996-99; Trustee: Big Issue Foundation -1999, Theatr Bara Caws -1999; Fellow, International Centre for Intercultural Studies, Institute of Education, London; Patron, Prince of Wales Trust – Bro; President, Bangor University; Surname changed from Thomas to Elis-Thomas by deed poll 1992. Welsh Politician of the Year 2008, ITV Wales. PC 2004.

Recreations: Welsh literature and art, music, theatre, films, hill- and mountain-walking, jogging.

Rt Hon the Lord Elis-Thomas, House of Lords, London SW1A 0PW
Tel: 020 7219 8701 *Email:* elisthomasd@parliament.uk
7 Bank Place, Porthmadog, Gwynedd LL49 9AA *Tel:* 01766 515028
Email: dafydd.elis-thomas@wales.gov.uk
Website: www.dafyddelis-thomas.plaidcymru.org *Twitter:* @ElisThomasD

ELTON, LORD

CONSERVATIVE

ELTON (2nd Baron, UK), Rodney Elton; cr. 1934. Born 2 March 1930; Son of Godfrey 1st Baron and Dedi Hartmann; Married Anne Tilney 1958 (divorced 1979) (1 son 3 daughters); married Richenda Gurney 1979 (CVO 1997, DCVO 2010).

Education: Eton College; New College, Oxford (MA modern history 1953).

Non-political career: 2nd Lieutenant, The Queens Bays 1950; Captain, Queen's Own Warwickshire and Worcestershire Yeomanry 1959; Major, Leicestershire and Derbyshire Yeomanry 1970. Farming 1957-73; Assistant mastership (history): Loughborough Grammar School 1962-67, Fairham Comprehensive School for Boys 1967-69; Lecturer, Bishop Lonsdale College of Education 1969-72; Director: Overseas Exhibitions Ltd 1977-79, Building Trades Exhibition Ltd 1977-79; Director and deputy chair, Andry Montgomery Ltd 1987-2002; DIVERT Trust: Founder and chair 1993-99, President 1999-2001; Licensed Lay Minister, Church of England 1998-. Assistant Masters Association 1962-69.

Political career: *House of Commons:* Contested (Conservative) Loughborough 1966 and 1970 general elections. *House of Lords:* First entered House of Lords 1973; Opposition Whip 1974-76; Opposition Spokesperson 1976-79; Parliamentary Under-Secretary of State for: Northern Ireland 1979-81, Department of Health and Social Security 1981-82, Home Office 1982-84; Minister of State: Home Office 1984-85, Department of the Environment 1985-86; Deputy Chairman of Committees 1997-2007; Elected hereditary peer 1999-; Deputy Speaker 1999-2008; Contested Lord Speaker election 2006. Member: Scrutiny of Delegated Powers 1994-97, Ecclesiastical Committee 2001-, Constitution 2003-07, Procedure 2005-09, Conventions Joint Committee 2006, EU Sub-committee B: Internal Market, Infrastructure and Employment 2013. *Other:* Vice-chair, Association of Conservative Peers 1988-93. *Councils and public bodies:* Member, Boyd Commission (South Rhodesia Independence Elections) 1979; Chair, Financial Intermediaries Managers and Brokers Regulatory Association 1987-90; Member, Panel on Takeovers and Mergers 1988-90; Chair, Inquiry into Discipline in Schools (Elton Report) 1988; Vice-President, Institute of Trading Standards Administration 1990-; Chair, Quality and Standards Committee, City and Guilds of London Institute 1999-2004.

Political interests: Juvenile justice, education; Norway.

Other: Chair, Intermediate Treatment Fund 1990-93; Trustee: The Airey Neave Trust 1991-96, City Parochial Foundation and Trust for London 1991-97; RSA; The DIVERT Trust. Honorary Fellow, City and Guilds of London 2000. TD 1970; Lord of the Manor of Adderbury; Beefsteak, Pratt's, Cavalry and Guards.

Recreations: Painting.

The Lord Elton TD, House of Lords, London SW1A 0PW
Tel: 020 7219 3165 *Fax:* 020 7219 0785

CROSSBENCH

ELYSTAN-MORGAN, LORD

ELYSTAN-MORGAN (Life Baron), Dafydd Elystan Elystan-Morgan; cr. 1981. Born 7 December 1932; Son of late Dewi, journalist, and Olwen Morgan; Married Alwen Roberts 1959 (died 2006) (1 son 1 daughter).

Education: Ardwyn Grammar School, Aberystwyth; University of Wales, Aberystwyth (LLB 1953).

Non-political career: Solicitor 1957; Partner in North Wales firm of solicitors 1958-68; Called to the Bar 1971 (Gray's Inn); Wales and Chester Circuit 1983-2003: Recorder 1983-87, Judge 1987-2003; Deputy High Court Judge 1989-2003.

Political career: *House of Commons:* MP (Labour) for Cardigan 1966-74. Joint Under-Secretary of State, Home Office 1968-70; Deputy Opposition Spokesperson for: Home Affairs 1970-72, Welsh Affairs 1972-74. *House of Lords:* Raised to the peerage as Baron Elystan-Morgan, of Aberteifi in the County of Dyfed 1981. Opposition Spokesperson for Home Affairs and Legal Affairs 1983-87. Member EU Sub-committee E: (Justice and Institutions) 2012, (Justice, Institutions and Consumer Protection) 2012-. *Other:* Chair, Welsh Parliamentary Party 1974. *Councils and public bodies:* Chair, Welsh Local Government Association 1966-74; President, Association of Welsh Local Authorities 1970-74; University of Wales, Aberystwyth: Vice-President 1990-97, President 1997-2007; President, School of Welsh Legal Studies 2001-.

Other: Honorary Fellow, University of Wales, Aberystwyth 1989.

The Lord Elystan-Morgan, House of Lords, London SW1A 0PW
Tel: 020 7219 5353
Carreg Afon, Dolau, Bow Street, Ceredigion SY24 5AE

CROSSBENCH

EMERTON, BARONESS

EMERTON (Life Baroness), Audrey Caroline Emerton; cr. 1997. Born 10 September 1935; Daughter of late George Emerton, and of Lily Emerton; Single.

Education: Tunbridge Wells Grammar School for Girls; St George's Hospital; Battersea College of Technology.

Non-political career: Senior tutor, St George's Hospital, London 1965-68; St John Ambulance: Kent County nursing officer 1967-85, County Commissioner 1985-88; Principal nursing officer, Education, Bromley Hospital Management Committee 1968-70; Chief nursing officer, Tunbridge Wells and Leybourne Hospital Management Committee 1970-73; Regional nursing officer, South East Thames RHA 1973-91; St John Ambulance: Chief nursing officer 1988-96, Chair, Medical Board 1993-96, Chief Officer, Care in the Community 1996-98, Chancellor, Chief Commander 1998-2002.

Political career: *House of Lords:* Raised to the peerage as Baroness Emerton, of Tunbridge Wells in the County of Kent and of Clerkenwell in the London Borough of Islington 1997. Member Science and Technology Sub-committees: I (Fighting Infection) 2003, I (Scientific Aspects of Ageing) 2005; Member Refreshment 2010-12. *Councils and public bodies:* DL, Kent 1992-2010; Chair, Brighton Health Care NHS Trust 1994-2000.

Political interests: Health – social care, voluntary services, defence medical welfare service, Jerusalem.

Other: President, chair several nursing, midwifery and health visiting organisations 1983-99, including: Trustee, Kent Community Housing Trust 1993-98; Honorary Vice-President, Royal College of Nursing 1994-99; Member, Court of Sussex University 1996-98; Lay Member, General Medical Council 1996-2001; Member, Burdett Nursing Trust 2001-03; Defence Medical Welfare Service: Trustee 2001-12, Patron 2013-; Chair, Association of Hospital and Community Friends 2003-06; President, Florence Nightingale Foundation 2004-; Prime Ministers Commission Nursing and Midwifery Commissioner; Fellow: Royal Society of Arts, Kings College London, Brighton University, Kingston, Christ Church Canterbury, Royal College of Nursing; Fellow, Royal College of Nursing; St John Ambulance; Order of St John of Jerusalem; Ophthalmic Hospital Jerusalem. Seven honorary doctorates. CStJ 1978; DBE 1989; DStJ 1993, Dame Grand Cross 2004.

Recreations: Walking, travel, reading.

The Baroness Emerton DBE, House of Lords, London SW1A 0PW
Tel: 020 7219 5035 *Email:* emertona@parliament.uk
Email: audrey.emerton@gmail.com

EMPEY, LORD

EMPEY (Life Baron), Reginald Norman Morgan Empey; cr 2011. Born 26 October 1947; Son of late Samuel Empey and late Emily Empey, née Morgan; Married Stella Donnan 1977 (1 son 1 daughter).

Education: Royal School, Armagh; Queen's University, Belfast (BSc Econ 1969).

Non-political career: 1970-1986: Industrial rubber products division, Goodyear International Corporation; House of Fraser/Switzer and Company; McMahon Co; Self-employed clothing retailer 1986-.

ULSTER UNIONIST PARTY

Political career: *House of Commons:* Contested (UUP) Belfast East 1997 and 2005 and (Ulster Conservatives and Unionists) South Antrim 2010 general elections. *House of Lords:* Raised to the peerage as Baron Empey, of Shandon in the City and County of Belfast 2011. Member Small- and Medium-Sized Enterprises 2012-13. *Other:* Member: Northern Ireland Convention 1975, UUP Talks Team, Brooke/Mayhew Talks 1991, UUP Talks Team, Castle Buildings Talks 1996-98; Northern Ireland Assembly: MLA for Belfast East 1998-2011, Minister for: Enterprise, Trade and Investment 1999-2002, Employment and Learning 2007-10. Member, UUP Negotiating Team: Brooke-Mayhew Talks 1991, Castle Building Talks 1996-98; Vice-president, Ulster Unionist Council 1996-2004; Ulster Unionist Party: Leader 2005-10, Chair 2012-. *Councils and public bodies:* Belfast City Council: Councillor 1985-2010, Mayor 1989, 1993; Member, Police Authority of Northern Ireland 1992-2001.

Political interests: Economic policy, education, UK-US relations, EU, small- and medium-sized enterprises; Canada, India, USA.

Other: Member, EU Committee of the Regions 1994-2002; Vice-President, The Institute of Export. OBE 1994; Kt 1999; Army and Navy.

Recreations: Walking, gardening.

The Lord Empey OBE, House of Lords, London SW1A 0PW
Tel: 020 7219 8482 *Email:* empeyr@parliament.uk

ERROLL, EARL OF

ERROLL (24th Earl of, S), Merlin Sereld Victor Gilbert Hay; cr. 1452. 25th Lord Hay (S) 1429, 24th Lord Slains (S) 1452; 12th Bt (NS) 1685; 28th Hereditary Lord High Constable of Scotland, 1314; 32nd Chief of The Hays since 1160 (Celtic title) Mac Garadh Mhor. Born 20 April 1948; Son of Sir Iain Moncreiffe of that Ilk, 11th Bt and Diana Denyse, Countess of Erroll (23rd in line); Married Isabelle Jacqueline Laline Astell 1982 (2 sons 2 daughters).

Education: Eton College; Trinity College, Cambridge.

Non-political career: Lieutenant, Atholl Highlanders 1974; TA 1975-90; Honorary Colonel, RMPTA 1992-97. Hayway Partners (Marketing) 1991-; Computer consultant -1993; Group director, Applications and Development, Girovend Holdings plc 1993-94; Chair: CRC Ltd 1995-, Fonem Ltd 2004-.

CROSSBENCH

Political career: *House of Lords:* First entered House of Lords 1978; Elected hereditary peer 1999-. Board Member of Parliamentary Office of Science and Technology 2000-; Council member PITCOM 2000-; Member Information 2003-05, 2007-08, 2009-12.

Political interests: Defence, ICT, science, Scotland, environment.

Other: Member, Queen's Body Guard for Scotland, Royal Company of Archers; Fishmongers Company Charitable Trust; Billingsgate Christian Mission; Trustee, Mar Estate Trust; Royal Caledonian Ball. Member, Court of Assistants of Fishmongers' Company, Prime Warden 2000-01. Freeman, City of London. Page to the Lord Lyon 1956; OStJ 1977; White's, Pratt's, Puffin's (Edinburgh).

Recreations: Country pursuits.

The Earl of Erroll, House of Lords, London SW1A 0PW
Tel: 020 7219 3885 *Email:* errollm@parliament.uk
Woodbury Hall, Everton, Sandy, Bedfordshire SG19 2HR *Tel:* 01767 650251

LABOUR

EVANS OF PARKSIDE, LORD

EVANS OF PARKSIDE (Life Baron), John Evans; cr. 1997. Born 19 October 1930; Son of late James and Margaret Evans; Married Joan Slater 1959 (2 sons 1 daughter).
Education: Jarrow Central School.
Non-political career: Royal Engineers 1949-50. Marine fitter, Tyneside shipyard worker. Joined AEU 1951.
Political career: *House of Commons:* MP (Labour) for Newton February 1974-83, for St Helens North 1983-97. Government Whip 1978-1979; Opposition Whip 1979-80; PPS to Michael Foot as Leader of Opposition 1980-83; Shadow Employment Minister 1983-87. *House of Lords:* Raised to the peerage as Baron Evans of Parkside, of St Helens in the County of Merseyside 1997. *Other:* European Parliament: MEP 1975-78, Chair, Regional Policy and Transport Committee 1976-78. Political Secretary, National Union of Labour and Socialist Clubs 1981-96; Member, Labour Party National Executive Committee 1982-96; Labour Party: Vice-chair 1990-91, Chair 1991-92. *Councils and public bodies:* Hebburn Urban District Council: Councillor 1962-74, Chair 1972-73, Leader 1969-74; Councillor, South Tyneside Metropolitan District Council 1973-74.
Political interests: Employment, energy, transport, manufacturing industries, industrial relations, licensed trade.
Other: Freeman, Metropolitan Borough of St Helens 1997; The Daten, Culcheth.
Recreations: Gardening, watching rugby and football.
The Lord Evans of Parkside, House of Lords, London SW1A 0PW
Tel: 020 7219 6541 *Fax:* 020 7219 1339

LABOUR

EVANS OF TEMPLE GUITING, LORD

EVANS OF TEMPLE GUITING (Life Baron), Matthew Evans; cr. 2000. Born 7 August 1941; Son of late George Evans and Florence Evans; Married Elizabeth Mead 1966 (2 sons) (divorced 1991); married Caroline Michel 1991 (2 sons 1 daughter).
Education: Friends' School, Saffron Walden; London School of Economics (BSc economics 1963).
Non-political career: Bookselling 1963-64; Faber & Faber Ltd 1964-2003: Managing director 1972-93, Chair 1981-2003; Director, Which? Ltd 1997-2000; Chair, E.F.G Private Bank 2008-.
Political career: *House of Lords:* Raised to the peerage as Baron Evans of Temple Guiting, of Temple Guiting in the County of Gloucestershire 2000. Government Whip 2002-07; Government Spokesperson for: Office of the Deputy Prime Minister 2002-03, Justice/Lord Chancellor's Department (Scotland and Wales) 2003-07, Trade and Industry 2003-04, Work and Pensions 2005-07, Treasury 2005-07, Cabinet Office 2007, Culture, Media and Sport 2007, Trade and Industry/Business, Enterprise and Regulatory Reform 2007, Environment, Food and Rural Affairs 2007; Opposition Spokesperson for Culture, Media and Sport 2010-11. *Councils and public bodies:* Chair, Library and Information Commission 1995-98; Member: Arts Council National Lottery Advisory Panel 1997-2000, University for Industry Advisory Group 1997, Sir Richard Eyre's Working Group on Royal Opera House 1997, Arts and Humanities Research Board 1998-2003; Chair, Museums, Libraries and Archives Council 2000-03.
Other: Council member, Publishers' Association 1978-84; BFI: Governor 1982-97, Vice-chair 1996-97; Chair: National Book League 1982-84, English Stage Company (Royal Court Theatre) 1984-90; Member, Literary Advisory Panel, British Council 1986-97; President, The British Antique Dealers' Association; FRSA 1990; Honorary FRCA 1999; Honorary FLA 1999. Honorary DLitt, Sunderland University. CBE 1998; Groucho.
The Lord Evans of Temple Guiting CBE, House of Lords, London SW1A 0PW
Tel: 020 7219 6631 *Email:* evansm@parliament.uk

LABOUR

EVANS OF WATFORD, LORD

EVANS OF WATFORD (Life Baron), David Charles Evans; cr. 1998. Born 30 November 1942; Son of Arthur Charles Evans and Phyllis Connie Evans; Married June Scaldwell 1966 (divorced) (2 sons 1 daughter).
Education: Hampden Secondary School; Watford College of Technology (Full Tech 1962).
Non-political career: Apprentice printer, Stone and Cox Ltd 1957; Sales executive and sales director at various printers; Centurion Press: Founder 1971, Chairman, and of subsidiary companies in UK, Netherlands and the USA -2002; Former chairman: Personnel Publications Ltd, Redactive Publishing Ltd, Indigo Publishing Ltd, Iconic Images Ltd; Chairman: Senate Consulting Ltd, TU Ink Ltd, Evans Mitchell Books, Care Capital plc, Kennedy Scott Ltd; Non-executive director, Partnership Sourcing Ltd. Amicus.

Political career: *House of Lords:* Raised to the peerage as Baron Evans of Watford, of Chipperfield in the County of Hertfordshire 1998. Departmental Liaison Peer for Department of Trade and Industry 1999-2004. Member Small- and Medium-Sized Enterprises 2012-13.
Political interests: Industrial relations, current affairs, education, travel, voluntary sector; Europe, Far East, USA.
Other: Honorary Fellow, Cancer Research UK; Assisted in creation of One World group (now One World Action); Voluntary lecturer for Postal Telegraph and Telephone International in trade union studies and media public relations; Non-executive director, Hendon Museum Enterprises Ltd; Trustee, Royal Air Force Museum; Fellow: Chartered Institute of Marketing, City and Guilds Institute; Cancer Research UK, Royal British Legion, British Red Cross, St Paul's Church, Chipperfield, Extension Appeal, CT Spiral Scanner Appeal, Watford Hospital, NCH Action For Children, Macmillan Cancer Care. Member, Worshipful Company of Marketors; Mortons.
Recreations: Theatre, the arts, reading, travel.
The Lord Evans of Watford, House of Lords, London SW1A 0PW
Tel: 020 7219 6184 *Fax:* 020 7219 1733
Senate Consulting Ltd, 86 Gloucester Place, London, Hertfordshire W1U 6HP *Tel:* 020 3617 8726
Email: lordevans@senateconsulting.co.uk

EZRA, LORD

EZRA (Life Baron), Derek Ezra; cr. 1983. Born 23 February 1919; Son of late David Ezra; Married Julia Elizabeth Wilkins 1950.
Education: Monmouth School; Magdalene College, Cambridge (MA, HM. Fellow).
Non-political career: Army Service 1939-47. National Coal Board 1947-82: Director General, marketing 1960-65, Board member 1965-67, Deputy chair 1967-71, Chair 1971-82; Chair, AHS-Emstar plc 1966-99; Member, advisory committee, Energy International SA 1975-90 Director: Solvay SA 1979-89, Redland plc 1981-89; Member, international advisory board: Banca del Lavoro 1981-2000, Creditanstalt Bankverein 1981-91; Member, advisory board, Petrofina SA 1981-90; Director, Aran Energy plc 1984-95; Chair, Throgmorton Trust 1985-90; Sheffield Heat & Power Ltd 1985-2000; Chair: Energy and Technical Services Group plc 1990-99, Micropower Ltd 2000-05.

LIBERAL DEMOCRAT

Political career: *House of Lords:* Raised to the peerage as Baron Ezra, of Horsham in the County of West Sussex 1983. Former Liberal Democrat Spokesperson for Economic Affairs; Spokesperson for Trade and Industry (Energy) 1998-2005. *Councils and public bodies:* Chair, Nationalised Industries Chairmen's Group 1972, 1980-81; President, Institute of Trading Standards Administration 1987-92.
Other: Former President, Coal Industry Society; Keep Britain Tidy Group: Chair 1979-85, President 1985-89; President, British Standards Institution 1983-86; Former Patron, Neighbourhood Energy Action; Patron (Past President), Combustion Engineering Association; Patron, Micropower Council 2005-; Vice-President (former President), National Home Improvement Council. Two honorary doctorates. MBE (Mil) 1945; Kt 1974; Order of Merit (Italy) 1979; Order of Merit (Luxembourg) 1981; Officer, Légion d'Honneur (France) 1981; National Liberal.
Publications: Coal and Energy (1978); The Energy Debate (1983).
The Lord Ezra MBE, House of Lords, London SW1A 0PW
Tel: 020 7219 3341 *Fax:* 020 7393 2752 *Email:* ezrad@parliament.uk

FALCONER OF THOROTON, LORD

Opposition Spokesperson for Justice

FALCONER OF THOROTON (Life Baron), Charles Leslie Falconer; cr. 1997. Born 19 November 1951; Son of late John Leslie Falconer and Anne Mansel Falconer; Married Marianna Catherine Thoroton Hildyard (later QC) 1985 (3 sons 1 daughter).
Education: Trinity College, Glenalmond; Queens' College, Cambridge.
Non-political career: Called to the Bar, Inner Temple 1974; QC 1991; Elected Master, Bench of the Inner Temple 1997; Senior Counsel, Gibson Dunn and Crutcher LLP.

LABOUR

Political career: *House of Lords:* Raised to the peerage as Baron Falconer of Thoroton, of Thoroton in the County of Nottinghamshire 1997. Solicitor General 1997-98; Minister of State and Government Spokesperson for: Cabinet Office 1998-2001, Department for Transport, Local Government and the Regions (Minister for Housing, Planning and Regeneration) 2001-02, Home Office (Criminal Justice, Sentencing and Law Reform) 2002-03; Secretary of State and Government Spokesperson for Constitutional Affairs/Justice and Lord Chancellor 2003-07; Opposition

Spokesperson for Justice (Constitutional Issues/DPM) 2010-. Adviser on Planning and Transition into Government 2013-. Member Procedure 2003-07. *Councils and public bodies:* Chair, Commission on Assisted Dying 2010-.
Other: Vice-President, Commonwealth Parliamentary Association (UK Branch). PC 2003.
Rt Hon the Lord Falconer of Thoroton QC, House of Lords, London SW1A 0PW
Tel: 020 7219 5159 *Email:* cfalconer@gibsondunn.com

FALKENDER, BARONESS

FALKENDER (Life Baroness), Marcia Matilda Falkender; cr. 1974. Born 10 March 1932; Daughter of late Harry Field; Married George Williams 1955 (divorced 1961) (2 sons).
Education: Northampton High School for Girls; Queen Mary College, London University (BA history).
Non-political career: Secretary to General Secretary, Labour Party HQ 1955-56; Private secretary to Harold Wilson MP 1956-64; Political secretary and head of political office to Harold Wilson as Leader of the Labour Party and Prime Minister 1964-70, 1974-76; Columnist, *Mail on Sunday* 1983-88; Local director, Cheltenham and Gloucester Building Society, Peckham; Director: South London Investment Mortgage Corporation 1986-91, Canvasback Productions 1988-91, Regent (GM) Laboratories 1996-.

LABOUR

Political career: *House of Lords:* Raised to the peerage as Baroness Falkender, of West Haddon in the County of Northamptonshire 1974.
Political interests: Exports, health, breast cancer, British film industry.
Other: Member: Film Industry Working Party 1975, Film Industry Action Committee 1977-85, British Screen Advisory Council 1985-, Royal Society of Arts; Former President, UN Unifem UK Trust; Trustee, The Silver Trust 1986-; Lay Governor, Queen Mary and Westfield College, London University 1987-93; The Silver Trust, Breast Cancer, Imperial Cancer Research. CBE 1983; Reform.
Publications: Inside No. 10 (1972); Perspective on Downing Street (1983).
Recreations: Films, reading, music.
The Baroness Falkender CBE, House of Lords, London SW1A 0PW
Tel: 020 7219 3156

FALKLAND, VISCOUNT OF

FALKLAND (15th Viscount of, S), Lucius Edward William Plantagenet Cary; cr. 1620; Lord Cary 1620. Born 8 May 1935; Son of 14th Viscount; Married Caroline Butler 1962 (divorced 1990) (1 son 2 daughters and 1 daughter deceased); married Nicole Mackey 1990 (1 son).
Education: Wellington College, Berkshire; French, German.
Non-political career: 2nd Lieutenant, 8th Hussars. Journalist, Theatrical agent, Chartered shipbroker; Chief executive, C T Bowring Trading (Holdings) Ltd 1974-80; Marketing consultant 1980-86.

CROSSBENCH

Political career: *House of Lords:* First entered House of Lords 1984; Liberal Democrat Deputy Chief Whip 1988-2001; Liberal Democrat Spokesperson for: National Heritage 1995-97, Culture, Media and Sport 1997-2005; Elected hereditary peer 1999-; Former Deputy Chair of Committees. Member: Overseas Trade 1984-85, Pre-legislative Gambling Joint Committee 2004-05; Works of Art: Member 2005-, Chair 2007-. *Other:* Resigned Liberal Democrat Whip March 2011. Now sits as Crossbench.
Political interests: Theatre, Europe, film industry, alcohol and drug addiction, transport (particularly motorcycling), racing and bloodstock; France, Sub-Saharan Africa.
Other: Tower Hamlets Mission; U Can Do It; Brooks's. Sunningdale Golf.
Recreations: Golf, cinema, motorcycling, reading, racing.
The Viscount of Falkland, House of Lords, London SW1A 0PW
Tel: 020 7219 3230
Email: lordfalkland@aol.com

LIBERAL DEMOCRAT

FALKNER OF MARGRAVINE, BARONESS

FALKNER OF MARGRAVINE (Life Baroness), Kishwer Falkner; cr. 2004. Born 9 March 1955; Daughter of Ahsan Mohammad Khan and Saeeda Ahsan; Married Robert Falkner 1996 (1 daughter).

Education: St Joseph's Convent School, Karachi, Pakistan; London School of Economics (BSc Econ international relations 1992); University of Kent (MA international relations and European studies 1994).

Non-political career: Deputy manager, Saudi Arabian Airlines, France and USA 1982-86; Senior researcher, Liberal Democrats, House of Commons 1992-93; Liberal Democrats: Director: International Affairs 1993-99, Policy 1997-98; Chief programme officer, Political Affairs Division, Commonwealth Secretariat 1999-2003; Chief executive, Student Partnerships Worldwide 2003-04. Commonwealth Secretariat Staff Association: Member 1999-2003, Vice-chair 2000-03.

Political career: *House of Commons:* Contested (Lib Dem) Kensington and Chelsea 2001 general election. *House of Lords:* Raised to the peerage as Baroness Falkner of Margravine, of Barons Court in the London Borough of Hammersmith and Fulham 2004. Liberal Democrat Spokesperson for: Home Office 2004-05, Communities and Local Government 2005-06, Children, Schools and Families 2007-08, Justice 2008-09, Foreign and Commonwealth Office 2009-10, Home Office 2009-10. Member Human Rights Joint Committee 2005; Co-opted member EU Sub-committee C (Foreign Affairs, Defence and Development Policy) 2005-06; Member: Draft Legal Services Bill Joint Committee 2006, Intergovernmental Organisations 2007-08, Human Rights Joint Committee 2009-10, Constitution 2010-11, 2012-. Chair, Liberal Democrat Parliamentary Party Committee on International Affairs (FCO) 2010-. *Other:* Contested London region 2004 European Parliament election. Member, Liberal Democrat Federal Policy Committee 1999-2001; Chair, policy, London Liberal Democrats 2000-04; Member, Federal Executive 2010-.

Political interests: European and foreign affairs, political Islam, diversity and equality, constitution, governance, transitional democracies; Middle East, USA.

Other: Chancellor, Northampton University 2008-.

Recreations: Travel, reading, cooking, running, cinema.

The Baroness Falkner of Margravine, House of Lords, London SW1A 0PW
Tel: 020 7219 2809 *Email:* falknerk@parliament.uk

LABOUR

FARRINGTON OF RIBBLETON, BARONESS

FARRINGTON OF RIBBLETON (Life Baroness), Josephine Farrington; cr. 1994. Born 29 June 1940; Daughter of late Ernest Joseph Cayless, and of Dorothy Cayless; Married Michael James Farrington 1960 (3 sons).

Political career: *House of Commons:* Contested (Labour) West Lancashire 1983 general election. *House of Lords:* Raised to the peerage as Baroness Farrington of Ribbleton, of Fulwood in the County of Lancashire 1994. Opposition Whip 1995-97; Government Whip 1997-2007; Government Spokesperson for: Local Government 1997-2001, Northern Ireland 1997-2007, Wales Office -2002, Environment and Rural Affairs 2001-07, Cabinet Office 2001-02, Women's Issues/Equality Agenda -2003; Government Whip 2008-10. Member: Leader's Group on Members Leaving the House 2010-, Delegated Powers and Regulatory Reform 2013-. *Councils and public bodies:* Councillor, Preston Borough Council 1973-76; Lancashire County Council: Councillor 1977-97, Chair, Education Committee 1981-91, Council Chair 1992-93; Association of County Councils: Leader, Labour Group 1987-94, Chair, Policy Committee 1993-94, Chair 1994-96; Member: Burnham Primary and Secondary and Further Education Committees, National Advisory Body for Public Sector Higher Education.

Other: Council member, Europe Standing Conference of Local and Regional Authorities 1981-94 and of new Congress: Chair, Council of Europe Culture, Education, Media and Sport Committee 1988-94; International observer at local elections in Poland, Ukraine and Albania; EU Committee of the Regions: Member 1994-, Chair, Education and Training Committee 1994. UK Woman of Europe 1994.

Recreations: Reading.

The Baroness Farrington of Ribbleton, House of Lords, London SW1A 0PW
Tel: 020 7219 3104

FAULKNER OF WORCESTER, LORD

FAULKNER OF WORCESTER (Life Baron), Richard Oliver Faulkner; cr. 1999. Born 22 March 1946; Son of late Harold and Mabel Faulkner; Married Susan Heyes 1968 (2 daughters). **Education:** Merchant Taylors' School, Northwood; Worcester College, Oxford (BA philosophy, politics and economics 1967, MA).

Non-political career: Graduate Armed Forces Parliamentary Scheme, attached to Royal Navy 2002-07. Research assistant and journalist, Labour Party 1967-69; Public relations officer, Construction Industry Training Board 1969-70; Editor, *Steel News* 1971; Account director, F J Lyons

LABOUR

(Public Relations) Ltd 1971-73; Director, PPR International 1973-76; Government relations adviser to various companies, unions, councils and bodies 1973-99; *The House Magazine*: Co-founder, Member Editorial Board 2003-; Communications adviser to Leader of the Opposition and Labour Party (unpaid) in general elections 1987, 1992, 1997; Communications adviser to the Bishop at Lambeth 1990; Deputy chair, Citigate Westminster 1997-99 (Joint Managing Director, Westminster Communications Group 1989-97); Cardiff Millennium Stadium plc: Director, 1997-2004, Deputy chair 2004-08; Strategy adviser, Littlewoods Leisure 1999-2009; Adviser, Alderney Gambling Control Commission 2005-08.

Political career: *House of Commons:* Contested (Labour) Devizes 1970, February 1974, Monmouth October 1974, Huddersfield West 1979 general elections. *House of Lords:* Raised to the peerage as Baron Faulkner of Worcester, of Wimbledon in the London Borough of Merton 1999. Departmental Liaison Peer: Department of the Environment, Transport and the Regions 2000-01, Cabinet Office 2001-05; Deputy Chairman of Committees 2007-09, 2010-; Deputy Speaker 2008-09, 2010-; Government Whip 2009-10. Member: Draft Gambling Bill Joint Scrutiny Committee 2003-04, London Local Authorities Private Bill 2006, Delegated Powers and Regulatory Reform 2007-09; Co-opted member European Union Sub-committee F (Home Affairs) 2009; Member: Administration and Works 2011-, Joint Committee on the Rookery South (Resource Recovery Facility) Order 2012-13, Selection 2013-, Olympic and Paralympic Legacy 2013-. *Councils and public bodies:* Councillor, Merton Borough Council 1971-78; Member, Court of University of Bedfordshire 1999-2009; ROSPA: President 2001-04, Vice-president 2004-; Chair, Inquiry into Betting on Sport 2004-05.

Political interests: Transport, sport, human rights, smoking and health, sex equality; Argentina, Caribbean, Denmark, Namibia, Norway, South Africa, Sweden, Taiwan.

Other: Member: Inter-Parliamentary Union, Executive committee, Commonwealth Parliamentary Association UK 2003-05; Various posts numerous sports, especially football, including directorships of four football clubs; Patron, Roy Castle Lung Cancer Foundation 1999-2003, 2006-; Vice-president, Transport 2000 Ltd 2001-; Director, West Somerset Railway 2004-05; Chair, Railway Heritage Committee 2004-09; Trustee: Foundation for Sports and the Arts 2000-, Gamcare 2005-09, National Museum for Science and Industry 2007-09, 2011-, National Football Museum 2007-09, 2012-; President, Heritage Railway Association 2011-; Vice-President, The Football Conference 2011-; President, Old Merchant Taylors' Society 2011-12. Honorary Fellow, Worcester College, Oxford 2002; Honorary Doctor of Law, Luton University 2003; Fellow, Worcester University 2008. Diplomatic Medal of Honour, Government of Taiwan 2004; Reform.

Recreations: Travelling by railway, collecting Lloyd George memorabilia, tinplate trains, watching Association Football.

The Lord Faulkner of Worcester, House of Lords, London SW1A 0PW
Tel: 020 7219 8503 *Fax:* 020 7219 1460 *Email:* faulknerro@parliament.uk
Website: www.lordfaulkner.net

FAULKS, LORD

FAULKS (Life Baron), Edward Peter Lawless Faulks; cr 2010. Born 19 August 1950; Son of His Honour Peter Faulks, MC and Pamela Faulks, née Lawless; Married Catherine Turner 1990 (2 sons).

Education: Wellington College, Berkshire; Jesus College, Oxford; French.

Non-political career: Called to the Bar, Middle Temple 1973; Literary agent, Curtis Brown 1980-81; QC 1996; Assistant recorder 1996-2000; Recorder 2000-; Bencher 2002; Chair, Professional Negligence Bar Association 2002-04; Special adviser to Department for Constitutional Affairs on

CONSERVATIVE

compensation culture 2005-06.

Political career: *House of Lords:* Raised to the peerage as Baron Faulks, of Donnington in the Royal County of Berkshire 2010. Member: Selection 2011, Joint Committees on: the Draft Detention of Terrorist Suspects (Temporary Extension) Bills 2011, Human Rights 2012-, the Draft Communications Data Bill 2012-13, Member Mental Capacity Act 2005 2013-.

Political interests: Legal issues, constitution, education, medicine, conservation, human rights; India, Sri Lanka, USA.

Publications: Contributing editor, Local Authority Liability (2012).

Recreations: Sports, the arts.

The Lord Faulks, House of Lords, London SW1A 0PW

Tel: 020 7219 5353

1 Chancery Lane, London WC2A 1LF *Tel:* 0845 634 6666 *Email:* efaulks@1chancerylane.com

FEARN, LORD

FEARN (Life Baron), Ronnie Cyril Fearn; cr. 2001. Born 6 February 1931; Son of late James Fearn and late Martha Fearn; Married Joyce Dugan 1955 (1 son 1 daughter).

Education: Norwood School; King George V Grammar School, Southport.

Non-political career: Royal Navy national service 1950-51. Banker, Royal Bank of Scotland 1947-87. Member, Association of Liberal Democrat Trade Unionists.

Political career: *House of Commons:* MP for Southport 1987-92 (Liberal 1987-88, Liberal Democrat 1988-92). Contested Southport 1992 general election. MP (Lib Dem) for Southport 1997-

LIBERAL DEMOCRAT 2001. Liberal Democrat: Deputy Chief Whip 1988-90, Spokesperson for: Tourism 1997-2001, Civil Service 1997-99, Constitution 1997. *House of Lords:* Raised to the peerage as Baron Fearn, of Southport in the County of Merseyside 2001. Co-opted member EU Sub-committee B (Energy, Industry and Transport/Internal Market) 2003-04; Member EU Sub-committee B: (Internal Market, Energy and Transport) 2010-12, (Internal Market, Infrastructure and Employment) 2012-. *Councils and public bodies:* Councillor and Leader of Liberal Democrat Group: Southport Borough Council 1963-74, Merseyside Metropolitan County Council 1974-86; Councillor, Sefton Metropolitan Borough Council 1974-.

Political interests: Tourism, health, transport, leisure, local government.

Other: Member: Inter-Parliamentary Union, Commonwealth Parliamentary Association, Liberal International; Voluntary Youth Leader in Southport 1960-81; President, Local Carers' Association 1974-80; Local President, Sue Ryder Association 1975-85; Honorary Member, LIFE; Vice-president, British Resorts Association 1987-; Member, Institute of Bankers 1970; Fellow, Chartered Institute of Bankers; Southport Offshore Life Boat; Southport Gladstone Liberal Club. OBE 1985; National Liberal. Southport and Waterloo Athletic Club.

Recreations: Amateur dramatics, badminton, athletics, community work.

The Lord Fearn OBE, House of Lords, London SW1A 0PW

Tel: 020 7219 5116 *Fax:* 01704 508635

FELDMAN, LORD

FELDMAN (Life Baron), Basil Feldman; cr. 1996. Born 23 September 1926; Son of late Philip and Tilly Feldman; Married Gita Julius 1952 (2 sons 1 daughter).

Education: Grocers' School, London; South East London Technical College (engineering); French, German.

Non-political career: Chair: Martlet Services Group Ltd 1973-81, Clothing Economic Development Committee (Clothing Little Neddy) 1978-85; Underwriting Member of Lloyds 1979-97; Chair, Solport Ltd 1980-85.

CONSERVATIVE **Political career:** *House of Lords:* Raised to the peerage as Baron Feldman, of Frognal in the London Borough of Camden 1996. Member Information 2009-12. *Other:* Vice-President, Greater London Young Conservatives 1975-77; National Union Executive Committee: Member 1975-99, Chair 1991-96; National Union of Conservative and Unionist Associations, Greater London Area: President 1981-85, Vice-President 1985-; Joint National Chair, Conservative Party's Impact 80s Campaign 1982-87; National Union of the Conservative Party: Chair 1985-86, Vice-President 1986-; Chair, National Union Executive Committee 1995-96; Party Treasurer 1996-; Renaissance Forum, Conservative Party: Chairman 1996-2010, President 2010-. *Councils and public bodies:* Member, Post Office Users' National Council 1978-81; Chair, Better Made in Britain 1983-98; Director, The Young Entrepreneurs Fund 1985-94; Member, English Tourist Board 1986-96; Chair: The Quality Mark 1987-92, Shopping Hours Reform Council 1988-94, Better Business Opportunities 1990-98, Market Opportunities Advisory Group, Department of Trade and Industry 1991-93, Festival of Arts and Culture 1994-95.

Political interests: Industry, arts, construction industry, retail industry, import substitution, tourism, sport; Austria, Germany, West Indies, USA.

Other: Fellow, Royal Society of Arts 1987; Governor, Sports Aid Foundation 1990-2002; Founder/Chairman, London Arts Season 1993-96; Conservative National Golf Tournament Charitable Settlement; Fresh Hope Trust; Chair: London Arts Season 1993-96, Salzburg Festival Trust 1997-2003. Freeman, City of London 1983. Marketing award, Marketing Society and Marketing Week 1985. Kt 1982; Carlton. Arsenal F.C.

Publications: Several publications, booklets and pamphlets for the Conservative Party; Constituency Campaigning (1977); Some Thoughts on Job Creation (NEDO, 1984).

Recreations: Golf, tennis, theatre, opera, travel, watching Football.

The Lord Feldman, House of Lords, London SW1A 0PW
Tel: 020 7219 0661
41 St James's Place, London SW1A 1NS *Tel:* 020 7493 3178 *Fax:* 020 7629 5189
Email: lordfeldman@aol.com

CONSERVATIVE

FELDMAN OF ELSTREE, LORD

FELDMAN OF ELSTREE (Life Baron), Andrew Simon Feldman; cr 2010. Born 25 February 1966; Malcolm and Marcia Feldman; Married Gabrielle Gourgey (2 sons 1 daughter).

Education: Haberdashers' Aske's School, Elstree; Brasenose College, Oxford (BA jurisprudence 1988).

Non-political career: Management consultant, Bain & Company 1988-90; Barrister, 1 Essex Court 1991-95; Chief executive, Jayroma 1995-.

Political career: *House of Lords:* Raised to the peerage as Baron Feldman of Elstree, of Elstree in the County of Hertfordshire 2010. *Other:* Conservative Party: Deputy treasurer 2005-08, Chief executive 2008-10, Co-chairman 2010-, Chairman, party board 2010-.

Recreations: Tennis, golf.

The Lord Feldman of Elstree, House of Lords, London SW1A 0PW
Tel: 020 7219 5353
The Conservative Party, 30 Millbank, London SW1P 4DP *Tel:* 020 7222 9000
Email: chairman@conservatives.com

CROSSBENCH

FELLOWES, LORD

FELLOWES (Life Baron), Robert Fellowes; cr. 1999. Born 11 December 1941; Son of late Sir William Fellowes, KCVO and Lady Fellowes; Married Lady Jane Spencer, daughter of 8th Earl Spencer, LVO, and Honorary Mrs Shand Kydd 1978 (1 son 2 daughters).

Education: Eton College.

Non-political career: Short Service Commission, Scots Guards 1960-63. Director, Allen Harvey & Ross Ltd 1968-77; Assistant Private Secretary to HM The Queen 1977-86, Deputy Private Secretary 1986-90, Private Secretary 1990-99; Barclays Private Bank: Vice-chair 1999-2000, Chair 2000-09; Non-executive director, SAB Miller 1999-2010; Secretary and registrar, Order of Merit 2003-; British Library Board 2007-.

Political career: *House of Lords:* Raised to the peerage as Baron Fellowes, of Shotesham in the County of Norfolk 1999. Member: Constitution 2001-04, Liaison 2009-13, Joint Committee on National Security Strategy 2010-.

Political interests: Prison reform; USA.

Other: Winston Churchill Memorial Trust: Trustee 2001-, Chair 2009-; Vice-chair, Commonwealth Education Trust 2007-; President, Advisory Council, Goodenough College 2008-; Trustee, King Edward VII Hospital, Sister Agnes 2010-; Rhodes Trust 2001-10; Chair, Prison Reform Trust 2001-08; Mandela-Rhodes Foundation 2003-10; Scots Guards 2006-. Liveryman, Goldsmith's Company. LVO 1983; CB 1987; KCVO 1989; PC 1990; KCB 1991; GCVO 1996; GCB 1998; QSO 1999; White's, Pratt's, Royal Overseas League. MCC.

Recreations: Golf, watching cricket, reading.

Rt Hon the Lord Fellowes GCB GCVO QSO, House of Lords, London SW1A 0PW
Tel: 020 7219 8754

FELLOWES OF WEST STAFFORD, LORD

FELLOWES OF WEST STAFFORD (Life Baron), Julian Alexander Kitchener-Fellowes; cr 2011. Born 17 August 1949; Son of late Peregrine Fellowes and Olwen Fellowes, née Stuart-Jones; Married Emma Kitchener LVO 1990 (1 son).
Education: Ampleforth College, Yorkshire; Magdalene College, Cambridge (BA); Webber Douglas Academy.
Non-political career: Actor: Joking Apart, Queen's Theatre 1978, Present Laughter, Vaudeville Theatre 1981, Futurists, Royal National Theatre, For the Greater Good 1991, Shadowlands 1993, Damage 1993, Our Friends in the North 1996, Tomorrow Never Dies 1997, Place Vendôme 1998, Aristocrats 1999, Monarch of the Glen 1999-2005; Producer, A Married Man 1982; Writer, Little Lord Fauntleroy 1994; Writer and co-producer, The Prince and the Pauper 1997; Writer, Gosford Park 2001; Writer and director, Separate Lies 2005; Writer: Vanity Fair 2005, The Young Victoria 2009; Writer and director, From Time to Time 2010; Writer and creator, Downton Abbey 2010-. Equity.

CONSERVATIVE

Political career: *House of Lords:* Raised to the peerage as Baron Fellowes of West Stafford, of West Stafford in the County of Dorset 2011. *Councils and public bodies:* Deputy Lieutenant, Dorset 2008.
Other: Chairman, Talking Books Appeal, RNIB 2003-; Vice-President, Weldmar Hospicecare Trust 2006-; President, Thomas Hardy Society 2007-; Ambassador: The Haven 2007-, Alzheimer's Society 2008-; Member, Appeal Council, National Memorial Arboretum 2009-; Vice-President, Catholic Association of Performing Arts 2010-; Member, National Advisory Council, The RicNic Trust 2011-; Vice-Patron, Priory of England and the Islands, of the Order of St. John; Patron: Rainbow Trust 2005-, Help the Aged/Age UK 2007-, Changing Faces 2007-, Moviola 2008-, Lewiston School Appeal 2009-, AdLib, Association of Friends of Dorset Libraries 2010-, Bay Theatre, Weymouth College 2010-; Honorary Patron, Sleaford Playhouse 2011-. Honorary DLitt, Bournemouth 2007; Honorary DArts, Southampton Solent 2010. Best Screenplay, New York Film Critics' Award 2001; Best Screenplay, National Film Critics' Award 2001; Screenwriter of the Year, ShoWest 2002; Best Original Screenplay, Writer's Guild Award 2002; Best Original Screenplay, Academy Award 2002; Best Directorial Debut, National Board of Review 2006; Best Writer, British Press Guild Awards 2011; Outstanding Writing for a Miniseries, Emmy Awards 2011; Boodle's, Pratt's, Annabel's.
Publications: Author: Snobs (2004), Past Imperfect (2008).
The Lord Fellowes of West Stafford, House of Lords, London SW1A 0PW
Tel: 020 7219 5353

FILKIN, LORD

FILKIN (Life Baron), David Geoffrey Nigel Filkin; cr. 1999. Born 1 July 1944; Son of late Donald and Winifred Filkin; Married Elizabeth Tompkins 1974 (divorced 1994) (3 daughters); married Brigitte Paupy 2005.
Education: King Edward VI School, Birmingham; Clare College, Cambridge (MA history 1966); Manchester University (DipTP 1972); Birmingham University (management in local government); French.
Non-political career: Teacher on Voluntary Services Overseas (VSO), Ghana 1966-67; Town planner, Redditch Development Corporation (New Town) 1969-72; Manager, Brent Housing Aid Centre, London Borough of Brent 1972-75; Deputy chief executive, Merseyside Improved Housing 1975-79; Borough housing officer, Ellesmere Port and Neston Borough Council 1979-82; Director of housing, London Borough of Greenwich 1982-88; Chief executive: Reading Borough Council 1988-91, Association of District Councils 1991-97; Local government adviser, Joseph Rowntree Foundation 1997-2001; Director, New Local Government Network 1997-2001; Policy analyst and writer 1997-2001; Adviser, Capgemini plc 2005-12; Non-executive director, Accord plc 2005-07; Adviser: Serco 2006-, NCP 2006-; Chair: Public Sector Reform Group 2005-08, St Alban's Cathedral Music Trust 2006-10; Foundation chair, 2020 Public Services Trust 2008-11.

LABOUR

Political career: *House of Lords:* Raised to the peerage as Baron Filkin, of Pimlico in the City of Westminster 1999. Government Spokesperson for: Transport, Local Government and the Regions 2001-02, Health 2001-02; Government Whip 2001-02; Parliamentary Under-Secretary of State and Government Spokesperson for: Home Office 2002-03, Department for Constitutional Affairs 2003-04, Department for Education and Skills and Department for Work and Pensions 2004-05. Chair Merits of Statutory Instruments 2005-09; Member Leader's Group on the Working Practices of the House of Lords 2010-11; Alternate member Procedure 2011-13; Chair Public Service and Demographic Change 2012-13; Member Procedure 2013-.
Political interests: Policy development, policy implementation, housing; Southern Africa, West Africa.

Other: Parliament Choir: Founder chair 2000-, Trustee; Trustee, Southbank Sinfonia; Former member, Royal Town Planning Institute; Former associate member, Institute of Housing; Honorary Fellow, Chartered Institute of Purchasing and Supplies. CBE 1997.

Publications: Best Value for the Public; Political Leadership of Best Value; Partnerships for Best Value; Modernising Local Government; Starting to Modernise; Achieving Best Value; Towards a New Localism; Winning the e-Revolution; Strategic Partnering for Local Services; Co-author: Public Matters – Renewing the Public Realm (Methuen, 2007), Better Outcomes (2009).

Recreations: Music, walking, swimming, singing, church.

The Lord Filkin CBE, House of Lords, London SW1A 0PW
Tel: 020 7219 0640 *Email:* gfilkin1@aol.com

FINK, LORD

FINK (Life Baron), Stanley Fink; cr 2011. Born 15 September 1957; Married Barbara Paskin (2 sons 2 daughters).

Education: Manchester Grammar School; Trinity Hall, Cambridge (LLB 1976).

Non-political career: Chartered accountancy training, Arthur Andersen 1980-82; Financial planning team, Mars Confectionery 1982-83; Vice-President, Citibank 1983-87; Man Group plc: Director, mergers acquisitions and treasury 1987-2000, Chief executive officer 2000, Deputy chairman 2008; Chief executive officer, International Standard Asset Management 2008-.

CONSERVATIVE

Political career: *House of Lords:* Raised to the peerage as Baron Fink, of Northwood in the County of Middlesex 2011. *Other:* Treasurer, Conservative Party 2010-12, 2012-13.

Other: Member, Institute of Chartered Accountants 1982. Honorary Fellow, King's College London 2011.

Recreations: Skiing, golf.

The Lord Fink, House of Lords, London SW1A 0PW
Tel: 020 7219 5353

FINKELSTEIN, LORD

FINKELSTEIN (Life Baron), Daniel William Finkelstein; cr 2013. Born 30 August 1962; Son of late Professor Ludwik Finkelstein OBE and Mirjam Emma Weiner; Married Dr Nicola Ruth 1993 (3 sons).

Education: Hendon Preparatory School; University College School; London School of Economics (BSc economics 1984); City University (MSc 1986).

Non-political career: Political adviser to Dr David Owen MP as Leader of the Social Democrat Party 1986-91; Journalist, *Network* Magazine 1987-89; Editor, Connexion 1989-92; Director: Social Market Foundation 1992-95, Conservative Party Research Department 1995-98, Polcy Unit, Conservative Central Office 1999-2001; *The Times:* Associate editor 2001-10, Comment editor 2004-08, Chief leader writer 2008-, Executive editor 2010-; Columnist, *Jewish Chronicle* 2004-; Editor, Comment Central, *Times* Online 2006-; Chair, Policy Exchange 2012-.

CONSERVATIVE

Political career: *House of Commons:* Contested Brent East (SDP/Alliance) 1987 and Harrow West 2001 (Conservative) general elections. *House of Lords:* Raised to the peerage as Baron Finkelstein, of Pinner in the County of Middlesex 2013.

Other: OBE 1997.

The Lord Finkelstein OBE, House of Lords, London SW1A 0PW
Tel: 020 7219 5353

FINLAY OF LLANDAFF, BARONESS

FINLAY OF LLANDAFF (Life Baroness), Ilora Gillian Finlay; cr 2001. Born 23 February 1949; Daughter of Charles Beaumont Benoy Downman and Thaïs Helène, née Barakan; Married Andrew Yule Finlay CBE 1972 (1 son 1 daughter).

Education: Wimbledon High School, London; St Mary's Hospital, London University (MB BS 1972); French.

Non-political career: General practitioner 1981-86; Palliative medicine 1987-; Member, Expert Advisory Group on Cancers 1993-97, Chair, Association for Palliative Medicine 1995-98; Velindre NHS Trust Cancer Centre, Cardiff 1994-; National Cancer Forum 1997-2000; Vice-dean, School of Medicine, University of Wales College of Medicine 2000-05; President: Medical Women's Federations 2001-02, Chartered Society of Physiotherapy 2002-; Vice-president, Marie Curie Cancer Care 2004-; President, Royal Society of Medicine 2006-08; Chair: Palliative Care

CROSSBENCH

Strategy (Wales) Implementation Board 2008-, Royal College of General Practitioners' Inquiry into Generalism 2011. Member, British Medical Association: Member, BMA Medical Ethics Committee 2009-.

Political career: *House of Lords:* Raised to the peerage as Baroness Finlay of Llandaff, of Llandaff in the County of South Glamorgan 2001. Contested Crossbench Convener election 2011. Member: Science and Technology 2003-08, Science and Technology Sub-committees: I (Fighting Infection) 2003, II (Science and the Regional Development Agencies) 2003, I (Science and International Agreements) 2003-04, I (Ageing) 2004-05, Assisted Dying for the Terminally Ill Bill 2004-05, Mental Health Bill 2004-05, Science and Technology Sub-committees: I (Avian Flu) 2005-06, II (Conservation Science) 2005-06; Chair Science and Technology Sub-committee I (Allergy) 2006-07; Co-opted member: Science and Technology Sub-committee II (Genomic Medicine) 2008-09, Science and Technology (Pandemic Influenza) 2008-09; Member Public Service and Demographic Change 2012-. *Councils and public bodies:* Non-executive director, Gwent Health Authority 1995-2001; Member: Cancer Research UK Science Committee 2002-04, Cancer Strategy Board, National Assembly for Wales 2006-07, End of Life Care Strategy Board, Department of Health 2007-09, UK Drugs Policy Commission 2008-.

Political interests: Women's careers, medical ethics, Welsh affairs, health and medicine; China (Hong Kong), France, Netherlands, Spain.

Other: President, vice-president, patron of several organisations, especially concerned with palliative care, end of life care, multiple sclerosis, music and Foodbanks Cymru; Royal College of Physicians; Royal College of General Practitioners; Royal College of Surgeons; Associate, Girls' Day School Trust 2005-; FRCP, FRCGP; Marie Curie Cancer Care; Changing Faces; MNDA; MS Cymru; Trussell Trust; CO Awareness. Honorary Doctor of Science, University of Glamorgan; Honorary Fellow, Cardiff University; Johanna Bijtel Professor, Gröningen University, Netherlands 2000-02; Honorary Doctor of Science, University of Wales; Honorary Fellow, University of Wales Institute, Cardiff. Welsh Woman of the Year 1996-97; Peer of the Year, Women in Public Life Awards 2008; Royal Society of Medicine.

Publications: Co-author Care of the Dying – a clinical handbook (Churchill Livingstone, 1984); Co-editor: Medical Humanities, (BMJ Press, 2001), The Effective Management of Cancer Pain (Aesculapius Medical Press, 2000, 2001); Oral Care in Advanced Disease (Oxford University Press, 2005); Communication in Cancer (Oxford University Press, 2010); Many chapters in books and papers on palliative medicine, medical education, ethics and service provision.

Recreations: Cycling, family events, hairdressing.

The Baroness Finlay of Llandaff, House of Lords, London SW1A 0PW
Tel: 020 7219 6693 *Fax:* 020 7219 1991 *Email:* finlayi@parliament.uk
Velindre Hospital NHS Trust, Whitchurch, Cardiff CF14 2TL *Tel:* 029 2019 6113
Fax: 029 2019 6115 *Email:* ilora.finlay@wales.nhs.uk

CROSSBENCH

FLATHER, BARONESS

FLATHER (Life Baroness), Shreela Flather; cr. 1990. Born 13 February 1934; Daughter of Aftab and Krishna Rai; Married Gary Flather 1965 (2 sons).

Education: University College, London (LLB 1956).

Non-political career: Called to the Bar, Inner Temple 1962; Infant teacher, ILEA 1965-67; Teacher of English as second language: Altwood Comprehensive School, Maidenhead 1968-74, Broadmoor Hospital 1974-78; Member, Committee of Management, Servite Houses Ltd 1987-94; Director: Meridian Broadcasting (MAI) Ltd 1990-2000, Marie Stopes International 1996-, Cable Corporation 1997-2000; Fellow, University College, London; Director, Kiss FM and Magic FM 1999-2002; Chair and Director, Club Asia 2002-06.

Political career: *House of Lords:* Raised to the peerage as Baroness Flather, of Windsor and Maidenhead in the Royal County of Berkshire 1990. Member: European Communities Sub-committee C 1990-95, Medical Ethics 1993-94, Intergovernmental Organisations 2007-08. *Other:* Member: Conservative Women's National Committee 1978-88, Anglo-Asian Conservative Society 1979-83, National Union Executive Committee of Conservative Party 1989-90; Resigned the Conservative Whip December 1998, rejoined November 1999, moved to crossbenches 2008. *Councils and public bodies:* JP, Maidenhead 1971-90; Royal Borough of Windsor and Maidenhead: Councillor 1976-91, Mayor 1986-87; Senior posts in numerous organisations involved in refugee, community, carer, race relations and prison work, including: Member: Commission for Racial Equality 1980-86, BBC South and East Regional Advisory Council 1987-89, Social Security Advisory Committee 1987-90; Vice-chair, Refugee Council 1991-94; Governor, Commonwealth Institute 1993-98; President, Ethics Committee Broadmoor Hospital 1993-97; DL, Berkshire 1994-2009; Chair, Alcohol Education and Research Council 1995-2001; Joint President, Family Planning Association 1995-98; Member, Council of University College London 2000-06.

Political interests: Role of four million Indians in two World Wars, empowerment of women in South Asia and Africa, assisted family planning; Indian sub-continent including Burma.

Other: UK Representative on EU Advisory Commission on Racism and Xenophobia 1995-97; UK Member, Economic and Social Committee, European Community 1987-90; Fellow, Royal Society of Arts; Trustee: Hillingdon Hospital 1990-98, Rajiv Gandhi (UK) Foundation 1993-2002; Member, Council of the Winston Churchill Memorial Trust 1993-2008; Patron, Cedar Centre (community centre Isle of Dogs) 1994-2007; Member, Council of St George's House, Windsor Castle 1996-2002; Chair, Memorial Gates Trust (memorial on Constitution Hill) 1998-2009; Fellow, Industry and Parliament Trust 1998; Seva Mandir (providing water in Rajsthan); Bookpower (providing low priced educational texts in developing countries) 2001-07; Pan African Health Foundation (auto disable syringe factory in Nigeria) 2004-; Member, Advisory Council, American Intercontinental University 2004-06; Patron, Population Matters 2011-; Memorial Gates Trust. Honorary DUniv, Open University 1994; Honorary LLD, Leeds University 2008; Honorary Doctorate, Northampton University 2010. Asian of the Year, *Asian Who's Who* 1996; Asian Jewel Award 2003; Pravasi Diwas Samman by President of India 2009.

Publications: Woman: Acceptable Exploitation for Profit (2010).

Recreations: Reading, cinema, travel.

The Baroness Flather DL, House of Lords, London SW1A 0PW
Tel: 020 7219 5353 *Fax:* 020 7219 5979

CONSERVATIVE

FLIGHT, LORD

FLIGHT (Life Baron), Howard Emerson Flight; cr 2011. Born 16 June 1948; Son of late Bernard Flight and late Doris Flight; Married Christabel Norbury 1973 (1 son 3 daughters).

Education: Brentwood School, Essex; Magdalene College, Cambridge (MA economics 1969); University of Michigan, USA (Power exchange scholar, MBA 1971); French.

Non-political career: Investment adviser, N M Rothschild 1970-73; Manager: Cayzer Ltd 1973-76, Wardley Ltd (HSBC) Hong Kong 1976-78, Merchant banking division, Hong Kong Bank, Bombay, India 1978-79; Director, investment division, Guinness Mahon 1979-86; Joint managing director, Guinness Flight Global Asset Management Ltd 1986-99; Chairman, Investec Asset Management 1999-2003; Director, Panmure Gordon & Co 2002-07; Chairman, Flight and Partners; Director, Investec Asset Management Limited; Chairman, CIM Investment Management Ltd; Director, Marechale Capital; Chairman: CorporActive Fund Ltd (Hong Kong), Downing Structured Opportunities VCT 1 plc; Director, Metrobank plc; Chairman, Aurora Investment Trust plc; Director, Edge Performance VCT plc; Chairman, EIS Association; Commissioner, Guernsey Financial Services Commission; Consultant: TISA, Kinetic Partners; Member, advisory board: Financial Services Forum, Guinness Renewable Energy EIS Fund.

Political career: *House of Commons:* Contested Southwark (Bermondsey) February and October 1974 general elections. MP (Conservative) for Arundel and South Downs 1997-2005; Whip withdrawn March 2005. Shadow Economic Secretary, HM Treasury 1999-2001; Shadow Paymaster General 2001-02; Shadow Chief Secretary to the Treasury 2002-04; Special envoy to City of London 2004-05. Member: Environment, Transport and Regional Affairs 1997-98, Environment, Transport and Regional Affairs (Environment Sub-Committee) 1997-98, Social Security 1998-99. Joint Secretary, Conservative Party Committee for International Development 1997-98; Joint Chairman, Conservative Party Committee for Hong Kong 1997-2005; Secretary, Conservative Party Committees for: Finance 1999-2005, Social Security 1999-2005. *House of Lords:* Raised to the peerage as Baron Flight, of Worcester in the County of Worcestershire 2011. Member EU Sub-committee A: (Economic and Financial Affairs and International Trade) 2011-12, (Economic and Financial Affairs) 2012-. *Other:* Chair, Cambridge University Conservative Association 1968-69; Vice-chair, Federation of Conservative Students 1969; Conservative City Circle: Chairman 2002-05, President 2006-10; Deputy Chairman, Conservative Party 2004-05. *Councils and public bodies:* Member, HMG Tax Consultative Committee to HM Treasury 1985-92; Governor and trustee, Brentwood School.

Political interests: Taxation, economic policy, farming, charities, venture capital, EMU, private finance initiative; China, India, South East Asia, USA.

Other: Trustee, Elgar Foundation 1979-; Fellow, Royal Society of Arts; Advisory Board, Institute for Economic Affairs; Trustee, Africa Research Institute 2006-; Council Member, Centre for Policy Studies 2008-; Chairman: 1900 Club 2008-, Croome Court (National Trust) Appeal Committee 2009-; Commissioner, Guernsey Financial Services Commission 2005-; Chairman, Enterprise Investment Scheme Association 2005-; National Trust Croome Court; Worcester Porcelein Museum; The Wedgewood Collection Trust. Liveryman, Carpenters' Company. Freeman, City of London 1999; Carlton; Pratt's; Boodles. Marden (Skiing).

Publications: All You Need to Know About Exchange Rates (1988).

Recreations: Skiing, classical music, antique collecting, gardening.

The Lord Flight, House of Lords, London SW1A 0PW
Tel: 020 7219 5353 *Email:* flighth@parliament.uk
Tel: 020 7222 7559 *Fax:* 020 7976 7059 *Email:* hflight@btinternet.com
Website: www.howardflight.com

FOOKES, BARONESS

FOOKES (Life Baroness), Janet Evelyn Fookes; cr. 1997. Born 21 February 1936; Daughter of late Lewis Fookes, company director, and late Evelyn Fookes, née Holmes; Single.
Education: Hastings and St Leonards Ladies' College; Hastings High School for Girls; Royal Holloway College, London University (BA history 1957).
Non-political career: History and English teacher in independent schools 1958-70.
Political career: *House of Commons:* MP (Conservative) for Merton and Morden 1970-74, for Plymouth Drake 1974-97. Deputy Speaker and Second Deputy Chairman of Ways and Means 1992-97; Sponsored as Private Member's Bill: Sexual Offences Act 1985, Dangerous Dogs Act 1989. Chair: Education, Arts and Home Affairs sub-committee 1975-79; Member: Panel of Chairs 1976-92, Home Affairs 1984-92. *House of Lords:* Raised to the peerage as Baroness Fookes, of Plymouth in the County of Devon 1997. Member, Armed Forces Parliamentary Scheme 2001-; Deputy Chair of Committees 2002-; Deputy Speaker 2002-; Contested Lord Speaker election 2006. Member: Consolidation, Etc, Bills Joint Committee 2000-10, Hybrid Instruments 2002-10; Chair Refreshments 2003-07; Member: Crossrail Bill 2008, Communications 2010-, Delegated Powers and Regulatory Reform 2013-. *Other:* Member, Association of Conservative Peers. *Councils and public bodies:* County Borough of Hastings: Councillor 1960-61, 1963-70, Chair, Education Committee 1967-70.
Political interests: Health, defence, animal welfare, equal opportunities; Canada, New Zealand.
Other: Fellow, Industry and Parliament Trust 1978; Member: Commonwealth War Graves Commission 1987-97, Council of Management, College of St Mark and St John 1989-2004, Art Fund; Chair, ambassadors group, Tomorrow's People; Governor, Kelly College, Tavistock 2002-; Honorary Fellow, Royal Holloway College; Member: RSPCA, SSAFA/Forces Help, Fellowship of St Nicholas, Mencap, NSPCC. Worshipful Company of Gardeners 2005-. Honorary Freeman, City of Plymouth 2000; Freeman, City of London 2005. Honorary DLitt, University of Plymouth; Honorary Fellow, Royal Holloway College. DBE 1989.
Recreations: Swimming, gardening, theatre, Yoga, opera.
The Baroness Fookes DBE, House of Lords, London SW1A 0PW
Tel: 020 7219 5899 *Email:* fookesj@parliament.uk

FORD, BARONESS

FORD (Life Baroness), Margaret Anne Ford; cr 2006. Born 16 December 1957; Daughter of Edward Garland and Susan Garland, née Townsley; Married David Bolger 1990 (1 son 1 daughter from previous marriage 1 stepson).
Education: St Michael's Academy, Kilwinning; Glasgow University (MA arts 1979, MPhil economics 1984).
Non-political career: Local government officer, Cunninghame District Council 1979-82; Scottish organiser, Banking Insurance and Finance Union 1982-87; Management consultant, Price Waterhouse & Co 1987-90; Director, Scottish Homes 1990-93; Founder and managing director, Eglinton Management Centre 1993-99; Founder and chief executive, Good Practice Ltd 2000-07; Managing director, Royal Bank of Canada Capital Markets 2007-09; Non-executive director: Thus plc 2002-05, Serco plc 2003-10, Grainger Trust plc 2008-, May Gurney Integrated Services plc 2011-, Barchester Healthcare Ltd 2012-. Branch secretary, NALGO 1979-82; Scottish organiser, BIFU 1982-87.
Political career: *House of Lords:* Raised to the peerage as Baroness Ford, of Cunninghame in North Ayrshire 2006. *Other:* Resigned Labour Whip February 2013. *Councils and public bodies:* Non-executive director, Scottish Prison Service 1993-97; Chair, Lothian Health Board 1997-2000; Non-executive director, Gas and Electrical Markets Authority (Ofgem) 2000-04; Chair: English Partnerships 2002-07, Olympic Park Legacy Company 2009-12.
Political interests: Regeneration, housing, planning, energy, public sector reform; Australia, USA.
Other: Member, Scottish Economic Council 1997-2000; President, British Epilepsy Association; Chair, Irvine Bay Urban Regeneration Company 2006-10; Honorary Member, Royal Institute of Chartered Surveyors; Epilepsy Action. D.BA, Napier University; D.Univ, Stirling University.
Publications: Contributor, Anatomy of New Scotland (Mainstream Publishing, 2002); Leadership Development: How Government Works (Audit Scotland, 2005).
Recreations: Family, fine art, music, gardening, sport (all kinds).
The Baroness Ford, House of Lords, London SW1A 0PW
Tel: 020 7219 5439 *Email:* fordm@parliament.uk

CONSERVATIVE

NON-AFFILIATED

FORSYTH OF DRUMLEAN, LORD

FORSYTH OF DRUMLEAN (Life Baron), Michael Bruce Forsyth; cr. 1999. Born 16 October 1954; Son of John T. Forsyth; Married Susan Clough 1977 (1 son 2 daughters).

Education: Arbroath High School; St Andrews University (MA).

Non-political career: Director, Robert Fleming & Co Ltd 1997-2000; J P Morgan 2000-: Vice-chair, investment banking Europe 2000-02, Deputy chair (UK) 2002-05; Non-executive director: J & J Denholm 2005-, Denholm Industrial Service (Holdings) Ltd 2006-; Evercore Partners: Senior adviser 2006-07, Senior managing director 2007-.

CONSERVATIVE

Political career: *House of Commons:* MP (Conservative) for Stirling 1983-97. PPS to Geoffrey Howe as Foreign Secretary 1986-87; Parliamentary Under-Secretary of State, Scottish Office 1987-90; Minister of State: Scottish Office with responsibility for Health, Education, Social Work and Sport 1990-92, Department of Employment 1992-94, Home Office 1994-95; Secretary of State for Scotland 1995-97. *House of Lords:* Raised to the peerage as Baron Forsyth of Drumlean, of Drumlean in Stirling 1999. Member: Monetary Policy of the Bank of England 2000-01, House of Lords Reform Joint Committee 2002-05, Barnett Formula 2008-09, Economic Affairs 2008-13, Soft Power and the UK's Influence 2013-. *Other:* President, St Andrews University Conservative Association 1973-76; Member, Executive Committee National Union of Conservative and Unionist Associations 1975-77; Chair: Federation of Conservative Students 1976-77, Scottish Conservative Party 1989-90. *Councils and public bodies:* Councillor, Westminster City Council 1978-83; Member: Commission on Strengthening Parliament 1999-2000, Development Board, National Portrait Gallery 2000-03; Chair, Tax Reform Commission 2005-06.

Political interests: Local government, privatisation, economics, healthcare, education, environment, constitution.

Other: Director, Centre for Policy Studies 2006-; Patron: Craighalbent Centre for Children with motor impairments, Children in Need Institute (UK), working in India 2008-; Save the Children, Debra, St Mungus. Highland Park/*The Spectator*: Member to Watch 1993, Parliamentarian of the Year 1996. PC 1995; KB 1997.

Publications: Various pamphlets on privatisation and local government.

Recreations: Mountaineering, photography, gardening, fly-fishing, astronomy.

Rt Hon the Lord Forsyth of Drumlean, House of Lords, London SW1A 0PW
Tel: 020 7219 4479 *Email:* forsythm@parliament.uk

FOSTER OF BISHOP AUCKLAND, LORD

FOSTER OF BISHOP AUCKLAND (Life Baron), Derek Foster; cr 2005. Born 25 June 1937; Son of Joseph Foster, shipyard worker; Married Florence Anne Bulmer 1972 (3 sons 1 daughter).

Education: Bede Grammar School, Sunderland; Oxford University (BA philosophy, politics and economics 1960); French, German.

Non-political career: Private sector marketing 1960-70; Durham County Council: Youth and community worker 1970-73, Further education organiser 1973-74; Assistant director of education, Sunderland Borough Council 1974-79. Member, National Union of Teachers.

LABOUR

Political career: *House of Commons:* MP (Labour) for Bishop Auckland 1979-2005. Opposition Whip 1981-82; Opposition Frontbench Spokesperson for Social Security 1982-83; PPS to Neil Kinnock as Leader of Opposition 1983-85; Opposition Chief Whip 1985-95; Shadow Chancellor of the Duchy of Lancaster 1995-97. Chair Employment Sub-Committee 1997-2001. *House of Lords:* Raised to the peerage as Baron Foster of Bishop Auckland, of Bishop Auckland in the County of Durham 2005. *Other:* Ex-officio member, Labour Party National Executive Committee 1985-95; Chair, Labour Manufacturing Industry Group. *Councils and public bodies:* Councillor: Sunderland County Borough Council 1972-74, Tyne and Wear County Council 1973-77; Chair: North of England Development Council 1974-76, National Prayer Breakfast 1998-99; Member, Advisory Committee for the Registration of Political Parties 1998; DL, Durham 2001-.

Political interests: Youth affairs, education and training, regional policy, socialist enterprise, transport, economics, finance, small businesses, education; Japan, USA.

Other: Uniformed member, Salvation Army; Vice-chair, Youthaid 1979-83; Fellow, Industry and Parliament Trust 1983; Vice-chair, Youth Affairs Lobby 1984-86; Honorary President, British Youth Council 1984-86; Vice-President, Christian Socialist Movement 1985-; Member, National Advisory Board of the Salvation Army 1995-; Chair: Pioneering Care Partnership 1997-, North Regional Information Society Initiative 1997-2000, National Prayer Breakfast 1998; Non-executive director, Northern Informatics 1998-; Chair: Regional Electronics Economy Project 2000-, Bishop Auckland Development Company Ltd; President, South West Dur-

ham Training; Chair, e-Learning Foundation North East; Trustee: Auckland Castle, National e-Learning Foundation; Member: Fabian Society, Christian Socialists Society; Companion of the Institution of Lighting Engineers 2001. PC 1993. Durham County Cricket.
Recreations: Brass bands, male voice choirs, cricket, soccer.
Rt Hon the Lord Foster of Bishop Auckland, House of Lords, London SW1A 0PW
Tel: 020 7219 6500

FOULKES OF CUMNOCK, LORD

FOULKES OF CUMNOCK (Life Baron), George Foulkes; cr 2005. Born 21 January 1942; Son of late George Horace Foulkes, engineer, and late Jessie Foulkes, principal nursing officer; Married Elizabeth Hope 1970 (2 sons 1 daughter).
Education: Keith Grammar School, Banff; Haberdashers' Aske's School; Edinburgh University (BSc psychology 1964) (President, Edinburgh University SRC 1963-64); Conversational Spanish.
Non-political career: Territorial Army 1961-64. President, Scottish Union of Students 1964-66; Director, ELEC 1966-68; Scottish organiser, European Movement 1968-69; Director: Enterprise Youth 1969-73, Age Concern Scotland 1973-79; Chairman, advisory committee, GovNet 2008-. Member, GMB.

LAB/CO-OP

Political career: *House of Commons:* Contested Edinburgh West 1970 and Edinburgh Pentlands October 1974 general elections. MP (Labour) for South Ayrshire 1979-83, for Carrick, Cumnock and Doon Valley 1983-2005. Opposition Frontbench Spokesperson for: Europe 1983-85, Foreign and Commonwealth Affairs 1985-92, Defence, Disarmament and Arms Control 1992-93, Overseas Development 1994-97; Parliamentary Under-Secretary of State, Department of International Development 1997-2001; Minister of State, Scotland Office 2001-02. *House of Lords:* Raised to the peerage as Baron Foulkes of Cumnock, of Cumnock in East Ayrshire 2005. Member, Intelligence and Security Committee 2007-10. Co-opted member European Union Sub-committee F (Home Affairs) 2006-07; Member: Joint Committee on National Security Strategy 2010-13, EU Sub-committee G (Social Policies and Consumer Protection) 2011-12, European Union 2011-, EU Sub-committee C (External Affairs) 2012-, Soft Power and the UK's Influence 2013-. *Other:* MSP for Lothians region 2007-11 (sat as George Foulkes). Chair, Labour Campaign for a Scottish Parliament -1997; Member, Co-operative Party. *Councils and public bodies:* Councillor: Edinburgh Corporation 1970-75, Lothian Regional Council 1974-79; Chair: Lothian Region Education Committee 1974-79, Education Committee, Convention of Scottish Local Authorities 1975-78; JP, Edinburgh 1975.
Political interests: International development, foreign affairs, devolution, energy, human rights, defence, Scotland, financial regulation; Latin America, Caribbean, China, EU, Russia.
Other: Delegate, Parliamentary Assemblies of the Council of Europe and Western European Union 1979-80, 2004-; Executive member: UK Branch of Commonwealth Parliamentary Association 1989-97, 2011-, British Section of Inter-Parliamentary Union 1989-97, Socialist International 2004-08; Rector's assessor, Edinburgh University 1968-71; Director, The Co-operative Press 1990-97; Chair, The John Wheatley Centre 1990-97; Trustee, Commonwealth Parliamentary Association Funds 1998-2008; Chair, Heart of Midlothian FC 2005-06; President, Caribbean Council 2011-; Age Concern; Ayrshire Hospice; Garvald Edinburgh. Wilberforce Medal 1998. PC 2000; Royal Scots Club, Edinburgh.
Publications: Editor, 80 Years On (History of Edinburgh University SRC); Chapters in: Scotland – A Claim of Right, Football and the Commons People.
Recreations: Boating, season ticket holder and shareholder Heart of Midlothian FC.
Rt Hon the Lord Foulkes of Cumnock, House of Lords, London SW1A 0PW
Tel: 020 7219 3474 *Email:* foulkesg@parliament.uk *Twitter:* @GeorgeFoulkes

FOWLER, LORD

FOWLER (Life Baron), (Peter) Norman Fowler; cr. 2001. Born 2 February 1938; Son of late N F and Katherine Fowler; Married Fiona Poole, née Donald 1979 (2 daughters).
Education: King Edward VI School, Chelmsford; Trinity Hall, Cambridge (BA economics and law 1961, MA).
Non-political career: Commissioned national service, Essex Regiment 1956-58. *The Times:* Special correspondent 1961-66, Home affairs correspondent 1966-70; Non-executive director, NFC plc 1990-97; Non-executive chair: Midland Independent Newspapers 1991-98, National House Building Council 1992-98, Regional Independent Media 1998-2002, Numark plc 1998-2005, Aggregate Industries plc 2000-06; Non-executive director, Holcim Ltd 2006-09; Member, Advisory Council, Electra QMC Europe Development Capital Fund plc 2006-08; Non-executive director: ABTA 2009-, Aggregate Industries 2010-.

CONSERVATIVE

Political career: *House of Commons:* MP (Conservative) for Nottingham South 1970-74, for Sutton Coldfield February 1974-2001. PPS to Minister of State for Northern Ireland 1972-74; Opposition Spokesperson for Home Affairs 1974-75; Chief Opposition Spokesperson for: Social Services 1975-76, Transport 1976-79; Minister of Transport 1979-81; Secretary of State for: Transport 1981, Social Services 1981-87, Employment 1987-90; Shadow Secretary of State for: Environment, Transport and the Regions 1997-98, the Home Department 1998-99. *House of Lords:* Raised to the peerage as Baron Fowler, of Sutton Coldfield in the County of West Midlands 2001. Chair: Review of the BBC Charter 2005-06, Communications 2007-10, HIV and AIDS in the UK 2010-11. *Other:* Chair, Cambridge University Conservative Association 1960; Editorial board, *Crossbow* 1962-70; Vice-chair, North Kensington Conservative Association 1967-68; Chair: East Midlands Conservative Political Centre 1970-73, Conservative Party 1992-94; Member, Executive Association of Conservative Peers 2001-04; Vice-chairman, Association of Conservative Peers 2005-10.

Political interests: HIV/AIDS, media; Middle East.

Other: Council member, Bow Group 1967-69; Chair, Thomson Foundation. Honorary Doctorate, City of Birmingham University 2011. PC 1979; Kt 1990; Garrick, Hurlingham, Seaview Yacht Club.

Publications: After the Riots (1979); Ministers Decide (1991); A Political Suicide (2008).

Rt Hon the Lord Fowler, House of Lords, London SW1A 0PW
Tel: 020 7219 3525 *Email:* fowlern@parliament.uk

FRAMLINGHAM, LORD

FRAMLINGHAM (Life Baron), Michael Nicholson Lord; cr 2011. Born 17 October 1938; Son of late John Lord, headmaster; Married Jennifer Childs 1965 (1 son 1 daughter).

Education: William Hulme's Grammar School, Manchester; Christ's College, Cambridge (MA agriculture 1962) (Cambridge Rugby Blue).

Non-political career: Farmer and agriculture tutor 1962-66; Director, Power Line Maintenance Ltd 1966-68; Founded Lords Tree Services Ltd 1968; Aboricultural Consultant 1983.

CONSERVATIVE

Political career: *House of Commons:* Contested Manchester Gorton 1979 general election. MP (Conservative) for Central Suffolk 1983-97, for Central Suffolk and North Ipswich 1997-2010. PPS to John MacGregor: as Minister of Agriculture, Fisheries and Food 1984-85, as Chief Secretary to the Treasury 1985-87; Second Deputy Chairman, Ways and Means and Deputy Speaker 1997-2010; Contested Speaker elections 2000, 2009. Ex-officio member: Chairmen's Panel 1997-2010, Court of Referees 1997-2010, Standing Orders 1998-2010, Unopposed Bills (Panel) 2000-10. *House of Lords:* Raised to the peerage as Baron Framlingham, of Eye in the County of Suffolk 2011. *Councils and public bodies:* North Bedfordshire Borough Council: Councillor 1974-77, Chair, Policy Committee 1974-77; Bedfordshire County Council: Councillor 1981-83, Chair, Further Education Committee 1981-83.

Political interests: Agriculture, forestry, environment.

Other: Parliamentary delegate, Council of Europe and Western European Union 1987-91; Member, Executive Committee, Inter-Parliamentary Union British Group 1995-97; President, Aboricultural Association 1989-95; Captain, Parliamentary Golfing Society 1999-2002; Fellowship: FArbA. KB 2001. Hawks Club.

Recreations: Golf, sailing, gardening.

The Lord Framlingham, House of Lords, London SW1A 0PW
Tel: 020 7219 5353

FREEMAN, LORD

FREEMAN (Life Baron), Roger Norman Freeman; cr. 1997; PC 1993. Born 27 May 1942; Son of Norman Freeman CBE and Marjorie Freeman; Married Jennifer Watson OBE 1969 (1 son 1 daughter).

Education: Whitgift School, Croydon; Balliol College, Oxford (BA philosophy, politics and economics 1964); Institute of Chartered Accountants, England and Wales (ACA 1968).

Non-political career: Managing director, Bow Publications Ltd 1968-69; Partner, Lehman Bros 1969-86; Director, Martini & Rossi UK Ltd and Baltic Leasing Group plc -1986; PricewaterhouseCoopers: Partner, Corporate Finance Division 1997-98, Adviser 1999-, Chair, UK Advisory Board, PWC 2000-; Chair, advisory board Thales UK plc 1999-2013; Director, Thales sa 1999-2012; Chair, Cambridge Enterprise Ltd 2006-10; Director: Chemring Group plc 2006-, Global Energy Development plc 2006-10; Director and former chair, Parity Group plc 2007-; Chair: Security Innovation and Technology Consortium Ltd (Public Sector Sponsored) 2008-11, Big DNA Ltd 2008-; Director: Saville Group plc 2008-, ITM Energy plc 2010-.

CONSERVATIVE

Political career: *House of Commons:* Contested Don Valley 1979 general election. MP (Conservative) for Kettering 1983-97. Parliamentary Under-Secretary of State: for the Armed Forces 1986-88, Department of Health 1988-90; Minister of State for: Public Transport, Department of Transport 1990-94, Defence Procurement, Ministry of Defence 1994-95; Chancellor of the Duchy of Lancaster and Cabinet Minister for Public Service 1995-97. *House of Lords:* Raised to the peerage as Baron Freeman, of Dingley in the County of Northamptonshire 1997. Co-opted member Science and Technology Sub-committee II (Innovations in Computer Processors/Microprocessing/ Science and the Regional Development Agencies) 2002-03; Member Speakership of the House 2003, 2005; Co-opted member EU Sub-committee C (Foreign Affairs, Defence and Development Policy) 2005-06; Member European Union 2006-10; Chair EU Sub-committee B (Internal Market) 2006-10; Member: Selection 2011, Joint Committee on the Draft Detention of Terrorist Suspects (Temporary Extension) Bills 2011, EU Sub-committee B (Internal Market, Infrastructure and Employment) 2013-. *Other:* President, Oxford University Conservative Association 1964; Chief financial officer, Conservative Central Office 1984-86; Special adviser on Candidates, Conservative Party 1997-2001; Member, Executive, Association of Conservative Peers 2005-09.

Political interests: International development, defence reservists, pensions, technology investment; Africa (Sierra Leone, Uganda).

Other: Treasurer, Bow Group 1967-68; President: Council of the UK Reserve Forces and Cadets Association 1999-2011, British International Freight Association 1999-2002; Chair: Busoga Trust 2000-10, Skill Force Development 2004-; Trustee, National Army museum 2005-11; Co-chair, UK-Sierra Leone Business Forum 2005-07; Fellow, Institute of Chartered Accountants, England and Wales; Busoga Trust (water well construction in Uganda, Africa). PC 1993; Carlton Club: Chairman 2010-13.

Publications: Fair Deal for Water (1986); Democracy in the Digital Age (1997); All Change, British Railway Privatisation (2000); Spin out Companies (2004).

Rt Hon the Lord Freeman, House of Lords, London SW1A 0PW
Tel: 020 7219 6364 *Email:* freemanr@parliament.uk
13 Little College Street, London SW1A 3SH

CONSERVATIVE

FREUD, LORD

Parliamentary Under-Secretary of State (Minister for Welfare Reform) and Government Spokesperson, Department for Work and Pensions

FREUD (Life Baron), David Anthony Freud; cr 2009. Born 24 June 1950; Son of late Anton Freud and late Annette Freud, née Krarup; Married Priscilla Dickinson 1978 (1 son 2 daughters).

Education: Whitgift School, Croydon; Merton College, Oxford (BA philosophy, politics and economics 1972).

Non-political career: Journalist 1972-83: *Western Mail* 1972-75, *Financial Times* 1976-83; Investment banker, Rowe and Pitman and successors, ultimately UBS AG 1984-2003; Chief executive, Portland Trust 2005-08; Adviser on welfare reform to Secretary of State for Work and Pensions 2008-09. Member, National Union of Journalists 1972-83.

Political career: *House of Lords:* Raised to the peerage as Baron Freud, of Eastry in the County of Kent 2009. Shadow Minister for Welfare Reform and Opposition Spokesperson for Work and Pensions 2009-10; Parliamentary Under-Secretary of State (Minister for Welfare Reform) and Government Spokesperson, Department for Work and Pensions 2010-.

Political interests: Welfare reform.

Publications: Freud in the City (Bene Factum Publishing, 2006); Reducing Dependency, Increasing Opportunity: Options for the Future of Welfare to Work (Independent Report to DWP).

Recreations: Cycling, swimming, skiing, tennis, history.

The Lord Freud, House of Lords, London SW1A 0PW
Tel: 020 7219 4907 *Email:* freudd@parliament.uk

Need additional copies?

Call 020 7593 5679

Visit www.dodsshop.co.uk

FREYBERG, LORD

FREYBERG (3rd Baron, UK), Valerian Bernard Freyberg; cr. 1951. Born 15 December 1970; Son of Colonel 2nd Baron, and Ivry Perronelle Katharine Guild; Married Dr Harriet Atkinson 2002 (1 son 2 daughters).

Education: Eton College; Camberwell College of Arts (BA 1994); Slade School of Fine Art (MA 2006).

Non-political career: Artist.

CROSSBENCH

Political career: *House of Lords:* First entered House of Lords 1994; Elected hereditary peer 1999-. Member House of Lords Offices Sub-committees: House of Lords Library and Computers 1995-98, Advisory Panel on Works of Art 1999-2002. *Councils and public bodies:* Member, Design Council 2001-04.

Political interests: Visual arts; New Zealand.

The Lord Freyberg, House of Lords, London SW1A 0PW
Tel: 020 7219 5101 *Email:* freybergv@parliament.uk

FRITCHIE, BARONESS

FRITCHIE (Life Baroness), Irene Tordoff Fritchie; cr 2005. Born 29 April 1942; Daughter of Charles Fennell and Eva, née Tordoff; Married Don Fritchie 1960 (1 son and 1 son deceased).

Education: Ribston Hall Grammar School for Girls.

Non-political career: Insurance 1970-76; Training posts Food and Drink Industry Training Board 1976-80; Consultant, Social Ecology Associates 1980-81; Director: Transform Ltd 1981-85, Rennie Fritchie Consultancy 1985-89; Managing director, Working Choices Ltd 1989-91; Consultant, Mainstream Development 1991-; Vice-chair, Stroud and Swindon Building Society 2004-08; Chair, Nominet 2010-.

CROSSBENCH

Political career: *House of Lords:* Raised to the peerage as Baroness Fritchie, of Gloucester in the County of Gloucestershire 2005. Member: Delegated Powers and Regulatory Reform 2007-09, Refreshment 2008-12. *Councils and public bodies:* Chair: Gloucester Health Authority 1988-92, South Western Regional Health Authority 1992-94, South and West Regional Health Authority 1994-96; Civil Service Commissioner 1999-2005; Commissioner for Public Appointments 1999-2005; Chair, Independent Appointments Selection Board, Royal Institution of Chartered Surveyors 2007-; Board member and deputy chair, Scottish Public Services Ombudsman Audit Advisory Board 2007-10; Chair, 2gether NHS Mental Health Foundation Trust 2008-12.

Countries of interest: China, New Zealand, Turkey, USA.

Other: President and founder member, Pennell Initiative, focusing on the health of women in later life 1997-; Gloucestershire Ambassador 2000-; Patron: The Pied Piper Appeal 2002-, Winston's Wish (grief support for children) 2002-; St Andrew's Ambassador 2004-; Vice-president, British Lung Foundation 2005-; President, Chronic Pain Policy Coalition 2005-08; Chair, advisory board, Web Science Research Initiative 2006-09; Patron, Women in Banking and Finance 2008-12; President, Hospital Caterers Association 2009-10; Companion, Institute of Management; Member, Royal Society of Medicine. Pro-chancellor, Southampton University 1998-2007; Chancellor, Gloucestershire University 2012. Seven honorary doctorates; Two fellowships. DBE 1996.

Publications: Working Choices (Dent, 1988), Co-author: The Business of Assertiveness (BBC Books, 1991), Resolving Conflicts in Organisations (Lemos & Crane, 1998), Career Life Planning – a tutor's guide (Manpower Services Commission), Interpersonal Skills for Managers, a tutor's guide (Manpower Services Commission), Women, Work and Training (Manpower Services Commission); Articles in training and management journals; Member, editorial board, Whitehall & Westminster World.

Recreations: Gardening, writing, reading, babysitting, the *Archers*.

The Baroness Fritchie DBE, House of Lords, London SW1A 0PW
Tel: 020 7219 5353 *Email:* fritchiei@parliament.uk
Tel: 01452 414542/01452-301266 *Fax:* 01452 414542/01452-304685
Email: renniefritchie@hotmail.com *Twitter:* @fritchiei

LABOUR

GALE, BARONESS

GALE (Life Baroness), Anita Gale; cr. 1999. Born 28 November 1940; Daughter of late Arthur Gale, coalminer and late Lillian Gale, housewife; Married Morcom Holmes 1959 (divorced 1983) (2 daughters).

Education: Treherbert Secondary Modern School; Pontypridd Technical College 1970-73; University College of Wales, Cardiff (BSc Econ politics 1976).

Non-political career: Sewing machinist, clothing factory 1956-57; Shop assistant 1957-59; Sewing machinist 1965-69; Wales Labour Party: Women's Officer and Assistant Organiser 1976-84, General Secretary 1984-99. Shop steward, Tailors and Garment Workers' Union 1967-70; GMB Labour Organisers' Branch 1976-: Chair, Wales and South West Section 1986-99, Equal opportunities officer 1991-99.

Political career: *House of Lords:* Raised to the peerage as Baroness Gale, of Blaenrhondda in the County of Mid Glamorgan 1999. Opposition Whip 2010-13. Member Statutory Instruments Joint Committee 2003-07; Co-opted member EU Sub-Committee G (Social Policy and Consumer Affairs) 2006-09; Member: Works of Art 2009-11, 2013-, Refreshment 2012-13. Vice-chair, PLP Departmental Group for Women 2006-10. *Other:* Vice-chair, Labour Animal Welfare Society 1995-; Member: Wales Labour Women's Committee 2000-; Labour Women's Network National Committee 2001-09. *Councils and public bodies:* Commissioner for Wales, Women's National Commission 2004-09.

Political interests: Animal welfare, women's equality, children's rights, Wales, devolution, smoking and health, environment; Taiwan, USA.

Other: Member: Inter-Parliamentary Union 1999-, Parliamentary Assembly of Council of Europe 2008-10, CPA 2005-; President, Royal British Legion Treherbert and District Branch 2003-; Patron, Kidney Wales Foundation 2008-; President, National Association of Old Age Pensioners in Wales 2010-; Honorary Vice-President, James Whale Fund for Kidney Cancer 2010-; NSPCC, Parkinson's Disease Society, British Legion. Welsh Woman of the Year, Val Feld award 2005.

Recreations: Swimming, walking, travel.

The Baroness Gale, House of Lords, London SW1A 0PW
Tel: 020 7219 8511 *Email:* galea@parliament.uk *Twitter:* @BaronessGale

LIBERAL DEMOCRAT

GARDEN OF FROGNAL, BARONESS

Government Spokesperson, Departments for Business, Innovation and Skills and Education and Ministry of Defence

GARDEN OF FROGNAL (Life Baroness), Susan Elizabeth Garden; cr 2007. Born 22 February 1944; Daughter of late Henry Button and Peggy, née Heslop; Married Timothy Garden (later Air Marshal Lord Garden KCB, died 2007) 1965 (2 daughters).

Education: Westonbirt School, Gloucestershire; St Hilda's College, Oxford (BA modern and medieval languages 1965, MA); French, Spanish.

Non-political career: Schoolteacher, various posts in England and Germany 1966-84; City & Guilds: Administrator/manager 1988-2000, Consultant 2000-08.

Political career: *House of Commons:* Contested (Lib Dem) Finchley and Golders Green 2005 general election. *House of Lords:* Raised to the peerage as Baroness Garden of Frognal, of Hampstead in the London Borough of Camden 2007. Liberal Democrat: Whip 2008-10, Spokesperson for: Children, Schools and Families 2008-09, Innovation, Universities and Skills 2009-10; Government Whip 2010-13; Government Spokesperson for: Business, Innovation and Skills (Higher Education) 2010-, Culture, Olympics Media and Sport (Olympics, Sport, Tourism and Lottery) 2010-12, Education 2010-, Defence 2012-. EU Sub-committee F (Home Affairs): Co-opted member 2008-10, Member 2010. *Other:* Member, Liberal Democrat Federal Conference Committee 2004-08; President, Camden Liberal Democrats 2007-.

Political interests: Education and skills.

Other: St Hilda's College Association 1965-: Chairman 1996-2000; President, Relate central Middlesex 1997-2001; Caseworker, SSAFA Forces Help 2000-05; Vice-chairman: Oxford University Society 2005-07; Council member, Air League 2012-; FRSA 1993; Fellow, City & Guilds 2010; Honorary FCIL 2012. Master World Traders' Livery Company 2008-09; National Liberal, Royal Air Force.

The Baroness Garden of Frognal, House of Lords, London SW1A 0PW
Tel: 020 7219 2747 *Email:* gardens@parliament.uk
Email: sue.garden@blueyonder.co.uk

CONSERVATIVE

GARDINER OF KIMBLE, LORD

Government Spokesperson, Departments for Culture, Media and Sport and Energy and Climate Change and Cabinet Office; Government Whip

GARDINER OF KIMBLE (Life Baron), John Eric Gardiner; cr 2010. Born 17 March 1956; Son of Anthony Gardiner and Heather Gardiner, née Robarts; Married Olivia Musgrave, sculptor, 2004.

Education: Uppingham School, Rutland; Royal Holloway College, London University (BA modern history and politics 1977).

Non-political career: Partner, family farm, Kimble, Buckinghamshire; Company director; British Field Sports Society/Countryside Alliance: Director of political affairs 1995-2004, Deputy chief executive 2004-10, Executive director and board member 2010-.

Political career: *House of Lords:* Raised to the peerage as Baron Gardiner of Kimble, of Kimble in the County of Buckinghamshire 2010. Party Whip 2010-12; Government Whip 2012-; Government Spokesperson for: Cabinet Office 2012-, Business, Innovation and Skills 2012-13, Energy and Climate Change 2012-, Culture, Media and Sport 2013-. Member HIV and AIDS in the UK 2010-11. *Other:* Private secretary to Chairmen of Conservative Party 1989-95: Rt Hon Kenneth Baker MP 1989-90, Rt Hon Chris Patten MP 1990-92, Rt Hon Sir Norman Fowler MP 1992-94, Rt Hon Jeremy Hanley MP 1994-95, Rt Hon Brian Mawhinney MP 1995; Member, Quality of Life Commission Rural Affairs Group, Conservative Party.

Political interests: Agriculture, rural affairs, housing, conservation, heritage; Australia, Greece, Ireland, Zimbabwe.

Other: Chair, Vale of Aylesbury with Garth and South Berks Hunt 1992-2006; Federation of Associations for Hunting and Conservation of the European Union: Chair (UK) 1998-, Treasurer (Europe) 2003-; President, Buckinghamshire County Show 2007; Pratt's.

Recreations: Hunting, gardening.

The Lord Gardiner of Kimble, House of Lords, London SW1A 0PW
Tel: 020 7219 5353 *Email:* gardinerj@parliament.uk

GARDNER OF PARKES, BARONESS

GARDNER OF PARKES (Life Baroness), (Rachel) Trixie Anne Gardner; cr. 1981. Born 17 July 1927; Daughter of late Honorary J. J. Gregory McGirr and late Rachel McGirr, OBE, LC; Married Kevin Gardner 1956 (died 2007) (3 daughters).

Education: Monte Sant Angelo College, north Sydney, Australia; East Sydney Technical College; Sydney University (BDS 1954); Cordon Bleu de Paris (Diploma 1956).

Non-political career: Came to UK 1954; Dentist in general practice 1955-90; Director: Gateway Building Society 1987-88, Woolwich Building Society 1988-93; Chair (UK), Plan International 1989-2003.

CONSERVATIVE

Political career: *House of Commons:* Contested (Conservative) Blackburn 1970 and North Cornwall February 1974 general elections. *House of Lords:* Raised to the peerage as Baroness Gardner of Parkes, of Southgate in Greater London and of Parkes in the State of New South Wales and Commonwealth of Australia 1981. Deputy Chair of Committees 1999-2002; Deputy Speaker 1999-2002. Member: Information 2003-05, Delegated Powers and Regulatory Reform 2005-09, 2010-. *Councils and public bodies:* Member: Inner London Executive Council NHS 1966-71, Standing Dental Advisory Committee for England and Wales 1968-76, Industrial Tribunal Panel for London 1974-97; Councillor, Westminster City Council 1968-78: Lady Mayoress of Westminster 1987-88; Councillor, GLC 1970-86; JP, North Westminster 1971-97; Member, Westminster, Kensington and Chelsea Area Health Authority 1974-81; Department of Employment's Advisory Committee on Women's Employment 1980-89; North Thames Gas Consumer Council 1980-82; Member: General Dental Council 1984-86, 1987-91, London Electricity Board 1984-90; Vice-chair, North East Thames Regional Health Authority 1990-94; Trustee, Parliamentary Advisory Council on Transport Safety 1992-98; Vice-President, National House Building Council 1992-99; Chair, Royal Free Hampstead NHS Trust 1994-97.

Political interests: Transport, housing, health, planning, energy; Commonwealth, Latin America, Scandinavia.

Other: British chair, European Union of Women 1978-82; UK representative on the UN Status of Women Commission 1982-88; Member, Executive Committee, Inter-Parliamentary Union, British Group -1997, 2008-11; UK representative to Euro-Mediterranean Women's Forum 2000-02; Governor: Eastman Dental Hospital 1971-80, National Heart Hospital 1974-90; Honorary President, War Widows' Association of Great Britain 1984-87; Sydney University UK Alumni Association: President 1990-2012, Patron 2012; President, British Fluoridation Society 1990-93; Chair, Suzy Lamplugh Trust 1993-96; President, Women's Guild of Friendship 1995-2011; Chair, The Cook

Society 1996; President, Married Women's Association 1998-2010; Honorary Vice-President, British Legion, Women's Section 2001-06; PLAN International UK; Multiple Sclerosis Trust. Freeman, City of London 1992. DU, Middlesex 1997; Fellow, University of Sydney, Australia 2005. International Achievement award, Sydney University; Peer Contribution to Central Lobby, *PoliticsHome* awards 2012. AM (Order of Australia) 2003.

Recreations: Family life, gardening, needlework, travel.

The Baroness Gardner of Parkes AM, House of Lords, London SW1A 0PW
Tel: 020 7219 6611 *Email:* gardnert@parliament.uk

CONSERVATIVE

GAREL-JONES, LORD

GAREL-JONES (Life Baron), (William Armand Thomas) Tristan Garel-Jones; cr. 1997. Born 28 February 1941; Son of Bernard Garel-Jones and Meriel Williams; Married Catalina Garrigues 1966 (4 sons 1 daughter).

Education: King's School, Canterbury; Spanish, Madrid University.

Non-political career: In business on the Continent 1960-70; Personal assistant to Michael Roberts MP at Cardiff North 1970 general election; Merchant banker 1971-74; Personal Assistant to Lord Thorneycroft 1978-79; Managing director, UBS.

Political career: *House of Commons:* Contested Caernarvon February 1974 and Watford October 1974 general elections. MP (Conservative) for Watford 1979-97. PPS to Barney Hayhoe as Minister of State, Civil Service Department 1981-82; Assistant Government Whip 1982-83; Government Whip 1983-89; Deputy Chief Whip 1989-90; Minister of State, Foreign and Commonwealth Office 1990-93. *House of Lords:* Raised to the peerage as Baron Garel-Jones, of Watford in the County of Hertfordshire 1997.

Political interests: European Union; Latin America, Spain.

Other: Canning House. PC 1992.

Recreations: Book collecting.

Rt Hon the Lord Garel-Jones, House of Lords, London SW1A 0PW
Tel: 020 7219 1855
Tel: 020 7568 1379 *Fax:* 020 7568 1468 *Email:* tristan.garel-jones@ubs.com

LABOUR

GAVRON, LORD

GAVRON (Life Baron), Robert Gavron; cr. 1999. Born 13 September 1930; Son of Nathaniel and Leah Gavron; Married Hannah Fyvel 1955 (died 1965) (1 son and 1 son deceased); married Nicolette Coates 1967 (divorced 1987) (2 daughters); married Katharine Gardiner, née Macnair 1989.

Education: Leighton Park School, Reading; St Peter's College, Oxford (BA jurisprudence 1953, MA).

Non-political career: National service Royal Army Education Corps 1949-50; Territorial Honourable Artillery Company 1950-53. Called to the Bar, Middle Temple 1955; St Ives Group: Founded 1964, Director 1964-98, Chair 1964-93; Director: Octopus Publishing plc 1975-87, Electra Management plc 1981-92; Proprietor, The Carcanet Press Ltd 1983-; Chair: The Folio Society 1982-, National Gallery Co Ltd (formerly National Gallery Publications Ltd) 1996-98, Guardian Media Group plc 1997-2000.

Political career: *House of Lords:* Raised to the peerage as Baron Gavron, of Highgate in the London Borough of Camden 1999. Member House of Lords Offices Sub-committee on Works of Art 2002-03, 2005-09.

Political interests: Entrepreneurialism, financial regulation, the arts.

Other: Trustee, Paul Hamlyn Foundation 1987-2005; Honorary Fellow, Royal College of Art 1990; Trustee, Institute for Public Policy Research 1991-2009; Chair, Open College of the Arts 1991-96; Director, Royal Opera House 1992-98; Trustee, National Gallery 1994-2001; Honorary Fellow, Royal Society of Literature 1996; Trustee, Scott Trust 1997-2000; Governor, London School of Economics 1997-2002; Honorary Member, The Poetry Society; Honorary Life Member, Barbados Cricket Association 2010-. Honorary Fellow, St Peter's College, Oxford 1992; Honorary PhD, Thames Valley University 1997. CBE 1990; MCC.

Publications: Co-author, The Entrepreneurial Society (1998).

Recreations: Books, music.

The Lord Gavron CBE, House of Lords, London SW1A 0PW
Tel: 020 7219 5353
44 Eagle Street, London WC1R 4FS *Tel:* 020 7400 4300 *Fax:* 020 7400 4245
Email: yvetted@foliosociety.com

GEDDES, LORD

CONSERVATIVE

GEDDES (3rd Baron, UK), Euan Michael Ross Geddes; cr. 1942. Born 3 September 1937; Son of 2nd Baron, KBE, DL; Married Gillian Butler 1966 (died 1995) (1 son 1 daughter); married Susan Hunter, née Carter 1996.

Education: Rugby School; Gonville and Caius College, Cambridge (BA history 1961, MA); Harvard Business School 1969.

Non-political career: Royal Navy 1956-58; Lieutenant-Commander, RNR (Rtd). Trinity College London: Chair 1992-2009, Life President.

Political career: *House of Lords:* First entered House of Lords 1975; Elected hereditary peer 1999-; Deputy Chair of Committees 2000-; Deputy Speaker 2002-. Member: European Union 1994-2000, EU Sub-committee A 1985-90, 2000-03; EU Sub-committee B: Member 1990-94, 1995-99, Chair 1996-99; Member: Science and Technology Sub-committee I 1990-92, Refreshment Sub-committee 2000-03, Procedure 2003-05, European Union 2003-07, EU Sub-committee B (Internal Market) 2003-07, Personal Bills 2003-09, Standing Orders (Private Bills) 2003-, Liaison 2003-08, Refreshment 2007-12, Intergovernmental Organisations 2007-08, Joint Committees on: Statutory Instruments 2012, the Rookery South (Resource Recovery Facility) Order 2012-13. *Other:* Executive of Association of Conservative Peers: Member 1999-, Treasurer 2000-.

Political interests: Shipping, Anglo-Chinese relations, immigration, energy, transport, industry, tourism; South East Asia, Hong Kong.

Other: Trustee, Portman. Honorary FTCL; Brooks's, Hong Kong, Noblemen and Gentlemen's Catch. Hong Kong Golf.

Recreations: Golf, music, bridge, gardening, shooting.

The Lord Geddes, House of Lords, London SW1A 0PW
Tel: 020 7219 6400 *Fax:* 020 7219 0034 *Email:* geddese@parliament.uk

GERMAN, LORD

LIBERAL DEMOCRAT

GERMAN (Life Baron), Michael James German; cr 2010. Born 8 May 1945; Son of Arthur Ronald German, retired, and Molly German, retired; Divorced (2 daughters); married Veronica Watkins (later AM as Veronica German 2010-11) 2006 (3 stepchildren).

Education: St Illtyd's College, Cardiff; St Mary's College London; Open University (BA educational studies 1972); Bristol Polytechnic (Post Graduate Diploma education management 1974); French.

Non-political career: Primary school teacher 1966-97; Secondary school teacher, Mostyn High School 1967-70; Head of music: Lady Mary High School, Cardiff 1970-86, Corpus Christi High School, Cardiff 1986-91; European director, Welsh Joint Education Committee 1991-99.

Political career: *House of Commons:* Contested Cardiff North 1974, and Cardiff Central 1979, 1983 and 1987 general elections. Co-chair, Liberal Democrat Parliamentary Committee on Work and Pensions. *House of Lords:* Raised to the peerage as Baron German, of Llanfrechfa in the County Borough of Torfaen 2010. Chair, Liberal Democrat Parliamentary Party Committee on Work and Pensions 2010-. *Other:* National Assembly for Wales: Contested Caerphilly constituency 1999 and Torfaen constituency 2003 National Assembly for Wales elections. AM for South Wales East region 1999-2010: Welsh Liberal Democrat: Spokesperson for Economic Development 1999-2001; Deputy First Minister 2000-01, 2002-03; Minister for: Economic Development 2000-01, Rural Development and Wales Abroad 2002-03; Welsh Liberal Democrat: Spokesperson for: Local Government 2004-05, Local Government and European Affairs 2005-07, Europe 2007-10; Shadow Minister for Environment 2010. Member: Liberal Party/Welsh Liberal Democrats 1974-, Federal Executive Committee 1989-91; General election director, Welsh Liberal Democrats 1992-97; Leader, Welsh Liberal Democrats in the National Assembly 1998-2008; Member, Liberal Democrat Federal Executive Committee 2001-03; Leader, Welsh Liberal Democrats 2007-08; Member, Federal Policy Committee 2010-. *Councils and public bodies:* Cardiff City Council: Councillor 1983-96, Group Leader 1983-96, Joint Leader 1987-91.

Political interests: Small businesses, education and skills, governance and constitutional affairs; European Union, Oman, Moldova, Sub-Saharan Africa.

Other: Executive member, Wales branch, Commonwealth Parliamentary Association 2004-10; Member, British-Irish Parliamentary Assembly 2004-10; President, Dolen Cymru (The Wales-Lesotho Link) 2008-; Parliament Choir: Chair and trustee 2011-13, Vice-chair 2013-; President, Monmouth, Brecon and Abergavenny Canals Trust 2011-. OBE 1996; National Liberal Club.

Recreations: Reading, music, travel.

The Lord German OBE, House of Lords, London SW1A 0PW
Tel: 020 7219 6942 *Email:* germanm@parliament.uk *Twitter:* @mjgerman

GIBSON OF MARKET RASEN, BARONESS

GIBSON OF MARKET RASEN (Life Baroness), Anne Gibson; cr. 2000. Born 10 December 1940; Daughter of Harry and Jessie Tasker; Married John Gibson 1962 (1 daughter); married John Bartell 1988 (1 stepdaughter).
Education: Caistor Grammar School, Lincolnshire; Chelmsford College of Further Education; Essex University (BA government 1976).
Non-political career: Secretary 1956-59; Bank cashier 1959-62; Organiser, Saffron Walden Labour Party 1966-70; Political researcher and advertising administrator, *House Magazine* 1976-77; Assistant secretary, Organisation and Industrial Relations Department, TUC 1977-87; National secretary, MSF (now Unite) 1987-2000. Member: AMICUS/Unite, TUC General Council 1989-2000.

LABOUR

Political career: *House of Lords:* Raised to the peerage as Baroness Gibson of Market Rasen, of Market Rasen in the County of Lincolnshire 2000. Deputy Speaker 2008-. Member: EU Sub-committee F (Social Affairs, Education and Home Affairs/Home Affairs) 2001-05, Joint Committee on House of Lords Reform 2002-03, Constitutional Reform Bill 2004, Review of the BBC Charter 2005-06, Information 2007-11, Constitutional Renewal Bill 2008-09, Joint Committees on: the Draft Enhanced Terrorism Prevention and Investigation Measures Bill 2012-13, Voting Eligibilty (Prisoners) Bill 2013-. *Other:* Member: Labour Party National Constitutional Committee 1997-2000, PLP Women's Committee 2000-, Labour Animal Welfare Society 2000-; Chair, BERR: Bullying at Work Partnership Committee 2003-08. *Councils and public bodies:* Member: Equal Opportunities Commission 1991-98, Department of Employment Advisory Group for Older Workers 1993-96, Health and Safety Commission 1996-2000, Occupational Health and Safety Commission 1996-2000; President, Royal Society for Prevention of Accidents 2004-08; Hon President, Dispensing Doctors Association 2009-.
Political interests: Industrial relations, equality issues, women's issues, health and safety at work, adoption, foreign affairs (especially Latin America), penal policy; China, France, Latin America, Portugal, Spain.
Other: ETUC Women's Committee 1977-2000: Chair, EC Committee on Violence at Work 1996-2000; ICFTU Women's Committee 1977-2000: Member: EC Committee on Health and Safety 1996-2000, Bilbao Agency 1996-2000; Member: Fawcett Society, Fabian Society, Air League Council 2006-, Air Cadet Council 2007-; Rare Breeds Society; National Asthma Campaign; National Osteoporosis Campaign; Action for Prisoners Families; End Child Poverty. Honorary Doctorate of Laws, Portsmouth University 2007. Distinguished service award for work in health and safety, Royal Society for Prevention of Accidents 2001. OBE 1998.
Publications: Numerous pamphlets on trade unions, workplace rights, equal pay, equal opportunities.
Recreations: Embroidery, reading, theatre.
The Baroness Gibson of Market Rasen OBE, House of Lords, London SW1A 0PW
Tel: 020 7219 5737 *Email:* gibsonan@parliament.uk

GIDDENS, LORD

GIDDENS (Life Baron), Anthony Giddens; cr. 2004. Born 18 January 1938; Son of Thomas George and Nell Maude Giddens; Married Alena Ledeneva 2005 (divorced).
Education: Minchenden Grammar School, London; Hull University (BA sociology and psychology 1959); London School of Economics (MA sociology 1961); University of Cambridge (PhD 1976); French, some German.
Non-political career: Lecturer in sociology, Leicester University 1961-70; Cambridge University: Sociology lecturer 1970-84, Reader/professor of sociology 1984-96, Fellow, King's College; London School of Economics: Director 1997-2004, Emeritus professor; Former chair and director, Polity Press Ltd 1985-.

LABOUR

Political career: *House of Lords:* Raised to the peerage as Baron Giddens, of Southgate in the London Borough of Enfield 2004. Co-opted member EU Sub-committee A (Economic and Financial Affairs) 2006-08; Member EU Sub-committee D: (Agriculture, Fisheries and Environment) 2010-12, (Agriculture, Fisheries, Environment and Energy) 2012-.
Political interests: Welfare, social policy, foreign policy, global issues; Latin America, China, EU, Russia.
Other: BBC Reith Lecturer 1998; Member, Academy of Social Sciences; Various universities. Numerous honorary doctorates from Europe, South America and China. Asturias Prize for Social Sciences 2002; Fellow American Academy of Arts and Sciences; Academician of the Russian Academy of Sciences. Order of the Southern Cross (Brazil); Orders of the Lion (Finland). Queen's Club.
Publications: Over forty books on sociology, politics and psychology.
Recreations: Watching Spurs, tennis, travel.
The Lord Giddens, House of Lords, London SW1A 0PW
Tel: 020 7219 6710

GLASGOW, EARL OF

GLASGOW (10th Earl of, S), Patrick Robin Archibald Boyle; cr. 1703; Viscount of Kelburn; 10th Lord Boyle (S) 1699/1703; 4th Baron Fairlie (UK) 1897. Born 30 July 1939; Son of Rear-Admiral 9th Earl, CB, DSC; Married Isabel James 1975 (1 son 1 daughter).

Education: Eton College; Sorbonne, Paris.

Non-political career: Royal Navy national service 1959-60; Sub-Lieutenant, RNR 1960. Television and film production: Assistant film director 1962-67, Documentary producer/director, Yorkshire TV 1968-70, Freelance television documentary producer 1971-86; Owner/manager, Kelburn Country Centre country park and visitor attraction. Former member, ACTT.

LIBERAL DEMOCRAT

Political career: *House of Lords:* First entered House of Lords 1990; Elected hereditary peer 2005-; Liberal Democrat Spokesperson for: Transport 2005-10, Culture, Media and Sport 2008-10. Member Works of Art 2005-09. *Councils and public bodies:* DL, Ayrshire and Arran 1995.

Political interests: Tourism, television, performing arts, small businesses, assisted dying.

Other: Arthritis Care.

Publications: Occasional articles for *The Spectator* and other magazines.

Recreations: Theatre, cinema, skiing.

The Earl of Glasgow DL, House of Lords, London SW1A 0PW
Tel: 020 7219 5419
Kelburn Country Centre, Fairlie, Ayrshire KA29 0BE *Tel:* 01475 568685 *Fax:* 01475 568121
Email: admin@kelburncountrycentre.com *Website:* www.kelburncastle.com

GLASMAN, LORD

GLASMAN (Life Baron), Maurice Mark Glasman; cr 2011. Born 1962; Married Catherine (3 sons 1 daughter).

Education: JFS Comprehensive School; St Katherine's College, Cambridge (BA modern history); York University (MA political philosophy); European University Institute, Florence (PhD unnecessary suffering 1989).

Non-political career: Senior lecturer in political theory, London Guildhall University; Senior lecturer in political theory and director of faith and citizenship programme, London Metropolitan University.

LABOUR

Political career: *House of Lords:* Raised to the peerage as Baron Glasman, of Stoke Newington and of Stamford Hill in the London Borough of Hackney 2011.

Other: London Citizens.

Publications: Unnecessary Suffering: Managing Market Utopia (Verso, 1996).

The Lord Glasman, House of Lords, London SW1A 0PW
Tel: 020 7219 5353

GLENARTHUR, LORD

GLENARTHUR (4th Baron, UK), Simon Mark Arthur; cr. 1918; 4th Bt of Carlung (UK) 1903. Born 7 October 1944; Son of 3rd Baron, OBE, DL; Married Susan Barry 1969 (1 son 1 daughter).

Education: Eton College.

Non-political career: Commissioned 10th Royal Hussars (PWO) 1963; ADC to High Commissioner, Aden 1964-65; Retired 1975 as Major; Major, The Royal Hussars (PWO) TAVR 1976-80; Honorary Colonel, 306 Hospital Support Medical Regiment (Volunteers) 2001-11; Honorary Air Commodore, 612 (County of Aberdeen) Squadron, Royal Auxiliary Air Force 2004-. Captain, British Airways Helicopters Ltd 1976-82; Director: Aberdeen and Texas Corporate Finance Ltd 1977-82, ABTEX Computer Systems Ltd 1979-82; Senior executive, Hanson plc 1989-96; Deputy chair, Hanson Pacific Ltd 1994-98; Director, Whirly Bird Services Ltd 1995-2004; Consultant, British Aerospace 1989-99; Director, Lewis Group plc 1993-94; Consultant, Chevron UK Ltd 1994-97; Director, Millennium Chemicals Inc 1996-2004; Consultant: Hanson plc 1996-99, Imperial Tobacco Group plc 1996-98; Audax Trading Ltd: Consultant 2001-02, Director 2003-05; Director: The Medical Defence Union 2002-06, Audax Global S.à.r.l. 2005-.

CONSERVATIVE

Political career: *House of Lords:* First entered House of Lords 1976; Government Whip 1982-83; Government Spokesperson for: the Treasury 1982-85, Home Office, Employment and Industry 1982-83, Defence 1983-89; Parliamentary Under-Secretary of State: Department of Health and Social Security 1983-85, Home Office 1985-86; Minister of State: Scottish Office 1986-87, Foreign and Commonwealth Office 1987-89; Elected hereditary peer 1999-. Member: Refreshment 2007-10, Ecclesiastical Committee 2010-. *Councils and public bodies:* DL, Aberdeenshire 1988;

Chair, St Mary's Hospital, Paddington, NHS Trust 1991-98; President, National Council for Civil Protection 1991-2003; Member, National Employers Liaison Committee for HM Reserve Forces 1996-2002; Governor, Nuffield Hospitals (now Nuffield Health) 2000-09; Commissioner, Royal Hospital, Chelsea 2001-07; Chair, National Employer Advisory Board for Britain's Reserve Forces 2002-09; King Edward VII's Hospital, Sister Agnes: Governor 2010-, Chairman of council 2012-; Governor, Sutton's Hospital, Charterhouse 2011-.

Political interests: Aviation, foreign affairs, defence, penal policy, health, Scotland; South Pacific.

Other: Member (Captain), Queen's Bodyguard for Scotland (Royal Company of Archers); Trustee, The Hanson Research Trust 1990-; Fellow, Royal Aeronautical Society 1992-2010; British Helicopter Association: Chair 1992-2004, President 2004-; Special Trustee, St Mary's Hospital, Paddington 1991-2000; Scottish Patron, The Butler Trust 1994-; Council member, Air League 1994-2009; Chair: European Helicopter Association 1996-2003, International Federation of Helicopter Associations 1997-2004; Trustee, The Philip Alison Foundation 2000-; Chartered Institute of Transport (now Chartered Institute of Logistics and Transport): Member 1978-2011, Fellow 1999-2011. Guild of Air Pilots and Air Navigators: Freeman 1992, Liveryman 1996-2011. Freeman, City of London 1996. Grand Cross, Order of Crown of Tonga; Order of St George, Tonga; Cavalry and Guards.

Recreations: Field sports, gardening, choral singing, organ playing, antique barometers.

The Lord Glenarthur DL, House of Lords, London SW1A 0PW
Tel: 020 7219 5429
PO Box 11012, Banchory, Kincardineshire AB31 6ZJ *Tel:* 01330 844467
Email: glenarthur@northbrae.co.uk

CONSERVATIVE

GLENDONBROOK, LORD

GLENDONBROOK (Life Baron), Michael David Bishop; cr 2011. Born 10 February 1942; Son of Clive Bishop.

Education: Mill Hill School.

Non-political career: Mercury Airlines, Manchester 1963; British Midland Airways 1964; Airtours plc: Director 1987-2001, Deputy Chairman 1996-2001; Wiliams plc 1993-2000; Chairman: Airlines of Britain Holdings/British Midland plc 1978-2009, British Regional Air Lines Group plc 1982-2001, Manx Airlines 1982-2001; Channel 4 Television: Deputy Chairman 1991-93, Chairman 1993-97; Non-executive director, Kidde plc 2000-02; Chairman, D'Oyly Carte Opera Trust Ltd 1989-2008.

Political career: *House of Lords:* Raised to the peerage as Baron Glendonbrook, of Bowdon in the County of Cheshire 2011. *Councils and public bodies:* Member, East Midlands Electricity Board 1980-83.

Other: Member, East Midlands Regional Board, Central Television 1981-89; Honorary member, Royal Society of Musicians of Great Britain 1989; Chair of Trustees, The Michael Bishop Foundation 1989-; Trustee and director, Friends in the UK, Royal Flying Doctor Service of Australia 2005. Liveryman, The Guild of Air Pilots and Air Navigators. CBE 1986; Kt 1991; Brooks's.

The Lord Glendonbrook CBE, House of Lords, London SW1A 0PW
Tel: 020 7219 5353

CONSERVATIVE

GLENTORAN, LORD

GLENTORAN (3rd Baron, UK), (Thomas) Robin Valerian Dixon; cr. 1939; 5th Bt of Ballymenoch (UK) 1903. Born 21 April 1935; Son of 2nd Baron, PC, KBE, and late Lady Diana Wellesley, daughter of 3rd Earl Cowley; Married Rona Colville 1959 (divorced 1975) (3 sons); married Alwyn Mason 1979 (divorced 1988); married Mrs Margaret Rainey 1990.

Education: Eton College; Grenoble University, France; French.

Non-political career: Grenadier Guards 1954-66, retired as Major. Redland (NI) Ltd: Managing director 1971-95, Chair 1995-98; Chair, Roofing Industry Alliance 1997-2003; Non-executive director, NHBC 2001-07; Betonsports plc 2004-07.

Political career: *House of Lords:* First entered House of Lords 1995; Elected hereditary peer 1999-; Opposition Spokesperson for: Northern Ireland 1999-2010, Industry 2004-05, Sport 2005-06, Olympics 2007-10, Wales 2007-10. *Councils and public bodies:* DL, Co. Antrim 1995-.

Political interests: Sport, environment, Northern Ireland, army, maritime affairs; India, Nepal, Ireland.

Other: Former member, British/Irish Inter-Parliamentary Body; Alternate Member, UK Delegation, Organisation for Security and Co-operation in Europe Parliamentary Assembly; Member, chair, president numerous organisations, especially related to sport, including: Member: Commission for Irish Lights 1985-2010, Millennium Commission 1994-2005; Chair: 'Paralympic World Cup' 2006-, BSSC 2006-; Royal Society of Ulster Architects; Parkinsons Society, Ocean Youth Club. Liveryman, Worshipful Company of Tylers and Bricklayers. Gold medal bobsleigh at Innsbruck Winter Olympic Games 1964. MBE 1969; CBE 1992; Royal Yacht Squadron (Cowes). Royal Portrush Golf; Irish Cruising.

Recreations: Sailing, travel, music, arts.

The Lord Glentoran CBE DL, House of Lords, London SW1A 0PW
Tel: 020 7219 5123 *Email:* glentoranr@parliament.uk

GLOUCESTER, LORD BISHOP OF

GLOUCESTER (40th Bishop of), Michael Francis Perham. Born 8 November 1947; Son of Raymond Perham and Marcelle Perham, née Barton; Married Alison Grove 1982 (4 daughters).

Education: Hardye's School, Dorchester; Keble College, Oxford (BA theology 1974, MA); Cuddesdon Theological College, Oxford.

Non-political career: Ordained priest 1977; Assistant curate, St Mary, Addington, Surrey 1976-81; Chaplain to Bishop of Winchester 1981-84; Rector, Oakdale Team Ministry, Poole, Dorset 1984-92; Norwich Cathedral 1992-98: Canon residentiary and precentor 1992-2004, Vice Dean

NON-AFFILIATED 1995-98; Provost, Dean of Derby 1998-2004; Bishop of Gloucester 2004-; Bishop Protector Society of St Francis 2005-.

Political career: *House of Lords:* Entered House of Lords 2009. *Councils and public bodies:* Member: Church of England Liturgical Commission 1986-2001, Archbishops' Commission on Church Music 1988-92, Church of England General Synod 1989-92, 1993-; Chair, Cathedrals' Liturgy Group 1994-2001; Member: Cathedrals' Fabric Commission for England 1996-2001, Archbishops' Council 1999-2004; Chair, Hospital Chaplaincies Council 2007-10.

Political interests: Education, universities, academics, overseas aid, equality issues, constitutional reform, church in society; Botswana, India, Sweden, Tanzania, USA.

Other: Pro-Chancellor, University of Gloucestershire. Honorary Fellow, Royal College of Church Music 2003; Honorary Doctor of Philosophy, University of Gloucestershire 2008.

Publications: Author, co-author and editor 16 books on liturgy and spirituality, most recently, The Hospitality of God (2011).

Recreations: Writing, reading, walking in Yorkshire Dales.

Rt Rev the Lord Bishop of Gloucester, House of Lords, London SW1A 0PW
Tel: 020 7219 5353
2 College Green, Gloucester GL1 2LR *Tel:* 01452 410022 *Fax:* 01452 308324
Email: bshpglos@glosdioc.org.uk *Website:* www.gloucester.anglican.org

GOFF OF CHIEVELEY, LORD

GOFF OF CHIEVELEY (Life Baron), Robert Lionel Archibald Goff; cr. 1986. Born 12 November 1926; Son of late Lieutenant Colonel L. T. Goff and Isobel Goff; Married Sarah Cousins 1953 (1 son 2 daughters and 1 son deceased).

Education: Eton College; New College, Oxford (BA jurisprudence 1950, MA 1953; DCL 1972).

Non-political career: Served Scots Guards 1945-48. Fellow and tutor, Lincoln College, Oxford 1951-55; Called to Bar, Inner Temple 1951; Bencher 1975; In practice at the Bar 1956-75; QC 1967; Member, General Council of the Bar 1971-74; Recorder 1974-75; Judge of the High Court, **NON-AFFILIATED** Queen's Bench Division 1975-82; Judge i/c Commercial Court 1979-81; Lord Justice of Appeal 1982-86.

Political career: *House of Lords:* Raised to the peerage as Baron Goff of Chieveley, of Chieveley in the Royal County of Berkshire 1986. Lord of Appeal in Ordinary 1986-98; Second Senior Law Lord 1994-96; Senior Law Lord 1996-98; On leave of absence.

Political interests: Comparative law.

Other: Chair, Council of Legal Education 1975-82; President Chartered Institute of Arbitrators 1986-91; Chair, Court of London University 1986-91; British Institute of International and Comparative Law: Chair 1986-2001, President 2001-; Chair, Pegasus Scholarship Trust of the Inner Temple 1987-2001; High Steward, Oxford University 1991-2001; Chair, Oxford Institute of European and Comparative Law 1995-2001; President, New College Society 1999-2001; DCL 1972 FBA 1987. Three honorary Oxford fellowships; Five honorary doctorates; Honorary fellow, American College of Trial Lawyers. Kt 1975; PC 1982 Grand Cross (First Class) of the Order of Merit (Germany) 1999.

Publications: Co-author, The Law of Restitution (1966); Maccabaean Lecture (British Academy, 1983); Lionel Cohen Memorial Lecture (Jerusalem, 1987); Cassel Lecture (Stockholm University, 1993).
Rt Hon the Lord Goff of Chieveley, House of Lords, London SW1A 0PW
Tel: 020 7219 5353

GOLD, LORD

GOLD (Life Baron), David Laurence Gold; cr 2011. Born 1 March 1951; Son of Michael and Betty Gold; Married Sharon Levy 1978 (1 daughter 2 sons).
Education: Westcliff High School for Boys; London School of Economics (LLB 1972).
Non-political career: Admitted solicitor 1975; Herbert Smith: Head of litigation 2003-05, Senior partner 2005-10; Corporate Monitor BAE Systems plc 2010-; Principal, David Gold and Associates 2011-.
Political career: *House of Lords:* Raised to the peerage as Baron Gold, of Westcliffe-on-Sea in the County of Essex 2011. Member Joint Committee on Privacy and Injunctions 2011-12. *Other:* Chairman, Conservative Party Disciplinary Committee 2010-12.
Other: Governor, London School of Economics 2010-; Law Society of England and Wales.
Recreations: Theatre, cinema, travel, family.
The Lord Gold, House of Lords, London SW1A 0PW
Tel: 020 7219 5353 *Email:* goldd@parliament.uk
3 Fitzhardinge Street, London W1H 6EF *Tel:* 020 3535 8989
Email: david.gold@davidgoldassociates.com *Website:* www.davidgoldassociates.com

CONSERVATIVE

GOLDIE, BARONESS – *Please see Addenda Page xi*

GOLDING, BARONESS

GOLDING (Life Baroness), (Llinos) Llin Golding; cr. 2001. Born 21 March 1933; Daughter of late Ness Edwards, MP for Caerphilly 1939 by-election to 1968; Married Dr Roland Lewis 1957 (1 son 2 daughters); married John Golding MP 1980 (died 1999).
Education: Caerphilly Girls Grammar School; Cardiff Royal Infirmary School of Radiography 1952.
Non-political career: Radiographer; Secretary and assistant to husband, John Golding, when an MP 1972-86. Former branch secretary, NUPE; Secretary, Newcastle Staffs and District Trades Council 1976-86.
Political career: *House of Commons:* MP (Labour) for Newcastle-under-Lyme 1986-2001. Opposition Whip 1987-92; Opposition Spokesperson for: Social Security 1992-93, Children and Families 1993-95, Food, Agriculture and Rural Affairs 1995-97. *House of Lords:* Raised to the peerage as Baroness Golding, of Newcastle-under-Lyme in the County of Staffordshire 2001. *Councils and public bodies:* Member: BBC Advisory Committee 1989-92, Commonwealth War Graves Commission 1992-2001; Administrative steward, British Boxing Board of Control 2004.
Political interests: Health service, trade unions, children, racing, gambling, fishing; Spain.
Other: Executive Committee Member, Inter-Parliamentary Union British Group 1996-99; Member, Board of Countryside Alliance 2002-; Chair, Countryside Alliance Fishing Committee 2004; Trustee, NSPCC 1988-2001; Chairman: Second Chance 1988-, Citizencard.
Recreations: Fishing.
The Baroness Golding, House of Lords, London SW1A 0PW
Tel: 020 7219 4209 *Email:* goldingll@parliament.uk

LABOUR

GOLDSMITH, LORD

GOLDSMITH (Life Baron), Peter Henry Goldsmith; cr. 1999. Born 5 January 1950; Son of late Sydney Goldsmith and Myra Nurick; Married Joy Elterman 1974 (3 sons 1 daughter).
Education: Quarry Bank High School, Liverpool; Gonville and Caius College, Cambridge (MA law 1971); University College, London (LLM 1972); French, German.
Non-political career: Called to the Bar, Gray's Inn 1972; In practice 1972-; QC 1987; Assistant Recorder, then Recorder of the Crown Court 1987-; Member, Paris Bar (Avocat a la Cour) 1997; Fellow, American Law Institute; European and Asian chair, Litigation Debevoise & Plimpton LLP 2007-.

LABOUR

Political career: *House of Lords:* Raised to the peerage as Baron Goldsmith, of Allerton in the County of Merseyside 1999. Attorney General and Government Spokesperson for Law Officers' Departments 2001-07. Member: Procedure 2009-12, Constitution 2010-. *Councils and public bodies:* Chair, Financial Reporting Review Panel 1997-2000.

Other: Prime Minister's Representative on Convention for a Charter of Fundamental Rights of the EU 1999-2000; Executive committee member, Great Britain China Centre 1996-2001; Council member, Public Concern at Work 1996-2001; Bar Pro Bono Unit: Founder 1996, President 2001-; Various offices international law organisations, including American Law Institute 1996-; Chairman, Access to Justice Foundation; Council member: Hong Kong International Arbitration Centre, CEELI (Central and Eastern European Law Initiative); Chair: Bar Council of England and Wales 1995, Bar Council International Relations Committee 1996, IBA Standing Committee on Globalisation 1996-98; Co-chair, IBA Human Pro Rights Institute 1998-2001; Fellow, University College London. City of London. Fellow, University College London. PC 2002.

Rt Hon the Lord Goldsmith QC, House of Lords, London SW1A 0PW
Tel: 020 7219 7500 *Email:* goldsmithp@parliament.uk
Debevoise & Plimpton LLP, Tower 42, Old Broad Street, London EC2N 1HQ *Tel:* 020 7786 9088
Fax: 020 7588 4180 *Email:* phgoldsmith@debevoise.com *Website:* www.debevoise.com

GOODHART, LORD

GOODHART (Life Baron), William Howard Goodhart; cr. 1997. Born 18 January 1933; Son of late Professor Arthur Goodhart, Honorary KBE, QC, FBA; Married Hon Celia McClare Herbert 1966 (1 son 2 daughters).

Education: Eton College; Trinity College, Cambridge (Scholar, MA law 1956); Harvard Law School (Commonwealth Fund Fellow, LLM 1958).

Non-political career: National Service Oxford and Bucks Light Infantry 1951-53. Called to the Bar, Lincoln's Inn 1957, QC 1979, Bencher 1986 (retired from practice 2003); Director, Bar

LIBERAL DEMOCRAT Mutual Indemnity Fund Ltd 1988-97; Has led reporting missions on human rights to Hong Kong 1991, Kashmir 1993, Israel and the West Bank 1994, Kenya 1996 and Sri Lanka 1997 and 2009.

Political career: *House of Commons:* Contested Kensington (SDP) 1983, (SDP/Alliance) 1987 general elections and (Lib Dem) July 1988 by-election and Oxford West and Abingdon 1992 general election. *House of Lords:* Raised to the peerage as Baron Goodhart, of Youlbury in the County of Oxfordshire 1997. Liberal Democrat Spokesperson for: Pensions 1998-2001, Lord Chancellor's Department 2000-04, Constitutional Affairs 2004-06; Liberal Democrat Shadow Lord Chancellor 2004-06. Co-opted member European Communities Sub-committee E 1997-2001; Member: Delegated Powers and Regulatory Reform 1998-2002, European Communities 1998-2001, Freedom of Information Bill 1999, Tax Simplification Joint Committee 2000-03, Procedure 2001-05, Reform of the House of Lords Joint Committee 2002-03, Economic Affairs 2003-07, Constitutional Reform Bill 2004-05, European Union 2005-06, European Union Sub-committee E (Law and Institutions) 2005-06, Tax Law Rewrite Bills Joint Committee 2005-10, Joint Committee on the Draft Bribery Bill 2009; Chair Delegated Powers and Regulatory Reform 2006-10; Member: Joint Committee on the Draft Detention of Terrorist Suspects (Temporary Extension) Bills 2011, Consumer Insurance (Disclosure and Representations) Bill 2011-12. *Other:* Chair: SDP Council Arrangements Committee 1982-88, Liberal Democrat Conference Committee 1988-91, Liberal Democrat Lawyers Association 1988-91; Liberal Democrat Policy Committee: Member 1988-97, Vice-chair 1995-97. *Councils and public bodies:* Member, Committee on Standards in Public Life 1997-2003.

Political interests: Human rights, constitutional reform; USA.

Other: International Commission of Jurists: Member, Executive Committee 1995-2002, Vice-President 2002-06, Honorary Member 2008-; Committee officer, Human Rights Institute 1995-2000; Member: Council of Legal Education 1986-92, Conveyancing Standing Committee, Law Commission 1987-89; Chair, Committee of Justice 1988-2004; Member: Trust Law Committee 1994-2005, Tax Law Review Committee 1994-2003; Council member, Royal Institute of International Affairs 1999-2002; Trustee: Airey Neave Trust 1999-2004, Fair Trials Abroad 2003-07; Chair of Council, Justice 2007-08; Justice. Kt 1989; Brooks's, Century Association (New York).

Publications: Co-author, Specific Performance (1986, 1996); Contributor to Halsbury's Laws of England; also articles in legal journals.

Recreations: Walking, skiing.

The Lord Goodhart QC, House of Lords, London SW1A 0PW
Tel: 020 7219 5449 *Email:* goodhartw@parliament.uk

CONSERVATIVE

GOODLAD, LORD

GOODLAD (Life Baron), Alastair Robertson Goodlad; cr 2005. Born 4 July 1943; Son of late Dr. John Goodlad and Isabel Goodlad, née Sinclair; Married Cecilia Hurst 1968 (2 sons).

Education: Marlborough College, Wiltshire; King's College, Cambridge (BA 1966, MA, LLB).

Non-political career: Former director, Bowater Overseas Holdings Ltd; President, Water Companies Association 1989; High Commissioner to Australia 2000-05.

Political career: *House of Commons:* Contested Crewe 1970 general election. MP (Conservative) for Northwich February 1974-83, for Eddisbury 1983-99. Government Whip 1981-84; Parliamentary Under-Secretary of State, Department of Energy 1984-87; Government Whip 1989-92; Minister of State, Foreign and Commonwealth Office 1992-95; Government Chief Whip 1995-97; Member, Shadow Cabinet 1997-98: Shadow Secretary of State for International Development 1997-98. Chairman, Conservative Party Committee for International Development 1997-98. *House of Lords:* Raised to the peerage as Baron Goodlad, of Lincoln in the County of Lincolnshire 2005. Contested Lord Speaker election 2011. Constitution Committee: Member 2007, Chair 2007-10; Chair: Merits of Statutory Instruments/Secondary Legislation Scrutiny 2010-, Leader's Group on the Working Practices of the House of Lords 2010-11.

Other: PC 1992; KCMG 1997; Brooks's, Beefsteak, Pratt's.

Rt Hon the Lord Goodlad KCMG, House of Lords, London SW1A 0PW
Tel: 020 7219 3427

GORDON OF STRATHBLANE, LORD

LABOUR

GORDON OF STRATHBLANE (Life Baron), James Stuart Gordon; cr. 1997. Born 17 May 1936; Son of late James and Elsie Gordon, née Riach; Married Margaret Anne Stevenson 1971 (1 daughter 2 sons).

Education: St Aloysius' College, Glasgow; Glasgow University (MA classics 1958).

Non-political career: Political editor, Scottish Television 1965-73; Managing director, Radio Clyde 1973-96; Scottish Advisory Board, BP 1990-2002; Scottish Radio Holdings: Chief executive 1991-96, Chair 1996-2005; Vice-chair, Melody Radio 1991-97; Director: Clydeport Holdings 1992-98, Johnston Press plc 1996-2007, AIM Trust plc (now Active Capital Trust) 1996-2009; Chair: Scottish Tourist Board 1998-2001, RAJAR (Radio Audience Research) 2003-06.

Political career: *House of Commons:* Contested East Renfrewshire (Labour) 1964 general election. *House of Lords:* Raised to the peerage as Baron Gordon of Strathblane, of Deil's Craig in Stirling 1997. Member Communications 2009-13. *Councils and public bodies:* Member, Scottish Development Agency 1981-90; Chair, Scottish Exhibition Centre 1983-89; Member, Court of University of Glasgow 1984-97; Chair, Advisory Group on Listed Events on TV 1997-98; Member, Independent Review Panel on Funding of BBC 1998-99; Board member, British Tourist Authority 1998-2001; Chair, Scottish Tourist Board 1998-2001.

Political interests: Broadcasting, tourism, constitutional affairs, Scotland; China, India, Middle East.

Other: Trustee, John Smith Memorial Trust 1995-2007; Board member, Scottish Tourist Board 1997-2001; Trustee, National Galleries of Scotland 1998-2001. Honorary DLitt, Glasgow Caledonian 1994; DUniv, Glasgow University 1998. Sony Award for outstanding services to radio 1984; Fellow, Radio Academy 1994; Lord Provost's Award for Public Service in Glasgow 1994. CBE 1984; New (Edinburgh), Glasgow Art. Prestwick Golf.

Recreations: Skiing, walking, genealogy.

The Lord Gordon of Strathblane CBE, House of Lords, London SW1A 0PW
Tel: 020 7219 1452 *Fax:* 020 7219 1993 *Email:* gordonj@parliament.uk

GOSCHEN, VISCOUNT

GOSCHEN (4th Viscount, UK), Giles John Harry Goschen; cr. 1900. Born 16 November 1965; Son of 3rd Viscount, KBE; Married Sarah Penelope Horsnail 1991 (2 daughters 1 son).

Education: Eton College.

Non-political career: Deutsche Bank 1997-2000; Director: Barchester Advisory 2000-02, Korn/Ferry International 2005-.

Political career: *House of Lords:* First entered House of Lords 1986; Government Whip (Lord-in-Waiting to HM The Queen) 1992-94; Government Spokesperson for Environment, Employment, Social Security, Transport and Trade and Industry 1992-94; Parliamentary Under-Secretary of State, Department of Transport 1994-97; Opposition Spokesperson for Environment, Transport and the Regions (Transport) 1997; Elected hereditary peer 1999-.

CONSERVATIVE

Countries of interest: Sub-Saharan Africa.
Other: Chair, Kasanka Trust; Air Squadron, Pratt's.
The Viscount Goschen, House of Lords, London SW1A 0PW
Tel: 020 7219 3198

GOUDIE, BARONESS

GOUDIE (Life Baroness), Mary Teresa Goudie; cr. 1998. Born 2 September 1946; Daughter of Martin and Hannah Brick; Married James Goudie QC 1969 (2 sons).

Education: Our Lady of The Visitation, Greenford; Our Lady of St Anselm, Hayes.

Non-political career: Assistant director, Brent People's Housing Association 1977-81; Director: The Hansard Society for Parliamentary Government 1985-90, *The House Magazine* 1989-90; European director of public affairs, World Wide Fund for Nature (UK) 1990-95; Independent public affairs consultant 1995-98; Strategic and management consultant 1998-; Member, global advisory board, WEConnect International 2012-; Director, Center for Talent Innovations 2012-. Member: APEX, GMB.

LABOUR

Political career: *House of Lords:* Raised to the peerage as Baroness Goudie, of Roundwood in the London Borough of Brent 1998. Co-opted member European Union Sub-committee E (Law and Institutions) 1998-2000; Member: Procedure 2001-04, House of Lords' Offices Finance and Staff Sub-committee 2002-03, Information Committee 2003-05, Statutory Instruments Joint Committee 2005-06, Selection 2008-13, Joint Committee on Tax Law Rewrite Bills 2009-10, Soft Power and the UK's Influence 2013-. Vice-chair, PLP Departmental Group for International Development 2010-. *Other:* Secretary, Labour Solidarity Campaign 1981-87; Campaign manager to Roy Hattersley MP, Labour Party Deputy leadership election 1983; Member, Labour Parliamentary general election campaign team 1998-2001; Vice-chair, Labour Peers 2001-03; Member: Society of Labour Lawyers, Labour Movement in Europe. *Councils and public bodies:* London Borough of Brent: Councillor 1971-78, Chair, Housing and Planning Committees, Deputy Whip.

Political interests: Women and children, regional development, human rights, charity law, human trafficking; Azerbaijan, Eire, Europe, India, Northern Ireland, Scotland, USA.

Other: Member, Inter-Parliamentary Union, British-Irish Inter-Parliamentary Committee; Chair, Women Leaders' Council to Fight Human Trafficking, UN; Member: Fabian Society, Smith Institute; Trustee: Piggybank Kids, Share Gift; Patron: National Childbirth Trust, Northern Ireland Community Foundation; Ambassador, World Wildlife Federation; Member, executive and board of directors, Vital Voices Global Partnership; Founding member, 30% Club 2010-; Trustee, El-Hibri Charitable Foundation 2012-. Honorary doctorate, Napier University 2000. Global Power award, Centre for Women Policy Studies 2012.

Recreations: Family, travelling, gardening, food and wine, art.
The Baroness Goudie, House of Lords, London SW1A 0PW
Tel: 020 7219 5880 *Website:* www.baronessgoudie.com *Twitter:* @BaronessGoudie

GOULD OF POTTERNEWTON, BARONESS

GOULD OF POTTERNEWTON (Life Baroness), Joyce Brenda Gould; cr. 1993. Born 29 October 1932; Daughter of late Sydney and Fanny Manson; Married Kevin Gould 1952 (separated) (1 daughter).

Education: Roundhay High School for Girls, Leeds; Bradford Technical College (pharmacy).

Non-political career: Pharmaceutical dispenser 1952-65; Organiser, Pioneer Women 1965; Clerical worker 1966-69; Labour Party 1969-93: Assistant regional organiser 1969-75, Assistant national agent and chief women's officer 1975-85, Director of organisation 1985-93. Member: TGWU, GMW.

LABOUR

Political career: *House of Lords:* Raised to the peerage as Baroness Gould of Potternewton, of Leeds in the County of West Yorkshire 1993. Opposition Whip 1994-97; Opposition Spokesperson for: Citizen's Charter 1994-96, Women 1996-97; Government Whip 1997; Deputy Chair of Committees 2002-12; Deputy Speaker 2002-. Member: Finance and Staffing 1994-97, EU Sub-committee C (Environmental Affairs) 1994-97, Constitution 2001-05, Speakership of the House 2003, Standing Orders (Private Bills) 2005-, Refreshment 2005-08, 2012-, Procedure 2008-12, 2012-13, HIV and AIDS in the UK 2010-11, Inquiries Act 2005 2013-. Vice-chair: Labour Party Departmental Committee/Group for Women 2001-06, 2011-, Labour Party Departmental Committee Office of the Deputy Prime Minister 2003-04, 2004-07. *Other:* Member: Regional Women's Advisory Committee 1960-69, National Labour Women's Committee 1960-69, Plant Committee on Electoral Systems 1990-92; Chair, Computing for Labour 1993-2002; Member: Labour Electoral Reform Association, Bevan Society, Labour, Arts and Heritage. *Councils and public bodies:*

Member: Jenkins Commission 1977-98, Commission on Conduct of Referendums 1990-94, Independent Commission on Electoral System 1997-98; Vice-chair and executive member, Hansard Society 1999-2007; Council member, Constitution Unit 2001-07; Chair: Independent Advisory Group on Sexual Health and HIV 2003-10, Women's National Commission 2007-10; Co-Chair, Sexual Health Forum, Department of Health 2011-.

Political interests: Women's equality, constitutional affairs, electoral affairs, race relations, population and development, disabled, sexual health; Bulgaria, China, USA.

Other: Vice-President, Socialist International Women 1978-85; Member: Inter-Parliamentary Union 1993-, Commonwealth Parliamentary Association 1993-; Member, secretary several anti-racist, women's and civil liberties bodies 1965-85; Member Fawcett Society; Fabian Society: Member, President Brighton and Hove branch; President and Trustee, Mary MacArthur Holiday Trust 1993-2007; Fellow, Industry and Parliamentary Trust 1996, 2001; Epilepsy Action: President 1996-2008, Honorary life member; Chair, H Chapman Society 1999-; Patron: Brighton and Hove Women's Centre 1999-, Forward 2000-; Vice-President, Speakability 2000-; President, fpa (formerly Family Planning Association) 2000-; Patron: Yorkshire MESMAC (gay and bisexual men's health charity) 2008-, Sussex Beacon, HIVsport; Trustee, Brighton and Hove Age UK 2011-; Industry Parliament Trust; British Association for Sexual Health and HIV; Faculty for Reproductive Health; Brighton and South Downs Women's Refuge; Red Card Appeal. Honorary Doctorate, Bradford University 1997; Honorary Fellow: Faculty of Sexual and Reproductive Healthcare (RCOG) 2006, British Association for Sexual Health and HIV 2007; Honorary Doctorates: Birmingham City University 2009, Greenwich University 2012. Health Champion Award, Charity Champion Awards 2007.

Publications: Editor, Include Women and Health (1989); Pamphlets on feminism, socialism and sexism, women's right to work, violence in society; Articles and reports on women's rights, electoral systems.

Recreations: Theatre, cinema, reading.

The Baroness Gould of Potternewton, House of Lords, London SW1A 0PW
Tel: 020 7219 3138 *Fax:* 020 7219 1372 *Email:* gouldj@parliament.uk

LABOUR

GRABINER, LORD

GRABINER (Life Baron), Anthony Stephen Grabiner; cr. 1999. Born 21 March 1945; Son of late Ralph and Freda Grabiner, née Cohen; Married Jane Portnoy 1983 (3 sons 1 daughter).

Education: Central Foundation Boys' Grammar School, London; London School of Economics (LLB 1966; LLM 1967); Lincoln's Inn (Hardwicke Scholar 1966, Droop Scholar 1968).

Non-political career: Called to the Bar, Lincoln's Inn 1968; Standing Junior Counsel to Department of Trade, Export Credits Guarantee Department 1976-81; Junior Counsel to the Crown 1978-81; QC 1981; Bencher 1989; Recorder of the Crown Court 1990-99; Deputy High Court Judge 1994-; Non-executive director, Next plc 2002; Non-executive chair, Arcadia Group Limited 2002-; Bank of England Financial Services Law Committee 2002-05.

Political career: *House of Lords:* Raised to the peerage as Baron Grabiner, of Aldwych in the City of Westminster 1999. Member Religious Offences 2002-03; Co-opted member European Union Sub-committee E (Law and Institutions) 2003-06; Member Joint Committee on Privacy and Injunctions 2011-12.

Political interests: Law reform, commercial and company law, city, pensions, higher education.

Other: Chair: Court of Governors, LSE 1998-, Management and Standards Committee, News Corporation 2011-; Garrick. Brocket Hall Golf; Non-executive director Wentworth Golf Club 2005-.

Publications: Co-editor, Sutton and Shannon on Contract (7th edition, 1970); The Informal Economy (Report to Chancellor of the Exchequer, March 2000).

Recreations: Golf, theatre, reading.

The Lord Grabiner QC, House of Lords, London SW1A 0PW
Tel: 020 7219 5353
1 Essex Court, Temple, London EC4Y 9AR *Tel:* 020 7583 2000 *Fax:* 020 7583 0118
Email: agrabiner@oeclaw.co.uk

Need additional copies?
Call 020 7593 5679
Visit www.dodsshop.co.uk

CONSERVATIVE

GRADE OF YARMOUTH, LORD

GRADE OF YARMOUTH (Life Baron), Michael Ian Grade; cr 2011. Born 8 March 1943; Son of Leslie Grade; Married Penelope Levinson 1967 (divorced 1981) (1 son 1 daughter); married Hon Sarah Lawson 1982 (divorced 1991); Married Francesca Leahy 1998 (1 son).

Education: St Dunstan's College, London; French.

Non-political career: *Daily Mirror*: Trainee journalist 1960s, Sports columnist 1964-66; Theatrical agent, Grade Organisation 1966; London Management and Representation: Joint managing director -1973, Deputy controller of programmes (entertainment), London Weekend Television 1973; Director of programmes 1977-81; President, Embassy Television 1981-84; Controller, BBC1 1984-86; Director of programmes, BBC TV 1986-87; Chief executive, Channel Four 1988-97; Director: ITN 1989-93, Delfont Macintosh Theatres Ltd 1994-99, Charlton Athletic FC 1997-, New Millennium Experience Co. 1997-2001; Chair, Pinewood-Shepperton plc 2000-; Camelot Group: Director 2000-04, Chair 2002-04; Director: Reel Enterprises Ltd 2002-04, SMG 2003-04, Television Corporation 2003-04; Chair, Ocado 2006-13; Executive chair and chief executive, ITV 2007-09; Chair, James Grant Group 2010-12; Director, WRG Group 2011-.

Political career: *House of Lords:* Raised to the peerage as Baron Grade of Yarmouth, of Yarmouth in the County of Isle of Wight 2011. Member: Joint Committee on the Draft Defamation Bill 2011, Small- and Medium-Sized Enterprises 2012-13. *Councils and public bodies:* Chairman, Fear of Crime Working Group 1989; Member, National Committee of Inquiry into Prevention of Child Abuse 1994-96; Chairman: Index on Censorship 2000-04, Board of Governors, BBC 2004-06; Member, Panel on Fair Access to the Professions 2009; Lay member, Press Complaints Commission; Trustee, Science Museum Group.

Political interests: Media, arts, business.

Other: Council member: LAMDA 1981-93, RADA 1996-2004; BAFTA: Council member 1981-82, 1986-88, Fellowship 1994, Vice-President 2004-; Member, British Screen Advisory Council 1986-97; Fellow, Royal Television Society 1991; Council member, Royal Albert Hall 1997-2004; Chair advisory board, National Media Museum; BAFTA 1994; The Healing Foundation; Samaritans; Royal National Lifeboat Institute; Tall Ships Trust. Honorary Professor, Thames Valley University (1994); Honorary LLD, Nottingham University (1997). CBE 1998. Royal Thames Yacht Club; Royal Solent Yacht Club.

Publications: It Seemed Like a Good Idea at the Time (autobiography, 1999).

Recreations: Sailing, theatre, opera, cricket.

The Lord Grade of Yarmouth CBE, House of Lords, London SW1A 0PW
Tel: 020 7219 5353
c/o Pagefield, The Old Courtyard, 18 Marshall Street, London W1F 7BE *Tel:* 020 3327 4102
Email: ros@mgrade.com

LAB/CO-OP

GRAHAM OF EDMONTON, LORD

GRAHAM OF EDMONTON (Life Baron), Thomas Edward Graham; cr. 1983. Born 26 March 1925; Son of Thomas Edward Graham; Married Margaret Golding 1950 (2 sons).

Education: Westgate Hill; WEA Co-operative College (Secretarial Diploma 1962; Managerial Diploma 1964); Open University (BA 1976).

Non-political career: Corporal, Royal Marines 1943-46. Various posts within Co-operative Movement 1939-74. Member, National Association of Co-operative Officials; Life member Prison Officers Association.

Political career: *House of Commons:* Contested Enfield West 1966 general election. MP (Labour) for Enfield, Edmonton 1974-83. PPS to Alan Williams as Minister of State, Department of Prices and Consumer Affairs 1974-76; Government Whip 1976-79; Opposition Whip 1979-81; Opposition Spokesperson for the Environment 1981-83. Member, Refreshments Committee 1990-. *House of Lords:* Raised to the peerage as Baron Graham of Edmonton, of Edmonton in Greater London 1983. Opposition Spokesperson for the Environment, Northern Ireland and Defence 1983-90; Opposition Whip 1983-90; Opposition Spokesperson for National Heritage (Tourism) 1990-95; Opposition Chief Whip 1990-97; Deputy Speaker 1990-97; Deputy Chair of Committees 1997-2000. Member: Privileges/Privileges and Conduct 2000-12, Merits of Statutory Instruments 2003-05. *Other:* Member, Co-operative Party 1997-2000; Chair, Labour Peers' Group 1997-2000. *Councils and public bodies:* Councillor and Labour leader, Enfield Borough Council 1961-68; Chair, Housing and Redevelopment Committee 1961-68; President, Co-operative Congress 1987-.

Political interests: Local government, consumer affairs, environment; Israel, USA.

Other: President, Institute of Meat; Patron, Ancient Order of Foresters; Fellow: Institute of British Management, Royal Society of Arts; Senate, Open University; National Association of Co-operative Officials; Charis, deals with drug and alcohol abuse; League Against Cruel Sports. Freeman, Worshipful Company of Butchers. Freedom, London Borough of Enfield. Honorary MA Open University 1989. PC 1998.

Publications: From Tyne to Thames via the Usual Channels (2005).

Recreations: Gardening, reading, relaxing.

Rt Hon the Lord Graham of Edmonton, House of Lords, London SW1A 0PW
Tel: 020 7219 6704
2 Clerks Piece, Loughton, Essex IG10 1NR *Tel:* 020 8508 9801

GRANTCHESTER, LORD

Opposition Whip

GRANTCHESTER (3rd Baron, UK), Christopher John Suenson-Taylor; cr. 1953. Born 8 April 1951; Son of 2nd Baron, CBE, QC and Berry, née Moores; Married Jacqueline Jaffé 1973 (divorced) (2 sons 2 daughters).

Education: Winchester College; London School of Economics (BSc economics 1973).

Non-political career: Dairy farmer and cattle breeder; Director: Littlewoods Organisation various companies 1993-97, Everton Football Club Company 1994-2000, Dairy Farmers of Britain 2003-09, Cheshire and Warrington Economic Alliance 2005-10; Chairman, Cheshire County, Country Land and Business Association 2002-04.

LABOUR

Political career: *House of Lords:* First entered House of Lords 1995; Elected hereditary peer 2003-; Opposition Whip 2010-. Member: EU Sub-Committee D Agriculture, Fisheries and Food 1996-99, Hybrid Instruments 2005-.

Political interests: Rural economy, the environment, sport, Merseyside, Cheshire and the North West; China, Denmark, Japan, Taiwan.

Other: Member of the Executive Council, Cheshire Agricultural Society 1986-99; Cheshire Representative to The Royal Agricultural Society of England 1994-97; President: Western Holstein Breeders Club 1999-2000, President, Royal Association of British Dairy Farmers 2001-03; Chairman, Local Football Partnership, Liverpool County FA 2001-06; Vice President, Oulton Park Cricket Club 2006; Trustee, The Foundation for Sports and the Arts 1997-; Chairman, The Everton Collection Charitable Trust 2005-; Vice President, The Wingate Special Children's Trust 2008.

Recreations: Sport (football, cricket, tennis); Everton Cricket Club; Oulton Park Cricket Club; countryside and gardens; the arts.

The Lord Grantchester, House of Lords, London SW1A 0PW
Tel: 020 7219 5421 *Fax:* 020 7219 5979 *Email:* grantchesterj@parliament.uk
Email: barbara@grantchesterfarms.co.uk

GREAVES, LORD

GREAVES (Life Baron), Anthony Robert Greaves; cr. 2000. Born 27 July 1942; Son of late Geoffrey Lawrence and Moyra Louise Greaves; Married Heather Ann Baxter 1968 (2 daughters).

Education: Queen Elizabeth Grammar School, Wakefield; Hertford College, Oxford (BA geography 1963).

Non-political career: Teacher; Lecturer; Organising secretary, Association of Liberal Councillors 1977-85; Manager, Liberal Party Publications 1985-90; Book dealer.

LIBERAL DEMOCRAT

Political career: *House of Commons:* Contested Nelson and Colne February and October 1974 and Pendle 1997 general elections. Member, Liberal Democrat Federal Policy Committee. *House of Lords:* Raised to the peerage as Baron Greaves, of Pendle in the County of Lancashire 2000. Liberal Democrat Spokesperson for: Environment, Food and Rural Affairs 2001-03, Deputy Prime Minister, Regional and Local Government 2003, Environment, Food and Rural Affairs 2005-10, Communities and Local Government 2007-10. Member: Standing Orders (Private Bills) 2000-05, Personal Bills 2005-09; Co-opted member European Union Sub-committee D (Environment and Agriculture) 2006-08. Chair, Liberal Democrat Parliamentary Party Committee on Energy and Climate Change; Environment, Food and Rural Affairs (Environment, Food and Rural Affairs) 2010-12. *Councils and public bodies:* Councillor: Colne Borough Council 1971-74, Pendle Borough Council 1973-92, 1994-98, 2004-, Lancashire County Council 1973-97; Vice-President, Local Government Association 2011-.

Political interests: Local government and democracy, environment, railways, elections, human rights, asylum seekers and refugees, countryside access; Bosnia-Herzegovina, Croatia, France.

Publications: Co-author, Merger: The Inside Story (1989).

Recreations: Climbing, mountaineering, botany, cycling.

The Lord Greaves, House of Lords, London SW1A 0PW
Tel: 020 7219 8620 *Email:* greavesa@parliament.uk
3 Hartington Street, Winewall, Colne, Lancashire BB8 8DB *Tel:* 01282 864346

CONSERVATIVE

GREEN OF HURSTPIERPOINT, LORD

Minister of State for Trade and Investment and Government Spokesperson, Department for Business, Innovation and Skills and Foreign and Commonwealth Office

GREEN OF HURSTPIERPOINT (Life Baron), Stephen Keith Green; cr 2010. Born 7 November 1948; Son of late Dudley and Rosamund Green; Married Janian Joy (1971) (2 daughters).

Education: Lancing College, West Sussex; Exeter College, Oxford (BA philosophy, politics and economics); Massachusetts Institute of Technology, USA (MSc political science); French, German.

Non-political career: Overseas Development Agency 1970-77; Foreign and Commonwealth Office; McKinsey & Co Inc. 1977-82; HSBC plc 1982-2010: Chief executive officer, Group Chairman 2006-10; Ordained deacon 1987; Priest 1988; Member, board of directors, BASF 2009-10.

Political career: *House of Lords:* Raised to the peerage as Baron Green of Hurstpierpoint, of Hurstpierpoint in the County of West Sussex 2010. Minister of State for Trade and Investment and Government Spokesperson, Department for Business, Innovation and Skills and Foreign and Commonwealth Office 2011-.

Countries of interest: France, Germany.

Other: Trustee, Archbishop of Canterbury's Anglican Communion Fund.

Publications: Serving God? Serving Mammon? (1996); Good Value: reflections on money, morality and an uncertain world (2009).

Recreations: Art, European literature, opera.

The Lord Green of Hurstpierpoint, House of Lords, London SW1A 0PW
Tel: 020 7219 5353

CROSSBENCH

GREENFIELD, BARONESS

GREENFIELD (Life Baroness) Professor Susan Adele Greenfield; cr 2001. Born 1 October 1950; Daughter of Reginald Greenfield and Doris Thorpe; Married Professor Peter Atkins 1991 (divorced 2003).

Education: Godolphin and Latymer Girls' School, London; St Hilda's College, Oxford (BA experimental psychology 1973, MA; DPhil pharmacology 1977); French.

Non-political career: Travelling scholarship to Israel ('Bridge in Britain') 1970; Medical Research Council (MRC) research scholarship, pharmacology department, Oxford 1973-76; MRC-INSERM exchange fellowship, College de France, Paris 1979-80; Junior research fellowship, Green College, Oxford 1981-84; Lecturer in synaptic pharmacology, Oxford 1985-96; Tutorial fellowship in medicine, Lincoln College, Oxford 1985-98; Deputy director, Squibb Projects 1988-95; Gresham Chair of Physics, Gresham College, London 1995-99; Visiting fellow, Neurosciences Institute, La Jolla, USA 1995; Professor of synaptic pharmacology, Oxford University and director, Institute for the Future of the Mind 1996-; Distinguished visiting scholar, Queen's University, Belfast 1996; Senior research fellowship, Lincoln College 1998; Director: The Royal Institution of Great Britain 1998-2010, Synaptica Ltd 1998-2003, BrainBoost Ltd 2003-06, Neurodiagnostics Ltd 2004-05; Thinker in Residence, Adelaide, South Australia 2004-05; Director: Enkephala 2005-13, MindWeavers 2006-09; Chair of Innovation, Queen's University, Belfast 2006; Director: Greenfield PPS Ltd 2007-, Mind Change 2011-13.

Political career: *House of Lords:* Raised to the peerage as Baroness Greenfield, of Ot Moor in the County of Oxfordshire 2001. Member Information 2005-08. *Councils and public bodies:* Board of Governors, Weizmann Institute of Science 2004-.

Political interests: Education, women's rights; Australia, Cyprus, France, India, Israel, Middle East, South Africa.

Other: Trustee, Science Museum 1998-2003; Vice-President, Association of Woman in Science and Engineering 2001; Chair, Women in Science Group 2002; President, Classical Association 2004-05; Fellow, James Martin Institute 2004-; Editorial Board, Common Knowledge 2004-;

Trustee: 'Plants and us' Charity 2004, Carnegie Mellon University Proposal 2004, John Porter National Trust 2004, Alexandria Library, Egypt 2006; Board of Trustees, Cyprus Research Institute 2006; Fellow: Royal Society of Edinburgh 2007-, Australian Davos Connection 2007-; Trustee: Institute for Food, Brain and Behaviour (formerly National Justice) 2007-, Science for Humanities 2007-; Science Media Centre Board, Australia 2007-, Royal Institution Australia 2008-; Fellow, Science Museum 2010-; Various posts in numerous organisations, particularly in fields of neurological illnesses and promotion of science; Honorary Fellow: The College of Teachers 2001, The Royal Society of South Australia 2005, British Association for the Advancement of Science 2006; Honorary Senior Fellow, Higher Education Academy 2007; Honorary Fellow, Royal College of Physicians 2000; Senior Research Fellow: Lincoln College, Department of Pharmacology, Oxford; The Royal Institution; Alzheimer's Research UK. Chancellor, Heriot-Watt University 2005-12. 30 honorary doctorates from UK, US, Israeli and Australian universities; Honorary Fellow, St Hilda's College, Oxford 1999. Dame Catherine Fulford Senior Scholarship, St Hugh's College, Oxford 1974; J.H. Burn Trust Scholarship, pharmacology department, Oxford 1977; MRC training fellowship, physiology department, Oxford 1977-81; Royal Society study visit award, College de France, Paris 1978; Woman of Distinction of the Year (Jewish Care) 1998; The Royal Society Michael Faraday Award 1998; *Observer* Woman of the Year 2000; Golden Plate Award, American Academy of Achievement 2003; Honorary Australian of the Year 2006; The British Inspiration Award – Science and Technology 2010; Australian Society for Medical Research Medal 2010. CBE 2000; Ordre National de la Légion d'Honneur (France) 2003; The Hospital Club.

Publications: Over 170 peer-reviewed scientific papers; Co-editor, Mindwaves: Thoughts on Intelligence, Identity and Consciousness (Basil Blackwell, 1987); Co-author, Journey to the Centres of the Brain (BBC Education Publishers, 1994); Editor, The Human Mind Explained (Reader's Digest, USA; Cassell UK, 1994); Author, The Human Brain: A Guided Tour (Weidenfield & Nicolson/Basic Books, 1997, Paperback Phoenix Press, 1998); Editor, Brainpower (Ivy Press, 1999); Author: The Private Life of the Brain (Penguin, 2000), Brain Story (BBC Books, 2000), Set Fair; a report on Women in Science, Engineering and Technology to the Secretary of State for Trade and Industry (2002), Tomorrow's People (Penguin, 2003); 'ID' The Quest for Identity in the 21st Century (Hodder & Stoughton, 2008); You and Me: Neuroscience and Identity (Notting Hill Education, 2011); 2121: A Tale from the Next Century (Head of Zeus, 2013).

Recreations: Squash, dancing.

Professor the Baroness Greenfield CBE, House of Lords, London SW1A 0PW
Tel: 020 7219 6451 *Email:* greenfieldsu@parliament.uk
Department of Pharmacology, Mansfield Road, Oxford OX1 3QT *Tel:* 01865 271852
Fax: 01865 271853 *Email:* susan.greenfield@pharm.ox.ac.uk
Website: www.susangreenfield.com

CROSSBENCH

GREENGROSS, BARONESS

GREENGROSS (Life Baroness), Sally Ralea Greengross; cr. 2000. Born 29 June 1935; Married Sir Alan Greengross 1959 (1 son 3 daughters).

Education: Brighton and Hove High School; London School of Economics (BA 1972); French, Spanish.

Non-political career: Formerly a linguist, executive in industry, lecturer and researcher; Age Concern England: Assistant director 1977-82, Deputy director 1982-87, Director-General (formerly director) 1987-2000; International Federation on Ageing: Secretary General 1982-87, Vice-President (Europe) 1987-2001; Joint chair, Age Concern Institute of Gerontology, King's College London 1987-2000; Chair, Experience Corps 2001-04; International Longevity Centre UK: Executive chair 2000-04, Chief executive 2004-; Co-president, ILC Global Alliance 2010-.

Political career: *House of Lords:* Raised to the peerage as Baroness Greengross, of Notting Hill in the Royal Borough of Kensington and Chelsea 2000. Co-opted member European Union Sub-committee F (Social Affairs, Education and Home Affairs) 2000-03; Member: European Union Sub-committee G (Social Policy and Consumer Affairs) 2003-07, Joint Committee on the Draft Care and Support Bill 2013. *Councils and public bodies:* Commissioner, Equality and Human Rights Commission 2006-; Vice-President, Local Government Association 2010-.

Other: Independent member, UN and WHO Networks on Ageing 1983-2000; Member, advisory council, European Movement 1992-; Vice-chair, Britain in Europe 2000-; Past and current member several advisory bodies concerned with the elderly; Founder and patron, Action on Elder Abuse 1994-; Vice-President, EXTEND 1996; Patron, Family Planning Association; President, Pensions Policy Institute; Royal Society for Public Health; Royal Society of Medicine; FRSH 1994; FRSA 1994; Patron to various charities. Eight honorary doctorates. UK Woman of Europe 1990. OBE 1993; Hurlingham; Reform.

Publications: Consultant, Journal of Educational Gerontology 1987-; Editor, Ageing: an adventure in living (1985); Has edited and contributed to other publications on ageing issues and social policy.

Recreations: Countryside, music.

The Baroness Greengross OBE, House of Lords, London SW1A 0PW

Tel: 020 7219 5494 *Email:* greengrosss@parliament.uk

GREENWAY, LORD

GREENWAY (4th Baron, UK), Ambrose Charles Drexel Greenway; cr. 1927; 4th Bt of Stanbridge Earls (UK) 1919. Born 21 May 1941; Son of 3rd Baron; Married Rosalynne Peta Schenk, née Fradgley 1985.

Education: Winchester College; Working French and German.

Non-political career: Marine photographer; Shipping consultant.

Political career: *House of Lords:* First entered House of Lords 1975; Elected hereditary peer 1999-. Member Statutory Instruments Joint Committee 2000-07.

CROSSBENCH   **Political interests:** Shipping, marine industry.

Other: Trinity House: Younger Brother 1987, Elder Brother 2007; Chair, The Marine Society 1994-2000; Vice-President, Sail Training Association 1995-2004; President, Cruise Europe 1996-2003; Chair, The World Ship Trust 2003-13; Honorary Fellow: Institute of Marine Engineering, Science and Technology, Nautical Institute; Mission to Seafarers; RNLI; Tall Ships Youth Trust; House of Lords Yacht.

Publications: Soviet Merchant Ships (1976); Comecon Merchant Ships (1978); A Century of Cross-Channel Passenger Ferries (1981); A Century of North Sea Passenger Steamers (1986); Cargo Liners (2009).

Recreations: Sailing, swimming.

The Lord Greenway, House of Lords, London SW1A 0PW

Tel: 020 7219 4943 *Email:* greenwaya@parliament.uk

GRENDER, BARONESS

GRENDER (Life Baroness), Rosalind (Olly) Grender; cr 2013.

Non-political career: Political co-ordinator and director for special projects to Lord Ashdown of Norton-sub-Hamdon as Chair of the Liberal Democrat's 2015 general election campaign 2012-.

Political career: *House of Lords:* Raised to the peerage as Baroness Grender, of Kingston upon Thames, in the London Borough of Kingston upon Thames 2013.

Other: MBE.

The Baroness Grender MBE, House of Lords, London SW1A 0PW

LIBERAL DEMOCRAT   *Tel:* 020 7219 5353

GRENFELL, LORD

GRENFELL (3rd Baron, UK), Julian Pascoe Francis St Leger Grenfell; cr. 1902; (Life) Baron Grenfell of Kilvey 2000. Born 23 May 1935; Son of 2nd Baron, CBE, TD; Married Loretta Reali 1961 (divorced 1970) (1 daughter); married Gabrielle Raab 1970 (divorced 1987) (2 daughters); married Mrs Elizabeth Porter 1987 (divorced 1992); married Dagmar Debreil, née Langbehn, 1993.

Education: Eton College; King's College, Cambridge (BA law 1959) (Union President 1959); French, German, Italian.

Non-political career: 2nd Lieutenant, KRRC (60th Rifles) 1954-56; Captain, Queen's Royal

LABOUR   Rifles, TA 1963. Television reporter, ATV Ltd 1960-63; World Bank 1965-95: Washington DC 1965-69, Paris 1969-74; Representative of World Bank to United Nations 1974-81; Senior adviser, Washington, DC 1983-90; Head of external affairs, European Office 1990-95.

Political career: *House of Lords:* Created a life peer as Baron Grenfell of Kilvey, of Kilvey in the County of Swansea 2000. First entered House of Lords 1976; Principal Deputy Chairman of Committees 2002-08; Deputy Speaker 2002-08; Contested Lord Speaker election 2006. European Union: Member 1999, 2000-08, Chair 2002-08; Procedure: Member 2003-07, Alternate member 2013-.

Political interests: European affairs, constitutional reform; Belgium, Croatia, France, Germany, Italy, Slovenia.

Other: Member, UK Delegation to Parliamentary Assemblies of Council of Europe and Western European Union 1997-99; President Anglo-Belgian Society of the UK. Chevalier de la Légion d'Honneur (France) 2005; Commander, Cross of the Order of Merit (Germany) 2008; Commander, Order of the Crown (Belgium) 2009; Royal Green Jackets.

Publications: Novels: Margot (1987), The Gazelle (2004).

Recreations: European history, writing fiction.

The Lord Grenfell, House of Lords, London SW1A 0PW
Tel: 020 7219 3601 *Email:* grenfellj@parliament.uk

GREY-THOMPSON, BARONESS

GREY-THOMPSON (Life Baroness), Tanni (Carys Davina) Grey-Thompson; cr 2010. Born 26 July 1969; Daughter of Peter Grey and Sulwen Grey, née Jones; Married Dr Ian Thompson 1999 (1 daughter).

Education: St Cyres School, Penarth; Loughborough University (BA politics and administration 1991).

Non-political career: Athlete; Development officer, UK Athletics 1996-2000; Director, Tanni Grey-Thompson Ltd; Board member: TfL 2008-, London Legacy Development Corporation 2012-.

CROSSBENCH

Political career: *House of Lords:* Raised to the peerage as Baroness Grey-Thompson, of Eaglescliffe in the County of Durham 2010. *Councils and public bodies:* Member: Sports Council for Wales 1996-2002, UK Sport 1998-2003; Board member, TfL 2008-; London Legacy Development Corporation 2013-.

Political interests: Sport, women's issues, disability rights; Developing countries.

Other: Council member, Winston Churchill Memorial Trust 2006-; Trustee and vice-chair, Laureus Sport for Good Foundation; Chair, Commission of the Future of Women's Sport; Non-executive director, UK Athletics 2007-12; Board member, London Marathon 2007-; President, Sports Leaders UK; Ambassador, International Inspiration; Trustee: Jane Tomlinson Trust, Tony Blair Sports Foundation, Snowdon Award Scheme 2012-; President, National Council for Voluntary Organisations; Member, executive committee, British Wheelchair Sports Foundation; Trustee: Spirit of 2012 Trust, Wembley National Stadium Trust; Trustee, V Charity. Freedom: City of Cardiff, Borough of Redcar and Cleveland. Pro-chancellor, Staffordshire University 2005. 27 honorary degrees. Bronze 400m medal Seoul Paralympics 1988; Gold 100m, 200m, 400m, 800m medals Barcelona Paralympics 1992; Gold 800m and Silver 100m, 200m, 400m medals Atlanta Paralympics 1996; Gold 100m, 200m, 400m, 800m medals Sydney Paralympics 2000; Gold 100m, 400m medals Athens Paralympics 2004. MBE 1993; OBE 2000; DBE 2005. Cardiff Amateur Athletics Club; New Marske Harriers; Cleveland Wheelers Cycling Club.

Publications: Seize the Day (autobiography, 2001); Aim High (2007).

Recreations: Handcycling, wheelchair sports.

The Baroness Grey-Thompson DBE, House of Lords, London SW1A 0PW
Tel: 020 7219 3143 *Email:* greythompsont@parliament.uk
Website: www.tanni.co.uk lordsoftheblog.net/category/baroness-grey-thompson
Twitter: @Tanni_GT

GRIFFITHS, LORD

GRIFFITHS (Life Baron), (William) Hugh Griffiths; cr. 1985. Born 26 September 1923; Son of late Sir Hugh Griffiths, CBE; Married Evelyn Krefting 1949 (died 1998) (1 son 3 daughters); married Baroness Brigstocke 2000 (died 2004); married Mrs Greta Fenston 2009.

Education: Charterhouse, Surrey; St John's College, Cambridge.

Non-political career: Commissioned Welsh Guards 1942. Called to the Bar, Inner Temple 1949; QC 1964; Recorder of: Margate 1962-64, Cambridge 1964-70; Judge of the High Court of Justice, Queen's Bench Division 1971-80; Lord Justice of Appeal 1980-85.

CROSSBENCH

Political career: *House of Lords:* Raised to the peerage as Baron Griffiths, of Govilon in the County of Gwent 1985. Lord of Appeal in Ordinary 1985-93; On leave of absence June 2012-. *Councils and public bodies:* Chair, Security Commission 1985-92.

Other: Honorary Member, Canadian Bar Association 1981; Honorary Fellow, American Institute of Judicial Administration 1985; American College of Trial Lawyers 1988; President, Bar Association for Commerce, Finance and Industry; Chairman, The Thalidomide Trust 1981-97. Hon LLD: University of Wales 1987; De Montfort University 1993. MC 1944; Kt 1971; PC 1980; Garrick, MCC (President 1990), Royal and Ancient (St Andrews) (Captain 1993).

Recreations: Golf, cricket, fishing.

Rt Hon the Lord Griffiths MC, House of Lords, London SW1A 0PW
Tel: 020 7219 5353

LABOUR

GRIFFITHS OF BURRY PORT, LORD

GRIFFITHS OF BURRY PORT (Life Baron), Leslie John Griffiths; cr. 2004. Born 15 February 1942; Son of Olwen Griffiths, née Thomas, and Sidney Griffiths; Married Margaret Rhodes 1969 (1 daughter 2 sons).

Education: Llanelli Grammar School; University College of Wales, Cardiff (BA medieval English 1963); Fitzwilliam College, Cambridge (MA theology 1969); School of Oriental and African Studies, London University (PhD 1987); French, Haitian Créole.

Non-political career: Assistant lecturer in English, University of Wales 1964-67; Methodist minister: Port-au-Prince, Haiti 1970-74, Reading, Berkshire 1974-77, Cap Haitien, Haiti 1997-80, Loughton, Essex 1980-86, West London Mission 1986-91; President Methodist Conference 1994-95; Methodist minister, Wesley's Chapel, City of London 1996-; Canon, St Paul's Cathedral 2000-. Member Association of University Teachers 1964-67.

Political career: *House of Lords:* Raised to the peerage as Baron Griffiths of Burry Port, of Pembrey and Burry Port in the County of Dyfed 2004. Member Ecclesiastical Committee 2010-.

Political interests: Education, international affairs, urban affairs, ethical issues; Cambodia, Dominican Republic, Fiji, Ghana, Haiti.

Other: Addiction Recovery Foundation 1989-2004, Patron 2004-; Christian Aid 1991-99; Birnbeck Housing Association 1991-96; Trustee, Sir Halley Stewart Trust 1999-; Art and Christianity Enquiry 1999-2008; Wesley House, Cambridge 2001-05; Central Foundation Schools of London 2002-; Abraham Path Initiative; Chairman, Central Foundation Schools of London; President, Boys' Brigade; Paul Harris fellow, Rotary International 2008; Associate member, Learned Society of Wales; Christian Aid; Shelter. Freedom of the City of London 1997. Fellow: Sarum College, Salisbury 2001, Sion College 2003, Cardiff University 2005, University of Wales, Lampeter 2006. Knight of the order of St John of Jerusalem 1989; Office of the order of Christopher Columbus (Dominican Republic) 2011; Graduate Centre, Cambridge.

Publications: History of Haitian Methodism (1991); Letters Home (Methodist Publishing House, 1995); The Aristide Factor (1996); Worship in Our Diverse World (1998); Voices from the Desert (Canterbury Press, 2003); World Without End? (Epworth Press, 2007); A View from the Edge (Continuum, 2010).

Recreations: Cricket, rugby union, the post-colonial world, poetry.

The Lord Griffiths of Burry Port, House of Lords, London SW1A 0PW
Tel: 020 7219 5353 *Email:* griffithslj@parliament.uk
Wesley's Chapel, 49 City Road, London EC1Y 1AU *Tel:* 020 7253 2262/020 7490 1820
Fax: 020 7608 3825 *Email:* superintendent@wesleyschapel.org.uk
Website: www.wesleyschapel.org.uk

CONSERVATIVE

GRIFFITHS OF FFORESTFACH, LORD

GRIFFITHS OF FFORESTFACH (Life Baron), Brian Griffiths; cr. 1991. Born 27 December 1941; Son of Ivor and Phyllis Griffiths; Married Rachel Jones 1965 (1 son 2 daughters).

Education: Dynevor Grammar School; London School of Economics (BScEcon 1963; MScEcon 1965).

Non-political career: Lecturer in economics, London School of Economics 1965-76; Professor of banking and Director of Centre, Banking and International Finance, City University 1977-82; Dean, Business School The City University 1982-85; Director, Bank of England 1983-85; Head, Prime Minister's Policy Unit and special adviser to Margaret Thatcher 1985-90; Director: Thorn EMI 1990-96, Herman Miller Inc. 1991-2011, Times Newspapers Ltd 1991-; International adviser, Goldman Sachs 1991-; Vice-chair, Goldman Sachs (International) 1991-; Director: Servicemaster 1992-2007, HTV 1992-93, Telewest 1995-98, English, Welsh, Scottish Railway 1996-2007; Chair: Trillium 1998-2000, Westminster Health Care 1999-2002, Trillium Land Securities 2000-08; Adviser, Telereal Trillium 2009-.

Political career: *House of Lords:* Raised to the peerage as Baron Griffiths of Fforestfach, of Fforestfach in the County of West Glamorgan 1991. Member: European Union Sub-committee F (Social Affairs, Education and Home Affairs) 1999-2003, Religious Offences 2002-03, Economic Affairs 2007-10, Economic Affairs Finance Bill Sub-Committee 2011, Public Service and Demographic Change 2012-13, Sub-committee on Economic Affairs Finance Bill 2012-, Economic Affairs 2013-. *Other:* Chairman, Centre for Policy Studies 1991-2001; Member, board of directors Conservative Christian Fellowship 2000-02. *Councils and public bodies:* Chair, Schools Examinations and Assessment Council 1991-93.

Political interests: Economic policy, education, broadcasting, social policy; China, Eastern and Central Europe.

Other: Freeman, City of London. Two honorary doctorates: The City University, University of Wales; University of Richmond; Fellow: Trinity College, Carmarthen 1996, Swansea Institute of Higher Education 2003, Swansea University 2006; Garrick.

Publications: Several books on economics including: The Creation of Wealth (1984); Morality and the Market Place (1989).

The Lord Griffiths of Fforestfach, House of Lords, London SW1A 0PW
Tel: 020 7219 5353

GROCOTT, LORD

GROCOTT (Life Baron), Bruce Joseph Grocott; cr. 2001. Born 1 November 1940; Son of late Reginald and Helen Grocott; Married Sally Ridgway 1965 (2 sons).

Education: Hemel Hempstead Grammar School; Leicester University (BA politics 1962); Manchester University (MA economics 1966).

Non-political career: Administrative officer, London County Council 1963-64; Tutor in politics, Manchester University 1964-65; Lecturer then senior lecturer in politics, Birmingham Polytechnic 1965-72; Principal lecturer, North Staffs Polytechnic 1972-74; Presenter then producer, Central Television 1979-87. Member: National Union of Journalists, Unite.

LABOUR

Political career: *House of Commons:* Contested South West Hertfordshire 1970 and Lichfield and Tamworth February 1974 general elections. MP (Labour) for Lichfield and Tamworth October 1974-79. Contested Lichfield and Tamworth 1979 and The Wrekin 1983 general elections. MP for The Wrekin 1987-97, for Telford 1997-2001. PPS to John Silkin: as Minister for Planning and Local Government 1975-76, as Minister of Agriculture 1976-78; Deputy Shadow Leader of the House and Deputy Campaigns Co-ordinator 1987-92; Opposition Frontbench Spokesperson for Foreign and Commonwealth Affairs 1992-93; PPS to Tony Blair: as Leader of the Labour Party 1994-2001, as Prime Minister 1997-2001. *House of Lords:* Raised to the peerage as Baron Grocott, of Telford in the County of Shropshire 2001. Government Spokesperson for: Defence 2001-02, Foreign and Commonwealth Office 2001-02, International Development 2001-02, Work and Pensions 2001-02; Government Whip 2001-02; Chief Whip 2002-08; Deputy Chair of Committees 2002-08; Deputy Speaker 2002-08. Member: Privileges 2002-08, Procedure 2002-08, Selection 2002-08, House of Lords' Offices Administration and Works Sub-committee 2002-08, Refreshment 2003-05, Communications 2008, Leader's Group on the Working Practices of the House of Lords 2010-11. *Councils and public bodies:* Councillor, Bromsgrove Urban District Council 1971-74.

Political interests: Foreign affairs, media, health service, machinery of government; Angola.

Other: Chairman, Hansard Society 2012-; Governor, Birmingham City University. Chancellor, Leicester University 2013-. Honorary Doctorates: Birmingham City University 2006, Leicester University 2011. PC 2002; Trench Labour.

Recreations: Steam railways, sport.

Rt Hon the Lord Grocott, House of Lords, London SW1A 0PW
Tel: 020 7219 5058 *Email:* grocottb@parliament.uk

GUTHRIE OF CRAIGIEBANK, LORD

GUTHRIE OF CRAIGIEBANK (Life Baron), Charles Ronald Llewelyn Guthrie GCB LVO OBE; cr 2001. Born 17 November 1938; Son of Ronald Guthrie and Nina Guthrie, née Llewelyn; Married Catherine Worrall 1971 (2 sons).

Education: Harrow School; RMA Sandhurst; Royal Military Academy, Sandhurst (Commission 1959).

Non-political career: Colonel, The Life Guards and Gold Stick, SAS 2001-10. 2nd lieutenant to captain, Welsh Guards 1959-65; Captain, 22 Special Air Service 1965-69; Lieutenant colonel, Welsh Guards 1977-80; Brigadier, 4th Armoured Brigade 1982-84; Major General, 2 Infantry Division 1986-87; Lieutenant General, 1 (BR) Corps 1987-91; Commander-in-chief, British Army of the Rhine 1992-94; Ministry of Defence: Chief of the General Staff 1994-97, Chief of the Defence Staff 1997-2001; Non-executive director: Sciens Capital, Petropavlovsk plc, Colt Defense (US); Consultant, NM Rothschild 2001-10; Gulf Keystone Petroleum; Petropavlovsk.

CROSSBENCH

Political career: *House of Lords:* Raised to the peerage as Baron Guthrie of Craigiebank, of Craigiebank in the City of Dundee 2001. *Councils and public bodies:* DL 2008.

Political interests: Defence, international relations, youth, medical ethics; India, Oman, Pakistan, Russia.

Other: International Institute of Strategic Studies; Institute of Strategic Dialogue; President: Federation of London Youth Clubs, Action Medical Research, Progressive Supranuclear Palsy Association; Chair: Hospital of St John and St Elizabeth, Advisory board, London School of Hygiene and Tropical Medicine; King's College London: Visiting Professor 2001-, Fellow 2002; Board member, Moscow School of Political Studies; Honorary Fellow, Kings College; Honorary Bencher, Middle Temple; Honorary Fellow, Cranfield; St Johns Hospice; Army Benevolent Fund; London Ferderation of Youth Clubs. Painter Stainers. City of London. Liverpool Hope University. LVO 1977; OBE 1980; KCB 1990; GCB 1994; Commander Legion of Merit (USA) 2001; White's. All-England Lawn Tennis.

Publications: Co-author, Just War (Bloomsbury, 2007).

Recreations: Tennis, opera, travel.

Field Marshal the Lord Guthrie of Craigiebank GCB LVO OBE, House of Lords, London SW1A 0PW
Tel: 020 7219 5353 *Email:* crlguthrie@gmail.com

HALE OF RICHMOND, BARONESS

HALE OF RICHMOND (Life Baroness), Brenda Marjorie Hale; cr. 2004. Born 31 January 1945; Daughter of Cecil Hale and Marjorie Hale, née Godfrey; Married Anthony Hoggett 1968 (divorced 1992) (1 daughter); married Dr Julian Farrand QC 1992 (1 stepson 2 stepdaughters).

Education: Richmond High School for Girls, Yorkshire; Girton College, Cambridge (BA law 1966, MA 1969); Gray's Inn (Barrister 1969).

Non-political career: Manchester University law faculty 1966-89: Assistant lecturer, Lecturer, Senior lecturer, Reader, Professor; Barrister 1969-1972; On leave 1984-89; Commissioner, Law Commission 1984-93; QC 1989; High Court judge 1994-99; Lord Justice of Appeal 1999-2004; Visitor, Girton College, Cambridge 2004-; Supreme Court of the United Kingdom: Justice 2009-13, Deputy President 2013-.

NON-AFFILIATED

Political career: *House of Lords:* Raised to the peerage as Baroness Hale of Richmond, of Easby in the County of North Yorkshire 2004. Lord of Appeal in Ordinary 2004-09; Disqualified from participation: As Justice of the Supreme Court 2009-13, Deputy President 2013-. *Councils and public bodies:* Member, Council on Tribunals 1980-84; Chair then President, National Family Mediation 1989-; Governor, Centre for Policy on Ageing 1990-93; Member: Human Fertilisation and Embryology Authority 1990-93, Judicial Studies Board, Civil and Family Committee 1990-94; Chair, Royal Courts of Justice Advice Bureau 2001-03.

Other: Managing trustee, Nuffield Foundation 1987-2002; Patron: Richmond Open Spaces Appeal 2004-, Hammersmith and Fulham Law Centre 2010-; President: Association of Women Barristers 1997-2005; UK Association of Women Judges 2003-; International Association of Women Judges: President-elect 2008-10, President 2010-12. Fellmongers Company of Richmond, North Yorkshire. Chancellor, Bristol University 2004-. 20 honorary law doctorates Honorary FBA Honorary FRC Psych. DBE 1994; PC 1999; Athenæum.

Publications: Women and the Law (Blackwell, 1984); Parents and Children (Sweet and Maxwell, 4th edition 1993); From the Test Tube to the Coffin (Stevens, 1996); The Family, Law and Society (Butterworth, 6th edition 2008); Mental Health Law (Sweet and Maxwell, 5th edition 2010).

Recreations: Domesticity, drama, duplicate bridge.

Rt Hon the Baroness Hale of Richmond DBE, House of Lords, London SW1A 0PW
Tel: 020 7219 5353
Supreme Court of the United Kingdom, Parliament Square, London SW1P 3BD
Tel: 020 7960 1960 *Fax:* 020 7960 1961 *Email:* justices@supremecourt.gsi.gov.uk

HALL OF BIRKENHEAD, LORD

HALL OF BIRKENHEAD (Life Baron), Anthony (Tony) William Hall; cr 2010. Born 3 March 1951; Son of late Donald Hall and Mary Hall; Married Cynthia Davis 1977 (1 son 1 daughter).

Education: King Edward's School, Birmingham; Birkenhead School; Keble College, Oxford (BA philosophy, politics and economics).

Non-political career: BBC 1973-2001: News trainee 1973, Producer, *World Tonight* 1976, Senior producer, *World at One* 1978, Output editor, *Newsnight* 1980, Senior producer, *Six O'Clock News* 1984, Assistant editor, *Nine O'Clock News* 1985, Editor, news and 1987 general election 1987; News and Current Affairs Department: Editor 1988-90, Director 1990-93, Managing director 1993-96; Chief executive: BBC News 1996-2001, Royal Opera House 2001-13; Non-executive director: HM Customs and Excise 2002-05, University for Industry 2003-06, Channel 4 Television 2005-; Director-General, BBC 2013-.

CROSSBENCH

Political career: *House of Lords:* Raised to the peerage as Baron Hall of Birkenhead, of Birkenhead in the County of Cheshire 2010. *Councils and public bodies:* Chair, Creative and Culture

Skills 2004-09; Member, Olympics Cultural Advisory Board, Department for Culture, Media and Sport 2006-08; Board member, London Organising Committee of the Olympic Games 2009-13; Chair, Cultural Olympiad Board 2009-13; Mayor of London's Cultural Forum.

Political interests: Arts, culture, broadcasting, skills; China, Italy.

Other: Fellow, Royal Society of Arts 1997; Chair, Theatre Royal, Stratford 2001-09; Trustee, British Council 2008-13. Honorary DLitt, London University 2009. CBE 2006.

Recreations: Ballet, TV and radio, gardening, walking, books, opera.

The Lord Hall of Birkenhead CBE, House of Lords, London SW1A 0PW
Tel: 020 7219 5353 *Email:* halla@parliament.uk
NBH 04A Director-General's Office, BBC Broadcasting House, Portland Place, London W1A 1AA *Tel:* 020 3614 2255 *Email:* tony.hall@bbc.co.uk

HAMEED, LORD

HAMEED (Life Baron), Khalid Hameed; cr 2007. Born 1 July 1941; Son of late Professor Dr M Abdul Hameed and Rashida Abdul Hameed; Married Dr Ghazala Afzal 1989 (3 daughters 3 sons).

Education: Colvin Taluqdars College, Lucknow, India; Lucknow University (BSc, DPA, MBBS 1966); London University (Diploma tropical medicine and hygiene 1972); Hindi, Urdu.

Non-political career: Clinical assistant, University College Hospital, London; Senior house officer, St George's Hospital, London; Registrar, St Mary's Hospital, London; Private and corporate medicine, London 1980-90; Chief executive officer, Cromwell Hospital, London 1990-2005; Chair, Alpha Hospitals 2003-; Chair and Chief Executive Officer, London International Hospital 2005-.

CROSSBENCH

Political career: *House of Lords:* Raised to the peerage as Baron Hameed, of Hampstead in the London Borough of Camden 2007. *Councils and public bodies:* Chair, Commonwealth Youth Exchange Council 1997-; High Sheriff of Greater London 2006-07; DL, Greater London 2007-.

Countries of interest: Commonwealth.

Other: Parliament of the World Religions, Brussels; Chair, Woolf Institute; President, Little Foundation; Vice-President, Friends of British Library; Trustee, International Students House; Member: Royal Society of Medicine, Medical Defence Union, General Medical Council; Honorary Fellow, Royal College of Physicians; Numerous, including: Save the Children; MacMillan Cancer Research; Royal Academy School of Art; British Red Cross; MENCAP; Commonwealth Youth Exchange Council. Freeman, City of London. DSc Lucknow University 1999; Honorary Fellow, Royal College of Physicians, London 2006; Honorary doctorates: Middlesex University 2008, Metropolitan University 2009. Several awards from UK and overseas organisations and universities. Padma Shri (India) 1992; Sitare Qaide Azam (Pakistan) 1996; Hilali-Quaid-i-Azam (Pakistan) 1999; PGDB (Nepal) 1999; Order of the Burning Spear (Kenya) 2001; CBE 2004; Padma Bhushan (India) 2009; Athaeneum; Marks; Mossiman Dining Club. Member, Guards Polo Club; Life Member: MCC, Lucknow Golf Club.

Publications: Published speeches on Interfaith Harmony.

Recreations: Chess, bridge, cricket, poetry, polo.

The Lord Hameed CBE, House of Lords, London SW1A 0PW
Tel: 020 7935 5012 *Fax:* 020 7431 4867 *Email:* hameed@parliament.uk
94 Harley Street, London W1G 7HX *Tel:* 020 7935 5012 *Fax:* 020 7486 6174

HAMILTON OF EPSOM, LORD

HAMILTON OF EPSOM (Life Baron), Archibald Gavin Hamilton; cr 2005. Born 30 December 1941; Son of late 3rd Baron Hamilton of Dalzell, GCVO, MC; Married Anne Napier 1968 (3 daughters).

Education: Eton College.

Non-political career: Coldstream Guards 1960-62, Lieutenant.

Political career: *House of Commons:* Contested Dagenham February and October 1974 general elections. MP (Conservative) for Epsom and Ewell 1978 by-election to 2001. PPS to David Howell: as Secretary of State for Energy 1979-81, as Secretary of State for Transport 1981-82; Assistant Government Whip 1982-84; Government Whip 1984-86; Parliamentary Under-Secretary of State for Defence Procurement 1986-87; PPS to Margaret Thatcher as Prime Minister 1987-88; Minister of State for the Armed Forces Ministry of Defence 1988-93; Member Committee on Intelligence and Security 1994-97. 1922 Committee: Member, Executive 1995-97, Chair 1997-2001; Member, Conservative Ethics and Integrity Committee 1999. *House of Lords:* Raised to the peerage as Baron Hamilton of Epsom, of West Anstey in the County of Devon 2005. Co-opted member EU Sub-committee C (Foreign Affairs, Defence and Development Policy) 2006-10;

CONSERVATIVE

Member EU Sub-committee A: (Economic and Financial Affairs and International Trade) 2010-12, (Economic and Financial Affairs) 2012-. *Councils and public bodies:* Councillor, Royal Borough of Kensington and Chelsea 1968-71.

Political interests: Finance, tax, economic policy, trade and industry, defence.

Other: Governor, Westminster Foundation for Democracy 1993-97; Council member, National Army Museum; President, Lest We Forget. PC 1991; Knighted 1994; White's.

Rt Hon the Lord Hamilton of Epsom, House of Lords, London SW1A 0PW
Tel: 020 7219 5353

HAMWEE, BARONESS

HAMWEE (Life Baroness), Sally Rachel Hamwee; cr. 1991. Born 12 January 1947; Daughter of late Alec and Dorothy Hamwee.

Education: Manchester High School for Girls; Girton College, Cambridge (BA law 1969, MA).

Non-political career: Admitted Solicitor 1972; Clintons Solicitors: Partner 1984-2004, Consultant 2004-10.

LIBERAL DEMOCRAT

Political career: *House of Lords:* Raised to the peerage as Baroness Hamwee, of Richmond upon Thames in the London Borough of Richmond upon Thames 1991. Liberal Democrat Spokesperson for: Local Government 1991-98, Housing and Planning 1993-98, Local Government and Planning 1998-2000, Environment, Transport and the Regions 1999-2000, Local Government and the Regions 2001-04, ODPM/Communities and Local Government 2004-10: Regional and Local Government 2006-09, Home Office 2009-. Member Economic Affairs 2008-10; Alternate member Procedure 2009-; Member: Leader's Group on Code of Conduct 2009, Merits of Statutory Instruments/Secondary Legislation Scrutiny 2010-, Leader's Group on the Working Practices of the House of Lords 2010-11, Adoption Legislation 2012-13, Inquiries Act 2005 2013-. Chair, Liberal Democrat Parliamentary Party Committee on Home Affairs, Justice and Equalities (Home Office) 2010-. *Other:* Member: National Executive, Liberal Party 1987-88, Federal Executive, Liberal Democrats 1989-91, Liberal Democrat general election teams, 1992 and 1997, Federal Policy Committee 1996-98. *Councils and public bodies:* Councillor, London Borough of Richmond upon Thames 1978-98: Chair: Planning Committee 1983-94, London Planning Advisory Committee 1986-94; Joint President, Association of London Government; London Assembly: Member 2000-08, Deputy chair 2000-01, 2002-03, 2004-05, 2006-07, Chair 2001-02, 2003-04, 2005-06, 2007-08; Joint President, London Councils.

Political interests: Local government, planning, London, arts, home affairs, immigration and asylum, penal policy.

Other: Council member, Parents for Children 1977-86; Legal adviser, Simon Community 1980-; Council member, Refuge 1991-2005; Member: Joseph Rowntree Foundation Inquiry, Planning for Housing 1991, Advisory board, Compact Advocacy Advisory Group, NCVO, Family Policy Studies Centre: Governing council -2000, Council member 1994-2001; Town and Country Planning Association: President 1995-2002, Vice-president 2002-; Chair, Xfm Ltd 1996-98; Member, advisory board, Centre for Public Scrutiny 2000-; Board member: Arts Council London 2006-08, Rose Theatre Kingston 2009-; Vice-President, Chartered Institute of Environmental Health; Member, advisory board, Equality and Diversity Forum, Human Rights Project.

The Baroness Hamwee, House of Lords, London SW1A 0PW
Tel: 020 7219 5353 *Email:* hamwees@parliament.uk

HANHAM, BARONESS

Government Spokesperson, Department for Communities and Local Government

HANHAM (Life Baroness), Joan Brownlow Hanham; cr. 1999. Born 23 September 1939; Daughter of late Alfred Spark and Mary Spark, née Mitchell; Married late Dr Iain Hanham, FRCP FRCR 1964 (1 son 1 daughter).

Education: Hillcourt School, Dublin.

CONSERVATIVE

Political career: *House of Lords:* Raised to the peerage as Baroness Hanham, of Kensington in the Royal Borough of Kensington and Chelsea 1999. Opposition Whip 2000-09; Opposition Spokesperson for: Transport, Local Government and the Regions 2001-02, Local Government and the Regions 2002, Office of the Deputy Prime Minister/Communities and Local Government 2003-07, Scotland 2003-07, Transport 2005-07, Home Affairs 2007-09, Health 2007-09, Transport 2009-10; Parliamentary Under-Secretary of State 2010-13; Government Spokesperson, Department for Communities and Local Government 2010-. Member Procedure -2002. *Councils and public bodies:* Royal

Borough of Kensington and Chelsea: Councillor 1970-2011, Mayor 1983-84, Chair: Town Planning Committee 1984-86, Social Services Committee 1987-89, Policy and Resources Committee 1989-2000, Leader of the Council 1989-2000; Member, Mental Health Act Commission 1983-90; Non-executive member, North West Thames Regional Health Authority 1983-94; JP: City of London Commission 1984-2009, Inner London Family Proceedings Court 1992-2009; Governor: Sir John Cass Foundation 1996-99, Sir John Cass Primary School 1997-99; Member, Policy Committee, London Government Association 1999-2001; Chair, St Mary's Hospital NHS Trust 2000-07.

Political interests: Local government, health, justice, environment, communities and families, housing and planning; Europe, USA.

Other: Member/alternate member, Committee of the Regions 1998-2010; Director, London First 1996-99; Vice-President, Commonwealth Institute 1999-2006; Friend, University of Grenada 2000-; Trustee, St Mary's Paddington Charitable Trust 2001-08; Chair, England Volunteering Development Council 2004-11; President, Volunteering England 2009-10; In Deep. Freeman: City of London 1984, Royal Borough of Kensington and Chelsea 2011. CBE 1997; The Hurlingham Club.

Recreations: Music, travel.

The Baroness Hanham CBE, House of Lords, London SW1A 0PW
Tel: 020 7219 5609 *Email:* hanhamj@parliament.uk

HANNAY OF CHISWICK, LORD

CROSSBENCH

HANNAY OF CHISWICK (Life Baron), David Hugh Alexander Hannay; cr 2001. Born 28 September 1935; Son of late Julian Hannay and late Eileen Hannay; Married Gillian Rex 1961 (4 sons).

Education: Craigflower School; Winchester College; New College, Oxford (BA modern history 1959); French.

Non-political career: National Service 1954-56 (2nd Lieutenant 8th King's Royal Irish Hussars). Foreign Office (FCO) 1959-95: London 1959-60, Language student, Tehran 1960-61, Oriental secretary, Kabul 1961-63, Second secretary, FCO 1963-65, First secretary, Brussels (EC) 1965-70, Brussels negotiating team 1970-72, Chef de Cabinet to Vice-President EC Commission 1973-77, FCO 1977-84: Head of: Energy, science and space department 1977-79, Middle East department 1979, Assistant under-secretary, EC 1979-84; Minister, Washington 1984-85, Ambassador, permanent representative to: EC 1985-90, UN, New York 1990-95; Special Representative for Cyprus 1996-2003; Non-executive director: Chime Communications 1999-2006, Aegis 2000-03; Member, advisory board, GPW 2011-. First Division Association 1959-95.

Political career: *House of Lords:* Raised to the peerage as Baron Hannay of Chiswick, of Bedford Park in the London Borough of Ealing 2001. Member: EU Sub-committee A (Economic and Financial Affairs, Trade and External Relations/Economic and Financial Affairs) 2001-05, European Union 2003-06, 2008-; EU Sub-committee C (Foreign Affairs, Defence and Development Policy): Member 2005-06, Co-opted member 2006-08; Member Intergovernmental Organisations 2007-08; EU Sub-committee F (Home Affairs): Member 2008-10, Chair 2010-12; Chair EU Sub-committee F (Home Affairs, Health and Education) 2012-. *Councils and public bodies:* Council member, Kent University 2009-.

Political interests: Foreign and development policy, EU, energy policy and climate change, higher education.

Other: Adviser to Executive Committee, World Federation of United Nations Associations 1995-2000; Advisory Board: Prospect 1995-2005, Centre for European Reform 1996-, European Foreign Affairs Review 1996-; Salzburg Seminar 2001-05; Chair, International Advisory Board, EDHEC Business School (France) 2002-09; TANGGUH Independent Advisory Panel 2002-09; Member, UN Secretary-General High Level Panel on Threats, Challenges and Change 2003-04; Judge, School of Management, Cambridge 2004-10; Governor, Ditchley Foundation 2005-; Chair, United Nations Association, UK 2006-11; Member, Top Level Group for Nuclear Disarmament and Non-proliferation 2011-; Children at Risk Foundation (UK). Pro-chancellor Birmingham University 2001-06. Honorary Fellow, New College, Oxford; Hon DLitt, Birmingham University. CMG 1981 KCMG 1986 GCMG 1995 CH 2003; Travellers Club.

Publications: Editor, Britain's Entry into the European Community, Report on the Negotiations (1970-72); Cyprus: The Search for a Solution (2004); New World Disorder – The UN after the Cold War, an Insider's View (2008); Britain's Quest for a Role: A Diplomatic Memoir from Europe to the UN (I.B. Tauris, 2012).

Recreations: Travel, photography, gardening, grandchildren.

The Lord Hannay of Chiswick GCMG CH, House of Lords, London SW1A 0PW
Tel: 020 7219 1358
3 The Orchard, London W4 1JZ *Tel:* 020 8987 9012 *Fax:* 020 8987 9012

NON-AFFILIATED

HANNINGFIELD, LORD

HANNINGFIELD (Life Baron), Paul Edward Winston White; cr. 1998. Born 16 September 1940; Son of late Edward Ernest William White and Irene Joyce Gertrude, née Williamson.

Education: King Edward VI Grammar School, Chelmsford; Nuffield Scholarship for Agriculture (research in USA specialising in marketing in farming).

Non-political career: Farmer.

Political career: *House of Lords:* Raised to the peerage as Baron Hanningfield, of Chelmsford in the County of Essex 1998. Opposition Whip 2003-07; Opposition Spokesperson for: Office of the Deputy Prime Minister/Communities and Local Government 2003-07, Education and Skills 2004-05, Transport 2005-09, Business, Innovation and Skills 2009-10; Suspended from membership July 2011-May 2012. *Other:* Chair: Conservative Party National Local Government Advisory Committee, Board of Conservative Party 1997-2001; Conservative Whip suspended February 2010. *Councils and public bodies:* Essex County Council: Councillor 1970-2010, Council Leader 1998-99, 2001-10, Leader, Conservative Group 2001-10; DL, Essex 1991-; Deputy Chair and Conservative Group Leader, Local Government Association 1997-2001.

Political interests: Local government, education, transport and infrastructure, agriculture, constitutional affairs, foreign policy.

Other: President, Assembly of European Regions Sub-Commission 1990-2005; EU Committee of the Regions: Leader, Conservative Group, UK Delegation -2005, Chair: Enlargement Group 1998-2005, Bulgarian Joint Consultative Committee 2002-05; Vice-President, Commission on Transport and the Information Society 1998-2000; Board member, Commonwealth Local Government Forum 2007-; Association of County Councils: Member 1981-97, Conservative Leader 1995-97; Chair: Council of Local Education Authorities 1990-92; Eastern Region Further Education Funding Council 1992-97; Chair and co-founder, Localis 2001-; Member of Court, Essex University; President, Society of Emergency Planning Officers 2003-; Vice-Patron, Helen Rollason Cancer Centre Appeal. Two honorary doctorates: Essex University, Anglia Ruskin University.

Publications: Several contributions to local government journals.

Recreations: Botany, politics and current affairs, travel, food and wine.

The Lord Hanningfield DL, House of Lords, London SW1A 0PW
Tel: 020 7219 5353

LABOUR

HANWORTH, VISCOUNT

HANWORTH (3rd Viscount, UK), David Stephen Geoffrey Pollock; cr. 1936; 3rd Baron Hanworth (UK) 1926; 3rd Bt of Hanworth (UK) 1922. Born 16 February 1946; Son of 2nd Viscount Hanworth; Married Elizabeth 1968 (2 daughters).

Education: Wellington College, Berkshire; Guildford Technical College; Sussex University (BSc economics 1969); Southampton University (MSc economics and statistics 1970); Amsterdam University (PhD 1988); French.

Non-political career: University of London 1972-2007: Lecturer, Reader; Professor, Leicester University 2007-.

Political career: *House of Lords:* First entered House of Lords 1996; Elected hereditary peer 2011-. Member: Partnerships (Prosecution) (Scotland) Bill 2013-, Joint Committee on Consolidation, Etc, Bills 2013-.

Political interests: Economic policy, financial regulation, energy, transport, environment, foreign affairs; Austria, France, Germany, Italy, Netherlands.

Publications: The Algebra of Econometrics (1979); Handbook of Time Series Analysis Signal Processing and Dynamics (1999); Co-author, Innovations in Multivariate Statistical Analysis (2000).

The Viscount Hanworth, House of Lords, London SW1A 0PW
Tel: 020 7219 5353 *Email:* pollockd@parliament.uk
Department of Economics, Astley Clarke Building, A108, University of Leicester, Leicester LE1 7RH *Website:* www.le.ac.uk/users/dsgp1

HARDIE, LORD

HARDIE (Life Baron), Andrew Rutherford Hardie; cr 1997. Born 8 January 1946; Son of late Andrew Rutherford and Elizabeth Currie Hardie; Married late Catherine Storrar Elgin 1971 (2 sons 1 daughter).

Education: St Modan's High School, Stirling; Edinburgh University (MA French and German 1966; LLB 1969).

Non-political career: Solicitor 1971; Member, Faculty of Advocates 1973; Advocate Depute 1979-83; QC (Scot) 1985; Treasurer, Faculty of Advocates 1989-94, Dean 1994-97; Lord Advo-

CROSSBENCH

cate 1997-2000; Senator of the College of Justice in Scotland 2000-13; Honorary Bencher, Lincoln's Inn.

Political career: *House of Lords:* Raised to the peerage as Baron Hardie, of Blackford in the City of Edinburgh 1997. Lord Advocate 1997-2000; As a senior member of the judiciary, disqualified from participation 2009-13. Chair Mental Capacity Act 2005 2013-.

Political interests: Law and the constitution, human rights, issues relating to families and children, care and rehabilitation of prisoners (particularly young offenders), disability issues, asylum and immigration, energy and environment; China, India, Sri Lanka, Taiwan.

Other: Non-practising member, Faculty of Advocates; Capability (Scotland), Children's Charities, Christian Aid. PC 1997.

Recreations: Cricket, travel, grandchildren.

Rt Hon the Lord Hardie, House of Lords, London SW1A 0PW
Tel: 020 7219 5353 *Email:* hardiera@parliament.uk

HARRIES OF PENTREGARTH, LORD

HARRIES OF PENTREGARTH (Life Baron), Richard Douglas Harries; cr 2006. Born 2 June 1936; Son of late Brigadier W. D. J. Harries, CBE; Married Josephine Bottomley, MB, BChir, DCH 1963 (1 son 1 daughter).

Education: Wellington College, Berkshire; RMA, Sandhurst; Selwyn College, Cambridge (MA theology 1965); Cuddesdon College, Oxford.

Non-political career: Lieutenant, Royal Corps of Signals 1955-58. Curate, Hampstead Parish Church 1963-69; Chaplain, Westfield College 1966-69; Lecturer, Wells Theological College 1969-72; Vicar, All Saints, Fulham 1972-81; Dean, King's College, London 1981-87; 41st Bishop

CROSSBENCH

of Oxford 1987-2006; Visiting Professor, Liverpool Hope University College 2002; Nuffield Council on Bioethics 2002-08; Honorary Professor of Theology, Kings College, London 2006-; Gresham College: Professor of Divinity 2008-12, Fellow and Emeritus Professor 2012-.

Political career: *House of Lords:* Raised to the peerage as Baron Harries of Pentregarth, of Ceinewydd in the County of Dyfed 2006. First entered House of Lords as Bishop of Oxford 1993, Convener of Bench of Bishops 1998-2006. Member House of Lords' Offices 1997-2001; Chair Stem Cell Research 2001-02; Member: Procedure 2007-12, Joint Committee on Privacy and Injunctions 2011-12, Works of Art 2012-12. *Councils and public bodies:* General Ordination examiner in Christian Ethics 1972-76; Director, Post Ordination Training, Kensington Jurisdiction 1973-79; Member, Home Office Advisory Committee for reform of sexual offences law 1981-85; Chair, Southwark Ordination Course 1982-87; Vice-chair, Council for Arms Control 1982-87; Chair: Council of Christians and Jews 1992-2001, Board of Social Responsibility for Church of England 1996-2001; Member, Royal Commission on Reform of House of Lords 1999-2000; Human Fertilisation and Embryo Authority 2003-09.

Political interests: Overseas aid and development, poverty, business ethics, arts, use of armed force, bioethics, the Dalits; Georgia, India, West Papua.

Other: Member, Anglican Consultative Council 1994-2003; Consultant, Anglican Peace and Justice Network 1984-94; Vice-chair, Council for Christian Action 1979-87; President, Johnson Society 1988-89; Board member, Christian Aid 1994-2000. Four honorary doctorates; Two honorary Oxbridge fellowships; Fellow, King's College, London; Honorary Fellow: Academy of Medical Sciences, Institute of Biology; Fellow: Learned Society of Wales, Royal Society of Literature. President's Medal, British Academy 2012.

Publications: Prayers of Hope (1975); Turning to Prayer (1978); Prayers of Grief and Glory (1979); Being a Christian (1981); Should Christians Support Guerillas? (1982); The Authority of Divine Love (1983); Praying Round the Clock (1983); Prayer and the Pursuit of Happiness (1985); Morning Has Broken (1985); Christianity and War in a Nuclear Age (1986); C. S. Lewis: the man and his God (1987); Christ is Risen (1988); Is There a Gospel for the Rich (1992); Art and the Beauty of God (1993); The Real God: A Response to Anthony Freeman (1994); Questioning

Belief (1995); A Gallery of Reflections – The Nativity in Art (1995); Co-editor, Two Cheers For Secularism (1998); In The Gladness of Today (2000); Co-editor, Christianity: Two Thousand Years (2001); God outside the Box: Why spiritual people object to Christianity (2002); After the Evil: Christianity and Judaism in the Shadow of the Holocaust (2003); The Passion in Art (2004); Praying the Eucharist (2004); The Re-enchantment of Morality (2008); Faith in Politics? Rediscovering the Christian Roots of our Political Values; Issues of Life and Death: Christian Faith and Medical Intervention; Co-editor, Reinhold Niebuhr and Contemporary Politics (2010); Reinhold Niebuhr Considered (2011); The Image of Christ in Modern Art (2013); Has edited and contributed to other Christian publications as well as articles in the press and periodicals.

Recreations: Theatre, literature, the visual arts, sport.

Rt Rev the Lord Harries of Pentregarth, House of Lords, London SW1A 0PW
Tel: 020 7219 2910 *Email:* harriesr@parliament.uk

HARRIS OF HARINGEY, LORD

HARRIS OF HARINGEY (Life Baron), (Jonathan) Toby Harris; cr. 1998. Born 11 October 1953; Son of late Professor Harry and Muriel Harris; Married Ann Herbert 1979 (2 sons 1 daughter).

Education: Haberdashers' Aske's School, Elstree; Trinity College, Cambridge (BA natural sciences and economics 1975) (Union President 1974).

Non-political career: Economics division, Bank of England 1975-79; Electricity Consumers' Council 1979-86: Deputy director 1983-86; Director, Association of Community Health Councils for England and Wales 1987-98; Senior associate, The King's Fund 1998-2004; Chair, Toby Harris Associates 1998-; Consultant adviser to: Harrogate Management Centre 1998-2004, Infolog Training 1998-2005, Vantage Point 1998-2001, KPMG 1999-2013, DEMSA 2001-03. Member, Unite.

LABOUR

Political career: *House of Lords:* Raised to the peerage as Baron Harris of Haringey, of Hornsey in the London Borough of Haringey 1998. Member: House of Lords Offices Finance and Staff Sub-committee 2000-02, Joint Committee on National Security Strategy 2010-; Chair Olympic and Paralympic Legacy 2013-. Member, Labour Peers' Co-ordinating Committee 2004-. *Other:* Chair: Cambridge University Labour Club 1973, Hornsey Labour Party 1978, 1979, 1980; Member: Labour Party National Policy Forum 1992-2004, Labour Party Local Government Committee 1993-2004, Greater London Labour Party Regional Board 1993-2004, Labour Peers Co-ordinating Committee 2004-; Labour Peers: Vice-chair 2008-12, Chair 2012-. *Councils and public bodies:* London Borough of Haringey: Councillor 1978-2002, Council Leader 1987-99; Deputy chair, National Fuel Poverty Forum 1981-86; Governor, National Institute for Social Work 1986-94; Member, London Drug Policy Forum 1990-98; Deputy chair, Association of Metropolitan Authorities 1991-97; Member: National Nursery Examination Board 1992-94, Home Office Advisory Council on Race Relations 1992-97; Chair: Association of London Authorities 1993-95, Local Government Anti-Poverty Unit 1994-97, Association of London Government 1995-2000; Member: Court of Middlesex University 1995-, Joint London Advisory Panel 1996-1997, London Ambulance Service NHS Trust 1998-2006, London Pension Fund Authority 1998-2000, Metropolitan Police Committee 1998-2000; Member, Executive: Local Government Association 1999-2003, Association of Police Authorities 2000-06; Member, Greater London Authority for Brent and Harrow 2000-04; Metropolitan Police Authority: Chair 2000-04, Member (representing the Home Secretary) 2004-12; Special adviser to Board, Transport for London 2004-08; Member, Public Sector Advisory Council, Anite 2005-06; Vice-President: Local Government Association 2005-10, Association of Police Authorities 2007-; Founding chair, Institute of Commissioning Professionals 2007-08; Member: Police Counter-Terrorism Board 2007-12, Police Counter-Terrorism Ministerial Advisory Group 2008-10; Chair: Independent Advisory Panel on Deaths in Custody 2009-, Audit Panel, Metropolitan Police and Mayor's Office for Policing and Crime 2012, National Trading Standards Board 2013-.

Political interests: Local government, health, policing, information technology, homeland security, consumer protection; Cyprus, France, USA.

Other: EU Committee of the Regions: Member 1994-98, Alternate member 1998-2002; Chair, Young Fabian Group 1976-77; Board member, London First 1993-2002; Executive council member, RNIB 1993-94; Trustee: Evening Standard Blitz Memorial Appeal 1995-99, Help for Health Trust 1995-97, The Learning Agency 1996-98; Chair, Wembley National Stadium Trust 1996-; Vice-patron: Artificial Heart Fund 2004, Vocaleyes 2004; Trustee, Safer London Foundation 2004-08; London Ambassador, Community Service Volunteers 2005-; The Burned Children's Club 2007; Trustee, Bilimankhwe Arts 2008-; Chair: The Freedom Trust 2010-, Advisory Council, Cities Security and Resilience Network 2011-; Fellow, British Computer Society 2011-; FRSA. Freeman, City of London 1998. Honorary doctorate, Middlesex University 1999.

Publications: Co-author, Why Vote Labour? (1979); Contributor to Economics of Prosperity (1980); Co-editor, Energy and Social Policy (1983).
Recreations: Reading, theatre, classical music, opera.
The Lord Harris of Haringey, House of Lords, London SW1A 0PW
Tel: 020 7219 8513 *Email:* toby@lordtobyharris.org.uk *Website:* www.lordtobyharris.org.uk
Twitter: @LordTobySays

HARRIS OF PECKHAM, LORD

HARRIS OF PECKHAM (Life Baron), Philip Charles Harris; cr. 1996. Born 15 September 1942; Son of Charles Harris, MC and Ruth Harris; Married Pauline Chumley (later DBE) 1960 (3 sons 1 daughter).
Education: Streatham Grammar School.
Non-political career: Harris Queensway plc: Chairman 1964-88, Chief executive 1987-88; Non-executive director: Great Universal Stores 1986-2004, Fisons plc 1986-94; Chairmn: Harris Ventures Ltd 1988-, C. W. Harris Properties 1988-97; Non-executive director, Molyneux Estates 1990-95; Chairman, Carpetright plc 1993-; Non-executive director: Matalan 2004-06, Arsenal FC 2005-.

CONSERVATIVE

Political career: *House of Lords:* Raised to the peerage as Baron Harris of Peckham, of Peckham in the London Borough of Southwark 1996. Member Works of Art 2005-09. *Other:* Deputy Chairman, Conservative Party Treasurers 1993. *Councils and public bodies:* Governor, United Medical and Dental School of Guy's and St Thomas's Hospitals 1983-98; Member, Court of Patrons, Royal College of Gynaecologists 1984-; Chair, Guy's and Lewisham NHS Trust 1991-93; Deputy chair, Lewisham NHS Trust 1993-97; Council member, University of London Court 1994-96; University College London Council 1996-99.

Other: British Showjumping Association 1974-; Chair: Prostate Cancer Charity: Investing in Life Campaign, Generation Trust, Guy's Hospital 1984-2004; Trustee: National Hospital for Neurology and Neurosurgery Development Foundation 1984-92, Westminster Abbey Trust 1987-96; Sponsor, Harris Federation of Schools 1989-; Director and co-sponsor, Bacon's City Technology College 1990-; Trustee, Tavistock Trust for Aphasia 1993-2003; NSPCC National Appeal Board and Executive Committee 1998-; Deputy chair, Full-Stop Campaign 1999-; President, Friends of Guy's Hospital 1999-; Trustee: Royal Academy of Arts 1999-2005, Outward Bound Trust 2001-03; Sponsor, Harris HospisCare, Orpington 2002-; Trustee, Bowel Cancer and Research Trust 2005-; Honorary Fellow, Royal College of Radiologists 1992; Great Ormond Street Hospital. Liveryman: Broderers' Company 1992, Clockmakers Company 2003. Freeman, City of London 1992. Three honorary doctorates; Four honorary University Fellowships. Hambro Business Man of the Year 1983; Ernst and Young Entrepreneur of the Year 2007. Kt 1985; Mark's Club; Mosimanns. Queens Club.
Recreations: Football, cricket, show jumping, tennis.
The Lord Harris of Peckham, House of Lords, London SW1A 0PW
Tel: 020 7219 5353
Carpetright plc, Harris House, Purfleet Bypass, Purfleet, Essex RM19 1TT *Tel:* 01708 802120
Fax: 01708 802130 *Email:* judy.willett@carpetright.co.uk *Website:* www.carpetright.co.uk

HARRIS OF RICHMOND, BARONESS

HARRIS OF RICHMOND (Life Baroness), Angela Felicity Harris; cr. 1999. Born 4 January 1944; Daughter of late Rev. G H Hamilton Richards and Eva Richards; Married 2nd John Harris 1976 (1 son from previous marriage).
Education: Canon Slade Grammar School, Bolton; Ealing Hotel and Catering College.
Political career: *House of Lords:* Raised to the peerage as Baroness Harris of Richmond, of Richmond in the County of North Yorkshire 1999. Liberal Democrat Whip 2000-08; Liberal Democrat Spokesperson for: Northern Ireland 2003-10, Home Office (police) 2005-10; Deputy Speaker 2008-; Deputy Chairman of Committees 2008-; Contested Lord Speaker election 2011. Member:

LIBERAL DEMOCRAT

European Union 2000-04, European Union Sub-committee F (Social Affairs, Education and Home Affairs/Home Affairs) 2000-04 (Chair 2000-04), Refreshment 2003-07, Administration and Works 2007-12. *Other:* Contested 1999 European Parliament elections . *Councils and public bodies:* Richmond Town Council (Yorkshire): Councillor 1978-81, 1991-99, Mayor 1993-94; Richmondshire District Council: Councillor 1979-89, Chair 1987-88; North Yorkshire County Council: Councillor 1981-2001, Chair 1991-92, Honorary Alderman 2002; JP 1982-98; Non-executive director, Northallerton NHS Trust 1989-97; DL, North Yorkshire 1994-; Chair, North Yorkshire Police Authority 1994-2001; Deputy Chair, National Association of Police Authorities 1997-2001; High Steward, Ripon Cathedral 2009-.

Political interests: Police, Northern Ireland; Canada, Ireland, Nepal, Qatar.

Other: Member: British-American Parliamentary Group 1999-, Inter-Parliamentary Union 2003-, British/Irish Parliamentary Assembly 2005-; University of York: Member, Court 1996-, Member, Nominations Committee 2012-; Patron, Herriot Hospice Homecare, Northallerton 1999-; The Police Rehabilitation Trust (Flint House) 2003-; Industry and Parliament Trust: Fellow 2003, Trustee 2006-, Chair of Trustees 2010-; President, National Association of Chaplains to the Police 2005-; Patron, Northern Ireland Hospice. Freeman, City of London; Honorary Freeman, Richmond, North Yorkshire 2004.

Recreations: Music, political biographies.

The Baroness Harris of Richmond DL, House of Lords, London SW1A 0PW
Tel: 020 7219 6709 *Email:* harrisa@parliament.uk

HARRISON, LORD

LABOUR

HARRISON (Life Baron), Lyndon Henry Arthur Harrison; cr. 1999. Born 28 September 1947; Son of late Charles and Edith Harrison; Married Hilary Plank 1980 (1 son 1 daughter).

Education: Oxford School; Warwick University (BA English and American studies 1970); Sussex University (MA American studies 1971); Keele University (MA American studies 1978).

Non-political career: Research officer, UMIST Union, Manchester 1975-78; Union manager, North East Wales Institute, Clwyd 1978-89. Member, GMB.

Political career: *House of Lords:* Raised to the peerage as Baron Harrison, of Chester in the County of Cheshire 1999. Departmental Liaison Peer for Northern Ireland 1999-2001. Member: EU Sub-committee C (Common Foreign and Security Policy) 1999-2003, Delegated Powers and Regulatory Reform 2003-07, EU Sub-committee G (Social Policy and Consumer Affairs) 2003-07, Hybrid Instruments 2003-, European Union 2004-08, 2010-; EU Sub-committee F (Home Affairs): Member 2006-08, Co-opted member 2008-10; Chair EU Sub-committee A: (Economic and Financial Affairs and International Trade) 2010-12, (Economic and Financial Affairs) 2012-. *Other:* European Parliament: MEP for Cheshire West 1989-94, and for Cheshire West and Wirral 1994-99; Secretary, European Parliamentary Labour Party 1991-94. *Councils and public bodies:* Councillor, Cheshire County Council 1981-90: Deputy Chair, North West Tourist Board 1986-89; Vice-President, Association of County Councils 1990-97.

Political interests: Small businesses, tourism, monetary union, children, European Union; Commonwealth, EU member and applicant countries, USA.

Other: Member: Inter-Parliamentary Union 1999-, Commonwealth Parliamentary Association 2007-; Vice-President, Cheshire Landscape Trust 1999-; President, Chester and District Parkinson's Disease Society 2005-; Honorary Council Member NSPCC.

Publications: Everything you wanted to know about the Euro...and were afraid to ask; Tourism means Jobs.

Recreations: Chess, the arts, sport, bridge.

The Lord Harrison, House of Lords, London SW1A 0PW
Tel: 020 7219 6424 *Fax:* 020 7219 5979 *Email:* harrisonlh@parliament.uk

HART OF CHILTON, LORD

LABOUR

HART OF CHILTON (Life Baron), Garry Richard Rushby Hart; cr. 2004. Born 29 June 1940; Son of late Dennis George Hart and Evelyn Hart, now Moore; Married Paula Shepherd 1966 (divorced 1985) (1 daughter 2 sons); married Valerie Davies 1986 (twin daughters).

Education: Northgate Grammar School, Ipswich; University College, London (LLB 1962).

Non-political career: Partner, Herbert Smith solicitors 1970-98; Special adviser to: Lord Irvine of Lairg as Lord Chancellor 1998-2003, Lord Falconer of Thoroton as Secretary of State for Constitutional Affairs/Justice and Lord Chancellor 2003-07; Fellow, University College London.

Political career: *House of Lords:* Raised to the peerage as Baron Hart of Chilton, of Chilton in the County of Suffolk 2004. Member Leaders Group on Code of Conduct 2009; House of Lords Appointments Commission 2010-. Member: Joint Committee on Draft Constitutional Renewal Bill 2007-08, Merits of Statutory Instruments/Secondary Legislation Scrutiny 2009-13, Constitution 2009-.

Political interests: Law, constitution, planning, arts, heritage; Caribbean, France, Italy, Spain.

Other: Council member, UCL 1994-2011; Trustee, Architectural Foundation 1996-2005; Almeida Theatre: Trustee 1997-2005, Chair 1997-2002; Trustee, British Architectural Library Trust 2001-10; Member, Building and Strategy Committee, V&A 2007-; Vice-Patron, Ipswich Society for the Blind 2008-; Member, Law Society; Honorary FRIBA; FRSA. Liveryman City of London Solicitors Company. Freeman, City of London. Chancellor, Greenwich University 2008-; Garrick; Beef Steak.

Publications: Co-author, Blundell and Dobry's Planning Appeals and Proceedings (Sweet and Maxwell, 4th edition 1990).
Recreations: Conservation, theatre, talking.
The Lord Hart of Chilton, House of Lords, London SW1A 0PW
Tel: 020 7219 5353
36 Alwyne Road, London N1 2HW *Tel:* 020 7226 5431 *Email:* hartofchilton@btinternet.com

---

HASKEL, LORD

LABOUR

HASKEL (Life Baron), Simon Haskel; cr. 1993. Born 8 October 1934; Son of late Isaac and Julia Haskel; Married Carole Lewis 1962 (1 son 1 daughter).
Education: Sedbergh School; Salford College of Advanced Technology (ARTCS textile technology 1955); French, Spanish.
Non-political career: National service commission, Royal Artillery 1957. Joined Perrotts Ltd 1961; Chairman, Perrotts Group plc and associated companies 1973-97.
Political career: *House of Lords:* Raised to the peerage as Baron Haskel, of Higher Broughton in the County of Greater Manchester 1993. Opposition Spokesperson for Trade and Industry 1994-97; Opposition Whip 1994-97; Government Whip 1997-98; Government Spokesperson for: Social Security 1997-98, Trade and Industry 1997-98, the Treasury 1997-98; Deputy Chair of Committees 2002-; Deputy Speaker 2002-; Board member, Parliamentary Office of Science and Technology (POST). Member: Science and Technology 1994-97, 1999-2002, 2005-10, Procedure 2002-05, Science and Technology Sub-committee I (Fighting Infection) 2002-03, EU Sub-committee B (Internal Market) 2003-07, Information 2003-07, Joint Committee on Tax Law Rewrite Bills 2005-10, Science and Technology Sub-committee I 2007-10 (Allergy/Waste Reduction 2007-08, Nanotechnologies and food 2008-10), Information 2009-, Delegated Powers and Regulatory Reform 2009-, EU Sub-committee B: (Internal Market, Energy and Transport) 2010-12, (Internal Market, Infrastructure and Employment) 2012-, Small- and Medium-Sized Enterprises 2012-13. *Other:* Labour Party Industry 1972 Group: Founder Member, Secretary 1976-81; Chair Labour Finance and Industry Group 1990-96.
Political interests: Trade and industry, science and technology, overseas development; Europe, USA.
Other: Chair, Thames Concerts Society 1982-90; Trustee: The Haskel Family Foundation 2000-, The Smith Institute 1998-2008; Patron: Chronic Disease Research Foundation 1999-2006, President, Environment Industries Commission 2000-; Society of Operations Engineers 2000-04; President, Institute for Jewish Policy research 2002-; International President, Textile Institute 2002-05; Honorary President, Materials UK 2006-. Honorary Doctorate, Bolton University 2007. Cyclists' Touring, Tandem.
Recreations: Music, cycling.
The Lord Haskel, House of Lords, London SW1A 0PW
Tel: 020 7219 4076
Email: haskels@parliament.uk lordsoftheblog.net/category/lord-haskel *Twitter:* @simon.haskel

---

HASKINS, LORD

CROSSBENCH

HASKINS (Life Baron), Christopher Robin Haskins; cr. 1998. Born 30 May 1937; Son of Robin and Margaret Haskins; Married Gilda Horsley 1959 (3 sons 2 daughters).
Education: St Columba's College, Dublin; Trinity College, Dublin (BA modern history 1959).
Non-political career: Ford Motor Company, Dagenham 1960-62; Northern Foods 1962-, Chairman 1986-2002; Chair, Express Dairies 1998-2002; Director, Yorkshire Television 2002-06; Adviser, Montrose Associates 2003-; Chair, Airtrack Railways Ltd 2004-09; Director, JSR Farms 1991-.
Political career: *House of Lords:* Raised to the peerage as Baron Haskins, of Skidby in the County of the East Riding of Yorkshire 1998. Member EU Sub-committee D (Environment, Agriculture, Public Health and Consumer Protection/Environment and Agriculture) 2003-06; EU Sub-committee A (Economic and Financial Affairs and International Trade): Co-opted member 2007-10, Member 2010-12; Member Small- and Medium-Sized Enterprises 2012-13. *Councils and public bodies:* Member: Commission for Social Justice 1992-94, UK Round Table on Sustainable Development 1995-97, Hampel Committee on Corporate Governance 1996-97, New Deal Advisory Task Force 1997-2001; Chairman, Better Regulation Task Force 1997-2002; Board member Yorkshire Forward Regional Development Agency 1998-2008; Chair Council, Open University 2005-; Member, Equality and Reform Group Board, Cabinet Office 2010-; Chair, Humber Local Enterprise Partnership 2011-.

Political interests: Europe, food and agriculture, countryside, regulation, universities, regionalism/devolution; France, Ireland, Italy, USA.

Other: Trustee: Runnymede Trust 1989-98, Demos 1993-2000, Civil Liberties Trust 1997-99, Legal Assistance Trust 1998-04, Lawes Agricultural Trust 2000-, Business Dynamics 2002-07; Oxfam, Unicef, Medical Aid for Palestine, Samaritans, One World, Médecins Sans Frontières, Safer World, Citizens Advice Bureau. Honorary doctorates: Trinity College, Dublin, Bradford University, Essex University, Cranfield University, Huddersfield University, Leeds Metropolitan University, Hull University, Lincoln University.

Recreations: Walking, writing.

The Lord Haskins, House of Lords, London SW1A 0PW
Tel: 020 7219 5353
Quarryside Farm, 46 Main Street, Skidby, Nr Cottingham, East Yorkshire HU16 5TG
Tel: 01482 842692 *Fax:* 01482 845249 *Email:* gshaskins@aol.com

HASTINGS OF SCARISBRICK, LORD

HASTINGS OF SCARISBRICK (Life Baron), Michael John Hastings; cr 2005. Born 29 January 1958; Son of late Petain Hastings and of Olive Hastings; Married Jane 1990 (2 daughters 1 son).

Education: Scarisbrick Hall School, Ormskirk; Cornwall College, Montego Bay, Jamaica; London School of Theology (BA theology and sociology 1979); Westminster College, Oxford (PGCE).

Non-political career: BBC 1994-2006: Political and parliamentary affairs department, Head of public affairs 1995-2006, Head of corporate social responsibility 2003-06; Chair, Crime Concern 1995-2008; Board member, Responsible and Sustainable Business Committee, BT 2004-; KPMG: International Director for Corporate Citizenship 2006-, Global Head, Citizenship and Diversity 2007-.

CROSSBENCH

Political career: *House of Lords:* Raised to the peerage as Baron Hastings of Scarisbrick, of Scarisbrick in the County of Lancashire 2005. Member Communications 2007-09. *Councils and public bodies:* Commissioner, Commission for Racial Equality 1993-2001; Member, Government Social Security Advisory Committee 1993-95; Founding member, Metropolitan Police Advisory Committee 1995-97.

Other: Patron: Zane, Child Brain Injury Trust; Founding chair: Childnet International, Springboard for Children; Trustee, Vodafone Group Foundation 2008-; Vice-President, Unicef; Chairman, Millenium Promise UK; Council member, Overseas Development Institute. Unicef award 2005. CBE 2002.

The Lord Hastings of Scarisbrick CBE, House of Lords, London SW1A 0PW
Tel: 020 7219 3781 *Email:* hastingsm@parliament.uk

HATTERSLEY, LORD

HATTERSLEY (Life Baron), Roy Sydney George Hattersley; cr. 1997. Born 28 December 1932; Son of late Frederick Roy and Enid Hattersley; Married Molly Loughran 1956 (divorced 2013).

Education: Sheffield City Grammar School; Hull University (BSc economics).

Non-political career: Member, NUJ.

Political career: *House of Commons:* Contested Sutton Coldfield 1959 general election. MP (Labour) for Birmingham Sparkbrook 1964-97. PPS to Minister of Pensions 1964-67; Parliamentary Secretary, Ministry of Labour 1967-68; Parliamentary Under-Secretary of State, Department of Employment and Productivity 1968-69; Minister of Defence for Administration 1969-70; Opposition Spokesperson for: Defence 1972, Education and Science 1972-74; Minister of State, Foreign and Commonwealth Affairs 1974-76; Secretary of State for Prices and Consumer Protection 1976-79; Principal Opposition Frontbench Spokesperson for: the Environment 1979-80, Home Affairs 1980-83; Deputy Leader Labour Party 1983-92; Principal Opposition Spokesperson for: Treasury and Economic Affairs 1983-87, Home Affairs 1987-92. *House of Lords:* Raised to the peerage as Baron Hattersley, of Sparkbrook in the County of West Midlands 1997. *Councils and public bodies:* Councillor, Sheffield City Council 1957-65.

LABOUR

Other: PC 1975; Garrick, Reform.

Publications: Nelson (1974); Goodbye to Yorkshire (essays 1976); Politics Apart (1982); Press Gang (1983); A Yorkshire Boyhood (1983); Endpiece Revisited (essays 1985); Choose Freedom: the future for Democratic Socialism (1987); Economic Priorities for a Labour Government (1987); The Maker's Mark (novel 1990); In that Quiet Earth (novel 1991); Between Ourselves (essays

1993); Who Goes Home? Scenes from a Political Life (1995); Fifty Years On (1997); Buster's Diaries (1998); Blood and Fire, the Story of William and Catherine Booth and their Salvation Army (1999); John Wesley: A Brand From The Burning (2001); The Edwardians (2004).

Recreations: Writing, watching football and cricket.

Rt Hon the Lord Hattersley, House of Lords, London SW1A 0PW
Tel: 020 7219 5353 *Email:* roy@royhattersley.com

HAUGHEY, LORD – *Please see Addenda Page xi*

HAWORTH, LORD

HAWORTH (Life Baron), Alan Robert Haworth; cr. 2004. Born 26 April 1948; Son of late John Haworth, retail grocer, and Hilma Haworth, née Westhead; Married Gill Cole 1973 (divorced); married Maggie Rae 1991.

Education: Blackburn Technical and Grammar School; Barking Regional College of Technology (BSc Soc London University external 1971).

Non-political career: North East London Polytechnic 1972-75: Registrar, Faculty of Art and Design 1972-73, Assistant to director of course development 1973-75; Parliamentary Labour Party: Committee Officer 1975-85, Senior Committee Officer 1985-92, Secretary 1992-2004. Member, Transport and General Workers' Union 1975-2005.

LABOUR

Political career: *House of Lords:* Raised to the peerage as Baron Haworth, of Fisherfield in Ross and Cromarty 2004.

Political interests: Energy, environment, transport, health, Royal Navy; Azerbaijan, Cambodia, Georgia, Iran, Kazakhstan, Kyrgyzstan, Laos, Russia, Tibet, Vietnam.

Other: Member: Munro Society, Mountain Bothies Association, Marine Conservation Society, Scottish Wild Land Group, National Trust for Scotland, RSPB, John Muir Trust, Mountaineering Council of Scotland, Wainwright Society, Wildfowl and Wetlands Trust, Ramblers.

Publications: Co-editor (with Baroness Hayter of Kentish Town), Men Who Made Labour (Routledge, 2006).

Recreations: Hill-walking, mountaineering, first member of Lords to have climbed all the Munros.

The Lord Haworth, House of Lords, London SW1A 0PW
Tel: 020 7219 6620 *Email:* hawortha@parliament.uk

HAYMAN, BARONESS

HAYMAN (Life Baroness), Helene Valerie Hayman; cr. 1996. Born 26 March 1949; Daughter of late Maurice and Maude Middleweek; Married Martin Hayman 1974 (4 sons).

Education: Wolverhampton High School for Girls; Newnham College, Cambridge (BA law 1969) (Union President 1969).

Non-political career: Shelter, National Campaign for the Homeless 1969-71; Social Services Department, London Borough of Camden 1971-74; Deputy director, National Council for One Parent Families 1974.

CROSSBENCH

Political career: *House of Commons:* Contested Wolverhampton South West February 1974 general election. MP (Labour) for Welwyn and Hatfield October 1974-79. Contested Welwyn and Hatfield 1979 general election. *House of Lords:* Raised to the peerage as Baroness Hayman, of Dartmouth Park in the London Borough of Camden 1996. Opposition Spokesperson for Health 1996-97; Parliamentary Under-Secretary of State: Department of the Environment, Transport and the Regions (Minister for Roads) 1997-98, Department of Health 1998-99; Minister of State, Ministry of Agriculture, Fisheries and Food 1999-2001; Lord Speaker 2006-11; Member, Parliamentary and Political Service Honours Committee 2012-. Member: Constitution 2005-06, Liaison 2005-06, Procedure 2006-11; Chair House 2006-11; Member Parliamentary and Political Service Honours Committee 2012-. *Councils and public bodies:* Member, Royal College of Gynaecologists Ethics Committee 1982-97; Committee on Ethics of Clinical Investigation, University College London/University College Hospital: Member 1987-97, Vice-chair 1990-97; Vice-chair: Bloomsbury Health Authority 1988-90, Bloomsbury and Islington Health Authority 1991-92; Council member, University College, London 1992-97; Chair, Whittington Hospital NHS Trust 1992-97; Member: Review Committee of Privy Counsellors of the Anti-terrorism, Crime and Security Act 2002-04, General Medical Council 2013-.

Political interests: Health, education, overseas development.

Other: Commonwealth Parliamentary Association (UK Branch): President 2006-11, Vice-President 2011-; Honorary President, Inter-Parliamentary Union, British Group 2006-11; Chair, Cancer Research UK 2001-04; Roadsafe: Board member 2001-05, Patron 2006-; Board of Trustees, Royal

Botanical Gardens, Kew 2002-06; Chair: Specialised Health Care Alliance 2004-06, Human Tissue Authority 2005-06; Trustee, Tropical Health and Education Trust 2005-06; Patron, Anne Frank Trust UK 2009-; President: Hansard Society 2010-11, Industry and Parliament Trust -2011, Parliament Choir -2011; Trustee: Sabin Vaccine Institute 2011-, Malaria Consortium 2013-. Two honorary fellowships; Two honorary doctorates. PC 2001; GBE 2012.

Rt Hon the Baroness Hayman GBE, House of Lords, London SW1A 0PW
Tel: 020 7219 5083 *Email:* haymanh@parliament.uk

HAYTER OF KENTISH TOWN, BARONESS

Opposition Whip; Opposition Spokesperson for Business, Innovation and Skills and for Cabinet Office

HAYTER OF KENTISH TOWN (Life Baroness); Dianne Hayter; cr 2010. Born 7 September 1949; Daughter of late Alec Hayter and late Nancy Hayter; Married Prof. David Caplin 1994.

Education: Penrhos College, Colwyn Bay; Aylesbury High School; Durham University (BA sociology and social administration 1970); London University (PhD 2004).

LABOUR

Non-political career: Research assistant: General and Municipal Workers Union 1970-72, European Trade Union Confederation, Brussels 1973; Research officer, Trade Union Advisory Committee to OECD, Paris 1973-74; Fabian Society: Assistant general secretary 1974-76, General secretary 1976-82, Member, executive committee 1986-95, Chair 1992-93; Journalist, *A Week in Politics*, Channel 4 1982-84; Director, Alcohol Concern 1984-90; Chief executive, European Parliamentary Labour Party 1990-96; Director of corporate affairs, Wellcome Trust 1996-99; Chief executive, Pelican Centre 1999-2001; Member, Board for Actuarial Standards 2006-11; Chair: Consumer panel, Bar Standards Board 2006-09, Property Standards Board 2008-10, Legal Services Consumer Panel 2009-11; Visiting Professor, University of Westminster 2012-. GMB.

Political career: *House of Lords:* Raised to the peerage as Baroness Hayter of Kentish Town, of Kentish Town in the London Borough of Camden 2010. Opposition Whip 2011-; Opposition Spokesperson for: Business, Innovation and Skills (Consumer Affairs) 2012-, Cabinet Office 2012-. Member: Joint Committee on the Draft Defamation Bill 2011. *Other:* Member: Executive committee, London Labour Party 1977-83, National Constitution Committee, Labour Party 1987-98; National Executive Committee, Labour Party: Member 1998-2010, Vice-chair 2006-07, Chair 2007-08; Chair, Holborn and St Pancras Labour Party 1990-93.

Political interests: Trade unions, consumer affairs, women; New Zealand, Sri Lanka.

Other: Member, Royal Commission on Criminal Procedure 1978-80; Vice-chair, Webb Memorial Trust 1997-; Member: National board, Patient Safety Agency 2001-04, Dr Foster Ethics Committee 2001-10; Financial Services Consumer Panel: Member 2001-05, Vice-chair 2003-05; Board member, National Consumer Council 2001-08; Member: Determinations Panel, Pensions Regulator 2005-10, Insolvency Practices Council 2006-10; Blenheim; Pelican Cancer Trust; Dartmouth Street Trust.

Publications: Author, Fightback! Labour's Traditional Right in the 1970s and 1980s (2005); Co-editor (with Lord Haworth), Men Who Made Labour (2006); Contributor, The Prime Ministers Who Never Were (2011).

Recreations: Reading, travel.

The Baroness Hayter of Kentish Town, House of Lords, London SW1A 0PW
Tel: 020 7219 8926 *Email:* hayterd@parliament.uk *Twitter:* @HayteratLords

HEALEY, LORD

HEALEY (Life Baron), Denis Winston Healey; cr. 1992. Born 30 August 1917; Son of late William Healey; Married Edna Edmunds 1945 (died 2010) (1 son 2 daughters).

Education: Bradford Grammar School; Balliol College, Oxford (BA mods and greats 1940, MA); French, Italian and German.

Non-political career: Served North Africa and Italy in Second World War (mentioned in despatches), Major RE. Member, GMB.

LABOUR

Political career: *House of Commons:* Contested (Labour) Pudsey and Otley 1945 general election. MP for South East Leeds 1952-55, for Leeds East 1955-92. Member Shadow Cabinet 1959-64; Secretary of State for Defence 1964-70; Member Shadow Cabinet 1970-74; Chancellor of the Exchequer 1974-79; Member Shadow Cabinet 1979-87; Opposition Spokesperson for Foreign Affairs 1983-87. *House of Lords:* Raised to the peerage as Baron Healey, of Riddlesden in the County of West Yorkshire 1992. *Other:* Secretary, International Department, Labour Party 1945-52; Member, Labour Party National Executive Committee 1970-75; Deputy Leader, Labour Party 1980-83. *Councils and public bodies:* Member, Council for Global Energy Studies 1989-2009; President, Birkbeck College, London University 1993-99.

Political interests: Foreign affairs, defence, arts.

Other: Chairman, IMF Interim Committee 1977-79; Member, Council for Global Energy Studies 1989-; President: National Trust Appeal Yorkshire Moors and Dales 1985-95, Corelli Ensemble 2010-13; National Trust. Freeman, City of Leeds 1991. Honorary Fellow, Balliol College, Oxford 1979; Three honorary degrees; Honorary Fellow, Birkbeck College 1999. MBE (Mil) 1945; PC 1964; CH 1979; Grand Cross of Order of Merit (Germany) 1979.

Publications: Several political works and Fabian essays; Healey's Eye (1980); The Time of My Life (autobiography 1989); When Shrimps Learn to Whistle (essays 1990); My Secret Planet (anthology 1992); Denis Healey's Yorkshire Dales (1995); Healey's World (2002).

Recreations: Music, painting, photography, gardening.

Rt Hon the Lord Healey CH MBE, House of Lords, London SW1A 0PW
Tel: 020 7219 3155

LABOUR

HEALY OF PRIMROSE HILL, BARONESS

HEALY OF PRIMROSE HILL (Life Baroness), Anna Mary Healy; cr 2010. Born 10 May 1955; Daughter of late Martin Healy and Kathleen Healy; Married Jon Cruddas, later MP (qv), 1992 (1 son).

Education: St Aloysius Convent; Royal Holloway College, London (BA modern history/economic history/politics 1976); Birkbeck College, London (MSc politics 1982); City University, London (Diploma journalism 1982-83).

Non-political career: Labour Party HQ 1978-88: Personal assistant to the international secretary 1978-81, Personal assistant to director of communications 1981-85; Press officer, later campaigns press officer 1985-88; Press office, Parliamentary Labour Party 1988-96; Press officer to Tony Blair MP as Leader of the Opposition 1996-97; Special adviser to: Mo Mowlam MP as Secretary of State for Northern Ireland 1997-98, Jack Cunningham MP as Minister for the Cabinet Office and Chancellor of the Duchy of Lancaster 1998-99; Communications strategist, Carlton TV 2000; Senior consultant, GPC 2000-01; Special adviser to Lord Macdonald of Tradeston as: Minister for Transport 2001, Minister for the Cabinet Office 2001-03; Head of office of Jon Cruddas MP 2003-07; Special adviser to Harriet Harman MP as Leader of the House of Commons and Lord Privy Seal 2007-10; Chief of staff to Harriet Harman MP as Leader of the Opposition 2010. Former member, NUJ; Member, Unite.

Political career: *House of Lords:* Raised to the peerage as Baroness Healy of Primrose Hill, of Primrose Hill in the London Borough of Camden 2010. Member: HIV and AIDS in the UK 2010-11, Joint Committee on Parliamentary Privilege 2013, Communications 2013-.

Political interests: Labour Party, health and welfare policies, penal reform; China, Ireland, Italy, Middle East, Spain, USA.

Other: Commonwealth Parliamentary Association; Anaphylaxis Campaign.

Recreations: Music, film, literature.

The Baroness Healy of Primrose Hill, House of Lords, London SW1A 0PW
Tel: 020 7219 8912 *Email:* healyab@parliament.uk

LABOUR

HENIG, BARONESS

HENIG (Life Baroness), Ruth Beatrice Henig; cr. 2004. Born 10 November 1943; Daughter of Kurt and Elfrieda Munzer; Married Stanley Henig 1966 (divorced 1993) (2 sons); married Jack Johnstone 1994.

Education: Wyggeston Girls' Grammar School, Leicester; Bedford College, London (BA history 1965); Lancaster University (PhD history 1978); French, German.

Non-political career: Lancaster University 1968-2002: History lecturer 1968-93, Senior history lecturer 1993-2002, Head of department 1995-97, Dean of arts and humanities 1997-2000; Chair, Security Industry Authority 2007-13. Member, AUT 1968-2002.

Political career: *House of Commons:* Contested Lancaster 1979 and 1992 general elections. *House of Lords:* Raised to the peerage as Baroness Henig, of Lancaster in the County of Lancashire 2004. Member: EU Sub-committee F (Home Affairs) 2005-09, Draft Legal Services Bill Joint Committee 2006, Refreshment 2009-10, 2011-; Co-opted member EU Sub-committee G (Social Policy and Consumer Affairs) 2009-10; Member EU Sub-committees: G (Social Policies and Consumer Protection) 2010-12, C (External Affairs) 2012-. Vice-chair, PLP Departmental: Committee for Home Affairs 2006-10, Group for Home Affairs 2010-. *Other:* Vice-chair, PLP Departmental Group for Home Affairs 2006-09, 2011-. *Councils and public bodies:* Lancashire County Council: Councillor 1981-2005, Chair 1999-2000; Magistrate, Lancaster Bench 1984-2005; Chair, Lancashire Police

Authority 1995-2005; Member, Lawrence Steering Group (Home Office) 1998-2005; Association of Police Authorities: Chair 1997-2005, President 2005-12; DL, Lancashire 2002; Member: Street Crime Action Group 2002-04, National Criminal Justice Board 2003-05.

Political interests: Policing and private security, criminal justice system, foreign affairs, Europe; China, Japan, Malaysia, Thailand.

Other: Chair, Storey Creative Industries Centre, Lancaster 2006-10; Royal National Lifeboat Institute; Save the Children; International Red Cross; Well-being of Women; Prince's Trust. Member, Worshipful Company of Security Professionals. Honorary Fellow, Lancaster University. Outstanding Contribution to Industry, Security Excellence Awards 2012; Imbert Prize for Security Industry Professional of the Year, ASC 2013. CBE 2000. Young Chelsea Bridge Club.

Publications: The League of Nations (Oliver and Boyd, 1973); Versailles and After (Routledge, 1984, 1995); Origins of the Second World War (Routledge, 1985); The Weimer Republic 1919-33 (Routledge, 1988); Origins of the First World War (Routledge, 1989, 1993, 2002); Co-author: Europe 1970-1945 (Longmans, 1997), Women and Political Power (Routledge, 2000); History of the League of Nations (Haus, 2010).

Recreations: Bridge, fell-walking, gardening, wine.

The Baroness Henig CBE, House of Lords, London SW1A 0PW
Tel: 020 7219 5133 *Email:* henigr@parliament.uk

HENLEY, LORD

CONSERVATIVE

HENLEY (8th Baron, I), Oliver Michael Robert Eden; cr. 1799; 6th Baron Northington (UK) 1885. Born 22 November 1953; Son of 7th Baron; Married Caroline Patricia Sharp 1984 (3 sons 1 daughter).

Education: Dragon School, Oxford; Clifton College, Bristol; Durham University (BA modern history 1975).

Non-political career: Called to the Bar, Middle Temple 1977.

Political career: *House of Lords:* First entered House of Lords 1977. Sits as Baron Northington; Government Whip 1989; Government Spokesperson for Health 1989; Joint Parliamentary Under-Secretary of State: Department of Social Security 1989-93, Department of Employment 1993-94, Ministry of Defence 1994-95; Minister of State, Department of Education and Employment 1995-97; Opposition Spokesperson for: Defence 1997, Education and Employment 1997, Treasury 1997-98, Home Affairs 1997-98, Constitutional Affairs 1998-99, Elected hereditary peer 1999-; Opposition Chief Whip 1998-2001; Deputy Speaker 1999-2001; Deputy Chairman of Committees 1999-2001; Opposition Spokesperson for: Cabinet Office June 1999-2000, Legal Affairs 2003-07, Constitutional Affairs 2005-07, Home Affairs 2006-07, Justice 2007-10; Parliamentary Under-Secretary of State and Government Spokesperson, Department for Environment, Food and Rural Affairs 2010-11; Government Spokesperson: Department for Business, Innovation and Skills 2011, Home Office 2011-12; Minister of State for Crime Prevention and Anti-Social Behaviour Reduction, Home Office 2011-12. Member: House of Lords Offices Administration and Works Sub-committee 1998-2001, Procedure 1998-2001, Privileges 1998-2002, Selection 1999-2001, House of Lords Offices -2001; Co-opted member European Union Sub-committee E (Law and Institutions) 2003-06. *Other:* Penrith and the Border Conservative Association: Chair 1987-89, President 1989-94. *Councils and public bodies:* President, Cumbria Association of Local Councils 1981-89; Councillor, Cumbria County Council 1986-89.

Other: PC 2013; Brooks's.

Rt Hon the Lord Henley, House of Lords, London SW1A 0PW
Tel: 020 7219 3108 *Email:* henleyo@parliament.uk

HENNESSY OF NYMPSFIELD, LORD

CROSSBENCH

HENNESSY OF NYMPSFIELD (Life Baron), Peter John Hennessy; cr 2010. Born 28 March 1947; Son of William Gerald and Edith Hennessy; Married Enid Candler 1969 (2 daughters).

Education: Marling School, Stroud; St John's College, Cambridge (BA 1969; PhD 1990); London School of Economics; Harvard University, USA.

Non-political career: Reporter: THES 1972-74, The Times 1974-76; Lobby Correspondent, Financial Times 1976; Whitehall Correspondent, The Times 1976-82; Journalist, The Economist 1982; Home leader writer and columnist, The Times 1982-84; Columnist: New Statesman 1986-87, The Independent 1987-91; Visiting professor of government, Strathclyde University 1989-94; Professor of contemporary history, Queen Mary University, London 1992-2000; Gresham professor of rhethoric 1994-97; Member, Steering group, Sharman Review of Audit and Accountability for Central Government 2001-01; Attlee professor of contemporary British history 2001-; Member, Cabinet office advisory group on security and intelligence records 2004-10; Mile End Institute of Contemporary British Government, Intelligence and Society, Queen Mary University, London: Director 2006-11, Patron 2011-.

Political career: *House of Lords:* Raised to the peerage as Baron Hennessy of Nympsfield, of Nympsfield in the County of Gloucestershire 2010. Member Joint Committee on the Draft House of Lords Reform Bill 2011-12.

Other: Vice-President, Politics Association 1985-90; Institute of Contemporary British History: Founder and co-director 1986-89, Board member 1989-98; Board member, Institute of Historical Research 1992-97; President, Johnian Society 1995; Chairman, Kennedy Memorial Trust 1995-2000; Vice-President, RHists 1996-2000; Governor, Ditchley Foundation 2001-; Director, The Tablet 2003-; Fellow, British Academy 2003-; Patron, Bletchley Park Trust 2011-; Trustee: Attlee Foundation 1985-98, Geffrye Museum 2002-04, Orwell Memorial Trust 2002-04; Visiting fellow: Policy Studies Institute 1986-91, Reading University 1988-94, Nottingham University 1989-95; Honorary research fellow, Department of Politics and Sociology, Birkbeck College, London 1990-91; Visiting scholar, Centre for Australian Public Sector Management, Griffith University, Brisbane 1991; Honorary fellow, Institute of Contemporary British History 1995; Fellow, Gresham College 1997. Honorary DLitt, Universities of: West of England 1995, Westminster 1996, Kingston 1998, Strathclyde 2005; Honorary Fellow, St Benet's Hall, Oxford 2008; DUniv, Open University 2009; Honorary DLitt, Reading University 2011; Honorary Master of the Bench, Middle Temple 2012. Duff Cooper Prize 1993; NCR Prize 1994; Orwell Prize for Political Writing 2007.

Publications: What the Papers Never Said (1985); Never Again: Britain 1945-51 (1992); The Hidden Wiring: Unearthing the British Constitution (1995); Muddling Through (1996); The Prime Minister: the office and its holders since 1945 (2000); The Secret State (2002, 2nd edn 2010); Having it So Good: Britain in the Fifties (2006); Editor, The New Protective State: Government, Intelligence and Terrorism (Continuum, 2007); Cabinets and the Bomb (2007); Distilling the Frenzy: Writing the History of One's Own Times (Biteback, 2012).

Professor the Lord Hennessy of Nympsfield, House of Lords, London SW1A 0PW
Tel: 020 7219 5790 *Email:* hennessyp@parliament.uk

HESELTINE, LORD

HESELTINE (Life Baron), Michael Ray Dibdin Heseltine; cr. 2001. Born 21 March 1933; Son of late Colonel R. D. Heseltine; Married Anne Williams 1962 (1 son 2 daughters).

Education: Shrewsbury School; Pembroke College, Oxford (BA philosophy, politics and economics 1954) (Union President).

Non-political career: Chairman: Haymarket Press (Magazine Publishers) 1964-70, Haymarket Media Group 1999-2009, Haymarket Group 2009-, Advisory Committee, Regional Growth Fund 2011-.

CONSERVATIVE

Political career: *House of Commons:* Contested Gower 1959 and Coventry North 1964 general elections. MP (Conservative) for Tavistock 1966-74, for Henley February 1974-2001. Parliamentary Secretary, Ministry of Transport June-October 1970; Parliamentary Under-Secretary of State, Department of the Environment 1970-72; Minister for Aerospace and Shipping, Department of Trade and Industry 1972-74; Opposition Spokesperson for: Industry 1974-76, The Environment 1976-79; Secretary of State for: the Environment 1979-83, Defence 1983-86, the Environment 1990-92; President of the Board of Trade and Secretary of State for Trade and Industry 1992-95; Deputy Prime Minister and First Secretary of State 1995-97. *House of Lords:* Raised to the peerage as Baron Heseltine, of Thenford in the County of Northamptonshire 2001. *Other:* Chair, Conservative Mainstream Group; President, Conservative Group for Europe; Contested Conservative Party leadership, November 1990; Patron, Tory Reform Group.

Other: Member, The Millennium Commission 1994-2001; Chair, Anglo/Chinese Forum 1998-2004; Vice-President, Royal Horticultural Society 2009-; Royal Institute of British Architects 1991; The 48 Group Club 2003. Freedom: City of Liverpool 2012, City of London 2012. Honorary Fellow, Pembroke College 1986; Honorary LLD, Liverpool University 1990; Honorary Degree, Aston University 2013; Honorary Doctorate, University of South Wales 2013; Honorary Fellow: University of Northampton 2013, Liverpool John Moores University 2013. PPA Marcus Morris Award 2003; Publicity Club of London Cup 2005; Lifetime Achievment, National Business Awards 2005; Goldie Oldie of the Year, The Oldie awards 2013. CH 1997; PC 1979; Carlton; Pratt's; Brooks's; White's.

Publications: Where There's a Will (1987); The Challenge of Europe: Can Britain Win? (1989); Life in the Jungle – the autobiography (2000); No Stone Unturned (2012).

Recreations: Gardening.

Rt Hon the Lord Heseltine CH, House of Lords, London SW1A 0PW
Tel: 020 7219 5353
Haymarket Group, 174 Hammersmith Road, London W6 7JP *Tel:* 020 8267 4213
Email: tracy.rodger@haymarket.com

CONSERVATIVE

HEYHOE FLINT, BARONESS

HEYHOE FLINT (Life Baroness), Rachael Heyhoe Flint; cr 2011. Born 11 June 1939; Daughter of Geoffrey and Roma Heyhoe, née Crocker; Married Derrick Flint 1971 (1 son 1 stepson 2 stepdaughters).

Education: Wolverhampton High School for Girls; Dartford College of Physical Education (Diploma physical education).

Non-political career: Head of physical education: Wolverhampton Municipal Grammar School 1960-62, Northicote School 1962-64; USA Field Hockey Association Coach 1964, 1965; Journalist, *Wolverhampton Express and Star* 1965-72; Sports editor, *Wolverhampton Chronicle* 1969-71; Sports reporter, ITV 1972; Sports writer, *Daily Telegraph* 1967-90; Women's Cricket Association: Vice-chair 1981-86, Public relations officer 1982-86; Consultant, La Manga Club 1983-; Wolverhampton Wanderers Football Club: Public relations executive 1990-2011, Director 1997-2004, Vice-President 2004-.

Political career: *House of Lords:* Raised to the peerage as Baroness Heyhoe Flint, of Wolverhampton in the County of West Midlands 2011. *Councils and public bodies:* DL, West Midlands 1997.

Political interests: Sport, education, charity, community; Bahamas, Singapore.

Other: England Hockey Representative 1964; Member, England Women's Cricket Team 1960-83; Trustee, Wolves Aid 1993-; President, Lady Taverners Charity 2000-11; Radio Wulfrun Hospital Broadcasting; Westcroft Special Needs Sports College; Birch Thompson Trust; West Midlands Air Ambulance. Freeman, City of Wolverhampton 2011. Honorary Fellow, Wolverhampton University 2002; Honorary BSc, Bradford University 2003; Honorary DSc, Greenwich University 2003; Honorary Doctorate of Sports Science, Leeds Metropolitan University 2006. ICC Hall of Fame 2010. MBE 1972; OBE 2008; Honorary Life Member, MCC 1998; Lord's Taverners. South Staffordshire Golf Club; La Manga Club, south east Spain.

Publications: Just for Kicks (Guide to Hockey Goalkeeping) (1966); Women's Hockey (1975); Co-author, Fair Play, The Story of Women's Cricket (1976); Heyhoe! (autobiography, 1978).

Recreations: Golf.

The Baroness Heyhoe Flint OBE, House of Lords, London SW1A 0PW
Tel: 020 7219 5353 *Email:* heyhoeflintr@parliament.uk
Email: flinters@talktalk.net

CONSERVATIVE

HIGGINS, LORD

HIGGINS (Life Baron), Terence Langley Higgins; cr. 1997. Born 18 January 1928; Son of late Reginald and Rose Higgins; Married Rosalyn Cohen 1961 (later QC and DBE and HE Judge Rosalyn Higgins, President of the International Court of Justice) (1 son 1 daughter).

Education: Alleyn's School, Dulwich, London; Gonville and Caius College, Cambridge (BA economics 1958, MA) (Union President 1958); Yale University, USA 1958-59.

Non-political career: Served in the RAF 1946-48. British Olympic Games Team 1948, 1952; New Zealand Shipping Co., in UK and New Zealand 1948-55; Commonwealth Games Team 1950; Economic specialist, Unilever Ltd 1958-64; Economic consultant, Lex Services Group plc 1975-80; Director: Warne Wright Group 1976-84, Lex Service Group 1980-92; First Choice Holidays plc (formerly Owners Abroad plc) 1991-97; Chair and trustee, Lex Services Pension Fund 1994-2003; Member, Claims Resolution Tribunal for Dormant Accounts in Switzerland 1998-2002.

Political career: *House of Commons:* MP (Conservative) for Worthing 1964-97. Minister of State, Treasury 1970-72; Financial Secretary, Treasury 1972-74. Chair: Procedure 1980-83, Treasury 1983-92, Liaison 1984-97. Member, Executive, 1922 Committee 1980-97. *House of Lords:* Raised to the peerage as Baron Higgins, of Worthing in the County of West Sussex 1997. Opposition Spokesperson for: Social Security/Work and Pensions 1997-2005, the Treasury 1997-2001. Member: Speakership 2005, Conventions Joint Committee 2006. *Councils and public bodies:* DL, West Sussex 1988.

Political interests: Finance, social security, transport, sport, horse welfare; Netherlands, New Zealand, USA.

Other: Council, Royal Institute of International Affairs, Chatham House 1980-85; Institute of Advanced Motorists: Council 1980-97, Fellow 1997; Council, National Institute for Economic and Social Research 1980-; Governor, Dulwich College 1980-95; Trustee, Industry and Parliament Trust 1987-92; Governor: National Institute Economic Social Research 1988-, Alleyn's School, Dulwich 1995-99; Hon member Keynes College University of Kent 1976-. Freeman, Worthing

1997. PC 1979; KBE 1993; Hawk's (Cambridge), Reform, Yale Club of London. Royal Blackheath Golf, Koninklijke Haagsche Golf; Patron Herne Hill Harriers.

Recreations: Golf, Sailing.

Rt Hon the Lord Higgins KBE DL, House of Lords, London SW1A 0PW
Tel: 020 7219 4164 *Fax:* 020 7219 6012 *Email:* higginst@parliament.uk

CONSERVATIVE

HILL OF OAREFORD, LORD

Leader of the House of Lords and Chancellor of the Duchy of Lancaster

HILL OF OAREFORD (Life Baron), Jonathan Hopkin Hill; cr 2010. Born 24 July 1960; Son of Rowland Hill and Paddy Henwood; Married Alexandra Nettelfield 1988 (1 son 2 daughters).

Education: Highgate School, London; Trinity College, Cambridge (BA history 1982).

Non-political career: RIT & Northern 1983; Hamish Hamilton 1984-85; Conservative Research Department 1985-86; Special adviser to Rt Hon Kenneth Clarke MP: as Paymaster General and Employment Minister 1986-87, as Chancellor of the Duchy of Lancaster and Minister of Trade and Industry 1987-88, as Secretary of State for Health 1988-89; Lowe Bell Communications 1989-91; Number 10 Policy Unit 1991-92; Political Secretary to Rt Hon John Major MP as Prime Minister 1992-94; Senior consultant, Bell Pottinger Consultants 1994-98; Founding director, Quiller Consultants 1998-2010.

Political career: *House of Lords:* Raised to the peerage as Baron Hill of Oareford, of Oareford in the County of Somerset 2010. Parliamentary Under-Secretary of State for Schools and Government Spokesperson, Department for Education 2010-13; Leader of the House of Lords 2013-; Chancellor of the Duchy of Lancaster 2013-. Member: House 2013-, Liaison 2013-, Privileges and Conduct 2013-, Procedure 2013-, Selection 2013-. *Councils and public bodies:* Governor: Highgate School 1995-2010, Hangford School 2004-10.

Other: Trustee, National Literacy Trust 1995-2009; Member, advisory board, Reform 2004-10. Resignation of the Year, *The Spectator* awards 2012. CBE 1995; PC 2013.

Recreations: Reading, gardening, walking on Exmoor.

Rt Hon the Lord Hill of Oareford CBE, House of Lords, London SW1A 0PW
Tel: 020 7219 3200

LABOUR

HILTON OF EGGARDON, BARONESS

HILTON OF EGGARDON (Life Baroness), Jennifer Hilton; cr. 1991. Born 12 January 1936; Daughter of late John Hilton, CMG and Margaret Hilton; Single.

Education: Bedales School, Hampshire; Manchester University (BA psychology 1970; MA (police scholarship) 1971); London University (Diploma criminology 1973; Diploma history of art 1980); French.

Non-political career: Metropolitan Police 1956-90; Directing staff, National Police Staff College; Metropolitan Police Management Services 1975-76; Superintendent/Chief Superintendent 1977-83; Senior Command Course, National Staff College 1979; New Scotland Yard 1983-87; North West London, responsible for Complaints/Discipline, Personnel, Community Relations 1987-88; Peel Centre, Hendon, responsible for all Metropolitan Police training 1988-90; Member: ACPOs Executive Committee, Equal Opportunities, Extended Interview Panel, Various Home Office Committees.

Political career: *House of Lords:* Raised to the peerage as Baroness Hilton of Eggardon, of Eggardon in the County of Dorset 1991. Opposition Whip 1991-95; Opposition Spokesperson for: the Environment 1991-97, Home Affairs 1994-97. EU Sub-committee D (Environment): Member 1991-97, Chair 1995-97; Member: Science and Technology 1992-95, 2010-, European Union 1997-99; Chair: EU Sub-committee C (Environment, Public Health and Consumer Protection) 1997-99, Advisory Panel on Works of Art 1998-2003, EU Sub-committee C (Foreign Affairs and Defence): Member 2000-03, Chair 2000-01; Member House of Lords Offices 2000-03, Science and Technology Sub-committees: I (Science and International Agreements) 2003-04, I (Scientific Aspects of Ageing) 2004-05, Works of Art 2007-09, Science and Technology Sub-committee I 2012-13.

Political interests: Environment, race relations, criminal justice; All countries of the old Russian empire.

Other: Member, UK Delegation, Organisation for Security and Co-operation in Europe Parliamentary Assembly. QPM 1989.

Publications: The Gentle Arm of the Law (1967); Co-author, Individual Development and Social Experience (1974).

Recreations: Gardening, travel, art.

The Baroness Hilton of Eggardon QPM, House of Lords, London SW1A 0PW
Tel: 020 7219 3182

HODGSON OF ABINGER, BARONESS – *Please see Addenda Page xi*

HODGSON OF ASTLEY ABBOTTS, LORD

CONSERVATIVE

HODGSON OF ASTLEY ABBOTTS (Life Baron), Robin Granville Hodgson; cr. 2000. Born 25 April 1942; Son of late Henry and Natalie Hodgson; Married Fiona Ferelith Allom 1982 (now Baroness Hodgson of Abinger) (3 sons 1 daughter and 1 twin son deceased).

Education: Shrewsbury School; Oxford University (BA modern history 1964); Wharton School of Finance, Pennsylvania University (MBA 1969).

Non-political career: Investment banker, New York and Montreal 1964-67; Industry in Birmingham 1969-72; Director, Johnson Brothers & Co Ltd, Walsall 1970-; Granville Baird Group: Director 1972-2003, Group chief executive 1979-95, Chair 1995-2002; Director: Domnick Hunter plc 1989-2003, Staffordshire Building Society 1995-2005, Community Hospitals plc 1995-2001; Chair: Market Touch plc 2001-02, Nova Capital Management 2002-, Carbo plc 2002-05; Director, Marstons plc (formerly Wolverhampton and Dudley Breweries plc) 2002-; Chair: RFIB Group Limited 2007-, Tenet Group Ltd 2007-12, EIS Optics Ltd 2009-11.

Political career: *House of Commons:* Contested Walsall North February and October 1974 general elections. MP (Conservative) for Walsall North November 1976-79. *House of Lords:* Raised to the peerage as Baron Hodgson of Astley Abbotts, of Nash in the County of Shropshire 2000. Opposition Spokesperson for: Home Office 2002-06, Trade and Industry 2002-06. EU Sub-committee F (Home Affairs): Co-opted member 2007-10, Member 2010-12; Member: Consumer Insurance (Disclosure and Representations) Bill 2011-12, EU Sub-committee E (Justice, Institutions and Consumer Protection) 2012-, Soft Power and the UK's Influence 2013-. *Other:* Chairman: National Union of Conservative Associations 1996-98, National Conservative Convention 1998-2000; Deputy Chairman, Conservative Party 1998-2000. *Councils and public bodies:* Member: Council for Securities Industry 1980-85, Securities and Investment Board 1985-89, West Midlands Industrial Development Board 1989-97, Securities and Futures Authority 1993-2001; President, National Council for Voluntary Organisation (NCVO) 2007-12; Official Reviewer of the Charities Act 2011-12.

Other: Chair, Armed Forces Charity Advisory Committee 2008-; Trustee, Fair Trials International 2012-; Salvation Army, Fair Trials International, Freedom from Torture, Howard League. Liveryman, Goldsmith's Company 1983. Trustee and Honorary Fellow, St Peter's College, Oxford. CBE 1992.

Publications: Britain's Home Defence Gamble (1978); Unshackling Good Neighbours (2011).

Recreations: Squash, fishing, theatre.

The Lord Hodgson of Astley Abbotts CBE, House of Lords, London SW1A 0PW
Tel: 020 7219 8526 *Fax:* 020 7219 1903 *Email:* hodgsonr@parliament.uk
Nova Capital Group, Cayzer House, 30 Buckingham Gate, London SW1E 6NN
Tel: 020 7901 1760 *Fax:* 020 7901 1761 *Email:* r.hodgson@nova-cap.com

HOFFMANN, LORD

CROSSBENCH

HOFFMANN (Life Baron), Leonard Hubert Hoffmann; cr. 1995. Born 8 May 1934; Married Gillian Lorna Sterner 1957 (2 daughters).

Education: South African College School, Cape Town; University of Cape Town (BA); The Queen's College, Oxford (Rhodes Scholar, MA, BCL, Vinerian Law Scholar).

Non-political career: Advocate of Supreme Court of South Africa 1958-60; Stowell Civil Law Fellow, University College, Oxford 1961-73; Called to the Bar, Gray's Inn 1964; QC 1977; Judge of the Courts of Appeal of Jersey and Guernsey 1980-85; Bencher 1984; Judge of the High Court of Justice, Chancery Division 1985-92; Lord Justice of Appeal 1992-95; Judge, Hong Kong Court of Final Appeal, 1998-; Chair, Financial Market Law Committee 2009-.

Political career: *House of Lords:* Raised to the peerage as Baron Hoffmann, of Chedworth in the County of Gloucestershire 1995. Lord of Appeal in Ordinary 1995-2009. Chair European Communities Sub-committee E (Law and Institutions) 1997-2000. *Councils and public bodies:* Member, Royal Commission on Gambling 1976-78; Council of Legal Education: Member 1983-92, Chair 1989-92.

Other: President, British-German Jurists Association 1991-2009; Director, English National Opera 1985-90, 1991-94. Honorary Fellow, The Queen's College, Oxford 1992; Three honorary doctorates; Honorary Fellow, University College, Oxford 1995. Kt 1985; PC 1992.

Publications: The South African Law of Evidence (1963).

Recreations: Music, cycling.

Rt Hon the Lord Hoffmann, House of Lords, London SW1A 0PW
Tel: 020 7219 6067
Surrey Lodge, 23 Keats Grove, London NW3 2RS

HOGG, BARONESS

HOGG (Life Baroness), Sarah Elizabeth Mary Hogg; cr. 1995. Born 14 May 1946; Daughter of late Rt Hon Baron Boyd-Carpenter; Married Rt Hon Douglas Martin Hogg (later MP, QC, 3rd Viscount Hailsham) 1968 (1 son 1 daughter).

Education: St Mary's Convent, Ascot; Lady Margaret Hall, Oxford (BA philosophy, politics and economics 1967).

CROSSBENCH

Non-political career: *The Economist* 1967-81: Literary editor 1970-77, Economics editor 1977-81; Economics editor, *The Sunday Times* 1981-82; Presenter, *Channel 4 News* 1982-83; Director, London Broadcasting Company 1982-90; Economics editor and deputy executive editor, finance and industry, *The Times* 1984-86; Assistant editor and business and city editor, *The Independent* 1986-89; Economics editor, *Daily Telegraph* and *Sunday Telegraph* 1989-90; Head, Prime Minister's Policy Unit, with rank of Second Permanent Secretary 1990-95; Director, London School of Economics 1995-97; Chair, London Economics 1997-99; Chairman, Frontier Economics Ltd 1999-, Foreign and Colonial Smaller Companies Trust: Non-executive director 1995-2002, Chairman 1997-2002; International advisory board, National Westminster Bank 1995-98; Advisory board, Bankinter 1995-98; NPI 1996-99; Non-executive director, The Energy Group 1996-98; GKN: Non-executive director 1996-2006, Deputy Chair 2003-06; 3i: Director 1997-, Deputy Chair 2000-01, Chair 2002-10; Non-executive director: Scottish Eastern Investment Trust 1998-99, Martin Currie Portfolio Trust 1999-2002, P&O 1999-2000, P&O Princess Cruises 2000-03, Carnival Corporation and Carnival plc 2003-08, BG Group plc 2005-; Cadbury plc 2008-10; Chairman, Financial Reporting Council 2010-, Non-executive director: HM Treasury Management Board 2010-, John Lewis Partnership 2011-.

Political career: *House of Lords:* Raised to the peerage as Baroness Hogg, of Kettlethorpe in the County of Lincolnshire 1995. Member: Science and Technology Committee 1996-99, Monetary Policy of the Bank of England/Economic Affairs 2000-03. *Councils and public bodies:* Governor, BBC 2000-04.

Other: Governor, Centre for Economic Policy Research 1985-92; Director, Royal National Theatre 1988-91; Fellow, Eton College 1996-2008; Council Member: Royal Economic Society 1996-2004, Institute for Fiscal Studies 1996-2005, Hansard Society for Parliamentary Government 1996-2000, Lincolnshire Foundation 1996-98, Lincoln University 2002-05; Governor, London Business School 2004-10; Financial Reporting Council: Member 2005-10, Chairman 2010-; Trustee: St Mary's School, Ascot 1994-, Trusthouse Charitable Foundation 2003-, Cicely Saunders International 2009-10. Honorary MA, Open University, 1987; Honorary DLitt, Loughborough, 1992; Honorary Fellow, Lady Margaret Hall, 1994; Honorary LLD, Lincoln, 2001; Honorary DPhil: City University, 2002, Cranfield, 2006. Wincott Foundation Financial Journalist of the Year 1985; CBI First Women Lifetime Award 2005.

Publications: Co-author, *Too Close to Call* (1995).

Viscountess Hailsham, The Baroness Hogg, House of Lords, London SW1A 0PW
Tel: 020 7219 5353

HOLLICK, LORD

HOLLICK (Life Baron), Clive Richard Hollick; cr. 1991. Born 20 May 1945; Son of late Leslie Hollick and Olive Hollick; Married Susan Woodford 1977 (3 daughters).

Education: Taunton's School, Southampton; Nottingham University (BA sociology 1966).

Non-political career: Hambros Bank: Joined 1967, Director 1973-96; Managing director, MAI plc 1974-96; Director, Mills and Allen Ltd 1975-89; Chair, Shepperton Studios Ltd 1976-84; Member, National Bus Company 1984-91; Director: Logica plc 1987-91, Avenir Havas Media SA (France) 1988-92, National Opinion Polls Ltd 1989-97, Satellite Information Services 1990-94;

LABOUR

Chair, Meridian Broadcasting 1991-96; Director, British Aerospace 1992-97; Member, Financial Law Panel 1993-97; Director, Anglia Television 1994-97; Member, Commission on Public Policy and British Business 1995-97; Chair, United Broadcasting and Entertainment Ltd 1995-2000; Chief executive, United Business Media plc 1996-2005; Special adviser to Margaret Beckett MP as President of the Board of Trade 1997-98; Director: Express Newspapers plc 1998-2000, TRW Inc 2000-02, Diageo plc 2001-; Chair, South Bank Centre 2002-08; Director, Honeywell International Inc 2003-; Kohlberg Kravis Roberts: Partner 2005-09, Senior adviser 2009-10; Partner, GP Bullhound 2010-; Senior adviser, Jefferies Inc 2011-.

Political career: *House of Lords:* Raised to the peerage as Baron Hollick, of Notting Hill in the Royal Borough of Kensington and Chelsea 1991. Member: Economic Affairs 2010-, Economic Affairs Finance Bill Sub-Committee 2011, Joint Committee on Privacy and Injunctions 2011-12, Sub-committee on Economic Affairs Finance Bill 2012-.

Political interests: Business, economic policy, constitutional affairs, transport, media.

Other: Founder, Institute for Public Policy Research 1988; Governor, London School of Economics and Political Science 1997-2002. Honorary LLD, Nottingham University 1993.

Recreations: Reading, countryside, cinema, theatre, tennis, golf.

The Lord Hollick, House of Lords, London SW1A 0PW

Tel: 020 7219 8942 *Email:* hollickrc@parliament.uk *Twitter:* @clivehollick

CROSSBENCH

HOLLINS, BARONESS

HOLLINS (Life Baroness), Sheila Clare Hollins; cr 2010. Born 22 June 1946; Daughter of late Captain Adrian Kelly and late Monica Kelly, née Edwards; Married Martin Prior Hollins 1969 (1 son 3 daughters).

Education: Notre Dame High School, Sheffield; St Thomas' Hospital Medical School, London (MB BS).

Non-political career: Senior registrar in child psychiatry, Earl's Court Child Guidance Unit and Westminster Child's Hospital 1979-81; Senior lecturer in psychiatry of learning disability 1981-90; Honorary Consultant 1981-2011: Wandsworth Community Health Trust, Richmond, Twickenham and Roehampton Healthcare Trust, South West London and St George's Mental Health Trust; Professor of psychiatry of disability, St George's, University of London 1990-; Policy adviser on learning disability, Department of Health (on secondment) 1992-93, 2001-03; Member, Minister's Advisory Group on Learning Disability 1999-2001; Chair: NHS Working Party on Breast and Cervical Screening in Learning Disability 1999-2000, Academic Division of Mental Health, St George's, University of London 2002-05; Deputy chair, National Specialist Commissioning Advisory Group 2006-08; Chair, External Advisory Group, National Confidential Inquiry into Suicides and Homicides 2007-11. President, BMA 2012-13; Chair, Board of Science 2013-.

Political career: *House of Lords:* Raised to the peerage as Baroness Hollins, of Wimbledon in the London Borough of Merton and of Grenoside in the County of South Yorkshire 2010. Member Mental Capacity Act 2005 2013-.

Political interests: Health and social care (especially mental health and learning disability), welfare reform, special education (long term conditions), human rights abuses of disabled people.

Other: Member: Community Care and Disability Subcommittee, Joseph Rowntree Foundation 1989-93, Academy of Medical Royal Colleges 2005-08; Executive chair, Books Beyond Word CIC; Patron, Respond 2011-; Honorary fellow and former vice-president, Institute of Psychotherapy and Disability; Patron, Wimbledon Bookfest 2010-; Royal College of Psychiatrists: Vice-President 2003-04, President 2005-08; MRCPsych 1978; FRCPsych 1988; FRCPCH 1990; Honorary FRCP 2007; FHEA; Honorary Fellow, Medical Women's Federation. Honorary Fellow, Colleges of Medecine, South Africa.

Publications: Over 200 academic and professional articles on mental health and learning disability.

Professor the Baroness Hollins, House of Lords, London SW1A 0PW

Tel: 020 7219 0520 *Email:* hollinss@parliament.uk

LABOUR

HOLLIS OF HEIGHAM, BARONESS

HOLLIS OF HEIGHAM (Life Baroness), Patricia Lesley Hollis; cr. 1990. Born 24 May 1941; Daughter of Harry Lesley George and Queenie Rosalyn Wells; Married James Martin Hollis (later Professor, FBA) 1965 (died 1998) (2 sons); partner Lord Howarth of Newport (qv).

Education: Plympton Grammar School; Cambridge University (BA history 1962, MA); University of California and Columbia University, New York (Harkness Fellow 1962-64); Nuffield College, Oxford (MA, DPhil 1967).

Non-political career: University of East Anglia: Modern history: Lecturer 1967, Senior lecturer 1979, Reader 1985, Dean School of English and American Studies 1988-90; Founder-director, Radio Broadland 1983-97. Member, AUT.

Political career: *House of Commons:* Contested (Labour) Great Yarmouth February and October 1974 and 1979 general elections. *House of Lords:* Raised to the peerage as Baroness Hollis of Heigham, of Heigham in the City of Norwich 1990. Opposition Whip 1990-95; Opposition Spokesperson for Environment and Social Security 1990-97; Parliamentary Under-Secretary of State and Government Spokesperson for: Department of Social Security 1997-2001, (Minister for Children and the Family), Department for Work and Pensions 2001-05. Member: Administration and Works 2006-07, Draft Human Tissue and Embryos Bill Joint Committee 2007, House 2007-13, Barnett Formula 2008-09, Procedure 2013-. *Councils and public bodies:* Norwich City Council: Councillor 1968-91, Leader 1983-88; Member: BBC Regional Advisory Council 1973-79, East Anglian Planning Council 1975-79, Regional Health Authority 1979-83; Councillor, Norfolk County Council 1981-85; Member, Press Council 1988-90, Commissioner, English Heritage 1988-91; Vice-President: Association of District Councils 1990-97, Association of Metropolitan Authorities 1990-97, Association of Environmental Health Officers 1992-97, National Federation of Housing Associations 1993-97; DL, Norfolk 1994-; Vice-President: Local Government Association 2005-10, Board, Pensions Advisory Service 2006-; President, Women's Local Government Society 2007-; Chair, Broadland Housing Association 2009-; Governor, Pensions Policy Institute 2010-.

Political interests: Local government, heritage, pensions, women's issues, housing.

Other: Patron: Norfolk Millennium Carers, St Martin's Housing Trust; Trustee, History of Parliament Trust; Fellow, Royal Historical Society. Freedom, City of Norwich. Three honorary doctorates; Honorary fellow, Girton College, Cambridge. Wolfson prize for History 1998; George Orwell prize for political biography 1998; Peer of the Year, Women in Public Life Awards 2009; Campaigining Politician, Channel 4 Political awards 2009. PC 1999.

Publications: The Pauper Press (1970); Class and Class Conflict 1815-50 (1973); Pressure from Without (1974); Women in Public, 1850-1900 (1979); Robert Lowry, Radical and Chartist (1979); Ladies Elect: women in English Local Government 1865-1914 (1987); Jennie Lee: a Life (1997).

Recreations: Boating, singing, domesticity.

Rt Hon the Baroness Hollis of Heigham DL, House of Lords, London SW1A 0PW
Tel: 020 7219 6784 *Email:* hollisp@parliament.uk
30 Park Lane, Norwich, Norfolk NR2 3EE *Tel:* 01603 621990

HOLMES OF RICHMOND, LORD – *Please see Addenda Page xi*

HOME, EARL OF

CONSERVATIVE

HOME (15th Earl of, S), David Alexander Cospatrick Douglas-Home; cr. 1604; Lord Dunglass; 20th Lord Home (S) 1473; 5th Baron Douglas (UK) 1875. Born 20 November 1943; Son of 14th Earl, KT, PC, DL, who disclaimed the earldom 1963 to become Prime Minister as Sir Alec Douglas-Home, and who was subsequently made a life peer as Baron Home of the Hirsel 1974; Married Jane Williams-Wynne 1972 (1 son 2 daughters).

Education: Eton College; Christ Church, Oxford (BA philosophy, politics and economics 1966).

Non-political career: Douglas and Angus Estates: Director 1966-, Chair 1995-; Director: Morgan Grenfell & Co. Ltd. 1974-99, Arab-British Chamber of Commerce 1975-84; Morgan Grenfell (Asia) Ltd.: Director 1978-82, Deputy chair 1979-82; Director: Arab Bank Investment Co. 1979-87, Agricultural Mortgage Corporation plc 1979-93; Tandem Group plc (formerly EFG plc): Director 1981-96, Chair 1993-96; Chair: Morgan Grenfell Export Services 1984-98, Morgan Grenfell (Scotland) 1986-98, Committee for Middle East Trade 1986-92, Morgan Grenfell International Ltd 1987-98; Director: Morgan Grenfell Asia (Hong Kong) Ltd/Deutsche Morgan Grenfell Hong Kong Ltd 1989-99, Morgan Grenfell Asia Holdings Pte Ltd/Deutsche Morgan Grenfell Asia Holdings Pte Ltd 1989-99, K & N Kenanga Holdings Bhd 1993-99; Non-executive director, Grosvenor Estate Holdings 1993-2000; Director: Kenanga DMG Futures Sdn Bhd/Kenanga Deutsche Futures Sdn Bhd 1995-99, Deutsche Morgan Grenfell Group plc 1996-99; Board member: Deva Group/Wheatsheaf Investments Ltd 1999-, Deva Holding Ltd/Deva Group 1999-2010; Chair: Coutts and Company 1999-, Coutts Switzerland Ltd/RBS Coutts/Coutts & Co Ltd. 2000-, MAN Ltd 2000-09; Board member: Oryx Fund 2004-07, Dubai Financial Services Authority 2005-12; Grosvenor Group Ltd: Board member 2005-10, Chair 2007-10.

Political career: *House of Lords:* First entered House of Lords 1995; Opposition Frontbench Spokesperson for: Trade 1997-98, the Treasury 1997-98; Elected hereditary peer 1999-. *Councils and public bodies:* Member, Export Guarantee Advisory Council, ECGD 1988-93.

Political interests: Foreign affairs, Scottish affairs, industry, agriculture; Australia, Middle and Far East.

Other: President, British Malaysian Society 2006-; Trustee: Grosvenor Estate 1993-2010, Royal Agricultural Society of England 1999-2003; Fellow, Chartered Institute of Bankers 1999-; Chairman: Coutts Charitable Trust, Coutts Foundation; Lymphoma Association. CBE 1991; CVO 1997; Turf.

Recreations: Outdoor sports.

The Earl of Home CVO CBE, House of Lords, London SW1A 0PW
Tel: 020 7219 3168
Coutts & Co, 440 Strand, London WC2R 0QS *Tel:* 020 7753 1000 *Fax:* 020 7753 1066
Email: linda.bracha@coutts.com

HOOPER, BARONESS

HOOPER (Life Baroness), Gloria Dorothy Hooper; cr. 1985. Born 25 May 1939; Daughter of late Frederick Hooper and late Frances Hooper, née Maloney; Single.

Education: La Sainte Union Convent; Royal Ballet School; Southampton University (BA law 1960); Universidad Central, Ecuador (Rotary Foundation Fellow 1965-66); Law Society; French, Spanish.

Non-political career: Assistant to chief registrar, John Lewis Partnership 1960-61; Editor, Current Law, Sweet & Maxwell, Law Publishers 1961-62; Information officer, Winchester City Council 1962-67; Assistant solicitor, Taylor and Humbert 1967-72; Legal adviser, Slater Walker France S.A. 1972-73; Partner, Taylor and Humbert (Solicitors), now Taylor Wessing 1974-84.

CONSERVATIVE

Political career: *House of Lords:* Raised to the peerage as Baroness Hooper, of Liverpool and St James's in the City of Westminster 1985. Government Whip 1985-87; Parliamentary Under-Secretary of State, Department of: Education and Science 1987-88, Energy 1988-89, Health 1989-92; Deputy Speaker 1993-; Deputy Chairman of Committees 1993-; PPS to William Hague as Leader of the Opposition 1999-2001. Member Intergovernmental Organisations 2008; EU Sub-committee A (Economic and Financial Affairs and International Trade): Co-opted member 2008-10, Member 2010-12; Member EU Sub-committees: A (Economic and Financial Affairs) 2012-13, B (Internal Market, Infrastructure and Employment) 2013-. *Other:* MEP (Conservative) for Liverpool 1979-84: Deputy chief whip, European Democratic Group. Member, Association of Conservative Peers 1985-; President, Greater London Women's Conservative Association 2006-.

Political interests: European Union, cultural heritage, education, energy, international relations; Mercosur countries, Andean Pact countries, CAFTA countries, Commonwealth countries, NAFTA countries, Council of Europe countries, Overseas Territories.

Other: Member: Parliamentary Delegation to Council of Europe and to Western European Union 1992-97, 2001-09, Council, Commonwealth Parliamentary Association, UK Branch 2008-, Executive Committee, Inter-Parliamentary Union, British Group 2010-; Member, The Law Society; President, British Educational Equipment and Supplies Association; Vice-President, Canning House (Hispanic and Luso Brazilian Council); President: Good Guy's Cancer Appeal, Friends of Colombia for Social Aid, European Foundation For Heritage Skills, The Friends of Gibraltar; Chair: Institute of the Americas UCL, Dance Teachers Benevolent Fund; Trustee/Governor, Centre for Global Energy Studies; Industry and Parliament Trust: Fellow 1983, Trustee 1996-2012; Trustee: The Tablet Trust 2004-, St George's House, Windsor Castle 2007-13; Member, The Law Society; Fellow: Royal Geographical Society, RSA. Honorary LLD, Southampton University 2009. Order of Francisco de Miranda (Venezuela) 1999; CMG 2003; Order of Boyaca Gran Cruz (Colombia) 2004; Order of Merit (Ecuador) 2004; Order of Bernardo O'Higgins (Chile) 2004; Dame of the Order of St Gregory the Great 2005; In and Out Club.

Recreations: Theatre, travel, gardening.

The Baroness Hooper CMG, House of Lords, London SW1A 0PW
Tel: 020 7219 5489 *Fax:* 020 7925 0625 *Email:* hooperg@parliament.uk

HOPE OF CRAIGHEAD, LORD

HOPE OF CRAIGHEAD (Life Baron), James Arthur David Hope; cr. 1995. Born 27 June 1938; Son of late Arthur Hope, OBE, WS; Married Mary Kerr 1966 (twin sons 1 daughter).

Education: Edinburgh Academy; Rugby School; St John's College, Cambridge (Scholarship 1956, BA classics 1962, MA); Edinburgh University (LLB 1965).

Non-political career: National service, Seaforth Highlanders 1957-59. Admitted Faculty of Advocates 1965; Standing Junior Counsel in Scotland to Board of Inland Revenue 1974-78; Advocate-Depute 1978-82; QC (Scotland) 1978; Legal Chairman, Pensions Appeal Tribunal 1985-86; Chairman, Medical Appeal Tribunals 1985-86; Dean, Faculty of Advocates 1986-89; Lord Justice General of Scotland and Lord President of the Court of Session 1989-96; Honorary Bencher: Gray's Inn 1989, Inn of Court of Northern Ireland 1995; Deputy President, Supreme Court of the United Kingdom 2009-13.

CROSSBENCH

Political career: *House of Lords:* Raised to the peerage as Baron Hope of Craighead, of Bamff in the District of Perth and Kinross 1995. Lord of Appeal in Ordinary 1996-2009: Second Senior Law Lord 2009; As Deputy President of the Supreme Court, disqualified from participation 2009-13. Member European Communities 1998-2001; Chair European Communities Sub-committee E (Law and Institutions) 1998-2001.

Other: Board of Trustees, National Library of Scotland 1989-96; Member, University of Strathclyde Charitable Foundation 1998-2001; Chair, Advisory Council, Institute of Advanced Legal Studies 1998-2013; President: The Stair Society 1993-2013, International Criminal Law Association 2000-13; Fellow: Strathclyde University 2000, Royal Society of Edinburgh 2003; Commonwealth Magistrates' and Judges' Association: President 2003-06, Life Vice-President; Chair, Botanic Cottage Trust, Edinburgh 2009-12. Chancellor, Strathclyde University 1998-2013. Honorary LLD: Aberdeen 1991, Strathclyde 1993, Edinburgh 1995, Glasgow 2013; Honorary Fellow, St John's College, Cambridge 1995. PC 1989; KT 2010; New Club (Edinburgh).

Publications: Co-editor, Gloag and Henderson's Introduction to the Law of Scotland (6th-9th eds 1956-87); Armour on Valuation for Rating (4th-5th eds, 1971, 1985); Co-author, The Rent (Scotland) Act (1984, 1986); Contributor, Stair Memorial Encyclopaedia of Scots Law; Gloag and Henderson's The Law of Scotland (11th ed, 2002); Court of Session Practice (2005) with regular updates.

Recreations: Walking, ornithology, music.

Rt Hon the Lord Hope of Craighead KT, House of Lords, London SW1A 0PW
Tel: 020 7219 5353

CROSSBENCH

HOPE OF THORNES, LORD

HOPE OF THORNES (Life Baron), David Michael Hope; cr 2005. Born 14 April 1940; Son of late Jack and Florence Hope.

Education: Queen Elizabeth Grammar School, Wakefield; Nottingham University (BA theology 1962); St Stephen's House, Oxford; Linacre College, Oxford (DPhil 1965).

Non-political career: Curate, St John, Tuebrook, Liverpool 1965-67, 1968-70; Chaplain, Church of the Resurrection, Bucharest 1967-68; Vicar, St Andrew, Orford, Warrington 1970-74; Principal, St Stephen's House, Oxford 1974-82; Vicar, All Saints, Margaret Street, London W1 1982-85; Diocesan Bishop of Wakefield 1985-91; Bishop of London 1991-95; Archbishop of York 1995-2005; Honorary Assistant Bishop: Bradford 2007, Europe 2007.

Political career: *House of Lords:* Raised to the peerage as Baron Hope of Thornes, of Thornes in the County of West Yorkshire 2005. First entered House of Lords as Bishop of Wakefield 1990; On leave of absence November 2012-. *Councils and public bodies:* Prelate of the Most Excellent Order of the British Empire 1991-95.

Political interests: Eastern Europe, inner cities, Africa.

Other: Honorary LLD CNAA; Honorary DD, Nottingham University; Honorary DD, Hull University. PC 1991; KCVO 1995; Athenæum.

Publications: The Leonine Sacramentary, The Living Gospel, Friendship with God.

Recreations: Music, fell walking, photography.

Rt Rev and Rt Hon the Lord Hope of Thornes KCVO, House of Lords, London SW1A 0PW
Tel: 020 7219 5353 *Email:* d.hope234@btinternet.com

CONSERVATIVE

HORAM, LORD

HORAM (Life Baron), John Rhodes Horam; cr 2013. Born 7 March 1939; Son of Sydney and Catherine Horam; Married Judith Jackson 1987 (2 sons from previous marriage).

Education: Silcoates School, Wakefield; St Catharine's College, Cambridge (MA economics 1960).

Non-political career: Market research officer, Rowntree & Co 1960-62; Leader and feature writer: *Financial Times* 1962-65, *The Economist* 1965-68; Managing director: Commodities Research Unit Ltd 1968-70, 1983-87, CRU Holdings Ltd 1988-92; Deputy chair, CRU International Ltd 1992-95, Honorary non-executive director, CRU International 1997-.

Political career: *House of Commons:* Contested (Labour) Folkstone and Hythe 1966 general election. MP for Gateshead West 1970-83 (Labour 1970-81, SDP 1981-83). Contested Newcastle upon Tyne Central (SDP/Alliance) 1983 general election. MP (Conservative) for Orpington 1992-2010. Parliamentary Under-Secretary of State, Department of Transport 1976-79; Labour Spokesperson for Economic Affairs 1979-81; SDP Spokesperson 1981-83; Parliamentary Secretary, Office of Public Service 1995; Parliamentary Under-Secretary of State, Department of Health 1995-97. Member: Public Accounts 1992-95, Liaison 1997-2003; Environmental Audit: Chair 1997-2003, Member 2003-05, Member: Foreign Affairs 2005-10. *House of Lords:* Raised to the peerage as Baron Horam, of Grimsargh in the County of Lancashire 2013. *Other:* Member, Executive, 1922 Committee 2004-07. *Councils and public bodies:* Electoral Commissioner 2012-.

Political interests: Economic policy, transport, health, environment, foreign affairs; France, Germany, USA.

Other: Globe.

Publications: Making Britain Competitive (1993).

Recreations: Opera, gardening, walking.

The Lord Horam, House of Lords, London SW1A 0PW
Tel: 020 7219 5353 *Website:* www.johnhoram.com

CONSERVATIVE

HOWARD OF LYMPNE, LORD

HOWARD OF LYMPNE (Life Baron), Michael Howard; cr 2010. Born 7 July 1941; Son of late Bernard and Hilda Howard; Married Sandra Paul 1975 (1 son 1 daughter 1 stepson).

Education: Llanelli Grammar School; Peterhouse, Cambridge (MA economics and law, LLB 1963).

Non-political career: Called to the Bar, Inner Temple 1964; Junior Counsel to the Crown 1980-82; QC 1982.

Political career: *House of Commons:* Contested Liverpool Edge Hill 1966 and 1970 general elections. MP (Conservative) for Folkestone and Hythe 1983-2010. PPS to Sir Patrick Mayhew as Solicitor-General 1984-85; Parliamentary Under-Secretary of State, Department of Trade and Industry 1985-87; Minister of State, Department of the Environment 1987-90; Secretary of State for: Employment 1990-92, the Environment 1992-93; Home Secretary 1993-97; Member, Shadow Cabinet 1997-99, 2001-05: Shadow Foreign Secretary 1997-99, Shadow Chancellor of the Exchequer 2001-03, Leader of the Opposition 2003-05. Chair, Conservative Policy Committee for Economic Affairs/Enterprise/Pensions/Social Affairs 2001-03. *House of Lords:* Raised to the peerage as Baron Howard of Lympne, of Lympne in the County of Kent 2010. *Other:* Chair, Coningsby Club 1972-73; Member, Conservative Policy Board 2001-03; Contested Conservative Party leadership June 1997; Leader, Conservative Party 2003-05; Patron, Tory Reform Group. *Councils and public bodies:* Member, House of Lords Appointments Commission 2010-.

Political interests: Home affairs, foreign affairs; USA.

Other: Chair, Bow Group 1970; President and founding chair, Atlantic Partnership 2003-. *The Spectator* Parliamentarian of the Year 2003. PC 1990; CH 2011; Carlton, Pratt's, Buck's.

Recreations: Football, baseball.

Rt Hon the Lord Howard of Lympne CH QC, House of Lords, London SW1A 0PW
Tel: 020 7219 3964 *Fax:* 0207 219 4551 *Email:* howardm@parliament.uk
Website: www.michaelhoward.org

CONSERVATIVE

HOWARD OF RISING, LORD

HOWARD OF RISING (Life Baron), Greville Patrick Charles Howard; cr. 2004. Born 22 April 1941; Son of Lt Col H R G Howard; Married Mary Cortland Culverwell 1981 (2 sons 1 daughter).

Education: Eton College.

Non-political career: Private secretary to J Enoch Powell MP 1968-70; Director: Keep Trust 1980-87, Fortress Trust 1989-93, Fortress Holdings 1993-2008.

Political career: *House of Lords:* Raised to the peerage as Baron Howard of Rising, of Castle Rising in the County of Norfolk 2004. Opposition Whip 2005-09; Opposition Spokesperson for: Treasury 2005-09, Work and Pensions 2005-06, Constitutional Affairs 2006, Cabinet Office 2006-09, Culture, Media and Sport 2006-10. Member: Joint Committee on Statutory Instruments 2005-07, Refreshment 2012-. *Councils and public bodies:* Councillor, King's Lynn and West Norfolk 2003-.

Publications: Editor, Enoch at 100 (Biteback, 2012).

The Lord Howard of Rising, House of Lords, London SW1A 0PW
Tel: 020 7219 5353

CROSSBENCH

HOWARTH OF BRECKLAND, BARONESS

HOWARTH OF BRECKLAND (Life Baroness), Valerie Georgina Howarth OBE; cr 2001. Born 5 September 1940; Daughter of George Howarth and Edith Steele.

Education: Abbeydale Girls Grammar School, Sheffield; Leicester University (Diploma social studies 1963; Certificate applied social studies); Home Office Certificate childcare.

Non-political career: Caseworker, Family Welfare Association 1963-68; London Borough of Lambeth 1968-82: Senior child care worker and training officer 1968-70, Area co-ordinator 1970-72, Chief co-ordinator of social work 1972-76, Assistant director of personal services 1976-82; Director of social services, London Borough of Brent 1982-86; Chief executive, ChildLine charity 1987-2001; Director and committee member, ICSTIS (Independent Committee for the Supervision of Telephone Information Systems) 1988-2000.

Political career: *House of Lords:* Raised to the peerage as Baroness Howarth of Breckland, of Parson Cross in the County of South Yorkshire 2001. EU Sub-committee G (Social Policy and Consumer Affairs): Member 2003-07, Chair 2007-10; Member: European Union 2007-12, EU Sub-committee D: (Agriculture, Fisheries and Environment) 2010-12, (Agriculture, Fisheries, Environment and Energy) 2012-, Adoption Legislation 2012-13. *Councils and public bodies:* UK Representative of European Forum for Child Welfare 1994-97; Chair, UK Group on Child Exploitation (linked with EFCW); Board member: Food Standards Agency 2000-07, National Care Standards Commission 2001-04, Meat Hygiene Services Board 2004-07; Cafcass (Children and Families Advisory and Support Services): Board member 2004-08, Chair 2008-12; Vice-President, Local Government Association 2010-.

Political interests: Social care, consumer affairs; Europe.

Other: Founder and first chair, King's Cross Homeless Project 1986-87; Founder member, London Homeless Forum 1986-87; Trustee and vice-chair, National Council for Voluntary Child Care Organisations 1990-95, Member NCH Commission considering Children as Abusers 1991-92; Trustee and vice-chair, Lucy Faithfull Foundation 1992-; Chair, 'Stop it Now' Steering Group - 2009; Trustee, National Children's Bureau 1993-94; Member, NSPCC Professional Advisory Panel 1993-95; Adviser and trustee, Sieff Foundation 1994-2004; Founder member and first chair, Telephone Helplines Association 1995-96; Patron, National Youth Advocacy Service 2000-; President, John Grooms Association for Disabled People and Chair of Care and Development Committee 2000-07; Patron and trustee, Little Hearts Matter 2002-; Chair, Children's International Helplines Association 2003-07; Patron, Voice 2006-; Chair/President, John Grooms – Shaftesbury (now Livability) 2007-; Patron, TRACKS 2011-; President, Child Helpline International; British Association of Social Workers; Association of Directors of Adult Social Care. Honorary Doctorate, Open University 2007. Children's Champion, Charity Champion awards 2012. OBE 1999.

Recreations: People, gardening, reading, walking.

The Baroness Howarth of Breckland OBE, House of Lords, London SW1A 0PW
Tel: 020 7219 8744 *Fax:* 020 7219 0269 *Email:* howarthv@parliament.uk

LABOUR

HOWARTH OF NEWPORT, LORD

HOWARTH OF NEWPORT (Life Baron), Alan Thomas Howarth; cr 2005. Born 11 June 1944; Son of late T. E. B. Howarth MC, TD, and Margaret Howarth, née Teakle; Married Gillian Chance 1967 (divorced 1996) (2 sons 2 daughters); partner Baroness Hollis of Heigham (qv).

Education: Rugby School; King's College, Cambridge (BA history 1965); French.

Non-political career: Senior research assistant to Field-Marshal Montgomery on *A History of Warfare* 1965-67; English and history teacher, Westminster School 1968-74; Private secretary to Conservative Party Chairmen William Whitelaw and Lord Thorneycroft 1975-79; Vice-chair and chief executive, Conservative Central Office 1979-81; Co-ordinated campaign planning for 1979 election; Director, Conservative Research Department 1979-81; Investment department, Baring Brothers 1982-87.

Political career: *House of Commons:* MP (Conservative June 1983-October 1995, Labour October 1995-May 2005) for Stratford-on-Avon 1983-97 and for Newport East 1997-2005. PPS to Sir Rhodes Boyson as Minister of State, Northern Ireland Office and Department of Environment 1985-87; Assistant Government Whip 1987-88; Government Whip 1988-89; Parliamentary Under-Secretary of State, Department for Education and Science 1989-92, Minister for Schools 1989-90, Minister for Higher Education and Science 1990-92; Resigned from Conservative Party and joined Labour Party, October 1995; Parliamentary Under-Secretary of State: Department for Education and Employment, Employment Minister and Minister for Disabled People 1997-98, Department for Culture, Media and Sport (Minister for the Arts) 1998-2001; Member, Intelligence and Security Committee 2001-05. *House of Lords:* Raised to the peerage as Baron Howarth of Newport, of Newport in the County of Gwent 2005. Member Intergovernmental Organisations 2007-08. Vice-chair PLP Departmental Committee for Culture, Media and Sport 2006-. *Other:* Vice-chair, Conservative Party 1980-81. *Councils and public bodies:* Vice-President, Local Government Association 2001-.

Political interests: Economic policy, education, disability, charities, voluntary sector, social security, arts, heritage, constituencies; Brazil, South Africa, Uganda, Vietnam.

Other: Leader, UK Parliamentary Trade Delegation to Washington 2003; Governor, Royal Shakespeare Company 1984-97; Founder and chair, Friends of the Huntington's Disease Association 1985-87; Board member: Retirement Security Ltd 1987, Institute of Historical Research 1992-97; Member, Constitution Unit Advisory Committee 1992-97; Vice-president, British Dyslexia Association 1992-97; Patron, Neurological Alliance 1992-97; Trustee, Employment Policy Institute 1992-97; Member, Executive Committee, Fabian Society 1995-96; Chair, Trustees and Governors, Friends of the Royal Pavilion, Brighton 2006-11; Board member, Norwich Heritage and Economic Regeneration Trust 2006-; Trustee: Poetry Archive 2006-13, Foundation for International Cultural Diplomacy 2006-11; Chair, Working Group on UK Literary Heritage 2006-12; Patron, Tourism for All UK 2006-; Vice-President, the Victorian Society 2009-; Hon Fellow, Royal Institute of British Architects 2004; Fellow, Society of Antiquaries 2007. CBE 1982; PC 2000.

Publications: Co-author: Changing Charity (1984), Monty at Close Quarters (1985), Save Our Schools (1986), The Arts: The Next Move Forward (1987); Articles in the *Guardian, Independent, Observer, Daily Telegraph.*
Recreations: The arts, heritage, reading, walking.
Rt Hon the Lord Howarth of Newport CBE, House of Lords, London SW1A 0PW
Tel: 020 7219 5077 *Email:* howartha@parliament.uk

HOWE, EARL

Parliamentary Under-Secretary of State and Government Spokesperson, Department of Health

CONSERVATIVE

HOWE (7th Earl, UK), Frederick Richard Penn Curzon; cr. 1821; 8th Viscount Curzon (UK) 1802; 9th Baron Howe (GB) 1788; 8th Baron Curzon (GB) 1794. Born 29 January 1951; Son of late Commander Chambré George William Penn Curzon, RN, grandson of 3rd Earl, GCVO, CB, and late Mrs Jane Curzon, née Fergusson; Married Elizabeth Stuart 1983 (1 son 3 daughters).
Education: Rugby School; Christ Church, Oxford (MA literae humaniores 1973).
Non-political career: Arable farmer; Director: Adam & Company plc 1987-90, Provident Life Association Ltd 1988-91; Barclays Bank plc 1973-87, Senior manager 1984-87; Chair, LAPADA 1999-2010; Director, Andry Montgomery Ltd 2000-10; Trustee, Portman Estate 2006-. Member, National Farmers' Union.
Political career: *House of Lords:* First entered House of Lords 1984; Government Whip 1991-92; Parliamentary Secretary, Ministry of Agriculture, Fisheries and Food 1992-95; Parliamentary Under-Secretary of State, Ministry of Defence 1995-97; Elected hereditary peer 1999-; Opposition Spokesperson for: Defence May-October 1997, Health October 1997-2010, the Family 2004-05; Parliamentary Under-Secretary of State (Quality) and Government Spokesperson, Department of Health 2010-.
Political interests: Agriculture, penal affairs and policy, healthcare.
Other: Governor, King William IV Naval Foundation 1984-; National Society for Epilepsy: Vice-President 1984-86, President 1986-2010; South Bucks Association for the Disabled 1984-, Chilterns Branch, RNLI 1985-; Governor, The Trident Trust 1985-2008; President, CPRE (Penn Country Branch) 1986-92; Trustee, Milton's Cottage 1986-2012; Member, RNLI Council 1997-; Trustee: Sir William Borlase's Grammar School, Marlow 1998-2010, Restoration of Appearance and Function Trust (RAFT) 1999-2010; Patron: Demand 1999-2010, The Chiltern Society 2001-; President, Institute of Clinical Research 2008-10; Associate, Chartered Institute of Bankers 1976-; Hon FRCP 2008-. Lords Minister of the Year, *House Magazine* awards 2012. PC 2013.
Recreations: Old films.
Rt Hon the Earl Howe, House of Lords, London SW1A 0PW
Tel: 020 7219 5353 *Email:* howef@parliament.uk

HOWE OF ABERAVON, LORD

CONSERVATIVE

HOWE OF ABERAVON (Life Baron), (Richard Edward) Geoffrey Howe; cr. 1992. Born 20 December 1926; Son of late Benjamin Edward Howe; Married Elspeth Rosamund Morton Shand (now Baroness Howe of Idlicote) 1953 (1 son 2 daughters).
Education: Winchester College (1945); Trinity Hall, Cambridge (Scholar, MA law 1951; LLB 1952).
Non-political career: Royal Signals 1945-48; Seconded to East African Signals 1947-48. Called to the Bar, Middle Temple 1952, QC 1965, Bencher 1969, Reader 1993; *Crossbow*: Managing Director 1957-60, Editor 1960-62; Deputy Chair, Glamorgan Quarter Sessions 1966-70; Director: AGB Research Group 1974-79, Sun Alliance and London Insurance Group 1974-79, EMI Ltd 1976-79, BICC plc 1991-97, Glaxo Wellcome 1991-96; Special Adviser on European and International Affairs to law firm of Jones, Day, Reavis and Pogue 1991-2001; Visitor at the School of Oriental and African Studies, London University 1991-2001; International Advisory Councils of: Stanford University's Institute for International Studies 1991-2004, J. P. Morgan & Co. 1992-2001; Chair, Framlington Russian Investment Fund 1994-2003; Fuji International European Advisory Board 1996-2003; Carlyle European Advisory Board 1996-2001; Chairman, Steering Committee Inland Revenue Tax Law Rewrite Project 1997-2005.
Political career: *House of Commons:* Contested Aberavon 1955 and 1959 general elections. MP (Conservative) for Bebington 1964-66, for Reigate 1970-74, for Surrey East 1974-92. Solicitor-General 1970-72; Minister for Trade and Consumer Affairs, Department of Trade and Industry 1972-74; Chancellor of the Exchequer 1979-83; Foreign Secretary 1983-89; Lord President of the

Council, Leader of the House of Commons and Deputy Prime Minister 1989-90. *House of Lords:* Raised to the peerage as Baron Howe of Aberavon, of Tandridge in the County of Surrey 1992. Member: House of Lords Reform Joint Committee 2002-03, Tax Law Rewrite Bills Joint Committee 2002-06, Privileges/Privileges and Conduct 2007-. *Other:* Chair, Cambridge University Conservative Association 1951; President, National Union of Conservative Associations 1983-84; Honorary Life member, Tory Reform Group; Senior Vice-President, United and Cecil Club 2009.

Political interests: Economic, foreign and constitutional policies; China, Commonwealth, EU, Japan, Russia, USA.

Other: Chairman, Interim Committee International Monetary Fund 1982-83; Vice-President, Commonwealth Parliamentary Association (UK Branch); Chair, Bow Group 1955; Member, General Council of the Bar 1957-61; Visitor, School of Oriental and African Studies 1991-2001; Member, Advisory Council of Presidium of Supreme Rada of Ukraine 1991-98; Thomson Foundation: Trustee 1991-2007, Chair 2003-07; President: Great Britain-China Centre 1992-, Consumers' Association 1993-2010; Paul Harris Fellow, Rotary International 1995; Patron, UK Metric Association 1999-; President The Academy of Experts 1996-2005, National Centre for Young People with Epilepsy (NCYPE) 2002-04; Honorary Fellow: American Bar Foundation 2000-, Chartered Institute of Taxation 2000-. Honorary Freeman of Tax Advisors Company 2004-. Freeman, Borough of Port Talbot 1992 (now Neath Port Talbot). Four honorary doctorates, three honorary university fellowships; Visiting Fellow, John F Kennedy School of Government, Harvard University, USA 1991-92; Honorary Fellow, Trinity Hall, Cambridge 1992; Herman Phleger Visiting Professor, Stanford Law School, USA. Joseph Bech Memorial Prize, Luxembourg 1993. Kt 1970; PC 1972; Grand Cross of the Order of Merit (Portugal) 1987; Grand Cross of the Order of Merit (Germany) 1992; CH 1996; Order of Public Service (Ukraine) 2001; Athenæum, Garrick.

Publications: Conflict of Loyalty (1994, 2007).

Recreations: Photography.

Rt Hon the Lord Howe of Aberavon CH QC, House of Lords, London SW1A 0PW
Tel: 020 7219 6986 *Fax:* 020 7219 0587 *Email:* howeg@parliament.uk

---

HOWE OF IDLICOTE, BARONESS

CROSSBENCH

BARONESS HOWE OF IDLICOTE (Life Baroness), Elspeth Rosamund Morton the Lady Howe of Aberavon CBE; cr 2001. Born 8 February 1932; Daughter of late Philip Shand and Sybil Shand; Married Geoffrey Howe (later Sir Geoffrey, now Lord Howe of Aberavon) 1953 (2 daughters 1 son).

Education: Bath High School; Wycombe Abbey; London School of Economics (BSc social science and administration 1985).

Non-political career: JP 1964-90; Chair, Inner London Juvenile Court 1970-90; Member: Briggs Committee on the Future of the Nursing Profession 1970-72, Parole Board for England and Wales 1972-75; Deputy chair, Equal Opportunities Commission 1975-79; President, Federation of Recruitment and Employment Services 1980-94; Governor, London School of Economics 1985-2007; Chair, BOC Foundation for the Environment 1990-2003; Institute of Business Ethics' Advisory Council: Member 1990-, Advisory Council Vice-President 2002-; Business in the Community: Chair, BITC's opportunity 2000 Target Team 1990-99, Board member 1992-98; Chair, Archbishop's Commission on Cathedrals 1992-94; Member, Department of Employment working group on women's issues 1992-97; Chair, Broadcasting Standards Commission 1993-99; President, UK Committee of Unicef 1993-2002; Council of the Open University: Member 1996-2003, Vice-chair 2001-03; Board member, Veolia (formerly Onyx) Environmental Trust plc 2003-.

Political career: *House of Lords:* Raised to the peerage as Baroness Howe of Idlicote, of Shipston-on-Stour in the County of Warwickshire 2001. Member: Review of the BBC Charter 2005-06, Communications 2007-10. *Councils and public bodies:* Co-opted member, Inner London Education Authority 1967-70; Vice-president, Institute of Business Ethics Advisory Council 2002-.

Political interests: Equal opportunities, education, environment, law, third age, communications.

Other: President, Peckham Settlement; Member, NCVO Advisory Council; Patron, Mary Ward Legal Centre; Trustee: Architectural Association, Ann Driver Trust; President, National Governors' Association 2007-; Unicef and other children's charities. Seven honorary doctorates; Honorary Fellow London School of Economics 2001. CBE 1999; Royal Society of Arts.

Publications: Under Five (CPC, 1966); Women and Credit (Equal Opportunities Commission, 1978); Women at the Top (Hansard Society, 1990).

Recreations: Bridge, theatre, grandchildren.

The Baroness Howe of Idlicote CBE, House of Lords, London SW1A 0PW
Tel: 020 7219 6581 *Fax:* 020 7219 1991 *Email:* howee@parliament.uk

HOWELL OF GUILDFORD, LORD

HOWELL OF GUILDFORD (Life Baron), David Arthur Russell Howell; cr. 1997. Born 18 January 1936; Son of late Arthur Howell, retired army officer and businessman; Married Davina Wallace 1967 (1 son 2 daughters).

Education: Eton College; King's College, Cambridge (BA economics 1959, MA).

Non-political career: Second Lieutenant, 2nd Btn Coldstream Guards 1954-56. Economic section, HM Treasury 1959-60; Leader writer, *Daily Telegraph* 1960-64; Editor, *Crossbow* 1962-64; Chair, UK-Japan 21st Century Group 1990-2000; Director, Trafalgar House 1990-2006; Visiting Fellow, Nuffield College, Oxford 1992-2000; Director: Monks Investment Trust 1993-2004, Jardine Insurance 1994-97; Advisory director, UBS-Warburg 1997-2000; Director, John Laing 2000-03; Financial advisory board, the Kuwait Investment Authority 2003-10, 2012-.

CONSERVATIVE

Political career: *House of Commons:* Contested Dudley 1964 general election. MP (Conservative) for Guildford 1966-97. Parliamentary Secretary, Civil Service Department 1970-72; Parliamentary Under-Secretary of State: Department of Employment 1971-72, Northern Ireland Office March-November 1972; Minister of State: Northern Ireland Office 1972-74, Department of Energy 1974; Secretary of State for: Energy 1979-81, Transport 1981-83. Chair Foreign and Commonwealth Affairs 1987-97. Chairman, The One Nation Group of Conservative MPs 1988-97. *House of Lords:* Raised to the peerage as Baron Howell of Guildford, of Penton Mewsey in the County of Hampshire 1997. Opposition Spokesperson for Foreign and Commonwealth Affairs 2000-10; Deputy Leader of the Opposition 2005-10; Minister of State and Government Spokesperson, Foreign and Commonwealth Office 2010-12. Member European Communities Sub-committee B (Energy, Industry and Transport) 1997-99; Chair: European Communities Sub-committee C (Defence and Foreign Policy) 1999-2000, Soft Power and the UK's Influence 2013-. *Other:* Director, Conservative Political Centre 1964-66.

Political interests: Economics, international finance, energy, oil, foreign affairs; All Central European countries, China, India, Japan, Middle East.

Other: Chair, Bow Group 1962; Board member, Shakespeare Globe Theatre 2000-10; Chair, Council of Commonwealth Societies; President, Royal Commonwealth Society. Liveryman, Clothworkers' Company. Grand Cordon of Order of Sacred Treasure (Japan) 2002. PC 1979; Beefsteak.

Publications: Co-author, Principles in Practice (1960); The Conservative Opportunity (1965); Freedom and Capital (1981); Blind Victory: a study in income, wealth and power (1986); The Edge of Now (2000); Out of the Energy Labyrinth (2007).

Recreations: Writing, travel, do-it-yourself.

Rt Hon the Lord Howell of Guildford, House of Lords, London SW1A 0PW
Tel: 020 7219 5415 *Email:* howelld@parliament.uk *Website:* www.lordhowell.com

HOWELLS OF ST DAVIDS, BARONESS

HOWELLS OF ST DAVIDS (Life Baroness), Rosalind Patricia-Anne Howells; cr 1999. Born 10 January 1931; Married John Charles Howells 1955 (died) (2 daughters).

Education: St Joseph's Convent, Grenada; South West London College (Certificate welfare and counselling); City University, Washington DC (community and race relations).

Non-political career: Former community and equal opportunities worker, with Moonshot Youth Club, Community Industry, then to Greenwich Racial Equality Council as equal opportunities director until retirement.

LABOUR

Political career: *House of Lords:* Raised to the peerage as Baroness Howells of St Davids, of Charlton in the London Borough of Greenwich 1999. Member Works of Art 2009-11, 2012-13.

Political interests: Community relations, international affairs (Africa/Caribbean), education, health; Algeria, China/Taiwan, Grenada, Nigeria, Saudi Arabia.

Other: Has been an active campaigner for justice in the field of race relations: The New Cross Fire, Roland Adams Campaign, Stephen Lawrence Family Campaign, SUS Campaign; Vice-chair, London Voluntary Services Council 1978-83; Former chair: Charlton Consortium, Carnival Liaison Committee, Greater London Action on Race Equality; Chair, Lewisham Racial Equality Council 1994-97, Director, Smithville Associates; President, Grenada Convent Past Pupils Association; Patron: Grenada Arts Council, Mediation Service; Member, Court of Governors, University of Greenwich; Has served on various committees including: Advisory Committee to the Home Secretary, Commonwealth Countries League, Greenwich Police/Community Consultative Group; Trustee: West Indian Standing Conference, Museum of Ethnic Arts, Women of the Year Committee, Stephen Lawrence Charitable Trust, City Parochial Foundation; Chair, Talawa Theatre Company 2004-06; Sickle Cell Anemia, Cancer Research. Chancellor, Bedfordshire University 2009-. Honorary DUniv, Greenwich 1998. Hansib Publications Award; The Voice Newspaper Community Award. OBE 1993.

Recreations: Food, music of all kinds, cricket, football.

The Baroness Howells of St Davids OBE, House of Lords, London SW1A 0PW
Tel: 020 7219 8655 *Fax:* 020 7219 8652

LABOUR

HOWIE OF TROON, LORD

HOWIE OF TROON (Life Baron), William Howie; cr. 1978. Born 2 March 1924; Son of late Peter and Annie Howie; Married Mairi Sanderson 1951 (died 2005) (2 daughters 2 sons).

Education: Marr College, Troon; Royal Technical College, Glasgow (BSc, DRTC civil engineering 1944).

Non-political career: Civil engineer 1944-63, 1970-73; Journalist and publisher 1973-96; Director: Internal relations of Thomas Telford Ltd, publishers 1976-95, SETO 1996-2001; Consultant: George S Hall Ltd, building services engineer 1999-, PMS 1995-2007, Parliamentary Perceptions: Consultant 2007-11, Chairman 2011-. Life member, National Union of Journalists.

Political career: *House of Commons:* Contested Cities of London and Westminster 1959 general election. MP (Labour) for Luton 1963 by-election to 1970. *House of Lords:* Raised to the peerage as Baron Howie of Troon, of Troon, Kyle and Carrick 1978. Member: Science and Technology 1992-95, 1997-2001, 2005-09, European Communities 1995-97; Member: Science and Technology Sub-committees: II (Science and Society) 1999-2000, I (Complementary and Alternative Medicine) 2000; European Union 2003-05, European Union Sub-committees: B (Energy, Industry and Transport) 2003, G (Social Policy and Consumer Affairs) 2003-06; Science and Technology Sub-committee I (Waste Reduction) 2007-08. *Councils and public bodies:* Member, Committee of Inquiry into Engineering Profession 1977-79.

Political interests: Construction industry, professional engineers, higher education.

Other: Member: Council of Institution of Civil Engineers 1965-68, Council of City University 1968-91; Vice-President, Periodical Publishers Association; Fellow, Industry and Parliamentary Trust 1983; Fellow, Institution of Civil Engineers; Member, Society of Engineers and Scientists (France); Honorary Fellow: Institution of Structural Engineers, Association of Building Engineers; Register of Engineers for Disaster Relief (RedR). Pro-Chancellor, City University 1984-91. Honorary DSc, City University; Honorary LLD, Strathclyde University. Institution of Civil Engineers Garth Watson Medal; St Stephens Club; Lighthouse Club.

Publications: Co-author, Public Sector Purchasing (1968); Trade Unions and the Professional Engineer (1977); Trade Unions in Construction (1981); Co-editor, Thames Tunnel to Channel Tunnel (1987).

Recreations: Opera.

The Lord Howie of Troon, House of Lords, London SW1A 0PW
Tel: 020 7219 3238
34 Temple Fortune Lane, London NW11 7UL *Tel:* 020 8455 0492 *Fax:* 020 8455 0492

LABOUR

HOYLE, LORD

HOYLE (Life Baron), (Eric) Douglas Harvey Hoyle; cr. 1997. Born 17 February 1930; Son of late William Hoyle; Married Pauline Spencer 1952 (died 1991) (1 son, Lindsay Hoyle MP).

Education: Adlington School; Horwich Technical College.

Non-political career: British Rail 1945-51; AEI 1951-53; Sales engineer, C. Weston Ltd, Salford 1953-74; Warrington Rugby League plc: Chair 1999-2009, President 2009-. ASTMS: Vice-President 1972-74, 1981-85, President 1977-81, 1985-88; Merged with TASS 1988; MSF: Joint President 1988-90, President 1990-91; Unite: Member, Chair, Lords Parliamentary Group.

Political career: *House of Commons:* Contested (Labour) Clitheroe 1964, Nelson and Colne 1970 and February 1974 general elections. MP (Labour) for Nelson and Colne October 1974-79, for Warrington 1981 by-election to 1983, for Warrington North 1983-97. Chair: PLP Trade and Industry Committee 1987-92, PLP 1992-97; Member, PLP Parliamentary Committee 2001-05. *House of Lords:* Raised to the peerage as Baron Hoyle, of Warrington in the County of Cheshire 1997. Government Spokesperson for: Defence 1997-99, Home Office 1997-99, Agriculture 1997-99; Government Whip 1997-99. Member Procedure 2003-05. *Other:* Member, Labour Party National Executive 1978-82, 1983-85. *Councils and public bodies:* JP 1958; Member, North West Regional Health Authority 1968-74.

Political interests: Trade, employment, industrial relations, health, immigration, arts, sport; Australia, Europe, Gibraltar, New Zealand, South Africa.

Other: Freedom of: Gibraltar, Warrington. Hon Doctorate, Chester University; Reform Club. President: Adlington Cricket Club 1974-, Chorley Rugby League Club 1989-96; Warrington Wolves RLFC: Chair 1999-2009, President 2010-.

Recreations: Cricket, rugby league, theatre, cinema, sport.

The Lord Hoyle, House of Lords, London SW1A 0PW
Tel: 020 7219 3196 *Fax:* 020 7219 3831

LABOUR

HUGHES OF STRETFORD, BARONESS

Opposition Spokesperson for Education

HUGHES OF STRETFORD (Life Baroness), Beverley June Hughes; cr 2010. Born 30 March 1950; Daughter of late Norman Hughes and late Doris Hughes; Married Thomas McDonald 1973 (1 son 2 daughters).

Education: Ellesmere Port Girls' Grammar School; Manchester University (BSc 1971; MSc 1978); Liverpool University (Diploma applied social studies 1974).

Non-political career: Trainee probation officer, Merseyside 1971; Probation officer, Merseyside 1972; Manchester University: Research associate 1976-81; Lecturer 1981-93, Senior lecturer and head of department 1993-97; Strategic adviser, WCL 2010-. Member, USDAW.

Political career: *House of Commons:* MP for Stretford and Urmston 1997-2010. PPS to Hilary Armstrong as Minister of State, Department of the Environment, Transport and the Regions (DETR) 1998-99; Parliamentary Under-Secretary of State, DETR 1999-2001; Home Office 2001-04: Parliamentary Under-Secretary of State 2001-02, Minister of State 2002-04: (for Citizenship, Immigration and Community Cohesion 2002-03, (Citizenship, Immigration and Counter Terrorism 2003-04); Minister of State, Department for Education and Skills/Children, Schools and Families 2005-09 (Children, Young People and Families 2005-07, Children and Youth Justice 2007-09) (attending cabinet 2008-09); Minister for the North West 2007-09. Member: Home Affairs 1997-98. Joint Vice-chair, PLP Departmental Committee for Women 1999-2000. *House of Lords:* Raised to the peerage as Baroness Hughes of Stretford, of Ellesmere Port in the County of Cheshire 2010. Opposition Spokesperson for Education 2010-. *Councils and public bodies:* Trafford Metropolitan Borough Council: Councillor 1986-97, Labour Group Leader 1992-97, Council Leader 1995-97; Director: Trafford Park Development Corporation 1992-97, Manchester Airport plc 1995-97.

Political interests: Economic regeneration, investment, local and regional government, health and community care, families, regional development, education, criminal justice, child protection and safety; Commonwealth countries, USA.

Other: PC 2004.

Publications: Older People and Community Care: Critical Theory and Practice (1995); Numerous academic and professional publications.

Recreations: Jazz, fell-walking.

Rt Hon the Baroness Hughes of Stretford, House of Lords, London SW1A 0PW
Tel: 020 7219 0956 *Email:* hughesb@parliament.uk *Twitter:* @BeverleyHughes1

LABOUR

HUGHES OF WOODSIDE, LORD

HUGHES OF WOODSIDE (Life Baron), Robert Hughes; cr. 1997. Born 3 January 1932; Son of Mitchell Hughes and Jessie Anderson; Married Ina Miller 1957 (2 sons 3 daughters).

Education: Robert Gordon's College, Aberdeen; Benoni High School, Transvaal, South Africa; Pietermaritzburgh Technical College, Natal, South Africa; Pietermaritzburg Technical College South Africa (Higher National Diploma engineering 1953).

Non-political career: Emigrated to South Africa 1947; Returned UK 1954; CF Wilson and Co (1932) Ltd, Aberdeen: Draughtsman 1954-64, Chief draughtsman 1964-70. Member, Unite.

Political career: *House of Commons:* Contested North Angus and Mearns 1959 general election. MP (Labour) for Aberdeen North 1970-97. Parliamentary Under-Secretary of State, Scottish Office 1974-75; Piloted the Rating (Disabled Persons) Act 1978 as Private Member's Bill. Chair Scottish Affairs 1991-94. *House of Lords:* Raised to the peerage as Baron Hughes of Woodside, of Woodside in the City of Aberdeen 1997. *Other:* Chairman, Aberdeen City Labour Party 1963-69. *Councils and public bodies:* Councillor, Aberdeen Town Council 1962-71; Member: North East Scotland Regional Hospital Board 1964-70, General Medical Council 1976-81.

Political interests: Anti-apartheid work, agriculture, fishing industry, transport, health service, overseas aid and development; South Africa.

Other: Founder member, CND; Anti-Apartheid Movement: Vice-chair 1976, Chair 1977-94; Action for Southern Africa: Chair 1994-98, Honorary President 1998-; Honorary President, Mozambique, Angola Committee 2001-; Sponsor Canon Collins Education Trust for Southern Africa. South African Government National Order, Grand Companion of Oliver Tambo 2004.

Recreations: Fishing.

The Lord Hughes of Woodside, House of Lords, London SW1A 0PW
Tel: 020 7219 1451 *Fax:* 020 7219 2772/020 7219 5979 *Email:* hughesr@parliament.uk

---

HUMPHREYS, BARONESS – *Please see Addenda Page xii*

HUNT OF CHESTERTON, LORD

LABOUR

HUNT OF CHESTERTON (Life Baron), Julian Charles Roland Hunt; cr. 2000. Born 5 September 1941; Son of Roland Hunt CMG and Pauline Hunt, née Garnett; Married Marylla Shephard 1965 (1 son 2 daughters).

Education: Westminster School; Trinity College, Cambridge (BA engineering 1963; PhD engineering 1967); Warwick University (engineering on secondment from Cambridge); French.

Non-political career: Cambridge University: Fellow 1966-, Senior research fellow 1998-99; Post-doctoral research, Cornell University, USA 1967; Research officer, Central Electricity Research Laboratories 1968-70; Trinity College: Lecturer in applied mathematics and in engineering 1970-78, Reader in fluid mechanics 1978-90, Professor 1990-92, Honorary Professor 1992-; Visiting professor: Colorado State University, USA 1975, National Center for Atmospheric Research, Boulder, Colorado, USA 1983; Cambridge Environmental Research Consultants Ltd: Founder director 1986-91, Director 1997-, Chair 2000-; Chief executive, Meteorological Office 1992-97; Visiting scientist, Cerfacs, Toulouse, France 1997, 1998, 2007, 2008; Visiting professor: Arizona State University, USA 1997-98, 2007-11, Stanford University, USA 1998, Delft University of Technology 1998-; Professor in climate modelling, and director, Lighthill Institute for Mathematical Science, University College, London 1999-2008, Emeritus 2008-; Visiting professor, Cornell University 2003-06; Pierre Fermat Visiting Professor, Toulouse 2007-08; Visiting fellow, Malaysian Commonwealth Studies Centre, Cambridge; Visiting professor, Hong Kong University 2011-; Chair, Advisory Committee Tokamak Solutions Ltd. Electrical Power Engineers Association: Member 1968-70, Branch secretary 1970; Member: AUT 1970-91, 1999-2008, IPCS 1992-97.

Political career: *House of Lords:* Raised to the peerage as Baron Hunt of Chesterton, of Chesterton in the County of Cambridgeshire 2000. Member: Animals in Scientific Procedures 2001-02, Science and Technology Sub-committees: II (Innovations in Microprocessing) 2002-03, I (Science and International Agreements) 2003-04. *Councils and public bodies:* Cambridge City Council: Councillor 1971-74, Leader, Labour Group 1972; President, National Society of Clean Air 2006-09.

Political interests: Environment, science, government – civil service issues, informational aspects; France, India, USA.

Other: Member, Management board, European Research Community for Flow Turbulence and Combustion 1988-95; Member, Executive council, World Meteorological Organisation 1992-97; President, Institute of Mathematics and its Applications 1993-95; Council member, Royal Society 1998-99; ACOPS (Advisory Committee on Protection of the Sea): Chair 2001-04, President 2004-; Vice-President, Globe International 2009-; Honorary Fellow: Institution of Civil Engineers, Institute of Mathematics and its applications, Royal Meteorological Society; FRS 1989; Oxfam; Unipal. Eight honorary doctorates from England, Scotland, France and Sweden. European Geophysical Society, LF Richardson Medal 2001. CB 1998; Meteorological.

Publications: Editor four volumes including London's Environment (Imperial College Press 2005); Articles in mathematical and scientific publications, and newspapers.

Recreations: Swimming, history, rough gardening.

Professor the Lord Hunt of Chesterton CB, House of Lords, London SW1A 0PW
Tel: 020 7219 6193
Department of Earth Sciences, University College London, Gower Street, London WC1E 6BT

LABOUR

HUNT OF KINGS HEATH, LORD

Shadow Deputy Leader of the House of Lords; Opposition Spokesperson for Health

HUNT OF KINGS HEATH (Life Baron), Philip Alexander Hunt; cr. 1997. Born 19 May 1949; Son of late Rev. Philip Hunt and Muriel Hunt; Married 1974 (divorced) (1 daughter); married Selina Stewart 1988 (3 sons 1 daughter).

Education: City of Oxford High School; Oxford School; Leeds University (BA political studies 1970).

Non-political career: Oxford Regional Hospital Board 1972-74; Nuffield Orthopaedic Centre 1974-75; Secretary, Edgware/Hendon Community Health Council 1975-78; National Association of Health Authorities: Assistant secretary 1978-79, Assistant director 1979-84, Director 1984-90; Director, National Association of Health Authorities and Trusts 1990-96; Chief executive, NHS Confederation 1996-97. Member, Unison.

Political career: *House of Lords:* Raised to the peerage as Baron Hunt of Kings Heath, of Birmingham in the County of West Midlands 1997. Government Spokesperson for Education and Employment 1998-99; Government Whip 1998-99; Parliamentary Under-Secretary of State and Government Spokesperson for: Department of Health 1999-2003, Department for Work and Pensions 2005-06; Minister of State for Quality, Department of Health and Government Spokesperson for Health 2006-07; Parliamentary Under-Secretary of State and Government Spokesperson, Ministry of Justice 2007-08; Minister of State and Government Spokesperson: Department for Environment, Food and Rural Affairs 2008-09, Department of Energy and Climate Change 2008-10; Deputy Leader of the House of Lords 2008-10; Opposition Spokesperson for: Cabinet Office 2010-12, Energy and Climate Change 2010, Home Office 2010-12; Shadow Deputy Leader of the House of Lords 2010-; Opposition Spokesperson for Health 2012-. Member Consolidation, Etc, Bills Joint Committee 1998; Chair Merits of Statutory Instruments 2003-05; Member Leader's Group on Members Leaving the House 2010-. *Councils and public bodies:* Councillor, Oxford City Council 1973-79; Member, Oxfordshire Area Health Authority 1975-77; Councillor, Birmingham City Council 1980-82; Chair, National Patient Safety Agency 2004-05; Chairman, Heart of England NHS Foundation Trust, Birmingham 2011-.

Political interests: Transport, constitutional affairs, energy and climate change.

Other: Council, International Hospital Federation 1986-91; Association for Public Health: Council 1992, Co-chair 1994-98; President: Family Planning Association 1997-98, Royal Society for Public Health 2010-; Oxfam; Living Streets; St Mary's Hospice, Birmingham; Birmingham Contemporary Music Group; City of Birmingham Symphony Orchestra. Honorary Doctorate: Birmingham University, Birmingham City University. OBE 1993; PC 2009. Warwickshire CCC.

Recreations: Cycling, swimming, Birmingham City FC, music.

Rt Hon the Lord Hunt of Kings Heath OBE, House of Lords, London SW1A 0PW
Tel: 020 7219 2030 *Email:* huntp@parliament.uk *Twitter:* @LordPhilofBrum

CONSERVATIVE

HUNT OF WIRRAL, LORD

HUNT OF WIRRAL (Life Baron), David James Fletcher Hunt; cr. 1997. Born 21 May 1942; Son of late Alan Hunt, OBE, shipping agent, and late Jessie Ellis Hunt; Married Paddy Orchard 1973 (2 sons 2 daughters).

Education: Liverpool College; Montpellier University, France 1962; Bristol University (LLB 1965); Guildford College of Law 1968.

Non-political career: Solicitor; Beachcroft LLP: Partner 1968-, Senior Partner 1996-2005, Chair, Financial Services Division 2005-; Director, BET Omnibus Services Ltd 1980-81; Chair, Beachcroft Regulatory Consulting 2002-08.

Political career: *House of Commons:* Contested Bristol South 1970 and Kingswood 1974 general elections. MP (Conservative) for Wirral 1976-83, for Wirral West 1983-97. Opposition Spokesperson for Shipping and Shipbuilding 1977-97; PPS to John Nott as Secretary of State for: Trade 1979-81, Defence 1981; Assistant Whip 1981-83; Government Whip 1983-84; Parliamentary Under-Secretary of State, Department of Energy 1984-87; Deputy Chief Whip (Treasurer of HM Household) 1987-89; Minister for Local Government and Inner Cities 1989-90; Secretary of State: for Wales 1990-93, for Employment 1993-94; Chancellor of the Duchy of Lancaster and Minister for Public Service and Science 1994-95. *House of Lords:* Raised to the peerage as Baron Hunt of Wirral, of Wirral in the County of Merseyside 1997. Opposition Spokesperson for Business, Enterprise and Regulatory Reform/Business, Innovation and Skills 2008-10. Member: Offices 1999-2001, European Communities Sub-committee E (Law and Institutions) 1999-2002, House 2003-

07; Chair Draft Legal Services Bill Joint Committee 2006; Alternate member Procedure 2007-08, 2008-11; Member EU Sub-committee G (Social Policies and Consumer Protection) 2010-12; Chair Leader's Group on Members Leaving the House 2010-. *Other:* Vice-chair, Bristol Conservative Association 1970; Chair, National Young Conservatives 1972-73; Vice-President, European Conservative and Christian Democratic Youth Community 1974-76; Vice-chair, Conservative Party 1983-84; Tory Reform Group: President 1991-97, Patron 1997-. *Councils and public bodies:* Chair, British Youth Council 1971-74; Member: South West Economic Planning Council 1972-76, Government Advisory Committee on Pop Festivals 1972-75; President, British Youth Council 1978-80; English Speaking Union: Governor 1998-2011, Deputy chair 2000-05, Chair 2005-11, International chair 2008-11; Board of the Chartered Insurance Institute: Professional Standards Board: Chair 2004-06, President 2007-08; Chair: McEdCo 2009-, Lending Standards Board 2011-, Press Complaints Commission 2011-.

Political interests: Europe, business and economy, skills; Commonwealth, European Union, USA.

Other: Governor, European Youth Foundation at Strasbourg 1972-75; Chair, British Atlantic Group of Young Politicians 1979-81; President, Atlantic Association for Young Political Leaders 1981-83; Vice-President and trustee, Holocaust Educational Trust 1995-; Honorary Fellow: International Institute of Risk and Safety Management 2000, Institute of Actuaries 2003, Chartered Insurance Institute 2004; Honorary Freedom of the Worshipful Company of Insurers 2009-. Hon LLD, University of Bristol 2008. MBE 1973; PC 1990; Hurlingham.

Recreations: Cricket, walking.

Rt Hon the Lord Hunt of Wirral MBE, House of Lords, London SW1A 0PW
Tel: 020 7219 6688 *Email:* lordhunt@dacbeachcroft.com
DAC Beachcroft LLP, 100 Fetter Lane, London EC4A 1BN *Tel:* 020 7894 6066
Fax: 020 7894 6758 *Email:* lordhunt@dacbeachcroft.com

CONSERVATIVE

HURD OF WESTWELL, LORD

HURD OF WESTWELL (Life Baron), Douglas Richard Hurd; cr. 1997. Born 8 March 1930; Son of late Baron Hurd (Life Peer); Married Tatiana Eyre 1960 (divorced 1982) (3 sons); married Judith Smart 1982 (died 2008) (1 son 1 daughter).

Education: Eton College; Trinity College, Cambridge (MA history 1952) (President, Cambridge Union 1952); French, Italian.

Non-political career: 2nd Lieutenant, Royal Artillery 1948-49. HM Foreign Service 1952-66: Peking 1954-56, UN, New York 1956-60, Rome 1963-66; Conservative Research Department 1966-68; Political Secretary to Edward Heath MP as leader of the Conservative Party and Prime Minister 1968-74; Deputy chair, Natwest Markets 1995-98; Chair, British Invisibles 1997-2000; Deputy chair, Coutts & Co 1998-2009; Senior adviser, Hawkpoint Partners 1999-2011; Chair, CEDR (Council for Effective Dispute Resolutions) 2001-05.

Political career: *House of Commons:* MP (Conservative) for Mid Oxon 1974-83, for Witney 1983-97. Opposition Spokesman for Europe 1976-79; Minister of State: Foreign and Commonwealth Office 1979-83, Home Office 1983-84; Secretary of State for Northern Ireland 1984-85; Home Secretary 1985-89, Foreign Secretary 1989-95. *House of Lords:* Raised to the peerage as Baron Hurd of Westwell, of Westwell in the County of Oxfordshire 1997. Member, Royal Commission on the Reform of the House of Lords 1999; House of Lords Appointments Commission 2000-10. *Other:* Contested Conservative Party leadership November 1990; Patron, Tory Reform Group. *Councils and public bodies:* Member, Constitutional Commission 1998-99; High Steward, Westminster Abbey 1999-2011; Chair, Archbishop of Canterbury's Review 2000-01.

Political interests: Foreign affairs, constitutional affairs, criminal justice.

Other: Vice-President, Commonwealth Parliamentary Association (UK Branch); Trustee, Prayer Book Society 1989-; Falkland Islands Association: Vice-President 1996-2000, President 2000-; Prison Reform Trust: Chair 1997-2001, Honorary President 2001-; Co-President, Royal Institute of International Affairs 2002-09. Honorary doctorate; Fellow, Nuffield College, Oxford; Two honorary degrees, Brunel and Aston Universities. CBE 1974; PC 1982; CH 1996; Beefsteak, Travellers', Pratt's.

Publications: The Arrow War (1967); Send Him Victorious (1968); The Smile on the Face of the Tiger (1969); Scotch on the Rocks (1971); Truth Game (1972); Vote to Kill (1975); An End to Promises (1979); War Without Frontiers (1982); Co-author, Palace of Enchantments (1985); The Search for Peace (1997); The Shape of Ice (1998); Ten Minutes to Turn the Devil (1999); Image in the Water (2001); Memoirs (2003); Robert Peel (2007); Choose Your Weapons (with Edward Young) 2010; Disraeli: or, the Two Lives (2013).

Recreations: Writing novels, history.

Rt Hon the Lord Hurd of Westwell CH CBE, House of Lords, London SW1A 0PW
Tel: 020 7219 5353

HUSSAIN, LORD

HUSSAIN (Life Baron), Qurban Hussain; cr 2011. Born 27 March 1956; Married (6 children).
Education: Rochdale College; Bedford College; Luton University.
Non-political career: Secretary, Luton TUC 1994-96.
Political career: *House of Commons:* Contested (Lib Dem) Luton South 2005 and 2010 general elections. *House of Lords:* Raised to the peerage as Baron Hussain, of Luton in the County of Bedfordshire 2011. *Other:* Member: Labour Party 1996-2003, Liberal Democrats 2003-. *Councils and public bodies:* Luton Borough Council: Councillor 2003-, Deputy leader 2005-07.

LIBERAL DEMOCRAT **Political interests:** Luton.
Other: Member: Luton Law Centre, Justice Foundation, Islamic Cultural Society.
Recreations: Badminton, swimming, walking, writing.
The Lord Hussain, House of Lords, London SW1A 0PW
Tel: 020 7219 3159 *Email:* hussainq@parliament.uk

HUSSEIN-ECE, BARONESS

HUSSEIN-ECE (Life Baroness), Meral Hussein Ece; cr 2010. Born 10 October 1953; Daughter of late Hasan Nihet Hussein and Ayshe Hussein (née Abdullah); 3 children.
Education: Edith Cavell Secondary School, Hackney; BA; Turkish.
Non-political career: Member, Government BME Women Councillors' Task Force 2008-; Special adviser to Nick Clegg MP on community cohesion and minority ethnic communities 2006-12.
Political career: *House of Lords:* Raised to the peerage as Baroness Hussein-Ece, of Highbury in the London Borough of Islington 2010. Member: HIV and AIDS in the UK 2010-11, Soft Power

LIBERAL DEMOCRAT and the UK's Influence 2013-. *Other:* Member, Executive, London Liberal Democrats 1998-2003; Member: Federal Policy Committee, Liberal Democrats 2005-06, Federal Executive, Liberal Democrats 2005-10; Chair, Ethnic Minority Liberal Democrats 2006-10. *Councils and public bodies:* London Borough of Hackney Council: Councillor 1994-2002, Deputy Leader 1995-96; London Borough of Islington Council: Councillor 2002-10, Cabinet Member for Health and Social Care 2002-06; Board member, Islington Primary Care Trust 2002-06; Non-executive director, Camden and Islington Mental Health and Social Care Trust 2004-06; Chair, Islington Health Partnership Board 2004-06; Commissioner, Equality and Human Rights Commission 2009-12.
Political interests: Local government, health, equality and diversity, women, youth, community cohesion, European and foreign affairs; Cyprus, Middle East, Turkey.
Other: Hon DLitt Coventry University 2012. OBE 2009.
The Baroness Hussein-Ece OBE, House of Lords, London SW1A 0PW
Tel: 020 7219 5353 *Email:* ecem@parliament.uk *Twitter:* @meralhece

HUTTON, LORD

HUTTON (Life Baron), (James) Brian Edward Hutton; cr. 1997. Born 29 June 1931; Son of late James and Mabel Hutton; Married Mary Murland 1975 (died 2000) (2 daughters); married Rosalind Nickols 2001 (2 stepsons 1 stepdaughter).
Education: Shrewsbury School; Balliol College, Oxford (BA jurisprudence 1953); Queen's University, Belfast 1954.
Non-political career: Called to Northern Ireland Bar 1954; Junior Counsel to Attorney-General for Northern Ireland 1969; QC (NI) 1970; Called to English Bar 1972; Legal Adviser to Ministry

CROSSBENCH of Home Affairs (NI) 1973; Senior Crown Counsel in NI 1973-79; Bencher, Inn of Court of Northern Ireland 1974; Judge of the High Court of Justice (NI) 1979-88; Honorary Bencher: Inner Temple 1988, King's Inn, Dublin 1988; Lord Chief Justice of Northern Ireland 1988-97; Visitor, Ulster University 1999-2003; Chair, Hutton Inquiry 2003-04.
Political career: *House of Lords:* Raised to the peerage as Baron Hutton, of Bresagh in the County of Down 1997. Lord of Appeal in Ordinary 1997-2004. *Councils and public bodies:* Member, Joint Law Enforcement Commission 1974; President, Northern Ireland Association for Mental Health 1983-90; Deputy chair, Boundary Commission (NI) 1985-88.
Other: Honorary Fellow, Balliol College, Oxford 1988; Two honorary law doctorates from NI universities. PC 1988; Kt 1988.
Rt Hon the Lord Hutton, House of Lords, London SW1A 0PW
Tel: 020 7219 5353

HUTTON OF FURNESS, LORD

HUTTON OF FURNESS (Life Baron), John Matthew Patrick Hutton; cr 2010. Born 6 May 1955; Son of late George Hutton, salesman and general labourer, and Rosemary Hutton, orthoptist; Married Rosemary Caroline Little 1978 (divorced 1993) (3 sons 1 daughter and 1 son deceased); married Heather Rogers OBE 2004.

Education: Westcliffe High School, Southend; Magdalen College, Oxford (BA law 1976; BCL 1978).

Non-political career: Legal assistant, CBI 1978-81; Research fellow, Templeton College, Oxford 1980-81; Senior law lecturer, Newcastle Polytechnic 1981-92; Non-executive director, Sirius Minerals 2012-; Special Adviser, PWC LLP 2013-.

LABOUR

Political career: *House of Commons:* Contested Penrith and the Border 1987 general election. MP for Barrow and Furness 1992-2010. PPS to Margaret Beckett: as President of the Board of Trade and Secretary of State for Trade and Industry 1997-98, as President of the Council and Leader of the House of Commons 1998; Department of Health: Parliamentary Under-Secretary of State 1998-99, Minister of State for Health 1999-2005; Chancellor of the Duchy of Lancaster and Minister for the Cabinet Office 2005; Secretary of State for: Work and Pensions 2005-07, Business, Enterprise and Regulatory Reform 2007-08, Defence 2008-09. Member: Home Affairs 1994-97. Chair PLP Departmental Committees for: Defence 1992-94, Home Affairs 1994-97. *House of Lords:* Raised to the peerage as Baron Hutton of Furness, of Aldingham in the County of Cumbria 2010. Member Public Service and Democratic Change 2012-13. *Other:* Contested Cumbria and North Lancashire 1989 European Parliament election. *Councils and public bodies:* Chair, Independent Public Service Pensions Commission 2010-.

Political interests: Defence, welfare state, home affairs, legal affairs.

Other: Chair: Royal United Services Institute 2010-, Nuclear Industry Association 2011-; Terence Higgins Trust. PC 2001.

Publications: Kitchener's Men (2008); August 1914 – Surrender at St Quentin (2010); A Doctor on the Western Front (2013).

Recreations: Cricket, football, films, music, history.

Rt Hon the Lord Hutton of Furness, House of Lords, London SW1A 0PW
Tel: 020 7219 5353

HYLTON, LORD

HYLTON (5th Baron, UK), Raymond Hervey Jolliffe; cr. 1866; 5th Bt of Merstham (UK) 1821. Born 13 June 1932; Son of 4th Baron; Married Joanna de Bertodano 1966 (4 sons 1 daughter).

Education: Eton College; Trinity College, Oxford (MA history 1955); French, some Italian.

Non-political career: National Service, commissioned Coldstream Guards 1951-52. Assistant Private Secretary to the Governor-General of Canada 1960-62; Farmer (organic), forester and land-owner.

CROSSBENCH

Political career: *House of Lords:* First entered House of Lords 1971; Private Member's Bills: Sexual Offences (Amendment) Bill, Overseas Domestic Workers (Protection) Bill; Elected hereditary peer 1999-. Member Selection 2008-13. *Councils and public bodies:* Councillor, Frome RDC 1968-72; DL, Somerset 1975-90; President Northern Ireland Association for Care and Resettlement of Offenders 1988-2009; Chairman Advisory Council Foundation for Reconciliation and Relief in Middle East (Iraq) 2006.

Political interests: Northern Ireland, housing, British-Irish relations, human rights, prisons, penal affairs and policy, conflict resolution, peace building, inter-faith relations, foreign affairs and policy; Caucasus (North and South), Europe, Iraq, Israel, Middle East, Moldova, Palestine, Russia, South East Europe, former Soviet Union.

Other: Chair, MICOM – Moldova Initiatives Committee of Management 1994; Foundation for Reconciliation and Relief in Middle East (Iraq); The Soul of Europe (Kosovo); Associated in various capacities since 1962 with: Abbeyfield Society, Catholic Housing Aid Society, The London Housing Aid Centre, National Federation of Housing Associations, Age Concern, L'Arche Ltd, Royal MENCAP, Foundation for Alternatives, Mendip Wansdyke Local Enterprise Group, Action around Bethlehem Children with Disability (ABCD); Housing Associations Charitable Trust; Trustee, Forward Thinking (Re Israel and Palestine etc); Acorn Christian Healing Trust 1976-99; Chair, St Francis and St Sergius Trust Fund (for the churches and youth in Russia) 1993-2001; Trustee and governor, Ammerdown Centre Ltd, near Bath; Associate, Royal Institute of Chartered Surveyors; ARICS 1960. Honorary DSocSci, Southampton University 1994; Lansdowne.

The Lord Hylton, House of Lords, London SW1A 0PW
Tel: 020 7219 3883 *Fax:* 020 7219 5979
Email: hyltonr@parliament.uk *Website:* lordsoftheblog.net/category/lord-hylton

IMBERT, LORD

CROSSBENCH

IMBERT (Life Baron), Peter Michael Imbert; cr. 1999. Born 27 April 1933; Son of late William Imbert, and of Frances Imbert, née Hodge; Married Iris Dove 1956 (1 son 2 daughters).

Education: Harvey Grammar School, Folkestone; Holborn College of Law, Languages and Commerce; Basic Russian.

Non-political career: Joined Metropolitan Police 1953; Metropolitan Police Anti-Terrorist Squad 1973-75; Police negotiator at Balcombe Street siege December 1975; Surrey Constabulary: Assistant Chief Constable 1976, Deputy Chief Constable 1977; Chief Constable, Thames Valley Police 1979-85; National Crime Committee-ACPO Council: Secretary 1980-83, Chair 1983-85; Metropolitan Police: Deputy Commissioner 1985-87, Commissioner 1987-93; Non-executive director: Securicor 1994-2000, Camelot plc 1994-2001; Non-executive chair, Retainagroup 1995-2002; Has lectured on terrorism and siege situations in UK, Europe, Australia and Canada; Chair, Capital Eye Ltd 1997-; Strategic adviser, Inkerman Group.

Political career: *House of Lords:* Raised to the peerage as Baron Imbert, of New Romney in the County of Kent 1999. *Councils and public bodies:* Member: General Advisory Council, BBC 1980-87, Criminal Justice Consultative Committee 1992-93, Ministerial Advisory Group, Royal Parks 1993-99, Public Policy Committee, RAC 1993-2000; Leader, International Criminal Justice Delegation to Russia 1993; Visiting International Fellow, Australian Police Staff College 1994 and 1997; Member, Mental Health Foundation, Committee of Inquiry into Care in the Community for the Severely Mentally Ill 1994; JP 1998-2005; Greater London: Lord Lieutenant 1998-2008, DL 2008-.

Political interests: Police, criminal justice; Russia.

Other: Life member, Association of Chief Police Officers; Trustee, Queen Elizabeth Foundation of St Catharine's 1988-2001; Chair, Surrey CCC Youth Trust 1993-96; Trustee, Police Federation; Member, International Police Association; Member, International Police Association; CIMgt (CBIM 1982); John Grooms; Crimestoppers Police Foundation. Security Professionals. Freeman: City of London, New Romney, Kent. Honorary DLitt, Reading University 1987; DBA, Buckingham University. QPM 1980; Kt 1988; CVO 2008; RAC, Saints and Sinners Club, London. Life Vice-President Surrey County CC.

Recreations: Bad bridge, coarse golf, talking about grandchildren.

The Lord Imbert CVO QPM, House of Lords, London SW1A 0PW
Tel: 020 7219 5353
3-4 Elwick Road, Ashford, Kent TN23 1RF *Tel:* 01233 614790
Email: peterimbert@btinternet.com

INGE, LORD

CROSSBENCH

INGE (Life Baron), Peter Anthony Inge; cr. 1997. Born 5 August 1935; Son of late Raymond and Grace Inge; Married Letitia Thornton-Berry 1960 (2 daughters).

Education: Summer Fields School; Wrekin College; RMA, Sandhurst.

Non-political career: Army Officer 1956-97: Commissioned Green Howards 1956; Served Hong Kong, Malaya, Germany, Libya and UK; ADC to GOC, 4 Division 1960-61; Adjutant, 1 Green Howards 1963-64; Student, Staff College 1966; Ministry of Defence 1967-69; Company Commander, 1 Green Howards 1969-70; Student, Joint Services Staff College 1971; BM, 11 Armoured Brigade 1972; Instructor, Staff College 1973-74; CO, 1 Green Howards 1974-76; Commandant, Junior Division, Staff College 1977-79; Commander, Task Force C/4 Armoured Brigade 1980-81; Chief of Staff, HQ 1 (BR) Corps 1982-83; Colonel, The Green Howards 1982-94; GOC, NE District and Commander 2nd Infantry Division 1984-86; Director General, Logistic Policy (Army), Ministry of Defence 1986-87; Commander, 1st (Br) Corps 1987-89; Colonel Commandant, Royal Military Police 1987-92; Commander, Northern Army Group and C-in-C, BAOR 1989-92; ADC General to HM The Queen 1991-94; Chief of the General Staff 1992-94; Field Marshal 1994; Chief of the Defence Staff 1994-97; Constable, HM Tower of London 1996-2001. Member, Intelligence Review Committee 2004.

Political career: *House of Lords:* Raised to the peerage as Baron Inge, of Richmond in the County of North Yorkshire 1997. Member EU Sub-committee C (Common Foreign and Security Policy/Foreign Affairs, Defence and Development Policy) 1999-2005; EU Sub-committee C (Foreign Affairs, Defence and Development Policy): Co-opted member 2008-10, Member 2010-12; Member EU Sub-committee C (External Affairs) 2012-13. *Councils and public bodies:* DL, North Yorkshire 1994.

Political interests: Defence; Europe, Middle and Far East, USA.

Other: Council member, International Institute for Strategic Studies; Vice-President, Not Forgotten Association; Patron, Royal United Services Institute; Army Benevolent Fund. Freeman, City of London. Honorary DCL, Newcastle University. KCB 1988; GCB (Mil) 1992; KG 2001; PC 2004; Boodle's, Beefsteak, Army and Navy, MCC, Travellers.

Recreations: Cricket, walking, music, reading.

Rt Hon Field Marshal the Lord Inge KG GCB DL, House of Lords, London SW1A 0PW
Tel: 020 7219 8706 *Email:* ingep@parliament.uk

INGLEWOOD, LORD

INGLEWOOD (2nd Baron, UK), (William) Richard Fletcher-Vane; cr. 1964. Born 31 July 1951; Son of 1st Baron, TD, DL and Mary, neé Proby; Married Cressida Pemberton-Pigott 1986 (1 son 2 daughters).

Education: Eton College; Trinity College, Cambridge (BA English/land economy 1973, MA); Cumbria College of Agriculture and Forestry (City and Guilds Levels III and IV 1982); French, German.

CONSERVATIVE

Non-political career: Called to the Bar, Lincoln's Inn 1975; CN Group: Non-executive director 1997-, Chair 2002-; Chair, Reviewing Committee on Export of Works of Art and Objects of Cultural Interest 2003-; Carrs Milling Industries plc: Non-executive director 2004, Chair 2005-13.

Political career: *House of Commons:* Contested (Conservative) Houghton and Washington 1983 general election. *House of Lords:* First entered House of Lords 1989; Government Whip 1994-95: Government Deputy Chief Whip 1995; Parliamentary Under-Secretary of State and Government Spokesperson, Department of National Heritage 1995-97; Opposition Spokesperson for Environment, Transport and the Regions 1997-98; Elected hereditary peer 1999-. Member: EU Sub-committees: E 1997-99, A 2004-07; Communications 2007-10; Co-opted member EU Sub-committee G (Social Policy and Consumer Affairs) 2008-10; Member EU Sub-committee G (Social Policies and Consumer Protection) 2010-11; Chair Communications 2010-. *Other:* Contested Durham 1984 European Parliament election. MEP (Conservative) for Cumbria and Lancashire North 1989-94. Contested Cumbria and Lancashire North 1994 European Parliament election. MEP for North West Region 1999-2004: Vice-President, EP-China Delegation 1999-2004. *Councils and public bodies:* Member, Lake District Special Planning Board 1984-90; Chair, Development Control Committee 1985-89; Member, North West Water Authority 1987-89; DL, Cumbria 1993; Chair, Reviewing Committee Export of Works of Art 2003- Governor, Skinners' Academy, Hackney 2008-11; Vice Lord-Lieutenant, Cumbria 2013-.

Political interests: Rural affairs, agriculture, environment, Europe, local and regional government, regional policy, legal affairs, media, arts, constitutional affairs; China, EU, Iceland, Turkey.

Other: Member, Royal Institution of Chartered Surveyors; FSA. Liveryman, Skinners' Company; Travellers', Pratt's.

The Lord Inglewood, House of Lords, London SW1A 0PW
Tel: 020 7219 3190 *Email:* inglewoodw@parliament.uk
Hutton-in-the-Forest, Penrith, Cumbria CA11 9TH *Tel:* 01768 484500 *Fax:* 01768 484571
Email: inglewood@hutton-in-the-forest.co.uk *Website:* www.hutton-in-the-forest.co.uk

IRVINE OF LAIRG, LORD

IRVINE OF LAIRG (Life Baron), Alexander Andrew Mackay Irvine; cr. 1987. Born 23 June 1940; Son of Alexander and Margaret Christina Irvine; Married Alison Mary McNair 1974 (2 sons).

Education: Inverness Royal Academy; Hutchesons' Boys' Grammar School, Glasgow; Glasgow University (MA, LLB); Christ's College, Cambridge (Scholar, BA, LLB).

Non-political career: University lecturer, London School of Economics 1965-69; Called to the Bar, Inner Temple 1967; QC 1978; Head, 11 King's Bench Walk Chambers 1981-97; Bencher of the Inner Temple, 1985; Recorder 1985-88; Deputy High Court Judge 1987-97.

LABOUR

Political career: *House of Commons:* Contested (Labour) Hendon North 1970 general election. *House of Lords:* Raised to the peerage as Baron Irvine of Lairg, of Lairg in the District of Sutherland 1987. Opposition Spokesperson for Legal Affairs and Home Affairs 1987-92; Shadow Lord Chancellor 1992-97; Lord Chancellor and Government Spokesperson for Legal Affairs and Lord Chancellor's Department 1997-2003; Lord of Appeal -2008. Member: Privileges/Privileges and Conduct 2008-, Sub-committee on Lords' Interests 2008-10, Constitution 2009-, Sub-committee on Lords' Conduct 2010-. *Councils and public bodies:* Church Commissioner.

Political interests: Legal affairs, home affairs, constitutional affairs.

Other: Vice-Patron, World Federation of Mental Health; Joint President: Inter-Parliamentary Union, Commonwealth Parliamentary Association; Vice-President, Commonwealth Parliamentary Association (UK Branch); President, Magistrates Association; Chair, Glasgow 2001 Committee; Member, Committee of the Slade School of Fine Art 1990-; Foundation trustee, Whitechapel Art Gallery 1990-97; Trustee: John Smith Memorial Trust 1992-97, Hunterian Collection 1997-; Joint President, Industry and Parliament Trust 1997-; Honorary Fellow, Society for Advanced Legal Studies; Fellow, US College of Trial Lawyers 1998-. Honorary Fellow, Christ's College, Cambridge 1996; Honorary LLD, Glasgow 1997; Honorary Bencher, Inn of Court of Northern Ireland 1998; Honorary Doctorate, Siena 2000; Fellowship, LSE 2000; Member, Polish Bar 2000. George and Thomas Hutchison Award 1998. PC 1997; Knight Commander of the Order of Merit of the Republic of Poland, with Star 2004; Garrick.

Publications: Articles on constitutional and legal topics in legal journals.

Recreations: Collecting paintings, travel, reading, cinema and theatre.

Rt Hon the Lord Irvine of Lairg, House of Lords, London SW1A 0PW
Tel: 020 7219 1446

NON-AFFILIATED

JACOBS, LORD

JACOBS (Life Baron) (David) Anthony Jacobs; cr. 1997. Born 13 November 1931; Son of Ridley and Ella Jacobs; Married Evelyn Patchett 1954 (1 son 1 daughter).

Education: Clifton College, Bristol; London University (BCom 1951).

Non-political career: Chairman: Nig Securities Group 1957-72, Tricoville Group 1961-90, 1992-94, British School of Motoring 1973-90.

Political career: *House of Lords:* Raised to the peerage as Baron Jacobs, of Belgravia in the City of Westminster 1997. Member House of Lords Offices Advisory Panel on Works of Art Sub-committee 2000-02. *Other:* Joint Treasurer, Liberal Party 1984-87; Vice-President, Social and Liberal Democrats 1988, Member, Federal Executive 1988. Resigned Liberal Democrat Whip December 2008. Now sits as a non-affiliated member. *Councils and public bodies:* Paving Commissioner, Crown Estate.

Political interests: Taxation; Israel.

Other: Chairman, Board of Governors, Haifa University, Israel 1993-2002; FCA; Tate Modern; Royal Opera House. Honorary Doctorate, Haifa University, Israel 2004. Kt 1988. Coombe Hill Golf (Surrey); Palm Beach County Club, Florida, USA.

Recreations: Golf, reading, theatre, opera, travel.

The Lord Jacobs, House of Lords, London SW1A 0PW
Tel: 020 7219 5353
9 Nottingham Terrace, London NW1 4QB *Tel:* 020 7486 6323 *Fax:* 020 7935 6598
Email: alordant@aol.com

CONSERVATIVE

JAMES OF BLACKHEATH, LORD

JAMES OF BLACKHEATH (Life Baron), David Noel James; cr 2006. Born 7 December 1937; Son of Captain Francis James and Alsina James, née Burdett; Married Caroline Webster 2004.

Education: Christ's College, Blackheath.

Non-political career: Lloyds Bank 1959-64; Ford Motor Co (UK) 1964-73; Rank Organisation plc 1974-81; Chairman: Central and Sherwood plc 1984-88, Eagle Trust 1989-97; LFP Group plc 1991-95, Henleys Group plc 1991-96, Robinson Group plc 1997-2001, New Millennium Experience Co 2000-01, Litigation Control Group Ltd 2002-06, Vidapulse Ltd 2003-.

Political career: *House of Lords:* Raised to the peerage as Baron James of Blackheath, of Wildbrooks in the County of West Sussex 2006. Co-opted member EU Sub-committee B (Internal Market) 2007-10; Member: Merits of Statutory Instruments 2007-10, Crossrail Bill 2008, EU Sub-committee B (Internal Market, Energy and Transport) 2010-12. *Other:* James Review of Taxpayer Value 2004-05.

Political interests: Horseracing industry, NHS finances, MoD procurement, funding and organisation of 2012 Olympics, renewable energy; Libya.

Other: Fellow, Institute of Directors; Trustee, David James Musical charity; Aphasia Society. Lifetime Achievement, Society of Turnaround Practitioners 2003. CBE 1992; Savile; Jockey Club Rooms. MCC, Lords' Taverners.

Publications: Future Capital Structure of Lloyd's of London (1996); James Report on Public Expenditure (2005).

Recreations: Opera, ballet, cricket, rugby, tennis, horseracing, golf.

The Lord James of Blackheath CBE, House of Lords, London SW1A 0PW
Tel: 020 7219 4954

JAMES OF HOLLAND PARK, BARONESS

JAMES OF HOLLAND PARK (Life Baroness), Phyllis Dorothy James; cr. 1991. Born 3 August 1920; Daughter of late Sydney and Dorothy James; Married Connor Bantry White 1941 (died 1964) (2 daughters).

Education: Cambridge High School for Girls.

Non-political career: Administrator, National Health Service 1949-68; Civil servant, Home Office: Police Department 1968-72, Criminal Policy Department 1972-79; Author; Honorary Bencher, Inner Temple 2009.

CONSERVATIVE

Political career: *House of Lords:* Raised to the peerage as Baroness James of Holland Park, of Southwold in the County of Suffolk 1991. *Councils and public bodies:* JP, Willesden and Inner London 1979-84; Governor, BBC 1988-93; Member, Arts Council 1988-92, Chair, Literature Advisory Panel 1988-92; Board member, British Council 1988-93.

Political interests: Literature, arts, criminal justice, broadcasting.

Other: Chairman, P D James Trust; Chair, Booker Panel of Judges 1987; President, Society of Authors 1997-; Fellow, Royal Society of Literature 1987; FRSA; Prayer Book Society. Seven honorary doctorates, five honorary fellowships; Associate fellow, Downing College, Cambridgeshire 1986. OBE 1983; Detection; Athenæum.

Publications: As P.D. James: Cover her Face (1962); A Mind to Murder (1963); Unnatural Causes (1967); Shroud for a Nightingale (1971); Co-author, The Maul and the Pear Tree (1971); An Unsuitable Job for a Woman (1972); The Black Tower (1975); Death of an Expert Witness (1977); Innocent Blood (1980); The Skull Beneath the Skin (1982); A Taste for Death (1986); Devices and Desires (1989); The Children of Men (1992); Original Sin (1994); A Certain Justice (1997); Time to be in Earnest (1999); Death in Holy Orders (2001); The Murder Room (2003); The Lighthouse (2005); The Private Patient (2008); Talking About Detective Fiction (2009); Death Comes to Pemberley (2011).

Recreations: Reading, exploring churches, walking by the sea.

The Baroness James of Holland Park OBE, House of Lords, London SW1A 0PW
Tel: 020 7219 5353
c/o Greene and Heaton Ltd, 37 Goldhawk Road, London W12 8QQ *Tel:* 020 8749 0315
Email: pdjames@dircon.co.uk

JANNER OF BRAUNSTONE, LORD

JANNER OF BRAUNSTONE (Life Baron), Greville Ewan Janner; cr. 1997. Born 11 July 1928; Son of late Baron Janner (Life Peer) and late Lady Janner, CBE; Married Myra Sheink 1955 (died 1996) (1 son 2 daughters).

Education: Bishop's College School, Canada; St Paul's School, London; Trinity Hall, Cambridge (MA economics and law 1952) (President Cambridge Union); Harvard Postgraduate Law School, USA 1953.

Non-political career: National Service 1946-48, RA, BAOR, War Crimes Investigator. Called to the Bar, Middle Temple 1954; QC 1971; Non-executive director, Ladbrokes plc 1986-95; Chairman, JSB Group and Effective Presentational Skills 1987-97; President, REACH 1989-. Life member, National Union of Journalists (London Freelance Branch); Honorary member, National Union of Mineworkers, Leicester.

LABOUR

Political career: *House of Commons:* Contested Wimbledon 1955 general election. MP (Labour) for Leicester North-West 1970-74, for Leicester West 1974-97. *House of Lords:* Raised to the peerage as Baron Janner of Braunstone, of Leicester in the County of Leicestershire 1997. Member Joint Committee on Consolidation, Etc, Bills 1998-2005, 2006-. *Other:* Chairman, Cambridge University Labour Club 1950; International Secretary, National Association of Labour Students 1952; Labour Friends of: Israel, India.

Political interests: Employment law, industrial relations, Jewish causes, inter community relations, human rights, consumer protection, Commonwealth; India, Middle East.

Other: Vice-President: Jewish Museum 1955-2001, Association for Jewish Youth 1970-; President: Board of Deputies of British Jews 1979-85, Commonwealth Jewish Council 1982-; Founder/ President, Interparliamentary Council Against Anti-Semitism 1985-; Chair: Holocaust Educational Trust 1988-, Lord Forte Charitable Trust; Vice-President, World Jewish Congress 1991-; Founder and President, Maimonides Foundation 1995-2002; Co-President, Coexistence Trust 2005-; President, Association of Jewish Ex-Servicemen 2009-; Fellow, Institute of Personnel Management and Development; Cancer Charities, Holocaust Educational Trust; Joint President, Political Council for Co-existence. Freeman: City of London, Gibraltar 2012. Honorary PhD, Haifa University, Israel; Honorary LLD, De Montfort University; Hon PhD, Leicester University 2008. Order of Lithuanian Grand Duke Gediminas.

Publications: Many books including: One Hand Alone Cannot Clap (1998); Janner's Complete Speechmaker (7th edition, 2003); To Life! (autobiography 2008).
Recreations: Swimming, member of the Magic Circle and International Brotherhood of Magicians, languages.
The Lord Janner of Braunstone QC, House of Lords, London SW1A 0PW
Tel: 020 7219 8988 *Email:* lordj@grevillejanner.org.uk *Website:* www.grevillejanner.org.uk

CROSSBENCH

JANVRIN, LORD

JANVRIN (Life Baron), Robin Berry Janvrin; cr 2007. Born 20 September 1946; Married Isabelle de Boissonneaux de Chevigny 1977 (2 sons 2 daughters).
Education: Marlborough College, Wiltshire; Brasenose College, Oxford (BA philosophy, politics and economics 1969).
Non-political career: Royal Navy 1964-75; HM Diplomatic Service 1975-87: First secretary, UK delegation to NATO 1976-78, New Delhi high commission 1981-84, Counsellor 1985; HM the Queen: Press secretary to 1987-90, Assistant private secretary to 1990-95, Deputy private secretary to 1996-99, Private secretary to and Keeper of the Queen's Archives 1999-2007, Permanent Lord-in-waiting 2007-.
Political career: *House of Lords:* Raised to the peerage as Baron Janvrin, of Chalford Hill in the County of Gloucestershire 2007. Member: Joint Committee on Privacy and Injunctions 2011-12, Soft Power and the UK's Influence 2013-.
Political interests: Constitutional issues, foreign and commonwealth affairs, philanthropy; France, India.
Other: Deputy chair, HSBC Private Bank (UK) Ltd; Trustee, National Portrait Gallery 2008-. LVO 1983; CVO 1994; CB 1997; PC 1998; KCVO 1998; KCB 2003; GCB 2007; GCVO 2007; QSO 2008.
Recreations: Family, painting.
Rt Hon the Lord Janvrin, House of Lords, London SW1A 0PW
Tel: 020 7219 6989 *Email:* janvrinr@parliament.uk

CROSSBENCH

JAY OF EWELME, LORD

JAY OF EWELME (Life Baron), Michael Hastings Jay; cr 2006. Born 19 June 1946; Son of late Alan Jay and of Vera Effa Vickery; Married Sylvia Mylroie 1975.
Education: Winchester College; Magdalen College, Oxford (BA philosophy, politics and economics 1968, MA); School of Oriental and African Studies, London University (MSc economic development 1969); French.
Non-political career: Volunteer teacher, Zambia 1965; Assistant principal, Ministry of Overseas Development (ODM) 1969-73; Technical assistant, UK delegation to International Monetary Fund and International Bank for Reconstruction and Development (World Bank), Washington DC 1973-75; Principal, ODM 1976-78; First Secretary (Development), New Delhi High Commission 1978-81; Foreign and Commonwealth Office (FCO), London 1981-85: Deputy Head, FCO Policy Planning Staff 1981-82, Private Secretary to Permanent Under Secretary 1982-85; Counsellor, European Secretariat, Cabinet Office 1985-87; Financial and Commercial Counsellor, British Embassy, Paris 1987-90; FCO 1990-96: Assistant Under-Secretary for European Affairs 1990-94, Deputy Under-Secretary of State for Economic and Economic Affairs 1994-96; Ambassador to France 1996-2001; Permanent Under-Secretary, FCO and Head of the Diplomatic Service 2002-06; Prime Minister's Personal Representative for G8 Presidency and Summits 2005-06; Non-executive director: Associated British Foods 2006-, Valeo SA 2007-, Credit Agricole SA 2007-11, Candover Investments plc 2008-, EDF 2009-.
Political career: *House of Lords:* Raised to the peerage as Baron Jay of Ewelme, of Ewelme in the County of Oxfordshire 2006. Co-opted member EU Sub-committee E (Law and Institutions) 2006-08; Member: Draft Climate Change Bill Joint Committee 2007, Intergovernmental Organisations 2007-08; EU Sub-committee C (Foreign Affairs, Defence and Development Policy): Co-opted member 2008-10, Member 2010-12; Member: EU Sub-committee C (External Affairs) 2012-13, Joint Committee on the Draft Enhanced Terrorism Prevention and Investigation Measures Bill 2012-13. *Councils and public bodies:* Chair, House of Lords Appointments Commission 2008-.
Political interests: Foreign and European policy, energy policy, environment and climate change, development; Africa, EU, India.

Other: Vice-chair, Business for New Europe 2006-; Chair: Merlin (international medical charity) 2007-, Culham Languages and Sciences (educational charity) 2009-11; Member, British Library Advisory Council 2011-. Senior associate member, St Antony's College, Oxford 1996; Honorary Fellow, Magdalen College, Oxford 2004. CMG 1992; KCMG 1997; GCMG 2006.

The Lord Jay of Ewelme GCMG, House of Lords, London SW1A 0PW
Tel: 020 7219 3941 *Email:* jaymh@parliament.uk

JAY OF PADDINGTON, BARONESS

JAY OF PADDINGTON (Life Baroness), Margaret Ann Jay; cr. 1992. Born 18 November 1939; Daughter of late James Callaghan, former Prime Minister, and Audrey Moulton; Married Hon Peter Jay 1961 (divorced 1986) (1 son 2 daughters); married Professor Michael Adler, CBE 1994.

Education: Blackheath High School, London; Somerville College, Oxford (BA philosophy, politics and economics 1961).

Non-political career: Various production posts with BBC Television in current affairs and further education 1965-77; Former reporter for: BBC Television's *Panorama*, Thames Television's *This* **LABOUR** *Week*; Founder director, The National AIDS Trust 1988-92; Non-executive director: Carlton Television 1996-97, Scottish Power 1996-97, Independent News and Media UK 2001-12, BT 2002-08; Political consultant to Currie and Brown 2004-07; Non-executive director, British Telecom Committee for Responsible and Sustainable Business 2008-. Member, National Union of Journalists.

Political career: *House of Lords:* Raised to the peerage as Baroness Jay of Paddington, of Paddington in the City of Westminster 1992. Opposition Spokesperson for Health 1992-97, Minister of State, Department of Health 1997-98; Deputy Leader, House of Lords 1997-98; Leader of the House of Lords and Lord Privy Seal Minister for Women 1998-2001; Opposition Whip 1992-95. Member: House of Lords Offices 1997-, Assisted Dying 2004-05, Leader's Group on Code of Conduct 2009; Constitution: Member 2009-10, Chair 2010-. *Other:* Member, Labour Party Donations Committee 2002-05; President, One Thousand Club 2002-06. *Councils and public bodies:* Member, Kensington and Chelsea and Westminster Health Authority 1993-97; Former Member, Central Research and Development Committee for NHS.

Political interests: Health, overseas aid and development, media, broadcasting.

Other: Former Member, President World Bank International Advisory Group on Health; Member, International Advisory Board Independent News and Media 2002-; Associate member, InterAction Council; Former Governor, South Bank University; Former Member, Governing Board: Queen Charlotte's Maternity Hospital, Chelsea Hospital for Women; Chair: Overseas Development Institute 2002-10; Bringing Research to Life Development Board, Great Ormond Street Hospital 2010-; Overseas Development Institute: Chair 2002-10, Council member; Trustee, Hansard Society 2012-; Member, Court of Governors, South Bank University 2012-. Two honorary degrees; Senior Honorary Fellow, Somerville College, Oxford; Honorary Fellow: Sunderland University, South Bank University. PC 1998.

Publications: How Rich Can We Get? (1972); Co-author, Battered – The Story of Child Abuse (1986).

Rt Hon the Baroness Jay of Paddington, House of Lords, London SW1A 0PW
Tel: 020 7219 4912 *Email:* jaym@parliament.uk

JENKIN OF KENNINGTON, BARONESS

JENKIN OF KENNINGTON (Life Baron), Anne Caroline Jenkin; cr 2011. Born 8 December 1955; Daughter of late Honorary Charles Stutt and Honorary Jean Stutt, née Davidson; Married Bernard Jenkin, later MP, 1988 (2 sons).

Political career: *House of Lords:* Raised to the peerage as Baroness Jenkin of Kennington, of Hatfield Peverel in the County of Essex 2011. Member Refreshment 2012-. *Other:* Founder and co-chair, Women2Win; Chair, Conservative Friends of International Development.

Other: Patron, Restless Development; Trustee, Unicef UK.

CONSERVATIVE The Baroness Jenkin of Kennington, House of Lords, London SW1A 0PW
Tel: 020 7219 5353 *Twitter:* @BaronessJenkin

JENKIN OF RODING, LORD

JENKIN OF RODING (Life Baron), Charles Patrick Fleeming Jenkin; cr. 1987. Born 7 September 1926; Son of late Charles Jenkin, industrial chemist; Married Alison Graham 1952 (2 sons 2 daughters).

Education: Clifton College; Jesus College, Cambridge (BA law 1951).

Non-political career: Served in the Cameron Highlanders, including service abroad 1945-48. Called to the Bar Middle Temple 1952; Practising barrister 1952-57; Distillers Co. Ltd 1957-70; Adviser, Andersen Consulting (Management Consultants) 1985-96; Member, UK Advisory Board, National Economic Research Associates Inc. 1985-98; UK-Japan 2000 Group: Member 1986-, UK Co-chair 1986-90, Board member 1990-99; Chair, Target Finland Ltd 1987-96; Crystalate Holdings plc: Non-executive director 1987-90, Chair 1988-90; Chair, Lamco Paper Sales Ltd 1987-93; Friends Provident Life Office: Director, Chair 1988-98; Adviser, Sumitomo Trust and Banking Co. Ltd 1989-2010; Member, Supervisory Board, Achmea Holding NV (Netherlands) 1992-98; Adviser, Thames Estuary Airport Co. Ltd. 1992-; Senior Vice-President, World Congress on Urban Growth and the Environment (Hong Kong) 1992-94; Member, International Advisory Board, Marsh and McLennan Group of Companies (US) 1993-99.

CONSERVATIVE

Political career: *House of Commons:* MP (Conservative) for Wanstead and Woodford 1964-87. Treasury Minister 1970-74: Financial Secretary 1970-72, Chief Secretary 1972-74; Minister for Energy 1974; Secretary of State for: Social Services 1979-81, Industry 1981-83, the Environment 1983-85. *House of Lords:* Raised to the peerage as Baron Jenkin of Roding, of Wanstead and Woodford in Greater London 1987. President, Parliamentary and Scientific Committee 2008-. Member Science and Technology Sub-committee on Managing Nuclear Waste 1988-89, 2001-02, 2003-04, 2006-07; Chair Science and Technology Sub-committee II (Science and Society) 1999-2000; Member: Science and Technology Sub-committees: II (Aircraft Cabin Environment) 2000-01, IIA (Human Genetic Databases) 2000-01, Joint Committee on Draft Human Tissue and Embryos Bill 2007; Co-opted member: Science and Technology (Pandemic Influenza) 2008-09, Science and Technology Sub-committee I (Radioactive Waste Management: a further update) 2010, Science and Technology -2012. *Other:* Greater London Area Conservatives: Vice-President 1987-89, President 1989-93; President, Saffron Walden Constituency Conservative Association 1994-2003; Executive Committee Member, ACP 1996-2000. *Councils and public bodies:* Councillor, Hornsey Borough Council 1960-63; Foundation for Science and Technology: Chair 1997-2006, President 2006-; Vice-President, Local Government Association 1997-; President, Association for Science Education 2002-03; Honorary President: National Skills Academy for Nuclear 2009-, Energy Industries Council 2009-.

Political interests: Economic policy, industry, science, technology, health, disabled, energy, housing, planning, financial services, statistics; Japan.

Other: Member: Inter-Parliamentary Union 1964-, Commonwealth Parliamentary Association 1964-; Member, Bow Group 1951-; Numerous charitable and voluntary organisations, including: Council member, Guide Dogs for the Blind Association 1987-97; Chair, Westfield College Trust 1989-2000; Patron: Redbridge Community Trust 1992-95, St Clare Hospice Trust 1992-; Chair, Forest Healthcare NHS Trust 1992-97; Trustee: Monteverdi Choir and Orchestra 1992-2001, Conservative Agents Superannuation Fund 1992-2000; Deputy chair, Imperial Cancer Research Fund 1994-97; Joint President, London Councils 1995-; Trustee, St Andrews Prize Trust 2001-06; Patron, Nuclear Institute 2011-; Bar Council; Honorary Fellow, Royal Society of Edinburgh 2001-. Freeman, City of London 1985; Honorary Freeman, London Borough of Redbridge 1988. Fellow, Queen Mary and Westfield College 1991-; Two honorary doctorates; Fellow, College of Optometrists 2003-. PC 1973.

Recreations: Gardening, DIY, bricklaying, sailing, music.

Rt Hon the Lord Jenkin of Roding, House of Lords, London SW1A 0PW
Tel: 020 7219 6966 *Fax:* 020 7219 0759 *Email:* jenkinp@parliament.uk

JOFFE, LORD

JOFFE (Life Baron), Joel Goodman Joffe; cr. 2000. Born 12 May 1932; Son of Abraham and Dena Joffe; Married Vanetta Pretorius 1962 (3 daughters).

Education: Marist Brothers' College, Johannesburg, South Africa; University of Witwatersrand, South Africa (BCom, LLB 1955).

Non-political career: Admitted Solicitor, Johannesburg 1956; Human rights lawyer 1958-65; Called to the Bar, South Africa 1962; Director and secretary, Abbey Life Assurance Company 1965-70; Director, joint managing director and deputy chair, Allied Dunbar, Life Assurance Company 1971-91; Chair, Swindon Private Hospital 1982-87; Oxfam: Honorary Secretary 1982-85, Executive Committee Chairman 1985-93, Chair 1995-2001; Special adviser to South African Minister of Transport 1997-98; Chair, The Giving Campaign 2001-04.

LABOUR

Political career: *House of Lords:* Raised to the peerage as Baron Joffe, of Liddington in the County of Wiltshire 2000. *Councils and public bodies:* Chair: Swindon Health Authority 1988-93, Swindon and Marlborough NHS Trust 1993-95; Member, Royal Commission on Long Term Care for the Elderly 1997-98.

Political interests: Human rights, developing world, financial services, consumer protection, assisted dying, philanthropy, voluntary sector; Southern Africa.

Other: Trustee, Joffe Charitable Trust 1968-; Chair, Allied Dunbar Charitable Trust 1974-93; Trustee: Oxfam 1979-2001, Action for Disability and Development 1984-98, Canon Collins Educational Trust for Southern Africa 1985-2007, International Alert 1994-2000, Legal Assistance Trust for Southern Africa 1995-2012, The Smith Institute 1999-2011, Management Accountancy for NGOs 2000-12; Oxfam. Five honorary doctorates. CBE 1999; Companion of O.R. Tambo (South Africa).

Publications: The State vs Nelson Mandela (2007).

Recreations: Tennis.

The Lord Joffe CBE, House of Lords, London SW1A 0PW
Tel: 020 7219 5353
Liddington Manor, Liddington, Swindon, Wiltshire SN4 0HD *Tel:* 01793 790203
Fax: 01793 791144 *Email:* joel@lidmanor.co.uk

JOLLY, BARONESS

Government Whip

JOLLY (Life Baroness), Judith Anne Jolly; cr 2010. Born 27 April 1951; Married (2 sons).

Education: The King's High School for Girls, Warwick; Leeds University (engineering); Nottingham University (PGCE).

Non-political career: Maths teacher 1974-1997; Chief of staff to Robin Teverson MEP 1997-1999; Taught English as a foreign language, British Council, Oman 1990s.

LIBERAL DEMOCRAT

Political career: *House of Lords:* Raised to the peerage as Baroness Jolly, of Congdon's Shop in the County of Cornwall 2010. Government Whip 2013-. Member: Ecclesiastical Committee 2012-, Joint Committee on the Draft Care and Support Bill 2013. Chair, Liberal Democrat Parliamentary Party Committee on Health and Social Care 2011-. *Other:* Member, Liberal Party/Liberal Democrats 1984-; Election agent to Paul Tyler, MP for North Cornwall, 1997; Vice-chair, parliamentary candidates assocation 1999-2008; Member, Federal Executive Committee 2002-10; Chair, Devon and Cornwall Regional Executive 2007-10. *Councils and public bodies:* Non-executive director, Mental Health and Learning Disability NHS Trust 1997-2007; Former chair, North and East Cornwall NHS Primary Care Trust; Former lay member, Commission for Health Improvement; President, Society of Chiropodists and Podiatrists 2013-; Chair, Digital Services Cornwall CIC.

Political interests: Poverty, rural affairs, global health, music; Oman.

Other: Trustee, Parliament Choir.

Recreations: Singing, reading modern novels.

The Baroness Jolly, House of Lords, London SW1A 0PW
Tel: 020 7219 1286 *Email:* jollyj@parliament.uk *Twitter:* @jollyjudith

JONES, LORD

JONES (Life Baron), (Stephen) Barry Jones; cr. 2001. Born 26 June 1937; Son of late Stephen Jones, steelworker, and late Grace Jones; Married Janet Davies (1 son).

Education: Hawarden Grammar School; Teacher training, Normal College, UCNW Bangor.

Non-political career: Head of English department, Deeside Secondary School, Flintshire; Regional officer, National Union of Teachers. National Union of Teachers; Transport and General Workers Union.

LABOUR

Political career: *House of Commons:* Contested Northwich, Cheshire 1966 general election. MP (Labour) for East Flint 1970-83, for Alyn and Deeside 1983-2001. PPS to Denis Healey as Chancellor of the Exchequer 1972-74; Parliamentary Under-Secretary of State for Wales 1974-79; Opposition Frontbench Spokesperson for Employment 1980-83; Member: Shadow Cabinet 1983-92, Prime Minister's Intelligence and Security Committee 1994-97, 1997-; Madam speaker's Chairman Panel 1997-2001; Chairman Welsh Grand Committee 1997-2001; Chairman Advisory Committee on Registration of Political Parties 1999-2001; Deputy Speaker, Westminster Hall 2001. *House of Lords:* Raised to the peerage as Baron Jones, of Deeside in the County of Clwyd 2001. Member EU Sub-committee A (Economic and Financial Affairs, Trade and External Relations/Economic and Financial Affairs) 2003-06; EU Sub-committee C (Foreign Affairs, Defence and Development Policy): Co-opted member 2008-10, Member 2010-12; Member Joint Committee on the Draft Communications Data Bill 2012-13. *Other:* Member, Executive of Labour Party, Wales 1966-70.

Political interests: Manufacturing industries, regional policy, NHS, education, aerospace; Austria, Germany.
Other: Member, Delegation of Council of Europe and Western European Union 1971-74; Honorary Life Member, Royal Liverpool Philharmonic Society 1980-; Governor: National Museum of Wales, National Library of Wales; Chair, Diocesan Board of Continuity Education, St Asaph 2004-; President: Flintshire Alzheimers Society, Deeside Hospital League of Friends, North East Wales Institute of Higher Education 2007-09, Neighbourhood Watch, Flintshire 2008-, Hawarden Singers, Saltney History Society; Vice-President, Federation of Economic Development Authorities; Chair, Diocesan Education Board (St Asaph); Dementia Champion Wales 2012-; President: Army Cadet Forces Wales 2013, Royal Buckley Town Band, Wrexham and Birkenhead Rail Users Association, Chester and East Clwyd Advanced Motorists, Deeside Industrial Park Forum, Arthritis Care, Flintshire, Sain Clwyd Sound (Talking Newspaper); Patron, Brain Injury Rehabilitation and Development Learning Centre, Chester; Trustee: Friends of Africa Foundation, Winnicot Clinic, Bodelwyddan Castle Trust (NPG Wales); Honorary Fellow: University of Bangor 2012, Gladstone's Library, Hawarden; Alzheimer's Disease Society, Mencap; Friend: Royal Academy, Tate Galleries, Merseyside Museum and Gallery; Patron: Welsh Association of ME and CFS Support (Wales Neurological Alliance), Cornerstone Flintshire (L'Arche UK). Chancellor, Glyndŵr University 2009-. PC 1999.
Recreations: Soccer, cricket, watching tennis.
Rt Hon the Lord Jones, House of Lords, London SW1A 0PW
Tel: 020 7219 3556

CROSSBENCH

JONES OF BIRMINGHAM, LORD

JONES OF BIRMINGHAM (Life Baron), Digby Marritt Jones; cr 2007. Born 28 October 1955; Son of late Derek Jones and of Bernice Jones; Married Patricia Moody 1990.
Education: Bromsgrove School, Worcestershire; University College, London (LLB 1977); College of Law, Chester; French.
Non-political career: University cadetship, Royal Navy 1974-77. Edge & Ellison, Solicitors 1978-98: Articled clerk 1978-80, Solicitor 1980-98, Partner 1984-98, Deputy senior partner 1990-95, Senior partner 1995-98; Vice-chair, corporate finance, KPMG Business Advisers 1998-2000; Director-general, Confederation of British Industry 2000-06; Director, Business in the Community 2000-06; Chair: Tourism Alliance 2001-06; extrinsic plc 2003-05; Non-executive director: Alba plc 2004-07; Mhl plc 2004-06, Iclean Systems plc 2005-07, Leicester Tigers plc 2005-; UK Skills Envoy 2006-07; Adviser: Wragge & Co, Solicitors 2006-07, Hugh James, Solicitors 2006-07; Senior adviser: Ford of Europe 2006-07, Barclays Capital 2006-07, Deloitte 2006-07, JCB 2006-07, Computer Science Corporation inc 2006-07; Member, advisory board, Thales 2006-07; Chairman: International Business Advisory Board, HSBC 2009-11, International Business Advisory Board, British Airways 2009-12, Grove Indistries 2012-, Triumph Motorcycles Limited 2009-, Neutrino Concepts Limited 2009-; Corporate Ambassador to Jaguar Cars 2009-; Corporate adviser to JCB 2009-; Senior Global Adviser Monitise plc 2009-; Business adviser to: ISeeU Limited 2009-10, Grove Industries Limited 2009-11, Barberry Developments Ltd 2009-, Business Ambassador for UK Trade & Investment 2008-; Adviser to: Duke of York as Special Representative to UK Trade & Investment 2009-10, BP PLC 2012-, SHP Limited 2013; Chairman: International business advisory board, British Airways 2009-12, Emergency services advisory board, Babcock International Group plc; Senior adviser, Harvey Nash plc; Chairman, advisory board: Jaguar academy of sport, Argentex Ltd 2012-; Non-executive director: Flybe plc 2012-, Spicers Ltd 2012-; Leicester Tigers PLC; Non-executive deputy chair, Unipart Expert Practices 2013-.
Political career: *House of Lords:* Raised to the peerage as Baron Jones of Birmingham, of Alvechurch and of Bromsgrove in the County of Worcestershire 2007. Minister of State (Trade and Investment) and Government Spokesperson, Foreign and Commonwealth Office and Department for Business, Enterprise and Regulatory Reform 2007-08. *Councils and public bodies:* Member, Commission for Racial Equality 2002-07; Director, VisitBritain 2003-05; Member, National Learning and Skills Council 2003-06; President, Diversity Works Initiative 2004-07; Chairman, Birmingham University Business School Advisory Board.
Countries of interest: Australia, India, Middle East, South Africa, USA.
Other: Corporate ambassador, Cancer Research UK 2004-; Chairman, Corporate Advisory Board, Sense 2004-07; Vice-President, Birmingham Hospice; Member, Development Trust CBSO; Vice-President, Birmingham Civic Society; Trustee, Millenium Point, Birmingham 2006-11; Corporate ambassador and member, Royal British Legion; Vice-President, Industrial Trust; Chairman, advisory board, Birmingham University Business School; Guardian, Birmingham Assay Office; Chairman, London Board, Sportaccord 2010-11; Member Law Society 1980; Honorary Fellow, Institute of Mechanical Engineers; Honorary Fellow: University College, London 2004, Cardiff University

2006, Visiting Professor, Hull University Business School, Cardiff Metropolitan University 2013; Get-a-Head Charitable Trust; Sense; Ovarian Cancer Action; Matt Hampson Foundation; Ladies Fighting Breast Cancer; Hospice of Hope, Romania; Help for Heroes; Birmingham St Mary's Hospice; Flying for Freedom; Avon River Trust; Birmingham Foundation. Freeman, City of London. Fifteen UK honorary doctorates: Univ. Central England 2002, Univ. Birmingham 2002, Univ. Manchester Instt.Sci.Techg 2003, Univ. Hertfordshire 2004, Univ. Middlesex 2005, Univ. Sheffield Hallam 2005, Univ. Aston 2006, Univ. Hull 2006, Queen Univ. Belfast 2006, Univ. Warwick 2006, Univ. Bradford 2006, Univ. Thames Valley 2006, Univ. Wolverhampton 2006, Univ. Loughborough 2007, Univ. Nottingham 2007. Kt 2005. Leicester Tigers.

Publications: Author, Fixing Britain: The Business of Reshaping Our Nation (John Wiley & Sons, 2011).

Recreations: Rugby (especially Leicester Tigers), Aston Villa, skiing, theatre, military history.

The Lord Jones of Birmingham, House of Lords, London, London SW1A 0PW

Tel: 0330 088 2030 *Email:* digby@digbylordjones.com *Website:* www.digbylordjones.com

JONES OF CHELTENHAM, LORD

JONES OF CHELTENHAM (Life Baron), Nigel David Jones; cr 2005. Born 30 March 1948; Son of late A J and Nora Jones; Married Katy Grinnell 1981 (1 son twin daughters).

Education: Prince Henry's Grammar School, Evesham; Arabic, French, German, Swedish.

Non-political career: Clerk; Computer operator, Westminster Bank 1965-67; Computer programmer, ICL Computers 1967-70; Systems analyst, Vehicle and General Insurance 1970-71; Systems programmer, Atkins Computing 1971; Systems designer; Consultant; Project manager, ICL Computers 1971-92.

LIBERAL DEMOCRAT

Political career: *House of Commons:* Contested Cheltenham 1979 general election. MP (Liberal Democrat) for Cheltenham 1992-2005. Liberal Democrat Spokesperson for: England, Local Government and Housing 1992-93, Science and Technology 1993-2005, Consumer Affairs 1995-97, Sport 1997-99, Science and Technology 1997-99, International Development 1999-2002. *House of Lords:* Raised to the peerage as Baron Jones of Cheltenham, of Cheltenham in the County of Gloucestershire 2005. Member: Information 2007-09, Crossrail Bill 2008. *Councils and public bodies:* Councillor, Gloucestershire County Council 1989-93.

Political interests: Trade and industry, transport, restructuring of defence industries, information technology, sport, international development; Africa, Bahrain, Botswana, Gambia, Ghana, Kenya, Kuwait, Lesotho, Malawi, Middle East, St Helena, Sierra Leone, Swaziland, Tanzania, Turks and Caicos Islands, Uganda, UAE, Zambia, Zimbabwe.

Other: Member, Executive Committee: Governing Body British Association for Central and Eastern Europe 1996-2001, Inter-Parliamentary Union British Group 1997-2005, Commonwealth Parliamentary Association UK Branch 1999-2005; NSPCC; Help the Aged; WWF; The Smile Train; National Liberal; Reform Club. Gloucestershire County Cricket Club; Cheltenham Town FC Season Ticket Holder.

Recreations: Watching Swindon Town and Cheltenham Town Football Club, playing cricket, gardening.

The Lord Jones of Cheltenham, House of Lords, London SW1A 0PW

Tel: 020 7219 4415 *Email:* jonesn@parliament.uk

JONES OF MOULESCOOMB, BARONESS – *Please see Addenda Page xii*

JONES OF WHITCHURCH, BARONESS

Opposition Spokesperson for Culture, Media and Sport, and for Education

JONES OF WHITCHURCH (Life Baroness), Margaret Beryl Jones; cr 2006. Born 22 May 1955; Daughter of Bill and Audrey Jones.

Education: Whitchurch High School, Cardiff; Sussex University (BA sociology 1976).

Non-political career: Inland Revenue Staff Federation 1977-78; National Union of Bank Employees 1978-79; National Union of Public Employees/Unison 1979-2006: Regional official 1979-89, National officer 1989-95, Director, policy and public affairs 1995-2006; Chair, Circle 33 Housing Association 2006-12; Non-executive board member, Circle Housing 2006-. Unison.

LABOUR

Political career: *House of Commons:* Contested (Labour) Blaenau Gwent 2005 general election. *House of Lords:* Raised to the peerage as Baroness Jones of Whitchurch, of Whitchurch in the County of South Glamorgan 2006. Opposition Spokesperson for Culture, Media and Sport 2010-; Opposition Whip 2010-11; Opposition Spokesperson for Education 2011-. Co-opted member EU Sub-committee D (Environment and Agriculture) 2006-09; Member Statutory Instruments Joint

Committee 2007-10; Co-opted member EU Sub-committee G (Social Policy and Consumer Affairs) 2009-10. *Other:* Member, Labour Party National Executive Committee trade union section 1993-2005; Chair, Labour Party: Local Government Committee 1996-2004, Housing, Transport and the Regions Commission 1999-2004; Chair: Labour Party 2000-01, Labour's Joint Policy Committee 2003-05. *Councils and public bodies:* General Medical Council, Fitness to Practice Panel 2006-; Chair, Ombudsman Services: Property 2007-; Non-executive director, Waste and Resources Action Programme 2007-.

Political interests: Housing, public service reform, food and nutrition, constitutional reform, culture and media; Burma, China.

Other: Trustee, Shelter 2003-09; Deputy chair, School Food Trust 2005-09; Farming and Countryside Education Strategy Group 2007-11; Member, Fabian Society; Patron, Empty Homes Agency 2010-; Fundraising Committee, The Passage Homeless Centre 2011-; Board member: Shelter, Empty Homes Agency.

Recreations: Walking, sailing, horse riding.

The Baroness Jones of Whitchurch, House of Lords, London SW1A 0PW
Tel: 020 7219 8272 *Email:* jonesmag@parliament.uk *Twitter:* @WhitchurchGirl

JOPLING, LORD

JOPLING (Life Baron), (Thomas) Michael Jopling; cr. 1997. Born 10 December 1930; Son of Mark Jopling; Married Gail Dickinson 1958 (2 sons).

Education: Cheltenham College; King's College, Newcastle upon Tyne (BSc agriculture Durham 1952).

Non-political career: Farmer.

Political career: *House of Commons:* Contested Wakefield 1959 general election. MP (Conservative) for Westmorland 1964-83, for Westmorland and Lonsdale 1983-97. Sponsored Private Member's Bill on Parish Councils 1969; PPS to James Prior as Minister of Agriculture, Fisheries and Food 1970-71; Government: Assistant Whip 1971-73, Whip 1973-74; Opposition Spokesman for Agriculture 1974-79; Shadow Minister for Agriculture 1975-76; Government Chief Whip 1979-83; Minister of Agriculture, Fisheries and Food 1983-87; Sponsored Private Member's Bills on: Children's Seat Belts 1990, Antarctica 1994. Chair, Select Committee on Sittings of the House (Jopling Report) 1991-92. *House of Lords:* Raised to the peerage as Baron Jopling, of Ainderby Quernhow in the County of North Yorkshire 1997. Member European Union 1999-2003, 2007-12; EU Sub-committee C (Common Foreign and Security Policy): Member 1999-2003, Chair 2000-03, Member: Procedure 2003-06, 2010-12, Merits of Statutory Instruments 2003-07; EU Sub-committee F (Home Affairs): Co-opted member 2006-07, Chair 2007-10; Member EU Sub-committee C: (Foreign Affairs, Defence and Development Policy) 2010-12, (External Affairs) 2012-. *Other:* Committee member, Association of Conservative Peers 1997-2000. *Councils and public bodies:* Councillor, Thirsk Rural District Council 1958-64; DL: Cumbria 1991-97, North Yorkshire 1998-2005.

CONSERVATIVE

Other: UK Branch of Commonwealth Parliamentary Association (CPA): Executive Committee 1974-79, 1987-97, Vice-chair 1977-78, Executive, CPA HQ 1988-89; President, EU Councils of Agriculture and Fishery Ministers 1986; North Atlantic Assembly and NATO Parliamentary Assembly: UK Delegate, 1987-97, 2001-, Chairman, Committee on Civilian Aspects of Security 2011-; OSCE Parliamentary Assembly: Leader, UK Delegation 1991-97, UK Delegate 2000-01; Member, Executive Committee, Inter-Parliamentary Union, British Group 1999-; Member, National Council of NFU 1962-65; Fellow, Industry and Parliament Trust 1979; Auto Cycle Union: President 1990-2004, President, Emeritus 2004-; President, Despatch Association 2002-07. Honorary DCL, Newcastle 1992. PC 1979; Honorary Member: Royal Automobile, Buck's.

Rt Hon the Lord Jopling DL, House of Lords, London SW1A 0PW
Tel: 020 7219 0801

JORDAN, LORD

JORDAN (Life Baron), William Brian Jordan; cr. 2000. Born 28 January 1936; Son of Walter and Alice Jordan; Married Jean Ann Livesey 1958 (3 daughters).

Education: Barford Road Secondary Modern School, Birmingham.

Non-political career: Convenor of shop stewards, Guest, Keen and Nettlefold 1966; Full-time AUEW divisional organiser 1976; President, AEU then AEEU 1986-95; Member, TUC General Council 1986-95; General Secretary, ICFTU (International Confederation of Free Trade Unions) 1995-2002. Member: AEEU England Amicus, Unite.

LABOUR

Political career: *House of Lords:* Raised to the peerage as Baron Jordan, of Bournville in the County of West Midlands 2000. Member EU Sub-committee A: (Economic and Financial Affairs) 2005-07, 2008-09, 2012-13, (Economic and Financial Affairs and International Trade) 2010-12.

Councils and public bodies: Member: National Economic Development Council 1986-92, Engineering Industry Training Board 1986-91, Council, Industrial Society 1987-, UK National Contact Point (NCP) Steering Board; Governor: LSE 1987-2002, Manchester Business School 1987-92, BBC 1988-98, Victim Support Advisory Committee 1990-2007; Board member, English Partnerships 1993-2002; Chair, Housing and Communities Agency Pension Scheme 2004-.

Political interests: Labour Party; Bahrain, India, Jordan.

Other: President: European Metal Workers Federation 1986-95, International Metal Workers Federation 1986-95; UN High Panel on Youth Employment 2001-; UN Global Compact Advisory Council 2001; Council member, Winston Churchill Trust; President, RoSPA; FRSA 1996. DUniv, Central England 1993; Honorary DSc, Cranfield 1995. CBE 1992.

Recreations: Reading, watching football.

The Lord Jordan CBE, House of Lords, London SW1A 0PW
Tel: 020 7219 5648 *Email:* jordanw@parliament.uk
352 Heath Road South, Northfield, Birmingham, West Midlands B31 2BH *Tel:* 0121-475 7319
Email: lordjordan@btinternet.com

LABOUR

JUDD, LORD

JUDD (Life Baron), Frank Ashcroft Judd; cr. 1991. Born 28 March 1935; Son of late Charles Judd, CBE, and late Helen Judd, JP; Married Christine Willington 1961 (2 daughters).

Education: City of London School; London School of Economics (BSc economics 1956).

Non-political career: Short Service Commission, RAF 1957-59. General Secretary, International Voluntary Service 1960-66; Associate director, International Defence and Aid Fund for Southern Africa 1979-80; Director: Voluntary Service Overseas 1980-85, Oxfam 1985-91; Chair, International Council of Voluntary Agencies 1986-90; Consultant (professional) to De Montfort University (Faculty of Health and Life Sciences and Scholarship Board) 1993-2012; Adviser to: Forbes Trust 1992-2000, Saferworld 1992-2002; Non-executive director, Portsmouth Harbour Renaissance 1998-2006. Member: Unite, GMB.

Political career: *House of Commons:* Contested Sutton and Cheam 1959 and Portsmouth West 1964 general elections. MP (Labour) for Portsmouth West 1966-74, for Portsmouth North 1974-79. PPS to: Anthony Greenwood as Minister of Housing 1967-70, Harold Wilson as Leader of Opposition 1970-72; Shadow Defence Team 1972-74; Parliamentary Under-Secretary of State (Navy), Ministry of Defence 1974-76; Minister of State: Overseas Development 1976-77, Foreign and Commonwealth Office 1977-79. *House of Lords:* Raised to the peerage as Baron Judd, of Portsea in the County of Hampshire 1991. Opposition Spokesperson for Foreign Affairs 1991-92; Principal Opposition Spokesperson for: Development and Co-operation 1992-97, Education 1992-94; Opposition Spokesperson for Defence 1995-97. Member: Procedure 2001-04, Ecclesiastical Committee 2002-, Joint Committee on Human Rights 2003-07, EU Sub-committee F: (Home Affairs) 2010-12, (Home Affairs, Health and Education) 2012-. *Councils and public bodies:* London School of Economics and Political Science: Member of the Court 1982-2012, Emeritus governor 2012-; Vice-President, Campaign for National Parks 1998-; Lancaster University Court: Member 2002-11, Life member 2011-; Newcastle University Court: Member 2004-13, Life member 2013-; Member, Advisory Board of Centre for Human Rights, LSE 2007-.

Political interests: Foreign affairs, Third World, defence, education, refugees, migration, race relations, penal affairs, environment policy, human rights.

Other: Member, Parliamentary Delegation to Council of Europe and WEU 1969-72, 1997-2005: Chair: Sub Committee on Refugees 1998-2001, Rapporteur and Co-chair, Ad Hoc Committee on the conflict in Chechnya, Council of Europe 1999-2003; Chair, Conference on the Future of Southern Africa, World Economic Forum 1990, 1991; Member, Commission on Global Governance 1992-2001; Vice-President, United Nations Association; Member: WHO Task Force on Health and Development 1994-98, Justice Richard Goldstone's Commission on Human Duties and Responsibilities 1997-99; President: YMCA (England) 1996-2005, Friends of the Royal Naval Museum 2002-12, Trustee: Saferworld 2002-, The Ruskin Foundation 2002-11; President: Friends of the Lake District 2005-12, Hospice at Home, West Cumbria 2008-; Member: British Council, Royal Institute for International Affairs; Fellow, Royal Society of Arts; Fabian Society: Former chair, Member; Member: Christian Socialist Movement, Advisory board, Institute for Global Challenges, Rutgers University, New Jersey, USA. Freeman, City of Portsmouth 1995. Honorary DLitt, Bradford University 1987; Honorary Fellow: Portsmouth University 1995, Selly Oak Colleges, Birmingham 1997; Honorary DLitt, Portsmouth University 1997; Honorary LLD, Greenwich University 1999; Honorary DLitt, De Montfort University 2006; Royal Overseas League.

Publications: Co-author: Radical Future (1967); Purpose in Socialism (1973); Imagining Tomorrow (2000).

Recreations: Walking, family holidays, music, theatre.

The Lord Judd, House of Lords, London SW1A 0PW
Tel: 020 7219 3205 *Fax:* 020 7219 5979/020 7630 7135

JUDGE, LORD

JUDGE (Life Baron), Igor Judge; cr 2008. Born 19 May 1941; Son of Raymond Judge and Rosa Judge, née Micallef; Married Judith Robinson 1965 (1 son 2 daughters).

Education: Sacred Heart Convent, St Julians, Malta; St Edward's College, Malta; Oratory School, Woodcote; Magdalene College, Cambridge (BA 1962); Middle Temple, London; Maltese.

Non-political career: Called to the Bar, Middle Temple 1963; Recorder 1976-88; QC 1979; Bencher Middle Temple 1987; Midland and Oxford Circuit: Leader 1988, High Court Judge, Queens Bench Division, Presiding Judge 1993-96; Lord Justice of Appeal 1996-2005; Senior Presiding Judge for England and Wales 1998-2003; Deputy Chief Justice of England and Wales 2003-05; President, QBD 2005-08; Lord Chief Justice of England and Wales 2008-13.

CROSSBENCH

Political career: *House of Lords:* Raised to the peerage as Baron Judge, of Draycote in the County of Warwickshire 2008. As a senior member of the judiciary, disqualified from participation 2009-13.

Countries of interest: Malta.

Other: Honorary LLD: Kingston University 2011, Cambridge University, Kings College University, Aberystwyth University, Swansea University, Nottingham Trent University, Northampton University. Kt 1988; PC 1996; Athenæum.

Recreations: History, music, cricket.

Rt Hon the Lord Judge, House of Lords, London SW1A 0PW
Tel: 020 7219 5353
Royal Courts of Justice, Strand, London WC2A 2LL *Tel:* 020 7947 6776 *Fax:* 020 7947 7512
Website: www.judiciary.gov.uk

KAKKAR, LORD

KAKKAR (Life Baron), Ajay Kumar Kakkar; cr 2010. Born 28 April 1964; Son of Prof. Vijay Vir Kakkar and Dr Savitri Kakkar; Married Nicola Lear 1993 (2 daughters).

Education: Alleyn's School, Dulwich, London; King's College School of Medicine and Dentistry (BSc 1985; MBBS 1988); Imperial College, London (PhD 1998).

Non-political career: House surgeon and physician, King's College Hospital 1988-89; Junior surgical trainee 1989-92; Hammersmith Hospital/Royal Postgraduate Medical School (Medical Research Council): Clinical training fellow 1993-96, Clinical scientist fellow 1996-99; Senior lecturer in surgery and consultant surgeon, Hammersmith Hospital 1999-2004; Professor of surgical sciences, St Barts and the London School of Medicine and Dentistry, Queen Mary University, London 2004-; Consultant surgeon: St Barts and the London NHS Trust 2004-, University College Hospitals NHS Foundation Trust 2006-; Director, Thrombosis Research Institute 2008-; Professor of surgery, University College, London.

CROSSBENCH

Political career: *House of Lords:* Raised to the peerage as Baron Kakkar, of Loxbeare in the County of Devon 2010. Member EU Sub-committee B (Internal Market, Infrastructure and Employment) 2012-. *Councils and public bodies:* Chair, governing board, Alleyn's School, Dulwich 2009-; Chair, House of Lords Appointments Commission 2013-.

Countries of interest: India, USA.

Other: Fellow, Royal College of Surgeons 1992; Trustee: Dulwich Estate, Thrombosis Research Institute; Wellcome lecturer, Royal Society of Medicine 2009; Vice-Patron: Smile, Power International; Patron, Partners Staff College, University College London; Trustee: London Pathway, Frederick Hugh House; Association of Surgeons of Great Britain and Ireland; General Medical Council; Royal College of Surgeons. Worshipful Company of Barbers. Honorary Fellow, Harris Manchester College, Oxford. James VI Association of Surgeons Fellow 1992; Hunterian Professor, Royal College of Surgeons of England 1996; David Patey Prize, Surgical Research Society of Great Britain and Ireland 1996; Knoll William Harvey Prize, International Society on Thrombosis and Haemostasis 1997; Athenæum.

Publications: Numerous academic publications.

Professor the Lord Kakkar, House of Lords, London SW1A 0PW
Tel: 020 7219 8933 *Email:* kakkara@parliament.uk

KALMS, LORD

KALMS (Life Baron), (Harold) Stanley Kalms; cr. 2004. Born 21 November 1931; Son of Charles and Cissie Kalms; Married Pamela Jimack 1954 (3 sons).

Education: Christ's College, Finchley.

Non-political career: Dixons Group/DSG International plc 1948-: Managing director 1962-72, Chair 1972-2002, President 2002-; Director, British Gas 1987-97; Chair, Volvere 2001-11.

Political career: *House of Lords:* Raised to the peerage as Baron Kalms, of Edgware in the London Borough of Barnet 2004. Member: Review of the BBC Charter 2005-06, Information 2006-09. *Other:* Treasurer, Conservative Party 2001-03. *Councils and public bodies:* Governor, Dixons Bradford City Technology College 1988-2002; Chair, Kings Healthcare NHS Trust 1993-96; Member, Funding Agency for Schools 1994-97.

INDEPENDENT CONSERVATIVE

Political interests: Preservation of sterling, Islamism; Europe, Israel.

Other: Director, Centre for Policy Studies 1991-2001; Trustee: Economic Trust 1993-2002, Industry in Education 1993-; Member, Business for Sterling 1998-2001; Chairman, Strategy Committee, Henry Jackson Society. Five honorary doctorates; Honorary fellow London Business School 1995. Kt 1996; Saville; Portland.

Publications: A Time for Change (1996).

Recreations: Opera, ballet, bridge.

The Lord Kalms, House of Lords, London SW1A 0PW
Tel: 020 7219 5353
39-40 St James's Place, London SW1A 1NS *Tel:* 020 7499 3494
Email: stanley.kalms@btinternet.com

KENNEDY OF CRADLEY, BARONESS – *Please see Addenda Page xii*

KENNEDY OF SOUTHWARK, LORD

KENNEDY OF SOUTHWARK (Life Baron), Roy Francis Kennedy; cr 2010. Born 9 November 1962; Son of John and Frances Kennedy; Married Alicia 2004 (no children).

Education: St Thomas the Apostle School, Peckham.

Non-political career: Commissioner, Electoral Commission 2010-. Member: GMB, Unite.

Political career: *House of Lords:* Raised to the peerage as Baron Kennedy of Southwark, of Newington in the London Borough of Southwark 2010. Opposition Whip 2011-12. Member: Joint Committee on Statutory Instruments 2010-, Refreshment 2013-. *Other:* Contested East Midlands 2009 European Parliament election. Member, Co-operative Party; Labour Party: Regional director, East Midlands 1997-2005, Director of Finance and Compliance 2005-10. *Councils and public bodies:* London Borough of Southwark Council: Councillor 1986-94, Former deputy leader, Former chair, Highways Committee.

LAB/CO-OP

Political interests: Low pay, credit unions, diabetes, co-operatives, mutuals; EU, Ireland.

Other: Member: Fabian Society, Diabetes UK, Ramblers Association, Amnesty International. Honorary Alderman, London Borough of Southwark.

Recreations: Reading, walking, theatre, football.

The Lord Kennedy of Southwark, House of Lords, London SW1A 0PW
Tel: 020 7219 5817 *Fax:* 020 7219 1506 *Email:* kennedyro@parliament.uk
Email: lordroykennedy@gmail.com *Twitter:* @LordRoyKennedy

KENNEDY OF THE SHAWS, BARONESS

KENNEDY OF THE SHAWS (Life Baroness), Helena Ann Kennedy; cr. 1997. Born 12 May 1950; Daughter of late Joshua Kennedy and of Mary Kennedy; Partner Roger Mitchell 1977-84 (1 son); married Dr Iain Hutchison 1986 (1 son 1 daughter).

Education: Holyrood Secondary School, Glasgow; Council of Legal Education.

Non-political career: Called to the Bar, Gray's Inn 1972; Established Chambers at: Garden Court 1974, Tooks Court 1984, Doughty Street 1990; Broadcaster: First female moderator, Hypotheticals (Granada) on surrogate motherhood and artificial insemination; Presenter: *Heart of the Matter*, BBC 1987, *Putting Women in the Picture*, BBC2 1987, *Time Gentlemen Please*, BBC Scotland 1994; QC 1991; Bencher of Gray's Inn 1999; Investigating Commissioner, Inquiry into Human Trafficking in Scotland, Equality and Human Rights Commission 2011.

LABOUR

Political career: *House of Lords:* Raised to the peerage as Baroness Kennedy of The Shaws, of Cathcart in the City of Glasgow 1997. Member Joint Committee on Human Rights 2012-.

Other: IBA's International Task Force on Terrorism 2001-02; Haldane Society: Chair 1983-86, Vice-President 1986-; Member, National Board, Women's Legal Defence Fund 1989-91; Council member, Howard League for Penal Reform 1989-; Board Member: New Statesman 1990-96, Counsel Magazine 1990-; Committee member, Association of Women Barristers 1991-92; Chair: Charter '88 1992-97, Standing Committee for Youth Justice, NACRO 1993-, London International Festival of Theatre 1993-2002, British Council 1998-, Human Genetics Commission 2000-07, Advisory Council, World Bank Institute; Member, Independent Newspaper Board; Chair of council, JUSTICE; Member, Bar Council 1990-93; Fellow, Royal Society of Arts; Honorary Fellow: Institute of Advanced Legal Studies 1997, City and Guilds London Institute, Institute of Advanced Legal Studies; Honorary Member, Paris-based Academie Universelle des Cultures; Vice-President Haldane Society; Patron Liberty; President National Children's Bureau. Chancellor, Oxford Brookes University 1994-2001. 18 honorary law doctorates. Women's Network Award for her work on women and justice 1992; UK Woman of Europe Award 1995; National Federation of Women's Institutes Making a World of Difference Award Institutes for her work on equal rights 1996; *The Times* (Joint) Lifetime Achievement Award 1997.

Publications: Co-author: The Bar on Trial (1978), Child Abuse Within the Family (1984), Balancing Acts (1989); Eve was Framed (1992); Leader of enquiry into health, environmental and safety aspects of Atomic Weapons Establishment Secrecy Versus Safety (1994); Inquiry into Violence in Penal Institutions for Young People (1995); Learning Works Official report for the FEFC on widening participation in Further Education (1997); Lectures; Has contributed articles on law, civil liberties and women.

Recreations: Theatre, spending time with family and friends.

The Baroness Kennedy of The Shaws QC, House of Lords, London SW1A 0PW
Tel: 020 7219 5353
c/o Hilary Hard, 12 Athelstan Close, Harold Wood, Essex RM3 0QJ
Twitter: @HelenaKennedyQC

KERR OF KINLOCHARD, LORD

CROSSBENCH

KERR OF KINLOCHARD (Life Baron), John Olav Kerr; cr. 2004. Born 22 February 1942; Son of Dr and Mrs J D O Kerr; Married Elizabeth Kalaugher 1965 (2 sons 3 daughters).

Education: Glasgow Academy; Pembroke College, Oxford (BA modern history 1963); French, Russian.

Non-political career: HM Diplomatic Service 1966-2002: Foreign Office, Moscow embassy, Rawalpindi, Pakistan High Commission, Foreign and Commonwealth Office (FCO), Private secretary to Permanent Under Secretary FCO 1974-79, Seconded to HM Treasury 1979-84: Principal private secretary to Sir Geoffrey Howe MP and Nigel Lawson MP as Chancellors of Exchequer 1981-84, Head of chancery, Washington DC, USA embassy 1984-87, Assistant Under-Secretary FCO 1987-90, Ambassador and UK Permanent Representative to EC/EU Brussels 1990-95, Ambassador to USA 1995-97, Permanent Under-Secretary and Head of Diplomatic Service, FCO 1997-2002; Secretary-General, European Convention 2002-03; Director: Scottish American Investment Trust 2002-, Shell Transport and Trading Co plc 2002-05, Rio Tinto plc 2003-; Deputy chairman, Royal Dutch Shell plc 2005-12; Member, Advisory Board, BAe Systems 2008-11; Scottish Power: Director 2009-12, Deputy Chairman 2012-; Adviser, Edinburgh Partners 2012-.

Political career: *House of Lords:* Raised to the peerage as Baron Kerr of Kinlochard, of Kinlochard in Perth and Kinross 2004. Member EU Sub-committee A: (Economic and Financial Affairs) 2006-08, 2012-, (Economic and Financial Affairs and International Trade) 2011-12; Member: European Union 2007-10, EU Sub-committee E: (Law and Institutions) 2008-10, (Justice and Institutions) 2010-11.

Political interests: International affairs, economic affairs; China, EU, Korea, Russia, USA.

Other: Trustee: Rhodes Trust 1997-2010, National Gallery 2002-10, Fulbright Commission 2004-09; Honorary President, Universities Association for Contemporary European Studies 2004-07; Trustee, Carnegie Trust for the Universities of Scotland 2005-; Chairman of Court/Council Imperial College, London 2005-11; Centre for European Reform: Member of Council 2005-, Chair 2008-; Member of Council, Business for New Europe 2006-; Vice-President, European Policy Centre 2007-; President, UK/Korea Forum for the Future 2007-; Honorary President, St Andrews Clinics for Children; Honorary Fellow: Pembroke College, Oxford 1991, Royal Society of Edinburgh 2006; Fellow, Imperial College, London 2012. Honorary LLD: St Andrews 1996, Glasgow University 1999; Honorary DLitt, Aston University 2010. CMG 1987; KCMG 1991; GCMG 2001.

Publications: Various articles.

Recreations: Travel, books, film, following Queen's Park Rangers F.C.

The Lord Kerr of Kinlochard GCMG, House of Lords, London SW1A 0PW
Tel: 020 7219 5353

KERR OF TONAGHMORE, LORD

KERR OF TONAGHMORE (Life Baron), Brian Francis Kerr; cr 2009. Born 22 February 1948; Son of James Kerr and Kathleen Kerr, née Murray; Married Gillian Widdowson 1970 (2 sons). **Education:** St Colman's College, Newry; Queen's University, Belfast (LLB 1969).

Non-political career: Called to Bar: Northern Ireland (NI) 1970, Gray's Inn 1974; Junior Crown Counsel, common law 1978-83; QC (NI) 1983; Senior Crown Counsel 1988-93; High Court Judge NI 1993-2004; Honorary Bencher, Gray's Inn 1997; Lord Chief Justice NI 2004-09; Honorary Bencher, King's Inn 2004; Justice of the Supreme Court of the United Kingdom 2009-.

NON-AFFILIATED **Political career:** *House of Lords:* Raised to the peerage as Baron Kerr of Tonaghmore, of Tonaghmore in the County of Down 2009. Lord of Appeal in Ordinary 2009-; As Justice of the Supreme Court, disqualified from participation 2009-. *Councils and public bodies:* Chair, Mental Health Commission for NI 1988; Member: Judicial Studies Board NI 1995-2004, Franco-British Judicial Co-operation Committee 1995-2001; Chair, Distinction and Meritorious Service Awards Committee NI 1997-2001.

Other: Eisenhower Exchange Fellow 1999; Honorary Fellow, American Board of Trial Advocates 2004. Honorary law doctorate, Queen's University, Belfast 2009. Kt 1993; PC 2003.

Recreations: Family, friends, France.

Rt Hon the Lord Kerr of Tonaghmore, House of Lords, London SW1A 0PW
Tel: 020 7219 5353
Supreme Court of the United Kingdom, Parliament Square, London SW1P 3BD
Tel: 020 7960 1956 *Email:* kaya.banerjee@supremecourt.gsi.gov.uk

KESTENBAUM, LORD

KESTENBAUM (Life Baron) Jonathan Andrew Kestenbaum; cr 2011. Born 5 August 1959; Son of Ralph and Gaby Kestenbaum; Married Deborah Zackon 1984 (3 sons 1 daughter).

Education: London School of Economics (BA 1982); Wolfson College, Cambridge; Hebrew University (MA 1989); Cass Business School (MBA 1994).

Non-political career: Chief executive: Office of Chief Rabbi 1991-96, UJIA 1996-2002, Portland Trust 2002-06; Chief of staff to Sir Ronald Cohen, chairman of Apax Partners 2002-06; Chief executive, National Endowment for Science, Technology and the Arts 2005-10; Chairman, Five Arrows Ltd 2010-; Chief operating officer, RIT Capital Partners plc 2011-.

LABOUR **Political career:** *House of Lords:* Raised to the peerage as Baron Kestenbaum, of Foxcote in the county of Somerset 2011.

Other: Governing Board, Royal Shakespeare Company; Rowley Lane Recreational Trust. Honorary Doctorate of Technology, University of Plymouth 2010; Honorary Fellowship, Royal College of Art 2011; MCC.

The Lord Kestenbaum, House of Lords, London SW1A 0PW
Tel: 020 7219 5353 *Website:* www.ritcap.com

KIDRON, BARONESS

KIDRON (Life Baroness), Beeban Tania Kidron; cr 2012. Born 2 May 1961; Daughter of Nina Kidron and late Michael Kidron; Married Lee Hall (1 son 1 daughter from previous).

Education: Camden School for Girls, London; National Film and Television School (1981-85; Postgraduate Diploma directing 1990).

Non-political career: Director, documentaries: *Carry Greenham Home* 1983, *Hookers, Hustlers, Pimps and their Johns* 1993, *Eve Arnold in Retrospect* 1996, *Antony Gormley: Making Space* 2007, *Storyville: Sex, Death and the Gods* 2011; Director, television: *Oranges Are Not the Only*

CROSSBENCH *Fruit* 1989, *Antonia and Jane* 1990, *Itch* 1991, *Texarkana* 1998, *Cinderella* 2000, *Murder* 2002; Director, films: *Vroom* 1990, *Used People* 1992, *Great Moments in Aviation* 1993, *To Wong Foo Thanks for Everything, Julie Newmar* 1995, *Swept from the Sea* 1997, *Bridget Jones: The Edge of Reason* 2004, *In Real Life* 2013.

Political career: *House of Lords:* Raised to the peerage as Baroness Kidron, of Angel in the London Borough of Islington 2012.

Political interests: Justice, arts, education, media, children and young people; China, India, Liberia, USA.

Other: Member: Directors' Guild of America 1990-, Directors UK, Academy of Motion Picture Sciences 1992-; UK Film Council: Trustee 2008-10, Board member 2008-11; Co-founder, FilmClub (educational charity) 2008-; Governor, BFI 2010-; Council member, Institute of Contemporary Art; Patron, Artangel; Mentor, Guiding Lights; Trustee, Paul Hamlyn Foundation; Directors' Guild of America 1990-; Directors UK; Academy of Motion Picture Sciences 1992-; Fellow, National Film and Television School; Co-founder and Vice-chair Film Club Educational Charity 2007-; UK Film Council 2008-10; Governor, BFI 2010-13; Council member, Institute of Contemporary Art 2011-; Trustee, Paul Hamlyn Foundation 2012-; President, Voluntary Arts 2013-; ICA. Honorary doctorate, Kingston University 2010. FIPA D'argent, Cannes Film Festival for Oranges Are Not the Only Fruit; Best Drama BAFTA for Oranges Are Not the Only Fruit; *Glamour* Woman of the Year 2005. OBE 2012.

The Baroness Kidron OBE, House of Lords, London SW1A 0PW
Tel: 020 7219 0586 *Email:* kidronb@parliament.uk

CROSSBENCH

KILCLOONEY, LORD

KILCLOONEY (Life Baron), John David Taylor; cr. 2001. Born 24 December 1937; Son of late George David Taylor, architect, and Georgina Taylor, née Baird; Married Mary Todd 1970 (1 son 5 daughters).

Education: Royal School, Armagh; Queen's University, Belfast (BSc applied science and technology 1950); French.

Non-political career: Company director; Chairman: West Ulster Estates Ltd 1965-, Alpha Newspaper Group 1977-, Sovereign Properties (NI) Ltd 1981-, Midland Tribune Ltd 2002-, Alpha Publications (Ireland) Ltd 2002-, Ballymena Radio Ltd 2005-; Northern Media Group Ltd 2006-.

Political career: *House of Commons:* MP (UUP) for Strangford 1983-2001. Spokesperson for: Trade and Industry 1992-97, Foreign and Commonwealth Affairs 1997-2001. *House of Lords:* Raised to the peerage as Baron Kilclooney, of Armagh in the County of Armagh 2001. *Other:* MP (South Tyrone) Stormont 1965-73: Parliamentary Secretary, Ministry of Home Affairs, Northern Ireland 1969-70; Minister of State, Home Affairs 1970-72, Member: Northern Ireland Assembly for Fermanagh and South Tyrone 1973-75, Northern Ireland Constitutional Convention for North Down 1976-77, Northern Ireland Assembly for North Down 1982-86; European Parliament: MEP for Northern Ireland 1979-89; Member Northern Ireland Forum for Political Dialogue 1996-98; Northern Ireland Assembly: MLA for Strangford 1998-2007. Chair: Queen's University Conservative and Unionist Association 1959-60, Ulster Young Unionist Council 1961-62; Ulster Unionist Party: Honorary Secretary 1994-96, Deputy Leader 1995-2001. *Councils and public bodies:* Governor, The Royal School, Armagh City 1973-; Castlereagh Borough Council: Councillor 1989-97, Leader, UUP 1989-94; Member, Northern Ireland Policing Board 2001-06.

Political interests: Irish politics, European Union, regional policy, agriculture; Asia, Cyprus, Gibraltar, Ireland, Latin America, Middle East, Taiwan, Turkey.

Other: Member: Council of Europe Assembly 1997-2005, Western European Union 1997-2011; Member: Board of Charles Sheils Charity Homes 1973-, Royal Horticultural Society, Elder, Presbyterian Church in Ireland, Loyal Orange Institution of Ireland; Amicei; Aminsthe; AMICEI; AMInstHE; Tear Fund. Eastern Mediterranean University, Famagusta (PhD international relations 1999). PC (Northern Ireland) 1970; Farmers (London), County (Armagh).

Publications: Ulster – The Economic Facts (1974).

Recreations: Antiques, Irish art, travelling, horticulture.

Rt Hon the Lord Kilclooney, House of Lords, London SW1A 0PW
Tel: 020 7219 6443 *Fax:* 020 7931 7211
Email: johnkilclooney@hotmail.co.uk

NON-AFFILIATED

KILPATRICK OF KINCRAIG, LORD

KILPATRICK OF KINCRAIG (Life Baron), Robert Kilpatrick; cr. 1996. Born 29 July 1926; Son of late Robert Kilpatrick; Married Elizabeth Gibson Page Forbes 1950 (2 sons 1 daughter).

Education: Buckhaven High School; Edinburgh University (MB, ChB 1949; MD 1960) (Ettles Scholar, Leslie Gold Medallist).

Non-political career: Medical registrar, Edinburgh 1951-54; Sheffield University: Lecturer 1955-66, Professor of clinical pharmacology and therapeutics 1966-75, Dean, Faculty of Medicine 1971-74; Chair: Society of Endocrinology 1975-78, Advisory Committee on Pesticides 1975-87; Leicester University 1975-89: Dean, Faculty of Medicine 1975-89, Professor and Head of Department of Clinical Pharmacology and Therapeutics 1975-83, Professor of medicine 1984-89; President: General Medical Council 1989-95, British Medical Association 1997-98.

Political career: *House of Lords:* Raised to the peerage as Baron Kilpatrick of Kincraig, of Dysart in the District of Kirkcaldy 1996. On leave of absence.

Political interests: Health, education, professional self-regulation.

Other: FRCP (Ed) 1963; FRCP 1975; FRCPGlas 1991; Honorary FRCS 1995; Honorary FRCP, Dublin 1995; Honorary FRCS, Edinburgh 1996; Honorary RC Path. 1996; Honorary FRCP (Ed) 1996; FRSE 1998; Lifeboat. Dr hc, Edinburgh 1987; Honorary LLD, Dundee 1992; Honorary DSc: Hull 1994, Leicester 1994; Honorary LLD, Sheffield 1995. CBE 1979; Kt 1986; Royal and Ancient (St Andrews), New (Edinburgh).

Publications: Several articles in medical and scientific journals.

Recreations: Golf.

The Lord Kilpatrick of Kincraig CBE, House of Lords, London SW1A 0PW
Tel: 020 7219 5353
12 Wester Coates Gardens, Edinburgh EH12 5LT *Tel:* 0131-337 7304

KIMBALL, LORD

KIMBALL (Life Baron), Marcus Richard Kimball; cr. 1985. Born 18 October 1928; Son of late Major Lawrence Kimball; Married June Fenwick 1956 (2 daughters).

Education: Eton College; Trinity College, Cambridge (BA history 1951).

Non-political career: Captain, Leicestershire and Derbyshire Yeomanry (TA). Director, The Royal Trust Bank 1970-93; Council of Lloyd's of London 1982-90; Chair: South East Assured Tenancies plc 1989-96, British Greyhound Racing Fund Ltd 1993-96.

CONSERVATIVE

Political career: *House of Commons:* Contested Derby South 1955 general election. MP (Conservative) for Gainsborough 1956-83. *House of Lords:* Raised to the peerage as Baron Kimball, of Easton in the County of Leicestershire 1985. On leave of absence June 2013-. Member: Liaison 1998-2007, Procedure 1999-2002, 2003-07, Statutory Instruments Joint Committee 2007-10. *Councils and public bodies:* Councillor, Rutland County Council 1955-62; DL: Leicestershire 1984-97, Rutland 1997-.

Political interests: Finance, agriculture; USA.

Other: Chair, British Field Sports Society 1966-82; Royal College of Veterinary Surgeons: Privy Council Representative 1969-82, Honorary Associate 1982; Chair: Firearms Consultation Committee 1989-94, University of Cambridge Veterinary School Trust 1989-97; President: National Light Horse Breeding Society 1990-91, Olympia International Show Jumping Championship 1991-2000; British Field Sports Society: President 1996-98, Deputy President 1998-; Hunt Servants' Benefit Society; The Countryside Foundation for Education. Kt 1981; White's, Pratt's.

Recreations: Fishing, hunting, shooting.

The Lord Kimball DL, House of Lords, London SW1A 0PW
Tel: 020 7219 5404 *Email:* kimballm@parliament.uk
Great Easton Manor, Great Easton, Market Harborough, Leicestershire LE16 8TB
Tel: 01536 770333 *Fax:* 01536 770008

KING OF BOW, BARONESS

KING OF BOW (Life Baroness), Oona Tamsyn King; cr 2011. Born 22 October 1967; Daughter of Preston King, professor of political science, and Hazel King, teacher; Married Tiberio Santomarco 1994 (1 adopted son 2 adopted daughters).

Education: Haverstock Comprehensive Secondary School, London; York University (BA politics 1990); Berkeley-University of California, USA (Scholarship); French, Italian.

Non-political career: Researcher, Socialist Group, European Parliament 1990; Political assistant to Glyn Ford MEP 1991-93; John Smith's Labour Party leadership campaign team 1992; Freelance speech-writer/ghost writer 1993-94; Political assistant to Glenys Kinnock MEP 1994-95; Trade union organiser, GMB Southern Region 1995-97; Freelance diversity executive, Channel 4 Television. Southern region equality officer, GMB.

LABOUR

Political career: *House of Commons:* MP (Labour) for Bethnal Green and Bow 1997-2005. Contested Bethnal Green and Bow 2005 general election. PPS to: Stephen Timms as Minister of State, Department of Trade and Industry 2002-03, Patricia Hewitt as Secretary of State for Trade and Industry 2003-05. Member: International Development 1997-2001, Transport, Local Government and the Regions 2001-02, Transport, Local Government and the Regions (Urban Affairs Sub-Committee) 2001-02. Member, Labour Party Departmental Committees for: Education and Employment 1997-99, Home Affairs 1997-2001. *House of Lords:* Raised to the peerage as Baroness King of Bow, of Bow in the London Borough of Tower Hamlets 2011. Member: Adoption Legislation 2012-13, Olympic and Paralympic Legacy 2013-. *Other:* Joint vice-chair, London Regional Group of Labour MPs 1997-2005; Chair, Labour Campaign for Electoral Reform; Contested Labour Party London Mayor candidacy 2010.

Political interests: Race relations, employment, education, health, development, equal opportunities, housing, European affairs, electoral reform, poverty; Bangladesh, France, Great Lakes Region, Italy, Nicaragua, Rwanda, South Africa, USA.

Other: Member: Oxfam, Amnesty International, Jewish Council for Racial Equality, One World Action, Fabian Society, Unicef; Member, 1990 Trust, Toynbee Hall; Vice-chair, British Council 1999-; Patron, Dane Ford Trust; Vice-chair, British Council 2001-; Patron: Positive Care Link, Council for Education in the World, Riverside Gallery; Associate fellow, Chatham House; Chair: Institute for Community Cohesion, Rich Mix Cultural Foundation.

Publications: Oona King Diaries (Bloomsbury, 2007).

Recreations: Music, cinema, cooking, history, walking.

The Baroness King of Bow, House of Lords, London SW1A 0PW
Tel: 020 7219 5353 *Email:* kingo@parliament.uk miahr@parliament.uk
Website: www.oonaking.com *Twitter:* @oona_king

KING OF BRIDGWATER, LORD

KING OF BRIDGWATER (Life Baron), Thomas (Tom) Jeremy King; cr. 2001. Born 13 June 1933; Son of John H King, JP; Married Jane Tilney 1960 (1 son 1 daughter).

Education: Rugby School; Emmanuel College, Cambridge (MA classics, archaeology and anthropology 1956).

Non-political career: Army national service 1952-53; Service in East Africa; TA 1953-56. E. S. and A. Robinson Ltd, Bristol 1956-69: Divisional General Manager 1964-69; Chair, Sale, Tilney & Co Ltd industrial holding company 1971-79; Non-executive director, Electra Investment Trust 1992-2008; London International Exhibition Centre plc: Chair 1994-2008, Non-executive director 2008-.

CONSERVATIVE

Political career: *House of Commons:* MP (Conservative) for Bridgwater 3 March 1970 by-election to 2001. PPS to Christopher Chataway: as Minister of Posts and Telecommunications 1970-72, as Minister for Industrial Development 1972-74; Opposition Spokesperson for: Industry 1975-76, Energy 1976-79; Minister for Local Government and Environmental Services 1979-83; Secretary of State for: Environment January-June 1983, Transport June-October 1983, Employment 1983-85, Northern Ireland 1985-89, Defence 1989-92; Chair, Intelligence and Security Committee 1994-2001. *House of Lords:* Raised to the peerage as Lord King of Bridgwater, of Bridgwater in the County of Somerset 2001. Member: Review of the BBC Charter 2005-06, Communications 2007-10, Joint Committee on the Draft Enhanced Terrorism Prevention and Investigation Measures Bill 2012-13, Inquiries Act 2005 2013-.

Other: PC 1979; CH 1992.

Recreations: Cricket, skiing.

Rt Hon the Lord King of Bridgwater CH, House of Lords, London SW1A 0PW
Tel: 020 7219 4467 *Email:* monroej@parliament.uk

KING OF LOTHBURY, LORD

KING OF LOTHBURY (Life Baron), Mervyn Allister; cr. 2013. Born 30 March 1948; Son of Eric King and Kathleen Passingham; Married Barbara Melander.

Education: Wolverhampton Grammar School; King's College, Cambridge (BA 1969); Harvard University (Kennedy scholar 1971-72); French; Economist.

Non-political career: Lecturer, Faculty of Economics, Cambridge 1976-77; Esmée Fairbairn professor of investment, Birmingham University 1977-84; Managing editor, Review of Economic Studies 1978-83; Associate editor, Journal of Public Economics 1982-98; Professor of economics, London School of Economics 1984-95; Associate editor, American Economic Review 1985-88; Bank of England: Non-executive director 1990-91, Chief economist and executive director 1991-98, Deputy Governor 1998-2003, Governor 2003-13.

CROSSBENCH

Political career: *House of Lords:* Raised to the peerage as Baron King of Lothbury, of Lothbury in the City of London 2013.

Other: Member, Meade Committee 1975-78; Council and executive, Royal Economic Society 1981-86, 1992-97; Visiting professor of economics: Harvard University 1982-83, 1990, Massachusetts Institute of Technology 1983-84, London School of Economics 1996-; Board member, The Securities Association 1987-89; Co-director, London of Economics Financial Markets Group 1987-91; Member, City Capital Markets Committee 1989-91; Trustee, Kennedy Memorial Trust 1990-2000; President, European Economic Association 1993; Member, Group of Thirty 1997-; President, Institute for Fiscal Studies 1999-2003; Monetary Policy Committee: Founder member 1997, Chair 2003-13; Member, Advisory Council, London Symphony Orchestra 2001-; Trustee,

National Gallery 2005-09; Chair, Interim Financial Policy Committee 2011-13; Vice-chair, European Systematic Risk Board 2011-13; President, Chance to Shine; GBE; Honorary fellow, King's College, Cambridge; Fellow, Econometric Society 1982; Visiting fellow, Nuffield College, Oxford 2002-; Athenæum, Brook's, Garrick, MCC, AELTC. Honorary President, Ekenäs Cricket Club, Finland; Patron, Worcestershire County Cricket Club 2004-.

Publications: Public Policy and the Corporation (1977); The British Tax System (1978); The Taxation of Income from Capital (1984).

The Lord King of Lothbury GBE, House of Lords, London SW1A 0PW
Tel: 020 7219 5353
Email: office@mervynking.com

KINGSDOWN, LORD

KINGSDOWN (Life Baron), Robin (Robert) Leigh-Pemberton; cr. 1993. Born 5 January 1927; Son of late Robert Douglas Leigh-Pemberton, MBE, MC; Married Rosemary Forbes, OBE, 1953 (4 sons and 1 son deceased).

Education: St Peter's Court, Broadstairs; Eton College; Trinity College, Oxford (MA greats 1950).

Non-political career: Served Grenadier Guards 1945-48; Honorary Colonel: Kent and Sharpshooters Yeomanry Squadron 1979-92, 265 (Kent and County of London Yeomanry) Signal Squadron (V) 1979-92, 5th Volunteer Battalion, The Queen's Regiment 1987-93. Called to Bar, Inner Temple 1954; Birmid Qualcast: Director 1966-83, Chairman 1975-77; Director, University Life Assurance Society 1967-78; National Westminster Bank: Director 1972-83, Deputy chair 1974-77, Chair 1977-83; Director: Redland Ltd 1972-83, Equitable Life Assurance Society 1979-83; Honorary Bencher, Inner Temple 1983; Governor, Bank of England 1983-93; Non-executive director: Hambros plc 1993-98, Glaxo Wellcome plc 1993-96, Redland plc 1993-98, Foreign and Colonial Investment Trust 1993-98.

NON-AFFILIATED

Political career: *House of Lords:* Raised to the peerage as Baron Kingsdown, of Pemberton in the County of Lancashire 1993. On leave of absence November 2010-. Member Economic Affairs 2005-08. *Councils and public bodies:* Kent County Council: Councillor 1961-77, Chair 1972-75, Member: South East Planning Council 1972-74, Prime Minister's Committee on Local Government Rules of Conduct 1973-74, Medway Ports Authority 1974-76, Committee on Police Pay 1977-79, Member, National Economic Development Council 1982-92; JP, Kent 1961-75, DL, Kent 1970-72, Vice-Lord-Lieutenant 1972-82, Lord-Lieutenant 1982-2002, Chair, Association of Lord-Lieutenants.

Political interests: Countryside and country life.

Other: Trustee, Glyndebourne Arts Trust 1977-83; Seneschal, Canterbury Cathedral 1983-; Governor, Ditchley Foundation 1987-2001; FRSA 1977-2002; FBIM 1977. Liveryman, Mercers' Company; Honorary Liveryman, Skinners' Company. Pro-Chancellor, University of Kent 1977-83. Honorary DCL, Kent 1983; Honorary Fellow, Trinity College, Oxford 1984; Honorary DLitt: City University 1988, Loughborough University 1990. PC 1987; KG 1994; Brooks's, Cavalry and Guards. Kent County Cricket.

Recreations: Country life.

Rt Hon the Lord Kingsdown KG, House of Lords, London SW1A 0PW
Tel: 020 7219 5353
Torry Hill, Sittingbourne, Kent ME9 0SP *Tel:* 01795 830258 *Fax:* 01795 830268
Email: lord.kingsdown@btinternet.com

KINGSMILL, BARONESS

KINGSMILL (Life Baroness), Denise Patricia Byrne Kingsmill; cr 2006. Born 24 April 1947; Daughter of Patrick Henry and Hester Jean Byrne; Married David Kingsmill 1970 (divorced 2002) (2 children); married Richard Wheatly 2006.

Education: Croesy Ceiliog Grammar School, Wales; Girton College, Cambridge (BA economics and anthropology 1968); Solicitor 1980.

Non-political career: ICI, International Wool Secretariat 1968-75; Robin Thompson & Partners 1979-82; Russell Jones and Walker 1982-85; Denise Kingsmill & Co 1985-90; Partner, D J Freeman 1990-93; Consultant, Denton Hall 1994-2000; Non-executive director, British Airways 2004-10; Chair, advisory forum, Laing O'Rourke 2004-06; Senior adviser, Royal Bank of Scotland 2005-08; Non-executive director: E.ON AG, Betfair plc 2011-12, APR Energy plc; Member, European Advisory Council, Microsoft 2007-12; Non-executive director, Korn/Ferry International 2009-12; Independent non-executive director, International Consolidated Airlines Group SA; Columnist, *Management Today*; Chair, European Advisory Board.

LABOUR

Political career: *House of Lords:* Raised to the peerage as Baroness Kingsmill, of Holland Park in the Royal Borough of Kensington and Chelsea 2006. Co-opted member European Union Sub-committee E (Law and Institutions) 2006-09; Member: Merits of Statutory Instruments 2007-09, Economic Affairs 2008-13. *Councils and public bodies:* Deputy chair, Monopolies and Mergers/ Competition Commission 1997-2003.

Political interests: International business, women; Australia, China, India, New Zealand, USA.

Other: Member, advisory board, IESE Business School. Pro-Chancellor, Brunel University 2002-06. Fellow, University of Wales 2000; Honorary LLD: Brunel University 2001, Stirling University 2003, Cranfield University 2007. CBE 2000.

Recreations: Fly-fishing, walking.

The Baroness Kingsmill CBE, House of Lords, London SW1A 0PW
Tel: 020 7219 4537 *Email:* kingsmilldp@parliament.uk
Tel: 020 7221 1700 *Fax:* 020 7727 8304 *Email:* tess@dkingsmill.com

LABOUR

KINNOCK, LORD

KINNOCK (Life Baron), Neil Gordon Kinnock; cr 2005. Born 28 March 1942; Son of late Gordon H Kinnock, steelworker and coalminer and Mary, née Howells, district nurse; Married Glenys Elizabeth Parry (later MEP, now Baroness Kinnock of Holyhead) (1 son 1 daughter).

Education: Lewis School, Pengam; University College of Wales, Cardiff (BA industrial relations and history 1966).

Non-political career: University College of Wales, Cardiff: President: Socialist Society 1963-65, Students' Union 1965-66; Tutor and organiser, Workers' Educational Association 1966-70; European Commission: Commissioner 1995-2004: Commissioner for Transport 1995-99, Vice-president for Administrative Reform, Internal Audit, Personnel, Language Services and Logistics 1999-2004. Member, Transport and General Workers Union 1966-.

Political career: *House of Commons:* MP (Labour) for Bedwellty 1970-83, for Islwyn 1983-95. PPS to Michael Foot as Secretary of State for Employment 1974-75; Principal Opposition Spokesperson for Education 1979-83; Leader of the Opposition 1983-92. *House of Lords:* Raised to the peerage as Baron Kinnock, of Bedwellty in the County of Gwent 2005. *Other:* Labour Party NEC, Member 1978-94, Chair 1987-88; Leader, Labour Party 1983-92. *Councils and public bodies:* Member, BBC Advisory Council 1976-79; Chair, British Council 2004-09.

Other: President of the Council (Chancellor) Cardiff University 1998-2009. PC 1983.

Publications: Making Our Way – Investing in Britain's Future (1986); Thorns and Roses (1992).

Recreations: Opera, male choral music, theatre, rugby, soccer, cricket, grandchildren.

Rt Hon the Lord Kinnock, House of Lords, London SW1A 0PW
Tel: 020 7219 8304 *Fax:* 020 7219 1903

LABOUR

KINNOCK OF HOLYHEAD, BARONESS

KINNOCK OF HOLYHEAD (Life Baroness); Glenys Elizabeth Kinnock; cr 2009. Born 7 July 1944; Daughter of Cyril Parry, railway signalman, and Elizabeth Parry; Married Neil Kinnock (later MP, Leader of the Labour Party, European Commissioner, now Lord Kinnock (qv)) 1967 (1 daughter 1 son).

Education: Holyhead Comprehensive School, Anglesey; University College of Wales, Cardiff (Degree history and education 1964; DipEd 1965); Welsh.

Non-political career: Primary and secondary school teacher 1965-93. Member: GMB, National Union of Teachers.

Political career: *House of Lords:* Raised to the peerage as Baroness Kinnock of Holyhead, of Holyhead in the County of Ynys Môn 2009. Minister of State and Government Spokesperson, Foreign and Commonwealth Office 2009-10: Minister for Europe 2009, Minister for Africa and UN 2009-10; Opposition Spokesperson for: Foreign and Commonwealth Office 2011, International Development 2011-12. *Other:* European Parliament: MEP for: South East Wales 1994-99, Wales 1999-2009; Labour party spokeswoman for International Development; Co-President, ACP-EU Joint Parliamentary Assembly. Co-president, Labour Campaign for International Development.

Political interests: International development, regions, gender issues, children's rights, education; African countries, Burma, Sudan, South Sudan.

Other: Patron, Saferworld; Fellow, Royal Society of Arts; Board member, Burma Campaign UK; Council member, Overseas Development Institute; Board member, European Centre for Development Policy Management, Maastricht, Netherlands; Member, advisory board, Global Witness; Various charities supported. Honorary Fellow: University of Wales, Newport, University of Wales, Bangor; Honorary Doctorate: Thames Valley University, Brunel University, Kingston University.

Publications: Voices for One World (Fontana, 1988); Eritrea – Images of War and Peace (Chatto and Windus, 1988); Namibia: Birth of a Nation (Quartet, 1990); By Faith and Daring (Virago, 1993); Changing States (Heinemann, 1996); Could do Better (1996); Zimbabwe on the Brink (Centurion, 2003).

Recreations: Grandchildren, cooking, theatre, cinema, reading.

The Baroness Kinnock of Holyhead, House of Lords, London SW1A 0PW
Tel: 020 7219 1297 *Email:* kinnockg@parliament.uk *Twitter:* @GlenysKinnock

KIRKHAM, LORD

KIRKHAM (Life Baron), Graham Kirkham; cr. 1999. Born 14 December 1944; Son of Tom and Elsie Kirkham; Married Pauline Fisher 1965 (1 son and 1 daughter).

Education: Maltby Grammar School.

Non-political career: DFS Furniture Company Ltd: Founded Company in 1969, Listed on UK Stock Exchange 1993, DFS de-listed and acquired by Kirkham Family and Trusts, Executive chair, Sold 2010; Director, Iceland Frozen Foods 2012-.

CONSERVATIVE

Political career: *House of Lords:* Raised to the peerage as Baron Kirkham, of Old Cantley in the County of South Yorkshire 1999. Member Administration and Works 2003-05. *Other:* Chairman, Conservative Party Treasurers 1997.

Political interests: Business, children.

Other: Chair of trustees, Duke of Edinburgh's Award Scheme; Deputy patron, Outward Bound Trust; Deputy president, Animal Health Trust; Duke of Edinburgh's Award, Outward Bound Trust, Animal Health Trust. Honorary Liveryman Worshipful Company of Furniture Makers 2007. Honorary Member, Emmanuel College, Cambridge 1995; Honorary Doctorate, Bradford University 1997. Kt 1995; CVO 2001.

The Lord Kirkham CVO, House of Lords, London SW1A 0PW
Tel: 020 7219 5353
Black Diamond Investments LP, Redhouse Interchange, Adwick-le-Street, Doncaster DN6 7FE
Tel: 01302 337215 *Fax:* 01302 573308 *Email:* lord.kirkham@bdinvestments.co.uk

KIRKHILL, LORD

KIRKHILL (Life Baron), John Farquharson Smith; cr. 1975. Born 7 May 1930; Son of late Alexander Findlay Smith and Ann Farquharson; Married Frances Reid 1965.

Non-political career: Lord Provost, Aberdeen 1971-75; Chairman, North of Scotland Hydro-Electric Board 1979-82.

Political career: *House of Lords:* Raised to the peerage as Baron Kirkhill, in the District of the City of Aberdeen 1975. Minister of State, Scottish Office 1975-78.

LABOUR

Other: Member, Assemblies of Council of Europe and of Western European Union 1987-91; Chairman, Legal Affairs and Human Rights Committee of the Parliamentary Assembly of the Council of Europe 1991-95. Honorary LLD, Aberdeen University 1974.

The Lord Kirkhill, House of Lords, London SW1A 0PW
Tel: 020 7219 3128
3 Rubislaw Den North, Aberdeen AB15 4AL

KIRKWOOD OF KIRKHOPE, LORD

KIRKWOOD OF KIRKHOPE (Life Baron), Archibald Johnstone Kirkwood; cr 2005. Born 22 April 1946; Son of David Kirkwood; Married Rosemary Chester 1972 (1 son 1 daughter).

Education: Cranhill School, Glasgow; Heriot-Watt University (BSc pharmacy 1971).

Non-political career: Aide to David Steel MP 1971-75, 1977-78; Solicitor.

Political career: *House of Commons:* MP (Liberal Democrat) for Roxburgh and Berwickshire 1983-2005. Liberal Spokesperson for: Health, Social Services and Social Security 1985-87, Scotland 1987-88; Alliance Spokesperson for Overseas Development 1987; Sponsored: Access to Per-

LIBERAL DEMOCRAT

sonal Files Act 1987 (Private Member's Bill), Access to Medical Reports Act 1988 (Private Member's Bill); Convenor and Spokesperson for Welfare and Social Security 1989-94; Liberal Democrat: Deputy Chief Whip 1989-92, Chief Whip 1992-97, Shadow Leader of the House 1994-97, Spokesperson for Community Care 1994-97; Member House of Commons Commission 1997-2005. Chair Social Security 1997-2001. *House of Lords:* Raised to the peerage as Baron Kirkwood of Kirkhope, of Kirkhope in Scottish Borders 2005. Liberal Democrat Spokesperson for Work and

Pensions 2007-10. Co-opted member EU Sub-committee G (Social Policy and Consumer Affairs) 2007-10; Information: Member 2009-10, Chair 2010-; Member EU Sub-committee G (Social Policies and Consumer Protection) 2010-11. *Other:* Social and Liberal Democrat Convenor on Welfare, Health and Education 1988-89.

Political interests: Freedom of information, health, social security, human rights.

Other: Joseph Rowntree Reform Trust: Trustee 1985-2007, Chair 1999-2006. Rowntree Political Fellow 1971. Kt 2003.

Publications: Co-author, Long Term Care – a Framework for Reform.

Recreations: Music, gardening.

The Lord Kirkwood of Kirkhope, House of Lords, London SW1A 0PW
Tel: 020 7219 4217

KNIGHT OF COLLINGTREE, BARONESS

KNIGHT OF COLLINGTREE (Life Baroness) (Joan Christabel) Jill Knight; cr. 1997. Born 9 July 1923; Daughter of late A. E. Christie and Alma Christie; Married James Knight 1947 (died 1986) (2 sons).

Education: King Edward Grammar School, Birmingham; French.

Non-political career: WAAF 1941-46. Director: Computeach International Ltd 1985-2002, Heckett Multiserv plc 1999-2002.

CONSERVATIVE

Political career: *House of Commons:* Contested Northampton 1959 and 1964 general elections. MP (Conservative) for Birmingham Edgbaston 1966-97. Chair, Conservative Backbench Committee on: Health and Social Services 1982-96, Health 1996-97; Vice-chair, 1922 committee 1988-97. *House of Lords:* Raised to the peerage as Baroness Knight of Collingtree, of Collingtree in the County of Northamptonshire 1997. Member: European Union Sub-committee F (Social Affairs, Education and Home Affairs) 2000-03, Personal Bills 2000-03, Adoption Legislation 2012-13. *Other:* Vice-chair, Association of Conservative Peers 2002-06. *Councils and public bodies:* Councillor, Northampton County Borough Council 1956-66.

Political interests: Health, social security, childcare, industry, Council of Europe and Western European Union; America, Cyprus, Taiwan.

Other: Parliamentary Assembly of Council of Europe and Assembly of Western European Union (WEU): Member 1977-88, 1999-2010, Chair: WEU Relations with Parliaments Committee 1984-88, British Inter-Parliamentary Union 1994-97; National Chair, Lifeline 1974-84; Vice-President, Townswomen's Guilds 1989-95; Fellow, Industry and Parliament Trust 1999; Vice-President: Fluoridation Society 2000-, Psoriasis Association 2007-; Sulgrave Manor Trust: Chair 2007-12, President 2012-; Alzheimer's Society. Freedom, San Francisco. Kentucky Colonel 1986; Nebraska Admiral 1989; Honorary DSc, Aston University 1998. MBE 1964; DBE 1985; Farmer's Club.

Publications: About the House (1995).

Recreations: Antique collecting, tapestry work, singing, theatre, cooking.

The Baroness Knight of Collingtree DBE, House of Lords, London SW1A 0PW
Tel: 020 7219 4470 *Fax:* 020 7219 5979

KNIGHT OF WEYMOUTH, LORD

Opposition Spokesperson for Environment, Food and Rural Affairs

KNIGHT OF WEYMOUTH (Life Baron), James Philip Knight; cr 2010. Born 6 March 1965; Son of Philip John Knight, accountant, and Hilary Jean Howlett, neé Harper, craftswoman; Married Anna Wheatley 1989 (1 daughter 1 son).

Education: Eltham College, London; Fitzwilliam College, Cambridge (BA geography, social and political sciences 1987); French.

Non-political career: Works Theatre Co-operative 1986-88; Manager Central Studio Basingstoke 1988-90; Director, West Wiltshire Arts Centre Ltd 1990-91; Dentons Directories Ltd 1991-2001: Sales executive 1991-96, General manager 1997-98, Director 1998-2000, Production manager 2000-01; Director, Egale Ltd; Board member, Arsenal Fanshare Society Ltd. Member: Unite 1995-2010, GMB 2001-.

LABOUR

Political career: *House of Commons:* Contested South Dorset 1997 general election. MP for South Dorset 2001-10. Contested South Dorset 2010 general election. PPS at Department of Health 2003-05: to Rosie Winterton as Minister of State 2003-04, Team PPS 2004-05; Parliamentary Under-Secretary of State, Department for Environment, Food and Rural Affairs 2005-06; Minister of State: Department for Education and Skills/Children, Schools and Families (Schools and Learners) 2006-09, Department for Work and Pensions 2009-10; Minister for the South West

2009-10. Member: Defence 2001-03. *House of Lords:* Raised to the peerage as Baron Knight of Weymouth, of Weymouth in the County of Dorset 2010. Opposition Spokesperson for: Work and Pensions 2010-11, Environment, Food and Rural Affairs 2011-. *Other:* Contested South West Region 1999 European Parliament election. Various posts local constituency party 1990-. *Councils and public bodies:* Frome Town Council: Councillor 1993-2001, Mayor 1998-2001; Mendip District Council: Councillor 1997-2001, Deputy leader 1999-2001, Labour group leader 1999-2001; Vice-President, Local Government Association 2010-13.

Political interests: International development, families, arts, sport, housing, rural affairs.

Other: Fellow, Royal Society of Arts; Chair and trustee, Online Centres Foundation; Trustee, E-Learning Foundation; Chair, HTI Education Trust; Board member, Apps For Good; Honorary Fellow, Institute of Employability Professionals. Visiting Professor, Institute of Education, University of London. Campaigner of the Year, *House Magazine* 2006. PC 2008.

Recreations: Football, tennis, cooking, cycling.

Rt Hon the Lord Knight of Weymouth, House of Lords, London SW1A 0PW
Tel: 020 7219 8209 *Email:* knightja@parliament.uk *Twitter:* @jimpknight

KNIGHTS, LORD

KNIGHTS (Life Baron), Philip Douglas Knights; cr. 1987. Born 3 October 1920; Son of late Thomas James Knights, market gardener, and late Ethel Ginn, schoolteacher; Married Jean Burman 1945 (died 2008).

Education: East Grinstead County School; King's School, Grantham; Police Staff College 1951.

Non-political career: RAF 1943-45. Police cadet, Lincolnshire Constabulary 1937; Police constable 1940; Seconded to Home Office (Sergeant) 1946; Inspector 1953; Superintendent 1955; Chief Superintendent 1957; Assistant Chief Constable, Birmingham 1959; Deputy Commandant, Police Staff College, Bramshill 1962-66; Deputy Chief Constable, Birmingham 1970; Chief Constable, Sheffield and Rotherham Constabulary 1972; Responsible for Police Force of the newly created County of South Yorkshire 1974; Chief Constable, West Midlands Police 1975-85; Member, Departmental Committee, chaired by Lord Devlin, which reported in 1976 on Identification Procedures; Formerly adviser, Police and Fire Committee of the Association of Municipal Authorities.

CROSSBENCH

Political career: *House of Lords:* Raised to the peerage as Baron Knights, of Edgbaston in the County of West Midlands 1987. *Councils and public bodies:* DL, West Midlands 1985.

Political interests: Law and order, prisons, inner cities, local government.

Other: Companion, Chartered Management Institute 1977; Founder trustee, Police Foundation 1979-98; Past President, Association of Chief Police Officers; Member, Council of: Aston University 1985-98, Cambridge Institute of Criminology 1986-2002; Police Dependants' Trust. Honorary DSc, Aston University 1996. First prize and gold medal, Queen's Police Gold Medal Essay Competition 1965. QPM 1964; OBE 1971; CBE 1976; Kt 1980; Royal Over-Seas League. Vice-President, Warwickshire County Cricket Club.

Recreations: Gardening, reading, travel, sport.

The Lord Knights CBE QPM DL, House of Lords, London SW1A 0PW
Tel: 020 7219 5353

KRAMER, BARONESS

Minister of State, Department for Transport

KRAMER (Life Baroness), Susan Veronica Kramer; cr 2010. Born 21 July 1950; Daughter of Harry Victor (Bill) Richards and Elisabeth Richards; Married John Kramer 1972 (died 2006) (1 daughter 1 son).

Education: St Paul's Girls' School, London; St Hilda's College, Oxford (BA philosophy, politics and economics 1972, MA); Illinois University, USA (MBA business/finance 1982).

Non-political career: Staff associate, National Academy of Engineering 1972-73; Second vice-president, Continental Bank, USA 1982-88; Vice-president, corporate finance, Citibank/Citicorp, USA 1988-92; Chief operating officer, Future Water International 1992-95; Partner, Kramer and Associates 1995-99; Board member, CAIB Infrastructure Project Advisers 1997-99; Director, Infrastructure Capital Partners Ltd 1999-2006; Board member, Transport for London 2000-05; Director, Speciality Scanners plc 2001-11.

LIBERAL DEMOCRAT

Political career: *House of Commons:* Contested (Lib Dem) Dulwich and West Norwood 1997 general election. MP for Richmond Park 2005-10. Contested Richmond Park 2010 general election. Liberal Democrat: Spokesperson for the Treasury 2005-06, Shadow Secretary of State for: International Development 2006, Trade and Industry 2006-07, Transport 2007, Shadow Minister for the Cabinet Office and Shadow Chancellor of the Duchy of Lancaster 2007-09. Member: Treasury 2005-06. *House of Lords:* Raised to the peerage as Baroness Kramer, of Richmond Park in the London Borough of Richmond upon Thames 2010. Minister of State, Department for Transport 2013-. Member: Economic Affairs Finance Bill Sub-Committee 2011, Consumer Insurance (Disclosure and Representations) Bill 2011-12, Small- and Medium-Sized Enterprises 2012-13, Parliamentary Commission on Banking Standards 2012-13, Sub-committee on Economic Affairs Finance Bill 2012-. Chair, Liberal Democrat Parliamentary Party Committee on Treasury 2012-. *Other:* Contested London region 1999 European Parliament election. Member: Women Liberal Democrats executive 1997-2000, London Region executive 1997-2003, Liberal Democrat federal executive 2001-04; Chair, Twickenham and Richmond Liberal Democrats 2001-02. *Councils and public bodies:* Contested London mayoral election 2000.

Political interests: Environment, finance, transport; Eastern Europe, USA.

Other: President, Oxford Union Trinity term 1971; Advisory board member, Centre for Reform 2001-04; Environment Trust; Three Wings Trust; Home Start; National Liberal.

Publications: Orange Book chapter 'Harnessing the Markets to Achieve Environmental Goals' (Profile Books 2004).

Recreations: Dog walking, opera, theatre, reading, rowing.

The Baroness Kramer, House of Lords, London SW1A 0PW
Tel: 020 7219 5353 *Email:* kramers@parliament.uk

CROSSBENCH

KREBS, LORD

KREBS (Life Baron), John Richard Krebs; cr 2007. Born 11 April 1945; Son of Sir Hans Adolf Krebs FRCP FRS, Nobel Prize winning scientist, and Margaret Cicely Krebs; Married Katharine Fullerton 1968 (divorced 2012) (2 daughters); married Sarah Margaret Phibbs 2013.

Education: City of Oxford High School; Pembroke College, Oxford (BA zoology 1966, MA; DPhil 1970); German.

Non-political career: Departmental demonstrator in ornithology, Edward Grey Institute, Oxford University 1969-70; Assistant professor of animal resource ecology, University of British Columbia, Canada 1970-73; Zoology lecturer, University College of North Wales, Bangor 1973-75; Oxford University 1975-: Research officer, Animal Behaviour Research Group 1975-76, Zoology lecturer, Edward Grey Institute 1976-88, Fellow, Wolfson College 1976-81, EP Abraham Fellow, Pembroke College 1981-88, Official Fellow, Pembroke College 1988-2005; Royal Society Professor Research 1988-2005: Seconded as Chief executive, National Environment Research Council 1994-99; Chair, Food Standards Agency 2000-05; Principal, Jesus College, Oxford 2005-.

Political career: *House of Lords:* Raised to the peerage as Baron Krebs, of Wytham in the County of Oxfordshire 2007. Board member, Parliamentary Office of Science and Technology (POST). Science and Technology: Member 2007, 2008-10, Chair 2010-; Chair Science and Technology Sub-committee I (Nanotechnologies and food) 2008-10; Member Science and Technology Sub-committees: II (Genomic Medicine) 2008-09, I 2012-13.

Political interests: Science, environment, food, education.

Other: Trustee, Nuffield Foundation; President, Campden BRI; Member, Committee on Climate Change 2010; Chair, Adaptation Sub-committee 2009-; FRS 1984; FMedSci 2004; Foreign member: US National Academy of Science, American Philosophical Society, American Academy of Arts and Science. 14 honorary fellowships; 16 honorary doctorates. Numerous awards, including: Linnean Society Bicentenary Medal 1983, Frink medal, Zoological Society 1997, Harben Gold Medal, Royal Institute of Public Health 2006. Kt 1999.

Publications: 250-plus books and articles on ecology and animal behaviour.

Recreations: Running, tennis, walking, food including cooking, music, gardening, family.

Professor the Lord Krebs FRS, House of Lords, London SW1A 0PW
Tel: 020 7219 5353
Jesus College, Oxford OX1 3DW *Tel:* 01865 279701 *Fax:* 01865 279696
Email: principal@jesus.ox.ac.uk

LAIRD, LORD

LAIRD (Life Baron), John Dunn Laird; cr. 1999. Born 23 April 1944; Son of late Dr Norman Laird, OBE, Northern Ireland MP, and late Councillor Margaret Laird; Married Caroline Ferguson 1971 (1 son 1 daughter).

Education: Royal Belfast Academical Institution; Ulster Scots.

Non-political career: Bank official 1963-67; Bank inspector 1967-68; Computer programmer 1968-73; Public relations consultant 1973-2005; Chair, John Laird Public Relations 1976-2005; Visiting professor of public relations, University of Ulster 1993-. National Union of Journalists.

NON-AFFILIATED **Political career:** *House of Lords:* Raised to the peerage as Baron Laird, of Artigarvan in the County of Tyrone 1999. *Other:* MP for St Annes, Belfast, Northern Ireland Parliament 1970-73; Member for West Belfast: Northern Ireland Assembly 1973-75, Northern Ireland Convention 1975-76. Member, Ulster Unionist Party; Resigned from the Ulster Unionist Party June 2013. *Councils and public bodies:* Member, North/South Language Implementation Board 1999-2004; Chair, Ulster/Scots Agency 1999-2004.

Political interests: Transport, dyslexia, Ulster Scots activity, new energy, new thinking.

Other: Chairman, advisory board, European Azerbaijan Society 2009-; Fellow, Royal Society of Arts 2012; Fellow, Chartered Institute of Public Relations 1991; Combat Cancer; NI Hospice. Freeman, City of London 2012. Lifetime Achievement Award, Certified Institute of Public Relations. Member Instonians, Belfast.

Publications: Videos and DVDs: Trolley Bus Day in Belfast (1992), Swansong of Steam in Ulster (1994), Twilight of Steam in Ulster (1995); Book: A Struggle to be Heard: By a True Ulster Liberal (Global & Western Publishing, 2010).

Recreations: Local history, railways, cricket.

The Lord Laird, House of Lords, London SW1A 0PW
Tel: 020 7219 8626 *Fax:* 020 7219 1657 *Email:* lairdj@parliament.uk
13 Little College Street, London SW1P 3SH

LAMING, LORD

Convener of the Crossbench Peers

LAMING (Life Baron), (William) Herbert Laming; cr. 1998. Born 19 July 1936; Son of William and Lillian Laming; Married Aileen Pollard 1962 (died 2010).

Education: Durham University (Diploma applied social sciences 1960); Rainer House (probation training 1960-61); London School of Economics (mental health course 1964-65).

Non-political career: Royal Navy 1954-56. Nottingham Probation Service: Probation officer 1961-66, Senior probation officer 1966-68; Assistant chief probation Officer, Nottingham City and County Probation Service 1968-71; Hertfordshire County Council Social Services: Deputy director 1971-75, Director 1975-91; Chair, Independent Inquiry for Somerset Health Authority 1989; Chief Inspector, Social Services Inspectorate, Department of Health 1991-98; Chair: Review of Management of the Prison Service 1999-2000, Independent Statutory Inquiry following the murder of Victoria Climbié 2001-03, Review of Protection of Children in England 2010.

CROSSBENCH

Political career: *House of Lords:* Raised to the peerage as Baron Laming, of Tewin in the County of Hertfordshire 1998. Convener of the Crossbench Peers 2011-. Member: Ecclesiastical Committee 2003-, House 2011-, Joint Committee on Security 2011-, Administration and Works 2011-, Liaison 2011-, Privileges and Conduct 2011-, Procedure 2011-, Sub-committee on Leave of Absence 2011-13, Selection 2011-. *Councils and public bodies:* DL, Hertfordshire 1999-; Vice-President, Local Government Association 2012-.

Political interests: Public services; China, Europe.

Other: President, Association of Directors of Social Services 1982-83; President and Patron of social care charities. Freeman, City of London 1996. Five honorary doctorates. CBE 1985; Kt 1996.

Publications: Lessons from America: the balance of services in social care (1985).

The Lord Laming CBE DL, House of Lords, London SW1A 0PW
Tel: 020 7219 1414 *Email:* bowyerj@parliament.uk

CONSERVATIVE

LAMONT OF LERWICK, LORD

LAMONT OF LERWICK (Life Baron), Norman Stewart Hughson Lamont; cr. 1998. Born 8 May 1942; Son of late Daniel Lamont and Helen Irene Lamont; Married Rosemary White 1971 (divorced) (1 son 1 daughter).

Education: Loretto School, Musselburgh (Scholar); Fitzwilliam College, Cambridge (BA economics 1965) (Union President 1964).

Non-political career: NM Rothschild and Sons Ltd 1968-79, 1993-95; Director: Rothschild Asset Management 1978-79, NM Rothschild and Sons 1993-95; Consultant to Monsanto Corporation 1994-99; Director, Balli Group plc 1995-; Adviser to Romanian Government 1995-97; Chair, East European Food Fund 1995-2006; Director: Cie International de Participations Bancaires et Financieres 1999-, Banca Commerciala Robank 2000-05; Consultant to Consensus Business Group 2001-; President, British Romanian Chamber of Commerce 2002-; Director, Scottish Re 2002-07; Consultant to Stanleybet 2004-; Member, advisory board, Merchant Bridge plc 2004-; Chair, British Iranian Chamber of Commerce 2004-; Director: RAB Capital 2004-11, Jupiter Second Split 2005-; Chair, Jupiter Adria 2006-; Consultant to Western Union Company 2006-08; Chair, advisory board, Uniastrum Bank 2006-08; Member, advisory board, Hermitage Global Fund 2007-; Chair, Smaller Companies Dividend Trust 2008-; Director, Phorm PLC.

Political career: *House of Commons:* Contested Kingston-upon-Hull East 1970 general election. MP (Conservative) for Kingston-upon-Thames 1972 by-election to 1997. PPS to Norman St John Stevas as Minister for the Arts 1974; Parliamentary Under-Secretary of State, Department of Energy 1979-81; Minister of State, Department of Trade and Industry 1981-85; Minister for Defence Procurement, Ministry of Defence 1985-86; HM Treasury 1986-93: Financial Secretary 1986-89, Chief Secretary 1989-90, Chancellor of the Exchequer 1990-93; Contested Harrogate and Knaresborough 1997 general election. *House of Lords:* Raised to the peerage as Baron Lamont of Lerwick, of Lerwick in the Shetland Islands 1998. Member: Economic Affairs 2005-08, Economic Affairs Taxation Sub-committee 2005-08, EU Sub-committee C: (Foreign Affairs, Defence and Development Policy) 2010-12, (External Affairs) 2012-. *Other:* Bruges Group: Vice-President 1994-2003, Co-chair 2003-07.

Political interests: Economics, European Union, foreign affairs; Chile, Iran, Middle East, Romania.

Other: Chair, Bow Group 1971-72; Trustee, Romanian Orthodox Church in London 2005-08; Chair: Clan Lamont Society 2006-08, Le Cercle 2007-08; Member, advisory board, Iran Heritage Foundation 2008-; President, Economic Research Council 2009-. PC 1986; Order of Faithful Service (Romania) 2010; Garrick, Beefsteak, White's.

Publications: Sovereign Britain (1995); In Office (1999).

Recreations: Theatre, history, ornithology.

Rt Hon the Lord Lamont of Lerwick, House of Lords, London SW1A 0PW
Tel: 020 7219 5353
Balli Group plc, 5 Stanhope Gate, London W1K 1AH *Tel:* 020 7306 2138 *Fax:* 020 7306 2072
Email: beverleyg@balli.co.uk

CROSSBENCH

LANE-FOX OF SOHO, BARONESS

LANE-FOX OF SOHO (Life Baroness), Martha Lane Fox; cr 2013. Born 10 February 1973.

Education: Oxford High School; Westminster School; Oxford University (BA ancient and modern history).

Non-political career: Co-founder, lastminute.com 1998; Founder and chair, Go On UK; Co-founder, LuckyVoice 2004; Founder, Antigone 2007; Non-executive Director, Efficiency and Reform Board, Cabinet Office 2010-12; Chair, MakieLab 2012; Government Digital Champion 2009-.

Political career: *House of Lords:* Raised to the peerage as Baroness Lane-Fox of Soho, of Soho in the City of Westminster 2013.

Other: Non-executive director: Marks and Spencer, Women's Prize for Fiction; Chair, Founders Forum for Good; Patron: AbilityNet, Reprieve, Just for Kids Law, Camfed. CBE 2013.

The Baroness Lane-Fox of Soho CBE, House of Lords, London SW1A 0PW
Tel: 020 7219 5353
Website: www.marthalanefox.com marthalanefoxblog.wordpress.com
Twitter: @Marthalanefox

LANG OF MONKTON, LORD

LANG OF MONKTON (Life Baron), Ian Bruce Lang; cr. 1997. Born 27 June 1940; Son of late James Lang, DSC; Married Sandra Montgomerie 1971 (2 daughters).

Education: Lathallan School, Montrose; Rugby School; Sidney Sussex College, Cambridge (BA history 1962).

Non-political career: Chairman, Marsh and McLennan Companies Inc and non-executive director of other companies.

Political career: *House of Commons:* Contested Ayrshire Central 1970 and Glasgow Pollok February 1974 general elections. MP (Conservative) for Galloway 1979-83, for Galloway and Upper Nithsdale 1983-97. Assistant Government Whip 1981-83; Government Whip 1983-86; Parliamentary Under-Secretary of State: Department of Employment 1986, Scottish Office 1986-87; Minister of State, Scottish Office 1987-90; Secretary of State for Scotland 1990-95; President of the Board of Trade and Secretary of State for Trade and Industry 1995-97. *House of Lords:* Raised to the peerage as Baron Lang of Monkton, of Merrick and the Rhinns of Kells in Dumfries and Galloway 1997. Member: Constitution 2001-05, 2012-, Barnett Formula 2008-09. *Councils and public bodies:* Governor, Rugby School 1997-2007; DL, Ayrshire and Arran 1998-; Prime Minister's Advisory Committee on Business Appointments: Member 2009-, Chairman 2009-.

Other: Member, Queen's Bodyguard for Scotland, Royal Company of Archers 1974-; President, Association for the Protection of Rural Scotland 1998-2001; Chair, Patrons of the National Galleries of Scotland 1999-2007. Officer of the Order of St John 1974; PC 1990; Pratt's. Prestwick Golf Club.

Publications: Blue Remembered Years (2002).

Rt Hon the Lord Lang of Monkton DL, House of Lords, London SW1A 0PW
Tel: 020 7219 5792

CONSERVATIVE

LAWRENCE OF CLARENDON, BARONESS

LAWRENCE OF CLARENDON (Life Baroness), Doreen Delceita Lawrence; cr 2013.

Non-political career: Founder, Stephen Lawrence Charitable Trust.

Political career: *House of Lords:* Raised to the peerage as Baroness Lawrence of Clarendon, of Clarendon in the Commonwealth Realm of Jamaica 2013.

Other: OBE 2003.

The Baroness Lawrence of Clarendon OBE, House of Lords, London SW1A 0PW
Tel: 020 7219 5353

LABOUR

LAWSON OF BLABY, LORD

LAWSON OF BLABY (Life Baron), Nigel Lawson; cr. 1992. Born 11 March 1932; Son of late Ralph Lawson and late Joan Lawson, née Davis; Married Vanessa Salmon 1955 (divorced 1980, she died 1985) (1 son 2 daughters and 1 daughter deceased); married Thérèse Maclear 1980 (divorced 2012) (1 son 1 daughter).

Education: Westminster School; Christ Church, Oxford (Scholar, BA philosophy, politics and economics 1954).

Non-political career: Royal Navy national service 1954-56; Sub-Lt RNVR, CO HMMTB Gay Charger. Member editorial staff, *Financial Times* 1956-60; City editor, *Sunday Telegraph* 1961-63; Special assistant to Sir Alec Douglas-Home as Prime Minister 1963-64; *Financial Times* columnist and BBC broadcaster 1965; Editor, *The Spectator* 1966-70; Director, Barclays Bank plc 1990-98; Chair: Central Europe Trust 1990-2012; Oxford Investment Partners 2006-13; Founding Chairman, Global Warming Policy Foundation 2009-; Mousquetaire d'Armagnac 2010-.

Political career: *House of Commons:* Contested Eton and Slough 1970 general election. MP (Conservative) for Blaby February 1974-92. Opposition Whip 1976-77; Opposition Spokesman on Treasury and Economic Affairs 1977-79; Financial Secretary to the Treasury 1979-81; Secretary of State for Energy 1981-83; Chancellor of the Exchequer 1983-89. *House of Lords:* Raised to the peerage as Baron Lawson of Blaby, of Newnham in the County of Northamptonshire 1992. Member: Economic Affairs 2005-08, 2010-, Barnett Formula 2008-09, Parliamentary Commission on Banking Standards 2012-13.

Political interests: Climate change, economics.

CONSERVATIVE

Other: President, British Institute of Energy Economics 1995-2004; Member, Governing Body, Westminster School 1999-2005. Honorary Student, Christ Church, Oxford 1996; Fellow, Westminster School 2005; Honorary DSc, Buckingham University 2011. IEA National Free Enterprise Award 2008. PC 1981; Beefsteak, Garrick, Pratt's.

Publications: Co-author, The Power Game (1976); The View from Number 11: (Memoirs 1992) [abridged and updated as Memoirs of a Tory Radical, 2010]; Co-author, The Nigel Lawson Diet Book (1996); An Appeal to Reason: A Cool Look at Global Warming (2008).

Rt Hon the Lord Lawson of Blaby, House of Lords, London SW1A 0PW
Tel: 020 7219 4464 *Email:* lawsonn@parliament.uk

LAYARD, LORD

LABOUR

LAYARD (Life Baron) (Peter) Richard Grenville Layard; cr. 2000 . Born 15 March 1934; Son of Dr John Layard and Doris Layard; Married Molly Meacher, née Reid (later Baroness Meacher) 1991.

Education: Eton College; King's College, Cambridge (BA history 1957); London School of Economics (MSc economics 1967).

Non-political career: History master, London comprehensive secondary schools 1959-61; Senior research officer, Robbins Committee on Higher Education 1961-63; London School of Economics 1964-: Deputy director, Higher Education Research Unit 1964-74, Lecturer in economics 1968-75, Reader in economics of labour 1975-80, Head, Centre for Labour Economics 1974-90, Professor of Economics 1980-99, Emeritus Professor of Economics 1999-; Director, Centre for Economic Performance 1990-2003; Economic Consultant to the Russian Government 1991-97; Consultant: Department for Education and Employment 1997-2001, Cabinet Office 2001; Programme director, Well-Being Programme, LSE Centre for Economic Performance 2003-; Adviser, Department of Health 2006-. Member, Association of University Teachers.

Political career: *House of Lords:* Raised to the peerage as Baron Layard, of Highgate in the London Borough of Haringey 2000. Member: European Union Sub-Committee A (Economic and Financial Affairs, Trade and External Relations) -2002, Economic Affairs 2005-08.

Political interests: Economic policy, employment, inequality, well-being, mental health; Bhutan.

Other: Member, UGC 1985-89; Chair, Employment Institute 1987-92; Fellow, British Academy 2003; Member, Good Childhood Inquiry Panel 2007-09; Fellow: European Economics Association 2004, Society of Labour Economists 2007. Honorary Fellow, London School of Economics 2000. WW Leontief Medal of the Russian Academy of Natural Sciences 2005; 12A Prize (Joint) in Labour Economics 2008; Royal College of Psychiatrists Medal 2010.

Publications: Co-author: The Causes of Graduate Unemployment in India (1969), The Impact of Robbins: Expansion in Higher Education (1969), Qualified Manpower and Economic Performance (1971); Editor, Cost-Benefit Analysis (1973, 1994); Co-author: Microeconomic Theory (1978), The Causes of Poverty (1978); Author: More Jobs, Less Inflation (1982), How to Beat Unemployment (1986); Co-author: Handbook of Labour Economics (1986), The Performance of the British Economy (1988), Unemployment: Macroeconomic Performance and the Labour Market (1991), Reform in Eastern Europe (1991), East-West Migration: the alternatives (1992), Post-Communist Russia: pain and progress (1993), Macroeconomics: a text for Russia (1994), The Coming Russian Boom (1996), Author, What Labour Can Do (1997); Co-author, Emerging from Communism: Lessons from Russia, China and Eastern Europe (1998); Author: Tackling Unemployment (1999), Tackling Inequality (1999); Co-author, What the Future Holds (2001); Author, Happiness (2005); Co-author: A Good Childhood: Searching for Values in a Competitive Age (2009), Combatting Unemployment (2011).

Recreations: Tennis, sailing.

Professor the Lord Layard, House of Lords, London SW1A 0PW
Tel: 020 7219 5353
Centre for Economic Performance, London School of Economics, Houghton Street,
London WC2A 2AE *Tel:* 020 7955 7048 *Fax:* 020 7955 7595
Email: r.layard@lse.ac.uk cep.lse.ac.uk/layard

LEA OF CRONDALL, LORD

LEA OF CRONDALL (Life Baron), David Edward Lea; cr. 1999. Born 2 November 1937; Son of late Edward and Lilian Lea.

Education: Farnham Grammar School, Surrey; Christ's College, Cambridge (MA economics 1961) (Inaugural chair Cambridge University Students Representative Council 1961); French.

Non-political career: National Service, Royal Horse Artillery 1955-57. Economist Intelligence Unit 1961-63; Trades Union Congress: Research/Economic Department 1964-67, Assistant secretary, Economic and Social Affairs 1968-70, Head, Economic and Social Affairs 1970-77, Assistant general secretary 1978-99. Member, TGWU 1962-; TUC: Member, Mission to Study Employment and Technology in the USA 1980, Secretary: Nuclear Energy Review Body 1986-88, Task Force on Representation at Work 1994-99; European TUC: Chair, Economic Committee 1980-90, Member, Executive Committee and Steering Group 1991-99, Vice-President 1997-99.

LABOUR

Political career: *House of Lords:* Raised to the peerage as Baron Lea of Crondall, of Crondall in the County of Hampshire 1999. Member: European Communities Sub-committees: A (Economic and Financial Affairs, Trade and External Relations) 2000-03, C (Foreign Affairs, Defence and Development Policy) 2003-07, G (Social Policy and Consumer Affairs) 2007-09. *Other:* President, Cambridge University Liberal Club 1960-61; Secretary, TUC-Labour Party: Liaison Committee 1972-86, Contact Group 1987-96. *Councils and public bodies:* Member: DTI Investment Mission in Japan 1974, Channel Tunnel Advisory Committee 1974-75, Bullock Committee on Industrial Democracy 1975-77, Royal Commission on the Distribution of Income and Wealth 1975-79, Delors Committee on Economic and Social Concepts in the Community 1977-79, Energy Commission 1977-79, UN Commission on Transnational Corporations 1977-82, NEDC Committee on Finance for Industry 1978-82, Franco-British Council 1982-99; Governor, National Institute of Economic and Social Research; Member: Retail Prices Index Advisory Committee 1985-99, Kreisky Commission on Employment Issues in Europe 1987-89, Tripartite Mission EU, Japan 1990, European Social Dialogue Joint Steering Committee 1992-, UK Delegation Earth Summit, Rio 1992, Round Table on Sustainable Development 1995-99, Advisory Committee on Vehicle Emissions 1998-99, EU High Level Group on Benchmarking 1998-99, Treasury Advisory Committee on EMU 1998-99, Central Arbitration Committee 2000-10; Council member, Britain in Europe 2000-05; Election monitor: Congo (DRC) 2007, Nepal 2008.

Political interests: European Union, employment, energy, economy, constitution; Bolivia, Africa, Madagascar, Nepal.

Other: Chair, Hammarskjold Inquiry Trust 2012-13; Editorial board member, New Economy (IPPR) 1991-99. OBE 1978. Bourne Club, Farnham, Lords/Commons Tennis and Ski Clubs.

Publications: Trade Unionism (1966); Co-author, Europe and Your Rights at Work (2006).

Recreations: Tennis, music, theatre, skiing.

The Lord Lea of Crondall OBE, House of Lords, London SW1A 0PW
Tel: 020 7219 8518 *Email:* lead@parliament.uk

LEACH OF FAIRFORD, LORD

LEACH OF FAIRFORD (Life Baron), (Charles Guy) Rodney Leach; cr 2006. Born 1 June 1934; Son of late Charles Harold Leach CBE; Married Felicity Ballantyne 1963 (divorced 1989) (3 daughters 2 sons); married Mrs Jessica Douglas-Home 1993 (2 stepsons).

Education: Harrow School; Balliol College, Oxford (BA classics, philosophy and ancient history 1955, MA).

Non-political career: N M Rothschild and Sons 1963-76: Partner 1968-76, Director 1970-76; Managing director, Trade Development Bank 1976-83; Director: Matheson & Co 1983-, Jardine Matheson Holdings 1984-, Jardine Strategic Holdings 1987-, Mandarin Oriental Holdings 1987-, Dairy Farm Holdings 1987-, Hongkong Land Holdings 1989-, British Library 1996-2004; Deputy chair, Jardine Lloyd Thompson Group 1997-; Director: Robert Fleming 1999-2000, Jardine Motors Group 2001-, Rothschilds Continuation AG 2006-; Chairman, Open Europe.

CONSERVATIVE

Political career: *House of Lords:* Raised to the peerage as Baron Leach of Fairford, of Fairford in the County of Gloucestershire 2006. Co-opted member European Union Sub-committee E (Law and Institutions) 2006-07.

Political interests: Finance, ethics, European Union; China, EU member states, Hong Kong, India, Singapore.

Other: Trustee: Post Office Pension Fund 1976-97, Mental Health Foundation 1984-98, Balliol College, Oxford 1986-, British Library 1996-2004.

Publications: Europe – A Concise Encyclopaedia of the European Union (Profile Books, 1998, 2004).

Recreations: Bridge, sport.

The Lord Leach of Fairford, House of Lords, London SW1A 0PW
Tel: 020 7219 5353
Matheson and Co Ltd, 3 Lombard Street, London EC3V 9AQ *Tel:* 020 7816 8278
Fax: 020 7623 5024 *Email:* rleach@matheson.co.uk

LIBERAL DEMOCRAT

LEE OF TRAFFORD, LORD

LEE OF TRAFFORD (Life Baron), John Robert Louis Lee; cr 2006. Born 21 June 1942; Son of Basil Lee, doctor; Married Anne Bakirgian 1975 (2 daughters).

Education: William Hulme's Grammar School, Manchester; Chartered accountant 1964.

Non-political career: Founding director, Chancery Consolidated Ltd (investment bankers), Manchester; Various non-executive directorships.

Political career: *House of Commons:* Contested Manchester Moss-side October 1974. MP (Conservative) for Nelson and Colne 1979-83, for Pendle 1983-92. Contested Pendle 1992 general election. PPS to: Kenneth Baker as Minister of State for Industry 1981-83, Cecil Parkinson as Secretary of State for Industry 1983; Parliamentary Under-Secretary of State: Ministry of Defence 1983-86, Department of Employment 1986-89; Minister for Tourism 1987-89. *House of Lords:* Raised to the peerage as Baron Lee of Trafford, of Bowdon in the County of Cheshire 2006. Liberal Democrat: Spokesperson for: Trade and Industry 2006-07, Culture, Media and Sport (Tourism) 2006-10, Defence 2007-10, Whip 2007-10. Co-opted member EU Sub-committee B (Internal Market) 2006-07; Member: Refreshment 2007-12, Joint Committee on National Security Strategy 2010-. Chair, Liberal Democrat Parliamentary Party Committee on International Affairs (Defence) 2010-12. *Other:* Chairman, Liberal Democrat Friends of Armed Forces 2010-12. *Councils and public bodies:* Chair, Association of Leading Visitor Attractions 1990-; Member, English Tourist Board 1992-99; Chair: Museum of Science and Industry, Manchester 1992-99, Christie Hospital NHS Trust 1992-98; DL, Greater Manchester 1995; High Sheriff, Greater Manchester 1998-99.

Political interests: Defence, tourism, trade and industry, investment; UK.

Other: Chairman, Association of Leading Visitor Attractions.

Publications: Portfolio Man (Willow Publishing, 2005).

Recreations: Golf, stock market, salmon fishing, antiques.

The Lord Lee of Trafford, House of Lords, London SW1A 0PW
Tel: 020 7219 3949 *Email:* leej@parliament.uk

NON-AFFILIATED

LEICESTER, LORD BISHOP OF

LEICESTER (6th Bishop of), Timothy John Stevens. Born 31 December 1946; Son of late Ralph and Ursula Stevens; Married Wendi Price 1973 (1 daughter 1 son).

Education: Chigwell School, Essex; Selwyn College, Cambridge (BA classics 1968; MA English 1972); Ripon Hall, Oxford (Diploma theology); French.

Non-political career: Senior management trainee, BOAC 1968-72; Second Secretary, Foreign and Commonwealth Office 1972-73; Ordained 1976; Curate East Ham 1976-79; Team vicar Upton Park 1979-80; Team rector Canvey Island 1980-88; Bishop of Chelmsford's urban officer 1988-91; Archdeacon of West Ham 1991-95; Bishop suffragan of Dunwich 1995-99; Bishop of Leicester 1999-.

Political career: *House of Lords:* Entered House of Lords 2003; Convener of Lords Spiritual 2009. Member Joint Committee on the Draft House of Lords Reform Bill 2011-12. *Councils and public bodies:* Member, board of governors, De Montfort University; Chair, board of governors, Westcott House Theological College.

Political interests: Constitutional reform, children and families, welfare reform.

Other: Chair, Children's Society 2002-10; Member: Archbishops' Council 2005-10, Standing Committee of House of Bishops 2005-10; Visiting Professor, Faith and Society, De Montfort University. Doctor of Laws, De Montfort University; Doctor of Letters, University of Leicester.

Recreations: Cricket, golf, walking in Yorkshire.

Rt Rev the Lord Bishop of Leicester, House of Lords, London SW1A 0PW
Tel: 020 7219 5353
Bishop's Lodge, 10 Springfield Road, Leicester LE2 3BD *Tel:* 0116-270 8985
Fax: 0116-270 3288 *Email:* bishop.tim@leccofe.org *Website:* www.leicester.anglican.org

LEIGH OF HURLEY, LORD – *Please see Addenda Page xii*

LEITCH, LORD

LABOUR

LEITCH (Life Baron), Alexander Park Leitch; cr. 2004. Born 20 October 1947; Son of Donald Leitch and Agnes Smith, née Park; Married (3 daughters), Married 2nd Noelle Kristin Dowd 2003 (1 daughter).
Education: Dunfermline High School.
Non-political career: Chief systems designer, National Mutual Life/Hambro Life 1969-88; Allied Dunbar plc: Chief executive 1993-96, Chair 1996-2001; Chair: Dunbar Bank 1994-2001, Eagle Star 1996-2004, Threadneedle Asset Management 1996-2004; Director, BAT Industries 1997-98; Chair, Association of British Insurers 1998-2000; Chief executive, Zurich Financial Services (UKISA Asia Pacific) 1998-2004; Chair: SANE 1999-2000, National Employment Panel 2000-07, Intrinsic FS 2005; Director, Lloyds TSB plc 2005; BUPA: Director 2006, Chair; Director: UBM plc 2005-09, Paternoster 2006-10; Scottish Widows plc: Director 2007, Chair; Deputy chair, Lloyds Banking Group plc.
Political career: *House of Lords:* Raised to the peerage as Baron Leitch, of Oakley in Fife 2004.
Countries of interest: Africa, China, France, India, Italy, Latin America, Spain, Switzerland, USA.
Other: Deputy chair, BITC 1996-2004; Chair, SANE 1999-2000; Trustee, National Galleries of Scotland 1999-2003; Deputy chair, Commonwealth Education Fund 2003; Vice-President, UK Cares 2004; Chair: Balance Foundation 2004-05, Leitch Review of UK Skills 2005-07, Medical Aid Films 2010; Trustee, Lloyds TSB Foundation 2011. Member, Worshipful Company of Insurers 2002. Freeman City of London 2002. Chancellor, Carnegie College, Dunfermline 2010. Fellow, Carnegie College; Honorary Doctorate, Sunderland University. Prince of Wales Ambassador's Award for Charitable Work 2001.
Recreations: Antiquarian books, antiques, poetry, malt whisky, art, painting.
The Lord Leitch, House of Lords, London SW1A 0PW
Tel: 020 7219 2929
5 The Sanctuary, Westminster, London SW1P 3JS *Tel:* 020 7222 3180 *Fax:* 020 7222 7913
Email: sandy.leitch@bupa.com

LESTER OF HERNE HILL, LORD

LIBERAL DEMOCRAT

LESTER OF HERNE HILL (Life Baron), Anthony Paul Lester; cr. 1993. Born 3 July 1936; Son of late Harry and Kate Lester; Married Catherine Wassey 1971 (1 son 1 daughter).
Education: City of London School; Trinity College, Cambridge (MA history and law 1962); Harvard Law School (LLM 1964); French.
Non-political career: 2nd Lieutenant, Royal Artillery 1955-57 (national service). Called to Bar, Lincoln's Inn 1963; QC 1975, QC (NI) 1984; Bencher 1985; Called to Bar of Northern Ireland 1984; Irish Bar 1983; Special adviser to: Home Secretary 1974-76, Standing Advisory Commission on Human Rights in Northern Ireland 1975-77; Honorary Visiting Professor, University College London 1983-; Recorder of the Crown Court 1987-93; Independent adviser to Jack Straw as Secretary of State for Justice on aspects of constitutional reform 2007-08.
Political career: *House of Lords:* Raised to the peerage as Baron Lester of Herne Hill, of Herne Hill in the London Borough of Southwark 1993. Liberal Democrat Spokesperson for: Discrimination Law Reform 2008-09, Women and Equality 2009-10. Member: Procedure 1995-97, European Communities Sub-committees E: Law and Institutions 1995-97, 1999-2003, 2005-06, 1996 Inter-Governmental Conference 1995-97, European Communities Sub-committee F (Social Affairs, Education and Home Affairs) 1997-99, Human Rights Joint Committee 2001-05, 2005-09, 2010-; Co-opted member EU Sub-committee E (Law and Institutions) 2006-08; Member Constitution 2013-. *Other:* Founder member, Social Democrat Party 1981; President, Liberal Democrat Lawyers' Association. *Councils and public bodies:* Governor, British Institute of Human Rights; Member, Council of Justice 1977-; President, Interights (International Centre for the Legal Protection of Human Rights) 1991-; European Roma Rights Centre: Executive Committee, Co-chair 1998-2001; Member, board of directors, Salzburg Seminar 1996-2000; Open Society Justice Initiative Board 2000-; Chair, Equal Rights Trust 2006-07; Vice-president, English PEN 2010; Commissioner, Bill of Rights Commission 2011-.
Political interests: Human rights, constitutional reform, law reform, equality and non-discrimination, media, European political integration; India, Ireland, South Africa, USA.
Other: Board member, Open Society Institute Justice Initiative 2000-; Overseas member, American Law Institute 1985-; Member, Bar Council of England and Wales; Honorary Fellow, Society for Advanced Legal Studies 1998-; Honorary Member, American Academy of Arts and Sciences

2002; Honorary Fellow, American Philosophical Society 2003; Honorary Member, Society of Legal Scholars 2008; Interights, Justice, Liberty. Seven honorary doctorates; Honorary Life Fellow, University College London 1998; Adj. Prof. of Law, University College Cork, Ireland 2006. Human Rights Lawyer of the Year, Liberty 1997; Lifetime Achievement Award, The Lawyer 2004; Peer of the Year, *House Magazine* 2006; Lifetime Achievement in Service of Human Rights, Liberty Judges Award 2008; Lifetime Achievement Award, Association of Muslim Lawyers 2008. Chevalier de la Légion d'Honneur (France) 2009; RAC.

Publications: Justice in the American South (Amnesty International, 1964); Co-editor, Shawcross and Beaumont on Air Law (3rd edition, 1964); Co-author, Race and Law (1972); Numerous articles on human rights law and constitutional reform; Contributor to other legal publications; Editor-in-Chief, Butterworths Human Rights Cases; Member, Editorial Board of Public Law; Consultant editor and contributor on 'Constitutional Law and Human Rights', Halsbury's Laws of England (4th edition, reissued 1996); Co-editor, Butterworths Human Rights Law and Practice (1999, 2004, 2009).

Recreations: Walking, sailing, watercolours.

The Lord Lester of Herne Hill QC, House of Lords, London SW1A 0PW
Tel: 020 7219 2999 *Email:* lestera@parliament.uk
The Odysseus Trust, 193 Fleet Street, London EC4A 2AH *Tel:* 020 7404 4712
Fax: 020 7405 7314 *Email:* info@odysseustrust.org *Website:* www.odysseustrust.org

LEVENE OF PORTSOKEN, LORD

LEVENE OF PORTSOKEN (Life Baron), Peter Keith Levene; cr. 1997. Born 8 December 1941; Son of late Maurice and Rose Levene; Married Wendy Fraiman 1966 (2 sons 1 daughter).

Education: City of London School; Manchester University (BA economics 1963); French, German, Italian.

CROSSBENCH

Non-political career: Honorary Col. Comdt, Royal Logistic Corps 1993-2006. United Scientific Holdings 1963-85: Managing director 1968-85, Chair 1982-85; Member, South East Asia Trade Advisory Group 1979-83; Defence Manufacturers' Association: Council member 1982-85, Chair 1984-85; Personal adviser to Michael Heseltine as Secretary of State for Defence 1984; Chief of Defence Procurement, Ministry of Defence 1985-91; UK National Armaments Director 1988-91; Chair, European National Armaments Directors 1989-90; Personal adviser to Michael Heseltine as Secretary of State for the Environment 1991-92, Chair, Docklands Light Railway Ltd 1991-94; Deputy chair, Wasserstein Perella & Co Ltd 1991-94; Personal adviser to Norman Lamont as Chancellor of the Exchequer on Competition and Purchasing 1992; Member, Citizen's Charter Advisory Panel 1992-93; Personal adviser to the President of the Board of Trade 1992-95; Adviser to John Major as Prime Minister on Efficiency and Effectiveness 1992-97; Chair and chief executive, Canary Wharf Ltd 1993-96; Senior adviser, Morgan Stanley & Co Ltd 1996-98; Director, Haymarket Group Ltd 1997-; Chair: Bankers Trust International plc 1998-99, Investment Banking Europe Deutsche Bank 1999-2001; Vice-chair, Deutsche Bank AG London 2001-02; Director, J. Sainsbury plc 2001-04; Chair: General Dynamics UK Ltd. 2001-, World Trade Centre Disaster Fund (UK) 2001-, Lloyd's 2002-11; Member, supervisory board, Deutsche Boerse ag 2004-05; Board member, TOTAL s.a. 2005-11; Director, China Construction Bank 2006-12; Chair: MDD Defence Reform Group 2010-11, NBNK Investments plc 2011-12; Starr Underwriting Agents Ltd 2012-; Board member, Eurotunnel S.A 2012-.

Political career: *House of Lords:* Raised to the peerage as Baron Levene of Portsoken, of Portsoken in the City of London 1997. Member: Economic Affairs 2008-13, Joint Committee on National Security Strategy 2013-. *Councils and public bodies:* Court of Common Council, City of London: Member 1983-84, Alderman 1984-2012; JP, City of London 1984-; Sheriff, City of London 1995-96; Lord Mayor of London 1998-99.

Other: Governor, City of London School 1986-; Chair: Board of management, London Homes for the Elderly 1990-93, Bevis Marks Trust; CIMgt; FCIPS; LEUKA 2000. Carmen's Company: Liveryman 1984-, Master 1992-93; Liveryman: Information Technologists 1992-, Management Consultant (Honorary) 2004-. Chancellor, City University 1998-99. Fellow, Queen Mary and Westfield College 1995; Two honorary doctorates. KBE 1989; KStJ 1998; Commandeur, Ordre National du Merite (France) 1996; Knight Commander Order of Merit (Germany) 1998; Middle Cross Order of Merit (Hungary) 1999; Guildhall, Royal Automobile, Walbrook.

Recreations: Skiing, watching football, travel.

The Lord Levene of Portsoken KBE, House of Lords, London SW1A 0PW
Tel: 020 7219 5353
140 Leadenhall Street, London EC3V 4QT *Tel:* 020 7398 5087
Email: peter.levene@starrcompanies.com

LABOUR

LEVY, LORD

LEVY (Life Baron), Michael Abraham Levy; cr. 1997. Born 11 July 1944; Son of Samuel and Annie Levy; Married Gilda Altbach 1967 (1 son 1 daughter).
Education: Hackney Downs Grammar School, London; FCA 1966.
Non-political career: Lubbock Fine (Chartered Accountants) 1961-66; Principal, M. Levy & Co. 1966-69; Partner, Wagner Prager Levy & Partners 1969-73; Chair, Magnet Group of Companies 1973-88; Vice-chair: Phonographic Performance Ltd 1979-84, British Phonographic Industry Ltd 1984-87; Chair: D & J Securities Ltd 1988-92, M & G Records Ltd 1992-97, Chase Music Ltd (formerly M & G Music Ltd) 1992-2008, Wireart Ltd 1992-2008; Principal, Global Consultancy Services.
Political career: *House of Lords:* Raised to the peerage as Baron Levy, of Mill Hill in the London Borough of Barnet 1997. Personal Envoy to the Prime Minister and Adviser on the Middle East 1998-2007. *Other:* Member, Labour Party Donations Committee 2002-07.
Political interests: Voluntary sector, social welfare, education, Middle East peace process; North Africa, Latin and Central America, Middle East, European countries, Kazakhstan.
Other: Fellow, Institute of Chartered Accountants; United Joint Israel Appeal: National Campaign Chair 1982-85, Honorary Vice-President 1994-2000, Honorary President 2000-; JFS (Jews Free School): Governor 1990-95, Honorary President 1995-2001, President 2001; Member: World Board of Governors of the Jewish Agency 1990-95, Keren Hayesod World Board of Governors 1991-95; World chair, Youth Aliyah Committee of Jewish Agency Board of Governors 1991-95; Chair, British Music Industry Trust Awards Committee 1992-95; Jewish Care: Chair 1992-97, President 1998-; Chair: Chief Rabbinate Awards for Excellence 1992-2007, Foundation for Education 1993-2006; Vice-chair, Central Council for Jewish Social Services 1994-2006; Patron, British Music Industry Trust Awards 1995; Chair, Jewish Care Community Foundation 1995-2010; Member: World Commission on Israel-Diaspora Relations 1995-, International Board of Governors, Peres Centre for Peace 1997-2009, Advisory Council, Foreign Policy Centre 1997-2006; Patron, Prostate Cancer Charitable Trust 1997-; President, Community Service Volunteers 1998-; Patron, Friends of Israel Educational Trust 1998-; Member: National Council for Voluntary Organisations Advisory Committee 1998-2011, Community Legal Service Champions Panel 1999-2010; Patron, Save A Child's Heart Foundation 2000-; Member, Honorary Committee, Israel Britain and the Commonwealth Association 2000-; Chair, board of trustees, New Policy Network Foundation 2000-07; Executive committee member, Chai-Lifeline 2001-02; Honorary Patron, Cambridge University Jewish Society 2002-; Patron, Simon Marks Jewish Primary School Trust 2002-; Former trustee and co-chair, Academy Sponsors Trust; President, Specialist Schools and Academics Trust 2005-08; Trustee and member, executive committee, Jewish Leadership Council (JLC) 2006-11; President, Jewish Lads' and Girls' Brigade (JLGB) 2006-; Member, development board, British Library 2008-11; Patron, Mathilda Marks-Kennedy Jewish Primary School; FCA 1966. Honorary Doctorate, Middlesex University 1999. B'nai B'rith First Lodge Award 1994; Friends of the Hebrew University of Jerusalem Scopus Award 1998; Israel Policy Forum (USA) Special Recognition Award 2003.
Publications: A Question of Honour (2008).
Recreations: Tennis, swimming.
The Lord Levy, House of Lords, London SW1A 0PW
Tel: 020 7219 1470 *Email:* ml@lordlevy.com

CROSSBENCH

LEWIS OF NEWNHAM, LORD

LEWIS OF NEWNHAM (Life Baron), Jack Lewis; cr. 1989. Born 13 February 1928; Son of late Robert Lewis; Married Elfreida Mabel Lamb 1951 (1 son 1 daughter).
Education: Barrow Grammar School; London University (BSc chemistry 1949; DSc 1961); Nottingham University (PhD chemistry 1952); Manchester University (MSc chemistry 1962); Sidney Sussex College, Cambridge (MA chemistry 1970; ScD chemistry 1977).
Non-political career: Chemistry lecturer: Sheffield University 1954-56, Imperial College, London 1956-57; Chemistry lecturer/reader, University College, London 1957-61; Professor of chemistry: Manchester University 1961-67, University College, London 1967-70, Cambridge University 1970-95; Member, Cambridge University 1970-; First Warden, Robinson College, Cambridge 1975-2001; Council member, SERC 1979-84; Royal Society: Council member 1982-84, 1996-98, Vice-President 1983-84; Chair: Visiting Committee, Cranfield Institute of Technology 1982-92, Royal Commission on Environmental Pollution 1986-92; President, Royal Society of Chemistry 1986-88; UK Science Representative on NATO Science Committee 1986-98; Director, The BOC Foundation 1990-2003; Council member, Royal Society of Chemistry 1992-95, 1996-98; President, National Society for Clean Air and Environmental Protection 1993-95; Chair, ESART Board 1998-2006.

Political career: *House of Lords:* Raised to the peerage as Baron Lewis of Newnham, of Newnham in the County of Cambridgeshire 1989. Chair: EU Sub-committee C 1993-95, Standing Committee on Structural Safety 1998-2002; Member: Science and Technology Sub-committee II (Aircraft Cabin Environment) 2000, Science and Technology 2000-05, Science and Technology Sub-committees: I (Fighting Infection) 2002-03, II (Innovations in Computer Processors/Microprocessing/Science and the Regional Development Agencies) 2002-03, II (Renewable Energy) 2003-04, EU Sub-committee D (Environment, Agriculture, Public Health and Consumer Protection/Environment and Agriculture) 2003-06, Science and Technology Sub-committee II (Energy Efficiency) 2004-; Co-opted member: Science and Technology Sub-committee I (Waste Reduction) 2007-08, EU Sub-committee D (Environment and Agriculture) 2009-10; Member EU Sub-committee D: (Agriculture, Fisheries and Environment) 2010-12, (Agriculture, Fisheries, Environment and Energy) 2012-.

Political interests: Education, environment.

Other: Foreign member, American Academy of Arts and Sciences 1983, Patron, Student Community Action Development Unit 1985-; Fellow, Indian National Science Academy 1985; Foreign associate, National Academy of Sciences, USA 1987; Foreign member, National Academy of Science (USA) 1987; Chair, Executive Committee of the Cambridge Overseas Trust 1988-2009; Trustee: Kennedy Memorial Trust 1989-99, Croucher Foundation 1989-98; Foreign fellow, Bangladesh Academy of Sciences 1992; Fellow, Royal Society of Arts; Foreign member: American Philosophical Society 1994, Accademia Nazionale dei Lincei, Italy 1995, Polish Academy of Arts and Sciences 1996-; Honorary President, Environmental Industries Commission 1996-2000; Honorary Member, Society of Chemical Industry 1996; Chair, The Leys School Governors 1997-2002; President: Arthritis Research Campaign 1998-, Veolia Environmental Trust 2001-; FRS 1973; Honorary Fellow CIWM 2010. Honorary Fellow: Sidney Sussex College, Fellow 1970-77, Australian Chemical Society 1988-, Royal Society of Chemistry 1998-; 19 honorary doctorates from the UK, Canada, Hong Kong, France and Ireland; Four honorary university fellowships. Kt 1982; Chevalier dans l'Ordre des Palmes Académiques 1993; Commander Cross of the Order of Merit (Poland) 1996; United Oxford and Cambridge University.

Publications: Sundry publications.

Recreations: Music, walking.

Professor the Lord Lewis of Newnham, House of Lords, London SW1A 0PW
Tel: 020 7219 5093
Robinson College, Grange Road, Cambridge CB3 9AN *Tel:* 01223 339198
Email: jl219@cam.ac.uk

LEXDEN, LORD

LEXDEN (Life Baron), Alistair Basil Cooke; cr 2010. Born 20 April 1945; Son of Dr Basil and Nancy Cooke; Single.

Education: Framlingham College, Suffolk; Peterhouse, Cambridge (BA, MA 1970); Queen's University, Belfast (PhD 1979).

Non-political career: Lecturer and tutor in modern history, Queen's University, Belfast 1971-77; Political adviser to Shadow Minister for Northern Ireland 1977-79; Conservative Research Department: Desk officer 1977-83, Assistant director 1983-85, Deputy director 1985-97; Director, Conservative Political Centre 1988-97; Official historian of the Conservative Party 2009-.

CONSERVATIVE

Political career: *House of Lords:* Raised to the peerage as Baron Lexden, of Lexden in the County of Essex and of Strangford in the County of Down 2010. Member: EU Sub-committee G (Social Policies and Consumer Protection) 2012, Constitution 2012-. *Other:* Co-chairman, Conservative History Group 2012-. *Councils and public bodies:* General Secretary, Independent Schools Council 1997-2004.

Political interests: Northern Ireland, education, constitutional and electoral affairs; All countries of the United Kingdom.

Other: President, Northern Ireland Schools Debating Competition 2001-; Co-Chairman, London Friends of the Belfast Buildings Preservation Trust 2006-; Vice-President, Council of British International Schools 2011-; President: Independent Schools Association 2013-, Council for Independent Education 2013-. OBE 1988; Carlton Club.

Publications: Joint-editor, Lord Carlingford's Journal (1971); Co-author, The Governing Passion: Cabinet Government and Party Politics in Britain 1885-86 (1974); Editor: The Ashbourne Papers 1869-1913 (1974), The Conservative Party's Campaign Guides, Seven Volumes (1987-2005), The Conservative Party: Seven Historical Studies (1997), The Conservative Research Department 1929-2004 (2004); Co-author, The Carlton Club 1832-2007 (2007); Tory Heroine: Dorothy Brant and the Rise of Conservative Women (2008); A Party of Change: A Brief History of the Conservatives (2008); Contributor, Between the Thin Blue Lines (2008); Editor and co-author, Tory Policy Making: The Conservative Research Department 1929-2009 (2009); A Gift from the Churchills: The Primrose League 1883-2004 (2010); Contributor, Enoch at 100: A Re-evaluation of Enoch Powell (2012).

Recreations: Writing letters to the press (and getting them published), collecting royal and political memorabilia, book reviewing.

The Lord Lexden OBE, House of Lords, London SW1A 0PW
Tel: 020 7219 8216 *Email:* lexdena@parliament.uk *Website:* www.alistairlexden.org.uk

NON-AFFILIATED

LICHFIELD, LORD BISHOP OF

LICHFIELD (98th Bishop of), Jonathan Michael Gledhill. Born 15 February 1949; Married Jane (later Dr) Street 1971 (1 son 1 daughter).

Education: Strode's School, Egham; Keele University (BA 1972); Bristol University (MA 1975); Trinity College, Bristol (certificate in theological studies 1975); French, German.

Non-political career: Ordained deacon 1975; Curate, All Saints, Marple, Greater Manchester 1975-78; Priest 1976; Priest-in-charge, St George's, Folkestone 1978-83; Vicar, St Mary Bredin, Canterbury 1983-96; Tutor, Canterbury School of Ministry/South East Institute for Theological Studies 1983-96; Rural dean, Canterbury 1988-94; Bishop suffragan of Southampton 1996-2003; Bishop of Lichfield 2003-.

Political career: *House of Lords:* Entered House of Lords 2009. *Councils and public bodies:* Member: Meissen Commission (Church of England and German evangelical church link) 1993-97, General Synod 1995-96, 2003-; Chair: National College of Evangelists 1998-2010, Anglican/ Old Catholic International Co-ordinating Council 1998-2013.

Political interests: West Midlands; France, Switzerland.

Other: Honorary doctorate Keele University 2007. Honorary canon, Canterbury Cathedral 1992-96.

Publications: Leading a Local Church in the Age of the Spirit (SPCK London, 2003).

Recreations: Sailing, skiing.

Rt Rev the Lord Bishop of Lichfield, House of Lords, London SW1A 0PW
Tel: 020 7219 5353
Bishop's House, 22 The Close, Lichfield, Staffordshire WS13 7LG *Tel:* 01543 306000
Fax: 01543 306009 *Email:* bishop.lichfield@lichfield.anglican.org
Website: www.lichfield.anglican.org

LABOUR

LIDDELL OF COATDYKE, BARONESS

LIDDELL OF COATDYKE (Life Baroness), Helen Lawrie Liddell; cr 2010. Born 6 December 1950; Daughter of Hugh and Bridget Reilly; Married Dr Alistair Liddell 1972 (1 son 1 daughter).
Education: St Patrick's High School, Coatbridge; Strathclyde University (BA economics 1972); French.

Non-political career: Head, Economic Department, Scottish TUC 1971-76; Economics correspondent, BBC Scotland 1976-77; General secretary, Labour Party in Scotland 1977-88; Director, personnel and public affairs, Scottish Daily Record and Sunday Mail (1986) Ltd 1988-92; Chief executive, Business Venture Programme 1993-94; High Commissioner, Australia 2005-09. GMB; NUJ.

Political career: *House of Commons:* Contested Fife East October 1974 general election. MP (Labour) for Monklands East 30 June 1994 by-election to 1997, and for Airdrie and Shotts 1997-2005. Opposition Spokesperson on Scotland 1995-97; Economic Secretary, HM Treasury 1997-98; Minister of State: Scottish Office (Minister for Education) 1998-99, Department of the Environment, Transport and the Regions (Minister for Transport) 1999, Department of Trade and Industry (Minister for Energy and Competitiveness in Europe) 1999-2001; Secretary of State for Scotland 2001-03. Member, Labour Party Departmental Committee for the Treasury 1997-2001. *House of Lords:* Raised to the peerage as Baroness Liddell of Coatdyke, of Airdrie in Lanarkshire 2010. Member: Selection 2011, Joint Committee on the Draft Detention of Terrorist Suspects (Temporary Extension) Bills 2011, EU Sub-committee E: Justice, Institutions and Consumer Protection 2013-, Partnerships (Prosecution) (Scotland) Bill 2013-. *Councils and public bodies:* Commissioner, BBC Privacy Commission 2011; Member, Inquiry into the Mull of Kintyre Helicopter Accident 2010-11.

Political interests: Media, foreign affairs, economic policy, trade and industry, small businesses, energy and climate change, defence and security; Australia, China, Europe, USA.

Other: Vice-chair, Rehab Scotland 1990-92; Chair, Independent Review into the future of the Scottish Symphony Orchestra and Orchestra of Scottish Opera 1993-94; Chair, UN5O: Scotland 1994; Associate member, BUPA 2010; Director, British-Australia Society 2011-; The Cook Society 2011-; Trustee: Northcote Educational Trust, Arthur Philip Trust; St Andrew's Hospice, Airdrie; Maggie's Centres. Honorary Doctor of Laws, University of Strathclyde 2005. PC 1998.

Publications: Elite (1990).

Recreations: Cooking, hill-walking, music, writing.

Rt Hon the Baroness Liddell of Coatdyke, House of Lords, London SW1A 0PW
Tel: 020 7219 6960 *Email:* liddellh@parliament.uk

LABOUR

LIDDLE, LORD

Opposition Spokesperson for Foreign and Commonwealth Office and for Business, Innovation and Skills

LIDDLE (Life Baron), Roger John Liddle; cr 2010. Born 14 June 1947; Son of late John Thwaites Liddle, railway clerk, and late Elizabeth Liddle, née Temple; Married Caroline Thomson 1983 (1 son).

Education: Carlisle Grammar School; Queen's College, Oxford (BA modern history 1968, MA; MPhil management studies 1970).

Non-political career: Oxford School of Social and Administrative Studies 1970-74; Industrial relations officer, Electricity Council 1974-76; Special adviser to Rt Hon William Rodgers MP 1976-81: as Secretary of State for Transport 1976-79; Director, Public Policy Centre 1982-87; Managing director, Prima Europe Ltd 1987-97; Special adviser to Rt Hon Tony Blair MP as Prime Minister 1997-2004; European Commission: Member of cabinet of Peter Mandelson as Trade Commissioner 2004-06, Principal adviser to the President of the European Commission 2006-07; Chair, advisory board, New Industry New Jobs Panel, Department for Business, Innovation and Skills 2008-10. Member, GMB.

Political career: *House of Lords:* Raised to the peerage as Baron Liddle, of Carlisle in the County of Cumbria 2010. Opposition Whip 2011-13; Opposition Spokesperson for: Foreign and Commonwealth Office (Europe) 2012-, Business, Innovation and Skills 2013-. Member: European Union 2010, EU Sub-committee G (Social Policies and Consumer Protection) 2011. *Other:* Member, National committee, Social Democratic Party 1981-86; Labour Campaign for Electoral Reform; Labour Movement for Europe. *Councils and public bodies:* Oxford City Council: Councillor 1971-76, Deputy Leader 1973-76; Councillor, Lambeth Borough Council 1982-86, 1994-95; Chair, Cumbria Vision 2007-10; Councillor, Cumbria County Council 2013-.

Political interests: Future of European Union, European social democracy, industrial economic questions, regional policy, future of welfare state, universities; France, Germany, Italy, Sweden, USA.

Other: Member: Fabian Society, Progress; Policy Network: Vice-chair 2007-09, Chair 2009-. Pro-Chancellor, Lancaster University 2013-; Reform.

Publications: Co-author (with Peter Mandelson), The Blair Revolution (1996); Author, The New Case for Europe (2005); Co-author: Global Europe, Social Europe (2006), Beyond New Labour (2009).

Recreations: Tennis, opera, reading history and politics, walking.

The Lord Liddle, House of Lords, London SW1A 0PW
Tel: 020 7219 5353 *Email:* liddler@parliament.uk
Policy Network, 11 Tufton Street, London SW1P 3QB *Tel:* 020 7340 2200
Email: erinloch@policy-network.net

CONSERVATIVE

LINDSAY, EARL OF

LINDSAY (16th Earl of, S), James Randolph Lindsay-Bethune; cr. 1633; Viscount Garnock (S) 1703; Lord Lindsay of the Byres (S) 1445; Lord Parbroath (S) 1633; Lord Kilbirnie, Kingsburn and Drumry (S) 1703. Born 19 November 1955; Son of 15th Earl and Honorary Mary-Clare Douglas Scott Montagu, daughter of 2nd Baron Montagu of Beaulieu, KCIE, CSI, DL; Married Diana Mary Chamberlayne-Macdonald 1982 (2 sons 3 daughters inc. twins).

Education: Eton College; Edinburgh University (BA economic history 1978, MA); University of California, Davis (Land use).

Non-political career: Chair, Assured British Meat Ltd 1997-2001; Non-executive director, UA Group plc 1998-2005; Chair: Scottish Quality Salmon 1999-2006, UA Properties Ltd 1999-2000, UA Forestry Ltd 1999-2000, Genesis Quality Assurance Ltd 2001-02, Elmwood College Board of Management 2001-09; Managing director, Marine Stewardship Council International 2001-04;

Non-executive director: Mining (Scotland) Ltd/Scottish Resources Group Ltd 2001-13, British Polythene Industries plc 2006-; Associate director, National Non-Food Crops Centre 2007-; Chair: Scottish Agricultural College Ltd/SRUC-Scotland's Rural College 2007-, British Polythene Pension Scheme 2009-.

Political career: *House of Lords:* First entered House of Lords 1989; Government Whip 1995; Parliamentary Under-Secretary of State, Scottish Office 1995-97; Opposition Spokesperson for Green Issues June-October 1997; Elected hereditary peer 1999-. Member: European Communities Sub-committee C (Environment and Social Affairs) 1993-95, 1997-98, Sustainable Development 1994-95, Science and Technology Sub-committee II (Energy Efficiency) 2004-, Partnerships (Prosecution) (Scotland) Bill 2013. *Councils and public bodies:* Board member, Cairngorms Partnership 1998-2003; Member: Secretary of State's Advisory Group on Sustainable Development 1998-99, UK Round Table on Sustainable Development 1998-99; Chair: United Kingdom Accreditation Service 1998-; Better Regulation Commission: Member 2006-08, Deputy chair 2007-08; DL, Fife 2007-; Member: Advisory board, Business and a Sustainable Environment 2007-, Commission on Scottish Devolution 2008-09, Risk and Regulation Advisory Council 2008-10.

Political interests: Environment, agriculture, rural affairs, energy, food industry, Scotland, regulation, accreditation, standards.

Other: Inter-Parliamentary Union Committee on Environment: Member 1993-95, Vice-chair 1994-95; Chair, Landscape Foundation 1992-95; International Tree Foundation: President 1995-2005, Vice-President 2005-; Vice-President, Royal Smithfield Club 1998-; Director, West Highland Rail Heritage Trust Ltd 1998-2006; RSPB: Chair, Scotland 1998-2003, UK vice-president 2004-; Royal Scottish Geographical Society: President 2005-12, Vice-President 2012-; President, Royal Highland Agriculture Society of Scotland 2005-06; Chair, Moorland Forum 2007-; Director and trustee, Leven Valley Development Trust 2009-; Honorary Fellow, Institute of Wastes Management 1998-; Fellow, Royal Agricultural Societies 2003. Honorary doctorate, Glasgow University 2012. Green Ribbon Political Award 1995; New (Edinburgh).

The Earl of Lindsay, House of Lords, London SW1A 0PW
Tel: 020 7219 5353 *Fax:* 020 7219 5979 *Email:* lindsayj@parliament.uk
Lahill, Upper Largo, Fife KY8 6JE

CONSERVATIVE

LINGFIELD, LORD

LINGFIELD (Life Baron), Robert George Alexander Balchin; cr 2010. Born 31 July 1942; Son of late Leonard George and Elizabeth Balchin; Married Jennifer Kinlay 1970 (twin sons, 1 deceased).

Education: Bec School; London University; Hull University.

Non-political career: Honorary Colonel, Humberside & South Yorkshire ACF 2004-12. Teacher 1964-69; Researcher, Institute of Education, Hull University 1969-71; Headmaster, Hill School 1972-80; Chairman, HSW Ltd 1980-2000; St John Ambulance: Assistant director-general 1982-84, Director-general 1984-90, Member, Chapter-General, Order of St John 1984-99; Joint founder and Treasurer, Catch 'em Young Project Trust 1984-98; Chairman: Grant-Maintained Schools Foundation 1989-99, Pardoe-Blacker (Publishing) Ltd 1989-99, CEFM Ltd 1994-; The Imperial Society of Knights Bachelor: Council Member 1995-, Knight Registrar 1998-2006, Knight Principal and Chairman of Knight Bachelors' Council 2006-, Knight President 2012-; President: English Schools Orchestra 1998-, League of Mercy 1999-; Deputy patron, National Association for Gifted Children 1999-; Patron, Gateway Training Centre for Homeless 1999-2010; Member, Court, Leeds University 1995-2000; Goldsmith' College, London: Council member 1997-2005, Deputy chair, council 1999-2005; Chairman: Blacker-Publishing Ltd 2003-09, Education Commission 2003-10, Government Review, Professionalism in Further Education 2012; Chartered Institution for Further Education 2014-.

Political career: *House of Lords:* Raised to the peerage as Baron Lingfield, of Lingfield in the County of Surrey 2010. Member EU Sub-committee F (Home Affairs, Health and Education) 2012-13. *Councils and public bodies:* Councillor, Surrey County Council 1981-85; Member, Funding Agency for Schools 1994-97; DL, Greater London 2001.

Political interests: Education; UK.

Other: Chairman: Balchin Family Society 1993-, ARNI Trust 2008-, The Maritime Heritage Foundation 2011-; FCP 1971; Honorary FHS 1987; Honorary FCP 1987; Honorary FCGI 1998. Goldsmiths' Company 1980; Broderers' Company 2004-12. Freeman, City of London 1980. Pro-chancellor, Brunel University 2008-13. DLitt, Hull University. KStJ 1984; SMOM 1987; Kt 1993; Athenæum.

Publications: Emergency Aid in Schools (1984); Choosing a State School (1989); Many articles on politics and education.

Recreations: Restoration of ancient house.

The Lord Lingfield Kt DL, House of Lords, London SW1A 0PW
Tel: 020 7219 5353

LINKLATER OF BUTTERSTONE, BARONESS

LINKLATER OF BUTTERSTONE (Life Baroness), Veronica Linklater; cr. 1997. Born 15 April 1943; Daughter of late Lt-Col Archibald Michael Lyle and late Elizabeth Sinclair, daughter of 1st Viscount Thurso; Married Magnus Linklater 1967 (2 sons 1 daughter).

Education: Cranborne Chase School; Sussex University (1962); London University (DipSoc admin 1966).

Non-political career: Childcare officer, London Borough of Tower Hamlets 1967-68; Co-founder, Visitors Centre, Pentonville Prison 1971-77; Prison Reform Trust, Winchester prison project 1981-82.

LIBERAL DEMOCRAT

Political career: *House of Commons:* Contested (Lib Dem) Perth and Kinross 1995 by-election. *House of Lords:* Raised to the peerage as Baroness Linklater of Butterstone, of Riemore in Perth and Kinross 1997. Liberal Democrat Spokesperson for Penal Affairs 2005-07. *Councils and public bodies:* JP, Inner London 1985-88; Member, Children's Panel, Edinburgh South 1989-97.

Political interests: Education, youth affairs, penal affairs and policy.

Other: Member, trustee, patron numerous organisations, especially relating to crime and punishment, including: The Visitors Centre, Pentonville Prison 1972-95; President, Society of Friends of Dunkeld Cathedral 1989-; Vice-chair, Pushkin Prizes, Scotland 1989-; Founder and President, The New School, Butterstone 1991-; Member, Beattie Committee on post-school provision for young people with special needs 1997-98; Trustee, Esmée Fairbairn Foundation; Foundation Patron, QM University College, Edinburgh 1998; Patron: Airborne Initiative (Scotland) Ltd 1998-2004, University of the Highlands and Islands 1999-2001, Mansfield Traquair 1999-; Patron, National Schizophrenia Fellowship, Scotland (Support in Mind since 2010) 2000-; Secretary, Scottish Peers Association 2000-07; Member, Scottish Committee, Barnado's 2001-04; Assessor to the Chancellor, Napier University Court 2001-04; Chair, Rethinking Crime and Punishment 2001-08; Vice-President, The Butler Trust 2001-; Trustee, Lyle Charitable Trust 2001-; Patron: National Family and Parenting Institute 2002-, Research Autism Trust 2004-, The Calyx 2004-08; Adviser, Koestler Award Trust 2004-; Patron, The Probation Boards Association 2005-; Member, The Scottish Association for the Study of Offending 2005-; Council member, Winston Churchill Memorial Trust 2005-; Patron: Action for Prisoners' Families 2005-, PUSH 2007-, Home Start 2007-, University of St Andrew's Medical Campaign Committee 2007-; President: Crime Reduction Initiative 2007-10, Supporting Others Through Voluntary Action 2009-; Patron: Tacade 2009-12, Epilepsy Scotland 2009-; The New School, Butterstone. One honorary degree.

Recreations: Family, music, theatre, reading.

The Baroness Linklater of Butterstone, House of Lords, London SW1A 0PW
Tel: 020 7219 6914 *Fax:* 020 7219 2377 *Email:* linklaterv@parliament.uk
Tel: 0131-557 5705 *Fax:* 0131-557 9757 *Email:* v.linklater@blueyonder.co.uk

LIPSEY, LORD

LIPSEY (Life Baron), David Lawrence Lipsey; cr. 1999. Born 21 April 1948; Son of late Lawrence Lipsey and Penelope Lipsey; Married Margaret Robson 1982 (1 daughter 2 stepsons).

Education: Bryanston School, Dorset; Magdalen College, Oxford (BA philosophy, politics and economics 1970).

Non-political career: Research assistant, GMWU 1970-72; Political adviser to Anthony Crosland (in Opposition, DoE and FCO) 1972-77; Adviser to 10 Downing Street 1977-79; *New Society:* Journalist 1979-80, Editor 1986-88; Journalist, then economics editor, *Sunday Times* 1980-86; Founder/deputy editor, *Sunday Correspondent* 1988-90; Associate (acting deputy) editor, *The Times* 1990-92; Journalist, political editor, public policy editor, *The Economist* 1992-99; Visiting professor, Ulster University 1993-98; Public interest director, Personal Investment Authority 1994-2000; Chairman: Impower 2001-03, Shadow Racing Trust 2002-07, British Greyhound Racing Board 2004-08; Non-executive director, LWT/ITV London 2004-06; Visiting professor, University of Salford 2008-12; Visiting fellow, Centre for European Studies, Havard University, USA 2011.

Political career: *House of Lords:* Raised to the peerage as Baron Lipsey, of Tooting Bec in the London Borough of Wandsworth 1999. Member, Speakers' Working Group on All-Party Groups 2011-12. Member: Economic Affairs 2009-, Sub-committee on Economic Affairs Finance Bill 2012-, Information 2013-. *Other:* Secretary, Streatham Labour Party 1970-72. *Councils and public bodies:* Member: Jenkins Commission on Electoral Reform 1998, Royal Commission on Long-term Care of the Elderly 1998-99, Davies Panel on BBC Licence Fee 1999; Council member, Advertising Standards Authority 1999-2005; Chair, Financial Services' Consumers Panel 2008.

Political interests: Horse racing, elderly people, electoral reform, broadcasting, machinery of government, greyhound welfare, gambling, financial services.

Other: Chair: Fabian Society 1982-83, Make Votes Count 1999-2006, Social Market Foundation 2000-10; Member, advisory council, Constitution Unit; President, British Harness Racing Club; Patron, Glasbury Arts Festival; Trustee: New Cambrian Orchestra Trust, Sidney Nolan Trust; Chair: Straight Statistics 2008-11, Trinity Laban Conservatoire of Music and Dance 2012-; President, Society of Later Life Advisers 2099-.

Publications: Labour and Land (1972); Editor, The Socialist Agenda (1981); The Name of the Rose (1992); The Secret Treasury (2000); In the Corridors of Power: An Autobiography (Biteback, 2012); Counter Coup.

Recreations: Golf, harness, horse and greyhound racing, opera, walking, cooking.

The Lord Lipsey, House of Lords, London SW1A 0PW
Tel: 020 7219 5353 *Email:* lipseyd@parliament.uk
Website: lordsoftheblog.net/category/lord-lipsey

LISTER OF BURTERSETT, BARONESS

LABOUR

LISTER OF BURTERSETT (Life Baroness), Margot Ruth Aline Lister; cr 2011. Born 3 May 1949; Daughter of Dr Werner Bernard and Daphne Lister; Single.

Education: Moreton Hall, Shropshire; Essex University (BA sociology 1970); Sussex University (MA multi-racial studies 1971); Rusty French and German.

Non-political career: Child Poverty Action Group: Legal research officer 1971-75, Assistant director 1975-77, Deputy director 1977-79, Director 1979-87; Professor of Applied Social Studies, Bradford University 1987-93; Loughborough University: Professor of Social Policy 1994-2010, Emeritus Professor of Social Policy 2010-; Donald Dewar Visiting Professor of Social Justice, Glasgow University 2005-06. University and College Union (when employed).

Political career: *House of Lords:* Raised to the peerage as Baroness Lister of Burtersett, of Nottingham in the County of Nottinghamshire 2011. Member Joint Committee on Human Rights 2012-.

Political interests: Poverty, social security, welfare reform, gender, children, refugees and asylum seekers; Australia, Japan, Nordic countries, USA.

Other: Vice-chair NVCO 1991-93; Founding Academician, Academy of Social Sciences 1999; Member: Opsahl Commission 1992-93, Commission for Social Justice 1992-94, Commission on Poverty, Participation and Power 1999-2000; Trustee, Community Development Foundation (Government appointment) 2000-10; Member: Fabian Commission on Life Chances and Child Poverty 2004-06, National Equality Panel (Government appointment) 2009-10; Fellow, British Academy 2009; Honorary President, Child Poverty Action Group 2010-; Vice-chair, Fair Pay Network 2011-; Board member, Smith Institute; Chair, management committee, Compass 2011-; Patron, Just Fair 2012-; Social Policy Association. Honorary LLD, Manchester University 1987; Honorary DLitt, Glasgow Caledonian University 2011; Honorary LLD, Brighton University 2012; DUniv, Essex University 2012; Honorary D.Sc., Lincoln University. Lifetime Achievement Award, Social Policy Association. CBE 1999.

Publications: Supplementary Benefit Rights (1974); Welfare Benefits (1981); The Exclusive Society (1990); Women's Economic Dependency and Social Security (1992); Citizenship: feminist perspectives (1997, 2003); Poverty (2004); Co-author, Gendering Citizenship in Western Europe (2007); Co-editor, Why Money Matters (2008); Understanding Theories and Concepts in Social Policy (2010).

Recreations: Walking, watching tennis, tai chi, music, films, theatre, mindfulness.

The Baroness Lister of Burtersett CBE, House of Lords, London SW1A 0PW
Tel: 020 7219 8984 *Email:* listerr@parliament.uk
Email: m.r.lister@lboro.ac.uk *Website:* www.lboro.ac.uk/departments/ss/staff/lister.html

LISTOWEL, EARL OF

CROSSBENCH

LISTOWEL (6th Earl of, I), Francis Michael Hare; cr. 1822; 6th Viscount Ennismore and Listowel (I) 1816; 6th Baron Ennismore (I) 1800; 4th Baron Hare (UK) 1869. Born 28 June 1964; Son of 5th Earl.

Education: Westminster School; Queen Mary and Westfield College, London (BA English literature 1992).

Political career: *House of Lords:* First entered House of Lords 1997. Sits as Baron Hare; Elected hereditary peer 1999-. Member: House of Lords Offices Library and Computers Sub-committee 2000-02, European Union Sub-committee F (Home Affairs) 2003-07.

Political interests: Young under-privileged; Angola.

Other: Trustee, Michael Sieff Foundation; Patron: Voice, The Who Cares? Trust, Caspari Foundation; Anna Freud Centre; Who Cares? Trust; Beanstalk. Honorary doctorate, University of East London; Reform.
Recreations: Singing, music, art.
The Earl of Listowel, House of Lords, London SW1A 0PW
Tel: 020 7219 2247 *Email:* listowelf@parliament.uk
Email: francis.listowel@googlemail.com

CONSERVATIVE

LIVERPOOL, EARL OF

LIVERPOOL (5th Earl of, UK), Edward Peter Bertram Savile Foljambe; cr. 1905; Viscount Hawkesbury; 5th Baron Hawkesbury (UK) 1893. Born 14 November 1944; Son of Captain Peter George William Savile Foljambe; Married Lady Juliana Noel 1970 (divorced 1994) (2 sons); married Comtesse Marie-Ange de Pierredon 1995 (divorced 2001); married Georgina Lederman 2002.
Education: Shrewsbury School; Perugia University, Italy (Studied Italian and Italian art 1963).
Non-political career: Melbourns Brewery Ltd, Stamford, Lincolnshire: Managing director 1971-76, Joint chair and managing director 1977-87; Director: Hilstone Developments Ltd 1986-91, Hart Hambleton plc 1986-92, Rutland Properties Ltd 1987-, J W Cameron & Co Ltd 1987-91; Chair and managing director, Maxador Ltd 1987-97; Chair, Rutland Management Ltd 1997-.
Political career: *House of Lords:* First entered House of Lords 1969; Elected hereditary peer 1999-. Member EU Sub-committee B (Internal Market, Infrastructure and Employment) 2012-.
Political interests: Environment, renewables, green energy, transport, IT, aviation.
Other: Turf, Pratt's, Air Squadron.
Recreations: Flying, golf, shooting.
The Earl of Liverpool, House of Lords, London SW1A 0PW
Tel: 020 7219 5406 *Fax:* 020 7219 0318 *Email:* liverpoole@parliament.uk

CONSERVATIVE

LIVINGSTON OF PARKHEAD, LORD

LIVINGSTON OF PARKHEAD (Life Baron), Ian Paul Livingston; cr 2013. Born 1964; Married Debbie (1 son 1 daughter).
Education: Manchester University (BA economics).
Non-political career: Arthur Andersen 1984-87; Bank of America International 1987-88; 3i Group plc 1988-91; Senior management roles 1991-96; Chief finance officer, Dixons Group plc 1996-2002; BT Group plc: Chief finance director 2002-05, Chief executive officer, BT Retail 2005-08; Chief executive officer 2008-13.
Political career: *House of Lords:* Raised to the peerage as Baron Livingston of Parkhead, of Parkhead in the City of Glasgow 2013.
Other: Associate, Institute of Chartered Accountants; Non-executive director, Freeserve plc 1999-2001, Hilton Group plc 2003-06, Celtic plc 2007-. Member, ICAEW (Institute of Chartered Accountants in England and Wales).
Recreations: Football.
The Lord Livingston of Parkhead, House of Lords, London SW1A 0PW
Tel: 020 7219 5353

CROSSBENCH

LLOYD OF BERWICK, LORD

LLOYD OF BERWICK (Life Baron), Anthony John Leslie Lloyd; cr. 1993. Born 9 May 1929; Son of late Edward Lloyd; Married Jane Shelford 1960.
Education: Eton College; Trinity College, Cambridge (MA classics and law 1952); Harvard Law School 1953.
Non-political career: Served Coldstream Guards (National Service) 1948. Called to Bar, Inner Temple 1955; QC 1967; Bencher 1976; Attorney-General to Prince of Wales 1969-77; Judge of the High Court of Justice, Queen's Bench Division 1978-84; Lord Justice of Appeal 1984-93; Security Commission: Vice-chair 1985-92, Chair 1992-99; Lord of Appeal in Ordinary 1993-99; Treasurer, Inner Temple 1999-2000.
Political career: *House of Lords:* Raised to the peerage as Baron Lloyd of Berwick, of Ludlay in the County of East Sussex 1993. Member House 2002-07; Chair Speakership of the House 2003-05; Ecclesiastical Committee: Chair 2008-10, 2011-, Member 2010-11; Chair Consumer Insurance (Disclosure and Representations) Bill 2011-12. *Councils and public bodies:* DL, East Sussex 1983-; Member: Top Salaries Review Body 1971-77, Committee on Royal Peculiars 2001.

Other: Director, Royal Academy of Music 1979-98; Vice-President, Corporation of the Sons of the Clergy 1996-2004; Trustee, Smith Charity 1971-91; Glyndebourne Arts Trust: Trustee 1973-, Chair 1975-94; Honorary FRAM 1985; Family Welfare Association. Salters' Company: Honorary Member 1988-, Master 2000-01. Choate Fellow, Harvard 1952; Fellow, Peterhouse, Cambridge 1953; Honorary Fellow, Peterhouse, Cambridge 1981; Honorary LLD: Queen's University Belfast 2005, Sussex University 2006. Kt 1978; PC 1984; Brooks's.

Publications: Report of Inquiry into Legislation on Terrorism (1995); Report of Public Inquiry into Gulf War Illnesses (2004).

Recreations: Music, carpentry.

Rt Hon the Lord Lloyd of Berwick DL, House of Lords, London SW1A 0PW
Tel: 020 7219 3169

LLOYD-WEBBER, LORD

CONSERVATIVE

LLOYD-WEBBER (Life Baron), Andrew Lloyd Webber; cr. 1997. Born 22 March 1948; Son of late William Southcombe Lloyd Webber, CBE, DMus, FRCM, FRCO, and late Jean Hermione Johnstone; Married Sarah Tudor 1971 (divorced 1983) (1 son 1 daughter); married Sarah Brightman 1984 (divorced 1990); married Madeleine Gurdon 1991 (2 sons 1 daughter).

Education: Westminster School; Royal College of Music.

Non-political career: Composer: Requiem, a setting of the Latin Requiem Mass 1985, Variations (based on A minor Caprice No 24 by Paganini) 1977, symphonic version 1986, Joseph and the Amazing Technicolour Dreamcoat (with lyrics by Timothy Rice) 1968, rev 1973, 1991, 2007, Jesus Christ Superstar (with lyrics by Timothy Rice) 1970, rev 1996, Gumshoe (film score) 1971, The Odessa File (film score) 1974, Jeeves (with lyrics by Alan Ayckbourn) 1975, Evita (with lyrics by Timothy Rice) 1976, (stage version 1978, 2006), Tell Me On a Sunday (with lyrics by Don Black) 1980, 2003, Cats (based on poems by T. S. Eliot) 1981, Song and Dance (with lyrics by Don Black) 1982, Starlight Express (with lyrics by Richard Stillgoe) 1984, Requiem Mass 1985, The Phantom of the Opera (with lyrics by Charles Hart and Richard Stilgoe) 1986, Aspects of Love (with lyrics by Don Black and Charles Hart) 1989, Sunset Boulevard (with lyrics by Don Black and Christopher Hampton) 1993, By Jeeves (with lyrics by Alan Ayckbourn) 1996, Whistle Down The Wind (with lyrics by Jim Steinman) 1996, The Beautiful Game (with lyrics by Ben Elton) 2000, The Woman in White 2004, Phantom Vegas 2006, Love Never Dies 2009; Producer: Joseph and the Amazing Technicolor Dreamcoat 1973, 1974, 1978, 1980, 1991, Jeeves Takes Charge 1975, Cats 1981, Song and Dance 1982, Daisy Pulls it Off 1983, 2002, The Hired Man 1984, Starlight Express 1984, On Your Toes 1984, The Phantom of the Opera 1986, Café Puccini 1986, The Resistable Rise of Arturo Ui 1987, Lend Me a Tenor 1988, Aspects of Love 1989, Shirley Valentine (Broadway) 1989, La Bete 1992, Sunset Boulevard 1993, By Jeeves 1996, Jesus Christ Superstar 1996, 1998, Whistle Down the Wind 1996, 1998, The Beautiful Game 2000, Bombay Dreams 2002, The Phantom of the Opera (film) 2004, The Sound of Music 2006, Love Never Dies 2009, The Wizard of Oz 2011; Film scores: Gumshoe 1971, The Odessa File 1974, Additional music: Evita 1996, The Wizard of Oz 2011.

Political career: *House of Lords:* Raised to the peerage as Baron Lloyd-Webber, of Sydmonton in the County of Hampshire 1997.

Political interests: Art, architecture.

Other: FRCM 1988. Star on the Hollywood Walk of Fame 1993; The American Society of Composers, Authors and Publishers Triple Play Award 'First recipient'; Seven Tony Awards; Five Drama Desk Awards; Three Grammy Awards; Seven Laurence Olivier Awards; Praemium Imperiale Award for Music 1995; Richard Rodger's Award for contributions to excellence in Musical Theatre 1996; Oscar and Golden Globe for Best Original Song *You Must Love Me* from Evita the movie; London Critics' Circle Award for Best Musical *The Beautiful Game* 2000; Two International Emmys; Kennedy Center Honor 2006; BASGA Fellowship 2012. Kt 1992.

Publications: Evita (with Tim Rice) (1978); Cats the book of the musical (1981); Joseph and the Amazing Technicolor Dreamcoat (with Tim Rice) (1982); The Complete Phantom of the Opera (1987); The Complete Aspects of Love (1989); Sunset Boulevard: From Movie to Musical (1993); Aspects of Andrew Lloyd Webber, The Essential Songbook.

Recreations: Architecture, art, food and wine.

The Lord Lloyd-Webber, House of Lords, London SW1A 0PW
Tel: 020 7219 5353

LABOUR

LOCKWOOD, BARONESS

LOCKWOOD (Life Baroness), Betty Lockwood; cr. 1978. Born 22 January 1924; Daughter of late Arthur and Edith Lockwood; Married Lieutenant-Colonel Cedric Hall 1978 (died 1988).

Education: East Borough Girls School, Dewsbury; Ruskin College, Oxford.

Non-political career: Labour Party: Assistant agent, Reading 1948-50, Secretary-Agent, Gillingham 1950-52, Yorkshire Regional Women's Officer 1952-67, Chief women's officer and assistant national agent 1967-75; Chair, Equal Opportunities Commission 1975-83.

Political career: *House of Lords:* Raised to the peerage as Baroness Lockwood, of Dewsbury in the County of West Yorkshire 1978. Deputy Speaker 1990-2007; Deputy Chair of Committees 1990-2007; On leave of absence 2013-. Member: Science and Technology 1983-89, European Communities 1985-93; Chair European Union Sub-committee on Social and Community Affairs 1990-93; Member: House of Lords Offices Finance and Staff Sub-committee 2001-02, Sub-committee on Lords' Interests 2007-08. Vice-chair PLP Departmental Committee for Education and Skills 2006-10. *Other:* Labour Party Parliamentary Group 1978-; Labour Peers' Group 1983-. *Councils and public bodies:* European Advisory Committee on Equal Opportunities for Women and Men 1982-83; Council member, Advertising Standards Authority 1983-92; President, Birkbeck College, London University 1983-89; Bradford University: Council member 1983-2005, Chancellor 1997-2005; Council member, Leeds University 1985-91; President, Hillcroft College 1987-94; DL, West Yorkshire 1987; Member, Leeds Development Corporation 1988-95; National Coal Mining Museum for England: Board member and chairman 1995-2007, President 2007-.

Political interests: Sex equality, education, industrial training, training, industry.

Other: Member, Council of Europe and WEU 1992-94; Fellow, Industry and Parliament Trust 1985; National Coal Mining Museum for England: Board member and chairman, 1995-2007, President 2007-; Member: National Trust, English Heritage, CPRE, Wildfowl and Wetlands Trust, Yorkshire Dales Society, RSPB, Wildlife Trust, Yorkshire, Yorkshire Dales National Park; President, Yorkshire Arthritis Research Campaign; Member, Soroptimist International. Bradford University: Pro-Chancellor 1987-97, Chancellor 1997-2005. Five honorary doctorates; Honorary Fellow: UMIST 1986, Birkbeck College, University of London 1987, RSA 1987, City and Guilds 2000; Soroptimist International.

Recreations: Yorkshire Dales, Opera North.

The Baroness Lockwood DL, House of Lords, London SW1A 0PW
Tel: 020 7219 3148 *Fax:* 020 7219 1372
6 Sycamore Drive, Addingham, Nr Ilkley, West Yorkshire LS29 0NY *Tel:* 01943 831098

NON-AFFILIATED

LONDON, LORD BISHOP OF

LONDON (132nd Bishop of), Richard John Carew Chartres. Born 11 July 1947; Son of late Richard Chartres and of Charlotte Chartres; Married Caroline Mary McLintock 1982 (2 sons 2 daughters).

Education: Hertford Grammar School; Trinity College, Cambridge (MA history 1968); Cuddesdon Theological College, Oxford; Lincoln Theological College (BD (Lambeth) 1984).

Non-political career: Deacon 1973; Priest 1974; Assistant Curate, St Andrew's, Bedford 1973-75; Bishop's Domestic Chaplain, St Albans 1975-80; Archbishop of Canterbury's Chaplain 1980-84; Vicar, St Stephen with St John, Westminster 1984-92; Director of Ordinands for the London Area 1985-92; Gresham Professor of Divinity 1986-92; Area Bishop of Stepney 1992-95; Honorary Bencher, Middle Temple; Bishop of London 1995-.

Political career: *House of Lords:* Entered House of Lords 1996. *Councils and public bodies:* Prelate Order of the British Empire 1995-; Prelate of the Imperial Society of Knights Bachelor; Dean of HM Chapels Royal 1996-; Chair: Church Buildings Division of Church of England, Church of England Shrinking the Footprint campaign, Church Commissioners' Board of Governors.

Political interests: London, environment, Europe; Europe.

Other: Member Court of Royal Foundation of St Katharine; Ecclesiastical Patron, The Prayer Book Society; Member: Ethics Committee of King Edward VII Hospital, St Ethelburga's Centre for Reconciliation and Peace (Founder and Life President), St Catherine's Sinai Foundation, St Andrew's Trust, All Saints Educational Trust, Sutton's Hospital in Charterhouse, Bromley and Sheppard's Colleges, C1 World Dialogue; President, The Bible Society; FSA 1999. Liveryman, Merchant Taylors' Company and Drapers' Company; Honorary Freeman: Weavers' Company, Leathersellers' Company, Woolmen Company, Vintners, Grocers, Water Conservators 2009. Freeman, City of London 1997. Honorary DD: London, City, Brunel Universities, King's College, London; Honorary DLitt, Guildhall London; Honorary doctorate, Sewanee: University of the South, Tennessee, USA. PC 1996; Ehrendomprediger (Germany) 2001; KCVO 2009; Garrick.

Publications: A Brief History of Gresham College (1997); Tree of Knowledge, Tree of Life (2004).
Recreations: Family.
Rt Rev and Rt Hon the Lord Bishop of London KCVO, House of Lords, London SW1A 0PW
Tel: 020 7219 5353
The Old Deanery, Dean's Court, London EC4V 5AA *Tel:* 020 7248 6233 *Fax:* 020 7248 9721
Email: bishop@londin.clara.co.uk *Website:* www.london.anglican.org

LOOMBA, LORD

LOOMBA (Life Baron), Rajinder Paul Loomba; cr 2011. Born 13 November 1943; Son of late Shri Jagiri Lal Loomba and late Shrimati Pushpa Wati Loomba; Married Veena (2 daughters 1 son).
Education: D.A.V. College, Jalandhar, India; State University of Iowa, USA (1962); Hindi, Punjabi.
Non-political career: Founder and chairman: Rinku Group 1980-, The Loomba Foundation 1997-.
Political career: *House of Lords:* Raised to the peerage as Baron Loomba, of Moor Park in the County of Hertfordshire 2011.
Political interests: Humanitarian causes, international development aid projects; South Asia, Bangladesh, Gabon, India, Kenya, Malawi, Nepal, Rwanda, South Africa, Sri Lanka, Uganda, UK, USA.

LIBERAL DEMOCRAT

Other: Vice-patron, Gates 1998-; Member: Rotary Club of London 2001-, Royal Institute of International Affairs 2002-09; Patron, Children in Need, India 2002-; Founding patron, World Punjabi Organisation 2002-; London First: Board member 2000-04, Member, President's Council 2004-06; Trustee, Maharajah Ranjit Singh Trust, India 2004-; Vice-president, Safer London Foundation 2006-; Chairman, Friends of the Three Faiths Forum 2007-; Member, Board of Governors, University of East London 2008-; Ambassador, Global Partnership Forum 2011-; Fellow, Royal Society of Arts; Oxfam, Barnardo's, YBI, Virgin Unite. Freeman, City of London 2000. International Excellence Award 1991; Hind Rattan Award 1991; Asian of the Year Award 1997; Pride of India Gold Medal 1998; Highly Commended New Initiative, Beacon Prize 2004; Priyadarshni Academy Global Award 2006; Charity of the Year, The Asian Who's Who awards 2006. CBE 2008. Moor Park Golf Club.
Recreations: Walking, reading, cooking.
The Lord Loomba CBE, House of Lords, London SW1A 0PW
Tel: 020 7219 3582 *Email:* loombar@parliament.uk
Loomba House, 622 Western Avenue, London W3 0TF *Tel:* 020 8896 9922 *Fax:* 020 8993 2736
Email: raj@loomba.com *Website:* www.theloombafoundation.org *Twitter:* @TheLoombaFndtn

LOTHIAN, MARQUESS OF

LOTHIAN (13th Marquess of, S), Michael Andrew Foster Jude Kerr; cr 1701; 14th Earl of Lothian (S) 1606; 15th Earl of Ancram (S) 1633; Viscount of Briene (S) 1701; Lord Newbottle (S) 1591; Lord Jedburgh (S) 1622; Lord Kerr (S) 1633; 8th Baron Ker (UK) 1821; (Life) Baron Kerr of Monteviot 2010. Born 7 July 1945; Son of late 12th Marquess of Lothian, KCVO, DL; Married Lady Jane Fitzalan-Howard daughter of 16th Duke of Norfolk 1975 (2 daughters).
Education: Ampleforth College, Yorkshire; Christ Church, Oxford (BA history 1966, MA); Edinburgh University (LLB 1968); French.

CONSERVATIVE

Non-political career: Advocate, Scottish Bar 1970; QC (Scot) 1996.
Political career: *House of Commons:* Contested (Conservative) West Lothian 1970 general election. MP for Berwickshire and East Lothian February-October 1974. Contested Berwickshire and East Lothian October 1974 general election. MP for Edinburgh South 1979-87. Contested Edinburgh South 1987 general election. MP for Devizes 1992-2010. Parliamentary Under-Secretary of State, Scottish Office 1983-87; Northern Ireland Office: Parliamentary Under-Secretary of State 1993-94, Minister of State 1994-97; Member Shadow Cabinet 1997-2005: Frontbench Spokesperson for Constitutional Affairs, with overall responsibility for Scottish and Welsh issues 1997-98, Deputy Leader of the Opposition 2001-05; Shadow Secretary of State for: Foreign and Commonwealth Affairs 2001-05, International Affairs 2003-05, Defence 2005; Member, Intelligence and Security Committee 2006-10. Member: Energy 1980-83, Public Accounts 1992-93. Chair: Conservative Parliamentary Constitutional Committee 1992-93, Conservative Party Committee for Constitutional Affairs, Scotland and Wales 1997-98, Conservative Defence/Foreign Affairs Policy Committee 2001-05. *House of Lords:* Created a life peer as Baron Kerr of Monteviot, of Monteviot in Roxburghshire 2010. Member Intelligence and Security Committee 2010-. *Other:* Chair, Conservative Party in Scotland 1980-83; Conservative Party: Deputy Chair June-October 1998, Chair 1998-2001, Contested leadership 2001; Member, Conservative Policy Board 2001-05. *Councils and public bodies:* DL, Roxburgh, Ettrick and Lauderdale 1990-.

Political interests: Housing, defence, agriculture; Middle East.
Other: Member, Board of Scottish Homes 1988-90; Chairman, Global Strategy Forum 2006-. Freedom: City of Gibraltar 2011, Devizes Town. PC 1996; New (Edinburgh), Whites, Beefsteak, Pratt's.
Publications: Numerous pamphlets published by Global Strategy Forum.
Recreations: Skiing, photography, folksinging.
Most Hon the Marquess of Lothian PC QC DL, House of Lords, London SW1A 0PW
Tel: 020 7219 5353 *Email:* lothianm@parliament.uk

CROSSBENCH

LOW OF DALSTON, LORD

LOW OF DALSTON (Life Baron), Colin MacKenzie Low; cr 2006. Born 23 September 1942; Son of Arthur Low and Catherine Cameron Low, née Anderson; Married Jill Irene Coton 1969 (1 son 1 daughter).
Education: Worcester College for the Blind; The Queen's College, Oxford (BA jursiprudence 1965, MA); Churchill College, Cambridge (Diploma criminology 1966).
Non-political career: Law lecturer, Leeds University 1968-84; Director, Disability Resource Team (initially within GLC) 1984-94; City University, London: Senior research fellow 1994-2000, Visiting professor 2001-. Member: Association of University Teachers 1968-84, 1994-, NALGO/ Unison 1984-94.
Political career: *House of Lords:* Raised to the peerage as Baron Low of Dalston, of Dalston in the London Borough of Hackney 2006. Member Procedure 2007-12. *Councils and public bodies:* Member: Special Educational Needs Tribunal 1994-, National Disability Council 1996-2000, Disability Rights Commission 2000-02.
Political interests: Disability, higher education, arts, music, broadcasting, crime and delinquency; Australia, South Africa, USA.
Other: Life member and holder of various offices, National Federation of the Blind 1969-92; Member and various positions, Association of Blind and Partially Sighted Teachers and Students 1970-; SKILL (National Bureau for Students with Disabilities): Member 1974-2011, Vice-president 2003-11; Disability Alliance: Chair 1991-97, President 1997-2010; Royal National Institute of the Blind: Chair 2000-09, Vice-President 2009-; President: European Blind Union 2003-11, International Council for the Education of all Visually Impaired People 2010-. Honorary doctorate, Open University 2011. CBE 2000.
Publications: Co-author: An Equal Say in Our Own Affairs (National Federation of the Blind of the United Kingdom [NFBUK] 1971), Educational Provision for the Visually Handicapped (NFBUK and Association of Blind and Partially Sighted Teachers and Students, 1973); Plus numerous articles on provision for the disabled, particularly education.
Recreations: Music, wine.
The Lord Low of Dalston CBE, House of Lords, London SW1A 0PW
Tel: 020 7219 4119 *Email:* lowc@parliament.uk
lordsoftheblog.net/category/lord-low

CONSERVATIVE

LUCAS OF CRUDWELL AND DINGWALL, LORD

LUCAS OF CRUDWELL (11th Baron, E) cr. 1663, and DINGWALL (de facto 8th Lord, 14th but for the attainder) (S) cr. 1609; Ralph Matthew Palmer. Born 7 June 1951; Son of late Major Honorary Robert Jocelyn Palmer, MC, and Anne Rosemary, Baroness Lucas of Crudwell (10th in line); Married Clarissa Lockett 1978 (divorced 1995) (1 son 1 daughter); married Amanda Atha 1995 (died 2000); married Antonia Rubinstein 2001 (1 daughter).
Education: Eton College; Balliol College, Oxford (BA physics 1972).
Non-political career: Articles with various firms once part of Arthur Andersen 1972-76; With S. G Warburg & Co. Ltd 1976-88; Director of various companies, principally those associated with the Good Schools Ltd.
Political career: *House of Lords:* First entered House of Lords 1991; Government Whip 1994-97; Government Spokesperson for: Education 1994-95, Social Security and the Welsh Office 1994-97, Agriculture, Fisheries and Food and Environment 1995-97; Elected hereditary peer 1999-; Opposition Spokesperson for: Agriculture, Fisheries and Food 1997, Constitutional Affairs, Scotland and Wales (Wales) 1997, Environment 1997, Environment, Transport and the Regions (Environment) 1997, International Development 1997-98. Member: Animals in Scientific Procedures 2001-02, Sub-committee

on House of Lords' Offices Library and Computers, Information -2003; Co-opted member European Union Sub-committee E (Law and Institutions) 2006-07; Member: Merits of Statutory Instruments 2007-11, Science and Technology Sub-committee I 2012-13.

Political interests: Education, liberty, planning, finance, electronic government, copyright.

Other: Safe Ground; Fellow, Institute of Chartered Accountants in England and Wales; FCA; Safe Ground – innovation in prison education. Liveryman, Mercers' Company.

The Lord Lucas of Crudwell and Dingwall, House of Lords, London SW1A 0PW
Tel: 020 7219 4177 *Email:* lucasr@parliament.uk
lordsoftheblog.net/category/lord-lucas *Twitter:* @LordLucasCD

CROSSBENCH

LUCE, LORD

LUCE (Life Baron), Richard Napier Luce; cr. 2000. Born 14 October 1936; Son of late Sir William Luce; Married Rose Nicholson 1961 (2 sons).

Education: Wellington College, Berkshire; Christ's College, Cambridge (BA history 1960); Wadham College, Oxford (overseas civil service course 1961).

Non-political career: Army national service 1955-57. District officer, Kenya 1961-63; Marketing manager: Gallaher Ltd 1963-65, Spirella 1965-67; Director, National Innovations Centre 1967-71; Vice-president, Institute of Patentees and Inventors 1974-79; Non-executive director, European Advisory Board, Corning Glass International SA 1976-79; Chair, Courtenay Stewart International Limited 1975-79; Non-executive director: Booker Tate 1991-96, Meridian Broadcasting 1991-97; Governor and Commander-in-chief, Gibraltar 1997-2000; Lord Chamberlain of the Queen's Household 2000-06; Permanent Lord in Waiting to HM the Queen 2007-.

Political career: *House of Commons:* Contested Hitchin 1970 general election. MP (Conservative) for West Sussex, Arundel and Shoreham 1971 by-election to February 1974, for Shoreham February 1974-92. PPS to Geoffrey Howe as Minister for Trade and Consumer Affairs 1972-74; Opposition Whip 1974-75; Parliamentary Under-Secretary of State for Foreign and Commonwealth Affairs 1979-81; Minister of State, Foreign and Commonwealth Office 1981-82 (resigned April 1982 on Falklands issue), 1983-85; Minister for Arts Privy Council Office 1985-90. *House of Lords:* Raised to the peerage as Baron Luce, of Adur in the County of West Sussex 2000. *Councils and public bodies:* DL, West Sussex 1991-; High Steward, Westminster Abbey 2011-; Chairman, Crown Nominations Commission 2012.

Political interests: International affairs, consumer affairs, constitutional affairs, the arts, civil service, higher education; Africa, Far East, Middle East.

Other: Chair: Atlantic Council of UK 1991-96, Commonwealth Foundation 1992-96; President, Voluntary Art Network 1993-2013; Trustee, Geographers' A-Z Map Trust 1993-; Emeritus trustee, Royal Academy of Arts; Member, court of governors, Royal Shakespeare Company 1994-2002; Trustee, Royal Collection Trust 2000-06; President: Royal Overseas League 2002-, King George V Fund for Actors and Actresses 2006-11; Patron, Sir William Luce Memorial Fund; President, Commonwealth Youth Orchestra and Choir 2010-13. Vice-chancellor, Buckingham University 1992-97. Honorary Fellow, Christ's College, Cambridge 2006; Honorary degree, Buckingham University 1998. PC 1986; Kt 1991; GCVO 2000; KG 2008; RAC; Royal Overseas League.

Publications: Memoir, Ringing the Changes (Michael Russell, 2007).

Recreations: Walking, reading, piano, painting, swimming.

Rt Hon the Lord Luce KG GCVO DL, House of Lords, London SW1A 0PW
Tel: 020 7219 6147

LIBERAL DEMOCRAT

LUDFORD, BARONESS

LUDFORD (Life Baroness), Sarah Ann Ludford; cr. 1997. Born 14 March 1951; Daughter of Joseph Campbell Ludford and Valerie Kathleen, née Skinner; Married Stephen Hitchins 1982.

Education: Portsmouth High School for Girls; London School of Economics (BSc Econ international history 1972, MSc Econ European studies 1977); Inns of Court School of Law; French, German.

Non-political career: Civil servant, Department of the Environment 1972-73; Independent Broadcasting Authority 1973-75; Called to the Bar, Gray's Inn 1979; Official, European Commission, Brussels 1979-85; European adviser, Lloyd's of London 1985-87; American Express Europe 1987-90; European affairs consultant 1990-99.

Political career: *House of Commons:* Contested Islington North 1992 and Islington South and Finsbury 1997 general elections. *House of Lords:* Raised to the peerage as Baroness Ludford, of Clerkenwell in the London Borough of Islington 1997. As an MEP, disqualified from participation

2009-. *Other:* Contested (Liberal Democrat) Hampshire East and Wight 1984 and London Central 1989 and 1994 European Parliament elections. MEP (Liberal Democrat) for London Region 1999- (sits as Sarah Ludford). Liberal Democrat Party: Member, Federal Policy Committee, Vice-president, Liberal Democrat LGBT Group. *Councils and public bodies:* Councillor London Borough of Islington 1991-99.

Political interests: Europe, justice and home affairs, foreign affairs; United States, Balkans, Turkey, Cyprus, Middle East.

Other: Member of council: Liberty, Justice, Federal Trust; Member, Royal Institute of International Affairs (Chatham House).

Recreations: Theatre, ballet.

The Baroness Ludford, House of Lords, London SW1A 0PW
Tel: 020 7219 5353
36b St Peter's Street, London N1 8JT *Tel:* 020 7288 2526 *Fax:* 020 7288 2524
Email: office@sarahludfordmep.org.uk *Website:* www.sarahludfordmep.org.uk
Twitter: @SarahLudfordMEP

CONSERVATIVE

LUKE, LORD

LUKE (3rd Baron, UK), Arthur Charles St John Lawson Johnston; cr. 1929. Born 13 January 1933; Son of 2nd Baron; Married Silvia Roigt 1959 (divorced 1971) (1 son 2 daughters); married Sarah Hearne 1971 (1 son).

Education: Eton College; Trinity College, Cambridge (BA history 1954).

Non-political career: Various managerial positions, Bovril Ltd 1955-71; Fine art dealer in watercolours 18th, 19th, 20th century 1972-.

Political career: *House of Lords:* First entered House of Lords 1996; Opposition Whip 1997-2010; Elected hereditary peer 1999-; Opposition Spokesperson for: Culture, Media and Sport (Tourism)2010, Wales 2000-06, Transport 2002-04, Defence 2004-10. Member: Hybrid Instruments 2001-, Standing Orders (Private Bills) 2001-; Works of Art: Member 2003-07, 2008-10, Chair 2010-11, 2012-13; Member Ecclesiastical Committee 2010-. *Councils and public bodies:* President, National Association of Warehouse-keepers 1962-78; Councillor, Bedfordshire County Council 1965-70; High Sheriff, Bedfordshire 1969-70; Member, Court of Corporation of Sons of the Clergy 1980-2005; DL, Bedfordshire 1989-2004.

Political interests: Art, heritage, church affairs, military history, river Thames, tourism, defence, motoring; Argentina.

Other: Member: CLA, Game Conservancy Association, Countryside Alliance. Drapers' Company: Member of Court 1993-, Master 2001-02. Freeman, City of London. KStJ; MCC.

Recreations: Watching cricket, shooting, fishing, watching motor sports.

The Lord Luke, House of Lords, London SW1A 0PW
Tel: 020 7219 3703 *Fax:* 020 7219 6069 *Email:* lukea@parliament.uk

CONSERVATIVE

LYELL, LORD

LYELL (3rd Baron, UK), Charles Lyell; cr. 1914; 3rd Bt of Kinnordy (UK) 1894. Born 27 March 1939; Son of 2nd Baron, VC.

Education: Eton College; Christ Church, Oxford (MA 1962).

Non-political career: 2nd Lieutenant Scots Guards 1957-59. Chartered accountant.

Political career: *House of Lords:* First entered House of Lords 1960; Opposition Whip 1974-79; Government Whip 1979-84; Government Spokesperson for: Health and Social Security, The Treasury 1982, Scotland 1982-84, Foreign Office Affairs 1983-84; Parliamentary Under-Secretary of State for Northern Ireland 1984-89; Deputy Speaker 1993-2008; Deputy Chair of Committees 1993-2007; Elected hereditary peer 1999-. Member Joint Committee on Statutory Instruments 2012-. *Councils and public bodies:* DL, Angus 1988.

Other: Member: North Atlantic Assembly 1973-79, UK Delegation to North Atlantic Assembly 1994-97; Member, Queen's Bodyguard for Scotland, Royal Company of Archers; Treasurer, Scottish Peers Association 1992-; Turf, White's. Chairman, Lords and Commons Ski Club 1990-93.

The Lord Lyell DL, House of Lords, London SW1A 0PW
Tel: 020 7219 3183 *Fax:* 020 7219 5979
Kinnordy House, Kirriemuir, Angus DD8 5ER *Tel:* 01575 572848 *Fax:* 01575 573921

LYTTON, EARL

LYTTON (5th Earl, UK), John Peter Michael Scawen Lytton; cr. 1880; Viscount Knebworth; 17th Baron Wentworth (E) 1529; 6th Baron Lytton (UK) 1866; 6th Bt of Knebworth (UK) 1838. Born 7 June 1950; Son of 4th Earl of Lytton; Married Ursula Alexandra (2 sons 1 daughter).

Education: Downside School, Somerset; College of Estate Management; Reading University (BSc estate management 1972).

Non-political career: Valuation officer, Inland Revenue 1975-81; Associate partner, Permutt Brown & Co. 1982-86; Cubitt and West 1986-87; Founder, John Lytton & Co. Chartered Surveyors (John Lytton & Co. Ltd 2009-) 1988-.

CROSSBENCH

Political career: *House of Lords:* First entered House of Lords 1985; Sponsor Party Wall etc. Bill 1996; Elected hereditary peer 2011-. Member Information 2012-. *Councils and public bodies:* President, National Association of Local Councils 1999-.

Political interests: Communities and local government finance, countryside conservation, agriculture, rural economy, town and country planning, property taxation.

Other: Council member, Country Landowners' Association 1993-; Horsham Chamber of Commerce: Chair 1993-95, President 1995-; Chairman: Leasehold Enfranchisement Advisory Service 1994-97, Leasehold Advisory Service 1997-; President: Newsted Abbey Byron Society, Institute of Heraldic and Genealogical Studies, 1st Shipley Scout Group, West Sussex, Sussex Association of Local Councils 1997-; Member, Countryside Alliance; Honorary Fellow, Association of Building Engineers; Member, Chartered Institute of Arbitrators; Trustee, Shipley Windmill Trust; FRICS; Elected member, Institute of Revenues, Rating and Valuation 1990.

The Earl of Lytton, House of Lords, London SW1A 0PW
Tel: 020 7219 5353

MACAULAY OF BRAGAR, LORD

MACAULAY OF BRAGAR (Life Baron), Donald Macaulay; cr. 1989. Born 14 November 1933; Son of late John and Henrietta Macaulay; Married Mary Morrison 1962 (2 daughters).

Education: Hermitage School, Helensburgh; Clydebank High School; Glasgow University (MA history, logic, French 1950; LLB 1956).

Non-political career: National Service, RASC 1958-60. Solicitor 1960-62; Called to Scottish Bar 1963; Advocate Depute (Crown Prosecutor) 1967-70, 1973-74; Standing Junior Counsel to Highlands and Islands Development Board; Chair: SACRO 1993-96, Supreme Court Legal Aid Committee; Member: Central Legal Aid Committee both during 1970s, Criminal Injuries Compensation Board; Scottish chair, Committee for Abolition of Paybeds in NHS; Founder member and former chair, Advocates' Criminal Law Group.

LABOUR

Political career: *House of Commons:* Contested (Labour) Inverness 1970 general election. *House of Lords:* Raised to the peerage as Baron Macaulay of Bragar, of Bragar in the County of Ross and Cromarty 1989. Former Opposition Spokesperson for Scottish Legal Affairs; On leave of absence February 2013-. Member: Computers, Crofting. *Councils and public bodies:* Member, Bryden Committee on Identification following Devlin Report.

Political interests: Scottish law, education, local government, sport, theatre.

Recreations: Art, music, theatre, football, golf, running.

The Lord Macaulay of Bragar QC, House of Lords, London SW1A 0PW
Tel: 020 7219 5353 *Email:* macaulayd@parliament.uk

McAVOY, LORD

Opposition Whip; Opposition Spokesperson for Northern Ireland and for Scotland

McAVOY (Life Baron), Thomas McLaughlin McAvoy; cr 2010. Born 14 December 1943; Son of late Edward McAvoy, steelworker, and late Frances McLaughlin McAvoy; Married Eleanor Kerr 1968 (4 sons).

Education: St Columbkilles Secondary School.

Non-political career: Hoover plc, Cambuslang 1974-87. USDAW: AEU shop steward 1974-87; Member, Unite 1974-.

LAB/CO-OP

Political career: *House of Commons:* MP for Glasgow Rutherglen 1987-2005, for Rutherglen and Hamilton West 2005-10. Opposition Whip 1991-93, 1996-97; Government Whip 1997-2010; Deputy Chief Whip 2008-10. Member: Northern Ireland Affairs 1994-96, Finance and Services

1997-2009, Selection 2008-10, Administration 2009, Members' Allowances 2009-10. PLP Departmental Committee on Northern Ireland: Member 1996-2010, Co-vice-chair 1996-97. *House of Lords:* Raised to the peerage as Baron McAvoy, of Rutherglen in the County of Lanarkshire 2010. Opposition Whip 2011-; Opposition Spokesperson for: Northern Ireland 2012-, Scotland 2012-. Member: Administration and Works 2012-, Partnerships (Prosecution) (Scotland) Bill 2013-. *Other:* Member, Co-operative Party. *Councils and public bodies:* Chair Rutherglen Community Council 1980-82; Councillor Strathclyde Regional Council 1982-87.

Political interests: Social services; Ireland, USA.

Other: PC 2003. South Lanarkshire Council, Eastfield Lifestyles.

Rt Hon the Lord McAvoy, House of Lords, London SW1A 0PW
Tel: 020 7219 5009 *Email:* mcavoytd@parliament.uk

CROSSBENCH

McCLUSKEY, LORD

McCLUSKEY (Life Baron), John Herbert McCluskey; cr. 1976. Born 12 June 1929; Son of late Francis John McCluskey and Margaret, née Doonan; Married Ruth Friedland 1956 (2 sons 1 daughter).

Education: St Bede's College, Manchester; Holy Cross Academy, Edinburgh; Edinburgh University (Harry Dalgety Bursar 1948, Vans Dunlop Scholar, MA arts 1950; LLB 1952).

Non-political career: RAF National Service 1952-54 (Sword of Honour, Spitalgate OCTU 1953). Admitted to Faculty of Advocates 1955; QC (Scot) 1967; Sheriff Principal of Dumfries and Galloway 1973-74; Senator of the College of Justice in Scotland 1984-2004; Reith Lecturer 1986.

Political career: *House of Lords:* Raised to the peerage as Baron McCluskey, of Churchill in the District of the City of Edinburgh 1976. Solicitor-General for Scotland 1974-79; Opposition Spokesperson for Scottish Legal Affairs 1979-84.

Political interests: Mental health, human rights; Former Soviet Union.

Other: Vice-chair: International Bar Association, IBA Human Rights Institute 1995-2000; Chair: Scottish Association for Mental Health 1985-94, Fairbridge in Scotland 1995-97, Age Concern Scotland 1999-2001; Chair, John Smith Memorial Trust 1997-2004; Amnesty International, Victims of Torture. Honorary LLD, Dundee 1989; Royal Air Force. Edinburgh Sports.

Publications: Law, Justice and Democracy (1987); Criminal Appeals (1992, 2000).

Recreations: Tennis, swimming.

The Lord McCluskey LLD QC, House of Lords, London SW1A 0PW
Tel: 020 7219 5353
Email: johnmccluskey1@btinternet.com

CONSERVATIVE

McCOLL OF DULWICH, LORD

McCOLL OF DULWICH (Life Baron), Ian McColl; cr. 1989. Born 6 January 1933; Son of late Frederick and Winifred McColl; Married Dr Jean Lennox, née McNair 1960 (1 son 2 daughters).

Education: Hutchesons' Grammar School, Glasgow; St Paul's School, London (Foundation Scholarship classics); London University (Master of Surgery 1965; MB BS 1957).

Non-political career: Honorary Group Captain, RAF, Armed Forces Parliamentary Scheme. Consultant surgeon and Sub Dean, St Bartholomew's Hospital 1967-71; Research fellow, Harvard Medical School 1967; Professor and Director of Surgery, Guy's Hospital 1971-98; Professor of Surgery, London University 1971-98; Consultant Surgeon to the Army 1980-98; Chair, Government Working Party on Artificial Limbs and Wheelchair Service (The McColl Report) 1984-86; Vice-chair, Disablement Services Authority 1987-91; Chair, Department of Surgery of the United Medical Schools of Guy's and St Thomas' Hospital 1988-92. BMA 1957-.

Political career: *House of Lords:* Raised to the peerage as Baron McColl of Dulwich, of Bermondsey in the London Borough of Southwark 1989. PPS to John Major as Prime Minister 1994-97; Deputy Speaker 1994-97, 1998-2002; Deputy Chairman of Committees 1994-97, 1998-2002; Opposition Spokesperson for Health 1997-2010. Member: European Communities Sub-committee F (Environment) 1991-94, Medical Ethics 1993-94, Science and Technology 2000-03, Science and Technology Sub-committees: IIA (Human Genetic Databases) 2000-01, II (Aircraft Cabin Environment) 2001, I (Systematic Biology and Biodiversity/Fighting Infection) 2002-03, I (Science and International Agreements) 2003-10, Patient-Assisted Dying for the terminally ill 2004, HIV and AIDS in the UK 2010-11. *Other:* Member, governing council, Conservative Christian Fellowship.

Political interests: Disability, higher education, health service, forestry, medicine, health; Benin, Gambia, Ghana, Liberia, Sierra Leone, Togo, Uganda.
Other: Vice-chair, International Board of Mercy Ships; Commonwealth Parliamentary Association UK Branch: Member, executive committee 1999-2005, 2006-, Vice-chair 2011-; Chair, UK Board of Mercy Ships; Governor-at-large for England, Board of Governors, American College of Surgeons 1982-86; Mildmay Mission Hospital: President 1985-2000, Vice-President 2000-; Council member, Royal College of Surgeons 1986-94; President: Society of Minimally Invasive Surgery 1991-94, National Association of Limbless Disabled 1992-; Vice-President, John Groom's Association for Disabled People 1992-; President: The Hospital Saving Association 1994-2001, Association of Endoscopic Surgery of Great Britain and Ireland 1994-96, Leprosy Mission 1996-; FRCS 1962; FACS; FKC; MS; The Shaftesbury Society. Master, Worshipful Company of Barbers. Fellow, King's College, London 2001; Honorary FDS RCS 2007. George and Thomas Hutchesons Award 2000; Great Scot Award for medical charity work 2002; National Maritime Historical Society Distinguished service award 2002. CBE 1997; Order of Mercy 2007; Royal College of Surgeons. Palace of Westminster; Jags of Dulwich.
Publications: Intestinal Absorption in Man (1976); NHS Data Book (1984); Government Report on Artificial Limb and Appliance Centre Service (1986); As well as articles in medical journals.
Recreations: Forestry, ornithology.
Professor the Lord McColl of Dulwich CBE, House of Lords, London SW1A 0PW
Tel: 020 7219 5141 *Fax:* 020 7219 6205 *Email:* mccolli@parliament.uk

LABOUR

McCONNELL OF GLENSCORRODALE, LORD

McCONNELL OF GLENSCORRODALE (Life Baron), Jack Wilson McConnell; cr 2010. Born 30 June 1960; Son of William Wilson McConnell, tenant farmer, and Elizabeth McConnell; Married Bridget McLuckie 1990 (1 son 1 daughter).
Education: Arran High School, Isle of Arran; Stirling University (BSc mathematics; Dip Ed 1983).
Non-political career: Maths teacher, Lornshill Academy 1983-92; General secretary, Scottish Labour Party 1992-98; Education adviser, Clinton Hunter Development Initiative 2007-11; Prime Minister's Special Representative for Peace-Building 2008-10; Member, advisory board, PricewaterhouseCoopers. Member, Community.
Political career: *House of Commons:* Contested Perth and Kinross 1987 general election. *House of Lords:* Raised to the peerage as Baron McConnell of Glenscorrodale, of the Isle of Arran in Ayrshire and Arran 2010. *Other:* Scottish Parliament: MSP for Motherwell and Wishaw constituency 1999-2011: Scottish Labour: Minister for: Finance 1999-2000, Education, Europe and External Affairs 2000-01; First Minister 2001-07. Member, Labour Scottish Executive 1989-92; General Secretary, Scottish Labour Party 1992-98; Leader, Scottish Labour Party 2001-07. *Councils and public bodies:* Stirling District Council: Councillor 1984-93, Treasurer 1988-92, Council leader 1990-92; Member: Scottish Constitutional Convention 1989-98, Convention of Scottish Local Authorities 1990-92.
Political interests: Education, economic policy, international development, conflict and peacebuilding; China, EU, Japan, Malawi, Rwanda, USA.
Other: Member: Congress of Local and Regional Authorities in Europe 1999-2001, EU Committee of the Regions 2000-07; President, European Regions with Legislative Power 2004; Board Member, UK-Japan 21st Century Group 2010-; Ambassador: Action for Children, SSE's Scotland Sustainable Fund Panel; Pump Aid; Patron: Positive Women, Diana Awards; Advisory board, Institute for Cultural Diplomacy; Chair: Radio Clyde Cash for Kids, McConnell International Foundation; Chair, SSE Community Funding Panel 2013-; 48 Group Club; various charities supporting international development and vulnerable children. Honorary Doctorate, Stirling University 2008. Scottish Politician of the Year 2001; UK Public Health Champion 2005; Scottish Politics Lifetime Achievement Award 2010. PC 2001. Lamlash Golf Clubs.
Recreations: Golf, music, sports, gardening.
Rt Hon the Lord McConnell of Glenscorrodale, House of Lords, London SW1A 0PW
Tel: 020 7219 8913 *Email:* mcconnellj@parliament.uk *Website:* www.jackmcconnell.org
Twitter: @LordMcConnell

LABOUR

McDONAGH, BARONESS

McDONAGH (Life Baroness), Margaret Josephine McDonagh; cr. 2004. Born 26 June 1961; Daughter of Breda, née Doogue, psychiatric nurse and Cumin McDonagh, building labourer.

Education: Holy Cross Secondary Modern, New Malden; Kingston College of Further Education, Surrey; Brunel University (BSc politics and modern history with statistics 1984); Kingston Business School (MA advanced marketing 1994); Harvard Business School, USA (advanced management programme 2002).

Non-political career: Labour Party 1987-2001: General election co-ordinator 1997, Secretary General 1998-2001; General manager, Express Newspapers 2001; Non-executive director: TBI plc 2004, Standard Life plc 2007. Amicus.

Political career: *House of Lords:* Raised to the peerage as Baroness McDonagh, of Mitcham and of Morden in the London Borough of Merton 2004. Member House 2013-.

The Baroness McDonagh, House of Lords, London SW1A 0PW
Tel: 020 7219 4438

LIBERAL DEMOCRAT

MACDONALD OF RIVER GLAVEN, LORD

MACDONALD OF RIVER GLAVEN (Life Baron), Kenneth Donald John Macdonald; cr 2010. Born 4 January 1953; Married Linda Zuck 1980 (2 sons 1 daughter).

Education: St Edmund Hall, Oxford (BA philosophy, politics and economics 1974).

Non-political career: Called to the Bar, Inner Temple 1978; Practising criminal lawyer 1978-; QC 1997; Recorder 2001-; Director of public prosecutions 2003-08; Bencher 2004; Member, Matrix Chambers 2008-; Visiting Professor of Law, London School of Economics 2009-; Warden, Wadham College, Oxford; Deputy High Court Judge 2010-.

Political career: *House of Lords:* Raised to the peerage as Baron Macdonald of River Glaven, of Cley-next-the-Sea in the County of Norfolk 2010. Member Constitution 2012-13. *Councils and public bodies:* Member: Treasury Counsel Selection Committee, Central Criminal Court 2001-03, Sentencing Guidelines Council 2003-08, Criminal Procedure Rules Committee 2003-08, Independent Commission on Youth Crime 2008-; Trustee, Index on Censorship 2009-; Advisory board, Centre for Criminology, University of Oxford.

Political interests: Security, criminal justice, civil liberties.

Other: Member, Bar Council 2000; Bar Public Affairs Group: Member 2001-03, Vice-chair 2001-02; Criminal Bar Association: Vice-chair 2002-03, Chair 2003-. Kt 2007.

The Lord Macdonald of River Glaven QC, House of Lords, London SW1A 0PW
Tel: 020 7219 5353

LABOUR

MACDONALD OF TRADESTON, LORD

MACDONALD OF TRADESTON (Life Baron), Angus John Macdonald; cr. 1998. Born 20 August 1940; Son of late Colin and Jean Macdonald; Married Alice Theresa McQuaid 1963 (2 daughters).

Education: Allan Glen's School, Glasgow; Apprenticeship, marine engineer.

Non-political career: Marine engineer 1956-63; Circulation manager, *Tribune* 1964-65; Feature writer, *The Scotsman* 1965-67; Executive, producer, presenter, Granada Television 1967-85; Scottish Television: Director of Programmes 1985-90, Managing director 1990-96; Director, GMTV 1991-97; Chair: Scottish Media Group plc 1996-98, Taylor and Francis plc 1997-98; Director, Bank of Scotland plc 1998; Adviser, Macquarie Group 2004-; Director, Scottish Power Ltd 2007-.

Political career: *House of Lords:* Raised to the peerage as Baron Macdonald of Tradeston, of Tradeston in the County of Glasgow 1998. Parliamentary Under-Secretary of State and Government Spokesperson for Scottish Office (Minister of Business and Industry) 1998-99; Minister of State and Government Spokesperson for Department of the Environment, Transport and the Regions (Minister for Transport) 1999-2001 (attending Cabinet); Minister and Government Spokesperson for Cabinet Office and Chancellor of Duchy of Lancaster 2001-03; Government Spokesperson for Transport 2002-03; Cabinet Office Advisory Committee on Business Appointments 2009-13. Member: Economic Affairs 2005-08, Communications 2008-12.

Political interests: Humanism, media, business, education.

Other: OECD, Member: Steering Group, Futures Project on Infrastructure 2005-11, Advisory board, International Transport Forum 2009-13; Chair, Edinburgh International Television Festival 1976-78; Governor, National Film and Television School 1985-97; Chair: Edinburgh Film Festival 1994-96, Cairngorms Partnership 1997-98; Board member, Scottish Enterprise 1997-98; Governor,

British Film Institute 1997-98; Council member, Sussex University 2006-08; Patron, Dystonia Society 2006-; Member, Court of Sussex University 2009-11. Chancellor, Glasgow Caledonian University 2007-12. Visiting professor of film and media studies, Stirling University 1985-98; Honorary doctorates: Stirling University 1992, Napier University 1997, Robert Gordon University 1998, Glasgow University 2001, Lincoln University 2007. BAFTA Award, Best Factual Television (*World in Action*) 1973; BAFTA Scotland Lifetime Achievement Award 1997; Scottish Business Elite Corporate Leader of the Year and Chairman of the Year 1997. CBE 1997; PC 1999; Royal Automobile.

Publications: Camera: Victorian eyewitness (1979).

Recreations: Pictures, music, sports.

Rt Hon the Lord Macdonald of Tradeston CBE, House of Lords, London SW1A 0PW
Tel: 020 7219 2239 *Email:* macdonaldaj@parliament.uk

McFALL OF ALCLUITH, LORD

McFALL OF ALCLUITH (Life Baron), John Francis McFall; cr 2010. Born 4 October 1944; Son of late John and Jean McFall; Married Joan Ward 1969 (3 sons 1 daughter).

Education: St Patrick's Secondary School, Dumbarton; Paisley College of Technology (BSc chemistry 1974); Strathclyde University (MBA); Open University (BA education).

Non-political career: Mathematics and chemistry teacher; Depute head teacher 1983-87.

LAB/CO-OP

Political career: *House of Commons:* MP (Labour) for Dumbarton 1987-2005, for West Dunbartonshire 2005-10. Member Public Accounts Commission -2010; Opposition Whip 1989-91; Opposition Spokesperson for Scottish Affairs 1992-97; Government Whip 1997-98; Parliamentary Under-Secretary of State, Northern Ireland Office 1998-99 (Minister for Education, Training and Employment, Health and Community Relations 1998-99, for Economy and Education 1999). Member: Public Administration 2000-01, Treasury (Treasury Sub-Committee) 2001-10; Chair: Treasury 2001-10; Member: Liaison 2001-10, Liaison Sub-committee 2007-10. *House of Lords:* Raised to the peerage as Baron McFall of Alcluith, of Dumbarton in the County of Dunbartonshire 2010. Member: Economic Affairs Finance Bill Sub-Committee 2011, Joint Committee on the Draft Financial Services Bill 2011-12, Economic Affairs 2012-, Parliamentary Commission on Banking Standards 2012-13. *Other:* Member, Co-operative Party.

Political interests: Defence, education, economic policy, co-operative development, Third World; Latin America, Middle East, Romania.

Other: Fellow, Industry and Parliament Trust 1989, 2003. DUniv: Strathclyde University 2010, Glasgow University 2011, Stirling University 2011; Honorary doctorate of business administration, BPP Business School, London 2011; DUniv, West of Scotland University 2012. PC 2004.

Recreations: Jogging, golf, reading.

Rt Hon the Lord McFall of Alcluith, House of Lords, London SW1A 0PW
Tel: 020 7219 3521 *Website:* www.johnmcfall.com *Twitter:* @McFallJF

MACFARLANE OF BEARSDEN, LORD

MACFARLANE OF BEARSDEN (Life Baron), Norman Somerville Macfarlane; cr. 1991. Born 5 March 1926; Son of late Daniel Robertson Macfarlane and Jessie Lindsay Somerville; Married Marguerite Campbell 1953 (1 son 4 daughters).

Education: High School of Glasgow.

Non-political career: Served in Palestine with RA 1945-47. Founded N. S. Macfarlane & Co. Ltd. 1949, Macfarlane Group (Clansman) plc 1973, Managing director 1973-90, Chair 1973-98, Honorary Life President 1999; The Fine Art Society plc: Chair 1976-98, Honorary Life President 1998-; Underwriting member, Lloyd's 1978-99; Director, Edinburgh Fund Managers plc 1980-97;

CONSERVATIVE

Clydesdale Bank plc: Director 1980-96, Deputy chair 1993-96; Director, General Accident Fire & Life Assurance Corporation 1984-96; Chair, Amercian Trust plc 1984-97; United Distillers UK plc: Chair 1987-96, Honorary Life President 1996-; Guinness plc: Chair 1987-89, Joint Deputy Chair 1989-92; Chair, Roger Billcliffe Fine Art Ltd 1991-; Honorary Life President, Diago (Scotland) 1999-.

Political career: *House of Lords:* Raised to the peerage as Baron Macfarlane of Bearsden, in the District of Bearsden and Milngavie 1991. *Councils and public bodies:* Council member, CBI Scotland 1975-81; Member, Court of Glasgow University 1979-87; Board member, Scottish Development Agency 1979-87; Member, Royal Fine Art Commission for Scotland 1980-82; Chair, Glasgow Development Agency (Formerly Glasgow Action) 1985-92; Lord High Commissioner to the General Assembly of the Church of Scotland 1992, 1993, 1997; DL, Dumbartonshire 1993.

Political interests: The arts, industry and commerce.

Other: President, Stationers Association of Great Britain and Ireland 1965; Scottish Ballet: Director 1975-87, Vice-chair 1983-87, President 2001-; President, Royal Glasgow Institute of the Fine Arts 1976-87; Director, Scottish National Orchestra 1977-82; Trustee: National Heritage Memorial Fund 1984-97, National Galleries of Scotland 1986-97; Honorary President, Chas Rennie McIntosh Society 1988-; President, High School of Glasgow 1992-; Patron, Scottish Licensed Trade Association 1992-; Regent, Royal College of Surgeons of Edinburgh 1997-; Honorary President, Glasgow School of Art 2001-; Honorary Patron, Queen's Park Football Club; Vice-President, Professional Golfers Association; Honorary Life Member, Scottish Football League 2006; Honorary FRIAS 1984; Honorary RSA 1987; Honorary RGI 1987; FRSE 1991; Honorary FRCPS (Glasgow) 1992; N.S. Macfarlane Charitable Trust. Freeman: Dumfries and Galloway 2006, City of Glasgow 2007. Seven honorary doctorates/fellowships. Kt 1983; KT 1996; Glasgow Art, Royal Scottish Automobile (Glasgow), New (Edinburgh). Glasgow Golf, North Berwick Golf, Honorary Company of Edinburgh Golfers.

Recreations: Golf, cricket, theatre, art.

The Lord Macfarlane of Bearsden KT DL, House of Lords, London SW1A 0PW
Tel: 020 7219 5353
Macfarlane Group (Clansman) plc, 21 Newton Place, Glasgow G3 7PY *Tel:* 0141-333 9666
Fax: 0141-333 1988

CONSERVATIVE

MacGREGOR OF PULHAM MARKET, LORD

MacGREGOR OF PULHAM MARKET (Life Baron), John Roddick Russell MacGregor; cr. 2001. Born 14 February 1937; Son of late Dr Norman MacGregor and Mary MacGregor, née Roddick; Married Jean Dungey 1962 (1 son 2 daughters).

Education: Merchiston Castle School, Edinburgh; St Andrews University (MA economics and history 1959); King's College, London University (LLB 1962).

Non-political career: Administrator, London University 1961-62; Editorial staff, *New Society* 1962-63; Special assistant to Prime Minister Sir Alec Douglas-Home 1963-64; Head of private office of Edward Heath, MP 1965-68; Business executive in the City 1968-79; Director: Hill Samuel Registrars Ltd 1971-79, Hill Samuel & Co. Ltd 1973-79; Deputy chair, Hill Samuel & Co. Ltd 1994-96; Director: Associated British Foods 1994-2007, Slough Estates/SEGRO 1995-2006, Unigate (now Uniq) 1996-2005, Friends Provident 1998-2007; Member, supervisory board, DAF Trucks NV 2000-09; Co-chair, UK Food and Agriculture Advisory Board, Rabobank International 2006-12; Chairman, pension fund trustees: SEGRO 2007-10, British Energy 2007-, Anglian Water Group 2009-, Eggborough Power Ltd 2011-.

Political career: *House of Commons:* MP (Conservative) for South Norfolk February 1974-2001. Opposition Whip 1977-79; Government Whip (Lord Commissioner of the Treasury) 1979-81; Parliamentary Under-Secretary of State for Industry 1981-83; Minister of State, Ministry of Agriculture, Fisheries and Food 1983-85; Chief Secretary to the Treasury 1985-87; Minister of Agriculture, Fisheries and Food 1987-89; Secretary of State for Education and Science 1989-90; Lord President of the Council and Leader of the House of Commons 1990-92; Secretary of State for Transport 1992-94. *House of Lords:* Raised to the peerage as Baron MacGregor of Pulham Market, of Pulham Market in the County of Norfolk 2001. Member: Constitution 2002-05, Regulators 2006-07; Economic Affairs: Member 2007-10, Chair 2010-; Member: Finance Bill Sub-committee 2008-11, Leader's Group on Code of Conduct 2009; Chair: Audit 2011-, Economic Affairs Finance Bill Sub-committee 2011, 2012-. *Other:* Chairman, Young Conservative External Relations Committee 1959-62; First President, Conservative and Christian Democratic Youth Community 1965; President, South Norfolk Conservative Association 2007-; Association of Conservative Peers: Vice-chair 2010-12, Chairman 2012-. *Councils and public bodies:* Council member, Institute of Directors 1995-2007; Vice-President, Association of County Councils 1995-97; Trustee, Foundation of Business Responsibilities 1996-2004; Conservative nominee, Committee on Standards in Public Life 1997-2003; Deputy chair, Governing Bodies Association (now Association of Governing Bodies of Independent Schools) 1998-2006; Member, Independent Schools Council 1998-2005; Chair, St Andrew's (Ecumenical) Trust 2006-12; Norwich Cathedral: High Steward 2007-, Chair of Cathedral Council 2012-.

Political interests: Economic and financial matters, agriculture, education, industry, housing, countryside; EU countries, USA.

Other: Chair, Bow Group 1961-62; Member: Council of King's College, London 1996-2002, Inner Magic Circle; Patron, New London Orchestra; Vice-President, COBISEC; President, Norfolk Association of Village Halls; Royal Norfolk Agricultural Association: President 1988, Trustee 2004-10. Fellow, King's College, London; Honorary LLD, Westminster University. OBE 1971; PC 1985.

Recreations: Music, theatre, gardening, travel, conjuring.

Rt Hon the Lord MacGregor of Pulham Market OBE, House of Lords, London SW1A 0PW
Tel: 020 7219 4439

LABOUR

McINTOSH OF HUDNALL, BARONESS

McINTOSH OF HUDNALL (Life Baroness), Genista Mary McIntosh; cr. 1999. Born 23 September 1946; Daughter of late Geoffrey and Maire Tandy; Married Neil McIntosh 1971 (divorced 1990) (1 son 1 daughter).

Education: Hemel Hempstead Grammar School; York University (BA philosophy and sociology 1968).

Non-political career: Press Secretary, York Festival of Arts 1968-69; Royal Shakespeare Company: Casting director 1972-77, Planning controller 1977-84, Senior administrator 1986-90, Associate producer 1990; Executive director, Royal National Theatre 1990-January 1997, October 1997-2002; Chief executive, Royal Opera House, Covent Garden 1997; Principal, Guildhall School of Music and Drama 2002-03.

Political career: *House of Lords:* Raised to the peerage as Baroness McIntosh of Hudnall, of Hampstead in the London Borough of Camden 1999. Deputy Chairman of Committees 2007-; Deputy Speaker 2008-. Member: Joint Scrutiny Committees on: Draft Mental Incapacity Bill 2003, Draft Charities Bill 2004, Draft Mental Health Bill 2004-05, Liaison 2005-09; Chair London Local Authorities Bill 2006; Member: Communications 2007-10, Administration and Works 2007-11, 2012-, House 2010-12, HIV and AIDS in the UK 2010-11, Mental Capacity Act 2005 2013-.

Political interests: Arts, public health, education, sustainable transport.

Other: Board member: The Roundhouse Trust, Southbank Sinfonia, Foundation for Sport and the Arts -2012, National Opera Studio; Patron: Helena Kennedy Bursary Scheme, firstsite:newsite; Fellow, Royal Society of Arts; Board member: Royal Shakespeare Company 2010-, Parliament Choir; Childline, National Trust, Cancer Research. Three honorary degrees; Honorary fellowship, Goldsmith's College 2003.

Recreations: Gardening, music.

The Baroness McIntosh of Hudnall, House of Lords, London SW1A 0PW
Tel: 020 7219 8732 *Email:* mcintoshg@parliament.uk

CONSERVATIVE

MACKAY OF CLASHFERN, LORD

MACKAY OF CLASHFERN (Life Baron), James Peter Hymers Mackay; cr. 1979. Born 2 July 1927; Son of late James Mackay, railwayman; Married Elizabeth Gunn Hymers 1958 (1 son 2 daughters).

Education: George Heriot's School, Edinburgh; Edinburgh University (MA mathematics and natural philosophy 1948; LLB 1955); Trinity College, Cambridge (BA maths 1952).

Non-political career: Lecturer in mathematics, St Andrews University 1948-50; Advocate 1955; QC (Scotland) 1965; Sheriff Principal, Renfrew and Argyll 1972-74; Director, Stenhouse Holdings Ltd 1976-78; Lord Clerk, Register of Scotland 2007-.

Political career: *House of Lords:* Raised to the peerage as Baron Mackay of Clashfern, of Eddrachillis in the District of Sutherland 1979. Lord Advocate 1979-84; Government Spokesperson for Legal Affairs in Scotland 1983-84; Lord of Appeal in Ordinary 1985-87; Lord High Chancellor 1987-97. Member Privileges/Privileges and Conduct; Chair Assisted Dying Bill; Member: Draft Human Tissue and Embryos Bill Joint Committee 2007, Joint Committee on the Draft Care and Support Bill 2013. *Other:* Chair, Conservative Party Constitutional Commission 1998-99.

Other: Vice-President, Commonwealth Parliamentary Association (UK Branch); Elder Brother, Trinity House; Dean, Faculty of Advocates 1976-79; Part-time member, Scottish Law Commission 1976-79; Member, Insurance Brokers' Registration Council 1978-79; Senator, College of Justice in Scotland 1984-85; Chair: Legal Reform Commission, Mauritius 1997-98, Legal Commission, Trinidad and Tobago 2000; Lord High Commission to General Assembly of Church of Scotland 2005, 2006; Honorary Fellow: Royal College of Surgeons of Edinburgh 1989, Royal Society of Edinburgh, RICE, Royal College of Physicians Edinburgh 1990, Royal College of Obstetrics and Gynaecology, Chartered Institute of Taxation; Cancer UK; Barnardo's; Army Benevolent Fund; Mission Aviation Fellowship; Mercy Ships. Honorary Freeman, Woolman's Company. Chancellor, Heriot-Watt University 1991-2005. Honorary Fellow: Trinity College, Cambridge, Girton College, Cambridge; Several Honorary Degrees. PC 1979; KT 1997; New (Edinburgh), Caledonian, Athenæum.

Publications: Senior editor, Armour: Valuation for Rating (third edition, 1961); General Editor-in-chief, Halsbury's Laws of England 1999-.

Recreations: Walking, travel.

Rt Hon the Lord Mackay of Clashfern KT, House of Lords, London SW1A 0PW
Tel: 020 7219 6041 *Email:* mackayjp@parliament.uk

MACKAY OF DRUMADOON, LORD

MACKAY OF DRUMADOON (Life Baron), Donald Sage Mackay; cr. 1995. Born 30 January 1946; Son of late Rev. Donald Mackintosh Mackay and late Jean Mackay; Married Lesley Waugh 1979 (1 son 2 daughters).

Education: George Watson's Boys' College, Edinburgh; Edinburgh University (LLB 1966; LLM 1968); University of Virginia, USA (LLM 1969).

Non-political career: Law apprentice 1969-71; Solicitor with Allan McDougall & Co., SSC, Edinburgh 1971-76; Called to the Scottish Bar 1976; Advocate Depute 1982-85; QC (Scot) 1987; Solicitor-General for Scotland 1995; Lord Advocate 1995-97; Senator of the College of Justice in Scotland 2000-13.

CROSSBENCH

Political career: *House of Lords:* Raised to the peerage as Baron Mackay of Drumadoon, of Blackwaterfoot in the District of Cunninghame 1995. Lord Advocate 1995-97; Government Spokesperson for Legal Affairs and for the Home and Scottish Offices 1995-97; Opposition Spokesperson for: Constitutional Affairs, Scotland 1997-2000, Home Affairs 1997-2000, Lord Advocate's Department 1997-99; Lord of Appeal 2000-09; As a senior member of the judiciary, disqualified from participation 2009-13. *Councils and public bodies:* Member, Criminal Injuries Compensation Board 1989-95.

Other: Faculty of Advocates, Scotland 1976-. PC 1996. Commons and Lords Rugby Club, Shiskine Golf and Tennis Club.

Recreations: Golf, gardening, Isle of Arran.

Rt Hon the Lord Mackay of Drumadoon QC, House of Lords, London SW1A 0PW
Tel: 020 7219 5353 *Email:* mackayd@parliament.uk

MACKENZIE OF CULKEIN, LORD

MACKENZIE OF CULKEIN (Life Baron), Hector Uisdean MacKenzie; cr. 1999. Born 25 February 1940; Son of late George MacKenzie, lighthouse keeper, and late Williamina Budge, née Sutherland; Married Anna Morrison 1961 (divorced 1991) (1 son 3 daughters).

Education: Isle of Erraid Public School, Argyll; Aird Public School, Isle of Lewis; Nicolson Institute, Stornoway, Isle of Lewis; Portree High School, Skye; Leverndale School of Nursing, Glasgow (RMN 1961); West Cumberland School of Nursing, Whitehaven (SRN 1966).

Non-political career: Student nurse, Leverndale Hospital 1958-61; Assistant lighthouse keeper, Clyde Lighthouses Trust 1961-64; West Cumberland Hospital: Student nurse 1964-66, Staff nurse 1966-69; Confederation of Health Service Employees: Assistant regional secretary 1969, Regional secretary, Yorkshire and East Midlands 1970-74, National officer 1974-83, Assistant General Secretary 1983-87, General Secretary 1987-93; Member, executive board, Public Services International 1987-2000; Associate General Secretary, Unison 1993-2000; Company secretary, UIA Insurance ltd 1996-2000; TUC: President 1998-99, Senior Vice-President 1999-2000. Member, Unison.

LABOUR

Political career: *House of Lords:* Raised to the peerage as Baron MacKenzie of Culkein, of Assynt in Highland 1999. *Other:* Member, Labour Party Policy: Forum 1997-2000, Commission on Health 1998-2000.

Political interests: Health, nursing, defence, aviation, maritime affairs, land reform; Australia, Falkland Islands, USA.

Other: First Substitute Member, World Executive of Public Services International 1987-2000; Inter-Parliamentary Union (British Group); Governor Member, RNLI; Trustee, COHSE 1974 Pension and Assurance Scheme; RGN; RMN. Lindsay Robertson Gold Medal for Nurse of the Year 1966; St Elpheges, Wallington; Ruskin Club, Croydon.

Recreations: Reading, Celtic music, shinty, aviation, travel.

The Lord MacKenzie of Culkein, House of Lords, London SW1A 0PW
Tel: 020 7219 8515 *Fax:* 020 7219 8712 *Email:* mackenzieh@parliament.uk

MACKENZIE OF FRAMWELLGATE, LORD

MACKENZIE OF FRAMWELLGATE (Life Baron), Brian Mackenzie; cr. 1998. Born 21 March 1943; Son of Frederick Mackenzie and Lucy Mackenzie, née Ward; Married Jean Seed 1965 (2 sons); married Deborah Glaister 2009 (divorced 2012).

Education: Eastbourne Boys' School, Darlington; London University (LLB 1974); FBI National Academy, Quantico, USA (Graduate 1985).

Non-political career: Durham Constabulary 1963-98: Chief Superintendent 1989-98. Member, Police Federation of England and Wales 1963-80; National President, Police Superintendents' Association 1995-98; Member, National Association of Retired Police Officers 1998-; Vice-President, BALPA 2003-.

NON-AFFILIATED

Political career: *House of Lords:* Raised to the peerage as Baron Mackenzie of Framwellgate, of Durham in the County of Durham 1998. EU Sub-committee F (Home Affairs): Co-opted member 2009-10, Member 2010-12; Member EU Sub-committee F (Home Affairs, Health and Education) 2012-13. *Other:* Labour Whip withdrawn June 2013.

Political interests: Police, home affairs, legal affairs; India, Poland, Russia, USA.

Other: Member: FBI National Academy Associates, International Association of Chiefs of Police; President/patron, various police, security, defence and hospice organisations; Honorary Billetmaster, City of Durham 1989-2004; Patron: Loomba Trust, Finchale Training College for Disabled, Durham; St Oswald's Hospice, Newcastle. OBE 1998; Dunelm, Durham City.

Publications: Two Lives of Brian – From Policing to Politics (autobiography) (Memoir Club, 2004).

Recreations: Herpetology, after-dinner speaking, swimming, fitness, singing.

The Lord Mackenzie of Framwellgate OBE, House of Lords, London SW1A 0PW
Tel: 020 7219 8632 *Fax:* 020 7219 1997 *Email:* mackenzieb@parliament.uk

LABOUR

McKENZIE OF LUTON, LORD

Opposition Spokesperson for Communities and Local Government and for Work and Pensions

McKENZIE OF LUTON (Life Baron), William David McKenzie; cr. 2004. Born 24 July 1946; Son of Elsie May Doust and George McKenzie; Married Diane Joyce Angliss 1972.

Education: Reading School; Bristol University (BA economics and accounting 1967).

Non-political career: Articled clerk to salaried partner Martin Rata and Partners 1968-73; Price Waterhouse, London 1973-86: Senior to senior manager 1973-80, Partner 1980-86; Sundry consultancy projects 1986-92; Price Waterhouse, Hong Kong 1992-98: Consultant 1992-93, Partner 1993-98, Partner in charge, Vietnam 1996-98. Member, GMB 1980s-.

Political career: *House of Commons:* Contested Luton South 1987 and 1992 general elections. *House of Lords:* Raised to the peerage as Baron McKenzie of Luton, of Luton in the County of Bedfordshire 2004. Government Spokesperson for: Trade and Industry 2005-07, Treasury 2005-07; Government Whip 2005-07; Parliamentary Under-Secretary of State and Government Spokesperson: Department for Work and Pensions 2007-10, Department for Communities and Local Government 2009-10; Opposition Spokesperson for: Communities and Local Government 2010-, Work and Pensions 2010-. Member Merits of Statutory Instruments 2005. *Other:* Various constituency posts. *Councils and public bodies:* Luton Borough Council: Councillor 1976-92, 1999-2005, Leader 1999-2003.

Political interests: Local government, local government finance, taxation systems, education, airports.

Other: FCA 1979.

Recreations: Swimming, reading.

The Lord McKenzie of Luton, House of Lords, London SW1A 0PW
Tel: 020 7219 6339 *Email:* mckenziew@parliament.uk

NON-AFFILIATED

MACKIE OF BENSHIE, LORD

MACKIE OF BENSHIE (Life Baron), George Yull Mackie; cr. 1974. Born 10 July 1919; Son of late Maitland Mackie, OBE, LLD; Married Lindsay Sharp 1944 (died 1985) (3 daughters and 1 son deceased); married Jacqueline Lane, née Rauch 1988.

Education: Aberdeen Grammar School; Aberdeen University (MA).

Non-political career: Served with RAF 1940-46; Squadron-Leader 1944; Air Staff 1944-45. Farming in Angus 1945-89; Former chair: Perth and Angus Fruit Growers Ltd, Caithness Glass Ltd; Benshie Cattle Company Ltd; Rector, Dundee University 1980-83; Cotswold Wine Ltd 1983-85. Member, NFU.

Political career: *House of Commons:* Contested South Angus 1959 general election. MP (Liberal) Caithness and Sutherland 1964-66. Scottish Whip 1964-66. *House of Lords:* Raised to the peerage as Baron Mackie of Benshie, of Kirriemuir in the County of Angus 1974. Liberal Democrat Spokesperson for Agriculture and Scottish Affairs 1975-2000; On leave of absence. *Other:* Scottish Liberal Party: Chair 1965-70, President 1983-88.

Political interests: Agriculture.

Other: Executive Committee Member, Inter-Parliamentary Union British Group; Member: Commonwealth Parliamentary Association, Council of Europe 1986-98, Western European Council 1986-98; Member, Scottish Farmers Union; Former President, Royal Agricultural and Highlands

Society; President, *205* Group Association RAF on Middle East; Member, Bomber Command Association; Honorary Adviser; Salvation Army. Honorary LLD, Dundee University 1982. DSO 1944; DFC 1944; CBE 1971; Garrick, Farmers', Royal Air Force.

Publications: Policy for Scottish Agriculture (1963); Flying Farming and Politics a Liberal Life (2004).

Recreations: Golf, social life, croquet.

The Lord Mackie of Benshie CBE DSO DFC, House of Lords, London SW1A 0PW
Tel: 020 7219 5353

MACLAURIN OF KNEBWORTH, LORD

MACLAURIN OF KNEBWORTH (Life Baron), Ian Charter MacLaurin; cr. 1996. Born 30 March 1937; Son of late Arthur George and Evelina Florence MacLaurin; Married Ann Margaret Collar 1961 (died 1999) (1 son 2 daughters); married Paula Brooke 2002 (2 stepdaughters).

Education: Malvern College.

Non-political career: National Service, RAF Flight Command 1956-58. Tesco plc 1959-97: Director 1970, Managing director 1973-85, Deputy chair 1983-85, Chair 1985-97; Director, Enterprise Oil 1984-90; Non-executive director: National Westminster Bank plc 1990-96, Gleneagles Hotels plc 1992-97; Vodafone Group plc: Non-executive director 1997-2006, Chair 1998-2006; Non-executive director: Whitbread plc 1997-2001, Evolution Group plc 2004-11, Fleet Support Group 2004-, Heineken NV 2006-10; Chair: Chartwell Group 2006-10, Vodafone Foundation 2006-09, Paperless Receipts 2012.

CONSERVATIVE

Political career: *House of Lords:* Raised to the peerage as Baron MacLaurin of Knebworth, of Knebworth in the County of Hertfordshire 1996. Member Economic Affairs 2007. *Councils and public bodies:* DL, Hertfordshire 1992-2007; Chair, UK Sports Council, resigned 1997; DL, Wiltshire 2007-12.

Political interests: Industry, sports; Europe, UK.

Other: Chair, Food Policy Group, Retail Consortium 1980-84; Committee member, MCC 1986-; President, Institute of Grocery Distribution 1989-92; Trustee, Royal Opera House Trust 1992; Chair, England and Wales Cricket Board (formerly Test and County Cricket Board) 1996-2002; Governor and Chairman of Council, Malvern College 2002-; Chair, Hope for Tomorrow; Trustee, Chance to Shine; Chair, Sport Honours Committee -2011; Chartered director, Institute of Directors; FRSA 1986; FIM 1987; Honorary FCGI 1992; Hope for Tomorrow. Liveryman, The Carmen's Company 1982-. Freeman, City of London 1981. Chancellor, University of Hertfordshire 1996-2005. Three honorary doctorates, universities of: Hertfordshire, Stirling, Bradford; Honorary Fellow, University of Wales. Kt 1989; Harry's Bar, Annabel's. Life President, Brocket Hall Golf; MCC; Royal and Ancient Golf Club; Royal St George's, Rye.

Publications: Tiger by the Tail (1999).

Recreations: Golf, cricket, walking the dogs.

The Lord MacLaurin of Knebworth DL, House of Lords, London SW1A 0PW
Tel: 020 7219 5353

MACLENNAN OF ROGART, LORD

MACLENNAN OF ROGART (Life Baron), Robert Adam Ross Maclennan; cr 2001. Born 26 June 1936; Son of late Sir Hector Maclennan; Married Mrs Helen Noyes 1968 (1 son 1 daughter 1 stepson).

Education: Glasgow Academy; Balliol College, Oxford (BA history 1958, MA); Trinity College, Cambridge (LLB 1962); Columbia University, New York.

Non-political career: Barrister.

LIBERAL DEMOCRAT

Political career: *House of Commons:* MP (Labour 1966-81, SDP 1981-88, Liberal Democrat 1988-2001) for Caithness and Sutherland 1966-97, Caithness, Sutherland and Easter Ross 1997-2001. PPS to George Thomson: as Minister without Portfolio 1967-69, as Chancellor of the Duchy of Lancaster 1969-70; Additional Opposition Spokesperson for: Scottish Affairs 1970-71, Defence 1971-72; Parliamentary Under-Secretary of State, Department of Prices and Consumer Protection 1974-79; Opposition Frontbench Spokesperson for Foreign and Commonwealth Affairs 1980-81; SDP Spokesperson for: Agriculture, Fisheries and Food 1981-87, Home and Legal Affairs 1983-87, Northern Ireland 1983-87, Scotland (jointly) 1982-87; Alliance Spokesperson for Agriculture and Fisheries and Food 1987; Liberal Democrat Spokesperson for: Home Affairs and National Heritage 1988-94, Constitutional Affairs and Culture 1994-2001. *House of Lords:* Raised to the peerage as Baron Maclennan of Rogart, of Rogart in Sutherland 2001. Liberal Democrat Spokesperson for: Europe 2001-04, European Constitution 2004-05, Scotland 2004-09, Cabinet Office 2005-10, Constitutional Affairs 2007-10. Member: European Union 2005-09, 2010-, EU Sub-committees: A (Economic and Financial Affairs and International Trade) 2005-08, E (Law and Institutions) 2008-10, Economic Affairs 2010, 2011, EU Sub-committee E (Justice and Institutions) 2010-12, Leader's Group on the Working Practices of the House of Lords 2010-11, EU Sub-committees: D (Agriculture, Fisheries, Environment and Energy) 2012-13, C (External Affairs) 2013-. Chair, Liberal Democrat Parliamentary Party Committees on: Constitutional and Political Reform (Cabinet Office) 2010-12, Scotland 2010-12. *Other:* Leader, SDP 1987-88; President, Liberal Democrat Party 1994-98.

Political interests: Constitutional reform, European Union, rural affairs, arts; all European countries, India, Pakistan, USA.

Other: Alternate National Parliamentary Representative, European Convention 2002-04; Council member, Northlands Creative Glass; Chair, North Highland Connections. Freeman, Caithness. PC 1997; Légion d'Honneur (France) 2004; Brooks's; RAC.

Publications: Librettos: The Lie (1992), Friend of The People (1999).

Recreations: Theatre, music, visual arts.

Rt Hon the Lord Maclennan of Rogart, House of Lords, London SW1A 0PW
Tel: 020 7219 4133 *Email:* maclennanr@parliament.uk

McNALLY, LORD

Deputy Leader of the House of Lords; Minister of State and Government Spokesperson, Ministry of Justice; Leader, Liberal Democrats in the House of Lords

McNALLY (Life Baron), Tom McNally; cr. 1995. Born 20 February 1943; Son of late John and Elizabeth McNally; Married Eileen Powell 1970 (divorced 1990); married Juliet Lamy Hutchinson 1990 (2 sons 1 daughter).

LIBERAL DEMOCRAT **Education:** College of St Joseph, Blackpool; University College, London (BSc economics 1966) (President, Students Union 1965-66).

Non-political career: Political adviser to James Callaghan: as Secretary of State for Foreign and Commonwealth Affairs 1974-76, as Prime Minister 1976-79; Public affairs adviser, GEC 1983-84; Director-General, Retail Consortium; Director, British Retailers Association 1985-87; Head of public affairs: Hill & Knowlton 1987-93, Shandwick 1993-96; Vice-chair, Weber Shandwick 1996-2004. Vice-President, National Union of Students 1966-67.

Political career: *House of Commons:* MP (Labour 1979-81, SDP 1981-83) for Stockport South. Contested (SDP) Stockport 1983 general election. SDP Spokesperson for Education and Sport 1981-83. Member: Industry and Trade 1979-83. *House of Lords:* Raised to the peerage as Baron McNally, of Blackpool in the County of Lancashire 1995. Liberal Democrat Spokesperson for: Broadcasting and Trade and Industry 1996-97, Home Affairs 1998-2002, Broadcasting 2002-04, Home Office 2004; Liberal Democrat peers: Deputy Leader 2001-04, Leader 2004-; Liberal Democrat Spokesperson for Constitutional Affairs 2006-10; Deputy Leader of the House of Lords 2010-; Minister of State and Government Spokesperson, Ministry of Justice 2010-. Member: Public Service 1996-97, Freedom of Information 1999, Draft Communications Bill Joint Committee 2002, Liaison 2005-, Privileges/Privileges and Conduct 2005-, Procedure 2005-, Selection 2005-, House 2005-, Conventions Joint Committee 2006. *Other:* Labour Party Researcher 1967-68; International Secretary, Labour Party 1969-74.

Countries of interest: China, EU, India, Tunisia.

Other: Assistant General Secretary, Fabian Society 1966-67; Fellow, Industry and Parliament Trust 1981; Fellow, Chartered Institute of Public Relations (FCIPR) 2000; Fellow, University College, London 1995. Fellow, University College London 1995-; Doctor of Law, Hertfordshire University 2011. PC 2004; National Liberal.

Recreations: Watching sport, reading political biographies.

Rt Hon the Lord McNally, House of Lords, London SW1A 0PW
Tel: 020 7219 5443 *Email:* mcnallyt@parliament.uk

LIBERAL DEMOCRAT

MADDOCK, BARONESS

MADDOCK (Life Baroness), Diana Maddock; cr. 1997. Born 19 May 1945; Daughter of late Reginald Derbyshire and of Margaret Evans; Married Robert Maddock 1966 (2 daughters); married Alan Beith MP (later Sir Alan) 2001.

Education: Brockenhurst Grammar School; Shenstone Training College (Cert Ed 1966); Portsmouth Polytechnic (Postgraduate Diploma linguistics 1978).

Non-political career: Geography teacher, Weston Park Girls' School, Southampton 1966-69; English as second language teacher: Extra-mural department, Stockholm University 1969-72, Sholing Girls' School, Southampton 1972-73, Anglo-Continental School of English, Bournemouth 1973-76, Greylands School of English (part time) 1990-91.

Political career: *House of Commons:* Contested Southampton Test 1992 general election. MP (Liberal Democrat) for Christchurch 29 July 1993 by-election to 1997. Liberal Democrat Spokesperson for Housing, Women's Issues and Family Policy 1994-97; Sponsored as Private Member's Bill, Home Energy Conservation Act 1995. *House of Lords:* Raised to the peerage as Baroness Maddock, of Christchurch in the County of Dorset 1997. Liberal Democrat Spokesperson for Housing 1998-2004. Member: European Union 2002-05, Merits of Statutory Instruments 2005-09, EU Sub-committee A: (Economic and Financial Affairs and International Trade) 2010-12, (Economic and Financial Affairs) 2012-, Works of Art 2012-13. *Other:* President, Liberal Democrat Party 1998-2000. *Councils and public bodies:* Southampton City Council: Councillor 1984-93, Leader, Liberal Democrat Group; Councillor: Northumberland County Council 2005-08, Berwick-upon-Tweed Borough Council 2007-09; Vice-President, Local Government Association 2010-.

Political interests: Education, local government, housing, environment; Denmark, Finland, Norway, Sweden.

Other: Vice-President: National Energy Action 2000-, National Home Improvement Council 2000-; President: MicroPower Council, Anglo-Swedish Society; National Association of Almshouses; St Mungos (St Mungo Community Housing Association Ltd); National Liberal; Northern Counties Club.

Recreations: Theatre, music, reading, travel.

The Baroness Maddock, House of Lords, London SW1A 0PW
Tel: 020 7219 1625 *Email:* maddockd@parliament.uk

CONSERVATIVE

MAGAN OF CASTLETOWN, LORD

MAGAN OF CASTLETOWN (Life Baron), George Morgan Magan; cr 2011. Born 14 November 1945; Son of Brigadier William Magan, CBE and Maxine Mitchell; Married Wendy Chilton 1972 (2 sons 1 daughter).

Education: Winchester College.

Non-political career: Peat Marwick Mitchell 1964-70; Kleinwort Benson Ltd 1971-74; Director, Morgan Grenfell and Co Ltd 1974-88; Co-founder and chair, JO Hambro Magan 1988-96; Chair: Hawkpoint Partners 1997-2001, eMuse 2001-, Lion Capital Partners 2001-08, Mallett plc 2001-08, Morgan Shipley Ltd (Dubai) 2001-; Director: Edmiston and Co. 2001-, Allied Investment Partners (Abu Dhabi) 2007-12.

Political career: *House of Lords:* Raised to the peerage as Baron Magan of Castletown, of Kensington in the Royal Borough of Kensington and Chelsea 2011. *Other:* Conservative Party: Deputy treasurer 2002-03, Treasurer 2003, Board member 2003; Conservative Party Foundation: Director 2003-13, Deputy chairman 2009-13. *Councils and public bodies:* Royal Opera House, Covent Garden 1995-2001.

Other: Trustee: London Philharmonic Orchestra 1992-2006, British Museum Development Trust 1999-2003; Royal Yacht Squadron.

The Lord Magan of Castletown, House of Lords, London SW1A 0PW
Tel: 020 7219 5353

MAGINNIS OF DRUMGLASS, LORD

MAGINNIS OF DRUMGLASS (Life Baron), Kenneth Wiggins Maginnis; cr 2001. Born 21 January 1938; Son of late Gilbert and Margaret Maginnis, née Wiggins; Married Joy Stewart 1961 (2 sons 2 daughters).

Education: Royal School, Dungannon; Stranmillis Teacher Training College, Belfast 1958.

Non-political career: Major (Rtd), 8 Battalion, Ulster Defence Regiment 1970-81. Teacher: Cookstown Secondary School 1959-60, Drumglass Primary School, Dungannon 1960-66; Principal, Pomeroy Primary School 1966-82.

**INDEPENDENT
ULSTER UNIONIST**

Political career: *House of Commons:* Contested Fermanagh and South Tyrone by-election August 1981. MP (UUP) for Fermanagh and South Tyrone 1983-2001 (Resigned December 1985 in protest against the Anglo-Irish Agreement; Re-elected by-election 23 January 1986; Retired 2001). UUP Spokesperson for: Defence and Home Office 1997-2000, Defence, Trade and Industry 2000-01. *House of Lords:* Raised to the peerage as Baron Maginnis of Drumglass, of Carnteel in the County of Tyrone 2001. *Other:* Member: Northern Ireland Assembly 1982, Northern Ireland Forum 1996-98. Treasurer, Ulster Unionist Council -2008; UUP Whip withdrawn June 2012; Resigned from UUP August 2012. *Councils and public bodies:* Dungannon and South Tyrone Borough Council: Councillor 1981-93, 2001-05, Member, Southern Health and Social Services Council 1989-93.

Political interests: Terrorism and internal security, defence, autism; Turkish Republic of Northern Cyprus.

Other: Chair: Moygashel Regeneration Group, Independent Review of Autism Services for DHSSPS(NI) 2008, Northern Ireland Regional ASD Reference Group 2009-11; Martin Residential Trust, Belfast (care of the profoundly mentally handicapped); Ulster Reform. President, Dungannon Rugby Club 2001-02.

Recreations: Rugby.

The Lord Maginnis of Drumglass, House of Lords, London SW1A 0PW
Tel: 020 7219 8189 *Email:* maginnisk@parliament.uk

MALLALIEU, BARONESS

MALLALIEU (Life Baroness), Ann Mallalieu; cr. 1991. Born 27 November 1945; Daughter of late Sir William Mallalieu and Lady Mallalieu; Married Timothy Cassel (later Sir Timothy Bt) 1979 (divorced 2007) (2 daughters).

Education: Holton Park Girls' Grammar School, Wheatley; Newnham College, Cambridge (MA, LLM law 1968).

Non-political career: Called to the Bar, Inner Temple 1970; Elected Member, General Council of the Bar 1973-75; Recorder 1985-94; Bencher 1992; QC.

LABOUR

Political career: *House of Lords:* Raised to the peerage as Baroness Mallalieu, of Studdridge in the County of Buckinghamshire 1991. Opposition Spokesperson for: Home Affairs 1992-97, Legal Affairs 1992-97. Member Joint Committees on: Consolidation, Etc, Bills 1998-2005, 2006-; Statutory Instruments 2013-. *Other:* Chair, Leave Country Sports Alone Labour Support Campaign 2000-. *Councils and public bodies:* Exmoor National Park Consultative Forum.

Political interests: Law, home affairs, agriculture, environment.

Other: Chair: Council of the Ombudsman for Corporate Estate Agents 1993-2000, Suzy Lamplugh Trust 1996-2000; President: Countryside Alliance May 1998-, British Hawking Association 1999-; Member, British Horseracing Board 2004-07 President, Horses Trust 2009-; Trustee: Racing Welfare 2009-, National Association of Stable Staff. Honorary Fellow, Newnham College, Cambridge 1992. Peer of the Year: *House Magazine* 2005, *The Spectator* 2005.

Recreations: Hunting, poetry, sheep, fishing, racing.

The Baroness Mallalieu QC, House of Lords, London SW1A 0PW
Tel: 020 7219 2000
Tel: 01494 482303 *Fax:* 01494 484339 *Email:* ann272727@aol.com

MALLOCH-BROWN, LORD

MALLOCH-BROWN (Life Baron), (George) Mark Malloch Brown; cr 2007. Born 16 September 1953; Son of late Robert Malloch-Brown and Ursula Malloch-Brown, née Pelly; Married Patricia Cronan 1989 (1 son 3 daughters).

Education: Marlborough College, Wiltshire; Magdalene College, Cambridge (BA history 1975); University of Michigan, USA (MA political science 1977).

Non-political career: Political correspondent, *Economist* 1977-79; Field operations for Cambodian refugees, Thailand 1979-81; Deputy chief emergency unit, UN High Commission for Refugees, Geneva 1981-83; Founder and editor, Economist Development Report 1983-86; Lead international partner, Sawyer-Miller Group 1986-94; World Bank 1994-99: Director, external affairs 1994-96, Vice-President, external affairs and UN affairs 1996-99; Administrator, UN Development Programme 1999-2005; UN 2005-06: Chef de Cabinet to Secretary-General Kofi Annan 2005-06, Deputy Secretary-General 2006; Vice-chair: Soros Fund Management 2007, Open Society Institute 2007, World Economic Forum 2009; Chairman, EMEA operations, FTI Consulting 2010-; Adviser, SouthWest Energy 2010-.

Political career: *House of Lords:* Raised to the peerage as Baron Malloch-Brown, of St Leonard's Forest in the County of West Sussex 2007. Minister of State for Africa, Asia and UN and Government Spokesperson, Foreign and Commonwealth Office (also attending Cabinet) 2007-09; On leave of absence June–December 2012.

Political interests: Development, foreign policy; Africa and Asia.

Other: Chair, Royal Africa Society; Board member: Open Society Institute, Save the Children International, Children's Investment Fund Foundation; Founder and board member, International Crisis Group 1995-; Board member: Centre for Global Development, Shell Foundation; Governor, Marlborough College. Honorary doctorates from three US and one Peruvian University; Honorary Fellow, Magdalene College, Cambridge. KCMG 2007; PC 2007.

Recreations: Reading, jogging and family.

Rt Hon the Lord Malloch-Brown KCMG, House of Lords, London SW1A 0PW
Tel: 020 7219 5353
Fifth Floor, Davidson Building, 5 Southampton Street, London WC2E 7HA *Tel:* 020 7632 5104
Email: mark.malloch-brown@fticonsulting.com camilla.decaires@fticonsulting.com

MANCE, LORD

MANCE (Life Baron), Jonathan Hugh Mance; cr 2005. Born 6 June 1943; Son of Sir Henry and Lady Mance, née Joan Erica Robertson Baker; Married Mary Arden, later Rt Hon Dame Mary Arden, Lady Justice Arden 1973 (1 son 2 daughters).

Education: Charterhouse, Surrey; University College, Oxford (BA jurisprudence 1964, MA); French, German, mainly reading Spanish.

Non-political career: Called to the Bar, Middle Temple 1965; Bencher 1965; QC 1982; Recorder 1990-93; Judge commercial list High Court Queen's Bench Division 1993-99; Lord Justice of Appeal 1999-2005; Justice of the Supreme Court of the United Kingdom 2009-.

Political career: *House of Lords:* Raised to the peerage as Baron Mance, of Frognal in the London Borough of Camden 2005. Lord of Appeal in Ordinary 2005-09; As Justice of the Supreme Court, disqualified from participation 2009-. European Union Sub-committee E (Law and Institutions): Co-opted member 2006-07, Chair 2007-09; Member European Union 2007-09. *Councils and public bodies:* Chair, various Banking Appeals Tribunals 1992-93.

Countries of interest: Europe, Democratic Republic of the Congo.

Other: UK Representative Judge, Council of Europe's Consultative Council of Judges -2011; Chair: International Law Association 2009-, British-German Jurists Association 2009-; Member, seven-person panel on the functioning of the European Union (established by Lisbon Treaty, under Article 255 TFEU); Member, The Judicial Integrity Group; Chair, Lord Chancellor's Advisory Committee on Private International Law; Trustee, European Law Academy -2011; High Steward, Oxford University 2012-; Member, British-German Jurists Association; Hampstead Counselling Service. Honorary Fellow: University College, Oxford, Liverpool John Moores University, John F Kennedy University, Buenos Aires, Argentina. Kt 1993; PC 1999.

Publications: Editor and author various legal works and articles.

Recreations: Languages, music, tennis, skiing.

Rt Hon the Lord Mance, House of Lords, London SW1A 0PW
Tel: 020 7219 5353
Supreme Court of the United Kingdom, Parliament Square, London SW1P 3BD *Tel:* 020 7960 1956 *Fax:* 020 7960 1961
Email: mancej@supremecourt.gsi.gov.uk kaya.banerjee@supremecourt.gsi.gov.uk

MANCROFT, LORD

MANCROFT (3rd Baron, UK), Benjamin Lloyd Stormont Mancroft; cr. 1937; 3rd Bt of Mancroft (UK) 1932. Born 16 May 1957; Son of 2nd Baron, KBE, TD and of late Diana, née Lloyd; Married Emma Peart 1990 (2 sons 1 daughter).

Education: Eton College.

Non-political career: Chair: Inter Lotto (UK) Ltd 1995-, Scratch-n-Win Lotteries Ltd 1995-98; Non-executive director: St Martin's Magazines plc, Rok Corporation (and deputy chair) 2003-; Chair, New Media Lottery Services plc 2006-.

CONSERVATIVE

Political career: *House of Lords:* First entered House of Lords 1987; Elected hereditary peer 1999-. Member: Statutory Instruments Joint Committee 2002-07, Pre-legislative Scrutiny Committee on Draft Gambling Bill 2003-04, Administration and Works 2009-. *Other:* Member: Executive National Union of Conservative Associations 1989-94, Executive Association of Conservative Peers 1989-94, 1999-. *Councils and public bodies:* Executive Committee, Lotteries Council 1999-.

Political interests: Drug addiction, alcoholism, rural affairs.

Other: President European Association for the Treatment of Addiction; Joint Master, Vale of White Horse Fox Hounds 1987-89; Chair, Addiction Recovery Foundation 1989-; Director, Phoenix House Housing Association 1991-96, Vice-Chairman 1992-96; Deputy chair, British Field Sports Society 1992-97; Chair, Drug and Alcohol Foundation 1994-; President, Alliance of Independent Retailers 1996-2000; Patron, Osteopathic Centre for Children 1996-; Chair, Mentor (UK) 2001-; Vice-chair, Countryside Alliance 2005-; Pratt's.

Recreations: Hunting, stalking, shooting, fishing.

The Lord Mancroft, House of Lords, London SW1A 0PW
Tel: 020 7219 5353
Host Europe House, Kendal Avenue, London W3 0XA

MANDELSON, LORD

MANDELSON (Life Baron); Peter Benjamin Mandelson; cr 2008. Born 21 October 1953; Son of late George Mandelson, and of Honorary Mary Joyce Morrison, daughter of late Baron Morrison of Lambeth.

Education: Hendon Grammar School; St Catherine's College, Oxford (BA philosophy, politics and economics 1976); French.

Non-political career: Producer, London Weekend Television 1982-85; Director, campaigns and communications, Labour Party 1985-90; Industrial consultant, SRU Group 1990-92; Economic department, Trade Union Congress (TUC) 1977-78; Member, GMB – Britain's General Union; Commissioner for Trade, European Commission 2004-08; Chairman, Global Counsel LLP; Senior Adviser, Lazard Ltd. Economic Department, TUC 1977-78; Member, GMB.

LABOUR

Political career: *House of Commons:* MP (Labour) for Hartlepool 1992-2004. Opposition Whip 1994-95; Opposition spokesperson: Civil service 1995-96, Election planning 1996-97; Minister without Portfolio 1997-98; Secretary of State for: Trade and Industry 1998, Northern Ireland 1999-2001. *House of Lords:* Raised to the peerage as Baron Mandelson, of Foy in the County of Herefordshire and Hartlepool in the County of Durham 2008. Secretary of State and Government Spokesperson for Business, Enterprise and Regulatory Reform/Business, Innovation and Skills 2008-10; First Secretary of State 2009-10; Lord President of the Council 2009-10. *Other:* Chair, Parliamentary Labour Party General Election Campaign (Planning) 1999-2001. *Councils and public bodies:* Councillor, London Borough of Lambeth 1979-82; High Steward, Hull 2013-.

Other: Chair, British Youth Council 1978-80; President, Central School of Speech and Drama 2001-; Chair, Policy Network 2001-; UK chair, UK-Japan 21st century Group; President, Hartlepool United FC. Hon Fellow, St Catherine's College, Oxford. Politicians' Politician, Channel 4 Political awards 2009. PC 1998.

Publications: Several books including Broadcasting and Youth (1980); Labour's Next Steps: Tackling Social Exclusion (Fabian Society, 1997); Co-author: The Blair Revolution – Can New Labour Deliver? (Faber and Faber, 1996); The Blair Revolution Revisited (Politico's, 2004); Author, The Third Man (Harper Press, 2010); Contributor, The Purple Book (Progress, 2011).

Recreations: Cinema, theatre.

Rt Hon the Lord Mandelson, House of Lords, London SW1A 0PW
Tel: 020 7219 5353

MANNINGHAM-BULLER, BARONESS

MANNINGHAM-BULLER (Life Baroness), Eliza(beth) Lydia Manningham-Buller; cr 2008. Born 14 July 1948; Daughter of 1st Viscount Dilhorne; Married.

Education: Northampton High School; Benenden School, Kent; Lady Margaret Hall, Oxford (BA English 1970).

Non-political career: Security Service 1974-2007: Deputy director-general 1997-2002, Director-general 2002-07.

Political career: *House of Lords:* Raised to the peerage as Baroness Manningham-Buller, of Northampton in the County of Northamptonshire 2008. Member Privileges/Privileges and Conduct 2008-13; Sub-committee on Lords' Interests: Member 2008-09: Chair 2009-10; Member Joint Committee on National Security Strategy 2010-13; Chair Sub-committee on Lords' Conduct 2010-; Member Science and Technology 2013-.

CROSSBENCH

Political interests: National security, foreign policy, defence, health, higher education.

Other: Governor, Wellcome Trust; Chair of council, Imperial College London. Honorary fellow: Lady Margaret Hall, Oxford, Northampton University, Cardiff University, City & Guilds; Five honorary doctorates: St Andrews University, Cranfield University, Open University, Oxford University, Leeds University 2012. Women in Public Life Awards: Outstanding Achievement award 2007, Public Servant of the Year 2007. DCB 2005.

Publications: Securing Freedom (Based on 2011 Reith lectures) (Profile Books, 2012).

The Baroness Manningham-Buller DCB, House of Lords, London SW1A 0PW
Tel: 020 7219 5353

MANZOOR, BARONESS

MANZOOR (Life Baroness), Zahida Parveen Manzoor; cr 2013. Born 25 May 1958; Married Dr Madassar Manzoor 1984 (2 daughters).

Education: Leeds University (1982); Bradford University (MA applied social studies 1989).

Non-political career: West Suffolk Area Health Authority 1977-80: Student nurse, Staff nurse; Health visitor, Durham Area Health Authority 1983-84; Lecturer, Thomas Danby College 1984-86, 1987-88; North east regional programme director, Common Purpose Charitable Trust 1990-92; Chair, Bradford Health Authority 1992-97; Regional chair, Northern and Yorkshire NHS, Department of Health 1997-2001; Legal Services Ombudsman 2003-11; Commissioner, Legal Services Complaints 2004-10; Managing director, Intellisys Ltd 2011-.

LIBERAL DEMOCRAT

Political career: *House of Lords:* Raised to the peerage as Baroness Manzoor, of Knightsbridge in the Royal Borough of Kensington and Chelsea 2013.

Other: Member, Bradford Congress 1992-96; Director, Bradford City Challenge 1993-96; Trustee: West Yorkshire Police Community Trust 1996-98, Uniting Britain Trust 1996-2000, NSPCC 1997; Member, Race Equality Advisory Panel, Home Office 2003-; Vice-patron, Regional Crime Stoppers 1998. CBE 1998.

The Baroness Manzoor CBE, House of Lords, London SW1A 0PW
Tel: 020 7219 5353

MAR, COUNTESS OF

MAR (Countess of, 31st in line, S), Margaret of Mar; cr. 1114, precedence 1404; Lady Garioch (24th in line, S) 1320. Born 19 September 1940; Daughter of 30th Earl; Married Edwin Artiss 1959 (1 daughter) (divorced 1976); married John Salton 1976 (divorced 1981); married John Jenkin 1982.

Education: Kenya High School for Girls, Nairobi, Kenya; Lewes County Grammar School for Girls.

Non-political career: Civil service, clerical officer 1959-63; Sales superintendent, Post Office/British Telecom 1969-82; Farmer and cheesemaker 1982-2010; Farmer 2010-. Vice-President, Association of Members of the Immigration Appeal Tribunal 2005-07.

CROSSBENCH

Political career: *House of Lords:* First entered House of Lords 1975; Deputy Chair of Committees 1997-2007, 2010-12; Deputy Speaker 1999-2007, 2011-; Elected hereditary peer 1999-; Contested Lord Speaker election 2006. Co-opted member European Communities Sub-committee C (Environment, Public Health and Consumer Protection) 1997-99; Member: EU Sub-committee D (Environment, Agriculture, Public Health and Consumer Protection/Environment and Agriculture) 2001-05, Refreshment 2005-09, Statutory Instruments Joint Committee 2007-10, Delegated Powers and Regulatory Reform 2013-.

Political interests: Health service, social security, agriculture, environment, pesticides, food standards; Africa.

Other: Numerous charitable organisations, especially ones involved in health; Chairman, Forward-Me. Laurent Perrier/Country Life Parliamentarian of the Year 1996; *BBC Wildlife Magazine* Green Ribbon Award 1997; Spectator Peer of the Year 1997; Honorary Assoc RCVS 2006; Honorary Assoc BVA 2006; Outstanding Achievement, Charity Champion Awards 2011. Holder of the Premier Earldom of Scotland; Recognised in the surname "of Mar" by warrant of the Court of the Lord Lyon 1967, when she abandoned her second Christian name of Alison; Farmers'.

Recreations: Gardening, goat keeping, reading.

The Countess of Mar, House of Lords, London SW1A 0PW
Tel: 020 7219 8627 *Fax:* 020 7219 1991 *Email:* marm@parliament.uk

MAR AND KELLIE, EARL OF

MAR (14th Earl of, S); cr. 1565, AND KELLIE (16th Earl of, S); cr. 1619, James (Jamie) Thorne Erskine; 16th Viscount Fentoun (S) 1606; 19th Lord Erskine (S) 1429; 16th Lord Erskine of Dirleton (S) 1604; 16th Lord Dirleton (S) 1606; (Life) Baron Erskine of Alloa Tower 2000. Born 10 March 1949; Son of 13th Earl; Married Mary Mooney, née Kirk 1974 (1 stepson 4 stepdaughters 1 deceased).

Education: Eton College; Moray House College of Education (Diploma social work; Diploma youth and community work 1971); Inverness College (Certificate building 1988).

SCOTTISH LIBERAL DEMOCRAT

Non-political career: RAuxAF Regiment 1979-86; Royal Naval Auxiliary Service 1986-88. Community service volunteer, York 1967-68; Youth worker, Craigmillar 1971-73; Senior social worker, Sheffield District Council 1973-76; Social worker: Grampian Regional Council 1976-78, Highland Regional Council 1978-87, HM Prison, Inverness 1979-81; Youth worker, Merkinch Centre 1982; Community service offenders supervisor, Inverness 1983-87; Slater, Kincardine 1989-91; Project worker, SACRO 1991-93; Canoe and small boat builder 1993-96; Estate worker 1993-. NALGO 1973-76.

Political career: *House of Lords:* Created a life peer as Baron Erskine of Alloa Tower, of Alloa in Clackmannanshire 2000. First entered House of Lords 1994; Chair, Strathclyde Tram Inquiry 1996; Commissioner, Burrell Collection (Lending) Inquiry 1997; Liberal Democrat Spokesperson for Scotland 2001-04; Liberal Democrat Whip 2002-07; Liberal Democrat Spokesperson for: Transport 2004-10, Home Office (Scottish home affairs) 2005-07; Liberal Democrat Whip 2009-10. Member: Transfer of Crofting Estates (Scotland) Bill 1996, The Constitution 2001-04, Religious Offences 2002-03, Administration and Works 2003-07, Barnett Formula 2008-09, Joint Committee on Statutory Instruments 2009-13. *Other:* Contested Ochil constituency 1999 Scottish Parliament election. *Councils and public bodies:* DL, Clackmannan 1991-.

Political interests: Scotland, probation, social policy, devolution, energy, transport, environment, Scottish political independence; Ireland, Scandinavia.

Other: Member, Scottish Independence Convention 2005-; Non-executive director: Clackmannanshire Heritage Trust, Ceteris -2011. Premier Viscount of Scotland; Hereditary Keeper of Stirling Castle; Page of Honour to HM the Queen 1962, 1963 (Order of the Thistle page); Farmers'.

Recreations: Canoeing, rowing, hill-walking, cycling, Alloa Tower, boat building, horticulture.

The Earl of Mar and Kellie DL, House of Lords, London SW1A 0PW
Tel: 020 7219 3469
Hilton Farm, Alloa, Clackmannan FK10 3PS *Tel:* 01259 212438

MARKS OF HENLEY-ON-THAMES, LORD

MARKS OF HENLEY-ON-THAMES (Life Baron), Jonathan Clive Marks; cr 2011. Born 19 October 1952; Son of late Geoffrey Marks and Patricia Marks, née Bowman; Married Sarah Russell 1982 (divorced 1991) (1 son 1 daughter); married Clementine Cafopoulous 1993 (3 sons 2 daughters).

Education: Harrow School; University College, Oxford (BA Jurisprudence 1974); Inns of Court School of Law (1975); French, Greek.

LIBERAL DEMOCRAT

Non-political career: Called to the Bar, Inner Temple 1975; Visiting lecturer in advocacy: Malaya University 1985, 1989-91, Mauritius University 1988, Sri Lanka University Law College 1992; Appointed Queens Counsel 1995; Barrister, 4 Pump Court Chambers; Arbitrator and Family Law Arbitration.

Political career: *House of Commons:* Contested (SDP) Weston-Super-Mare 1983 and Falmouth and Camborne 1987 general elections. Co-chair, Liberal Democrat Parliamentary Committee on Home Affairs, Justice and Equalities. *House of Lords:* Raised to the peerage as Baron Marks of

Henley-on-Thames, of Henley-on-Thames in the County of Oxfordshire 2011. Liberal Democrat Spokesperson for Justice 2012-. Member: Joint Committee on the Draft Defamation Bill 2011, Delegated Powers and Regulatory Reform 2012-. Chair, Liberal Democrat Parliamentary Party Committee on Home Affairs, Justice and Equalities (Justice) 2012-. *Other:* Contested Cornwall and Plymouth 1984 European Parliament election. Member, Liberal Democrat Committee for England 1988-89; Chair, Liberal Democrat Lawyers Association 2001-07; Member, Federal Policy Committee, Liberal Democrat 2004-10, 2012-.

Political interests: Justice issues, constitutional reform, human rights, education, health; Greece.

Other: Vice-patron, Jubilee; Sailing Trust; Fellow, Chartered Institute of Arbitrators 2012-. Worshipful Company of Pattenmakers; Royal Automobile.

Recreations: Tennis, skiing, theatre, opera, travel.

The Lord Marks of Henley-on-Thames QC, House of Lords, London SW1A 0PW
Tel: 020 7219 6270 *Email:* marksj@parliament.uk
4 Pump Court, London EC4Y 7AN *Tel:* 020 7842 5555 *Email:* jmarks@4pumpcourt.com
Website: www.4pumpcourt.com

MARLAND, LORD

CONSERVATIVE

MARLAND (Life Baron), Jonathan Peter Marland; cr 2006. Born 14 August 1956; Son of Peter Greaves Marland and Audrey Joan Marland; Married Penelope Mary Lamb 1983 (2 sons 2 daughters).

Education: Shrewsbury School.

Non-political career: Director, Lloyd Thompson 1982-99; Partner, JLT Risk Solutions 1999-2006; Chair: Herriot Ltd 2000-10, Janspeed Performance Exhaust Systems Ltd 2002-10; Non-executive director, Clareville Capital LLP 2006-10; Director: Insurance Capital Partners LLP, Hunter Boot Ltd 2007-10; Chair, Jubilee/Appleclaim; Non-executive director: Essex Court Management, WH Ireland Ltd, Test Match Extra.

Political career: *House of Commons:* Contested (Conservative) Somerset and Frome 2001 general election. *House of Lords:* Raised to the peerage as Baron Marland, of Odstock in the County of Wiltshire 2006. Opposition Whip 2009-10; Opposition Spokesperson for: Cabinet Office 2009-10, Energy and Climate Change 2009-10; Parliamentary Under-Secretary of State and Government Spokesperson, Department for: Energy and Climate Change 2010-12, Business, Innovation and Skills 2012-13. *Other:* Conservative Party: Treasurer 2003-07, Board member 2005-07; Director, C&UCO Properties (Party property company) 2006-05; Treasurer, Boris Johnson's London Mayoral Campaign 2007-08. *Councils and public bodies:* Royal Academy of Arts Development Committee 2008-10.

Political interests: Sport, arts, environment, business, finance.

Other: Advisory committee member, Airey Neave Trust 1992-; J P Marland Charitable Trust 1995-; Harnham Water Meadows Trust 2001-10; Trustee: Atlantic Partnership 2001-, Guggenheim (Museum) UK 2002-, Invercauld Estate 2002-, The Sports Nexus 2003-; President, Salisbury FC 2008-; Trustee, International Churchill Society 2009-; FRSA 2008-; Chair, Sports Nexus; RSA, MCC, Brooks's.

Recreations: Sport, British art.

The Lord Marland, House of Lords, London SW1A 0PW
Tel: 020 7219 8738 *Email:* marland@parliament.uk
6 Wilton Place, London SW1X 8RH *Tel:* 020 7752 0177 *Fax:* 020 7245 0778
Email: marland@odstock.net

MARLESFORD, LORD

CONSERVATIVE

MARLESFORD (Life Baron), Mark Shuldham Schreiber; cr. 1991. Born 11 September 1931; Son of late John Shuldham Schreiber, AE, DL and Maureen Schreiber, née Dent; Married 1969, Gabriella Federica, daughter of Count Teodoro Veglio di Castelletto d'Uzzone (2 daughters).

Education: Eton College; Trinity College, Cambridge (BA economics 1956, MA); French.

Non-political career: National Service, Coldstream Guards, 2nd Lieutenant 1950-51. Fisons Ltd 1957-63; Conservative Research Department 1963-70; Special adviser: to HM Government 1970-74, to Leader of the Opposition 1974-75; *The Economist:* Editorial consultant 1974-91, Lobby correspondent 1976-91; Director, Eastern Group plc 1990-96; Adviser to Mitsubishi Corporation International NV 1990-2003; Independent national director, Times Newspaper Holdings 1991-; Adviser to Board, John Swire and Sons Ltd 1992-2009; Non-executive director, Baring New Russia Fund 1996-2007; Adviser, Sit Investment Associates, Minneapolis, USA 2001-; Non-executive director, Gave-Kal Research (Hong Kong) 2004-.

Political career: *House of Lords:* Raised to the peerage as Baron Marlesford, of Marlesford in the County of Suffolk 1991. Member EU Sub-committee A: (Economic and Financial Affairs, Trade and External Relations/Economic and Financial Affairs) 2000-05, (Economic and Financial Affairs and International Trade) 2010-12, (Economic and Financial Affairs) 2012-; Member European Union 2003-07, 2012-; EU Sub-committee F (Home Affairs): Member 2005-07, Co-opted member 2007-09. *Councils and public bodies:* Councillor, East Suffolk County Council 1968-70; Chair, Marlesford Parish Council 1978-; Member: Countryside Commission 1980-92, Rural Development Commission 1985-93; DL, Suffolk 1991-.

Political interests: Conservation, defence, EU economy; China, Hong Kong, Iran.

Other: Chair, Council for the Protection of Rural England 1993-98; President: Suffolk ACRE 1995-2004, Suffolk Preservation Society 1997-; Pratt's.

Recreations: Planting trees and hedges, collecting minerals.

The Lord Marlesford DL, House of Lords, London SW1A 0PW
Tel: 020 7219 5480 *Fax:* 020 7219 5979 *Email:* marlesford@parliament.uk
Marlesford Hall, Woodbridge, Suffolk IP13 0AU

MARTIN OF SPRINGBURN, LORD

MARTIN OF SPRINGBURN (Life Baron), Michael John Martin; cr 2009. Born 3 July 1945; Son of Michael Martin, merchant seaman, and Mary McNeill, school cleaner; Married Mary McLay 1966 (1 son 1 daughter).

Education: St Patrick's Boys' School, Glasgow.

Non-political career: Metal worker, Rolls-Royce Engineering 1970-76; Full-time trades union official 1976-79. Shop steward, AUEW 1970-74; Trade union organiser, NUPE 1976-79; Member, AEEU (Craft Sector)/Unite; Sponsored as MP by AEEU.

CROSSBENCH

Political career: *House of Commons:* MP (Labour 1979-2000, Speaker 2000-09) for Glasgow Springburn 1979-2005, for Glasgow North East 2005-09. PPS to Denis Healey as Deputy Leader of the Labour Party 1980-83; First Deputy Chairman, Ways and Means (Deputy Speaker) 1997-2000; Speaker 2000-09; Ex-officio chair House of Commons Commission 2000-09; Former chair Speaker's Committee on the Electoral Commission. Chair: Chairmen's Panel 1987-2000, Administration 1992-97, Liaison 1993-97; Member: Court of Referees 1997-2000, Unopposed Bills (Panel) 1997-2000, Standing Orders 1998-2000. *House of Lords:* Raised to the peerage as Baron Martin of Springburn, of Port Dundas in the City of Glasgow 2009. *Councils and public bodies:* Councillor: Glasgow Corporation 1973-74, Glasgow District Council 1974-79.

Political interests: Trade and industry, drug abuse, industrial relations, equal opportunities, care of the elderly, human rights, housing, apprenticeships; Canada, Italy, USA.

Other: Fellow, Industry and Parliament Trust 1984. Honorary doctorate, Glasgow University. PC 2000.

Recreations: Hill-walking, folk music, local history, playing the Highland Pipes and member of the College of Piping.

Rt Hon the Lord Martin of Springburn, House of Lords, London SW1A 0PW
Tel: 020 7219 1892 *Email:* martinm@parliament.uk

MASHAM OF ILTON, BARONESS

MASHAM OF ILTON (Life Baroness), Susan Lilian Primrose Cunliffe-Lister; cr. 1970. Born 14 April 1935; Daughter of late Major Sir Ronald Sinclair, 8th Bt, TD, DL; Married Lord Masham, later 2nd Earl of Swinton 1959 (died 2006) (1 son 1 daughter both adopted).

Education: Heathfield School, Ascot; London Polytechnic.

Non-political career: Voluntary social work/health matters. Member, NFU.

Political career: *House of Lords:* Raised to the peerage as Baroness Masham of Ilton, of Masham in the North Riding of the County of Yorkshire 1970. Chair Home Office Crime Prevention Work-

CROSSBENCH

ing Group on Young People and Alcohol 1987. Member: Science and Technology Sub-committee I (Resistance to Anti-Microbial Agents) 1997-98, Administration and Works 2005-09, HIV and AIDS in the UK 2010-11. *Councils and public bodies:* Member: Peterlee and Newton Aycliffe Corporation 1973-85, Yorkshire Regional Health Authority 1982-90; DL, North Yorkshire 1991-; Member: North Yorkshire Family Health Service Authority 1990-96, Board of Visitors Wetherby Young Offenders Institute.

Political interests: Health, disability, penal affairs and policy, drug abuse, farming, horticulture; Europe.

Other: North Yorkshire Red Cross: President 1963-88, Patron 1989-; Council member, Winston Churchill Trust 1980-2005; Honorary President, Ripon St Cecilia Orchestra 2008; Chair, Howard League Inquiry into Girls in Prison; Patron: International Spinal Research Trust, Northern Counties Trust for People Living with HIV/AIDS; Animal Health Trust; John Mordaunt Trust; Yorkshire Wildlife Trust; Highland Pony Society; Vice-President, Ponies UK; Former and current president, patron, chair, member of numerous charities, especially in areas of health and disability; Honorary Fellowship: RCGP 1981, Chartered Society of Physiotherapy 1996. Freedom: Ripon 1960, Harrogate 1989. Six honorary degrees; four honorary fellowships. Rome Paralympics 1968: Gold 25m breaststroke swimming medal, Silver 25m backstroke swimming medal, Bronze women's doubles table tennis medal; Tokyo Paralympics 1964: Gold women's doubles table tennis medal, Silver 25m breaststroke swimming, 25m freestyle prone swimming, 25m freestyle supine swimming and women's singles table tennis medals; Tel Aviv Paralympics 1968: Silver women's doubles table tennis medal, Bronze women's singles tabletennis medal.

Publications: The World Walks By (1986).

Recreations: Breeding Highland ponies, long haired dachshunds, gardening, swimming.

The Countess of Swinton, Baroness Masham of Ilton DL, House of Lords, London SW1A 0PW *Tel:* 020 7219 6302 *Fax:* 020 7219 5979

Dykes Hill House, Masham, Nr Ripon, North Yorkshire HG4 4NS *Tel:* 01765 689241 *Fax:* 01765 688184 *Email:* susan@masham1935.fsnet.co.uk mashamridingcentre.com

MASON OF BARNSLEY, LORD

MASON OF BARNSLEY (Life Baron), Roy Mason; cr. 1987. Born 18 April 1924; Son of late Joseph Mason, miner; Married Marjorie Sowden 1945 (2 daughters).

Education: Carlton and Royston Elementary Schools; London School of Economics (TUC Scholarship 1951-52).

Non-political career: Coal miner 1938-53. Member, Yorkshire Miners' Council 1949-53; Chair, Parliamentary Triple Alliance of Miners, Railway and Steel Union MPs 1979-80.

LABOUR

Political career: House of Commons: MP (Labour) for Barnsley 1953-83, for Barnsley Central 1983-87. Minister of State (Shipping), Board of Trade 1964-67; Minister of Defence Equipment 1967-68; Postmaster General April-June 1968; Minister of Power 1968-69; President, Board of Trade 1969-70; Secretary of State for: Defence 1974-76; Northern Ireland 1976-79. House of Lords: Raised to the peerage as Baron Mason of Barnsley, of Barnsley in South Yorkshire 1987. On leave of absence June 2012-. Other: Chair: Yorkshire Group of Labour MPs 1970-74, 1981-84, Miners' Group of Labour MPs 1973-74, 1980-81. Councils and public bodies: DL, South Yorkshire 1992-.

Political interests: Coal industry, human rights, Northern Ireland, defence, anti-pollution matters.

Other: Member, Council of Europe and Western European Union 1970-71; President: Yorkshire Salmon and Trout Association, Yorkshire Water Colour Society; Vice-President, South Yorkshire Foundation (Charity); Chair: Barnsley Business and Innovation Centre Ltd, Prince's Youth Business Trust, South Yorkshire 1987-2002; Member: National Council of The Scouts Association, National Rivers Authority Advisory Committee 1988, National Rivers Authority 1989-92; President, Lords and Commons Pipe and Cigar Club; Cancer Research, York's Area. Two honorary doctorates, including Northumbria University 2005. PC 1968; Life Membership: Carlton Village Working Men's Club, Barnsley Gawber Road Working Men's Club, Barnsley Trades and Labour Club. President, Lords and Commons Fly Fishing Club.

Publications: Paying the Price (autobiography, 1999).

Recreations: Fly-fishing, golf, tie designing (cravatology), specialist philately.

Rt Hon the Lord Mason of Barnsley DL

MASSEY OF DARWEN, BARONESS

MASSEY OF DARWEN (Life Baroness), Doreen Elizabeth Massey; cr. 1999. Born 5 September 1938; Daughter of late Jack and Mary Ann Hall, née Sharrock; Married Dr Leslie Massey 1966 (2 sons 1 daughter).

Education: Darwen Grammar School, Lancashire; Birmingham University (BA French 1961; DipEd 1962); London University (MA health education 1985); French, some Russian.

Non-political career: Graduate service overseas, Gabon 1962-63; French teacher, South Hackney School 1964-67; French and English teacher, Springside School, Philadelphia 1967-69; Running

LABOUR

community playgroup 1970-77; Teacher/Head of year/Senior teacher in charge of health education, Walsingham School, London 1979-83; Director of training, Family Planning Association

(FPA) 1981-89; Adviser in personal, social and health education, Inner London Education Authority 1983-85; Director of Young People's Programme, Health Education Authority 1985-87; Director, FPA 1989-94; Independent consultant in health education 1994-2001; Chair, National Treatment Agency for Substance Misuse 2002-. Former member: NUT, MSF.

Political career: *House of Lords:* Raised to the peerage as Baroness Massey of Darwen, of Darwen in the County of Lancashire 1999. Member: Selection 2005-08, Ecclesiastical Committee 2005-10, Works of Art 2007-11, Information 2010-. Vice-chair, PLP Departmental Group for Education 2010-.

Political interests: Education, health, children and young people, sport, substance misuse; Central Asia, France, Russia, USA.

Other: Unicef; Member, Lady Taverners; President, Brook Advisory Centres; Patron, Family Planning Association; Advisory Council for Alcohol and Drug Education; Trust for the Study of Adolescence; Board of Unicef UK; Patron, Women and Children First; FRSA; ENO; Opera North; Tacade; Terrence Higgins Trust; Stonewall; Brook Advisory; Women and Children First; FPA. Fellow, University of Central Lancashire 2005; Farmers' Club; Lady Taverners.

Publications: Teaching About HIV/AIDS (1988); Co-author, Sex Education Factpack (1988); Sex Education: Why, What and How (1988); Editor, The Sex Education Source Book (1995); Lovers' Guide Encyclopaedia (1996); Articles on health education in a variety of journals.

Recreations: Theatre, opera, reading, walking, pilates, travel, sports.

The Baroness Massey of Darwen, House of Lords, London SW1A 0PW
Tel: 020 7219 8653 *Email:* masseyd@parliament.uk

MAWHINNEY, LORD

CONSERVATIVE

MAWHINNEY (Life Baron), Brian Stanley Mawhinney; cr 2005. Born 26 July 1940; Son of Frederick and Coralie Mawhinney; Married Betty Oja 1965 (2 sons 1 daughter).

Education: Royal Belfast Academical Institution; Queen's University, Belfast (BSc physics 1963); Michigan University, USA (MSc radiation biology 1964); London University (PhD radiation biology 1968).

Non-political career: Assistant professor of radiation research, Iowa University, USA 1968-70; Lecturer (subsequently senior lecturer), Royal Free Hospital School of Medicine 1970-84. Life Member, AUT.

Political career: *House of Commons:* Contested Teesside Stockton October 1974 general election. MP (Conservative) for Peterborough 1979-97, for North West Cambridgeshire 1997-2005. PPS: to Barney Hayhoe as Minister of State HM Treasury 1982-84; to Tom King as Secretary of State for: Employment 1983-85, Northern Ireland 1984-86; Northern Ireland Office: Parliamentary Under-Secretary of State 1986-90, Minister of State 1990-92; Minister of State, Department of Health 1992-94; Secretary of State for Transport 1994-95; Minister without Portfolio 1995-97; Shadow Home Secretary 1997-98. Chair, Conservative Party Committee for Home Affairs 1997-98. *House of Lords:* Raised to the peerage as Baron Mawhinney, of Peterborough in the County of Cambridgeshire 2005. Chair Joint Committee on the Draft Defamation Bill 2011; Member: Joint Committee on Privacy and Injunctions 2011-12, Public Service and Demographic Change 2012-13. *Other:* National President, Conservative Trade Unionists 1987-90; Chair, Conservative Party 1995-97; Member, governing council, Conservative Christian Fellowship. *Councils and public bodies:* Deputy chair, England 2018 World Cup Bid 2009-10.

Political interests: Health, Northern Ireland, Anglo-American relations, trade and industry; Middle East, USA.

Other: Member: Medical Research Council 1979-83, National Council, National Society for Cancer Relief 1981-85; Fellow, Industry and Parliament Trust 1984; Member, General Synod of Church of England 1985-90; Review Committee of Privy Counsellors of the Anti-terrorism, Crime and Security Act 2002-; Football League: Chair 2003-10, Honorary President 2010-13; Director, Football Association 2006-08; Honorary member, Institute of Physics; Peterborough Association for the Blind, Evangelical Alliance Relief Fund, Macmillan Cancer Relief, More Than Gold. Freedom of Peterborough 2008. Visiting Parliamentary Fellow, St Anthony's College, Oxford 2004-05; Honorary LLD Queen's University, Belfast 2008. PC 1994; Kt 1997. Member, Etton Furze Golf Club.

Publications: Co-author, Conflict and Christianity in Northern Ireland (1972); In the Firing Line – Politics, Faith, Power and Forgiveness (1999); Just a Simple Belfast Boy (2013).

Recreations: Sport, reading.

Rt Hon the Lord Mawhinney, House of Lords, London SW1A 0PW
Tel: 020 7219 5211 *Fax:* 020 7219 0034
53 Ledbury Road, Peterborough PE3 9RF *Tel:* 01733 261868 *Email:* judith5@waitrose.com

CROSSBENCH

MAWSON, LORD

MAWSON (Life Baron), Andrew Mawson; cr 2007. Born 8 November 1954; Son of Jack and Mary Mawson; Married Susan Barnes 1975 (1 daughter 2 sons).

Education: Hanson Boys' School, Bradford; Manchester University (BA theology 1979; MPhil urban spirituality 1990).

Non-political career: Ordained minister, United Reformed Church 1979; Founder and director, Church Action on Central America 1980-92; Founder, chief executive, chair, president, Bromley by Bow Centre (community and primary care facilities) 1984-; Co-founder, executive director, president, Community Action Network 1998-; Director: Andrew Mawson Partnerships, St Paul's Way CIC, Water City CIC, St Paul's Way Transformation Project; Founder: Poplar Harca, Leaside Regeneration; Non-executive director, London Legacy Development Corporation.

Political career: *House of Lords:* Raised to the peerage as Baron Mawson, of Bromley-by-Bow in the London Borough of Tower Hamlets 2007. EU Sub-committee F (Home Affairs): Co-opted member 2007-10, Member 2010-12; Member: Small- and Medium-Sized Enterprises 2012-13, Refreshment 2012-, Joint Committee on the Draft Deregulation Bill 2013-.

Political interests: Public services, international affairs, health, education, enterprise; Europe, UK.

Other: Honorary doctorate. OBE 2000.

Recreations: Music, walking, travel.

The Lord Mawson OBE, House of Lords, London SW1A 0PW
Tel: 020 7219 6949
Ground Floor, 46 Loman Street, London SE1 0EH *Tel:* 020 7620 6000
Email: andrew@amawsonpartnerships.com *Website:* www.amawsonpartnerships.com
Twitter: @AndrewMawson

LABOUR

MAXTON, LORD

MAXTON (Life Baron), John Alston Maxton; cr. 2004. Born 5 May 1936; Son of late John Maxton, agricultural economist, and late Jenny Maxton; Married Christine Waine 1970 (3 sons).

Education: Lord William's Grammar School, Thame; University College, Oxford (BA modern history 1960; DipEd 1961).

Non-political career: Teacher, Glasgow Academy 1961-70; Lecturer in social studies, Hamilton College 1970-79. Member: MSF, Educational Institute of Scotland.

Political career: *House of Commons:* MP (Labour) for Glasgow Cathcart 1979-2001. Opposition Scottish and Treasury Whip 1985; Opposition Frontbench Spokesperson for Scotland 1985-92. Chair PLP National Heritage/Culture, Media and Sport Committee, Member 1992-97. *House of Lords:* Raised to the peerage as Baron Maxton, of Blackwaterfoot in Ayrshire and Arran 2004. Member: Review of the BBC Charter 2005-06, Communications 2007-10, Information 2011-.

Political interests: Broadcasting, internet; France, Spain.

Other: Member: Association of Lecturers in Colleges of Education, Socialist Educational Association. Shiskine Golf and Tennis Club; Virgin Active; Hamilton Rugby Club.

Recreations: Listening to Jazz, fitness, holiday golf on the Isle of Arran, technology.

The Lord Maxton, House of Lords, London SW1A 0PW
Tel: 020 7219 6475 *Email:* maxtonj@parliament.uk maxtonj@yahoo.co.uk

CROSSBENCH

MAY OF OXFORD, LORD

MAY OF OXFORD (Life Baron), Robert McCredie May; cr 2001. Born 8 January 1936; Son of Henry May and Kathleen May, née McCredie; Married Judith Feiner 1962 (1 daughter).

Education: Sydney Boys' High School; Sydney University, Australia (BSc theoretical physics 1957; PhD 1959).

Non-political career: Gordon Mackay lecturer in applied mathematics, Harvard University, USA 1959-61; Sydney University: Senior lecturer 1961-64, Reader 1964-69, Professor of theoretical physics 1969-73; Princeton University, USA: Class of 1877 professor of zoology 1973-88, Vice-president for research 1977-88; Royal Society research professor, Oxford University and Imperial College, London 1988-; Chief scientific adviser to UK Government and Head of UK Office of Science and Technology 1995-2000.

Political career: *House of Lords:* Raised to the peerage as Baron May of Oxford, of Oxford in the County of Oxfordshire 2001. Member: Science and Technology 2006-12, Science and Technology Sub-committee I (Scientific Aspects of Ageing 2005, Allergy/Waste Reduction 2007-08, Nanotechnologies and Food 2008-10, Behavioural Change 2010-11), Systematics and Taxonomy Enquiry 2008, Draft Climate Change Bill Joint Committee 2007, HIV and AIDS in the UK 2010-

11, Economic Affairs 2013-. *Councils and public bodies:* Chair of trustees, Natural History Museum 1993-98; President, The Royal Society 2000-05; Non-executive board member, Defence, Science and Technology Laboratory 2002-12; Member, Climate Change Committee (DECC); Adviser, Tesco's Sustainable Consumption Institute; President, British Science Association 2009-10; Board member, British Council.

Political interests: Science and technology; energy and environment, climate change, education, economy and finance, financial ecosystems.

Other: Non-executive member, HSBC Corporate Sustainability Board, Member, Committee on Climate Change. The Salters Company 2003. City of London 2003. Merton College, Oxford University: Fellow, Emeritus; Fellow: Royal Society 1979, Australian Academy of Sciences 1991, US National Academy of Sciences 1992; Honorary Fellow: Australian Academy of Technological Sciences and Engineering 2001, Royal Academy of Engineering 2004; Numerous other honorary fellowships from scientific institutions in UK, USA and Australia; Numerous honorary degrees, including Oxford and many other UK universities, Harvard, Upsalla, Princeton, Sydney, Yale, ETH Zurich. Numerous, including: Royal Swedish Academy of Science, Crafoord Prize 1996, Balzan Prize 1998, Blue Planet Prize 2001, Royal Society Copley Medal 2007. Kt 1996; Companion Order of Australia (AC) 1998; OM 2002. Oxford University Tennis.

Publications: Several hundred scientific papers; Scientific journalism for journals, radio and television; Stability and Complexity in Model Ecosystems (Princeton University Press, 1973, 2000); Co-author, Infectious Diseases of Humans: Dynamics and Control (OUP, 1991); Editor: Large Scale Ecology and Conservation Biology (Blackwell, 1994), Extinction Rates (OUP, 1995), Evolution of Biological Diversity (OUP, 1999); Co-author, Virus Dynamics: the Mathematical Foundations of Immunology and Virology (OUP, 2000); Theoretical Ecology (3rd edn OUP, 2006); Co-author, Systematic Risk in Banking Ecosystems (Nature 469, 2011).

Recreations: Hiking, running, tennis.

The Lord May of Oxford OM, House of Lords, London SW1A 0PW
Tel: 020 7219 6958
Department of Zoology, Tinbergen Building, South Parks Road, Oxford OX1 3PS

MAYHEW OF TWYSDEN, LORD

MAYHEW OF TWYSDEN (Life Baron), Patrick Barnabas Burke Mayhew; cr. 1997. Born 11 September 1929; Son of late AGH Mayhew MC and Sheila MB Mayhew, née Roche; Married Revd. Jean Gurney, OBE 1963 (4 sons).

Education: Tonbridge School; Mons Officer Cadet School, Aldershot; Balliol College, Oxford (BA jurisprudence 1953, MA); Basic French.

Non-political career: National service 1948-49, commissioned 4th/7th Royal Dragoon Guards; Captain, Army Emergency Reserve 1954-65. Called to the Bar Middle Temple 1955; QC 1972; Bencher 1976; Reader 2000; Non-executive director, Western Provident Association 1997-2007.

CONSERVATIVE

Political career: *House of Commons:* Contested (Conservative) Camberwell-Dulwich 1970 general election. MP (Conservative) for Tunbridge Wells 1974-97. Parliamentary Under-Secretary of State, Department of Employment 1979-81; Minister of State, Home Office 1981-83; Solicitor-General 1983-87; Attorney General 1987-92; Secretary of State for Northern Ireland 1992-97. *House of Lords:* Raised to the peerage as Baron Mayhew of Twysden, of Kilndown in the County of Kent 1997. Member: Deregulation and Devolved Legislation 1997-2001, 2003-05, Parliamentary Privilege Joint Committee 1997-2003, European Union Sub-committee E (Law and Institutions) 2001-05, Parliamentary Joint Scrutiny Committee on: 2nd Draft Mental Health Bill 2004-05, Draft Bribery Bill 2009, Delegated Powers and Regulatory Reform 2009-. *Other:* Executive member, Association Conservative Peers 1998-2006. *Councils and public bodies:* President: West Kent College of Further Education 1997-2012, National Fruit Show 1999-2007; Chair: Prime Minister's Advisory Committee on Business Appointments 1999-2008, Rochester Cathedral Council 2000-07; DL, Kent 2001.

Political interests: Northern Ireland, criminal justice, constitutional matters, defence; all Arab countries, Iran.

Other: President: The Airey Neave Trust 1997-2012, St Paul's Trust Centre, Liverpool; President, Kent Scouts Council 2000-09; Member, General Council of the Bar of England and Wales. Liveryman, Worshipful Company of Skinners 1956-; Honorary Liveryman, Worshipful Company of Fruiterers 2001-. Kt 1983; PC 1986; Pratt's, Beefsteak, Garrick, Tunbridge Wells Constitutional. Tunbridge Wells RFC.

Recreations: Country life, travel, reading.

Rt Hon the Lord Mayhew of Twysden QC DL, House of Lords, London SW1A 0PW
Tel: 020 7219 5858 *Fax:* 020 7219 2709

CROSSBENCH

MEACHER, BARONESS

MEACHER (Life Baron), Molly Christine Meacher; cr 2006. Born 15 May 1940; Daughter of William Frederick and Lucy Marie Reid; Married Michael Meacher 1962 (later MP (qv), divorced 1987) (2 sons 2 daughters); married Professor Richard Layard (later Lord Layard (qv)) 1991.

Education: Berkhamsted School for Girls; York University (BA economics 1970); London University (CQSW 1980).

Non-political career: Manager, National Association of Citizens Advice Bureaux 1982-84; Parliamentary officer, British Association of Social Workers 1984-86; Director, Campaign for Work 1986-91; Chief adviser to Russian Government on employment 1991-94; Member and deputy chair, Police Complaints Authority 1994-2002; Chair: Security Industry Authority 2002-04, East London NHS Foundation 2004-12.

Political career: *House of Lords:* Raised to the peerage as Baroness Meacher, of Spitalfields in the London Borough of Tower Hamlets 2006. *Councils and public bodies:* Commissioner, Mental Health Act 1987-92; Non-executive director, Tower Hamlets Healthcare Trust 1994-98; Chair: Home Office Forum for Forensic Physicians 2002-04, Clinical Ethics Committee, Central and North West London Mental Health Trust 2004-08.

Political interests: Mental health, criminal justice, welfare benefits, social care; Russia.

Other: Russian European Trust; Taxaid.

Publications: Scrounging on the Welfare (Hutchinson, 1972); To Him Who Hath (Penguin, 1977); New Methods of Mental Health Care (Penguin, 1979); Contributor: The Mentally Disordered Offender (Butterworth-Heinemann, 1991), Mental Health Services Today and Tomorrow (Radcliffe Publishing Oxford, 2008).

Recreations: Music, golf.

The Baroness Meacher, House of Lords, London SW1A 0PW
Tel: 020 7219 4081 *Email:* meachermc@parliament.uk

LABOUR

MENDELSOHN, LORD

MENDELSOHN (Life Baron), Jonathan Neil Mendelsohn; cr 2013. Born 1967.

Non-political career: Managing Director, FTI Strategic Communications 2007; Director of general election resources, Labour Party.

Political career: *House of Lords:* Raised to the peerage as Baron Mendelsohn, of Finchley in the London Borough of Barnet 2013.

The Lord Mendelsohn, House of Lords, London SW1A 0PW
Tel: 020 7219 5353

LIBERAL DEMOCRAT

METHUEN, LORD

METHUEN (7th Baron, UK), Robert Alexander Holt Methuen; cr. 1838. Born 22 July 1931; Son of 5th Baron; Married Mary Catherine Jane Hooper 1958 (2 daughters) (divorced 1993); married Margrit Andrea Hadwiger 1994.

Education: Shrewsbury School; Trinity College, Cambridge (BA engineering 1957).

Non-political career: Design engineer, Westinghouse Brake and Signal Company 1957-67; Computer systems engineer: IBM UK Ltd 1968-75, Rolls-Royce plc 1975-94.

Political career: *House of Lords:* First entered House of Lords 1994; Deputy Chair of Committees 1999-2001; Elected hereditary peer 1999-. Member: Science and Technology 1999-2003, 2007-10, Science and Technology Sub-committee II 2002-04 (Innovations in Microprocessing/Science and the Regional Development Agencies 2002-03, Renewable Energy 2003-04), Information - 2003, 2005-09, Merits of Statutory Instruments 2003-07, Joint Committee on Consolidation, Etc, Bills 2007-, Science and Technology Sub-committee I 2007- (Waste Reduction 2007-08, Nanotechnologies and food 2008-10, Radioactive Waste Management: a further update 2010), Merits of Statutory Instruments/Secondary Legislation Scrutiny 2009-.

Political interests: Environment, transport, technology, information and communications technology; Austria, Turkey.

Other: Patron, Lady Margaret Hungerford Charity.

Recreations: Walking, horse trekking, industrial archaeology.

The Lord Methuen, House of Lords, London SW1A 0PW
Tel: 020 7219 1220 *Email:* methuenr@parliament.uk

LIBERAL DEMOCRAT

MILLER OF CHILTHORNE DOMER, BARONESS

MILLER OF CHILTHORNE DOMER (Life Baroness), Susan Elisabeth Miller; cr. 1998. Born 1 January 1954; Daughter of Frederick Taylor and Norah Langham; Married John Miller 1980 (divorced 1998) (2 daughters 1 deceased); married Humphrey Temperley 1999.

Education: Sidcot School, Winscombe, Somerset; Oxford Polytechnic (book publishing 1975); French.

Non-political career: In publishing: David & Charles, Weidenfeld & Nicolson, Penguin Books 1975-79; Bookshop owner 1979-89; Vineyard owner 2009-.

Political career: *House of Lords:* Raised to the peerage as Baroness Miller of Chilthorne Domer, of Chilthorne Domer in the County of Somerset 1998. Liberal Democrat Spokesperson for: Agriculture and Rural Affairs 1999-2001, Environment, Food and Rural Affairs 2001-07, Home Affairs 2007-09. Member: European Union Sub-committee D (Environment and Agriculture) 2005-07, Draft Climate Change Bill Joint Committee 2007, Draft Marine Bill Joint Committee 2008. *Other:* Member, Liberal Democrat Federal Policy Committee 2004-. *Councils and public bodies:* South Somerset District Council: Councillor 1991-98, Leader 1996-98; Councillor, Somerset County Council 1997-2005.

Political interests: Environment, street children, human rights, nutrition and food, sovereignty; Central and South America, France.

Other: Member: Inter-Parliamentary Union, Parliamentarians for Nuclear Non-proliferation and Disarmament (PNND); Vice-President: British Trust for Conservation Volunteers, Wildlife Link; Patron, ECOS Homes; TCF; Charlotte Miller Art Project; International Children's Trust (Juconi); Save the Children; Marine Conservation Society; Baby Milk Action; Wildlife Trusts; Oxfam; War on Want. Fellow, Joint University (Exeter and Bournemouth).

Publications: Stuck or Spiked – What Happened to eco-labelling in the UK (2002); Hungry for Change – A UK Food Policy (2004).

Recreations: Horse riding, reading, friends, gardening vegetables, wine.

The Baroness Miller of Chilthorne Domer, House of Lords, London SW1A 0PW

Tel: 020 7219 6042 *Email:* millers@parliament.uk *Website:* www.suemiller.org.uk

CONSERVATIVE

MILLER OF HENDON, BARONESS

MILLER OF HENDON (Life Baroness), Doreen Miller; cr. 1993. Born 13 June 1933; Daughter of Bernard and Hetty Feldman; Married Henry Miller 1955 (3 sons).

Education: Brondesbury and Kilburn High School; London School of Economics; Hull University (MA 2009).

Non-political career: Managing director/chair, Universal Beauty Club Ltd 1972-88; Managing director: Cosmetic Club International GmbH (Germany) 1974-88, Universal Beauty Club (Pty) Australia 1976-88; Director, group of property investment companies.

Political career: *House of Lords:* Raised to the peerage as Baroness Miller of Hendon, of Gore in the London Borough of Barnet 1993. Government Whip 1994-97; Government Spokesperson for: Health 1995-97, Education and Employment 1996-97, Trade and Industry 1996-97, Office of Public Service 1996, Environment 1996-97; Opposition Whip 1997-99; Opposition Spokesperson for: Environment, Transport and the Regions 1997-2000, Department of Trade and Industry 1997-2006, Employment 2000-03, Education and Skills 2001-03. Member Information 2007-08; Co-opted member EU Sub-Committee G (Social Policy and Consumer Affairs) 2009-10; Member EU Sub-committee G (Social Policies and Consumer Protection) 2010-11. *Other:* Contested London South Inner 1984 European Parliament election. Member, Conservative Board of Finance and its Training and Fund Raising Sub-Committees 1990-93; Greater London Area Conservative and Unionist Associations: Chair 1993-96, President 1996-98; President, Hampstead and Highgate Women's Committee 1993-96; Conservative Women's National and General Purposes Committees: Member 1993-96, Patron 1996-; President, Greenwich and Woolwich Conservative Association 1996-; Patrons for Conservative Association: Eltham and Woolwich 1996-, Hackney North 1996-, North Thanet 1996-, Hendon 2006-, Finchley and Golders Green 2006-; Vice-President, Chipping Barnet Conservative Association 2006-. *Councils and public bodies:* JP, Brent 1971; National chairman and executive director, 300 Group 1985-88; Chair, Women into Public Life Campaign 1986-92; Human rights adviser, Soroptomist International 1987-90; Non-executive director, Crown Agents 1990-94; Chair, Barnet Family Health Services Authority 1990-94; Member, Monopolies and Mergers Commission 1992-93; Chair, National Association of Hospital and Community Friends 1997-2003.

Political interests: Women's issues, health, law and order, small businesses; Israel, USA.

Other: Patron, Minerva Educational Trust; Fellow, Institute of Marketing; FRSA. MBE 1989; Carlton.

Publications: Let's Make Up (1974).
Recreations: Reading, football, politics.
The Baroness Miller of Hendon MBE, House of Lords, London SW1A 0PW
Tel: 020 7219 3164 *Fax:* 020 7219 1465 *Email:* millerd@parliament.uk

MILLETT, LORD

MILLETT (Life Baron), Peter Julian Millett; cr. 1998. Born 23 June 1932; Son of late Denis Millett and Adele Millett; Married Ann Mireille Harris 1959 (2 sons and 1 son deceased).
Education: Harrow School; Trinity Hall, Cambridge (Scholar, MA classics and law 1954).
Non-political career: Flying Officer, RAF national service 1955-57. Called to the Bar, Middle Temple 1955; At Chancery Bar 1958-86; Called to the Bar, Lincoln's Inn 1959; QC 1973; Called to the Bar: Singapore 1976, Hong Kong 1979; Lincoln's Inn: Bencher 1980, Treasurer 2004; Judge of the High Court of Justice 1986-94; Lord Justice of Appeal 1994-98; Non-Permanent Judge of the Court of Final Appeal, Hong Kong 2000-.

CROSSBENCH

Political career: *House of Lords:* Raised to the peerage as Baron Millett, of St Marylebone in the City of Westminster 1998. Lord of Appeal in Ordinary 1998-2004; On leave of absence June 2012-. Member Tax Law Rewrite Bills Joint Committee 2005-10. *Councils and public bodies:* Examiner and lecturer in practical conveyancing, Council of Legal Education 1962-76; Junior counsel to Department of Trade and Industry in Chancery matters 1967-73; Outside member, Law Commission on working party on co-ownership of the matrimonial home 1972-73; Member, Department of Trade Insolvency Law Review Committee 1977-82.

Other: Member, Insol International; President, West London Synagogue of British Jews 1991-95; Member, General Council of the Bar 1971-75; Hammerson House (for the Elderly); Harrow School Memorial Trust; Barristers' Benevolent Association; World Jewish Relief; Lincoln's Inn Denning Fund. Honorary Fellow, Trinity Hall, Cambridge 1994; Honorary doctorate, London University 2000. Kt 1986; PC 1994; Home House.

Publications: Contributor to several legal publications including Halsbury's Law of England; Editor-in-Chief, Encyclopaedia of Forms and Precedents.
Recreations: Philately, bridge, *The Times* crossword.
Rt Hon the Lord Millett, House of Lords, London SW1A 0PW
Tel: 020 7219 5353

MITCHELL, LORD

MITCHELL (Life Baron), Parry Andrew Mitchell; cr. 2000. Born 6 May 1943; Son of late Leon Mitchell and Rose Mitchell; Married Doreen Hargreaves 1972 (divorced) (1 daughter); married Hannah Lowy 1988 (twin sons).
Education: Christ's College Grammar School, London; London University (BSc economics 1964); Graduate School of Business, Columbia University, New York (MBA 1966).
Non-political career: Information technology entrepreneur; Chair and founder: United Leasing plc 1976-87, Syscap plc 1992-2006; Zuse Inc New York 2012-.

LABOUR

Political career: *House of Lords:* Raised to the peerage as Baron Mitchell, of Hampstead in the London Borough of Camden 2000. Opposition Spokesperson for Business, Innovation and Skills 2012-13. Member: House of Lords Offices Library and Computers Sub-committee 2001-03; Science and Technology Sub-committee II (Innovations in Computer Processors/Microprocessors/Science and the Regional Development Agencies) 2002-03, Science and Technology Committee 2003-06; Chair Science and Technology Sub-committee I (Science and International Agreements) 2003-04; Member Science and Technology Sub-committee I (Scientific Aspects of Ageing) 2004-05; Co-opted member: EU Sub-committee B (Internal Market) 2006-10, Science and Technology Sub-committee I (Nanotechnologies and food) 2009-10; Member Small- and Medium-Sized Enterprises 2012. *Other:* Labour's Business Ambassador 2013-; Adviser to Shadow Ministerial Business, Innovation and Skills team 2013-.

Political interests: Information technology, small businesses, foreign affairs, education, alcohol abuse; Israel, USA.

Other: Trustee, Lowy Mitchell Foundation. Honorary fellow, College of Teachers 2011; Players Club, New York.

Recreations: Scuba diving, theatre, jazz, opera.
The Lord Mitchell, House of Lords, London SW1A 0PW
Tel: 020 7219 8657 *Email:* mitchellp@parliament.uk *Twitter:* @lordparry

CROSSBENCH

MOGG, LORD

MOGG (Life Baron), John Frederick Mogg; cr 2008. Born 5 October 1943; Married Anne Smith 1967 (1 daughter 1 son).

Education: Bishop Vesey's Grammar School, Sutton Coldfield; Birmingham University (BA history 1965).

Non-political career: Rediffusion Ltd 1965-74; Principal: Office of Fair Trading 1974-76, Department of Trade 1976-79; First secretary, UK Permanent Representation to EC, Brussels 1979-82; Department of Trade and Industry 1982-89: Assistant secretary, minerals and metals division 1982-85, Principal private secretary to Secretaries of State Norman Tebbit, Leon Brittan and Paul Channon 1985-86, Under-secretary: European policy division 1986-87, Industrial materials market division 1987-89; Deputy head, European secretariat, Cabinet Office 1989-90; European Commission 1990-2003: Deputy director-general, DG III Internal Market and Industrial Affairs 1990-93, Director-general, DG XV, later DG Internal Market and Financial Services 1993-2003.

Political career: *House of Lords:* Raised to the peerage as Baron Mogg, of Queen's Park in the County of East Sussex 2008. *Councils and public bodies:* Non-executive chair and member, Gas and Electricity Markets Authority 2003-13.

Political interests: Business industry and consumers, economy and finance, education; European Union, USA.

Other: President, Council of European Energy Regulators 2005-; Special adviser to President, Office for Harmonisation in the International Market 2009-12; Chair: International Confederation of Energy Regulators 2010-, Board of Regulators, Agency for the Co-operation of European Regulators 2011-; Member, Advisory Board of Electric Power Research Institute 2012-; Chair, Advisory Board of the European Union Observatory on Infringements of Intellectual Property Rights 2012-; Chair of Governors, Brighton University 2006-. KCMG 2003.

The Lord Mogg KCMG, House of Lords, London SW1A 0PW
Tel: 020 7219 5353 *Email:* moggj@parliament.uk
Tel: 020 7901 7203 *Fax:* 020 7901 7395 *Email:* john.mogg@ofgem.gov.uk

CROSSBENCH

MOLYNEAUX OF KILLEAD, LORD

MOLYNEAUX OF KILLEAD (Life Baron), James Henry Molyneaux; cr. 1997. Born 27 August 1920; Son of late William Molyneaux.

Education: Aldergrove School, Co. Antrim.

Non-political career: RAF 1941-46.

Political career: *House of Commons:* MP (UUP) for Antrim South 1970-83, for Lagan Valley 9 June 1983 general election to 17 December 1985 (resigned seat in protest against Anglo-Irish Agreement), from 23 January 1986 by-election to May 1997. UUP Spokesperson for Treasury 1995-97. *House of Lords:* Raised to the peerage as Baron Molyneaux of Killead, of Killead in the County of Antrim 1997. Former spokesperson for Northern Ireland; On leave of absence June 2012-. *Other:* Honorary Secretary, South Antrim Unionist Association 1964-70; Chair, Antrim division Unionist Association 1971-74; Leader: United Ulster Unionist Coalition 1974-77, Ulster Unionist Parliamentary Party 1974-95, Ulster Unionist Party 1979-95. *Councils and public bodies:* JP, Co. Antrim 1957-86; Antrim County Councillor 1964-73.

Political interests: Constitutional affairs, mental health, local government.

Other: Vice-chair, Eastern Special Care Hospital Committee 1966-73; Chair, Antrim Mental Health Branch 1967-70; Sovereign Grand Master, British Commonwealth Royal Black Institution 1971-98; Chair, Crumlin Branch, Royal British Legion 1985-99; Vice-President, Federation of Economic Development Authorities. PC 1983; KBE 1996.

Recreations: Gardening, music.

Rt Hon the Lord Molyneaux of Killead KBE, House of Lords, London SW1A 0PW
Fax: 020 7219 5353

VACHER'S QUARTERLY
The most up-to-date contact details throughout the year
Call 020 7593 5644 or visit www.dodsshop.co.uk

MONKS, LORD

MONKS (Life Baron), John Stephen Monks; cr 2010. Born 5 August 1945; Married Francine Schenk 1970 (2 sons 1 daughter).

Education: Ducie Technical High School, Manchester; Nottingham University (BA economics 1967); French.

Non-political career: Trades Union Congress 1969-2003: Head of organisation and industrial relations department 1977-87, Deputy General Secretary 1987-93, General Secretary 1993-2003; General Secretary, European Trades Union Confederation 2003-11; Non-executive director, Thompsons' Solicitors 2010-; Special adviser to José Manuel Barroso as President, European Commission 2011-; Trustee director, NOW:Pensions 2011-.

LABOUR

Political career: *House of Lords:* Raised to the peerage as Baron Monks, of Blackley in the County of Greater Manchester 2010. *Councils and public bodies:* Council member, ACAS 1979-95, Vice-chair, Learning and Skills Council 2001-04; Chairman, Co-operative Commission 2001.

Countries of interest: Europe.

Other: Council member, Economic and Social Research Council 1988-91; People's History Museum: Trustee 1988-, Chair of trustees 2004-. Honorary doctorates: Nottingham University, Salford University, Manchester University, Cranfield University, Cardiff University, Kingston University, Southampton University, Open University; Fellow, City & Guilds of London.

Recreations: Music, film, football, cricket, rugby (especially league).

The Lord Monks, House of Lords, London SW1A 0PW
Tel: 020 7219 6943 *Email:* monksj@parliament.uk

MONTAGU OF BEAULIEU, LORD

MONTAGU OF BEAULIEU (3rd Baron, UK), Edward John Barrington Douglas-Scott-Montagu; cr. 1885. Born 20 October 1926; Son of 2nd Baron, KCIE, CSI, DL; Married Belinda Crossley 1959 (1 son 1 daughter) (divorced 1974); married Fiona Herbert 1974 (1 son).

Education: Ridley College, Ontario, Canada; Eton College; New College, Oxford (history).

Non-political career: Lieutenant, Grenadier Guards 1945-48. Author, museum founder, historic house entrepreneur; Founder and editor, *Veteran and Vintage Magazine* 1956-79; Founded Montagu Motor Museum 1952, which became the National Motor Museum 1972; President, Fédération Internationale des Voitures Anciennes 1980-83; Development Commissioner 1980-84; Chair: Report on Britain's Historic Buildings: A Policy for their Future Use 1980, English Tourist Board's Committee of Enquiry publishing Britain's Zoos 1981 (published 1983); First chair, Historic Buildings and Monuments Commission (English Heritage) 1984-92.

CONSERVATIVE

Political career: *House of Lords:* First entered House of Lords 1947; Elected hereditary peer 1999-.

Political interests: Heritage, museums and galleries, road transport, motor industry, tourism; Canada, USA.

Other: Member: Commission Historique Internationale de FIA (Federation Internationale de l'Automobile), International Council of Museums; President, Historic Commercial Vehicle Society 1957; First President, Historic Houses Association 1973-78; President, Southern Tourist Board 1977-2004; First President, European Union of Historic Houses Associations 1978-81; President, Museums Association 1982-84; Chancellor, Wine Guild UK 1983-; President, Federation of British Historic Vehicle Clubs 1988-; President Emeritus, Tourism Society 1991-2000; Honorary Vice-President, Veteran Car Club of Great Britain 1993-; Governor, Countryside Education Trust; President: Disabled Motoring UK, National Motor Museum Trust Limited, British Military Powerboat Trust, United Kingdom Vineyards Association 1996-, Millennium Institute of Journalists 2000; FRSA; FMA; Honorary RICS; FMI; FIMI; FIPR. Freeman, City of London. Honorary DTech 1998. Officer, Order of St John; RAC, Beefsteak. Commodore, Beaulieu River Sailing Club; Vice-Commodore, House of Lords Yacht Club; Commodore, Nelson Boat Owners' Club.

Publications: Jaguar: A Biography (1961); Gilt and the Gingerbread (1967); More Equal than Others (1970); Daimler Century (1995); Wheels Within Wheels – an Unconventional Life (2000); And many other motoring books and books on motoring history and historic houses.

Recreations: Water and field sports, theatre, cinema, music, travel, opera.

The Lord Montagu of Beaulieu, House of Lords, London SW1A 0PW
Tel: 020 7219 5353
Palace House, Beaulieu, Brockenhurst, Hampshire SO42 7ZN *Tel:* 01590 614 701
Fax: 01590 612623 *Email:* lord.montagu@beaulieu.co.uk *Website:* www.beaulieu.co.uk

CROSSBENCH

MONTGOMERY OF ALAMEIN, VISCOUNT

MONTGOMERY OF ALAMEIN (2nd Viscount, UK), David Bernard Montgomery; cr. 1946. Born 18 August 1928; Son of Field Marshal 1st Viscount, KG, GCB, DSO, DL and Elizabeth Carver, née Hobart; Married Mary Connell 1953 (divorced 1967) (1 son 1 daughter); married Tessa Browning 1970.

Education: Winchester College; Trinity College, Cambridge (BA engineering 1950); Spanish.

Non-political career: 2nd Lt 1st Royal Tank Regiment 1947-48. Shell International 1950-62; Director, Yardley International 1962-74; Managing director, Terimar Services 1974-2000; Quarterly contributor, Vision Interamericana 1974-94; Director, Korn/Ferry International 1977-93; Chair, Antofagasta (Chile) and Bolivia Railway Co. 1980-82; Director, Northern Engineering Industries 1981-87; Chair, Baring Puma Fund 1991-2002.

Political career: *House of Lords:* First entered House of Lords 1976; Elected hereditary peer 2005-; Chair House of Lords London Group 2007-12. Member Refreshment 2007-10; Alternate member Procedure 2010-. *Other:* Sat as Conservative 1976-99; Elected as Crossbench peer 2005. *Councils and public bodies:* Councillor, Royal Borough of Kensington and Chelsea 1974-78; President, British Industrial Exhibition: Sao Paulo 1974, Caracas 1977, Mexico 1978; President, Anglo-Argentine Society 1976-87; Hispanic and Luso Brazilian Council, Canning House: Chair 1978-80, President 1987-94; Chair, Brazilian Chamber of Commerce in Great Britain 1980-82; President: Restaurateurs Association of Great Britain 1982-99, Centre for International Briefing, Farnham Castle 1985-2003, Anglo-Belgian Society 1994-2006, Cambridge University Engineers Association 2001-06.

Political interests: Consumer affairs, London; Latin America.

Other: Member, Executive Committee, Inter-Parliamentary Union, British Group 1987-99, 2008-; Delegate, Organisation for Security and Co-operation in Europe Parliamentary Assembly 1992-99; Trustee, Overlord Embroidery Trust 1984-2009. Mercers. CBE 1975; CMG 2000; Decorations from Germany, Belgium, Spain, Chile, Argentina, Brazil, Mexico, Venezuela and Colombia; Garrick, Canning.

Publications: Co-author, The Lonely Leader: Monty 1944-45 (1994).

Recreations: Walking.

The Viscount Montgomery of Alamein CMG CBE, House of Lords, London SW1A 0PW
Tel: 020 7219 5353
2/97 Onslow Square, London SW7 3LU *Tel:* 020 7589 8747

CONSERVATIVE

MONTROSE, DUKE OF

MONTROSE (8th Duke of, S), James Graham; cr. 1707; Marquis of Montrose (S) 1644; Marquess of Graham and Buchanan (S) 1707; Earl of Montrose (S) 1505; Earl of Kincardine (S) 1707; Earl Graham (GB) 1722; Viscount Dundaff (S) 1707; Lord Graham (S) 1445; Lord Aberuthven, Mugdock and Fintrie (S) 1707; Baron Graham (GB) 1722; 12th Bt of Braco (NA) 1625. Born 6 April 1935; Son of 7th Duke and late Isobel Sellar; Married Catherine MacDonnell, née Young 1970 (2 sons 1 daughter).

Education: Loretto School, Musselburgh.

Non-political career: Farmer, landowner.

Political career: *House of Lords:* First entered House of Lords 1996; Elected hereditary peer 1999-; Opposition Spokesperson for: Scotland 2001-10, Environment 2001-06, 2008-10, Food and Rural Affairs 2001-10; Opposition Whip 2001-10; Opposition Spokesperson for: Northern Ireland 2007, Wales 2007-08, 2009-10. Member Partnerships (Prosecution) (Scotland) Bill 2013-. *Councils and public bodies:* Chair, Buchanan Community Council 1982-93; Vice-chair, Secretary of State's Working Party for Loch Lomond and the Trossachs.

Political interests: Europe, agriculture, rural affairs; Ethiopia, Sudan.

Other: Member: Inter-Parliamentary Union 1997-, Commonwealth Parliamentary Association 1997-; Queen's Bodyguard for Scotland (Royal Company of Archers): Member 1965-, Captain 2006; Hereditary Sheriff, Dunbartonshire; Member: Council of Scottish National Farmers Union 1981-90, Royal Scottish Pipers Society; President, Royal Highland and Agricultural Society 1997-98; Scottish Landowners Federation; Royal Agricultural Benevolent Society; President, National Sheep Association; Royal Agricultural Benevolent Society. OStJ 1978; Farmers.

Recreations: Walking, shooting, golf.

His Grace the Duke of Montrose, House of Lords, London SW1A 0PW
Tel: 020 7219 4487 *Fax:* 020 7219 5979 *Email:* montrosej@parliament.uk
Montrose Estates Ltd, Buchanan Castle, Drymen G63 0HY *Tel:* 01360 660307 *Fax:* 01360 660993

LAB/CO-OP

MOONIE, LORD

MOONIE (Life Baron), Lewis George Moonie; cr 2005. Born 25 February 1947; Son of late George Moonie, accountant, and of Eva Moonie; Married Sheila Burt 1971 (2 sons).

Education: Grove Academy, Dundee; St Andrews University (MB, ChB 1970); Edinburgh University (DPM 1975; MRCPsych 1979; MSc community medicine 1981; MFCM 1984); French, Dutch.

Non-political career: Registrar training in psychiatry 1973-75; Full-time research clinical pharmacologist and medical adviser in pharmaceutical industry in Netherlands, Switzerland and Edinburgh 1975-80; Trainee community medicine, Fife Health Board 1980-84; Community medicine specialist, Fife Health Board 1984-87. Member: TGWU, MSF.

Political career: *House of Commons:* MP (Labour) for Kirkcaldy 1987-2005. Opposition Frontbench Spokesperson for: Technology, Trade and Industry 1989-92, Science and Technology 1992-94, Trade and Industry 1994-95, Broadcasting and Telecommunications 1995-97; Member House of Commons Commission 1997-2000; Parliamentary Under-Secretary of State (Minister for Veterans), Ministry of Defence 2000-03. *House of Lords:* Raised to the peerage as Baron Moonie, of Bennochy in Fife 2005. Member: Economic Affairs 2007-12, Finance Bill Sub-committee 2008-10, Economic Affairs Finance Bill Sub-Committee 2011. *Other:* Member, Co-operative Party. *Councils and public bodies:* Councillor, Fife Regional Council 1982-86.

Political interests: Industry, technology, economic policy, defence.

Other: RSPB, Oxfam.

Recreations: Fishing, walking, golf, bridge.

The Lord Moonie, House of Lords, London SW1A 0PW
Tel: 020 7219 4097 *Email:* mooniel@parliament.uk

CONSERVATIVE

MOORE OF LOWER MARSH, LORD

MOORE OF LOWER MARSH (Life Baron), John Edward Michael Moore; cr. 1992. Born 26 November 1937; Son of late Edward Moore; Married Sheila Tillotson 1962 (died 2008) (2 sons 1 daughter).

Education: Licensed Victuallers' School, Slough; London School of Economics (BSc Econ 1961).

Non-political career: Commissioned army national service with Royal Sussex Regiment in Korea 1955-57. Dean Witter (International) Ltd: Chair 1975-79, Director 1968-79; Advisory board member, Marvin and Palmer Inc. 1989-; Director, Monitor Inc. 1990-2006, Chair, European Executive Committee; Member, advisory board, Sir Alexander Gibb & Co. 1990-95; Chair, Credit Suisse Asset Management 1992-2000; Director: Swiss American NY Inc 1992-96, GTECH 1993-2001, Blue Circle Industries plc 1993-2001, Camelot Holdings plc 1993-98; Rolls-Royce plc: Director 1994-2005, Deputy chair 1996-2003, Chair 2003-05; Supervisory board member, ITT Automotive Europe GMBH, Germany 1994-97; Director: Central European Growth Fund Ltd 1995-2000, BEA (NY) 1996-98, TIG Holdings Inc (NY) 1997-99, Private Client Bank (Zurich) 1999-2003.

Political career: *House of Commons:* MP (Conservative) for Croydon Central February 1974-92. Parliamentary Under-Secretary of State for Energy 1979-83; Economic Secretary to the Treasury 1983; Financial Secretary to the Treasury 1983-86; Secretary of State for: Transport 1986-87, Social Services 1987-88, Social Security 1988-89. *House of Lords:* Raised to the peerage as Baron Moore of Lower Marsh, of Lower Marsh in the London Borough of Lambeth 1992. *Other:* Chair: Conservative Association LSE 1958, Stepney Green Conservative Association 1968; Vice-chair, Conservative Party with responsibility for Youth 1975-79. *Councils and public bodies:* Councillor, London Borough of Merton 1971-74; Member, Court of Governors, LSE 1977-2002.

Other: Council Member, Institute of Directors 1991-99; Energy Savings Trust: Chair 1992-95, President 1995-2001. PC 1986; Royal Automobile.

Rt Hon the Lord Moore of Lower Marsh, House of Lords, London SW1A 0PW
Tel: 020 7219 5353 *Email:* jemmoore@o2.co.uk

DO YOU NEED THIS INFORMATION ONLINE?
visit www.dodspeople.com or call 020 7593 5675
to register for a free trial

CROSSBENCH

MORAN, LORD

MORAN (2nd Baron, UK), (Richard) John McMoran Wilson; cr. 1943. Born 22 September 1924; Son of 1st Baron, MC, MD, FRCP, and late Dorothy, née Dufton; Married Shirley Rowntree, née Harris 1948 (2 sons 1 daughter).

Education: Eton College; King's College, Cambridge (history).

Non-political career: RNVR 1943-45: Ordinary Seaman, HMS Belfast 1943, Sub-Lieutenant, Motor Torpedo Boats and HM Destroyer Oribi 1944-45. Foreign and Commonwealth Office 1945-84: Served in Ankara, Tel Aviv, Rio de Janeiro, Washington and South Africa, Head of West African Department, Foreign Office 1968-73, Concurrently non-resident Ambassador to Chad 1970-73, Ambassador to: Hungary 1973-76, Portugal 1976-81; High Commissioner to Canada 1981-84.

Political career: *House of Lords:* First entered House of Lords 1977; Elected hereditary peer 1999-. *Councils and public bodies:* Chair, Regional Fisheries Advisory Committee for the Welsh Region, National Rivers Authority 1989-94.

Political interests: Conservation, farming, fisheries, relations with Europe, countryside, heritage, crime, social issues; Canada, Portugal, Hungary, France, Russia, USA.

Other: Vice-chair, Atlantic Salmon Trust 1988-95; President, Welsh Salmon and Trout Angling Association 1988-95, 2000-; Chair, Wildlife and Countryside Link 1990-95; President, Radnorshire Wildlife Trust 1994-; Vice-President, RSPB 1996-97; Salmon and Trout Association: Chair 1997-2000, Executive Vice-President 2000-; Chair, Fisheries Policy and Legislation Working Group (The Moran Committee) 1997-; Salvation Army. CMG 1970; Grand Cross Order of the Infante (Portugal) 1978; KCMG 1981; Flyfishers' (President 1987-88).

Publications: C.B. – A Life of Sir Henry Campbell-Bannerman (1973) (Whitbread Award for Biography); Fairfax (1985); Co-author, William Robert Grove, The Lawyer who Invented the Fuel Cell.

Recreations: Fly-fishing, bird-watching.

The Lord Moran KCMG, House of Lords, London SW1A 0PW
Tel: 020 7219 5353 *Fax:* 020 7219 5979

LABOUR

MORGAN, LORD

MORGAN (Life Baron), Kenneth Owen Morgan; cr. 2000. Born 16 May 1934; Son of late David Morgan and Margaret Morgan, née Owen; Married Jane Keeler 1973 (died 1992) (1 son 1 daughter); married Dr Elizabeth Gibson 2009.

Education: University College School, Hampstead; Oriel College, Oxford (BA modern history 1955, MA; DPhil 1958; DLitt 1985).

Non-political career: Lecturer, later senior lecturer in history, University College of Wales, Swansea 1958-66; Columbia University: Visiting Fellow 1962-63, Visiting Professor 1965; Fellow and praelector, modern history and politics, The Queen's College, Oxford 1966-89; Visiting Professor, University of South Carolina 1972; O'Donnell lecturer, University of Wales 1981-82; Neale lecturer, University College, London 1986; Principal, then Vice-Chancellor, University College of Wales, Aberystwyth; University of Wales: Professor 1989-95, Senior Vice-Chancellor 1993-95, Emeritus Professor 1999; AH Dodd lecturer, University of Wales, Bangor 1992, 2004; Lloyd George Memorial lecturer 1993; Visiting lecturer, University of Texas (Austin) 1994, 1999, 2007, 2010; Faculty lecturer, Oxford University 1995-; BBC (Wales) annual lecturer 1995; Prothero lecturer, Royal Historical Society 1996; Callaghan lecturer, University College of Wales, Swansea 1996; Visiting Professor, Witwatersrand University, South Africa 1997, 1998, 2000; British Academy lecturer 1998; Benjamin Meaker Visiting Professor, Bristol University 2000; Merlyn-Rees lecturer, University of Glamorgan 2002; Presidential lecturer, University of Rouen 2003; Ford special lecturer, Oxford University 2005; London Guildhall lecturer 2006, 2007; Gresham College Lecturer 2007; Visiting Professor, King's College, London 2011-; Speaker's House lecture 2011; King's College London annual lecture 2012; SAES lecture, Limoges 2012. Member, AUT -1995.

Political career: *House of Lords:* Raised to the peerage as Baron Morgan, of Aberdyfi in the County of Gwynedd 2000. Member Constitution 2001-04; Joint Committee on Draft Constitutional Bill 2008.

Political interests: Education, Europe, foreign affairs, constitutional reform, civil liberties, children; France, India, South Africa, Wales, USA.

Other: Chair, Curatorium, Celtic Studies Centre, Tubingen University 1998-2005; President, Committee for Advanced Studies, Rouen University 2002-; Vice-President, Hon Society Cymmrodorion, Llafur, International Eisteddfod of Llangollen; Yr Academi Gymreig; Middlesex County Cricket Club; Board member, Celtic Studies 1972-2003; Council member, Royal Historical Society 1983-86; Trustee, St. Deiniol's, Hawarden 1989-96; Council member, National Library of Wales 1991-95; Academic assessor, Leverhulme Devolution project 1999-2002; Chair, Fabian

Society Commission on the Monarchy 2002-03; Trustee, History of Parliament Trust 2002-; Fellow: Royal Historical Society 1964, British Academy 1983; Founding Fellow, Learned Society of Wales 2009; Honorary Fellow: The Queen's College, Oxford 1992, Oriel College, Oxford 2003; Imperial Cancer Research; Royal Institute for the Deaf. Honorary Fellow: The Queen's College, Oxford 1992, Oriel College, Oxford 2003; Three honorary university fellowships (Swansea, Cardiff; Trinity College; Carmarthen); Three honorary doctorates (Wales; Glamorgan; Greenwich). ACLS Fellowship, Columbia University 1962-63; Honorary Druid, Welsh National Eisteddfod 2008; Gold medal for lifetime achievement, Honourable Society of Cymmrodorion 2009; Reform. Member, Middlesex County Cricket Club.

Publications: Editor, Welsh History Review 1961-2003; Wales in British Politics 1868-1922 (1963, 1992); David Lloyd George: Welsh radical as world statesman (1963); Freedom or Sacrilege? (1967); Keir Hardie (1967); The Age of Lloyd George (1971); Editor, Lloyd George Family Letters (1973); Lloyd George (1974); Keir Hardie, Radical and Socialist (1975) (Arts Council prize); Consensus and Disunity (1979); Co-author, Portrait of a Progressive (1980); Rebirth of a Nation: Wales 1880-1980 (1981) (Arts Council prize); David Lloyd George (1981); Labour in Power, 1945-1951 (1984); Editor, The Oxford Illustrated History of Britain (1984, new updated edn, 2009); Labour People (1987); Editor, The Oxford History of Britain (1988, 2001, updated 2010); The Red Dragon and the Red Flag (1989); The People's Peace (1990, 2001); Co-editor, Twentieth Century British History (1994-99); Modern Wales: politics, places and people (1995); Britain and Europe (1995); Editor, The Young Oxford History of Britain and Ireland (1996, 2006); Callaghan: a life (1997); Co-editor, Crime, Protest and Police in Modern British Society (1999); The Twentieth Century (2000); The Great Reform Act (2001); 25 contributions to Oxford Dictionary of National Biography (2004) and supplements (2009) and (2014); Michael Foot: a Life (2007); Ages of Reform (2011); Editor, David Lloyd George (2013); Author and editor of many other works, as well as articles and reviews; Frequent broadcaster on history, politics and Welsh affairs.

Recreations: Music, travel, sport (cricket), architectural history.

Professor the Lord Morgan, House of Lords, London SW1A 0PW
Tel: 020 7219 8616 *Email:* kenneth.morgan@hotmail.co.uk

MORGAN OF DREFELIN, BARONESS

MORGAN OF DREFELIN (Life Baroness), Delyth Jane Morgan; cr. 2004. Born 30 August 1961; Daughter of David Elias Julian Morgan and Ann George, née Stedman; Married Jim Shepherd 1991 (1 daughter).

Education: Elliott Comprehensive, London; Putney College of Further Education; University College, London (BSc Physiology 1986).

Non-political career: President, London University Union 1985-86; Campaigns organiser, Shelter 1986-88; Director, Workplace Nurseries Campaign 1988-92; Director of communications, National Asthma Campaign 1992-96; Chief executive, Breakthrough Breast Cancer 1996-2005; Fellow: University College London, Cardiff University, Institute of Cancer Research, London University; Chief executive, Breast Cancer Campaign 2011-.

CROSSBENCH

Political career: *House of Lords:* Raised to the peerage as Baroness Morgan of Drefelin, of Drefelin in the County of Dyfed 2004. Government Whip 2007-08; Government Spokesperson for: Communities and Local Government 2007-08, Work and Pensions 2007-08, Scotland 2007-08, Wales 2007-08; Parliamentary Under-Secretary of State (Intellectual Property and Quality) and Government Spokesperson, Department for Innovation, Universities and Skills 2008; Government Spokesperson for Cabinet Office 2008; Government Whip 2008; Parliamentary Under-Secretary of State and Government Spokesperson, Department for Children, Schools and Families 2008-10; Opposition Spokesperson for Education 2010-11. Member: Merits of Statutory Instruments 2005-07, Draft Children (Contact and Adoption) Bill Joint Committee 2005. *Other:* Labour until July 2011 (on taking up position of chief executive of Breast Cancer Campaign); Crossbench July 2011-.

Political interests: Science, health, women, children, voluntary sector; Wales.

Other: Chair, Childcare Umbrella 1989-92; Member: Cancer Task Force 2000-05, NHS Modernisation Board 2002-05; Chair, Choice in Primary Care 2003-04; Patron, Sheila McKechnie Foundation 2004-; Chair, Patient Voices 2005-07; Member, Ethics Committee, Royal College of Obstetricians and Gynaecologists 2006-07; Patron, Breast Cancer Campaign 2007; Long Term Conditions Alliance: Trustee 1994-2000, Chair of trustees 1996-98; Association of Medical Research Charities Trustee 2001-04; Chair of trustees, Foundations UK 2004-07; Trustee, Children with Leukaemia 2005-07.

Recreations: Photography, singing, reading, watching rugby.

The Baroness Morgan of Drefelin, House of Lords, London SW1A 0PW
Tel: 020 7219 8727 *Email:* morgand@parliament.uk *Twitter:* @delythjmorgan

MORGAN OF ELY, BARONESS

Opposition Whip; Opposition Spokesperson for Wales

MORGAN OF ELY (Life Baroness), Mair Eluned Morgan; cr 2011. Born 16 February 1967; Daughter of Rev Bob Morgan and Elaine Morgan; Married Rhys Jenkins 1996 (1 son 1 daughter). **Education:** Atlantic College; Glantaf Welsh Language Comprehensive; Hull University (BA European studies); French, Spanish, Welsh.

Non-political career: Programme sales 1991; TV reporter 1992-93; Documentaries researcher, BBC 1993-94; Director of national business development, Wales, Scottish and Southern Energy plc. Member, Unite.

LABOUR

Political career: *House of Lords:* Raised to the peerage as Baroness Morgan of Ely, of Ely in the City of Cardiff 2011. Opposition Whip 2013-; Opposition Spokesperson for Wales 2013-. *Other:* European Parliament: MEP for: Mid and West Wales 1994-99, Wales 1999-2009: Labour spokesperson on: Budgetary control, Energy.

Political interests: European Union reform and economic development, devolution, tourism, minority languages, business, energy; Nicaragua, Russia.

Other: Fellow, Trinity College Carmarthen; Honorary Distinguished Professor, Cardiff University.

Recreations: Walking, reading.

The Baroness Morgan of Ely, House of Lords, London SW1A 0PW
Tel: 020 7219 5353 *Twitter:* @Eluned_Morgan

MORGAN OF HUYTON, BARONESS

MORGAN OF HUYTON (Life Baroness), Sally Morgan; cr. 2001. Born 28 June 1959; Daughter of Albert Morgan and Margaret Morgan; Married John Lyons 1984 (2 sons).

Education: Belvedere School for Girls, Liverpool; Van Mildert College, Durham University (BA geography 1980); King's College, London (PGCE 1981); Institute of Education, London (MA education 1988).

Non-political career: Secondary school geography teacher 1981-85; Labour Party: Student organiser 1985-88, Key seats organiser 1989-92, Director of campaigns and elections 1993-95, Head of party liaison to Tony Blair as Leader of the Opposition 1995-97; Prime Minister's Office 1997-2005: Political secretary to Tony Blair as Prime Minister 1997-2001; Director, government relations 2001-05; Adviser to ARK (Absolute Return for Kids) 2005-; Non-executive director, Carphone Warehouse plc 2005-; Chair, Office for Standards in Education (OFSTED) 2011-; Member, advisory board, Virgin Holdings. Member, GMB.

LABOUR

Political career: *House of Lords:* Raised to the peerage as Baroness Morgan of Huyton, of Huyton in the County of Merseyside 2001. Minister of State, Cabinet Office 2001; Government Spokesperson for Women's Issues, Cabinet Office 2001. Co-opted member EU Sub-committee G (Social Policy and Consumer Affairs) 2006-09; Member Public Service and Demographic Change 2012-13. *Councils and public bodies:* Councillor, Wandsworth Borough Council 1986-90; Trustee, Olympic Delivery Authority 2006-; Chair, Future Leaders (head teacher training); Member, University of London, Institute of Education Advisory Board.

Political interests: Equality issues, education, health.

Other: Trustee, Mayor's Fund 2009-; Children's charities.

Recreations: Gardening, family, cooking, theatre.

The Baroness Morgan of Huyton, House of Lords, London SW1A 0PW
Tel: 020 7219 5500 *Email:* morgan@parliament.uk

MORRIS OF ABERAVON, LORD

MORRIS OF ABERAVON (Life Baron), John Morris; cr. 2001. Born 5 November 1931; Son of late D W Morris and late M O A Lewis, formerly Morris; Married Margaret Lewis 1959 (3 daughters).

Education: Ardwyn School, Aberystwyth; University College of Wales, Aberystwyth (LLB 1952); Gonville and Caius College, Cambridge (LLM 1953); Gray's Inn (Holker Senior Exhibitioner); Welsh.

Non-political career: Commissioned Welch Regiment and served Royal Welch Fusiliers. Called to the Bar, Gray's Inn 1954; QC 1973; Recorder of Crown Court 1982-97; Bencher, Gray's Inn 1984. Member, GMB.

LABOUR

Political career: *House of Commons:* MP (Labour) for Aberavon 1959-2001. Parliamentary Secretary, Ministry of Power 1964-1966; Joint Parliamentary Secretary, Ministry of Transport 1966-1968; Minister of Defence for Equipment 1968-70; Secretary of State for Wales 1974-79; Shadow Attorney General and Principal Opposition Frontbench Spokesperson for Legal Affairs 1979-81,

1983-97; Attorney General 1997-99. *House of Lords:* Raised to the peerage as Baron Morris of Aberavon, of Aberavon in the County of West Glamorgan and of Ceredigion in the County of Dyfed 2001. Member: European Union Sub-committee C (Common Foreign and Security Policy/ Foreign Affairs, Defence and Development Policy) 2002-05, Constitution 2006-09, Joint Committee on the Draft Defamation Bill 2011, EU Sub-committee E (Justice and Institutions) 2011-12, Inquiries Act 2005 2013-. *Councils and public bodies:* Chair: Joint Review of British Railways 1966-67, National Road Safety Advisory Council 1967-68; Committee member, Implementation of Nolan Report 1997; Member, Prime Minister's Advisory Committee on Business Appointments 2002-09; Lord Lieutenant, Dyfed 2002-06.

Political interests: Legal matters, armed forces, steel industry, agriculture; Spain.

Other: Member: UK Delegation, Consultative Assemblies Council of Europe and Western European Union 1963-64, 1982-83, UK Delegates to North Atlantic Assembly 1970, Executive Committee, Inter-Parliamentary Union, British Group, UK Delegation to US Senate (British-American Parliamentary Group) 2011; President, London Welsh Association 2001-08; Member, Prince's Trust Council (Cymru) 2002-08; Patron: London Welsh Lawyers Association 2010-, Edmund-Davies Charitable Trust. Freeman, Borough of Port Talbot 1992. Chancellor, University of Glamorgan 2001-13. Honorary LLD, University of Wales; Honorary Fellow: University College, Aberystwyth, Trinity College, Carmarthen, University College, Swansea, Gonville and Caius College, Cambridge, University College, Lampeter. Lifetime Achievement, *Wales Yearbook* awards 2011. PC 1970; Kt 1999; KG 2003.

Publications: Endowed Lecture, David Lloyd George Memorial (Honorary Society of Cymrodorion, London, 2005); Autobiography, Fifty Years in Politics and the Law (University of Wales Press, Cardiff, 2011); Youard Lecture, The Development by Attorney Generals of the Doctrine of Armed Intervention by States, without Security Council Authorisation, to Avert an Overwhelming Human Catastrophe (Swansea University, 2011).

Recreations: Fishing, shooting.

Rt Hon the Lord Morris of Aberavon KG QC, House of Lords, London SW1A 0PW
Tel: 020 7219 3470 *Fax:* 020 7219 0785 *Email:* stevensonmm@parliament.uk

---

MORRIS OF BOLTON, BARONESS

MORRIS OF BOLTON (Life Baroness), Patricia Morris; cr. 2004. Born 16 January 1953; Daughter of late James Sydney and Alice Whittaker; Married William Patrick Morris 1978 (1 daughter 1 son).

Education: Bolton School; Clifton and Didsbury Colleges of Education.

Non-political career: PA to: Northern Regional Director, Slater Walker Ltd 1974-75, Chevalier Dr Harry D. Schultz 1975; Fund manager, PPS 1975-77; Technical analyst: Foster & Braithwaite 1977-78, Charlton, Seal, Dimmock & Co 1979-83; Policy and political adviser to Conservative Member of European Parliament 1999-2001.

CONSERVATIVE

Political career: *House of Commons:* Contested (Conservative) Oldham Central and Royton 1992 general election. *House of Lords:* Raised to the peerage as Baroness Morris of Bolton, of Bolton in the County of Greater Manchester 2004. Opposition Spokesperson for: Health 2004-06, Education and Skills 2004-07; Opposition Whip 2004-10; Opposition Spokesperson for: Women 2005-10, Children, Schools and Families 2007-09, Health 2009-10, Work and Pensions 2009-10; Deputy Chairman of Committees 2010-; Deputy Speaker 2011-; Trade envoy to Jordan, Kuwait and Palestinian Territories 2012-. Member: Joint Committee on Human Rights 2010-11, Adoption Legislation 2012-13, Soft Power and the UK's Influence 2013-. *Other:* Member, National Union Executive Committee of Conservative Party 1991-96; Chair, North West Area Conservative Women's Committee 1993-96; Member: Conservative Conferences Committee 1998-2001, Field Operations Panel 1998-2001, Conservative Agents' Remuneration Panel 1998-2001; Vice-chair, Conservative Party (Candidates) 2001-05. *Councils and public bodies:* Deputy chair, Salford Royal Hospitals NHS Trust 1993-97; Adviser to Abbot of Ampleforth 1998-2004; Co-chair, Women in Public Policy 2007-; Vice-President, Catholic Union of Great Britain 2008-; Deputy Lieutenant, Greater Manchester 2008-.

Other: Chair, Bolton Cancer Research Campaign 1992-1995; Trustee, Bolton Lads and Girls Club 1994-2002; Member, advisory board, Women 2 Win 2005-; President, National Benevolent Institution 2006-; Patron, Oxford Parent Infant Project (OXPIP) 2006-; Trustee: Agbis 2006-, Disability Partnership 2007-, Unicef UK 2007-. OBE; Special Forces.

Recreations: Music, reading, football – Bolton Wanderers.

The Baroness Morris of Bolton OBE, House of Lords, London SW1A 0PW
Tel: 020 7219 5353 *Email:* morrispa@parliament.uk

MORRIS OF HANDSWORTH, LORD

MORRIS OF HANDSWORTH (Life Baron), William (Bill) Manuel Morris; cr 2006. Born 19 October 1938; Son of William Morris and Una Cornwall; Married Minetta Smith 1957 (died 1990) (2 sons); partner Eileen Ware.

Education: Mizpah School, Manchester, Jamaica; Handsworth Technical College (day release mechanical engineering).

LABOUR

Non-political career: Hardy Spicers 1955-73: Transport and General Workers' Union 1958-2003: District organiser, Nottingham/Derby 1973-76, District secretary, Northampton 1976-79, National secretary, Passenger Services Trade Group 1979-86, Deputy general secretary 1986-91, General secretary 1992-2003; Non-executive director: Unity Trust Bank 1992-2003, Bank of England 1998-2006; Vice-chair, Jamaican National Money Services 2007-11; Chair, Midland Heart Housing Association 2007-. Transport and General Workers' Union: Member 1958-, Shop steward at Hardy Spicers 1963-73; Member: T&G General Executive Council 1971-72, TUC General Council 1988-2003.

Political career: *House of Lords:* Raised to the peerage as Baron Morris of Handsworth, of Handsworth in the County of West Midlands 2006. Member: Joint Committee on Human Rights 2007-12, Adoption Legislation 2012-13, EU Sub-committee F (Home Affairs, Health and Education) 2013-. *Other:* Chair: Conference Arrangements Committee, Labour Party/Trade Union Liaison Committee. *Councils and public bodies:* Chair, Morris Inquiry Metropolitan Police Authority 2004; Member: Commission for Racial Equality 1977-87, IBA General Advisory Council 1981-86, Road Transport Industries Training Board 1986-92, BBC General Advisory Council 1987-88, Employment Appeal Tribunal 1988-2008, ACAS (the Advisory Conciliation and Arbitration Service) 1997-2003, Royal Commission on House of Lords Reform 1999, Commission for Integrated Transport 1999-2005, Architects Registration Board 2001-05, Panel of Mergers and Take Overs 2005-08; DL, Staffordshire 2008.

Political interests: Social justice, trade unions, the economy, international affairs, diversity.

Other: Member: Board International Transport Federation 1986-2003, Economic and Social Committee EC 1990-92; Member, Prince's Youth Business Trust 1987-90; Non-executive director, England and Wales Cricket Board 2005-; Trustee, Performance Birmingham Ltd 2008-. Chancellor: University of Technology, Jamaica 2000-10, Staffordshire University, England 2004-11. Order of Jamaica (OJ) 2002; Kt 2003.

Recreations: Family life, walking, gardening, music.

The Lord Morris of Handsworth OJ, House of Lords, London SW1A 0PW
Tel: 020 7219 3485 *Email:* morrisw@parliament.uk *Website:* www.billmorris.info

MORRIS OF YARDLEY, BARONESS

MORRIS OF YARDLEY (Life Baroness), Estelle Morris; cr 2005. Born 17 June 1952; Daughter of late Charles Morris, former MP 1963-83, and Pauline Morris, née Dunn; Single.

Education: Whalley Range High School, Manchester; Coventry College of Education (BEd Warwick University 1974).

Non-political career: Teacher, Sidney Stringer School and Community College 1974-92. Member, CWU.

LABOUR

Political career: *House of Commons:* MP (Labour) for Birmingham Yardley 1992-2005. Opposition Whip 1994-95; Opposition Spokesperson for Education and Employment 1995-97; Department for Education and Employment/Skills 1997-2002: Parliamentary Under-Secretary of State 1997-98, Minister of State 1998-2001; Secretary of State for Education and Skills 2001-02; Minister of State (Minister for the Arts), Department for Culture, Media and Sport 2003-05. *House of Lords:* Raised to the peerage as Baroness Morris of Yardley, of Yardley in the County of West Midlands 2005. Member Merits of Statutory Instruments/Secondary Legislation Scrutiny 2009-. *Councils and public bodies:* Warwick District Council: Councillor 1979-91, Leader, Labour Group 1982-89.

Political interests: Education and training, political engagement, arts.

Other: Chair, National Coalmining Museum; Trustee, Hamlyn Foundation; Fellow, Industry and Parliament Trust 1994; Trustee, The Roundhouse; Chair, Goldsmiths Council. Honorary doctorate; Seven honorary degrees. PC 1999.

Rt Hon the Baroness Morris of Yardley, House of Lords, London SW1A 0PW
Tel: 020 7219 5353 *Email:* morrise@parliament.uk

**DEMOCRATIC
UNIONIST PARTY**

MORROW, LORD

MORROW (Life Baron), Maurice George Morrow; cr 2006. Born 27 September 1948; Son of Ernest and Eliza Jane Morrow; Married Jennifer Reid 1976 (2 daughters).

Education: Drumglass High School; East Tyrone College of Further and Higher Education.

Non-political career: Self-employed auctioneer, estate agent and valuer.

Political career: *House of Lords:* Raised to the peerage as Baron Morrow, of Clogher Valley in the County of Tyrone 2006. *Other:* Member, Northern Ireland Forum for Political Dialogue 1996-98; Northern Ireland Assembly: MLA for Fermanagh and South Tyrone 1998- (sits as Maurice Morrow); Minister for Social Development 2000-01; DUP Chief Whip -2002; Member, Preparation for Government Committee 2006-07; Chair: Assembly Committees on: Procedures 2007-10, Justice 2010-11. Chair, Democratic Unionist Party. *Councils and public bodies:* Councillor, Dungannon and South Tyrone Borough Council 1973-.

Countries of interest: Israel, USA.

Other: Alternate member, EU Committee of the Regions 2006-10; Member, Apprentice Boys of Derry; Director: Moygashel Development Association, Dungannon Enterprise Centre.

Recreations: Field sports.

The Lord Morrow, House of Lords, London SW1A 0PW
Tel: 020 7219 5353

CROSSBENCH

MOSER, LORD

MOSER (Life Baron), Claus Adolf Moser KCB CBE; cr 2001. Born 24 November 1922; Son of Dr Ernest Moser and Lotte Moser; Married Mary Oxlin 1949 (2 daughters 1 son).

Education: Frensham Heights School, Surrey; London School of Economics (BSc Econ statistics 1943); German.

Non-political career: London School of Economics 1946-67: Latterly professor of social statistics; Head, Government Statistical Service 1967-78; Vice-chair, N M Rothschild 1978-84; Warden Wadham College, Oxford 1984-93; British Museum 1988-2004: Trustee 1988-2001, Chair, Development Trust 1994-2004; Chair, Basic Skills Agency 1997-2002. Association of University Teachers 1946-67.

Political career: *House of Lords:* Raised to the peerage as Baron Moser, of Regents Park in the London Borough of Camden 2001. Member: EU Sub-committee G (Social Policy and Consumer Affairs) 2005-07, Liaison 2005-08; EU Sub-committee A (Economic and Financial Affairs and International Trade): Co-opted member 2007-10, Member 2010-12; Member: Barnett Formula 2008-09, Selection 2013-.

Political interests: Arts, education, social policy, migration, statistics; Germany, Switzerland, USA.

Other: Chair: Royal Opera House, Oxford Playhouse, Music at Oxford, London Symphony Orchestra Education Committee, *The Economist*, Equity and Law; Trustee: Paul Hamlyn Trust, Rayne Foundation. Chancellor: Keele University 1986-2002, Open University of Israel 1994-2004. Sixteen honorary doctorates; Three honorary university fellowships; Honorary Fellow, RIBA 2005. CBE 1965; FBA 1969; KCB 1973; Commander National Order of Merit (France) 1976; Commander's Cross, Order of Merit (Germany) 1985; Garrick.

Publications: Numerous articles in statistics professional journals; The Measurement of Levels of Living: with special reference to Jamaica (HMSO, London 1957); Survey Methods in Social Investigations (William Heinemann Ltd, 1958); Co-author, A Survey of Social Conditions in England and Wales: as illustrated by statistics (Clarendon Press, 1958); British Towns: a statistical study of their social and economic conditions (Oliver and Boyd, Edinburgh and London, 1961); Co-author, The Impact of Robbins (Penguin, London 1969).

Recreations: Music.

The Lord Moser KCB CBE FBA, House of Lords, London SW1A 0PW
Tel: 020 7219 3283
3 Regents Park Terrace, London NW1 7EE *Tel:* 020 7485 1619 *Fax:* 020 7485 7502

CONSERVATIVE

MOYNIHAN, LORD

MOYNIHAN (4th Baron, UK), Colin Berkeley Moynihan; cr. 1929; 4th Bt of Carr Manor (UK) 1922. Born 13 September 1955; Son of 2nd Baron; Married Gaynor-Louise Metcalf 1992 (2 sons 1 daughter).

Education: Monmouth School (Music Scholar); University College, Oxford (BA philosophy, politics and economics 1977, MA 1982) (President of the Oxford Union); Brasenose College, Oxford (J A Fiddian Research Scholarship 1977); French.

Non-political career: Personal assistant to chairman, Tate and Lyle Ltd 1978-80; Manager, Tate and Lyle Agribusiness 1980-82; Ridgways Tea and Coffee Merchants: Chief executive 1982-83, Chair 1983-87; Chair, CMA Consultants 1993-; Managing director, Independent Power Corporation plc 1996-2001; Director, Rowan Group of Companies 1996-; Chair and chief executive, Consort Resources Group of Companies 2000-03; Director, Clipper Windpower UK Ltd 2001-07, Executive chair, Clipper UK Ltd 2004-07, Chair, Clipper EU Ltd 2004-07; Non-executive chair, Pelamis Wave Energy Ltd 2005-11; Chair, British Olympic Association 2005-12; Director, London Organising Committee for Olympic Games (LOCOG) 2006-12; Member: International Olympic Committee (IOC) International Relations Commission 2008-, IOC Candidature Acceptance Working Group for the 2016 Olympic Games 2008-; Non-executive chairman, Hydrodec 2012-.

Political career: *House of Commons:* MP (Conservative) for Lewisham East 1983-92. Contested Lewisham East 1992 general election. PPS to Rt Hon Kenneth Clarke MP: as Minister of Health 1985, as Paymaster-General 1985-87; Parliamentary Under-Secretary of State: Department of Environment (Minister for Sport) 1987-90, Department of Energy 1990-92. *House of Lords:* First entered House of Lords 1997; Senior Opposition Spokesperson for Foreign and Commonwealth Affairs 1997-2000; Elected hereditary peer 1999-; Shadow Minister for Sport 2003-05. Co-opted member European Union Sub-committee D (Environment and Agriculture) 2006-07; Member Olympic and Paralympic Legacy 2013-. *Councils and public bodies:* Governor, Sports Aid Foundation (London and South East) 1980-82.

Political interests: Foreign affairs, trade and industry, sport, inner cities, refugees, overseas aid and development.

Other: Member, The Bow Group 1978-: Chair, Trade and Industry Standing Committee 1983-87; Director, Canterbury Festival 1999-2001; Executive council member, Association of National Olympic Committees (ANOC) 2006-; Ex-officio member, Olympic Board; Spinal Injuries Association. Liveryman, Worshipful Company of Haberdashers 1981; Court of Assistants 2003-. Freeman, City of London 1978. Honorary doctorate, London Metropolitan University 2007. Oxford Double Blue, Rowing and Boxing 1976 and 1977; World Gold Medal for Lightweight Rowing, International Rowing Federation 1978; Silver Medal for Rowing at Moscow Olympic Games 1980; World Silver Medal for Rowing 1981; Brooks's, Vincent's (Oxford). London Rowing, Leander.

Recreations: Reading, sport, music.

The Lord Moynihan, House of Lords, London SW1A 0PW
Tel: 020 7219 5879 *Fax:* 020 7219 5213 *Email:* moynihanc@parliament.uk

CROSSBENCH

MURPHY, BARONESS

MURPHY (Life Baroness), Elaine Murphy; cr. 2004. Born 16 January 1947; Daughter of Roger Lawson, engineer, and Nell Lawson, née Allitt; Married John Murphy 1969 (divorced 2001); married Michael Robb 2001.

Education: West Bridgford Grammar School, Nottingham; Manchester University (MB ChB 1971, MD 1979); University College, London (PhD history of medicine 2000).

Non-political career: Professor of old age psychiatry Guy's Hospital, United Medical Schools, University of London 1983-96; Chair: City and Hackney Community Services NHS Trust 1995-98, East London and City Health Authority 1998-2001, North East London Strategic Health Authority 2001-06, St George's Hospital Medical School, University of London 2006-10.

Political career: *House of Lords:* Raised to the peerage as Baroness Murphy, of Aldgate in the City of London 2004. Member: Science and Technology Sub-committee I (Scientific Aspects of Ageing) 2005, Leader's Group on Members Leaving the House 2010-. *Councils and public bodies:* Commissioner, Commission on Assisted Dying 2010-.

Political interests: Mental health, National Health Service, learning disability, ageing, higher education; Italy.

Other: Vice-President, Alzheimer's Society; Centre of the Cell, Queen Mary's College, London University; Bethlem Hospital Archives and Museum Trust; MRCPsych 1976; FRCPsych 1983; Alzheimer's Society; Oxfam. Three honorary doctorates.

Publications: 100-plus publications in learned journals; Eight books, including: After the Asylums (Faber, 1991); Co-author, The Falling Shadow (Duckworth, 1995).

Recreations: Italy, Norfolk, entertaining friends.

The Baroness Murphy, House of Lords, London SW1A 0PW

Tel: 020 7219 5353 *Email:* murphyel@parliament.uk lordsoftheblog.net/category/baroness-murphy

CROSSBENCH

MUSTILL, LORD

MUSTILL (Life Baron), Michael John Mustill; cr. 1992. Born 10 May 1931; Son of late Clement William and Marion Mustill; Married Beryl Davies 1960 (divorced 1983, she died 2012); married Mrs Caroline Phillips 1991 (2 sons 1 stepdaughter).

Education: Oundle School, Northamptonshire; St John's College, Cambridge (LLD 1992).

Non-political career: Served Royal Artillery 1949-51. Called to the Bar, Gray's Inn 1955; Founding member, Four Essex Court (now Essex Court Chambers) 1961-; QC 1968; Deputy chair, Hampshire Quarter Sessions 1971; Chair, Civil Service Appeal Tribunal 1971-78; Recorder of the Crown Court 1972-78; Bencher 1976; Judge of the High Court, Queen's Bench Division 1978-85; Presiding Judge, NE Circuit 1981-84; Chair: Judicial Studies Board 1985-89, Departmental Committee on Law of Arbitration 1985-90; Lord Justice of Appeal 1985-92.

Political career: *House of Lords:* Raised to the peerage as Baron Mustill, of Pateley Bridge in the County of North Yorkshire 1992. Lord of Appeal in Ordinary 1992-97; On leave of absence October 2012-.

Other: FBA. Kt 1978; PC 1985.

Publications: Several legal works and articles in legal journals.

Rt Hon the Lord Mustill, House of Lords, London SW1A 0PW

Tel: 020 7219 5353

Essex Court Chambers, 24 Lincoln's Inn Fields, London WC2A 3EG *Tel:* 020 7813 8000

LABOUR

MYNERS, LORD

MYNERS (Life Baron), Paul Myners; cr 2008. Born 1 April 1948; Married 2nd Alison Macleod 1995 (1 son 1 daughter; 3 daughters from previous marriage).

Education: Truro School, Cornwall; London University Institute of Education (BEd); Stanford Executive Program, Stanford School of Business, USA.

Non-political career: *Daily Telegraph* 1970-74; N M Rothschild & Sons Ltd 1974-85; Gartmore plc 1985-2001: Chief executive 1985-93, 1999-2000, Chair 1987-2001; Deputy chair, Powergen plc 1999-2001; Director, National Westminster Bank 1997-2000; Chair, Guardian Media Group 2000-; Personal accounts delivery authority, Department for Work and Pensions 2007-09; Chair and managing partner, Cevian Capital 2011-.

Political career: *House of Lords:* Raised to the peerage as Baron Myners, of Truro in the County of Cornwall 2008. Financial Services Secretary and Government Spokesperson, HM Treasury 2008-10. Member: Joint Committee on Privacy and Injunctions 2011-12, Works of Art 2012-13. Vice-chair, PLP Departmental Group for Treasury 2010-. *Councils and public bodies:* Member: Financial Reporting Council 1995-2004, Company Law Review Consultative Committee 1998-2000; Court of Directors, Bank of England 2005-; Chair, Low Pay Commission 2006-.

Other: Trustee, Royal Academy Trust 2000-03; Tate Gallery: Trustee 2003-, Chair 2004-; Trustee: Glyndbourne 2003-, Smith Institute 2003- National Gallery 2007-. CBE 2003.

The Lord Myners CBE, House of Lords, London SW1A 0PW

Tel: 020 7219 6760

CONSERVATIVE

NASEBY, LORD

NASEBY (Life Baron), Michael Wolfgang Laurence Morris; cr. 1997. Born 25 November 1936; Son of late Cyril Morris and Margaret Morris; Married Dr Ann Appleby 1960 (2 sons 1 daughter).

Education: Bedford School; St Catharine's College, Cambridge (BA economics 1960, MA); French.

Non-political career: National service pilot (RAF and NATO) 1955-57. Marketing manager, Reckitt and Colman Group 1960-64; Director: Service Advertising 1964-71, Benton & Bowles Ltd 1971-81; Chairman: Children's Mutual 1997-2005, Invesco Recovery Trust 2011 1995-2011; Non-executive director, Mansell Ltd 1998-2003.

Political career: *House of Commons:* Contested Islington North 1966 general election. MP (Conservative) for Northampton South 1974-97. PPS to Hugh Rossi and Michael Alison as Ministers of State, Northern Ireland 1979-81; Deputy Speaker and Chairman of Ways and Means 1992-97. *House of Lords:* Raised to the peerage as Baron Naseby, of Sandy in the County of Bedfordshire

1997. Member: Standing Orders (Private Bills) 2003-, Administration and Works 2005-09; EU Sub-committee F (Home Affairs): Co-opted member 2009-10, Member 2010-11; Member Joint Committee on the Draft Deregulation Bill 2013-. *Councils and public bodies:* London Borough of Islington: Councillor 1968-74, Leader 1969-71, Alderman 1971-74.

Political interests: Energy, health service, exports, marketing, parliamentary procedure, financial services, questioning government of the day; Brunei, Cayman Islands, Chile, France, India, Maldives, Singapore, Sri Lanka.

Other: Member, Council of Europe and Western European Union 1983-91; Trustee, Parliamentary Contributory Pension Fund 2005-; Patron, Naseby Battlefield Project Trust 2008-; President, Lords and Commons Golf Society 2010-; Bedford School Foundation. Honorary fellow in history, Northampton University 2007. PC 1994; Sri Lanka Ratna 2005; Carlton Club; Chamberlain, Ordre des Cofeaux de Champagne; Confrérie des Chevalier du Tasterin; Chevalier, Commanderie de Bordeaux à Londres; Chairman, Cofradia del Vino Chileno. John O'Gaunt Golf, Port Stanley Golf, All England Lawn Tennis, Lords Taverners, President, Northamptonshire County Cricket, MCC, John O'Gaunt Golf Club.

Publications: Helping The Exporter (1967); Co-author, Marketing Below The Line (1970); The Disaster of Direct Labour (1978).

Recreations: Golf, tennis, forestry, wine, cricket.

Rt Hon the Lord Naseby, House of Lords, London SW1A 0PW
Tel: 020 7219 5613 *Fax:* 020 7219 6633
Caesar's Camp, Sandy, Bedfordshire SG19 2AD *Tel:* 01767 680388 *Fax:* 01767 692099
Email: amnaseby@btinternet.com

CONSERVATIVE

NASH, LORD

Parliamentary Under-Secretary of State for Schools and Government Spokesperson, Department for Education

NASH (Life Baron), John Alfred Stoddard; cr 2013. Born 22 March 1949; Married Caroline 1983 (1 son 1 daughter).

Education: Milton Abbey School, Dorset; Corpus Christi College, Oxford (MA law 1971).

Non-political career: Barrister, Inner Temple 1972-74; William Brandts Sons & Co Ltd 1974-75; Lazard Brothers & Co Ltd 1975-83: Assistant director 1981-83; Advent Ltd 1983-88: Managing director 1987-88; Nash, Sells & Partners/Sovereign Capital Partners 1988-: Founder 1988, Chairman 1988-2010, Non-executive partner 2010-13; Non-executive director, Department for Education 2010-13.

Political career: *House of Lords:* Raised to the peerage as Baron Nash, of Ewelme in the County of Oxfordshire 2013. Parliamentary Under-Secretary of State for Schools and Government Spokesperson, Department for Education 2013-.

Political interests: Education.

Other: Chairman, British Venture Capital Association 1988-89; Corpus Christi College, Oxford: Foundation Fellow, Member, Investment Committee 2005-, Deputy Chairman, Development Committee 2005-; Chairman: Future (charity) 2005-, Pimlico Academy 2008-; Board member, Centre for Policy Studies 2003-13; Foundation fellow, Corpus Christi College, Oxford; Future. Sunningdale Golf Club; Pine Valley Golf Club, USA.

Recreations: Golf, tennis, skiing.

The Lord Nash, House of Lords, London SW1A 0PW
Tel: 020 7219 5353

CROSSBENCH

NEILL OF BLADEN, LORD

NEILL OF BLADEN (Life Baron), Francis Patrick Neill; cr. 1997. Born 8 August 1926; Son of late Sir Thomas Neill, JP, and late Lady (Annie) Neill; Married Caroline Susan Debenham 1954 (died 2010) (4 sons 1 daughter and 1 daughter deceased).

Education: Highgate School, London; Magdalen College, Oxford (BA law 1950, MA); All Souls College, Oxford (BCL 1951).

Non-political career: Served Rifle Brigade 1944-47 (Captain); GSO III (Training) British Troops, Egypt 1947. Fellow, All Souls, Oxford 1950-77; Called to the Bar, Gray's Inn 1951; Lecturer in law, LSE 1955-58; QC 1966; Bencher, Gray's Inn 1971; All Souls, Oxford: Sub-Warden 1972-74, Warden 1977-95; Chair, Senate of the Inns of Court and the Bar 1974-75; Recorder of the Crown

Court 1975-78; Judge of the Courts of Appeal of Jersey and Guernsey 1977-94; Chair, DTI Committee of Inquiry into Regulatory Arrangements at Lloyd's 1986-87; Independent National Director, Times Newspaper Holdings 1988-97; Gray's Inn: Vice-treasurer 1989, Treasurer 1990.

Political career: *House of Lords:* Raised to the peerage as Baron Neill of Bladen, of Briantspuddle in the County of Dorset 1997. Member: European Union 2003-06, European Union Sub-committee E (Law and Institutions) 2003-06, Draft Legal Services Bill Joint Committee 2006. *Councils and public bodies:* Chair: Press Council 1978-83, Council for the Securities Industry 1978-85 (member of the Takeover Panel); Vice-chair, Committee of Vice-Chancellors and Principals of the Universities of the United Kingdom 1987-90; Chair: Feltrim Loss Review Committee at Lloyd's 1991-92, Committee on Standards in Public Life 1997-2001; Visitor, Buckingham University 1997-.

Other: Bar Council: Member 1967-71, Chair 1974-75, Honorary fellow 1995-. Vice-Chancellor, Oxford University 1985-89. Honorary Professor of Legal Ethics, Birmingham University 1983-84; Honorary Fellow, Magdalen College, Oxford 1988; Three honorary law doctorates (Hull, Oxford, Buckingham); Honorary Fellow, All Souls College, Oxford 1995. Kt 1983; Athenæum, Garrick, Beefsteak.

Publications: Administrative Justice: some necessary reforms (OUP, 1988).

Recreations: Music, forestry.

The Lord Neill of Bladen QC, House of Lords, London SW1A 0PW
Tel: 020 7219 5353
20 Essex Street, London WC2R 3AL *Tel:* 020 7842 1200 *Fax:* 020 7842 1270
Email: pneill@20essexst.com

CROSSBENCH

NEUBERGER, BARONESS

NEUBERGER (Life Baroness), Julia Babette Sarah Neuberger; cr. 2004. Born 27 February 1950; Daughter of late Walter Schwab, civil servant, and Alice Schwab, née Rosenthal, art collector; Married Anthony Neuberger 1973 (1 daughter 1 son).

Education: South Hampstead High School, London; Newnham College, Cambridge (BA Hebrew/Assyriology 1973, MA); Leo Baeck College, London (rabbinic ordination 1977).

Non-political career: Rabbi, author, broadcaster; Rabbi, South London Liberal Synagogue 1977-89; Visiting fellow: King's Fund Institute 1989-91, Harvard Medical School (Harkness fellowship) 1991-92; Consultant, Clore Duffield Foundation 2004-; Adviser to Trustees Sainsbury Centre for Mental Health 2006-11; Bloomberg Professor, Harvard Divinity School, spring semester 2006; Senior Rabbi, West London Synagogue 2011-.

Political career: *House of Commons:* Contested (Liberal Democrat) Tooting 1983 general election. *House of Lords:* Raised to the peerage as Baroness Neuberger, of Primrose Hill in the London Borough of Camden 2004. Liberal Democrat Spokesperson for Health 2004-07; Prime Minister's Champion for Volunteering 2007-10. Member: EU Sub-committee G (Social Policy and Consumer Affairs) 2005-08, Draft Human Tissue and Embryos Bill Joint Committee 2007, Science and Technology Sub-committee I (Nanotechnologies and food) 2008-10, Science and Technology 2009-12; Chair Science and Technology Sub-committee I (Behaviour Change) 2010-11; Member Science and Technology Sub-committee I 2012-13. *Other:* Liberal Democrat until September 2011 (on taking up position of Senior Rabbi of West London Synagogue); Crossbench September 2011-. *Councils and public bodies:* Chair, Camden and Islington Community Health Services NHS Trust 1993-97; Civil Service Commissioner 2001-02; Member, Committee on Standards in Public Life 2001-04; One Housing Group 2008-12; Responsible Gambling Strategy Board 2008-11; Advisory Panel, Judicial Diversity 2009-10.

Political interests: Health, citizens' rights, asylum and refugees; Ireland.

Other: Numerous, including: Patron, North London Hospice, Chief executive, King's Fund 1997-2004, Trustee: Imperial War Museum 1999-2006, Booker Prize Foundation 2002-11, British Council 2004-07, Liberal Democrats 2004-08, New Philanthropy Capital 2008-11, Van Leer Group Foundation 2012-; Board member and trustee, Social Market Foundation 2012-13. Chancellor, University of Ulster 1994-2000. 13 honorary doctorates; 5 honorary fellowships. DBE 2004.

Publications: Caring for Dying Patients of Different Faiths (1986, 1994, 2004); The Story of Judaism (for children) (Dinosaur/Collins, 1987); Whatever's Happening to Women? (Kyle Cathie, 1991); Ethics and Healthcare: Research Ethics Committees in the UK (Kings Fund Institute, 1992); The Things That Matter; An Anthology of Women's Spiritual Poetry (Kyle Cathie, 1993);

On Being Jewish (Heinemann, 1996); Dying Well: a guide to enabling a good death (1999, 2004); The Moral State We're In (HarperCollins, 2006); Not Dead Yet: A Manifesto for Old Age (HarperCollins, 2008); Is That All There Is? (Rider, 2011); Frequent broadcaster and press contributor.

Recreations: Opera, gardening, Irish life, novels, food, sailing.

The Baroness Neuberger DBE, House of Lords, London SW1A 0PW
Tel: 020 7219 2716 *Email:* neubergerj@parliament.uk
West London Synagogue, 33 Seymour Place, London W1H 5AU *Tel:* 020 7535 0255
Fax: 020 7224 8258 *Email:* julia.neuberger@wls.org.uk   *Website:* www.wls.org.uk

NEUBERGER OF ABBOTSBURY, LORD

NON-AFFILIATED

NEUBERGER OF ABBOTSBURY (Life Baron), David Edmond Neuberger; cr. 2006. Born 10 January 1948; Son of Professor Albert Neuberger CBE FRS and Lilian Dreyfus; Married Angela Holdsworth 1976 (2 sons 1 daughter).

Education: Westminster School; Christ Church, Oxford (BA chemistry 1970, MA); French.

Non-political career: NM Rothschild & Sons 1970-73; Called to the Bar, Lincoln's Inn 1974; QC 1987; Recorder 1990-96; Bencher 1993; High Court Judge, Chancery Division 1996-2004; Supervisory Chancery Judge, Midland, Wales and Chester, and Western Circuits 2001-04; Lord Justice of Appeal 2004-07; Judge in charge of Modernisation 2004-06; Lord of Appeal in Ordinary 2007-09; Master of the Rolls 2009-12; President of the Supreme Court 2012-.

Political career: *House of Lords:* Raised to the peerage as Baron Neuberger of Abbotsbury, of Abbotsbury in the County of Dorset 2006. Lord of Appeal in Ordinary 2007-09; As a senior member of the judiciary, disqualified from participation 2009-. *Councils and public bodies:* Chair, Advisory Committee on Spoliation of Art during the Holocaust 1997-; Governor, University of the Arts, London 2000-10.

Other: Chair, Schizophrenia Trust 2003-. Freeman, Company of Drapers 2011. Kt 1996; PC 2004; Garrick.

Rt Hon the Lord Neuberger of Abbotsbury, House of Lords, London SW1A 0PW
Tel: 020 7219 5353
Supreme Court of the United Kingdom, Parliament Square, London SW1P 3BD
Tel: 020 7960 1966 *Email:* jackie.sears@supremecourt.gsi.gov.uk
Website: www.supremecourt.gov.uk

NEVILLE-JONES, BARONESS

CONSERVATIVE

NEVILLE-JONES (Life Baroness), (Lilian) Pauline Neville-Jones; cr 2007. Born 2 November 1939; Daughter of Roland Neville-Jones and Cecilia Winn.

Education: Leeds Girls' High School; Lady Margaret Hall, Oxford (BA modern history 1961); French, German, some Spanish.

Non-political career: HM Diplomatic Service 1963-96: Third secretary, Salisbury, Rhodesia High Commission 1964-65, Third, second secretary, Singapore High Commission 1965-68, Foreign and Commonwealth Office, London (FCO) 1968-71, First secretary, Washington DC embassy 1971-75, FCO 1975-77, Member/chef de cabinet to European Commissioner Christopher Tugendhat, Brussels 1977-82, Head of planning staff FCO 1983-87, Bonn embassy 1987-91: Minister (economics) 1987-88, Minister 1988-91, Seconded as Deputy Secretary to the Cabinet and Head of Defence and Overseas Secretariat, Cabinet Office 1991-94; Chair, Joint Intelligence Committee 1993-94; Political director, FCO 1994-96; Seconded as senior adviser to High Representative for Bosnia 1996; BBC International Governor 1998-2004; Chair: Information Assurance Advisory Council 2004-07, Qinetiq Group plc 2002-05.

Political career: *House of Lords:* Raised to the peerage as Baroness Neville-Jones, of Hutton Roof in the County of Cumbria 2007. Shadow Minister for Security and National Security Adviser to the Leader of the Opposition 2007-10; Minister of State for Security and Government Spokesperson, Home Office 2010-11; Special Representative to Business on Cyber Security 2011-. Member: Joint Committees on the: National Security Strategy 2012-, Draft Enhanced Terrorism Prevention and Investigation Measures Bill 2012-13.

Political interests: National security issues; Asia, Middle East.

Other: Cyclotion Trust (particle therapy); Unique (chromosome disorder). Freeman, City of London. Honorary doctorates: University of London, Open University, City University; Honorary fellow, Lady Margaret Hall, Oxford. CMG 1987; DCMG 1996; Légion d'Honneur (France) 2009; PC 2010.

Rt Hon the Baroness Neville-Jones DCMG, House of Lords, London SW1A 0PW
Tel: 020 7219 3208 *Email:* nevillejonesp@parliament.uk

CONSERVATIVE

NEVILLE-ROLFE, BARONESS

NEVILLE-ROLFE (Life Baroness), Lucy Jeanne Neville-Rolfe; cr 2013. Born 2 January 1953; Daughter of Edmund and late Margaret Neville-Rolfe; Married Sir Richard Packer (4 sons).

Education: Somerville College, Oxford (BA philosophy, politics and economics).

Non-political career: Private Secretary to Peter Walker as Minister of Agriculture, Fisheries and Food 1977-79; Member, Prime Minister's Policy Unit 1992-94; Director, Deregulation Unit (Department of Trade and Industry)/Better Regulation Unit (Cabinet Office) 1995-97; Tesco plc: Group director of corporate affairs 1997-2006, Company Secretary 2003-06, Executive director, corporate and legal affairs 2006-12; Board of Management, Foreign and Commonwealth Office 2000-05; Member, Deputy Prime Minister's Local Government Funding Committee 2003-04; Efficiency Board, Cabinet Office 2010-.

Political career: *House of Lords:* Raised to the peerage as Baroness Neville-Rolfe, of Chilmark in the County of Wiltshire 2013.

Other: Non-executive director, John Laing Construction 1991-92; EuroCommerce: Vice-president 1998-2008, President 2012-; Corporate Leaders Group on Climate Change 2005-; Foresight Obesity Project 2005-07; China Britain Business Council 2005-; Chair, Dobbies Garden Centres plc 2007-11; Non-executive director, Carbon Trust 2008-; UK India Business Council 2008-; Non-executive director, ITV plc 2010-; Strategic Advisory Group, UK Trade & Investment 2011-. CMG 2005; DBE 2012.

The Baroness Neville-Rolfe DBE CMG, House of Lords, London SW1A 0PW
Tel: 020 7219 5353

LIBERAL DEMOCRAT

NEWBY, LORD

Deputy Chief Whip (Captain of the Queen's Bodyguard of the Yeomen of the Guard); Government Spokesperson, HM Treasury

NEWBY (Life Baron), Richard Mark Newby; cr 1997. Born 14 February 1953; Son of Frank and Kathleen Newby; Married Ailsa Ballantyne Thomson 1978 (2 sons).

Education: Rothwell Grammar School; St Catherine's College, Oxford (BA philosophy, politics and economics 1974, MA).

Non-political career: HM Customs and Excise: Administration trainee 1974, Private secretary to Permanent Secretary 1977-79, Principal, Planning Unit 1979-81; Secretary, SDP Parliamentary Committee 1981; SDP headquarters 1981-88: National Secretary 1983-88; Corporate affairs director, Rosehaugh plc 1988-92; Director: Matrix Communications Consultancy Ltd 1992-99, Flagship Group Ltd 1999-2001; Chief of Staff to Charles Kennedy, MP 1999-2006; Chair: Live Consulting 2001-12, Live Sport CIC 2009-12.

Political career: *House of Lords:* Raised to the peerage as Baron Newby, of Rothwell in the County of West Yorkshire 1997. Liberal Democrat Spokesperson for: Trade and Industry 1998-2000, The Treasury 1998-2010; Sponsored Public Services (Social Value) Act 2012; Deputy Chief Whip (Captain of the Queen's Bodyguard of the Yeomen of the Guard) 2012-; Government Spokesperson, HM Treasury 2012-. Member: Monetary Policy of the Bank of England/Economic Affairs 1998-2003, Ecclesiastical Committee 2002-12, Economic Affairs Sub-committee on Financial Bill 2004, Joint Committee on the Draft Financial Services Bill 2011-12, Administration and Works 2012-, Privileges and Conduct 2012-, Procedure 2012-, Sub-committee on Leave of Absence 2012-13, Selection 2012-, Refreshment 2012-, Joint Committee on Security 2012-. Chair, Liberal Democrat Parliamentary Party Committee on Treasury 2010-12. *Other:* Deputy Chair, Liberal Democrat General Election Team 1995-97; Liberal Democrat Campaigns and Communications Committee 1995-2006; Chief of Staff to Charles Kennedy as Leader of the Liberal Democrats 1999-2006.

Political interests: Europe, regional development; Eastern Caribbean, Pakistan, South Africa.

Other: FRSA 2006; The Prince's Trust. OBE 1990. MCC.

Recreations: Football, cricket, tennis.

The Lord Newby OBE, House of Lords, London SW1A 0PW
Tel: 020 7219 8501 *Email:* newbyr@parliament.uk *Twitter:* @RichardNewby3

NEWCASTLE, LORD BISHOP OF

NEWCASTLE (11th Bishop of), (John) Martin Wharton. Born 6 August 1944; Son of John and Marjorie Wharton; Married Marlene Duckett 1970 (1 daughter 2 sons).

Education: Ulverston Grammar School; Van Mildert College, Durham (BA economics, politics, sociology 1969); Linacre College, Oxford (BA theology 1971, MA); Ripon Hall, Oxford.

Non-political career: Curate: St Peter Spring Hill, Birmingham 1972-75, St John the Baptist, Croydon 1975-77; Director of Pastoral Studies, Ripon College, Cuddesdon, Oxford 1977-83; Director of Ministry and Training, Diocese of Bradford and Residentiary Canon of Bradford Cathedral 1983-92; Bishop of Kingston upon Thames 1992-97; Bishop of Newcastle 1997-.

NON-AFFILIATED

Political career: *House of Lords:* Entered House of Lords 2002.

Political interests: International relations, environment; Botswana, India, Norway.

Other: President, Azure 1998. CBE 2011. Lancashire County Cricket Club.

Publications: Co-author, Knowing Me, Knowing You (SPCK, 1993).

Recreations: Cricket, football, rugby.

Rt Rev the Lord Bishop of Newcastle, House of Lords, London SW1A 0PW
Tel: 020 7219 5353 *Email:* whartonm@parliament.uk
Bishop's House, 29 Moor Road South, Newcastle upon Tyne NE3 1PA *Tel:* 0191-285 2220
Fax: 0191-284 6933 *Email:* bishop@newcastle.anglican.org

NEWLOVE, BARONESS

NEWLOVE (Life Baroness), Helen Margaret Newlove; cr 2010. Born 28 December 1961; Married Garry Newlove 1986 (died 2007) (3 daughters).

Non-political career: Campaigner Against Anti-Social Behaviour.

Political career: *House of Lords:* Raised to the peerage as Baroness Newlove, of Warrington in the County of Cheshire 2010. Government Champion for Active, Safer Communities, Department for Communities and Local Government 2011-; Victims' Commissioner for England and Wales 2013-.

CONSERVATIVE

Political interests: Community, policing, volunteering, anti-social behaviour, alcohol, victims and justice.

Other: Founder, Newlove Warrington Campaign 2009; Patron, Warrington Wolves Foundation 2013. Cheshire Woman of the Year 2009.

The Baroness Newlove, House of Lords, London SW1A 0PW
Tel: 020 7219 6464 *Email:* newloveh@parliament.uk
Website: www.helennewlove.co.uk www.newlovewarrington.co.uk *Twitter:* @HelenNewlove

NICHOLLS OF BIRKENHEAD, LORD

NICHOLLS OF BIRKENHEAD (Life Baron), Donald James Nicholls; cr. 1994. Born 25 January 1933; Son of late William Greenhow and Eleanor Nicholls; Married Jennifer Mary Thomas 1960 (2 sons 1 daughter).

Education: Birkenhead School; Liverpool University (LLB 1956); Trinity Hall, Cambridge (BA law tripos, LLB 1958).

Non-political career: 2nd Lieutenant, Royal Army Pay Corps 1952-53. Called to the Bar, Middle Temple 1958; In practice, Chancery Bar 1958-83; QC 1974; Member, Senate of Inns of Court and the Bar 1974-76; Bencher 1981; Judge of the High Court of Justice, Chancery Division 1983-86; Lord Justice of Appeal 1986-91; Treasurer, Middle Temple 1997; Vice-Chancellor of the Supreme Court 1991-94; Chair, Lord Chancellor's Advisory Committee on Legal Education and Conduct 1996-97; Non-permanent member, Court of Final Appeal of Hong Kong 1998-2004.

CROSSBENCH

Political career: *House of Lords:* Raised to the peerage as Baron Nicholls of Birkenhead, of Stoke D'Abernon in the County of Surrey 1994. Lord of Appeal in Ordinary 1994-2007; Second Senior Lord of Appeal in Ordinary 2002-07; On leave of absence June 2013-. Chair Parliamentary Privilege Joint Committee 1997-99.

Other: President, Birkenhead School 1986-; Patron, Cayman Islands Law School 1994-2006. Honorary Fellow, Trinity Hall, Cambridge 1986; Honorary LLD, Liverpool University 1987. Kt 1983; PC 1986; Athenæum.

Recreations: Walking, history, music.

Rt Hon the Lord Nicholls of Birkenhead, House of Lords, London SW1A 0PW
Tel: 020 7219 5353 *Email:* nichollsd@parliament.uk

NICHOLSON OF WINTERBOURNE, BARONESS

NICHOLSON OF WINTERBOURNE (Life Baroness), Emma Harriet Nicholson; cr. 1997. Born 16 October 1941; Daughter of late Sir Godfrey Nicholson, 1st and last Bt and late Lady Katharine Lindsay, daughter of 27th Earl of Crawford, KT, PC; Married Sir Michael Harris Caine 1987 (died 1999) (2 stepchildren).

LIBERAL DEMOCRAT

Education: Portsdown Lodge School, Bexhill; St Mary's School, Wantage; Royal Academy of Music (LRAM 1962, ARCM); French.

Non-political career: ICL 1961-64; Computer consultant, John Tyzack and Partners 1964-69; Computer management consultant, McLintock Mann and Whinney Murray 1969-74; Save the Children Fund 1974-85: Director of Fundraising 1977-85; Consultant inter alia Dr Barnardos, Westminster Children's Hospital, The Duke of Edinburgh's Award Scheme, Foster Parents Plan 1985-87; St Antony's College, Oxford: Visiting fellow 1995-96, Senior associate member 1997-98, 1998-99.

Political career: *House of Commons:* Contested (Conservative) Blyth 1979 general election. MP (Conservative 1987 to December 1995, Liberal Democrat 1995-97) for Devon West and Torridge 1987-97. PPS to Michael Jack as Minister of State: at Home Office 1992-93, at Ministry of Agriculture, Fisheries and Food 1993-95, at The Treasury 1995; Liberal Democrat Spokesperson for Overseas Development and Human Rights 1996-97. *House of Lords:* Raised to the peerage as Baroness Nicholson of Winterbourne, of Winterbourne in the Royal County of Berkshire 1997. Member, Liberal Democrat Foreign Affairs Team 1997-; Front Bench Spokesperson for Data Protection 1998-99. Member Soft Power and the UK's Influence 2013-. *Other:* European Parliament: MEP for South East Region 1999-2009 (sat as Emma Nicholson): Whip, Liberal Democrat Party 1999-2001; Vice-chair, Foreign Affairs, Human Rights, Common Defence and Security Policy/Foreign Affairs Committee 1999-2007. Former treasurer, Positive European Group (Conservative); Vice-chair, Conservative Party 1983-87; Member, Liberal Democrats Federal Executive Committee 1999-2003.

Political interests: Information technology, human rights, education, health, foreign affairs, Islamic world, refugees/displaced people, poverty reduction, freedom of information, intellectual property; Armenia, Bulgaria, Georgia, Iran, Iraq, Kuwait, Lebanon, Moldova, Romania, Saudi Arabia, Syria, Turkey, Yemen.

Other: Treasurer, Positive European Group 1990-95; Member, UK Delegation to the Parliamentary Assembly of the Council of Europe; Many and varied past honorary positions with UK registered charities helping the disadvantaged; Executive chair, AMAR International Charitable Foundation; President, Association Children's High Level Group; Trustee, chair, fellow, member of a number of charitable trusts, particularly concerned with refugees, children and the disabled; Trustee, Booker Prize for English fiction and Booker Prize for Russian fiction; President, Caine Prize for African Writing; Fellow, Industry and Parliament Trust 1990; Executive chairman, Iraq-Britain Business Council; Director, Islamic Finance Centre; LRAM; ARCM; FRSA; Honorary D. Freeman, Worshipful Company of Information Technologists. Freeman, City of London. Five honorary doctorates, Universities of: Oklahoma City, USA, Birmingham, London Metropolitan, Victor Babes University of Medicine and Pharmacy, Romania, Dimitrie Cantemir Christian University, Bucharest, Romania; Reform; Royal Overseas League.

Publications: Why Does the West Forget? (1993); Secret Society – Inside and Outside the Conservative Party (1996); Co-editor, The Haqi Marshlands (2002).

The Baroness Nicholson of Winterbourne, House of Lords, London SW1A 0PW
Tel: 020 7219 5353

NICKSON, LORD

NICKSON (Life Baron), David Wigley Nickson; cr. 1994. Born 27 November 1929; Son of late Geoffrey Wigley Nickson and of late Janet Dobie; Married Helen Cockcraft 1952 (3 daughters); Married Eira Drysdale 2013.

Education: Eton College; RMA, Sandhurst.

CROSSBENCH

Non-political career: Commissioned Coldstream Guards 1949-54. William Collins Sons & Co. Ltd publishers 1954-82: Director 1961-85, Joint managing director 1967, Vice-chair 1976-83, Group managing director 1979-82; Director, Scottish United Investors plc 1970-83; General Accident Fire and Life Assurance Corporation plc: Director 1971-98, Deputy chair 1993-98; Clydesdale Bank plc: Director 1981-89, 1990-98, Deputy chair 1990-91, Chair 1991-98; Scottish & Newcastle Breweries plc: Director 1981-95, Deputy chair 1982-83, Chair 1983-89; Chairman, Pan Books Ltd 1982; Director: Radio Clyde plc 1982-85, Edinburgh Investment Trust plc 1983-94, Hambro's plc 1989-98, National Australia Bank Ltd 1991-96.

Political career: *House of Lords:* Raised to the peerage as Baron Nickson, of Renagour in the District of Stirling 1994. *Councils and public bodies:* Member, Scottish Committee, Design Council 1978-81; Stirling and Falkirk: DL 1982-97, Vice-Lieutenant 1997-2004; Chair, Countryside Commission for Scotland 1983-85; Member, National Economic Development Council 1985-88; Chair: Senior Salaries Review Body 1989-95, Scottish Development Agency 1989-92, Scottish Enterprise 1992-94; Independent adviser, Secretary of State for Scotland's Appointments Committee 1996-99; Chair, Secretary of State for Scotland's Scottish Salmon Strategy Task Force 1997-.

Other: Chairman, CBI in Scotland 1979-81; Member, Scottish Economic Council 1980-95; President, CBI 1986-88; Captain, Queen's Body Guard for Scotland, The Royal Company of Archers; Atlantic Salmon Trust: Chairman 1989-95, Vice-President 1995-2005; Trustee: Prince's Youth Business Trust 1987-90, Game Conservancy 1988-91, Princess Royal's Trust for Carers 1990-94; President, Association of Scottish District Salmon Fishery Boards 1996-2011; Scottish Advisory Committee, Imperial Cancer Research Fund: Chair 1994-2002, Life Governor; CIMgt; FRSE 1987. Honorary Freeman, Fishmongers' Company 1999-. Freeman, City of London. Chancellor, Glasgow Caledonian University 1993-2002. Four honorary doctorates from Scottish Universities. CBE 1981; KBE 1987; Boodle's, Flyfishers'.

Publications: Autobiography, Two at a Time (2004).

Recreations: Fishing, shooting, birdwatching.

The Lord Nickson KBE, House of Lords, London SW1A 0PW
Tel: 020 7219 5353   *Email:* wignick@btinternet.com

NICOL, BARONESS

NICOL (Life Baroness), (Olive Mary) Wendy Nicol; cr. 1982. Born 21 March 1923; Daughter of late James and Harriet Rowe-Hunter; Married Alexander Douglas Ian Nicol 1947 (died 2009) (2 sons 1 daughter).

Education: Cahir School, Co Tipperary, Ireland.

Non-political career: Clerical officer, Inland Revenue 1942-44; Inspector Admiralty 1944-48; Supplementary Benefits Tribunal 1976-78; Co-operative Board 1976-85: President 1981-85; Careers Service Consultative Panel 1978-81.

LAB/CO-OP

Political career: *House of Lords:* Raised to the peerage as Baroness Nicol, of Newnham in the County of Cambridge 1982. Member Lord Chancellor's Advisory Committee 1982-88; Opposition Spokesperson for Green issues 1983-92; Opposition Whip 1983-87; Opposition Deputy Chief Whip 1987-89; Opposition Spokesperson for Energy 1988-89; Deputy Speaker 1995-2002, Deputy Chair of Committees 1995-2002; Board member Parliamentary Office of Science and Technology (POST) 1998-2000; On leave of absence June 2012-. *Other:* Member, Co-operative Party. *Councils and public bodies:* JP, Cambridge Bench 1972-86; Cambridge City Council: Councillor 1972-82, Deputy Mayor 1974.

Political interests: Commerce, conservation, environment, energy, forestry.

Other: Various school governing bodies and other public service areas, including Granta Housing Association; Chair, United Charities 1967-86; Council member, RSPB 1989-94; Vice-President: Marine Conservation Society, RSPB, Council for National Parks; FRGS 1990-2001; RSPB. Senior Member, Robinson College, Cambridge 1995-; Honorary Fellow, Institute of Wastes Management.

Recreations: Reading, walking, gardening.

The Baroness Nicol, House of Lords, London SW1A 0PW
Tel: 020 7219 5353

NOAKES, BARONESS

NOAKES (Life Baroness), Sheila Valerie Noakes; cr. 2000. Born 23 June 1949; Daughter of Albert and Iris Masters; Married (Colin) Barry Noakes 1985.

Education: Eltham Hill Grammar School; Bristol University (LLB 1970).

Non-political career: Peat Marwick Mitchell & Co/KPMG/KPMG Peat Marwick 1970-2000: Partner 1983-2000; Seconded to: HM Treasury 1979-81, Department of Health, as Director of Finance, NHS Management Executive 1988-91; Bank of England: Director 1994-2001, Senior non-executive director 1998-2001; Non-executive director: Carpetright plc 2001-, SThree plc 2001-07,

CONSERVATIVE Hanson plc 2001-07, English National Opera 2001-08, John Laing plc 2002-04, Imperial Chemical Industries plc 2004-08, Severn Trent plc 2008-, Royal Bank of Scotland Group plc 2011-.

Political career: *House of Lords:* Raised to the peerage as Baroness Noakes, of Goudhurst in the County of Kent 2000. Opposition Spokesperson for: Health 2001-03, Work and Pensions 2001-06, Treasury 2003-10. Member: Economic Affairs Finance Bill Sub-Committee 2011, Audit 2011-, Sub-committee on Economic Affairs Finance Bill 2012-, Joint Committee on Voting Eligibilty (Prisoners) Bill 2013-, Communications 2013-. *Councils and public bodies:* Member: Inland Revenue Management Board 1992-99, NHS Policy Board 1992-95, Chancellor of the Exchequer's Private Finance Panel 1993-97; Commissioner, Public Works Loan Board 1995-2001; Member, Public Services Productivity Panel 1998-2000; Governor: London Business School 1998-2001, Eastbourne College 2000-04.

Political interests: Health, public finance, trade and industry, public service management, horse racing, rural issues.

Other: Trustee, Thomson Reuters Founder Share Company 1998-; Board member, Social Market Foundation 2002-05; Institute of Chartered Accountants of England and Wales: Fellow, Council member 1987-2002, President 1999-2000; Board member, Companions, Institute of Management 1996-2002; FCA; Childrens Society, Dogs Trust, Cats Protection Society. Freeman, City of London. Three honorary doctorates. DBE 1996; Farmers'.

Recreations: Skiing, horse racing, opera, early classical music.

The Baroness Noakes DBE, House of Lords, London SW1A 0PW
Tel: 020 7219 5230 *Fax:* 020 7219 4215 *Email:* noakess@parliament.uk

NOON, LORD

LABOUR

NOON (Life Baron), Gulam Kaderbhoy Noon; cr 2011. Born 24 January 1936; Son of Kaderbhoy Ebrahimjee and Safiabai Kaderbhoy; Married Mohini Kert 1998 (2 daughters).

Gujarati, Hindi, Urdu.

Non-political career: Royal Sweets 1953; Managing director, Bombay Halwa Ltd 1972-; Noon Products Ltd: Founder 1988, Chairman 1989-2005, Non-executive chairman 2005-; Chairman, Noon Group 1995-; Board member: Care International UK 2002-06, Transport for London 2004-08; Director, Britain in Europe 2004-07; Member of the advisory board, Naturalisation and Integration (ABNI), Home Office 2004-08; Non-executive director: NeutraHealth plc 2004-, Obento Limited 2004-; Independent director, Zee Telefilms Ltd 2006-; Non-executive director, Zee Entertainment Studios Ltd 2008-.

Political career: *House of Lords:* Raised to the peerage as Baron Noon, of St John's Wood in the London Borough of Camden 2011.

Political interests: Immigration, prevention of extremism, education; South East Asia, Middle East.

Other: Asian Business Association: Founder and chairman 1995, Board member 1998-, President 2002-; Trustee and Chairman, Noon Foundation 1995-; Director of Board, Covent Garden Market Authority 1995-2000; Trustee: Arpana Charitable Trust UK 1996-2006, Memorial Gates Trust 1998-; Member: Advisory council, Prince's Trust 1996-, Ethnic Business Forum 2000-03; London Chamber of Commerce and Industry 2002-05; Founder member, Cancer Research UK 2002-; Trustee, the Maimonides Foundation 2002-08; Honorary Life Vice-President, Surrey County Cricket Club 2005-; Member, advisory board, British Olympic Association 2007; Founder and Chief Trustee, The Noon Hospital and Research Centre (Zeen-Zar Charitable Foundation Trust) 2008-; Prince's Trust. Chancellor, University of East London 2012-. MUniv Surrey University 1998; Honorary DBA, London Guildhall 2001; Honorary doctorate, University of Central England 2002; DUniv, Middlesex 2002; Honorary doctorate, Business Administration, University of East London 2009; Honorary doctorate, Laws, Warwick University 2010; Honorary DLitt, De Montfort University 2011; Honorary doctorate, University of West London 2011. Asian of the Year 1994; Carlton Television Multicultural Achievement Award for Outstanding Contribution to British Business 2002; Asian Jewel Award 2003; Best Business Leader Award, Sage 2003; Asian Business Award 2004; Pravasi Bharatiya Samman Award by Government of India 2006; Watford and Northwest London Business Person of the Year Award 2006; Global Indian, Rajiv Gandhi Award 2007. MBE 1996; Kt 2002; Reform Club; Gymkhana Club; St Stephen's Club.

Publications: Autobiography, Noon, with a View (Whittles Publishing, 2008).

Recreations: Cricket.

The Lord Noon MBE, House of Lords, London SW1A 0PW
Tel: 020 7219 5353 *Email:* noong@parliament.uk
25 Queen Anne's Gate, London SW1H 9BU *Tel:* 020 7654 1600 *Fax:* 020 7654 1601
Email: gkn@noongroup.co.uk *Website:* www.noon.co.uk

CROSSBENCH

NORFOLK, DUKE OF

NORFOLK (18th Duke of, E), Edward William Fitzalan-Howard; cr. 1483; 29th Earl of Arundel (E) 1139/1289; Earl of Surrey (E) 1483; 16th Earl of Norfolk (E) 1644; 13th Baron Beaumont (E) 1309; 20th Baron Maltravers (E) 1330; 16th Baron FitzAlan, Clun, and Oswaldestre (E) 1627; 5th Baron Howard of Glossop (UK) 1869; DL. Born 2 December 1956; Son of Major-General 17th Duke, KG, GCVO, CB, MC, DL; Married Georgina Susan Temple Gore 1987 (3 sons 2 daughters).

Education: Ampleforth College, Yorkshire; Lincoln College, Oxford (BA philosophy, politics and economics 1978, MA).

Non-political career: Chair: Sigas Ltd 1979-88, Parkwood Group Ltd 1989-2002.

Political career: *House of Lords:* Entered House of Lords 2002; On leave of absence June 2012-. *Councils and public bodies:* DL, West Sussex 2002-.

Other: Premier Duke and Earl of England; Earl Marshal and Hereditary Marshal and Chief Butler of England; British Racing Drivers Club (Silverstone).

Recreations: Skiing, motor-racing, shooting.

His Grace the Duke of Norfolk DL, House of Lords, London SW1A 0PW
Tel: 020 7219 5353
Arundel Castle, Arundel, West Sussex BN18 9AB *Tel:* 01903 883400 *Fax:* 01903 884482

CROSSBENCH

NORTHBOURNE, LORD

NORTHBOURNE (5th Baron, UK), Christopher George Walter James; cr. 1884; 6th Bt of Langley Hall (GB) 1791. Born 18 February 1926; Son of 4th Baron and Katherine Louise, née Nickerson; Married Marie Sygne Aliki Claudel 1959 (3 sons 1 daughter).

Education: Eton College; Magdalen College, Oxford (MA 1959).

Non-political career: Farmer and businessman including overseas agriculture; Chair, Betteshanger Farms Ltd (UK); Nchima Tea and Tung Estates (Malawi).

Political career: *House of Lords:* First entered House of Lords 1982; Elected hereditary peer 1999-;. *Councils and public bodies:* DL, Kent 1996-.

Political interests: Education, disadvantaged and excluded children, parents, family, agriculture, horticulture; Australia, France, Indonesia, Malawi.

Other: FRICS; Stepney Childrens' Fund (Toynbee); Brooks's, Royal Yacht Squadron (Cowes), House of Lords Yacht Club.

Recreations: Painting, sailing, gardening.

The Lord Northbourne DL, House of Lords, London SW1A 0PW
Tel: 020 7219 3884 *Fax:* 020 7219 5933 *Email:* northbournec@parliament.uk

CONSERVATIVE

NORTHBROOK, LORD

NORTHBROOK (6th Baron, UK), Francis Thomas Baring; cr. 1866; 8th Bt of The City of London (GB) 1793. Born 21 February 1954; Son of 5th Baron; Married Amelia Taylor 1987 (divorced 2006) (3 daughters).

Education: Winchester College; Bristol University (BA 1976).

Non-political career: Trainee accountant, Dixon Wilson & Co. 1976-80; Baring Bros & Co. Ltd 1981-89; Senior investment manager, Taylor Young Investment Management Ltd 1990-93; Investment fund manager, Smith and Williamson 1993-95; Managing director, Cabincity Ltd 1995-; Director, Mars Asset Management 1996-.

Political career: *House of Lords:* First entered House of Lords 1990; Elected hereditary peer 1999-; Opposition Whip 1999-2000.

Political interests: City, agriculture, foreign affairs.

Other: Trustee, Winchester Medical Trust; White's.

Recreations: Cricket, skiing, shooting.

The Lord Northbrook, House of Lords, London SW1A 0PW
Tel: 020 7219 4090

LIBERAL DEMOCRAT

NORTHOVER, BARONESS

Government Spokesperson, Departments for Culture, Media and Sport, Environment, Food and Rural Affairs, Health, International Development, and for Women and Equalities; Government Whip

NORTHOVER (Life Baroness), Lindsay Patricia Northover; cr. 2000. Born 21 August 1954; Daughter of Charles and Patricia Granshaw; Married John Northover 1988 (separated) (2 sons 1 daughter).

Education: Brighton and Hove High School; St Anne's College, Oxford (BA modern history 1976, MA); Bryn Mawr College, Pennsylvania University, USA (MA history and philosophy of science 1978; PhD 1981).

Non-political career: Research Fellow: University College London and St Mark's Hospital 1980-83, St Thomas's Hospital Medical School, London 1983-84; Lecturer, University College London 1984-91; Historian of twentieth century medicine, Wellcome Institute, London 1984-91. Member, AUT 1984-91.

Political career: *House of Commons:* Contested Welwyn Hatfield 1983 and 1987 and Basildon 1997 general elections. *House of Lords:* Raised to the peerage as Baroness Northover, of Cissbury in the County of West Sussex 2000. Liberal Democrat Spokesperson for: Health 2001-02, International Development 2002-10, Equality Bill 2009-10; Government Whip 2010-; Government Spokesperson for: Health 2010-, Justice 2010-12, Law Officers 2010, Wales 2010, Women and Equalities 2010-, Advocate General for Scotland 2010, International Development 2010-, Environment, Food and Rural Affairs 2012-, Culture, Media and Sport 2013-. Member: Stem Cell Research 2001-02, EU Sub-committee C (Foreign Affairs, Defence and Development Policy) 2003-04, Procedure 2005-09, EU Sub-committee A (Economic and Financial Affairs and International Trade) 2008-10. *Other:* Chair: SDP Health and Social Welfare Association 1987-88, Liberal Democrats' Parliamentary Candidates Association 1988-91, Women Liberal Democrats 1992-95; Trustee, Liberal Democrats 2009-11.

Other: Vice-chair, Commonwealth Parliamentary Association; Trustee, Bryn Mawr College Association, Great Britain; Council member, Overseas Development Institute 2005-10; Trustee: Tropical Health and Education Trust 2007-10, Unicef UK 2009-10. English-Speaking Union award to study in USA 1972; St Anne's College Exhibition 1973; Herbert Plumer Bursary for postgraduate study overseas 1976; English-speaking Union Fellowship 1976-79; Mrs Giles Whiting Fellowship in the Humanities 1979-80.

Publications: Various academic publications.

The Baroness Northover, House of Lords, London SW1A 0PW
Tel: 020 7219 8623 *Email:* northoverl@parliament.uk

CONSERVATIVE

NORTON OF LOUTH, LORD

NORTON OF LOUTH (Life Baron), Philip Norton; cr. 1998. Born 5 March 1951; Youngest son of late George and Ena Norton.

Education: King Edward VI Grammar School, Louth; Sheffield University (BA political theory and institutions 1972; PhD 1977) (Nalgo Prize); University of Pennsylvania (Thouron Scholar, MA political science 1975).

Non-political career: Hull University: Politics lecturer 1977-82, Senior lecturer 1982-84, Reader 1984-86, Professor of Government 1986-, Director, Centre of Legislative Studies 1992-, Head of Department of Politics and International Studies 2002-07; Editor, Journal of Legislative Studies 1995-.

Political career: *House of Lords:* Raised to the peerage as Baron Norton of Louth, of Louth in the County of Lincolnshire 1998. Chair Constitution 2001-04; Co-opted member EU Sub-committee E (Law and Institutions) 1999-2001, 2006-09; Member: Regulators 2006-07, Constitution 2007-12, Joint Committee on Draft Constitutional Bill 2008, Merits of Statutory Instruments/Secondary Legislation Scrutiny 2009-, Joint Committees on: the Draft House of Lords Reform Bill 2011-12, Voting Eligibilty (Prisoners) Bill 2013-. *Other:* Chair, Conservative Academic Group 2000-; Executive Committee, Conservative History Group 2003-. *Councils and public bodies:* Chair, Standards Committee, Kingston-upon-Hull City Council 1999-2003.

Political interests: Constitutional affairs, parliamentary reform, legislatures, British politics, American politics, education.

Other: Executive committee member: Study of Parliament Group 1981-93, 2012-, Political Studies Association 1983-89; Member, Society and Politics Research Development Group, Economic and Social Research Council 1987-90; Associate editor, *Political Studies* 1987-93; President, British Politics Group (USA) 1988-90; Warden, King Edward VI Grammar School, Louth 1990-93; President, Politics Association 1993-2008; Co-chair, Research Committee of Legislative Specialists, International Political Science Association 1994-2003; Hansard Society: Council member 1997-, Director of Studies 2002-; Chair, Commission to Strengthen Parliament 1999-2001; Vice-President, Political Studies Association 1999-; Trustee: History of Parliament Trust 1999-, Jo Carby-Hall Poland and Cyprus Scholarships/Fellowships 2009-; Member, advisory board, Opposition Studies Forum 2009-; FRSA 1995; ACSS 2001. Honorary LLD, Lincoln University 2011; Royal Overseas League.

Publications: Author or editor: Dissension in the House of Commons 1945-74 (1975); Conservative Dissidents (1978); Dissension in the House of Commons 1974-79 (1980); The Commons in Perspective (1981); Co-author, Conservatives and Conservatism (1981); The Constitution in Flux (1982); Law and Order and British Politics (1984); The British Polity (1984, 5th edition 2010); Parliament in the 1980s (1985); Co-editor, The Political Science of British Politics (1986); Legislatures (1990); Parliaments in Western Europe (1990); New Directions in British Politics? (1991); Co-editor, Parliamentary Questions (1993); Co-author, Back from Westminster (1993); Does Parliament Matter? (1993); National Parliaments and the European Union (1996); Co-editor, The New Parliaments of Central and Eastern Europe (1996); The Conservative Party (1996); Legislatures and Legislators (1998); Parliaments and Governments in Western Europe (1998); Parliaments and Pressure Groups in Western Europe (1998); Co-editor, Parliaments in Asia (1999); Parliaments and Citizens in Western Europe (2002); Co-editor: Post-Communist and Post-Soviet Legislatures: The Initial Decade (2007), The Internet and Parliamentary Democracy in Europe (2008); A Century of Constitutional Reform (2011); Eminent Parliamentarians (2012); Parliament in British Politics (2nd edition 2013); Co-author, Politics UK (8th edition 2013).

Recreations: Table tennis, walking, writing.

Professor the Lord Norton of Louth, House of Lords, London SW1A 0PW
Tel: 020 7219 0669 *Fax:* 020 7219 1465 *Email:* nortonp@parliament.uk
Department of Politics, Hull University, Hull HU6 7RX *Tel:* 01482 465863 *Fax:* 01482 466208
Email: p.norton@hull.ac.uk *Website:* www.hull.ac.uk/pas/pnorton.htm
nortonview.wordpress.com lordsoftheblog.net/category/lord-norton
Twitter: @LordNortonLouth

NORWICH, LORD BISHOP OF

NORWICH (71st Bishop of), Graham Richard James. Born 19 January 1951; Son of late Rev Lionel James and Florence James, née James; Married Julie Freemantle 1978 (1 daughter 1 son 1 daughter deceased).

Education: Northampton Grammar School; Lancaster University (BA history 1972); Oxford University (DipTh 1974); Cuddesdon Theological College, Oxford.

Non-political career: Deacon 1975; Assistant curate, Christ the Carpenter, Peterborough 1975-78; Priest 1976; Christ the King, Digswell, Hertfordshire 1979-83; Advisory Council for the Church's Ministry 1983-87: Selection Secretary and Secretary for Continuing Education 1983-85, Senior Selection Secretary 1985-87; Chaplain to Archbishop of Canterbury 1987-93; Bishop Suffragan of St Germans Diocese of Truro 1993-99; Bishop of Norwich 1999-.

NON-AFFILIATED

Political career: *House of Lords:* Entered House of Lords 2004. Member: Communications 2011-. *Councils and public bodies:* Member, Church of England General Synod 1995-; Chair, Rural Bishops Panel 2001-06; Board member: Countryside Agency 2001-06, Norfolk County Strategic Partnership 2003-11; Chair: Central Religious Advisory Committee of BBC 2004-08, Norfolk Community Foundation 2005-10; President, Royal Norfolk Agricultural Association 2005; Member, Archbishops' Council 2006-10; Chair: Ministry Division, Church of England 2006-12, Standing Conference on Religion and Belief, BBC 2009-11.

Political interests: Rural issues, broadcasting, education and training.

Other: Athanaeum, London; Norfolk, Norwich; Strangers, Norwich.

Publications: Editor, New Soundings (DLT, 1997).

Recreations: Theatre, cricket, rugby, discovering second-hand bookshops.

Rt Rev the Lord Bishop of Norwich, House of Lords, London SW1A 0PW
Tel: 020 7219 5353
Bishop's House, Norwich NR3 1SB *Tel:* 01603 629001 *Fax:* 01603 761613
Email: bishop@norwich.anglican.org *Website:* www.norwich.anglican.org

NYE, BARONESS

NYE (Life Baroness), Susan Jane Nye; cr 2010. Born 17 May 1955; Married Gavyn Davies (2 sons 1 daughter).

Non-political career: Civil servant: Department of Employment 1974-76, Downing Street 1976-79; Office of the Leader of the Opposition 1979-92; Office manager to Gordon Brown MP as Shadow Chancellor of the Exchequer 1992-97; Political secretary to Gordon Brown MP as Chancellor of the Exchequer 1997-2007; Director of government relations, Downing Street 2007-10.

Political career: *House of Lords:* Raised to the peerage as Baroness Nye, of Lambeth in the London Borough of Lambeth 2010.

LABOUR

The Baroness Nye, House of Lords, London SW1A 0PW
Tel: 020 7219 5353

OAKESHOTT OF SEAGROVE BAY, LORD

OAKESHOTT OF SEAGROVE BAY (Life Baron), Matthew Alan Oakeshott; cr. 2000. Born 10 January 1947; Son of late Keith Oakeshott CMG, diplomat, and late Jill Oakeshott; Married Dr Philippa Poulton 1976 (2 sons 1 daughter).

Education: Charterhouse, Surrey (Senior Foundation Scholar); University and Nuffield Colleges, Oxford (BA philosophy, politics and economics 1968, MA); French, German, Spanish.

Non-political career: ODI/Nuffield Fellow, Kenya Ministry of Finance and Economic Planning 1968-70; Special adviser to Roy Jenkins MP 1972-76; Director, Warburg Investment Management 1976-81; Manager, Courtaulds Pension Fund 1981-85; Founder director, OLIM Ltd and Investment director, Value and Income Trust plc 1986-; Chairman, OLIM Property Ltd 2012.

LIBERAL DEMOCRAT

Political career: *House of Commons:* Contested (Labour) Horsham and Crawley October 1974 and (Alliance) Cambridge 1983 general elections. *House of Lords:* Raised to the peerage as Baron Oakeshott of Seagrove Bay, of Seagrove Bay in the County of the Isle of Wight 2000. Liberal Democrat Spokesperson for: Treasury 2001-11, Work and Pensions 2002-10; Chair, Business Advisory Group to Vince Cable as Secretary of State for Business, Innovation and Skills 2010. Member: Economic Affairs 2001-04, House of Lords' Offices Finance and Staff Sub-committee 2001-02, Reform of House of Lords Joint Committee 2002-03, Economic Affairs 2007-08. *Other:* Member: SDP National Committee 1981-82, SDP National Economic Policy Committee 1981-85, Liberal Democrat Taxation Group 2007-10. *Councils and public bodies:* Oxford City Councillor 1972-76.

Political interests: Economic policy, housing, overseas development; Kenya.

Other: Governor and council member, National Institute of Economic and Social Research; Council member, Overseas Development Institute; Chair, Coltstaple Trust; Chairman, Coltstaple Trust.

Publications: Chapter in By-Elections in British Politics (1973).

Recreations: Music, elections, Arsenal F.C.

The Lord Oakeshott of Seagrove Bay, House of Lords, London SW1A 0PW
Tel: 020 7439 4400 *Email:* oakeshottm@parliament.uk *Twitter:* @oakeshottm

O'CATHAIN, BARONESS

O'CATHAIN (Life Baroness), Detta O'Cathain; cr. 1991. Born 3 February 1938; Daughter of late Caoimhghin and Margaret O'Cathain; Married William Bishop 1968 (died 2001).

Education: Laurel Hill, Limerick; University College, Dublin (BA economics, English and French 1961).

Non-political career: Assistant economist, Aer Lingus 1959-66; Group economist, Tarmac 1966-69; Economic adviser to Chair, Rootes Motors/Chrysler 1969-72; Senior economist, Carrington Viyella 1972; British Leyland: Economic adviser 1973-74, Director, Market Planning 1974-76; Corporate planning executive, Unigate plc 1976-81; Milk Marketing Board 1981-88: Managing director 1985-88; Managing director, Barbican Centre 1990-95; Numerous non-executive directorships.

CONSERVATIVE

Political career: *House of Lords:* Raised to the peerage as Baroness O'Cathain, of The Barbican in the City of London 1991. Member: Monetary Policy of the Bank of England/Economic Affairs 1998-2005, European Communities Sub-committee B (Energy, Industry and Transport) 1998-2002, European Union 1999-2001, 2010-, Joint Committee on House of Lords Reform 2002-05, Constitution 2005-08; Co-opted member EU Sub-committee E (Law and Institutions) 2007-10; Chair EU Sub-committee B: (Internal Market, Energy and Transport) 2010-12, (Internal Market, Infrastructure and Employment) 2012-; Member: Leader's Group on the Working Practices of the

House of Lords 2010-11, Consumer Insurance (Disclosure and Representations) Bill 2011-12. *Other:* Chair, Conservative Friends of Azerbaijan. *Councils and public bodies:* Past President, Agricultural Section British Association for the Advancement of Science; Member: Design Council 1978-80, Engineering Council 1980-83; Council member, Industrial Society 1986-92; Patron, Women in Banking and Finance 2000-07.

Political interests: Arts, agriculture, industry, commerce, finance, retail industry, disabled, economic policy, family, energy; Azerbaijan, EU, Ireland, Israel, USA.

Other: Fellow: Royal Society of Arts 1986, Chartered Institute of Marketing 1987; Chair, Chichester Cathedral Council 2010-; President, Chartered Institute of Marketing 1998-2001; Sight Savers International 2002-. Freeman, City of London. Honorary Fellow, Harris Manchester College, Oxford 2009. OBE 1983; Commander: Royal Norwegian Order 1993, Order of the Lion of Finland 1994, Order of Friends of Azerbaijan 2011; Athenæum.

Recreations: Music, reading, swimming, walking, gardening.

The Baroness O'Cathain OBE, House of Lords, London SW1A 0PW
Tel: 020 7219 0662 *Email:* ocathaind@parliament.uk

CROSSBENCH

O'DONNELL, LORD

O'DONNELL (Life Baron), Augustine (Gus) Thomas O'Donnell; cr 2012. Born 1 October 1952; Son of James O'Donnell and Helen McLean, both deceased; Married Melanie Timmis 1979 (1 daughter).

Education: Salesian College, Battersea; Warwick University (BA economics 1973); Nuffield College, Oxford (MPhil economics 1975).

Non-political career: Lecturer in political economy, Glasgow University 1975-79; HM Treasury 1979-2005: Economist 1979-85, First Secretary (Economic), Washington DC embassy 1985-88, Senior Economic Adviser 1988-89, Press Secretary to John Major: as Chancellor of Exchequer 1989-90, as Prime Minister 1990-94, Under Secretary, Monetary Group 1994-95, Deputy Director, Macroeconomic Policy and Prospects Directorate 1995-96, UK's Executive Director to IMF and World Bank 1997-98, Economic Minister, Washington DC embassy 1997-98, Director, Macroeconomic Policy and Prospects 1998-99, Head of Government Economic Service 1998-2003, Managing Director, Macroeconomic Policy and International Finance Directorate 1999-2002, Permanent Secretary and Chair HMT Management Board 2002-05; Secretary of the Cabinet and Head of the Home Civil Service, Cabinet Office 2005-11, Secretary of the Cabinet and Head of the Civil Service 2011; Chair, Main Honours Advisory Committee -2012; Senior fellow, Civil Service College, Singapore; Strategic adviser to the chief executive, Toronto Dominion Bank 2012-; Senior adviser, Frontier Economics 2012-.

Political career: *House of Lords:* Raised to the peerage as Baron O'Donnell, of Clapham in the London Borough of Wandsworth 2012.

Political interests: Public sector, especially the civil service, economic and financial issues, wellbeing, behavioural science; Bhutan, Canada, New Zealand, USA.

Other: Trustee, *The Tablet*; Member, Economist Trust; Chair, Commission on Wellbeing Policy, Legatum Institute 2012-; Fellow, Institute for Government 2012-; Society of Business Economists; ProBono economics; Anchor House; Paul's Charity; Shine. City of London. Honorary degrees from Glasgow and Warwick universities; Honorary fellow, Nuffield College, Oxford. CB 1994; KCB 2005; GCB 2011. All England Lawn Tennis Club.

Recreations: Tennis, opera, golf.

The Lord O'Donnell GCB, House of Lords, London SW1A 0PW
Tel: 020 7219 5353 *Email:* odonnellg@parliament.uk

CROSSBENCH

O'LOAN, BARONESS

O'LOAN (Life Baroness), Nuala Patricia O'Loan; cr 2009. Born 20 December 1951; Daughter of Gerard Herbert and Sara Herbert; Née St Clair-Herbert; married Declan O'Loan (later MLA 2007-11) 1975 (5 sons).

Education: Holy Child School, Harrogate; King's College, London (LLB 1973); College of Law, London (1976).

Non-political career: Articled clerk, Stephenson Harwood solicitors, London 1974-76; Law lecturer, Ulster Polytechnic 1976-80; Raised family in Kenya where her husband was teaching 1980-83: Teacher, St Patrick's School, Iten, Kenya 1982-83; Ulster University 1984-2000: Law lecturer, then senior lecturer 1984-92, Jean Monnet chair, European law 1992-2000; External examiner, Aberystwyth University and IPSERA 1996-2000; Visiting professor, School of Law, Ulster University; Member, Independent Group for Dialogue and Peace, Basque Country 2007-10; Ireland's roving ambassador for conflict resolution and special envoy to Timor Leste 2008-; UN special envoy, women and peace-keeping 2009-11; Roving ambassador and special envoy of Ireland, women, peace and security 2009-11; Member, International Contact Group, Basque 2011-; Chair, Governing Authority, National University of Ireland, Maynooth.

Political career: *House of Lords:* Raised to the peerage as Baroness O'Loan, of Kirkinriola in the County of Antrim 2009. Member: Delegated Powers and Regulatory Reform 2010-, EU Sub-committee E: (Justice and Institutions) 2011-12, (Justice, Institutions and Consumer Protection) 2012-, Joint Committee on Human Rights 2012-. *Councils and public bodies:* Member: General Consumer Council, Northern Ireland 1991-96, UK Domestic Coal Consumers Council 1992-95, Ministerial Working Group on Green Economy 1993-95, Northern Health and Social Services Board 1993-97, Northern Ireland Police Authority 1997-2000; Chair, Northern Ireland Consumer Committee for Electricity 1997-2000; Strategy group 2010, Department for Economic Development 1998-99; Police Ombudsman for Northern Ireland 1999-2007; Special Commissioner, Commission for Racial Equality 2004-05; Chair, human rights inquiry, Equality and Human Rights Commission 2008-09; Independent Review for Home Office 2009-10.

Countries of interest: Africa, South East Asia, Spain.

Other: Member, Consumers Consultative Council, European Commission 1994-95; Associate member, British-Irish Parliamentary Assembly; NetPLUSS, Club of Madrid; Member, Commonwealth Parliamentary Association; Member: Society of Public Teachers of Law 1992-2000, Irish Association of Law Teachers 1992-2000, International Purchasing and Supply Educational Research Association 1992-2000; Patron: Living and Dying Well, Drumalis Retreat Centre, British Irish Association; Member, Royal Irish Academy 2013-; Member: Law Society of England and Wales, Solicitor of Supreme Court England and Wales, Association of Women Solicitors; Trustee, CONCERN Worldwide 2008-12. Honorary Doctor of Laws: Ulster University 2008, National University of Ireland, Maynooth 2008, Higher Education and Technical Awards Council, Ireland, Queen's University, Belfast 2010. Outstanding Achievement Award, American Association for the Civilian Oversight of Law Enforcement 2007; Northern Ireland Woman of the Year, Irish Tatler Awards 2007; Person of the Year, RTE Awards 2008. DBE 2008.

Publications: Many (80+) in reviewed journals, books and papers; Review editor and member of editorial board, Public Procurement Law Review (Sweet and Maxwell) 1991-96.

Recreations: Reading.

The Baroness O'Loan DBE, House of Lords, London SW1A 0PW
Tel: 020 7219 8724 *Email:* oloann@parliament.uk
Email: nualaoloan@googlemail.com

O'NEILL OF BENGARVE, BARONESS

CROSSBENCH

O'NEILL OF BENGARVE (Life Baroness), Onora Sylvia O'Neill; cr. 1999. Born 23 August 1941; Daughter of late Honorary Sir Con O'Neill, GCMG and late Lady Garvey, née Pritchard; Married Edward Nell 1963 (divorced 1976) (2 sons).

Education: St Paul's Girls' School, London; Somerville College, Oxford (BA philosophy, psychology and physiology 1962, MA); Harvard University (PhD philosophy 1969); French, German.

Non-political career: Philosophy assistant, then associate professor, Barnard College, Columbia University 1970-77; Essex University: Philosophy lecturer 1977-78, Senior lecturer 1978-83, Reader 1983-87, Professor of philosophy 1987-92; Principal, Newnham College, Cambridge 1992-2006.

Political career: *House of Lords:* Raised to the peerage as Baroness O'Neill of Bengarve, of The Braid in the County of Antrim 1999. Member: Stem Cell Research 2002, BBC Charter Review 2005-06; Co-opted member: Science and Technology Sub-committee II (Genomic Medicine) 2008-09, Science and Technology Sub-committee I (Nanotechnologies and Food) 2009-10; Science and Technology Sub-committee I (Behavioural Change) 2010-11; Member: Sub-committee on Lords' Interests 2009-10, Sub-committee on Lords' Conduct 2010-. *Councils and public bodies:* Chair, Equalities and Human Rights Commission 2012-.

Political interests: Constitutional reform, education especially higher education, medical ethics, languages, communication, copyright and publishing; Germany, Northern Ireland, Republic of Ireland.

Other: Fellow, Wissenschaftskolleg, Berlin 1989-90; Foreign Honorary Member: American Academy of Arts and Sciences 1993-, Austrian Academy of Sciences 2002-; Foreign Member American Philosophical Society 2003-; Honorary Member Royal Irish Academy 2003-; Foreign Member: Leopoldina 2004-, Norwegian Academy of Sciences 2006-; President, Aristotelian Society 1988-89; Member, Animal Procedures Committee 1990-94; Nuffield Council on Bioethics:

Member 1991-98, Chair 1996-98; Human Genetics Advisory Commission: Member 1996-99, Chair 1998-99; Chair, Nuffield Foundation 1998-2010; The Ditchley Foundation: Governor 2001-11, Council member 2003-11; President, Mind Association 2003-04; Trustee, Sense about Science 2004-; President, British Academy 2005-09; Trustee, American University of Sharjah 2005-; Board member, Medical Research Council 2012-; British Philosophical Association; FBA 1993, PBA 2005-09; F Med Sci 2002; Honorary FRS 2007. Over twenty honorary degrees. CBE 1995.

Publications: Faces of Hunger (1986); Constructions of Reason (1989), Towards Justice and Virtue (1996); Bounds of Justice (2000); Autonomy and Trust in Bioethics (2002); A Question of Trust (2002); Acting on Principle (2nd edition 2013); Co-author, Rethinking Informed Consent in Bioethics; Numerous articles on philosophy in learned journals.

Recreations: Walking and talking.

The Baroness O'Neill of Bengarve CBE, House of Lords, London SW1A 0PW
Tel: 020 7219 4120

O'NEILL OF CLACKMANNAN, LORD

O'NEILL OF CLACKMANNAN (Life Baron), Martin John O'Neill; cr 2005. Born 6 January 1945; Son of John O'Neill, fitter and turner; Married Elaine Samuel 1973 (2 sons).

Education: Trinity Academy, Edinburgh; Heriot-Watt University (BA economics); Moray House College of Education, Edinburgh; French (basic).

Non-political career: Insurance clerk 1963-67; President, Scottish Union of Students 1970-71; Open University Tutor.

LABOUR

Political career: *House of Commons:* Contested Edinburgh North October 1974 general election. MP (Labour) for Stirlingshire East and Clackmannan 1979-83, for Clackmannan 1983-97, for Ochil 1997-2005. Opposition Frontbench Spokesperson for: Scotland 1980-84, Defence and Disarmament and Arms Control 1984-88; Principal Opposition Frontbench Spokesperson for Defence 1988-92; Opposition Frontbench Spokesperson for Trade and Industry (Energy) 1992-95. Chair Trade and Industry 1995-2005. *House of Lords:* Raised to the peerage as Baron O'Neill of Clackmannan in Clackmannanshire 2005. Member Science and Technology 2006-07, 2007-10, 2012-; Science and Technology Sub-committee I: Chair (Waste Reduction) 2007-08, Member (Nanotechnologies and food) 2008-10. *Other:* Held most party positions in constituency and local government organisations.

Political interests: Education, defence, trade and industry; Argentina.

Other: Chair, Nuclear Industry Association 2008-11.

Recreations: Cinema, jazz.

The Lord O'Neill of Clackmannan, House of Lords, London SW1A 0PW
Tel: 020 7219 5059 *Fax:* 020 7219 0528 *Email:* oneillm@parliament.uk

OPPENHEIM-BARNES, BARONESS

OPPENHEIM-BARNES (Life Baroness), Sally Oppenheim-Barnes; cr. 1989. Born 26 July 1930; Daughter of late Mark Viner; Married Henry Oppenheim 1949 (died 1980) (1 son 2 daughters); married John Barnes 1984 (died 2004).

Education: Sheffield High School; Royal Academy of Dramatic Art.

Non-political career: Non-executive director, The Boots Co. plc 1981-93; Chair, National Consumer Council 1987-89; Director, Fleming High Income Trust plc 1989-97; Non-executive director, HFC Bank plc 1990-98; Former Vice-President, South Wales and West Fire Liaison Panel.

CONSERVATIVE

Political career: *House of Commons:* MP (Conservative) for Gloucester 1970-87. Opposition Spokesperson for Prices and Consumer Protection 1974-79; Member of the Shadow Cabinet 1975-79; Minister of State for Consumer Affairs 1979-82. *House of Lords:* Raised to the peerage as Baroness Oppenheim-Barnes, of Gloucester in the County of Gloucestershire 1989. Member House of Lords' Offices 2000-02. *Other:* President, Conservative Club of Gloucester 1970. *Councils and public bodies:* Former National Vice-President, National Mobile Homes Residents' Association; Former Vice-President: National Union of Townswomen's Guilds 1973-79, Western Centre of Public Health Inspectors; President, National Waterways Trust to 1990.

Political interests: Consumer affairs.

Other: MNDA, Dogs Trust. PC 1979; House of Lords Bridge Club. Vanderbilt Racquet Club.

Recreations: Bridge, tennis.

Rt Hon the Baroness Oppenheim-Barnes, House of Lords, London SW1A 0PW
Tel: 020 7219 5353

OUSELEY, LORD

OUSELEY (Life Baron), Herman George Ouseley; cr 2001. Born 24 March 1945; Married Margaret (1 son 1 daughter).

Education: William Penn School, south London; Catford College (Diploma municipal administration).

Non-political career: Town planning administrator 1963-70; Homes for elderly management 1970-73; Community development policy co-ordinator 1970-81; Principal race relations adviser to Greater London Council 1981-84; Assistant chief executive, London Borough of Lambeth 1984-86; Director of education and chief executive, Inner London Education Authority 1986-90; Chief executive, London Borough of Lambeth 1990-93; Chair and chief executive, Commission for Racial Equality 1993-2000; Director: Brooknight Security 1996-2005, Focus Consultancy Ltd 2000-11; Chair: Different Realities Partnership Ltd 2000-07, Solicitors Regulation Authority Advisory Group 2008-.

Political career: *House of Lords:* Raised to the peerage as Baron Ouseley, of Peckham Rye in the London Borough of Southwark 2001. *Councils and public bodies:* Local Government Association: President 2000-02, Vice-President 2010-.

Political interests: Public services, poverty, equality.

Other: Council member, Institute of Race Relations 1990-; Chair: Kick It Out 1994-, Policy Research Institute on Ageing and Ethnicity 1997-2011, PRESET education and employment charitable trust 1997-; Council member, Football Association 2006-13; Trustee: Daneford Trust, Manchester United Foundation; Institute of Race Relations; Fellow, Chartered Institute of Personnel Development; Unicef. Thirteen honorary degrees. Kt 1997.

Publications: The System (1981).

The Lord Ouseley, House of Lords, London SW1A 0PW
Tel: 020 7219 8725 *Email:* ouseleyh@parliament.uk

OWEN, LORD

OWEN (Life Baron), David Anthony Llewellyn Owen; cr. 1992. Born 2 July 1938; Son of late Dr John Owen, general practitioner, and Alderman Molly Owen; Married Deborah Schabert 1968 (2 sons 1 daughter).

Education: Bradfield College; Sidney Sussex College, Cambridge (BA natural sciences 1959; MB BChir 1962); St Thomas's Hospital, London 1956-61.

Non-political career: Various house appointments, St Thomas's Hospital 1962-64; Neurological and psychiatric registrar 1964-66; Research Fellow, Medical Unit 1966-68; Director, Deborah Owen Ltd 1972-; Non-executive director: New Crane Publishing 1992-2005, Coats Viyella 1994-2001; Executive chair, Global Natural Energy plc 1995-2006; Director, Abbott Laboratories plc 1995-2011; Chair, NEU Ltd 1999-2005; Non-executive chair, Europe-Steel Company 2000-; Chair, Yukos International UK BV 2002-05; Member, Supervisory Council of Mazeikiu Nafta Oil Refinery, Lithuania 2002-05; Director: Intelligent Energy 2003-05, Hyperdynamics Corporation 2009-.

Political career: *House of Commons:* Contested Torrington 1964 general election. MP (Labour 1966-81, SDP 1981-92) for Plymouth Sutton 1966-74, for Plymouth Devonport 1974-92. PPS to Gerry Reynolds as Minister of Defence 1966-68; Parliamentary Under-Secretary of State for Defence (Royal Navy) 1968-70; Opposition Spokesperson for Defence 1970-72; Parliamentary Under-Secretary of State, Department of Health and Social Security 1974, Minister of State 1974-76; Minister of State, Foreign Office 1976-77; Secretary of State for Foreign and Commonwealth Affairs 1977-79; Principal Opposition Spokesperson for Energy 1979-80. *House of Lords:* Raised to the peerage as Baron Owen, of the City of Plymouth 1992. *Other:* One of the founders of the Social Democratic Party, March 1981; Chairman, Parliamentary Committee 1981-82; Deputy Leader of the Party 1982-83, Leader 1983-87, Resigned over merger with Liberal Party; Re-elected SDP Leader 1988-90.

Political interests: International affairs (foreign and defence).

Other: Member: Palme Commission on Disarmament and Security Issues 1980-89, Independent Commission on International Humanitarian Issues 1983-88; EU Co-chair, International Conference on former Yugoslavia 1992-95; Carnegie Commission on Preventing Deadly Conflict 1994-99; Director, Center for International Humanitarian Co-operation 1996-; Eminent Persons Group on curbing illicit traffic in small arms and light weapons 1999-2001; Vice-President, Commonwealth Parliamentary Association (UK Branch); Patron: Social Market Foundation 1989-, James Callaghan Centre for Conflict Studies, University of Wales 2002-, Greenham Common Community Trust 2004-; President, River Thames Society 2009-; Chairman of Trustees, Daedalus Trust 2010-; Fellow, Royal College of Physicians 2005. Freeman, City of Plymouth 2000. Chancellor, Liverpool University 1996-2009. Three honorary degrees. PC 1976; CH 1994.

Publications: A Unified Health Service (1968); The Politics of Defence (1972); In Sickness and in Health (1976); Human Rights (1978); Face the Future (1981); A Future that will Work (1984); A United Kingdom (1986); Personally Speaking (to Kenneth Harris) (1987); Our NHS (1988); Time to Declare (autobiography 1991); Seven Ages (poetry anthology 1992); Balkan Odyssey (1995); The Hubris Syndrome (2007); In Sickness and in Power: Illness in Heads of Government during the last 100 years (2008, revised edition 2011); Time to Declare: Second Innings (updated and abridged autobiography, 2009); Nuclear Papers (2009); Europe Restructured (2012); Bosnia and Herzegovina: The Vance Owen Peace Plan (2013).
Recreations: Sailing.
Rt Hon the Lord Owen CH, House of Lords, London SW1A 0PW
Tel: 020 7219 5353
4 Curzon Square, London W1J 7FW *Tel:* 01442 872617/020 7947 3021 *Fax:* 01442 876108
Email: davidowen@lorddavidowen.co.uk *Website:* www.lorddavidowen.co.uk

OXBURGH, LORD

CROSSBENCH

OXBURGH (Life Baron), (Ernest) Ronald Oxburgh; cr. 1999. Born 2 November 1934; Son of Ernest Oxburgh and Violet, née Bugden; Married Ursula Mary Brown 1958 (1 son 2 daughters).
Education: Liverpool Institute; Oxford University (BA natural sciences (geology) 1957, MA); Princeton University, USA (PhD geology 1960).
Non-political career: Oxford University: Departmental demonstrator 1960-61, Lecturer in geology 1961-78, Fellow, St Edmund Hall 1964-78, Emeritus Fellow 1978; California Institute of Technology: Visiting Professor 1967-68, Fairchild Fellow 1995-96; Visiting Professor, Stanford and Cornell Universities 1973-74; Cambridge University: Professor of mineralogy and petrology 1978-91, Head of Department of Earth Sciences 1980-88, Fellow of Trinity Hall 1978-82, President, Queens' College 1982-89, Professorial Fellow 1989-91; Chief scientific adviser, Ministry of Defence 1988-93; Rector, Imperial College of Science, Technology and Medicine, London 1993-2001; Chair: SETNET 2002-05, Shell Transport and Trading plc 2004-05, D1 Oils plc 2007-08, 2OC 2007-, Falck Renewables 2007-10; Adviser: Climate Change Capital 2005-, Deutsche Bank 2008-, McKinsey 2010-; Non-executve director, Green Energy Options 2011-.
Political career: *House of Lords:* Raised to the peerage as Baron Oxburgh, of Liverpool in the County of Merseyside 1999. Board member, Parliamentary Office of Science and Technology (POST) 2000-. Science and Technology: Member 1999-2005, Chair 2001-05, Co-opted member - 2012; Member: Science and Technology Sub-committees: II (Science and Society) 1999-2000, II (Aircraft Cabin Environment) 2000-01; Chair Science and Technology Sub-committee IIA (Human Genetic Databases) 2000-01; Member Science and Technology Sub-committees: I (Fighting Infection) 2002-03, II (Innovations in Computer Processors/Microprocessing/Science and the Regional Development Agencies) 2002-03, I (Science and International Agreements) 2003-04; Chair Science and Technology Sub-committee II (Renewable Energy) 2003-04; Member Science and Technology Sub-committees: I (Scientific Aspects of Ageing) 2004-05, II (Energy Efficiency) 2004-05, Opposed Private Bills Committee (Broads) 2009; Co-opted member Science and Technology Sub-committee I (Radioactive Waste Management: a further update) 2010. *Councils and public bodies:* Member, National Committee of Inquiry into Higher Education (Dearing Committee) 1996-97; Council member, Foundation for Science and Technology; Chair, Scientific Programme Review Committee British Antarctic Survey.
Political interests: Higher education, health, energy, research and development, climate change; China, Singapore, USA.
Other: Member: ASTAR Singapore, SERC Singapore; President, European Union of Geosciences 1985-87; Member, geological and scientific academies and societies in USA, Germany, Austria, Australia and Venezuela; Natural History Museum: Trustee 1995-2002, Chairman 1999-2002; Vice-President, Globe UK; Council member, Winston Churchill Memorial Trust 1995-2008; President, Geological Society 1999-2001; Chair, Friends of Natural History Museum 2004-07; President, Carbon Capture and Storage Association 2006-; FRS 1978, Honorary FIMechE 1993, Honorary FCGI 1996, Honorary FREng 2000, Foreign Associate, US Academy of Sciences 2001, American Philosophical Society 2005. Honorary Fellow: Trinity Hall, Cambridge 1982, University College, Oxford 1983, St Edmund Hall, Oxford 1986; Queens' College, Cambridge 1992; Ten honorary doctorates. Bigsby Medal, Geological Society 1979. KBE 1992; Officier, Ordre des Palmes Académiques (France) 1995; Public Service Medal (Singapore) 2009; Honorary Citizen (Singapore) 2012; Athenæum. Climbers, West Anglia Orienteering.
Publications: Contributor to geological, defence and scientific journals.
Recreations: Mountaineering, theatre, orienteering.
The Lord Oxburgh KBE, House of Lords, London SW1A 0PW
Tel: 020 7219 4341 *Fax:* 020 7219 5979 *Email:* oxburghe@parliament.uk

NON-AFFILIATED

OXFORD, LORD BISHOP OF

OXFORD (42nd Bishop of), John Lawrence Pritchard. Born 22 April 1948; Son of late Revd Canon Neil Pritchard and late Winifred Pritchard; Married Susan Claridge 1972 (2 daughters).

Education: Arnold School, Blackpool; St Peter's College Oxford (MA Law 1973); St John's College, Durham (MLitt Theology 1993).

Non-political career: Assistant Curate, St Martin's-in-the Bull Ring, Birmingham 1972-76; Diocesan Youth Chaplain and Assistant Director of Education, diocese of Bath and Wells 1976-80; Vicar, St George's Wilton, Taunton 1980-88; Cranmer Hall, St John's College Durham: Director of Pastoral Studies 1989-93, Warden 1993-96; Archdeacon of Canterbury 1996-2001; Bishop of Suffragan of Jarrow 2002-07; Bishop of Oxford 2007-.

Political career: *House of Lords:* Entered House of Lords 2010. *Councils and public bodies:* Member, General Synod 1999-2001, 2007-.

Political interests: Education, world development, environment, Camp Ashraf; South Africa, Sweden (Diocesan links).

Other: Board, Church Amy 2003-10; President: Guild of Health 2003-, St John's College Durham 2006-11; Society for Promoting Christian Knowledge: Governor 2010, Chair 2011; Chair, Education Board, National Society 2011-; Christian Aid; Church Army; Friends of the Earth; Amnesty International; British Heart Foundation. Honorary fellow: St Peter's College, Oxford 2007, St John's College, Durham University 2012.

Publications: Practical Theology in Action (1996); The Intercessions Handbook (1997); Beginning Again (2000); Living the Gospel Stories Today (2001); How to Pray (2002); The Second Intercessions Handbook (2004); Living Easter through the Year (2005); Leading Intercessions (2005); How to Explain Your Faith (2006); The Life and Work of a Priest (2007); Going to Church: a user's guide (2009); Living Jesus (2010); God Lost and Found (2011); Living Faithfully (2013).

Recreations: Walking, photography, travel, music, sport, film.

Rt Rev the Lord Bishop of Oxford, House of Lords, London SW1A 0PW
Tel: 020 7219 5353
Diocesan Church House, North Hinksey Lane, Oxford OX2 0NB *Tel:* 01865 208222
Email: bishopoxon@oxford.anglican.org *Website:* www.oxford.anglican.org

LIBERAL DEMOCRAT

PADDICK, LORD

PADDICK (Life Baron), Brian Leonard Paddick; cr 2013.

Education: Queen's College, Oxford (BA philosophy, politics and economics 1986); Warwick Business School (MBA 1990); Fitzwilliam College, Cambridge (Diploma applied criminology and policing).

Non-political career: Metropolitan Police: Constable 1977-80, Sergeant 1980-83, Inspector 1983-89, Chief Inspector 1989-96, Superintendent 1997-2000, Commander 2001-03, Deputy Assistant Commissioner; Senior consultant, Policing and Public Sector, Public Partners.

Political career: *House of Lords:* Raised to the peerage as Baron Paddick, of Brixton in the London Borough of Lambeth 2013. *Councils and public bodies:* Contested Liberal Democrat London Mayor candidacy 2008 and 2012.

Other: Visiting fellow, Ashridge Business School.

The Lord Paddick, House of Lords, London SW1A 0PW
Tel: 020 7219 5353

DEMOCRATIC UNIONIST PARTY

PAISLEY OF ST GEORGE'S, BARONESS

PAISLEY OF ST GEORGE'S (Life Baroness), Eileen Emily Paisley; cr 2006. Born 2 November 1931; Daughter of Thomas James and Emily Jane Cassells; Married Ian Paisley (later MP, MEP, MLA, leader DUP, now Lord Bannside (qv)) 1956 (twin sons 3 daughters).

Education: Belfast Shorthand Institute and Business Training College.

Non-political career: Secretarial positions in several companies.

Political career: *House of Lords:* Raised to the peerage as Baroness Paisley of St George's, of St George's in the County of Antrim 2006. On leave of absence June 2013-. *Other:* Member: Northern Ireland Assembly 1973, Northern Ireland Convention 1975. Honorary Vice-President, DUP. *Councils and public bodies:* Councillor, Belfast Corporation 1967.

Political interests: Women, children, health, education.

Recreations: Gardening, reading, sewing, needlework.

The Baroness Paisley of St George's, House of Lords, London SW1A 0PW
Tel: 020 7219 5353

CROSSBENCH

PALMER, LORD

PALMER (4th Baron, UK), Adrian Bailie Nottage Palmer; cr. 1933; 4th Bt of Grosvenor Crescent (UK) 1916. Born 8 October 1951; Son of Colonel Hon Sir Gordon Palmer, KCVO and Hon Lady Palmer, DL; Married Cornelia Wadham 1977 (divorced 2004) (2 sons 1 daughter); married Loraine McMurrey 2006.

Education: Eton College; Edinburgh University (Certificate farming practice 1979); French.

Non-political career: Apprentice, Huntley and Palmers Ltd 1970-73; Sales manager, southern Belgium and Luxembourg 1974-77; Scottish representative to European Landowning Organisation 1986-91; Farmer. Member: National Farmers Union of Scotland, Scottish Landowners' Federation, Historic Houses Association.

Political career: *House of Lords:* First entered House of Lords 1990; Elected hereditary peer 1999-. Member: Advisory Panel on Works of Art 1995-98, 2000-02, 2005-09, Refreshment 1997-2000, 2003-05, Standing Orders (Private Bills) 2005-; Co-opted member EU Sub-committee D (Environment and Agriculture) 2000-03, 2007-10; Procedure: Member 2007, Alternate Member 2007-10. *Councils and public bodies:* Member: Executive Council Historic Houses Association 1981-99, Council Scottish Landowners' Federation 1986-92; Secretary, Royal Caledonian Hunt 1989-2005; President, Palm Tree Silk Co (St Lucia) 1992-; Historic Houses Association for Scotland: Vice-chair 1993-94, Chair 1994-99; President: British Association of Biofuels and Oils 1999-, Renewable Energy Authority (transport division) 2006-.

Political interests: Agriculture, environment, heritage, media, tourism; St Lucia, Scotland, Zimbabwe.

Other: Member, Queen's Bodyguard for Scotland (Royal Company of Archers) 1990-96; Chair, Country Sports Defence Trust 1994-; Secretary, Scottish Peers Association 2007-; New (Edinburgh); Pratt's; Convenor, Lords and Commons Cigar Club. Patron, Manderston Cricket Club 1978-.

Recreations: Gardening.

The Lord Palmer, House of Lords, London SW1A 0PW
Tel: 020 7219 6452 *Fax:* 020 7219 0785/020 7219 5979 *Email:* palmerad@parliament.uk
Manderston, Duns, Borders TD11 3PP *Tel:* 01361 883450/01361 882636 *Fax:* 01361 882010
Email: palmer@manderston.co.uk

LIBERAL DEMOCRAT

PALMER OF CHILDS HILL, LORD

PALMER OF CHILDS HILL (Life Baron), Monroe Edward Palmer; cr 2011. Born 30 November 1938; Son of William and Sybil Polikoff; Married Susette Cardash 1962 (2 sons 1 daughter).

Education: Orange Hill Grammar School; Open University (BA 2005).

Non-political career: Chartered accountant 1963; Treasurer, Disablement Association, London Borough of Barnet 1971-88; Citizens Advice Bureau: Chair, Hendon 1981-83, Barnet: Vice-chair 1986-88, Chair; Director, Barnet Homes 1994-2010.

Political career: *House of Commons:* Contested (Liberal) Hendon South 1979, (Lib/All) 1983 and 1987 and (Lib Dem) Hastings and Rye 1992 and 1997 general elections. Co-chair, Liberal Democrat Parliamentary Party Committee on International Affairs. *House of Lords:* Raised to the peerage as Baron Palmer of Childs Hill, of Childs Hill in the London Borough of Barnet 2011. Liberal Democrat Spokesperson on Defence. Member Refreshment 2012-. Chair, Liberal Democrat Parliamentary Party Committee on International Affairs (Defence) 2012-. *Other:* Joint Treasurer, Liberal Parliamentary Party 1977-83; Liberal Democrat Friends of Israel: Chair 1987-2010, Vice-President 2010-; Treasurer, London Region, Liberal Democrats 2008-09. *Councils and public bodies:* London Borough of Barnet Council: Councillor 1986-94, 1998-, Chair, Audit Committee 2010-.

Political interests: Defence, taxation, local government; Israel, Middle East, Palestine.

Other: Fellow, Institute of Chartered Accountants. OBE 1982; National Liberal Club. LA Fitness.

Recreations: Horseriding, reading, music.

The Lord Palmer of Childs Hill OBE, House of Lords, London SW1A 0PW
Tel: 020 7219 2561 *Email:* palmerm@parliament.uk

PALUMBO, LORD

CONSERVATIVE

PALUMBO (Life Baron), Peter Garth Palumbo; cr. 1991. Born 20 July 1935; Son of late Rudolph Palumbo and Elsie Palumbo; Married Denia Wigram 1959 (died 1986) (1 son 2 daughters); married Hayat Morowa 1986 (1 son 2 daughters).

Education: Eton College; Worcester College, Oxford (MA law 1954).

Political career: *House of Lords:* Raised to the peerage as Baron Palumbo, of Walbrook in the City of London 1991. *Councils and public bodies:* Governor, London School of Economics and Political Science 1976-94; Chair: Tate Gallery Foundation 1986-87, Arts Council of Great Britain 1989-94, Serpentine Gallery 1994-; Council member, Royal Albert Hall 1995-99; Governor, The Royal Shakespeare Theatre 1995-2000; Whitgift School: Governor 2002-10, Adviser emeritus to the Board of Governors 2010-; Chair, Pritzker Architecture Prize Jury 2004-.

Political interests: Arts, education, defence; Middle East, South America.

Other: Trustee: Mies van der Rohe Archive 1977-, Tate Gallery 1978-85, Whitechapel Arts Gallery Foundation 1981-87; Trustee and Honorary Treasurer, Writers and Scholars Educational Trust 1984-99; Chair, Painshill Park Trust Appeal 1986-96; Trustee: Natural History Museum 1994-2004, Design Museum 1995-2005; Honorary FRIBA; Honorary FFB 1994; Honorary FIStructE 1994. Liveryman, Salters' Company. Chancellor, Portsmouth University 1992-07. Honorary DLitt, Portsmouth University 1993. Patronage of the Arts Award, Cranbrook Academy of Arts, Detroit, USA 2002. National Order of the Southern Cross (Brazil); White's, Pratt's, Athenæum, Knickerbocker (New York), Garrick.

Recreations: Music, travel, gardening, reading.

The Lord Palumbo, House of Lords, London SW1A 0PW
Tel: 020 7219 5353
49 Oakley House, 103 Sloane Street, London SW3 3RU *Tel:* 020 7245 0809 *Fax:* 020 7245 0292
Email: anne@palumbo.demon.co.uk

PALUMBO OF SOUTHWARK, LORD – *Please see Addenda Page xii*

PANNICK, LORD

CROSSBENCH

PANNICK (Life Baron), David Philip Pannick; cr 2008. Born 7 March 1956; Son of late Maurice Pannick and late Rita Pannick; Married Denise Sloam 1978 (died 1999) (2 sons 1 daughter); married Nathalie Trager-Lewis 2003 (1 son 2 daughters).

Education: Bancroft's School, Essex; Hertford College, Oxford (MA 1977; BCL 1978); Gray's Inn, London.

Non-political career: Called to the Bar 1979; Junior counsel to Crown (Common Law) 1988-92; QC 1992; Bencher, Gray's Inn 1998; Deputy High Court Judge 1998-2005.

Political career: *House of Lords:* Raised to the peerage as Baron Pannick, of Radlett in the County of Hertfordshire 2008. Member Constitution 2008-13.

Political interests: Legal matters; Israel, USA.

Other: Chair, Legal Friends of the Hebrew University, Jerusalem. Fellow, All Souls College, Oxford 1978-; Honorary fellow: Hertford College, Oxford, Hebrew University of Jerusalem; Honorary Doctorate, University of Hertfordshire.

Recreations: Cinema, theatre, Arsenal FC.

The Lord Pannick QC, House of Lords, London SW1A 0PW
Tel: 020 7219 5353
Blackstone Chambers, Temple, London EC4Y 9BW *Tel:* 020 7583 1770 *Fax:* 020 7822 7350
Email: davidpannick@blackstonechambers.com

PAREKH, LORD

LABOUR

PAREKH (Life Baron), Bhikhu Chhotalal Parekh; cr. 2000. Born 4 January 1935; Son of Chhotalal and Gajaraben Parekh; Married Pramila Dalal 1959 (3 sons).

Education: HDS High School, Amalsad, India; Bombay University (BA economics 1954; MA political science 1956); London University (PhD the idea of equality in English political thought 1966); Gujarati, Hindi.

Non-political career: Politics tutor, London School of Economics 1962-63; Assistant lecturer in politics, Glasgow University 1963-64; Hull University: Politics lecturer, senior lecturer and reader 1964-82, Professor of political theory 1982-2001, Emeritus Professor 2000-; Visiting Professor: University of British Columbia, Canada 1974-75, McGill University 1976-77, Harvard University 1996, Institute for Advanced Study, Vienna 1997, University of Pompeu Fabra, Barcelona 1997, University of Pennsylvania 1998, École des Hautes Études en Sciences Sociales 2000; Centennial Professor, London School of Economics 2001-03; Westminster University: Professor of political philosophy 2001-09, Emeritus Professor of Political Philosophy 2009-.

Political career: *House of Lords:* Raised to the peerage as Baron Parekh, of Kingston upon Hull in the East Riding of Yorkshire 2000. Member Human Rights Joint Committee 2001-03. *Councils and public bodies:* Member, Rampton/Swann Committee of Inquiry into Educational Problems of Ethnic Minority Children 1978-82; Deputy chair, Commission for Racial Equality 1985-90; Vice-President, UK Council for Overseas Students Affairs 1989-99; Chair, Commission on Future of Multi-Ethnic Britain 1998-2001; President, British Association of South Asia Scholars 2004-07.

Political interests: Race relations, higher education, ethnic conflicts, global justice, international politics, multiculturalism; Canada, India, USA.

Other: Founding Member and Past President, Research Committee on Political Philosophy of International Political Science Association; Council Member, Policy Studies Institute 1985-90; Runnymede Trust: Trustee 1986-2003, Patron 2003, Gandhi Foundation: Trustee 1988, Patron 2002-, President 2012-; Council member, Institute for Public Policy Research 1990-96; Trustee: Anne Frank Educational Trust 1992-, Nirman Foundation 2000-; Fellow, Asiatic Society India 2003; Trustee: Rathbone Society 2003-, Black Umbrella 2005-; Patron: Institute of Advanced Study, Durham University 2008-10, Whistling Woods International, Mumbai 2008-; FRSA 1988; Fellow, British Academy 2003; President, Academy of Learned Societies for the Social Sciences 2004-08; Fellow, European Academy 2009; Cancer Research Society; Royal Society for the Blind; Barnardo's. Vice-chancellor, University of Baroda, India 1981-84. Sixteen honorary doctorates; Honorary Professor, University of Wales; Distinguished Professorial Fellow, Centre for the Study of Developing Societies, Delhi; Distinguished Visiting Professor, Cardozo Law School, New York; Distinguished Visiting Fellow, University of Maine, USA. British Asian of the Year 1991; Gujarati of the Year 1994; BBC's Special Lifetime Achievement Award for Asians 1999; Sir Isaiah Berlin Prize for Lifetime Contribution to Political Studies 2003; Pravasi Bharatiya Samman, by President of India 2005; Interdependence Prize, Campaign for Democracy, New York 2006; Pride of India 2006; Distinguished Global Thinker, India International Centre, Delhi 2006; Padma Bhushan, President of India 2007; Royal Society of Arts.

Publications: Politics and Experience (1968); Dissent and Disorder (1971); The Morality of Politics (1972); Knowledge and Belief in Politics (1973); Bentham's Political Thought (1973); Colour, Culture and Consciousness (1974); Jeremy Bentham: ten critical essays (1974); The Concept of Socialism (1975); Hannah Arendt and the Search for a new Political Philosophy (1981); Karl's Marx's Theory of Ideology (1982); Contemporary Political Thinkers (1982); Political Discourse (1986); Gandhi's Political Philosophy (1989); Colonialism, Tradition and Reform (1989); Jeremy Bentham: critical assessments (1993); The Decolonisation of Imagination (1995); Crisis and Change in Contemporary India (1995); Gandhi (1997); Race Relations in Britain (1998); Rethinking Multiculturalism (2000); The Future of Multi Ethnic Britain: The Parekh Report (2000); Culture and Economy in the Indian Diaspora (2003); A New Politics of Identity (2008); Conversations with Bhikhu Parekh (2012) Numerous articles in various learned journals.

Recreations: Reading, music, walking.

Professor the Lord Parekh, House of Lords, London SW1A 0PW
Tel: 020 7219 5353 *Fax:* 020 7219 5979
211 Victoria Avenue, Hull HU5 3EF *Tel:* 01482 345530 *Fax:* 01482 345530
Email: profparekh@gmail.com

PARKINSON, LORD

PARKINSON (Life Baron), Cecil Edward Parkinson; cr. 1992. Born 1 September 1931; Son of Sydney Parkinson; Married Ann Mary Jarvis 1957 (3 daughters).

Education: Royal Grammar School, Lancaster; Emmanuel College, Cambridge (MA English and law 1955).

Non-political career: Chartered accountant; Company director.

CONSERVATIVE

Political career: *House of Commons:* MP (Conservative) for Enfield West 1970-74, for Hertfordshire South 1974-83, for Hertsmere 1983-92. PPS to Michael Heseltine as Minister for Aerospace and Shipping, Department of Trade and Industry 1972-74; Assistant Government Whip 1974; Opposition Whip 1974-79; Opposition Spokesperson for Trade 1976-79; Minister for Trade, Department of Trade 1979-81; Paymaster General 1981-83; Chancellor, Duchy of Lancaster 1982-83; Secretary of State for: Trade and Industry June-October 1983, Energy 1987-89, Transport 1989-90; Member, Shadow Cabinet 1997-98. *House of Lords:* Raised to the peerage as Baron Parkinson, of Carnforth in the County of Lancashire 1992. *Other:* Chairman, Conservative Party 1981-83, 1997-98.

Political interests: Energy, transport, World Trade Organization, European Union.

Other: Treasurer, The Wordsworth Trust 1997-2003; President, Chemical Dependency Centre. PC 1983; Beefsteak, Garrick, Pratt's, Hawks (Cambridge). Achilles, Ashridge Golf Club, Chart Hills Golf Club.

Publications: Right at the Centre: An Autobiography (1992).

Recreations: Reading, golf, skiing.

Rt Hon the Lord Parkinson, House of Lords, London SW1A 0PW

Tel: 020 7219 5353

Tel: 07956 531325 *Fax:* 01707 660501 *Email:* suzanne.odonnell2@btinternet.com

LIBERAL DEMOCRAT

PARMINTER, BARONESS

PARMINTER (Life Baroness), Kathryn Jane Parminter; cr 2010. Born 24 June 1964; Daughter of James and June Parminter; Married Neil Sherlock 1994 (2 daughters).

Education: Millais School, West Sussex; Collyers Sixth Form College, Horsham; Lady Margaret Hall, Oxford (BA theology 1986, MA).

Non-political career: Graduate trainee, Nestle 1986-88; Parliamentary researcher to Simon Hughes MP 1988-89; Account executive, Juliette Hellman Public Relations 1989-90; Royal Society for the Prevention of Cruelty to Animals: Public relations officer 1990-92, Head of campaigns and events 1992-95, Head of public affairs 1995-96, Head of press and public affairs 1996-98; Chief executive, Campaign to Protect Rural England 1998-2004; Freelance consultant advising corporations and charities on CSR and charitable issues 2004-10.

Political career: *House of Lords:* Raised to the peerage as Baroness Parminter, of Godalming in the County of Surrey 2010. Member EU Sub-committee D: (Agriculture, Fisheries and Environment) 2010-12, (Agriculture, Fisheries, Environment and Energy) 2012-; Member European Union 2013-. Chair, Liberal Democrat Policy Committees on: Energy and Climate Change; Environment, Food and Rural Affairs (Environment, Food and Rural Affairs) 2012, Environment, Food and Rural Affairs 2012-. *Other:* Liberal Democrat: Policy Review Group 2005-07, Reform Commission 2008, Federal Executive 2008-10; Trustee, Liberal Democrat Party 2011-. *Councils and public bodies:* Councillor, Horsham District Council 1987-95.

Political interests: Environment, equality issues, food policy.

Other: Chair, Campaign for Protection of Hunted Animals 1997-98; Trustee, Institute for Public Policy Research 2007-; Advisory group, Every Child A Reader 2007-10; Vice-president, RSPCA 2011-; Patron, Meath Trust; National Liberal Club.

Recreations: Walking.

The Baroness Parminter, House of Lords, London SW1A 0PW

Tel: 020 7219 4195 *Email:* parminterk@parliament.uk *Twitter:* @kateparminter

CROSSBENCH

PATEL, LORD

PATEL (Life Baron), Naren Babubhai Patel; cr. 1999. Born 11 May 1938; Son of Babubhai and Lalita Patel; Married Dr Helen Dally 1970 (twin sons 1 daughter).

Education: Government Secondary School, Dar Es Salaam, Tanzania; Harrow High School; St Andrews University (MB ChB 1964).

Non-political career: Consultant obstetrician, Ninewells Hospital, Dundee 1974-2003; Professor, Dundee University.

Political career: *House of Lords:* Raised to the peerage as Baron Patel, of Dunkeld in Perth and Kinross 1999. Member: Science and Technology 1999-2003, 2005-09, 2010-, Science and Technology Sub-committees: II (Aircraft Cabin Environment) 2000-02, IIA (Human Genetic Databases) 2000-01, I (Fighting Infection) 2002-10, II (Innovations in Computer Processors/Microprocessing) 2002; Chair Science and Technology Sub-committee II (Science and the Regional Development Agencies) 2003; Member Science and Technology Sub-committee II: (Renewable Energy/Energy Efficiency) 2003-04, (Water Management) 2006, (Pandemic Influenza) 2006; Chair Science and Technology Sub-committee II (Genomic Medicine) 2008-09; Member: Procedure 2012-, Science and Technology Sub-committee I 2012-13. *Councils and public bodies:* President, Royal College of Obstetricians 1995-98; Chair, Academy of Medical Royal Colleges 1996-98; Council, General Medical Council 1998-2003; Chair: Specialist Training Authority of Medicine 1998-2001, NHS Quality Improvement, Scotland 1999-2006, Clinical Standards Board of Scotland 1999-2002; Member, Armed Forces Pay Review Body 2000-06; Chair: UK Stem Cell Oversight Committee 2005-10, National Patient Safety Agency 2006-10, Armed Forces Diversity and Equality Committee 2006-09, UK National Stem Cell Network 2007-09; Council member, Medical Research Council 2008-12.

Political interests: Women's health, higher education, regulation of medicine, ethnic minority issues, standards in medicine, care of obstetric fistulas worldwide, NHS, medical research; France, India, South Africa, Sweden, Tanzania, USA.

Other: European Board of Obstetrics and Gynaecology 2000-03; Vice-President, International Federation of Obstetrics and Gynaecology 2000-03; President, European Association of Obstetricians and Gynaecologists 2005-07; FMedSci; FRCOG; FRSE; Fistula Fund; WellBeing; Safe Hands; South Asia Health Foundation. Chancellor, Dundee University 2006. Numerous honorary degrees and fellowships from universities in UK and worldwide. Kt 1997; KT 2010.

Publications: Several books, chapters, articles on maternal/foetal medicine, epidemiology, obstetrics, gynaecology, quality healthcare etc.

Recreations: Walking, travel.

The Lord Patel KT, House of Lords, London SW1A 0PW
Tel: 020 7219 8702

PATEL OF BLACKBURN, LORD

PATEL OF BLACKBURN (Life Baron), Adam Hafejee Patel; cr. 2000. Born 7 June 1940; Son of late Hafejee Ismail Patel and of Aman Hafejee Patel; Married Ayesha Adam Bholabhai 1964 (4 sons 4 daughters).

Education: The Pioneer High School, Bharuch, Gujarat, India; MS Baroda University, India (Bachelor of Commerce 1964); Gujarati, Hindi, Urdu.

Non-political career: Accountant, Ivan Jacques Chartered Accountants 1967-72; Newscaster (Gujrati), Blackburn Radio Inc 1971-74; Chief Internal Auditor 1975-76; Director: Comet Cash and Carry 1977-97, Enterprise plc, Blackburn City Challenge, Blackburn Partnership 1977-95, East Lancashire Training Enterprise Council 1987-95, Lancashire Enterprises.

LABOUR

Political career: *House of Lords:* Raised to the peerage as Baron Patel of Blackburn, of Langho in the County of Lancashire 2000. *Councils and public bodies:* President: Indian Worker's Association 1968-, Lancashire Council of Mosques 1987-95; Vice-President, Blackburn Community Relations Council 1995; Counsellor, Muslim Council of Britain 1984-95; Magistrate, Blackburn 1984-95; Chair: Blackburn Racial Equality Council 1989-95, British Hajj Delegation and Committee 2001-10.

Political interests: Community and social work, education, race relations, economy and regeneration; Bangladesh, India, Kuwait, Pakistan, Qatar, Saudi Arabia, Swaziland, UAE, Zambia.

Other: Member, Commonwealth Parliamentary Association; Vice-President, Bopio; President, Lancashire Scouts 2005-; Bharuch Muslim Hospital. Honorary Doctorate of Social Science, Bolton University 2010; Honorary Fellowship: Bolton Institute, University of Central Lancashire. High Commissioner of India 2000; Lifetime achievement Jewel Award, Asian Jewel Awards 2005; Services to Muslim Community, Lancashire Council of Mosques 2008; Dedicated Services to Mankind, Ali Jauhar Foundation, Lucknow, India. Blackburn Rovers Football Club.

Recreations: Gardening, watching football and cricket, charity work, philanthropy.

The Lord Patel of Blackburn, House of Lords, London SW1A 0PW
Tel: 020 7219 5353 *Fax:* 020 7219 5979
36 Derwent House, Southern Grove, Mile End, London E3 4PU *Tel:* 020 8980 8252
Email: lordadampatel@hotmail.com

PATEL OF BRADFORD, LORD

PATEL OF BRADFORD (Life Baron), Kamlesh Kumar Patel; cr 2006. Born 28 September 1960; Son of Sudhindra Kumar and Savita Devi Patel; Married Yasmin Saloojee 1998 (2 sons 2 step-daughters).

Education: Belle Vue Boys Grammar School, Bradford; Huddersfield Polytechnic (CQSW 1987).

Non-political career: West Yorkshire Police Service 1981-91; Ambulanceman West Yorkshire Ambulance Service 1981-83; Bradford Social Services: Social worker 1983-87, Specialist caseworker (alcohol and drugs team) 1987-89; Manager, Bridge Project (drugs and mental health care organisation) 1989-95; University of Central Lancashire 1995-2010: Senior lecturer in social work 1995-97, Senior researcher in health 1997-98, Principal lecturer/research in health 1998-99, Professor and Head of Centre for Ethnicity and Health and of Institute for Philosophy, Diversity and Mental Health 1999-2008; Seconded as national strategic director, National Institute for Mental Health England 2003-04; Seconded as national director, Department of Health national delivering race equality mental health programme 2004-07; Ministerial adviser to Hazel Blears as Secretary of State for Communities and Local Government 2008-09; Professor and Head of International School for Communities, Rights and Inclusion 2008-10; Professor, senior management team, De Montfort University March-October 2010; Director of strategic partnerships and senior adviser to the Vice-Chancellor, University of East London 2010-.

LABOUR

Political career: *House of Lords:* Raised to the peerage as Baron Patel of Bradford, of Bradford in the County of West Yorkshire 2006. Government Whip 2008-09; Opposition Spokesperson for Communities and Local Government 2010-11. Member Mental Capacity Act 2005 2013-. *Councils and public bodies:* Home Office Advisory Council for the Misuse of Drugs: Member, Criminal Justice Advisory Working Group 1990-96, Council member 1993-96; Mental Health Act Commission 1995-2008: Non-executive board member 1995-2001, Member 1995-2001, Vice-chair 2001-02, Chair 2002-08; Non-executive board member, Central Council for Education and Training and Social Work 1997-98; National Treatment Agency for Substance Misuse: Non-executive board member 2001-08, Chair, Audit and Risk Committee 2001-08; Non-executive board member, Healthcare Commission 2003-05; Commissioner and trustee, UK Drug Policy Commission 2007-09; Chair, National Prison Drug Treatment Review Group 2008-10; Leicestershire Partnership NHS Trust: Associate non-executive director 2008-, Adviser to Communities, Rights and Inclusion Programme 2008-, Chair, Communities, Rights and Inclusion Governance Committee 2010-; Chair, Integrated Equality and Human Rights Committee, Leicestershire County and Rutland NHS Trust 2010-.

Countries of interest: Africa, India, Middle East.

Other: UK Member, Unicef's Global Task Force on Water, Sanitation and Hygiene 2006-10; Patron: National Men's Health Forum 2003-, Sharing Voices 2007-12, Bridge Project 2008-; President, Bradford Magistrates Chaplaincy Service 2008-; Patron: Westminster Health Forum 2009-, British Muslim Heritage Centre 2009-, Equity Partnership 2009-, Bradford Cryrenians 2010-, Safe Inside – Safe Outside 2010-; Chair: International Deaf 2010-, International Forum for Community Innovations 2011-; Patron: Mental Health First Aid 2011-, Awaaz 2011-, Engage Communities 2012-, Lily Project 2012-, Intercultural Communication and Leadership School 2012-; Professorial fellow: Mental Health (Institute of Mental Health), Public Health (Royal Society of Public Health) 2012-. Two honorary doctorates. Long Service Medal, West Yorkshire Police 1991; Plaque of Recognition for Contributions to the Enhancement of Human Welfare and International Understanding, India High Commission, London 1999; Glory of India Award and Certificate of Excellence, India International Friendship Society 2009; Achievement Award for Services to Education, India International Foundation 2009. OBE 1999. Northowram Fields Community Cricket Club.

Publications: Numerous on substance abuse, mental health, equality, extremism, human rights and diversity.

Recreations: Member of several cricket clubs.

The Lord Patel of Bradford OBE, House of Lords, London SW1A 0PW
Tel: 020 7219 4557 *Email:* patelkk@parliament.uk
Director of Strategic Partnerships and Senior Adviser to the Vice-Chancellor, University of East London, Docklands Campus, University Way, London E16 2RD *Tel:* 020 8223 7932
Email: k.patel@uel.ac.uk *Twitter:* @LordKPatel

PATTEN, LORD

PATTEN (Life Baron), John Haggitt Charles Patten; cr. 1997. Born 17 July 1945; Son of late Jack Patten; Married Louise Alexandra Virginia Charlotte Rowe 1978 (1 daughter).

Education: Wimbledon College, London; Sidney Sussex College, Cambridge (MA; PhD).

Non-political career: Oxford University: University lecturer 1969-79, Fellow and tutor, Hertford College 1972-81, Supernumary Fellow, Hertford College 1981-94; Business adviser and company director 1995-.

CONSERVATIVE

Political career: *House of Commons:* MP (Conservative) for Oxford 1979-83, for Oxford West and Abingdon 1983-97. PPS to the Ministers of State at the Home Office 1980-81; Parliamentary Under-Secretary of State for: Northern Ireland 1981-83, Health 1983-85; Minister of State: Department of Environment 1985-87, Home Office 1987-92; Secretary of State for Education 1992-94. *House of Lords:* Raised to the peerage as Baron Patten, of Wincanton in the County of Somerset 1997. *Councils and public bodies:* Oxford City Councillor 1973-76.

Other: Liveryman, Drapers' Company. Honorary Fellow, Harris Manchester College, Oxford. PC 1990.

Publications: Co-editor, The Conservative Opportunity (1976); Things to Come: The Tories in the 21st Century (1995) and other volumes.

Recreations: Talking with my wife and daughter.

Rt Hon the Lord Patten, House of Lords, London SW1A 0PW
Tel: 020 7219 1282

PATTEN OF BARNES, LORD

CROSSBENCH

PATTEN OF BARNES (Life Baron), Christopher Francis Patten; cr 2005. Born 12 May 1944; Son of late Francis Patten, music publisher, and Joan McCarthy; Married Mary St Leger, née Thornton 1971 (3 daughters).

Education: St Benedict's School, West London; Balliol College, Oxford (BA modern history 1965, MA).

Non-political career: Conservative Research Department: Research officer 1966-70, Director 1974-79; Research officer: Cabinet Office 1970-72, Home Office 1972; Governor and Commander-in-Chief, Hong Kong 1992-97; Chair, Independent Commission on Policing in Northern Ireland 1998-99; European Commissioner for External Relations 1999-2004.

Political career: *House of Commons:* MP (Conservative) for Bath 1979-92. Contested Bath 1992 general election. PPS: to Norman St John Stevas as Leader of the House of Commons and Chancellor of the Duchy of Lancaster 1979-81, to Patrick Jenkin as Secretary of State for Social Services 1981; Parliamentary Secretary, Northern Ireland Office 1983-85; Minister of State: Department of Education and Science 1985-86, for Overseas Development, Foreign and Commonwealth Office 1986-89; Secretary of State for the Environment 1989-90; Chancellor of the Duchy of Lancaster 1990-92. *House of Lords:* Raised to the peerage as Baron Patten of Barnes, of Barnes in the London Borough of Richmond 2005. *Other:* Personal assistant to Chairman Conservative Party 1972-74; Chair, Conservative Party 1990-92; Patron, Tory Reform Group. *Councils and public bodies:* Chairman, BBC Trust 2011-.

Other: Member, advisory council, Hague Institute for Global Justice, Netherlands 2012-. Chancellor: Newcastle University 1999-2009, Oxford University 2003-. Honorary Fellow: Balliol College, Oxford, St Antony's College, Oxford; Nine honorary doctorates. PC 1989; CH 1998.

Publications: The Tory Case (1983); East and West (1998); Not Quite the Diplomat (2005); What Next? Surviving the 21st Century (2008).

Rt Hon the Lord Patten of Barnes CH, House of Lords, London SW1A 0PW
Tel: 020 7219 8736 *Email:* pattenc@parliament.uk

PAUL, LORD

NON-AFFILIATED

PAUL (Life Baron), Swraj Paul; cr. 1996. Born 18 February 1931; Son of late Payare Paul and of Mongwati Paul; Married Aruna Vij 1956 (3 sons 1 daughter and 1 daughter deceased).

Education: Foreman Christian College, Lahore, Pakistan; Punjab University (BSc physics, chemistry and maths 1949); Massachusetts Institute of Technology (BSc, MSc 1952, mechanical engineering); English, Hindi.

Non-political career: Partner in family firm in India, Apeejay Surrendra Group 1953; Came to the UK in 1966, establishing first business Natural Gas Tubes Ltd; Caparo Group Ltd formed in 1978; Chairman, Caparo Group Ltd 1978-.

Political career: *House of Lords:* Raised to the peerage as Baron Paul, of Marylebone in the City of Westminster 1996. Deputy Speaker 2008-10; Deputy Chairman of Committees 2008-10; Suspended from membership October 2010-February 2011. Member: European Communities Sub-committee B (Energy, Industry and Transport) 1997-2001, Monetary Policy of the Bank of England/Economic Affairs 2000, 2001-03, 2005-09, Science and Technology 2003-07, Science and Technology Sub-committee II (Energy Efficiency) 2004-05; EU Sub-committee B (Internal Market): Co-opted member 2007-08, Member 2008-10; Member: Finance Bill Sub-committee 2008-10, European Union 2008-10, EU Sub-committee B (Internal Market, Energy and Transport) 2010. *Other:* Resigned Labour Whip October 2010. *Councils and public bodies:* Member: London Development Agency 2000-08, London 2012 2003-05; Chairman, Olympic Delivery Committee 2005-08.

Political interests: Foreign affairs, economic affairs, education; Austria, China, Dubai, Germany, India, Poland, Spain, Switzerland, Turkey, USA.

Other: Founder and chair, Ambika Paul Foundation 1978-; Chair: Piggy Bank Kids 2002-, Piggy Bank Kids Projects Ltd 2002-; Royal Society of Arts 1984-; Magic Bus; Chance to Shine; Hospices; ZSL. Freeman, City of London 1998. Thames Valley University: Pro-chancellor 1998-2000, Chancellor 2000-01; Chancellor: Wolverhampton University 1999-, Westminster University 2006-. Fifteen honorary doctorates from England, Switzerland, Russia, USA and India. Corporate Leadership Award, MIT 1987. Padma Bhushan (Government of India) 1983; PC 2009. Royal Calcutta Turf; Royal Calcutta Golf; Cricket of India (Bombay); MCC.

Publications: Indira Gandhi (1984); Beyond Boundaries (autobiography, 1998).

Recreations: Grandchildren.

Rt Hon the Lord Paul, House of Lords, London SW1A 0PW
Tel: 020 7219 5353
Caparo Group Ltd, Caparo House, 103 Baker Street, London W1U 6LN *Tel:* 020 7486 1417
Fax: 020 7224 4109 *Email:* lpoffice@caparo.com *Website:* www.caparo.com

PEARSON OF RANNOCH, LORD

PEARSON OF RANNOCH (Life Baron), Malcolm Everard MacLaren Pearson; cr. 1990. Born 20 July 1942; Son of late Colonel John MacLaren Pearson; Married Francesca Frua de Angeli 1965 (divorced 1970) (1 daughter); married Honorary Mary Charteris 1977 (divorced 1995) (2 daughters); married Caroline St Vincent Rose 1997.

Education: Eton College.

Non-political career: Founded PWS Group of reinsurance brokers 1964.

Political career: *House of Lords:* Raised to the peerage as Baron Pearson of Rannoch, of Bridge of Gaur in the District of Perth and Kinross 1990. Member European Communities and Sub-committee on Social Affairs and the Environment 1992-96. *Other:* Leader, UKIP 2009-10. *Councils and public bodies:* Council for National Academic Awards: Member 1983-93, Honorary Treasurer 1986-93.

Political interests: European Union, intellectual impairment, Islamism, education.

Other: Co-founder, Global Britain; Patron, Register of Chinese Herbal Medicine; Founded Rannoch Charitable Trust 1984; Patron, RESCARE (Society for Children and Adults with Learning Disabilities and their Families) 1994-. Honorary LLD, CNAA 1992; White's. Swinley Forest Golf.

Recreations: Stalking, fishing, shooting, golf.

The Lord Pearson of Rannoch, House of Lords, London SW1A 0PW
Tel: 020 7219 8686
Email: lordpearsonofrannoch@gmail.com

PEEL, EARL

Lord Chamberlain

PEEL (3rd Earl, UK), William James Robert Peel; cr. 1929. 4th Viscount Peel (UK) 1895; Viscount Clanfield (UK) 1929; 8th Bt of Drayton Manor (GB) 1800. Born 3 October 1947; Son of 2nd Earl; Married Veronica Timpson 1973 (divorced 1987) (1 son 1 daughter); married Honorary Charlotte Hambro, née Soames 1989 (1 daughter).

Education: Ampleforth College, Yorkshire; Tours University, France; Royal Agricultural College, Cirencester.

Non-political career: Lord Chamberlain of the Queen's Household and Chancellor of the Royal Victorian Order 2006-.

Political career: *House of Lords:* First entered House of Lords 1979; Elected hereditary peer 1999-. Co-opted member European Union Sub-committee D (Environment and Agriculture Policy) 2003-06. *Councils and public bodies:* DL, North Yorkshire 1998-.

Other: Chair, North of England Grouse Research Project 1979-96; Member: Yorkshire Dales National Parks Committee 1981-87, Moorland Association Executive Committee 1988-2006; President, Yorkshire Wildlife Trust 1989-96; Council member, Nature Conservancy Council for England, then English Nature 1991-96; President, Gun Trade Association 1993-99; Member, Princes Council Duchy of Cornwall 1993-96; Lord Warden of the Stannaries, Duchy of Cornwall 1994-2006; Game and Wildlife Conservation Trust: Chair 1994-2000, President 2000-08, Vice-President 2008-; Chair, Standing Conference on Country Sports 2001-06. GCVO 2006; PC 2006; White's.

Recreations: Shooting, cricket, photography, ornithology.

Rt Hon the Earl Peel GCVO DL, House of Lords, London SW1A 0PW
Tel: 020 7219 5353
Lord Chamberlain, Buckingham Palace, London SW1A 1AA

PENDRY, LORD

PENDRY (Life Baron), Thomas Pendry; cr 2001. Born 10 June 1934; Son of late Leonard Pendry; Married Moira Smith 1966 (separated 1983) (1 son 1 daughter).

Education: St Augustine's School, Ramsgate; Plater Hall, Oxford University.

Non-political career: RAF national service 1955-57. Boxed for Oxford University 1957-59; Middleweight Colonial boxing champion, Hong Kong 1957; Full-time official, National Union of Public Employees 1960-70. Member, AEEU.

Political career: *House of Commons:* MP (Labour) for Stalybridge and Hyde 1970-2001. Opposition Whip 1971-74; Government Whip 1974-77 (resigned); Parliamentary Under-Secretary of State, Northern Ireland Office 1978-79; Opposition Frontbench Spokesperson for: Northern Ireland 1979-82, Regional Affairs and Devolution 1982-92, National Heritage (Sport and Tourism) 1992-97. *House of Lords:* Raised to the peerage as Baron Pendry, of Stalybridge in the County of Greater Manchester 2001. *Other:* Chair, Derby Labour Party 1966. *Councils and public bodies:* Councillor, Paddington Borough Council 1962-65.

Political interests: Industrial relations, housing, sport, recreation, finance, social security, environment; Hong Kong, Malta, USA.

Other: Member, Council of Europe and Western European Union 1973-75; President: Stalybridge Public Band, Football Foundation; Patron, Football Supporter's Federation; Fellow, Industry and Parliament Trust 1979, 1988; President, Ramsgate FC; Teenage Cancer Trust. Freeman: Borough of Tameside, Lord Mottram of Longendale. PC 2001; Knight of Malta; Royal Air Force Club; Garrick. Lord's Taverners; MCC; Vincent's, Oxford University.

Recreations: Watching all sport, meeting sportspersons, jazz.

Rt Hon the Lord Pendry, House of Lords, London SW1A 0PW
Tel: 020 7219 4590 *Fax:* 020 7219 4419 *Email:* pendryt@parliament.uk

---

PERRY OF SOUTHWARK, BARONESS

CONSERVATIVE

PERRY OF SOUTHWARK (Life Baroness), Pauline Perry; cr. 1991. Born 15 October 1931; Daughter of late John and Elizabeth Welch; Married George Perry 1952 (died 2008) (3 sons 1 daughter).

Education: Wolverhampton High School for Girls; Girton College, Cambridge (BA moral sciences (philosophy) 1952, MA); French, Latin.

Non-political career: Philosophy lecturer, University of Manitoba, Canada 1956-59; High school teacher, Andover, Massachusetts 1959-61; Part-time Philosophy lecturer: University of Massachusetts, USA 1960-62, Exeter University 1962-65; Part-time education lecturer, Oxford University 1966-70; Access Course Tutor, Abingdon 1966-70; HM Inspectorate Department of Education and Science 1970-86: Chief Inspector 1981-86; Vice-Chancellor and chief executive, South Bank Polytechnic/University 1986-93; Chair, South Bank University Enterprises Ltd 1989-93; Member, Board of Directors, Greater London Enterprise 1990-91; Director, South Bank Arts Centre 1991-94; President, Lucy Cavendish College, Cambridge University 1994-2001.

Political career: *House of Lords:* Raised to the peerage as Baroness Perry of Southwark, of Charlbury in the County of Oxfordshire 1991. Party Whip 2010-. Member: Science and Technology 1992-97, 2003-07, 2010-, Scrutiny of Delegated Powers 1993-97, Relations between Central and Local Government 1995-96, Stem Cell Research 2001-02, Human Rights Joint Committee 2000-03, Religious Offences 2002-03; Chair Science and Technology Sub-committee I (Energy Efficiency) 2004-05; Member: Ecclesiastical Committee 2006-, Liaison 2007-12; Co-opted member: EU Sub-committee G (Social Policy and Consumer Affairs) 2007-09, Science and Technology Sub-committee II (Genomic Medicine) 2008-09; Member Science and Technology Sub-committees: I (Radioactive Waste Management: a further update) 2010, I 2012-13. *Other:* Association of Conservative Peers: Member 1991-, Executive Committee 2003-06, 2009-12; President, Cambridge City Conservative Association 1998-; Co-chair, Policy Commission on Public Service Improvement 2006-07; Vice-chairman, Conservative Academics Group. *Councils and public bodies:* Member: Committee on International Co-operation in Higher Education, British Council 1987-96, Economic and Social Research Council 1989-93; Academic adviser, Home Office, Police Training Council 1990-92; Chair, DTI Committee for Education and Training Exports 1993-98; Member, Citizen's Charter Advisory Panel 1993-97; Chair, Charter Mark Judging Panel 1997-2004; Addenbrookes NHS Trust: Non-executive director 1998-2001, Research Governance Committee 2001-11; Chair: Church of England Review of Crown Appointments Commission 1999-2001, Council, Roehampton University 2000-05; President: Council for Independent Further Education 2000-13, Westminster and City Branch Chartered Management Institute 2000-13; Chair, Church of England Inquiry into Crown Appointments Commission 2001-03, President, Foundation for Higher Education 2002-06; Chair, Nuffield Council for Bio-Ethics Inquiry into Animals in Scientific Research 2003-05.

Political interests: Education, international affairs; Korea, Israel, Taiwan, United Arab Emirates.

Other: British Council Committee on International Co-operation in Higher Education 1989-96; Chair, DTI Export Group for Education and Training 1993-98; Member: Overseas Projects Board, DTI 1993-98, British-Thai Business Group 1993-2000, Singapore-British Business Group 1993-98, Indo-British Partnership 1993-98, Korea Trade Advisory Group 1995-2002, British-Israel Business Group 1995-98, UK-Korean Forum for the Future 1999-2005, Inter-Parliamentary Union; Patron, Women's Engineering Society 1987-97, Rector's Warden, Southwark Cathedral 1990-94; Patron, British Youth Opera 1990-; Member of the Court, Bath University 1991-98; Trustee, Bacon's City Technology College 1991-2009; Patron, Alzheimers Research UK 1993-;

Vice-President, City and Guilds of London Institute 1994-99; Member, Board of Patrons, Royal Society Appeal 1996-99; Chair, Friends of Southwark Cathedral 1996-2002; Trustee: Cambridge Foundation 1996-2005, Southwark Cathedral Millennium Project; Governor (Board Member), English Speaking Union 1997-2003; British Friends of Neve-Shalom-Wahat-al-Salaam 2000-; Member, Institute of Directors; Companion, Institute of Management (now Chartered Management Institute); Honorary fellow: Royal College of Teachers, City and Guilds Institute, Girton College, Cambridge, Lucy Cavendish College, Cambridge, Royal Society of Arts; Alzheimer's Research UK; British Youth Opera; Village of Peace, Israel. Liveryman, Worshipful Company of Bakers; Honorary Freeman, Worshipful Company of Fishmongers. Freedom, City of London 1991. Pro-Chancellor, Surrey University 2001-06. Thirteen honorary doctorates and fellowships; Institute of Directors.

Publications: Four books, chapters in eleven other books, numerous articles in educational journals and national press; participated in international seminars and study visits on education.

Recreations: Gardening, walking, listening to music, French countryside, food and literature.

The Baroness Perry of Southwark, House of Lords, London SW1A 0PW
Tel: 020 7219 5474 *Email:* perryp@parliament.uk

PESTON, LORD

LABOUR

PESTON (Life Baron), Maurice Harry Peston; cr. 1987. Born 19 March 1931; Son of late Abraham and Yetta Peston; Married Helen Conroy 1958 (2 sons 1 daughter).

Education: Belle Vue High School, Bradford; Hackney Downs School; London School of Economics (BSc economics); Princeton University, USA.

Non-political career: Scientific and senior scientific officer, Army Operations Research Group 1954-57; Assistant lecturer, lecturer, reader in economics London School of Economics 1957-65; Economic adviser, HM Treasury 1962-64; Queen Mary College, London University: Professor of economics 1965-88, Emeritus Professor 1988-; Editor, *Applied Economics* 1972-; Special adviser to Secretary of State for: Education and Science 1974-75, Prices 1976-79; Chair: Pools Panel 1991-94, National Foundation for Education Research 1991-97, Office of Health Economics 1991-2000.

Political career: *House of Lords:* Raised to the peerage as Baron Peston, of Mile End in Greater London 1987. Opposition Spokesperson for: Energy 1987-97, Education and Science 1987-97, Treasury 1990-92, Trade and Industry 1992-97. Chair Monetary Policy of the Bank of England/ Economic Affairs 1998-2005; Member: Review of the BBC Charter 2005-06, Constitution 2005-09, Joint Committees on: Security 2010-, Voting Eligibilty (Prisoners) Bill 2013-; Science and Technology 2013-. *Councils and public bodies:* Member, Council for National Academic Awards 1967-73, Chair: Economics Board, Economics Board Social Science Research Council 1976-79.

Other: Member, Council Royal Pharmaceutical Society of Great Britain 1986-96; Vice-President, Speakability; Honorary Member, Royal Pharmaceutical Society of Great Britain 1996; Communications Forum; Nightingale House. Honorary DEd, University of East London 1984; Honorary Fellow: Portsmouth University 1987, Queen Mary and Westfield College 1992, London School of Economics 1995; Honorary DPhil, London Guildhall University 1999.

Publications: Elementary Matrices for Economics (1969); Public Goods and the Public Sector (1972); Theory of Macroeconomic Policy (1974); Whatever Happened to Macroeconomics? (1980); The British Economy (1982).

The Lord Peston, House of Lords, London SW1A 0PW
Tel: 020 7219 3122 *Email:* pestonmh@parliament.uk

PHILLIPS OF SUDBURY, LORD

LIBERAL DEMOCRAT

PHILLIPS OF SUDBURY (Life Baron), Andrew Wyndham Phillips; cr. 1998. Born 15 March 1939; Son of Alan Phillips and Dorothy, née Wyndham; Married Penelope Ann Bennett 1968 (1 son 2 daughters).

Education: Sudbury School; Culford School; Uppingham School; Trinity Hall, Cambridge (BA economics and law 1962); Workable French.

Non-political career: Solicitor 1964; Founded Bates, Wells & Braithwaite (London) 1970: Senior Partner -1998; Consultant: Bates, Wells & Braithwaite (Sudbury), Bates, Wells & Braithwaite LLP (London); Many non-executive directorships; Freelance journalist and broadcaster, *Legal Eagle* on BBC Radio 2 Jimmy Young Show 1976-2001; Presenter, *The London Programme*, London Weekend Television 1980-81; Occasional presenter, current affairs programmes, Anglia Television.

Political career: *House of Commons:* Contested (Labour) Harwich 1970 general election. Expelled as Lab candidate for North Norfolk 1973. Contested (Liberal) Saffron Walden 1977 by-election and 1979 general election and (Liberal/Alliance) Gainsborough 1983 general election.

House of Lords: Raised to the peerage as Baron Phillips of Sudbury, of Sudbury in the County of Suffolk 1998. Liberal Democrat Spokesperson for Home Office (ID Cards Bill and Charities Bill) 2005-06; On leave of absence 2006-10. Member Consolidation, Etc, Bills 2000-06. *Other:* Contested (Liberal) North East Essex 1979 European Parliament election. *Councils and public bodies:* Member, National Lottery Charities Board 1994-96; Appointments Commissioner, Press Complaints Commission 2005-10.

Political interests: Voluntary sector, legal services, magistracy, citizenship, crime/punishment, libertarian issues, rural/country town problems, theatre/arts, tourism, heritage matters; Democratic Republic of Congo, Iran, Israel-Palestine, Syria.

Other: Co-founder and chair, Legal Action Group 1971-76; Co-founder, Parlex Group of European Lawyers 1971; Initiated, Lawyers in the Community Scheme 1987; Founder, then president, Citizenship Foundation 1989-; Trustee: Phillips Fund 1990-, Scott Trust (owner of *Guardian/ Observer*) 1991-2001; Member, Charter 88 Committee from inception -1994; Trustee: Gainsborough's House 1995-, Age Concern Funeral Trust 1996-; Founder, then president, Solicitors Pro Bono Group (LawWorks) 1996-; President: Sudbury Society 2000-, British-Iranian Chamber of Commerce 2001-; Fellow, Royal Society of Arts; Patron of numerous national and East Anglian charities. Chancellor, Essex University 2003-. Privacy International 'Winston' Parliamentarian of Year 2001; Third Sector Luke Fitzherbert Lifetime Achievement Award 2009; Public Interest Law Institute Lifetime Award 2010. OBE 1996. Sudbury Cricket, Newton Green Golf, Sudbury Rugby.

Publications: The Living Law; Co-author, Charitable Status – A Practical Handbook (5th edition); Justice Beyond Reach; Co-author, Charity Investment – Law and Practice; A Review of the Bingham Report (1978).

Recreations: Theatre, local history (especially Suffolk), arts, architecture (especially parish churches), golf, walking, reading, family and friends.

The Lord Phillips of Sudbury OBE, House of Lords, London SW1A 0PW
Tel: 020 7219 5353
Tel: 020 7551 7777 *Fax:* 020 7551 7800 *Email:* a.phillips@bwbllp.com

CROSSBENCH

PHILLIPS OF WORTH MATRAVERS, LORD

PHILLIPS OF WORTH MATRAVERS (Life Baron), Nicholas Addison Phillips; cr. 1999. Born 21 January 1938; Son of Michael Pennington Phillips and Dora Phillips, née Hassid; Married Christylle Marie-Thérèse Rouffiac, née Doreau 1972 (2 daughters 1 stepson 1 stepdaughter).

Education: Bryanston School; King's College, Cambridge (BA law 1961, MA).

Non-political career: Royal Navy national service commissioned RNVR 1956-58. Called to the Bar, Middle Temple (Harmsworth Scholar) 1962; In practice at the Bar 1962-87; Junior Counsel to Ministry of Defence and to Treasury in Admiralty matters 1973-78; QC 1978; Recorder 1982-87; Judge of the High Court of Justice (Queen's Bench Division) 1987-95; Lord Justice of Appeal 1995-98; Chairman of the BSE Inquiry 1998-2000; Master of the Rolls 2000-05; Head of Civil Justice 2000-05; Lord Chief Justice 2005-08; President of the Supreme Court of the United Kingdom 2009-12.

Political career: *House of Lords:* Raised to the peerage as Baron Phillips of Worth Matravers, of Belsize Park in the London Borough of Camden 1999. Lord of Appeal in Ordinary 1999-2000; Senior Lord of Appeal in Ordinary 2008-09; As President of the Supreme Court, disqualified from participation 2009-12. Member Joint Committee on Voting Eligibilty (Prisoners) Bill 2013-. *Councils and public bodies:* Member, Panel of Wreck Commissioners 1979; Chair: Law Advisory Committee, British Council 1991-97; Council of Legal Education 1992-97; Advisory Council of Institute of European and Comparative Law 1999-; Council of Management, British Institute of International and Comparative Law 1999-; Chair, Lord Chancellor's Advisory Committee on Public Records 2000-05; President, British Maritime Law Association 2005-; Chair: Sentencing Guidelines Council 2005-08, Criminal Procedure Rules Committee 2005-08.

Other: The Draper's Company; Worshipful Company of Shipwrights. Freeman, City of London. Chancellor, Bournemouth University. Honorary LLD, Exeter 1998; Honorary Fellow, Society for Advanced Legal Studies 1999; Visitor: Nuffield College, Oxford 2000-05, University College, London 2000-05; Honorary Fellow, King's College, Cambridge 2003; Doctor of Civil Law, City University, London; Honorary LLD: London University, Birmingham University; Visitor, Darwin College, Cambridge 2005; International Maritime Law Institute 2007. Kt 1987; PC 1995; KG 2011; Brooks's; Garrick.

Recreations: Sea, mountains.

Rt Hon the Lord Phillips of Worth Matravers KG, House of Lords, London SW1A 0PW
Tel: 020 7219 5353
Email: phillipsofworth@gmail.com

LABOUR

PITKEATHLEY, BARONESS

PITKEATHLEY (Life Baroness), Jill Elizabeth Pitkeathley; cr. 1997. Born 4 January 1940; Daughter of Roland and May Bisson; Married W. Pitkeathley 1961 (divorced 1978) (1 son 1 daughter); married David Emerson 2008.

Education: Ladies' College, Guernsey; Bristol University (BA economics 1960).

Non-political career: Social worker 1961-68; Voluntary service co-ordinator, West Berkshire Health Authority 1970-83; National Consumer Council 1983-86; Director, National Council for Carers 1986 until merger with Association of Carers 1988; Carers National Association: Chief executive 1988-98, Vice-President 2001-; Chair: Children and Families Court Advisory and Support Service 2003-08, Council for Health Care Regulatory Excellence/Professional Standards Authority 2009-; Trustee, Big Society Trust 2011-.

Political career: *House of Lords:* Raised to the peerage as Baroness Pitkeathley, of Caversham in the Royal County of Berkshire 1997. Deputy Speaker 2002-; Deputy Chair of Committees 2002-. Member: House of Lords' Offices Refreshment Sub-committee 2001-09, Information 2010-13, Joint Committee on the Draft Care and Support Bill 2013. *Councils and public bodies:* Adviser to Griffith's Review of Community Care 1986-88; Community Council for Berkshire: Vice-President 1990-98, President 1998-; President, Community Council for Berkshire 1998-; Chair: New Opportunities Fund 1998-2004, Future Builders Advisory Panel 2005-08, Office of Third Sector Advisory Board 2008-10; Interim chair, General Social Care Council 2008.

Political interests: Health, social care, voluntary sector, charities; Channel Islands.

Other: Vice-President, Carers UK 1998-; Patron, Bracknell CVS 2000-; Trustee, Cumberland Lodge; Honorary RCGP; Honorary City and Guilds 2009; Carers UK. DL: Bristol 2002, London Metropolitan 2002. OBE 1993.

Publications: When I Went Home (1978); Mobilising Voluntary Resources (1984); Supporting Volunteers (1985); It's my duty, isn't it? (1989); Co-author: Age Gap Relationships (1996), Only Child (1994); Fiction: Cassandra and Jane (2004), Dearest Cousin Jane (2009).

Recreations: Gardening, grand-children, writing.

The Baroness Pitkeathley OBE, House of Lords, London SW1A 0PW
Tel: 020 7219 0358 *Email:* pitkeathleyj@parliament.uk

LABOUR

PLANT OF HIGHFIELD, LORD

PLANT OF HIGHFIELD (Life Baron), Raymond Plant; cr. 1992. Born 19 March 1945; Son of late Stanley Plant and of Marjorie Plant; Married Katherine Dixon 1967 (3 sons).

Education: Havelock School, Grimsby; King's College, London (BA philosophy 1966); Hull University (PhD political philosophy 1971); French, German.

Non-political career: Lecturer, then senior lecturer in philosophy, Manchester University 1967-79; Philosophy lecturer in several universities 1981-91; Professor of politics, Southampton University 1979-94; Master, St Catherine's College, Oxford 1994-2000; Professor of: European politics Southampton University 2000-02, Law and philosophy King's College, London 2002-; Head of Law School 2006-08; Visiting Professor of Law and Philosophy, Institut d'Etudes Politiques, Paris 2008; Honorary Professor of Humanities, Winchester University; Part-time Professor of Law, Tallinn University, Estonia.

Political career: *House of Lords:* Raised to the peerage as Baron Plant of Highfield, of Weelsby in the County of Humberside 1992. Opposition Spokesperson for Home Affairs 1992-96. Member: Relations between Central and Local Government 1995-96, European Communities Sub-committee E 2000-03, Joint Committee on Human Rights 2003-07, Merits of Statutory Instruments/Secondary Legislation Scrutiny 2010-, Joint Committee on the Draft Enhanced Terrorism Prevention and Investigation Measures Bill 2012-13. *Other:* Chair, Labour Party Commission on Electoral Systems 1991-93.

Countries of interest: France, Germany, Portugal, Russia.

Other: President, National Council for Voluntary Organisations (NCVO) 1998-2002; Fellow, Industry and Parliament Trust 1998; Chair: Hope Medical Trust, Southampton 2000-06, Centrepoint 2001-04; Chair, Southampton University Development Trust 2007-08; FRSA 1992; ACSS (Academy of Learned Societies in the Social Sciences); Centrepoint, Hope. Pro-Chancellor, Southampton University 1996-2000. Six honorary doctorates; Fellow: King's College, London, Catherine's College, Oxford, Cardiff University, Harris Manchester College, Oxford. Isiah Berlin prize 2010; Athenæum.

Publications: Hegel (1974); Community and Ideology (1974); Political Philosophy and Social Welfare (1981); Philosophy, Politics and Citizenship (1984); Contributor to *The Times* (1988-91); Conservative Capitalism in Britain and the United States: a critical appraisal (1988); Modern Political Thought (1991); Politics, Theology and History (2001); The Neo-liberal State (OUP, 2009).

Recreations: Music, opera, reading.
Professor the Lord Plant of Highfield, House of Lords, London SW1A 0PW
Tel: 020 7219 5424
School of Law, King's College, Strand, London WC2R 2LS *Tel:* 020 7836 5454
Fax: 020 7848 2465 *Email:* raymond.plant@kcl.ac.uk

NON-AFFILIATED

PLATT OF WRITTLE, BARONESS

PLATT OF WRITTLE (Life Baroness), Beryl Catherine Platt; cr. 1981. Born 18 April 1923; Daughter of late Ernest and Dorothy Myatt; Married Stewart Platt 1949 (died 2003) (1 son 1 daughter).
Education: Westcliff High School for Girls; Girton College, Cambridge (BA mechanical sciences 1943, MA).
Non-political career: Technical assistant: Hawker Aircraft 1943-46, British European Airways 1946-49; Chair, Equal Opportunities Commission 1983-88.
Political career: *House of Lords:* Raised to the peerage as Baroness Platt of Writtle, of Writtle in the County of Essex 1981. On leave of absence October 2010-. Member: Murder and Life Imprisonment 1988-89, Science and Technology 1982-85, 1990-94, 1996-2001, 2003-07, Relations between Central and Local Government 1995-96, Science and Technology Sub-committee II: (Science and Society) 1999-2000, (Aircraft Cabin Environment) 2000-01, Stem Cell Research 2001-02, Science and Technology Sub-committee II (Energy Efficiency) 2004-05, Energy and the Renewables 2005, Science and Heritage 2005-06, Water Management 2005-06, Allergy 2006-07; Co-opted member Science and Technology Sub-committee I (Waste Reduction) 2007-08. *Other:* Member, Association of Conservative Peers. *Councils and public bodies:* Councillor, Chelmsford RDC 1958-73; Essex County Council 1965-86: Alderman 1969-74, Council Vice-chair 1980-83; DL, County of Essex 1983; Honorary Alderman 2005.
Political interests: Education, women's opportunities in engineering, local government.
Other: Member: European Communities Advisory Committee on Equal Opportunities for Women and Men 1983-88; UK Delegation to Nairobi for UN Decade for Women World Conference 1985; Trustee, Homerton College 1970-81; Fellow: Fellowship of Engineering (FREng) (now Royal Academy of Engineering) 1987, Royal Aeronautical Society; European Engineer (EurIng) 1987; Fellow, Institution of Gas Engineers 1990; Companion: Institute of Energy, Institute of Personnel Development 1995; British and Overseas Aid; Technical and Medical, Men, Women and Children. Worshipful Company of Engineers: Liveryman 1988, Assistant to the Court 1996-2002, Assistant Emeritus of the Court 2002. Freeman, City of London 1988. First Chancellor, Middlesex University 1993-2000. 23 honorary doctorates and fellowships, including Royal Aeronautical Society 1994. City and Guilds of London Insignia Award 1988; Royal Society of Chemistry Parliamentary Award 2007. CBE 1978.
Recreations: Reading.
The Baroness Platt of Writtle CBE DL, House of Lords, London SW1A 0PW
Tel: 020 7219 5353

CONSERVATIVE

PLUMB, LORD

PLUMB (Life Baron), (Charles) Henry Plumb; cr. 1987. Born 27 March 1925; Son of late Charles Plumb; Married Marjorie Dunn 1947 (1 son 2 daughters, 1 deceased).
Education: King Edward VI School, Nuneaton.
Non-political career: NFU: Council member 1959, Vice-President 1964-65, Deputy President 1966-69, President 1970-79; Non-executive director, Lloyds Bank, United Biscuits, Fisons 1979-94; Chair, Agricultural Mortgage Corporation 1994-95.
Political career: *House of Lords:* Raised to the peerage as Baron Plumb, of Coleshill in the County of Warwickshire 1987. EU Sub-committee D (Environment and Agriculture): Member 2005-06, 2007-08, Co-opted member 2006-07; Member: European Union 2008-12, EU Sub-committee B: (Internal Market) 2008-10, (Internal Market, Energy and Transport) 2010-12, (Internal Market, Infrastructure and Employment) 2012-13; Member EU Sub-committee D: Agriculture, Fisheries, Environment and Energy 2013-. *Other:* European Parliament: MEP (Conservative) for Cotswolds 1979-99: Chair: Agricultural Committee 1979-82, European Democratic Group 1982-87, 1994-99, President, European Parliament 1987-89, Honorary MEP 1999-; EU-ACP Joint Assembly: Co-president 1994-99, Honorary president 1999-; President, FMA (Former Members Association) 2001-07. President, North Warwickshire Conservative Association 1988-2000. *Councils and public bodies:* Member, Duke of Northumberland's Committee of Enquiry, Foot and Mouth Disease 1967-68; DL, Warwick 1977.

Political interests: Europe, agriculture, environment, international trade, farming; Africa, Commonwealth, USA.

Other: President, Comité des Organisations Professionnelles Agricoles de la CEE (COPA) 1975-77; Chair, British Agricultural Council 1975-79; President, Royal Agricultural Society of England 1977; Chair, president numerous national and international organisations related to food, agriculture and environment; Henry Plumb Trust; The Royal Agricultural Benevolent Institute; Farm Africa. Master, Farmers' Company; Honorary Liveryman, Worshipful Company of Fruiterers. Freeman, City of London; Honorary Freedom of the Borough of North Warwickshire 2002. Chancellor, Coventry University 1995-2007. Honorary Fellow: Duchy College, Royal Agricultural College, Wye College 1995; Six honorary doctorates. RASE Gold Medal 1978. Kt 1973; Knight Commander's Cross of the Order of Merit (Federal Republic of Germany) 1976; Ordén de Merito (Portugal) 1987; Order of Merit (Luxembourg) 1988; Grand Cross of the Order of Civil Merit (Spain) 1989; Grand Order of the Phoenix (Greece) 1997; Medal Mediterraneum, European Institute, Florence (Italy) 1998; St Stephen's Constitutional, Farmers.

Publications: The Plumb Line (Greycoat Press, 2001).

Recreations: Shooting, country pursuits.

The Lord Plumb DL, House of Lords, London SW1A 0PW
Tel: 020 7219 1233 *Email:* plumbh@parliament.uk
Maxstoke, Coleshill, Warwickshire B46 2QJ *Tel:* 01675 464156 *Fax:* 01675 464156

LABOUR

PONSONBY OF SHULBREDE, LORD

PONSONBY OF SHULBREDE (4th Baron, UK), Frederick Matthew Thomas Ponsonby; cr. 1930; (Life) Baron Ponsonby of Roehampton 2000. Born 27 October 1958; Son of 3rd Baron; Married Sarah Jackson 1995 (1 daughter 1 son).

Education: Holland Park Comprehensive School; University College, Cardiff (BSc physics 1980); Imperial College, London (MSc DIC petroleum engineering 1983).

Non-political career: Member, Unite.

Political career: *House of Lords:* Created a life peer as Baron Ponsonby of Roehampton, of Shulbrede in the County of West Sussex 2000. First entered House of Lords 1990; Opposition Spokesperson for Education 1992-97. Member: Science and Technology 1998-99, Science and Technology Sub-committee II (Science and Society) 1999, Constitution 2001. *Councils and public bodies:* Councillor, London Borough of Wandsworth 1990-94; JP: Westminster bench 2006-11, Inner London Youth Panel 2008-11, Central London bench 2012-, Central London youth bench 2012-, Greater London family panel 2012-.

Political interests: Foreign affairs.

Other: Delegate to: Council of Europe 1997-2001, Western European Union 1997-2001; Organisation for Security and Co-operation in Europe 2001-10; FIMM.

The Lord Ponsonby of Shulbrede, House of Lords, London SW1A 0PW
Tel: 020 7219 0071

CONSERVATIVE

POPAT, LORD

Government Spokesperson Departments for Business, Innovation and Skills and Transport; Government Whip

POPAT (Life Baron), Dolar Amarshi Popat; cr 2010. Born 14 June 1953; Son of Amarshibhai Haridas Popat and Parvatiben Amarshibhai Popat; Married Sandhya Popat 1980 (3 sons).

Education: Manjasi High School, Torono, Uganda; Harrow Technical College; Kilburn Polytechnic; City of London Polytechnic, Moorgate; Chartered Institute of Management Accounting (management accounting 1977); Gujarati, Hindi, Swahili.

Non-political career: Practising accountant 1980-82; Harrow Chamber of Commerce 1982-1987; Chief executive, Fast Finance plc 1982-91; Harrow Grange Hospice 1984-; Founder and chief executive, TLC Group 1991-2010.

Political career: *House of Lords:* Raised to the peerage as Baron Popat, of Harrow in the London Borough of Harrow 2010. Government Whip 2013-; Government Spokesperson: Business, Innovation and Skills 2013-, Transport 2013-. Member Small- and Medium-Sized Enterprises 2012-13. *Other:* Secretary, Anglo-Asian Conservative Association; Chair, One Nation Forum, Barnet; President, Harrow East Conservative Association; Member, Conservative Ethnic Diversity Council; Co-chair, Conservative Friends of India 2012-13.

Political interests: International affairs, international development, small- and medium-sized businesses, banking and finance, community, exports; Africa, India, Kenya, Malawi, Tanzania, Uganda.

Other: Vice-chair, subsequently chair, Strangers Gallery (a private parliamentary club for business community); Affiliate member, Institute of Chartered Management Accountants; Dolar Popat Foundation Trust; Dolar Popat Foundation; St Luke's Hospice; Nightingale Trust; Akshaya Patra Foundation UK.

Recreations: Reading, tennis, walking, community work, travelling, Tottenham Hotspur F.C.

The Lord Popat, House of Lords, London SW1A 0PW
Tel: 020 7219 8321 *Email:* popatd@parliament.uk

CROSSBENCH

POWELL OF BAYSWATER, LORD

POWELL OF BAYSWATER (Life Baron), Charles David Powell; cr. 2000. Born 6 June 1941; Son of late Air Vice Marshal John Powell, OBE; Married Carla Bonardi 1964 (2 sons).

Education: King's School, Canterbury; New College, Oxford (BA modern history 1963); Finnish, French, German, Italian.

Non-political career: Diplomatic Service 1963-83; Private Secretary to Prime Ministers: Margaret Thatcher 1983-90, John Major 1990-91; Director: Matheson & Co 1991-, Mandarin Oriental Hotel Group 1991-, Hong Kong Land Holdings 1991-2001, 2008-, Jardine Matheson Holdings 1991-2001, National Westminster Bank 1991-2000, J Rothschild Name Company 1992-2003, Said Holdings 1993-2000, Arjo Wiggins Appleton 1993-2000, Louis Vuitton Moët Hennessy 1995-, British Mediterranean Airways 1997-2007; Chairman: International advisory board, GEMS 1999-2013, Phillips de Pury Luxembourg 2000-02, Sagitta Asset Management 2001-05; Director: Caterpillar Inc 2001-, Textron Corporation 2001-, Yell Group 2002-09; Member, international advisory board, Barrick Gold 2002-; Director, Northern Trust Global Services 2004-; Member, international advisory board: Thales UK 2004-, Alfa Capital 2005-10, ACE Insurance 2006-; Chairman: International advisory board, Rolls Royce 2006-, Capital Generation Partners 2006-13, Magna Holdings International 2006-, Bowmark advisory board 2008-.

Political career: *House of Lords:* Raised to the peerage as Baron Powell of Bayswater, of Canterbury in the County of Kent 2000. Co-opted member EU Sub-committee C (Common Foreign and Security Policy/Foreign Affairs, Defence and Development Policy) 2000-04; Member: Economic Affairs 2005-07, European Union 2006-10, EU Sub-committee B (Internal Market) 2006-10, Finance Bill Sub-committee 2006-11, Constitution 2010-. *Councils and public bodies:* Co-chairman, Asia Task Force 2007-.

Political interests: Foreign affairs, defence, intelligence, trade ; Asia, Europe, North America.

Other: President, China-Britain Business Council 1997-2007; Chair, Singapore British Business Council 1997-2001; Trustee, Aspen Institute, USA 1995-; Chair, Trustees Oxford University Business School 1997-; Trustee, British Museum Trust 2011-; Chair, Atlantic Partnership 2000-; Trustee, International Institute of Strategic Studies 2010-; Member, International Advisory Board, Council on Foreign Relations 2011-; Honorary Fellow, Ashmolean Museum, Oxford; Aspen Institute. KCMG 1990; Public Service Star (Singapore) 2001.

Recreations: Walking.

The Lord Powell of Bayswater KCMG, House of Lords, London SW1A 0PW
Tel: 020 7219 5451
LVMH House, 15 St George Street, London W1S 1FH *Tel:* 020 7408 7426 *Fax:* 020 7408 7428
Email: suzie@charlespowell.com

CROSSBENCH

PRASHAR, BARONESS

PRASHAR (Life Baroness), Usha Kumari Prashar; cr. 1999. Born 29 June 1948; Daughter of late Naurhia Lal and Durga Devi Prashar; Married Vijay Kumar Sharma 1973.

Education: Duchess of Gloucester School, Nairobi, Kenya; Wakefield Girls' High School, Yorkshire; Leeds University (BA political science 1970); Glasgow University (Dip Soc Admin 1971); Hindi.

Non-political career: Conciliation officer, Race Relations Board 1971-75; Director, Runnymede Trust 1976-84; Research fellow, Policy Studies Institute 1984-86; National Council of Voluntary Organisations: Director 1986-91; National Literacy Trust: Deputy chair 1992-2000, Chair 2000-05; Executive chairman, Parole Board of England and Wales 1997-2000; First Civil Service Commissioner 2000-05; Non-executive director, Unite plc 2000-04; Chair, Judicial Appointments Commission 2005-10.

Political career: *House of Lords:* Raised to the peerage as Baroness Prashar, of Runnymede in the County of Surrey 1999. Member: Joint Committee on Human Rights 2000-04, 2008-10, Privileges 2008-09; Chair Sub-committee on Lords' Interests 2008-09; Member EU Sub-committee F (Home Affairs, Health and Education) 2012-. *Councils and public bodies:* Member: Arts Council of Great Britain 1979-81, 1994-97, Study Commission on the Family 1980-83, Social Security Advisory Committee 1980-83, London Food Commission 1984-90, BBC Educational Broadcasting Council 1987-89, Solicitor's Complaints Bureau 1989-90, Royal Commission on Criminal Justice 1991-93; Part-time Civil Service Commissioner 1991-96; Member, Lord Chancellor's Advisory Committee on Legal Education and Conduct 1991-97; Non-executive director, Channel Four 1992-98; Chair: Royal Commonwealth Society 2002-08, ITV Board 2005-10; Member, Iraq Inquiry 2009-; Deputy Chair, British Council.

Political interests: Education, criminal justice, human rights, race relations, international affairs; Africa, Europe, India, Mauritius.

Other: Board member, Salzburg Seminar 2000-04; Member, executive committee, Child Poverty Action Group 1984-85; Honorary Vice-President, Council for Overseas Student Affairs 1986-; Trustee, Camelot Foundation 1995-2000; Governor, De Montfort University 1996-2006; Management Board, King's Fund 1997-2002; Trustee, Ethnic Minority Foundation 1997-2002; Tara Arts 1999-; Chair, National Literacy Trust 2000-05; Trustee, BBC World Service Trust 2002-05; Wise Thoughts 2002-; Governor and member, Management Committee, Ditchley Foundation 2003; Trustee, Ditchley Foundation 2004-; President: Community Foundation Network, National Literacy Trust; Trustee, Miriam Rothschild and John Foster Trust 2007-10; Cumberland Lodge 2007-; Senior Fellow, Salzberg Global Seminar; Companion, Chartered Management Institute; Fellow, Royal Society of Arts. Chancellor, De Montfort University 2000-06. Honorary Fellow, Goldsmith's College, London University; Ten honorary doctorates; Elected Master of the Bench of Inner Temple 2011. CBE 1994; PC 2009; Royal Commonwealth Society. Foxhills Golf Club.

Publications: Contributor to several publications on health and race relations.

Recreations: Golf, music, art, reading.

Rt Hon the Baroness Prashar CBE, House of Lords, London SW1A 0PW
Tel: 020 7219 6792 *Email:* prasharu@parliament.uk

PRESCOTT, LORD

PRESCOTT (Life Baron), John Leslie Prescott; cr 2010. Born 31 May 1938; Son of late John Herbert Prescott, railway controller, and late Phyllis Prescott; Married Pauline Tilston 1961 (2 sons).

Education: Ellesmere Port Secondary Modern School; Ruskin College, Oxford (DipEcon/Pol 1965); Hull University (BSc Econ 1968).

Non-political career: Steward, Merchant Navy 1955-63; Union official, National Union of Seamen 1968-70. TU Official, National Union of Seamen, RMT (resigned 2002).

Political career: *House of Commons:* Contested Southport 1966 general election. MP (Labour) for Kingston-upon-Hull East 1970-83, for Hull East 1983-2010. PPS to Peter Shore as Secretary of State for Trade 1974-76; Opposition Spokesperson for: Transport 1979-81, Regional Affairs and Devolution 1981-83; Member Shadow Cabinet 1983-97: Shadow Secretary of State for: Transport 1983-84, Employment 1984-87, Energy 1987-89, Transport 1988-93, Employment 1993-94; Deputy Prime Minister 1997-2007; Secretary of State for the Environment, Transport and the Regions 1997-2001; First Secretary of State 2001-07. *House of Lords:* Raised to the peerage as Baron Prescott, of Kingston upon Hull in the County of East Yorkshire 2010. *Other:* Deputy Leader: Labour Party 1994-2007, Labour Party National Executive Committee 1997-2007; Contested Labour Party treasurer 2010.

Political interests: Climate change; China.

Other: Member, Council of Europe 1972-75; Delegate, EEC Parliamentary 1975; Leader: Labour Party Delegation to European Parliament 1976-79, UK Delegation Parliamentary Assembly of the Council of Europe/Western European Union 2007-. Honorary Professor on Climate Change, Xiamen University; Honorary Degree: Ningbo University, University of Notthingham. North of England Zoological Society Gold Medal 1999; Priyadarshni Award 2002; Political Tweeter of the Year, *PoliticsHome* awards 2012. PC 1994 (resigned July 2013).

Publications: Prezza: Pulling No Punches (2008).

Recreations: Jazz, theatre, music, aqua diving.

The Lord Prescott, House of Lords, London SW1A 0PW
Tel: 020 7219 5353 *Twitter:* @johnprescott

NON-AFFILIATED

PRIOR, LORD

PRIOR (Life Baron), James Michael Leathes Prior; cr. 1987. Born 11 October 1927; Son of late Charles Bolingbroke Leathes Prior, JP; Married Jane Gifford, née Lywood 1954 (3 sons 1 daughter). **Education:** Charterhouse, Surrey; Pembroke College, Cambridge (BA estate management 1950).

Non-political career: Commissioned Service Royal Norfolk Regiment 1946; Served in India and Germany. Farmer and land agent 1950; Chair: General Electric Company plc 1984-98, Allders Ltd 1984-94; Director: United Biscuits plc 1984-94, J Sainsbury 1984-94, Barclays Bank 1985-90; Member, Tenneco Europe Ltd (Advisory Committee) 1986-98; Palgrave Farming Co Ltd 1990-2008; South Pickenham Estate Co Ltd 1990-2008; Member, American International Group (Advisory Council) 1992-2006; Chair: East Anglia Radio plc 1992-95, African Cargo Handling Ltd 1998-2000; Deputy chair, MSI Cellular Investments BV 2000-05; Ascot Underwriting Ltd 2001-06.

Political career: *House of Commons:* MP (Conservative) for Lowestoft 1959-83, for Waveney 1983-87. PPS: to President of the Board of Trade 1962-63, to Minister of Power 1963-64, to Edward Heath as Leader of the Opposition 1965-70; Minister of Agriculture, Fisheries and Food 1970-72; Lord President and Leader of the House 1972-74; Opposition Spokesperson for Employment 1974-79; Secretary of State for: Employment 1979-81, Northern Ireland 1981-84. *House of Lords:* Raised to the peerage as Baron Prior, of Brampton in the County of Suffolk 1987. On leave of absence since May 2010. *Other:* Conservative Party: Vice-chair 1965, Deputy Chair 1972-74; Honorary Life member, Tory Reform Group. *Councils and public bodies:* Chairman: Council for Industry and Higher Education 1985-92, Archbishops' Commission on Rural Areas 1988-91.

Political interests: Agriculture, industry, education, health.

Other: Chair, Arab-British Chamber of Commerce 1996-2004; Chair: Royal Veterinary College 1990-99, Industry and Parliament Trust 1990-94, NAC Rural Housing Trust 1990-99, London Playing Fields Association 1998-2001; Chair, Special Trustees 1989-95, Wishing Well Appeal (Great Ormond Street Children's Hospital) 1986-89. Chancellor, Anglia Polytechnic University 1993-99. Honorary Fellow, Pembroke College, Cambridge; Two honorary doctorates. PC 1970; MCC. Izingari Cricket Club, Butterflies Cricket Club.

Publications: A Balance of Power (1986).

Recreations: Country sports, cricket, football, gardening, breeding of South Devon cattle.

Rt Hon the Lord Prior, House of Lords, London SW1A 0PW
Tel: 020 7219 5353

LABOUR

PROSSER, BARONESS

PROSSER (Life Baroness), Margaret Theresa Prosser; cr. 2004. Born 22 August 1937; Daughter of Frederick James and Lilian James, née Barry; Divorced (1 son 2 daughters). **Education:** St Philomena's Convent, Carshalton, Surrey; North East London Polytechnic (Postgraduate Diploma housing, law and social security 1977).

Non-political career: Advice centre organiser, Southwark Community Development Project 1974-77; Legal adviser, Southwark Law Project 1977-83; Transport and General Workers' Union 1983-2002: District organiser 1983-84, National women's secretary 1984-92, National organiser 1992-98, Deputy secretary-general 1998-2002; President, Trades Union Congress 1995-96; Chair: Women's National Commission 2002-07, Women and Work Commission 2004-06. Member, Unite (T&G) 1977-.

Political career: *House of Lords:* Raised to the peerage as Baroness Prosser, of Battersea in the London Borough of Wandsworth 2004. Member Information 2005-09; Co-opted member EU Sub-committee G (Social Policy and Consumer Affairs) 2009-10; Member EU Sub-committees: G (Social Policies and Consumer Protection) 2010-12, A (Economic and Financial Affairs) 2012-13; Member Soft Power and the UK's Influence 2013-. *Other:* National treasurer, Labour Party 1996-2001. *Councils and public bodies:* Member: Equal Opportunities Commission 1985-92, Low Pay Commission 2000-05; Deputy chair, Equality and Human Rights Commission 2006-12.

Political interests: World of work, equalities, equal pay; Middle East, USA.

Other: Fellow, Royal Society of Arts 1996-; Director, Trade Union Fund Managers 1998-; Non-executive director, Royal Mail Holdings 2004-10; Trustee: Industry and Parliament Trust 2012-, Involvement and Participation Association 2013-. Two honorary doctorates from London universities. OBE 1997.

Recreations: Walking, cooking.

The Baroness Prosser OBE, House of Lords, London SW1A 0PW
Tel: 020 7219 4694 *Fax:* 020 7219 0699 *Email:* prosserm@parliament.uk

PRYS-DAVIES, LORD

LABOUR

PRYS-DAVIES (Life Baron), Gwilym Prys-Davies; cr 1982. Born 8 December 1923; Son of late William Davies; Married Llinos Evans 1951 (died 2010) (3 daughters).

Education: Tywyn School, Gwynedd; University College of Wales, Aberystwyth (LLB 1949; LLM 1952).

Non-political career: Solicitor; Consultant and Partner, Morgan Bruce & Hardwickes, Cardiff and Pontypridd 1959-93; Special Adviser to Secretary of State for Wales 1974-78.

Political career: *House of Lords:* Raised to the peerage as Baron Prys-Davies, of Llanegryn in the County of Gwynedd 1982. Opposition Frontbench Spokesperson for: Health 1983-87, Welsh Office 1987-97, Northern Ireland 1982-93; On leave of absence September 2011-. *Councils and public bodies:* Chair, Welsh Hospitals Board 1968-74; President, University of Wales, Swansea 1997-2001.

Political interests: Devolution, Welsh language legislation.

Other: Member: Economic and Social Committee, EEC 1978-82, British-Irish Parliamentary Body 1990-97. Five honorary university fellowships; Two honorary doctorates.

The Lord Prys-Davies, House of Lords, London SW1A 0PW
Tel: 020 7219 5353
Lluest, 78 Church Road, Tonteg, Pontypridd, Mid Glamorgan CF38 1EN *Tel:* 01443 202462

PURVIS OF TWEED, LORD – *Please see Addenda Page xiii*

PUTTNAM, LORD

LABOUR

PUTTNAM (Life Baron), David Terence Puttnam; cr. 1997. Born 25 February 1941; Son of late Leonard and Marie Puttnam; Married Patricia Jones 1961 (1 son 1 daughter).

Education: Minchenden Grammar School, London; City and Guilds 1958-62.

Non-political career: Advertising 1958-68; Film production 1968-98; Producer of films including: *Bugsy Malone*, 1976 (four BAFTA Awards), *Midnight Express*, 1978 (two Academy Awards, three BAFTA Awards), *Chariots of Fire*, 1981 (four Academy Awards, three BAFTA Awards including awards for best film), *Local Hero*, 1982 (two BAFTA Awards); *The Killing Fields*, 1984 (three Academy Awards, seven nominations: eight BAFTA Awards including Best Film); *The Mission*, 1986 (Palme D'Or, Cannes, one Academy Award, seven nominations: three BAFTA Awards); *Memphis Belle*, 1990, as well as many others; Chair, Enigma Productions Ltd 1978-; Director: National Film Finance Corporation 1980-85, Anglia Television Group 1982-99; Visiting Professor, Bristol University 1983-97; Chair and chief executive officer, Columbia Pictures 1986-88; Village Roadshow plc 1988-99; Adviser, Department for Children, Schools and Families 1997-2010; Visiting lecturer, London School of Economics 1997-2002; Non-executive chair, Spectrum Management Consultants 1998-2007; Deputy chair, Channel 4 2006-12; Chair, Futurelab 2005-11; Deputy chair, Profero; Non-executive director, Huntsworth plc 2007-12; Senior non-executive director, Promethean World; Visting Professor, Institute of Education, London University 2008-; Chairman: Atticus Education 2012-, Prime Hotels (UK) Ltd. Advisory Board; Director, EMPGI Ireland. Honorary Member, BECTU.

Political career: *House of Lords:* Raised to the peerage as Baron Puttnam, of Queensgate in the Royal Borough of Kensington and Chelsea 1997. Trade envoy to Vietnam, Laos and Cambodia 2012-. Chair Draft Communications Bill Joint Committee 2002; Member Information 2005-09; Chair Draft Climate Change Bill Joint Committee 2007. *Other:* Digital Champion, Republic of Ireland 2012-. *Councils and public bodies:* Chair, British Council TV and Video Advisory Panel 1987-97; Member: British Screen Advisory Council 1988-98, Arts Council Lottery Panel 1995-98; Member, Government's Education Standards Task Force 1997-2001; Chair: British Council Arts Advisory Committee 2002-04, Hansard Commission "Parliament in the Public Eye" 2004-05.

Political interests: Education, culture, environment; Ireland, USA.

Other: Fellow, World Economic Forum, Davos, Switzerland; President, Unicef UK 2002-09; National Film and Television School: Governor 1974-, Chair 1988-96; Chair, Producers and Directors Section ACCT 1975-77; Council for the Protection of Rural England: President 1985-92, Vice-President 1997-2008; Trustee: Sundance Institute 1985-90, Tate Gallery 1985-92; Governor, American Film Institute 1986-88; Trustee: National Aids Trust 1988-, Landscape Foundation; Chair, National Memorial Arboretum Trustees 1992-2003, Vice-President, BAFTA 1993-2002; Chair, National Museum of Photography, Film and Television 1994-2003; Trustee, Science Museum 1996-2003; Member, Court of Governors: London School of Economics 1997-2002, London Institute 1997-2002; Vice-President, Royal Geographical Society 1997-99; Trustee and fellow, World Economic Forum 1997-2008; Member: Academic Board, Bristol University, Arts and Humanities Research Board, UK-China Forum 1998-2002; Chair: Teaching Awards Trust 1998-2008, National Endowment for Science, Technology and Arts 1998-2003, General Teaching Council 1999-2002, BAFTA Trustees 2000-04; Trustee: Institute for Public Policy Reform, Thompson Foundation 2003-; Chair, The Sage Gateshead (North Music Trust) 2007-; President, Film Distributors Association 2009-; Trustee: Eden Project 2009-, Transformation Trust 2009-, Baker Dearing Educational Trust 2010-13; Chair, TSL Advisory Board 2010-; FRGS; FRSA; FRPS; FCGI; Fellow: The British Film Institute, Royal Television Society; Unicef. Freeman, City of Sunderland 2007. Chancellor: Sunderland University 1997-2007, Open University 2006-. Over 40 honorary doctorates and fellowships in UK and overseas. Ten Academy awards, 25 BAFTA awards and ten Golden Globes, and numerous other awards, including: BAFTA Michael Balcon Award for outstanding contribution to British Film Industry 1982, RSA Benjamin Franklin Award 1996, World Economic Forum Crystal Award 1997, Honorary BECTU 1998, President's Medal, Royal Photographic Society 2003, BAFTA Fellowship 2006, RSA Bicentenary Medal 2007, New Media Consortium Fellows Award (USA) 2012. CBE 1983; Chevalier de l'Ordre des Arts et des Lettres (France) 1985; Officier de l'Ordre des Arts et des Lettres (France) 1992; Kt 1995; Commander de l'Ordre des Arts et des Lettres (France) 2006; Chelsea Arts, Athenæum. Trustee, Sunderland AFC Foundation; MCC.

Publications: Contributor, The Third Age of Broadcasting (1982); Co-author, Rural England (1988); A Submission to the EC Think Tank on Audio-Visual Policy (1994); The Creative Imagination in 'What Needs to Change' (1996); The Undeclared War (1997); Movies and Money (1998); Members Only? Parliament in the Public Eye: Report of the Hansard Society Commission on the Communication of Parliamentary Democracy (Hansard Society, 2005); Parliament in the Public Eye 2006: Coming into Focus? (Hansard Society, 2006).

Recreations: Reading, cinema, landscape gardening.

The Lord Puttnam CBE, House of Lords, London SW1A 0PW
Tel: 020 7219 6822 *Fax:* 020 7219 5794 *Email:* puttnamd@parliament.uk

LABOUR

QUIN, BARONESS

QUIN (Life Baroness), Joyce Gwendolen Quin; cr. 2006. Born 26 November 1944; Daughter of late Basil Godfrey Quin, schoolmaster, and late Ida Quin, neé Ritson, teacher; Married (Francis) Guy MacMullen 2010.

Education: Whitley Bay Grammar School; Newcastle University (BA French 1967); London School of Economics (MSc international relations 1969); French, some Italian, German and Spanish.

Non-political career: Lecturer in French, Bath University 1972-76; Tutor and lecturer in French and politics, Durham University 1976-79. Member, TGWU/Unite.

Political career: *House of Commons:* MP (Labour) for Gateshead East 1987-97, for Gateshead East and Washington West 1997-2005. Opposition Spokesperson for: Trade and Industry 1989-92, Employment 1992-93, Foreign and Commonwealth Affairs 1993-97; Minister of State: Home Office 1997-98, Foreign and Commonwealth Office 1998-99; Minister of State and Deputy Minister, Ministry of Agriculture, Fisheries and Food 1999-2001. Member Joint Committee on House of Lords Reform 2003-05. Chair, PLP Regional Government Group 2001-05. *House of Lords:* Raised to the peerage as Baroness Quin, of Gateshead in the County of Tyne and Wear 2006. Opposition Spokesperson for Environment, Food and Rural Affairs 2010-11. Member: Constitution 2007-10, EU Sub-committee C (External Affairs) 2013-. *Other:* European Parliament: MEP for Tyne and Wear 1979-89. Research officer, International Department, Labour Party HQ 1969-72. *Councils and public bodies:* Member, Review Committee of Privy Counsellors of Anti-terrorism, Crime and Security Act 2002-05.

Political interests: European affairs, industrial policy, regional policy; Europe (including Eastern Europe).

Other: Chair, Franco-British Council 2008-; President, Northumberland Pipers Society 2009-. Honorary Freeman, Borough of Gateshead 2006. Honorary Fellow: Sunderland Polytechnic 1986, St Mary's College, Durham University 1996. PC 1998; Officier de la Légion d'Honneur (France) 2010.

Publications: Author, The British Constitution – Continuity and Change (Northern Writers, 2010).

Recreations: North East local history, walking, music, reading, cycling, playing Northumbrian pipes.

Rt Hon the Baroness Quin, House of Lords, London SW1A 0PW
Tel: 020 7219 4009 *Email:* quinjg@parliament.uk

QUIRK, LORD

QUIRK (Life Baron), (Charles) Randolph Quirk; cr. 1994. Born 12 July 1920; Son of late Thomas and Amy Randolph Quirk; Married Jean Williams 1946 (2 sons) (divorced 1979, she died 1995); married Gabriele Stein 1984.

Education: Douglas High School, Isle of Man; University College, London (BA English 1947, MA; PhD; DLitt); Yale University, USA (Post-Doctoral Studies 1951-52).

Non-political career: Served RAF 1940-45. Lecturer in English, University College, London 1947-54; Commonwealth Fund Fellow, Yale University and University of Michigan 1951-52; Durham University: Reader in English language and literature 1954-58, Professor 1958-60; Professor, London University 1960-68; Quain Professor of English language and literature, University College, London 1968-81; President: Institute of Linguistics 1982-86, Royal College of Speech and Language Therapists 1987-91.

Political career: *House of Lords:* Raised to the peerage as Baron Quirk, of Bloomsbury in the London Borough of Camden 1994. Member: Science and Technology 1998-2003, Science and Technology Sub-committees: II (Science and Society) 1999-2000, I (Complementary and Alternative Medicine) 2000-01, I (Systematic Biology and Biodiversity) 2002, Hybrid Instruments 2005-. *Councils and public bodies:* Chair, Committee of Enquiry in Speech Therapy Services 1969-72; Member of Senate, London University 1970-85; Governor, British Institute of Recorded Sound 1975-80; Member, BBC Archives Committee 1975-81; Board member, British Council 1983-91; Chair: Anglo-Spanish Foundation 1983-85, British Library Advisory Committee 1984-97; Member, RADA Council 1985-2004; President, British Academy 1985-89; Academic Governor, Richmond American University 1985-2006; Trustee: City Technology Colleges 1986-98, Wolfson Foundation 1987-; Royal Commissioner, 1851 Exhibition 1987-95; President, North of England Educational Conference 1989.

Political interests: Education, public communication, health, speech pathology, broadcasting, media.

Other: Member: Linguistic Society of America, Modern Language Association, Philological Society; FBA 1975. Vice-Chancellor, London University 1981-85. Honorary LLD, DLitt, DSc. from universities in the United Kingdom, USA and Europe; Jubilee Medal, Institute of Linguistics 1973; Foreign Fellow, Royal Belgian Academy of Science 1975; Honorary Fellow three London University Colleges. Jubilee Medal, Institute of Linguistics 1973. CBE 1975; Kt 1985; Athenæum.

Publications: Co-author of several works on English, notably A Comprehensive Grammar of the English Language (1985); The Concessive Relation in Old English Poetry (1954); Essays on the English Language – Medieval and Modern (1968); The English Language and Images of Matter (1972); The Linguist and the English Language (1974); Style and Communication in the English Language (1984); Words at Work – Lectures on Textual Structures (1986); Grammatical and Lexical Variance in English (1995); Has contributed to conference proceedings and learned journals.

Professor the Lord Quirk CBE FBA, House of Lords, London SW1A 0PW
Tel: 020 7219 2226 *Fax:* 020 7219 5979
University College London, Gower Street, London WC1E 6BT

RADICE, LORD

RADICE (Life Baron), Giles Heneage Radice; cr. 2001. Born 4 October 1936; Married Lisanne Koch 1971.

Education: Winchester College; Magdalen College, Oxford (BA history 1960); French.

Non-political career: Head of research department, General and Municipal Workers Union 1966-73. Member, GMB.

Political career: *House of Commons:* Contested Chippenham 1964 and 1966 general elections. MP (Labour) for Chester-le-Street 1 March 1973 by-election to 1983, for Durham North 1983-2001. PPS to Shirley Williams as Secretary of State for Education and Science 1978-1979; Opposition Frontbench Spokesperson for: Foreign Affairs 1981, Employment 1982-83, Education 1983-87; Member, Shadow Cabinet 1983-87. Chair: Public Service 1996-97, Treasury 1997-2001. *House of Lords:* Raised to the peerage as Baron Radice, of Chester-le-Street in the County of Durham 2001. Member European Union 2003-06; Chair EU Sub-committee A (Economic and Financial Affairs, Trade and External Relations/Economic and Financial Affairs) 2003-06; Member EU Sub-committee C: (Foreign Affairs, Defence and Development Policy) 2010-12, (External Affairs) 2012-.

Political interests: Economic and European affairs, Labour Party policy revision, foreign policy; France, Germany, India, Italy, Poland, Sweden.

Other: Chair: European Movement 1995-2001, Franco British Council 2002-07; Chair: British Association for Central and Eastern Europe 1997-2008, Policy Network 2007-09. Parliamentary Fellow, St Anthony's College Oxford 1994-95. Order of Merit (Germany) 1995, Légion d'Honneur (France) 2005. PC 1999.

Publications: Democratic Socialism (1965); Co-editor, More Power to People (1968); Co-author, Will Thorne (1974); The Industrial Democrats (1978); Co-author, Socialists in the Recession: a Survey of European Socialism (1986); Labour's Path to Power: the New Revisionism (1989); Offshore – Britain and the European Idea (1992); The New Germans (1995); Editor, What Needs to Change (1996); Friends and Rivals (2002); Diaries 1980-2001 (2004); The Tortoise and the Hares (2008); Trio: Blair, Brown and Mandelson (2010).

Recreations: Reading, tennis, gardening.

Rt Hon the Lord Radice, House of Lords, London SW1A 0PW
Tel: 020 7219 4194 *Email:* gh@radice.plus.com

LABOUR

RAMSAY OF CARTVALE, BARONESS

RAMSAY OF CARTVALE (Life Baroness), Meta Ramsay; cr. 1996. Born 12 July 1936; Daughter of Alexander Ramsay and Sheila, née Jackson; Single.

Education: Hutchesons' Girls' Grammar School, Glasgow; Glasgow University (MA 1958; MEd 1961); Graduate Institute for International Affairs, Geneva 1967-68.

Non-political career: HM Diplomatic Service 1969-91: Stockholm embassy 1970-73, Helsinki embassy 1981-85, Counsellor, FCO London 1986-91; Foreign policy adviser to John Smith as Leader of the Labour Party 1992-94; Special adviser to John Cunningham as Shadow Secretary of State for Trade and Industry 1994-95. Member, GMB.

Political career: *House of Lords:* Raised to the peerage as Baroness Ramsay of Cartvale, of Langside in the City of Glasgow 1996. Government Spokesperson for: Culture, Media and Sport 1997-98, Health 1997-98, Scotland 1997-2001; Government Whip December 1997-2001; Member Intelligence and Security Committee 1997, 2001-06; Foreign Affairs and Europe 1998-2001; Deputy Speaker 2002-08. Member Joint Committee on National Security Strategy 2010-. *Other:* Member: Co-operative Party, Labour Finance and Industry Group, Labour Movement in Europe, Labour Party. *Councils and public bodies:* Member, Lewisham Community Health Council 1992-94.

Political interests: Foreign affairs, defence, intelligence, women's affairs, Scotland; Finland, Israel, Sweden.

Other: Member, British Delegation to the: Parliamentary Assembly of Organisation for Security and Co-operation in Europe 1997, NATO Parliamentary Assembly 2003-; Trustee, Smith Institute 1996-2008; Chair, Atlantic Council of the United Kingdom 1997, 2001-10; Member: Fabian Society, RIIA, Institute for Jewish Policy Research, 300 Group; Chair: Wyndham Deedes Trust, Kenneth Lindsay Trust; FRSA; Blind Veterans UK. Three honorary doctorates: Bradford University 1997, Glasgow University 2004, Stirling University 2009. Commander of the Order of the White Rose of Finland 2002; University Women's, Reform.

Recreations: Theatre, opera, ballet.

The Baroness Ramsay of Cartvale, House of Lords, London SW1A 0PW
Tel: 020 7219 3145 *Fax:* 020 7219 5979 *Email:* ramsaym@parliament.uk

CROSSBENCH

RAMSBOTHAM, LORD

RAMSBOTHAM (Life Baron), David John Ramsbotham; cr 2005. Born 6 November 1934; Son of late Rev John Alexander Ramsbotham, Bishop of Wakefield, and Eirian Morgan-Owen; Married Susan Dickinson 1958 (2 sons).

Education: Haileybury College, Hertford; Corpus Christi College, Cambridge (BA history 1957, MA 1971).

Non-political career: Army national service 1952-54; Rifle Brigade UK and Germany 1957-62; Seconded to King's African Rifles 1962-63; Staff College 1964; Service in Far East 1965; 7 Armoured Brigade 1966-68; Royal Green Jackets, Germany 1968-71; Military assistant to Chief of the General Staff 1971-73; Commanding officer 2 Royal Green Jackets 1974-76; 4 Armoured Division, Germany 1982-84; Commander 39 Infantry Brigade 1978-80; Royal College of Defence Studies 1981; Director of Public Relations (Army) 1982-84; Commander 3 Armoured Division 1984-87; Commander UK Field Army and Inspector General Territorial Army 1987-90; Adjutant General 1990-93; ADC General to HM the Queen 1990-93. Director of International Affairs, DSL Ltd 1994-99.

Political career: *House of Lords:* Raised to the peerage as Baron Ramsbotham, of Kensington in the Royal Borough of Kensington and Chelsea 2005. Member: Regulators 2006-07, Soft Power and the UK's Influence 2013-. *Councils and public bodies:* Chair, Hillingdon Hospital NHS Trust 1994-95; Chief Inspector of Prisons for England and Wales 1995-2001.

Political interests: Penal reform, youth justice, education and employment, UN peace keeping and reform, mental health particularly in prisons, post conflict reconstruction including demining.

Other: Advisory Board, Youth at Risk 1999-; Vice-chair: Prisoners Education Trust 2001-, National Justice 2003-; President, UNLOCK (National Association of Ex Prisoners) 2004-; Vice-chair, NAOPV (National Association of Official Prison Visitors) 2005-; Trustee, International Centre for Prison Studies 2010-; Patron of several penal organisations. Honorary Liveryman: Worshipful Company of Weavers 2008-, The Skinners' Company 2008-. Seven honorary doctorates; Honorary bencher, Grey's Inn 2001; Honorary fellow, Corpus Christi Cambridge 2001. OBE 1971; CBE 1980; KCB 1987; GCB 1993; MCC, Beefsteak.

Publications: Prisongate (2003).

Recreations: Sailing, walking, arts, art history.

General the Lord Ramsbotham GCB CBE, House of Lords, London SW1A 0PW
Tel: 020 7219 8752 *Email:* ramsbothamd@parliament.uk

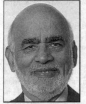

CROSSBENCH

RANA, LORD

RANA (Life Baron), Diljit Singh Rana; cr. 2004. Born 20 September 1938; Son of Paras Ram Rana; Married Uma Kumari Passi 1966 (died 2002) (2 sons); married Shruti 2009 (divorced).

Education: AS High School, Khanna, Punjab, India; Punjab University (BA economics 1958); Hindi, Punjabi, Urdu.

Non-political career: Café and restaurant owner; Property developer, hotel owner, Belfast; Founder, Andras House Ltd office, hotel and retail property management company 1981; Founder and chair, Indian Business Forum 1985; President: Belfast Chamber of Trade 1991-92, Northern Ireland Chamber of Commerce 2004-06; Founder: Cordia Technologies Software Development, Europe India Chamber of Commerce; Indian Community Centre.

Political career: *House of Lords:* Raised to the peerage as Baron Rana, of Malone in the County of Antrim 2004.

Political interests: International development, global living wage, education, poverty alleviation, rural development, healthcare, human rights, non-violence, peaceful resolution of problems; India, Ireland, Mauritius, Namibia, Taiwan.

Other: Member, Confederation of British Industry; Northern Ireland Chamber of Commerce; Founder, Rana Charitable Trust 1996; Chair, Thanksgiving Square 2002-; JD Memorial Trust, India 2005-; President, Global Organisation for People of Indian Origin 2009-; Shardhanjali Trust, India; Member, Institute of Directors. Three honorary doctorates: University of Ulster 1999, Queen's University, Belfast 2003, Bengal Engineering and Science University 2009. MBE 1996; Honorary Consul of India in Northern Ireland 2004; Non-resident Indian of the Year Award 2005; Samman Bharat Divas Award 2007; Honorary Consul of Namibia in Northern Ireland 2012.

Recreations: Community activities, charitable work, travel.

The Lord Rana MBE, House of Lords, London SW1A 0PW
Tel: 020 7219 3295 *Email:* ranad@parliament.uk
Andras House, 60 Great Victoria Street, Belfast BT2 7BB *Tel:* 028 9087 8787 *Fax:* 028 9087 8797 *Email:* mail@andrashouse.co.uk *Website:* www.diljitrana.com

LIBERAL DEMOCRAT

RANDERSON, BARONESS

Parliamentary Under-Secretary of State and Government Spokesperson, Wales Office; Government Spokesperson for Northern Ireland Office

RANDERSON (Life Baroness), Jennifer Elizabeth Randerson; cr 2011. Born 26 May 1948; Married Dr Peter Randerson 1970 (1 son 1 daughter).

Education: Wimbledon High School, London; Bedford College, London University (BA history 1969); London University Institute of Education (PGCE 1970); French, Welsh learner.

Non-political career: History, economics and politics teacher: Sydenham High School 1970-72, Spalding High School 1972-74, Llanishen High School, Cardiff 1974-76; Coleg Glan Hafren, Cardiff: Business studies lecturer 1976-, Manager 1994-99. Former branch chair and member, Association for College Management.

Political career: *House of Commons:* Contested Cardiff South 1987 and Cardiff Central 1992 and 1997 general elections. *House of Lords:* Raised to the peerage as Baroness Randerson, of Roath Park in the City of Cardiff 2011. Parliamentary Under-Secretary of State and Government Spokesperson, Wales Office 2012-; Government Spokesperson for Northern Ireland 2012-. Chair, Liberal Democrat Parliamentary Party Committee on Wales 2011-12. *Other:* National Assembly for Wales: AM for Cardiff Central constituency 1999-2011: Welsh Liberal Democrat: Whip 1999-2000; Spokesperson for Education (under-16) 1999-2000; Minister for Culture, Sports and Welsh Language 2000-03; Acting Deputy First Minister 2001-02; Chair, Committees on: Business Committee 2003-07, Standing Orders -2007; Spokesperson for: Economic Development, Finance and Transport 2003-05, Health and Finance/Health, Finance and Equal Opportunities 2005-07, Finance, Health and Well-being 2007-08; Shadow Minister for: Enterprise, Transport and Education 2008-09, Economy, Transport and Education 2009-10, Economy and Education 2010-11; Chair, Committee on Legislation Number 4 2010-11; Shadow Minister for Transport 2011. Former member: Welsh Campaigns and Candidates Committee, Federal Executive, Federal Policy Committee, Welsh Policy Committee; Contested Welsh Liberal Democrats leadership election 2008. *Councils and public bodies:* Cardiff City Council: Councillor 1983-2000, Opposition Leader 1995-99; JP (Supplemental list).

Political interests: Education, culture, the arts, Europe, local government, health, equal opportunities; Australia, Canada, Europe, France.

Other: Patron: Cardiff and Vale of Glamorgan Youth Wind Band, African Mothers' Foundation, Wales Council for Deaf People; Member: Friends of Synfonia Cymru, Friends of Nant Fawr; Vice-President, Cardiff Business Club; RNID; British Deaf Association; Alzheimers Society; Mencap; Kidney Wales Foundation; The Living Room. Honorary Fellowship, Cardiff University 2011; National Liberal Club.

Recreations: Travel, concert and theatre going, walking, gardening.

The Baroness Randerson, House of Lords, London SW1A 0PW
Tel: 020 7219 2538 *Email:* randersonj@parliament.uk *Twitter:* @jennyranderson

CONSERVATIVE

RAWLINGS, BARONESS

RAWLINGS (Life Baroness), Patricia Elizabeth Rawlings; cr. 1994. Born 27 January 1939; Daughter of late Louis Rawlings and Mary Rawlings, née Boas de Winter; Married Sir David Wolfson 1962 (later Baron Wolfson of Sunningdale) (divorced 1967).

Education: Le Manoir, Lausanne, Switzerland; Oak Hall, Haslemere, Surrey; Florence University; University College, London (BA English 1979); London School of Economics (Postgraduate Diploma international relations 1983).

Non-political career: Nurse, Westminster Hospital; Director: California Dress Company 1969-82, Rheims and Laurent, French Fine Art Auctioneers 1969-71, Nigel Greenwood Inc 1969-86; Member: Peace through NATO Council 1985-88, British Video Classification Council 1986-89; Special adviser to Sir David Trippier, Minister for Inner Cities, Department of the Environment 1987-88; Board member, British Association for Central and Eastern Europe 1994-2008.

Political career: *House of Commons:* Contested (Conservative) Sheffield Central 1983 and Doncaster Central 1987 general elections. *House of Lords:* Raised to the peerage as Baroness Rawlings, of Burnham Westgate in the County of Norfolk 1994. Opposition Whip 1997-98; Opposition Spokesperson for: Culture, Media and Sport 1997-98, Foreign and Commonwealth Affairs December 1998-2010, International Development December 1998-2010; Government Whip (Baroness in Waiting) 2010-12; Government Spokesperson for: Scotland 2010-12, Culture, Olympics, Media and Sport (Arts, Culture, and Media) 2010-12, Attorney General's Office 2010-12, Advocate General for Scotland 2010-12. Member: House of Lords Offices Sub-committee: Advisory Panel on Works of Art 2000-02, Information 2013-. *Other:* MEP (Conservative) for Essex South West 1989-94. Contested Essex West and Hertfordshire East 1994 European Parliament election.

Political interests: International affairs, culture, heritage, media; Brazil, Bulgaria, Oman, Russia.

Other: Member, LCC Children's Care Committee 1959-61; British Red Cross Society: Member 1964-, Chair, Appeals, London Branch, Honorary Vice-President 1988-; Director, English Chamber Orchestra and Music Society 1980-2001; Governor, American University in Bulgaria 1991-; Member, British Council 1997-; Council member, NACF; Member: RIIA, IISS, European Academy of Sciences and Arts, Advisory Council, The Prince's Youth Business Trust; Chair of Council, King's College, London -2007; Trustee, The Chevening Estate 2002-; Patron, Afghan Mother and Child Health Care 2002; President: NCVO 2002-07, British Antique Dealers Association 2005-12; Chairman of Governors, English College in Prague 2008-; President, Friends of BADA.

Honorary DLitt, University of Buckingham; Fellow: King's College, London, University College, London. National Badge of Honour, British Red Cross 1987. Order of the Rose (Silver) (Bulgaria) 1991; Grand Official, Order of the Southern Cross (Brazil) 1997; Hon Plaquette National Assembly of Republic of Bulgaria 2007; Honorary Secretary, Grillions. Royal West Norfolk Golf.

Recreations: Music, art, architecture, gardening, travel, golf.

The Baroness Rawlings, House of Lords, London SW1A 0PW
Tel: 020 7219 5353 *Email:* rawlingsp@parliament.uk

LIBERAL DEMOCRAT

RAZZALL, LORD

RAZZALL (Life Baron), Edward Timothy Razzall; cr. 1997. Born 12 June 1943; Son of Leonard Razzall and Muriel Razzall; Married Deirdre Bourke 1982 (divorced 2003) (1 son 1 daughter from previous marriage); partner Baroness Bonham-Carter of Yarnbury.

Education: St Paul's School, London; Open Scholar Worcester College, Oxford (BA jurisprudence 1965).

Non-political career: Teaching associate, North Western University, Chicago, USA 1965-66; Frere Cholmeley Bischoff, solicitors 1966-96: Partner 1973-96; Director, Cala plc 1973-99; Chair, Abaco Investments plc 1974-90; Partner, Argonaut Associates 1996-; Director, Erinaceous Group plc 2002-09.

Political career: *House of Lords:* Raised to the peerage as Baron Razzall, of Mortlake in the London Borough of Richmond 1997. Liberal Democrat Spokesperson for Trade and Industry/Business, Enterprise and Regulatory Reform 1998-2010. Member: Joint Committee on Consolidation, Etc, Bills 1998-2005, 2006-, Delegated Powers and Regulatory Reform 2007-10, Communications 2010-. Chair, Liberal Democrat Parliamentary Party Committee on Business, Innovation and Skills 2010-. *Other:* Treasurer: Liberal Party 1986-87, Liberal Democrats 1987-2000; Member, Liberal Democrat Federal Executive Committee 1987-2010; President, Association of Liberal Democrat Councillors 1990-95; Chair: Liberal Democrats General Election Campaign 1999-2006, Campaigns and Communications Committee 2000-06. *Councils and public bodies:* London Borough of Richmond: Councillor 1974-98, Deputy Leader 1983-96.

Countries of interest: Greenland, Iceland, Sub-Saharan Africa.

Other: European Lawyer of the Year 1992. CBE 1993; National Liberal, MCC, Soho House.

Recreations: All sports.

The Lord Razzall CBE, House of Lords, London SW1A 0PW
Tel: 020 7219 5888
Email: tim@argonaut-associates.net

LABOUR

REA, LORD

REA (3rd Baron, UK), (John) Nicolas Rea; cr. 1937; 3rd Bt of Eskdale (UK) 1935. Born 6 June 1928; Son of late Honorary James Rea and Betty Rea, née Bevan; Married Elizabeth Robinson 1951 (divorced 1991) (4 sons); partner Jane Conniff (1 daughter); partner Katya Benjamin (1 daughter); married Judith Powell 1991.

Education: Dartington Hall School; Belmont Hill School, Massachusetts, USA; Dauntsey's School; Christ's College, Cambridge (MA natural sciences; MB, BChir 1954; MD 1969); University College Hospital, London (DObst, DCH, DPH 1956-65); Primitive French and Spanish.

Non-political career: Acting Sergeant, Suffolk Regiment, National Service 1946-48. Junior hospital posts 1954-57; Research fellow in paediatrics in Ibadan and Lagos, Nigeria 1962-65; Lecturer in social medicine, St Thomas' Hospital Medical School, London 1966-68; General practitioner, North London 1957-62, 1968-93. Member, Unite.

Political career: *House of Lords:* First entered House of Lords 1982; Deputy Opposition Spokesperson for Health and International Development 1992-97; Elected hereditary peer 1999-. Member: Science and Technology 1987-88, 1997-2002, Science and Technology Sub-committees: Non Food Crops/NHS Research and Development/Antibiotic Resistance/Medicinal Use of Cannabis 1997-2003, I (Complementary and Alternative Medicine) 2000, IIA (Human Genetic Databases) 2000-02, I (Systematic Biology and Biodiversity/Fighting Infection) 2002-03, I (Allergy) 2007, HIV and AIDS in the UK 2010-11. Vice-chair PLP Departmental Committee for International Development 2006-10.

Political interests: Health, food and nutrition, international development, human rights; Subsaharan Africa, Latin America, Russia (Chechnya), Turkey (Kurdish question).

Other: Member: Inter-Parliamentary Union 1985-, Commonwealth Parliamentary Association 1985-; Member: Mary Ward Centre, Mother and Child Foundation, Caroline Walker Trust, National Heart Forum; Member, British Medical Association; FRCGP; FRSA; Oxfam; War on Want; Voluntary Services Overseas (VSO); World Development Movement. Honorary Degree, London Metropolitan University (formerly University of North London) 2002; Royal Society of Medicine.

Publications: Papers on epidemiology, medical education etc in various medical journals 1970-97.

Recreations: Music (bassoon), gardening, photography.

The Lord Rea, House of Lords, London SW1A 0PW
Tel: 020 7219 5353 *Fax:* 020 7219 5969 *Email:* reajn@parliament.uk

LIBERAL DEMOCRAT

REDESDALE, LORD

REDESDALE (6th Baron, UK), Rupert Bertram Mitford; cr. 1902; (Life) Baron Mitford 2000. Born 18 July 1967; Son of 5th Baron; Married Helen Shipsey 1998 (2 sons 2 daughters).

Education: Highgate School, London; Newcastle University (BA archaeology 1989).

Non-political career: Chairman: Anaerobic Digestion and Biogas Association 2009-, Carbon Management Association 2012-, Energy Managers Association 2012-.

Political career: *House of Lords:* Created a life peer as Baron Mitford, of Redesdale in the County of Northumberland 2000. First entered House of Lords 1991; Liberal Democrat Spokesperson for: Overseas Development 1994-99, Northern Ireland 1999, Tourism 2000, International Development 2000-01, Defence 2001-05, Energy 2005-09; Agriculture 2006-09; Contested Lord Speaker elections 2006, 2011.

Political interests: Environment, archaeology; Qatar.

Other: York Archaelogical Trust; Council member, Institute of Advanced Motorists 1994-2010; Fellow, Society of Antiquaries; Patron: Kids Kabin, Rainbow Trust.

Recreations: Caving, climbing, skiing.

The Lord Redesdale, House of Lords, London SW1A 0PW
Tel: 020 7219 4342 *Email:* redesdaler@parliament.uk

CROSSBENCH

REES OF LUDLOW, LORD

REES OF LUDLOW (Life Baron), Martin John Rees; cr 2005. Born 23 June 1942; Son of late Reginald Jackson Rees and Joan Rees, née Bett; Married Professor Caroline Humphrey (later Dame) 1986.

Education: Shrewsbury School; Trinity College, Cambridge (BA mathematics 1963; PhD 1967).

Non-political career: Research associate, California Institute of Technology, USA 1967-68, 1971; Member, Institute for Advanced Study Princeton University, USA 1969-70; Professor, Sussex University 1972-73; Cambridge University 1973-: Professor of astronomy and experimental philosophy 1973-91; Research professor, Royal Society 1992-2003; Astronomer Royal 1995-; Visiting professor, Leicester University and Imperial College, London 2000-; Cambridge University: Professor of cosmology and astrophysics 2002-09, Master, Trinity College 2004-12; President, Royal Society 2005-10.

Political career: *House of Lords:* Raised to the peerage as Baron Rees of Ludlow, of Ludlow in the County of Shropshire 2005. Member: Science and Technology 2010-, Science and Technology Sub-committee I 2012-13.

Political interests: Science and technology, education, developing world, energy.

Other: Trustee: British Museum 1994-2000, Institute for Advanced Studies 1996-; Kennedy Memorial Trust 1999-2004; IPPR 2000-09; National Museum of Science and Industry 2002-; Gates Trust 2005-; Royal Institution 2008-09. Numerous honorary doctorates and fellowships; Honorary Member: US National Academy of Science, Russian Academy of Science, American Philosophical Society, Pontifical Academy of Science and other foreign academies. Numerous UK and international awards; Templeton Prize 2011. FRS 1979; Officer Order des Artes et lettres (France) 1991; Kt 1992; OM 2007.

Publications: Scientific and general articles, plus seven books.

Recreations: Writing, music, rural pursuits.

Professor the Lord Rees of Ludlow OM FRS, House of Lords, London SW1A 0PW
Tel: 020 7219 5353
Trinity College, Cambridge CB2 1TQ *Tel:* 01223 338412 *Fax:* 01223 337520
Email: mjr36@cam.ac.uk

LABOUR

REID OF CARDOWAN, LORD

REID OF CARDOWAN (Life Baron), John Reid; cr 2010. Born 8 May 1947; Son of late Thomas Reid, postman, and late Mary Reid, factory worker; Married Cathie McGowan 1969 (died 1998) (2 sons); married Carine Adler 2002.

Education: St Patrick's Senior Secondary School, Coatbridge; Stirling University (MA history 1978; PhD economic history 1987); French.

Non-political career: Fellow, Armed Forces Parliamentary Scheme 1990-. Insurance clerk late 1960s; Scottish research officer, Labour Party 1979-83; Adviser to Neil Kinnock MP as Leader of Labour Party 1983-85; Scottish organiser, Trade Unionists for Labour 1985-87; Honorary Prof, University College London. Member, TGWU.

Political career: *House of Commons:* MP (Labour) for Motherwell North 1987-97, for Hamilton North and Bellshill 1997-2005, for Airdrie and Shotts 2005-10. Deputy Opposition Spokesperson for: Children 1989-90, Defence, Disarmament and Arms Control 1990-97; Shadow Deputy Secretary of State for Defence 1995-97; Minister of State, Ministry of Defence (Minister for the Armed Forces) 1997-98; Minister of State, Department of the Environment, Transport and the Regions (Minister for Transport) 1998-99; Secretary of State for: Scotland 1999-2001, Northern Ireland 2001-02; Minister without Portfolio and Party Chair 2002-03; Leader of the House of Commons and President of the Council 2003; Secretary of State for: Health 2003-05, Defence 2005-06, the Home Department (Home Secretary) 2006-07. Chair: Modernisation of the House of Commons 2003. *House of Lords:* Raised to the peerage as Baron Reid of Cardowan, of Stepps in Lanarkshire 2010. *Other:* Member, Labour Party National Executive Committee 2002-03.

Political interests: Security, foreign affairs, defence, cyber.

Other: Chair, Institute for Security and Resilience Studies. Honorary doctorate, Stirling University 2009. Best Scot at Westminster 2001; Peace Person of the Year (Northern Ireland) 2002; Minister to Watch 2005; Politician of the Year, *The Spectator* 2006. PC 1998.

Publications: Co-author, Cyber Doctrine: Towards a framework for learning resilience (2011).

Recreations: Football, crosswords.

Rt Hon the Lord Reid of Cardowan, House of Lords, London SW1A 0PW
Tel: 020 7219 8537 *Email:* reidja@parliament.uk

LABOUR

RENDELL OF BABERGH, BARONESS

RENDELL OF BABERGH (Life Baroness), Ruth Barbara Rendell; cr. 1997. Born 17 February 1930; Daughter of Arthur and Ebba Grasemann; Married Donald Rendell 1950 (divorced 1975, re-married 1977, he died 1999) (1 son).

Education: Loughton County High School.

Non-political career: Author and crime novelist 1964-. Member Society of Authors.

Political career: *House of Lords:* Raised to the peerage as Baroness Rendell of Babergh, of Aldeburgh in the County of Suffolk 1997. Member: Ecclesiastical Committee 2002-10, Refreshment 2003-05, 2007-12, Works of Art 2012-13.

Other: FRSL, ActionAid, Refuge, RNIB, London Black Women's Health Action Group, Medical Foundation for the Victims of Torture. Honorary DLitt: University of Bowling Green (Ohio), University of Essex, University of East Anglia; Honorary MLitt, University of East London; Honorary DLitt, University of Middlesex. Arts Council National Book Award for Genre Fiction 1981; *Sunday Times* Award for Literary Excellence 1990; Crime Writers' Association Gold Dagger (4 times) and Diamond Dagger; Mystery Writers of America three Edgar Allan Poe Awards. CBE 1996; Groucho, Detection.

Publications: From Doon with Death (1964); To Fear a Painted Devil (1965); Vanity Dies Hard (1966); A New Lease of Death (1967); Wolf to the Slaughter (1967); The Secret House of Death (1968); The Best Man to Die (1969); A Guilty Thing Surprised (1970); One Across Two Down (1971); No More Dying Then (1972); Murder Being Once Done (1972); Some Lie and Some Die (1973); The Face of Trespass (1974); Shake Hands for Ever (1975); A Demon in my View (1976); A Judgement in Stone (1977); A Sleeping Life (1978); Make Death Love Me (1979); The Lake of Darkness (1980); Put on by Cunning (1981); Master of the Moor (1982); The Speaker of Mandarin (1983); The Killing Doll (1984); The Tree of Hands (1984); An Unkindness of Ravens (1985); Live Flesh (1986); Heartstones (1987); Talking to Strange Men (1987); Editor A Warning to the Curious – The Ghost Stories of M R James (1987); The Veiled One (1988); The Bridesmaid (1989); Ruth Rendell's Suffolk (1989); Co-author Undermining the Central Line (1989); Going Wrong (1990); Kissing the Gunner's Daughter (1992); The Crocodile Bird (1993); Simisola (1994); Editor The Reason Why (1995); The Keys to the Street (1996); Road Rage (1997); A Sight for Sore Eyes (1998); Harm Done (1999); Piranha to Scurfy (2000); Adam and Eve and Pinch Me (2001); The Babes in the Wood (2002); Thirteen Steps Down (2004); End in Tears (2005); The Water's Lovely (2006) Collected Short Stories vol 1 (2006); Not in the Flesh (2007); Collected Short Stories (2008); Portobello (2008); As Barbara Vine: A Dark-Adapted Eye (1986); A Fatal Inversion (1987); The House of Stairs (1988); Gallowglass (1990); King Solomon's Carpet (1991); Asta's Book (1993); No Night is Too Long (1994); The Brimstone Wedding (1996); The Chimney Sweeper's Boy (1998); Grasshopper (2001); The Blood Doctor (2002); The Minotaur (2005); The Birthday Present (2008); The Vault (2011).

Recreations: Reading, walking, opera.

The Baroness Rendell of Babergh CBE, House of Lords, London SW1A 0PW
Tel: 020 7219 2185
11 Maida Avenue, Little Venice, London W2 1SR

RENFREW OF KAIMSTHORN, LORD

RENFREW OF KAIMSTHORN (Life Baron), (Andrew) Colin Renfrew; cr. 1991. Born 25 July 1937; Son of late Archibald and Helena Renfrew; Married Jane Margaret Ewbank 1965 (2 sons 1 daughter).

Education: St Albans School; St John's College, Cambridge (Exhibitioner, BA archaeology and anthropology 1962, MA; PhD 1965, ScD 1976); British School of Archaeology, Athens; French, Greek.

CONSERVATIVE

Non-political career: RAF national service 1956-58 . Sheffield University 1965-72: Lecturer in prehistory and archaeology 1965-70, Senior lecturer 1970-72, Reader 1972; Visiting lecturer, University of California 1967; Professor of archaeology, Southampton University 1972-81; Cambridge University: Disney Professor of Archaeology 1981-2004, Research director, McDonald Institute for Archaeological Research 2013; St John's College, Cambridge: Professional fellow 1981-86, Honorary fellow 2004-; Jesus College, Cambridge: Master 1986-97, Fellow 1986-2004, Honorary fellow 2004-, Emeritus fellow 2004-; Has lectured on archaeology in numerous British and American universities; Has excavated in Greece and the United Kingdom.

Political career: *House of Commons:* Contested (Conservative) Sheffield Brightside 1968 by-election. *House of Lords:* Raised to the peerage as Baron Renfrew of Kaimsthorn, of Hurlet in the District of Renfrew 1991. Chair Library and Computing Sub-committee 1995-2003; Member House 2003-07. *Councils and public bodies:* Chair, Hampshire Archaeological Committee 1974-81; Member: Ancient Monuments Board for England 1974-84, Royal Commission for Historical Monuments (England) 1977-87; Vice-president, Royal Archaeological Institute 1982-85; Member: Historical Buildings and Monuments Commission for England 1984-86, Ancient Monuments Advisory Committee 1984-2001, UK National Commission for UNESCO 1984-86; Board member, Parliamentary Office of Science and Technology (POST) 1997-98; Member, executive committee, National Art Collections Fund Committee 2001-10.

Political interests: National heritage, arts, museums and galleries, education, foreign affairs; France, Greece, USA.

Other: Foreign associate, US National Academy of Sciences 1997; Corresponding Member: Austrian Academy of Sciences 2000, German Archaeological Institute 2004; Foreign member, Russian Academy of Sciences 2006; Trustee, British Museum 1991-2000; Antiquity Trust; FSA; Hon FSA (Scotland); FBA 1980; Hon FRSE 2001. Freeman, City of London. Seven honorary doctorates. Huxley Memorial Medal 1991; Fyssen Prize 1996; European Science Foundation Latsis Prize 2003; Balzan Foundation Prize 2004; Athenæum, United Oxford and Cambridge University.

Publications: The Emergence of Civilisation (1972); Editor The Explanation of Culture Change (1973); Before Civilisation (1973); Editor British Prehistory, a New Outline (1974); Investigations in Orkney (1979); Problems in European Prehistory (1979); An Island Polity (1982); Approaches to Social Archaeology (1984); The Prehistory of Orkney (1985); The Archaeology of Cult (1985); Archaeology and Language (1987); The Cycladic Spirit (1991); Loot, Legitimacy and Ownership: the Ethical Crisis in Archaeology (2000); Figuring It Out (2003); Prehistory, the Making of the Human Mind (2008); Collaboration with other authors on archaeological subjects, as well as contributions to archaeological journals.

Recreations: Contemporary art.

Professor the Lord Renfrew of Kaimsthorn FBA FSA, House of Lords, London SW1A 0PW
Tel: 020 7219 5353
McDonald Institute for Archaeological Research, Downing Street, Cambridge CB2 3ER
Tel: 01223 333521 *Fax:* 01223 333536 *Email:* acr10@cam.ac.uk

**LIBERAL DEMO-
CRAT INDEPENDENT**

RENNARD, LORD

RENNARD (Life Baron), Christopher John Rennard; cr. 1999. Born 8 July 1960; Son of late Cecil and Jean Rennard; Married Ann McTegart 1989.

Education: Liverpool Blue Coat School; Liverpool University (BA politics and economics 1982).

Non-political career: Liberal Party agent, Liverpool, Mossley Hill 1982-84; Liberal Party regional agent, East Midlands 1984-88; Social and Liberal Democrats election co-ordinator 1988-89; Director of campaigns and elections, Liberal Democrats 1989-2003; Chief executive, Liberal Democrats 2003-09.

Political career: *House of Lords:* Raised to the peerage as Baron Rennard, of Wavertree in the County of Merseyside 1999. Liberal Democrat Spokesperson for: Communities and Local Government 2009-10, Constitutional Affairs 2009-10. Member: Information 2009-, Constitution 2011-12. *Other:* Liberal Democrat Whip withdrawn (pending investigation) March 2013. *Councils and public bodies:* Vice-President, Local Government Association 2011-.

Other: Member: Inter-Parliamentary Union, Commonwealth Parliamentary Association; Vice-president, Liberal International; Member, Electoral Reform Society. MBE 1989.

Recreations: Cooking, wine, France.

The Lord Rennard MBE, House of Lords, London SW1A 0PW
Tel: 020 7219 6717 *Fax:* 020 7219 2458 *Email:* rennardc@parliament.uk
Website: lordsoftheblog.net/category/lord-rennard *Twitter:* @LordRennard

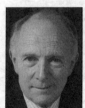

CONSERVATIVE

RENTON OF MOUNT HARRY, LORD

RENTON OF MOUNT HARRY (Life Baron), (Ronald) Timothy Renton; cr. 1997. Born 28 May 1932; Son of late R. K. D. Renton, CBE and of late Eila Renton, MBE; Married Alice Fergusson 1960 (2 sons 2 daughters 1 daughter deceased).

Education: Eton College (Kings Scholar); Magdalen College, Oxford (Roberts Gawen Scholar BA modern history 1953, MA).

Non-political career: C. Tennant Sons & Co. Ltd, Canada 1957-62; Managing director, Tennant Trading Ltd 1964-71; Director: Silvermines Ltd 1966-84, ANZ Banking Group Ltd 1969-76, J. H. Vavasseur & Co. Ltd 1971-74; Fleming Continental European Investment Trust: Director 1992-, Chair 1999-2005; Partner, Mount Harry Vines 2007-. Member, APEX 1977-90.

Political career: *House of Commons:* Contested (Conservative) Sheffield Park 1970 general election. MP (Conservative) for Sussex Mid 1974-97. PPS: to John Biffen: as Chief Secretary to the Treasury 1979-81, as Secretary of State for Trade 1981, to Sir Geoffrey Howe as Chancellor of the Exchequer 1983; Parliamentary Under-Secretary of State, Foreign and Commonwealth Office 1984-85; Minister of State: Foreign and Commonwealth Office 1985-87, Home Office 1987-89; Government Chief Whip 1989-90; Minister for the Arts Privy Council Office 1990-92. *House of Lords:* Raised to the peerage as Baron Renton of Mount Harry, of Offham in the County of East Sussex 1997. Member: European Communities Sub-committees: A (Economic and Financial Affairs, Trade and External Relations/Economic and Financial Affairs and International Trade) 1997-2001, 2007-10, D (Environment, Agriculture, Public Health and Consumer Protection) 2002-03, European Union 2003-06; Chair: EU Sub-committee D (Environment and Agriculture) 2003-06, Information 2007-10; Co-opted member EU Sub-committee E (Law and Institutions) 2009-10; Member: EU Sub-committee E (Justice and Institutions) 2010-12, Constitution 2010-12, EU Sub-committee D (Agriculture, Fisheries, Environment and Energy) 2012-. *Other:* President, Conservative Trade Unionists 1980-84. *Councils and public bodies:* Member, Know How Fund Advisory Board 1992-99; British Council: Vice-chair 1992-97, Board Member 1997-99; Chair: Outsider Art Archive and Collection 1993-99, Sussex Downs Conservative Board 1997-2005; President: Roedean School 1997-2005, Federation of Sussex Amenity Societies 2000-; Council member, Sussex University 2000-07; DL 2004; Chair, South Downs Joint Committee 2005-09; President, Brighton College 2007-12.

Political interests: Arts, privatisation, financial institutions, conservation, environment.

Other: Fellow, Industry and Parliament Trust 1980; Hope from Homes. PC 1989.

Publications: The Dangerous Edge (1994); Hostage to Fortune (1997); Chief Whip (2004); Articles published in journals and newspapers.

Recreations: Writing, mucking about in boats, arguing about opera, touring France on a bicycle, tasting wine.

Rt Hon the Lord Renton of Mount Harry, House of Lords, London SW1A 0PW
Tel: 020 7219 3308 *Email:* rentont@parliament.uk

CROSSBENCH

RENWICK OF CLIFTON, LORD

RENWICK OF CLIFTON (Life Baron), Robin William Renwick; cr. 1997. Born 13 December 1937; Son of the late Richard and Clarice Renwick; Married Annie Giudicelli 1965 (1 son 1 daughter).

Education: St Paul's School, London; Jesus College, Cambridge (MA history 1962); University of Paris (Sorbonne).

Non-political career: Army national service 1956-58. Entered Foreign Service 1963; Dakar 1963-64; FO 1964-66; New Delhi 1966-70; Private Secretary to Minister of State, FCO 1970-72; First Secretary, Paris 1972-76; Counsellor, Cabinet Office 1976-78; Rhodesia Department, FCO 1978-80; Political adviser to Governor of Rhodesia 1980; Head of Chancery, Washington 1981-84; Assistant Under-Secretary of State, FCO 1984-87; Ambassador to: South Africa 1987-91, USA 1991-95; Deputy chair, Robert Fleming Holdings 1995-2000; Director: Compagnie Financiere Richemont AG 1995-, British Airways plc 1996-2005; Chair, Fluor Ltd 1996-2011; Director: Fluor Corporation 1997-2008, BHP Billiton plc 1997-2005, SAB Miller plc 1999-2008, Harmony Gold 1999-2004; Deputy chair, Fleming Family and Partners 2000-; Vice-chair, Investment Banking, JP Morgan Europe, JP Morgan Cazenove 2000-; Director: Kazakhmys plc 2005-, Gem Diamonds Ltd 2007-09, BUMI plc 2011-.

Political career: *House of Lords:* Raised to the peerage as Baron Renwick of Clifton, of Chelsea in the Royal Borough of Kensington and Chelsea 1997.

Political interests: Defence, foreign affairs; France, South Africa, USA.

Other: Trustee: The Economist 1996-2010, The Hakluyt Foundation 2000-07; FRSA. Visiting Fellow, Center for International Affairs, Harvard University 1980-81; Honorary DLitt, University of the Witwatersrand, South Africa 1990; Honorary Fellow, Jesus College 1992; Honorary DLitt: College of William and Mary, USA 1993, Oglethorpe University 1995. CMG 1980; KCMG 1988; Brooks's, Hurlingham.

Publications: Economic Sanctions (1981); Fighting with Allies (1996); Unconventional Diplomacy (1997).

Recreations: Tennis, fly-fishing.

The Lord Renwick of Clifton KCMG, House of Lords, London SW1A 0PW
Tel: 020 7219 5353
J P Morgan plc, 10 Aldermanbury, London EC2V 7RF *Tel:* 020 7155 4801
Email: robin.renwick@jpmorgan.com

CONSERVATIVE

RIBEIRO, LORD

RIBEIRO (Life Baron), Bernard Francisco Ribeiro; cr 2010. Born 20 January 1944; Son of late Miguel and Matilda Ribeiro; Married Elisabeth Orr 1968 (1 son 3 daughters including twins).

Education: Dean Close School, Cheltenham; Middlesex Hospital Medical School, London University (MBBS, LRCP 1967).

Non-political career: Drum Major, Combined Cadet Force 1958-62. Registrar, then senior registrar, Middlesex Hospital 1972-78; Lecturer in urology, Ghana Medical School, Accra 1974; Consultant General Surgeon, Basildon University Hospital 1979-2008; Surgical adviser to Expert Advisory Group on Aids (EAGA) and UK Advisory Panel for health care workers infected with blood-borne viruses (UKAP), Department of Health 1994-2003; President, Royal College of Surgeons of England 2005-08; Visiting professor, University of North Carolina at Chapel Hill, USA 2006-07; Chairman, Independent Reconfiguration Panel 2012-.

Political career: *House of Lords:* Raised to the peerage as Baron Ribeiro, of Achimota in the Republic of Ghana and of Ovington in the County of Hampshire 2010. *Other:* Member, Executive Committee, Association of Conservative Peers. *Councils and public bodies:* Member, board of visitors, HM Prison Chelmsford 1982-92; Council member, Dean Close School, Cheltenham 2006-.

Political interests: Health, education, prison reform; Africa (Ghana), USA.

Other: Royal College of Surgeons: Member 1967-, Fellow 1972-, Council member 1998-2008, Member, court of examiners 1998-2004, Chairman, Quality Assurance and Inspection 2000-05, Senior vice-president 2004-05, Chair, Honours Committee 2005-13, President 2005-08; Association of Surgeons of Great Britain and Ireland: Honorary secretary 1991-96, President 1999-2000, Chair, Distinction Awards Committee 2000-04; Consultant to advisory board, Health Policy Research Institute, American College of Surgeons 2000-10; Medical vice-chair, East of England Advisory Committee on Clinical Excellence Awards 2002-05; Member, Test and Itchen Association; Chair, Research Review Panel, Pelican Foundation 2009-; Member: Royal Society of Medicine, British

Medical Association, Association of Surgeons of Great Britain and Ireland. Honorary Liveryman, Worshipful Company of Cutlers 2008-; Worshipful Company of Barbers: Middle Warden 2011-12, Upper Warden 2012-13, Master 2013-14. Freeman, City of London 1991. Fellow ad hominem, Royal College of Surgeons, Edinburgh 2000; Honorary Fellow, Ghana College of Physicians and Surgeons 2006; Fellow: Royal College of Physicians 2006, Academy of Medicine of Malaysia 2006; Honorary Fellow, Caribbean College of Surgeons 2007; Honorary Member, Académie Chirurgie de Paris 2008; Honorary Fellow: Royal College of Surgeons in Ireland 2008, Royal College of Physicians and Surgeons of Glasgow 2008, American College of Surgeons 2008; Fellow, College of Anaesthetists 2008; Honorary DSc, Anglia Ruskin University 2008; Honorary DEng, Bath University 2012. CBE 2004; Charles Saint Medal (South Africa) 2007; Arthur Li Oration (Hong Kong) 2007; Officer, Order of the Volta 2008; Kt 2009; Surgical Sixty Club. Flyfishers' Club.

Publications: Chapters in surgical textbooks; Papers on rectal cancer and biliary manometry; Contributions to Royal College of Surgeons bulletins.

Recreations: Fishing, shooting, history of warfare.

The Lord Ribeiro CBE FRCS, House of Lords, London SW1A 0PW
Tel: 020 7219 4819 *Email:* ribeirob@parliament.uk

LABOUR

RICHARD, LORD

RICHARD (Life Baron), Ivor Seward Richard; cr. 1990. Born 30 May 1932; Son of Seward Thomas Richard; Married Geraldine Moore 1956 (divorced 1962) (1 son); married Alison Imrie 1962 (divorced) (1 son 1 daughter); married Janet Jones 1989 (1 son).

Education: St Michael's School, Bryn, Llanelly; Cheltenham College; Pembroke College, Oxford (Wightwick Scholar, BA jurisprudence 1953).

Non-political career: Called to the Bar, Inner Temple 1955; Bencher 1985; Practised in London 1955-74; QC 1971; UK Permanent Representative to UN 1974-79; EEC Commissioner 1981-85; Chair: World Trade Centre (Wales) Ltd 1985-97, World Trade Centre (London) Ltd 2010-.

Political career: *House of Commons:* Contested South Kensington 1959 general election. MP (Labour) for Barons Court 1964-74. PPS to Denis Healey as Secretary of State for Defence 1966-67; Parliamentary Under-Secretary of State (Army), Ministry of Defence 1969-70; Opposition Spokesperson for Broadcasting, Posts and Telecommunications 1970-71; Deputy Spokesperson for Foreign Affairs 1971-74. *House of Lords:* Raised to the peerage as Baron Richard, of Ammanford in the County of Dyfed 1990. Opposition Spokesperson for: Home Office affairs 1990-92, The Civil Service 1992-97, European Affairs 1992-97, The Treasury and Economic Affairs 1992-93; Leader of the Opposition 1992-97; Lord Privy Seal and Leader of the House of Lords 1997-98; Contested Lord Speaker election 2006. Chair Constitutional Reform Bill 2004; Member: Liaison 2006-09, European Union 2008-13, EU Sub-committee F (Home Affairs) 2008-12; Chair: Barnett Formula 2008-09, Joint Committee on the Draft House of Lords Reform Bill 2011-12; Member: EU Sub-committee F (Home Affairs, Health and Education) 2012-13, Inquiries Act 2005 2013-. *Councils and public bodies:* Chair, Commission on the Powers and Electoral Management of the NAW 2002-04.

Other: Honorary Fellow, Pembroke College, Oxford 1981. PC 1993.

Publications: Co-author, Europe or the Open Sea (1971); We, the British (1983); Co-author, Unfinished Business – the Reform of the House of Lords (1999); As well as articles in political journals.

Recreations: Music, talking.

Rt Hon the Lord Richard QC, House of Lords, London SW1A 0PW
Tel: 020 7219 1495/020 7219 6158 *Email:* richardi@parliament.uk

CROSSBENCH

RICHARDSON OF CALOW, BARONESS

RICHARDSON OF CALOW (Life Baroness), Kathleen Margaret Richardson; cr. 1998. Born 24 February 1938; Daughter of Francis and Margaret Fountain; Married Ian Richardson 1964 (3 daughters).

Education: St Helena School, Chesterfield; Stockwell College (Teaching Certificate 1958); Wesley Deaconess College 1961-63; Wesley House, Cambridge (theological education 1977-79).

Non-political career: First Woman President of the Methodist Conference 1992-93; Moderator, Free Churches Council 1995-99; President, Churches Together In England 1995-99.

Political career: *House of Lords:* Raised to the peerage as Baroness Richardson of Calow, of Calow in the County of Derbyshire 1998. *Councils and public bodies:* Moderator of Churches Commission for Inter-faith Relations 2000-06.

Political interests: Church affairs, inter-faith relations.

Other: Former Vice-President, National Children's Homes; Chair: London Ecumenical Aids Trust 2000-11, British and Foreign Schools Society 2004-10; President, Christian Education 2004-10; Chair, Board of Management for Methodist Schools and Colleges 2004-11; Vice-President, Council of Christians and Jews; Langley House, Walsingham Homes, Methodist Homes, Action for Children, Embrace. Three honorary doctorates. OBE 1994.

Recreations: Reading, needlework.

Rev the Baroness Richardson of Calow OBE, House of Lords, London SW1A 0PW
Tel: 020 7219 0314 *Email:* richardsonk@parliament.uk

RIDLEY, VISCOUNT

RIDLEY, (5th Viscount, UK) Matthew White Ridley; cr 1900; Baron Wensleydale; 9th Bt of Blagdon (GB) 1756. Born 7 February 1958; Son of 4th Viscount and Lady Anne Lumley; Married Anya Hurlbert 1989 (1 son 1 daughter).

Education: Eton College; Magdalen College, Oxford (BA zoology 1979; DPhil zoology 1983).

Non-political career: *The Economist* 1983-92: Science editor 1983-87, Washington correspondent 1987-90, American editor 1990-92; Columnist, *Daily Telegraph* and *Sunday Telegraph* 1993-2000; Northern Rock: Director 1994-2007, Non-executive chairman 2004-07; Director, Northern Investors 1994-2007; Founding chairman, International Centre for Life 1996-2003; Chairman, Northern 2 VCT 1999-2008; PA Holdings Ltd 1999-2008; Columnist: *Wall Street Journal*, *The Times*.

CONSERVATIVE

Political career: *House of Lords:* Elected hereditary peer 2013-. *Councils and public bodies:* DL, Northumberland.

Other: Fellow: Royal Society of Literature, Academy of Medical Sciences; Foreign honorary member, American Academy of Arts and Sciences. Honorary DCL: Buckingham University 2003, Newcastle University 2007; Honorary DSc, Cold Spring Harbor Laboratory 2006.

Publications: Warts and All: The Men Who Would be Bush (Viking, 1989); The Red Queen: The Sex and the Evolution of Human Nature (Prentice Hall & IBD, 1994); The Origins of Virtue (Viking, 1996); Genome: The Auto-biography of a Species in 23 Chapters (Fourth Estate, 1999); Nature via Nurture: Genes, Experience and What Makes us Human (Fourth Estate, 2003); Francis Crick: Discoverer of the Genetic Code (Harper Press, 2006); The Rational Optimist: How Prosperity Evolves (Fourth Estate, 2010).

The Viscount Ridley, House of Lords, London SW1A 0PW
Tel: 020 7219 5353 *Email:* ridleywm@parliament.uk
Blagdon Estate Office, Seaton Burn, Newcastle NE13 6DD *Tel:* 01670 789325
Website: www.rationaloptimist.com   *Twitter:* @mattwridley

RIPON AND LEEDS, LORD BISHOP OF

RIPON AND LEEDS (Bishop of), John Richard Packer. Born 10 October 1946; Son of Canon John and Muriel Packer; Married Barbara Jack 1971 (1 daughter 2 sons).

Education: Manchester Grammar School; Keble College, Oxford (BA modern history 1967; BA theology, MA 1975); Ripon Hall, Oxford (ministerial training).

Non-political career: Deacon 1970; Curate, St Helier, Southwark, London 1970-73; Ordained priest 1971; Chaplain, Abingdon St Nicolas, Oxford 1973-77; Tutor: Ripon Hall, Oxford 1973-75, Ripon College, Cuddeson 1975-77; Vicar, Wath-upon-Dearne with Adwick-upon-Dearne 1977-86; Rural dean, Wath 1983-86; Team rector, Sheffield Manor 1986-91; Rural dean, Attercliffe 1990-91; Archdeacon, West Cumberland, Carlisle 1991-96; Priest-in-charge, Bridekirk 1995-96; Suffragan Bishop, Warrington 1996-2000; Bishop of Ripon and Leeds 2000-.

NON-AFFILIATED

Political career: *House of Lords:* Entered House of Lords 2006.

Political interests: Social, educational and ethical issues, asylum, combating racism; Sri Lanka.

Recreations: History, walking.

Rt Rev the Lord Bishop of Ripon and Leeds, House of Lords, London SW1A 0PW
Tel: 020 7219 5353
Hollin House, Weetwood Avenue, Leeds LS16 5NG *Tel:* 0113-224 2789 *Fax:* 0113-230 5471
Email: bishop@riponleeds-diocese.org.uk

CONSERVATIVE

RISBY, LORD

RISBY (Life Baron), Richard John Grenville Spring; cr 2010. Born 24 September 1946; Son of late H. J. A. Spring and of late Marjorie Watson-Morris; Married Honorary Jane Henniker-Major 1979 (divorced 1993) (1 son 1 daughter).

Education: Rondebosch, Cape Town, South Africa; University of Cape Town; Magdalene College, Cambridge (BA economics, MA); French (basic).

Non-political career: Merrill Lynch Ltd 1971-86: Vice-President 1976-86; Deputy managing director, Hutton International Associates 1986-88; Executive director, Shearson Lehman Hutton 1988-90; Managing director, Xerox Furman Selz 1990-92.

Political career: *House of Commons:* Contested (Conservative) Ashton-Under-Lyne 1983 general election. MP for Bury St Edmunds 1992-97, for West Suffolk 1997-2010. PPS to: Sir Patrick Mayhew as Secretary of State for Northern Ireland 1994-95, Tim Eggar as Minister for Trade and Industry 1995-96, Nicholas Soames and James Arbuthnot as Ministers of State, Ministry of Defence 1996-97; Opposition Spokesperson for: Culture, Media and Sport November 1997-2000, Foreign Affairs 2000-04; Shadow Minister for the Treasury 2004-05. Member: Northern Ireland Affairs 1995-97, Health 1995-96, Deregulation 1997, Home Affairs 2006-07. *House of Lords:* Raised to the peerage as Baron Risby, of Haverhill in the County of Suffolk 2010. Trade envoy to Algeria 2012-. *Other:* Various offices in Westminster Conservative Association 1976-87, including CPC Chair 1990; Vice-chair: Conservative Industrial Fund 1993-96, Conservative Party (Business) 2005-10.

Political interests: Treasury, small business, foreign affairs; China, Europe, Middle East, Pacific Rim, South Africa, USA.

Other: Deputy chair, Small Business Bureau 1992-; Fellow, Industry and Parliament Trust 1994; Governor, Westminster Foundation for Democracy 2001-10; Director, British Syria Society 2005-11; Chairman, British-Ukrainian Society 2007-; Boodle's.

Recreations: Country pursuits, tennis, swimming.

The Lord Risby, House of Lords, London SW1A 0PW
Tel: 020 7219 8996 *Email:* risbyr@parliament.uk

CROSSBENCH

RIX, LORD

RIX (Life Baron), Brian Norman Roger Rix; cr. 1992. Born 27 January 1924; Son of late Herbert and Fanny Rix; Married Elspet Gray, actress, 1949 (died 2013) (2 sons, 1 daughter and 1 daughter deceased).

Education: Bootham School, York.

Non-political career: Served in RAF and as Bevin Boy. Actor 1942-; Actor manager 1947-77 (mostly at the Whitehall Theatre and Garrick Theatre, London); MENCAP (Royal Society for Mentally Handicapped Children and Adults, now the Royal Mencap Society): Secretary-General 1980-87, Chair 1988-98, President 1998-. Life Member, British Actors' Equity Association.

Political career: *House of Lords:* Raised to the peerage as Baron Rix, of Whitehall in the City of Westminster and of Hornsea in Yorkshire 1992. Member Joint Committees: Draft Mental Incapacity Bill 2003, Draft Disability Discrimination Bill 2004, Draft Mental Health Bill 2004-05. *Councils and public bodies:* Chair, Independent Development Council for People with Mental Handicap 1981-86; Member, Arts Council 1986-93; Chair, Drama Panel 1986-93; Greater London: DL 1987-88, 1997- (for life), Vice-Lord-Lieutenant 1988-97; Chair, Monitoring Committee, Arts and Disabled People 1988-93.

Political interests: Arts, disability, theatre, voluntary sector, charities, cricket, higher education.

Other: Fellow, Hong Kong Association for Scientific Study of Mental Handicap; Friends of Normansfield/Normansfield and Richmond Foundation: Chair 1973-2003, President 2003-; Mencap City Foundation (later Rix-Thompson-Rothenberg Foundation): Founder and governor 1984, Chair 1988-; Chair, Libertas Group of Charities 1988-2006; Mencap City Insurance Services: Chair 1993-2003, President 2003-07; Chair, Family Charities Ethical Trust Advisory Panel 1994-2001; Life Vice-President, Radio Society of Great Britain; President: Roy Kinnear Memorial Trust, Langdon-Down Centre Trust, Friends of Richmond Park, Royal Mencap Society; Patron, Rix Centre, University of East London; Honorary FRSM, Honorary FRCPsch; Supporter: British Heart Foundation, St Raphael's Hospice, Medic Alert, Imperial Society of Knight's Bachelor, Orange Tree Theatre, Rose Theatre, Kingston upon Thames, RTR Foundation; Normansfield and Richmond Foundation. University of East London: Chancellor 1997-2011, Chancellor Emeritus 2012-. Ten honorary degrees and five fellowships. Evian Health Award 1988; RNID Communicator of the Year Award 1990; *The Spectator* Campaigner of the Year Award 1999; Yorkshire Lifetime Achievement Award 1999; Lifetime Achievement UK Charity Awards 2001; Award for Public Service, British Neuroscience Association 2001; ePolitix Charity Champions Lifetime Achievement Award 2004. CBE 1977; Kt 1986; Garrick, Lord's Taverners (Honorary Member, Past President). MCC, Yorkshire CCC.

Publications: My Farce from My Elbow (autobiography, 1975); Farce about Face (autobiography, 1989); Tour de Farce (history of theatre touring, 1992); Life in the Farce Lane (history of farce, 1995); Editor and contributor: Gullible's Travails (1996), All About Us! (history of learning disability and Mencap [60th anniversary] 2006).

Recreations: Cricket, amateur radio, gardening.

The Lord Rix CBE DL, House of Lords, London SW1A 0PW
Tel: 020 7219 5353
Mencap (Royal Mencap Society), 123 Golden Lane, London EC1Y 0RT *Tel:* 020 7696 5614
Fax: 020 7696 5548 *Email:* leigh.banks@mencap.org.uk
Fax: 01372 476768 *Email:* lordrix@btinternet.com

ROBERTS OF CONWY, LORD

ROBERTS OF CONWY (Life Baron), (Ieuan) Wyn Pritchard Roberts; cr. 1997. Born 10 July 1930; Son of late Rev. Evan Pritchard Roberts; Married Enid Williams 1956 (3 sons).

Education: Beaumaris County School; Harrow School; University College, Oxford (BA history 1952, MA).

Non-political career: Intelligence Corps 1948-49. Sub-editor, *Liverpool Daily Post* 1952-54; News assistant, BBC 1954-57; Executive: TWW Ltd 1957-68, Harlech TV Ltd 1968-69.

CONSERVATIVE

Political career: *House of Commons:* MP (Conservative) for Conwy 1970-97. PPS to Peter Thomas as Secretary of State for Wales 1970-74; Opposition Spokesperson for Welsh Affairs 1974-79; Welsh Office: Parliamentary Under-Secretary of State 1979-87, Minister of State 1987-94. *House of Lords:* Raised to the peerage as Baron Roberts of Conwy, of Talyfan in the County of Gwynedd 1997. Opposition Spokesperson for: Welsh Affairs 1997-2007, Home Office 2002-04. *Other:* President, Welsh Conservative Clubs 1991-2003. *Councils and public bodies:* Member, Royal National Eisteddfod Gorsedd of Bards; President, University of Wales College of Medicine 1997-2004; Vice-President, Cardiff University 2004-07.

Political interests: Education, health, training, tourism, small businesses, transport, economics, conservation, Welsh affairs; Germany, Ghana, Russia.

Other: Life Member, Commonwealth Parliamentary Association; Rheumatoid Arthritis Association; Diabetics UK; Almshouses Association. Honorary Fellow, University Colleges of Wales, Bangor and Aberystwyth; Honorary Doctorate of Laws, University of Wales 2005. Kt 1990; PC 1991; Savile, Cardiff and County (Cardiff).

Publications: Autobiography, Right from the Start (University of Wales Press, 2006).

Recreations: Fishing, walking.

Rt Hon the Lord Roberts of Conwy, House of Lords, London SW1A 0PW
Tel: 020 7219 2410 *Email:* robertsw@parliament.uk

ROBERTS OF LLANDUDNO, LORD

ROBERTS OF LLANDUDNO (Life Baron), (John) Roger Roberts; cr. 2004. Born 23 October 1935; Son of Thomas Charles and Alice Ellen Roberts; Married Eirlys Ann 1962 (died 1995) (2 daughters 1 son).

Education: John Bright Grammar School, Llandudno; University College of North Wales (BA history, biblical history 1957); Handsworth Methodist College; Welsh.

Non-political career: Methodist Church 1959-: Superintendent minister: Llangollen 1965-70, Llandudno 1983-2002; Minister, Toronto Welsh Church 2003-04; Part-time lecturer, Llandrillo College.

LIBERAL DEMOCRAT

Political career: *House of Commons:* Contested Conwy 1979, 1983, 1987, 1992 and 1997 general elections. *House of Lords:* Raised to the peerage as Baron Roberts of Llandudno, of Llandudno in the County of Gwynedd 2004. Liberal Democrat: Spokesperson for: International Development 2004-10, Wales 2004-10, Whip 2005-10. Member Works of Art 2010-11, 2012-13. *Other:* Contested Wales 1999 European Parliament election. Chair, Union of University Liberal Societies 1956-57; Former president: Welsh Liberal Party, Welsh Liberal Democrats; Deputy president, UK Liberal Democrats. *Councils and public bodies:* Group leader, Aberconwy Borough Council 1976-87; Former Vice-President, Local Government Association.

Political interests: Human rights, international affairs, Welsh affairs, child welfare, asylum seekers, migrant workers; Canada, Israel, Poland, Uganda.

Other: President, Wales International; Trustee, Fund for Human Need; Patron, Bite the Ballot; Chair, Grassroutes; Director, Commonwealth Carnival of Music; Vice-President, Llangollen International Music Eisteddford.

Publications: Author, Hel Tai (Gwasg y Bwthyn, 2010).

Recreations: Music, travel, walking.

The Lord Roberts of Llandudno, House of Lords, London SW1A 0PW
Tel: 020 7219 8739 *Email:* robertsr@parliament.uk

LABOUR

ROBERTSON OF PORT ELLEN, LORD

ROBERTSON OF PORT ELLEN (Life Baron), George Islay MacNeill Robertson; cr. 1999. Born 12 April 1946; Son of the late George Robertson, police inspector, and late Marion Robertson; Married Sandra Wallace 1970 (2 sons 1 daughter).

Education: Dunoon Grammar School, Argyll; Dundee University (MA economics 1968).

Non-political career: Research assistant, Tayside Study, Economics Group 1968-69; Scottish organiser, GMWU 1969-78; Secretary-General, North Atlantic Treaty Organisation 1999-2003; Executive Deputy Chair, Cable and Wireless plc 2004-06; Chair, Cable and Wireless International 2006-08; Senior counsellor, Cohen Group 2004-; Non-executive director: Weir Group plc 2004-, The Smiths Group 2004-06; Special adviser, BP plc 2006-; Non-executive director, Western Ferries (Clyde) Ltd 2006-13; Deputy Chair, TNK-BP 2006-13; Senior international adviser, Cable and Wireless Communications plc 2008-. Member, GMB 1965-.

Political career: *House of Commons:* MP (Labour) for Hamilton May 1978 by-election to 1997, for Hamilton South 1997 to 24 August 1999. PPS to David Ennals as Secretary of State for Social Services February-May 1979; Opposition Frontbench Spokesperson for: Scotland 1979-80, Defence 1980-81, Foreign and Commonwealth Affairs 1981-93, European and Community Affairs 1985-93; Shadow Secretary of State for Scotland 1993-97; Secretary of State for Defence 1997-99. *House of Lords:* Raised to the peerage as Baron Robertson of Port Ellen, of Islay in Argyll and Bute 1999. Secretary of State for Defence August-October 1999. *Other:* Chair, Scottish Labour Party 1977-78. *Councils and public bodies:* Vice-President, Raleigh International 1984-; Vice-chair, British Council 1985-94; Chair: Commission on Global Road Safety 2006-, Commission on National Security (IPPR) 2007-; Joint President, UK Atlantic Council 2008-.

Political interests: Foreign affairs, defence, road safety.

Other: Fellow, Industry and Parliament Trust 1983; Hon Reg Col, London-Scottish (Volunteers) 2000-; Joint President, Royal Institute of International Affairs 2001-11; Elder Brother, Corporation of Trinity House 2002-; Chair: John Smith Memorial Trust 2004-08, Maggies (Cancer Care) Centre, Lanarkshire Appeal 2004-; Trustee, British Forces Foundation 2004-; Patron: Glasgow Islay Association 2004-, Alzheimer's Research UK 2004-; Member, advisory board: Centre for European Reform 2004-, European Council for Foreign Affairs 2007-; Patron: Scottish Burned Children's Club 2008-, Islay Book Festival 2008-; Chair, Ditchley Foundation 2009-; Patron: The Dunblane Centre 2010-, The Disabilities Trust 2010-; FRSA 1999; Hon FRSE 2003. Chancellor, Order of St Michael and St George 2011-. 14 honorary doctorates from UK, Azerbaijan, Kyrgyzstan, Romania and Armenia; Honorary Professor, politics department, Stirling University 2009-. International Academy of Achievement, Golden Plate Award 2000; English Speaking Union Winston Churchill Medal of Honour 2003; Atlantic Council of USA Distinguished International Leadership Award 2003; Parliamentarian of the Year (Jt) 2003; Licentiate, Royal Photographic Society 2010. PC 1997; Honours from Italy, Germany, Poland, Hungary, Luxembourg, Netherlands, Spain, Belgium, Portugal, Lithuania, Romania, Bulgaria, Croatia, Estonia, Ukraine, Slovakia, Latvia, Slovenia; Presidential Medal of Freedom (USA) 2003; Distinguished Service Medal, US Department of Defence 2003; KT 2004; GCMG 2004; Army and Navy. Hamilton Rugby; Islay Golf; Dunblane New Golf.

Publications: Author, Islay and Jura: Photographs (Birlinn, 2006).

Recreations: Photography, golf, reading.

Rt Hon the Lord Robertson of Port Ellen KT GCMG, House of Lords, London SW1A 0PW
Tel: 020 7219 6235 *Email:* robertsong@parliament.uk

RODGERS OF QUARRY BANK, LORD

RODGERS OF QUARRY BANK (Life Baron), William Thomas Rodgers; cr. 1992. Born 28 October 1928; Son of William and Gertrude Rodgers; Married Silvia Szulman 1955 (died 2006) (3 daughters).

Education: Sudley Road Council School; Quarry Bank High School, Liverpool; Magdalen College, Oxford (Open Exhibitioner, BA modern history 1951).

Non-political career: National Service 1947-49. General Secretary: The Fabian Society 1953-60, Publishing 1960-64, 1970-72; Director-General, Royal Institute of British Architects 1987-94; **LIBERAL DEMOCRAT** Chair, Advertising Standards Authority 1995-2000.

Political career: *House of Commons:* Contested Bristol West 1957 general election. MP (Labour) for Stockton-on-Tees 1962-74, for Teesside, Stockton 1974-83 (Labour 1974-81, SDP 1981-83). Contested (SDP) Stockton North 1983 and (SDP/Alliance) Milton Keynes 1987 general elections. Parliamentary Under-Secretary of State: Department of Economic Affairs 1964-67, Foreign Office 1967-68; Minister of State: Board of Trade 1968-69, HM Treasury 1969-70, Ministry of Defence 1974-76; Secretary of State for Transport 1976-79; Shadow Secretary of State for Defence 1979-80. *House of Lords:* Raised to the peerage as Baron Rodgers of Quarry Bank, of Kentish Town in the London Borough of Camden 1992. Liberal Democrat Spokesperson for Home Office Affairs 1994-97. Member: House of Lords' Offices 1998-2001, Liaison 1998-2001, Privileges 1998-2001, Procedure 1998-2001, Selection 1998-2001, House 2003-05, Constitution 2007-12, Standing Orders (Private Bills) 2013. *Other:* Social Democratic Party: Joint founder 1981, Vice-president 1982-87; Leader, Liberal Democrat Peers 1998-2001. *Councils and public bodies:* Borough Councillor, St Marylebone 1958-62.

Other: Leader, UK Delegation to the Council of Europe and WEU 1967-68; Honorary FRIBA; Honorary FIStructE. Honorary LLD, Liverpool University; Honorary Fellow, Liverpool John Moore University. PC 1975.

Publications: Editor, Hugh Gaitskell 1906-1963 (1964); Co-author, The People into Parliament (1966); The Politics of Change (1982); Editor, Government and Industry (1986); Fourth Among Equals (2000).

Rt Hon the Lord Rodgers of Quarry Bank, House of Lords, London SW1A 0PW
Tel: 020 7219 3607

ROGAN, LORD

ROGAN (Life Baron), Dennis Robert David Rogan; cr. 1999. Born 30 June 1942; Son of late Robert Henderson Rogan; Married Lorna Colgan 1968 (2 sons).

Education: The Wallace High School; Belfast Institute of Technology; The Open University (BA economics, politics 1976).

Non-political career: Honorary Colonel, 40 Signal Regiment. Moygashel Ltd 1960-69; William Ewart & Sons Ltd 1969-72; Lamont Holdings plc 1972-78; Managing director Dennis Rogan Assoc 1978-; Chair: Associated Processors Ltd 1985-, Events Management 2002-, Stakeholder **ULSTER UNIONIST** Group 2005-; Council member, TLFCA-NI; Member, International Advisory Board, Parker Green **PARTY** International 2008-.

Political career: *House of Lords:* Raised to the peerage as Baron Rogan, of Lower Iveagh in the County of Down 1999. Leader in the Lords, Ulster Unionist Party 2001-. *Other:* Chair: Ulster Young Unionist Council 1968-69, South Belfast Constituency Association 1992-96; Ulster Unionist Party: Chair 1996-2001, Honorary secretary 2001-04, President 2004-06, Party officer 2012-. *Councils and public bodies:* Chair, Lisburn Unit of Management Health Board 1984-85; Member, Northern Ireland Police Fund 2001-05.

Political interests: Northern Ireland, trade and industry, defence.

Other: Member: CPA (UK) 2000-, IPU (UK) 2001-; Patron, The Somme Association 1999-; Honorary Col. 40 (Ulster) Signal Regiment (Volunteers) 2008-; Friend of the Salvation Army; Army Benevolent Fund; Ulster Reform, Belfast; Army and Navy, London.

Recreations: Rugby football, oriental carpets, gardening, shooting.

The Lord Rogan, House of Lords, London SW1A 0PW
Tel: 020 7219 8625
31 Notting Hill, Malone Road, Belfast BT9 5NS *Tel:* 028 9066 2468

LABOUR

ROGERS OF RIVERSIDE, LORD

ROGERS OF RIVERSIDE (Life Baron), Richard George Rogers; cr. 1996. Born 23 July 1933; Son of Dada Geiringer and Nino Rogers; Married Su Brumwell 1961 (3 sons); married Ruth Elias, later MBE, 1973 (2 sons, 1 deceased).

Education: Kingswood House School, Epsom, Surrey; Downs Lodge, Sutton; St John's School, Leatherhead; Architectural Association (AA Dip 1959); Yale University (MArch, Fulbright, Edward D. Stone and Yale Scholar 1961-62); RIBA; French, Italian.

Non-political career: Team 4 1963-67; Richard & Su Rogers 1968-70; Piano + Rogers 1970-78; Visiting professor, Yale University and University College, London 1978; Chair, Richard Rogers Architects Ltd 1978- (Rogers Stirk Harbour + Partners from 2006); Gave the BBC Reith Lectures entitled 'Cities for a Small Planet' 1995; Masterplans for many city centres, including Shanghai, Berlin, Mallorca, Paris and London; Buildings designed include: Centre Georges Pompidou, Paris (with Renzo Piano); Lloyd's of London; European Court of Human Rights, Strasbourg; Kabuki-Cho Tower, Tokyo; Channel 4 headquarters, London; Millennium Dome, Greenwich, London; Law Courts, Bordeaux, France; Lloyd's Registry of Shipping, London; 88 Wood Street, London; Broadwick House, Soho; Waterside, Paddington Basin; Barajas Airport, Madrid; Law Courts, Antwerp, Belgium; Hotel Hesperia and Conference Centre, Barcelona, Spain; National Assembly for Wales, Cardiff; Mossbourne City Academy, London; Minami Yamashiro Secondary School, nr Kyoto, Japan; Terminal 5, Heathrow Airport, London; Oxley Woods housing, Milton Keynes; Bodegas Protos winery, Penafiel, Spain; 300 New Jersey Avenue, Washington DC, USA; Campus Palmas Altas, Seville, Spain. Current projects include: Bullring, Barcelona; 122 Leadenhall Street, London; The Berkeley Hotel, London; Tower 3 on World Trade Centre site, New York; One Hyde Park, London; British Museum, London World Conservation and Exhibitions Centre; Chifley Square, Sydney, Australia; Canary Riverside South, London; Barangaroo Masterplan, Sydney, Australia; NEO Bankside Residential, London; Millers Point, Sydney, Australia. Adviser to the Mayor, Barcelona Urban Strategies Council; Greater London Authority: Mayor's Chief Adviser on Architecture and Urbanism 2000-08; Member, Mayor of London's Advisory Cabinet 2008-09; UK Business Ambassador 2008-.

Political career: *House of Lords:* Raised to the peerage as Baron Rogers of Riverside, of Chelsea in the Royal Borough of Kensington and Chelsea 1996. *Councils and public bodies:* Vice-chair, Arts Council of England 1994-96.

Political interests: Sustainable built environment, arts, New York City; Brazil, Italy, Mexico, UK.

Other: Member, Barcelona Urban Strategy Council; Director, River Cafe; Member, United Nations Architects' Committee; Patron, Society of Black Architects; Trustee, Doctors of the World, UK Board; Membre de l'Acadamie d'Architecture 1983; Member, RIBA Council and Policy Committees 1984-87; Chair, Board of Trustees, Tate Gallery 1984-88; Honorary member, Bund Deutscher Architekten 1989; President, National Communities Resource Centre 1991-; Chair, Architecture Foundation 1991-2001; Honorary Trustee, MOMA; Chair, Urban Task Force 1997-99; United Nations World Commissions on 21st Century Urbanisations; Member, Royal Institute of British Architects; Honorary Fellow: Royal Academy of Art, The Hague, American Institute of Architects 1983; Royal Academian, Royal Academy of London 1984; Honorary Fellow, Tokyo Society of Architects and Building Engineers 1996; Fellow, Royal Society for the Arts 1996; Academician, International Academy of Architecture; Fellow: The Royal Academy of Engineering 2005, University of Wales Institute, Wales 2007; Patron: Maggie's Centres, Reprieve; Trustee, Doctors of the World. Honorary degrees from British, Chinese, Czech and Spanish universities. International Union of Architects August Perret Prize for most outstanding international work (Centre Pompidon) 1975-78; Royal Gold Medal for Architecture 1985; American Academy and Institute of Arts and Letters, Arnold W Brunner Memorial Prize 1989; Friend of Barcelona 1997; Thomas Jefferson Memorial Foundation Medal in Architecture 1999; Japan Art Association Praemium Imperiale Award for Architecture 2000; Golden Lion for Lifetime Achievement 2006; Pritzker Architecture Prize Laureate 2007. Kt 1991; Chevalier l'Ordre National de la Légion d'Honneur (France) 1986; Officier de l'Ordre des Arts et des Lettres (France) 1995; CH 2008.

Publications: Richard Rogers + Architects (1985); A + U: Richard Rogers 1978-88 (1988); Architecture: A Modern View (1990); (jointly) A New London (1992); Richard Rogers (1995); Cities for a Small Planet (1997); Towards an Urban Renaissance (Urban Task Force, 1999); Richard Rogers, Complete Works, Vol 1 (1999); Paying for an Urban Renaissance (2000); Co-author Cities for a Small Country (2000); Richard Rogers, Complete Works, Vol 2 (2001); Delivering an Urban Renaissance (2002); Towards a Strong Urban Renaissance (2005); Richard Rogers, Architecture of the Future (2005); Richard Rogers, Complete Works, Vol 3 (2006); Richard Rogers + Architects, From the House to the City (2010).

Recreations: Friends, food, art, architecture, travel.

The Lord Rogers of Riverside CH, House of Lords, London SW1A 0PW
Tel: 020 7219 5353
Rogers Stirk Harbour and Partners, Thames Wharf, Rainville Road, London W6 9HA
Tel: 020 7746 0408/020 7746 0411 *Fax:* 020 7385 8409 *Email:* enquiries@rsh-p.com
Website: www.rsh-p.com

ROOKER, LORD

ROOKER (Life Baron), Jeffrey William Rooker; cr. 2001. Born 5 June 1941; Son of late William Rooker and Mary Rooker; Married Angela Edwards 1972 (died 2003); married Helen Hughes 2010.
Education: Aldridge Road Secondary Modern; Handsworth Technical School; Handsworth Technical College 1957-60; Aston University (BSc production engineering 1964); Warwick University (MA industrial relations 1972).
Non-political career: Apprentice toolmaker, Kings and Heath Engineering Company 1957-63; Manager, Geo Salter & Co 1964-67; Production manager, Rola Celestion Ltd 1967-70; Lecturer, Lanchester Polytechnic, Coventry 1972-74. Member, Community 2010.

LABOUR

Political career: *House of Commons:* MP (Labour) for Birmingham Perry Barr February 1974-2001. PPS to Peter Archer as Solicitor General 1974-77; Opposition Frontbench Spokesperson for: Social Services 1979-80, Social Security 1980-83, Treasury and Economic Affairs 1983-84, Environment 1984-88, Community Care and Social Services 1990-92, Education 1992-93; Shadow Deputy Leader of the House of Commons 1994-97; Minister of State and Deputy Minister, Ministry of Agriculture, Fisheries and Food (Minister for Food Safety) 1997-99; Minister of State, Department of Social Security 1999-2001. *House of Lords:* Raised to the peerage as Baron Rooker, of Perry Barr in the County of West Midlands 2001. Minister of State and Government Spokesperson for: Home Office 2001-02, Office of the Deputy Prime Minister 2002-05; Minister of State, Northern Ireland Office 2005-06; Government Spokesperson for Northern Ireland 2005-08; Deputy Leader of the Lords 2005-08; Minister of State and Government Spokesperson, Department for Environment, Food and Rural Affairs 2006-08. Member: Procedure 2005-07, Barnett Formula 2008-09, Joint Committee on the Draft House of Lords Reform Bill 2011-12; Chair Joint Committee on the Draft Deregulation Bill 2013-. *Councils and public bodies:* Birmingham Education Committee 1972-74; Council member, Institution of Production Engineers 1975-80; Lay Member of Council, Aston University 2008-10; Chair, Food Standards Agency 2009-13.
Political interests: Food, agriculture, planning, constitutional affairs, science and technology, housing, energy, fairness; New Zealand, Sweden.
Other: Trustee, National Benevolent Society for Aged; Chair: British Motorsport Training Trust 2011-, Castle Vale Partnership Board; Fellow, Institution Engineering and Technology; Member, Institute of Management. DSc, Aston University 2001; DUniv, University of Central England 2002. Minister of the Year, *House Magazine* awards 2004; Peer of Year, Channel 4 2007; Lords Minister of the Year, *House Magazine* awards 2008. PC 1999.
Recreations: Walking, reading, motorsport (spectator).
Rt Hon the Lord Rooker, House of Lords, London SW1A 0PW
Tel: 020 7219 6469 *Email:* rookerj@parliament.uk

ROPER, LORD

ROPER (Life Baron), John Francis Hodgess Roper; cr. 2000. Born 10 September 1935; Son of late Rev. Frederick Mabor Hodgess Roper and late Ellen Frances Roper; Married Valerie Hope Edwards 1959 (died 2003) (1 daughter).
Education: William Hulme's Grammar School, Manchester; Reading School; Magdalen College, Oxford (BA philosophy, politics and economics 1959); University of Chicago (economics).
Non-political career: Commissioned RNVR (National Service) 1954-56. Harkness Fellow, Commonwealth Fund 1959-61; Manchester University 1961-70: Research fellow in economic statistics 1961, Assistant lecturer in economics 1962-64, Lecturer 1964-70, Faculty tutor 1968-70; Director: CWS 1969-74, Co-op Insurance Society 1973-74; RIIA: Editor, *International Affairs* 1983-88, Head of International Security Programme 1985-88, 1989-90, Head of WEU Institute for Security Studies, Paris 1990-95; Visiting Professor, College of Europe, Bruges 1997-2001.

LIBERAL DEMOCRAT

Political career: *House of Commons:* Contested (Labour) High Peak, Derbyshire 1964 general election. MP (Lab/Co-op 1970-81, SDP 1981-83) for Farnworth 1970-83. Contested (SDP) Worsley 1983 general election. PPS to Minister of State, Department of Industry 1978-79; Opposition Spokesperson for Defence 1979-81. *House of Lords:* Raised to the peerage as Baron Roper, of Thorney Island in the City of Westminster 2000. Liberal Democrat Chief Whip 2001-05; Deputy Speaker 2008-; Principal Deputy Chairman of Committees 2008-12. EU Sub-committee C (Common Foreign and Security Policy/Foreign Affairs, Defence and Development Policy): Member 2000-08, Chair 2006-08; Member: Procedure 2000-05, 2013- House of Lords' Offices 2001-02,

House of Lords' Offices Administration and Works Sub-committee 2001-05, Liaison 2001-02, Privileges 2003-05, Selection -2005, EU Sub-committee B (Internal Market) 2005-06; European Union: Member 2006-08, Chair 2008, 2011-12; Member Administration and Works 2012-. *Other:* Honorary Treasurer, Fabian Society 1976-81; Chair, Labour Committee for Europe 1976-80.

Other: Council of Europe: Consultant 1965-6, Member, Consultative Assembly 1973-80, Chair, Committee on Culture and Education 1979-80; President, General Council, UNA 1972-78; Member, Western European Union Assembly 1973-80: Chair, Committee on Defence Questions and Armaments 1977-80; Vice-President, Manchester Statistical Society 1971-; Trustee, History of Parliament Trust 1974-84; Council member, Institute for Fiscal Studies 1975-90. PC 2005; Légion d'Honneur (France) 2005; Oxford and Cambridge University.

Publications: Towards Regional Co-operatives (1967); The Teaching of Economics at University Level (1970); The Future of British Defence Policy (1985); Editor (with others) of publications on European Defence.

Rt Hon the Lord Roper, House of Lords, London SW1A 0PW
Tel: 020 7219 8663 *Fax:* 020 7219 0860 *Email:* roperj@parliament.uk

LABOUR

ROSSER, LORD

Opposition Spokesperson for Home Office, for Defence and for Transport

ROSSER (Life Baron), Richard Andrew Rosser; cr. 2004. Born 5 October 1944; Son of Gordon Rosser and Kathleen Rosser, née Moon; Married Sheena Denoon 1973 (2 sons 1 daughter).

Education: St Nicholas Grammar School for Boys, Northwood; University of London (BSc(Econ) economics 1970).

Non-political career: London Transport: Clerk 1962-65, PA to operating manager (railways) 1965-66, Transport Salaried Staffs' Association: Research officer 1966-76, Finance and organising officer 1976-77, London Midland regional division secretary 1977-82, Assistant general secretary 1982-89, General secretary 1989-2004; Non-executive director, Correctional Services Board/National Offender Management Service Board 2000-09; Chair, Prison Service/National Offender Management Service Audit Committee 2003-09. Transport Salaried Staffs' Association (TSSA) 1963-; GMB 1966-; Member, TUC general council 2000-04.

Political career: *House of Commons:* Contested (Labour) Croydon Central 1974 general election. *House of Lords:* Raised to the peerage as Baron Rosser, of Ickenham in the London Borough of Hillingdon 2004. Opposition Whip 2010-11; Opposition Spokesperson for: Home Office 2011-, Defence 2011-, Transport 2011-. Member Procedure 2005-09; Co-opted member EU Sub-committee E (Law and Institutions) 2007-10; Merits of Statutory Instruments: Member 2008-10, Chair 2009-10. Vice-chair PLP Departmental Committee for Work and Pensions 2006-10. *Other:* Member, Labour Party NEC 1988-98; Chair, Labour Party 1997-98. *Councils and public bodies:* London Borough of Hillingdon: Councillor 1971-78, Chair, Labour Group 1975-78; Justice of the Peace 1978.

Political interests: Transport, employment, criminal justice system, treatment of offenders; Taiwan.

Other: Honorary Vice-president, Ryman Isthmian Football League 2008-; Vice-president, National Association of Disabled Supporters (Football) 2009-; Trustee, White Rose Children's Charity; Chartered member, Institute of Logistics and Transport (formerly Institute of Transport) 1967.

Recreations: Walking, reading, going to non-league football matches.

The Lord Rosser, House of Lords, London SW1A 0PW
Tel: 020 7219 4589 *Email:* rosserr@parliament.uk

CROSSBENCH

ROSSLYN, EARL OF

ROSSLYN (7th Earl of, UK), Peter St Clair-Erskine; cr. 1801; 7th Baron Loughborough (GB) 1795; 11th Bt of Alva (NS) 1666. Born 31 March 1958; Son of 6th Earl; Married Helen Watters 1982 (2 sons 2 daughters).

Education: Eton College; Bristol University (BA Hispanic and Latin American studies 1980); Cambridge University (MSt applied criminology 2002).

Non-political career: Metropolitan Police 1980-94; Thames Valley Police 1994-2000; Commander, Metropolitan Police 2000-: Royalty and diplomatic protection department 2003-.

Political career: *House of Lords:* First entered House of Lords 1979; Elected hereditary peer 1999-.

Other: Member, Queen's Body Guard for Scotland, Royal Company of Archers; Trustee, Dunimarle Museum; Chair of Governors, Ludgrove School. Queen's Police Medal 2009; White's.

The Earl of Rosslyn QPM, House of Lords, London SW1A 0PW
Tel: 020 7219 5353

CONSERVATIVE

ROTHERWICK, LORD

ROTHERWICK (3rd Baron, UK), (Herbert) Robin Cayzer; cr. 1939; 6th Bt of Gartmore (UK) 1904; 3rd Bt of Tylney (UK) 1924. Born 12 March 1954; Son of 2nd Baron; Married Sara Jane McAlpine 1982 (divorced 1994) (2 sons 1 daughter); married Tania Fox 2000 (1 son 1 daughter).

Education: Harrow School; RMA, Sandhurst; Royal Agricultural College, Cirencester (Diploma agriculture 1982).

Non-political career: Acting Captain, The Life Guards 1973-76; Household Cavalry, Territorial 1977-83; Member, Armed Forces Parliamentary Scheme 2010-12. Barings Bank 1976-78; Bristol Helicopters 1978-80; Farming and estate management 1982-.

Political career: *House of Lords:* First entered House of Lords 1996; Elected hereditary peer 1999-; Opposition Whip 2001-05; Opposition Spokesperson for: Education and Skills, Work and Pensions 2001-03, Environment, Food and Rural Affairs 2003-05, Transport 2004-05.

Political interests: Defence, aviation, agriculture.

Other: Member: Council of Europe (COE) 2000-01, Western European Union 2000-01; Vice-chair, Popular Flying Association 1999-2001; President, General Aviation Awareness Council; Board director, Cayzer Continuation PCC Ltd 2004-; Fellow, Industry and Parliamentary Trust 2005; Non-executive chair, Air Touring Ltd 2006-11; Director: Light Aviation Association, Cornbury Estates Company Limited, Cornbury Maintenance Company Limited. Succeeded his kinsman as 6th Bt of Gartmore 2012; White's.

Recreations: Flying, Conservation.

The Lord Rotherwick, House of Lords, London SW1A 0PW
Tel: 020 7219 0660
Cornbury Park, Charlbury, Oxfordshire OX7 3EH *Tel:* 01608 811276 *Fax:* 01608 811252
Email: r@cpark.co.uk

CROSSBENCH

ROWE-BEDDOE, LORD

ROWE-BEDDOE (Life Baron), David Sydney Rowe-Beddoe; cr 2006. Born 19 December 1937; Son of late Sydney and Dolan Rowe-Beddoe, née Evans; Married Malinda Collison 1962 (divorced 1982) (3 daughters); married Madeleine Harrison 1984.

Education: Cathedral School, Llandaff; Stowe School, Buckinghamshire; St John's College, Cambridge (BA economics/law 1961); Graduate School of Business Administration, Harvard University (PMD 1974).

Non-political career: Royal Navy national service 1956-58; Royal Naval Reserve 1958-66. Thomas De la Rue & Co 1961-76: Chief executive 1971-76, Executive director, De la Rue plc 1974-76; President, Revlon Inc 1976-81: Latin America and Caribbean 1976-77, Europe, Middle East and Africa 1977-81; President: GFTA Trendanalysen 1981-87, Morgan Stanley-GFTA Ltd 1983-91; Consultant, Cavendish Services Ltd 1987-93; Chair, EHC International Ltd 2001-; Deputy chair, Toye & Company plc 2002-; Director, Newport Networks Group plc 2004-09; Chair, GFTA – The Euro/Dollar Technology Co. Ltd 2005-.

Political career: *House of Lords:* Raised to the peerage as Baron Rowe-Beddoe, of Kilgetty in the County of Dyfed 2006. Co-opted member EU Sub-committee B (Internal Market) 2007-10; Member: Barnett Formula 2008-09, Administration and Works 2009-, EU Sub-committee B (Internal Market, Energy and Transport) 2010-12, Economic Affairs 2012-, Sub-committee on Economic Affairs Finance Bill 2012-. *Councils and public bodies:* Chairman: Welsh Development Agency 1993-2001, Development Board for Rural Wales 1994-98; Wales Millennium Centre: Chairman 2001-10, Life President 2010-; Chairman, Representative Body of the Church in Wales 2002-; Member, Governing Body, Church in Wales 2002-; DL, Gwent 2003; President, Royal Welsh College of Music and Drama 2004-; Deputy Chairman, UK Statistics Authority 2008-.

Political interests: Arts and heritage, management, university, armed forces, faith and society; Argentina, Brazil, Central America, Latin America, Mexico, North Korea, United Arab Emirates.

Other: Commonwealth Parliamentary Association; President, British-Australia Society (Wales Branch). Pro-chancellor, University of Glamorgan. Two honorary doctorates: Fellow: University of Wales, Cardiff University, Aberystwyth University, Newport University. Kt 2000; Order of the Rising Sun, Gold Rays with Neck Ribbon (Japan) 2008; The Garrick, Cardiff and County, The Brook (New York).

Recreations: Music, theatre, country pursuits.

The Lord Rowe-Beddoe DL, House of Lords, London SW1A 0PW
Tel: 020 7219 5353
Wales Millennium Centre, Bute Place, Cardiff CF10 5AL *Website:* www.wmc.org.uk

ROWLANDS, LORD

LABOUR

ROWLANDS (Life Baron), Edward (Ted) Rowlands; cr. 2004. Born 23 January 1940; Son of William Samuel Rowlands, Clerk of Works; Married Janice Williams 1968 (died 2004) (2 sons 1 daughter).

Education: Rhondda Grammar School; Wirral Grammar, Cheshire; King's College, London (BA history 1962).

Non-political career: Research student 1962; Research assistant, History of Parliament Trust 1963-65; Lecturer: Modern history and government, Welsh College of Advanced Technology 1965-66, Law Department, London School of Economics 1972-74. Member: Association of University Teachers 1965-72, ASTMS 1972-2001.

Political career: *House of Commons:* MP (Labour) for Cardiff North 1966-70, for Merthyr Tydfil 13 April 1972 by-election to 1983, for Merthyr Tydfil and Rhymney 1983-2001. Parliamentary Under-Secretary of State (PUS), Welsh Office 1969-70, 1974-75; Foreign and Commonwealth Office 1975-79: PUS 1975-76, Minister of State 1976-79; Opposition Frontbench Spokesperson for: Foreign and Commonwealth Affairs 1979-80, Energy 1981-87. Member: Foreign Affairs 1987-2001; Former chair: Quadripartite Committee. *House of Lords:* Raised to the peerage as Baron Rowlands, of Merthyr Tydfil and Rhymney in the county of Mid Glamorgan 2004. Member: Constitution 2005-09, EU Sub-committee E: (Justice and Institutions) 2010-12, (Justice, Institutions and Consumer Protection) 2012-. *Councils and public bodies:* Member, Richard Commission 2003-04.

Political interests: International energy, constitution; South Africa, Botswana, former Soviet Eastern Europe.

Other: Fellow, Industry and Parliament Trust 1982; Judge, Booker McConnel Novel of the Year Competition 1984; Council member, Winston Churchill Memorial Trust 1989-2010; History of Parliamentary Trust: Chair 1993-2001, Trustee; President, National Training Federation for Wales; WaterAid. Honorary degree, Glamorgan University. CBE 2003.

Publications: 'Something Must be Done' South Wales v Whitehall 1921-1951 (TTC books); Robert Harley and the Battle for Power in Radnorshire 1690-1693 (Welsh History Review, 1990); A Golden Age – Peer Power in the Early Eighteenth Century (TTC Books, 2008).

Recreations: Gardening, golf.

The Lord Rowlands CBE, House of Lords, London SW1A 0PW
Tel: 020 7219 3842

ROYALL OF BLAISDON, BARONESS

Shadow Leader of the House of Lords

LABOUR

ROYALL OF BLAISDON (Life Baroness), Janet Anne Royall; cr. 2004. Born 20 August 1955; Daughter of Basil and Myra Royall; Married Stuart Hercock 1980 (died 2010) (1 daughter 2 sons).

Education: Royal Forest of Dean Grammar School; Westfield College, London University (BA Spanish and French 1977); French, Spanish, some Italian.

Non-political career: Continental Farms (Europe) Ltd 1978; Secretary-General, British Labour Group European Parliament 1979-85 Policy adviser/PA to Neil Kinnock as Leader of the Opposition 1986-92; Researcher/Press officer to Neil Kinnock as MP 1992-95; Member, Cabinet of Neil Kinnock as: European Commissioner for Transport 1995-99, Vice-president of the Commission 1999-2001; Parliamentary co-ordinator, European Commission Press and communications directorate-general 2001-03; Head of European Commission Office in Wales 2003-04. USDAW.

Political career: *House of Lords:* Raised to the peerage as Baroness Royall of Blaisdon, of Blaisdon in the County of Gloucestershire 2004. Government Spokesperson for: Health 2005-08, International Development 2005-08, Foreign and Commonwealth Office 2005-08; Government Whip 2005-08; Chief Whip 2008; Leader of the House of Lords 2008-10; Lord President of the Council 2008-09; Government Spokesperson for: Equality 2008-10, Northern Ireland 2008-10, Cabinet Office 2009-10; Chancellor of the Duchy of Lancaster 2009-10; Shadow Leader of the House of Lords 2010-; Opposition Spokesperson for: Cabinet Office 2010-12, Education 2010, Northern Ireland 2010-11, Work and Pensions 2010, Equalities Office 2010-12, International Development 2012-13. Member: Merits of Statutory Instruments 2005, Administration and Works 2008, Privileges/Privileges and Conduct 2008-, Procedure 2008-, Liaison 2008-, House 2008-, Selection 2008-.

Political interests: Foreign policy, development, carers, democratic engagement, penal affairs, youth policies; Central and Latin America, Australia, Balkans, European Union, India, New Zealand, South Africa, USA.

Other: Vice-president, Party of European Socialists 2012-; Former Patron, Kidney Wales Foundation; Former President, Autism Cymru; Former Trustee: IPPR, National Botanic Garden of Wales, Generation Europe. PC 2008.

Recreations: Reading, travel, gardening, swimming.

Rt Hon the Baroness Royall of Blaisdon, House of Lords, London SW1A 0PW
Tel: 020 7219 6370 *Email:* royallj@parliament.uk *Twitter:* @LabourRoyall

RYDER OF WENSUM, LORD

RYDER OF WENSUM (Life Baron), Richard Ryder; cr. 1997. Born 4 February 1949; Son of Stephen Ryder, JP, DL, farmer; Married Caroline Stephens (later CVO MBE) 1981 (1 daughter 1 son deceased).

Education: Radley College; Magdalene College, Cambridge (BA history 1971).

Non-political career: Former journalist; Director of family business in Suffolk; Political Secretary to Margaret Thatcher as Leader of the Opposition and Prime Minister 1975-81; Founding chair, Eastern Counties Radio 1997-2001; Vice-chairman and acting chairman, BBC 2002-04;

CONSERVATIVE Chair: Institute of Cancer Research 2005-13, UCanDolt 2011-, Child Bereavement UK 2013-.

Political career: *House of Commons:* Contested Gateshead East February and October 1974 general elections. MP (Conservative) for Norfolk Mid 1983-97. PPS to: John Moore as Financial Secretary to the Treasury 1984, Geoffrey Howe as Foreign Secretary 1984-86; Government Whip 1986-88; Parliamentary Secretary, Ministry of Agriculture, Fisheries and Food 1988-89; HM Treasury: Economic Secretary 1989-90, Paymaster General July-November 1990; Government Chief Whip 1990-95. *House of Lords:* Raised to the peerage as Baron Ryder of Wensum, of Wensum in the County of Norfolk 1997. Co-opted member EU Sub-committee B (Internal Market) 2008-10; Member EU Sub-committee B (Internal Market, Energy and Transport) 2010-12. *Other:* Chairman, Conservative Foreign and Commonwealth Council 1984-89. *Councils and public bodies:* BBC Governors: Vice-chair 2002-04, Acting chair 2004-05.

Other: OBE 1981; PC 1990.

Rt Hon the Lord Ryder of Wensum OBE, House of Lords, London SW1A 0PW
Tel: 020 7219 5353

SAATCHI, LORD

SAATCHI (Life Baron), Maurice Saatchi; cr. 1996. Born 21 June 1946; Son of Nathan and Daisy Saatchi; Married Josephine Hart 1984 (died 2011) (1 son 1 stepson).

Education: Tollington Grammar School, Muswell Hill, London; London School of Economics (BSc economics 1967); French.

Non-political career: Co-founder, Saatchi & Saatchi 1970; Partner, M & C Saatchi 1995-.

Political career: *House of Lords:* Raised to the peerage as Baron Saatchi, of Staplefield in the County of West Sussex 1996. Opposition Spokesperson for: Treasury 1999-2003, Cabinet Office

CONSERVATIVE 2001-03. *Other:* Co-chair, Conservative Party 2003-05. *Councils and public bodies:* Governor, London School of Economics 1985-.

Countries of interest: UK.

Other: Director, Museum of Garden History; Centre for Policy Studies: Director 1999-, Chair 2009-.

Publications: The War of Independence (1999); Happiness Can't Buy Money (1999); The Bad Samaritan (2000); The Science of Politics (2001); Poor People! Stop Paying Tax! (2001); If this is Conservatism, I am a Conservative (2005); In Praise of Ideology (2007); Enemy of the People (2008); The Myth of Inflation Targeting (2009).

The Lord Saatchi, House of Lords, London SW1A 0PW
Tel: 020 7219 6401
M & C Saatchi plc, 36 Golden Square, London W1F 9EE *Tel:* 020 7543 4510 *Fax:* 020 7543 4502
Email: maurices@mcsaatchi.com

Need additional copies?
Call 020 7593 5679
Visit www.dodsshop.co.uk

SACKS, LORD

SACKS (Life Baron), Jonathan Henry Sacks; cr 2009. Born 8 March 1948; Son of late Louis David Sacks; Married Elaine Taylor 1970 (1 son 2 daughters).

Education: Christ's College, Finchley; Gonville and Caius College, Cambridge (BA 1972, MA); New College, Oxford; London University (PhD 1981); Jews' College, London (rabbinical ordination 1976); Yeshivat Etz Hayyim, London.

CROSSBENCH

Non-political career: Moral philosophy lecturer, Middlesex Polytechnic 1971-73; Jews' College, London 1973-90: Jewish philosophy lecturer 1973-76, Talmud and philosophy lecturer 1976-82, First Chief Rabbi Sir Immanuel Jakobovits professor of modern Jewish thought 1982-, Director, rabbinic faculty 1983-90, Principal 1984-90; Rabbi: Golders Green Synagogue 1978-82, Marble Arch Synagogue 1983-90; Chief Rabbi, United Hebrew Congregations of the Commonwealth 1991-2013.

Political career: *House of Lords:* Raised to the peerage as Baron Sacks, of Aldgate in the City of London 2009. *Councils and public bodies:* Member, Central Advisory Committee, BBC and Independent Broadcasting Authority 1987-90.

Other: Nine honorary doctorates from UK, Israeli and US universities. Jerusalem Prize 1995. Kt 2005.

Publications: Numerous religious and philosophical works. Latest publications: The Home We Build Together: Recreating Society (Continuum, 2007); The Great Partnership: God, Science and the Search for Meaning (Hodder and Stoughton, 2011).

Chief Rabbi the Lord Sacks, House of Lords, London SW1A 0PW

Tel: 020 7219 5353

Office of the Chief Rabbi, 305 Ballards Lane, London N12 8GB *Tel:* 020 8343 6301
Fax: 020 8343 6310 *Email:* info@chiefrabbi.org *Website:* www.chiefrabbi.org
Twitter: @chiefrabb

SAINSBURY OF PRESTON CANDOVER, LORD

SAINSBURY OF PRESTON CANDOVER (Life Baron), John Davan Sainsbury; cr. 1989. Born 2 November 1927; Son of late Lord Sainsbury (Life Peer); Married Anya Eltenton 1963 (2 sons 1 daughter).

Education: Stowe School, Buckinghamshire; Worcester College, Oxford (BA history).

Non-political career: Served Life Guards 1945-48. Joined J. Sainsbury in buying departments 1950: Director 1958-92, Vice-chair 1967-69, Chair and chief executive 1969-92, President 1992-; Director, *The Economist* 1972-80.

NON-AFFILIATED

Political career: *House of Lords:* Raised to the peerage as Baron Sainsbury of Preston Candover, of Preston Candover in the County of Hampshire 1989. On leave of absence 2010-. Member Joint Parliamentary Scrutiny Committee on Draft Charities Bill 2004-05. *Councils and public bodies:* Member, National Committee for Electoral Reform 1976-85.

Political interests: Commerce, arts.

Other: Governor, Royal Ballet School 1965-76, 1987-91; Contemporary Arts Society: Honorary secretary 1965-71, Vice-chair 1971-74, Vice-President 1984-96, Vice-Patron 1998-2006; Royal Opera House, Covent Garden: Director 1969-85, Chair 1987-91, Vice-President 2009-; Chair, Council of Friends of Covent Garden 1969-81; Joint Honorary Treasurer, European Movement 1972-75; Director, Royal Opera House Trust 1974-84, 1987-97; Trustee: National Gallery 1976-83, Westminster Abbey Trust 1977-83; President's Committee, CBI 1982-84; Trustee: Tate Gallery 1982-83, Rhodes Trust 1984-98; Honorary Bencher, Inner Temple 1985; Chair, Benesh Institute of Choreology 1986-87; Royal Ballet: Governor 1987-2003, Chair of governors 1995-2003; President, Sparsholt College, Hampshire 1993-2000; Dulwich Picture Gallery: Chair of trustees 1994-2000, Patron 2004-; Director, Friends of the Nelson Mandela Children's Fund 1996-2000; Chair of trustees, Royal Opera House Endowment Fund 2001-05; Rambert School, chairman: Development committee 2002-03, Steering committee 2005-09; Visitor, Ashmolean Museum 2003-; Trustee, Said Business School Foundation 2003; Director, Rambert School of Ballet and Contemporary Dance 2003-05; Patron, Sir Harold Hillier Gardens and Arboretum 2005-; Chairman, Rambert School Trust 2005-10; Director, Centre for Policy Studies 2009-; British Retail Consortium: Council member 1975-79, President 1993-97; Fellow, Institute of Grocery Distribution 1973-; Honorary FRIBA 1993. Honorary Fellow, Worcester College, Oxford 1982; Honorary DSc, Economics (London) 1985; Honorary DLitt, South Bank University 1992; Honorary LLD, Bristol University 1993; Honorary D.EconSc, Cape Town 2000; Honorary Fellow, British School at Rome 2002. Albert Medal, Royal Society of Arts 1989; Hadrian Award 2000; Prince of Wales Medal for Arts Philanthropy 2008; Sheldon Medal, Oxford University 2010. Kt 1980; KG 1992; Garrick, Beefsteak.

The Lord Sainsbury of Preston Candover KG, House of Lords, London SW1A 0PW
Tel: 020 7219 5353

LABOUR

SAINSBURY OF TURVILLE, LORD

SAINSBURY OF TURVILLE (Life Baron), David John Sainsbury; cr 1997. Born 24 October 1940; Son of late Sir Robert and Lady Lisa Sainsbury; Married Susan Reid 1973 (3 daughters).

Education: Eton College; King's College, Cambridge (BA history and psychology 1963); Columbia University, New York (MBA 1971).

Non-political career: Joined J. Sainsbury plc 1963: Finance director 1973-90, Deputy chair 1988-92, Chief executive 1992-97, Chair 1992-98; Visiting Fellow, Nuffield College, Oxford 1987-95.

Political career: *House of Lords:* Raised to the peerage as Baron Sainsbury of Turville, of Turville in the County of Buckinghamshire 1997. Parliamentary Under-Secretary of State and Government Spokesperson, Department of Trade and Industry (Minister for Science and Innovation) 1998-2006; On leave of absence July 2013-. *Other:* Trustee, Social Democratic Party 1982-90. *Councils and public bodies:* Member, Committee of Review of Post Office (Carter Committee) 1975-77; London Business School: Member, governing body 1985-, Chair 1991-98.

Political interests: Science and innovation, policy, industry and education; Africa, China, India, USA.

Other: Settlor Gatsby Charitable Foundation; Chair, Institute for Government 2009-; Gatsby Charitable Foundation. Chancellor, Cambridge University 2011-. Honorary doctorate from Universities of Cambridge, Oxford and Manchester, and Imperial College; Honorary Fellowship, London Business School 1990; Honorary FREng 1994; Honorary FRS 2008; Honorary Fellow, Academy of Medical Sciences 2008. Andrew Carnegie Medal of Philanthropy (on behalf of Sainsbury Family) 2003.

Publications: Government and Industry: a new partnership (1981); Co-author, Wealth Creation and Jobs (1987); The Race to the Top – report for the Government on its science and innovation policies (2007).

The Lord Sainsbury of Turville, House of Lords, London SW1A 0PW
Tel: 020 7219 5353

CROSSBENCH

ST JOHN OF BLETSO, LORD

ST JOHN OF BLETSO (21st Baron, E), Anthony Tudor St John; cr. 1558; 18th Bt of Bletso (E) 1660. Born 16 May 1957; Son of 20th Baron, TD; Married Dr Helen Jane Westlake 1994 (divorced 2012) (2 sons 2 daughters).

Education: Diocesan College, Cape Town, South Africa; University of Cape Town (BSocSc 1977; BA law 1979; BProc law 1982); London University (LLM 1983); Afrikaans, German, Xhosa.

Non-political career: Solicitor; Financial Consultant; Attorney in South Africa 1983-85; Oil Analyst/Stockbroker, County Natwest 1985-88; Consultant to Merrill Lynch 1988-2008; Chair, Estate and General 1993-2012; Managing director, Globix 1997-2002; Non-executive director: WMRC plc 2000-02, Regal Petroleum 2003-09; Strategic Adviser, 2e2 Group 2003-; Non-executive chairman: Spiritel plc 2004-10, Equest Balkan Properties 2004-08; Non-executive director, Albion Enterprise VCT 2007-; Member, Advisory Board, Infinity SDC 2007-10; Director, Sharp Interpak 2008-10; Adviser, Chayton Capital Africa Agricultural Fund 2009-12; Non-executive director: Obtala Resources plc 2009-, Carbon Desk plc 2009-2011;.

Political career: *House of Lords:* First entered House of Lords 1978; Extra Lord in Waiting to HM The Queen 1998-; Elected hereditary peer 1999-. Member: European Communities/Union Sub-committee A (Economic and Financial Affairs, Trade and External Relations) 1997-2003, Library and Computers Sub-committee 1998-2000, European Union Sub-committee B (Internal Market) 2003-07, Information 2008-13, Communications 2009-.

Political interests: Foreign affairs, finance, legal affairs, sport, information technology, environment; Southern Africa, Balkans, China.

Other: Chair: Governing Board of Certification International, Sierra Leone Business Forum; Trustee: TUSK 1997-2012, Citizens-on-Line 2000-08, TVE (Television for the Environment) 2002-12, Life Neurological Trust 2004, M'Afrika Tikkun 2006-, Alexandra Rose Charities 2008-, Christel House, Co-existence Trust, Helen Feather Memorial Trust; Unicef; Alfreds. Sunningdale Golf; Hurlingham; Royal Cape Golf.

Recreations: Skiing, golf, tennis, bridge.

The Lord St John of Bletso, House of Lords, London SW1A 0PW
Tel: 020 7219 3886 *Email:* stjohna@parliament.uk asj1957@ocra.com

NON-AFFILIATED

SALISBURY, MARQUESS OF

SALISBURY (7th Marquess, GB), Robert Michael James Gascoyne-Cecil; cr. 1789; 13th Earl of Salisbury (E) 1605; 13th Viscount Cranborne (E) 1604; 13th Baron Cecil (E) 1603; (Life) Baron Gascoyne-Cecil 1999. Born 30 September 1946; Son of 6th Marquess of Salisbury, DL and Marjorie Olein, née Wyndham-Quin; Married Hannah Ann Stirling 1970 (2 sons 3 daughters).

Education: Eton College; Christ Church, Oxford (BA history 1968).

Non-political career: Bank of California, San Francisco 1968-70; Williams & Glyn's Bank, London 1970-75; Chairman: Combined Clinical Science Foundation 2004-, Thames Diamond Jubilee Foundation 2011-.

Political career: *House of Commons:* MP (Conservative) for Dorset South 1979-87. *House of Lords:* Created a life peer as Baron Gascoyne-Cecil, of Essendon in the County of Rutland 1999. Summoned to the Upper House in his father's barony of Cecil, of Essendon in the County of Rutland, by a Writ of Acceleration 1992; First entered House of Lords 1992; Parliamentary Under-Secretary of State for Defence 1992-94; Lord Privy Seal and Leader of the House of Lords 1994-97; Member, Shadow Cabinet 1997-98: Opposition Spokesperson for the Public Service 1997-98, Leader of the Opposition 1997-98; On leave of absence 2002-. Member: Ecclesiastical Committee 2000-01, Constitution 2001-02. *Councils and public bodies:* DL: Dorset 1987-2006, Hertfordshire 2006-.

Political interests: Constitutional affairs, EU, foreign policy; Central Asia, USA, France.

Other: President British Pig Association; Co-president Anglo-French Student Alliance; Chairman of Council, Royal Veterinary College 1999-2007; President: Friends of British Library 2005-, Royal Agricultural Society of England 2008, Game and Wildlife Conservation Trust 2008-; Chairman, Friends of Lambeth Palace Library 2008-; Governor, Charterhouse School 2009-; Chairman, court of patrons, Thrombosis Research Institute 2010-. Chancellor University of Hertfordshire 2005-. Honorary degree. PC 1994; KCVO 2012; White's, Pratt's, Beefsteak.

Most Hon the Marquess of Salisbury KCVO PC DL, House of Lords, London SW1A 0PW
Tel: 020 7219 5353

CROSSBENCH

SALTOUN OF ABERNETHY, LADY

SALTOUN OF ABERNETHY (Lady, 20th in line, S), Flora Marjory Fraser; cr. 1445. Born 18 October 1930; Daughter of 19th Lord, MC; Married Captain Alexander Ramsay of Mar, DL 1956 (died 2000) (3 daughters).

Education: St Mary's School, Wantage; Cordon Bleu Diploma in Cookery 1950.

Political career: *House of Lords:* First entered House of Lords 1979; Elected hereditary peer 1999-. Member House of Lords Offices Sub-committee Advisory Panel on Works of Art 2000-02, 2005-09.

Political interests: Scottish affairs, defence, forestry, children, rural issues, fisheries.

Other: Member, Standing Council of Scottish Chiefs; Chief of the Name of Fraser; New Club, Edinburgh.

Recreations: Reading, music, needlework, cooking, gardening.

The Lady Saltoun of Abernethy, House of Lords, London SW1A 0PW
Tel: 020 7219 0313

LIBERAL DEMOCRAT

SANDBERG, LORD

SANDBERG (Life Baron), Michael Graham Ruddock Sandberg; cr. 1997. Born 31 May 1927; Son of Gerald and Ethel Sandberg; Married Carmel Donnelly 1954 (2 sons 2 daughters).

Education: St Edward's School, Oxford.

Non-political career: 6th Lancers (Indian Army) and First King's Dragoon Guards 1945. Hong Kong and Shanghai Banking Corporation 1949-86: Chair 1977-86.

Political career: *House of Lords:* Raised to the peerage as Baron Sandberg, of Passfield in the County of Hampshire 1997. On leave of absence June 2012-. Member: Personal Bills 2000-09, Hybrid Instruments 2003-11, 2011-12, 2013-.

Political interests: Foreign affairs, finance; Hong Kong, Latin America.

Other: Commonwealth Parliamentary Association; British Council Associate Parliamentary Group; Inter-Parliamentary Union British Group; Member, Executive Council, Hong Kong 1978-86; Treasurer, University of Hong Kong 1977-86; Patron, Dame Vera Lynn Trust; FCIB; FRSA 1983. Member of the Court, Clockmakers' Company. Freeman, City of London. Two honorary doctorates. OBE 1977; CBE 1982; Kt 1986; White's. President, Surrey County Cricket Club 1988; Member MCCC; Patron Liphook and Ripsley Cricket Club.

Publications: The Sandberg Watch Collection (1998).

Recreations: Horse racing, cricket, horology.

The Lord Sandberg CBE, House of Lords, London SW1A 0PW
Tel: 020 7219 5353

CONSERVATIVE

SANDERSON OF BOWDEN, LORD

SANDERSON OF BOWDEN (Life Baron), (Charles) Russell Sanderson; cr. 1985. Born 30 April 1933; Son of late Charles Plummer Sanderson; Married Elizabeth Macaulay 1958 (1 son 2 daughters and 1 son deceased).

Education: St Mary's School, Melrose; Glenalmond College, Perthshire; Bradford Technical College (textile design and management); Scottish College of Textiles, Galashiels (HND design 1955); French.

Non-political career: Army national service 1951-53: Commissioned Royal Signals 1952; King's Own Scottish Borderers: Commissioned 1955-58, Trustee 2000-11. Partner, Charles P. Sanderson wool and yarn merchants 1958-87; Director: Johnston of Elgin 1980-87, Illingworth Morris 1982-87; Chair: Edinburgh Financial Trust plc 1983-87, Shires Investment plc 1983-87; Clydesdale Bank plc: Director 1986-2004, Chair 1999-2004; Hawick Cashmere Co.: Chair 1991-2013, Director 2013-; Scottish Mortgage and Trust plc: Director 1991-, Chair 1993-2003; Director: Woolcombers plc 1992-95, Edinburgh Woollen Mills 1992-97, United Auctions Ltd 1992-99, Watson-Philip plc 1993-99, Morrison Construction 1995-2001, Develica Deutschland plc 2006-09, Accsys Technologies plc 2007-.

Political career: *House of Lords:* Raised to the peerage as Baron Sanderson of Bowden, of Melrose in the District of Ettrick and Lauderdale 1985. Minister of State, Scottish Office 1987-90. *Other:* President, Scottish Conservative and Unionist Association 1977-79; Vice-President, National Union of Conservative and Unionist Associations 1979-81; Chair: National Union Executive Committee 1981-86, Scottish Conservative Party 1990-93; Honorary President, Scottish

Conservative Unionist Association 2010-; Chairman, Sanderson Commission of Scottish Conservative Party 2010. *Councils and public bodies:* Chair, Council of Glenalmond College 1994-2000; Member of Court, Napier University, Edinburgh 1994-2001; President, Royal Highland Agricultural Society of Scotland 2002-03; Roxburgh, Ettrick and Lauderdale: Deputy Lieutenant 1990-2003, Vice Lieutenant 2003-08.

Political interests: Industry, textile industry, small businesses, Scottish affairs, housing, transport; China, Hong Kong.

Other: Chair: Scottish Peers Association 1998-2000, The Abbotsford Trust 2009-; Friends of Bowden Kirk Trust Fund. Liveryman, Worshipful Company of Framework Knitters: Master 2005-06. Two honorary degrees: Glasgow University, Napier University. Kt 1981; Caledonian. Honorary Company of Edinburgh Golfers.

Recreations: Golf, fishing.

The Lord Sanderson of Bowden DL, House of Lords, London SW1A 0PW
Tel: 020 7219 5353

CROSSBENCH

SANDWICH, EARL OF

SANDWICH (11th Earl of, E), John Edward Hollister Montagu; cr. 1660; Viscount Hinchingbrooke and Baron Montagu. Born 11 April 1943; Son of Rosemary Maud Peto and Victor Montagu, 10th Earl, formerly Viscount Hinchingbrooke MP, who disclaimed the earldom and other honours for life in 1964; Married (Susan) Caroline Hayman 1968 (2 sons 1 daughter).

Education: Eton College; Trinity College, Cambridge (BA history and modern language Tripos 1965, MA); Open University (Certificate European studies 1973); French, German.

Non-political career: Assistant editor, The Bodley Head 1966-68; Editor, India Tourism Development Corporation 1968-69; Christian Aid: Information officer 1974-85, Research officer 1985-86, Board 1999-2004; Joint owner/administrator, Mapperton Estate, Dorset 1982-; Consultant, CARE Britain 1987-93; Editor, Save the Children 1990-92. Former member, National Union of Journalists.

Political career: *House of Lords:* First entered House of Lords 1995; Elected hereditary peer 1999-. Member: Standing Orders (Private Bills) 2000-01, Library and Computers Sub-committee 2001-04, Constitution 2005-07; Co-opted member EU Sub-committee E (Law and Institutions) 2009-10; Member: European Union 2010-, EU Sub-committee E: (Justice and Institutions) 2010-12, (Justice, Institutions and Consumer Protection) 2012-13, EU Sub-committee C (External Affairs) 2013-.

Political interests: Aid and development, international affairs, national heritage; Afghanistan, India, Mozambique, Nepal, South Africa, Sudan, Uganda, Zimbabwe.

Other: President, Samuel Pepys Club 1985-; Associate, Care International 1993-; Trustee, Britain-Afghanistan Trust 1994-2001; Council, Anti-Slavery International 1997-2006; Vice-President, Worldaware 1997-2001; International Development Affairs Committee, Church House 1997-2001; Patron: Trust for Africa's Orphans 2000-, Haslar Visitors 2002-; Independent Asylum Commission 2007-09; Dorset Expeditionary Society 2011-.

Publications: Author or editor: The Book of the World (1971); Prospects for Africa (1988); Prospects for Africa's Children (1990); Children at Crisis Point (1992); Co-editor, Hinch: A Celebration (1997).

Recreations: Walking, tennis, sailing, skiing.

The Earl of Sandwich, House of Lords, London SW1A 0PW
Tel: 020 7219 3882 *Email:* sandwichj@parliament.uk

CONSERVATIVE

SASSOON, LORD

SASSOON (Life Baron), James Meyer Sassoon; cr 2010. Born 11 September 1955; Son of Hugh Sassoon and Marion Sassoon, née Schiff; Married Sarah Barnes 1981 (1 son 2 daughters).

Education: Eton College; Christ Church, Oxford (BA philosophy, politics and economics 1977, MA).

Non-political career: Thomson McLintock & Co (KPMG) 1977-86; S G Warburg & Co 1987-95: Director 1991-95; Warburg Dillon Read/UBS Warburg: Managing director 1995-2002, Vice-chair, Corporate Finance 2000-02; HM Treasury (HMT) 2002-08: Managing Director, Finance Regulation and Industry Directorate 2002-06, HMT Representative for Promotion of the City 2006-08; Member: Financial Stability Forum 2002-06, EU Financial Services Committee 2003-06; President, Financial Action Task Force 2007-08; Adviser to George Osborne MP as Shadow Chancellor of the Exchequer 2008-10; Member, Economic Recovery Committee, Shadow Cabinet 2009-10; Executive director, Jardine Matheson 2013-.

Political career: *House of Lords:* Raised to the peerage as Baron Sassoon, of Ashley Park in the County of Surrey 2010. Commercial Secretary and Government Spokesperson, HM Treasury 2010-13. Member Consumer Insurance (Disclosure and Representations) Bill 2011-12.

Political interests: Trade and investment, financial services; The UK's major trading partners and inward/outward investors.

Other: Director, Partnerships UK 2002-06; Trustee, National Gallery Trust 2002-09; Merchants Trust plc: Director 2006-10, Chair 2010; Director, Nuclear Liabilities Fund 2008-10; Chair, ifs School of Finance 2009-10; Trustee, British Museum 2009-10; Chairman, China-Britain Business Council 2013-; FCA. Kt 2008.

Publications: Author, The Tripartite Review (2009).

Recreations: Travel, the arts, gardening.

The Lord Sassoon, House of Lords, London SW1A 0PW
Tel: 020 7219 5353 *Email:* sassoonjm@parliament.uk

SAVILLE OF NEWDIGATE, LORD

SAVILLE OF NEWDIGATE (Life Baron), Mark Oliver Saville; cr. 1997. Born 20 March 1936; Son of Kenneth and Olivia Saville; Married Jill Gray 1961 (2 sons).

Education: Rye Grammar School; Brasenose College, Oxford (Vinerian Scholar, BA law 1959; BCL 1960).

Non-political career: Second Lieutenant, Royal Sussex Regiment 1954-56. Called to the Bar, Middle Temple 1962, Bencher 1983; QC 1975; Judge of the High Court, Queen's Bench Division 1985-93; Lord Justice of Appeal 1994-97; Justice of the Supreme Court of the United Kingdom 2009-10.

CROSSBENCH

Political career: *House of Lords:* Raised to the peerage as Baron Saville of Newdigate, of Newdigate in the County of Surrey 1997. Lord of Appeal in Ordinary 1997-2009; As Justice of the Supreme Court, disqualified from participation 2009-10.

Other: Two honorary law doctorates. Kt 1985; PC 1994; Garrick.

Recreations: Sailing, flying, gardening, computers.

Rt Hon the Lord Saville of Newdigate, House of Lords, London SW1A 0PW
Tel: 020 7219 5353

SAWYER, LORD

SAWYER (Life Baron), Lawrence Sawyer; cr. 1998. Born 12 May 1943.

Education: Dodmire School; Eastbourne School; Darlington Technical School and College.

Non-political career: Engineering apprentice, Robert Stephenson and Hawthorne 1958-63; Engineering inspector, Lockhead Brakes, Leamington Spa 1963-65; Engineering inspection and work study officer, Cummins Engines, Darlington 1965-71; NUPE Officer 1971-75, Northern Regional Officer 1975-81, Deputy General Secretary, NUPE/Unison 1981-94; Director: Investors in People UK 1998-2005, Reed Executive plc 1998-2001; Britannia Building Society 1999-2009; Visiting Professor, Cranfield Business School 1999-2013; Notting Hill Housing Association 1999-2004; Union Income Benefit Advisory Board 2000-; Royal Mail Partnership Board 2001-08; Reed Healthcare plc 2001-04; Thompsons Solicitors Supervisory Board 2001-10; Chair, Norlife 2004-. Member, Unison: Deputy General Secretary 1982-94.

LABOUR

Political career: *House of Lords:* Raised to the peerage as Baron Sawyer, of Darlington in the County of Durham 1998. *Other:* Labour Party: Member, National Executive 1982-94, 1998-2001, Party Chair 1992; Chair, Labour Home Policy Committee 1994-98; General Secretary 1994-98.

Political interests: Housing, employment, education, Royal Mail; Americas, Europe.

Other: Member: Post Office Northern Advisory Board 1997-99, Nurses' and Midwives' Whitley Council 1997-99, NJIC for Manual Workers 1997-99. Chancellor, Teesside University 2005-; Royal Commonwealth Society, Royal Overseas League.

Recreations: Antiquarian book dealer and collector.

The Lord Sawyer, House of Lords, London SW1A 0PW
Tel: 020 7219 8668

SCOTLAND OF ASTHAL, BARONESS

SCOTLAND OF ASTHAL (Life Baroness), Patricia Janet Scotland; cr. 1997. Born 19 August 1955; Daughter of Arthur and Dellie Marie Scotland; Married Richard Mawhinney 1985 (2 sons). **Education:** Walthamstow School for Girls; London University (LLB 1976).

Non-political career: Called to the Bar, Middle Temple 1977; Founding member, later head of chambers, 1 Gray's Inn Square 1979-; QC 1991; Assistant recorder 1992; Bencher 1997; Barrister specialising in family and administrative law 1997-91; Recorder 2000; Member, Antigua Bar and Commonwealth of Dominica.

LABOUR

Political career: *House of Lords:* Raised to the peerage as Baroness Scotland of Asthal, of Asthal in the County of Oxfordshire 1997. Parliamentary Under-Secretary of State and Government Spokesperson for Foreign and Commonwealth Office 1999-2001; Parliamentary Secretary, Lord Chancellor's Department and Government Spokesperson for Law Officers' Department 2001-03; Minister of State and Government Spokesperson for Home Office 2003-07; Government Spokesperson for: Trade and Industry 2004-05, Women's Issues/Equal Agenda; Attorney General and Government Spokesperson for the Law Officers (attending cabinet) 2007-10; Shadow Attorney General 2010-11; Opposition Spokesperson for the Law Officers 2010-11; Trade envoy to South Africa 2012-. Member: Privileges and Conduct 2012-, Communications 2013-. *Councils and public bodies:* Former member, Commission for Racial Equality.

Other: Alternate UK Government Representative, European Convention 2002-; Member: Millennium Commission 1994-99, Thomas More Society, Lawyers' Christian Fellowship; Patron: Margaret Beaufort Institute, GAP; Vice-patron: CFAB, Almshouses Association. Five honorary doctorates, Universities of Westminster, Buckingham, Leicester, East London and West Indies; Honorary Fellow: Wolfson College, Cambridge, Cardiff University. Peer of the Year, *House Magazine* awards 2004; Peer of the Year, Channel 4 2004; Parliamentarian of the Year, Political Studies Association 2004; Parliamentarian of the Year, *The Spectator* 2005; Kathleen Carlin Justice Seekers award 2008; Lifetime Achievement award, Black Solicitors Network 2009; Female Personality of the Year award, GV Media Group 2009; Anti-corruption award, Doha 2009; European Women in Business Law Lifetime Achievement award, Euromoney Legal Media Group 2011. PC 2001.

Rt Hon the Baroness Scotland of Asthal QC, House of Lords, London SW1A 0PW
Tel: 020 7219 5700 *Twitter:* @PScotlandQC

SCOTT OF FOSCOTE, LORD

SCOTT OF FOSCOTE (Life Baron), Richard Rashleigh Folliott Scott; cr. 2000. Born 2 October 1934; Son of Lieutenant-Colonel C. W. F. Scott, 2/9th Gurkha Rifles and Katharine Scott; Married Rima Elisa Ripoll 1959 (2 sons 2 daughters). **Education:** Michaelhouse College, Natal, South Africa; Cape Town University (BA 1954); Trinity College, Cambridge (BA, LLB 1957); Bigelow Fellow, University of Chicago, USA 1958-59.

Non-political career: Inner Temple: Called to the Bar 1959, Bencher 1981; In practice, Chancery Bar 1960-83; QC 1975; Duchy and County Palatine of Lancaster: Attorney General 1980-83, Vice-Chancellor 1987-91; Chairman of the Bar 1982-83; Judge of the High Court of Justice, Chancery Division 1983-91; Lord Justice of Appeal 1991-94; Inquiry into defence related exports to Iraq and related prosecutions (The Scott Report) 1992-96; Vice-Chancellor of the Supreme Court 1994-2000; Head of Civil Justice 1995-2000; Non-Permanent Judge, Hong Kong Court of Final Appeal 2003-12; Justice of the Civil and Commercial Court of Qatar 2010-.

CROSSBENCH

Political career: *House of Lords:* Raised to the peerage as Baron Scott of Foscote, of Foscote in the County of Buckinghamshire 2000. Lord of Appeal in Ordinary 2000-09. Member European Union 2001-05; Chair European Union Sub-committee E (Law and Institutions) 2001-05; Member: Merits of Statutory Instruments/Secondary Legislation Scrutiny 2009-, Privileges/Privileges and Conduct 2009-. *Councils and public bodies:* Chair, advisory council, Society for Advanced Legal Studies.

Countries of interest: Panama, South Africa, Spain.

Other: Chair: Grafton Hunt 1987-93, 2010-, Michaelhouse UK Trust; Patron, Harrison Homes; Honorary Member: American Bar Association 1983, Canadian Bar Association 1983, American College of Trial Lawyers 2006, Society of Legal Scholars; Harrison Homes, Hunt Servants Benevolent Society. Honorary doctorates: Buckingham University, Birmingham University. Kt 1983; PC 1991; Hawks (Cambridge).

Publications: Articles in legal journals.

Recreations: Tennis, bridge, hunting (foxhounds and bloodhounds), riding horses.

Rt Hon the Lord Scott of Foscote, House of Lords, London SW1A 0PW
Tel: 020 7219 6373 *Email:* rrfscott.foscote@gmail.com

LIBERAL DEMOCRAT

SCOTT OF NEEDHAM MARKET, BARONESS

SCOTT OF NEEDHAM MARKET (Life Baroness), Rosalind Carol Scott; cr. 2000. Born 10 August 1957; Daughter of Kenneth Vincent and Carol Leadbeater; Married Mark Valladares 2008 (1 son 1 daughter from previous marriage).

Education: Whitby Grammar School; Kent School; University of East Anglia (BA European studies 1999).

Political career: *House of Lords:* Raised to the peerage as Baroness Scott of Needham Market, of Needham Market in the County of Suffolk 2000. Liberal Democrat: Whip 2001-02, Deputy Chief Whip 2002, Spokesperson for: Transport, Local Government and the Regions 2001-02, Transport 2002-04, Office of the Deputy Prime Minister/Communities and Local Government 2004-09; House of Lords Appointments Commission 2010-. Member: Liaison 2003-07, Delegated Powers and Regulatory Reform 2005-07, Communications 2007-10, Leader's Group on Members Leaving the House 2010-, EU Sub-Committee G (Social Policies and Consumer Protection) 2011-12, Joint Committee on the Draft House of Lords Reform Bill 2011-12, European Union 2012-, EU Sub-committee B (Internal Market, Infrastructure and Employment) 2012-13; Chair EU Sub-committee D (Agriculture, Fisheries, Environment and Energy) 2013-. *Other:* President, Liberal Democrat Party 2008-10. *Councils and public bodies:* Councillor, Mid Suffolk District Council 1991-94; Suffolk County Council: Councillor 1993-2005, Vice-chair 1996-97, Chair, Transport Committee, Local Government Association 2002-04.

Political interests: Transport; Commonwealth, India, USA.

Other: Member: North Sea Commission 1997-2005, Council of European Municipalities and Regions 1997-2003, Congress of Local and Regional Authorities in Europe 1997-2003, EU Committee of the Regions 1998-2002, Inter-Parliamentary Union 2000-; Commonwealth Parliamentary Association 2000-; Fellow, Industry and Parliament Trust; Honorary Member, Chartered Institute Highways and Transportation; Suffolk Foundation; Royal Commonwealth Society.

Recreations: Walking, political biography, genealogy.

The Baroness Scott of Needham Market, House of Lords, London SW1A 0PW
Tel: 020 7219 8660 *Email:* scottrc@parliament.uk *Twitter:* @BaronessRos

CONSERVATIVE

SECCOMBE, BARONESS

SECCOMBE (Life Baroness), Joan Anna Dalziel Seccombe; cr. 1991. Born 3 May 1930; Daughter of late Robert Owen and Olive Barlow Owen; Married Henry Seccombe 1950 (died 2008) (2 sons).

Education: St Martin's, Solihull.

Political career: *House of Lords:* Raised to the peerage as Baroness Seccombe, of Kineton in the County of Warwickshire 1991. Opposition Whip 1997-2001; Opposition Deputy Chief Whip 2001-10 Opposition Spokesperson for: Education and Skills 2003-04, Legal Affairs 2003-06, Home Affairs 2004-07; Extra Baroness in Waiting to HM The Queen 2004-; Opposition Spokesperson for: Constitutional Affairs 2005-06, Constitutional and Legal Affairs/Justice 2006-10; Party Whip 2010-. Member: Information 2012-. *Other:* Chairman: West Midlands Conservative Women's Committee 1975-78, Conservative Women's National Committee 1981-84; National Union of Conservative and Unionist Associations: Chairman 1987-88, Vice-chairman 1984-87, Member of Executive 1975-97; Chairman, Conservative Party Annual Conference, Blackpool 1987; Vice-chairman, Conservative Party with special responsibility for Women 1987-97. *Councils and public bodies:* JP, Solihull 1968-2000, Chairman of Bench 1981-84; Chairman, Lord Chancellor's Advisory Committee, Solihull 1975-93; Councillor, West Midlands County Council 1977-81, Chairman, Trading Standards Committee 1979-81; Member, Women's National Commission 1984-90; Governor, Nuffield Hospitals 1988-2001; Vice-President, Institute of Trading Standards Administration 1992-.

Political interests: Women's issues, family, criminal justice.

Other: Chair, Trustees of Nuffield Hospitals Pension Scheme 1992-2001. DBE 1984. President, St Enedoc Golf Club 1992-.

Recreations: Golf, needlework.

The Baroness Seccombe DBE, House of Lords, London SW1A 0PW
Tel: 020 7219 4558 *Fax:* 020 7219 3602 *Email:* seccombej@parliament.uk

SELBORNE, EARL OF

SELBORNE (4th Earl of, UK), John Roundell Palmer; cr. 1882; Viscount Wolmer; 4th Baron Selborne (UK) 1872. Born 24 March 1940; Son of Captain Viscount Wolmer (died on active service 1942), son of 3rd Earl, PC, CH; Married Joanna Van Antwerp, née James 1969 (3 sons 1 daughter).
Education: Eton College; Christ Church, Oxford (BA history 1961, MA).
Non-political career: Director: Lloyds Bank plc 1994-95, Lloyds TSB Group plc 1995-2004; Vice-chair, Science and Technology in Agriculture 2008-; Chair, Partners Board, Living with Environmental Change Programme 2008-12.

CONSERVATIVE

Political career: *House of Lords:* Succeeded the Peerage 1971; First entered House of Lords 1972; Elected hereditary peer 1999-. Chair European Communities Sub-committee D 1991-93, 1999-2003; Science and Technology: Member 1992-97, 2005-, Chair 1993-97; Member European Union 1999-2003; Co-opted member Science and Technology Sub-committee I (Systematic Biology and Biodiversity) 2002; Member House of Lords Reform Joint Committee 2002-03; Chair Science and Technology Sub-committee I (Water Management) 2005-07; Member: Draft Climate Change Bill Joint Committee 2007, Science and Technology Sub-committee I 2007-10 (Allergy/Waste Reduction 2007-08, Nanotechnologies and food 2008-10), Communications 2011-. *Councils and public bodies:* Member, Apple and Pear Development Council 1969-73; Chair: Hops Marketing Board 1978-82, Agricultural and Food Research Council 1982-89; DL, Hampshire 1982; President: Royal Agricultural Society of England 1987-88, Royal Institute of Public Health and Hygiene 1991-97; Chair, Joint Nature Conservation Committee 1991-97; Member: NEDC Food Sector Group 1991-92, Royal Commission on Environmental Pollution 1993-98; President, Royal Geographical Society (with the Institute of British Geographers) 1997-2000; Chair, Foundation for Science and Technology 2006-.
Political interests: Science, agriculture, education, conservation; Kazakhstan.
Other: World Commission on the Ethics of Science and Technology, UNESCO 1999-2003; Chair of Trustees, Royal Botanic Gardens, Kew 2003-09; FRS 1991; FSB; Fellow, Linnean Society. Master, Mercers' Company 1989. Chancellor, Southampton University 1996-2006. Five honorary doctorates. KBE 1987; GBE 2011; Travellers'.
The Earl of Selborne GBE FRS DL, House of Lords, London SW1A 0PW
Tel: 020 7219 6171 *Email:* selbornejr@parliament.uk
Temple Manor, Selborne, Alton, Hampshire GU34 3LR *Tel:* 01420 473646 *Fax:* 01420 473646

SELKIRK OF DOUGLAS, LORD

SELKIRK OF DOUGLAS (Life Baron), James Alexander Douglas-Hamilton; cr. 1997. Born 31 July 1942; Son of late 14th Duke of Hamilton and Brandon, KT, PC, GCVO, AFC, DL, and late Lady Elizabeth Percy, OBE, DL, daughter of 8th Duke of Northumberland, KG, CBE, MVO; Married Hon Susan Buchan 1974 (4 sons including twins).
Education: Eton College; Balliol College, Oxford (BA modern history 1964) (Oxford Boxing Blue 1961; President, Oxford Union Society Summer 1964); Edinburgh University (LLB Scots law 1967).

CONSERVATIVE

Non-political career: Officer 6/7th Btn, Cameronians TA 1961-66; 2nd Btn Lowland Volunteers, TAVR 1971-74; Captain Cameronians TA 1973; Honorary Air Commodore No 2 (City of Edinburgh), Maritime Headquarters Unit 1995; Honorary Air Commodore No 603 (City of Edinburgh) Squadron 2000. Scots Advocate (and Interim Procurator Fiscal Depute at Scottish Bar) 1968-76; QC 1996.
Political career: *House of Commons:* MP (Conservative) for Edinburgh West 1974-97. Contested Edinburgh West 1997 general election. Opposition Whip 1976-79; Government Whip 1979-81; PPS to Malcolm Rifkind: as Minister of State, Foreign Office 1983-85, as Secretary of State for Scotland 1986-87; Scottish Office 1987-95: Parliamentary Under-Secretary of State 1987-95, Minister of State 1995-97. *House of Lords:* Raised to the peerage as Baron Selkirk of Douglas, of Cramond in the City of Edinburgh 1997. EU Sub-committee C (Foreign Affairs, Defence and Development Policy): Co-opted member 2008-10, Member 2011-12; Member Joint Committees on: Statutory Instruments 2012-, Draft Deregulation Bill 2013-. *Other:* Scottish Parliament: Contested Edinburgh West constituency 1999 and 2003 elections. MSP for Lothians 1999-2007 (contested the seat as Lord James Douglas-Hamilton): Member, Parliamentary Bureau 1999-2001; Business Manager (Chief Whip Conservative Group) 1999-2001; Conservative Spokesperson for: Justice 2001-03, Education 2003-07. President, Oxford University Conservative Association Winter 1963. *Councils and public bodies:* Councillor, Edinburgh Corporation 1972-74; President: Royal Commonwealth Society in Scotland 1979-87, Scottish National Council, UN Association 1981-87; Member, Commission on Scottish Devolution (Calman Commission) 2008-09.

Political interests: Foreign affairs, defence, Scottish affairs, law reform, conservation, arts, housing, health, education, local government, environment, heritage; Africa, Asia, Australasia, Europe, Middle East, North America.

Other: Honorary President, Scottish Boxing Association 1975-98; President, International Rescue Corps 1995-; Edinburgh Support Group of Hope and Homes for Children: Chairman 2002-07, Patron 2007-; President: The Scottish Veterans' Garden City Association 2007-, Trefoil Centre 2007; Chair, Scottish Advisory Committee, SkillForce; Member, Royal Company of Archers, the Queen's Bodyguard for Scotland; Lord High Commissioner, General Assembly, Church of Scotland 2012-; Trustee, Selkirk Charitable Trust. Disclaimed the Earldom of Selkirk, November 1994; PC 1996; Pratt's, New (Edinburgh). Member, Muirfield (Honorable Company of Edinburgh Golfers).

Publications: Motive for a Mission: The Story Behind Hess's Flight to Britain (1971); The Air Battle for Malta: The Diaries of a Fighter Pilot (1981); Roof of the World: Man's First Flight over Everest (1983); The Truth About Rudolph Hess (1993); After You, Prime Minister (Stacey International, 2010).

Recreations: Golf, boxing, forestry, debating, history.

Rt Hon the Lord Selkirk of Douglas QC, House of Lords, London SW1A 0PW
Tel: 020 7219 2131 *Email:* selkirkj@parliament.uk

CONSERVATIVE

SELSDON, LORD

SELSDON (3rd Baron, UK), Malcolm McEacharn Mitchell-Thomson; cr. 1932; 4th Bt of Polmood (UK) 1900. Born 27 October 1937. Born of 2nd Baron, DSC; Married Patricia Anne Smith 1965 (1 son) (divorced); married Gabrielle Tesseron, née Williams 1995.

Education: Winchester College; French, German.

Non-political career: Sub-Lieutenant RNVR, Royal Navy 1956-58. Plastics products manager, Universal Asbestos (UAM) 1959-63; Director, market analysis and research services, London Press Exchange Group 1964-72; Singer and Friedlanden (CT Bowring Troup) 1972-76; Midland Bank Group 1976-90: Director international banking, Samuel Montagu and Co, EEC and public finance adviser; International board member, Merloni Group, Italy 1978-98; Peasant farmer, Provence, France (vineyard and olive groves) 1987-; Deputy chairman, Comcap plc 1988-93; UK board member, Raab Karcher, Germany 1994-98; Director, MJ Gleeson Group plc 1996-2006.

Political career: *House of Lords:* First entered House of Lords 1963; Elected hereditary peer 1999-. Member: EC Sub-committee B (Internal Market, Energy and Transport) 1974-76, EC Sub-committee A (Economic and Financial Affairs and International Trade) 1974-84, Draft Human Tissue and Embryos Bill Joint Committee 2007, Information 2008-13. *Other:* Treasurer, Conservative Group on Europe. *Councils and public bodies:* Chair: Greater London and South East Council for Sport and Recreation 1977-83, Committee for Middle East Trade 1979-86; Member: British Overseas Trade Board 1983-86, East European Trade Council 1983-87.

Political interests: Trade and industry, foreign affairs, defence, economic and finance, health and technology, construction and planning; Africa, China, Commonwealth and overseas territories, EU, Middle East, Russia and former Soviet Union.

Other: British Delegate, Council of Europe and Western European Union 1972-78; President: British Exporters' Association 1992-98, Anglo Swiss Society 2001-; MCC 1958-. Honorary Secretary and treasurer, House of Lords Yacht Club.

Recreations: Skiing, sailing, tennis, lawn tennis, golf.

The Lord Selsdon, House of Lords, London SW1A 0PW
Tel: 020 7219 6668 *Email:* selsdonm@parliament.uk

NON-AFFILIATED

SEWEL, LORD

Chairman of Committees

SEWEL (Life Baron), John Buttifant Sewel; cr. 1996. Born 15 January 1946; Son of late Leonard Sewel and late Hilda Ivy Sewel; Married Jennifer Ann 2005 (1 son 1 daughter 2 stepdaughters).

Education: Hanson Boys' Grammar School, Bradford; Durham University (BA 1967); University College of Wales, Swansea (MSc economics 1969); Aberdeen University (PhD 1977).

Non-political career: Research assistant, Department of Sociology and Anthropology, University College of Wales, Swansea 1967-69; Aberdeen University 1969-2004: Successively research fellow, lecturer, senior lecturer, Dean, Faculty of Economic and Social Sciences 1989-94, Vice-principal and Dean, Faculty of Social Sciences and Law 1995-97, Professor and Vice-principal 1999-2001, Senior Vice-principal 2001-04.

Political career: *House of Lords:* Raised to the peerage as Baron Sewel, of Gilcomstoun in the District of the City of Aberdeen 1996. Opposition Spokesperson for Scotland 1996-97; Parliamentary Under-Secretary of State, Scottish Office (Minister for Agriculture, the Environment and Fisheries) 1997-99; Opposition Spokesperson for Scotland 2010; Chairman of Committees 2012-; Deputy Speaker 2012-. Chair EU Sub-committee D (Environment and Agriculture) 2006-09; Member: European Union 2006-10, Barnett Formula 2008-09, EU Sub-committee C (Foreign Affairs, Defence and Development Policy) 2009-12; Chair: Hybrid Instruments 2012-13; Administration and Works 2012-, Liaison 2012-, Privileges and Conduct 2012-, Procedure 2012-, Subcommittee on Leave of Absence 2012-13, Refreshment 2012-, Selection 2012-, Standing Orders (Private Bills) 2012-13; Member House 2012-. *Councils and public bodies:* Aberdeen City Council: Councillor 1974-84, Leader 1977-80; President, Convention of Scottish Local Authorities 1982-84; Member: Accounts Commission for Scotland 1987-97, Scottish Constitutional Commission 1994-95.

Political interests: Scotland, higher education, Europe, constitutional affairs; Central and Eastern Europe.

Other: UK representative to NATO Parliamentary Assembly 1999-2002, 2005-; Chair, NATO Sub-Committee Transatlantic Economic Relations 2006-. Honorary LLD, Aberdeen University 2008. CBE 1984.

Publications: Books and learned articles mainly on politics and development in Scotland.

Recreations: Hill-walking, skiing.

The Lord Sewel CBE, House of Lords, London SW1A 0PW
Tel: 020 7219 3217 *Email:* sewelj@parliament.uk

SHACKLETON OF BELGRAVIA, BARONESS

CONSERVATIVE

SHACKLETON OF BELGRAVIA (Life Baroness), Fiona Sara Shackleton; cr 2010. Born 26 May 1956; Daughter of late Jonathan Charkham CBE; Married Ian Shackleton (2 daughters).

Education: Francis Holland School; Benenden School; Exeter University (LLB 1977).

Non-political career: Articled clerk, Herbert Smith 1978-80; Admitted solicitor 1980; Partner: Brecher and Co. 1981-84, Farrer and Co. 1987-2000; Personal solicitor to: The Prince of Wales 1996-2005, Prince William of Wales 1996-, Prince Harry of Wales 1996-; Partner, Payne Hicks Beach Solicitors.

Political career: *House of Lords:* Raised to the peerage as Baroness Shackleton of Belgravia, of Belgravia in the City of Westminster 2010. *Councils and public bodies:* Governor, Benenden School 1986-2007.

Other: Inaugural member, International Academy of Matrimonial Lawyers 1986-; Trustee: Broad Cairn Foundation, Glen Beg Foundation, Sir Frank Lowe's Football Trust, Royal Opera House Endowment Fund; Director, Diana, Princess of Wales Memorial Fund Trustee Company; Member, advisory council, London Philharmonic Orchestra. Honorary LLD, Exeter University 2010; Elected Master of the Bench of the Inner Temple 2011. LVO 2005.

Publications: Co-author, The Divorce Handbook (1992).

The Baroness Shackleton of Belgravia LVO, House of Lords, London SW1A 0PW
Tel: 020 7219 5353
Email: fshackleton@phb.co.uk

SHARKEY, LORD

LIBERAL DEMOCRAT

SHARKEY (Life Baron), John Kevin Sharkey; cr 2010. Born 24 September 1947; Married (3 daughters).

Education: Maths degree.

Non-political career: Benton & Bowles, KMP; Saatchi & Saatchi: Joined 1984, Deputy chairman 1986, Managing director 1987; Chairman, Broad Street Group, BDDP; Founder, joint chairman and chief executive, Bainsfair Sharkey Trott/BST-BDDP 1990-97; Joint chairman, BDDP GGT 1997-98; Managing director, Europe Manpower plc 1998; Chairman, Sharkey Associates Ltd; Honorary treasurer, Hansard Society 2008-; Chief executive, Blue Arrow plc; Political adviser to Deputy Prime Minister.

Political career: *House of Lords:* Raised to the peerage as Baron Sharkey, of Niton Undercliff in the County of Isle of Wight 2010. Member: EU Sub-committee F (Home Affairs, Health and Education) 2012-, Joint Committee on the Draft Deregulation Bill 2013-. *Other:* Liberal Democrats: Chair, general election campaign 2010, Campaign director, YES to Fairer Votes for the 2011 Referendum.

Other: Non-executive chair, Highland Partners Europe; Hansard Society: Member 2004-, Honorary Treasurer 2007-.

The Lord Sharkey, House of Lords, London SW1A 0PW
Tel: 020 7219 5353

LIBERAL DEMOCRAT

SHARMAN, LORD

SHARMAN (Life Baron), Colin Morven Sharman; cr. 1999. Born 19 February 1943; Son of Colonel Terence John Sharman; Married Angela Timmins 1966 (1 son 1 daughter).
Education: Bishops Wordsworth School, Salisbury, Wiltshire.
Non-political career: Chartered Accountant 1965; KPMG and predecessors 1966-99: Partner 1973, Senior Partner (National Marketing and Industry Groups) 1987-90, UK Senior Partner 1994-98, Chair, KPMG International 1998-99; Director: Reed Elsevier plc 2000-10, B G International plc 2000-10, Liberal Democrat (Trustees) Ltd; Chair: Le Gavroche Ltd, Aviva plc 2005-12.
Political career: *House of Lords:* Raised to the peerage as Baron Sharman, of Redlynch in the County of Wiltshire 1999. Liberal Democrat Spokesperson for Trade and Industry/Business, Enterprise and Regulatory Reform 2001-10; Trade envoy to Morocco 2012-. Member: House 2005, Audit 2005-.
Countries of interest: Morocco.
Other: Member, Industry Society; Companion, British Institute of Management; FCA; CIMgt; Honorary Fellow Securities Institute; Salisbury Cathedral; Eve Appeal. Company of Gunmakers: Master, Liveryman; Liveryman, Company of Management Consultants. Freeman, City of London. Honorary Doctorate, Cranfield School of Management 1998. OBE 1979; Flyfishers'; Reform. Royal Yacht Squadron.
Publications: Holding to Account (Review of audit and accountability in central government); Turning the Corner (Report of Foresight Panel on Crime Prevention); Co-author, Living Culture; Going Concern and Liquidity Risks: Lessons for Companies and Auditors (Report of the Sharman Panel of Inquiry, 2012).
Recreations: Shooting, fishing, sailing, opera, food and wine.
The Lord Sharman OBE, House of Lords, London SW1A 0PW
Tel: 020 7219 8622 *Email:* csharman43@gmail.com

LIBERAL DEMOCRAT

SHARP OF GUILDFORD, BARONESS

SHARP OF GUILDFORD (Life Baroness), Margaret Lucy Sharp; cr. 1998. Born 21 November 1938; Daughter of Osmund Hailstone and Sydney Hailstone; Married Thomas Sharp 1962.
Education: Tonbridge Girls' Grammar School; Newnham College, Cambridge (BA economics 1960); French, a little German.
Non-political career: Civil servant, Board of Trade and Industry 1960-63; Lecturer, London School of Economics 1964-72; Economic adviser, National Economic Development Office 1977-81; Sussex University: Research fellow 1981-84, Senior research fellow 1984-92, Economic and Social Research Council: Director 1992-99, Visiting fellow 2000-. Member, Association of University Teachers.
Political career: *House of Commons:* Contested Guildford (SDP/All) 1983, 1987 and (Lib Dems) 1992 and 1997 general elections. *House of Lords:* Raised to the peerage as Baroness Sharp of Guildford, of Guildford in the County of Surrey 1998. Liberal Democrat Spokesperson for: Higher Education 2000, Education and Employment/Skills 2000-04, Further Education, Higher Education and Skills 2004-07, Innovation, Universities and Skills 2007-09, Science and Technology 2009-10. Member: European Communities Sub-committee A (Economic and Financial Affairs, Trade and External Relations) 1998-2002, Science and Technology 2003-07, 2012-, Science and Heritage Sub-committee II (Energy Efficiency) 2004-05; Chair: Science and Heritage 2005-06, Science and Heritage Sub-committee II (Internet Security) 2006-07; EU Sub-committee D (Environment and Agriculture): Member 2007-08, Co-opted member 2008-10; Co-opted member Science and Technology Sub-committee I (Waste Reduction) 2007-08; Member: European Union 2009-10, 2011, EU Sub-committee D (Agriculture, Fisheries and Environment) 2010-12. *Other:* Founder Member: Social Democrat Party 1981, Liberal Democrats 1988; Liberal Democrat Federal Policy Committee: Member 1992-2004, Vice-chair 1995-96, 1998-99; Liberal Democrat History Group; Centre for Reform. *Councils and public bodies:* Save British Science: Executive committee member 1988-97, Advisory Board 1997-; Governor, Weyfield Community Primary School 2005-; Member of corporation, Guildford College of Further and Higher Education 2006-13.

Political interests: Economic policy, industrial issues, science and technology, education; Australia, Canada, New Zealand, USA.

Other: Member, Inter-Parliamentary Union 2000-; Trustee, Nancy Seear Trust 1998-2005; Age Concern Surrey: Trustee 2001-09, Chair 2005-08; Fellow, Industry and Parliament Trust 2006; Transformation Trust 2009-; Fellow, Royal Economic Society; Shelter, Crisis, Oxfam, Challengers (Stoke Park, Guildford). Honorary fellow, City and Guilds Institute 2004; Honorary doctorate, Sussex University 2005; Honorary fellow, Birkbeck College 2006; Associate fellow, Newnham College, Cambridge 2007-10.

Publications: The State, the Enterprise and the Individual (1974); Editor, Europe and the New Technologies (1985); Co-author, Managing Change in British Industry (1986); Co-editor, Strategies for New Technologies (1987); Editorial board member, *Political Quarterly* 1987-92; Co-author: Technology and the Future of Europe (1992); Technology Policy in the European Union (1998); Plus numerous articles, book chapters etc in learned journals on issues relating to science and technology policy.

Recreations: Reading, walking, theatre and concert going.

The Baroness Sharp of Guildford, House of Lords, London SW1A 0PW
Tel: 020 7219 3121 *Email:* sharpm@parliament.uk

CONSERVATIVE

SHARPLES, BARONESS

SHARPLES (Life Baroness), Pamela Sharples; cr. 1973. Born 11 February 1923; Daughter of late Lieutenant-Commander K. W. Newall, RN; Married Major Richard C. Sharples, OBE, MC 1946 (later Sir Richard Sharples, Governor of Bermuda, assassinated 1973) (2 sons 2 daughters); married Patrick D. de Laszlo 1977 (died 1980); married Robert Douglas Swan 1983 (died 1995).

Education: Southover Manor, Lewes; Florence; French, some Italian.

Non-political career: WAAF 1941-46. Director, TVS 1982-93; Former publican.

Political career: *House of Lords:* Raised to the peerage as Baroness Sharples, of Chawton in the County of Hampshire 1973. Member Leader's Group on Members Leaving the House 2010-. *Councils and public bodies:* Member Review Body on Armed Services Pay 1979-81.

Political interests: Small businesses, cheque-book journalism, prisoners' wives, pet quarantine, defence; South Africa.

Other: Member, Wessex Medical Trust 1997-2000. Defence Medal; War Medal; Mid-Ocean Bermuda. Parliamentary Golf, Rushmoor Park.

Recreations: Golf, walking, gardening.

The Baroness Sharples, House of Lords, London SW1A 0PW
Tel: 020 7219 4456 *Email:* sharplesp@parliament.uk

CONSERVATIVE

SHAW OF NORTHSTEAD, LORD

SHAW OF NORTHSTEAD (Life Baron), Michael Norman Shaw; cr. 1994. Born 9 October 1920; Son of late Norman Shaw, FCA; Married Joan Mowat 1951 (3 sons).

Education: Sedbergh School.

Non-political career: Chartered accountant.

Political career: *House of Commons:* MP (Conservative) for Brighouse and Spenborough 17 March 1960 by-election to 1964, for Scarborough and Whitby 1966-74, for Scarborough 1974-92. PPS: to John Hare as Minister of Labour 1962-63, to John Davies: as Secretary of State for Trade and Industry 1970-72, as Chancellor of the Duchy of Lancaster 1972-74. *House of Lords:* Raised to the peerage as Baron Shaw of Northstead, of Liversedge in the County of West Yorkshire 1994. Member: Administration and Works 2002-05, Delegated Powers and Regulatory Reform 2005-08, Ecclesiastical Committee 2006-, Constitution 2008-12. *Other:* MEP 1974-79. Chair, later President, (former) Yorkshire Area Conservative Association; Member, Association of Conservative Peers. *Councils and public bodies:* JP, Dewsbury 1953; DL, West Yorkshire 1977.

Other: ACA 1945; FCA 1952. Kt 1982; Carlton.

Recreations: Golf, opera, music.

The Lord Shaw of Northstead DL, House of Lords, London SW1A 0PW
Tel: 020 7219 4178
Duxbury Hall, Liversedge, West Yorkshire WF15 7NR *Tel:* 01924 402270

NON-AFFILIATED

SHEFFIELD, LORD BISHOP OF

SHEFFIELD (7th Bishop of), Steven John Lindsay Croft. Born 29 May 1957; Son of James and Marian Croft; Married Ann Baker 1978 (2 sons 2 daughters).

Education: Worcester College, Oxford (BA 1980, MA); St John's College, Durham (PhD 1984).

Non-political career: Ordained deacon 1983; Priest 1984; Curate, St Andrew's, Enfield 1983-87; Vicar, St George's, Ovenden 1987-96; Mission consultant, Diocese of Wakefield 1993-96; Priest-in-charge, St Augustine, Halifax 1994-96; Warden, Cranmer Hall, St John's College, Durham 1996-2004; Archbishop's Missioner and Team Leader, Fresh Expressions 2004-09; Bishop of Sheffield 2009-.

Political career: *House of Lords:* Entered House of Lords 2013.

Publications: The Identity of the Individual in the Psalms (1987); Growing New Christians (1993); Making New Disciples (1994); Co-author, Emmaus, The Way of Faith volumes one to six (1996), volumes seven to eight (1998); Man to Man: friendship and faith (1999); Co-author, Travelling Well (2000); The Lord is Risen (2001); Missionary Journeys, Missionary Church (2001); Transforming Communities: re-imagining the Church for the 21st-century (2002); Co-author, Learning for Ministry: making the most of study and training (2005); Moving On in a Mission-Shaped Church (2005); The Advent Calendar (2006); Editor: The Future of the Parish System (2006), Mission-shaped Questions (2008); Jesus' People: what the church should do next (2009); Editor, Fresh Expressions in the Sacramental Tradition (2010); Exploring God's Mercy (2011); Exploring God's Love (2011).

Recreations: Walking, cooking, films.

Rt Rev the Lord Bishop of Sheffield, House of Lords, London SW1A 0PW
Tel: 020 7219 5353

CONSERVATIVE

SHEIKH, LORD

SHEIKH (Life Baron), Mohamed Iltaf Sheikh; cr 2006. Born 13 June 1941; Son of Mohamed Abdullah Sheikh and Kalsum Ara, née Bux; Married Shaida Begum Thantrey 1986 (1 daughter from previous marriage).

Education: Government Secondary School, Mbale, Uganda; City of London College (associateship Chartered Insurance Institute 1966); Holborn College (FCII 1968).

Non-political career: Section manager, Sun Alliance Insurance Co 1962-66; Accident underwriter, Household and General Insurance Company 1966-68; Principal officer, Guardian Royal Exchange 1968-78; Chair and chief executive, Camberford Law plc 1978-.

Political career: *House of Lords:* Raised to the peerage as Baron Sheikh, of Cornhill in the City of London 2006. *Other:* Chair, Conservative: Muslim Forum 2004-, Ethnic Diversity Council 2005-. *Councils and public bodies:* Regional chair, British Insurance Brokers Association (BIBA) 1991-92, 1996-97; Director: South London Training and Enterprise Council 1998-99, 1999-2003, British Insurance Brokers Association (BIBA).

Political interests: Ethnic issues, environment, financial services, economy, home and international affairs, pensions.

Other: President, chair, council member several financial, especially insurance, bodies; Chair, Ethnic Diversity Council 2005-. Freeman City of London 1995.

Recreations: Keep fit, walking, countryside, travel.

The Lord Sheikh, House of Lords, London SW1A 0PW
Tel: 020 7219 4542 *Email:* sheikhm@parliament.uk

LABOUR

SHELDON, LORD

SHELDON (Life Baron), Robert Edward Sheldon; cr 2001. Born 13 September 1923; Married Eileen Shamash 1945 (died 1969) (1 son 1 daughter); married Mary Shield 1971.

Education: London University (External graduate, Whitworth Scholar).

Non-political career: Engineer. Member, T&G.

Political career: *House of Commons:* Contested Manchester Withington 1959 general election. MP (Labour) for Ashton-under-Lyne 1964-2001. Opposition Frontbench Spokesperson for Civil Service, Treasury Matters and Machinery of Government 1970-74; Minister of State: Department of Civil Service 1974, HM Treasury 1974-75; Financial Secretary to HM Treasury 1975-79; Deputy Opposition Frontbench Spokesperson for Treasury and Economic Affairs 1981-83; Chairman: Public Accounts Committee 1983-97, Standards and Privileges Committee 1997-2001, Liaison Committee 1997-2001, Public Accounts Commission 1997-2001. *House of Lords:* Raised to the peerage as Baron Sheldon, of Ashton-under-Lyne in the County of Greater Manchester 2001. Member: Economic Affairs 2003-08, Economic Affairs Taxation Sub-committee 2003-. *Other:* Chair, North West Group Labour MPs 1970-74.

Political interests: Economy, Treasury.

Other: PC 1977.

Rt Hon the Lord Sheldon, House of Lords, London SW1A 0PW
Tel: 020 7219 6993 *Email:* sheldonr@parliament.uk

SHEPHARD OF NORTHWOLD, BARONESS

SHEPHARD OF NORTHWOLD (Life Baroness), Gillian Patricia Shephard; cr 2005. Born 22 January 1940; Daughter of late Reginald and Bertha Watts; Married Thomas Shephard 1975 (2 stepsons).

Education: North Walsham Girls' High School; St Hilda's College, Oxford (BA modern languages 1961, MA); French, rusty German.

Non-political career: Education officer and schools inspector, Norfolk County Council 1963-75; Part-time lecturer, Workers' Educational Association and Cambridge Extra Mural Board 1965-87; Anglia TV 1975-77.

CONSERVATIVE

Political career: *House of Commons:* MP (Conservative) for South West Norfolk 1987-2005. PPS to Peter Lilley as Economic Secretary to the Treasury 1988-89; Parliamentary Under-Secretary of State, Department of Social Security 1989-90; Minister of State, HM Treasury 1990-92; Secretary of State for Employment and for Women's Issues 1992-93; Minister of Agriculture, Fisheries and Food 1993-94; Secretary of State for Education (and Employment) 1995-97; Shadow Leader of the House of Commons 1997-98; Member House of Commons Commission 1997-99; Shadow Chancellor of the Duchy of Lancaster 1997-98, Shadow Secretary of State for the Environment, Transport and the Regions 1998-99. *House of Lords:* Raised to the peerage as Baroness Shephard of Northwold, of Northwold in the County of Norfolk 2005. Member, Speakers' Working Group on All-Party Groups 2011-12. Member: Selection 2007-10, Procedure 2007-10, Joint Committee on the Draft House of Lords Reform Bill 2011-12, Public Service and Demographic Change 2012-13, Mental Capacity Act 2005 2013-. *Other:* Joint deputy chair, Conservative Party 1991-92; Head, Conservative Candidates Development Unit 2001-03; Deputy chair, Conservative Party 2002-03; Conservative nominee, Committee on Standards in Public Life 2003-07; Chair, Association of Conservative Peers 2007-12; Member, Conservative Party Board 2007-12. *Councils and public bodies:* JP 1973-; Norfolk County Council: Councillor 1977-89, Deputy Leader 1982-87; Government co-chair, Women's National Commission 1990; DL, Norfolk 2003-; President, Norfolk Association of Local Councils 2009-.

Political interests: Constitution, education, agriculture and rural affairs; Latin America, France.

Other: Member, Franco-British Council 2000-07; Chair, Franco-British Society 2005-11; Council member, Oxford University 2002-06; Member: Continuing Education Board, Oxford University 2004-, Fawcett Commission 2005-; Patron, WEA 2006-; Royal Veterinary College: Chair of council 2006-, Fellow 2012-; Chair, Oxford University Society 2009-; Chair of council, Institute of Education 2010-; Council member, Royal Norfolk Agricultural Association; Trustee, Norwich Cathedral; Deputy chair, Social Mobility Commission 2013-; Fellow, Royal Veterinary College; EDP We Care Appeal. Honorary fellow: St Hilda's College, Oxford, Queen Mary, University of London. PC 1992; Légion d'Honneur (France) 2009; The Norfolk Club.

Publications: Reforming Local Government (1999); Shephard's Watch (2000); Knapton Remembered (2007); Twentieth Century Village Voices (2011); The Real Iron Lady – Working with Margaret Thatcher (2013).

Recreations: Music, gardening, France.

Rt Hon the Baroness Shephard of Northwold, House of Lords, London SW1A 0PW
Tel: 020 7219 4457/020 7219 6241 *Email:* westm@parliament.uk

SHEPPARD OF DIDGEMERE, LORD

SHEPPARD OF DIDGEMERE (Life Baron), Allen John George Sheppard; cr. 1994. Born 25 December 1932; Son of late John and Lily Sheppard; Married Peggy Jones 1959 (divorced 1980); married Mary Stewart 1980.

Education: Ilford County School; London School of Economics (BSc Econ business administration 1953).

Non-political career: Ford Motor Company 1958-68; Rootes/Chrysler 1968-71; British Leyland 1971-75; Grand Metropolitan plc 1975-96: Group managing director 1982-86, Chief executive 1986-93, Chair 1987-96; Chair: UBM Group 1981-85, Mallinson-Denny Group 1985-87; Meyer

CONSERVATIVE

International plc: Director 1989-92, Deputy chair 1992-94; Non-executive director, Bowater plc

1994-95; Non-executive chair: Group Trust plc 1994-2001, Bright Reasons Group plc 1995-96, McBride plc 1995-2007, Unipart Group 1996-2012; Non-executive chair, GB Railways plc 1996-2004; Director, High-Point Rendel Group plc 1997-2003; Non-executive chair, One Click HR plc 1999-2010; Director: Gladstone plc 1999-2001, Nyne plc 2000-07, Transware plc 2001-03; Non-executive chair: Namibian Resources plc 2004-, Global Tote Ltd 2005-09.

Political career: *House of Lords:* Raised to the peerage as Baron Sheppard of Didgemere, of Roydon in the County of Essex 1994. Member: Economic Affairs 2003-07, Sub-committee on Finance Bill 2003-04, 2004-05, 2006-07, 2007-08, 2008-09. *Other:* Member, Board of Management, Conservative Party 1993-98. *Councils and public bodies:* Governor/Honorary Governor, London School of Economics 1989-; Deputy chair, International Business Leaders' Forum 1990-96; Chair, Advisory Board, British-American Chamber of Commerce 1991-94; London First: Chair 1992-2002, President 2002-; Vice-President/board member, several trade and business organisations.

Other: Trustee, Animal Health Trust 1990-2005; Chair: Board of Trustees, Prince's Youth Business Trust 1990-94, Administrative Council, Prince of Wales' Trusts 1995-98; FCIM; FCMA; FCIS; ATII; FRSA; Animal Health Trust, Blue Cross. Chancellor, Middlesex University 2000-. Six honorary doctorates; Three fellowships. Institute of Management Gold Medal 1993; Marketing Society International Hall of Fame Award 1994; British-American Chamber of Commerce Trans-Atlantic Business Award 1995. Kt 1990; KCVO 1997; Athenæum.

Publications: Your Business Matters (1958); Maximum Leadership (1995).

Recreations: Gardens, reading, red setter dogs.

The Lord Sheppard of Didgemere KCVO, House of Lords, London SW1A 0PW
Tel: 020 7219 5353
Tel: 01279 792819 *Fax:* 01279 792030 *Email:* lord_allen_sheppard@unipart.co.uk

CONSERVATIVE

SHERBOURNE OF DIDSBURY, LORD

SHERBOURNE OF DIDSBURY (Life Baron), Stephen Ashley Sherbourne; cr 2013. Born 15 October 1945; Son of the late Jack and Blanche Sherbourne.

Education: Burnage Grammar School, Manchester; St Edmund Hall, Oxford (BA philosophy, politics and economics).

Non-political career: Conservative Research Department: Head of economic section 1973-74, Assistant director 1974-75; Head of office for Edward Heath 1975-76; Special adviser to Patrick Jenkin as Secretary of State for Industry 1982-83; Political secretary to the Prime Minister 1983-88; Senior corporate communications consultant, Lowe Bell Communications 1988-92; Managing director, Lowe Bell Consultants/Bell Pottinger Consultants 1992-99; Chair, Lowe Bell Political/Bell Pottinger Public Affairs 1994-2001; Director, Chime Communications plc 2001-03; Chief of Staff to Michael Howard as Leader of the Opposition 2003-05; Director: Smithfield Consultants 2006-, Newscounter 2007-10.

Political career: *House of Lords:* Raised to the peerage as Baron Sherbourne of Didsbury, of Didsbury in the City of Manchester 2013.

Other: CBE 1988; Kt 2006.

The Lord Sherbourne of Didsbury CBE, House of Lords, London SW1A 0PW
Tel: 020 7219 5353

LABOUR

SHERLOCK, BARONESS

Opposition Whip; Opposition Spokesperson for Work and Pensions

SHERLOCK (Life Baroness), Maeve Christina Mary Sherlock; cr 2010. Born 10 November 1960; Daughter of Roisin and William Sherlock.

Education: Our Lady's Senior School, Abingdon; Liverpool University (BA sociology 1984); Open University (MBA 1997); Durham University (MA theology 2007).

Non-political career: Treasurer, Liverpool University Guild 1984-85; National Union of Students: Executive officer 1985-86, Treasurer 1986-88, President 1988-90; Director, Endsleigh Insurance 1986-90; UKCOSA: Deputy director 1990-91, Director 1991-97; Director, National Council for One Parent Families 1997-2000; Special adviser to Gordon Brown MP as Chancellor of the Exchequer 2000-03; Chief executive, British Refugee Council 2003-06.

Political career: *House of Lords:* Raised to the peerage as Baroness Sherlock, of Durham in the County of Durham 2010. Opposition Whip 2013-; Opposition Spokesperson for Work and Pensions 2013-. *Councils and public bodies:* Member, Equality and Human Rights Commission 2007-10; Board member, Financial Ombudsman Service 2008-; Non-executive director, Child Maintenance and Enforcement Commission 2008-10; Member, Riot Communities and Victims Panel 2011-.

Political interests: Families with children, poverty, welfare state, health, communities, faith and politics.

Other: Court member, Warwick University 1993-95, Executive board member, European Association for International Education 1994-97, Assembly member, Greenwich University 1995-97; Governor, Sheffield Hallam University 1997-2000; Trustee: National Family and Parenting Institute 1999-2000, Demos 2004-07; Member: Advisory board, Naturalisation and Integration 2004-, National Refugee Integration Forum 2006-; Chair, National Students Forum 2008-10; Council member, St John's College, Durham University 2009-; NEPACS; Chapel St. DUniv, Sheffield Hallam University; Honorary fellow, St Chad's College, Durham University. OBE 2000.

Recreations: Cookery, music, books.

The Baroness Sherlock OBE, House of Lords, London SW1A 0PW
Tel: 020 7219 8905 *Email:* sherlockm@parliament.uk *Twitter:* @maevesherlock

LIBERAL DEMOCRAT

SHIPLEY, LORD

SHIPLEY (Life Baron), John Warren Shipley; cr 2010. Born 5 July 1946; Son of Edward Shipley and Grace Shipley, née Horton; Married Margaret Pattison 1969 (1 son 1 daughter).

Education: Whitby Grammar School; University College London (history 1969) (Union President 1968-69).

Non-political career: Brand management, Procter and Gamble 1969-71; Administrator, various roles then retired as regional director for the north of England and EU, Open University 1971-2005.

Political career: *House of Commons:* Contested (as Liberal) Blyth February and October 1974, Hexham 1979, (as Liberal/SDP Alliance) Newcastle North 1983 and 1987 general elections. *House of Lords:* Raised to the peerage as Baron Shipley, of Gosforth in the County of Tyne and Wear 2010. Member: Economic Affairs 2010-, Economic Affairs Finance Bill Sub-Committee 2011. *Other:* Member, Liberal Democrat Manifesto Working Group 2013-. *Councils and public bodies:* Newcastle City Council: Councillor 1975-2012, Opposition Leader 1988-98, Council Leader 2006-10; Member: Northumbria Police Authority 1980s, Tyne and Wear Passenger Transport Authority 1990s, 2004-06; Former board member, Newcastle International Airport Local Authority Holding Company 2004-06; Board member, One North East 2005-12; Vice-President, Local Government Association 2010-.

Political interests: Local government, regeneration, child poverty, housing; Central and eastern Europe.

Other: Former director: Northern Development Company 1990s, Tyne and Wear Development Company 1990s, 2004-08; Executive member, Universities for the North East; Former board member: NewcastleGateshead City Development Company (1NG), Newcastle Science City Company, Newcastle Local Strategic Partnership, Northern Way Transport Compact, Newcastle Theatre Royal Trust; Chair, Prince's Trust (North East). Doctor of Civil Law, Northumbria University 2011. OBE 1995; National Liberal.

Recreations: Classical music, theatre, First World War, Sunderland AFC.

The Lord Shipley OBE, House of Lords, London SW1A 0PW
Tel: 020 7219 5353 *Email:* shipleyj@parliament.uk

CONSERVATIVE

SHREWSBURY AND WATERFORD, EARL OF

SHREWSBURY (22nd Earl of, E), cr. 1442, AND WATERFORD (22nd Earl of, I), cr. 1446; Charles Henry John Benedict Crofton Chetwynd Chetwynd-Talbot; Earl Talbot and Viscount Ingestre (GB) 1784; Baron Talbot (GB) 1733. Born 18 December 1952; Son of 21st Earl; Married Deborah Hutchinson 1974 (2 sons 1 daughter).

Education: Harrow School.

Non-political career: Honorary Colonel, 'A' Squadron RMLY 2003-06. Landowner; Joint Deputy Chairman, Britannia Building Society 1987-92; Director, Richmount Enterprise Zone Trust 1988-94; Director: PMI Limited 1996-98, Banafix Limited 1996-98, Minibusplus 1997-2001.

Political career: *House of Lords:* First entered House of Lords 1980; Elected hereditary peer 1999-. Member Works of Art 2009-10, 2012-13. *Other:* Member, Association of Conservative Peers. *Councils and public bodies:* DL, Staffordshire 1994-; Chair, Firearms Consultative Committee 1994-99.

Political interests: Agriculture, environment, construction industry, property, West Midlands, mineral extraction, firearms and shooting sports, fishing; Scotland.

Other: President and National Executive Director, British Institute of Innkeeping 1996-98; Honorary President, Gun Trade Association 2002-; British Shooting Sports Council: Chair 2002-08, President 2008-; Deputy chair, Standing Conference on Country Sports 2011-; President, Building

Societies Association 1993-97; St Giles' Hospice, Lichfield. Member: Worshipful Company of Weavers, Worshipful Company of Gunmakers. Chancellor, Wolverhampton University 1993-99. Honorary LLD, Wolverhampton University 1994. Premier Earl on Rolls of both England and Ireland; Hereditary Lord High Steward of Ireland; Army and Navy, Pratt's Club.

Recreations: Shooting, fishing.

The Earl of Shrewsbury and Waterford DL, House of Lords, London SW1A 0PW
Tel: 020 7219 3158 *Email:* shrewsburyc@parliament.uk
Throstles House, Birdsgrove Lane, Ashbourne, Derbyshire DE6 2BP

SHUTT OF GREETLAND, LORD

SHUTT OF GREETLAND (Life Baron), David Trevor Shutt; cr. 2000. Born 16 March 1942; Son of late Edward Angus Shutt and Ruth Satterthwaite, née Berry; Married Margaret Pemberton 1965 (2 sons 1 daughter).

Education: Pudsey Grammar School.

Non-political career: Chartered accountant; Articled clerk, Smithson Blackburn and Company, Leeds 1959-66; Bousfield Waite and Company, Halifax: Taxation assistant, Partner 1970-94, Consultant 1994-2001; Non-executive director: Job Ownership Ltd 1978-85, Bradford Community Radio *Pennine Radio* 1984-89, Pluto Press Ltd 1985-86, New Society Ltd, *New Society* 1986-88, Statesman and Nation Publishing Company Ltd, *New Statesman* 1988-90, Gerald Duckworth and Co. Ltd 1990-95, Marcher Sound Ltd 1997-2000; Northern Broadsides 2002-10; X-Pert Health CIC 2007-10.

LIBERAL DEMOCRAT

Political career: *House of Commons:* Contested Sowerby (Lib) 1970, February and October 1974 and 1979, and Calder Valley (Lib/Alliance) 1983 and 1987, and Pudsey (Lib Dem) 1992 general elections. *House of Lords:* Raised to the peerage as Baron Shutt of Greetland, of Greetland and Stainland in the County of West Yorkshire 2000. Liberal Democrat Spokesperson for: Northern Ireland 2001-05, International Development 2001-04; Liberal Democrat Whip 2001-10: Deputy Chief Whip 2002-05, Chief Whip 2005-10; Deputy Chief Whip (Captain of the Queen's Bodyguard of the Yeomen of the Guard) 2010-12; Government Spokesperson for: Culture, Media and Sport 2010, Northern Ireland 2010-12, Transport 2010-12, Wales 2010-12. Member: European Union 2003-05, Administration and Works 2005-12, Privileges/Privileges and Conduct 2005-12, Procedure 2005-12, Selection 2005-12, Refreshment 2010-12, Joint Committee on Security 2010-12, Sub-committee on Leave of Absence 2011-12, Joint Committee on Parliamentary Privilege 2013; Chair Inquiries Act 2005 2013-. *Councils and public bodies:* Calderdale MBC: Councillor 1973-90, 1995-2003, Leader, Liberal Democrat Group 1979-82, 1995-2000, Mayor of Calderdale 1982-83.

Political interests: Transport, charities; Dependent territories, Ireland, Zimbabwe.

Other: Pennine Heritage 1976-2010; Historic Chapels Trust -2010; Member, Society of Friends (Quakers); Trustee: Joseph Rowntree Reform Trust Ltd 1975-2010, Joseph Rowntree Charitable Trust 1984-2010, The Irish Peace Institute 1990-2010; Chair and founder, Calderdale Community Foundation 1990-99; Treasurer, Institute for Citizenship Studies 1995-2001; Whitefield Regeneration Partnership 2005-10; Treasurer and trustee, Parliament Choir -2013; Fellow, Institute of Chartered Accountants in England and Wales; FCA; Calderdale Community Foundation. Freeman, Metropolitan Borough of Calderdale 2000. Citoyen d'Honneur de la Ville de Riorges (France) 1983; Paul Harris Fellow 1999. OBE 1992; PC 2009.

Recreations: Travel, transport.

Rt Hon the Lord Shutt of Greetland OBE, House of Lords, London SW1A 0PW
Tel: 020 7219 8624 *Email:* shuttd@parliament.uk
197 Saddleworth Road, Greetland, Halifax HX4 8LZ *Tel:* 01422 375276
Email: davidshutt@btinternet.com

SIMON, VISCOUNT

SIMON (3rd Viscount, UK), Jan David Simon; cr. 1940. Born 20 July 1940; Son of 2nd Viscount, CMG; Married Mary Burns 1969 (1 daughter).

Education: Westminster School; School of Navigation, Southampton University; Sydney Technical College.

Political career: *House of Lords:* First entered House of Lords 1993; Deputy Chairman of Committees 1998-; Deputy Speaker 1999-; Elected hereditary peer 1999-. Member: Dangerous Dogs (Amendment) Bill 1995-96, London Local Authorities Bill 1998, Procedure 1999-2002, Personal Bills 2004-09, Standing Orders (Private Bills) 2004-; Co-opted member Science and Technology Sub-committee I (Allergy) 2006-07.

LABOUR

Political interests: Disability, motor industry, police, road safety, science and technology, aviation; Australia, Qatar.

Other: Trustee, Guild of Experienced Motorists, Road Safety Charity 1999-; President: Driving Instructors Association 2000-, GEM Motoring Assist 2004-; Younger Brother, Trinity House 2007-.

Recreations: Photography, baroque music.

The Viscount Simon, House of Lords, London SW1A 0PW
Tel: 020 7219 6527 *Email:* simonj@parliament.uk

SIMON OF HIGHBURY, LORD

SIMON OF HIGHBURY (Life Baron), David Alec Gwyn Simon; cr. 1997. Born 24 July 1939; Son of late Roger Simon; Married Hanne Mohn 1964 (divorced 1987) (2 sons); married Sarah Roderick Smith 1992.

Education: Christ's Hospital, Horsham; Gonville and Caius College, Cambridge (BA modern languages 1961, MA); INSEAD (MBA 1966); Dutch, French, German, Norwegian.

Non-political career: British Petroleum Co plc 1961-97: Marketing co-ordinator, European Region 1975-80, Director, BP Oil UK and Chairman, National Benzole Company 1980-82, Managing director, BP Oil International 1982-85, Managing director 1985-95, Chief operating officer 1990-92, Deputy chair 1990-95, Chief group executive 1992-95, Chair 1995-97; Non-executive director, Grand Metropolitan plc 1989-97; Member, advisory board, Deutsche Bank 1991-97; Non-executive director, RTZ Corporation plc 1995-97; Member: International advisory council, Allianz AG Holding 1993-97, Court of Bank of England 1995-97; Unilever: Director 2000-09, Deputy chairman 2006-09; Senior adviser, Morgan Stanley International 2000-; Director, Suez Group 2001-; Member, international advisory committee, Fitch global financial rating agency 2001-06; Advisory board, Danagas 2006-; Chair, advisory board, Montrose Associates Ltd 2009-; Senior adviser, MWM Consulting 2010-.

Political career: *House of Lords:* Raised to the peerage as Baron Simon of Highbury, of Canonbury in the London Borough of Islington 1997. Minister for Trade and Competitiveness in Europe and Government Spokesperson for Trade and Industry 1997-99; On leave of absence 2005-08, 2010-. *Councils and public bodies:* Member: Sports Council 1988-92, 1994-95, President's Committee, CBI 1992-97.

Countries of interest: China, EU.

Other: Member, European Union Competitive Advisory Group 1995-97; Adviser to European Commission President 1999-2000; Vice-chair, European Round Table 1995-97; International Council, INSEAD 2000-08; Chair, Cambridge Foundation 2001-05; Board member, Hertie Foundation, Hessen, Germany 2001-; Cicely Saunders Foundation 2003-; Cambridge University Council 2004-10: Deputy chair 2007-10; Governor, Institute for Government; Council member, Centre for European Reform; Board member, Centre for European Policy Studies; Christ's Hospital School; RAF Benevolent Fund. Liveryman: Tallow Chandlers, Carmen. Four honorary doctorates. CBE 1991; Kt 1995; Commander Order of Leopold (Belgium) 2001; Grand Officer Order of Leopold II (Belgium) 2005; Brooks's, Athenæum. Highgate Golf; Royal West Norfolk Golf; Hunstanton Golf; Royal and Ancient Golf Club, St Andrews.

Recreations: Golf, books, music.

The Lord Simon of Highbury CBE, House of Lords, London SW1A 0PW
Tel: 020 7219 5353
1 St James's Square, London SW1Y 4PD *Tel:* 020 7496 4431 *Fax:* 020 7496 4436
Email: sjs1@bp.com

SIMPSON OF DUNKELD, LORD

SIMPSON OF DUNKELD (Life Baron), George Simpson; cr. 1997. Born 2 July 1942; Son of late William and Elizabeth Simpson; Married Eva Chalmers 1964 (1 son 1 daughter).

Education: Morgan Academy, Dundee; Dundee Institute of Technology.

Non-political career: Senior accountant, gas industry, Scotland 1962-69; Central audit manager, British Leyland 1969-73; Financial controller, Leyland Bus and Truck Division 1973-76; Accounting director, Leyland Cars 1976-78; Finance and systems director, Leyland Trucks 1978-80; Managing director: Coventry Climax Ltd 1980-83, Freight Rover Ltd 1983-86; Chief executive officer, Leyland DAF 1986-88; Rover Group: Managing director 1989-91, Chief executive 1991-92, Chair 1991-94; British Aerospace: Director 1990-94, Deputy chief executive 1992-94; Chair, Ballast Nedam Construction Ltd 1992-94; Non-executive director: Pilkington plc 1992-99, Northern Venture Capital 1992-, Pro Share 1992-94; Chair, Arlington Securities 1993-94; Chief executive, Lucas Industries plc 1994-96; Non-executive director, ICI plc 1995-2001; Chief execu-

NON-AFFILIATED

LABOUR

tive, General Electric Company plc (now Marconi plc) 1996-2001; Non-executive director: Nestlé SA 1999-2004, Alstom SA 1998-; Industrial Professor at Warwick University; Governor, London Business School; Board of Institute for Manufacturing; Non-executive director: Bank of Scotland 2000-01, Triumph Group Inc 2002-.

Political career: *House of Lords:* Raised to the peerage as Baron Simpson of Dunkeld, of Dunkeld in Perth and Kinross 1997. On leave of absence 2004-10, June 2012-.

Political interests: Trade and industry.

Other: Governor, Economic Forum; Member, European Round Table; Society of Motor Manufacturers and Traders: Member, Executive Committee 1986-, Vice-President 1986-95, President 1995-96; ACIS; FCCA; MENCAP. Liveryman, Worshipful Company of Coachmakers. Honorary Degrees: Warwick University, Abertay University, Aston University; Royal Automobile Club. Royal Birkdale, Gleneagles Golf, New Zealand Golf, Kenilworth Rugby Football, Pine Valley Golf, Blairgowrie Golf, Royal Perth Golf.

Recreations: Golf, squash, watching rugby.

The Lord Simpson of Dunkeld, House of Lords, London SW1A 0PW
Tel: 020 7219 5353
Tel: 01250 870625 *Fax:* 01250 870625 *Email:* lordsimps@aol.com

SINGH OF WIMBLEDON, LORD

SINGH OF WIMBLEDON (Life Baron); Indarjit Singh cr. 2011. Born 17 September 1932; Married Dr Kanwaljit Kaur 1962 (2 daughters).

Education: Bishop Vesey's Grammar School, Sutton Coldfield; Birmingham University (MCom; MBA); CEng 1967; French, Hindu, Punjabi.

Non-political career: Head of Sikh Armed Services Chaplaincy. National Coal Board 1955-59, 1965-67; Mines manager, India 1959-65; Costain 1967-75; Management consultant, London 1975-; Editor, *Sikh Messenger* 1984-; Director, Network of Sikh Organisations UK 1995-.

CROSSBENCH

Political career: *House of Lords:* Raised to the peerage as Baron Singh of Wimbledon, of Wimbledon in the London Borough of Merton 2011. *Councils and public bodies:* JP, Wimbledon 1984; Adviser, Commission for Racial Equality.

Political interests: Resolution of conflict, liaising with all political parties to ensure greater weightage of ethical considerations in decision-making; Canada, India, USA.

Other: Prison Chaplaincy and Director, Sikh Chaplaincy Service UK; Member, Institution of Mining Engineers 1967; Amnesty International; Save the Children Fund; Unicef. Honorary DLitt, Coventry University 2002; Honorary DLaws, Leicester University 2004; Honorary DArts, Leeds Metropolitan University 2007. Promotion of Inter-faith Understanding, UK Templeton Prize 1989; Inter-faith Medallion for Services to Religious Broadcasting 1991; Jewel of Punjab Award, World Punjabi Organisation. OBE 1996; CBE 2009.

The Lord Singh of Wimbledon CBE, House of Lords, London SW1A 0PW
Tel: 020 7219 8951

SKELMERSDALE, LORD

SKELMERSDALE (7th Baron, UK), Roger Bootle-Wilbraham; cr. 1828. Born 2 April 1945; Son of Brigadier 6th Baron and late Ann Quilter; Married Christine Morgan 1972 (1 son 1 daughter).

Education: Eton College; Lord Wandsworth College, Odiham; Somerset Farm Institute; Hadlow College of Agriculture and Horticulture; Dutch (rusty), French.

Non-political career: Voluntary Service Overseas, Zambia 1969-71; Horticulturist; Broadleigh Nurseries Ltd: Managing director 1972-81, Director 1991-; Parliamentary affairs adviser 1992-96.

CONSERVATIVE

Political career: *House of Lords:* Succeeded his father 1973; First entered House of Lords 1975; Government Whip 1981-86; Government Spokesperson on various topics 1981-86; Parliamentary Under-Secretary of State: Department of the Environment 1986-87, Department of Health and Social Security 1987-88, Department of Social Security 1988-89, Northern Ireland Office 1989-90; Deputy Chair of Committees 1991-94, 2010-; Deputy Speaker 1994-2003, 2011-; Elected hereditary peer 1999-; Opposition Whip 2003-05; Opposition Spokesperson for: Health 2003-04, Work and Pensions 2003-09, Trade and Industry 2004-05, Home Office 2009-10. Co-opted member European Union Sub-committee B (Energy, Industry and Transport) 1997-2000, 2001-03; Member: Statutory Instruments Joint Committee 1998-2005, Procedure 1998-2000, Communications 2010-, Leader's Group on the Working Practices of the House of Lords 2010-11.

Political interests: Horticulture, Post Office, energy, environment, privatised utilities, health; Belize, Colombia, Zambia.

Other: Vice-chair, Co-En-Co (Council for Environmental Conservation) 1979-81; President: British Naturalists Association 1979-95, Somerset Opera 1980-, Somerset Trust for Nature Conservation 1980-; Governor, Castle School, Taunton 1992-96; Chair of Council, The Stroke Association 1993-2003; Trustee, Hestercombe Gardens Trust 2001-08; President, Somerset Contract Bridge Association 2007-; Royal Horticultural Society, Stroke Association, Somerset Opera, Voluntary Service Overseas. Former Liveryman, Worshipful Company of Gardeners.

Recreations: Bridge, gardening, reading, walking.

The Lord Skelmersdale, House of Lords, London SW1A 0PW
Tel: 020 7219 3224 *Fax:* 020 7219 5798 *Email:* skelmersdaler@parliament.uk
Broadleigh Gardens, Bishops Hull, Taunton TA4 1AE *Tel:* 020 7630 0088

CROSSBENCH

SKIDELSKY, LORD

SKIDELSKY (Life Baron), Robert Jacob Alexander Skidelsky; cr. 1991. Born 25 April 1939; Son of late Boris Skidelsky and Galia Skidelsky, née Sapelkin; Married Augusta Hope 1970 (2 sons 1 daughter).

Education: Brighton College; Jesus College, Oxford (BA modern history 1961); Nuffield College, Oxford (DPhil 1968).

Non-political career: Research fellow, Nuffield College, Oxford 1965-68; Associate professor, School of Advanced International Studies, Johns Hopkins University, Washington DC 1970-76; Head of department of history, philosophy and European studies, Polytechnic of North London 1976-78; Warwick University: Professor of: International studies 1978-90, Political economy 1990-2006; Director, Janus Capital 2001-11; Founder and chair, Centre for Global Studies 2002-; Director: Greater Europe Fund 2005-09, Sistema JSC 2008-10, Rusnano Capital 2010-. Member, AUT.

Political career: *House of Lords:* Raised to the peerage as Baron Skidelsky, of Tilton in the County of East Sussex 1991. Opposition Spokesperson for: Culture, Media and Sport 1997-98, the Treasury 1998-99. Member: Economic Affairs 2003-08, 2012-, Refreshment 2009-, EU Sub-committee G (Social Policies and Consumer Protection) 2010-12, Joint Committee on the Draft Financial Services Bill 2011-12. *Councils and public bodies:* Member: Lord Chancellor's Advisory Council on Public Records 1987-92, School Examinations and Assessment Council 1992-93; Governor, Portsmouth University 1994-97; Brighton College: Governor 1998-, Chair 2004-; Governor, Moscow School of Political Studies 1999-; Founder member, World Political Forum 2002-; Member, Academic Council, Wilton Park 2002-09.

Political interests: Education, economic policy, Europe, transition economies, arts; China, Russia.

Other: Member, Inter-Parliamentary Union; Fellow: Royal Historical Society 1973, Royal Society of Literature 1978, Chair: Charleston Trust 1987-92, Social Market Foundation 1991-2001; Fellow, British Academy 1994; Trustee, Daedatus Trust 2011-. Freeman, Knocksville, Tennessee, USA 1998. Honorary DLitt, University of Buckingham; Honorary Fellow, Jesus College, Oxford 1997; Honorary doctorate, University of Rome 2001; Honorary DLitt, Warwick University 2011. Wolfson Prize for History 1992; Duff Cooper Prize for *Fighting for Britain, 1937-1946*, 2000; Lionel Gelber Prize for International Relations 2001; Council on Foreign Relations Prize 2002; James Tait Black Memorial Prize for *Fighting for Britain, 1937-1946*, 2002. Cavaliere di gran Croce (Italy) 2010; Grillion.

Publications: Include: Politicians and the Slump (1967); English Progressive Schools (1969); Oswald Mosley (1975); Biographies of John Maynard Keynes: Hopes Betrayed, 1883-1920 (1983), The Economist as Saviour, 1920-1937 (1992), Fighting for Britain, 1937-1946 (2000), (abridged, single volume edition 2003); The World After Communism (1995); Keynes – The Return of the Master (2009); Co-author, How Much Is Enough? (Allen Lane, 2012).

Recreations: Opera, listening to music, tennis, table tennis, good conversation.

Professor the Lord Skidelsky, House of Lords, London SW1A 0PW
Tel: 020 7219 8721 *Email:* skidelskyr@parliament.uk
Room 207, Fielden House, 13 Little College Street, London SW1P 3SH *Tel:* 020 7219 8721
Email: skidelskyr@parliament.uk *Website:* www.skidelskyr.com
Twitter: @RSkidelsky

CROSSBENCH

SLIM, VISCOUNT

SLIM (2nd Viscount, UK), John Douglas Slim; cr. 1960. Born 20 July 1927; Son of Field Marshal 1st Viscount, KG, GCB, GCMG, GCVO, GBE, DSO, MC; Married Elisabeth Spinney 1958 (2 sons 1 daughter).

Education: Prince of Wales Royal Indian Military College, Dehra Dun; IMEDE, Switzerland (1971).

Non-political career: Regular Army 1944-72: Indian Army 6th Gurkha Rifles 1944, Argyll and Sutherland Highlanders 1948, Special Air Service 1952; Staff College Camberley 1961; Joint Services Staff College 1964. Morgan Crucible Company 1972-76; Peek plc: Chair 1976-91, Deputy chair 1991-96, Consultant 1996-2003; Director, Trailfinders Ltd 1985-2007, and other companies; Independent security consultant.

Political career: *House of Lords:* First entered House of Lords 1971; Founder member, House of Lords Defence Study Group 1971-; Elected hereditary peer 1999-. Member Selection 2001-05; Procedure: Member 2005-07, Alternate member 2007-10. *Councils and public bodies:* DL, Greater London 1988.

Political interests: Foreign affairs, defence, exports, industry, veterans and war widows.

Other: Foundation for Aviation and Sustainable Tourism (New Delhi); Parliamentary and Scientific Committee; Trustee, Royal Commonwealth Ex-Services League; President, Burma Star Association 1971-; Britain-Australia Society: Vice-President, Former chair; Vice-chair, Arab-British Chamber of Commerce 1977-96; Fellow, Royal Geographical Society 1983; SAS Association: President 2000-10, Patron 2010-; Patron, Prospect Burma; Clothworkers' Foundation; Indian Army Association; Burma Forces Welfare Association; Burma Children's Fund. Master, The Clothworkers' Company 1995-96. Freeman, City of London 1953. Ebbe Munk Award, Denmark 1995; Shiramani Award, India 2002; Pingat Jasa, Malaysia 2007. OBE (Mil) 1973; White's, Special Forces.

The Viscount Slim OBE DL, House of Lords, London SW1A 0PW
Tel: 020 7219 2122

LAB/CO-OP

SMITH OF BASILDON, BARONESS

Opposition Deputy Chief Whip; Opposition Spokesperson for Home Office

SMITH OF BASILDON (Life Baroness), Angela Evans Smith; cr 2010. Born 7 January 1959; Daughter of Patrick Evans, retired factory worker, and Emily Evans, neé Russell, supervisor of church pre-school; Married Nigel Smith 1978.

Education: Chalvedon Comprehensive, Basildon; Leicester Polytechnic (BA public administration).

Non-political career: Trainee accountant, London Borough of Newham 1982-83; League Against Cruel Sports, finally head of political and public relations 1983-95; Research assistant to Alun Michael MP 1995-97. Member, Unite.

Political career: *House of Commons:* Contested Southend West 1987 general election. MP (Lab/Co-op) for Basildon 1997-2010. Contested South Basildon and East Thurrock 2010 general election. PPS to Paul Boateng as Minister of State, Home Office 1999-2001; Assistant Government Whip 2001-02; Parliamentary Under-Secretary of State: Northern Ireland Office 2002-06, Department for Communities and Local Government 2006-07; PPS to Gordon Brown as Prime Minister 2007-09; Minister of State, Cabinet Office 2009-10. Joint Vice-chair, PLP Departmental Committee for International Development 1999-2000. *House of Lords:* Raised to the peerage as Baroness Smith of Basildon, of Basildon in the County of Essex 2010. Opposition Spokesperson for: Energy and Climate Change 2010-13, Northern Ireland 2011-12, Home Office 2012-; Opposition Deputy Chief Whip 2012-. *Councils and public bodies:* Essex County Council: Councillor 1989-97, Chief Whip 1993-96; Vice-President Local Government Association 2011-.

Political interests: Home affairs, animal welfare, international development, employment, third sector, fire service; Cuba, Germany, Ireland, Liechtenstein, Switzerland, USA.

Other: Patron, Basildon Women's Aid; Vice-chair, Cuba Solidarity Campaign; President, Basildon Ladies Football Club. PC 2009.

Recreations: Swimming, reading, theatre, watching Coronation Street.

Rt Hon the Baroness Smith of Basildon, House of Lords, London SW1A 0PW
Tel: 020 7219 6273 *Email:* smithangela@parliament.uk *Twitter:* @LadyBasildon

LIBERAL DEMOCRAT

SMITH OF CLIFTON, LORD

SMITH OF CLIFTON (Life Baron), Trevor Arthur Smith; cr. 1997. Born 14 June 1937; Son of late Arthur Smith and late Vera Smith; Married Brenda Eustace 1960 (divorced 1973) (2 sons); married Julia Bullock 1979 (1 daughter).

Education: Hounslow College; Chiswick Polytechnic; London School of Economics (BSc economics 1958).

Non-political career: Secondary school teacher, London 1958-59; Temporary political science assistant lecturer, Exeter University 1959-60; Acton Society Trust: Research officer 1960-62, Trustee 1975-87; Lecturer in politics, Hull University 1962-67; Visiting associate professor, California State University, Los Angeles 1969; Queen Mary Westfield College, London: Head of department 1972-85, Dean of social studies 1979-82, Pro-principal 1983-87, Lecturer, senior lecturer, professor in political studies 1967-91, Senior pro-principal 1987-89, Senior vice-principal 1989-91; Director: Job Ownership Ltd 1978-85, New Society Ltd 1986-88; Statesman and Nation Publishing Company Ltd: Director 1988-90, Chair 1990; Director, Gerald Duckworth & Co 1990-95; Visiting Professor of Politics: York University 1999-2003, Portsmouth University 2000-01; Director, Democratic Audit Ltd 2007-11.

Political career: *House of Lords:* Raised to the peerage as Baron Smith of Clifton, of Mountsandel in the County of Londonderry 1997. Liberal Democrat Spokesperson for: Northern Ireland 2000-10, Constitutional Affairs 2007-10. Member Science and Technology Sub-committee I (Complementary and Alternative Medicine) 1999-2000; Co-opted member European Union Sub-committee E (Law and Institutions) 2000-; Chair Animals in Scientific Procedures 2000-02; Member: Information 2003-07, Constitution 2005-08, Sub-committee on Lords' Interests 2006-08, Barnett Formula 2008-09, Works of Art 2009-10, Economic Affairs 2010-. Chair, Liberal Democrat Policy Committee on Northern Ireland 2010-11. *Other:* Member, Liberal Party Executive 1958-59. *Councils and public bodies:* Member, Tower Hamlets District Health Authority 1987-91; Member of Senate, London University 1987-91; Non-executive director, North Yorkshire Regional Health Authority 2000-02.

Political interests: Northern Ireland, health, transport (aircraft), higher education, constitutional reform, corporate governance; China, Scandinavia.

Other: British-Irish Interparliamentary Assembly 2000-11; Joseph Rowntree Reform Trust Ltd: Director 1975-06, Chair 1987-99; Governor, University of Haifa, Israel 1985-91; Trustee, Employment Institute 1987-92; Political Studies Association of UK: Chair 1988-89, Vice-President 1989-91, 1993-, President 1991-93; Vice-chair, Board of Governors, Princess Alexandra and Newnham College of Nursing and Midwifery 1990-91; Institute of Citizenship 1991-2001; UK Socrates Council: Member 1993-99, Chair 1996-99; President, Belfast Civic Trust 1995-99; Member: Administrative Board, International Association of Universities 1995-96, Editorial Board, Government and Opposition 1995-2013, Board, A Taste of Ulster 1996-99; Chair, Hampden Trust 1999-2001; Stroke Association 2002-05; Board Member, Democratic Audit 2006-11; FRHistS; CCIM (CBIM 1992); FICPD; FRSA; AcSS; Intermediate Technology Development Group (now Practical Action); Blood Pressure Association; Diabetes UK; Camfed. Vice-chancellor, Ulster University 1991-99. Six honorary doctorates; Honorary Professor Ulster University 1991; Honorary Fellow Queen Mary Westfield College, London 2003. Kt 1996; Reform. Easingwold CC.

Publications: Co-author: Training Managers (1962), Town Councillors (1964), Direct Action and Democratic Politics (1972); Town and County Hall (1966); Anti-Politics: consensus and reform (1972); The Politics of the Corporate Economy (1979); The Fixers (1996); Various articles and papers, book reviews and broadcasts.

Recreations: Water colour painting.

Professor the Lord Smith of Clifton, House of Lords, London SW1A 0PW
Tel: 020 7219 3563 *Fax:* 020 7219 5979 *Email:* smitht@parliament.uk

SMITH OF FINSBURY, LORD

SMITH OF FINSBURY (Life Baron), Christopher (Chris) Robert Smith; cr 2005. Born 24 July 1951; Son of Colin Smith, civil servant and Gladys Smith, teacher.

Education: George Watson's College, Edinburgh; Pembroke College, Cambridge (BA English 1972; PhD 1979) (President, Cambridge Union 1972); Harvard University (Kennedy Scholar 1975-76); French, German (rusty).

Non-political career: Housing Corporation 1976-77; Shaftesbury Society Housing Association 1977-80; Society for Co-operative Dwellings 1980-83; Senior adviser, The Walt Disney Company 2001-07; Visiting professor, University of the Arts London 2002-; Chair, Environment Agency 2008-. ASTMS: Branch secretary 1977-80, Branch chair 1980-83.

NON-AFFILIATED

Political career: *House of Commons:* Contested Epsom and Ewell 1979 general election. MP (Labour) for Islington South and Finsbury 1983-2005. Opposition London Whip 1986-87; Shadow Treasury Minister 1987-92; Shadow Secretary of State for: Environmental Protection 1992-94, National Heritage 1994-95, Social Security 1995-96, Health 1996-97; Sponsored Environment and Safety Information Act 1988 (Private Member's Bill); Secretary of State for: National Heritage May-July 1997, Culture, Media and Sport July 1997-2001; Chair, Millennium Commission 1997-2001. *House of Lords:* Raised to the peerage as Baron Smith of Finsbury, of Finsbury in the London Borough of Islington 2005. *Other:* Chair, Labour Campaign for Criminal Justice 1985-88; Vice-President, Christian Socialist Movement 1987-; President, SERA 1992-2007. *Councils and public bodies:* Islington Borough Council: Councillor 1978-83, Chief Whip 1978-79, Chair of Housing 1981-83; Co-opted member, Council for National Parks 1980-89; Member, Committee on Standards in Public Life 2001-05; Senior associate, Judge Institute, Cambridge University 2001-06; Member, Review Committee of Privy Counsellors of the Anti-terrorism, Crime and Security Act 2002-03; Founding director, Clore Leadership Programme 2003-08; Chair: London Cultural Consortium 2004-08, Advertising Standards Authority 2007-.

Political interests: Culture, media, sport, housing, local and regional government, foreign affairs, environment, civil liberties, criminal justice, economic policy, social security, health; Argentina, Australia, Brazil, China, Cyprus, Europe, Hong Kong, New Zealand, South Africa, USA.

Other: Tribune Group: Secretary 1984-88, Chair 1988-89, Chair, Board of *Tribune* newspaper 1990-93; Member: Shelter Board 1986-92, Executive of National Council for Civil Liberties 1986-88; Sadlers Wells Theatre: Board member 1986-92, Governor 1992-97; Vice-President, Wildlife Link 1986-90; Fabian Society: Member, Executive 1990-98, Vice-chair 1995-96, Chair 1997-98; Trustee, John Muir Trust 1992-97; Chair, Board of *New Century* Magazine 1993-96; Executive Committee, National Trust 1994-96; Honorary Fellow, Royal Institute of British Architects 2000-; The Wordsworth Trust: Trustee 2001-, Chair 2002-; Board member, Royal National Theatre 2001-09; Chair, Classic FM Consumer Panel 2001-07; Donmar Warehouse: Board member 2001-, Chair 2003-; Board member: Terrence Higgins Trust 2001-05, The Poetry Archive 2002-07; Chair of Judges, Man Brooker Prize 2004; Governor, University of the Arts London 2005-08; Windsor Leadership Trust 2006-08; Board member, Phonographic Performance Ltd 2007-; International Advisory Committee, Russian State Museum, St Petersburg 2008-; Chair of Judges, Museum of the Year Prize 2012; Trustee, The Sixteen 2013-; Freeman, London Borough of Islington 2011. Honorary Doctor of Arts, City University 2003; Honorary fellow, Pembroke College, Cambridge 2004-; Senior Fellow, Royal College of Art 2007; Visiting fellow, Ashridge Business School 2007-; Honorary Fellow: King's College London 2008, University of Cumbria 2010; Honorary doctorate, Lancaster University 2011. PC 1997.

Publications: National Parks (Fabian Society, 1977); New Questions for Socialism (Fabian Society, 1996); Creative Britain (Faber, 1998); Co-author, Suicide of the West (Continuum, 2006).

Recreations: Mountaineering, literature, theatre, music, art.

Rt Hon the Lord Smith of Finsbury, House of Lords, London SW1A 0PW
Tel: 020 7219 5119 *Email:* smithcr@parliament.uk

SMITH OF GILMOREHILL, BARONESS

SMITH OF GILMOREHILL (Life Baroness), Elizabeth Margaret Smith; cr. 1995. Born 4 June 1940; Daughter of late Frederick William Moncrieff Bennett, and of late Elizabeth Waters Irvine Shanks; Married John Smith 1967, MP 1970-94, Leader of the Labour Party 1992-94 (died 1994) (3 daughters).

Education: Hutchesons' Girls' Grammar School, Glasgow; Glasgow University (MA French and Russian 1962).

Non-political career: Chair, Lamda Development Board -2001; Non-executive director: Deutsche Bank, Scotland -2004, City Inn Ltd -2011; BP Advisory Board for Scotland -2004.

LABOUR

Political career: *House of Lords:* Raised to the peerage as Baroness Smith of Gilmorehill, of Gilmorehill in the District of the City of Glasgow 1995. Opposition Spokeswoman on National Heritage (Tourism) 1996-97. *Councils and public bodies:* Member, Press Complaints Commission 1995-2001; DL, City of Edinburgh 1996.

Political interests: Arts; Russia, Former Soviet Union.

Other: Executive Committee Member, Inter-Parliamentary Union British Group -2002; Board member, Edinburgh International Festival -1999; Council member, Britain in Europe Campaign; Member: British Heart Foundation -2000, Future of Europe Trust -2000, John Smith Memorial Trust, Know How Fund Advisory Board -2000; Trustee, Hakluyt Foundation -2001; Member: English Speaking Union, Russo-British Chamber of Commerce, Centre for European Reform -2004; 21st Century Trust -2008; President, Scottish Opera -2012; Chair, Edinburgh Festival

Fringe -2012; Member: RIIA – Chatham House Mariinsky Theatre Trust; John Smith Memorial Trust; Mariinsky Theatre Trust; Dash Arts. Chancellor, Birkbeck College, London 1998-2003. Honorary LLD, University of Glasgow.

The Baroness Smith of Gilmorehill DL, House of Lords, London SW1A 0PW
Tel: 020 7219 5353 *Email:* smithlady@parliament.uk

SMITH OF KELVIN, LORD

SMITH OF KELVIN (Life Baron), Robert Haldane Smith; cr 2008. Born 8 August 1944; Married Alison Bell 1969 (2 daughters).

Education: Allan Glen's School, Glasgow; Articles, Rubb Ferguson & Co 1963-68. Qualified chartered accountant 1968.

Non-political career: Industrial and Commercial Finance Corporation 1968-82; Managing director, National Commercial & Glyns Ltd 1983-85; General manager, Corporate Finance Division, Royal Bank of Scotland plc; Managing director, Charterhouse Development Capital Ltd 1985-89; Morgan Grenfell Development Capital Ltd 1989-2001: Chair 1989-2001, Chief executive 1989-96; Chief executive, Morgan Grenfell Asset Management Ltd 1996-2000; Vice-chair, Deutsche Asset Management 2000-02; Chair, Weir Group plc 2002-13; Director, Standard Bank Group 2003-; Chair: Scottish and Southern Energy plc 2005-, The Smith Group 2005-12, UK Green Investment Bank 2012-.

CROSSBENCH

Political career: *House of Lords:* Raised to the peerage as Baron Smith of Kelvin, of Kelvin in the City of Glasgow 2008. *Councils and public bodies:* Member, Museums Advisory Board 1983-85; National Museums of Scotland: Trustee 1985-2002, Chair, Board of Trustees 1993-2002; Museums and Galleries Commission: Commissioner 1988-98, Vice-chair 1997-98; Member, Financial Services Authority 1997-2000; Financial Reporting Council: Member 2001-04, Chair, FRC Group on Audit Committees Combined Code of Guidance – "The Smith Report" 2003; Member: Judicial Appointments Board for Scotland 2002-07, Council of Economic Advisers to First Minister of Scotland 2007-10; Chair, Glasgow 2014 Commonwealth Games Organising Committee 2008-.

Countries of interest: South Africa.

Other: Director and treasurer, Sussex Heritage Trust 1975-82; President: British Association of Friends and Museums 1995-2005, Institute of Chartered Accountants of Scotland 1996-97; Member, Board of Trustees, British Council 2002-05; Patron, Scottish Community Foundation 2008-; President, Royal Highland and Agricultural Society of Scotland 2010-. Chancellor: University of the West of Scotland 2003-13, Strathclyde University 2013-. Honorary degree: Edinburgh University 1999, Glasgow University 2001, Paisley University 2003; Honorary Fellowship, Institute of Internal Auditors 2010. British Venture Capital Association Hall of Fame 2006; Business Leader of the Year, Elite Insider 2008; Lifetime Achievement Award, Scottish Accounts Association 2010. Kt 1999.

Publications: Co-author, Managing Your Company's Finances.

The Lord Smith of Kelvin, House of Lords, London SW1A 0PW
Tel: 020 7219 5353 *Email:* robert.smith@weir.co.uk

SMITH OF LEIGH, LORD

SMITH OF LEIGH (Life Baron), Peter Richard Charles Smith; cr. 1999. Born 24 July 1945; Son of Ronald and Kathleen Smith; Married Joy Booth 1968 (1 daughter).

Education: Bolton School; London School of Economics (BSc economics 1967); Garnett College, London University (CertEd(FE) 1969); Salford University (MSc Urban Studies 1983).

Non-political career: Lecturer: Walbrook College, London 1969-74, Manchester College of Art and Technology (part-time 1991-2000) 1974-2000; Manchester Airport plc: Board director 1986-2001, Chair 1989-90; Board director, Manchester Airport Group 2001-09. Member, NATFHE - 2001.

LABOUR

Political career: *House of Lords:* Raised to the peerage as Baron Smith of Leigh, of Wigan in the County of Greater Manchester 1999. Vice-chair: PLP Departmental Committee for Office of the Deputy Prime Minister 2006-07, PLP Departmental Group for Communities and Local Government 2010-. *Councils and public bodies:* Wigan Metropolitan Borough Council: Councillor 1978-, Chair, Finance Committee 1982-91, Council Leader 1991-; Member: Association of Metropolitan Authorities Policy Committee 1991-97, Local Government Association Policy and Strategy Committee 1997-2000; Vice-chair, Special Interest Group for Municipal Authorities 1997-; Member, Improvement and Development Agency 1999-2003; North West Regional Assembly: Chair 1999-2000, Executive Board 2005-09; Chair, Association of Greater Manchester Authorities 2000-; Vice-President, Local Government Association 2010-; Chairman, Greater Manchester Combined Authority 2011-.

Political interests: Local government, regionalism, airports, health; Australia/New Zealand, France, USA.
Other: Oxfam, Wigan and Leigh Hospice. Freeman, Wigan Metropolitan Borough 2011. Doctor of Laws, Manchester Metropolitan University.
Recreations: Gardening, sport, jazz.
The Lord Smith of Leigh, House of Lords, London SW1A 0PW
Tel: 020 7219 8631 *Email:* smithprc@parliament.uk
Town Hall, Library Street, Wigan WN1 1YN *Tel:* 01942 827001 *Fax:* 01942 827365
Email: leader@wigan.gov.uk

SNAPE, LORD

LABOUR

SNAPE (Life Baron), Peter Charles Snape; cr. 2004. Born 12 February 1942; Son of late Thomas Snape, Railway Chargeman; Married Winifred Grimshaw 1963 (divorced 1980) (2 daughters); married Janet Brenda Manley 2004.
Education: Dial Stone Secondary Modern School, Cheshire.
Non-political career: Regular Army service 1961-67: Royal Engineers 1961-64, Royal Corps of Transport 1964-67. British Railways/Rail: Railway signalman 1957-60, Goods guard 1967-70, Clerical officer 1970-74; Travel West Midlands: Non-executive director 1992-95, Chair 1995-2000; Transport consultants 2000-. National Union of Railwaymen: Member 1957-61, 1969-94, Branch chair 1970-74; Member, Rail Maritime and Transport Union 1994-.
Political career: *House of Commons:* MP (Labour) for West Bromwich East 1974-2001. Assistant Government Whip 1975-77; Government Whip 1977-79; Opposition Frontbench Spokesperson on: Defence 1979-82, Home Affairs 1982-84, Transport 1984-92. *House of Lords:* Raised to the peerage as Baron Snape, of Wednesbury in the County of West Midlands 2004. Member: Procedure 2005-07, Crossrail Bill 2008. *Councils and public bodies:* Bredbury and Romiley Urban District Council: Leader 1971-74, Chair, Finance Committee 1972-74.
Political interests: Transport.
Recreations: Golf, football.
The Lord Snape, House of Lords, London SW1A 0PW
Tel: 020 7219 5877

SNOWDON, EARL OF

CROSSBENCH

SNOWDON (1st Earl of, UK), Antony Charles Robert Armstrong-Jones; cr. 1961; Viscount Linley; (Life) Baron Armstrong-Jones 1999. Born 7 March 1930; Son of late Ronald Owen Lloyd Armstrong-Jones, MBE, QC, DL, and late Anne, Countess of Rosse; Married HRH The Princess Margaret 1960 (divorced 1978, she died 2002) (1 son 1 daughter); married Mrs Lucy Lindsay-Hogg 1978 (1 daughter).
Education: Eton College; Jesus College, Cambridge (architecture 1948-50, no degree).
Non-political career: Constable of Caernarfon Castle, Wales 1963-; Artistic adviser to the: *Sunday Times* and Sunday Times Publications Ltd 1962-90, *Daily Telegraph* Magazine 1990-95; Consultative adviser, Design Council, London 1962-87; Editorial adviser, *Design Magazine* 1962-87; President for England, International Year for Disabled People 1981; Television films: *Don't Count the Candles* 1968 (2 Hollywood EMMY Awards); *Love of a Kind* 1969; *Born To Be Small* 1971 (Chicago Hugo Awards); *Happy Being Happy* 1973; *Mary Kingsley* 1975; *Burke and Wills* 1975; *Peter, Tina and Steve* 1977; *Snowdon on Camera* (BAFTA nomination) 1981; Exhibitions: Photocall 1957, Assignments 1972, Serendipity 1989; Designer of: Mobile chair for disabled people (The Chairmobile) 1972, Snowdon Aviary for London Zoo 1965 (Listed Grade II* starred 1998); Retrospective Exhibition: National Portrait Gallery 2000, Edinburgh 2000, Vienna 2001, Yale 2001. Member, NUJ.
Political career: *House of Lords:* Created a life peer as Baron Armstrong-Jones, of Nymans in the County of West Sussex 1999. First entered House of Lords 1961; Elected hereditary peer 1999-; On leave of absence June 2012-.
Political interests: Art and design.
Other: President: Contemporary Art Society for Wales, Welsh Theatre Company; Council member, National Fund for Research into Crippling Diseases; Patron: National Youth Theatre 1962-87, Metropolitan Union of YMCAs, British Water Ski Federation, Welsh National Rowing Club, Physically Handicapped and Able Bodied, Circle of Guide Dog Owners; Started Snowdon award scheme for further education of disabled students 1981; Member, Prince of Wales Advisory Group on Disability; President, Civic Trust for Wales; Senior Fellow, Royal College of Art 1986; Fellow:

Manchester College of Art and Design; Chartered Society of Designers (London), Royal Photographic Society (London), Royal Society of Arts; FRSA, RDI; Patron: Polio Plus 1988, British Disabled Water Ski Association; Provost, Royal College of Art 1995-2004; Snowdon Award Scheme for Further Education of Disabled Students. Liveryman, Cloth Workers' Company. Honorary LLD: Bradford University 1989, Bath University 1989, Portsmouth University 1993. GCVO 1969; Buck's. Leander (Henley-on-Thames), Hawks.

Publications: Malta (in collaboration with Sacheverell Sitwell) (1958); London (1958); Assignments (1972); A View of Venice (1972); Integrating the disabled – The Snowdon Report (1976); Inchcape Review (1977); Personal View (1979); Co-author: Private View (1965), Pride of the Shires (1979); Tasmania Essay (1981); Sittings (1983); Israel – A First View (1986); Co-author, My Wales (1986); Stills (1987); Personal Appearances (1992); Wild Flowers (1995); Hong Kong – Portraits of Power (1995); Snowdon On Stage (1996); Wild Fruit (1997); London Sight Unseen (1999); Snowdon: a retrospective (2000); Snowdon on Russia (2003); Snowdon on India (2008); Snowdon Blue (2012).

Recreations: Photography.

The Earl of Snowdon GCVO, House of Lords, London SW1A 0PW
Tel: 020 7219 5353
22 Launceston Place, London W8 5RL *Tel:* 020 7937 1524 *Fax:* 020 7938 1727
Email: lordsnowdon@btinternet.com

SOLEY, LORD

LABOUR

SOLEY (Life Baron), Clive Stafford Soley; cr 2005. Born 7 May 1939; Son of Joseph Soley and Doris Despard; Rosslyn Brown (1 son 1 daughter).

Education: Downshall Secondary Modern, Ilford; Newbattle Abbey Adult Education College; Strathclyde University (BA politics and psychology 1968); Southampton University (Diploma applied social studies 1970).

Non-political career: RAF national service 1959-61. British Council, London and Madrid 1968-69; Probation officer and senior probation officer, Inner London Probation Service 1970-79; Chairman and director, Good Governance Foundation (a community interest company) 2011-. Member, GMB.

Political career: *House of Commons:* MP (Labour) for Hammersmith North 1979-83, for Hammersmith 1983-97, for Ealing, Acton and Shepherds Bush 1997-2005. Opposition Spokesperson for: Northern Ireland 1982-85, Home Affairs 1985-87, Housing and Local Government 1987-89, Housing and Planning 1989-92. Chair Northern Ireland Affairs 1995-97; Member: Joint Committee on House of Lords Reform 2002-05, Constitutional Affairs 2003-05. *House of Lords:* Raised to the peerage as Baron Soley, of Hammersmith in the London Borough of Hammersmith and Fulham 2005. Chair Intergovernmental Organisations 2007-08; Member: Delegated Powers and Regulatory Reform 2009-13, Inquiries Act 2005 2013-. *Other:* Chair: Labour Campaign for Criminal Justice 1983-97, Parliamentary Labour Party 1997-2001; Member, Labour Party National Executive Committee 1998-2001; Chair, London Selection Board for Labour candidate for Mayor 1999. *Councils and public bodies:* Councillor, Hammersmith and Fulham Council 1974-78; Chair: Alcohol Education Centre, Maudsley Hospital 1974-84, Mary Seacole Memorial Statue Appeal 2004-, Arab-Jewish Forum 2005-; Campaign director, Future Heathrow 2005-10.

Political interests: Environment, civil liberties, foreign policy, aviation policy, good governance; China, South East Asia.

Other: International Observer at: First national elections in Mongolia 1990, Peruvian general election 1995; Leader, Westminster Foundation Group to Kosovo 1999; Fellow, Industry and Parliament Trust 1984; Commonwealth Club.

Publications: 'The Politics of the Family' in Rewriting the Sexual Contract (Institute of Community Studies, 1997); Co-author, Regulating the Press (Pluto Press, 2000).

Recreations: Walking, photography, scuba diving.

The Lord Soley, House of Lords, London SW1A 0PW
Tel: 020 7219 5118 *Email:* soleyc@parliament.uk lordsoftheblog.net/category/lord-soley

---

CONSERVATIVE

SOULSBY OF SWAFFHAM PRIOR, LORD

SOULSBY OF SWAFFHAM PRIOR (Life Baron), (Ernest Jackson) Lawson Soulsby; cr. 1990. Born 23 June 1926; Son of late William George Lawson Soulsby; Married Margaret Macdonald 1950 (1 son 1 daughter); married Georgina Williams 1962.

Education: Queen Elizabeth Grammar School, Penrith; Edinburgh University (MRCVS veterinary medicine 1948; DVSM 1949; PhD immunology 1952); Cambridge University (MA 1954); Conversational German.

Non-political career: Veterinary practitioner, Cumbria 1948-50; Veterinary officer, City of Edinburgh 1949-52; Lecturer in: Clinical parasitology, Bristol University 1952-54, Animal pathology, Cambridge University 1954-63; Expert adviser to several UN Agencies and overseas governments 1963-; Ford Foundation Visiting Professor, University of Ibadan 1964; Professor of parasitology, University of Pennsylvania 1964-78; Cambridge University: Professor of animal pathology 1978-93, Dean, Veterinary Faculty 1978-93, Emeritus professor 1993-; Member, EEC Advisory Committee on Veterinary Training 1981-86; Veterinary Advisory Committee Horserace Betting Levy Board: Member 1984, Chair 1985-98; Member, Agriculture and Food Research Council 1984-88; Chair, Animal Research Grants Board 1986-89; Member, Home Office Animal Procedures Committee 1987-95; Chair: Ethics Committee, British Veterinary Association 1994-2006, Companion Animal Welfare Council 1998-.

Political career: *House of Lords:* Raised to the peerage as Baron Soulsby of Swaffham Prior, of Swaffham Prior in the County of Cambridgeshire 1990. Chair Science and Technology Sub-committee I: (Antibiotic Resistance) 1997-98, (Fighting Infection) 2002-03; Member Science and Technology Sub-committee I: (Science and International Agreements) 2003-04, (Scientific Aspects of Ageing) 2004-05, (Allergy) 2006-07; Co-opted member Science and Technology 2008. *Other:* Member, Association of Conservative Peers.

Political interests: Higher education, environment, agriculture, animal welfare, foreign affairs, biotechnology; Africa south of Sahara, South America, China, India, Malaysia.

Other: Advisory, General Parasitology, World Health Organisation, Geneva; Royal College of Veterinary Surgeons: Council member 1978-92, President 1984; Corresponding member, Academie Royale de Médicine de Belgique; President, Pet Advisory Committee 1996-; President, Royal Society of Medicine 1998-2000; Windward Islands Research and Educational Foundation: Trustee 1999-, Chair 2001-06, President 2008-; Member, Home Office Committee of Inquiry into Hunting with Dogs 2000-01; Patron: Wildlife Information Network 2000-, Veterinary Benevolent Fund 2000-, Fund for the Replacement of Animals in Medical Research; President: Royal Institute of Public Health 2004-08, Royal Society for Public Health 2008-; Honorary Member parasitology societies in Germany, Mexico, Argentina, UK and USA; FRCVS; Honorary Fellow, Royal Society of Medicine 1996; Fellow, Institute Medical Sciences 1998; Honorary Fellow: Institute of Biology 2002, Royal College of Pathologists; Red Cross; Veterinary Benevolent Fund. Member, Worshipful Company of Farriers. Freeman, City of London. Nine honorary degrees; Wolfson College, Cambridge: Emeritus Fellow 1993-, Honorary Fellow 2004. R. N. Chaudhury Gold Medal, Calcutta School of Tropical Medicine 1976; Behring-Bilharz Prize, Cairo 1977; Ludwig-Schunk Prize, Justus Liebig University, Germany 1979; Mussemmeir Medal, Humboldt University, Berlin 1991; British Veterinary Association Centaur Award 1999; St George's University, Grenada: Distinguished Service Award 2006, Mike Fisher Award 2006; British Small Animal Veterinary Association Wight Award 2009; Farmers'.

Publications: Include: Textbook of Veterinary Clinical Parasitology (1965); Biology of Parasites (1966); Reaction of the Host to Parasitism (1968); Helminths, Anthropods and Protozoa of Domesticated Animals (7th edition, 1982); Immune Response to Parasitic Infections (3 volumes 1987); Zoonoses (1998, 2nd edition 2011); As well as other works, articles in journals of parasitology, immunology and pathology.

Recreations: Gardening, travel.

The Lord Soulsby of Swaffham Prior, House of Lords, London SW1A 0PW
Tel: 020 7219 8500 *Fax:* 020 7219 8602 *Email:* soulsbyl@parliament.uk

---

CONSERVATIVE

SPICER, LORD

SPICER (Life Baron), William Michael Hardy Spicer; cr 2010. Born 22 January 1943; Son of late Brigadier L. H. Spicer; Married Patricia Ann Hunter 1967 (1 son 2 daughters).

Education: Wellington College, Berkshire; Emmanuel College, Cambridge (MA economics 1964).

Non-political career: Assistant to editor *The Statist* 1964-66; Conservative Research Department 1966-68; Director, Conservative Systems Research Centre 1968-70; Managing director, Economic Models Limited 1970-80.

Political career: *House of Commons:* Contested Easington 1966 and 1970 general elections. MP (Conservative) for South Worcestershire 1974-97, for West Worcestershire 1997-2010. PPS to Sally Oppenheim as Minister for Trade and Consumer Affairs 1979-81; Parliamentary Under-Secretary of State for Transport 1984-87; Aviation Minister 1985-87; Parliamentary Under-Secretary of State, Department of Energy 1987-90; Minister of State, Housing and Planning, Department of Environment 1990. Chair: Parliamentary and Scientific Committee 1996-99; Member: Treasury 1997-2001; Chair: Treasury (Treasury Sub-Committee) 1999-2001. *House of Lords:* Raised to the peerage as Baron Spicer, of Cropthorne in the County of Worcestershire 2010. Chairman, Parliamentary and Political Service Honours Committee 2012-. Chair Parliamentary and Political Service Honours Committee 2012-. *Other:* Conservative Party: Vice-chair 1981-83, Deputy Chair 1983-84, Board member 2001-; Chair 1922 Committee 2001-10; Chairman Conservative Party Finance and Audit Committee 2007-10. *Councils and public bodies:* President Association of Electricity Producers 1991-; Governor Wellington College 1992-2004.

Political interests: Economic policy; USA.

Other: Chair, European Research Group 1992-2001; Joint chairman, Congress of Democracy. Kt 1996; PC 2013; Pratts, Garrick.

Publications: A Treaty Too Far: A New Policy For Europe (1992); The Challenge from the East: The Rebirth of the West (1996); The Spicer Diaries (Biteback, 2012); Six novels.

Recreations: Tennis, writing novels, painting, bridge.

Rt Hon the Lord Spicer, House of Lords, London SW1A 0PW
Tel: 020 7219 5353

CROSSBENCH

STAIR, EARL OF

STAIR (14th Earl of, S), John David James Dalrymple; cr. 1703; Viscount Dalrymple and Lord Newliston, Glenluce and Stranraer; 15th Viscount Stair and Lord Glenluce and Stranraer (S) 1690; 7th Baron Oxenfoord (UK) 1841; 15th Bt of Stair (S) 1664; 11th Bt of Killock (S) 1698. Born 4 September 1961; Son of 13th Earl; Married Hon Emily Stonor 2006 (1 son 1 daughter).

Education: Harrow School; Royal Military Academy, Sandhurst.

Non-political career: Commissioned Scots Guards 1982.

Political career: *House of Lords:* First entered House of Lords 1996; Elected hereditary peer 2008-. Member EU Sub-committee F (Home Affairs, Health and Education) 2012-. *Councils and public bodies:* Board member: Scottish Enterprise Dumfries and Galloway 1999-2008, Scottish Environment Protection Agency 2002-09.

Political interests: Scottish affairs, agriculture, tourism, defence.

The Earl of Stair, House of Lords, London SW1A 0PW
Tel: 020 7219 5353 *Email:* dalrymplej@parliament.uk

CONSERVATIVE

STEDMAN-SCOTT, BARONESS

STEDMAN-SCOTT (Life Baroness), Deborah Stedman-Scott; cr 2010. Born 23 November 1955; Daughter of Jack Scott and Doreen-Margaret Scott; Civil partner Gabrielle Joy Stedman-Scott 2006.

Education: Ensham Secondary School for Girls; Southwark Technical College (1972).

Non-political career: Chief executive, Tomorrow's People Trust 1984-.

Political career: *House of Lords:* Raised to the peerage as Baroness Stedman-Scott, of Rolvenden in the County of Kent 2010. Member: Information 2011-, Joint Committee on Parliamentary Privilege 2013. *Councils and public bodies:* DL, East Sussex.

Political interests: Unemployment, young people; New Zealand.

Other: IWF; Member, advisory board, International Centre for Drugs Policy 2004-07; Member, CBI: Employment Advisory Group 2004-09, Public Service Industry Forum; Employment Related Services Association: Founding member, Chair 2007-09; Deputy chair, Social Justice Policy Group; Fellow, Royal Society; Board member, New Philanthropy Capital; Member, Association of Chief Executives of National Voluntary Organisations; Companion, Chartered Management Institute 2010; Patron: Gloucester House, Salvation Army, Rye Studio School. Charity Principal of the Year 2005; Regional Entrepreneur of the Year, Ernst and Young 2010; Outstanding Leadership Award, Private Equity Foundation 2011. OBE 2008.

Recreations: Reading, travelling, art, particularly Lowry.

The Baroness Stedman-Scott OBE, House of Lords, London SW1A 0PW
Tel: 020 7219 8919 *Email:* stedmanscottd@parliament.uk

STEEL OF AIKWOOD, LORD

STEEL OF AIKWOOD (Life Baron), David Martin Scott Steel; cr. 1997. Born 31 March 1938; Son of the late Very Rev. Dr David Steel, Moderator of the General Assembly of the Church of Scotland 1974-75; Married Judith MacGregor 1962 (2 sons 1 daughter).

Education: Prince of Wales School, Nairobi; George Watson's College, Edinburgh; Edinburgh University (MA 1960; LLB 1962); French, Swahili.

Non-political career: President, Edinburgh University Students' Representative Council 1961; Broadcaster; Journalist; BBC Television interviewer in Scotland 1964-65; Rector, Edinburgh University 1982-85.

LIBERAL DEMOCRAT

Political career: *House of Commons:* Contested (Liberal) Roxburgh, Selkirk and Peebles October 1964 general election. MP (Liberal) for Roxburgh, Selkirk and Peebles 24 March 1965 by-election to 1983, for Tweeddale, Ettrick and Lauderdale 1983-97 (Liberal Democrat 1988-97). Sponsor, Abortion Act 1967; Liberal Chief Whip 1970-74. *House of Lords:* Raised to the Peerage as Baron Steel of Aikwood, of Ettrick Forest in The Scottish Borders 1997. *Other:* Scottish Parliament: MSP for Lothians region 1999-2003 (as Sir David Steel), Presiding Officer 1999-2003. President, Edinburgh University Liberal Club 1960; Assistant Secretary, Scottish Liberal Party 1962-64; Leader, Liberal Party 1976-88; Joint Founder, Social and Liberal Democrats 1988. *Councils and public bodies:* DL, Roxburgh, Ettrick and Lauderdale 1990-2013.

Political interests: International democracy; Africa, China, Middle East, Taiwan.

Other: President, Liberal International 1992-94; President, Anti-Apartheid Movement in GB 1966-70; Chair, Scottish Advisory Council of Shelter 1968-72; President, Medical Aid for the Palestinians 1997-2004; Vice-President, Countryside Alliance 1998-99; President: Scottish Castles Association 2003-11, Jaguar Drivers' Club 2008-; Trustee, St Giles' Cathedral Restoration Trust; Visiting fellow, St Antony's College, Oxford 2013; Honorary fellow, Royal College of Obstetricians and Gynaecologists 2013; Former President, Medical Aid for the Palestinians; Prostate Cancer, Scotland; Cancer Research International. Freeman: Tweeddale 1987, Ettrick and Lauderdale 1989. Ten honorary doctorates from British universities; Chubb fellow, Yale University, USA 1989. Queen's Lord High Commissioner to the General Assembly of the Church of Scotland 2003 and 2004. PC 1977; KBE 1990; Commander's Cross of the Order of Merit (Germany) 1992; Chevalier Légion d'Honneur (France) 2003; KT 2004; National Liberal, London; Royal Overseas League, Edinburgh.

Publications: No Entry, A House Divided; Editor, Partners in One Nation; David Steel's Border Country; Co-author, Mary Stuart's Scotland; Against Goliath (autobiography, 1989).

Recreations: Angling, classic car rallying.

Rt Hon the Lord Steel of Aikwood KT KBE, House of Lords, London SW1A 0PW
Tel: 020 7219 4433

STEPHEN, LORD

STEPHEN (Life Baron), Nicol Ross Stephen; cr 2011. Born 23 March 1960; Son of Nicol Stephen, teacher, and Sheila Stephen, teacher; Married Caris Doig 1996 (2 sons 2 daughters).

Education: Robert Gordon's College, Aberdeen; Aberdeen University (LLB 1980); Edinburgh University (Diploma legal practice 1981); French.

Non-political career: Trainee solicitor, C & P H Chalmers 1981-83; Solicitor, Milne & Mackinnon 1983-88; Senior manager, Touche Ross Corporate Finance 1988-91; Director, Glassbox Ltd 1992-99.

LIBERAL DEMOCRAT

Political career: *House of Commons:* Contested Kincardine and Deeside 1987 general election. MP for Kincardine and Deeside November 1991 by-election to 1992. Contested Kincardine and Deeside 1992 and Aberdeen South 1997 general elections. *House of Lords:* Raised to the peerage as Baron Stephen, of Lower Deeside in the City of Aberdeen 2011. Member Partnerships (Prosecution) (Scotland) Bill 2013-. Chair, Liberal Democrat Parliamentary Party Committee on Scotland 2012-. *Other:* Scottish Parliament: MSP for Aberdeen South constituency 1999-2011: Scottish Liberal Democrat: Deputy Minister for Enterprise and Lifelong Learning 1999-2000; Minister for Higher Education 1999-2000; Deputy Minister for: Education, Europe and External Affairs 2000-01, Education and Young People 2001-03; Minister for Transport 2003-05; Deputy

First Minister 2005-07; Minister for Enterprise and Lifelong Learning 2005-07. General election agent, Kincardine and Deeside 1983; Scottish Liberal Democrat Spokesperson for Health 1995-97; Party Spokesperson for Education and Heritage, Team Leader; Leader, Scottish Liberal Democrats 2005-08. *Councils and public bodies:* Councillor, Grampian Regional Council 1982-92.

Political interests: Economic development, education, health; China, India, Japan, USA.

Other: EU Committee of the Regions: Member 2002-05, Alternate member 2010-11; Former chair: CREATE (Campaign for Rail Electrification Aberdeen to Edinburgh), STAR Campaign (Save Tor-na-Dee Hospital and Roxburghe House); Founding director, Grampian Enterprise; Director, Grampion Youth Orchestra. Deeside Golf.

Recreations: Golf.

The Lord Stephen, House of Lords, London SW1A 0PW
Tel: 020 7219 2964 *Email:* stephenn@parliament.uk

CONSERVATIVE

STERLING OF PLAISTOW, LORD

STERLING OF PLAISTOW (Life Baron), Jeffrey Maurice Sterling; cr. 1991. Born 27 December 1934; Son of late Harry and Alice Sterling; Married Dorothy Smith 1985 (1 daughter).

Education: Reigate Grammar School; Preston Manor County School, Brent; Guildhall School of Music, London.

Non-political career: RAF National Service; Royal Naval Reserve: Honorary Captain 1991, Honorary Rear Admiral 2010. Paul Schweder and Co. (Stock Exchange) 1955-57; G. Eberstadt & Co. 1957-62; Financial director, General Guarantee Corporation 1962-64; Managing director, Gula Investments Ltd 1964-69; Chair, Sterling Guarantee Trust plc 1969, merging with P&O 1985; Board member, British Airways 1979-82; Executive chair, Peninsular and Oriental Steam Navigation Company 1983-2005; Special adviser to: Patrick Jenkin MP as Secretary of State for Industry 1982-83, Secretaries of State for Trade and Industry 1983-90; P&O Princess Cruises plc: Chair 2000-03, Life President 2003-; Chair: Swan Hellenic 2007-, Hebridean Island Cruises 2009-.

Political career: *House of Lords:* Raised to the peerage as Baron Sterling of Plaistow, of Pall Mall in the City of Westminster 1991. Member Joint Committee on National Security Strategy 2010-. *Councils and public bodies:* President: General Council of British Shipping 1990-91, European Community Shipowners' Associations 1992-94.

Political interests: Shipping, economics, disability, arts, music, international affairs.

Other: Organisation for Rehabilitation through Training (ORT): Vice-President, British ORT 1978-; Deputy chair and Honorary treasurer, London Celebrations Committee, Queen's Silver Jubilee 1975-83; Chair, Young Vic Company 1975-83; Motability: Joint founder 1977, Chair 1994-; Chair of Governors, Royal Ballet School 1983-99; Governor, Royal Ballet 1986-99; Elder Brother, Trinity House 1991-; Chair: Board of Trustees, National Maritime Museum (which incorporates The Royal Observatory Greenwich and Royal Museums Greenwich) 2005-, Cutty Sark Trust 2011-; President, Ajex; Honorary Fellow: Institute of Marine Engineers 1991, Institute of Chartered Shipbrokers 1992; Honorary Member, Royal Institute of Chartered Surveyors 1993; Fellow, Incorporated Society of Valuers and Auctioneers 1995; Honorary Fellow, Royal Institute of Naval Architects 1997; Motability. Worshipful Company of Coopers. Freeman, City of London. Three honorary doctorates. Interfaith Medallion 2003. CBE 1977; Kt 1985; KStJ 1998; GCVO 2002 Grand Officer Order of May (Argentina) 2002; Officer's Cross Order of Merit (Germany) 2004; Officier de l'Ordre National de Légion d'Honneur (France) 2005; Garrick; Hurlingham.

Recreations: Music, swimming.

The Lord Sterling of Plaistow GCVO CBE, House of Lords, London SW1A 0PW
15 St James's Place, London SW1A 1NP *Tel:* 020 7647 8522 *Email:* bstar@lordsterling.co.uk

CROSSBENCH

STERN, BARONESS

STERN (Life Baroness) Vivien Helen Stern; cr. 1999. Born 25 September 1941; Daughter of Frederick Stern and Renate Mills; Married Professor Andrew Coyle CMG.

Education: Kent College, Pembury, Kent; Bristol University (BA English literature 1963; MLitt 1964; CertEd 1965).

Non-political career: Lecturer in education 1970; Principal officer, Community Relations Commission 1970-77; Director, NACRO 1977-96; Visiting fellow, Nuffield College, Oxford 1984-91; Senior research fellow, International Centre for Prison Studies, King's College London 1997-2010; Visiting professor, Essex University 2011-.

Political career: *House of Lords:* Raised to the peerage as Baroness Stern, of Vauxhall in the London Borough of Lambeth 1999. Member: European Union 2000-03, Joint Committee on Human Rights 2004-08, Joint Committee on Statutory Instruments 2010-, Inquiries Act 2005 2013-. *Councils and public bodies:* Committee Member, Prison Disciplinary System 1984-85.

Political interests: Criminal justice, foreign affairs, human rights, international development, penal reform, prisons, rape and sexual violence, death penalty; Afghanistan, Algeria, Argentina, Chile, Dominican Republic, Kazakhstan, Kenya, Kyrgyzstan, Takjikistan, Uzbekistan.

Other: Penal Reform International: Honorary secretary-general 1989-2006, Honorary president 2006-; Board member, Association for Prevention of Torture, Geneva 1993-2000; Trustee, Milton S. Eisenhower Foundation, Washington 1993-2007; Vice-president, Comité de Soutien, Français Incarcérés au Loin (FIL) 2001-07; Member, advisory council: Legal Policy Research Centre, Kazakhstan 2008-, International Legal Foundation, New York 2009-; Member: Special Programmes Board, Manpower Services Commission 1980-82, Youth Training Board 1982-88, General Advisory Council, IBA 1982-87, Advisory Council, PSI 1993-96; Member, Law Advisory Committee, British Council 1995-2000; Patron: Clean Break 1998-, Prisoners' Education Trust 1998-; President, New Bridge 2001-06; Patron, Rethink (formerly the National Schizophrenia Fellowship) 2002-; Vice-President, RPS Rainer 2002-; Governance Advisory Committee, British Council 2002-06; Convener, Scottish Consortium on Crime and Criminal Justice 2003-09; President, Association of Members of Independent Monitoring Boards 2005-; Patron: Amicus 2007-, Alternatives to Violence Project 2010-, The Venture Trust 2010-, UK Network of Sex Work Projects 2011-, London Havens (Sexual Assault Referral Centres) 2012-; Survivors' Network, Brighton 2013. Five honorary doctorates; Honorary Fellow, LSE 1996. Peer of the Year, Women in Public Life Awards 2010. CBE 1992.

Publications: Bricks of Shame (1987); Imprisoned by Our Prisons (1989); Deprived of their Liberty, a report for Caribbean Rights (1990); A Sin Against the Future: imprisonment in the world (1998); Alternatives to Prison in Developing Countries (1999); Editor, Sentenced to Die: The Problems of TB in Prisons in Eastern Europe and Central Asia (2000); Creating Criminals: People and Prisons in a Market Society (2006); The Stern Review (2010).

The Baroness Stern CBE, House of Lords, London SW1A 0PW
Tel: 020 7219 5353 *Email:* sternvh@parliament.uk
International Centre for Prison Studies, Victoria Charity Centre, 11 Belgrave Road,
London SW1V 1RB *Tel:* 020 3667 7883 *Email:* helen.fair@icps.essex.ac.uk

STERN OF BRENTFORD, LORD

STERN OF BRENTFORD (Life Baron), Nicholas Herbert Stern; cr 2007. Born 22 April 1946; Son of late Adalbert and Marion Stern, née Swann; Married Susan Ruth Chesterton 1968 (1 daughter 2 sons).

Education: Peterhouse, Cambridge (BA mathematics 1967); Nuffield College, Oxford (DPhil economics 1972); French.

Non-political career: Lecturer in industrial mathematics, Oxford, and Fellow in economics, St Catherine's College, Oxford 1970-77; Professor of economics: London School of Economics and Political Science (LSE) 1999-2003, Warwick University 1978-85; Sir John Hicks Professor of Economics, LSE 1986-94; Chief Economist and Special Counsellor to the President, European Bank for Reconstruction and Development 1994-99; Chief Economist and Senior Vice-President, World Bank, Washington DC 2000-03; HM Treasury 2003-07: Managing director, Budget and Public Finance 2003-05, Second Permanent Secretary 2003-05, Head of Government Economic Service 2003-07, Adviser on Economics of Climate Change and Development (Stern Review) 2005-06; IG Patel Chair, LSE 2007-.

CROSSBENCH

Political career: *House of Lords:* Raised to the peerage as Baron Stern of Brentford, of Elsted in the County of West Sussex and of Wimbledon in the London Borough of Merton 2007.

Other: Fellow: British Academy, Econometric Society 1978; Member, United Nations High Level Group on Development Strategy and Management of the Market Economy 1997. 11 honorary doctorates. Foreign Honorary Member, American Academy of Arts and Sciences; Great Briton of the Year (Environment) 2006; Royal Geographical Society Patron's Royal Medal 2009; Asahi Glass Foundation Blue Planet Prize 2009. Kt 2004.

Publications: Crime, the Police and Criminal Statistics (1979); Editor, Journal of Public Economics 1981-97; Palanpur: The Economy of an Indian Village (1982); The Theory of Taxation for Developing Countries (World Bank, 1987); The Role of the State in Economic Development (1991); The Theory and Practice of Tax Reform in Developing Countries (1991); Economic Development in Palanpur over Five Decades (1998); A Case for Aid (World Bank, 2002); A Strategy for Development (World Bank, 2002); Co-author, Growth and Empowerment (2005); A Blueprint for a Safer Planet (2009).

Recreations: Walking, reading, football.

Professor the Lord Stern of Brentford, House of Lords, London SW1A 0PW
Tel: 020 7219 1300

CROSSBENCH

STEVENS OF KIRKWHELPINGTON, LORD

STEVENS OF KIRKWHELPINGTON (Life Baron), John Arthur Stevens QPM; cr 2005. Born 21 October 1942; Married (2 sons 1 daughter).

Education: St Lawrence College, Ramsgate; Leicester University (LLB, LLD 2000); Southampton University.

Non-political career: Metropolitan Police 1963-83; Directing staff, Police Staff College 1983-84; Assistant Chief Constable, Hampshire Constabulary 1986-89; Deputy Chief Constable, Cambridgeshire Constabulary 1989-91; Chief Constable, Northumbria 1991-96; HM Inspector of Constabulary 1996-98; Metropolitan Police 1998-2005: Deputy Commissioner 1998-99, Commissioner 2000-05; Senior international security adviser to Prime Minister 2007-.

Political career: *House of Lords:* Raised to the peerage as Baron Stevens of Kirkwhelpington, of Kirkwhelpington in the County of Northumberland 2005. *Other:* Chair, Independent Review into the Future of Policing in England and Wales 2011-. *Councils and public bodies:* Chair: Stevens Enquiries (into NI security faces and paramilitary collusion) 1989-92, 1999-2003, Joint Committee on Offender Profiling 1991, Inquiry into death of Princess Diana 2003-06, Strategic Advisory Panel Interpol 2005-.

Other: Freeman, City of London 2002. Chancellor, Northumbria University 2005. QPM 1992; Kt 2000.

The Lord Stevens of Kirkwhelpington QPM, House of Lords, London SW1A 0PW
Tel: 020 7219 5488

**CONSERVATIVE
INDEPENDENT**

STEVENS OF LUDGATE, LORD

STEVENS OF LUDGATE (Life Baron), David Robert Stevens; cr. 1987. Born 26 May 1936; Son of late A. Edwin Stevens, CBE and of Kathleen James; Married Patricia Rose 1961 (divorced 1971) (1 son 1 daughter); married Melissa Sadoff, née Milicevic 1977 (died 1989); married Meriza Giori, née Dzienciolsky 1990.

Education: Stowe School, Buckinghamshire; Sidney Sussex College, Cambridge (BA economics 1959, MA); French.

Non-political career: Second Lieutenant, Royal Artillery, National Service, Hong Kong 1954-56. Management trainee, Elliot Automation 1959; Hill Samuel Securities 1959-68; Drayton Group 1968-74; Chair: City and Foreign/Alexander Proudfoot 1976-95, Drayton Far East 1976-93, English and International 1976-89, Consolidated Venture 1979-93, Drayton Consolidated 1980-92, Drayton Japan 1980-88; MIM Britannia Ltd (formerly Montagu Investment Management Ltd): Chair and chief executive 1980-89, Chair 1989-93; United News and Media plc (formerly United Newspapers): Director 1974-, Chair 1981-99; Chair, Express Newspapers plc 1985-99; Deputy chair, Britannia Arrow Holdings plc 1987-89; Chair: Invesco MIM plc (formerly Britannia Arrow Holdings) 1989-92, Oak Industries 1989-1995, Premier Asset Management 1997-2001, Express National Newspapers Ltd 1998-99, The Personal Number Company 1998-2003.

Political career: *House of Lords:* Raised to the peerage as Baron Stevens of Ludgate, of Ludgate in the City of London 1987. *Councils and public bodies:* Chair, EDC for Civil Engineering 1984-86.

Political interests: European Union, tax and financial affairs; France, Italy, USA.

Other: Director, English National Opera 1980-87; Chair, Helicopter Emergency Rescue Services 1988-90; Patron, Royal College of Surgeons; National Association of Almshouses; Action Against Cancer; St George's Hospital (Cancer) Charity; Cancer Research. Honorary Fellow, Sidney Sussex College, Cambridge 1991. Grand Official, Order of the Southern Cross (Brazil) 1993; White's. Sunningdale Golf, Swinley Forest Golf.

Recreations: Gardening, golf.

The Lord Stevens of Ludgate, House of Lords, London SW1A 0PW
Tel: 020 7219 5353 *Fax:* 020 7436 9741 *Email:* stevensdavid@parliament.uk

LABOUR

STEVENSON OF BALMACARA, LORD

Opposition Whip; Opposition Spokesperson for Business, Innovation and Skills and for Culture, Media and Sport

STEVENSON OF BALMACARA (Life Baron), Robert Wilfrid (Wilf) Stevenson; cr 2010. Born 19 April 1947; Son of late James Stevenson and late Elizabeth Macrae; Married Jennifer Antonio 1972 (divorced 1979); married Ann Minogue (1 son 2 daughters).

Education: Edinburgh Academy; University College, Oxford (BA natural sciences, chemistry, MA); Napier Polytechnic (FCCA).

Non-political career: Research officer, Edinburgh University Students' Association 1970-74; Secretary, Napier College, Edinburgh 1974-87; British Film Institute: Deputy director 1987-88,

Director 1988-97; Director, Smith Institute 1997-2008; Senior policy adviser, Prime Minister's Office 2008-10. Member, Unite 1974-.

Political career: *House of Lords:* Raised to the peerage as Baron Stevenson of Balmacara, of Little Missenden in the County of Buckinghamshire 2010. Opposition Whip 2011-; Opposition Spokesperson for: Business, Innovation and Skills 2011-, Culture, Media and Sport 2011-. Member Communications 2011.

Political interests: Constitutional issues, the Arts, Scotland; Eire.

Other: Chair, Foundation for Credit Counselling/StepChange Debt Charity 2010-; Member, ACCA (retired); Hyposadias UK. Honorary DArts Napier University 2008.

Publications: Editor: Gordon Brown Speeches (2006), Moving Britain Forward (2006), The Change We Choose: Speeches 2007-2009 (2010).

Recreations: Cinema, gardening, beekeeping.

The Lord Stevenson of Balmacara, House of Lords, London SW1A 0PW
Tel: 020 7219 8914/0777 8465103 *Email:* stevensonw@parliament.uk
Missenden House, Little Missenden, Amersham, Buckinghamshire HP7 0RD *Tel:* 01494 890689
Email: wilf@wilfstevenson.co.uk *Twitter:* @missenden50

CROSSBENCH

STEVENSON OF CODDENHAM, LORD

STEVENSON OF CODDENHAM (Life Baron), (Henry Dennistoun) Dennis Stevenson; cr. 1999. Born 19 July 1945; Son of late Alexander and Sylvia Stevenson, née Ingleby; Married Charlotte Susan Vanneck 1972 (4 sons).

Education: Trinity College, Glenalmond; King's College, Cambridge (MA classics 1970).

Non-political career: Chair, SRU Group of Companies 1972-96; Non-executive director, Manpower Inc 1988-2006; Chair: Sinfonia 21 1989-99, Pearson plc 1996-05, Halifax plc 1999-2008, HBOS plc 2001-08, Non-executive director: The Western Union Company 2006-, Culture and Sport Glasgow 2007-09, Loudwater Investment Partners Ltd 2007-.

Political career: *House of Lords:* Raised to the peerage as Baron Stevenson of Coddenham, of Coddenham in the County of Suffolk 1999. Member Works of Art 2009-10, 2012-13. *Councils and public bodies:* Chair, House of Lords Appointments Commission 2000-08.

Countries of interest: Holland, Japan, Sierra Leone, USA.

Other: Chair: Government Working Party on role of voluntary movements and youth in the environment 1971, Newton Aycliffe and Peterlee New Town Development Corporation 1971-80, Independent Advisory Committee on Pop Festivals 1972-76, National Association of Youth Clubs 1973-81; Director, National Building Agency 1977-81; Adviser on agricultural marketing to Minister of Agriculture 1979-83; Director, London Docklands Development Corporation 1981-88; Chair: Intermediate Technology Development Group 1983-90, Trustees, Tate Gallery 1988-98; Member, Panel on Takeovers and Mergers 1992-2000; Board member, British Council 1996-2003; Governor: London School of Economics 1996-2002, London Business School 1996-2002; Director, Glyndebourne Productions 1998-; Honorary Member, The Royal Society of Musicians of Great Britain 1998-; Trustee, Tate Gallery Foundation 1998-; Chair, Aldeburgh Music Ltd 2000-; Trustee, Horse's Mouth 2006-. Chancellor, University of the Arts, London 2000-10. CBE 1981; Kt 1998; Brooks's, MCC.

Publications: Stevenson Commission Information and Communications Technology in UK Schools Report (1997).

The Lord Stevenson of Coddenham CBE, House of Lords, London SW1A 0PW
Tel: 020 7219 5353
Little Tufton House, 3 Dean Trench Street, London SW1P 3HB *Tel:* 020 7340 0650 *Fax:* 020 7340 0653 *Email:* dennis@hdstevenson.co.uk

STEWARTBY, LORD

STEWARTBY (Life Baron), (Bernard Harold) Ian Halley Stewart; cr. 1992. Born 10 August 1935; Son of late Professor Harold Stewart of Stewartby, CBE, MD, DL, KStJ, FRSE; Married Honorary Deborah Buchan, JP, daughter of 3rd Baron Tweedsmuir 1966 (1 son 2 daughters).

Education: Haileybury College, Hertford; Jesus College, Cambridge (BA classics 1959, MA; DLitt 1978).

Non-political career: Served RNVR 1954-56; Lieutenant-Commander RNR. Brown Shipley & Co. Ltd 1960-83: Director 1971-83; Chair, Throgmorton Trust plc 1990-2005; Deputy chair, Standard Chartered plc 1993-2004; Director, Financial Services Authority 1993-97; Deputy chair: Amlin plc 1995-2006, Portman Building Society 1999-2002.

CONSERVATIVE

Political career: *House of Commons:* Contested North Hammersmith 1970 general election. MP (Conservative) for Hitchin 1974-83, for Hertfordshire North 1983-92. Opposition Spokesperson for the Banking Bill 1978-79; PPS to Geoffrey Howe as Chancellor of the Exchequer 1979-83; Parliamentary Under-Secretary of State (Procurement), Ministry of Defence 1983; Economic Secretary to the Treasury 1983-87; Minister of State: Armed Forces, MoD 1987-88, Northern Ireland Office 1988-89. *House of Lords:* Raised to the peerage as Baron Stewartby, of Portmoak in the District of Perth and Kinross 1992. *Councils and public bodies:* Director, British Numismatic Society 1965-75; Numismatic adviser, National Art Collections Fund 1989-; Chair: British Academy Committee for the Sylloge of Coins of the British Isles 1993-2003, Treasure Valuation Committee 1996-2001.

Political interests: Financial markets, tax, charities, foreign affairs, defence; China, EU, India.

Other: Life Governor, Haileybury 1977; County Vice-President, St John Ambulance Brigade for Hertfordshire 1978-; Chair, Economic Standing Committee, Bow Group 1978-83; Trustee, Parliamentary Pension Fund 2000-05; President: Sir Halley Stewart Trust 2002-, The Stewart Society 2007-; FSA (Council Member 1974-76); FBA 1981; FRSE 1986. Jesus College, Cambridge: DLitt 1978, Honorary Fellow 1994. Royal Numismatic Society Medal 1996. RD 1972; PC 1989; Kt 1991; KStJ 1992; New (Edinburgh), Beefsteak, Hawks (Cambridge). Lords and Commons Cricket Club; MCC.

Publications: The Scottish Coinage (1955, 1967); Scottish Mints (1971); Co-author: Studies in Numismatic Method (1983), Coinage in Tenth Century England (1989), New History of the Royal Mint (1992); Author, English Coins 1180-1551 (2009).

Recreations: Archaeology, tennis, cricket.

Rt Hon the Lord Stewartby, House of Lords, London SW1A 0PW
Tel: 020 7219 6418 *Fax:* 020 7821 6455

STEYN, LORD

CROSSBENCH

STEYN (Life Baron), Johan van Zyl Steyn; cr. 1995. Born 15 August 1932; Son of Van Zyl Steyn and Janet Steyn; Married Susan Lewis 1977 (2 sons and 2 daughters from previous marriage; 1 stepson and 1 stepdaughter).

Education: Jan van Riebeeck School, Cape Town, South Africa; University of Stellenbosch, South Africa (BA law 1957; LLB 1957); University College, Oxford (MA law 1957) Cape Province Rhodes Scholar 1955.

Non-political career: Commenced practice at the South African Bar 1958; Senior Counsel of Supreme Court of South Africa 1970; English Bar 1973; QC 1979; Bencher, Lincoln's Inn 1985; Judge of the High Court, Queen's Bench Division 1985-91; Member, Supreme Court Rule Committee 1985-89; Departmental Advisory Committee on Arbitration Law 1986-89, Chair 1990-94; Chair, Race Relations Committee of the Bar 1987-88; Presiding Judge, Northern Circuit 1989-91; President, British Insurance Law Association 1992-94; Lord Justice of Appeal 1992-95; Chair: Advisory Council, Centre for Commercial Law Studies, Queen Mary and Westfield College, London 1993-94, Lord Chancellor's Advisory Committee on Legal Education and Conduct 1994-96, Appeal Board of the Takeover Panel 2006-.

Political career: *House of Lords:* Raised to the peerage as Baron Steyn, of Swafield in the County of Norfolk 1995. Lord of Appeal in Ordinary 1995-2005.

Other: Honorary Member: American Law Institute 1999, Society of Legal Scholars 2002. Three honorary doctorates; Honorary fellow: University College, Oxford 1985, University College, London 2005. Kt 1985; PC 1992.

Publications: Democracy Through Law collected essays (Ashgate, 2004).

Rt Hon the Lord Steyn, House of Lords, London SW1A 0PW
Tel: 020 7219 5353

STIRRUP, LORD

CROSSBENCH

STIRRUP (Life Baron), Graham Eric (Jock) Stirrup; cr 2011. Born 4 December 1949; Son of William Stirrup and Jacqueline Stirrup, née Coulson; Married Mary Elliott 1976 (1 son).

Education: Merchant Taylors' School, Northwood; Royal Air Force College.

Non-political career: Qualified as flying instructor 1971; Service in the Sultan of Oman's Air Force 1973-75; Fighter reconnaissance pilot 1976-78; US Air Force 1978-81; Flight Commander 1982-84; Officer Commanding (OC) No II (Army Co-operation) Squadron 1985-87; Personal Staff Officer to Chief of the Air Staff 1987-90; OC RAF Marham 1990-92; Royal College of Defence Studies 1993; Director, Air Force Plans and Programmes, MoD 1994-97; Air OC No I 1997-98; Assistant Chief of Air Staff 1998-2000; Deputy Commander-in-Chief, Strike Command;

Commander NATO Combined Air Operations Centre 9 and Director, European Air Group 2000-02; Deputy Chief of Defence Staff (Equipment Capability) 2002-03; Chief of the Air Staff 2003-06; Chief of the Defence Staff 2006-10;.

Political career: *House of Lords:* Raised to the peerage as Baron Stirrup, of Marylebone in the City of Westminster 2011. Member House 2013-.

Countries of interest: Australia, Middle East, USA.

Other: Director, City of London Sinfonia; Governor, Wellington College; FRAeS; FIMgt. Honorary DSc, Cranfield University 2005. AFC 1982. CB 2000; KCB 2002; GCB 2005; KG 2013; Royal Air Force; Beefsteak.

Recreations: History, music, theatre, golf.

Air Chief Marshal the Lord Stirrup KG GCB AFC ADC, House of Lords, London SW1A 0PW
Tel: 020 7219 5979 *Email:* stirrupg@parliament.uk

STODDART OF SWINDON, LORD

STODDART OF SWINDON (Life Baron), David Leonard Stoddart; cr. 1983. Born 4 May 1926; Son of Arthur Stoddart, coal miner, and Queenie Stoddart; Married 2nd Jennifer Percival-Alwyn 1961 (2 sons) (1 daughter by previous marriage).

Education: St Clement Danes Grammar School; Henley Grammar School.

Non-political career: British Railways; NHS; Power station clerical worker 1951-70. NALGO 1951-70; EETPU (later AEEU, now Unite) 1953-.

**INDEPENDENT
LABOUR**

Political career: *House of Commons:* Contested Newbury 1959 and 1964 general elections. MP (Labour) for Swindon 1970-83. PPS to Reg Freeson as Minister for Housing and Construction 1974-75; Assistant Government Whip 1975-76; Government Whip 1976-77. *House of Lords:* Raised to the peerage as Baron Stoddart of Swindon, of Reading in the Royal County of Berkshire 1983. Opposition Spokesperson for Energy 1983-88; Opposition Whip 1983-88. *Councils and public bodies:* Reading County Borough Council: Councillor 1954-72, Council Leader 1967-72; Member, various boards inc. Thames Valley Water Board and Police Authority.

Political interests: Commonwealth, economic policy, energy, European Union, housing, industry, local government, transport.

Other: Member, Court and Council of Reading University 1964-68; Treasurer, Anzac Group 1985-2002; Chair: Campaign for an Independent Britain 1989-2007, Anti-Maastricht Alliance/ Alliance against the European constitution 1991-2007; Founder member, Global Britain; Phylis Court, Henley-on-Thames.

The Lord Stoddart of Swindon, House of Lords, London SW1A 0PW
Tel: 020 7219 5402

STONE OF BLACKHEATH, LORD

STONE OF BLACKHEATH (Life Baron), Andrew Zelig Stone; cr. 1997. Born 7 September 1942; Son of Sydney and Louise Stone; Married Vivienne Lee 1973 (1 son 2 daughters).

Education: Cardiff High School.

Non-political career: Marks and Spencer plc 1966-99: Personal assistant to chair 1978-80, Director 1990-, Joint managing director 1994-2000; Director: N Brown 2002-13, Ted Baker plc 2002-04, McDonalds Advisory Board 2005-07, Deal Group Media plc 2005-07; Deputy chair, Sindicatum Carbon Capital Holdings Ltd 2005-09; Director, Falcon Power Holdings 2012-.

LABOUR

Political career: *House of Lords:* Raised to the peerage as Baron Stone of Blackheath, of Blackheath in the London Borough of Greenwich 1997. Departmental Liaison Peer to Baroness Jay as Leader of the House of Lords 1999-2001. Member House of Lords Offices Refreshment Sub-committee 2000-02.

Political interests: Conflict resolution, art and science, health, ecology; China, Middle East.

Other: British Overseas Trade Board for Israel: Chair 1991-99, President 1995-2000; Governor, Weizmann Institute Foundation 1993-; Council member, Arts and Business 1994-2001; Member, national advisory committee, Creative and Cultural Education 1998-2000; Director, Science Media Centre 2001-05; Governor, Tel Aviv University 2001-04; Honorary Vice-President, The Movement for Reform Judaism; Chair, Dipex (Direct Patient Experiences) 2005-; Trustee Olive Tree Trust 2005-09; Governor, British University of Egypt 2006-; Member, Risk Commission (RSA); Chair, Sindicatum Climate Change Foundation 2009-11; Trustee, Prism the Gift Fund 2009-; Orphaids, Gauchers Association, DIPEX. Two honorary degrees.

Recreations: Reading, walking, thinking, meditating.

The Lord Stone of Blackheath, House of Lords, London SW1A 0PW
Tel: 020 7219 4556 *Fax:* 020 7219 5979 *Email:* stonea@parliament.uk

STONEHAM OF DROXFORD, LORD

STONEHAM OF DROXFORD (Life Baron), Benjamin Russell Mackintosh Stoneham; cr 2011. Born 24 August 1948; Son of Major B.J.R. Stoneham and Beryl Stoneham; Married Anne 1975 (2 sons 1 daughter).

Education: Harrow School; Christ's College, Cambridge (BA economics 1970); Warwick University (MA industrial relations 1971).

Non-political career: Research officer, Social and Administrative Studies Department, Oxford University 1971-74; NCB 1974-78; National officer, National Union of Railwaymen 1979-82; **LIBERAL DEMOCRAT** Portsmouth and Sunderland Newspapers 1982-89; Managing director, Portsmouth Publishing and Printing Ltd 1989-99; Group production and personnel director, News International 2000-03; Operations director, Liberal Democrat HQ 2003-10; Chair and director, First Wessex Housing Group Ltd 2007-12; Chairman, Housing 21 2011-.

Political career: *House of Commons:* Contested (Labour) Saffron Walden 1977 and 1979 and (SDP/All) Stevenage 1983 and 1987 general elections. *House of Lords:* Raised to the peerage as Baron Stoneham of Droxford, of the Meon Valley in the County of Hampshire 2011. Liberal Democrat Whip 2011-. Member: EU Sub-committee E (Justice, Institutions and Consumer Protection) 2012-; Olympic and Paralympic Legacy 2013-. *Councils and public bodies:* Councillor, Hertfordshire County Council 1985-89.

Political interests: Pensions, housing and regeneration, media; France, South Africa, USA.

Other: Director, Make Votes Count; Trustee, Coltstaple Trust.

The Lord Stoneham of Droxford, House of Lords, London SW1A 0PW
Tel: 020 7219 8629

STOREY, LORD

STOREY (Life Baron), Michael John Storey; cr 2011. Born 25 May 1949; Married (1 daughter).
Education: Liverpool University (BEd).

Non-political career: Teacher: Prescot CoE Primary School, Prescot; New Hutte Primary School, Halewood; Deputy headteacher, Halsnead Primary School, Whiston; Headteacher 1986-: St Gabriel's CoE Primary School, Huyton, Plantation County Primary School, Halewood.

Political career: *House of Lords:* Raised to the peerage as Baron Storey, of Childwall in the City of Liverpool 2011. Liberal Democrat Whip 2011-. Member Small- and Medium-Sized Enterprises **LIBERAL DEMOCRAT** 2012-13. Chair, Liberal Democrat Parliamentary Committee for Education, Families and Young People 2013-. *Councils and public bodies:* Liverpool City Council: Councillor 1973-2011, Leader, Liberal Democrat opposition 1991-98, Council Leader 1998-2005, Lord Mayor of Liverpool 2009-10.

Political interests: Education, arts, local authorities, Merseyside; France, Germany, Switzerland, USA.

Other: OBE 1994; CBE 2002.

Recreations: Reading, theatre, cinema, gardening.

The Lord Storey CBE, House of Lords, London SW1A 0PW
Tel: 020 7219 1972 *Email:* storeym@parliament.uk *Twitter:* @LordStorey

STOWELL OF BEESTON, BARONESS

Parliamentary Under-Secretary of State, Department for Communities and Local Government

STOWELL OF BEESTON (Life Baroness), Tina Wendy Stowell; cr 2011. Born 2 July 1967; Daughter of David Stowell and Margaret Stowell; Single (no children).

Education: Chilwell Comprehensive School; Broxtowe College of Further Education 1985.

Non-political career: Civil servant 1986-96: Ministry of Defence 1986-88, British Embassy, **CONSERVATIVE** Washington DC 1988-91, Downing Street Press Office 1991-96; Private Sector (various, including Paradine Productions, Granada Media) 1996-98; Deputy Chief of Staff to William Hague MP as Leader of the Conservative Party 1998-2001; British Broadcasting Corporation: Deputy Secretary 2001-03, Head of communications to the Chairman and Board of Governors/BBC Trust 2003-08, Head of corporate affairs 2008-10; Consultant, Tina Stowell Associates 2010-11.

Political career: *House of Lords:* Raised to the peerage as Baroness Stowell of Beeston, of Beeston in the County of Nottinghamshire 2011. Party Whip 2011; Government Whip 2011-13; Government Spokesperson for: Energy and Climate Change 2011-12, International Development 2011-12, Home Office 2011-, Culture, Media and Sport 2012-13, Northern Ireland September-October 2012, Women and Equalities 2012-, Work and Pensions 2012-13; Parliamentary Under-Secretary of State, Department for Communities and Local Government 2013-. Member Joint Committee on: Human Rights 2011, Security 2012-. *Other:* Deputy Chairman (Political), Finchley and Golders Green Conservative Association 2011-.

Political interests: Social mobility, political reform; USA.

Other: MBE 1996.

Recreations: Running (when not injured).

The Baroness Stowell of Beeston MBE, House of Lords, London SW1A 0PW

Tel: 020 7219 5353 *Email:* stowellt@parliament.uk *Website:* www.tinastowell.co.uk

Twitter: @tinastowell

LIBERAL DEMOCRAT

STRASBURGER, LORD

STRASBURGER (Life Baron), Paul Cline Strasburger; cr 2011. Born 31 July 1946; Married (1 daughter).

Non-political career: IT and security industries; Property management.

Political career: *House of Lords:* Raised to the peerage as Baron Strasburger, of Langridge in the County of Somerset 2011. Member Joint Committee on the Draft Communications Data Bill 2012-13.

Political interests: Civil law, justice and rights, liberating potential (particularly in young people with a bad start in life), freedom, environment, fighting privilege and greed.

Other: The Prince's Trust. MCC.

Recreations: All music (almost), sport, theatre, adventure.

The Lord Strasburger, House of Lords, London SW1A 0PW

Tel: 020 7219 5081 *Email:* strasburgerp@parliament.uk *Twitter:* @LordStras

CONSERVATIVE

STRATHCLYDE, LORD

STRATHCLYDE (2nd Baron, UK), Thomas Galloway Dunlop du Roy de Blicquy Galbraith; cr. 1955. Born 22 February 1960; Son of late Honorary Sir Thomas Galbraith, KBE, MP, eldest son of 1st Baron, PC; Married Jane Skinner 1992 (3 daughters).

Education: Wellington College, Berkshire; University of East Anglia 1978-82; University of Aix-en-Provence 1981.

Non-political career: Lloyd's insurance broker; Bain Clarkson Ltd 1982-88; Chair, Trafalgar Capital Management Ltd 2001-10; Director: Scottish Mortgage Investment Trust plc 2004-10, Galena Asset Management Ltd 2004-10, Marketform Group Ltd 2004-10, Hampden Agencies Ltd 2008-10; Director, Trafigura Beheer BV Supervisory Board 2013-.

Political career: *House of Lords:* First entered House of Lords 1985; Government Spokesperson for Department of Trade and Industry (DTI), Treasury and Scotland 1988-89; Government Whip 1988-89; Parliamentary Under-Secretary of State: Department of Employment (Tourism) 1989-90, Department of Environment 1990, DTI 1993-94; Scottish Office (Agriculture and Fisheries) 1990-92; Parliamentary Under-Secretary of State: Department of Environment 1992-93, Minister of State DTI 1994; Government Chief Whip 1994-97; Member, Shadow Cabinet 1997-2010; Opposition Chief Whip 1997-98; Deputy Speaker 1997-98; Deputy Chairman of Committees 1997-98; Leader of the Opposition 1998-2010; Opposition Spokesperson for Constitutional Affairs December 1998-2005; Elected hereditary peer 1999-; Leader of the House of Lords 2010-13; Chancellor of the Duchy of Lancaster 2010-13. Member: House -2013, Liaison -2013, Privileges/Privileges and Conduct -2013, Procedure -2013, Selection -2013. *Other:* Contested Merseyside East 1984 European Parliament election. Chair, Commission on the Future Structure of the Scottish Conservative and Unionist Party 1997-98.

Other: President, Quoted Companies Alliance 2003-09. Peer of 2000 Channel 4 and *The House Magazine*; Peer of the Year, *The Spectator* 2004. PC 1995; CH 2013.

Publications: New Frontiers for Reform (CPS, 2001); Working in Harness: parliamentary government and the role of the Lords (Politeia, 2005).

Rt Hon the Lord Strathclyde CH, House of Lords, London SW1A 0PW

Tel: 020 7219 5353 *Fax:* 020 7219 3051

SUGAR, LORD

SUGAR (Life Baron), Alan Michael Sugar; cr 2009. Born 24 March 1947; Married Ann Simons 1968 (2 sons 1 daughter).

Non-political career: Amstrad and post-1997 successors Betacom and Viglen: Founder chair 1968-97, Chair 1991-2001, Chief executive 1998-2000; Presenter, *The Apprentice* BBC TV 2005-.

Political career: *House of Lords:* Raised to the peerage as Baron Sugar, of Clapton in the London Borough of Hackney 2009. Government Enterprise Champion 2009-10.

Other: Kt 2000.

LABOUR

The Lord Sugar, House of Lords, London SW1A 0PW
Tel: 020 7219 5353 *Twitter:* @Lord_Sugar

SUTHERLAND OF HOUNDWOOD, LORD

SUTHERLAND OF HOUNDWOOD (Life Baron), Stewart Ross Sutherland; cr 2001. Born 25 February 1941; Son of late George Sutherland and Ethel, née Masson; Married Sheena Robertson 1964 (2 daughters 1 son).

Education: Woodside School, Aberdeen; Robert Gordon's College, Aberdeen; Aberdeen University (MA philosophy 1963); Corpus Christi College, Cambridge (BA philosophy of religion 1965, MA).

Non-political career: Assistant lecturer, University College of North Wales, Bangor 1965-68; Lecturer, reader, Stirling University 1968-77; King's College, London: Professor of history and philosophy of religion 1977-85, Vice-principal 1981-85, Titular professor 1985-94, Principal 1985-90; Inspector of Schools and founder, Office for Standards in Education (OFSTED) 1992-94; Principal and Vice-chancellor, Edinburgh University 1994-2002; Non-executive director, NHP 2001-05; Chair: YTL Education (UK) Ltd 2003-, Frogtrade 2013-.

CROSSBENCH

Political career: *House of Lords:* Raised to the peerage as Baron Sutherland of Houndwood, of Houndwood in the Scottish Borders 2001. Member Science and Technology 2003-07; Chair: Science and Technology Sub-committee I (Scientific Aspects of Ageing) 2004-05, Science and Technology 2007-10; Member: Science and Technology Sub-committee I 2007- (Waste Reduction 2007-08, Nanotechnologies and food 2008-10, Radioactive Waste Management: a further update 2010), Science and Technology Sub-committee II (Genomic Medicine) 2008-09. *Councils and public bodies:* Member, Council for Science and Technology 1993-2000; Chair, Committee on Appeal Court Procedure (Scotland) 1994-96; Member, Higher Education Funding Council for England 1995-2001; Chair, Royal Commission on Long Term Care of the Elderly 1997-99; Provost, Gresham College 2002-08.

Political interests: Education, care of the elderly, research policy.

Other: Member, Hong Kong University Grants Committee 1995-2004; Honorary President, Alzheimer's and Dementia (Scotland) 2000-; Chair, Scottish Care 2001-; Honorary President, Saltire Society 2002-05; Chair, Quarry Products Association 2002-05; Board member, Courtauld Institute of Art 2002-07; President, Royal Society of Edinburgh 2002-05; Council member: British Academy 2002-05, Foundation for Science and Technology 2003-; President, David Hume Institute 2005-08; Chair, Associated Board of Royal Schools of Music 2006-12; Patron, University College London Centre for Dementia Care 2008-; Chair, Chartered Institute of Education Assessors 2009-11; FBA 1992; FRSE 1995; Eight honorary fellowships; Ethiopian Gemini Trust. Goldsmiths' Company: Court of Assistants 2000-, Prime Warden 2012-13. London University: Vice-chancellor 1990-94, Pro-chancellor 2006-08. 19 honorary degrees. Kt 1995; KT 2002; New Club, Edinburgh.

Publications: Criminal Appeals and Alleged Miscarriages of Justice (1996); With Respect to Old Age (Royal Commission Report, 1999); Higher Education in Hong Kong (2003); Independent Review of Free Personal and Nursing Care in Scotland (2008); The Sutherland Inquiry into SATS (2009); Various books and academic articles.

Recreations: Rough gardening, jazz, Tassie Medallions, theatre.

The Lord Sutherland of Houndwood KT, House of Lords, London SW1A 0PW
Tel: 020 7219 1618 *Email:* sutherlands@parliament.uk

SUTTIE, BARONESS – *Please see Addenda px*

SWINFEN, LORD

SWINFEN (3rd Baron, UK), Roger Mynors Swinfen Eady; cr. 1919. Born 14 December 1938; Son of 2nd Baron; Married Patricia Blackmore 1962 (1 son 3 daughters).

Education: Westminster School; RMA, Sandhurst.

Non-political career: Lieutenant, The Royal Scots (The Royal Regiment). Director, Swinfen Charitable Trust 1998-.

Political career: *House of Lords:* First entered House of Lords 1977; Elected hereditary peer 1999-. Member: Greater Manchester Bill 1979, European Communities House of Lords: Sub-committees: C 1990-94, B 2004-05; Co-opted member: EU Sub-committees: B (Internal Market) 2005-06, C (Foreign Affairs, Defence and Development Policy) 2007-10; Member: Hybrid Instruments 2010-, Joint Committee on Consolidation, Etc, Bills 2010-, Mental Capacity Act 2005 2013-. *Councils and public bodies:* JP, Kent 1983-85.

CONSERVATIVE

Political interests: Disability, telemedicine.

Other: President, South East Region British Sports Association for the Disabled; Member, Direct Mail Services Standards Board 1983-97; Fellow, Industry and Parliament Trust 1983; Patron: Disablement Income Group 1988-, Labrador Rescue South East 1996-; Director, Swinden Charitable Trust 1998-; Patron: World Orthopaedic Concern, MOET Iraq (Management of Obstetric Emergency Trauma), KunDe Foundation; Director, American Telemedicine Association 2009-13. Liveryman, Worshipful Company of Drapers. Honorary Research Fellow, Centre for Online Health, University of Queensland 2001-10.

Publications: Co-author An Evaluation of the First Year's Experience with a Low-cost Telemedicine Link in Bangladesh (2001), Store-and-Forward Teleneurology in Developing Countries (2001), Experience with a Low-cost Telemedicine System in Three Developing Countries (2001); Low Cost Telemedicine in the Developing World (2002); Telemedicine: The Way Ahead for Medicine in the Developing World (2003); Prospective Case Review of a Global E-health System for Doctors in Developing Countries (2004); Telemedicine Support for Iraq (2005); Low-cost Telemedicine in Iraq: analysis of referrals in the first 15 months (2005); Supporting Hospital Doctors in the Middle East by Email Telemedicine: Something the industrial world can do (2007).

Recreations: Gardening, painting, reading history.

The Lord Swinfen, House of Lords, London SW1A 0PW
Tel: 020 7219 3500 *Email:* swinfenr@parliament.uk

SYMONS OF VERNHAM DEAN, BARONESS

SYMONS OF VERNHAM DEAN (Life Baroness), Elizabeth Conway Symons; cr. 1996. Born 14 April 1951; Daughter of Ernest Vize Symons and Elizabeth Megan, née Jenkins ; Married Philip Bassett 2001 (1 son).

Education: Putney High School for Girls; Girton College, Cambridge (MA history 1974).

Non-political career: Research, Girton College, Cambridge 1972-74; Administration trainee, Department of the Environment 1974-77; Inland Revenue Staff Federation: Assistant secretary 1977-78, Deputy general secretary 1978-89; General secretary, Association of First Division Civil Servants 1989-97. Member, General Council, TUC 1989-96.

LABOUR

Political career: *House of Lords:* Raised to the peerage as Baroness Symons of Vernham Dean, of Vernham Dean in the County of Hampshire 1996. Parliamentary Under-Secretary of State, Foreign and Commonwealth Office 1997-99; Minister of State for: Defence Procurement, Ministry of Defence 1999-2001, International Trade and Investment, Foreign and Commonwealth Office and Department of Trade and Industry 2001-03; Government Spokesperson for: Foreign and Commonwealth Office 2001-05, Trade and Industry 2001-05; Deputy Leader of the Lords 2001-05; Minister of State for Middle East, Foreign and Commonwealth Office 2003-05; Opposition Spokesperson for Foreign and Commonwealth Office 2010-11. Member: EU Sub-committee C (Foreign Affairs, Defence and Development Policy): Co-opted member 2005-06, Member 2006-09; Member: Conventions Joint Committee 2006, European Union 2006-10; Co-opted member EU Sub-committee D (Environment and Agriculture) 2009-10; Member: National Security Strategy Joint Committee 2010, Joint Committee on the Draft House of Lords Reform Bill 2011-12. *Other:* Member, Parliamentary Labour Party Parliamentary Committee 2001-10. *Councils and public bodies:* Member, Employment Appeal Tribunal 1995-97.

Other: Council member, RIPA 1989-97; Governor. Polytechnic of North London 1989-94; Honorary Associate, National Council of Women 1989; Member: Executive Council, Campaign for Freedom of Information 1989-97, Hansard Society Council 1992-97, Advisory Council, Civil Service College 1992-97; Governor, London Business School 1993-97; Council member: Industrial Society 1994-97, Open University 1994-97; FRSA. Lords Select Committee Member of the Year, *House Magazine* awards 2012. PC 2001.

Recreations: Reading, gardening.

Rt Hon the Baroness Symons of Vernham Dean, House of Lords, London SW1A 0PW
Tel: 020 7219 5837

CROSSBENCH

TANLAW, LORD

TANLAW (Life Baron), Simon Brooke Mackay; cr. 1971. Born 30 March 1934; Son of late 2nd Earl of Inchcape; Married Joanna Susan Hirsch 1959 (1 son 2 daughters and 1 son deceased); married Rina Siew Yong Tan 1976 (1 son 1 daughter).

Education: Eton College; Trinity College, Cambridge (BA medieval history, archaeology and anthropology 1957, MA).

Non-political career: Commissioned army national service, XII Royal Lancers, Malaya 1952-54. Inchcape Group of Companies, India and Far East 1960-66: Managing director 1967-71, Director 1971-92; Chair, Fandstan Group of Companies 1973-; Member, Executive Committee of the Great Britain-China Centre 1981-88.

Political career: *House of Commons:* Contested (Liberal) Galloway 1959, 1960 and 1964 general elections. *House of Lords:* Raised to the peerage as Baron Tanlaw, of Tanlawhill in the County of Dumfries 1971. *Councils and public bodies:* President, Sarawak Association 1973-75, 1997-99, 2012-; Member, Court of Governors, London School of Economics 1980-96.

Political interests: Time, space, countryside, daylight saving; Malaysia, Singapore.

Other: Honorary Treasurer, Scottish Peers Association 1979-86; Royal Observatory Greenwich Appeal Board 2004-05; Fellow: British Horological Institute, Royal Astronomical Society; President, Sarawak Association 2012-; Fellow, Buckingham University; Elizabeth Fitzroy Support for people with learning difficulties; Tanlaw Foundation. Member: Worshipful Company of Fishmongers, Worshipful Company of Clockmakers. Chancellor, Buckingham University 2010-13. Honorary DUniversity, Buckingham University 1983; White's, Oriental, Puffin's (Edinburgh). Houghton Club.

Publications: Articles in Horological Journal.

Recreations: Fishing, horology.

The Lord Tanlaw, House of Lords, London SW1A 0PW
Tel: 020 7219 4613 *Email:* tanlaws@parliament.uk lordtanlaw@gmail.com

LIBERAL DEMOCRAT

TAVERNE, LORD

TAVERNE (Life Baron), Dick Taverne; cr. 1996. Born 18 October 1928; Son of late Dr N. J. M. Taverne and of Mrs L. V. Taverne; Married Janice Hennessey 1955 (2 daughters).

Education: Charterhouse, Surrey; Balliol College, Oxford (Greats 1951).

Non-political career: Called to the Bar, Middle Temple 1954; QC 1965; Institute for Fiscal Studies: Director 1970-79, Director-General 1979-81, Chair 1981-83; Axa Equity and Law: Director 1972-2001, Chair 1997-2001; Director, BOC Group 1975-95; PRIMA Europe Ltd: Director 1987-, Chair 1991-93, President 1993-98; Chair, OLIM Investment Trust 1989-99; Deputy chair, Central European Growth Fund 1994-2000; Chair, monitoring board, Axa Sun Life plc 2001-; President, Research Defence Society 2003-08; Chair, IFG Developments Initiative Ltd 2004-07.

Political career: *House of Commons:* Contested Wandsworth, Putney 1959 general election. MP (Labour) for Lincoln 1962-72 (resigned), (Democratic Labour) for Lincoln March 1973 to September 1974. Contested (SDP) Southwark, Peckham 1982 by-election and Dulwich 1983 general election. Parliamentary Under-Secretary of State, Home Office 1966-68; HM Treasury: Minister of State 1968-69, Financial Secretary 1969-70. *House of Lords:* Raised to the peerage as Baron Taverne, of Pimlico in the City of Westminster 1996. Liberal Democrat Spokesperson for: Treasury 1998-2005, (Euro) 2001-05. Member: Monetary Policy of the Bank of England 2000-03, Animals in Scientific Procedures 2001-02, European Union Sub-committee A (Economic and Financial Affairs, Trade and External Relations/Economic and Financial Affairs) 2003-05, Science and Technology 2004-09, Science and Technology Sub-committee II (Genomic Medicine) 2008-09; Co-opted member Science and Technology 2009. *Other:* Member: National Committee, Social Democratic Party 1981-87; Federal Policy Committee, Liberal Democrats 1989-90. *Councils and public bodies:* Chair: Public Policy Centre 1983-87, Alcohol and Drug Abuse Prevention and Treatment Ltd 1996-2008, Sense About Science 2002-.

Political interests: Science and technology, European Union, crime and drugs, tax, economic policy.

Other: Member, International Independent Review Body to review workings of European Commission 1979. Association of British Science Writers Parliamentary Science Communicator of the Year 2006; Cruising Association. Cruising Association.

Publications: The Future of the Left: Lincoln and after (1974); The March of Unreason – Science, Democracy and the New Fundamentalism (2005).

Recreations: Sailing.

The Lord Taverne QC, House of Lords, London SW1A 0PW

Tel: 020 7219 3341

25 Tufton Court, Tufton Street, London SW1P 3QH *Tel:* 020 7233 2409

TAYLOR OF BLACKBURN, LORD

LABOUR

TAYLOR OF BLACKBURN (Life Baron), Thomas Taylor; cr. 1978. Born 10 June 1929; Son of James and Edith Gladys Taylor; Married Kathleen Nurton 1950 (1 son).

Education: Blakey Moor Elementary School.

Non-political career: Department of social administration, Manchester University; Consultant: Initial Electronic Security Systems Ltd, BAE Systems plc 1994-2005; Adviser, several energy and other businesses: Electronic Data Systems Ltd 1996-2009, Experian 1999-2009, Lucent 2003-09, NPL Estates 2004-09, Canatxx Energy Ventures Ltd 2004-09; Non-executive director: Adivision 2005-09, Eisis 2005-; Adviser, BT plc 2007-09; President, Wrens Hotel Group; Member, Norweb Board. Member, USDAW 1946-79.

Political career: *House of Lords:* Raised to the peerage as Baron Taylor of Blackburn, of Blackburn in the County of Lancaster 1978. Suspended from membership May-November 2009. *Other:* Member, Labour North West Group. *Councils and public bodies:* Blackburn Council: Councillor 1954-76, Council Leader -1976; JP, Blackburn 1960; Member of Council, Lancaster University 1961-95; President, Free Church Council 1962-63; Chair, Electricity Consumers Council for North West 1977-80; DL, Lancashire 1994-2009.

Political interests: Education, North West, railways, Commonwealth, energy, local government; Croatia.

Other: Member Commonwealth Parliamentary Association 1978-; Vice-President, Association of Lancastrians in London 1994-; Patron/President of several voluntary organisations; FRGS 1994; FICPD 1998. Freeman: Borough of Blackburn 1992, City of London 1999. Deputy Pro-Chancellor, Lancaster University 1961-95. Honorary LLD, Lancaster 1996. OBE 1969; CBE 1974.

Publications: A New Partnership for our Schools (1977).

Recreations: Gardening, radio, books, music.

The Lord Taylor of Blackburn CBE, House of Lords, London SW1A 0PW

Tel: 020 7219 5130 *Fax:* 020 7219 5979

TAYLOR OF BOLTON, BARONESS

LABOUR

TAYLOR OF BOLTON (Life Baroness), Ann Taylor; cr 2005. Born 2 July 1947; Daughter of late John Walker and late Doreen Bowling; Married David Taylor 1966 (1 son 1 daughter).

Education: Bolton School; Bradford University (BSc politics and economic history 1969); Sheffield University (MA economic history 1970).

Non-political career: Part-time tutor, Open University 1971-74; Monitoring officer, Housing Corporation 1985-87; Member, Intelligence Review Committee 2004; Parliamentary Fellowship, St Anthony's College, Oxford; Member, advisory board, Thales UK 2010-. Member: Association of University Teachers GMB.

Political career: *House of Commons:* Contested Bolton West February 1974 general election. MP (Labour) for Bolton West October 1974-83. Contested Bolton North East 1983 general election. MP (Labour) for Dewsbury 1987-2005. PPS to Fred Mulley: as Secretary of State for Education and Science 1975-76, as Secretary of State for Defence 1976-77; Government Whip 1977-79; Opposition Frontbench Spokesperson for: Education 1979-81, Housing 1981-83, Home Office 1987-88, Environment 1988-92; Shadow Secretary of State for Education 1992-94; Shadow Chancellor of the Duchy of Lancaster 1994-95; Shadow Leader of the House 1994-97: Member House of Commons Commission 1994-98, President of the Council and Leader of the House of Commons 1997-98; Member Public Accounts Commission 1997-98; Government Chief Whip 1998-2001. Chair Intelligence and Security Committee 2001-05. *House of Lords:* Raised to the peerage as Baroness Taylor of Bolton, of Bolton in the County of Greater Manchester 2005. Parliamentary Under-Secretary of State and Government Spokesperson: Ministry of Defence 2007-10 (Defence

Equipment and Support 2007-08, International Defence and Security 2008-10), Foreign and Commonwealth Office 2009-10. Member Joint Committee on National Security Strategy 2010-. *Councils and public bodies:* Holmfirth UDC 1972-74.

Political interests: Education, Home Office, intelligence and security, defence.

Other: Honorary Fellow, Birkbeck College, London University; Honorary Doctorate, Bradford University. PC 1997.

Publications: Choosing Our Future – Practical Politics of the Environment (1992).

Recreations: Bolton Wanderers football club.

Rt Hon the Baroness Taylor of Bolton, House of Lords, London SW1A 0PW
Tel: 020 7219 5183 *Email:* taylora@parliament.uk

TAYLOR OF GOSS MOOR, LORD

LIBERAL DEMOCRAT

TAYLOR OF GOSS MOOR (Life Baron), Matthew Owen John Taylor; cr 2010. Born 3 January 1963; Son of late Ken Taylor, screenwriter, and Jill Taylor, née Black; Married Victoria Garner 2009 (3 sons).

Education: Treliske School, Truro; University College School, London; Lady Margaret Hall, Oxford (BA politics, philosophy and economics 1986, MA).

Non-political career: Sabbatical President, Oxford University Student Union 1985-86; Economic policy researcher, Parliamentary Liberal Party, attached to David Penhaligon MP 1986-87; Director, Taylor & Garner Ltd (family business); Chair, National Housing Federation 2009-; Non-executive director, South West Water 2010-; Chair, St Austell Ecotown Strategic Partnership Board 2010-; Non-executive director, Mayfield Towns Ltd 2013-; Chair, Bridgehall Real Estate 2013-.

Political career: *House of Commons:* MP (Liberal 1987-88, Lib Dem 1988-2010) for Truro 12 March 1987 by-election to 1997, for Truro and St Austell 1997-2010. Liberal Spokesperson for Energy 1987-88; Liberal Democrat Spokesperson for: England (Local Government, Housing and Transport) 1988-89, Trade and Industry 1989-90, Education 1990-92, Citizen's Charter 1992-94; Principal Spokesperson for: Environment 1994-97, the Environment and Transport 1997-99, Economy 1999-2003, Cabinet Office and Social Exclusion 2006-07. Member: Broadcasting 1992-94, Environment 1996-97. *House of Lords:* Raised to the peerage as Baron Taylor of Goss Moor, of Truro in the County of Cornwall 2010. *Other:* Chair, Liberal Democrat: Campaigns and Communications 1989-95, Parliamentary Party 2003-05.

Political interests: Environment, economy, education, international development, rural communities, housing, sustainable development, planning.

Publications: Living Working Countryside (DCLG Review of Rural Housing and Rural Economy, 2008); The Rural Challenge (2010); Planning Practice Guidance Review (DCLG, 2013).

The Lord Taylor of Goss Moor, House of Lords, London SW1A 0PW
Tel: 020 7219 5353 *Website:* www.matthewtaylor.info

TAYLOR OF HOLBEACH, LORD

Parliamentary Under-Secretary of State (Criminal Information) and Home Office

CONSERVATIVE

TAYLOR OF HOLBEACH (Life Baron), John Derek Taylor; cr 2006. Born 12 November 1943; Son of late Percy Taylor and Ethel Taylor, née Brocklehurst; Married Julia Cunnington 1968 (2 sons).

Education: Bedford School; Conversational French and Dutch.

Non-political career: Director, Taylors Bulbs of Spalding 1968-2010. Member, NFU Bulb subcommittee 1982-87.

Political career: *House of Commons:* Contested Chesterfield February and October 1974 general elections. *House of Lords:* Raised to the peerage as Baron Taylor of Holbeach, of South Holland in the County of Lincolnshire 2006. Opposition Whip 2006-10; Opposition Spokesperson for: Environment 2006-07, Wales 2006-07, Work and Pensions 2006-10, Environment, Food and Rural Affairs 2007-10; Government Whip 2010-11; Government Spokesperson for: Cabinet Office 2010-11, Energy and Climate Change 2010-11, Work and Pensions 2010-11; Parliamentary Under-Secretary of State: Department for Environment, Food and Rural Affairs 2011-12, (Criminal Information), Home Office 2012-. *Other:* Contested Nottingham 1979 European Parliament election. Member, Executive Committee, East Midlands Conservative Council 1966-98; Chair, Candidates Committee 1997-98, 2002-05; Member, Conservative Board of: Finance 1985-89, Management 1996-98, 2000-03; President and Conservative Conference Chair 1997-98; Deputy chair, Conservative Party 2000-03; Chair: National Conservative Convention 2000-03, Conservatives Abroad 2001-09, Conservative Agents Superannuation Fund 2006-10. *Councils and public bodies:* Member, Horticulture Development Council 1986-91; Minister of Agriculture's Regional Panel: Eastern Region 1990-92, East Midlands Region 1992-96, Lincoln Diocesan Assets Committee 1995-2001, 2004-.

Political interests: Agriculture and horticulture, environment, energy, waste, freight, democracy and political parties; France, Netherlands, Slovenia.

Other: Member, EC Working Party on European Bulb Industry 1982; Fellow, Royal Society of Arts 1994; Associate, Royal Agricultural Society 2012; Institute of Horticulture 2012. Worshipful Company of Gardeners; Worshipful Company of Farmers. Peer of the Year, *House Magazine* awards 2011; Personality of the Year, *Farm Business Magazine* 2012. CBE 1992; Farmers.

Publications: Taylors Bulb Book.

Recreations: Travel, arts, literature, music.

The Lord Taylor of Holbeach CBE, House of Lords, London SW1A 0PW
Tel: 020 7219 4051 *Email:* taylorjl@parliament.uk

TAYLOR OF WARWICK, LORD

NON-AFFILIATED

TAYLOR OF WARWICK (Life Baron), John David Beckett Taylor; cr. 1996. Born 21 September 1952; Son of late Derief Taylor, Warwickshire professional cricketer, and Mrs Enid Taylor, nurse; Married Dr Katherine Taylor 1981 (1 son 2 daughters).

Education: Moseley Church of England School, Birmingham; Moseley Grammar School; Keele University (BA law 1977); Gray's Inn, Inns of Court School of Law.

Non-political career: Barrister-at-Law, called Gray's Inn 1978; Television and radio presenter, writer and company director; Non-executive director: Currencies Direct Ltd -2010, Asia Now Resources Inc, Canada; Part-time Judge 2001-06. Member, NUJ.

Political career: *House of Commons:* Contested (Conservative) Cheltenham 1992 general election. *House of Lords:* Raised to the peerage as Baron Taylor of Warwick, of Warwick in the County of Warwickshire 1996. Introduced the Criminal Evidence (Amendment) Bill which came into force March 1997 as the Criminal Evidence (Amendment) Act 1997; Suspended from membership May 2011-June 2012. Member Information 2007-11. *Other:* Member, Association of Conservative Peers -2010; Resigned Conservative Whip July 2010. *Councils and public bodies:* Councillor, Solihull Borough Council 1986-91; Member: North West Thames Regional Health Authority 1992-93, Greater London Further Education Funding Council 1992-95; Vice-President, British Board of Film Classification 1998-; Member, Independent Football Commission 2002-03.

Political interests: Law, broadcasting, film; China, Italy, Jamaica, Japan, USA.

Other: Member: Inter-Parliamentary Union, Commonwealth Parliamentary Association; Life Patron, West Indian Senior Citizens Association (WISCA); Patron: Parents Need Children Adoption Charity, Kidscape Charity; Executive Committee Member, Sickle Cell Anaemia Relief Charity; Member: Royal Television Society, Radio Academy; Vice-President, National Small Business Bureau; President, African Caribbean Westminster Business Initiative; Barker, Variety Club of Great Britain; Director, The Warwick Leadership Foundation Charity; Vice-President, British Board of Film Classification 1998-; Member, Industry and Parliament Trust; Member: Bar Council, Institute of Directors; Variety Club of Great Britain, SCAR (Sickle Cell Anaemia Relief Charity), Director, The Warwick Leadership Foundation 1999-. City of London 1998; City of Lexington, Kentucky, USA 2004; City of Las Vegas, USA 2007. Chancellor, Bournemouth University 2002-07. Honorary LLD: Warwick University 2001, Asbury College, Kentucky, USA 2004. Gray's Inn Advocacy Prize 1978. Aston Villa Football Club; Honorary President, Ilford Town Football Club.

Publications: The System on Trial (BBC Publications, 1996).

Recreations: Singing, soccer and cricket, spending time with my family.

The Lord Taylor of Warwick, House of Lords, London SW1A 0PW
Tel: 020 7219 5353 *Email:* taylorjdb@parliament.uk *Website:* www.lordtaylor.org
Twitter: @LordJohnTaylor

CONSERVATIVE

TEBBIT, LORD

TEBBIT (Life Baron), Norman Beresford Tebbit; cr. 1992. Born 29 March 1931; Son of late Leonard Albert Tebbit; Married Margaret Daines 1956 (2 sons 1 daughter).

Education: Edmonton County Grammar School.

Non-political career: RAF pilot, 1949-51, Commissioned; Served RAuxAF 604 Squadron 1952-55. Journalist 1947-49; Publicist and publisher 1951-53; Airline pilot 1953-70; Assistant director of information, National Federation of Building Trades Employers 1975-79; Company director: Sears Holdings plc 1987-99, British Telecom 1987-96, BET 1987-96, Spectator (1828) Ltd 1989-2004; Political commentator on Sky Television's Target programme 1989-98; Company director, Onix Ltd 1990-92; Columnist: *The Sun* 1995-97, *Mail on Sunday* 1997-2001; Former director and adviser to JCB Excavators Ltd; Blogger, *Daily Telegraph* 2010-. Member and office holder, BALPA.

Political career: *House of Commons:* MP (Conservative) for Epping 1970-74, for Chingford 1974-92. PPS to Robin Chichester-Clarke as Minister of State, Department of Employment 1972-73; Parliamentary Under-Secretary of State, Department of Trade 1979-81; Minister of State for Industry 1981; Secretary of State for: Employment 1981-83, Trade and Industry and President of the Board of Trade 1983-85; Chancellor of the Duchy of Lancaster 1985-87. *House of Lords:* Raised to the peerage as Baron Tebbit, of Chingford in the London Borough of Waltham Forest 1992. *Other:* Chair, Conservative Party 1985-87.

Political interests: Europe, industrial relations, aviation; UK.

Other: President, Air League 1994-98; Chair, Battle of Britain London Monument Appeal 2003-06; President: The Nuffield Ortholics Appeal 2005-, Nuffield Orthopaedic Appeal 2005-; Member, Royal Aeronautical Society 2005-; Member, The Guild of Air Pilots and Air Navigators; Nuffield Orthopaedic Appeal. Liveryman, Guild of Air Pilots and Air Navigators. Freeman, City of London. PC 1981; CH 1987; Royal Air Force, Beefsteak, The Other Club.

Publications: Upwardly Mobile (1988); Unfinished Business (1991); The Game Cook (2009).

Recreations: Shooting.

Rt Hon the Lord Tebbit CH, House of Lords, London SW1A 0PW
Tel: 020 7219 5353 *Email:* tebbitn@parliament.uk

CROSSBENCH

TEMPLEMAN, LORD

TEMPLEMAN (Life Baron), Sydney William Templeman; cr. 1982. Born 3 March 1920; Son of late Herbert William Templeman; Married Margaret Rowles 1946 (died 1988) (2 sons); married Mrs Sheila Edworthy 1996 (died 2008).

Education: Southall Grammar School; St John's College, Cambridge (BA history 1940; law 1947).

Non-political career: Served Second World War 1939-45; Commissioned 4/1st Gurkha Rifles 1941; NW Frontier 1942; Arakan 1943; Imphal 1944 (despatches, Honorary Major); Burma 1945. Called to the Bar, Middle Temple and Lincoln's Inn 1947; Attorney-General of the Duchy of Lancaster 1970-72; Judge of the High Court of Justice, Chancery Division 1972-78; Lord Justice of Appeal 1978-82; Treasurer, Middle Temple 1987.

Political career: *House of Lords:* Raised to the peerage as Baron Templeman, of White Lackington in the County of Somerset 1982. Lord of Appeal in Ordinary 1982-94; On leave of absence October 2012-. Member: Ecclesiastical 1997-2002, Personal Bills -2009. *Councils and public bodies:* President, Senate of the Inns of Court and the Bar 1974-76; Member, Royal Commission on Legal Services 1976-79.

Other: Member, Bar Council 1961-65. Honorary Fellow, St John's College, Cambridge 1982; Six honorary doctorates. MBE (Mil) 1946; Kt 1972; PC 1978.

Rt Hon the Lord Templeman MBE, House of Lords, London SW1A 0PW
Tel: 020 7219 5353
Mellowstone, 1 Rosebank Crescent, Exeter EX4 6EJ *Tel:* 01392 275428

Need additional copies?
Call 020 7593 5679
Visit www.dodsshop.co.uk

TEMPLE-MORRIS, LORD

TEMPLE-MORRIS (Life Baron), Peter Temple-Morris; cr 2001. Born 12 February 1938; Son of late His Honorary Sir Owen Temple-Morris, QC; Married Tahere Alam 1964 (2 sons 2 daughters). **Education:** Malvern College; St Catharine's College, Cambridge (BA law 1961, MA 1965); French.

Non-political career: Barrister, Inner Temple 1962; Solicitor 1989-; Consultant solicitor with Moon Beever, solicitors, of Bloomsbury.

LABOUR

Political career: *House of Commons:* Contested (Conservative) Newport 1964 and 1966, and Norwood Lambeth 1970 general elections. MP for Leominster February 1974-2001 (Conservative February 1974 to October 1997, Independent October 1997 to June 1998, Labour October 1998-2001). PPS to Norman Fowler as Minister of Transport 1979. *House of Lords:* Raised to the peerage as Baron Temple-Morris, of Llandaff in the County of South Glamorgan and of Leominister in the County of Herefordshire 2001. Member: Delegated Powers and Regulatory Reform 2003-07, EU Sub-committee E: (Justice and Institutions) 2010-12, (Justice, Institutions and Consumer Protection) 2012-13. *Other:* Chair, Cambridge University Conservative Association 1961; Society of Conservative Lawyers: Member, executive committee 1968-71, 1990-97, Chair 1995-97. *Councils and public bodies:* Member, governing council, Malvern College 1978-2002; Chevalier du Tastevin (Chat. de Vougeot) 1988-; Chair, Lords and Commons Solicitors Group 1992-97; President, Iran Society Council 1995-2009; Member, advisory council, British Institute of Persian Studies 1997-2009; Jurade De St Emilion 1999-; Chair, British-Iranian Chamber of Commerce 2002-04; President, St Catharine's College, Cambridge Society 2004; Member, Lord Chancellor's Advisory Committee on National Records and Archives 2008-09; Chief Steward, City of Hereford 2009-.

Political interests: Foreign affairs, Irish affairs, European Union, constitutional and legal affairs; Iran, Middle East, Netherlands.

Other: Executive British Branch of Inter-Parliamentary Union: Member 1977-97, Chair 1982-85; Member, Parliamentary Delegation to United Nations 1980, 1984 (leader); Vice-chair, GB-USSR Association 1985-93; Honorary Vice-President, United Nations Association 1987-2005; British-Irish Parliamentary Body: Founding Co-chair 1990-97, Member 1997-2005; Vice-chair, GB-Russia and Eastern Europe Centre 1993-98; Commonwealth Parliamentary Association: Member, executive 1994-98, Vice-chair 1996; Member, Cambridge Afro-Asian Expedition 1961; Chair: Standing Committee on Home Affairs, Bow Group 1975-80, Afghanistan Support Committee 1981-82; Fellow, Industry and Parliament Trust 1988; Member: Academic Council, Wilton Park (FCO) 1990-97, Lord Chancellor's Advisory Committee on National Records and Archives Office (Kew) 2008; NSPCC. Freedom: City of London 1969, New Orleans, USA, Havana, Cuba. Honorary Citizen: New Orleans, USA, Havana, Cuba; Honorary Member, National Party of Australia, Queensland; Chief Steward, City of Hereford 2009-. Knight of the Order of Orange Nassau (Netherlands) 2007; Cardiff and County (Cardiff); Reform Club: Committee member 2007-, Chair, Wine Committee 2008-10.

Publications: Motoring Justice (1979), Various articles on foreign affairs and Ireland.

Recreations: Wine and food, travel, theatre, cinema, art galleries.

The Lord Temple-Morris, House of Lords, London SW1A 0PW

Tel: 020 7219 4181 *Fax:* 020 7219 6388 *Email:* templemorrisp@parliament.uk

TENBY, VISCOUNT

TENBY (3rd Viscount, UK), William Lloyd-George; cr. 1957. Born 7 November 1927; Son of 1st Viscount, PC, TD; Married Ursula Medlicott 1955 (1 son 2 daughters).

Education: Eastbourne College; St Catharine's College, Cambridge (Late Exhibitioner) (BA history 1949).

Non-political career: Captain, Royal Welch Fusiliers: National service 1949-51, TA 1951-58. Editorial assistant, Herbert Jenkins Ltd 1951-54; Advertisement department, Associated Newspapers 1954-57; Group advertising manager, United Dominions Trust Ltd 1957-74; Public relations adviser to Chairman, Kleinwort Benson Ltd 1974-87; Consultant, Williams Lea Group 1985-93; Director, Ugland International plc 1993-95.

CROSSBENCH

Political career: *House of Lords:* First entered House of Lords 1983; Elected hereditary peer 1999-. Member: Administration and Works Sub-committee 1992-95, Procedure 1995-98, House of Lords Offices Refreshment Sub-committee 2000-02, Internal Lords Reform Committee 2001-02, Ad Hoc Committee on Smoking, Selection 2005-08. *Councils and public bodies:* JP, Hampshire, 1971-97; Member, Hampshire Police Authority 1985-94.

Political interests: Communications industry, magistracy, railways, environment.

Other: Trustee, Byways Residential Home; President, Aldershot Group Riding For The Disabled.
Recreations: Ornithology, music (choral singing), reading, countryside.
The Viscount Tenby, House of Lords, London SW1A 0PW
Tel: 020 7219 5403

TEVERSON, LORD

TEVERSON (Life Baron), Robin Teverson; cr 2006. Born 31 March 1952; Son of Dr Crofton and Joan Teverson; Married Rosemary Young 1975 (2 daughters); married Terrye Lynn Jones 2006 (3 stepdaughters).

Education: Chigwell School, Essex; Waltham Forest Technical College; Exeter University (BA economics 1973).

Non-political career: Director, Exel Logistics 1986-89; Managing director: SPD Ltd 1986-89, Rationale Ltd supply chain consultancy 1989-2002; Chair, Finance South West Ltd 1999-2002; Chief executive, Finance Cornwall 2002-06; Director: Finance South West Ltd 2004-06, Devon and Cornwall Business Council 2006-, KCS Print Ltd 2006-, UK-Japan 21st Century Group Ltd 2007-, Thornparks Ltd 2008-09; Chair, Wessex Investors Ltd 2008-.

LIBERAL DEMOCRAT

Political career: *House of Commons:* Contested South East Cornwall 1992 general election. *House of Lords:* Raised to the peerage as Baron Teverson, of Tregony in the County of Cornwall 2006. Liberal Democrat: Whip 2006-09, Spokesperson for: Environment, Food and Rural Affairs 2006-08, Energy and Climate Change 2008-10. Co-opted member EU Sub-committee F (Home Affairs) 2006-08; Member: Draft Climate Change Bill Joint Committee 2007, European Union 2008-13; Chair EU Sub-committee C: (Foreign Affairs, Defence and Development Policy) 2008-12, (External Affairs) 2012-13. Chair, Liberal Democrat Parliamentary Party Committees on: Energy and Climate Change; Environment, Food and Rural Affairs (Energy and Climate Change) 2010-12, Energy and Climate Change 2012-. *Other:* European Parliament: MEP for Cornwall and West Plymouth 1994-99. Contested South West region 1999 election. Chair, Federal Finance and Administration Committee 1999-2002; Member, Federal Executive 1999-2002, 2005-. *Councils and public bodies:* Member, Cornwall Council 2009-.

Political interests: Business, transport, Europe, financial markets, international affairs; Australia, Chile, Denmark, India, Ireland.

Other: Member, The Securities and Investment Institute (MSI).

Recreations: Running, history, science.

The Lord Teverson, House of Lords, London SW1A 0PW
Tel: 020 7219 3566 *Twitter:* @lordtev

THOMAS OF GRESFORD, LORD

THOMAS OF GRESFORD (Life Baron), (Donald) Martin Thomas; cr. 1996. Born 13 March 1937; Son of late Hywel Thomas and of Olwen Thomas; Married Nan Thomas, née Kerr 1961 (died 2000) (3 sons 1 daughter); married Baroness Walmsley 2005.

Education: Grove Park Grammar School, Wrexham; Peterhouse, Cambridge (MA classics; LLB).

Non-political career: Solicitor, Wrexham 1961-66; Lecturer in law 1966-68; Called to the Bar, Gray's Inn 1967, Bencher 1989; Barrister, Wales and Chester Circuit 1968-; Deputy Circuit Judge 1974-76; Recorder of the Crown Court 1976-2002; QC 1979; Deputy High Court Judge 1985-.

LIBERAL DEMOCRAT

Political career: *House of Commons:* Contested (Liberal) West Flintshire 1964, 1966, 1970, and Wrexham February and October 1974, 1979, 1983, 1987 general elections. *House of Lords:* Raised to the peerage as Baron Thomas of Gresford, of Gresford in the County Borough of Wrexham 1996. Liberal Democrat: Spokesperson for: Welsh Affairs -2004, Home Office -2004; Shadow: Attorney General 2004-06, Lord Chancellor 2006-07, Attorney General 2007-10, Spokesperson for Justice 2007-10. Member Joint Committee on Privacy and Injunctions 2011-12. Chair, Liberal Democrat Parliamentary Party Committees on Home Affairs, Justice and Equalities (Justice) 2010-12, Wales 2012-. *Other:* Welsh Liberal Party: Vice-chair 1967-69, Chair 1969-74; President: Wrexham Liberal Association 1975-, Welsh Liberal Party 1977, 1978, 1979; Welsh Liberal Democrats: Vice-President 1991-93, President 1993. *Councils and public bodies:* Member, Criminal Injury Compensation Board 1985-93.

Political interests: Criminal justice; China, Hong Kong, Wales.

Other: Marcher Sound: Chair 1991-2000, Vice-chair 1983-91; President: Gresford Memorial Trust 1993-, London Welsh Chorale 2000-. OBE 1982; Reform, Western (Glasgow).

Recreations: Rugby football, rowing, golf, fishing, cooking, harp, piano, bagpipes, singing.

The Lord Thomas of Gresford OBE QC, House of Lords, London SW1A 0PW
Tel: 020 7219 5453 *Email:* thomasm@parliament.uk

THOMAS OF MACCLESFIELD, LORD

LAB/CO-OP

THOMAS OF MACCLESFIELD (Life Baron), Terence James Thomas; cr. 1997. Born 19 October 1937; Son of late William Emrys Thomas, and of Mildred Evelyn Thomas; Married Lynda Stevens 1963 (3 sons).

Education: Queen Elizabeth Grammar School, Carmarthen; School of Management, Bath University (Postgraduate Diploma 1971); INSEAD (AMP) 1987.

Non-political career: National Provincial Bank (later National Westminster) 1962-71; Market research manager, later national sales manager, Joint Credit Card Company 1971-73; Co-operative Bank plc 1973-97: Executive director 1984-88, Managing director 1988-97; Visiting professor, Stirling University 1988-91; Various company directorships including: Unity Trust Bank plc 1983-95, Co-operative Commercial Ltd 1985-87, Co-operative City Investments Ltd 1988-90, Vector Investments Ltd 1992-95 (Chair), Stanley Leisure Organisation plc 1994-98, Venture Technic (Cheshire) Ltd (Chair), FI Group Shareholders Trust (Chair); Rathbone CI 1997-98; Capita Group 1997-98; Chair, North West Development Agency 1998-2002.

Political career: *House of Lords:* Raised to the peerage as Baron Thomas of Macclesfield, of Prestbury in the County of Cheshire 1997. On leave of absence June 2012-.

Political interests: North West England.

Other: President, International Co-operative Banking Association (ICBA) 1988-95; Chief examiner, Chartered Institute of Bankers 1983-85; Fellow and member, General Council of the Institute of Bankers FCIB; Member: British Invisibles European Committee (Bank of England appointment), Court of Governors, UMIST 1996-; President, Society for Co-operative Studies 1997; Patron: Macclesfield Museums Trust 1997, West Lancs Disability Helpline 1997-2008; Trustee, Board of Unicef 1998; Patron: Red Rose Community Forest 2000-08, Youth Charter for Sport, Art and Culture; FCIB; CIMgt; MCIM; NSPCC. Two honorary doctorates; Honorary Degree Business Management. Mancunian of the Year 1998. CBE 1997.

Publications: An Inclusive Community with Integrity (2008).

The Lord Thomas of Macclesfield CBE, House of Lords, London SW1A 0PW
Tel: 020 7219 5353

THOMAS OF SWYNNERTON, LORD

CROSSBENCH

THOMAS OF SWYNNERTON (Life Baron), Hugh Swynnerton Thomas; cr. 1981. Born 21 October 1931; Son of late Hugh Whitelegge Thomas, CMG, Secretary for Native Affairs, Gold Coast (now Ghana), and Margery Swynnerton, Colonial Nursing Service; Married Hon Vanessa Jebb 1961 (2 sons 1 daughter).

Education: Sherborne School, Dorset; Queens' College, Cambridge (scholar, BA history 1953) Sorbonne, Paris 1954; French, Spanish.

Non-political career: Professor of history, Reading University 1966-76; Chair, Centre for Policy Studies 1979-90; King Juan Carlos I Professor of Spanish Civilisation, New York University 1995-96; Professor, University Professors' Programme, Boston University, USA 1996-2000.

Political career: *House of Lords:* Raised to the peerage as Baron Thomas of Swynnerton, of Notting Hill in Greater London 1981. Member Works of Art 2007-.

Countries of interest: France, Italy, Mexico, Spain, USA.

Other: Member, Academia de Bellas Artes, Sevilla; Trustee, Fundación Medinaceli. Honorary Fellow, Queens' College, Cambridge 2008. Somerset Maugham Prize 1962; Arts Council Prize for History 1980; Gabarrón Prize for Humanity, Valladolid, Spain 2008; Nonino Prize 2009; Boccaccio Prize 2009; Félix Carrer Prize 2009; Lifetime Achievement in Literature, PEN Prize, Mexico 2011; Literary and Historical Achievement, Houses of Parliament Archives of History Committee prize 2011; Joaquin Romero Murube Prize, Seville 2013. Grand Cross of the Order of Isabel la Católica (Spain); Order of the Aztec Eagle (Mexico); Commandeur Ordre des Arts et des Lettres (France) 2008; Athenæum, Beefsteak.

Publications: The Spanish Civil War (1961, 1976); The Suez Affair (1967); Cuba or The Pursuit of Freedom (1971); John Strachey (1973); Goya and the Third of May (1973); An Unfinished History of the World (1979); Havannah! (1984); Armed Truce (1986); Ever Closer Union: Britain's Destiny in Europe (1991); The Conquest of Mexico (1993); The Slave Trade (1997); The Future of Europe (1997); Who's Who of the Conquistadors (2000); Rivers of Gold (2003); Letter from Asturias (2006); Beaumarchais in Seville (2006); Don Eduardo (2008); The Golden Age: The Spanish Empire of Charles V (Allen Lane, 2011).

The Lord Thomas of Swynnerton, House of Lords, London SW1A 0PW
Tel: 020 7219 5353

LIBERAL DEMOCRAT

THOMAS OF WALLISWOOD, BARONESS

THOMAS OF WALLISWOOD (Life Baroness), Susan Petronella Thomas; cr. 1994. Born 20 December 1935; Daughter of John Arrow, and of Mrs Ebba Fordham; Married David Churchill Thomas (later CMG) 1958 (1 son 2 daughters).

Education: Cranborne Chase School; Lady Margaret Hall, Oxford University (BA history 1957); French, Spanish.

Non-political career: National Economic Development Office 1971-74; Chief executive, British Clothing Industries, Council for Europe 1974-78.

Political career: *House of Commons:* Contested (Liberal Alliance) Mole Valley 1983 and 1987 general elections. *House of Lords:* Raised to the peerage as Baroness Thomas of Walliswood, of Dorking in the County of Surrey 1994. Liberal Democrat Spokesperson for: Transport 1994-2001, Women's Issues 2001-06; Deputy Chair of Committees 2002-07; Deputy Speaker 2002-07; Liberal Democrat Spokesperson for Women and Equality 2007-09. Member: Personal Bills -2005, European Union Sub-committee E (Law and Institutions) 2001-05, European Union 2005-07, Standing Orders (Private Bills) 2005-13; Chair European Union Sub-committee G (Social Policy and Consumer Affairs) 2005-07. *Other:* Contested (Liberal Democrat) Surrey 1994 European Parliament election. Former President, Women Liberal Democrats; Member, Liberal International 1999-. *Councils and public bodies:* Surrey County Council: Councillor 1985-97, Vice-Chair 1993-96, Chair 1996-97; Member, East Surrey Community Health Council 1989-92; Non-executive director, East Surrey Hospital and Community Healthcare Trust 1992-96; Chair, Highways and Transport Committee 1993-96; Surrey County Representative, Association of County Councils 1993-97; DL, Surrey 1996; Member: Surrey Probation Committee 1997-2001, Surrey Probation Board 2001-04.

Political interests: Equality issues, women and health in developing countries, liberty of the individual; Latin America, especially Peru, Cuba, former Soviet bloc EU members.

Other: Member, Inter-Parliamentary Union. OBE 1989.

Recreations: Gardening, reading, ballet, theatre, travel.

The Baroness Thomas of Walliswood OBE DL, House of Lords, London SW1A 0PW
Tel: 020 7219 5353

LIBERAL DEMOCRAT

THOMAS OF WINCHESTER, BARONESS

THOMAS OF WINCHESTER (Life Baroness), Celia Marjorie Thomas; cr 2006. Born 14 October 1945; Daughter of David Thomas and Marjorie Thomas, née Best.

Education: St Swithun's School, Winchester.

Non-political career: Winchester Diocesan Board of Finance 1963-65; Winchester Cathedral Appeal 1965-66; The Pilgrims' School, Winchester 1967-72; Christ Church Cathedral School, Oxford 1972-74; Liberal/Liberal Democrat Lords Whips Office 1977-2006: Head of Office.

Political career: *House of Lords:* Raised to the peerage as Baroness Thomas of Winchester, of Winchester in the County of Hampshire 2006. Liberal Democrat Spokesperson for Work and Pensions 2007-10. Member: Liaison 2007-10, Merits of Statutory Instruments 2007-10, Refreshment 2007-12; Procedure: Member 2007, 2009-, Alternate member 2008-09; Chair Delegated Powers and Regulatory Reform 2010-. *Other:* Liberal/Liberal Democrat election agent: Winchester October 1974, Brecon and Radnor 1987 and 1992; Chair, Liberal Summer School, now Keynes Forum 2001-; Vice-President, Lloyd George Society 2005-; President, Winchester Liberal Democrats.

Political interests: Disability, prisons, bee health, voting reform.

Other: Vice-president and trustee, Muscular Dystrophy; Patron: Winchester Campaign Churches Nightshelter, Avonbrook Projects Abroad, Thrive; Management Board, Centre Forum 2006-09; Patron, Pinotage Youth Development Academy, SA; Vice-president, Lloyd George Society; Muscular Distrophy Campaign; Target Ovarian Cancer; Thrive; Butterfly Conservation; Plantlife. Health Champion, Charity Champion awards 2012. MBE 1985.

Recreations: Music, theatre, gardening, butterfly conservation, watching cricket.

The Baroness Thomas of Winchester MBE, House of Lords, London SW1A 0PW
Tel: 020 7219 5353

THORNTON, BARONESS

Opposition Spokesperson for Equalities Office

THORNTON (Life Baroness), (Dorothea) Glenys Thornton; cr. 1998. Born 16 October 1952; Daughter of Peter and Jean Thornton; Married John Carr 1977 (1 son 1 daughter). **Education:** Thornton Secondary School, Bradford; London School of Economics (BSc economics 1976).

Non-political career: National co-ordinator, Gingerbread 1977-79; Area officer, Citizens Advice Bureau 1979-81; Public affairs adviser, Co-operative Wholesale Society 1981-93; Director of development and general secretary, Fabian Society 1993-96; Chair, Pall Mall Consult 2001-08. Member, GMB.

LAB/CO-OP

Political career: *House of Commons:* Member, European Union Sub-committee C (Environment, Public Health and Consumer Protection) 1999-2000. *House of Lords:* Raised to the peerage as Baroness Thornton, of Manningham in the County of West Yorkshire 1998. Government Whip 2008-10; Government Spokesperson for: Work and Pensions 2008, Equality 2008, Health 2008, 2009-10; Parliamentary Under-Secretary of State, Department of Health 2010; Opposition Spokesperson for: Health 2010-12, Work and Pensions 2010, Equalities Office 2010-. *Other:* Member, Co-operative Party 1974-; Chair, Greater London Labour Party 1986-91; Labour Party Policy Forum 2005-08. *Councils and public bodies:* Member, Court of Governors, London School of Economics 1999-.

Political interests: Children, media, social enterprise, Yorkshire.

Other: RSA; NCH; Circusspace; One World Action; Theodora Childrens Trust; Patron, Social Enterprise UK.

Recreations: Canoeing, hill-walking in Yorkshire.

The Baroness Thornton, House of Lords, London SW1A 0PW
Tel: 020 7219 8502 *Email:* thorntong@parliament.uk
Website: lordsoftheblog.net/category/baroness-thornton *Twitter:* @GlenysThornton

TOMBS, LORD

TOMBS (Life Baron), Francis Leonard Tombs; cr. 1990. Born 17 May 1924; Son of late Joseph and Jane Tombs; Married Marjorie Evans 1949 (died 2008) (3 daughters). **Education:** Elmore Green School, Walsall; Birmingham College of Technology (HNC electrical engineering 1943); London University (BSc economics 1963).

Non-political career: Apprentice and planning engineer, GEC 1939-45; Graduate trainee and junior shift engineer, Birmingham Corporation 1946-47; Grid control posts and operations engineer, Ince power station: British Electricity Authority, Midlands, Central Electricity Authority, Merseyside and North Wales 1948-57; General Manager, GEC, Erith 1958-67; Director and general manager, James Howden and Co., Glasgow 1967-68; Successively director of engineering, deputy chair and chair, South of Scotland Electricity Board 1969-77; Chair: The Electricity Council 1977-80, The Weir Group 1981-83; Director, N M Rothschild & Sons Ltd 1981-94; Chair, Turner and Newall 1982-89; Rolls-Royce plc: Director 1982-92, Chair 1985-92; Director, Shell UK 1983-94.

CROSSBENCH

Political career: *House of Lords:* Raised to the peerage as Baron Tombs, of Brailes in the County of Warwickshire 1990. Member Science and Technology 1992-94, 1997-2000; Chair: Sustainable Development Committee 1994-95, Science and Technology Sub-committee II (Management of Nuclear Waste) 1998-99; Member: Science and Technology Sub-committee II (Science and Society) 1999-2000, Delegated Powers and Deregulation 2000-05, Science and Technology Sub-committee II (Renewable Energy) 2003-04; Co-opted member Science and Technology Sub-committee I (Radioactive Waste Management: a further update) 2010; Member Joint Committee on Consolidation, Etc, Bills 2010-.

Political interests: Science, technology, engineering.

Other: The Molecule Theatre of Science: Chair 1985-92, President 1992-94; Chair, Brooklands Museum Trust 1994-2001; FRAEng 1977; Honorary FIChemE 1985; Honorary FICE 1986; Honorary FIProdE 1986; Honorary FIMechE 1989; Honorary FIEE 1991; Honorary FRAeS 1995; Honorary FRSE 1996. Goldsmiths' Company: Liveryman 1981-, Prime Warden 1994-95. Freeman, City of London. Chancellor, Strathclyde University 1991-98. 14 honorary doctorates from British and Polish universities. Kt 1978.

Publications: Power Politics (I.B Tauris, 2011).

Recreations: Music.

The Lord Tombs, House of Lords, London SW1A 0PW
Tel: 020 7219 5353 *Email:* tombsf@parliament.uk

LAB/CO-OP

TOMLINSON, LORD

TOMLINSON (Life Baron), John Edward Tomlinson; cr. 1998. Born 1 August 1939; Son of Frederick and Doris Tomlinson; Married 2nd Paulette Fuller 1998.

Education: Westminster City School; Co-operative College, Loughborough (Diploma political, economic and social studies 1961); Brunel University (health services management 1974-76); Warwick University (MA industrial relations 1982).

Non-political career: Head of research, AUEW 1968-70; Senior lecturer in industrial relations and management, Solihull College of Technology 1979-84. Member, TGWU.

Political career: *House of Commons:* MP (Labour) for Meriden 1974-79. PPS to Harold Wilson as Prime Minister 1975-76; Parliamentary Under-Secretary of State, Foreign and Commonwealth Office 1976-79; Parliamentary Secretary, Ministry of Overseas Development 1977-79. *House of Lords:* Raised to the peerage as Baron Tomlinson, of Walsall in the County of West Midlands 1998. Member European Union 1998-2002, 2005-08, 2010-; EU Sub-committee A (Economic and Financial Affairs, Trade and External Relations): Member 1998-2002, Chair 2000-01; Member: House of Lords' Offices 2001-02, EU Sub-committee C (Foreign Affairs, Defence and Development Policy) 2003-07, Joint Committee on Conventions 2006; EU Sub-committee E (Law and Institutions): Member 2007-08, Co-opted member 2008-10; Member: EU Sub-committee F (Home Affairs) 2010-12, Audit 2011-, EU Sub-committee F (Home Affairs, Health and Education) 2012-13. *Other:* European Parliament: MEP for Birmingham West 1984-99. *Councils and public bodies:* Councillor, Sheffield City Council 1963-67; Dartford Borough Council: Councillor 1970-74, Deputy Leader.

Political interests: Finance, Europe, international development, foreign policy.

Other: House of Lords Representative on Convention on Future of Europe 2002-03; Member Parliamentary Assembly: Council of Europe, Western European Union; Vice-chair, Election of Judges Committee to the European Court of Human Rights; Industry and Parliament Trust: Trustee 1987, Chair of Trustees -2007; Vice-President, Hansard Society -2006; Chair, advisory board, London School of Commerce 2004-; President: British Fluoridation Society 2004-11, Association of Independent Higher Education Providers 2005-13; Anglia Ruskin University: Board of Governors 2008-, Chair 2010-; Chair of council, Association of Business Executives. Honorary doctorate, Birmingham University; Honorary Fellowship, University of Wales Institute, Cardiff 2007; West Bromwich Labour.

Publications: Left, Right: The March of Political Extremism in Britain (Calders, 1981).

Recreations: Walking, reading, sport.

The Lord Tomlinson, House of Lords, London SW1A 0PW
Tel: 020 7219 3770

INDEPENDENT LIBERAL DEMOCRAT

TONGE, BARONESS

TONGE (Life Baroness), Jenny (Jennifer) Louise Tonge; cr 2005. Born 19 February 1941; Daughter of late Sidney Smith, school teacher, and late Violet Smith, school teacher; Married Keith Tonge 1964 (2 sons 1 daughter deceased).

Education: Dudley Girls' High School; University College, London (MB, BS 1964); French.

Non-political career: General practice/family planning 1968-78, 1987-92; Senior medical officer, Women's Services (Ealing) 1982-87; Manager, Community Health Services (Ealing) 1992-96. South West Thames Representative, BMA Public and Community Health Committee 1992-96.

Political career: *House of Commons:* Contested Richmond and Barnes 1992 general election. MP (Liberal Democrat) for Richmond Park 1997-2005. Liberal Democrat Spokesperson for International Development 1997-2003. *House of Lords:* Raised to the peerage as Baroness Tonge, of Kew in the London Borough of Richmond upon Thames 2005. Liberal Democrat Spokesperson for Health 2005-10. Co-opted member European Union Sub-committee F (Home Affairs) 2007-08; Member HIV and AIDS in the UK 2010-11. *Other:* Chair, Richmond and Barnes Liberal Party 1978-80; Resigned the Liberal Democrat Whip February 2012; Now sits as an Independent Liberal Democrat. *Councils and public bodies:* London Borough of Richmond-on-Thames: Councillor 1981-90, Chair, Social Services 1983-87.

Political interests: Health, environment, international development; Afghanistan, Bangladesh, Colombia, Iraq, Palestine, Rwanda, Sudan.

Other: Organisation for Security and Co-operation in Europe: Parliamentary Assembly: Delegate 1998-2000, Deputy 2000-05; European Parliamentary Forum: Vice-chair 2009-, President 2013-; Kew Society; Welfare Association UK; Fellow, Royal Society for Public Health; HACAN Clear-Skies; Board member, British Institute of Technology and E-Commerce; BMAS; MFFP; Fellow, Royal Society for Public Health; Visiting Parliamentary Fellow, St Anthony's College, Oxford

1999-2000; Christian Aid. Honorary Fellow, Faculty of Reproductive and Sexual Health, Royal College of Obstetricians and Gynaecologists. *ePolitix* Charity Award 2004. Honorary Member, Richmond Football Club (Rugby).

Recreations: Birdwatching, looking after grandchildren.

The Baroness Tonge, House of Lords, London SW1A 0PW
Tel: 020 7219 5563 *Email:* tongej@parliament.uk

LIBERAL DEMOCRAT

TOPE, LORD

TOPE (Life Baron), Graham Norman Tope; cr. 1994. Born 30 November 1943; Son of late Leslie Tope; Married Margaret East 1972 (2 sons).

Education: Whitgift School, Croydon.

Non-political career: London Scottish TA 1962-64. Company secretary and insurance manager 1965-72; Deputy general secretary, Voluntary Action Camden 1975-90; Chair, Community Investors Ltd 1995-98.

Political career: *House of Commons:* MP (Liberal) Sutton and Cheam 7 December 1972 by-election to February 1974. Contested (Liberal) Sutton and Cheam February and October 1974 general elections. Liberal Spokesperson for Environment 1972-74. Co-chair, Liberal Democrat Parliamentary Committee on Communities and Local Government 2010-. *House of Lords:* Raised to the peerage as Baron Tope, of Sutton in the London Borough of Sutton 1994. Liberal Democrat: Spokesperson for Education 1994-2000, Assistant Whip 1998-2000, Spokesperson for Communities and Local Government 2008-10. Member: Relations between Central and Local Government 1995-96, EU Sub-committee F (Home Affairs) 2011-12, Public Service and Demographic Change 2012-13. Chair, Liberal Democrat Parliamentary Party Committee on Communities and Local Government 2010-. *Other:* Member, Liberal Party National Council 1970-76; National League of Young Liberals: Vice-chair 1971-73, President 1973-75; President, London Liberal Democrats 1991-2000. *Councils and public bodies:* London Borough of Sutton: Councillor 1974-, Leader, Liberal (later Liberal Democrat) Group 1974-99, Opposition Leader 1984-86, Council Leader 1986-99, Executive Councillor for Community Safety Leisure and Libraries 1999-2012; Member, London Fire and Civil Defence Authority 1995-97; Vice-President, Local Government Association 1997-2005; Vice-chair, Association of London Government 1997-2000; London Assembly: Member 2000-08, Leader, Liberal Democrat Group 2000-06, Member, Metropolitan Police Authority 2000-08, Chair, Finance 2000-08, Mayor of London Cabinet 2000-04; Member: Croydon Strategic Partnership Board 2002-08, Sutton Strategic Partnership Board 2003-12, Safer Croydon Partnership Board 2004-08, Safer Sutton Partnership Board: Member 2004-12, Chair 2009-12; Chair, Local Government Group for Europe 2005-; Vice-president, Local Government Association 2013-.

Political interests: Local government, Europe, London; Bermuda, EU, Western Balkans.

Other: EU Committee of the Regions: Member 1994-, Vice-chair, UK Delegation 1996-, Bureau member 1996-, President: European Liberal Democrat and Reform Group 1998-2002, Constitutional Affairs and European Governance Commission 2002-04, Political co-ordinator, ALDE Group 2007-, Member, Political Monitoring Group 2008-10, Western Balkans Working Group 2008-; Member, Congress of Local and Regional Authorities in Europe, Council of Europe 1996-2000; Rapporteur, Smarter Regulation 2010-11; Member, EU High Level Group of Independent Stakeholders on Administrative Burdens, European Commission 2011-. Member, Needle Makers Company. Freeman, City of London 1998. CBE 1991.

Publications: Co-author: Liberals and the Community (1974), A Political Life (2011).

Recreations: Garden, history, walking, stamps.

The Lord Tope CBE, House of Lords, London SW1A 0PW
Tel: 020 7219 3098 *Email:* topeg@parliament.uk

LIBERAL DEMOCRAT

TORDOFF, LORD

TORDOFF (Life Baron), Geoffrey Johnson Tordoff; cr. 1981. Born 11 October 1928; Son of late Stanley Acomb Tordoff; Married Mary Swarbrick 1953 (died 2013) (2 sons 3 daughters).

Education: Manchester Grammar School; Manchester University.

Non-political career: Sgt, RAOC (National Service) 1948-49. Sgt, RAoc (National Service) 1948-49. Shell 1950-83: Marketing executive, Shell Chemicals, Public affairs manager (Chemicals), Shell UK.

Political career: *House of Commons:* Contested (Liberal) Northwich 1964, and Knutsford 1966 and 1970 general elections. *House of Lords:* Raised to the peerage as Baron Tordoff, of Knutsford in the County of Cheshire 1981. Liberal Democrat Transport Spokesperson 1988-94; Liberal: Deputy Whip 1983-84, Chief Whip 1984-88; Liberal Democrat Chief Whip 1988-94; Principal

Deputy Chairman of Committees 1994-2001; Deputy Speaker 1994-2008; Chairman of Committees 2001-02; Deputy Chair of Committees 2002-08; Extra Lord in Waiting to HM The Queen 2004-. Chair European Communities/Union 1994-2001; House of Lords' Offices: Member 1997-2002, Chair 2001-02; Chair: Administration and Works Sub-committee 2001-02, Finance and Staff Sub-committee 2001-02, Hybrid Instruments 2001-02, Liaison 2001-02, Personal Bills 2001-02, Privileges 2001-02, Procedures 2001-02, Selection 2001-02, Standing Orders (Private Bills) 2001-02; Member: Advisory Panel on Works of Art 2003-05, Speakership of the House 2003, House 2005-10. *Other:* Liberal Party: Chair, Assembly Committee 1974-76, Chair 1976-79, Chair, Campaigns and Elections Committee 1980-82, President 1983-84. *Councils and public bodies:* Honorary President, British Youth Council 1986-92; Chair, Middle East Committee, Refugee Council 1990-94; Member, Press Complaints Commission 1995-2002.

Political interests: Foreign affairs, Europe.

Other: National Liberal.

The Lord Tordoff, House of Lords, London SW1A 0PW
Tel: 020 7219 6613 *Email:* tordoffg@parliament.uk

LAB/CO-OP

TOUHIG, LORD

TOUHIG (Life Baron), James Donnelly (Don) Touhig; cr 2010. Born 5 December 1947; Son of late Michael and Catherine Touhig; Married Jennifer Hughes 1968 (2 sons 2 daughters).

Education: St Francis School, Abersychan; East Monmouth College.

Non-political career: Apprentice radio and tv engineer; Journalist 1968-76; Editor, Free Press of Monmouthshire 1976-90; General manager and editor in chief, Free Press Group of Newspapers 1988-92; General manager (business development): Bailey Group 1992-93, Bailey Print 1993-95. Member, TGWU.

Political career: *House of Commons:* Contested Richmond and Barnes 1992 general election. MP for Islwyn 16 February 1995 by-election to 2010. Public Interest Disclosure (Private Member's Bill) 1995; PPS to Gordon Brown as Chancellor of the Exchequer 1997-99; Assistant Government Whip 1999-2001; Parliamentary Under-Secretary of State, Wales Office 2001-05; Parliamentary Under-Secretary of State and Minister for Veterans, Ministry of Defence 2005-06; Member, Speaker's Committee for the Independent Parliamentary Standards Authority 2009-10. Member: European Standing Committee B 1995-96, Welsh Affairs 1996-97, Public Accounts 2006-10, Liaison 2009-10; Chair: Members' Allowances 2009-10. Honorary Secretary, PLP Welsh Regional Group 1995-99, 2007-08. *House of Lords:* Raised to the peerage as Baron Touhig, of Islwyn and Glansychan in the County of Gwent 2010. Member: Public Service and Demographic Change 2012, Liaison 2013-. *Other:* Member: Labour Leadership Campaign Team (responsible for Devolution in Wales) 1996-97, Co-operative Party; Chair Co-operative Party Parliamentary Group 1999, 2010. *Councils and public bodies:* Gwent County Council: Councillor 1973-95, Chair, Finance Committee 1992-94.

Political interests: Treasury, employment, health, education, local and regional government; France.

Other: Past President, South Wales Newspaper Society; Member: MENSA, MENCAP, Amnesty International; President: Islwyn Community Credit Union, Caerphilly County Borough Access Group, Blackwood Amateur Operatic Society, Caerphilly Citizens Advice Bureau, Newbridge and District Ladies Choir, Cancercareline; Fellow Industry and Parliament Trust 2003; Patron, Everyone's Child Romania. Freeman, City of London 2013. Papal Knight of the Order of St Sylvester 1991; PC 2006.

Recreations: Reading, cooking for family and friends, music, walking.

Rt Hon the Lord Touhig, House of Lords, London SW1A 0PW
Tel: 020 7219 7248 *Email:* touhigjd@parliament.uk

CROSSBENCH

TREES, LORD

TREES (Life Baron), Alexander John Trees; cr 2012. Born 12 June 1946; Son of John Trees, chemical engineer, and Margaret Trees, née Bell; Married Frances McAnally 1970 (1 daughter).

Education: Brigg Grammar School, Lincolnshire; Edinburgh University (BVMS 1969; PhD 1976); French, Italian.

Non-political career: Assistant in general veterinary practice, Derby 1970-71; Research assistant, Edinburgh University 1971-76; Elcano Products Ltd, Rome, Italy: Veterinary adviser 1977-80, Head of animal science 1980; Liverpool School of Tropical Medicine, Liverpool University: Lecturer, Department of Veterinary Parasitology 1980-91, Senior lecturer 1991-94, Head of Veterinary Parasitology 1992-2001, Parasite and Vector Biology Division 1994-97, Professor of Veterinary Parasitology 1994-2011, Faculty of Veterinary Science: Dean 2001-08, Emeritus professor 2011-;

Glasgow University: Visiting professor, School of Veterinary Medicine, Professor James McCall Memorial Lecture 2010; Editor-in-chief, *Veterinary Record* 2011-; Chair, Moredun Research Institute 2011-.

Political career: *House of Lords:* Raised to the peerage as Baron Trees, of The Ross in Perth and Kinross 2012.

Political interests: Veterinary matters, animal health and welfare, aspects of public health, tropical medicine and overseas development, higher education, professional regulation, the environment; Africa, Middle East.

Other: European Veterinary Parasitology College: Founding diplomate 2003, Vice-president 2006-09; Executive council, World Association of Veterinary Parasitology 2007-; British Society of Parasitology 1980-; Royal Society of Tropical Medicine and Hygiene: Fellow 1986-, Council 1997-2000; Royal College of Veterinary Surgeons: Member 1969-, Council member 2000, Junior vice-president 2008-09, President 2009-10, Senior vice-president; President, Association of Veterinary Teachers and Research Workers 1996-97 British Veterinary Association: Member 1980-, Veterinary Policy Group 1997-2001, Chair, Education Group; Royal Society of Tropical Medicine and Hygiene; Honorary fellow, Myerscough College. DVM, Royal Veterinary College, University of London. Peter Bridge Award, BCVA; Selborne medal, Association of Veterinary Teachers and Research Workers 2005; Wooldridge lecture and medal, British Veterinary Association 2009; Amoroso award, British Small Animal Veterinary Association 2011; Farmers' Club.

Publications: 140+ papers in peer-reviewed academic journals.

Recreations: Natural history, outdoors, mountaineering, DIY.

Professor the Lord Trees, House of Lords, London SW1A 0PW
Tel: 020 7219 7278 *Fax:* 020 7219 1991 *Email:* treesa@parliament.uk

CONSERVATIVE

TREFGARNE, LORD

TREFGARNE (2nd Baron, UK), David Garro Trefgarne; cr. 1947. Born 31 March 1941; Son of 1st Baron; Married Rosalie Lane 1968 (2 sons 1 daughter).

Education: Haileybury College, Hertford; Princeton University, USA.

Non-political career: Non-executive director, Siebe plc 1991-98; Chairman: Engineering and Marine Training Authority (now SEMTA) 1994-2006, Scotty Group plc 2006-11.

Political career: *House of Lords:* First entered House of Lords 1962; Opposition Whip 1977-79; Government Whip 1979-80; Parliamentary Under-Secretary of State: Department of Trade 1980-81, Foreign and Commonwealth Office 1981-82, Department of Health and Social Security 1982-83, for the Armed Forces June 1983-85; Minister of State: for Defence Support 1985-86, for Defence Procurement 1986-89, Department of Trade and Industry (Minister for Trade) 1989-90; Elected hereditary peer 1999-. Member: Procedure 2000-03, Privileges 2002-05, Speakership of the House 2003; Co-opted member EU Sub-committee G (Social Policy and Consumer Affairs) 2006-08; Member: EU Sub-committee A (Economic and Financial Affairs and International Trade) 2010-11, Joint Committee on the Draft House of Lords Reform Bill 2011-12, Inquiries Act 2005 2013-. *Other:* Association of Conservative Peers: Treasurer 1997-2000, Chair 2000-04.

Political interests: Aviation.

Other: President, Mechanical and Metal Trades Confederation 1990-; Governor, Guildford School of Acting 1992-2001; Member, Mary Rose Trust 1992-2001; Honorary President, Popular Flying Association 1992-2003; Life Governor and council member, Haileybury 1993-2001; Honorary President, British Association of Aviation Consultants 1993-; Vice-chair, Army Cadet Force 1993-2001; Patron, Catering Equipment Suppliers Association 2000-; Director, Arab-British Chamber of Commerce 2000-; Chair, Brooklands Museum Trust 2001-; Director, UK Skills 2001-05; Chair, Libyan British Business Council 2003-; President, TWI 2006; Honorary fellowship, IET. Honorary doctorate. Royal Aero Club Bronze Medal 1963. PC 1989.

Recreations: Photography.

Rt Hon the Lord Trefgarne, House of Lords, London SW1A 0PW
Tel: 020 7219 5450 *Email:* trefgarned@parliament.uk
Broolands Museum, Brooklands Road, Weybridge, Surrey KT13 0QN *Tel:* 01932 857381

DO YOU NEED THIS INFORMATION ONLINE?
visit www.dodspeople.com or call 020 7593 5675
to register for a free trial

CONSERVATIVE

TRENCHARD, VISCOUNT

TRENCHARD (3rd Viscount, UK), Hugh Trenchard; cr. 1936; 3rd Baron Trenchard (UK) 1930; 3rd Bt of Wolfeton (UK) 1919. Born 12 March 1951; Son of 2nd Viscount, MC and Patricia Bailey; Married Fiona, daughter of 2nd Baron Margadale, 1975 (2 sons 2 daughters).

Education: Eton College; Trinity College, Cambridge (BA archaeology and anthropology 1973); German, Japanese.

Non-political career: Captain, 4th Battalion, The Royal Green Jackets, TA 1972-80; Honorary Air Commodore, 600 (City of London) Squadron, Royal Auxiliary Air Force 2006-. Kleinwort Benson Ltd 1973-96: Chief Representative in Japan 1980-85, Director 1986-96; Director, Dover Japan Inc. 1985-87; Kleinwort Benson International Incorporated: General manager (Tokyo branch) 1985-88, President 1988-95, Deputy chair 1995-96; Director, ACP Holdings Ltd 1990-94; Securities Committee, European Business Community in Japan: Chair 1993-95, Vice-chair of Council 1995; Director: Japan Securities Dealers Association 1994-95, Bond Underwriters Association of Japan 1994-95, Robert Fleming and Co Ltd 1996-98, Robert Fleming International Ltd 1998-2000; Non-executive director, Berkeley Technology Limited 1999-2011; Director, Westhall Capital Limited (formerly AC European Finance Limited) 2001-03; Non-executive chair, The Dejima Fund Ltd 2001-09; Senior adviser, Prudential Financial, Inc 2002-08; Non-executive director, Dryden Wealth Management Limited 2004-05; Stratton Street PCC Limited: Non-executive director 2005-, Chair 2009-, Director general, European Fund and Asset Management Association 2006; Director, Standon Lordship Ltd 2006-; Managing director, Mizuho International plc 2007-12; Director: Bache Global Series 2008-, UK Koyu Corporation Ltd 2009-, Lotte Chemical UK Ltd 2010-; Consultant and senior adviser, Mizuho Bank Ltd. 2013-; Consultant, Robertson Robey Associates LLP 2013-.

Political career: *House of Lords:* First entered House of Lords 1987; Elected hereditary peer 2004-. Member Joint Committee on Financial Services and Markets 1999. *Other:* Chair, Conservatives Abroad in Japan 1986-88; President, North East Hertfordshire Conservative Association 2001-. *Councils and public bodies:* DL, Hertfordshire 2008-.

Political interests: Financial services, defence, foreign affairs; China, Japan, Korea, USA.

Other: Member, Japan Association of Corporate Executives 1987-95; Chair, Japan Society 2000-04; Chair of Council and Board of Trustees, RAF Benevolent Fund 2006-; Brooks's, Pratt's, Cavalry and Guards, Tokyo Club.

Recreations: Shooting, fishing, skiing.

The Viscount Trenchard DL, House of Lords, London SW1A 0PW
Tel: 020 7219 5353 *Email:* trenchardh@parliament.uk
Mizuho Bank Ltd, Bracken House, 1 Friday Street, London EC4M 9JA *Tel:* 020 7090 6067 *Email:* hugh.trenchard@mhcb.co.uk

LABOUR

TRIESMAN, LORD

Opposition Spokesperson for Foreign and Commonwealth Office

TRIESMAN (Life Baron), David Maxim Triesman; cr. 2004. Born 30 October 1943; Son of Michael Triesman and Rita Triesman, née Lubran; Married Lucy Hooberman 2004 (1 daughter).

Education: Stationers' Company's School, London; Essex University (BA social sciences 1968; MA philosophy of science 1969); King's College, Cambridge (postgraduate research 1970-73); French.

Non-political career: Senior researcher, addiction research unit, London University 1970-74; Senior lecturer and co-ordinator of postgraduate research, South Bank Polytechnic 1975-84; Non-executive chair, Mortgage Credit Corp (UBS) 1975-97; Visiting professor of economics, S Lawrence University, USA 1977; National negotiating secretary and deputy general secretary, NATFHE 1984-93; Chair, Victoria Management Ltd 1989-2001; Visiting scholar in economics, Cambridge University; General secretary and chief executive officer, Association of University Teachers 1993-2001; Visiting fellow in economics, Wolfson College, Cambridge 2000-; General secretary, Labour Party 2001-03; Senior associate fellow, Manufacturing Group, Warwick University 2003-; Senior visiting fellow in politics, London School of Economics 2005-; Chair, Board of Advisers, Templewood Merchant Bank 2010-; Board member, Augur Buchler 2010-; Chairman, Triesman Associates 2011-. AUT/University and College Union 1970-: General secretary 1993-2001.

Political career: *House of Lords:* Raised to the peerage as Baron Triesman, of Tottenham in the London Borough of Haringey 2004. Government Spokesperson for: Education and Skills 2004-05, Trade and Industry 2004-05, Transport 2004, International Development 2004-05; Government Whip 2004-05; Foreign and Commonwealth Office: Government Spokesperson 2004-07, Parliamentary Under-Secretary of State 2005-07; Parliamentary Under-Secretary of State (Intellectual Property and Quality) and Government Spokesperson, Department for Innovation, Universities and Skills 2007-08; Opposition Spokesperson for: Business, Innovation and Skills 2010-11, Foreign and Commonwealth Office 2011-. *Councils and public bodies:* Member: Home Office Committee on Prison Education 1980-83, Greater London Manpower Board 1981-86; Chair, Burnham FHE Committee Teachers' Side 1985-86; Member: Bett Inquiry into Higher Education 1998-99, Ruskin College Governors 1999-2002, Better Regulations Task Force 2000-01, HM Treasury Public Services Productivity Panel 2000-02; Chair: The Football Association 2008-10, England 2018/2022 FIFA World Cup bid -2010.

Political interests: Economics, industry, banking, foreign affairs, intelligence, broadcasting, higher education, public diplomacy, sports, arts, governance and ethics; Africa, The Americas, Caribbean, China, Commonwealth, Europe, India, Middle East, UK Overseas Territories.

Other: British North American Committee; Chair, The Usecolour Foundation 2000-02; Trustee, Public Management Foundation 2000-02; The Football Foundation 2008-; Tottenham Hotspurs Foundation 2008-; Fellow: Royal Statistical Society 1984, Royal Society of Arts 1992; One World Action, Piggy Bank Kids. Fellow, Northampton University 1996; Honorary Doctor of Laws, London Southbank University 2009; Honorary Doctorate, Essex University 2010; Reform; Charles Rennie Mackintosh Society. Tottenham Hotspur Supporters Club; Middlesex County Cricket Club.

Publications: Co-author, Football Mania (Ocean Books, 1972); Reconstructing Social Psychology (Penguin Books, 1974); Five Ring Circus: The Olympics (Pluto Press, 1984); College Administration (Longmans, 1988); c.50 academic papers in economics and epidemology.

Recreations: Football, blues and rock guitar, mountain walking, reading.

The Lord Triesman, House of Lords, London SW1A 0PW
Tel: 020 7219 6224 *Email:* triesmand@parliament.uk

TRIMBLE, LORD

CONSERVATIVE

TRIMBLE (Life Baron), (William) David Trimble; cr 2006. Born 15 October 1944; Son of late William and Ivy Trimble; Married Daphne Orr 1978 (2 sons 2 daughters).

Education: Bangor Grammar School; Queen's University, Belfast (LLB 1968).

Non-political career: Queen's University, Belfast: Lecturer in Law 1968-77, Senior Lecturer 1977-90.

Political career: *House of Commons:* MP (UUP) for Upper Bann 1990 by-election to 2005. UUP Spokesperson for: Constitutional Affairs, Treasury 2002-05, Trade and Industry 2004-05, Work and Pensions 2004-05. *House of Lords:* Raised to the peerage as Baron Trimble, of Lisnagarvey in the County of Antrim 2006. Ulster Unionist 2006-07; Conservative 2007. EU Sub-committee A (Economic and Financial Affairs and International Trade): Co-opted member 2007-08, Member 2008-10; Member: European Union 2008-13, Barnett Formula 2008-09, EU Sub-committee C (Foreign Affairs, Defence and Development Policy) 2010-12, Joint Committee on the Draft House of Lords Reform Bill 2011-12, EU Sub-committee C (External Affairs) 2012-, Inquiries Act 2005 2013-. *Other:* Member: Northern Ireland Constitutional Convention for South Belfast 1975-76, Northern Ireland Forum for Political Dialogue 1996-98; Northern Ireland Assembly: MLA for Upper Bann 1998-2007, First Minister 1998-July 2001, November 2001-03. Chair, Lagan Valley Unionist Association 1985-90; Leader, Ulster Unionist Party 1995-2005; Patron, Tory Reform Group.

Political interests: Legal affairs, arts and culture, foreign policy.

Other: Chair, Ulster Society 1985-90. Several honorary degrees. Nobel Peace Prize (jointly) 1998; Major Political Achievement House Award, Channel 4 and *The House* Magazine 1999; Parliamentarian of the Year, *The Spectator* 2001; St Angela's Peace and Justice Group Award 2002. PC 1998; Légion d'Honneur (France) 2002.

Recreations: Music, reading.

Rt Hon the Lord Trimble, House of Lords, London SW1A 0PW
Tel: 020 7219 2421 *Fax:* 020 7219 5979 *Website:* www.davidtrimble.org

---

CONSERVATIVE

TRUE, LORD

TRUE (Life Baron), Nicholas Edward True; cr 2010. Born 31 July 1951; Son of Edward and Kathleen True; Married Anne-Marie Hood 1979 (2 sons 1 daughter).

Education: Nottingham High School; Peterhouse, Cambridge (BA 1973); Italian.

Non-political career: Member, Conservative Research Department 1975-82; Assistant to Conservative Party Deputy Leader 1978-82; Special adviser to Secretary of State for Health and Social Security 1982-86; Director, Public Policy Unit 1986-90; Deputy head, Prime Minister's Policy Unit 1991-95; Special adviser, Prime Minister's Office 1997; Private Secretary to Leader of the Opposition 1997-2010; Director, Opposition Whips' Office 1997-2010.

Political career: *House of Lords:* Raised to the peerage as Baron True, of East Sheen in the County of Surrey 2010. Procedure: Member 2011-12, Alternate member 2012-; Member House 2012-. *Other:* Conservative Councillors' Association. *Councils and public bodies:* Royal Borough of Richmond-upon-Thames Council: Councillor 1986-90, 1998-, Deputy Leader 2002-06, Opposition Leader 2006-10, Council Leader 2010-.

Political interests: Local government, education, constitution, arts; Guatemala, Italy.

Other: Olga Havel Foundation 1990-94; Sir Harold Hood's Charitable Trust 1996-; Richmond Civic Trust 2006-10; Patron, Venice in Peril Foundation. CBE 1993; Beefsteak, Brook's, Traveller's.

Recreations: Books, history, art, gardens.

The Lord True CBE, House of Lords, London SW1A 0PW
Tel: 020 7219 5353 *Email:* truen@parliament.uk
Leader of the Council, York House, Twickenham, Middlesex *Tel:* 020 8487 5001
Email: cllr.lordtrue@richmond.gov.uk

CONSERVATIVE

TRUMPINGTON, BARONESS

TRUMPINGTON (Life Baroness), Jean Alys Barker; cr. 1980. Born 23 October 1922; Daughter of Major Arthur Campbell-Harris and Doris Robson; Married William Alan Barker 1954 (died 1988) (1 son).

Education: Privately in England and France; French, German, some Italian.

Non-political career: Landgirl to David Lloyd George 1939-41; Naval intelligence, Bletchley Park 1941-45; Bletchley Park, FCO 1941-46. European Central Inland Transport Organisation (in London and Paris) 1946-49; Secretary to Viscount Hinchingbrooke, MP 1949-52; Copywriter in advertising agency, New York City 1952-54.

Political career: *House of Lords:* Raised to the peerage as Baroness Trumpington, of Sandwich in the County of Kent 1980. Government Whip 1983-85; Parliamentary Under-Secretary of State, Department for Health and Social Security 1985-87; Ministry of Agriculture, Fisheries and Food: Parliamentary Secretary 1987-89, Minister of State 1989-92; Extra Baroness in Waiting to HM The Queen 1998-; Government Whip 1992-97; Government Spokesperson for: Office of Public Service 1996-97, Department of National Heritage, Agriculture. Member: House of Lords' Offices Advisory Panel on Works of Art 2001-05, Works of Art 2007-. *Other:* Chair, Cambridge City Conservative Association 1969-71. *Councils and public bodies:* Cambridge City Council: Councillor 1963-73; Mayor of Cambridge 1971-72; Councillor, Cambridgeshire County Council 1973-75; JP: Cambridgeshire 1972-75, South Westminster 1975-82; Member: Board of visitors, HM Prison, Pentonville 1975-81, Mental Health Review Tribunal 1975-1981; General Commissioner of Taxes 1975-83; United Kingdom representative to the United Nations Status of Women Commission 1979-81; Chair, Airline Users Committee 1979-80.

Political interests: Agriculture, House of Lords heritage, medical; France, Italy, Madagascar, Mongolia, Spain, USA.

Other: President, Association of Heads of Independent Schools 1980-90; Steward, Folkestone Racecourse 1980-92; Member, Council and Executive Committee of the Animal Health Trust 1981-87; Honorary Fellow, Royal College of Pathologists; Vice-president, International League for the Protection of Horses 1990-99; Honorary Associate, Royal College of Veterinary Surgeons 1994; Honorary Member, British Veterinary Association; Board member, Crimestoppers 2004-10; Fine Cell Work. Honorary Fellow, Lucy Cavendish College, Cambridge 1980. Peer of the Year, *Oldie* awards 2012. PC 1992; DCVO 2005; Officier de l'Ordre du Mérite (France) 2005; Grillions, Farmers'.

Recreations: Antiques, bridge, cookery, needlepoint, racing.

Rt Hon the Baroness Trumpington DCVO, House of Lords, London SW1A 0PW
Tel: 020 7219 5353

TRURO, LORD BISHOP OF

TRURO (15th Bishop of), Timothy Martin Thornton. Born 14 April 1957; Son of late John and late May Thornton; Married Sian Evans 1978 (1 son 1 daughter).

Education: Devonport High School for Boys; Southampton University (BA theology 1978); St Stephen's House, Oxford (Certificate theology 1978); King's College London (MA ecclesiastical theology 1997).

Non-political career: Ordained Deacon 1980; Assistant curate, Todmorden 1980-83; Ordained Priest 1981; Priest, Walsden 1983-85; Chaplain, University College Cardiff 1985-87; Bishop's chaplain: Wakefield 1987-91, London 1991-94; Principal, North Thames Ministerial Training Course 1994-98; Vicar of Kensington, London 1998-2001; Area Bishop of Sherborne 2001-08; Bishop of Truro 2008-.

NON-AFFILIATED

Political career: *House of Lords:* Entered House of Lords 2013. *Councils and public bodies:* DL, Dorset 2007-09.

Other: Chair of Trustees, The Children's Society.

Recreations: Running, reading.

Rt Rev the Lord Bishop of Truro, House of Lords, London SW1A 0PW
Tel: 020 7219 5353 *Email:* thorntonmt@parliament.uk
Lis Escop, Feock, Truro TR3 6QQ *Tel:* 01872 862657 *Email:* info@truro.anglican.org
Website: www.trurodiocese.org.uk

TRUSCOTT, LORD

TRUSCOTT (Life Baron), Peter Derek Truscott; cr. 2004. Born 20 March 1959; Son of Late Derek and Dorothy Truscott; Married Svetlana Chernikova 1991.

Education: Newton Abbot Grammar School; Knowles Hill Comprehensive School, Newton Abbot; Exeter College, Oxford (BA modern history 1981, MA; DPhil 1985).

Non-political career: Political organiser, Labour Party 1986-89; National Association for the Care and Resettlement of Offenders (NACRO) 1989-94; Author 1997-; Senior expert, European Commission 1999; Institute for Public Policy Research (IPPR): Visiting research fellow 1999-2000, Associate research fellow 2001-06; Associate fellow, Royal United Services Institute for Defence and Security Studies 2005-06, 2008-. Formerly TGWU, various posts in TU movement.

NON-AFFILIATED

Political career: *House of Commons:* Contested Torbay (Labour) 1992 general election. *House of Lords:* Raised to the peerage as Baron Truscott, of St James's in the City of Westminster 2004. Parliamentary Under-Secretary of State for Energy and Government Spokesperson, Department of Trade and Industry 2006-07; Ministry of Defence Liaison Peer 2005-06; Suspended from membership May-November 2009. Member European Union Sub-committee C (Foreign Affairs, Defence and Development) 2007-09. *Other:* European Parliament: MEP for Hertfordshire 1994-99: Vice-president, Security Committee 1996-99. Contested Eastern Region 1999 election. Member, NEC Domestic and International Policy Sub-committee 1997-99; National Labour Party Membership Champion 1997-; Formerly member, Co-operative Party. *Councils and public bodies:* Councillor, Colchester Borough Council 1988-92.

Political interests: Foreign affairs, defence, energy, international trade; Russia and former Soviet Union, EU.

Other: Election expert, Organisation for Security and Co-operation in Europe 1995, 1996, 1999, 2003; Fellow, Industry and Parliament Trust 2006; Children's Fire and Burn Trust.

Publications: Russia First (1997); European Defence (IPPR, 2000); Kursk: Russia's Lost Pride (Simon and Schuster, 2002); Putin's Progress (Simon and Schuster, 2004); The Ascendancy of Political Risk Management (RUSI, 2006); European Energy Security (RUSI, 2009); Numerous articles.

Recreations: Walking, swimming, theatre, travel.

The Lord Truscott, House of Lords, London SW1A 0PW
Tel: 020 7219 3241

DO YOU NEED THIS INFORMATION ONLINE?
visit www.dodspeople.com or call 020 7593 5675
to register for a free trial

CONSERVATIVE

TUGENDHAT, LORD

TUGENDHAT (Life Baron), Christopher Samuel Tugendhat; cr. 1993. Born 23 February 1937; Son of late Dr Georg and Mairé Tugendhat; Married Julia Dobson 1967 (2 sons).

Education: Ampleforth College, Yorkshire; Gonville and Caius College, Cambridge (BA history 1960, MA).

Non-political career: Army national service Essex Regiment 1955-57. Journalist, *Financial Times* 1960-70; Director: Sunningdale Oils 1971-76, Phillips Petroleum International (UK) Ltd 1972-76, EEC Commission: Commissioner for Budget and Financial Control, Financial Institutions Personnel and Administration 1977-85: Vice-President 1981-85; Director: National Westminster Bank 1985-91, The BOC Group 1985-96; Chair, Civil Aviation Authority 1986-91; Director, Commercial Union Assurance 1988-91; Deputy chair, National Westminster Bank 1990-91; Director, LWT (Holdings) plc 1991-94, Chairman: Abbey National plc 1991-2002, Blue Circle Industries plc 1996-2001; Non-executive chair, Eurotunnel plc 1991-2003; Director, Rio Tinto plc 1997-2004; Chairman: Lehman Brothers, Europe 2002-06, Lehman Brothers European Advisory Board 2006-07, Imperial College Healthcare NHS Trust 2007-11.

Political career: *House of Commons:* MP (Conservative) for Cities of London and Westminster 1970-74, for City of London and Westminster South 1974-76. *House of Lords:* Raised to the peerage as Baron Tugendhat, of Widdington in the County of Essex 1993. Member: Economic Affairs 2008-13, Sub-committee on Economic Affairs Finance Bill 2012-, European Union 2013-; Chair EU Sub-committee C (External Affairs) 2013-.

Political interests: Health, economy, Europe.

Other: Chair, The Royal Institute for International Affairs, Chatham House 1986-95; Governor, Council of Ditchley Foundation 1986-2010; Chair, European Policy Forum 1997-; Member, advisory board, OMFIF 2012-. Freeman, City of London. Chancellor, Bath University 1998-. Honorary LLD, Bath University 1998; Honorary DLitt, UMIST 2002. Kt 1990; Athenæum.

Publications: Oil: the biggest business (1968); The Multinationals (1971); Making Sense of Europe (1986); Co-author Options for British Foreign Policy in the 1990s (1988).

Recreations: Family, reading, conversation.

The Lord Tugendhat, House of Lords, London SW1A 0PW
Tel: 020 7219 5353 *Email:* tugendhatc@parliament.uk cstug@btinternet.com

LABOUR

TUNNICLIFFE, LORD

Opposition Deputy Chief Whip

TUNNICLIFFE (Life Baron), Denis Tunnicliffe; cr 2004. Born 17 January 1943; Son of Harold and Nellie Tunnicliffe; Married Susan Dale 1968 (2 sons, 1 deceased).

Education: Henry Cavendish School, Derby; University College, London (BSc mathematics 1965); College of Air Training, Hamble.

Non-political career: BOAC/British Airways 1966-86: Co-pilot 1966-72, Chief executive, International Leisure Group, Aviation Division 1986-88; London Underground Ltd: Managing director 1988-98, Chair 1998-2000; Chief executive, London Transport 1998-2000; Chair: United Kingdom Atomic Energy Authority 2002-04, Rail Safety and Standards Board 2003-08. Member, British Airline Pilots Association 1966-72.

Political career: *House of Lords:* Raised to the peerage as Baron Tunnicliffe, of Bracknell in the Royal County of Berkshire 2004. Government Whip 2008-10; Government Spokesperson for: International Development 2008-09, Work and Pensions 2008; Opposition Spokesperson for Defence 2010-11; Opposition Deputy Chief Whip 2010-; Opposition Spokesperson for Business, Innovation and Skills 2012. Member: Merits of Statutory Instruments 2005-08, Refreshment 2013, Joint Committee on Security 2010-. *Councils and public bodies:* Councillor: Royal Borough of New Windsor 1972-75, Royal County of Berkshire 1974-78; Bracknell District Council: Councillor 1983-87, Leader 1985-87.

Political interests: Finance, justice, defence, climate change; Antigua.

Other: Trustee, Homerton College Cambridge 1998-2008; Council member, Royal Holloway College, University of London 2004-08; Board member, ACT (a property company that gives its profits to charity) 2004-08; Non-executive director, Defence Equipment and Support 2007-08. CBE 1993; RAC and RAF.

Recreations: Theatre, boating and flying.

The Lord Tunnicliffe CBE, House of Lords, London SW1A 0PW
Tel: 020 7219 4326 *Email:* tunnicliffed@parliament.uk

TURNBERG, LORD

LABOUR

TURNBERG (Life Baron), Leslie Arnold Turnberg; cr. 2000. Born 22 March 1934; Son of Hyman and Dora Turnberg; Married Edna Barme 1968 (1 son deceased 1 daughter).
Education: Stand Grammar School, Whitefield; Manchester University (MB, ChB 1957; MD 1966).
Non-political career: Junior medical posts 1957-61, 1964-66: Manchester Jewish Hospital, Northern Hospital, Ancoats Hospital, Manchester Royal Infirmary; Registrar, University College Hospital, London 1961-64; Lecturer, Royal Free Hospital, London 1967; Research fellow, University of Texas South-Western Medical School, Dallas, Texas 1968; Manchester University: Lecturer, then senior lecturer 1968-73, Professor of medicine 1973-97, Dean, Faculty of medicine 1986-89; Scientific adviser, Association of Medical Research Charities 1997-; Board member, Renovo 2006-11.
Political career: *House of Lords:* Raised to the peerage as Baron Turnberg, of Cheadle in the County of Cheshire 2000. Member: Science and Technology 2001-06, Science and Technology Sub-committees: I (Systematic Biology and Biodiversity/Fighting Infection) 2002-03, II (Renewable Energy) 2003-04, I (Scientific Aspects of Ageing) 2004-05, Draft Human Tissue and Embryos Bill Joint Committee 2007; Co-opted member Science and Technology 2013, Member Mental Capacity Act 2005 2013-. *Other:* Member, Labour Friends of Israel. *Councils and public bodies:* Member: Salford Health Authority 1974-81, 1990-92, North West Regional Health Authority 1986-89; Chair: Conference of Medical Royal Colleges 1994-96, Specialist Training Authority 1996-98, Public Health Laboratory Service Board 1997-2002; President: Medical Council on Alcoholism 1997-2002, Medical Protection Society 1997-2007; Chair, Medical Advisory Board, Nations Healthcare 2004-07.
Political interests: Health Service, medical education, research; Middle East, Israel.
Other: Trustee: Haddasah UK 1996-, Wolfson Foundation 1997-; Vice-president, Academy of Medical Sciences 1998-2004; Chair, Health Quality Service 1999-2004; President: British Society of Gastroenterology 1999-2000, Association of Physicians 2000; Trustee: Foulkes Foundation 2000-, Dipex 2004-10; Chairman, National Centre for Replacement, Reduction and Refinement of use of Animals in Research 2004-07; Trustee: Ovarian Cancer Action 2007-, Weizmann UK 2010-; Vice-president, Academy of Medical Services 1998-2004; President, Royal College of Physicians 1992-97; MRCP 1961; FRCP 1973; FRCPE 1993; FRCP(I) 1993; Honorary Fellow: Academy of Medicine, Singapore 1994, College of Medicine, South Africa 1994; FRCPSGlas 1994; FCPPak 1994; Hong Kong Coll of Physns 1995; FRAustCP 1995; FRCS 1996; FRCOphth 1996; FRCOG 1996; FRCPsych 1997; Malaysia Coll of Med 1997; FMedSci 1998; Physiological Society 2005. Four honorary doctorates. Kt 1994.
Publications: Author of publications on intestinal research and clinical gastroenterology.
Recreations: Reading, antiquarian books, painting, Chinese ceramics, walking.
The Lord Turnberg, House of Lords, London SW1A 0PW
Tel: 020 7219 5353

TURNBULL, LORD

CROSSBENCH

TURNBULL (Life Baron), Andrew Turnbull; cr 2005. Born 21 January 1945; Son of Anthony and Mary Turnbull; Married Diane Clarke 1967 (2 sons).
Education: Enfield Grammar School; Christ's College, Cambridge (BA economics 1967).
Non-political career: Economist, Government Republic of Zambia 1968-70; HM Treasury (HMT) 1970-94: Seconded to International Monetary Fund 1976-78, Private Secretary (Economics) to Margaret Thatcher as Prime Minister 1983-85, Head, General Expenditure Policy Group 1985-88; Principal Private Secretary to Margaret Thatcher as Prime Minister 1988-92; Deputy Secretary, Public Finance and Monetary Policy 1992-93; Second Permanent Secretary, Public Expenditure 1993-94; Permanent Secretary: Department of the Environment 1994-97, Department of Environment, Transport and the Regions 1997-98, HMT 1998-2002; Secretary of the Cabinet and Head of the Home Civil Service 2002-05; Non-executive director: Prudential plc 2006-, British Land Company plc 2006-, Frontier Economics 2006-, BH Global Ltd (Chair) 2008-12.
Political career: *House of Lords:* Raised to the peerage as Baron Turnbull, of Enfield in the London Borough of Enfield 2005. Member: Audit 2011-, Parliamentary Commission on Banking Standards 2012-13.
Political interests: Public services, the economy, financial services, energy, climate change; Zambia.
Other: Chair of Governors, Dulwich College; Trustee, Global Warming Policy Foundation. Honorary doctorates: Middlesex University, Cranfield University; Honorary fellow, Christ's College, Cambridge. CB 1990; CVO 1992; KCB 1998. Tottenham Hotspur.
Recreations: Golf, opera, sailing, walking.
The Lord Turnbull KCB CVO, House of Lords, London SW1A 0PW
Tel: 020 7219 5353

LABOUR

TURNER OF CAMDEN, BARONESS

TURNER OF CAMDEN (Life Baroness), Muriel Turner; cr. 1985. Born 18 September 1927; Daughter of Edward Price; Married Wing-Commander Reginald Turner, MC, DFC 1955 (died 1995).

Non-political career: Assistant General Secretary, Association of Scientific, Technical and Managerial Staffs 1970-87; Member, TUC General Council 1980-87.

Political career: *House of Lords:* Raised to the peerage as Baroness Turner of Camden, of Camden in Greater London 1985. Opposition Spokesperson for: Social Security 1987-96, Employment 1987-96; Deputy Chair of Committees 1997-2008; Deputy Speaker 2002-08. Co-opted member European Communities Sub-committee F (Social Affairs, Education and Home Affairs) 1997-2009; Member House of Lords' Offices 1997-98. *Councils and public bodies:* Member: Occupational Pensions Board 1977-93, Equal Opportunities Commission 1982-88; Council member, OPAS (Pension Advisory Service) 1989-2007; Chair, PIA Ombudsman Council 1994-97.

Political interests: Employment, social security, pensions.

Other: Council member, Save The Children Fund 1991-98; Save The Children Fund. Honorary LLD, Leicester University 1991; RAF.

Recreations: Reading, music.

The Baroness Turner of Camden, House of Lords, London SW1A 0PW
Tel: 020 7219 5353 *Email:* muriel.m.turner@btinternet.com

CROSSBENCH

TURNER OF ECCHINSWELL, LORD

TURNER OF ECCHINSWELL (Life Baron), (Jonathan) Adair Turner; cr 2005. Born 5 October 1955; Son of Geoffrey Turner and Kathleen Turner, née Broadhurst; Married Orna Ni Chionna 1985 (2 daughters).

Education: Glenalmond School, Perthshire; Gonville and Caius College, Cambridge (BA history and economics 1978, MA) (Union President).

Non-political career: Economics supervisor (part-time), Gonville and Caius College, Cambridge 1979-82; BP 1979; Chase Manhattan Bank 1979-82; McKinsey & Co 1982-95: Director 1994-95; Director-general, Confederation of British Industry 1995-99; Vice-chair, Merrill Lynch Europe 2000-06; Director, United Business Media 2000-08; Chair: Low Pay Commission 2002-06, Pension Commission 2003-06; Director: Standard Chartered Bank 2006-08, Paternoster 2006-08; Chair: ESRC 2007-08, ODI 2007-10, Financial Services Authority 2008-13, Committee on Climate Change 2008-12; Senior fellow, Institute of New Economic Thinking (INET) 2013-.

Political career: *House of Lords:* Raised to the peerage as Baron Turner of Ecchinswell, of Ecchinswell in the County of Hampshire 2005. Member Economic Affairs 2007-08.

Countries of interest: China.

Other: Fellow, World Wide Fund for Nature (WWF) UK; Chair, Committee on Climate Change 2008-12; Honorary fellow, Royal Society of Edinburgh; Trustee, British Museum; Council member, Overseas Development Institute; Save the Children; WWF UK. Visiting professor: London School of Economics, Cass Business School; Honorary fellow, London Business School.

Publications: Author, Just Capital (MacMillan, 2001); Declining Populations in Philosophical Transactions of the Royal Society (2009); Economics After the Crisis (Lionel Robbins Memorial Lectures, MIT, 2012).

The Lord Turner of Ecchinswell, House of Lords, London SW1A 0PW
Tel: 020 7219 5353

LIBERAL DEMOCRAT

TYLER, LORD

TYLER (Life Baron), Paul Archer Tyler; cr 2005. Born 29 October 1941; Son of Oliver and Grace Tyler; Married Nicola Ingram 1970 (1 daughter 1 son).

Education: Sherborne School, Dorset; Exeter College, Oxford (BA modern history 1963, MA).

Non-political career: Director, public affairs, Royal Institute of British Architects 1972-73; Board member, Shelter: National Campaign for the Homeless 1975-76; Managing director, Cornwall Courier Newspaper Group 1976-81; Public affairs division, Good Relations plc: Chief executive 1984-86, Chair 1986-87; Senior consultant, Public Affairs 1987-92; Director, Western Approaches Public Relations Ltd 1987-92. National Union of Journalists 1973-82.

Political career: *House of Commons:* Contested (Liberal) Totnes 1966 and Bodmin 1970 general elections. MP (Liberal) for Bodmin February-October 1974. Contested Bodmin 1979 general election and Beaconsfield 1982 by-election. MP (Liberal Democrat) for North Cornwall 1992-2005.

Liberal Democrat: Spokesperson for: Agriculture and Rural Affairs 1992-97, Agriculture, Tourism, Transport and Rural Affairs 1994-96, Food 1997-99, Chief Whip 1997-2001, Shadow Leader of the House 1997-2005, Spokesperson for Constitutional Reform 2001-05. Co-chair, Liberal Democrat Parliamentary Policy Committee on Constitutional and Political Reform 2010-. *House of Lords:* Raised to the peerage as Baron Tyler, of Linkinhorne in the County of Cornwall 2005. Liberal Democrat Spokesperson for: Constitutional Affairs 2006-10, Environment, Food and Rural Affairs 2008-09. Member: Conventions Joint Committee 2006, Draft Constitutional Renewal Bill Joint Committee 2008, Procedure 2008-13, Joint Committee on the Draft House of Lords Reform Bill 2011-12. Chair, Liberal Democrat Parliamentary Party Committee on Constitutional and Political Reform 2010-. *Other:* Contested (SLD) Cornwall and Plymouth 1989 European Parliament election. Chair: Devon and Cornwall Region Liberal Party 1981-82, Liberal Party National Executive Committee 1983-86; Campaign adviser to David Steel MP in 1983 and 1987 general elections. *Councils and public bodies:* Councillor, Devon County Council 1964-70; Member, Devon and Cornwall Police Authority 1965-70; Vice-chair, Dartmoor National Park Committee 1965-70; DL, Cornwall 2005-10.

Political interests: Tourism, rural affairs, constitutional reform; Australia, Canada, Finland, Germany, Sweden.

Other: Chair, Council for the Protection of Rural England Working Party on the future of the village 1974-81; Vice-President: British Resorts and Destinations Association 1995-, Youth Hostels Association 1996-; Director, Make Votes Count 2005-10; Chair, Faiths and Civil Society Unit, Goldsmiths College, London 2008-; Vice-chair, Hansard Society 2009-; Chair, advisory board, Interclimate Network 2010-; Patron, Joe Homan Charity 2011-; Ambassador, Concern Universal 2012-; Shelter. Parliamentarian of the Year, *Country Life* 1997. CBE 1985.

Publications: Co-author, Power to the Provinces (1968); A New Deal for Rural Britain (1978); Country Lives, Country Landscapes (1996); Britain's Democratic Deficit (2003); Co-author: Reforming the House of Lords – Breaking the Deadlock (2005), Beating the Retreat – The Government's Flight from Constitutional Reform (2008); Constitutional Renewal Bill (2009); Lords Reform: A Guide for MPs (2012); Funding a Democracy: Breaking the Deadlock (2013).

Recreations: Sailing, gardening, walking.

The Lord Tyler CBE, House of Lords, London SW1A 0PW
Tel: 020 7219 6355 *Email:* tylerp@parliament.uk *Website:* www.paultyler.libdems.org

TYLER OF ENFIELD, BARONESS

TYLER OF ENFIELD (Life Baroness) Claire Tyler; cr 2011. Born 4 June 1957.
Education: Latymer Grammar School, Edmonton; Southampton University (BA law and politics); Diploma (management studies).
Non-political career: Greater London Council/Inner London Education Authority 1978-88; Department of Employment 1988-2000: Assistant Regional Director, Government Office for London, Head, 16-19 Policy Unit; Deputy Chief Executive, Connexions Service 2000-02; Director, Social Exclusion Unit, Office of the Deputy Prime Minister/Department for Communities and Local Government 2002-06; Director, Vulnerable Children's Group, Department for Education and Skills 2006-07.

LIBERAL DEMOCRAT

Political career: *House of Lords:* Raised to the peerage as Baroness Tyler of Enfield, of Enfield in the London Borough of Enfield 2011. Member Public Service and Demographic Change 2012-13.
Other: Fellow, Chartered Institute for Personnel and Development; Member, Joseph Rowntree Foundation Poverty and Disadvantage Committee.
The Baroness Tyler of Enfield, House of Lords, London SW1A 0PW
Tel: 020 7219 5353

UDDIN, BARONESS

UDDIN (Life Baroness), Pola Manzila Uddin; cr. 1998. Born 17 July 1959; Daughter of Mr and Mrs Khan; Married Komar Uddin 1976 (4 sons 1 daughter).
Education: Plashet School for Girls, Newham; Polytechnic of North London (Diploma social work 1990).
Non-political career: Youth and Community Worker, YWCA 1980-82; Liaison officer, Tower Hamlets Social Services 1982-84; Manager, Women's Health Project 1984-88; Asian Family Counselling Service 1989-90; Social worker, subsequently management consultant, Social Services Department, London Borough of Newham Council 1993-98; Non-executive director, Carlton Media Group 1999-2001; Project Leader, Addaction.

NON-AFFILIATED

Political career: *House of Lords:* Raised to the peerage as Baroness Uddin, of Bethnal Green in the London Borough of Tower Hamlets 1998. Suspended from membership October 2010-May 2012. Co-opted member European Union Sub-committee G (Social Policy and Consumer Affairs) 2006-08. *Other:* Labour Whip suspended October 2010. *Councils and public bodies:* London Borough of Tower Hamlets: Councillor 1990-98, Deputy Leader 1994-96.

Political interests: Women, international affairs, human rights and equality; Bangladesh, Morocco, Qatar, Saudi Arabia, Tunisia, UAE.

Other: Patron: Bethnal Green and Victoria Park Housing Association, Social Action for Health, Women's Aid, Black Women's Health Project, Disability Trust, Student Partnership Worldwide, ORBIS International; NSPCC, East London Asian Family Counselling. Honorary degrees, universities of East London and Exeter.

The Baroness Uddin, House of Lords, London SW1A 0PW
Tel: 020 7219 8506 *Email:* uddinm@parliament.uk

ULLSWATER, VISCOUNT

CONSERVATIVE

ULLSWATER (2nd Viscount, UK), Nicholas James Christopher Lowther; cr. 1921. Born 9 January 1942; Son of late Lieutenant John Lowther, MVO, RNVR, grandson of 1st Viscount, PC, GCB; Married Susan Weatherby 1967 (2 sons 2 daughters).

Education: Eton College; Trinity College, Cambridge (BA agriculture 1963, MA).

Non-political career: Captain, Royal Wessex Yeomanry, Retired. Chair, Wincanton Races Co. Ltd 1986-93; Private Secretary and Comptroller to Princess Margaret, Countess of Snowdon 1998-2002.

Political career: *House of Lords:* First entered House of Lords 1963; Government Whip 1989-90; Parliamentary Under-Secretary of State, Department of Employment 1990-93; Government Chief Whip 1993-94; Minister of State, Department of the Environment (Construction and Planning) 1994-95; Elected hereditary peer 2003-; Deputy Speaker 2004-; Deputy Chair of Committees 2004-; Contested Lord Speaker election 2006. Co-opted member EU Sub-Committee F (Home Affairs) 2003-07; Member: Merits of Statutory Instruments 2003-05, Administration and Works 2005-09; Co-opted member EU Sub-committee D (Environment and Agriculture) 2006-10; Member: Procedure 2009-, Liaison 2010-. *Councils and public bodies:* JP 1971-88; Councillor, King's Lynn and West Norfolk Borough Council 2003-11.

Other: Wiltshire Association of Boys Clubs: Chair 1966-74, Vice-President 1975-. PC 1994; LVO 2002; Jockey (Newmarket), Pratt's.

Recreations: Racing, golf.

Rt Hon the Viscount Ullswater LVO, House of Lords, London SW1A 0PW
Tel: 020 7219 5219 *Email:* ullswatern@parliament.uk
Whiteacres, Cross Lane, Brancaster, King's Lynn, Norfolk PE31 8AE *Tel:* 01485 210488

VADERA, BARONESS

LABOUR

VADERA (Life Baroness), Shriti Vadera; cr 2007. Born 23 June 1962.

Non-political career: Executive director, UBS Warburg 1984-99; Adviser to the Chancellor and member, Council of Economic Advisers, HM Treasury 1999-2007.

Political career: *House of Lords:* Raised to the peerage as Baroness Vadera, of Holland Park in the London Borough of Kensington and Chelsea 2007. Parliamentary Under-Secretary of State and Government Spokesperson: Department for International Development 2007-08, Department for Business, Enterprise and Regulatory Reform/Business, Innovation and Skills (Minister for Economic Competitiveness, Small Business and Enterprise) 2008-09, Cabinet Office 2008-09; On leave of absence December 2011-. *Councils and public bodies:* Adviser at Republic of Korea as Chair G20 2009-10.

Other: PC 2009.

Rt Hon the Baroness Vadera, House of Lords, London SW1A 0PW
Tel: 020 7219 5353

CROSSBENCH

VALENTINE, BARONESS

VALENTINE (Life Baroness), Josephine (Jo) Clare Valentine; cr 2005. Born 8 December 1958; Daughter of Michael and Shirley Valentine; Married Simon Acland 1990 (2 daughters).

Education: St Paul's Girls' School, London; St Hugh's College, Oxford (BA maths and philosophy 1981); Casual French.

Non-political career: Manager, Barings 1981-88; Chief executive officer, Blackburn Partnership 1988-90; Senior manager, BOC Group 1990-95; Chief executive officer, Central London Partnership 1995-97; London First 1997-: Chief operating officer 2000-03; Chief executive officer 2003-; Non-executive director: TP70 2008 (ii), VCT plc, Peabody Trust.

Political career: *House of Lords:* Raised to the peerage as Baroness Valentine, of Putney in the London Borough of Wandsworth 2005. Member: Works of Art 2009-10, 2012-13, EU Sub-committee B: (Internal Market, Energy and Transport) 2010-12, (Internal Market, Infrastructure and Employment) 2012-.

Political interests: Maintaining London as a world city, Olympics, transport, skills and employment, party conference.

Other: Honorary fellow, St Hugh's College, Oxford.

Recreations: Piano, bridge, travel.

The Baroness Valentine, House of Lords, London SW1A 0PW
Tel: 020 7219 5353
3 Whitcomb Street, London WC2H 7HA *Tel:* 020 7665 1500
Email: jvalentine@londonfirst.co.uk

LIBERAL DEMOCRAT

VALLANCE OF TUMMEL, LORD

VALLANCE OF TUMMEL (Life Baron), Iain David Thomas Vallance; cr. 2004. Born 20 May 1943; Married Elizabeth McGonnigill 1967 (1 daughter 1 son).

Education: Edinburgh Academy; Dulwich College, London; Glasgow Academy; Brasenose College, Oxford (BA English language and literature 1965); London Business School (MSc business administration 1972).

Non-political career: Post Office 1966-81: Director: Central finance 1976-78, Telecommunications finance 1978-79, Materials department 1979-81; British Telecommunications (BT) 1981-2002: Chief of operations 1985-86, Chief executive 1986-95, Chair 1987-2001, President emeritus 2001-02; Vice-chair, Royal Bank of Scotland Group plc 1994-2005; Chair, European advisory committee, New York Stock Exchange 1995-2005; Director, Mobil Corporation 1996-99; Member, international advisory board, Allianz AG 1996-; Chair, European Services Forum 2003-08; Member: Supervisory board, Siemens AG 2003-13, European advisory council, Rothschild Group 2003-08.

Political career: *House of Lords:* Raised to the peerage as Baron Vallance of Tummel, of Tummel in Perth and Kinross 2004. Liberal Democrat Spokesperson for Trade and Industry/Business, Enterprise and Regulatory Reform 2005-10. Economic Affairs: Member 2005-07, Chair 2007-10; Chair Finance Bill Sub-committee 2008-10; Member EU Sub-committee A: (Economic and Financial Affairs and International Trade) 2010-12, (Economic and Financial Affairs) 2012-. *Councils and public bodies:* CBI President's Committee: Member 1988-, President 2000-02; Board member, Scottish Enterprise 1998-2001; Deputy chair, Financial Reporting Council 2001-02.

Political interests: Business, economics, Europe.

Other: Member: European Foundation for Quality Management 1988-96, International advisory board, British-American Chamber of Commerce 1991-2002; Member, President's Committee, Business in the Community 1988-2002; Princess Royal Trust for Carers: Chair 1991-98, Vice-President 1999-2012; Chair: Nations Healthcare 2005-07, Amsphere Ltd 2006-, Royal Scottish Academy of Music and Drama 2007-; Fellow, Chartered Institute of Bankers in Scotland. Honorary Fellow Brasenose College, Oxford Fellow, London Business School Fellow, Royal Society of Arts; Seven honorary doctorates. Kt 1994.

Recreations: Hill-walking, music.

The Lord Vallance of Tummel, House of Lords, London SW1A 0PW
Tel: 020 7219 2715

VERJEE, LORD – *Please see Addenda px*

CONSERVATIVE

VERMA, BARONESS

Parliamentary Under-Secretary of State and Government Spokesperson, Department of Energy and Climate Change

VERMA (Life Baroness), Sandip Verma; cr 2006. Born 30 June 1959; Daughter of Shivcharan Singh Rana and Ravinder Rana; Married Ashok Kumar Verma 1977 (1 daughter 1 son).

Education: Leicester; De Montfort University, Leicester (Deferred Degree business management); Hindi, Punjabi.

Non-political career: Managing director: Domiciliary Care Services UK Ltd 2000-, DCS (West Midlands) Ltd; Director, DCS Foods Ltd.

Political career: *House of Commons:* Contested (Conservative) Hull East 2001 and Wolverhampton South West 2005 general elections. *House of Lords:* Raised to the peerage as Baroness Verma, of Leicester in the County of Leicestershire 2006. Opposition Whip 2006-10; Opposition Spokesperson for: Health 2006-07, Education and Skills 2006-07, Innovation, Universities and Skills 2007-09, Children, Schools and Families 2007-08, 2009-10, Universities and Skills 2009-10; Government Whip 2010-12; Government Spokesperson for: Cabinet Office 2010-12, International Development 2010-11, Women and Equalities 2010-12, Business, Innovation and Skills 2011-12; Parliamentary Under-Secretary of State and Government Spokesperson, Department of Energy and Climate Change 2012-. *Other:* Area chair, Conservative Women 2001-02; Area officer 2001-03; Executive National Conservative (Women) 2001-03; Chair, Leicester South Conservative Association 2006-08; President, City of Leicester Conservative Association 2008-09, 2010-11; Patron: Tory Reform Group, British Asian Conservative Link, Friends of Conservative Society of Indians; Vice-chair, Syston branch, Rutland Conservative Association.

Political interests: Health, education, overseas development, home affairs; Africa, Europe, South Asia.

Other: Patron: CST – Protecting the Jewish Community, India Association, The British Sikh Association, Bucks Punjabi Society, Pakistan-India and UK-Friendship Forum, Punjab Link Council; Extraordinary Champion, Roko Cancer (Breast Cancer); Board member, Football Foundation; NRI Institute, India; Trustee, Ellie Bishop Trust Fund; Punjab House Trust; Patron, Dil Trust UK; FRSA; Distinguished Fellowship, Institute of Directors, India. Freedom, City of London. Honorary Doctorate, Wolverhampton University. Pravasi Bharatiya Saman, President of India 2011.

Recreations: Socialising, walking, travel.

The Baroness Verma, House of Lords, London SW1A 0PW
Tel: 020 7219 5216 *Email:* vermas@parliament.uk

CROSSBENCH

VINCENT OF COLESHILL, LORD

VINCENT OF COLESHILL (Life Baron), Richard Frederick Vincent; cr. 1996. Born 23 August 1931; Son of late Frederick Vincent and Frances Elizabeth, née Coleshill; Married Jean Stewart 1955 (1 son 1 daughter and 1 son deceased).

Education: Aldenham School, Hertfordshire; Royal Military College of Science 1963-64.

Non-political career: Commissioned, Royal Artillery, National Service 1951, Germany 1951-55, Gunnery Staff 1959; Radar Research Establishment, Malvern 1960-61; BAOR 1962, Technical Staff Training 1963-64; Staff College 1965; Commonwealth Brigade, Malaysia 1966-68; Ministry of Defence 1968-70; Commanded 12th Light Air Defence Regiment, Germany, UK and Northern Ireland 1970-72; Instructor, Staff College 1972-73; Greenlands Staff College, Henley 1974; Military Director of Studies, Royal Military College of Science 1974-75; Commanded 19th Airportable Brigade 1975-77; Royal College of Defence Studies 1978; Deputy Military Secretary 1979-80; Commandant, Royal Military College of Science 1980-83; Colonel Commandant, REME 1981-87; Master General of the Ordnance, Ministry of Defence 1983-87; Colonel Commandant, RA 1983-2000; Vice-Chief of Defence Staff 1987-91; Chief of Defence Staff 1991-92; Chair, Military Committee, NATO 1993-96; Master Gunner, St James's Park 1996-2000. Director, Vickers Defence Systems 1996-2002; Chair: Imperial College of Science, Technology and Medicine 1996-2004, Hunting Defence Ltd 1996-2003, Hunting Engineering Ltd 1998-2001, Hunting – BRAE 1998-2003; Director, INSYS Ltd 2001-05.

Political career: *House of Lords:* Raised to the peerage as Baron Vincent of Coleshill, of Shrivenham in the County of Oxfordshire 1996. Adviser to Secretary of State on Strategic Defence Review 1997-98; On leave of absence June 2012-. *Councils and public bodies:* Aldenham School: Governor 1987-2009, Governor Emeritus 2009-.

Political interests: Foreign affairs, security, defence, education; NATO member countries.

Other: Member, The Pilgrims 1996-2011; Past and present member, president, chair numerous organisations, especially those concerned with military, education and sport, including: Chair, Imperial College London 1995-2003; Member, Commission on Britain and Europe (Royal Institute of International Affairs) 1996-98; Defence Manufacturers Association: Vice-President 1996-2000, President 2000-05; Governor, The Ditchley Foundation 1996-2007; President: Old Aldenhamian Society 1999-2003, Cranfield Trust 2000-11; Patron: National Service Veterans Association 2007-, INSPIRE Foundation; FRAeS 1990; FIMechE 1990; FIC 1996; Royal Artillery Charitable Fund, Inspire, The Cranfield Trust. Member, The Guild of Freemen of the City of London; Freeman, Worshipful Company of Wheelwrights 1997. Freeman, City of London 1992. Chancellor, Cranfield University 1998-2010. Honorary DSc, Cranfield 1985; Visiting Fellow, Australian College of Defence and Strategic Studies 1995-99; Fellow, Imperial College of Science, Technology and Medicine 1996; Honorary Fellow, City and Guilds of London Institute; Senior Fellow, Cranfield University 2010. DSO 1972; KCB 1984; GBE 1990; Jordanian Order of Military Merit 1992; Commander, Legion of Merit (USA) 1993; Army and Navy, Royal Scots, Cavalry and Guards.

Publications: Has contributed to military journals and publications.

Recreations: Grandchildren.

Field Marshal the Lord Vincent of Coleshill GBE KCB DSO, House of Lords,
London SW1A 0PW
Tel: 020 7219 5353

CONSERVATIVE

VINSON, LORD

VINSON (Life Baron), Nigel Vinson; cr. 1985. Born 27 January 1931; Son of late Ronald Vinson, farmer; Married Yvonne Collin 1972 (3 daughters).

Education: Nautical College, Pangbourne.

Non-political career: Lieutenant, Queen's Royal Regiment 1948-50. Founder, Plastic Coatings Ltd 1952 (floated on London Stock Exchange 1970); Director, British Airports Authority 1973-80; Co-founder and director, Centre for Policy Studies 1974-80; Director, Barclays Bank UK 1982-87; Deputy chair, Electra Investment Trust 1990-98; Chair: St Cuthbert's Newcastle Estates 1990-2000, Fleming Income and Growth Trust 1995-2000.

Political career: *House of Lords:* Raised to the peerage as Baron Vinson, of Roddam Dene in the County of Northumberland 1985. Member: Pollution 1997-98, Monetary Policy of the Bank of England/Economic Affairs 1998-2004, Draft Climate Change Bill Joint Committee 2007. *Other:* President, Berwick upon Tweed Conservative Association 2000-05. *Councils and public bodies:* Member: Crafts Advisory Committee 1971-77, Design Council 1973-80; President, Industrial Participation Association 1979-90; Chair, Rural Development Commission 1980-90; DL, Northumberland 1990.

Political interests: Small businesses, deregulation, tax, pensions; UK.

Other: CBI: Member, Grand Council 1975-, Deputy Chair, Smaller Firms Council 1979-84; Honorary Director, Queen's Silver Jubilee Appeal 1976-78; Member, Regional Committee, National Trust 1977-84; Northumbrian National Parks: Member, Countryside Committee 1977-87; Chair, Rural Development Committee 1980-90; Member, Industry Year Steering Committee, Royal Society of Arts 1985; Institute of Economic Affairs: Chair of trustees 1988-95, Vice-President 1995-; Trustee, St George's House, Windsor 1990-96; Member, Foundation of Science and Technology 1991-; Chair: North East Civic Trust 1996-2001, Prince's Trust (NE) 1997-99; Trustee: Civitas 2003-, Chillingham Wild Cattle Association 2008; Council member, Freedom Association; CBIM; FRSA; Nigel Vinson Charitable Trust (gives mostly to freedom supporting institutes). Queen's Award to Industry 1971. LVO 1979; Boodle's, Pratt's.

Publications: Personal Pensions for All (1984); Take Upon Retiring (Late Extra) (2005).

Recreations: Objets d'art, farming, horses.

The Lord Vinson LVO DL, House of Lords, London SW1A 0PW
Tel: 020 7219 5353
34 Kynance Mews, London SW7 4QR *Tel:* 020 7937 4183 *Fax:* 01668 217356
Email: roddamdene@btinternet.com

CONSERVATIVE

WADDINGTON, LORD

WADDINGTON (Life Baron), David Charles Waddington; cr. 1990. Born 2 August 1929; Son of late Charles Waddington, JP; Married Gillian Green 1958 (3 sons 2 daughters).

Education: Sedbergh School; Hertford College, Oxford (MA law 1950).

Non-political career: Second Lieutenant, 12th Royal Lancers 1951-53; Captain, Duke of Lancaster's Yeomanry 1953-60. Called to Bar, Gray's Inn 1951; QC 1971; Bencher 1985; Recorder of the Crown Court 1972; Governor and Commander-in-Chief, Bermuda 1992-97.

Political career: *House of Commons:* Contested Farnworth 1955, Nelson and Colne 1964 and Heywood and Royton 1966 general elections. MP (Conservative) for Nelson and Colne 1968-74, for Clitheroe 1979-83, for Ribble Valley 1983-90. Government Whip 1979-81; Parliamentary Under-Secretary of State, Department of Employment 1981-83; Minister of State, Home Office 1983-87; Government Chief Whip 1987-89; Home Secretary 1989-90. *House of Lords:* Raised to the peerage as Baron Waddington, of Read in the County of Lancashire 1990. Lord Privy Seal and Leader of the House of Lords 1990-92. Member: Parliamentary Privilege (Joint Committee) 1997-98, Delegated Powers and Deregulation 1999-2002, Procedure 2000-03, Works of Art 2008-10. *Other:* President, Oxford University Conservative Association 1950; Chair, Clitheroe Constituency Young Conservatives 1953. *Councils and public bodies:* DL, Lancashire 1991-.

Political interests: Legal affairs, textile industry, Lancashire; Australia, Bermuda, St Helena.

Other: President: Hertford Society 1997-2003, OSPA (Overseas Service Pensioners Association) 1998-; Vice-chair, Bermuda Society 1999-2006; Scouts. Honorary Fellow, Hertford College, Oxford. PC 1987; GCVO 1994; Buck's.

Publications: Memoirs (Biteback, 2012).

Recreations: Sailing.

Rt Hon the Lord Waddington GCVO DL QC, House of Lords, London SW1A 0PW
Tel: 020 7219 6448 *Fax:* 020 7219 6807 *Email:* waddingtond@parliament.uk

WADE OF CHORLTON, LORD

WADE OF CHORLTON (Life Baron), (William) Oulton Wade; cr. 1990. Born 24 December 1932; Son of late Samuel Wade, farmer, and late Joan Ferris Wade, née Wild; Married Gillian Leete 1959 (1 son 1 daughter).

Education: Birkenhead School; Queen's University, Belfast (agriculture).

Non-political career: Farmer and cheesemaster; Chair, Cheese Export Council 1982-84; Member, Food From Britain Export Council 1984-88; Chair: William Wild and Son (Mollington) Ltd, NIM-TECH, Risingstars Growth Fund Ltd, Rocktron Ltd, International Open View Exchange Ltd; Deputy chair, MAM Funds plc; Director, MAM Funds plc/MITON Group plc.

CONSERVATIVE

Political career: *House of Lords:* Raised to the peerage as Baron Wade of Chorlton, of Chester in the County of Cheshire 1990. Chair Science and Technology Sub-committee II (Chips for Everything Opportunities in Micro Processors) 2002; Member: Science and Technology -2003, 2010-, Science and Technology Sub-committee II (Energy Efficiency) 2005, European Union 2008-09; EU Sub-committee G (Social Policy and Consumer Affairs): Co-opted member 2006-07, 2009-10, Member 2007-09. *Other:* Member, National Union Executive Committee 1975-90; Chair, North West Area Conservative Association 1976-81; Joint Honorary Treasurer, Conservative Party 1982-90. *Councils and public bodies:* JP, Cheshire 1965; Councillor, Cheshire County Council 1973-77.

Political interests: Food industry, agriculture, industry, planning, technology, innovation, venture capital.

Other: President, CHPA 1992-2006; Chair, Historic Cheshire Churches Preservation Trust 1993-2012. Member, Worshipful Company of Farmers. Freeman, City of London 1980. Two honorary doctorates: Liverpool University, Chester University. Kt 1982; The City (Chester), Portico Library, Manchester.

Recreations: Shooting, reading, farming.

The Lord Wade of Chorlton, House of Lords, London SW1A 0PW
Tel: 020 7219 5499 *Email:* wadew@parliament.uk

NON-AFFILIATED

WAKEFIELD, LORD BISHOP OF

WAKEFIELD (12th Bishop of); Stephen George Platten. Born 17 May 1947; Son of George Henry Platten, advertising manager, and Marjory Platten; Married Rosslie Thompson 1972 (2 sons).

Education: Stationers' Company School; London University (BEd 1972); Trinity College, Oxford (Dip Theol 1974; BD 2003); Cuddesdon Theological College; French, German.

Non-political career: Management trainee, Shell International Chemical Company 1966-68; Ordained deacon 1975, priest 1976; Assistant curate, St Andrew's Church, Headington, Oxford 1975-78; Chaplain and tutor in ethics, Lincoln Theological College 1978-82; Director of ordinands and canon residentiary, Portsmouth Cathedral 1983-89; Director post-ordination training, Portsmouth diocese 1984-89; Archbishop of Canterbury's secretary for ecumenical affairs and honorary canon, Canterbury Cathedral 1990-95; Dean of Norwich 1995-2003; Bishop of Wakefield 2003-.

Political career: *House of Lords:* Entered House of Lords 2009. *Councils and public bodies:* Chair, Society for Study of Christian Ethics 1983-89; Anglican secretary, Anglican-Roman Catholic International Commission 1990-95; Chair, Liturgical Commission 2005-; Member: Cathedrals Fabric Commission for England, Faith and Order Commission.

Political interests: Defence and foreign affairs, higher education, agriculture and rural affairs; Australia, Georgia, Germany, Sweden, Tanzania.

Other: SCM Press Ltd: Board member 1989-, Chair 1995-; Member, Hymns Ancient and Modern Trust 1998-; Chair of Governors, Anglican Centre in Rome 2005-; Trustee, Media Standards Trust 2005-; Member, Inter-Anglican Liturgical Consultation 2005-; Fellow, Guild of Church Musicians 2012-; Society for Study of Christian Ethics; Association of Teachers of Moral Theology; A large variety of church and socially orientated charities. Liveryman and court member, Worshipful Company of Stationers and Newspaper Makers. Freeman, City of London. DLitt, University of East Anglia 2003; Athenæum.

Publications: Co-author, Spirit and Tradition (Canterbury Press, 1996); Pilgrims (Fount, 1996); Augustine's Legacy (Darton, Longman and Todd, 1997); Pilgrim Guide to Norwich Cathedral (Canterbury Press, 1998); Cathedrals and Abbeys OF England (Jarrold Publishing, 1999); Rebuilding Jerusalem: The Church's Hold on Hearts and Minds (SPCK, 2007); Vocation: Singing the Lord's Song (SPCK, 2007); Co-editor, Reinhold Niebuhr and Contemporary Politics (OUP, 2010); Cathedrals and Abbeys of England (Revised edition, History Press, 2011); Co-author, editor and contributor to 14 more books; 70-plus articles in learned journals; 140-plus book reviews.

Recreations: Reading, walking, music, Northumberland, Landrovers, railways.

Rt Rev the Lord Bishop of Wakefield, House of Lords, London SW1A 0PW
Tel: 020 7219 5353 *Email:* plattens@parliament.uk
Bishop's Lodge, Woodthorpe Lane, Wakefield WF2 6JL *Tel:* 01924 255349 *Fax:* 01924 250202
Email: bishop@bishopofwakefield.org.uk *Website:* www.wakefield.anglican.org

CONSERVATIVE

WAKEHAM, LORD

WAKEHAM (Life Baron), John Wakeham; cr. 1992. Born 22 June 1932; Son of late Major Walter John Wakeham; Married Anne Bailey 1965 (died 1984) (2 sons); married Alison Ward, MBE DL 1985 (1 son).

Education: Charterhouse School.

Non-political career: Army national service 1955-57, commissioned Royal Artillery. Chair: Genner Holdings 1994-, Press Complaints Commission 1995-2002, British Horseracing Board 1996-98.

Political career: *House of Commons:* Contested Coventry East 1966 and Putney 1970 general elections. MP (Conservative) for Maldon 1974-83, for South Colchester and Maldon 1983-92. Assistant Government Whip 1979-81; Government Whip 1981; Parliamentary Under-Secretary of State, Department of Industry 1981-82; Minister of State, HM Treasury 1982-83; Government Chief Whip 1983-87; Lord Privy Seal and Leader of the House of Commons 1987-88; Lord President of the Council and Leader of the House of Commons 1988-89; Secretary of State for Energy 1989-92; Given additional responsibility for co-ordinating the development and presentation of Government policies 1990-92. *House of Lords:* Raised to the peerage as Baron Wakeham, of Maldon in the County of Essex 1992. Lord Privy Seal and Leader of the House of Lords 1992-94. Economic Affairs: Member 2003-09, Chair 2005-07, Member: Procedure 2003-07, 2010-, Liaison 2007-10, House 2007-13, Finance Bill Sub-committee 2008-10, Selection 2010-, Joint Committee on Security 2010-, Economic Affairs Finance Bill Sub-Committee 2011, Sub-committee on Economic Affairs Finance Bill 2012-. *Councils and public bodies:* JP, Inner London 1972; DL, Hampshire 1997; Chair, Royal Commission on the Reform of the House of Lords 1999.

Political interests: Economic affairs, energy, reform of the constitution.

Other: Member, Governing Body, Charterhouse 1986-2004; Governor, Sutton's Hospital, Charterhouse 1992-; Trustee: Management, RNLI 1995-2003, HMS Warrior 1860 1997-; President: GamCare 1997-2003, Brendoncare Foundation 1998-2011, Printers' Charitable Corporation 1998; Chair: Alexandra Rose Day 1998-2010, Cothill Education Trust 1998-2011; Trustee, Council of RNLI 2003-05; Chartered Accountant; FCA. Chancellor, Brunel University 1997-2012. Honorary PhD, Anglia Ruskin University 1992; Honorary DUniv, Brunel University 1998. PC 1983; Buck's, St Stephen's Constitutional, Garrick, Royal Yacht Squadron (Cowes); Chair, Carlton Club 1992-98.

Recreations: Sailing, racing, reading.

Rt Hon the Lord Wakeham DL, House of Lords, London SW1A 0PW
Tel: 020 7219 3162 *Fax:* 020 7219 6807 *Email:* wakehamj@parliament.uk

WALDEGRAVE OF NORTH HILL, LORD

WALDEGRAVE OF NORTH HILL (Life Baron), William Arthur Waldegrave; cr. 1999. Born 15 August 1946; Son of 12th Earl Waldegrave, KG, GCVO, TD, DL and Mary Hermione Grenfell; Married Caroline Burrows OBE 1977 (1 son 3 daughters).

Education: Eton College; Corpus Christi College, Oxford (Open Scholar, BA literae humaniores 1969) (Union President 1968); Harvard University (Kennedy Scholar) 1969-70.

Non-political career: Fellow, All Souls, Oxford 1971-86, 1999-; Member: Central Policy Review Staff, Cabinet Office 1971-73, Political Staff at 10 Downing Street 1973-74; Leader of Opposition's Office 1974-75; With GEC Ltd 1975-81; Non-executive director: Waldegrave Farms Ltd 1975-, Bristol and West plc (formerly Bristol and West Building Society) 1997-2006, Biotech Growth Trust plc (formerly Finsbury Life Sciences Investment Trust plc) 1997-, Henry Sotheran Ltd 1998-; Dresdner Kleinwort Wasserstein 1998-2003: Managing director, Investment Banking, UBS; Vice-chairman and managing director, Investment Banking 2003-08; Non-executive director, Bank of Ireland UK Holdings plc 2002-06; Member: International Advisory Board, Teijin Ltd 2006-08, Remuneration and Nomination Committee, Bergeson Worldwide Gas ASA 2006-08; Provost, Eton College 2009-; Chair, Biotech Growth Trust plc 2012-.

CONSERVATIVE

Political career: *House of Commons:* MP (Conservative) for Bristol West 1979-97. Parliamentary Under-Secretary of State: Department of Education and Science 1981-83, Department of Environment (DoE) 1983-85; Minister of State: DoE 1985-88, Foreign and Commonwealth Office 1988-90; Secretary of State for Health 1990-92; Chancellor of the Duchy of Lancaster and Minister for Public Service and Science 1992-94; Minister of Agriculture, Fisheries and Food 1994-95; Chief Secretary to HM Treasury 1995-97. *House of Lords:* Raised to the peerage as Baron Waldegrave of North Hill, of Chewton Mendip in the County of Somerset 1999. President Parliamentary and Scientific Committee 2000-03. Member Joint Committee on National Security Strategy 2010-. *Other:* Honorary Life member, Tory Reform Group. *Councils and public bodies:* JP, Inner London Juvenile Court 1975-79.

Other: Rhodes Trust: Trustee 1992-2011, Chair 2002-11; Trustee: Beit Memorial Fellowships 1998-2006, Strawberry Hill Trust 2002-; Chair, National Museum of Science and Industry 2002-10; Trustee, Mandela Rhodes Foundation, South Africa 2003-11; President, Royal Bath and West Society 2006; Trustee, Cumberland Lodge, Windsor 2008-. Liveryman, The Merchant Taylors' Company. Freeman: City of London, City of Bristol. Honorary Fellow, Corpus Christi College, Oxford. Royal Society of Chemistry Parliamentary Award 2001. PC 1990; Whites, Beefsteak, Pratt's, Clifton (Bristol), Leander. Eton Vikings.

Publications: The Binding of Leviathan (1978); Various pamphlets.

Rt Hon the Lord Waldegrave of North Hill, House of Lords, London SW1A 0PW
Tel: 020 7219 5353
Eton College, Windsor, Berkshire SL4 6DH *Tel:* 01753 671234 *Fax:* 01753 671283
Email: provostsecretary@etoncollege.org.uk

WALKER OF ALDRINGHAM, LORD

WALKER OF ALDRINGHAM (Life Baron), Michael John Dawson Walker; cr. 2006. Born 7 July 1944; Son of William Walker and Dorothy Walker; Married Victoria Holme 1973 (2 sons 1 daughter).

Education: Milton School, Bulawayo, Zimbabwe; Woodhouse Grove School, Yorkshire; RMA Sandhurst (commissioned 1966).

Non-political career: Regimental and staff duties Royal Anglian Regiment 1966-82; Military Assistant to Chief of the General Staff 1982-85; Commanding Officer, 1 Royal Anglian Regiment 1985-87; Commander, 20th Armoured Brigade 1987-89; Chief of Staff 1 (Br) Corps 1989-91; Colonel Commandant, Queen's Division 1991-2000; General Officer Commanding: North East Dis-

CROSSBENCH

trict and Commander 2nd Infantry Division 1991-92, Eastern District 1992; Assistant Chief of the General Staff, Ministry of Defence 1992-94; Commander, Allied Command Europe Rapid Reaction Corps 1994-97; Colonel Commandant, Army Air Corps 1994-2004; Commander, Land Component Peace Implementation Force, Bosnia 1995-96; Commander-in-Chief, Land Command 1997-2000; Colonel, Royal Anglian Regiment 1997-2002; Aide de Camp General to the Queen 1997-2006; Chief of the General Staff 2000-03; Chief of the Defence Staff 2003-06; Governor Royal Hospital Chelsea 2006-11.

Political career: *House of Lords:* Raised to the peerage as Baron Walker of Aldringham, of Aldringham in the County of Suffolk 2006. *Councils and public bodies:* DL, Greater London 2007-; Member, Prime Minister's Advisory Committee on Business Appointments.

Political interests: Defence, foreign affairs, international relations, country sports, sports; Africa, eastern Europe.

Other: Patron, British South Africa Police Association; Former chair, Army Benevolent Fund; Chair, Tutu Foundation UK; President, Sir Oswald Stoll Foundation. Honorary Doctor of Civil Law, University of East Anglia 2002; Honorary Doctor of Science in Social Science, Cranfield University 2003. OBE 1982; CBE 1990; KCB 1995; CMG 1997; Legion of Merit (USA) 1997; GCB 2000; Cross of Merit (Czechoslovakia) 2001.

Recreations: Golf, shooting, tennis, sailing, motorcycling, skiing.

The Lord Walker of Aldringham GCB CMG CBE DL, House of Lords, London SW1A 0PW
Tel: 020 7219 5353 *Email:* walkermjd@parliament.uk

WALKER OF GESTINGTHORPE, LORD

WALKER OF GESTINGTHORPE (Life Baron), Robert Walker; cr. 2002. Born 17 March 1938; Son of late Ronald Robert Antony Walker and late Mary Helen Walker, née Welsh; Married Suzanne Diana Leggi 1962 (3 daughters 1 son).

Education: Downside School, Somerset; Trinity College, Cambridge (BA classics and law 1959); French, Italian.

Non-political career: 2nd Lieutenant R.A (National Service) 1959-61. Barrister, Lincoln's Inn 1960; QC 1982; High Court Judge, Chancery Division 1994-97; Lord Justice of Appeal 1997-2002; Justice of the Supreme Court of the United Kingdom 2009-13; Non-permanent Judge, Court of Final Appeal, Hong Kong 2009-.

CROSSBENCH

Political career: *House of Lords:* Raised to the peerage as Baron Walker of Gestingthorpe, of Gestingthorpe in the County of Essex 2002. Lord of Appeal in Ordinary 2002-09; As Justice of the Supreme Court, disqualified from participation 2009-13.

Other: Honorary fellow, Trinity College, Cambridge 2006; Honorary doctorate, London Metropolitan University 2008. Kt 1994; PC 1997.

Publications: Articles in legal periodicals.

Recreations: Walking, gardening.

Rt Hon the Lord Walker of Gestingthorpe QC, House of Lords, London SW1A 0PW
Tel: 020 7219 5353

WALL OF NEW BARNET, BARONESS

WALL OF NEW BARNET (Life Baroness), Margaret Mary Wall; cr. 2004. Born 14 November 1941; Daughter of Thomas Mylott and Dorothy Mylott , née Walker; Married Peter Wall 1962 (divorced 1990) (1 son); married Edwin Holdsworth 1992.

Education: Druids Cross Independent School; Notre Dame High School, Liverpool; Ruskin College, Liverpool University; Cranfield Business College.

Non-political career: Worked for large chemical company, north west England; MSF/Amicus: National secretary 1995-98, Director, political policy 1999-2003; Consultant, Department for Education and Skills and successors 2004. Unite.

LABOUR

Political career: *House of Lords:* Raised to the peerage as Baroness Wall of New Barnet, of New Barnet in the London Borough of Barnet 2004. Member Procedure 2008-13. Vice-chair PLP Departmental Committee/Group for Education and Skills 2005-06, 2010-. *Other:* Member, National Policy Forum, Labour Party. *Councils and public bodies:* Chair, Barnet and Chase Farm NHS Trust.

Political interests: Education and skills, NHS; Middle East, South Africa.

Other: Member: Fabian Society, Progress; North London Hospice. Wainwright Trust.

Recreations: Walking, reading, National Trust.

The Baroness Wall of New Barnet, House of Lords, London SW1A 0PW
Tel: 020 7219 6526 *Email:* wallm@parliament.uk

LIBERAL DEMOCRAT

WALLACE OF SALTAIRE, LORD

Government Spokesperson, Foreign and Commonwealth Office and Cabinet Office; Government Whip

WALLACE OF SALTAIRE (Life Baron), William John Lawrence Wallace; cr. 1995. Born 12 March 1941; Son of late William Edward Wallace and late Mary Agnes Tricks; Married Helen Rushworth 1968 (1 son 1 daughter).

Education: Westminster Abbey Choir School; St Edward's School, Oxford; King's College, Cambridge (BA history 1962); Cornell University, USA (PhD government 1968); Nuffield College, Oxford (MA 1965).

Non-political career: Lecturer in government, Manchester University 1967-77; Director of studies, Royal Institute of International Affairs 1978-90; Walter F. Hallstein Fellow, St Antony's College, Oxford 1990-95; London School of Economics 1995-: International relations reader 1995-99, Professor 1999-2005, Emeritus Professor 2005-.

Political career: *House of Lords:* Raised to the peerage as Baron Wallace of Saltaire, of Shipley in the County of West Yorkshire 1995. Liberal Democrat Spokesperson for: Defence 1997-2001, Foreign and Commonwealth Affairs 1998-2010; Deputy Leader Liberal Democrat peers 2004-10; Liberal Democrat Spokesperson for Justice 2007-08; Government Whip 2010-; Government Spokesperson for: Education (Higher Education) 2010, Foreign and Commonwealth Office 2010-, Defence 2010-12, Business, Innovation and Skills 2010, Home Office (Security) 2010-11, Cabinet Office 2011-. Member: Ecclesiastical Committee 1997-2010, European Union 1997-2000, 2001-02; Chair European Union Sub-committee F (Social Affairs, Education and Home Affairs) 1997-2000; Member European Union Sub-committee C (Common Foreign and Security Policy) 2001-02.

Political interests: Foreign affairs, defence, Europe, constitutional affairs; Armenia, EU member states, Georgia, Russia, Ukraine, USA.

Other: Doctorate hc, Université Libre de Bruxelles 1992. Chevalier, Ordre pour le Mérite (France) 1995; Légion d'Honneur (France) 2005; PC 2012. Saltaire Tennis Club.

Publications: The Foreign Policy Process in Britain (1977); The Transformation of Europe (1990); The Dynamics of European Integration (1990); Regional Integration – The West European Experience (1994); Policy-making in the European Union, with Helen Wallace (1996, 2000, 2005); Why Vote Liberal Democrat? (1997).

Recreations: Singing, swimming, walking, gardening.

Rt Hon the Lord Wallace of Saltaire, House of Lords, London SW1A 0PW
Tel: 020 7219 3125/020 7219 3778 *Email:* wallacew@parliament.uk

LIBERAL DEMOCRAT

WALLACE OF TANKERNESS, LORD

Advocate General for Scotland; Government Spokesperson, Law Officers and Scotland Office

WALLACE OF TANKERNESS (Life Baron), James Robert Wallace; cr 2007. Born 25 August 1954; Son of John Fergus Thomson Wallace and Grace Wallace, née Maxwell; Married Rosemary Fraser 1983 (2 daughters).

Education: Annan Academy, Dumfriesshire; Downing College, Cambridge (BA economics and law 1975, MA); Edinburgh University (LLB law 1977).

Non-political career: Called to the Scottish Bar 1979; QC (Scot) 1997; Jim Wallace Consultancy Ltd 2007-10; Honorary Professor, Institute of Petroleum Engineering, Heriot-Watt University 2007-10; Advocate, Terra Firma Chambers, Edinburgh 2010; Honorary Bencher, Lincoln's Inn 2012.

Political career: *House of Commons:* Contested Dumfries 1979 general election. MP for Orkney and Shetland 1983-2001 (Liberal 1983-88, Liberal Democrat 1988-2001). *House of Lords:* Raised to the peerage as Baron Wallace of Tankerness, of Tankerness in Orkney 2007. Liberal Democrat Spokesperson for: Justice 2009-10, Scotland 2009-10; Equality Bill 2009-10; Advocate General for Scotland 2010-; Government Spokesperson for: Scotland 2010-, Wales 2010-12, Attorney General's Office/Law Officers 2010-. Co-opted member EU Sub-committee D (Environment and Agriculture) 2008; Member: Constitution 2008-10, Partnerships (Prosecution) (Scotland) Bill 2013-. *Other:* Contested South Scotland 1979 European Parliament election; Scottish Parliament: MSP for Orkney 1999-2007; Deputy First Minister 1999-2005; Minister for: Justice 1999-2003, Enterprise and Lifelong Learning 2003-05. Member, Scottish Liberal Party Executive 1976-85; Vice-chair (Policy), Scottish Liberal Party 1982-85; Honorary President, Scottish Young Liberals 1984-85; Leader, Scottish Liberal Democrats 1992-2005. *Councils and public bodies:* Member: Scottish Office Consultative Steering Group on Scottish Parliament 1998, Commission on Scottish Devolution 2008-09.

Political interests: Constitutional reform, Scottish home rule and federalism, Scottish law, rural development, energy conservation, shipping, Amnesty International, renewable energy; China, New Zealand, Norway, USA.

Other: Chair, Relationships Scotland 2008-10; Co-convener, Scottish Poverty Truth Commission 2009-10; Member, Faculty of Advocates; RNLI, Christian Aid, Amnesty International, British Red Cross. DLitt, Heriot-Watt University 2007; DUniv, Open University 2009; Doctor honoris causa, Edinburgh University 2009. Joint recipient Saltire Society's Andrew Fletcher Award for Services to Scotland 1998; Scottish Politician of the Year, *Herald* 2000; Devolved Politician of the Year, Channel Four 2002; Lifetime Achievement Award, *Herald* 2008. PC 2000; Caledonian, Scottish Liberal.

Recreations: Golf, travel, music.

Rt Hon the Lord Wallace of Tankerness QC, House of Lords, London SW1A 0PW
Tel: 020 7219 3526 *Email:* wallacej@parliament.uk

LIBERAL DEMOCRAT

WALMSLEY, BARONESS

WALMSLEY (Life Baroness), Joan Margaret Walmsley; cr. 2000. Born 12 April 1943; Daughter of Leo and Monica Watson; Married John Richardson 1966 (divorced 1980); married Christopher Walmsley 1986 (died 1995) (1 son 1 daughter 1 stepson 2 stepdaughters); married Lord Thomas of Gresford (qv) 2005 (3 stepsons 1 stepdaughter).

Education: Notre Dame High School, Liverpool; Liverpool University (BSc biology 1966); Manchester Polytechnic (PGCE 1979).

Non-political career: Cytologist, Christie Hospital, Manchester 1965-67; Teacher, Buxton College, Derbyshire 1979-86; Public relations consultant 1987-2003.

Political career: *House of Commons:* Contested (Liberal Democrat) Leeds South and Morley 1992 and Congleton 1997 general elections. *House of Lords:* Raised to the peerage as Baroness Walmsley, of West Derby in the County of Merseyside 2000. Liberal Democrat Spokesperson for: Early Years Education, Education and Skills 2001-03, Home Office 2003-04, Education and Children/Children, Schools and Families 2004-10. Member Science and Technology 2000-05; Chair Science and Technology Sub-committee I (Systematic Biology and Biodiversity) 2002; Member Science and Technology Sub-committees: I (Fighting Infection) 2002-03, I (Science and International Agreements) 2003-04, I (Scientific Aspects of Ageing) 2004-05; Co-opted member Science and Technology 2008; Member, Adoption Legislation 2012-13. Chair, Liberal Democrat Parliamentary Party Committee on Education, Families and Young People 2010-12. *Other:* Member, Liberal Democrat Conference Committee 2000-03; President, Women Liberal Democrats 2002-04; Member, Liberal Democrats Federal Executive 2003-04.

Political interests: Child protection, young offenders, prisoner education, environment, early years education.

Other: Patron: Family Planning Association, Helena Kennedy Trust; Infant Trust; Ambassador for NSPCC; Chair, Botanic Gardens Conservation International; Honorary fellow, Unicef; Member, Parliament Choir; SKCV Children's Trust (Indian Street Children), Amnesty International. Rex Boat Club.

Publications: Chaired report What on Earth? The threats to the Science Underpinning Conservation (2002).

Recreations: Music, theatre, gardening, rowing, good company, bee-keeping.

The Baroness Walmsley, House of Lords, London SW1A 0PW
Tel: 020 7219 6047 *Fax:* 020 7219 0967 *Email:* walmsleyj@parliament.uk
Website: www.joanwalmsley.org.uk

CROSSBENCH

WALPOLE, LORD

WALPOLE (10th Baron, GB), (Robert) Robin Horatio Walpole; cr. 1723; 8th Baron Walpole of Wolterton (GB) 1756. Born 8 December 1938; Son of 9th Baron, TD; Married Judith Schofield 1962 (divorced 1979, she died 1993) (2 sons 2 daughters); married Laurel Celia Ball 1980 (2 sons 1 daughter).

Education: Eton College; King's College, Cambridge (MA natural sciences; DipAgric 1961); French, Norfolk.

Political career: *House of Lords:* First entered House of Lords 1989; Elected hereditary peer 1999-. Member: Ecclesiastical Committee 2006-, Statutory Instruments Joint Committee 2007-10, 2013-; Co-opted member EU Sub-committee B (Internal Market) 2007-10; Member, EU Sub-committee B (Internal Market, Energy and Transport) 2010-12,. *Councils and public bodies:* Councillor, Norfolk County Council 1970-81; JP, Norfolk 1972; Vice-President, Local Government Association 2010-.

Political interests: Agriculture, arts, tourism, conservation; Australia, Europe.

Other: Chair: Area Museums Service for South East England 1976-79, Norwich School of Art 1977-87, Textile Conservation Centre 1981-88, President 1988-2003, East Anglian Tourist Board 1982-88; Member: CPRE, RSPB; Vice president RNRS; President North Norfolk Orbital Railway. Liveryman, Carpenter's Company. Honorary Fellow, St Mary's University College, Strawberry Hill 1997.

Recreations: Natural history and family.

The Lord Walpole, House of Lords, London SW1A 0PW
Tel: 020 7219 3173 *Email:* walpolerh@parliament.uk
Mannington Hall, Norwich, Norfolk NR11 7BB *Tel:* 01263 584175/01263 768444

CROSSBENCH

WALTON OF DETCHANT, LORD

WALTON OF DETCHANT (Life Baron), John Nicholas Walton; cr. 1989. Born 16 September 1922; Son of late Herbert and Eleanor Walton; Married Mary Elizabeth (Betty) Harrison 1946 (died 2003) (1 son 2 daughters).

Education: Alderman Wraith Grammar School, Spennymoor; Medical School, King's College, Newcastle upon Tyne (Durham University) (MB BS 1945; MD 1952; DSc 1972; MA Oxon); French.

Non-political career: RAMC 1947-49; Colonel (late RAMC) and Officer Commanding 1 (N) General Hospital (TA) 1963-66; Honorary Colonel 1968-73. Nuffield Foundation Fellow in Neurology, Massachusetts General Hospital, Boston USA 1953-54; King's College Travelling Fellow in Medicine, National Hospital, London 1954-55; First assistant in neurology, King's College and Royal Infirmary, Newcastle 1956-58; Newcastle General Hospital: Consultant neurologist 1958-83, Director, Muscular Dystrophy Group Research Laboratories 1965-83; Newcastle University: Lecturer in neurology 1966-68, Professor of neurology 1968-83, Dean of medicine 1971-81; Warden, Green College, Oxford 1983-89. Member, BMA.

Political career: *House of Lords:* Raised to the peerage as Baron Walton of Detchant, of Detchant in the County of Northumberland 1989. Member Science and Technology 1992-96, 1997-2001; Chair Medical Ethics 1993-94.

Political interests: Medicine, health, science, education; Australia, Canada, France, New Zealand, USA.

Other: World Federation of Neurology: First Vice-President 1987-89, President 1989-97; Chair, Muscular Dystrophy Group of Great Britain and Northern Ireland 1971-95, now Life President; Member, Medical Research Council 1974-78; President: British Medical Association 1980-82, General Medical Council 1982-89, Royal Society of Medicine 1984-86, Association of British Neurologists 1987-88; President, Bamburgh Castle golf club 1990-; FRCP; Honorary FRCPEd; Honorary FRCPC; Honorary FRCPsych; Honorary FRCPath; Honorary FRCPCH; FMedSci; Muscular Dystrophy Campaign. Honorary Freeman, Newcastle upon Tyne 1980; Freeman, City of London 1981 . 11 honorary degrees from British, French, Italian and Thai universities; Honorary fellow: Norwegian Academy of Science and letters, Russian Academy of Medical Sciences, Institute of Education, London. TD 1962; Kt 1979; Athenæum, United Oxford and Cambridge University, Royal Society of Medicine. President, Bamburgh Castle Golf Club; Member, MCC.

Publications: Several medical titles including: Essentials of Neurology (6 eds 1961-93); Brain's Disease of the Nervous System (1993); Disorders of Voluntary Muscle (eds 1-6 1964-93); Oxford Companion to Medicine (1988, 1993); The Spice of Life (autobiography) (1993); as well as numerous chapters in books and articles in scientific journals.

Recreations: Golf, cricket, reading, music, opera.

The Lord Walton of Detchant TD, House of Lords, London SW1A 0PW
Tel: 020 7219 3102 *Fax:* 020 7219 5979
15 Croft Way, Belford, Northumberland NE70 7ET *Tel:* 01668 219009 *Fax:* 01668 219010 *Email:* waldetch@aol.com

LABOUR

WARNER, LORD

WARNER (Life Baron), Norman Reginald Warner; cr. 1998. Born 8 September 1940; Son of Albert and Laura Warner; Married Anne Lawrence 1961 (divorced 1981) (1 son 1 daughter); married Suzanne Reeve 1990 (1 son).

Education: Dulwich College, London; University of California, Berkeley (MPH) (Harkness Fellowship 1971-73).

Non-political career: Ministry of Health/DHSS 1959-85: Assistant private secretary: to Minister of Health 1967-68; to Secretary of State for Social Services 1968-69; Executive Councils Division 1969-71; NHS Reorganisation 1973-74; Principal private secretary to Secretary of State for Social Services 1974-76; Supplementary Benefits Division 1976-78; Management services 1979-81;

Controller, Wales and South Western Region 1981-83; Under-Secretary, Supplementary Benefits Division 1984-85; Director of social services, Kent County Council 1985-91; Managing director, Warner Consultancy and Training Services Ltd 1991-97; Senior policy adviser to Home Secretary 1997-; Chair: Youth Justice Board for England and Wales 1998-2003, London Sports Board 2003.

Political career: *House of Lords:* Raised to the peerage as Baron Warner, of Brockley in the London Borough of Lewisham 1998. Department of Health: Government Spokesperson 2003-06, Parliamentary Under-Secretary of State 2003-05, Minister of State: (NHS Delivery) 2005-06, (NHS Reform) 2006. Member: Science and Technology 2008-12, Science and Technology Sub-committee II (Genomic Medicine) 2008-09, Science and Technology Sub-committee I (Radioactive Waste Management: a further update) 2010, Adoption Legislation 2012-13, Joint Committee on the Draft Care and Support Bill 2013. *Councils and public bodies:* Chair: City and East London FHSA 1991-94, National Inquiry into Selection, Development and Management of Staff in Children's Homes 1991-92; Member, Local Government Commission 1995-96; Chair, NHS London Provider Agency 2007-09; Member, Commission on Funding of Care and Support (Dilnot Commission) 2010-11.

Political interests: Law and order, children, social and healthcare, end of life; Commonwealth countries, North Africa/Middle East, USA.

Other: Member, Carers National Association 1991-94; Royal Philanthropic Society: Member 1991-, Chair 1993-98; Trustee: Leonard Cheshire Foundation 1994-96, MacIntyre Care 1994-97; Chair: Expert Panel for UK Harkness Fellowships 1994-97, Residential Forum, in Association with National Institute for Social Work 1994-97; National Council for Voluntary Organisations 2001-03; Harkness Fellowship 1971-73; Oxfam, Amnesty International, Samaritans. Gwilym Gibbon Fellow, Nuffield College, Oxford 1984. PC 2006.

Publications: Editor, Commissioning Community Alternatives in European Social and Health Care (1993); Articles in specialised journals and national newspapers; A Suitable Case for Treatment: The NHS and Reform (2011).

Recreations: Reading, cinema, theatre, exercise, travel.

Rt Hon the Lord Warner, House of Lords, London SW1A 0PW
Tel: 020 7219 4540 *Email:* warnern@parliament.uk

WARNOCK, BARONESS

WARNOCK (Life Baroness), Helen Mary Warnock; cr. 1985. Born 14 April 1924; Daughter of late Archibald Wilson and Ethel Schuster; Married Sir Geoffrey Warnock 1949 (died 1995) (2 sons 3 daughters (1 deceased)).

Education: St Swithun's, Winchester; Prior's Field, Godalming; Lady Margaret Hall, Oxford (MA literae humariores 1948, BPhil); French.

Non-political career: Fellow and tutor in philosophy, St Hugh's College, Oxford 1952-66, Headmistress, Oxford High School 1966-72; Research Fellow: Lady Margaret Hall, Oxford 1966-72, St Hugh's College, Oxford 1972-84; Mistress, Girton College, Cambridge 1985-91; Gifford Lecturer, Glasgow University 1991-92; Visiting Professor, Gresham College 2000-01; Presidential Lecturer, Case Western Reserve University, Cleveland, Ohio, USA 2004.

CROSSBENCH

Political career: *House of Lords:* Raised to the peerage as Baroness Warnock, of Weeke in the City of Winchester 1985. Member: Medical Ethics 1993-94, Dangerous Dogs 1996, Animals in Scientific Procedures 2001-02, Procedures 2003-05. *Councils and public bodies:* Member, Independent Broadcasting Authority 1972-83; Chair, Committee of Inquiry into Special Education 1974-78; Member, Royal Commission on Environmental Pollution 1979-84; Chair: Committee of Inquiry on Human Fertilisation and Embryology 1982-84, Home Office Committee on Animal Experimentation 1984-89, Advisory Panel on Spoliation 1998-; Archbishop of Canterbury's Medical Ethics Board 1998-2001.

Political interests: Education, broadcasting, medicine, environment, constitution, law on assisted dying.

Other: President: British Dyslexia Association, Sound Start Children's Radio, ATE Chiltern's Holidays; Fellow, College of Teachers (formerly College of Preceptors); Honorary FRCM; Honorary Fellow: Royal Society of Physicians, Scotland, British Academy 2000, Royal College of Physicians 2002; Hertford College, Oxford Development Fund; Girton College, Cambridge Development Fund; National Autistic Society; Alzheimer's Society; British Red Cross. 15 honorary degrees from UK and Australia; Six honorary university fellowships including: Lady Margaret Hall, Oxford, St Hugh's College, Oxford, Hertford College, Oxford; Life Fellow, Girton College, Cambridge; Honorary Bencher, Gray's Inn. Albert Medalist, Royal Society of Arts 1998. DBE 1984.

Publications: Author of books on ethics and education and philosophy of mind; Co-author (with Dr Elisabeth MacDonald), Easeful Death: Is There a Case for Assisted Dying? (OUP, 2008); Dishonest to God (2010).

Recreations: Music, gardening.

The Baroness Warnock DBE, House of Lords, London SW1A 0PW
Tel: 020 7219 8619 *Email:* warnockh@parliament.uk

WARSI, BARONESS

Senior Minister of State (Faith and Communities) and Government Spokesperson, Department for Communities and Local Government and Foreign and Commonwealth Office

WARSI (Life Baroness), Sayeeda Hussain Warsi; cr 2007. Born 28 March 1971; Married (divorced) 1 daughter; Married Iftikhar (4 stepchildren).

Education: Dewsbury College; Leeds University (LLB 1992).

CONSERVATIVE

Non-political career: Trainee solicitor, Crown Prosecution Service 1994-96; Solicitor, Whitfield Hallam Goodall Solicitors 1996-97; Managing partner, George Warsi Solicitors 1997-2002; Legal draftsman, Ministry of Law, Pakistan 2002-03.

Political career: *House of Commons:* Contested (Conservative) Dewsbury 2005 general election. *House of Lords:* Raised to the peerage as Baroness Warsi, of Dewsbury in the County of West Yorkshire 2007. Shadow Minister for: Community Cohesion 2007-10, Social Action 2007-10; Minister without Portfolio 2010-12; Government Spokesperson for Cabinet Office 2011-12; Senior Minister of State (Faith and Communities) and Government Spokesperson, Department for Communities and Local Government and Foreign and Commonwealth Office 2012-. *Other:* Vice-chairman, Conservative Party with responsibility for cities 2005-07; Chairman, Conservative Party 2010-12.

Political interests: Foreign affairs, faith, integration, freedom of religion, social action; Afghanistan, Central Asia, Bangladesh, Pakistan.

Other: Founder and chair, Savayra Foundation, UK 2003-. PC 2010.

Recreations: Writing, family life.

Rt Hon the Baroness Warsi, House of Lords, London SW1A 0PW
Tel: 020 7219 6097 *Email:* warsis@parliament.uk *Website:* www.sayeedawarsi.com
Twitter: @SayeedaWarsi

WARWICK OF UNDERCLIFFE, BARONESS

WARWICK OF UNDERCLIFFE (Life Baroness), Diana Warwick; cr. 1999. Born 16 July 1945; Daughter of Jack and Olive Warwick; Married Sean Bowes Young 1969.

Education: St Joseph's College, Bradford; Bedford College, London University (BA 1967).

Non-political career: Technical assistant to general secretary, NUT 1969-72; Assistant secretary, Civil and Public Services Association 1972-83; General secretary, Association of University Teachers 1983-92; Chief executive: Westminster Foundation for Democracy 1992-95, Universities UK (previously Committee of Vice-Chancellors and Principals/Universities UK) 1995-2009; Non-executive director: Lattice plc 2000-02, Universities Superannuation Scheme Ltd 2001-09; Chair, Human Tissue Authority 2010-. Member, TUC General Council 1989-92.

LABOUR

Political career: *House of Lords:* Raised to the peerage as Baroness Warwick of Undercliffe, of Undercliffe in the County of West Yorkshire 1999. Member: Science and Technology 1999-2005, Science and Technology Sub-committees: II (Aircraft Cabin Environment) 2000-01, (Stem Cell Research) 2001-02, II (Innovations in Computer Processors) 2001-02, I (Fighting Infection) 2002-03, (Science and International Agreements) 2003-04, Advisory Panel on Works of Art 2003-05. *Councils and public bodies:* Board member, British Council 1985-95; Member: Employment Appeal Tribunal 1987-99, Executive and Council, Industrial Society 1987-97, Commonwealth Institute 1988-95, Nolan/Neill Committee on Standards in Public Life 1994-99, OST Technology Foresight Steering Group 1997-2000.

Political interests: Higher education, science and technology, health, heritage, international development, pensions, corporate social responsibility.

Other: Member: Inter-Parliamentary Union 1999-, Commonwealth Parliamentary Association 1999-, British American Parliamentary Group 1999-; Trustee, Royal Anniversary Trust 1991-93; Council member, Duke of Edinburgh's Seventh Commonwealth Study Conference 1991; Voluntary Service Overseas: Chair 1994-2003, Life Vice-president 2003-; Member, RIIA 1995-;

Trustee, St Catherine's Foundation, Windsor 1996-2008; Chair of trustee, International Students House 2000-; Chair, Modern Records Centre, Warwick University 2009-; Council member, University College London 2010-; Board member, Pensions Protection Fund 2011-; FRSA 1984; Voluntary Services Overseas (VSO), Womankind Worldwide. Five honorary doctorates.

Recreations: Theatre, opera, looking at pictures.

The Baroness Warwick of Undercliffe, House of Lords, London SW1A 0PW
Tel: 020 7219 5086 *Email:* warwickd@parliament.uk
151 Buckingham Palace Road, London SW1W 9SZ

CONSERVATIVE

WASSERMAN, LORD

WASSERMAN (Life Baron), Gordon Joshua Wasserman; cr 2011. Born 26 July 1938; Son of late John Wasserman QC and Professor Rachel Wasserman; Married Cressida Frances 1964.

Education: Westmount High School, Montreal, Canada; New College, Oxford (BA); McGill University, Canada (Rhodes Scholar 1959).

Non-political career: Senior research scholar, St Antony's College, Oxford 1961-64; Lecturer in economics, Merton College, Oxford 1963-64; Research Fellow, New College Oxford 1964-67; Home Office: Economic adviser 1967, Senior economic adviser 1972, Assistant secretary 1977-81; Head, Urban Deprivation Unit 1973-77; Civil service travelling fellowship, USA 1977-78; Under Secretary, Central Policy Review Staff, Cabinet Office 1981-83; Assistant Under Secretary of State, Home Office 1983-95; Special adviser (science and technology) to Police Commissioner, New York 1996-98; Chief of staff to Police Commissioner, New York 1998-2002; Special adviser to Police Commissioner, Philadelphia 1998-2003; Chair, ION Track Inc. 2000-02; Chair and chief executive officer, Gordon Wasserman Group LLC 2003-.

Political career: *House of Lords:* Raised to the peerage as Baron Wasserman, of Pimlico in the City of Westminster 2011. Government Adviser on Policing and Criminal Justice 2011-. Member EU Sub-committee F (Home Affairs, Health and Education) 2013-.

Other: Executive member, ELITE Group 1993-96; Board member, SEARCH Group Inc. 1994-2000; Member, US Justice Department Advisory Panel on Science and Technology 1996-2003; Vice-President, English Basketball Association 1983-86.

The Lord Wasserman, House of Lords, London SW1A 0PW
Tel: 020 7219 5353

LABOUR

WATSON OF INVERGOWRIE, LORD

WATSON OF INVERGOWRIE (Life Baron), Michael (Mike) Goodall Watson; cr. 1997. Born 1 May 1949; Son of late Clarke and late Senga Watson, née Goodall; Married Lorraine McManus 1986 (divorced); married Clare Thomas 2004 (1 son).

Education: Dundee High School; Heriot-Watt University, Edinburgh (BA economics and industrial relations 1974); French.

Non-political career: Development officer, Workers Educational Association East Midlands District 1974-77; MSF: Full-time official 1977-89, Industrial officer 1977-79, Regional officer based in Glasgow 1979-89; Director, PS Communication Consultants Ltd, Edinburgh 1997-99; Associate director, Caledonia Consulting, Edinburgh 2007-12. Member, Unite 1975-.

Political career: *House of Commons:* MP (Labour) for Glasgow Central 1989-97. Chairman, Parliamentary Labour Party Committee on Overseas Development Aid 1991-97. *House of Lords:* Raised to the peerage as Baron Watson of Invergowrie, of Invergowrie in Perth and Kinross 1997. *Other:* Scottish Parliament: MSP for Glasgow Cathcart constituency 1999-2005 (contested the seat as Mike Watson); Minister for Tourism, Culture and Sport 2001-03. Member, Labour Party Scottish Executive Committee 1987-90; Re-admitted to Labour Party November 2012.

Political interests: Economy, social inclusion policy, overseas aid and development, extension of devolution throughout the UK; France.

Other: Fellow, Industry and Parliament Trust 1999; Visiting Research Fellow, Department of Government, Strathclyde University 1993-96, 1999-2002; Oxfam, Epilepsy Action Scotland, Shelter. Honorary LLD, University of Abertay Dundee 1998. Director, Dundee United Football Company Ltd 2003-05.

Publications: Rags to Riches: The Official History of Dundee United FC (1985); The Tannadice Encyclopedia (1997); Year Zero: An Inside View of the Scottish Parliament (2001).

Recreations: Dundee United FC, cycling, running.

The Lord Watson of Invergowrie, House of Lords, London SW1A 0PW
Tel: 020 7219 8731 *Email:* watsonm@parliament.uk

WATSON OF RICHMOND, LORD

WATSON OF RICHMOND (Life Baron), Alan John Watson; cr. 1999. Born 3 February 1941; Son of Rev. John William Watson and Edna Mary, née Peters; Married Karen Lederer 1965 (2 sons).

Education: Diocesan College, Cape Town, South Africa; Kingswood School, Bath; Jesus College, Cambridge (Open Scholar history 1959; State Scholar 1959, MA 1963) (Vice-President, Cambridge Union); German.

Non-political career: Research assistant, Cambridge University 1962-64; BBC 1965-68: General trainee 1965-66, Reporter, BBC TV, The Money Programme 1966-68; Chief public affairs commentator, London Weekend Television 1969-70; Presenter: Panorama, BBC TV 1971-74, The Money Programme 1974-75; Head of TV, radio, audio-visual division, EEC, and Editor, European Community Newsreel service to Lomé Convention Countries 1975-79; Charles Barker City Ltd: Director 1980-85, Chief executive 1980-83; Deputy chair, Sterling Public Relations 1985-86; Chair: City and Corporate Counsel Ltd 1987-94, Threadneedle Publishing Group 1987-94, Corporate Vision Ltd 1989-98; Presenter: BBC 1 1990 *You and 92*, Documentary Series *The Germans*, Channel 4 1992; Chair, Corporate Television Networks 1992-; Member, Y&R Partnership Board; Chair: Burson-Marsteller UK 1994-2004, Burson-Marsteller Europe 1996-2007, The Cola Cola Company European Advisory Board 2002-06, Raisin Social Ltd (Wine Importers) 2005-, Nexus Publishing 2007-, Havas Media/Havas Media Group 2008-.

Political career: *House of Commons:* Contested Richmond, Surrey (Liberal) 1974 and 1979 and Richmond and Barnes (Liberal/Alliance) 1983 and 1987 general elections. *House of Lords:* Raised to the peerage as Baron Watson of Richmond, of Richmond in the London Borough of Richmond upon Thames 1999. Liberal Democrat Spokesperson for: Foreign and Commonwealth Affairs (Europe) 2000-01, 2002-05, Universities 2007-09. Member EU Sub-committee C (Common Foreign and Security Policy) 2000-03; Co-opted member EU Sub-committee A (Economic and Financial Affairs) 2006-10. *Other:* President, Cambridge University Liberal Club 1961-; Chair, Liberal Party Parliamentary Association 1982-84; Member, Liberal Party National Executive 1982-86; President, Liberal Party 1984-85.

Political interests: Worldwide use of English, EU enlargement, transatlantic relationship; Germany, Romania, Russia, USA.

Other: Member, executive board, Unicef 1985-92; Chair, British-German Association 1992-2000; Vice-chair, European Movement 1995-2001; Chair, English Speaking Union 2000-06; President, British-German Association 2000-; Member, High Level EU-Romania Group 2000-02; Chair: UK Steering Committee of Koenigswinter Conference 2003-, Emeritus English-speaking Union International Council, Council of Commonwealth Societies 2005-12; Chair of Governors, Westminster College, Oxford 1988-94; Chair, Royal Television Society 1990-91; Visiting Fellow, Louvanium International Business Centre, Brussels 1990-95; Visiting Erasmus Professor in European studies, Louvain University 1990; President, Heathrow Association for Control of Aircraft Noise 1992-95; Prince of Wales Business Leaders Forum 1996-; Honorary Professor, German Studies, Birmingham University 1997-; Council member, British Studies Centre, Humboldt University, Berlin 1998-; Chair, Father Thames Trust 1999-; English Speaking Union: Chair 1999-2005, International chair Emeritus 2006-, Vice-President 2012-, Co-chair, British Jamestown Committee 2005-07; Trustee and Patron, Richmond Museum 2002-; Patron, Richmond Society 2002-; Visiting Fellow, Oriel College, Oxford 2003-; Chair, Chemistry Advisory Board, Cambridge 2004-; Honorary Fellow, Jesus College Cambridge 2004-; Chair, Cambridge Foundation 2005-; High Steward, Cambridge University 2010-; FRSA; FIPR; FIVCA; FRTS; Marsh Memorial Homes, Cape Town, South Africa. Ten honorary doctorates from Russian, Romania, Moldovan, US and UK Universities; Honorary professor; Honorary Fellowship Jesus College, Cambridge; Visiting fellow, Oriel College Oxford. Jean Monnet Prize for European TV coverage 1974; The Churchill Medal 2005. CBE 1985; Order of Merit (Germany) 1995; Grand Cross Order of Merit (Germany) 2001, Grand Cross Order of Merit (Romania) 2004; Knights Grand Cross (Germany) 2007; Brooks's, Royal Automobile, Kennel, Beefsteak. House of Lords Yacht Club.

Publications: Europe at risk (1972); The Germans: who are they now? (1992); Thatcher and Kohl: old rivalries revisited (1996); Jamestown: The Voyage of English (2007); The Queen and the USA (2012).

Recreations: Boating, wines, foreign travel, art.

The Lord Watson of Richmond CBE, House of Lords, London SW1A 0PW
Tel: 020 7219 8661
CTN Communications, 114 St Martin's Lane, London WC2N 4BE *Tel:* 020 7395 4485
Fax: 020 7395 4461 *Email:* alan.watson@ctn.co.uk *Twitter:* @LordWatson1

CROSSBENCH

WAVERLEY, VISCOUNT

WAVERLEY (3rd Viscount, UK), John Desmond Forbes Anderson; cr. 1952. Born 31 October 1949; Son of 2nd Viscount; Engaged to Philippa Way 2012.

Education: Malvern College.

Non-political career: Adviser, The CCC Group.

Political career: *House of Lords:* First entered House of Lords 1993; Elected hereditary peer 1999-.

Political interests: International affairs; Central Asia.

Other: Member, Royal Institute of International Affairs; Honorary co-chairman, International Tax and Investment Center, Washington DC, USA. Order of San Carlos (Grand Cross) (Colombia) 1998; Jubilee Medal (Kazakhstan) 2002; Chieftaincy (Yoruba) 2010; Anniversary Medal (Kyrgyzstan) 2010. Rye Golf.

Recreations: Golf, walking.

The Viscount Waverley, House of Lords, London SW1A 0PW

Tel: 020 7219 3174

Email: jd@lordwaverley.com *Website:* lordwaverley.com

CONSERVATIVE

WEI, LORD

WEI (Life Baron), Nathanael Ming-Yan Wei; cr 2010. Born 19 January 1977; Son of Rev Edward Wei and Mrs Meggy Wei; Married Cynthia Wei 2003 (2 sons).

Education: Sir Frank Markham School, Milton Keynes; Jesus College, Oxford (BA modern languages 1999).

Non-political career: Consultant, McKinsey 1999-2001; Co-founder: Teach First 2001-05, Future Leaders 2005-07, The Challenge Network; Co-founder and partner, Shaftesbury Partnership 2006-10; Head of new ventures and strategic adviser, Absolute Return for Kids 2007-10; Community Foundation Network 2011-.

Political career: *House of Lords:* Raised to the peerage as Baron Wei, of Shoreditch in the London Borough of Hackney 2010. Government adviser, Big Society (unpaid), Cabinet Office 2010-11.

Other: Fellow, Young Foundation 2005-10.

The Lord Wei, House of Lords, London SW1A 0PW

Tel: 020 7219 5353 *Email:* wein@parliament.uk *Twitter:* @natwei

CROSSBENCH

WEIDENFELD, LORD

WEIDENFELD (Life Baron), (Arthur) George Weidenfeld; cr. 1976. Born 13 September 1919; Son of late Max Weidenfeld; Married Jane Sieff 1952 (1 daughter); married Mrs Barbara Connolly 1956 (divorced 1961, she died 1996); married Mrs Sandra Meyer 1966 (divorced 1976); married Annabelle Whitestone 1992.

Education: Piaristen Gymnasium, Vienna, Austria; Vienna University (Diplomatic Academy, Vienna) ; German, French, Italian.

Non-political career: BBC Monitoring Service 1939-42; News commentator, BBC Empire and North American Service 1942-46; Columnist, *News Chronicle* 1943-44; Chair, Weidenfeld and Nicolson Ltd, Publishers 1948-; Political adviser and chief of cabinet to President Weizmann of Israel 1949-50; Columnist, *Die Welt* and *Die Welt am Sonntag* 1999-; Chair, Cheyne Capital Management Limited 2000-07.

Political career: *House of Lords:* Raised to the peerage as Baron Weidenfeld, of Chelsea in the County of Greater London 1976. SDP Spokesperson for Foreign Affairs, the Arts, Broadcasting 1983-90.

Political interests: International affairs, especially Europe, Middle East and transatlantic relations, the arts and media; Central Europe, Germany, Italy, Israel, Middle East, USA.

Other: Governor: Weizmann Institute of Science 1964-, Tel Aviv University 1980-, Jerusalem Foundation; Member, South Bank Board 1986-99; Board member, English National Opera 1988-98; Consultant, Bertelsmann Foundation 1992-2010; Vice-President, Oxford University Development Programme 1995-2010; Ben Gurion University of the Negev, Beer-Sheva, Israel: Chairman, Board of Governors 1996-2004, Honorary chairman 2004-; Chair, Trialogue Educational Trust (Club of Three), (later Weidenfeld Institute for Strategic Dialogue) 1996-2006; Board member, Diplomatic Academy, Vienna 1997-; Trustee, Quandt Stiftung, Bad Homburg 1999-2009; Founder and president, Weidenfeld Institute for Strategic Dialogue 2006-; Trustee Emeritus, Aspen Foundation; Former Trustee, National Portrait Gallery; British Museum Development Trust; Board member, Encyclopedia Britannica 2011-. Freeman, cities of: London, San Francisco, Jerusalem. Honorary PhD, Ben Gurion University of the Negev 1984; Honorary MA, Oxon 1992; Honorary Fellow: St Peter's College, Oxford 1992, St Anne's College, Oxford 1993; Honorary Senator (Ehrensenator), Bonn University 1996; Magister, Diplomatic College, Vienna University 1 1999; Honorary DLitt, Exeter University 2001; Fellow, King's College London 2007; Honorary DLitt, Oxford 2010. Charlemagne Medal for European Media (Germany) 2000; London Book Fair/Trilogy Lifetime Achievement Award for International Publishing 2007; Teddy Kollek Lifetime Achievement Award 2009; Significant Life's Work Award, M100 Sanssouci Media 2011; Tolerence Ring, European Academy of Science and the Arts 2012. Kt 1969; Golden Knight's Cross with Star of the Austrian Order of Merit 1989; Chevalier de l'Ordre National de la Légion d'Honneur (France) 1990; Knight Commander's Cross (Badge and Star) of the Order of Merit of Germany 1991; Cross of Honour First Class for Arts and Science of Austria 2002; Decoration of Honour in Gold for Services to the County of Vienna 2003; Honour of City of Vienna 2003; Italian Grand Officer of the Order of Merit 2005; Order of Merit or the Land Baden-Württemberg 2008; GBE 2011; Benemerito Distinction (Poland) 2011; Garrick.

Publications: The Goebbels Experiment (1943); Remembering My Good Friends (1994).

Recreations: Travel, opera.

The Lord Weidenfeld GBE, House of Lords, London SW1A 0PW
Tel: 020 7219 5353
Weidenfeld and Nicolson, Orion House, 5 Upper St Martin's Lane, London WC2H 9EA
Tel: 020 7520 4411 *Fax:* 020 7379 1604 *Email:* george.weidenfeld@orionbooks.co.uk,
Weidenfeld Institute for Strategic Dialogue, 48 Charles Street, London W1J 5EN
Tel: 020 7493 9333 *Fax:* 020 7493 4909 *Email:* info@strategicdialogue.org

WEST OF SPITHEAD, LORD

LABOUR

WEST OF SPITHEAD (Life Baron), Alan William John West; cr 2007. Born 21 April 1948; Son of Walter West, Admiralty civil servant, and Jacqueline West, née Bliss; Married Rosemary Linington Childs 1973 (2 sons 1 daughter).

Education: Windsor Grammar School; Clydebank High School; Dartmouth (Britannia Royal Naval College); RN staff course 1978; Royal College of Defence Studies 1992; Higher Command and Staff course 1993; Basic French.

Non-political career: Active List, Royal Navy. Royal Navy 1965-2006: Seagoing posts 1966-73; Commanding officer (CO) HMS Yarnton 1973; HMSs Juno 1976, Ambuscade 1977, Norfolk 1979; CO HMS Ardent 1980; Naval Staff, Ministry of Defence (MoD) 1982; CO HMS Bristol 1987; Defence Intelligence Staff, MoD 1989; MoD 1993-96: Director Naval Staff Duties 1993, Naval Secretary 1994-96; Commander UK Task Group and of Anti-submarine Warfare Striking Force 1996-97; Chief of Defence Intelligence, MoD 1997-2001; Commander-in-Chief Fleet and East Atlantic and Commander Allied Naval Forces North 2001-02; Chief of Naval Staff and First Sea Lord, MoD 2002-06; Chairman, defence advisory board, QinetiQ 2006-07; Member, foreign advisory board, HSBC 2010-11; Strategic adviser, Primetake plc 2011-12; Chairman, Magic Industries Ltd 2012-13.

Political career: *House of Lords:* Raised to the peerage as Baron West of Spithead, of Seaview in the County of Isle of Wight 2007. Parliamentary Under-Secretary of State (Security and Counter-terrorism) and Government Spokesperson, Home Office 2007-10.

Political interests: Security, defence, foreign affairs, shipping/maritime; Gulf/South West Asia, Japan, Pakistan, Scandinavian countries, Ukraine.

Other: Younger Brother, Trinity House 1986-; President, Merchant Navy Medal Fund 2006-; Trustee, Imperial War Museum 2007-; Chairman, National Security Forum 2008-10; Member, RUSI; St Anne's Lime House; Chauncy Maples; Bollington Sea Cadet Unit. Liveryman, Honourable Company of Master Mariners; Company of Watermen and Lightermen of the River Thames; The Cachalots. Chancellor, Southampton Solent University. Honorary doctorate 2006. Trench Gascoigne prize winner. DSC 1982; KCB 2000; GCB 2004; PC 2010; Navy Club of 1765 & 85; Royal Naval Club; Royal Yacht Squadron.

Publications: Seaford House Paper (2002); Contributor, The Oxford Handbook of War.

Recreations: Boating, military history, OMRS.

Rt Hon Admiral the Lord West of Spithead GCB, House of Lords, London SW1A 0PW
Tel: 020 7219 5953 *Email:* westaa@parliament.uk westbuzz1@btinternet.com

WHEATCROFT, BARONESS

CONSERVATIVE

WHEATCROFT (Life Baroness), Patience Jane Wheatcroft; cr 2010. Born 28 September 1951; Daughter of Anthony and Ruth Wheatcroft; Married Anthony Salter 1976 (2 sons 1 daughter).
Education: Wolverhampton High School for Girls; Queen Elizabeth's Grammar School, Tamworth; Birmingham University (LLB 1972).
Non-political career: Deputy city editor, *The Times* 1984-86; Assistant city editor, *Daily Mail* 1986-88; Editor, *Retail Week* 1988-93; Deputy city editor, *Mail on Sunday* 1994-97; Business and city editor, *The Times* 1997-2006; Editor, *Sunday Telegraph* 2006-07; Non-executive director: Barclays plc 2008-09, Shaftesbury plc 2008-09; Editor-in-chief, *Wall Street Journal Europe* 2009-10; Non-executive director: St James's Place plc, Fiat; Member, UK advisory board, Huawei Technologies; Business consultant, DLA Piper; Member, advisory board, Pelham Bell Pottinger.
Political career: *House of Lords:* Raised to the peerage as Baroness Wheatcroft, of Blackheath in the London Borough of Greenwich 2010. Member: EU Sub-committee G (Social Policies and Consumer Protection) 2011-12, Joint Committee on the Draft Financial Services Bill 2011-12, Constitution 2012-, Sub-committee on Economic Affairs Finance Bill 2012-, Olympic and Paralympic Legacy 2013-.
Political interests: Business, finance, economics, arts; China, India.
Other: Trustee: Policy Exchange, British Museum, Member, UK-India Round Table; Director, Association of Leading Visitor Attractions; Action Aid; Samaritans. Honorary Doctorate, City University, London.
Recreations: Opera, skiing, theatre.
The Baroness Wheatcroft, House of Lords, London SW1A 0PW
Tel: 020 7219 5353
Email: patiencewheatcroft@googlemail.com

WHEELER, BARONESS

Opposition Whip

LABOUR

WHEELER (Life Baroness), Margaret Eileen Joyce Wheeler; cr 2010. Born 25 March 1949; Partner (no children).
Education: St Ursula's Convent School, Greenwich; Nottingham University (BA politics and psychology 1971).
Non-political career: Publishing/editorial trainee, Routledge and Kegan Paul 1971-73; Confederation of Health Service Employees 1973-93: 1973-88: Head of editorial department, Press officer, Campaigns strategies, Parliamentary and international officer, Director of specialist and support services 1988-93; Unison: Director of organisation development 1993-97, Director of organisation and staff development 1997-2010; Natural carers strategy implementation team, Department of Health 2009-10. Member: National Union of Journalists 1972-2010, Unison 1997-2010.
Political career: *House of Lords:* Raised to the peerage as Baroness Wheeler, of Blackfriars in the City of London 2010. Opposition Whip 2010-. Member Consumer Insurance (Disclosure and Representations) Bill 2011-12. *Councils and public bodies:* Former member: Commission on Social Justice, Enquiry panel into productivity and high performance, Department of Trade and Industry/Work Foundation; Investors in People Advisory Board, UK Commission for Employment and Skills.
Political interests: Health and social care; disabilities; China, India.
Other: Trustee and board member: One World Action, Carer Support, Elmbridge; Chair and board member, Blackfriars Settlement; One World Action; Christian Aid. MBE.
Recreations: Walking, theatre, arts, music.
The Baroness Wheeler MBE, House of Lords, London SW1A 0PW
Tel: 020 7219 8909 *Email:* wheelerm@parliament.uk

WHITAKER, BARONESS

LABOUR

WHITAKER (Life Baroness), Janet Alison Whitaker; cr. 1999. Born 20 February 1936; Daughter of Alan Stewart and Ella Stewart, née Saunders; Married Ben Whitaker CBE 1964 (2 sons 1 daughter).
Education: Nottingham High School for Girls; Girton College, Cambridge (BA English 1957); Bryn Mawr College, USA (MA English 1959); Harvard University, USA (Radcliffe Fellow 1960).
Non-political career: Editor, André Deutsch (Publishers) 1961-66; Various posts, Health and Safety Executive 1974-88; Department of Education and Employment 1988-96: Head of sex equality branch 1992-96; Consultant: Commission for Racial Equality 1995-96, Commonwealth Secretariat 1996; Assessor, Citizens' Charter Chartermark 1996; Consultant, Committee of Reference, Friends Provident Group 2000-08. Member, FDA.

Political career: *House of Lords:* Raised to the peerage as Baroness Whitaker, of Beeston in the County of Nottinghamshire 1999. International Development Liaison Peer 1999-2007; Chair: Design in Public Procurement Inquiry 2009, Design Education Inquiry 2011. Member: Joint Committee on Human Rights 2000-03, Joint Committee on Draft Corruption Bill 2003, Intergovernmental Organisations 2007-08, Joint Committee on Draft Bribery Bill 2009. *Councils and public bodies:* Magistrate 1985-2006; Member, Employment Tribunal 1995-2000; Deputy chair and chair, Camden Racial Equality Council 1996-99; Non-executive director, Tavistock and Portman NHS Trust 1997-2001; Member, Immigration Complaints Audit Committee 1998-99.

Political interests: Architecture and design, international development, race relations; Africa, Asia, Europe.

Other: Member: Inter-Parliamentary Union, Commonwealth Parliamentary Association, UK advisory panel, United Nations Association 2006-; Member/associate, Fabian Society 1962; Council member, SOS Sahel 1997-2011; Chair, Working Men's College for Men and Women 1998-2001; Advisory council, Transparency International (UK) 2001-09; Deputy chair, ITC 2001-03; Patron, Runnymede Trust 2001-; Council member, Overseas Development Institute 2003-; Trustee, Unicef UK 2003-09; Patron, British Stammering Association 2003-; Practical Action (formerly Intermediate Technology Development Group) 2004-10; Vice-President: British Humanist Association 2004-, One World Trust 2004-; Advisory board, British Institute of Human Rights 2005-; Patron, Student Partnerships Worldwide 2005-; Fellow, Royal Society of Arts; President, South Downs Society 2012-; FRIBA; Fellow of the Working Men's College; Reform.

Recreations: Travel, walking, art, music, reading.

The Baroness Whitaker, House of Lords, London SW1A 0PW
Tel: 020 7219 5353

WHITBY, LORD

WHITBY (Life Baron), Michael John Whitby; cr 2013.

Political career: *House of Lords:* Raised to the peerage as Baron Whitby, of Harborne in the City of Birmingham 2013. *Councils and public bodies:* Birmingham City Council: Councillor 1997-, Leader, Conservative Group.

Other: General Assembly, Local Government Association; West Midlands Police and Crime Panel.

The Lord Whitby, House of Lords, London SW1A 0PW

CONSERVATIVE   *Tel:* 020 7219 5353

WHITTY, LORD

WHITTY (Life Baron), John Lawrence (Larry) Whitty; cr. 1996. Born 15 June 1943; Son of late Frederick James and Kathleen May Whitty; Married Tanya Gibson 1969 (divorced 1986) (2 sons); married Angela Forrester 1993.

Education: Latymer Upper School, London; St John's College, Cambridge (BA economics 1965); French, German.

Non-political career: Hawker Siddeley Aviation 1960-62; Ministry of Aviation and Ministry of Technology 1965-70; Trades Union Congress 1970-73; General, Municipal, Boilermakers and Allied Trade Union 1973-85; Chair, Cofeely East London Energy 2005-10. Member, GMB.

LABOUR

Political career: *House of Lords:* Raised to the peerage as Baron Whitty, of Camberwell in the London Borough of Southwark 1996. Government Whip 1997-98; Government Spokesperson for European Affairs, International Development, Foreign and Commonwealth Affairs, Education and Employment 1997-98; Parliamentary Under-Secretary of State and Government Spokesperson: Department of the Environment, Transport and the Regions (Minister for Roads and Road Safety) 1998-2001, Department for Environment, Food and Rural Affairs 2001-05. Member Draft Climate Change Bill Joint Committee 2007; Co-opted member EU Sub-committee B (Internal Market) 2007-10; Member EU Sub-committees: G (Social Policies and Consumer Protection) 2010-12, D (Agriculture, Fisheries, Environment and Energy) 2012-. Vice-chair, PLP Departmental Group for Energy and Climate Change 2010-. *Other:* Labour Party: General Secretary 1985-94, European Co-ordinator 1994-97. *Councils and public bodies:* Chair, National Consumer Council 2006-08; Member, National Water Regulation Authority (Ofwat) 2006; Non-executive director, Environment Agency 2006-12; Chair, Consumer Focus 2008-10.

Political interests: Employment, energy, environment, food, Europe, consumers, education; China, France, Germany, Ireland, Italy, Japan.

Other: Member: Friends of the Earth, Fabian Society; President, Combined Heat and Power Association 2005-11; Alzheimer's Society. PC 2005.
Recreations: Theatre, cinema, swimming.
Rt Hon the Lord Whitty, House of Lords, London SW1A 0PW
Tel: 020 7219 3118 *Email:* whittyl@parliament.uk

WIGLEY, LORD

WIGLEY (Life Baron), Dafydd Wigley; cr 2011. Born 1 April 1943; Son of Elfyn and Myfanwy Wigley; Married Elinor Bennett 1967 (1 son 1 daughter two sons deceased).
Education: Caernarfon Grammar School; Rydal School, Colwyn Bay; Manchester University (BSc physics 1964); English (fluent), Welsh (fluent), French (modest).
Non-political career: Finance staff, Ford Motor Co 1964-67; Chief cost accountant and financial planning manager, Mars Ltd 1967-71; Financial controller, Hoover Ltd, Merthyr Plant 1971-74; Chair, Alpha-Dyffryn Ltd (Electronics) 1987-91; Board member, S4C 2003-06. Former member, Association of Scientific, Technical and Managerial Staffs (ASTMS).

PLAID CYMRU

Political career: *House of Commons:* Contested Merioneth 1970 general election. MP (Plaid Cymru) for Caernarfon February 1974-2001. Sponsor Disabled Persons Act 1981; Plaid Cymru: Whip 1987-91, Spokesman for Constitutional Affairs 1997-2000. *House of Lords:* Raised to the peerage as Baron Wigley, of Caernarfon in the County of Gwynedd 2011. Member Olympic and Paralympic Legacy 2013-. *Other:* Contested North Wales region 1994 European Parliament election; National Assembly for Wales: AM for Caernarfon constituency 1999-2003: Shadow First Minister 1999-2000, Shadow Secretary for Finance 1999-2000. Contested North Wales region 2007 National Assembly for Wales election. Leader and president, Plaid Cymru 1981-84, 1991-2000. *Councils and public bodies:* Councillor, Merthy Tydfil County Borough Council 1972-74.
Political interests: Industry, employment, disability, Europe, minority languages; Argentina, Ireland, New Zealand, Slovenia, USA.
Other: Vice-President, Wales Council for the Disabled; President, Spastic Society for Wales 1985-90; Member, Mencap Profound Mental Handicap Study Committee 1987-97; Vice-President: Mencap in Wales 1990-, Federation of Economic Development Authorities (FEDA); Patron, Autism Wales 2003-; President: Gwynedd Family History Society 2005-, National Library of Wales 2008-12; Honorary member, Welsh Gorsedd of Bards; Honorary fellowship, Bangor University; NSPCC; Mencap Wales; Contact a Family. Freedom: Borough of Arfon 1996, Town of Caernarfon 2001. Pro-chancellor, University of Wales 2003-06. Honorary LLB University of Wales. National Federation of the Blind Grimshaw Memorial Award 1981. PC 1997; Clwb y Castell, Caernarfon. Caernarfon Town Football Club.
Publications: Co-author: An Economic Plan for Wales (1970), O Ddifri (1992), A Democratic Wales in an United Europe (1994) A Fair Choice for Wales (1996); Columnist, *Daily Post* 2009-.
Recreations: Chess, walking, soccer, rugby, gardening.
Rt Hon the Lord Wigley, House of Lords, London SW1A 0PW
Tel: 020 7219 5021 *Email:* wigleyd@parliament.uk

WILCOX, BARONESS

WILCOX (Life Baroness), Judith Ann Wilcox; cr. 1996. Born 31 October 1940; Daughter of John and Elsie Freeman; Married Keith Davenport 1961 (divorced 1986) (1 son); married Sir Malcom Wilcox, CBE (died 1986).
Education: St Dunstan's Abbey, Devon; St Mary's Convent, Wantage; University of Plymouth.
Non-political career: Management of family business in Devon 1969-79; Founder/financial director, Capstan Fisheries Ltd, Devon 1979-84; Founder/chair, Channel Foods Ltd, Cornwall 1984-89; President Directeur-General, Pecheries de la Morinie, Boulogne-sur-Mer, France 1989-91; Chair: National Consumer Council 1990-96, Morinie et Cie, Boulogne-sur-Mer, France 1991-94; Board member, Automobile Association 1991-2001; Non-executive member, Inland Revenue Board 1992-95; Member, Prime Minister's Advisory Panel to Citizen's Charter Unit 1992-97; Commissioner, Local Government Commission 1992-95; Chair, Citizen's Charter Complaints Task Force 1993-95; Port of London Authority: Board member 1993-2000, Vice-chair 2000-05; Director: Cadbury Schweppes plc 1997-2007, Carpetright plc 1997-2010, Elexon Ltd 2000-02, Johnson Services plc 2003-09.

CONSERVATIVE

Political career: *House of Lords:* Raised to the peerage as Baroness Wilcox, of Plymouth in the County of Devon 1996. Opposition Whip 2002-05; Opposition Spokesperson for: the Treasury 2003-05, Cabinet Office 2005-06, Trade and Industry/Business, Enterprise and Regulatory Reform 2006-08; Energy and Climate Change 2008-10; Parliamentary Under-Secretary of State (Parliamentary Secretary for Business, Innovation and Skills) and Government Spokesperson, Department for Business, Innovation and Skills 2010-12. Member: European Union Sub-committee D

(Environment, Public Health and Consumer Protection) 1997-2000, Ecclesiastical Committee 1997-2010, Science and Technology Sub-committee II (Science and Society) 1999-2000, Science and Technology 2000-02, Science and Technology Sub-committee IIA (Human Genetic Databases) 2000-; Chair Science and Technology Sub-committee II (Aircraft Cabin Environment) 2000; Member: Liaison 2000-05, Science and Technology Sub-committees: I (Fighting Infection) 2002-03, II (Innovation in Computer Processors/Microprocessing) 2002-03, Ecclesiastical Standing Committee 2002-. *Councils and public bodies:* Member: General Advisory Council of the BBC 1996-2000, Lord Chancellor's Review of the Court of Appeal 1996-97, Tax Law Review Committee 1996-2000.

Political interests: Fishing industry, mariculture, consumer affairs, finance, intellectual property; Australia, France.

Other: Delegate, Council of Europe 2013-; Council member, Institute of Directors 1991-98; Member, Governing Body of Institute of Food Research 1996-2002; President: National Federation of Consumer Groups 1996-, Institute of Trading Standards Administration (ITSA) 1996-; Chair, London Diocesan Advisory Committee 2000-02; Governor, Imperial College 2006-; FIMgt; FRSA; Royal National Mission to Deep Sea Fishermen; Children's Hospice South West. Liveryman, Fishmongers' Company 2006. Freeman, City of London; Athenæum Club; Nobody's Friends; Gardeners. St Mawes Sailing.

Recreations: Sailing, birdwatching, calligraphy.

The Baroness Wilcox, House of Lords, London SW1A 0PW
Tel: 020 7219 4458 *Email:* wilcoxj@parliament.uk

LABOUR

WILKINS, BARONESS

WILKINS (Life Baroness), Rosalie Catherine Wilkins; cr. 1999. Born 6 May 1946; Daughter of late Eric and Marjorie Wilkins; Civil partner Maria Brenton 2006.

Education: Dr Challoner's Grammar School, Amersham; St Helen's School, Northwood; Manchester University (BA government and sociology 1969).

Non-political career: PA to director, Central Council for the Disabled 1971-74; Information officer, MIND (National Association for Mental Health) 1974-78; Researcher/presenter, The Link Programme (magazine programme for disabled people), ATV Network/Central Television 1975-88; Freelance video and documentary producer 1988-96; Information officer, National Centre for Independent Living 1997-99. Former member BECTU.

Political career: *House of Lords:* Raised to the peerage as Baroness Wilkins, of Chesham Bois in the County of Buckinghamshire 1999. Member: Hybrid Instruments 2000-05, Joint Committee on Draft Mental Incapacity Bill 2003-04, Administration and Works 2003-07, Joint Committee on Draft Disability Discrimination Bill 2004, Leader's Group on the Working Practices of the House of Lords 2010-11. *Councils and public bodies:* Member: Central Health Services Council 1974-76, BBC General Advisory Council 1976-78.

Political interests: Disability, housing, social care.

Other: Member, Prince of Wales' Advisory Group on Disability 1982-90; President, College of Occupational Therapists 2003-08; Patron: Integrated Neurological Services 2006-, Candoco Dance Company 2009-, SPIRIT (spinal injuries charity) 2011-; SIA (Spinal Injuries Association), Medical Foundation for the Victims of Torture, Crisis, Wateraid. The Snowdon Award 1983.

Publications: Contributor Able Lives – Women's Experience of Paralysis (1989).

Recreations: Friends, gardening, theatre, genealogy.

The Baroness Wilkins, House of Lords, London SW1A 0PW
Tel: 020 7219 8522 (pm) *Email:* wilkinsrc@parliament.uk

CROSSBENCH

WILLIAMS OF BAGLAN, LORD

WILLIAMS OF BAGLAN (Life Baron), Michael Charles Williams; cr 2010. Born 11 June 1949; Married Margaret Rigby 1974 (divorced 1984) (1 daughter); married Isobelle Jaques 1992 (1 son).

Education: Sandfields Comprehensive School, Port Talbot; University College, London (BSc international relations 1971; School of Oriental and African Studies, London (MSc politics 1971; PhD politics 1984); Dutch, French, Indonesian.

Non-political career: Researcher, Amnesty International 1977-78; Politics lecturer, University of East Anglia 1978-80; Head of Asia research, Amnesty International 1980-84; Senior commentator/editor, BBC World Service 1984-92; Human rights director, UN Mission to Cambodia 1992-93; Information director, UN Mission to Former Yugoslavia 1993-95; Senior fellow, International Institute for Strategic Studies 1996-98; Consultant, UNHCR 1998-; Director, Office for Children and Armed Conflict, UN, New York 1998-99; Special adviser to Foreign Secretaries: Robin Cook MP 2000-01, Jack Straw MP 2001-05; UN, New York: Director, Middle East and Africa 2005-06, Assistant Secretary-General and special adviser on the Middle East 2006-07; UK special representative on the Middle East and special projects, Foreign and Commonwealth Office 2007-08; UN special co-ordinator for Lebanon 2008-.

Political career: *House of Lords:* Raised to the peerage as Baron Williams of Baglan, of Neath Port Talbot in Glamorgan 2010. On leave of absence October 2010-October 2011. *Other:* Labour Party until December 2011 (on taking up position as trustee, BBC Trust); Crossbench December 2011-. *Councils and public bodies:* Trustee, BBC Trust 2011-; Member, Council of Swansea University 2011-; Governor, School of Oriental and African Studies, London 2012-.

Political interests: Foreign affairs, defence, social welfare; Balkans, France, Germany, Middle East including Iran, southeast Asia, especially Indonesia, Vietnam, and Burma, USA.

Other: Royal Institute of International Affairs, Chatham House: Member 1978-, Council member and executive committee member 2000-06; International Institute for Strategic Studies 1990-; Distinguished Visiting Fellow, Royal Institute of International Affairs, Chatham House 2011; British Lung Foundation; Salvation Army. National Order of the Cedar, Commander Grade (Lebanon); Athenæum.

Publications: Vietnam at the Crossroads (RIIA Chatham House, 1992); Civil-Military Relations and Peacekeeping (Oxford University Press/IISS, 1998).

Recreations: Reading especially history, travel.

Dr the Lord Williams of Baglan, House of Lords, London SW1A 0PW
Tel: 020 7219 5353 *Email:* williamsmc3@parliament.uk

WILLIAMS OF CROSBY, BARONESS

WILLIAMS OF CROSBY (Life Baroness), Shirley Vivian Teresa Brittain Williams; cr. 1993. Born 27 July 1930; Daughter of late Professor Sir George Catlin and late Vera Brittain; Married Professor Sir Bernard Williams FBA 1955 (divorced 1974) (1 daughter); married Professor Richard Neustadt 1987 (died 2003) (1 stepson deceased 1 stepdaughter).

Education: St Paul's Girls' School, London and schools in UK and US; Somerville College, Oxford (Scholar, BA philosophy, politics and economics 1951, MA); Columbia University, New York (Fulbright Scholarship 1951).

LIBERAL DEMOCRAT   **Non-political career:** Journalist: *Daily Mirror* 1952-54, *Financial Times* 1954-58; Fabian Society: General Secretary, 1960-64, Chair 1980-81; Institute of Politics, Harvard University: Fellow 1979-80, Acting Director 1987-88; John F. Kennedy School of Government, Harvard University: Professor of Elective Politics 1988-2000, Professor Emeritus 2000-; Various lectureships in UK and USA; Associate: Center for European Studies, Harvard, Belfer Center for Science and International Affairs. Member, NUGMW 1960-.

Political career: *House of Commons:* Contested (as Labour) Harwich 1954 and 1955 and Southampton Test 1959 general elections. MP (Labour) for Hitchin 1964-74, for Hertford and Stevenage 1974-79. Contested (as Labour) Hertford and Stevenage 1979 general election. MP (SDP) for Crosby November 1981 by-election to 1983. Contested (as SDP) Crosby 1983 and (as SDP/Alliance) Cambridge 1987 general elections. PPS to Kenneth Robinson as Minister of Health 1964-66; Parliamentary Secretary, Ministry of Labour 1966-67; Minister of State: Department of Education and Science 1967-69, Home Office 1969-70; Secretary of State for: Prices and Consumer Protection 1974-76, Education and Science 1976-79; Paymaster General 1976-79. *House of Lords:* Raised to the peerage as Baroness Williams of Crosby, of Stevenage in the County of Hertfordshire 1993. Liberal Democrat peers: Deputy Leader 1999-2001, Leader 2001-04; Liberal Democrat Spokesperson for Foreign and Commonwealth Affairs 1998-2001. Member: European Communities 1997-99, European Communities Sub-committee A (Economic and Financial Affairs, Trade and External Relations) 1997-99, House of Lords' Offices 2001-02, Liaison 2001-05, Privileges 2001-05, Procedure 2001-05, Selection 2001-05, House of Lords' Offices Finance and Staff Sub-committee 2001-02. *Other:* Joined the Labour Party 1946; Member, Labour Party National Executive Committee 1970-81; Social Democratic Party: Co-founder 1981, President 1982-88. *Councils and public bodies:* Visiting Fellow, Nuffield College, Oxford 1967-75; Director, Turing Institute, Glasgow 1985-90; Board member, Rand Corporation, Europe 1993-2001; Governor, Ditchley Foundation 1994-; Member, Advisory Committee on Business Appointments 1999-2001; Board member: Nuclear Threat Initiative (USA) 2002-, Oxford Centre for Islamic Studies; Member, advisory committee, Century Foundation.

Political interests: Globalisation, human rights, international affairs, civil liberties.

Other: Board member: Moscow School of Political Studies 1992-, European Movement 1993-; Member, International Advisory Committee Council on Foreign Relations, New York 1994-2006; President, British-Russian Society and East-West Centre 1996-2000; Co-chair, Anglo-Dutch Society 1998-2001; Council member, Britain in Europe; Board Member: International Crisis Group, Brussels 1998-2001, Overseers of John F Kennedy School of Government, Harvard University 2001-; Commissioner, International Commission on Nuclear Proliferation and Nuclear Disarmament 2008-10; Trustee: Century Foundation, New York 1976-, IPPR, London 2002-10; Refugee Council, Oxfam, Cafod, Action Aid, RNIB, Church Charities, Gatwick Detainees Welfare Group. Honorary Fellow: Somerville College, Oxford 1970, Newnham College, Cambridge 1977, Liverpool University 2008, Cambridge University 2009; Twelve honorary doctorates from British, European and US universities. Silver Medal, Royal Society of Arts; Women in Public Life Awards: Peer of the Year 2011, Lifetime Achievement Award 2011; Parliamentarian of the Year, *Spectator* awards 2011; Peer of the Year, *PoliticsHome* awards 2012. PC 1974; Grand Cross (second class) (Federal Republic of Germany); The Other Club. LivingWell.

Publications: Shirley Williams in Conversation, BBC TV series 1979; Jobs for the 1980s; Youth Without Work (1981); Politics is for People (1981); Co-author, Unemployment and Growth in the Western Economies (1984); A Job to Live (1985); Snakes and Ladders – A Political Diary, BBC radio series (1996); Women in the House, BBC Radio Four (1998); Chapter on Human Rights in Europe in Human Rights Policy: What Works? (2000); Making Globalisation Good in The Moral Responsibility of the Rich to the Poor (OUP, 2003); God and Caesar (Continuum, 2003); Climbing the Bookshelves (Little Brown, 2009); Numerous newspaper articles and broadcasts.

Recreations: Music, hill-walking, poetry.

Rt Hon the Baroness Williams of Crosby, House of Lords, London SW1A 0PW
Tel: 020 7219 5850 *Fax:* 020 7219 1174 *Email:* williamss@parliament.uk

WILLIAMS OF ELVEL, LORD

WILLIAMS OF ELVEL (Life Baron), Charles Cuthbert Powell Williams; cr. 1985. Born 9 February 1933; Son of late Dr N. P. Williams, DD, Lady Margaret Professor of Divinity at Oxford and Muriel de Lérisson, née Cazenove; Married Jane Gillian Welby, née Portal 1975 (1 stepson, the Most Rev and Rt Hon the Archbishop of Canterbury).

Education: Westminster School; Christ Church, Oxford (BA literae humaniores 1955, MA); London School of Economics (BSc Econ Part I 1964); French, German, Italian.

LABOUR

Non-political career: Army national service 1955-57, Subaltern KRRC (60th Rifles) HQ Battalion (Winchester) and 1st Battalion Derna (Libya). Various management posts, British Petroleum Co. Ltd 1958-64; Personal assistant to manager, Guatemala branch, Bank of London and Montreal 1964-66; Manager, mergers and acquisitions, Eurofinance SA, Paris 1966-70; Baring Bros & Co. Ltd 1970-77: Managing director 1971-77; Chair, Price Commission 1977-79; Managing director: Henry Ansbacher & Co. Ltd 1979-82, Henry Ansbacher Holdings 1982-85; Director, Mirror Group Newspapers plc 1985-92.

Political career: *House of Lords:* Raised to the peerage as Baron Williams of Elvel, of Llansantffraed in Elvel in the County of Powys 1985. Opposition Spokesperson for Trade and Industry 1987-92; Deputy Leader of the Opposition 1989-92; Opposition Spokesperson for: Defence 1990-97, the Environment 1992-97. Member: Ecclesiastical Committee 1997-2013, European Union 1999-2002, EU Sub-committee C (Common Foreign and Security Policy) 1999-2003, Procedure 2005-08; EU Sub-committee C (Foreign Affairs, Defence and Development): Co-opted member 2009-10, Member 2010-12; Member EU Sub-committees: C (External Affairs) 2012-13, D (Agriculture, Fisheries, Environment and Energy) 2013-.

Political interests: Banking, finance, environment; France, Germany, Italy, Russia, Spain.

Other: Chair, Academy of St Martin-in-the-Fields 1988-90; Campaign for the Protection of Rural Wales: President 1989-95, Vice-President 1995-, President, Radnor Branch 1995-; Chair, Mid Wales Chamber Orchestra 2008-13; Busby Trustee, Westminster School 1989-99; Macmillan Cancer Relief. CBE 1980; PC 2013; Beefsteak, Reform. MCC.

Publications: The Last Great Frenchman: a life of General de Gaulle (1993); Bradman: an Australian Hero (1996); Adenauer: the Father of the New Germany (2000); Pétain (2005); Harold Macmillan (2009); Gentlemen and Players (2012).

Recreations: Cricket, music.

Rt Hon the Lord Williams of Elvel CBE, House of Lords, London SW1A 0PW
Tel: 020 7219 6054 *Email:* williamscc@parliament.uk

WILLIAMS OF OYSTERMOUTH, LORD

CROSSBENCH

WILLIAMS OF OYSTERMOUTH (Life Baron), Rowan Douglas Williams; cr 2013. Born 14 June 1950; Son of Aneurin and Delphine Williams; Married (Hilary) Jane Paul 1981 (1 son 1 daughter). **Education:** Dynevor School, Swansea; Christ's College, Cambridge (BA theology 1971, MA); Christ Church and Wadham Colleges, Oxford (DPhil 1975; DD 1989); French, German, Welsh. **Non-political career:** Lecturer, College of the Resurrection, Mirfield 1975-77; Tutor and director of studies, Westcott House, Cambridge 1977-80; Ordained priest 1978; Honorary curate, Chesterton St George, Ely 1980-83; Divinity lecturer, Cambridge 1980-86; Canon theologian, Leicester Cathedral 1981-82; Dean and Chaplain, Clare College, Cambridge 1984-86; Lady Margaret professor of divinity and canon of Christ Church, Oxford 1986-92; Bishop of Monmouth 1992-2002; Archbishop of Wales 1999-2002; Archbishop of Canterbury 2002-12.

Political career: *House of Lords:* Raised to the peerage as Baron Williams of Oystermouth, of Oystermouth in the City and County of Swansea 2013. First entered the House of Lords as Archbishop of Canterbury 2002.

Political interests: Children and family issues, development; Africa, Middle East.

Other: Fellow: British Academy 1990, Royal Society of Literature 2004, Learned Society of Wales 2010; Honorary board member, Cardinal Willebrands Research Centre; Chair, Christian Aid; Christian Aid. Honorary Liveryman, Worshipful Company of Wax Chandlers; Patron: The Stationers' Company, Parish Clerks. Freeman: City of Swansea 2010, City of Canterbury 2012. Chancellor, University of South Wales. Honorary fellow: Clare College, Cambridge, Wadham College, Oxford, Newport University, Swansea University; Honorary doctorates from German and US universities, plus: Aberdeen University, Cambridge University, Durham University, Exeter University, Kent University, King's College, London, Oxford University, Roehampton University, Wales University. Order of St. John of Jerusalem, Priory for Wales (Confrere); PC 2002; Royal Victorian Chain 2012; Athenæum. Honorary Member, Kent County Cricket Club.

Publications: The Wound of Knowledge (1979); Resurrection (1982); The Truce of God (1983); Arius: heresy and tradition (1987); Editor The Making of Orthodoxy (1989); Teresa of Avila (1991); Open to Judgement (1994); Sergii Bulgakov (1999); On Christian Theology (2000); Lost Icons (2000); Christ on Trial (2000); Poems of Rowan Williams (2002); Ponder these things (2002); Writing in the Dust (2002); Silence and Honey Cakes (2003); The Dwelling of the Light (2003); Anglican Identities (2004); Grace and Necessity (2005); Why Study the Past? (2005); Tokens of Trust (2007); Wrestling with Angels (2007); Headwaters (poems 2008); Dostoevsky: Language, Faith and Fiction (2008); A Margin of Silence/Une Marge de Silence (2008); Co-editor, Crisis and Recovery: Ethics, Economics and Justice (Palgrave Macmillan, 2010); Co-author, For All That Has Been: Thanks: Growing a Sense of Gratitude (2010).

Recreations: Music, fiction, languages.

Most Rev and Rt Hon the Lord Williams of Oystermouth, House of Lords, London SW1A 0PW *Tel:* 020 7219 5353
Magdalene College, Cambridge CB3 0AG *Tel:* 01223 332144 *Email:* jeh34@cam.ac.uk

WILLIAMS OF TRAFFORD, BARONESS – *Please see Addenda Page xiii*

WILLIAMSON OF HORTON, LORD

CROSSBENCH

WILLIAMSON OF HORTON (Life Baron), David Francis Williamson; cr. 1999. Born 8 May 1934; Son of late Samuel and Marie Williamson; Married Patricia Smith 1961 (2 sons). **Education:** Tonbridge School; Exeter College, Oxford (BA literae humaniores 1956, MA); French.

Non-political career: Second Lieutenant, Royal Signals 1956-58. Ministry of Agriculture, Fisheries and Food (MAFF) 1958-62: Private Secretary to Permanent Secretary and to successive Parliamentary Secretaries 1960-62; HM Diplomatic Service as First Secretary (Agriculture and Food) Geneva, for Kennedy Round Trade Negotiations 1965-67; MAFF 1967-83: Principal Private Secretary to successive Ministers of Agriculture, Fisheries and Food 1967-70, Head of Milk and Milk Products Division, Marketing Policy Division and Food Policy Division 1970-74, Under-Secretary: General Agricultural Policy Group 1974-76, EEC Group 1976-77; Deputy Director-General, Agriculture, European Commission 1977-83; Deputy Secretary, Cabinet Office 1983-87; Secretary-General, European Commission 1987-97; Visiting Professor, Bath University 1997-2001; Non-executive director, Whitbread plc 1998-2005.

Political career: *House of Lords:* Raised to the peerage as Baron Williamson of Horton, of Horton in the County of Somerset 1999. Convenor of the Crossbench Peers 2004-07. Member: European Union Sub-committee C (Common Foreign and Security Policy) 1999-2003, European Union 2000-04; Chair European Union Sub-committee G (Social Policy and Consumer Affairs) 2003-04; Member: House 2004-07, Administration and Works 2004-07, Liaison 2004-07, Privileges 2004-

07, Procedure 2004-07, Selection 2004-07, Joint Committee on the draft Constitutional Reform Bill 2008; Joint Committee on the draft Bribery Bill 2009. *Councils and public bodies:* Chair, Somerset Strategic Partnership 2000-04.

Other: Member, Wessex Regional Committee, National Trust 1998-2004; President, University Association for Contemporary European Studies 2000-03; Trustee, Thomson Foundation 2001-05; Rethink; Centrepoint. Four honorary doctorates. CB 1984; Knight Commander's Cross of the Order of Merit (Germany) 1991; GCMG 1998; Commander Grand Cross of the Royal Order of the Polar Star (Sweden) 1998; Commandeur de la Légion d'Honneur (France) 1999; PC 2007.

Rt Hon the Lord Williamson of Horton GCMG CB, House of Lords, London SW1A 0PW
Tel: 020 7219 3583 *Email:* williamsond@parliament.uk

WILLIS OF KNARESBOROUGH, LORD

WILLIS OF KNARESBOROUGH (Life Baron), Philip George Willis; cr 2010. Born 30 November 1941; Son of late George Willis, postman, and late Norah Willis, nurse; Married Heather Sellars 1974 (1 son 1 daughter).

Education: Burnley Grammar School; City of Leeds and Carnegie College (Cert Ed 1963); Birmingham University (BPhil education 1978); French.

Non-political career: Head teacher: Ormesby School, Cleveland 1978-82, John Smeaton Community High School, Leeds 1983-97. Member, Secondary Heads Association.

LIBERAL DEMOCRAT **Political career:** *House of Commons:* MP (Lib Dem) for Harrogate and Knaresborough 1997-2010. Liberal Democrat: Whip 1997-99, Spokesperson for Further, Higher and Adult Education 1997-99, Principal Spokesperson for Education and Employment 1999-2000, Shadow Secretary of State for Education and Skills 2000-05. Member: Education and Employment (Education Sub-Committee) 1999-2000, Education and Employment 1999-2000, Liaison 2005-10; Chair: Science and Technology 2005-07, Joint Committee on the Draft Human Tissue and Embryos Bill 2007, Innovation, Universities[, Science] and Skills/Science and Technology 2007-10. *House of Lords:* Raised to the peerage as Baron Willis of Knaresborough, of Harrogate in the County of North Yorkshire 2010. Science and Technology: Co-opted member 2010-11, Member 2011-; Member Science and Technology Sub-committee I 2012-13. *Other:* Member, Association of Liberal Democrat Councillors. *Councils and public bodies:* Harrogate Borough Council: Councillor 1988-99, First Liberal Democrat Leader 1990-97; North Yorkshire County Council: Councillor 1993-97, Deputy Group Leader 1993-97; Vice-President, Local Government Association 2010-11.

Political interests: Inclusive education, health, local and regional government, science policy, higher education reform; Ireland.

Other: Council member: Foundation for Science and Technology, National Environment Research Council; Chair, e-Learning Foundation; President, AOC Charitable Trust; Chair, Association of Medical Research Charities; National Children's Homes, St Michael's Hospice, Harrogate; Horticap, Bluecoat Wood Nursery, Harrogate. Man of the Year, *Times Educational Supplement* 2002. Leeds United Football Club.

Recreations: Theatre, music, dance (especially ballet), football (Leeds United).

The Lord Willis of Knaresborough, House of Lords, London SW1A 0PW
Tel: 020 7219 5709 *Email:* willisg@parliament.uk *Website:* www.philwillis.org.uk
Twitter: @philwillis_exmp

WILLOUGHBY DE BROKE, LORD

WILLOUGHBY DE BROKE (21st Baron, E), (Leopold) David Verney; cr. 1491. Born 14 September 1938; Son of 20th Baron, MC, AFC; Married Petra Aird 1965 (divorced 1989) (3 sons); married Mrs Alexandra du Luart 2003.

Education: Le Rosey, Switzerland; New College, Oxford (BA modern languages 1961).

Non-political career: Chair: St Martin's Magazines 1992-2008, SM Theatre Ltd 1992-; President, Heart of England Tourist Board 1999-04.

UK INDEPENDENCE **Political career:** *House of Lords:* First entered House of Lords 1986; Elected hereditary peer **PARTY** 1999-. Member: European Union 1997-2000, European Union Sub-committee D (Environment, Agriculture, Public Health and Consumer Protection) 1997-2001. *Other:* Vice-President, Conservatives Against a Federal Europe (CAFE) 1997-2007. *Councils and public bodies:* DL, Warwickshire 1999-.

Political interests: Rural affairs, EU; Europe, Hong Kong, Tibet.

Other: Patron, Warwickshire Association of Boys' Clubs 1990-04; Honorary governor, Royal Shakespeare Theatre 1992-; President, CPRE Warwickshire 2002-; Chair, Warwickshire Hunt Ltd 2005, 2012-. All England Lawn Tennis.

The Lord Willoughby de Broke DL, House of Lords, London SW1A 0PW
Tel: 020 7219 4941 *Email:* willoughbyl@parliament.uk
Ditchford Farm, Moreton in Marsh, Gloucestershire GL56 9RD *Tel:* 01608 661990
Fax: 01608 663565

WILLS, LORD

WILLS (Life Baron), Michael David Wills; cr 2010. Born 20 May 1952; Son of late Stephen Wills
and Elizabeth Wills; Married Jill Freeman 1984 (3 sons 2 daughters).
Education: Haberdashers' Aske's, Elstree; Clare College, Cambridge (BA history 1973).
Non-political career: Third secretary, later second secretary, HM Diplomatic Service 1976-80;
Researcher, later producer, London Weekend Television 1980-84; Director, Juniper Productions
TV production company 1984-97. Member, TGWU.
Political career: *House of Commons:* MP (Labour) for North Swindon 1997-2010. Parliamentary
Under-Secretary of State: Department of Trade and Industry (Minister for Small Firms, Trade and
LABOUR Industry) 1999, Department for Education and Employment 1999-2001; Parliamentary Secretary,
Lord Chancellor's Department 2001-02; Parliamentary Under-Secretary of State, Home Office
2002-03: (for Criminal Justice System IT 2002, Information Technology in the Criminal Justice
System 2003); Minister of State, Ministry of Justice 2007-10. *House of Lords:* Raised to the peer-
age as Baron Wills, of North Swindon in the County of Wiltshire and Woodside Park in the Lon-
don Borough of Barnet 2010.
Other: PC 2008.
Rt Hon the Lord Wills, House of Lords, London SW1A 0PW
Tel: 020 7219 5353

WILSON OF DINTON, LORD

WILSON OF DINTON (Life Baron), Richard Thomas James Wilson; cr. 2002. Born 11 October
1942; Son of late Richard Ridley and Frieda Bell Wilson, née Finlay; Married Caroline Margaret
Lee 1972 (1 son 1 daughter).
Education: Radley College; Clare College, Cambridge (BA law 1964; LLM 1965).
Non-political career: Called to Bar, Middle Temple 1965; Assistant principal, Board of Trade 1966-
71; Principal, Cabinet Office 1971-73; Department of Energy 1974-86: Principal establishment and
finance officer 1983-86; Seconded to Cabinet Office 1986-90: Head, economic secretariat 1987-90;
Deputy secretary, industry, HM Treasury 1990-92; Permanent Secretary, Department of the Environ-
CROSSBENCH ment 1992-94; Permanent Under-Secretary, Home Office 1994-97; Cabinet Secretary and Head,
Home Civil Service 1998-2002; Master of Emmanuel College, Cambridge University 2002-12.
Political career: *House of Lords:* Raised to the peerage as Baron Wilson of Dinton, of Dinton in
the County of Buckinghamshire 2002.
Other: Trustee, Ewing Foundation 1995-; Non-executive director, BSkyB 2003-12; Trustee, Cic-
ely Saunders Foundation 2004-; President, Chartered Institute of Personnel and Development
2004-06; Chairman, Radley College 2004-10; Trustee, Syndic Fitzwilliam Museum 2005-11;
Chairman; C Hoare & Co, Bankers 2006-, Prince's Teaching Institute 2006-09; Trustee, Cam-
bridge Arts Theatre 2008-12. CB 1991; KCB 1997; GCB 2001.
Recreations: Home, garden.
The Lord Wilson of Dinton GCB, House of Lords, London SW1A 0PW
Tel: 020 7219 5353 *Email:* rw272@cam.ac.uk

WILSON OF TILLYORN, LORD

WILSON OF TILLYORN (Life Baron), David Clive Wilson; cr. 1992. Born 14 February 1935;
Son of late Rev. William Skinner Wilson and late Enid Wilson; Married Natasha Alexander 1967
(2 sons).
Education: Trinity College, Glenalmond; Keble College, Oxford (Scholar, BA history 1958,
MA); London University (PhD modern Chinese history 1973); Chinese (Mandarin), French.
Non-political career: Army national service (Black Watch) 1953-55. Foreign Service 1958-68:
Served Vientiane, Laos 1959-60, Language student, Hong Kong 1960-62, First Secretary, Peking
Embassy 1963-65, FCO 1965-68; Editor, *China Quarterly* 1968-74; Visiting Scholar, Columbia
CROSSBENCH University, New York 1972; Rejoined Diplomatic Service 1974-92: Seconded to Cabinet Office
1974-77, Political adviser, Hong Kong 1977-81; FCO 1981-87: Head of Southern European
Department 1981-84, Assistant Under-Secretary of State 1984-87; Governor and Commander-in-
Chief, Hong Kong 1987-92; Chair, Scottish Hydro Electric plc (now Scottish and Southern Energy
plc) 1993-2000); Master, Peterhouse, Cambridge 2002-08.

Political career: *House of Lords:* Raised to the peerage as Baron Wilson of Tillyorn, of Finzean in the District of Kincardine and Deeside and of Fanling in Hong Kong 1992. Chair Revised Red Deer Act (Scotland) 1996; Co-opted member European Union Sub-committee B (Energy, Industry and Transport) 2000-02; Member EU Sub-committee B (Internal Market, Infrastructure and Employment) 2012-. *Councils and public bodies:* Member, Board of British Council 1993-2002; Chair, Scottish Committee of the British Council 1993-2002; Prime Minister's Advisory Committee on Public Appointments: Member 2000-09, Chair 2008-09.

Political interests: Scottish affairs, education; China (including Hong Kong SAR), East and South East Asia.

Other: Member: Oxford University Expedition to Somaliland 1957, British Mount Kongur Expedition (North West China) 1981; Council member, CBI Scotland 1993-2000; President: Bhutan Society of the UK 1993-2008, Hong Kong Society 1994-2012, Hong Kong Association 1994-; Glenalmond College: Council member 1994-2005, Chair 2000-05; Vice-President, Royal Scottish Geographical Society 1996-; Scottish Peers Association: Vice-chair 1998-2000, Chair 2000-02; Member, Royal Society for Asian Affairs; Royal Society of Edinburgh: Council member 2000-04, President 2008-11; Registrar, Order of Saint Michael and Saint George 2001-10; Chair, Advisory Council, St Paul's Cathedral 2009-; Member, Hopetoun House Preservation Trust 1993-98; Trustee, Scotland's Churches Scheme (later Scotland's Churches Trust) 1999-2002, 2009-; Museums of Scotland: Trustee 1999-2006, Chair 2002-06; Carnegie Trust for the Universities of Scotland 2000-; FRSE. Chancellor, Aberdeen University 1997-2013; Deputy vice-chancellor, Cambridge University 2005-08. Six honorary doctorates; Honorary Fellow: Keble College, Oxford 1987, Peterhouse, Cambridge 2008. CMG 1985; KCMG 1987; KStJ 1987; GCMG 1991; KT 2000; Alpine, New (Edinburgh); Royal Northern and University (Aberdeen).

Recreations: Mountaineering, reading, theatre.

The Lord Wilson of Tillyorn KT GCMG, House of Lords, London SW1A 0PW
Tel: 020 7219 3161 *Email:* wilsondc@parliament.uk

WINCHESTER, LORD BISHOP OF

WINCHESTER (97th Bishop of), Tim Dakin. Born 6 February 1958; Married Sally (1 son 1 daughter).

Education: University College of Saint Mark and St John, Plymouth; King's College, London; Christ Church, Oxford.

Non-political career: Principal, Carlile College, Kenya 1993-2000; Curate, Nairobi Cathedral 1993-2000; General secretary, Church Mission Society 2000-12; Honorary Canon Theologian, Coventry Cathedral 2001-; Bishop of Winchester 2012-.

NON-AFFILIATED **Political career:** *House of Lords:* Entered House of Lords 2012.

Countries of interest: Burundi, Democratic Republic of Congo, Kenya, Rwanda, Uganda.

Recreations: Reading, walking, films.

Rt Revd Bishop of Winchester, House of Lords, London SW1A 0PW
Tel: 020 7219 5353 *Email:* dakint@parliament.uk
Wolvesey, Winchester SO23 9ND *Tel:* 01962 854050 *Email:* bishop.tim@winchester.anglican.org
Website: www.cofewinchester.org.uk

WINSTON, LORD

WINSTON (Life Baron), Robert Maurice Lipson Winston; cr. 1995. Born 15 July 1940; Son of late Laurence Winston and Ruth Winston-Fox, MBE; Married Lira Helen Feigenbaum 1973 (2 sons 1 daughter).

Education: St Paul's School, London; London Hospital Medical College, London University (MB, BS 1964).

Non-political career: Wellcome research senior lecturer, Institute of Obstetrics and Gynaecology 1974-78; Other posts in UK, Belgium and USA; Consultant obstetrician and gynaecologist, Hammersmith Hospital 1978-2005; Past Dean, Institute of Obstetrics and Gynaecology, Royal Postgraduate Medical School (RPMS), London; Past Chair, British Fertility Society; Institute of Obstetrics and Gynaecology, PPMS, London University: Professor of Fertility Studies 1987-2005, Professor Emeritus 2005-; Professor of Science and Society, Imperial College, London 2008; Presenter: *Making Babies*, BBC TV 1995, *The Human Body*, BBC TV 1998, *Secret Life of Twins*, BBC TV 1999; *The Superhuman*, BBC TV 2000; *Child of our Time*, BBC TV 2000-05, *Human Instinct*, BBC TV 2002, *Threads of Life*, BBC TV 2002, *Human Mind*, BBC TV 2003, *Walking with Cavemen*, BBC TV 2003, *The Story of God* 2005; President, British Association for Advancement of Science 2005.

LABOUR

Political career: *House of Lords:* Raised to the peerage as Baron Winston, of Hammersmith in the London Borough of Hammersmith and Fulham 1995. Parliamentary Office of Science and Technology (POST): Member 1998-, Vice-chair 2006-. Science and Technology: Member 1996-2006, 2010-, Chair 1998-2001; Member: Innovation Exploitation Barrier 1997, Science and Technology Sub-committees: II (Cannabis) 1998, II (Antibiotic Resistance) 1999-2000, I (Non-food Crops) 1999, II (Science and Society) 1999-2000, II (Aircraft Cabin Environment) 2000-01, IIA (Human Genetic Databases) 2000-01; Chair Science and Technology Sub-committee I (Science in Schools) 2000-01; Member Science and Technology Sub-committees: II (Renewable Energy) 2003-04, II (Science and RDAs) 2003, II (Energy Efficiency) 2004-; Member Draft Human Tissue and Embryos Bill Joint Committee 2007; Co-opted member Science and Technology Sub-committee II (Genomic Medicine) 2008-09; Chair Science and Technology Sub-committee I 2012-13.

Political interests: Health, science and technology, education, arts.

Other: Chair, Council of Royal College of Music; Commissioner, UK Pavilion Expo 2001; Council member, Cancer Research UK -2007; Board member, Lyric Theatre, Hammersmith; Chair, Genesis Research Trust; Academy of Medical Sciences; Royal Academy of Engineering; Hon FREng; FRCOG 1983; FRCP; FRSA; FMedSci; FRCSE; FRCPS; Natural History Museum; Cheltenham Science Festival; Royal College of Music; Glyndebourne Opera; Royal Opera House. Chancellor, Sheffield Hallam University 2001-. Honorary Fellow, Queen Mary Westfield College; Twenty honorary doctorates. Cedric Carter Medal, Clinical Genetics Society 1993; Victor Bonney Triennial Prize, Royal College of Surgeons of England 1993; Gold Medal, Royal Society for Promotion of Health 1998; Michael Faraday Gold Medal, Royal Society 1999; Robert Menzies Medal 2001; Edwin Stevens Medal, Royal Society of Medicine 2003; Gold Medal, North of England Zoological Society 2004; Peer of the Year, *House Magazine* 2008; Athenæum; MCC; Garrick.

Publications: Reversibility of Sterilization (1978); Co-author Tubal Infertility (1981); Infertility, a Sympathetic Approach (1987); The IVF Revolution (1999); The Superhuman (2000); Human Instinct (2002); The Human Mind (2003); What Makes Me, Me (2004); The Story of God (2005); A Child Against All Odds (2006); Bad Ideas (2010) Over 300 papers in scientific journals on human and experimental reproduction.

Recreations: Theatre, broadcasting, music, wine.

Professor the Lord Winston, House of Lords, London SW1A 0PW
Tel: 020 7219 6020
11 Denman Drive, London NW11 6RE *Tel:* 020 8455 7475 *Email:* r.winston@imperial.ac.uk
Website: www.robertwinston.org *Twitter:* @ProfRWinston

WOLFSON OF ASPLEY GUISE, LORD

WOLFSON OF ASPLEY GUISE (Life Baron), Simon Adam Wolfson; cr 2010. Born 27 October 1967; Son of David Wolfson, now Lord Wolfson of Sunningdale (qv), and Susan Davis; Married Eleanor Shawcross, special adviser to George Osborne MP, 2012.

Education: Radley College; Trinity College, Cambridge (LLB 1989).

Non-political career: Next plc: Director 1997-, Managing director 1999-2001, Chief executive 2001-.

Political career: *House of Lords:* Raised to the peerage as Baron Wolfson of Aspley Guise, of Aspley Guise in the County of Bedfordshire 2010.

CONSERVATIVE   **Political interests:** Industry, economy.

Other: Trustee: Charles Wolfson Charitable Trust, Policy Exchange.

The Lord Wolfson of Aspley Guise, House of Lords, London SW1A 0PW
Tel: 020 7219 5353

WOLFSON OF SUNNINGDALE, LORD

WOLFSON OF SUNNINGDALE (Life Baron), David Wolfson; cr. 1991. Born 9 November 1935; Son of late Charles and Hylda Wolfson; Married Patricia Rawlings 1962 (later Baroness Rawlings) (divorced 1967); married Susan Davis 1967 (2 sons 1 daughter).

Education: Clifton College, Bristol; Trinity College, Cambridge (MA economics and law 1956); Stanford University, California, USA (MBA 1959).

Non-political career: Great Universal Stores: Director 1973-78, 1993-2000, Chair 1996-2000; Secretary to Shadow Cabinet 1978-79; Chief of Staff, Political Office, 10 Downing Street 1979-85; Chair: Alexon Group plc 1982-86, Next plc 1990-98, William Baird 2002-03; Fibernet: Non-executive director 2001-, Chair 2002-06; Non-executive director, Compco 1995-2003.

CONSERVATIVE   **Political career:** *House of Lords:* Raised to the peerage as Baron Wolfson of Sunningdale, of Trevose in the County of Cornwall 1991.

Political interests: Health.

Other: Chair: Charles Wolfson Charitable Trust, Benesco Charity Ltd; Honorary FRCR; Honorary FRCOG. Honorary Fellow, Hughes Hall, Cambridge 1989. Kt 1984; Portland. Sunningdale Golf, Woburn Golf, Trevose Golf.

Recreations: Golf, bridge.

The Lord Wolfson of Sunningdale, House of Lords, London SW1A 0PW
Tel: 020 7219 5353
c/o 8-10 Hallam Street, London W1W 6NS *Tel:* 020 7636 0604 *Email:* dwolfson01@gmail.com

LABOUR

WOOD OF ANFIELD, LORD

Shadow Minister without Portfolio, Cabinet Office

WOOD OF ANFIELD (Life Baron), Stewart Martin Wood; cr 2011. Born 25 March 1968; Son of Brian and Gisela Wood; Married Camilla Bustani 1998 (2 sons).

Education: Judd School, Tonbridge; University College, Oxford (BA philosophy, politics and economics); Harvard University (Fulbright Scholar, government department, PhD 1997); French, German.

Non-political career: Junior research fellow, St John's College, Oxford University 1996; Fellow in politics and lecturer, Magdalen College, Oxford University 1996-; Special adviser to Gordon Brown: as Chancellor of the Exchequer 2001-07, as Prime Minister 2007-10; Adviser to Ed Miliband as Leader of the Opposition 2010-. Community.

Political career: *House of Lords:* Raised to the peerage as Baron Wood of Anfield, of Tonbridge in the County of Kent 2011. Opposition Spokesperson for Cabinet Office 2011-12; Shadow Minister without Portfolio, Cabinet Office 2011-. *Other:* Ed Miliband Labour leadership campaign 2010; Member, Co-operative Party 2010-.

Political interests: Foreign policy, economic policy, sport, media and creative industries, Northern Ireland; China, EU, Germany, Russia, USA.

Other: Co-Founder and co-director, Nexus 1996-99; Member, National Film Theatre; Board member, English Stage Company, Royal Court Theatre, London 2008-; Patron, Camden Psychotherapy Unit; Board member, YouGov. Member, Liverpool Football Club.

Publications: Numerous articles and chapters on political economy, West European politics, education policy.

Recreations: Alt-country music, film and movie history, cricket, football.

Dr the Lord Wood of Anfield, House of Lords, London SW1A 0PW
Tel: 020 7219 7304 *Email:* stewart.wood@parliament.uk *Twitter:* @StewartWood

CROSSBENCH

WOOLF, LORD

WOOLF (Life Baron), Harry Kenneth Woolf; cr. 1992. Born 2 May 1933; Son of late Alexander and Leah Woolf; Married Marguerite Sassoon 1961 (3 sons).

Education: Fettes College, Edinburgh; University College, London (LLB 1954).

Non-political career: Commissioned (National Service) 15/19th Royal Hussars 1954; Seconded to Army Legal Services 1954; Captain 1955. Called to Bar, Inner Temple 1954, Bencher 1976; Started practice at Bar 1956; Recorder of the Crown Court 1972-79; Junior Counsel, Inland Revenue 1973-74; First Treasury Junior Counsel (Common Law) 1974-79; Judge of the High Court of Justice, Queen's Bench Division 1979-86; Presiding Judge, South Eastern Circuit 1981-84; Member: Senate, Inns of Court and Bar 1981-85, Board of Management, Institute of Advanced Legal Studies 1985-93; Chair, Lord Chancellor's Advisory Committee on Legal Education 1986-90; Lord Justice of Appeal 1986-92; Chair, Board of Management, Institute of Advanced Legal Studies 1986-93; Held inquiry into: Prison disturbances 1990, part II with Judge Tumim, report 1991, Access to Justice 1994-96 (interim report 1995, final report and rules 1996); Master of the Rolls 1996-2000; Chair, Advisory Committee on Public Records 1996; Visitor: University College, London 1996-2000, Nuffield College, Oxford 1996-2000; Lord Chief Justice of England and Wales 2000-05; Visitor, Downing College, Cambridge 2005-; Judge of final appeal, Hong Kong; President, Qatar Financial Services Court; Chair of Council, University College London 2005-07; Chair, Woolf Committee 2007-08; President of the Civil and Commercial Court of Qatar.

Political career: *House of Lords:* Raised to the peerage as Baron Woolf, of Barnes in the London Borough of Richmond 1992. Lord of Appeal in Ordinary 1992-2006. Chair Sub-committee on Lords' Interests 2006-08; Member: Constitution 2006-10, Privileges 2007-08, Inquiries Act 2005 2013-.

Other: President: Association of Law Teachers 1985-89, South West London Magistrates Association 1987-92, Central Council of Jewish Social Services 1989-99; Governor, Oxford Centre of Hebrew Studies (Emeritus) 1990-93; Butler Trust: Chair 1992-96, President 1996-; Trustee, St Mary's Hospital Special Trustees 1993-97; Mogen Dovid Adom 1995-; FBA. Honorary Liveryman, Drapers' Company. Pro Chancellor, London University 1994-2002; Chancellor, Open University of Israel 2005-. Fellow: University College, London 1981, British Academy 2000; Twelve honorary doctorates; Honorary Fellow: Leeds Municipal University, Academy of Medical Sciences 2002-. Kt 1979; PC 1986; Garrick, Royal Automobile.

Publications: Protection of the public: A New Challenge (Hamlyn lecture, 1990); Co-author: Zamir and Woolf: The Declaratory Judgement (2nd edition, 1993), De Smith, Woolf and Jowell (5th edition, 1995), Principles of Judicial Review; De Smith Administrative Law (6th edition, 2008); The Pursuit of Justice (Oxford University Press); Ethical Conduct in BAE Systems plc – The Way Forward.

Recreations: Theatre, music.

Rt Hon the Lord Woolf, House of Lords, London SW1A 0PW
Tel: 020 7219 1788/020 7219 3156 *Fax:* 020 7219 0785 *Email:* stevensonmm@parliament.uk

WOOLMER OF LEEDS, LORD

LABOUR

WOOLMER OF LEEDS (Life Baron), Kenneth John Woolmer; cr. 1999. Born 25 April 1940; Son of late Joseph Woolmer; Married Janice Chambers 1961 (3 sons).

Education: Kettering Grammar School; Leeds University (BA economics 1961).

Non-political career: Research Fellow, University of the West Indies 1961-62; Teacher, Friern Road Secondary Modern School, London 1963; Lecturer: Leeds University (economics) 1963-66, University of Ahmadu Bello, Nigeria 1966-68, Leeds University 1968-79; Principal, Halton Gill Associates 1979-96; Parliamentary adviser, Inland Revenue Staff Federation 1979-83; Leeds University Business School: Director of MBA Programmes 1991-97, Dean of External Relations 1997, Dean of Business School 1997-2000; Partner, Hilton Gill Associates 1998-2009; Non-executive director, Thornfield Developments Ltd 1999-2002; Partner, Anderson McGraw 2001-06; Non-executive director: Courtcom Ltd 2001-03, Thornfield Ventures Ltd 2002-04. Member, AUT.

Political career: *House of Commons:* MP (Labour) for Batley and Morley 1979-83. Contested Batley and Spen (Labour) 1983 and 1987 general elections. Frontbench Opposition Spokesperson for: Trade, Aviation, Shipping, Film Industry 1981-82, Prices and Consumer Protection 1982. *House of Lords:* Raised to the peerage as Baron Woolmer of Leeds, of Leeds in the County of West Yorkshire 1999. Chair Yorkshire and Humber Regional Peers Group 2002-09. EU Sub-committee B (Energy, Industry and Transport/Internal Market): Member 1999-2002, Chair 2002-06; Member: European Union 2002-06, Draft Climate Change Bill Joint Committee 2007; EU Sub-committee A (Economic and Financial Affairs and International Trade): Co-opted member 2007-10, Member 2010-12; Member Secondary Legislation Scrutiny 2013-. *Councils and public bodies:* Leeds County Borough Council: Councillor 1970-74, Deputy Leader 1972-74; Councillor, Leeds Metropolitan District Council 1973-78; West Yorkshire Metropolitan County Council: Councillor 1973-80, Deputy Leader 1973-75, Leader 1975-77, Leader of the Opposition 1977-79; Chair: Planning and Transportation Committee of Association of Metropolitan Authorities 1974-77, Regional Energy Forum, Yorkshire Forward 2001-04.

Political interests: Energy, financial markets; China, EU accession states, India, Japan.

Other: Fellow, Industry and Parliament Trust 1980; Director: Leeds United AFC 1991-96, UK Japan 21st Century Group 2005-10; International Advisory Board, White Rose East Asia Centre 2007-; Chair, Board of Governors, Leeds Metropolitan University 2010-; Warwick Business School Advisory Board 2012-. Leeds United AFC supporter, Yorkshire CCC supporter.

Recreations: Football, cricket.

The Lord Woolmer of Leeds, House of Lords, London SW1A 0PW
Tel: 020 7219 8520 *Email:* woolmerk@parliament.uk

WORCESTER, LORD BISHOP OF

WORCESTER (113th Bishop of), John Geoffrey Inge. Born 1955.

Education: Kent College, Canterbury; St Chads College, Durham (BSc chemistry); Keble College, Oxford (PGCE); College of the Resurrection, Mirfield, Yorkshire.

Non-political career: Chemistry teacher, Lancing College; Diocese of Chichester: Ordained deacon 1983, Ordained priest 1984; Chaplain: Lancing College, Harrow School; Vicar, St Luke's Church, Wallsend; Ely Cathedral: Residentiary Canon, Vice Dean 1999-2003; Bishop of Huntingdon 2003-08; Bishop of Worcester 2008-.

NON-AFFILIATED   **Political career:** *House of Lords:* Entered House of Lords 2012. *Councils and public bodies:* Lord High Almoner to HM The Queen 2013-.

Other: Member: World Development Movement, Amnesty International; Trustee, Common Purpose.

Publications: A Christian Theology of Place (Ashgate, 2003); Living Love: In Conversation with the No. 1 Ladies' Detective Agency (Inspire, 2007).

Rt Rev the Lord Bishop of Worcester, House of Lords, London SW1A 0PW
Tel: 020 7219 5353
The Old Palace, Deansway, Worcester WR1 2JE *Tel:* 01905 20537
Email: generalinfo@cofe-worcester.org.uk *Website:* www.cofe-worcester.org.uk

WORTHINGTON, BARONESS

Opposition Whip; Opposition Spokesperson for Energy and Climate Change

WORTHINGTON (Life Baroness) Bryony Katherine Worthington; cr 2011. Born 19 September 1971; Married Dr Srivas Chennu 2010 (1 son).

Education: Queens' College, Cambridge (BA English literature 1993).

Non-political career: Fundraiser, Operation Raleigh; Wildlife and Countryside Link; Campaigner, Friends of the Earth; Department of Energy and Climate Change (on secondment); Policy adviser, Scottish and Southern Electricity; Founder and director, Sandbag 2008-.

LABOUR   **Political career:** *House of Lords:* Raised to the peerage as Baroness Worthington, of Cambridge in the County of Cambridgeshire 2011. Opposition Whip 2012-; Opposition Spokesperson for Energy and Climate Change 2013-.

Political interests: Environment, climate change.

The Baroness Worthington, House of Lords, London SW1A 0PW
Tel: 020 7219 8987 *Email:* worthingtonb@parliament.uk *Twitter:* @bryworthington

WRIGGLESWORTH, LORD

WRIGGLESWORTH (Life Baron), Ian William Wrigglesworth; cr 2013. Born December 1939; Son of late Edward Wrigglesworth; Married Patricia Truscott 1967 (2 sons 1 daughter).

Education: Stockton Grammar School; Stockton-Billingham Technical College; College of St Mark and St John, Chelsea.

Non-political career: Personal assistant to Sir Ronald Gould as General Secretary of National Union of Teachers; Press and public affairs manager, National Giro; Divisional director, Smith's Industries 1976-2000; Deputy chair, John Livingston and Sons Ltd 1987-95; Director, CIT Holdings Ltd 1987-2003; Chair: Northern Business Forum, UK Land Estates 1995-2008, Government Policy Consultants Ltd 1998-2000; Director, Tyne Tees TV 2002-06; Chair: Newcastle-Gateshead Initiative 1999-2004, Baltic Centre for Contemporary Art 2004-09.

LIBERAL DEMOCRAT

Political career: *House of Commons:* MP for Teesside, Thornaby 1974-87 (Labour 1974-81, SDP 1981-87). PPS to: Alex Lyon as Minister of State, Home Office March-November 1974, Roy Jenkins as Home Secretary 1974-76; Opposition Spokesperson on the Civil Service 1979-80; Social Democrats Spokesperson on Economic Affairs and Taxation, Trade and Industry, Energy, Small Businesses and Consumer Affairs. *House of Lords:* Raised to the peerage as Baron Wrigglesworth, of Norton on Tees in the County of Durham 2013. *Other:* Research officer, Co-operative Party; Member, Labour Party -1981; Founder member, Social Democrats 1981; Liberal Democrats: President 1988-90, Treasurer 2012-. *Councils and public bodies:* DL, Tyne and Wear 2005.

Other: Kt 1991.

The Lord Wrigglesworth Kt DL, House of Lords, London SW1A 0PW
Tel: 020 7219 5353

CROSSBENCH

WRIGHT OF RICHMOND, LORD

WRIGHT OF RICHMOND (Life Baron), Patrick Richard Henry Wright; cr. 1994. Born 28 June 1931; Son of late Herbert and Rachel Wright; Married Virginia Gaffney 1958 (2 sons 1 daughter). **Education:** Marlborough College, Wiltshire; Merton College, Oxford (BA literae humaniores 1955); Arabic, French.

Non-political career: Army national service (Royal Artillery) 1950-51. Diplomatic Service 1955-91: Middle East Centre for Arab Studies 1956-57; Third Secretary, Beirut Embassy 1958-60; Private Secretary and later First Secretary, Washington DC Embassy 1960-65; Private Secretary to Permanent Under-Secretary, Foreign Office 1965-67; First Secretary and Head of Chancery, Cairo Embassy 1967-70; Deputy Political Resident, Bahrain 1971-72; Head of Middle East Department, FCO 1972-74; Private Secretary (Overseas Affairs) to Prime Ministers Harold Wilson and James Callaghan 1974-77; Ambassador to: Luxembourg 1977-79, Syria 1979-81; Deputy Under-Secretary of State, FCO and chair, Joint Intelligence Committee 1982-84; Ambassador to Saudi Arabia 1984-86; Permanent Under-Secretary of State and Head of the Diplomatic Service 1986-91; Director: Barclays Bank plc 1991-96, British Petroleum Co. (now BP plc) 1991-2001, De La Rue: Director 1991-2000, Consultant 2001-10; Advisory director, Unilever 1991-99; Director, BAA 1992-98; Member, Security Commission 1993-2002.

Political career: *House of Lords:* Raised to the peerage as Baron Wright of Richmond, of Richmond upon Thames in the London Borough of Richmond upon Thames 1994. Member: EU Sub-committee F (Home Affairs) 2001-07 (Chair 2004-07), Science and Technology Sub-committee I (Science and International Agreements) 2003-04, European Union 2004-08, Conventions Joint Committee 2006, EU Sub-committee E (Law and Institutions) 2007-08, Co-opted member 2008-10; Member EU Sub-committee E (Justice and Institutions) 2010-11.

Political interests: Foreign affairs (particularly Middle East), public service; Middle East and Islamic world.

Other: Governor: Ditchley Foundation 1986-2011, Wellington College 1991-2001; OStJ: Registrar 1991-95, Director of Overseas Relations 1995-97; Royal College of Music: Council member 1991-2001, Fellow 1994-; Council member, Atlantic College 1993-2000; Chair, Council of Royal Institute of International Affairs 1995-99; Home-Start International: Chairman 2004-07, Honorary President 2008-11; Governor, Edward VII Hospital (Sister Agnes) 2005-07; Fellow, Wellington College 2009; St John Hospital; Medical Aid for Palestinians. Honorary Fellow, Merton College, Oxford 1987. Parliamentary Speech of the Year, *House Magazine* 2004. CMG 1978; KCMG 1984; GCMG 1989; KStJ 1990; Oxford and Cambridge.

Recreations: Piano duets, philately.

The Lord Wright of Richmond GCMG, House of Lords, London SW1A 0PW
Tel: 020 7219 5353 *Email:* prhwright@btinternet.com

NON-AFFILIATED

YORK, LORD ARCHBISHOP OF

YORK (97th Archbishop of), John Mugabi Tucker Sentamu. Born 10 June 1949; Son of late John and Ruth Walakira; Married Margaret Wanambwa 1973.

Education: Kitante and Old Kampala Secondary Schools, Uganda; Makerere University, Uganda (LLB 1971); Diploma in legal practice, Uganda 1972; Selwyn College, Cambridge (BA 1976; PhD 1984); Ridley Hall, Cambridge.

Non-political career: Advocate, High Court of Uganda 1971-; Ordained 1979; Assistant chaplain, Selwyn College, Cambridge 1979; Chaplain, HM Remand Centre, Latchmere House 1979-82; Assistant curate: St Andrew, Ham 1979-82, St Paul, Herne Hill, London 1982-83; Holy Trinity and St Mathias, Tulse Hill London: Respectively priest and vicar 1983-84; Vicar 1985-96; Member, General Synod 1985-96, 2002-; Priest, St Saviour, Brixton Hill, London 1987-89; Honorary Canon, Southwark Cathedral 1993-96; Stepney Area Bishop, London 1996-2002; Bishop of Birmingham 2002-05; Archbishop of York 2005-; Honorary Master Bencher, Gray's Inn.

Political career: *House of Lords:* Entered House of Lords 2005.

Political interests: Legal, community, young people, faith; The continent of Africa.

Other: President: YMCA England, Youth for Christ; Chair, Sickle Cell and Thalassaemia Screening Programme 2001-; Sponsor, York Fairness Commission; Fellow, Royal Society of Arts. Freeman: City of London 2000, Montego Bay, Jamaica 2007. Chancellor: York St John University 2006-, Cumbria University 2007-. 18 honorary doctorates from UK, Canada, Caribbean and US universities; Fellow: University College Christ Church, Canterbury 2001, Queen Mary College, University of London 2001; Honorary fellow, Selwyn College, Cambridge 2005. Midlander of the Year 2003; Yorkshire Man of the Year 2007; Speaker of the Year 2007; York Ambassador, York Tourism Awards 2010. PC 2005.

Recreations: Cooking, music, rugby, football, athletics.
Most Rev and Rt Hon the Archbishop of York, House of Lords, London SW1A 0PW
Tel: 020 7219 5353
Bishopthorpe Palace, Bishopthorpe, York YO23 2GE *Tel:* 01904 707021 *Fax:* 01904 772389
Email: office@archbishopofyork.org *Website:* www.archbishopofyork.org
Twitter: @JohnSentamu

YOUNG OF GRAFFHAM, LORD

CONSERVATIVE

YOUNG OF GRAFFHAM (Life Baron), David Ivor Young; cr. 1984. Born 27 February 1932; Son
of late Joseph Young; Married Lita Marianne Shaw 1956 (2 daughters).
Education: Christ's College, Finchley; University College, London (LLB 1954).
Non-political career: Solicitor 1956; Executive, Great Universal Stores 1956-61; Chair: Eldon-
wall Ltd 1961-75, Manufacturers Hanover Property Services Ltd 1974-84; Industrial adviser/spe-
cial adviser, Department of Industry 1979-82; Chair, Manpower Services Commission 1982-84;
Fellow, University College London 1988; Executive Chair, Cable and Wireless plc 1990-95;
Director, Salomon Inc 1990-94; Chair of several companies, including: Young Associates Ltd
1996-, Pixology Ltd 1997-, Newhaven Management Services 1997-, Spectrum Interactive plc,
TSSI Ltd, Camcon Ltd; Director: Deeptek Ltd, Kashflow Software Ltd.
Political career: *House of Lords:* Raised to the peerage as Baron Young of Graffham, of Graffham
in the County of West Sussex 1984. Cabinet Minister without Portfolio 1984-85; Secretary of State
for: Employment 1985-87, Trade and Industry 1987-89; Adviser to the Prime Minister on: Health
and Safety Law and Practice 2010, Enterprise 2010, 2011-. Member: Science and Technology
2003-06, Science and Technology Sub-committees: II (Science and the Regional Development
Agencies) 2003, II (Renewable Energy) 2003-04, II (Energy Efficiency) 2004-. *Other:* Deputy
chair, Conservative Party 1989-90. *Councils and public bodies:* DL, West Sussex 1999-.
Other: Chair, West Sussex Economic Forum 1993-2001; President, Institute of Directors 1993-
2004; Chair of Council, University College, London 1995-2005; Chair, Chichester Festival Theatre
Ltd 1997-; The Prince's Trust: Chair, Development Board 2003-07, Trustees council member
2004-07; Chair and trustee, The Peter Cruddas Foundation 2006-; Trustee, MBI AL Jaber Founda-
tion 2007-; President and trustee, Chai Cancer Care 2007-. Honorary Doctorate of Science, Cran-
field University 1986; Doctor of Laws, Honoris Causa, University College London 2006. PC 1984.
Publications: The Enterprise Years (1990).
Recreations: Photography, music, book collecting, fishing.
Rt Hon the Lord Young of Graffham DL, House of Lords, London SW1A 0PW
Tel: 020 7219 5353 *Twitter:* @TheLordYoung

YOUNG OF HORNSEY, BARONESS

CROSSBENCH

YOUNG OF HORNSEY (Life Baroness), Margaret Omolola (Lola) Young; cr. 2004. Born 1 June
1951; Daughter of Maxwell Fela Young and Yele Santos; Married Barrie Birch 1984 (1 son).
Education: Parliament Hill School for Girls, London; New College of Speech and Drama
(Diploma dramatic art 1975; Teaching Certificate 1976); Middlesex Polytechnic/University (BA
contemporary cultural studies 1988; PhD British film 1995).
Non-political career: Residential social worker, London Borough of Islington 1971-73; Professional actor 1976-84; Co-director and training and development manager, Haringey Arts Council
1985-89; Freelance lecturer and arts consultant 1989-1991; Lecturer in media studies, Polytechnic
of West London/Thames Valley University 1990-92; Middlesex University 1992-2001: Lecturer,
Senior lecturer, Principal lecturer, Professor of cultural studies, Emeritus professor; Project director, Archives and Museum of Black Heritage 1997-2001; Head of culture, Greater London Authority 2002-04; Visiting professor, Birkbeck College, London; Founder, Cultural Brokers Arts and
Heritage Consultancy 2004-.
Political career: *House of Lords:* Raised to the peerage as Baroness Young of Hornsey, of Horn-
sey in the London Borough of Haringey 2004. Co-opted member EU Sub-committee G (Social
Policy and Consumer Affairs) 2007-10; Chair EU Sub-committee G (Social Policies and Con-
sumer Protection) 2010-12; Member: European Union 2010-, Joint Committee on the Draft House
of Lords Reform Bill 2011-12, EU Sub-committee C (External Affairs) 2012-.
Political interests: Arts and culture, children and young people in care, mental health, equalities,
London, North and South West England; Commonwealth, Sub-saharan Africa, USA.
Other: Commissioner, Royal Commission on Historical Manuscripts 2000-01; Board member:
National Theatre 2000-03, South Bank Centre 2002-08; Chair: Arts Advisory Committee British
Council 2004-08, Nitro Theatre Company 2004-09; Patron, Post-adoption Centre 2004-; Council

member, RSA 2005-08; Patron, Josephine Wolf Trust, 2007-; Chair, Commonwealth group on Culture and Development 2008-12; Commissioner, English Heritage 2011-; FRSA 2000. Freeman, Tallow Chandlers Company. OBE 2001; The Hospital Club; RSA.

Publications: Numerous newspaper articles and radio and television broadcasts; Fear of the Dark: 'Race', Gender and Sexuality in Cinema (Routledge, 1996).

Recreations: Walking, cinema, theatre, visual arts, gardening, reading.

Professor the Baroness Young of Hornsey OBE, House of Lords, London SW1A 0PW
Tel: 020 7219 5991 *Email:* younglo@parliament.uk
Email: lola.young@culturalbrokers.co.uk *Website:* lordsoftheblog.net/category/baroness-young
Twitter: @LolaHornsey

YOUNG OF NORWOOD GREEN, LORD

Opposition Spokesperson for Business, Innovation and Skills

YOUNG OF NORWOOD GREEN (Life Baron), Anthony Ian Young; cr. 2004. Born 16 April 1942; Son of late Henry and Sheila Young; Married Doreen Goodman (divorced 1984) (1 son 2 daughters); married Margaret Newnham 1985 (1 son 1 daughter).

Education: Harrow County Grammar School.

Non-political career: GPO (General Post Office) telecommunications apprentice 1958; Post Office Engineering Union: Union branch officer 1967, Member, National Executive Committee 1989-95; General secretary, National Communications Union 1989-95; Communication Workers' Union: Joint General secretary 1995-98, Senior deputy general secretary 1998-2002; Trades Union Council: Member, General Council 1989-2002, President 2001-02;. Communication Workers Union (CWU).

LABOUR

Political career: *House of Lords:* Raised to the peerage as Baron Young of Norwood Green, of Norwood Green in the London Borough of Ealing 2004. Parliamentary Under-Secretary of State (Skills and Apprenticeships 2008-09; Postal Affairs and Employment Relations 2009-10) and Government Spokesperson, Department for Innovation, Universities and Skills/Business, Innovation and Skills 2008-10; Government Whip 2008-10; Opposition Spokesperson for Business, Innovation and Skills 2010-. Co-opted member European Union Sub-committee F (Home Affairs) 2007-08; Member Crossrail Bill 2008. *Councils and public bodies:* Member: Wilton Park Academic Council 1996-2005, Employment Tribunal Steering Board 1997-2003; Governor, BBC 1998-2002; Vice-chair, Ethical Trading Initiative; Chair, One World Broadcasting Trust 2002-09; Member, Armed Forces Pay Review Board -2008; School Governor, Three Bridges Primary School.

Countries of interest: China, Italy, USA.

Other: Kt 2002.

Recreations: Cycling, tennis, table tennis, reading, gardening.

The Lord Young of Norwood Green, House of Lords, London SW1A 0PW
Tel: 020 7219 3176 *Email:* younga@parliament.uk

YOUNG OF OLD SCONE, BARONESS

YOUNG OF OLD SCONE (Life Baroness), Barbara Scott Young; cr. 1997. Born 8 April 1948; Daughter of late George Young and late Mary Young.

Education: Perth Academy; Edinburgh University (MA classics 1970); Strathclyde University (DipSocSci 1971); DipHSM 1974.

Non-political career: Sector administrator, Glasgow Health Board 1973-78; Director of planning and development, St Thomas' Health District, London 1978-79; District general administrator, Kensington and Chelsea and Westminster Area Health Authority 1979-82; District administrator, Haringey Health Authority (HA), London 1982-85; District general manager: Paddington and North Kensington HA 1985-88, Parkside HA 1988-91; Chief executive, Royal Society for the Protection of Birds 1991-98; Chair, English Nature 1998-2000; Vice-chair, BBC 1998-2000; Non-executive director, Anglian Water 1998-2000; Chief executive, Environment Agency 2000-08; Chair, Care Quality Commission 2008-09; Chief executive, Diabetes UK 2010-.

NON-AFFILIATED

Political career: *House of Lords:* Raised to the peerage as Baroness Young of Old Scone, of Old Scone in Perth and Kinross 1997. *Councils and public bodies:* Member: BBC General Advisory Council 1985-88, Committee, Secretary of State for the Environment's Going for Green Initiative 1994-96, UK Round Table on Sustainability 1995-2000, Commission on the Future of the Voluntary Sector 1995-97, Committee on the Public Understanding of Science 1996-97; Commissioner, Commission on Assisted Dying 2010-.

Political interests: Environment, broadcasting, health and social care, equality and rights.

Other: President, Institute of Health Services Management 1987-88; Patron, Institute of Ecological and Environment Management 1993-; Trustee, National Council for Voluntary Organisations 1994-98; Vice-President: Flora and Fauna International 1998-, World Council, Birdlife International 1999-, Plantlife 2000-, RSPB 2000-; Trustee, Institute for Public Policy Research 2000-09; President: Beds, Cambs, Northants and Peterborough Wildlife Trust 2001-, British Trust of Ornithology 2004-, South Georgia Heritage Trust; Honorary member, RICS; Honorary fellow: Geologists Association, Linnean Society; Eminent fellow, IAgrE; CIWEM Chartered Environmentalist; CIWM; RSPB, Action Aid, Plantlife, Dignity in Dying, Diabetes UK, Birdlife International, South Georgia Heritage Trust. Chancellor, Cranfield University. Fifteen honorary doctorates; Honorary Fellow Sydney Sussex College.

Recreations: Cinema, gardening, dressage.

The Baroness Young of Old Scone, House of Lords, London SW1A 0PW
Tel: 020 7219 1000 *Email:* youngb@parliament.uk *Twitter:* @youngb48

YOUNGER OF LECKIE, VISCOUNT

CONSERVATIVE

Parliamentary Under-Secretary of State and Government Spokesperson, Department for Business, Innovation and Skills

YOUNGER OF LECKIE (5th Viscount, UK), James Edward George Younger; cr. 1923; 5th Bt of Leckie (UK) 1911. Born 11 November 1955; Son of 4th Viscount and Diana Tuck; Married Jennie Wootton 1988 (1 son 2 daughters).

Education: Cargilfield School, Edinburgh; Winchester College; St Andrews University (MA Hons medieval history 1979); Henley Management College (MBA 1993).

Non-political career: Personnel manager, Coats Patons 1979-84; Recruitment consultant, Angela Mortimer Ltd 1984-86; Executive search consultant, Stephens Consultancies 1986-92; Director, McInnes Younger 1992-94; Human Resources director, UBS Wealth Management 1994-2004; Director, Culliford Edmunds Associates 2004-07; Consultant, Eban Ltd 2007-10.

Political career: *House of Lords:* Elected Hereditary peer 2010-; Party Whip 2010-12; Government Whip 2012-13; Government Spokesperson for: Culture, Olympics, Media and Sport/Culture, Media and Sport 2012-13, Scotland 2012-13, Attorney General's Office 2012, Advocate General for Scotland 2012, Law Officers 2012-13, Transport 2012-13; Parliamentary Under-Secretary of State and Government Spokesperson, Department for Business, Innovation and Skills 2013-. Member Public Service and Demographic Change 2012. *Other:* Chair, Buckingham Conservative Constituency Association 2006-10; Member, Association of Conservative Peers 2006-; Elected member, area board, Oxfordshire and Buckinghamshire Conservatives 2009-; Chair, Milton Keynes Conservative Association 2010-13.

Political interests: Big Society, tourism, War Widows Association, localism, sports in schools, diversity and corporate responsibility, human resources, employment law, intergenerational; Scotland.

Other: Member, Queen's Bodyguard for Scotland; Highland Society of London: Director 2005-12, President 2012-; Member, Parliamentary Choir; President of Life Members, The Kate Kennedy Club; Vice-President, War Widows Association; Member: Chartered Institute of Marketing, Association of MBAs; Trustee, Mrs W Wootton Trust; Pace, Aylesbury; Garsington Opera; Kate Kennedy Club; Aylesbury Museum. White Hunter Cricket Club.

Recreations: Sailing, cricket, running, tennis, DIY, highland dancing, country pursuits.

The Viscount Younger of Leckie, House of Lords, London SW1A 0PW
Tel: 020 7219 5353 *Email:* youngerj@parliament.uk

ANALYSIS OF PEERS

Committees and Offices

Peers' Political Interests

For precise details of individuals' stated interests, see relevant biography. The interests listed are supplied by Peers themselves.

Animals
See also:
Animal rights and welfare

Business and finance
See also:
Business, banking and finance
Capital and financial markets
Corporate governance
Economy
Enterprise
Euro and EMU
European Union economy
Exports
Financial services
Financial services regulation
Food industry
Globalisation
Investment
Manufacturing
Pensions
PFI/PPP
Property investments
Public finance
Retail industry
Small businesses
Steel industry
Tax
Textile industry
Trade and industry
Venture capital

Communities, planning and local government
See also:
Built environment
Community cohesion
Conservation areas
Construction industry
Housing
Local government
Local government finance
London
North West
Planning
Regeneration
Rural communities
Urban renewal
West Midlands

Culture, recreation and sport
See also:
Architecture
Cricket
Culture and creativity

Cycling
Design
Films and film-making
Heritage
Historic buildings
Horse racing
Museums and galleries
Music
Olympics 2012
Performing arts
Theatre
Tourism
Visual arts

Defence and security
See also:
British armed forces
Defence procurement
Royal Navy
Terrorism

Education and skills
See also:
Adoption
Child care
Children's rights
Further and higher education
Medical schools
School sports
Skills and competences
Special educational needs
Universities
Youth affairs

Employment and welfare
See also:
Apprenticeships
Benefits
Employment rights
Equality
Equal pay
Health and safety at work
Pay
Trade unions
Unemployment and jobseeking

Energy and Utilities
See also:
Climate change
Coal
Environmental impact of energy
Renewables

Environment, food and rural affairs
See also:
   Agriculture
   Countryside recreation
   Fisheries
   Forestry in the UK
   Rural environment

Government, politics and public administration
See also:
   Constitution
   Constitutional reform
   Democracy and elections
   Devolved government
   Electoral reform
   Labour Party
   Machinery of government
   National security
   Northern Ireland
   Policy-making
   Political parties
   Public services
   Reform of public services
   Regional policy
   Regulatory Reform
   Scotland
   Wales
   Women's issues

Healthcare and pharmaceuticals
See also:
   Addiction
   AIDS and HIV
   Alcohol abuse
   Autism
   Breast cancer
   Cancer
   Care for the elderly
   Complementary medicine
   Disabilities
   Dyslexia
   Family planning services
   Healthcare
   Learning disabilities
   Medical ethics
   Mental health
   National Health Service (NHS)
   NHS finances
   Nursing
   Palliative care
   Public health
   Smoking and health
   Social care
   Telehealth
   Women's health

Home affairs
See also:
   Asylum
   Charities and volunteers
   Charity law
   Child protection
   Children and families
   Citizenship
   Consumer rights
   Crime
   Crime and punishment
   Crime prevention
   Immigration, migration and nationality
   Islam
   Judaism
   Justice system
   Legal aid
   Legal services
   Magistrates courts
   Migrant workers
   Police
   Prisons
   Probation
   Race relations
   Refugees and asylum seekers
   Religion
   Young offenders
   Youth justice

Information and communications
See also:
   Copyright
   Freedom of information
   Information and communication technology
   Intellectual property
   Internet
   Media
   Post Office
   Television

International affairs
See also:
   Africa
   Common Agricultural Policy
   Commonwealth
   Europe
   European affairs
   European enlargement
   European Union
   Foreign policy
   Human rights
   Humanitarian aid
   International development and aid
   Middle East
   Poverty
   Sexual health
   Transatlantic relations
   United Nations

Lord Rooker	*Lab*	p917
Lord Selsdon	*Con*	p931
Lord Shipley	*Lib Dem*	p938
Lord Stoneham of Droxford	*Lib Dem*	p958
Baroness Warsi	*Con*	p996
Lord Wright of Richmond	*CB*	p1015
Archbishop of York	*Non-Affiliated*	p1015
Viscount Younger of Leckie	*Con*	p1018

Community cohesion

Baroness Hussein-Ece	*Lib Dem*	p776

Complementary medicine

Earl Baldwin of Bewdley	*CB*	p616
Lord Colwyn	*Con*	p670
Baroness Corston	*Lab*	p673

Conservation areas

Lord Eatwell	*Lab*	p697
Lord Faulks	*Con*	p708
Lord Gardiner of Kimble	*Con*	p722
Lord Marlesford	*Con*	p842
Lord Moran	*CB*	p855
Baroness Nicol	*Lab/Co-op*	p869
Lord Renton of Mount Harry	*Con*	p908
Lord Roberts of Conwy	*Con*	p913
Earl of Selborne	*Con*	p930
Lord Selkirk of Douglas	*Con*	p930
Lord Walpole	*CB*	p993

Constitution

Lord Armstrong of Ilminster	*CB*	p608
Lord Bannside	*DUP*	p617
Lord Birt	*CB*	p628
Baroness Boothroyd	*CB*	p633
Lord Boyd of Duncansby	*Non-Affiliated*	p637
Lord Brittan of Spennithorne	*Con*	p643
Lord Brown of Eaton-under-Heywood	*CB*	p647
Lord Browne of Ladyton	*Lab*	p647
Lord Butler of Brockwell	*CB*	p651
Lord Carswell	*CB*	p658
Lord Elis-Thomas	*PlC*	p700
Baroness Falkner of Margravine	*Lib Dem*	p707
Lord Faulks	*Con*	p708
Lord Forsyth of Drumlean	*Con*	p716
Lord German	*Lib Dem*	p724
Lord Gordon of Strathblane	*Lab*	p731
Baroness Gould of Potternewton	*Lab*	p732
Lord Hanningfield	*Non-Affiliated*	p746
Lord Hardie	*CB*	p747
Lord Hart of Chilton	*Lab*	p750
Lord Hollick	*Lab*	p761
Lord Howe of Aberavon	*Con*	p768

Lord Hunt of Kings Heath	*Lab*	p774
Lord Hurd of Westwell	*Con*	p775
Lord Inglewood	*Con*	p779
Lord Irvine of Lairg	*Lab*	p779
Lord Janvrin	*CB*	p782
Lord Lea of Crondall	*Lab*	p807
Bishop of Leicester	*Non-Affiliated*	p808
Lord Lexden	*Con*	p812
Lord Luce	*CB*	p823
Lord Marks of Henley-on-Thames	*Lib Dem*	p841
Lord Mayhew of Twysden	*Con*	p847
Lord Molyneaux of Killead	*CB*	p851
Lord Norton of Louth	*Con*	p872
Lord Rooker	*Lab*	p917
Lord Rowlands	*Lab*	p920
Marquess of Salisbury	*Non-Affiliated*	p924
Lord Sewel	*Non-Affiliated*	p931
Baroness Shephard of Northwold	*Con*	p936
Lord Temple-Morris	*Lab*	p967
Lord True	*Con*	p978
Lord Wallace of Saltaire	*Lib Dem*	p992
Baroness Warnock	*CB*	p995

Constitutional reform

Baroness Clark of Calton	*Non-Affiliated*	p664
Bishop of Gloucester	*Non-Affiliated*	p728
Lord Goodhart	*Lib Dem*	p730
Lord Grenfell	*Lab*	p738
Baroness Jones of Whitchurch	*Lab*	p787
Lord Lester of Herne Hill	*Lib Dem*	p809
Lord Maclennan of Rogart	*Lib Dem*	p834
Lord Morgan	*Lab*	p855
Lord Norton of Louth	*Con*	p872
Baroness O'Neill of Bengarve	*CB*	p876
Lord Smith of Clifton	*Lib Dem*	p944
Baroness Stowell of Beeston	*Con*	p958
Lord Tyler	*Lib Dem*	p982
Lord Wakeham	*Con*	p989
Lord Wallace of Tankerness	*Lib Dem*	p992

Construction industry

Baroness Chalker of Wallasey	*Con*	p661
Lord Feldman	*Con*	p709
Lord Howie of Troon	*Lab*	p771
Lord Selsdon	*Con*	p931
Earl of Shrewsbury and Waterford	*Con*	p938

Consumer rights

Lord Deben	*Con*	p686
Lord Graham of Edmonton	*Lab/Co-op*	p734
Lord Harris of Haringey	*Lab*	p748

Education and skills

Electoral reform

Lord Lipsey	Lab	p816

Employment and welfare

Baroness Anelay of St Johns	Con	p606
Lord Bach	Lab	p614
Baroness Barker	Lib Dem	p618
Lord Beecham	Lab	p620
Lord Best	CB	p623
Lord Bichard	CB	p625
Lord Bilston	Lab/Co-op	p627
Baroness Blackstone	Lab	p629
Viscount Bridgeman	Con	p640
Lord Briggs	CB	p641
Lord Brooke of Alverthorpe	Lab	p644
Baroness Campbell of Surbiton	CB	p654
Earl of Clancarty	CB	p664
Baroness Coussins	CB	p674
Lord Curry of Kirkharle	CB	p681
Lord Davies of Abersoch	Lab	p683
Lord Davies of Oldham	Lab	p684
Lord Davies of Stamford	Lab	p685
Lord Dixon	Lab	p691
Lord Eames	CB	p696
Baroness Emerton	CB	p702
Lord Evans of Parkside	Lab	p704
Lord Giddens	Lab	p725
Lord Griffiths of Fforestfach	Con	p740
Lord Higgins	Con	p758
Lord Howarth of Newport	Lab	p767
Lord Hoyle	Lab	p771
Lord Hutton of Furness	Lab	p777
Lord Kirkwood of Kirkhope	Lib Dem	p799
Baroness Knight of Collingtree	Con	p800
Lord Layard	Lab	p806
Lord Lea of Crondall	Lab	p807
Lord Levy	Lab	p811
Lord Lipsey	Lab	p816
Baroness Lister of Burtersett	Lab	p817
Earl of Listowel	CB	p817
Lord McAvoy	Lab/Co-op	p825
Countess of Mar	CB	p840
Earl of Mar and Kellie	Scottish Lib Dem	p841
Lord Moran	CB	p855
Lord Moser	CB	p860
Lord Pendry	Lab	p888
Baroness Prosser	Lab	p897
Bishop of Ripon and Leeds	Non-Affiliated	p911
Lord Roberts of Conwy	Con	p913
Lord Rosser	Lab	p918
Baroness Royall of Blaisdon	Lab	p920
Lord Sawyer	Lab	p927
Baroness Smith of Basildon	Lab/Co-op	p943
Lord Smith of Finsbury	Non-Affiliated	p944
Lord Touhig	Lab/Co-op	p974
Baroness Turner of Camden	Lab	p982
Baroness Valentine	CB	p985
Lord Watson of Invergowrie	Lab	p997
Lord Whitty	Lab	p1002
Viscount Younger of Leckie	Con	p1018

Employment rights

Lord Brookman	Lab	p645
Lord Janner of Braunstone	Lab	p781
Viscount Younger of Leckie	Con	p1018

Energy and utilities

Lord Birt	CB	p628
Lord Black of Brentwood	Con	p628
Lord Broers	CB	p643
Lord Browne of Madingley	CB	p648
Earl Cathcart	Con	p659
Lord Cunningham of Felling	Non-Affiliated	p680
Lord Deben	Con	p686
Lord Evans of Parkside	Lab	p704
Baroness Ford	Non-Affiliated	p715
Lord Foulkes of Cumnock	Lab/Co-op	p717
Baroness Gardner of Parkes	Con	p722
Lord Geddes	Con	p724
Viscount Hanworth	Lab	p746
Lord Hardie	CB	p747
Lord Haworth	Lab	p753
Baroness Hooper	Con	p764
Lord Howell of Guildford	Con	p770
Lord Jay of Ewelme	CB	p782
Lord Jenkin of Roding	Con	p784
Lord Laird	Non-Affiliated	p803
Lord Lea of Crondall	Lab	p807
Earl of Lindsay	Con	p814
Earl of Mar and Kellie	Scottish Lib Dem	p841
Lord May of Oxford	CB	p846
Lord Naseby	Con	p862
Baroness Nicol	Lab/Co-op	p869
Baroness O'Cathain	Con	p874
Lord Oxburgh	CB	p879
Lord Parkinson	Con	p883
Lord Rees of Ludlow	CB	p905
Lord Rooker	Lab	p917
Lord Rowlands	Lab	p920
Lord Skelmersdale	Con	p941
Lord Stoddart of Swindon	Ind Lab	p957
Lord Taylor of Blackburn	Lab	p963
Lord Taylor of Holbeach	Con	p964
Lord Truscott	Non-Affiliated	p979
Lord Turnbull	CB	p981
Lord Wakeham	Con	p989
Lord Whitty	Lab	p1002
Lord Woolmer of Leeds	Lab	p1013

Engineering

Earl Attlee	*Con*	p613
Lord Tombs	*CB*	p971

Enterprise

Lord Bates	*Con*	p620
Lord Mawson	*CB*	p846

Environment, food and rural affairs

Lord Barber of Tewkesbury	*CB*	p618
Baroness Byford	*Con*	p652
Lord Eatwell	*Lab*	p697
Lord Flight	*Con*	p714
Baroness Jones of Whitchurch	*Lab*	p787
Lord Krebs	*CB*	p802
Countess of Mar	*CB*	p840
Baroness Masham of Ilton	*CB*	p843
Baroness Miller of Chilthorne Domer	*Lib Dem*	p849
Lord Moran	*CB*	p855
Baroness Noakes	*Con*	p869
Lord Northbourne	*CB*	p871
Baroness Parminter	*Lib Dem*	p884
Lord Plumb	*Con*	p893
Lord Rana	*CB*	p902
Lord Rea	*Lab*	p904
Lord Skelmersdale	*Con*	p941
Lord Wallace of Tankerness	*Lib Dem*	p992
Lord Whitty	*Lab*	p1002
Baroness Wilcox	*Con*	p1003

Environmental impact of energy

Lord Wallace of Tankerness	*Lib Dem*	p992

Environmental issues

Lord Alton of Liverpool	*CB*	p604
Baroness Armstrong of Hill Top	*Lab*	p608
Earl Baldwin of Bewdley	*CB*	p616
Lord Barber of Tewkesbury	*CB*	p618
Lord Bassam of Brighton	*Lab/Co-op*	p619
Lord Beecham	*Lab*	p620
Lord Berkeley	*Lab*	p622
Lord Boateng	*Lab*	p632
Lord Bradshaw	*Lib Dem*	p639
Viscount Bridgeman	*Con*	p640
Lord Browne of Madingley	*CB*	p648
Lord Cameron of Dillington	*CB*	p653
Earl Cathcart	*Con*	p659
Lord Cavendish of Furness	*Con*	p659
Lord Chorley	*CB*	p663
Lord Clinton-Davis	*Lab*	p667
Lord Coe	*Con*	p668
Earl of Courtown	*Con*	p674
Lord Crickhowell	*Con*	p678
Lord Cunningham of Felling	*Non-Affiliated*	p680
Lord Deben	*Con*	p686
Lord Dixon-Smith	*Con*	p691
Lord Elis-Thomas	*PlC*	p700
Earl of Erroll	*CB*	p703

Lord Forsyth of Drumlean	*Con*	p716
Lord Framlingham	*Con*	p718
Baroness Gale	*Lab*	p721
Lord Glentoran	*Con*	p727
Lord Graham of Edmonton	*Lab/Co-op*	p734
Lord Greaves	*Lib Dem*	p735
Baroness Hanham	*Con*	p744
Viscount Hanworth	*Lab*	p746
Lord Hardie	*CB*	p747
Lord Haworth	*Lab*	p753
Baroness Hilton of Eggardon	*Lab*	p759
Baroness Howe of Idlicote	*CB*	p769
Lord Hunt of Chesterton	*Lab*	p773
Lord Inglewood	*Con*	p779
Lord Jay of Ewelme	*CB*	p782
Lord Judd	*Lab*	p789
Lord Krebs	*CB*	p802
Lord Lewis of Newnham	*CB*	p811
Earl of Lindsay	*Con*	p814
Earl of Liverpool	*Con*	p818
Bishop of London	*Non-Affiliated*	p820
Baroness Maddock	*Lib Dem*	p836
Baroness Mallalieu	*Lab*	p837
Countess of Mar	*CB*	p840
Earl of Mar and Kellie	*Scottish Lib Dem*	p841
Lord Marland	*Con*	p842
Lord May of Oxford	*CB*	p846
Lord Methuen	*Lib Dem*	p848
Baroness Miller of Chilthorne Domer	*Lib Dem*	p849
Bishop of Newcastle	*Non-Affiliated*	p867
Baroness Nicol	*Lab/Co-op*	p869
Lord Palmer	*CB*	p881
Baroness Parminter	*Lib Dem*	p884
Lord Pendry	*Lab*	p888
Lord Plumb	*Con*	p893
Lord Prescott	*Lab*	p896
Lord Puttnam	*Lab*	p898
Lord Redesdale	*Lib Dem*	p905
Lord Renton of Mount Harry	*Con*	p908
Lord St John of Bletso	*CB*	p924
Lord Selkirk of Douglas	*Con*	p930
Lord Sheikh	*Con*	p935
Earl of Shrewsbury and Waterford	*Con*	p938
Lord Skelmersdale	*Con*	p941
Lord Smith of Finsbury	*Non-Affiliated*	p944
Lord Soley	*Lab*	p948
Lord Soulsby of Swaffham Prior	*Con*	p949
Lord Strasburger	*Lib Dem*	p959
Lord Taylor of Goss Moor	*Lib Dem*	p964
Lord Taylor of Holbeach	*Con*	p964
Viscount Tenby	*CB*	p967

Baroness Tonge	*Ind*	
	Lib Dem	p972
Lord Trees	*CB*	p974
Baroness Walmsley	*Lib Dem*	p993
Baroness Warnock	*CB*	p995
Lord Whitty	*Lab*	p1002
Lord Williams of Elvel	*Lab*	p1006
Baroness Young of Old Scone	*Non-*	
	Affiliated	p1017

Equality

Lord Ahmed	*Non-*	
	Affiliated	p601
Baroness Benjamin	*Lib Dem*	p621
Baroness Berridge	*Con*	p623
Lord Boswell of Aynho	*Non-*	
	Affiliated	p635
Baroness Bottomley of		
Nettlestone	*Con*	p635
Lord Collins of Highbury	*Lab*	p669
Baroness Corston	*Lab*	p673
Baroness Crawley	*Lab*	p678
Lord Davies of Abersoch	*Lab*	p683
Baroness Falkner of		
Margravine	*Lib Dem*	p707
Lord Faulkner of Worcester	*Lab*	p708
Baroness Fookes	*Con*	p715
Baroness Gibson of		
Market Rasen	*Lab*	p725
Bishop of Gloucester	*Non-*	
	Affiliated	p728
Lord Griffiths of Burry Port	*Lab*	p740
Baroness Howe of Idlicote	*CB*	p769
Baroness Hussein-Ece	*Lib Dem*	p776
Lord Layard	*Lab*	p806
Lord Lester of Herne Hill	*Lib Dem*	p809
Baroness Lockwood	*Lab*	p820
Lord Martin of Springburn	*CB*	p843
Baroness Morgan of Huyton	*Lab*	p857
Lord Morris of Handsworth	*Lab*	p859
Lord Parekh	*Lab*	p882
Baroness Parminter	*Lib Dem*	p884
Lord Phillips of Sudbury	*Lib Dem*	p890
Baroness Prosser	*Lab*	p897
Bishop of Ripon and Leeds	*Non-*	
	Affiliated	p911
Lord Rooker	*Lab*	p917
Lord Sheikh	*Con*	p935
Lord Singh of Wimbledon	*CB*	p941
Baroness Thomas of		
Walliswood	*Lib Dem*	p970
Lord Williams of Baglan	*CB*	p1004
Baroness Young of Hornsey	*CB*	p1016
Baroness Young of Old Scone	*Non-*	
	Affiliated	p1017

Equal pay

Baroness Prosser	*Lab*	p897

Euro and EMU

Lord Flight	*Con*	p714
Lord Harrison	*Lab*	p750

Europe

Lord Astor of Hever	*Con*	p611
Baroness Billingham	*Lab*	p626
Viscount of Falkland	*CB*	p706
Baroness Falkner of		
Margravine	*Lib Dem*	p707
Lord Haskins	*CB*	p751
Baroness Henig	*Lab*	p755
Lord Hope of Thornes	*CB*	p765
Lord Hunt of Wirral	*Con*	p774
Lord Inglewood	*Con*	p779
Lord Lester of Herne Hill	*Lib Dem*	p809
Bishop of London	*Non-*	
	Affiliated	p820
Baroness Ludford	*Lib Dem*	p823
Duke of Montrose	*Con*	p853
Lord Moran	*CB*	p855
Lord Morgan	*Lab*	p855
Lord Newby	*Lib Dem*	p866
Lord Plumb	*Con*	p893
Lord Sewel	*Non-*	
	Affiliated	p931
Lord Skidelsky	*CB*	p942
Lord Tebbit	*Con*	p966
Lord Teverson	*Lib Dem*	p968
Lord Tomlinson	*Lab/Co-op*	p972
Lord Tope	*Lib Dem*	p973
Lord Tordoff	*Lib Dem*	p973
Lord Tugendhat	*Con*	p980
Lord Vallance of Tummel	*Lib Dem*	p985
Lord Wallace of Saltaire	*Lib Dem*	p992
Lord Weidenfeld	*CB*	p999
Lord Whitty	*Lab*	p1002

European affairs

Lord Brittan of Spennithorne	*Con*	p643
Lord Deben	*Con*	p686
Lord Grenfell	*Lab*	p738
Baroness Quin	*Lab*	p899

European Union

Lord Ahmad of Wimbledon	*Con*	p600
Lord Blackwell	*Con*	p630
Lord Boswell of Aynho	*Non-*	
	Affiliated	p635
Baroness Crawley	*Lab*	p678
Lord Dykes	*Lib Dem*	p696
Lord Garel-Jones	*Con*	p723
Lord Hannay of Chiswick	*CB*	p745
Lord Harrison	*Lab*	p750
Baroness Hooper	*Con*	p764
Lord Kilclooney	*CB*	p794
Lord Lamont of Lerwick	*Con*	p804
Lord Lea of Crondall	*Lab*	p807
Lord Leach of Fairford	*Con*	p807

Healthcare

Healthcare and pharmaceuticals

Baroness Uddin	Non-Affiliated	p983
Viscount Waverley	CB	p999
Lord Weidenfeld	CB	p999
Baroness Williams of Crosby	Lib Dem	p1005

International development and aid

Lord Ahmad of Wimbledon	Con	p600
Baroness Andrews	Lab	p606
Baroness Armstrong of Hill Top	Lab	p608
Lord Attenborough	Lab	p612
Earl Attlee	Con	p613
Lord Bilston	Lab/Co-op	p627
Lord Boateng	Lab	p632
Baroness Chalker of Wallasey	Con	p661
Lord Chidgey	Lib Dem	p662
Lord Clarke of Hampstead	Lab	p665
Lord Davies of Stamford	Lab	p685
Lord Desai	Lab	p689
Viscount Eccles	Con	p698
Lord Foulkes of Cumnock	Lab/Co-op	p717
Lord Freeman	Con	p718
Lord Harries of Pentregarth	CB	p747
Baroness Hayman	CB	p753
Lord Hughes of Woodside	Lab	p772
Lord Jay of Ewelme	CB	p782
Baroness Jay of Paddington	Lab	p783
Lord Joffe	Lab	p784
Lord Jones of Cheltenham	Lib Dem	p787
Lord Judd	Lab	p789
Baroness Kinnock of Holyhead	Lab	p798
Lord Knight of Weymouth	Lab	p800
Lord McConnell of Glenscorrodale	Lab	p827
Lord Malloch-Brown	CB	p838
Lord Moynihan	Con	p861
Lord Oakeshott of Seagrove Bay	Lib Dem	p874
Lord Popat	Con	p894
Lord Ramsbotham	CB	p901
Lord Rana	CB	p902
Lord Rea	Lab	p904
Lord Rees of Ludlow	CB	p905
Baroness Royall of Blaisdon	Lab	p920
Earl of Sandwich	CB	p926
Baroness Smith of Basildon	Lab/Co-op	p943
Baroness Stern	CB	p952
Lord Taylor of Goss Moor	Lib Dem	p964
Lord Tomlinson	Lab/Co-op	p972
Baroness Tonge	Ind Lib Dem	p972
Lord Trees	CB	p974
Baroness Verma	Con	p986
Baroness Warwick of Undercliffe	Lab	p996
Lord Watson of Invergowrie	Lab	p997
Baroness Whitaker	Lab	p1001
Lord Williams of Oystermouth	CB	p1007

Internet

Lord Maxton	Lab	p846
Lord Reid of Cardowan	Lab	p906

Investment

Baroness Hughes of Stretford	Lab	p772
Lord Lee of Trafford	Lib Dem	p808

Islam

Lord Kalms	Non-Affiliated	p791
Baroness Nicholson of Winterbourne	Lib Dem	p868
Lord Pearson of Rannoch	UKIP	p888

Judaism

Lord Janner of Braunstone	Lab	p781

Justice system

Lord Ahmed	Non-Affiliated	p601
Lord Bach	Lab	p614
Lord Christopher	Lab	p663
Baroness Clark of Calton	Non-Affiliated	p664
Lord Collins of Highbury	Lab	p669
Bishop of Coventry	Non-Affiliated	p674
Lord Dubs	Lab	p695
Lord Glenarthur	Con	p726
Lord Goff of Chieveley	Non-Affiliated	p728
Lord Grabiner	Lab	p733
Baroness Hanham	Con	p744
Baroness Healy of Primrose Hill	Lab	p755
Baroness Henig	Lab	p755
Earl Howe	Con	p768
Lord Hylton	CB	p777
Lord Judd	Lab	p789
Baroness Kidron	CB	p793
Baroness Linklater of Butterstone	Lib Dem	p816
Lord Low of Dalston	CB	p822
Lord Lucas of Crudwell and Dingwall	Con	p822
Lord Marks of Henley-on-Thames	Lib Dem	p841
Baroness Masham of Ilton	CB	p843
Baroness Neuberger	CB	p864
Baroness Newlove	Con	p867
Lord Parekh	Lab	p882
Lord Phillips of Sudbury	Lib Dem	p890
Lord Ramsbotham	CB	p901
Lord Rana	CB	p902
Lord Rosser	Lab	p918
Baroness Sharples	Con	p934
Lord Soley	Lab	p948
Baroness Stern	CB	p952
Lord Tunnicliffe	Lab	p980

Labour Party

Baroness Healy of Primrose Hill	*Lab*	p755

Learning disabilities

Baroness Browning	*Con*	p649
Baroness Murphy	*CB*	p861
Lord Pearson of Rannoch	*UKIP*	p888

Legal aid

Lord Beecham	*Lab*	p620

Legal services

Lord Anderson of Swansea	*Lab*	p605
Lord Browne of Ladyton	*Lab*	p647
Baroness Buscombe	*Con*	p651
Baroness Butler-Sloss	*CB*	p652
Lord Cameron of Lochbroom	*CB*	p653
Lord Carlile of Berriew	*Lib Dem*	p656
Lord Clement-Jones	*Lib Dem*	p666
Lord Clinton-Davis	*Lab*	p667
Baroness Deech	*CB*	p687
Lord Faulks	*Con*	p708
Lord Grabiner	*Lab*	p733
Lord Hardie	*CB*	p747
Lord Hart of Chilton	*Lab*	p750
Baroness Howe of Idlicote	*CB*	p769
Lord Hutton of Furness	*Lab*	p777
Lord Inglewood	*Con*	p779
Lord Irvine of Lairg	*Lab*	p779
Lord Lester of Herne Hill	*Lib Dem*	p809
Lord Mackenzie of Framwellgate	*Non-Affiliated*	p832
Baroness Mallalieu	*Lab*	p837
Lord Morris of Aberavon	*Lab*	p857
Lord Norton of Louth	*Con*	p872
Lord Pannick	*CB*	p882
Lord Phillips of Sudbury	*Lib Dem*	p890
Lord St John of Bletso	*CB*	p924
Lord Selkirk of Douglas	*Con*	p930
Lord Taylor of Warwick	*Non-Affiliated*	p965
Lord Trimble	*Con*	p977
Lord Waddington	*Con*	p988
Lord Wallace of Tankerness	*Lib Dem*	p992
Archbishop of York	*Non-Affiliated*	p1015

Local government

Lord Bach	*Lab*	p614
Lord Bassam of Brighton	*Lab/Co-op*	p619
Lord Beecham	*Lab*	p620
Bishop of Birmingham	*Non-Affiliated*	p627
Lord Bowness	*Con*	p636
Lord Bradley	*Lab*	p638
Viscount Bridgeman	*Con*	p640
Baroness Cumberlege	*Con*	p679
Viscount Eccles	*Con*	p698
Lord Evans of Parkside	*Lab*	p704
Lord Fearn	*Lib Dem*	p709
Lord Forsyth of Drumlean	*Con*	p716

Lord Graham of Edmonton	*Lab/Co-op*	p734
Lord Greaves	*Lib Dem*	p735
Baroness Hamwee	*Lib Dem*	p744
Baroness Hanham	*Con*	p744
Lord Hanningfield	*Non-Affiliated*	p746
Lord Harris of Haringey	*Lab*	p748
Baroness Hollis of Heigham	*Lab*	p762
Baroness Hughes of Stretford	*Lab*	p772
Baroness Hussein-Ece	*Lib Dem*	p776
Lord Inglewood	*Con*	p779
Lord Knights	*CB*	p801
Lord Macaulay of Bragar	*Lab*	p825
Lord McKenzie of Luton	*Lab*	p833
Baroness Maddock	*Lib Dem*	p836
Lord Molyneaux of Killead	*CB*	p851
Baroness Platt of Writtle	*Non-Affiliated*	p893
Lord Selkirk of Douglas	*Con*	p930
Lord Shipley	*Lib Dem*	p938
Lord Smith of Finsbury	*Non-Affiliated*	p944
Lord Smith of Leigh	*Lab*	p946
Lord Stoddart of Swindon	*Ind Lab*	p957
Lord Storey	*Lib Dem*	p958
Lord Taylor of Blackburn	*Lab*	p963
Lord Taylor of Holbeach	*Con*	p964
Lord Tope	*Lib Dem*	p973
Lord Touhig	*Lab/Co-op*	p974
Lord True	*Con*	p978
Lord Willis of Knaresborough	*Lib Dem*	p1008

Local government finance

Lord McKenzie of Luton	*Lab*	p833

London

Lord Birt	*CB*	p628
Lord Bowness	*Con*	p636
Baroness Hamwee	*Lib Dem*	p744
Bishop of London	*Non-Affiliated*	p820
Lord Luke	*Con*	p824
Viscount Montgomery of Alamein	*CB*	p853
Lord Tope	*Lib Dem*	p973
Baroness Valentine	*CB*	p985
Baroness Young of Hornsey	*CB*	p1016

Machinery of government

Lord Denham	*Con*	p688
Lord Grocott	*Lab*	p741
Lord Lipsey	*Lab*	p816

Magistrates courts

Lord Phillips of Sudbury	*Lib Dem*	p890
Viscount Tenby	*CB*	p967

Manufacturing

Lord Bhattacharyya	*Lab*	p624
Lord Bilimoria	*CB*	p625
Lord Brookman	*Lab*	p645
Lord Evans of Parkside	*Lab*	p704
Lord Jones	*Lab*	p785

Maritime industries

Lord Dixon	Lab	p691
Lord Glentoran	Con	p727
Lord MacKenzie of Culkein	Lab	p832

Media

Earl of Arran	Con	p609
Baroness Benjamin	Lib Dem	p621
Lord Birt	CB	p628
Lord Black of Brentwood	Con	p628
Lord Bragg	Lab	p639
Viscount Colville of Culross	CB	p670
Baroness Cumberlege	Con	p679
Lord Currie of Marylebone	CB	p680
Baroness Dean of Thornton-le-Fylde	Lab	p685
Baroness Deech	CB	p687
Lord Eames	CB	p696
Lord Fowler	Con	p717
Lord Gordon of Strathblane	Lab	p731
Lord Grade of Yarmouth	Con	p734
Lord Griffiths of Fforestfach	Con	p740
Lord Grocott	Lab	p741
Lord Hall of Birkenhead	CB	p742
Lord Haskins	CB	p751
Lord Hollick	Lab	p761
Baroness Howe of Idlicote	CB	p769
Lord Inglewood	Con	p779
Baroness James of Holland Park	Con	p781
Baroness Jay of Paddington	Lab	p783
Baroness Kidron	CB	p793
Lord Lester of Herne Hill	Lib Dem	p809
Baroness Liddell of Coatdyke	Lab	p813
Lord Lipsey	Lab	p816
Lord Low of Dalston	CB	p822
Lord Luce	CB	p823
Lord Macdonald of Tradeston	Lab	p828
Lord Maxton	Lab	p846
Lord Naseby	Con	p862
Bishop of Norwich	Non-Affiliated	p873
Lord Palmer	CB	p881
Lord Quirk	CB	p900
Baroness Rawlings	Con	p903
Baroness Sharples	Con	p934
Lord Smith of Finsbury	Non-Affiliated	p944
Lord Stoneham of Droxford	Lib Dem	p958
Lord Taylor of Warwick	Non-Affiliated	p965
Baroness Thornton	Lab/Co-op	p971
Baroness Warnock	CB	p995
Baroness Young of Old Scone	Non-Affiliated	p1017

Medical ethics

Baroness Campbell of Surbiton	CB	p654
Baroness Finlay of Llandaff	CB	p712
Baroness O'Neill of Bengarve	CB	p876

Medical schools

Lord Turnberg	Lab	p981

Medical science

Earl Baldwin of Bewdley	CB	p616
Lord Faulks	Con	p708
Lord McColl of Dulwich	Con	p826
Baroness Trumpington	Con	p978
Lord Walton of Detchant	CB	p994
Baroness Warnock	CB	p995

Mental health

Lord Alderdice	Lib Dem	p602
Baroness Browning	Con	p649
Lord Carlile of Berriew	Lib Dem	p656
Lord Layard	Lab	p806
Lord McCluskey	CB	p826
Baroness Meacher	CB	p848
Lord Molyneaux of Killead	CB	p851
Baroness Murphy	CB	p861
Baroness Young of Hornsey	CB	p1016

Middle East

Lord Weidenfeld	CB	p999
Lord Wright of Richmond	CB	p1015

Migrant workers

Lord Roberts of Llandudno	Lib Dem	p913

Museums and galleries

Lord Armstrong of Ilminster	CB	p608
Viscount Eccles	Con	p698
Lord Montagu of Beaulieu	Con	p852
Lord Renfrew of Kaimsthorn	Con	p907

Music

Baroness Jolly	Lib Dem	p785
Lord Low of Dalston	CB	p822
Lord Sterling of Plaistow	Con	p952

National Health Service (NHS)

Baroness Cumberlege	Con	p679
Baroness Murphy	CB	p861

National security

Baroness Manningham-Buller	CB	p840
Baroness Neville-Jones	Con	p865

NHS finances

Lord James of Blackheath	Con	p780

North West

Lord Campbell-Savours	Lab	p655
Lord Storey	Lib Dem	p958
Lord Taylor of Blackburn	Lab	p963
Lord Thomas of Macclesfield	Lab/Co-op	p969
Baroness Thornton	Lab/Co-op	p971
Lord Waddington	Con	p988

Northern Ireland

Lord Alderdice	Lib Dem	p602
Lord Alton of Liverpool	CB	p604
Lord Brooke of Sutton Mandeville	Con	p644
Viscount Brookeborough	CB	p645
Lord Browne of Belmont	DUP	p647

Probation

Earl of Mar and Kellie	Scottish Lib	
	Dem	p841

Property

Earl of Courtown	Con	p674
Earl of Shrewsbury and		
Waterford	Con	p938

Public finance

Baroness Noakes	Con	p869

Public health

Baroness McIntosh of Hudnall	Lab	p831

Public services

Lord Blackwell	Con	p630
Lord Laming	CB	p803
Lord Mawson	CB	p846
Lord Turnbull	CB	p981

Race relations

Lord Ahmed	Non-	
	Affiliated	p601
Lord Dubs	Lab	p695
Baroness Gould of		
Potternewton	Lab	p732
Baroness Hilton of Eggardon	Lab	p759
Lord Judd	Lab	p789
Lord Parekh	Lab	p882
Lord Patel of Blackburn	Lab	p885
Baroness Prashar	CB	p895
Baroness Whitaker	Lab	p1001

Rail transport

Lord Greaves	Lib Dem	p735
Lord Taylor of Blackburn	Lab	p963
Viscount Tenby	CB	p967

Reform of public services

Lord Freud	Con	p719
Bishop of Leicester	Non-	
	Affiliated	p808
Baroness Lister of Burtersett	Lab	p817

Refugees and asylum seekers

Lord Alton of Liverpool	CB	p604
Lord Greaves	Lib Dem	p735
Lord Judd	Lab	p789
Baroness Lister of Burtersett	Lab	p817
Lord Moynihan	Con	p861
Baroness Neuberger	CB	p864
Baroness Nicholson of		
Winterbourne	Lib Dem	p868
Lord Roberts of Llandudno	Lib Dem	p913

Regeneration

Lord Adebowale	CB	p599
Lord Best	CB	p623
Baroness Ford	Non-	
	Affiliated	p715

Regional policy

Baroness Armstrong of Hill Top	Lab	p608

Lord Beecham	Lab	p620
Lord Cunningham of Felling	Non-	
	Affiliated	p680
Lord Foster of		
Bishop Auckland	Lab	p716
Baroness Goudie	Lab	p732
Baroness Hughes of Stretford	Lab	p772
Lord Inglewood	Con	p779
Lord Jones	Lab	p785
Lord Kilclooney	CB	p794
Baroness Kinnock of Holyhead	Lab	p798
Lord Newby	Lib Dem	p866
Baroness Quin	Lab	p899

Regulatory reform

Baroness Bottomley of		
Nettlestone	Con	p635

Religion

Lord Bannside	DUP	p617
Baroness Berridge	Con	p623
Lord Bilimoria	CB	p625
Lord Birt	CB	p628
Baroness Butler-Sloss	CB	p652
Bishop of Gloucester	Non-	
	Affiliated	p728
Lord Hylton	CB	p777
Lord Luke	Con	p824
Lord Macdonald of Tradeston	Lab	p828
Baroness Richardson of Calow	CB	p910
Lord Rowe-Beddoe	CB	p919
Archbishop of York	Non-	
	Affiliated	p1015

Renewables

Lord James of Blackheath	Con	p780
Earl of Liverpool	Con	p818
Lord Wallace of Tankerness	Lib Dem	p992

Retail industry

Lord Feldman	Con	p709
Baroness O'Cathain	Con	p874

Road safety

Lord Brougham and Vaux	Con	p646
Lord Robertson of Port Ellen	Lab	p914
Viscount Simon	Lab	p939

Road transport

Lord Montagu of Beaulieu	Con	p852

Royal Navy

Lord Haworth	Lab	p753

Rural communities

Lord Taylor of Goss Moor	Lib Dem	p964

Rural Environment

Lord Bragg	Lab	p639
Lord Cameron of Dillington	CB	p653
Earl Cathcart	Con	p659
Lord Chorley	CB	p663
Lord Elis-Thomas	PlC	p700

Peers' Countries of Interest

For precise details of individuals' stated interests, see relevant biography. The interests listed are supplied by Peers themselves.

Afghanistan

Lord Avebury	Lib Dem	p613
Lord Browne of Ladyton	Lab	p647
Baroness D'Souza	Lord Speaker	p694
Earl of Sandwich	CB	p926
Baroness Stern	CB	p952
Baroness Tonge	Ind Lib Dem	p972

Africa

Lord Ahmed	Non-Affiliated	p601
Lord Alton of Liverpool	CB	p604
Baroness Amos	Non-Affiliated	p605
Baroness Armstrong of Hill Top	Lab	p608
Lord Bhatia	Non-Affiliated	p624
Lord Boateng	Lab	p632
Lord Cameron of Dillington	CB	p653
Baroness Campbell of Loughborough	CB	p654
Baroness Chalker of Wallasey	Con	p661
Lord Chidgey	Lib Dem	p662
Lord Christopher	Lab	p663
Lord Dannatt	CB	p682
Lord Davies of Abersoch	Lab	p683
Lord Dholakia	Lib Dem	p690
Baroness D'Souza	Lord Speaker	p694
Viscount of Falkland	CB	p706
Lord Filkin	Lab	p711
Lord German	Lib Dem	p724
Viscount Goschen	Con	p731
Lord Jay of Ewelme	CB	p782
Lord Joffe	Lab	p784
Lord Jones of Cheltenham	Lib Dem	p787
Baroness King of Bow	Lab	p795
Baroness Kinnock of Holyhead	Lab	p798
Lord Lea of Crondall	Lab	p807
Lord Leitch	Lab	p809
Lord Levy	Lab	p811
Lord Luce	CB	p823
Lord Malloch-Brown	CB	p838
Countess of Mar	CB	p840
Baroness O'Loan	CB	p875
Lord Patel of Bradford	Lab	p885
Lord Plumb	Con	p893
Lord Popat	Con	p894
Baroness Prashar	CB	p895
Lord Razzall	Lib Dem	p904
Lord Rea	Lab	p904
Lord Sainsbury of Turville	Lab	p923

Lord St John of Bletso	CB	p924
Lord Selkirk of Douglas	Con	p930
Lord Selsdon	Con	p931
Lord Soulsby of Swaffham Prior	Con	p949
Lord Steel of Aikwood	Lib Dem	p951
Lord Triesman	Lab	p976
Baroness Verma	Con	p986
Lord Walker of Aldringham	CB	p990
Lord Warner	Lab	p994
Baroness Whitaker	Lab	p1001
Lord Williams of Oystermouth	CB	p1007
Archbishop of York	Non-Affiliated	p1015
Baroness Young of Hornsey	CB	p1016

Albania

Lord Bates	Con	p620

Algeria

Baroness Howells of St Davids	Lab	p770
Baroness Stern	CB	p952

Angola

Lord Grocott	Lab	p741
Earl of Listowel	CB	p817

Antigua and Barbuda

Lord Tunnicliffe	Lab	p980

Argentina

Lord Faulkner of Worcester	Lab	p708
Lord Luke	Con	p824
Lord O'Neill of Clackmannan	Lab	p877
Lord Rowe-Beddoe	CB	p919
Lord Smith of Finsbury	Non-Affiliated	p944
Baroness Stern	CB	p952
Lord Wigley	PlC	p1003

Armenia

Baroness Cox	CB	p675
Baroness Nicholson of Winterbourne	Lib Dem	p868
Lord Wallace of Saltaire	Lib Dem	p992

Asia

Lord Ahmed	Non-Affiliated	p601
Baroness Campbell of Loughborough	CB	p654
Lord Carlile of Berriew	Lib Dem	p656
Lord Chidgey	Lib Dem	p662
Lord Clement-Jones	Lib Dem	p666
Lord Dannatt	CB	p682
Lord Davies of Abersoch	Lab	p683
Lord de Mauley	Con	p688
Lord Dholakia	Lib Dem	p690
Lord Flight	Con	p714

Lord Geddes	*Con*	p724
Lord Kilclooney	*CB*	p794
Lord Loomba	*Lib Dem*	p821
Lord Malloch-Brown	*CB*	p838
Baroness Massey of Darwen	*Lab*	p844
Baroness Neville-Jones	*Con*	p865
Lord Noon	*Lab*	p870
Baroness O'Loan	*CB*	p875
Lord Powell of Bayswater	*CB*	p895
Marquess of Salisbury	*Non-*	
	Affiliated	p924
Lord Selkirk of Douglas	*Con*	p930
Lord Soley	*Lab*	p948
Baroness Verma	*Con*	p986
Viscount Waverley	*CB*	p999
Baroness Whitaker	*Lab*	p1001
Lord Wilson of Tillyorn	*CB*	p1009

Australia

Lord Archer of	*Non-*	
Weston-Super-Mare	*Affiliated*	p607
Lord Bassam of Brighton	*Lab/Co-op*	p619
Lord Broers	*CB*	p643
Baroness Dean of		
Thornton-le-Fylde	*Lab*	p685
Lord Desai	*Lab*	p689
Baroness Ford	*Non-*	
	Affiliated	p715
Lord Gardiner of Kimble	*Con*	p722
Baroness Greenfield	*CB*	p736
Earl of Home	*Con*	p763
Lord Hoyle	*Lab*	p771
Lord Jones of Birmingham	*CB*	p786
Baroness Kingsmill	*Lab*	p797
Baroness Liddell of Coatdyke	*Lab*	p813
Baroness Lister of Burtersett	*Lab*	p817
Lord Low of Dalston	*CB*	p822
Lord MacKenzie of Culkein	*Lab*	p832
Lord Northbourne	*CB*	p871
Baroness Randerson	*Lib Dem*	p902
Baroness Royall of Blaisdon	*Lab*	p920
Baroness Sharp of Guildford	*Lib Dem*	p933
Viscount Simon	*Lab*	p939
Lord Smith of Finsbury	*Non-*	
	Affiliated	p944
Lord Smith of Leigh	*Lab*	p946
Lord Stirrup	*CB*	p956
Lord Teverson	*Lib Dem*	p968
Lord Tyler	*Lib Dem*	p982
Lord Waddington	*Con*	p988
Bishop of Wakefield	*Non-*	
	Affiliated	p989
Lord Walpole	*CB*	p993
Lord Walton of Detchant	*CB*	p994
Baroness Wilcox	*Con*	p1003

Austria

Lord Feldman	*Con*	p709
Viscount Hanworth	*Lab*	p746

Lord Jones	*Lab*	p785
Lord Methuen	*Lib Dem*	p848
Lord Paul	*Non-*	
	Affiliated	p887

Azerbaijan

Baroness Goudie	*Lab*	p732
Lord Haworth	*Lab*	p753
Baroness O'Cathain	*Con*	p874

Bahamas

Baroness Heyhoe Flint	*Con*	p758

Bahrain

Lord Avebury	*Lib Dem*	p613
Lord Jones of Cheltenham	*Lib Dem*	p787
Lord Jordan	*Lab*	p788

Bangladesh

Lord Ahmad of Wimbledon	*Con*	p600
Lord Avebury	*Lib Dem*	p613
Lord Bhatia	*Non-*	
	Affiliated	p624
Lord Desai	*Lab*	p689
Baroness King of Bow	*Lab*	p795
Lord Loomba	*Lib Dem*	p821
Lord Patel of Blackburn	*Lab*	p885
Baroness Tonge	*Ind*	
	Lib Dem	p972
Baroness Uddin	*Non-*	
	Affiliated	p983

Belgium

Lord Grenfell	*Lab*	p738

Belize

Lord Skelmersdale	*Con*	p941

Benin

Lord McColl of Dulwich	*Con*	p826

Bermuda

Lord Tope	*Lib Dem*	p973
Lord Waddington	*Con*	p988

Bhutan

Lord Layard	*Lab*	p806
Lord O'Donnell	*CB*	p875

Bolivia

Lord Lea of Crondall	*Lab*	p807

Bosnia and Herzegovina

Lord Cormack	*Con*	p672
Lord Greaves	*Lib Dem*	p735

Botswana

Bishop of Gloucester	*Non-*	
	Affiliated	p728
Lord Jones of Cheltenham	*Lib Dem*	p787
Bishop of Newcastle	*Non-*	
	Affiliated	p867
Lord Rowlands	*Lab*	p920

Brazil

Baroness Bakewell	*Lab*	p615
Lord Browne of Belmont	*DUP*	p647

Croatia

Lord Bates	*Con*	p620
Lord Browne of Belmont	*DUP*	p647
Lord Cormack	*Con*	p672
Lord Greaves	*Lib Dem*	p735
Lord Grenfell	*Lab*	p738
Lord Taylor of Blackburn	*Lab*	p963

Cuba

Baroness Coussins	*CB*	p674
Baroness Smith of Basildon	*Lab/Co-op*	p943
Baroness Thomas of Walliswood	*Lib Dem*	p970

Cyprus

Lord Dixon	*Lab*	p691
Baroness Greenfield	*CB*	p736
Lord Harris of Haringey	*Lab*	p748
Baroness Hussein-Ece	*Lib Dem*	p776
Lord Kilclooney	*CB*	p794
Baroness Knight of Collingtree	*Con*	p800
Baroness Ludford	*Lib Dem*	p823
Lord Maginnis of Drumglass	*Ind UUP*	p837
Lord Smith of Finsbury	*Non-Affiliated*	p944

Denmark

Lord Faulkner of Worcester	*Lab*	p708
Lord Grantchester	*Lab*	p735
Baroness Maddock	*Lib Dem*	p836
Lord Teverson	*Lib Dem*	p968

Dominican Republic

Lord Griffiths of Burry Port	*Lab*	p740
Baroness Stern	*CB*	p952

East Timor

Lord Avebury	*Lib Dem*	p613
Baroness Cox	*CB*	p675

Eastern Europe

Lord Carlile of Berriew	*Lib Dem*	p656
Baroness Eaton	*Con*	p697
Lord Griffiths of Fforestfach	*Con*	p740
Baroness Kramer	*Lib Dem*	p801
Baroness Quin	*Lab*	p899
Lord Rowlands	*Lab*	p920
Lord Sewel	*Non-Affiliated*	p931
Lord Shipley	*Lib Dem*	p938
Lord Walker of Aldringham	*CB*	p990

Ecuador

Lord Allan of Hallam	*Lib Dem*	p603

Egypt

Baroness Chalker of Wallasey	*Con*	p661
Lord Christopher	*Lab*	p663

Eritrea

Lord Avebury	*Lib Dem*	p613

Ethiopia

Lord Avebury	*Lib Dem*	p613

Europe

Baroness Bonham-Carter of Yarnbury	*Lib Dem*	p633
Duke of Montrose	*Con*	p853

Europe

Lord Barnett	*Lab*	p619
Lord Boswell of Aynho	*Non-Affiliated*	p635
Lord Bowness	*Con*	p636
Viscount Brookeborough	*CB*	p645
Lord Chidgey	*Lib Dem*	p662
Lord Clinton-Davis	*Lab*	p667
Lord Cunningham of Felling	*Non-Affiliated*	p680
Lord de Mauley	*Con*	p688
Lord Dykes	*Lib Dem*	p696
Lord Evans of Watford	*Lab*	p704
Baroness Goudie	*Lab*	p732
Lord Griffiths of Fforestfach	*Con*	p740
Baroness Hanham	*Con*	p744
Lord Haskel	*Lab*	p751
Baroness Howarth of Breckland	*CB*	p766
Lord Howell of Guildford	*Con*	p770
Lord Hoyle	*Lab*	p771
Lord Hylton	*CB*	p777
Lord Inge	*CB*	p778
Lord Kalms	*Non-Affiliated*	p791
Lord Laming	*CB*	p803
Lord Levy	*Lab*	p811
Baroness Liddell of Coatdyke	*Lab*	p813
Bishop of London	*Non-Affiliated*	p820
Lord MacLaurin of Knebworth	*Con*	p834
Lord Maclennan of Rogart	*Lib Dem*	p834
Lord Mance	*Non-Affiliated*	p838
Baroness Masham of Ilton	*CB*	p843
Lord Mawson	*CB*	p846
Lord Monks	*Lab*	p852
Lord Powell of Bayswater	*CB*	p895
Baroness Prashar	*CB*	p895
Baroness Quin	*Lab*	p899
Baroness Randerson	*Lib Dem*	p902
Lord Risby	*Con*	p912
Lord Sawyer	*Lab*	p927
Lord Selkirk of Douglas	*Con*	p930
Lord Smith of Finsbury	*Non-Affiliated*	p944
Lord Triesman	*Lab*	p976
Baroness Verma	*Con*	p986
Lord Walpole	*CB*	p993
Lord Weidenfeld	*CB*	p999
Baroness Whitaker	*Lab*	p1001
Lord Willoughby de Broke	*UKIP*	p1008

European Union

Lord Anderson of Swansea	*Lab*	p605
Lord Berkeley	*Lab*	p622

Baroness Billingham	*Lab*	p626
Lord Cobbold	*CB*	p667
Baroness Coussins	*CB*	p674
Lord Davies of Stamford	*Lab*	p685
Lord Foulkes of Cumnock	*Lab/Co-op*	p717
Lord German	*Lib Dem*	p724
Lord Giddens	*Lab*	p725
Lord Harrison	*Lab*	p750
Lord Howe of Aberavon	*Con*	p768
Lord Hunt of Wirral	*Con*	p774
Lord Inglewood	*Con*	p779
Lord Jay of Ewelme	*CB*	p782
Lord Kennedy of Southwark	*Lab/Co-op*	p791
Lord Kerr of Kinlochard	*CB*	p792
Lord Leach of Fairford	*Con*	p807
Lord McConnell of Glenscorrodale	*Lab*	p827
Lord MacGregor of Pulham Market	*Con*	p830
Lord McNally	*Lib Dem*	p835
Lord Mogg	*CB*	p851
Baroness O'Cathain	*Con*	p874
Baroness Royall of Blaisdon	*Lab*	p920
Lord Simon of Highbury	*Non-Affiliated*	p940
Lord Stewartby	*Con*	p955
Lord Tope	*Lib Dem*	p973
Lord Truscott	*Non-Affiliated*	p979
Lord Wallace of Saltaire	*Lib Dem*	p992
Lord Wood of Anfield	*Lab*	p1012

Falkland Islands

Lord MacKenzie of Culkein	*Lab*	p832

Fiji

Lord Griffiths of Burry Port	*Lab*	p740

Finland

Lord Cormack	*Con*	p672
Baroness Maddock	*Lib Dem*	p836
Baroness Ramsay of Cartvale	*Lab*	p901
Lord Tyler	*Lib Dem*	p982

France

Baroness Afshar	*CB*	p600
Lord Anderson of Swansea	*Lab*	p605
Lord Armstrong of Ilminster	*CB*	p608
Lord Astor of Hever	*Con*	p611
Baroness Benjamin	*Lib Dem*	p621
Baroness Blackstone	*Lab*	p629
Lord Bradley	*Lab*	p638
Lord Bragg	*Lab*	p639
Lord Briggs	*CB*	p641
Baroness Brinton	*Lib Dem*	p642
Lord Brougham and Vaux	*Con*	p646
Lord Browne of Belmont	*DUP*	p647
Archbishop of Canterbury	*Non-Affiliated*	p655
Earl of Clancarty	*CB*	p664

Baroness Cohen of Pimlico	*Lab*	p669
Baroness Coussins	*CB*	p674
Lord Drayson	*Lab*	p694
Viscount of Falkland	*CB*	p706
Baroness Finlay of Llandaff	*CB*	p712
Baroness Gibson of Market Rasen	*Lab*	p725
Lord Greaves	*Lib Dem*	p735
Lord Green of Hurstpierpoint	*Con*	p736
Baroness Greenfield	*CB*	p736
Lord Grenfell	*Lab*	p738
Viscount Hanworth	*Lab*	p746
Lord Harris of Haringey	*Lab*	p748
Lord Hart of Chilton	*Lab*	p750
Lord Haskins	*CB*	p751
Lord Hunt of Chesterton	*Lab*	p773
Lord Janvrin	*CB*	p782
Baroness King of Bow	*Lab*	p795
Lord Leitch	*Lab*	p809
Bishop of Lichfield	*Non-Affiliated*	p813
Lord Liddle	*Lab*	p814
Baroness Massey of Darwen	*Lab*	p844
Lord Maxton	*Lab*	p846
Baroness Miller of Chilthorne Domer	*Lib Dem*	p849
Lord Moran	*CB*	p855
Lord Morgan	*Lab*	p855
Lord Naseby	*Con*	p862
Lord Northbourne	*CB*	p871
Lord Patel	*CB*	p884
Lord Plant of Highfield	*Lab*	p892
Lord Radice	*Lab*	p900
Baroness Randerson	*Lib Dem*	p902
Lord Renfrew of Kaimsthorn	*Con*	p907
Lord Renwick of Clifton	*CB*	p909
Marquess of Salisbury	*Non-Affiliated*	p924
Baroness Shephard of Northwold	*Con*	p936
Lord Smith of Leigh	*Lab*	p946
Lord Stevens of Ludgate	*Con Ind*	p954
Lord Stoneham of Droxford	*Lib Dem*	p958
Lord Storey	*Lib Dem*	p958
Lord Taylor of Holbeach	*Con*	p964
Lord Thomas of Swynnerton	*CB*	p969
Lord Touhig	*Lab/Co-op*	p974
Baroness Trumpington	*Con*	p978
Lord Walton of Detchant	*CB*	p994
Lord Watson of Invergowrie	*Lab*	p997
Lord Whitty	*Lab*	p1002
Baroness Wilcox	*Con*	p1003
Lord Williams of Baglan	*CB*	p1004
Lord Williams of Elvel	*Lab*	p1006

Gabon

Lord Loomba	*Lib Dem*	p821

Archbishop of Canterbury	Non-Affiliated	p655
Baroness Corston	Lab	p673
Lord Jones of Cheltenham	Lib Dem	p787
Lord Loomba	Lib Dem	p821
Lord Oakeshott of Seagrove Bay	Lib Dem	p874
Lord Popat	Con	p894
Baroness Stern	CB	p952
Bishop of Winchester	Non-Affiliated	p1010

Korea, North

Lord Alton of Liverpool	CB	p604
Baroness Cox	CB	p675
Baroness D'Souza	Lord Speaker	p694
Lord Eames	CB	p696
Lord Rowe-Beddoe	CB	p919

Korea, South

Baroness Benjamin	Lib Dem	p621

Kuwait

Lord Jones of Cheltenham	Lib Dem	p787
Baroness Nicholson of Winterbourne	Lib Dem	p868
Lord Patel of Blackburn	Lab	p885

Kyrgzstan

Lord Haworth	Lab	p753
Baroness Stern	CB	p952

Laos

Baroness D'Souza	Lord Speaker	p694
Lord Haworth	Lab	p753

Latin America

Baroness Andrews	Lab	p606
Lord Bach	Lab	p614
Lord Blyth of Rowington	Con	p632
Lord Foulkes of Cumnock	Lab/Co-op	p717
Baroness Gardner of Parkes	Con	p722
Lord Garel-Jones	Con	p723
Baroness Gibson of Market Rasen	Lab	p725
Lord Giddens	Lab	p725
Lord Kilclooney	CB	p794
Lord Leitch	Lab	p809
Lord Levy	Lab	p811
Lord McFall of Alcluith	Lab/Co-op	p829
Viscount Montgomery of Alamein	CB	p853
Lord Rea	Lab	p904
Lord Rowe-Beddoe	CB	p919
Baroness Royall of Blaisdon	Lab	p920
Lord Sandberg	Lib Dem	p925
Baroness Shephard of Northwold	Con	p936
Baroness Thomas of Walliswood	Lib Dem	p970

Lebanon

Lord Eden of Winton	Con	p699
Baroness Nicholson of Winterbourne	Lib Dem	p868

Lesotho

Lord Jones of Cheltenham	Lib Dem	p787

Liberia

Lord McColl of Dulwich	Con	p826

Libya

Lord Avebury	Lib Dem	p613
Lord James of Blackheath	Con	p780

Liechtenstein

Baroness Smith of Basildon	Lab/Co-op	p943

Lithuania

Lord Cormack	Con	p672

Madagascar

Lord Lea of Crondall	Lab	p807
Baroness Trumpington	Con	p978

Malawi

Bishop of Birmingham	Non-Affiliated	p627
Lord Jones of Cheltenham	Lib Dem	p787
Lord Loomba	Lib Dem	p821
Lord McConnell of Glenscorrodale	Lab	p827
Lord Northbourne	CB	p871
Lord Popat	Con	p894

Malaysia

Lord Avebury	Lib Dem	p613
Baroness Butler-Sloss	CB	p652
Lord Desai	Lab	p689
Baroness Henig	Lab	p755
Lord Soulsby of Swaffham Prior	Con	p949
Lord Tanlaw	CB	p962

Maldives

Lord Naseby	Con	p862

Mali

Lord Avebury	Lib Dem	p613

Malta

Lord Judge	Non-Affiliated	p790
Lord Pendry	Lab	p888

Mauritius

Lord Desai	Lab	p689
Baroness Prashar	CB	p895
Lord Rana	CB	p902

Mexico

Lord Avebury	Lib Dem	p613
Lord Rogers of Riverside	Lab	p916
Lord Rowe-Beddoe	CB	p919
Lord Thomas of Swynnerton	CB	p969

Middle East

Lord Ahmad of Wimbledon	Con	p600
Lord Ahmed	Non-Affiliated	p601

Nigeria

Lord Adebowale	CB	p599
Lord Avebury	Lib Dem	p613
Baroness Barker	Lib Dem	p618
Baroness Berridge	Con	p623
Archbishop of Canterbury	Non-Affiliated	p655
Bishop of Coventry	Non-Affiliated	p674
Baroness Cox	CB	p675
Baroness Howells of St Davids	Lab	p770

North America

Lord Powell of Bayswater	CB	p895
Lord Sawyer	Lab	p927
Lord Selkirk of Douglas	Con	p930
Lord Triesman	Lab	p976

Northern Ireland

Baroness Goudie	Lab	p732
Baroness O'Neill of Bengarve	CB	p876

Norway

Lord Anderson of Swansea	Lab	p605
Lord Elton	Con	p701
Lord Faulkner of Worcester	Lab	p708
Baroness Maddock	Lib Dem	p836
Bishop of Newcastle	Non-Affiliated	p867
Lord Wallace of Tankerness	Lib Dem	p992

Oman

Lord German	Lib Dem	p724
Lord Guthrie of Craigiebank	CB	p741
Baroness Jolly	Lib Dem	p785
Baroness Rawlings	Con	p903

Pakistan

Lord Ahmad of Wimbledon	Con	p600
Lord Ahmed	Non-Affiliated	p601
Lord Avebury	Lib Dem	p613
Lord Bhatia	Non-Affiliated	p624
Baroness Butler-Sloss	CB	p652
Lord Desai	Lab	p689
Lord Guthrie of Craigiebank	CB	p741
Lord Maclennan of Rogart	Lib Dem	p834
Lord Newby	Lib Dem	p866
Lord Patel of Blackburn	Lab	p885
Baroness Warsi	Con	p996
Lord West of Spithead	Lab	p1000

Palestine

Baroness Blackstone	Lab	p629
Baroness Brinton	Lib Dem	p642
Archbishop of Canterbury	Non-Affiliated	p655
Lord Carey of Clifton	CB	p656
Lord Cope of Berkeley	Con	p671
Bishop of Coventry	Non-Affiliated	p674

Lord Hylton	CB	p777
Lord Palmer of Childs Hill	Lib Dem	p881
Lord Phillips of Sudbury	Lib Dem	p890
Baroness Tonge	Ind	
	Lib Dem	p972

Panama

Lord Scott of Foscote	CB	p928

Papua New Guinea

Bishop of St Edmundsbury and Ipswich	Non-Affiliated	p923

Peru

Lord Avebury	Lib Dem	p613
Baroness Coussins	CB	p674
Baroness Thomas of Walliswood	Lib Dem	p970

Poland

Baroness Cox	CB	p675
Baroness Deech	CB	p687
Lord Mackenzie of Framwellgate	Non-Affiliated	p832
Lord Paul	Non-Affiliated	p887
Lord Radice	Lab	p900
Lord Roberts of Llandudno	Lib Dem	p913

Portugal

Lord Bach	Lab	p614
Lord Briggs	CB	p641
Baroness Gibson of Market Rasen	Lab	p725
Lord Moran	CB	p855
Lord Plant of Highfield	Lab	p892

Qatar

Baroness Harris of Richmond	Lib Dem	p749
Lord Patel of Blackburn	Lab	p885
Lord Redesdale	Lib Dem	p905
Viscount Simon	Lab	p939
Baroness Uddin	Non-Affiliated	p983

Romania

Lord Lamont of Lerwick	Con	p804
Lord McFall of Alcluith	Lab/Co-op	p829
Baroness Nicholson of Winterbourne	Lib Dem	p868
Lord Watson of Richmond	Lib Dem	p998

Russia

Lord Aberdare	CB	p598
Lord Ahmad of Wimbledon	Con	p600
Lord Ahmed	Non-Affiliated	p601
Lord Chalfont	Non-Affiliated	p660
Viscount Colville of Culross	CB	p670
Lord Davies of Stamford	Lab	p685
Lord Foulkes of Cumnock	Lab/Co-op	p717
Lord Giddens	Lab	p725

Lord Moser	*CB*	p860
Lord Paul	*Non-Affiliated*	p887
Baroness Smith of Basildon	*Lab/Co-op*	p943
Lord Storey	*Lib Dem*	p958

Syria

Bishop of Coventry	*Non-Affiliated*	p674
Baroness Nicholson of Winterbourne	*Lib Dem*	p868
Lord Phillips of Sudbury	*Lib Dem*	p890

Taiwan

Lord Faulkner of Worcester	*Lab*	p708
Baroness Gale	*Lab*	p721
Lord Grantchester	*Lab*	p735
Lord Hardie	*CB*	p747
Baroness Howells of St Davids	*Lab*	p770
Lord Kilclooney	*CB*	p794
Baroness Knight of Collingtree	*Con*	p800
Baroness Perry of Southwark	*Con*	p889
Lord Rana	*CB*	p902
Lord Rosser	*Lab*	p918
Lord Steel of Aikwood	*Lib Dem*	p951

Tajikistan

Baroness Stern	*CB*	p952

Tanzania

Baroness Armstrong of Hill Top	*Lab*	p608
Bishop of Gloucester	*Non-Affiliated*	p728
Lord Jones of Cheltenham	*Lib Dem*	p787
Lord Patel	*CB*	p884
Lord Popat	*Con*	p894
Bishop of St Edmundsbury and Ipswich	*Non-Affiliated*	p923
Bishop of Wakefield	*Non-Affiliated*	p989

Thailand

Baroness Henig	*Lab*	p755

Togo

Lord McColl of Dulwich	*Con*	p826

Trinidad and Tobago

Baroness Berridge	*Con*	p623

Tunisia

Lord McNally	*Lib Dem*	p835
Baroness Uddin	*Non-Affiliated*	p983

Turkey

Baroness Bakewell	*Lab*	p615
Lord Bhattacharyya	*Lab*	p624
Lord Clement-Jones	*Lib Dem*	p666
Baroness Fritchie	*CB*	p720

Baroness Hussein-Ece	*Lib Dem*	p776
Lord Inglewood	*Con*	p779
Lord Kilclooney	*CB*	p794
Baroness Ludford	*Lib Dem*	p823
Lord Methuen	*Lib Dem*	p848
Baroness Nicholson of Winterbourne	*Lib Dem*	p868
Lord Paul	*Non-Affiliated*	p887
Lord Rea	*Lab*	p904

Turks and Caicos Islands

Lord Jones of Cheltenham	*Lib Dem*	p787

Uganda

Baroness Armstrong of Hill Top	*Lab*	p608
Baroness Cox	*CB*	p675
Lord Freeman	*Con*	p718
Lord Howarth of Newport	*Lab*	p767
Lord Jones of Cheltenham	*Lib Dem*	p787
Lord Loomba	*Lib Dem*	p821
Lord McColl of Dulwich	*Con*	p826
Lord Popat	*Con*	p894
Lord Roberts of Llandudno	*Lib Dem*	p913
Earl of Sandwich	*CB*	p926
Bishop of Winchester	*Non-Affiliated*	p1010

Ukraine

Lord Wallace of Saltaire	*Lib Dem*	p992
Lord West of Spithead	*Lab*	p1000

United Arab Emirates

Lord Clement-Jones	*Lib Dem*	p666
Lord Jones of Cheltenham	*Lib Dem*	p787
Lord Patel of Blackburn	*Lab*	p885
Lord Paul	*Non-Affiliated*	p887
Baroness Perry of Southwark	*Con*	p889
Lord Rowe-Beddoe	*CB*	p919
Baroness Uddin	*Non-Affiliated*	p983
Baroness Warsi	*Con*	p996

United Kingdom

Lord Baker of Dorking	*Con*	p615
Viscount Brookeborough	*CB*	p645
Earl Cathcart	*Con*	p659
Lord Lee of Trafford	*Lib Dem*	p808
Lord Lexden	*Con*	p812
Lord Lingfield	*Con*	p815
Lord Loomba	*Lib Dem*	p821
Lord MacLaurin of Knebworth	*Con*	p834
Lord Mawson	*CB*	p846
Lord Rogers of Riverside	*Lab*	p916
Lord Saatchi	*Con*	p921
Lord Tebbit	*Con*	p966
Lord Vinson	*Con*	p987

United States of America

Lord Aberdare	*CB*	p598
Lord Adebowale	*CB*	p599
Lord Ahmad of Wimbledon	*Con*	p600
Lord Ahmed	*Non-Affiliated*	p601
Lord Allan of Hallam	*Lib Dem*	p603
Lord Armstrong of Ilminster	*CB*	p608
Lord Astor of Hever	*Con*	p611
Lord Bach	*Lab*	p614
Lord Barnett	*Lab*	p619
Lord Bassam of Brighton	*Lab/Co-op*	p619
Lord Bates	*Con*	p620
Baroness Benjamin	*Lib Dem*	p621
Baroness Billingham	*Lab*	p626
Lord Birt	*CB*	p628
Baroness Blackstone	*Lab*	p629
Lord Blyth of Rowington	*Con*	p632
Lord Boateng	*Lab*	p632
Baroness Bonham-Carter of Yarnbury	*Lib Dem*	p633
Lord Borwick	*Con*	p634
Lord Bradley	*Lab*	p638
Lord Bragg	*Lab*	p639
Lord Briggs	*CB*	p641
Lord Brittan of Spennithorne	*Con*	p643
Lord Broers	*CB*	p643
Lord Brooke of Sutton Mandeville	*Con*	p644
Lord Clinton-Davis	*Lab*	p667
Lord Cormack	*Con*	p672
Baroness Corston	*Lab*	p673
Lord Crathorne	*Con*	p676
Lord Cunningham of Felling	*Non-Affiliated*	p680
Lord Davies of Stamford	*Lab*	p685
Baroness Dean of Thornton-le-Fylde	*Lab*	p685
Lord Dear	*CB*	p686
Baroness Deech	*CB*	p687
Lord Desai	*Lab*	p689
Lord Dobbs	*Con*	p691
Baroness Doocey	*Lib Dem*	p693
Lord Dykes	*Lib Dem*	p696
Lord Eames	*CB*	p696
Lord Empey	*UUP*	p703
Lord Evans of Watford	*Lab*	p704
Baroness Falkner of Margravine	*Lib Dem*	p707
Lord Feldman	*Con*	p709
Lord Fellowes	*CB*	p710
Lord Flight	*Con*	p714
Baroness Ford	*Non-Affiliated*	p715
Lord Foster of Bishop Auckland	*Lab*	p716
Baroness Fritchie	*CB*	p720

Baroness Gale	*Lab*	p721
Bishop of Gloucester	*Non-Affiliated*	p728
Lord Goodhart	*Lib Dem*	p730
Baroness Goudie	*Lab*	p732
Baroness Gould of Potternewton	*Lab*	p732
Lord Graham of Edmonton	*Lab/Co-op*	p734
Baroness Hanham	*Con*	p744
Lord Harris of Haringey	*Lab*	p748
Lord Harrison	*Lab*	p750
Lord Haskel	*Lab*	p751
Lord Haskins	*CB*	p751
Baroness Healy of Primrose Hill	*Lab*	p755
Lord Higgins	*Con*	p758
Lord Howard of Lympne	*Con*	p766
Lord Howe of Aberavon	*Con*	p768
Baroness Hughes of Stretford	*Lab*	p772
Lord Hunt of Chesterton	*Lab*	p773
Lord Hunt of Wirral	*Con*	p774
Lord Inge	*CB*	p778
Lord Jones of Birmingham	*CB*	p786
Lord Kakkar	*CB*	p790
Lord Kerr of Kinlochard	*CB*	p792
Lord Kimball	*Con*	p795
Baroness King of Bow	*Lab*	p795
Baroness Kingsmill	*Lab*	p797
Baroness Knight of Collingtree	*Con*	p800
Baroness Kramer	*Lib Dem*	p801
Lord Leitch	*Lab*	p809
Lord Lester of Herne Hill	*Lib Dem*	p809
Baroness Liddell of Coatdyke	*Lab*	p813
Lord Liddle	*Lab*	p814
Baroness Lister of Burtersett	*Lab*	p817
Lord Loomba	*Lib Dem*	p821
Lord Low of Dalston	*CB*	p822
Baroness Ludford	*Lib Dem*	p823
Lord McAvoy	*Lab/Co-op*	p825
Lord McConnell of Glenscorrodale	*Lab*	p827
Lord MacGregor of Pulham Market	*Con*	p830
Lord MacKenzie of Culkein	*Lab*	p832
Lord Mackenzie of Framwellgate	*Non-Affiliated*	p832
Lord Maclennan of Rogart	*Lib Dem*	p834
Lord Martin of Springburn	*CB*	p843
Baroness Massey of Darwen	*Lab*	p844
Lord Mawhinney	*Con*	p845
Baroness Miller of Hendon	*Con*	p849
Lord Mitchell	*Lab*	p850
Lord Mogg	*CB*	p851
Lord Montagu of Beaulieu	*Con*	p852
Lord Moran	*CB*	p855
Lord Morgan	*Lab*	p855
Lord Morrow	*DUP*	p860

Lord Moser	CB	p860
Baroness O'Cathain	Con	p874
Lord O'Donnell	CB	p875
Lord Oxburgh	CB	p879
Lord Pannick	CB	p882
Lord Parekh	Lab	p882
Lord Patel	CB	p884
Lord Paul	Non-Affiliated	p887
Lord Pendry	Lab	p888
Lord Plumb	Con	p893
Baroness Prosser	Lab	p897
Lord Puttnam	Lab	p898
Lord Renfrew of Kaimsthorn	Con	p907
Lord Renwick of Clifton	CB	p909
Lord Ribeiro	Con	p909
Lord Risby	Con	p912
Baroness Royall of Blaisdon	Lab	p920
Lord Sainsbury of Turville	Lab	p923
Marquess of Salisbury	Non-Affiliated	p924
Baroness Scott of Needham Market	Lib Dem	p929
Baroness Sharp of Guildford	Lib Dem	p933
Lord Singh of Wimbledon	CB	p941
Baroness Smith of Basildon	Lab/Co-op	p943
Lord Smith of Finsbury	Non-Affiliated	p944
Lord Smith of Leigh	Lab	p946
Lord Spicer	Con	p950
Lord Stevens of Ludgate	Con Ind	p954
Lord Stevenson of Coddenham	CB	p955
Lord Stirrup	CB	p956
Lord Stoneham of Droxford	Lib Dem	p958
Lord Storey	Lib Dem	p958
Baroness Stowell of Beeston	Con	p958
Lord Taylor of Warwick	Non-Affiliated	p965
Lord Thomas of Swynnerton	CB	p969
Viscount Trenchard	Con	p976
Baroness Trumpington	Con	p978
Lord Wallace of Saltaire	Lib Dem	p992
Lord Wallace of Tankerness	Lib Dem	p992
Lord Walton of Detchant	CB	p994
Lord Warner	Lab	p994
Lord Watson of Richmond	Lib Dem	p998

Lord Weidenfeld	CB	p999
Lord Wigley	PlC	p1003
Lord Williams of Baglan	CB	p1004
Lord Wood of Anfield	Lab	p1012
Baroness Young of Hornsey	CB	p1016
Lord Young of Norwood Green	Lab	p1017

Uzbekistan

Baroness Stern	CB	p952

Vanuatu

Bishop of Chester	Non-Affiliated	p662
Bishop of St Edmundsbury and Ipswich	Non-Affiliated	p923

Vietnam

Baroness D'Souza	Lord Speaker	p694
Lord Haworth	Lab	p753
Lord Howarth of Newport	Lab	p767
Lord Williams of Baglan	CB	p1004

Wales

Lord Aberdare	CB	p598
Lord Elis-Thomas	PlC	p700
Lord Morgan	Lab	p855
Baroness Morgan of Drefelin	CB	p856
Lord Thomas of Gresford	Lib Dem	p968

Yemen

Lord Avebury	Lib Dem	p613
Baroness Nicholson of Winterbourne	Lib Dem	p868

Zambia

Lord Jones of Cheltenham	Lib Dem	p787
Lord Patel of Blackburn	Lab	p885
Lord Skelmersdale	Con	p941
Lord Turnbull	CB	p981

Zimbabwe

Lord Avebury	Lib Dem	p613
Baroness Bonham-Carter of Yarnbury	Lib Dem	p633
Lord Gardiner of Kimble	Con	p722
Lord Jones of Cheltenham	Lib Dem	p787
Lord Palmer	CB	p881
Earl of Sandwich	CB	p926
Lord Shutt of Greetland	Lib Dem	p939

MPs who are now Peers

Irene Adams
Baroness Adams of Craigielea

Richard Allan
Lord Allan of Hallam

David Alton
Lord Alton of Liverpool

Michael Ancram
Marquess of Lothian

Donald Anderson
Lord Anderson of Swansea

Jeffrey Archer
Lord Archer of Weston-Super-Mare

Hilary Armstrong
Baroness Armstrong of Hill Top

Paddy Ashdown
Lord Ashdown of Norton-sub-Hamdon

Kenneth Baker
Lord Baker of Dorking

Joel Barnett
Lord Barnett

Michael Bates
Lord Bates

Paul Boateng
Lord Boateng

Betty Boothroyd
Baroness Boothroyd

Tim Boswell
Lord Boswell of Aynho

Virginia Bottomley
Baroness Bottomley of Nettlestone

Keith Bradley
Lord Bradley

Leon Brittan
Lord Brittan of Spennithorne

Peter Brooke
Lord Brooke of Sutton Mandeville

Des Browne
Lord Browne of Ladyton

Angela Browning
Baroness Browning

John Burnett
Lord Burnett

Dale Campbell-Savours
Lord Campbell-Savours

Alexander Carlile
Lord Carlile of Berriew

Matthew Carrington
Lord Carrington of Fulham

Lynda Chalker
Baroness Chalker of Wallasey

David Chidgey
Lord Chidgey

David Clark
Lord Clark of Windermere

Lynda Clark
Baroness Clark of Calton

Stanley Clinton-Davis
Lord Clinton-Davis

Sebastian Coe
Lord Coe

John Cope
Lord Cope of Berkeley

Patrick Cormack
Lord Cormack

Jean Corston
Baroness Corston

Brian Cotter
Lord Cotter

Jack Cunningham
Lord Cunningham of Felling

Bryan Davies
Lord Davies of Oldham

Quentin Davies
Lord Davies of Stamford

Donald Dixon
Lord Dixon

James Douglas-Hamilton
Lord Selkirk of Douglas

Alf Dubs
Lord Dubs

Hugh Dykes
Lord Dykes

John Eden
Lord Eden of Winton

Nicholas Edwards
Lord Crickhowell

Dafydd Elis-Thomas
Lord Elis-Thomas

Dafydd Elystan-Morgan
Lord Elystan-Morgan

John Evans
Lord Evans of Parkside

Ronnie Fearn
Lord Fearn

Howard Flight
Lord Flight

Janet Fookes
Baroness Fookes

Michael Forsyth
Lord Forsyth of Drumlean

Derek Foster
Lord Foster of Bishop Auckland

George Foulkes
Lord Foulkes of Cumnock

Norman Fowler
Lord Fowler

Roger Freeman
Lord Freeman

Tristan Garel-Jones
Lord Garel-Jones

Robert Gascoyne-Cecil
Marquess of Salibsury

Llin Golding
Baroness Golding

Alastair Goodlad
Lord Goodlad

Edward Graham
Lord Graham of Edmonton

Bruce Grocott
Lord Grocott

John Gummer
Lord Deben

Archie Hamilton
Lord Hamilton of Epsom

Roy Hattersley
Lord Hattersley

Helene Hayman
Baroness Hayman

Denis Healey
Lord Healey

Michael Heseltine
Lord Heseltine

Terence Higgins
Lord Higgins

Robin Hodgson
Lord Hodgson of Astley Abbotts

John Horam
Lord Horam

Michael Howard
Lord Howard of Lympne

Alan Howarth
Lord Howarth of Newport

Geoffrey Howe
Lord Howe of Aberavon

David Howell
Lord Howell of Guildford

William Howie
Lord Howie of Troon

Douglas Hoyle
Lord Hoyle

Beverly Hughes
Baroness Hughes of Stretford

Robert Hughes
Lord Hughes of Woodside

David Hunt
Lord Hunt of Wirral

Douglas Hurd
Lord Hurd of Westwell

John Hutton
Lord Hutton of Furness

Greville Janner
Lord Janner of Braunstone

Patrick Jenkin
Lord Jenkin of Roding

Barry Jones
Lord Jones

Nigel Jones
Lord Jones of Cheltenham

Michael Jopling
Lord Jopling

Frank Judd
Lord Judd

Marcus Kimball
Lord Kimball

Oona King
Baroness King of Bow

Tom King
Lord King of Bridgwater

Neil Kinnock
Lord Kinnock

Archy Kirkwood
Lord Kirkwood of Kirkhope

Jill Knight
Baroness Knight of Collingtree

Jim Knight
Lord Knight of Weymouth

Susan Kramer
Baroness Kramer

Norman Lamont
Lord Lamont of Lerwick

Ian Lang
Lord Lang of Monkton

Nigel Lawson
Lord Lawson of Blaby

John Lee
Lord Lee of Trafford

Helen Liddell
Baroness Liddell of Coatdyke

Robert Lindsay
Earl of Crawford and Balcarres

Michael Lord
Lord Framlingham

Eric Lubbock
Lord Avebury

Richard Luce
Lord Luce

Thomas McAvoy
Lord McAvoy

John McFall
Lord McFall of Alcluith

John MacGregor
Lord MacGregor of Pulham Market

George Mackie
Lord Mackie of Benshie

David Maclean
Lord Blencathra

Robert Maclennan
Lord Maclennan of Rogart

Tom McNally
Lord McNally

Diana Maddock
Baroness Maddock

Ken Maginnis
Lord Maginnis of Drumglass

Michael Martin
Lord Martin of Springburn

Roy Mason
Lord Mason of Barnsley

Brian Mawhinney
Lord Mawhinney

John Maxton
Lord Maxton

Patrick Mayhew
Lord Mayhew of Twysden

James Molyneaux
Lord Molyneaux of Killead

Lewis Moonie
Lord Moonie

John Moore
Lord Moore of Lower Marsh

Estelle Morris
Baroness Morris of Yardley

John Morris
Lord Morris of Aberavon

Michael Morris
Lord Naseby

Maurice Morrow
Lord Morrow

Colin Moynihan
Lord Moynihan

Emma Nicholson
Baroness Nicholson of Winterbourne

Martin O'Neill
Lord O'Neill of Clackmannan

Sally Oppenheim-Barnes
Baroness Oppenheim-Barnes

David Owen
Lord Owen

Ian Paisley
Lord Bannside

Cecil Parkinson
Lord Parkinson

Christopher Patten
Lord Patten of Barnes

John Patten
Lord Patten

Tom Pendry
Lord Pendry

John Prescott
Lord Prescott

James Prior
Lord Prior

Joyce Quin
Baroness Quin

Giles Radice
Lord Radice

John Reid
Lord Reid of Cardowan

Timothy Renton
Lord Renton of Mount Harry

Ivor Richard
Lord Richard

Wyn Roberts
Lord Roberts of Conwy

George Robertson
Lord Robertson of Port Ellen

William Rodgers
Lord Rodgers of Quarry Bank

Jeffrey Rooker
Lord Rooker

John Roper
Lord Roper

Ted Rowlands
Lord Rowlands

Richard Ryder
Lord Ryder of Wensum

Michael Shaw
Lord Shaw of Northstead

Robert Sheldon
Lord Sheldon

Gillian Shephard
Baroness Shephard of Northwold

Angela Smith
Baroness Smith of Basildon

Chris Smith
Lord Smith of Finsbury

Peter Snape
Lord Snape

Clive Soley
Lord Soley

Michael Spicer
Lord Spicer

Richard Spring
Lord Risby

David Steel
Lord Steel of Aikwood

Nicol Stephen
Lord Stephen

Ian Stewart
Lord Stewartby

David Stoddart
Lord Stoddart of Swindon

Dick Taverne
Lord Taverne

Ann Taylor
Baroness Taylor of Bolton

John David Taylor
Lord Kilclooney

Matthew Taylor
Lord Taylor of Goss Moor

Norman Tebbit
Lord Tebbit

Peter Temple-Morris
Lord Temple-Morris

John Tomlinson
Lord Tomlinson

Jenny Tonge
Baroness Tonge

Graham Tope
Lord Tope

Don Touhig
Lord Touhig

David Trimble
Lord Trimble

Christopher Tugendhat
Lord Tugendhat

Dennis Turner
Lord Bilston

Paul Tyler
Lord Tyler

David Waddington
Lord Waddington

John Wakeham
Lord Wakeham

William Waldegrave
Lord Waldegrave of North Hill

Jim Wallace
Lord Wallace of Tankerness

Mike Watson
Lord Watson of Invergowrie

Dafydd Wigley
Lord Wigley

Shirley Williams
Baroness Williams of Crosby

Phil Willis
Lord Willis of Knaresborough

Michael Wills
Lord Wills

Kenneth Woolmer
Lord Woolmer of Leeds

Ian Wrigglesworth
Lord Wrigglesworth

Hereditary Peer Members

Under the 1999 House of Lords Act, which abolished the right of most hereditary peers to sit in the Upper Chamber, 92 hereditary peers retained their seats. These include two hereditary office holders, the Duke of Norfolk (Earl Marshal), and the Marquess of Cholmondeley (Lord Great Chamberlain).

Peers of Ireland are marked*, with their British honours in parenthesis.

A number of other peers sit under their hereditary titles, although they are members by virtue of life peerages, the titles of which appear in bold.

Lord Aberdare cr. 1873

Lord Addington cr. 1887

Viscount Allenby of Megiddo cr. 1919

Earl of Arran cr. 1762* (Baron Sudley)

Lord Ashton of Hyde cr.1911

Viscount Astor cr. 1917

Lord Astor of Hever cr. 1956

Earl Attlee cr. 1955

Lord Avebury cr. 1900

Earl Baldwin of Bewdley cr. 1937

Lord Berkeley cr. 1421 (LP **Baron Gueterbock** 2000)

Lord Borwick cr. 1922

Lord Brabazon of Tara cr. 1942

Viscount Bridgeman cr. 1929

Lord Bridges cr. 1957

Viscount Brookeborough cr. 1952

Lord Brougham and Vaux cr. 1860

Earl of Caithness cr. 1455

Lord Carrington cr. 1796* (LP **Baron Carington of Upton** 1999) (Baron Carrington)

Earl Cathcart cr. 1814

Viscount Chandos cr. 1954 (LP **Baron Lyttelton of Aldershot** 2000)

Marquess of Cholmondeley cr. 1815

Lord Chorley cr. 1945

Earl of Clancarty cr. 1803* (Baron Trench)

Lord Cobbold cr. 1960

Viscount Colville of Culross cr. 1902

Lord Colwyn cr. 1917

Earl of Courtown cr. 1762* (Baron Saltersford)

Viscount Craigavon cr. 1927

Lord Crathorne cr. 1959

Earl of Crawford and Balcarres cr. 1398/1651 (LP **Baron Balniel** 1974)

Lord de Mauley cr. 1838

Lord Denham cr. 1937

Earl of Dundee cr. 1660

Viscount Eccles cr. 1964

Lord Elton cr. 1934

Earl of Erroll cr. 1452

Viscount of Falkland cr. 1620

Lord Freyberg cr. 1951

Lord Geddes cr. 1942

Earl of Glasgow cr. 1703

Lord Glenarthur cr. 1918

Lord Glentoran cr. 1939

Viscount Goschen cr. 1900

Lord Grantchester cr. 1953

Lord Greenway cr. 1927

Lord Grenfell cr. 1902 (LP **Baron Grenfell of Kilvey** 2000)

Viscount Hanworth cr. 1936

Lord Henley cr. 1799* (Baron Northington)

Earl of Home cr. 1604

Earl Howe cr. 1821

Lord Hylton cr. 1866

Lord Inglewood cr. 1964

Earl of Lindsay cr. 1633

Earl of Listowel cr. 1822* (Baron Hare)

Earl of Liverpool cr. 1905

Marquess of Lothian cr. 1701 (LP **Baron Kerr of Monteviot** 2010)

Lord Lucas of Crudwell and Dingwall cr. 1663/ 1609

Lord Luke cr. 1929

Lord Lyell cr. 1914

Earl of Lytton cr. 1880

Lord Mancroft cr. 1937

Countess of Mar cr. 1114

Earl of Mar and Kellie cr. 1565/1619 (LP **Baron Erskine of Alloa Tower** 2000)

Lord Methuen cr. 1838

Lord Montagu of Beaulieu cr. 1885

Viscount Montgomery of Alamein cr. 1946

Duke of Montrose cr. 1707

Lord Moran cr. 1943

Lord Moynihan cr. 1929

Duke of Norfolk cr. 1483

Lord Northbourne cr. 1884

Lord Northbrook cr. 1866

Lord Palmer cr. 1933

Earl Peel cr. 1929

Lord Ponsonby of Shulbrede cr. 1930 (LP **Baron Ponsonby of Roehampton** 2000)

Lord Rea cr. 1937

Lord Redesdale cr. 1902 (LP **Baron Mitford** 2000)

Viscount Ridley cr. 1900

Earl of Rosslyn cr. 1801

Lord Rotherwick cr. 1939

Lord St John of Bletso cr. 1558

Marquess of Salisbury cr. 1789 (LP **Baron Gascoyne-Cecil** 1999)

Lady Saltoun of Abernethy cr. 1445
Earl of Sandwich cr. 1660
Earl of Selborne cr. 1882
Lord Selsdon cr. 1932
Earl of Shrewsbury and Waterford cr. 1442/1446
Viscount Simon cr. 1940
Lord Skelmersdale cr. 1828
Viscount Slim cr. 1960
Earl of Snowdon cr. 1961 (LP **Baron Armstrong-Jones** 1999)
Earl of Stair cr. 1703

Lord Strathclyde cr. 1955
Lord Swinfen cr. 1919
Viscount Tenby cr. 1957
Lord Trefgarne cr. 1947
Viscount Trenchard cr. 1936
Viscount Ullswater cr. 1921
Lord Walpole cr. 1723
Viscount Waverley cr. 1952
Lord Willoughby de Broke cr. 1491
Viscount Younger of Leckie cr. 1923

Bishops

By ancient usage the two Anglican archbishops and the bishops of London, Durham and Winchester automatically have seats in the House of Lords. Since the mid-nineteenth century the number of bishops in the House (known as lords spiritual as opposed to lords temporal) has been limited to 26. The remaining diocesan bishops qualify for membership according to seniority, the longest serving bishop outside the Lords succeeding to a vacancy among the lords spiritual.

ARCHBISHOPS (2) AND DIOCESAN BISHOPS (2) EX-OFFICIO

Most Rev. Justin Welby	Canterbury
Most Rev. John Sentamu	York
Rt Rev. Richard Chartres	London
Rt Rev. Tim Dakin	Winchester

BISHOPS IN ORDER OF SENIORITY (22)*

		Entered Lords
Rt Rev. Peter Forster	Chester	2001
Rt Rev. Martin Wharton	Newcastle	2002
Rt Rev. Tim Stevens	Leicester	2003
Rt Rev. Graham James	Norwich	2004
Rt Rev. John Richard Packer	Ripon and Leeds†	2006
Rt Rev. Stephen Platten	Wakefield‡	2009
Rt Rev. Michael Hill	Bristol	2009
Rt Rev. Jonathan Gledhill	Lichfield	2009
Rt Rev. Michael Perham	Gloucester	2009
Rt Rev. Alastair Redfern	Derby	2010
Rt Rev. David Urquhart	Birmingham	2010
Rt Rev. John Pritchard	Oxford	2010
Rt Rev. John Inge	Worcester	2012
Rt Rev. Christopher Cocksworth	Coventry	2013
Rt Rev. Tim Thornton	Truro	2013
Rt Rev. Steven Croft	Sheffield	2013
Rt Rev. Alan Smith	St Albans	2013
Rt Rev. James Newcome	Carlisle	2013
Rt Rev. Paul Butler	Southwell and Nottingham	2013*
Rt Rev. Donald Allister	Peterborough	2013
Rt Rev. Christopher Foster	Portsmouth	2013-14
Rt Rev. Stephen Cottrell	Chelmsford	2014

* Bishop of Southwell and Nottingham is to be introduced as the Bishop of Durham in early 2014.

†Bishop of Ripon and Leeds is to retire after Easter recess and will be replaced by the Rt Rev. James Langstaff the Bishop of Rochester.

‡Bishop of Wakefield is to retire after Easter recess and will be replaced by the Rt Rev. Stephen Conway the Bishop of Ely.

NB: Please note Bishops of St Albans, Carlisle, Southwell and Nottingham, Peterborough, Portsmouth, and Chelmsford have no biographies as they were not introduced to the House of Lords at the time of going to press.

Law Lords

Senior members of the judiciary are unable to sit or vote in the House of Lords until they retire.

Supreme Court Justices:

Lord Clarke of Stone-cum-Ebony
Baroness Hale of Richmond
Lord Kerr of Tonaghmore

Lord Mance
Lord Neuberger of Abbotsbury

Lord Chief Justice of England and Wales: Rt Hon Sir John Thomas has been appointed. Not introduced to the House of Lords at time of going to press.
Senators of the College of Justice in Scotland: Lord Boyd of Duncansby, Baroness Clark of Carlton

Peers on leave of absence (43)

Baroness Amos	NA	Lord Millett	CB
Baroness Ashton of Upholland	NA	Lord Molyneaux of Killead	CB
Lord Attenborough	Lab	Lord Mustill	CB
Lord Bannside	DUP	Lord Nicholls of Birkenhead	CB
Lord Barber of Tewkesbury	CB	Baroness Nicol	Lab/Co-op
Lord Black of Crossharbour	NA	Duke of Norfolk	CB
Lord Blyth of Rowington	Con	Baroness Paisley of St George's	DUP
Lord Bridges	CB	Baroness Platt of Writtle	NA
Lord Briggs	CB	Lord Prior	NA
Lord Chalfont	NA	Lord Prys-Davies	Lab
Marquess of Cholmondeley	NA	Lord Sainsbury of Preston Candover	NA
Earl of Crawford and Balcarres	Con	Lord Sainsbury of Turville	Lab
Lord Goff of Chieveley	NA	Marquess of Salisbury	NA
Lord Griffiths	CB	Lord Sandberg	Lib Dem
Lord Hope of Thornes	CB	Lord Simon of Highbury	NA
Lord Kilpatrick of Kincraig	NA	Lord Simpson of Dunkeld	Lab
Lord Kimball	Con	Earl of Snowdon	CB
Lord Kingsdown	NA	Lord Templeman	CB
Baroness Lockwood	Lab	Lord Thomas of Macclesfield	Lab/Co-op
Lord Macaulay of Bragar	Lab	Baroness Vadera	Lab
Lord Mackie of Benshie	NA	Lord Vincent of Coleshill	CB
Lord Mason of Barnsley	Lab		

Women Members (192)

Women were first admitted into the House of Lords by the Life Peerage Act, 1958. Women peers by succession (indicated with an asterisk) were not admitted into the Upper House until 1963.

Baroness Adams of Craigielea	Lab	Baroness Bonham-Carter of Yarnbury	Lib Dem
Baroness Afshar	CB	Baroness Boothroyd	CB
Baroness Amos	NA	Baroness Bottomley of Nettlestone	Con
Baroness Andrews	Lab	Baroness Brinton	Lib Dem
Baroness Anelay of St Johns	Con	Baroness Browning	Con
Baroness Armstrong of Hill Top	Lab	Baroness Buscombe	Con
Baroness Ashton of Upholland	NA	Baroness Butler-Sloss	CB
Baroness Bakewell	Lab	Baroness Byford	Con
Baroness Bakewell of Hardington Mandeville	Lib Dem	Baroness Campbell of Loughborough	CB
		Baroness Campbell of Surbiton	CB
Baroness Barker	Lib Dem	Baroness Chalker of Wallasey	Con
Baroness Benjamin	Lib Dem	Baroness Clark of Calton	NA
Baroness Berridge	Con	Baroness Cohen of Pimlico	Lab
Baroness Billingham	Lab	Baroness Corston	Lab
Baroness Blackstone	Lab	Baroness Coussins	CB
Baroness Blood	Lab	Baroness Cox	CB

Baroness Crawley	*Lab*	Baroness Jenkin of Kennington	*Con*
Baroness Cumberlege	*Con*	Baroness Jolly	*Lib Dem*
Baroness Dean of Thornton-le-Fylde	*Lab*	Baroness Jones of Moulsecoomb	*Green*
Baroness Deech	*CB*	Baroness Jones of Whitchurch	*Lab*
Baroness Donaghy	*Lab*	Baroness Kenndey of Cradley	*Lab*
Baroness Doocey	*Lib Dem*	Baroness Kennedy of The Shaws	*Lab*
Baroness Drake	*Lab*	Baroness Kidron	*CB*
Baroness D'Souza	*Lord Speaker*	Baroness King of Bow	*Lab*
Baroness Eaton	*Con*	Baroness Kingsmill	*Lab*
Baroness Eccles of Moulton	*Con*	Baroness Kinnock of Holyhead	*Lab*
Baroness Emerton	*CB*	Baroness Knight of Collingtree	*Con*
Baroness Falkender	*Lab*	Baroness Kramer	*Lib Dem*
Baroness Falkner of Margravine	*Lib Dem*	Baroness Lane-Fox of Soho	*CB*
Baroness Farrington of Ribbleton	*Lab*	Baroness Lawrence of Clarendon	*Lab*
Baroness Finlay of Llandaff	*CB*	Baroness Liddell of Coatdyke	*Lab*
Baroness Flather	*CB*	Baroness Linklater of Butterstone	*Lib Dem*
Baroness Fookes	*Con*	Baroness Lister of Burtersett	*Lab*
Baroness Ford	*NA*	Baroness Lockwood	*Lab*
Baroness Fritchie	*CB*	Baroness Ludford	*Lib Dem*
Baroness Gale	*Lab*	Baroness McDonagh	*Lab*
Baroness Garden of Frognal	*Lib Dem*	Baroness McIntosh of Hudnall	*Lab*
Baroness Gardner of Parkes	*Con*	Baroness Maddock	*Lib Dem*
Baroness Gibson of Market Rasen	*Lab*	Baroness Mallalieu	*Lab*
Baroness Goldie	*Con*	Baroness Manningham-Buller	*CB*
Baroness Golding	*Lab*	Baroness Manzoor	*Lib Dem*
Baroness Goudie	*Lab*	Countess of Mar*	*CB*
Baroness Gould of Potternewton	*Lab*	Baroness Masham of Ilton	*CB*
Baroness Greenfield	*CB*	Baroness Massey of Darwen	*Lab*
Baroness Greengross	*CB*	Baroness Meacher	*CB*
Baroness Grender	*Lib Dem*	Baroness Miller of Chilthorne Domer	*Lib Dem*
Baroness Grey-Thompson	*CB*	Baroness Miller of Hendon	*Con*
Baroness Hale of Richmond	*NA*	Baroness Morgan of Drefelin	*CB*
Baroness Hamwee	*Lib Dem*	Baroness Morgan of Ely	*Lab*
Baroness Hanham	*Con*	Baroness Morgan of Huyton	*Lab*
Baroness Harris of Richmond	*Lib Dem*	Baroness Morris of Bolton	*Con*
Baroness Hayman	*CB*	Baroness Morris of Yardley	*Lab*
Baroness Hayter of Kentish Town	*Lab*	Baroness Murphy	*CB*
Baroness Healy of Primrose Hill	*Lab*	Baroness Neuberger	*CB*
Baroness Henig	*Lab*	Baroness Neville-Jones	*Con*
Baroness Heyhoe Flint	*Con*	Baroness Neville-Rolfe	*Con*
Baroness Hilton of Eggardon	*Lab*	Baroness Newlove	*Con*
Baroness Hodgson of Abinger	*Con*	Baroness Nicholson of Winterbourne	*Lib Dem*
Baroness Hogg	*CB*	Baroness Nicol	*Lab/Co-op*
Baroness Hollins	*CB*	Baroness Noakes	*Con*
Baroness Hollis of Heigham	*Lab*	Baroness Northover	*Lib Dem*
Baroness Hooper	*Con*	Baroness Nye	*Lab*
Baroness Howarth of Breckland	*CB*	Baroness O'Cathain	*Con*
Baroness Howe of Idlicote	*CB*	Baroness O'Loan	*CB*
Baroness Howells of St Davids	*Lab*	Baroness O'Neill of Bengarve	*CB*
Baroness Hughes of Stretford	*Lab*	Baroness Oppenheim-Barnes	*Con*
Baroness Humphreys	*Lib Dem*	Baroness Paisley of St George's	*DUP*
Baroness Hussein-Ece	*Lib Dem*	Baroness Parminter	*Lib Dem*
Baroness James of Holland Park	*Con*	Baroness Perry of Southwark	*Con*
Baroness Jay of Paddington	*Lab*	Baroness Pitkeathley	*Lab*

Baroness Platt of Writtle	NA	Baroness Thomas of Walliswood	Lib Dem
Baroness Prashar	CB	Baroness Thomas of Winchester	Lib Dem
Baroness Prosser	Lab	Baroness Thornton	Lab/Co-op
Baroness Quin	Lab	Baroness Tonge	Ind Lib Dem
Baroness Ramsay of Cartvale	Lab	Baroness Trumpington	Con
Baroness Randerson	Lib Dem	Baroness Turner of Camden	Lab
Baroness Rawlings	Con	Baroness Tyler of Enfield	Lib Dem
Baroness Rendell of Babergh	Lab	Baroness Uddin	NA
Baroness Richardson of Calow	CB	Baroness Vadera	Lab
Baroness Royall of Blaisdon	Lab	Baroness Valentine	CB
Lady Saltoun of Abernethy*	CB	Baroness Verma	Con
Baroness Scotland of Asthal	Lab	Baroness Wall of New Barnet	Lab
Baroness Scott of Needham Market	Lib Dem	Baroness Walmsley	Lib Dem
Baroness Seccombe	Con	Baroness Warnock	CB
Baroness Shackleton of Belgravia	Con	Baroness Warsi	Con
Baroness Sharp of Guildford	Lib Dem	Baroness Warwick of Undercliffe	Lab
Baroness Sharples	Con	Baroness Wheatcroft	Con
Baroness Shephard of Northwold	Con	Baroness Wheeler	Lab
Baroness Sherlock	Lab	Baroness Whitaker	Lab
Baroness Smith of Basildon	Lab/Co-op	Baroness Wilcox	Con
Baroness Smith of Gilmorehill	Lab	Baroness Wilkins	Lab
Baroness Stedman-Scott	Con	Baroness Williams of Crosby	Lib Dem
Baroness Stern	CB	Baroness Williams of Trafford	Con
Baroness Stowell of Beeston	Con	Baroness Worthington	Lab
Baroness Suttie	Lib Dem	Baroness Young of Hornsey	CB
Baroness Symons of Vernham Dean	Lab	Baroness Young of Old Scone	NA
Baroness Taylor of Bolton	Lab		

Peers by Age
(Ages as at 1 September 2013)

	Conservative	%	Labour	%	Lib Dem	%	CB	%	Other*	%	Total
30–39	1	0.5	0	0.0	0	0.0	0	0.0	0	0.0	1
40–49	9	4.1	8	3.5	3	3.1	5	2.6	0	0.0	25
50–59	30	13.8	23	10.0	18	18.8	17	8.7	14	17.9	102
60–69	55	25.2	73	31.9	31	32.3	61	31.1	32	41	252
70–79	76	34.9	86	37.6	33	34.4	65	33.2	17	21.8	277
80–89	41	18.8	36	15.7	10	10.4	39	19.9	12	15.4	138
Over 90	6	2.8	3	1.3	1	1	9	4.6	3	3.8	22
	218		229		96		196		78		817
Average age	**69.9**		**69.9**		**67.7**		**71.8**		**68.8**		**70.0**

Peers who have not supplied date of birth

Baroness Bakewell of Hardington Mandeville
Baroness Eaton
Baroness Grender
Lord Holmes of Richmond
Baroness Kennedy of Cradley

Baroness Lawrence of Clarendon
Lord Leigh of Hurley
Lord Paddick
Lord Verjee
Lord Whitby

Lord Wei	36	Lord Adonis	50
Lord Purvis of Tweed	39	Lord Glasman	50/51
Baroness Lane-Fox of Soho	40	Lord Kennedy of Southwark	50
Baroness Berridge	41	Lord Taylor of Goss Moor	50
Baroness Worthington	41	Lord Adebowale	51
Lord Freyberg	42	Lord Bilimoria	51
Baroness Warsi	42	Lord Finkelstein	51
Baroness Grey-Thompson	44	Baroness Newlove	51
Lord Ahmad of Wimbledon	45	Earl of Stair	51
Baroness King of Bow	45	Baroness Vadera	51
Lord Mendelsohn	45/46	Baroness Barker	52
Baroness Suttie	45	Lord Bates	52
Lord Wolfson of Aspley Guise	45	Baroness Kidron	52
Lord Wood of Anfield	45	Baroness McDonagh	52
Baroness Morgan of Ely	46	Baroness Morgan of Drefelin	52
Lord Redesdale	46	Lord Patel of Bradford	52
Baroness Stowell of Beeston	46	Baroness Sherlock	52
Baroness Williams of Trafford	46	Marquess of Cholmondeley	53
Lord Allan of Hallam	47	Viscount Colville of Culross	53
Lord Feldman of Elstree	47	Lord Darzi of Denham	53
Viscount Goschen	47	Lord Drayson	53
Lord Alli	48	Lord Hill of Oareford	53
Lord Knight of Weymouth	48	Lord McConnell of Glenscorrodale	53
Lord Livingston of Parkhead	48/49	Lord Rennard	53
Lord Black of Brentwood	49	Lord Stephen	53
Lord Carter of Barnes	49	Lord Strathclyde	53
Lord Kakkar	49	Baroness Campbell of Surbiton	54
Earl of Listowel	49	Bishop of Coventry	54
Baroness Parminter	49	Lord Kestenbaum	54
Lord Palumbo of Southwark	49/50	Baroness Morgan of Huyton	54
Lord Addington	50		

Lord Ponsonby of Shulbrede	54	Baroness Royall of Blaisdon	58
Baroness Smith of Basildon	54	Baroness Scotland of Asthal	58
Lord Truscott	54	Baroness Amos	59
Baroness Uddin	54	Baroness Buscombe	59
Baroness Valentine	54	Earl of Courtown	59
Baroness Verma	54	Lord Harris of Haringey	59
Lord Ashton of Hyde	55	Lord Henley	59
Baroness Bonham-Carter of Yarnbury	55	Baroness Hussein-Ece	59
Lord Fink	55	Lord Malloch-Brown	59
Baroness Ford	55	Lord Mandelson	59
Lord Hastings of Scarisbrick	55	Baroness Miller of Chilthorne Domer	59
Baroness Manzoor	55	Lord Northbrook	59
Viscount Ridley	55	Baroness Northover	59
Earl of Rosslyn	55	Lord Rotherwick	59
Bishop of Winchester	55	Lord Wallace of Tankerness	59
Lord Ahmed	56	Lord Bassam of Brighton	60
Lord Allen of Kensington	56	Lord Blair of Boughton	60
Earl Attlee	56	Lord Blencathra	60
Lord Coe	56	Lord Boyd of Duncansby	60
Lord de Mauley	56	Earl Cathcart	60
Lord Mancroft	56	Viscount Chandos	60
Duke of Norfolk	56	Lord Davies of Abersoch	60
Lord St John of Bletso	56	Lord Macdonald of River Glaven	60
Baroness Scott of Needham Market	56	Lord Marks of Henley-on-Thames	60
Bishop of Sheffield	56	Baroness Morris of Bolton	60
Bishop of Truro	56	Baroness Neville-Rolfe	60
Baroness Tyler of Enfield	56	Lord Newby	60
Baroness Ashton of Upholland	57	Lord O'Donnell	60
Archbishop of Canterbury	57	Lord Popat	60
Lord Deighton	57	Earl of Shrewsbury and Waterford	60
Lord Gardiner of Kimble	57	Lord Taylor of Warwick	60
Lord Hussain	57	Baroness Thornton	60
Baroness Jenkin of Kennington	57	Viscount Astor	61
Lord Jones of Birmingham	57	Bishop of Birmingham	61
Earl of Lindsay	57	Lord Blackwell	61
Lord Marland	57	Lord Bourne of Aberystwyth	61
Lord Moynihan	57	Viscount Brookeborough	61
Lord Pannick	57	Lord Browne of Ladyton	61
Lord Sassoon	57	Earl of Clancarty	61
Baroness Shackleton of Belgravia	57	Lord Crisp	61
Baroness Stedman-Scott	57	Lord Falconer of Thoroton	61
Lord Turner of Ecchinswell	57	Baroness Morris of Yardley	61
Bishop of Worcester	57/58	Baroness O'Loan	61
Viscount Younger of Leckie	57	Lord Palmer	61
Lord Alderdice	58	Lord Teverson	61
Lord Borwick	58	Baroness Wheatcroft	61
Baroness Brinton	58	Lord Wills	61
Lord Collins of Highbury	58	Lord Alton of Liverpool	62
Baroness Falkner of Margravine	58	Lord Boateng	62
Lord Forsyth of Drumlean	58	Baroness Coussins	62
Baroness Healy of Primrose Hill	58	Lord Dannatt	62
Lord Hutton of Furness	58	Lord Davidson of Glen Clova	62
Baroness Jones of Whitchurch	58	Lord Gold	62
Lord Mawson	58	Lord Grantchester	62
Baroness Nye	58		

Baroness Greenfield	62
Lord Hall of Birkenhead	62
Earl Howe	62
Lord Inglewood	62
Baroness Jolly	62
Baroness Liddell of Coatdyke	62
Lord Lucas of Crudwell and Dingwall	62
Baroness Ludford	62
Lord Norton of Louth	62
Bishop of Norwich	62
Lord Smith of Finsbury	62
Baroness Symons of Vernham Dean	62
Viscount Trenchard	62
Baroness Young of Hornsey	62
Lord True	62
Baroness Benjamin	63
Lord Bew	63
Lord Bradley	63
Lord Cameron of Dillington	63
Bishop of Chester	63
Lord Clement-Jones	63
Baroness Crawley	63
Lord Elder	63
Lord Faulks	63
Lord Freud	63
Baroness Goldie	63
Lord Goldsmith	63
Baroness Hayter of Kentish Town	63
Baroness Hughes of Stretford	63
Baroness Kennedy of The Shaws	63
Baroness Kramer	63
Earl of Lytton	63
Baroness Neuberger	63
Bishop of St Edmundsbury and Ipswich	63
Lord Stirrup	63
Viscount Waverley	63
Lord Williams of Oystermouth	63
Bishop of Bristol	64
Earl of Caithness	64
Baroness Campbell of Loughborough	64
Baroness Clark of Calton	64
Lord Dobbs	64/65
Earl of Dundee	64
Lord Fellowes of West Stafford	64
Baroness Finlay of Llandaff	64
Lord Green of Hurstpierpoint	64
Baroness Hayman	64
Lord Hunt of Kings Heath	64
Baroness Jones of Moulsecoomb	64
Bishop of Lichfield	64
Baroness Lister of Burtersett	64
Earl of Mar and Kellie	64
Lord Morrow	64
Lord Nash	64
Baroness Noakes	64
Lord Ryder of Wensum	64
Lord Storey	64
Lord Watson of Invergowrie	64
Baroness Wheeler	64
Lord Williams of Baglan	64
Archbishop of York	64
Baroness Adams of Craigielea	65
Lord Berkeley of Knighton	65
Baroness Bottomley of Nettlestone	65
Lord Brabazon of Tara	65
Lord Browne of Belmont	65
Lord Browne of Madingley	65
Lord Carlile of Berriew	65
Lord Carrington of Fulham	65
Bishop of Derby	65
Baroness Doocey	65
Baroness Drake	65
Lord Empey	65
Earl of Erroll	65
Lord Flight	65
Bishop of Gloucester	65
Lord Harrison	65
Lord Haworth	65
Lord Jones of Cheltenham	65
Lord Kerr of Tonaghmore	65
Lord King of Lothbury	65
Lord Leitch	65
Lord Lipsey	65
Lord Lloyd-Webber	65
Baroness Manningham-Buller	65
Lord Myners	65
Lord Neuberger of Abbotsbury	65
Bishop of Oxford	65
Earl Peel	65
Baroness Prashar	65
Baroness Randerson	65
Lord Sacks	65
Lord Sharkey	65
Lord Stoneham of Droxford	65
Lord Touhig	65
Lord West of Spithead	65
Baroness Young of Old Scone	65
Lord Aberdare	66
Baroness Anelay of St Johns	66
Lord Bach	66
Lord Bichard	66
Baroness Browning	66
Lord Condon	66
Lord Currie of Marylebone	66
Lord Edmiston	66
Lord Elis-Thomas	66
Baroness Goudie	66
Baroness Hamwee	66
Lord Hennessy of Nympsfield	66

Lord Janvrin	66	Lord Kirkham	68
Baroness Kingsmill	66	Lord Krebs	68
Bishop of Leicester	66	Lord Lexden	68
Lord Liddle	66	Earl of Liverpool	68
Bishop of London	66	Marquess of Lothian	68
Baroness McIntosh of Hudnall	66	Lord McFall of Alcluith	68
Lord Moonie	66	Baroness Maddock	68
Baroness Murphy	66	Lord Martin of Springburn	68
Lord Oakeshott of Seagrove Bay	66	Lord Monks	68
Lord Reid of Cardowan	66	Lord O'Neill of Clackmannan	68
Bishop of Ripon and Leeds	66	Lord Ouseley	68
Lord Risby	66	Lord Patten	68
Marquess of Salisbury	66	Lord Plant of Highfield	68
Lord Stevenson of Balmacara	66	Baroness Quin	68
Lord Sugar	66	Lord Rosser	68
Baroness Taylor of Bolton	66	Lord Skelmersdale	68
Bishop of Wakefield	66	Lord Smith of Leigh	68
Baroness Armstrong of Hill Top	67	Lord Stevenson of Coddenham	68
Lord Ashcroft	67	Lord Trimble	68
Lord Astor of Hever	67	Lord Turnbull	68
Lord Burnett	67	Baroness Warwick of Undercliffe	68
Lord Carter of Coles	67	Baroness Afshar	69
Lord Faulkner of Worcester	67	Lord Balfe	69
Viscount Hanworth	67	Lord Ballyedmond	69
Lord Hardie	67	Lord Black of Crossharbour	69
Baroness Hogg	67	Lord Burns	69
Baroness Hollins	67	Viscount Craigavon	69
Lord Jay of Ewelme	67	Lord Curry of Kirkharle	69
Lord Kirkwood of Kirkhope	67	Lord Davies of Stamford	69
Lord Mackay of Drumadoon	67	Baroness D'Souza	69
Lord McKenzie of Luton	67	Lord Filkin	69
Lord Magan of Castletown	67	Baroness Garden of Frognal	69
Baroness Mallalieu	67	Baroness Harris of Richmond	69
Lord Robertson of Port Ellen	67	Baroness Henig	69
Lord Saatchi	67	Earl of Home	69
Lord Sewel	67	Lord Howarth of Newport	69
Lord Sherbourne of Didsbury	67	Baroness Kinnock of Holyhead	69
Lord Shipley	67	Lord Laird	69
Lord Stern of Brentford	67	Lord Levy	69
Lord Strasburger	67	Lord Loomba	69
Baroness Thomas of Winchester	67	Lord McAvoy	69
Lord Trees	67	Lord Mogg	69
Lord Waldegrave of North Hill	67	Bishop of Newcastle	69
Baroness Wilkins	67	Lord Patten of Barnes	69
Lord Bamford	68	Lord Ribeiro	69
Lord Beecham	68	Lord Smith of Kelvin	69
Lord Best	68	Lord Taylor of Holbeach	69
Lord Birt	68	Lord Tope	69
Baroness Donaghy	68	Lord Triesman	69
Lord Eatwell	68	Lord Walker of Aldringham	69
Lord German	68	Baroness Andrews	70
Lord Glenarthur	68	Baroness Blackstone	70
Lord Grabiner	68	Lord Boswell of Aynho	70
Baroness Hale of Richmond	68	Lord Bowness	70
Lord Hollick	68		

Lord Boyce	70
Lord Campbell-Savours	70
Lord Clarke of Stone-cum-Ebony	70
Baroness Cumberlege	70
Baroness Dean of Thornton-le-Fylde	70
Baroness Deech	70
Lord Evans of Watford	70
Lord Goodlad	70
Lord Grade of Yarmouth	70
Lord Harris of Peckham	70
Baroness Linklater of Butterstone	70
Lord Low of Dalston	70
Lord Mackenzie of Framwellgate	70
Lord McNally	70
Lord Mance	70
Lord Mitchell	70
Lord Razzall	70
Earl of Sandwich	70
Lord Sawyer	70
Lord Sharman	70
Lord Spicer	70
Lord Stevens of Kirkwhelpington	70
Lord Stone of Blackheath	70
Lord Tunnicliffe	70
Lord Vallance of Tummel	70
Baroness Walmsley	70
Lord Whitty	70
Lord Wigley	70
Lord Wilson of Dinton	70
Lord Bell	71
Lord Bilston	71
Lord Brennan	71
Lord Brooke of Alverthorpe	71
Lord Cavendish of Furness	71
Lord Chadlington	71
Baroness Chalker of Wallasey	71
Lord Chidgey	71
Lord Colwyn	71
Baroness Corston	71
Lord Fellowes	71
Lord Foulkes of Cumnock	71
Lord Freeman	71
Baroness Fritchie	71
Lord Glendonbrook	71
Lord Greaves	71
Lord Griffiths of Burry Port	71
Lord Griffiths of Fforestfach	71
Lord Hamilton of Epsom	71
Lord Hodgson of Astley Abbotts	71
Lord Hunt of Chesterton	71
Lord Hunt of Wirral	71
Lord Kerr of Kinlochard	71
Lord Kinnock	71
Lord Lamont of Lerwick	71
Lord Lee of Trafford	71
Lord Levene of Portsoken	71
Lord Lingfield	71
Baroness Nicholson of Winterbourne	71
Lord Pearson of Rannoch	71
Lord Rees of Ludlow	71
Lord Rogan	71
Lord Selkirk of Douglas	71
Lord Shutt of Greetland	71
Lord Simpson of Dunkeld	71
Lord Snape	71
Baroness Stern	71
Lord Tyler	71
Viscount Ullswater	71
Baroness Wall of New Barnet	71
Lord Willis of Knaresborough	71
Lord Young of Norwood Green	71
Lord Ashdown of Norton-sub-Hamdon	72
Baroness Byford	72
Lord Collins of Mapesbury	72
Lord Evans of Temple Guiting	72
Baroness Gale	72
Lord Garel-Jones	72
Baroness Gibson of Market Rasen	72
Lord Greenway	72
Lord Grocott	72
Lord Hameed	72
Lord Hanningfield	72
Baroness Hollis of Heigham	72
Lord Howard of Lympne	72
Lord Howard of Rising	72
Baroness Howarth of Breckland	72
Lord Judge	72
Countess of Mar	72
Baroness O'Neill of Bengarve	72
Lord Powell of Bayswater	72
Lord Puttnam	72
Lord Rooker	72
Lord Sainsbury of Turville	72
Lord Sheikh	72
Lord Sutherland of Houndwood	72
Baroness Tonge	72
Lord Trefgarne	72
Lord Wallace of Saltaire	72
Lord Warner	72
Lord Watson of Richmond	72
Baroness Wilcox	72
Lord Archer of Weston-Super-Mare	73
Lord Berkeley	73
Lord Bhattacharyya	73
Lord Blyth of Rowington	73
Lord Bragg	73
Lord Brittan of Spennithorne	73
Lord Clark of Windermere	73

Baroness Cohen of Pimlico	73
Lord Crathorne	73
Lord Davies of Oldham	73
Lord Deben	73
Lord Desai	73
Baroness Farrington of Ribbleton	73
Baroness Hanham	73
Lord Hart of Chilton	73
Lord Hope of Thornes	73
Lord Irvine of Lairg	73
Baroness Jay of Paddington	73
Lord Lang of Monkton	73
Lord Macdonald of Tradeston	73
Lord MacKenzie of Culkein	73
Lord Mawhinney	73
Baroness Meacher	73
Baroness Neville-Jones	73
Lord Patel of Blackburn	73
Baroness Pitkeathley	73
Lord Rowlands	73
Earl of Selborne	73
Baroness Shephard of Northwold	73
Viscount Simon	73
Baroness Smith of Gilmorehill	73
Lord Winston	73
Lord Woolmer of Leeds	73
Lord Wrigglesworth	73/74
Lord Anderson of Swansea	74
Baroness Billingham	74
Lord Broers	74
Lord Cormack	74
Lord Cunningham of Felling	74
Lord Dykes	74
Lord Framlingham	74
Earl of Glasgow	74
Lord Guthrie of Craigiebank	74
Baroness Heyhoe Flint	74
Baroness Hooper	74
Lord Horam	74
Lord Lyell	74
Baroness Massey of Darwen	74
Lord Morris of Handsworth	74
Lord Palmer of Childs Hill	74
Lord Phillips of Sudbury	74
Lord Rana	74
Baroness Rawlings	74
Baroness Sharp of Guildford	74
Lord Simon of Highbury	74
Lord Skidelsky	74
Lord Soley	74
Lord Swinfen	74
Lord Tomlinson	74
Lord Walpole	74
Lord Willoughby de Broke	74

Earl of Arran	75
Earl Baldwin of Bewdley	75
Baroness Blood	75
Lord Brougham and Vaux	75
Lord Butler of Brockwell	75
Lord Dear	75
Lord Fowler	75
Lord Geddes	75
Lord Giddens	75
Lord Hope of Craighead	75
Lord James of Blackheath	75
Lord Kilclooney	75
Lord Lea of Crondall	75
Lord Maginnis of Drumglass	75
Lord Moore of Lower Marsh	75
Baroness O'Cathain	75
Lord Owen	75
Lord Patel	75
Lord Phillips of Worth Matravers	75
Lord Prescott	75
Lord Renwick of Clifton	75
Baroness Richardson of Calow	75
Lord Rowe-Beddoe	75
Lord Selsdon	75
Lord Steel of Aikwood	75
Lord Temple-Morris	75
Lord Thomas of Macclesfield	75
Lord Walker of Gestingthorpe	75
Lord Wasserman	75
Lord Bradshaw	76
Lord Brookman	76
Lord Brown of Eaton-under-Heywood	76
Lord Cobbold	76
Lord Cope of Berkeley	76
Baroness Cox	76
Lord Dholakia	76
Lord Eames	76
Lord Foster of Bishop Auckland	76
Lord Haskins	76
Lord Jones	76
Lord Luce	76
Lord MacGregor of Pulham Market	76
Lord MacLaurin of Knebworth	76
Lord Naseby	76
Baroness Prosser	76
Lord Radice	76
Lord Renfrew of Kaimsthorn	76
Lord Smith of Clifton	76
Lord Thomas of Gresford	76
Lord Tugendhat	76
Lord Carey of Clifton	77
Lord Cotter	77
Lord Cullen of Whitekirk	77
Baroness Emerton	77

Baroness Fookes	77
Lord Gordon of Strathblane	77
Lord Hannay of Chiswick	77
Lord Harries of Pentregarth	77
Baroness Hilton of Eggardon	77
Lord Howell of Guildford	77
Lord Jordan	77
Lord Laming	77
Lord Lester of Herne Hill	77
Lord Maclennan of Rogart	77
Lord Maxton	77
Lord May of Oxford	77
Lord Noon	77
Baroness Ramsay of Cartvale	77
Lord Roberts of Llandudno	77
Lord Roper	77
Lord Saville of Newdigate	77
Lord Stevens of Ludgate	77
Baroness Thomas of Walliswood	77
Baroness Whitaker	77
Lord Wolfson of Sunningdale	77
Lord Baker of Dorking	78
Lord Davies of Coity	78
Lord Dixon-Smith	78
Lord Donoughue	78
Viscount of Falkland	78
Lord Glentoran	78
Baroness Greengross	78
Lord Grenfell	78
Lord Haskel	78
Lord Inge	78
Lord Judd	78
Baroness Masham of Ilton	78
Duke of Montrose	78
Lord Oxburgh	78
Lord Palumbo	78
Lord Parekh	78
Lord Ramsbotham	78
Lord Scott of Foscote	78
Lord Sterling of Plaistow	78
Lord Stewartby	78
Lord Wilson of Tillyorn	78
Lord Brooke of Sutton Mandeville	79
Lord Carswell	79
Lord Crickhowell	79
Baroness Eccles of Moulton	79
Baroness Flather	79
Lord Hoffmann	79
Lord Layard	79
Lord Leach of Fairford	79
Lord Macaulay of Bragar	79
Lord Morgan	79
Lord Pendry	79
Lord Tanlaw	79

Lord Turnberg	79
Lord Williamson of Horton	79
Baroness Bakewell	80
Baroness Butler-Sloss	80
Lord Dubs	80
Lord Elystan-Morgan	80
Baroness Golding	80
Lord Goodhart	80
Baroness Gould of Potternewton	80
Lord Hattersley	80
Lord Heseltine	80
Lord Imbert	80
Lord King of Bridgwater	80
Lord Luke	80
Lord McColl of Dulwich	80
Baroness Miller of Hendon	80
Lord Nicholls of Birkenhead	80
Lord Rogers of Riverside	80
Lord Sanderson of Bowden	80
Lord Sheppard of Didgemere	80
Lord Singh of Wimbledon	80
Lord Wade of Chorlton	80
Lord Williams of Elvel	80
Lord Woolf	80
Lord Alliance	81
Lord Bhatia	81
Lord Clarke of Hampstead	81
Baroness Falkender	81
Baroness Howe of Idlicote	81
Lord Hughes of Woodside	81
Lord Hylton	81
Lord Jacobs	81
Lord Joffe	81
Lord Kalms	81
Lord Lawson of Blaby	81
Lord Marlesford	81
Lord Millett	81
Lord Morris of Aberavon	81
Baroness Paisley of St George's	81
Baroness Perry of Southwark	81
Lord Renton of Mount Harry	81
Lord Richard	81
Lord Steyn	81
Lord Thomas of Swynnerton	81
Lord Wakeham	81
Lord Young of Graffham	81
Viscount Allenby of Megiddo	82
Lord Borrie	82
Viscount Bridgeman	82
Lord Cameron of Lochbroom	82
Viscount Eccles	82
Lord Evans of Parkside	82
Lord Fearn	82
Lord Gavron	82

Baroness Howells of St Davids	82	Lord Feldman	86
Lord Hutton	82	Baroness Gardner of Parkes	86
Lord Jopling	82	Lord Goff of Chieveley	86
Lord Methuen	82	Lord Howe of Aberavon	86
Lord Mustill	82	Lord Jenkin of Roding	86
Lord Parkinson	82	Lord Kingsdown	86
Lord Paul	82	Lord Mackay of Clashfern	86
Lord Peston	82	Lord Montagu of Beaulieu	86
Lady Saltoun of Abernethy	82	Lord Sandberg	86
Lord Tebbit	82	Viscount Slim	86
Lord Vincent of Coleshill	82	Lord Bannside	87
Lord Vinson	82	Lord Eden of Winton	87
Lord Wright of Richmond	82	Lord Kilpatrick of Kincraig	87
Baroness Boothroyd	83	Lord Macfarlane of Bearsden	87
Lord Browne-Wilkinson	83	Lord Neill of Bladen	87
Lord Chorley	83	Lord Northbourne	87
Lord Craig of Radley	83	Lord Soulsby of Swaffham Prior	87
Lord Elton	83	Lord Stoddart of Swindon	87
Lord Hoyle	83	Lord Christopher	88
Lord Hurd of Westwell	83	Lord Graham of Edmonton	88
Lord Kirkhill	83	Lord Moran	88
Lord Mayhew of Twysden	83	Lord Plumb	88
Lord Nickson	83	Lord Barnett	89
Baroness Oppenheim-Barnes	83	Lord Griffiths	89
Baroness Rendell of Babergh	83	Lord Howie of Troon	89
Lord Roberts of Conwy	83	Baroness Lockwood	89
Baroness Seccombe	83	Lord Mason of Barnsley	89
Earl of Snowdon	83	Lord Prys-Davies	89
Baroness Williams of Crosby	83	Lord Rix	89
Lord Avebury	84	Lord Sheldon	89
Lord Clinton-Davis	84	Lord Tombs	89
Lord Dixon	84	Baroness Warnock	89
Lord Kimball	84	Lord Attenborough	90
Lord Lloyd of Berwick	84	Baroness Knight of Collingtree	90
Lord McCluskey	84	Lord Moser	90
Lord Rodgers of Quarry Bank	84	Baroness Nicol	90
Lord Taverne	84	Baroness Platt of Writtle	90
Lord Taylor of Blackburn	84	Baroness Sharples	90
Lord Tordoff	84	Baroness Trumpington	90
Lord Waddington	84	Lord Walton of Detchant	90
Lord Bridges	85	Lord Briggs	92
Lord Denham	85	Lord Knights	92
Lord Higgins	85	Lord Shaw of Northstead	92
Lord Janner of Braunstone	85	Lord Chalfont	93
Lord Lewis of Newnham	85	Baroness James of Holland Park	93
Viscount Montgomery of Alamein	85	Lord Molyneaux of Killead	93
Lord Prior	85	Lord Quirk	93
Lord Rea	85	Lord Templeman	93
Lord Sainsbury of Preston Candover	85	Lord Weidenfeld	93
Viscount Tenby	85	Lord Carrington	94
Baroness Turner of Camden	85	Lord Ezra	94
Lord Armstrong of Ilminster	86	Lord Mackie of Benshie	94
Lord Brooks of Tremorfa	86	Lord Barber of Tewkesbury	95
Earl of Crawford and Balcarres	86	Lord Healey	96

Peers by Party

Labour*

ADAMS OF CRAIGIELEA Baroness
ADONIS Lord
ALLEN OF KENSINGTON LORD
ALLI Lord
ANDERSON OF SWANSEA Lord
ANDREWS Baroness
ARMSTRONG OF HILL TOP Baroness
ATTENBOROUGH Lord
BACH Lord
BAKEWELL Baroness
BARNETT Lord
BASSAM OF BRIGHTON Lord
BEECHAM Lord
BERKELEY Lord
BHATTACHARYYA Lord
BILLINGHAM Baroness
BILSTON Lord
BLACKSTONE Baroness
BLOOD Baroness
BOATENG Lord
BORRIE Lord
BRADLEY Lord
BRAGG Lord
BRENNAN Lord
BROOKE OF ALVERTHORPE Lord
BROOKMAN Lord
BROOKS OF TREMORFA Lord
BROWNE OF LADYTON Lord
CAMPBELL-SAVOURS Lord
CARTER OF BARNES Lord
CARTER OF COLES Lord
CHANDOS Viscount
CHRISTOPHER Lord
CLARK OF WINDERMERE Lord
CLARKE OF HAMPSTEAD Lord
CLINTON-DAVIS Lord
COHEN OF PIMLICO Baroness
COLLINS OF HIGHBURY Lord
CORSTON Baroness
CRAWLEY Baroness
DARZI OF DENHAM Lord
DAVIDSON OF GLEN CLOVA Lord
DAVIES OF ABERSOCH Lord
DAVIES OF COITY Lord
DAVIES OF OLDHAM Lord
DAVIES OF STAMFORD Lord
DEAN OF THORNTON-LE-FYLDE Baroness
DESAI Lord
DIXON Lord
DONAGHY Baroness

DONOUGHUE Lord
DRAKE Baroness
DRAYSON Lord
DUBS Lord
EATWELL Lord
ELDER Lord
EVANS OF PARKSIDE Lord
EVANS OF TEMPLE GUITING Lord
EVANS OF WATFORD Lord
FALCONER OF THOROTON Lord
FALKENDER Baroness
FARRINGTON OF RIBBLETON Baroness
FAULKNER OF WORCESTER Lord
FILKIN Lord
FOSTER OF BISHOP AUCKLAND Lord
FOULKES OF CUMNOCK Lord
GALE Baroness
GAVRON Lord
GIBSON OF MARKET RASEN Baroness
GIDDENS Lord
GLASMAN Lord
GOLDING Baroness
GOLDSMITH Lord
GORDON OF STRATHBLANE Lord
GOUDIE Baroness
GOULD OF POTTERNEWTON Baroness
GRABINER Lord
GRAHAM OF EDMONTON Lord
GRANTCHESTER Lord
GRENFELL Lord
GRIFFITHS OF BURRY PORT Lord
GROCOTT Lord
HANWORTH Viscount
HARRIS OF HARINGEY Lord
HARRISON Lord
HART OF CHILTON Lord
HASKEL Lord
HATTERSLEY Lord
HAUGHEY Lord
HAWORTH Lord
HAYTER OF KENTISH TOWN Baroness
HEALEY Lord
HEALY OF PRIMROSE HILL Baroness
HENIG Baroness
HILTON OF EGGARDON Baroness
HOLLICK Lord
HOLLIS OF HEIGHAM Baroness
HOWARTH OF NEWPORT Lord
HOWELLS OF ST DAVIDS Baroness
HOWIE OF TROON Lord

HOYLE Lord
HUGHES OF STRETFORD Baroness
HUGHES OF WOODSIDE Lord
HUNT OF CHESTERTON Lord
HUNT OF KINGS HEATH Lord
HUTTON OF FURNESS Lord
IRVINE OF LAIRG Lord
JANNER OF BRAUNSTONE Lord
JAY OF PADDINGTON Baroness
JOFFE Lord
JONES Lord
JONES OF WHITCHURCH Baroness
JORDAN Lord
JUDD Lord
KENNEDY OF CRADLEY Baroness
KENNEDY OF SOUTHWARK Lord
KENNEDY OF THE SHAWS Baroness
KESTENBAUM Lord
KING OF BOW Baroness
KINGSMILL Baroness
KINNOCK Lord
KINNOCK OF HOLYHEAD Baroness
KIRKHILL Lord
KNIGHT OF WEYMOUTH Lord
LAWRENCE OF CLARENDON Baroness
LAYARD Lord
LEA OF CRONDALL Lord
LEITCH Lord
LEVY Lord
LIDDELL OF COATDYKE Baroness
LIDDLE Lord
LIPSEY Lord
LISTER OF BURTERSETT Baroness
LOCKWOOD Baroness
MACAULAY OF BRAGAR Lord
McAVOY Lord
McCONNELL OF GLENSCORRODALE Lord
McDONAGH Baroness
MACDONALD OF TRADESTON Lord
McFALL OF ALCLUITH Lord
McINTOSH OF HUDNALL Baroness
MacKENZIE OF CULKEIN Lord
McKENZIE OF LUTON Lord
MALLALIEU Baroness
MANDELSON Lord
MASON OF BARNSLEY Lord
MASSEY OF DARWEN Baroness
MAXTON Lord
MENDELSOHN Lord
MITCHELL Lord
MONKS Lord
MOONIE Lord
MORGAN Lord

MORGAN OF ELY Baroness
MORGAN OF HUYTON Baroness
MORRIS OF ABERAVON Lord
MORRIS OF HANDSWORTH Lord
MORRIS OF YARDLEY Baroness
MYNERS Lord
NICOL Baroness
NOON Lord
NYE Baroness
O'NEILL OF CLACKMANNAN Lord
PAREKH Lord
PATEL OF BLACKBURN Lord
PATEL OF BRADFORD Lord
PENDRY Lord
PESTON Lord
PITKEATHLEY Baroness
PLANT OF HIGHFIELD Lord
PONSONBY OF SHULBREDE Lord
PRESCOTT Lord
PROSSER Baroness
PRYS-DAVIES Lord
PUTTNAM Lord
QUIN Baroness
RADICE Lord
RAMSAY OF CARTVALE Baroness
REA Lord
REID OF CARDOWAN Lord
RENDELL OF BABERGH Baroness
RICHARD Lord
ROBERTSON OF PORT ELLEN Lord
ROGERS OF RIVERSIDE Lord
ROOKER Lord
ROSSER Lord
ROWLANDS Lord
ROYALL OF BLAISDON Baroness
SAINSBURY OF TURVILLE Lord
SAWYER Lord
SCOTLAND OF ASTHAL Baroness
SHELDON Lord
SHERLOCK Baroness
SIMON Viscount
SIMPSON OF DUNKELD Lord
SMITH OF BASILDON Baroness
SMITH OF GILMOREHILL Baroness
SMITH OF LEIGH Lord
SNAPE Lord
SOLEY Lord
STEVENSON OF BALMACARA Lord
STONE OF BLACKHEATH Lord
SUGAR Lord
SYMONS OF VERNHAM DEAN Baroness
TAYLOR OF BLACKBURN Lord
TAYLOR OF BOLTON Baroness

TEMPLE-MORRIS Lord
THOMAS OF MACCLESFIELD Lord
THORNTON Baroness
TOMLINSON Lord
TOUHIG Lord
TRIESMAN Lord
TUNNICLIFFE Lord
TURNBERG Lord
TURNER OF CAMDEN Baroness
VADERA Baroness
WALL OF NEW BARNET Baroness
WARNER Lord
WARWICK OF UNDERCLIFFE Baroness

WATSON OF INVERGOWRIE Lord
WEST OF SPITHEAD Lord
WHEELER Baroness
WHITAKER Baroness
WHITTY Lord
WILKINS Baroness
WILLIAMS OF ELVEL Lord
WILLS Lord
WINSTON Lord
WOOD OF ANFIELD Lord
WOOLMER OF LEEDS Lord
WORTHINGTON Baroness
YOUNG OF NORWOOD GREEN Lord

* Includes 15 Labour/Co-operative peers.

Conservative

AHMAD OF WIMBLEDON Lord
ANELAY OF ST JOHNS Baroness
ARRAN Earl of
ASHCROFT Lord
ASHTON OF HYDE Lord
ASTOR Viscount
ASTOR OF HEVER Lord
ATTLEE Earl
BAKER OF DORKING Lord
BALFE Lord
BALLYEDMOND Lord
BAMFORD Lord
BATES Lord
BELL Lord
BERRIDGE Baroness
BLACK OF BRENTWOOD Lord
BLACKWELL Lord
BLENCATHRA Lord
BLYTH OF ROWINGTON Lord
BORWICK Lord
BOTTOMLEY OF NETTLESTONE Baroness
BOURNE OF ABERYSTWYTH Lord
BOWNESS Lord
BRABAZON OF TARA Lord
BRIDGEMAN Viscount
BRITTAN OF SPENNITHORNE Lord
BROOKE OF SUTTON MANDEVILLE Lord
BROUGHAM AND VAUX Lord
BROWNING Baroness
BUSCOMBE Baroness
BYFORD Baroness
CAITHNESS Earl of
CARRINGTON Lord
CARRINGTON OF FULHAM Lord
CATHCART Earl
CAVENDISH OF FURNESS Lord
CHADLINGTON Lord

CHALKER OF WALLASEY Baroness
COE Lord
COLWYN Lord
COPE OF BERKELEY Lord
CORMACK Lord
COURTOWN Earl of
CRATHORNE Lord
CRAWFORD AND BALCARRES Earl of
CRICKHOWELL Lord
CUMBERLEGE Baroness
DEBEN Lord
DEIGHTON Lord
DE MAULEY Lord
DENHAM Lord
DIXON-SMITH Lord
DOBBS Lord
DUNDEE Earl of
EATON Baroness
ECCLES Viscount
ECCLES OF MOULTON Baroness
EDEN OF WINTON Lord
EDMISTON Lord
ELTON Lord
FAULKS Lord
FELDMAN Lord
FELDMAN OF ELSTREE Lord
FELLOWES OF WEST STAFFORD Lord
FINK Lord
FINKELSTEIN Lord
FLIGHT Lord
FOOKES Baroness
FORSYTH OF DRUMLEAN Lord
FOWLER Lord
FRAMLINGHAM Lord
FREEMAN Lord
FREUD Lord
GARDINER OF KIMBLE Lord

GARDNER OF PARKES Baroness
GAREL-JONES Lord
GEDDES Lord
GLENARTHUR Lord
GLENDONBROOK Lord
GLENTORAN Lord
GOLD Lord
GOLDIE Baroness
GOODLAD Lord
GOSCHEN Viscount
GRADE OF YARMOUTH Lord
GREEN OF HURSTPIERPOINT Lord
GRIFFITHS OF FFORESTFACH Lord
HAMILTON OF EPSOM Lord
HANHAM Baroness
HARRIS OF PECKHAM Lord
HENLEY Lord
HESELTINE Lord
HEYHOE FLINT Baroness
HIGGINS Lord
HILL OF OAREFORD Lord
HODGSON OF ASTLEY ABBOTTS Lord
HODGSON OF ABINGER Baroness
HOLMES OF RICHMOND Lord
HOME Earl of
HOOPER Baroness
HORAM Lord
HOWARD OF LYMPNE Lord
HOWARD OF RISING Lord
HOWE Earl
HOWE OF ABERAVON Lord
HOWELL OF GUILDFORD Lord
HUNT OF WIRRAL Lord
HURD OF WESTWELL Lord
INGLEWOOD Lord
JAMES OF BLACKHEATH Lord
JAMES OF HOLLAND PARK Baroness
JENKIN OF KENNINGTON Baroness
JENKIN OF RODING Lord
JOPLING Lord
KIMBALL Lord
KING OF BRIDGWATER Lord
KIRKHAM Lord
KNIGHT OF COLLINGTREE Baroness
LAMONT OF LERWICK Lord
LANG OF MONKTON Lord
LAWSON OF BLABY Lord
LEACH OF FAIRFORD Lord
LEIGH OF HURLEY Lord
LEXDEN Lord
LINDSAY Earl of
LINGFIELD Lord
LIVERPOOL Earl of

LIVINGSTON OF PARKHEAD Lord
LLOYD-WEBBER Lord
LOTHIAN Marquess of
LUCAS OF CRUDWELL AND DINGWALL
Lord
LUKE Lord
LYELL Lord
McCOLL OF DULWICH Lord
MACFARLANE OF BEARSDEN Lord
MacGREGOR OF PULHAM MARKET Lord
MACKAY OF CLASHFERN Lord
MacLAURIN OF KNEBWORTH Lord
MAGAN OF CASTLETOWN Lord
MANCROFT Lord
MARLAND Lord
MARLESFORD Lord
MAWHINNEY Lord
MAYHEW OF TWYSDEN Lord
MILLER OF HENDON Baroness
MONTAGU OF BEAULIEU Lord
MONTROSE Duke of
MOORE OF LOWER MARSH Lord
MORRIS OF BOLTON Baroness
MOYNIHAN Lord
NASEBY Lord
NASH Lord
NEVILLE-JONES Baroness
NEVILLE-ROLFE Baroness
NEWLOVE Baroness
NOAKES Baroness
NORTHBROOK Lord
NORTON OF LOUTH Lord
O'CATHAIN Baroness
OPPENHEIM-BARNES Baroness
PALUMBO Lord
PARKINSON Lord
PATTEN Lord
PERRY OF SOUTHWARK Baroness
PLUMB Lord
POPAT Lord
RAWLINGS Baroness
RENFREW OF KAIMSTHORN Lord
RENTON OF MOUNT HARRY Lord
RIBEIRO Lord
RIDLEY Viscount
RISBY Lord
ROBERTS OF CONWY Lord
ROTHERWICK Lord
RYDER OF WENSUM Lord
SAATCHI Lord
SANDERSON OF BOWDEN Lord
SASSOON Lord
SECCOMBE Baroness

SELBORNE Earl of
SELKIRK OF DOUGLAS Lord
SELSDON Lord
SHACKLETON OF BELGRAVIA Baroness
SHARPLES Baroness
SHAW OF NORTHSTEAD Lord
SHEIKH Lord
SHEPHARD OF NORTHWOLD Baroness
SHEPPARD OF DIDGEMERE Lord
SHERBOURNE OF DIDSBURY Lord
SHREWSBURY AND WATERFORD Earl of
SKELMERSDALE Lord
SOULSBY OF SWAFFHAM PRIOR Lord
SPICER Lord
STEDMAN-SCOTT Baroness
STERLING OF PLAISTOW Lord
STEWARTBY Lord
STOWELL OF BEESTON Baroness
STRATHCLYDE Lord
SWINFEN Lord
TAYLOR OF HOLBEACH Lord
TEBBIT Lord
TREFGARNE Lord

TRENCHARD Viscount
TRIMBLE Lord
TRUE Lord
TRUMPINGTON Baroness
TUGENDHAT Lord
ULLSWATER Viscount
VERMA Baroness
VINSON Lord
WADDINGTON Lord
WADE OF CHORLTON Lord
WAKEHAM Lord
WALDEGRAVE OF NORTH HILL Lord
WARSI Baroness
WASSERMAN Lord
WEI Lord
WHEATCROFT Baroness
WHITBY Lord
WILCOX Baroness
WILLIAMS OF TRAFFORD Baroness
WOLFSON OF ASPLEY GUISE Lord
WOLFSON OF SUNNINGDALE Lord
YOUNG OF GRAFFHAM Lord
YOUNGER OF LECKIE Viscount

Crossbench

ABERDARE Lord
ADEBOWALE Lord
AFSHAR Baroness
ALLENBY OF MEGIDDO Viscount
ALTON OF LIVERPOOL Lord
ARMSTRONG OF ILMINSTER Lord
BALDWIN OF BEWDLEY Earl
BARBER OF TEWKESBURY Lord
BERKELEY OF KNIGHTON Lord
BEST Lord
BEW Lord
BICHARD Lord
BILIMORIA Lord
BIRT Lord
BLAIR OF BOUGHTON Lord
BOOTHROYD Baroness
BOYCE Lord
BRIDGES Lord
BRIGGS Lord
BROERS Lord
BROOKEBOROUGH Viscount
BROWN OF EATON-UNDER-HEYWOOD
Lord
BROWNE OF MADINGLEY Lord
BROWNE-WILKINSON Lord
BURNS Lord
BUTLER OF BROCKWELL Lord
BUTLER-SLOSS Baroness

CAMERON OF DILLINGTON Lord
CAMERON OF LOCHBROOM Lord
CAMPBELL OF LOUGHBOROUGH Baroness
CAMPBELL OF SURBITON Baroness
CAREY OF CLIFTON Lord
CARSWELL Lord
CHORLEY Lord
CLANCARTY Earl of
COBBOLD Lord
COLVILLE OF CULROSS Viscount
CONDON Lord
COUSSINS Baroness
COX Baroness
CRAIG OF RADLEY Lord
CRAIGAVON Viscount
CRISP Lord
CULLEN OF WHITEKIRK Lord
CURRIE OF MARYLEBONE Lord
CURRY OF KIRKHARLE Lord
DANNATT Lord
DEAR Lord
DEECH Baroness
EAMES Lord
ELYSTAN-MORGAN Lord
EMERTON Baroness
ERROLL Earl of
FALKLAND Viscount of
FELLOWES Lord

FINLAY OF LLANDAFF Baroness
FLATHER Baroness
FREYBERG Lord
FRITCHIE Baroness
GREENFIELD Baroness
GREENGROSS Baroness
GREENWAY Lord
GREY-THOMPSON Baroness
GRIFFITHS Lord
GUTHRIE OF CRAIGIEBANK Lord
HALL OF BIRKENHEAD Lord
HAMEED Lord
HANNAY OF CHISWICK Lord
HARDIE Lord
HARRIES OF PENTREGARTH Lord
HASKINS Lord
HASTINGS OF SCARISBRICK Lord
HAYMAN Baroness
HENNESSY OF NYMPSFIELD Lord
HOFFMANN Lord
HOGG Baroness
HOLLINS Baroness
HOPE OF CRAIGHEAD Lord
HOPE OF THORNES Lord
HOWARTH OF BRECKLAND Baroness
HOWE OF IDLICOTE Baroness
HUTTON Lord
HYLTON Lord
IMBERT Lord
INGE Lord
JANVRIN Lord
JAY OF EWELME Lord
JONES OF BIRMINGHAM Lord
JUDGE Lord
KAKKAR Lord
KERR OF KINLOCHARD Lord
KIDRON Baroness
KILCLOONEY Lord
KING OF LOTHBURY Lord
KNIGHTS Lord
KREBS Lord
LAMING Lord
LANE-FOX OF SOHO Baroness
LEVENE OF PORTSOKEN Lord
LEWIS OF NEWNHAM Lord
LISTOWEL Earl of
LLOYD OF BERWICK Lord
LOW OF DALSTON Lord
LUCE Lord
LYTTON Earl
McCLUSKEY Lord
MACKAY OF DRUMADOON Lord
MALLOCH-BROWN Lord

MANNINGHAM-BULLER Baroness
MAR Countess of
MARTIN OF SPRINGBURN Lord
MASHAM OF ILTON Baroness
MAWSON Lord
MAY OF OXFORD Lord
MEACHER Baroness
MILLETT Lord
MOGG Lord
MOLYNEAUX OF KILLEAD Lord
MONTGOMERY OF ALAMEIN Viscount
MORAN Lord
MORGAN OF DREFELIN Baroness
MOSER Lord
MURPHY Baroness
MUSTILL Lord
NEILL OF BLADEN Lord
NEUBERGER Baroness
NICHOLLS OF BIRKENHEAD Lord
NICKSON Lord
NORFOLK Duke of
NORTHBOURNE Lord
O'DONNELL Lord
O'LOAN Baroness
O'NEILL OF BENGARVE Baroness
OUSELEY Lord
OWEN Lord
OXBURGH Lord
PALMER Lord
PANNICK Lord
PATEL Lord
PATTEN OF BARNES Lord
PEEL Earl
PHILLIPS OF WORTH MATRAVERS Lord
POWELL OF BAYSWATER Lord
PRASHAR Baroness
QUIRK Lord
RAMSBOTHAM Lord
RANA Lord
REES OF LUDLOW Lord
RENWICK OF CLIFTON Lord
RICHARDSON OF CALOW Baroness
RIX Lord
ROSSLYN Earl of
ROWE-BEDDOE Lord
SACKS Lord
ST JOHN OF BLETSO Lord
SALTOUN OF ABERNETHY Lady
SANDWICH Earl of
SAVILLE OF NEWDIGATE Lord
SCOTT OF FOSCOTE Lord
SINGH OF WIMBLEDON Lord
SKIDELSKY Lord

SLIM Viscount
SMITH OF KELVIN Lord
SNOWDON Earl of
STAIR Earl of
STERN Baroness
STERN OF BRENTFORD Lord
STEVENS OF KIRKWHELPINGTON Lord
STEVENSON OF CODDENHAM Lord
STEYN Lord
STIRRUP Lord
SUTHERLAND OF HOUNDWOOD Lord
TANLAW Lord
TEMPLEMAN Lord
TENBY Viscount
THOMAS OF SWYNNERTON Lord
TOMBS Lord
TREES Lord
TURNBULL Lord

TURNER OF ECCHINSWELL Lord
VALENTINE Baroness
VINCENT OF COLESHILL Lord
WALKER OF ALDRINGHAM Lord
WALKER OF GESTINGTHORPE Lord
WALPOLE Lord
WALTON OF DETCHANT Lord
WARNOCK Baroness
WAVERLEY Viscount
WEIDENFELD Lord
WILLIAMS OF BAGLAN Lord
WILLIAMS OF OYSTERMOUTH Lord
WILLIAMSON OF HORTON Lord
WILSON OF DINTON Lord
WILSON OF TILLYORN Lord
WOOLF Lord
WRIGHT OF RICHMOND Lord
YOUNG OF HORNSEY Baroness

Liberal Democrat

ADDINGTON Lord
ALDERDICE Lord
ALLAN OF HALLAM Lord
ALLIANCE Lord
ASHDOWN OF NORTON-SUB-HAMDON Lord
AVEBURY Lord
BAKEWELL OF HARDINGTON MANDEVILLE Baroness
BARKER Baroness
BENJAMIN Baroness
BONHAM-CARTER OF YARNBURY Baroness
BRADSHAW Lord
BRINTON Baroness
BURNETT Lord
CARLILE OF BERRIEW Lord
CHIDGEY Lord
CLEMENT-JONES Lord
COTTER Lord
DHOLAKIA Lord
DOOCEY Baroness
DYKES Lord
EZRA Lord
FALKNER OF MARGRAVINE Baroness
FEARN Lord
GARDEN OF FROGNAL Baroness
GERMAN Lord
GLASGOW Earl of
GOODHART Lord
GREAVES Lord
GRENDER Baroness

HAMWEE Baroness
HARRIS OF RICHMOND Baroness
HUMPHREYS Baroness
HUSSAIN Lord
HUSSEIN-ECE Baroness
JOLLY Baroness
JONES OF CHELTENHAM Lord
KIRKWOOD OF KIRKHOPE Lord
KRAMER Baroness
LEE OF TRAFFORD Lord
LESTER OF HERNE HILL Lord
LINKLATER OF BUTTERSTONE Baroness
LOOMBA Lord
LUDFORD Baroness
MACDONALD OF RIVER GLAVEN Lord
MACLENNAN OF ROGART Lord
McNALLY Lord
MADDOCK Baroness
MANZOOR Baroness
MAR AND KELLIE Earl of
MARKS OF HENLEY-ON-THAMES Lord
METHUEN Lord
MILLER OF CHILTHORNE DOMER Baroness
NEWBY Lord
NICHOLSON OF WINTERBOURNE Baroness
NORTHOVER Baroness
OAKESHOTT OF SEAGROVE BAY Lord
PADDICK Lord
PALMER OF CHILDS HILL Lord
PALUMBO OF SOUTHWARK Lord
PARMINTER Baroness
PHILLIPS OF SUDBURY Lord

RANDERSON Baroness
RAZZALL Lord
REDESDALE Lord
ROBERTS OF LLANDUDNO Lord
RODGERS OF QUARRY BANK Lord
ROPER Lord
SANDBERG Lord
SCOTT OF NEEDHAM MARKET Baroness
SHARKEY Lord
SHARMAN Lord
SHARP OF GUILDFORD Baroness
SHIPLEY Lord
SHUTT OF GREETLAND Lord
SMITH OF CLIFTON Lord
STEEL OF AIKWOOD Lord
STEPHEN Lord
STONEHAM OF DROXFORD Lord
STOREY Lord
STRASBURGER Lord
SUTTIE Baroness

TAVERNE Lord
TAYLOR OF GOSS MOOR Lord
TEVERSON Lord
THOMAS OF GRESFORD Lord
THOMAS OF WALLISWOOD Baroness
THOMAS OF WINCHESTER Baroness
TOPE Lord
TORDOFF Lord
TYLER Lord
TYLER OF ENFIELD Baroness
VALLANCE OF TUMMEL Lord
VERJEE Lord
WALLACE OF SALTAIRE Lord
WALLACE OF TANKERNESS Lord
WALMSLEY Baroness
WATSON OF RICHMOND Lord
WILLIAMS OF CROSBY Baroness
WILLIS OF KNARESBOROUGH Lord
WRIGGLESWORTH Lord

Non-Affiliated

AHMED Lord
AMOS Baroness
ARCHER OF WESTON-SUPER-MARE Lord
ASHTON OF UPHOLLAND Baroness
BHATIA Lord
BIRMINGHAM Lord Bishop of
BLACK OF CROSSHARBOUR Lord
BOSWELL OF AYNHO Lord
BOYD OF DUNCANSBY Lord
BRISTOL Lord Bishop of
CANTERBURY Lord Archbishop of
CHALFONT Lord
CHESTER Lord Bishop of
CHOLMONDELEY Marquess of
CLARK OF CALTON Baroness
CLARKE OF STONE-CUM-EBONY Lord
COLLINS OF MAPESBURY Lord
COVENTRY Lord Bishop of
CUNNINGHAM OF FELLING Lord
DERBY Lord Bishop of
FORD Baroness
GLOUCESTER Lord Bishop of
GOFF OF CHIEVELEY Lord
HALE OF RICHMOND Baroness
HANNINGFIELD Lord
JACOBS Lord
KALMS Lord
KERR OF TONAGHMORE Lord
KILPATRICK OF KINCRAIG Lord
KINGSDOWN Lord
LAIRD Lord
LEICESTER Lord Bishop of

LICHFIELD Lord Bishop of
LONDON Lord Bishop of
MACKENZIE OF FRAMWELLGATE Lord
MACKIE OF BENSHIE Lord
MANCE Lord
NEUBERGER OF ABBOTSBURY Lord
NEWCASTLE Lord Bishop of
NORWICH Lord Bishop of
OXFORD Lord Bishop of
PAUL Lord
PLATT OF WRITTLE Baroness
PRIOR Lord
RIPON AND LEEDS Lord Bishop of
SAINSBURY OF PRESTON CANDOVER
Lord
ST EDMUNDSBURY AND IPSWICH Lord
Bishop of
SALISBURY Marquess of
SEWEL Lord
SHEFFIELD Lord Bishop of
SIMON OF HIGHBURY Lord
SMITH OF FINSBURY Lord
TAYLOR OF WARWICK Lord
TRURO Lord Bishop of
TRUSCOTT Lord
UDDIN Baroness
WAKEFIELD Lord Bishop of
WINCHESTER Lord Bishop of
WORCESTER Lord Bishop of
YORK Lord Archbishop of
YOUNG OF OLD SCONE Baroness

Democratic Unionist Party
BANNSIDE Lord
BROWNE OF BELMONT Lord

MORROW Lord
PAISLEY OF ST GEORGE'S Baroness

Plaid Cymru
ELIS-THOMAS Lord
WIGLEY Lord

UK Independence Party
PEARSON OF RANNOCH Lord
WILLOUGHBY DE BROKE Lord

Ulster Unionist Party
EMPEY Lord
ROGAN Lord

Conservative Independent
STEVENS OF LUDGATE Lord

Green
JONES OF MOULESCOOMB Baroness

Independent Labour
STODDART OF SWINDON Lord

Independent Liberal Democrat
TONGE Baroness

Independent Ulster Unionist
MAGINNIS OF DRUMGLASS Lord

Liberal Democrat Independent
RENNARD Lord

Lord Speaker
D'SOUZA Baroness

Select Committees

Legislative Committees

Constitution

Examines constitutional implications of all public bills; reviews operation of the constitution.

Tel: 020 7219 1228 Fax: 020 7219 4931
Email: beslyn@parliament.uk
www.parliament.uk/hlconstitution

Baroness Jay of Paddington (Chair)	Lab
Lord Crickhowell	Con
Lord Cullen of Whitekirk	CB
Baroness Falkner of Margravine	Lib Dem
Lord Goldsmith	Lab
Lord Hart of Chilton	Lab
Lord Irvine of Lairg	Lab
Lord Lang of Monkton	Con
Lord Lester of Herne Hill	Lib Dem
Lord Lexden	Con
Lord Powell of Bayswater	CB
Baroness Wheatcroft	Con

Staff: Nicolas Besly (Clerk), Luke Wilcox (Policy Analyst), Helen Gibson (Committee Assistant)

Delegated Powers and Regulatory Reform

Reports whether the provisions of any bill inappropriately delegate legislative powers or whether they subject the exercise of legislative power to an inappropriate degree of parliamentary scrutiny.

Tel: 020 7219 3233 Fax: 020 7219 2571
Email: dprr@parliament.uk

Baroness Thomas of Winchester (Chair)	Lib Dem
Baroness Andrews	Lab
Baroness Farrington of Ribbleton	Lab
Baroness Fookes	Con
Baroness Gardner of Parkes	Con
Lord Haskel	Lab
Countess of Mar	CB
Lord Marks of Henley-on-Thames	Lib Dem
Lord Mayhew of Twysden	Con
Baroness O'Loan	CB

Staff: Christine Salmon Percival (Clerk)

Hybrid Instruments

Tel: 020 7219 3231

Lord Brabazon of Tara (Chair)	Con
Lord Grantchester	Lab
Lord Harrison	Lab
Lord Luke	Con
Prof. Lord Quirk	CB
Lord Sandberg	Lib Dem
Lord Swinfen	Con

Staff: To be appointed (Clerk)

Secondary Legislation Scrutiny

Tel: 020 7219 8821
Email: seclegscrutiny@parliament.uk

Lord Goodlad (Chair)	Con
Lord Bichard	CB
Lord Blackwell	Con
Rt Rev Lord Eames	CB
Baroness Hamwee	Lib Dem
Lord Methuen	Lib Dem
Baroness Morris of Yardley	Lab
Prof. Lord Norton of Louth	Con
Prof. Lord Plant of Highfield	Lab
Lord Scott of Foscote	CB
Lord Woolmer of Leeds	Lab

Staff: Mark Gladwell (Contact)

Standing Orders (Private Bills)

Reviews compliance with standing orders.

Tel: 020 7219 5438

Lord Brabazon of Tara (Chair)	Con
Lord Geddes	Con
Baroness Gould of Potternewton	Lab
Lord Luke	Con
Lord Naseby	Con
Lord Palmer	CB
Viscount Simon	Lab

Joint Committees

See Lords and Commons Joint Select Committees on p1100

House Committees

Administration and Works

Tel: 020 7219 3736
Email: jonessa@parliament.uk

Lord Sewel (Chair)	Non-Affiliated

Baroness Anelay of St Johns	Con
Lord Brougham and Vaux	Con
Lord Cameron of Dillington	CB
Rt Rev Dr Bishop of Chester	Non-Affiliated
Lord Faulkner of Worcester	Lab

Lord Laming	*CB*
Lord McAvoy	*Lab/Co-op*
Baroness McIntosh of Hudnall	*Lab*
Lord Mancroft	*Con*
Lord Newby	*Lib Dem*
Lord Roper	*Lib Dem*
Lord Rowe-Beddoe	*CB*

Staff: Sarah Jones (Clerk), Jennifer Mitchley (Secretary)

Audit

Tel: 020 7219 5961
Email: daviesma@parliament.uk

Lord MacGregor of Pulham Market (Chair)	*Con*
Baroness Noakes	*Con*
Lord Sharman	*Lib Dem*
Lord Tomlinson	*Lab/Co-op*
Lord Turnbull	*CB*

House

Tel: 020 7219 6644
Email: whittlej@parliament.uk

Baroness D'Souza (Chair)	*Lord Speaker*
Lord Alderdice	*Lib Dem*
Lord Campbell-Savours	*Lab*
Lord Cope of Berkeley	*Con*
Lord Hill of Oareford	*Con*
Lord Laming	*CB*
Baroness McDonagh	*Lab*
Lord McNally	*Lib Dem*
Baroness Royall of Blaisdon	*Lab*
Lord Sewel	*Non-Affiliated*
Air Chief Marshal Lord Stirrup	*CB*
Lord True	*Con*

Staff: James Whittle (Clerk)

Information

Tel: 020 7219 4840
Email: daviesma@parliament.uk

Lord Kirkwood of Kirkhope (Chair)	*Lib Dem*
Lord Aberdare	*CB*
Lord Best	*CB*
Lord Black of Brentwood	*Con*
Lord Haskel	*Lab*
Lord Lipsey	*Lab*
Earl of Lytton	*CB*
Baroness Massey of Darwen	*Lab*
Lord Maxton	*Lab*
Baroness Rawlings	*Con*
Lord Rennard	*Lib Dem Ind*
Baroness Seccombe	*Con*
Baroness Stedman-Scott	*Con*

Staff: Mark Davies (Clerk)

Liaison

Co-ordinates and allocates resources for committee work.

Tel: 020 7219 3130
Email: tudorfp@parliament.uk

Lord Sewel (Chair)	*Non-Affiliated*
Lord Alderdice	*Lib Dem*
Baroness Browning	*Con*
Lord Campbell-Savours	*Lab*
Marshal of the RAF	
Lord Craig of Radley	*CB*
Lord Hill of Oareford	*Con*
Lord Laming	*CB*
Lord McNally	*Lib Dem*
Baroness Royall of Blaisdon	*Lab*
Lord Touhig	*Lab/Co-op*
Viscount Ullswater	*Con*

Staff: Philippa Tudor (Clerk), Helena Ali (Committee Assistant)

Privileges and Conduct

Tel: 020 7219 8796

Lord Sewel (Chair)	*Non-Affiliated*
Baroness Anelay of St Johns	*Con*
Lord Bassam of Brighton	*Lab/Co-op*
Lord Brooke of	
Sutton Mandeville	*Con*
Lord Brown of	
Eaton-under-Heywood	*CB*
Rt Rev Lord Eames	*CB*
Lord Hill of Oareford	*Con*
Lord Howe of Aberavon	*Con*
Lord Irvine of Lairg	*Lab*
Lord Laming	*CB*
Lord Mackay of Clashfern	*Con*
Lord McNally	*Lib Dem*
Lord Newby	*Lib Dem*
Baroness Royall of Blaisdon	*Lab*
Baroness Scotland of Asthal	*Lab*
Lord Scott of Foscote	*CB*

Staff: To be appointed (Clerk)

Sub-committee on Lords' Conduct

Tel: 020 7219 1228
Email: lordsconduct@parliament.uk

Baroness Manningham-Buller (Chair)	*CB*
Lord Cope of Berkeley	*Con*
Lord Dholakia	*Lib Dem*
Lord Irvine of Lairg	*Lab*
Baroness O'Neill of Bengarve	*CB*

Staff: To be appointed (Clerk)

Procedure

Tel: 020 7219 8796

Lord Sewel (Chair)	*Non-Affiliated*
Baroness Anelay of St Johns	*Con*
Lord Bassam of Brighton	*Lab/Co-op*
Lord Blencathra	*Con*
Lord Butler of Brockwell	*CB*
Lord Campbell-Savours	*Lab*
Baroness D'Souza	*Lord Speaker*
Lord Filkin	*Lab*
Lord Hill of Oareford	*Con*
Baroness Hollis of Heigham	*Lab*
Lord Laming	*CB*
Lord McNally	*Lib Dem*
Lord Newby	*Lib Dem*
Lord Patel	*CB*
Lord Roper	*Lib Dem*
Baroness Royall of Blaisdon	*Lab*
Baroness Thomas of Winchester	*Lib Dem*
Viscount Ullswater	*Con*
Lord Wakeham	*Con*
Alternate members:	
Viscount Craigavon	*CB*
Lord Grenfell	*Lab*
Baroness Hamwee	*Lib Dem*
Viscount Montgomery of Alamein	*CB*
Lord True	*Con*

Staff: Christopher Johnson (Clerk)

Refreshment

Tel: 020 7219 3736
Email: jonessa@parliament.uk

Lord Sewel (Chair)	*Non-Affiliated*
Lord Colwyn	*Con*
Baroness Doocey	*Lib Dem*
Baroness Gould of Potternewton	*Lab*
Baroness Henig	*Lab*
Lord Howard of Rising	*Con*
Baroness Jenkin of Kennington	*Con*
Lord Kennedy of Southwark	*Lab/Co-op*
Lord Mawson	*CB*
Lord Newby	*Lib Dem*
Lord Palmer of Childs Hill	*Lib Dem*
Prof. Lord Skidelsky	*CB*

Staff: Sarah Jones, Jennifer Mitchley (Clerks)

Selection

Selects members for select committees and other bodies.

Tel: 020 7219 3736

Lord Sewel (Chair)	*Non-Affiliated*
Baroness Anelay of St Johns	*Con*
Lord Bassam of Brighton	*Lab/Co-op*
Baroness Goudie	*Lab*
Lord Hylton	*CB*
Lord Laming	*CB*
Lord McNally	*Lib Dem*
Lord Newby	*Lib Dem*
Baroness Royall of Blaisdon	*Lab*
Lord Strathclyde	*Con*
Lord Wakeham	*Con*

Staff: To be appointed (Clerk)

Investigative Committees

Communications

Tel: 020 7219 6076 Fax: 020 7219 4931
Email: holcommunications@parliament.uk
www.parliament.uk/hlcommunications

Lord Inglewood (Chair)	*Con*
Baroness Bakewell	*Lab*
Lord Clement-Jones	*Lib Dem*
Baroness Deech	*CB*
Lord Dubs	*Lab*
Baroness Fookes	*Con*
Baroness Healy of Primrose Hill	*Lab*
Rt Rev Bishop of Norwich	*Non-Affiliated*
Lord Razzall	*Lib Dem*
Lord St John of Bletso	*CB*
Baroness Scotland of Asthal	*Lab*
Earl of Selborne	*Con*
Lord Skelmersdale	*Con*

Staff: Anna Murphy (Clerk), Alan Morrison (Policy Analyst), Rita Logan (Committee Assistant)

Economic Affairs

Tel: 020 7219 5358 Fax: 020 7219 4931
Email: economicaffairs@parliament.uk
www.parliament.uk/hleconomicaffairs

Lord MacGregor of Pulham Market (Chair)	*Con*
Baroness Blackstone	*Lab*
Lord Griffiths of Fforestfach	*Con*
Lord Hollick	*Lab*
Lord Lawson of Blaby	*Con*
Lord Lipsey	*Lab*
Lord McFall of Alcluith	*Lab/Co-op*
Lord May of Oxford	*CB*
Baroness Noakes	*Con*
Lord Rowe-Beddoe	*CB*

Lord Shipley — *Lib Dem*
Prof. Lord Skidelsky — *CB*
Lord Smith of Clifton — *Lib Dem*
Staff: Bill Sinton (Clerk), Stephen Seawright (Policy Analyst), Kiren Mirza (Committee Assistant)

Sub-committee on Economic Affairs Finance Bill
Tel: 020 7219 5358 Fax: 020 7219 4931
Email: economicaffairs@parliament.uk
www.parliament.uk/hlfinancebill

Lord MacGregor of Pulham Market (Chair) — *Con*
Lord Bilimoria — *CB*
Lord Griffiths of Fforestfach — *Con*
Lord Hollick — *Lab*
Baroness Kramer — *Lib Dem*
Lord Lipsey — *Lab*
Baroness Noakes — *Con*
Lord Rowe-Beddoe — *CB*
Lord Tugendhat — *Con*
Lord Wakeham — *Con*
Baroness Wheatcroft — *Con*
Staff: Bill Sinton (Clerk), Kiren Mirza (Committee Assistant)

European Union
Tel: 020 7219 6083 Fax: 020 7219 6715
Email: euclords@parliament.uk
www.parliament.uk/hleu

Lord Boswell of Aynho (Chair) — *Non-Affiliated*
Lord Bowness — *Con*
Lord Cameron of Dillington — *CB*
Lord Carter of Coles — *Lab*
Baroness Corston — *Lab*
Lord Dear — *CB*
Baroness Eccles of Moulton — *Con*
Lord Foulkes of Cumnock — *Lab/Co-op*
Lord Hannay of Chiswick — *CB*
Lord Harrison — *Lab*
Lord Maclennan of Rogart — *Lib Dem*
Lord Marlesford — *Con*
Baroness O'Cathain — *Con*
Baroness Parminter — *Lib Dem*
Earl of Sandwich — *CB*
Baroness Scott of Needham Market — *Lib Dem*
Lord Tomlinson — *Lab/Co-op*
Lord Tugendhat — *Con*
Prof. Baroness Young of Hornsey — *CB*
Staff: Jake Vaughan (First Clerk), Christopher Atkinson (Second Clerk), Hazel Scott (Committee Assistant)

Sub-committee A: Economic and Financial Affairs
Tel: 020 7219 3616 Fax: 020 7219 6715
Email: stoners@parliament.uk
www.parliament.uk/hleua

Lord Harrison (Chair) — *Lab*
Viscount Brookeborough — *CB*
Earl of Caithness — *Con*
Lord Carter of Coles — *Lab*
Lord Davies of Stamford — *Lab*
Lord Dear — *CB*
Lord Flight — *Con*
Lord Hamilton of Epsom — *Con*
Lord Kerr of Kinlochard — *CB*
Baroness Maddock — *Lib Dem*
Lord Marlesford — *Con*
Lord Vallance of Tummel — *Lib Dem*
Staff: Stuart Stoner (Clerk), Rose Crabtree (Policy Analyst), Sarah Yusuf (Committee Assistant)

Sub-committee B: Internal Market, Infrastructure and Employment
Tel: 020 7219 4840 Fax: 020 7219 6715
Email: masonn@parliament.uk
www.parliament.uk/hleub

Baroness O'Cathain (Chair) — *Con*
Lord Brooke of Alverthorpe — *Lab*
Lord Clinton-Davis — *Lab*
Lord Cotter — *Lib Dem*
Lord Fearn — *Lib Dem*
Lord Freeman — *Con*
Lord Haskel — *Lab*
Baroness Hooper — *Con*
Prof. Lord Kakkar — *CB*
Earl of Liverpool — *Con*
Baroness Valentine — *CB*
Lord Wilson of Tillyorn — *CB*
Staff: Nicole Mason (Clerk), Paul Dowling (Policy Analyst), Deborah Bonfante (Committee Assistant)

Sub-committee C: External Affairs
Tel: 020 7219 3616 Fax: 020 7219 6715
Email: stoners@parliament.uk
www.parliament.uk/hleuc

Lord Tugendhat (Chair) — *Con*
Baroness Bonham-Carter of Yarnbury — *Lib Dem*
Baroness Coussins — *CB*
Lord Foulkes of Cumnock — *Lab/Co-op*
Baroness Henig — *Lab*
Lord Jopling — *Con*
Lord Lamont of Lerwick — *Con*
Lord Maclennan of Rogart — *Lib Dem*
Baroness Quin — *Lab*
Lord Radice — *Lab*
Earl of Sandwich — *CB*

Lord Trimble — Con
Prof. Baroness Young of Hornsey — CB
Staff: Stuart Stoner (Clerk), Roshani Palamakumbura (Policy Analyst), Edward Bolton (Committee Assistant)

Sub-committee D: Agriculture, Fisheries, Environment and Energy

Tel: 020 7219 3015 Fax: 020 7219 6715
Email: speera@parliament.uk
www.parliament.uk/hleud

Baroness Scott of Needham Market (Chair)	*Lib Dem*
Lord Bowness	*Con*
Baroness Byford	*Con*
Lord Cameron of Dillington	*CB*
Lord Giddens	*Lab*
Baroness Howarth of Breckland	*CB*
Prof. Lord Lewis of Newnham	*CB*
Baroness Parminter	*Lib Dem*
Lord Plumb	*Con*
Lord Renton of Mount Harry	*Con*
Lord Whitty	*Lab*
Lord Williams of Elvel	*Lab*

Staff: Aaron Speer (Clerk), Alistair Dillon (Policy Analyst), Kate Chapman (Committee Assistant)

Sub-committee E: Justice, Institutions and Consumer Protection

Tel: 020 7219 3194 Fax: 020 7219 6715
Email: rubioe@parliament.uk
www.parliament.uk/hleue

Baroness Corston (Chair)	*Lab*
Lord Anderson of Swansea	*Lab*
Lord Blair of Boughton	*CB*
Lord Dykes	*Lib Dem*
Viscount Eccles	*Con*
Baroness Eccles of Moulton	*Con*
Lord Elystan-Morgan	*CB*
Lord Hodgson of Astley Abbotts	*Con*
Baroness Liddell of Coatdyke	*Lab*
Baroness O'Loan	*CB*
Lord Rowlands	*Lab*
Lord Stoneham of Droxford	*Lib Dem*

Staff: Elisa Rubio (Clerk), Mike Thomas (Legal Adviser), Arnold Ridout (Deputy Legal Adviser), Tim Mitchell (Assistant Legal Adviser), Amanda McGrath (Committee Assistant)

Sub-committee F: Home Affairs, Health and Education

Tel: 020 7219 8650 Fax: 020 7219 6715
Email: torrancem@parliament.uk
www.parliament.uk/hleuf

Lord Hannay of Chiswick (Chair)	*CB*
Baroness Benjamin	*Lib Dem*
Lord Blencathra	*Con*
Viscount Bridgeman	*Con*
Lord Judd	*Lab*
Lord Morris of Handsworth	*Lab*
Baroness Prashar	*CB*
Lord Sharkey	*Lib Dem*
Earl of Stair	*CB*
Lord Wasserman	*Con*

Staff: Michael Torrance (Clerk), Paul Dowling (Policy Analyst), Alice Ryder (Committee Assistant)

Science and Technology

Tel: 020 7219 4963 Fax: 020 7219 4931
Email: hlscience@parliament.uk
www.parliament.uk/hlscience

Prof. Lord Krebs (Chair)	*CB*
Lord Dixon-Smith	*Con*
Baroness Hilton of Eggardon	*Lab*
Baroness Manningham-Buller	*CB*
Lord O'Neill of Clackmannan	*Lab*
Lord Patel	*CB*
Baroness Perry of Southwark	*Con*
Lord Peston	*Lab*
Lord Rees of Ludlow	*CB*
Earl of Selborne	*Con*
Baroness Sharp of Guildford	*Lib Dem*
Lord Wade of Chorlton	*Con*
Lord Willis of Knaresborough	*Lib Dem*
Prof. Lord Winston	*Lab*

Staff: Christopher Clarke (Clerk), Katherine Bainbridge (Policy Analyst), Cerise Burnett-Stuart (Committee Assistant)

Other Committees

Leader's Group on Members Leaving the House

Lord Hunt of Wirral (Chair)	*Con*
Baroness Farrington of Ribbleton	*Lab*
Lord Hunt of Kings Heath	*Lab*
Baroness Murphy	*CB*
Baroness Scott of Needham Market	*Lib Dem*
Baroness Sharples	*Con*

Partnerships (Prosecution) (Scotland) Bill

Tel: 020 7219 3154 Fax: 020 7219 5933
Email: pbhol@parliament.uk

Lord Cullen of Whitekirk (Chair)	CB
Earl Attlee	Con
Lord Bates	Con
Lord Browne of Ladyton	Lab
Viscount Hanworth	Lab
Baroness Liddell of Coatdyke	Lab
Earl of Lindsay	Con
Lord McAvoy	Lab/Co-op
Duke of Montrose	Con
Lord Stephen	Lib Dem
Lord Wallace of Tankerness	Lib Dem

Principal Office Holders and Staff

Lord Speaker: Rt Hon Baroness D'Souza CMG
Chairman of Committees: Lord Sewel CBE
Principal Deputy Chairman of Committees: Lord Boswell of Aynho
Clerk of the Parliaments: David Beamish 020 7219 3181
Clerk Assistant: Edward Ollard 020 7219 3171
Reading Clerk and Clerk of the Overseas Office: Rhodri Walters DPhil 020 7219 3187
Gentleman Usher of the Black Rod: Lt Gen David Leakey 020 7219 3100
Commissioner for Standards: P. R. Kernaghan CBE QPM 020 7219 7152
Registrar of Members' Interests: Brendan Keith 020 7219 3112/020 7219 3120
Clerk of Committees: Dr Philippa Tudor 020 7219 3130
Director of Information Services and Librarian: Dr Elizabeth Hallam Smith 020 7219 3240
Director of Facilities: Carl Woodall 020 7219 5501
Finance Director: Andrew Makower 020 7219 6219
Director of Human Resources: Tom Mohan 020 7219 3185
Clerk of Legislation: Simon Burton 020 7219 3152
Examiners of Petitions for Private Bills: Peter Davis, Peter Milledge, Simon Patrick,
Christine Salmon Percival
Change Manager: Mary Ollard 020 7219 3828
Clerk of the Journals: Chloe Mawson 020 7219 8796
Director of Library Services: Alex Brocklehurst 020 7219 5805
Director of the Parliamentary Archives: Dr Caroline Shenton 020 7219 3071
Director of Public Information: Benet Hiscock 020 7219 0671
Editor of the Official Report: John Vice 020 7219 3397
Counsel to the Chairman of Committees:
Peter Milledge 020 7219 2251, Michael Thomas 020 7219 3043
Deputy Counsel to the Chairman of Committees: Nicholas Beach 020 7219 3243
Assistant Counsel to the Chairman of Committees: John Crane 020 7219 3243
Legal Adviser to the Human Rights Committee: Murray Hunt 020 7219 3033
Director of Parliamentary ICT Service: Joan Miller 020 7219 2001
Head of Catering and Retail Services: Timothy Lamming 020 7219 4222
Head of Property and Office Services: Fiona Smith 020 7219 3757
Staff Adviser: Beverley Pye 020 7219 6018
Head of Internal Audit: Paul Thompson 020 7219 3353
Internal Communications Manager: Alison Couch 020 7219 4155
Freedom of Information and Data Protection Officer: Frances Grey 020 7219 0100
Private Secretary to the Lord Speaker: James Whittle 020 7219 6644
Private Secretary to the Chairman of Committees: Sarah Jones 020 7219 3736
Private Secretary to the Clerk of the Parliaments: Talitha Rowland 020 7219 4536
Principal Clerk of Select Committees: Jake Vaughan 020 7219 5458
Chief Clerks of Committee Office: Christopher Johnson DPhil, Duncan Sagar
Deputy Head of Legislation Office: Christine Salmon Percival
Chief Clerk (on secondment to the Office of the Leader of the House of Lords): Andrew Mackersie

House of Lords Information Office

Westminster, London SW1A 0PW
Tel: 020 7219 3107
Website: www.parliament.uk/lords

Director of Public Information: Benet Hiscock 020 7219 0671
Head of Enquiry Service: Mark Simpson 020 7219 3107
Head of Outreach: Seonaid Whitley 020 7219 5317
Head of Press and Media: Owen Williams 020 7219 8659

Political Offices

Government
Email: holgovernmentwhips@parliament.uk Website: www.lordswhips.org.uk
Leader of the House of Lords' Office 020 7219 3200
Government Whips' Office 020 7219 3131/020 7219 5846

Official Opposition
Leader's Office 020 7219 3237
Opposition Chief Whip's Office 020 7219 3237

Crossbenchers
Email: lordscrossbenchconvenor@parliament.uk Website: www.crossbenchpeers.org.uk
Convenor: Lord Laming CBE DL
Tel: 020 7219 1414
Private Secretary: James Bowyer Email: bowyerj@parliament.uk

PARLIAMENT

Joint Committees

Joint Committee on Consolidation, &c, Bills

These Bills fall into five categories:

Consolidation Bills, whether public or private, which are limited to re-enacting existing law; Statute Law Revision Bills, which are limited to repeal of obsolete, spent, unnecessary or superseded enactments;

Bills presented under the Consolidation of Enactments (Procedure) Act 1949, which include corrections and minor improvements to the existing law;

Bills to consolidate any enactments with amendments to give effect recommendations made by the Law Commissions;

Bills prepared by the Law Commissions to promote the reform of the Statute Law by the repeal of enactments which are no longer of practical utility.

Tel: 020 7219 3154
www.parliament.uk/business/committees/
committees-a-z/joint-select/consolidation-
committee

Lord Carswell (Chair)	CB
Robert Buckland	Con
Martin Caton	Lab
Jenny Chapman	Lab
Lord Christopher	Lab
Damian Collins	Con
Jim Dobbin	Lab/Co-op
Stephen Dorrell	Con
Earl of Dundee	Con
Rt Rev Lord Eames	CB
Charlie Elphicke	Con
Paul Farrelly	Lab
Yvonne Fovargue	Lab
Viscount Hanworth	Lab
Lord Janner of Braunstone	Lab
Baroness Mallalieu	Lab
Lord Methuen	Lib Dem
Jesse Norman	Con
Lord Razzall	Lib Dem
Sir Robert Smith	Lib Dem
Lord Swinfen	Con
Lord Tombs	CB
Justin Tomlinson	Con

Staff: Simon Blackburn (Clerk, Lords), David Slater (Clerk, Commons)

Joint Committee on the Draft Deregulation Bill

Tel: 020 7219 3103
Email: draftderegulationbill@parliament.uk
www.parliament.uk/business/committees/
committees-a-z/joint-select/draft-deregulation-bill

Lord Rooker (Chair)	Lab
Baroness Andrews	Lab
Andrew Bridgen	Con
James Duddridge	Con
John Hemming	Lib Dem
Kelvin Hopkins	Lab
Ian Lavery	Lab
Lord Mawson	CB
Lord Naseby	Con
Priti Patel	Con
Lord Selkirk of Douglas	Con
Lord Sharkey	Lib Dem

Staff: Christine Salmon Percival (Clerk, Lords)

Joint Committee on Human Rights

Tel: 020 7219 2797 Fax: 020 7219 8393
Email: jchr@parliament.uk
www.parliament.uk/jchr

Dr Hywel Francis (Chair)	Lab
Baroness Berridge	Con
Robert Buckland	Con
Rehman Chishti	Con
Lord Faulks	Con
Simon Hughes	Lib Dem
Baroness Kennedy of The Shaws	Lab
Lord Lester of Herne Hill	Lib Dem
Baroness Lister of Burtersett	Lab
Baroness O'Loan	CB
Virendra Sharma	Lab
Sir Richard Shepherd	Con

Staff: Mike Hennessy (Clerk, Commons), Megan Conway (Clerk, Lords), Murray Hunt (Legal Adviser), Natalie Wease (Assistant Legal Adviser), Liz Parratt (Media Officer), Lisa Wrobel (Senior Committee Assistant), Michelle Owens (Committee Assistant), Holly Knowles (Committee Support Assistant), Keith Pryke (Office Support Assistant)

Joint Committee on the National Security Strategy

Tel: 020 7219 3267 Fax: 020 7219 6952
www.parliament.uk/business/committees/
committees-a-z/joint-select/national-security-
strategy

Margaret Beckett (Chair)	*Lab*
James Arbuthnot	*Con*
Adrian Bailey	*Lab/Co-op*
Sir Alan Beith	*Lib Dem*
Sir Malcolm Bruce	*Lib Dem*
Lord Clark of Windermere	*Lab*
Lord Fellowes	*CB*
Fabian Hamilton	*Lab*
Lord Harris of Haringey	*Lab*
Lord Lee of Trafford	*Lib Dem*
Lord Levene of Portsoken	*CB*
Paul Murphy	*Lab*
Baroness Neville-Jones	*Con*
Richard Ottaway	*Con*
Mark Pritchard	*Con*
Baroness Ramsay of Cartvale	*Lab*
Sir Malcolm Rifkind	*Con*
Lord Sterling of Plaistow	*Con*
Baroness Taylor of Bolton	*Lab*
Keith Vaz	*Lab*
Lord Waldegrave of North Hill	*Con*
Tim Yeo	*Con*

Staff: Philippa Helme (Clerk, Commons), Christopher Atkinson (Clerk, Lords), Emma Graham (Committee Specialist, Commons), Alex Paterson (Media Officer), Christine Randall (Senior Committee Assistant, Commons), Jacqui Cooksey (Committee Assistant, Commons), Rita Logan (Committee Assistant, Lords)

Joint Committee on Statutory Instruments

Commons members of the Joint Committee also meet separately as the Select Committee on Statutory Instruments.

Tel: 020 7219 2026 Fax: 020 7219 2441
Email: jcsi@parliament.uk
www.parliament.uk/jcsi

George Mudie (Chair)	*Lab*
Lord Avebury	*Lib Dem*
Robert Buckland	*Con*
Michael Ellis	*Con*

John Hemming	*Lib Dem*
Lord Kennedy of Southwark	*Lab/Co-op*
Ian Liddell-Grainger	*Con*
Lord Lyell	*Con*
Baroness Mallalieu	*Lab*
Toby Perkins	*Lab*
Lord Selkirk of Douglas	*Con*
Baroness Stern	*CB*
Lord Walpole	*CB*

Staff: Sarah Petit (Clerk, Commons), Jane White (Clerk, Lords), Peter Brooksbank, Philip Davies, Peter Davis, Daniel Greenberg (Legal Advisers, Commons), Nicholas Beach, Peter Milledge (Legal Advisers, Lords), Liz Booth (Committee Assistant), Paula Saunderson (Office Support Assistant)

Joint Committee on Voting Eligibilty (Prisoners) Bill

Tel: 020 7219 8675
Email: prisonervoting@parliament.uk
www.parliament.uk/business/committees/
committees-a-z/joint-select/draft-voting-
eligibility-prisoners-bill

Nick Gibb (Chair)	*Con*
Crispin Blunt	*Con*
Steve Brine	*Con*
Lorely Burt	*Lib Dem*
Lord Dholakia	*Lib Dem*
Baroness Gibson of Market Rasen	*Lab*
Sir Alan Meale	*Lab*
Baroness Noakes	*Con*
Prof. Lord Norton of Louth	*Con*
Lord Peston	*Lab*
Lord Phillips of Worth Matravers	*CB*
Derek Twigg	*Lab*

Staff: Sîan Woodward (Clerk, Commons), Christopher Johnson (Clerk, Lords), Rob Dinsdale (Committee Assistant, Commons), Stephanie Johnson (Committee Assistant, Lords), Owen Williams (Press Officer)

Statutory Committees

These committees are not select committees or committees of Parliament, but statutory committees of parliamentarians, which are required by law to be made up of Members of the two Houses. Generally, however, they model their procedure closely on that of select committees, and, with the exception of the Intelligence and Security Committee and Parliamentary and Political Service Honours Committee, draw their secretariats from parliamentary staff.

Ecclesiastical Committee

This Committee examines draft Measures presented to it by the Legislative Committee of the General Synod of the Church of England. It reports to Parliament on whether or not it considers the measures to be expedient. The members of the Committee are appointed by the Speaker and Lord Speaker for the duration of each Parliament.

Tel: 020 7219 3152 Fax: 020 7219 5933
Email: burtons@parliament.uk
www.parliament.uk/business/committees/
committees-a-z/other-committees/
ecclesiastical-committee

Lord Lloyd of Berwick (Chair)	CB
Sir Tony Baldry	Con
Lord Bilston	Lab/Co-op
Sir Peter Bottomley	Con
Ben Bradshaw	Lab
Baroness Butler-Sloss	CB
Lord Davies of Coity	Lab/Co-op
Lord Elton	Con
Frank Field	Lab
Lord Glenarthur	Con
Helen Goodman	Lab
Lord Griffiths of Burry Port	Lab
Sir Alan Haselhurst	Con
Sharon Hodgson	Lab
Simon Hughes	Lib Dem
Baroness Jolly	Lib Dem
Lord Judd	Lab
Lord Laming	CB
David Lammy	Lab
Lord Luke	Con
Gordon Marsden	Lab
Patrick Mercer	Ind
Baroness Perry of Southwark	Con
Laura Sandys	Con
Andrew Selous	Con
Lord Shaw of Northstead	Con
Gary Streeter	Con
Lord Walpole	CB

Staff: Margaret McKinnon (Secretary, Commons), Simon Burton (Secretary, Lords)

Speaker's Committee on the Electoral Commission

The Speaker's Committee is a statutory body established under the Political Parties, Elections and Referendums Act 2000.

Of the six appointed members, one is a Member of the House of Commons who is a Minister with responsibilities in relation to local government. This appointment is made by the Prime Minister. The other five appointed members are Members of the House of Commons who are not Ministers and are appointed by the Speaker. Appointed members serve for the full length of the Parliament, unless they cease to be Members of the House, resign from the Committee, or another member is appointed in their place. They may be reappointed.

Nick Clegg, Graham Allen and Mark Prisk are *ex-officio* members.

Tel: 020 7219 3351
www.parliament.uk/business/committees/
committees-a-z/other-committees/speakers-
committee-on-the-electoral-commission

John Bercow (Chair)	Speaker
Graham Allen	Lab
Nick Clegg	Lib Dem
Sir Gerald Kaufman	Lab
Eleanor Laing	Con
Naomi Long	All
Bridget Phillipson	Lab
Mark Prisk	Con
Gary Streeter	Con

Staff: Elizabeth Hunt (Secretary), Jim Camp (Committee Assistant), Sam Colebrook (Committee Support Assistant)

Intelligence and Security Committee of Parliament

Tel: 020 7276 1215
Email: committee@isc.x.gsi.gov.uk
isc.independent.gov.uk

Sir Malcolm Rifkind (Chair)	Con
Hazel Blears	Lab
Lord Butler of Brockwell	CB
Sir Menzies Campbell	Lib Dem
Mark Field	Con
Paul Goggins	Lab

George Howarth	*Lab*
Dr Julian Lewis	*Con*
Most Hon Marquess of Lothian	*Con*

Staff: Emma-Louise Avery (Clerk)

Parliamentary and Political Service Honours Committee

Lord Spicer (Chair)	*Con*
Lord Butler of Brockwell	*CB*
Alistair Carmichael	*Lib Dem*
Baroness Hayman	*CB*
Rosie Winterton	*Lab*
Sir George Young	*Con*

Non-parliamentary Members:
Diane Bevan
Dame Mary Keegan
Rt Hon Peter Riddell

Staff: Richard Tilbrook (Head of Honours and Appointments Secretariat)

Public Accounts Commission

The Commission's principal duties are to examine the National Audit Office Estimates and (if satisfied) present them to the House of Commons, to consider Reports from the appointed auditor for the National Audit Office, and to report from time to time. The Leader of the House and Chair of the Public Accounts Committee are *ex-officio* members.

Tel: 020 7219 3299 Fax: 020 7219 2622
Email: twiggerrj@parliament.uk
www.parliament.uk/parliamentary_committees/
public_accounts_commission.cfm

Sir Edward Leigh (Chair)	*Con*
Richard Bacon	*Con*
Dr Stella Creasy	*Lab/Co-op*
Margaret Hodge	*Lab*
Andrew Lansley	*Con*
Anne McGuire	*Lab*
Austin Mitchell	*Lab*

Dr John Pugh	*Lib Dem*
Andrew Tyrie	*Con*

Staff: Bob Twigger (Secretary)

Speaker's Committee for the Independent Parliamentary Standards Authority

The Committee considers the candidates proposed by the Speaker, following fair and open competition, for the posts of Chair and members of the Independent Parliamentary Standards Authority (IPSA). The candidates for these posts must then be considered by the House of Commons before their appointment by the Queen.

The Committee also reviews the IPSA's annual estimate of the resources it needs.

The Speaker, the Leader of the House and the Chair of the Committee on Standards and Privileges are *ex-officio* members.

Tel: 020 7219 3351
Email: scipsa@parliament.uk
www.parliament.uk/scipsa

John Bercow (Chair)	*Speaker*
Kevin Barron	*Lab*
Nick Brown	*Lab*
Angela Eagle	*Lab*
Andrew Lansley	*Con*
Sir Bob Russell	*Lib Dem*
Laura Sandys	*Con*
Charles Walker	*Con*

Lay Members:
Dame Janet Gaymer
Sir Anthony Holland
Elizabeth McMeikan

Staff: Elizabeth Hunt (Secretary), Lee Bridges (Media Officer), Jim Camp (Committee Assistant), Sam Colebrook (Committee Support Assistant)

Advisory Committees

Joint Committee on Security

The Committee is an advisory committee of Members of both Houses appointed by Mr Speaker and the House Committee of the House of Lords to make recommendations to Mr Speaker and the Lord Speaker on the security of the Parliamentary Estate.

Tel: 020 7219 2712
www.parliament.uk/business/committees/
committees-a-z/other-committees/joint-
committee-on-security

John Randall (Chair)	*Con*
Sir Paul Beresford	*Con*
Alan Campbell	*Lab*
Alistair Carmichael	*Lib Dem*
Lord Laming	*CB*
Lord Newby	*Lib Dem*
Lord Peston	*Lab*
Baroness Stowell of Beeston	*Con*
Gary Streeter	*Con*
Mark Tami	*Lab*
Lord Tunnicliffe	*Lab*
Lord Wakeham	*Con*

Staff: Philippa Helme (Clerk, Commons), James Whittle (Clerk, Lords), Susan Ramsay (Committee Assistant)

Speaker's Advisory Committee on Works of Art

The Committee is an advisory committee whose members are appointed by the Speaker to advise on matters relating to works of art in the House of Commons.

Tel: 020 7219 4151 Fax: 020 7219 2622
Email: art@parliament.uk
www.parliament.uk/acwa

Frank Doran (Chair)	*Lab*
Sir Alan Haselhurst	*Con*
George Hollingbery	*Con*
Dr Tristram Hunt	*Lab*
Charles Kennedy	*Lib Dem*
David Lammy	*Lab*
Ian Liddell-Grainger	*Con*
Alison McGovern	*Lab*
Caroline Nokes	*Con*
Hon Jacob Rees-Mogg	*Con*
Hywel Williams	*PlC*

Staff: Helen Wood (Secretary), Lee Bridges (Media Officer), Jennifer Kelly (Committee Assistant)

Party Committees

Conservative Party 1922 Committee

The 1922 Committee exists to give Conservative Backbench MPs a voice and as a mechanism for consultation between the backbenches and the government.

The 1922 conducts the early stages of leadership elections in the Party and the Chairman has the role of the Returning Officer throughout the process which includes a vote by the entire countrywide membership of the Conservative Party.

In Opposition, the membership extends to all members of the Parliamentary Party whether front- or backbenchers. Conservative Peers are invited to all 1922 meetings. When in Government, the 1922 is comprised of all the backbenchers of the Party; the Whips come to the weekly meetings by invitation, as do other Government Ministers.

Chairman: Graham Brady
Vice-chairmen: Charles Walker, John Whittingdale
Treasurer: Brian Binley
Secretaries: Robert Buckland, Nick de Bois
Members, Executive: Steve Baker, Guto Bebb, Graham Evans, Robert Halfon, Simon Hart, Bernard Jenkin, Jason McCartney, Karl McCartney, Penny Mordaunt, Sheryll Murray, Priti Patel, Heather Wheeler

Backbench Policy Committees

Economic Affairs (including BIS and Welfare)
Chairman: John Redwood

Environment (including DEFRA, DCLG, Energy and Climate Change)
Chairman: Neil Parish

Foreign Affairs (including Defence and International Development)
Chairman: Edward Leigh

Home Affairs and Constitution (including DPM, DCMS, Scotland, Wales, Northern Ireland and Justice)
Chairman: Eleanor Laing

Public Services (including Health, Education and Transport)
Chairman: Steve Baker

Liberal Democrat Policy Committees

Business, Innovation and Skills
Chairs: Gordon Birtwistle, Lord Razzall

Communities and Local Government
Chairs: Annette Brooke, Lord Tope

Constitutional and Political Reform
Chairs: John Thurso, Lord Tyler

Culture, Media and Sport
Chairs: Baroness Bonham-Carter of Yarnbury, John Leech

Education, Families and Young People
Chairs: Dan Rogerson, Lord Storey

Energy and Climate Change
Chairs: Mike Crockart, Lord Teverson

Environment, Food and Rural Affairs
Chairs: Baroness Parminter, Roger Williams

Health and Social Care
Chairs: Baroness Jolly, John Pugh

Home Affairs, Justice and Equalities
Chairs: Julian Huppert, Baroness Hamwee *(Home Office)*, Lord Marks of Henley-on-Thames *(Justice)*

International Affairs
Chairs: Martin Horwood *(FCO, MoD and DFID)*, Baroness Falkner of Margravine *(FCO)*, Lord Palmer of Childs Hill *(Defence)*, Lord Chidgey *(International Development)*

Northern Ireland
Chairs: Lord Alderdice, Stephen Lloyd

Scotland
Chairs: Lord Stephen, John Thurso

Transport
Chairs: Lord Bradshaw, Alan Reid

Treasury
Chairs: Baroness Kramer, Stephen Williams

Wales
Chairs: Lord Thomas of Gresford, Mark Williams

Work and Pensions
Chairs: Lord German, Greg Mulholland

Parliamentary Labour Party Departmental Groups

Business, Innovation and Skills
Chair: Seema Malhotra
Vice-chairs: Lord Haskel, Valerie Vaz, Baroness Wall of New Barnet

Communities and Local Government
Chair: Ian Mearns
Vice-chair: Lord Smith of Leigh

Culture, Olympics, Media and Sport
Chair: Steve Rotheram
Vice-chairs: Lord Howarth of Newport, Ian Murray

Defence
Chair: Gisela Stuart
Vice-chair: Lord Clark of Windermere

DPM/Constitutional Affairs
Chair: Kelvin Hopkins
Vice-chairs: Nic Dakin, Lord Dubs

Education
Chair: Steve Reed
Vice-chairs: Baroness Massey of Darwen, Lindsay Roy, Baroness Wall of New Barnet

Energy and Climate Change
Chair: Alan Whitehead
Vice-chairs: Barry Gardiner, Lord Whitty

Environment, Food and Rural Affairs
Chair: Barry Gardiner
Vice-chairs: Baroness Gibson of Market Rasen, Alan Whitehead

Foreign and Commonwealth Affairs
Chair: Mike Gapes
Vice-chairs: Lord Anderson of Swansea, Sandra Osborne

Health and Social Services
Chair: Debbie Abrahams
Vice-chair: Lord Rea

Home Affairs
Chair: Steve McCabe
Vice-chairs: Fabian Hamilton, Baroness Henig

International Development
Chair: Michael McCann
Vice-chair: Baroness Goudie

Justice
Chair: To be appointed
Vice-chairs: Geraint Davies, Lord Dubs

Northern Ireland
Chair: Paul Murphy
Vice-chairs: Lord Dubs, Tom Greatrex

Transport
Chair: Brian Donohoe
Vice-chairs: Lord Brooke of Alverthorpe, Rachel Reeves, Alison Seabeck

Treasury
Chair: Andy Love
Vice-chairs: Luciana Berger, Lord Myners

Women
Chair: Fiona Mactaggart
Vice-chairs: Baroness Gould of Potternewton, Yasmin Qureshi

Work and Pensions
Chair: Sheila Gilmore
Vice-chairs: Baroness Drake, Yvonne Fovargue

VACHER'S QUARTERLY
The most up-to-date contact details throughout the year

Call 020 7593 5644 or visit www.dodsshop.co.uk

All-Party Groups

Subject Groups

All-party groups are unofficial, and have a membership from both Houses. The groups tend to change frequently according to the Members' interests and with the topicality of the various subjects.

Accident Prevention

Chair: Lord Jordan — Lab
Vice-chairs:
Lord Brougham and Vaux — Con
Baroness Masham of Ilton — CB
Secretary: Russell Brown — Lab
Treasurer: Lord Faulkner of Worcester — Lab

Contact: Russell Brown, House of Commons, London SW1A 0AA Tel: 020 7219 4429

Adoption and Fostering

Chair: Craig Whittaker — Con
Vice-chair: Bill Esterson — Lab
Secretary: Jessica Lee — Con
Treasurer: Lisa Nandy — Lab

Contact: Craig Whittaker, House of Commons, London SW1A 0AA Tel: 020 7219 7031

Adventure and Recreation in Society

President: Frank Dobson — Lab
Chairs:
Julian Brazier — Con
Lord Greaves — Lib Dem
Stephen Pound — Lab
Treasurer: Earl of Erroll — CB

Contact: Julian Brazier, House of Commons, London SW1A 0AA Tel: 020 7219 5178

Aerospace

Chair: Emma Reynolds — Lab
Vice-chairs:
Steve Baker — Con
Brian Donohoe — Lab
Lord Empey — UUP
Secretary: Chris Williamson — Lab
Treasurer: Lord Jones — Lab

Contact: Emma Reynolds, House of Commons, London SW1A 0AA Tel: 020 7219 6919

Ageing and Older People

Chairs:
Baroness Greengross — CB
Penny Mordaunt — Con
Greg Mulholland — Lib Dem
Secretary: Stephen Lloyd — Lib Dem

Contact: Penny Mordaunt, House of Commons, London SW1A 0AA Tel: 020 7219 7129
centrallobby.politicshome.com/members/member-page/sites/age-uk/pages/all-party-parliamentary-group-1

Agriculture and Food for Development

Chair: Lord Cameron of Dillington — CB
Vice-chairs:
Heidi Alexander — Lab
Lord Boateng — Lab
Lord Chidgey — Lib Dem
Mark Durkan — SDLP
Pauline Latham — Con
Countess of Mar — CB
Laura Sandys — Con
Roger Williams — Lib Dem

Contact: Roger Williams, House of Commons, London SW1A 0AA Tel: 020 7219 8324
www.appg-agdev.co.uk

Agro-Ecology

Chairs:
Andrew George — Lib Dem
Baroness Miller of Chilthorne Domer — Lib Dem
Vice-chairs:
Baroness Jenkin of Kennington — Con
Countess of Mar — CB
Secretary and Treasurer:
Baroness Miller of Chilthorne Domer — Lib Dem

Contact: Andrew George, House of Commons, London SW1A 0AA Tel: 020 7219 4588

Ahmadiyya Muslim Community

Chair: Siobhain McDonagh — Lab
Vice-chairs:
Sir Peter Bottomley — Con
Jane Ellison — Con
Secretary: Lord Tope — Lib Dem
Treasurer: Mike Gapes — Lab/Co-op

Contact: Siobhain McDonagh, House of Commons, London SW1A 0AA
Tel: 020 7219 4678

Air Ambulances

Chair: Guy Opperman — Con
Vice-chairs:
Sir Alan Beith — Lib Dem
Tracey Crouch — Con
Jim Fitzpatrick — Lab
Nia Griffith — Lab
Duncan Hames — Lib Dem
Marcus Jones — Con
Jason McCartney — Con
Karl McCartney — Con
Lord Stevens of Ludgate — Con Ind

Secretaries:
Mark Pawsey   *Con*
Julian Sturdy   *Con*

Contact: Guy Opperman, House of Commons,
London SW1A 0AA Tel: 020 7219 7113

Alcohol Misuse

Chair: Tracey Crouch   *Con*
Vice-chairs:
Lord Brooke of Alverthorpe   *Lab*
Fiona Bruce   *Con*
Secretary: Baroness Finlay of Llandaff   *CB*
Treasurer: Russell Brown   *Lab*

Contact: Tracey Crouch, House of Commons,
London SW1A 0AA Tel: 020 7219 7203

Allergy

Acting Chair: Jon Cruddas   *Lab*
Vice-chair: Baroness Finlay of Llandaff   *CB*
Secretary: Stephen McPartland   *Con*

Contact: Jon Cruddas, House of Commons,
London SW1A 0AA Tel: 020 7219 8161

Aluminium Industry

Chair: David Mowat   *Con*
Vice-chairs:
Lord Brookman   *Lab*
Baroness Gardner of Parkes   *Con*
Secretary: Lord Davies of Coity   *Lab/Co-op*

Contact: David Mowat, House of Commons,
London SW1A 0AA Tel: 020 7219 7178

American Football

Chair: Richard Fuller   *Con*
Vice-chair: Gregg McClymont   *Lab*
Secretary: George Hollingbery   *Con*
Treasurer: Peter Bone   *Con*

Contact: Richard Fuller, House of Commons,
London SW1A 0AA Tel: 020 7219 7012

Angling

Chair: George Hollingbery   *Con*
Vice-chair: Charles Walker   *Con*
Secretary: Baroness Golding   *Lab*
Treasurer: Jon Cruddas   *Lab*

Contact: George Hollingbery, House of
Commons, London SW1A 0AA
Tel: 020 7219 7109

Animal Welfare

Chair: Neil Parish   *Con*
Vice-chairs:
Jim Fitzpatrick   *Lab*
Mike Hancock   *Ind*
Dr Caroline Lucas   *Green*
Secretary: Andrew Rosindell   *Con*
Treasurer: Lord Soulsby of Swaffham Prior   *Con*

Contact: Neil Parish, House of Commons,
London SW1A 0AA Tel: 020 7219 7172
www.apgaw.org

Animals in Medical Experimentation

Chair: Nic Dakin   *Lab*
Vice-chairs:
Annette Brooke   *Lib Dem*
Diana Johnson   *Lab*
Henry Smith   *Con*
Secretaries:
Jim Dowd   *Lab*
Fabian Hamilton   *Lab*
Treasurer:
Baroness Smith of Basildon   *Lab/Co-op*

Contact: Nic Dakin, House of Commons,
London SW1A 0AA Tel: 01724 842000

Antibiotics

Chair: Jamie Reed   *Lab*
Vice-chair: Kevin Barron   *Lab*
Secretary: Baroness Masham of Ilton   *CB*
Treasurer: Zac Goldsmith   *Con*

Contact: Jamie Reed, House of Commons,
London SW1A 0AA Tel: 020 7219 4706
antibiotic-action.com/appg-on-antibiotics

Anti-Corruption

Chairs:
Catherine McKinnell   *Lab*
Anas Sarwar   *Lab*
Vice-chairs:
Pauline Latham   *Con*
Lord Phillips of Sudbury   *Lib Dem*
Secretary: Sir Tony Baldry   *Con*

Contact: Anas Sarwar, House of Commons,
London SW1A 0AA Tel: 020 7219 7076
www.anticorruptionappg.org

Anti-Semitism

Presidents:
Lord Hunt of Wirral   *Con*
Lord Janner of Braunstone   *Lab*
Vice-Presidents:
Louise Ellman   *Lab/Co-op*
Mike Freer   *Con*
Chair: John Mann   *Lab*
Vice-chairs:
Lord Boswell of Aynho   *Non-Affiliated*
Tom Brake   *Lib Dem*
Phil Wilson   *Lab*
Secretary: Lady Hermon   *Ind*
Treasurer: Dr Matthew Offord   *Con*

Contact: John Mann, House of Commons,
London SW1A 0AA Tel: 020 7219 8345
www.antisemitism.org.uk/parliament

Apprenticeships

Chair: Gordon Birtwistle   *Lib Dem*
Vice-chairs:
Lord Aberdare   *CB*
Jake Berry   *Con*
Paul Blomfield   *Lab*
Richard Harrington   *Con*
Andrew Jones   *Con*
Stephen Lloyd   *Lib Dem*
Jack Lopresti   *Con*
Catherine McKinnell   *Lab*
David Simpson   *DUP*
Secretary: Guy Opperman   *Con*

Contact: Gordon Birtwistle, House of
Commons, London SW1A 0AA
Tel: 020 7219 7028

Arch Cru Investment Scheme

Chairs:
Alun Cairns   *Con*
Tom Greatrex   *Lab/Co-op*
Vice-chairs:
Mark Durkan   *SDLP*
Jonathan Edwards   *PlC*
Duncan Hames   *Lib Dem*
Lady Hermon   *Ind*
Naomi Long   *All*
Jim Sheridan   *Lab*
Secretary: Guy Opperman   *Con*

Contact: Guy Opperman, House of Commons,
London SW1A 0AA Tel: 020 7219 7113

Archaeology

Chair: Prof. Lord Renfrew of Kaimsthorn   *Con*
Secretary: Lord Redesdale   *Lib Dem*
Treasurer: Paul Flynn   *Lab*

Contact: Paul Flynn, House of Commons,
London SW1A 0AA Tel: 020 7219 3478
www.appag.org.uk

Architecture and Planning

Chair: Peter Aldous   *Con*
Honorary Chair: Lord Rogers of Riverside   *Lab*
Vice-chairs:
Clive Betts   *Lab*
Nick Raynsford   *Lab*
Treasurer: Lord Palmer   *CB*

Contact: Peter Aldous, House of Commons,
London SW1A 0AA Tel: 020 7219 7182

Archives and History

Chair: Dr Hywel Francis   *Lab*
Vice-chairs:
Lord Boswell of Aynho   *Non-Affiliated*
Lord Clark of Windermere   *Lab*
Dr Tristram Hunt   *Lab*

Paul Murphy   *Lab*
Chris Skidmore   *Con*
Secretary: Lord Bew   *CB*

Contact: Dr Hywel Francis, House of Commons,
London SW1A 0AA Tel: 020 7219 8121

Armed Forces

Chair: James Gray   *Con*
Deputy Chairs:
Bob Ainsworth   *Lab*
Lord Lee of Trafford   *Lib Dem*
Mark Pritchard   *Con*
Angus Robertson   *SNP*
Vice-chairs:
(Army): Bob Stewart   *Con*
(Royal Air Force): Madeleine Moon   *Lab*
(Royal Marines): Oliver Colvile   *Con*
(Royal Navy): Caroline Dinenage   *Con*
Secretary: Jonathan Reynolds   *Lab/Co-op*
Treasurers:
Lord Moonie   *Lab/Co-op*
Sir Bob Russell   *Lib Dem*

Contact: James Gray, House of Commons,
London SW1A 0AA Tel: 020 7219 6237

Arms Length Management Organisations (ALMOs)

Chair: Clive Betts   *Lab*
Vice-chair: Heidi Alexander   *Lab*
Secretary: Sarah Newton   *Con*

Contact: Clive Betts, House of Commons,
London SW1A 0AA Tel: 020 7219 5114

Art, Craft and Design in Education

Chair: Sharon Hodgson   *Lab*
Vice-chairs:
Earl of Clancarty   *CB*
Lord Cormack   *Con*

Contact: Sharon Hodgson, House of Commons,
London SW1A 0AA Tel: 020 7219 6916

Arts and Heritage

Chair: Lord Crathorne   *Con*
Vice-chair: Gordon Marsden   *Lab*
Secretary: Lord Crathorne   *Con*
Treasurer: Baroness Noakes   *Con*

Contact: Gordon Marsden, House of Commons,
London SW1A 0AA Tel: 020 7219 1262

Atrial Fibrillation

Chair: Glyn Davies   *Con*
Vice-chairs:
Lord Colwyn   *Con*
Lord Jones of Cheltenham   *Lib Dem*

Contact: Glyn Davies, House of Commons,
London SW1A 0AA Tel: 020 7219 3806

Autism

Chair: Robert Buckland   Con
Vice-chairs:
Steve Brine   Con
Annette Brooke   *Lib Dem*
Robert Flello   *Lab*
Jonathan Reynolds   *Lab/Co-op*
Secretary: Russell Brown   *Lab*
Treasurer: Charlotte Leslie   Con
Contact: Robert Buckland, House of Commons,
London SW1A 0AA Tel: 020 7219 7168
www.appga.org.uk

Aviation

Chair: Brian Donohoe   *Lab*
Vice-chair: Anne McIntosh   Con
Secretary: Mark Pritchard   Con
Contact: Brian Donohoe, House of Commons,
London SW1A 0AA Tel: 020 7219 6230

Friends of the Bahá'ís

Chair: Lord Avebury   *Lib Dem*
Vice-chairs:
Nic Dakin   *Lab*
Jonathan Evans   Con
Secretary: Mark Williams   *Lib Dem*
Treasurer: Louise Ellman   *Lab/Co-op*
Contact: Mark Williams, House of Commons,
London SW1A 0AA Tel: 020 7219 8469

Basketball

Chair: Sharon Hodgson   *Lab*
Vice-chairs:
Oliver Colvile   Con
Stephen Mosley   Con
Gary Streeter   Con
Treasurer: George Howarth   *Lab*
Contact: Sharon Hodgson, House of Commons,
London SW1A 0AA Tel: 020 7219 5160

BBC

Chair: Gareth Johnson   Con
Vice-chairs:
Lord Gordon of Strathblane   *Lab*
Jason McCartney   Con
Mark Menzies   Con
Tom Watson   *Lab*
Secretary: Dame Anne Begg   *Lab*
Treasurer: Dr Therese Coffey   Con
Contact: Dame Anne Begg, House of Commons,
London SW1A 0AA Tel: 020 7219 2140

Beef and Lamb

Chair: Neil Parish   Con
Vice-chairs:
Andrew George   *Lib Dem*
Huw Irranca-Davies   *Lab*

Mark Spencer   Con
Rory Stewart   Con
Roger Williams   *Lib Dem*
Secretary: Baroness Gibson of Market Rasen *Lab*
Contact: Neil Parish, House of Commons,
London SW1A 0AA Tel: 020 7219 7172

Beer

Chair: Andrew Griffiths   Con
Vice-chairs:
Nigel Adams   Con
Dr Therese Coffey   Con
Sir Tony Cunningham   *Lab*
Thomas Docherty   *Lab*
Clive Efford   *Lab*
Graham Evans   Con
Lord Kennedy of Southwark   *Lab/Co-op*
Charlotte Leslie   Con
Dan Rogerson   *Lib Dem*
Contact: Andrew Griffiths, House of Commons,
London SW1A 0AA Tel: 020 7219 7029

Betting and Gaming

Chairs:
Philip Davies   Con
Baroness Golding   *Lab*
Vice-chairs:
Lord Lipsey   *Lab*
Lord Mancroft   Con
Secretary: Lord Donoughue   *Lab*
Treasurer: Viscount of Falkland   CB
Contact: Philip Davies, House of Commons,
London SW1A 0AA Tel: 020 7219 8264

Bingo

Chair: Brian Binley   Con
Vice-chair: Philip Davies   Con
Secretary: Luciana Berger   *Lab/Co-op*
Treasurer: John Hemming   *Lib Dem*
Contact: Luciana Berger, House of Commons,
London SW1A 0AA Tel: 020 7219 7102

Biodiversity

Chair: Barry Gardiner   *Lab*
Vice-chairs:
Katy Clark   *Lab*
Nic Dakin   *Lab*
Mary Glindon   *Lab*
Tom Harris   *Lab*
Prof. Lord Hunt of Chesterton   *Lab*
Huw Irranca-Davies   *Lab*
Dr Caroline Lucas   *Green*
Dr Matthew Offord   Con
Lord Oxburgh   CB
Laura Sandys   Con
Sir Andrew Stunell   *Lib Dem*
Contact: Barry Gardiner, House of Commons,
London SW1A 0AA Tel: 020 7219 4046

Biomass

Chair: Nigel Adams	Con
Vice-chair: David Anderson	Lab
Secretary: Jackie Doyle-Price	Con
Treasurer: Karen Bradley	Con

Contact: Nigel Adams, House of Commons,
London SW1A 0AA Tel: 020 7219 7141

Boarding Schools

Chair: Philip Davies	Con
Vice-chair: Julian Smith	Con
Secretary: David Nuttall	Con
Treasurer: Margot James	Con

Contact: Philip Davies, House of Commons,
London SW1A 0AA Tel: 020 7219 8264

Body Image

Chair: Caroline Nokes	Con
Vice-chair: Stephen Williams	Lib Dem
Secretary: Mary Glindon	Lab
Treasurer: Caroline Dinenage	Con

Contact: Caroline Nokes, House of Commons,
London SW1A 0AA Tel: 020 7219 1468
www.ymca.co.uk/bodyimage/parliament

Bowls

Chair: John Woodcock	Lab/Co-op
Vice-chairs:	
Jenny Chapman	Lab
Jim Fitzpatrick	Lab
Secretary: Ian Davidson	Lab/Co-op
Treasurer: Lorraine Fullbrook	Con

Contact: John Woodcock, House of Commons,
London SW1A 0AA Tel: 020 7219 2859

Boxing

Chair: Charlotte Leslie	Con
Vice-chairs:	
John Cryer	Lab
Baroness Golding	Lab
Stephen Hepburn	Lab
Kate Hoey	Lab
Dr Phillip Lee	Con
Jack Lopresti	Con
Greg Mulholland	Lib Dem
Secretary: Steve Barclay	Con
Treasurer: Penny Mordaunt	Con

Contact: Charlotte Leslie, House of Commons,
London SW1A 0AA Tel: 020 7219 7026

Brain Tumours

Chair: Andrew Selous	Con
Vice-chairs:	
Kevin Brennan	Lab
Lord Carlile of Berriew	Lib Dem
Secretary: Rebecca Harris	Con

Treasurer: Graeme Morrice	Lab

Contact: James Arbuthnot, House of Commons,
London SW1A 0AA Tel: 020 7219 4649

Breast Cancer

Chairs:	
Steve Brine	Con
Annette Brooke	Lib Dem
Sharon Hodgson	Lab
Vice-chair: Baroness Morgan of Drefelin	CB

Contact: Annette Brooke, House of Commons,
London SW1A 0AA Tel: 020 7219 8193
www.breakthrough.org.uk/our_work/
appg_on_breast_cancer

Bridge

Chair: Baroness Henig	Lab
Vice-chairs:	
Bob Blackman	Con
Lord Harrison	Lab
Secretary: Lord Hamilton of Epsom	Con
Treasurer: Stephen Mosley	Con

Contact: Bob Blackman, House of Commons,
London SW1A 0AA Tel: 020 7219 7082

British Economy

Chairs:	
Dr Tristram Hunt	Lab
David Mowat	Con
Secretary: Andy Sawford	Lab/Co-op

Contact: Dr Tristram Hunt, House of Commons,
London SW1A 0AA Tel: 020 7219 1179

British Museum

Chair: Tim Loughton	Con
Vice-chairs:	
Dr Tristram Hunt	Lab
Lord Lea of Crondall	Lab
Mark Pritchard	Con
Rory Stewart	Con
Gisela Stuart	Lab
Secretary: Angus MacNeil	SNP
Treasurer: Peter Luff	Con

Contact: Tim Loughton, House of Commons,
London SW1A 0AA Tel: 020 7219 4471

British Property Owners in Cyprus

Chair: William Cash	Con
Vice-chair: Paul Goggins	Lab
Secretary: Tessa Munt	Lib Dem

Contact: William Cash, House of Commons,
London SW1A 0AA Tel: 020 7219 6330

Built Environment

Acting Chair: Oliver Colvile	Con
Vice-chairs:	
Earl of Lytton	CB
Nick Raynsford	Lab

Secretary: Oliver Colvile   Con
Treasurer: Lord Howie of Troon   Lab

Contact: Oliver Colvile, House of Commons,
London SW1A 0AA Tel: 020 7219 7219

Bullying

Chairs:
Baroness Brinton   Lib Dem
Barry Sheerman   Lab/Co-op
Vice-chairs:
Baroness Walmsley   Lib Dem
Chris White   Con
Secretary:
Baroness Sharp of Guildford   Lib Dem
Treasurer: Baroness Howe of Idlicote   CB

Contact: Barry Sheerman, House of Commons,
London SW1A 0AA Tel: 020 7219 5037

Business, Finance and Accountancy

Chair: Iain Wright   Lab
Vice-chairs:
Nigel Mills   Con
Toby Perkins   Lab
Secretary: Alok Sharma   Con

Contact: Iain Wright, House of Commons,
London SW1A 0AA Tel: 020 7219 5587

CAFOD

(Catholic Agency for Overseas Development)
Chair: Tom Clarke   Lab
Vice-chairs:
Paul Goggins   Lab
Sir Edward Leigh   Con
Dr John Pugh   Lib Dem
Baroness Williams of Crosby   Lib Dem
Secretary: Jim Dobbin   Lab/Co-op
Treasurer: Lord Alton of Liverpool   CB

Contact: Tom Clarke, House of Commons,
London SW1A 0AA Tel: 020 7219 5007

Cancer

Chair: John Baron   Con
Vice-chairs:
Paul Burstow   Lib Dem
Baroness Finlay of Llandaff   CB
Baroness Masham of Ilton   CB
Stephen Metcalfe   Con
Baroness Morgan of Drefelin   CB
Grahame Morris   Lab

Contact: John Baron, House of Commons,
London SW1A 0AA Tel: 020 7219 2352
www.macmillan.org.uk/getinvolved/appg/
appg.aspx

Cannabis and Children

Chair: Charles Walker   Con
Vice-chairs:
Robert Buckland   Con
George Howarth   Lab
Secretary: Nic Dakin   Lab
Treasurer: Russell Brown   Lab

Contact: Charles Walker, House of Commons,
London SW1A 0AA Tel: 020 7219 0338

Carbon Monoxide

Chairs:
Baroness Finlay of Llandaff   CB
Jason McCartney   Con
Baroness Maddock   Lib Dem
Barry Sheerman   Lab/Co-op

Contact: Barry Sheerman, House of Commons,
London SW1A 0AA Tel: 020 7219 5037
www.policyconnect.org.uk/appcog

Cardiac Risk in the Young

Chair: Kevan Jones   Lab
Vice-chairs:
Sir Roger Gale   Con
Dr John Pugh   Lib Dem
Secretary: George Howarth   Lab
Treasurer: David Amess   Con

Contact: Kevan Jones, House of Commons,
London SW1A 0AA Tel: 020 7219 8219

Carers

Chairs:
Sir Tony Baldry   Con
Baroness Pitkeathley   Lab
Vice-chairs:
Paul Burstow   Lib Dem
Tim Farron   Lib Dem
Dr Hywel Francis   Lab
Laura Sandys   Con
Dr Eilidh Whiteford   SNP
Secretary: Alex Cunningham   Lab
Treasurer: Cathy Jamieson   Lab/Co-op

Contact: Alex Cunningham, House of
Commons, London SW1A 0AA
Tel: 020 7219 7157

Carpet Industry

Chair: Mark Garnier   Con
Vice-chairs:
John Glen   Con
Lord Rogan   UUP
Secretary: Neil Parish   Con
Treasurer: David Nuttall   Con

Contact: Mark Garnier, House of Commons,
London SW1A 0AA Tel: 020 7219 7198

Channel 4

Chair: Nadhim Zahawi	Con
Vice-chair: Lord Lipsey	Lab
Secretary: Luciana Berger	Lab/Co-op

Treasurer:
Baroness Bonham-Carter of Yarnbury   *Lib Dem*

Contact: Nadhim Zahawi, House of Commons, London SW1A 0AA Tel: 020 7219 7159

Cheese

Chair: Dan Rogerson	Lib Dem
Vice-chair: Mark Williams	Lib Dem
Secretary: Andrew Percy	Con
Treasurer: Russell Brown	Lab

Contact: Dan Rogerson, House of Commons, London SW1A 0AA Tel: 020 7219 4707

Chemical Industry

Chair: Ian Swales	Lib Dem
Vice-chairs:	
Michael Connarty	Lab
Graham Evans	Con
Secretary:	
Lord Willis of Knaresborough	Lib Dem
Treasurer: Nic Dakin	Lab

Contact: Ian Swales, House of Commons, London SW1A 0AA Tel: 020 7219 4576

Child Abduction

Chairs:	
Sir John Stanley	Con
Stephen Timms	Lab
Secretary: Aidan Burley	Con

Contact: Stephen Timms, House of Commons, London SW1A 0AA Tel: 020 7219 4000

Child and Youth Crime

Chair: Stephen McPartland	Con
Vice-chairs:	
David Burrowes	Con
Vernon Coaker	Lab
Andrew Griffiths	Con
Secretary: Sadiq Khan	Lab
Treasurer: John Leech	Lib Dem

Contact: Stephen McPartland, House of Commons, London SW1A 0AA
Tel: 020 7219 7156

Child Health and Vaccine Preventable Diseases

Chairs:	
Lord Avebury	Lib Dem
Lord Boswell of Aynho	Non-Affiliated
Jim Dobbin	Lab/Co-op
Vice-chair: Lord Dholakia	Lib Dem
Secretary: Ian Liddell-Grainger	Con

Treasurer: Stephen McPartland	Con

Contact: Jim Dobbin, House of Commons, London SW1A 0AA Tel: 020 7219 4530

Child Protection

Chair: Meg Munn	Lab/Co-op
Vice-chairs:	
Andrea Leadsom	Con
Tim Loughton	Con
Secretary: Baroness Grey-Thompson	CB
Treasurer: Mark Williams	Lib Dem

Contact: Meg Munn, House of Commons, London SW1A 0AA Tel: 020 7219 8316

Children

Chair: Baroness Massey of Darwen	Lab
Vice-chairs:	
Baroness Berridge	Con
Baroness Blood	Lab
Bill Esterson	Lab
Jessica Lee	Con
Baroness Walmsley	Lib Dem
Secretary: Baroness Howarth of Breckland	CB
Treasurer: Earl of Listowel	CB

Contact: Jessica Lee, House of Commons, London SW1A 0AA Tel: 020 7219 7067

Children in Wales

Chair: Jessica Morden	Lab
Vice-chair: Mark Williams	Lib Dem
Secretary: Siân James	Lab

Contact: Jessica Morden, Room 2, Floor 7, Clarence House, Clarence Place, Newport, Monmouthshire NP19 7AA Tel: 01633 841726

Children's Media and the Arts

Chair: Baroness Benjamin	Lib Dem
Vice-chairs:	
Damian Hinds	Con
Tom Watson	Lab
Secretary: Dan Rogerson	Lib Dem

Contact: Damian Hinds, House of Commons, London SW1A 0AA Tel: 020 7219 7057

Chinese in Britain

Chair: Barry Gardiner	Lab
Vice-chairs:	
David Davies	Con
Lord Triesman	Lab
Secretary: Nigel Dodds	DUP

Contact: Barry Gardiner, House of Commons, London SW1A 0AA Tel: 020 7219 2104

Choice at the End of Life

Chair: Heidi Alexander	Lab
Vice-chairs:	
Andrew George	Lib Dem

Baroness Greengross	*CB*
Baroness Jay of Paddington	*Lab*
Dr Caroline Lucas	*Green*
Guy Opperman	*Con*
Secretary: Lord Joffe	*Lab*

Contact: Heidi Alexander, House of Commons, London SW1A 0AA Tel: 020 7219 7099

Choir

Chair: Caroline Spelman *Con*
Vice-chairs:

Baroness Corston	*Lab*
Lord German	*Lib Dem*
Bernard Jenkin	*Con*
Treasurer: Lord Shutt of Greetland	*Lib Dem*

Contact: Bernard Jenkin, House of Commons, London SW1A 0AA Tel: 020 7219 4029
www.parliamentchoir.org.uk

Christian and Jewish Relations

Chair: Rev Baroness Richardson of Calow *CB*
Vice-chairs:

John Howell	*Con*
Stephen Timms	*Lab*

Contact: John Howell, House of Commons, London SW1A 0AA Tel: 020 7219 6676

Christians in Parliament

Chair: Gary Streeter *Con*
Vice-chairs:

Lord Bates	*Con*
Baroness Brinton	*Lib Dem*
Jeffrey Donaldson	*DUP*
Tim Farron	*Lib Dem*
Baroness Sherlock	*Lab*
Gavin Shuker	*Lab/Co-op*
Secretary: Sharon Hodgson	*Lab*
Treasurer: Stephen Timms	*Lab*

Contact: Gary Streeter, House of Commons, London SW1A 0AA Tel: 020 7219 5033
www.christiansinparliament.org.uk

Chronic Pain

Chair: Linda Riordan *Lab/Co-op*
Secretary: Baroness Masham of Ilton *CB*

Contact: Linda Riordan, House of Commons, London SW1A 0AA Tel: 020 7219 5399

Cider

Chair: Ian Liddell-Grainger *Con*
Treasurer: Jesse Norman *Con*

Contact: Ian Liddell-Grainger, House of Commons, London SW1A 0AA
Tel: 020 7219 8149

Citizens Advice

Chairs:

Jonathan Edwards	*PlC*
Stephen Lloyd	*Lib Dem*

Sarah Newton	*Con*
Fiona O'Donnell	*Lab*
Vice-chair: Huw Irranca-Davies	*Lab*
Secretary: Pamela Nash	*Lab*
Treasurer: Baroness Howe of Idlicote	*CB*

Contact: Pamela Nash, House of Commons, London SW1A 0AA Tel: 020 7219 7003

City Regions' Transport

Chair: Graham Stringer *Lab*
Vice-chairs:

Philip Davies	*Con*
Greg Mulholland	*Lib Dem*

Contact: Graham Stringer, House of Commons, London SW1A 0AA Tel: 020 7219 5235

Civic Societies

Chair: Laura Sandys	*Con*
Vice-chair: Eric Ollerenshaw	*Con*
Secretary: Heather Wheeler	*Con*
Treasurer: Steve Baker	*Con*

Contact: Laura Sandys, House of Commons, London SW1A 0AA Tel: 020 7219 8302

Civil Society and Volunteering

Chairs:

Andrew George	*Lib Dem*
Susan Elan Jones	*Lab*
Baroness Pitkeathley	*Lab*

Vice-chairs:

Lord Best	*CB*
Lord Hodgson of Astley Abbotts	*Con*
Mark Spencer	*Con*
Secretary: Lord Rix	*CB*
Treasurer: Baroness Masham of Ilton	*CB*

Contact: Susan Elan Jones, House of Commons, London SW1A 0AA Tel: 020 7219 0920

Classical Music

Chair: Lord Lipsey *Lab*
Vice-chairs:

Jonathan Evans	*Con*
Lord Maclennan of Rogart	*Lib Dem*
Secretary: Barbara Keeley	*Lab*
Treasurer: Baroness McIntosh of Hudnall	*Lab*

Contact: Jonathan Evans, House of Commons, London SW1A 0AA Tel: 020 7219 7205

Clean Coal

Chairs:

Brian Binley	*Con*
Ian Lavery	*Lab*
Vice-chair: William Cash	*Con*
Secretary: David Anderson	*Lab*
Treasurer: Thomas Docherty	*Lab*

Contact: Brian Binley, House of Commons, London SW1A 0AA Tel: 020 7219 4447

Cleaning and Hygiene

Chair: Jim Dobbin   *Lab/Co-op*
Vice-chairs:
Lord Evans of Parkside   *Lab*
David Mowat   *Con*
Elizabeth Truss   *Con*
Secretary and Treasurer: David Crausby   *Lab*

Contact: Jim Dobbin, House of Commons, London SW1A 0AA Tel: 020 7219 4530

Climate Change

Chair: Joan Walley   *Lab*
Vice-chair: Lord Redesdale   *Lib Dem*
Secretary: Dr Caroline Lucas   *Green*
Treasurer: Tim Yeo   *Con*

Contact: Joan Walley, House of Commons, London SW1A 0AA Tel: 020 7219 6985

Clinical Physiology

Chair: Baroness Masham of Ilton   *CB*
Vice-chairs:
Jim Dobbin   *Lab/Co-op*
Lord Rea   *Lab*

Contact: Jim Dobbin, House of Commons, London SW1A 0AA Tel: 020 7219 1000

Coalfield Communities

Chair: David Anderson   *Lab*
Vice-chairs:
Sir Alan Beith   *Lib Dem*
Brian Binley   *Con*
Ann Clwyd   *Lab*
David Hamilton   *Lab*
Secretary: Ian Lavery   *Lab*
Treasurer: Cathy Jamieson   *Lab/Co-op*

Contact: David Anderson, House of Commons, London SW1A 0AA Tel: 020 7219 4843

Coeliac Disease and Dermatitis Herpetiformis

Chair: Kevan Jones   *Lab*
Vice-chairs:
Lord Brookman   *Lab*
Lord Dholakia   *Lib Dem*
Secretary: Gordon Banks   *Lab*

Contact: Gordon Banks, House of Commons, London SW1A 0AA Tel: 020 7219 8275

Commercial Radio

Chair: Dame Anne Begg   *Lab*
Vice-chairs:
Andrew Bingham   *Con*
Lord Kilclooney   *CB*
Secretary and Treasurer:
Lord Gordon of Strathblane   *Lab*

Contact: Dame Anne Begg, House of Commons, London SW1A 0AA Tel: 020 7219 2140

Commonwealth

Chair: Henry Bellingham   *Con*
Vice-chairs:
Rushanara Ali   *Lab*
Rehman Chishti   *Con*
Richard Graham   *Con*
Baroness Hooper   *Con*
Baroness Howells of St Davids   *Lab*
Chi Onwurah   *Lab*
Baroness Prashar   *CB*
Laura Sandys   *Con*
Nicholas Soames   *Con*
Secretary: Robin Walker   *Con*
Treasurer: Lord Hussain   *Lib Dem*

Contact: Henry Bellingham, House of Commons, London SW1A 0AA Tel: 020 7219 8234

Communications

Chair: John Robertson   *Lab*
Vice-chair: John Thurso   *Lib Dem*
Secretary: Jim Sheridan   *Lab*
Treasurer: Earl of Erroll   *CB*

Contact: John Robertson, House of Commons, London SW1A 0AA Tel: 020 7219 6964

Community Development in Europe

Chair: Earl of Dundee   *Con*
Vice-chair: Lord Grenfell   *Lab*
Secretary: Lord Grenfell   *Lab*

Contact: Robert Walter, House of Commons, London SW1A 0AA Tel: 020 7219 6981

Complex Needs and Dual Diagnosis

Chairs:
Lord Adebowale   *CB*
David Burrowes   *Con*

Contact: David Burrowes, House of Commons, London SW1A 0AA Tel: 020 7219 8144

Conception to Age Two – The First 1001 Days

Chairs:
Frank Field   *Lab*
Andrea Leadsom   *Con*
Vice-chairs:
Mark Durkan   *SDLP*
Sharon Hodgson   *Lab*
Liz Kendall   *Lab*
Earl of Listowel   *CB*
Dr Caroline Lucas   *Green*
Claire Perry   *Con*
Secretary: Lucy Powell   *Lab/Co-op*
Treasurer: Damian Hinds   *Con*

Contact: Andrea Leadsom, House of Commons, London SW1A 0AA Tel: 020 7219 7149

Conflict Issues
Chairs:
Lord Alderdice — *Lib Dem*
George Howarth — *Lab*
Gary Streeter — *Con*
Vice-chairs:
Lord Bates — *Con*
Simon Hughes — *Lib Dem*
Secretary: Jeffrey Donaldson — *DUP*
Treasurer: Andy Slaughter — *Lab*
Contact: Simon Hughes, House of Commons,
London SW1A 0AA Tel: 020 7219 6256

Connecting Communities
Chair: Claire Perry — *Con*
Vice-chair: Sir Peter Bottomley — *Con*
Contact: Claire Perry, House of Commons,
London SW1A 0AA Tel: 020 7219 7050

Conservation and Wildlife
Chair: Angela Smith — *Lab*
Vice-chairs:
Sir Peter Bottomley — *Con*
Baroness Miller of Chilthorne Domer — *Lib Dem*
Madeleine Moon — *Lab*
Lord Moran — *CB*
Roger Williams — *Lib Dem*
Secretary: Mark Pritchard — *Con*
Contact: Angela Smith, House of Commons,
London SW1A 0AA Tel: 020 7219 6713

Constitution
Chair: Prof. Lord Norton of Louth — *Con*
Vice-chairs:
Lord Howarth of Newport — *Lab*
Lord Rennard — *Lib Dem Ind*
Secretary: Lord Hunt of Kings Heath — *Lab*
Treasurer: Christopher Chope — *Con*
Contact: Christopher Chope, House of Commons,
London SW1A 0AA Tel: 020 7219 5808

Consumer Affairs and Trading Standards
Chair: Austin Mitchell — *Lab*
Vice-chair and Secretary:
Stephen Lloyd — *Lib Dem*
Contact: Stephen Lloyd, House of Commons,
London SW1A 0AA Tel: 020 7219 7061

Continence Care
Chair: Baroness Greengross — *CB*
Vice-chairs:
Jim Dobbin — *Lab/Co-op*
Baroness Finlay of Llandaff — *CB*
Laura Sandys — *Con*
Baroness Tonge — *Ind Lib Dem*
Secretary: Rosie Cooper — *Lab*
Treasurer: Baroness Masham of Ilton — *CB*
Contact: Rosie Cooper, House of Commons,
London SW1A 0AA Tel: 020 7219 5278
www.appgcontinence.org.uk

Corporate Governance
President: Lord Gordon of Strathblane — *Lab*
Chair: Andrew Tyrie — *Con*
Vice-chairs:
Lord Harrison — *Lab*
Kwasi Kwarteng — *Con*
Lord McFall of Alcluith — *Lab/Co-op*
Acting Secretary: Jonathan Djanogly — *Con*
Treasurer: Lord Wade of Chorlton — *Con*
Contact: Kwasi Kwarteng, House of Commons,
London SW1A 0AA Tel: 020 7219 3000
www.appcgg.co.uk

Corporate Responsibility
Chair: Baroness Greengross — *CB*
Acting Vice-chairs:
Jonathan Djanogly — *Con*
Baroness Gibson of Market Rasen — *Lab*
Baroness Howe of Idlicote — *CB*
John Robertson — *Lab*
Lord Sheppard of Didgemere — *Con*
Secretary: Martin Horwood — *Lib Dem*
Contact: John Robertson, House of Commons,
London SW1A 0AA Tel: 020 7219 6964
www.apcrg.org.uk

Couple Relationships
Chair: Andrew Selous — *Con*
Vice-chairs:
Graham Allen — *Lab*
Baroness Tyler of Enfield — *Lib Dem*
Contact: Andrew Selous, House of Commons,
London SW1A 0AA Tel: 020 7219 8134

Credit Unions
Chair: Damian Hinds — *Con*
Vice-chairs:
Mark Durkan — *SDLP*
Simon Hughes — *Lib Dem*
Lord Kennedy of Southwark — *Lab/Co-op*
Madeleine Moon — *Lab*
Secretary: Yvonne Fovargue — *Lab*
Treasurer: Chris Evans — *Lab/Co-op*
Contact: Damian Hinds, House of Commons,
London SW1A 0AA Tel: 020 7219 7057

Cricket
Chair: Sir Alan Haselhurst — *Con*
Vice-chairs:
Lord Kilclooney — *CB*
Baroness Massey of Darwen — *Lab*
Andrew Miller — *Lab*
Secretary: Nigel Adams — *Con*
Treasurer: Matthew Hancock — *Con*
Contact: Nigel Adams, House of Commons,
London SW1A 0AA Tel: 020 7219 7141

Cricket Club
Vice-Presidents:

Graham Allen	*Lab*
Crispin Blunt	*Con*
William Cash	*Con*
Sir Alan Haselhurst	*Con*
Lord King of Bridgwater	*Con*

Secretaries:

Nigel Adams	*Con*
Lord Razzall	*Lib Dem*

Treasurer: Henry Bellingham *Con*

Contact: Nigel Adams, House of Commons, London SW1A 0AA Tel: 020 7219 7141

Crossrail
Chair: Mike Gapes *Lab/Co-op*
Vice-chairs:

Lord Brougham and Vaux	*Con*
Robert Wilson	*Con*

Secretary: Earl of Glasgow *Lib Dem*
Treasurer: Angie Bray *Con*

Contact: Mike Gapes, House of Commons, London SW1A 0AA Tel: 020 7219 6485

Cycling
Patron: Ben Bradshaw *Lab*
Chairs:

Ian Austin	*Lab*
Dr Julian Huppert	*Lib Dem*

Vice-chairs:

Steve Brine	*Con*
Jim Fitzpatrick	*Lab*
Fabian Hamilton	*Lab*
Meg Hillier	*Lab/Co-op*
Jason McCartney	*Con*

Secretary: Lord Berkeley *Lab*
Treasurer: Dr Sarah Wollaston *Con*

Contact: Ian Austin, House of Commons, London SW1A 0AA Tel: 020 7219 8012
allpartycycling.org

Dalits
(Discrimination against Dalits, the former 'untouchables' caste in India)

Chair: Rt Rev Lord Harries of Pentregarth	*CB*
Vice-chair: Earl of Sandwich	*CB*
Secretary: Jeremy Corbyn	*Lab*
Treasurer: Prof. Lord Kakkar	*CB*

Contact: Jeremy Corbyn, House of Commons, London SW1A 0AA Tel: 020 7219 3545

Dance
Chair: Sir Gerald Kaufman *Lab*
Vice-chairs:

Christopher Heaton-Harris	*Con*
Baroness Hooper	*Con*

Secretary: Frank Doran *Lab*

Contact: Frank Doran, House of Commons, London SW1A 0AA Tel: 020 7219 3481

Deafness
Chair: Sir Malcolm Bruce *Lib Dem*
Vice-chairs:

Sir Peter Bottomley	*Con*
Rosie Cooper	*Lab*
Stephen Lloyd	*Lib Dem*
Stephen Phillips	*Con*
Baroness Wilkins	*Lab*

Contact: Sir Malcolm Bruce, House of Commons, London SW1A 0AA
Tel: 020 7219 6233

Death Penalty
Chair: Baroness Stern *CB*
Vice-chairs:

Lord Faulkner of Worcester	*Lab*
Lord Macdonald of River Glaven	*Lib Dem*
Greg Mulholland	*Lib Dem*

Secretary: Chris Williamson *Lab*
Treasurer: Lord Dubs *Lab*

Contact: Chris Williamson, House of Commons, London SW1A 0AA Tel: 020 7219 7049

Debt and Personal Finance
Chair: Yvonne Fovargue *Lab*
Vice-chairs:

Lorely Burt	*Lib Dem*
Tracey Crouch	*Con*
Mike Weir	*SNP*

Secretary and Treasurer: Nic Dakin *Lab*

Contact: Yvonne Fovargue, House of Commons, London SW1A 0AA Tel: 01942 824029
www.citizensadvice.org.uk/index/parliament/debtgroup.htm

Defence and Diplomacy in the Middle East and North Africa
Chair: Dai Havard *Lab*
Secretary: John Glen *Con*

Contact: Dai Havard, Unit 4, Triangle Business Park, Pentrebach, Merthyr Tydfil CF48 4TQ
Tel: 01685 379247

Dementia
Chair: Baroness Greengross *CB*
Vice-chairs:

Hazel Blears	*Lab*
David Blunkett	*Lab*
Tracey Crouch	*Con*
Tim Farron	*Lib Dem*
Mike Hancock	*Ind*
Stephen Lloyd	*Lib Dem*

Contact: Tracey Crouch, House of Commons, London SW1A 0AA Tel: 020 7219 7203 www.alzheimers.org.uk/appg

Democracy in Bahrain

Chair: Andy Slaughter	*Lab*
Vice-chair: David Amess	*Con*

Contact: Andy Slaughter, House of Commons, London SW1A 0AA Tel: 020 7219 4990

Dentistry

Chair: Sir Paul Beresford	*Con*
Vice-chairs:	
Kevin Barron	*Lab*
Lord Colwyn	*Con*
Steve Gilbert	*Lib Dem*
Alison Seabeck	*Lab*

Contact: Sir Paul Beresford, House of Commons, London SW1A 0AA Tel: 020 7219 2223 www.appgdentistry.org

Design and Innovation

President: Lord Rogers of Riverside	*Lab*
Chairs:	
Barry Sheerman	*Lab/Co-op*
Gavin Williamson	*Con*
Vice-chairs:	
Lord Bichard	*CB*
Baroness Whitaker	*Lab*

Contact: Barry Sheerman, House of Commons, London SW1A 0AA Tel: 020 7219 5037 www.policyconnect.org.uk/apdig

Diabetes

Chair: Adrian Sanders	*Lib Dem*
Vice-chairs:	
Lord Harrison	*Lab*
Anne McIntosh	*Con*
Keith Vaz	*Lab*

Contact: Adrian Sanders, House of Commons, London SW1A 0AA Tel: 020 7219 6304

Disability

Chairs:	
Baroness Campbell of Surbiton	*CB*
Anne McGuire	*Lab*
Vice-chairs:	
Baroness Thomas of Winchester	*Lib Dem*
Baroness Wilkins	*Lab*
Secretary: Chris Skidmore	*Con*

Contact: Anne McGuire, House of Commons, London SW1A 0AA Tel: 020 7219 5014

Disability Sports

Chair: Gerry Sutcliffe	*Lab*
Vice-chair: Jason McCartney	*Con*
Secretary: Linda Riordan	*Lab/Co-op*

Treasurer: Stuart Andrew	*Con*

Contact: Gerry Sutcliffe, Gumption Centre, Glydegate, Bradford BD5 0BQ Tel: 01274 400027

Domestic and Sexual Violence

Chair: Baroness Scotland of Asthal	*Lab*
Vice-chairs:	
Eleanor Laing	*Con*
Baroness Stern	*CB*
Secretary: Bridget Phillipson	*Lab*
Treasurer: Fiona Mactaggart	*Lab*

Contact: Bridget Phillipson, House of Commons, London SW1A 0AA Tel: 020 7219 7087

Down's Syndrome

Chair: Dr Hywel Francis	*Lab*
Vice-chairs:	
Virendra Sharma	*Lab*
Lord Touhig	*Lab/Co-op*
Secretary: Dan Rogerson	*Lib Dem*
Treasurer: Lord Wigley	*PlC*

Contact: Dr Hywel Francis, House of Commons, London SW1A 0AA Tel: 020 7219 8121

Drones

Chair: Tom Watson	*Lab*
Vice-chairs:	
Zac Goldsmith	*Con*
Baroness Stern	*CB*
Secretary: David Anderson	*Lab*
Treasurer: John Hemming	*Lib Dem*

Contact: Tom Watson, House of Commons, London SW1A 0AA Tel: 020 7219 8123

Drug Misuse

Chair: Lord Mancroft	*Con*
Vice-chairs:	
Paul Flynn	*Lab*
Baroness Masham of Ilton	*CB*
Lord Rea	*Lab*
Secretary: Andrew Griffiths	*Con*

Contact: Andrew Griffiths, House of Commons, London SW1A 0AA Tel: 020 7219 7029

Drug Policy Reform

Chair: Baroness Meacher	*CB*
Vice-chairs:	
Paul Flynn	*Lab*
Dr Julian Huppert	*Lib Dem*
Baroness Stern	*CB*
Treasurer: Lord Howarth of Newport	*Lab*

Contact: Dr Julian Huppert, House of Commons, London SW1A 0AA Tel: 020 7219 0647 www.drugpolicyreform.net

Dying Well

Chairs:
Jim Dobbin | *Lab/Co-op*
Baroness Finlay of Llandaff | *CB*
Vice-chairs:
Fiona Bruce | *Con*
Robert Flello | *Lab*

Contact: Jim Dobbin, House of Commons,
London SW1A 0AA Tel: 020 7219 4530
www.dyingwell.org.uk

Dyslexia and Specific Learning Difficulties

Chair: Ian Liddell-Grainger | *Con*
Vice-chair: Kelvin Hopkins | *Lab*
Treasurer: Brian Binley | *Con*

Contact: Ian Liddell-Grainger, House of
Commons, London SW1A 0AA
Tel: 020 7219 8149

Earth and Environmental Sciences

Chair: Martin Caton | *Lab*
Vice-chair: Duke of Montrose | *Con*
Secretary: Roger Williams | *Lib Dem*
Treasurer: Lord Oxburgh | *CB*

Contact: Martin Caton, House of Commons,
London SW1A 0AA Tel: 020 7219 5111
www.bgs.ac.uk/esef/all_party/
all_party_home.htm

East Asian Business

Honorary Presidents:
Lord Mandelson | *Lab*
Lord Powell of Bayswater | *CB*
Chair: Lord Wei | *Con*
Vice-chairs:
Kevan Jones | *Lab*
Lord Risby | *Con*
Secretary: Roger Godsiff | *Lab*
Treasurers:
Margot James | *Con*
Priti Patel | *Con*

Contact: Priti Patel, House of Commons,
London SW1A 0AA Tel: 020 7219 3528

East-West Rail

Chair: Iain Stewart | *Con*
Vice-chairs:
Lord Faulkner of Worcester | *Lab*
Dr Julian Huppert | *Lib Dem*

Contact: Iain Stewart, House of Commons,
London SW1A 0AA Tel: 020 7219 7230

Economics, Money and Banking

Chair: Steve Baker | *Con*
Vice-chairs:
Frank Dobson | *Lab*
Mark Garnier | *Con*

Secretary: Alun Cairns | *Con*
Secretary and Treasurer: Steve Baker | *Con*

Contact: Steve Baker, House of Commons,
London SW1A 0AA Tel: 020 7219 3547

Education

Chairs:
Nic Dakin | *Lab*
Fabian Hamilton | *Lab*
Vice-chairs:
Martin Horwood | *Lib Dem*
Baroness Perry of Southwark | *Con*

Contact: Fabian Hamilton, House of Commons,
London SW1A 0AA Tel: 020 7219 3493
www.educationappg.org.uk

Education Governance and Leadership

Chair: Neil Carmichael | *Con*
Vice-chair: Robin Walker | *Con*

Contact: Neil Carmichael, House of Commons,
London SW1A 0AA Tel: 020 7219 7163

Eggs, Pigs and Poultry

Chair: Neil Parish | *Con*
Vice-chairs:
Thomas Docherty | *Lab*
Dan Rogerson | *Lib Dem*
Mark Spencer | *Con*
Dr Eilidh Whiteford | *SNP*

Contact: Neil Parish, House of Commons,
London SW1A 0AA Tel: 020 7219 7172

Emergency Services

Chair: Mark Pawsey | *Con*
Vice-chairs:
Sir Paul Beresford | *Con*
Fiona Mactaggart | *Lab*

Contact: Mark Pawsey, House of Commons,
London SW1A 0AA Tel: 020 7219 7136

Employee Ownership

Chair: Jesse Norman | *Con*
Vice-chairs:
Martin Horwood | *Lib Dem*
Lindsay Roy | *Lab*
Secretary: Lord Brooke of Alverthorpe | *Lab*
Treasurer: Lord Best | *CB*

Contact: Jesse Norman, House of Commons,
London SW1A 0AA Tel: 020 7219 3000

Energy Costs

Chair: Lord Palmer | *CB*
Vice-chairs:
Lord Deben | *Con*
Laura Sandys | *Con*

Secretary: Julie Elliott   *Lab*
Treasurer: Stephen Hepburn   *Lab*
Contact: Julie Elliott, House of Commons, London SW1A 0AA Tel: 020 7219 7165

Energy Intensive Industries
Chair: Dr Tristram Hunt   *Lab*
Vice-chairs:
Huw Irranca-Davies   *Lab*
Ian Swales   *Lib Dem*
Secretary: Angela Smith   *Lab*
Treasurer: Graham Evans   *Con*
Contact: Dr Tristram Hunt, House of Commons, London SW1A 0AA Tel: 020 7219 1179

Energy Studies
Chair: Ian Liddell-Grainger   *Con*
Vice-chairs:
Simon Hughes   *Lib Dem*
Lord Hunt of Kings Heath   *Lab*
Lord O'Neill of Clackmannan   *Lab*
Lord Skelmersdale   *Con*
Secretaries:
Ian Lavery   *Lab*
John Thurso   *Lib Dem*
Treasurers:
Lord Oxburgh   *CB*
Neil Parish   *Con*
Contact: Ian Lavery, House of Commons, London SW1A 0AA Tel: 020 7219 7177

Engineering
Chair: Prof. Lord Broers   *CB*
Vice-chairs:
Dr Julian Huppert   *Lib Dem*
Meg Munn   *Lab/Co-op*
Lord Willis of Knaresborough   *Lib Dem*
Secretary: Laurence Robertson   *Con*
Treasurer: Stephen Williams   *Lib Dem*
Contact: Laurence Robertson, House of Commons, London SW1A 0AA
Tel: 020 7219 4196

Entrepreneurship
Chair: Earl of Erroll   *CB*
Vice-chairs:
Lord Ahmed   *Non-Affiliated*
Lorely Burt   *Lib Dem*
Anne Marie Morris   *Con*
Baroness Morris of Bolton   *Con*
Secretary: Baroness Morris of Bolton   *Con*
Contact: Anne Marie Morris, House of Commons, London SW1A 0AA
Tel: 020 7219 7232
www.allpartyenterprise.co.uk

Environment
Chair: Dan Byles   *Con*
Vice-chairs:
Jack Dromey   *Lab*
Martin Horwood   *Lib Dem*
Dr Phillip Lee   *Con*
Mike Weir   *SNP*
Dr Alan Whitehead   *Lab*
Baroness Young of Old Scone   *Non-Affiliated*
Contact: Dan Byles, House of Commons, London SW1A 0AA Tel: 020 7219 7179

Environmental Health
Chair: Joan Walley   *Lab*
Secretary: Baroness Hamwee   *Lib Dem*
Contact: Joan Walley, House of Commons, London SW1A 0AA Tel: 020 7219 6985

Epilepsy
Chair: Laura Sandys   *Con*
Vice-chairs:
Baroness Ford   *Non-Affiliated*
Paul Maynard   *Con*
Lord Walton of Detchant   *CB*
Secretary: Valerie Vaz   *Lab*
Treasurer: Teresa Pearce   *Lab*
Contact: Laura Sandys, House of Commons, London SW1A 0AA Tel: 020 7219 7170

Equalities
Chair: Sandra Osborne   *Lab*
Vice-chair: Lord Lester of Herne Hill   *Lib Dem*
Secretary and Treasurer:
Baroness Greengross   *CB*
Contact: Sandra Osborne, House of Commons, London SW1A 0AA Tel: 020 7219 6402

Equitable Life Policy Holders
Chairs:
Bob Blackman   *Con*
Fabian Hamilton   *Lab*
Secretary: Stephen Lloyd   *Lib Dem*
Contact: Bob Blackman, House of Commons, London SW1A 0AA Tel: 020 7219 7082

Ethics and Sustainability in Fashion
Chair: Prof. Baroness Young of Hornsey   *CB*
Vice-chairs:
Baroness Jones of Whitchurch   *Lab*
Alison McGovern   *Lab*
Secretary: Baroness Prosser   *Lab*
Treasurer: Baroness Parminter   *Lib Dem*
Contact: Alison McGovern, House of Commons, London SW1A 0AA
Tel: 020 7219 7190

European Reform

Chairs:
Thomas Docherty	Lab
Andrea Leadsom	Con

Vice-chairs:
Harriett Baldwin	Con
George Eustice	Con
Frank Field	Lab
Mark Garnier	Con
Christopher Heaton-Harris	Con
Margot James	Con
Karen Lumley	Con
Baroness Nicholson of Winterbourne	Lib Dem
David Ruffley	Con
Gisela Stuart	Lab
Secretary: Priti Patel	Con
Treasurer: Anne Marie Morris	Con

Contact: Andrea Leadsom, House of Commons, London SW1A 0AA Tel: 020 7219 7149

European Secure Vehicle Alliance

(Reduction of vehicle crime and fraud in the UK and Europe)

Chair: Lord Brougham and Vaux	Con

Vice-chairs:
Mark Reckless	Con
Viscount Simon	Lab
Secretary: Steve McCabe	Lab

Contact: Steve McCabe, House of Commons, London SW1A 0AA Tel: 020 7219 3509

European Union

Chairs:
Robert Buckland	Con
Mike Gapes	Lab/Co-op
Steve Gilbert	Lib Dem

Vice-chairs:
Lord Dykes	Lib Dem
Lord Hannay of Chiswick	CB
Lord Lea of Crondall	Lab
Baroness Quin	Lab
Secretary: Robert Walter	Con

Contact: Robert Buckland, House of Commons, London SW1A 0AA Tel: 020 7219 7168

European Union Referendum

Chair: John Baron	Con

Vice-chairs:
Ian Davidson	Lab/Co-op
Nigel Dodds	DUP
David Nuttall	Con
Keith Vaz	Lab

Contact: John Baron, House of Commons, London SW1A 0AA Tel: 020 7219 8138

European Union-United States Trade and Investment

Chair: John Healey	Lab

Vice-chairs:
Jonathan Evans	Con
Lilian Greenwood	Lab
Nadhim Zahawi	Con
Secretary: Guto Bebb	Con
Treasurer: Luciana Berger	Lab/Co-op

Contact: John Healey, House of Commons, London SW1A 0AA Tel: 020 7219 6359

Events Industry

Chair: Nick de Bois	Con
Vice-chair: Don Foster	Lib Dem
Secretary: Paul Uppal	Con
Treasurer: Steve Brine	Con

Contact: Nick de Bois, House of Commons, London SW1A 0AA Tel: 020 7219 5234

Extractive Industry

Chair: Pauline Latham	Con
Vice-chair: Eric Joyce	Ind
Secretary: Robin Walker	Con

Contact: Pauline Latham, House of Commons, London SW1A 0AA Tel: 020 7219 7110
www.extractiveindustry.co.uk/
Extractive_industry/APPG_EI.html

Extraordinary Rendition

Chair: Andrew Tyrie	Con
Vice-chair: Lord Tyler	Lib Dem
Treasurer: Lord Hodgson of Astley Abbotts	Con

Contact: Andrew Tyrie, House of Commons, London SW1A 0AA Tel: 020 7219 6371
www.extraordinaryrendition.org

Eye Health and Visual Impairment

Chair: Lord Low of Dalston	CB
Vice-chair: Annette Brooke	Lib Dem

Contact: Annette Brooke, House of Commons, London SW1A 0AA Tel: 020 7219 8193

Fair Fuel for Motorists and Hauliers

Chair: Robert Halfon	Con

Vice-chairs:
Angus MacNeil	SNP
Caroline Nokes	Con
Treasurer: Martin Vickers	Con

Contact: Robert Halfon, House of Commons, London SW1A 0AA Tel: 020 7219 7223

Fairs and Showgrounds

Chairs:
Brian Binley	Con
Brian Donohoe	Lab

Vice-chairs:
Sir Peter Bottomley   Con
Jim Dobbin   Lab/Co-op
Secretary: David Crausby   Lab
Treasurer: Kwasi Kwarteng   Con

Contact: Brian Donohoe, House of Commons,
London SW1A 0AA Tel: 020 7219 6230

Faith and Society

Chair: Stephen Timms   Lab
Vice-chairs:
Tim Farron   Lib Dem
Sharon Hodgson   Lab
Baroness Neuberger   CB
Baroness Sherlock   Lab
Gary Streeter   Con
Secretary: David Lammy   Lab
Treasurer: Lord Singh of Wimbledon   CB

Contact: Stephen Timms, House of Commons,
London SW1A 0AA Tel: 020 7219 4000

Family Business

Chair: Chris Kelly   Con
Vice-chairs:
Andrew Bridgen   Con
Lord Cotter   Lib Dem
Nadine Dorries   Con
Mary Glindon   Lab
Stephen Lloyd   Lib Dem
Lindsay Roy   Lab

Contact: Chris Kelly, House of Commons,
London SW1A 0AA Tel: 020 7219 7053
www.ifb.org.uk/representation/appg-for-family-
business.aspx

Family Law and the Court of Protection

Chair: John Hemming   Lib Dem
Vice-chair: Baroness Deech   CB

Contact: John Hemming, House of Commons,
London SW1A 0AA Tel: 020 7219 6314

Fashion and Textile

Chair: Damian Collins   Con
Vice-chair: Lord Davies of Coity   Lab/Co-op
Secretary: Tessa Munt   Lib Dem
Treasurer: Nadhim Zahawi   Con

Contact: Damian Collins, House of Commons,
London SW1A 0AA Tel: 020 7219 7072

Fatherhood

Chair: David Lammy   Lab
Vice-chairs:
John Hemming   Lib Dem
Andrew Selous   Con
Charles Walker   Con

Secretaries:
Annette Brooke   Lib Dem
Chris Leslie   Lab/Co-op

Contact: David Lammy, House of Commons,
London SW1A 0AA Tel: 020 7219 0899

Film Industry

Chair: Kevin Barron   Lab
Vice-chair: Richard Harrington   Con
Secretary: Brandon Lewis   Con
Treasurer: Ian Lucas   Lab

Contact: Kevin Barron, House of Commons,
London SW1A 0AA Tel: 020 7219 6306

Financial Education for Young People

Chair: Justin Tomlinson   Con
Vice-chairs:
Fiona Bruce   Con
Nic Dakin   Lab
Mark Garnier   Con
Duncan Hames   Lib Dem
Andrew Percy   Con

Contact: Justin Tomlinson, House of Commons,
London SW1A 0AA Tel: 020 7219 7167

Financial Markets and Services

Chair: Jonathan Evans   Con
Vice-chairs:
Baroness Cohen of Pimlico   Lab
David Ruffley   Con
Lord Teverson   Lib Dem
Secretary: Alun Cairns   Con
Treasurer: Andy Love   Lab/Co-op

Contact: Jonathan Evans, House of Commons,
London SW1A 0AA Tel: 020 7219 7205
www.apgfms.org.uk

Fire Safety and Rescue

Chairs:
David Amess   Con
Roger Williams   Lib Dem
Secretary: Jim Fitzpatrick   Lab
Treasurer: Peter Aldous   Con

Contact: David Amess, House of Commons,
London SW1A 0AA Tel: 020 7219 3452

First Aid

Chair: Sir Bob Russell   Lib Dem
Vice-chairs:
Lord Aberdare   CB
Dr Julian Huppert   Lib Dem
Jessica Morden   Lab
Priti Patel   Con
Secretary: Anne Marie Morris   Con

Contact: Sir Bob Russell, Magdalen Hall,
Wimpole Road, Colchester CO1 2DE
Tel: 01206 506600

Fisheries
Chair: Austin Mitchell — *Lab*
Vice-chairs:
Peter Aldous — *Con*
Andrew George — *Lib Dem*
Angus MacNeil — *SNP*
Secretary: Frank Doran — *Lab*
Treasurer: Sir Robert Smith — *Lib Dem*
Contact: Frank Doran, House of Commons, London SW1A 0AA Tel: 020 7219 3481

Flags and Heraldry
Chair: Andrew Rosindell — *Con*
Deputy Chair:
Admiral Lord West of Spithead — *Lab*
Vice-chairs:
Nigel Dodds — *DUP*
Philip Hollobone — *Con*
Lord Kilclooney — *CB*
Angus MacNeil — *SNP*
Tom Watson — *Lab*
Secretary: Robert Halfon — *Con*
Treasurer: Henry Smith — *Con*
Contact: Andrew Rosindell, House of Commons, London SW1A 0AA Tel: 020 7219 8475

Flood Prevention
Chair: Anne McIntosh — *Con*
Vice-chairs:
Nia Griffith — *Lab*
Laurence Robertson — *Con*
Secretary: Anne Marie Morris — *Con*
Contact: Anne McIntosh, House of Commons, London SW1A 0AA Tel: 020 7219 3541

Folk Arts
Chair: Kevin Brennan — *Lab*
Vice-chairs:
Jenny Chapman — *Lab*
Sir Bob Russell — *Lib Dem*
Secretary: Chris Ruane — *Lab*
Treasurer: Peter Wishart — *SNP*
Contact: Kevin Brennan, House of Commons, London SW1A 0AA Tel: 029 2022 3207

Food and Drink Manufacturing
Chair: John Stevenson — *Con*
Vice-chair: Russell Brown — *Lab*
Secretary: Mark Spencer — *Con*
Treasurer: Lord Dykes — *Lib Dem*
Contact: John Stevenson, House of Commons, London SW1A 0AA Tel: 020 7219 7035
www.appgfooddrink.org.uk/appg

Food and Health
Chair:
Baroness Miller of Chilthorne Domer — *Lib Dem*
Vice-chairs:
Countess of Mar — *CB*
Lord Rea — *Lab*
Roger Williams — *Lib Dem*
Secretary: Earl Baldwin of Bewdley — *CB*
Treasurer:
Baroness Gibson of Market Rasen — *Lab*
Contact: Roger Williams, House of Commons, London SW1A 0AA Tel: 020 7219 8145
www.fhf.org.uk

Football
Chair: Clive Betts — *Lab*
Vice-chairs:
Lord Faulkner of Worcester — *Lab*
Mark Field — *Con*
Joan Walley — *Lab*
Secretary: Stephen Hepburn — *Lab*
Treasurer: Christopher Heaton-Harris — *Con*
Contact: Clive Betts, House of Commons, London SW1A 0AA Tel: 020 7219 5114

Football Club
Chair: Clive Betts — *Lab*
Vice-chairs:
Christopher Heaton-Harris — *Con*
John Leech — *Lib Dem*
Steve Rotheram — *Lab*
Secretary: Stephen Hepburn — *Lab*
Treasurer: Jim Sheridan — *Lab*
Contact: Clive Betts, House of Commons, London SW1A 0AA Tel: 020 7219 3588

Foreign Affairs
Chair:
Baroness Nicholson of Winterbourne — *Lib Dem*
Vice-chairs:
Lord Alton of Liverpool — *CB*
Lord Burnett — *Lib Dem*
Prof. Lord Desai — *Lab*
Lord Ryder of Wensum — *Con*
Admiral Lord West of Spithead — *Lab*
Secretaries:
Lord Foulkes of Cumnock — *Lab/Co-op*
Hon Jacob Rees-Mogg — *Con*
Rory Stewart — *Con*
Treasurers:
Lord Boateng — *Lab*
Lord Clement-Jones — *Lib Dem*
Baroness Falkner of Margravine — *Lib Dem*
Lord Sheikh — *Con*
Contact: Hon Jacob Rees-Mogg, House of Commons, London SW1A 0AA Tel: 020 7219 7118

Forestry

Chair: Lord Clark of Windermere   *Lab*
Vice-chairs:
Lord Boswell of Aynho   *Non-Affiliated*
Roger Williams   *Lib Dem*
Secretary: Dr Therese Coffey   *Con*
Treasurer: Baroness Sharples   *Con*
Contact: Roger Williams, House of Commons, London SW1A 0AA Tel: 020 7219 8145

Freelance Sector

Chair: Brian Binley   *Con*
Vice-chair: John Glen   *Con*
Secretary: Steve Gilbert   *Lib Dem*
Treasurer: Jim Dowd   *Lab*
Contact: Brian Binley, House of Commons, London SW1A 0AA Tel: 020 7219 8298

Freight Transport

Chair: Robert Flello   *Lab*
Secretary: Kelvin Hopkins   *Lab*
Treasurer: Andrew Bridgen   *Con*
Contact: Kelvin Hopkins, House of Commons, London SW1A 0AA Tel: 020 7219 6670

Fruit Industry

Chair: Earl of Selborne   *Con*
Vice-chair: Sarah Newton   *Con*
Secretary: Laura Sandys   *Con*
Contact: Laura Sandys, House of Commons, London SW1A 0AA Tel: 020 7219 7170

Fuel Poverty and Energy Efficiency

Chairs:
Rebecca Harris   *Con*
Kelvin Hopkins   *Lab*
Dr Caroline Lucas   *Green*
Vice-chair: Gordon Henderson   *Con*
Secretary: Margaret Ritchie   *SDLP*
Treasurer: Laura Sandys   *Con*
Contact: Dr Caroline Lucas, House of Commons, London SW1A 0AA Tel: 020 7219 7025 www.nea.org.uk/fpeeg/fpeeg

Funerals and Bereavement

Chair: Lorely Burt   *Lib Dem*
Vice-chairs:
David Amess   *Con*
Rosie Cooper   *Lab*
Mark Pawsey   *Con*
Contact: Lorely Burt, House of Commons, London SW1A 0AA Tel: 020 7219 8269

Furniture Industry

Chair: Stephen McPartland   *Con*
Vice-chair: Lord Davies of Coity   *Lab/Co-op*

Executive Officers:
Duncan Hames   *Lib Dem*
Jessica Lee   *Con*
Contact: Stephen McPartland, House of Commons, London SW1A 0AA
Tel: 020 7219 7156

Further Education, Skills and Lifelong Learning

Chairs:
Stephen Lloyd   *Lib Dem*
Baroness Wall of New Barnet   *Lab*
Vice-chairs:
Robert Halfon   *Con*
Baroness Sharp of Guildford   *Lib Dem*
Treasurer: Baroness Brinton   *Lib Dem*
Contact: Stephen Lloyd, House of Commons, London SW1A 0AA Tel: 020 7219 7061

Game and Wildlife Conservation

Chair: Nicholas Soames   *Con*
Vice-chair: Roger Williams   *Lib Dem*
Secretary: Baroness Byford   *Con*
Contact: Nicholas Soames, House of Commons, London SW1A 0AA Tel: 020 7219 4143

Gardening and Horticulture

Chair: Baroness Fookes   *Con*
Vice-chairs:
Cheryl Gillan   *Con*
Lord Kilclooney   *CB*
Lord Kirkwood of Kirkhope   *Lib Dem*
Lord Palmer   *CB*
Baroness Royall of Blaisdon   *Lab*
Roger Williams   *Lib Dem*
Secretary: Brian Donohoe   *Lab*
Treasurer: Earl of Courtown   *Con*
Contact: Brian Donohoe, House of Commons, London SW1A 0AA Tel: 020 7219 6230

Genital Mutilation

Chair: Jane Ellison   *Con*
Vice-chair: Ann Clwyd   *Lab*
Treasurer: Amber Rudd   *Con*
Contact: Jane Ellison, House of Commons, London SW1A 0AA Tel: 020 7219 7010

Genocide and Crimes against Humanity

Chair: Michael McCann   *Lab*
Vice-chairs:
Lord Carlile of Berriew   *Lib Dem*
Dr Matthew Offord   *Con*
Secretary: Stephen Twigg   *Lab/Co-op*
Treasurer: Lord Dubs   *Lab*
Contact: Michael McCann, House of Commons, London SW1A 0AA Tel: 020 7219 7058

Global Education for All

Chairs:

Baroness Goudie	*Lab*
Mark Williams	*Lib Dem*

Vice-chairs:

David Blunkett	*Lab*
Annette Brooke	*Lib Dem*
Christopher Heaton-Harris	*Con*
Lord Low of Dalston	*CB*
Jason McCartney	*Con*
Alison McGovern	*Lab*
Pamela Nash	*Lab*
Fiona O'Donnell	*Lab*
Andrew Percy	*Con*
Baroness Sharp of Guildford	*Lib Dem*

Contact: Mark Williams, House of Commons, London SW1A 0AA Tel: 020 7219 8469 www.appg-educationforall.org.uk

Global Health

Chairs:

Lord Crisp	*CB*
Meg Hillier	*Lab/Co-op*

Vice-chairs:

Kevin Barron	*Lab*
Hugh Bayley	*Lab*
Prof. Lord Darzi of Denham	*Lab*
Stephen Dorrell	*Con*
Lord Ribeiro	*Con*
Baroness Tonge	*Ind Lib Dem*
Treasurer: Prof. Lord Kakkar	*CB*

Contact: Meg Hillier, House of Commons, London SW1A 0AA Tel: 020 7219 5325

Global Security and Non-Proliferation

Conveners:

Mike Gapes	*Lab/Co-op*
Lord Hannay of Chiswick	*CB*

Vice-Conveners:

Sir Peter Bottomley	*Con*
Baroness Falkner of Margravine	*Lib Dem*
Austin Mitchell	*Lab*
Secretary: Lord Lea of Crondall	*Lab*

Contact: Mike Gapes, House of Commons, London SW1A 0AA Tel: 020 7219 6485

Global Uncertainties

Chair: John Glen	*Con*
Vice-chair: Dai Havard	*Lab*

Contact: John Glen, House of Commons, London SW1A 0AA Tel: 020 7219 7138

Globe UK

(Promotes policy, legislation and understanding on green economy and sustainable development)

President: Lord Deben	*Con*

Vice-Presidents:

Sir Malcolm Bruce	*Lib Dem*
Zac Goldsmith	*Con*
Lord Prescott	*Lab*
Baroness Worthington	*Lab*
Tim Yeo	*Con*
Chair: Graham Stuart	*Con*

Vice-chair:

Prof. Lord Hunt of Chesterton	*Lab*

Contact: Graham Stuart, House of Commons, London SW1A 0AA Tel: 020 7219 4340

Green Deal

Chairs:

Barry Gardiner	*Lab*
Laura Sandys	*Con*

Vice-chairs:

Earl of Lindsay	*Con*
Lord Teverson	*Lib Dem*
Lord Whitty	*Lab*

Secretary and Treasurer:

Simon Wright	*Lib Dem*

Contact: Simon Wright, House of Commons, London SW1A 0AA Tel: 020 7219 3482 www.appg-greendealgroup.org.uk

Greenbelt

Chair: Chris Skidmore	*Con*

Vice-chairs:

Andrew Jones	*Con*
Julian Sturdy	*Con*
Secretary: Guy Opperman	*Con*
Treasurer: Gavin Williamson	*Con*

Contact: Chris Skidmore, House of Commons, London SW1A 0AA Tel: 020 7219 7094

Greyhound

Chairs:

Lord Bilston	*Lab/Co-op*
Andrew Rosindell	*Con*

Vice-chairs:

Lord Evans of Parkside	*Lab*
Dame Angela Watkinson	*Con*
Secretary: Ian Lavery	*Lab*
Treasurer: Baroness Golding	*Lab*

Contact: Andrew Rosindell, House of Commons, London SW1A 0AA Tel: 020 7219 8475

Gypsies Travellers Roma

Chair: Andrew George — *Lib Dem*
Vice-chair: Baroness Whitaker — *Lab*
Secretary: Lord Avebury — *Lib Dem*

Contact: Andrew George, House of Commons, London SW1A 0AA Tel: 020 7219 4588

Haemophilia and Contaminated Blood

Chairs:
Diana Johnson — *Lab*
Jason McCartney — *Con*

Contact: Diana Johnson, House of Commons, London SW1A 0AA Tel: 020 7219 5647

Hazara

(Hazara communities in Pakistan and Afghanistan)

Chair: John Denham — *Lab*
Secretary: Iain Stewart — *Con*

Contact: John Denham, House of Commons, London SW1A 0AA Tel: 020 7219 0067

Headache Disorders

Chair: Jim Fitzpatrick — *Lab*
Vice-chairs:
Pauline Latham — *Con*
John Leech — *Lib Dem*
Lord Rea — *Lab*
Viscount Simon — *Lab*
Secretary: Baroness Masham of Ilton — *CB*

Contact: Jim Fitzpatrick, House of Commons, London SW1A 0AA Tel: 020 7219 6215

Health

Chairs:
Kevin Barron — *Lab*
Paul Burstow — *Lib Dem*
Sarah Champion — *Lab*
Baroness Cumberlege — *Con*
Andrew George — *Lib Dem*
Baroness Masham of Ilton — *CB*
Dr Sarah Wollaston — *Con*
Secretary: Neil Carmichael — *Con*
Treasurer: Lord Hunt of Kings Heath — *Lab*

Contact: Neil Carmichael, House of Commons, London SW1A 0AA Tel: 020 7219 7163
www.healthinparliament.org.uk

Heart Disease

Chair: Chris Ruane — *Lab*
Vice-chairs:
Nigel Dodds — *DUP*
Michael Dugher — *Lab*
Baroness Masham of Ilton — *CB*
Jessica Morden — *Lab*

Justin Tomlinson — *Con*
Secretary: Lord Elder — *Lab*
Treasurer: Baroness Gardner of Parkes — *Con*

Contact: Chris Ruane, House of Commons, London SW1A 0AA Tel: 020 7219 6378

Hepatology

Chairs:
David Amess — *Con*
Baroness Masham of Ilton — *CB*
Vice-chairs:
Jason McCartney — *Con*
Virendra Sharma — *Lab*

Contact: David Amess, House of Commons, London SW1A 0AA Tel: 020 7219 3452

Heritage Rail

Chair: Mark Garnier — *Con*
Vice-chairs:
Karen Bradley — *Con*
Lord Faulkner of Worcester — *Lab*
Lord Grocott — *Lab*
Susan Elan Jones — *Lab*
Earl of Mar and Kellie — *Scottish Lib Dem*
Treasurer: Martin Vickers — *Con*

Contact: Mark Garnier, House of Commons, London SW1A 0AA Tel: 020 7219 7198

High Speed Rail

Chairs:
Stuart Andrew — *Con*
Graham Stringer — *Lab*
Vice-chairs:
Lord Adonis — *Lab*
Graham Evans — *Con*
Secretary: Gisela Stuart — *Lab*

Contact: Stuart Andrew, House of Commons, London SW1A 0AA Tel: 020 7219 7130

Highway Maintenance

Chair: Christopher Chope — *Con*
Vice-chair: Viscount Simon — *Lab*
Secretary: Lord Davies of Coity — *Lab/Co-op*
Treasurer: Heather Wheeler — *Con*

Contact: Christopher Chope, House of Commons, London SW1A 0AA
Tel: 020 7219 5808

Hill Farming

Chair: Tim Farron — *Lib Dem*
Vice-chairs:
Julian Smith — *Con*
John Woodcock — *Lab/Co-op*
Secretary: Rory Stewart — *Con*

Contact: Tim Farron, House of Commons, London SW1A 0AA Tel: 020 7219 8498

Hillsborough Disaster

Chair: Alison McGovern — *Lab*
Vice-chairs:
Stephen Mosley — *Con*
Dr John Pugh — *Lib Dem*
Secretary: Derek Twigg — *Lab*

Contact: Alison McGovern, House of Commons, London SW1A 0AA Tel: 020 7219 7190

Historic Churches

Chair: Frank Dobson — *Lab*
Vice-chair: William Cash — *Con*
Secretaries:
Sir Alan Beith — *Lib Dem*
Lord Phillips of Sudbury — *Lib Dem*

Contact: Frank Dobson, House of Commons, London SW1A 0AA Tel: 020 7219 5840

Historic Vehicles

Chair: Greg Knight — *Con*
Vice-chair: Kelvin Hopkins — *Lab*
Secretary: Christopher Chope — *Con*
Treasurer: John Cryer — *Lab*

Contact: Greg Knight, House of Commons, London SW1A 0AA Tel: 020 7219 8417

HIV and AIDS

Chair: Pamela Nash — *Lab*
Vice-chairs:
Stuart Andrew — *Con*
Russell Brown — *Lab*
Lord Fowler — *Con*
Steve Gilbert — *Lib Dem*
Simon Kirby — *Con*
Baroness Masham of Ilton — *CB*
Secretary: Russell Brown — *Lab*
Treasurer: Simon Kirby — *Con*

Contact: Pamela Nash, House of Commons, London SW1A 0AA Tel: 020 7219 7003
www.appghivaids.org.uk

Hockey

Chair: Tim Loughton — *Con*
Secretary: Meg Munn — *Lab/Co-op*

Contact: Tim Loughton, House of Commons, London SW1A 0AA Tel: 020 7219 4471

Holy See

Chairs:
Conor Burns — *Con*
Sir Edward Leigh — *Con*
Vice-chairs:
Joe Benton — *Lab*
Mark Pritchard — *Con*
Secretaries:
Baroness Hooper — *Con*
Dan Rogerson — *Lib Dem*

Treasurers:
Jim McGovern — *Lab*
Angus MacNeil — *SNP*

Contact: Conor Burns, House of Commons, London SW1A 0AA Tel: 020 7219 7021

Home Education

Chair: Graham Stuart — *Con*
Vice-chair: Andrew Griffiths — *Con*
Secretary: Tim Farron — *Lib Dem*
Treasurer: David Anderson — *Lab*

Contact: Graham Stuart, House of Commons, London SW1A 0AA Tel: 020 7219 4848

Home Safety

Chairs:
Baroness Finlay of Llandaff — *CB*
Barry Sheerman — *Lab/Co-op*

Contact: Barry Sheerman, Office F18, The Media Centre, 7 Northumberland Street, Huddersfield HD1 1RL Tel: 01484 487970

Homeland Security

Chair: Bernard Jenkin — *Con*
Vice-chairs:
Lord Carlile of Berriew — *Lib Dem*
Lord Reid of Cardowan — *Lab*
Secretary: Lord Harris of Haringey — *Lab*
Treasurer: James Morris — *Con*

Contact: Bernard Jenkin, House of Commons, London SW1A 0AA Tel: 020 7219 4029
homeland-security.org.uk

Honour Based Abuse

Chairs:
Baroness Afshar — *CB*
Baroness Cox — *CB*
Vice-chair: Virendra Sharma — *Lab*
Secretary and Treasurer:
Lord Carlile of Berriew — *Lib Dem*

Contact: Virendra Sharma, House of Commons, London SW1A 0AA Tel: 020 7219 6080

Horse

Chair: Baroness Mallalieu — *Lab*
Vice-chairs:
Sir Tony Cunningham — *Lab*
Ian Liddell-Grainger — *Con*
Secretary: Roger Williams — *Lib Dem*
Treasurer: Baroness Masham of Ilton — *CB*

Contact: Roger Williams, House of Commons, London SW1A 0AA Tel: 020 7219 8145

Hospice and Palliative Care

Chair: Fabian Hamilton — *Lab*
Vice-chairs:
Baroness Finlay of Llandaff — *CB*
Margot James — *Con*

Secretary: Jim Dobbin   *Lab/Co-op*
Treasurer: Stuart Andrew   *Con*

Contact: Fabian Hamilton, House of Commons, London SW1A 0AA Tel: 020 7219 3493

Housing

Chairs:
Annette Brooke   *Lib Dem*
Graham Jones   *Lab*
Vice-chair: Stephen Pound   *Lab*
Secretary: Lord Best   *CB*
Treasurer: Graham Jones   *Lab*

Contact: Annette Brooke, House of Commons, London SW1A 0AA Tel: 020 7219 8193

Housing and Care for Older People

Chair: Lord Best   *CB*
Vice-chairs:
Baroness Barker   *Lib Dem*
Sarah Newton   *Con*
Nick Raynsford   *Lab*
Secretary: Baroness Howarth of Breckland   *CB*

Contact: Nick Raynsford, House of Commons, London SW1A 0AA Tel: 020 7219 5895

Housing and Planning

Chairs:
Clive Betts   *Lab*
Tim Yeo   *Con*
Vice-chair: Andrew George   *Lib Dem*
Secretary: Lord Howarth of Newport   *Lab*

Contact: Tim Yeo, House of Commons, London SW1A 0AA Tel: 020 7219 4175

Housing in the North

Chair: Ian Mearns   *Lab*
Vice-chairs:
Kris Hopkins   *Con*
David Ward   *Lib Dem*
Secretary: Grahame Morris   *Lab*
Treasurer: Graham Jones   *Lab*

Contact: Ian Mearns, 12 Regents Terrace, Gateshead, Tyne and Wear NE8 1LU Tel: 0191-477 0651

Human Rights

Chair: Ann Clwyd   *Lab*
Vice-chairs:
Lord Avebury   *Lib Dem*
Jeremy Corbyn   *Lab*
Robert Walter   *Con*
Secretary: Dr Sarah Wollaston   *Con*
Treasurer: Mark Durkan   *SDLP*

Contact: Ann Clwyd, House of Commons, London SW1A 0AA Tel: 020 7219 6609

Human Trafficking and Modern Day Slavery

Chairs:
Baroness Butler-Sloss   *CB*
Fiona Mactaggart   *Lab*
Vice-chairs:
Fiona Bruce   *Con*
Michael Connarty   *Lab*
Baroness Nicholson of Winterbourne   *Lib Dem*
Secretaries:
Emma Reynolds   *Lab*
Andrew Selous   *Con*
David Simpson (acting)   *DUP*
Treasurers:
Mark Durkan   *SDLP*
Frank Field   *Lab*

Contact: Fiona Mactaggart, House of Commons, London SW1A 0AA Tel: 020 7219 3416 www.allpartygrouphumantrafficking.org

Humanist

Chair: Lord Warner   *Lab*
Vice-chairs:
Baroness Flather   *CB*
Lord Garel-Jones   *Con*
Kelvin Hopkins   *Lab*
Dr Julian Huppert   *Lib Dem*
Lord Taverne   *Lib Dem*
Secretary: Baroness Massey of Darwen   *Lab*
Treasurer: Lord Dubs   *Lab*

Contact: Kelvin Hopkins, House of Commons, London SW1A 0AA Tel: 020 7219 6670 humanism.org.uk/about/humanists-in-parliament

Huntington's Disease

Chair: Lord Walton of Detchant   *CB*
Secretary: Frank Dobson   *Lab*
Treasurer: Mark Field   *Con*

Contact: Frank Dobson, House of Commons, London SW1A 0AA Tel: 020 7219 5840

Infertility

Chair: Andrew Griffiths   *Con*
Vice-chair: Karl McCartney   *Con*

Contact: Andrew Griffiths, House of Commons, London SW1A 0AA Tel: 020 7219 7029

Infrastructure

Chair: Nick Raynsford   *Lab*
Vice-chairs:
Lord Chidgey   *Lib Dem*
Naomi Long   *All*
Stephen Pound   *Lab*
Secretary: Mark Garnier   *Con*
Treasurer: Lord Berkeley   *Lab*

Contact: Nick Raynsford, House of Commons, London SW1A 0AA Tel: 020 7219 2773

Insurance and Financial Services

Chair: Jonathan Evans   *Con*
Vice-chairs:
Lord Hunt of Wirral   *Con*
Andy Love   *Lab/Co-op*
Secretaries:
Sir Edward Leigh   *Con*
Heather Wheeler   *Con*

Contact: Jonathan Evans, House of Commons,
London SW1A 0AA Tel: 020 7219 7205
www.incisivemedia.com/incisive-media/profile/
2101279/party-parliamentary-insurance-
financial-services

Integrated Healthcare

President: Lord Colwyn   *Con*
Chair: David Tredinnick   *Con*
Vice-chairs:
Penny Mordaunt   *Con*
Valerie Vaz   *Lab*
Secretary: Oliver Colvile   *Con*

Contact: David Tredinnick, House of Commons,
London SW1A 0AA Tel: 020 7219 4474

Intellectual Property

Chair: John Whittingdale   *Con*
Vice-chairs:
Lord Clement-Jones   *Lib Dem*
Jim Dowd   *Lab*
Peter Wishart   *SNP*
Secretary: Mike Weatherley   *Con*
Treasurer: Lord Razzall   *Lib Dem*

Contact: John Whittingdale, House of
Commons, London SW1A 0AA
Tel: 020 7219 3557 www.allpartyipgroup.org.uk

Intelligent Energy

Chair: Peter Aldous   *Con*
Vice-chair: Lord Redesdale   *Lib Dem*
Secretary: Dr Alan Whitehead   *Lab*
Treasurer: Mike Weir   *SNP*

Contact: Peter Aldous, House of Commons,
London SW1A 0AA Tel: 020 7219 7182

Interest Rate Swap Mis-Selling

Chair: Guto Bebb   *Con*
Vice-chairs:
Steve Brine   *Con*
Nick de Bois   *Con*
Andrea Leadsom   *Con*
Dr Caroline Lucas   *Green*
Emma Reynolds   *Lab*
Secretary: David Ruffley   *Con*
Treasurer: Mark Williams   *Lib Dem*

Contact: Guto Bebb, House of Commons,
London SW1A 0AA Tel: 020 7219 7002

Inter-Faith

Chair: Rt Rev Lord Harries of Pentregarth   *CB*
Vice-chairs:
Baroness Afshar   *CB*
Lord Ahmed   *Non-Affiliated*
Secretary: Baroness Neuberger   *CB*
Treasurer: Jack Straw   *Lab*

Contact: Jack Straw, House of Commons,
London SW1A 0AA Tel: 020 7219 5070

Intergenerational Futures

Chair: Baroness Greengross   *CB*
Vice-chair: John Leech   *Lib Dem*
Secretary: Baroness Howe of Idlicote   *CB*
Treasurer:
Baroness Thomas of Walliswood   *Lib Dem*

Contact: John Leech, House of Commons,
London SW1A 0AA Tel: 020 7219 8353

International Corporate Responsibility: Business, Human Rights and the Environment

Chair: Lisa Nandy   *Lab*
Vice-chairs:
Jon Cruddas   *Lab*
Martin Horwood   *Lib Dem*
Dr Caroline Lucas   *Green*
Secretary: Teresa Pearce   *Lab*
Treasurer: Virendra Sharma   *Lab*

Contact: Lisa Nandy, House of Commons,
London SW1A 0AA Tel: 020 7219 7188 appg-
icr.org

International Development and the Environment

Chairs:
Mark Durkan   *SDLP*
Martin Horwood   *Lib Dem*
Baroness Jenkin of Kennington   *Con*
Mark Lazarowicz   *Lab/Co-op*
Dr Caroline Lucas   *Green*
Michael Meacher   *Lab*
Laura Sandys   *Con*
Lord Teverson   *Lib Dem*
Vice-chairs:
Sir Peter Bottomley   *Con*
Lord Cameron of Dillington   *CB*
Lord Foulkes of Cumnock   *Lab/Co-op*
Lord Hannay of Chiswick   *CB*
Baroness Kinnock of Holyhead   *Lab*
Pauline Latham   *Con*
Baroness Miller of Chilthorne Domer   *Lib Dem*
Dr Eilidh Whiteford   *SNP*

Contact: Martin Horwood, House of Commons,
London SW1A 0AA Tel: 020 7219 4784
www.appgide.org

International Relations

Chair: Khalid Mahmood   *Lab*
Vice-chairs:
Lord Ahmed   *Non-Affiliated*
Mark Pritchard   *Con*
Secretary: David Anderson   *Lab*

Contact: Khalid Mahmood, House of Commons, London SW1A 0AA Tel: 020 7219 8141

Internet and Communications Technology

President: John Bercow   *Speaker*
Chairs:
Stephen Mosley   *Con*
Chi Onwurah   *Lab*
Vice-chairs:
Nigel Adams   *Con*
Dr Julian Huppert   *Lib Dem*
Stephen McPartland   *Con*
Andrew Miller   *Lab*
Treasurer: Lord Harris of Haringey   *Lab*

Contact: Stephen Mosley, House of Commons, London SW1A 0AA Tel: 020 7219 7207
www.pictfor.org.uk

Irish in Britain

Chair: Chris Ruane   *Lab*
Vice-chairs:
Sir Peter Bottomley   *Con*
Simon Hughes   *Lib Dem*
Margaret Ritchie   *SDLP*
Secretary: Paul Farrelly   *Lab*
Treasurer: Lord Dubs   *Lab*

Contact: Chris Ruane, House of Commons, London SW1A 0AA Tel: 020 7219 6378

Islamic Finance and Diversity in Financial Markets

Chair: Roger Williams   *Lib Dem*
Vice-chairs:
Lord Alderdice   *Lib Dem*
Lord Sheikh   *Con*
Andy Slaughter   *Lab*
Secretary: Lord Smith of Clifton   *Lib Dem*
Treasurer:
Baroness Nicholson of Winterbourne   *Lib Dem*

Contact: Roger Williams, House of Commons, London SW1A 0AA Tel: 020 7219 8145

Islamophobia

Chairs:
Stuart Andrew   *Con*
Simon Hughes   *Lib Dem*
Khalid Mahmood   *Lab*
Vice-chair: Jack Straw   *Lab*
Treasurer: Nigel Dodds   *DUP*

Contact: Simon Hughes, House of Commons, London SW1A 0AA Tel: 020 7219 6256

ITV

Chair: Lord Dubs   *Lab*
Vice-chair: Dr Therese Coffey   *Con*
Secretary:
Baroness Bonham-Carter of Yarnbury   *Lib Dem*
Treasurer: Richard Ottaway   *Con*

Contact: Richard Ottaway, House of Commons, London SW1A 0AA Tel: 020 7219 6392

Jazz Appreciation

Chairs:
Lord Colwyn   *Con*
Michael Connarty   *Lab*
Vice-chair: Kelvin Hopkins   *Lab*
Secretary: Baroness Coussins   *CB*
Treasurer: Mike Gapes   *Lab/Co-op*

Contact: Michael Connarty, House of Commons, London SW1A 0AA Tel: 020 7219 5071

Kidney

Chairs:
Glyn Davies   *Con*
Madeleine Moon   *Lab*
Vice-chairs:
Lord Davies of Coity   *Lab/Co-op*
Duncan Hames   *Lib Dem*
Secretary: Rosie Cooper   *Lab*

Contact: Madeleine Moon, House of Commons, London SW1A 0AA Tel: 020 7219 0814

Landmines and Unexploded Weapons of Conflict

Chair: Pauline Latham   *Con*
Vice-chairs:
Martin Caton   *Lab*
Caroline Dinenage   *Con*
Mark Durkan   *SDLP*
Lord Elton   *Con*
Gen Lord Ramsbotham   *CB*
Secretary: Paul Goggins   *Lab*
Treasurer: Dr Matthew Offord   *Con*

Contact: Pauline Latham, House of Commons, London SW1A 0AA Tel: 020 7219 7110

Learning Disability

Chairs:
Tom Clarke   *Lab*
Lord Rix   *CB*
Vice-chairs:
Prof. Baroness Hollins   *CB*
Grahame Morris   *Lab*
Secretary: Viscount Tenby   *CB*
Treasurer: Baroness Wilkins   *Lab*

Contact: Tom Clarke, House of Commons, London SW1A 0AA Tel: 020 7219 5007
www.mencap.org.uk/campaigns/westminster-watch/all-party-parliamentary-group-appgld

Legal Aid

Chair: Yvonne Fovargue — *Lab*
Vice-chair: Lord Carlile of Berriew — *Lib Dem*
Secretary: Robert Buckland — *Con*
Treasurer: Lord Bach — *Lab*

Contact: Yvonne Fovargue, House of Commons, London SW1A 0AA Tel: 020 7219 7108
www.appg-legalaid.org

Legal and Constitutional Affairs

Chair: Lord Hunt of Wirral — *Con*
Vice-chairs:
Lord Bach — *Lab*
Lord Brennan — *Lab*
Lord Burnett — *Lib Dem*
Lord Clinton-Davis — *Lab*
Lord Goodhart — *Lib Dem*
Lord Neill of Bladen — *CB*
Keith Vaz — *Lab*
Secretary: Rehman Chishti — *Con*
Treasurer: Yasmin Qureshi — *Lab*

Contact: Rehman Chishti, House of Commons, London SW1A 0AA Tel: 020 7219 7075

Leisure

Chair: Gerry Sutcliffe — *Lab*
Vice-chairs:
Mark Pritchard — *Con*
Mike Weatherley — *Con*

Contact: Gerry Sutcliffe, House of Commons, London SW1A 0AA Tel: 020 7219 3247

Libraries

Chair: Justin Tomlinson — *Con*
Vice-chairs:
Lisa Nandy — *Lab*
Andrew Percy — *Con*
Lord Tope — *Lib Dem*

Contact: Justin Tomlinson, House of Commons, London SW1A 0AA Tel: 020 7219 7167
www.cilip.org.uk/about-us/librariesappg/pages/default.aspx

Life Transitions

Chairs:
David Blunkett — *Lab*
Lord Wei — *Con*
Vice-chair: Lord Rennard — *Lib Dem Ind*
Secretary: Robert Halfon — *Con*
Treasurer: Chris White — *Con*

Contact: Chris White, House of Commons, London SW1A 0AA Tel: 020 7219 7201

Light Rail

Chair: John Leech — *Lib Dem*
Vice-chair: Graham Stringer — *Lab*

Secretary: Kelvin Hopkins — *Lab*

Contact: John Leech, 8 Gansworth Avenue, Didsbury, Manchester M20 5NF
Tel: 0161-434 3334 www.applrguk.co.uk

Lighting

(Industry and technology)
Chairs:
Sir Tony Baldry — *Con*
Joan Walley — *Lab*
Secretary: Clive Efford — *Lab*

Contact: Joan Walley, House of Commons, London SW1A 0AA Tel: 020 7219 6985

Limb Loss

Chairs:
Steve McCabe — *Lab*
Prof. Lord McColl of Dulwich — *Con*
Lord Rennard — *Lib Dem Ind*
Alison Seabeck — *Lab*
Secretary: Dame Anne Begg — *Lab*

Contact: Dame Anne Begg, House of Commons, London SW1A 0AA Tel: 020 7219 2140
www.apllg.eu

Literacy

Chair: Robert Halfon — *Con*
Vice-chairs:
Lord Knight of Weymouth — *Lab*
Stephen McPartland — *Con*

Contact: Robert Halfon, House of Commons, London SW1A 0AA Tel: 020 7219 7223

Local Democracy

Chair: Rory Stewart — *Con*
Deputy Chair: Fiona Bruce — *Con*
Vice-chairs:
Lord Greaves — *Lib Dem*
Dr Tristram Hunt — *Lab*
Secretary: Julian Smith — *Con*
Treasurer: Dan Rogerson — *Lib Dem*

Contact: Rory Stewart, House of Commons, London SW1A 0AA Tel: 020 7219 7127

Local Government

Chair: Heather Wheeler — *Con*
Vice-chairs:
Lord Best — *CB*
Dr Roberta Blackman-Woods — *Lab*
Dr Julian Huppert — *Lib Dem*
Secretary: Andy Sawford — *Lab/Co-op*
Treasurer: Eric Ollerenshaw — *Con*

Contact: Heather Wheeler, House of Commons, London SW1A 0AA Tel: 01283 225365

Local Growth, Local Enterprise Partnerships and Enterprise Zones

Chairs:
Caroline Dinenage — Con
James Morris — Con
Vice-chairs:
Ian Mearns — Lab
Anne Marie Morris — Con
Secretary: Baroness Kramer — Lib Dem
Treasurer: Andy Sawford — Lab/Co-op

Contact: Caroline Dinenage, House of Commons, London SW1A 0AA
Tel: 020 7219 7078 appglocalgrowth.org

London-Stansted-Cambridge Corridor

Chairs:
Nick de Bois — Con
David Lammy — Lab
Vice-chair: Dr Julian Huppert — Lib Dem
Secretary: Lord Adonis — Lab

Contact: David Lammy, House of Commons, London SW1A 0AA Tel: 020 7219 0767

Looked After Children and Care Leavers

Chair: Craig Whittaker — Con
Vice-chairs:
Earl of Listowel — CB
Lisa Nandy — Lab
Secretary and Treasurer: Jessica Lee — Con

Contact: Craig Whittaker, House of Commons, London SW1A 0AA Tel: 020 7219 7031
www.thewhocarestrust.org.uk/pages/the-all-party-parliamentary-group-for-looked-after-children-and-care-leavers.html

Malaria and Neglected Tropical Diseases

Chair: Jeremy Lefroy — Con
Vice-chairs:
Kevin Barron — Lab
Baroness Hayman — CB
Eleanor Laing — Con
Pauline Latham — Con
Lord Rea — Lab
Secretary: Fiona Bruce — Con
Treasurer: Andrew George — Lib Dem

Contact: Jeremy Lefroy, House of Commons, London SW1A 0AA Tel: 020 7219 7154
www.appmg-malaria.org.uk

Management

Chair: Barry Sheerman — Lab/Co-op
Vice-chairs:
Sir Peter Bottomley — Con
Lorely Burt — Lib Dem
Lord Haskel — Lab
Lord Hodgson of Astley Abbotts — Con

Baroness Kingsmill — Lab
Contact: Barry Sheerman, House of Commons, London SW1A 0AA Tel: 020 7219 5037

Manufacturing

Chairs:
Barry Sheerman — Lab/Co-op
Chris White — Con
Vice-chairs:
Caroline Dinenage — Con
Jonathan Reynolds — Lab/Co-op
Baroness Wall of New Barnet — Lab
Secretary: John Stevenson — Con
Treasurer: Gordon Birtwistle — Lib Dem

Contact: Chris White, House of Commons, London SW1A 0AA Tel: 020 7219 7201

Maritime and Ports

Chairs:
Julian Brazier — Con
Lord Greenway — CB
Vice-chairs:
Dr Therese Coffey — Con
Dr Alan Whitehead — Lab
Secretary: Lord Berkeley — Lab

Contact: Julian Brazier, House of Commons, London SW1A 0AA Tel: 020 7219 5178

Markets

Chair: Ann Coffey — Lab
Vice-chairs:
Lord Bilston — Lab/Co-op
Lorely Burt — Lib Dem
Jenny Chapman — Lab
Baroness Dean of Thornton-le-Fylde — Lab
Marcus Jones — Con
Nicky Morgan — Con
Lord Wade of Chorlton — Con
Secretaries:
Jim Fitzpatrick — Lab
Jim Dobbin — Lab/Co-op

Contact: Ann Coffey, House of Commons, London SW1A 0AA Tel: 020 7219 4546

Maternity

Chair: David Amess — Con
Vice-chairs:
Baroness Cumberlege — Con
Lord Patel — CB
Secretary: Lilian Greenwood — Lab
Treasurer: Annette Brooke — Lib Dem

Contact: David Amess, House of Commons, London SW1A 0AA Tel: 020 7219 3452
www.appg-maternity.org.uk

ME (Myalgic Encephalomyelitis)

Chair: Annette Brooke — *Lib Dem*
Vice-chairs:
Countess of Mar — *CB*
Ian Swales — *Lib Dem*
Secretary: Russell Brown — *Lab*

Contact: Annette Brooke, House of Commons, London SW1A 0AA Tel: 020 7219 8193

Media

Chair: Austin Mitchell — *Lab*
Vice-chairs:
Dame Anne Begg — *Lab*
Sir Roger Gale — *Con*
Lord Lipsey — *Lab*
Honorary Secretaries:
Sir Peter Bottomley — *Con*
Alun Cairns — *Con*

Contact: Austin Mitchell, House of Commons, London SW1A 0AA Tel: 020 7219 4559

Media Reform

Chair: Lord Fowler — *Con*
Vice-chair: George Eustice — *Con*
Secretary: Paul Farrelly — *Lab*
Treasurer: Adrian Sanders — *Lib Dem*

Contact: Paul Farrelly, House of Commons, London SW1A 0AA Tel: 020 7219 8391

Medical Research

Chair: Lord Turnberg — *Lab*
Vice-chair: Prof. Lord Kakkar — *CB*
Secretary: Lord Davies of Coity — *Lab/Co-op*
Treasurer: Dr Julian Huppert — *Lib Dem*

Contact: Dr Julian Huppert, House of Commons, London SW1A 0AA Tel: 020 7219 0647 www.amrc.org.uk/news-policy--debate_appg-on-medical-research

Non-Profit Making Members' Clubs

Chairs:
Brian Binley — *Con*
Stephen Hepburn — *Lab*
Vice-chairs:
David Crausby — *Lab*
Andrew Griffiths — *Con*
David Ward — *Lib Dem*
Secretary: Lord Bilston — *Lab/Co-op*
Treasurer: David Crausby — *Lab*

Contact: Brian Binley, House of Commons, London SW1A 0AA Tel: 020 7219 8298

Men's Health

Chair: Lord Patel of Bradford — *Lab*
Vice-chairs:
Baroness Masham of Ilton — *CB*

Paul Uppal — *Con*

Contact: Paul Uppal, House of Commons, London SW1A 0AA Tel: 020 7219 7195

Mental Health

Chair: James Morris — *Con*
Vice-chairs:
Paul Burstow — *Lib Dem*
Gloria De Piero — *Lab*
Secretary: Prof. Baroness Hollins — *CB*
Treasurer: Lord Alderdice — *Lib Dem*

Contact: James Morris, House of Commons, London SW1A 0AA Tel: 020 7219 8715

Metal Theft

Chairs:
Graham Jones — *Lab*
Chris Kelly — *Con*
Vice-chairs:
Lord Faulkner of Worcester — *Lab*
Mark Garnier — *Con*
Stewart Jackson — *Con*
Margot James — *Con*
Robin Walker — *Con*

Contact: Chris Kelly, House of Commons, London SW1A 0AA Tel: 020 7219 7053

Methodist

Chair: Meg Munn — *Lab/Co-op*
Vice-chair: Sir Alan Beith — *Lib Dem*
Secretary: Annette Brooke — *Lib Dem*
Treasurer: Lord Griffiths of Burry Port — *Lab*

Contact: Meg Munn, House of Commons, London SW1A 0AA Tel: 020 7219 8316

Micro Businesses

Chairs:
Anne Marie Morris — *Con*
Julian Smith — *Con*
Secretary: Admiral Lord West of Spithead — *Lab*
Treasurer: Mark Pawsey — *Con*

Contact: Anne Marie Morris, House of Commons, London SW1A 0AA Tel: 020 7219 8928

Microfinance

Chairs:
Guto Bebb — *Con*
Lord Boateng — *Lab*
Stephen Lloyd — *Lib Dem*
Vice-chairs:
Annette Brooke — *Lib Dem*
Mary Macleod — *Con*

Contact: Stephen Lloyd, House of Commons, London SW1A 0AA Tel: 020 7219 7061 www.appg-microfinance.org

Middle Way
(In relation to hunting and other field sports)
Chairs:
Baroness Golding	*Lab*
Sir Edward Leigh	*Con*
Roger Williams	*Lib Dem*
Vice-chair: Sir Alan Beith	*Lib Dem*

Secretaries:
Lord Carlile of Berriew	*Lib Dem*
Kate Hoey	*Lab*
Treasurer: Baroness Sharples	*Con*

Contact: Roger Williams, House of Commons, London SW1A 0AA Tel: 020 7219 1586
www.appmwg.org.uk

Migration
Chair: Jack Dromey   *Lab*
Vice-chairs:
Lord Boswell of Aynho	*Non-Affiliated*
Jon Cruddas	*Lab*
Kate Green	*Lab*
Lord Roberts of Llandudno	*Lib Dem*

Contact: Jack Dromey, House of Commons, London SW1A 0AA Tel: 020 7219 0903
www.appgmigration.org.uk

Minerals
Chair: Roger Williams   *Lib Dem*
Vice-chairs:
Tom Blenkinsop	*Lab*
James Gray	*Con*

Contact: Roger Williams, House of Commons, London SW1A 0AA Tel: 020 7219 8145

Mobile Homes
Chair: Christopher Chope   *Con*
Vice-chairs:
Steve Brine	*Con*
Annette Brooke	*Lib Dem*

Acting Secretary:
Lord Graham of Edmonton	*Lab/Co-op*
Treasurer: Lord Evans of Parkside	*Lab*

Contact: Christopher Chope, House of Commons, London SW1A 0AA
Tel: 020 7219 4971

Modern Languages
Chair: Baroness Coussins   *CB*
Vice-chairs:
Luciana Berger	*Lab/Co-op*
Paul Maynard	*Con*
Baroness Sharp of Guildford	*Lib Dem*

Contact: Paul Maynard, House of Commons, London SW1A 0AA Tel: 020 7219 7017

Motor
(Motor and motorsport industries)
Chair: Richard Burden   *Lab*
Vice-chairs:
Lorely Burt	*Lib Dem*
Lord Drayson	*Lab*
Heather Wheeler	*Con*
Secretary: Gavin Shuker	*Lab/Co-op*
Treasurer: Neil Carmichael	*Con*

Contact: Richard Burden, House of Commons, London SW1A 0AA Tel: 020 7219 2318
motorappg.com

Motor Neurone Disease
Chair: Gavin Williamson   *Con*
Vice-chairs:
Paul Blomfield	*Lab*
Greg Mulholland	*Lib Dem*
Secretary: Chris Evans	*Lab/Co-op*
Treasurer: Karl McCartney	*Con*

Contact: Gavin Williamson, House of Commons, London SW1A 0AA
Tel: 020 7219 7150

Motorcycle Speedway
Chair: Nick Brown   *Lab*
Vice-chairs:
Sir Tony Cunningham	*Lab*
Justin Tomlinson	*Con*
Secretary and Treasurer: Mark Pawsey	*Con*

Contact: Nick Brown, House of Commons, London SW1A 0AA Tel: 020 7219 6814

Motorcycling
Chair: Steve Baker   *Con*
Vice-chairs:
Jim Fitzpatrick	*Lab*
John Leech	*Lib Dem*
Treasurer: Stephen Pound	*Lab*

Contact: Steve Baker, House of Commons, London SW1A 0AA Tel: 020 7219 3547

Mountain Rescue
Chair: Rory Stewart   *Con*
Vice-chairs:
Lord Clark of Windermere	*Lab*
Sir Tony Cunningham	*Lab*
Lord Dubs	*Lab*
Tim Farron	*Lib Dem*
David Rutley	*Con*
Angela Smith	*Lab*
Secretary: John Woodcock	*Lab/Co-op*
Treasurer: Andrew Bingham	*Con*

Contact: Rory Stewart, House of Commons, London SW1A 0AA Tel: 020 7219 1663

Mountaineering

Chairs:
John Mann	Lab
David Rutley	Con

Vice-chairs:
Lilian Greenwood	Lab
Angela Smith	Lab
Secretary: Lord Howarth of Newport	Lab
Treasurer: Kris Hopkins	Con

Contact: David Rutley, House of Commons, London SW1A 0AA Tel: 020 7219 7106

MS (Multiple Sclerosis)

Chair: Paul Burstow	Lib Dem

Vice-chairs:
David Amess	Con
Lord Dubs	Lab
Stephen Lloyd	Lib Dem
Secretary: Russell Brown	Lab
Treasurer: Pamela Nash	Lab

Contact: David Amess, House of Commons, London SW1A 0AA Tel: 020 7219 3452

Munitions Workers

Chair: Huw Irranca-Davies	Lab

Vice-chairs:
Sir Peter Bottomley	Con
Tim Farron	Lib Dem
Madeleine Moon	Lab
Secretary: Robert Flello	Lab
Treasurer: Paul Flynn	Lab

Contact: Robert Flello, House of Commons, London SW1A 0AA Tel: 020 7219 6744

Muscular Dystrophy

Chair: David Anderson	Lab

Vice-chairs:
John Leech	Lib Dem
Paul Maynard	Con
Dan Rogerson	Lib Dem
Secretary: Lord Walton of Detchant	CB

Treasurer:
Baroness Thomas of Winchester	Lib Dem

Contact: David Anderson, St Cuthbert's Hall, Shibdon Road, Blaydon on Tyne NE21 5PT Tel: 0191-414 2488

Music

Chairs:
John Robertson	Lab
Mike Weatherley	Con

Vice-chairs:
Luciana Berger	Lab/Co-op
Andrew Bingham	Con
Sharon Hodgson	Lab
Kerry McCarthy	Lab

Secretary: Jim Sheridan	Lab
Treasurer: Lord German	Lib Dem

Contact: John Robertson, House of Commons, London SW1A 0AA Tel: 020 7219 6964

Music Education

Chair: Mike Weatherley	Con
Vice-chair: Diana Johnson	Lab

Secretary and Treasurer:
Baroness Finlay of Llandaff	CB

Contact: Mike Weatherley, House of Commons, London SW1A 0AA Tel: 020 7219 7216

Mutuals

Chair: Jonathan Evans	Con

Vice-chairs:
Cathy Jamieson	Lab/Co-op
Andy Love	Lab/Co-op
Baroness Maddock	Lib Dem
Lord Naseby	Con
Secretary: Russell Brown	Lab
Treasurer: Kelvin Hopkins	Lab

Contact: Jonathan Evans, House of Commons, London SW1A 0AA Tel: 020 7219 7205
www.mutuo.co.uk/category/appg

National Citizen Service and Volunteering

Chair: Charlotte Leslie	Con
Vice-chair: David Blunkett	Lab
Secretary: Sarah Newton	Con
Treasurer: Chris White	Con

Contact: Charlotte Leslie, House of Commons, London SW1A 0AA Tel: 020 7219 7026

National Parks

Chair: Clive Betts	Lab

Vice-chairs:
Lord Clark of Windermere	Lab
Lord Judd	Lab
Lord Renton of Mount Harry	Con
Roger Williams	Lib Dem
Secretary: David Rutley	Con

Contact: Clive Betts, House of Commons, London SW1A 0AA Tel: 020 7219 5114

New Media

Chair: John Hemming	Lib Dem
Secretary: Tom Watson	Lab

Contact: John Hemming, House of Commons, London SW1A 0AA Tel: 020 7219 6314

Nuclear Energy

Chair: John Robertson	Lab

Vice-chairs:
Ian Liddell-Grainger	Con
Stephen Mosley	Con
David Mowat	Con

Secretary: Michael Connarty — *Lab*
Treasurer: Jim Sheridan — *Lab*
Contact: John Robertson, House of Commons, London SW1A 0AA Tel: 020 7219 6964

Nuisance Calls
Chairs:
Alun Cairns — *Con*
Mike Crockart — *Lib Dem*
Vice-chairs:
Fiona Bruce — *Con*
Martin Vickers — *Con*
Simon Wright — *Lib Dem*
Contact: Mike Crockart, House of Commons, London SW1A 0AA Tel: 020 7219 7063

Obesity
Chair: Rosie Cooper — *Lab*
Vice-chair: David Amess — *Con*
Treasurer: Jackie Doyle-Price — *Con*
Contact: Rosie Cooper, Suite 108 Malthouse Business Centre, 48 Southport Road, Ormskirk L39 1QR Tel: 01695 570094

Occupational Safety and Health
President: Lord Hunt of Wirral — *Con*
Chair: Jim Sheridan — *Lab*
Secretary: Ian Lavery — *Lab*
Contact: Jim Sheridan, House of Commons, London SW1A 0AA Tel: 020 7219 8314

Off-Gas Grid
Chairs:
Dr Therese Coffey — *Con*
Patricia Glass — *Lab*
Secretary: Alan Reid — *Lib Dem*
Treasurer: Jim Shannon — *DUP*
Contact: Dr Therese Coffey, House of Commons, London SW1A 0AA Tel: 020 7219 7164

Offshore Oil and Gas Industry
Chair: Dame Anne Begg — *Lab*
Vice-chairs:
Sir Robert Smith — *Lib Dem*
Mike Weir — *SNP*
Secretary: Michael Connarty — *Lab*
Treasurer: Frank Doran — *Lab*
Contact: Dame Anne Begg, House of Commons, London SW1A 0AA Tel: 020 7219 2140

Opera
Chair: Sir Gerald Kaufman — *Lab*
Vice-chairs:
Lord Aberdare — *CB*
Lord Trimble — *Con*
Baroness Whitaker — *Lab*

Secretary: Andy Love — *Lab/Co-op*
Treasurer: Mark Pritchard — *Con*
Contact: Andy Love, House of Commons, London SW1A 0AA Tel: 020 7219 6377

Osteoporosis
Chairs:
Baroness Cumberlege — *Con*
Gordon Marsden — *Lab*
Vice-chair: Lorely Burt — *Lib Dem*
Secretary: Linda Riordan — *Lab/Co-op*
Treasurer: Sarah Newton — *Con*
Contact: Gordon Marsden, House of Commons, London SW1A 0AA Tel: 020 7219 1262

Outsourcing and Shared Services
Chair: Bob Blackman — *Con*
Vice-chairs:
Tom Blenkinsop — *Lab*
Siobhain McDonagh — *Lab*
Secretary: Ian Swales — *Lib Dem*
Contact: Bob Blackman, House of Commons, London SW1A 0AA Tel: 020 7219 7082

Ovarian Cancer
Chair: Sharon Hodgson — *Lab*
Vice-chairs:
Lord Clement-Jones — *Lib Dem*
Tim Farron — *Lib Dem*
Dr Sarah Wollaston — *Con*
Treasurer: Russell Brown — *Lab*
Contact: Sharon Hodgson, House of Commons, London SW1A 0AA Tel: 020 7219 6916
www.targetovariancancer.org.uk/
page.asp?section=333&sectiontitle=the+all+party
+parliamentary+group+on+ovarian+cancer

Overseas Development
Chair: Baroness Kinnock of Holyhead — *Lab*
Vice-chairs:
Sir Tony Baldry — *Con*
Lord McFall of Alcluith — *Lab/Co-op*
Secretary: Nicola Blackwood — *Con*
Treasurer: Tom Clarke — *Lab*
Contact: Tom Clarke, House of Commons, London SW1A 0AA Tel: 020 7219 6997
www.apgood.org.uk

Packaging Manufacturing Industry
Chair: Mark Pawsey — *Con*
Vice-chair: Dan Rogerson — *Lib Dem*
Secretary: Dr John Pugh — *Lib Dem*
Treasurer: Russell Brown — *Lab*
Contact: Mark Pawsey, House of Commons, London SW1A 0AA Tel: 020 7219 7136

Pancreatic Cancer

Chair: Lord Patel   *CB*
Vice-chair: Baroness Morgan of Drefelin   *CB*
Secretary: Eric Ollerenshaw   *Con*
Treasurer: Nic Dakin   *Lab*
Contact: Eric Ollerenshaw, House of Commons,
London SW1A 0AA Tel: 020 7219 7096
www.pancreaticcancer.org.uk/campaigning/
parliamentary-activity/appg-on-pancreatic-cancer

Parents and Families

Chair: Lord Northbourne   *CB*
Vice-chairs:
Sharon Hodgson   *Lab*
Baroness Morris of Bolton   *Con*
Claire Perry   *Con*
Baroness Tyler of Enfield   *Lib Dem*
Secretary: Baroness Sharp of Guildford *Lib Dem*
Treasurer: Earl of Listowel   *CB*
Contact: Sharon Hodgson, House of Commons,
London SW1A 0AA Tel: 020 7219 5160
www.familyandparenting.org/our_work/policy-
and-public-affairs/associate-parliamentary-group

Parkinson's Disease

Chair: Baroness Gale   *Lab*
Vice-chairs:
Steve Brine   *Con*
Baroness Finlay of Llandaff   *CB*
Secretaries:
Lord Brooke of Sutton Mandeville   *Con*
Madeleine Moon   *Lab*
Treasurer: Duncan Hames   *Lib Dem*
Contact: Duncan Hames, House of Commons,
London SW1A 0AA Tel: 020 7219 7039
www.parkinsons.org.uk/appg

Parliament First

Chair: Michael Meacher   *Lab*
Vice-chair: Zac Goldsmith   *Con*
Secretary: Dr Caroline Lucas   *Green*
Treasurer: John Hemming   *Lib Dem*
Contact: Michael Meacher, House of Commons,
London SW1A 0AA Tel: 020 7219 4532

Patient and Public Involvement in Health and Social Care

Chairs:
Huw Irranca-Davies   *Lab*
Dr John Pugh   *Lib Dem*
Vice-chair: Baroness Masham of Ilton   *CB*
Contact: Dr John Pugh, House of Commons,
London SW1A 0AA Tel: 020 7219 8318

Peak Oil and Gas

(Non-renewable energy sources' production peaks)
Chair: John Hemming   *Lib Dem*
Vice-chair: Dr Caroline Lucas   *Green*
Secretary: Stephen Williams   *Lib Dem*
Treasurer: Mark Williams   *Lib Dem*
Contact: John Hemming, House of Commons,
London SW1A 0AA Tel: 020 7219 6314

Penal Affairs

Chairs:
Paul Goggins   *Lab*
Gen Lord Ramsbotham   *CB*
Vice-chairs:
Claire Perry   *Con*
Ian Swales   *Lib Dem*
Secretary: Lord Hodgson of Astley Abbotts *Con*
Contact: Claire Perry, House of Commons,
London SW1A 0AA Tel: 020 7219 7050
www.prisonreformtrust.org.uk/presspolicy/
parliament/allpartyparliamentarypenal
affairsgroup

Pensions

Chair: Richard Graham   *Con*
Vice-chairs:
Harriett Baldwin   *Con*
Lord Davies of Coity   *Lab/Co-op*
Baroness Drake   *Lab*
Secretary: Mark Durkan   *SDLP*
Treasurer: Stephen Lloyd   *Lib Dem*
Contact: Richard Graham, House of Commons,
London SW1A 0AA Tel: 020 7219 7077

Perfomers' Alliance

Chair: Kerry McCarthy   *Lab*
Vice-chairs:
Lord Clement-Jones   *Lib Dem*
Michael Connarty   *Lab*
Secretary: Peter Wishart   *SNP*
Treasurer: John Whittingdale   *Con*
Contact: Kerry McCarthy, House of Commons,
London SW1A 0AA Tel: 020 7219 8117

Pharmaceutical Industry

Chair: Ian Liddell-Grainger   *Con*
Vice-chair: Lord Hunt of Kings Heath   *Lab*
Secretary: Ian Liddell-Grainger   *Con*
Contact: Ian Liddell-Grainger, House of
Commons, London SW1A 0AA
Tel: 020 7219 8149

Pharmacy

Chair: Kevin Barron   *Lab*
Vice-chairs:
Oliver Colvile   *Con*

Baroness Cumberlege   *Con*
Secretary: Stephen Lloyd   *Lib Dem*
Treasurer: Margot James   *Con*
Contact: Kevin Barron, House of Commons,
London SW1A 0AA Tel: 020 7219 6306
www.appg.org.uk

Philately

Chair: Andrew Rosindell   *Con*
Vice-chair: Admiral Lord West of Spithead   *Lab*
Secretary: Lord Jones of Cheltenham   *Lib Dem*
Treasurer: Lee Scott   *Con*
Contact: Andrew Rosindell, House of
Commons, London SW1A 0AA
Tel: 020 7219 8475

Photography

Chair: Austin Mitchell   *Lab*
Vice-chairs:
Viscount Allenby of Megiddo   *CB*
Baroness Hilton of Eggardon   *Lab*
Sir Gerald Howarth   *Con*
Andrew Miller   *Lab*
Secretaries:
Sir Peter Bottomley   *Con*
Lord Crathorne   *Con*
Contact: Austin Mitchell, House of Commons,
London SW1A 0AA Tel: 020 7219 4559

Policing

Chairs:
Sir Paul Beresford   *Con*
Lord Harris of Haringey   *Lab*
Vice-chairs:
Sir Tony Baldry   *Con*
Steve McCabe   *Lab*
Dr Matthew Offord   *Con*
Secretaries:
Baroness Harris of Richmond   *Lib Dem*
Mark Reckless   *Con*
Contact: Steve McCabe, House of Commons,
London SW1A 0AA Tel: 020 7219 3509

Population, Development and Reproductive Health

Chair: Baroness Tonge   *Ind Lib Dem*
Vice-chairs:
Richard Ottaway   *Con*
Heather Wheeler   *Con*
Secretary: Baroness Flather   *CB*
Treasurer: Geoffrey Clifton-Brown   *Con*
Contact: Richard Ottaway, House of Commons,
London SW1A 0AA Tel: 020 7219 6392
www.appg-popdevrh.org.uk

Post Offices

Chair: Russell Brown   *Lab*
Vice-chairs:
Jason McCartney   *Con*
Sir Robert Smith   *Lib Dem*
Secretary: Richard Graham   *Con*
Treasurer: Alan Reid   *Lib Dem*
Contact: Russell Brown, House of Commons,
London SW1A 0AA Tel: 020 7219 4429

Poverty

Chair: Kate Green   *Lab*
Vice-chair: Chris White   *Con*
Secretary: Paul Goggins   *Lab*
Treasurer: Baroness Sherlock   *Lab*
Contact: Kate Green, House of Commons,
London SW1A 0AA Tel: 020 7219 7162

Primary Care and Public Health

Chairs:
Kevin Barron   *Lab*
Nick de Bois   *Con*
Julie Elliott   *Lab*
Secretary: Baroness Masham of Ilton   *CB*
Executive Officer:
Baroness Gardner of Parkes   *Con*
Contact: Kevin Barron, House of Commons,
London SW1A 0AA Tel: 020 7219 4432

Print

Chair: Lord O'Neill of Clackmannan   *Lab*
Vice-chair: Stephen Metcalfe   *Con*
Secretary: Gerry Sutcliffe   *Lab*
Contact: Gerry Sutcliffe, Gumption Centre,
Glydegate, Bradford BD5 0BQ Tel: 01274 400007

Private Equity and Venture Capital

Chair: Mark Field   *Con*
Vice-chair: Lord Newby   *Lib Dem*
Contact: Mark Field, House of Commons,
London SW1A 0AA Tel: 020 7219 8155

Private Rented Sector

Chair: Oliver Colvile   *Con*
Vice-chairs:
Paul Goggins   *Lab*
David Ward   *Lib Dem*
Contact: Oliver Colvile, House of Commons,
London SW1A 0AA Tel: 020 7219 6839

Pro-Bono Work

Chair: Jessica Lee   *Con*
Vice-chairs:
Anne Marie Morris   *Con*
Valerie Vaz   *Lab*
Contact: Jessica Lee, House of Commons,
London SW1A 0AA Tel: 020 7219 7067

Pro-Life

(In relation to abortion, euthanasia and research on the human embryo)

Chairs:

Fiona Bruce	Con
Jim Dobbin	Lab/Co-op

Vice-chairs:

Robert Flello	Lab
Baroness Hooper	Con
Baroness Masham of Ilton	CB
Mark Pritchard	Con
Dr John Pugh	Lib Dem

Secretaries:

Joe Benton	Lab
Margaret Ritchie	SDLP

Treasurers:

Jeffrey Donaldson	DUP
Sir Edward Leigh	Con

Contact: Jim Dobbin, House of Commons, London SW1A 0AA Tel: 020 7219 0968

Prostitution and the Global Sex Trade

Chair: Gavin Shuker	Lab/Co-op
Secretary: Fiona Mactaggart	Lab
Treasurer: Claire Perry	Con

Contact: Gavin Shuker, House of Commons, London SW1A 0AA Tel: 020 7219 1130 appgprostitution.org

Save the Pub

Chair: Greg Mulholland	Lib Dem

Vice-chairs:

Lord Bilston	Lab/Co-op
Brian Binley	Con
Grahame Morris	Lab

Contact: Greg Mulholland, House of Commons, London SW1A 0AA Tel: 020 7219 3833

Publishing

Chair: Dr Tristram Hunt	Lab
Vice-chair: Lord Heseltine	Con

Contact: Dr Tristram Hunt, House of Commons, London SW1A 0AA Tel: 020 7219 1179

Queen's Diamond Jubilee

Chair: Michael Ellis	Con

Vice-chairs:

Lord Cormack	Con
Dr Tristram Hunt	Lab
Andrew Rosindell	Con
Baroness Sharples	Con
Secretary: John Thurso	Lib Dem
Treasurer: Mary Macleod	Con

Contact: Michael Ellis, House of Commons, London SW1A 0AA Tel: 020 7219 7220

Race and Community

Chair: David Lammy	Lab

Vice-chairs:

Debbie Abrahams	Lab
Baroness Hussein-Ece	Lib Dem
Lord Sheikh	Con
Baroness Whitaker	Lab
Secretary: Sir Peter Bottomley	Con
Treasurer: Gavin Barwell	Con

Contact: David Lammy, House of Commons, London SW1A 0AA Tel: 020 7219 0767

Racing and Bloodstock Industries

Chairs:

Sir Alan Meale	Lab
Laurence Robertson	Con

Vice-chairs:

Viscount of Falkland	CB
Grahame Morris	Lab
Secretary: Lord Donoughue	Lab
Treasurer: Baroness Golding	Lab

Contact: Laurence Robertson, House of Commons, London SW1A 0AA Tel: 020 7219 4196

Rail

Chair: Martin Vickers	Con

Vice-chairs:

Lord Bradshaw	Lib Dem
Kelvin Hopkins	Lab
Lord Snape	Lab
Secretary: Lord Berkeley	Lab
Treasurer: Lord Faulkner of Worcester	Lab

Contact: Martin Vickers, House of Commons, London SW1A 0AA Tel: 020 7219 7212

Rail in the North

Chair: Julie Hilling	Lab

Vice-chairs:

Andrew Jones	Con
Jason McCartney	Con
Ian Mearns	Lab

Contact: Julie Hilling, House of Commons, London SW1A 0AA Tel: 020 7219 7020

Rail in Wales

Chair: Siân James	Lab
Vice-chair: Simon Hart	Con
Secretary: Mark Williams	Lib Dem
Treasurer: Hywel Williams	PlC

Contact: Mark Williams, House of Commons, London SW1A 0AA Tel: 020 7219 8469

Refugees

Chair: Sarah Teather	Lib Dem

Vice-chairs:

Jeremy Corbyn	Lab

Dr Julian Huppert   *Lib Dem*
Secretary: Lord Dubs   *Lab*
Contact: Sarah Teather, House of Commons, London SW1A 0AA Tel: 020 7219 8147

Regeneration through Innovation
Chair: Richard Graham   *Con*
Vice-chairs:
Michael McCann   *Lab*
Ian Swales   *Lib Dem*
David Ward   *Lib Dem*
Secretary: Lord Aberdare   *CB*
Treasurer: Robin Walker   *Con*
Contact: Richard Graham, House of Commons, London SW1A 0AA Tel: 020 7219 7077

Religious Education
Chair: Stephen Lloyd   *Lib Dem*
Vice-chairs:
Baroness Brinton   *Lib Dem*
Fiona Bruce   *Con*
Mike Crockart   *Lib Dem*
Mary Glindon   *Lab*
Contact: Stephen Lloyd, House of Commons, London SW1A 0AA Tel: 020 7219 7061

Religious Freedom or Belief
Chair: Baroness Berridge   *Con*
Vice-chairs:
Lord Alton of Liverpool   *CB*
Baroness Cox   *CB*
Naomi Long   *All*
Lord Singh of Wimbledon   *CB*
Secretary: Angie Bray   *Con*
Treasurer: Jim Dobbin   *Lab/Co-op*
Contact: Angie Bray, House of Commons, London SW1A 0AA Tel: 020 7219 7055
anorphanedright.net/about

Renewable and Sustainable Energy
Chair: Dr Alan Whitehead   *Lab*
Vice-chairs:
Peter Aldous   *Con*
Sir Malcolm Bruce   *Lib Dem*
Dr Caroline Lucas   *Green*
Secretary: Baroness Maddock   *Lib Dem*
Treasurer: Ian Mearns   *Lab*
Contact: Dr Alan Whitehead, House of Commons, London SW1A 0AA Tel: 020 7219 5517

Reserve Forces and Cadets
Chair: Julian Brazier   *Con*
Vice-chairs:
Sir Tony Baldry   *Con*
Andrew Miller   *Lab*
Madeleine Moon   *Lab*

Secretaries:
Dr Therese Coffey   *Con*
Robert Flello   *Lab*
Treasurer: David Crausby   *Lab*
Contact: Julian Brazier, House of Commons, London SW1A 0AA Tel: 020 7219 5178

Respiratory Health
Chair: Stephen McPartland   *Con*
Vice-chair: John Woodcock   *Lab/Co-op*
Contact: Stephen McPartland, House of Commons, London SW1A 0AA
Tel: 020 7219 7156

Responsible Investment
Chair: Jon Cruddas   *Lab*
Vice-chairs:
Martin Horwood   *Lib Dem*
Dr Caroline Lucas   *Green*
Secretary: Lord Harrison   *Lab*
Contact: Jon Cruddas, House of Commons, London SW1A 0AA Tel: 020 7219 8161

Retail
President:
Lord Graham of Edmonton   *Lab/Co-op*
Chairs:
Ann Coffey   *Lab*
Jane Ellison   *Con*
Vice-chairs:
Philip Davies   *Con*
Kate Green   *Lab*
Gareth Johnson   *Con*
Justin Tomlinson   *Con*
Secretary: Lord Dykes   *Lib Dem*
Contact: Ann Coffey, House of Commons, London SW1A 0AA Tel: 020 7219 4546

Road Passenger Transport
Chairs:
Brian Donohoe   *Lab*
Lord Snape   *Lab*
Honorary Treasurer: Sir Bob Russell *Lib Dem*
Contact: Brian Donohoe, House of Commons, London SW1A 0AA Tel: 020 7219 6230

Roofing Industry
Chair: David Hanson   *Lab*
Vice-chairs:
Lord Davies of Coity   *Lab/Co-op*
Baroness Maddock   *Lib Dem*
Contact: David Hanson, House of Commons, London SW1A 0AA Tel: 020 7219 5064

Rowing

Chairs:
Sir Peter Bottomley   *Con*
Lord Thomas of Gresford   *Lib Dem*
Secretary: Sir Edward Leigh   *Con*

Contact: Sir Edward Leigh, House of Commons, London SW1A 0AA Tel: 020 7219 6480

Royal Television Society

Chair: Lord Fowler   *Con*
Vice-chair: Tessa Jowell   *Lab*
Secretary:
Baroness Bonham-Carter of Yarnbury   *Lib Dem*
Treasurer: Sir Peter Bottomley   *Con*

Contact: Tessa Jowell, House of Commons, London SW1A 0AA Tel: 020 7219 3409

Rugby League

President: Lord Hoyle   *Lab*
Chair: Greg Mulholland   *Lib Dem*
Vice-chairs:
James Clappison   *Con*
Lindsay Hoyle   *Lab*
David Mowat   *Con*
Secretary: Gerry Sutcliffe   *Lab*
Treasurer: Lord Smith of Leigh   *Lab*

Contact: Greg Mulholland, House of Commons, London SW1A 0AA Tel: 020 7219 3833
www.apprlg.org.uk

Rugby Union

Chair: Sir Tony Cunningham   *Lab*
Vice-chairs:
Lord Addington   *Lib Dem*
Paul Farrelly   *Lab*
Don Foster   *Lib Dem*
Robert Walter   *Con*
Secretary: Stephen Mosley   *Con*
Treasurer: Dai Havard   *Lab*

Contact: Stephen Mosley, House of Commons, London SW1A 0AA Tel: 020 7219 7207

Rugby Union Football Club

Chair: Mark Pawsey   *Con*
Vice-chairs:
Aidan Burley   *Con*
Ian Davidson   *Lab/Co-op*
Paul Farrelly   *Lab*
Secretary: Lord Addington   *Lib Dem*
Treasurer: Stephen Mosley   *Con*

Contact: Mark Pawsey, House of Commons, London SW1A 0AA Tel: 020 7219 7136

Runaway and Missing Children and Adults

Chair: Ann Coffey   *Lab*
Vice-chairs:
Lord Boswell of Aynho   *Non-Affiliated*

Baroness Kramer   *Lib Dem*
Secretary: Annette Brooke   *Lib Dem*

Contact: Ann Coffey, House of Commons, London SW1A 0AA Tel: 020 7219 4546

Rural Services

Chair: Graham Stuart   *Con*
Vice-chairs:
Lord Dear   *CB*
Grahame Morris   *Lab*
Dan Rogerson   *Lib Dem*
Secretary: Baroness Byford   *Con*
Treasurer: Rory Stewart   *Con*

Contact: Graham Stuart, House of Commons, London SW1A 0AA Tel: 020 7219 4340

Sailing and Marine Leisure

Chair: Sir Peter Bottomley   *Con*
Vice-chair: Richard Ottaway   *Con*
Secretary: Jake Berry   *Con*
Treasurer: Robert Walter   *Con*

Contact: Sir Peter Bottomley, House of Commons, London SW1A 0AA
Tel: 020 7219 5060

St George's Day

Presidents:
David Blunkett   *Lab*
Chris Kelly   *Con*
Lord Tebbit   *Con*
Chair: Andrew Rosindell   *Con*
Vice-chairs:
Philip Davies   *Con*
John Mann   *Lab*
Greg Mulholland   *Lib Dem*
Chris Skidmore   *Con*
Henry Smith   *Con*
Tom Watson   *Lab*
Admiral Lord West of Spithead   *Lab*
Secretary: Sir Peter Bottomley   *Con*
Treasurer: Jack Lopresti   *Con*

Contact: Andrew Rosindell, House of Commons, London SW1A 0AA
Tel: 020 7219 8475

School Food

Chair: Sharon Hodgson   *Lab*
Vice-chairs:
Dr Roberta Blackman-Woods   *Lab*
Amber Rudd   *Con*
Secretary: Diana Johnson   *Lab*

Contact: Sharon Hodgson, House of Commons, London SW1A 0AA Tel: 020 7219 6916

Science

Chair: Andrew Miller   *Lab*
Vice-chair: Tom Blenkinsop   *Lab*

Secretary: Stephen Mosley   *Con*
Treasurer:
Lord Willis of Knaresborough   *Lib Dem*
Contact: Andrew Miller, House of Commons,
London SW1A 0AA Tel: 020 7219 3580
www.vmine.net/scienceinparliament

Science and Technology in Agriculture

Chair: George Freeman   *Con*
Vice-chairs:
Lord Haskins   *CB*
Huw Irranca-Davies   *Lab*
Earl of Selborne   *Con*
Mark Spencer   *Con*
Roger Williams   *Lib Dem*
Contact: George Freeman, House of Commons,
London SW1A 0AA Tel: 020 7219 1940
www.appg-agscience.org.uk

Scotch Whisky and Spirits

Chair: Jim Sheridan   *Lab*
Vice-chairs:
Anne McIntosh   *Con*
Alan Reid   *Lib Dem*
Angus Robertson   *SNP*
Secretary: Brian Donohoe   *Lab*
Treasurer: Gemma Doyle   *Lab/Co-op*
Contact: Brian Donohoe, House of Commons,
London SW1A 0AA Tel: 020 7219 6230

Scout

Honorary President:
Baroness Morgan of Huyton   *Lab*
Chairs:
Graham Evans   *Con*
Gareth Thomas   *Lab/Co-op*
Vice-chairs:
Nicola Blackwood   *Con*
Lord Jones of Cheltenham   *Lib Dem*
Secretary: Steve Gilbert   *Lib Dem*
Contact: Steve Gilbert, House of Commons,
London SW1A 0AA Tel: 020 7219 7153

Severn Barrage and Tidal Energy

Chair: Peter Hain   *Lab*
Vice-chair: Ian Liddell-Grainger   *Con*
Secretary: Sir Nick Harvey   *Lib Dem*
Treasurer: Elfyn Llwyd   *PlC*
Contact: Peter Hain, House of Commons,
London SW1A 0AA Tel: 020 7219 3925

Sex Equality

Chair: Amber Rudd   *Con*
Vice-chairs:
Baroness Prosser   *Lab*
Lord Smith of Clifton   *Lib Dem*

Secretary: Lorely Burt   *Lib Dem*
Treasurer: Sir Peter Bottomley   *Con*
Contact: Amber Rudd, House of Commons,
London SW1A 0AA Tel: 020 7219 7229

Sexual and Reproductive Health in the UK

Chair: Baroness Gould of Potternewton   *Lab*
Vice-chairs:
Baroness Flather   *CB*
Emily Thornberry   *Lab*
Baroness Tonge   *Ind Lib Dem*
Treasurer: Baroness Blood   *Lab*
Contact: Emily Thornberry, House of Commons,
London SW1A 0AA Tel: 020 7219 5676

Shipbuilding and Ship Repair

Chair: John Robertson   *Lab*
Vice-chairs:
Stephen Hepburn   *Lab*
Iain McKenzie   *Lab*
Penny Mordaunt   *Con*
Jim Sheridan   *Lab*
John Woodcock   *Lab/Co-op*
Secretary: Ian Davidson   *Lab/Co-op*
Contact: Ian Davidson, House of Commons,
London SW1A 0AA Tel: 0141-621 2216

Shooting and Conservation

Chair: Geoffrey Clifton-Brown   *Con*
Vice-chair:
Lord Cunningham of Felling   *Non-Affiliated*
Secretary: John Thurso   *Lib Dem*
Treasurer: Ian Liddell-Grainger   *Con*
Contact: Geoffrey Clifton-Brown, House of
Commons, London SW1A 0AA
Tel: 020 7219 5147

Sickle Cell and Thalassaemia

Chair: Diane Abbott   *Lab*
Vice-chairs:
Baroness Benjamin   *Lib Dem*
David Burrowes   *Con*
Lord Smith of Clifton   *Lib Dem*
Secretary: Bob Blackman   *Con*
Contact: Diane Abbott, House of Commons,
London SW1A 0AA Tel: 020 7219 4426

British Sikhs

Chair: Fabian Hamilton   *Lab*
Vice-chairs:
Mike Gapes   *Lab/Co-op*
Fiona Mactaggart   *Lab*
Caroline Nokes   *Con*
Lee Scott   *Con*
Secretary: Emma Reynolds   *Lab*
Treasurer: Paul Uppal   *Con*
Contact: Fabian Hamilton, House of Commons,
London SW1A 0AA Tel: 020 7219 3493

Sixth Form Colleges

Chair: Kelvin Hopkins   *Lab*
Vice-chairs:
Nic Dakin   *Lab*
Sir Gerald Howarth   *Con*
Dr Caroline Lucas   *Green*
Sir Bob Russell   *Lib Dem*
Secretary and Treasurer: David Nuttall   *Con*

Contact: Kelvin Hopkins, House of Commons, London SW1A 0AA Tel: 020 7219 6670

Skills and Employment

Chairs:
Fiona Bruce   *Con*
Nic Dakin   *Lab*
Charlotte Leslie   *Con*
Vice-chairs:
Lord Boswell of Aynho   *Non-Affiliated*
Eric Joyce   *Ind*
Baroness Sharp of Guildford   *Lib Dem*
Secretary: Stephen Williams   *Lib Dem*

Contact: Nic Dakin, House of Commons, London SW1A 0AA Tel: 020 7219 7139

Skin

(As health issue)
Chair: Sir Paul Beresford   *Con*
Vice-chairs:
Cheryl Gillan   *Con*
Baroness Masham of Ilton   *CB*
Secretary: Russell Brown   *Lab*

Contact: Sir Paul Beresford, House of Commons, London SW1A 0AA Tel: 020 7219 5018

Small Business

President:
Lord MacGregor of Pulham Market   *Con*
Chair: Brian Binley   *Con*
Vice-chairs:
Lord Cotter   *Lib Dem*
Lord Harrison   *Lab*
Andy Love   *Lab/Co-op*
Secretary: Margot James   *Con*
Treasurer: Lorely Burt   *Lib Dem*

Contact: Brian Binley, House of Commons, London SW1A 0AA Tel: 020 7219 4447

Small Shops

Chair: Priti Patel   *Con*
Vice-chair: Lord Cotter   *Lib Dem*
Secretary: Peter Aldous   *Con*
Treasurer: Andrew Percy   *Con*

Contact: Priti Patel, House of Commons, London SW1A 0AA Tel: 020 7219 3528

Smoking and Health

Chair: Stephen Williams   *Lib Dem*
Vice-chairs:
Kevin Barron   *Lab*
Baroness Finlay of Llandaff   *CB*
Baroness O'Cathain   *Con*
Lord Patel   *CB*
Lord Rennard   *Lib Dem Ind*
John Robertson   *Lab*
Secretary: Bob Blackman   *Con*
Treasurer: Ian Mearns   *Lab*

Contact: Stephen Williams, House of Commons, London SW1A 0AA Tel: 020 7219 8416
www.ash.org.uk/about-ash/all-party-parliamentary-group-on-smoking-and-health

Social Care

Chair: Barbara Keeley   *Lab*
Vice-chair: Sarah Newton   *Con*
Treasurer: Alex Cunningham   *Lab*

Contact: Barbara Keeley, House of Commons, London SW1A 0AA Tel: 020 7219 8025

Social Enterprise

Chair: Chris White   *Con*
Vice-chairs:
Hazel Blears   *Lab*
Margot James   *Con*
Secretary: Baroness Thornton   *Lab/Co-op*

Contact: Chris White, House of Commons, London SW1A 0AA Tel: 020 7219 7201

Social Mobility

Chair: Damian Hinds   *Con*
Vice-chairs:
Hazel Blears   *Lab*
Mike Crockart   *Lib Dem*
Patricia Glass   *Lab*
Meg Hillier   *Lab/Co-op*
Jack Lopresti   *Con*
Baroness Morris of Yardley   *Lab*
Eric Ollerenshaw   *Con*
Baroness Tyler of Enfield   *Lib Dem*

Contact: Damian Hinds, House of Commons, London SW1A 0AA Tel: 020 7219 7057
www.appg-socialmobility.org

Social Science and Policy

Chair: Kelvin Hopkins   *Lab*
Vice-chair: Sir Peter Bottomley   *Con*

Contact: Kelvin Hopkins, House of Commons, London SW1A 0AA Tel: 020 7219 6670

Social Tourism

Chair: Paul Maynard   *Con*
Vice-chair: Baroness Rendell of Babergh   *Lab*

Contact: Paul Maynard, House of Commons, London SW1A 0AA Tel: 020 7219 7017

Social Work

Chair: Ann Clwyd	Lab
Vice-chair: Mike Wood	Lab
Secretary: Hywel Williams	PlC
Treasurer: Sir Peter Bottomley	Con

Contact: Ann Clwyd, House of Commons, London SW1A 0AA Tel: 020 7219 6609

Space

Patron: Nigel Evans	Ind
Chair: Adam Afriyie	Con
Executive Vice-chairs:	
Prof. Lord Hunt of Chesterton	Lab
Dr Phillip Lee	Con
Simon Wright	Lib Dem
Vice-chairs:	
Mark Garnier	Con
Stephen McPartland	Con
David Morris	Con
Pamela Nash	Lab
Chi Onwurah	Lab
Mark Pritchard	Con
Membership Secretary: Laura Sandys	Con
Honorary Secretary: Sir Alan Meale	Lab
Treasurer: Pamela Nash	Lab

Contact: Adam Afriyie, House of Commons, London SW1A 0AA Tel: 020 7219 8023
www.parliamentaryspacecommittee.com

Speech and Language Difficulties

Chair: Gen Lord Ramsbotham	CB
Vice-chairs:	
Kevin Barron	Lab
Robert Buckland	Con
Secretary: Geraint Davies	Lab/Co-op

Contact: Geraint Davies, House of Commons, London SW1A 0AA Tel: 020 7219 7166

Spinal Cord Injury

Chair: Ian Lucas	Lab
Vice-chairs:	
Kevin Barron	Lab
Baroness Wilkins	Lab
Secretary: Dr John Pugh	Lib Dem
Treasurer: Baroness Masham of Ilton	CB

Contact: Ian Lucas, House of Commons, London SW1A 0AA Tel: 020 7219 8346
www.spinal.co.uk/page/appg-sia-sci

Sport

President: Lord Pendry	Lab
Chair: Gerry Sutcliffe	Lab
Vice-chairs:	
Lord Addington	Lib Dem
Andrew Bingham	Con
Baroness Grey-Thompson	CB
Secretary: Charlotte Leslie	Con

Contact: Gerry Sutcliffe, House of Commons, London SW1A 0AA Tel: 020 7219 3247
www.sportandrecreation.org.uk/appgsport

Srebrenica

(To raise awareness of the Srebrenica Genocide)

Chair: Yasmin Qureshi	Lab
Vice-chair: Andrew Stephenson	Con
Secretary: Lord Hussain	Lib Dem
Treasurer: Jackie Doyle-Price	Con

Contact: Yasmin Qureshi, House of Commons, London SW1A 0AA Tel: 020 7219 7019

Stalking and Harassment

Chair: Elfyn Llwyd	PlC
Vice-chairs:	
Baroness Brinton	Lib Dem
Robert Buckland	Con
Jenny Chapman	Lab
Cheryl Gillan	Con
Gordon Henderson	Con
Baroness Howe of Idlicote	CB
Sandra Osborne	Lab
Barry Sheerman	Lab/Co-op

Contact: Elfyn Llwyd, House of Commons, London SW1A 0AA Tel: 020 7219 5021

Statistics

Chair: Lord Lipsey	Lab
Vice-chair: Sir Peter Bottomley	Con
Secretary: Baroness Kramer	Lib Dem
Treasurer: Rachel Reeves	Lab

Contact: Sir Peter Bottomley, House of Commons, London SW1A 0AA
Tel: 020 7219 5060

Steel and Metal Related Industry

Chair: Tom Blenkinsop	Lab
Vice-chairs:	
Gordon Henderson	Con
Jessica Morden	Lab
Ian Swales	Lib Dem
Secretary: Nia Griffith	Lab
Treasurer: Angela Smith	Lab

Contact: Nia Griffith, House of Commons, London SW1A 0AA Tel: 020 7219 3410

Stem Cell Transplantation

Chairs:	
David Burrowes	Con
Mark Tami	Lab
Vice-chairs:	
Fiona Bruce	Con
Jim Dobbin	Lab/Co-op
Baroness Masham of Ilton	CB
Secretary: Chris Ruane	Lab

Contact: Mark Tami, House of Commons, London SW1A 0AA Tel: 020 7219 8174

Street Children

Chairs:
Russell Brown *Lab*
Baroness Miller of Chilthorne Domer *Lib Dem*
Craig Whittaker *Con*

Contact: Russell Brown, House of Commons, London SW1A 0AA Tel: 020 7219 4429

Stroke

Chair: Helen Jones *Lab*
Vice-chairs:
Lord Clinton-Davis *Lab*
Andrew Jones *Con*
Lord Rodgers of Quarry Bank *Lib Dem*
Secretary: Andrew Turner *Con*
Treasurer: Lord Walton of Detchant *CB*

Contact: Helen Jones, House of Commons, London SW1A 0AA Tel: 020 7219 4048

Suicide and Self Harm Prevention

Chair: Madeleine Moon *Lab*
Vice-chairs:
Baroness Finlay of Llandaff *CB*
Greg Mulholland *Lib Dem*
Charles Walker *Con*
Secretary: Lord Carlile of Berriew *Lib Dem*
Treasurer: James Gray *Con*

Contact: Madeleine Moon, House of Commons, London SW1A 0AA Tel: 020 7219 4417

Sure Start Children's Centres

Chair: Andrea Leadsom *Con*
Vice-chairs:
Sharon Hodgson *Lab*
Earl of Listowel *CB*
Secretary and Treasurer:
Richard Harrington *Con*

Contact: Andrea Leadsom, House of Commons, London SW1A 0AA Tel: 020 7219 7149

Sustainable Housing

Chairs:
Nick Raynsford *Lab*
Iain Stewart *Con*
Vice-chairs:
Peter Aldous *Con*
Dr Caroline Lucas *Green*
Secretary: Pamela Nash *Lab*

Contact: Nick Raynsford, House of Commons, London SW1A 0AA Tel: 020 7219 2773
www.appg-sustainablehousing.org.uk

Sustainable Resource

Chairs:
Baroness Jenkin of Kennington *Con*
Prof. Lord Lewis of Newnham *CB*
Dan Rogerson *Lib Dem*

Mark Spencer *Con*
Dr Alan Whitehead *Lab*
Secretary: Barry Sheerman *Lab/Co-op*

Contact: Barry Sheerman, House of Commons, London SW1A 0AA Tel: 020 7219 5037
www.policyconnect.org.uk/apsrg

Tamils

Chair: Lee Scott *Con*
Vice-chairs:
Simon Hughes *Lib Dem*
Siobhain McDonagh *Lab*
Virendra Sharma *Lab*
Secretary and Treasurer: Robert Halfon *Con*

Contact: Lee Scott, House of Commons, London SW1A 0AA Tel: 020 7219 8326

Taxation

Chair: Ian Liddell-Grainger *Con*
Vice-chair: Kelvin Hopkins *Lab*
Secretary: Ian Liddell-Grainger *Con*

Contact: Ian Liddell-Grainger, House of Commons, London SW1A 0AA
Tel: 020 7219 8149

Telehealth

Chair: Dr John Pugh *Lib Dem*
Vice-chairs:
Mark Garnier *Con*
Baroness Masham of Ilton *CB*
Secretary: Laurence Robertson *Con*
Treasurer: Nick de Bois *Con*

Contact: Laurence Robertson, House of Commons, London SW1A 0AA
Tel: 020 7219 4196

Tennis

Chair: Baroness Billingham *Lab*
Vice-chairs:
Chris Leslie *Lab/Co-op*
Andrew Miller *Lab*
Mark Pritchard *Con*
Secretary: Meg Munn *Lab/Co-op*
Treasurer: Lord Naseby *Con*

Contact: Meg Munn, House of Commons, London SW1A 0AA Tel: 020 7219 8316

Terrorism

Chair: Khalid Mahmood *Lab*
Vice-chairs:
Andrew Rosindell *Con*
Jim Sheridan *Lab*
Lord Steel of Aikwood *Lib Dem*

Contact: Khalid Mahmood, House of Commons, London SW1A 0AA Tel: 020 7219 8141

Textile Manufacturing

Chair: David Ward   *Lib Dem*
Vice-chairs:
Stuart Andrew   *Con*
Barry Sheerman   *Lab/Co-op*
Secretary: Jake Berry   *Con*
Treasurer: Lord Woolmer of Leeds   *Lab*
Contact: David Ward, House of Commons,
London SW1A 0AA Tel: 020 7219 7213

Thalidomide

Chair: Alec Shelbrooke   *Con*
Vice-chair: Martin Caton   *Lab*
Contact: Alec Shelbrooke, House of Commons,
London SW1A 0AA Tel: 020 7219 5049

Thameslink Route

Chair: Dr Matthew Offord   *Con*
Vice-chairs:
Gavin Shuker   *Lab/Co-op*
Chuka Umunna   *Lab*
Secretary: Paul Burstow   *Lib Dem*
Treasurer: Heidi Alexander   *Lab*
Contact: Dr Matthew Offord, House of
Commons, London SW1A 0AA
Tel: 020 7219 7083

Third World Solidarity

Chair: David Anderson   *Lab*
Vice-chairs:
Lord Ahmed   *Non-Affiliated*
Lord Hussain   *Lib Dem*
Charlotte Leslie   *Con*
Secretary: Anas Sarwar   *Lab*
Treasurer: Khalid Mahmood   *Lab*
Contact: David Anderson, St Cuthbert's Hall,
Shibdon Road, Blaydon,
Tyne and Wear NE21 5PT Tel: 0191-414 2488

Thorium Energy

Chair:
Lord Lucas of Crudwell and Dingwall   *Con*
Vice-chair: Dr Julian Huppert   *Lib Dem*
Treasurer: Viscount Hanworth   *Lab*
Contact: Dr Julian Huppert, House of Commons,
London SW1A 0AA Tel: 020 7219 0647
www.appg-thorium.org.uk

Thrombosis

Chair: Andrew Gwynne   *Lab*
Vice-chairs:
David Amess   *Con*
Michael McCann   *Lab*
Secretary: Russell Brown   *Lab*
Contact: Andrew Gwynne, House of Commons,
London SW1A 0AA Tel: 020 7219 4652

Tidy Britain

Chair: Anne McIntosh   *Con*
Vice-chairs:
Jim Fitzpatrick   *Lab*
Baroness Miller of Chilthorne Domer   *Lib Dem*
Contact: Anne McIntosh, House of Commons,
London SW1A 0AA Tel: 020 7219 3541

Tour de France

Chairs:
Fabian Hamilton   *Lab*
Greg Mulholland   *Lib Dem*
Julian Smith   *Con*
Vice-chairs:
Nigel Adams   *Con*
Sarah Champion   *Lab*
Dr Julian Huppert   *Lib Dem*
Andrew Jones   *Con*
Jason McCartney   *Con*
Julian Sturdy   *Con*
Contact: Julian Smith, House of Commons,
London SW1A 0AA Tel: 020 7219 7145
www.juliansmithmp.co.uk/tdf

Tourism

Chair: Lord Lee of Trafford   *Lib Dem*
Vice-chairs:
Lord Fowler   *Con*
Mark Pritchard   *Con*
John Thurso   *Lib Dem*
Secretary: Lord Harrison   *Lab*
Treasurer: Paul Maynard   *Con*
Contact: John Thurso, House of Commons,
London SW1A 0AA Tel: 020 7219 1752

Tourism and Hospitality Industry in Wales

Chair: Mark Williams   *Lib Dem*
Vice-chairs:
Guto Bebb   *Con*
Jessica Morden   *Lab*
Lord Wigley   *PIC*
Secretary: Glyn Davies   *Con*
Treasurer: Lord Aberdare   *CB*
Contact: Mark Williams, House of Commons,
London SW1A 0AA Tel: 020 7219 8469

Town Centres

Chair: Marcus Jones   *Con*
Vice-chairs:
Peter Aldous   *Con*
Ann Coffey   *Lab*
Stephen Lloyd   *Lib Dem*
Justin Tomlinson   *Con*
Contact: Marcus Jones, House of Commons,
London SW1A 0AA Tel: 020 7219 4880

Trade and Investment

Chair: Margot James   Con
Vice-chairs:
Nick de Bois   Con
Pat McFadden   Lab
David Ward   Lib Dem
Secretary: Geoffrey Clifton-Brown   Con
Treasurer: Lord Wei   Con

Contact: Margot James, House of Commons,
London SW1A 0AA Tel: 020 7219 7226

Trade out of Poverty

Chair: Peter Lilley   Con
Vice-chair: Sir Menzies Campbell   Lib Dem
Secretary: Robin Walker   Con
Treasurer: Lord Hastings of Scarisbrick   CB

Contact: Peter Lilley, House of Commons,
London SW1A 0AA Tel: 020 7219 4577

Tranquilliser Addiction

Chair: Jim Dobbin   Lab/Co-op
Vice-chair: Earl of Sandwich   CB
Secretary and Treasurer: David Crausby   Lab

Contact: Jim Dobbin, House of Commons,
London SW1A 0AA Tel: 020 7219 4530

Transatlantic and International Security

Chair: Gisela Stuart   Lab
Vice-chairs:
Henry Smith   Con
Derek Twigg   Lab
Secretary: Damian Collins   Con
Treasurer: David Ruffley   Con

Contact: Gisela Stuart, House of Commons,
London SW1A 0AA Tel: 020 7219 5051
www.transatlanticsecurity.org

Transport Safety

Chairs:
Sir Peter Bottomley   Con
Jim Fitzpatrick   Lab
John Leech   Lib Dem
Vice-chairs:
Lord Bradshaw   Lib Dem
Viscount Simon   Lab
Secretary: Barry Sheerman   Lab/Co-op

Contact: Barry Sheerman, House of Commons,
London SW1A 0AA Tel: 020 7219 5037

Tribal Peoples

Chair: Martin Horwood   Lib Dem
Vice-chair: Andrew George   Lib Dem
Treasurer: Lisa Nandy   Lab

Contact: Martin Horwood, House of Commons,
London SW1A 0AA Tel: 020 7219 4784

Tuberculosis (TB)

Chairs:
Nick Herbert   Con
Andrew George   Lib Dem
Virendra Sharma   Lab
Vice-chairs:
Annette Brooke   Lib Dem
Mark Lancaster   Con
Baroness Masham of Ilton   CB

Contact: Andrew George, House of Commons,
London SW1A 0AA Tel: 020 7219 4588
www.appg-tb.org.uk

Unconventional Oil and Gas

Chair: Dan Byles   Con
Vice-chairs:
Steve Baker   Con
Charles Hendry   Con
Mark Menzies   Con
Nigel Mills   Con
Tessa Munt   Lib Dem
Christopher Pincher   Con
John Robertson   Lab

Contact: Dan Byles, House of Commons,
London SW1A 0AA Tel: 020 7219 7179
www.appgunconventionaloilandgas.com

United Kingdom

(Future of the United Kingdom)

Chair: Eleanor Laing   Con
Vice-chairs:
Jim Fitzpatrick   Lab
Bernard Jenkin   Con
Secretary: Tom Harris   Lab
Treasurer: Sir Malcolm Bruce   Lib Dem

Contact: Eleanor Laing, House of Commons,
London SW1A 0AA Tel: 020 7219 2086

United Nations

Chair: Lord Hannay of Chiswick   CB
Vice-chairs:
Baroness Coussins   CB
Baroness Kinnock of Holyhead   Lab
Julian Smith   Con

Contact: Julian Smith, House of Commons,
London SW1A 0AA Tel: 020 7219 7145
www.una.org.uk/un-appg

United Nations Women

Chair: Pauline Latham   Con
Vice-chairs:
Rushanara Ali   Lab
Sir Peter Bottomley   Con
Baroness Falkner of Margravine   Lib Dem
Dawn Primarolo   Lab
Secretary: Baroness Hussein-Ece   Lib Dem

Treasurer: Baroness Gould of Potternewton *Lab*
Contact: Pauline Latham, House of Commons, London SW1A 0AA Tel: 020 7219 7110

University
Chairs:
Dr Roberta Blackman-Woods *Lab*
Prof. Lord Norton of Louth *Con*
Lord Willis of Knaresborough *Lib Dem*
Vice-chairs:
Huw Irranca-Davies *Lab*
Baroness Maddock *Lib Dem*
Robert Wilson *Con*
Secretary: Paul Blomfield *Lab*
Treasurer: Baroness Sharp of Guildford *Lib Dem*
Contact: Dr Roberta Blackman-Woods, House of Commons, London SW1A 0AA
Tel: 020 7219 4982
www.appg-universities.org.uk

Uranium
Chair: Katy Clark *Lab*
Vice-chair: To be appointed
Secretary: John McDonnell *Lab*
Contact: Katy Clark, House of Commons, London SW1A 0AA Tel: 020 7219 4113

Urban Development
Chair: Paul Uppal *Con*
Honorary Chair: Nick Raynsford *Lab*
Vice-chairs:
Lord Best *CB*
Ian Davidson *Lab/Co-op*
Secretary: Clive Betts *Lab*
Contact: Paul Uppal, House of Commons, London SW1A 0AA Tel: 020 7219 7195

Vaccine Damaged People
Chair: Russell Brown *Lab*
Vice-chair: Sir Alan Beith *Lib Dem*
Secretary: Tom Clarke *Lab*
Contact: Russell Brown, 5 Friars Vennel, Dumfries DG12RQ Tel: 01387 247902

Vascular Disease
Chair: Neil Carmichael *Con*
Vice-chairs:
Sir Peter Bottomley *Con*
Chi Onwurah *Lab*
Contact: Neil Carmichael, House of Commons, London SW1A 0AA Tel: 020 7219 7163

Veterans
Chair: Gordon Marsden *Lab*
Vice-chairs:
Oliver Colvile *Con*

Jeffrey Donaldson *DUP*
Robert Flello *Lab*
Contact: Gordon Marsden, House of Commons, London SW1A 0AA Tel: 020 7219 1262

Veterans' Pensions
Chair: Katy Clark *Lab*
Secretary: Sir Bob Russell *Lib Dem*
Contact: Katy Clark, House of Commons, London SW1A 0AA Tel: 020 7219 4113

Victims and Witnesses of Crime
Chairs:
Robert Flello *Lab*
Baroness Newlove *Con*
Secretary: Jenny Chapman *Lab*
Treasurer: Catherine McKinnell *Lab*
Contact: Jenny Chapman, House of Commons, London SW1A 0AA Tel: 020 7219 7046

Video Games
Chair: Justin Tomlinson *Con*
Vice-chairs:
Luciana Berger *Lab/Co-op*
Dan Rogerson *Lib Dem*
Chris White *Con*
Contact: Justin Tomlinson, House of Commons, London SW1A 0AA Tel: 020 7219 7167

Visteon Pensioners
(To support the pensioners of the former Visteon UK)
Chair: Stephen Metcalfe *Con*
Vice-chair: Siân James *Lab*
Secretary: Geraint Davies *Lab/Co-op*
Treasurer: Jackie Doyle-Price *Con*
Contact: Stephen Metcalfe, House of Commons, London SW1A 0AA Tel: 020 7219 7009

Volatile Substance Abuse
Chair: David Hanson *Lab*
Vice-chairs:
William Cash *Con*
Jeremy Lefroy *Con*
Contact: David Hanson, House of Commons, London SW1A 0AA Tel: 020 7219 5064

War Heritage
Chair: Lord Faulkner of Worcester *Lab*
Vice-chairs:
Lord Cope of Berkeley *Con*
Nigel Dodds *DUP*
Baroness Golding *Lab*
Lord Roper *Lib Dem*
Treasurer: Jeffrey Donaldson *DUP*
Contact: Jeffrey Donaldson, House of Commons, London SW1A 0AA Tel: 020 7219 5679
www.wargravesheritage.org.uk

Water

Chair: Anne McIntosh	Con
Vice-chair: Nia Griffith	Lab
Treasurer: Earl of Selborne	Con

Contact: Anne McIntosh, House of Commons, London SW1A 0AA Tel: 020 7219 3541

Water and Sanitation in the Third World

Chair: William Cash	Con
Vice-chairs:	
Philip Davies	Con
Lord Steel of Aikwood	Lib Dem
Secretary: Jim Dobbin	Lab/Co-op
Treasurer: James Clappison	Con

Contact: William Cash, House of Commons, London SW1A 0AA Tel: 020 7219 6330

Waterways

Chairs:	
Sir Tony Baldry	Con
Huw Irranca-Davies	Lab
Vice-chairs:	
Lord Graham of Edmonton	Lab/Co-op
Dr Tristram Hunt	Lab
Roger Williams	Lib Dem
Secretary: Susan Elan Jones	Lab
Treasurer: Lord German	Lib Dem

Contact: Huw Irranca-Davies, House of Commons, London SW1A 0AA Tel: 020 7219 4027

Weapons and Protection of Civilians

Chair: Martin Caton	Lab
Vice-chairs:	
Lord Dubs	Lab
Lord Elton	Con
Nia Griffith	Lab
Dr Caroline Lucas	Green
Hywel Williams	PlC
Secretary: Tessa Munt	Lib Dem

Contact: Martin Caton, House of Commons, London SW1A 0AA Tel: 020 7219 5111

Weight Watchers

Chair: Adrian Bailey	Lab/Co-op
Vice-chair: Baroness Walmsley	Lib Dem

Contact: Adrian Bailey, House of Commons, London SW1A 0AA Tel: 020 7219 6060

Wellbeing Economics

Chair: David Lammy	Lab
Vice-chairs:	
Dr Julian Huppert	Lib Dem
Baroness Tyler of Enfield	Lib Dem
Secretary: Dr Caroline Lucas	Green
Treasurer: Helen Goodman	Lab

Contact: David Lammy, House of Commons, London SW1A 0AA Tel: 020 7219 0899
www.parliamentarywellbeinggroup.org.uk

West Coast Main Line

Chair: Russell Brown	Lab
Vice-chair: John Stevenson	Con
Secretary: Lord Taylor of Blackburn	Lab
Treasurer:	
Earl of Mar and Kellie	Scottish Lib Dem

Contact: Russell Brown, 5 Friars Venner, Dumfries DG1 2RQ Tel: 01387 247902

West Midlands

Chairs:	
Ian Austin	Lab
Lorely Burt	Lib Dem
Mark Garnier	Con
Secretaries:	
Richard Burden	Lab
Jeremy Lefroy	Con
Treasurer: Paul Uppal	Con

Contact: Mark Garnier, House of Commons, London SW1A 0AA Tel: 01562 746771

Wine and Spirit

Chairs:	
Lord Anderson of Swansea	Lab
Geoffrey Clifton-Brown	Con
Vice-chair: Lord Brougham and Vaux	Con
Secretary: John Thurso	Lib Dem
Treasurer: Sir Peter Bottomley	Con

Contact: Geoffrey Clifton-Brown, House of Commons, London SW1A 0AA Tel: 020 7219 5147

Women and Enterprise

Chair: Lorely Burt	Lib Dem
Vice-chair: Meg Munn	Lab/Co-op

Contact: Lorely Burt, House of Commons, London SW1A 0AA Tel: 020 7219 8269

Women in Parliament

Chair: Mary Macleod	Con
Vice-chairs:	
Baroness Goudie	Lab
Baroness Jenkin of Kennington	Con
Tessa Munt	Lib Dem
Caroline Spelman	Con
Secretary: Baroness Uddin	Non-Affiliated
Treasurer: Harriett Baldwin	Con

Contact: Mary Macleod, House of Commons, London SW1A 0AA Tel: 020 7219 7023

Women, Peace and Security

Chair: Nicola Blackwood	Con
Vice-chairs:	
Madeleine Moon	Lab

Brooks Newmark   Con
Baroness Stern   CB
Contact: Nicola Blackwood, House of
Commons, London SW1A 0AA
Tel: 020 7219 7126 www.gaps-uk.org/apg.php

Women in the Penal System
Chair: Baroness Corston   Lab
Vice-chairs:
Kate Green   Lab
Elfyn Llwyd   PlC
Secretary: Claire Perry   Con
Treasurer: Baroness Stern   CB
Contact: Elfyn Llwyd, House of Commons,
London SW1A 0AA Tel: 020 7219 3555

Women's Sport and Fitness
Chairs:
Baroness Grey-Thompson   CB
Barbara Keeley   Lab
Vice-chair: Tracey Crouch   Con
Secretary: Luciana Berger   Lab/Co-op
Contact: Barbara Keeley, House of Commons,
London SW1A 0AA Tel: 020 7219 8025

Wood Panel Industry
Chair: Anne McGuire   Lab
Vice-chairs:
Susan Elan Jones   Lab
Guy Opperman   Con
Secretary: Roger Williams   Lib Dem
Treasurer: Gregory Campbell   DUP
Contact: Anne McGuire, House of Commons,
London SW1A 0AA Tel: 020 7219 5829
www.appgwoodpanelindustry.org

World Governance
Chair: Mark Pritchard   Con
Vice-chair: Jim Sheridan   Lab
Secretary: Graham Stuart   Con
Treasurer: Brian Binley   Con
Contact: Mark Pritchard, House of Commons,
London SW1A 0AA Tel: 020 7219 8494

Writers
Chair: John Whittingdale   Con
Vice-chair: Lord Clement-Jones   Lib Dem
Secretary: Baroness Rendell of Babergh   Lab
Treasurer: Jim Dowd   Lab
Contact: John Whittingdale, House of Commons,
London SW1A 0AA Tel: 020 7219 3557
www.allpartywritersgroup.co.uk

Yorkshire and Northern Lincolnshire
Chairs:
Andrew Percy   Con
Barry Sheerman   · Lab/Co-op

Vice-chairs:
Jason McCartney   Con
Meg Munn   Lab/Co-op
David Ward   Lib Dem
Secretary: Linda Riordan   Lab/Co-op
Treasurer: Martin Vickers   Con
Contact: Andrew Percy, House of Commons,
London SW1A 0AA Tel: 020 7219 7208

Young Disabled People
Chair: Paul Maynard   Con
Vice-chair: John Woodcock   Lab/Co-op
Contact: Paul Maynard, House of Commons,
London SW1A 0AA Tel: 020 7219 7017

Youth Affairs
Chair: Julie Hilling   Lab
Vice-chairs:
Simon Hughes   Lib Dem
James Morris   Con
Secretary: Sir Peter Bottomley   Con
Contact: James Morris, House of Commons,
London SW1A 0AA Tel: 020 7219 7080
www.ncvys.org.uk/appg.html

Youth Hostelling
Chair: John Mann   Lab
Vice-chair: Sir Bob Russell   Lib Dem
Contact: John Mann, House of Commons,
London SW1A 0AA Tel: 020 7219 8345

Youth Unemployment
Chair: Pamela Nash   Lab
Vice-chair: Stuart Andrew   Con
Secretary: Baroness Stedman-Scott   Con
Treasurer: Lord Reid of Cardowan   Lab
Contact: Pamela Nash, House of Commons,
London SW1A 0AA Tel: 020 7219 7003

Zoos and Aquariums
Chair: Andrew Rosindell   Con
Vice-chairs:
Nigel Dodds   DUP
Simon Hart   Con
Lord Hoyle   Lab
Angus MacNeil   SNP
Sir Bob Russell   Lib Dem
Charles Walker   Con
Secretary: Stephen Mosley   Con
Treasurer: David Amess   Con
Contact: Andrew Rosindell, House of
Commons, London SW1A 0AA
Tel: 020 7219 8475

Country Groups

Most all-party country groups are formed under the auspices of the Commonwealth Parliamentary Association or the Inter-Parliamentary Union. These organisations have a UK branch, CPA and IPU, which contains affiliated groups of members interested in a particular country.

Afghanistan

Chairs:

Tobias Ellwood	Con
Sandra Osborne	Lab
Sir Robert Smith	Lib Dem

Vice-chairs:

Dai Havard	Lab
Viscount Waverley	CB

Secretary: Madeleine Moon — Lab
Treasurer: Earl of Sandwich — CB

Contact: Tobias Ellwood, House of Commons, London SW1A 0AA Tel: 020 7219 3396

Africa

Honorary President:

Lord Steel of Aikwood	Lib Dem

Honorary Vice-Presidents:

Baroness Chalker of Wallasey	Con
Baroness Kinnock of Holyhead	Lab

Chair: James Duddridge — Con
Vice-chairs:

Hugh Bayley	Lab
Lord Chidgey	Lib Dem
Pauline Latham	Con
Lord Lea of Crondall	Lab
Earl of Sandwich	CB

Secretary: Jeremy Lefroy — Con
Treasurer:

Lord Brooke of Sutton Mandeville	Con

Contact: James Duddridge, House of Commons, London SW1A 0AA Tel: 01702 616135

African Great Lakes Region

Chair: Lord McConnell of Glenscorrodale — Lab
Vice-chairs:

Geoffrey Clifton-Brown	Con
Jeremy Corbyn	Lab
Mary Glindon	Lab
Mark Pritchard	Con

Secretary: Russell Brown — Lab
Treasurer: Jeremy Corbyn — Lab

Contact: Jeremy Corbyn, House of Commons, London SW1A 0AA Tel: 020 7219 3545
www.appggreatlakes.org

Albania

Chair: Stewart Jackson — Con
Vice-chairs:

Brian Binley	Con
Stephen Pound	Lab

Secretary: To be appointed

Treasurer: Virendra Sharma — Lab

Contact: Stewart Jackson, House of Commons, London SW1A 0AA Tel: 020 7219 8286

Algeria

Chair: Mark Menzies — Con
Vice-chairs:

Lord Foulkes of Cumnock	Lab/Co-op
Lord Kilclooney	CB
Baroness Stern	CB

Secretary: Adam Holloway — Con
Treasurer: James Wharton — Con

Contact: Mark Menzies, House of Commons, London SW1A 0AA Tel: 020 7219 7073

America

Presidents:

John Bercow	Speaker
Baroness D'Souza	Lord Speaker

Vice-Presidents:

Margaret Beckett	Lab
Baroness Boothroyd	CB
Lord Carrington	Con
Nick Clegg	Lib Dem
Iain Duncan Smith	Con
Lord Falconer of Thoroton	Lab
William Hague	Con
Lord Howard of Lympne	Con
Lord Howe of Aberavon	Con
Lord Hurd of Westwell	Con
Lord Jopling	Con
Charles Kennedy	Lib Dem
Lord Mackay of Clashfern	Con
Lord Martin of Springburn	CB
Ed Miliband	Lab
Lord Molyneaux of Killead	CB
Lord Morris of Aberavon	Lab
Lord Owen	CB
Jack Straw	Lab

Chair: David Cameron — Con
Vice-chairs:

Douglas Alexander	Lab
Andrew Mitchell	Con

Honorary Secretary: Brian Donohoe — Lab
Honorary Treasurers:

Greg Knight	Con
John Spellar	Lab

Contact: Brian Donohoe, House of Commons, London SW1A 0AA Tel: 020 7219 6230
www.bapg.org.uk

Argentina

President: Viscount Montgomery of Alamein *CB*
Chair: Robin Walker   *Con*
Vice-chairs:
Baroness Gibson of Market Rasen   *Lab*
Baroness Hooper   *Con*
Mark Pritchard   *Con*
Baroness Stern   *CB*
Secretary: Lord Faulkner of Worcester   *Lab*
Treasurer: Chris Bryant   *Lab*

Contact: Robin Walker, House of Commons, London SW1A 0AA Tel: 020 7219 7196

Armenia

Chair: Baroness Cox   *CB*
Vice-chairs:
Lord Alton of Liverpool   *CB*
Lord Avebury   *Lib Dem*
Baroness Flather   *CB*
Lord Harrison   *Lab*
Stephen Pound   *Lab*
John Whittingdale   *Con*

Contact: John Whittingdale, House of Commons, London SW1A 0AA Tel: 020 7219 3557

Australia and New Zealand

Chairs:
Austin Mitchell   *Lab*
Andrew Rosindell   *Con*
Vice-chairs:
Sir Paul Beresford   *Con*
Nigel Dodds   *DUP*
Jane Ellison   *Con*
Lord Faulkner of Worcester   *Lab*
Roger Godsiff   *Lab*
Teresa Pearce   *Lab*
Viscount Simon   *Lab*
John Spellar   *Lab*
Secretary: Andrew Percy   *Con*

Contact: Andrew Rosindell, House of Commons, London SW1A 0AA Tel: 020 7219 8475

Austria

Chair: Angus Robertson   *SNP*
Vice-chairs:
John Mann   *Lab*
Ben Wallace   *Con*
Secretary: Lord Dubs   *Lab*
Treasurer: Lord Methuen   *Lib Dem*

Contact: Angus Robertson, House of Commons, London SW1A 0AA Tel: 020 7219 8259

Azerbaijan

Chair: Christopher Pincher   *Con*
Vice-chairs:
Lord Addington   *Lib Dem*
Mike Gapes   *Lab/Co-op*
Lord German   *Lib Dem*
Baroness O'Cathain   *Con*
Secretary: Bob Blackman   *Con*
Treasurer: Lord Kilclooney   *CB*

Contact: Christopher Pincher, House of Commons, London SW1A 0AA
Tel: 020 7219 7169 www.appg-azerbaijan.org

Bahrain

Chair: Conor Burns   *Con*
Vice-chairs:
Thomas Docherty   *Lab*
Lord Jones of Cheltenham   *Lib Dem*
Lord Kilclooney   *CB*
Ian Liddell-Grainger   *Con*
Priti Patel   *Con*
Bob Stewart   *Con*

Contact: Conor Burns, House of Commons, London SW1A 0AA Tel: 020 7219 7021

Bangladesh

Chair: Anne Main   *Con*
Vice-chairs:
Rushanara Ali   *Lab*
Mark Field   *Con*
Jim Fitzpatrick   *Lab*
Lord Sheikh   *Con*
Secretary: Nick de Bois   *Con*
Treasurer: Lord Ahmed   *Non-Affiliated*

Contact: Anne Main, House of Commons, London SW1A 0AA Tel: 020 7219 8270

Belarus

Chair: Pamela Nash   *Lab*
Vice-chair: John Whittingdale   *Con*

Contact: Pamela Nash, House of Commons, London SW1A 0AA Tel: 020 7219 7003

Belgium

Chair: Robert Walter   *Con*
Vice-chairs:
Mike Gapes   *Lab/Co-op*
Viscount Montgomery of Alamein   *CB*
Secretary: Lord Grenfell   *Lab*
Treasurer: Baroness Hooper   *Con*

Contact: Robert Walter, House of Commons, London SW1A 0AA Tel: 020 7219 6981

Belize

Chair: Lord Foulkes of Cumnock   *Lab/Co-op*
Vice-chairs:
Graham Brady   *Con*
Baroness Gale   *Lab*
Lord Kilclooney   *CB*
Secretary: Andrew Rosindell   *Con*
Treasurer: Lord Brookman   *Lab*

Contact: Andrew Rosindell, House of Commons, London SW1A 0AA Tel: 020 7219 8475

Bermuda

Chair: Ian Davidson	Lab/Co-op

Vice-chairs:

David Amess	Con
Paul Farrelly	Lab
Andrew Rosindell	Con
Secretary: David Crausby	Lab
Treasurer: Lord Tope	Lib Dem

Contact: Ian Davidson, House of Commons, London SW1A 0AA Tel: 0141-621 2216

Bolivia

Chair: Baroness Gibson of Market Rasen	Lab

Vice-chairs:

Lord Kilclooney	CB
Lord Lea of Crondall	Lab
Secretary: Jeremy Corbyn	Lab

Contact: Jeremy Corbyn, House of Commons, London SW1A 0AA Tel: 020 7219 3545

Bosnia and Herzegovina

Chair: Karen Lumley	Con
Vice-chair: Bob Stewart	Con
Secretary: Mark Williams	Lib Dem
Treasurer: Mark Hendrick	Lab/Co-op

Contact: Karen Lumley, House of Commons, London SW1A 0AA Tel: 020 7219 2704

Botswana

Chair: Roger Godsiff	Lab

Vice-chairs:

Lord Chidgey	Lib Dem
Ian Davidson	Lab/Co-op
John Spellar	Lab
Secretary: Lord Jones of Cheltenham	Lib Dem
Treasurer: Andrew Rosindell	Con

Contact: Roger Godsiff, House of Commons, London SW1A 0AA Tel: 020 7219 5191
Email: godsiffr@parliament.uk

Brazil

Chair: Robert Halfon	Con

Vice-chairs:

Baroness Hooper	Con
Daniel Kawczynski	Con
Viscount Montgomery of Alamein	CB
Gerry Sutcliffe	Lab
David Watts	Lab
Secretary: Lord Rogan	UUP
Treasurer: Jim Sheridan	Lab

Contact: Robert Halfon, House of Commons, London SW1A 0AA Tel: 020 7219 7223

Bulgaria

Chair: Kevin Barron	Lab
Vice-chair: Mark Pritchard	Con
Secretary: Lord Dubs	Lab

Treasurer: Lord Jones of Cheltenham	Lib Dem

Contact: Kevin Barron, House of Commons, London SW1A 0AA Tel: 020 7219 6306

Burma

Chair: Baroness Kinnock of Holyhead	Lab
Vice-chair: Lord Avebury	Lib Dem
Secretary: Sir Peter Bottomley	Con

Contact: Sir Peter Bottomley, House of Commons, London SW1A 0AA Tel: 020 7219 5060

Cambodia

Chair: Ann Clwyd	Lab
Vice-chair: Lord Griffiths of Burry Port	Lab
Secretary: Cathy Jamieson	Lab/Co-op
Treasurer: Lord Kilclooney	CB

Contact: Ann Clwyd, House of Commons, London SW1A 0AA Tel: 020 7219 6609

Canada

Chair: Andrew Rosindell	Con

Vice-chairs:

Charles Kennedy	Lib Dem
Lord Kilclooney	CB
Andy Love	Lab/Co-op
David Morris	Con
David Ruffley	Con
Virendra Sharma	Lab
Andrew Stephenson	Con
Secretary: Andrew Percy	Con
Treasurer: Lord Faulkner of Worcester	Lab

Contact: Andrew Rosindell, House of Commons, London SW1A 0AA Tel: 020 7219 8475

Caribbean

Chair: Diane Abbott	Lab

Vice-chairs:

Baroness Hooper	Con
Baroness Howells of St Davids	Lab
Secretary: Diane Abbott	Lab
Treasurer: Robert Walter	Con

Contact: Diane Abbott, House of Commons, London SW1A 0AA Tel: 020 7219 4426

Cayman Islands

Chair: Graham Brady	Con

Vice-chairs:

Brian Donohoe	Lab
Andrew Rosindell	Con
Treasurer: Baroness Golding	Lab

Contact: Graham Brady, House of Commons, London SW1A 0AA Tel: 020 7219 1260

Central America

President: Viscount Montgomery of Alamein	CB
Chair: Andrew Rosindell	Con

Vice-chairs:

Baroness Hooper	Con
John Robertson	Lab
Secretary: Daniel Kawczynski	Con
Treasurer: Lord Kilclooney	CB

Contact: Andrew Rosindell, House of Commons, London SW1A 0AA Tel: 020 7219 8475

Chagos Islands

(British Indian Overseas Territory)

Chair: Jeremy Corbyn	Lab
Vice-chairs:	
Lord Avebury	Lib Dem
Gen Lord Ramsbotham	CB
Andrew Rosindell	Con
Henry Smith	Con
Secretary and Treasurer:	
Andrew George	Lib Dem

Contact: Jeremy Corbyn, House of Commons, London SW1A 0AA Tel: 020 7219 3545

Channel Islands

Chair: Jim Dobbin	Lab/Co-op
Vice-chairs:	
Thomas Docherty	Lab
Lord Kilclooney	CB
Andrew Rosindell	Con
Secretary: David Crausby	Lab
Treasurer: John Whittingdale	Con

Contact: Jim Dobbin, House of Commons, London SW1A 0AA Tel: 020 7219 4530

China

Chair: Richard Graham	Con
Deputy Chairs:	
Sir Tony Baldry	Con
Lord Clement-Jones	Lib Dem
Lord Steel of Aikwood	Lib Dem
Vice-chairs:	
Lord Bates	Con
Alun Cairns	Con
Duncan Hames	Lib Dem
Mark Hendrick	Lab/Co-op
Adam Holloway	Con
Anne McGuire	Lab
Madeleine Moon	Lab
Neil Parish	Con
Priti Patel	Con
David Simpson	DUP
Heather Wheeler	Con
Secretary: Lord Cotter	Lib Dem
Treasurer: Robin Walker	Con

Contact: Richard Graham, House of Commons, London SW1A 0AA Tel: 020 7219 7077 www.appcg.org.uk

Croatia

Chair: Earl of Dundee	Con
Vice-chair: Robert Walter	Con
Secretary: Lord Grenfell	Lab

Contact: Robert Walter, House of Commons, London SW1A 0AA Tel: 020 7219 6981

Cuba

Chair: Baroness Smith of Basildon	Lab/Co-op
Vice-chairs:	
Viscount Montgomery of Alamein	CB
Andrew Rosindell	Con
Secretary: Cathy Jamieson	Lab/Co-op
Treasurer: Baroness Hooper	Con

Contact: Cathy Jamieson, House of Commons, London SW1A 0AA Tel: 020 7219 8456

Cyprus

Chair: Dr Matthew Offord	Con
Vice-chairs:	
David Burrowes	Con
Nick de Bois	Con
Sir Alan Meale	Lab
Secretary: Jim Dobbin	Lab/Co-op
Treasurer: Ian Lavery	Lab

Contact: Dr Matthew Offord, House of Commons, London SW1A 0AA Tel: 020 7219 7083 www.cyprusappg.co.uk

Turkish Republic of Northern Cyprus

Chair: Lord Sharkey	Lib Dem
Vice-chair: Lord Harrison	Lab

Contact: George Howarth, House of Commons, London SW1A 0AA Tel: 020 7219 6902

Denmark

Chair: Anne McIntosh	Con
Vice-chairs:	
Helen Goodman	Lab
Lord Teverson	Lib Dem
Secretary: Viscount Craigavon	CB
Treasurer: Andrew Rosindell	Con

Contact: Anne McIntosh, House of Commons, London SW1A 0AA Tel: 020 7219 3541

Dominican Republic

Chair: Mark Menzies	Con
Vice-chairs:	
Lord Foulkes of Cumnock	Lab/Co-op
Baroness Hooper	Con
Lord Kilclooney	CB
Viscount Montgomery of Alamein	CB
Baroness Stern	CB
Secretary: Gareth Johnson	Con

Contact: Gareth Johnson, House of Commons, London SW1A 0AA Tel: 020 7219 7047

Estonia

Chair: Gordon Marsden — Lab
Vice-chairs:
Sir Malcolm Bruce — Lib Dem
Ian Davidson — Lab/Co-op
Andrew Rosindell — Con

Contact: Gordon Marsden, House of Commons, London SW1A 0AA Tel: 020 7219 1262

Ethiopia and Djibouti

Chair: Laurence Robertson — Con
Vice-chairs:
Lord Dholakia — Lib Dem
Jeffrey Donaldson — DUP
David Watts — Lab
Secretary: Mark Pritchard — Con
Treasurer: Joe Benton — Lab

Contact: Laurence Robertson, House of Commons, London SW1A 0AA
Tel: 020 7219 4196

European Union Enlargement

Chair: Lord Dubs — Lab
Vice-chairs:
Lord Bowness — Con
Baroness Nicholson of Winterbourne — Lib Dem
Secretary: Robert Walter — Con
Treasurer: Wayne David — Lab

Contact: Robert Walter, House of Commons, London SW1A 0AA Tel: 020 7219 6081

Falkland Islands

Chair: Derek Twigg — Lab
Vice-chairs:
David Crausby — Lab
Lord Jones of Cheltenham — Lib Dem
Lord Kilclooney — CB
Sir Jim Paice — Con
Secretary: Andrew Rosindell — Con
Treasurer: Madeleine Moon — Lab

Contact: Andrew Rosindell, House of Commons, London SW1A 0AA
Tel: 020 7219 8475

Faroe Islands

Chair: Angus MacNeil — SNP
Vice-chairs:
Dame Anne Begg — Lab
Lord Faulkner of Worcester — Lab
Charles Kennedy — Lib Dem
Ian Mearns — Lab
Andrew Rosindell — Con
Secretary: Lord Lea of Crondall — Lab
Treasurer: Jeffrey Donaldson — DUP

Contact: Angus MacNeil, House of Commons, London SW1A 0AA Tel: 020 7219 3225

Finland

Chair: Baroness Ramsay of Cartvale — Lab
Vice-chairs:
Simon Hughes — Lib Dem
Andrew Rosindell — Con
Secretary: Viscount Craigavon — CB
Treasurer: Angela Smith — Lab

Contact: Simon Hughes, House of Commons, London SW1A 0AA Tel: 020 7219 6256

France

Chair: Sir Edward Leigh — Con
Vice-chairs:
Paul Murphy — Lab
Mark Pritchard — Con
Baroness Taylor of Bolton — Lab
Secretary: Robert Neill — Con
Treasurer: Lord Anderson of Swansea — Lab

Contact: Robert Neill, House of Commons, London SW1A 0AA Tel: 020 7219 2537

Georgia

Chair: Mark Reckless — Con
Vice-chairs:
Lord Bowness — Con
Dr Liam Fox — Con
Lord Haworth — Lab
Baroness Nicholson of Winterbourne — Lib Dem
Secretary: Patrick Mercer — Ind
Treasurer:
Rt Rev Lord Harries of Pentregarth — CB

Contact: Mark Reckless, House of Commons, London SW1A 0AA Tel: 020 7219 7135

Germany

Chair: Paul Farrelly — Lab
Vice-chairs:
Lord Anderson of Swansea — Lab
Ian Davidson — Lab/Co-op
Lord Dykes — Lib Dem
Lord Roper — Lib Dem
Stephen Timms — Lab
Secretary: David Davies — Con
Treasurer: Mark Hendrick — Lab/Co-op

Contact: Paul Farrelly, House of Commons, London SW1A 0AA Tel: 020 7219 8262

Ghana

Chair: Lord Boateng — Lab
Vice-chairs:
Sir Tony Baldry — Con
Prof. Lord McColl of Dulwich — Con
Mark Pritchard — Con
Virendra Sharma — Lab
Lord Steel of Aikwood — Lib Dem
Secretary: Lord Chidgey — Lib Dem

Treasurers:
Lord Anderson of Swansea — Lab
Lord Ribeiro — Con
Contact: Sir Tony Baldry, House of Commons,
London SW1A 0AA Tel: 020 7219 4491

Gibraltar
Chair: Jim Dobbin — Lab/Co-op
Vice-chairs:
David Crausby — Lab
Simon Hughes — Lib Dem
Lord Kilclooney — CB
Andrew Rosindell — Con
Secretary: Jack Lopresti — Con
Treasurer: Lord Hoyle — Lab
Contact: Jim Dobbin, House of Commons,
London SW1A 0AA Tel: 020 7219 4530

Greece
Chair: Sir Roger Gale — Con
Vice-chairs:
Andrew George — Lib Dem
Sir Alan Meale — Lab
Secretaries:
Joe Benton — Lab
Mark Pritchard — Con
Contact: Sir Roger Gale, House of Commons,
London SW1A 0AA Tel: 020 7219 4087

Guinea-Bissau
Chair: Lord Teverson — Lib Dem
Vice-chairs:
Ian Paisley — DUP
Mark Pritchard — Con
Keith Vaz — Lab
Treasurer: Lorely Burt — Lib Dem
Contact: Lorely Burt, House of Commons,
London SW1A 0AA Tel: 020 7219 8269
www.guineabissau.org.uk

Gulf Co-operation Council States
Chair: James Wharton — Con
Vice-chair: Admiral Lord West of Spithead — Lab
Secretary: Mark Garnier — Con
Treasurer: David Morris — Con
Contact: James Wharton, House of Commons,
London SW1A 0AA Tel: 020 7219 7236

Haiti
Chair: Lord Griffiths of Burry Port — Lab
Vice-chair: Sir Peter Bottomley — Con
Secretary: Caroline Dinenage — Con
Treasurer: Lord Alton of Liverpool — CB
Contact: Sir Peter Bottomley, House of
Commons, London SW1A 0AA
Tel: 020 7219 5060

Hungary
Chair: Andrew Miller — Lab
Vice-chairs:
David Amess — Con
David Davies — Con
Robert Neill — Con
Secretary: Paul Farrelly — Lab
Treasurer: Mark Pritchard — Con
Contact: Andrew Miller, House of Commons,
London SW1A 0AA Tel: 020 7219 3580

Iceland
Chair: Austin Mitchell — Lab
Vice-chairs:
Sir Alan Beith — Lib Dem
Paul Farrelly — Lab
Andrew Rosindell — Con
Secretary: Viscount Craigavon — CB
Treasurer: Fabian Hamilton — Lab
Contact: Austin Mitchell, House of Commons,
London SW1A 0AA Tel: 020 7219 4559

India
Chair: Virendra Sharma — Lab
Vice-chairs:
Lord Bilimoria — CB
Peter Luff — Con
Priti Patel — Con
Secretary: Bob Blackman — Con
Membership Secretary: Stephen Pound — Lab
Treasurer: Andy Love — Lab/Co-op
Contact: Virendra Sharma, House of Commons,
London SW1A 0AA Tel: 020 7219 6080

Indonesia
Chair: Richard Graham — Con
Vice-chairs:
Alun Cairns — Con
Khalid Mahmood — Lab
Lord Rogan — UUP
John Spellar — Lab
Baroness Uddin — Non-Affiliated
Secretary: Baroness Cox — CB
Treasurer: Tobias Ellwood — Con
Contact: Richard Graham, House of Commons,
London SW1A 0AA Tel: 020 7219 7077

Iran
Chairs:
Jack Straw — Lab
Ben Wallace — Con
Vice-chairs:
Lord Ahmed — Non-Affiliated
Lord Kilclooney — CB
David Ruffley — Con
Secretary: Fabian Hamilton — Lab
Treasurer: Stewart Jackson — Con
Contact: Ben Wallace, House of Commons,
London SW1A 0AA Tel: 020 7219 5804

Iraq

Chair: Ann Clwyd	*Lab*
Vice-chair: Lord Kilclooney	*CB*
Secretary: Nadhim Zahawi	*Con*
Treasurer: Dr Andrew Murrison	*Con*

Contact: Ann Clwyd, House of Commons, London SW1A 0AA Tel: 020 7219 6609

Kurdistan Region in Iraq

Chairs:

Meg Munn	*Lab/Co-op*
Nadhim Zahawi	*Con*

Vice-chairs:

Lord Clement-Jones	*Lib Dem*
Robert Halfon	*Con*
Fabian Hamilton	*Lab*
Stephen Metcalfe	*Con*
Secretary: David Anderson	*Lab*

Contact: David Anderson, House of Commons, London SW1A 0AA Tel: 020 7219 4843
www.appgkurdistan.org.uk

Isle of Man

Chair: Andrew Rosindell	*Con*

Vice-chairs:

Lord Bach	*Lab*
Baroness Harris of Richmond	*Lib Dem*
Lord Kilclooney	*CB*
Angus MacNeil	*SNP*
Ian Paisley	*DUP*
Prof. Lord Quirk	*CB*
James Wharton	*Con*
Secretary: David Morris	*Con*
Treasurer: Jim Dobbin	*Lab/Co-op*

Contact: Andrew Rosindell, House of Commons, London SW1A 0AA Tel: 020 7219 8475

Israel

Chair: Lord Janner of Braunstone	*Lab*
Vice-chair: Louise Ellman	*Lab/Co-op*
Secretary: Dr Matthew Offord	*Con*
Treasurer: Mike Freer	*Con*

Contact: Louise Ellman, House of Commons, London SW1A 0AA Tel: 020 7219 5210

Italy

Chair: Sir Tony Baldry	*Con*

Vice-chairs:

Jim Dobbin	*Lab/Co-op*
Lord Dykes	*Lib Dem*
Mark Pritchard	*Con*
Sir Richard Shepherd	*Con*
Secretary: Paul Farrelly	*Lab*
Treasurer: Robert Flello	*Lab*

Contact: Sir Tony Baldry, House of Commons, London SW1A 0AA Tel: 020 7219 6465

Jamaica

Chair: Diane Abbott	*Lab*
Vice-chair: Henry Bellingham	*Con*
Secretary: Diane Abbott	*Lab*
Treasurer: Sarah Teather	*Lib Dem*

Contact: Diane Abbott, House of Commons, London SW1A 0AA Tel: 020 7219 4426

Japan

Chair: Roger Godsiff	*Lab*

Vice-chairs:

Paul Farrelly	*Lab*
Fabian Hamilton	*Lab*
Baroness Hooper	*Con*
Mark Pritchard	*Con*
John Spellar	*Lab*
Sir John Stanley	*Con*
Viscount Trenchard	*Con*
David Wright	*Lab*
Secretary: Steve McCabe	*Lab*
Treasurer: Robert Walter	*Con*

Contact: Roger Godsiff, House of Commons, London SW1A 0AA Tel: 020 7219 5191
www.bjpg.co.uk

Jordan

Chair: Richard Burden	*Lab*

Vice-chairs:

Lord Jordan	*Lab*
Lord Kilclooney	*CB*
Baroness Nicholson of Winterbourne	*Lib Dem*
Mark Pritchard	*Con*
Secretary: David Ruffley	*Con*
Treasurer: Lord Dubs	*Lab*

Contact: Richard Burden, House of Commons, London SW1A 0AA Tel: 020 7219 2318

Kashmir

Chair: Andrew Griffiths	*Con*
Senior Vice-chair: Debbie Abrahams	*Lab*

Vice-chairs:

Steve Baker	*Con*
Lord Hussain	*Lib Dem*

Secretaries:

Richard Harrington	*Con*
Marcus Jones	*Con*
Chris Leslie	*Lab/Co-op*

Treasurers:

Simon Danczuk	*Lab*
Gavin Shuker	*Lab/Co-op*

Contact: Richard Harrington, House of Commons, London SW1A 0AA
Tel: 020 7219 7180

Kenya

Chair: William Cash	*Con*
Vice-chair: Bob Ainsworth	*Lab*

Secretary: Andrew Rosindell — Con
Treasurer: Brian Binley — Con
Contact: William Cash, House of Commons, London SW1A 0AA Tel: 020 7219 6330

North Korea
(Democratic People's Republic of Korea)

Chair: Lord Alton of Liverpool — CB
Vice-chairs:
Lord Bates — Con
Fiona Bruce — Con
Baroness Cox — CB
Jim Dobbin — Lab/Co-op
Lord German — Lib Dem
Gary Streeter — Con
Secretaries:
Baroness Berridge — Con
Mark Pritchard — Con
Treasurers:
David Amess — Con
Lord Clarke of Hampstead — Lab
Contact: Jim Dobbin, House of Commons, London SW1A 0AA Tel: 020 7219 4530

South Korea
(Republic of Korea)

Chair: Sir John Stanley — Con
Vice-chair: Mike Gapes — Lab/Co-op
Secretary: Sir Peter Bottomley — Con
Contact: Sir John Stanley, House of Commons, London SW1A 0AA Tel: 020 7219 5977

Kosovo

Chair: Sir Tony Baldry — Con
Vice-chair: Mark Pritchard — Con
Secretary: Andy Slaughter — Lab
Contact: Sir Tony Baldry, House of Commons, London SW1A 0AA Tel: 020 7219 6465

Kyrgyzstan

Chair: John Mann — Lab
Vice-chair: Baroness Stern — CB
Contact: John Mann, House of Commons, London SW1A 0AA Tel: 020 7219 8345

Laos

Chair: Mark Pritchard — Con
Vice-chairs:
David Crausby — Lab
Lord Dholakia — Lib Dem
Lord Kilclooney — CB
Secretary: John Spellar — Lab
Treasurer: Stewart Jackson — Con
Contact: Mark Pritchard, House of Commons, London SW1A 0AA Tel: 020 7219 8494

Latin America

Chair: Baroness Hooper — Con
Vice-chairs:
Jeremy Corbyn — Lab
Baroness Gibson of Market Rasen — Lab
Baroness Miller of Chilthorne Domer — Lib Dem
Viscount Montgomery of Alamein — CB
Mark Pritchard — Con
Secretary: Jeremy Corbyn — Lab
Acting Treasurer: Robin Walker — Con
Contact: Jeremy Corbyn, House of Commons, London SW1A 0AA Tel: 020 7219 3545

Latvia

Chair: Christopher Pincher — Con
Vice-chairs:
Lord Cormack — Con
Angus MacNeil — SNP
Secretary: Neil Parish — Con
Contact: Christopher Pincher, House of Commons, London SW1A 0AA Tel: 020 7219 7169

Lebanon

Chair: Andy Love — Lab/Co-op
Vice-chairs:
Richard Burden — Lab
Mark Pritchard — Con
Contact: Andy Love, House of Commons, London SW1A 0AA Tel: 020 7219 6377

Libya

Chair: Daniel Kawczynski — Con
Vice-chairs:
Lord Kilclooney — CB
Baroness Uddin — Non-Affiliated
Secretary: Khalid Mahmood — Lab
Treasurer: Andrew Rosindell — Con
Contact: Daniel Kawczynski, House of Commons, London SW1A 0AA Tel: 020 7219 6249

Liechtenstein

President: Sir Edward Garnier — Con
Chair: Andrew Rosindell — Con
Vice-chairs:
Fabian Hamilton — Lab
Lady Hermon — Ind
Daniel Kawczynski — Con
Lord Temple-Morris — Lab
Robert Wilson — Con
Secretary: Mark Menzies — Con
Treasurer: Angus MacNeil — SNP
Contact: Andrew Rosindell, House of Commons, London SW1A 0AA Tel: 020 7219 8475

Macedonia

Chair: Karen Lumley	Con
Vice-chair: Nigel Mills	Con
Secretary: Lord Dubs	Lab
Treasurer: Mark Williams	Lib Dem

Contact: Karen Lumley, House of Commons, London SW1A 0AA Tel: 020 7219 2704

Malaysia

Chair: William Cash	Con
Vice-chair: Peter Bone	Con
Secretary: Ian Liddell-Grainger	Con
Treasurer: Lord Rogan	UUP

Contact: William Cash, House of Commons, London SW1A 0AA Tel: 020 7219 6330

Maldives

Chair: David Amess	Con
Vice-chairs:	
Rosie Cooper	Lab
Karen Lumley	Con
Mark Pritchard	Con
Treasurer: Graham Brady	Con

Contact: David Amess, House of Commons, London SW1A 0AA Tel: 020 7219 3452

Malta

Chair: Mark Pritchard	Con
Vice-chair: Baroness Hooper	Con
Secretary: Stewart Jackson	Con
Treasurer: Lord Dholakia	Lib Dem

Contact: Mark Pritchard, House of Commons, London SW1A 0AA Tel: 020 7219 8494

Mauritius

Chair: Lord Steel of Aikwood	Lib Dem
Vice-chairs:	
David Amess	Con
Roger Godsiff	Lab
Lord Kilclooney	CB
Andrew Rosindell	Con
Treasurer: Virendra Sharma	Lab

Contact: Andrew Rosindell, House of Commons, London SW1A 0AA Tel: 020 7219 8475

Mexico

Chair: Jeremy Corbyn	Lab
Vice-chairs:	
Lord Brennan	Lab
Meg Munn	Lab/Co-op
Mark Pritchard	Con
Secretary: Andy Love	Lab/Co-op
Treasurer: Baroness Hooper	Con

Contact: Jeremy Corbyn, House of Commons, London SW1A 0AA Tel: 020 7219 3545

Moldova

Chair: Lord Dubs	Lab
Vice-chairs:	
Karen Lumley	Con
Mark Pritchard	Con
Secretary: Lord Bowness	Con

Contact: Karen Lumley, House of Commons, London SW1A 0AA Tel: 020 7219 7133

Mongolia

President: Baroness Trumpington	Con
Chairs:	
Andrew Rosindell	Con
Viscount Waverley	CB
Vice-chairs:	
Lord Kilclooney	CB
John Mann	Lab
Secretary: Daniel Kawczynski	Con
Treasurer: Rory Stewart	Con

Contact: Andrew Rosindell, House of Commons, London SW1A 0AA Tel: 020 7219 8499

Montserrat

Chair: Andrew Rosindell	Con
Vice-chairs:	
Graham Brady	Con
Jim Dobbin	Lab/Co-op
Nigel Dodds	DUP
Lord Jones of Cheltenham	Lib Dem
Secretary: Thomas Docherty	Lab
Treasurer: Baroness Hooper	Con

Contact: Andrew Rosindell, House of Commons, London SW1A 0AA Tel: 020 7219 8475

Morocco

Chair: Ian Liddell-Grainger	Con
Vice-chairs:	
Lord Janner of Braunstone	Lab
Lord Kilclooney	CB
Mark Pritchard	Con
Robert Walter	Con
Secretary: Graham Jones	Lab
Treasurer: Lord Anderson of Swansea	Lab

Contact: Ian Liddell-Grainger, House of Commons, London SW1A 0AA Tel: 020 7219 8149

Mozambique

Chair: Ian Davidson	Lab/Co-op
Vice-chairs:	
Roger Godsiff	Lab
Lord Jones of Cheltenham	Lib Dem
Mark Pritchard	Con
Secretary: Madeleine Moon	Lab

Treasurer: Lord Chidgey   *Lib Dem*

Contact: Ian Davidson, House of Commons, London SW1A 0AA Tel: 0141-621 2216

Namibia

Chair: Ian Davidson   *Lab/Co-op*
Vice-chairs:
Lord Chidgey   *Lib Dem*
Lord Jones of Cheltenham   *Lib Dem*
Lord Kilclooney   *CB*
Lord Rana   *CB*
Mark Pritchard   *Con*
Secretary: Roger Godsiff   *Lab*

Contact: Ian Davidson, House of Commons, London SW1A 0AA Tel: 0141-621 2216

Nepal

Chair: Sir John Stanley   *Con*
Vice-chair: Virendra Sharma   *Lab*
Secretary: Mark Lancaster   *Con*

Contact: Sir John Stanley, House of Commons, London SW1A 0AA Tel: 020 7219 5977

Netherlands

Chair: Clive Betts   *Lab*
Vice-chairs:
Lord Anderson of Swansea   *Lab*
Sir Edward Garnier   *Con*
Robert Walter   *Con*
Secretary: Lord Harrison   *Lab*
Treasurer: Lord Temple-Morris   *Lab*

Contact: Clive Betts, House of Commons, London SW1A 0AA Tel: 020 7219 5114

Nigeria

Chair: Meg Hillier   *Lab/Co-op*
Vice-chairs:
Richard Fuller   *Con*
Chi Onwurah   *Lab*
Secretary: James Duddridge   *Con*
Treasurer: Heidi Alexander   *Lab*

Contact: Meg Hillier, House of Commons, London SW1A 0AA Tel: 020 7219 5325

Norway

Chair: Sir Alan Beith   *Lib Dem*
Vice-chairs:
Lord Anderson of Swansea   *Lab*
Viscount Craigavon   *CB*
Lord Elton   *Con*
Kelvin Hopkins   *Lab*
Secretary: Lord Faulkner of Worcester   *Lab*
Treasurer: Paul Farrelly   *Lab*

Contact: Sir Alan Beith, House of Commons, London SW1A 0AA Tel: 020 7219 3540

Oman

Chair: Kate Hoey   *Lab*
Vice-chairs:
Lord Chidgey   *Lib Dem*
Philip Hollobone   *Con*
Baroness Jolly   *Lib Dem*
Lord Kilclooney   *CB*
Secretary: Lord German   *Lib Dem*
Treasurer: Lord Rogan   *UUP*

Contact: Kate Hoey, House of Commons, London SW1A 0AA Tel: 020 7219 5803

Overseas Territories

(Anguilla, Bermuda, British Antarctic Territory, British Indian Ocean Territory, British Virgin Islands, Cayman Islands, Falkland Islands, Gibraltar, Montserrat, Pitcairn Islands, St Helena, Ascension and Tristan da Cunha, South Georgia and the Sandwich Islands, Sovereign Base Areas of Akrotiri and Dhekelia, Turks and Caicos Islands)

Chair: Andrew Rosindell   *Con*
Vice-chairs:
Lord Ashcroft   *Con*
Graham Brady   *Con*
Oliver Colvile   *Con*
Ian Davidson   *Lab/Co-op*
Jim Dobbin   *Lab/Co-op*
Thomas Docherty   *Lab*
Nigel Dodds   *DUP*
Lord Jones of Cheltenham   *Lib Dem*
Austin Mitchell   *Lab*
Lord Rogan   *UUP*
Henry Smith   *Con*
Derek Twigg   *Lab*
Secretary: Lord Kilclooney   *CB*
Treasurer: Baroness Hooper   *Con*

Contact: Andrew Rosindell, House of Commons, London SW1A 0AA Tel: 020 7219 8475

Pakistan

Chair: Andrew Stephenson   *Con*
Vice-chairs:
Simon Danczuk   *Lab*
Andrew Griffiths   *Con*
Secretary and Treasurer: David Ward   *Lib Dem*

Contact: Andrew Stephenson, House of Commons, London SW1A 0AA Tel: 020 7219 7222

Palestine

Chair: Richard Burden   *Lab*
Vice-chairs:
Baroness Morris of Bolton   *Con*
Lord Steel of Aikwood   *Lib Dem*
Secretary: Andy Slaughter   *Lab*
Treasurer: Stephen Williams   *Lib Dem*

Contact: Richard Burden, House of Commons, London SW1A 0AA Tel: 020 7219 2318

Peru

Chair: Michael Connarty — *Lab*
Vice-chairs:
Lord Alderdice — *Lib Dem*
Baroness Thomas of Walliswood — *Lib Dem*
Secretary: Baroness Gardner of Parkes — *Con*
Treasurer: Lord Avebury — *Lib Dem*

Contact: Michael Connarty, House of Commons, London SW1A 0AA Tel: 020 7219 5071

Pitcairn Islands

Chair: Andrew Rosindell — *Con*
Vice-chairs:
Fabian Hamilton — *Lab*
Christopher Heaton-Harris — *Con*
Lord Jones of Cheltenham — *Lib Dem*
Lord Kilclooney — *CB*
Austin Mitchell — *Lab*
Secretary and Treasurer:
Baroness Hooper — *Con*

Contact: Andrew Rosindell, House of Commons, London SW1A 0AA Tel: 020 7219 8475

Poland

Chair: Dr Alan Whitehead — *Lab*
Vice-chairs:
Dr Julian Lewis — *Con*
Lord Grenfell — *Lab*
Mark Lazarowicz — *Lab/Co-op*
Secretary: Stephen Pound — *Lab*

Contact: Dr Alan Whitehead, House of Commons, London SW1A 0AA
Tel: 020 7219 6338

Polar Regions

(Arctic and Antarctic)

President: Earl of Selborne — *Con*
Chair: Andrew Rosindell — *Con*
Vice-chairs:
Earl of Courtown — *Con*
James Gray — *Con*
Dr Julian Huppert — *Lib Dem*
Gareth Johnson — *Con*
Lord Jones of Cheltenham — *Lib Dem*
Gavin Shuker — *Lab/Co-op*
Secretary: Oliver Colvile — *Con*
Treasurer: Baroness Jay of Paddington — *Lab*

Contact: Andrew Rosindell, House of Commons, London SW1A 0AA
Tel: 020 7219 8475

Portugal

Chair: Lord Dubs — *Lab*
Vice-chairs:
Graham Brady — *Con*

Lord Davies of Stamford — *Lab*
Lord Rogan — *UUP*
Secretary:
Lord Boswell of Aynho — *Non-Affiliated*
Treasurer: Mark Pritchard — *Con*

Contact: Graham Brady, House of Commons, London SW1A 0AA Tel: 020 7219 1620

Qatar

Chair: Baroness Morris of Bolton — *Con*
Vice-chairs:
Lord Kilclooney — *CB*
David Ruffley — *Con*
Baroness Uddin — *Non-Affiliated*
Secretary: Lord Redesdale — *Lib Dem*
Treasurer: Cathy Jamieson — *Lab/Co-op*

Contact: Cathy Jamieson, House of Commons, London SW1A 0AA Tel: 020 7219 8456

Romania

Chair: Lord Davies of Stamford — *Lab*
Vice-chairs:
Lord Bowness — *Con*
Paul Flynn — *Lab*
Robert Walter — *Con*
Secretary and Treasurer:
Lord Woolmer of Leeds — *Lab*

Contact: Paul Flynn, House of Commons, London SW1A 0AA Tel: 020 7219 3478

Russia

Chair: Chris Bryant — *Lab*
Vice-chairs:
Harriett Baldwin — *Con*
Emma Reynolds — *Lab*
Secretary: David Ruffley — *Con*
Treasurer:
Baroness Gibson of Market Rasen — *Lab*

Contact: Chris Bryant, House of Commons, London SW1A 0AA Tel: 020 7219 1894

Saudi Arabia

Chair: Daniel Kawczynski — *Con*
Deputy Chairs:
Lord Ahmed — *Non-Affiliated*
Rehman Chishti — *Con*
Lord Rogan — *UUP*
Baroness Uddin — *Non-Affiliated*
Secretary: Khalid Mahmood — *Lab*
Treasurer: Paul Uppal — *Con*

Contact: Khalid Mahmood, House of Commons, London SW1A 0AA
Tel: 0121-356 8268

Serbia

Chair: Karen Lumley — *Con*
Vice-chair: Lord Dubs — *Lab*

Secretary: Stuart Andrew   Con
Treasurer: Mark Williams   Lib Dem

Contact: Karen Lumley, House of Commons,
London SW1A 0AA Tel: 020 7219 2704

Singapore

Chair: John Spellar   Lab
Vice-chairs:
Alun Cairns   Con
Brian Donohoe   Lab
Jim Fitzpatrick   Lab
Mark Hendrick   Lab/Co-op
Lord Naseby   Con
Lord Rogan   UUP
Secretary: Graham Brady   Con
Treasurer: Richard Ottaway   Con

Contact: John Spellar, House of Commons,
London SW1A 0AA Tel: 020 7219 5800

Slovenia

Chair: Neil Parish   Con
Vice-chairs:
Lord Dubs   Lab
Mike Gapes   Lab/Co-op
Christopher Pincher   Con
Mark Pritchard   Con
Secretary: Sheryll Murray   Con

Contact: Neil Parish, House of Commons,
London SW1A 0AA Tel: 020 7219 7172

Somaliland and Somalia

Chairs:
Sir Tony Baldry   Con
Clive Betts   Lab
Vice-chairs:
Lord Anderson of Swansea   Lab
Lord Avebury   Lib Dem
Mark Hendrick   Lab/Co-op
Secretary: Kerry McCarthy   Lab

Contact: Clive Betts, House of Commons,
London SW1A 0AA Tel: 020 7219 5114

South Africa

Chair: Anne McIntosh   Con
Vice-chairs:
Lord Chidgey   Lib Dem
Ian Davidson   Lab/Co-op
Helen Jones   Lab
Elfyn Llwyd   PlC
Lord St John of Bletso   CB
Lord Steel of Aikwood   Lib Dem
Secretary: Roger Godsiff   Lab
Treasurer: Lord Jones of Cheltenham   Lib Dem

Contact: Anne McIntosh, House of Commons,
London SW1A 0AA Tel: 020 7219 3541

South Pacific

Chair: Meg Munn   Lab/Co-op
Vice-chairs:
Angus MacNeil   SNP
Austin Mitchell   Lab
Ian Paisley   DUP
Andrew Percy   Con
Lord Roper   Lib Dem
Secretary: Andrew Rosindell   Con
Treasurer: Lord Jones of Cheltenham   Lib Dem

Contact: Meg Munn, House of Commons,
London SW1A 0AA Tel: 020 7219 8316

Spain

Chair: Lord Brennan   Lab
Vice-chairs:
Lord Dykes   Lib Dem
Baroness Hooper   Con
Lord Kilclooney   CB
Viscount Montgomery of Alamein   CB
Secretary: Chris Bryant   Lab
Treasurers:
Luciana Berger   Lab/Co-op
Baroness Golding   Lab

Contact: Chris Bryant, House of Commons,
London SW1A 0AA Tel: 020 7219 1894

Sri Lanka

Chairs:
Andy Love   Lab/Co-op
Lord Naseby   Con
Vice-chairs:
Stephen Hammond   Con
Mark Pritchard   Con
Secretaries:
Brian Binley   Con
James Wharton   Con

Contact: Andy Love, House of Commons,
London SW1A 0AA Tel: 020 7219 6377

Sudan and South Sudan

Chair: Willie Bain   Lab
Vice-chairs:
Sir Tony Baldry   Con
Hilary Benn   Lab
Lord Chidgey   Lib Dem
Baroness Cox   CB
Mark Durkan   SDLP
Sir Roger Gale   Con
Baroness Kinnock of Holyhead   Lab
Baroness Tonge   Ind Lib Dem
Secretary: Lord Alton of Liverpool   CB
Treasurer: Earl of Sandwich   CB

Contact: Sir Roger Gale, House of Commons,
London SW1A 0AA Tel: 020 7219 4087
www.sudanapg.tumblr.com

Sweden

Chair: Baroness Maddock · Lib Dem
Vice-chairs:
Sir Alan Beith · Lib Dem
Kelvin Hopkins · Lab
Robert Walter · Con
Secretary: Viscount Craigavon · CB
Treasurer: John Mann · Lab

Contact: Sir Alan Beith, House of Commons,
London SW1A 0AA Tel: 020 7219 3540

Switzerland

Chairs:
Earl of Courtown · Con
Andrew Rosindell · Con
Vice-chairs:
Steve Barclay · Con
Lord Davies of Stamford · Lab
Viscount Montgomery of Alamein · CB
Secretary: Tim Loughton · Con
Treasurers:
Mark Menzies · Con
Mike Weatherley · Con

Contact: Andrew Rosindell, House of
Commons, London SW1A 0AA
Tel: 020 7219 8475

Syria

Chair: Roger Godsiff · Lab
Vice-chairs:
Lord Dubs · Lab
Lord Kilclooney · CB
Secretary: Andrew Rosindell · Con
Treasurer: Robert Walter · Con

Contact: Roger Godsiff, House of Commons,
London SW1A 0AA Tel: 020 7219 5191

Taiwan

Chairs:
Lord Faulkner of Worcester · Lab
Lord Steel of Aikwood · Lib Dem
Vice-chairs:
Lord Dholakia · Lib Dem
Brian Donohoe · Lab
Baroness Gale · Lab
Baroness Howells of St Davids · Lab
Baroness Perry of Southwark · Con
Lord Rogan · UUP
Secretary and Treasurer: Heather Wheeler · Con

Contact: Heather Wheeler, House of Commons,
London SW1A 0AA Tel: 020 7219 7237
www.taiwanappg.org.uk

Tajikistan

Chair: Baroness Stern · CB
Vice-chair: John Mann · Lab

Secretary: Nigel Mills · Con
Contact: John Mann, House of Commons,
London SW1A 0AA Tel: 020 7219 8345

Tanzania

Chair: Jeremy Lefroy · Con
Vice-chairs:
Kevin Barron · Lab
William Cash · Con
Pauline Latham · Con
Treasurer: Luciana Berger · Lab/Co-op

Contact: Jeremy Lefroy, House of Commons,
London SW1A 0AA Tel: 020 7219 7154

Thailand

Chair: Roger Godsiff · Lab
Vice-chairs:
Geraint Davies · Lab/Co-op
Mike Hancock · Ind
Mark Hendrick · Lab/Co-op
John Spellar · Lab
Secretary: Brian Binley · Con
Treasurer: Graham Brady · Con

Contact: Roger Godsiff, House of Commons,
London SW1A 0AA Tel: 020 7219 5191

Tibet

Chair: Fabian Hamilton · Lab
Vice-chairs:
Lord Alton of Liverpool · CB
Lord Avebury · Lib Dem
James Gray · Con
Kate Hoey · Lab
Lord Steel of Aikwood · Lib Dem
Secretary: Mark Pritchard · Con
Treasurer: Martin Horwood · Lib Dem

Contact: Fabian Hamilton, House of Commons,
London SW1A 0AA Tel: 020 7219 2535

Trinidad and Tobago

Chair: Baroness Benjamin · Lib Dem
Vice-chairs:
Baroness Berridge · Con
Baroness Hussein-Ece · Lib Dem
Secretary: Jeremy Lefroy · Con
Treasurer:
Baroness Howells of St Davids · Lab

Contact: Jeremy Lefroy, House of Commons,
London SW1A 0AA Tel: 020 7219 7154

Turkey

Chair: Fabian Hamilton · Lab
Vice-chairs:
Lord Clement-Jones · Lib Dem
Baroness Hussein-Ece · Lib Dem

Mark Pritchard	*Con*
Lord Rogan	*UUP*
Secretary: Robert Walter	*Con*
Treasurer: Lord Dubs	*Lab*

Contact: Fabian Hamilton, House of Commons, London SW1A 0AA Tel: 020 7219 3493

Turks and Caicos Islands

Chair: Thomas Docherty	*Lab*
Vice-chairs:	
Lord Bilston	*Lab/Co-op*
Lord Jones of Cheltenham	*Lib Dem*
Robert Walter	*Con*
Secretary: Andrew Rosindell	*Con*
Treasurer: Andrew Percy	*Con*

Contact: Andrew Rosindell, House of Commons, London SW1A 0AA Tel: 020 7219 8475

Uganda

Chair: William Cash	*Con*
Vice-chair: Mark Pritchard	*Con*
Secretary: Brian Binley	*Con*
Treasurer: Lord Steel of Aikwood	*Lib Dem*

Contact: William Cash, House of Commons, London SW1A 0AA Tel: 020 7219 6330

Ukraine

Chair: John Whittingdale	*Con*
Vice-chairs:	
Lord Howe of Aberavon	*Con*
Simon Hughes	*Lib Dem*
Secretaries:	
Mark Pritchard	*Con*
Lord Risby	*Con*
Treasurer: Helen Goodman	*Lab*

Contact: John Whittingdale, House of Commons, London SW1A 0AA Tel: 020 7219 5828

United Arab Emirates

Chair: Lord Howard of Lympne	*Con*
Vice-chairs:	
Lord Clement-Jones	*Lib Dem*
Kevan Jones	*Lab*
Secretary: Mark Tami	*Lab*
Treasurer: Priti Patel	*Con*

Contact: Kevan Jones, House of Commons, London SW1A 0AA Tel: 020 7219 8219

Vietnam

Chair: George Howarth	*Lab*
Vice-chairs:	
Mark Hendrick	*Lab/Co-op*
Mark Pritchard	*Con*
David Ruffley	*Con*
Secretaries:	
Roger Godsiff	*Lab*
Ian Liddell-Grainger	*Con*
Treasurer: Chris Ruane	*Lab*

Contact: George Howarth, House of Commons, London SW1A 0AA Tel: 020 7219 6902

Western Sahara

Chair: Jeremy Corbyn	*Lab*
Vice-chairs:	
Ann Clwyd	*Lab*
Cathy Jamieson	*Lab/Co-op*
Secretary: Mark Williams	*Lib Dem*
Treasurer: Roger Williams	*Lib Dem*

Contact: Jeremy Corbyn, House of Commons, London SW1A 0AA Tel: 020 7219 3545

Zambia and Malawi

Chairs:	
Tom Greatrex	*Lab/Co-op*
Lord Skelmersdale	*Con*
Vice-chairs:	
Ian Davidson	*Lab/Co-op*
James Duddridge	*Con*
Lord McConnell of Glenscorrodale	*Lab*
Stephen Mosley	*Con*
Secretary: Oliver Colvile	*Con*

Contact: Tom Greatrex, House of Commons, London SW1A 0AA Tel: 020 7219 8974

Zimbabwe

Chair: Kate Hoey	*Lab*
Vice-chairs:	
Lord Chidgey	*Lib Dem*
Oliver Colvile	*Con*
Secretary: Lord Hughes of Woodside	*Lab*

Contact: Kate Hoey, House of Commons, London SW1A 0AA Tel: 020 7219 5989

Privy Counsellors

Privy Counsellors historically advised the monarch. The title is now largely honorary; it is given automatically to all cabinet members and the Speaker, the archbishops of Canterbury and York and the Bishop of London and to holders of certain judicial appointments. Leaders of the main political parties are conventionally nominated. The appointment is for life, unless withdrawn, and holders are addressed as 'Right Honourable' (Rt Hon).

The following lists members of the UK Parliaments and Assemblies who are Privy Counsellors.

Lord Adonis	2009	Lord Cameron of Lochbroom	1984
Bob Ainsworth	2005	Sir Menzies Campbell	1999
Danny Alexander	2010	Archbishop of Canterbury	2013
Douglas Alexander	2005	Lord Carey of Clifton	1991
Baroness Amos	2003	Alistair Carmichael	2010
Lord Anderson of Swansea	2000	Lord Carrington	1959
Baroness Anelay of St Johns	2009	Lord Carswell	1993
James Arbuthnot	1998	Lord Chalfont	1964
Baroness Armstrong of Hill Top	1999	Baroness Chalker of Wallasey	1987
Lord Ashcroft	2012	Lord Clark of Windermere	1997
Lord Ashdown of Norton-sub-Hamdon	1989	Greg Clark	2010
Baroness Ashton of Upholland	2006	Lord Clarke of Stone-cum-Ebony	1998
Lord Baker of Dorking	1984	Kenneth Clarke	1984
Ed Balls	2007	Tom Clarke	1997
Lord Bannside	2005	Nick Clegg	2008
Gregory Barker	2012	Lord Clinton-Davis	1998
Lord Barnett	1975	Ann Clwyd	2004
Kevin Barron	2001	Lord Collins of Mapesbury	2007
Lord Bassam of Brighton	2009	Yvette Cooper	2007
Margaret Beckett	1993	Lord Cope of Berkeley	1988
Sir Alan Beith	1992	Baroness Corston	2003
Hilary Benn	2003	Earl of Crawford and Balcarres	1972
John Bercow	2009	Lord Crickhowell	1979
Baroness Blackstone	2001	Lord Cullen of Whitekirk	1997
Hazel Blears	2005	Lord Cunningham of Felling	1993
Lord Blencathra	2001	Alistair Darling	1997
David Blunkett	1997	Lord Darzi of Denham	2009
Lord Boateng	1999	Edward Davey	2012
Baroness Boothroyd	1992	Lord Davies of Oldham	2006
Baroness Bottomley of Nettlestone	1992	David Davis	1997
Lord Boyd of Duncansby	2000	Baroness Dean of Thornton-le-Fylde	1998
Lord Brabazon of Tara	2013	Lord Deben	1985
Lord Bradley	2001	Lord Denham	1981
Ben Bradshaw	2009	John Denham	2000
Tom Brake	2011	Lord Dholakia	2010
Lord Brittan of Spennithorne	1981	Lord Dixon	1996
Lord Brooke of Sutton Mandeville	1988	Frank Dobson	1997
Gordon Brown	1996	Nigel Dodds	2010
Nick Brown	1997	Jeffrey Donaldson	2007
Lord Brown of Eaton-under-Heywood	1992	Stephen Dorrell	1994
Lord Browne of Ladyton	2005	Lord Drayson	2008
Lord Browne-Wilkinson	1983	Baroness D'Souza	2009
Sir Malcolm Bruce	2006	Alan Duncan	2010
Andy Burnham	2007	Iain Duncan Smith	2001
Simon Burns	2011	Lord Eden of Winton	1972
Paul Burstow	2012	Lord Elis-Thomas	2004
Lord Butler of Brockwell	2004	Lord Falconer of Thoroton	2003
Baroness Butler-Sloss	1988	Michael Fallon	2012
Liam Byrne	2008	Lord Fellowes	1990
Vincent Cable	2010	Alex Fergusson	2010
Earl of Caithness	1990	Frank Field	1997
David Cameron	2005	Caroline Flint	2008

Lord Forsyth of Drumlean	1995	Lord Hutton of Furness	2001
Lord Foster of Bishop Auckland	1993	Lord Inge	2004
Don Foster	2010	Lord Irvine of Lairg	1997
Lord Foulkes of Cumnock	2002	Lord Janvrin	1998
Lord Fowler	1979	Baroness Jay of Paddington	1998
Liam Fox	2010	Lord Jenkin of Roding	1973
Mark Francois	2010	Alan Johnson	2003
Lord Freeman	1993	Carwyn Jones	2010
Lord Garel-Jones	1992	David Jones	2012
Cheryl Gillan	2010	Lord Jones	1999
Lord Goff of Chieveley	1982	Lord Jopling	1979
Paul Goggins	2009	Dame Tessa Jowell	1998
Lord Goldsmith	2002	Lord Judge	1996
Lord Goodlad	1992	Sir Gerald Kaufman	1978
Michael Gove	2010	Charles Kennedy	1999
Lord Graham of Edmonton	1998	Lord Kerr of Tonaghmore	2003
Chris Grayling	2010	Sadiq Khan	2009
Damian Green	2012	Lord King of Bridgwater	1979
Justine Greening	2011	Lord Kingsdown	1987
Dominic Grieve	2010	Lord Kinnock	1983
Lord Griffiths	1980	Greg Knight	1995
Lord Grocott	2002	Lord Knight of Weymouth	2008
William Hague	1995	David Lammy	2008
Peter Hain	2001	Lord Lamont of Lerwick	1986
Baroness Hale of Richmond	1999	Lord Lang of Monkton	1990
Lord Hamilton of Epsom	1991	Andrew Lansley	2010
Philip Hammond	2010	David Laws	2010
David Hanson	2007	Lord Lawson of Blaby	1981
Lord Hardie	1997	Oliver Letwin	2002
Harriet Harman	1997	Baroness Liddell of Coatdyke	1998
Sir Alan Haselhurst	1999	David Lidington	2010
Lord Hattersley	1975	Peter Lilley	1990
John Hayes	2013	Lord Lloyd of Berwick	1984
Baroness Hayman	2000	Elfyn Llwyd	2011
Lord Healey	1964	Bishop of London	1995
John Healey	2008	Marquess of Lothian	1996
Lord Henley	2013	Lord Luce	1986
Nick Herbert	2010	Lord McAvoy	2003
Lord Heseltine	1979	Lord McConnell of Glenscorrodale	2001
Lord Higgins	1979	Lord Macdonald of Tradeston	1999
Lord Hill of Oareford	2013	Pat McFadden	2008
Margaret Hodge	2003	Lord McFall of Alcluith	2004
Lord Hoffmann	1992	Lord MacGregor of Pulham Market	1985
Baroness Hollis of Heigham	1999	Anne McGuire	2008
Lord Hope of Craighead	1989	Lord Mackay of Clashfern	1979
Lord Hope of Thornes	1991	Lord Mackay of Drumadoon	1996
Lord Howard of Lympne	1990	Lord Maclennan of Rogart	1997
Lord Howarth of Newport	2000	Patrick McLoughlin	2005
George Howarth	2005	Lord McNally	2005
Earl Howe	2013	Lord Malloch-Brown	2007
Lord Howe of Aberavon	1972	Lord Mance	1999
Lord Howell of Guildford	1979	Lord Mandelson	1998
Lindsay Hoyle	2013	Lord Martin of Springburn	2000
Baroness Hughes of Stretford	2004	Tricia Marwick	2012
Simon Hughes	2010	Lord Mason of Barnsley	1968
Jeremy Hunt	2010	Francis Maude	1992
Lord Hunt of Kings Heath	2009	Lord Mawhinney	1994
Lord Hunt of Wirral	1980	Theresa May	2003
Lord Hurd of Westwell	1982	Lord Mayhew of Twysden	1986
Lord Hutton	1988	Michael Meacher	1997

Ed Miliband	2007	Lord Selkirk of Douglas	1996
Maria Miller	2012	Grant Shapps	2010
Lord Millett	1994	Lord Sheldon	1977
Andrew Mitchell	2010	Baroness Shephard of Northwold	1992
Lord Molyneaux of Killead	1983	Lord Shutt of Greetland	2009
Lord Moore of Lower Marsh	1986	Andrew Smith	1997
Michael Moore	2010	Baroness Smith of Basildon	2009
Lord Morris of Aberavon	1970	Lord Smith of Finsbury	1997
Baroness Morris of Yardley	1999	Nicholas Soames	2011
David Mundell	2010	John Spellar	2001
Jim Murphy	2008	Caroline Spelman	2010
Paul Murphy	1999	Lord Spicer	2013
Lord Mustill	1985	Sir John Stanley	1984
Lord Naseby	1994	Lord Steel of Aikwood	1977
Lord Neuberger of Abbotsbury	2004	Lord Stewartby	1989
Baroness Neville-Jones	2010	Lord Steyn	1992
Lord Nicholls of Birkenhead	1995	Lord Strathclyde	1995
Stephen O'Brien	2013	Jack Straw	1997
Baroness Oppenheim-Barnes	1979	Sir Andrew Stunell	2012
George Osborne	2010	Desmond Swayne	2011
Lord Owen	1976	Hugo Swire	2010
Sir Jim Paice	2010	Baroness Symons of Vernham Dean	2001
Lord Parkinson	1981	Sir Peter Tapsell	2011
Owen Paterson	2010	Baroness Taylor of Bolton	1997
Lord Patten	1990	Lord Tebbit	1981
Lord Patten of Barnes	1989	Lord Templeman	1978
Lord Paul	2009	Stephen Timms	2006
Earl Peel	2006	Lord Touhig	2006
Lord Pendry	2000	Lord Trefgarne	1989
Lord Phillips of Worth Matravers	1995	Lord Trimble	1997
Eric Pickles	2010	Baroness Trumpington	1992
Baroness Prashar	2009	Viscount Ullswater	1994
Dawn Primarolo	2002	Baroness Vadera	2009
Lord Prior	1970	Keith Vaz	2006
Baroness Quin	1998	Theresa Villiers	2010
Lord Radice	1999	Lord Waddington	1987
John Randall	2010	Lord Wakeham	1983
Nick Raynsford	2001	Lord Waldegrave of North Hill	1990
John Redwood	1993	Lord Walker of Gestingthorpe	1997
Lord Reid of Cardowan	1998	Lord Wallace of Saltaire	2012
Lord Renton of Mount Harry	1989	Lord Wallace of Tankerness	2000
Lord Richard	1993	Lord Warner	2006
Sir Malcolm Rifkind	1986	Baroness Warsi	2010
Andrew Robathan	2010	Lord West of Spithead	2010
Hugh Robertson	2012	Lord Whitty	2005
Lord Roberts of Conwy	1991	Lord Wigley	1997
Lord Robertson of Port Ellen	1997	David Willetts	2010
Peter Robinson	2007	Baroness Williams of Crosby	1974
Lord Rodgers of Quarry Bank	1975	Lord Williams of Elvel	2013
Lord Rooker	1999	Lord Williams of Oystermouth	2002
Lord Roper	2005	Lord Williamson of Horton	2007
Baroness Royall of Blaisdon	2008	Lord Wills	2008
Dame Joan Ruddock	2010	Rosie Winterton	2006
Lord Ryder of Wensum	1990	Shaun Woodward	2007
Marquess of Salisbury	1994	Lord Woolf	1986
Alex Salmond	2007	Archbishop of York	2005
Lord Saville of Newdigate	1994	Sir George Young	1993
Baroness Scotland of Asthal	2001	Lord Young of Graffham	1984
Lord Scott of Foscote	1991		

Political Parties

Conservative and Unionist Party

30 Millbank, London SW1P 4DP
Tel: 020 7222 9000 Fax: 020 7222 1135
Website: www.conservatives.com Twitter: @Conservatives

Leader: David Cameron MP
Chairmen: Lord Feldman of Elstree, Grant Shapps MP
Deputy Chairman: Sarah Newton MP
Vice-chairmen:
  BME Communities: Alok Sharma MP
  Business: Alan Lewis
  Target Seats Campaigning: Richard Harrington MP
  Social Action: Wendy Morton
  International: Geoffrey Clifton-Brown MP
  Local Government: Robert Neill MP
  Parliamentary Campaigning: Michael Fabricant MP
  Youth: Rebecca Harris MP
Treasurers: Michael Farmer, James Lupton
Chair, National Convention: Emma Pidding

Labour Party

One Brewer's Green, London SW1H 0RH
Tel: 0845 092 2299/020 7783 1299 Fax: 020 7783 1234
Website: www.labour.org.uk Twitter: @UKLabour

Leader: Ed Miliband MP
Deputy Leader and Party Chair: Harriet Harman MP
General Secretary: Iain McNicol
Treasurer: Diana Holland
Director of Communications: Bob Roberts
Deputy Director of Communications: Patrick Hennessy
General Election Campaign Director: Spencer Livermore

National Executive Committee

Leader: Ed Miliband MP
Deputy Leader and Party Chair: Harriet Harman MP
Treasurer: Diana Holland
Members:
  Frontbench: Angela Eagle MP, Sadiq Khan MP, Jon Ashworth MP
  European Parliament Labour Party Leader: Glenis Willmott MEP
  Ex-officio as General Secretary: Iain McNicol
  Ex-officio as Opposition Chief Whip: Rosie Winterton MP
  Young Labour: Bex Bailey

Division I – Trade Unions

Members:
  Community: Susan Lewis
  CWU: Andy Kerr
  GMB: Mary Turner, Andy Worth
  TSSA: Harriet Yeo
  Ucatt: Jim Kennedy
  Unison: Keith Birch, Wendy Nichols
  Unite: Jennie Formby, Martin Mayer
  Usdaw: Paddy Lillis

Division II – Socialist Societies

Members: Conor McGinn, Keith Vaz MP

Division III – Constituency Labour Parties

Members: Johanna Baxter, Ann Black, Ken Livingstone, Ellie Reeves, Christine Shawcroft, Peter Wheeler

Division IV – Local Government

Members: Ann Lucas, Dave Sparks

Division V – Parliamentary Labour Party/European Parliamentary Labour Party

Members: Margaret Beckett MP, Steve Rotheram MP, Dennis Skinner MP

Parliamentary Labour Party

Chair: David Watts MP
Secretary and Director of Unit: Wesley Ball 020 7219 4552

Co-operative Party

77 Weston Street, London SE1 3SD
Tel: 020 7367 4150 Fax: 020 7407 4476
Email: mail@party.coop Website: www.party.coop Twitter: @CoopParty

Chair: Gareth Thomas MP
Vice-chair: Stuart Ramsay
General Secretary: Karin Christiansen
Head of External and Political Affairs: Claire McCarthy
Chair, Parliamentary Group: Cathy Jamieson MP

Liberal Democrats

Fourth Floor, 8-10 Great George Street, London SW1P 3AE
Tel: 020 7222 7999 Fax: 020 7799 2170
Email: info@libdems.org uk Website: www.libdems.org.uk Twitter: @LibDems

Leader: Nick Clegg MP
President: Tim Farron MP
Vice-Presidents: Peter Ellis *(England)*, Craig Harrow *(Scotland)*, John Last *(Wales)*
Treasurer: Lord Wrigglesworth
Chief Executive: Tim Gordon
Directors:
   Finance and Operations: Nigel Bliss
   Digital: Steve Pitman
   Communications: Tim Snowball 020 7229 1388 Email: tim.snowball@libdems.org.uk
   Elections and Field: Hilary Stephenson
   Fundraising: Ibrahim Taguri
Heads:
   Candidates and Diversity: Jemima Jefferson
   Conference: Lucy Billingsley
   Digital Campaigns: Jake Holland
   Ground Communications: Shaun Roberts
   International: Iain Gill
   Media: James Holt
   Member and Supporter Development: Austin Rathe
   Parliamentary Support Team: Jamie Saddler
   Policy: Christian Moon
   Strategic Research: Tom Smithard
   Strategic Seats: Victoria Marsom
   Commons Whips' Office: Hollie Voyce
   Lords Whips' Office: Laura Gilmore

Alliance

88 University Street, Belfast BT7 1HE
Tel: 028 9032 4274 Fax: 028 9033 3147
Email: alliance@allianceparty.org Website: www.allianceparty.org Twitter: @allianceparty

Assembly Office, Room 220 Parliament Buildings, Stormont, Belfast BT4 3XX
Tel: 028 9052 1314 Fax: 028 9052 1313

Leader: David Ford MLA
Deputy Leader: Naomi Long MP
Chair: Andrew Muir Email: andrew.muir@allianceparty.org
General Secretary: Sharon Lowry Email: sharon.lowry@allianceparty.org
Joint Hon Treasurers:
Mervyn Jones Email: mervyn.jones@allianceparty.org
Dan McGuinness Email: dan.mcguinness@allianceparty.org
Press Officer: David Young 028 9052 1977 Email: david.young@allianceparty.org

Democratic Unionist Party
91 Dundela Avenue, Belfast BT4 3BU
Tel: 028 9047 1155 Fax: 028 9052 1289
Email: info@dup.org.uk Website: www.mydup.com Twitter: @duponline
Assembly Office, Room 207 Parliament Buildings, Stormont, Belfast BT4 3XX
Tel: 028 9052 1323 Fax: 028 9052 1289
Leader: Peter Robinson MLA
Deputy Leader: Nigel Dodds MP
Chair: Lord Morrow MLA
Vice-chair: Dr William McCrea MP
Secretary: Michelle McIlveen MLA
Treasurer: Gregory Campbell MP, MLA
Director, Communications: John Robinson 07901 914006 Email: johnrobinson@dup.org.uk

Green Party
Development House, 56-64 Leonard Street, London EC2A 4LT
Tel: 020 7549 0310 Fax: 020 7549 0318
Email: office@greenparty.org.uk Website: www.greenparty.org.uk Twitter: @TheGreenParty
Leader: Natalie Bennett
Deputy Leader: Will Duckworth

Plaid Cymru (The Party of Wales)
Tŷ Gwynfor, Marine Chambers, Anson Court, Atlantic Wharf, Cardiff CF10 4AL
Tel: 029 2047 2272
Email: post@plaidcymru.org Website: www.plaidcymru.org Twitter: @plaid_cymru
Assembly Office:
Tel: 029 2089 8761 Fax: 029 2089 8260
Leader: Leanne Wood AM
Chief Executive: Rhuanedd Richards 029 2047 2272
Treasurer: Dr Dafydd Trystan 029 2047 2272

Respect Party
PO Box 167, Manchester M19 0AH
Email: office@respectparty.info Website: www.respectparty.org
Chair: To be appointed
National Secretary: Ron McKay

Scottish National Party
Gordon Lamb House, 3 Jackson's Entry, Edinburgh EH8 8PJ
Tel: 0800 633 5432 Fax: 0131-525 8901
Email: info@snp.org Website: www.snp.org Twitter: @thesnp
Leader: Alex Salmond MSP
Depute Leader: Nicola Sturgeon MSP
President: Ian Hudghton MEP
Chief Executive: Peter Murrell
Director, Strategic Communications: Kevin Pringle
Head, Communications and Research, Scottish Parliament:
Ross Ingebrigtsen 0131-348 5679 Email: ross.ingebrigtsen@scottish.parliament.uk

Sinn Féin

44 Parnell Square, Dublin 1, Ireland
Tel: +353 1 8726932 Fax: +353 1 8733441
Email: sfadmin@eircom.net Website: www.sinnfein.ie Twitter: @sinnfeinireland

53 Falls Road, Belfast BT12 4PD
Tel: 028 9034 7350 Fax: 028 9022 3001

Assembly Office:
Tel: 028 9052 1471/028 9052 1470 Fax: 028 9052 1488

President: Gerry Adams
Vice-President: Mary Lou McDonald
Chair: Declan Kearney
General Secretary: Dawn Doyle
Treasurers: Jonathan O'Brien, Ted Howell
Director, Publicity: Sean MacBradaigh

Social Democratic and Labour Party

121 Ormeau Road, Belfast BT7 1SH
Tel: 028 9024 7700 Fax: 028 9023 6699
Email: info@sdlp.ie Website: www.sdlp.ie Twitter: @sdlplive

Assembly Office:
Tel: 028 9052 1319

Press Office:
Tel: 028 9052 1837

Leader: Dr Alasdair McDonnell MP, MLA
Deputy Leader: Dolores Kelly MLA
Chair: Joe Byrne MLA
Vice-chairs: Fearghal McKinney MLA, Cathal Mulligan
General Secretary: Gerry Cosgrove Email: gerry.cosgrove@sdlphq.ie

Ulster Unionist Party

Strandtown Hall, 2-4 Belmont Road, Belfast BT4 2AN
Tel: 028 9047 4630 Fax: 028 9065 2149
Email: uup@uup.org Website: www.uup.org Twitter: @uuponline

Assembly Office, Room 214 Parliament Buildings, Stormont, Belfast BT4 3XX
Tel: 028 9052 1423 Fax: 028 9052 1883

Policy Unit:
Tel: 028 9052 1892

Leader: Mike Nesbitt MLA
Chair: Lord Empey
Vice-chair: Roy McCune
Treasurer: Mark Cosgrove
Party Officers: Tom Elliott MLA, Jim Nicholson MEP, Alexander Redpath, Lord Rogan, Joy Rollston, Philip Smith, Robin Swann MLA, George White, Trevor Wilson
Communications and Policy Co-ordinator: John Moore 028 9052 1328 Email: john.moore@uup.org
Press Officer: Stephen Barr 028 9052 1890 Email: stephen.barr@party.niassembly.gov.uk

UK Independence Party

PO Box 408, Newton Abbot, Devon TQ12 9BG
Tel: 01626 831290 Fax: 01626 831348
Email: mail@ukip.org Website: www.ukip.org Twitter: @UKIP

Leader: Nigel Farage MEP
Deputy Leader: Paul Nuttall MEP
Treasurer: Stuart Wheeler
General Secretary: Jonathan Arnott

Parliamentary Press Gallery

The Parliamentary Lobby Journalists are those journalists authorised to work in Parliament.
Members of the Lobby are marked with an asterisk.
Tel: 020 7219 4700; for individual desk numbers prefix 020 7219 in most cases.
Attendants: 020 7219 5371
Press Bar: 020 7219 4284
Website: www.pressgallery.org.uk

Chairman	Christopher Hope (Daily Telegraph)	4960
Honorary Secretary	Jason Beattie (Daily Mirror)	3639
Honorary Treasurer	Rob Hutton (Bloomberg News)	3526
Administrator	Elizabeth Johnson	4395
	press.gallery@virgin.net	
Lobby Journalists' Chairman	James Chapman (Daily Mail)	
Honorary Secretary	Jon Craig (Sky News)	
Honorary Treasurer	Nigel Morris (Independent)	4392

National Daily Newspapers

Daily Express
Political Editor: Macer Hall 3389
*Martyn Brown 6149
*Alison Little 3387
Administrator: Jackie Murray 020 7925 2708

Daily Mail
Political Editor: James Chapman 6140
Deputy Political Editor: Tim Shipman 3679
Quentin Letts 020 7233 2413
*Daniel Martin 6561
*Tamara Cohen 6561
*Jason Groves 0616
*Gerri Peev 3683
Administrator: Nicole Worth 6894

Daily Mirror
Political Editor: Jason Beattie 3639
Deputy Political Editor: James Lyons 4377
*Tom McTague 4359
*Kevin Maguire 6733
Paul Routledge 4583

Daily Record
*Torcuil Crichton 3336

Daily Star
Political Editor: Gary Nicks 6764

Daily Telegraph
Political Editor: Robert Winnett 3687
Deputy Political Editor: James Kirkup 6890
Senior Political Correspondent:
Christopher Hope 4960
*Tim Ross 5719

Michael Deacon 4927
*Peter Dominiczak
Administrator: Kate Mayer 3685

Evening Standard
Political Editor: Joe Murphy 5718
Deputy Political Editor: Nic Cecil 6730
*Pippa Crerar 6724
*Joe Watts
Administrator: Caroline Robertson

Financial Times
Political Editor: George Parker 4380
*Jim Pickard 6892
*Elizabeth Rigby 6893
*Kiran Stacey 6142

Guardian
Political Editor: Patrick Wintour 3681
Assistant Editor: Michael White 6143
Chief Political Correspondent:
Nicholas Watt 6891
*Rajeev Syal 6738
*Rowena Mason
Simon Hoggart 6738
Administrator: Flora MacQueen 0026

GUARDIAN UNLIMITED
Senior Political Correspondent: Andrew
Sparrow 020 7886 9760

Herald
Political Editor: Mike Settle 0156
*Kate Devlin 6722

Independent
Political Editor: Andrew Grice 4665
Deputy Political Editor: Nigel Morris 4392
*Oliver Wright 4392
Don MacIntyre
*Andy McSmith 2037
*Steve Richards

Morning Star
Political Editor: Roger Bagley 0369

Scotsman
Westminster Editor: David Maddox 4370

Sun
Political Editor: Tom Newton Dunn 3337
Associate Editor: Trevor Kavanagh 6144

*Graeme Wilson 4638
*Kevin Schofield 0431
*Emily Ashton 0140
*Craig Woodhouse 3339
Political Editor (Sunday edition):
David Wooding 3339

The Times
Political Editor: Francis Elliott 5241
Deputy Political Editor: Sam Coates
*Michael Savage 5284
*Laura Pitel 6543
Ann Treneman 5284

UK Metro
Chief Political Correspondent: John Higginson

National Sunday Newspapers

Independent on Sunday
Political Editor: Jane Merrick
Whitehall Editor: Brian Brady 2058
Jim Cusick
*John Rentoul

Mail on Sunday
Political Editor: Simon Walters 4531
*Brendan Carlin 3025
*Glen Owen 4386

Observer
Political Editor: Toby Helm 3380
*Andrew Rawsley
Whitehall Editor: Daniel Boffey 3380

People
Editor: James Scott
Political Editor: Nigel Nelson 6904

Scottish Sunday Post
*James Millar

Sunday Express
Political Editor: Kirsty Buchanan 5596
Marco Giannangeli
Adam Helliker

Sunday Mirror
Political Editor: Vincent Moss 5544

Sunday Telegraph
Political Editor: To be appointed

Sunday Times
Political Editor: Isabel Oakshott 3477
Whitehall Editor: Marie Woolf
*Jack Grimston

Regional Press

Birmingham Evening Mail/Birmingham Post
*Jon Walker 3765

Bradford Telegraph and Argus
*Rob Merrick 5287

City AM
James Waterson 020 7015 1253

Eastern Daily Press
*Annabelle Dickson

Newcastle Journal
Political Editor: Adrian Pearson

Northcliffe Newspapers
*David Torrance 4691

Press and Journal
*Calum Ross 4390

Southern Daily Echo (Southampton)
*Rob Merrick 5287

Western Mail
Political Editor: David Williamson 4382

Western Morning News
London Editor: Graeme Demianyk 6742

Yorkshire Post
Political Editor: Jack Blanchard 3674

Magazines

Civil Service World
Editor: Matt Ross 020 7593 5589

Economist
*Janan Ganesh
*Andrew Miller

House Magazine
Jess Bowie 020 7593 5808

New Statesman
Editor: Jason Cowley 020 7592 3625
*Rafael Behr

Spectator
Editor: Fraser Nelson
Political Editor: James Forsyth 3689
*Isabel Hardman

Total Politics
Editor: Sam Macrory 020 7593 5665

Tribune
Editor: Chris McLaughlin 020 7433 6415
*David Hencke 2093

News Agencies

Associated Press
*Cassandra Vinograd 020 7427 4211

Bloomberg News
*Rob Hutton 020 7222 5241
*Kitty Donaldson 020 7976 1795
Thomas Penny 020 7233 3462
*Svenja O'Donnell

Dow Jones
*Ainsley Thomson 1132
*Nick Winning 1132

Gallery News
*Robert Gibson 2035
*Nick Assinder

Parliament Today
*Mike Peters
*Julian Robinson

Press Association (PA News)
Political Editor: Andrew Woodcock
*James Tapsfield
*Sam Lister
Soraya Kishtwari
Tim Sculthorpe
Theo Usherwood
Arjun Singh
*David Hughes
*Joe Churcher
*Gavin Cordon
*Chris Moncrieff

Reuters
Andrew Osborn 5389
Peter Griffiths 5389
David Milliken 5389

Broadcasting

BBC (British Broadcasting Corporation)

BBC EAST
Regional Political Correspondent:
Deborah McGurran 03744 679244

BBC EAST MIDLANDS
Regional Political Correspondent:
John Hess 07801 317273

BBC NORTH
Regional Political Correspondent:
Len Tingle 4700

BBC NORTH EAST
Regional Political Correspondent:
Richard Moss 07736 481129

BBC NORTH WEST
Political Editor: Arif Ansari

BBC NORTHERN IRELAND
*Regional Political Correspondent:
Lisa Costello

BBC POLITICAL PROGRAMMES
Head of Political Programmes: Sue Inglish
Editor, Political News:
Stephen Mawhinney 020 7973 6016
*Political Editor: Nick Robinson 020 7973 6001
*Deputy Political Editor: James Landale
*Regional Political Editor:
Bob Ledwidge 020 7973 6170
Political Correspondents: 020 7973 6050
*John Pienarr
*Paul Rowley
*Norman Smith
*Carole Walker
Joanne Coburn
*Vicky Young
*Sean Curran
Mark Darcy
Susan Hulme
David Wilby
*Gary O'Donaghue
Rob Watson (BBC World Service)

BBC SCOTLAND
*National Regional Correspondent:
David Porter 020 7973 6187

BBC SOUTH
Political Editor: Peter Henley 023 807 4202

BBC SOUTH EAST
Regional Political Correspondents:
*Paul Siegert
Tim Donavan 020 7973 6167

BBC SOUTH WEST
Regional Political Correspondent:
Chris Rogers 01752 234331

BBC WALES
*National Regional Correspondent:
David Cornock 020 7973 6245

BBC WEST
Regional Political Correspondent:
Dave Harvey 07810 854035

BBC WEST MIDLANDS
Regional Political Correspondent:
Patrick Burns 0121-432 8308

Channel 4 Television
CHANNEL 4 NEWS
*Political Editor: Gary Gibbon 3334
*Michael Crick
*Robert Hamilton
*Rob Thomson

Five News
Political Editor: Andy Bell 020 7705 3232

Independent Television News
Tel: Press Gallery: 020 7219 3334/4387
News Desk (Gray's Inn Road): 020 7430 4551

CHANNEL 4 NEWS
*Political Editor: Gary Gibbon 3334
*Michael Crick
*Robert Hamilton
*Rob Thomson

ITV NEWS
*Political Editor: Tom Bradby
*News Editor: Samana Haq
*Carl Dinnen
*Libby Wiener
*Chris Ship
Producers: *Dan Hewitt, Anne Lingley, Claire
Bidmead, Fenella Meyer

Israel Radio
Jerry Lewis 0452

ITV
DAYBREAK
*Sue Jamieson
*Anne Alexander 3678

ITV ANGLIA
*Emma Hutchinson

ITV CENTRAL
*Westminster News Editor of ITV Regions:
Simon Mares 020 7233 0203
*Alison MacKenzie

ITV GRANADA
*Dan Hewitt

ITV MERIDIAN
*Phil Hornby 020 7976 3360

ITV TYNE TEES/BORDER
Helen Ford

ITV WALES
*Adrian Masters

ITV WEST/WEST COUNTRY
*Bob Constantine

ITV YORKSHIRE
Paul Brand

London News Network
*Simon Harris

RTE – Irish Broadcasting
*Brian O'Connell 4700

Scottish Television
Westminster Correspondent: Harry Smith

Sky News
Political Editor: Adam Boulton 020 7705 5500
*Jon Craig
Clare Parry
*Peter Spencer
*Joey Jones
*Amber Elliott
*Sophy Ridge

UTV
*Ken Reid

Women's Parliamentary Radio
Boni Sones
Linda Fairbrother

Websites

Conservative Home
Editor: Paul Goodman
Contributing Editor: Andrew Gimson

Huffington Post
*Ned Simons

Politics.co.uk
Editor: Ian Dunt
Deputy Editor, Politics:
Alex Stevenson 020 7517 2204

PoliticsHome
Editor: Paul Waugh
Parliamentary Editor:
Tony Grew 07595 082773

Parliamentary Agents

Parliamentary Agents provide general information on Parliament to both individuals and firms, fully reporting on progress of Bills. There are two types of Agent, those registered to propose and oppose bills on behalf of their clients and those who only oppose Bills.

Berwin Leighton Paisner LLP

Adelaide House, London Bridge, London EC4R 9HA
Tel: 020 3400 1000
Email: helen.kemp@blplaw.com daniel.greenberg@blplaw.com Website:www.blplaw.com
Parliamentary Agent: Helen Kemp Email: helen.kemp@blplaw.com
Partner: Tim Pugh Email: tim.pugh@blplaw.com
Parliamentary Counsel: Daniel Greenberg Email: daniel.greenberg@blplaw.com

Bircham Dyson Bell LLP

50 Broadway, London SW1H 0BL
Tel: 020 7227 7000
Email: enquirieslondon@bdb-law.co.uk Website:www.bdb-law.co.uk Twitter: @BDB_Law
Parliamentary Agents: Ian McCulloch, Paul Thompson, Nicholas Brown
Head of Public Policy: Jonathan Bracken 020 7783 3408 Email: jonathanbracken@bdb-law.co.uk

Eversheds LLP

One Wood Street, London EC2V 7WS
Tel: 0845 497 9797 Fax: 0845 497 4919
Email: monicapeto@eversheds.com Website:www.eversheds.com Twitter: @eversheds
Parliamentary Agents:
Joe Durkin Email: joedurkin@eversheds.com
Stephen Collings Email: stephencollings@eversheds.com
Monica Peto Email: monicapeto@eversheds.com

Sharpe Pritchard

Elizabeth House, Fulwood Place, London WC1V 6HG
Tel: 020 7405 4600
Email: alewis@sharpepritchard.co.uk Website:www.sharpepritchard.co.uk
Partner and Parliamentary Agent: Alastair Lewis 020 7405 4600 Email: alewis@sharpepritchard.co.uk

Veale Wasbrough Vizards

Barnards Inn, 86 Fetter Lane, London EC4A 1AD
Tel: 020 7405 1234 Fax: 020 7405 4171
Website:www.vwv.co.uk Twitter: @vwvlawfirm
Partner: Ronald Perry Email: rperry@vwv.co.uk

Winckworth Sherwood

Minerva House, 5 Montague Close, London SE1 9BB
Tel: 020 7593 5000 Fax: 020 7593 5099
Email: agorlov@wslaw.co.uk Website:www.wslaw.co.uk Twitter: @ws_law
Parliamentary Agents: Paul Irving, Alison Gorlov, Chris Vine, Stephen Wiggs

DEVOLVED PARLIAMENT AND ASSEMBLIES

Salaries
From 1 April 2013

Scottish Parliament

	Ministerial £	Total Ministerial salary (including MSP's salary of £58,097) £
First Minister	84,160	142,257
Cabinet Secretary	43,660	101,757
Minister	27,348	85,445
Presiding Officer	43,660	101,757
Deputy Presiding Officer	27,348	85,445
Lord Advocate	57,038	115,135
Solicitor General	41,246	99,343

The annual salary for an MSP who holds a dual mandate is £19,366.

National Assembly for Wales

	Ministerial £	Total salary (including AM's salary of £53,852) £
First Minister	80,870	134,722
Cabinet Minister	41,949	95,801
Deputy Minister	26,385	80,237
Leader of the Opposition	41,949	95,801
Presiding Officer	41,949	95,801
Deputy Presiding Officer	26,385	80,237

It was decided in November 2010 to freeze salaries at their current level until 2015.

Northern Ireland Assembly

	Ministerial £	Total salary (including MLA's salary of £48,000) £
First Minister	72,000	120,000
Deputy First Minister	72,000	120,000
Minister	38,000	86,000
Junior Minister	12,000/ 14,710*	60,000/ 62,710*
Speaker	44,000	92,000
Principal Deputy Speaker	9,000	57,000
Deputy Speaker	9,000	57,000

MLAs who draw a salary from Westminster, as an MP, are not paid a MLA's salary but may claim an Office Holder's allowance if applicable.

*A Junior Minister who held that office on 1 April 2012.

Scottish Parliament

Scottish Parliament, Edinburgh EH99 1SP
Tel: 0131-348 5000/0800 092 7500 Textphone: 0800 092 7100
Email: sp.info@scottish.parliament.uk Website: www.scottish.parliament.uk Twitter: @scotparl

Scottish Government

Cabinet

First Minister	Rt Hon **Alex Salmond**
Deputy First Minister and Cabinet Secretary for Infrastructure, Investment and Cities	**Nicola Sturgeon**
Cabinet Secretary for Finance, Employment and Sustainable Growth	**John Swinney**
Cabinet Secretary for Health and Wellbeing	**Alex Neil**
Cabinet Secretary for Education and Lifelong Learning	**Michael Russell**
Cabinet Secretary for Justice	**Kenny MacAskill**
Cabinet Secretary for Rural Affairs and Environment	**Richard Lochhead**
Cabinet Secretary for Culture and External Affairs	**Fiona Hyslop**

Also attending Cabinet

Minister for Parliamentary Business	**Joe FitzPatrick**
Lord Advocate	Rt Hon **Frank Mulholland** QC
Solicitor General	**Lesley Thomson** QC

Ministerial Responsibilities and Staff

Office of the First Minister

St Andrew's House, Regent Road, Edinburgh EH1 3DG
Tel: 0131-556 8400
Email: firstminister@scotland.gsi.gov.uk Twitter: @scotgov

First Minister Rt Hon **Alex Salmond** MSP

Head of the devolved Scottish Government; responsible for development, implementation and presentation of Government policy; constitutional affairs, including Referendum Bill; promoting and representing Scotland.

Parliamentary Liaison Officers	Joan McAlpine MSP	0131-348 6885
	Email: joan.mcalpine.msp@scottish.parliament.uk	
	Mark McDonald MSP	0131-348 6522
	Email: mark.mcdonald.msp@scottish.parliament.uk	
Special Advisers	Geoff Aberdein	0131-244 5190
	Email: geoff.aberdein@scotland.gsi.gov.uk	
	Malcolm Fleming	
	Email: malcolm.fleming@scotland.gsi.gov.uk	
	Alexander Anderson	0131-244 3361
	Email: alexander.anderson@scotland.gsi.gov.uk	
Principal Private Secretary	Joe Griffin	0131-244 5218
	Email: firstminister@scotland.gsi.gov.uk	

Minister for Parliamentary Business **Joe FitzPatrick** MSP

(reports to the First Minister and Deputy First Minister) Management of Government's interests in the Parliament; liaison between Ministers and the Parliamentary Group.

Private Secretary	Nicola Dove	0131-348 5572
	Email: nicola.dove@scotland.gsi.gov.uk	

Infrastructure, Investment and Cities
St Andrew's House, Regent Road, Edinburgh EH1 3DG
Tel: 0131-244 1821
Email: dfm@scotland.gsi.gov.uk

Cabinet Secretary for Infrastructure, Investment and Cities (with responsibility for Government Strategy and the Constitution) **Nicola Sturgeon** MSP

Infrastructure and capital investment; transport policy; housing policy; Scottish Water; procurement; European Structural Funds; Scottish Futures Trust; cities strategy; welfare reform; developing Government strategy and co-ordinating policy delivery across portfolios; responsible for constitution policy, including preparations for the Referendum; UK relations; Freedom of Information.

Parliamentary Liaison Officers	Jim Eadie MSP	0131-348 6283
	Email: jim.eadie.msp@scottish.parliament.uk	
	Annabelle Ewing MSP	0131-348 5066
	Email: annabelle.ewing.msp@scottish.parliament.uk	
Special Adviser	Noel Dolan	0131-244 5090
	Email: noel.dolan@scotland.gsi.gov.uk	
Private Secretary	Beth Elliot	0131-244 1821
	Email: dfm@scotland.gsi.gov.uk	

Minister for Transport and Veterans **Keith Brown** MSP

Transport policy; transport delivery; public transport; roads; rail services; air and ferry services; veterans.

Private Secretary	Martyn McDonald	0131-348 5570/0131-244 7005
	Email: ministerfortransportandveterans@scotland.gsi.gov.uk	

Minister for Housing and Welfare **Margaret Burgess** MSP

Housing; communities; anti-poverty measures; welfare.

Private Secretary	Gavin McDougall	0131-244 5027
	Email: ministerforhousingandwelfare@scotland.gsi.gov.uk	

Finance, Employment and Sustainable Growth
St Andrew's House, Regent Road, Edinburgh EH1 3DG
Tel: 0131-244 5227
Email: cabsecfesg@scotland.gsi.gov.uk

Cabinet Secretary for Finance, Employment and Sustainable Growth **John Swinney** MSP

The economy; Scottish Budget; employment; public service reform; deregulation; local government; public service delivery; community planning; Registers of Scotland; Scottish Public Pensions Agency; relocation; e-government; budgetary monitoring; business and industry, including Scottish Enterprise; Highlands and Islands Enterprise; trade and inward investment; corporate social responsibility; voluntary sector and the social economy; community business and co-operative development; energy; renewables; tourism; building standards; land use planning system.

Parliamentary Liaison Officers	Stewart Stevenson MSP	
	Mike Mackenzie MSP	0131-348 5057
	Email: mike.mackenzie.msp@scottish.parliament.uk	

Special Advisers
(Energy)

Malcolm Fleming
Email: malcolm.fleming@scotland.gsi.gov.uk

(Finance and Constitution)

Liz Lloyd
Email: liz.lloyd@scotland.gsi.gov.uk

Private Secretary

Gabriella Pieraccini   0131-244 5227
Email: cabsecfesg@scotland.gsi.gov.uk

Minister for Energy, Enterprise and Tourism **Fergus Ewing** MSP

Energy and energy consents; voluntary sector and social economy; Accountant in Bankruptcy; Highlands and Islands Enterprise; Scottish Enterprise; trade and inward investment, including Scottish Development International; business and industry, including manufacturing; Registers of Scotland.

Private Secretary

Kevin Veitch   0131-348 5580
Email: ministereet@scotland.gsi.gov.uk

Minister for Local Government and Planning **Derek Mackay** MSP

Local government; community planning; business improvement; elections; planning; building standards.

Private Secretary

Darren Dickson   0131-244 0402
Email: lgpminister@scotland.gsi.gov.uk

Health and Wellbeing

St Andrew's House, Regent Road, Edinburgh EH1 3DG
Tel: 0131-244 2125 Fax: 0131-244 3563
Email: cabsechealth@scotland.gsi.gov.uk   Twitter: @scotgovhealth

Cabinet Secretary for Health and Wellbeing **Alex Neil** MSP

NHS; health service reform; allied healthcare services; acute and primary services; performance; quality and improvement framework; health promotion; sport; Commonwealth Games; public health; health improvement; pharmaceutical services; food safety; dentistry; community care; older people; mental health; learning disability; carers; Social Care and Social Work Improvement Scotland; substance misuse; social inclusion; equalities.

Parliamentary Liaison Officer

Dr Aileen McLeod MSP   0131-348 5084
Email: aileen.mcleod.msp@scottish.parliament.uk

Special Adviser

David Hutchison   0131-244 4892
Email: david.hutchison@scotland.gsi.gov.uk

Private Secretary

Joni Smith   0131-244 2125
Email: cabsechealth@scotland.gsi.gov.uk

Minister for Commonwealth Games and Sport **Shona Robison** MSP

Sport; Commonwealth Games; obesity; physical activity; equalities.

Private Secretary

Gemma Park   0131-244 2186
Email:
ministerforcommonwealthgamesandsport@scotland.gsi.gov.uk

Minister for Public Health **Michael Matheson** MSP

Public health; health protection; dentistry; healthy working lives; sexual health; child and maternal health; medical records; adult care and support; drug misuse; social inclusion.

Private Secretary

Laura Hitchings   0131-244 5539
Email: ministerforpublichealth2@scotland.gsi.gov.uk

Education and Lifelong Learning

St Andrew's House, Regent Road, Edinburgh EH1 3DG
Tel: 0131-556 8400
Email: cabsecell@scotland.gsi.gov.uk

Cabinet Secretary for Education and Lifelong Learning **Michael Russell** MSP

Further and higher education; science and lifelong learning; school education; early years; training and skills; Education Scotland; Scottish Qualifications Authority; nurseries and childcare; children's services; children's hearings; social work; youth employment; Gaelic and Scots.

Parliamentary Liaison Officer	George Adam MSP	0131-348 5869
	Email: george.adam.msp@scottish.parliament.uk	
Special Adviser	Colin McAllister	0131-244 3248
	Email: colin.mcallister@scotland.gsi.gov.uk	
Private Secretary	Ellen MacKinnon	0131-244 1556
	Email: cabsecell@scotland.gsi.gov.uk	

Minister for Children and Young People **Aileen Campbell** MSP

Social Services workforce; early years/early intervention; protection of vulnerable groups; child protection; adoption and fostering; Kerelaw and historic abuse.

Private Secretary	Lauren Drummond	0131-244 0953
	Email: ministerforchildrenandyoungpeople@scotland.gsi.gov.uk	

Minister for Learning, Science and Scotland's Languages Dr **Alasdair Allan** MSP

Gaelic and Scots; modern languages and scottish studies; Scottish Education Quality and Improvement Agency; Scottish Qualifications Authority; behaviour; bullying; skills strategy; non-advanced vocational skills.

Private Secretary	Grant Moncur	0131-244 1469
	Email: minforlssl@scotland.gsi.gov.uk	

Minister for Youth Employment **Angela Constance** MSP

Employability for 16-24 year olds; ministerial oversight of Skills Development Scotland activity; engagement with employers and employer bodies on youth employment; engagement with DWP, third sector bodies and local authorities on support for young people; co-ordinating cross-government activity to support young people into work.

Parliamentary Liaison Officer	Gordon MacDonald MSP	0131-348 5741
	Email: gordon.macdonald.msp@scottish.parliament.uk	
Private Secretary	Jill Rosie	0131-244 7821
	Email: ministerforyouthemployment@scotland.gsi.gov.uk	

Justice

St Andrew's House, Regent Road, Edinburgh EH1 3DG
Tel: 0131-556 8400
Email: cabinetsecretaryforjustice@scotland.gsi.gov.uk

Cabinet Secretary for Justice **Kenny MacAskill** MSP

Criminal law and procedure; youth justice; criminal justice social work; police; prisons and sentencing policy; legal aid; legal profession; courts and law reform; fire and rescue services; civil contingencies; liquor licensing; vulnerable witnesses; victim support; life sentence prisoner casework; reducing reoffending; cashback.

Parliamentary Liaison Officer	Sandra White MSP	0131-348 5688 Fax: 0131-348 5945
	Email: sandra.white.msp@scottish.parliament.uk	
Private Secretary	Saira Kapasi	0131-244 5147
	Email: cabinetsecretaryforjustice@scotland.gsi.gov.uk	

Minister for Community Safety and Legal Affairs **Roseanna Cunningham** MSP

Community safety and anti-social behaviour; sectarianism; violence; human rights; drugs; civil law; charity law; fire and rescue; religious and faith organisations; tribunals and administrative justice; arbitration; law reform arbitration.

Private Secretary	Alison Dewar	0131-244 4579
	Email:	
	ministerforcommunitysafetyandlegalaffairs@scotland.gsi.gov.uk	

Rural Affairs and Environment

St Andrew's House, Regent Road, Edinburgh EH1 3DG
Tel: 0131-556 8400
Email: cabsecrae@scotland.gsi.gov.uk ministerforenvironment@scotland.gsi.gov.uk

Cabinet Secretary for Rural Affairs and Environment **Richard Lochhead** MSP

Agriculture; marine; rural development; food and drink; fisheries; environment; forestry; natural heritage; water quality regulation; sustainable development and rural communitites; waste.

Parliamentary Liaison Officer	Angus MacDonald MSP	0131-348 5489 Fax: 0131-348 5677
	Email: angus.macdonald.msp@scottish.parliament.uk	
Special Adviser		
(Rural affairs and environment)	Malcolm Fleming	0131-244 2338
	Email: malcolm.fleming@scotland.gsi.gov.uk	
Private Secretary	John Davidson	0131-244 4456
	Email: john.davidson@scotland.gsi.gov.uk	

Minister for Environment and Climate Change **Paul Wheelhouse** MSP

Forestry Commission Scotland; biodiversity; crofting; national parks; environmental justice; flooding; Scottish Natural Heritage; Scottish Environment Protection Agency; aquaculture; climate change; land reform.

Private Secretary	Marissa Gallagher	0131-244 4425
	Email: marissa.gallagher@scotland.gsi.gov.uk	

Culture and External Affairs

St Andrew's House, Regent Road, Edinburgh EH1 3DG
Tel: 0131-244 7716/0131-244 0627
Email: cabseccea@scotland.gsi.gov.uk mea@scotland.gsi.gov.uk

Cabinet Secretary for Culture and External Affairs **Fiona Hyslop** MSP

Europe; external affairs; culture and the arts; broadcasting; architecture; built heritage; Historic Scotland and lottery funding; National Records of Scotland; major events strategy; digital participation.

Parliamentary Liaison Officer	Clare Adamson MSP	0131-348 6377
	Email: clare.adamson.msp@scottish.parliament.uk	
Special Adviser	Alexander Anderson	0131-244 3361
	Email: alexander.anderson@scotland.gsi.gov.uk	
Private Secretary	Caroline Mair	0131-244 7716
	Email: cabseccea@scotland.gsi.gov.uk	

Minister for External Affairs and International Development **Humza Yousaf** MSP

Europe; external affairs; international development; culture and the arts; broadcasting; architecture; built heritage; Historic Scotland and lottery funding; National Records of Scotland; major events strategy.

Private Secretary   Billy Wright   0131-244 4820
Email: mea@scotland.gsi.gov.uk

Whips

Chief Whip	**Bill Kidd**
Depute Whips	**Graeme Dey**
	James Dornan
	Fiona McLeod

Opposition

Scottish Labour

Shadow Cabinet

Leader	**Johann Lamont**
Parliamentary Business Manager	**Paul Martin**
Chief Whip	**Lewis Macdonald**
Shadow Cabinet Secretary for Finance, Employment and Sustainable Growth	**Iain Gray**
Shadow Cabinet Secretary for Health and Wellbeing	**Neil Findlay**
Shadow Cabinet Secretary for Education and Lifelong Learning	**Kezia Dugdale**
Shadow Cabinet Secretary for Local Government and Planning	**Sarah Boyack**
Shadow Cabinet Secretary for Infrastructure, Investment and Cities	**James Kelly**
Shadow Cabinet Secretary for Social Justice, Equalities and Welfare	**Jackie Baillie**
Shadow Cabinet Secretary for Justice	**Graeme Pearson**
Shadow Cabinet Secretary for Rural Affairs and Environment	**Claire Baker**
Shadow Cabinet Secretary for Culture, Sport and External Affairs	**Patricia Ferguson**
Shadow Cabinet Secretary for Constitution	**Drew Smith**
Shadow Minister for Youth Employment and Deputy Minister for Finance	**Jenny Marra**

Party Deputy Leader, Anas Sarwar MP, and Shadow Secretary of State for Scotland, Margaret Curran MP, also attend Shadow Cabinet meetings.

Shadow Ministers

Shadow Minister for Wellbeing	**Rhoda Grant**
Shadow Minister for Public Health	Dr **Richard Simpson**
Shadow Deputy Minister for Education	**Neil Bibby**
Shadow Minister for Children and Young People	**Jayne Baxter**
Shadow Minister for Transport and Veterans	**Mark Griffin**
Shadow Minister for Housing	**Mary Fee**

Shadow Minister for Community Safety and Legal Affairs	Dr **Elaine Murray**
Shadow Minister for Environment and Climate Change	**Claudia Beamish**
Deputy Whips	**Margaret McCulloch** **John Pentland**

Scottish Conservatives

Leader	**Ruth Davidson**
Deputy Leader; Spokesperson for Health	**Jackson Carlaw**
Chief Whip and Business Manager	**John Lamont**
Spokesperson for Finance, Employment and Sustainable Growth	**Gavin Brown**
Spokesperson for Justice	**Margaret Mitchell**
Spokesperson for Education and Lifelong Learning	**Mary Scanlon**
Spokesperson for Enterprise, Energy and Tourism	**Murdo Fraser**
Spokesperson for Culture, Sport and Young People	**Elizabeth Smith**
Spokesperson for Rural Affairs	Rt Hon **Alex Fergusson**
Spokesperson for Constitution	**Annabel Goldie**
Spokesperson for Local Government and Planning	**Cameron Buchanan**
Spokesperson for Environment, Fishing and External Affairs	Sir **Jamie McGrigor**
Spokesperson for Infrastructure, Capital Investment, Housing and Transport	**Alex Johnstone**
Spokesperson for Public Health	**Nanette Milne**

Scottish Liberal Democrats

Leader; Spokesperson for Economy, Business and Infrastructure	**Willie Rennie**
Spokesperson for Justice; Business Manager	**Alison McInnes** OBE
Spokesperson for Health and Housing	**Jim Hume**
Spokesperson for Transport, Rural Affairs, Fisheries, Environment and Sport	**Tavish Scott**
Spokesperson for Energy, Young People and Education	**Liam McArthur**

Members (MSPs)

State of the Parties (September 2013)

	Constituency	Regional	Total
Scottish National Party	51*	14	65
Scottish Labour Party	15†	22	37
(includes Scottish Labour/Co-operative Party)			
Scottish Conservative and Unionist Party	3†	12	15
Scottish Liberal Democrats	2	3	5
Independent	0	3	3
Scottish Green Party	0	2	2
Presiding Officer	1	0	1
	72‡	56	128 seats‡

* Excludes the Presiding Officer who has no party allegiance while in post.
† Includes a deputy Presiding Officer who can participate and vote fully in the Parliament when not in the chair.
‡ By-election pending in Dunfermline.

Changes since 2011 Scottish Parliament election

RESIGNATIONS

John Park	Mid Scotland and Fife – *Lab*	8 December 2012
Mark McDonald	North East Scotland – *SNP*	14 May 2013
Bill Walker	Dunfermline – *Ind*	9 September 2013

DEATHS

Brian Adam	Aberdeen Donside – *SNP*	25 April 2013
David McLetchie	Lothian – *Con*	12 August 2013

REPLACEMENTS

Jayne Baxter	Mid Scotland and Fife – *Lab*	Returned 11 December 2012 following the resignation of John Park
Christian Allard	North East Scotland – *SNP*	Returned 15 May 2013 following the resignation of Mark McDonald
Cameron Buchanan	Lothian – *Con*	Returned 4 September 2013 following the death of David McLetchie

CHANGE OF PARTY

John Finnie	Highlands and Islands	Resigned SNP Whip October 2012, now Independent
Jean Urquhart	Highlands and Islands	Resigned SNP Whip October 2012, now Independent

BY-ELECTION

ABERDEEN DONSIDE

20 June 2013 due to the death of the Scottish National Party MSP Brian Adam

SNP	Mark McDonald	9,814
Lab	Willie Young	7,789
Lib Dem	Christine Jardine	1,940
Con	Ross Thomson	1,791

UKIP Otto Inglis 1,128, *Green* Rhonda Reekie 410, *NF* David MacDonald 249, *SCP* Tom Morrow 222, *SDA* James Trolland 35

SNP majority 2,025 – SNP hold (9.1% from SNP to Lab)
Electorate 60,242 – Total vote 23,396 – Turnout 38.84%

MSPs' Directory

Con	Conservative
Green	Green Party
Ind	Independent
Lab	Labour
Lab/Co-op	Labour/Co-operative
Lib Dem	Liberal Democrat
Pres Off	Presiding Officer
SNP	Scottish National Party

ADAM, George   *SNP*   **Paisley**
Parliamentary Liaison Officer to Michael Russell as Cabinet Secretary for Education and Lifelong Learning
Tel: 0131-348 5869 Email: george.adam.msp@scottish.parliament.uk
Constituency office: 4 Johnston Street, Paisley PA1 1XG
Tel: 0141-887 8075
Website: www.paisleysmsp.org Twitter: @georgeadam

ADAMSON, Clare   *SNP*   **Central Scotland**
Parliamentary Liaison Officer to Fiona Hyslop as Cabinet Secretary for Culture and External Affairs
Tel: 0131-348 6377 Email: clare.adamson.msp@scottish.parliament.uk
Regional office: Unit 19, Enterprise House, Dalziel Street, Motherwell ML1 1PJ
Tel: 01698 337540 Fax: 01698 337450
Website: www.clareadamsonmsp.com Twitter: @clareadamsonmsp

ALLAN, Dr Alasdair   *SNP*   **Na h-Eileanan an Iar**
Minister for Learning, Science and Scotland's Languages
Email: alasdair.allan.msp@scottish.parliament.uk
Ministerial office: Education and Lifelong Learning, St Andrew's House, Regent Road, Edinburgh EH1 3DG Switchboard: 0131-556 8400
Constituency office: 31 Bayhead, Stornoway, Isle of Lewis HS1 2DU
Tel: 01851 702272 Fax: 01851 701767
Website: www.alasdairallanmsp.net Twitter: @alasdairallan

ALLARD, Christian   *SNP*   **North East Scotland**
Tel: 0131-348 5764 Email: christian.allard.msp@scottish.parliament.uk
Regional office: 84 North Street, Inverurie AB51 4QX
Tel: 01467 625404 Twitter: @Christia_Allard

BAILLIE, Jackie   *Lab*   **Dumbarton**
Scottish Labour Shadow Cabinet Secretary for Social Justice, Equalities and Welfare
Tel: 0131-348 5905 Fax: 0131-348 5986 Email: jackie.baillie.msp@scottish.parliament.uk
Constituency office: 11 Castle Street, Dumbarton G82 1QS
Tel: 01389 734214 Fax: 01389 761498
Website: www.jackiebaillie.co.uk Twitter: @jackiebmsp

BAKER, Claire   *Lab*   **Mid Scotland and Fife**
Scottish Labour Shadow Cabinet Secretary for Rural Affairs and Environment
Tel: 0131-348 6769 Fax: 0131-348 6761 Email: claire.baker.msp@scottish.parliament.uk
Regional office: Carlyle House, Carlyle Road, Kirkcaldy KY1 1DB
Tel: 01592 568678 Fax: 01592 566401 Email: claire-baker@live.co.uk
Website: www.clairebaker.org Twitter: @clairebakermsp

BAKER, Richard   *Lab*   **North East Scotland**
Tel: 0131-348 5916 Fax: 0131-348 5979 Email: richard.baker.msp@scottish.parliament.uk
Regional office: 80 Rosemount Place, Aberdeen AB25 2XN
Tel: 01224 641171 Fax: 01224 645450
Website: www.richardbakermsp.org.uk

BAXTER, Jayne *Lab*   **Mid Scotland and Fife**
Scottish Labour Shadow Minister for Children and Young People
Tel: 0131-348 6753 Fax: 0131-348 6755 Email: jayne.baxter.msp@scottish.parliament.uk
Regional office: Carlyle House, Carlyle Road, Kirkcaldy, Fife KY1 1DB
Tel: 01592 568678 Fax: 01592 566401
Website: www.jaynebaxter.org Twitter: @jayniebax

BEAMISH, Claudia *Lab/Co-op*   **South Scotland**
Scottish Labour Shadow Minister for Environment and Climate Change
Tel: 0131-348 6889 Fax: 0131-348 5978 Email: claudia.beamish.msp@scottish.parliament.uk
Regional office: 12 St Vincent Place, Lanark ML11 7LA
Tel: 01555 664065
Website: www.claudiabeamish.com Twitter: @claudiabeamish

BEATTIE, Colin *SNP*   **Midlothian North and Musselburgh**
Tel: 0131-348 6374 Fax: 0131-348 6280 Email: colin.beattie.msp@scottish.parliament.uk
Constituency office: 164 High Street, Dalkeith EH22 1AY
Tel: 0131-454 0204
Website: colinbeattiemsp.org Twitter: @uartlach

BIAGI, Marco *SNP*   **Edinburgh Central**
Tel: 0131-348 6482 Email: marco.biagi.msp@scottish.parliament.uk
Constituency office: 77 Buccleuch Street, Edinburgh EH8 9LS
Tel: 0131-668 3642 Twitter: @marcobiagimsp

BIBBY, Neil *Lab*   **West Scotland**
Scottish Labour Shadow Deputy Minister for Education
Tel: 0131-348 6385 Email: neil.bibby.msp@scottish.parliament.uk
Regional office: 4 St Mirren Street, Paisley PA1 1UA
Tel: 0141-889 0457 Fax: 0141-840 2510 Email: contact@neilbibby.com
Website: www.neilbibby.com Twitter: @neilbibby

BOYACK, Sarah *Lab*   **Lothian**
Scottish Labour Shadow Cabinet Secretary for Local Government and Planning
Tel: 0131-348 5751 Email: sarah.boyack.msp@scottish.parliament.uk
Regional office: No regional office
Website: www.sarahboyack.com Twitter: @sarahboyackmsp

BRODIE, Chic *SNP*   **South Scotland**
Tel: 0131-348 6882 Email: chic.brodie.msp@scottish.parliament.uk
Regional office: 8 Sandbed, Hawick, Roxburghshire TD9 0HE
Tel: 01450 379572 Email: cbrodie@calstrat.freeserve.co.uk Twitter: @chicbrodiemsp

BROWN, Gavin *Con*   **Lothian**
Scottish Conservatives Spokesperson for Finance, Employment and Sustainable Growth
Tel: 0131-348 6931 Fax: 0131-348 5935 Email: gavin.brown.msp@scottish.parliament.uk
Regional office: 13 Mentone Gardens, Edinburgh EH9 2DJ
Tel: 0131-662 8577 Email: info@gavinbrown.org
Website: www.gavinbrown.org

BROWN, Keith *SNP*   **Clackmannanshire and Dunblane**
Minister for Transport and Veterans
Email: keith.brown.msp@scottish.parliament.uk
Ministerial office: Infrastructure, Investment and Cities, St Andrew's House, Regent Road,
Edinburgh EH1 3DG Switchboard: 0131-244 1821
Constituency office: Unit 4, Townhead Institute, 39 Drysdale Street, Alloa FK10 1JA
Tel: 01259 219333 Twitter: @keithbrownmsp

BUCHANAN, Cameron *Con*   **Lothian**
Scottish Conservatives Spokesperson for Local Government and Planning
Email: cameron.buchanan.msp@scottish.parliament.uk
Regional office: Currently being set up

BURGESS, Margaret *SNP*   **Cunninghame South**
Minister for Housing and Welfare
Email: margaret.burgess.msp@scottish.parliament.uk
Ministerial office: Infrastructure, Investment and Cities, St Andrew's House, Regent Road,
Edinburgh EH1 3DG Switchboard: 0131-244 1821
Constituency office: 14 Eglinton Street, Irvine KA12 8AS
Tel: 01294 276730
Website: margaretburgessmsp.org Twitter: @mgtburgessmsp

CAMPBELL, Aileen *SNP*   **Clydesdale**
Minister for Children and Young People
Tel: 0131-348 6707 Fax: 0131-348 6709 Email: aileen.campbell.msp@scottish.parliament.uk
Ministerial office: Education and Lifelong Learning, St Andrew's House, Regent Road,
Edinburgh EH1 3DG Switchboard: 0131-556 8400
Constituency office: Room 9, Kirkton Chambers, 12 Kirkton Street, Carluke ML8 4AB
Tel: 01555 750249 Fax: 01555 750249
Website: www.aileencampbell.com Twitter: @clydesdaileen

CAMPBELL, Roderick *SNP*   **North East Fife**
Tel: 0131-348 6524 Email: roderick.campbell.msp@scottish.parliament.uk
Constituency office: Unit F1, The Granary Business Centre, Coal Road, Cupar, Fife KY15 5YQ
Tel: 01334 844971
Website: roderickcampbell.org Twitter: @RCampbellMSP

CARLAW, Jackson *Con*   **West Scotland**
Deputy Leader, Scottish Conservative and Unionist Party; Scottish Conservatives Spokesperson for
Health
Tel: 0131-348 6800 Fax: 0131-348 6803 Email: jackson.carlaw.msp@scottish.parliament.uk
Regional office: 69 Ayr Road, Newton Mearns, Glasgow G77 6SP
Tel: 0141-639 8929
Website: www.jacksoncarlawmsp.com Twitter: @jacksonmsp

CHISHOLM, Malcolm *Lab*   **Edinburgh Northern and Leith**
Tel: 0131-348 5908 Fax: 0131-348 5974 Email: malcolm.chisholm.msp@scottish.parliament.uk
Constituency office: 5 Croall Place, Leith Walk, Edinburgh EH7 4LT
Tel: 0131-558 8358 Fax: 0131-557 6781 Email: malcolm.chisholm@hotmail.com
Website: www.malcolmchisholm.org.uk Twitter: @malcolmchisholl

COFFEY, Willie *SNP*   **Kilmarnock and Irvine Valley**
Tel: 0131-348 6515 Fax: 0131-348 6517 Email: willie.coffey.msp@scottish.parliament.uk
Constituency office: 53 Titchfield Street, Kilmarnock KA1 1QS
Tel: 01563 537300 Fax: 01563 537300 Email: willie.coffey@msp-office.co.uk

CONSTANCE, Angela *SNP*   **Almond Valley**
Minister for Youth Employment
Email: angela.constance.msp@scottish.parliament.uk
Ministerial office: Education and Lifelong Learning, St Andrew's House, Regent Road,
Edinburgh EH1 3DG Switchboard: 0131-556 8400
Constituency office: Unit 5, Ochil House, Owen Square, Livingston EH54 6PW
Tel: 01506 460403
Website: www.angelaconstancemsp.org Twitter: @aconstancemsp

CRAWFORD, Bruce *SNP* **Stirling**
Tel: 0131-348 5687 Email: bruce.crawford.msp@scottish.parliament.uk
Constituency office: Suite 3:3, Wallace House, Maxwell Place, Stirling FK8 1JU
Tel: 01786 471899
Website: www.brucecrawfordmsp.org Twitter: @rhbrucecrawford

CUNNINGHAM, Roseanna *SNP* **Perthshire South and Kinross-shire**
Minister for Community Safety and Legal Affairs
Tel: 0131-348 5697 Fax: 0131-348 5563 Email: roseanna.cunningham.msp@scottish.parliament.uk
Ministerial office: Justice, St Andrew's House, Regent Road, Edinburgh EH1 3DG
Switchboard: 0131-556 8400
Constituency office: 9 York Place, Perth PH2 8EP
Tel: 01738 639598 Fax: 01738 587637
Website: www.roseannacunningham.com Twitter: @strathearnrose

DAVIDSON, Ruth *Con* **Glasgow**
Leader, Scottish Conservative and Unionist Party
Tel: 0131-348 6370 Email: ruth.davidson.msp@scottish.parliament.uk
Regional office: 1373 Argyle Street, Glasgow G3 8AF
Tel: 0141-357 2739 Twitter: @ruthdavidsonmsp

DEY, Graeme *SNP* **Angus South**
SNP Depute Whip
Tel: 0131-348 6292 Email: graeme.dey.msp@scottish.parliament.uk
Constituency office: 282-284 High Street, Arbroath, Angus DD11 1JF
Tel: 01241 873058
Website: www.graemedeymsp.co.uk

DON, Nigel *SNP* **Angus North and Mearns**
Tel: 0131-348 5996 Fax: 0131-348 6998 Email: nigel.don.msp@scottish.parliament.uk
Constituency office: 6a Cameron Street, Stonehaven AB39 2BL
Tel: 01569 767206 Email: nigel@nigeldon.com
Website: www.nigeldon.com

DORIS, Bob *SNP* **Glasgow**
Tel: 0131-348 6547 Fax: 0131-348 6549 Email: bob.doris.msp@scottish.parliament.uk
Regional office: Third Floor, Empire House, 131 West Nile Street, Glasgow G1 2RX
Tel: 0141-353 0784
Website: www.bobdoris.com Twitter: @glasgowmsp

DORNAN, James *SNP* **Glasgow Cathcart**
SNP Depute Whip
Tel: 0131-348 5683 Email: james.dornan.msp@scottish.parliament.uk
Constituency office: 4 Kings Park Road, Glasgow G44 4TU
Tel: 0141-632 5238
Website: www.jamesdornanmsp.org Twitter: @glasgowcathcart

DUGDALE, Kezia *Lab/Co-op* **Lothian**
Scottish Labour Shadow Cabinet Secretary for Education and Lifelong Learning
Tel: 0131-348 6894 Email: kezia.dugdale.msp@scottish.parliament.uk
Regional office: No regional office
Website: www.keziadugdale.com Twitter: @kdugdalemsp

EADIE, Helen *Lab/Co-op* **Cowdenbeath**
Tel: 0131-348 5749 Fax: 0131-348 6948 Email: helen.eadie.msp@scottish.parliament.uk
Constituency office: 25 Church Street, Inverkeithing, Fife KY11 1LG
Tel: 01383 412856 Fax: 01383 412855
Website: heleneadie.wordpress.com Twitter: @heleneadie007

EADIE, Jim *SNP*   **Edinburgh Southern**
Parliamentary Liaison Officer to Nicola Sturgeon as Deputy First Minister and Cabinet Secretary for
Infrastructure, Investment and Cities
Tel: 0131-348 6283 Email: jim.eadie.msp@scottish.parliament.uk
Constituency office: 13-15 Morningside Drive, Edinburgh EH10 5NX
Tel: 0131-466 5950

EWING, Annabelle *SNP*   **Mid Scotland and Fife**
Parliamentary Liaison Officer to Nicola Sturgeon as Deputy First Minister and Cabinet Secretary for
Infrastructure, Investment and Cities
Tel: 0131-348 5066 Email: annabelle.ewing.msp@scottish.parliament.uk
Regional office: 113 High Street, Cowdenbeath KY4 9QA
Tel: 01383 611067

EWING, Fergus *SNP*   **Inverness and Nairn**
Minister for Energy, Enterprise and Tourism
Tel: 0131-348 5732 Email: fergus.ewing.msp@scottish.parliament.uk
Ministerial office: Finance, Employment and Sustainable Growth, St Andrew's House, Regent Road,
Edinburgh EH1 3DG Switchboard: 0131-244 5227
Constituency office: Highland Rail House, Station Square, Inverness IV1 1LE
Tel: 01463 713004 Email: fergus@fergusewing.com
Website: www.fergusewing.com Twitter: @fergusewingmsp

FABIANI, Linda *SNP*   **East Kilbride**
Tel: 0131-348 5698 Fax: 0131-348 6473 Email: linda.fabiani.msp@scottish.parliament.uk
Constituency office: 1/3 Strathmore House, East Kilbride G74 1LF
Tel: 01355 232800 Fax: 01355 232770
Website: www.lindafabiani.co.uk Twitter: @lindafabianisnp

FEE, Mary *Lab*   **West Scotland**
Scottish Labour Shadow Minister for Housing
Tel: 0131-348 6391 Email: mary.fee.msp@scottish.parliament.uk
Regional office: 4 St Mirren Street, Paisley PA1 1UA
Tel: 0141-889 4828 Fax: 0141-840 2510
Website: maryfeemsp.com Twitter: @maryfeemsp

FERGUSON, Patricia *Lab*   **Glasgow Maryhill and Springburn**
Scottish Labour Shadow Cabinet Secretary for Culture, Sport and External Affairs
Fax: 0131-348 5925 Email: patricia.ferguson.msp@scottish.parliament.uk
Constituency office: 43 Atlas Road, Glasgow G21 4TA
Tel: 0141-558 9483
Website: www.patriciaferguson.labour.co.uk

FERGUSSON, Rt Hon Alex *Con*   **Galloway and West Dumfries**
Scottish Conservatives Spokesperson for Rural Affairs
Tel: 0131-348 5638 Fax: 0131-348 5932 Email: alex.fergusson.msp@scottish.parliament.uk
Constituency office: Constituency Office, New Market Street, Castle Douglas DG7 1HY
Tel: 01556 504991 Fax: 01556 503059
Website: www.alexfergusson.org.uk

FINDLAY, Neil *Lab*   **Lothian**
Scottish Labour Shadow Cabinet Secretary for Health and Wellbeing
Tel: 0131-348 6896 Email: neil.findlay.msp@scottish.parliament.uk
Regional office: 4 Northfield Court, West Calder EH55 8DS
Tel: 01506 873242
Website: www.neilfindlaymsp.com Twitter: @neil_findlaymsp

FINNIE, John *Ind* **Highlands and Islands**
Tel: 0131-348 6898 Email: john.finnie.msp@scottish.parliament.uk
Regional office: Second Floor, Highland Railhouse, Station Square, Inverness IV1 1LE
Website: johnfinniemsp.org Twitter: @johnfinniemsp

FitzPATRICK, Joe *SNP* **Dundee City West**
Minister for Parliamentary Business
Email: parliament@joefitzpatrick.net
Ministerial office: Office of the First Minister, St Andrew's House, Regent Road, Edinburgh EH1 3DG
Switchboard: 0131-556 8400
Constituency office: 8 Old Glamis Road, Dundee DD3 8HP
Tel: 01382 623200 Fax: 01382 903205 Email: dundee@joefitzpatrick.net
Website: www.joefitzpatrick.net Twitter: @joefitzsnp

FRASER, Murdo *Con* **Mid Scotland and Fife**
Scottish Conservatives Spokesperson for Enterprise, Energy and Tourism
Tel: 0131-348 5293 Fax: 0131-348 5933 Email: murdo.fraser.msp@scottish.parliament.uk
Regional office: Control Tower, Perth Airport, Scone, Perth PH2 6PL
Tel: 01738 553990 Fax: 01738 553967 Email: pkconservatives@gmail.com
Website: www.murdofraser.com Twitter: @murdo_fraser

GIBSON, Kenneth *SNP* **Cunninghame North**
Tel: 0131-348 6536 Fax: 0131-348 6539 Email: kenneth.gibson.msp@scottish.parliament.uk
Constituency office: 15 Main Street, Dalry KA24 5DL
Tel: 01294 833687

GIBSON, Rob *SNP* **Caithness, Sutherland and Ross**
Tel: 0131-348 5726 Fax: 0131-348 5943 Email: rob.gibson.msp@scottish.parliament.uk
Constituency office: 4 Grant Street, Wick, Caithness KW1 5AY
Tel: 01955 605016 Fax: 01955 604963 Email: niall.macdonald@scottish.parliament.uk
Website: www.robgibson.org Twitter: @robgibsonmsp

GOLDIE, Annabel *Con* **West Scotland**
Scottish Conservatives Spokesperson for Constitution
Tel: 0131-348 5662 Fax: 0131-348 5937 Email: annabel.goldie.msp@scottish.parliament.uk
Regional office: Upper Floor, 10 Shuttle Street, Paisley PA1 1YD
Tel: 0141-887 6161 Fax: 0141-889 0223

GRAHAME, Christine *SNP* **Midlothian South, Tweeddale and Lauderdale**
Tel: 0131-348 5729 Fax: 0131-348 5954 Email: christine.grahame.msp@scottish.parliament.uk
Constituency office: 69 Bank Street, Galashiels TD1 1EL
Tel: 01896 759575
Website: www.christinegrahame.com

GRANT, Rhoda *Lab* **Highlands and Islands**
Scottish Labour Shadow Minister for Wellbeing
Tel: 0131-348 5766 Fax: 0131-348 5767 Email: rhoda.grant.msp@scottish.parliament.uk
Regional office: Queensgate Business Centre, 1-3 Fraser Street, Inverness IV1 1DW
Tel: 01463 716299 Fax: 01463 716572
Website: www.rhodagrant.org.uk Twitter: @rhodagrant

GRAY, Iain *Lab* **East Lothian**
Scottish Labour Shadow Cabinet Secretary for Finance, Employment and Sustainable Growth
Tel: 0131-348 5839 Fax: 0131-348 6359 Email: iain.gray.msp@scottish.parliament.uk
Constituency office: c/o East Lothian Labour Party, 65 High Street, Tranent EH33 1LN
Tel: 01875 616610 Fax: 01875 616610 Email: eastlothianlabour@btconnection.com
Website: www.iaingraymsp.co.uk

GRIFFIN, Mark *Lab* Central Scotland
Scottish Labour Shadow Minister for Transport and Veterans
Tel: 0131-348 6397 Email: mark.griffin.msp@scottish.parliament.uk
Regional office: Unit 32, Coatbridge Business Centre, 204 Main Street, Coatbridge ML5 3RB
Tel: 01236 423555
Website: www.markgriffinmsp.org.uk Twitter: @markgriffinmsp

HARVIE, Patrick *Green* Glasgow
Co-convener, Scottish Green Party
Tel: 0131-348 6363 Fax: 0131-348 5972 Email: patrick.harvie.msp@scottish.parliament.uk
Regional office: Room 4/2, 52 St Enoch Square, Glasgow G1 4AA
Tel: 0141-248 3850
Website: www.patrickharviemsp.com Twitter: @patrickharvie

HENRY, Hugh *Lab* Renfrewshire South
Email: hugh.henry.msp@scottish.parliament.uk
Constituency office: St James Business Centre, Linwood Road, Paisley PA3 3AT
Tel: 0141-848 7361
Website: www.hughhenry.blogspot.com Twitter: @hughhenrymsp

HEPBURN, Jamie *SNP* Cumbernauld and Kilsyth
Tel: 0131-348 6574 Fax: 0131-348 6575 Email: jamie.hepburn.msp@scottish.parliament.uk
Constituency office: 13 The Wynd, Cumbernauld G67 2ST
Tel: 01236 453969 Twitter: @jamiehepburn

HUME, Jim *Lib Dem* South Scotland
Scottish Liberal Democrats Spokesperson for Health and Housing
Tel: 0131-348 6703 Fax: 0131-348 6705 Email: jim.hume.msp@scottish.parliament.uk
Regional office: No regional office
Website: www.jimhume.org Twitter: @jimhumelibdem

HYSLOP, Fiona *SNP* Linlithgow
Cabinet Secretary for Culture and External Affairs
Tel: 0131-348 5921 Email: fiona.hyslop.msp@scottish.parliament.uk
Ministerial office: Culture and External Affairs, St Andrew's House, Regent Road,
Edinburgh EH1 3DG Switchboard: 0131-244 7716
Constituency office: 59 West Main Street, Whitburn, West Lothian EH47 0QD
Tel: 01501 749941 Email: mary.dickson@scottish.parliament.uk
Website: www.fionahyslop.com Twitter: @fionahyslop

INGRAM, Adam *SNP* Carrick, Cumnock and Doon Valley
Tel: 0131-348 5733 Fax: 0131-348 5563 Email: adam.ingram.msp@scottish.parliament.uk
Constituency office: Office 1, 4 The Square, Cumnock KA18 1BG
Tel: 01290 425874
Website: www.adamingrammsp.com

JOHNSTONE, Alex *Con* North East Scotland
Scottish Conservatives Spokesperson for Infrastructure, Capital Investment, Housing and Transport
Tel: 0131-348 5647 Fax: 0131-348 5656 Email: alex.johnstone.msp@scottish.parliament.uk
Regional office: 265a High Street, Arbroath, Angus DD11 1EE
Tel: 01241 430467 Fax: 01241 430476 Email: alex.johnstone@btconnect.com
Website: www.alexjohnstone.msp.org.uk/alex.html

JOHNSTONE, Alison *Green* Lothian
Tel: 0131-348 6364 Email: alison.johnstone.msp@scottish.parliament.uk
Regional office: No regional office
Website: alisonjohnstonemsp.com Twitter: @alisonjohnstone

KEIR, Colin *SNP* **Edinburgh Western**
Tel: 0131-348 5860 Email: colin.keir.msp@scottish.parliament.uk
Constituency office: 14 Featherhall Place, Corstorphine, Edinburgh EH12 7TN
Tel: 0131-334 9926
Website: www.colinkeirmsp.com

KELLY, James *Lab/Co-op* **Rutherglen**
Scottish Labour Shadow Cabinet Secretary for Infrastructure, Investment and Cities
Tel: 0131-348 6510 Fax: 0131-348 6513 Email: james.kelly.msp@scottish.parliament.uk
Constituency office: 51 Stonelaw Road, Rutherglen, South Lanarkshire G73 3TN
Tel: 0141-647 0707 Fax: 0141-643 1491 Twitter: @jamesklabmsp

KIDD, Bill *SNP* **Glasgow Anniesland**
SNP Chief Whip
Tel: 0131-348 5691/0131-348 6593 Fax: 0131-348 5945 Email: bill.kidd.msp@scottish.parliament.uk
Constituency office: Room 116, Anniesland College, 19 Hatfield Drive, Glasgow G12 0YE
Tel: 0141-339 3277

LAMONT, Johann *Lab/Co-op* **Glasgow Pollok**
Leader, Scottish Labour Party; Leader of the Opposition
Tel: 0131-348 5847 Email: johann.lamont.msp@scottish.parliament.uk
Constituency office: Unit 8, The Wedge, 1066 Barrhead Road, Glasgow G53 5AB
Tel: 0141-270 1890 Fax: 0141-270 1891 Email: celine.lauter@scottish.parliament.uk
Website: www.johannlamontmsp.co.uk Twitter: @johannlamont

LAMONT, John *Con* **Ettrick, Roxburgh and Berwickshire**
Scottish Conservatives Chief Whip and Business Manager
Tel: 0131-348 6533 Fax: 0131-348 6534 Email: john.lamont.msp@scottish.parliament.uk
Constituency office: 25 High Street, Hawick TD9 9BU
Tel: 01450 375948 Fax: 01450 379613 Email: john.lamont@scottishconservatives.com
Website: www.johnlamont.org Twitter: @john2win

LOCHHEAD, Richard *SNP* **Moray**
Cabinet Secretary for Rural Affairs and Environment
Tel: 0131-348 5712 Fax: 0131-348 5737 Email: richard.lochhead.msp@scottish.parliament.uk
Ministerial office: Rural Affairs and Environment, St Andrew's House, Regent Road,
Edinburgh EH1 3DG Switchboard: 0131-556 8400
Constituency office: 9 Wards Road, Elgin, Moray IV30 1NL
Tel: 01343 551111 Fax: 01343 556355
Website: www.richardlochhead.org Twitter: @richardlochhead

LYLE, Richard *SNP* **Central Scotland**
Tel: 0131-348 6394 Fax: 0131-348 6798 Email: richard.lyle.msp@scottish.parliament.uk
Regional office: Unit 19, Enterprise House, Dalziel Street, Motherwell ML1 1PJ
Tel: 01698 337541 Fax: 01698 337451 Twitter: @richardlylesnp

McALPINE, Joan *SNP* **South Scotland**
Parliamentary Liaison Officer to Alex Salmond as First Minister
Tel: 0131-348 6885 Email: joan.mcalpine.msp@scottish.parliament.uk
Regional office: Unit 7, Loreburne Shopping Centre, High Street, Dumfries DG1 2BD
Tel: 01387 255334
Website: joanmcalpine.typepad.com Twitter: @joanmcalpine

McARTHUR, Liam *Lib Dem* **Orkney Islands**
Scottish Liberal Democrats Spokesperson for Energy, Young People and Education
Tel: 0131-348 5815 Fax: 0131-348 5807 Email: liam.mcarthur.msp@scottish.parliament.uk
Constituency office: 14 Palace Road, Kirkwall, Orkney KW15 1PA
Tel: 01856 876541 Fax: 01856 876162 Email: msp@msporkney.com
Website: www.liammcarthurmsp.org.uk

MacASKILL, Kenny *SNP* **Edinburgh Eastern**
Cabinet Secretary for Justice
Tel: 0131-348 5012 Fax: 0131-348 5563 Email: kenny.macaskill.msp@scottish.parliament.uk
Ministerial office: Justice, St Andrew's House, Regent Road, Edinburgh EH1 3DG
Switchboard: 0131-556 8400
Constituency office: 16a Willowbrae Road, Edinburgh EH8 7DB
Tel: 0131-661 9546 Fax: 0131-661 9546 Email: kenny.macaskill@edinburghsnp.org
Website: www.kennymacaskill.co.uk Twitter: @kennymacaskill

McCULLOCH, Margaret *Lab* **Central Scotland**
Scottish Labour Deputy Whip
Tel: 0131-348 6381 Email: margaret.mcculloch.msp@scottish.parliament.uk
Regional office: Unit 32, Coatbridge Business Centre, 204 Main Street, Coatbridge ML5 3RB
Tel: 01236 423555
Website: margaretmcculloch.org Twitter: @magmsp

MacDONALD, Angus *SNP* **Falkirk East**
Parliamentary Liaison Officer to Richard Lochhead as Cabinet Secretary for Rural Affairs and
Environment
Tel: 0131-348 5489 Fax: 0131-348 5677 Email: angus.macdonald.msp@scottish.parliament.uk
Constituency office: 2 York Arcade, Grangemouth FK3 8BA
Tel: 01324 482100
Website: www.angusmacdonald.info Twitter: @angus4falkirke

MacDONALD, Gordon *SNP* **Edinburgh Pentlands**
Parliamentary Liaison Officer to Angela Constance as Minister for Youth Employment
Tel: 0131-348 5741 Email: gordon.macdonald.msp@scottish.parliament.uk
Constituency office: 69 Inglis Green Road, Edinburgh EH14 2EZ
Tel: 0131-466 5810
Website: www.gordonmacdonaldmsp.info Twitter: @gmacdonaldmsp

MACDONALD, Lewis *Lab* **North East Scotland**
Scottish Labour Chief Whip
Tel: 0131-348 5915 Fax: 0131-348 5958 Email: lewis.macdonald.msp@scottish.parliament.uk
Regional office: 80 Rosemount Place, Aberdeen AB25 2XN
Tel: 01224 646333 Fax: 01224 645450
Website: www.lewismacdonald.info

MacDONALD, Margo *Ind* **Lothian**
Tel: 0131-348 5714 Fax: 0131-348 6271 Email: margo.macdonald.msp@scottish.parliament.uk
Regional office: No regional office

McDONALD, Mark *SNP* **Aberdeen Donside**
Parliamentary Liaison Officer to Alex Salmond as First Minister
Tel: 0131-348 6522 Email: mark.mcdonald.msp@scottish.parliament.uk
Constituency office: 825-827 Great Northern Road, Aberdeen AB24 2BR
Tel: 01224 789457
Website: www.markmcdonald.org Twitter: @markmcdsnp

McDOUGALL, Margaret *Lab* **West Scotland**
Tel: 0131-348 6426 Email: margaret.mcdougall.msp@scottish.parliament.uk
Regional office: 29a Eglinton Street, Irvine KA12 8AS
Tel: 01294 311976
Website: margaretmcdougallmsp.org Twitter: @margmsp

McGRIGOR, Sir Jamie　*Con*　　　　　　　　　　**Highlands and Islands**
Scottish Conservatives Spokesperson for Environment, Fishing and External Affairs
Tel: 0131-348 5616 Fax: 0131-348 5656 Email: jamie.mcgrigor.msp@scottish.parliament.uk
Regional office: 61 Chalmers Street, Ardrishaig, Argyll PA30 8DX
Tel: 01546 606586 Fax: 01546 605387 Email: douglas.pattullo@scottish.parliament.uk
Website: www.jamiemcgrigormsp.com　Twitter: @jamiemcgrigor

McINNES, Alison, OBE　*Lib Dem*　　　　　　　**North East Scotland**
Scottish Liberal Democrats Spokesperson for Justice; Business Manager
Tel: 0131-348 5463 Fax: 0131-348 5465 Email: alison.mcinnes.msp@scottish.parliament.uk
Regional office: Ellon Business Centre, Broomiesburn Road, Ellon AB41 9RD
Tel: 01358 729962 Fax: 01358 725615
Website: www.alisonmcinnes.co.uk

MACINTOSH, Ken　*Lab*　　　　　　　　　　　　**Eastwood**
Email: ken.macintosh.msp@scottish.parliament.uk
Constituency office: Suite 4/5, 1 Spiersbridge Way, Thornliebank, Glasgow G46 8NG
Tel: 0141-620 6310
Website: www.kenmacintosh.co.uk　Twitter: @kenmacintoshmsp

MACKAY, Derek　*SNP*　　　　　　　　**Renfrewshire North and West**
Minister for Local Government and Planning
Email: derek.mackay.msp@scottish.parliament.uk
Ministerial office: Finance, Employment and Sustainable Growth, St Andrew's House, Regent Road,
Edinburgh EH1 3DG Switchboard: 0131-244 5227
Constituency office: 37 Hairst Street, Renfrew PA4 8QU
Tel: 0141-885 2076
Website: www.therealmackay.org　Twitter: @derekmackaymsp

McKELVIE, Christina　*SNP*　　　　**Hamilton, Larkhall and Stonehouse**
Tel: 0131-348 6680 Fax: 0131-348 6683 Email: christina.mckelvie.msp@scottish.parliament.uk
Constituency office: Barncluith Business Centre, Townhead Street, Hamilton ML3 7DP
Tel: 01698 403311 Fax: 01698 403313
Website: www.christinamckelviemsp.org.uk　Twitter: @christinasnp

MACKENZIE, Mike　*SNP*　　　　　　　　　　**Highlands and Islands**
Parliamentary Liaison Officer to John Swinney as Cabinet Secretary for Finance, Employment and
Sustainable Growth
Tel: 0131-348 5057 Email: mike.mackenzie.msp@scottish.parliament.uk
Regional office: 31 Combie Street, Oban, Argyll PA31 4HS
Tel: 01631 571359　Twitter: @mmackenziesnp

McLEOD, Dr Aileen　*SNP*　　　　　　　　　　**South Scotland**
Parliamentary Liaison Officer to Alex Neil as Cabinet Secretary for Health and Wellbeing
Tel: 0131-348 5084 Email: aileen.mcleod.msp@scottish.parliament.uk
Regional office: Unit 7, Loreburne Shopping Centre, High Street, Dumfries DG1 2BD
Tel: 01387 255334
Website: www.aileenmcleod.org

McLEOD, Fiona　*SNP*　　　　　　　　　**Strathkelvin and Bearsden**
SNP Depute Whip
Tel: 0131-348 5867 Email: fiona.mcleod.msp@scottish.parliament.uk
Constituency office: Suite 13, Enterprise House, Donaldson Street, Kirkintilloch G66 1XQ
Tel: 0141-776 2091
Email: gillian.renwick@scottish.parliament.uk　claire.renwick@scottish.parliament.uk
Website: fionamcleodmsp.com　Twitter: @fionamcleodmsp

McMAHON, Michael *Lab*   **Uddingston and Bellshill**
Tel: 0131-348 5828 Fax: 0131-348 6941 Email: michael.mcmahon.msp@scottish.parliament.uk
Constituency office: 188 Main Street, Bellshill, Lanarkshire ML4 1AE
Tel: 01698 304501 Fax: 01698 300223
Website: michaelmcmahonmsp.snappages.com Twitter: @m_mcmahon_msp

McMAHON, Siobhan *Lab*   **Central Scotland**
Tel: 0131-348 6388 Fax: 0131-348 6949 Email: siobhan.mcmahon.msp@scottish.parliament.uk
Regional office: Unit 32, Coatbridge Business Centre, 204 Main Street, Coatbridge ML5 3RB
Tel: 01236 423555
Website: siobhanmcmahon.org Twitter: @smcmahon_msp

McMILLAN, Stuart *SNP*   **West Scotland**
Tel: 0131-348 6807 Email: stuart.mcmillan.msp@scottish.parliament.uk
Regional office: Unit 3003, Mile End Mill, Abbey Mill Business Centre, 12 Seedhill Road,
Paisley PA1 1JS
Tel: 0141-889 9519 Fax: 0141-889 4693
Website: www.stuart-mcmillan.net Twitter: @stumcmillansnp

McNEIL, Duncan *Lab*   **Greenock and Inverclyde**
Tel: 0131-348 5912 Email: duncan.mcneil.msp@scottish.parliament.uk
Constituency office: 20 Union Street, Greenock, Inverclyde PA16 8JL
Tel: 01475 791820 Fax: 01475 791821
Website: www.duncanmcneil.com Twitter: @duncanmcneilmsp

McTAGGART, Anne *Lab*   **Glasgow**
Tel: 0131-348 6211 Email: anne.mctaggart.msp@scottish.parliament.uk
Regional office: 333 Woodlands Road, Glasgow G3 6NG
Tel: 0141-218 4647
Website: www.annemctaggart.co.uk Twitter: @anmctmsp

MALIK, Hanzala *Lab*   **Glasgow**
Tel: 0131-348 6204 Fax: 0131-348 5968 Email: hanzala.malik.msp@scottish.parliament.uk
Regional office: 333 Woodlands Road, Glasgow G3 6NG
Tel: 0141-218 4567 Fax: 0141-334 0234

MARRA, Jenny *Lab*   **North East Scotland**
Scottish Labour Shadow Minister for Youth Employment and Deputy Minister for Finance
Tel: 0131-348 6427 Email: jenny.marra.msp@scottish.parliament.uk
Regional office: 15/16 Springfield, Dundee DD1 4JE
Tel: 01382 202584 Email: jenny@jennymarra.com
Website: www.jennymarra.com Twitter: @jennymarra

MARTIN, Paul *Lab*   **Glasgow Provan**
Scottish Labour Parliamentary Business Manager
Email: paul.martin.msp@scottish.parliament.uk
Constituency office: 604 Alexandra Parade, Glasgow G31 3BS
Tel: 0141-564 1364
Website: www.paulmartinmsp.org.uk Twitter: @paulmartinmsp

MARWICK, Rt Hon Tricia *Pres Off*   **Mid Fife and Glenrothes**
Fax: 0131-348 5301 Email: tricia.marwick.msp@scottish.parliament.uk
Constituency office: 12 Commercial Street, Markinch, Fife KY7 6DE
Tel: 01592 764815 Fax: 01592 759223

MASON, John *SNP* **Glasgow Shettleston**
Email: john.mason.msp@scottish.parliament.uk
Constituency office: 1335 Gallowgate, Parkhead Cross, Glasgow G31 4DN
Tel: 0141-550 4327
Website: www.john-mason.org Twitter: @johnmasonmsp

MATHESON, Michael *SNP* **Falkirk West**
Minister for Public Health
Email: michael.matheson.msp@scottish.parliament.uk
Ministerial office: Health and Wellbeing, St Andrew's House, Regent Road, Edinburgh EH1 3DG
Switchboard: 0131-244 2125
Constituency office: 15a East Bridge Street, Falkirk FK1 1YB
Tel: 01324 629271 Fax: 01324 635576 Email: andrew.maclachlan@scottish.parliament.uk
Website: michaelmatheson.org Twitter: @mathesonmichael

MAXWELL, Stewart *SNP* **West Scotland**
Tel: 0131-348 5669 Fax: 0131-348 6479 Email: stewart.maxwell.msp@scottish.parliament.uk
Regional office: Unit 3003, Mile End Mill, Abbey Mill Business Centre, 12 Seedhill Road,
Paisley PA1 1JS
Tel: 0141-887 2607 Fax: 0141-887 2626
Email: fraser.brown@scottish.parliament.uk colin.macdonald@scottish.parliament.uk
Website: www.stewartmaxwellmsp.com Twitter: @maxwellsnp

MILNE, Nanette *Con* **North East Scotland**
Scottish Conservatives Spokesperson for Public Health
Tel: 0131-348 5651 Fax: 0131-348 6480 Email: nanette.milne.msp@scottish.parliament.uk
Regional office: 7 Northern Road, Kintore, Aberdeenshire AB51 0YL
Tel: 01467 633062 Email: nanette.milne@scottishconservatives.com
Website: www.nanettemilne.co.uk

MITCHELL, Margaret *Con* **Central Scotland**
Scottish Conservatives Spokesperson for Justice
Tel: 0131-348 5639 Fax: 0131-348 6483 Email: margaret.mitchell.msp@scottish.parliament.uk
Regional office: 104 Cadzow Street, Hamilton ML3 6HP
Tel: 01698 282815 Fax: 01698 281533 Email: liz.mclean@scottish.parliament.uk
Website: www.margaretmitchellmsp.org

MURRAY, Dr Elaine *Lab* **Dumfriesshire**
Scottish Labour Shadow Minister for Community Safety and Legal Affairs
Tel: 0131-348 5826 Fax: 0131-348 5834 Email: elaine.murray.msp@scottish.parliament.uk
Constituency office: 5 Friars Vennel, Dumfries DG1 2RQ
Tel: 01387 279205 Fax: 01387 279206 Twitter: @elainemurraymsp

NEIL, Alex *SNP* **Airdrie and Shotts**
Cabinet Secretary for Health and Wellbeing
Tel: 0131-348 5703 Fax: 0131-348 5895 Email: alex.neil.msp@scottish.parliament.uk
Ministerial office: Health and Wellbeing, St Andrew's House, Regent Road, Edinburgh EH1 3DG
Switchboard: 0131-244 2125
Constituency office: One Wellwynd, 35 Wellwynd, Airdrie ML6 0BN
Tel: 01236 439331
Website: www.alexneilmsp.net Twitter: @alexneilsnp

PATERSON, Gil *SNP* **Clydebank and Milngavie**
Tel: 0131-348 6812 Fax: 0131-348 6814 Email: gil.paterson.msp@scottish.parliament.uk
Constituency office: Unit 16, Clyde Business Centre, Clydebank G81 1PF
Tel: 0141-952 9677 Fax: 0141-952 9677
Website: www.gilmsp.com

PEARSON, Graeme *Lab* **South Scotland**
Scottish Labour Shadow Cabinet Secretary for Justice
Tel: 0131-348 6887 Fax: 0131-348 5978 Email: graeme.pearson.msp@scottish.parliament.uk
Regional office: No regional office
Website: www.graemepearsonmsp.com

PENTLAND, John *Lab* **Motherwell and Wishaw**
Scottish Labour Deputy Whip
Tel: 0131-348 5773 Email: john.pentland.msp@scottish.parliament.uk
Constituency office: 265 Main Street, Wishaw ML2 7NE
Tel: 01698 303040
Website: johnpentland.org Twitter: @johnpentlandmsp

RENNIE, Willie *Lib Dem* **Mid Scotland and Fife**
Leader, Scottish Liberal Democrats; Scottish Liberal Democrats Spokesperson for Economy, Business
and Infrastructure
Tel: 0131-348 5803 Email: willie.rennie.msp@scottish.parliament.uk
Regional office: North East Fife Liberal Democrats, 16 Millgate, Cupar KY15 5EG
Tel: 01334 656361 Twitter: @willie_rennie

ROBERTSON, Dennis *SNP* **Aberdeenshire West**
Tel: 0131-348 6201 Email: dennis.robertson.msp@scottish.parliament.uk
Constituency office: Units 10-11, Craigearn Business Park, Morrison Way, Kintore,
Aberdeenshire AB51 0TH
Tel: 01467 631364
Website: www.dennisrobertsonmsp.net Twitter: @DRobertsonSNP

ROBISON, Shona *SNP* **Dundee City East**
Minister for Commonwealth Games and Sport
Fax: 0131-348 5562 Email: shona.robison.msp@scottish.parliament.uk
Ministerial office: Health and Wellbeing, St Andrew's House, Regent Road, Edinburgh EH1 3DG
Switchboard: 0131-244 2125
Constituency office: 8 Old Glamis Road, Dundee DD3 8HP
Tel: 01382 623200 Fax: 01382 903205 Email: dundee@shonarobison.com
Website: www.dundeesnp.org www.shonarobison.com Twitter: @shonarobison

RUSSELL, Michael *SNP* **Argyll and Bute**
Cabinet Secretary for Education and Lifelong Learning
Tel: 0131-348 6326 Fax: 0131-348 6689 Email: michael.russell.msp@scottish.parliament.uk
Ministerial office: Education and Lifelong Learning, St Andrew's House, Regent Road,
Edinburgh EH1 3DG Switchboard: 0131-556 8400
Constituency office: 81 Argyll Street, Dunoon, Argyll PA23 7DH
Tel: 01369 702011
Website: michaelrussellmsp.org Twitter: @feorlean

SALMOND, Rt Hon Alex *SNP* **Aberdeenshire East**
First Minister; Leader, Scottish National Party
Email: alex.salmond.msp@scottish.parliament.uk
Ministerial office: Office of the First Minister, St Andrew's House, Regent Road, Edinburgh EH1 3DG
Switchboard: 0131-556 8400
Constituency office: 84 North Street, Inverurie, Aberdeenshire AB51 4QX
Tel: 01467 670070 Twitter: @alexsalmond

SCANLON, Mary *Con* **Highlands and Islands**
Scottish Conservatives Spokesperson for Education and Lifelong Learning
Tel: 0131-348 5460 Email: mary.scanlon.msp@scottish.parliament.uk
Regional office: 14a Ardross Street, Inverness IV3 5NS
Tel: 01463 241004
Website: www.maryscanlonmsp.com

SCOTT, John *Con*   **Ayr**
Deputy Presiding Officer
Tel: 0131-348 5664 Fax: 0131-348 5617 Email: john.scott.msp@scottish.parliament.uk
Constituency office: 17 Wellington Square, Ayr KA7 1EZ
Tel: 01292 286251 Fax: 01292 280480

SCOTT, Tavish *Lib Dem*   **Shetland Islands**
Scottish Liberal Democrats Spokesperson for Transport, Rural Affairs, Fisheries, Environment and
Sport
Tel: 0131-348 6296 Fax: 0131-348 5807 Email: tavish.scott.msp@scottish.parliament.uk
Constituency office: 171 Commercial Street, Lerwick, Shetland ZE1 0HX
Tel: 01595 690044 Fax: 01595 690055 Email: tscott@supanet.com
Website: www.tavishscott.com Twitter: @tavishscott

SIMPSON, Dr Richard *Lab*   **Mid Scotland and Fife**
Scottish Labour Shadow Minister for Public Health
Tel: 0131-348 6330 Fax: 0131-348 6758 Email: richard.simpson.msp@scottish.parliament.uk
Regional office: 22 Viewfield Street, Stirling FK8 1UA
Tel: 01786 446515 Fax: 01786 446513 Email: richard@richardsimpson.info
Website: richardsimpson.info Twitter: @rsimpsonmsp

SMITH, Drew *Lab*   **Glasgow**
Scottish Labour Shadow Cabinet Secretary for Constitution
Tel: 0131-348 6208 Email: drew.smith.msp@scottish.parliament.uk
Regional office: 333 Woodlands Road, Glasgow G3 6NG
Tel: 0141-218 4646
Website: www.drewsmith.org.uk Twitter: @drewsm1th

SMITH, Elaine *Lab*   **Coatbridge and Chryston**
Deputy Presiding Officer
Tel: 0131-348 5824 Fax: 0131-348 6942 Email: elaine.smith.msp@scottish.parliament.uk
Constituency office: Unit 65, Fountain Business Centre, Ellis Street, Coatbridge ML5 3AA
Tel: 01236 449122 Fax: 01236 449137

SMITH, Elizabeth *Con*   **Mid Scotland and Fife**
Scottish Conservatives Spokesperson for Culture, Sport and Young People
Tel: 0131-348 6762 Fax: 0131-348 6764 Email: elizabeth.smith.msp@scottish.parliament.uk
Regional office: Control Tower, Perth Airport, Scone, Perth PH2 6PL
Tel: 01738 553990 Fax: 01738 553967 Email: osp@scottishtories.com
Website: www.ospconservatives.com

STEVENSON, Stewart *SNP*   **Banffshire and Buchan Coast**
Parliamentary Liaison Officer to John Swinney as Cabinet Secretary for Finance, Employment and
Sustainable Growth
Constituency office: Unit 8, Burnside Business Centre, Burnside Road, Peterhead,
Aberdeenshire AB42 3AW
Tel: 01779 470444 Fax: 01779 822025 Email: msp@stewartstevenson.net
Website: www.stewartstevenson.net Twitter: @zsstevens

STEWART, David *Lab*   **Highlands and Islands**
Tel: 0131-348 5766 Fax: 0131-348 5767 Email: david.stewart.msp@scottish.parliament.uk
Regional office: Highlands and Islands Labour MSPs' Office, PO Box 5717, Inverness IV1 1YT
Tel: 01463 716299 Fax: 01463 716572
Website: www.davidstewart.org.uk Twitter: @davidstewartmsp

STEWART, Kevin *SNP*   **Aberdeen Central**
Tel: 0131-348 6382 Email: kevin.stewart.msp@scottish.parliament.uk
Constituency office: Third Floor, 27 John Street, Aberdeen AB25 1BT
Tel: 01224 624719 Twitter: @kevinstewartmsp

STURGEON, Nicola *SNP*   **Glasgow Southside**
Deputy First Minister and Cabinet Secretary for Infrastructure, Investment and Cities
Email: nicola.sturgeon.msp@scottish.parliament.uk
Ministerial office: Infrastructure, Investment and Cities, St Andrew's House, Regent Road,
Edinburgh EH1 3DG Switchboard: 0131-244 1821
Constituency office: 627 Pollockshaws Road, Glasgow G41 2QG
Tel: 0141-424 1174 Fax: 0141-427 0650
Website: www.nicolasturgeon.org Twitter: @nicolasturgeon

SWINNEY, John *SNP*   **Perthshire North**
Cabinet Secretary for Finance, Employment and Sustainable Growth
Tel: 0131-348 5717 Email: john.swinney.msp@scottish.parliament.uk
Ministerial office: Finance, Employment and Sustainable Growth, St Andrew's House, Regent Road,
Edinburgh EH1 3DG Switchboard: 0131-244 5227
Constituency office: 35 Perth Street, Blairgowrie PH10 6DL
Tel: 01250 876576 Fax: 01250 876991
Website: www.johnswinneymsp.com Twitter: @johnswinney

THOMPSON, Dave *SNP*   **Skye, Lochaber and Badenoch**
Tel: 0131-348 5325 Fax: 0131-348 5327 Email: dave.thompson.msp@scottish.parliament.uk
Constituency office: Thorfin House, Bridgend Business Park, Dingwall IV15 9SL
Tel: 01349 864701 Fax: 01349 866327
Website: www.davethompson.snp.org

TORRANCE, David *SNP*   **Kirkcaldy**
Tel: 0131-348 6892 Email: david.torrance.msp@scottish.parliament.uk
Constituency office: 53 Kirk Wynd, Kirkcaldy, Fife KY1 1EH
Tel: 01592 200349

URQUHART, Jean, MBE *Ind*   **Highlands and Islands**
Tel: 0131-348 5053 Email: jean.urquhart.msp@scottish.parliament.uk
Regional office: No regional office
Website: jeanurquharthighlandsandislandsmsp.wordpress.com Twitter: @jeanurquhartmsp

WATT, Maureen *SNP*   **Aberdeen South and North Kincardine**
Tel: 0131-348 6675 Fax: 0131-348 6676 Email: maureen.watt.msp@scottish.parliament.uk
Constituency office: 51 Victoria Road, Torry, Aberdeen AB11 9LS
Tel: 01224 876743 Email: stephen.flynn@scottish.parliament.uk
Website: www.maureenwatt.com

WHEELHOUSE, Paul *SNP*   **South Scotland**
Minister for Environment and Climate Change
Tel: 0131-348 6891 Email: paul.wheelhouse.msp@scottish.parliament.uk
Ministerial office: Rural Affairs and Environment, St Andrew's House, Regent Road,
Edinburgh EH1 3DG Switchboard: 0131-556 8400
Regional office: 8 Sandbed, Hawick, Roxburghshire TD9 0HE
Tel: 01450 379572 Twitter: @paulwheelhouse

WHITE, Sandra *SNP*   **Glasgow Kelvin**
Parliamentary Liaison Officer to Kenny MacAskill as Cabinet Secretary for Justice
Tel: 0131-348 5688 Fax: 0131-348 5945 Email: sandra.white.msp@scottish.parliament.uk
Constituency office: 1274 Argyle Street, Glasgow G3 8AA
Tel: 0141-339 7693
Website: www.sandra-white.org Twitter: @sandrawhitesnp

WILSON, John *SNP*   **Central Scotland**
Tel: 0131-348 6684 Fax: 0131-348 6686 Email: john.wilson.msp@scottish.parliament.uk
Regional office: Unit 19, Enterprise House, Dalziel Street, Motherwell ML1 1PJ
Tel: 01698 337542 Fax: 01698 337452
Website: www.johnwilsonmsp.com

YOUSAF, Humza *SNP* **Glasgow**
Minister for External Affairs and International Development
Tel: 0131-348 6210 Email: humza.yousaf.msp@scottish.parliament.uk
Ministerial office: Culture and External Affairs, St Andrew's House, Regent Road,
Edinburgh EH1 3DG Switchboard: 0131-244 7716
Regional office: Third Floor, Empire House, 131 West Nile Street, Glasgow G1 2RX
Tel: 0141-353 1593
Website: www.humzayousaf.org Twitter: @humzayousaf

Women MSPs (46)

ADAMSON Clare	*SNP*	McALPINE Joan	*SNP*
BAILLIE Jackie	*Lab*	McCULLOCH Margaret	*Lab*
BAKER Claire	*Lab*	MacDONALD Margo	*Ind*
BAXTER Jayne	*Lab*	McDOUGALL Margaret	*Lab*
BEAMISH Claudia	*Lab/Co-op*	McINNES Alison	*Lib Dem*
BOYACK Sarah	*Lab*	McKELVIE Christina	*SNP*
BURGESS Margaret	*SNP*	McLEOD Aileen	*SNP*
CAMPBELL Aileen	*SNP*	McLEOD Fiona	*SNP*
CONSTANCE Angela	*SNP*	McMAHON Siobhan	*Lab*
CUNNINGHAM Roseanna	*SNP*	McTAGGART Anne	*Lab*
DAVIDSON Ruth	*Con*	MARRA Jenny	*Lab*
DUGDALE Kezia	*Lab/Co-op*	MARWICK Tricia	*Pres Off*
EADIE Helen	*Lab/Co-op*	MILNE Nanette	*Con*
EWING Annabelle	*SNP*	MITCHELL Margaret	*Con*
FABIANI Linda	*SNP*	MURRAY Elaine	*Lab*
FEE Mary	*Lab*	ROBISON Shona	*SNP*
FERGUSON Patricia	*Lab*	SCANLON Mary	*Con*
GOLDIE Annabel	*Con*	SMITH Elaine	*Lab*
GRAHAME Christine	*SNP*	SMITH Elizabeth	*Con*
GRANT Rhoda	*Lab*	STURGEON Nicola	*SNP*
HYSLOP Fiona	*SNP*	URQUHART Jean	*Ind*
JOHNSTONE Alison	*Green*	WATT Maureen	*SNP*
LAMONT Johann	*Lab/Co-op*	WHITE Sandra	*SNP*

Constituencies

			Majority	%
Aberdeen Central	Kevin Stewart	SNP	617	2.45
Aberdeen Donside	Mark McDonald	SNP	2,025	8.66
Aberdeen South and North Kincardine	Maureen Watt	SNP	6,323	22.07
Aberdeenshire East	Alex Salmond	SNP	15,295	50.5
Aberdeenshire West	Dennis Robertson	SNP	4,112	14.36
Airdrie and Shotts	Alex Neil	SNP	2,001	8.37
Almond Valley	Angela Constance	SNP	5,542	18.03
Angus North and Mearns	Nigel Don	SNP	7,286	29.24
Angus South	Graeme Dey	SNP	10,583	38.28
Argyll and Bute	Michael Russell	SNP	8,543	32.27
Ayr	John Scott	Con	1,113	3.34
Banffshire and Buchan Coast	Stewart Stevenson	SNP	12,220	48.87
Caithness, Sutherland and Ross	Rob Gibson	SNP	7,458	26.08
Carrick, Cumnock and Doon Valley	Adam Ingram	SNP	2,581	8.99
Clackmannanshire and Dunblane	Keith Brown	SNP	3,609	13.16
Clydebank and Milngavie	Gil Paterson	SNP	714	2.52
Clydesdale	Aileen Campbell	SNP	4,216	14.08
Coatbridge and Chryston	Elaine Smith	Lab	2,741	11.77
Cowdenbeath	Helen Eadie	Lab/Co-op	1,246	4.85
Cumbernauld and Kilsyth	Jamie Hepburn	SNP	3,459	13.7

Cunninghame North	Kenneth Gibson	SNP	6,117	20.71
Cunninghame South	Margaret Burgess	SNP	2,348	10.65
Dumbarton	Jackie Baillie	Lab	1,639	5.75
Dumfriesshire	Elaine Murray	Lab	3,156	9.89
Dundee City East	Shona Robison	SNP	10,679	41.47
Dundee City West	Joe FitzPatrick	SNP	6,405	26.18
Dunfermline	**By-election on 24th October 2013**			
East Kilbride	Linda Fabiani	SNP	1,949	6.52
Eastwood	Ken Macintosh	Lab	2,012	6.3
Edinburgh Central	Marco Biagi	SNP	237	0.82
Edinburgh Eastern	Kenny MacAskill	SNP	2,233	7.27
Edinburgh Northern and Leith	Malcolm Chisholm	Lab	595	1.93
Edinburgh Pentlands	Gordon MacDonald	SNP	1,758	5.85
Edinburgh Southern	Jim Eadie	SNP	693	2.05
Edinburgh Western	Colin Keir	SNP	2,689	8.04
Ettrick, Roxburgh and Berwickshire	John Lamont	Con	5,334	18.51
Falkirk East	Angus MacDonald	SNP	3,535	12.55
Falkirk West	Michael Matheson	SNP	5,745	20.37
Mid Fife and Glenrothes	Tricia Marwick	Pres Off*	4,188	15.92
North East Fife	Roderick Campbell	SNP	2,592	8.73
Galloway and West Dumfries	Alex Fergusson	Con	862	2.87
Glasgow Anniesland	Bill Kidd	SNP	7	0.03
Glasgow Cathcart	James Dornan	SNP	1,592	6.07
Glasgow Kelvin	Sandra White	SNP	882	3.59
Glasgow Maryhill and Springburn	Patricia Ferguson	Lab	1,292	6.29
Glasgow Pollok	Johann Lamont	Lab/Co-op	623	2.72
Glasgow Provan	Paul Martin	Lab	2,079	10.84
Glasgow Shettleston	John Mason	SNP	586	2.76
Glasgow Southside	Nicola Sturgeon	SNP	4,349	19.24
Greenock and Inverclyde	Duncan McNeil	Lab	511	1.81
Hamilton, Larkhall and Stonehouse	Christina McKelvie	SNP	2,213	8.73
Inverness and Nairn	Fergus Ewing	SNP	9,745	29.77
Kilmarnock and Irvine Valley	Willie Coffey	SNP	5,993	18.81
Kirkcaldy	David Torrance	SNP	182	0.65
Linlithgow	Fiona Hyslop	SNP	4,091	11.97
East Lothian	Iain Gray	Lab	151	0.47
Midlothian North and Musselburgh	Colin Beattie	SNP	2,996	10.05
Midlothian South, Tweeddale and Lauderdale	Christine Grahame	SNP	4,924	15.46
Moray	Richard Lochhead	SNP	10,944	38.27
Motherwell and Wishaw	John Pentland	Lab	587	2.4
Na h-Eileanan an Iar	Alasdair Allan	SNP	4,772	36.68
Orkney Islands	Liam McArthur	Lib Dem	860	10.55
Paisley	George Adam	SNP	248	0.97
Perthshire North	John Swinney	SNP	10,353	34.56
Perthshire South and Kinross-shire	Roseanna Cunningham	SNP	7,166	22.96
Renfrewshire North and West	Derek Mackay	SNP	1,564	5.69
Renfrewshire South	Hugh Henry	Lab	2,577	9.58
Rutherglen	James Kelly	Lab/Co-op	1,779	6.56
Shetland Islands	Tavish Scott	Lib Dem	1,617	17.22
Skye, Lochaber and Badenoch	Dave Thompson	SNP	4,995	15.65
Stirling	Bruce Crawford	SNP	5,670	18.65
Strathkelvin and Bearsden	Fiona McLeod	SNP	1,802	5.34
Uddingston and Bellshill	Michael McMahon	Lab	714	2.86

* elected as SNP

Regions

			Count elected on
Central Scotland	Clare Adamson	SNP	7
Central Scotland	Mark Griffin	Lab	2
Central Scotland	Richard Lyle	SNP	3
Central Scotland	Margaret McCulloch	Lab	5
Central Scotland	Siobhan McMahon	Lab	1
Central Scotland	Margaret Mitchell	Con	4
Central Scotland	John Wilson	SNP	6
Glasgow	Ruth Davidson	Con	3
Glasgow	Bob Doris	SNP	6
Glasgow	Patrick Harvie	Green	4
Glasgow	Anne McTaggart	Lab	7
Glasgow	Hanzala Malik	Lab	1
Glasgow	Drew Smith	Lab	5
Glasgow	Humza Yousaf	SNP	2
Highlands and Islands	John Finnie	Ind*	4
Highlands and Islands	Rhoda Grant	Lab	1
Highlands and Islands	Jamie McGrigor	Con	2
Highlands and Islands	Mike Mackenzie	SNP	7
Highlands and Islands	Mary Scanlon	Con	6
Highlands and Islands	David Stewart	Lab	3
Highlands and Islands	Jean Urquhart	Ind*	5
Lothian	Sarah Boyack	Lab	1
Lothian	Gavin Brown	Con	7
Lothian	Cameron Buchanan	Con	
Lothian	Kezia Dugdale	Lab/Co-op	3
Lothian	Neil Findlay	Lab	6
Lothian	Alison Johnstone	Green	4
Lothian	Margo MacDonald	Ind	5
Mid Scotland and Fife	Claire Baker	Lab	3
Mid Scotland and Fife	Jayne Baxter	Lab	
Mid Scotland and Fife	Annabelle Ewing	SNP	7
Mid Scotland and Fife	Murdo Fraser	Con	1
Mid Scotland and Fife	Willie Rennie	Lib Dem	6
Mid Scotland and Fife	Richard Simpson	Lab	5
Mid Scotland and Fife	Elizabeth Smith	Con	4
North East Scotland	Christian Allard	SNP	
North East Scotland	Richard Baker	Lab	1
North East Scotland	Alex Johnstone	Con	2
North East Scotland	Lewis Macdonald	Lab	6
North East Scotland	Alison McInnes	Lib Dem	5
North East Scotland	Jenny Marra	Lab	3
North East Scotland	Nanette Milne	Con	4
South Scotland	Claudia Beamish	Lab/Co-op	1
South Scotland	Chic Brodie	SNP	7
South Scotland	Jim Hume	Lib Dem	6
South Scotland	Joan McAlpine	SNP	2
South Scotland	Aileen McLeod	SNP	3
South Scotland	Graeme Pearson	Lab	4
South Scotland	Paul Wheelhouse	SNP	5
West Scotland	Neil Bibby	Lab	5
West Scotland	Jackson Carlaw	Con	3
West Scotland	Mary Fee	Lab	2
West Scotland	Annabel Goldie	Con	1
West Scotland	Margaret McDougall	Lab	7
West Scotland	Stuart McMillan	SNP	6
West Scotland	Stewart Maxwell	SNP	4

*Elected as SNP

Parliamentary Committees

Conveners' Group

The Conveners' Group comprises the conveners of the mandatory and subject committees of the Parliament but is not itself a Parliamentary committee

Tel: 0131-348 5202
Email: phillipa.booth@scottish.parliament.uk
www.scottish.parliament.uk/parliamentary
business/21516.aspx

Elaine Smith (Convener)	*Lab*
Nigel Don	*SNP*
Murdo Fraser	*Con*
Kenneth Gibson	*SNP*
Rob Gibson	*SNP*
Christine Grahame	*SNP*
Hugh Henry	*Lab*
Margaret McCulloch	*Lab*
Christina McKelvie	*SNP*
Michael McMahon	*Lab*
Duncan McNeil	*Lab*
Stewart Maxwell	*SNP*
David Stewart	*Lab*
Kevin Stewart	*SNP*
Dave Thompson	*SNP*
Maureen Watt	*SNP*

Staff: Susan Duffy (Clerk)

Mandatory Committees

Delegated Powers and Law Reform

Tel: 0131-348 5175
Email: dplr.committee@scottish.parliament.uk
www.scottish.parliament.uk/parliamentary
business/currentcommittees/64215.aspx

Nigel Don (Convener)	*SNP*
Stewart Stevenson (Deputy Convener)	*SNP*
Christian Allard	*SNP*
Richard Baker	*Lab*
Margaret McCulloch	*Lab*
Mike Mackenzie	*SNP*
John Scott	*Con*

Staff: Euan Donald (Clerk)

Equal Opportunities

Tel: 0131-348 5408
Email:
equal.opportunities@scottish.parliament.uk
www.scottish.parliament.uk/parliamentary
business/currentcommittees/29807.aspx

Margaret McCulloch (Convener)	*Lab*
Marco Biagi (Deputy Convener)	*SNP*
Christian Allard	*SNP*
John Finnie	*Ind*
Alex Johnstone	*Con*
Siobhan McMahon	*Lab*
John Mason	*SNP*

Staff: Douglas Thornton (Clerk), Ailsa Kilpatrick (Assistant Clerk), Debra Gourlay (Committee Assistant)

European and External Relations

Tel: 0131-348 5226
Email: europe@scottish.parliament.uk
www.scottish.parliament.uk/parliamentary
business/currentcommittees/29814.aspx

Christina McKelvie (Convener)	*SNP*
Hanzala Malik (Deputy Convener)	*Lab*
Clare Adamson	*SNP*
Roderick Campbell	*SNP*
Willie Coffey	*SNP*
Helen Eadie	*Lab/Co-op*
Jamie McGrigor	*Con*

Staff: Katy Orr (Clerk)

Finance

Tel: 0131-348 5451
Email:
finance.committee@scottish.parliament.uk
www.scottish.parliament.uk/parliamentary
business/currentcommittees/29822.aspx

Kenneth Gibson (Convener)	*SNP*
John Mason (Deputy Convener)	*SNP*
Gavin Brown	*Con*
Malcolm Chisholm	*Lab*
Jamie Hepburn	*SNP*
Michael McMahon	*Lab*
Jean Urquhart	*Ind*

Staff: James Johnston (Clerk)

Public Audit

Tel: 0131-348 5390
Email: pa.committee@scottish.parliament.uk
www.scottish.parliament.uk/parliamentary
business/currentcommittees/29860.aspx

Hugh Henry (Convener)	*Lab*
Mary Scanlon (Deputy Convener)	*Con*
Colin Beattie	*SNP*
Willie Coffey	*SNP*
Bob Doris	*SNP*
James Dornan	*SNP*

Colin Keir — *SNP*
Ken Macintosh — *Lab*
Tavish Scott — *Lib Dem*
Staff: Fergus Cochrane (Clerk)

Public Petitions

Tel: 0131-348 5254
Email: petitions@scottish.parliament.uk
www.scottish.parliament.uk/parliamentary
business/currentcommittees/29869.aspx

David Stewart (Convener) — *Lab*
Chic Brodie (Deputy Convener) — *SNP*
Jackson Carlaw — *Con*
Angus MacDonald — *SNP*
Anne McTaggart — *Lab*
David Torrance — *SNP*
John Wilson — *SNP*
Staff: Anne Peat (Clerk)

Standards, Procedures and Public Appointments

Tel: 0131-348 6924
Email: sppa.committee@scottish.parliament.uk
www.scottish.parliament.uk/parliamentary
business/currentcommittees/29890.aspx

Dave Thompson (Convener) — *SNP*
Helen Eadie (Deputy Convener) — *Lab/Co-op*
George Adam — *SNP*
Cameron Buchanan — *Con*
Richard Lyle — *SNP*
Margaret McDougall — *Lab*
Fiona McLeod — *SNP*
Staff: Gillian Baxendine, Alison Walker (Clerks)

Subject Committees

Economy, Energy and Tourism

Tel: 0131-348 5214
Email: eet@scottish.parliament.uk
www.scottish.parliament.uk/parliamentary
business/currentcommittees/29793.aspx

Murdo Fraser (Convener) — *Con*
Dennis Robertson (Deputy Convener) — *SNP*
Marco Biagi — *SNP*
Chic Brodie — *SNP*
Alison Johnstone — *Green*
Mark McDonald — *SNP*
Margaret McDougall — *Lab*
Mike Mackenzie — *SNP*
Hanzala Malik — *Lab*
Staff: Jane Williams (Clerk)

Education and Culture

Tel: 0131-348 5222
Email: ec.committee@scottish.parliament.uk
www.scottish.parliament.uk/parliamentary
business/currentcommittees/29800.aspx

Stewart Maxwell (Convener) — *SNP*
Neil Bibby (Deputy Convener) — *Lab*
George Adam — *SNP*
Clare Adamson — *SNP*
Jayne Baxter — *Lab*
Colin Beattie — *SNP*
Joan McAlpine — *SNP*
Liam McArthur — *Lib Dem*
Elizabeth Smith — *Con*
Staff: Terry Shevlin (Clerk)

Health and Sport

Tel: 0131-348 5410
Email:
healthandsport.committee@scottish.parliament.uk
www.scottish.parliament.uk/parliamentary
business/currentcommittees/29829.aspx

Duncan McNeil (Convener) — *Lab*
Bob Doris (Deputy Convener) — *SNP*
Rhoda Grant — *Lab*
Richard Lyle — *SNP*
Mark McDonald — *SNP*
Aileen McLeod — *SNP*
Nanette Milne — *Con*
Gil Paterson — *SNP*
Richard Simpson — *Lab*
Staff: Eugene Windsor (Clerk)

Infrastructure and Capital Investment

Tel: 0131-348 5229
Email: ici.committee@scottish.parliament.uk
www.scottish.parliament.uk/parliamentary
business/currentcommittees/29837.aspx

Maureen Watt (Convener) — *SNP*
Adam Ingram (Deputy Convener) — *SNP*
Jim Eadie — *SNP*
Mary Fee — *Lab*
Mark Griffin — *Lab*
Alex Johnstone — *Con*
Gordon MacDonald — *SNP*
Staff: Steve Farrell (Clerk)

Justice

Tel: 0131-348 5047
Email: justice.committee@scottish.parliament.uk
www.scottish.parliament.uk/parliamentary
business/currentcommittees/29845.aspx

Christine Grahame (Convener)	SNP
Elaine Murray (Deputy Convener)	Lab
Roderick Campbell	SNP
John Finnie	Ind
Colin Keir	SNP
Alison McInnes	Lib Dem
Margaret Mitchell	Con
John Pentland	Lab
Sandra White	SNP
Staff: Irene Fleming (Clerk)	

Justice Sub-committee on Policing

Tel: 0131-348 5220
Email: justice.committee@scottish.parliament.uk
www.scottish.parliament.uk/parliamentary
business/currentcommittees/61065.aspx

Christine Grahame (Convener)	SNP
John Finnie	Ind
Alison McInnes	Lib Dem
Margaret Mitchell	Con
Graeme Pearson	Lab
Kevin Stewart	SNP
Staff: Joanne Clinton (Clerk)	

Local Government and Regeneration

Tel: 0131-348 5223
Email: lgr.committee@scottish.parliament.uk
www.scottish.parliament.uk/parliamentary
business/currentcommittees/29852.aspx

Kevin Stewart (Convener)	SNP
John Wilson (Deputy Convener)	SNP
Richard Baker	Lab
Cameron Buchanan	Con

Stuart McMillan	SNP
Anne McTaggart	Lab
Stewart Stevenson	SNP
Staff: David Cullum (Clerk)	

Rural Affairs, Climate Change and Environment

Tel: 0131-348 5242
Email: racce.committee@scottish.parliament.uk
www.scottish.parliament.uk/parliamentary
business/currentcommittees/29876.aspx

Rob Gibson (Convener)	SNP
Graeme Dey (Deputy Convener)	SNP
Jayne Baxter	Lab
Claudia Beamish	Lab/Co-op
Nigel Don	SNP
Alex Fergusson	Con
Jim Hume	Lib Dem
Richard Lyle	SNP
Angus MacDonald	SNP
Staff: Lynn Tullis (Clerk), Nick Hawthorne (Senior Assistant Clerk)	

Welfare Reform

Tel: 0131-348 5228
Email:
welfarereformcommittee@scottish.parliament.uk
www.scottish.parliament.uk/parliamentary
business/currentcommittees/46339.aspx

Michael McMahon (Convener)	Lab
Jamie Hepburn (Deputy Convener)	SNP
Annabelle Ewing	SNP
Linda Fabiani	SNP
Alex Johnstone	Con
Ken Macintosh	Lab
Kevin Stewart	SNP
Staff: Simon Watkins (Clerk)	

Bill and Other Committees

Burrell Collection (Lending and Borrowing) (Scotland) Bill

Tel: 0131-348 6234
Email: private.bills@scottish.parliament.uk
www.scottish.parliament.uk/parliamentary
business/currentcommittees/64708.aspx

Joan McAlpine (Convener)	SNP
Jackson Carlaw (Deputy Convener)	Con
Mark Griffin	Lab
Gordon MacDonald	SNP
Staff: Joanna Hardy (Clerk)	

City of Edinburgh Council (Leith Links and Surplus Fire Fund) Bill

www.scottish.parliament.uk/parliamentary
business/currentcommittees/67594.aspx

To be appointed (Convener)	
To be appointed (Deputy Convener)	
Bruce Crawford	SNP
John Lamont	Con
Anne McTaggart	Lab
Sandra White	SNP
Staff: To be appointed (Clerk)	

City of Edinburgh Council (Portobello Park) Bill

Tel: 0131-348 5209
Email: private.bills@scottish.parliament.uk
www.scottish.parliament.uk/parliamentary
business/currentcommittees/63954.aspx

Siobhan McMahon (Convener)	*Lab*
James Dornan (Deputy Convener)	*SNP*
Alison McInnes	*Lib Dem*
Fiona McLeod	*SNP*

Staff: Mary Dinsdale (Clerk)

Referendum (Scotland) Bill

Tel: 0131-348 6124
Email:
referendum.committee@scottish.parliament.uk

www.scottish.parliament.uk/parliamentary
business/currentcommittees/55798.aspx

Bruce Crawford (Convener)	*SNP*
Lewis Macdonald (Deputy Convener)	*Lab*
Annabelle Ewing	*SNP*
Linda Fabiani	*SNP*
Rob Gibson	*SNP*
Annabel Goldie	*Con*
Patrick Harvie	*Green*
Stuart McMillan	*SNP*
Stewart Maxwell	*SNP*
Tavish Scott	*Lib Dem*
Drew Smith	*Lab*

Staff: Andrew Mylne (Clerk)

Scottish Commission for Public Audit

The Scottish Commission for Public Audit is not formally a parliamentary committee. The Commission was established under section 12 of the Public Finance and Accountability (Scotland) Act 2000 and is made up of five MSPs.

Tel: 0131-348 5236
Email: scpa@scottish.parliament.uk
www.scottish.parliament.uk/parliamentary
business/1704.aspx

Colin Beattie (Convener)	*SNP*
John Pentland (Deputy Convener)	*Lab*
Hugh Henry	*Lab*
Alex Johnstone	*Con*
Angus MacDonald	*SNP*

Staff: Fergus Cochrane (Secretary)

Principal Officers and Officials

Office of the Presiding Officer

Presiding Officer Rt Hon **Tricia Marwick** MSP

Principal Private Secretary	**Billy McLaren**	0131-348 5302
	Email: billy.mclaren@scottish.parliament.uk	

Deputy Presiding Officers **John Scott** MSP (Con), **Elaine Smith** MSP (Lab)

Scottish Parliamentary Corporate Body

(responsible for administration)

Chair	Rt Hon **Tricia Marwick** (Pres Off)
Members	**Linda Fabiani** (SNP)
	Liam McArthur (Lib Dem)
	Mary Scanlon (Con)
	David Stewart (Lab)

Secretariat

Officers	Lori Gray	0131-348 6222
	Email: lori.gray@scottish.parliament.uk	
	Judith Proudfoot	0131-348 5307
	Email: judith.proudfoot@scottish.parliament.uk	

Parliamentary Bureau

(responsible for all-party business programme and forward planning)

Chair	Rt Hon **Tricia Marwick** (Pres Off)

Members	John Finnie (Ind/Green Grouping)
	Joe FitzPatrick (SNP)
	John Lamont (Con)
	Alison McInnes OBE (Lib Dem)
	Paul Martin (Lab)

Leadership Group

Clerk/Chief Executive	Paul Grice 0131-348 5255
	Email: paul.grice@scottish.parliament.uk
Solicitor to the Scottish Parliament	Lynda Towers 0131-348 6649
	Email: lynda.towers@scottish.parliament.uk
Assistant Clerks/Chief Executives	Stewart Gilfillan 0131-348 5163
	Email: stewart.gilfillan@scottish.parliament.uk
	Bill Thomson 0131-348 5168
	Email: bill.thomson@scottish.parliament.uk

Heads	
Business Information Technology and Broadcasting	Alan Balharrie 0131-348 6535
	Email: alan.balharrie@scottish.parliament.uk
Human Resources and Security	Colin Chisholm 0131-348 6630
	Email: colin.chisholm@scottish.parliament.uk
Financial Resources	Derek Croll 0131-348 6819
	Email: derek.croll@scottish.parliament.uk
Facilities, Events and Visitor Services	Jerry Headley 0131-348 5106
	Email: jerry.headley@scottish.parliament.uk
Communications and Research	Michelle Hegarty 0131-348 6070
	Email: michelle.hegarty@scottish.parliament.uk
Committees and Outreach	Ken Hughes 0131-348 5201
	Email: ken.hughes@scottish.parliament.uk
Chamber and Reporting	David McGill 0131-348 5173
	Email: david.mcgill@scottish.parliament.uk

Scottish Government

Permanent Secretary's Office

St Andrew's House, Regent Road, Edinburgh EH1 3DG
Tel: 0131-556 8400/0845 774 1741
Email: ceu@scotland.gsi.gov.uk Website: www.scotland.gov.uk Twitter: @scotgov
Permanent Secretary: Sir Peter Housden KCB 0131-244 4026 Email: permsec@scotland.gsi.gov.uk

Strategy and External Affairs Directorate-General

St Andrews House, Regent Road, Edinburgh EH1 3DG
Tel: 0131 244 0170
Director-General: Ken Thomson 0131-244 6923 Email: dgsea@scotland.gsi.gov.uk

Enterprise, Environment and Digital Directorate-General

St Andrew's House, Regent Road, Edinburgh, Lothian EH1 3DG
Tel: 0131-556 8400/0845 774 1741
Website: www.scotland.gov.uk
Director-General: Graeme Dickson 0131-244 5598 Email: dgeed@scotland.gsi.gov.uk

Finance Directorate-General

St Andrew's House, Regent Road, Edinburgh, Lothian EH1 3DG
Tel: 0131-556 8400 Fax: 08457 741741
Website: www.scotland.gov.uk
Director-General: Alyson Stafford CBE 0131-244 7286 Email: dgf@scotland.gsi.gov.uk

Governance and Communities Directorate-General
R1 Spur, Saughton House, Broomhouse Drive, Edinburgh, Lothian EH11 3XD
Tel: 0131-244 6021

Director-General: Paul Gray 0131-244 6021 Email: dggc@scotland.gsi.gov.uk

Health and Social Care Directorate-General
St Andrew's House, Regent Road, Edinburgh, Lothian EH1 3DG
Tel: 0131-556 8400/0845 774 1741 Website: www.scotland.gov.uk

Director-General: John Connaghan 0131-244 2790 Email: dghsc@scotland.gsi.gov.uk

Learning and Justice Directorate-General
St Andrew's House, Regent Road, Edinburgh, Lothian EH1 3DG
Tel: 0131-556 8400/0845 774 1741
Email: dglj@scotland.gsi.gov.uk Website: www.scotland.gov.uk

Director-General: Leslie Evans 0131-244 2814 Email: dglj@scotland.gsi.gov.uk

Crown Office and Procurator Fiscal Service
25 Chambers Street, Edinburgh, Lothian EH1 1LA
Tel: 0844 561 3000 Fax: 0844 561 4069
Email: ps/copfs@scotland.gsi.gov.uk Website: www.copfs.gov.uk

Lord Advocate: Rt Hon Frank Mulholland QC 0844 561 3790
Email: lordadvocate@scotland.gsi.gov.uk
Solicitor General for Scotland: Lesley Thomson QC 0131-226 2626
Email: solicitorgeneral@scotland.gsi.gov.uk
Crown Agent and Chief Executive: Catherine Dyer 0844 561 3201 Email: psceca@copfs.gsi.gov.uk
Deputy Chief Executive: Dr Peter Collings 0844 561 4201 Email: peter.collings@copfs.gsi.gov.uk

Executive Agencies

Accountant in Bankruptcy
1 Pennyburn Road, Kilwinning, Ayrshire KA13 6SA
Tel: 0300 200 2600 Fax: 0300 200 2601
Email: aib@aib.gsi.gov.uk Website: www.aib.gov.uk Twitter: @AiB_updates
Number of staff: 158

Chief Executive: Rosemary Winter-Scott 0300 200 2900 Email: ce@aib.gsi.gov.uk
Sponsored by: Enterprise, Environment and Digital Directorate-General, Scottish Government

Disclosure Scotland
1 Pacific Quay, Glasgow G51 1BZ
Tel: 0870 609 6006
Email: info@disclosurescotland.co.uk Website: www.disclosurescotland.co.uk
PO Box 250, Glasgow G51 1YU
Tel: 0870 609 6006
Number of staff: 185

Sponsored by: Health and Social Care Directorate-General, Scottish Government

Education Scotland
Denholm House, Almondvale Business Park, Almondvale Way, Livingston, West Lothian EH54 6GA
Tel: 0141-282 5000
Email: enquiries@educationscotland.gov.uk Website: www.educationscotland.gov.uk
Twitter: @EducationScot
Number of staff: 373

Sponsored by: Learning and Justice Directorate-General, Scottish Government

Forest Enterprise Scotland
Forest Enterprise Scotland HQ, 1 Highlander Way, Inverness Business Park, Inverness, Highlands and Islands IV2 7GB
Tel: 01463 232811
Email: fescotland@forestry.gsi.gov.uk Website: www.forestry.gov.uk
South Scotland Area Office, 55/57 Moffat Road, Dumfries, Dumfriesshire DG1 1NP
Tel: 01387 272440 Fax: 01387 251491
Chief Executive: Simon Hodge
Sponsored by: Forestry Commission Scotland, Forestry Commission of Great Britain, Non-Ministerial Departments

Historic Scotland
Longmore House, Salisbury Place, Edinburgh, Lothian EH9 1SH
Tel: 0131-668 8600 Fax: 0131-668 8789
Email: hs.website@scotland.gsi.gov.uk Website: www.historic-scotland.gov.uk
Twitter: @welovehistory
Number of staff: 1,200
Acting Chief Executive: Ian Walford 0131-668 8693 Email: hschiefexecutive@scotland.gsi.gov.uk
Sponsored by: Governance and Communities Directorate-General, Scottish Government

Scottish Housing Regulator
Highlander House, 58 Waterloo Street, Glasgow G2 7DA
Tel: 0141-271 3810
Email: shr@scottishhousingregulator.gsi.gov.uk Website: www.scottishhousingregulator.gov.uk
Number of staff: 56
Chief Executive: Michael Cameron 0141-305 4055
Email: elizabeth.stewart@scottishhousingregulator.gsi.gov.uk
Sponsored by: Governance and Communities Directorate-General, Scottish Government

Scottish Prison Service
Calton House, 5 Redheughs Rigg, Edinburgh, Lothian EH12 9HW
Tel: 0131-244 8747 Fax: 0131-244 8774
Email: gaolinfo@sps.pnn.gov.uk Website: www.sps.gov.uk
Number of staff: 4,223
Chief Executive: Colin McConnell 0131-244 8523 Email: colin.mcconnell@sps.pnn.gov.uk
Sponsored by: Learning and Justice Directorate-General, Scottish Government

Scottish Public Pensions Agency
7 Tweedside Park, Tweedbank, Galashiels TD1 3TE
Tel: 01896 893000 Fax: 01896 893214
Website: www.sppa.gov.uk
Number of staff: 260
Chief Executive: Neville Mackay 01896 893232 Email: neville.mackay@scotland.gsi.gov.uk
Sponsored by: Finance Directorate-General, Scottish Government

Student Awards Agency for Scotland
Gyleview House, 3 Redheughs Rigg, Edinburgh EH12 9HH
Tel: 0300 555 0505
Email: saasceoffice@scotland.gsi.gov.uk Website: www.saas.gov.uk
Number of staff: 230
Chief Executive: David Wallace 0131-244 5867 Email: david.wallace@scotland.gsi.gov.uk
Sponsored by: Learning and Justice Directorate-General, Scottish Government

Transport Scotland
Buchanan House, 58 Port Dundas Road, Glasgow G4 0HF
Tel: 0141-272 7100
Email: info@transportscotland.gsi.gov.uk Website: www.transportscotland.gov.uk
Twitter: @transcotland
Number of staff: 386

Chief Executive: David Middleton 0141-272 7110
Email: chiefexecutive@transportscotland.gsi.gov.uk
Sponsored by: Enterprise, Environment and Digital Directorate-General, Scottish Government

Non-Ministerial Departments

National Records of Scotland
Website: www.nrscotland.gov.uk www.scotlandspeople.gov.uk
HM General Register House, 2 Princes Street, Edinburgh, Lothian EH1 3YY
Tel: 0131-535 1314
Ladywell House, Ladywell Road, Edinburgh, Lothian EH12 7TF
Tel: 0131-334 0380
Number of staff: 450

Registrar General for Scotland and Keeper of the Records of Scotland: Tim Ellis

Registers of Scotland
Meadowbank House, 153 London Road, Edinburgh, Lothian EH8 7AU
Tel: 0131-659 6111 Fax: 0131-479 3688
Email: customer.services@ros.gov.uk Website: www.ros.gov.uk Twitter: @RoStweets
Number of staff: 1,014
Keeper of the Registers of Scotland and Chief Executive: Sheenagh Adams 0131-659 6111 ext 3299
Email: sheenagh.adams@ros.gov.uk

Office of the Scottish Charity Regulator
Second Floor, Quadrant House, 9 Riverside Drive, Dundee DD1 4NY
Tel: 01382 220446 Fax: 01382 220314
Email: info@oscr.org.uk Website: www.oscr.org.uk
Number of staff: 54
Chief Executive: David Robb 01382 220446

Scottish Court Service
Saughton House, Broomhouse Drive, Edinburgh, Lothian EH11 3XD
Tel: 0131-444 3352 Fax: 0131-443 2610
Email: enquiries@scotcourts.gov.uk Website: www.scotcourts.gov.uk
Number of staff: 1,625

Forestry Commission Scotland
Silvan House, 231 Corstorphine Road, Edinburgh, Lothian EH12 7AT
Tel: 0131-334 0303 Fax: 0131-314 6152
Email: fcscotland@forestry.gsi.gov.uk Twitter: @fcsotland
Director: Dr Bob McIntosh 0131 314 6456 Email: bob.mcintosh@forestry.gsi.gov.uk

Political Parties

Scottish National Party

Gordon Lamb House, 3 Jackson's Entry, Edinburgh EH8 8PJ
Tel: 0800 633 5432 Fax: 0131-525 8901
Email: info@snp.org Website: www.snp.org Twitter: @thesnp

Leader: Alex Salmond MSP
Depute Leader: Nicola Sturgeon MSP
President: Ian Hudghton MEP
Chief Executive: Peter Murrell
Director of Strategic Communications: Kevin Pringle
Head of Communications and Research, Scottish Parliament: Ross Ingebrigtsen 0131-348 5679
Email: ross.ingebrigtsen@scottish.parliament.uk

Scottish Labour

290 Bath Street, Glasgow G2 4RE
Tel: 0141-572 6900 Fax: 0141-572 2566
Email: scotland@labour.org.uk Website: www.scottishlabour.org.uk Twitter: @scottishlabour

Leader: Johann Lamont MSP
Deputy Leader: Anas Sarwar MP
General Secretary: Ian Price

Scottish Conservative and Unionist Party

67 Northumberland Street, Edinburgh EH3 6JG
Tel: 0131-524 0030
Email: info@scottishconservatives.com Website: www.scottishconservatives.com
Twitter: @scottories

Leader: Ruth Davidson MSP
Chairman: David Mundell MP
Conference Convener: Pat McPhee
Director: Mark McInnes
Honorary Secretary: Robert Forman
Treasurer: James Stewart

Scottish Liberal Democrats

4 Clifton Terrace, Edinburgh EH12 5DR
Tel: 0131-337 2314 Fax: 0131-337 3566
Email: hq@scotlibdems.org.uk Website: www.scotlibdems.org.uk Twitter: @scotlibdems

Leader: Willie Rennie MSP
Deputy Leader: Alistair Carmichael MP
President: Sir Malcolm Bruce MP
Party Manager: Linda Wilson
Chief of Staff, Scottish Parliament: Matthew Clark 0131-348 5818
Email: matthew.clark@scottish.parliament.uk
Press Officer: Natalie Coupar 0131-348 5810 Email: natalie.coupar@scottish.parliament.uk

Scottish Green Party

Bonnington Mill, 72 Newhaven Road, Edinburgh EH6 5QG
Tel: 08700 772207
Email: info@scottishgreens.org.uk Website: www.scottishgreens.org.uk Twitter: @scotgp

Co-conveners: Patrick Harvie MSP, Martha Wardrop
Vice-convener: Dr Eleanor Scott
Head of Media: Jason Rose 0131-348 6360 Email: greencomms@scottish.parliament.uk

National Assembly for Wales

Cynulliad Cenedlaethol Cymru

Cardiff Bay, Cardiff CF99 1NA
Tel: 0845 010 5500/Textphone: 0845 010 5678
Email: assembly.info@wales.gov.uk Website:www.assemblywales.org Twitter: @assemblywales

Welsh Government

Welsh Government, Fifth floor, Tŷ Hywel, Cardiff Bay, CF99 1NA Switchboard: 0300 060 3300
Twitter: @WelshGovernment

Cabinet

First Minister	Rt Hon **Carwyn Jones**
Minister for Economy, Science and Transport	**Edwina Hart** MBE
Minister for Health and Social Services	**Mark Drakeford**
Minister for Communities and Tackling Poverty	**Jeff Cuthbert**
Minister for Local Government and Government Business	**Lesley Griffiths**
Minister for Finance	**Jane Hutt**
Minister for Culture and Sport	**John Griffiths**
Minister for Education and Skills	**Huw Lewis**
Minister for Housing and Regeneration	**Carl Sargeant**
Minister for Natural Resources and Food	**Alun Davies**
Chief Whip	**Janice Gregory**
Also attending Cabinet	
Counsel General	**Theodore Huckle** QC

Ministerial Responsibilities and Staff

First Minister

First Minister Rt Hon **Carwyn Jones** AM

Legislative programme; Delivery Unit; policy development and co-ordination; relationships with the rest of the United Kingdom, Europe and internationally; Welsh Government's offices abroad; European Union policy matters; Freedom of Information; civil contingencies; Economic Research Advisory Panel; energy facilities; major events; communications; staffing and civil service; public appointments; Ministerial Code; Welsh language.

Principal Private Secretary	Desmond Clifford	029 2089 8765
	Email: desmond.clifford@wales.gsi.gov.uk	
Senior Special Adviser	Jo Kiernan	029 2089 8690
	Email: jo.kiernan@wales.gsi.gov.uk	
Cabinet Secretary and Head of Cabinet Division	Peter Greening	029 2089 8036
	Email: peter.greening@wales.gsi.gov.uk	
Senior Private Secretary	Rose Stewart	029 2089 8764 Fax: 029 2089 8198
	Email: ps.firstminister@wales.gsi.gov.uk	

Economy, Science and Transport

Minister for Economy, Science and Transport **Edwina Hart** MBE AM

The establishment, growth, modernisation and development of business in Wales; Finance Wales; promoting Wales as a location for business and investment; Welsh exports; business property issues and environmental improvements; entrepreneurships; social enterprise; tourism; business rates; Economic Research Advisory Panel; transport policy; road transport and safety; rail services through Wales and Borders franchise; science; National Science Academy; innovation; Research Centres of Excellence and Technium network.

Special Adviser	Dr Andrew Bold	029 2089 8798
	Email: andrew.bold@wales.gsi.gov.uk	
Senior Private Secretary	David Fletcher	029 2089 8768
	Email: ps.minister.for.et@wales.gsi.gov.uk	

Health and Social Services

Minister for Health and Social Services **Mark Drakeford** AM

NHS in Wales; public health; Food Standards Agency in Wales; poisons; substance misuse; genetically-modified food; responding to reports from the Health Care Inspectorate for Wales; Wales Audit Office's activities relating to the NHS in Wales; research and development in health and social care; postgraduate medical education; Medicine Act 1968 in Wales; Prison Service health service.

Special Adviser	Jonathan Davies	029 2089 8965
	Email: jonathan.davies@wales.gsi.gov.uk	
Senior Private Secretary	Rory Powell	029 2089 8386
	Email: ps.minister.for.hss@wales.gsi.gov.uk	

Deputy Minister for Social Services **Gwenda Thomas** AM

Care in the community; social services; adoption and fostering services in Wales; Care Council for Wales; responding to reports from the Care and Social Services Inspectorate for Wales; health improvement; carers; Older People's Commissioner for Wales; Children and Family Court Advisory Support Service.

Specialist Policy Adviser	Andrew Pithouse	029 2089 8480
	Email: andy.pithouse@wales.gsi.gov.uk	
Private Secretary	Ruth Parness	029 2089 8631
	Email: ps.deputyminister.for.ss@cymru-wales.gsi.gov.uk	

Communities and Tackling Poverty

Minister for Communities and Tackling Poverty **Jeff Cuthbert** AM

Sustainable development; welfare reform; equalities; asylum, immigration, migrant workers and community cohesion; gypsies and travellers; voluntary sector; Communities First; Tackling Poverty Action Plan; children and young people; Children's Commissioner for Wales; Families First; childcare; Post Office and Royal Mail in Wales.

Special Adviser	Chris Roberts	029 2089 8611
	Email: chris.roberts2@wales.gsi.gov.uk	
Senior Private Secretary	Imelda Francombe	029 2089 8107
	Email: ps.minister.for.ctp@wales.gsi.gov.uk	

Deputy Minister for Tackling Poverty **Vaughan Gething** AM

Overall responsibility for delivering the Tackling Poverty Action Plan.

Private Secretary	Sarah Gwilliam	029 2082 1820
	Email: ps.minister.for.tp@wales.gsi.gov.uk	

Local Government and Government Business

Minister for Local Government and Government Business **Lesley Griffiths** AM

Council tax; local authority and police authority funding; local authority accounting issues; Valuation Office Agency and Valuation Tribunal Service; councillors' allowances and standards of conduct; burial grounds and crematoria; by-laws; timing of local elections; improvement and co-ordination of public service delivery; public sector reform; community safety; youth justice; domestic violence; Fire and Rescue Services; Armed Forces in Wales and veterans; Welsh Government business in the Assembly.

Special Adviser	To be appointed
Senior Private Secretary	Glyn Stapleton 029 2089 8774
	Email: ps.minister.for.lg@wales.gsi.gov.uk

Finance

Minister for Finance **Jane Hutt** AM

Financial direction and management of the Welsh Government's resources; publishing and consulting on the Welsh Government's budget proposals; National Statistics; Census in Wales; European Union structural funds; development of a Welsh Treasury function; strategic communications.

Special Policy Adviser	Jeff Andrews 029 2089 8193
	Email: jeff.andrews@wales.gsi.gov.uk
Senior Private Secretary	Eleanor Vaughan 029 2089 8467
	Email: ps.minister.for.finance@wales.gsi.gov.uk

Culture and Sport

Minister for Culture and Sport **John Griffiths** AM

National parks; access to the countryside and coasts; Welsh heritage; Royal Commission on Ancient Monuments; Welsh Archaeological Trusts; Arts Council of Wales; Sports Council for Wales; National Museum Wales; National Library of Wales; Wales Millennium Centre; sport; broadcasting policy; Welsh Books Council; Lottery funding; National Botanic Garden of Wales; walking and cycling promotion (Active Travel Bill); allotments.

Special Advisers	Dr Andrew Bold 029 2089 8798
	Email: andrew.bold@wales.gsi.gov.uk
(Active Travel (Wales) Bill)	Chris Roberts 029 2089 8611
	Email: chris.roberts2@wales.gsi.gov.uk
Senior Private Secretary	Peter Kellam 029 2089 8458
	Email: ps.minister.for.cs@wales.gsi.gov.uk
Private Secretary	Kate Bacon 029 2089 8895
	Email: ps.minister.for.cs@wales.gsi.gov.uk

Education and Skills

Minister for Education and Skills **Huw Lewis** AM

Mainstream education from early years to higher education; higher education fees; School Effectiveness Framework; dyslexia; complaints against Local Education Authorities and school governing bodies; teacher performance management.

Special Adviser	Matt Greenough 029 2089 8673
	Email: matt.greenough@wales.gsi.gov.uk
Senior Private Secretary	Helen Childs 029 2089 8783
	Email: ps.mfes@wales.gsi.gov.uk
Private Secretary	Matthew Mithan 029 2089 8771
	Email: ps.mfes@wales.gsi.gov.uk

Deputy Minister for Skills and Technology **Ken Skates** AM

Apprenticeship policy and delivery; Chair of Wales Employment and Skills Board; vocational qualifications for all ages; key and essential skills qualifications for all ages; workforce skills development; youth employment; Jobs Growth Wales; careers services in Wales; prisoner learning; Digital Wales; broadband and ICT infrastructure; High Performance Computing for Wales Project; Academia for Business; Software Alliance Wales.

Private Secretary   Helen Palmer   029 2089 8717
Email: ps.deputyminister.for.st@wales.gsi.gov.uk

Housing and Regeneration

Minister for Housing and Regeneration **Carl Sargeant** AM

Housing activities of local authorities and housing associations; homelessness; social landlords; private rented sector; Disabled Facilities Grants and Physical Adaptation Grants; regeneration; Physical Regeneration Fund; Groundwork Wales; Coalfields' Regeneration Trust; planning policy; building regulations; Wales Spatial Plan.

Specialist Policy Adviser   Tamsin Stirling   029 2089 8072
Email: tamsin.stirling@wales.gsi.gov.uk

Senior Private Secretary   Suzanne Pomeroy   029 2089 8769
Email: ps.minister.for.hrh@wales.gsi.gov.uk

Natural Resources and Food

Minister for Natural Resources and Food **Alun Davies** AM

Climate change; flood prevention; air pollution (except vehicle emissions) and marine pollution; nature conservation; water quality; reservoirs; waste management; energy policy; Natural Resources Wales; animal welfare and diseases; importation of livestock; zoo licensing; pest control; slaughterhouse regulation; plant health and diseases; approval of genetically modified crops in cultivation, importation in the European Union and trial licensing; agri-food sector; provision of support to farmers in Wales; management of Welsh fisheries.

Specialist Policy Adviser   Anna McMorrin   029 2089 8592
Email: anna.mcmorrin@wales.gsi.gov.uk

Senior Private Secretary   Peredur John   029 2089 8767
Email: ps.minister.for.nrf@wales.gsi.gov.uk

Counsel General

Counsel General **Theodore Huckle** QC

Make appropriate representations about matters affecting Wales; bring, defend or appear in legal proceedings to promote or protect the public interest; refer to the Supreme Court whether a provision of an Assembly Bill is within the Assembly's legislative competence; bring legal proceedings to have a "devolution issue" decided or defend if brought by other Law Officers; provide legal advice, represent and oversee the Welsh Government in legal proceedings; liaise with Law Officers, judiciary and members of the legal profession; improve accessibility of devolved legislation in Wales; respond to the Law Commission and other proposals/consultations; facilitate public debate on a separate Welsh legal jurisdiction.

Senior Private Secretary   David Rich   029 2082 3508
Email: pscounselgeneral@wales.gsi.gov.uk

Opposition

Welsh Conservatives

Leader, Welsh Conservative Group in the National Assembly	**Andrew R T Davies**
Deputy Leader, Welsh Conservative Group in the National Assembly; Shadow Minister for Finance	**Paul Davies**
Shadow Minister for Business, Enterprise and Technology	**Nick Ramsay**
Shadow Minister for Education	**Angela Burns**
Shadow Minister for Health and Social Services	**Darren Millar**
Shadow Minister for Environment and Sustainable Development	**Russell George**
Shadow Minister for Equalities and Sport	**Mohammad Asghar**
Shadow Minister for Local Government	**Janet Finch-Saunders**
Shadow Minister for Welsh Language and Culture	**Suzy Davies**
Shadow Minister for Transport and Regeneration; Shadow Whip	**Byron Davies**
Business Manager; Chief Whip	**William Graham**
Shadow Minister for North Wales, Social Justice and Housing	**Mark Isherwood**
Shadow Minister for Rural Affairs	**Antoinette Sandbach**

Plaid Cymru

Leader; Spokesperson for Welfare, Constitution and International Affairs	**Leanne Wood**
Deputy Leader, Assembly Group; Business Manager; Chief Whip; Spokesperson for Health	**Elin Jones**
Spokesperson for Women, Young People, Housing and Finance	**Jocelyn Davies**
Spokesperson for Local Government and Regeneration	**Rhodri Glyn Thomas**
Spokesperson for Education, Skills and Welsh Language	**Simon Thomas**
Spokesperson for Business, Economy, Science and Development	**Alun Ffred Jones**
Spokesperson for Transport and Society	Rt Hon **Dafydd Elis-Thomas**
Spokesperson for Social Services, Equality and Older People	**Lindsay Whittle**
Spokesperson for Environment, Energy and Agriculture	**Llyr Gruffydd**
Spokesperson for Broadcasting, Sport, Culture and Heritage	**Bethan Jenkins**

Welsh Liberal Democrats

Leader; Shadow Minister for Health and Social Care	**Kirsty Williams** CBE
Shadow Minister for Local Government, Heritage, Housing and Finance	**Peter Black**
Shadow Minister for Enterprise, Transport, Europe and Business	**Eluned Parrott**
Shadow Minister for Environment, Sustainability and Rural Affairs	**William Powell**
Shadow Minister for Children, Education and Welsh Language; Business Manager	**Aled Roberts**

Members (AMs)

State of the Parties (September 2013)

	Constituency	Regional	Total
Labour	27*	2	29
(includes Labour/Co-operative Party)			
Conservative	6†	8	14
Plaid Cymru	5	6	11
Liberal Democrat	1	4	5
Presiding Officer	1	0	1
	40	**20**	**60 seats**

*Excludes a Presiding Officer who can participate and vote fully in the Assembly when not in the Chair.
†Includes the Deputy Presiding Officer.

Changes since 2011 National Assembly for Wales election

DISQUALIFICATION
John Dixon   South Wales Central – *Lib Dem*   17 May 2011

RESIGNATION
Ieuan Wyn Jones   Ynys Môn – *PlC*   20 June 2013

REPLACEMENT
Eluned Parrott   South Wales Central – *Lib Dem*   Returned 6 July 2011
following the disqualification of John Dixon

BY-ELECTION

YNYS MÔN

1 August 2013 due to the resignation of the Plaid Cymru AM Ieuan Wyn Jones

PlC	Rhun ap Iorwerth		12,601
Lab	Tal Michael		3,435
UKIP	Nathan Gill		3,099
Con	Neil Fairlamb		1,843

SLP Kathrine Jones 348, *Lib Dem* Steve Churchman 309
PlC majority 9,166 – PlC hold (13.6% from Lab to PlC)
Electorate 51,080 – Total vote 21,682 – Turnout 42.45%

AMs' Directory

Con	Conservative
Lab	Labour
Lab/Co-op	Labour/Co-operative
Lib Dem	Liberal Democrat
PlC	Plaid Cymru
Pres Off	Presiding Officer

ANDREWS, Leighton   *Lab*   **Rhondda**
Tel: 029 2089 8784 Email: leighton.andrews@wales.gov.uk
Constituency office: Oxford House, Dunraven Street, Tonypandy, Rhondda CF40 1AU
Tel: 01443 685261
Website: www.leightonandrews.com Twitter: @leightonandrews

ANTONIW, Mick   *Lab/Co-op*   **Pontypridd**
Tel: 029 2089 8134 Email: mick.antoniw@wales.gov.uk
Constituency office: GMB House, Morgan Street, Pontypridd CF37 2DS
Tel: 01443 406400 Fax: 01443 406402
Website: www.mickantoniw.co.uk Twitter: @mickantoniwam

AP IORWERTH, Rhun *PlC* **Ynys Môn**
Tel: 029 2089 8270 Email: rhun.apiorwerth@wales.gov.uk
Constituency Office: 27 Church Street, Llangefni, Ynys Môn LL77 7DU
Tel: 01248 723599
Website: www.rhunapiorwerth.plaidcymru.org Twitter: @RhunapIorwerth

ASGHAR, Mohammad *Con* **South Wales East**
Welsh Conservatives Shadow Minister for Equalities and Sport
Tel: 029 2089 8319 Email: mohammad.asghar@wales.gov.uk
Regional office: First Floor, Fairoak House, 15-17 Church Road, Newport, Gwent NP19 7EJ
Tel: 01633 220022 Fax: 01633 220611
Website: www.mohammadasgharam.co.uk Twitter: @mohammadasghar

BLACK, Peter *Lib Dem* **South Wales West**
Welsh Liberal Democrats Shadow Minister for Local Government, Heritage, Housing and Finance
Tel: 029 2089 8744 Fax: 029 2089 8363 Email: peter.black@wales.gov.uk
Regional office: 110 Walter Road, Swansea SA1 5QQ
Tel: 01792 536353 Fax: 01792 536354
Website: peterblack.blogspot.com www.peter-black.net Twitter: @peterblackwales

BURNS, Angela *Con* **Carmarthen West and South Pembrokeshire**
Welsh Conservatives Shadow Minister for Education
Tel: 029 2089 8384 Fax: 029 2089 8974 Email: angela.burns@wales.gov.uk
Constituency office: 14 Market Square, Narberth, Pembrokeshire SA67 7AU
Tel: 01834 862725
Website: www.angelaburns.org.uk Twitter: @angelaburnsam

BUTLER, Rosemary *Pres Off* **Newport West**
Tel: 029 2089 8470 Email: rosemary.butler@wales.gov.uk
Constituency office: 72 Caerau Road, Newport NP20 4HJ
Tel: 01633 222523
Website: www.rosemarybutleram.com Twitter: @rosemarybutler

CHAPMAN, Christine *Lab/Co-op* **Cynon Valley**
Tel: 029 2089 8364 Email: christine.chapman@wales.gov.uk
Constituency office: Bank Chambers, 28a Oxford Street, Mountain Ash CF45 3EU
Tel: 01443 478098 Fax: 01443 478311
Website: www.christinechapman4cynon.com Twitter: @chrischapmanam

CUTHBERT, Jeff *Lab* **Caerphilly**
Minister for Communities and Tackling Poverty
Tel: 029 2089 8314 Fax: 029 2089 8310 Email: jeff.cuthbert@wales.gov.uk
Ministerial office: Communities and Tackling Poverty, Welsh Government, Fifth floor, Tŷ Hywel,
Cardiff Bay CF99 1NA
Constituency office: Bargoed YMCA, Aeron Place, Gilfach, Bargoed CF81 8JA
Tel: 01443 838542 Fax: 01443 838726
Twitter: @jeffcuthbert

DAVIES, Alun *Lab/Co-op* **Blaenau Gwent**
Minister for Natural Resources and Food
Tel: 029 2089 8300 Fax: 029 2089 8302 Email: alun.davies@wales.gov.uk
Ministerial office: Natural Resources and Food, Welsh Government, Fifth floor, Tŷ Hywel,
Cardiff Bay CF99 1NA
Constituency office: 23 Beaufort Street, Brynmawr, Blaenau Gwent NP23 4AQ
Twitter: @alundaviesam

DAVIES, Andrew R T *Con* **South Wales Central**
Leader, Welsh Conservatives Group in the National Assembly
Tel: 029 2089 8747 Fax: 029 2089 8371 Email: andrew.davies2@wales.gov.uk
Regional office: 79 Eastgate, Cowbridge, Vale of Glamorgan CF71 7AA
Website: www.andrewrtdavies.com Twitter: @andrewrtdavies

DAVIES, Byron *Con*South Wales West
Welsh Conservatives Shadow Minister for Transport and Regeneration; Whip
Tel: 029 2089 8929 Email: byron.davies@wales.gov.uk
Regional office: Ground Floor, 11 St James' Gardens, Uplands, Swansea SA1 6DY
Tel: 01792 654049
Website: www.byrondavies.org.uk Twitter: @byron_davies

DAVIES, Jocelyn *PlC*South Wales East
Plaid Cymru Spokesperson for Women, Young People, Housing and Finance
Email: jocelyn.davies@wales.gov.uk
Regional office: 1 Griffiths Building, Victoria Terrace, Newbridge NP11 4ET
Tel: 01495 241100 Email: jocelyndavies@plaidcymru.org
Website: www.jocelyndavies.plaidcymru.org

DAVIES, Keith *Lab*Llanelli
Tel: 029 2082 1997 Email: keith.davies@wales.gov.uk
Constituency office: 6 Queen Victoria Road, Llanelli SA15 2TL
Tel: 01554 774902
Website: keithdavies.org.uk Twitter: @keithdaviesac

DAVIES, Paul *Con*Preseli Pembrokeshire
Deputy Leader, Welsh Conservatives Group in the National Assembly; Shadow Minister for Finance
Tel: 029 2089 8725 Email: paul.davies@wales.gov.uk
Constituency office: 20 Upper Market Street, Haverfordwest SA61 1QA
Tel: 01437 766425 Fax: 01437 766425
Website: www.pauldaviesam.co.uk

DAVIES, Suzy *Con*South Wales West
Welsh Conservatives Shadow Minister for Welsh Language and Culture
Tel: 029 2089 8883 Fax: 029 2089 8391 Email: suzy.davies@wales.gov.uk
Regional offices: 11 St James' Gardens, Uplands, Swansea SA1 6DY
Tel: 01792 654049
1a Station Hill, Bridgend CF31 1EA
Tel: 01656 646432
Website: www.suzydaviesam.com Twitter: @suzydavies

DRAKEFORD, Mark *Lab*Cardiff West
Minister for Health and Social Services
Tel: 029 2089 8724 Email: mark.drakeford@wales.gov.uk
Ministerial office: Health and Social Services, Welsh Government, Fifth floor, Tŷ Hywel,
Cardiff Bay CF99 1NA
Constituency office: 33-35 Cathedral Road, Cardiff CF11 6LB
Tel: 029 2022 3207
Website: www.markdrakeford.com Twitter: @markdrakeford

ELIS-THOMAS, Rt Hon Dafydd *PlC*Dwyfor Meirionnydd
Plaid Cymru Spokesperson for Transport and Society
Tel: 029 2089 8709 Fax: 029 2089 8777 Email: dafydd.elis-thomas@wales.gov.uk
Constituency office: 7 Bank Place, Porthmadog, Gwynedd LL49 9AA
Tel: 01766 515028
Website: www.dafyddelis-thomas.plaidcymru.org Twitter: @ElisThomasD

EVANS, Rebecca *Lab*Mid and West Wales
Tel: 029 2089 8288 Email: rebecca.evans@wales.gov.uk
Regional office: Unit 1, Ferry Lane Works, Ferry Lane, Pembroke Dock SA71 4RE
Tel: 01646 622145
Website: www.rebeccaevansam.com Twitter: @rebeccaevansam

FINCH-SAUNDERS, Janet *Con*   Aberconwy
Welsh Conservatives Shadow Minister for Local Government
Tel: 029 2089 8734 Email: janet.finchsaunders@wales.gov.uk
Constituency office: 29 Madoc Street, Llandudno LL30 2TL
Tel: 01492 871198
Website: www.janetfinchsaunders.org.uk Twitter: @jfinchsaunders

GEORGE, Russell *Con*   Montgomeryshire
Welsh Conservatives Shadow Minister for Environment and Sustainable Development
Tel: 029 2089 8733 Email: russell.george@wales.gov.uk
Constituency office: 13 Parker's Lane, Newtown, Powys SY16 2LT
Tel: 01686 610887
Website: www.russellgeorge.com Twitter: @russ_george

GETHING, Vaughan *Lab/Co-op*   Cardiff South and Penarth
Deputy Minister for Tackling Poverty
Tel: 029 2089 8276 Fax: 029 2089 8377 Email: vaughan.gething@wales.gov.uk
Ministerial office: Communities and Tackling Poverty, Welsh Government, Fifth floor, Tŷ Hywel, Cardiff Bay CF99 1NA
Constituency office: No constituency office
Website: www.vaughangething.co.uk Twitter: @vaughangething

GRAHAM, William *Con*   South Wales East
Welsh Conservatives Business Manager and Chief Whip
Tel: 029 2089 8348 Fax: 029 2089 8347 Email: william.graham@wales.gov.uk
Regional office: 19a East Street, Newport NP20 4BR
Tel: 01633 250455 Fax: 01633 222694 Twitter: @williamgrahamam

GREGORY, Janice *Lab*   Ogmore
Chief Whip
Tel: 029 2089 8748 Fax: 029 2089 8375 Email: janice.gregory@wales.gov.uk
Constituency office: 44a Penybont Road, Pencoed, Bridgend CF35 5RA
Tel: 01656 860034 Fax: 01656 860189
Website: www.janicegregoryam.co.uk Twitter: @janice4ogmore

GRIFFITHS, John *Lab/Co-op*   Newport East
Minister for Culture and Sport
Tel: 029 2089 8315 Email: john.griffiths@wales.gov.uk
Ministerial office: Culture and Sport, Welsh Government, Fifth floor, Tŷ Hywel, Cardiff Bay CF99 1NA
Constituency office: Seventh Floor, Clarence House, Clarence Place, Newport NP19 7AA
Tel: 01633 222302 Fax: 01633 246575
Website: www.johngriffithsam.com Twitter: @j_griffithsam

GRIFFITHS, Lesley *Lab*   Wrexham
Minister for Local Government and Government Business
Tel: 029 2089 8536 Email: lesley.griffiths@wales.gov.uk
Ministerial office: Local Government and Government Business, Welsh Government, Fifth floor, Tŷ Hywel, Cardiff Bay CF99 1NA
Constituency office: Vernon House, 41 Rhosddu Road, Wrexham LL11 2NS
Tel: 01978 355743
Website: www.lesleygriffiths.org Twitter: @lesley4wrexham

GRUFFYDD, Llyr *PlC*   North Wales
Plaid Cymru Spokesperson for Environment, Energy and Agriculture
Email: llyr.gruffydd@wales.gov.uk
Regional office: Plaid Cymru, Regent Street, Wrexham LL11 1RE
Tel: 01978 365512
Website: www.llyrgruffydd.com Twitter: @llyrgruffydd

HART, Edwina, MBE *Lab* **Gower**
Minister for Economy, Science and Transport
Tel: 029 2089 8400 Email: edwina.hart@wales.gov.uk
Ministerial office: Economy, Science and Transport, Welsh Government, Fifth floor, Tŷ Hywel,
Cardiff Bay CF99 1NA
Constituency office: 9 Pontardulais Road, Gorseinon, Swansea SA4 4FE
Tel: 01792 895481 Fax: 01792 895646 Email: diane.thomas@wales.gov.uk
Website: www.edwinahart.com

HEDGES, Mike *Lab* **Swansea East**
Tel: 029 2089 8317 Email: mike.hedges@wales.gov.uk
Constituency office: 97 Pleasant Street, Morriston, Swansea SA6 6HJ
Tel: 01792 790621 Fax: 01792 794802
Website: www.mikehedges.org.uk Twitter: @mikehedgesam

HUTT, Jane *Lab* **Vale of Glamorgan**
Minister for Finance
Tel: 029 2089 8469 Fax: 029 2089 8129 Email: jane.hutt@wales.gov.uk
Ministerial office: Finance, Welsh Government, Fifth floor, Tŷ Hywel, Cardiff Bay CF99 1NA
Constituency office: 115 High Street, Barry CF62 7DT
Tel: 01446 740981 Fax: 01446 747106
Website: www.janehutt.co.uk Twitter: @janehutt

ISHERWOOD, Mark *Con* **North Wales**
Welsh Conservatives Shadow Minister for North Wales, Social Justice and Housing
Tel: 029 2089 8730 Fax: 029 2089 8323 Email: mark.isherwood@wales.gov.uk
Regional office: 5 Halkyn Street, Holywell CH8 7TX
Tel: 01352 710232
Website: www.markisherwood.com

JAMES, Julie *Lab* **Swansea West**
Tel: 029 2089 8132 Email: julie.james@wales.gov.uk
Constituency office: 30-31 High Street, Swansea SA1 1LG
Tel: 01792 460836 Fax: 01792 460836 Email: sandra.richards@wales.gov.uk
Website: www.juliejames4swanseawest.com Twitter: @juliejamesam

JENKINS, Bethan *PlC* **South Wales West**
Plaid Cymru Spokesperson for Broadcasting, Sport, Culture and Heritage
Tel: 029 2089 8713 Email: bethan.jenkins@wales.gov.uk
Regional office: 75 Briton Ferry Road, Melin Cryddan, Neath SA11 1AR
Tel: 01639 643549 Email: philippa.richards@wales.gov.uk
Website: www.bethanjenkins.plaidcymru.org Twitter: @bethanjenkins

JONES, Alun Ffred *PlC* **Arfon**
Plaid Cymru Spokesperson for Business, Economy, Science and Development
Tel: 029 2089 8414 Email: alunffred.jones@wales.gov.uk
Constituency office: 8 Castle Street, Caernarfon, Gwynedd LL55 1SE
Tel: 01286 672076
Website: www.alunffredjones.plaidcymru.org Twitter: @alunffredplaid

JONES, Ann *Lab/Co-op* **Vale of Clwyd**
Tel: 029 2089 8753 Email: ann.jones@wales.gov.uk
Constituency office: 25 Kinmel Street, Rhyl, Denbighshire LL18 1AH
Tel: 01745 332813 Fax: 01745 369038
Website: www.annjones.org.uk Twitter: @ann_jonesam

JONES, Rt Hon Carwyn   *Lab*   **Bridgend**
First Minister; Leader, Labour Party in the National Assembly
Tel: 029 2089 8468 Email: carwyn.jones@wales.gov.uk
Ministerial office: First Minister, Welsh Government, Fifth floor, Tŷ Hywel, Cardiff Bay CF99 1NA
Constituency office: First and Second Floor Suites, 3 Cross Street, Bridgend CF31 1EX
Tel: 01656 664320 Email: christopher.mainwaring@wales.gov.uk
Website: www.carwynjonesam.co.uk Twitter: @fmwales

JONES, Elin   *PlC*   **Ceredigion**
**Deputy Leader, Plaid Cymru Assembly Group; Business Manager; Chief Whip; Spokesperson for
Health**
Email: elin.jones@wales.gov.uk
Constituency office: Ty Goronwy, 32 Heol y Wig, Aberystwyth, Ceredigion SY23 2LN
Tel: 01970 624516 Fax: 01970 624473
Website: www.elinjones.com Twitter: @elinceredigion

LEWIS, Huw   *Lab/Co-op*   **Merthyr Tydfil and Rhymney**
Minister for Education and Skills
Tel: 029 2089 8752 Email: huw.lewis@wales.gov.uk
Ministerial office: Education and Skills, Welsh Government, Fifth floor, Tŷ Hywel, Cardiff Bay CF99 1NA
Constituency office: Venture Wales Building, Pentrebach, Merthyr Tydfil CF48 4DR
Tel: 01443 692299 Fax: 01443 691847
Website: www.huwlewis.org.uk Twitter: @huwlewis

MELDING, David   *Con*   **South Wales Central**
Deputy Presiding Officer
Tel: 029 2089 8732 Email: david.melding@wales.gov.uk
Regional office: 29 High Street, Barry CF62 7EB
Tel: 01446 744126 Fax: 01446 744126 Email: sarah.sharpe@wales.gov.uk Twitter: @davidmeldingam

MEWIES, Sandy   *Lab/Co-op*   **Delyn**
Tel: 029 2089 8736 Fax: 029 2089 8281 Email: sandy.mewies@wales.gov.uk
Constituency office: Transport House, 64 Chester Street, Flint CH6 5DH
Tel: 01352 763398 Fax: 01352 763474
Website: www.sandymewies.org.uk Twitter: @sandymewiesam

MILLAR, Darren   *Con*   **Clwyd West**
Welsh Conservatives Shadow Minister for Health and Social Services
Tel: 029 2089 8731 Fax: 029 2089 8326 Email: darren.millar@wales.gov.uk
Constituency office: North Wales Business Park, Abergele LL22 8LJ
Tel: 01745 839117
Website: www.darrenmillaram.com Twitter: @darrenmillaram

MORGAN, Julie   *Lab*   **Cardiff North**
Tel: 029 2089 8297 Email: julie.morgan@wales.gov.uk
Constituency office: 17 Plasnewydd, Whitchurch, Cardiff CF14 1NR
Tel: 029 2061 4577
Website: www.juliemorgan.org Twitter: @juliemorganlab

NEAGLE, Lynne   *Lab/Co-op*   **Torfaen**
Tel: 029 2089 8151 Email: lynne.neagle@wales.gov.uk
Constituency office: 73 Upper Trosnant Street, Pontypool, Torfaen NP4 8AU
Tel: 01495 740022 Fax: 01495 755776

PARROTT, Eluned   *Lib Dem*   **South Wales Central**
Welsh Liberal Democrats Shadow Minister for Enterprise, Transport, Europe and Business
Tel: 029 2089 8343 Email: eluned.parrott@wales.gov.uk
Regional office: 38 The Parade, Roath, Cardiff CF24 3AD
Tel: 029 2046 2326
Website: www.elunedparrott.com Twitter: @elunedparrottam

POWELL, William *Lib Dem* **Mid and West Wales**
Welsh Liberal Democrats Shadow Minister for Environment, Sustainability and Rural Affairs
Tel: 029 2089 8718 Email: william.powell@wales.gov.uk
Regional offices: 3 Park Street, Newtown, Powys SY16 1EE
Tel: 01686 625527 Email: post@mwwlibdems.org.uk
83a Water Street, Carmarthen SA31 1PZ
Tel: 0333 344 0270
Website: www.williampowell.org.uk Twitter: @williampowellam

PRICE, Gwyn *Lab* **Islwyn**
Tel: 029 2089 8309 Email: gwyn.price@wales.gov.uk
Constituency office: 208 High Street, Blackwood NP12 1AJ
Tel: 01495 225162

RAMSAY, Nick *Con* **Monmouth**
Welsh Conservatives Shadow Minister for Business, Enterprise and Technology
Tel: 029 2089 8735 Email: nicholas.ramsay@wales.gov.uk
Constituency office: The Grange, 16 Maryport Street, Usk, Monmouthshire NP15 1AB
Tel: 01291 674898 Email: katherine.jordan@wales.gov.uk
Website: www.nickramsay.org.uk Twitter: @nickramsayam

RATHBONE, Jenny *Lab* **Cardiff Central**
Tel: 029 2089 8287 Email: jenny.rathbone@wales.gov.uk
Constituency office: 165 Albany Road, Cardiff CF24 3NT
Tel: 029 2025 6255/029 2049 0352 Email: jenny@jennyrathbone.com
Website: jennyrathbone.wordpress.com Twitter: @jennyrathbone

REES, David *Lab* **Aberavon**
Tel: 029 2089 8751 Fax: 029 2089 8383 Email: david.rees@wales.gov.uk
Constituency office: Unit 6, Water Street Business Centre, Gwyn Terrace, Aberafan,
Port Talbot SA12 6LG
Tel: 01639 870779 Fax: 01639 870779
Website: david-rees.com Twitter: @davidreesam

ROBERTS, Aled *Lib Dem* **North Wales**
Welsh Liberal Democrats Business Manager; Shadow Minister for Children, Education and Welsh
Language
Tel: 029 2089 8129 Fax: 029 2089 8354 Email: aled.roberts@wales.gov.uk
Regional office: 18 High Street, Johnstown, Wrexham LL14 2SN
Tel: 01978 843300 Twitter: @aledrobertsam

SANDBACH, Antoinette *Con* **North Wales**
Welsh Conservatives Shadow Minister for Rural Affairs
Tel: 029 2089 8755 Fax: 029 2089 8416 Email: antoinette.sandbach@wales.gov.uk
Regional office: 37 High Street, Denbigh LL16 3HY
Tel: 01745 813345
Website: www.antoinettesandbach.org.uk Twitter: @asandbacham

SARGEANT, Carl *Lab* **Alyn and Deeside**
Minister for Housing and Regeneration
Tel: 029 2089 8716 Email: carl.sargeant@wales.gov.uk
Ministerial office: Housing and Regeneration, Welsh Government, Fifth floor, Tŷ Hywel,
Cardiff Bay CF99 1NA
Constituency office: 70 High Street, Connah's Quay, Flintshire CH5 4DD
Tel: 01244 823547 Fax: 01244 823547 Twitter: @carlsargeant1

SKATES, Ken *Lab* Clwyd South
Deputy Minister for Skills and Technology
Tel: 029 2089 8136 Email: ken.skates@wales.gov.uk
Ministerial office: Education and Skills, Welsh Government, Fifth floor, Tŷ Hywel,
Cardiff Bay CF99 1NA
Constituency office: Unit 19, The Malthouse Business Centre, Regent Street, Llangollen LL20 8HS
Tel: 01978 869058
Website: www.kenskates.co.uk Twitter: @kenskatesam

THOMAS, Gwenda *Lab* Neath
Deputy Minister for Social Services
Tel: 029 2089 8750 Fax: 029 2089 8380 Email: gwenda.thomas@wales.gov.uk
Ministerial office: Health and Social Services, Welsh Government, Fifth floor, Tŷ Hywel,
Cardiff Bay CF99 1NA
Constituency office: 7 High Street, Pontardawe, Swansea SA8 4HU
Tel: 01792 869993 Fax: 01792 869993
Website: www.gwendathomas.com Twitter: @gwendathomas

THOMAS, Rhodri Glyn *PlC* Carmarthen East and Dinefwr
Plaid Cymru Spokesperson for Local Government and Regeneration
Tel: 029 2089 8055 Email: rhodri.thomas@wales.gov.uk
Constituency office: 37 Wind Street, Ammanford, Carmarthenshire SA18 3DN
Tel: 01269 597677 Fax: 01269 591334 Email: rhodriglynthomas@plaidcymru.org
Website: www.rhodriglynthomas.org Twitter: @rhodriglynplaid

THOMAS, Simon *PlC* Mid and West Wales
Plaid Cymru Spokesperson for Education, Skills and Welsh Language
Tel: 029 2089 8476 Email: simon.thomas@wales.gov.uk
Regional office: Bres House, Bres Road, Llanelli SA15 1UA
Tel: 01554 774393
Website: www.simonthomas.plaidcymru.org Twitter: @simonthomasaber

WATSON, Joyce *Lab* Mid and West Wales
Tel: 029 2089 8614 Fax: 029 2089 8419 Email: joyce.watson@wales.gov.uk
Regional office: 3 Red Street, Carmarthen SA31 1QL
Tel: 01267 233448
Website: www.joycewatson.co.uk

WHITTLE, Lindsay *PlC* South Wales East
Plaid Cymru Spokesperson for Social Services, Equality and Older People
Tel: 029 2089 8719 Email: lindsay.whittle@wales.gov.uk
Regional office: 2 Portland Buildings, Commercial Street, Pontypool NP4 6JS
Tel: 01495 763278 Email: lindsaywhittle@plaidcymru.org

WILLIAMS, Kirsty, CBE *Lib Dem* Brecon and Radnorshire
Leader, Welsh Liberal Democrats; Shadow Minister for Health and Social Care
Tel: 029 2089 8743 Email: kirsty.williams@wales.gov.uk
Constituency office: 4 Water Gate, Brecon LD3 9AN
Tel: 01874 625739
Website: www.kirstywilliams.org.uk Twitter: @kirsty_williams

WOOD, Leanne *PlC* South Wales Central
Leader, Plaid Cymru; Spokesperson for Welfare, Constitution and International Affairs
Tel: 029 2089 8256 Email: leanne.wood@wales.gov.uk
Regional office: 32 Gelliwastad Road, Pontypridd, Rhondda Cynon Taff CF37 2BN
Tel: 01443 480291
Website: www.leannewood.org Twitter: @leannewood

Women AMs (25)

BURNS Angela	Con	JONES Ann	Lab/Co-op
BUTLER Rosemary	Pres Off	JONES Elin	PlC
CHAPMAN Christine	Lab/Co-op	MEWIES Sandy	Lab/Co-op
DAVIES Jocelyn	PlC	MORGAN Julie	Lab
DAVIES Suzy	Con	NEAGLE Lynne	Lab/Co-op
EVANS Rebecca	Lab	PARROTT Eluned	Lib Dem
FINCH-SAUNDERS Janet	Con	RATHBONE Jenny	Lab
GREGORY Janice	Lab	SANDBACH Antoinette	Con
GRIFFITHS Lesley	Lab	THOMAS Gwenda	Lab
HART Edwina	Lab	WATSON Joyce	Lab
HUTT Jane	Lab	WILLIAMS Kirsty	Lib Dem
JAMES Julie	Lab	WOOD Leanne	PlC
JENKINS Bethan	PlC		

Constituencies

			Majority	%
Aberavon	David Rees	Lab	9,311	49.32
Aberconwy	Janet Finch-Saunders	Con	1,567	7.72
Alyn and Deeside	Carl Sargeant	Lab	5,581	24.51
Arfon	Alun Ffred Jones	PlC	5,394	30.54
Blaenau Gwent	Alun Davies	Lab/Co-op	9,120	45.12
Brecon and Radnorshire	Kirsty Williams	Lib Dem	2,757	9.73
Bridgend	Carwyn Jones	Lab	6,775	28.19
Caerphilly	Jeff Cuthbert	Lab	4,924	19.26
Cardiff Central	Jenny Rathbone	Lab	38	0.16
Cardiff North	Julie Morgan	Lab	1,782	5.18
Cardiff South and Penarth	Vaughan Gething	Lab/Co-op	6,259	22.78
Cardiff West	Mark Drakeford	Lab	5,901	21.28
Carmarthen East and Dinefwr	Rhodri Glyn Thomas	PlC	4,148	14.91
Carmarthen West and South Pembrokeshire	Angela Burns	Con	1,504	5.34
Ceredigion	Elin Jones	PlC	1,777	6.11
Clwyd South	Ken Skates	Lab	2,659	13.27
Clwyd West	Darren Millar	Con	4,248	16.89
Vale of Clwyd	Ann Jones	Lab/Co-op	4,011	17.4
Cynon Valley	Christine Chapman	Lab/Co-op	6,515	34.73
Delyn	Sandy Mewies	Lab/Co-op	2,881	12.42
Dwyfor Meirionnydd	Dafydd Elis-Thomas	PlC	5,417	26.11
Vale of Glamorgan	Jane Hutt	Lab	3,775	11.35
Gower	Edwina Hart	Lab	4,864	18.17
Islwyn	Gwyn Price	Lab	7,589	36.3
Llanelli	Keith Davies	Lab	80	0.31
Merthyr Tydfil and Rhymney	Huw Lewis	Lab/Co-op	7,051	36.5
Monmouth	Nick Ramsay	Con	6,117	20.39
Montgomeryshire	Russell George	Con	2,324	10.13
Neath	Gwenda Thomas	Lab	6,390	26.79
Newport East	John Griffiths	Lab/Co-op	5,388	27.69
Newport West	Rosemary Butler	Pres Off[*]	4,220	18.34
Ogmore	Janice Gregory	Lab	9,576	47.26
Pontypridd	Mick Antoniw	Lab/Co-op	7,694	32.97

* elected as Labour

			Majority	*%*
Preseli Pembrokeshire	Paul Davies	Con	2,175	7.99
Rhondda	Leighton Andrews	Lab	6,739	33.65
Swansea East	Mike Hedges	Lab	8,281	43.79
Swansea West	Julie James	Lab	4,654	21.34
Torfaen	Lynne Neagle	Lab/Co-op	6,088	27.27
Wrexham	Lesley Griffiths	Lab	3,337	17.86
Ynys Môn	Rhun ap Iorwerth	PlC	9,166	42.27

Regions

			Count elected on
Mid and West Wales	Rebecca Evans	Lab	2
Mid and West Wales	William Powell	Lib Dem	4
Mid and West Wales	Simon Thomas	PlC	3
Mid and West Wales	Joyce Watson	Lab	1
North Wales	Llyr Huws Gruffydd	PlC	2
North Wales	Mark Isherwood	Con	1
North Wales	Aled Roberts	Lib Dem	4
North Wales	Antoinette Sandbach	Con	3
South Wales Central	Andrew R T Davies	Con	1
South Wales Central	David Melding	Con	3
South Wales Central	Eluned Parrott	Lib Dem	4
South Wales Central	Leanne Wood	PlC	2
South Wales East	Mohammad Asghar	Con	3
South Wales East	Jocelyn Davies	PlC	1
South Wales East	William Graham	Con	2
South Wales East	Lindsay Whittle	PlC	4
South Wales West	Peter Black	Lib Dem	4
South Wales West	Byron Davies	Con	3
South Wales West	Suzy Davies	Con	1
South Wales West	Bethan Jenkins	PlC	2

Assembly Committees

Business

Tel: 029 2089 8009
Email: business.committee@wales.gov.uk
www.senedd.assemblywales.org/
mgcommitteedetails.aspx?id=144

Rosemary Butler (Chair)	*Pres Off*
William Graham	*Con*
Lesley Griffiths	*Lab*
Elin Jones	*PlC*
Aled Roberts	*Lib Dem*

Staff: Aled Elwyn Jones (Clerk)

Children and Young People

Tel: 029 2089 8505
Email: cypcommittee@wales.gov.uk
www.senedd.assemblywales.org/
mgcommitteedetails.aspx?id=224

Ann Jones (Chair)	*Lab/Co-op*
Angela Burns	*Con*
Keith Davies	*Lab*
Suzy Davies	*Con*
Rebecca Evans	*Lab*
Bethan Jenkins	*PlC*
Lynne Neagle	*Lab/Co-op*
David Rees	*Lab*
Aled Roberts	*Lib Dem*
Simon Thomas	*PlC*

Staff: Marc Wyn Jones (Clerk)

Communities, Equality and Local Government

Tel: 029 2089 8032
Email: celg.committee@wales.gov.uk
www.senedd.assemblywales.org/
mgcommitteedetails.aspx?id=226

Christine Chapman (Chair)	*Lab/Co-op*
Leighton Andrews	*Lab*
Peter Black	*Lib Dem*
Janet Finch-Saunders	*Con*
Mike Hedges	*Lab*
Mark Isherwood	*Con*
Gwyn Price	*Lab*
Jenny Rathbone	*Lab*
Rhodri Glyn Thomas	*PlC*
Lindsay Whittle	*PlC*

Staff: Sarah Beasley (Clerk)

Constitutional and Legislative Affairs

Tel: 029 2089 8008
Email: cla.committee@wales.gov.uk
www.senedd.assemblywales.org/
mgcommitteedetails.aspx?id=219

David Melding (Chair)	*Con*
Suzy Davies	*Con*

Julie James	*Lab*
Eluned Parrott	*Lib Dem*
Simon Thomas	*PlC*

Staff: Gareth Williams (Clerk)

Enterprise and Business

Tel: 029 2089 8582
Email: enterprise.committee@wales.gov.uk
www.senedd.assemblywales.org/
mgcommitteedetails.aspx?id=228

Nick Ramsay (Chair)	*Con*
Rhun ap Iorwerth	*PlC*
Mick Antoniw	*Lab/Co-op*
Byron Davies	*Con*
Keith Davies	*Lab*
Julie James	*Lab*
Alun Ffred Jones	*PlC*
Eluned Parrott	*Lib Dem*
David Rees	*Lab*
Joyce Watson	*Lab*

Staff: Siân Phipps (Clerk)

Environment and Sustainability

Tel: 029 2089 8639
Email: es.comm@wales.gov.uk
www.senedd.assemblywales.org/
mgcommitteedetails.aspx?ID=225

Dafydd Elis-Thomas (Chair)	*PlC*
Mick Antoniw	*Lab/Co-op*
Russell George	*Con*
Llyr Huws Gruffydd	*PlC*
Julie James	*Lab*
Julie Morgan	*Lab*
William Powell	*Lib Dem*
Antoinette Sandbach	*Con*
Joyce Watson	*Lab*

Staff: Alun Davidson (Clerk)

Finance

Tel: 029 2089 8409
Email: financecommittee@wales.gov.uk
www.senedd.assemblywales.org/
mgcommitteedetails.aspx?id=229

Jocelyn Davies (Chair)	*PlC*
Peter Black	*Lib Dem*
Christine Chapman	*Lab/Co-op*
Paul Davies	*Con*
Mike Hedges	*Lab*
Ann Jones	*Lab/Co-op*
Julie Morgan	*Lab*
Simon Thomas	*PlC*

Staff: Gareth Price (Clerk)

Health and Social Care

Tel: 029 2089 8403
Email: hsccommittee@wales.gov.uk
www.senedd.assemblywales.org/
mgcommitteedetails.aspx?id=227

David Rees (Chair)	*Lab*
Leighton Andrews	*Lab*
Rebecca Evans	*Lab*
William Graham	*Con*
Elin Jones	*PlC*
Darren Millar	*Con*
Lynne Neagle	*Lab/Co-op*
Gwyn Price	*Lab*
Lindsay Whittle	*PlC*
Kirsty Williams	*Lib Dem*

Staff: Llinos Madeley (Clerk)

Petitions

Tel: 029 2089 8421
Email: petition@wales.gov.uk
www.senedd.assemblywales.org/
mgcommitteedetails.aspx?id=218

William Powell (Chair)	*Lib Dem*
Russell George	*Con*
Bethan Jenkins	*PlC*
Joyce Watson	*Lab*

Staff: Steve George (Clerk)

Public Accounts

Tel: 029 2089 8041
Email: publicaccounts.comm@wales.gov.uk
www.senedd.assemblywales.org/
mgcommitteedetails.aspx?id=230

Darren Millar (Chair)	*Con*
Mohammad Asghar	*Con*
Jocelyn Davies	*PlC*
Mike Hedges	*Lab*
Sandy Mewies	*Lab/Co-op*
Julie Morgan	*Lab*
Jenny Rathbone	*Lab*
Aled Roberts	*Lib Dem*

Staff: Fay Buckle (Clerk)

Scrutiny of the First Minister

Tel: 029 2089 8242
Email: fm.scrutiny@wales.gov.uk
www.senedd.assemblywales.org/
mgcommitteedetails.aspx?id=302

David Melding (Chair)	*Con*
Paul Davies	*Con*
Elin Jones	*PlC*
Eluned Parrott	*Lib Dem*
Ken Skates	*Lab*

Staff: Steve George (Clerk)

Standards of Conduct

Tel: 029 2089 8506
Email: standards@wales.gov.uk
www.senedd.assemblywales.org/
mgcommitteedetails.aspx?id=231

Mick Antoniw (Chair)	*Lab/Co-op*
Llyr Huws Gruffydd	*PlC*
Mark Isherwood	*Con*
Kirsty Williams	*Lib Dem*

Staff: Meriel Singleton (Clerk)

Common Agricultural Policy Task and Finish Group

Tel: 029 2089 8639
Email: es.comm@wales.gov.uk
www.senedd.assemblywales.org/
mgcommitteedetails.aspx?id=268

Vaughan Gething (Chair)	*Lab/Co-op*
Dafydd Elis-Thomas	*PlC*
Llyr Huws Gruffydd	*PlC*
William Powell	*Lib Dem*
Antoinette Sandbach	*Con*

Staff: Alun Davidson (Clerk)

Common Fisheries Policy Task and Finish Group

Tel: 029 2089 8639
Email: es.comm@wales.gov.uk
www.senedd.assemblywales.org/
mgcommitteedetails.aspx?id=269

Julie James (Chair)	*Lab*
Dafydd Elis-Thomas	*PlC*
Llyr Huws Gruffydd	*PlC*
William Powell	*Lib Dem*
David Rees	*Lab*
Antoinette Sandbach	*Con*

Staff: Alun Davidson (Clerk)

Smoke-free Premises etc. (Wales) (Amendment) Regulations 2012 Sub-committee

Tel: 029 2082 1821
www.senedd.assemblywales.org/
mgcommitteedetails.aspx?id=311

Nick Ramsay (Chair)	*Con*
Vaughan Gething	*Lab/Co-op*
Alun Ffred Jones	*PlC*
Elin Jones	*PlC*
Darren Millar	*Con*
Lynne Neagle	*Lab/Co-op*
Eluned Parrott	*Lib Dem*
David Rees	*Lab*
Ken Skates	*Lab*

Staff: Lara Date (Clerk)

Principal Officers and Officials

Office of the Presiding Officer

Presiding Officer **Rosemary Butler** AM

Principal Private Secretary	Craig Stephenson 029 2089 8230 Email: craig.stephenson@wales.gov.uk

Deputy Presiding Officer **David Melding** AM (Con)

Assembly Commission

Chair	**Rosemary Butler** (Pres Off)
Members	**Peter Black** (Lib Dem)
	Angela Burns (Con)
	Sandy Mewies (Lab/Co-op)
	Rhodri Glyn Thomas (PlC)

Senior Management Team

Chief Executive and Clerk of the Assembly	Claire Clancy 029 2089 8233 Email: claire.clancy@wales.gov.uk
Directors	
Assembly Business	Adrian Crompton 029 2089 8264 Email: adrian.crompton@wales.gov.uk
ICT	Dave Tosh 029 2089 8171 Email: david.tosh@wales.gov.uk
Heads of Service	
Communications	Dr Non Gwilym 029 2089 8647 Email: non.gwilym@wales.gov.uk
Legislation and Chamber Services	Siân Wilkins 029 2089 8224 Email: sian.wilkins@wales.gov.uk
Members' Research Service	Kathryn Potter 029 2089 8038 Email: kathryn.potter@wales.gov.uk
Assembly Committees	Virginia Hawkins 029 2089 8238 Email: virginia.hawkins@wales.gov.uk Sulafa Thomas 029 2089 8238 Email: sulafa.thomas@wales.gov.uk
Estates	Mike Snook 029 2089 8660 Email: michael.snook@wales.gov.uk
Assembly Resources	Steve O'Donoghue 029 2089 8746 Email: steven.o'donoghue@wales.gov.uk
Translation and Reporting Service	Mair Parry-Jones 029 2089 8218 Email: mair.parry-jones@wales.gov.uk
Commission and Member Support	Craig Stephenson 029 2089 8230 Email: craig.stephenson@wales.gov.uk
Strategic Transformation	Anna Daniel 029 2089 8144 Email: anna.daniel@wales.gov.uk

Welsh Government

Welsh Government, Cathays Park, Cardiff, South Glamorgan CF10 3NQ
Tel: 0300 060 3300/0845 010 3300
Email: [firstname.surname]@wales.gsi.gov.uk Website: www.wales.gov.uk
Llywodraeth Cymru, Parc Cathays, Caerdydd, South Glamorgan CF10 3NQ
Tel: 0300 060 4400/0845 010 4400

Permanent Secretary's Division
Website: www.wales.gov.uk
Permanent Secretary: Derek Jones CB 029 2082 3289 Email: derek.jones@wales.gsi.gov.uk
ps.permanentsecretary@wales.gsi.gov.uk

Department for Business, Enterprise, Technology and Science
Website: www.wales.gov.uk/about/civilservice/directorates/bets
Director-General: James Price 029 2082 6646 Email: james.price@wales.gsi.gov.uk
Chief Scientific Adviser for Wales: To be appointed

Department for Education and Skills
Website: www.wales.gov.uk/about/civilservice/directorates/educationandskills
Director-General: Owen Evans 029 2082 5381 Email: owen.evans3@wales.gsi.gov.uk

Department for Health, Social Services and Children
Website: www.wales.gov.uk/about/civilservice/directorates/hsscdirectorate
Director-General and Chief Executive, NHS Wales: David Sissling 029 2080 1182
Email: david.sissling@wales.gsi.gov.uk

Local Government and Communities Directorate
Website: www.wales.gov.uk/about/civilservice/directorates/lgc
Director-General: Dr June Milligan 029 2082 5727 Email: june.milligan@wales.gsi.gov.uk

People, Places and Corporate Services Directorate
Website: www.wales.gov.uk/about/civilservice/directorates/ppcs
Director-General: Bernard Galton 029 2082 3695 Email: bernard.galton@wales.gsi.gov.uk

Department for Strategic Planning, Finance and Performance
Website: www.wales.gov.uk/about/civilservice/directorates/spfp
Director-General: Michael Hearty 029 2082 3494 Email: michael.hearty@wales.gsi.gov.uk
Chief Executive, Welsh European Funding Office: Damien O'Brien 0300 062 8334
Email: damien.obrien@wales.gsi.gov.uk
Acting Chief, Statistical Services: Glyn Jones 029 2082 6691 Email: glyn.jones@wales.gsi.gov.uk

Sustainable Futures Directorate
Website: www.wales.gov.uk/about/civilservice/directorates/sustainablefutures
Director-General: Gareth Jones OBE 029 2082 6925 Email: gareth.jones2@wales.gsi.gov.uk
Adviser on Energy to the Welsh Government: Ron Loveland 029 2082 3497
Email: ron.loveland@wales.gsi.gov.uk

Legal Services Department
Website: www.wales.gov.uk/about/civilservice/directorates/other/legalservices
Director: Jeffrey Godfrey 029 2080 1105 Email: jeffrey.godfrey@wales.gsi.gov.uk
First Legislative Counsel: Dylan Hughes 029 2082 1649 Email: dylan.hughes@wales.gsi.gov.uk

Non-Ministerial Department

Estyn – HM Inspectorate for Education and Training in Wales
Anchor Court, Keen Road, Cardiff CF24 5JW
Tel: 029 2044 6446 Fax: 029 2044 6448
Email: enquiries@estyn.gov.uk Website: www.estyn.gov.uk/english Twitter: @EstynHMI

Llys Angor, Heol Keen, Caerdydd CF24 5JW
Tel: 029 2044 6446 Fax: 029 2044 6448
Email: ymholiadau@estyn.gov.uk Website: www.estyn.gov.uk/cymraeg

Number of staff: 120

HM Chief Inspector of Education and Training in Wales: Ann Keane 029 2044 6523
Email: chief-inspector@estyn.gov.uk

Political Parties

Welsh Labour (Llafur Cymru)

Unite the Union Building, 1 Cathedral Road, Cardiff CF11 9HA
Tel: 029 2087 7700 Fax: 029 2022 1153
Email: wales@labour.org.uk Website: www.welshlabour.org.uk Twitter: @welshlabour

Labour Group Office:
Tel: 029 2089 8548

First Minister and Leader of Labour in the National Assembly: Carwyn Jones AM
General Secretary: David Hagendyk
Press Officer: Huw Price

Welsh Conservatives (Ceidwadwyr Cymreig)

Welsh Conservative Campaign Headquarters, Ground Floor, Rhymney House, 1-2 Copse Walk,
Cardiff Gate Business Park, Cardiff CF23 8RB Tel: 029 2073 6562
Email: info@welshconservatives.com Website: www.welshconservatives.com
Twitter: @welshconserv

Chairman: Jeff James
Deputy Chairmen: Lyndon Jones, Paul Morris
Director: Roger Pratt 029 2073 6562
Senior Media Officers:
Mike Jackson 029 2089 8395 Email: mike.jackson@wales.gov.uk
Richard John 029 2089 8976 Email: richard.john@wales.gov.uk

Plaid Cymru (The Party of Wales)

Tŷ Gwynfor, Marine Chambers, Anson Court, Atlantic Wharf, Cardiff CF10 4AL Tel: 029 2047 2272
Email: post@plaidcymru.org Website: www.plaidcymru.org Twitter: @plaid_cymru

Assembly Office:
Tel: 029 2089 8761 Fax: 029 2089 8260

Leader: Leanne Wood AM
Chief Executive: Rhuanedd Richards 029 2047 2272
Treasurer: Dr Dafydd Trystan 029 2047 2272

Welsh Liberal Democrats (Democratiaid Rhyddfrydol Cymru)

38 The Parade, Cardiff CF24 3AD Tel: 029 2031 3400
Email: enquiries@welshlibdems.org.uk Website: www.welshlibdems.org.uk Twitter: @welshlibdems

Assembly Office:
Tel: 029 2089 8741

Leader: Kirsty Williams AM Email: kirsty.williams@welshlibdems.org.uk
Deputy Leader: Roger Williams MP Email: williamsr@parliament.uk
Chief Executive: Richard Thomas Email: richard.thomas@welshlibdems.org.uk
Party Manager: Ian Walton Email: ian.walton@welshlibdems.org.uk
Campaigns Officer: Jon Aylwin Email: jon.aylwin@welshlibdems.org.uk
Policy Officer: Morgan Griffith-David 029 2031 3649
Email: morgan.griffith-david@welshlibdems.org.uk
Head of Communications: Myrddin Edwards 029 2031 3400
Email: myrddin.edwards@welshlibdems.org.uk

Northern Ireland Assembly

Parliament Buildings, Stormont, Belfast BT4 3XX
Tel: 028 9052 1137/Textphone: 028 9052 1209 Fax: 028 9052 1961
Email: info@niassembly.gov.uk Website:www.niassembly.gov.uk Twitter: @niassembly

Executive Committee of Ministers

First Minister	Rt Hon **Peter Robinson** (DUP)
Deputy First Minister	**Martin McGuinness** (Sinn Féin)
Minister of Agriculture and Rural Development	**Michelle O'Neill** (Sinn Féin)
Minister of Culture, Arts and Leisure	**Carál Ní Chuilín** (Sinn Féin)
Minister for Education	**John O'Dowd** (Sinn Féin)
Minister for Employment and Learning	Dr **Stephen Farry** (All)
Minister of Enterprise, Trade and Investment	**Arlene Foster** (DUP)
Minister of Environment	**Mark H Durkan** (SDLP)
Minister of Finance and Personnel	**Simon Hamilton** (DUP)
Minister of Health, Social Services and Public Safety	**Edwin Poots** (DUP)
Minister of Justice	**David Ford** (All)
Minister for Regional Development	**Danny Kennedy** (UUP)
Minister for Social Development	**Nelson McCausland** (DUP)

Ministerial Responsibilities and Staff

Office of the First Minister and Deputy First Minister

Stormont Castle, Stormont Estate, Belfast BT4 3TT
Tel: 028 9052 8400 Fax: 028 9052 2814
Email: ps.ministers@ofmdfmni.gov.uk Website: www.ofmdfmni.gov.uk

Support for the Executive, and liaison with the Assembly, the North-South Ministerial Council, British-Irish Council, Civic Forum and UK Departments; international relations; Programme for Government and the Executive's economic policies; promoting and monitoring implementation of equality of opportunity/good relations, tackling poverty and social exclusion, children and young people, victims and survivors, sustainable development; Maze/Long Kesh Regeneration; Review of Public Administration; Information Service; emergency planning; improving investment in infrastructure and the Statutory Publications Office.

First Minister Rt Hon **Peter Robinson** MLA (DUP)

Principal Private Secretary	Jeremy Gardner	028 9037 8080
	Email: jeremy.gardner@ofmdfmni.gov.uk	

Deputy First Minister **Martin McGuinness** MLA (Sinn Féin)

Principal Private Secretary	Anne Dickson	028 9037 8075
	Email: anne.dickson@ofmdfmni.gov.uk	

Junior Minister **Jonathan Bell** MLA (DUP)

Private Secretary	Sean Kerr	028 9037 8097
	Email: sean.kerr@ofmdfmni.gov.uk	

Junior Minister **Jennifer McCann** MLA (Sinn Féin)

Private Secretary	Kathy Monaghan	028 9037 8125
	Email: kathy.monaghan@ofmdfmni.gov.uk	

Department of Agriculture and Rural Development

Dundonald House, Upper Newtownards Road, Ballymiscaw, Belfast BT4 3SB
Tel: 028 9052 4999/Textphone: 028 9052 4420 Fax: 028 9052 4170
Email: dardhelpline@dardni.gov.uk Website: www.dardni.gov.uk

Minister of Agriculture and Rural Development **Michelle O'Neill** MLA (Sinn Féin)

Development of the agri-food, forestry and fishing industries in Northern Ireland; lead Department for
rural development in Northern Ireland; policy on research and development in agriculture and food;
education and training; provision of a veterinary service and administration of animal health and
welfare policies; agent of the Department for Environment, Food and Rural Affairs in the administration
in Northern Ireland of schemes affecting the whole of the United Kingdom; involvement with the
application to Northern Ireland of the agricultural policy of the EU.

Assembly Private Secretary	To be appointed	
Special Adviser	Conor Heaney	028 9052 4119
	Email: private.office@dardni.gov.uk	
Private Secretary	Paula Magill	028 9052 4011
	Email: paula.magill@dardni.gov.uk	

Department of Culture, Arts and Leisure

Causeway Exchange, 1-7 Bedford Street, Belfast BT2 7FB
Tel: 028 9051 5202 Fax: 028 9082 3450
Website: www.dcalni.gov.uk

Minister of Culture, Arts and Leisure **Carál Ní Chuilín** MLA (Sinn Féin)

Arts and creativity; sport and leisure; inland fisheries; inland waterways; public libraries and museums;
language diversity; Public Record Office of Northern Ireland; Advising on National Lottery policy.

Assembly Private Secretary	Barry McElduff MLA	
	(Sinn Féin)	028 9052 1624 Fax: 028 9052 1622
	Email: barry.mcelduff@mla.niassembly.gov.uk	
Special Adviser	Jarlath Kearney	028 9051 5206
	Email: spad.dcal@dcalni.eu	
Private Secretary	Paul Loughlin	028 9051 5202
	Email: private.office@dcalni.gov.uk	

Department of Education

Rathgael House, Balloo Road, Rathgill, Bangor BT19 7PR
Tel: 028 9127 9279 Fax: 028 9127 9100
Email: mail@deni.gov.uk Website: www.deni.gov.uk

Minister for Education **John O'Dowd** MLA (Sinn Féin)

Schools funding and administrations; pre-school, primary, post-primary and special education; the youth
service; the promotion of community relations within and between schools; teacher education and salaries.

Assembly Private Secretary	To be appointed	
Special Adviser	Mark Mullan	028 9052 1068
	Email: SpAd@deni.eu	
Private Secretary	Claire McKee	028 9052 0486
	Email: claire.mckee@deni.gov.uk	

Department for Employment and Learning

Adelaide House, 39-49 Adelaide Street, Belfast BT2 8FD
Tel: 028 9025 7791
Website: www.delni.gov.uk

Minister for Employment and Learning Dr **Stephen Farry** MLA (All)

Higher education; further education; vocational training; employment services; employment law and labour relations; student support and postgraduate awards; careers advice and guidance; skills strategy; STEM Strategy.

Special Adviser	Christine Robinson	028 9025 7767
	Email: christine.robinson@delni.gov.uk	
Private Secretary	Rory Muldrew	028 9025 7791
	Email: rory.muldrew@delni.gov.uk	

Department of Enterprise, Trade and Investment

Netherleigh House, Massey Avenue, Belfast BT4 2JP
Tel: 028 9052 9900 Fax: 028 9052 9545
Website: www.detini.gov.uk

Minister of Enterprise, Trade and Investment **Arlene Foster** MLA (DUP)

Economic development policy, including business development, energy, telecoms, tourism; economic advice and research; research and statistics services; business regulation, including company law/registry, insolvency service, consumer affairs, trading standards; health and safety at work; social economy; mineral development; geological survey of NI; Invest NI; NI Tourist Board; Intertrade Ireland and Tourism Ireland; Health and Safety Executive for NI; the Consumer Council for NI.

Assembly Private Secretary	Alastair Ross MLA (DUP)	028 9052 1322/028 9052 9452
	Email: alastair.ross@mla.niassembly.gov.uk	
	alastair.ross@detini.gov.uk	
Private Secretary	Glynis Aiken	028 9052 9452
	Email: glynis.aiken@detini.gov.uk	

Department of the Environment

Eighth Floor, Goodwood House, 44-58 May Street, Belfast BT1 4NN
Tel: 028 9025 6019
Email: private.office@doeni.gov.uk Website: www.doeni.gov.uk

Minister of Environment **Mark H Durkan** MLA (SDLP)

Planning control; environment and heritage; protection of the countryside; waste management; pollution control; wildlife protection; local government; local government reform; mineral resources (planning aspects); driver and vehicle testing and licensing; road safety; transport licensing and enforcement.

Assembly Private Secretary	Colum Eastwood MLA (SDLP)	028 9041 8357
	Email: colum.eastwood@mla.niassembly.gov.uk	
Special Adviser	Michael McKernan	
	Email: spad@doeni.gov.uk	
Private Secretary	Joann Hanna	028 9025 6019
	Email: joann.hanna@doeni.gov.uk	

Department of Finance and Personnel

Craigantlet Buildings, Stormont Estate, Belfast BT4 3SX
Tel: 028 9016 3371
Email: private.office@dfpni.gov.uk Website: www.dfpni.gov.uk

Minister of Finance and Personnel **Simon Hamilton** MLA (DUP)

Finance; personnel; Civil Law Reform Division; Land Registers; General Registers Office and Building Regulations; Central Procurement; Land and Property Services Agency; civil service accommodation; legal services; Official Statistics Northern Ireland; NI Statistics and Research Agency (NISRA).

Assembly Private Secretary	To be appointed	
Special Adviser	Allan Ewart	028 9016 3387
	Email: spad@dfpni.gov.uk	
Private Secretary	Siobhan Tweedie	028 9016 3371
	Email: siobhan.tweedie@dfpni.gov.uk	

Department of Health, Social Services and Public Safety

Castle Buildings, Stormont, Belfast BT4 3SJ
Tel: 028 9052 0500 Fax: 028 9052 0557
Website: www.dhsspsni.gov.uk

Minister of Health, Social Services and Public Safety **Edwin Poots** MLA (DUP)

Public health; primary care services and community health and personal social services; family practitioner services; elderly and community care; child care and child protection; family policy; mental health; learning disability; physical and sensory disability; provision of hospital services and clinics; accident and emergency services; public safety; ambulance and fire and rescue services.

Assembly Private Secretary	Alex Easton MLA (DUP)	028 9058 8379
	Email: alex.easton@mla.niassembly.gov.uk	
Special Adviser	Dr Philip Weir	028 9076 5613
	Email: philip.weir@dhsspsni.gov.uk	
Private Secretary	Pamela Baxter	028 9052 0643
	Email: pamela.baxter@dhsspsni.gov.uk	

Department of Justice

Block B, Castle Buildings, Belfast BT4 3SG
Tel: 028 9052 2704 Fax: 028 9052 8434
Website: www.dojni.gov.uk

Minister of Justice **David Ford** MLA (All)

Providing resources and a legislative framework for its agencies and arms length bodies; ensuring there is a fair and effective justice system; increasing public confidence; tackling avoidable delay within the criminal justice system; building safer communities; addressing the needs of victims and witnesses; reducing re-offending and managing offenders; DoJ agencies, including the Northern Ireland Prison Service, Northern Ireland Courts and Tribunals Service, Compensation Agency, Forensic Science Agency and the Youth Justice Agency.

Special Adviser	Richard Good	028 9052 3424
	Email: richard.good@dojni.x.gsi.gov.uk	
Private Secretary	Steven McKee	028 9052 2704/028 9052 5975
	Email: steven.mckee@dojni.x.gsi.gov.uk	

Department for Regional Development

Clarence Court, 10-18 Adelaide Street, Belfast BT2 8GB
Tel: 028 9054 0540 Fax: 028 9054 0028
Website: www.drdni.gov.uk

Minister for Regional Development **Danny Kennedy** MLA (UUP)

Strategic planning; transportation strategy; ports and public transport; roads and water policy; providing and maintaining roads; water and sewerage services.

Assembly Private Secretary	Jo-Anne Dobson MLA (UUP)	028 9052 1925
	Email: jo-anne.dobson@mla.niassembly.gov.uk	
Special Adviser	Rodney McCune (UUP)	028 9054 0346
	Email: spad@drdni.gov.uk	
Private Secretary	Máire Cairns	028 9054 0105
	Email: maire.cairns@drdni.gov.uk	

Department for Social Development
Lighthouse Building, 1 Cromac Place, Gasworks Business Park, Ormeau Road, Belfast BT7 2JB
Tel: 028 9082 9000 Fax: 028 9082 9548
Email: private.office@dsdni.gov.uk Website: www.dsdni.gov.uk

Minister for Social Development **Nelson McCausland** MLA (DUP)

Housing, urban regeneration, community and voluntary sector development; social security legislation, social security benefits and child maintenance.

Assembly Private Secretary	William Humphrey MLA	
	(DUP)	028 9052 1322
	Email: william.humphrey@mla.niassembly.gov.uk	
Special Adviser	Stephen Brimstone	
	Email: stephen.brimstone@dsdni.gov.uk	
Private Secretary	Emma Murray	028 9082 9034
	Email: emma.murray@dsdni.gov.uk	

Opposition

Sinn Féin

Leader, Assembly Group; Spokesperson for Justice	**Raymond McCartney**
Spokesperson for Agriculture	**Oliver McMullan**
Spokesperson for Culture, Arts and Leisure	**Cathal Ó hOisín**
Spokesperson for Economy	**Daithí McKay**
Spokesperson for Education	**Chris Hazzard**
Spokesperson for Employment and Learning and Equality	**Bronwyn McGahan**
Spokesperson for Enterprise and Tourism	**Phil Flanagan**
Spokesperson for Environment	**Barry McElduff**
Spokesperson for Families, Youth, Children and Young People	**Megan Fearon**
Spokesperson for Governance	**Michaela Boyle**
Spokesperson for Health	**Sue Ramsey**
Spokesperson for Housing	**Fra McCann**
Spokesperson for Infrastructure and Transport	**Declan McAleer**
Spokesperson for International Affairs	**Pat Sheehan**
Spokesperson for Irish Language and Youth Justice and Community Safety	**Rosie McCorley**
Spokesperson for Planning, Road Safety and Review of Public Administration	**Cathal Boylan**
Spokesperson for Policing; Deputy Chief Whip	**Gerry Kelly**
Spokesperson for Regional Development	**Seán Lynch**
Spokesperson for Social Development	**Alex Maskey**
Spokesperson for Social Economy and Victims and Truth	**Maeve McLaughlin**
Spokesperson for Welfare and Older People	**Mickey Brady**
Chief Whip	**Caitríona Ruane**

Ulster Unionist Party

Leader; Spokesperson for Office of the First Minister and Deputy First Minister and Victims	**Mike Nesbitt**
Spokesperson for Agriculture	**Jo-Anne Dobson**
Spokesperson for Culture, Arts and Leisure	**Michael McGimpsey**
Spokesperson for Education	**Danny Kinahan**
Spokesperson for Employment and Learning and Parading; Chief Whip	**Robin Swann**
Spokesperson for Enterprise, Trade and Investment and Children and Young People; Deputy Whip	**Sandra Overend**
Spokesperson for Finance	**Leslie Cree** MBE
Spokesperson for Health	**Roy Beggs**
Spokesperson for Justice and Environment	**Tom Elliott**
Spokesperson for Older People	**Samuel Gardiner** MBE
Spokesperson for Regional Development	**Ross Hussey**
Spokesperson for Social Development and Voluntary and Community Sector	**Michael Copeland**

Social Democratic and Labour Party

Leader	Dr **Alasdair McDonnell**
Deputy Leader; Spokesperson for Environment	**Dolores Kelly**
Spokesperson for Agriculture and Rural Development	**Joe Byrne**
Spokesperson for Culture, Arts and Leisure	**Karen McKevitt**
Spokesperson for Education	**Seán Rogers**
Spokesperson for Employment and Learning; Chief Whip	**Pat Ramsey**
Spokesperson for Enterprise, Trade and Investment	**Patsy McGlone**
Spokesperson for Finance and Personnel	**Dominic Bradley**
Spokesperson for Health, Social Services and Public Safety and Policing	**To be appointed**
Spokesperson for Justice	**Alban Maginness**
Spokesperson for Office of the First Minister and Deputy First Minister	**Colum Eastwood**
Spokesperson for Regional Development	**John Dallat**

Alliance Party

Leader	**David Ford**
Spokesperson for Culture, Arts and Leisure and Environment	**Anna Lo** MBE
Spokesperson for Education, Enterprise, Trade and Investment and Agriculture	**Trevor Lunn**
Spokesperson for Employment and Learning and Office of the First Minister and Deputy First Minister	**Chris Lyttle**
Spokesperson for Finance and Personnel	**Judith Cochrane**
Spokesperson for Health and Regional Development	**Kieran McCarthy**
Spokesperson for Justice and Social Development; Chief Whip	**Stewart Dickson**

Members (MLAs)

State of the Parties (September 2013)

	Total
Democratic Unionist Party	37*
Sinn Féin	29†
Social Democratic and Labour Party	14†
Ulster Unionist Party	13†
Alliance	8
NI21	2
Green Party	1
Independent	1
Traditional Unionist Voice	1
UK Independence Party	1
The Speaker	1
	108 seats

*Excludes the Speaker who has no party allegiance while in post.
†Includes a Deputy Speaker who can participate and vote fully in the Assembly when not in the Chair.

Changes since 2011 Northern Ireland Assembly election

RESIGNATIONS

Margaret Ritchie	South Down – *SDLP*	31 March 2012
Willie Clarke	South Down – *Sinn Féin*	12 April 2012
Martina Anderson	Foyle – *Sinn Féin*	11 June 2012
Pat Doherty	West Tyrone – *Sinn Féin*	2 July 2012
Michelle Gildernew	Fermanagh and South Tyrone – *Sinn Féin*	2 July 2012
Paul Maskey	Belfast West – *Sinn Féin*	2 July 2012
Conor Murphy	Newry and Armagh – *Sinn Féin*	2 July 2012
Francie Molloy	Mid Ulster – *Sinn Féin*	7 April 2013
Conall McDevitt	Belfast South – *SDLP*	4 September 2013

REPLACEMENTS

Seán Rogers	South Down – *SDLP*	Returned 1 April 2012 following the resignation of Margaret Ritchie
Chris Hazzard	South Down – *Sinn Féin*	Returned 13 April 2012 following the resignation of Willie Clarke
Maeve McLaughlin	Foyle – *Sinn Féin*	Returned 14 June 2012 following the resignation of Martina Anderson
Megan Fearon	Newry and Armagh – *Sinn Féin*	Returned 2 July 2012 following the resignation of Conor Murphy
Declan McAleer	West Tyrone – *Sinn Féin*	Returned 2 July 2012 following the resignation of Pat Doherty
Rosie McCorley	Belfast West – *Sinn Féin*	Returned 2 July 2012 following the resignation of Paul Maskey
Bronwyn McGahan	Fermanagh and South Tyrone – *Sinn Féin*	Returned 2 July 2012 following the resignation of Michelle Gildernew
Ian Milne	Mid Ulster – *Sinn Féin*	Returned 8 April 2013 following the resignation of Francie Molloy
Fearghal McKinney	Belfast South – *SDLP*	Returned 13 September 2013 following the resignation of Conall McDevitt

CHANGE OF PARTY

David McNarry	Strangford	Resigned from UUP Assembly Group 30 January 2012, now UK Independence Party
John McCallister	South Down	Resigned from UUP 14 February 2013, now NI21
Basil McCrea	Lagan Valley	Resigned from UUP 15 February 2013, now NI21

MLAs' Directory

All	Alliance
DUP	Democratic Unionist Party
Green	Green Party
Ind	Independent
NI21	NI21
SDLP	Social Democratic and Labour Party
Speaker	The Speaker
TUV	Traditional Unionist Voice
UKIP	UK Independence Party
UUP	Ulster Unionist Party

AGNEW, Steven   *Green*   **North Down**
Leader, Green Party in Northern Ireland
Tel: 028 9052 1790 Email: steven.agnew@mla.niassembly.gov.uk
Constituency office: 76 Abbey Street, Bangor, Co Down BT20 4JB
Tel: 028 9145 9110 Email: stevenagnewgpni@hotmail.co.uk
Website: www.stevenagnew.net Twitter: @stevenagnew

ALLISTER, Jim   *TUV*   **North Antrim**
Leader, Traditional Unionist Voice
Tel: 028 9052 1175 Email: jim.allister@mla.niassembly.gov.uk
Constituency offices: 38 Henry Street, Ballykeel, Ballymena, Co Antrim BT42 3AH
Tel: 028 2564 0250 Email: info@jimallister.org
1 Charles Street, Ballymoney, Co Antrim BT53 6DX
Tel: 028 2723 8393
Website: www.jimallister.org Twitter: @jimallister

ANDERSON, Sydney   *DUP*   **Upper Bann**
Tel: 028 9052 0320 Email: sydney.anderson@mla.niassembly.gov.uk
Constituency offices: 8 Rathfriland Street, Ballyvally, Banbridge, Co Down BT32 3LA
Tel: 028 4066 2426
13 Thomas Street, Portadown, Co Armagh BT62 3NP
Tel: 028 3833 2234

ATTWOOD, Alex   *SDLP*   **Belfast West**
Tel: 028 9052 1319 Email: alex.attwood@mla.niassembly.gov.uk
Constituency office: 60 Andersontown Road, Ballydownfine, Belfast, Co Antrim BT11 9AN
Tel: 028 9080 7808 Fax: 028 9080 7370 Email: a.attwood@sdlp.ie attwoodalex@yahoo.co.uk

BEGGS, Roy   *UUP*   **East Antrim**
Deputy Speaker; UUP Spokesperson for Health
Tel: 028 9052 1546 Email: roy.beggs@mla.niassembly.gov.uk
Constituency offices: 3 St Brides Street, Carrickfergus, Co Antrim BT38 8AF
Tel: 028 9336 2995 Fax: 028 9336 8048 Email: roybeggs.office@btopenworld.com
41 Station Road, Inver, Larne, Co Antrim BT40 3AA
Tel: 028 2827 3258 Fax: 028 2827 3258 Email: roybeggs.office3@btopenworld.com
Website: www.roybeggs.co.uk Twitter: @roybeggs

BELL, Jonathan   *DUP*   **Strangford**
Junior Minister, Office of the First Minister and Deputy First Minister
Email: jonathan.bell@mla.niassembly.gov.uk
Ministerial office: Office of the First Minister and Deputy First Minister, Stormont Castle, Stormont
Estate, Belfast BT4 3TT Switchboard: 028 9052 8400
Constituency office: 12 North Street, Newtownards, Co Down BT23 4DE
Tel: 028 9182 7701 Fax: 028 9182 7703 Email: joanathanrobinson@dup.org.uk
Twitter: @jonathanfbell

BOYLAN, Cathal *Sinn Féin* **Newry and Armagh**
Sinn Féin Spokesperson for Planning, Road Safety and Review of Public Administration
Tel: 028 9041 8351 Email: cathal.boylan@mla.niassembly.gov.uk
Constituency office: 1 Ogle Street, Armagh, Co Armagh BT61 7EN
Tel: 028 3751 1797 Email: armaghsinnfein@gmail.com Website: www.newryarmaghsf.com

BOYLE, Michaela *Sinn Féin* **West Tyrone**
Sinn Féin Spokesperson for Governance
Tel: 028 9041 8383 Email: michaela.boyle@mla.niassembly.gov.uk
Constituency office: 1a Melvin Road, Ballycolman, Strabane, Co Tyrone BT82 9PP
Tel: 028 7188 6464 Email: micheala.boyle@sinn-fein.ie Twitter: @boyler4

BRADLEY, Dominic *SDLP* **Newry and Armagh**
SDLP Spokesperson for Finance and Personnel
Tel: 028 9058 8352 Email: dominic.bradley@mla.niassembly.gov.uk
Constituency offices: 19 Cathedral Road, Armagh BT61 7QX
Tel: 028 3752 6800
15 Trevor Hill, Newry BT34 1DN
Tel: 028 3026 7933 Email: dominicobrolchain@btinternet.com
Website: www.dominicbradleymla.com Twitter: @dbradleymla

BRADLEY, Paula *DUP* **Belfast North**
Tel: 028 9052 1335 Email: paula.bradley@mla.niassembly.gov.uk
Constituency office: 3 Portland Avenue, Glengormley, Newtownabbey BT36 5EY
Tel: 028 9083 0066

BRADY, Mickey *Sinn Féin* **Newry and Armagh**
Sinn Féin Spokesperson for Welfare and Older People
Tel: 028 9052 0356 Email: mickey.brady@mla.niassembly.gov.uk
Constituency office: 1 Kilmorey Terrace, Newry, Co Down BT35 8DW
Tel: 028 3026 1693 Email: mickey.brady@sinn-fein.ie

BROWN, Pam *DUP* **South Antrim**
Email: pam.brown@mla.niassembly.gov.uk
Constituency office: 12a Beverley Road, Newtownabbey BT36 6QD
Tel: 028 9034 2234 Twitter: @pbrownmla

BUCHANAN, Thomas *DUP* **West Tyrone**
Tel: 028 9058 8368 Email: thomas.buchanan@mla.niassembly.gov.uk
Constituency office: 5 Dublin Road, Omagh, Co Tyrone BT78 1ES
Tel: 028 8224 7702 Fax: 028 8225 9919 Email: cllrthomasbuchananmla@hotmail.com

BYRNE, Joe *SDLP* **West Tyrone**
SDLP Spokesperson for Agriculture and Rural Development
Tel: 028 9052 1702 Email: joe.byrne@mla.niassembly.gov.uk
Constituency office: 9b Dromore Road, Omagh, Co Tyrone BT78 1QZ
Tel: 028 8225 0060 Twitter: @joebyrnemla

CAMPBELL, Gregory *DUP* **East Londonderry**
Tel: 028 9052 1322 Email: gregory.campbell@mla.niassembly.gov.uk
Constituency offices: 25 Bushmills Road, Coleraine, Co Londonderry BT52 2BP
Tel: 028 7032 7327 Fax: 028 7032 7328 Email: wilkinsonh@parliament.uk
6-8 Catherine Street, Limavady, Co Londonderry BT49 9DB
Tel: 028 7776 6060 Fax: 028 7776 9531

CLARKE, Trevor *DUP* **South Antrim**
Tel: 028 9052 1191 Fax: 028 9052 1832 Email: trevor.clarke@mla.niassembly.gov.uk
Constituency office: 1 Lough Road, Antrim, Co Antrim BT41 4DG
Tel: 028 9446 3273 Fax: 028 9446 9143 Email: trevor.clarke62@btinternet.com
Twitter: @trevorclarkemla

COCHRANE, Judith *All* Belfast East
Alliance Party Spokesperson for Finance and Personnel
Tel: 028 9052 0351 Email: judith.cochrane@mla.niassembly.gov.uk
Constituency office: 56 Upper Newtownards Road, Belfast, Co Down BT4 3EL
Tel: 028 9047 2004 Email: judith.cochrane@allianceparty.org
Website: www.judithcochrane.com Twitter: @judithcochrane

COPELAND, Michael *UUP* Belfast East
UUP Spokesperson for Social Development and for the Voluntary and Community Sector
Tel: 028 9052 1291 Email: michael.copeland@mla.niassembly.gov.uk
Constituency office: 174 Albertbridge Road, Ballymacarrett, Belfast BT5 4GS
Tel: 028 9046 3900
Website: www.michaelcopelandmla.com Twitter: @mcopelandmla

CRAIG, Jonathan *DUP* Lagan Valley
Tel: 028 9052 1822 Email: jonathan.craig@mla.niassembly.gov.uk
Constituency offices: The Old Town Hall, 29 Castle Street, Lisburn, Co Antrim BT27 4DH
Tel: 028 9266 8378 Fax: 028 9267 1845 Email: jonathan.craig@laganvalleydup.co.uk
Website: www.laganvalleydup.co.uk
3 Church Street, Ballymaganlis, Dromore, Co Down BT25 1AA
Tel: 028 9269 8866

CREE, Leslie, MBE *UUP* North Down
UUP Spokesperson for Finance
Tel: 028 9041 8391 Email: leslie.cree@mla.niassembly.gov.uk
Constituency office: 20 Hamilton Road, Bangor, Co Down BT20 4LE
Tel: 028 9147 0300 Fax: 028 9147 0301 Email: leslie.cree@co.niassembly.gov.uk
Website: www.lesliecreemla.co.uk

DALLAT, John *SDLP* East Londonderry
Deputy Speaker; SDLP Spokesperson for Regional Development
Tel: 028 9052 1319 Email: john.dallat@mla.niassembly.gov.uk
Constituency offices: 11 Bridge Street, Kilrea, Co Derry BT51 5RR
Tel: 028 2954 1880 Fax: 028 2954 1881
20a Linenhall Street, Limavady BT49 0HQ
Tel: 028 7776 3391 Email: lim2avady-sdlp@btconnect.com Twitter: @johndallat

DICKSON, Stewart *All* East Antrim
Alliance Party Spokesperson for Justice and for Social Development; Chief Whip
Tel: 028 9052 1315 Email: stewart.dickson@mla.niassembly.gov.uk
Constituency offices: 8 West Street, Carrickfergus, Co Antrim BT38 7AR
Tel: 028 9335 0286
97c Main Street, Larne BT40 1HJ
Website: stewartdicksonmla.com Twitter: @stewartcdickson

DOBSON, Jo-Anne *UUP* Upper Bann
Assembly Private Secretary to Danny Kennedy as Minister for Regional Development; UUP
Spokesperson for Agriculture
Tel: 028 9052 1925 Email: jo-anne.dobson@mla.niassembly.gov.uk
Constituency office: 18 Rathfriland Street, Ballyvally, Banbridge, Co Down BT32 3LA
Tel: 028 4066 9004 Twitter: @joanne_dobson

DOUGLAS, Sammy, MBE *DUP* Belfast East
Tel: 028 9052 1249 Email: sammy.douglas@mla.niassembly.gov.uk
Constituency office: 274 Newtownards Road, Belfast, Co Down BT4 1HE
Tel: 028 9046 7926 Email: david.douglas@party.niassembly.gov.uk
Website: sammydouglas.com Twitter: @sammydouglasmla

DUNNE, Gordon *DUP* **North Down**
Tel: 028 9042 3322 Email: gordon.dunne@mla.niassembly.gov.uk
Constituency office: 8 Church Road, Holywood, Co Down BT18 9BU
Tel: 028 9042 3322 Email: info@gordondunne.org
Website: www.gordondunne.org Twitter: @gordondunnemla

DURKAN, Mark H *SDLP* **Foyle**
Minister of Environment
Tel: 028 9041 8354 Email: markh.durkan@mla.niassembly.gov.uk
Ministerial office: Department of the Environment, Eighth Floor, Goodwood House, 44-58 May Street,
Belfast BT1 4NN Switchboard: 028 9025 6019
Constituency office: 141h Strand Road, Derry, Co Derry BT48 7PB
Tel: 028 7136 5516 Email: mhdurkan@sdlp.ie Twitter: @markhdurkan

EASTON, Alex *DUP* **North Down**
Assembly Private Secretary to Edwin Poots as Minister of Health, Social Services and Public Safety
Tel: 028 9058 8379 Email: alex.easton@mla.niassembly.gov.uk
Constituency office: 7 High Street, Donaghadee, Co Down BT21 0AA
Tel: 028 9188 9620 Website: www.nddup.org.uk

EASTWOOD, Colum *SDLP* **Foyle**
Assembly Private Secretary to Mark H Durkan as Minister of Environment; SDLP Spokesperson for
Office of the First Minister and Deputy First Minister
Tel: 028 9041 8357 Email: colum.eastwood@mla.niassembly.gov.uk
Constituency office: Northside Village Centre, Glengalliagh Road, Derry BT48 8NN
Tel: 028 7135 0045 Email: colum.eastwood@sdlp.ie Twitter: @columeastwood

ELLIOTT, Tom *UUP* **Fermanagh and South Tyrone**
UUP Spokesperson for Environment and for Justice
Tel: 028 9041 8372 Email: tom.elliott@mla.niassembly.gov.uk
Constituency offices: 1 Regal Pass, Enniskillen, Co Fermanagh BT74 7NT
Tel: 028 6632 2028 Fax: 028 6634 2846 Email: fstuup@btconnect.com
20 Brooke Street, Dungannon, Co Tyrone BT71 7AN
Tel: 028 8772 3265 Fax: 028 8772 3265 Email: southtyrone1@btconnect.com Twitter: @telliott_uup

FARRY, Dr Stephen *All* **North Down**
Minister for Employment and Learning
Tel: 028 9052 1314 Email: stephen.farry@mla.niassembly.gov.uk
Ministerial office: Department for Employment and Learning, Adelaide House, 39-49 Adelaide Street,
Belfast BT2 8FD Switchboard: 028 9025 7791
Constituency office: 58 Abbey Street, Bangor BT20 4JB
Tel: 028 9185 9475 Email: stephen.farry@allianceparty.org

FEARON, Megan *Sinn Féin* **Newry and Armagh**
Sinn Féin Spokesperson for Families, Youth, Children and Young People
Email: megan.fearon@mla.niassembly.gov.uk
Constituency office: 10 Newry Street, Crossmaglen BT35 9JH
Tel: 028 3086 1948 Twitter: @mfearon91

FLANAGAN, Phil *Sinn Féin* **Fermanagh and South Tyrone**
Sinn Féin Spokesperson for Enterprise and Tourism
Tel: 028 9041 8381
Constituency office: Bobby Sands Centre, 7 Market Street, Enniskillen, Co Fermanagh BT74 7DS
Tel: 028 6632 8214 Email: phil.flanagan1@gmail.com
Website: dearcadheile.blogspot.com Twitter: @philflanagan

FORD, David *All*   **South Antrim**
Leader, Alliance Party; Minister of Justice
Tel: 028 9052 1314 Fax: 028 9052 1313 Email: david.ford@mla.niassembly.gov.uk
Ministerial office: Department of Justice, Block B, Castle Buildings, Belfast BT4 3SG
Switchboard: 028 9052 2704
Constituency office: Unit 2, 21a Carnmoney Road, Newtownabbey, Co Antrim BT36 6HL
Tel: 028 9084 0930 Fax: 028 9083 7774 Email: south.antrim@davidford.org
Website: www.davidford.org

FOSTER, Arlene *DUP*   **Fermanagh and South Tyrone**
Minister of Enterprise, Trade and Investment
Tel: 028 9041 8366
Ministerial office: Department of Enterprise, Trade and Investment, Netherleigh House, Massey
Avenue, Belfast BT4 2JP Switchboard: 028 9052 9900
Constituency office: 32a New Street, Enniskillen, Co Fermanagh BT74 6AH
Tel: 028 6632 0722 Fax: 028 6632 0123 Email: arlene@arlenefoster.org.uk
Website: www.arlenefoster.org.uk

FREW, Paul *DUP*   **North Antrim**
Tel: 028 9041 8392 Email: paul.frew@mla.niassembly.gov.uk
Constituency office: 9-11 Church Street, Ballymena, Co Antrim BT43 6DD
Tel: 028 2564 1421 Fax: 028 2565 7296 Email: frew637@btinternet.com

GARDINER, Samuel, MBE *UUP*   **Upper Bann**
UUP Spokesperson for Older People
Tel: 028 9041 8367 Fax: 028 9052 1743 Email: samuel.gardiner@mla.niassembly.gov.uk
Constituency office: 58a High Street, Lurgan, Craigavon BT66 8AU
Tel: 028 3831 0011 Fax: 028 3831 0012

GIRVAN, Paul *DUP*   **South Antrim**
Assembly Private Secretary to Peter Robinson as First Minister
Tel: 028 9041 8348 Email: paul.girvan@mla.niassembly.gov.uk
Constituency office: 5-7 School Street, Ballyclare BT39 9BE
Tel: 028 9334 0111 Fax: 028 9334 9111

GIVAN, Paul *DUP*   **Lagan Valley**
Tel: 028 9041 8389 Email: paul.givan@mla.niassembly.gov.uk
Constituency office: The Old Town Hall, 29 Castle Street, Lisburn, Co Antrim BT27 4DH
Tel: 028 9266 1100 Email: paul@laganvalley.net

HALE, Brenda *DUP*   **Lagan Valley**
Tel: 028 9052 1823 Email: brenda.hale@mla.niassembly.gov.uk
Constituency office: 3 Church Street, Dromore, Co Down BT25 1AA
Tel: 028 9269 8866 Fax: 028 9269 3679

HAMILTON, Simon *DUP*   **Strangford**
Minister of Finance and Personnel
Email: simon.hamilton@mla.niassembly.gov.uk
Ministerial office: Department of Finance and Personnel, Craigantlet Buildings, Stormont Estate,
Belfast BT4 3SX Switchboard: 028 9016 3371
Constituency offices: 7 The Square, Comber, Co Down BT23 5DX
Tel: 028 9187 0900 Email: simonhamilton@dup.org.uk
82 Main Street, Saintfield, Co Down BT24 7AB
Tel: 028 9751 0545
Website: www.simonhamilton.org Twitter: @simonhamilton

HAY, William *Speaker*   **Foyle**
Tel: 028 9052 1181 Fax: 028 9052 1959 Email: speaker@niassembly.gov.uk
Constituency office: 9 Ebrington Terrace, Waterside, Londonderry, Co Londonderry BT47 6JS
Tel: 028 7134 6271 Fax: 028 7132 9550 Email: williamhaydup@btconnect.com
Website: www.duplondonderry.co.uk

HAZZARD, Chris *Sinn Féin*   **South Down**
Sinn Féin Spokesperson for Education
Email: chris.hazzard@mla.niassembly.gov.uk
Constituency office: 2 Circular Road, Castlewellan BT31 9ED
Tel: 028 4377 0185 Email: sfcastlewellanoffice@gmail.com Twitter: @chrishazzardsf

HILDITCH, David *DUP*   **East Antrim**
Tel: 028 9052 1322 Email: david.hilditch@mla.niassembly.gov.uk
Constituency offices: 31 Lancasterian Street, Carrickfergus, Co Antrim BT38 7AB
Tel: 028 9332 9980 Email: davyhilditch@gmail.com
116 Main Street, Larne, Co Antrim BT40 1RG
Tel: 028 9332 9980
Website: www.davidhilditch.org Twitter: @dwh_crfc

HUMPHREY, William *DUP*   **Belfast North**
Assembly Private Secretary to Nelson McCausland as Minister for Social Development
Tel: 028 9052 1322 Email: william.humphrey@mla.niassembly.gov.uk
Constituency office: Park Gate House, 35 Woodvale Road, Belfast BT13 3BN
Tel: 028 9074 4008 Email: williamhy@dup-belfast.co.uk

HUSSEY, Ross *UUP*   **West Tyrone**
UUP Spokesperson for Regional Development
Tel: 028 9052 1292 Email: ross.hussey@mla.niassembly.gov.uk
Constituency office: 64 Market Street, Omagh BT78 1EN
Tel: 028 8224 5568 Email: info@rosshusseymla.com
Website: www.rosshusseymla.com Twitter: @rosshusseymla

IRWIN, William *DUP*   **Newry and Armagh**
Tel: 028 9052 0313 Email: william.irwin@mla.niassembly.gov.uk
Constituency offices: 8-10 Main Street, Richhill, Co Antrim BT61 9PW
Tel: 028 3887 0500 Fax: 028 3887 0054
19 Church Street, Tandragee BT62 2AF
Tel: 028 3884 9000 Fax: 028 3884 9444 Email: william.irwin@armagh.gov.uk

KELLY, Dolores *SDLP*   **Upper Bann**
Deputy Leader, Social Democratic and Labour Party; SDLP Spokesperson for Environment
Tel: 028 9058 8355 Email: dolores.kelly@mla.niassembly.gov.uk
Constituency office: 7 William Street, Lurgan, Co Antrim BT66 6JA
Tel: 028 3832 2140 Fax: 028 3831 6996 Email: d.kelly@sdlp.ie doloreskellysdlp@btconnect.com
Twitter: @doloreskelly

KELLY, Gerry *Sinn Féin*   **Belfast North**
Sinn Féin Spokesperson for Policing; Deputy Chief Whip
Tel: 028 9052 1471 Email: gerry.kelly@mla.niassembly.gov.uk
Constituency office: 291 Antrim Road, Belfast, Co Antrim BT15 2GZ
Tel: 028 9074 0817 Fax: 028 9074 0814 Email: gerry.kelly@sinn-fein.ie Twitter: @gerrykellymla

KENNEDY, Danny *UUP*   **Newry and Armagh**
Minister for Regional Development
Tel: 028 9052 1336 Email: danny.kennedy@mla.niassembly.gov.uk
Ministerial office: Department for Regional Development, Clarence Court, 10-18 Adelaide Street,
Belfast BT2 8GB Switchboard: 028 9054 0540
Constituency office: 47 Main Street, Markethill, Co Armagh BT60 1PH
Tel: 028 3755 2831 Email: danny.kennedymla@hotmail.co.uk

KINAHAN, Danny *UUP* South Antrim
UUP Spokesperson for Education
Tel: 028 9052 0394 Email: danny.kinahan@mla.niassembly.gov.uk
Constituency offices: Castle Upton, Templepatrick, Co Antrim BT39 0AH
Tel: 028 9443 3480
24 Fountain Street, Antrim, Co Antrim BT52 4BB
Tel: 028 9446 1211
Website: dannykinahan.com Twitter: @ddebk

LO, Anna, MBE *All* **Belfast South**
Alliance Party Spokesperson for Environment and for Culture, Arts and Leisure
Tel: 028 9052 1560 Fax: 028 9052 0304 Email: anna.lo@mla.niassembly.gov.uk
Constituency office: 88 University Street, Belfast, Co Antrim BT7 1HE
Tel: 028 9033 0811 Fax: 028 9033 3147
Email: catherine.curran@allianceparty.org jenna.maghie@allianceparty.org
Website: www.annalo.org

LUNN, Trevor *All* **Lagan Valley**
Alliance Party Spokesperson for Education, for Enterprise, Trade and Investment and for Agriculture
Tel: 028 9052 1139 Email: trevor.lunn@mla.niassembly.gov.uk
Constituency office: 17 Graham Gardens, Lisburn, Co Antrim BT28 1XE
Tel: 028 9267 1177 Fax: 028 9267 1157 Email: trevor.lunn@allianceparty.org

---

LYNCH, Seán *Sinn Féin* **Fermanagh and South Tyrone**
Sinn Féin Spokesperson for Regional Development
Tel: 028 9052 0350 Email: sean.lynch@mla.niassembly.gov.uk
Constituency office: 115 Main Street, Lisnaskea, Co Fermanagh BT92 0JE
Tel: 028 6772 1642 Email: sean.lynch@sinn-fein.ie

LYTTLE, Chris *All* **Belfast East**
Alliance Party Spokesperson for Office of the First Minister and Deputy First Minister and for Employment and Learning
Tel: 028 9052 1314 Email: chris.lyttle@mla.niassembly.gov.uk
Constituency office: 56 Upper Newtownards Road, Belfast, Co Down BT4 3EL
Tel: 028 9047 2004 Fax: 028 9065 6408 Email: chris.lyttle@co.niassembly.gov.uk
Website: www.chrislyttle.com Twitter: @chris_lyttle

McALEER, Declan *Sinn Féin* **West Tyrone**
Sinn Féin Spokesperson for Infrastructure and Transport
Email: declan.mcaleer@mla.niassembly.gov.uk
Constituency office: 4-5 James Street, Omagh BT78 1DH
Tel: 028 8225 3040 Fax: 028 8225 3041 Email: declanmcaleer@yahoo.com

---

McCALLISTER, John *NI21* **South Down**
Tel: 028 9058 8373 Email: john.mccallister@mla.niassembly.gov.uk
Constituency office: 29a Central Promenade, Newcastle BT33 0AA
Tel: 028 4372 7085 Twitter: @johnmccallister

McCANN, Fra *Sinn Féin* **Belfast West**
Sinn Féin Spokesperson for Housing
Tel: 028 9052 1471 Email: fra.mccann@mla.niassembly.gov.uk
Constituency office: 53 Falls Road, Belfast, Co Antrim BT12 4PD
Tel: 028 9050 8989 Fax: 028 9050 8988 Email: framccann@hotmail.com Twitter: @framccannmla

McCANN, Jennifer   *Sinn Féin*   **Belfast West**
Junior Minister, Office of the First Minister and Deputy First Minister
Tel: 028 9052 1471 Email: jennifer.mccann@mla.niassembly.gov.uk
Ministerial office: Office of the First Minister and Deputy First Minister, Stormont Castle, Stormont
Estate, Belfast BT4 3TT Switchboard: 028 9052 8400
Constituency office: Unit W2, Dairy Farm Centre, Stewartstown Road, Belfast, Co Antrim BT17 0AW
Tel: 028 9061 1176 Email: jennifermccann1@googlemail.com

McCARTHY, Kieran   *All*   **Strangford**
Alliance Party Spokesperson for Health and for Regional Development
Tel: 028 9052 1542 Fax: 028 9052 1053 Email: kieran.mccarthy@mla.niassembly.gov.uk
Constituency office: 14 South Street, Newtownards, Co Down BT23 4JT
Tel: 028 9182 2004 Email: kieran.mccarthy@allianceparty.org
Website: kieranmccarthy.blogspot.co.uk

McCARTNEY, Raymond   *Sinn Féin*   **Foyle**
Leader, Sinn Féin Assembly Group; Spokesperson for Justice
Tel: 028 9052 0322 Email: raymond.mccartney@mla.niassembly.gov.uk
Constituency office: Ráth Mór Business Park, Derry BT48 0LZ
Tel: 028 7137 7551 Email: foyleassembly@gmail.com

McCAUSLAND, Nelson   *DUP*   **Belfast North**
Minister for Social Development
Tel: 028 9052 1322 Email: nelson.mccausland@mla.niassembly.gov.uk
Ministerial office: Department for Social Development, Lighthouse Building, 1 Cromac Place,
Gasworks Business Park, Ormeau Road, Belfast BT7 2JB Switchboard: 028 9082 9000
Constituency office: 256 Ballysillan Road, Belfast BT14 6RB
Tel: 028 9071 7072 Fax: 028 9071 8575 Email: nelsonmccausland@dup-belfast.co.uk
Website: theministerspen.blogspot.co.uk

McCLARTY, David   *Ind*   **East Londonderry**
Tel: 028 9052 0310 Fax: 028 9052 0309 Email: david.mcclarty@mla.niassembly.gov.uk
Constituency office: 1 Upper Abbey Street, Coleraine, Co Londonderry BT51 1BF
Tel: 028 7032 7294 Fax: 028 7032 7474 Email: david.mcclarty.eld@gmail.com
Website: www.davidmcclarty.co.uk Twitter: @davidmcclarty

McCORLEY, Rosie   *Sinn Féin*   **Belfast West**
Sinn Féin Spokesperson for Irish Language and for Youth Justice and Community Safety
Email: rosie.mccorley@mla.niassembly.gov.uk
Constituency office: Connolly House, 147 Andersonstown Road, Belfast BT11 9BW
Tel: 028 9080 8404

McCREA, Basil   *NI21*   **Lagan Valley**
Tel: 028 9052 1803 Email: basil.mccrea@mla.niassembly.gov.uk
Constituency office: 19 Market Square, Dromore BT25 1AW
Tel: 028 9269 3594 Email: basil.mccrea@btinternet.com Twitter: @basilmccrea

McCREA, Ian   *DUP*   **Mid Ulster**
Tel: 028 9052 1543 Email: ian.mccrea@mla.niassembly.gov.uk
Constituency office: 34 Fairhill Road, Cookstown, Co Tyrone BT80 8AG
Tel: 028 8676 4952 Email: cookstown@ianmccrea.com
Website: www.ianmccrea.com Twitter: @ianmccrea_mla

McDONNELL, Dr Alasdair   *SDLP*   **Belfast South**
Leader, Social Democratic and Labour Party
Tel: 028 9052 0329 Email: alasdair.mcdonnell@mla.niassembly.gov.uk
Constituency office: 120a Ormeau Road, Belfast, Co Antrim BT7 2EB
Tel: 028 9024 2474 Fax: 028 9043 9935 Email: mcdonnella@parliament.uk
Website: www.alasdairmcdonnell.com

McELDUFF, Barry   *Sinn Féin*   **West Tyrone**
Assembly Private Secretary to Carál Ní Chuilín as Minister for Culture, Arts and Leisure; Sinn Féin
Spokesperson for Environment
Tel: 028 9052 1624 Fax: 028 9052 1622 Email: barry.mcelduff@mla.niassembly.gov.uk
Constituency office: 4-5 James Street, Omagh, Co Tyrone BT78 1DH
Tel: 028 8225 3040 Fax: 028 8225 3041 Email: barry.mcelduff@sinn-fein.ie Twitter: @barrymcelduff

McGAHAN, Bronwyn   *Sinn Féin*   **Fermanagh and South Tyrone**
Sinn Féin Spokesperson for Employment and Learning and for Equality
Email: bronwyn.mcgahan@mla.niassembly.gov.uk
Constituency office: Thomas Clarke House, 60 Irish Street, Dungannon BT70 1DQ
Tel: 028 8772 2776 Twitter: @bronwynmcgahan

McGIMPSEY, Michael   *UUP*   **Belfast South**
UUP Spokesperson for Culture, Arts and Leisure
Tel: 028 9052 1361 Email: michael.mcgimpsey@mla.niassembly.gov.uk
Constituency office: 127-145 Sandy Row, Belfast, Co Antrim BT12 5ET
Tel: 028 9024 5801 Fax: 028 9024 5801 Email: michaelmcgimpsey@live.co.uk
Website: mmcgimpsey.org Twitter: @mmcgimpsey

McGLONE, Patsy   *SDLP*   **Mid Ulster**
SDLP Spokesperson for Enterprise, Trade and Investment
Tel: 028 9052 0347
Constituency office: 54a William Street, Cookstown, Co Tyrone BT80 8NB
Tel: 028 8675 8175 Fax: 028 8676 4611 Email: patsy.mcglone@sdlp.ie patsymcglonemla@yahoo.ie
Website: www.patsymcglone.com Twitter: @patsymcglone

McGUINNESS, Martin   *Sinn Féin*   **Mid Ulster**
Deputy First Minister
Tel: 028 9052 1671 Email: martin.mcguinness@mla.niassembly.gov.uk
Ministerial office: Office of the First Minister and Deputy First Minister, Stormont Castle,
Stormont Estate, Belfast BT4 3TT Switchboard: 028 9052 8400
Constituency office: 32 Burn Road, Cookstown, Co Tyrone BT80 8DN
Tel: 028 8676 5850 Fax: 028 8676 6734 Email: martin.mcguinness@sinn-fein.ie

McILVEEN, David   *DUP*   **North Antrim**
Tel: 028 9052 1829 Email: david.mcilveen@mla.niassembly.gov.uk
Constituency office: 9-11 Church Street, Ballymena, Co Antrim BT43 6DD
Tel: 028 2564 1421 Fax: 028 2565 7296
Website: www.davidmcilveen.org.uk Twitter: @davidrmcilveen

McILVEEN, Michelle   *DUP*   **Strangford**
Tel: 028 9052 1557 Email: michelle.mcilveen@mla.niassembly.gov.uk
Constituency office: 7 The Square, Comber, Co Down BT23 5DX
Tel: 028 9187 1441 Email: mail@michellemcilveen.org.uk
Website: www.michellemcilveen.org.uk Twitter: @mmcilveenmla

McKAY, Daithí   *Sinn Féin*   **North Antrim**
Sinn Féin Spokesperson for Economy
Tel: 028 9052 1471 Email: daithi.mckay@mla.niassembly.gov.uk
Constituency office: 162 Tullaghans Road, Dunloy, Ballymena, Co Antrim BT44 9AF
Tel: 028 2765 7198 Email: daithimckay@btinternet.com
Website: daithimckay.blogspot.com Twitter: @daithimckay

McKEVITT, Karen   *SDLP*   **South Down**
SDLP Spokesperson for Culture, Arts and Leisure
Tel: 028 9041 8353 Email: karen.mckevitt@mla.niassembly.gov.uk
Constituency office: 11-14 Newry Street, Warrenpoint, Co Down BT34 3JZ
Tel: 028 4177 4386 Twitter: @karen_mckevitt

McKINNEY, Fearghal *SDLP* **Belfast South**
Tel: 028 9052 1319 Email: fearghal.mckinney@mla.niassembly.gov.uk
Constituency office: Currently being set up Email: fearghal.mckinney@sdlp.ie Twitter: @fearghalsdlp

McLAUGHLIN, Maeve *Sinn Féin* **Foyle**
Sinn Féin Spokesperson for Social Economy and for Victims and Truth
Email: maeve.mclaughlin@mla.niassembly.gov.uk
Constituency office: Ráth Mór Business Park, Derry BT48 0LZ
Tel: 028 7137 7551 Email: foyleassembly@gmail.com

McLAUGHLIN, Mitchel *Sinn Féin* **South Antrim**
Principal Deputy Speaker
Tel: 028 9052 1612 Email: mitchel.mclaughlin@mla.niassembly.gov.uk
Constituency office: Unit 1, 2 Main Street, Randalstown, Co Antrim BT41 3AB
Tel: 028 9447 3972 Email: misteal@btinternet.com

McMULLAN, Oliver *Sinn Féin* **East Antrim**
Sinn Féin Spokesperson for Agriculture
Tel: 028 9052 1471 Email: oliver.mcmullan@mla.niassembly.gov.uk
Constituency office: 19 High Street, Carnlough, Co Antrim BT44 0EP
Tel: 028 2888 5800 Email: omcmullan@yahoo.com

McNARRY, David *UKIP* **Strangford**
Tel: 028 9052 1853 Email: david.mcnarry@mla.niassembly.gov.uk
Constituency office: 35 Saintfield Mill, Saintfield Parks, Saintfield, Co Down BT24 7FH
Tel: 028 9751 0705 Email: davidmcnarry@btconnect.com
Website: www.davidmcnarry.com

McQUILLAN, Adrian *DUP* **East Londonderry**
Tel: 028 9052 1850 Email: adrian.mcquillan@mla.niassembly.gov.uk
Constituency office: 54 Main Street, Garvagh, Coleraine, Co Londonderry BT5 5AE
Tel: 028 2955 8045 Fax: 028 2955 8046 Email: garvaghdup@hotmail.co.uk

MAGINNESS, Alban *SDLP* **Belfast North**
SDLP Spokesperson for Justice
Tel: 028 9052 1319 Email: alban.maginness@mla.niassembly.gov.uk
Constituency office: 228 Antrim Road, Belfast, Co Antrim BT15 2AN
Tel: 028 9022 0520 Fax: 028 9022 0522 Email: a.maginness@sdlp.ie
Website: www.albanmaginness.com Twitter: @albanmaginness

MASKEY, Alex *Sinn Féin* **Belfast South**
Sinn Féin Spokesperson for Social Development
Tel: 028 9052 1224 Email: alex.maskey@mla.niassembly.gov.uk
Constituency office: 178 Ormeau Road, Belfast, Co Antrim BT7 2ED
Tel: 028 9024 3194 Fax: 028 9023 9471 Email: alex.maskey@sinn-fein.ie
Website: www.sebelfastsinnfein.com

MILNE, Ian *Sinn Féin* **Mid Ulster**
Email: ian.milne@mla.niassembly.gov.uk
Constituency office: 79 Quarry Road, Gulladuff, Co Derry BT45 8NT
Tel: 028 7964 4550

MORROW, Maurice *DUP* **Fermanagh and South Tyrone**
Tel: 028 9052 1568 Email: maurice.morrow@mla.niassembly.gov.uk
Constituency office: 19 Church Street, Dungannon, Co Tyrone BT71 6AB
Tel: 028 8775 2799 Fax: 028 8775 2802 Email: mauricemorrow@hotmail.com

MOUTRAY, Stephen *DUP* **Upper Bann**
Tel: 028 9041 8370 Fax: 028 9052 1752 Email: stephen.moutray@mla.niassembly.gov.uk
Constituency office: 31 High Street, Lurgan, Craigavon, Co Armagh BT66 8AU
Tel: 028 3831 0088 Fax: 028 3831 0099 Email: stephenmoutray@btinternet.com
Twitter: @stephenmoutray

NESBITT, Mike *UUP*   **Strangford**
Leader, Ulster Unionist Party; Spokesperson for Office of the First Minister and Deputy First Minister
and for Victims
Tel: 028 9052 1861 Email: mike.nesbitt@mla.niassembly.gov.uk
Constituency office: 16 South Street, Newtownards, Co Down BT23 4JT
Tel: 028 9182 1587
Website: mikenesbitt.co.uk Twitter: @mikenesbittni

NEWTON, Robin, MBE *DUP*   **Belfast East**
Tel: 028 9052 1322 Email: robin.newton@mla.niassembly.gov.uk
Constituency office: 59 Castlereagh Road, Belfast BT5 5FB
Tel: 028 9045 9500 Fax: 028 9052 1912 Email: mail@robinnewton.co.uk
Website: www.robinnewton.co.uk Twitter: @robinnewtonmla

NÍ CHUILÍN, Carál *Sinn Féin*   **Belfast North**
Minister of Culture, Arts and Leisure
Tel: 028 9052 1471 Email: caral.nichuilin@mla.niassembly.gov.uk
Ministerial office: Department of Culture, Arts and Leisure, Causeway Exchange, 1-7 Bedford Street,
Belfast BT2 7FB Switchboard: 028 9051 5202
Constituency office: 291 Antrim Road, Belfast, Co Antrim BT15 2GZ
Tel: 028 9074 0817 Fax: 028 9074 0414 Email: caral.nichuilin@sinn-fein.ie

O'DOWD, John *Sinn Féin*   **Upper Bann**
Minister for Education
Tel: 028 9052 1471 Email: john.odowd@mla.niassembly.gov.uk
Ministerial office: Department of Education, Rathgael House, Balloo Road, Rathgill, Bangor BT19 7PR
Switchboard: 028 9127 9279
Constituency office: 77 North Street, Lurgan, Co Armagh BT67 9AH
Tel: 028 3834 9675 Fax: 028 3832 2610 Email: johnodowd@hotmail.com
Website: www.upperbannsf.com Twitter: @johnodowdsf

Ó HOISÍN, Cathal *Sinn Féin*   **East Londonderry**
Sinn Féin Spokesperson for Culture, Arts and Leisure
Tel: 028 9052 1471 Email: cathal.ohoisin@mla.niassembly.gov.uk
Constituency offices: 81 Main Street, Dungiven BT47 4LE
Tel: 028 7774 2488 Email: cathal.ohoisin@sinn-fein.ie
10 Church Street, Kilrea, Co Derry BT51 5QU
Tel: 028 2954 2464

O'NEILL, Michelle *Sinn Féin*   **Mid Ulster**
Minister of Agriculture and Rural Development
Tel: 028 9052 0463 Email: michelle.oneill@mla.niassembly.gov.uk
Ministerial office: Department of Agriculture and Rural Development, Dundonald House, Upper
Newtownards Road, Ballymiscaw, Belfast BT4 3SB Switchboard: 028 9052 4999
Constituency office: 7-9 The Square, Coalisland, Co Tyrone BT71 4LN
Tel: 028 8774 8689 Fax: 028 8774 6903 Email: michelle.oneill@dstbc.org

OVEREND, Sandra *UUP*   **Mid Ulster**
UUP Deputy Whip; UUP Spokesperson for Enterprise, Trade and Investment and for Children and
Young People
Tel: 028 9052 0305 Email: sandra.overend@mla.niassembly.gov.uk
Constituency office: 1 High Street, Moneymore, Co Londonderry BT45 7PB
Tel: 028 8674 8090 Website: www.sandraoverend.co.uk Twitter: @over2sandra

POOTS, Edwin *DUP*   **Lagan Valley**
Minister of Health, Social Services and Public Safety
Tel: 028 9052 1114 Email: edwin.poots@mla.niassembly.gov.uk
Ministerial office: Department of Health, Social Services and Public Safety, Castle Buildings, Stormont,
Belfast BT4 3SJ Switchboard: 028 9052 0500

Constituency offices: The Old Town Hall, 29 Castle Street, Lisburn, Co Antrim BT27 4DH
Tel: 028 9260 3003 Fax: 028 9267 1845 Email: edwin@edwinpoots.co.uk
3 Church Street, Dromore, Co Down BT25 1AA
Tel: 028 9269 8866
Website: www.edwinpoots.co.uk

RAMSEY, Pat *SDLP*   **Foyle**
SDLP Chief Whip and Spokesperson for Employment and Learning
Tel: 028 9052 1288 Fax: 028 9052 1700 Email: pat.ramsey@mla.niassembly.gov.uk
Constituency office: Level Two, The Embassy Building, 3 Strand Road, Derry BT48 7BH
Tel: 028 7136 1444 Email: p.ramsey@sdlp.ie
Website: www.patramsey.ie Twitter: @patramseymla

RAMSEY, Sue *Sinn Féin*   **Belfast West**
Sinn Féin Spokesperson for Health
Tel: 028 9052 1471 Email: sue.ramsey@mla.niassembly.gov.uk
Constituency office: Connolly House, 147 Andersonstown Road, Belfast, Co Antrim BT11 9BW
Tel: 028 9080 8404 Email: sueramsaymla@googlemail.com Twitter: @sueramseymla

ROBINSON, George *DUP*   **East Londonderry**
Tel: 028 9052 1322 Email: george.robinson@mla.niassembly.gov.uk
Constituency office: 6-8 Catherine Street, Limavady, Co Londonderry BT49 9DB
Tel: 028 7776 9191 Fax: 028 7776 9111 Email: limavadyhq@dup.org.uk Twitter: @g_rob44

ROBINSON, Rt Hon Peter *DUP*   **Belfast East**
First Minister; Leader, Democratic Unionist Party
Tel: 028 9052 1322 Email: peter.robinson@mla.niassembly.gov.uk
Ministerial office: Office of the First Minister and Deputy First Minister, Stormont Castle,
Stormont Estate, Belfast BT4 3TT Switchboard: 028 9052 8400
Constituency office: Strandtown Hall, 96 Belmont Avenue, Belfast, Co Down BT4 3DE
Tel: 028 9047 3111 Fax: 028 9047 1797 Email: rt.hon.peter.robinson@btconnect.com
Website: www.peterrobinson.org Twitter: @dupleader

ROGERS, Seán *SDLP*   **South Down**
SDLP Spokesperson for Education
Email: sean.rogers@mla.niassembly.gov.uk
Constituency offices: 60 Main Street, Castlewellan, Co Down BT31 9DJ
Tel: 028 4377 8833
8 Railway Street, Newcastle BT33 0AL
Tel: 028 4372 2443 Twitter: @sean_rogers_mla

ROSS, Alastair *DUP*   **East Antrim**
Assembly Private Secretary to Arlene Foster as Minister of Enterprise, Trade and Investment
Tel: 028 9052 1322 Email: alastair.ross@mla.niassembly.gov.uk
Constituency offices: 31 Lancasterian Street, Carrickfergus, Co Antrim BT38 7AB
Tel: 028 9332 9980 Fax: 028 9332 9979 Email: office@alastairross.org
116 Main Street, Larne, Co Antrim BT40 1RG
Tel: 028 2826 7722 Fax: 028 2826 9922
Website: www.alastairross.org Twitter: @alastairianross

RUANE, Caitríona *Sinn Féin*   **South Down**
Sinn Féin Chief Whip
Tel: 028 9052 1471 Email: caitriona.ruane@mla.niassembly.gov.uk
Constituency office: 3 Dock Street, Warrenpoint BT34 3LZ
Tel: 028 4175 4448 Email: caitriona.ruane@sinn-fein.ie Website: www.southdownsinnfein.com

SHEEHAN, Pat   *Sinn Féin*   Belfast West
Sinn Féin Spokesperson for International Affairs
Tel: 028 9052 1471 Email: pat.sheehan@mla.niassembly.gov.uk
Constituency office: 2a Monagh Crescent, Ballymurphy, Belfast, Co Antrim BT11 8EB
Email: patsheehan@ymail.com

SPRATT, Jimmy   *DUP*   Belfast South
Tel: 028 9052 0317 Email: jimmy.spratt@mla.niassembly.gov.uk
Constituency office: 15 Cregagh Road, Belfast, Co Down BT6 8PX
Tel: 028 9045 5936 Email: jimmyspratt@dup.org.uk
Website: www.jimmyspratt.org

STOREY, Mervyn   *DUP*   North Antrim
Tel: 028 9052 1322 Email: mervyn.storey@mla.niassembly.gov.uk
Constituency office: 3 Market Street, Ballymoney BT53 6EA
Tel: 028 2766 9753 Fax: 028 2766 6143 Email: mervynstorey@btconnect.com

SWANN, Robin   *UUP*   North Antrim
UUP Spokesperson for Employment and Learning and Parading; UUP Chief Whip
Tel: 028 9052 1766 Email: robin.swann@mla.niassembly.gov.uk
Constituency office: 13-15 Queen Street, Harryville, Ballymena, Co Antrim BT42 2BB
Tel: 028 2565 9595 Email: robin.swannmla@gmail.com
Website: www.robinswannmla.com Twitter: @robinkells

WEIR, Peter   *DUP*   North Down
DUP Chief Whip
Tel: 028 9052 1296 Fax: 028 9052 1287 Email: peter.weir@mla.niassembly.gov.uk
Constituency office: 94 Abbey Street, Bangor, Co Down BT20 4JB
Tel: 028 9145 4500 Fax: 028 9145 8895 Email: pjweir@hotmail.com
Website: www.peterweir.net Twitter: @peterweirmla

WELLS, Jim   *DUP*   South Down
DUP Spokesperson for Health
Tel: 028 9052 1110 Fax: 028 9052 1820 Email: jim.wells@mla.niassembly.gov.uk
Constituency office: 12 Bridge Street, Kilkeel, Co Down BT34 4AD
Tel: 028 4176 9900 Fax: 028 3832 1837 Email: jimwells6@gmail.com Twitter: @jim_wells_mla

WILSON, Sammy   *DUP*   East Antrim
Tel: 028 9052 1322 Email: sammy.wilson@mla.niassembly.gov.uk
Constituency offices: 31 Lancasterian Street, Carrickfergus, Co Antrim BT38 7AB
Tel: 028 9332 9980 Fax: 028 9332 9979
116 Main Street, Larne, Co Antrim BT40 1RG
Tel: 028 2826 7722 Fax: 028 2826 9922
Website: www.sammywilson.org

Women MLAs (21)

BOYLE Michaela	*Sinn Féin*	McCORLEY Rosie	*Sinn Féin*
BRADLEY Paula	*DUP*	McGAHAN Bronwyn	*Sinn Féin*
BROWN Pam	*DUP*	McILVEEN Michelle	*DUP*
COCHRANE Judith	*All*	McKEVITT Karen	*SDLP*
DOBSON Jo-Anne	*UUP*	McLAUGHLIN Maeve	*Sinn Féin*
FEARON Megan	*Sinn Féin*	NÍ CHUILÍN Carál	*Sinn Féin*
FOSTER Arlene	*DUP*	O'NEILL Michelle	*Sinn Féin*
HALE Brenda	*DUP*	OVEREND Sandra	*UUP*
KELLY Dolores	*SDLP*	RAMSEY Sue	*Sinn Féin*
LO Anna	*All*	RUANE Caitríona	*Sinn Féin*
McCANN Jennifer	*Sinn Féin*		

Constituencies

			Count elected on
East Antrim	Roy Beggs	UUP	9
East Antrim	Stewart Dickson	All	9
East Antrim	David Hilditch	DUP	2
East Antrim	Oliver McMullan	Sinn Féin	10
East Antrim	Alastair Ross	DUP	6
East Antrim	Sammy Wilson	DUP	1
North Antrim	Jim Allister	TUV	9
North Antrim	Paul Frew	DUP	1
North Antrim	David McIlveen	DUP	8
North Antrim	Daithí McKay	Sinn Féin	1
North Antrim	Mervyn Storey	DUP	1
North Antrim	Robin Swann	UUP	9
South Antrim	Pam Brown	DUP	4
South Antrim	Trevor Clarke	DUP	1
South Antrim	David Ford	All	2
South Antrim	Paul Girvan	DUP	1
South Antrim	Danny Kinahan	UUP	3
South Antrim	Mitchel McLaughlin	Sinn Féin	1
Belfast East	Judith Cochrane	All	7
Belfast East	Michael Copeland	UUP	11
Belfast East	Sammy Douglas	DUP	11
Belfast East	Chris Lyttle	All	9
Belfast East	Robin Newton	DUP	2
Belfast East	Peter Robinson	DUP	1
Belfast North	Paula Bradley	DUP	7
Belfast North	William Humphrey	DUP	7
Belfast North	Gerry Kelly	Sinn Féin	1
Belfast North	Nelson McCausland	DUP	1
Belfast North	Alban Maginness	SDLP	6
Belfast North	Carál Ní Chuilín	Sinn Féin	6
Belfast South	Anna Lo	All	1
Belfast South	Alasdair McDonnell	SDLP	2
Belfast South	Michael McGimpsey	UUP	5
Belfast South	Fearghal McKinney	SDLP	–
Belfast South	Alex Maskey	Sinn Féin	5
Belfast South	Jimmy Spratt	DUP	5
Belfast West	Alex Attwood	SDLP	10
Belfast West	Fra McCann	Sinn Féin	10
Belfast West	Jennifer McCann	Sinn Féin	1
Belfast West	Rosie McCorley	Sinn Féin	–
Belfast West	Sue Ramsey	Sinn Féin	11
Belfast West	Pat Sheehan	Sinn Féin	11
North Down	Steven Agnew	Green	11
North Down	Leslie Cree	UUP	10
North Down	Gordon Dunne	DUP	2
North Down	Alex Easton	DUP	1
North Down	Stephen Farry	All	10
North Down	Peter Weir	DUP	2
South Down	Chris Hazzard	Sinn Féin	–
South Down	John McCallister	NI21*	6
South Down	Karen McKevitt	SDLP	8
South Down	Seán Rogers	SDLP	1
South Down	Caitríona Ruane	Sinn Féin	2
South Down	Jim Wells	DUP	5

* elected as UUP

Fermanagh and South Tyrone	Tom Elliott	UUP	1
Fermanagh and South Tyrone	Phil Flanagan	Sinn Féin	6
Fermanagh and South Tyrone	Arlene Foster	DUP	1
Fermanagh and South Tyrone	Seán Lynch	Sinn Féin	6
Fermanagh and South Tyrone	Bronwyn McGahan	Sinn Féin	–
Fermanagh and South Tyrone	Maurice Morrow	DUP	5
Foyle	Mark H Durkan	SDLP	4
Foyle	Colum Eastwood	SDLP	7
Foyle	William Hay	Speaker†	1
Foyle	Raymond McCartney	Sinn Féin	7
Foyle	Maeve McLaughlin	Sinn Féin	–
Foyle	Pat Ramsey	SDLP	7
Lagan Valley	Jonathan Craig	DUP	5
Lagan Valley	Paul Givan	DUP	6
Lagan Valley	Brenda Hale	DUP	7
Lagan Valley	Trevor Lunn	All	6
Lagan Valley	Basil McCrea	NI21*	1
Lagan Valley	Edwin Poots	DUP	1
East Londonderry	Gregory Campbell	DUP	1
East Londonderry	John Dallat	SDLP	6
East Londonderry	David McClarty	Ind	7
East Londonderry	Adrian McQuillan	DUP	7
East Londonderry	Cathal Ó hOisín	Sinn Féin	6
East Londonderry	George Robinson	DUP	7
Newry and Armagh	Cathal Boylan	Sinn Féin	1
Newry and Armagh	Dominic Bradley	SDLP	1
Newry and Armagh	Mickey Brady	Sinn Féin	6
Newry and Armagh	Megan Fearon	Sinn Féin	–
Newry and Armagh	William Irwin	DUP	3
Newry and Armagh	Danny Kennedy	UUP	1
Strangford	Jonathan Bell	DUP	1
Strangford	Simon Hamilton	DUP	5
Strangford	Kieran McCarthy	All	1
Strangford	Michelle McIlveen	DUP	1
Strangford	David McNarry	UKIP*	6
Strangford	Mike Nesbitt	UUP	6
West Tyrone	Michaela Boyle	Sinn Féin	4
West Tyrone	Thomas Buchanan	DUP	5
West Tyrone	Joe Byrne	SDLP	5
West Tyrone	Ross Hussey	UUP	5
West Tyrone	Declan McAleer	Sinn Féin	–
West Tyrone	Barry McElduff	Sinn Féin	1
Mid Ulster	Ian McCrea	DUP	1
Mid Ulster	Patsy McGlone	SDLP	5
Mid Ulster	Martin McGuinness	Sinn Féin	1
Mid Ulster	Ian Milne	Sinn Féin	–
Mid Ulster	Michelle O'Neill	Sinn Féin	7
Mid Ulster	Sandra Overend	UUP	6
Upper Bann	Sydney Anderson	DUP	5
Upper Bann	Jo-Anne Dobson	UUP	7
Upper Bann	Samuel Gardiner	UUP	7
Upper Bann	Dolores Kelly	SDLP	7
Upper Bann	Stephen Moutray	DUP	5
Upper Bann	John O'Dowd	Sinn Féin	1

* elected as UUP
† elected as DUP

Assembly Committees

Chairpersons' Liaison Group

Tel: 028 9052 1216
Email: committee.office@niassembly.gov.uk
www.niassembly.gov.uk/assembly-business/
committees/chairperson-liaison-group

Robin Swann (Chair)	UUP
Patsy McGlone (Deputy Chair)	SDLP
Michaela Boyle	Sinn Féin
Paul Frew	DUP
Paul Givan	DUP
Gerry Kelly	Sinn Féin
Danny Kinahan	UUP
Anna Lo	All
Michelle McIlveen	DUP
Daithí McKay	Sinn Féin
Maeve McLaughlin	Sinn Féin
Alex Maskey	Sinn Féin
Stephen Moutray	DUP
Mike Nesbitt	UUP
Alastair Ross	DUP
Jimmy Spratt	DUP
Mervyn Storey	DUP

Staff: Kathy O'Hanlon (Clerk)

Departmental Committees

Agriculture and Rural Development

Tel: 028 9052 1475
Email:
committee.agriculture@niassembly.gov.uk
www.niassembly.gov.uk/assembly-business/
committees/agriculture-and-rural-development

Paul Frew (Chair)	DUP
Joe Byrne (Deputy Chair)	SDLP
Thomas Buchanan	DUP
Jo-Anne Dobson	UUP
William Irwin	DUP
Trevor Lunn	All
Declan McAleer	Sinn Féin
Michelle McIlveen	DUP
Oliver McMullan	Sinn Féin
Ian Milne	Sinn Féin
Robin Swann	UUP

Staff: Stella McArdle (Clerk)

Culture, Arts and Leisure

Tel: 028 9052 1718
Email: committee.cal@niassembly.gov.uk
www.niassembly.gov.uk/assembly-business/
committees/culture-arts-and-leisure

Michelle McIlveen (Chair)	DUP
William Irwin (Deputy Chair)	DUP
Dominic Bradley	SDLP
David Hilditch	DUP
William Humphrey	DUP
Rosie McCorley	Sinn Féin
Basil McCrea	NI21
Michael McGimpsey	UUP
Karen McKevitt	SDLP
Oliver McMullan	Sinn Féin
Cathal Ó hOisín	Sinn Féin

Staff: Peter Hall (Clerk)

Education

Tel: 028 9052 1821
Email: committee.education@niassembly.gov.uk
www.niassembly.gov.uk/assembly-business/
committees/education

Mervyn Storey (Chair)	DUP
Danny Kinahan (Deputy Chair)	UUP
Michaela Boyle	Sinn Féin
Jonathan Craig	DUP
Jo-Anne Dobson	UUP
Chris Hazzard	Sinn Féin
Trevor Lunn	All
Stephen Moutray	DUP
Robin Newton	DUP
Seán Rogers	SDLP
Pat Sheehan	Sinn Féin

Staff: Peter McCallion (Clerk)

Employment and Learning

Tel: 028 9052 1448
Email: cel@niassembly.gov.uk
www.niassembly.gov.uk/assembly-business/
committees/employment-and-learning

Robin Swann (Chair)	UUP
Thomas Buchanan (Deputy Chair)	DUP
Sammy Douglas	DUP
Phil Flanagan	Sinn Féin
David Hilditch	DUP
Chris Lyttle	All
Fra McCann	Sinn Féin
David McClarty	Ind
Bronwyn McGahan	Sinn Féin
Pat Ramsey	SDLP
Alastair Ross	DUP

Staff: Cathie White (Clerk)

Enterprise, Trade and Investment

Tel: 028 9052 1230
Email: committee.eti@niassembly.gov.uk
www.niassembly.gov.uk/assembly-business/
committees/enterprise-trade-and-investment

Patsy McGlone (Chair)	SDLP
Phil Flanagan (Deputy Chair)	Sinn Féin
Steven Agnew	Green
Sydney Anderson	DUP
Sammy Douglas	DUP
Gordon Dunne	DUP
Paul Frew	DUP
Fearghal McKinney	SDLP
Maeve McLaughlin	Sinn Féin
Sandra Overend	UUP
Sue Ramsey	Sinn Féin
Staff: Jim McManus (Clerk)	

Environment

Tel: 028 9052 1783
Email:
committee.environment@niassembly.gov.uk
www.niassembly.gov.uk/assembly-business/
committees/environment

Anna Lo (Chair)	All
Pam Brown (Deputy Chair)	DUP
Cathal Boylan	Sinn Féin
Colum Eastwood	SDLP
Tom Elliott	UUP
Ian McCrea	DUP
Barry McElduff	Sinn Féin
Alban Maginness	SDLP
Ian Milne	Sinn Féin
Maurice Morrow	DUP
Peter Weir	DUP
Staff: Sheila Mawhinney (Clerk)	

Finance and Personnel

Tel: 028 9052 1843
Email:
committee.financepersonnel@niassembly.gov.uk
www.niassembly.gov.uk/assembly-business/
committees/finance-and-personnel

Daithí McKay (Chair)	Sinn Féin
Dominic Bradley (Deputy Chair)	SDLP
Judith Cochrane	All
Leslie Cree	UUP
Megan Fearon	Sinn Féin
Paul Girvan	DUP
John McCallister	NI21
Ian McCrea	DUP
Mitchel McLaughlin	Sinn Féin
Adrian McQuillan	DUP
Peter Weir	DUP
Staff: Shane McAteer (Clerk)	

Health, Social Services and Public Safety

Tel: 028 9052 1841
Email: committee.hssps@niassembly.gov.uk
www.niassembly.gov.uk/assembly-business/
committees/health-social-services-and-public-safety

Maeve McLaughlin (Chair)	Sinn Féin
Jim Wells (Deputy Chair)	DUP
Roy Beggs	UUP
Mickey Brady	Sinn Féin
Pam Brown	DUP
Gordon Dunne	DUP
Samuel Gardiner	UUP
Kieran McCarthy	All
David McIlveen	DUP
Fearghal McKinney	SDLP
Staff: Kathryn Bell (Clerk)	

Justice

Tel: 028 9052 1629
Email: committee.justice@niassembly.gov.uk
www.niassembly.gov.uk/assembly-business/
committees/justice

Paul Givan (Chair)	DUP
Raymond McCartney (Deputy Chair)	Sinn Féin
Sydney Anderson	DUP
Stewart Dickson	All
Tom Elliott	UUP
William Humphrey	DUP
Seán Lynch	Sinn Féin
Rosie McCorley	Sinn Féin
Patsy McGlone	SDLP
Alban Maginness	SDLP
Jim Wells	DUP
Staff: Christine Darrah (Clerk)	

Office of the First Minister and Deputy First Minister

Tel: 028 9052 0379
Email: committee.ofmdfm@niassembly.gov.uk
www.niassembly.gov.uk/assembly-business/
committees/office-of-the-first-minister-and-deputy-first-minister

Mike Nesbitt (Chair)	UUP
Chris Lyttle (Deputy Chair)	All
Alex Attwood	SDLP
Leslie Cree	UUP
Megan Fearon	Sinn Féin
Brenda Hale	DUP
Bronwyn McGahan	Sinn Féin
Alex Maskey	Sinn Féin
Stephen Moutray	DUP
George Robinson	DUP
Jimmy Spratt	DUP
Staff: Shauna Mageean (Clerk)	

Regional Development

Tel: 028 9052 1063
Email: committee.regionaldevelopment
@niassembly.gov.uk
www.niassembly.gov.uk/assembly-business/
committees/regional-development

Jimmy Spratt (Chair)	DUP
Seán Lynch (Deputy Chair)	Sinn Féin
Kieran McCarthy	All
John Dallat	SDLP
Alex Easton	DUP
Brenda Hale	DUP
Ross Hussey	UUP
Declan McAleer	Sinn Féin
Joe Byrne	SDLP
David McNarry	UKIP
Cathal Ó hOisín	Sinn Féin

Staff: Paul Carlisle (Clerk)

Social Development

Tel: 028 9052 1864
Email:
committee.socialdevelopment@niassembly.gov.uk
www.niassembly.gov.uk/assembly-business/
committees/social-development

Alex Maskey (Chair)	Sinn Féin
Mickey Brady (Deputy Chair)	Sinn Féin
Jim Allister	TUV
Paula Bradley	DUP
Gregory Campbell	DUP
Trevor Clarke	DUP
Michael Copeland	UUP
Stewart Dickson	All
Dolores Kelly	SDLP
Fra McCann	Sinn Féin
Sammy Wilson	DUP

Staff: Kevin Pelan (Clerk)

Standing Committees

Assembly and Executive Review

Tel: 028 9052 1787
Email: committee.assembly&executivereview
@niassembly.gov.uk
www.niassembly.gov.uk/assembly-business/
committees/assembly-and-executive-review

Stephen Moutray (Chair)	DUP
Pat Sheehan (Deputy Chair)	Sinn Féin
Alex Attwood	SDLP
Roy Beggs	UUP
Gregory Campbell	DUP
Paul Givan	DUP
Simon Hamilton	DUP
Trevor Lunn	All
Raymond McCartney	Sinn Féin
Seán Rogers	SDLP
Caitríona Ruane	Sinn Féin

Staff: John Simmons (Clerk)

Audit

Tel: 028 9052 0333
Email: committee.audit@niasssembly.gov.uk
www.niassembly.gov.uk/assembly-business/
committees/audit

Danny Kinahan (Chair)	UUP
David Hilditch (Deputy Chair)	DUP
Michaela Boyle	Sinn Féin
Dominic Bradley	SDLP
Anna Lo	All

Staff: Paul Gill (Clerk)

Business

Tel: 028 9052 1534
Email: business.office@niassembly.gov.uk
www.niassembly.gov.uk/assembly-business/
committees/business

William Hay (Chair)	Speaker
Stewart Dickson	All
Gerry Kelly	Sinn Féin
Karen McKevitt	SDLP
Maurice Morrow	DUP
Sandra Overend	UUP
Pat Ramsey	SDLP
Caitríona Ruane	Sinn Féin
Robin Swann	UUP
Peter Weir	DUP

Staff: Loretta Gordon (Clerk)

Procedures

Tel: 028 9052 1436
Email:
committee.procedures@niassembly.gov.uk
www.niassembly.gov.uk/assembly-business/
committees/procedures

Gerry Kelly (Chair)	Sinn Féin
Trevor Clarke (Deputy Chair)	DUP
Jim Allister	TUV
Paula Bradley	DUP
Samuel Gardiner	UUP
Kieran McCarthy	All
Barry McElduff	Sinn Féin
Oliver McMullan	Sinn Féin
Alban Maginness	SDLP
Maurice Morrow	DUP
George Robinson	DUP

Staff: Alison Ross (Clerk)

Public Accounts

Tel: 028 9052 1208
Email: pac.committee@niassembly.gov.uk
www.niassembly.gov.uk/assembly-business/
committees/public-accounts

Michaela Boyle (Chair)	Sinn Féin
John Dallat (Deputy Chair)	SDLP
Trevor Clarke	DUP
Michael Copeland	UUP
Alex Easton	DUP
Paul Girvan	DUP
Chris Hazzard	Sinn Féin
Ross Hussey	UUP
Daithí McKay	Sinn Féin
Adrian McQuillan	DUP
Seán Rogers	SDLP

Staff: Aoibhinn Treanor (Clerk)

Standards and Privileges

Tel: 028 9052 0333
Email: committee.standards&privileges
@niassembly.gov.uk
www.niassembly.gov.uk/assembly-business/
committees/standards-and-privileges

Alastair Ross (Chair)	DUP
Anna Lo (Deputy Chair)	All
Steven Agnew	Green
Cathal Boylan	Sinn Féin
Paula Bradley	DUP
Colum Eastwood	SDLP
Declan McAleer	Sinn Féin
Fra McCann	Sinn Féin
Ian McCrea	DUP
Sandra Overend	UUP
Mervyn Storey	DUP

Staff: Paul Gill (Clerk)

Principal Officers and Officials

Office of the Speaker

Speaker **William Hay** MLA (Speaker)

Private Secretary	Frances Leneghan	028 9052 1377
	Email: frances.leneghan@niassembly.gov.uk	
Adviser	Robin Ramsey	028 9052 1551
	Email: robin.ramsey@niassembly.gov.uk	

Principal Deputy Speaker **Mitchel McLaughlin** MLA (Sinn Féin)

Deputy Speakers **Roy Beggs** MLA (UUP), **John Dallat** MLA (SDLP)

Assembly Commission

Chair	**William Hay** (Speaker)
Members	**Judith Cochrane** (All)
	Leslie Cree MBE (UUP)
	Pat Ramsey (SDLP)
	Caitríona Ruane (Sinn Féin)
	Peter Weir (DUP)

Principal Officers

Clerk to the Assembly/Director General	Trevor Reaney
Directors	
Clerking and Reporting	Gareth McGrath
Corporate Services	Richard Stewart
Facilities	Stephen Welch
Information and Outreach	John Stewart
Legal Services	Hugh Widdis
Examiner of Statutory Rules	Gordon Nabney
Clerk Assistants	Nuala Dunwoody
	Damien Martin

Editor of Debates	Simon Burrowes
Clerk to the Commission	Tony Logue
Comptroller and Auditor General	Kieran Donnelly
Assembly Ombudsman	Dr Thomas Frawley CBE

Northern Ireland Civil Service

Office of the First Minister and Deputy First Minister
Stormont Castle, Stormont, Belfast BT4 3TT
Tel: 028 9037 8158
Email: pauline.boyle@ofmdfmni.gov.uk ps.ministers@ofmdfmni.gov.uk
Website: www.ofmdfmni.gov.uk
Head of Northern Ireland Civil Service and Secretary to the Executive:
Dr Malcolm McKibbin 028 9037 8133 Email: hocs@ofmdfmni.gov.uk

Department of Agriculture and Rural Development
Dundonald House, Upper Newtownards Road, Belfast, Belfast BT4 3SB
Tel: 028 9052 0100
Email: marion.white@dardni.gov.uk Website: www.dardni.gov.uk
Permanent Secretary: Noel Lavery 028 9052 4608 Email: noel.lavery@dardni.gov.uk

Department of Culture, Arts and Leisure
Causeway Exchange, 1-7 Bedford Street, Belfast BT2 7EG
Tel: 028 9051 5177 Fax: 028 9082 3450
Email: anne.wallace@dcalni.gov.uk Website: www.dcalni.gov.uk
Acting Permanent Secretary: Peter May 028 9051 5177 Email: peter.may@dcalni.gov.uk

Department of Education
Rathgael House, Balloo Road, Bangor BT19 7PR
Tel: 028 9127 9279
Email: brenda.nixon@deni.gov.uk mail@deni.gov.uk Website: www.deni.gov.uk
Permanent Secretary: Paul Sweeney 028 9127 9310 Email: paul.sweeney@deni.gov.uk

Department for Employment and Learning
Adelaide House, 39-49 Adelaide Street, Belfast BT2 8FD
Tel: 028 9025 7777
Email: alison.dawson@delni.gov.uk Website: www.delni.gov.uk
Permanent Secretary: Derek Baker 028 9025 7833 Email: permanent.secretary.office@delni.gov.uk

Department of Enterprise, Trade and Investment
Netherleigh House, Massey Avenue, Belfast BT4 2JP
Tel: 028 9052 9900/Textphone: 028 9052 9304 Fax: 028 9052 9273
Email: janice.hill@detini.gov.uk Website: www.detini.gov.uk
Permanent Secretary: David Sterling 028 9052 9441 Email: david.sterling@detini.gov.uk

Department of the Environment
Clarence Court, 10-18 Adelaide Street, Belfast BT2 8GB
Tel: 028 9054 0540
Email: enquiries@doeni.gov.uk Website: www.doeni.gov.uk
Permanent Secretary: Leo O'Reilly 028 9025 6020 Email: leo.oreilly@doeni.gov.uk

Department of Finance and Personnel
Rathgael House, Balloo Road, Bangor BT19 7NA
Tel: 028 9185 8111
Email: helen.frazer@dfpni.gov.uk Website: www.dfpni.gov.uk
Permanent Secretary: Stephen Peover 028 9127 7601 Email: stephen.peover@dfpni.gov.uk

Department of Health, Social Services and Public Safety
Castle Buildings, Stormont Estate, Belfast BT4 3SQ
Tel: 028 9052 0500 Fax: 028 9052 0573
Email: tracey.walsh@dhsspsni.gov.uk Website: www.dhsspsni.gov.uk
Permanent Secretary: Dr Andrew McCormick 028 9052 0559
Email: andrew.mccormick@dhsspsni.gov.uk

Department of Justice
Block B, Castle Buildings, Stormont Estate, Belfast BT4 3SG
Tel: 028 9076 3000/028 9052 7668 (text phone) Fax: 028 9052 7668
Email: coleen.patton@dojni.x.gsi.gov.uk Website: www.dojni.gov.uk
Permanent Secretary: Nick Perry 028 9052 2992 Email: nick.perry@dojni.x.gsi.gov.uk

Department for Regional Development
Clarence Court, 10-18 Adelaide Street, Belfast BT2 8GB
Tel: 028 9054 0540 Fax: 028 9054 0024
Email: sandra.hinds@drdni.gov.uk Website: www.drdni.gov.uk
Permanent Secretary: Richard Pengelly 028 9054 1175 Email: richard.pengelly@drdni.gov.uk

Department for Social Development
Fifth Floor, Lighthouse Building, 1 Cromac Place, Gasworks Business Park, Ormeau Road,
Belfast BT7 2JB
Tel: 028 9082 9464
Email: sheila.o'connor@dsdni.gov.uk Website: www.dsdni.gov.uk
Permanent Secretary: Will Haire 028 9082 9002
Email: will.haire@dsdni.gov.uk perm.sec@dsdni.gov.uk

Office of the Attorney General for Northern Ireland
PO Box 1272, Belfast BT1 9LU
Tel: 028 9072 5333
Email: contact@attorneygeneralni.gov.uk Website: www.attorneygeneralni.gov.uk
Attorney General for Northern Ireland: John Larkin QC

Executive Agencies

Compensation Services
Sixth Floor, Millennium House, Great Victoria Street, Belfast BT2 7AQ
Tel: 0300 200 7887 Fax: 028 9024 6956
Email: comp-agency@nics.gov.uk Website: www.compensationni.gov.uk
Number of staff: 60
Head: Marcella McKnight 028 9026 1374 Email: marcella.mcknight@dojni.x.gsi.gov.uk
Sponsored by: Department of Justice, Northern Ireland Civil Service

Driver and Vehicle Agency

148-158 Corporation Street, Belfast BT1 3DH
Website: www.nidirect.gov.uk/motoring www.dvani.gov.uk

66 Balmoral Road, Belfast BT12 6QL
Tel: 0845 601 4094 (Driver and Vehicle Testing) Fax: 028 7034 1422
Email: dvta@doeni.gov.uk

County Hall, Castlerock Road, Coleraine, Co Londonderry BT51 3HS
Tel: 0845 402 4000 (Driver and Vehicle Licensing) Fax: 028 7034 1422 (Vehicle Licensing)/
028 7034 1398 (Driver Licensing)
Email: dvlni@doeni.gov.uk

Number of staff: 1,062

Chief Executive: Paul Duffy 028 9025 4125 Email: paul.duffy2@doeni.gov.uk
chief.executivedva@doeni.gov.uk

Sponsored by: Road Safety and Corporate Services Group, Department of the Environment, Northern Ireland Civil Service

Forensic Science Northern Ireland

151 Belfast Road, Carrickfergus BT38 8PL
Tel: 028 9036 1888 Fax: 028 9036 1900
Email: generalenquiries@fsni.x.gsi.gov.uk Website: www.fsni.gov.uk

Number of staff: 211

Chief Executive: Stan Brown 028 9036 1801

Sponsored by: Department of Justice, Northern Ireland Civil Service

Forest Service

Dundonald House, Upper Newtownards Road, Ballymiscaw, Belfast BT4 3SB
Tel: 028 6634 3165 Fax: 028 6634 3144
Email: customer.forestservice@dardni.gov.uk Website: www.dardni.gov.uk/forestservice
www.nidirect.gov.uk/forests

Number of staff: 217

Chief Executive: Malcolm Beatty 028 9052 4463 Email: malcolm.beatty@dardni.gov.uk

Sponsored by: Department of Agriculture and Rural Development, Northern Ireland Civil Service

Invest Northern Ireland

Bedford Square, Bedford Street, Belfast BT2 7ES
Tel: 028 9023 9090 Fax: 028 9043 6536
Email: info@investni.com Website: www.investni.com Twitter: @InvestNINews

Number of staff: 648

Chair: Mark Ennis

Sponsored by: Department of Enterprise, Trade and Investment, Northern Ireland Civil Service

Northern Ireland Courts and Tribunals Service

Laganside House, 23–27 Oxford Street, Belfast BT1 3LA
Tel: 028 9032 8594
Website: www.courtsni.gov.uk

Number of staff: 800

Chief Executive: Jacqui Durkin Email: jacqui.durkin@courtsni.gov.uk

Sponsored by: Department of Justice, Northern Ireland Civil Service

Northern Ireland Environment Agency
Klondyke Building, Gasworks Business Park, Lower Ormeau Road, Belfast BT7 2JA
Tel: 0845 302 0008
Website: www.ni-environment.gov.uk

Number of staff: 767
Chief Executive: Terry A'Hearne 028 9056 9210 Email: caroline.lyons@doeni.gov.uk
Sponsored by: Environment and Marine Group, Department of the Environment, Northern Ireland Civil Service

Northern Ireland Prison Service
Dundonald House, Upper Newtownards Road, Belfast BT4 3SU
Tel: 028 9052 2922 Fax: 028 9052 5284
Email: info@niprisonservice.gov.uk Website: www.niprisonservice.gov.uk

Number of staff: 2,036
Director-General: Sue McAllister Email: sue.mcallister@dojni.x.gsi.gov.uk
Sponsored by: Department of Justice, Northern Ireland Civil Service

Northern Ireland Statistics and Research Agency
McAuley House, 2-14 Castle Street, Belfast BT1 1SA
Tel: 028 9034 8100 Fax: 028 9034 8106
Email: info.nisra@dfpni.gov.uk [firstname.surname]@dfpni.gov.uk Website: www.nisra.gov.uk

Number of staff: 440
Registrar General and Chief Executive: Dr Norman Caven 028 9034 8102
Email: norman.caven@dfpni.gov.uk
Sponsored by: Department of Finance and Personnel, Northern Ireland Civil Service

Rivers Agency
Hydebank, 4 Hospital Road, Ballydollaghan, Belfast BT8 8JP
Tel: 028 9260 6100 Fax: 028 9260 6111
Email: rivers.registry@dardni.gov.uk Website: www.dardni.gov.uk/riversagency

Number of staff: 400
Chief Executive: Catherine McCallum 028 9025 3440 Email: catherine.mccallum@dardni.gov.uk
Sponsored by: Department of Agriculture and Rural Development, Northern Ireland Civil Service

Social Security Agency
Lighthouse Building, Gasworks Park, 1 Cromac Place, Ormeau Road, Belfast BT7 2JB
Tel: 028 9082 9108
Email: ssa@nics.gov.uk Website: www.dsdni.gov.uk/ssa

Chief Executive: Tommy O'Reilly 028 9082 9003 Email: tommy.o'reilly@dsdni.gsi.gov.uk
june.salmon@dsdni.gov.uk
Sponsored by: Department for Social Development, Northern Ireland Civil Service

Youth Justice Agency
41-43 Waring Street, Belfast BT1 2DY
Tel: 028 9031 6400 Fax: 028 9031 6402/3
Email: info@yjani.gov.uk Website: www.youthjusticeagencyni.gov.uk

Number of staff: 350
Chief Executive: Paula Jack 028 9031 6450 Email: paula.jack@dojni.x.gsi.gov.uk
Sponsored by: Department of Justice, Northern Ireland Civil Service

Non-Ministerial Department

Public Prosecutions Service

Headquarters and Belfast Region, Belfast Chambers, 93 Chichester Street, Belfast BT1 3JR
Tel: 028 9054 2444
Email: info@ppsni.gsi.gov.uk Website: www.ppsni.gov.uk
Director of Public Prosecutions: Barra McGrory QC

Political Parties

Democratic Unionist Party

91 Dundela Avenue, Belfast BT4 3BU
Tel: 028 9047 1155 Fax: 028 9052 1289
Email: info@dup.org.uk Website: www.mydup.com Twitter: @duponline
Assembly Office, Room 207 Parliament Buildings, Stormont, Belfast BT4 3XX
Tel: 028 9052 1323 Fax: 028 9052 1289

Leader: Peter Robinson MLA
Deputy Leader: Nigel Dodds MP
Chair: Lord Morrow MLA
Vice-chair: Dr William McCrea MP
Secretary: Michelle McIlveen MLA
Treasurer: Gregory Campbell MP, MLA
Director of Communications: John Robinson 07901 914006 Email: johnrobinson@dup.org.uk

Sinn Féin

44 Parnell Square, Dublin 1, Ireland
Tel: +353 1 8726932 Fax: +353 1 8733441
Email: sfadmin@eircom.net Website: www.sinnfein.ie Twitter: @sinnfeinireland
53 Falls Road, Belfast BT12 4PD
Tel: 028 9034 7350 Fax: 028 9022 3001
Assembly Office:
Tel: 028 9052 1471/028 9052 1470 Fax: 028 9052 1488

President: Gerry Adams
Vice-President: Mary Lou McDonald
Chair: Declan Kearney
General Secretary: Dawn Doyle
Treasurers: Jonathan O'Brien, Ted Howell
Director of Publicity: Sean MacBradaigh

Ulster Unionist Party

Strandtown Hall, 2-4 Belmont Road, Belfast BT4 2AN
Tel: 028 9047 4630 Fax: 028 9065 2149
Email: uup@uup.org Website: www.uup.org Twitter: @uuponline
Assembly Office, Room 214 Parliament Buildings, Stormont, Belfast BT4 3XX
Tel: 028 9052 1423 Fax: 028 9052 1883
Policy Unit:
Tel: 028 9052 1892

Leader: Mike Nesbitt MLA
Chair: Lord Empey OBE
Vice-chair: Roy McCune
Treasurer: Mark Cosgrove

Party Officers: Tom Elliott MLA, Jim Nicholson MEP, Alexander Redpath, Lord Rogan, Joy Rollston, Philip Smith, Robin Swann MLA, George White, Trevor Wilson
Communications and Policy Co-ordinator: John Moore 028 9052 1328 Email: john.moore@uup.org
Press Officer: Stephen Barr 028 9052 1890 Email: stephen.barr@party.niassembly.gov.uk

Social Democratic and Labour Party

121 Ormeau Road, Belfast BT7 1SH
Tel: 028 9024 7700 Fax: 028 9023 6699
Email: info@sdlp.ie Website: www.sdlp.ie Twitter: @sdlplive

Assembly Office:
Tel: 028 9052 1319

Press Office:
Tel: 028 9052 1837

Leader: Dr Alasdair McDonnell MP, MLA
Deputy Leader: Dolores Kelly MLA
Chair: Joe Byrne MLA
Vice-chairs: Fearghal McKinney MLA, Cathal Mulligan
General Secretary: Gerry Cosgrove Email: gerry.cosgrove@sdlphq.ie

Alliance

88 University Street, Belfast BT7 1HE
Tel: 028 9032 4274 Fax: 028 9033 3147
Email: alliance@allianceparty.org Website: www.allianceparty.org Twitter: @allianceparty

Assembly Office, Room 220 Parliament Buildings, Stormont, Belfast BT4 3XX
Tel: 028 9052 1314 Fax: 028 9052 1313

Leader: David Ford MLA
Deputy Leader: Naomi Long MP
Chair: Andrew Muir Email: andrew.muir@allianceparty.org
General Secretary: Sharon Lowry Email: sharon.lowry@allianceparty.org
Joint Hon Treasurers:
Mervyn Jones Email: mervyn.jones@allianceparty.org
Dan McGuinness Email: dan.mcguinness@allianceparty.org
Press Officer: David Young 028 9052 1977 Email: david.young@allianceparty.org

NI21

19 Market Square, Dromore BT25 1AW
Tel: 028 9269 3594
Email: info@ni21.com Website: ni21.com Twitter: @ni21official

Leader: Basil McCrea MLA
Deputy Leader: John McCallister MLA
Chair: Tina McKenzie

Green Party

First Floor, 76 Abbey Street, Bangor BT20 4JB
Tel: 028 9145 9110
Email: info@greenpartyni.org Website: www.greenpartyni.org Twitter: @greenpartyni

Assembly Office:
Tel: 028 9052 1790

Leader, Green Party in Northern Ireland: Steven Agnew MLA
Chair: Mark Bailey
Press Officer: Joanna Braniff 028 9052 1141 Email: joanna.braniff@party.niassembly.gov.uk

Traditional Unionist Voice
38 Henry Street, Ballymena BT42 3AH
Tel: 028 2564 0250
Website: www.tuv.org.uk

1 Charles Street, Ballymoney BT53 6DZ
Tel: 028 2723 8393

Assembly Office:
Tel: 028 9052 1461

Leader: Jim Allister MLA
President: William Ross
Chair: Ivor McConnell
Treasurer: Kenny Loughrin
Press Officer: Samuel Morrison

UK Independence Party
PO Box 408, Newton Abbot, Devon TQ12 9BG
Tel: 01626 831290 Fax: 01626 831348
Email: mail@ukip.org Website: www.ukip.org Twitter: @UKIP

Leader: Nigel Farage MEP
Deputy Leader: Paul Nuttall MEP
Treasurer: Stuart Wheeler
General Secretary: Jonathan Arnott

EUROPEAN UNION

European Parliament
Rue Wiertz, 1047 Brussels, Belgium
Tel: +32 2 284 21 11 Fax: +32 2 284 92 01
Email: [firstname.surname]@europarl.europa.eu Website:www.europarl.europa.eu
Twitter: @europarl_en

Allée du Printemps, 67070 Strasbourg Cedex, France
Tel: +33 3 88 17 40 01 Fax: +33 3 88 17 92 01

Plateau du Kirchberg, 2929 Luxembourg
Tel: +352 4300 1 Fax: +352 4300 22457

United Kingdom Offices
Europe House, 32 Smith Square, London SW1P 3EU
Tel: 020 7227 4300 Fax: 020 7227 4302
Email: eplondon@europarl.europa.eu Website:www.europarl.org.uk

Head of UK Office: Björn Kjellström
Tel: 020 7227 4325 Email: bjorn.kjellstrom@europarl.europa.eu

Head of Media: Paola Buonadonna
Tel: 020 7227 4335 Email: paola.buonadonna@europarl.europa.eu

Head of Outreach: Gergely Polner
Tel: 020 7227 4316 Email: gergely.polner@europarl.europa.eu

Head of Scotland Office: James Temple-Smithson
The Tun, 4 Jackson's Entry, Holyrood Road, Edinburgh EH8 8PJ
Tel: 0131-557 7866 Fax: 0131-557 4977 Email: epedinburgh@europarl.europa.eu

Cabinet of the President
Rue Wiertz, 1047 Brussels, Belgium
Tel: +32 2 284 21 11 Fax: +32 2 284 92 01
Email: [firstname.surname]@europarl.europa.eu Website:www.europarl.europa.eu

President	Martin Schulz (Ger)	
Head of Cabinet	Markus Winkler	+32 2 284 07 37/+33 3 88 17 49 38
Assistant to Head of Cabinet	Marie-Jeanne Olejniczak	+32 2 284 31 20/+33 3 88 17 28 83
Deputy Head of Cabinet	Herwig Kaiser	+32 2 284 38 26/+33 3 88 17 43 80
Assistant to Deputy Head of Cabinet	Aleksandra Heflich	+32 2 284 60 87/+33 3 88 17 21 02
Advisers		
Relations with Institutions	Maria José Martinez Iglesias	+32 2 284 31 50/+33 3 88 17 40 54
Administration	Lorenzo Mannelli	+32 2 284 24 35/+33 3 88 17 40 13
Adviser and Speechwriter	Silvia Pelz	+32 2 284 87 12/+33 3 88 17 81 64
Advisers		
Private Office and Protocol	Estelle Goeger	+32 2 283 41 54/+33 3 88 17 48 81
Internal Policies	Sonia Wollny	+32 2 283 10 65/+33 3 88 17 48 70
	Monika Strasser	+32 2 284 06 23/+33 3 88 16 41 03
	Edouard Dirrig	+32 2 284 44 37/+33 3 88 17 29 70
Diplomatic Adviser	Alexandre Stutzmann	+32 2 284 34 39/+33 3 88 17 47 69
Advisers		
External Policies	Marc Jütten	+32 2 284 36 43/+33 3 88 17 49 33
	Arnoldas Pranckevičius	+32 2 283 25 69/+33 3 88 17 27 10
	Djamila Chikhi	+32 2 284 24 73/+33 3 88 17 33 13
President's Spokesperson	Armin Machmer	+32 2 284 41 51/+33 3 88 17 41 34
Press Officer	Andreas Kleiner	+32 2 283 22 66/+33 3 88 17 23 36
Press Officer/Webmaster	Richard Freedman	+32 2 284 14 48/+33 3 88 17 37 85
Press Officers	Marcin Grajewski	+32 2 284 60 88/+33 3 88 17 37 85
	Raffaella De Marte	+32 2 283 12 47/+33 3 88 17 32 44

UK Members (MEPs)

State of the Parties (September 2013)

	Total
Conservative	26
Labour	13
Liberal Democrat	12
UK Independence Party	9
Independent	3
Green Party	2
Scottish National Party	2
British National Party	1
Democratic Unionist Party	1
Plaid Cymru	1
Sinn Féin	1
Ulster Conservatives and Unionists–New Force	1
We Demand A Referendum	1
	73 seats

State of European Party Groups (September 2013)

	Total
European Conservatives and Reformists Group (ECR)	27
Progressive Alliance of Socialists and Democrats (S&D)	13
Alliance of Liberals and Democrats for Europe (ALDE)	12
Europe of Freedom and Democracy Group (EFD)	8
Non-attached Group (NA)	7
Greens-European Free Alliance (Greens-EFA)	5
European United Left-Nordic Green Left Confederal Group	1
	73 seats

UK MEPs' Directory

Within the MEP contact directory we have only included MEPs' room numbers and buildings for the Parliaments' offices in Brussels and Strasbourg, but not the remainder of the addresses, which do not vary and are as follows:

Brussels: European Parliament, 60 Rue Wiertz, 1047 Brussels, Belgium
Strasbourg: European Parliament, Avenue du Président Robert Schuman 1, CS 91024, 67070 Strasbourg Cedex, France

ALDE	Alliance of Liberals and Democrats for Europe
ECR	European Conservatives and Reformists Group
EFD	Europe of Freedom and Democracy Group
EUL-NGL	European United Left-Nordic Green Left Confederal Group
Greens-EFA	Greens-European Free Alliance
NA	Non-attached Group
S&D	Progressive Alliance of Socialists and Democrats

AGNEW, Stuart   *UKIP/EFD*   **Eastern**
UK office: Rochester House, 145 New London Road, Chelmsford CM2 0QT
Tel: 01245 266466 *Fax:* 01245 252071 *Email:* stuartagnewmep@ukip.org
Website: www.stuartagnewmep.co.uk
Brussels office: 04F143, Bâtiment Altiero Spinelli
Tel: +32 2 284 54 04 *Fax:* +32 2 284 94 04 *Email:* johnstuart.agnew@europarl.europa.eu
Strasbourg office: M03103, Bâtiment Winston Churchill
Tel: +33 3 88 17 54 04 *Fax:* +33 3 88 17 94 04

ANDERSON, Martina *Sinn Féin/EUL-NGL*   **Northern Ireland**
UK office: Unit 2, Spencer House, 18-22 Spencer Road, Derry BT47 6QA
Tel: 028 7131 8683 Website: martinamep.eu
Brussels office: 07F247, Bâtiment Altiero Spinelli
Tel: +32 2 284 52 22 *Fax:* +32 2 284 92 22 *Email:* martina.anderson@europarl.europa.eu
Strasbourg office: T05011, Bâtiment Louise Weiss
Tel: +33 3 88 17 52 22 *Fax:* +33 3 88 17 92 22

ANDREASEN, Marta *Con/ECR*   **South East**
UK office: Fides House, 10 Chertsey Road, Woking GU21 5AB
Tel: 01483 729077 *Email:* marta@martaandreasen.com Website: www.martaandreasen.com
Twitter: @mandreasen
Brussels office: 06F258, Bâtiment Altiero Spinelli
Tel: +32 2 284 57 26 *Fax:* +32 2 284 97 26 *Email:* marta.andreasen@europarl.europa.eu
Strasbourg office: T06086, Bâtiment Louise Weiss
Tel: +33 3 88 17 57 26 *Fax:* +33 3 88 17 97 26

ASHWORTH, Richard *Con/ECR*   **South East**
UK office: Email: john@richardashworth.org Website: www.richardashworth.org
Brussels office: 06M105, Bâtiment Willy Brandt
Tel: +32 2 284 53 09 *Fax:* +32 2 284 93 09 *Email:* richard.ashworth@europarl.europa.eu
Strasbourg office: T11028, Bâtiment Louise Weiss
Tel: +33 3 88 17 53 09 *Fax:* +33 3 88 17 93 09

ATKINS, Rt Hon Sir Robert *Con/ECR*   **North West**
UK office: Manor House, Lancaster Road, Garstang PR3 1JA
Tel: 01995 602225 *Fax:* 01995 605690 *Email:* ratsmep@sir-robertatkins.org
Website: www.sir-robertatkins.org
Brussels office: 06M107, Bâtiment Willy Brandt
Tel: +32 2 284 53 73 *Fax:* +32 2 284 93 73 *Email:* robert.atkins@europarl.europa.eu
Strasbourg office: T11030, Bâtiment Louise Weiss
Tel: +33 3 88 17 53 73 *Fax:* +33 3 88 17 93 73

BATTEN, Gerard *UKIP/EFD*   **London**
UK office: PO Box 2409, Ilford IG1 8ES
Tel: 020 7403 7174/020 7403 7175 Website: www.gerardbattenmep.co.uk Twitter: @gerardbattenmep
Brussels office: 04F243, Bâtiment Altiero Spinelli
Tel: +32 2 284 59 20 *Fax:* +32 2 284 99 20 *Email:* gerard.batten@europarl.europa.eu
Strasbourg office: T06014, Bâtiment Louise Weiss
Tel: +33 3 88 17 59 20 *Fax:* +33 3 88 17 99 20

BEARDER, Catherine *Lib Dem/ALDE*   **South East**
UK office: 27 Park End Street, Oxford OX1 1HU
Tel: 01865 249838 *Email:* catherine@bearder.eu Website: www.bearder.eu Twitter: @catherinemep
Brussels office: 10G218, Bâtiment Altiero Spinelli
Tel: +32 2 284 56 32 *Fax:* +32 2 284 96 32 *Email:* catherine.bearder@europarl.europa.eu
Strasbourg office: M02006, Bâtiment Winston Churchill
Tel: +33 3 88 17 56 32 *Fax:* +33 3 88 17 96 32

BENNION, Phil *Lib Dem/ALDE*   **West Midlands**
UK office: 6b Bolebridge Street, Tamworth B79 7PA
Tel: 01827 312100 *Email:* office@philbennion.org Website: philbennion.org
Brussels office: 10G258, Bâtiment Altiero Spinelli
Tel: +32 2 284 55 21 *Fax:* +32 2 284 95 21 *Email:* phil.bennion@europarl.europa.eu
Strasbourg office: M02003, Bâtiment Winston Churchill
Tel: +33 3 88 17 55 21 *Fax:* +33 3 88 17 95 21

BLOOM, Godfrey *Ind/NA*   **Yorkshire & Humber**
UK office: 108 Main Street, Wressle, Selby YO8 6ET
Tel: 01757 630778 *Fax:* 01757 630395 *Email:* gbloom@ukip.org
Website: www.godfreybloommep.co.uk Twitter: @goddersukip

Brussels office: 04F155, Bâtiment Altiero Spinelli
Tel: +32 2 284 54 69 *Fax:* +32 2 284 94 69 *Email:* godfrey.bloom@europarl.europa.eu
Strasbourg office: T06012, Bâtiment Louise Weiss
Tel: +33 3 88 17 54 69 *Fax:* +33 3 88 17 94 69

BOWLES, Sharon *Lib Dem/ALDE*   **South East**
UK office: Felden House, Dower Mews, High Street, Berkhamsted HP4 2BL
Tel: 01442 875962 *Fax:* 01442 872860 *Email:* info@sharonbowles.org.uk
Website: www.sharonbowles.org.uk Twitter: @sharonbowlesmep
Brussels office: 10G201, Bâtiment Altiero Spinelli
Tel: +32 2 284 52 21 *Fax:* +32 2 284 92 21 *Email:* sharon.bowles@europarl.europa.eu
Strasbourg office: M02029, Bâtiment Winston Churchill
Tel: +33 3 88 17 52 21 *Fax:* +33 3 88 17 92 21

BRADBOURN, Philip, OBE *Con/ECR*   **West Midlands**
UK office: 285 Kenilworth Road, Balsall Common, Coventry CV7 7EL
Tel: 01676 530621 *Fax:* 01676 530658 *Email:* press@torymeps.com Website: www.torymeps.com
Brussels office: 03F370, Bâtiment Altiero Spinelli
Tel: +32 2 284 74 07 *Fax:* +32 2 284 94 07 *Email:* philip.bradbourn@europarl.europa.eu
Strasbourg office: T11302, Bâtiment Louise Weiss
Tel: +33 3 88 17 74 07 *Fax:* +33 3 88 17 94 07

BRONS, Andrew *Ind/NA*   **Yorkshire & Humber**
UK office: Office 300, 57 Great George Street, Leeds LS1 3AJ
Tel: 0113-251 5651 Website: www.andrewbronsmep.eu Twitter: @andrewbronsmep
Brussels office: 03F258, Bâtiment Altiero Spinelli
Tel: +32 2 284 57 73 *Fax:* +32 2 284 97 73 *Email:* andrew.brons@europarl.europa.eu
Strasbourg office: M02048, Bâtiment Winston Churchill
Tel: +33 3 88 17 57 73 *Fax:* +33 3 88 17 97 73

BUFTON, John *UKIP/EFD*   **Wales**
UK office: UKIP Wales, 1 Caspian Point, Pierhead Strret, Cardiff CF10 4DQ
Tel: 029 2044 4060 *Fax:* 029 2044 4061 *Email:* jbufton@ukipwales.org Website: www.johnbufton.eu
Brussels office: 04F247, Bâtiment Altiero Spinelli
Tel: +32 2 284 57 30 *Fax:* +32 2 284 97 30 *Email:* john.bufton@europarl.europa.eu
Strasbourg office: M03104, Bâtiment Winston Churchill
Tel: +33 3 88 17 57 30 *Fax:* +33 3 88 17 97 30

CALLANAN, Martin *Con/ECR*   **North East**
UK office: Aston House, Redburn Road, Newcastle upon Tyne NE5 1NB
Tel: 0191-214 6744 *Fax:* 0191-214 5497 Website: www.martincallanan.com
Brussels office: 06M095, Bâtiment Willy Brandt
Tel: +32 2 284 57 01 *Fax:* +32 2 284 97 01 *Email:* martin.callanan@europarl.europa.eu
Strasbourg office: T06055, Bâtiment Louise Weiss
Tel: +33 3 88 17 57 01 *Fax:* +33 3 88 17 97 01

CAMPBELL BANNERMAN, David *Con/ECR*   **Eastern**
UK office: 153 St Neots Road, Hardwick CB23 7QJ
Tel: 01954 210333/07796 225237 Website: www.dcbmep.org
Brussels office: 03M113, Bâtiment Willy Brandt
Tel: +32 2 284 57 33 *Fax:* +32 2 284 97 33 *Email:* david.campbellbannerman@europarl.europa.eu
Strasbourg office: T11018, Bâtiment Louise Weiss
Tel: +33 3 88 17 57 33 *Fax:* +33 3 88 17 97 33

CASHMAN, Michael, CBE *Lab/S&D*   **West Midlands**
UK office: West Midlands Labour European Office, Terry Duffy House, Thomas Street,
West Bromwich B70 6NT
Tel: 0121-569 1923 *Fax:* 0121-553 1898 *Email:* michaelcashman@phonecoop.coop
Website: michael-cashman.eu Twitter: @mcashmanmep

Brussels office: 13G205, Bâtiment Altiero Spinelli
Tel: +32 2 284 57 59 *Fax:* +32 2 284 97 59 *Email:* michael.cashman@europarl.europa.eu
Strasbourg office: T07026, Bâtiment Louise Weiss
Tel: +33 3 88 17 57 59 *Fax:* +33 3 88 17 97 59

CHICHESTER, Giles *Con/ECR*   South West
UK office: Longridge, West Hill, Ottery St Mary EX11 1UX
Tel: 01404 851106 *Fax:* 01404 850752 *Email:* giles@gileschichestermep.org.uk
Website: www.gileschichestermep.org.uk
Brussels office: 06M121, Bâtiment Willy Brandt
Tel: +32 2 284 52 96 *Fax:* +32 2 284 92 96 *Email:* giles.chichester@europarl.europa.eu
Strasbourg office: T11036, Bâtiment Louise Weiss
Tel: +33 3 88 17 52 96 *Fax:* +33 3 88 17 92 96

CLARK, Derek *UKIP/EFD*   East Midlands
UK office: Rowan House, 23 Billing Road, Northampton NN1 5AT
Tel: 01604 620064 *Fax:* 01604 636002 *Email:* mep@derekclarkmep.org.uk
Website: www.derekclarkmep.org.uk Twitter: @derekclarkmep
Brussels office: 04F163, Bâtiment Altiero Spinelli
Tel: +32 2 284 55 52 *Fax:* +32 2 284 95 52 *Email:* derekroland.clark@europarl.europa.eu
Strasbourg office: T05032, Bâtiment Louise Weiss
Tel: +33 3 88 17 55 52 *Fax:* +33 3 88 17 95 52

COLMAN, Trevor *UKIP/NA*   South West
UK office: Lexdrum House, Old Newton Road, Newton Abbot, Devon TQ12 6UT
Tel: 01626 830630 *Fax:* 01626 830619
Brussels office: 04F136, Bâtiment Altiero Spinelli
Tel: +32 2 284 57 63 *Fax:* +32 2 284 97 63 *Email:* trevor.colman@europarl.europa.eu
Strasbourg office: T05038, Bâtiment Louise Weiss
Tel: +33 3 88 17 57 63 *Fax:* +33 3 88 17 97 63

DARTMOUTH, William *UKIP/EFD*   South West
UK office: The Old Stores Cottage, Brooms Green, Dymock GL18 2DP
Tel: 01531 890180 *Fax:* 01531 890180 Website: www.williamdartmouth.com
Brussels office: 04F142, Bâtiment Altiero Spinelli
Tel: +32 2 284 57 35 *Fax:* +32 2 284 97 35 *Email:* william.dartmouth@europarl.europa.eu
Strasbourg office: M03106, Bâtiment Winston Churchill
Tel: +33 3 88 17 57 35 *Fax:* +33 3 88 17 97 35

DAVIES, Chris *Lib Dem/ALDE*   North West
UK office: 87a Castle Street, Edgeley, Stockport SK3 9AR
Tel: 0161-477 7070 *Fax:* 0161-477 7007 *Email:* chris@chrisdaviesmep.org.uk
Website: www.chrisdaviesmep.org.uk Twitter: @chrisdaviesmep
Brussels office: 10G169, Bâtiment Altiero Spinelli
Tel: +32 2 284 53 53 *Fax:* +32 2 284 93 53 *Email:* chris.davies@europarl.europa.eu
Strasbourg office: M02005, Bâtiment Winston Churchill
Tel: +33 3 88 17 53 53 *Fax:* +33 3 88 17 93 53

DEVA, Nirj *Con/ECR*   South East
UK office: 96 Vine Lane, Hillingdon, London UB10 0BE
Tel: 01895 470463 *Email:* office@nirjdeva.com Website: www.nirjdeva.com Twitter: @nirjdeva
Brussels office: 04M099, Bâtiment Willy Brandt
Tel: +32 2 284 72 45 *Fax:* +32 2 284 92 45 *Email:* nirj.deva@europarl.europa.eu
Strasbourg office: T11038, Bâtiment Louise Weiss
Tel: +33 3 88 17 72 45 *Fax:* +33 3 88 17 92 45

DODDS, Diane *DUP/NA* Northern Ireland
UK office: DUP European Office, Garvey Studios, Longstone Street, Lisburn BT28 1TP
Tel: 028 9266 7733 *Email:* ddodds@dup-belfast.co.uk Website: www.dianedodds.co.uk
Twitter: @dianedoddsmep
Brussels office: 11G206, Bâtiment Altiero Spinelli
Tel: +32 2 284 57 70 *Fax:* +32 2 284 97 70 *Email:* diane.dodds@europarl.europa.eu
Strasbourg office: T06045, Bâtiment Louise Weiss
Tel: +33 3 88 17 57 70 *Fax:* +33 3 88 17 97 70

DUFF, Andrew *Lib Dem/ALDE* Eastern
UK office: Orwell House, Cowley Road, Cambridge CB4 0PP
Tel: 01223 566700 *Fax:* 01223 566698 *Email:* mep@andrewduffmep.org Website: andrewduff.eu
Twitter: @andrew_duff_mep
Brussels office: 10G346, Bâtiment Altiero Spinelli
Tel: +32 2 284 59 98 *Fax:* +32 2 284 99 98 *Email:* andrew.duff@europarl.europa.eu
Strasbourg office: M02010, Bâtiment Winston Churchill
Tel: +33 3 88 17 59 98 *Fax:* +33 3 88 17 99 98

ELLES, James *Con/ECR* South East
UK office: Beaconsfield Constituency Conservative Association, Disraeli House, 12 Aylesbury End,
Beaconsfield HP9 1LW
Tel: 01494 673745 *Fax:* 01494 670428 Website: www.jameselles.com
Brussels office: 04M091, Bâtiment Willy Brandt
Tel: +32 2 284 59 51 *Fax:* +32 2 284 99 51 *Email:* james.elles@europarl.europa.eu
Strasbourg office: T01140, Bâtiment Louise Weiss
Tel: +33 3 88 17 59 51 *Fax:* +33 3 88 17 99 51

EVANS, Jill *PlC/Greens-EFA* Wales
UK office: 45 Gelligaled Road, Ystrad, Rhondda Cynon Taf CF41 7RQ
Tel: 01443 441 395 *Fax:* 01443 440 999 Website: www.jillevans.net Twitter: @jillevansmep
Brussels office: 08H153, Bâtiment Altiero Spinelli
Tel: +32 2 284 51 03 *Fax:* +32 2 284 91 03 *Email:* jill.evans@europarl.europa.eu
Strasbourg office: T05139, Bâtiment Louise Weiss
Tel: +33 3 88 17 51 03 *Fax:* +33 3 88 17 91 03

FARAGE, Nigel *UKIP/EFD* South East
UK office: The Old Grain Store, Church Lane, Lyminster BN17 7QJ
Tel: 01903 885573 *Fax:* 01903 885574 *Email:* ukipse@ukip.org Website: www.nigelfaragemep.co.uk
Twitter: @nigel_farage
Brussels office: 04F158, Bâtiment Altiero Spinelli
Tel: +32 2 284 58 55 *Fax:* +32 2 284 98 55 *Email:* nigel.farage@europarl.europa.eu
Strasbourg office: T06007, Bâtiment Louise Weiss
Tel: +33 3 88 17 58 55 *Fax:* +33 3 88 17 98 55

FORD, Vicky *Con/ECR* Eastern
UK office: 153 St Neots Road, Hardwick CB23 7QJ
Tel: 01954 211722 *Fax:* 01954 212455 *Email:* office@vickyford.org Website: www.vickyford.org
Twitter: @vickyford
Brussels office: 05M083, Bâtiment Willy Brandt
Tel: +32 2 284 56 72 *Fax:* +32 2 284 96 72 *Email:* vicky.ford@europarl.europa.eu
Strasbourg office: T11042, Bâtiment Louise Weiss
Tel: +33 3 88 17 56 72 *Fax:* +33 3 88 17 96 72

FOSTER, Jacqueline *Con/ECR* North West
UK office: Thursby House, 1 Thursby Road, Croft Business Park, Bromborough, Wirral CH62 3PW
Tel: 0151-346 2108 *Email:* office@jacquelinefostermep.com Website: www.jacquelinefostermep.com
Twitter: @jfostermep

Brussels office: 06M113, Bâtiment Willy Brandt
Tel: +32 2 284 56 74 *Fax:* +32 2 284 96 74 *Email:* jacqueline.foster@europarl.europa.eu
Strasbourg office: T11044, Bâtiment Louise Weiss
Tel: +33 3 88 17 56 74 *Fax:* +33 3 88 17 96 74

FOX, Ashley *Con/ECR*   **South West**
UK office: 5 Westfield Park, Bristol BS6 6LT
Tel: 0117-973 7050 *Email:* ashley@ashleyfoxmep.co.uk Website: www.ashleyfoxmep.co.uk
Brussels office: 05M075, Bâtiment Willy Brandt
Tel: +32 2 284 76 77 *Fax:* +32 2 284 96 77 *Email:* ashley.fox@europarl.europa.eu
Strasbourg office: T11046, Bâtiment Louise Weiss
Tel: +33 3 88 17 76 77 *Fax:* +33 3 88 17 96 77

GIRLING, Julie *Con/ECR*   **South West**
UK office: Gloucestershire Conservatives, Regent Court, Gloucester Business Park,
Hucclecote GL3 4AD
Tel: 01386 882491 *Email:* linda@juliegirling.com Website: www.juliegirling.com
Twitter: @juliegirling
Brussels office: 05M091, Bâtiment Willy Brandt
Tel: +32 2 284 56 78 *Fax:* +32 2 284 96 78 *Email:* julie.girling@europarl.europa.eu
Strasbourg office: T11048, Bâtiment Louise Weiss
Tel: +33 3 88 17 56 78 *Fax:* +33 3 88 17 96 78

GRIFFIN, Nick *BNP/NA*   **North West**
UK office: PO Box 107, Wigton CA7 0YA
Tel: 01697 344480 *Email:* contact@nickgriffinmep.eu Website: nickgriffinmep.eu
Twitter: @nickgriffinmep
Brussels office: 03F266, Bâtiment Altiero Spinelli
Tel: +32 2 284 57 72 *Fax:* +32 2 284 97 72 *Email:* nick.griffin@europarl.europa.eu
Strasbourg office: M02047, Bâtiment Winston Churchill
Tel: +33 3 88 17 57 72 *Fax:* +33 3 88 17 97 72

HALL, Fiona, MBE *Lib Dem/ALDE*   **North East**
UK office: 55a Old Elvet, Durham DH1 3HN
Tel: 0191-383 0119 *Fax:* 0191-375 7519 *Email:* fiona@fionahallmep.co.uk
Website: www.fionahall.org.uk Twitter: @fionahallmep
Brussels office: 10G246, Bâtiment Altiero Spinelli
Tel: +32 2 284 55 61 *Fax:* +32 2 284 95 61 *Email:* fiona.hall@europarl.europa.eu
Strasbourg office: M02004, Bâtiment Winston Churchill
Tel: +33 3 88 17 55 61 *Fax:* +33 3 88 17 95 61

HANNAN, Daniel *Con/ECR*   **South East**
UK office: PO Box 99, Hassocks BN6 0DY
Email: office@hannan.co.uk Website: www.hannan.co.uk Twitter: @danhannanmep
Brussels office: 05M089, Bâtiment Willy Brandt
Tel: +32 2 284 51 37 *Fax:* +32 2 284 91 37 *Email:* daniel.hannan@europarl.europa.eu
Strasbourg office: T11050, Bâtiment Louise Weiss
Tel: +33 3 88 17 51 37 *Fax:* +33 3 88 17 91 37

HARBOUR, Malcolm, CBE *Con/ECR*   **West Midlands**
UK office: 285 Kenilworth Road, Balsall Common, Coventry CV7 7EL
Tel: 01676 530682 *Fax:* 01676 530658 *Email:* bharding@torymeps.com Website: www.torymeps.com
Brussels office: 13E130, Bâtiment Altiero Spinelli
Tel: +32 2 284 51 32 *Fax:* +32 2 284 91 32 *Email:* malcolm.harbour@europarl.europa.eu
Strasbourg office: T12018, Bâtiment Louise Weiss
Tel: +33 3 88 17 51 32 *Fax:* +33 3 88 17 91 32

HELMER, Roger *UKIP/EFD* **East Midlands**
UK office: 21 Manor Walk, Coventry Road, Market Harborough LE16 9BP
Twitter: @rogerhelmermep
Brussels office: 04F151, Bâtiment Altiero Spinelli
Tel: +32 2 284 57 64 *Fax:* +32 2 284 97 64 *Email:* roger.helmer@europarl.europa.eu
Strasbourg office: T11063, Bâtiment Louise Weiss
Tel: +33 3 88 17 57 64 *Fax:* +33 3 88 17 97 64

HONEYBALL, Mary *Lab/S&D* **London**
UK office: 4G Shirland Mews, London W9 3DY
Tel: 020 8964 9815 *Fax:* 020 8960 0150 *Email:* mary@maryhoneyball.net
Website: thehoneyballbuzz.com Twitter: @maryhoneyball
Brussels office: 13G258, Bâtiment Altiero Spinelli
Tel: +32 2 284 52 09 *Fax:* +32 2 284 92 09 *Email:* mary.honeyball@europarl.europa.eu
Strasbourg office: T07048, Bâtiment Louise Weiss
Tel: +33 3 88 17 52 09 *Fax:* +33 3 88 17 92 09

HOWITT, Richard *Lab/S&D* **Eastern**
UK office: Labour European Office, Unit 3, Frohock House, 222 Mill Road, Cambridge CB1 3NF
Tel: 01223 240202 *Fax:* 01223 241900 *Email:* richard@richardhowittmep.com
Website: www.richardhowittmep.com Twitter: @richardhowitt
Brussels office: 13G246, Bâtiment Altiero Spinelli
Tel: +32 2 284 54 77 *Fax:* +32 2 284 94 77 *Email:* richard.howitt@europarl.europa.eu
Strasbourg office: T07044, Bâtiment Louise Weiss
Tel: +33 3 88 17 54 77 *Fax:* +33 3 88 17 94 77

HUDGHTON, Ian *SNP/Greens-EFA* **Scotland**
UK office: 8 Old Glamis Road, Dundee DD3 8HP
Tel: 01382 623200 *Fax:* 01382 903205 Website: www.hudghtonmep.com
Brussels office: 08H161, Bâtiment Altiero Spinelli
Tel: +32 2 284 54 99 *Fax:* +32 2 284 94 99 *Email:* ian.hudghton@europarl.europa.eu
Strasbourg office: T05137, Bâtiment Louise Weiss
Tel: +33 3 88 17 54 99 *Fax:* +33 3 88 17 94 99

HUGHES, Stephen *Lab/S&D* **North East**
UK office: North East European Constituency Office, Room 38/4, County Hall, Durham DH1 5UR
Tel: 0191-384 9371 *Fax:* 0191-384 6100 *Email:* stephen-hughes@btconnect.com
Website: www.stephenhughesmep.org
Brussels office: 13G242, Bâtiment Altiero Spinelli
Tel: +32 2 284 54 08 *Fax:* +32 2 284 94 08 *Email:* stephen.hughes@europarl.europa.eu
Strasbourg office: T07046, Bâtiment Louise Weiss
Tel: +33 3 88 17 54 08 *Fax:* +33 3 88 17 94 08

KAMALL, Syed *Con/ECR* **London**
UK office: 3 Bridle Close, Kingston upon Thames KT1 2JW
Tel: 020 8546 2398 *Fax:* 020 3292 1601 Website: www.syedkamall.com Twitter: @syedkamall
Brussels office: 05M073, Bâtiment Willy Brandt
Tel: +32 2 284 57 92 *Fax:* +32 2 284 97 92 *Email:* syed.kamall@europarl.europa.eu
Strasbourg office: T11052, Bâtiment Louise Weiss
Tel: +33 3 88 17 57 92 *Fax:* +33 3 88 17 97 92

KARIM, Sajjad *Con/ECR* **North West**
UK office: 14b Wynford Square, West Ashton Street, Salford M50 2SN
Tel: 01282 613616 *Fax:* 01282 616177 *Email:* info@sajjadkarim.eu Website: www.sajjadkarim.eu
Twitter: @shkmep
Brussels office: 04M107, Bâtiment Willy Brandt
Tel: +32 2 284 56 40 *Fax:* +32 2 284 96 40 *Email:* sajjad.karim@europarl.europa.eu
Strasbourg office: T11054, Bâtiment Louise Weiss
Tel: +33 3 88 17 56 40 *Fax:* +33 3 88 17 96 40

KIRKHOPE, Timothy *Con/ECR*   **Yorkshire & Humber**
UK office: Beechwood Farm, Main Street, Scotton, Knaresborough HG5 9HY
Tel: 01423 866001 *Fax:* 01423 860640 *Email:* timothy.kirkhope@btinternet.com
Website: www.kirkhope.org.uk
Brussels office: 09G305, Bâtiment Altiero Spinelli
Tel: +32 2 284 53 21 *Fax:* +32 2 284 93 21 *Email:* timothy.kirkhope@europarl.europa.eu
Strasbourg office: T11026, Bâtiment Louise Weiss
Tel: +33 3 88 17 53 21 *Fax:* +33 3 88 17 93 21

LAMBERT, Jean *Green/Greens-EFA*   **London**
UK office: CAN Mezzanine, 49-51 East Road, London N1 6AH
Tel: 020 7250 8416 *Email:* jeanlambert@greenmeps.org.uk Website: www.jeanlambertmep.org.uk
Twitter: @greenjeanmep
Brussels office: 08G107, Bâtiment Altiero Spinelli
Tel: +32 2 284 55 07 *Fax:* +32 2 284 95 07 *Email:* jean.lambert@europarl.europa.eu
Strasbourg office: T05087, Bâtiment Louise Weiss
Tel: +33 3 88 17 55 07 *Fax:* +33 3 88 17 95 07

LUDFORD, Sarah *Lib Dem/ALDE*   **London**
UK office: 36B St Peter's Street, London N1 8JT
Tel: 020 7288 2526 *Fax:* 020 7288 2526 *Email:* office@sarahludfordmep.org.uk
Website: www.sarahludfordmep.org.uk Twitter: @SarahLudfordMEP
Brussels office: 10G165, Bâtiment Altiero Spinelli
Tel: +32 2 284 51 04 *Fax:* +32 2 284 91 04 *Email:* sarah.ludford@europarl.europa.eu
Strasbourg office: M02009, Bâtiment Winston Churchill
Tel: +33 3 88 17 51 04 *Fax:* +33 3 88 17 91 04

LYON, George *Lib Dem/ALDE*   **Scotland**
UK office: Mirren Court (One), 119 Renfrew Road, Paisley PA3 4EA
Tel: 0141-887 5332 *Email:* george@georgelyon.org.uk Website: www.georgelyon.org.uk
Twitter: @georgelyonmep
Brussels office: 10G210, Bâtiment Altiero Spinelli
Tel: +32 2 284 76 28 *Fax:* +32 2 284 96 28 *Email:* george.lyon@europarl.europa.eu
Strasbourg office: M02008, Bâtiment Winston Churchill
Tel: +33 3 88 17 76 28 *Fax:* +33 3 88 17 96 28

McAVAN, Linda *Lab/S&D*   **Yorkshire & Humber**
UK office: Labour Constituency Office, 79 High Street, Wath upon Dearne S63 7QB
Tel: 01709 875665 *Email:* lindamcavan@lindamcavanmep.org.uk
Website: www.lindamcavanmep.org.uk Twitter: @lindamcavanmep
Brussels office: 13G346, Bâtiment Altiero Spinelli
Tel: +32 2 284 54 38 *Fax:* +32 2 284 94 38 *Email:* linda.mcavan@europarl.europa.eu
Strasbourg office: T07040, Bâtiment Louise Weiss
Tel: +33 3 88 17 54 38 *Fax:* +33 3 88 17 94 38

McCARTHY, Arlene *Lab/S&D*   **North West**
UK office: Express Networks, 1 George Leigh Street, Manchester M4 5DL
Tel: 0161-906 0801 *Fax:* 0161-906 0802 *Email:* arlene.mccarthy@easynet.co.uk
Website: www.arlenemccarthy.labour.co.uk Twitter: @euromp_arlenemc
Brussels office: 13G351, Bâtiment Altiero Spinelli
Tel: +32 2 284 55 01 *Fax:* +32 2 284 95 01 *Email:* arlene.mccarthy@europarl.europa.eu
Strasbourg office: T07034, Bâtiment Louise Weiss
Tel: +33 3 88 17 55 01 *Fax:* +33 3 88 17 95 01

McCLARKIN, Emma   *Con/ECR*   **East Midlands**
UK office: Three Crowns Yard, High Street, Market Harborough LE16 7AF
Tel: 01858 419709 *Fax:* 01858 432855 Website: www.emmamcclarkin.com
Twitter: @emmamcclarkin
Brussels office: 04M105, Bâtiment Willy Brandt
Tel: +32 2 284 56 84 *Fax:* +32 2 284 96 84 *Email:* emma.mcclarkin@europarl.europa.eu
Strasbourg office: T11055, Bâtiment Louise Weiss
Tel: +33 3 88 17 56 84 *Fax:* +33 3 88 17 96 84

McINTYRE, Anthea   *Con/ECR*   **West Midlands**
UK office: The Chapel, Wythall Estate, Walford, Ross-on-Wye HR9 5SD
Tel: 01989 769544 *Email:* anthea@antheamcintyre.com Website: www.antheamcintyre.com
Brussels office: 05M081, Bâtiment Willy Brandt
Tel: +32 2 284 71 06 *Fax:* +32 2 284 91 06 *Email:* anthea.mcintyre@europarl.europa.eu
Strasbourg office: T11034, Bâtiment Louise Weiss
Tel: +33 3 88 17 71 06 *Fax:* +33 3 88 17 91 06

McMILLAN-SCOTT, Edward   *Lib Dem/ALDE*   **Yorkshire & Humber**
UK office: 460 Killinghall Road, Bradford BD2 4SL
Tel: 01274 911450 Website: www.emcmillanscott.com Twitter: @emcmillanscott
Brussels office: 13G130, Bâtiment Altiero Spinelli
Tel: +32 2 284 59 59 *Fax:* +32 2 284 99 59 *Email:* edward.mcmillan-scott@europarl.europa.eu
Strasbourg office: T12027, Bâtiment Louise Weiss
Tel: +33 3 88 17 59 59 *Fax:* +33 3 88 17 99 59

MARTIN, David   *Lab/S&D*   **Scotland**
UK office: Midlothian Innovation Centre, Pentlandfield, Roslin, Midlothian EH25 9RE
Tel: 0131-440 9040 *Email:* david@martinmep.com Website: www.martinmep.com
Twitter: @davidmartinmep
Brussels office: 13G354, Bâtiment Altiero Spinelli
Tel: +32 2 284 55 39 *Fax:* +32 2 284 95 39 *Email:* david.martin@europarl.europa.eu
Strasbourg office: T07036, Bâtiment Louise Weiss
Tel: +33 3 88 17 55 39 *Fax:* +33 3 88 17 95 39

MORAES, Claude   *Lab/S&D*   **London**
UK office: 65 Barnsbury Street, London N1 1EJ
Tel: 020 7609 5005 *Email:* office@claudemoraes.com Website: www.claudemoraes.com
Twitter: @claudemoraesmep
Brussels office: 13G342, Bâtiment Altiero Spinelli
Tel: +32 2 284 75 53 *Fax:* +32 2 284 95 53 *Email:* claude.moraes@europarl.europa.eu
Strasbourg office: T07042, Bâtiment Louise Weiss
Tel: +33 3 88 17 55 53 *Fax:* +33 3 88 17 95 53

NATTRASS, Mike   *Ind/NA*   **West Midlands**
UK office: 48 Fentham Road, Hampton-In-Arden B92 0AY
Tel: 0121-333 7737 *Email:* ukipmep@hotmail.co.uk Website: www.ukipmep.org
Brussels office: 04F258, Bâtiment Altiero Spinelli
Tel: +32 2 284 51 33 *Fax:* +32 2 284 91 33 *Email:* michaelhenry.nattrass@europarl.europa.eu
Strasbourg office: M03058, Bâtiment Winston Churchill
Tel: +33 3 88 17 51 33 *Fax:* +33 3 88 17 91 33

NEWTON DUNN, Bill   *Lib Dem/ALDE*   **East Midlands**
UK office: 10 Church Lane, Navenby, Lincoln LN5 0EG
Tel: 01522 810812/07939 250473 Website: www.newton-dunn.com Twitter: @billnewtondunn
Brussels office: 08G142, Bâtiment Altiero Spinelli
Tel: +32 2 284 57 12 *Fax:* +32 2 284 97 12 *Email:* bill.newtondunn@europarl.europa.eu
Strasbourg office: M03105, Bâtiment Winston Churchill
Tel: +33 3 88 17 57 12 *Fax:* +33 3 88 17 97 12

NICHOLSON, Jim *UCUNF/ECR* **Northern Ireland**
UK office: Strandtown Hall, 2-4 Belmont Road, Belfast BT4 2AN
Tel: 028 9097 4634 *Fax:* 028 9065 2149 *Email:* jim.nicholson@uup.org
Website: www.jim-nicholson.eu *Twitter:* @jnicholsonmep
Brussels office: 04M097, Bâtiment Willy Brandt
Tel: +32 2 284 59 33 *Fax:* +32 2 284 99 33 *Email:* james.nicholson@europarl.europa.eu
Strasbourg office: T11057, Bâtiment Louise Weiss
Tel: +33 3 88 17 59 33 *Fax:* +33 3 88 17 99 33

NUTTALL, Paul *UKIP/EFD* **North West**
UK office: Riverway House, Morecambe Road, Lancaster LA1 5JA
Tel: 01524 387690 *Website:* www.paulnuttallmep.com *Twitter:* @paulnuttallukip
Brussels office: 04F167, Bâtiment Altiero Spinelli
Tel: +32 2 284 57 40 *Fax:* +32 2 284 97 40 *Email:* paul.nuttall@europarl.europa.eu
Strasbourg office: M03107, Bâtiment Winston Churchill
Tel: +33 3 88 17 57 40 *Fax:* +33 3 88 17 97 40

SIMPSON, Brian *Lab/S&D* **North West**
UK office: Alexandra Park, Prescot Road, St Helens WA10 3TT
Tel: 01744 451609 *Email:* briansimpson.labour@virgin.net *Website:* www.briansimpsonmep.co.uk
Brussels office: 13G306, Bâtiment Altiero Spinelli
Tel: +32 2 284 55 10 *Fax:* +32 2 284 95 10 *Email:* brian.simpson@europarl.europa.eu
Strasbourg office: T06015, Bâtiment Louise Weiss
Tel: +33 3 88 17 55 10 *Fax:* +33 3 88 17 95 10

SINCLAIRE, Nicole *WDAR/NA* **West Midlands**
UK office: PO Box 15262, Solihull B90 9FY
Tel: 0330 440 8434 *Email:* nikkimep@googlemail.com *Website:* www.yourmep.org
Twitter: @nsinclairemep
Brussels office: 04F254, Bâtiment Altiero Spinelli
Tel: +32 2 284 57 56 *Fax:* +32 2 284 97 56 *Email:* nikki.sinclaire@europarl.europa.eu
Strasbourg office: T05034, Bâtiment Louise Weiss
Tel: +33 3 88 17 57 56 *Fax:* +33 3 88 17 97 56

SKINNER, Peter *Lab/S&D* **South East**
UK office: Suites 4 and 5, New Road, Rochester ME1 1DU
Tel: 01634 840930 *Fax:* 01634 840930 *Email:* southeast@peterskinnermep.eu
Website: www.peterskinnermep.eu *Twitter:* @pwskinnermep
Brussels office: 13G317, Bâtiment Altiero Spinelli
Tel: +32 2 284 54 58 *Fax:* +32 2 284 94 58 *Email:* peter.skinner@europarl.europa.eu
Strasbourg office: T07038, Bâtiment Louise Weiss
Tel: +33 3 88 17 54 58 *Fax:* +33 3 88 17 94 58

SMITH, Alyn *SNP/Greens-EFA* **Scotland**
UK office: c/o SNP Headquarters, Gordon Lamb House, 3 Jackson's Entry, Edinburgh EH8 8PJ
Tel: 0131-525 8926 *Website:* www.alynsmith.eu *Twitter:* @alynsmithmep
Brussels office: 08H149, Bâtiment Altiero Spinelli
Tel: +32 2 284 51 87 *Fax:* +32 2 284 91 87 *Email:* alyn.smith@europarl.europa.eu
Strasbourg office: T05135, Bâtiment Louise Weiss
Tel: +33 3 88 17 51 87 *Fax:* +33 3 88 17 91 87

STEVENSON, Struan *Con/ECR* **Scotland**
UK office: Scottish Conservative and Unionist Central Office, 67 Northumberland Street,
Edinburgh EH3 6JG
Tel: 0131-524 0033 *Email:* struanmep@aol.com *Website:* www.struanstevenson.com

Brussels office: 12G302, Bâtiment Altiero Spinelli
Tel: +32 2 284 57 10 *Fax:* +32 2 284 97 10 *Email:* struan.stevenson@europarl.europa.eu
Strasbourg office: T11058, Bâtiment Louise Weiss
Tel: +33 3 88 17 57 10 *Fax:* +33 3 88 17 97 10

STIHLER, Catherine   *Lab/S&D*   Scotland
UK office: 25 Church Street, Inverkeithing KY11 1LG
Tel: 01383 417799 *Fax:* 01383 413335 *Email:* cstihlermep@btconnect.com
Website: www.cstihlermep.com   Twitter: @c_stihler_mep
Brussels office: 13G309, Bâtiment Altiero Spinelli
Tel: +32 2 284 54 62 *Fax:* +32 2 284 94 62 *Email:* catherine.stihler@europarl.europa.eu
Strasbourg office: T07032, Bâtiment Louise Weiss
Tel: +33 3 88 17 54 62 *Fax:* +33 3 88 17 94 62

STURDY, Robert   *Con/ECR*   Eastern
UK office: 153 St Neot's Road, Hardwick, Cambridge CB23 7QJ
Tel: 01954 211790 *Email:* rwsturdy@btconnect.com Website: www.robertsturdymep.com
Brussels office: 04M089, Bâtiment Willy Brandt
Tel: +32 2 284 52 94 *Fax:* +32 2 284 92 94 *Email:* robert.sturdy@europarl.europa.eu
Strasbourg office: T11059, Bâtiment Louise Weiss
Tel: +33 3 88 17 52 94 *Fax:* +33 3 88 17 92 94

SWINBURNE, Kay   *Con/ECR*   Wales
UK office: Rhumney House, Copse Walk, Cardiff Gate Business Park, Cardiff CF23 8RB
Tel: 029 2054 0895 *Email:* kayswinburnemep@welshconservatives.com
Website: www.kayswinburne.co.uk
Brussels office: 04M083, Bâtiment Willy Brandt
Tel: +32 2 284 56 87 *Fax:* +32 2 284 96 87 *Email:* kay.swinburne@europarl.europa.eu
Strasbourg office: T11061, Bâtiment Louise Weiss
Tel: +33 3 88 17 56 87 *Fax:* +33 3 88 17 96 87

TANNOCK, Charles   *Con/ECR*   London
UK office: 1a Chelsea Manor Street, London SW3 5RP
Tel: 020 7349 6946 *Fax:* 020 7351 5885 *Email:* charles@charlestannock.com
Website: www.charlestannock.com   Twitter: @charlestannock
Brussels office: 04M081, Bâtiment Willy Brandt
Tel: +32 2 284 58 70 *Fax:* +32 2 284 98 70 *Email:* charles.tannock@europarl.europa.eu
Strasbourg office: T11065, Bâtiment Louise Weiss
Tel: +33 3 88 17 58 70 *Fax:* +33 3 88 17 98 70

TAYLOR, Keith   *Green/Greens-EFA*   South East
UK office: Office of the Green MEPs, CAN Mezzanine, 49-51 East Road, London N1 6AH
Tel: 020 7250 8415 *Email:* keithoffice@greenmeps.org.uk Website: www.keithtaylormep.org.uk
Twitter: @greenkeithmep
Brussels office: 08G103, Bâtiment Altiero Spinelli
Tel: +32 2 284 51 53 *Fax:* +32 2 284 91 53 *Email:* keith.taylor@europarl.europa.eu
Strasbourg office: T05089, Bâtiment Louise Weiss
Tel: +33 3 88 17 51 53 *Fax:* +33 3 88 17 91 53

TAYLOR, Rebecca   *Lib Dem/ALDE*   Yorkshire & Humber
UK office: Unit 10, Newlands House, Newlands Science Park, Inglemire Lane, Hull HU6 7TQ
Tel: 01482 850155 *Email:* office@rebeccataylor.eu Website: www.rebeccataylor.eu
Twitter: @rtaylor_mep
Brussels office: 10G254, Bâtiment Altiero Spinelli
Tel: +32 2 284 52 01 *Fax:* +32 2 284 92 01 *Email:* rebecca.taylor@europarl.europa.eu
Strasbourg office: M02101, Bâtiment Winston Churchill
Tel: +33 3 88 17 52 01 *Fax:* +33 3 88 17 92 01

VAN ORDEN, Geoffrey *Con/ECR*   **Eastern**
UK office: Conservative Office, 88 Rectory Lane, Chelmsford CM1 1RF
Tel: 01245 345188 *Fax:* 01245 269757 Website: www.geoffreyvanorden.com
Brussels office: 04M075, Bâtiment Willy Brandt
Tel: +32 2 284 53 32 *Fax:* +32 2 284 93 32 *Email:* geoffrey.vanorden@europarl.europa.eu
Strasbourg office: T11067, Bâtiment Louise Weiss
Tel: +33 3 88 17 53 32 *Fax:* +33 3 88 17 93 32

VAUGHAN, Derek *Lab/S&D*   **Wales**
UK office: Fourth Floor, Transport House, 1 Cathedral Road, Cardiff CF11 9SD
Tel: 029 2022 7660 *Email:* contact@derekvaughanmep.org.uk
Website: www.derekvaughanmep.org.uk Twitter: @derekvaughan
Brussels office: 13G254, Bâtiment Altiero Spinelli
Tel: +32 2 284 54 19 *Fax:* +32 2 284 94 19 *Email:* derek.vaughan@europarl.europa.eu
Strasbourg office: T07030, Bâtiment Louise Weiss
Tel: +33 3 88 17 54 19 *Fax:* +33 3 88 17 94 19

WATSON, Sir Graham *Lib Dem/ALDE*   **South West**
UK office: The Liberty, Old Kelways, Langport, Somerset TA10 9SJ
Tel: 01458 252265 *Fax:* 01458 253430 *Email:* info@grahamwatsonmep.org
Website: www.grahamwatsonmep.org Twitter: @grahamwatsonmep
Brussels office: 09G205, Bâtiment Altiero Spinelli
Tel: +32 2 284 56 26 *Fax:* +32 2 284 96 26 *Email:* graham.watson@europarl.europa.eu
Strasbourg office: M02106, Bâtiment Winston Churchill
Tel: +33 3 88 17 56 26 *Fax:* +33 3 88 17 96 26

WILLMOTT, Glenis *Lab/S&D*   **East Midlands**
UK office: Harold Wilson House, 23 Barratt Lane, Attenborough, Nottingham NG9 6AD
Tel: 0115-922 9717 *Fax:* 0115-922 4439 *Email:* office@gleniswillmott.org.uk
Website: www.gleniswillmott.eu Twitter: @gleniswillmott
Brussels office: 13G305, Bâtiment Altiero Spinelli
Tel: +32 2 284 54 59 *Fax:* +32 2 284 94 59 *Email:* glenis.willmott@europarl.europa.eu
Strasbourg office: T07028, Bâtiment Louise Weiss
Tel: +33 3 88 17 54 59 *Fax:* +33 3 88 17 94 59

YANNAKOUDAKIS, Marina *Con/ECR*   **London**
UK office: Margaret Thatcher House, 212 Ballards Lane, London N3 2LX
Tel: 020 8445 8055 Website: www.marinayannakoudakis.com Twitter: @marinamep
Brussels office: 04M073, Bâtiment Willy Brandt
Tel: +32 2 284 56 92 *Fax:* +32 2 284 96 92 *Email:* marina.yannakoudakis@europarl.europa.eu
Strasbourg office: T11069, Bâtiment Louise Weiss
Tel: +33 3 88 17 56 92 *Fax:* +33 3 88 17 96 92

European Commission
1049 Brussels, Belgium
Tel: +32 2 299 11 11
Email: [firstname.surname]@ec.europa.eu Website:www.ec.europa.eu Twitter: @eu_commission

United Kingdom
32 Smith Square, London SW1P 3EU
Tel: 020 7973 1992 Fax: 020 7973 1900
Email: comm-uk-press@ec.europa.eu Website: ec.europa.eu/unitedkingdom Twitter: @eulondonrep
Head of Representation, London: Jacqueline Minor

9 Alva Street, Edinburgh EH2 4PH
Tel: 0131-225 2058 Fax: 0131-226 4105
Head of Representation, Edinburgh: Graham Blythe

2 Caspian Point, Caspian Way, Cardiff CF10 4QQ
Tel: 029 2089 5020 Fax: 029 2089 5035
Head of Representation, Cardiff: David Hughes

74-76 Dublin Road, Belfast BT2 7HP
Tel: 028 9024 0708 Fax: 028 9024 8241
Head of Representation, Belfast: Colette Fitzgerald

College of Commissioners

President of the European Commission	José Manuel Barroso (Por)
External Relations	Catherine Ashton (UK)
Justice, Fundamental Rights and Citizenship	Viviane Reding (Lux)
Competition	Joaquín Almunia (Spa)
Transport	Siim Kallas (Est)
Digital Agenda	Neelie Kroes (Nth)
Industry and Entrepreneurship	Antonio Tajani (Ita)
Inter-Institutional Relations and Administration	Maroš Šefčovič (Slk)
Economic and Monetary Affairs and the Euro	Olli Rehn (Fin)
Employment, Social Affairs and Inclusion	László Andor (Hun)
Internal Market and Services	Michel Barnier (Fra)
Agriculture and Rural Development	Dacian Cioloş (Rom)
Health	Tonio Borg (Mal)
Maritime Affairs and Fisheries	Maria Damanaki (Gre)
Trade	Karel de Gucht (Bel)
Enlargement and European Neighbourhood Policy	Štefan Füle (Cze)
Research, Innovation and Science	Máire Geoghegan-Quinn (Irl)
International Co-operation, Humanitarian Aid and Crisis Response	Kristalina Georgieva (Bul)
Regional Policy	Johannes Hahn (Aut)
Climate Action	Connie Hedegaard (Den)
Financial Programming and Budget	Janusz Lewandowski (Pol)
Home Affairs	Cecilia Malmström (Swe)
Consumer Policy	Neven Mimica (Cro)
Energy	Günther Oettinger (Ger)
Development	Andris Piebalgs (Lat)
Environment	Janez Potočnik (Sln)
Taxation, Customs, Statistics, Audit and Anti-Fraud	Algirdas Šemeta (Lit)
Education, Culture, Multilingualism and Youth	Androulla Vassiliou (Cyp)

European Council and the Council of the EU

EUROPEAN COUNCIL

Rue de la Loi 175, 1048 Brussels, Belgium
Tel: +32 2 281 61 11 Fax: +32 2 281 69 99
Email: herman.vanrompuy@consilium.europa.eu Website:www.consilium.europa.eu
Twitter: @eucouncilpress

Since the implementation of the Lisbon Treaty in 2009, the Council is chaired by the permanent president of the European Council; the head of government or state of the country holding the rotating Council presidency deputises for the president in his absence.

President: Herman Van Rompuy (Bel)

Heads of Government and Heads of State sitting on the Council

Austria	Federal Chancellor Werner Faymann
Belgium	Prime Minister Elio Di Rupo
Bulgaria	Prime Minister Plamen Oresharski
Croatia	Prime Minister Zoran Milanović
Cyprus	President Nicos Anastasiades
Czech Republic	Prime Minister Jiří Rusnok
Denmark	Prime Minister Helle Thorning-Schmidt
Estonia	Prime Minister Andrus Ansip
Finland	Prime Minister Jyrki Katainen
France	President François Hollande
Germany	Federal Chancellor Angela Merkel
Greece	Prime Minister Antonis Samaras
Hungary	Prime Minister Viktor Orbán
Ireland	Prime Minister Enda Kenny
Italy	Prime Minister Enrico Letta
Latvia	Prime Minister Valdis Dombrovskis
Lithuania	President Dalia Grybauskaitė
Luxembourg	Prime Minister Jean-Claude Juncker
Malta	Prime Minister Joseph Muscat
Netherlands	Prime Minister Mark Rutte
Poland	Prime Minister Donald Tusk
Portugal	Prime Minister Pedro Passos Coelho
Romania	President Traian Băsescu
Slovakia	Prime Minister Robert Fico
Slovenia	Prime Minister Alenka Bratušek
Spain	Prime Minister Mariano Rajoy
Sweden	Prime Minister Fredrik Reinfeldt
United Kingdom	Prime Minister David Cameron

Presidency of the Council

www.eu2013.lt

Each Member State presides over the Council for a period of six months in turn, in partnership with the permanent President of the Council, in accordance with a pre-established rota. The Presidency of the Council organises the work of the institution and organises and chairs all meetings. It facilitates legislative and political decision-making and brokers compromises between the Member States.

For the period 2013-14, the order of succession is:

2013
Second half: Lithuania

2014
First half: Greece
Second half: Italy

COUNCIL OF THE EUROPEAN UNION

Rue de la Loi 175, 1048 Brussels, Belgium
Tel: +32 2 281 61 11 Fax: +32 2 281 69 99
Email: public.info@consilium.europa.eu Website:www.consilium.europa.eu

The Council of Ministers has one representative from each Member State. Ministers who attend its meetings vary depending on the subject under discussion: finance ministers on financial affairs, agricultural ministers on agricultural matters, etc.

The Council meetings and deliberations are prepared by the Committee of Representatives (Coreper), which is composed of the Member States' ambassadors to the Union. A staff of national civil servants assists each ambassador.

Permanent Representatives

Austria
Avenue de Cortenbergh 30, 1040 Brussels
Tel: +32 2 234 51 00 Fax: +32 2 235 63 00
Email: bruessel-ov@bmeia.gv.at
www.bmeia.gv.at/en/austrian-mission/
brussels.html
Permanent Representative: Walter Grahammer

Belgium
Rue de la Loi 61-63, 1040 Brussels
Tel: +32 2 233 21 21 Fax: +32 2 231 10 75
Email: dispatch.belgoeurop@diplobel.fed.be
www.diplomatie.belgium.be/belgium_eu/
Permanent Representative: Dirk Wouters

Bulgaria
Square Marie-Louise 49, 1000 Brussels
Tel: +32 2 235 83 00 Fax: +32 2 374 91 88
Email: mission.brusselseu@bg-permrep.eu
www.mfa.bg/embassies/belgiumpp/en/301/
index.html
Permanent Representative: Dimiter Tzantchev

Croatia
Avenue des Arts 50, 1000 Brussels
Tel: +32 2 507 54 11 Fax: +32 2 646 56 64
Email: cromiss.eu@mvep.hr
www.eu.mfa.hr
Ambassador: Mato Škrabalo

Cyprus
Avenue de Cortenbergh 61, 1000 Brussels
Tel: +32 2 739 51 11 Fax: +32 2 735 45 52
Email: cy.perm.rep@mfa.gov.cy
www.mfa.gov.cy/permrepeu
Permanent Representative:
Kornelios Korneliou

Czech Republic
Rue Caroly 15, 1050 Brussels
Tel: +32 2 213 91 11 Fax: +32 2 213 91 85
Email: eu.brussels@embassy.mzv.cz
www.mzv.cz/representation_brussels/en/
index.html
Permanent Representative: Martin Povejšil

Denmark
Rue d'Arlon 73, 1040 Brussels
Tel: +32 2 233 08 11 Fax: +32 2 230 93 84
Email: brurep@um.dk
www.eu.um.dk/en/
Permanent Representative:
Jeppe Tranholm-Mikkelsen

Estonia
Rue Guimard 11-13, 1040 Brussels
Tel: +32 2 227 39 10 Fax: +32 2 227 39 25
Email: permrep.eu@mfa.ee
www.eu.estemb.be/eng
Permanent Representative: Matti Maasikas

Finland
Avenue de Cortenbergh 80, 1000 Brussels
Tel: +32 2 287 84 11 Fax: +32 2 287 84 00
Email: sanomat.eue@formin.fi
www.finland.eu/public/default.aspx?culture=en-
US&contentlan=2 Twitter: @finpermrepeu
Permanent Representative:
Pilvi-Sisko Vierros-Villeneuve

France
Place de Louvain 14, 1000 Brussels
Tel: +32 2 229 82 11 Fax: +32 2 229 82 82
Email: presse.bruxelles-dfra@diplomatie.gouv.fr
www.rpfrance.eu Twitter: @rpuefrance
Permanent Representative: Philippe Etienne

Germany
Rue Jacques de Lalaing 8-14, 1040 Brussels
Tel: +32 2 787 10 00 Fax: +32 2 787 20 00
Email: pol-101-eu@brue.auswaertiges-amt.de
www.bruessel-eu.diplo.de
Permanent Representative: Peter Tempel

Greece
Rue Jacques De Lalaing 19-21, 1040 Brussels
Tel: +32 2 551 56 11 Fax: +32 2 551 56 51
Email: mea.bruxelles@rp-grece.be
Permanent Representative:
Theodoros N. Sotiropoulos

Hungary
Rue de Trèves 92-98, 1040 Brussels
Tel: +32 2 234 12 00 Fax: +32 2 372 07 84
Email: sec.beu@mfa.gov.hu
www.mfa.gov.hu/kulkepviselet/brussels_eu/en/
mainpage.htm
Permanent Representative: Péter Györkös

Ireland
Rue Froissart 50, 1040 Brussels
Tel: +32 2 230 85 80 Fax: +32 2 230 32 03
Email: irlprb@dfa.ie
www.irelandrepbrussels.be
Twitter: @irelandrepbru
Permanent Representative: Rory Montgomery

Italy
Rue du Marteau 7-15, 1000 Brussels
Tel: +32 2 220 04 11
Email: rpue@rpue.esteri.it
www.italiaue.esteri.it
Ambassador: Stefano Sannino

Latvia
Avenue des Arts 23, 1000 Brussels
Tel: +32 2 238 31 00 Fax: +32 2 238 32 50
Email: permrep.eu@mfa.gov.lv
www.mfa.gov.lv/en/brussels
Permanent Representative: Ilze Juhansone

Lithuania
Rue Belliard 41-43, 1040 Brussels
Tel: +32 2 771 01 40 Fax: +32 2 771 45 97
Email: office@eu.mfa.lt
www.eurep.mfa.lt/index.php?569282635
Twitter: @eu2013ltpress
Ambassador and Permanent Representative:
Raimundas Karoblis

Luxembourg
Avenue de Cortenbergh 75, 1000 Brussels
Tel: +32 2 737 56 00 Fax: +32 2 737 14 29
Email: bruxelles.rp@mae.etat.lu
Permanent Representative: Christian Braun

Malta
Rue Archimède 25, 1000 Brussels
Tel: +32 2 343 01 95 Fax: +32 2 343 01 06
Email: maltarep@gov.mt
www.foreign.gov.mt/Default.aspx?MDIS=104
Permanent Representative: Marlene Bonnici

Netherlands
Avenue de Cortenbergh 4-10, 1040 Brussels
Tel: +32 2 679 15 11 Fax: +32 2 679 17 75
Email: bre@minbuza.nl
www.eu.nlmission.org
Permanent Representative: Pieter de Gooijer

Poland
Rue Stevin 139, 1000 Brussels
Tel: +32 2 780 42 00 Fax: +32 2 780 42 97
Email: bebrustpe@msz.gov.pl
www.brukselaue.msz.gov.pl/en
Twitter: @plpermrepeu
Permanent Representative: Marek Prawda

Portugal
Avenue de Cortenbergh 12, 1040 Brussels
Tel: +32 2 286 42 11 Fax: +32 2 231 00 26
Email: reper@reper-portugal.be
www.reper.mne.pt/en
Permanent Representative:
Domingos Fezas Vital

Romania
Rue Montoyer 12, 1000 Brussels
Tel: +32 2 700 06 40 Fax: +32 2 700 06 41
Email: bru@rpro.eu
www.ue.mae.ro/en
Permanent Representative: Mihnea Ioan Motoc

Slovakia
Avenue de Cortenbergh 79, 1000 Brussels
Tel: +32 2 743 68 11 Fax: +32 2 743 68 88
Email: eu.brussels@mzv.sk
www.eubrussels.mfa.sk/App/WCM/ZU/
BruselEU/main.nsf?Open
Permanent Representative: Ivan Korčok

Slovenia

Rue du Commerce 44, 1000 Brussels
Tel: +32 2 213 63 00 Fax: +32 2 213 63 01
Email: spbr@gov.si
www.brussels.representation.si/
index.php?id=14&L=1

Permanent Representative: Rado Genorio

Spain

Boulevard du Régent 52, 1000 Brussels
Tel: +32 2 509 86 11 Fax: +32 2 511 19 40/+32 2
511 26 30
Email: reper.bruselasue@reper.maec.es
www.es-ue.org/default.asp?lg=1

Permanent Representative:
Alfonso Dastis Quecedo

Sweden

Square de Meeûs 30, 1000 Brussels
Tel: +32 2 289 56 11 Fax: +32 2 289 56 00
Email: representationen.bryssel@gov.se
www.sweden.gov.se/sb/d/2250
Twitter: @swe_eupress

Ambassador and Permanent Representative:
Dag Hartelius

United Kingdom

Avenue d'Auderghem 10, 1040 Brussels
Tel: +32 2 287 82 11 Fax: +32 2 287 83 98
Email: ukrep@fco.gov.uk
www.gov.uk/world/uk-eu Twitter: @ukineu

Permanent Representative: Ivan Rogers

General Secretariat

Rue de la Loi 175, 1048 Brussels, Belgium
Tel: +32 2 281 61 11 Fax: +32 2 281 69 34
Email: press.office@consilium.europa.eu Website:www.consilium.europa.eu

Secretary-General: Uwe Corsepius +32 2 281 62 15 Email: uwe.corsepius@consilium.europa.eu
High Representative for Foreign Affairs and Security Policy: Catherine Ashton
Email: catherine.ashton@eeas.europa.eu

Dods Contacts

Do you need to contact Members of Parliament, the House of Lords or local councillors?

Dods' definitive data provides you with direct access to those who shape policy and legislation in the UK. Constantly updated to ensure the most current information is available, renting Dods data gives you full contact details of all 650 MPs, 800 Peers and over 20,000 councillors.

Lists available include:

Person Type	Quantity	Cost per record
Members of Parliament	650	75p
House of Lords	806*	75p
Members of the European Parliament	736	75p
Councillors	20,000*	75p

*Subject to change

Minimum order £350 for single use; all orders are subject to VAT.

To discuss your requirements, please contact Lucy Williams on 020 7593 5644 email lucy.williams@dods.co.uk or visit www.dodsshop.co.uk

GOVERNMENT AND PUBLIC OFFICES

Permanent Secretaries

Departments of State

Business, Innovation and Skills
Permanent Secretary
Martin Donnelly CMG

Cabinet Office
Head of the Civil Service
Sir Bob Kerslake
Cabinet Secretary
Sir Jeremy Heywood KCB CVO
Permanent Secretary
Richard Heaton CB

Communities and Local Government
Permanent Secretary
Sir Bob Kerslake

Culture, Media and Sport
Permanent Secretary
Sue Owen

Defence
Permanent Secretary
Jon Thompson

Education
Permanent Secretary
Chris Wormald

Energy and Climate Change
Permanent Secretary
Stephen Lovegrove CB

Environment, Food and Rural Affairs
Permanent Secretary
Bronwyn Hill CBE

Foreign and Commonwealth Office
Permanent Under-Secretary
Simon Fraser CMG

Health
Permanent Secretary
Una O'Brien CB

Home Office
Permanent Secretary
Mark Sedwill CMG

International Development
Permanent Secretary
Mark Lowcock CB

Justice
Permanent Secretary
Dame Ursula Brennan DCB

Transport
Permanent Secretary
Philip Rutnam

Treasury
Permanent Secretary
Sir Nicholas Macpherson KCB
Second Permanent Secretaries
Tom Scholar
John Kingman

Work and Pensions
Permanent Secretary
Robert Devereux

Devolved Parliament and Assemblies

Northern Ireland Executive
Head of Northern Ireland Civil Service and Secretary to the Executive
Dr Malcolm McKibbin

Scottish Government
Permanent Secretary
Sir Peter Housden KCB

Welsh Government
Permanent Secretary
Derek Jones CB

Departments of State

Prime Minister's Office

10 Downing Street, London SW1A 2AA
Tel: 020 7930 4433
Email: [initialsurname]@no10.x.gsi.gov.uk Website: www.gov.uk/number10 Twitter: @number10gov
Prime Minister, First Lord of the Treasury and Minister for the Civil Service:
Rt Hon **David Cameron** MP

For staff see p14

Department for Business, Innovation and Skills

1 Victoria Street, London SW1H 0ET
Tel: 020 7215 5000 Fax: 020 7215 0105
Email: enquiries@bis.gov.uk Website: www.gov.uk/bis Twitter: @bisgovuk

Ministers

Secretary of State: Rt Hon Dr Vincent Cable MP
Minister of State for Universities and Science: Rt Hon David Willetts MP
Minister of State for Business and Enterprise: Rt Hon Michael Fallon MP
Minister of State for Trade and Investment: Lord Green of Hurstpierpoint
Parliamentary Under-Secretary of State: Viscount Younger of Leckie
Parliamentary Under-Secretary of State (Minister for Employment Relations and Consumer Affairs): Jo Swinson MP
Parliamentary Under-Secretary of State: Matthew Hancock MP
Head of Parliamentary Unit: Ian Webster 020 7215 6630
House of Lords Spokespeople: Baroness Garden of Frognal, Lord Green of Hurstpierpoint, Lord Popat, Viscount Younger of Leckie

Civil Servants

Permanent Secretary: Martin Donnelly CMG 020 7215 5536 Email: perm.sec@bis.gsi.gov.uk
Government Chief Scientific Adviser and Head of Government Office for Science:
Sir Mark Walport FMedSci 020 7215 1995 Email: mpst.walport@bis.gsi.gov.uk
Chief Scientific Adviser: Prof John Perkins CBE 020 7215 6305 Email: mpst.perkins@bis.gsi.gov.uk
john.perkins@bis.gsi.gov.uk
Director-General, Business and Skills Group: Rachel Sandby-Thomas CB 020 7215 3039
Email: rachel.sandby-thomas@bis.gsi.gov.uk
Director-General, Finance and Commercial: Howard Orme 020 7215 5369
Email: howard.orme@bis.gsi.gov.uk
Director-General, Knowledge and Innovation: Prof Sir John O'Reilly 020 7215 1219
Email: john.oreilly@bis.gsi.gov.uk
Director-General, Markets and Local Growth Group: Bernadette Kelly CB 020 7215 6858
Email: bernadette.kelly@bis.gsi.gov.uk
Acting Director-General, Strategy, Analysis and Better Regulation: Amanda Rowlatt CBE
020 7215 6042 Email: amanda.rowlatt@bis.gsi.gov.uk
Director-General, People, Communications and Effectiveness Group: Dr Philippa Lloyd
020 7215 5517 Email: philippa.lloyd@bis.gsi.gov.uk
Director-General, Legal Services: Rachel Sandby-Thomas CB 020 7215 3039
Email: rachel.sandby-thomas@bis.gsi.gov.uk
Chairman of Shareholder Executive: Patrick O'Sullivan 020 7215 6435
Email: patrick.o'sullivan@bis.gsi.gov.uk
Chief Executive, Shareholder Executive: Mark Russell 020 7215 5699
Email: mark.russell@bis.gsi.gov.uk

Chief Executive, UK Trade & Investment: Nick Baird CMG CVO   020 7215 4300
Email: nick.baird@ukti.gsi.gov.uk
Director, Office of Manpower Economics: Geoff Dart   020 7271 0482
Email: geoff.dart@bis.gsi.gov.uk
Executive Agencies: Companies House; Insolvency Service; HM Land Registry; Met Office; National Measurement Office; Ordnance Survey; Skills Funding Agency; UK Intellectual Property Office; UK Space Agency

Export Credits Guarantee Department (UK Export Finance)
1 Horse Guard Road, London SW1A 2HQ
Tel: 020 7271 8000 Fax: 020 7271 8001
Email: enquiries@ecgd.gsi.gov.uk Website: www.gov.uk/uk-export-finance

Non-Executive Chair: Guy Beringer QC
Acting Chief Executive: David Havelock   020 7271 8100 Email: david.havelock@ecgd.gsi.gov.uk
Director, Finance Group: Nigel Addison Smith   020 7271 8124
Email: nigel.addison.smith@ecgd.gsi.gov.uk
Director, Business Group: Steve Dodgson   020 7271 8074 Email: steve.dodgson@ecgd.gsi.gov.uk
Director, Credit Risk Group: David Havelock   020 7512 7051
Email: david.havelock@ecgd.gsi.gov.uk
Head, Human Resources: Sue Johnson   Email: sue.johnson@ecgd.gsi.gov.uk
Non-Executive Directors: David Godfrey, Jon Harding, David Harrison CBE, Sir Eric Peacock

Cabinet Office
70 Whitehall, London SW1A 2AS
Tel: 020 7276 1234
Email: publiccorrespondence@cabinet-office.gsi.gov.uk Website: www.gov.uk/cabinet-office
Twitter: @cabinetofficeuk

Ministers
Deputy Prime Minister: Rt Hon Nick Clegg MP
Minister for the Cabinet Office; Paymaster General: Rt Hon Francis Maude MP
Minister for Government Policy: Rt Hon Oliver Letwin MP
Minister of State: Rt Hon David Laws MP
Parliamentary Secretary (Minister for Civil Society): Nick Hurd MP
Parliamentary Secretary (Minister for Political and Constitutional Reform): Chloe Smith MP
Parliamentary Secretary (based at No 10): Jo Johnson MP
Minister without portfolio: Rt Hon Kenneth Clarke QC MP
Minister without portfolio: Rt Hon Grant Shapps MP
Minister without portfolio: Rt Hon John Hayes MP
Parliamentary Clerk: Stuart Doubleday 020 7276 0415
House of Lords Spokespeople: Lord Gardiner of Kimble, Lord Wallace of Saltaire

Civil Servants
Head of the Civil Service: Sir Bob Kerslake 020 7276 0101 Email: hocs@cabinet-office.gsi.gov.uk
Cabinet Secretary: Sir Jeremy Heywood CVO 020 7276 0101
Email: cabinet.secretary@cabinet-office.gsi.gov.uk
Permanent Secretary: Richard Heaton CB 020 7276 6571
Email: permanent.secretary@cabinet-office.gsi.gov.uk
Chief Operating Officer for Government: Stephen Kelly   020 7271 0805
Email: coo@cabinet-office.gsi.gov.uk
Director-General, Economic and Domestic Affairs Secretariat: Melanie Dawes CB   020 7276 0083
Email: melanie.dawes@cabinet-office.gsi.gov.uk
Director-General, Deputy Prime Minister's Office: Philip Rycroft   020 7276 3988
Email: philip.rycroft@cabinet-office.gsi.gov.uk
Director-General, Civil Service Reform: Katherine Kerswell   020 7271 2954
Email: katherine.kerswell@cabinet-office.gsi.gov.uk

Prime Minister's Adviser on Europe and Global Issues: Ivan Rogers   020 7276 1130
Email: irogers@no10.x.gsi.gov.uk
Prime Minister's National Security Adviser: Sir Kim Darroch KCMG   020 7276 2012
Email: nsaaction@cabinet-office.x.gsi.gov.uk
Chairman, Joint Intelligence Committee and Professional Head of Intelligence Analysis: Jon Day CBE
020 7276 6042   Email: jicchairman@cabinet-office.x.gsi.gov.uk

Department for Communities and Local Government

Eland House, Bressenden Place, London SW1E 5DU
Tel: 0303 444 0000
Email: contactus@communities.gsi.gov.uk   Website: www.gov.uk/dclg   Twitter: @communitiesuk

Ministers
Secretary of State: Rt Hon Eric Pickles MP
Senior Minister of State (Faith and Communities): Rt Hon Baroness Warsi
Minister of State for Housing: Mark Prisk MP
Parliamentary Under-Secretary of State (Planning): Nick Boles MP
Parliamentary Under-Secretary of State: Rt Hon Don Foster MP
Parliamentary Under-Secretary of State: Brandon Lewis MP
Parliamentary Under-Secretary of State: Baroness Hanham CBE

Parliamentary Clerk: Chris Woolf 030 3444 3407
House of Lords Spokespeople: Lord Ahmad of Wimbledon, Baroness Hanham, Baroness Warsi

Civil Servants
Permanent Secretary: Sir Bob Kerslake 0303 444 2785
Email: pspermanentsecretary@communities.gsi.gov.uk
Director-General, Localism: Helen Edwards CB CBE   0303 444 2143
Email: helen.edwards@communities.gsi.gov.uk
Director-General, Finance and Corporate Services: Susan Higgins   0303 444 4439
Email: sue.higgins@communities.gsi.gov.uk
Director-General, Neighbourhoods: Peter Schofield   0303 444 2746
Email: peter.schofield@communities.gsi.gov.uk
Director-General, Troubled Families Team: Louise Casey CB   0303 444 1131
Email: louise.casey@communities.gsi.gov.uk families.team@communities.gsi.gov.uk
Acting Chief Scientific Adviser: Stephen Aldridge CB   0303 444 3339
Email: stephen.aldridge@communities.gsi.gov.uk
Director, Strategy and Programme Team: Andrew Campbell CB   0303 444 2536
Email: andrew.campbell@communities.gsi.gov.uk
Executive Agencies: Planning Inspectorate; Queen Elizabeth II Conference Centre

Department for Culture, Media and Sport

100 Parliament Street, London SW1A 2BQ
Tel: 020 7211 6000 Fax: 020 7211 6032
Email: enquiries@culture.gov.uk Website: www.gov.uk/dcms Twitter: @DCMS

Ministers
Secretary of State: Rt Hon Maria Miller MP
Minister of State for Sport and Tourism: Rt Hon Hugh Robertson MP
Parliamentary Under-Secretary of State (Minister for Culture, Communications and Creative Industries): Hon Ed Vaizey MP
Parliamentary Under-Secretary of State (Women and Equalities): Helen Grant MP
Parliamentary Under-Secretary of State (Women and Equalities): Jo Swinson MP
Parliamentary Clerk: David Goss 020 7211 6068
House of Lords Spokespeople: Lord Gardiner of Kimble, Baroness Northover

Civil Servants

Permanent Secretary: Sue Owen CB Email: sue.owen@culture.gsi.gov.uk
Director: David Brooker 020 7211 6503 Email: david.brooker@culture.gsi.gov.uk
Director: Rachel Clark 020 7211 6075 Email: rachel.clark@culture.gsi.gov.uk
Director: Helen MacNamara 020 7211 6411 Email: helen.macnamara@culture.gsi.gov.uk
Director: Clare Pillman 020 7211 6411 Email: clare.pillman@culture.gsi.gov.uk
Director: Jon Zeff 020 7211 6450 Email: jon.zeff@culture.gsi.gov.uk
Director, Finance: Sam Foley 020 7211 6077 Email: sam.foley@culture.gsi.gov.uk
Director (on maternity leave): Rita French 020 7211 6411 Email: rita.french@culture.gsi.gov.uk
Executive Agency: Royal Parks

Ministry of Defence

Main Building, Whitehall, London SW1A 2HB
Tel: 020 7218 9000 Fax: 020 7218 6538
Website: www.gov.uk/mod Twitter: @DefenceHQ

Ministers

Secretary of State: Rt Hon Philip Hammond MP
Minister of State for the Armed Forces: Rt Hon Andrew Robathan MP
Minister of State for Defence Personnel, Welfare and Veterans: Rt Hon Mark Francois MP
Parliamentary Under-Secretary of State (International Security Strategy): Dr Andrew Murrison MP
Parliamentary Under-Secretary of State (Defence Equipment, Support and Technology):
Philip Dunne MP
Parliamentary Under-Secretary of State: Lord Astor of Hever DL
Parliamentary Clerk: Teresa Andrews 020 7218 1991
House of Lords Spokespeople: Lord Astor of Hever, Baroness Garden of Frognal

Civil Servants

Permanent Secretary: Jon Thompson 020 7218 2193 Email: pus-privateoffice@mod.uk
jon.thompson791@mod.uk
Chief of the Defence Staff: Gen Sir Nicholas Houghton GCB CBE ADC Gen 020 7218 6190
Email: cds-privateoffice@mod.uk
Vice Chief of Defence Staff: Air Chief-Marshal Stuart Peach KCB CBE 020 7218 7899
Email: vcds-pa@mod.uk
Director-General, Finance: David Williams 020 7218 6361 Email: dgfinance-dgfinance@mod.uk
Director-General, Transformation and Corporate Strategy: Jonathan Slater 020 7218 4077
Email: transformation-dgcts@mod.uk
Director-General, Security Policy: Tom McKane 020 7218 3832
Email: dgsecpol-privateoffice@mod.uk
Director, Media and Communication: Stephen Jolly 020 7218 0546
Email: dmc-executiveassistant@mod.uk
Director, Central Legal Services: Frances Nash 020 7218 0723 Email: cls-d@mod.uk
Chief of Defence Materiel: Bernard Gray 020 7218 7995 Email: descdm-ps@mod.uk

Executive Agencies: Defence Science and Technology Laboratory; Defence Support Group;
Intelligence Collection Group; Ministry of Defence Police and Guarding Agency; Service Children's
Education; Service Personnel and Veterans Agency; UK Hydrographic Office

Department for Education

Sanctuary Buildings, Great Smith Street, London, London SW1P 3BT
Tel: 0370 000 2288 Fax: 01928 738248
Email: inforequests@education.gsi.gov.uk Website: www.gov.uk/dfe Twitter: @educationgovuk

Ministers

Secretary of State: Rt Hon Michael Gove MP
Minister of State: Rt Hon David Laws MP

Parliamentary Under-Secretary of State for Schools: Lord Nash
Parliamentary Under-Secretary of State: Matthew Hancock MP
Parliamentary Under-Secretary of State: Edward Timpson MP
Parliamentary Under-Secretary of State: Elizabeth Truss MP
Parliamentary Clerk: To be appointed
House of Lords Spokespeople: Baroness Garden of Frognal, Lord Nash

Civil Servants

Permanent Secretary: Chris Wormald 020 7925 6937 Email: permanent.secretary@education.gsi.gov.uk
Director-General, Education Standards: Shona Dunn 020 7340 7732
Email: shona.dunn@education.gsi.gov.uk
Acting Director-General, Infrastructure and Funding: Andrew McCully 020 7340 8075
Email: andrew.mccully@education.gsi.gov.uk
Legal Adviser: Claire Johnston 020 7783 8199 Email: claire.johnston@education.gsi.gov.uk
Director, Corporate Finance and Commercial: Simon Judge 020 7340 7502
Email: simon.judge@education.gsi.gov.uk
Director, Strategy and Performance: Hilary Spencer 020 7783 8574
Email: hilary.spencer@education.gsi.gov.uk

Department of Energy and Climate Change

3 Whitehall Place, London SW1A 2AW
Tel: 0300 060 4000
Email: correspondence@decc.gsi.gov.uk Website: www.gov.uk/decc Twitter: @deccgovuk

Ministers

Secretary of State: Rt Hon Edward Davey MP
Minister of State for Climate Change: Rt Hon Gregory Barker MP
Minister of State for Energy: Rt Hon Michael Fallon MP
Parliamentary Under-Secretary of State: Baroness Verma

Parliamentary Clerk: Derek Turner 0300 068 5991

House of Lords Spokespeople: Lord Gardiner of Kimble, Baroness Verma

Civil Servants

Permanent Secretary: Stephen Lovegrove CB 0300 068 5963 Email: perm.sec@decc.gsi.gov.uk
Acting Chief Operating Officer: Vanessa Nicholls 0300 068 2825
Email: vanessa.nicholls@decc.gsi.gov.uk
Director-General, Energy Markets and Infrastructure: Simon Virley 0300 068 5668
Email: simon.virley@decc.gsi.gov.uk
Director-General, International Climate Change and Energy Efficiency: Stephen Speed
0300 068 5199 Email: stephen.speed@decc.gsi.gov.uk
Chief Scientific Adviser: Prof David Mackay 0300 068 6505 Email: csa@decc.gsi.gov.uk
Director, Corporate Strategy and Change: Jo Shanmugalingam 0300 068 2870
Email: jo.shanmugalingam@decc.gsi.gov.uk
Director, Finance and Information Services: Vanessa Howlison 0300 068 6579
Email: vanessa.howlison@decc.gsi.gov.uk
Director, Nuclear Decommissioning and Security: Stefanie Murphy 0300 068 5909
Email: stefanie.murphy@decc.gsi.gov.uk
Director, Performance and Planning: Scott McPherson Email: scott.mcpherson@decc.gsi.gov.uk

Department for Environment, Food and Rural Affairs

Nobel House, 17 Smith Square, London SW1P 3JR
Tel: 020 7238 6000 Fax: 0845 933 5577
Email: defra.helpline@defra.gsi.gov.uk Website: www.gov.uk/defra Twitter: @Defragovuk

Ministers

Secretary of State: Rt Hon Owen Paterson MP
Minister of State for Agriculture and Food: David Heath CBE MP

Parliamentary Under-Secretary of State (Natural Environment, Water and Rural Affairs):
Richard Benyon MP
*Parliamentary Under-Secretary of State (Resource Management, the Local Environment and
Environmental Science):* Lord de Mauley TD
Parliamentary Clerk: Deirdre Kennedy 020 7238 5455
House of Lords Spokespeople: Lord de Mauley, Baroness Northover

Civil Servants

Permanent Secretary: Bronwyn Hill CBE 020 7238 5446 Email: ps.bronwyn.hill@defra.gsi.gov.uk
Chief Scientific Adviser: Prof Ian Boyd 020 7238 1645 Email: ian.boyd@defra.gsi.gov.uk
Director-General, Strategy, Evidence and Customers: Katrina Williams 020 7238 5578
Email: katrina.williams@defra.gsi.gov.uk
Director-General, Policy Delivery Group: Peter Unwin CB 020 7238 5601
Email: peter.unwin@defra.gsi.gov.uk
Chief Operating Officer: Ian Trenholm 020 7238 4831 Email: ian.trenholm@defra.gsi.gov.uk
Chief Veterinary Officer: Nigel Gibbens 020 7238 6495 Email: nigel.gibbens@defra.gsi.gov.uk
Director, Communications: Kim Worts 020 7238 5528 Email: kim.worts@defra.gsi.gov.uk
Director, Human Resources: To be appointed
Director, Finance and Performance: Tom Taylor 020 7238 1502 Email: tom.taylor@defra.gsi.gov.uk
Acting Chief Information Officer: Julie Pierce 01905 768736 Email: julie.pierce@defra.gsi.gov.uk

Executive Agencies: Animal Health and Veterinary Laboratories Agency; Centre for Environment,
Fisheries and Aquaculture Science; Food and Environment Research Agency; Rural Payments Agency;
Veterinary Medicines Directorate

Foreign and Commonwealth Office

King Charles Street, Whitehall, London SW1A 2AH
Tel: 020 7008 1500
Email: fcocorrespondence@fco.gov.uk Website: www.gov.uk/fco Twitter: @foreignoffice

Ministers

First Secretary of State: Rt Hon William Hague MP
Senior Minister of State: Rt Hon Baroness Warsi
Minister of State: Rt Hon David Lidington MP
Minister of State: Rt Hon Hugo Swire MP
Minister of State for Trade and Investment : Lord Green of Hurstpierpoint
Parliamentary Under-Secretary of State: Mark Simmonds MP
Parliamentary Under-Secretary of State: Alistair Burt MP
Parliamentary Clerk: Susan Geary 020 7008 2094
House of Lords Spokespeople: Lord Green of Hurstpierpoint, Lord Wallace of Saltaire, Baroness Warsi

Civil Servants

Permanent Under-Secretary and Head of HM Diplomatic Service: Simon Fraser CMG 020 7008 2150
Email: pus.action@fco.gov.uk
Director-General, Chief Operating Officer: Matthew Rycroft CBE 020 7008 0410
Email: matthew.rycroft@fco.gov.uk
Director-General, Defence and Intelligence: Robert Hannigan CMG 020 7008 2176
Email: robert.hannigan@fco.gov.uk
Director-General, Economic and Consular: Barbara Woodward CMG OBE 020 7008 2206
Email: barbara.woodward@fco.gov.uk
Director-General, Political: Simon Gass CMG CVO Email: simon.gass@fco.gov.uk
Director-General, Finance: Iain Walker 020 7008 1062 Email: iain.walker@fco.gov.uk
Legal Adviser: Iain Macleod 020 7008 3052 Email: iain.macleod@fco.gov.uk
Chief Information Officer: Colin Martin-Reynolds 020 7008 4655
Email: colin.martin-reynolds@fco.gov.uk

Chief Scientific Adviser: Prof Robin Grimes 020 7008 4073 Email: robin.grimes@fco.gov.uk
Director, Human Resources: Menna Rawlings Email: menna.rawlings@fco.gov.uk
Director, Strategy: Peter Hill Email: peter.hill@fco.gov.uk
Executive Agencies: FCO Services; Wilton Park

Department of Health
Richmond House, 79 Whitehall, London SW1A 2NS
Tel: 020 7210 4850 Fax: 020 7210 5952
Email: [firstname.surname]@dh.gsi.gov.uk Website: www.gov.uk/dh Twitter: @DHgovuk

Ministers
Secretary of State: Rt Hon Jeremy Hunt MP
Minister of State for Care and Support: Norman Lamb MP
Parliamentary Under-Secretary of State (Public Health): Anna Soubry MP
Parliamentary Under-Secretary of State: Dr Daniel Poulter MP
Parliamentary Under-Secretary of State (Quality): Rt Hon Earl Howe
Parliamentary Clerk: Tim Elms 020 7210 5808
House of Lords Spokespeople: Earl Howe, Baroness Northover

Civil Servants
Permanent Secretary: Una O'Brien CB 020 7210 5762 Email: una.o'brien@dh.gsi.gov.uk
Chief Medical Officer: Prof Dame Sally C Davies DBE
Director-General, Policy, Strategy and Finance: Richard Douglas CB 020 7210 5429
Email: richard.douglas@dh.gsi.gov.uk
Director-General, Social Care, Local Government and Care Partnerships: Jon Rouse 020 7210 5348
Email: jon.rouse@dh.gsi.gov.uk
Director-General, Group Operations and Assurance: Karen Wheeler CBE 020 7210 2755
Email: karen.wheeler@dh.gsi.gov.uk
Director-General, External Relations: Charlie Massey 020 7210 5368
Email: charlie.massey@dh.gsi.gov.uk
Director, Communications: Sam Lister 020 7210 5212 Email: sam.lister@dh.gsi.gov.uk
Director, Human Resources: Shirley Pointer 020 7972 1570 Email: shirley.pointer@dh.gsi.gov.uk
Head, Procurement, Investment and Commercial Division: Peter Coates CBE 020 7972 5579
Email: peter.coates@dh.gsi.gov.uk
Executive Agencies: Medicines and Healthcare products Regulatory Agency; Public Health England

Home Office
2 Marsham Street, London SW1P 4DF
Tel: 020 7035 4848 Fax: 020 7035 4745
Email: public.enquiries@homeoffice.gsi.gov.uk Website: www.gov.uk/home-office
Twitter: @UKHomeOffice

Ministers
Secretary of State: Rt Hon Theresa May MP
Minister of State for Immigration: Mark Harper MP
Minister of State for Policing and Criminal Justice: Rt Hon Damian Green MP
Minister of State for Crime Prevention: Jeremy Browne MP
Parliamentary Under-Secretary of State (Crime and Security): James Brokenshire MP
Parliamentary Under-Secretary of State (Criminal Information): Lord Taylor of Holbeach CBE
Parliamentary Clerk: Joanne Dawes 020 7035 8838
House of Lords Spokespeople: Earl Attlee, Baroness Stowell of Beeston

Civil Servants

Permanent Secretary: Mark Sedwill CMG 020 7035 0197
Email: permanentsecretary.submissions@homeoffice.gsi.gov.uk
Chief Scientific Adviser: Prof Bernard Silverman 020 7035 3344
Email: bernard.silverman@homeoffice.gsi.gov.uk
Director-General, Human Resources: Kevin White CB 020 7035 6186
Email: kevin.white@homeoffice.gsi.gov.uk
Director-General, Crime and Policing Group: Stephen Rimmer 020 7035 1439
Email: stephen.rimmer@homeoffice.gsi.gov.uk
Director-General, Financial and Commercial: Helen Kilpatrick CB 020 7035 0989
Email: helen.kilpatrick@homeoffice.gsi.gov.uk
Director-General, Strategy, Immigration and International Group: Mike Anderson 020 7035 1096
Email: mike.anderson@homeoffice.gsi.gov.uk
Director-General, Office for Security and Counter-Terrorism: Charles Farr CMG OBE 020 7035 8882
Email: dg.osct@homeoffice.x.gsi.gov.uk charles.farr@homeoffice.x.gsi.gov.uk
Director-General, Border Force: Sir Charles Montgomery
Email: dgborderforce.submissions@homeoffice.gsi.gov.uk
Director, Communication: Simon Wren CBE 020 7035 4101
Email: simon.wren@homeoffice.gsi.gov.uk
Senior Legal Adviser: Jonathan Jones 020 7035 1393
Email: jonathan.jones10@homeoffice.gsi.gov.uk
Chief Information Officer: Justin Holliday 020 7035 8256
Email: justin.holliday4@homeoffice.gsi.gov.uk

Executive Agencies: National Crime Agency; National Fraud Authority; HM Passport Office

Department for International Development
22 Whitehall, London SW1A 2EG
Tel: 020 7023 0000
Email: enquiry@dfid.gov.uk Website: www.gov.uk/dfid Twitter: @DFID_UK

Abercrombie House, Eaglesham Road, East Kilbride, Glasgow G75 8EA
Tel: 01355 844000 Fax: 01355 844099

Ministers

Secretary of State: Rt Hon Justine Greening MP
Minister of State: Rt Hon Alan Duncan MP
Parliamentary Under-Secretary of State: Lynne Featherstone MP

Parliamentary Clerk: Rob Foot 020 7023 0559

House of Lords Spokespeople: Lord Ahmad of Wimbledon, Baroness Northover

Civil Servants

Permanent Secretary: Mark Lowcock CB 020 7023 0500 Email: pspermsec@dfid.gov.uk
Director-General, Finance and Corporate Performance: Richard Calvert 020 7023 0417
Email: r-calvert@dfid.gov.uk
Acting Director-General, Policy and Global Programmes: Nick Dyer 020 7023 0970
Email: n-dyer@dfid.gov.uk
Director-General, Country Programmes: Joy Hutcheon 020 7023 0407
Email: j-hutcheon@dfid.gov.uk
Director-General, Humanitarian, Security, Conflict and International Finance: Mark Bowman
020 7023 1300 Email: m-bowman@dfid.gov.uk

Ministry of Justice

102 Petty France, London SW1H 9AJ
Tel: 020 3334 3555 Fax: 020 3334 4455
Email: general.queries@justice.gsi.gov.uk Website: www.gov.uk/moj Twitter: @MoJGovUK

Ministers

Lord Chancellor and Secretary of State for Justice: Rt Hon Chris Grayling MP
Minister of State and Deputy Leader of the House of Lords: Rt Hon Lord McNally
Minister of State for Policing and Criminal Justice: Rt Hon Damian Green MP
Parliamentary Under-Secretary of State (Minister for Victims and the Courts): Helen Grant MP
Parliamentary Under-Secretary of State (Minister for Prisons and Rehabilitation):
Jeremy Wright MP
Parliamentary Clerk: Ann Nixon 020 3334 3635
House of Lords Spokespeople: Lord Ahmad of Wimbledon, Lord McNally

Civil Servants

Permanent Secretary: Dame Ursula Brennan DCB 020 3334 3708 Email: psecretary1@justice.gsi.gov.uk
Group Director, HR: Debbie Alder 0203 334 4607 Email: debbie.alder@justice.gsi.gov.uk
Director-General, Justice Policy: Catherine Lee CBE 020 3334 6806
Email: catherine.lee@justice.gsi.gov.uk
Director-General, Transforming Justice: Antonia Romeo 020 3334 6599
Email: antonia.romeo@justice.gsi.gov.uk
Director-General, Finance and Corporate Services: Ann Beasley CBE 020 3334 6505
Email: ann.beasley@justice.gsi.gov.uk
Director, Human Resources, National Offender Management Service: Carol Carpenter 0300 047 5160
Email: carol.carpenter@noms.gsi.gov.uk
Chief Executive, National Offender Management Service: Michael Spurr 0300 047 5164
Email: ceonoms@noms.gsi.gov.uk
Chief Executive, HM Courts and Tribunals Service: Peter Handcock CBE 020 3334 3012
Email: hmcts.chiefexecutive@hmcts.gsi.gov.uk
Executive Agencies: HM Courts & Tribunals Service; Legal Aid Agency; National Archives; National Offender Management Service; Office of the Public Guardian

Law Officers

Attorney General's Office, 20 Victoria Street, London SW1H 0NF
Tel: 020 7271 2492 Fax: 020 7271 2453
Email: [firstname.surname]@attorneygeneral.gsi.gov.uk Website: www.gov.uk/ago
Office of the Advocate General for Scotland, Dover House, 66 Whitehall, London SW1A 2AU
Tel: 020 7270 6720 Fax: 020 7270 6813
Email: privateoffice@advocategeneral.gsi.gov.uk [firstname.surname]@advocategeneral.gsi.gov.uk
Website: www.gov.uk/oag

Ministers

Attorney General: Rt Hon Dominic Grieve QC MP
Solicitor General: Oliver Heald MP
Advocate General for Scotland: Rt Hon Lord Wallace of Tankerness QC
Parliamentary Clerk: Michael Dawes 020 7271 2490

Civil Servants

Legal Secretary to the Law Officers: Rowena Collins-Rice 020 7271 2401
Email: rowena.collins-rice@attorneygeneral.gsi.gov.uk
Solicitor to the Advocate General for Scotland: Michael Chalmers 0131-244 0359
Email: michael.chalmers@advocategeneral.gsi.gov.uk
Executive Agency: Treasury Solicitor's Department

Northern Ireland Office

Stormont House, Stormont Estate, Belfast BT4 3ST
Tel: 028 9052 0700/028 9052 7668 (Textphone)

1 Horseguards Road, Whitehall, London SW1A 2HQ
Tel: 020 9052 0700
Email: nioweb.editor@nio.x.gsi.gov.uk goggs.reception@hmtreasury.gsi.gov.uk
Website: www.gov.uk/nio

Ministers
Secretary of State: Rt Hon Theresa Villiers MP
Minister of State: Mike Penning MP
Parliamentary Clerk: Ben Sneddon 020 7210 6551
House of Lords Spokespeople: Earl Attlee, Baroness Randerson

Civil Servants
Director-General: Julian King CMG CVO 020 7210 0850/028 9052 7769 (Belfast)
Email: julian.king@nio.x.gsi.gov.uk

Privy Council Office

2 Carlton Gardens, London SW1Y 5AA
Tel: 020 7747 5310 Fax: 020 7747 5311
Email: pcosecretariat@pco.x.gsi.gov.uk Website: privycouncil.independent.gov.uk

Ministers
Lord President of the Council: Rt Hon Nick Clegg MP

Civil Servants
Clerk of the Council: Richard Tilbrook 020 7276 5310
Head of Secretariat and Senior Clerk: Ceri King 020 7747 5300 Email: ceri.king@pco.x.gsi.gov.uk
Senior Clerk: Christopher Berry 020 7747 5301 Email: christopher.berry@pco.x.gsi.gov.uk

Scotland Office

Dover House, Whitehall, London SW1A 2AU
Tel: 020 7270 6754 Fax: 020 7270 6812
Email: [firstname.surname]@scotlandoffice.gsi.gov.uk Website: www.gov.uk/scotland-office
Twitter: @scotlandoffice

1 Melville Crescent, Edinburgh EH3 7HW
Tel: 0131-244 9010

Ministers
Secretary of State: Rt Hon Michael Moore MP
Parliamentary Under-Secretary of State: Rt Hon David Mundell MP
Parliamentary Clerk: Ben Sneddon 020 7270 6746
House of Lords Spokespeople: Earl Attlee, Lord Wallace of Tankerness

Civil Servants
Director: Alun Evans 020 7270 6883/0131-244 9022 Email: alun.evans@scotlandoffice.gsi.gov.uk

Department for Transport

Great Minster House, 33 Horseferry Road, London SW1P 4DR
Tel: 0300 330 3000
Email: [firstname.surname]@dft.gsi.gov.uk Website: www.gov.uk/dft Twitter: @transportgovuk

Ministers
Secretary of State: Rt Hon Patrick McLoughlin MP

Minister of State: Rt Hon Simon Burns MP
Parliamentary Under-Secretary of State: Norman Baker MP
Parliamentary Under-Secretary of State: Stephen Hammond MP
Parliamentary Clerk: James Langston 020 7944 4472
House of Lords Spokespeople: Earl Attlee, Lord Popat

Civil Servants

Permanent Secretary: Philip Rutnam 020 7944 5010 Email: philip.rutnam@dft.gsi.gov.uk
Director-General, International, Strategy and Environment Group: Lucy Chadwick 020 7944 6948
Email: lucy.chadwick@dft.gsi.gov.uk
Director-General, Domestic Group: Steve Gooding 020 7944 5459
Email: steve.gooding@dft.gsi.gov.uk
Director-General, Corporate Group: Jonathan Moor CBE 020 7944 6409
Email: jonathan.moor@dft.gsi.gov.uk
Director-General, High Speed 2: David Prout 020 7944 2112 Email: david.prout@dft.gsi.gov.uk
Director-General, Rail: Clare Moriarty 020 7944 2931 Email: clare.moriarty@dft.gsi.gov.uk
Executive Agencies: Driver and Vehicle Licensing Agency; Driving Standards Agency; Highways
Agency; Maritime and Coastguard Agency; Vehicle and Operator Services Agency; Vehicle
Certification Agency

HM Treasury

1 Horse Guards Road, London SW1A 2HQ
Tel: 020 7270 5000 Fax: 020 7270 5148
Email: public.enquiries@hmtreasury.gsi.gov.uk Website: www.gov.uk/treasury
Twitter: @HMTreasury

Ministers

Chancellor of the Exchequer: Rt Hon George Osborne MP
Chief Secretary to the Treasury: Rt Hon Danny Alexander MP
Financial Secretary: Rt Hon Greg Clark MP
Exchequer Secretary: David Gauke MP
Economic Secretary: Sajid Javid MP
Commercial Secretary: Lord Deighton KBE
Parliamentary Clerk: Stephen Wiles 020 7270 4520
House of Lords Spokespeople: Lord Deighton, Lord Newby

Civil Servants

Permanent Secretary: Sir Nicholas Macpherson KCB 020 7270 4360
Email: action.permsec@hmtreasury.gsi.gov.uk
Second Permanent Secretary: John Kingman 020 7270 1599
Email: john.kingman@hmtreasury.gsi.gov.uk
Second Permanent Secretary: Tom Scholar 020 7270 5202 Email: pa.scholar@hmtreasury.gsi.gov.uk
Chief Scientific Adviser: Dr James Richardson 020 7270 4748
Email: james.richardson@hmtreasury.gsi.gov.uk
Director-General, International and European Union: Michael Ellam 020 7270 6637
Email: michael.ellam@hmtreasury.gsi.gov.uk
Director-General, Chief Economic Adviser and Head of Government Economic Service:
Dave Ramsden CBE 020 7270 4318 Email: dave.ramsden@hmtreasury.gsi.gov.uk
Director-General, Public Spending: Sharon White 020 7270 5504
Email: sharon.white@hmtreasury.gsi.gov.uk
Director, Corporate Services: Alison Cottrell 020 7270 4440
Email: alison.cottrell@hmtreasury.gsi.gov.uk
Director, Financial Services: Alison Cottrell 020 7270 4440
Email: alison.cottrell@hmtreasury.gsi.gov.uk

Director, Strategy, Planning and Budget: James Bowler CB   020 7270 5524
Email: james.bowler@hmtreasury.gsi.gov.uk
Head of Government Finance Profession: Richard Douglas CB   020 7270 4554
Email: maria.taulli@hmtreasury.gsi.gov.uk
Treasury Legal Adviser: Stephen Parker   020 7270 5666   Email: stephen.parker@hmtreasury.gsi.gov.uk
Executive Agencies: National Savings and Investments; UK Debt Management Office

Wales Office

Gwydyr House, Whitehall, London SW1A 2NP
Tel: 020 7270 0565/020 7270 1362
Email: correspondence@walesoffice.gsi.gov.uk   Website: www.gov.uk/wales-office
Twitter: @walesoffice
1 Caspian Point, Caspian Way, Cardiff CF10 4DQ
Tel: 029 2092 4220

Ministers

Secretary of State: Rt Hon David Jones MP
Parliamentary Under-Secretary of State: Stephen Crabb MP
Parliamentary Under-Secretary of State: Baroness Randerson
Parliamentary Clerk: Ben Sneddon   020 7270 0584/020 7210 6551
House of Lords Spokespeople: Earl Attlee, Baroness Randerson

Civil Servants

Head, Communications: Tricia Quiller-Croasdell 020 7270 0565
Email: tricia.quiller-croasdell@walesoffice.gsi.gov.uk
Director: Glynne Jones   020 7270 0558   Email: glynne.jones@walesoffice.gsi.gov.uk
Head, Communications: Tricia Quiller-Croasdell   020 7270 0565
Email: tricia.quiller-croasdell@walesoffice.gsi.gov.uk

Department for Work and Pensions

Caxton House, Tothill Street, London SW1H 9DA
Tel: 020 7449 7892
Email: enquiries@dwp.gsi.gov.uk   ministers@dwp.gsi.gov.uk   Website: www.gov.uk/dwp
Twitter: @dwppressoffice

Ministers

Secretary of State: Rt Hon Iain Duncan Smith MP
Minister of State for Employment: Mark Hoban MP
Minister of State for Pensions: Steve Webb MP
Parliamentary Under-Secretary of State (Minister for Welfare Reform): Lord Freud
Parliamentary Under-Secretary of State (Minister for Disabled People): Esther McVey MP
Parliamentary Clerk: James Rowe   020 3267 5053
House of Lords Spokespeople: Lord Freud, Baroness Stowell of Beeston

Civil Servants

Permanent Secretary: Robert Devereux 020 3267 5013   Email: robert.devereux@dwp.gsi.gov.uk
Director-General, Transformation: Gill Aitken   020 7449 7248   Email: gill.aitken@dwp.gsi.gov.uk
Chief Information Officer and Director-General, Corporate Information Technology: Andy Nelson
Director-General, Operations: Noel Shanahan
Director-General, Professional Services: Gill Aitken   020 7449 7248   Email: gill.aitken@dwp.gsi.gov.uk
Director-General, Group Finance and Chief Financial Officer: Mike Driver   020 7449 5780
Email: mike.driver@dwp.gsi.gov.uk
Director-General, Human Resources: Chris Last   020 7340 4193   Email: chris.last@dwp.gsi.gov.uk
Director-General, Strategy: Sue Owen CB   020 7449 5516   Email: sue.owen@dwp.gsi.gov.uk
Director, Health and Wellbeing and Chief Medical Adviser: Dr Bill Gunnyeon CBE   020 7449 5598
Email: bill.gunnyeon@dwp.gsi.gov.uk

Executive Agencies

Animal Health and Veterinary Laboratories Agency
Corporate Headquarters, AHVLA Weybridge, Woodham Lane, Addlestone, Surrey KT15 3NB
Tel: 01932 341111 Fax: 01932 347046
Email: corp.weybridge@ahvla.gsi.gov.uk Website: www.defra.gov.uk/ahvla Twitter: @AHVLA

Number of staff: 2,250
Chief Executive: Chris Hadkiss 01932 341111 Email: corp.weybridge@ahvla.gsi.gov.uk
Sponsored by: Department for Environment, Food and Rural Affairs

Centre for Environment, Fisheries and Aquaculture Science
Pakefield Road, Lowestoft, Suffolk NR33 0HT
Tel: 01502 562244 Fax: 01502 513865
Email: reception@cefas.co.uk Website: www.cefas.defra.gov.uk

Weymouth Laboratory, The Nothe, Barrack Road, Weymouth, Dorset DT4 8UB
Tel: 01305 206600 Fax: 01305 206602

Number of staff: 529
Sponsored by: Department for Environment, Food and Rural Affairs

Companies House
Crown Way, Cardiff CF14 3UZ
Tel: 0303 123 4500 Fax: 029 2038 0517
Email: enquiries@companieshouse.gov.uk Website: www.companieshouse.gov.uk
Twitter: @CompaniesHouse

Number of staff: 913
Chairman: Brian Landers 029 2038 0400 Email: blanders@companieshouse.gov.uk
Sponsored by: Department for Business, Innovation and Skills

HM Courts & Tribunals Service
102 Petty France, London, London SW1H 9AJ
Tel: 020 3334 3555
Email: hmcts.communications@hmcts.gsi.gov.uk
Website: www.gov.uk/government/organisations/hm-courts-and-tribunals-service

Number of staff: 18,000
Chief Executive: Peter Handcock CBE 020 3334 3012 Email: hmcts.chiefexecutive@hmcts.gsi.gov.uk
Sponsored by: Ministry of Justice

Defence Equipment and Support
Mail Point #2219, Abbey Wood, Bristol BS34 8JH
Tel: 0117-913 0000 Fax: 0117-913 0900
Email: DESCDM-CDMCoSouteroffice@mod.uk

Number of staff: 20,000
Chief of Defence Materiel: Bernard Gray 020 7218 7995 Email: descdm-outeroffice@mod.uk

Defence Science and Technology Laboratory
Porton Down, Salisbury, Wiltshire SP4 0JQ
Tel: 01980 613 121 Fax: 01980 658 400
Email: centralenquiries@dstl.gov.uk Website: www.dstl.gov.uk

Number of staff: 3,800
Chairman: Sir Richard Mottram GCB
Sponsored by: Ministry of Defence

Defence Support Group
Sedgemoor Building, Monxton Road, Andover SP11 8HT
Tel: 01264 383295 Fax: 01264 385458
Email: info@dsg.mod.uk Website: www.dsg.mod.uk
Number of staff: 2,500
Chair: Alex Jablonowski
Sponsored by: Ministry of Defence

Driver and Vehicle Licensing Agency
Longview Road, Morriston, Swansea SA6 7JL
Tel: 0300 790 6801 (Drivers)/0300 790 6802 (Vehicles)
Fax: 0300 123 0784 (Drivers)/0300 123 0798 (Vehicles)
Email: www.gov.uk/contact-the-dvla Website: www.gov.uk/dvla Twitter: @dvla.gov
Number of staff: 6,174
(Acting) Chief Executive and Accounting Officer: Malcolm Dawson OBE 01792 783014
Email: malcolm.dawson@dvla.gsi.gov.uk
Sponsored by: Department for Transport

Driving Standards Agency
The Axis, 112 Upper Parliament Street, Nottingham, Nottinghamshire NG1 6LP
Tel: 0115-936 6666
Email: customer.services@dsa.gsi.gov.uk Website: www.dsa.gov.uk Twitter: @DSAgovuk
Number of staff: 2,417
Chief Executive: Rosemary Thew 0115-936 6010 Email: rosemary.thew@dsa.gsi.gov.uk
Sponsored by: Department for Transport

Education Funding Agency
Number of staff: 750
Chief Executive: Peter Lauener CB 024 7666 0272 Email: peter.lauener@education.gsi.gov.uk
Sponsored by: Infrastructure and Funding Directorate, Department for Education

FCO Services
Hanslope Park, Milton Keynes MK19 7BH
Tel: 01908 515789
Email: fcoservices.customercontactcentre@fco.gov.uk Website: www.fcoservices.gov.uk
Number of staff: 1,300
Chief Executive: Christopher Moxey 020 7008 0051 Email: chris.moxey@fco.gov.uk
Sponsored by: Foreign and Commonwealth Office

Food and Environment Research Agency
Sand Hutton, York YO41 1LZ
Tel: 01904 462000 Fax: 01904 462111
Email: info@fera.gsi.gov.uk Website: www.defra.gov.uk/fera Twitter: @FeraGovUK
Number of staff: 900
Chief Executive: Adrian Belton 01904 462400 Email: adrian.belton@fera.gsi.gov.uk
Sponsored by: Department for Environment, Food and Rural Affairs

Forest Enterprise England
620 Bristol Business Park, Coldharbour Lane, Bristol BS16 1EJ
Tel: 0117-906 6000 Fax: 0117-931 2859 Email: fe.england@forestry.gsi.gov.uk
Number of staff: 981
Chief Executive: Simon Hodgson 0117-372 1049 Email: simon.hodgson@foresty.gsi.gov.uk
Sponsored by: England Executive Board, Forestry Commission of Great Britain

Forest Research
Alice Holt Lodge Research Station, Farnham, Surrey GU10 4LH
Tel: 01420 22255 Fax: 01420 23653
Email: research.info@forestry.gsi.gov.uk Website: www.forestry.gov.uk/forestresearch
Northern Research Station, Roslin, Midlothian EH25 9SY
Tel: 0131-445 2176 Fax: 0131-445 5124
Email: nrs@forestry.gsi.gov.uk
Forest Research in Wales, Welsh Government Offices, Rhodfa Padarn, Llanbadarn Fawr, Aberystwyth, Ceredigion SY23 3UR
Tel: 0300 068 0300 (Welsh Government) Fax: 0300 068 0301
Email: fcwenquiries@forestry.gsi.gov.uk
Number of staff: 170
Chief Executive: Dr James Pendlebury 0131-445 8710 Email: james.pendlebury@forestry.gsi.gov.uk
Sponsored by: Forestry Commission of Great Britain

Government Procurement Service
Ninth Floor, The Capital, Old Hall Street, Liverpool L3 9PP
Rosebery Court, St Andrews Business Park, Norwich, Norfolk NR7 0HS
Room 2Y92, Concept House, Cardiff Road, Newport, Mid and West Wales NP10 8QQ
Tel: 0345 410 2222 Fax: 0151-227 3315
Email: info@gps.gsi.gov.uk Website: gps.cabinetoffice.gov.uk
1 Horse Guards Road, London SW1A 2HQ
Number of staff: 398
Chief Procurement Officer for Government: Bill Crothers
Email: bill.crothers@cabinet-office.gsi.gov.uk
Sponsored by: Efficiency and Reform Group, Cabinet Office

Highways Agency
Federated House, London Road, Dorking, Surrey RH4 1SZ
Tel: 0300 123 5000 (enquiries)/0845 955 6575 (switchboard)
Email: ha_info@highways.gsi.gov.uk Website: www.highways.gov.uk Twitter: @Highways_Agency
Number of staff: 3,500
Chief Executive: Graham Dalton 01306 878667 Email: helen.nelson@highways.gsi.gov.uk
graham.dalton@highways.gsi.gov.uk
Sponsored by: Department for Transport

Insolvency Service
4 Abbey Orchard Street, London SW1P 2HT
Tel: 020 7637 1110
Email: insolvency.enquiryline@insolvency.gsi.gov.uk
Website: www.bis.gov.uk/insolvency www.insolvency.gov.uk
Number of staff: 1,951
Acting Inspector General and Chief Executive: Dr Richard Judge 0207 291 6713
Email: richard.judge@insolvency.gsi.gov.uk
Sponsored by: Department for Business, Innovation and Skills

Intelligence Collection Group
Watson Building, Elmwood Avenue, Feltham TW13 7AH
Tel: 020 8818 2136 Fax: 020 8818 2246
Number of staff: 3,225
Chief of Staff: 020 8818 2377 Email: icg-cos@icg.mod.uk
Sponsored by: Ministry of Defence

HM Land Registry
Trafalgar House, 1 Bedford Park, Croydon, London CR0 2AQ
Tel: 0300 006 0004/0844 892 1111 Fax: 0300 006 0024
Email: customersupport@landregistry.gsi.gov.uk Website: www.landregistry.gov.uk
Twitter: @LandRegGov
Number of staff: 4,536
Non-Executive Chair: Mark Boyle 0300 006 3418 Email: mark.boyle@landregistry.gsi.gov.uk
Sponsored by: Department for Business, Innovation and Skills

Legal Aid Agency
102 Petty France, London SW1H 9AJ
Website: www.justice.gov.uk/legal-aid
Number of staff: 1,516
Sponsored by: Ministry of Justice

Maritime and Coastguard Agency
Spring Place, 105 Commercial Road, Southampton, Hampshire SO15 1EG
Tel: 023 8032 9100 Fax: 023 8032 9404
Email: infoline@mcga.gov.uk Website: www.dft.gov.uk/mca Twitter: @MCA_media
Number of staff: 1,122
Chief Executive: Vice Admiral (Retd) Sir Alan Massey CBE KCB 02380 329103
Email: alan.massey@mcga.gov.uk
Sponsored by: Department for Transport

Medicines and Healthcare products Regulatory Agency
151 Buckingham Palace Road, London SW1W 9SZ
Tel: 020 3080 6000
Email: info@mhra.gsi.gov.uk Website: www.mhra.gov.uk Twitter: @MHRAGovUkPress
Number of staff: 900
Chair: Sir Gordon W Duff 020 3080 6875 Email: jude.thompson@mhra.gsi.gov.uk
Sponsored by: Department of Health

Met Office
FitzRoy Road, Exeter, Devon EX1 3PB
Tel: 0870 900 0100/01392 885680 Fax: 0870 900 5050/01392 885681
Email: enquiries@metoffice.gov.uk Website: www.metoffice.gov.uk Twitter: @metoffice
Number of staff: 1,876
Chief Executive: John Hirst 01392 884610 Email: john.hirst@metoffice.gov.uk
Sponsored by: Department for Business, Innovation and Skills

Ministry of Defence Police and Guarding Agency
Wethersfield, Braintree CM7 4AZ
Tel: 01371 854000 Fax: 01371 854060
Email: centreoffice@mdpga.mod.uk Website: www.mod.uk
Number of staff: 7,000
Chief Constable: Stephen Love QPM 01371 854316 Email: stephen.love977@mdpga.mod.uk
Sponsored by: Ministry of Defence

National Archives
Kew, Richmond TW9 4DU
Tel: 020 8876 3444 Fax: 020 8878 8905
Website: www.nationalarchives.gov.uk Twitter: @UKNatArchive

Number of staff: 563
Chief Executive and Keeper: Oliver Morley 020 8392 5220
Email: oliver.morley@nationalarchives.gsi.gov.uk
Sponsored by: Ministry of Justice

National College for School Leadership

Triumph Road, Nottingham, Nottinghamshire NG8 1DH
Tel: 0845 609 0009 Fax: 0115-945 6803
Email: enquiries@nationalcollege.org.uk Website: www.nationalcollege.org.uk

Number of staff: 233
Sponsored by: Education Standards Directorate, Department for Education

National Crime Agency

Director-General: Chief Constable Keith Bristow QPM
Sponsored by: Home Office

National Fraud Authority

Third Floor, Fry Building, 2 Marsham Street, London SW1P 4DF
Tel: 020 7035 3431
Email: nfacontact@nfa.gsi.gov.uk
Website: www.gov.uk/government/organisations/national-fraud-authority www.actionfraud.police.uk
Twitter: @nfa_uk

Number of staff: 42
Chief Executive: Stephen Harrison 020 7035 3431 Email: stephen.harrison@nfa.gsi.gov.uk
Sponsored by: Home Office

National Measurement Office

Stanton Avenue, Teddington TW11 0JZ
Tel: 020 8943 7272 Fax: 020 8943 7270
Email: info@nmo.gov.uk Website: www.bis.gov.uk/nmo

Number of staff: 74
Chief Executive: Peter Mason 020 8943 7211 Email: peter.mason@nmo.gov.uk
Sponsored by: Department for Business, Innovation and Skills

National Offender Management Service

Clive House, 70 Petty France, London, London SW1H 9EX
Tel: 0300 047 6325
Email: public.enquiries@noms.gsi.gov.uk Website: www.justice.gov.uk/about/noms

Number of staff: 50,000
Chief Executive: Michael Spurr 0300 047 5164 Email: ceonoms@noms.gsi.gov.uk
Sponsored by: Ministry of Justice

National Savings and Investments

1 Drummond Gate, Pimlico, London SW1V 2QX
Tel: 020 7932 6600
Website: www.nsandi.com

Number of staff: 160
Chief Executive: Jane Platt CBE 020 7932 6601 Email: jane.platt@nsandi.com
Sponsored by: HM Treasury

Office for National Statistics
Government Buildings, Cardiff Road, Newport, Gwent NP10 8XG
Tel: 0845 601 3034
Email: info@ons.gsi.gov.uk [firstname.surname]@ons.gsi.gov.uk Website: www.ons.gov.uk
Twitter: @statisticsONS

Number of staff: 4,000
National Statistician and Principal Accounting Officer: Jil Matheson 01633 455306
Email: national.statistician@statistics.gsi.gov.uk jil.matheson@statistics.gsi.gov.uk
Sponsored by: UK Statistics Authority

Ordnance Survey
Explorer House, Adanac Drive, Southampton, Hampshire SO16 0AS
Tel: 0845 605 0505 Fax: 0845 099 0494
Email: customerservices@ordnancesurvey.co.uk Website: www.ordnancesurvey.co.uk
Twitter: @OrdnanceSurvey

Number of staff: 1,100
Sponsored by: Department for Business, Innovation and Skills

HM Passport Office
Globe House, 89 Eccleston Square, London SW1V 1PN
Tel: 0300 222 0000
Email: info@passport.gov.uk Website: www.gov.uk/ips

Number of staff: 3,961
Registrar General for England and Wales: Sarah Rapson 020 7901 7575
Email: sarah.rapson@ips.gsi.gov.uk
(Acting) Chief Executvie: Paul Pugh Email: paul.pugh@ips.gsi.gov.uk
Sponsored by: Home Office

Planning Inspectorate
Temple Quay House, 2 The Square, Temple Quay, Bristol BS1 6PN
Tel: 0303 444 5000
Email: enquiries@pins.gsi.gov.uk Website: www.planningportal.gov.uk/planninginspectorate

Number of staff: 700
Chief Executive: Sir Michael Pitt 0303 444 5648 Email: simone.cowdery@pins.gsi.gov.uk
Sponsored by: Department for Communities and Local Government

Office of the Public Guardian
PO Box 16185, Birmingham B2 2WH
Tel: 0300 456 0300 Fax: 0870 739 5780
Email: customerservices@publicguardian.gsi.gov.uk Website: www.justice.gov.uk/about/opg.htm

Number of staff: 706
Chief Executive and Public Guardian: Alan Eccles 0121-631 6534
Email: alan.eccles@publicguardian.gsi.gov.uk
Sponsored by: Ministry of Justice

Public Health England
Wellington House, 133-155 Waterloo Road, London SE1 8UG
Tel: 0207 654 8000
Website: www.gov.uk/phe

Chief Executive: Duncan Selbie Email: duncan.selbie@phe.gov.uk
Sponsored by: Department of Health

Queen Elizabeth II Conference Centre
Broad Sanctuary, Westminster, London SW1P 3EE
Tel: 020 7222 5000 Fax: 020 7798 4200
Email: info@qeiicc.co.uk Website: www.qeiicc.co.uk

Number of staff: 4,000

Sponsored by: Department for Communities and Local Government

The Royal Parks
The Old Police House, Hyde Park, London W2 2UH
Tel: 0300 061 2000 Fax: 0300 061 2005
Email: hq@royalparks.gsi.gov.uk Website: www.royalparks.org.uk

Number of staff: 100

Sponsored by: Department for Culture, Media and Sport

Rural Payments Agency
Northgate House, 21-23 Valpy Street, PO Box 69, Reading, Berkshire RG1 1AF
Tel: 0118-958 3626 Fax: 0118-968 7599
Email: enquiries@rpa.gsi.gov.uk Website: www.rpa.gsi.gov.uk

Number of staff: 2,400

Chief Executive: Mark Grimshaw 0118-968 7555 Email: chiefexecutive'soffice@rpa.gsi.gov.uk
mark.grimshaw@rpa.gsi.gov.uk

Sponsored by: Department for Environment, Food and Rural Affairs

Service Children's Education
Building 5, Military Comlex, BFPO 40 Wegberg, Germany
Tel: +49 2161 908 2372
Email: info@sceschools.com Website: www.sceschools.com www.mod.uk/sce

Number of staff: 720

Chief Executive Officer: To be appointed

Sponsored by: Ministry of Defence

Service Personnel and Veterans Agency
Centurion Building, Grange Road, Gosport PO13 9XA

Service Contacts, Joint Personnel Administration Centre
Tel: 0800 085 3600

Veterans Contacts
Tel: 0800 169 2277 Fax: 01253 332014
Email: veterans.help@spva.gsi.gov.uk Website: www.veterans-uk.info

Number of staff: 2,000

Chief Executive: Kathy Barnes 023 9270 2320 Email: chiefexecutive@spva.mod.uk

Sponsored by: Ministry of Defence

Skills Funding Agency
Cheylesmore House, Quinton Road, Coventry CV1 2WT
Tel: 0845 019 4170/0845 377 5000 Fax: 024 7682 3675
Email: info@skillsfundingagency.bis.gov.uk Website: skillsfundingagency.bis.gov.uk
Twitter: @skillsfunding

Number of staff: 1,295

Acting Chief Executive: Kim Thorneywork 0845 377 5000
Email: kim.thorneywork@skillsfundingagency.bis.gov.uk

Sponsored by: Department for Business, Innovation and Skills

Standards and Testing Agency
53-55 Butts Road, Earlsdon Park, Coventry CV1 3BH
Tel: 0370 000 2288
Email: assessments@education.gov.uk Website: www.education.gov.uk/sta
Number of staff: 95
Chief Executive: Ian Todd 020 7340 8024 Email: ian.todd@education.gsi.gov.uk
Sponsored by: Education Standards Directorate, Department for Education

Treasury Solicitor's Department
One Kemble Street, London WC2B 4TS
Tel: 020 7210 3000 Fax: 020 7210 3420
Email: thetreasurysolicitor@tsol.gsi.gov.uk Website: www.tsol.gov.uk
Number of staff: 1,050
HM Procurator-General and Treasury Solicitor: Sir Paul Jenkins KCB QC 020 7210 3050
Email: thetreasurysolicitor@tsol.gsi.gov.uk
Sponsored by: Law Officers

UK Debt Management Office
Eastcheap Court, 11 Philpot Lane, London EC3M 8UD
Tel: 020 7862 6500 Fax: 020 7862 6509
Email: [firstname.surname]@dmo.gsi.gov.uk Website: www.dmo.gov.uk
Number of staff: 106
Chief Executive: Robert Stheeman CB 020 7862 6500 Email: robert.stheeman@dmo.gsi.gov.uk
Sponsored by: HM Treasury

UK Hydrographic Office
Admiralty Way, Taunton TA1 2DN
Tel: 01823 337900 Fax: 01823 284077
Email: customerservices@ukho.gov.uk Website: www.ukho.gov.uk
Number of staff: 1,100
Non-Executive Chair: Sandra Rogers 01823 337900 ext 4810 Email: sandra.rogers@ukho.gov.uk
Sponsored by: Ministry of Defence

UK Intellectual Property Office
Concept House, Cardiff Road, Newport NP10 8QQ
Tel: 0300 300 2000 Fax: 01633 817777
Email: information@ipo.gov.uk Website: www.ipo.gov.uk Twitter: @The_IPO
Number of staff: 1,000
Chief Executive and Comptroller General: John Alty CB 01633 814500 Email: john.alty@ipo.gov.uk
Sponsored by: Department for Business, Innovation and Skills

UK Space Agency
Polaris House, North Star Avenue, Swindon SN2 1SZ
Tel: 020 7215 5000
Email: ukspaceagencyinfo@ukspaceagency.bis.gsi.gov.uk Website: www.ukspaceagency.bis.gov.uk
Twitter: @spacegovuk
Number of staff: 48
Chief Executive: Dr David Parker 020 7215 6049 Email: david.parker@ukspaceagency.bis.gsi.gov.uk
Sponsored by: Department for Business, Innovation and Skills

Valuation Office Agency
Wingate House, 93-107 Shaftesbury Avenue, London W1D 5BU
Tel: 03000 501 501 (England)/03000 505 505 (Wales) Fax: 0300 050 0690
Email: customerservices@voa.gsi.gov.uk Website: www.voa.gov.uk

Number of staff: 3,800

Sponsored by: HM Revenue & Customs

Vehicle and Operator Services Agency
Berkeley House, Croydon Street, Bristol BS5 0DA
Tel: 0117-954 3200
Email: enquiries@vosa.gov.uk Website: www.vosa.gov.uk

Number of staff: 2,200

Chief Executive: Alastair Peoples 0117-954 3211 Email: alastair.peoples@vosa.gsi.gov.uk

Sponsored by: Department for Transport

Vehicle Certification Agency
1 The Eastgate Office Centre, Eastgate Road, Bristol BS5 6XX
Tel: 0117-951 5151 Fax: 0117-952 4103
Email: enquiries@vca.gov.uk Website: www.vca.gov.uk

Number of staff: 157

Chief Executive: Paul Markwick 0117-952 4100 Email: paul.markwick@vca.gov.uk

Sponsored by: Department for Transport

Veterinary Medicines Directorate
Woodham Lane, New Haw, Addlestone, Surrey KT15 3LS
Tel: 01932 336911 Fax: 01932 336618
Email: postmaster@vmd.defra.gsi.gov.uk Website: www.vmd.defra.gov.uk

Number of staff: 160

Chief Executive: Prof Peter Borriello 01932 338301 Email: p.borriello@vmd.defra.gsi.gov.uk

Sponsored by: Department for Environment, Food and Rural Affairs

Wilton Park
Wiston House, Steyning BN44 3DZ
Tel: 01903 815020 Fax: 01903 816373
Email: admin@wiltonpark.org.uk Website: www.wiltonpark.org.uk Twitter: @Wilton Park

Number of staff: 70

Chief Executive: Richard Burge 01903 817766 Email: richard.burge@wiltonpark.org.uk

Sponsored by: Foreign and Commonwealth Office

Non-Ministerial Departments

Non-Ministerial Departments are headed by office-holders, boards or Commissioners with specific statutory responsibilities

Charity Commission

Charity Commission Direct, PO Box 1227, Liverpool, Merseyside L69 3UG
Twitter: @ChtyCommission

Number of staff: 300

Chair: William Shawcross CVO 020 7674 2503
Email: william.shawcross@charitycommission.gsi.gov.uk
Chief Executive: Sam Younger CBE 020 7674 2503
Email: sam.younger@charitycommission.gsi.gov.uk

Office of Communications

Riverside House, 2a Southwark Bridge Road, London SE1 9HA
Tel: 020 7981 3000/0300 123 3000 Fax: 020 7981 3333
Email: contact@ofcom.org.uk Website: www.ofcom.org.uk Twitter: @Ofcom

Number of staff: 700

Chief Executive: Ed Richards 020 7981 3800 Email: ed.richards@ofcom.org.uk
Chief Operating Officer and Director, Operations Group: Jill Ainscough 020 7987 3351
Email: jill.ainscough@ofcom.org.uk

The Crown Estate

16 New Burlington Place, London W1S 2HX
Tel: 020 7851 5000 Fax: 020 7851 5128
Email: enquiries@thecrownestate.co.uk Website: www.thecrownestate.co.uk
Twitter: @TheCrownEstate

Number of staff: 400

Chair and First Commissioner: Sir Stuart Hampson 020 7851 5002
Email: stuart.hampson@thecrownestate.co.uk
Chief Executive and Second Commissioner: Alison Nimmo CBE
Email: alison.nimmo@thecrownestate.co.uk
Director, Finance: John Lelliott 020 7851 5010 Email: john.lelliott@thecrownestate.co.uk
Director, Corporate Affairs and General Counsel: Vivienne King 020 7851 5168
Email: vivienne.king@thecrownestate.co.uk
Director, Energy and Infrastructure: Rob Hastings 020 7851 5192
Email: rob.hastings@thecrownestate.co.uk
Director, Investment and Asset Management: Paul Clark 020 7851 5215
Email: paul.clark@thecrownestate.co.uk
Director, Rural and Coastal: Ken Jones   Email: ken.jones@thecrownestate.co.uk

Crown Prosecution Service

Rose Court, 2 Southwark Bridge, London SE1 9HS
Tel: 020 3357 0000
Email: enquiries@cps.gsi.gov.uk Website: www.cps.gov.uk Twitter: @cpsuk

Number of staff: 6,999

Director of Public Prosecutions: Alison Saunders CB 020 3357 0883
Email: privateoffice@cps.gsi.gov.uk
Chief Executive: Peter Lewis CB 020 3357 0892 Email: privateoffice@cps.gsi.gov.uk

Office of Fair Trading
Fleetbank House, 2-6 Salisbury Square, London EC4Y 8JX
Tel: 020 7211 8000 Fax: 020 7211 8800
Email: enquiries@oft.gsi.gov.uk Website: www.oft.gov.uk Twitter: @OFTgov

Number of staff: 665

Chairman: Philip Collins 020 7211 8279 Email: chairman@oft.gsi.gov.uk
Chief Executive: Clive Maxwell 020 7211 8920 Email: ceo@oft.gsi.gov.uk

Food Standards Agency
Aviation House, 125 Kingsway, London WC2B 6NH
Tel: 020 7276 8000
Email: helpline@foodstandards.gsi.gov.uk Twitter: @foodgov

Number of staff: 1,800

Chair: Rt Hon Lord Rooker 020 7276 8010 Email: jeff.rooker@foodstandards.gsi.gov.uk
Chief Executive: Catherine Brown 020 7276 8201 Email: catherine.brown@foodstandards.gsi.gov.uk
Deputy Chair: Tim Bennett 020 7276 8020 Email: tim.bennett@foodstandards.gsi.gov.uk
Chief Scientist, Chief Scientist Group: Andrew Wadge 020 7276 8511
Email: andrew.wadge@foodstandards.gsi.gov.uk
Director, FSA Scotland: Prof Charles Milne 01224 285101 Email: scotland@foodstandards.gsi.gov.uk
Director, Legal Services: Rod Ainsworth 020 7276 8500
Email: rod.ainsworth@foodstandards.gsi.gov.uk
Director, Operations: Andrew Rhodes 020 7276 8615
Email: andrew.rhodes@foodstandards.gsi.gov.uk
Director, Food Safety Group: Steve Wearne 020 7276 8400
Email: steve.wearne@foodstandards.gsi.gov.uk
Director, FSA Northern Ireland: Gerry McCurdy 028 9041 7719
Email: gerry.mccurdy@foodstandards.gsi.gov.uk
Director, FSA Wales: Geoff Ogle 029 2067 8914 Email: wales@foodstandards.gsi.gov.uk
Director, Human Resources: Lynne Bywater 01904 455503
Email: lynne.bywater@foodstandards.gsi.gov.uk
Director, Communications: Stephen Humphreys 020 7276 8812
Email: stephen.humphreys@foodstandards.gsi.gov.uk

Forestry Commission of Great Britain
Forestry Commission GB Functions, Silvan House, 231 Corstorphine Road, Edinburgh EH12 7AT
Tel: 0131-334 0303 Fax: 0131-334 3047
Email: enquiries@forestry.gsi.gov.uk Website: www.forestry.gov.uk

Number of staff: 3,600

Director-General and Deputy Chair: Tim Rollinson CBE 0131-314 6424
Email: tim.rollinson@forestry.gsi.gov.uk

Office of Gas and Electricity Markets
9 Millbank, London SW1P 3GE
Tel: 020 7901 7000 Fax: 020 7901 7066
Email: consumeraffairs@ofgem.gov.uk Website: www.ofgem.gov.uk Twitter: @ofgem

Number of staff: 367

Chair of the Gas and Electricity Markets Authority: John Gray 020 7901 7203
Chief Executive, Ofgem Group: Alistair Buchanan CBE 020 7901 7357
Email: alistair.buchanan@ofgem.gov.uk sue.hidson@ofgem.gov.uk
Group Finance Director: To be appointed
Director, GB External Relations, Scotland and Wales: Charles Gallacher 0141-331 6000
Email: charles.gallacher@ofgem.gov.uk

Government Actuary's Department

Finlaison House, 15-17 Furnival Street, London EC4A 1AB
Tel: 020 7211 2601 Fax: 020 7211 2650
Email: enquiries@gad.gov.uk Website: www.gad.gov.uk
Number of staff: 130
Government Actuary: Trevor Llanwarne CB

Office of Qualifications and Examinations Regulation

Spring Place, Coventry Business Park, Herald Avenue, Coventry CV5 6UB
Tel: 0300 303 3344 Fax: 0300 303 3348
Email: info@ofqual.gov.uk Website: www.ofqual.gov.uk Twitter: @ofqual
Chair: Amanda Spielman 024 7671 6741 Email: amanda.spielman@ofqual.gov.uk
Chief Regulator: Glenys Stacey 024 7671 6741 Email: diane.francis@ofqual.gov.uk

Office of Rail Regulation

One Kemble Street, London WC2B 4AN
Tel: 020 7282 2000 Fax: 020 7282 2040
Email: contact.cct@orr.gsi.gov.uk Website: www.rail-reg.gov.uk
Number of staff: 286
Chair: Anna Walker CB 020 7282 3696 Email: anna.walker@orr.gsi.gov.uk
Chief Executive: Richard Price 020 7282 3889 Email: richard.price@orr.gsi.gov.uk
Director, Legal Services: Juliet Lazarus 020 7282 2089 Email: juliet.lazarus@orr.gsi.gov.uk
Director, Railway Safety: Ian Prosser 020 7282 2187 Email: ian.prosser@orr.gsi.gov.uk
Director, Strategy and Policy: Daniel Brown 020 7282 3824 Email: daniel.brown@orr.gsi.gov.uk
Director, Corporate Operations: Alastair Gilchrist 020 7282 3847
Email: alastair.gilchrist@orr.gsi.gov.uk
Acting Director, Communications: Richard Emmott 020 7282 3862
Email: richard.emmott@orr.gsi.gov.uk
Director, Railway Planning and Performance: Alan Price 020 7282 2073
Email: alan.price@orr.gsi.gov.uk
Director, PR13 Programme: John Larkinson 020 7282 2193 Email: john.larkinson@orr.gsi.gov.uk

HM Revenue & Customs

100 Parliament Street, London SW1A 2BQ
Tel: 020 7147 0000
Email: [firstname.surname]@hmrc.gsi.gov.uk Website: www.hmrc.gov.uk Twitter: @HMRCgovuk
Chief Executive and Permanent Secretary: Lin Homer CB 020 7147 2153
Email: lin.homer@hmrc.gsi.gov.uk
Second Permanent Secretary and Tax Assurance Commissioner: Edward Troup 020 7147 3072
Email: edward.troup@hmrc.gsi.gov.uk

Scottish Housing Regulator

Highlander House, 58 Waterloo Street, Glasgow G2 7DA
Tel: 0141-271 3810
Email: shr@scottishhousingregulator.gsi.gov.uk Website: www.scottishhousingregulator.gov.uk
Number of staff: 56
Chief Executive: Michael Cameron 0141-305 4055
Email: elizabeth.stewart@scottishhousingregulator.gsi.gov.uk
Director, Regulation, Finance and Risk Division: Ian Brennan
Email: ian.brennan@scottishhousingregulator.gsi.gov.uk

Director, Regulation, Governance and Performance Division: Christine Macleod
Email: christine.macleod@scottishhousingregulator.gsi.gov.uk
Director, Strategy and Communications: Iain Muirhead
Email: iain.muirhead@scottishhousingregulator.gsi.gov.uk

Serious Fraud Office
2-4 Cockspur Street, London SW1Y 5BS
Tel: 020 7239 7272 Fax: 020 7837 1689
Email: public.enquiries@sfo.gsi.gov.uk Website: www.sfo.gov.uk

Number of staff: 330

Director: David Green CB QC 020 7239 7101 Email: john.peck@sfo.gsi.gov.uk
General Counsel: Alun Milford Email: alun.milford@sfo.gsi.gov.uk
Chief Investigating Officer: Kevin Davis Email: kevin.davis@sfo.gsi.gov.uk

Office for Standards in Education, Children's Services and Skills
Aviation House, 125 Kingsway, London WC2B 6SE
Tel: 0300 123 1231
Email: enquiries@ofsted.gov.uk Website: www.ofsted.gov.uk Twitter: @Ofstednews

Number of staff: 1,430

HM Chief Inspector of Education, Children's Services and Skills: Sir Michael Wilshaw 0300 013 1064
Email: michael.wilshaw@ofsted.gov.uk
Chair: Baroness Morgan of Huyton 0300 013 1064 Email: sally.morgan@ofsted.gov.uk

UK Statistics Authority
Statistics House, Tredegar Park, Newport NP10 8XG
Tel: 0845 604 1857 Fax: 01633 456179
Email: authority.enquiries@statistics.gsi.gov.uk Website: www.statisticsauthority.gov.uk
Twitter: @UKStatsAuth

Number of staff: 40

Chair: Sir Andrew Dilnot CBE 020 7592 8673 Email: andrew.dilnot@statistics.gsi.gov.uk
National Statistician and Permanent Secretary: Jil Matheson 01633 455306
Email: national.statistician@statistics.gsi.gov.uk jil.matheson@statistics.gsi.gov.uk
Deputy Chair, Official Statistics: Prof David Rhind CBE

UK Supreme Court
Parliament Square, London SW1P 3BD
Tel: 020 7960 1900/020 7960 1500 Fax: 020 7960 1901
Email: enquiries@supremecourt.gsi.gov.uk Website: www.supremecourt.gov.uk
Twitter: @UKSupremeCourt

Number of staff: 40

Chief Executive: Jenny Rowe CB 020 7960 1906 Email: jenny.rowe@supremecourt.gsi.gov.uk
President of the Supreme Court: Rt Hon Lord Neuberger of Abbotsbury
Registrar of the Supreme Court: Louise di Mambro 020 7960 1985
Email: louise.dimambro@supremecourt.gsi.gov.uk

UK Trade & Investment
1 Victoria Street, London SW1H 0ET
Tel: 020 7215 8000
Email: enquiries@ukti.gsi.gov.uk [firstname.surname]@ukti.gsi.gov.uk Website: www.gov.uk/ukti
Twitter: @UKTI

Number of staff: 2,400

Chief Executive: Nick Baird CMG CVO 020 7215 4300 Email: nick.baird@ukti.gsi.gov.uk

Water Services Regulation Authority

Centre City Tower, 7 Hill Street, Birmingham, West Midlands B5 4UA
Tel: 0121-644 7500 Fax: 0121-644 7559
Email: mailbox@ofwat.gsi.gov.uk casemanagementoffice@ofwat.gsi.gov.uk
Website: www.ofwat.gov.uk Twitter: @Ofwat

Number of staff: 202

Chair: Jonson Cox   Email: jonson.cox@ofwat.gsi.gov.uk
Chief Executive: Regina Finn 0121-644 7748 Email: regina.finn@ofwat.gsi.gov.uk
Chief Regulation Officer: Sonia Brown 0121-644 7500 Email: sonia.brown@ofwat.gsi.gov.uk
Senior Director, Finance and Networks: Keith Mason 0121-644 7677
Email: keith.mason@ofwat.gsi.gov.uk
Senior Director, Corporate Services and Programme Management: Stuart Crawford 0121-644 7694
Email: stuart.crawford@ofwat.gsi.gov.uk

Ombudsmen and Complaint-handling Bodies

Adjudicator's Office
Eighth Floor, Euston Tower, 286 Euston Road, London NW1 3US
Tel: 0300 057 1111 Fax: 0300 057 1212
Website: www.adjudicatorsoffice.gov.uk

Number of staff: 50
Adjudicator: Judy Clements OBE
Head of Office: Margaret Allcock 0300 057 1829

Advertising Standards Authority
Mid City Place, 71 High Holborn, London WC1V 6QT
Tel: 020 7492 2222 Fax: 020 7242 3696
Email: enquiries@asa.org.uk Website: www.asa.org.uk Twitter: @ASA_UK

Number of staff: 115
Chair: Chris Smith
Chief Executive: Guy Parker

Commissioner for Children and Young People in Scotland
85 Holyrood Road, Edinburgh, Lothian EH8 8AU
Tel: 0131-558 3733
Email: info@sccyp.org.uk Website: www.sccyp.org.uk Twitter: @rightssccyp

Number of staff: 15
Commissioner: Tam Baillie Email: tam.baillie@sccyp.org.uk

Commission for Ethical Standards in Public Life in Scotland
39 Drumsheugh Gardens, Edinburgh, Lothian EH3 7SW
Tel: 0300 011 0550
Email: info@ethicalstandards.org.uk Website: www.ethicalstandards.org.uk

Number of staff: 16
Commissioner for Public Standards and Public Appointments in Scotland: Stuart Allan 0131-226 8138
Email: appointments@ethicalstandards.org.uk investigations@ethicalstandards.org.uk

European Ombudsman
Avenue du Président Robert Schuman 1, CS 30403, 67001 Strasbourg Cedex, France
Tel: +33 3 88 17 23 13 Fax: +33 3 88 17 90 62
Email: eo@ombudsman.europa.eu Website: www.ombudsman.europa.eu

Number of staff: 76
Ombudsman: P. Nikiforos Diamandouros Email: nikiforos.diamandouros@ombudsman.europa.eu
Head of Cabinet: Zinovia Assimakopoulou +33 3 88 17 22 62
Email: zinovia.assimakopoulou@ombudsman.europa.eu

Financial Ombudsman Service
South Quay Plaza, 183 Marsh Wall, London E14 9SR
Tel: 020 7964 1000/0800 023 4567 (consumer) Fax: 020 7964 1001
Email: complaint.info@financial-ombudsman.org.uk Website: www.financial-ombudsman.org.uk
Twitter: @Financialombuds

Number of staff: 3,000

Chief Executive and Chief Ombudsman: Natalie Ceeney CBE 020 3222 9680
Email: jordan.baker@financial-ombudsman.org.uk
Deputy Chief Executive and Deputy Chief Ombudsman: Tony Boorman 020 7964 0690
Email: tony.boorman@financial-ombudsman.org.uk

Financial Services Ombudsman Scheme for the Isle of Man
Government Building, Lord Street, Douglas, Isle of Man IM1 1LE
Tel: 01624 686500 Fax: 01624 686504
Email: ombudsman@iomoft.gov.im Website: www.gov.im/oft/ombudsman
Number of staff: 3
Senior Adjudicator: Norman Teare Email: ombudsman@iomoft.gov.im

Gibraltar Ombudsman
Office of the Ombudsman, 10 Governor's Lane, Gibraltar
Tel: +350 200 46001 Fax: +350 200 46002
Email: ombudsman@gibraltar.gi Website: www.ombudsman.org.gi Twitter: @GibratarOmbuds
Number of staff: 5
Ombudsman: Mario M Hook +350 200 46001 Email: ombudsman@gibraltar.gi

Groceries Code Adjudicator
Adjudicator Designate: Christine Tacon CBE

Housing Ombudsman Service
81 Aldwych, London WC2B 4HN
Tel: 0300 111 3000 Fax: 020 7831 1942
Email: info@housing-ombudsman.org.uk Website: www.housing-ombudsman.org.uk
Number of staff: 50
Ombudsman: Dr Michael Biles

Independent Case Examiner
Jupiter Drive, Chester West Employment Park, Chester, Cheshire CH70 8DR
Tel: 0845 606 0777 Fax: 0151-221 6601
Email: ice@dwp.gsi.gov.uk Website: www.ind-case-exam.org.uk
Number of staff: 90
Independent Case Examiner: Joanna Wallace

Independent Complaints Reviewer
Dover House, 66 Whitehall, London SW1A 2AU
Tel: 020 7930 0749 Fax: 020 7321 0406
Email: enquiries@icr.gsi.gov.uk Website: www.icrev.org.uk
Number of staff: 5
Independent Complaints Reviewer for the National Archives, the Children's Commissioner for Wales and Joint Independent Complaints Reviewer for the Youth Justice Agency: Jodi Berg OBE
Independent Complaints Reviewer for Land Registry and Joint Independent Complaints Reviewer for the Youth Justice Agency: Elizabeth Derrington

Information Commissioner's Office
Wycliffe House, Water Lane, Wilmslow SK9 5AF
Tel: 0303 123 1113 Fax: 01625 524510
Email: casework@ico.gsi.gov.uk Website: www.ico.gov.uk
Number of staff: 400

Deputy Commissionerand Director, Data Protection: David Smith
Email: david.smith@ico.gsi.gov.uk
Deputy Commissioner and Director, Freedom of Information for the ICO: Graham Smith
Email: graham.smith@ico.gsi.gov.uk

Legal Ombudsman

PO Box 6806, Wolverhampton WV1 9WJ
Tel: 0300 555 0333
Email: enquiries@legalombudsman.org.uk Website: www.legalombudsman.org.uk
Twitter: @Legal_Ombudsman @OmbudServices

Number of staff: 279

Chief Ombudsman: Adam Sampson Email: christina.goodin@legalombudsman.org.uk
Deputy Chief Ombudsman: Gary Garland 0121-245 3111
Email: kay.kershaw@legalombudsman.org.uk
Chief Operating Officer: Rob Hezel Email: rob.hezel@legalombudsman.org.uk
holly.richardson@legalombudsman.org.uk

Local Government Ombudsman

LGO Advice Team, PO Box 4771, Coventry CV4 0EH
Tel: 0300 061 0614/0845 602 1983 Fax: 024 7682 0001
Email: advice@lgo.org.uk Website: www.lgo.org.uk

Vice-chair and Ombudsman: Anne Seex 01904 380200
Chair and Ombudsman: Dr Jane Martin 024 7682 0019 Email: r.toora@lgo.org.uk

Northern Ireland Ombudsman

Progressive House, 33 Wellington Place, Belfast BT1 6HN
Tel: 028 9023 3821/(Freephone) 0800 343 424 Fax: 028 9023 4912
Email: ombudsman@ni-ombudsman.org.uk Website: www.ni-ombudsman.org.uk

Number of staff: 35

Ombudsman: Dr Thomas Frawley CBE

Office of the Independent Adjudicator for Higher Education

Third Floor, Kings Reach, 38-50 Kings Road, Reading, Berkshire RG1 3AA
Tel: 0118-959 9813 Fax: 0118-955 9099
Email: enquiries@oiahe.org.uk Website: www.oiahe.org.uk

Number of staff: 50

Independent Adjudicator and Chief Executive: Robert Behrens Email: enquiries@oiahe.org.uk
Secretary: Ben Elger 0118-959 9813

Office of the Schools Adjudicator

Mowden Hall, Staindrop Road, Darlington DL3 9BG
Tel: 01325 735303
Email: osa.team@osa.gsi.gov.uk Website: www.education.gov.uk/schoolsadjudicator

Number of staff: 6

Chief Schools Adjudicator: Dr Elizabeth Passmore OBE 01325 735303

Ombudsman Association

PO Box 308, Twickenham, Middlesex TW1 9BE
Tel: 020 8894 9272
Email: secretary@ombudsmanassociation.org Website: www.ombudsmanassociation.org

Secretary: Ian Pattison

Ombudsman Services

Wilderspool Park, Greenall's Avenue, Warrington, Cheshire WA4 6HL
Tel: 0330 440 1624/01925 530263
Email: enquiries@os-communications.org Website: www.ombudsman-services.org
Chief Ombudsman: Lewis Shand Smith

Pensions Ombudsman

Sixth Floor, 11 Belgrave Road, London SW1V 1RB
Tel: 020 7630 2200 Fax: 020 7821 0065
Email: enquiries@pensions-ombudsman.org.uk Website: www.pensions-ombudsman.org.uk
Number of staff: 39

Ombudsman: Tony King 020 7630 2223

Police Ombudsman for Northern Ireland

New Cathedral Buildings, 11 Church Street, Belfast BT1 1PG
Tel: 028 9082 8600/0845 601 2931 Fax: 028 9082 8659
Email: info@policeombudsman.org Website: www.policeombudsman.org
Number of staff: 150

Chief Executive: Adrian McAllister 028 9082 8680
Email: adrian.macallister@policeombudsman.org

Prisons and Probation Ombudsman for England and Wales

Ashley House, 2 Monck Street, London SW1P 2BQ
Tel: 020 7035 2876/Lo-call: 0845 010 7938 Fax: 020 7035 2860
Email: mail@ppo.gsi.gov.uk Website: www.ppo.gov.uk
Number of staff: 100

Ombudsman: Nigel Newcomen CBE 020 7035 2851 Email: nigel.newcomen1@ppo.gsi.gov.uk
Deputy Ombudsman, Prisons, Probation and Immigration Removal Centre Complaints:
Elizabeth Moody 020 7035 2046 Email: elizabeth.moody@ppo.gsi.gov.uk
Deputy Ombudsman, Fatal Incidents Investigations: Michael Loughlin 020 7035 2741
Email: michael.loughlin1@ppo.gsi.gov.uk

The Property Ombudsman

Milford House, 43-55 Milford Street, Salisbury SP1 2BP
Tel: 01722 333306 Fax: 01722 332296
Email: admin@tpos.co.uk Website: www.tpos.co.uk Twitter: @TPOmb
Number of staff: 60

Chair: Lord Best OBE
Ombudsman: Christopher Hamer 01722 430 027 Email: christopher.hamer@tpos.co.uk
stephanie.spencer@tpos.co.uk

Commissioner for Public Appointments Northern Ireland

Dundonald House, Annexe B, Stormont Estate, Upper Newtownards Road, Belfast, Belfast BT4 3SB
Tel: 028 9052 4820
Email: info@publicappointmentsni.org Website: www.publicappointmentsni.org
Number of staff: 4

Commissioner: John Keanie MBA 028 9052 4820 Email: info@publicappointmentsni.org
Compliance Adviser: Pat Neeson

Public Services Ombudsman for Wales
1 Ffordd yr Hen Gae, Pencoed, Mid Glamorgan CF35 5LJ
Tel: 01656 641150 Fax: 01656 641199
Email: ask@ombudsman-wales.org.uk Website: www.ombudsman-wales.org.uk
Number of staff: 55
Public Services Ombudsman for Wales: Peter Tyndall

Scottish Human Rights Commission
4 Melville Street, Edinburgh EH3 7NS
Tel: 0131-240 2989
Email: hello@scottishhumanrights.com Website: www.scottishhumanrights.com
Twitter: @ScotHumanRights
Number of staff: 13
Chair: Prof Alan Miller

Scottish Information Commissioner
Kinburn Castle, Doubledykes Road, St Andrews, Fife KY16 9DS
Tel: 01334 464610 Fax: 01334 464611
Email: enquiries@itspublicknowledge.info Website: www.itspublicknowledge.info
Number of staff: 21
Commissioner: Rosemary Agnew

The Scottish Legal Complaints Commission
The Stamp Office, 10-14 Waterloo Place, Edinburgh EH1 3EG
Tel: 0131-201 2130 Fax: 0131-201 2131
Email: enquiries@scottishlegalcomplaints.org.uk Website: www.scottishlegalcomplaints.org.uk
Number of staff: 42
Chair: To be appointed
Chair: Bill Brackenridge
Chief Executive: Matthew Vickers

Scottish Public Services Ombudsman
4 Melville Street, Edinburgh EH3 7NS
Tel: 0800 377 7330 Fax: 0800 377 7331
Website: www.spso.org.uk
Number of staff: 50
Ombudsman: Jim Martin

UK Parliamentary Ombudsman and Health Service Ombudsman for England
Millbank Tower, Millbank, London SW1P 4QP
Tel: 0345 015 4033 Fax: 0300 061 4000
Email: phso.enquiries@ombudsman.org.uk Website: www.ombudsman.org.uk
Ombudsman: Dame Julie Mellor DBE 0300 061 4211 Email: privateoffice@ombudsman.org.uk

---

VACHER'S QUARTERLY
The most up-to-date contact details throughout the year
Call 020 7593 5644 or visit www.dodsshop.co.uk

Political and Parliamentary Organisations

Armed Forces Parliamentary Scheme
13 Cowley Street, London SW1P 3LZ
Tel: 020 7222 0480 Fax: 020 7222 7783
Email: lesley.snape1@btinternet.com Website: af-ps.info
Chair: Sir Neil Thorne OBE TD DL

Audit Scotland
110 George Street, Edinburgh EH2 4LH
Tel: 0845 146 1010
Email: info@audit-scotland.gov.uk Website: www.audit-scotland.gov.uk Twitter: @auditscotland
Auditor General for Scotland: Caroline Gardner
Chair, Accounts Commission for Scotland: Prof John Baillie

Boundary Commission for England
Room 3/21, 1 Horse Guards Road, London SW1A 2HQ
Tel: 020 7276 1102
Email: information@bcommengland.gsi.gov.uk
Website: www.boundarycommissionforengland.independent.gov.uk
Chairman: Rt Hon John Bercow MP
Deputy Chairman: Hon Mr Justice Sales
Acting Secretary: Tony Bellringer 020 7276 1402 Email: tony.bellringer@bcommengland.gsi.gov.uk

Boundary Commission for Northern Ireland
Forestview, Purdy's Lane, Newtownbreda, Belfast BT8 7AR
Tel: 028 9069 4800
Email: bcni@belfast.org.uk Website: www.boundarycommission.org.uk
Chairman: Rt Hon John Bercow MP
Deputy Chairman: Hon Mr Justice McCloskey
Secretary: Elizabeth Benson

Boundary Commission for Scotland
Thistle House, 91 Haymarket Terrace, Edinburgh EH12 5HD
Tel: 0131-538 7510 Fax: 0131-538 7511
Email: bcs@scottishboundaries.gov.uk Website: www.bcomm-scotland.independent.gov.uk
Chairman: Rt Hon John Bercow MP
Deputy Chairman: Hon Lord Woolman
Secretary: Dr Hugh Buchanan Email: hugh.buchanan@scottishboundaries.gov.uk

Boundary Commission for Wales
Hastings House, Fitzalan Court, Cardiff CF24 0BL
Tel: 029 2046 4819 Fax: 029 2046 4823
Email: bcomm.wales@wales.gsi.gov.uk Website: www.bcomm-wales.gov.uk
Chairman: Rt Hon John Bercow MP
Deputy Chairman: Hon Mr Justice Williams

Commonwealth Parliamentary Association, United Kingdom Branch
Westminster Hall, Houses of Parliament, London SW1A 0AA
Tel: 020 7219 5373 Fax: 020 7233 1202
Email: cpa@parliament.uk Website: www.parliament.uk/cpauk

Presidents: Rt Hon John Bercow MP, Rt Hon Baroness D'Souza CMG
Vice-Presidents: Rt Hon Baroness Boothroyd OM, Rt Hon Lord Carrington KG GCMG CH MC DL, Rt Hon Lord Falconer of Thoroton QC, Rt Hon William Hague MP, Rt Hon Baroness Hayman GBE, Rt Hon Lord Howe of Aberavon CH QC, Rt Hon Lord Hurd of Westwell CH CBE, Rt Hon Lord Irvine of Lairg, Rt Hon Lord Mackay of Clashfern, Rt Hon Lord Owen CH, Rt Hon Jack Straw MP
Chairman of the Executive Committee: Rt Hon Sir Alan Haselhurst MP
Chairman of the Branch: Rt Hon David Cameron MP
Vice-chairmen: Dr Roberta Blackman-Woods MP, Pauline Latham OBE MP, Professor Lord McColl of Dulwich CBE
Hon Treasurer: Rt Hon Kevin Barron MP
Secretary: Andrew Tuggey DL

Confederation of British Industry

Centre Point, 103 New Oxford Street, London WC1A 1DU
Tel: 020 7395 8041/020 7395 8239 (Press Office) Fax: 020 7836 0645
Email: parliament@cbi.org.uk press.office@cbi.org.uk Website: www.cbi.org.uk
Twitter: @CBItweets

President: Sir Michael Rake
Director-General: John Cridland CBE
Principal Political Adviser: Richard Maughan 020 7395 8004 Email: richard.maughan@cbi.org.uk

Electoral Commission

3 Bunhill Row, London EC1Y 8YZ
Tel: 020 7271 0500 Fax: 020 7271 0505
Email: info@electoralcommission.org.uk Website: www.electoralcommission.org.uk
www.aboutmyvote.org.uk Twitter: @ElectoralCommUK

Chair of Commission Board: Jenny Watson
Commissioners: Anna Carragher, Gareth Halliwell, Tony Hobman, Lord Horam, David Howarth, Lord Kennedy of Southwark, John McCormick, Rt Hon Sir George Reid
Chief Executive: Peter Wardle
Secretary to the Commission Board: Kairen Zonena

Electoral Office for Northern Ireland

St Anne's House, 15 Church Street, Belfast BT1 1ER
Tel: 0800 4320 712 Fax: 028 9033 0661
Email: [firstname.surname]@eoni.org.uk Website: www.eoni.org.uk
Chief Electoral Officer: Graham Shields Email: graham.shields@eoni.org.uk

Electoral Reform Society

Thomas Hare House, 6 Chancel Street, Blackfriars, London SE1 0UU
Tel: 020 7928 1622 Fax: 020 7401 7789
Email: ers@electoral-reform.org.uk Website: www.electoral-reform.org.uk Twitter: @electoralreform

Chair: Amy Dodd
Vice-chair: Jessica Asato
Chief Executive: Katie Ghose Email: katie.ghose@electoral-reform.org.uk
Treasurer: Chris Carrigan

Hansard Society

Fifth Floor, 9 King Street, London EC2V 8EA
Tel: 020 7710 6070 Fax: 020 7710 6088
Email: contact@hansardsociety.org.uk Website: www.hansardsociety.org.uk
Twitter: @HansardSociety

Presidents: Rt Hon John Bercow MP, Rt Hon Baroness D'Souza CMG
Vice-Presidents: Rt Hon David Cameron MP, Rt Hon Nick Clegg MP, Rt Hon Ed Miliband MP
Chairman: Rt Hon Lord Grocott 020 7710 6070
Hon Treasurer: Roshana Arasaratnam 020 7710 6070
Director and Head of Research: Ruth Fox 020 7710 6070 Email: ruth.fox@hansardsociety.org.uk
Director of Learning: Michael Raftery Email: michael.raftery@hansardsociety.org.uk
Head of Communications: Virginia Gibbons 020 7710 6079 Email: comms@hansardsociety.org.uk

Independent Parliamentary Standards Authority
Portland House, Bressenden Place, London SW1E 5BH
Tel: 020 7811 6400
Email: info@parliamentarystandards.org.uk Website: www.parliamentarystandards.org.uk
Chair: Prof Sir Ian Kennedy
Chief Executive: Dr Andrew McDonald
Board Members: Sir Neil Butterfield, Elizabeth Padmore, Anne Whitaker, Prof Tony Wright

Industry and Parliament Trust
Suite 101, 3 Whitehall Court, London SW1A 2EL
Tel: 020 7839 9400 Fax: 020 7839 9401
Email: industryandparliamenttrust@ipt.org.uk Website: www.ipt.org.uk
Presidents: Rt Hon John Bercow MP, Rt Hon Baroness D'Souza CMG, Rt Hon Chris Grayling MP
Chairman, Board of Trustees: Baroness Harris of Richmond DL
Chairman, Management Board: Rosemary Brook
Chief Executive: Nick Maher
Executive Assistant: Sheila Palmer 020 7839 9400 Email: sheilapalmer@ipt.org.uk

British Group Inter-Parliamentary Union
Palace of Westminster, London SW1A 0AA
Tel: 020 7219 3011/2/3 Fax: 020 7219 8780
Email: bgipu@parliament.uk Website: www.bgipu.org
Honorary Presidents: Rt Hon John Bercow MP, Rt Hon Baroness D'Souza CMG
Chair: Robert Walter MP
Vice-chairs: Rt Hon Ann Clwyd MP, Stewart Jackson MP
Treasurer: Mike Gapes MP
Director: Rick Nimmo

National Audit Office
157-197 Buckingham Palace Road, Victoria, London SW1W 9SP
Tel: 020 7798 7000 Press: 020 7798 7400 Fax: 020 7828 7070
Email: enquiries@nao.gsi.gov.uk Website: www.nao.org.uk
Comptroller and Auditor General: Amyas Morse
Chief Operating Officer: Michael Whitehouse
Executive Leaders: Gabrielle Cohen, Ed Humpherson, Martin Sinclair
Director, Parliamentary Relations: Ashley McDougall

Police Service Parliamentary Scheme
13 Cowley Street, London SW1P 3LZ
Tel: 020 8501 1673 Fax: 020 8500 6854
Email: ej_hunt@hotmail.com Website: af-ps.info
Chair: Sir Neil Thorne OBE TD DL

Committee on Standards in Public Life
Room G.05, 1 Horse Guards Road, London SW1A 2HQ
Tel: 020 7271 0855
Email: public@standards.gsi.gov.uk Website: www.public-standards.gov.uk
Chair: Lord Bew
Members: Lord Alderdice, Margaret Beckett DBE MP, Sheila Drew Smith OBE, Patricia Moberly,
Sir Derek Morris DPhil, Dame Denise Platt DBE, Richard Thomas CBE, Dame Angela Watkinson DBE MP
Secretary: Ruth Thompson Email: ruth.thompson@standards.gsi.gov.uk

Trades Union Congress
Congress House, Great Russell Street, London WC1B 3LS
Tel: 020 7636 4030
Email: ilarkin@tuc.org.uk Website: www.tuc.org.uk Twitter: @tucnews
General Secretary: Frances O'Grady
Assistant General Secretaries: Kay Carberry, Paul Nowak
Head of Management Services and Administration Department: David Hemington
Head of Economic and Social Affairs Department: Nicola Smith
Head of Campaigns and Communications Department: Nigel Stanley Email: nstanley@tuc.org.uk
Head of European Union and International Relations Department: Owen Tudor
Head of Equality and Employment Rights Department: Sarah Veale
Director of unionlearn: Tom Wilson

Wales Audit Office
24 Cathedral Road, Cardiff CF11 9LJ
Tel: 029 2032 0500 Fax: 029 2032 0600
Email: info@wao.gov.uk Website: www.wao.gov.uk Twitter: @walesaudit
Auditor-General for Wales: Huw Vaughan Thomas

Whitehall and Industry Group
80 Petty France, London SW1H 9EX
Tel: 020 7222 1166 Fax: 020 7222 1167
Email: info@wig.co.uk Website: www.wig.co.uk
Chief Executive: Mark Gibson CB

DIPLOMATIC REPRESENTATION

Diplomatic Representation

British Embassies and High Commissions

Afghanistan

British Embassy, 15th Street, Roundabout Wazir Akbar Khan, PO Box 334, Kabul
Tel: +93 700 102 000 Fax: +93 700 102 250
Website: www.gov.uk/government/world/organisations/british-embassy-kabul
Ambassador: HE Sir Richard Stagg KCMG

Albania

British Embassy, Rruga Skenderbeg 12, Tirana
Tel: +355 4 223 4973 Fax: +355 4 224 7697
Website: www.gov.uk/government/world/organisations/british-embassy-tirana
Ambassador: HE Nicholas Cannon OBE

Algeria

British Embassy, 3 Chemin Capitaine Hocine Slimane (ex Chemin des Glycines), Hydra, Algiers
Tel: +213 770 085 000 Fax: +213 770 085 099
Email: britishembassy.algiers@fco.gov.uk
Website: www.gov.uk/government/world/organisations/british-embassy-algiers Twitter: @ukinalgeria
Ambassador: HE Martyn Roper OBE

Andorra – see Spain

Angola

Non-resident: São Tomé and Príncipe
British Embassy, Rua 17 de Setembro, No 4, Caixa, 1244 Luanda
Tel: +244 222 334 582 Fax: +244 222 333 331
Email: postmaster.luand@fco.gov.uk
Website: www.gov.uk/government/world/organisations/british-embassy-luanda
Ambassador (until February 2014): HE Richard Wildash LVO
Ambassador (from February 2014): HE John Dennis

Antigua and Barbuda – see Barbados

Argentina

British Embassy, Dr Luis Agote 2412, 1425 Buenos Aires
Tel: +54 11 4808 2200 Fax: +54 11 4808 2274
Email: askinformation.baires@fco.gov.uk
Website: www.gov.uk/government/world/organisations/british-embassy-buenos-aires
Ambassador: HE Dr John Freeman

Armenia

British Embassy, 34 Baghramyan Avenue, 0019 Yerevan
Tel: +374 10 264 301 Fax: +374 10 264 318
Email: enquiries.yerevan@fco.gov.uk
Website: www.gov.uk/government/world/organisations/british-embassy-armenia
blogs.fco.gov.uk/ukinarmenia
Ambassadors: HE Jonathan Aves, HE Katherine Leach

Australia
British High Commission, Commonwealth Avenue, Yarralumla, Canberra ACT 2600
Tel: +61 2 6270 6666
Website: www.gov.uk/government/world/organisations/british-high-commission-canberra
blogs.fco.gov.uk/paulmadden Twitter: @ukinaustralia
High Commissioner: HE Paul Madden CMG

Austria
British Embassy, Jaurèsgasse 12, 1030 Vienna
Tel: +43 1 716130 Fax: +43 1 71613 2900
Email: press@britishembassy.at
Website: www.gov.uk/government/world/organisations/british-embassy-vienna
Ambassador: HE Susan le Jeune d'Allegeershecque CMG

Azerbaijan
British Embassy, 45 Khagani Street, AZ1010 Baku
Tel: +994 12 4377878 Fax: +994 12 4977434
Email: generalenquiries.baku@fco.gov.uk
Website: www.gov.uk/government/world/organisations/british-embassy-baku
Twitter: @ukinazerbaijan
Ambassador: HE Irfan Siddiq OBE

Bahamas – see Jamaica

Bahrain
British Embassy, 21 Government Avenue, PO Box 114, Manama 306
Tel: +973 17574100 Fax: +973 17574161
Website: www.gov.uk/government/world/organisations/british-embassy-manama
Twitter: @ukinbahrain
Ambassador: HE Iain Lindsay OBE

Bangladesh
British High Commission, United Nations Road, Baridhara, PO Box 6079, Dhaka 1212
Tel: +880 2 882 2705
Email: press.dhaka@fco.gov.uk
Website: www.gov.uk/government/world/organisations/british-high-commission-dhaka
Twitter: @ukinbangladesh
High Commissioner: HE Robert Gibson CMG

Barbados
Non-resident: Antigua and Barbuda, Commonwealth of Dominica, Grenada, St Kitts and Nevis, St Lucia, St Vincent and the Grenadines
British High Commission, Lower Collymore Rock, PO Box 676, Bridgetown
Tel: +1 246 430 7800
Email: ukinbarbados@fco.gov.uk
Website: www.gov.uk/government/world/organisations/british-high-commission-barbados
Twitter: @ukincaribbean
High Commissioner: HE Victoria Dean

Belarus

British Embassy, 37 Karl Marx Street, 220030 Minsk
Tel: +375 17 229 8200 Fax: +375 17 229 8206
Email: ukin.belarus@fconet.fco.gov.uk
Website: www.gov.uk/government/world/organisations/british-embassy-minsk
blogs.fco.gov.uk/brucebucknell
Ambassador: HE Bruce Bucknell

Belgium

British Embassy, Avenue d'Auderghem 10, 1040 Brussels
Tel: +32 2 287 62 11 Fax: +32 2 287 62 50
Email: public.brussels@fco.gov.uk
Website: www.gov.uk/government/world/organisations/british-embassy-brussels
Twitter: @ukinbelgium
Ambassador: HE Jonathan Brenton (until August 2014)
Ambassador: HE Alison Rose (from August 2014)

Belize

British High Commission, Embassy Square, PO Box 91, Belmopan
Tel: +501 822 2981
Email: brithicom@btl.net
Website: www.gov.uk/government/world/organisations/british-high-commission-belmopan
High Commissioner: HE Peter Hughes OBE

Benin – see Ghana

Bolivia

British Embassy, Avenida Arce 2732, La Paz
Tel: +591 2 243 3424 Fax: +591 2 243 1073
Email: ukinbolivia@gmail.com
Website: www.gov.uk/government/world/organisations/british-embassy-bolivia Twitter: @ukinbolivia
Ambassador: HE Ross Denny

Bosnia and Herzegovina

British Embassy, 39a Hamdije Cemerlica Street, 71000 Sarajevo
Tel: +387 33 282 200 Fax: +387 33 282 203
Email: britemb@bih.net.ba
Website: www.gov.uk/government/world/organisations/british-embassy-sarajevo
Ambassador: HE Nigel Casey MVO

Botswana

British High Commission, Plot 1079-1084 Main Mall, off Queens Road, Gaborone
Tel: +267 395 2841 Fax: +267 395 6105
Email: bhc@botsnet.bw
Website: www.gov.uk/government/world/organisations/british-high-commission-gaborone
High Commissioner: HE Nicholas Pyle OBE

Brazil

British Embassy, Setor de Embaixadas Sul, Quadra 801, Lote 8, CEP 70408-900, Brasilia-DF
Tel: +55 61 3329 2300 Fax: +55 61 3329 2369
Email: press.brasilia@fco.gov.uk
Website: www.gov.uk/government/world/organisations/british-embassy-brazil Twitter: @ukinbrazil
Ambassador: HE Alex Ellis

Brunei

British High Commission, 2.01, Second Floor, Block D, Kompleks Bangunan Yayasan Sultan Haji, Hassanal Bokiah, BS8711 Bandar Seri Begawan
Tel: +673 2 222231 Fax: +673 2 234315
Email: brithc@brunet.bn
Website: www.gov.uk/government/world/organisations/british-high-commission-bandar-seri-begawan
Twitter: @ukinbrunei
High Commissioner: HE David Campbell

Bulgaria

British Embassy, 9 Moskovska Street, 1000 Sofia
Tel: +359 2 933 9222 Fax: +359 2 933 9250
Email: britishembassysofia@fco.gov.uk
Website: www.gov.uk/government/world/organisations/british-embassy-sofia Twitter: @ukinbulgaria
Ambassador: HE Jonathan Allen

Burkina Faso – see Ghana

Burma (Myanmar)

British Embassy, 80 Strand Road, PO Box No 638, Rangoon
Tel: +95 1 380322 Fax: +95 1 370866
Website: www.gov.uk/government/world/organisations/british-embassy-rangoon Twitter: @ukinburma
Ambassador: HE Andrew Patrick

Burundi – see Rwanda

Cambodia

British Embassy, 27-29 Street 75, Sangkat Srah Chak, Khan Daun Penh, 12201 Phnom Penh
Tel: +855 23 427124 Fax: +855 23 427125
Email: britemb@online.com.kh
Website: www.gov.uk/government/world/organisations/british-embassy-phnom-penh
Ambassador (until January 2014): HE Mark Gooding
Ambassador (from January 2014): HE Bill Longhurst

Cameroon

Non-resident: Central African Republic, Chad, Equatorial Guinea, Gabon

British High Commission, Avenue Winston Churchill, BP 547, Yaoundé
Tel: +237 22 22 07 96 Fax: +237 2222 01 48
Email: bhc.yaounde@fco.gov.uk
Website: www.gov.uk/government/world/organisations/british-high-commission-yaounde
Twitter: @ukincameroon
High Commissioner: HE Brian Olley

Canada

British High Commission, 80 Elgin Street, Ottawa K1P 5K7
Tel: +1 613 237 1530 Fax: +1 613 237 7980
Email: ukincanada@fco.gov.uk
Website: www.gov.uk/government/world/organisations/british-high-commission-ottawa
blogs.fco.gov.uk/ukincanada Twitter: @ukincanada
High Commissioner: HE Howard Drake OBE

Cape Verde – see Senegal

Central African Republic – see Cameroon

Chad – see Cameroon

Chile
British Embassy, Avda El Bosque Norte 0125, Las Condes, Santiago
Tel: +56 2 370 4100 Fax: +56 2 370 4160
Email: embsan@britemb.cl
Website: www.gov.uk/government/world/organisations/british-embassy-chile Twitter: @ukinchile
Ambassador (until February 2014): HE Jon Benjamin
Ambassador (from February 2014): HE Fiona Clouder

China
British Embassy, 11 Guang Hua Lu, Jian Guo Men Wai, Beijing 100 600
Tel: +86 10 5192 4000 Fax: +86 10 5192 4239
Website: www.gov.uk/government/world/organisations/british-embassy-beijing Twitter: @ukinchina
Ambassador: HE Sebastian Wood CMG

Colombia
British Embassy, Carrera 9 No 76-49, Piso 8, Edificio ING Barings, Bogotá
Tel: +57 1 326 8300
Email: embajadabritanica.bogota@fco.gov.uk
Website: www.gov.uk/government/world/organisations/british-embassy-colombia
Twitter: @ukincolombia
Ambassador: HE Lindsay Croisdale-Appleby

Comoros – see Mauritius

Democratic Republic of Congo
Non-resident: Republic of Congo
British Embassy, 83 Avenue Roi Baudoin, Gombe, Kinshasa
Tel: +243 81 556 6200 Fax: +243 81 346 4291
Email: ambassade.britannique@fco.gov.uk
Website: www.gov.uk/government/world/organisations/british-embassy-kinshasa Twitter: @ukindrc
Ambassador: HE Diane Corner

Republic of Congo – see Democratic Republic of Congo

Costa Rica
British Embassy, Edificio Centro Colón, Paseo Colón and Streets 38 and 40, San José
Tel: +506 2258 2025 Fax: +506 2256 8574
Website: www.gov.uk/government/world/organisations/british-embassy-in-costa-rica
Ambassador: HE Sharon Campbell

Côte d'Ivoire
British Embassy, Cocody Quartier Ambassades, Rue l'Impasse du Belier, Rue A58, 01 BP 2581 Abidjan 01
Tel: +225 22 44 26 69 Fax: +225 22 48 95 48
Email: uk_abidjan@yahoo.fr
Website: www.gov.uk/government/world/organisations/british-embassy-abidjan
Ambassador: HE Simon Tonge

Croatia
British Embassy, Ivana Lučića 4, 10000 Zagreb
Tel: +385 1 6009 100 Fax: +385 1 6009 111
Website: www.gov.uk/government/world/organisations/british-embassy-zagreb Twitter: @ukincroatia
Ambassador: HE David Slinn CMG OBE

Cuba
British Embassy, Calle 34 no. 702e/7ma, Miramar, La Habana
Tel: +53 7 214 2200 Fax: +53 7 214 2218
Email: embrit@ceniai.inf.cu
Website: www.gov.uk/government/world/organisations/british-embassy-havana
Twitter: @ukincaribbean
Ambassador: HE Tim Cole

Cyprus
British High Commission, Alexander Pallis Street, PO Box 21978, Nicosia 1587
Tel: +357 2 861100 Fax: +357 2 861125
Email: brithc.2@cytanet.com.cy
Website: www.gov.uk/government/world/organisations/british-high-commission-nicosia
Twitter: @ukincyprus
High Commissioner (until April 2014): HE Matthew Kidd
High Commissioner (from April 2014): HE Ric Todd

Czech Republic
British Embassy, Thunovská 14, 118 00 Prague 1
Tel: +420 257 402 111 Fax: +420 257 402 296
Email: ukinczechrepublic@fco.gov.uk
Website: www.gov.uk/government/world/organisations/british-embassy-prague
Ambassador: HE Jan Thompson OBE

Denmark
British Embassy, Kastelsvej 36-40, 2100 Copenhagen Ø
Tel: +45 35 44 52 00
Email: enquiry.copenhagen@fco.gov.uk
Website: www.gov.uk/government/world/organisations/british-embassy-copenhagen
Ambassador: HE Vivien Life

Djibouti – see Ethiopia

Dominica – see Barbados

Dominican Republic
Non-resident: Haiti
British Embassy, Ave 27 de Febrero No 233, Edificio Corominas Pepin, Santo Domingo
Tel: +1 809 472 7111 Fax: +1 809 472 7190
Email: brit.emb.sadom@codetel.net.do
Website: www.gov.uk/government/world/organisations/british-embassy-santo-domingo
Twitter: @ukindomrep
Ambassador: HE Steven Fisher

Ecuador

British Embassy, 14th Floor, Citiplaza Building, Naciones Unidas Avenue and República de El Salvador, PO Box 17-17-830, Quito
Tel: +593 2 2970 800
Website: www.gov.uk/government/world/organisations/british-embassy-in-ecuador
Twitter: @ukinecuador

Ambassador: HE Patrick Mullee

Egypt

British Embassy, 7 Ahmed Ragheb Street, Garden City, Cairo
Tel: +20 2 2791 6000 Fax: +20 2 2791 6131
Email: cairo.press@fco.gov.uk
Website: www.gov.uk/government/world/organisations/british-embassy-cairo
blogs.fco.gov.uk/jameswatt Twitter: @ukinegypt

Ambassador: HE James Watt CVO

El Salvador

British Embassy, Edifico Torre Futura, 14th Floor, Colonia Escalon, San Salvador
Tel: +503 2511 5757
Email: britishembassy.elsalvador@fco.gov.uk
Website: www.gov.uk/government/world/organisations/british-embassy-san-salvador
Twitter: @ukinelsalvador

Ambassador: HE Linda Cross MBE

Equatorial Guinea – see Cameroon

Eritrea

British Embassy, 66-68 Mariam Ghimbi Street, Zip Code 174, PO Box 5584, Asmara
Tel: +291 120 28 39 Fax: +291 112 01 04
Email: asmara.enquiries@fco.gov.uk
Website: www.gov.uk/government/world/organisations/british-embassy-asmara

Ambassador: HE Dr Amanda Tanfield

Estonia

British Embassy, Wismari 6, 10136 Tallinn
Tel: +372 667 4700 Fax: +372 667 4755
Email: infotallinn@fco.gov.uk
Website: www.gov.uk/government/world/organisations/british-embassy-tallin

Ambassador: HE Christopher Holtby OBE

Ethiopia

Non-resident: Djibouti

British Embassy, Comoros Street, PO Box 858, Addis Ababa
Tel: +251 11 661 2354 Fax: +251 11 661 0588
Email: britishembassy.addisababa@fco.gov.uk
Website: www.gov.uk/government/world/organisations/british-embassy-addis-ababa
blogs.fco.gov.uk/gregdorey

Ambassador: HE Gregory Dorey CVO

Fiji
Non-resident: Kiribati, Marshall Islands, Micronesia, Nauru, Tonga and Tuvalu
British High Commission, 47 Gladstone Road, Suva
Tel: +679 322 9100 Fax: +679 322 9132
Email: publicdiplomacy@fco.gov.uk
Website: www.gov.uk/government/world/organisations/british-high-commission-suva
High Commissioner: HE Roderick Drummond

Finland
British Embassy, Itäinen Puistotie 17, 00140 Helsinki
Tel: +358 9 2286 5100 Fax: +358 9 2286 5284
Email: info.helsinki@fco.gov.uk
Website: www.gov.uk/government/world/organisations/british-embassy-helsinki
Twitter: @ukinfinland
Ambassador (until January 2014): HE Matthew Lodge
Ambassador (from January 2014): HE Sarah Price

France
Non-resident: Monaco
British Embassy, 35 rue du Faubourg St Honoré, 75363 Paris Cedex 08
Tel: +33 1 44 51 31 00 Fax: +33 144 51 31 09
Email: public.paris@fco.gov.uk
Website: www.gov.uk/government/world/organisations/british-embassy-paris
blogs.fco.gov.uk/peterricketts Twitter: @ukinfrance
Ambassador: HE Sir Peter Ricketts GCMG

Gabon – see Cameroon

The Gambia
British High Commission, 48 Atlantic Road, Fajara, PO Box 507, Banjul
Tel: +220 4494508 Fax: +220 4496134
Email: bhcbanjul@fco.gov.uk
Website: www.gov.uk/government/world/organisations/british-high-commission-banjul
High Commissioner: HE David Morley

Georgia
British Embassy, 51 Krtsanisi Street, Tbilisi 0114
Tel: +995 32 2274747 Fax: +995 32 2274792
Email: british.embassy.tbilisi@fco.gov.uk
Website: www.gov.uk/government/world/organisations/british-embassy-tbilisi
Ambassador: HE Alexandra Hall Hall

Germany
British Embassy, Wilhelmstrasse 70, 10117 Berlin
Tel: +49 30 204570
Email: ukingermany@fco.gov.uk
Website: www.gov.uk/government/world/organisations/british-embassy-berlin Twitter: @ukingermany
Ambassador: HE Simon McDonald CMG

Ghana

Non-resident: Benin, Burkina Faso, Togo

British High Commission, Osu Link, off Gamel Abdul Nasser Avenue, PO Box 296, Accra
Tel: +233 302 213250 Fax: +233 302 213274
Website: www.gov.uk/government/world/organisations/british-high-commission-accra
Twitter: @ukinghana
High Commissioner: HE Peter Jones

Greece

British Embassy, 1 Ploutarchou Street, 106 75 Athens
Tel: +30 1 7272 600
Email: information.athens@fco.gov.uk
Website: www.gov.uk/government/world/organisations/british-embassy-athens
Twitter: @ukingreece
Ambassador: HE John Kittmer

Grenada – see Barbados

Guatemala

Non-resident: Honduras

British Embassy, Edificio Torre Internacional, Nivel 11, 16 Calle 0-55, Zona 10, Guatemala City
Tel: +502 2380 7300
Website: www.gov.uk/government/world/organisations/british-embassy-guatemala
Twitter: @ukinguatemala
Ambassador: HE Sarah Dickson

Guinea

British Embassy, Villa 1, Residence 2000, Corniche Sud, Conakry
Tel: +224 63 35 53 29
Email: britembconakry@hotmail.com
Website: www.gov.uk/government/world/organisations/british-embassy-conakry
Ambassador: HE Graham Styles

Guinea-Bissau – see Senegal

Guyana

Non-resident: Suriname

British High Commission, 44 Main Street, Georgetown
Tel: +592 226 5881 Fax: +592 225 3555
Email: bhcguyana@networksgy.com
Website: www.gov.uk/government/world/organisations/british-high-commission-georgetown
High Commissioner: HE Andrew Ayre

Haiti

Ambassador resident in Dominican Republic

British Embassy, Entre 73 et 75 Delmas, Port-au-Prince
Tel: +1 509 2812 9191
Website: www.gov.uk/government/world/organisations/british-embassy-port-au-prince
Non-resident Ambassador: HE Steven Fisher

Holy See
British Embassy, Via XX Settembre 80a, 00187 Rome
Tel: +39 06 4220 4000 Fax: +39 06 4220 4205
Email: holysee@fco.gov.uk
Website: www.gov.uk/government/world/organisations/british-embassy-holy-see
blogs.fco.gov.uk/nigelbaker Twitter: @ukinholysee
Ambassador: HE Nigel Baker OBE MVO

Honduras – see Guatemala

Hungary
British Embassy, Harmincad Utca 6, 1051 Budapest
Tel: +36 1 266 2888 Fax: +36 1 266 0907
Email: info@britemb.hu
Website: www.gov.uk/government/world/organisations/british-embassy-budapest
blogs.fco.gov.uk/jonathanknott Twitter: @ukinhungary
Ambassador: HE Jonathan Knott

Iceland
British Embassy, Laufásvegur 31, 101 Reykjavík
Tel: +354 550 5100 Fax: +354 550 5105
Email: info@britishembassy.is
Website: www.gov.uk/government/world/organisations/british-embassy-reykjavik
Ambassador: HE Stuart Gill

India
British High Commission, Shantipath, Chanakyapuri, New Delhi 110021
Tel: +91 11 2419 2100 Fax: +91 11 2419 2411
Email: web.newdelhi@fco.gov.uk
Website: www.gov.uk/government/world/organisations/british-high-commission-new-delhi
Twitter: @ukinindia
High Commissioner: HE Sir James Bevan KCMG

Indonesia
Non-resident: Timor-Leste
British Embassy, Jalan M H Thamrin No 75, Jakarta 10310
Tel: +62 21 2356 5200 Fax: +62 21 2356 5351
Email: jakarta.mcs@fco.gov.uk
Website: www.gov.uk/government/world/organisations/british-embassy-jakarta
blogs.fco.gov.uk/markcanning Twitter: @ukinindonesia
Ambassador: HE Mark Canning CMG

Iraq
British Embassy, International Zone, Baghdad
Tel: +964 790 192 6280
Website: www.gov.uk/government/world/organisations/british-embassy-baghdad Twitter: @ukiniraq
Ambassador: HE Simon Collis

Ireland
British Embassy, 29 Merrion Road, Ballsbridge, Dublin 4
Tel: +353 1 205 3700 Fax: +351 1 205 3885
Website: www.gov.uk/government/world/organisations/british-embassy-dublin
Twitter: @britembdublin
Ambassador: HE Dominick Chilcott CMG

Israel

British Embassy, 192 Hayarkon Street, 63405 Tel Aviv
Tel: +972 3 725 1222 Fax: +972 3 725 1203
Email: webmaster.telaviv@fco.gov.uk
Website: www.gov.uk/government/world/organisations/british-embassy-tel-aviv Twitter: @ukinisrael
Ambassador: HE Matthew Gould

Italy

Non-resident: San Marino

British Embassy, Via XX Settembre 80/a, 00187 Rome
Tel: +39 6 4220 0001
Email: inforome@fco.gov.uk
Website: www.gov.uk/government/world/organisations/british-embassy-rome Twitter: @ukinitaly
Ambassador: HE Christopher Prentice CMG

Ivory Coast – see Côte d'Ivoire

Jamaica

Non-resident: Bahamas

British High Commission, PO Box 575, 28 Trafalgar Road, Kingston 10
Tel: +1 876 936 0700 Fax: +1 876 510 0737
Email: ppa.kingston@fco.gov.uk
Website: www.gov.uk/government/world/organisations/british-high-commission-jamaica
blogs.fco.gov.uk/ukinjamaica Twitter: @ukincaribbean
High Commissioner: HE David Fitton

Japan

British Embassy, No 1 Ichiban-cho, Chiyoda-ku, 102-8381 Tokyo
Tel: +81 3 5211 1100 Fax: +81 3 5275 3164
Email: public-enquiries.tokyo@fco.gov.uk
Website: www.gov.uk/government/world/organisations/british-embassy-tokyo Twitter: @ukinjapan
Ambassador: HE Timothy Hitchens CMG LVO

Jordan

British Embassy, (PO Box 87) Abdoun, 11118 Amman
Tel: +962 6 590 9200 Fax: +962 6 590 9279
Email: amman.enquiries@fco.gov.uk
Website: www.gov.uk/government/world/organisations/british-embassy-amman Twitter: @ukinjordan
Ambassador: HE Peter Millett CMG

Kazakhstan

British Embassy, 62 Kosmonavtov Street, Astana 010000
Tel: +7 7172 556200 Fax: +7 7272 556211
Email: ukinkz@fco.gov.uk
Website: www.gov.uk/government/world/organisations/british-embassy-astana Twitter: @ukinkz
Ambassador: HE Dr Carolyn Browne

Kenya

British High Commission, Upper Hill Road, PO Box 30465-00100, Nairobi
Tel: +254 20 287 3000
Email: nairobi.enquiries@fco.gov.uk
Website: www.gov.uk/government/world/organisations/british-high-commission-nairobi
Twitter: @ukinkenya
High Commissioner: HE Dr Christian Turner

Kiribati - see Fiji

Democratic People's Republic of Korea (North)
British Embassy, Munsu-dong Diplomatic Compound, Pyongyang
Tel: +850 2 381 7980 Fax: +850 2 381 7985
Website: www.gov.uk/government/world/organisations/british-embassy-pyonyang
Ambassador: HE Michael Gifford

Republic of Korea (South)
British Embassy, Sejong-daero 19-gil 24, Jung-gu, 100-120 Seoul
Tel: +82 2 3210 5500 Fax: +82 2 725 1738
Email: enquiry.seoul@fco.gov.uk
Website: www.gov.uk/government/world/organisations/british-embassy-seoul
blogs.fco.gov.uk/scottwightman Twitter: @ukinkorea
Ambassador: HE Scott Wightman CMG

Kosovo
British Embassy, Ismail Qemajli 6, Arberi, Dragodan, Pristina
Tel: +381 38 254 700 Fax: +381 38 249 799
Email: britishembassy.pristina@fco.gov.uk
Website: www.gov.uk/government/world/organisations/british-embassy-pristina
Ambassador: HE Ian Cliff OBE

Kuwait
British Embassy, PO Box 2, 13001, Safat
Tel: +965 2259 4320 Fax: +965 2259 4339
Email: kuwait.generalenquiries@fco.gov.uk
Website: www.gov.uk/government/world/organisations/british-embassy-kuwait
blogs.fco.gov.uk/frankbaker Twitter: @ukinkuwait
Ambassador: HE Francis Baker OBE

Kyrgyzstan
British Embassy, 21 Erkindik Boulevard, Office 404, 720040 Bishkek
Tel: +996 312 303647
Email: ukin.kyrgyzrepublic@fco.gov.uk
Website: www.gov.uk/government/world/organisations/british-embassy-bishkek
Ambassador: HE Judith Farnworth

Laos
British Embassy, Rue J Nehru Phonexay, Saysettha District, Vientaine
Tel: +856 30 777 1065
Email: bevientaine@gmail.com
Website: www.gov.uk/government/world/organisations/british-embassy-vientiane
blogs.fco.gov.uk/philipmalone Twitter: @ukinlaos
Ambassador: HE Philip Malone LVO

Latvia
British Embassy, 5 J Alunana Street, LV-1010 Riga
Tel: +371 6774 4700 Fax: +371 6777 4707
Email: britishembassy.riga@fco.gov.uk
Website: www.gov.uk/government/world/organisations/british-embassy-riga Twitter: @ukinlatvia
Ambassador: HE Sarah Cowley

Lebanon

British Embassy, Embassies Complex, Armies Street, Zkak Al-Blat, Serail Hill, PO Box 11-471 Beirut
Tel: +961 1 960800 Fax: +961 1 960855
Website: www.gov.uk/government/world/organisations/british-embassy-beirut Twitter: @ukinlebanon
Ambassador: HE Tom Fletcher CMG

Lesotho – see South Africa

Liberia

Leone Compound, 12th Street Beach-side, Sinkor, Monrovia
Tel: +231 77530320
Email: ukemb.liberia@gmail.com
Website: www.gov.uk/government/world/organisations/british-embassy-monrovia
Ambassador: HE Fergus Cochrane-Dyet

Libya

British Embassy, 24th Floor, Tripoli Towers (formerly Bourj al Fateh), Tripoli
Tel: +218 21 335 1084
Website: www.gov.uk/government/world/organisations/british-embassy-tripoli Twitter: @ukinlibya
Ambassador: HE Michael Aron

Liechtenstein – see Switzerland

Lithuania

British Embassy, Antakalnio str. 2, LT-10308 Vilnius
Tel: +370 5 246 29 00 Fax: +370 5 246 29 01
Email: be-vilnius@britain.lt
Website: www.gov.uk/government/world/organisations/british-embassy-vilnius
Ambassador: HE David Hunt

Luxembourg

British Embassy, Boulevard Joseph II 5, 1840 Luxembourg
Tel: +352 22 98 64 Fax: +352 22 98 67
Email: britemb@internet.lu
Website: www.gov.uk/government/world/organisations/british-embassy-in-luxembourg
Ambassador: HE the Hon Alice Walpole

Former Yugoslav Republic of Macedonia

British Embassy, Todor Aleksandrov No. 165, 1000 Skopje
Tel: +389 2 3299 299 Fax: +389 2 3179 726
Email: britishembassyskopje@fco.gov.uk
Website: www.gov.uk/government/world/organisations/british-embassy-skopje
Twitter: @ukinmacedonia
Ambassador (until summer 2014): HE Christopher Yvon
Ambassador (from summer 2014): HE Charles Garrett

Madagascar

British Embassy, Ninth Floor Tour Zital, Ravoninahitriniarivo Street, Ankorondrano, Antananarivo 101
Tel: +261 20 22 330 53
Email: beantananarivo@moov.mg
Website: www.gov.uk/government/world/organisations/british-embassy-antananarivo
Ambassador: HE Timothy Smart

Malawi

British High Commission, PO Box 30042, Lilongwe 3
Tel: +265 772 400 Fax: +265 772 657
Email: bhclilongwe@fco.gov.uk
Website: www.gov.uk/government/world/organisations/british-high-commission-lilongwe
High Commissioner: HE Michael Nevin

Malaysia

British High Commission, 185 Jalan Ampang, 50450 Kuala Lumpur
Tel: +60 3 2170 2200 Fax: +60 3 2170 2370
Email: press.kualalumpur@fco.gov.uk
Website: www.gov.uk/government/world/organisations/british-high-commission-kuala-lumpur
Twitter: @ukinmalaysia
High Commissioner: HE Simon Featherstone CMG

Maldives – see Sri Lanka

Mali

Non-resident: Niger
British Embassy, Immeuble Semega, Koulikoro Road, Hippodrome PO Box 2069, Bamako
Tel: +223 2021 3412 Fax: +223 2021 8377
Ambassador: HE Dr Phil Boyle

Malta

British High Commission, Whitehall Mansions, Ta'Xbiex Seafront, Ta'Xbiex XBX 1026
Tel: +356 2323 0000 Fax: +356 2323 2216
Website: www.gov.uk/government/world/organisations/british-high-commission-malta
blogs.fco.gov.uk/robluke
High Commissioner: HE Robert Luke

Marshall Islands – see Fiji

Mauritania – see Morocco

Mauritius

Non-resident: Comoros
British High Commission, Seventh Floor, Les Cascades Building, Edith Cavell Street, Port Louis
Tel: +230 202 9400 Fax: +230 202 9408
Email: bhc@intnet.mu
Website: www.gov.uk/government/world/organisations/british-high-commission-port-louis
High Commissioner (until August 2014): HE Nicholas Leake
High Commissioner (from August 2014): HE Jonathan Drew MBE

Mexico

British Embassy, Río Lerma 71, Col Cuauhtémoc, 06500 Mexico City
Tel: +52 55 1670 3200 Fax: +52 55 1670 3217
Email: ukinmexico@fco.gov.uk
Website: www.gov.uk/government/world/organisations/british-embassy-mexico-city
Twitter: @ukinmexico
Ambassador: HE Duncan Taylor CBE

Micronesia – see Fiji

Moldova

British Embassy, 18 Nicolae Iorga str., 2012 Chisinau
Tel: +373 22 22 59 02 Fax: +373 22 25 18 59
Email: enquiries.chisinau@fco.gov.uk
Website: www.gov.uk/government/world/organisations/british-embassy-chisinau
Twitter: @ukinmoldova
Ambassador: HE Philip Batson

Monaco – see France

Mongolia

British Embassy, Peace Avenue 30, Bayanzurkh District, Ulaanbaatar 13381
Tel: +976 11 458133 Fax: +976 11 458036
Website: www.gov.uk/government/world/organisations/british-embassy-ulaanbaatar
Ambassador: HE Christopher Stuart

Montenegro

British Embassy, Ulcinjska 8, Gorica C, 81000 Podgorica
Tel: +382 20 618 010 Fax: +382 20 618 020
Email: podgorica@fco.gov.uk
Website: www.gov.uk/government/world/organisations/british-embassy-podgorica
Twitter: @ukinmontenegro
Ambassador: HE Ian Whitting CVO OBE

Morocco

Non-resident: Mauritania

British Embassy, 28 Avenue S.A.R. Sidi Mohammed, Souissi, 10105 (BP 45) Rabat
Tel: +212 537 63 33 33 Fax: +212 537 75 87 09
Website: www.gov.uk/government/world/organisations/british-embassy-rabat
Ambassador: HE Clive Alderton

Mozambique

British High Commission, Avenida Vladimir Lenine 310, PO Box 55, Maputo
Tel: +258 21 356 000 Fax: +258 21 356 060
Email: bhcgeneral@gmail.com
Website: www.gov.uk/government/world/organisations/british-high-commission-maputo
High Commissioner: HE Shaun Cleary

Myanmar – see Burma

Namibia

British High Commission, 116 Robert Mugabe Avenue, PO Box 22202, Windhoek
Tel: +264 61 274800 Fax: +264 61 228895
Email: general.windhoek@fco.gov.uk
Website: www.gov.uk/government/world/organisations/british-high-commission-windhoek
blogs.fco.gov.uk/marianneyoung
High Commissioner: HE Marianne Young

Nauru – see Fiji

Nepal
British Embassy, PO Box 106, Lainchaur, Kathmandu
Tel: +977 1 4410583 Fax: +977 1 4411789
Email: bekathmandu@fco.gov.uk
Website: www.gov.uk/government/world/organisations/british-embassy-kathmandu Twitter: @ukinnepal
Ambassador: HE Andrew Sparkes CMG

Netherlands
British Embassy, Lange Voorhout 10, 2514 ED The Hague
Tel: +31 70 4270 427 Fax: +31 70 4270 345
Email: ukinnl@fco.gov.uk
Website: www.gov.uk/government/world/organisations/british-embassy-the-hague
blogs.fco.gov.uk/paularkwright Twitter: @ukinnl
Ambassador: HE Sir Geoffrey Adams KCMG

New Zealand
Non-resident: Samoa; Governor: Pitcairn, Henderson, Ducie and Oeno Islands

British High Commission, 44 Hill Street, Wellington 6011
Tel: +64 4 924 2888 Fax: +64 4 473 4982
Website: www.gov.uk/government/world/organisations/british-high-commission-wellington
Twitter: @ukinnz
High Commissioner: HE Victoria Treadell CMG MVO

Nicaragua
Ambassador resident in Costa Rica

c/o British Embassy San José, Edificio Centro Colón and Streets 38 and 40, 1007 San José, Costa Rica
Tel: +506 2258 2025
Website: www.gov.uk/government/world/organisations/british-embassy-in-costa-rica
Non-resident Ambassador: HE Christopher Campbell

Niger – see Mali

Nigeria
British High Commission, 19 Torrens Close, Maitama, Abuja
Tel: +234 9 462 2200 Fax: +234 9 462 2263
Email: ppainformation.abuja@fco.gov.uk
Website: www.gov.uk/government/world/organisations/british-high-commission-abuja
Twitter: @ukinnigeria
High Commissioner: HE Dr Andrew Pocock CMG

Norway
British Embassy, Thomas Heftyesgate 8, 0264 Oslo
Tel: +47 23 13 27 00 Fax: +47 23 13 27 41
Email: britemb@online.no
Website: www.gov.uk/government/world/organisations/british-embassy-oslo Twitter: @ukinnorway
Ambassador: HE Jane Owen

Oman
British Embassy, PO Box 185, 116 Mina Al Fahal, Muscat
Tel: +968 2460 9000 Fax: +968 2460 9010
Email: muscat.enquiries@fco.gov.uk
Website: www.gov.uk/government/world/organisations/british-embassy-muscat Twitter: @ukinoman
Ambassador: HE Jamie Bowden CMG OBE

Pakistan

British High Commission, Diplomatic Enclave, Ramna-5, PO Box 1122, Islamabad
Tel: +92 51 201 2000
Email: islamabad-general.enquiries@fco.gov.uk
Website: www.gov.uk/government/world/organisations/british-high-commission-islamabad
blogs.fco.gov.uk/ukinpakistan Twitter: @ukinpakistan
High Commissioner: HE Adam Thomson CMG

Palau – see Philippines

Panama

British Embassy, Fourth Floor, MMG Tower, Calle 53, Marbella, (PO Box 0816-07946), Panama City
Tel: +507 297 6550 Fax: +507 297 6588
Website: www.gov.uk/government/world/organisations/british-embassy-panama-city
Twitter: @ukinpanama
Ambassador (from December 2013): HE Dr Ian Collard

Papua New Guinea

British High Commission, Sec 411, Lot 1 and 2, Kiroki Street, Waigani, Port Moresby
Tel: +675 325 1677 Fax: +675 325 3547
Email: ukinpng@datec.net.pg
Website: www.gov.uk/government/world/organisations/british-high-commission-port-moresby
High Commissioner: HE Jacqueline Barson MBE

Paraguay

British Embassy, Edificio Citicenter Piso 5, Av. Mariscal López y Cruz del Chaco, Asuncion
Tel: +595 21 328 5507
Email: be-asuncion.enquiries@fco.gov.uk
Website: www.gov.uk/government/world/organisations/british-embassy-asuncion
Ambassador: HE Dr Jeremy Hobbs

Peru

British Embassy, Torre Parque Mar (Piso 22), Avenida José Larco, 1301 Miraflores, Lima
Tel: +51 1 617 3000 Fax: +51 1 617 3100
Email: belima@fco.gov.uk
Website: www.gov.uk/government/world/organisations/british-embassy-peru
blogs.fco.gov.uk/ukinperu Twitter: @ukinperu
Ambassador: HE James Dauris

Philippines

Non-resident: Marshall Islands, Micronesia, Palau
British Embassy, 120 Upper McKinley Road, McKinley Hill, Taguig City, 1634 Manila
Tel: +63 2 858 2200 Fax: +63 2 858 2313
Email: ukinthephilippines@fco.gov.uk
Website: www.gov.uk/government/world/organisations/british-embassy-manila
Twitter: @ukinphilippines
Ambassador: HE Asif Ahmad

Poland
British Embassy, ul. Kawalerii 12, 00-468 Warsaw
Tel: +48 22 311 00 00 Fax: +48 22 311 03 13
Email: info@britishembassy.pl
Website: www.gov.uk/government/world/organisations/british-embassy-warsaw
blogs.fco.gov.uk/robinbarnett Twitter: @ukinpoland
Ambassador: HE Robin Barnett CMG OBE

Portugal
British Embassy, Rua de São Bernardo 33, 1249-082 Lisbon
Tel: +351 21 392 4000 Fax: +351 21 392 4021
Email: ppa.lisbon@fco.gov.uk
Website: www.gov.uk/government/world/organisations/british-embassy-lisbon Twitter: @ukinportugal
Ambassador: HE Jill Gallard

Qatar
British Embassy, West Bay, PO Box 3, off Wahda Street near Rainbow roundabout, Doha
Tel: +974 496 2000 Fax: +974 496 2086
Email: embassy.qatar@fco.gov.uk
Website: www.gov.uk/government/world/organisations/british-embassy-doha Twitter: @ukinqatar
Ambassador: HE Nicholas Hopton

Romania
British Embassy, 24 Strada Jules Michelet, 010463 Bucharest
Tel: +40 21 201 7200
Email: press.bucharest@fco.gov.uk
Website: www.gov.uk/government/world/organisations/british-embassy-bucharest
blogs.fco.gov.uk/martinharris Twitter: @ukinromania
Ambassador (until August 2014): HE Martin Harris OBE
Ambassador (from August 2014): HE Paul Brummell

Russia
British Embassy, Smolenskaya Naberezhnaya 10, 121099 Moscow
Tel: +7 495 956 7200 Fax: +7 495 956 7481
Email: ukinrussia@fco.gov.uk
Website: www.gov.uk/government/world/organisations/british-embassy-moscow Twitter: @ukinrussia
Ambassador: HE Timothy Barrow CMG LVO MBE

Rwanda
Non-resident Ambassador: Burundi
British High Commission, Parcelle No 1131, Boulevard de l'Umuganda, Kacyiru-Sud, BP 576, Kigali
Tel: +250 252 556000 Fax: +250 252 582044
Email: bhc.kigali@fco.gov.uk
Website: www.gov.uk/government/world/organisations/british-high-commission-kigali
Twitter: @ukinrwanda
High Commissioner: HE Benedict Llewellyn-Jones OBE

St Kitts and Nevis – see Barbados

St Lucia – see Barbados

St Vincent and the Grenadines – see Barbados

Samoa – see New Zealand

San Marino – see Italy

São Tomé and Príncipe – see Angola

Saudi Arabia
British Embassy, PO Box 94351, Riyadh 11693
Tel: +966 1 4819 100 Fax: +966 1 481 9350
Website: www.gov.uk/government/world/organisations/british-embassy-riyadh
Twitter: @ukinsaudiarabia
Ambassador: HE Sir John Jenkins KCMG LVO

Senegal
Non-resident: Cape Verde, Guinea-Bissau
British Embassy, 20 Rue du Docteur Guillet, BP 6025, Dakar
Tel: +221 33 823 73 92 Fax: +221 33 823 27 66
Email: britemb@orange.sn
Website: www.gov.uk/government/world/organisations/british-embassy-dakar
Ambassador: HE John Marshall

Serbia
British Embassy, Resavska 46, 11000 Belgrade
Tel: +381 11 3060 900 Fax: +381 11 3061 070
Email: belgrade.ppd@fco.gov.uk
Website: www.gov.uk/government/world/organisations/british-embassy-belgrade
Ambassador: To be appointed
Chargé d'Affaires: David McFarlane

Seychelles
British High Commission, Third Floor, Oliaji Trade Centre, Francis Rachel Street, Victoria, Mahé
Tel: +248 283 666 Fax: +248 283 657
Email: bhcvictoria@fco.gov.uk
Website: www.gov.uk/government/world/organisations/high-commission-victoria
High Commissioner: HE Lindsay Skoll

Sierra Leone
British High Commission, 6 Spur Road, Freetown
Tel: +232 78124451 Fax: +232 22232070
Email: freetown.general.enquiries@fco.gov.uk
Website: www.gov.uk/government/world/organisations/british-high-commission-freetown
High Commissioner: HE Peter West

Singapore
British High Commission, 100 Tanglin Road, 247919 Singapore
Tel: +65 6424 4200
Website: www.gov.uk/government/world/organisations/british-high-commission-singapore
Twitter: @ukinsingapore
High Commissioner: HE Anthony Phillipson

Slovakia

British Embassy, Panská 16, 811 01 Bratislava
Tel: +421 2 5998 2000 Fax: +421 2 5998 2237
Email: bebra@internet.sk
Website: www.gov.uk/government/world/organisations/british-embassy-bratislava
Ambassador: To be appointed
Chargé d'Affaires: Gill Fraser

Slovenia

British Embassy, Fourth Floor, Trg Republike 3, 1000 Ljubljana
Tel: +386 1 200 3910 Fax: +386 1 425 0174
Email: info@british-embassy.si
Website: www.gov.uk/government/world/organisations/british-embassy-ljubljana
Twitter: @ukinslovenia
Ambassador (until February 2014): HE Andrew Page
Ambassador (from February 2014): HE Sophie Honey

Solomon Islands

Non-resident: Vanuatu
British High Commission, PO Box 676, Telekom House, Mendana Avenue, Honiara
Tel: +677 21705 Fax: +677 21549
Email: bhc@solomon.com.sb
Website: www.gov.uk/government/world/organisations/british-high-commission-honiara
High Commissioner: HE Dominic Meiklejohn OBE

Somalia

c/o British High Commission Nairobi, Upper Hill Road, PO Box 30465-00100 GPO, Nairobi
Tel: +254 20 284 4000
Website: www.gov.uk/government/world/organisations/british-embassy-mogadishu
Twitter: @ukinsomalia
Ambassador: HE Neil Wigan

South Africa

Non-resident: Lesotho, Swaziland
British High Commission, 255 Hill Street, Arcadia 0028, Pretoria
Tel: +27 12 421 7500
Email: media.pretoria@fco.gov.uk
Website: www.gov.uk/government/world/organisations/british-high-commission-pretoria
Twitter: @ukinsouthafrica
High Commissioner: HE Judith MacGregor CMG LVO

South Sudan

British Embassy, EU Compound, Kololo Road, Thom Ping, Juba
Tel: +211 91 232 3712
Email: ukin.southsudan@fco.gov.uk
Website: www.gov.uk/government/world/organisations/british-embassy-juba
Twitter: @ukinsouthsudan
Ambassador: HE Ian Hughes

Spain

Non-resident: Andorra
British Embassy, Torre Espacio, Paseo de la Castellana 259D, 28046 Madrid
Tel: +34 91 714 63 00 Fax: +34 91 714 63 01
Website: www.gov.uk/government/world/organisations/british-embassy-madrid Twitter: @ukinspain
Ambassador: HE Simon Manley CMG

Sri Lanka

Non-resident: Maldives

British High Commission, 389 Bauddhaloka Mawatha, Colombo 7
Tel: +94 11 5390639 Fax: +94 11 5390694
Email: colombo.general@fco.gov.uk
Website: www.gov.uk/government/world/organisations/british-high-commission-colombo
Twitter: @ukinsrilanka

High Commissioner: HE John Rankin

Sudan

British Embassy, off Sharia Al Baladia, Khartoum East, PO Box No 801
Tel: +249 156 775500 Fax: +249 183 776457
Email: information.khartoum@fco.gov.uk
Website: www.gov.uk/government/world/organisations/british-embassy-khartoum
blogs.fco.gov.uk/petertibber

Ambassador: HE Dr Peter Tibber

Suriname – see Guyana

Swaziland – see South Africa

Sweden

British Embassy, Skarpögatan 6-8, Box 27819, 115 93 Stockholm
Tel: +46 8 671 3000 Fax: +46 8 662 9989
Email: stockholm@fco.gov.uk
Website: www.gov.uk/government/world/organisations/british-embassy-stockholm
blogs.fco.gov.uk/pauljohnston Twitter: @ukinsweden

Ambassador: HE Paul Johnston

Switzerland

Non-resident: Liechtenstein

British Embassy, Thunstrasse 50, 3005 Berne
Tel: +41 31 359 77 00 Fax: +41 31 359 77 01
Email: info.berne@fco.gsi.gov.uk
Website: www.gov.uk/government/world/organisations/british-embassy-berne

Ambassador (from December 2013): HE David Moran

Tajikistan

British Embassy, 65 Mirzo Tursunzade Street, 734002 Dushanbe
Tel: +992 372 24 2221 Fax: +992 372 27 1726
Email: dushanbe.reception@fco.gov.uk
Website: www.gov.uk/government/world/organisations/british-embassy-dushanbe
blogs.fco.gov.uk/ukintajikistan Twitter: @ukintajikistan

Ambassador: HE Robin Ord-Smith MVO

Tanzania

British High Commission, Umoja House, Garden Avenue, PO Box 9200, Dar es Salaam
Tel: +255 22 229 0000 Fax: +225 22 211 0102
Email: bhc.dar@fco.gov.uk
Website: www.gov.uk/government/world/organisations/british-high-commission-dar-es-salaam
Twitter: @ukintanzania

High Commissioner: HE Dianna Melrose

Thailand
British Embassy, 14 Wireless Road, Lumpini, Pathumwan, 10330 Bangkok
Tel: +66 2 305 8333 Fax: +66 2 255 9278
Email: info.bangkok@fco.gov.uk
Website: www.gov.uk/government/world/organisations/british-embassy-bangkok
Twitter: @ukinthailand
Ambassador: HE Mark Kent

Timor Leste – see Indonesia

Togo – see Ghana

Tonga – see Fiji

Trinidad and Tobago
British High Commission, 19 St Clair Avenue, St Clair, Port of Spain
Tel: +1 868 350 0444 Fax: +1 868 350 0425
Website: www.gov.uk/government/world/organisations/british-high-commission-trinidad-and-tobago
blogs.fco.gov.uk/arthursnell Twitter: @ukintt
High Commissioner: HE Arthur Snell

Tunisia
British Embassy, Rue du Lac Windermere, Les Berges du Lac, 1053 Tunis
Tel: +216 71 108 700 Fax: +216 71 108 749
Email: british.embassy@planet.tn
Website: www.gov.uk/government/world/organisations/british-embassy-tunis Twitter: @ukintunisia
Ambassador: HE Hamish Cowell

Turkey
British Embassy, Şehit Ersan Caddesi 46/A, Çankaya, Ankara
Tel: +90 312 455 3344 Fax: +90 312 455 3352
Email: info.officer@fco.gov.uk
Website: www.gov.uk/government/world/organisations/british-embassy-ankara Twitter: @ukinturkey
Ambassador (until January 2014): HE Sir David Reddaway KCMG MBE
Ambassador (from January 2014): HE Richard Moore

Turkmenistan
British Embassy, Four Points Ak Altin Hotel, 301-308 Office Building, 744001 Ashgabat
Tel: +993 12 363462 Fax: +993 12 363465
Email: beasb@online.tm
Website: www.gov.uk/government/world/organisations/british-embassy-ashgabat
Ambassador: HE Sanjay Wadvani OBE

Tuvalu – see Fiji

Uganda
British High Commission, 4 Windsor Loop, PO Box 7070, Kampala
Tel: +256 31 2312000 Fax: +256 41 4257304
Email: kampala.bhcinfo@fco.gov.uk
Website: www.gov.uk/government/world/organisations/british-high-commission-kampala
Twitter: @ukinuganda
High Commissioner: HE Alison Blackburne

Ukraine

British Embassy, 9 Desyatynna Street, 01025 Kyiv
Tel: +380 44 490 3660 Fax: +380 44 490 3662
Email: ukembinf@gmail.com
Website: www.gov.uk/government/world/organisations/british-embassy-kyiv
blogs.fco.gov.uk/simonsmith
Ambassador: HE Simon Smith

United Arab Emirates

British Embassy, Khalid bin Al Waleed Street (Street 22), PO Box 248, Abu Dhabi
Tel: +971 2 610 1100 Fax: +971 2 610 1586
Website: www.gov.uk/government/world/organisations/british-embassy-abu-dhabi
blogs.fco.gov.uk/dominicjermey Twitter: @ukinuae

British Embassy, Al Seef Street, PO Box 65, Dubai
Tel: +971 4 309 4444 Fax: +971 4 309 4301
Website: www.gov.uk/government/world/organisations/british-embassy-dubai
Ambassador: HE Dominic Jermey OBE

United States of America

British Embassy, 3100 Massachusetts Avenue NW, Washington DC 20008
Tel: +1 202 588 6500
Email: britishembassyenquiries@gmail.com
Website: www.gov.uk/government/world/organisations/british-embassy-washington
blogs.fco.gov.uk/usa Twitter: @ukinusa
Ambassador: HE Sir Peter Westmacott KCMG LVO

Uruguay

British Embassy, Calle Marco Bruto 1073, 11300 Montevideo
Tel: +598 2622 3630 Fax: +598 2622 7815
Email: ukinuruguay@adinet.com.uy
Website: www.gov.uk/government/world/organisations/british-embassy-montevideo
Twitter: @ukinuruguay
Ambassador: HE Ben Lyster-Binns

Uzbekistan

British Embassy, 67 Gulyamov Street, 100000 Tashkent
Tel: +99 871 120 1500
Email: ukin.uzbekistan@fco.gov.uk
Website: www.gov.uk/government/world/organisations/british-embassy-tashkent
Twitter: @ukinuzbekistan
Ambassador: HE George Edgar OBE

Vanuatu – see Solomon Islands

Venezuela

British Embassy, Torre La Castellana, Piso 11, Avenida La Principal de la Castellana, (Av Eugenio Mendoza) La Castellana, 1061 Caracas
Tel: +58 21 2 263 8411 Fax: +58 21 2 267 1275
Email: ukinvenezuela@fco.gov.uk
Website: www.gov.uk/government/world/organisations/british-embassy-venezuela
Twitter: @ukinvenezuela
Ambassador: HE Catherine Nettleton

Vietnam
British Embassy, Fourth Floor, 31 Hai Ba Trung, Hanoi
Tel: +84 4 936 0500 Fax: +84 4 936 0561
Email: generalenquiries.vietnam@fco.gov.uk
Website: www.gov.uk/government/world/organisations/british-embassy-hanoi
blogs.fco.gov.uk/antonystokes
Ambassador: HE Dr Antony Stokes LVO

Yemen
British Embassy, 938 Thahr Himyar Street, PO Box 1287, East Ring Road, near Mövenpick Hotel, Sana'a
Tel: +967 1 308 114 Fax: +967 1 302 454
Email: britishembassysanaa@fco.gov.uk
Website: www.gov.uk/government/world/organisations/british-embassy-sana-a
Twitter: @ukinyemen
Ambassador: HE Jane Marriott OBE

Zambia
British High Commission, 5210 Independence Avenue, PO Box 50050, 15101 Ridgeway, Lusaka
Tel: +260 211 423200 Fax: +260 211 423291
Email: lusakageneralenquiries@fco.gov.uk
Website: www.gov.uk/government/world/organisations/british-high-commission-lusaka
Twitter: @ukinzambia
High Commissioner: HE James Thornton

Zimbabwe
British Embassy, 3 Norfolk Road, Mount Pleasant, PO Box 4490, Harare
Tel: +263 4 8585 5200 Fax: +263 4 8585 5284
Email: ukinfo.harare@fco.gov.uk
Website: www.gov.uk/government/world/organisations/british-embassy-harare
Ambassador: HE Deborah Bronnert CMG

UK Permanent Representations

UK Delegation to the Council of Europe
Rue Gottfried 18, 67000 Strasbourg, France
Tel: +33 3 88 35 00 78 Fax: +33 3 88 36 74 39
Email: ukdelstrasbourg@fco.gov.uk
Website: www.gov.uk/government/world/organisations/uk-delegation-to-the-council-of-europe
UK Permanent Representative: HE Matthew Johnson

UK Permanent Representation to the EU
Avenue d'Auderghem 10, 1040 Brussels, Belgium
Tel: +32 2 287 82 11
Email: ukrep@fco.gov.uk
Website: www.gov.uk/government/world/organisations/uk-representation-to-the-eu
Twitter: @ukineu
UK Permanent Representative: HE Ivan Rogers

Political and Security Committee
UK Permanent Representative: HE Julian Braithwaite

UK Joint Delegation to NATO

NATO, Boulevard Leopold III, 1110 Brussels, Belgium
Tel: +32 2 707 75 01 Fax: +32 2 707 75 96
Email: ukdel.natogeneralenquiries@fco.gsi.gov.uk
Website: www.gov.uk/government/world/organisations/uk-joint-delegation-to-nato Twitter: @uknato
UK Permanent Representative to the North Atlantic Council: HE Dame Mariot Leslie DCMG

UK Delegation to the OECD

Rue du Faubourg Saint-Honoré 35, 75363 Paris CEDEX, France
Tel: +33 1 44 51 31 00 Fax: +33 1 44 51 31 83
Email: ukoecd@fco.gov.uk
Website: www.gov.uk/government/world/organisations/uk-permanent-delegation-to-the-oecd
blogs.fco.gov.uk/nicholasbridge Twitter: @ukoecd
Ambassador: HE Nick Bridge

UK Delegation to the OSCE

Jaurèsgasse 12, 1030 Vienna, Austria
Tel: +43 1 716130
Email: ukdel@britishembassy.at
Website:
www.gov.uk/government/world/organisations/organisation-for-security-and-co-opertation-in-europe
Twitter: @ukosce
Head of UK Delegation: HE Dominic Schroeder

UK Mission to the UN and other International Organisations (Geneva)

Avenue Louis Casaï 58, Case Postale 6, 1216 Cointrin, Geneva, Switzerland
Tel: +41 22 918 23 00 Fax: +41 22 918 23 33
Website: www.gov.uk/government/world/organisations/uk-mission-to-the-united-nations-geneva
Twitter: @ukmissiongeneva
UK Permanent Representative: HE Karen Pierce CMG

UK Mission to the UN (New York)

One Dag Hammarskjöld Plaza, 885 Second Avenue, New York 10017, USA
Tel: +1 212 745 9200 Fax: +1 212 745 9316
Website: www.gov.uk/government/world/organisations/uk-mission-to-un-in-new-york
Twitter: @ukun_newyork
Ambassador and Permanent Representative: HE Sir Mark Lyall Grant KCMG

UK Mission to the UN and other International Organisations (Vienna)

Jaurèsgasse 12, 1030 Vienna, Austria
Tel: +43 1 716 130 Fax: +43 1 716 134 900
Email: ukmis.vienna@fco.gov.uk
Website: www.gov.uk/government/world/organisations/united-kingdom-mission-to-the-united-nations
Twitter: @ukmissionvienna
UK Permanent Representative: HE Susan le Jeune d'Allegeershecque CMG

London Embassies and High Commissions

Afghanistan

Embassy of the Islamic Republic of Afghanistan, 31 Prince's Gate, London SW7 1QQ
Tel: 020 7589 8891 Fax: 020 7581 3452
Email: info@afghanistanembassy.org.uk Website: www.afghanistanembassy.org.uk
Ambassador: HE Dr Mohammad Daud Yaar

Albania

Embassy of the Republic of Albania, 33 St George's Drive, London SW1V 4DG
Tel: 020 7828 8897 Fax: 020 7828 8869
Email: embassy.london@mfa.gov.al Website: www.albanianembassy.co.uk
Ambassador: HE Mal Berisha

Algeria

Embassy of the People's Democratic Republic of Algeria, 1-3 Riding House Street,
London W1W 7DR
Tel: 020 7299 7077 Fax: 020 7299 7076
Email: info@algerianembassy.org.uk Website: www.algerianembassy.org.uk
Ambassador: HE Amar Abba

Angola

Embassy of the Republic of Angola, 22 Dorset Street, London W1U 6QY
Tel: 020 7299 9850 Fax: 020 7486 9397
Email: embassy@angola.org.uk Website: www.angola.org.uk
Ambassador: HE Miguel Fernandes Neto

Antigua and Barbuda

High Commission for Antigua and Barbuda, Second Floor, 45 Crawford Place, London W1H 4LP
Tel: 020 7258 0070 Fax: 020 7258 7486
Email: enquiries@antigua-barbuda.com Website: www.antigua-barbuda.com
High Commissioner: HE Dr Carl Roberts CMG

Argentina

Embassy of the Argentine Republic, 65 Brook Street, London W1K 4AH
Tel: 020 7318 1300 Fax: 020 7318 1301
Email: info@argentine-embassy-uk.org Website: www.argentine-embassy-uk.org
Ambassador: HE Alicia Castro

Armenia

Embassy of the Republic of Armenia, 25a Cheniston Gardens, London W8 6TG
Tel: 020 7938 5435 Fax: 020 7938 2595
Email: armemb@armenianembassyuk.com Website: www.armenianembassyuk.com
Ambassador: To be appointed
Chargé d'Affaires: Ara Margarian

Australia

Australian High Commission, Australia House, Strand, London WC2B 4LA
Tel: 020 7379 4334 Fax: 020 7240 5333
Email: generalenquiries.lhlh@dfat.gov.au Website: www.uk.embassy.gov.au
Twitter: @aushouselondon
High Commissioner: HE Michael Rann

Austria

Embassy of Austria, 18 Belgrave Mews West, London SW1X 8HU
Tel: 020 7344 3250 Fax: 020 7344 0292
Email: london-ob@bmeia.gv.at Website: www.bmeia.gv.at/en/embassy/london.html
Ambassador: HE Dr Emil Brix

Azerbaijan
Embassy of the Republic of Azerbaijan, 4 Kensington Court, London W8 5DL
Tel: 020 7938 3412 Fax: 020 7937 1783
Email: london@mission.mfa.gov.az Website: www.azembassy.org.uk
Ambassador: HE Fakhraddin Gurbanov

Bahamas
High Commission of the Commonwealth of the Bahamas, 10 Chesterfield Street, London W1J 5JL
Tel: 020 7408 4488 Fax: 020 7499 9937
Email: information@bahamashclondon.net Website: www.bahamashclondon.net
High Commissioner: HE Eldred Bethel

Bahrain
Embassy of the Kingdom of Bahrain, 30 Belgrave Square, London SW1X 8QB
Tel: 020 7201 9170 Fax: 020 7201 9183
Email: information@bahrainembassy.co.uk Website: www.bahrainembassy.co.uk
Ambassador: HE Alice Samaan

Bangladesh
High Commission for the People's Republic of Bangladesh, 28 Queen's Gate, London SW7 5JA
Tel: 020 7584 0081 Fax: 020 7581 7477
Email: info@bhclondon.org.uk Website: www.bhclondon.org.uk
High Commissioner: HE Dr Mijarul Quayes

Barbados
Barbados High Commission, 1 Great Russell Street, London WC1B 3ND
Tel: 020 7631 4975 Fax: 020 7323 6872
Email: london@foreign.gov.bb
High Commissioner: HE Hugh Arthur OBE

Belarus
Embassy of the Republic of Belarus, 6 Kensington Court, London W8 5DL
Tel: 020 7937 3288 Fax: 020 7361 0005
Email: uk.london@mfa.gov.by Website: uk.mfa.gov.by/en
Ambassador: HE Sergei Aleinik

Belgium
Embassy of Belgium, 17 Grosvenor Crescent, London SW1X 7EE
Tel: 020 7470 3700 Fax: 020 7470 3795
Email: london@diplobel.fed.be Website: www.diplomatie.be/london
Ambassador: HE Johan Verbeke

Belize
Belize High Commission, Third Floor, 45 Crawford Place, London W1H 4LP
Tel: 020 7723 3603 Fax: 020 7723 9637
Email: bzhc-lon@btconnect.com Website: www.belizehighcommission.com
High Commissioner: HE Perla Perdomo

Benin
No London Embassy
Embassy of the Republic of Benin, 87 Avenue Victor Hugo, 75116 Paris, France
Tel: +33 1 45 00 98 82 Fax: +33 1 45 01 82 02
Email: contact@ambassade-benin.fr Website: www.ambassade-benin.fr
Ambassador: HE Albert Agossou

UK Consulate
Millennium House, Humber Road, London NW2 6DW
Tel: 020 8830 8612 Fax: 020 7435 0665
Email: beninconsulate@hotmail.co.uk Website: beninconsulate.co.uk/index.html
Honorary Consul: Lawrence Landau

Bhutan
No London Embassy
UK Consulate
2 Windacres Warren Road, Guildford GU1 2HG
Tel: 01483 538189
Email: mrutland@aol.com
Honorary Consul: Michael Rutland

Bolivia
Embassy of Bolivia, 106 Eaton Square, London SW1W 9AD
Tel: 020 7235 4248 Fax: 020 7235 1286
Email: embol@bolivianembassy.co.uk Website: www.bolivianembassy.co.uk
Ambassador: To be appointed
Chargé d'Affaires: Veronica Paola Melendres Argote

Bosnia and Herzegovina
Embassy of Bosnia and Herzegovina, 5-7 Lexham Gardens, London W8 5JJ
Tel: 020 7373 0867 Fax: 020 7373 0871
Email: embassy@bhembassy.co.uk Website: www.bhembassy.co.uk
Ambassador: HE Mustafa Mujezinović

Botswana
Botswana High Commission, 6 Stratford Place, London W1C 1AY
Tel: 020 7499 0031 Fax: 020 7495 8595
Email: bohico@govbw.com
High Commissioner: HE Roy Blackbeard

Brazil
Embassy of Brazil, 14-16 Cockspur Street, London SW1Y 5BL
Tel: 020 7747 4525 Fax: 020 7747 4555
Email: info@brazil.org.uk Website: www.brazil.org.uk
Ambassador: HE Roberto Jaguaribe

Brunei
Brunei Darussalam High Commission, 19-20 Belgrave Square, London SW1X 8PG
Tel: 020 7581 0521 Fax: 020 7235 9717
Email: info@bdhcl.co.uk
High Commissioner: HE Mohd Aziyan Abdullah

Bulgaria
Embassy of the Republic of Bulgaria, 186-188 Queen's Gate, London SW7 5HL
Tel: 020 7581 3144 Fax: 020 7584 4948
Email: info@bulgarianembassy.org.uk Website: www.bulgarianembassy-london.org
Ambassador: HE Konstantin Dimitrov

Burkina Faso

No London Embassy

Embassy of the Republic of Burkina Faso, Place Guy d'Arezzo 16, 1180 Brussels, Belgium
Tel: +32 2 345 99 12 Fax: +32 2 345 06 12
Email: ambassade.burkina@skynet.be Website: www.ambassadeduburkina.be
Ambassador: HE Frédéric Assomption Korsaga

UK Consulate

The Lilacs, Stane Street, Ockley, Surrey RH5 5LU
Tel: 01306 627225
Email: consul@colinseelig.co.uk Website: www.burkinafasovisa.co.uk
Honorary Consul: Colin Seelig

Burma (Myanmar)

Embassy of the Republic of the Union of Myanmar, 19a Charles Street, London W1J 5DX
Tel: 020 3397 4463 Fax: 020 7409 7043
Email: melondon@btconnect.com Website: www.myanmarembassyuk.co.uk
Ambassador: HE Kyaw Myo Htut

Burundi

Embassy of the Republic of Burundi, Second Floor, Uganda House, 58-59 Trafalgar Square,
London WC2N 5DX
Tel: 0207 930 4958 Fax: 0207 930 4957
Email: info@burundiembassy.org.uk Website: www.burundiembassy.org.uk
Ambassador: To be appointed
Chargé d'Affaires: Bernard Ntahiraja

Cambodia

Royal Embassy of Cambodia, 64 Brondesbury Park, Willesden Green, London NW6 7AT
Tel: 020 8451 7997 Fax: 020 8451 7594
Email: cambodianembassy@btconnect.com Website: www.cambodianembassy.org.uk
Ambassador: HE Nambora Hor

Cameroon

High Commission for the Republic of Cameroon, 84 Holland Park, London W11 3SB
Tel: 020 7727 0771 Fax: 020 7792 9353
Email: info@cameroonhighcommission.co.uk Website: www.cameroonhighcommission.co.uk
High Commissioner: HE Nkwelle Ekaney

Canada

Canadian High Commission, Macdonald House, 1 Grosvenor Square, London W1K 4AB
Tel: 020 7258 6600 Fax: 020 7258 6333
Email: ldn@international.gc.ca Website: www.unitedkingdom.gc.ca
High Commissioner: HE Gordon Campbell

Cape Verde

No London Embassy

Embassy of the Republic of Cape Verde, Avenue Jeane 29, 1050 Brussels, Belgium
Tel: +32 2 643 62 70 Fax: +32 2 646 33 85
Ambassador: To be appointed
Chargé d'Affaires: Maria de Jesus Mascarenhas

UK Consulate
7a The Grove, London N6 6JU
Tel: 07876 232305
Email: capeverde@jonathanlux.co.uk
Honorary Consul: Johnathan Lux

Central African Republic
No London Embassy
Embassy of the Central African Republic, 30 rue des Perchamps, 75016 Paris, France
Ambassador: HE Jean Willybiro Sako

Chad
No London Embassy
Embassy of the Republic of Chad, Boulevard Lambermont 52, 1030 Brussels, Belgium
Tel: +32 2 215 19 75 Fax: +32 2 216 35 26
Email: ambassade.tchad@chello.be
Ambassador: HE Ahmat Awad Sakine

Chile
Embassy of Chile, 37-41 Old Queen Street, London SW1H 9JA
Tel: 020 7222 2361 Fax: 020 7222 0861
Email: embachile@embachile.co.uk Website: chileabroad.gov.cl/reino-unido/en
Ambassador: HE Tomás Müller Sproat

China
Embassy of the People's Republic of China, 49-51 Portland Place, London W1B 1JL
Tel: 020 7299 4049
Website: www.chinese-embassy.org.uk
Ambassador: HE Liu Xiaoming

Colombia
Embassy of Colombia, 3 Hans Crescent, London SW1X 0LN
Tel: 020 7589 5037 Fax: 020 7581 1829
Email: elondres@cancilleria.gov.co Website: www.colombianembassy.co.uk
Twitter: @colombianembuk
Ambassador: HE Dr Mauricio Rodríguez Múnera

Democratic Republic of Congo
Embassy of the Democratic Republic of Congo, 45-49 Great Portland Street, London W1W 7LD
Tel: 020 7580 3931 Fax: 020 7580 8713
Email: info@ambardc-londres.gov.cd
Ambassador: HE Dr Barnabé Kikaya Bin Karubi

Republic of Congo
No London Embassy
Embassy of the Republic of Congo, 37 bis Rue Paul Valéry, 75116 Paris, France
Tel: +33 1 45 00 60 57 Fax: +33 1 40 67 17 33
Ambassador: HE Henri Marie Joseph Lopes

UK Consulate
The Arena, 24 Southwark Bridge Road, London SE1 9HF
Tel: 020 7922 0695 Fax: 020 7401 2566
Website: consulateofthecongobrazzaville.webs.com
Honorary Consul: Louis Muzzu

Costa Rica
Embassy of Costa Rica, 14 Lancaster Gate, London W2 3LH
Tel: 020 7706 8844 Fax: 020 7706 8655
Email: info@costaricanembassy.co.uk Website: www.costaricanembassy.co.uk
Ambassador: HE Pilar Saborío Rocafort

Côte d'Ivoire
Embassy of the Republic of Côte d'Ivoire, 2 Upper Belgrave Street, London SW1X 8BJ
Tel: 020 7235 6991 Fax: 020 7259 5320
Ambassador: HE Claude Bouah-Kamon

Croatia
Embassy of the Republic of Croatia, 21 Conway Street, London W1T 6BN
Tel: 020 7387 2022 Fax: 020 7387 0310
Email: vrhlon@mvep.hr Website: uk.mfa.hr
Ambassador: HE Ivan Grdešić

Cuba
Embassy of the Republic of Cuba, 167 High Holborn, London WC1V 6PA
Tel: 020 7240 2488 Fax: 020 7836 2602
Email: secembajador@uk.embacuba.cu
Website: www.cubadiplomatica.cu/reinounido/en/home.aspx
Ambassador: HE Esther Armenteros Cárdenas

Cyprus
High Commission of the Republic of Cyprus, 13 St James's Square, London SW1Y 4LB
Tel: 020 7321 4100 Fax: 020 7321 4164
Email: cyphclondon@btconnect.com Website: www.mfa.gov.cy/mfa/highcom/highcom_london.nsf/
dmlindex_en/dmlindex_en?opendocument
High Commissioner: To be appointed
Deputy High Commissioner: Yiorgos Christofides

Czech Republic
Embassy of the Czech Republic, 26 Kensington Palace Gardens, London W8 4QY
Tel: 020 7243 1115 Fax: 020 7727 9654
Email: london@embassy.mzv.cz Website: www.czechembassy.org.uk
Ambassador: HE Michael Žantovský

Denmark
Royal Danish Embassy, 55 Sloane Street, London SW1X 9SR
Tel: 020 7333 0200 Fax: 020 7333 0270
Email: lonamb@um.dk Website: www.denmark.org.uk Twitter: @denmarkinuk
Ambassador: Claus Grube

Djibouti
No London Embassy
Embassy of the Republic of Djibouti, 26 Rue Emilie Ménier, 75116 Paris, France
Tel: +33 1 47 27 49 22 Fax: +33 1 45 53 50 53
Email: webmaster@amb-djibouti.org
Ambassador: HE Rachad Farah

Dominica
High Commission for the Commonwealth of Dominica, 1 Collingham Gardens, London SW5 0HW
Tel: 020 7370 5194 Fax: 020 7373 8743
Email: info@dominicahighcommission.co.uk Website: www.dominicahighcommission.co.uk
High Commissioner: HE Francine Baron-Royer

Dominican Republic
Embassy of the Dominican Republic, 139 Inverness Terrace, London W2 6JF
Tel: 020 7727 7091 Fax: 020 7727 3693
Email: info@dominicanembassy.org.uk Website: www.dominicanembassy.org.uk
Ambassador: HE Dr Federico Alberto Cuello Camilo

Ecuador
Embassy of Ecuador, Flat 3b, 3 Hans Crescent, London SW1X 0LS
Tel: 020 7584 1367 Fax: 020 7590 2509
Email: eecugranbretania@mmrree.gov.ec Website: www.ecuadorembassyuk.org.uk
Twitter: @ceculondres
Ambassador: HE Juan Falconi Puig

Egypt
Embassy of the Arab Republic of Egypt, 26 South Street, London W1K 1DW
Tel: 020 7499 3304 Fax: 020 7491 1542
Email: eg.emb_london@mfa.gov.eg Twitter: @egyptconsulatuk
Ambassador: HE Ashraf Elkholy

El Salvador
Embassy of El Salvador, 8 Dorset Square, London NW1 6PU
Tel: 020 7224 9800 Fax: 020 7224 9878
Email: embajadalondres@rree.gob.sv Twitter: @elsembassy
Ambassador: HE Werner Romero

Equatorial Guinea
Embassy of the Republic of Equatorial Guinea, 13 Park Place, London SW1A 1LP
Tel: 020 7499 6867 Fax: 020 7499 6782
Email: embarege-londres@embarege-londres.org
Ambassador: HE Maricruz Evuna Andeme

Eritrea
Embassy of the State of Eritrea, 96 White Lion Street, London N1 9PF
Tel: 020 7713 0096 Fax: 020 7713 0161
Email: eriemba@eriembauk.com
Ambassador: HE Tesfamicael Gerahtu Ogbaghiorghis

Estonia
Embassy of the Republic of Estonia, 16 Hyde Park Gate, London SW7 5DG
Tel: 020 7589 3428 Fax: 020 7589 3430
Email: london@mfa.ee Website: www.estonia.gov.uk Twitter: @estembassyuk
Ambassador: HE Aino Lepik von Wirén

Ethiopia
Embassy of the Federal Democratic Republic of Ethiopia, 17 Prince's Gate, London SW7 1PZ
Tel: 020 7589 7212 Fax: 020 7584 7054
Email: info@ethioembassy.org.uk Website: www.ethioembassy.org.uk
Ambassador: HE Berhanu Kebede

Fiji

High Commission of the Republic of the Fiji Islands, 34 Hyde Park Gate, London SW7 5DN
Tel: 020 7584 3661 Fax: 020 7584 2838
Email: mail@fijihighcommission.org.uk Website: www.fijihighcommission.org.uk
High Commissioner: HE Solo Mara

Finland

Embassy of Finland, 38 Chesham Place, London SW1X 8HW
Tel: 020 7838 6200 Fax: 020 7235 3680
Email: sanomat.lon@formin.fi Website: www.finemb.org.uk Twitter: @finlandinuk
Ambassador: HE Pekka Huhtaniemi

France

Embassy of France, 58 Knightsbridge, London SW1X 7JT
Tel: 020 7073 1000 Fax: 020 7073 1004
Website: www.ambafrance-uk.org
Ambassador: HE Bernard Emié

Gabon

Embassy of the Gabonese Republic, 27 Elvaston Place, London SW7 5NL
Tel: 020 7823 9986 Fax: 020 7584 0047
Website: gabonembassyuk.org
Ambassador: HE Omer Piankali

The Gambia

The Gambia High Commission, 92 Ledbury Road, London W11 2AH
Tel: 020 7229 8066 Fax: 020 7229 9225
Email: gambiahighcomuk@btconnect.com
High Commissioner: HE Elizabeth Ya Eli Harding

Georgia

Embassy of Georgia, 4 Russell Gardens, London W14 8EZ
Tel: 020 7348 1941 Fax: 020 7603 6682
Email: embassy@geoemb.plus.com Website: www.uk.mfa.gov.ge
Ambassador: To be appointed
Chargé d'Affaires: Tamar Kapanadze

Germany

Embassy of the Federal Republic of Germany, 23 Belgrave Square, London SW1X 8PZ
Tel: 020 7824 1300 Fax: 020 7824 1449
Email: info@london.diplo.de Website: www.london.diplo.de Twitter: @germanembassy
Ambassador: To be appointed
Chargé d'Affaires: Dr Rudolf Adam

Ghana

High Commission for Ghana, 13 Belgrave Square, London SW1X 8PN
Tel: 020 7201 5921 Fax: 020 7245 9552
Email: ghmfa31@yahoo.com Website: www.ghanahighcommissionuk.com
High Commissioner: HE Prof Kwaku Danso-Boafo

Greece
Embassy of Greece, 1a Holland Park, London W11 3TP
Tel: 020 7229 3850 Fax: 020 7229 7221
Email: political@greekembassy.org.uk Website: www.mfa.gr/uk/en
Ambassador: HE Konstantinos Bikas

Grenada
High Commission for Grenada, The Chapel, Archel Road, London W14 9QH
Tel: 020 7385 4415 Fax: 020 7381 4807
Email: office@grenada-highcommission.co.uk Website: www.grenadahclon.co.uk
Twitter: @grenadahcuk
High Commissioner: HE Joslyn Whiteman

Guatemala
Embassy of Guatemala, 13 Fawcett Street, London SW10 9HN
Tel: 020 7351 3042 Fax: 020 7376 5708
Email: embassy.gtm@btconnect.com
Ambassador: HE Acisclo Valladares Molina

Guinea
Embassy of the Republic of Guinea, 258 Belsize Road, London NW6 4BT
Tel: 020 7316 1861 Fax: 020 7316 1861
Email: office@ambaguinee-london.co.uk
Ambassador: To be appointed
Chargé d'Affaires: Sangare Ramatoulaye

Guinea-Bissau
No London Embassy
Embassy of the Republic of Guinea-Bissau, Rue St Lazare 94, 75009 Paris, France
Tel: +33 1 48 74 36 39
Ambassador: To be appointed

Guyana
High Commission for Guyana, 3 Palace Court, Bayswater Road, London W2 4LP
Tel: 020 7229 7684 Fax: 020 7727 9809
Email: guyanahc1@btconnect.com Website: www.guyanahclondon.co.uk
High Commissioner: HE Laleshwar Singh

Haiti
Embassy of the Republic of Haiti, 14 Cavendish Place, London W1G 9DJ
Tel: 020 7637 8985 Email: amb.royaumeuni@diplomatie.ht
Ambassador: To be appointed
Chargé d'Affaires: Valerie Pompee

Holy See
Apostolic Nunciature, 54 Parkside, London SW19 5NE
Tel: 020 8944 7189 Fax: 020 8947 2494
Email: nuntius@globalnet.co.uk
Apostolic Nuncio: HE Archbishop Antonio Mennini

Honduras
Embassy of Honduras, 115 Gloucester Place, London W1U 6JT
Tel: 020 7486 4880 Fax: 020 7486 4550
Email: hondurasuk@lineone.net
Ambassador: HE Ivan Romero-Martinez

Hungary

Embassy of Hungary, 35 Eaton Place, London SW1X 8BY
Tel: 020 7204 3440 Fax: 020 7823 1348
Email: mission.lon@mfa.gov.hu Website: www.mfa.gov.hu/emb/london
Ambassador: HE János Csák

Iceland

Embassy of Iceland, 2a Hans Street, London SW1X 0JE
Tel: 020 7259 3999 Fax: 020 7245 9649
Email: icemb.london@utn.stjr.is Website: www.iceland.is/uk Twitter: @icelandinuk
Ambassador: HE Benedikt Jónsson

India

High Commission for India, India House, Aldwych, London WC2B 4NA
Tel: 020 7836 8484 Fax: 020 7836 4331
Email: hc.office@hcilondon.in Website: hcilondon.in
Acting High Commissioner: Dr Virander Paul

Indonesia

Embassy of the Republic of Indonesia, 38 Grosvenor Square, London W1K 2HW
Tel: 020 7499 7661 Fax: 020 7491 4993
Email: kbri@btconnect.com Website: www.indonesianembassy.org.uk
Ambassador: HE Teuku Hamzah Thayeb

Iraq

Embassy of the Republic of Iraq, 21 Queen Gate, London SW7 5JE
Tel: 020 7590 7650 Fax: 020 7590 7679
Website: www.mofamission.gov.iq/grb/en/articles.aspx
Ambassador: HE Faik Nerweyi

Ireland

Embassy of Ireland, 17 Grosvenor Place, London SW1X 7HR
Tel: 020 7235 2171 Fax: 020 7589 8450
Email: londonembassymail@dfa.ie Website: www.embassyofireland.co.uk Twitter: @irelandembgb
Ambassador: HE Dan Mulhall

Israel

Embassy of Israel, 2 Palace Green, London W8 4QB
Tel: 020 7957 9500 Fax: 020 7957 9555
Email: info@london.mfa.gov.il Website: www.embassyofisrael.co.uk Twitter: @israelinuk
Ambassador: HE Daniel Taub

Italy

Embassy of Italy, 14 Three Kings Yard, Davies Street, London W1K 4EH
Tel: 020 7312 2200 Fax: 020 7312 2230
Email: ambasciata.londra@esteri.it Website: www.amblondra.esteri.it Twitter: @stampaamblondra
Ambassador: HE Pasquale Terracciano

Ivory Coast – see Côte d'Ivoire

Jamaica

Jamaican High Commission, 1-2 Prince Consort Road, London SW7 2BZ
Tel: 020 7823 9911 Fax: 020 7589 5154
Email: jamhigh@jhcuk.com Website: www.jhcuk.org
High Commissioner: HE Aloun Ndombet-Assamba

Japan

Embassy of Japan, 101-104 Piccadilly, London W1J 7JT
Tel: 020 7465 6500 Fax: 020 7491 9348
Email: info@ld.mofa.go.jp Website: www.uk.emb-japan.go.jp Twitter: @japaninuk
Ambassador: HE Keiichi Hayashi

Jordan

Embassy of the Hashemite Kingdom of Jordan, 6 Upper Phillimore Gardens, London W8 7HA
Tel: 020 7937 3685 Fax: 020 7937 8795
Email: london@fm.gov.jo Website: www.jordanembassy.org.uk
Ambassador: HE Mazen Kemal al-Homoud

Kazakhstan

Embassy of the Republic of Kazakhstan, 33 Thurloe Square, London SW7 2DS
Tel: 020 7590 3490 Fax: 020 7584 8481
Email: london@kazembassy.org.uk Website: www.kazembassy.org.uk
Ambassador: HE Kairat Abusseitov

Kenya

Kenya High Commission, 45 Portland Place, London W1B 1AS
Tel: 020 7636 2371 Fax: 020 7323 6717
Email: info@kenyahighcommission.net Website: www.kenyahighcommission.net
High Commissioner: HE Ephraim Ngare

Kiribati

No London High Commission
Kiribati High Commissioner, c/o Office of the President, PO Box 68, Bairiki, Tarawa, Kiribati
Acting High Commissioner: Makurita Baaro

UK Consulate

The Great House, Llandewi Rydderch, Monmouthshire NP7 9UY
Tel: 01873 840375 Fax: 01873 840375
Email: mravellwalsh@btopenworld.com
Honorary Consul: Michael Ravell Walsh

Democratic People's Republic of Korea (North)

Embassy of the Democratic People's Republic of Korea, 73 Gunnersbury Avenue, London W5 4LP
Tel: 020 8992 4965 Fax: 020 8992 2053
Email: dprkrepmission@yahoo.co.uk
Ambassador: HE Hyon Hak Bong

Republic of Korea (South)

Embassy of the Republic of Korea, 60 Buckingham Gate, London SW1E 6AJ
Tel: 020 7227 5500 Fax: 020 7227 5503
Email: koreanembinuk@mofat.go.kr Website: gbr.mofat.go.kr/english/eu/gbr/main/index.jsp
Ambassador: HE Sungnam Lim

Kosovo

Embassy of the Republic of Kosovo, 100 Pall Mall, London SW1Y 5NQ
Tel: 020 7659 6140 Fax: 020 7659 6137
Email: embassy.uk@ks-gov.net Website: www.ambasada-ks.net/gb
Ambassador: HE Lirim Greiçevci

Kuwait

Embassy of the State of Kuwait, 2 Albert Gate, London SW1X 7JU
Tel: 020 7590 3400 Fax: 020 7823 1712
Ambassador: HE Khaled Al Duwaisan GCVO

Kyrgyzstan

Embassy of the Kyrgyz Republic, Ascot House, 119 Crawford Street, London W1U 6BJ
Tel: 020 7935 1462 Fax: 020 7935 7449
Email: mail@kyrgyz-embassy.org.uk Website: www.kyrgyz-embassy.org.uk
Twitter: @kyrgyzembassy
Ambassador: To be appointed
Chargé d'Affaires: Aibek Tilebaliev

Laos

No London Embassy
Embassy of the Lao People's Democratic Republic, 74 Avenue Raymond-Poincaré, 75116 Paris,
France
Tel: +33 1 45 53 02 98 Fax: +33 1 47 27 57 89
Email: ambalaoparis@wanadoo.fr Website: www.laoparis.com
Ambassador: HE Khouanta Phalivong

Latvia

Embassy of the Republic of Latvia, 45 Nottingham Place, London W1U 5LY
Tel: 020 7312 0041 Fax: 020 7312 0042
Email: embassy.uk@mfa.gov.lv Website: www.london.mfa.gov.lv
Ambassador: HE Andris Teikmanis

Lebanon

Embassy of Lebanon, 21 Palace Gardens Mews, London W8 4RB
Tel: 020 7229 7265 Fax: 020 7243 1699
Email: emb.leb@btinternet.com Website: lebaneseembassyuk.org
Ambassador: HE Inaam Osseiran

Lesotho

High Commission of the Kingdom of Lesotho, 7 Chesham Place, London SW1X 8HN
Tel: 020 7235 5686 Fax: 020 7235 5023
Email: lhc@lesotholondon.org.uk Website: www.lesotholondon.org.uk
Acting High Commissioner: Maanna Mapetja

Liberia

Embassy of the Republic of Liberia, 23 Fitzroy Square, London W1 6EW
Tel: 020 7388 5489 Fax: 020 7388 2899
Email: info@embassyofliberia.org.uk Website: www.embassyofliberia.org.uk
Ambassador: HE Wesley Johnson

Libya
Embassy of Libya, 15 Knightsbridge, London SW1X 7LY
Tel: 020 7201 8280 Fax: 020 7245 0588
Website: www.libyanembassy.org
Ambassador: HE Mahmud Nacua

Lithuania
Embassy of the Republic of Lithuania, Lithuania House, 2 Bessborough Gardens, London SW1V 2JE
Tel: 020 7592 2840 Fax: 020 7592 2864
Email: amb.uk@urm.lt Website: uk.mfa.lt
Ambassador: HE Asta Skaisgirytė Liauškienė

Luxembourg
Embassy of Luxembourg, 27 Wilton Crescent, London SW1X 8SD
Tel: 020 7235 6961 Fax: 020 7235 9734
Email: londres.amb@mae.etat.lu Website: londres.mae.lu/en
Ambassador: HE Patrick Engelberg

Former Yugoslav Republic of Macedonia
Embassy of the Republic of Macedonia, Suites 2.1-2.2, Buckingham Court, 75-83 Buckingham Gate, London SW1E 6PE
Tel: 020 7066 0535 Fax: 020 7976 0539
Email: info@macedonianembassy.org.uk Website: www.macedonianembassy.org.uk
Ambassador: HE Jovan Donev

Madagascar
No London Embassy
Embassy of the Republic of Madagascar, 4 Avenue Raphael, 75016 Paris, France
Tel: +33 1 45 04 62 11 Fax: +33 1 45 03 58 70
Email: accueil@ambassade-madagascar.fr Website: ambassade-madagascar.fr
Ambassador: To be appointed

Malawi
High Commission for the Republic of Malawi, 36 John Street, London WC1N 2AT
Tel: 020 7421 6010 Fax: 020 7831 9273
Email: malawi@malawihighcommission.co.uk Website: www.malawihighcommission.co.uk
High Commissioner: HE Bernard Sande

Malaysia
Malaysian High Commission, 45 Belgrave Square, London SW1X 8QT
Tel: 020 7235 8033 Fax: 020 7235 5161
Email: mwlondon@btinternet.com
High Commissioner: HE Datuk Zakaria bin Sulong

Maldives
High Commission of the Republic of Maldives, 22 Nottingham Place, London W1U 5NJ
Tel: 020 7224 2135 Fax: 020 7224 2157
Email: info@maldiveshighcommission.org Website: www.maldiveshighcommission.org
Acting High Commissioner: Ahmed Shiaan

Mali

No London Embassy

Embassy of the Republic of Mali, Avenue Molière 487, 1050 Brussels, Belgium
Tel: +32 2 345 74 32 Fax: +32 2 344 57 00
Email: info@amba-mali.be Website: www.amba-mali.be
Ambassador: HE Ibrahim Bocar Ba

Malta

Malta High Commission, Malta House, 36-38 Piccadilly, London W1J 0LE
Tel: 020 7292 4800 Fax: 020 7292 4803
Email: maltahighcommission.london@gov.mt Website: www.foreign.gov.mt/default.aspx?mdis=403
High Commissioner: Norman Hamilton

Mauritania

No London Embassy

Embassy of the Islamic Republic of Mauritania, 5 Rue de Montevideo, 75116 Paris, France
Tel: +33 1 45 04 83 54
Ambassador: To be appointed
Chargé d'Affaires: Mohamed Yahya Sidi Haiba

Mauritius

Mauritius High Commission, 32-33 Elvaston Place, London SW7 5NW
Tel: 020 7581 0294 Fax: 020 7823 8437
Email: londonmhc@btinternet.com
High Commissioner: HE Abhimanu Kundasamy

Mexico

Embassy of Mexico, 16 St George Street, London W1S 1FD
Tel: 020 7499 8586 Fax: 020 7495 4035
Email: embgbretana@sre.gob.mx Website: www.sre.gob.mx/reinounido Twitter: @embamexru
Ambassador: To be appointed
Chargé d'Affaires: Alejandro Estivill Castro

Moldova

Embassy of the Republic of Moldova, 5 Dolphin Square, Edensor Road, London W4 2ST
Tel: 020 8995 6818 Fax: 020 8995 6927
Email: embassy.london@mfa.md Website: www.britania.mfa.gov.md
Ambassador: HE Iulian Fruntaşu

Monaco

Embassy of the Principality of Monaco, 7 Upper Grosvenor Street, London W1K 2LX
Tel: 020 7318 1081 Fax: 020 7493 4563
Email: embassy@gouv.mc Website: www.monaco-embassy-uk.gouv.mc
Ambassador: HE Evelyne Genta

Mongolia

Embassy of Mongolia, 7 Kensington Court, London W8 5DL
Tel: 020 7937 0150 Fax: 020 7937 1117
Email: office@embassyofmongolia.co.uk Website: www.embassyofmongolia.co.uk
Ambassador: HE Narkhuu Tulgu

Montenegro
Embassy of Montenegro, 18 Callcott Street, London W8 7SU
Tel: 020 7727 6007 Fax: 020 7243 9358
Email: unitedkingdom@mfa.gov.me
Ambassador: HE Prof Ljubiša Stanković

Morocco
Embassy of the Kingdom of Morocco, 49 Queen's Gate Gardens, London SW7 5NE
Tel: 020 7581 5001 Fax: 020 7225 3862
Email: ambalondres@maec.gov.ma Website: www.moroccanembassylondon.org.uk
Ambassador: HE HH Princess Lalla Joumala Alaoui

Mozambique
High Commission for the Republic of Mozambique, 21 Fitzroy Square, London W1T 6EL
Tel: 020 7383 3800 Fax: 020 7383 3801
Website: www.mozambiquehighcommission.org.uk
High Commissioner: HE Carlos dos Santos

Myanmar – see Burma

Namibia
High Commission for the Republic of Namibia, 6 Chandos Street, London W1G 9LU
Tel: 020 7636 6244 Fax: 020 7637 5694
Email: info@namibiahc.org.uk Website: www.namibiahc.org.uk
High Commissioner: To be appointed
Minister Counsellor: Michael Ndivayele

Nauru
No London High Commission
High Commissioner: To be appointed

UK Consulate
Romshed Courtyard, Underriver, nr Sevenoaks, Kent TN15 0SD
Tel: 01732 746061 Fax: 01732 746062
Email: nauru@weald.co.uk
Honorary Consul: Martin Weston

Nepal
Embassy of Nepal, 12a Kensington Palace Gardens, London W8 4QU
Tel: 020 7229 1594 Fax: 020 7792 9861
Email: eon@nepembassy.org.uk Website: www.nepembassy.org.uk
Ambassador: HE Dr Suresh Chalise

Netherlands
Royal Netherlands Embassy, 38 Hyde Park Gate, London SW7 5DP
Tel: 020 7590 3200 Fax: 020 7225 0947
Email: lon@minbuza.nl Website: www.dutchembassyuk.org Twitter: @dutchembassyuk
Ambassador: HE Laetitia van den Assum

New Zealand
New Zealand High Commission, New Zealand House, 80 Haymarket, London SW1Y 4TQ
Tel: 020 7930 8422 Fax: 020 7839 4580
Email: aboutnz@newzealandhc.org.uk Website: www.nzembassy.com/uk
High Commissioner: HE Dr Lockwood Smith

Nicaragua

Embassy of Nicaragua, Suite 31, Vicarage House, 58-60 Kensington Church Street, London W8 4DB
Tel: 020 7938 2373 Fax: 020 7937 0952
Email: embaniclondon@btconnect.com
Ambassador: HE Dr Carlos Argüello-Gómez

Niger

No London Embassy
Embassy of the Republic of Niger, 154 Rue de Longchamp, 75116 Paris, France
Tel: +33 1 45 04 80 60 Fax: +33 1 45 04 79 73
Website: ambassadeniger-fr.org
Ambassador: HE Adamou Seydou

UK Consulate

MPC House, 15 Maple Mews, London NW6 5UZ
Tel: 020 7328 8180 Fax: 020 7328 8120
Email: consulate@nigerconsulateuk.org Website: www.nigerconsulateuk.org
Honorary Consul: Muhammadu Dikko Ladan

Nigeria

High Commission for the Federal Republic of Nigeria, Nigeria House, 9 Northumberland Avenue,
London WC2N 5BX
Tel: 020 7839 1244 Fax: 020 7839 8746
Email: information@nigeriahc.org.uk Website: www.nigeriahc.org.uk
High Commissioner: HE Dr Dalhatu Tafida

Norway

Royal Norwegian Embassy, 25 Belgrave Square, London SW1X 8QD
Tel: 020 7591 5500 Fax: 020 7591 5501
Email: emb.london@mfa.no Website: www.norway.org.uk Twitter: @norwayinuk
Ambassador: HE Kim Traavik

Oman

Embassy of the Sultanate of Oman, 167 Queen's Gate, London SW7 5HE
Tel: 020 7225 0001 Fax: 020 7589 2505
Email: theembassy@omanembassy.org.uk Website: www.omanembassy.org.uk
Ambassador: HE Abdul Aziz Al Hinai

Pakistan

High Commission for the Islamic Republic of Pakistan, 35-36 Lowndes Square, London SW1X 9JN
Tel: 020 7664 9200 Fax: 020 7664 9224
Website: www.pakmission-uk.gov.pk
Acting High Commissioner: Syed Zulfiqar Gardezi

Palau

No London Embassy

UK Consulate

Bankfoot Square, Bankfoot Street, Batley WF17 5LH
Tel: 01924 470786 Fax: 01924 474747
Website: palauconsulate.org.uk
Honorary Consul: Mr Q Mohammed

Panama
Embassy of Panama, 40 Hertford Street, London W1J 7SH
Tel: 020 7493 4646 Fax: 020 7493 4333
Email: panama1@btconnect.com Website: www.panamaconsul.co.uk
Ambassador: HE Ana Delgado

Papua New Guinea
Papua New Guinea High Commission, Ground Floor, 14 Waterloo Place, London SW1Y 4AR
Tel: 020 7930 0922 Fax: 020 7930 0828
Email: info@png.org.uk Website: www.pnghighcomm.org.uk
High Commissioner: HE Winnie Kiap

Paraguay
Embassy of the Republic of Paraguay, Third Floor, 344 Kensington High Street, London W14 8NS
Tel: 020 7610 4180 Fax: 020 7371 4297
Email: embaparuk@btconnect.com Website: www.paraguayembassy.co.uk
Ambassador: HE Miguel Angel Solano López Casco

Peru
Embassy of Peru, 52 Sloane Street, London SW1X 9SP
Tel: 020 7235 1917 Fax: 020 7235 4463
Email: postmaster@peruembassy-uk.com Website: www.peruembassy-uk.com
Ambassador: HE Julio Muñoz-Deacon

Philippines
Embassy of the Republic of the Philippines, 6-8 Suffolk Street, London SW1Y 4HG
Tel: 020 7451 1780 Fax: 020 7930 9787
Email: embassy@philemb.co.uk Website: philembassy-uk.org Twitter: @philemblondon
Ambassador: HE Enrique Manalo

Poland
Embassy of the Republic of Poland, 47 Portland Place, London W1B 1JH
Tel: 020 7291 3520 Fax: 020 7291 3575
Email: london@msz.gov.pl Website: london.polemb.net Twitter: @polishembassyuk
Ambassador: HE Witold Sobków

Portugal
Embassy of Portugal, 11 Belgrave Square, London SW1X 8PP
Tel: 020 7235 5331 Fax: 020 7245 1287
Email: londres@me.pt
Ambassador: HE João de Vallera

Qatar
Embassy of the State of Qatar, 1 South Audley Street, London W1K 1NB
Tel: 020 7493 2200 Fax: 020 7493 2819
Website: www.qatarembassy.info
Ambassador: HE Khalid Rashid Salem Al-Homoudi Al-Mansouri

Romania
Embassy of Romania, Arundel House, 4 Palace Green, London W8 4QD
Tel: 020 7937 9666 Fax: 020 7937 8069
Email: roemb@roemb.co.uk Website: londra.mae.ro
Ambassador: HE Dr Ion Jinga

Russia

Embassy of the Russian Federation, 6-7 Kensington Palace Gardens, London W8 4QP
Tel: 020 7229 6412 Fax: 020 7727 8625
Email: office@rusemblon.org Website: www.great-britain.mid.ru Twitter: @russianembassy
Ambassador: HE Alexander Yakovenko

Rwanda

High Commission for the Republic of Rwanda, 120-122 Seymour Place, London W1H 1NR
Tel: 020 7224 9832 Fax: 020 7724 8642
Email: uk@ambarwanda.org.uk Website: www.rwandahc.org Twitter: @rwandahcuk
High Commissioner: HE Williams Nkurunziza

St Kitts and Nevis

High Commission for Saint Christopher and Nevis, 10 Kensington Court, London W8 5DL
Tel: 020 7937 9718 Fax: 020 7937 7484
Email: info@sknhc.co.uk Website: www.stkittsnevisuk.com
High Commissioner: HE Kevin Isaac

St Lucia

High Commission for Saint Lucia, 1 Collingham Gardens, London SW5 0HW
Tel: 020 7370 7123 Fax: 020 7370 1905
Email: enquiries@stluciahcuk.org Website: www.stluciahcuk.org
High Commissioner: HE Dr Ernest Hilaire

St Vincent and the Grenadines

High Commission for Saint Vincent and the Grenadines, 10 Kensington Court, London W8 5DL
Tel: 020 7460 1256 Fax: 020 7937 6040
Email: info@svghighcom.co.uk Website: www.svghighcom.co.uk Twitter: @svghighcom
High Commissioner: HE Cenio Lewis

Samoa

No London High Commission
Embassy of Samoa, Avenue de l'Orée 20, 1000 Brussels, Belgium
Tel: +32 2 660 84 54 Fax: +32 2 675 03 36
Email: info@samoaembassy.be Website: www.samoaembassy.be
High Commissioner: HE Fatumanava Dr Pa'olelei Luteru

UK Consulate

Church Cottage, Pedlinge, nr Hythe, Kent CT21 5JL
Tel: 01303 260541 Fax: 01303 238058
Honorary Consul: Prunella Scarlett LVO

San Marino

No London Embassy
Embassy of the Republic of San Marino, Department of Foreign Affairs, Palazzo Begni – Contrada
Omerelli, 47890 San Marino
Tel: +378 0549 992018
Email: dipartimentoaffariesteri@pa.sm
Ambassador: HE Federica Bigi

UK consulate
Flat 51, 162 Sloane Street, London SW1X 9BS
Tel: 020 7823 4768 Fax: 020 7823 4768
Email: consolato.londra.sm@gmail.com
Honorary Consul: Teodorani Fabbri

São Tomé and Príncipe
No London Embassy
Embassy of São Tomé and Principé, Avenue de Tervuren 175, 1150 Brussels, Belgium
Tel: +32 2 734 89 66 Fax: +32 2 734 88 15
Email: ambassade@saotomeeprincipe.be
Ambassador: To be appointed
Chargé d'Affaires: Armindo de Brito Fernandes

UK Consulate
Flat 8, Marsham Court, 58 Victoria Drive, London SW19 6BB
Tel: 020 8788 6139
Honorary Consul: Nathalie Galland-Burkl

Saudi Arabia
Royal Embassy of Saudi Arabia, 30 Charles Street, London W1J 5DZ
Tel: 020 7917 3000
Email: ukemb@mofa.gov.sa Website: www.saudiembassy.org.uk
Ambassador: HE HRH Prince Mohammed bin Nawaf Al Saud

Senegal
Embassy of the Republic of Senegal, 39 Marloes Road, London W8 6LA
Tel: 020 7938 4048 Fax: 020 7938 2546
Email: senegalembassy@hotmail.co.uk
Ambassador: HE Abdou Sourang

Serbia
Embassy of the Republic of Serbia, 28 Belgrave Square, London SW1X 8QB
Tel: 020 7235 9049 Fax: 020 7235 7092
Email: london@serbianembassy.org.uk Website: www.serbianembassy.org.uk
Ambassador: To be appointed
Chargé d'Affaires: Nebojša Radojičić

Seychelles
High Commission of the Republic of Seychelles, Fourth Floor, 130-132 Buckingham Palace Road, London SW1W 9SA
Tel: 020 7245 0680 Fax: 020 7235 7509
Email: seyhc.london@btconnect.com
High Commissioner: HE Marie-Pierre Lloyd

Sierra Leone
Sierra Leone High Commission, 41 Eagle Street, London WC1R 4TL
Tel: 020 7404 0140 Fax: 020 7430 9862
Email: info@slhc-uk.org.uk Website: www.slhc-uk.org.uk
High Commissioner: HE Edward Turay

Singapore
High Commission for the Republic of Singapore, 9 Wilton Crescent, London SW1X 8SP
Tel: 020 7235 8315 Fax: 020 7245 6583
Email: singhc_lon@sgmfa.gov.sg Website: www.mfa.gov.sg/london Twitter: @shclon
High Commissioner: HE Thambynathan Jasudasen

Slovakia
Embassy of the Slovak Republic, 25 Kensington Palace Gardens, London W8 4QY
Tel: 020 7313 6470 Fax: 020 7313 6481
Email: emb.london@mzv.sk Website: www.mzv.sk/londyn
Ambassador: HE Miroslav Wlachovský

Slovenia
Embassy of the Republic of Slovenia, 10 Little College Street, London SW1P 3SH
Tel: 020 7222 5400 Fax: 020 7222 5277
Email: vlo@gov.si Website: www.london.embassy.si Twitter: @sl_embassyuk
Ambassador: HE Iztok Jarc

Solomon Islands
No London High Commission
High Commission for the Solomon Islands, Avenue Edouard Lacombe 17b, 1040 Brussels, Belgium
Tel: +32 2 732 70 85 Fax: +32 2 732 68 85
High Commissioner: HE Joseph Ma'ahanua

South Africa
South African High Commission, South Africa House, Trafalgar Square, London WC2N 5DP
Tel: 020 7451 7299 Fax: 020 7839 5670
Email: london.general@foreign.gov.za Website: www.southafricahouseuk.com
High Commissioner: HE Dr Zola Skweyiya

South Sudan
Embassy of the Republic of South Sudan, 28-32 Wellington Road, London NW8 9SP
Tel: 020 7483 9260 Fax: 020 7483 9256
Email: info@embrss.org.uk Website: embrss.org.uk
Ambassador: HE Sabit Abbe Alley

Spain
Embassy of Spain, 39 Chesham Place, London SW1X 8SB
Tel: 020 7235 5555 Fax: 020 7259 5392
Email: emb.londres@maec.es Website: www.maec.es/subwebs/embajadas/londres/en/home
Ambassador: HE Federico Trillo-Figueroa Martínez-Conde

Sri Lanka
High Commission for the Democratic Socialist Republic of Sri Lanka, 13 Hyde Park Gardens,
London W2 2LU
Tel: 020 7262 1841 Fax: 020 7262 7970
Email: mail@slhc-london.co.uk Website: www.srilankahighcommission.co.uk
High Commissioner: HE Dr Chrisantha Nonis

Sudan
Embassy of the Republic of the Sudan, 3 Cleveland Row, London SW1A 1DD
Tel: 020 7839 8080 Fax: 020 7839 7560
Email: admin@sudanembassy.co.uk Website: www.sudanembassy.co.uk
Ambassador: HE Abdullahi Hamad Ali Alazreg

Suriname
No London Embassy
Embassy of the Republic of Suriname, 2 Alexander Gogelweg, 2517JH The Hague, Netherlands
Tel: +31 70 365 0844 Fax: +31 70 361 7445
Email: ambassade.suriname@wxs.nl
Ambassador: HE Harvey Naarendorp

UK Consulate

89 Pier House, 31 Cheyne Walk, London SW3 5HN
Tel: 07768 196326 Fax: 020 7349 0663
Honorary Consul: Dr Amwedhkar Jethu

Swaziland

Kingdom of Swaziland High Commission, 20 Buckingham Gate, London SW1E 6LB
Tel: 020 7630 6611 Fax: 020 7630 6564
Email: enquiries@swaziland.org.uk
High Commissioner: HE Dumsile Sukati

Sweden

Embassy of Sweden, 11 Montagu Place, London W1H 2AL
Tel: 020 7917 6400 Fax: 020 7724 4174
Email: ambassaden.london@gov.se Website: www.swedenabroad.com/london
Twitter: @swedeninuk
Ambassador: HE Nicola Clase

Switzerland

Embassy of Switzerland, 16-18 Montagu Place, London W1H 2BQ
Tel: 020 7616 6000 Fax: 020 7724 7001
Email: lon.vertretung@eda.admin.ch Website: www.swissembassy.org.uk Twitter: @swissembassyuk
Ambassador: HE Dominik Furgler

Tajikistan

Embassy of the Republic of Tajikistan, 26-28 Hammersmith Grove, London W6 7BA
Tel: 020 8834 1003 Fax: 020 8834 1100
Email: info@tajembassy.org.uk Website: www.tajembassy.org.uk
Ambassador: HE Erkin Kasymov

Tanzania

High Commission for the United Republic of Tanzania, 3 Stratford Place, London W1C 1AS
Tel: 020 7569 1470 Fax: 020 7495 8817
Email: balozi@tanzania-online.gov.uk Website: www.tanzania-online.gov.uk
High Commissioner: HE Peter Kallaghe

Thailand

Royal Thai Embassy, 29-30 Queen's Gate, London SW7 5JB
Tel: 020 7589 2944 Fax: 020 7823 7492
Email: thaiduto@btinternet.com Website: www.thaiembassyuk.org.uk
Ambassador: HE Pasan Teparak

Togo

No London Embassy

Embassy of the Republic of Togo, Rue Alfred Roll 8, 75017 Paris, France
Tel: +33 1 43 80 12 13 Fax: +33 1 43 80 06 05
Ambassador: HE Calixte Madjoulba

Tonga

Tonga High Commission, 36 Molyneux Street, London W1H 5BQ
Tel: 020 7724 5828 Fax: 020 7723 9074
Acting High Commissioner: Sione Sonata Tupou

Trinidad and Tobago

High Commission of the Republic of Trinidad and Tobago, 42 Belgrave Square, London SW1X 8NT
Tel: 020 7245 9351 Fax: 020 7823 1065
Email: tthc@btconnect.net Website: www.tthighcommission.co.uk Twitter: @tnt_london
High Commissioner: HE Garvin Nicholas

Tunisia

Embassy of Tunisia, 29 Prince's Gate, London SW7 1QG
Tel: 020 7584 8117 Fax: 020 7584 3205 Email: london@tunisianembassy.co.uk
Ambassador: HE Nabil Ammar

Turkey

Embassy of the Republic of Turkey, 43 Belgrave Square, London SW1X 8PA
Tel: 020 7393 0202 Fax: 020 7393 0066
Email: embassy.london@mfa.gov.tr Website: london.emb.mfa.gov.tr
Ambassador: HE Ünal Çeviköz

Turkmenistan

Embassy of Turkmenistan, 131 Holland Park Avenue, London W11 4UT
Tel: 020 7610 5239 Fax: 020 7751 1903
Email: tkm-embassy-uk@btconnect.org.uk Website: www.turkmenembassy.org.uk
Ambassador: HE Yazmurad Seryaev

Tuvalu

No London High Commission
High Commissioner: To be appointed

UK consulate

Tuvalu House, 230 Worple Road, London SW20 8RH
Tel: 020 8879 0985 Fax: 020 8879 0985
Honorary Consul: Dr Iftikhar Ayaz

Uganda

Uganda High Commission, Uganda House, 58-59 Trafalgar Square, London WC2N 5DX
Tel: 020 7839 5783 Fax: 020 7839 8925
Email: info@ugandahighcommission.co.uk Website: www.ugandahighcommission.co.uk
High Commissioner: HE Prof Joyce Kakuramatsi Kikafunda

Ukraine

Embassy of Ukraine, 60 Holland Park, London W11 3SJ
Tel: 020 7727 6312 Fax: 020 7792 1708
Email: emb_gb@mfa.gov.ua Website: www.ukremb.org.uk
Ambassador: HE Volodymyr Khandogiy

United Arab Emirates

Embassy of the United Arab Emirates, 30 Prince's Gate, London SW7 1PT
Tel: 020 7581 1281 Fax: 020 7581 9616
Email: informationuk@mofa.gov.ae Website: www.uae-embassy.ae
Ambassador: HE Abdulrahman Ghanem Almutaiwee

United States of America

American Embassy, 24 Grosvenor Square, London W1K 6AH
Tel: 020 7499 9000
Website: london.usembassy.gov Twitter: @usainuk
Ambassador: HE Matthew Barzun

Uruguay
Embassy of Uruguay, Fourth Floor, 150 Brompton Road, Knightsbridge, London SW3 1HX
Tel: 020 7584 4200 Fax: 020 7584 2947
Email: emburuguay@emburuguay.org.uk
Ambassador: HE Julio Moreira Morán

Uzbekistan
Embassy of the Republic of Uzbekistan, 41 Holland Park, London W11 3RP
Tel: 020 7229 7679 Fax: 020 7229 7029
Email: info@uzbekembassy.org Website: www.uzbekembassy.org Twitter: @uzbekembassy
Ambassador: HE Otabek Akbarov

Vanuatu
No London High Commission
High Commission of Vanuatu, Avenue de Tervueren 380, Chemin de Ronde, 1150 Brussels, Belgium
Tel: +32 2 771 74 94 Fax: +32 2 771 74 94
Email: info@vanuatuembassy.net
High Commissioner: HE Roy Mickey Joy

Venezuela
Embassy of the Bolivarian Republic of Venezuela, 1 Cromwell Road, London SW7 2HW
Tel: 020 7584 4206 Fax: 020 7589 8887
Email: info@venezlon.co.uk Website: www.embavenez-uk.org
Ambassador: To be appointed
Chargé d'Affaires: Álvaro Sánchez

Vietnam
Embassy of the Socialist Republic of Vietnam, 12-14 Victoria Road, London W8 5RD
Tel: 020 7937 1912 Fax: 020 7937 6108
Website: www.vietnamembassy.org.uk
Ambassador: HE Vu Quang Minh

Yemen
Embassy of the Republic of Yemen, 57 Cromwell Road, London SW7 2ED
Tel: 020 7584 6607 Fax: 020 7589 3350
Email: yemen.embassy@btconnect.com Website: www.yemenembassy.org.uk
Ambassador: HE Abdulla Ali Mohamed Al-Radhi

Zambia
High Commission for the Republic of Zambia, Zambia House, 2 Palace Gate, London W8 5NG
Tel: 020 7589 6655 Fax: 020 7581 1353
Email: zhcl@btconnect.com Website: zambiahc.org.uk
High Commissioner: HE Paul Lumbi

Zimbabwe
Embassy for the Republic of Zimbabwe, Zimbabwe House, 429 Strand, London WC2R 0JR
Tel: 020 7836 7755 Fax: 020 7379 1167
Website: www.zimlondon.gov.zw
Ambassador: HE Gabriel Mharadze Machinga

Royal Households

HER MAJESTY'S HOUSEHOLD
Buckingham Palace, London SW1A 1AA
Tel: 020 7930 4832
Website: www.royal.gov.uk Twitter: @BritishMonarchy
Private Secretary to HM The Queen: Rt Hon Sir Christopher Geidt KCVO OBE

HRH THE PRINCE PHILIP, DUKE OF EDINBURGH
Buckingham Palace, London SW1A 1AA
Tel: 020 7930 4832
Private Secretary and Treasurer: Brig. Archie Miller-Bakewell

TRH THE PRINCE OF WALES AND THE DUCHESS OF CORNWALL
Clarence House, London SW1A 1BA
Tel: 020 7930 4832
Website: www.princeofwales.gov.uk Twitter: @ClarenceHouse
Principal Private Secretary: William Nye

TRH THE DUKE AND DUCHESS OF CAMBRIDGE
Kensington Palace, London W8 4PU
Tel: 020 7930 4832
Principal Private Secretary: To be appointed

HRH PRINCE HENRY OF WALES
Kensington Palace, London, London W8 4PU
Tel: 020 7930 4832
Private Secretary: Edward Lane-Fox

HRH THE DUKE OF YORK
Buckingham Palace, London SW1A 1AA
Tel: 020 7930 4832 Twitter: @TheDukeofYork
Private Secretary and Treasurer: Amanda Thirsk

TRH THE EARL AND COUNTESS OF WESSEX
Bagshot Park, Bagshot, Surrey GU19 5PL
Tel: 01276 707040/01276 707043
Private Secretary: Brig. John Smedley LVO

HRH THE PRINCESS ROYAL
Buckingham Palace, London SW1A 1AA
Tel: 020 7930 4832
Private Secretary: Capt. Nick Wright CVO RN

TRH THE DUKE AND DUCHESS OF GLOUCESTER
Kensington Palace, London W8 4PU
Tel: 020 7368 1000
Private Secretary and Comptroller: Lt Col Alastair Todd

HRH THE DUKE OF KENT
St James's Palace, London SW1A 1BQ
Tel: 020 7930 4872
Private Secretary: Nicholas Marden

HRH THE DUCHESS OF KENT
Wren House, Palace Green, London W8 4PY
Tel: 020 7937 2730
Secretary: Chloe Hill

TRH PRINCE AND PRINCESS MICHAEL OF KENT
Kensington Palace, London W8 4PU
Tel: 020 7938 3519
Website: www.princemichael.org.uk
Private Secretary: Nicholas Chance LVO

HRH PRINCESS ALEXANDRA, THE HONOURABLE LADY OGILVY
Buckingham Palace, London SW1A 1AA
Tel: 020 7024 4270
Private Secretary and Comptroller: Diane Duke

HM Lord Lieutenants

ENGLAND

Bedfordshire	Helen Nellis
Berkshire	Hon Mary Bayliss
Bristol	Mary Prior MBE
Buckinghamshire	Sir Henry Aubrey-Fletcher Bt
Cambridgeshire	Hugh Duberly CBE
Cheshire	David Briggs MBE
Cornwall	Colonel Edward Bolitho OBE
Cumbria	Claire Hensman
Derbyshire	William Tucker
Devon	Sir Eric Dancer KstJ CBE
Dorset	Valerie Lane-Fox Pitt-Rivers
Durham	Susan Snowdon
Essex	Lord Petre
Gloucestershire	Dame Janet Trotter DBE
Hampshire	Dame Mary Fagan DCVO
Herefordshire	Countess of Darnley
Hertfordshire	Countess of Verulam
Isle of Wight	Major-General Martin Spencer White CB CBE
Kent	Viscount De L'Isle MBE
Lancashire	Lord Shuttleworth KCVO
Leicestershire	Lady Gretton
Lincolnshire	Anthony Worth
Greater London	Sir David Brewer CMG
Greater Manchester	Warren Smith
Merseyside	Dame Lorna Muirhead DBE
Norfolk	Richard Jewson
Northamptonshire	Lady Juliet Townsend LVO
Northumberland	Duchess of Northumberland
Nottinghamshire	Sir John Peace
Oxfordshire	Tim Stevenson OBE
Rutland	Dr Laurence Howard OBE
Shropshire	Algernon Heber-Percy
Somerset	Lady Gass
Staffordshire	Ian Dudson CBE
Suffolk	Lord Tollemache
Surrey	Dame Sarah Goad DCVO
East Sussex	Peter Field
West Sussex	Susan Pyper
Tyne and Wear	Nigel Sherlock KstJ OBE
Warwickshire	Timothy Cox
West Midlands	Paul Sabapathy CBE
Wiltshire	Sarah Troughton
Worcestershire	Lt Col Patrick Holcroft LVO OBE
East Riding of Yorkshire	Hon Susan Cunliffe-Lister
North Yorkshire	Lord Crathorne
South Yorkshire	David Moody
West Yorkshire	Dr Ingrid Roscoe

SCOTLAND

The Lord Provosts for the time being of the four City Districts (Aberdeen, Dundee, Edinburgh and Glasgow) are Lord-Lieutenants of those districts ex-officio

Aberdeen City	Lord Provost ex-officio George Adam
Aberdeenshire	James Ingleby
Angus	Georgiana Osborne
Argyll and Bute	Patrick Stewart MBE
Ayrshire and Arran	John Duncan QPM
Banffshire	Clare Russell
Berwickshire	Major Alexander Trotter
Caithness	Anne Dunnett
Clackmannan	Rt Hon Sir George Reid
Dumfries	Jean Tulloch
Dunbartonshire	Rear Admiral Michael Gregory OBE
Dundee	Lord Provost ex-officio Robert Duncan
Edinburgh	Lord Provost ex-officio Donald Wilson
Fife	Margaret Dean
Glasgow	Lord Provost ex-officio Sadie Docherty
Inverness	Donald Cameron of Lochiel (the Younger)
Kincardineshire	Carol Kinghorn
Lanarkshire	Mushtaq Ahmad OBE
East Lothian	Michael Williams (acting)
Midlothian	Patrick Prenter CBE
West Lothian	Isobel Brydie MBE
Moray	Lieutenant-Colonel Sir Grenville Johnston OBE TD KCSG
Nairn	Ewen Brodie of Lethen
Orkney	To be appointed
Perth and Kinross	Brigadier Melville Stewart Jameson CBE
Renfrewshire	Guy Clark
Ross and Cromarty	Janet Bowen
Roxburgh, Ettrick and Lauderdale	Captain The Hon Gerald Maitland-Carew
Shetland	Robert Hunter
Stewartry of Kirkcudbright	Lieutenant-Colonel Sir Malcolm Ross GCVO OBE
Stirling and Falkirk	Marjory McLachlan
Sutherland	Dr Monica Main
Tweeddale	Captain David Younger LVO
Western Isles	Alexander Matheson OBE
Wigtown	Marion Teresa Brewis

WALES

Clwyd	Henry Fetherstonhaugh OBE
Dyfed	Hon Robin Lewis OBE
Mid Glamorgan	Kathrin Thomas CVO
South Glamorgan	Dr Peter Beck
West Glamorgan	Byron Lewis
Gwent	Simon Boyle
Gwynedd	His Honour Huw Morgan Daniel
Powys	Hon Shän Legge-Bourke LVO

NORTHERN IRELAND

Antrim	Joan Christie OBE
Armagh	Earl of Caledon
Belfast	Dame Mary Peters DBE
Down	David Lindsay
Fermanagh	Viscount Brookeborough
Londonderry	Dr Angela Garvey
Londonderry City	Sir Donal Keegan OBE
Tyrone	Robert Scott OBE

Association of Lord-Lieutenants

Chairman	Lord Shuttleworth
Secretary	Andrew Mackersie
	House of Lords, London SW1A 0PW
	E-mail: lord-lieutenants@parliament.uk

British Overseas Territories Governors and Commanders-in-Chief

Anguilla	HE Christina Scott (*Governor*)
Bermuda	HE George Fergusson (*Governor*)
British Antarctic Territory	Dr Peter Hayes (*Commissioner*) (Non-resident)
British Indian Ocean Territory	Dr Peter Hayes (*Commissioner*) (Non-resident)
British Virgin Islands	HE Boyd McCleary CMG CVO (*Governor*)
Cayman Islands	HE Helen Kilpatrick CB (*Governor*)
Falkland Islands	HE Nigel Haywood CVO (*Governor*); Colin Roberts CVO (from April 2014)
Gibraltar	Lt Gen Sir James Dutton KCB CBE (*Governor and Commander-in-Chief*) (from December 2013)
Montserrat	HE Adrian Davis (*Governor*)
Pitcairn, Henderson, Ducie and Oeno Islands	HE Victoria Treadell MVO (*Governor*) (Non-resident) see New Zealand – British Embassies and High Commissions Overseas section
St Helena and Dependencies	HE Mark Capes (*Governor*)
South Georgia and South Sandwich Islands	HE Nigel Haywood CVO (*Commissioner*) (Non-resident); Colin Roberts CVO (from April 2014)
Turks and Caicos Islands	HE Peter Beckingham (*Governor*)

The Commonwealth

Of the 54 member countries of the Commonwealth, Queen Elizabeth II is Head of State of 16 (including the United Kingdom), 33 are republics, and 5 are monarchies with other sovereigns. The Queen remains symbolically Head of the Commonwealth.

GOVERNORS-GENERAL

In the overseas realms of which she is Queen, Her Majesty is represented by a Governor-General

Antigua and Barbuda HE Dame Louise Lake-Tack GCMG
Prime Minister: Hon Dr Baldwin Spencer

Australia	HE Quentin Bryce AC CVO
	Prime Minister: Hon Tony Abbott
Bahamas	HE Sir Arthur Foulkes GCMG
	Prime Minister: Rt Hon Perry Christie
Barbados	HE Sir Elliott Belgrave GCMG KA
	Prime Minister: Hon Freundel Stuart
Belize	HE Sir Colville Young GCMG MBE
	Prime Minister: Hon Dean Barrow
Canada	HE Rt Hon David Johnston
	Prime Minister: Rt Hon Stephen Harper
Grenada	HE Dame Cécile La Grenade GCMG OBE
	Prime Minister: Rt Hon Dr Keith Mitchell
Jamaica	HE Most Hon Sir Patrick Allenon GCMG
	Prime Minister: Most Hon Portia Simpson Miller ON
New Zealand	HE Lt Gen Rt Hon Sir Jerry Mateparae
	Prime Minister: Rt Hon John Key
Papua New Guinea	HE Sir Michael Ogio GCMG CBE
	Prime Minister: Hon Peter O'Neill CMG
***St Christopher**	HE Sir Edmund Lawrence GCMG OBE
and Nevis	*Prime Minister:* Rt Hon Dr Denzil Douglas
***St Lucia**	HE Dame Pearlette Louisy GCMG
	Prime Minister: Hon Dr Kenny Anthony
***St Vincent and**	HE Sir Frederick Ballantyne
The Grenadines	*Prime Minister:* Hon Dr Ralph Gonsalves
Solomon Islands	HE Sir Frank Kabui GCMG OBE
	Prime Minister: Hon Gordon Darcy Lilo ˙
Tuvalu	HE Sir Iakoba Italeli GCMG
	Prime Minister: Enele Sopoaga

*Eastern Caribbean States.

REPUBLICS AND OTHER COMMONWEALTH MONARCHIES HEADS OF STATE AND HEADS OF GOVERNMENT

Bangladesh	*President and Head of State:* HE Abdul Hamid
	Prime Minister: Hon Sheikh Hasina
Botswana	*President and Head of State:* HE Lt Gen Seretse Khama Ian Khama
Brunei Darussalam	*Sultan and Head of Government:* HM Sultan Hassanal Bolkiah of Brunei
Cameroon	*President and Head of State:* HE Paul Biya
	Prime Minister and Head of Government: Philémon Yang
Cyprus	*President and Head of State:* HE Nicos Anastasiades
Dominica	*President and Head of State:* HE Eliud Williams
	Prime Minister and Head of Government: Hon Roosevelt Skerritt
†**Fiji Islands**	*President and Head of State:* HE Ratu Epeli Nailatikau
	Prime Minister and Head of Government: Commodore Voreqe Bainimarama
‡**The Gambia**	*President and Head of Government:*
	HE Sheikh Professor Alhaji Dr Yahya A J J Jammeh
Ghana	*President and Head of State:* HE John Dramani Mahama
Guyana	*President and Head of State:* HE Donald Ramotar
	Prime Minister and Head of Government: Hon Samual Hinds
India	*President and Head of State:* HE Shri Pranab Mukherjee
	Prime Minister and Head of Government: Hon Dr Manmohan Singh

†Currently suspended.

‡On 4 October 2013 The Gambia announced it would be leaving the Commonwealth.

Kenya	*President and Head of State:* HE Uhuru Kenyatta
	Prime Minster and Head of Government: Hon Raila Odinga
Kiribati	*President and Head of State:* HE Anote Tong
Lesotho	*Head of State:* HM King Letsie III
	Prime Minister and Head of Government:
	Rt Hon Dr Motsoahae Thomas Thabane
Malawi	*President and Head of State:* HE Joyce Banda
Malaysia	*Head of State:* HM Sultan Abdul Halim Mu'adzam Shah (King of Malaysia)
	Prime Minister and Head of Government:
	Hon Dato'Sri Mohd Najib bin Tun Abdul Razak
Maldives	*President and Head of State:* HE Dr Mohammed Waheed Hassan
Malta	*President and Head of State:* HE Dr George Abela
	Prime Minister and Head of Government: Hon Dr Joseph Muscat
Mauritius	*President and Head of State:* HE Rajkeswur Purryag
	Prime Minister and Head of Government: Hon Dr Navinchandra Ramgoolam
Mozambique	*President and Head of State:* HE Armando Guebuza
Namibia	*President and Head of State:* HE Hifikepunye Pohamba
Nauru	*President and Head of Government:* HE Baron Waqa
Nigeria	*President and Head of State:* HE Goodluck Ebele Jonathan
Pakistan	*President and Head of State:* HE Mamnoon Hussain
	Prime Minister and Head of Government: Nawaz Sharif
Rwanda	*President and Head of State:* HE Paul Kagame
	Prime Minister and Head of Government: Rt Hon Dr Pierre Habumuremyi
Samoa	*Head of State:* HE Tui Atua Tupua Tamasese
	Prime Minister and Head of Government: Hon Tuilaepa Sailele Malielegaoi
Seychelles	*President and Head of State:* HE James Michel
Sierra Leone	*President and Head of Government:* HE Ernest Bai Koroma
Singapore	*President and Head of State:* HE Dr Tony Tan Keng Yam
	Prime Minister and Head of Government: Hon Lee Hsien Loong
South Africa	*President and Head of State:* HE Jacob Zuma
Sri Lanka	*President and Head of State:* HE Mahinda Rajapakse
	Prime Minister and Head of Government: Hon D M Jayaratne
Swaziland	*Head of State:* HM King Mswati III
	Prime Minister and Head of Government: Dr Barnabas Sibusiso Dlamini
Tanzania	*President and Head of State:* HE Jakaya Kikwete
	Prime Minister and Head of Government: Mizengo Pinda
Tonga	*Head of State:* HM King George Tupou VI
	Prime Minister and Head of Government: Hon Lord Tu'ivakano
Trinidad and	*President and Head of State:* HE Anthony Carmona
Tobago	*Prime Minister and Head of Government:* Hon Kamla Persad-Bissessar
Uganda	*President and Head of State:* HE Yoweri Museveni
	Prime Minister and Head of Government: Rt Hon Amama Mbabazi
Vanuatu	*President and Head of State:* HE Iolu Abil
	Prime Minister and Head of Government: Hon Moana Carcasses Kalosil
Zambia	*President and Head of State:* HE Michael Sata

Forms of Address

Formal modes of address become less formal every year but there are occasions when a person may want to address someone with strict formality. The first form of address given is that which should always be used on the envelope, the second is the formal salutation and conclusion and the third is the less formal salutation and conclusion, respectively (1), (2) and (3).

The honorific prefix 'The Right Honourable' is not now generally used for Peers other than Privy Counsellors.

The courtesy titles Honourable, Lady and Lord to which sons and daughters of Peers (depending on the rank of their father) are not prefixed by the definite article. These are the practices adopted by the Earl Marshal's Office and that of the Lord Chamberlain of the Household and consequently have been followed here.

In the formal mode of address the conclusion '... Obedient Servant' has been used. This is a matter of choice as it can be 'humble and obedient servant' or simply 'I am, Sir (my Lord or whatever) Yours faithfully'.

AMBASSADOR—(1) His Excellency Mr., Dr., etc. as appropriate, (Esquire is never used), Ambassador of the Italian Republic, (the name of the country in full i.e. not The Italian Ambassador). (2) Your Excellency, conclude I am Your Excellency's Obedient Servant. (3) Dear Mr Ambassador, conclude Yours sincerely. A list of Ambassadors is given towards the end of the book. In conversation an Ambassador is addressed as 'Your Excellency', but once is sufficient, thereafter 'Sir' is normal.

AMBASSADOR'S WIFE—(1) As an ordinary married woman. She is not 'Your Excellency' nor 'Ambassadress'.

ARCHBISHOP—(1) The Most Rev The Lord Archbishop of York. Or, The Most Rev John Smith, Lord Archbishop of York. (2) Your Grace or My Lord Archbishop, conclude I am Your Grace's Obedient Servant. (3) Dear Archbishop, conclude Yours sincerely. The Archbishops of Canterbury and York are Privy Counsellors and are therefore addressed as The Most Reverend and Right Honourable.

BARON—(1) The Lord Barton. (2) My Lord, conclude I am, My Lord, Your Obedient Servant. (3) Dear Lord Barton, conclude Yours sincerely.

BARONESS IN HER OWN RIGHT OR BARON'S WIFE —(1) The Lady Barton or, in the case of Baronesses in their own right, most prefer to be styled The Baroness Barton (see biographies of Members of the House of Lords). (2) Dear Madam, conclude Yours faithfully. (3) Dear Lady Barton or Dear Baroness Barton, conclude Yours sincerely.

BARONETS—(1) Sir John Smith, Bt. (the abbreviation Bart. is not much used today but is not incorrect). (2) Dear Sir, conclude Yours faithfully. (3) Dear Sir John, conclude Yours sincerely.

BISHOP WITH A SEAT IN THE HOUSE OF LORDS—(1) The Right Reverend The Lord Bishop of Buxton. Or, The Right Reverend John Smith, Lord Bishop of Buxton. (2) My Lord Bishop, conclude I am, My Lord, Your Obedient Servant. (3) Dear Lord Bishop, Dear Bishop or Dear Bishop of Buxton, conclude Yours sincerely. The Lord and Lord are not used for Bishops not sitting in the Lords. Bishops suffragan are addressed by courtesy in the same way as diocesan bishops.

COUNTESS—(1) The Countess of Poole. (2) Dear Madam, conclude Yours faithfully. (3) Dear Lady Poole, conclude Yours sincerely.

DAME—(1) Dame Mary Smith, followed by appropriate post-nominal letters (e.g. DBE). (2) Dear Madam, conclude Yours faithfully. (3) Dear Dame Mary, conclude Yours sincerely.

DUCHESS—(1) Her Grace The Duchess of Avon. (2) Your Grace, conclude I am, Your Grace's Obedient Servant. (3) Dear Duchess of Avon, conclude Yours sincerely.

DUKE—(1) His Grace The Duke of Avon. (2) Your Grace, or My Lord Duke, conclude I am, Your Grace's Obedient Servant. (3) Dear Duke of Avon, conclude Yours sincerely.

EARL—(1) The Earl of Hethe. (2) My Lord, conclude I am my Lord Your Obedient Servant. (3) Dear Lord Hethe, conclude Yours sincerely.

GOVERNORS GENERAL, GOVERNORS AND LIEUTENANT GOVERNORS—As for Ambassadors but followed by description of office, such as Governor General and Commander-in-Chief of New Zealand. (3) Dear Governor General, Governor or Lieutenant-Governor, conclude Yours sincerely. The Lieutenant-Governors of Guernsey, Jersey and the Isle of Man enjoy this style. The Governor General of Canada has the style 'The Right Honourable' for life and a

Lieutenant-Governor of a Canadian Province is 'His Honour' for life.

JUDGE (LORD JUSTICE OF APPEAL)—(1) The Right Honourable Sir John Smith, as he is invariably a Privy Counsellor and a Knight, or the Right Honourable Lord Justice Smith. (2) My Lord, conclude I am My Lord, Your Obedient Servant. (3) Dear Sir John, conclude Yours sincerely.

JUDGE (JUSTICE OF THE HIGH COURT)—(1) The Honourable Sir John Smith, as he is invariably a Knight, or The Honourable Mr Justice Smith. (2) and (3) as for a Lord Justice of Appeal.

JUDGE (CIRCUIT JUDGE)—(1) His Honour Judge Smith. (2) Your Honour, conclude I have the honour to be Your Honour's Obedient Servant. (3) Dear Sir (or Judge Smith), conclude Yours sincerely.

JUDGE (WOMEN JUDGES)—(1) The Right Honourable Dame Ann Smith, DBE (if a Lord of Appeal), The Honourable Dame Anne Smith, DBE (if a High Court Judge). (2) and (3) as for a male Judge with suitable gender changes.

KNIGHT—(1) Sir John Smith, if a Knight Bachelor there is no post-nominal addition in this respect but if a Knight or Knight Grand Cross or Grand Commander of an Order of Chivalry the appropriate post-nominal letters should be added. A Knight may be so addressed when his knighthood is announced, there is now no need to wait for the accolade to have been conferred. (2) Dear Sir, conclude Yours faithfully. (3) Dear Sir John, conclude Yours sincerely.

LORD LIEUTENANT—(1) The normal form of address, followed by, for courtesy, H.M.'s Lord Lieutenant for the County of Newshire. (2) My Lord Lieutenant, conclude I have the honour to be my Lord Lieutenant, Your Obedient Servant. (3) Dear Lord (Sir John or Mr. as appropriate), conclude Yours sincerely.

LORD OF SESSION IN SCOTLAND—(1) The Honourable (or Right Honourable if a Privy Counsellor), Lord Glentie. (2) My Lord, conclude I have the honour to be My Lord, Your Obedient Servant. (3) Dear Lord Glentie, conclude Yours sincerely. Note: The wife of a Lord of Session is styled as the wife of a Baron but her children have no courtesy titles. The Lord Justice General or Lord Justice Clerk is usually so addressed in correspondence, rather than by his juridical title.

MEMBER OF NATIONAL ASSEMBLY FOR WALES—Address according to rank with the addition of the letters AM after the name.

MEMBER OF NORTHERN IRELAND ASSEMBLY—Address according to rank with the addition of the letters MLA after the name.

MEMBER OF PARLIAMENT—(1) Address according to rank with the addition of the letters MP after the name. Privy Counsellors have the prefix 'The Right Honourable'. Letters to Ministers may start Dear Minister.

MEMBER OF SCOTTISH PARLIAMENT—Address according to rank with the addition of the letters MSP after the name.

PRIME MINISTER—The Prime Minister has the prefix 'The Right Honourable', as a Member of the Privy Council and the letters MP after the name, as a Member of Parliament. Letters to the Prime Minister may start Dear Prime Minister.

PRINCE—(1) HRH The Prince Henry of Wales or, if a Duke, HRH The Duke of Kent; the children of the Sovereign use the definite article before Prince (e.g. The Prince Edward). (2) Your Royal Highness or Sir, conclude I have the honour to be Your Royal Highness's Obedient Servant. In conversation address as Your Royal Highness but once is sufficient, thereafter Sir is normal.

PRINCESS—(1) HRH Princess Beatrice of York, or, if the wife of a Royal Duke, HRH The Duchess of Kent; a daughter of the Sovereign uses the definite article before Princess (e.g. The Princess Anne). (2) Your Royal Highness or Madam, conclude I have the honour to be Your Royal Highness's Obedient Servant. In conversation address as Your Royal Highness but once is sufficient, thereafter Ma'am (pronounced so as to rhyme with lamb) is normal.

PRIVY COUNSELLOR—(1) The Right Honourable prefixes the name and style except in respect of Marquesses and Dukes when the letters PC are placed after the name. The letters follow those indicating membership of Orders of Chivalry. (2) Address according to rank. (See also Member of Parliament).

QUEEN—(1) Her Majesty the Queen, although letters are usually addressed to The Private Secretary to Her Majesty the Queen. (2) Your Majesty or 'May it please your Majesty', conclude I have the honour to be Your Majesty's Obedient Subject. (3) Madam, conclude With my humble duty to Your Majesty. In conversation address as Your Majesty at first thereafter as Ma'am (see Princess).

Parliamentary Terms and Proceedings

For further details see Dod's *Handbook of House of Commons Procedure* by Paul Evans (8th edition, 2012) and Dod's *Handbook of House of Lords Procedure* by Mary Robertson and Thomas Elias (2nd edition, 2006).

References in *bold italics* have entries of their own.

accounting officer: the person (usually the permanent secretary of a government department or chief executive of an agency) responsible for accounting to Parliament, in respect of each of the *Estimates* (or part of such Estimate), for the resources voted by Parliament for the public service.

address: a motion for an address usually involves either House asking for some matter or request to be communicated to the sovereign.

adjournment motion: although technically a motion moved for the purpose of bringing to a conclusion a sitting, when it is rarely debated, such a motion is often used as a procedural device in the Commons for enabling a debate to take place without having to come to a conclusion in terms (see also *general debate*).

adjournment debate: a debate on an *adjournment motion* (see also *daily adjournment* and *general debate*).

affirmation: see *oath*.

allocation of time motion: see *guillotine*.

allotted days: in the Commons, the days allotted to debate a bill under a programme order or a guillotine, also the 20 days allotted each session as opposition days and the 35 days allotted in each session to **backbench business**.

ambit: the description of the scope of expenditure covered by an *Estimate* for moneys voted by Parliament for the public services (see also *appropriation* and *Estimates*).

amendment: a proposal to change the terms of a motion or to alter a *bill*.

annunciator: the television screens situated around Parliament and its precincts on which details of the current proceedings and future business of either House are shown.

appropriation: the allocation of money by Parliament to specified purposes. The Resource Accounts are the *Comptroller & Auditor General*'s audited accounts showing that money has been spent in accordance with Parliament's instructions embodied in the *Supply and Appropriation Acts* (see also *Consolidated Fund* and *Estimates*).

backbench: the backbenches are the places where Members who are not government Ministers or official opposition *shadows* sit in each Chamber, hence *backbencher*, the term used to describe a Member who holds no official position in government or in his or her party and who is therefore not bound by the convention of collective responsibility: such a Member may more formally be referred to as a private Member though, strictly speaking, this term applies to any Member not in receipt of a ministerial salary.

backbench business: in the Commons there are 35 days in each session allotted to business which is chosen by the *Backbench Business Committee* (27 in the main Chamber and 8 – in the form of 16 Thursday afternoon sessions – in Westminster Hall) which is not government business, *opposition days* or private Members' business.

Backbench Business Committee: the committee of the Commons of seven *backbench* Members elected by secret ballot of the whole House which is charged with choosing the business to be taken on the days allotted to *backbench business*.

ballot: the term is used in the House of Commons to refer to the draw for private Members' bills. There is also provision for secret ballots in the House's proceedings relating to the election of its *Speaker*, the *Deputy Speakers*, the *Backbench Business Committee* and the Chairs of the principal *select committees*.

Bar of the House: in the Commons, the line across the floor of the Chamber which marks its formal threshold: the Bar is also marked by a rail (now invariably retracted) to which, in former times, *strangers* might be summoned to address the House or to be arraigned before it: in the Lords, this bar (about waist height) is where Members of the Commons stand to hear the **Queen's Speech** at the State Opening and on **prorogation**.

bill: a proposal for legislation formally presented to either House of Parliament; a bill may be a *private bill* or a *public bill*.

Black Rod: the Gentleman Usher of the Black Rod, a member of the royal household, the broad equivalent in the Lords of the *Serjeant at Arms*, responsible for the security of the House and sent to summon the Commons to the Lords at the opening and closing of *sessions*.

book entry: in the Commons, an entry in the *Votes and Proceedings* which records as a procedural event something which occurred without any actual proceedings taking place on the floor of the House.

breach of privilege: an abuse of one of the privileges of either House or an attempt to impede or frustrate either House or one of their Members in the exercise of one of their privileges.

budget resolutions: the series of financial resolutions, passed by the House of Commons at the conclusion of the debate on the *budget statement*, on which the *Finance Bill* is founded.

budget statement: the annual statement made by the Chancellor of the Exchequer (usually in March or April) setting out the government's tax and spending plans and proposals for their reconciliation for the forthcoming financial year: at the end of the debate on the budget, the *budget resolutions* are passed and the *Finance Bill* is introduced.

business motion: a motion proposing to regulate the time available to the Commons for consideration of a specified item of business at a specified sitting; in the Lords, a business of the House motion is moved by the Leader of the House to allow its standing orders to be suspended or varied or to make other arrangements for organising debates.

business question: in the Commons, the question addressed each Thursday to the *Leader of the House* under the urgent question procedure in reply to which the main items of business to be taken on each sitting day for the next week or so are announced.

by-election: an election in a single constituency to fill a vacancy caused by the death or *disqualification*, etc. of a Member of Parliament (or in the Lords, to fill a vacancy amongst the elected hereditary peers).

C&AG: see *Comptroller & Auditor General*.

Cabinet: the inner circle of the government to which the Minister in charge of each government department belongs (and certain other Ministers), presided over by the *Prime Minister*.

casting vote: in the Commons, where any *division* (either in the House or in a *general committee*) results in a tie, it is decided on the vote of the occupant of the Chair, which is given in accordance with precedent.

Central Lobby: the main public area of the Palace of Westminster, equidistant from the two Houses of Parliament, where members of the public are received by Members.

Chairman of Committees: in the Lords, the first Deputy Speaker and chairman of the panel of deputy speakers; also chairs the Committee of Selection, the Liaison Committee and the Procedure Committee, and has special responsibilities for *private business* and committees of the whole House.

Chairman of Ways and Means: in the Commons, the first Deputy Speaker, with particular responsibilities for *private business* and *committees of the whole House* and *sittings in Westminster Hall*.

Chief Whip: the senior *Whip* in each party in each House: the government chief whips attend meetings of the Cabinet.

Chiltern Hundreds: the steward or bailiff of the three Chiltern Hundreds is the mythical 'office of profit under the Crown' to which Members of the Commons are appointed when wishing to resign their seats by disqualifying themselves from membership of the House (see *disqualification*): the Stewardship of the Manor of Northstead is also used for this purpose.

Clandestine Outlawries Bill: the bill presented *proforma* in the Commons on the first day of each session; in the Lords the Select Vestries Bill; they each signify the right of Parliament to legislate on matters not included in the Queen's Speech.

Clerk Assistant: in each House, the second *Clerk at the Table*, and first deputy to the *Clerk of the House* and the *Clerk of the Parliaments*.

Clerks at the Table: the senior clerks in each Clerk of the House's Department who sit at the *Table* of the House.

Clerk of the House: the principal permanent officer of the House of Commons and principal adviser to the Speaker on the law, procedure and practice of the Commons; also the *accounting officer* for the House of Commons Vote and Chief Executive of the House's permanent service.

Clerk of the Parliaments: the principal permanent officer of the House of Lords, and principal adviser to the Lord Speaker on the law, procedure and practice of the Lords. Also the House's *accounting officer*.

closure: a procedural device for bringing a debate to a conclusion.

code of conduct: the codes adopted by each House to guide Members on questions relating to the interpretation of its resolutions in respect of the declarations in the *Register of Members' Interests* (*Register of Members' Financial Interests* in the Commons), relating to financial and other relationships with outside persons and bodies.

command paper: a government publication (more often than not a *White Paper*) presented to Parliament by 'command of Her Majesty'.

Commissioner for Standards: the officer of each House appointed to supervise the *Register of Members' Financial Interests*, to advise Members on the interpretation of the *code of conduct* and to assist the *Committee on Standards and Privileges* in its work.

committal: the act of sending a *bill* to a committee of one kind or another after it has received a *second reading*; in the Lords also called 'commitment'.

committee: see *committee of the whole House, general committee, grand committee, joint committee, public bill committee, select committee*.

Committee for Privileges: in the Lords, the Committee which investigates allegations of breaches of privilege or contempts and peerage claims; it has a sub-committee on Lords' Interests.

Committee of Selection: in the Commons, the committee which appoints Members to *general committees* and proposes Members to *select committees*; in the Lords the committee which proposes Members to most select committees.

Committee on Standards and Privileges: in the Commons, the select committee which investigates allegations of *breaches of privilege, contempts* and, with the assistance of the *Commissioner for Standards*, matters relating to the *code of conduct*, in particular complaints about Members in relation to outside financial interests and related matters.

committee of the whole House: either House forms itself into a committee of all its Members when it decides to take the committee stage of a *bill* on the floor of the House.

committee stage: the next stage of a bill's progress after it has been given a *second reading* and committed; it is the stage at which a bill receives the most detailed examination. In the Commons, this generally takes place in a *public bill committee*, sometimes in *committee of the whole House*, and very occasionally in another type of committee. In the Lords, this may take place in committee of the whole House or in a Grand Committee, or very occasionally some other type of committee. After a bill has completed its committee stage it is reported back to the House for its *report stage*.

Commons Amendments: amendments proposed by the Commons to a *bill* which has been sent to it by the Lords.

Comptroller & Auditor General: the officer of the House of Commons responsible for the running of the *National Audit Office* and for assisting the *Public Accounts Committee* in its scrutiny of public expenditure.

consideration: the more formal title for the *report stage* of a bill.

Consolidated Fund: the general fund into which almost all government receipts (in the form of taxes, duties, etc.) are paid (under section 10 of the Exchequer and Audit Act 1866) and out of which almost all government expenditure is met: Parliament passes the regular *Supply & Appropriation Bills* which appropriate to the government service out of the Fund the total sums voted for particular purposes by way of the *Estimates*.

consolidation bill: a *bill* which consolidates much of the existing law on a particular subject into one convenient statute: because such bills do not (except within strict and very narrow limits) change the law, they are subject to special procedures distinct from the general procedures applying to public bills.

constituency: each Member of Parliament is elected by the voters in a single geographical division of the UK which is known as a constituency: each has a unique name given by the Boundary Commission, which also recommends the boundaries of each constituency and periodically reviews these. At present each has generally between 60,000 and 80,000 electors (though at the extremes there are wide variations for historical and geographical reasons and the provisions of the Parliamentary Voting Systems and Constituencies Act 2011, if implemented, will narrow this range of variation and reduce the number of constituencies to 600. At present the UK is divided into 650 constituencies.

contempt: disobedience to, or defiance of, an order of either House, or some other insult to either House or its dignity or a *breach of privilege*.

Crossbenches: Peers who do not take the Whip of any party in the House of Lords, otherwise 'independents', sit on the crossbenches which face the throne, and are known as 'Crossbench Peers'; however, not all independent peers join the group, which works as an administrative but not political collective. In the Commons those sitting on the few crossbenches are not recognised to speak by the Chair.

crown prerogative: essentially, prerogative actions are those which the executive may take without the sanction of Parliament: they include *prorogation* and *dissolution* of Parliament (though the latter will become a statutory matter under the provisions proposed in the 2011 Fixed-term Parliaments Bill), the grant of honours, the declaration of war and, in some circumstances, the making of treaties with foreign governments.

CWH: see *committee of the whole House*.

daily adjournment: the half-hour debate at the end of each day's sitting in the House of Commons at which a *backbench* Member has the opportunity to raise a matter with a Minister.

delegated legislation: legislation made by Ministers under powers granted to them in Acts of Parliament, usually by means of a *statutory instrument*.

delegated legislation committees: in the Commons, the *general committees* which consider items of *delegated legislation* referred to them by the House.

departmental select committees: the select committees of the House of Commons established under standing orders to oversee the work of individual government departments.

Deputy Chairmen: the First and Second Deputy Chairmen of Ways and Means in the Commons, who with the *Chairman of Ways and Means* share with the *Speaker* the duties of presiding over the House. In the Lords, there is a panel of Deputy Chairmen who assist the *Chairman of Committees*. There is a First Deputy Chairman, who chairs the European Union Committee.

Deputy Speakers: see **Chairman of Ways** and Means and **Deputy Chairmen**.

despatch box: two despatch boxes are situated at either side of the *Table* in each House and serve as lecterns for those leading debate (or answering questions) from the government and official opposition frontbenches.

dilatory motion: in the Commons a motion for the adjournment of debate or for the adjournment of the House or a committee moved for the purpose of superseding the business in hand.

Director of Parliamentary Broadcasting: the officer of both Houses responsible for day to day oversight of the broadcasting of their proceedings.

disqualification: there are a large number of offices the holding of which disqualify a person from sitting as a Member of the House of Commons. Broadly speaking these fall within the general disqualifying category of 'offices of profit under the Crown', though the holders of ministerial office (up to a maximum of 95) are exempt (see also *Chiltern Hundreds*). There are also general disqualifications for civil servants, police officers, members of the armed forces, some judges and members of non-Commonwealth overseas legislatures. Also disqualified, in general terms, are persons ineligible to vote in a general election, for example Peers entitled to sit in the House of Lords, aliens, persons under the age of 18, sentenced prisoners and persons detained under the Mental Health Act. So too are bankrupts, under the Insolvency Act 1986. Members may also be disqualified after an election for breach of electoral law. In the Lords, peers under the age of 21, aliens, bankrupts and those convicted of treason are disqualified from membership.

dissolution: at present, on the advice of the Prime Minister, the Queen may at any time dissolve Parliament, thereby initiating a general election. Under the terms of the Fixed-term Parliaments Bill of 2010/11, this process would be regulated by statute. Under the Bill's proposals a dissolution normally takes place 17 days before the date fixed by statute for the next general election (the first Thursday in May in the fifth year following the last general election) unless an earlier dissolution is triggered by either a vote of two-thirds of the Members of the House of Commons or a vote of no confidence in the government followed by a failure to express confidence in a new government within a fortnight.

division: a vote, that is the means by which either House or one of their committees ascertains the number of Members for and against a proposition before it when the Chair's opinion as to which side is in the majority on a *Question* is challenged. A division in the House of Commons on a question which might otherwise take place after the moment of interruption may, in certain circumstances, be automatically deferred; deferred divisions are then taken by collecting voting papers from members on the following Wednesday afternoon.

division bell area: the area from within which it is deemed to be possible to reach the *division lobbies* within the period from the ringing of the *division bells* to the closing of the lobby doors during a *division*.

division bells: the bells, situated in the House and its precincts and outbuildings which are rung to summon Members to vote in a *division*. Their function has been largely superseded off the premises by electronic devices, activated by the *Whips* offices.

division lobbies: the lobbies running down either side of each Chamber through which Members must pass to register their votes in a *division*.

draft bill: a bill presented to Parliament, and published more generally, in draft form (usually as a *command paper*), to enable consultation on its form and contents to take place before a **bill** is formally introduced into one or other House; the number published has increased in recent years though not steadily; they are now regularly referred to a joint committee or taken up by a select committee for consideration and report.

early day motions: expressions of opinion by Members of the Commons on almost any subject which are published in the form of motions printed in the Notice Paper part of the *Vote Bundle*, to which other Members may add their names to indicate support. They are not debated.

Ecclesiastical Committee: the statutory committee of Members of both Houses which considers Church of England *Measures*.

Editor: the officer of the House of Commons in charge of the publication of the *Official Report* of debates in the Chamber and in *general committees* (aka *Hansard*). The Lords has its own Hansard, overseen by the Editor of Debates.

EDM: see *early day motions*.

Electoral Commission: the statutory body established under the Political Parties, Elections and Referendums Act 2000 which has wide-ranging responsibilities in respect of the conduct of elections and referendums and the registration of political parties and related matters. Its funding and work are overseen by a statutory committee of elected parliamentarians called the Speaker's Committee on the Electoral Commission.

Erskine May: Erskine May's *Treatise on the Law, Privileges, Proceedings and Usage of Parliament*, first published by the then Assistant Librarian and subsequently *Clerk of the House*, Thomas Erskine May in 1844, and revised by his successors as Clerk ever since: it is acknowledged as the authoritative text book on the law and practice of both Houses of Parliament: the latest edition is the 24th, edited by Sir Malcolm Jack (LexisNexis, London, 2011).

Estimates: the form in which the government presents, for approval by the Commons, its requests for the resources needed to cover recurring public expenditure.

Estimates days: the three days in each session set aside in the Commons for consideration of the Estimates, in practice used for debate on one or more select committee reports chosen by the *Liaison Committee*.

European Committees: in the Commons, the group of *general committees* which consider documents referred to them by the European Scrutiny Committee relating to the EU.

Examiner of Petitions: the officer of each House with responsibility for examining certain matters relating to private bills and hybrid bills for compliance with the standing orders relating to *private business*.

exempted business: business which, under standing orders or under a specific order of the House of Commons, may be carried on after the *moment of interruption*.

Father of the House: see *Senior Member*.

Finance Bill: the annual bill, founded on the *budget resolutions*, which embodies the government's statutory power to levy most taxes and duties, and which may include other provisions relating to taxes management.

financial privilege: the right to approve proposals for taxation or for government expenditure which the Commons asserts as its exclusive privilege, not shared with the Lords.

financial resolutions: the collective term for *money resolutions*, *ways and means resolutions*, and *supply resolutions*.

first reading: the formal first stage of a *bill*'s progress, which occurs without debate or vote after it has been introduced to either House.

frontbench: the frontbenches are where Ministers and their official opposition *shadows* sit in each Chamber, hence *frontbencher* or *frontbench spokesman* (in the Commons the government frontbench is also known as the *Treasury Bench*).

general committees: the family of committees in the Commons (known until recently as "standing committees") which proceed principally by debate rather than inquiry; it includes *delegated legislation committees*, *European Committees*, *grand committees* and *public bill committees*.

general debate: debates of a general nature which take place on the motion "that this House has considered [a specified matter]"; the motion is not amendable.

general election: an event initiated by the *dissolution* of Parliament on the advice of the Prime Minister (or in future under the provisions proposed in the Fixed-term Parliaments Bill), when all seats are automatically vacated and elections must be held in each *constituency* to elect a new Member of Parliament.

grand committees: in the Commons there are three grand committees for Scotland, Wales and Northern Ireland; they are general committees on which all Members having their constituency in the relevant country have an automatic place; in the case of Wales and Northern Ireland additional members from outside those countries may be added; the grand committees generally debate matters (including legislative proposals) relevant to the specific country; they may also conduct other types of proceedings including oral questions and statements. They sometimes meet away from Westminster. The term has a different meaning in the House of Lords, where it is applied to any proceedings of a *committee of the whole House* held in parallel with sittings in the main chamber.

guillotine: an order of the House of Commons which limits the time available to debate any stage or stages of a bill, now largely superseded by *programme* orders.

Hansard: the colloquial name for the *Official Report*, the publication containing the accurate and full (though not strictly verbatim as often claimed) reports of what is said and done in the debates of each House and their committees (other than select committees).

health service commissioner: the officer of the House of Commons who acts as the ombudsman for the NHS in England who also holds the office of *PCA* and who reports to the Public Administration Select Committee: there are separate commissioners for Wales and Scotland reporting to the devolved legislatures.

House of Commons Commission: the executive body of Members responsible for the running of the House.

insistence: when one House insists on its own version of the text of a bill or amendment during the exchange of messages ('ping pong') without offering an alternative or compromise.

instruction: after *committal* of a bill, either House may give an instruction to any committee to which it is committed to do certain things that the committee might not otherwise be empowered to do.

Joint Committee on Human Rights: a joint select committee of both Houses charged with examining bills, *remedial orders* and other matters relating to human rights in the UK.

joint committees: select committees which include Members of both Houses.

Journals: the *Votes and Proceedings* of the House of Commons and the *Minute* of the House of Lords are each consolidated into the Journals on a sessional basis and these form the authoritative record of the decisions of each House.

law commissions: the law commissions for England and Wales and for Scotland prepare proposals for reform of the law and also for its rationalisation by means of *consolidation bills* and statute law repeal bills.

Leader of the House: the Cabinet Minister charged with special responsibility for the management of the House of Commons and its business, part of the *usual channels*. He or she is a member, *ex officio*, of the *House of Commons Commission*. He or she also has responsibility for the cabinet committees dealing with the management of the government's legislative programme. His or her name will frequently appear on motions relating to the business of the House, and he or she will initiate government proposals for the reform of its procedures. His or her most public role is the period of questioning which, each Thursday, follows the *business question*. The Leader of the House of Lords is also a minister in the Cabinet and has similar responsibilities to those of the Leader of the Commons except that he or she also has a responsibility to the House as well as a responsibility to the Government.

leader of the opposition: the person elected leader of the second largest party in the House of Commons is the leader of the official opposition. He or she receives official recognition in this role in the receipt of a ministerial salary and appointment to the Privy Council. The leader of the opposition has certain well-entrenched conventional rights to initiate certain kinds of business, in particular to demand, and to expect in most circumstances to receive, an opportunity to move a motion of no confidence in the government. He also has certain rights under standing orders (see *official opposition*). In the Lords, the Leader of the Opposition is the leader of the second largest party in the Commons. He or she receives a salary.

leave: there are a number of types of proceeding which may only be done by leave of the House (or a committee). These include to speak more than once to a Question other than in committee, to withdraw a motion before the House or a committee and to move certain types of motion. Generally leave must be unanimous, that is, any single objection from any Member in the House or in a committee means that leave is thereby denied.

Liaison Committee: in the Commons the select committee consisting mainly of the Chairs of other select committees, which under standing orders has certain powers and duties in relation to the proceedings of the House, as well as a more informal role exercising oversight of the work, and as an advocate of the interests, of select committees in general. It also has a power to examine the Prime Minister on matters of public policy, and certain duties relating to National Policy Statements proposed to be made under the Planning Act 2008. The Lords also has a Liaison Committee, chaired by the Chairman of Committees, which oversees the work of its committees.

lobby correspondents: certain representatives of the various news media who have the authority of the *Serjeant at Arms* to enter the *Members' Lobby* when the House of Commons is sitting and who enjoy certain other privileges of access to areas of the Palace otherwise closed to persons apart from Members and permanent staff. They also subscribe to a code of conduct relating to the disclosure of the sources of their information (hence the expression 'on lobby terms').

Lord Speaker: Speaker of the House of Lords, having taken the role over from the Lord Chancellor in 2006. Elected by the House from amongst its Members.

Lords Amendments: the amendments proposed by the Lords to a *bill* which has been passed by the Commons.

Lords Commissioners: the Peers appointed by the Queen to deliver her *proclamation* proroguing Parliament and her *royal assent* to Acts agreed just before *prorogation* and any other Commission she chooses to send.

Loyal Address: the motion moved in reply to the *Queen's Speech* on which the debate on the Queen's Speech takes place.

Mace: the symbol of the Crown's authority in Parliament, which is displayed in each House whenever the House is in session.

maiden speech: the first speech delivered by a Member after he or she first enters the House. By convention, in the Commons, it includes a tribute to his or her predecessor, an encomium to his or her *constituency*, and avoids controversy (though this latter tradition shows signs of dying out). Also, by tradition, it is heard without interruption from other Members. The latter two points apply also to maiden speeches in the House of Lords.

manuscript amendment: an amendment of which no *notice* has been given, which (in the Commons) is presented to the Chair during debate or (in the Lords) is circulated to Members in manuscript or typescript form.

marshalled list: a list of *amendments* proposed to a *bill* which has been arranged in the order in which the amendments will be considered at *committee stage*, *report stage* or, in the Lords, third reading, rather than in the order in which they were received.

Measure: legislation made by the General Synod of the Church of England.

Member in charge: the Member in charge of a bill is the one who introduces it to the House, and he or she has certain prerogatives in relation to that bill. In the case of a government bill, any Minister (including a *Whip*) may exercise the rights of the Member in charge.

Members' lobby: the area immediately outside the Commons Chamber generally reserved to Members and *lobby correspondents* and staff of the House when the House is sitting. The equivalent in the Lords is the 'Peers Lobby'.

Minister: a member of the government, usually entitled to receive a ministerial salary and bound by the convention of collective responsibility for decisions of government. For procedural purposes, the members of the government (including *Whips*) are each regarded as being able to act on behalf of any other Minister.

Minute: the document produced after each sitting of the House of Lords recording decisions taken at that sitting and also setting out future business, questions for written answers and other information on the progress of procedural business.

moment of interruption: the time set by standing orders in the House of Commons at which the main business of a day's sitting normally ends after which business may only be taken if it is *exempted business* or unopposed business. Currently the moment of interruption is 10 pm on Mondays and Tuesdays, 7 pm on Wednesdays, 6 pm on Thursdays and 2.30 pm on Fridays.

money bill: a bill which is concerned exclusively with raising or spending public money and which, under the terms of the *Parliament Acts*, cannot be amended by the Lords.

money resolution: a *resolution* of the House of Commons, agreed on a motion which may only be moved by a *Minister*, authorising the provisions of a *bill* which entail novel forms of public expenditure.

naming: a Member who persistently defies the authority of the Chair in the House of Commons may be *named* by the Chair, which immediately causes a motion to be moved to suspend the Member from the service of the House.

National Audit Office: the office under the direction of the *Comptroller & Auditor General* which audits the expenditure of government departments.

National Policy Statement Committee: a select committee designated by the Commons *Liaison Committee* to consider a proposal for a National Policy Statement which a Minister has laid before the House under 5.9 of the Planning Act 2008. It has between 7 and 14 members drawn from the Communities and Local Government; Energy and Climate Change; Environment, Food and Rural Affairs; Transport and Welsh Affairs Committees.

Northstead, Manor of: see *Chiltern Hundreds.*

notice: where it is a requirement of standing orders or the rules of the House that a motion requires notice, it means that such a motion cannot be moved unless it appears on the *Order Paper.* In most circumstances, the latest time for giving notice of a motion to appear on a Paper for the next sitting day is the rising of the House on the previous day. While there is no formal requirement for notice of amendments to bills in committee or on report, the Chair will generally not select *manuscript amendments* or *starred amendments* for debate. This does not apply in the Lords where manuscript amendments may be moved on Committee and at Report stage without notice. Written notice is required of oral and written *PQ*s except *urgent questions* (Private Notice Questions in the Lords) and *topical questions* in the Commons. In the Commons, but not in the Lords, notice is required of presentation of bills.

Notice Paper: the blue pages of the **Vote Bundle** include the Notice Papers for notices of questions, notices of motions for future days, notices of early day motions and notices of amendments to bills.

oath: on their election at a general election or a *by-election,* each Member of the Commons is required to take the parliamentary oath or to make the required affirmation before taking his or her seat. Witnesses before a committee of the House may also be required to take an oath before giving evidence, though this requirement is generally only imposed on witnesses before a private bill committee. In the Lords, Members take the oath on their first introduction and at the start of each *session.*

official opposition: the party with the second largest number of Members in the House of Commons is the official opposition, a status which gains it certain privileges by long-standing convention (such as the right of its official spokespeople to sit on the *frontbench* and to address the House from the *despatch box*) as well as certain rights under the standing orders (to initiate debate on the majority of *opposition days*) and by statute (such as for certain of its officers to receive ministerial salaries). To an extent, the privileges are shared by members of that same party in the House of Lords.

Official Report: see *Hansard.*

ombudsman: see *Parliamentary Commissioner for Administration.*

opposition days: the 20 days each session set aside under standing orders of the House of Commons on which the opposition parties have the right to choose the business for debate.

oral question: see *PQ.*

order: when either House agrees a motion that something should happen (such as a bill being set down for a second reading or for consideration) it becomes an order of the House (see also *resolution*). The word is also commonly used in the House of Commons to connote procedural regularity (as in the expression 'in order') or to correct parliamentary behaviour (as in the Chair's call of 'Order, order', which is also used as a form of oral procedural 'punctuation'). In the Lords the word "undesirable" has the same meaning as "out of Order" in the Commons.

Order Paper: the paper, published each sitting day (except the first day of a *session*), which lists the business of each House and for any sitting in Westminster Hall (or in a Grand Committee of the Lords) for that day, as well as *parliamentary questions* (PQs) for oral answer to be asked that day, PQs for written answer that day, and certain other items such as notices of *written statements,* committee notices, *remaining orders* (in the Commons) and lists of future business.

Outlawries Bill: see *Clandestine Outlawries Bill.*

PAC: see *Public Accounts Committee.*

Parliament Acts: the Parliament Act 1911 as amended and supplemented by the Parliament Act 1949 restrict the powers of the Lords to amend *money bills* or reject or delay other *bills* agreed by the Commons.

Panel of Chairs: in the Commons, the body of Members appointed by the *Speaker* from among whom he chooses the Chair of each *general committee.* They receive an additional payment for this work. In the Lords, there is a panel of Deputy Chairmen who assist the *Chairman of Committees.*

Parliamentary Commissioner for Administration: the officer of the House of Commons appointed under statute to investigate complaints of maladministration leading to injustice in the public service, commonly known as the ombudsman. Her work is overseen by the Public Administration Select Committee (see also *health service commissioner*).

Parliamentary Commissioner for Standards: see *Commissioner for Standards.*

Parliamentary Counsel: the civil servants (all lawyers) who draft *bills* on the instruction of the government, not to be confused with the *Speaker's Counsel* or Counsel of the Chairman of Committees or other lawyers working directly to either House.

parliamentary question: a question addressed (generally) to a Minister for answer orally on the floor of the House at question time, or in writing in *Hansard.*

PCA: see *Parliamentary Commissioner for Administration.*

PNQ: see *urgent question.*

PQ: see *parliamentary question.*

point of order: properly, a request by a Member of the Commons to the Chair for elucidation of, or a ruling on, a question of procedure, but not infrequently misused by Members who do not have the floor of the House or of a committee to interrupt proceedings for other purposes.

prayers: each sitting of each House begins with prayers, conducted by the Speaker's Chaplain in the Commons or a Bishop in the Lords. The term is also used colloquially to describe a motion to annul a *statutory instrument* subject to negative resolution procedure; and to designate the final paragraph of a *public petition.*

prerogative: see *Crown prerogative.*

press gallery: the gallery of the Chamber of the Commons above and behind the Speaker's Chair reserved to accredited representatives of the various news media, also used more generally to describe the large area outside and behind this gallery given over to the use of journalists etc. and also to describe collectively the accredited members of the press gallery (see also *lobby correspondents*). In the Lords there is a much smaller Press Gallery, at the far end from the Throne.

Prime Minister: the First Lord of the Treasury and the head of the government; the person who is elected the leader of the party which can sustain a majority (either alone or in coalition) in the Commons.

Prince of Wales's consent: see *Queen's consent.*

private bill: a bill to confer on individuals, or more commonly corporate bodies of one kind or another, powers in excess of or in contradiction to the general law.

private business: the business of each House for the most part relating directly or indirectly to *private bills.*

private Member's bill: a *public bill* introduced to either House by a Member who is not a *Minister.*

private notice question: the former name for what is now called an *urgent question* in the Commons. The term is still used in the House of Lords.

privilege: a privilege enjoyed by either House collectively or its Members individually in excess of the general law, which enables it or them to fulfil the functions and duties of the House.

Privy Counsellor: a Member of the Queen's Privy Council, the body of senior royal advisers which in former times was something equivalent to the *Cabinet*, membership of which is now conferred automatically on Cabinet Ministers and also on certain senior judges; it is also by convention granted to the leaders of parties of any size in the Commons and is occasionally conferred as a mark of honour on senior backbenchers and occasionally others outside these circles. The Council retains certain judicial functions and residual executive functions. Membership once conferred is for life, unless withdrawn. It entitles the holder to the courtesy of the title 'Right Honourable' as in 'the Right Honourable Member for Witney'. In written form this is usually abbreviated to 'Rt Hon'.

Procedure Committee: *select committees* of each House appointed to consider proposals for the reform of their procedures.

proclamation: the Queen issues proclamations for the **prorogation** and summoning Parliament.

programme: an order made by the House of Commons after a *bill's second reading* to timetable the subsequent proceedings on that bill.

prorogation: the end of a *session*.

Public Accounts Commission: the statutory committee of elected parliamentarians which has oversight of the *National Audit Office*.

Public Accounts Committee: the *select committee* of the House of Commons, which works closely with the *Comptroller & Auditor General* and the *National Audit Office*, with particular responsibility for ensuring propriety, efficiency, economy and effectiveness in the spending of public money.

public bill: a proposal for legislation to change the general law; most bills introduced into either House by the government or by private Members are public bills; a minority are *private bills*.

public bill committee: in the Commons the *committee stage* of proceedings on a public bill is usually taken in a public bill committee (until recently a 'standing committee'). Each committee is appointed *ad hoc* to consider each bill and ceases to exist once that bill is reported back to the House. Public bill committees are *general committees*, but exceptionally in this category, they have power to take written and oral evidence from witnesses, in the manner of *select committees*, at some of their sittings.

Public Bill Office: the office in each House with particular responsibility for the management of legislation and (in the Commons) for clerking the *public bill committees* and other *general committees* of the House.

public gallery: the gallery of each Chamber in which members of the public may sit to observe its proceedings; there is also an area designated for the same purpose in each committee room and at *sittings in Westminster Hall*.

public petition: a petition to either House (but generally to the Commons) for redress of a grievance or other relief.

Queen's consent: where the legislation proposed in a *bill* touches on the prerogatives or private interests of the Crown, her consent is required for the bill to proceed: this may be required to be given either before the *second reading* or *third reading* (or, conceivably, before *first reading*), depending on the nature of the interest and the extent to which it is fundamental to the bill's purposes. Consent must be obtained from the Queen by a Minister and must be signified at the appropriate time by a *Privy Counsellor*. The Prince of Wales's consent may also be required, as the heir to the throne, before certain bills may be debated at certain stages.

Queen's recommendation: only the government can propose increases in public expenditure and the recommendation of the 'Crown' is therefore required for a motion in the Commons which proposes to increase or widen the scope of public expenditure: such a motion can therefore be moved only by a Minister.

Queen's Speech: the speech read by the Queen from her throne in the Lords Chamber on the first day of each *session* setting out, among other matters, details of the government's proposed legislative programme. In July 2007, for the first time, the Prime Minister gave notice of the expected contents of the legislative programme in a statement to the House in advance of the Queen's Speech, and this was done again in subsequent years but it is not yet established whether this practice will be adopted by the present government.

question: see *parliamentary question*.

Question: in procedural jargon, the matter before either House or a committee awaiting decision at any time.

Questions Book: a daily publication of the House of Commons divided into two parts: Part 1 lists all questions for written answer on that day, Part 2 lists all outstanding PQs for oral or written answer on future days.

question time: the period set aside for *PQs* to be asked and answered orally on the floor of either House.

quorum: The minimum number of members needed to be present at a sitting to make proceedings valid. The quorum of the House of Commons is 40 but only for divisions; the quorum for a *sitting in Westminster Hall* is three; the quorum of a *general committee* (except a *European Committee*) is one-third of its members, with fractions rounded up; the quorum of a European Committee is three of its appointed members, not including the Chair; the quorum of a *select committee* is one-third of its membership or three, whichever is the greater, unless otherwise set out in the standing orders or its order of appointment. The quorum of the Lords is 30 for legislative business or otherwise three.

reasoned amendment: an amendment proposed to the motion to give a *bill* a *second reading* or *third reading*.

recess: strictly speaking, the period when Parliament is prorogued; now used to refer to either House's regular holiday adjournments at Christmas, in February, at Easter, at Whitsun and in the summer.

Register of Members' Financial Interests: (in the Lords, Register of Members' Interests) the registers, published annually, in which Members of either House record their outside financial interests and the receipt of gifts, free travel, etc.

Registrar of Members' Financial Interests: (in the Lords, Registrar of Members' Interests) the officers of each House responsible for the maintenance of the *Register of Members' Financial Interests*.

remaining orders: the list of forthcoming government business published with the *Order Paper* of the House of Commons each day.

remedial order: a form of *delegated legislation* which remedies an incompatibility between UK law and the European Convention on Human Rights.

report stage: the stage of a *bill's* progress in each House between its *committee stage* and its *third reading*, at which further detailed amendments may be made.

resolution: when a motion is agreed by either House, it becomes a resolution (unless it is an *order*).

resource accounts: the audited accounts of *voted expenditure* authorised by the *Estimates*.

return: an answer or response to an address from either House for the deposit of same document.

royal assent: the Queen's assent to a *bill* agreed to by both Houses of Parliament is the final act which makes that bill an Act of Parliament.

royal recommendation: see *Queen's recommendation*.

seconder: no seconder is required for a motion to be proposed to either House, but by tradition the motion for the *Loyal Address* is seconded.

second reading: the first stage at which a *bill* is debated (and possibly voted on) in each House.

select committees: committees established by either House to inquire into particular matters or subject areas and to report back their findings and recommendations. In the Commons most are appointed permanently, and have members who remain on them for a Parliament unless replaced (and for most of them their Chairs are separately elected by secret ballot of the whole House); some are appointed ad hoc and cease to exist once they have reported on the matter which the House has referred to them. In the Lords most committees are appointed each session. Members remain on them for several *sessions* but are subject to a rotation rule.

Select Vestries Bill – see *Clandestine Outlawries Bill*.

Senior Member: the Member of the House of Commons who has the longest *continuous* period of service in the House, also known as the *Father of the House*.

Serjeant at Arms: the officer of the House of Commons responsible for security and ceremonial.

session: the period between the state opening of Parliament and its prorogation or dissolution, in the past this has generally been a year running from November to November, but was often altered by the timing of general elections; the present government has indicated its intention to run sessions normally from May to April.

shadow: broadly speaking, the official opposition appoints or elects Members of its party to 'shadow' each government Minister, that is, to take particular responsibility for presenting in and out of Parliament the policies of the opposition for the areas which are that *Minister's* responsibility, hence 'Shadow Home Secretary' etc (also called *frontbench spokesmen or spokeswomen or spokesperson*).

shuffle: the process by which the *PQs* for oral answer in the Commons are randomly sorted to determine which Members' questions will be printed on the *Order Paper* on any given day, and in what order.

sitting: a single meeting of either House or one of their committees.

sittings in Westminster Hall: the 'parallel chamber' of the House of Commons which meets in the Grand Committee Room off Westminster Hall on Tuesdays, Wednesdays and Thursdays. On Tuesdays and Wednesdays it debates subjects chosen by *backbench* Members in timed slots of either an hour-and-a-half or half-an-hour; on Thursdays it debates reports from *select committees* chosen by the *Liaison Committee*, or subjects selected by the *Backbench Business Committee*, for three hours. No decisions are taken at sittings in Westminster Hall, and all its proceedings take place as *adjournment debates*.

Speaker: the impartial presiding officer of the House of Commons: in the Lords the Lord Speaker and her deputies have far fewer formal powers than their Commons equivalents.

Speaker's Counsel: officers of the House who head its **legal services office**, including those lawyers providing legal advice to the **Speaker** and to certain of the committees of the House.

standing committee: see *general committees*.

standing orders: the rules formulated by each House to regulate their own proceedings.

starred amendment: an amendment to a bill which has not appeared on a notice paper sufficiently before the sitting at which it is to be considered; as a rule, the Chair in the Commons will not select such an amendment for debate (see also *notice*). No such problem arises in the Lords.

state opening: the occasion on the first day of each *session* on which the Queen usually attends in the House of Lords to deliver the *Queen's Speech*.

statutory instruments: the form in which most *delegated legislation* is made.

strangers: the traditional and now obsolete appellation for anyone who is not a Member, officer or official of the House.

Supply and Appropriation Bills/Acts: the twice yearly Acts of Parliament which give statutory authority to the appropriations made by the House of Commons in agreeing the *Estimates*.

supply resolution: one of the *resolutions* on which the *Supply and Appropriation bills* are founded.

Table: the Table of the House, situated between the government and opposition *frontbenches*, in each House; in former times this was the place where motions, questions, reports etc. were delivered into the possession of the House *via* the Clerks, hence 'tabled' or 'laid upon the Table'.

Table Office: in the Commons the office, situated outside the Chamber of the Commons behind the Speaker's Chair, in which *PQs* and *EDMs* are tabled; it also deals with all matters relating to the business on the floor of the House other than legislation. In the Lords, the office situated near the Prince's Chamber where all business is tabled (including questions) and where the *Minute* is compiled.

ten-minute-rule bill: a *bill* introduced into the Commons where the Member seeking the *leave* of the House to introduce the bill, and a Member who opposes granting it, may each make a short speech before the House comes to a decision on whether to allow the bill to proceed.

Test Roll: the Test Roll must be signed by each new Member after he or she has taken the *oath* or affirmed after being elected or appointed to either House.

third reading: the final stage of a whole *bill*'s passage through either House, though Lords Amendments or Commons Amendments to the bill may subsequently be considered.

topical debate: a debate on a motion "That this House has considered [a specified matter]", on a topic chosen by the *Backbench Business Committee*. It may last no more than 1½ hours and both frontbench and backbench speeches are time-limited. In practice, the Backbench Business Committee has not made use of them in this Parliament.

topical questions: a procedure whereby the last few minutes of oral question time to particular Ministers are devoted to questions of which no notice needs to be given of the terms of the question; the choice of Members who have the opportunity to ask a topical question is determined by an electronic ballot (see *shuffle*) of those who have entered their names for a particular question time in advance.

urgent question: an oral parliamentary question in the Commons asked with the consent of the Speaker without published *notice* relating to an urgent and important matter. In the Lords, called a Private Notice Question, or PNQ.

usual channels: the colloquial name for the discussions about the business of each House which take place between the *Whips* and the Leaders of each House, and in the Lords sometimes (but not always) including the Convenor of the Crossbench Peers.

voted expenditure: the Commons' agreement to an *Estimate* followed by a *Supply and Appropriation Act* represents the detailed *appropriation* of public money to the public service by Parliament.

Votes and Proceedings: the daily minute of the Commons' proceedings.

Vote Bundle: the papers published each day on which the House of Commons sits, including among other things the *Order Paper*, the *remaining orders*, the *Votes and Proceedings*, and the *notice* papers (in the Lords the *Minute* serves the same general purpose).

ways and means resolution: a *resolution* authorising a charge on the people, that is, for the most part, taxes and duties: the *Finance Bill* is founded on ways and means resolutions.

Westminster Hall: the oldest remaining part of the Palace of Westminster, now used solely as a public area and for occasional ceremonial purposes (see also *sittings in Westminster Hall*.)

Whips: the officers of each party in each House with particular responsibilities for party management and organisation of the business of the House and its committees.

White Paper: a *command paper* embodying some statement of government policy, often including proposals for legislation.

writ: the issue of a writ is the formal process for initiating a **by-election** (or indeed a general election) in the Commons. In the Lords, new Members are summoned by writ, and all Members receive a writ of summons at the beginning of a new Parliament.

written statement: a vehicle which may be used by a *minister* to inform either House on various types of matter relating to his or her responsibilities; they are published in *Hansard*.

Abbreviations

ABRO	Army Base Repair Organisation
ACA	Associate, Institute of Chartered Accountants
ACAS	Advisory, Conciliation and Arbitration Service
ACPO	Association of Chief Police Officers
ACRE	Action with Communities in Rural England
AcSS	Academy of Learned Societies for the Social Statistics
AEEU	Amalgamated Engineering and Electrical Union
AEF	Amalgamated Union of Engineering and Foundry Workers
AEU	Amalgamated Engineering Union
AFC	Air Force Cross
AIB	Associate, Institute of Bankers
AIESC	Association Internationale des Étudiants en Sciences Économiques et Commerciales
AII	Alliance Party of Northern Ireland
AM	Assembly Member (National Assembly for Wales)
AMP	Advanced Management Program; Air Member for Personnel
APEX	Association of Professional, Executive, Clerical and Computer Staff
ARA	Associate, Royal Academy
ARCM	Associate, Royal College of Music
ARCS	Associate, Royal College of Science
ARICS	Professional Associate, Royal Institution of Chartered Surveyors
ASBAH	Association for Spina Bifida and Hydrocephalus
ASLEF	Associated Society of Locomotive Engineers and Firemen
ATII	Associate Member, Incorporated Institute of Taxation
AUEW	Amalgamated Union of Engineering Workers
BA	Bachelor of Arts
BAFTA	British Academy of Film and Television Arts
BALPA	British Air Line Pilots' Association
BAOR	British Army on the Rhine
BChir	Bachelor of Surgery
BCL	Bachelor of Civil Law
BCom	Bachelor of Commerce
BD	Bachelor of Divinity
BDS	Business Development Service
BE	Bachelor of Engineering
BEc	Bachelor of Economics
BECTU	Broadcasting, Entertainment, Cinematograph and Theatre Union
BEd	Bachelor of Education
BEM	British Empire Medal
BFI	British Film Institute
BIC	British-Irish Council
BIGC	British-Irish Governmental Conference
BIS	Department for Business, Innovation and Skills
BLitt	Bachelor of Literature
BMA	British Medical Association
BMus	Bachelor of Music
BOAC	British Overseas Airways Corporation
BP	British Petroleum
BS	Bachelor of Surgery
BSocSci	Bachelor of Social Science
Bt	Baronet
BT	British Telecom
BVC	Bar Vocational Course

CAFCASS	Children and Family Court Advisory and Support Service
CAFOD	Catholic Aid Fund for Overseas Development
CAMRA	Campaign for Real Ale
CAP	Common Agricultural Policy
CB	Companion of the Order of the Bath
CBC	County Borough Council
CBE	Commander of the Order of the British Empire
CBI	Confederation of British Industry
CBIM	Companion, British Institute of Management
CCHQ	Conservative Party Campagn Headquarters
CCIM	Certified Commercial Investment Member
CDipAF	Certified Diploma in Accounting and Finance
CEFAS	Centre for Environment, Fisheries and Aquaculture Science
CEng	Chartered Engineer
Cert Ed	Certificate of Education
CH	Companion of Honour
ChB	Bachelor of Surgery
ChM	Master of Surgery
CIE	Companion of the Order of the Indian Empire
CIMA	Chartered Institute of Management Accountants
CIMgt	Companion, Institute of Management
CIPFA	Chartered Institute of Public Finance and Accountancy
CIS	Institute of Chartered Secretaries and Administrators
CLP	Constituency Labour Party
CMG	Companion of the Order of St Michael and St George
CND	Campaign for Nuclear Disarmament
CoE	Church of England
COI	Central Office of Information
CPA	Commonwealth Parliamentary Association
CPE	Common Professional Examination
CPRE	Campaign to Protect Rural England
CPS	Crown Prosecution Service
CPhys	Chartered Physicist
CPsychol	Chartered Psychologist
CQSW	Certificate of Qualification in Social Work
cr	Created
CSA	Child Support Agency; Chief Scentific Adviser
CSCE	Conference on Security and Co-operation in Europe
CSI	Committee on the Intelligence Services; Companion of the Order of the Star of India
CSL	Central Science Laboratory
CStJ	Commander, Most Venerable Order of the Hospital of St. John of Jerusalem
CVO	Commander of the Royal Victorian Order
CWU	Communication Workers Union
DARA	Defence Aviation Repair Agency
DASA	Defence Analytical Services Agency
DBA	Doctor of Business Administration
DBE	Dame Commander of the Order of the British Empire
DCB	Dame Commander of the Order of the Bath
DCL	Doctor of Civil Law
DCM	Distinguished Conduct Medal
DCMG	Dame Commander of the Order of St Michael and St George
DCMS	Department for Culture, Media and Sport
DCSA	Defence Communication Services Agency

DCSF	Department for Children, Schools and Families
DCVO	Dame Commander of the Royal Victorian Order
DD	Doctor of Divinity
DECC	Department of Energy and Climate Change
DEFRA	Department of the Environment, Food and Rural Affairs
DFC	Distinguished Flying Cross
DFID	Department for International Development
DFM	Distinguished Flying Medal
DfT	Department for Transport
DH	Department of Health
DHSS	Department of Health and Social Security
DipAgriSci	Diploma in Agricultural Science
DipEd	Diploma in Education
DipObst	Diploma in Obstetrics
DIUS	Department for Innovation, Universities and Skills
DL	Deputy Lieutenant
Dlitt	Doctor of Letters; Doctor of Literature
DMS	Diploma in Management Studies
DoE	Department of Environment
DPM	Diploma, Personnel Management; Diploma, Psychological Medicine
DPH	Diploma in Public Health
DPhil	Doctor of Philosophy
DSC	Distinguished Service Cross
DSc	Doctor of Science
DSDA	Defence Storage and Distribution Agency
DSO	Distinguished Service Order
DSocSci	Doctor of Social Science
DST	Defence Science and Technology
DStJ	Dame of Grace/or Dame of Justice, Order of the Hospital of St John of Jerusalem
Dstl	Defence Science and Technology Laboratory
DTI	Department of Trade and Industry
DTMA	Defence Transport and Movements Agency
DU	Doctor of the University
DUniv	Doctor of the University
DUP	Democratic Unionist Party
DVA	Defence Vetting Agency
EC	European Community
ECGD	Export Credits Guarantee Department
ECHR	European Convention on Human Rights
Econ	Economics
EFCW	European Forum for Child Welfare
EIA	Environmental Investigation Agency
EMU	Economic and Monetary Union
EPLP	European Parliament Labour Party
ERD	Emergency Reserve Decoration (Army)
ESRC	Economic and Social Research Council
ETS	Employment Tribunals Service
ETUC	European Trade Union Confederation
FACS	Fellow, American College of Surgeons
FArbA	Fellow, Arboricultural Association
FBA	Fellow, British Academy
FBIM	Fellow, British Institute of Management
FCA	Fellow, Chartered Accountant

FCCA	Fellow, Chartered Association of Certified Accountants
FCGI	Fellow, City and Guilds
FCILT	Fellow, Chartered Institute of Logistics and Transport
FCIM	Fellow, Chartered Institute of Marketing
FCIPS	Fellow, Chartered Institute of Purchasing and Supply
FCIT	Fellow, Chartered Institute of Transport
FCMA	Fellow, Chartered Institute of Management Accountants
FCO	Foreign and Commonwealth Office
FCP	Fellow, College of Physicians
FCPA	Fellow, Australian Society of Certified Practising Accountants
FCPaed	Fellow, College of Paediatrics
FCPsych	Fellow, College of Psychiatrists
FDA	Association of First Division Civil Servants
FHCIMA	Fellow, Hotel, Catering and Institutional Management Association
FICE	Fellow, Institution of Civil Engineers
FICPD	Fellow, Institute of Continuing Professional Development
FIEE	Fellow, Institution of Electrical Engineers
FILA	Fellow, Institute of Landscape Architects
FIMechE	Fellow, Institution of Mechanical Engineers
FIMgt	Fellow, Institute of Management
FIMI	Fellow, Institute of the Motor Industry
FIMM	Fellow, Institute of Mining and Metallurgy
FIMT	Fellow, Institute of the Motor Trade
FInstD	Fellow, Institute of Directors
FInstM	Fellow, Institute of Marketing
FInstP	Fellow, Institute of Physics
FIPA	Fellow, Institute of Practitioners in Advertising
FInstPet	Fellow, Institute of Petroleum
FInstPS	Fellow, Institute of Purchasing and Supply
FIPR	Fellow, Institute of Public Relations
FIQA	Fellow, Institute of Quality Assurance
FIRTE	Fellow, Institute of Road Transport Engineers
FKC	Fellow, King's College, London
FLA	Fellow, Library Association
FMA	Fellow, Museums Association
FMedSci	Fellow, Academy of Medical Sciences
FMI	Foundation for Manufacturing and Industry
FO	Foreign Office
FRAeS	Fellow, Royal Aeronautical Society
FRAM	Fellow, Royal Academy of Music
FRAME	Fund for the Replacement of Animals in Medical Experiments
FRCA	Fellow, Royal College of Anaesthetists; Fellow, Royal College of Art
FRCN	Fellow, Royal College of Nursing
FRCOG	Fellow, Royal College of Obstetricians and Gynaecologists
FRCOphth	Fellow, Royal College of Ophthalmologists
FRCP	Fellow, Royal College of Physicians
FRCPath	Fellow, Royal College of Pathologists
FRCPCH	Fellow, Royal College of Paediatrics and Child Health
FRCPsych	Fellow, Royal College of Pshychiatrists
FRCS	Fellow, Royal College of Surgeons of England
FRCVS	Fellow, Royal College of Veterinary Surgeons
FREng	Fellow, Royal Academy of Engineering
FRGS	Fellow, Royal Geographical Society
FRHistS	Fellow, Royal Historical Society

FRIBA	Fellow, Royal Institute of British Architects
FRCPSGlas	Fellow, Royal College of Physicians and Surgeons, Glasgow
FRCPsych	Fellow, Royal College of Psychiatrists
FRPS	Fellow, Royal Photographic Society
FRRME	Foundation for Relief and Reconciliation in the Middle East
FRS	Fellow, The Royal Society
FRSA	Fellow, Royal Society of Arts
FRSE	Fellow, Royal Society of Edinburgh
FRSH	Fellow, Royal Society for the Promotion of Health
FRSS	Fellow of the Royal Statistical Society
FSA	Fellow, Society of Antiquaries; Financial Services Authority
FSAA	Fellow, Society of Incorporated Accountants and Auditors
FSB	Fellow, Society of Biology
GBE	Knight or Dame Grand Cross of the Order of the British Empire
GC	George Cross
GCB	Knight or Dame Grand Cross of the Order of the Bath
GCHQ	Government Communication Headquarters
GCIE	Knight Grand Commander, Order of the Indian Empire
GCMG	Knight or Dame Grand Cross of the Order of St Michael and St George
GCSI	Knight Grand Commander, Order of the Star of India
GCVO	Knight or Dame Grand Cross of the Royal Victorian Order
GLC	Greater London Council
GMB	General Municipal Boilermakers Union
GMBATU	General, Municipal, Boilermakers and Allied Trades Union (see GMB)
GMW	General Municipal Boilermakers and Allied Trades Union
GMWU	General Municipal Workers' Union
GNN	Government News Network
GPMU	Graphical, Paper, Media Union
GPO	General Post Office
Green	Green Party
GSM	General Service Medal
HCIMA	Hotel and Catering International Management Association
HE	His/Her Excellency; Higher Education
HMCI	Her Majesty's Chief Inspector
HMMTB	Her Majesty's Motor Torpedo Boat
HMT	Her Majesty's Treasury
Hon	Honorary; Honourable
ICAEW	Institute of Chartered Accountants in England and Wales
ICFTU	International Confederation of Free Trade Unions
ICI	Imperial Chemical Industries
IDeA	Improvement and Development Agency for Local Government
IFAW	International Fund for Animal Welfare
IISS	International Institute of Strategic Studies
ILEA	Inner London Education Authority
IMEDE	Institut pour l'Etude des Methodes de Direction de l'Entreprise
IMF	International Monetary Fund
INSEAD	Institut Européen d'Administration des Affaires
IPU	Inter-Parliamentary Union
ITU	International Telecommunication Union (UN)
JCR	Junior Common Room
JIC	Joint Intelligence Committee
JP	Justice of the Peace
JSD	Doctor of Juristic Science
KBE	Knight Commander of the Order of the British Empire

KCB	Knight Commander of the Order of the Bath
KCIE	Knight Commander of the Order of the Indian Empire
KCMG	Knight Commander of the Order of St Michael and St George
KCSI	Knight Commander of the Order of the Star of India
KCVO	Knight Commander of the Royal Victorian Order
KG	Knight of the Order of the Garter
KM	Knight of Malta
KP	Knight, Order of St Patrick
KRRC	King's Royal Rifle Corps
KStJ	Knight of the Most Venerable Order of the Hospital of St John of Jerusalem
KT	Knight of the Order of the Thistle
Kt	Knight Bachelor; knighted
Lab/Co-op	Labour Co-operative
LAMDA	London Academy of Music and Dramatic Art
LAPADA	Association for Professional Art and Antiques Dealers
LCC	London County Council
LCO	Legislative Competence Order
LDS	Licentiate in Dental Surgery
LEA	Local Education Authority
LEAF	Linking Environment And Farming
LG	Lady Companion, Order of the Garter
LGSM&D	Licentiate, Guildhall School of Music and Drama
LIBiol	Licentiate, Institute of Biology
LLB	Bachelor of Laws
LLD	Doctor of Laws
LLM	Master of Laws
LRAM	Licentiate, Royal Academy of Music
LRCP	Licentiate, Royal College of Physicians, London
LSE	London School of Economics
LVO	Lieutenant of the Royal Victorian Order
MA	Master of Arts
MAFF	Ministry of Agriculture, Fisheries and Food
MALD	Master of Arts in Law and Diplomacy
MB	Bachelor of Medicine
MBA	Master of Business Administration
MBC	Metropolitan Borough Council
MBE	Member of the Order of the British Empire
MBL	Master in Business Leadership
MC	Military Cross
MCC	Marylebone Cricket Club
MD	Doctor of Medicine
MDC	Metropolitan District Council
ME	Myalgic Encephalomyelitis
MEd	Master of Education
MENA	Middle East North Africa
MENCAP	Royal Society for Mentally Handicapped Children and Adults
MEP	Member of the European Parliament
MFCM	Member, Faculty of Community Medicine
MIBiol	Member, Institute of Biology
MICE	Member, Institution of Civil Engineers
MIMechE	Member, Institution of Mechanical Engineers
MIMinE	Member, Institution of Mining Engineers
MInstP	Member, Institute of Physics
MIPD	Member, Institute of Personnel and Development

MLA	Member of Legislative Assembly (Northern Ireland Assembly)
Mlitt	Master of Letters
MM	Military Medal
MoD	Ministry of Defence
MoJ	Ministry of Justice
MP	Member of Parliament
MPH	Master of Public Health
MPhil	Master of Philosophy
MRCGP	Member, Royal College of General Practitioners
MRCP	Member, Royal College of Physicians
MRCPsych	Member, Royal College of Psychiatrists
MRCS	Member, Royal College of Surgeons
MS	Master of Surgery
MSF	Manufacturing Science Finance Union
MSP	Member of Scottish Parliament
MVO	Member of the Royal Victorian Order
NA	National Academician (USA)
NACF	National Art Collections Fund
NAO	National Audit Office
NATO	North Atlantic Treaty Organisation
NATS	National Air Traffic Services
NCB	National Coal Board
NCVQ	National Council for Vocational Qualifications
NCVO	National Council for Voluntary Organisations
NDPB	Non-Departmental Public Body
NEDC	National Economic Development Council
NFU	National Farmers' Union
NGO	Non-governmental Organisation
NHS LIFT	NHS Local Improvement Finance Trust
NHSPASA	NHS Purchasing and Supply Agency
NI	Northern Ireland
NIO	Northern Ireland Office
NIPS	Northern Ireland Prison Service
NUJ	National Union of Journalists
NUM	National Union of Mineworkers
NUR	National Union of Railwaymen
NSPCC	National Society for Prevention of Cruelty to Children
NUT	National Union of Teachers
NVQ	National Vocational Qualification
OBE	Officer of the Order of the British Empire
OC	Officer, Order of Canada
OCSC	Office of the Civil Service Commissioners
ODI	Overseas Development Institute
OECD	Organisation for Economic Co-Operation and Development
OFCOM	Office of Communications
Ofgem	Office of Gas and Electricity Markets
OFSTED	Office for Standards in Education
OFT	Office of Fair Trading
OFWAT	Office of Water Services
OGC	Office of Government Commerce
OM	Order of Merit
OSCE	Organisation on Security and Co-operation in Europe
OStJ	Officer of the Most Venerable Order of the Hospital of St John of Jerusalem
OUP	Oxford University Press

PC	Privy Counsellor
PCC	Press Complaints Commission
PFI	Private Finance Initiative
PGCE	Post Graduate Certificate of Education
PhD	Doctor of Philosophy
PlC	Plaid Cymru
PLP	Parliamentary Labour Party
PMOS	Prime Minister's Official Spokesman
POST	Parliamentary Office of Science and Technology
PPP	Public Private Partnerships
PPS	Parliamentary Private Secretary
PR	Proportional Representation; public relations
PSA	Public Services Agreement
PUP	Progressive Unionist Party
PUS	Parliamentary Under-Secretary; Permanent Under-Secretary
QC	Queen's Counsel
QPM	Queen's Police Medal
QSO	Queen's Service Order (New Zealand)
RA	Royal Academician; Royal Regiment of Artillery
RAC	Royal Automobile Club; Royal Agricultural College; Royal Armoured Corps
RADA	Royal Academy of Dramatic Art
RAFVR	Royal Air Force Volunteer Reserve
RAMC	Royal Army Medical Corps
RC	Roman Catholic
RCAC	Royal Canadian Armoured Corps
RCDS	Royal College of Defence Studies
RCVS	Royal College of Veterinary Surgeons
RD	Royal Naval and Royal Marine Forces Reserve Decoration
RDC	Rural District Council
RFC	Rugby Football Club
RGS	Royal Geographical Society
RICS	Royal Institution of Chartered Surveyors
RIIA	Royal Institute of International Affairs
RMA	Royal Military Academy
RMN	Registered Mental Nurse
RMT	Rail, Maritime and Transport Union
RNLI	Royal National Lifeboat Institute
RNR	Royal Navy Reserve
RNVR	Royal Naval Volunteer Reserve
RoSPA	Royal Society for the Prevention of Accidents
RPA	Rural Payments Agency
RPMS	Royal Postgraduate Medical School
RSA	Royal Society of Arts
RSC	Royal Society of Chemistry
RSO	Resident Surgical Officer
RSPCA	Royal Society for Prevention of Cruelty to Animals
RTS	Royal Television Society
RUFC	Rugby Union Football Club
RUSI	Royal United Services Institute
SBS	Small Business Service
SCAA	School Curriculum and Assessment Authority
SCCRC	Scottish Criminal Cases Review Commission
ScD	Doctor of Science
SCE	Service Children's Education

SCS	Senior Civil Servant
SDA	Scottish Development Agency
SDLP	Social Democratic and Labour Party
SDP	Social Democratic Party
SF	Sinn Féin
SFO	Serious Fraud Office
SLD	Scottish Liberal Democrats; Social and Liberal Democrats
SNP	Scottish National Party
SOGAT	Society of Graphical and Allied Trades
SpAds	Special Advisers
SQA	Scottish Qualifications Authority
SRB	Single Regeneration Budget
SRC	Science Research Council
SSA	Standard Spending Assessment
SSAFA	Soldiers, Sailors, Airmen and Families Association
SSC	Solicitor before Supreme Court (Scotland)
SSRC	Social Science Research Council
STV	Single Transferable Vote
SVQ	Scottish Vocational Qualification
TA	Territorial Army
TD	Territorial Efficiency Decoration
TGWU	Transport and General Workers Union
TLB	Top Level Budget
TUC	Trades Union Congress
TUV	Traditional Unionist Voice Party
UCATT	Union of Construction, Allied Trades and Technicians
UDC	Urban District Council
UKIP	United Kingdom Independence Party
UMIST	University of Manchester Institute of Science and Technology
UNA	United Nations Association
UNCTAD	United Nations Conference on Trade and Development
UNDP	United Nations Development Programme
UNEP	United Nations Environment Programme
UNESCO	United Nations Educational, Scientific and Cultural Organisation
UNHCR	United Nations High Commissioner for Refugees
UNICEF	United Nations Children's Fund
UPW	Union of Postal Workers
USDAW	Union of Shop Distributive and Allied Workers
UUP	Ulster Unionist Party
UUUC	United Ulster Unionist Coalition
VAT	Value Added Tax
VC	Victoria Cross
VR	Volunteer Reserve
VRD	Royal Naval Volunteer Reserve Officers' Decoration
VSO	Voluntary Service Overseas
WAAF	Women's Auxiliary Air Force
WEA	Workers' Educational Association
WEU	Western European Union
WHO	World Health Organisation (UN)
WMO	World Meteorological Organisation (UN)
WS	Writer to the Signet
WWF	World Wide Fund for Nature
YMCA	Young Men's Christian Association

Index of Members of Parliaments and Assemblies

Index

VACHER'S QUARTERLY

The most up-to-date contact details throughout the year

Call 020 7593 5644 or visit www.dodsshop.co.uk